Chambers
Student Learners'
Dictionary

r intermediate learners of English

Chambers

CHAMBERS
An imprint of Chambers Harrap Publishers Ltd
7 Hopetoun Crescent, Edinburgh, EH7 4AY

Chambers Harrap is an Hachette UK company

© Chambers Harrap Publishers Ltd 2009

Chambers® is a registered trademark of Chambers Harrap Publishers Ltd

First published by Chambers Harrap Publishers Ltd 2009

A CIP catalogue record for this book is available from the British Library.

UK edition ISBN 978 0550 10424 3
French edition ISBN 978-0245-50947-6
Egyptian edition ISBN 978-977-304-362-3   Legal Deposit Number: 10723/2009

10 9 8 7 6 5 4 3 2 1

Publishing Manager
Morven Dooner

Managing Editors
Elizabeth Walter
Kate Woodford

Editors
Pat Bulhosen
Penny Hands
Lucy Hollingworth
Ginny Klein
Julie Moore

www.chambersharrap.co.uk

Designed by Sharon Mcteir
Typeset in Bliss by Charlesworth
Printed and bound in Italy by Legoprint

Contents

Preface   5

How to use this dictionary   6-7

Parts of speech   8

Grammar in the dictionary   9

Special use of words   10

British and US English   10

Collocations   11-12

Study pages

   Modal verbs   13-14

   Punctuation   15-16

   Word building   17-18

   Articles   19

Chambers Student Learners' Dictionary   1

Preface

The *Chambers Student Learners' Dictionary* is a new dictionary for anyone learning English. It contains all the important words you will need for study, work or simply for life, explained in a clear, simple way, using words you will already know.

When you open the book, you will probably notice the symbol ⊕, which appears at many entries. This is the sign we have used to show one of the most important aspects of English: collocation. Collocation means the way words go together. For example, if there are a lot of cars on the road, we say there is **'heavy traffic'**, and if someone does something illegal, we say they have **'committed a crime'**. These word combinations can often be impossible to guess, but learning them is probably the most important thing you can do to make your English sound fluent and natural, and this dictionary will help you to do it.

Unlike many learners' dictionaries, *Chambers Student Learners' Dictionary* does not have complicated grammar codes, but the most important and common words all have examples which show clearly how to use them. Because the book has been written by experienced teachers, you will also find special notes to help you avoid common mistakes.

The information in this dictionary is based on the evidence provided by the *Chambers Harrap International Corpus,* a collection of millions of words of English, taken from all types of language, from newspapers to novels to ordinary conversation. It helps us to see how words are used in real life and to make sure that the dictionary is completely up to date.

You will also find a useful Study Section, which gives information and help with English grammar.

We hope you enjoy using the *Chambers Student Learners' Dictionary* at home, in the classroom or wherever you may be!

How to use this dictionary

Every word has a **part of speech**, showing if it is a noun, verb, adjective, etc. For an explanation of these words, see page 8.

Entry words are in alphabetical order.

The **plural** of all nouns is shown.

All **verb inflections** are shown.

Phrasal verbs are shown after the other verbs in an entry.

lap /læp/ ▶ NOUN [plural laps]
1 the top part of a person's legs when they are in a sitting position □ *Jessie sat on her mother's lap.*
2 one complete journey around a race track □ *He crashed out on the first lap of the race.*
◆ IDIOM in the lap of luxury in a very comfortable situation, with expensive things around you
▶ VERB [laps, lapping, lapped]
1 to drink something with the tongue sticking out □ *The cat was lapping milk from a saucer.*
2 if water laps, it moves gently against rocks or onto a beach □ *The waves were lapping at our feet.*
3 to pass someone more than once as you go round a race track
◆ PHRASAL VERB lap something up to enjoy experiencing or hearing something very much □ *She lapped up the compliments about her new dress.*

Common **idioms** are shown.

Numbers show where a word has different **meanings**.

Every word has a **pronunciation** using the International Phonetic Alphabet. You can find an explanation of these symbols inside the front cover.

Entry words like this are the **most common and useful** words to learn and use.

Words belonging to the same **word families** are shown under the main entry if they are in alphabetical order.

eager /'iːgə(r)/ ADJECTIVE wanting very much to do or have something □ + to do something Imran seems eager to learn.
● eagerly /'iːgəlɪ/ ADVERB in an eager way ⊞ *This is the eagerly awaited new film from the Spanish director.*
● eagerness /'iːgənɪs/ NOUN, NO PLURAL being eager □ *In his eagerness to get there, he fell over.*

This dictionary has thousands of **example sentences** showing typical uses of the entry words.

Simple **grammar patterns** are shown for these common words. They are always attached to an example, clearly showing you how to use the word. For an explanation of all the grammar codes, see page 9.

The **comparative** and **superlative** forms of adjectives and adverbs are shown. These are used when you want to say that something or someone has more of a quality or most of a quality, compared to other things or people.

lonely /'ləʊnlɪ/ ADJECTIVE [lonelier, loneliest]
1 unhappy because you are alone, with no friends around you ⏛ She suddenly felt very lonely. ⏛ I get lonely at the weekends.
2 far from other places and with very few people □ He lived in a lonely cottage on the hillside.

Collocations (words that go together) are a very important feature of this dictionary. For more information, see page 11.

This dictionary uses simple words in all the entries, but where a more difficult word is necessary, a **short explanation** is given.

duodenum /ˌdjuː'diːnəm/ NOUN [plural duodenums or duodena] the first part of the small intestine (=tube that food goes into to be digested), just below the stomach. A biology word.

Because this dictionary is for use at school as well as at home, words used in the **school subjects** maths, physics, chemistry, biology, geography and computing are shown.

If you need to be careful using a word, for instance because it is formal or informal, this is shown in the explanation. For a list of words that describe these characteristics, see 10.

abeyance /ə'beɪəns/ NOUN in abeyance not happening or not being used at present. A formal word.

If a word is always used in a particular **phrase**, that phrase is shown before the explanation, and the explanation describes the whole phrase.

Usage notes give advice about using words. In particular, they help you avoid mistakes which learners of English often make.

picnic /'pɪknɪk/ ▶ NOUN [plural picnics] a meal that you take with you to eat outdoors ⏛ We had a picnic on the beach. ⏛ There's a beautiful picnic area in the forest.

➤ Note that you **have** a picnic. You do not 'make' a picnic:
✓ We had a picnic in the park.
✗ We made a picnic in the park.

▶ VERB [picnics, picnicking, picnicked] to have a picnic
• **picnicker** /'pɪknɪkə(r)/ NOUN [plural picnickers] someone who is having a picnic

Some words have more than one possible **spelling**.

lasagne or lasagna /lə'zænjə/ NOUN [plural lasagnes or lasagnas] an Italian food made up of layers of pasta, and layers of meat or vegetables with a white sauce and cheese

This dictionary is written in British English. The spellings in explanations and examples are British. However, US spellings and common US words are shown.

diaper /'daɪəpə(r)/ NOUN [plural diapers] the US word for nappy

Parts of speech

These are the parts of speech used in this dictionary:

abbreviation	a short form of a word or words, using their first letters	*l (litre), UK (United Kingdom)*
adjective	a word that describes a noun	*pretty, hot, uncomfortable*
adverb	a word that describes a verb or an adjective	*slowly, extremely, honestly*
auxiliary verb	a verb used to make tenses, negatives and questions	*be, do, have*
conjunction	a word that connects parts of a sentence	*and, but, however*
determiner	a word used before a noun to show how the noun is being used	*the, this, those*
exclamation	something you say suddenly or loudly	*hey, ouch*
modal verb	a verb used to show ideas such as being possible, necessary, certain, etc.	*might, ought, will*
noun	a word that refers to a person, a thing, or a quality	*dog, table, car*
noun, no plural	a noun that cannot be used in a plural form	*air, happiness, ham*
number	a number	*eleven, twenty, million*
past participle	the past of the verb that indicates the past	*sung, watched, eaten*
past tense	the word used to talk about the past	*sang, watched, ate*
plural noun	a noun that often refers to several things and needs a plural verb	*trousers, outskirts*
prefix	letters added to the beginning of a word to make another meaning	*anti-, eco-, hydro-*
preposition	a word used to show things such as position, time or method	*by, under, with*
pronoun	a word that can be used in place of a noun	*they, it, those*
suffix	letters added to the end of a word to make another word	*-ful, -able*
verb	a word that says what something or someone does	*speak, increase, allow*

Grammar in the dictionary

In order to make this dictionary as easy to use as possible, grammar codes are used only on the most important and common words. That is because these are the words you are most likely to *use* and not just want to understand.

You will see that wherever there is a grammar code, there is also an example which shows you what it means.

This is a list of the codes that are used in this dictionary:

+ ing	the word is followed by a verb using an –ing form	e.g. **like** + ing: *I like playing computer games.*
+ question word	the word is followed by a word such as who, what, why	e.g. **understand** + question word: *I don't understand why he's so upset.*
+ that	the word is followed by part of a sentence beginning with that	e.g. **promise** + that: *I promise that I'll pay you back later.*
+ to do something	the word is followed by an infinitive verb	e.g. **forget** + to do something: *I forgot to lock the door.*
no plural	this meaning of the word cannot be used in a plural form even though other meanings of the same word can	e.g. **hair** I *no plural* all the hairs that grow on your head
+ in/over/up, etc.	this word is followed by a preposition	e.g. **truth** + **about**: *We're determined to learn the truth about his disappearance.*

Special use of words

Sometimes a word that can be used in one situation is not suitable for another situation. For example, we do not use the same language when we are talking to our friends as we do when we are writing an essay.

These differences are clearly shown in the explanations of words in this dictionary. These are the words we use to describe them:

formal formal words are suitable for serious writing and official situations. They would sound slightly strange if you used them in an ordinary conversation.

> **longevity** /lɒnˈdʒevətɪ/ NOUN, NO PLURAL when someone lives for a long time. A formal word
> □ *Improvements in diet have led to an increase in longevity.*

informal informal words are not suitable for serious writing or official situations. They are more likely to be used with people you know well.

> **tubby** /ˈtʌbɪ/ ADJECTIVE [**tubbier, tubbiest**] an informal word meaning slightly fat

old-fashioned This dictionary does not include words which are not used any more, but there are some words which are still in use, but not used much by young people.

> **spinster** /ˈspɪnstə(r)/ NOUN [*plural* **spinsters**] an old-fashioned word for a woman who is not married

literary literary words are usually found in poetry or novels.

> • **riches** /ˈrɪtʃɪz/ PLURAL NOUN a literary word meaning a lot of money and expensive things

British and US English

This dictionary is written in British English. The spelling and words in the explanations and the example sentences are British. However, common US words have also been included:

> **sidewalk** /ˈsaɪdwɔːk/ NOUN [*plural* **sidewalks**] the US word for pavement

Sometimes just one meaning of a word is US, for instance meaning number 5 here:

> **after** /ˈɑːftə(r)/ ▶ PREPOSITION
> **1** when something has happened □ *I'll do it after dinner.* □ *It rained day after day.*
> **5** used in US English to talk about the time when it is minutes past the hour □ *It's ten after eight.*

Many words have a different spelling in British and US English, and this is explained in the dictionary:

> **sulfur** /ˈsʌlfə(r)/ NOUN, NO PLURAL the US spelling of sulphur

Collocations

What are collocations?

Collocations are sometimes known as 'word partners' because they are the words that go together with the word you are using. For instance, if it is raining a lot, we talk about '*heavy* rain', and if two people love each other very much, we say they are '*madly* in love'.

These words appear together more often than they would do just by chance, or just because of their meanings. For instance, it is correct to say that someone can 'steal a car', but this is not a collocation because 'steal' can be used with many different nouns. However, if we talk about someone '*committing* a crime', we are using a collocation, because those words go together so strongly, and if you need a verb to go with 'crime' it *has* to be 'commit' – a verb like 'do' would not be correct.

Sometimes we can guess the collocations we want, but often it is difficult. Why do we '*pay* attention' or '*draw* conclusions'? Why do we '*tell* lies' but '*make* promises'?

That is why we have been careful to show the most useful collocations of words in this dictionary. Collocations are shown with this symbol 뫄, to make it easy for you to see the words you need to learn together with the word you have looked up.

Why is it so important to learn collocations?

Words are not usually used on their own. As well as learning just one word, you need to learn the words that go around it; the words that allow you to use your word in a clear and natural way.

- *Knowing collocations will help you to speak and write more fluent and natural English*. For example, you may know the meaning of a word like 'exam', but it is also important to know which verbs to use with it. Although it is possibly to say 'I have to do an exam at the end of the year', it is much more natural to say 'I have to *take* an exam at the end of the year'. And although people will understand if you say 'I was successful in my exam', a native speaker of English would not be likely to say that. They would say 'I *passed* my exam'.

- *Knowing collocations will make your English more interesting and help you to express yourself better.* For instance, it is fine to say 'I was very disappointed', but if you know how to say 'I was *bitterly* disappointed', your sentence has much more force, and sounds more impressive.

- *Knowing collocations will help you avoid mistakes*. Although it is sometimes possible to guess which words to use, it is also easy to make mistakes. For instance, many learners of English say things like 'We decided to make a party for him'. This is not correct English: you should say 'We decided to *have* a party for him', or even better 'We decided to *throw* a party for him'.

- *Knowing collocations will improve your exam results*. Many common English exams test your knowledge of collocation. You will lose marks if you use the wrong ones, and gain marks if you use correct, interesting ones.

Finding and learning collocations

Collocations are such an important part of learning a language, it is a good idea to try to learn them right from the beginning.

Look at the following simple sentences, for instance, to see how important they are, even for the type of ideas and activities we talk about nearly every day:

I brush my teeth every morning.
I need to do my homework.
He watches TV every evening.
It was raining heavily yesterday.
My sister wears glasses.

When you look up a word in the dictionary, try to look for its collocations and learn them together with the word.

What sort of collocations are there?

adjective + noun	e.g. *strong accent, detailed account, heavy traffic*
verb + noun	e.g. *gain acceptance, open an account, commit a crime*
verb + adverb	e.g. *go abroad, chop finely*
noun + verb	e.g. *standards slip, war breaks out*
adverb + adjective	e.g. *hopelessly lost, pleasantly surprised*
verb + adjective	e.g. *fall asleep, get married*
noun + preposition + noun	e.g. *a sense of achievement, a piece of advice*
noun + noun	e.g. *travel arrangements, management skills*

Intensifying adverb collocations

If you look in the dictionary, you will see that there is often a much more interesting way of saying 'very' or 'extremely'.

For instance, if someone is very ill, we can say they are ***seriously ill***, and if someone is very shy, we can say they are ***painfully shy***. Adverbs like 'seriously' and 'painfully' are called 'intensifying adverbs' because they make words more intense, or stronger in meaning. They are useful collocations to learn, because they can make your English more interesting.

Study Pages

Modal verbs

A modal verb is an extra verb which is used before the main verb and gives more information about the main verb. An example of a modal verb is the verb 'can'. 'Can' goes before another verb and shows that someone is able to do something. For example, in the sentence 'Lucy can swim', 'can' shows that Lucy *is able to* swim. The main English modal verbs are *can, could, may, might, must, shall, will, would* and *should*. *Have to, have got to* and *need to* are also used as modal verbs.

Some facts about modal verbs

1. Modal verbs are used before the basic form of the main verb (the 'infinitive') and are used without 'to':

✓ Julia *could go* instead of me.
✗ Julia *could to go* instead of me.

2. Modal verbs do not take 's' in the 3rd person singular:

✓ She *must* get there early
✗ She *musts* get there early.

3. The modal verb 'will' is often shortened to ''ll', especially in speech:
Don't worry - I*'ll* help.

Below are the main ways in which modal verbs are used:

1. Showing ability (modal verbs: can, could)
Used to show that someone is able to do something. (*Can* is used to show that someone is able to do something now and *could* is used to show that someone was able to do something in the past):
  I can run faster than you.
  I could run faster when I was a child.

2. Saying what is necessary (modal verbs: must, have to/have got to, need to)
Used to say that it is necessary to do something:
  I must call my mum.
  I have to finish my essay by tomorrow.
  I have got to finish my essay by tomorrow.
  I need to go now.

3. Saying what is possible (modal verbs: may/might/could)
Used to say that it is possible that something will happen or possible that something is true:
  We may come if we've got time.
  Jim might know what time it starts.
  He could be right about that.

4. Saying what is probable (modal verbs must, will, should)
Used to say that something will probably happen or that something is probably true:
  Here's Anna's coat so she must be here.
  She will be here at the usual time.
  He should call – he usually does at this time.

5. Asking for permission (modal verbs: could, may, can)
Used to ask if you can do or have something:
  Could I borrow your pen, please?

May I have another biscuit, please?
Can I take this chair, please?

Note that *could* and *may* are more polite than *can*.

6. Making requests (modal verbs: could, can, would)
Used to ask someone to do something:
Could you tell her to call me?
Can you write down any messages, please?
Would you give these to Louisa, please?

Note that *could* and *would* are more polite than *can*.

7. Giving advice and asking for advice (modal verb: should)
Used to make suggestions about what someone does or to ask someone for suggestions:
You should complain to the manager.
Should I tell her?

8. Making offers (modal verbs: shall, will, can)
Used to say that you will do something for someone:
Shall I bring some food?
I'll help (= I will help).
I can take Juliana home if you'd like.

Punctuation

Capital letters (A, B, C, etc.) are used:	• at the beginning of sentences	*The car came towards me.*
	• for names, titles, and organizations	*Jane, Mr Smith, Lord Jones, British Gas*
	• for countries and languages	*England, France, Chinese*
	• for days and months	*Monday, Saturday, July*
	• for most abbreviations	*BBC, WHO*
	• for the pronoun 'I'	*I am tired*
Full stops (.) are used:	• at the end of sentences	*I read the letter.*
	• in e-mail and website addresses (*pronounced 'dot'*)	*www.chambersharrap.co.uk*
	• in some abbreviations, especially ones made by making words shorter	*Smith & Co., Dr. Smith*
Question marks (?) are used:	• at the end of questions	*Do you know his name?*
Exclamation marks (!) are used:	• to express surprise, shock, anger, loud noises, etc.	*I've won! Get out of my house!*
Commas (,) are used:	• to show a pause in a long sentence	*After a good night's sleep, I was ready for work.*
	• to divide things in a list	*I bought eggs, milk, butter and cheese.*
	• to add extra information in a sentence	*My mother, who is nearly eighty, enjoyed the show very much.*
	• in large numbers, to separate groups of three numbers	*1,000, £234,500*
Apostrophes (') are used:	• for showing where letters are missing	*I'm, there'll*
	• for showing who or what something belongs to	*Kate's dog, the car's engine*
Quotation marks – also called inverted commas - (" or "") are used:	• around speech	*"Go away," she said.*
	• around thoughts	*'I must phone John,' he thought.*
	• to show something that someone else said or wrote	*He said that the work was 'not satisfactory'.*
	• to show that a word is new, unusual or interesting	*They play a style of music known as 'classical punk'.*

Brackets (()) are used:	• to add information and keep it separate from the rest of a sentence	*I have many hobbies (e.g. sailing, jazz, cinema) and I go out a lot.*
Colons (:) are used:	• before lists	*You will need: cardboard, paint, glue.*
	• to show that the reader must look at what follows	*Answer the following questions:*
Semicolons (;) are used:	• to divide two parts of a sentence	*My mother hated birthday parties; we children loved them of course.*
	• to separate things in a list where the items are long or already include commas	*Choose from the following: egg and chips; ham, egg and chips; sausage and chips.*
Hyphens (-) are used:	• in some words that are made from two words put together	*half-sister, one-sided*
	• when you need to divide a word at the end of a line	*I will give you my telephone number.*
Dashes (-) are used:	• to put an extra part into a sentence	*I helped Ella – not that she really needs help – to wrap the presents.*
	• to add an extra part to the end of a sentence	*She told me that Sara had been injured – it was a terrible shock.*
	• to show that a sentence has been interrupted	*We're expecting Louis to arrive at – oh, here he is!*

Word building

These two pages deal with the way in which groups of letters are added to words to make different words.

Prefixes

Sometimes a group of letters is added to the *beginning* of a word. This group of letters is called a **prefix**. There are many prefixes. Some common prefixes that you might have noticed are 'dis-', meaning *not*, for example in the word 'dishonest', and 'inter-', meaning *between*, for example in the word 'international'.

Here is a list of common prefixes with an explanation of what each prefix means and examples of words that contain those prefixes.

Prefix	What the prefix means	Words containing the prefix
anti-	'against' or 'preventing'	*antisocial, antifreeze*
auto-	to do with yourself	*autobiography*
bi-	'two' or 'twice'	*bicycle, bilingual*
co-	'together with' or 'working with'	*co-star, cooperate*
de-	1. removing something	*defrost*
	2. the opposite of	*decompose*
dis-	not	*dislike*
eco-	to do with the environment	*eco-friendly*
inter-	between	*international*
mini-	'small' or 'short'	*minibus, miniskirt*
mis-	'bad' or 'badly' or 'wrong' or 'wrongly'	*misbehave, misunderstand*
non-	not	*a non-smoker*
over-	'too' or 'too much'	*overconfident, overcrowded*
post-	after	*postwar*
pre-	before	*prehistoric*
re-	again	*reappear*
sub-	below	*submarine*
super-	'above' or 'extreme'	*superhuman, superpower*
under-	1. below	*underground*
	2. not enough	*undernourished*

Notice that some prefixes, for example 'de-' and 'under-' have more than one meaning.

Suffixes

Sometimes a group of letters is added to the *end* of a word. This group of letters is called a **suffix**. A suffix often changes a word into a different part of speech. For example the suffix '-ness' is added to the end of an adjective such as 'happy' to make the noun 'happiness'. Another example is the suffix '-ful' which changes a noun such as 'hope' into the adjective 'hopeful', meaning 'having a lot of hope'.

Here is a list of common suffixes with an explanation of what each suffix means and whether it changes the part of speech. There are also examples of words that contain those prefixes.

Suffix	What the suffix means	words containing the suffix
-able	used to make adjectives meaning 'able to be'	*preventable*

-ful	used to make adjectives meaning 'full of'	*hopeful*
-ism	used to make nouns to do with beliefs or qualities	*communism, heroism*
-ist	1. used to make nouns to do with people who do a particular thing	*artist*
	2. used to make nouns to do with people who have particular beliefs	*communist*
-ize or -ise	used to make verbs to do with making something become a particular way	*computerize*
-less	used to make adjectives meaning 'without'	*hopeless, thoughtless*
-ment	added to the end of verbs to make nouns relating to the results of the actions or processes of the verb	*accomplishment*
-ness	added to the end of adjectives to make nouns relating to the qualities or states of the adjectives	*sadness*
-proof	added to the end of words to mean 'protected against'	*waterproof*
-ship	used to make nouns relating to the relationships between people	*friendship*

Notice that some suffixes, for example '-ist', have more than one meaning.

Articles

Articles are the words 'a', 'an' and 'the'. It can often be difficult to know when to use them and when they are not needed, but there are some rules you can follow.

The words 'a' and 'an' are called 'indefinite articles'. We use 'an' before words beginning with vowels (a, e, i, o, u) and 'a' before words beginning with consonants (all the other letters.) Some words beginning with 'u' are pronounced /juː/, and these words have 'a' before them, eg *a ukulele*.

'The' is called a 'definite article'. We use 'the' to talk about a **particular** thing, or to refer to something we have already talked about. Look at these examples:

She went to buy a new coat.
The coat she bought was red.

In the first example, we do not know which coat she went to buy – just that she would buy a coat of some sort. In the second example, we are talking about a **particular** coat – the one that was already talked about.

We also use 'the' when it is already clear who or what we are talking about. Look at these examples:

Put your books on the table.
The doctor told me to drink plenty of water.

In the first example it is clear that you mean a table that you can see or that is near you. In the second example, it is clear that the person is talking about the doctor they have spoken to.

A*a*

A or **a** /eɪ/ the first letter of the alphabet

a or **an** /ən/ DETERMINER
1 used before a noun to refer to one person or thing but not a particular person or thing □ *I need a pen.* □ *I'd love to have a baby.*
2 one □ *a hundred miles*
3 each or every □ *He gets £5 a week.*

➤ Remember to use **an** (and not **a**) before a word that begins with a vowel, or a word that sounds as if it begins with a vowel: □ *a bag* □ *an apple* □ *an hour*

aback /əˈbæk/ ADVERB taken aback surprised or shocked □ *I was taken aback by the change in Dan.*

abacus /ˈæbəkəs/ NOUN [plural **abacuses**] a frame with small balls used for counting and calculations

abandon /əˈbændən/ VERB [**abandons, abandoning, abandoned**]
1 to leave someone or something, often not intending to go back □ *He abandoned the car and walked the rest of the way.* □ *How could she abandon her family like that?*
2 to stop something before it is finished □ *If it rains, we'll just abandon the whole trip.*

abashed /əˈbæʃt/ ADJECTIVE shy and embarrassed

abate /əˈbeɪt/ VERB [**abates, abating, abated**] a formal word meaning to become less strong □ *At last the storm abated.*

abattoir /ˈæbətwɑː(r)/ NOUN [plural **abattoirs**] a place where animals are killed to make meat

abbey /ˈæbɪ/ NOUN [plural **abbeys**]
1 the buildings where monks and nuns (= religious men and women) live
2 a church that monks or nuns use

abbot /ˈæbət/ NOUN [plural **abbots**] a monk (= religious man) who is in charge of an abbey

abbreviate /əˈbriːvɪeɪt/ VERB [**abbreviates, abbreviating, abbreviated**] to make a word or a phrase shorter □ *Everyone abbreviates Alistair James's name to A.J.*
• **abbreviation** /əˌbriːvɪˈeɪʃən/ NOUN [plural **abbreviations**] a short form of a word or phrase □ **+ of** *UK is an abbreviation of United Kingdom.*

ABC /ˌeɪbiːˈsiː/ NOUN [plural **ABCs**] the alphabet □ *The children were learning their ABC.*

abdicate /ˈæbdɪkeɪt/ VERB [**abdicates, abdicating, abdicated**]
1 to decide to stop being king or queen

2 **abdicate responsibility for something** to stop being responsible for something you should be responsible for □ *He has abdicated all responsibility for the children.*
• **abdication** /ˌæbdɪˈkeɪʃən/ NOUN [plural **abdications**]
1 when a king or queen decides to stop being king or queen
2 when someone stops taking responsibility for something

abdomen /ˈæbdəmən/ NOUN [plural **abdomens**]
1 the part of an animal or person's body that contains the stomach
2 the end part of an insect's body. A biology word.
• **abdominal** /æbˈdɒmɪnəl/ ADJECTIVE to do with the abdomen. A biology word. □ *abdominal pain*

abduct /æbˈdʌkt/ VERB [**abducts, abducting, abducted**] to take someone away by using force □ *Two more tourists have been abducted from their hotel room.*
• **abduction** /æbˈdʌkʃən/ NOUN [plural **abductions**] taking someone away using force □ *He faces charges of child abduction and murder.*

aberration /ˌæbəˈreɪʃən/ NOUN [plural **aberrations**] a situation or someone's behaviour that is different from usual, usually in a bad way. A formal word.

abeyance /əˈbeɪəns/ NOUN **in abeyance** not happening or not being used at present. A formal word.

abhor /əbˈhɔː(r)/ VERB [**abhors, abhorring, abhorred**] to hate someone or something □ *I abhor violence.*
• **abhorrence** /əbˈhɒrəns/ NOUN, NO PLURAL very strong dislike
• **abhorrent** /əbˈhɒrənt/ ADJECTIVE morally very bad □ *I find his views on immigration abhorrent.*

abide /əˈbaɪd/ VERB [**abides, abiding, abided**] **can't abide something/someone** if you can't abide something or someone, you dislike them very much □ *I can't abide people who smoke in restaurants.*
◆ PHRASAL VERB **abide by something** to obey a rule or a decision □ *Please abide by the rules of the game.*
• **abiding** /əˈbaɪdɪŋ/ ADJECTIVE lasting a long time 🖫 *My abiding memory of him is his loud laugh.*

ability /əˈbɪlətɪ/ NOUN [plural **abilities**] someone who has the ability to do something is able to do it or has the skill to do it □ **+ to do something** *Not everyone has the ability to play a musical instrument.*

> ➤ Remember that **ability** is followed by the structure **to do something**:
> ✓ her ability to drive
> ✗ her ability of driving

abject /ˈæbdʒekt/ ADJECTIVE
1 abject failure/poverty, etc. when someone is extremely unsuccessful/poor, etc.
2 abject behaviour shows that you are very afraid or ashamed □ an abject coward
• **abjectly** /ˈæbdʒektlɪ/ ADVERB showing that you are very afraid or ashamed □ He apologized abjectly.

ablaze /əˈbleɪz/ ADJECTIVE, ADVERB
1 burning strongly □ The bomb set several buildings ablaze.
2 shining very brightly □ The children's eyes were ablaze with excitement.

able /ˈeɪbəl/ ADJECTIVE
1 able to do something if you are able to do something, you can do it □ He wasn't able to run fast enough. □ Will you be able to help me?
2 an able person is good at doing something □ an able student

-able /əbəl/ SUFFIX -able is added to the end of words to mean 'able to be' □ manageable □ preventable

able-bodied /ˈeɪbəlˈbɒdɪd/ ▶ ADJECTIVE physically healthy
▶ NOUN the able-bodied people who are physically healthy

ably /ˈeɪblɪ/ ADVERB if you do something ably, you do it well □ It is an unusual film, ably directed by George Clooney.

abnormal /æbˈnɔːməl/ ADJECTIVE not normal, especially in way that worries you □ This is abnormal behaviour for a five-year-old.
• **abnormality** /ˌæbnɔːˈmælɪtɪ/ NOUN [plural abnormalities] something that is not normal
• **abnormally** /æbˈnɔːməlɪ/ ADVERB in a way that is not normal and which worries you □ an abnormally fast heartbeat

aboard /əˈbɔːd/ PREPOSITION, ADVERB on or onto a bus, train, ship or aeroplane □ He was one of the team aboard the shuttle. □ We all climbed aboard the boat.

abode /əˈbəʊd/ NOUN [plural abodes] an old or formal word for the place where someone lives ⊞ He had no fixed abode (= no permanent place to live) and had to sleep on the street.

abolish /əˈbɒlɪʃ/ VERB [abolishes, abolishing, abolished] to to get rid of a rule or a way of doing something □ The school has abolished its uniform.
• **abolition** /ˌæbəˈlɪʃən/ NOUN, NO PLURAL getting rid of a law or a way of doing something □ the abolition of slavery

abominable /əˈbɒmɪnəbəl/ ADJECTIVE very evil or unpleasant □ He was an abominable man.
• **abominably** /əˈbɒmɪnəblɪ/ ADVERB in an evil or unpleasant way □ She behaved abominably this evening.

Aboriginal /ˌæbəˈrɪdʒənəl/ or **Aborigine** /ˌæbəˈrɪdʒənɪ/ NOUN [plural **Aboriginals** or **Aborigines**] one of the people who lived in Australia before anyone arrived from other countries
• **Aboriginal** /ˌæbəˈrɪdʒənəl/ ADJECTIVE to do with or belonging to Aboriginals □ Aboriginal art

abort /əˈbɔːt/ VERB [aborts, aborting, aborted] to abort a plan or process is to stop it □ Severe storms forced NASA to abort the launch of the space shuttle.
• **abortive** /əˈbɔːtɪv/ ADJECTIVE an abortive plan or attempt is one that fails ⊞ They made an abortive attempt to rescue the child.

abound /əˈbaʊnd/ VERB [abounds, abounding, abounded] if things abound, there are a lot of them □ Stories abound of girls forced to become servants.

about /əˈbaʊt/ ▶ PREPOSITION
1 on the subject of □ a book about bats □ a talk about Spain
2 in different parts of a place □ Clothes were scattered about the room.
3 What about/How about something? used to make a suggestion □ How about going for a walk?
▶ ADVERB
1 not exactly but almost the number or amount given □ about five years ago □ about four centimetres
2 in or to different parts of a place □ We started moving things about. □ They were running about all day.
3 about to do something if you are about to do something, you are going to do it very soon □ I was about to leave when the phone rang. □ I think it's about to rain.

about-turn or **about-face** /əbaʊtˈfeɪs/ NOUN, NO PLURAL a complete change of plan or opinion

above /əˈbʌv/ PREPOSITION, ADVERB
1 in a higher position than something else □ the shelf above the sink □ clouds in the sky above
2 more than an amount or level □ two degrees above zero □ in the class above me
3 earlier in a piece of writing □ See instruction 5 above.
4 above all more than anything else □ Above all, I'm grateful to my parents.
5 not above doing something if someone is not above doing something, they will do it, even if it is wrong or embarrassing □ James was not above asking for his ten pence back.

above-board /əbʌvˈbɔːd/ ADJECTIVE fair and honest

abrasion /əˈbreɪʒən/ NOUN [plural abrasions] an area where skin has been slightly cut by something rough

abrasive /əˈbreɪsɪv/ ADJECTIVE
1 abrasive substances scratch things that they rub against
2 abrasive people are rude and seem as if they do not care about other people's feelings

abreast /ə'brest/ ADVERB

1 two/three, etc. abreast with two/three, etc. people or things moving next to each other □ *They were walking three abreast.*

2 keep abreast of something if you keep abreast of information or changes, you make sure you know about them

abridge /ə'brɪdʒ/ VERB [abridges, abridging, abridged] to make a book or story shorter

• **abridgement** or **abridgment** /ə'brɪdʒmənt/ NOUN [*plural* abridgements or abridgments] a book or story that has been made shorter

abroad /ə'brɔːd/ ADVERB in or to a foreign country ⊞ *We always go abroad for our holidays.* □ *She's abroad at the moment.*

abrupt /ə'brʌpt/ ADJECTIVE

1 sudden and unexpected □ *The driver made an abrupt change of direction.*

2 rude and unfriendly ⊞ *She has rather an abrupt manner.*

• **abruptly** /ə'brʌptlɪ/ ADVERB

1 suddenly and unexpectedly □ *He turned abruptly and walked out.*

2 in a rude and unfriendly way

abscess /'æbsɪs, 'æbsəs/ NOUN [*plural* abscesses] a painful swollen area on your body that is filled with pus (= white or yellow liquid)

abscond /əb'skɒnd/ VERB [absconds, absconding, absconded]

1 a formal word meaning to leave a place without permission □ *He absconded from jail.*

2 if someone absconds with something, they steal it and go away. A formal word.

abseil /'æbseɪl/ VERB [abseils, abseiling, abseiled] to move down a rope with your feet against a wall or other surface

• **abseiling** /'æbseɪlɪŋ/ NOUN, NO PLURAL the sport of moving down a rope with your feet against a wall or other surface

absence /'æbsəns/ NOUN [*plural* absences] being away from a place □ *Your absence from the meeting was noticed.*

• **absent** /'æbsənt/ ADJECTIVE not at a place where you are expected to be □ **+ from** *She has been absent from school twice this week.* □ *Is anyone absent today?*

• **absentee** /ˌæbsən'tiː/ NOUN [*plural* absentees] a person who is absent

• **absently** /'æbsəntlɪ/ ADVERB without giving much attention to what you are doing □ *She picked up the book absently and put it down again.*

absent-minded /ˌæbsənt'maɪndɪd/ ADJECTIVE an absent-minded person often forgets things

absolute /'æbsəluːt/ ADJECTIVE complete □ *I have absolute trust in her.* □ *That's absolute rubbish!*

• **absolutely** /'æbsəluːtlɪ/ ADVERB

1 completely □ *Are you absolutely sure you locked the door?*

2 extremely □ *This cake is absolutely delicious!* □ *That's absolutely ridiculous!*

3 used to agree or to give permission □ *'We should write and thank them.' 'Absolutely.'*

➤ **Absolutely** meaning 'extremely' is only used before adjectives with very strong meanings:
✓ *That's absolutely crazy.*
✗ *That's absolutely silly.*
✓ *She's absolutely beautiful.*
✗ *She's absolutely pretty.*

absolute zero /ˌæbsəluːt 'zɪərəʊ/ NOUN, NO PLURAL the lowest temperature that scientists think is possible. A physics word.

absolution /ˌæbsə'luːʃən/ NOUN, NO PLURAL in the Christian Church, a statement that someone has been forgiven

absolve /əb'zɒlv/ VERB [absolves, absolving, absolved] to say formally that someone is not guilty of something or responsible for something

absorb /əb'sɔːb/ VERB [absorbs, absorbing, absorbed]

1 to take up liquid and keep it inside □ *The bath mat will absorb the splashes.*

2 be absorbed in something to be giving all your attention to something □ *We were so absorbed in our game, we didn't hear the bell.*

• **absorbency** /əb'sɔːbənsɪ/ NOUN, NO PLURAL how much liquid a substance can absorb

• **absorbent** /əb'sɔːbənt/ ADJECTIVE an absorbent material is able to take up liquid and keep it inside □ *absorbent kitchen towels*

• **absorbing** /əb'sɔːbɪŋ/ ADJECTIVE very interesting and taking all your attention □ *an absorbing puzzle*

• **absorption** /əb'sɔːpʃən/ NOUN, NO PLURAL when a substance absorbs liquid

abstain /əb'steɪn/ VERB [abstains, abstaining, abstained] to choose not to vote yes or no

♦ PHRASAL VERB **abstain from something** to stop doing or having something that you enjoy. A formal word. □ *You will have to abstain from all forms of exercise.*

abstemious /æb'stiːmɪəs/ ADJECTIVE an abstemious person is careful not to eat or drink too much. A formal word.

abstention /əb'stenʃən/ NOUN [*plural* abstentions] when someone abstains (= does not vote yes or no) in a vote

abstinence /'æbstɪnəns/ NOUN, NO PLURAL when you do not do or have something that you enjoy

abstract /'æbstrækt/ ADJECTIVE

1 based on ideas and not real things or situations □ *Her writing is too abstract for me.*

2 abstract art uses shapes and colours instead of pictures of real things

abstruse /æb'struːs/ ADJECTIVE an abstruse subject or argument is difficult to understand. A formal word.

absurd /əb'sɜːd/ ADJECTIVE very silly □ *What an absurd idea!*

- **absurdity** /əb'sɜ:dɪtɪ/ NOUN [plural **absurdities**] something that is very silly
- **absurdly** /əb'sɜ:dlɪ/ ADVERB in a very silly way □ The questions were absurdly easy.

abundance /ə'bʌndəns/ NOUN, NO PLURAL
1 an abundance of something is a lot of it. A formal word. □ There is an abundance of information on the subject.
2 in abundance if something exists in abundance, there is a lot of it □ There was food in abundance.
- **abundant** /ə'bʌndənt/ ADJECTIVE existing in large amounts □ an abundant harvest
- **abundantly** /ə'bʌndəntlɪ/ ADVERB
1 in large amounts □ Fruit grows abundantly in the area.
2 very □ It is abundantly clear that he is lying.

abuse ▶ NOUN /ə'bju:s/ [abuses]
1 using something the wrong way for a bad reason □ This is an abuse of power. □ alcohol abuse (= drinking too much alcohol)
2 violence or bad treatment □ child abuse
3 insults □ They shouted abuse at us.
▶ VERB /ə'bju:z/ [abuses, abusing, abused]
1 to use something the wrong way for a bad purpose □ She abused people's trust in order to steal money from them.
2 to hurt someone or to treat them badly □ He was abused in prison.
- **abusive** /ə'bju:sɪv/ ADJECTIVE rude or insulting □ abusive language

➤ The noun **abuse** ends with an **ss** sound. The verb **abuse** ends with a **z** sound.

abysmal /ə'bɪzməl/ ADJECTIVE very bad □ abysmal exam results
- **abysmally** /ə'bɪzməlɪ/ ADVERB very badly □ The team played abysmally.

abyss /ə'bɪs/ NOUN [plural **abysses**]
1 a very deep hole
2 a very bad situation

academic /ˌækə'demɪk/ ▶ ADJECTIVE
1 to do with studying and education □ academic qualifications □ the academic year
2 good at studying and learning □ He loves school but he isn't very academic.
3 not having anything to do with a real situation □ Whether she has the qualifications is academic - she can't take the job because she has to look after the children.
▶ NOUN [plural **academics**] a teacher at a college or university or someone who is paid to study there
- **academically** /ˌækə'demɪkəlɪ/ ADVERB in a way that is to do with studying and learning □ Not all students can succeed academically.

academy /ə'kædəmɪ/ NOUN [plural **academies**]
1 a school or college where you learn about a particular subject □ a science academy

2 an organization that supports a particular subject □ the Academy of Ancient Music

accede /æk'si:d/ VERB [accedes, acceding, acceded] a formal word meaning to agree to a plan or something you have been asked to do

accelerate /ək'seləreɪt/ VERB [accelerates, accelerating, accelerated]
1 to drive faster □ She accelerated round the corner.
2 to happen faster or to make something happen faster □ Air travel is accelerating global warming.
- **acceleration** /ˌəkˌselə'reɪʃən/ NOUN, NO PLURAL when something moves faster or happens faster □ You'll be pushed back into your seat during acceleration.
- **accelerator** /ək'seləreɪtə(r)/ NOUN [plural **accelerators**] the part of a vehicle you press with your foot to make it go faster

accent ▶ NOUN /'æksent/ [plural **accents**]
1 the way people from a particular area pronounce words □ I have a Scottish accent. 🔊 I speak German with a strong English accent.
2 a mark over a letter that shows how to pronounce it, for example in the word 'café'
3 the emphasis on part of a word or a note of music □ Put the accent on the third syllable in the word 'preparation'.
▶ VERB /æk'sent/ [accents, accenting, accented] to put the emphasis on part of a word or a note of music □ Make sure you accent the first syllable.

accentuate /æk'sentjueɪt/ VERB [accentuates, accentuating, accentuated] to make something more obvious

accept /ək'sept/ VERB [accepts, accepting, accepted]
1 to take something that someone offers you □ + **from** He accepted some food from us. □ She won't accept help from anyone.
2 to say yes to an invitation □ We've accepted his invitation to lunch.
3 to agree that something is true □ + **that** I accept that I was wrong and I'm sorry.
4 to allow someone to join an organization □ Raj has been accepted to study medicine.
- **acceptable** /ək'septəbəl/ ADJECTIVE good enough □ This kind of behaviour just isn't acceptable! □ + **to** The offer is not acceptable to families of the victims.
- **acceptance** /ək'septəns/ NOUN, NO PLURAL
1 taking something that is given or offered to you □ We are delighted about her acceptance of the job.
2 when you agree that something is true, good or necessary 🔊 His ideas on education never gained acceptance.
- **accepted** /ək'septɪd/ ADJECTIVE agreed to by most people □ Long hours are an accepted part of the job.

access /'ækses/ ▶ NOUN, NO PLURAL
1 when you are able to see or use something □ + **to** They don't have access to a doctor. 🔊 Do you have Internet access?
2 a way of getting to or entering a place □ + **to** The

builders will need access to the house while you're out at work.

▶ VERB [**accesses, accessing, accessed**]
1 to be able to see or use something □ *This file was last accessed yesterday.* □ *I was able to access all the information I needed.*
2 to be able to get to or enter a place □ *The castle is accessed by the sea.*
• **accessible** /ək'sesəbəl/ ADJECTIVE
1 easy to get to □ *The house is not very accessible.*
2 easy to see and use □ *We make the information accessible to the public.*
3 easy to understand □ *Make sure you use clear, accessible language.*

accession /æk'seʃən/ NOUN, NO PLURAL
1 the accession of a king or queen is the official start of their rule
2 when a country or organization becomes part of an international organization □ *the accession of Romania to the EU*

accessory /ək'sesəri/ NOUN [*plural* **accessories**]
1 an extra part that can be used with something □ *a hairdryer with lots of accessories*
2 something like a bag or piece of jewellery, that goes with your clothes □ *a little black dress with bright pink accessories*
3 a person who helps someone commit a crime □ *an accessory to murder*

access provider /'ækses prə'vaɪdə(r)/ NOUN [*plural* **access providers**] a company that you pay so that you can use the Internet and e-mail. A computing word.

accident /'æksɪdənt/ NOUN [*plural* **accidents**]
1 a bad thing that happens that is not intended
🔀 *Don's had an accident.* 🔀 *a serious/fatal accident*
□ *She was injured in a road traffic accident.* □ *I'm sorry I broke your clock - it was an accident.*
2 by accident if something happens by accident, it is not intended □ *I dropped the glass by accident and it smashed.*
• **accidental** /ˌæksɪ'dentəl/ ADJECTIVE not intended
🔀 *There was a lot of accidental damage.*
• **accidentally** /ˌæksɪ'dentəli/ ADVERB by accident
□ *I accidentally shut the car door and locked my keys inside.*

Accident and Emergency /'æksɪdənt ənd ɪ'mɜːdʒənsɪ/ NOUN, NO PLURAL the hospital department that looks after people who have been injured or have suddenly become very ill

acclaim /ə'kleɪm/ NOUN, NO PLURAL praise
□ *international acclaim*
• **acclaimed** /ə'kleɪmd/ ADJECTIVE praised by many people □ *an acclaimed television show*

acclimatize *or* **acclimatise** /ə'klaɪmətaɪz/ VERB [**acclimatizes, acclimatizing, acclimatized**] to start to feel comfortable with a type of weather or a situation
□ *It didn't take him long to acclimatize to Singapore's humidity.*

accommodate /ə'kɒmədeɪt/ VERB [**accommodates, accommodating, accommodated**]
1 to find someone a place to stay □ *The whole group can be accommodated in the same hotel.*
2 to be big enough for someone or something □ *This room could easily accommodate ten people.*
3 to provide what someone wants or needs
• **accommodating** /ə'kɒmədeɪtɪŋ/ ADJECTIVE helpful and willing to change your plans
• **accommodation** /əˌkɒmə'deɪʃən/ NOUN, NO PLURAL somewhere to stay or live 🔀 *She's staying in rented accommodation.* 🔀 *Does the college provide accommodation?*

> ▶ In UK English **accommodation** is never used in the plural:
> ✓ *Accommodation is very expensive.*
> ✗ *Accommodations are very expensive.*

accompaniment /ə'kʌmpənɪmənt/ NOUN [*plural* **accompaniments**]
1 the music that someone plays for a person to sing or play an instrument with □ *a love song with a guitar accompaniment*
2 food or drink that is good with another type of food or drink □ *This wine is the perfect accompaniment to fish.*

accompanist /ə'kʌmpənɪst/ NOUN [*plural* **accompanists**] someone who plays a musical accompaniment

accompany /ə'kʌmpəni/ VERB [**accompanies, accompanying, accompanied**]
1 to go with someone □ **+ to** *We accompanied him to the station.*
2 to exist or come with something □ *The tickets were accompanied by a book on travel safety.*
3 to play an instrument, especially the piano, while someone else sings a song or plays another instrument □ *Her sister usually accompanies her on the piano.*

accomplice /ə'kʌmplɪs/ NOUN [*plural* **accomplices**] someone who helps a person to do something bad

accomplish /ə'kʌmplɪʃ/ VERB [**accomplishes, accomplishing, accomplished**] to manage to do something □ *Most children accomplished the task in a few minutes.*
• **accomplished** /ə'kʌmplɪʃt/ ADJECTIVE having a lot of skill □ *an accomplished artist*
• **accomplishment** /ə'kʌmplɪʃmənt/ NOUN [*plural* **accomplishments**]
1 when you finish something successfully
2 something you are good at □ *Cooking is just one of her many accomplishments.*

accord /ə'kɔːd/ NOUN of your own accord if you do something of your own accord, you do it without being asked or told □ *I was surprised that he thanked me of his own accord.*

accordance /ə'kɔːdəns/ NOUN, NO PLURAL in accordance with something obeying a rule, wish, etc. □ *He tries to live in accordance with Christian principles.*

accordingly /əˈkɔːdɪŋlɪ/ ADVERB

1 in a way that is suitable for a situation □ *The sun was shining and Jake dressed accordingly.* □ *They weigh the vegetables and we are paid accordingly.*

2 a formal word meaning for that reason □ *Their behaviour did not improve. Accordingly, I had to ask them to leave.*

according to /əˈkɔːdɪŋ tuː/ PREPOSITION

1 as said or written by someone □ *Hannah's ill, according to Lucy.* □ *According to the dictionary, there are two m's in 'accommodation'.*

2 using a particular measurement or system □ *You'll be paid according to how much work you have done.* 🔁 *Everything went according to plan* (= happened as intended).

accordion /əˈkɔːdɪən/ NOUN [plural **accordions**] a musical instrument that you play by pressing in and out a folding box with a small keyboard on its side

accost /əˈkɒst/ VERB [accosts, accosting, accosted] if you are accosted by someone, they come close to you and speak to you, often rudely

account /əˈkaʊnt/ NOUN [plural **accounts**]

1 a description of something that has happened 🔁 *He gave a humorous account of his journey.* 🔁 *The report gives a detailed account of their work.*

2 an arrangement with a bank to keep money there 🔁 *I opened a savings account.* □ *Which account do you want to pay this cheque into?*

3 an agreement with a shop to pay later for what you have bought

4 take something into account to consider something when you are thinking about a situation or a decision □ *Will they take my age into account when they decide who can go?*

5 on no account certainly not □ *On no account are you to stay out after ten o'clock.*

➡ go to **accounts**

◆ PHRASAL VERB [accounts, accounting, accounted] **account for something**

1 to be the reason for something □ *The fact that it's her birthday accounts for all the visitors she's had today.*

2 to be a certain amount of a total □ *Tourism accounts for over 50% of the country's income.*

accountability /əˌkaʊntəˈbɪlɪtɪ/ NOUN, NO PLURAL the state of being responsible for something

accountable /əˈkaʊntəbəl/ ADJECTIVE

1 if you are accountable for something, you are responsible for it 🔁 *Employers should be held accountable for safety in their factories.*

2 if you are accountable to someone, they judge and control what you do

accountancy /əˈkaʊntənsɪ/ NOUN, NO PLURAL the job of keeping records of a person's or an organization's money

• **accountant** /əˈkaʊntənt/ NOUN [plural **accountants**] someone whose job is to keep or examine records of a person's or an organization's money

• **accounting** /əˈkaʊntɪŋ/ NOUN, NO PLURAL the work of an accountant

accounts /əˈkaʊnts/ PLURAL NOUN written records of the money received and spent by a person or organization

accrue /əˈkruː/ VERB [accrues, accruing, accrued] to increase over a period of time

accumulate /əˈkjuːmjʊleɪt/ VERB [accumulates, accumulating, accumulated] to collect a number or amount of something, or to increase in number or amount □ *Greenhouse gases are accumulating in the Earth's atmosphere.*

• **accumulation** /əˌkjuːmjʊˈleɪʃən/ NOUN [plural **accumulations**] when things have been accumulated □ *the accumulation of knowledge*

accuracy /ˈækjʊrəsɪ/ NOUN, NO PLURAL being exactly correct □ *Please check the accuracy of this measurement.*

• **accurate** /ˈækjʊrət/ ADJECTIVE exactly correct 🔁 *an accurate description* 🔁 *accurate measurements* 🔁 *Their account of what happened was pretty accurate.*

• **accurately** /ˈækjʊrətlɪ/ ADVERB in an accurate way □ *Copy the shape as accurately as possible.*

accusation /ˌækjuːˈzeɪʃən/ NOUN [plural **accusations**] a statement saying that someone has done something bad 🔁 *She has made some accusations against me.* 🔁 *These are serious accusations.*

• **accuse** /əˈkjuːz/ VERB [accuses, accusing, accused] to say that someone has done something bad □ **+ of** *He was accused of murder.* □ *Are you accusing me of lying?*

• **accused** /əˈkjuːzd/ NOUN **the accused** the person or people who are accused of a crime in court

• **accuser** /əˈkjuːzə(r)/ NOUN [plural **accusers**] a person who makes an accusation

• **accusing** /əˈkjuːzɪŋ/ ADJECTIVE showing that you think someone has done something wrong □ *She gave me an accusing stare.*

• **accusingly** /əˈkjuːzɪŋlɪ/ ADVERB in an accusing way □ *'Look at that scratch on the door,' she said accusingly.*

accustom /əˈkʌstəm/ VERB [accustoms, accustoming, accustomed] **accustom yourself** to do or experience something often enough for it to become normal to you □ *I'm gradually accustoming myself to the new software.*

• **accustomed** /əˈkʌstəmd/ ADJECTIVE having done or experienced something often enough for it to become normal to you □ *I became accustomed to having to wait.*

ace /eɪs/ ► NOUN [plural **aces**]

1 a playing card with one symbol on it which has the highest or lowest value in games □ *the ace of spades*

2 when a tennis player hits their first shot and the other player cannot hit it back

3 an informal word for someone who is very good at something □ *a Brazilian soccer ace*

▶ ADJECTIVE an informal word that means very good □ *an ace golfer*

ache /eɪk/ ▶ NOUN [*plural* **aches**] a pain which is not strong but continues for a long time 🖬 *I started getting aches and pains.* □ *She could feel an ache in her back.*

▶ VERB [**aches, aching, ached**] to hurt for a long time, especially in a way which is not strong □ *My arm aches from playing too much tennis.*

achieve /ə'tʃiːv/ VERB [**achieves, achieving, achieved**] to succeed in doing or getting something good, especially by trying hard □ *We have achieved everything we set out to do.* □ *She has achieved a very high standard.*

• **achievement** /ə'tʃiːvmənt/ NOUN [*plural* **achievements**]

1 a success or a good result □ *Reaching the finals is a great achievement.*

2 *no plural* having success generally 🖬 *You get an enormous sense of achievement when you finish a project.*

acid /'æsɪd/ NOUN [*plural* **acids**] a type of chemical. Strong acids can dissolve metals. A chemistry word.

• **acidic** /ə'sɪdɪk/ ADJECTIVE

1 containing acid

2 with a strong, sour taste

• **acidity** /ə'sɪdəti/ NOUN, NO PLURAL how much acid a substance contains. A chemistry word.

acid rain /'æsɪd 'reɪn/ NOUN, NO PLURAL rain that contains chemicals from air pollution

acid test /'æsɪd 'test/ NOUN [*plural* **acid tests**] something that will prove something, especially whether something works or not □ *The acid test for the system will be when the public start using it.*

acknowledge /ək'nɒlɪdʒ/ VERB [**acknowledges, acknowledging, acknowledged**]

1 to admit that something is true □ *I acknowledge that you were right.*

2 to tell someone that you have got something they sent you □ *They never acknowledge my letters.*

• **acknowledgement** /ək'nɒlɪdʒmənt/ NOUN [*plural* **acknowledgements**]

1 a message to tell someone that you have received something □ *I sent two letters but only got one acknowledgement.*

2 when you admit that something is true □ *There has been no acknowledgement of the mistake.*

acne /'ækni/ NOUN, NO PLURAL a skin problem that causes spots, usually on someone's face

acorn /'eɪkɔːn/ NOUN [*plural* **acorns**] a type of nut that grows on oak trees

acoustic /ə'kuːstɪk/ ADJECTIVE

1 to do with sound and hearing □ *an acoustic signal*

2 an acoustic musical instrument does not need electricity to work 🖬 *an acoustic guitar*

• **acoustics** /ə'kuːstɪks/ PLURAL NOUN the way a room can make music or speech sound better or worse □ *The concert hall has wonderful acoustics.*

acquaint /ə'kweɪnt/ VERB [**acquaints, acquainting, acquainted**] to tell someone about something. A formal word. □ *Let me acquaint you with the facts.*

• **acquaintance** /ə'kweɪntəns/ NOUN [*plural* **acquaintances**]

1 someone you have met but do not know well □ *He was an acquaintance of the family.*

2 **make someone's acquaintance** to meet someone for the first time. A formal phrase.

• **acquainted** /ə'kweɪntɪd/ ADJECTIVE

1 **be acquainted with someone** to know someone □ *He became acquainted with several well-known writers.*

2 **be acquainted with something** to know about something □ *I am not acquainted with her work.*

acquiesce /ˌækwɪ'es/ VERB [**acquiesces, acquiescing, acquiesced**] a formal word meaning to agree to something, especially when you do not want to □ *He finally acquiesced to their demands.*

• **acquiescence** /ˌækwɪ'esəns/ NOUN, NO PLURAL when you agree to something, especially when you do not want to. A formal word.

acquire /ə'kwaɪə(r)/ VERB [**acquires, acquiring, acquired**]

1 a formal word meaning to get or to buy something □ *I managed to acquire a copy of the tape.* □ *A Russian billionaire recently acquired a 25% stake in the company.*

2 to learn something or to develop something 🖬 *He acquired some new skills.* 🖬 *She soon acquired a taste for Italian food.*

• **acquisition** /ˌækwɪ'zɪʃən/ NOUN [*plural* **acquisitions**]

1 when you get, buy or learn something □ *People protested about the acquisition of land for industry.* □ *language acquisition*

2 something that you get or buy □ *The painting is one of the museum's newest acquisitions.*

• **acquisitive** /ə'kwɪzɪtɪv/ ADJECTIVE always wanting to get and own more things

acquit /ə'kwɪt/ VERB [**acquits, acquitting, acquitted**] to decide in a court that someone did not commit a crime

• **acquittal** /ə'kwɪtəl/ NOUN [*plural* **acquittals**] when someone is acquitted of a crime

acre /'eɪkə(r)/ NOUN [*plural* **acres**] a unit for measuring the area of land, equal to 4840 square yards

acrid /'ækrɪd/ ADJECTIVE an acrid taste or smell is strong and unpleasantly bitter □ *The room began to fill with acrid smoke.*

acrimonious /ˌækrɪ'məʊniəs/ ADJECTIVE an acrimonious discussion or disagreement is full of anger and unfriendly feelings

• **acrimony** /'ækrɪməni/ NOUN, NO PLURAL unfriendly

feelings and disagreement between people □ *Their money discussions usually ended in acrimony.*

acrobat /ˈækrəbæt/ NOUN [plural **acrobats**] someone who performs skilful physical movements, like jumping and balancing, to entertain people

● **acrobatic** /ˌækrəˈbætɪk/ ADJECTIVE to do with skilful physical movements, especially jumping

● **acrobatics** /ˌækrəˈbætɪks/ PLURAL NOUN skilful physical movements like jumping and balancing

acronym /ˈækrənɪm/ NOUN [plural **acronyms**] a word made from the first letters of other words □ *NATO is an acronym for North Atlantic Treaty Organization.*

across /əˈkrɒs/ PREPOSITION, ADVERB

1 from one side of something to the other □ *a bridge across the river* □ *I ran across the road.* □ *Don't run, but walk across quickly.* □ *clouds moving across the sky*
2 on the opposite side □ *Their house is across the river from ours.*

acrylic /əˈkrɪlɪk/ ► NOUN, NO PLURAL a substance used for making some paints and different types of plastic materials

► ADJECTIVE made with acrylic □ *an acrylic sweater*

act /ækt/ ► VERB [**acts, acting, acted**]

1 to behave in a particular way ☐ *Stop acting like a baby!* ☐ *Police thought the man was acting suspiciously.*
2 to do something ☐ *The hospital acted quickly to solve the problem.* □ *We must act now to save the planet!* □ *+ on We were acting on medical advice.*
3 to perform in a film or in the theatre □ *+ in He has acted in more than 50 films.*

◆ PHRASAL VERBS **act as something** to have a particular effect or to do a particular job □ *The security cameras act as a deterrent.* □ *Our local driver also acted as interpreter.* **act up** to behave badly □ *Sam's been acting up at school.*

► NOUN [plural **acts**]

1 something that someone does ☐ *a terrorist act* ☐ *He was accused of committing a criminal act.* □ *+ of an act of kindness*
2 a law ☐ *an act of parliament*
3 a part of a theatre performance □ *He appears in the third act of the play.*
4 a short performance, or the people in the performance □ *a comedy act*

◆ IDIOM **get your act together** to start to do things better and achieve more □ *If you want to keep this job, you'd better get your act together.*

● **acting** /ˈæktɪŋ/ ► NOUN, NO PLURAL performing in films or in the theatre □ *There was some brilliant acting in the film.*

► ADJECTIVE doing someone else's job for a time while they are away □ *the acting headmaster*

action /ˈækʃən/ NOUN [plural **actions**]

1 something you do ☐ *We must take urgent action to prevent a disaster.* ☐ *They need to decide on a course*

of action (= what to do). □ *He has to take responsibility for his actions.*
2 no plural things which are happening □ *Let's see some action around here!*
3 a movement someone or something makes □ *Hit the ball with a swinging action.*
4 a legal process ☐ *She has threatened to take legal action.* □ *a libel action*
5 fighting in a war ☐ *Both soldiers were killed in action.* ☐ *the threat of military action*
6 the action what happens in the story of a film, book or theatre play □ *Most of the action takes place in America.*
7 out of action not working □ *My car's out of action at the moment.*

action replay /ˈækʃən ˈriːpleɪ/ NOUN [plural **action replays**] when part of a film of a sports match is shown again, often more slowly

action stations /ˈækʃən ˈsteɪʃənz/ PLURAL NOUN used to tell people to get into positions ready to do something, especially soldiers getting ready to fight

activate /ˈæktɪveɪt/ VERB [**activates, activating, activated**] to make something start working □ *Someone activated the fire alarm.*

active /ˈæktɪv/ ADJECTIVE

1 busy doing things or involved in an activity □ *+ in Her mum's very active in the drama club.* ☐ *He remained politically active throughout his life.* ☐ *Fathers are taking a more active role in childcare.*
2 moving around a lot ☐ *She's still physically active.* ☐ *Try to keep active as you grow older.*
3 in grammar, an active verb or sentence has a subject that performs the action of the verb, for example in the sentence 'The cat chased the mouse'.

● **actively** /ˈæktɪvli/ ADVERB in a way that involves doing things and trying to have an effect ☐ *We actively encourage patients to ask questions.* ☐ *I became actively involved in local politics.*

activist /ˈæktɪvɪst/ NOUN [plural **activists**] someone who tries to change society by doing things that people notice □ *animal rights activists*

activity /ækˈtɪvəti/ NOUN [plural **activities**]

1 something you do, especially something you do for fun, in an organized way ☐ *Outdoor activities include sailing and waterskiing.* ☐ *a variety of sporting activities*
2 no plural being active or busy generally ☐ *Children need regular physical activity.* ☐ *There was a flurry of activity (= a lot of things happening) for a few days.*

actor /ˈæktə(r)/ NOUN [plural **actors**] someone who performs in a film or in the theatre

actress /ˈæktrɪs/ NOUN [plural **actresses**] a woman who performs in a film or in the theatre

actual /ˈæktʃuəl/ ADJECTIVE

1 really true or exact ☐ *We guessed there were about 100 people but the actual number was 110.*

2 in actual fact used to emphasize the real situation □ *It may look easy, but in actual fact it takes a lot of hard work.*

➤ **Actual** means 'true' or 'exact'. It does not mean 'existing now'. Adjectives that mean 'existing now' are 'present' and 'current':
✓ *My current job involves a lot of travel.*
✗ *My actual job involves a lot of travel.*

● **actuality** /ˌæktʃuˈælətɪ/ NOUN, NO PLURAL
1 a formal word for what is real or a fact
2 in actuality a formal phrase emphasizing that something is true □ *There are fewer cases of real poverty than you'd expect, in actuality.*

● **actually** /ˈæktʃuəlɪ/ ADVERB
1 used to emphasize what is true □ *Actually, I haven't read any of his books.* □ *We haven't actually chosen a name yet.*
2 used to emphasize something surprising □ *Instead of improving, things have actually got worse.*

acumen /ˈækjumən/ NOUN, NO PLURAL someone's ability to judge a situation quickly and correctly and make the right decisions 🕮 *He has business acumen and can turn any idea into a business plan.*

acupuncture /ˈækjupʌŋktʃə(r)/ NOUN, NO PLURAL a treatment for illness where very thin needles are put into your skin at different places on your body

● **acupuncturist** /ˈækjupʌŋktʃərɪst/ NOUN [plural **acupuncturists**] someone who does acupuncture

acute /əˈkjuːt/ ADJECTIVE
1 an acute problem, especially an illness, is very bad □ *acute appendicitis* □ *an acute shortage of nurses*
2 quick to notice or understand something □ *an acute mind* □ *acute eyesight*
3 an acute angle is less than 90°. A maths word.

acute accent /əˈkjuːt ˈæksent/ NOUN [plural **acute accents**] a mark (′) put over a vowel in certain languages, such as French, showing pronunciation, as in 'début' and 'élite'.

acutely /əˈkjuːtlɪ/ ADVERB extremely □ *I felt acutely embarrassed.*

AD /ˌeɪˈdiː/ ABBREVIATION used before or after a date to show that the date was after the birth of Jesus Christ □ *95 AD*

ad /æd/ NOUN [plural **ads**] an informal short way to say or write advertisement

adamant /ˈædəmənt/ ADJECTIVE having a strong opinion or a fixed plan that you will not change □ *I told her it was a bad idea but she was adamant.*

● **adamantly** /ˈædəməntlɪ/ ADVERB in an adamant way □ *She adamantly refused to move.*

Adam's apple /ˈædəmz ˈæpəl/ NOUN [plural **Adam's apples**] the lump you can see at the front of a man's neck

adapt /əˈdæpt/ VERB [adapts, adapting, adapted]
1 to change so that you become more happy or comfortable in a new situation □ *It didn't take long to adapt to the heat.*
2 to change something to make it more suitable □ *The design can be adapted for use in a variety of situations.*

● **adaptable** /əˈdæptəbəl/ ADJECTIVE able to deal with new or different situations

● **adaptation** /ˌædæpˈteɪʃən/ NOUN [plural **adaptations**] a film, TV programme, etc. that is made from a book □ *He is working on a television adaptation of a Roald Dahl novel.*

● **adaptor** /əˈdæptə(r)/ NOUN [plural **adaptors**] something that you attach to the plug (= object with metal pins) of a piece of electrical equipment that allows you to use that equipment in a different country, or allows you to connect many pieces of electrical equipment to one electrical supply

add /æd/ VERB [adds, adding, added]
1 to put things together □ **+ to** *Add the sugar to the egg mixture.*
2 to put two or more numbers or amounts together □ *Add two and two.*
3 to say or write something more □ *'You could take the letter yourself - if you didn't mind?' he added.* □ **+ that** *A police spokesman added that the two arrests weren't linked.*
4 to make something better, bigger, stronger, etc. □ *The latest incident has added to an already nervous atmosphere.* 🕮 *Having the baby has added a new dimension to my life.*

◆ PHRASAL VERBS **add up** to gradually increase to make a large amount □ *All those little costs soon add up.*
add (something) up to find the total of numbers put together □ *Can you add these numbers up in your head?*

adder /ˈædə(r)/ NOUN [plural **adders**] a poisonous snake which lives in the north of Europe and Asia

addict /ˈædɪkt/ NOUN [plural **addicts**]
1 someone who cannot stop taking a drug 🕮 *a drug addict*
2 someone who cannot stop doing or having something they enjoy □ *I'm a sugar addict.*

● **addicted** /əˈdɪktɪd/ ADJECTIVE
1 not able to stop taking a drug □ *He became addicted to drugs.*
2 not able to stop doing or having something you enjoy □ *I'm completely addicted to computer games.*

● **addiction** /əˈdɪkʃən/ NOUN [plural **addictions**]
1 not being able to stop taking a drug □ *alcohol addiction*
2 not being able to stop doing or having something you enjoy

● **addictive** /əˈdɪktɪv/ ADJECTIVE if something is addictive, it makes you want to have it or do it more and more □ *an addictive computer game*

addition /əˈdɪʃən/ NOUN [plural **additions**]
1 in addition (to something) extra or added to

something □ *The schools offer extra subjects in addition to the core curriculum.*

2 *no plural* the process of adding numbers together □ *Pupils learn simple addition and subtraction.*

3 something that has been added or when something is added ⊞ *There are four new additions to our menu.* ⊞ *The changes include the addition of a swimming pool.*

• **additional** /ə'dɪʃənəl/ ADJECTIVE extra □ *They requested additional information.* ⊞ *There are no additional costs.*

• **additionally** /ə'dɪʃənəlɪ/ ADVERB as well as something else □ *Additionally, you have to pay to get in.*

additive /'ædɪtɪv/ NOUN [*plural* **additives**] a substance that is added to food or drinks to make them taste better or stay fresh for longer □ *Our organic cheeses are free from additives.*

add-on /'æd,ɒn/ NOUN [*plural* **add-ons**] a piece of software that is used with other software to make it able to do something extra. A computing word.

address /ə'drɛs/ ► NOUN [*plural* **addresses**]

1 the details of the building, the street and the town where someone lives □ *I'll give you my address and telephone number.* ⊞ *Here is a list of the names and addresses of all the members.*

2 the numbers, letters and symbols that are used to send e-mails or to find pages on the Internet. A computing word ⊞ *What's your e-mail address?* ⊞ *Our web address is in the brochure.*

3 a formal speech

► VERB [**addresses, addressing, addressed**]

1 to write an address on an envelope

2 to deal with a problem ⊞ *The government has failed to address this problem.*

3 to speak to someone □ *Were you addressing me?*

address book /ə'drɛs ,bʊk/ NOUN [*plural* **address books**]

1 a small book in which people's addresses are written

2 a place on a computer where e-mail addresses are kept. A computing word.

adept /ə'dɛpt/ ADJECTIVE very good or skilful at something □ *She'd become adept at hiding her feelings.*

adequate /'ædɪkwət/ ADJECTIVE enough □ *Three rooms should be adequate for our family.* □ *There's an adequate supply of clean water.*

• **adequately** /'ædɪkwətlɪ/ ADVERB in an adequate way □ *The staff were not adequately trained.*

adhere /əd'hɪə(r)/ VERB [**adheres, adhering, adhered**] a formal word meaning to stick firmly to something □ *This glue will adhere to any surface.*

• PHRASAL VERB **adhere to something**

1 to obey a rule or to keep to a plan, arrangement, etc. □ *Visitors must adhere to a strict dress code.*

2 to continue to have a belief, opinion, etc.

• **adherence** /əd'hɪərəns/ NOUN, NO PLURAL when you obey a rule or keep to a plan. A formal word.

• **adherent** /əd'hɪərənt/ NOUN [*plural* **adherents**] a loyal supporter of a political party, belief, etc.

adhesive /əd'hiːsɪv/ ► NOUN [*plural* **adhesives**] a substance used to stick things together

► ADJECTIVE sticky □ *adhesive tape*

ad hoc /,æd'hɒk/ ADJECTIVE used only for a particular situation and not permanent or regular ⊞ *The committee meets on an ad hoc basis to discuss issues which crop up.*

adjacent /ə'dʒeɪsənt/ ADJECTIVE a formal word meaning next to □ *There is a car park adjacent to the hospital.*

adjective /'ædʒɪktɪv/ NOUN [*plural* **adjectives**] a word that tells you something about a noun. For example, *difficult, good* and *stupid* are adjectives.

adjoin /ə'dʒɔɪn/ VERB [**adjoins, adjoining, adjoined**] a formal word that means to be joined to □ *The bathroom adjoins the bedroom.*

• **adjoining** /ə'dʒɔɪnɪŋ/ ADJECTIVE next to and joined to something ⊞ *an adjoining room*

adjourn /ə'dʒɜːn/ VERB [**adjourns, adjourning, adjourned**] to stop a meeting or a court trial which will continue at another time

• **adjournment** /ə'dʒɜːnmənt/ NOUN [*plural* **adjournments**] when a meeting or a trial is adjourned

adjudicate /ə'dʒuːdɪkeɪt/ VERB [**adjudicates, adjudicating, adjudicated**]

1 a formal word meaning to be the official judge of a competition □ *She was invited to adjudicate at the dancing championships.*

2 a formal word meaning to decide officially how a disagreement should be solved

• **adjudicator** /ə'dʒuːdɪkeɪtə(r)/ NOUN [*plural* **adjudicators**] someone who makes official decisions

adjust /ə'dʒʌst/ VERB [**adjusts, adjusting, adjusted**]

1 to change something slightly □ *I adjusted the clock by two minutes.*

2 to get used to a new situation □ *It was difficult to adjust to living in a flat.*

• **adjustable** /ə'dʒʌstəbəl/ ADJECTIVE able to be adjusted to fit something □ *adjustable seat belts*

• **adjustment** /ə'dʒʌstmənt/ NOUN [*plural* **adjustments**]

1 a slight change ⊞ *We've made a few adjustments to the schedule this week.*

2 when someone becomes familiar with a new situation □ *You'll be fine after a short period of adjustment.*

ad-lib /,æd'lɪb/ ► ADVERB done or said without preparation □ *I admire people who can just get up and speak ad-lib in public.*

► VERB [**ad-libs, ad-libbing, ad-libbed**] to speak without preparation, especially in a speech or performance □ *I completely forgot my lines and had to ad-lib for a bit.*

admin /'ædmɪn/ NOUN, NO PLURAL a short way to say and write **administration** (= managing an organization)

administer /əd'mɪnɪstə(r)/ VERB [administers, administering, administered]
1 to manage a company, an organization or a project □ *The free health care service is administered by the regional government.*
2 a formal word meaning to give a medicine to someone □ *The drug should be administered by a doctor.*
• **administration** /əd,mɪnɪ'streɪʃən/ NOUN [plural administrations]
1 the work of planning, organizing and managing an organization □ *So much of my time is taken up with administration, I hardly have time to actually do any work.*
2 the politicians who govern a country □ *the Bush administration*
3 the process of giving something such as medicine to someone
• **administrative** /əd'mɪnɪstrətɪv/ ADJECTIVE to do with the administration of an organization □ *He was hired to take on the administrative work.*
• **administrator** /əd'mɪnɪstreɪtə(r)/ NOUN [plural administrators] someone who does administrative work
admirable /'ædmərəbəl/ ADJECTIVE admirable behaviour is very good and respected by others □ *The way he behaved was admirable.*
• **admirably** /'ædmərəbli/ ADVERB very well □ *She coped admirably in a difficult situation.*
admiral /'ædmərəl/ NOUN [plural admirals] one of the most important officers in the navy
admiration /,ædmə'reɪʃən/ NOUN, NO PLURAL a feeling of admiring someone or something □ *+ for I have the greatest admiration for her work.*
admire /əd'maɪə(r)/ VERB [admires, admiring, admired]
1 to like and respect someone or something very much □ *He was someone I admired greatly.* □ *+ for I admired her for her courage in speaking out.*
2 to enjoy looking at something ▣ *We stopped at the top of the hill to admire the view.*
• **admirer** /əd'maɪərə(r)/ NOUN [plural admirers] a person who likes someone or something very much
• **admiring** /əd'maɪərɪŋ/ ADJECTIVE showing admiration □ *admiring glances*
admissible /əd'mɪsəbəl/ ADJECTIVE a formal word meaning acceptable or allowed □ *evidence that is admissible in a court of law*
admission /əd'mɪʃən/ NOUN [plural admissions]
1 when someone goes into a place or joins a club, university, etc. □ *A sign on the door said 'No admission'.* □ *the university admissions process*
2 no plural the cost of going into a place □ *We don't charge admission here.* □ *Adult admission is £10.*
3 when you admit that something bad is true □ *+ that We were surprised by his admission that he had done it.* ▣ *He had, by his own admission, played badly.* □ *+ of They have made no admission of guilt.*

admit /əd'mɪt/ VERB [admits, admitting, admitted]
1 to agree that you have done something bad □ *+ (that) I admit that I should have told you sooner.* □ *+ to She admitted to cheating.* □ *He admitted his mistake.*
2 to agree that something is true □ *I admit that this is a difficult exercise, but do your best.*
3 to allow someone to go into a place or to take someone to hospital □ *They won't admit anyone wearing trainers.* □ *+ to The next morning he was admitted to hospital.*
• **admittance** /əd'mɪtəns/ NOUN, NO PLURAL being allowed to go into a place □ *No admittance for anyone under 18.*
• **admittedly** /əd'mɪtɪdli/ ADVERB used to say that you agree that something is true □ *Admittedly, I wasn't there at the time, but I believe him.*

admonish /əd'mɒnɪʃ/ VERB [admonishes, admonishing, admonished] a formal word meaning to tell someone that they have done something wrong □ *He was officially admonished for wasting the club's money.*
ado /ə'duː/ NOUN without further/more ado without waiting any longer
adolescence /,ædə'lesəns/ NOUN, NO PLURAL the time between being a child and being an adult
• **adolescent** /,ædə'lesənt/ ▶ NOUN [plural adolescents] someone older than a child, but not yet an adult ▶ ADJECTIVE to do with adolescents □ *adolescent girls/boys*
adopt /ə'dɒpt/ VERB [adopts, adopting, adopted]
1 to take someone else's child into your family and legally become their parent □ *I was ten before I knew I had been adopted.*
2 to start doing something in a new way □ *We must adopt new methods of fighting crime.*
• **adoption** /ə'dɒpʃən/ NOUN [plural adoptions]
1 when a child is adopted
2 starting to use something new
• **adoptive** /ə'dɒptɪv/ ADJECTIVE being a relation because of an adoption □ *my adoptive mother/ parents* □ *an adoptive son/daughter*
adorable /ə'dɔːrəbəl/ ADJECTIVE if something or someone is adorable, they are very attractive and you like them very much □ *an adorable baby boy*
adoration /,ædə'reɪʃən/ NOUN, NO PLURAL loving someone or something very much □ *a look of adoration*
adore /ə'dɔː(r)/ VERB [adores, adoring, adored] to love something or someone very much □ *She just adores her father.*
• **adoring** /ə'dɔːrɪŋ/ ADJECTIVE showing great love □ *Her adoring fans crowded the streets.*
adorn /ə'dɔːn/ VERB [adorns, adorning, adorned] to decorate something □ *Their hair was adorned with flowers.*
• **adornment** /ə'dɔːnmənt/ NOUN [plural

adornments] a decoration, or the process of decorating something

adrenalin *or* **adrenaline** /ə'drenəlɪn/ NOUN, NO PLURAL a chemical your body produces when you are afraid, angry or excited. A biology word.

adrift /ə'drɪft/ ADJECTIVE, ADVERB a boat that is adrift is not tied up and is floating in the water □ *They spent three weeks adrift on the ocean.*

adulation /ˌædjʊ'leɪʃən/ NOUN, NO PLURAL a lot of praise from people

adult /'ædʌlt/ ▶ NOUN [*plural* **adults**]
1 someone who is no longer a child □ *The activity is suitable for adults and children.*
2 an animal that is completely grown □ *adult rabbits*
▶ ADJECTIVE to do with or for adults □ *adult sizes* □ *It's aimed at a more adult audience.*

adulterate /ə'dʌltəreɪt/ VERB [**adulterates, adulterating, adulterated**] to make something, for example food or drink, less pure by adding something to it □ *The cooking oil had been adulterated with a poisonous substance.*

adulthood /'ædʌlthʊd/ NOUN, NO PLURAL the period of time in your life when you are an adult

advance /əd'vɑːns/ ▶ NOUN [*plural* **advances**]
1 in advance before something is needed or before a particular time □ *I arrived in advance to make sure everything was ready.* □ *We prepared all the food in advance.*
2 progress or new things □ *technological advances* □ *We have to keep up with the latest advances in medicine.*
3 money paid before the usual time □ *I asked for an advance of £50 on my salary.*
4 a movement towards a place by an army □ *The troops continued their advance on the city.*
▶ VERB [**advances, advancing, advanced**]
1 to make progress □ *Technology is advancing rapidly.*
2 to move forwards □ *The crowd advanced towards us.* □ *The army is advancing on our borders.*
▶ ADJECTIVE happening before an event 🔁 *If you want to bring a friend, can you give us some advance warning?*

• **advanced** /əd'vɑːnst/ ADJECTIVE
1 the newest or most developed □ *the most technologically advanced facilities*
2 at a high academic level □ *an advanced Spanish course* □ *advanced students*
3 if an illness is at an advanced stage, it is already very bad

advantage /əd'vɑːntɪdʒ/ NOUN [*plural* **advantages**]
1 something good or helpful about a situation □ *+ of* the advantages of working from home □ *Being tall does have some advantages.*
2 something that makes you more likely to succeed □ *+ over* Max had an advantage over the others as he already spoke Italian. 🔁 *Her long legs give her an advantage in the high jump.* 🔁 *an unfair advantage*

3 take advantage of something to use a situation well □ *We took advantage of the sunshine to get the clothes dry.*
4 take advantage of someone to get what you want from someone in an unfair way □ *She's very generous and her children take advantage of her.*

• **advantageous** /ˌædvən'teɪdʒəs/ ADJECTIVE helping you to succeed □ *It would not be advantageous for you to go abroad at this stage in your career.*

advent /'ædvənt/ NOUN, NO PLURAL
1 the start of something □ *the advent of television*
2 Advent the four weeks before Christmas

adventure /əd'ventʃə(r)/ NOUN [*plural* **adventures**] something exciting that happens to you □ *A jungle visit would be a real adventure for us.*

• **adventurous** /əd'ventʃərəs/ ADJECTIVE an adventurous person likes to do exciting new things □ *He's more adventurous than his brother.*

adverb /'ædvɜːb/ NOUN [*plural* **adverbs**] a word that you use to describe a verb or an adjective. For example, *really, badly, abroad* and *often* are adverbs.

adversary /'ædvəsəri/ NOUN [*plural* **adversaries**] a formal word for an enemy or someone you compete against

adverse /'ædvɜːs/ ADJECTIVE negative or causing you problems 🔁 *All this worry is likely to have an adverse effect on her health.* 🔁 *It's amazing how the schoolchildren learn anything in such adverse conditions.*

• **adversely** /'ædvɜːsli/ ADVERB in a negative way □ *I'm afraid their advertising campaign has affected our sales adversely.*

adversity /əd'vɜːsəti/ NOUN, NO PLURAL a formal word for a very difficult situation 🔁 *She struggled on bravely in the face of adversity.*

advert /'ædvɜːt/ NOUN [*plural* **adverts**] a short word for an advertisement

advertise /'ædvətaɪz/ VERB [**advertises, advertising, advertised**]
1 to tell people about something in order to persuade them to buy it or use it □ *They advertise their products in magazines.*
2 if you advertise for something, you put information in a newspaper, on the Internet, etc. to try to get something you want □ *We decided to advertise for a gardener.*

• **advertisement** /əd'vɜːtɪsmənt/ NOUN [*plural* **advertisements**] a picture, short article or film about something to persuade people to buy it or use it 🔁 *television/newspaper advertisement* □ *+ for* I saw an advertisement for a new chocolate bar.

• **advertiser** /'ædvətaɪzə(r)/ NOUN [*plural* **advertisers**] someone who advertises something

• **advertising** /'ædvətaɪzɪŋ/ NOUN, NO PLURAL the business of making advertisements □ *She works in advertising.* 🔁 *an advertising campaign*

advice /əd'vaɪs/ NOUN, NO PLURAL suggestions about what you think someone should do 🕮 *She gave me some good advice.* 🕮 *I decided to take Jane's advice and go to the doctor's.* 🕮 *May I offer a piece of advice?* □ **+ on** *They provide expert advice on career development.*

> ► Remember that **advice** with a **c** is a noun and **advise** with an **s** is a verb: □ *Can you give me some advice?* □ *Can you advise me?*

> ► Remember also that you say **any/some advice** and not 'an advice':
> ✓ *Can I give you some advice?*
> ✗ *Can I give you an advice?*
> ► To talk about one particular suggestion, use **piece of advice**: □ *Can I give you a piece of advice?*

advisable /əd'vaɪzəbəl/ ADJECTIVE if something is advisable, it will avoid problems if you do it □ *It is advisable to book tickets early.*

advise /əd'vaɪz/ VERB [**advises, advising, advised**] to tell someone what you think they should do □ **+ to do something** *They are advising motorists to drive carefully.* □ **+ against** *We advise against all travel to the region.* □ **+ on** *He advises us on financial matters.*
• **adviser** *or* **advisor** /əd'vaɪzə(r)/ NOUN [*plural* **advisers** *or* **advisors**] someone whose job is to give advice about a particular subject □ *financial/security advisers*
• **advisory** /əd'vaɪzəri/ ADJECTIVE to do with giving advice □ *an advisory body*

advocate ► VERB /'ædvəkeɪt/ [**advocates, advocating, advocated**] to express support for an idea □ *We don't advocate giving up meat completely.*
► NOUN /'ædvəkət/ [*plural* **advocates**]
1 someone who supports an idea □ *He is an outspoken advocate of tax cuts.*
2 in Scotland, a lawyer

aerate /'eəreɪt/ VERB [**aerates, aerating, aerated**] to put air into something such as soil or a liquid. A biology word.

aerial /'eəriəl/ ► NOUN [*plural* **aerials**] a piece of metal equipment for getting or sending radio or television signals 🕮 *a television aerial*
► ADJECTIVE from the air □ *an aerial photograph*

aero- /'eərə/ PREFIX aero- is added to the start of words to mean 'to do with air or flying' □ *aeroplane*

aerobatics /ˌeərəʊ'bætɪks/ PLURAL NOUN flying with skilful movements in an aeroplane

aerobic /eə'rəʊbɪk/ ADJECTIVE
1 aerobic exercise makes your heart and lungs stronger
2 using or needing oxygen. A biology word.

aerobic respiration /eə'rəʊbɪk respə'reɪʃən/ NOUN, NO PLURAL when the body uses oxygen to make energy from food. A biology word.

aerobics /eə'rəʊbɪks/ PLURAL NOUN exercises for the whole body that make your heart and lungs work hard

aerodrome /'eərədrəʊm/ NOUN [*plural* **aerodromes**] a small airport for private aeroplanes

aerodynamic /ˌeərəʊdaɪ'næmɪk/ ADJECTIVE aerodynamic objects are able to move easily through the air. A physics word. □ *an aerodynamic design*
• **aerodynamically** /ˌeərəʊdaɪ'næmɪklɪ/ ADVERB in a way that moves easily through the air. A physics word.
• **aerodynamics** /ˌeərəʊdaɪ'næmɪks/ PLURAL NOUN the study of the way objects move through the air. A physics word.

aeroplane /'eərəpleɪn/ NOUN [*plural* **aeroplanes**] a flying vehicle that has wings and an engine □ *The aeroplane took off at midday.*

aerosol /'eərəsɒl/ NOUN [*plural* **aerosols**] a container with a part that you press to let out very small drops of liquid

aesthetic /iːs'θetɪk/ ADJECTIVE to do with beauty, art and the appearance of things
• **aesthetically** /iːs'θetɪkəlɪ/ ADVERB in a way that is to do with beauty and appearance □ *an aesthetically pleasing design*

afar /ə'fɑː(r)/ ADVERB from afar a formal phrase meaning from a long distance away

affair /ə'feə(r)/ NOUN [*plural* **affairs**]
1 affairs events or activities in a particular area of life, business, politics, etc. 🕮 *He is very interested in foreign affairs* (= international politics). 🕮 *She was responsible for the financial affairs of the club.*
2 a situation or an event, especially a problem or something bad □ *Some people have criticized the way he handled the affair.*
3 a sexual relationship between two people, especially when one or both of them is married to someone else 🕮 *She had an affair with an older man.*
4 be someone's (own) affair used to say that something is personal and private □ *Her private life is her own affair.*

affect /ə'fekt/ VERB [**affects, affecting, affected**] to change, influence or cause harm to someone or something □ *The accident affected his eyesight.* □ *Were you affected by the floods?*

> ► Be careful not to confuse **affect**, which is a verb, with **effect**, which is a noun: □ *One thing affects another.* □ *One thing has an effect on another.*

affectation /ˌæfek'teɪʃən/ NOUN [*plural* **affectations**] behaviour that is not natural and is done only to impress other people □ *Her silly laugh is clearly an affectation.*

affection /ə'fekʃən/ NOUN, NO PLURAL a strong feeling of liking someone or something □ *I have great affection for the town.* □ *My father rarely showed his affection.*
• **affectionate** /ə'fekʃənət/ ADJECTIVE showing that

you like or love someone □ *Her mother gave her an affectionate kiss.*

• **affectionately** /ə'fekʃənətlɪ/ ADVERB in an affectionate way □ *Joe scratched the cat's head affectionately.*

affiliated /ə'fɪlɪeɪtɪd/ ADJECTIVE officially connected with another organization □ *The school is affiliated to the local college.*

• **affiliation** /ə,fɪlɪ'eɪʃən/ NOUN [plural **affiliations**] a connection between two or more organizations

affinity /ə'fɪnətɪ/ NOUN [plural **affinities**] a feeling of close connection with someone or something □ *She had always felt a deep affinity with horses.*

affirm /ə'fɜ:m/ VERB [**affirms, affirming, affirmed**] a formal word meaning to say clearly that something is true □ *He affirmed his continued support for the team's manager.*

• **affirmation** /,æfə'meɪʃən/ NOUN, NO PLURAL when you show that you agree with something □ *She signalled her affirmation with a nod.*

affirmative /ə'fɜ:mətɪv/ ▶ ADJECTIVE an affirmative reply, word or gesture (= body movement) is one that says 'yes'. A formal word.

▶ NOUN [plural **affirmatives**]

1 the word 'yes', or any word or gesture (= body movement) meaning 'yes'. A formal word.

2 in the affirmative by saying 'yes' or showing agreement □ *Peter answered in the affirmative.*

affix ▶ VERB /ə'fɪks/ [**affixes, affixing, affixed**] a formal word meaning to attach something □ *Affix stamp here.*

▶ NOUN /'æfɪks/ [plural **affixes**] a part added to the beginning or the end of a word to give it an extra meaning

afflict /ə'flɪkt/ VERB [**afflicts, afflicting, afflicted**] a formal word meaning to make someone suffer from something □ *This is a disease that can afflict anyone.*

• **affliction** /ə'flɪkʃən/ NOUN [plural **afflictions**] an illness or problem that makes someone suffer

affluence /'æfluəns/ NOUN, NO PLURAL having a lot of money to spend □ *There was greater affluence after the war.*

• **affluent** /'æfluənt/ ADJECTIVE having a lot of money □ *an affluent area of the city*

afford /ə'fɔ:d/ VERB [**affords, affording, afforded**]

1 if you can afford something, you have enough money to pay for it □ *I can't afford a new dress.* □ + *to do something We couldn't afford to go abroad.*

2 to be able to do something without it causing problems □ + *to do something We can't afford to make any mistakes.* □ *We can afford to wait a bit longer.*

• **affordable** /ə'fɔ:dəbəl/ ADJECTIVE at a low enough price for most people □ *affordable accommodation*

affront /ə'frʌnt/ ▶ VERB [**affronts, affronting, affronted**] to offend someone □ *Brenda was affronted by his remark.*

▶ NOUN [plural **affronts**] something that offends

someone □ *They see the book as an affront to their culture.*

afield /ə'fiːld/ ADVERB far/further afield a long distance away ⊞ *Some people had travelled from as far afield as Australia and South Africa.*

afloat /ə'fləʊt/ ADVERB

1 floating on water ⊞ *He held on to a piece of wood to stay afloat.*

2 with enough money to continue a business ⊞ *He's struggling to keep his business afloat.*

afoot /ə'fʊt/ ADJECTIVE happening now or being planned □ *Plans are afoot for a concert in Beijing.*

afraid /ə'freɪd/ ADJECTIVE

1 frightened or worried □ *There's no need to be afraid.* □ + *of Small children are often afraid of dogs.* □ + *that I was afraid that I'd fall.* □ + *to do something Don't be afraid to tell me if you don't understand.*

2 I'm afraid used to tell someone in a polite way that you cannot do something or to give them bad news □ *I'm afraid I don't know.* □ *Helen can't come, I'm afraid.* □ + *that I'm afraid that I can't tell you any more now.*

afresh /ə'freʃ/ ADVERB once again □ *Throw that away and begin afresh.*

African /'æfrɪkən/ ▶ ADJECTIVE belonging to or from Africa □ *an African country*

▶ NOUN [plural **Africans**] a person from Africa

Afro- /'æfrəʊ/ PREFIX Afro- is added to the start of words to mean 'from or to do with Africa' □ *Afro-Caribbean* (= with African and Caribbean origins)

after /'ɑ:ftə(r)/ ▶ PREPOSITION

1 when something has happened □ *I'll do it after dinner.* □ *It rained day after day.*

2 after an hour/three days, etc. when an hour/three days, etc. have passed

3 following in order □ *Your name's after mine on the list.*

4 following someone or something □ *We ran after the man.*

5 used in US English to talk about the time when it is minutes past the hour □ *It's ten after eight.*

6 after all used to talk about something that happened or was true although you did not expect it to be □ *I decided to go to the party after all.*

▶ ADVERB following in time □ *Can you come the week after?*

▶ CONJUNCTION when something has happened □ *Mrs Shaw died after we moved.* □ *After we'd said goodbye, we felt quite sad.*

► Use the phrases **a week/month, etc. from now** or **in a week's/month's, etc. time** to talk about a time in the future that you are measuring from now. Do not say 'after a week/month, etc.' to mean this □ *A week from now my exams will all be finished.*

✓ *In a week's time my exams will all be finished.*

✗ *After a week my exams will all be finished.*

after- /'ɑːftə(r)/ PREFIX after- is added to the start of words to mean 'after' or 'later' □ *afternoon* □ *afterthought*

after-effects /'ɑːftərɪˌfekts/ PLURAL NOUN bad things that happen after and because of something else

aftermath /'ɑːftəmæθ/ NOUN, NO PLURAL the aftermath the situation that exists after something bad has happened 🔄 *There was panic and confusion in the aftermath of the earthquake.*

afternoon /ˌɑːftə'nuːn/ ▶ NOUN [plural afternoons]
1 the time between the middle of the day and the evening □ *I saw him on Monday afternoon.* □ *We finish at 4 o'clock in the afternoon.* 🔄 *What are you doing this afternoon?*
2 **Good afternoon** used to say 'hello' when you meet someone in the afternoon
▶ ADJECTIVE happening in the afternoon □ *afternoon classes*

aftershave /'ɑːftəʃeɪv/ NOUN, NO PLURAL a liquid with a pleasant smell which men put on their skin after shaving

aftershock /'ɑːftəʃɒk/ NOUN [plural aftershocks] a small earthquake (= when the ground shakes) that happens after a larger earthquake

afterthought /'ɑːftəθɔːt/ NOUN [plural afterthoughts] something you do or say later 🔄 *'You could come too,' he suggested as an afterthought.*

afterwards /'ɑːftəwədz/ ADVERB later or after something else □ *He's busy now but I'll speak to him afterwards.* □ *They moved to Paris and soon afterwards they got married.*

again /ə'gen/ ADVERB
1 once more □ *Do it again!* □ *Will I see you again?*
2 in the same place or situation as before □ *Can we go home again now?*
3 **again and again** many times □ *I've told you again and again to tidy your room!*

> ► Remember that **again** meaning 'once more' usually comes after the object in a sentence:
> ✓ *I'd like to visit France again.*
> ✗ *I'd like to visit again France.*
> ✓ *We could have pizza again.*
> ✗ *We could have again pizza.*

against /ə'genst/ PREPOSITION
1 leaning on, touching or hitting something □ *She was throwing a ball against the wall.* □ *He was sitting with his back against a tree.*
2 competing or fighting with someone □ *Liverpool are playing against Barcelona.* □ *We all support the fight against racism.*
3 disagreeing with a plan or situation □ *I'm against the ban on hunting.*
4 **against the law/rules** not allowed by the laws/rules □ *Smoking on the train is against the law.*

age /eɪdʒ/ ▶ NOUN [plural ages]
1 how old someone or something is 🔄 *Zoe will start school at the age of four.* 🔄 *He's 19 years of age.* □ **+ of** *Do you know the age of the building?* 🔄 *It's suitable for children of all ages.* 🔄 *He reaches retirement age next year.*
2 **ages/an age** an informal word meaning a very long time □ *I haven't seen Alex for ages.* 🔄 *You took ages to finish.* □ *The tickets sold out ages ago.* □ *We had to wait an age for him to come out.*
3 a period of time in history □ *the Stone Age*
4 **under age** not legally old enough to do something □ *You can't buy beer – you're under age.*
5 **come of age** to become an adult
▶ VERB [ages, aging or ageing, aged] to become older or to look older □ *She's aged a lot recently.*
● **aged** /eɪdʒd/ ADJECTIVE used to say how many years old someone is □ *They have two children aged eight and three.* 🔄 *young people aged between 18 and 25*
● **aged** /'eɪdʒɪd/ ▶ ADJECTIVE very old □ *She looks after her aged mother.*
▶ NOUN **the aged** old people
● **ageing** /'eɪdʒɪŋ/ ADJECTIVE becoming or looking older □ *an ageing actor*
● **ageism** /'eɪdʒɪzəm/ NOUN, NO PLURAL treating old people unfairly because of their age

agency /'eɪdʒənsɪ/ NOUN [plural agencies]
1 a business that provides a particular service □ *an employment agency* □ *an advertising agency*
2 an organization that is part of a government or is controlled by a government □ *the UN refugee agency*
➡ go to **travel agency**

agenda /ə'dʒendə/ NOUN [plural agendas]
1 a list of things to be discussed at a meeting 🔄 *What's on the agenda today?*
2 things that need to be done or discussed 🔄 *Getting more schools built is high on the country's agenda.*

agent /'eɪdʒənt/ NOUN [plural agents]
1 someone who does business for another person or company □ *Our overseas agents sell the books for us.*
2 someone who collects secret information for a government 🔄 *a secret agent*
3 a substance that has a particular effect □ *a cleaning agent*
➡ go to **travel agent**, **estate agent**

aggravate /'ægrəveɪt/ VERB [aggravates, aggravating, aggravated]
1 to make something worse □ *He aggravated the injury during training.*
2 to annoy someone □ *He really aggravates me sometimes.*
● **aggravation** /ˌægrə'veɪʃən/ NOUN, NO PLURAL annoying problems □ *That man has caused a lot of aggravation today.*

aggregate /'ægrɪgət/ NOUN [plural aggregates] a total

aggression /əˈɡreʃən/ NOUN, NO PLURAL behaviour that is angry and threatening

• **aggressive** /əˈɡresɪv/ ADJECTIVE angry and threatening 🔁 *aggressive behaviour*

• **aggressively** /əˈɡresɪvli/ ADVERB in a threatening way □ *He was shouting aggressively.*

• **aggressor** /əˈɡresə(r)/ NOUN [plural **aggressors**] someone who attacks someone else

aggrieved /əˈɡriːvd/ ADJECTIVE upset because someone has been unfair to you

aghast /əˈɡɑːst/ ADJECTIVE very surprised and shocked □ *She stared at him, aghast.*

agile /ˈædʒaɪl/ ADJECTIVE

1 good at moving about quickly and easily □ *He's an agile climber.*

2 able to think quickly □ *an agile mind*

• **agility** /əˈdʒɪləti/ NOUN, NO PLURAL being agile

aging /ˈeɪdʒɪŋ/ ADJECTIVE the US spelling of ageing

agitate /ˈædʒɪteɪt/ VERB [**agitates, agitating, agitated**]

1 to try to get social or political changes □ *We must agitate for a change in the law.*

2 to make someone nervous and upset

• **agitated** /ˈædʒɪteɪtɪd/ ADJECTIVE nervous and upset □ *I started to get agitated when nobody answered the door.*

• **agitation** /ˌædʒɪˈteɪʃən/ NOUN, NO PLURAL a feeling of being nervous and upset □ *She tried to hide her agitation.*

AGM /ˌeɪdʒiːˈem/ ABBREVIATION annual general meeting; an important meeting that an organization has once a year

agnostic /æɡˈnɒstɪk/ NOUN [plural **agnostics**] someone who believes nobody can know if God exists or not

ago /əˈɡəʊ/ ADVERB used to say how long in the past something happened □ *I last saw Lily ten years ago.* 🔁 *That all seems a long time ago.*

agog /əˈɡɒɡ/ ADJECTIVE excited and interested □ *The audience were agog with curiosity.*

agonize or **agonise** /ˈæɡənaɪz/ VERB [**agonizes, agonizing, agonized**] to worry about making a difficult decision □ *She agonized over what to say to him.*

• **agonizing** or **agonising** /ˈæɡənaɪzɪŋ/ ADJECTIVE

1 extremely difficult or upsetting □ *an agonizing decision*

2 extremely painful

agony /ˈæɡəni/ NOUN, NO PLURAL very great pain □ *You could see he was in agony.*

agoraphobia /ˌæɡərəˈfəʊbiə/ NOUN, NO PLURAL people who have agoraphobia are afraid of being in open spaces or of going outside

• **agoraphobic** /ˌæɡərəˈfəʊbɪk/ ADJECTIVE suffering from agoraphobia

agree /əˈɡriː/ VERB [**agrees, agreeing, agreed**]

1 to have the same opinion as someone else about something □ **+ with** *She never agrees with him about anything.* □ **+ about** *I'm glad we agree about something.*

2 to say that you will do what someone has asked you to □ **+ to do something** *I only agreed to come if you came too.*

3 to decide something together with someone □ **+ on** *They couldn't agree on a name for the baby.* □ *Doctors have agreed a pay deal.*

• **agreeable** /əˈɡriːəbəl/ ADJECTIVE

1 possible to agree on □ *We need to find a solution that is agreeable to both sides.*

2 pleasant □ *He was very agreeable.*

• **agreeably** /əˈɡriːəbli/ ADVERB in a pleasant way □ *The holidays passed very agreeably.*

• **agreement** /əˈɡriːmənt/ NOUN [plural **agreements**]

1 a decision or a promise between two or more people □ **+ between** *a trade agreement between Canada and the US* □ **+ with** *We have an agreement with the local sports club.* 🔁 *The two companies have reached an agreement.*

2 no plural when people have the same opinion □ *There was no agreement about what to do.*

3 in agreement if people are in agreement, they agree with each other

agricultural /ˌæɡrɪˈkʌltʃərəl/ ADJECTIVE to do with farming □ *agricultural land*

agriculture /ˈæɡrɪˌkʌltʃə(r)/ NOUN, NO PLURAL the work of farming

aground /əˈɡraʊnd/ ADJECTIVE, ADVERB if a ship is aground it is stuck because the water is not deep enough 🔁 *The boat ran aground in stormy weather.*

ahead /əˈhed/ ADVERB

1 in front □ *Run on ahead and tell them we're coming.* 🔁 *Our house is straight ahead.*

2 in the future □ **+ of** *We've got a long journey ahead of us.* 🔁 *We're planning for the year ahead.*

3 in a better position in a race, competition, etc. □ **+ of** *They are four points ahead of their main rivals.* □ *Jones put United ahead with a goal in the first half.*

4 before □ **+ of** *Everyone was nervous ahead of the first performance.*

AI /ˈeɪˈaɪ/ ABBREVIATION artificial intelligence; the use of computers that try to act like human brains

aid /eɪd/ NOUN [plural **aids**]

1 help 🔁 *He can walk with the aid of a stick.* 🔁 *Mr Oliver came to our aid* (= helped us).

2 money, food, etc. that is sent to places that need it □ *Many countries will send aid to the disaster area.*

3 in aid of someone/something in order to collect money for someone/something □ *a collection in aid of the crash victims*

4 something you use to help you do something □ *a teaching aid*

▶ VERB [**aids, aiding, aided**] to help someone □ *Gentle exercise will aid your recovery.*

aide /eɪd/ NOUN [plural **aides**] someone whose job is to give help and advice, especially to a politician

AIDS or **Aids** /eɪdz/ ABBREVIATION Acquired Immune Deficiency Syndrome; an illness that makes the body unable to fight disease

ailing /'eɪlɪŋ/ ADJECTIVE ill or weak □ *He knew he should visit his ailing mother.* □ *an ailing business*

ailment /'eɪlmənt/ NOUN [*plural* **ailments**] an illness 🔁 *a minor ailment*

aim /eɪm/ ► VERB [**aims, aiming, aimed**]
1 to intend or to hope to do something □ *+ to do something We aim to help all our customers.* □ *+ for She's aiming for a medal at the next Olympics.*
2 be aimed at someone/something to be intended for a particular person, group or purpose □ *The magazine is aimed at 16 to 24-year-olds.* □ *+ ing The scheme is aimed at cutting traffic.*
3 to point a weapon at someone or something □ *+ at Paul was aiming at the target but missed it completely.*
► NOUN [*plural* **aims**]
1 what you are trying to achieve □ *+ of The aim of the project is to encourage healthy eating.* 🔁 *My main aim is to get fit.* 🔁 *We have achieved our aim.*
2 someone's ability to hit something when they throw, shoot, etc. □ *He has a good aim.*
3 take aim to point a weapon at someone or something □ *+ at He took aim at the open window.*
• **aimless** /'eɪmlɪs/ ADJECTIVE having no purpose □ *an aimless stroll*
• **aimlessly** /'eɪmlɪslɪ/ ADVERB without a reason □ *She walked aimlessly around the house.*

ain't /eɪnt/ an informal short way to say and write 'am not', 'are not', 'is not', 'has not' or 'have not' □ *Ain't he clever?* □ *You ain't lived yet.*

air /eə(r)/ ► NOUN
1 *no plural* the gases around us that we breathe in 🔁 *Kelly went outside to get some fresh air.* □ *The air carries the seeds for miles.*
2 the air the space above you □ *He put his hand in the air.* □ *Police fired into the air.*
3 *no plural* travel in an aircraft □ *The food is transported by air.* 🔁 *air travel*
4 an appearance or quality □ *+ of She has an air of mystery about her.*
5 on (the) air being broadcast on radio or television
♦ IDIOM up in the air not decided yet □ *Our holiday plans are still up in the air.*
► VERB [**airs, airing, aired**]
1 to broadcast something on television or radio □ *The show airs twice a week.* □ *The interview was aired on television.*
2 to tell people your opinion 🔁 *Everyone will have a chance to air their views.*
3 to hang clothes somewhere to make them completely dry
4 to let some fresh air into a room

airbag /'eəbæg/ NOUN [*plural* **airbags**] a bag that fills with air to protect passengers in a car accident
airbed /'eəbed/ NOUN [*plural* **airbeds**] a mattress (= soft thing to sleep on) filled with air

airborne /'eəbɔ:n/ ADJECTIVE
1 when an aircraft is airborne, it is flying
2 moving in the air □ *airborne diseases*

air-conditioned /'eəkən,dɪʃənd/ ADJECTIVE air-conditioned vehicles or buildings have a system for keeping the air cool □ *an air-conditioned office*
• **air conditioning** /'eəkən,dɪʃənɪŋ/ NOUN, NO PLURAL a system for keeping the air cool in vehicles or buildings

aircraft /'eəkrɑ:ft/ NOUN [*plural* **aircraft**] a vehicle that can fly 🔁 *a commercial aircraft* 🔁 *a military aircraft*

aircraft carrier /'eəkrɑ:ft ˈkærɪə(r)/ NOUN [*plural* **aircraft carriers**] a military ship on which aircraft can take off and land

airfield /'eəfi:ld/ NOUN [*plural* **airfields**] a place used by private or military aircraft for taking off and landing

air force /'eə ˈfɔ:s/ NOUN [*plural* **air forces**] a military organization that uses aircraft

air freshener /'eə ˈfreʃənə(r)/ NOUN [*plural* **air fresheners**] a substance that is used to get rid of bad smells from rooms, cars, etc.

airgun /'eəgʌn/ NOUN [*plural* **airguns**] a gun that uses air pressure to fire bullets

airing /'eərɪŋ/ NOUN [*plural* **airings**] when something is discussed in public or broadcast on television or radio □ *The film gets its first airing on British television this week.*

airing cupboard /'eərɪŋ ˈkʌbəd/ NOUN [*plural* **airing cupboards**] a heated cupboard for putting clean clothes in to dry completely

airless /'eəlɪs/ ADJECTIVE an airless room does not have enough fresh air

airlift /'eəlɪft/ ► VERB [**airlifts, airlifting, airlifted**] to take people or things somewhere by aircraft □ *The soldiers were airlifted to safety*
► NOUN [*plural* **airlifts**] when goods or people are airlifted

airline /'eəlaɪn/ NOUN [*plural* **airlines**] a company that takes people or goods to places by plane 🔁 *a low-cost airline* 🔁 *an airline ticket* 🔁 *an airline pilot*
• **airliner** /'eəlaɪnə(r)/ NOUN [*plural* **airliners**] a large aeroplane for passengers

airmail /'eəmeɪl/ NOUN, NO PLURAL the system of sending letters and packages by aeroplane □ *I'll send you the book by airmail.*

airplane /'eəpleɪn/ NOUN [*plural* **airplanes**] the US word for an aeroplane

airport /'eəpɔ:t/ NOUN [*plural* **airports**] a place where passengers get on and off aircraft □ *She arrived at the city's international airport.*

air raid /'eə ˈreɪd/ NOUN [*plural* **air raids**] an attack by military aircraft

airship /'eəʃɪp/ NOUN [*plural* **airships**] a large aircraft filled with a light gas for carrying things or people

airspace /ˈeəspeɪs/ NOUN, NO PLURAL the part of the sky over a particular country

airtight /ˈeətaɪt/ ADJECTIVE made so that air cannot pass in or out 🔁 *an airtight container*

air-traffic control /ˈeə ˈtræfɪk kənˈtrəʊl/ NOUN, NO PLURAL the system of making sure aircraft can land or take off safely, or the people who do this
• **air traffic controller** /ˈeə ˈtræfɪk kənˈtrəʊlə(r)/ NOUN [*plural* **air traffic controllers**] a person whose job is to do air traffic control

airwaves /ˈeəweɪvz/ PLURAL NOUN radio waves used for sending radio and television broadcasts □ *It's the only topic of debate on the nation's airwaves.*

airy /ˈeərɪ/ ADJECTIVE [**airier, airiest**]
1 with a lot of space and air □ *The room is bright and airy.*
2 showing that you are not worried about anything □ *an airy wave*

airy-fairy /ˈeərɪ ˈfeərɪ/ ADJECTIVE not based on real life or practical ideas

aisle /aɪl/ NOUN [*plural* **aisles**] the space that you can walk along between rows of seats or shelves in a church, supermarket, etc.

ajar /əˈdʒɑː(r)/ ADJECTIVE, ADVERB slightly open □ *David left the door ajar on purpose.*

aka /ˌeɪkeɪˈeɪ/ ABBREVIATION also known as; used before another name for someone □ *William H Bonney, aka Billy the Kid*

akimbo /əˈkɪmbəʊ/ ADVERB **with arms akimbo** with your hands on your hips and your elbows pointing out

alarm /əˈlɑːm/ ► NOUN [*plural* **alarms**]
1 a loud noise to warn people about something 🔁 *the fire alarm* 🔁 *My alarm goes off at 7 o'clock.* 🔁 *If the alarm sounds, leave the building.*
2 *no plural* a sudden feeling of fear and worry □ *He jumped back in alarm.* 🔁 *Everyone stay calm, there's no cause for alarm.*
3 **raise/sound the alarm** to warn people about something dangerous □ *His brother raised the alarm when he didn't return home last night.*
➡ *go to* **false alarm**
► VERB [**alarms, alarming, alarmed**] to frighten and worry someone suddenly □ *It's okay, don't be alarmed.*

alarm clock /əˈlɑːm ˈklɒk/ NOUN [*plural* **alarm clocks**] a clock that makes a noise to wake you up 🔁 *His alarm clock went off* (= rang) *at 6 am.*

alarming /əˈlɑːmɪŋ/ ADJECTIVE frightening and making you worry □ *alarming reports*
• **alarmingly** /əˈlɑːmɪŋlɪ/ ADVERB in an alarming way □ *The floor shook alarmingly.*

alas /əˈlæs/ EXCLAMATION a formal way of saying that you are sad □ *Alas, she didn't live that long.*

albatross /ˈælbətrɒs/ NOUN [*plural* **albatrosses**] a large white sea bird

albeit /ɔːlˈbiːɪt/ CONJUNCTION although □ *It was her first success, albeit a modest one.*

albino /ælˈbiːnəʊ/ NOUN [*plural* **albinos**] a person or animal with no natural colour in their hair, skin or eyes. A biology word.

album /ˈælbəm/ NOUN [*plural* **albums**]
1 a book for keeping photographs, stamps, etc. 🔁 *a photo album*
2 a collection of songs or pieces of music on a CD, record, etc. □ *the band's new album*

albumen /ˈælbjʊmɪn/ NOUN, NO PLURAL the colourless part of an egg that is white when cooked. A biology word.

alcohol /ˈælkəhɒl/ NOUN, NO PLURAL
1 drinks like wine and beer that can make you drunk 🔁 *He doesn't drink alcohol.*
2 a substance in wine and beer that is also in some chemicals and medicines. A chemistry word.
• **alcoholic** /ˌælkəˈhɒlɪk/ ► ADJECTIVE containing alcohol 🔁 *alcoholic drinks*
► NOUN [*plural* **alcoholics**] someone who regularly drinks too much alcohol
• **alcoholism** /ˈælkəhɒlɪzəm/ NOUN, NO PLURAL the state of being an alcoholic

alcove /ˈælkəʊv/ NOUN [*plural* **alcoves**] a space in a room where part of the wall is further back than the rest

ale /eɪl/ NOUN [*plural* **ales**] a type of beer

alert /əˈlɜːt/ ► ADJECTIVE quick to notice what is around you and to react to it □ *Stay alert - the enemy could attack at any time.*
► VERB [**alerts, alerting, alerted**] to warn someone about a danger □ *If you see a suspicious package, alert the police at once.* □ *We should alert the public to the risks.*
► NOUN [*plural* **alerts**]
1 a warning about something 🔁 *Weather experts issued a flood alert.*
2 **on alert** ready to deal with problems 🔁 *Security forces are on full/high alert.* 🔁 *Police are on the alert for another attack.*

A level /ˈeɪ ˈlevəl/ NOUN [*plural* **A levels**] an exam that students in England, Wales and Northern Ireland take at about age eighteen in a particular subject □ *She's got* (= has been successful in) *3 A levels.*

algae /ˈældʒiː/ PLURAL NOUN plants that grow near or in water and do not have stems, leaves or flowers

algebra /ˈældʒɪbrə/ NOUN, NO PLURAL a type of mathematics that uses letters and signs instead of numbers

algorithm /ˈælgərɪðəm/ NOUN [*plural* **algorithms**] a set of rules that are used for doing a calculation, especially in computing. A computing word.

alias /ˈeɪlɪəs/ ► ADVERB also known as □ *Norman Cook, alias Fatboy Slim*
► NOUN [*plural* **aliases**] another name that someone uses 🔁 *She uses an alias when she travels abroad.*

alibi /ˈælɪbaɪ/ NOUN [*plural* **alibis**] proof that someone could not have committed a crime, because they were somewhere else at the time

alien /ˈeɪljən/ ▶ NOUN [plural **aliens**]
1 a creature from another planet
2 someone who is not from the country they are living in 🔲 *an illegal alien*
▶ ADJECTIVE
1 strange and not familiar 🔲 *The idea of taking orders from a woman was totally alien to him.*
2 to do with creatures from another planet 🔲 *an alien spaceship*

alienate /ˈeɪljəneɪt/ VERB [**alienates, alienating, alienated**]
1 to make someone start to dislike you 🔲 *She had alienated most of her former friends.*
2 to make someone feel that they do not belong somewhere 🔲 *We don't want to alienate older viewers.*
● **alienated** /ˈeɪljəneɪtɪd/ ADJECTIVE feeling that you do not belong 🔲 *Many young immigrants feel alienated.*
● **alienation** /ˌeɪljəˈneɪʃən/ NOUN, NO PLURAL a feeling that you do not belong 🔲 *a sense of alienation*

alight /əˈlaɪt/ ▶ ADJECTIVE burning 🔲 *The whole building was alight.*
▶ ADVERB burning 🔲 *They poured petrol over the car and set it alight.*
▶ VERB [**alights, alighting, alighted**] a formal word meaning to get off a train or bus 🔲 *Alight here for the airport.*

align /əˈlaɪn/ VERB [**aligns, aligning, aligned**]
1 to put things in a straight line 🔲 *Align the words down the left side of the page.*
2 be aligned with something/someone to support a political idea or group 🔲 *Many local police are aligned with the rebels.*
● **alignment** /əˈlaɪnmənt/ NOUN, NO PLURAL the position of things in a straight line 🔲 *The wheels need to be in alignment.*

alike /əˈlaɪk/ ▶ ADJECTIVE like one another
🔲 *The twins aren't at all alike in character.*
▶ ADVERB
1 in the same way 🔲 *Dad treats us both alike.*
2 used to refer to two people or things equally 🔲 *It's popular with adults and children alike.*

alimentary canal /ˌælɪˈmentərɪ kəˈnæl/ NOUN [plural **alimentary canals**] the parts of the body (the oesophagus, stomach and intestines) that carry food through the body. A biology word.

alimony /ˈælɪmənɪ/ NOUN, NO PLURAL a mainly US word for money that is paid to a husband or wife you are no longer married to

alive /əˈlaɪv/ ADJECTIVE
1 living 🔲 *He was seriously injured, but still alive.*
🔲 *She didn't know whether he was alive or dead.*
2 still existing 🔲 *They have to win to keep alive their chances of reaching the finals.*
3 full of activity 🔲 *The city really comes alive at night.*

alkali /ˈælkəlaɪ/ NOUN [plural **alkalis**] the type of chemical that behaves in the opposite way to an acid. A chemistry word.
● **alkaline** /ˈælkəlaɪn/ ADJECTIVE containing an alkali. A chemistry word.

all /ɔːl/ ▶ PRONOUN, DETERMINER
1 every one 🔲 *All the children stood up.* 🔲 *I want to see them all.* 🔲 **+ of** *All of the animals were healthy.*
2 every part 🔲 *We ate all the cake.* 🔲 *Don't spend it all.* 🔲 *We've been working all day.*
3 the only thing 🔲 *All he's interested in is football.*
4 at all used to emphasize a negative statement 🔲 *You haven't eaten anything at all.*
➡ *go to* be all *talk* (and no action)
▶ ADVERB
1 completely 🔲 *His shirt was all dirty.*
2 all over (a) in every place or part of something 🔲 *His clothes were all over the place.* (b) finished 🔲 *I'll be glad when it's all over.*

Allah /ˈælə/ NOUN the Muslim name for God

allay /əˈleɪ/ VERB [**allays, allaying, allayed**] a formal word meaning to reduce fears or worry 🔲 *The chairman tried to allay fears over job losses.*

allegation /ˌælɪˈgeɪʃən/ NOUN [plural **allegations**] when you say that someone has done something wrong or illegal 🔲 *allegations of corruption* 🔲 *He denies all the allegations.*

allege /əˈledʒ/ VERB [**alleges, alleging, alleged**] to say that someone has done something wrong or illegal 🔲 *The boys allege that they are being bullied.*
● **alleged** /əˈledʒd/ ADJECTIVE said to exist or be true, but without proof 🔲 *an alleged plot to bomb an airliner*
● **allegedly** /əˈledʒɪdlɪ/ ADVERB if something is allegedly true, people say it but there is no proof 🔲 *He allegedly stole money out of the till.*

allegiance /əˈliːdʒəns/ NOUN [plural **allegiances**] strong loyalty 🔲 *The soldiers all swear allegiance to their country.*

allegory /ˈælɪgərɪ/ NOUN [plural **allegories**] a story, picture, etc. that represents an idea 🔲 *His plays are mostly political allegories.*

allergic /əˈlɜːdʒɪk/ ADJECTIVE having an allergy to something 🔲 *an allergic reaction* 🔲 *I'm allergic to cats.*

allergy /ˈælədʒɪ/ NOUN [plural **allergies**] a condition where your body reacts badly to something you touch, breathe, eat or drink 🔲 *a peanut allergy* 🔲 *I have an allergy to dairy products.*

alleviate /əˈliːvɪeɪt/ VERB [**alleviates, alleviating, alleviated**] to make a problem, pain, etc. less serious 🔲 *The medicine should alleviate the symptoms.*

alley /ˈælɪ/ or **alleyway** /ˈælɪweɪ/ NOUN [plural **alleys**] a narrow passage between buildings

alliance /əˈlaɪəns/ NOUN [plural **alliances**] an agreement between organizations or countries to work together 🔲 *The US car maker has formed an alliance with a Chinese manufacturer.*

allied /'ælaɪd/ ADJECTIVE
1 Allied to do with countries joined by an agreement, especially Britain and other countries in the First and Second World Wars □ the Allied invasion
2 related or connected □ They do say genius is closely allied to madness.

alligator /'ælɪɡeɪtə(r)/ NOUN [plural **alligators**] a large reptile like a crocodile, with thick skin, a long body and a big mouth with sharp teeth

alliteration /ə,lɪtə'reɪʃən/ NOUN, NO PLURAL the use of the same sound repeated at the beginning of several words

allocate /'æləkeɪt/ VERB [allocates, allocating, allocated] to give someone something for them to use □ Now we'll allocate the rooms you will be staying in. □ We need to allocate more money for schools.

• **allocation** /ælə'keɪʃən/ NOUN [plural **allocations**]
1 giving or sharing something between people or things □ the allocation of resources
2 something that has been given to someone □ Both teams have the same allocation of tickets for the cup final.

allot /ə'lɒt/ VERB [allots, allotting, allotted] to give someone a particular amount of something □ It was hard to finish the exam in the time allotted.

• **allotment** /ə'lɒtmənt/ NOUN [plural **allotments**]
1 a small piece of land where someone can grow vegetables
2 the process of giving someone a particular amount of something

all-out /'ɔːl 'aʊt/ ADJECTIVE complete □ We want an all-out ban on smoking.

allow /ə'laʊ/ VERB [allows, allowing, allowed]
1 to give permission for something □ + to do something Will you allow me to come in now? □ We do not allow smoking in the house. □ Prisoners are allowed out to exercise.
2 to make something possible □ + to do something The new technology allows them to stay in touch with their families. □ Social networking sites allow users to set up their own home pages.
3 to plan or give a certain amount of time, money, etc. for something □ You should allow extra time for your journey.
4 to not stop something from happening □ They allowed the grass to grow very long.
♦ PHRASAL VERB **allow for something** to include something in your plans or calculations □ Add 5% to allow for inflation.

> ► Do not use the phrase **it is not allowed to do something** as this is not correct English. Instead use either of these phrases: □ You are not allowed to talk in a written exam. □ Talking is not allowed in a written exam.

• **allowable** /ə'laʊəbəl/ ADJECTIVE allowed according to a rule □ Radiation was way above the allowable limit.

• **allowance** /ə'laʊəns/ NOUN [plural **allowances**]
1 an amount of money that someone is given regularly □ Adam gets an allowance of £50 a month from his father.
2 the amount of something you are allowed □ There's a baggage allowance that you mustn't go over.
3 make allowances for someone/something to expect less from someone because you know they have a problem, disadvantage, etc. □ We'll make allowances for the fact that you've never done anything like this before.

alloy /'ælɔɪ/ NOUN [plural **alloys**] a mixture of two or more metals. A chemistry word.

all-purpose /'ɔːl 'pɜːpəs/ ADJECTIVE designed or used for many different purposes □ Aspirin became an all-purpose remedy.

all right /'ɔːl 'raɪt/ ► ADJECTIVE, ADVERB
1 quite good but not very good □ The party was all right I suppose.
2 safe or well □ I'm all right. How are you? □ I'm glad you're all right – we heard there had been an accident.
3 acceptable or not a problem □ Is it all right if I go out tonight? □ It's all right - it wasn't your fault.
4 That's all right. used when someone has thanked you for something
► EXCLAMATION used to agree to something □ All right, I'll go then.

all-round /'ɔːl 'raʊnd/ ADJECTIVE good at or including a lot of different things □ an all-round athlete □ a good all-round education

• **all-rounder** /'ɔːl 'raʊndə(r)/ NOUN [plural **all-rounders**] someone who is good at many different things

all-time /'ɔːl ,taɪm/ ADJECTIVE if something is at an all-time best/high/low, etc., it is better/higher/lower than it has ever been

allude /ə'luːd/
♦ PHRASAL VERB [alludes, alluding, alluded] **allude to something** to refer to something without talking about it directly □ 'I'm moving much better now,' he said, alluding to his recent back problem.

allure /ə'ljʊə(r)/ NOUN, NO PLURAL something that you find attractive about something or someone □ the allure of life at sea

• **alluring** /ə'ljʊərɪŋ/ ADJECTIVE attractive

allusion /ə'luːʒən/ NOUN [plural **allusions**] when you refer to something without talking about it directly 🔁 He made an allusion to the war.

alluvial /ə'luːvɪəl/ ADJECTIVE made from earth left by rivers or floods. A geography word.

• **alluvium** /ə'luːvɪəm/ NOUN, NO PLURAL earth left by rivers or floods. A geography word.

ally ► NOUN /'ælaɪ/ [allies] a person or country that supports another 🔁 He is one of the president's closest allies. □ Britain has been a strong political ally of the United States.
► VERB /ə'laɪ/ [allies, allying, allied] to support or work

with another person, country, etc. □ *The rebels are allied to a local military group.*

almighty /ɔː'maɪtɪ/ ▶ ADJECTIVE
1 very loud, strong, serious, etc. 🖫*We heard an almighty bang.*
2 very powerful □ *almighty God*
▶ NOUN the Almighty God

almond /'ɑːmənd/ NOUN [*plural* **almonds**] a long narrow nut

almost /'ɔːlməʊst/ ADVERB nearly but not quite or not completely □ *She is almost ten years old.* 🖫*Almost all the children go to state schools.* □ *He's almost as tall as his father.* □ *It's almost impossible to predict.* □ *I almost missed my flight.*

aloft /ə'lɒft/ ADVERB high up in the air 🖫*Bernard held the cup aloft.*

alone /ə'ləʊn/ ADJECTIVE, ADVERB
1 without anyone else □ *I live alone.* 🖫*I was all alone with no one to talk to.* 🖫*A young woman sat alone in the waiting room.* □ *I felt completely alone.*
2 used to emphasize that only one person or thing is involved □ *The ticket alone will use up all my money.*
3 leave something **alone** to not touch something □ *Leave my sweets alone!*
4 leave someone **alone** to not talk to or annoy someone □ *Leave her alone - she's had enough of your moaning.*
5 not **alone** in something not the only person to be experiencing something bad □ *He's not alone in feeling disappointed.*

▶ Note that **alone** only means 'without anyone else'. It does not mean 'feeling sad because you are without other people'. The word for this is **lonely** □ *I was alone in the house.* □ *I felt lonely without my family around me.*

---

along /ə'lɒŋ/ ▶ PREPOSITION
1 from one part of something to another □ *Shona walked along the street.*
2 by the side of something long □ *Hari's house is somewhere along this street.*
▶ ADVERB
1 forwards □ *Move along, please.* □ *He was driving along, singing.*
2 with someone 🖫*We're going swimming - why don't you come along?* 🖫*Adam brought a friend along.*
3 along with together with □ *We'd packed drinks along with the sandwiches.*
4 be coming **along** to be making good progress □ *The building work is really coming along now.*

alongside /əlɒŋ'saɪd/ PREPOSITION, ADVERB
1 next to □ *A police car pulled up alongside us.*
2 if you work **alongside** someone, you work together with them

aloof /ə'luːf/ ADJECTIVE staying apart from other people or not friendly 🖫*She remained aloof from the others.*

aloud /ə'laʊd/ ADVERB so that other people can hear 🖫*She almost laughed aloud.* 🖫*Edith read the letter aloud to the boys.*

alphabet /'ælfəbet/ NOUN [*plural* **alphabets**] all the written letters of a language 🖫*Z is the last letter of the alphabet.*
• **alphabetical** /ˌælfə'betɪkəl/ ADJECTIVE with the first letters in the order of the alphabet 🖫*The books are in alphabetical order.* □ *an alphabetical index*
• **alphabetically** /ˌælfə'betɪkəlɪ/ ADVERB with the first letters in the order of the alphabet □ *The list has been arranged alphabetically.*

alphanumeric /ˌælfənjuː'merɪk/ ADJECTIVE using letters and numbers. A computing word.

alpine /'ælpaɪn/ ADJECTIVE to do with high mountains □ *an alpine meadow*

already /ɔːl'redɪ/ ADVERB
1 before now or before a particular time □ *I had already gone when Bob arrived.* □ *We've already booked our summer holiday.*
2 now, before the expected time □ *Is he here already?* □ *I'm already tired.*

alright /ɔːl'raɪt/ ADJECTIVE, ADVERB another spelling of all right

alsatian /æl'seɪʃən/ NOUN [*plural* **alsatians**] a large dog with short brown and black fur, often used by the police

also /'ɔːlsəʊ/ ADVERB in addition □ *Bernie speaks French and also Italian.* □ *My sister also attends this school.* 🖫*The process is not only slow, but also very expensive.*

altar /'ɔːltə(r)/ NOUN [*plural* **altars**] a special table used for religious ceremonies in a church

alter /'ɔːltə(r)/ VERB [**alters, altering, altered**] to change, or to change something □ *The town has altered a lot recently.* □ *Can you alter this skirt to fit me?*
• **alteration** /ɔːltə'reɪʃən/ NOUN [*plural* **alterations**] a change, or the process of being changed □ *There have been a few alterations to our plans.* □ *The museum is closed for alteration.*

alternate[1] /ɔːl'tɜːnət/ ADJECTIVE
1 happening on one day, week, etc. but not the next □ *I have to work on alternate Saturdays.*
2 with one thing, then another, then the first thing again, in a repeated pattern □ *alternate stripes of red and green*
3 a US word for **alternative**

alternate[2] /'ɔːltəneɪt/ VERB [**alternates, alternating, alternated**] if two things alternate, one happens or is used first, then the other, then the first again, etc. □ *She alternates between being too strict and being too soft.* □ *He alternates between the guitar and the violin.*

alternative /ɔːl'tɜːnətɪv/ ▶ ADJECTIVE
1 giving you another choice or possibility □ *If you*

cannot come on Tuesday you can suggest an alternative day. □ Drivers are advised to use an alternative route.

2 not usual or traditional □ an alternative lifestyle

▶ NOUN [plural **alternatives**] another possibility or choice □ Is there an alternative to chips on the menu? □ There are cheaper alternatives.

• **alternatively** /ɔːˈtɜːnətɪvlɪ/ ADVERB used to offer another suggestion □ Alternatively, we could go to the cinema.

alternative medicine /ɔːˈtɜːnətɪv ˈmedsɪn/ NOUN, NO PLURAL treating diseases with methods which are different from usual Western medicine

alternator /ˈɔːltəneɪtə(r)/ NOUN [plural **alternators**] a piece of equipment that produces an electric current that keeps changing its direction. A physics word.

although /ɔːlˈðəʊ/ CONJUNCTION

1 despite the fact that □ I did go to the show, although I'd said I wouldn't. □ Although he was a clever kid, he didn't do well in exams.

2 but □ He's retired from professional athletics, although he's still very fit.

altitude /ˈæltɪtjuːd/ NOUN [plural **altitudes**] the height of a place above the level of the sea □ We are flying at an altitude of 20,000 metres.

alto /ˈæltəʊ/ NOUN [plural **altos**] the lowest singing voice for a woman

altogether /ɔːltəˈgeðə(r)/ ADVERB

1 completely □ Finally, he stopped altogether. 🗗 I'm not altogether happy. □ They're from altogether different cultures.

2 in total □ We raised £100 altogether. □ There are six of us altogether.

3 in general □ Altogether, it was a great holiday.

altruism /ˈæltruːɪzəm/ NOUN, NO PLURAL behaving in a way that shows you care more about others than yourself. A formal word. □ an act of altruism

• **altruistic** /ˌæltruːˈɪstɪk/ ADJECTIVE involving altruism. A formal word. □ He did it for purely altruistic reasons.

aluminium /ˌæljuˈmɪnɪəm/ NOUN, NO PLURAL a very light metal that is a silver colour

aluminum /əˈluːmɪnəm/ NOUN, NO PLURAL the US word for aluminium

alveolus /ælˈvɪələs/ NOUN [plural **alveoli**] alveoli are structures in the lungs like very small bags, that take oxygen into the blood. A biology word.

always /ˈɔːlweɪz/ ADVERB

1 at all times □ I always work hard. 🗗 You look lovely, as always.

2 at all times in the past □ She's always lived in the same village. □ He hasn't always been so successful.

3 forever □ I'll always remember that day.

4 repeatedly □ + ing I'm always getting this wrong.

Alzheimer's disease /ˈæltsˌhaɪməz dɪˌziːz/ NOUN, NO PLURAL a serious illness that affects the brain of

older people, making them forget things and become confused

am[1] /æm/ VERB the present tense of the verb be when it is used with I □ I am happy.

➤ Note that instead of I am, people often say and write the short form I'm □ I'm very pleased.

am[2] /eɪˈem/ or **a.m.** ABBREVIATION used after the time to show that it is in the morning □ My flight is at 6 am.

amalgamate /əˈmælgəˌmeɪt/ VERB [amalgamates, amalgamating, amalgamated] if two organizations amalgamate, they join together □ The two firms amalgamated last year.

• **amalgamation** /əˌmælgəˈmeɪʃən/ NOUN, NO PLURAL the joining of two or more organizations □ The new union is an amalgamation of three smaller unions.

amass /əˈmæs/ VERB [amasses, amassing, amassed] to collect a lot of something □ The family has amassed a lot of furniture over the years.

amateur /ˈæmətə(r)/ ▶ NOUN [plural **amateurs**]

1 someone who does something because they enjoy it, not for money □ The team is made up of enthusiastic amateurs.

2 someone who is not very good at doing something □ They're complete amateurs.

▶ ADJECTIVE doing something for fun and not to be paid □ an amateur photographer □ amateur athletics

• **amateurish** /ˈæmətərɪʃ/ ADJECTIVE done or made without much skill □ an amateurish video

amaze /əˈmeɪz/ VERB [amazes, amazing, amazed] to surprise someone very much □ It amazes me how stupid you can be.

• **amazed** /əˈmeɪzd/ ADJECTIVE very surprised □ + at We were all amazed at how easy it was. □ + that I'm amazed that no one was hurt. □ Mum looked amazed when he walked in.

• **amazement** /əˈmeɪzmənt/ NOUN, NO PLURAL great surprise 🗗 To my amazement, Dad agreed with me. □ He shook his head in amazement.

• **amazing** /əˈmeɪzɪŋ/ ADJECTIVE

1 very surprising □ an amazing sight □ It's amazing how quickly the weather can change.

2 very pleasant, exciting or enjoyable □ We saw the most amazing sunset. □ It's a pretty amazing feeling.

• **amazingly** /əˈmeɪzɪŋlɪ/ ADVERB in a very surprising way □ The cake was amazingly good. □ Amazingly, it didn't rain for our picnic.

ambassador /æmˈbæsədə(r)/ NOUN [plural **ambassadors**] someone who officially represents their government in a foreign country □ the British ambassador to Japan

amber /ˈæmbə(r)/ NOUN, NO PLURAL

1 a colour between yellow and orange □ The traffic lights were on amber.

2 a clear yellow-brown substance that is used to make jewellery

ambi- /ˈæmbɪ/ PREFIX ambi- is added to the start of words to mean 'to do with both parts' or 'to do with two of something' □ ambidextrous

ambidextrous /ˌæmbɪˈdekstrəs/ ADJECTIVE able to use both of your hands equally well

ambience /ˈæmbɪəns/ NOUN, NO PLURAL the atmosphere of a place □ *The restaurant has a pleasant ambience.*

ambiguity /ˌæmbɪˈgjuːətɪ/ NOUN [plural **ambiguities**] when something can have more than one meaning □ *We need to make sure there is no ambiguity in the contract.*

• **ambiguous** /æmˈbɪgjuəs/ ADJECTIVE having more than one possible meaning □ *His comments on her performance were rather ambiguous.*

• **ambiguously** /æmˈbɪgjuəslɪ/ ADVERB in an ambiguous way □ *an ambiguously worded statement*

ambition /æmˈbɪʃən/ NOUN [plural **ambitions**]
1 something that you want to achieve ⊞ *I have an ambition to see the pyramids.* ⊞ *He achieved his ambition of performing on Broadway.*
2 no plural wanting to be very successful □ *He shows a lack of ambition.*

• **ambitious** /æmˈbɪʃəs/ ADJECTIVE
1 wanting to be very successful in life □ *an ambitious and talented young player*
2 difficult to achieve □ *an ambitious plan*

ambivalence /æmˈbɪvələns/ NOUN, NO PLURAL when you have two different, often opposite, feelings about something □ *This shows the public's ambivalence about the monarchy.*

• **ambivalent** /æmˈbɪvələnt/ ADJECTIVE having two different, often opposite, feelings about something □ *She had ambivalent feelings about marriage.*

amble /ˈæmbəl/ VERB [**ambles, ambling, ambled**] to walk in a slow and relaxed way □ *They were ambling along, chatting.*

ambulance /ˈæmbjʊləns/ NOUN [plural **ambulances**] a vehicle for taking ill or injured people to hospital

ambush /ˈæmbʊʃ/ ▶ NOUN [plural **ambushes**] an attack by someone who was hidden □ *a deadly ambush*

▶ VERB [**ambushes, ambushing, ambushed**] to attack someone from a hidden position □ *Four masked men ambushed the security guard.*

ameba /əˈmiːbə/ NOUN [plural **amebas** or **amebae**] the US spelling of amoeba

amen /ɑːˈmen/ EXCLAMATION something that is said by Christians at the end of a prayer

amend /əˈmend/ VERB [**amends, amending, amended**] to make changes to something written □ *We need to amend the guidelines.*

• **amendment** /əˈmendmənt/ NOUN [plural **amendments**] a change to something written, for example a law

• **amends** /əˈmendz/ PLURAL NOUN make amends to do something good to show you are sorry for something you did wrong □ *Now we'll see if he can make amends for letting in that goal.*

amenity /əˈmiːnətɪ/ NOUN [plural **amenities**] something such as a shop or park that is available for people to use ⊞ *Newlands has excellent local amenities.*

American /əˈmerɪkən/ ▶ ADJECTIVE belonging to or from America, especially the United States of America □ *an American accent*
▶ NOUN [plural **Americans**] a person from America, especially the United States of America

amethyst /ˈæmɪθɪst/ NOUN [plural **amethysts**] a valuable purple stone used in jewellery

amiable /ˈeɪmɪəbəl/ ADJECTIVE friendly and relaxed □ *a very amiable man*

• **amiably** /ˈeɪmɪəblɪ/ ADVERB in a friendly, relaxed way □ *They chatted amiably.*

amicable /ˈæmɪkəbəl/ ADJECTIVE friendly and without any argument ⊞ *an amicable agreement/settlement*

• **amicably** /ˈæmɪkəblɪ/ ADVERB in a friendly way □ *This problem can be resolved amicably.*

amid /əˈmɪd/ or **amidst** /əˈmɪdst/ ADVERB a formal word meaning 'in the middle of' □ *It was a moment of calm amid great excitement.*

amino acid /əˈmiːnəʊ ˈæsɪd/ NOUN [plural **amino acids**] one of the substances in the body that join together to make proteins. A biology word.

amiss /əˈmɪs/ ADVERB if something is amiss, there is something wrong □ *He didn't notice anything amiss.*

ammonia /əˈməʊnɪə/ NOUN, NO PLURAL a substance that can be a gas or a liquid and has a very strong smell. A chemistry word.

ammunition /ˌæmjʊˈnɪʃən/ NOUN, NO PLURAL bullets or bombs that you can fire from a weapon

amnesia /æmˈniːzɪə/ NOUN, NO PLURAL a medical condition that makes you forget things

amnesty /ˈæmnəstɪ/ NOUN [plural **amnesties**] a period of time when the usual punishments for people are stopped □ *The government announced an amnesty for political prisoners.*

amniotic fluid /ˌæmnɪˈɒtɪk ˈfluːɪd/ NOUN, NO PLURAL the liquid that surrounds a baby in the mother's womb (= place where the baby grows). A biology word.

amoeba /əˈmiːbə/ NOUN [plural **amoebas** or **amoebae**] a microorganism made from a single cell. A biology word.

amok /əˈmɒk/ ADVERB run amok to behave in an uncontrolled way and do a lot of damage □ *Rioters ran amok in the city.*

among /əˈmʌŋ/ or **amongst** /əˈmʌŋst/ PREPOSITION
1 surrounded by or in the middle of □ *You are among friends.*
2 between people in a group □ *Divide the chocolate among yourselves.*
3 in a group of □ *The band is popular among teenagers.*

amoral /eɪˈmɒrəl/ ADJECTIVE not caring about moral principles

amorous /ˈæmərəs/ ADJECTIVE full of love and sexual feeling □ *amorous behaviour*

• **amorously** /ˈæmərəslɪ/ ADVERB in an amorous way □ He clasped her hand amorously.

amount /əˈmaʊnt/ NOUN [plural **amounts**] a quantity □ + of a small amount of money □ These drinks contain large amounts of sugar.

➤ Remember that 'large' and 'small' are used before the word **amount** but not 'big' or 'little' □ A large amount of this food is wasted. □ A small amount of salt is necessary.

◆ PHRASAL VERB [**amounts, amounting, amounted**]
amount to something
1 to be the same as something □ Her lawyer said the behaviour amounted to blackmail.
2 to add up to a total □ What I've spent amounts to exactly $10.

amp /æmp/ NOUN [plural **amps**]
1 the unit used to measure electric current. A physics word.
2 a short informal way to say or write amplifier

ampere /ˈæmpeə(r)/ NOUN [plural **amperes**] a formal word for amp. A physics word.

ampersand /ˈæmpəsænd/ NOUN [plural **ampersands**] the sign '&', which means and

amphibian /æmˈfɪbɪən/ NOUN [plural **amphibians**]
1 an animal that lives on land and in water. A biology word. □ Frogs are amphibians.
2 a vehicle that can travel on land and on water

• **amphibious** /æmˈfɪbɪəs/ ADJECTIVE able to go or live on land and in water

amphitheatre /ˈæmfɪˌθɪətə(r)/ NOUN [plural **amphitheatres**] a large theatre with no roof that has seats in a circle around an area in the centre

ample /ˈæmpəl/ ADJECTIVE enough or more than enough □ We had ample opportunity to ask questions. □ an ample supply of water

amplifier /ˈæmplɪfaɪə(r)/ NOUN [plural **amplifiers**] a piece of electrical equipment that makes sounds louder

amplify /ˈæmplɪfaɪ/ VERB [**amplifies, amplifying, amplified**]
1 to make something louder □ The sounds are amplified.
2 to make something stronger or clearer □ The incident amplified concerns about safety.

amply /ˈæmplɪ/ ADVERB very well or more than necessary □ We were amply rewarded with tea and chocolate cake.

amputate /ˈæmpjuteɪt/ VERB [**amputates, amputating, amputated**] to cut off a part of the body in a medical operation □ He had to have his left leg amputated.

• **amputation** /ˌæmpjʊˈteɪʃən/ NOUN [plural **amputations**] when a part of the body is amputated

amuse /əˈmjuːz/ VERB [**amuses, amusing, amused**]
1 to make someone smile or laugh □ He told jokes to amuse his classmates.

2 to keep someone happy and interested □ Would you amuse the children for half an hour? □ She amused herself playing word games.

• **amused** /əˈmjuːzd/ ADJECTIVE
1 finding something funny □ He smiled, amused at John's silly mistake. □ an amused expression 🔁He was clearly not amused (= he was annoyed) by the decision.
2 happy and interested 🔁 Playing with the dog kept them amused for hours.

• **amusement** /əˈmjuːzmənt/ NOUN [plural **amusements**]
1 the feeling that makes you smile or laugh □ He smiled with obvious amusement.
2 something you do for entertainment □ What did you do for amusement? □ There were various amusements and food stalls.

• **amusing** /əˈmjuːzɪŋ/ ADJECTIVE making you want to smile or laugh □ an amusing story 🔁 She found the whole thing quite amusing.

• **amusingly** /əˈmjuːzɪŋlɪ/ ADVERB in an amusing way □ It was an amusingly written article.

an /ən/ DETERMINER used instead of a before words beginning with a vowel, or before words beginning with 'h' when it is not pronounced □ an apple □ an elephant □ an honest person

anachronism /əˈnækrənɪzəm/ NOUN [plural **anachronisms**] something old-fashioned □ Some view the Royal Family as an anachronism.

• **anachronistic** /əˌnækrəˈnɪstɪk/ ADJECTIVE old-fashioned □ His political views are anachronistic.

anaemia /əˈniːmɪə/ NOUN, NO PLURAL a condition where someone does not have enough red blood cells and looks pale

• **anaemic** /əˈniːmɪk/ ADJECTIVE suffering from anaemia

anaerobic /ˌænəˈrəʊbɪk/ ADJECTIVE not needing or using oxygen. A biology word.

anaerobic respiration /ˌænəˈrəʊbɪk ˌrespəˈreɪʃən/ NOUN, NO PLURAL respiration (= making energy) that uses little or no oxygen. A biology word.

anaesthesia /ˌænɪsˈθiːzɪə/ NOUN, NO PLURAL giving someone a drug to stop them feeling pain or to make them unconscious

• **anaesthetic** /ˌænɪsˈθetɪk/ NOUN [plural **anaesthetics**] a drug that stops you feeling pain or makes you unconscious 🔁 The operation will be carried out under general anaesthetic (= one which makes you unconscious). 🔁a local anaesthetic (= one which stops pain in only one part of the body)

• **anaesthetist** /əˈniːsθətɪst/ NOUN [plural **anaesthetists**] a doctor whose job is to give people anaesthetics

• **anaesthetize** or **anaesthetise** /æˈniːsθətaɪz/ VERB [**anaesthetizes, anaesthetizing, anaesthetized**] to give someone an anaesthetic before an operation

anagram /ˈænəgræm/ NOUN [plural **anagrams**] a word or phrase that has the same letters as another word or phrase, but in a different order □ *'Stone' is an anagram of 'notes'.*

analogous /ə'næləgəs/ ADJECTIVE similar in some way □ *The way the cells combine is analogous to how a key fits in a lock.*

analogue /'ænəlɒg/ ADJECTIVE
1 using a continuously changing signal, such as sound or electric current. A physics word. □ *The TV is capable of receiving both analogue and digital signals.*
2 an analogue watch or clock has hands that move around a clock face to show the time

analogy /ə'nælədʒɪ/ NOUN [plural **analogies**] a comparison with something similar that helps to explain something 🔁 *To use a football analogy, it's like scoring the winning goal in extra time.*

analysis /ə'næləsɪs/ NOUN [plural **analyses**] when you examine something carefully in order to understand it 🔁 *a statistical analysis* 🔁 *We carried out a detailed analysis of the project.*

• **analyst** /'ænəlɪst/ NOUN [plural **analysts**]
1 someone who examines something carefully in order to understand it 🔁 *a political analyst* 🔁 *a legal analyst*
2 someone whose job is talking to people to find out why they are unhappy

• **analytical** /ænə'lɪtɪkəl/ or **analytic** /ænə'lɪtɪk/ ADJECTIVE using a careful method to examine and understand something 🔁 *an analytical mind*

• **analytically** /ænə'lɪtɪkəlɪ/ ADVERB in an analytical way

analyze or **analyse** /'ænəlaɪz/ VERB [**analyzes, analyzing, analyzed**] to examine something carefully in order to understand it 🔁 *We need to analyze the data.* □ *Researchers analyzed a thousand samples.*

anarchist /'ænəkɪst/ NOUN [plural **anarchists**] someone who believes it is not necessary to have any government in a country

• **anarchy** /'ænəkɪ/ NOUN, NO PLURAL a situation where people do not obey normal rules or laws □ *There is a growing state of anarchy in the city.*

anathema /ə'næθəmə/ NOUN, NO PLURAL a formal word for something you hate □ *Sitting in the sun was anathema to him.*

anatomy /ə'nætəmɪ/ NOUN, NO PLURAL
1 the body of a person or animal 🔁 *a knowledge of human anatomy*
2 the study of the body and its structure □ *a professor of anatomy*

ancestor /'ænsestə(r)/ NOUN [plural **ancestors**] a member of your family who lived in the past □ *His distant ancestors came from India.*

• **ancestral** /æn'sestrəl/ ADJECTIVE belonging to your family in the past □ *the Duke's ancestral home*

• **ancestry** /'ænsestrɪ/ NOUN, NO PLURAL your family's past □ *We can trace our ancestry back to the twelfth century.* □ *a French citizen of Moroccan ancestry*

anchor /'æŋkə(r)/ ▶ NOUN [plural **anchors**]
1 a heavy piece of metal attached to a boat that is dropped into the water to stop it from moving away

🔁 *The captain dropped anchor.*
2 the main person who talks on a television news programme 🔁 *the CBS news anchor*
▶ VERB [**anchors, anchoring, anchored**]
1 to drop the anchor of a boat to stop it moving away □ *The ship is anchored in Sydney harbour.*
2 to fix something firmly in a position □ *Steel rods anchor the statue in place.*
3 to present a television news programme □ *Jennings was picked to anchor the evening news.*

• **anchorage** /'æŋkərɪdʒ/ NOUN [plural **anchorages**] a place where ships can stop

anchovy /'æntʃəvɪ/ NOUN [plural **anchovies**] a type of small fish with a very salty taste

ancient /'eɪnʃənt/ ADJECTIVE
1 from a very long time ago 🔁 *ancient history* 🔁 *the remains of an ancient civilization*
2 old □ *The building's ancient heating system had broken.*

and /ænd/ CONJUNCTION
1 a word that is used to join parts of sentences □ *bread and butter* □ *I saw Alice and Peter.* □ *Go and get ready.*
2 added to □ *Two and two make four.*

android /'ændrɔɪd/ NOUN [plural **androids**] a robot (= machine that moves) that looks like a human being

anecdote /'ænɪkdəʊt/ NOUN [plural **anecdotes**] a short story you tell about something that happened to you □ *He was full of amusing anecdotes.*

anemia /ə'niːmɪə/ NOUN, NO PLURAL the US spelling of anaemia

• **anemic** /ə'niːmɪk/ ADJECTIVE the US spelling of anaemic

anemone /ə'nemənɪ/ NOUN [plural **anemones**] a type of flower that often grows in woods

anesthesia /ænɪs'θiːzɪə/ NOUN, NO PLURAL the US spelling of anaesthesia

• **anesthetic** /ænɪs'θetɪk/ NOUN [plural **anesthetics**] the US spelling of anaesthetic

• **anesthetist** /ə'niːsθətɪst/ NOUN [plural **anesthetists**] the US spelling of anaesthetist

• **anesthetize** /æ'niːsθətaɪz/ VERB [**anesthetizes, anesthetizing, anesthetized**] the US spelling of anaesthetize

anew /ə'njuː/ ADVERB again from the beginning, usually in a different way 🔁 *This is an opportunity to start anew.*

angel /'eɪndʒəl/ NOUN [plural **angels**]
1 a creature, usually shown like a person with wings, which is believed to bring messages from God
2 a very good person □ *Thanks for doing all that - you're an angel!*

• **angelic** /æn'dʒelɪk/ ADJECTIVE very beautiful and good

anger /'æŋgə(r)/ ▶ NOUN, NO PLURAL the strong, bad feeling you get about someone or something that annoys you □ *The fans expressed their anger at the*

decision. □ There's a lot of anger and frustration among local people. □ He was shaking with anger.
▶ VERB [angers, angering, angered] to make someone feel angry □ The plans have angered green campaigners.

angle /ˈæŋɡəl/ ▶ NOUN [plural angles]
1 the shape that is made at the point where two straight lines meet, measured in degrees □ a 90-degree angle
2 at an angle in a position that is not straight or normal □ Slice the vegetables at an angle. □ His injured leg was at an awkward angle.
3 a way of thinking about something □ + on What's your angle on this? 🖰 We're covering all the angles of this story.
4 the direction that something comes from □ He looked at it from every angle. □ Wright shot from a narrow angle.
▶ VERB [angles, angling, angled]
1 to put something in a position or direction that is not straight □ Angle your head back.
2 to try to get something without asking directly □ Did you hear her angling to borrow my new coat?

angler /ˈæŋɡlə(r)/ NOUN [plural anglers] someone who catches fish for sport or a hobby

Anglican /ˈæŋɡlɪkən/ ▶ ADJECTIVE to do with or belonging to the Church of England
▶ NOUN [plural Anglicans] a member of the Church of England

angling /ˈæŋɡlɪŋ/ NOUN, NO PLURAL the sport or hobby of catching fish

Anglo- /ˈæŋɡləʊ/ PREFIX Anglo- is added to the start of words to mean 'to do with or England' □ the Anglo-French trade agreement □ She calls herself an Anglo-American.

Anglo-Saxon /ˌæŋɡləʊˈsæksən/ ▶ NOUN [plural Anglo-Saxons]
1 one of the people who came to live in England in the 5th century
2 the English language before about 1150
▶ ADJECTIVE belonging to or to do with the Anglo-Saxon people or their language

angrily /ˈæŋɡrəlɪ/ ADVERB in an angry way
□ A young woman came in, shouting angrily. □ He reacted angrily.

angry /ˈæŋɡrɪ/ ADJECTIVE [angrier, angriest] very annoyed □ + about They're angry about the way they were treated. □ + with I'm not angry with you. □ an angry crowd 🖰 Then Mike got very angry. 🖰 That kind of thing makes me so angry.

anguish /ˈæŋɡwɪʃ/ NOUN, NO PLURAL a strong feeling of unhappiness and suffering □ a cry of anguish 🖰 She suffered a lot of mental anguish.
• **anguished** /ˈæŋɡwɪʃt/ ADJECTIVE very unhappy and suffering □ an anguished look

angular /ˈæŋɡjʊlə(r)/ ADJECTIVE with straight lines and pointed □ an angular face

animal /ˈænɪməl/ NOUN [plural animals]
1 a living creature that is not a human 🖰 a wild animal 🖰 a farm animal □ The charity helps to protect endangered animals.
2 any living creature that can feel and move □ Humans and insects – we're all animals.

animate /ˈænɪmət/ ADJECTIVE alive or having life

animated /ˈænɪmeɪtɪd/ ADJECTIVE
1 in an animated film, pictures or objects look as if they are moving 🖰 a short animated film
2 behaving or talking in an interested and excited way □ an animated conversation □ He had never seen them so animated.
• **animatedly** /ˈænɪmeɪtɪdlɪ/ ADVERB in an interested and excited way □ The two men were talking animatedly.
• **animation** /ˌænɪˈmeɪʃən/ NOUN [plural animations]
1 the process of making a film in which pictures or objects look as if they are moving, or a film which is made like this 🖰 The film used computer animation.
2 interest and excitement □ She was talking with great animation.
• **animator** /ˈænɪmeɪtə(r)/ NOUN [plural animators] someone who makes animated films

animosity /ˌænɪˈmɒsɪtɪ/ NOUN, NO PLURAL a feeling of strong dislike towards someone □ There is deep animosity between the two men.

aniseed /ˈænɪsiːd/ NOUN, NO PLURAL a seed with a strong taste, used in making sweets, drinks and medicines

ankle /ˈæŋkəl/ NOUN [plural ankles] the place where your foot joins your leg □ She fell over and sprained her left ankle.

annex[1] /ˈæneks/ or **annexe** NOUN [plural annexes] an extra part of a building that is added on to it

annex[2] /æˈneks/ VERB [annexes, annexing, annexed] to take control of an area or country next to your own □ After the war, the region was annexed by the Soviet Union.

annihilate /əˈnaɪəleɪt/ VERB [annihilates, annihilating, annihilated] to destroy someone or something completely
• **annihilation** /əˌnaɪəˈleɪʃən/ NOUN, NO PLURAL destroying someone or something completely

anniversary /ˌænɪˈvɜːsərɪ/ NOUN [plural anniversaries] a date when you celebrate something that happened on the same date in the past 🖰 a wedding anniversary □ + of Today is the anniversary of the King's death. 🖰 The celebrations will mark the 60th anniversary of the country's independence.

annotated /ˈænəteɪtɪd/ ADJECTIVE an annotated text includes notes to help you understand it

announce /əˈnaʊns/ VERB [announces, announcing, announced] to tell people something, especially loudly or forcefully 🖰 The government has *announced plans to build four new hospitals.* 🖰 *Have they announced their engagement yet?* □ **+ that** *The minister has announced that he is retiring.*

• **announcement** /ə'naʊnsmənt/ NOUN [*plural* **announcements**]

1 something that people are told, especially publicly or officially 🖰 *I want to make an announcement.* 🖰 *a formal/official announcement*

2 *no plural* when something is announced □ *We tried to delay the announcement of the news.*

• **announcer** /ə'naʊnsə(r)/ NOUN [*plural* **announcers**] someone who introduces programmes on television or the radio

annoy /ə'nɔɪ/ VERB [**annoys, annoying, annoyed**] to make someone angry □ *It really annoys me when she wastes food.*

• **annoyance** /ə'nɔɪəns/ NOUN [*plural* **annoyances**]

1 a feeling of being annoyed 🖰 *She completely ignored him, much to his annoyance.* □ *She gave him a look of annoyance.*

2 something that annoys you

• **annoyed** /ə'nɔɪd/ ADJECTIVE angry □ **+ with** *I could tell he was annoyed with me.*

• **annoying** /ə'nɔɪɪŋ/ ADJECTIVE making you feel annoyed 🖰 *an annoying habit* □ *Jo can be so annoying!*

annual /'ænjuəl/ ▶ ADJECTIVE

1 an annual event happens once every year □ *an annual meeting of shareholders*

2 measured over a period of one year □ *annual rainfall* □ *What is your annual income?*

▶ NOUN [*plural* **annuals**]

1 a book that is published every year

2 a plant that lives for only one year

• **annually** /'ænjuəlɪ/ ADVERB happening once every year

anode /'ænəʊd/ NOUN [*plural* **anodes**] the negative electrode (= part where an electric current enters or leaves) in a battery. A physics word.

anomalous /ə'nɒmələs/ ADJECTIVE different from what is normal or expected. A formal word.

• **anomaly** /ə'nɒməlɪ/ NOUN [*plural* **anomalies**] something that is anomalous. A formal word. □ *Experts have spotted some anomalies in the data.*

anonymity /ænə'nɪmətɪ/ NOUN, NO PLURAL when someone's name is kept secret □ *The police informant insisted on anonymity.*

• **anonymous** /ə'nɒnɪməs/ ADJECTIVE without giving a name □ *She started receiving anonymous phone calls.*

• **anonymously** /ə'nɒnɪməslɪ/ ADVERB by someone whose name is kept secret □ *The money has been given anonymously.*

anorak /'ænəræk/ NOUN [*plural* **anoraks**] a thick jacket with a hood (= part that goes over the head)

anorexia /ænə'reksɪə/ NOUN, NO PLURAL an illness in which someone does not eat enough

• **anorexic** /ænə'reksɪk/ ▶ ADJECTIVE suffering from anorexia and very thin

▶ NOUN [*plural* **anorexics**] someone who is suffering from anorexia

another /ə'nʌðə(r)/ DETERMINER, PRONOUN

1 one more person or thing □ *Have another piece of chocolate.* □ *He had two gold medals and now he has another.*

2 a different person or thing □ *We'll finish this game another time.* □ *If that pen's broken, use another one.* □ *I lost my coat and I haven't got another.*

answer /'ɑːnsə(r)/ ▶ VERB [**answers, answering, answered**]

1 to reply when someone asks you a question or sends you a letter □ *I waited for him to answer.* □ *She tried to answer truthfully.* □ *I'm just going to answer his letter.*

2 to pick up the telephone when it rings, or to open the door when someone is there □ *A child answered the telephone.* □ *I knocked at the door and an old woman answered.*

3 to write or say the answer to a question in an exam or a competition □ *You have an hour to answer all four questions.*

◆ PHRASAL VERB **answer (someone) back** to reply rudely to someone who has criticized you □ *His teacher told him off for answering back.*

▶ NOUN [*plural* **answers**]

1 a reply □ **+ to** *I couldn't find an answer to my question.* 🖰 *He gave a detailed answer.*

2 the solution to a problem □ *If you can't afford a car, then a car sharing scheme could be the answer.*

3 in answer to as a reply □ *In answer to my question, he handed me the document to read.*

4 what you write or say to answer a question in an exam or a competition 🖰 *the correct/wrong answer*

► Remember to use the preposition **to** after the noun **answer**:
  ✓ *What's the answer to question six?*
  ✗ *What's the answer for question six?*

• **answerable** /'ɑːnsərəbəl/ ADJECTIVE answerable to someone if you are answerable to someone for something, you are responsible for it, and you will have to explain to them if anything goes wrong

answerphone /'ɑːnsəˌfəʊn/ or **answering machine** /'ɑːnsərɪŋ mə'ʃiːn/ NOUN [*plural* **answerphones** or **answering machines**] a machine that automatically answers your telephone and records messages for you

ant /ænt/ NOUN [*plural* **ants**] a small, usually black, insect that lives in organized groups

antagonism /æn'tægənɪzəm/ NOUN, NO PLURAL a feeling of wanting to fight against a person or an idea □ *We couldn't understand their antagonism towards us.*

• **antagonistic** /æn,tægə'nɪstɪk/ ADJECTIVE wanting to fight or argue against a person or an idea

• **antagonize** or **antagonise** /æn'tægənaɪz/ VERB [**antagonizes, antagonizing, antagonized**] to make someone want to fight or argue with you

Antarctic /ænt'ɑːktɪk/ ▶ NOUN the Antarctic the area of the world round the South Pole
▶ ADJECTIVE to do with the Antarctic □ *Antarctic exploration* □ *the Antarctic winter*

ante- /,æntɪ/ PREFIX ante- is added to the beginning of words to mean 'before' □ *antenatal*

antelope /'æntɪləʊp/ NOUN [*plural* **antelope** or **antelopes**] an animal like a deer, that has long horns and runs very fast

antenatal /,æntɪ'neɪtəl/ ADJECTIVE to do with the time when a woman is pregnant, before the baby is born 🖫 *antenatal classes*

antenna /æn'tenə/ NOUN [*plural* **antennae** or **antennas**]
1 one of two long thin parts on the head of an insect or a sea animal, used for feeling
2 a thin piece of metal that is used for getting television or radio signals

anthem /'ænθəm/ NOUN [*plural* **anthems**] a song that praises a country or an organization, for example a football team
➡ **go to** national anthem

anthology /æn'θɒlədʒɪ/ NOUN [*plural* **anthologies**] a book that is a collection of stories, poems or songs by different writers

anthropologist /,ænθrə'pɒlədʒɪst/ NOUN [*plural* **anthropologists**] someone who studies the way humans live

• **anthropology** /,ænθrə'pɒlədʒɪ/ NOUN, NO PLURAL the study of the way humans live

anti- /'æntɪ/ PREFIX anti- is added to the beginning of words to mean 'against' or 'preventing' □ *antisocial* □ *antifreeze*

antibiotic /,æntɪbaɪ'ɒtɪk/ NOUN [*plural* **antibiotics**] a medicine that kills bacteria that can cause infections □ *The doctor's put me on antibiotics.*

antibody /'æntɪ,bɒdɪ/ NOUN [*plural* **antibodies**] a substance that is produced in your blood to fight disease. A biology word.

anticipate /æn'tɪsɪ,peɪt/ VERB [**anticipates, anticipating, anticipated**] to expect something to happen, and often to prepare for it □ *We don't anticipate any problems.*

• **anticipation** /æn,tɪsɪ'peɪʃən/ NOUN, NO PLURAL
1 excitement about something that is going to happen □ *There was a sense of anticipation in the hall.*
2 in anticipation of something in order to prepare for something □ *The school has closed in anticipation of heavy snow.*

anticlimax /,æntɪ'klaɪmæks/ NOUN [*plural* **anticlimaxes**] when something ends in a way that is less exciting than you expected or less exciting than what happened before it □ *After all the publicity, the show was a bit of an anticlimax.*

anticlockwise /,æntɪ'klɒkwaɪz/ ADJECTIVE, ADVERB going in the opposite direction to the hands (= parts that point) of a clock □ *Turn the top of the bottle anticlockwise.*

antics /'æntɪks/ PLURAL NOUN someone's antics are the funny or annoying things that they do

antidote /'æntɪdəʊt/ NOUN [*plural* **antidotes**]
1 an antidote to something something that stops the harmful effects of something else □ *Laughter is the best antidote to stress.*
2 a medicine that stops the effects of poison

antifreeze /'æntɪfriːz/ NOUN, NO PLURAL a chemical that you add to a liquid to stop it from freezing

antigen /'æntɪdʒən/ NOUN [*plural* **antigens**] a substance that makes the body produce antibodies (= substances that fight disease). A biology word.

antihistamine /,æntɪ'hɪstəmɪn/ NOUN [*plural* **antihistamines**] a medicine that is used to treat allergies (= bad reactions to something you have eaten or touched)

anti-oxidant /,æntɪ'ɒksɪdənt/ NOUN [*plural* **anti-oxidants**] a substance, for example a vitamin from a healthy food, that removes harmful molecules (= groups of atoms) from your body

antipathy /æn'tɪpəθɪ/ NOUN, NO PLURAL a feeling of dislike □ *He had a deep antipathy towards the modern world.*

antiperspirant /,æntɪ'pɜːspərənt/ NOUN [*plural* **antiperspirants**] a substance that stops you sweating

antiquated /'æntɪkweɪtɪd/ ADJECTIVE too old-fashioned □ *The factory was using antiquated machinery.*

antique /æn'tiːk/ ▶ NOUN [*plural* **antiques**] an object that is old and valuable □ *a collector of antiques*
▶ ADJECTIVE old and valuable □ *antique jewellery*

► Remember that **antique** is used for old objects, such as furniture and jewellery. It is not used for old buildings. For buildings, use **old** or **ancient**. □ *They have a lot of very valuable antique furniture.* □ *We visited the ancient monuments.*

anti-Semitic /,æntɪsɪ'mɪtɪk/ ADJECTIVE showing hate towards Jewish people □ *anti-Semitic views*

• **anti-Semitism** /,æntɪ'semɪtɪzəm/ NOUN, NO PLURAL hate or unfair treatment of Jewish people

antiseptic /,æntɪ'septɪk/ NOUN [*plural* **antiseptics**] a substance that is used to clean injuries in order to prevent infections

antisocial /,æntɪ'səʊʃəl/ ADJECTIVE
1 antisocial behaviour is unpleasant or harmful to other people
2 antisocial people do not enjoy being with other people

anti-spam /ˌæntɪˈspæm/ ADJECTIVE anti-spam software stops you getting e-mails that you do not want, especially advertising. A computing word.

antithesis /ænˈtɪθɪsɪs/ NOUN [plural **antitheses**] the antithesis of something the complete opposite of something. A formal word. □ His new book is the antithesis of his previous gloomy, intellectual novels.

antivirus /ˈæntɪˌvaɪrəs/ ADJECTIVE antivirus software stops other software from harming your computer. A computing word.

antler /ˈæntlə(r)/ NOUN [plural **antlers**] a horn that divides like branches and grows on the head of a deer

antonym /ˈæntənɪm/ NOUN [plural **antonyms**] a word that means the opposite of another word

anus /ˈeɪnəs/ NOUN [plural **anuses**] the opening in your bottom through which you get rid of solid waste from your body

anxiety /æŋˈzaɪətɪ/ NOUN [plural **anxieties**] a feeling of worry □ The parents of these soldiers suffered a lot of anxiety.

• **anxious** /ˈæŋkʃəs/ ADJECTIVE
1 worried □ + **about** He's anxious about missing his train. □ She gave me an anxious glance.
2 wanting very much to do something or wanting something to happen □ + **to do something** We're anxious to make sure the work is finished on time.

• **anxiously** /ˈæŋkʃəslɪ/ ADVERB in a worried way □ He looked anxiously at his watch.

any /ˈenɪ/ ▶ DETERMINER, PRONOUN
1 used in questions and negative statements to mean 'some' □ Have we got any sweets? □ We had lots of food, but there isn't any left now.
2 one or a piece of something, but not a particular one □ Let me know if you have any questions. □ Choose any colour you like. □ The children all know the answers - ask any of them.
▶ ADVERB
1 at all □ Are you feeling any better? □ Can't you walk any faster?
2 any more if something does not happen any more, it has stopped happening □ Ricky doesn't work here any more. □ The children don't get free milk any more.

anybody /ˈenɪˌbɒdɪ/ PRONOUN
1 used in questions and negatives to mean 'a person' or 'people' □ Has anybody seen my glasses? □ I didn't speak to anybody.
2 any person □ Anybody is allowed to enter.

anyhow /ˈenɪhaʊ/ ADVERB
1 used to add another reason to what you have just said □ I missed lunch but I wasn't hungry anyhow.
2 despite that □ Two of our players are injured, but anyhow we have a very good team.

anyone /ˈenɪwʌn/ PRONOUN
1 used in questions and negatives to mean 'a person' or 'people' □ Has anyone got a mobile? □ There isn't anyone left.
2 any person □ Anyone can bake a cake. □ He'll talk to anyone.

► Remember that 'anyone' is singular so the verb following it must be singular □ If anyone calls, tell them I'll be back in ten minutes. □ Anyone is welcome to come.

anyplace /ˈenɪpleɪs/ ADVERB the US word for anywhere

anything /ˈenɪθɪŋ/ PRONOUN
1 used in questions and negative statements to mean 'something' □ We didn't have anything to eat. □ Is there anything I can do to help? ⤷ Is there anything else I should know?
2 something of any type □ He's capable of anything. □ We can do anything we like while our teacher is away.

anyway /ˈenɪweɪ/ ADVERB
1 used to add another reason to what you have just said □ I can give you a lift. I'm going that way anyway.
2 despite that □ Leon couldn't go with me but I enjoyed the party anyway.
3 used to start a new part of a conversation □ Anyway, how have you been lately?
4 used to change something you have just said slightly □ I'm not going to leave - not yet, anyway.

anywhere /ˈenɪweə(r)/ ADVERB
1 in or to any place □ I'm willing to travel anywhere. □ You can buy these anywhere in the world. □ Don't go anywhere near Dad - he's in a terrible mood.
2 used in questions and negative statements to mean 'a place' □ Have you got anywhere to stay? □ There isn't anywhere to hide.
3 anywhere near used in questions and negative statements to mean 'almost in a particular state' □ The building isn't anywhere near completion. □ Are you anywhere near finishing with the computer?

aorta /eɪˈɔːtə/ NOUN [plural **aortas**] the main tube that takes blood from your heart to the rest of your body. A biology word.

apart /əˈpɑːt/ ADVERB
1 separated by distance or time □ Stand with your feet apart. □ We had two classes, a week apart.
2 into pieces ⤷ The seams of this jacket have come apart. □ We had to take the lamp apart to mend it.
3 apart from except for □ Apart from us, nobody's interested. □ I've had nothing to eat apart from a biscuit.
4 tell apart if you cannot tell two people apart, you cannot see any differences in their appearance

apartheid /əˈpɑːthaɪt/ NOUN, NO PLURAL the system in the past in South Africa, where black and white people lived separately and were treated differently by law

apartment /əˈpɑːtmənt/ NOUN [plural **apartments**] a mainly US word for **flat** (= set of rooms on one level) □ an apartment block

apathetic /ˌæpə'θetɪk/ ADJECTIVE not interested in anything

• **apathy** /'æpəθɪ/ NOUN, NO PLURAL being apathetic

ape /eɪp/ ▶ NOUN [plural **apes**] a large animal like a monkey with no tail

▶ VERB [**apes, aping, aped**] to copy the way someone else speaks or behaves

aperitif /əperə'tiːf/ NOUN [plural **aperitifs**] an alcoholic drink that you have before a meal

apex /'eɪpeks/ NOUN [plural **apexes** or **apices**] the top point of something, especially a triangle

aphid /'eɪfɪd/ NOUN [plural **aphids**] a small insect that eats plants

apiece /ə'piːs/ ADVERB each □ We bought five chairs at £30 apiece.

aplomb /ə'plɒm/ NOUN, NO PLURAL if you do something with aplomb, you do it well and with confidence □ She delivered her speech with aplomb.

apocryphal /ə'pɒkrɪfəl/ ADJECTIVE an apocryphal story is not true, although many people think it is

apolitical /ˌeɪpə'lɪtɪkəl/ ADJECTIVE not interested in politics, or not connected to any political beliefs

apologetic /əˌpɒlə'dʒetɪk/ ADJECTIVE showing that you are sorry for doing something wrong □ She gave me an apologetic smile.

apologize or **apologise** /ə'pɒlədʒaɪz/ VERB [**apologizes, apologizing, apologized**] to say sorry for doing something wrong □ + **for** I had to apologize for being late.

• **apology** /ə'pɒlədʒɪ/ NOUN [plural **apologies**] when someone apologizes ▣ He made a public apology. ▣ She demanded an apology from the newspaper's editor. □ + **for** I owe you an apology for forgetting your birthday again.

apostle /ə'pɒsəl/ NOUN [plural **apostles**] one of the first twelve men who followed Jesus Christ

apostrophe /ə'pɒstrəfɪ/ NOUN [plural **apostrophes**]

1 the symbol (') that shows where a letter or letters have been missed out □ Jane's (= Jane is) late again. □ I think it'll (= it will) rain later.

2 the symbol (') that is used before the letter s to show who something belongs to □ I borrowed Ralf's bicycle.

appal /ə'pɔːl/ VERB [**appals, appalling, appalled**] if you are appalled by something, you are shocked and upset by it □ I was appalled by her language.

• **appalling** /ə'pɔːlɪŋ/ ADJECTIVE shocking and very bad □ an appalling accident □ appalling weather

apparatus /ˌæpə'reɪtəs/ NOUN, NO PLURAL the equipment that you need for a particular task □ breathing apparatus

apparent /ə'pærənt/ ADJECTIVE

1 easy to see ▣ Then, for no apparent reason, he began to cry.

2 seeming to be true □ We were shocked by his apparent lack of regret.

• **apparently** /ə'pærəntlɪ/ ADVERB

1 used to tell people about something you have been told, although you are not sure if it is true

□ Apparently there's going to be an announcement later.

2 used to talk about something that seems to be true □ The cause of the illness is apparently unknown.

apparition /ˌæpə'rɪʃən/ NOUN [plural **apparitions**] a strange thing that someone sees, especially a ghost (= spirit of a dead person)

appeal /ə'piːl/ ▶ VERB [**appeals, appealing, appealed**]

1 to ask for something, often forcefully or publicly □ The police have appealed to the public for more information.

2 if something appeals to you, you think you would enjoy it □ Diving doesn't appeal to me one bit.

3 to try to get a legal decision changed officially □ They will appeal against the sentence.

▶ NOUN [plural **appeals**]

1 when someone appeals for something □ Their appeals for calm were ignored. □ Their appeal raised £3,000 for the hospice.

2 the quality that makes something attractive □ I don't understand the appeal of stamp collecting.

3 when someone appeals against a legal decision □ His appeal was rejected.

appear /ə'pɪə(r)/ VERB [**appears, appearing, appeared**]

1 to seem □ + **that** It appears that his wife knew nothing of his crimes. □ + **to do something** The man appeared to punch his victim. ▣ I appear to be the only one who has read the book. □ He appears determined to win.

2 to arrive or start to be able to be seen □ Greta appeared round the corner. □ A car appeared in the distance.

3 to start to exist □ The first signs of the disease appeared in June.

4 to be present somewhere, especially officially ▣ He appeared in court charged with assault. □ Bax failed to appear at the meeting.

5 if an actor appears in a film or a play, they are in it

• **appearance** /ə'pɪərəns/ NOUN [plural **appearances**]

1 the way someone or something looks □ He was described as being of Asian appearance. □ We thought carefully about the appearance of the room.

2 when someone appears in public ▣ He is making his first appearance for AC Milan. ▣ This is her first public appearance since her divorce. ▣ He has already had several court appearances.

3 when someone or something arrives or starts to be seen □ We were thrilled by the appearance of dolphins near our boat. □ The appearance of a police officer frightened the youths away.

4 the way something seems to be □ We like to give the appearance of efficiency. ▣ To all appearances (= everyone thought) they were the ideal couple. ▣ We don't have much money, but we try to keep

up appearances (= make it seem that everything is good).

appease /ə'piːz/ VERB [appeases, appeasing, appeased] to make someone feel less angry by doing what they want

appendicitis /ə,pendɪ'saɪtɪs/ NOUN, NO PLURAL an illness where your appendix becomes infected and has to be removed

appendix[1] /ə'pendɪks/ NOUN [plural appendixes] a small body part that has no purpose, just below the stomach. A biology word.

appendix[2] /ə'pendɪks/ NOUN [plural appendices] an extra part at the end of a book or document that gives more details about something

appetite /'æpɪtaɪt/ NOUN [plural appetites] the feeling of being hungry 🕮 *Elly has lost her appetite since she's been ill.* 🕮 *You'll spoil your appetite if you eat all those biscuits.*

• **appetizer** *or* **appetiser** /'æpɪtaɪzə(r)/ NOUN [plural appetizers] something small to eat before a meal

• **appetizing** *or* **appetising** /'æpɪtaɪzɪŋ/ ADJECTIVE appetizing food smells or looks good

applaud /ə'plɔːd/ VERB [applauds, applauding, applauded] to hit your hands together to show that you enjoyed something □ *The audience applauded loudly.*

• **applause** /ə'plɔːz/ NOUN, NO PLURAL when people applaud

apple /'æpəl/ NOUN [plural apples] a hard, round fruit with red, green or yellow skin

♦ IDIOM **the apple of someone's eye** if someone is the apple of your eye, you love them and are very proud of them

appliance /ə'plaɪəns/ NOUN [plural appliances] a piece of electrical equipment 🕮 *kitchen appliances*

applicable /ə'plɪkəbəl/ ADJECTIVE if something is applicable to a person or a situation, it is to do with them or affects them □ *Managers must understand the laws that are applicable to their companies.*

applicant /'æplɪkənt/ NOUN [plural applicants] someone who applies for something such as a job or university place

application /,æplɪ'keɪʃən/ NOUN [plural applications]
1 a written document asking for something such as a job
2 a computer program that does a particular job. A computing word.
3 a particular use for something □ *This research could have several applications in medicine.*
4 *no plural* an effort to do something well □ *He could pass the exam with a little more application.*
5 when you put something such as paint or cream on a surface □ *Let the paint dry between applications.*

applicator /'æplɪkeɪtə(r)/ NOUN [plural applicators] a device that helps you put something in the right place □ *Spread the glue with the applicator on the top.*

applied /ə'plaɪd/ ADJECTIVE applied maths/science mathematics or science that has a practical use

apply /ə'plaɪ/ VERB [applies, applying, applied]
1 to officially ask for something, especially a job or a place on a course □ *+ for* *I've applied for a new job.* □ *+ to* *Maria's applying to university this year.*
2 to spread a substance on a surface □ *Apply the cream to the affected skin three times a day.*
3 to affect a particular person or people □ *+ to* *Do these rules apply to all of us?*
4 **apply yourself** to work hard

appoint /ə'pɔɪnt/ VERB [appoints, appointing, appointed] to officially give someone a job □ *The committee has appointed Mark Burns as manager.*

• **appointment** /ə'pɔɪntmənt/ NOUN [plural appointments]
1 a time when you have arranged to meet someone 🕮 *I've made an appointment with the nurse.* 🕮 *I have a doctor's appointment.* 🕮 *I've arranged a dental appointment.*
2 choosing someone for a job □ *We hope to secure the appointment of a new music teacher this month.*
3 an important job □ *academic appointments*

> ➤ An **appointment** is an arranged meeting with a doctor, dentist, etc. It is not a meeting with a friend. To say that you are meeting a friend, say **I'm seeing x** or **I have arranged to see x**:
> ✓ *I'm seeing Maria this afternoon.*
> ✗ *I have an appointment with Maria this afternoon.*

appraisal /ə'preɪzəl/ NOUN [plural appraisals]
1 when you consider something and form an opinion about it
2 when you formally judge how well someone is doing their job

appraise /ə'preɪz/ VERB [appraises, appraising, appraised] to consider something and form an opinion about it □ *She appraised the situation.*

appreciable /ə'priːʃəbəl/ ADJECTIVE big or obvious enough to be noticed □ *The next day there was an appreciable drop in temperature.*

• **appreciably** /ə'priːʃəblɪ/ ADVERB enough to be noticed

appreciate /ə'priːʃɪeɪt/ VERB [appreciates, appreciating, appreciated]
1 to feel grateful for something □ *I really appreciate all the time you've spent on this.*
2 to enjoy or understand something that is of good quality □ *I bought Ava the more expensive perfume because I know she appreciates it.*
3 to understand that a situation is difficult □ *I appreciate that you have had a lot of problems to deal with.*

4 to become more valuable □ *The painting has appreciated in value over the years.*

● **appreciation** /əˌpriːʃɪˈeɪʃən/ NOUN, NO PLURAL
1 when you are grateful to someone □ *Here's a little gift to show our appreciation of all your help.*
2 when you enjoy or understand something that is of good quality □ *the appreciation of good food*
3 increasing value

● **appreciative** /əˈpriːʃɪətɪv/ ADJECTIVE
1 grateful to someone
2 showing enjoyment or understanding □ *an appreciative audience*

apprehension /ˌæprɪˈhenʃən/ NOUN, NO PLURAL
worry about something that is going to happen

● **apprehensive** /ˌæprɪˈhensɪv/ ADJECTIVE worried about something that is going to happen □ *She's a bit apprehensive about her interview.*

● **apprehensively** /ˌæprɪˈhensɪvlɪ/ ADVERB in a worried way

apprentice /əˈprentɪs/ NOUN [plural **apprentices**] someone who is learning how to do a skilled job from someone who can already do it

● **apprenticeship** /əˈprentɪʃɪp/ NOUN [plural **apprenticeships**] the time when someone is learning their job

approach /əˈprəʊtʃ/ ▶ VERB [approaches, approaching, approached]
1 to come towards a place, person or thing □ *Approach the animals very slowly.* □ *The plane was approaching Paris from the south.*
2 to ask someone for something □ *If you want more money you'll have to approach your boss.*
3 to deal with something □ *What's the best way to approach the problem?*
▶ NOUN [plural **approaches**]
1 a way of trying to deal with something □ + *to It's a sensible approach to the problem.* ▣ *We could take a different approach.*
2 when something or someone gets closer □ *the approach of spring* □ *At the approach of the train, everyone pushed forward.*
3 a road or path that takes you to a building □ *a tree-lined approach*

● **approachable** /əˈprəʊtʃəbəl/ ADJECTIVE an approachable person is easy to talk to

appropriate /əˈprəʊprɪət/ ADJECTIVE suitable □ *Please wear appropriate clothing.*

● **appropriately** /əˈprəʊprɪətlɪ/ ADVERB in a suitable way □ *appropriately dressed*

approval /əˈpruːvəl/ NOUN, NO PLURAL
1 when someone thinks something is good □ *I've always wanted my father's approval.*
2 permission to do something □ *We need your approval before we can send the money.*

approve /əˈpruːv/ VERB [approves, approving, approved]
1 approve of something/someone to think

something or someone is good □ *They don't approve of her boyfriend.*
2 to formally agree to something □ *Has he approved the proposal yet?*

● **approving** /əˈpruːvɪŋ/ ADJECTIVE showing that you think something or someone is good □ *He gave an approving nod.*

● **approvingly** /əˈpruːvɪŋlɪ/ ADVERB in an approving way

approximate /əˈprɒksɪmət/ ADJECTIVE not exact but close □ *Can you tell me the approximate number of chairs we'll need?* □ *This is the approximate size of the rug.*

● **approximately** /əˈprɒksɪmətlɪ/ ADVERB not exactly although close to □ *There will be approximately sixty people there.*

● **approximation** /əˌprɒksɪˈmeɪʃən/ NOUN [plural **approximations**] a number or amount that someone has guessed and which is not exact □ *The number quoted was only an approximation.*

apricot /ˈeɪprɪkɒt/ ▶ NOUN [plural **apricots**] a small, light orange fruit with a soft skin and a stone inside
▶ ADJECTIVE having a light orange colour, like an apricot

April /ˈeɪprəl/ NOUN the fourth month of the year, after March and before May □ *We're getting married in April.*

apron /ˈeɪprən/ NOUN [plural **aprons**] something that you wear over your normal clothes, especially when you are cooking, which keeps your clothes clean

apt /æpt/ ADJECTIVE
1 apt to do something if you are apt to do something, you often do it □ *He is apt to fly into a temper.*
2 suitable □ *an apt description*

aptitude /ˈæptɪtjuːd/ NOUN [plural **aptitudes**] a natural ability to do something □ *She never showed much aptitude for the piano.*

aptly /ˈæptlɪ/ ADVERB in a way that is suitable □ *They bought a house by the river, very aptly named 'River's Edge'.*

aqua- /ˈækwə/ PREFIX aqua- is added to the start of words to mean 'to do with water' □ *aquarium*

aquamarine /ˌækwəməˈriːn/ ADJECTIVE having a pale, blue-green colour

aquarium /əˈkweərɪəm/ NOUN [plural **aquariums**] a glass box or a building, for example in a zoo, for keeping fish or water animals

aquatic /əˈkwætɪk/ ADJECTIVE to do with water □ *aquatic sports* □ *aquatic plants*

aqueduct /ˈækwɪdʌkt/ NOUN [plural **aqueducts**] a bridge that carries a river or canal (= river made by men) across a valley

Arabic numeral /ˈærəbɪk ˈnjuːmərəl/ NOUN [plural **Arabic numerals**] a number such as 0, 1, 2, 3, 4, 5, 6, 7, 8 or 9
➡ *go to* Roman numeral

arable /ˈærəbəl/ ADJECTIVE used for or to do with growing crops

arbiter /ˈɑːbɪtə(r)/ NOUN [plural **arbiters**] a person or an organization that acts as a judge, for example in a disagreement between people or countries

arbitrary /ˈɑːbɪtrərɪ/ ADJECTIVE an arbitrary decision or choice is one that you make without a good reason □ Our choice of hotel was purely arbitrary.

arbitrate /ˈɑːbɪtreɪt/ VERB [arbitrates, arbitrating, arbitrated] to be a judge when people are arguing

• **arbitration** /ˌɑːbɪˈtreɪʃən/ NOUN, NO PLURAL when someone official tries to solve an argument between other people

arc /ɑːk/ NOUN [plural **arcs**] a curve that is like part of a circle

arcade /ɑːˈkeɪd/ NOUN [plural **arcades**]
1 a place with a lot of machines that you can play games on 🔲 an amusement arcade
2 a covered street with shops on both sides 🔲 a shopping arcade

arch /ɑːtʃ/ ▶ NOUN [plural **arches**]
1 a curved structure that sometimes gives support to something, for example a bridge
2 the curved part on the under side of your foot
▶ VERB [arches, arching, arched] to make a curved shape □ The cat arched its back.

archaeological /ˌɑːkɪəˈlɒdʒɪkəl/ ADJECTIVE to do with archaeology

archaeologist /ˌɑːkɪˈɒlədʒɪst/ ADJECTIVE [archaeologists] someone who studies things from ancient societies that have been found

• **archaeology** /ˌɑːkɪˈɒlədʒɪ/ NOUN, NO PLURAL the study of ancient societies by looking at things from that time that have been found

archaic /ɑːˈkeɪɪk/ ADJECTIVE very old, and often no longer used □ archaic language

archangel /ˈɑːkˌeɪndʒəl/ NOUN [plural **archangels**] a very important angel (= creature like a person with wings)

archbishop /ˌɑːtʃˈbɪʃəp/ NOUN [plural **archbishops**] the most important priest in some Christian churches

archeological /ˌɑːkɪəˈlɒdʒɪkəl/ ADJECTIVE the US spelling of archaeological

archeologist /ˌɑːkɪˈɒlədʒɪst/ NOUN [plural **archeologists**] the US spelling of archaeologist

• **archeology** /ˌɑːkɪˈɒlədʒɪ/ NOUN, NO PLURAL the US spelling of archaeology

archer /ˈɑːtʃə(r)/ NOUN [plural **archers**] someone who shoots arrows with a bow (= piece of curved wood with string attached)

• **archery** /ˈɑːtʃərɪ/ NOUN, NO PLURAL the sport of shooting arrows with a bow (= piece of curved wood with string attached)

archetypal /ˌɑːkɪˈtaɪpəl/ ADJECTIVE very typical □ an archetypal 1930s cinema

• **archetype** /ˈɑːkɪtaɪp/ NOUN [plural **archetypes**] a typical example of a particular type of person or thing □ He seemed to me the archetype of an academic.

archipelago /ˌɑːkɪˈpelɪɡəʊ/ NOUN [plural **archipelagoes** or **archipelagos**] a group of small islands. A geography word.

architect /ˈɑːkɪtekt/ NOUN [plural **architects**] someone whose job is to design buildings

• **architectural** /ˌɑːkɪˈtektʃərəl/ ADJECTIVE to do with the design of buildings □ architectural features

• **architecturally** /ˌɑːkɪˈtektʃərəlɪ/ ADVERB in a way that is to do with the design of buildings □ Architecturally, the city is very interesting.

• **architecture** /ˈɑːkɪtektʃə(r)/ NOUN, NO PLURAL
1 designing buildings □ He studied architecture.
2 a style of building □ modern architecture

archive /ˈɑːkaɪv/ ▶ NOUN [plural **archives**]
1 a collection of historical records about a place, organization, family, etc. □ The information is kept in the company archives.
2 a place on a computer where files that are not often used are stored. A computing word.
▶ VERB [archives, archiving, archived] to put paper or computer documents in an archive. A computing word.

archway /ˈɑːtʃweɪ/ NOUN [plural **archways**] an entrance or a passage with an arch (= curved structure) over it

Arctic /ˈɑːktɪk/ ▶ NOUN the Arctic the area of the world around the North Pole
▶ ADJECTIVE
1 to do with the Arctic □ the Arctic Ocean
2 arctic extremely cold □ They camped in arctic conditions.

ardent /ˈɑːdənt/ ADJECTIVE having strong feelings □ an ardent football fan

arduous /ˈɑːdjuəs/ ADJECTIVE difficult or physically hard 🔲 an arduous journey/task

are /ɑː(r)/ VERB the present tense of the verb be when it is used with you, we and they □ They are hungry. □ Are we late?

> ► Note that instead of **you are**, **we are** and **they are**, people often say or write the short forms, **you're**, **we're** and **they're** □ You're late. □ We're here! □ They're over there.

area /ˈeərɪə/ NOUN [plural **areas**]
1 a part of a place □ There are a lot of farms in this area. □ We work with children from deprived areas of the city.
2 a subject or activity □ What area of medicine do you specialize in?
3 the size of a surface, that you measure in square units of measurement □ A carpet that is 5 metres by 5 metres has an area of 25 square metres.
4 a part of a building or place used for a particular purpose □ a children's play area □ a cooking area

arena /əˈriːnə/ NOUN [plural **arenas**] a large space for sports or concerts with seats all around it

aren't /ɑːnt/ a short way to say and write 'are not' □ These aren't my boots.

arguable /'ɑ:gjuəbəl/ ADJECTIVE if something is arguable, it is possible that it is true □ *It is arguable that prison was good for him.*
• **arguably** /'ɑ:gjuəblɪ/ ADVERB something is arguably true if it is possible to believe it □ *He is arguably the best player we've ever had.*

argue /'ɑ:gju:/ VERB [argues, arguing, argued]
1 to speak in an angry way with someone because you disagree with them □ **+ with** *The children never stop arguing with each other.* □ **+ about/over** *They were arguing about where to go on holiday.*
2 to give reasons for thinking or believing something □ **+ that** *The manager argued that the shop would have to close.* □ **+ for** *They argued for an increase in their pay.*
• **argument** /'ɑ:gjumənt/ NOUN [plural **arguments**]
1 an angry discussion 🔁 *The kids were having an argument.* 🔁 *a heated argument* (= a very angry argument) □ **+ about** *an argument about money*
2 a reason for having a particular point of view □ **+ against** *My argument against the plan is that we just don't have the money.*
• **argumentative** /,ɑ:gju'mentətɪv/ ADJECTIVE an argumentative person often argues with other people

aria /'ɑ:rɪə/ NOUN [plural **arias**] a song in an opera for one person to sing
arid /'ærɪd/ ADJECTIVE very dry □ *arid regions*
arise /ə'raɪz/ VERB [arises, arising, arose, arisen] to happen □ *A small problem has arisen.*
aristocracy /,ærɪ'stɒkrəsɪ/ NOUN [plural **aristocracies**] people of a country's highest social class, often connected to royal families □ *Only members of the aristocracy are invited to these occasions.*
• **aristocrat** /'ærɪstəkræt/ NOUN [plural **aristocrats**] someone from a family of a very high social class, who often have a title like *Lord* or *Lady*
• **aristocratic** /,ærɪstə'krætɪk/ ADJECTIVE belonging to or typical of the aristocracy □ *an aristocratic family*
arithmetic /ə'rɪθmətɪk/ NOUN, NO PLURAL mathematics that involves processes such as adding and multiplying □ *simple arithmetic*
• **arithmetical** /,ærɪθ'metɪkəl/ ADJECTIVE to do with calculating numbers □ *an arithmetical problem*
ark /ɑ:k/ NOUN [plural **arks**] the boat that carried Noah, his family and two of every animal during the flood in the Bible story

arm¹ /ɑ:m/ NOUN [plural **arms**]
1 the part of your body between your shoulder and your hand □ *I put my arm round his shoulder.* 🔁 *She folded her arms* (= crossed one over the other close to her body).
2 the arm of a piece of clothing is the sleeve
3 the part of a chair that you rest your arms on
4 **arm in arm** holding someone's arm □ *They walked arm in arm along the beach.*
➡ go to **arms**

arm² /ɑ:m/ VERB [arms, arming, armed] to give someone a weapon to fight with □ *The crowd was armed with sticks and knives.*
armaments /'ɑ:məmənts/ PLURAL NOUN weapons and other military equipment

armchair /'ɑ:mtʃeə(r)/ NOUN [plural **armchairs**] a comfortable chair with sides for resting your arms on

armed /ɑ:md/ ADJECTIVE carrying a weapon
🔁 *heavily armed* 🔁 *armed robbery/burglary*

armed forces /ɑ:md 'fɔ:sɪz/ PLURAL NOUN the **armed forces** the military groups of a country, for example its army
armistice /'ɑ:mɪstɪs/ NOUN [plural **armistices**] an agreement between enemies to stop fighting in a war
armor /'ɑ:mə(r)/ NOUN, NO PLURAL the US spelling of **armour**
• **armored** /'ɑ:məd/ ADJECTIVE the US spelling of **armoured**
armour /'ɑ:mə(r)/ NOUN, NO PLURAL
1 metal covers worn by soldiers in the past to protect their bodies 🔁 *a suit of armour*
2 metal covers used to protect military vehicles
• **armoured** /'ɑ:məd/ ADJECTIVE an armoured vehicle is protected by layers of metal
armpit /'ɑ:mpɪt/ NOUN [plural **armpits**] the part under your arm where it joins your body
arms /ɑ:mz/ PLURAL NOUN weapons 🔁 *the arms race* (= when countries try to get more and better weapons than each other) □ *arms manufacturers*
• IDIOM **be up in arms** to be very angry about something and trying to stop it □ *Local people are up in arms over proposals for a nuclear power station.*

army /'ɑ:mɪ/ NOUN [plural **armies**]
1 an organization of soldiers 🔁 *He joined the army after leaving school.* □ *the US army* □ *an army officer*
2 a large number of people □ *An army of decorators transformed the building.*

aroma /ə'rəumə/ NOUN [plural **aromas**] a nice smell, especially of food
aromatherapy /ə,rəumə'θerəpɪ/ NOUN, NO PLURAL using the oils of plants and flowers that have different smells to treat people who are not well
aromatic /,ærə'mætɪk/ ADJECTIVE having a good smell □ *aromatic plants*
arose /ə'rəuz/ PAST TENSE OF **arise**

around /ə'raund/ PREPOSITION, ADVERB
1 on all sides □ *We were sitting around the table.*
2 in or to different parts of a place □ *We walked around the city.* □ *There were clothes lying around everywhere.* □ *The children are allowed to run around all over the place.*
3 to several different people □ *We passed the drinks around.*
4 about □ *They should arrive at around 4 o'clock.* □ *I weigh around sixty kilos.*

5 to face the opposite direction □ *He turned around and pointed the gun at me.*
6 in a circular movement □ *Twist the knife around in the hole.*
7 near □ *Is there a teacher around?*

arouse /əˈrauz/ VERB [arouses, arousing, aroused] to make someone have a particular feeling □ *His strange behaviour aroused my suspicion.*

arrange /əˈreɪndʒ/ VERB [arranges, arranging, arranged]
1 to make plans or to prepare for something □ *Who is arranging the wedding?* □ **+ to do something** *He's arranged to go out with his mates tonight.* □ **+ for** *I've arranged for a taxi to pick him up later.*
2 to put things in a particular order □ *Arrange the flowers in the vase.* □ *All his books are arranged in alphabetical order by author.*
• **arrangement** /əˈreɪndʒmənt/ NOUN [plural arrangements]
1 a plan that is made so that something can happen the way you want it to ⊞ *They made arrangements to meet back at the car.* □ *If he's not back in time, we'll have to make other arrangements.*
2 an agreement with someone ⊞ *We managed to come to an arrangement about who should do the cooking.* □ *I have an arrangement with my sister to look after the children on Fridays.*
3 a group of things that are in a particular order or position □ *a flower arrangement*

array /əˈreɪ/ NOUN [plural arrays] a large group of things □ *He owns a vast array of electronic equipment.*

arrears /əˈrɪəz/ PLURAL NOUN **in arrears** owing money on regular payments □ *He's in arrears with his rent.*

arrest /əˈrest/ ▶ VERB [arrests, arresting, arrested] if the police arrest someone, they take them to the police station because they may have committed a crime □ **+ for** *He was arrested for causing a disturbance.*
▶ NOUN [plural arrests]
1 when the police arrest someone ⊞ *Police have made three arrests in connection with the murder.*
2 under arrest someone is under arrest when the police are keeping them because they may have committed a crime

arrival /əˈraɪvəl/ NOUN [plural arrivals]
1 *no plural* when someone reaches a place □ *We are all looking forward to Alice's arrival.*
2 on arrival when you arrive □ *On arrival, go straight to the meeting room.*
3 a person or thing that has come to a place or started to exist □ *Come and meet the new arrivals.* □ *the arrival of spring*

arrive /əˈraɪv/ VERB [arrives, arriving, arrived]
1 to reach a place □ **+ at** *Please arrive at the station by 5.30.* □ **+ in** *We arrived in Warsaw on Friday.* □ *If they don't arrive soon, we'll have to go without them.*

2 to start to happen or exist □ *Would her birthday ever arrive?*

➤ Remember that you **arrive in** a city or country:
✓ We arrived in Madrid at 10 o'clock that night.
✗ We arrived to Madrid at 10 o'clock that night.

♦ PHRASAL VERB **arrive at something** to manage to make an agreement, decision, etc. □ *We haven't really arrived at any conclusions.*

arrogance /ˈærəgəns/ NOUN, NO PLURAL a feeling of being better or more important than other people
• **arrogant** /ˈærəgənt/ ADJECTIVE arrogant people think they are better or more important than other people □ *He's an extremely arrogant man.*

arrow /ˈærəʊ/ NOUN [plural arrows]
1 a pointed shape used to show a particular direction □ *Follow the red arrows to the X-ray department.*
2 a thin, pointed stick that is used as a weapon

arsenal /ˈɑːsənəl/ NOUN [plural arsenals] a store for weapons

arsenic /ˈɑːsnɪk/ NOUN, NO PLURAL a strong poison

arson /ˈɑːsən/ NOUN, NO PLURAL the crime of setting fire to a building on purpose
• **arsonist** /ˈɑːsənɪst/ NOUN [plural arsonists] someone who sets fire to a building on purpose

art /ɑːt/ NOUN [plural arts]
1 *no plural* the beautiful things that people make and invent in painting, music, writing, etc.
2 a skill that you use to do or make something □ *the art of conversation*
3 the arts subjects that you can study that are not sciences

artefact / ˈɑːtɪfækt/ NOUN [plural artefacts] a very old object that tells us something about history

artery /ˈɑːtəri/ NOUN [plural arteries] a tube that takes blood from your heart to the rest of your body. A biology word.

artful /ˈɑːtfʊl/ ADJECTIVE clever in a slightly dishonest way

arthritic /ɑːˈθrɪtɪk/ ADJECTIVE swollen and painful because of arthritis □ *her arthritic hip*

arthritis /ɑːˈθraɪtɪs/ NOUN, NO PLURAL a disease that makes your joints (= knees, hips, etc.) swollen and painful

artichoke /ˈɑːtɪtʃəʊk/ NOUN [plural artichokes] a round green vegetable with thick pointed leaves that you cook and eat the bottom part of

article /ˈɑːtɪkəl/ NOUN [plural articles]
1 a piece of writing in a magazine or newspaper ⊞ *Maya wrote an article for the school magazine.* ⊞ *I read an interesting article in the newspaper.* □ **+ about/on** *an article about farming*
2 a thing ⊞ *There were a few articles of clothing on the floor.*
3 in grammar, the words 'a' and 'the'

articulate /ɑːˈtɪkjuleɪt/ VERB [articulates, articulating, articulated] to express your ideas and feelings clearly in words. A formal word. □ *His books articulate his vision for a better world.*

articulated /ɑːˈtɪkjuleɪtɪd/ ADJECTIVE an articulated truck has two parts which are joined together to make turning easier

articulation /ɑːˌtɪkjuˈleɪʃən/ NOUN, NO PLURAL how clearly someone speaks

artifact /ˈɑːtɪfækt/ NOUN [plural **artifacts**] another spelling of **artefact**

artificial /ˌɑːtɪˈfɪʃəl/ ADJECTIVE looking natural, but made by a person or machine □ *artificial snow*

artificial intelligence /ˌɑːtɪˈfɪʃəl ɪnˈtelɪdʒəns/ NOUN, NO PLURAL the use of computers that try to act like human brains

artificially /ˌɑːtɪˈfɪʃəli/ ADVERB not naturally □ *artificially sweetened drinks*

artificial respiration /ˌɑːtɪˈfɪʃəl ˌrespəˈreɪʃən/ NOUN, NO PLURAL the process of blowing air into the nose or mouth of someone who has stopped breathing in order to make them start breathing again

artillery /ɑːˈtɪləri/ NOUN, NO PLURAL big guns that an army uses

artisan /ˌɑːtɪˈzæn/ NOUN [plural **artisans**] someone who is skilled at making something with their hands

artist /ˈɑːtɪst/ NOUN [plural **artists**]
1 someone who paints or draws things □ *the well-known French artist, Claude Monet*
2 a performer, for example a singer or a dancer

artiste /ɑːˈtiːst/ NOUN [plural **artistes**] a performer such as a dancer or a singer

artistic /ɑːˈtɪstɪk/ ADJECTIVE
1 to do with art □ *The ballet was one of his greatest artistic achievements.*
2 good at art □ *Emma's very artistic.*
• **artistically** /ɑːˈtɪstɪkəli/ ADVERB done in a way that is nice to look at □ *an artistically decorated room*

artistry /ˈɑːtɪstri/ NOUN, NO PLURAL the skill of a painter, musician, poet, etc.

as /əz/ CONJUNCTION, PREPOSITION
1 as ... as used to compare things □ *Are you as tall as me?* □ *This restaurant's not as cheap as the other one.*
2 while □ *As we climbed, the air got colder.*
3 used to talk about the purpose or job of something or someone □ *She works as a teacher.* □ *I use this room as my study.*
4 as if/as though used to talk about how something seems □ *He looks as if he's going to faint.* □ *She cried as if her heart was broken.*
5 because □ *I went first as I was the youngest.*
6 in the same way □ *As I thought, most people had already left.*

asap /ˌeɪeseɪˈpiː/ ABBREVIATION as soon as possible

asbestos /æsˈbestəs/ NOUN, NO PLURAL a grey poisonous material that does not burn

ASBO /ˈæzˌbəʊ/ ABBREVIATION antisocial behaviour order; an official order from a court in the UK that says that someone must stop their bad behaviour or they will be punished

ascend /əˈsend/ VERB [ascends, ascending, ascended]
1 a formal word that means to climb something □ *She began to ascend the narrow staircase.*
2 a formal word that means to go up □ *a bird ascending into the sky*
• **ascending** /əˈsendɪŋ/ ADJECTIVE in ascending order with the lowest, worst, etc. first and the highest, best, etc. last □ *Arrange the points in ascending order of importance.*
• **ascent** /əˈsent/ NOUN [plural **ascents**] a movement or climb up □ *The plane will now begin its ascent to 50,000 feet.*

ascertain /ˌæsəˈteɪn/ VERB [ascertains, ascertaining, ascertained] a formal word meaning to find something out □ *It should be possible to ascertain where he was born.*

ascribe /əˈskraɪb/
♦ PHRASAL VERB [ascribes, ascribing, ascribed] **ascribe something to something/someone** to say that something is caused by something or someone □ *He ascribed the failure of his business to lack of trained staff.*

asexual reproduction /ˌeɪˈsekʃuəl ˌriːprəˈdʌkʃən/ NOUN, NO PLURAL when an animal or plant creates new animals or plants without sex. A biology word.

ash /æʃ/ NOUN [plural **ashes**]
1 the white powder that remains after something is burnt
2 a tree with silver-grey bark (= hard outer covering)

ashamed /əˈʃeɪmd/ ADJECTIVE feeling embarrassed or guilty about something □ + *of* I *am deeply ashamed of everything I said, and I apologize.* ⏎*You should be ashamed of yourself, behaving like that.* □ + *that* I *felt ashamed that I had never visited him in hospital.*

ashore /əˈʃɔː(r)/ ADVERB onto the land at the edge of a sea, river, etc. □ *We went ashore for dinner and returned to the ship later.*

ashtray /ˈæʃtreɪ/ NOUN [plural **ashtrays**] a small dish for the ash from people's cigarettes

Asian /ˈeɪʒən, ˈeɪʃən/ ▶ ADJECTIVE to do with Asia, or from Asia □ *Asian art*
▶ NOUN [plural **Asians**] someone who comes from Asia

aside /əˈsaɪd/ ADVERB to or on one side ⏎*Please stand aside and let us through.*

ask /ɑːsk/ VERB [asks, asking, asked]
1 to say something as a question □ *She asked how old I was.* □ + *about* *They asked us about our families.*
2 to say that you want someone to give you something □ + *for* I *asked Joanne for some food.*

3 to say that you want someone to do something □ + *to do something* He asked me to close the door.
4 to invite □ + *to* We've asked twenty people to our party.

> ➤ Remember that you **ask someone**. You do not **ask to someone**:
> ✔ He asked me the time.
> ✗ He asked to me the time.

◆ PHRASAL VERBS **ask after someone** to ask about someone's health and what they are doing □ Rob was asking after you. **ask someone out** to invite someone to go somewhere, often as a way of starting a romantic relationship

askew /ə'skju:/ ADVERB not straight □ Dom's collar was open and his tie was askew.

asleep /ə'sli:p/ ADJECTIVE
1 if you are asleep, you are sleeping □ Don't wake her if she's asleep. ⊞ The baby was fast asleep (= deeply asleep) in her pram. ⊞ She got out of bed, still half asleep (= very tired).
2 fall asleep to start sleeping □ He fell asleep in front of the television.

asparagus /ə'spærəgəs/ NOUN, NO PLURAL a vegetable with long green stems

aspect /'æspekt/ NOUN [plural aspects] a part of a situation or subject □ Newspapers have examined every aspect of her life.

aspersions /ə'spɜː.ʃənz/ PLURAL NOUN **cast aspersions on something/someone** to criticize something or someone □ Are you casting aspersions on my driving skills?

asphalt /'æsfælt/ NOUN, NO PLURAL a black substance used for making roads

asphyxiate /əs'fɪksɪeɪt/ VERB [asphyxiates, asphyxiating, asphyxiated] if someone is asphyxiated, they die because air cannot get into their lungs
● **asphyxiation** /əs,fɪksɪ'eɪʃən/ NOUN, NO PLURAL when someone is asphyxiated

aspiration /,æspə'reɪʃən/ NOUN [plural aspirations] a hope that you will get or achieve something □ She has aspirations to be a lawyer.

aspire /ə'spaɪə(r)/ VERB [aspires, aspiring, aspired] **aspire to something/to do something** to hope that you will get or achieve something □ He aspires to be prime minister one day.

aspirin /'æsprɪn/ NOUN [plural aspirin or aspirins]
1 *no plural* a medicine that stops pain ⊞ He takes aspirin every day.
2 a pill that contains this medicine ⊞ I've just taken a couple of aspirins for my headache.

ass /æs/ NOUN [plural asses] an old-fashioned word for a donkey

assailant /ə'seɪlənt/ NOUN [plural assailants] a formal word for someone who attacks someone

assassin /ə'sæsɪn/ NOUN [plural assassins] someone who kills an important person, for example a politician
● **assassinate** /ə'sæsɪneɪt/ VERB [assassinates, assassinating, assassinated] to kill a famous person
● **assassination** /ə,sæsɪ'neɪʃən/ NOUN [plural assassinations] the murder of a famous person

assault /ə'sɔːlt/ ► NOUN [plural assaults] an attack ⊞ It was a violent assault on an elderly woman.
► VERB [assaults, assaulting, assaulted] to attack someone

assemble /ə'sembəl/ VERB [assembles, assembling, assembled]
1 to bring several things or people together □ We've assembled a choir for the concert.
2 to come together in a group □ Please assemble in the hall after the show.
3 to make something by putting several parts together □ Where are the instructions for assembling the bookcase?
● **assembly** /ə'semblɪ/ NOUN [plural assemblies]
1 making something by joining several parts together □ These are the assembly instructions.
2 a regular meeting for everyone in a school
3 a group of people who make decisions for a country or an organization □ the General Assembly of the United Nations

assent /ə'sent/ ► NOUN, NO PLURAL a formal word that means agreement
► VERB [assents, assenting, assented] a formal word that means to agree

assert /ə'sɜːt/ VERB [asserts, asserting, asserted]
1 assert yourself to behave in a very confident way
2 assert your authority/independence, etc. to show that you are in control/independent, etc.
3 to say that something is true □ He asserted that he had done nothing wrong.
● **assertion** /ə'sɜː.ʃən/ NOUN [plural assertions] something that someone says is true □ We know Nigel broke the TV in spite of his assertions to the contrary.
● **assertive** /ə'sɜː.tɪv/ ADJECTIVE confident and not afraid to say what you think

assess /ə'ses/ VERB [assesses, assessing, assessed] to examine something and make a judgment about it □ One of our agents will assess the damage to your car.
● **assessment** /ə'sesmənt/ NOUN [plural assessments] an opinion based on examining something □ What is your assessment of the situation?

asset /'æset/ NOUN [plural assets]
1 someone or something that helps you succeed □ Sam is a tremendous asset to the team.
2 money or property that a person or a company owns

assiduous /ə'sɪdjuəs/ ADJECTIVE working very hard and carefully. A formal word.

assign /əˈsaɪn/ VERB [assigns, assigning, assigned]
1 to give someone a job or a responsibility □ *He had been assigned to work on the project.*
2 to give someone something or an amount of something □ *Each passenger was assigned a small amount of food.*
● **assignment** /əˈsaɪnmənt/ NOUN [plural **assignments**] a job someone has given you to do □ *I've got three homework assignments to finish by Friday.*

assimilate /əˈsɪmɪleɪt/ VERB [assimilates, assimilating, assimilated]
1 to learn and understand new information, skills, etc.
2 to become part of a group or society □ *The immigrants were keen to assimilate into Dutch society.*

assist /əˈsɪst/ ▶ VERB [assists, assisting, assisted] to help □ *Villagers assisted in the search for the girl.*
● **assistance** /əˈsɪstəns/ NOUN, NO PLURAL help ⊞ *The charity provides financial assistance to people in need.* ⊞ *Can I be of any assistance (= can I help)?*
● **assistant** /əˈsɪstənt/ NOUN [plural **assistants**]
1 someone whose job is to help someone else ⊞ *She's a teaching assistant at the local school.* ⊞ *You can speak to the assistant manager.*
2 someone who works in a shop ⊞ *She worked as a shop assistant.*

associate ▶ VERB /əˈsəʊʃieɪt/ [associates, associating, associated]
1 to be related to or caused by something □ *Heavy pollution is associated with increased road travel.*
2 to connect two things in your mind □ *He has the manners that we associate with an English gentleman.*
◆ PHRASAL VERB **associate with someone** to spend time with someone
▶ NOUN /əˈsəʊʃiət/ [plural **associates**] someone who you know from your work ⊞ *business associates*
● **associated** /əˈsəʊʃieɪtɪd/ ADJECTIVE related □ *a disease with associated problems*
● **association** /əˌsəʊsiˈeɪʃən/ NOUN [plural **associations**]
1 an organization for people with similar interests □ *a professional association for teachers*
2 a connection □ *He stresses the association between obesity and early death.*
3 in association with working together with □ *They produced the programme in association with an American company.*

assonance /ˈæsənəns/ NOUN, NO PLURAL when parts of words have similar sounds

assorted /əˈsɔːtɪd/ ADJECTIVE of different types □ *assorted flavours*
● **assortment** /əˈsɔːtmənt/ NOUN [plural **assortments**] a mixture of different types □ *a strange assortment of people*

assume /əˈsjuːm/ VERB [assumes, assuming, assumed]
1 to think something is true, although you have no proof □ *Oh sorry, I assumed that you had met each other before.*
2 **assume control/power/responsibility**, etc. to take control/power/responsibility, etc. □ *Jones will assume responsibility for the Paris office.*
● **assumed** /əˈsjuːmd/ ADJECTIVE an assumed name is a false one
● **assuming** /əˈsjuːmɪŋ/ CONJUNCTION if □ *Assuming he's not too tired, we could take him out for a meal.*
● **assumption** /əˈsʌmpʃən/ NOUN [plural **assumptions**]
1 something you think is true ⊞ *You can't make any assumptions about the weather on the mountain.*
2 when someone takes control, power, responsibility, etc.

assurance /əˈʃʊərəns/ NOUN [plural **assurances**]
1 a promise ⊞ *He gave me an assurance that the work would be completed.*
2 confidence □ *Tim plays tennis with complete assurance.*

assure /əˈʃʊə(r)/ VERB [assures, assuring, assured] to tell someone that something is certainly true or will certainly happen □ *Mr Harris has assured us that the car will be ready tomorrow.*
● **assured** /əˈʃʊəd/ ADJECTIVE
1 confident □ *an assured manner*
2 **be assured of something** to be certain to get something □ *You can be assured of a warm welcome at the hotel.*

asterisk /ˈæstərɪsk/ NOUN [plural **asterisks**] a mark (*), used in writing

asteroid /ˈæstərɔɪd/ NOUN [plural **asteroids**] a large piece of rock that moves around in space

asthma /ˈæsmə/ NOUN, NO PLURAL an illness that makes breathing difficult
● **asthmatic** /æsˈmætɪk/ ▶ ADJECTIVE suffering from asthma
▶ NOUN [plural **asthmatics**] someone who has asthma

astonish /əˈstɒnɪʃ/ VERB [astonishes, astonishing, astonished] to surprise someone very much □ *His arrest has astonished neighbours and friends.*
● **astonished** /əˈstɒnɪʃt/ ADJECTIVE very surprised □ *I was astonished at how much the place had changed.*
● **astonishing** /əˈstɒnɪʃɪŋ/ ADJECTIVE very surprising □ *Her mind worked with astonishing speed.*
● **astonishment** /əˈstɒnɪʃmənt/ NOUN, NO PLURAL the state of being astonished □ *To my great astonishment, she agreed that I could stay.* □ *We stared in astonishment at the painting.*

astound /əˈstaʊnd/ VERB [astounds, astounding, astounded] to surprise or shock someone very much □ *The information astounded us all.*
● **astounded** /əˈstaʊndɪd/ ADJECTIVE very surprised or shocked □ *He was astounded at the price.*
● **astounding** /əˈstaʊndɪŋ/ ADJECTIVE very surprising or shocking □ *Her knowledge of Chinese is astounding.*

astray /əˈstreɪ/ ADVERB
1 **go astray** to become lost □ *Too many letters are going astray in the post.*

2 lead someone astray to encourage someone to do bad things

astride /ə'straɪd/ PREPOSITION with one leg on each side □ *sitting astride a horse*

astro- /'æstrə/ PREFIX astro- is added to the start of words to mean 'to do with the stars or space' □ *astronomer*

astrologer /ə'strɒlədʒə(r)/ NOUN [plural astrologers] someone who tells people what may happen to them, by looking at the movement of stars

• **astrology** /ə'strɒlədʒɪ/ NOUN, NO PLURAL the study of how the movement of stars may affect our lives

astronaut /'æstrənɔ:t/ NOUN [plural astronauts] someone who travels into space

astronomer /ə'strɒnəmə(r)/ NOUN [plural astronomers] someone who studies stars and planets

astronomical /ˌæstrə'nɒmɪkəl/ ADJECTIVE
1 very large □ *The cost was astronomical.*
2 to do with astronomy
• **astronomically** /ˌæstrə'nɒmɪkəlɪ/ ADVERB very much □ *Prices have risen astronomically.*

astronomy /ə'strɒnəmɪ/ NOUN, NO PLURAL the study of stars and planets

astute /ə'stju:t/ ADJECTIVE quick to understand things and able to take advantage of them □ *His remarks were politically astute.*

asylum /ə'saɪləm/ NOUN, NO PLURAL when someone is allowed to stay in a country because they are in danger in their own country 🔁 *Many people seek asylum in this country.* 🔁 *He was granted asylum in 2006.*

asylum seeker /ə'saɪləm 'si:kə(r)/ NOUN [plural asylum seekers] someone who is trying to get asylum in a country

asymmetrical /ˌeɪsɪ'metrɪkəl/ ADJECTIVE not the same shape on both sides

at /ət/ PREPOSITION

1 used to show the position of something or something □ *Meet me at the station.* □ *The car is at Clara's house.* □ *He's still at work.*
2 used to show the time or period that something happens □ *School finishes at 4 o'clock.* □ *Will you be here at the weekend?* □ *I always visit my parents at Christmas.*
3 towards □ *He threw a bucket of water at me.* □ *Look at me!* □ *She drove the car straight at him.*
4 **bad/good at something** used to show someone's level of ability □ *He's good at football.*
5 used to show the price, speed, level, etc. of something □ *We bought four bottles at 75p each.* □ *The car was travelling at 70 miles an hour.*
6 used to describe someone's reaction □ *He broke down at the news.*
7 **at all** used for emphasis, for example when talking about something that does not exist □ *Doesn't he have any friends at all?* □ *I'm not looking forward to the party at all.*

ate /eɪt/ PAST TENSE OF **eat**

atheism /'eɪθɪɪzəm/ NOUN, NO PLURAL the belief that there is no god
• **atheist** /'eɪθɪɪst/ NOUN [plural atheists] someone who does not believe in a god

athlete /'æθli:t/ NOUN [plural athletes] someone who is good at sports such as running 🔁 *She is one of the country's top athletes.* 🔁 *He was an Olympic athlete in 1928.*
• **athletic** /æθ'letɪk/ ADJECTIVE
1 fit and good at sports
2 to do with the sports of running, jumping and throwing □ *athletic events*
• **athletics** /æθ'letɪks/ NOUN, NO PLURAL the sports that include running, jumping and throwing □ *Lee is very good at athletics.*

atlas /'ætləs/ NOUN [plural atlases] a book of maps

ATM /ˌeɪti:'em/ ABBREVIATION automated teller machine; a machine, usually in the wall outside a bank, where you can get money using a small plastic card

atmosphere /'ætmə,sfɪə(r)/ NOUN [plural atmospheres]
1 the feeling that a place or situation has □ *The atmosphere in the company was very friendly.* □ **+ of** *Increased crime is creating an atmosphere of fear.* 🔁 *We are trying to create a relaxed atmosphere.*
2 the air around a planet □ *the Earth's atmosphere*
• **atmospheric** /ˌætməs'ferɪk/ ADJECTIVE to do with the air or the atmosphere □ *atmospheric pressure*

atoll /'ætɒl/ NOUN [plural atolls] an island made from a ring of coral (= very small pink bones of sea creatures). A geography word.

atom /'ætəm/ NOUN [plural atoms] the smallest part of a chemical element □ *Water contains two hydrogen atoms and one oxygen atom.*
• **atomic** /ə'tɒmɪk/ ADJECTIVE
1 using the power that is created when atoms are broken 🔁 *an atomic bomb* 🔁 *atomic energy*
2 to do with atoms □ *the atomic structure of crystals*

atomic mass /ə'tɒmɪk 'mæs/ NOUN, NO PLURAL the amount of matter in an atom of a particular substance. A chemistry word.

atomic number /ə'tɒmɪk 'nʌmbə(r)/ NOUN, NO PLURAL the number of protons (= parts with a positive electrical charge) in the nucleus of a substance. A chemistry word.

atomic weight /ə'tɒmɪk 'weɪt/ NOUN, NO PLURAL the amount of matter in an atom of a particular substance. A chemistry word.

atone /ə'təʊn/ VERB [atones, atoning, atoned] to do something to show that you are sorry for something bad you have done □ *She tried to atone for her rudeness by being extra helpful in the house.*

atrium /'eɪtrɪəm/ NOUN [plural atriums]
1 a high space or an open space in the centre of a building

2 one of the two upper spaces in your heart that push blood around your body. A biology word.

atrocious /əˈtrəʊʃəs/ ADJECTIVE very bad □ *atrocious weather*

● **atrocity** /əˈtrɒsətɪ/ NOUN [*plural* **atrocities**] a very cruel or violent event □ *The bombing was Britain's worst terrorist atrocity.*

attach /əˈtætʃ/ VERB [**attaches, attaching, attached**]

1 to join one thing to another thing □ + *to* *They attached a rope to the car.*

2 if you attach a document to an e-mail, you send the document with the e-mail. A computing word.

● **attached** /əˈtætʃt/ ADJECTIVE **be attached to someone/something** to like someone or something very much □ *Teachers often become attached to their students.*

● **attachment** /əˈtætʃmənt/ NOUN [*plural* **attachments**]

1 a feeling of liking someone or something very much 🕮 *He felt an emotional attachment to the place.*

2 a document or picture that you send with an e-mail. A computing word. 🕮 *Don't open an attachment if you don't know who it's from.*

3 an extra part that you can add to a machine to make it do something different

attack /əˈtæk/ ▶ VERB [**attacks, attacking, attacked**]

1 to suddenly try to hurt someone □ + *with* *He attacked her with a knife.* □ *A man was attacked and robbed on Friday.*

2 to try to destroy a place using weapons □ *A violent crowd tried to attack the embassy.*

3 to criticize someone or something □ *He attacked the government for failing to improve standards in schools.*

▶ NOUN [*plural* **attacks**]

1 a violent act against a place or person 🕮 *The attack was carried out by four men.* 🕮 *Terrorist attacks have killed thousands of people.* □ + *on* *The attack on police officers began when an angry crowd started throwing bottles.*

2 strong criticism □ + *on* *He launched a personal attack on the President.*

3 a sudden illness or bad feeling 🕮 *He had an asthma attack.* □ + *of* *I always get an attack of nerves before a performance.*

● **attacker** /əˈtækə(r)/ NOUN [*plural* **attackers**] a person who tries to hurt someone violently □ *Ravi was able to describe his attacker to police.*

attain /əˈteɪn/ VERB [**attains, attaining, attained**] to achieve something □ *He attained a high level of fitness.*

● **attainable** /əˈteɪnəbəl/ ADJECTIVE possible to achieve □ *Set yourself challenging but attainable goals.*

● **attainment** /əˈteɪnmənt/ NOUN [*plural* **attainments**] achievement □ *Levels of educational attainment are low.*

attempt /əˈtempt/ ▶ VERB [**attempts, attempting, attempted**] to try to do something □ + *to do something* *He attempted to explain what he meant.*

▶ NOUN [*plural* **attempts**] when you try to do something 🕮 *Doctors made a desperate attempt to save her life.* 🕮 *She made no attempt to escape.* □ + *to do something* *I will resist any attempts to force me to move.*

attend /əˈtend/ VERB [**attends, attending, attended**]

1 to go to an event. A formal word. □ *More than 100 people attended the meeting.*

2 to go regularly to a school, church, etc. A formal word. □ *James attended a private school.*

> ► People **attend** formal meetings but people usually **come to** or **go to** parties, friends' houses, football matches, etc:
> ✓ *Did Jamie come to the wedding?*
> ✗ *Did Jamie attend the wedding?*

◆ PHRASAL VERB **attend to someone/something** to deal with someone or something □ *She was attending to the funeral arrangements.*

● **attendance** /əˈtendəns/ NOUN, NO PLURAL

1 being present somewhere □ *She was given an award for 100% attendance at school.*

2 the number of people who go to an event or who go to a place regularly □ *Church attendance is declining.*

● **attendant** /əˈtendənt/ NOUN [*plural* **attendants**] someone whose job is to help people in a public place □ *a parking attendant*

attention /əˈtenʃən/ NOUN, NO PLURAL

1 **pay attention** to listen or watch carefully □ + *to* *He paid close attention to what was happening.* □ + *to* *Pay attention to what I'm saying, please.*

2 interest and thought that you give to something 🕮 *The story attracted attention from all over the world.*

3 **get someone's attention** to make someone notice you □ *I waved at her to get her attention.*

4 action to stop a problem 🕮 *If the symptoms continue, seek medical attention.*

● **attentive** /əˈtentɪv/ ADJECTIVE listening or watching carefully □ *an attentive student*

attest /əˈtest/ VERB [**attests, attesting, attested**] to give proof that something is true. A formal word. □ *As his many friends will attest, he was a quiet man.*

attic /ˈætɪk/ NOUN [*plural* **attics**] the space in the roof of a house

attire /əˈtaɪə(r)/ NOUN, NO PLURAL a formal word for the clothes someone is wearing □ *casual attire*

● **attired** /əˈtaɪə(r)d/ ADJECTIVE wearing something. A formal word. □ *She was elegantly attired in a black dress.*

attitude /ˈætɪtjuːd/ NOUN [*plural* **attitudes**] the way someone thinks about something 🕮 *He has a very positive attitude.* 🕮 *He needs to change his attitude* *and start working hard.* □ + *to/towards Jane has a relaxed attitude to life.*

attorney /ə'tɜ:nɪ/ NOUN [*plural* **attorneys**] a lawyer

attract /ə'trækt/ VERB [**attracts, attracting, attracted**]

1 to make someone feel interested in or like someone or something □ *It was his smile that first attracted me.* □ + *to They were attracted to the idea of filming in Sydney because of the weather.*

2 to make people come somewhere or do something □ *The museum attracts visitors from all around the world.* □ *The programme attracted 15 million viewers.*

3 to make people have a particular reaction 🔁 *The show attracted strong criticism.* 🔁 *The painting will attract interest from private collectors.*

4 to pull something towards something else using a natural force □ *A magnet attracts iron filings.*

• **attraction** /ə'trækʃən/ NOUN [*plural* **attractions**]

1 *no plural* a feeling of liking someone and finding them physically attractive □ + *between The attraction between them was immediate.*

2 something that people want to visit or do 🔁 *The Eiffel Tower is a popular tourist attraction.* 🔁 *The town's main attraction is its castle.*

3 a reason for liking something or wanting to do it □ + *of I can't see the attraction of fast cars.* 🔁 *One of the main attractions of the design is its simplicity.*

4 *no plural* the natural force that pulls things together

• **attractive** /ə'træktɪv/ ADJECTIVE

1 nice to look at □ *She was an attractive woman in her late thirties.* □ *The hotel is set in attractive gardens.*

2 interesting and worth having or doing 🔁 *It's a very attractive offer.*

• **attractively** /ə'træktɪvlɪ/ ADVERB in a pleasant way □ *The house is attractively decorated.*

attribute¹ /ə'trɪbju:t/

♦ PHRASAL VERBS [**attributes, attributing, attributed**]
attribute something to someone to think that something was made, painted, written, etc. by a particular person □ *The statue had been wrongly attributed to Bernini.* **attribute something to something** to say that something is caused by something □ *He attributed his success to determination.*

attribute² /'ætrɪbju:t/ NOUN [*plural* **attributes**] a quality or feature □ *He was chosen for his physical attributes rather than his acting ability.*

attuned /ə'tju:nd/ ADJECTIVE

1 if you are attuned to something, you understand it and know how to deal with it □ *They were very attuned to each other's moods.*

2 if you are attuned to a sound, you hear and recognize it very quickly □ *Babies are attuned to the sound of their mother's voice.*

aubergine /'əʊbəʒi:n/ NOUN [*plural* **aubergines**] a vegetable with a smooth, shiny, dark purple skin

auburn /'ɔ:bən/ ADJECTIVE auburn hair is reddish-brown

auction /'ɔ:kʃən/ ▶ NOUN [*plural* **auctions**] a sale in which the person who offers the most money buys something

▶ VERB [**auctions, auctioning, auctioned**] to sell something to the person who offers the most money for it

• **auctioneer** /ˌɔ:kʃə'nɪə(r)/ NOUN [*plural* **auctioneers**] someone whose job is to sell things to the person who offers the most money for them

audacious /ɔ:'deɪʃəs/ ADJECTIVE brave and taking risks □ *an audacious plan* □ *an audacious young man*

• **audacity** /ɔ:'dæsətɪ/ NOUN, NO PLURAL audacious behaviour

audible /'ɔ:dəbəl/ ADJECTIVE able to be heard □ *His voice was barely audible.*

audience /'ɔ:dɪəns/ NOUN [*plural* **audiences**]

1 the people who listen to or watch a performance 🔁 *My father was in the audience tonight.* 🔁 *Many audience members left before the end of the show.*

2 the people who watch a particular television programme, read a particular magazine, etc. 🔁 *The programme attracted an audience of 13 million people.* 🔁 *The magazine's target audience is young women.*

audio- /'ɔ:dɪəʊ/ PREFIX audio- is added to the start of words to mean 'to do with hearing'

audio-visual /ˌɔ:dɪəʊ'vɪʒuəl/ ADJECTIVE to do with both hearing and seeing □ *The tour begins with an audio-visual presentation.*

audit /'ɔ:dɪt/ ▶ NOUN [*plural* **audits**] an official examination of a company's financial records

▶ VERB [**audits, auditing, audited**] to officially examine a company's financial records

audition /ɔ:'dɪʃən/ ▶ NOUN [*plural* **auditions**] a short performance that an actor, dancer, etc. does so that someone else can decide if they are good enough to be in a play, musical group, etc. 🔁 *They're holding auditions for the show next week.*

▶ VERB [**auditions, auditioning, auditioned**]

1 to do a short performance so that someone can see if you are good enough to be in a play, musical group, etc.

2 to watch and listen to performers and try to choose the best ones for something like a play or musical group □ *We auditioned over 100 actors for the part.*

auditor /'ɔ:dɪtə(r)/ NOUN [*plural* **auditors**] someone who officially examines an organization's financial records

auditorium /ˌɔ:dɪ'tɔ:rɪəm/ NOUN [*plural* **auditoriums**] the part of a theatre where the audience sits

augment /ɔ:g'ment/ VERB [**augments, augmenting, augmented**] a formal word that means to increase something

August /'ɔ:gəst/ NOUN the eighth month of the year, after July and before September □ *We'll visit you in August.*

aunt /ɑːnt/ or **auntie** or **aunty** /ˈɑːnti/ NOUN [plural **aunts, aunties**]
1 the sister of one of your parents □ My aunt and uncle live in Canada. □ Auntie Emily came to stay.
2 your uncle's wife

au pair /ˌəʊˈpeə(r)/ NOUN [plural **au pairs**] someone who lives with a family in a foreign country and looks after their children

aura /ˈɔːrə/ NOUN [plural **auras**] a quality that seems to surround a person, place or situation 🔒 There was an aura of mystery around him.

aural /ˈɔːrəl/ ADJECTIVE to do with your ears or hearing □ an aural examination

auspices /ˈɔːspɪsɪz/ PLURAL NOUN **under the auspices of something** with the help and support of a particular organization. A formal phrase. □ The 'Enjoy Reading' scheme was being run under the auspices of the British Council.

auspicious /ɔːˈspɪʃəs/ ADJECTIVE showing signs that something is going to be successful □ Their 5-0 win last weekend was an auspicious start to the season.

austere /ɒˈstɪə(r)/ ADJECTIVE
1 simple and not comfortable □ an austere lifestyle
2 unfriendly and severe □ He was an austere, private man.
3 plain and with no decoration □ an austere dining room
• **austerity** /ɒˈsterəti/ NOUN, NO PLURAL an austere quality

authentic /ɔːˈθentɪk/ ADJECTIVE real □ an authentic wartime uniform
• **authenticate** /ɔːˈθentɪkeɪt/ VERB [**authenticates, authenticating, authenticated**] to prove that something is real or true □ They weren't able to authenticate the document.
• **authenticity** /ˌɔːθenˈtɪsəti/ NOUN, NO PLURAL how real or true something is □ It's difficult to prove the authenticity of this story.

author /ˈɔːθə(r)/ NOUN [plural **authors**] a writer □ Atkinson is the author of four novels.

authoritarian /ɔːˌθɒrɪˈteəriən/ ▶ ADJECTIVE trying to control everything and stop people from making their own decisions □ an authoritarian government
▶ NOUN [plural **authoritarians**] someone who tries to control everything and stop people from making their own decisions

authoritative /ɔːˈθɒrɪtətɪv/ ADJECTIVE
1 based on information that is correct □ It's an authoritative account of what happened.
2 able to make people obey you □ 'Come here at once!' he said in an authoritative voice.

authority /ɔːˈθɒrəti/ NOUN [plural **authorities**]
1 no plural power and control 🔒 People who are in a position of authority need to behave appropriately. □ + to do something As chairman, he has the authority to make decisions. □ + over This law gives the government more authority over the police force.
2 an official organization or government department that controls something 🔒 Some local authorities do not have enough money for repairing roads.
3 the authorities the police and people who have the power to make people obey laws □ The British authorities raised concerns over the deal
4 an expert □ + on She's a leading authority on climate change.
• **authorization** or **authorisation** /ˌɔːθəraɪˈzeɪʃən/ NOUN, NO PLURAL official permission □ We need to get authorization for the project.
• **authorize** or **authorise** /ˈɔːθəraɪz/ VERB [**authorizes, authorizing, authorized**] to give official permission for something □ The government authorized the use of military force.

autism /ˈɔːtɪzəm/ NOUN, NO PLURAL a medical condition in which someone finds it difficult to react to other people and communicate with them
• **autistic** /ɔːˈtɪstɪk/ ADJECTIVE having autism

auto /ˈɔːtəʊ/ ADJECTIVE to do with cars □ the American auto industry

auto- /ˈɔːtəʊ/ PREFIX
1 auto- is added to the beginning of words to mean 'to do with yourself' □ autobiography
2 auto- is added to the beginning of words to mean 'on its own without human help' □ automatic

autobiographical /ˌɔːtəˌbaɪəˈɡræfɪkəl/ ADJECTIVE to do with someone's own life □ Many of the events in Barrie's story are autobiographical.
• **autobiography** /ˌɔːtəbaɪˈɒɡrəfi/ NOUN [plural **autobiographies**] the story of someone's own life

autocrat /ˈɔːtəkræt/ NOUN [plural **autocrats**] a ruler with complete power
• **autocratic** /ˌɔːtəˈkrætɪk/ ADJECTIVE to do with or behaving like an autocrat □ autocratic behaviour

autograph /ˈɔːtəɡrɑːf/ ▶ NOUN [plural **autographs**] the name of a famous person, written by them 🔒 Please can I have your autograph?
▶ VERB [**autographs, autographing, autographed**] to write your autograph on something □ The whole team autographed the football.

automate /ˈɔːtəmeɪt/ VERB [**automates, automating, automated**] to use machines or computers to do something, and not people 🔒 Our bottle production is fully automated.

automatic /ˌɔːtəˈmætɪk/ ▶ ADJECTIVE
1 an automatic machine works without a person operating it 🔒 automatic doors 🔒 Our heating system is fully automatic.
2 always happening because of a rule or a system □ After two years, you get automatic promotion.
3 an automatic action is something you do without thinking □ My automatic response was to cover my face.
▶ NOUN [plural **automatics**]
1 a car which changes gears itself
2 a gun that keeps firing bullets when you press the trigger (= device that causes bullets to fire)
• **automatically** /ˌɔːtəˈmætɪkəli/ ADVERB

1 without a person operating something □ *The doors open automatically.*
2 because of a rule or a system □ *If you get caught speeding again, you will automatically lose your licence.*
3 without thinking □ *When I saw the stone coming I automatically ducked.*

automation /ˌɔːtəˈmeɪʃən/ NOUN, NO PLURAL using machines to do things instead of people

automobile /ˈɔːtəməbiːl/ ► NOUN [*plural* **automobiles**] a US word for **car**
► ADJECTIVE a US word meaning to do with cars □ *the automobile industry*

autonomous /ɔːˈtɒnəməs/ ADJECTIVE
1 an automonous country, area or organization governs or controls itself
2 an autonomous person can make decisions and act without asking anyone else what to do
● **autonomy** /ɔːˈtɒnəmɪ/ NOUN, NO PLURAL
1 when a country, area or organization governs or controls itself □ *Many of the administrative regions are seeking more autonomy.*
2 the ability to make decisions and act without asking anyone else what to do

autopsy /ˈɔːtɒpsɪ/ NOUN [*plural* **autopsies**] an examination of a dead person's body to find out why they died

autumn /ˈɔːtəm/ NOUN [*plural* **autumns**] the season after summer, when the leaves change colour and fall □ *I love the colours of autumn leaves.*
● **autumnal** /ɔːˈtʌmnəl/ ADJECTIVE typical of autumn □ *trees in their autumnal colours*

auxiliary /ɔːgˈzɪljərɪ/ ► NOUN [*plural* **auxiliaries**]
1 an auxiliary verb
2 someone whose job is to help and support another group of workers □ *He's a hospital auxiliary.*
► ADJECTIVE helping and supporting another group of workers □ *auxiliary nurses/police officers*

auxiliary verb /ɔːgˈzɪljərɪ ˈvɜːb/ NOUN [*plural* **auxiliary verbs**] a verb like *be*, *have* or *do* that you use to make tenses, negatives or questions

avail /əˈveɪl/ NOUN **to no avail** without success □ *Our attempt to hide was to no avail.*
◆ PHRASAL VERB [**avails, availing, availed**] **avail yourself of something** to make use of something □ *I availed myself of the opportunity to catch up on some sleep.*

availability /əˌveɪləˈbɪlətɪ/ NOUN, NO PLURAL
1 how possible it is to get something □ *Please can you check the availability of tickets for Thursday?*
2 the times when someone is free to do something

available /əˈveɪləbəl/ ADJECTIVE
1 if something is available, you can get it or buy it 🕮 *Guns are readily available* (= easy to get) *here.*
🕮 *The government plans to make more college places available to poor students.* □ *Judging by the available information, the man died over a week ago.*

2 if someone is available, they are free to do something □ **+ to do something** *I'm sorry, there's nobody available to help you at the moment.*

avalanche /ˈævəlɑːnʃ/ NOUN [*plural* **avalanches**]
1 a large amount of snow and rocks sliding down the side of a mountain
2 a large amount of something □ *The paper received an avalanche of protests after its article on racism.*

avant-garde /ˌævɒnˈɡɑːd/ ADJECTIVE very modern and new □ *avant-garde paintings/theories*

avarice /ˈævərɪs/ NOUN, NO PLURAL when someone wants more money and things than they need. A formal word.
● **avaricious** /ˌævəˈrɪʃəs/ ADJECTIVE wanting more money and things than you need. A formal word.

avatar /ˈævətɑː(r)/ NOUN [*plural* **avatars**] a picture that represents you in computer games, discussion websites, etc. A computing word.

avenge /əˈvendʒ/ VERB [**avenges, avenging, avenged**] to do something bad to someone to punish them for something bad they did to you or someone else □ *She vowed to avenge her sister's death.*

avenue /ˈævənjuː/ NOUN [*plural* **avenues**]
1 a wide street, usually with trees on both sides
2 a way of achieving something 🕮 *If TV advertising doesn't work, there are other avenues we can explore.*

average /ˈævərɪdʒ/ ► ADJECTIVE
1 usual or ordinary □ *How much do you earn in an average week?*
2 an average amount is the amount you get by adding amounts together and dividing by the number of amounts □ *average temperatures* □ *the average wage*
3 not very good quality □ *The food was pretty average.*
► NOUN [*plural* **averages**]
1 the amount you get by adding amounts together and dividing by the number of amounts.
2 the normal amount □ *We spend an average of £100 a week on food.*
3 on average usually, or based on an average amount □ *On average, adults in this country watch three hours of TV every day.*
4 above/below average more/less than the average amount □ *Temperatures are below average for the time of year.*
► VERB [**averages, averaging, averaged**] to have a particular amount as an average □ *I usually average around 6 miles per hour when I run.*

averse /əˈvɜːs/ ADJECTIVE
1 not averse to something not against doing or having something □ *We're not averse to lending the children money if it's for a worthwhile purpose.*
2 averse to something not liking or wanting something □ *They are very averse to the idea of women priests.*
● **aversion** /əˈvɜːʃən/ NOUN **an aversion to something** a dislike of something

avert /ə'vɜːt/ VERB [averts, averting, averted]
1 to manage to stop something bad happening
🔁 avert a crisis/war
2 to turn away 🔁 avert your eyes/gaze

aviary /'eɪvjərɪ/ NOUN [plural aviaries] a large cage or building for keeping birds

aviation /ˌeɪvɪ'eɪʃən/ NOUN, NO PLURAL making and flying aircraft 🔁 the aviation industry

avid /'ævɪd/ ADJECTIVE very enthusiastic 🔁 an avid reader

avocado /ˌævə'kɑːdəʊ/ NOUN [plural avocados]
1 a fruit shaped like a pear, that is not sweet and has dark green skin and a large stone in the middle
2 a light green colour

avoid /ə'vɔɪd/ VERB [avoids, avoiding, avoided]
1 to stay away from somewhere or someone □ Have you been avoiding me? □ I left early to avoid the rush hour traffic.
2 to prevent something bad happening □ I usually do the housework, just to avoid arguments. □ If you keep your joints supple, it can avoid problems in later life.
3 to manage not to do something □ + ing It's hard to avoid offending her.
• **avoidable** /ə'vɔɪdəbəl/ ADJECTIVE able to be avoided □ This was an avoidable tragedy.

await /ə'weɪt/ VERB [awaits, awaiting, awaited]
1 to wait for something or someone 🔁 He is in prison, awaiting trial for murder.
2 to be going to happen to someone □ She could never have imagined the triumph that awaited her in New York.

awake /ə'weɪk/ ▶ ADJECTIVE not sleeping 🔁 I tried to stay awake. 🔁 Stop talking - you're keeping me awake. 🔁 She's wide awake (= completely awake) by six every morning.
▶ VERB [awakes, awaking, awoke, awoken] to wake up or to make someone wake up. A formal word. □ Gloria awoke early.

➤ Awake is used mainly as an adjective. The verb awake is formal and not often used. Instead, use the phrasal verb wake up:
✓ I woke up early this morning.
✗ I awoke early this morning.

• **awaken** /ə'weɪkən/ VERB [awakens, awakening, awakened]
1 to cause a feeling or emotion to start □ The sight of the injured cat awakened a great tenderness in him.
2 to wake up or to make someone wake up. A formal word. □ We were awakened by the bombs.
• **awakening** /ə'weɪknɪŋ/ NOUN [plural awakenings]
1 when a feeling or an emotion starts
2 a rude awakening a shock when someone discovers the truth about something

award /ə'wɔːd/ ▶ NOUN [plural awards]
1 a prize for someone who has achieved something

🔁 Joe won an award for his contribution to football.
2 an amount of money that is paid to someone because of a legal decision
▶ VERB [awards, awarding, awarded]
1 to give someone a prize or something good because of what they have achieved □ She was awarded the Nobel Prize for literature.
2 to give someone money or something they want because of a legal decision 🔁 She was awarded damages (= money paid because she was harmed) of £50,000. 🔁 He was awarded custody of the children (= allowed to have them living with him).

aware /ə'weə(r)/ ADJECTIVE if you are aware of something, you know about it □ + of Katya became aware of someone else in the room. 🔁 He's well aware (= very aware) of all the problems. □ + that I'm perfectly aware that you've been waiting a long time.
• **awareness** /ə'weənɪs/ NOUN, NO PLURAL being aware of something 🔁 We are hoping to raise awareness of the disease.

awash /ə'wɒʃ/ ADJECTIVE
1 be awash with something to contain a lot of something □ The village was suddenly awash with reporters.
2 covered with a liquid □ The streets of Perth are awash tonight after heavy rain.

away /ə'weɪ/ ▶ ADVERB
1 to a different place or in a different place □ He walked away. □ We'll be away for three weeks.
2 at a distance □ How far away is the school? □ The exam is only a week away.
3 in the opposite direction □ Peter turned away.
4 not at work or school □ Tina was away today.
5 in the place where something is kept □ Could you put the books away, please?
6 continuously □ They've been working away all night.
▶ ADJECTIVE an away game or match is one a team has to travel to

awe /ɔː/ NOUN, NO PLURAL
1 a feeling of great admiration and often fear □ The children gazed at their hero in awe.
2 be in awe of someone to admire someone and be slightly afraid of them

awe-inspiring /'ɔːɪnˌspaɪərɪŋ/ ADJECTIVE if something is awe-inspiring, it is very surprising and you admire and respect it very much

awesome /'ɔːsəm/ ADJECTIVE
1 if something is awesome, you admire and respect it, and are often slightly afraid of it □ We were shocked by the awesome power of their weapons. □ an awesome responsibility
2 an informal word meaning very good □ Her show was awesome.

awestruck /'ɔːˌstrʌk/ ADJECTIVE filled with feelings of admiration and often fear

awful /ˈɔːfʊl/ ADJECTIVE
1 very bad □ an awful headache ⬚ The food was absolutely awful.
2 very great □ There is an awful lot of ice on the roads. □ Looking after their dogs is an awful nuisance.
• **awfully** /ˈɔːflɪ/ ADVERB
1 very □ It's an awfully long way. □ She's awfully shy.
2 very badly □ We played awfully.

awkward /ˈɔːkwəd/ ADJECTIVE
1 difficult to manage or use □ I find this keyboard a bit awkward.
2 an awkward person causes difficulties for others □ Just stop being awkward and say you'll come.
3 embarrassed or embarrassing □ I feel really awkward when she asks me for money. □ an awkward silence
4 awkward movements are not easy and relaxed
• **awkwardly** /ˈɔːkwədlɪ/ ADVERB in an awkward way □ He fell awkwardly and broke his leg. □ They shuffled awkwardly when we asked them to tell the truth.
• **awkwardness** /ˈɔːkwədnɪs/ NOUN, NO PLURAL being awkward □ You soon get used to the awkwardness of using the headphones.

awoke /əˈwəʊk/ PAST TENSE OF awake
awoken /əˈwəʊkən/ PAST PARTICIPLE OF awake

awry /əˈraɪ/ ADJECTIVE, ADVERB
1 go awry to not happen in the way that was planned □ We don't want the schedule to go awry again.
2 not in the correct position □ Your skirt is a bit awry.

axe /æks/ ▶ NOUN [plural axes]
1 a tool for cutting wood
2 the axe when someone or something is got rid of or stopped □ Three hundred jobs are due to get the axe next week.
▶ VERB [axes, axing, axed] to stop a plan or a service, close a business or get rid of workers □ Thousands of jobs were axed.

axis /ˈæksɪs/ NOUN [plural axes]
1 the imaginary line that an object like a planet seems to turn around
2 the line up the side or along the bottom of a graph used to show measurements and find positions. A maths word.

axle /ˈæksəl/ NOUN [plural axles] a long metal bar that connects two wheels on a vehicle

ayatollah /ˌaɪəˈtɒlə/ NOUN [plural ayatollahs] a Muslim religious leader in Iran

aye /eɪ/ EXCLAMATION another word for yes, used especially in Scotland and the North of England

azure /ˈæʒʊər/ ADJECTIVE having a bright blue colour

B*b*

B *or* **b** /biː/ the second letter of the alphabet

babble /ˈbæbəl/ VERB [**babbles, babbling, babbled**]
1 to talk quickly in a way that is not easy to understand
2 if a stream (= small river) babbles, it makes a nice, gentle sound

babe /beɪb/ NOUN [*plural* **babes**]
1 a baby
2 an informal word used for talking to someone □ *Are you all right, babe?*

baboon /bəˈbuːn/ NOUN [*plural* **baboons**] a type of large monkey with a long pointed nose and long teeth

baby /ˈbeɪbɪ/ ► NOUN [*plural* **babies**]
1 a very young child ⊞ *Paola has had a baby.* □ *a baby boy*
2 an older child or an adult who is crying or behaving like a baby □ *Don't be such a baby, it's only a little spider!*
► ADJECTIVE very young □ *a baby elephant*
• **babyish** /ˈbeɪbɪɪʃ/ ADJECTIVE suitable for babies or younger children □ *This game is probably too babyish for most ten-year-olds.*

babysit /ˈbeɪbɪˌsɪt/ VERB [**babysits, babysitting, babysat**] to look after a baby or child when its parents are not in the house □ *Could you babysit for me on Saturday?*
• **babysitter** /ˈbeɪbɪˌsɪtə(r)/ NOUN [*plural* **babysitters**] someone who looks after a baby or a child when its parents are not in the house

bachelor /ˈbætʃələ(r)/ NOUN [*plural* **bachelors**] a man who has never married

back /bæk/ ► NOUN [*plural* **backs**]
1 the part of something that is furthest away from the front □ *Nina hid her diary at the back of a drawer.*
2 the part of the body that goes from the shoulders to the bottom □ *I always sleep on my back.*
3 in football and hockey, a player who tries to stop the other team scoring a goal
4 in **back of** the American way of saying 'behind' □ *She was sitting in back of me.*
♦ IDIOM **back to front** the wrong way, so that the part that should be at the back is now at the front □ *You've got your sweater on back to front!*
► ADJECTIVE away from the front □ *Ben's had one of his back teeth out.*
► ADVERB
1 to the place where a person or thing was before

□ *What time is he coming back?* □ *Could you give Maria her book back, please?*
2 in the direction that is the opposite of forwards □ *I stood back to let her pass.* □ *She sat back in her chair.*
3 as a reply to something □ *Can I call you back in an hour?*
4 to the condition someone or something was in before □ *I went back to sleep.*
5 to an earlier time □ *Thinking back to that day, she was obviously unhappy.*
► VERB [**backs, backing, backed**]
1 to support or help someone or something □ *He is backing the female candidate in the election.*
2 to move backwards, usually in a car □ *She backed into the drive.*
♦ PHRASAL VERBS **back someone up** to support someone □ *If you complain to the teacher, I'll back you up.* **back something up** to make an extra copy of information on a computer. A computing word. □ *Are the files all backed up?* **back down** to admit that you are wrong □ *He backed down when I pointed out that his figures were wrong.*

backache /ˈbækeɪk/ NOUN, NO PLURAL pain in the back □ *She suffers from backache.*

backbench /ˈbækbentʃ/ ► ADJECTIVE a backbench MP (= member of the government) does not have an important job in the government
► NOUN **the backbenches** the place where backbench MPs sit
• **backbencher** /ˌbækˈbentʃə(r)/ NOUN [*plural* **backbenchers**] a backbench MP

backbiting /ˈbækˌbaɪtɪŋ/ NOUN, NO PLURAL when people say bad and unkind things about a person who is not there

backbone /ˈbækbəʊn/ NOUN [*plural* **backbones**] the row of bones down the middle of your back

backbreaking /ˈbækˌbreɪkɪŋ/ ADJECTIVE backbreaking work is physically very hard and makes you tired

backdate /ˌbækˈdeɪt/ VERB [**backdates, backdating, backdated**] if you backdate a cheque or a payment, you make it start from an earlier date □ *Claims for benefit can be backdated for up to 52 weeks.*

backdoor /ˈbækdɔː(r)/ ADJECTIVE backdoor activities are secret and not official □ *backdoor negotiations*

backdrop /ˈbækdrɒp/ NOUN [*plural* **backdrops**]
1 the situation that exists when something happens

□ *The trial took place against a backdrop of political violence.*

2 the things you can see behind the main thing you are looking at □ *The hotel is set against a backdrop of stunning mountains.*

3 a cloth with a picture on it that is hung at the back of a stage in a theatre

backer /'bækə(r)/ NOUN [*plural* **backers**] someone who supports a person, business or organization by giving them money

backfire /ˌbæk'faɪə(r)/ VERB [**backfires, backfiring, backfired**]

1 if a plan backfires, it goes wrong and has the opposite effect from what you wanted

2 if a car backfires, its fuel burns too quickly, causing a sudden loud noise

backgammon /'bæk.gæmən/ NOUN, NO PLURAL a game where two players move pieces on a board with triangular patterns

background /'bækɡraʊnd/ NOUN [*plural* **backgrounds**]

1 the part of a picture which is behind the main people or objects 🖽 *Here's a photo of us with Ben Nevis in the background.*

2 a person's background is their family and the things they have done in the past □ *These children are from very poor backgrounds.*

3 the background of an event is all the things that happened before it and caused it to happen □ *+ to the background to the English civil war.*

backhand /'bækhænd/ NOUN [*plural* **backhands**] in games like tennis, a way of hitting the ball by holding the racket (= round part with a stick) across the front of your body

backing /'bækɪŋ/ NOUN, NO PLURAL

1 support or money for a person or plan in order to make them successful □ *Research of this type has the backing of industry.*

2 music or singing that goes with a main singer's voice 🖽 *a backing singer*

backlash /'bæklæʃ/ NOUN, NO PLURAL a sudden violent reaction to an event or situation □ *a backlash against the feminist movement*

backlog /'bæklɒɡ/ NOUN, NO PLURAL a large amount of work that you have not done and must now do 🖽 *We've got to work this weekend to try to clear the backlog.*

backpack /'bækpæk/ ▶ NOUN [*plural* **backpacks**] a large bag that you carry on your back □ *I was carrying the tent in my backpack.*

▶ VERB [**backpacks, backpacking, backpacked**] to travel to a lot of different places carrying the things you need in a bag on your back 🖽 *I went backpacking when I was a student.*

backpedal /ˌbæk'pedəl/ VERB [**backpedals, backpedalling/US backpedaling, backpedalled/US backpedaled**] to try to change something that you

have started doing or something that you said □ *They are backpedalling on promises for better funding.*

backrest /'bækrest/ NOUN [*plural* **backrests**] the part of a piece of furniture that supports your back

backslash /'bækslæʃ/ NOUN [*plural* **backslashes**] the symbol '\'

backslide /ˌbæk'slaɪd/ VERB [**backslides, backsliding, backslid**] to start to do bad things again after a period of not doing them

backspace /'bækspeɪs/ ▶ NOUN [*plural* **backspaces**] the key on a computer that you press to move back one space. A computing word.

▶ VERB [**backspaces, backspacing, backspaced**] to move back one space by pressing a key on a computer. A computing word.

backstage /ˌbæk'steɪdʒ/ ADJECTIVE, ADVERB things that happen backstage in a theatre happen where the audience cannot see them, for example behind the stage □ *The play started late because of a problem backstage.*

backstroke /'bækstrəʊk/ NOUN, NO PLURAL a way of swimming in which you lie on your back and move your arms backwards over your shoulders

backtrack /'bæktræk/ VERB [**backtracks, backtracking, backtracked**]

1 to say that you will not do something that you said you would do earlier □ *He was accused of backtracking on promises to help them.*

2 to return to a subject you were talking about earlier

backup /'bækʌp/ NOUN [*plural* **backups**]

1 extra people or equipment that you can use if you need them

2 an extra copy of information on a computer. A computing word.

backward /'bækwəd/ ▶ ADJECTIVE

1 towards the back □ *a backward look*

2 slow to learn or develop

▶ ADVERB backwards □ *She was looking backward over her shoulder.*

backwards /'bækwədz/ ADVERB

1 in the direction behind you □ *I stepped backwards to give her some room.*

2 in the wrong position, with the back part at the front □ *I think my skirt is on backwards.*

3 in the opposite way to the usual way □ *Tom can say the alphabet backwards.*

bacon /'beɪkən/ NOUN, NO PLURAL thin pieces of salty meat from a pig

bacteria /bæk'tɪərɪə/ PLURAL NOUN very small living things that sometimes cause disease in humans and animals

bad /bæd/ ADJECTIVE [**worse, worst**]

1 not of a good standard □ *I've had a really bad haircut.* □ *The food was so bad I couldn't eat it.*

2 unpleasant, causing problems or worry □ *Bad weather can spoil a holiday.* □ *I had some bad news this morning.*

3 not bad satisfactory or good enough □ *We made over three hundred pounds so that's not bad.* □ *'How are you doing, Maria?' 'Not bad, thanks.'*
4 bad for someone harmful to your body, making you not healthy □ *It's bad for you to eat too much sugar.*
5 bad at something not able to do something well □ *I'm very bad at maths.*
6 food which is bad does not taste or smell good because it is old □ *This meat is bad - throw it away.*
7 evil or cruel □ *He's not a bad man.*

➤ Remember that **bad** is an adjective and not an adverb. To describe the way that someone does something, use the adverb **badly**:
✓ *He behaved very badly.*
✗ *He behaved very bad.*

bade /bæd, beɪd/ PAST TENSE OF **bid²** □ *I bade him goodbye.*
badge /bædʒ/ NOUN [plural **badges**] a small object with words or pictures that you put on your clothes to show something, for example your name
badger /'bædʒə(r)/ NOUN [plural **badgers**] an animal with black and white stripes on its face, which lives underground

badly /'bædlɪ/ ADVERB [**worse, worst**]
1 seriously □ *The car was badly damaged in the crash.*
2 in a way that is not good □ *Both children behaved badly.*
3 very much 🕮 *I badly wanted a new pair of trainers.*

badly-off /ˌbædlɪ'ɒf/ ADJECTIVE [**worse-off, worst-off**]
1 poor □ *With my father in prison, we were fairly badly-off.*
2 badly-off for something needing more of something □ *We're quite badly-off for equipment.*
badminton /'bædmɪntən/ NOUN, NO PLURAL a sport in which two or four players hit a shuttlecock (= light object with feathers) across a net
bad-tempered /ˌbæd'tempəd/ ADJECTIVE speaking or behaving angrily or rudely □ *Perhaps you wouldn't be so bad-tempered in the morning if you got more sleep.*
baffle /'bæfəl/ VERB [**baffles, baffling, baffled**] if you are baffled by a situation, you do not understand it □ *Police were baffled by the crime.*
• **baffling** /'bæflɪŋ/ ADJECTIVE if a situation is baffling, you do not understand it □ *a baffling problem*

bag /bæg/ ➤ NOUN [plural **bags**]
1 an object that you put things in and carry with you □ *a leather bag* □ *a bag of crisps*
2 bags of an informal way of saying a lot of something □ *We've got bags of time before the bus comes.*
➤ VERB [**bags, bagging, bagged**] to put things into a bag or bags □ *We helped Dad bag all the garden rubbish.*

bagel /'beɪgəl/ NOUN [plural **bagels**] a piece of hard bread in the shape of a ring
bagful /'bægful/ NOUN [plural **bagfuls**] the amount that a bag holds □ *a bagful of sweets*

baggage /'bægɪdʒ/ NOUN, NO PLURAL the cases and bags that a person takes with them when they travel □ *The baggage is stored in the back of the coach.*

➤ Remember that the noun **baggage** is never used in the plural:
✓ *I had so much baggage.*
✗ *I had so many baggages.*

baggy /'bægɪ/ ADJECTIVE [**baggier, baggiest**] baggy clothes are too big for the person wearing them and hang loosely from their body □ *a baggy sweater*
bagpipes /'bægpaɪps/ PLURAL NOUN a musical instrument made up of a bag with pipes attached. You play it by blowing down a pipe.
baguette /bæ'get/ NOUN [plural **baguettes**] a long, thin loaf of bread
bail /beɪl/ ➤ NOUN, NO PLURAL money that must be paid to a court so that someone who has been arrested for a crime can leave a prison until their trial 🕮 *He was released on bail.*
➤ VERB [**bails, bailing, bailed**] to let someone go free because bail has been paid
♦ PHRASAL VERB **bail someone out** to help a person or organization by giving them money
bailiff /'beɪlɪf/ NOUN [plural **bailiffs**] someone whose job is to take away the things that belong to a person who has not paid money they owe
bait /beɪt/ NOUN, NO PLURAL food that you use for catching a fish or an animal

bake /beɪk/ VERB [**bakes, baking, baked**]
1 to cook things like bread, cakes or biscuits in an oven □ *I baked a cake this afternoon.* □ *I love to bake with the children.*
2 to bake things that are soft is to make them hard in the sun or in an oven

baked beans /ˌbeɪkt 'biːnz/ PLURAL NOUN small white beans in a red tomato sauce, usually sold in tins (= metal containers) □ *baked beans on toast*
baker /'beɪkə(r)/ NOUN [plural **bakers**]
1 someone who bakes bread and cakes
2 baker's a shop that makes and sells bread and cakes
• **bakery** /'beɪkərɪ/ NOUN [plural **bakeries**] a shop or factory where bread and cakes are made

balance /'bæləns/ ➤ NOUN, NO PLURAL
1 when you have the same amount of weight on each side of the body so that you do not fall over 🕮 *I lost my balance and fell over.* 🕮 *I find it hard to keep my balance in high heels.*
2 a good situation in which you have or do the right amount of two or more things □ *I try to achieve a balance between work and family life.*
3 the amount of money that is in a bank account
➤ VERB [**balances, balancing, balanced**] to stay in a

position where you do not fall to either side, or to put something in a position where it will not fall □ *Lisa balanced the book on her head.*

balance sheet /'bæləns 'ʃiːt/ NOUN [*plural* **balance sheets**] a document that shows what a business has earned and what it has spent

balcony /'bælkənɪ/ NOUN [*plural* **balconies**]
1 a part of a high building which is on the outside wall. You can sit or stand in it □ *We sat on the balcony and watched the sun go down.*
2 in a theatre, the area upstairs where the seats are above the rest of the audience

bald /bɔːld/ ADJECTIVE [**balder, baldest**]
1 with little or no hair on the head ⊞ *He's going bald.* ⊞ *Dan has a bald patch.*
2 said clearly, in only a few words □ *a bald statement.*
• **balding** /'bɔːldɪŋ/ ADJECTIVE starting to lose the hair on your head □ *He was grey and balding.*
• **baldness** /'bɔːldnɪs/ NOUN, NO PLURAL being bald

bale /beɪl/ NOUN [*plural* **bales**] a lot of something, for example cloth or hay (= dried grass), pressed and tied together tightly
♦ PHRASAL VERB [**bales, baling, baled**] **bale out** to escape from a dangerous situation □ *The pilot had baled out of the burning aircraft.*

balk /bɔːk/ VERB [**balks, balking, balked**] another spelling of baulk

ball /bɔːl/ NOUN [*plural* **balls**]
1 a round object that you use for playing games like football, hockey and tennis
2 anything that has a round shape □ *a ball of string* □ *The hedgehog had rolled itself into a ball.*
3 a big formal party where people dance
♦ IDIOM **be on the ball** to be quick to understand what is happening

ballad /'bæləd/ NOUN [*plural* **ballads**] a slow song about love

ballast /'bæləst/ NOUN, NO PLURAL any heavy substance such as sand or water which is put in ships to stop them turning over

ball bearing /'bɔːl 'beərɪŋ/ NOUN [*plural* **ball bearings**] one of many small metal balls that are put between machine parts so that the parts move easily over each other

ballerina /ˌbælə'riːnə/ NOUN [*plural* **ballerinas**] a female ballet dancer

ballet /'bæleɪ/ NOUN [*plural* **ballets**]
1 *no plural* a type of dancing that tells a story and uses smooth, attractive movements which are very difficult to do ⊞ *a ballet dancer* □ *Sarah does ballet and tap dancing.*
2 a story which is told using ballet □ *My favourite ballets are The Nutcracker and Swan Lake.*

ballistics /bə'lɪstɪks/ NOUN, NO PLURAL the study of the way that objects move through the air. A physics word.

balloon /bə'luːn/ ► NOUN [*plural* **balloons**] a very light, round, rubber object that is filled with air or gas □ *The children were holding balloons.*
► VERB [**balloons, ballooning, ballooned**] to become larger and rounder □ *The sail ballooned out in the breeze.*

ballot /'bælət/ ► NOUN [*plural* **ballots**] a way of voting in secret by marking a paper and putting it into a special box ⊞ *They held a ballot to decide who would be leader.*
► VERB [**ballots, balloting, balloted**] to ballot a group of people is to get votes from them by ballot □ *The workers were balloted and voted to strike.*

ballot box /'bælət 'bɒks/ NOUN [*plural* **ballot boxes**] a box which people who have just voted put their ballot papers into

ballot paper /'bælət 'peɪpə(r)/ NOUN [*plural* **ballot papers**] a piece of paper on which you make a mark to show who you are voting for

ballpark /'bɔːlpɑːk/ ADJECTIVE a ballpark amount or number has been guessed using the information available, but not calculated exactly ⊞ *Do you have ballpark figures for the building costs?*

ballpoint pen /'bɔːlpɔɪnt 'pen/ NOUN [*plural* **ballpoint pens**] a pen with a very small metal ball at the end where the ink comes out

ballroom dancing /'bɔːlrʊm 'dɑːnsɪŋ/ NOUN, NO PLURAL a formal, old-fashioned type of dancing in which two people hold each other and do a pattern of steps

balm /bɑːm/ NOUN, NO PLURAL oil or cream that you put on sore skin to make it feel better □ *lip balm*

balmy /'bɑːmɪ/ ADJECTIVE [**balmier, balmiest**] describes weather than is warm and pleasant □ *a balmy evening*

balsa /'bɔːlsə/ NOUN, NO PLURAL a very light, soft wood that people use for making model boats and aircraft

bamboo /bæm'buː/ NOUN, NO PLURAL a tall Asian grass that has hard, round stems that are used to make furniture

bamboozle /bæm'buːzəl/ VERB [**bamboozles, bamboozling, bamboozled**] to confuse or trick someone

ban /bæn/ ► VERB [**bans, banning, banned**] to not allow people to do something □ *Cycling is banned in the park.*
► NOUN [*plural* **bans**] an order that people are not allowed to do something □ *There's a ban on smoking in public places.*

banal /bə'nɑːl/ ADJECTIVE boring and not original □ *She found his conversation rather banal.*
• **banality** /bə'nælətɪ/ NOUN, NO PLURAL when something is banal

banana /bə'nɑːnə/ NOUN [plural bananas] a long, curved, yellow fruit which is white inside 🔊 I watched him peel a banana.

band /bænd/ NOUN [plural bands]
1 a group of musicians who play together □ a rock band
2 a long, thin piece of material used for putting round something 🔊 a rubber band
3 a line of colour which is different from the colour around it □ Her hat had a band of red around it.
4 a group □ a band of robbers
◆ PHRASAL VERB [bands, banding, banded] **band together** to join together as a group to do something □ All the parents banded together to demand improvements in the school.

bandage /'bændɪdʒ/ ▶ NOUN [plural bandages] a long piece of cloth that you put around a part of your body that has been cut or hurt □ He had a bandage around his arm.
▶ VERB [bandages, bandaging, bandaged] to put a bandage around a part of your body □ The nurse bandaged his wrist.

bandit /'bændɪt/ NOUN [plural bandits] someone who attacks people who are travelling and takes money and possessions from them

bandwagon /'bændwægən/ NOUN
◆ IDIOM **climb/jump on the bandwagon** to start to do something only because other people are doing it or it is fashionable □ Once one company has a success with a product, other companies jump on the bandwagon and start producing a similar product.

bandwidth /'bændwɪdθ/ NOUN [plural bandwidths] a measurement of how much information an Internet connection can send in an amount of time. A computing word.

bandy /'bændɪ/ ADJECTIVE [bandier, bandiest] bandy legs curve out at the knees

bane /beɪn/ NOUN **the bane of your life** something that causes you a lot of trouble □ Hay fever is the bane of my life!

bang /bæŋ/ ▶ NOUN [plural bangs]
1 a sudden loud noise □ There was a loud bang and all the lights went out.
2 when you knock part of your body against something □ She's had a bang on the head and is feeling a bit dizzy.
▶ VERB [bangs, banging, banged]
1 to make a sudden loud noise by hitting against something □ The door banged shut in the wind.
2 to knock part of your body against something □ Neil banged his head on the shelf.

banger /'bæŋə(r)/ NOUN [plural bangers]
1 a type of very loud firework (= object that explodes in the sky and makes a noise and colours)
2 an informal word for sausage 🔊 bangers and mash (= sausages and crushed potatoes)
3 an informal word for an old car that is in bad condition

bangle /'bæŋgəl/ NOUN [plural bangles] a ring of metal, wood or plastic that you wear on your wrist (= part between hand and arm)

banish /'bænɪʃ/ VERB [banishes, banishing, banished]
1 to make someone leave their country or their home as a punishment
2 to make you stop thinking or feeling a particular way □ You must banish all thoughts of revenge.
● **banishment** /'bænɪʃmənt/ NOUN, NO PLURAL being banished

banisters /'bænɪstəz/ PLURAL NOUN a bar that you can hold as you walk up or down stairs and the poles that support the bar

banjo /'bændʒəʊ/ NOUN [plural banjos or banjoes] a musical instrument with strings, like a small guitar but with the main part round in shape

bank /bæŋk/ ▶ NOUN [plural banks]
1 a business that looks after other people's money and also lends money 🔊 I must go to the bank.
2 a place where a lot of one thing is stored so that it can be used later □ a blood bank
3 an area of ground which is next to a river or lake □ We camped on the banks of Loch Lomond.
4 an area of ground which is raised □ There's a steep wooded bank behind the house.
▶ VERB [banks, banking, banked] to have a bank account with a particular bank □ I've banked with them for years.
◆ PHRASAL VERB **bank on something** to depend on something □ He might help you but don't bank on it.

bank account /'bæŋk 'əkaʊnt/ NOUN [plural bank accounts] an arrangement that you have with a bank for keeping money there, and for taking it out when you need it 🔊 I must open a bank account.

bank balance /'bæŋk 'bæləns/ NOUN [plural bank balances] the amount of money you have in a bank account

bank card /'bæŋk 'kɑːd/ NOUN [plural bank cards] a small piece of plastic that you use to pay for things or to get money out of a machine

banker /'bæŋkə(r)/ NOUN [plural bankers] someone who has an important job in a bank

bank holiday /'bæŋk 'hɒlɪdeɪ/ NOUN [plural bank holidays] a public holiday when the banks are closed

banking /'bæŋkɪŋ/ NOUN, NO PLURAL the business that banks do

banknote /'bæŋknəʊt/ NOUN [plural banknotes] a piece of paper money □ a £20 banknote

bankrupt /'bæŋkrʌpt/ ADJECTIVE if a person or business is bankrupt, they are not able to pay the money they owe 🔊 The business went bankrupt because costs rose.
● **bankruptcy** /'bæŋkrʌptsɪ/ NOUN [plural bankruptcies] being bankrupt 🔊 The business is facing bankruptcy. □ The number of bankruptcies went up last year.

bank statement /'bæŋk 'steɪtmənt/ NOUN [plural bank statements] a list that your bank sends you, which shows all the money that you have put into your bank account, and the money you have taken out of your bank account during a particular period

banner /'bænə(r)/ NOUN [plural banners] a large piece of cloth with writing on it which people carry on poles □ The anti-war protesters were carrying banners.

banquet /'bæŋkwɪt/ NOUN [plural banquets] a formal meal for a lot of people on an important occasion

banter /'bæntə(r)/ NOUN, NO PLURAL talk in which people tell jokes and laugh at each other

baptism /'bæptɪzəm/ NOUN [plural baptisms] a Christian ceremony in which someone has water put on their head to show that they are joining the Christian religion

baptize /bæp'taɪz/ or **baptise** VERB [baptizes, baptizing, baptized] to make someone a member of the Christian religion by putting water on their head in a special ceremony

bar /bɑː(r)/ ▶ NOUN [plural bars]
1 a place that sells alcoholic drinks □ The city is full of cafés and bars.
2 a long narrow piece of metal □ an iron bar
3 a restaurant that serves a particular type of food □ a burger bar
4 a large piece of something such as chocolate or soap □ + of a bar of chocolate
5 a bar to something something that prevents something else from happening □ The disease should not be a bar to success.
6 one of the parts that a line of music is divided into □ There were four beats in each bar.
▶ VERB [bars, barring, barred]
1 if someone is barred from a place or barred from doing something, they are not allowed in or are not allowed to do it □ + from Anyone over the age of 12 is barred from the competition.
2 to prevent someone from going somewhere by standing in their way □ Over a hundred protestors barred the entrance to the building.
3 to lock a door or window by putting a metal bar across it

barb /bɑːb/ NOUN [plural barbs] a curved point on an arrow or a fish hook (= used for catching fish) that makes it difficult to remove

barbarian /bɑː'beərɪən/ NOUN [plural barbarians] someone who behaves badly and shows no respect for things like art and education

barbaric /bɑː'bærɪk/ ADJECTIVE cruel or violent □ barbaric acts of terrorism

barbecue /'bɑːbɪkjuː/ ▶ NOUN [plural barbecues]
1 a piece of equipment used for cooking food outdoors □ She was trying to light the barbecue. 🔁 Put some more sausages on the barbecue.
2 a party or meal outdoors where food is cooked on a barbecue 🔁 We're having a barbecue tonight.
▶ VERB [barbecues, barbecuing, barbecued] to cook food on a barbecue

barbed wire /'bɑːbd 'waɪə(r)/ NOUN, NO PLURAL wire with sharp points on it, used to stop people getting into a place

barber /'bɑːbə(r)/ NOUN [plural barbers]
1 a man whose job is to cut men's hair
2 barber's a shop where men have their hair cut

bar chart /'bɑː(r) 'tʃɑːt/ NOUN [plural bar charts] a graph (= picture in maths) which shows different amounts as thick lines of different lengths. A maths word.

bar code /'bɑː(r) 'kəʊd/ NOUN [plural bar codes] many printed black lines on a product, which a computer uses to get information, for example the price of the product

bare /beə(r)/ ADJECTIVE [barer, barest]
1 not covered with anything 🔁 It's too cold to go out with bare legs. □ The wall looks really bare without any pictures on it.
2 basic and with nothing extra 🔁 Her bag was packed with the bare essentials. 🔁 We try to keep prices to a bare minimum.

bareback /'beəbæk/ ADVERB if you ride bareback, you ride a horse without a saddle (= a leather seat)

barefaced /'beəfeɪst/ ADJECTIVE done in a way that shows you are not embarrassed about behaving badly 🔁 a barefaced lie

barefoot /'beəfʊt/ ADJECTIVE, ADVERB not wearing any shoes or socks □ barefoot children □ They were running barefoot on the beach.

barely /'beəlɪ/ ADVERB almost not □ She was old and barely able to walk. □ They had barely arrived when they had to leave again.

bargain /'bɑːgɪn/ ▶ NOUN [plural bargains]
1 something that is cheap or cheaper than usual □ These jeans were a real bargain.
2 an agreement in which each person or group promises to do something 🔁 She tried to strike a bargain with (= make an agreement with) him.
▶ VERB [bargains, bargaining, bargained]
1 to try to persuade someone to sell something to you for less money
2 get more than you bargained for to be different from what you expected, especially in a way that is worse

barge /bɑːdʒ/ ▶ NOUN [plural barges] a boat with a flat bottom, used on canals (= passages of water) and rivers
▶ VERB [barges, barging, barged] to go somewhere so quickly that you push people out of your way or hit things □ Matt barged into the room knocking all the books over as he came. □ He barged past me to get to the front of the queue.

baritone /'bærɪtəʊn/ NOUN [plural baritones]
1 a male singing voice which is low but not the lowest
2 a man with this singing voice

barium /'beərɪəm/ NOUN, NO PLURAL a soft metal element. A chemistry word.

bark /bɑːk/ ► NOUN [plural **barks**]
1 the short, loud sound that a dog makes
2 the rough wood on the outside of a tree
► VERB [**barks, barking, barked**]
1 when a dog barks, it makes a short, loud sound
2 to say something in a loud, angry voice □ 'Hurry up, you lot!' he barked.

barley /'bɑːlɪ/ NOUN, NO PLURAL a grain used for food and for making beer

barman /'bɑːmən/ NOUN [plural **barmen**] a man who serves drinks at a bar

bar mitzvah /ˌbɑː(r) 'mɪtsvə/ NOUN [plural **bar mitzvahs**] a religious ceremony for a Jewish boy when he is 13. It marks the time when he starts to have the religious responsibilities of an adult.

barmy /'bɑːmɪ/ ADJECTIVE an informal word meaning very silly or mad

barn /bɑːn/ NOUN [plural **barns**] a large building on a farm, for keeping crops or animals in

barnacle /'bɑːnəkəl/ NOUN [plural **barnacles**] a type of small shellfish (= sea creature) that sticks to rocks and the bottoms of boats

barometer /bə'rɒmɪtə(r)/ NOUN [plural **barometers**] an instrument for measuring the pressure of air and showing changes in the weather

baron /'bærən/ NOUN [plural **barons**] a name given to some men who belong to the highest social class

baroness /'bærənɪs/ NOUN [plural **baronesses**] a female baron or a baron's wife □ Baroness Thatcher

baroque /bə'rɒk/ ADJECTIVE to do with the style of art, music and buildings used in Europe in the 17th and 18th centuries □ baroque churches

barrack /'bærək/ VERB [**barracks, barracking, barracked**] to shout at someone who is speaking or performing in public, because you do not like what they are saying or doing □ He was barracked by several members of the audience.

barracks /'bærəks/ PLURAL NOUN a group of buildings where soldiers live and work

barracuda /ˌbærə'kuːdə/ NOUN [plural **barracudas**] a large fierce sea fish with big teeth, found in the Caribbean and other warm seas

barrage /'bærɑːʒ/ NOUN [plural **barrages**]
1 a continuous firing of guns
2 a barrage of sth a lot of questions or complaints said all at the same time by a lot of different people □ He has faced a barrage of criticism.

barrel /'bærəl/ NOUN [plural **barrels**]
1 a wooden or metal container with curved sides, used for holding liquids such as beer
2 the barrel of a gun is the metal tube through which the bullet is fired

barren /'bærən/ ADJECTIVE barren land has very little or nothing growing on it

barricade /'bærɪˌkeɪd/ ► NOUN [plural **barricades**] something that is put across a road or door to stop people getting through □ Police smashed barricades which had been erected by protesters.
► VERB [**barricades, barricading, barricaded**]

1 to put something across a road or door to stop people getting through
2 barricade yourself somewhere to stay inside a place and put something across the door so that people cannot get in □ They've barricaded themselves inside the house.

barrier /'bærɪə(r)/ NOUN [plural **barriers**]
1 a gate or fence used to stop people getting past □ There is a barrier at the exit of the car park, and you need a ticket to get out.
2 something that stops you from making progress or stops you from being successful □ Nowadays, being a woman isn't a barrier to a career in the navy.
3 something that prevents people from communicating or working well together ⊞ The language barrier can be a real problem when people go to live abroad.

barring /'bɑːrɪŋ/ PREPOSITION unless something happens □ Barring accidents, he should win the competition.

barrister /'bærɪstə(r)/ NOUN [plural **barristers**] a lawyer who works in a court

barrow /'bærəʊ/ NOUN [plural **barrows**] a container on wheels that you push

barter /'bɑːtə(r)/ VERB [**barters, bartering, bartered**] to exchange one thing for another thing, without using any money □ They bartered crops for milk in nearby villages.

basalt /'bæsɔːlt/ NOUN, NO PLURAL a type of rock made from hot liquid rock from a volcano (= mountain that explodes). A geography word.

base /beɪs/ ► NOUN [plural **bases**]
1 the lowest part of something □ + of He broke a bone at the base of his spine.
2 something which is under something else and which supports it □ The shed stood on a concrete base.
3 the main place where someone works or stays □ + for The hotel is an ideal base for walking holidays.
4 a place where people in the army, navy, etc. live and work □ a British military base in Germany
5 a situation or idea from which something can develop □ + for The conditions provide a good base for economic strength.
6 the number used as the most important unit in a system of counting, for example 10 in the decimal system. A maths word.
► VERB [**bases, basing, based**] if a person or organization is based in a particular place, that is where they live or do their work □ **usually passive** The company is based in Moscow. □ a London-based organization
♦ PHRASAL VERB **base something on something** to use an idea, situation, fact etc. as the thing that you develop something else from □ **often passive** The court's decision was based on facts.

baseball /'beɪsbɔːl/ NOUN [plural **baseballs**]
1 no plural a game for two teams who hit a ball with a long bat (= wooden stick) and run to four different

places 🕮 *He taught me how to play baseball.* □ *a baseball game*
2 a small ball used in the game of baseball

baseless /ˈbeɪslɪs/ ADJECTIVE not based on facts or good reasons. A formal word. □ *baseless accusations*

basement /ˈbeɪsmənt/ NOUN [plural **basements**] the lowest level of a building, under the ground □ *There is a restaurant in the basement.* □ *a basement flat*

bases /ˈbeɪsiːz/ PLURAL OF **basis** *and* **base**

bash /bæʃ/ ▶ VERB [bashes, bashing, bashed] an informal word meaning to hit something or someone very hard □ *The ball bashed him in the face.*
▶ NOUN [plural **bashes**]
1 an informal word meaning a hard hit
2 an informal word meaning a party
3 an informal word meaning a try at something 🕮 *The club allows members to have a bash at various sports.*

bashful /ˈbæʃful/ ADJECTIVE shy and becoming embarrassed very easily □ *Lily, suddenly bashful, could think of nothing to say.*

basic /ˈbeɪsɪk/ ADJECTIVE
1 being the main or most important part of something □ *He taught us the basic principles of karate.* □ *basic training/skills*
2 without any extra or special features □ *The cottage was pretty basic - it didn't even have a proper bath.*
• **basically** /ˈbeɪsɪkəli/ ADVERB used when you are stating the most important fact and not giving all the details □ *Joe's basically a good person.* □ *Basically, I was sick of the job.*
• **basics** /ˈbeɪsɪks/ PLURAL NOUN the most important things that you need □ *John taught her the basics of sailing.* □ *We spend most of our money on basics like food and clothes.*

basil /ˈbæzəl/ NOUN, NO PLURAL a herb that is used in cooking with leaves that smell sweet

basin /ˈbeɪsən/ NOUN [plural **basins**]
1 a bowl with taps (= objects you turn to get water) for washing your hands and face in
2 a bowl used in the kitchen for holding food □ *a pudding basin*
3 an area of land from which water flows into a river □ *the Amazon basin*

basis /ˈbeɪsɪs/ NOUN [plural **bases**]
1 **on a regular/part-time/unpaid, etc. basis** used to express the method or system used for arranging or organizing something □ *The team meets on a weekly basis.* □ *I work there on a voluntary basis.*
2 **on the basis of something** used to show the reason why something is done in a particular way □ *Medical treatment should not be refused on the basis of age.*
3 the thing on which something is based 🕮 *Sweets can*

be eaten occasionally but should not form the basis of your diet.

bask /bɑːsk/ VERB [basks, basking, basked]
1 to sit or lie enjoying the warmth of the sun □ *We basked in the warm sunshine.*
2 if you bask in other people's praise or attention, you enjoy it □ *Amrish had scored the winning goal and was basking in the admiration of his friends.*

basket /ˈbɑːskɪt/ NOUN [plural **baskets**] a container for storing or carrying things, made of thin pieces of material such as wood or plastic 🕮 *a shopping basket* 🕮 *a laundry basket* □ **+ of** *a basket of fruit*

basketball /ˈbɑːskɪtbɔːl/ NOUN [plural **basketballs**]
1 *no plural* a game played by two teams who try to throw a ball through a net
2 a large ball used to play basketball

basmati /bæsˈmætɪ/ NOUN, NO PLURAL a type of rice that is often used in South Asian cooking

bass /beɪs/ ▶ NOUN [plural **basses**]
1 the lowest range of notes in music
2 an electric guitar that plays low notes
3 a double bass (= very large instrument with strings)
4 a man with the lowest type of singing voice
▶ ADJECTIVE of or making the lowest range of musical notes □ *singing the bass part*

bass clef /ˌbeɪs ˈklef/ NOUN [plural **bass clefs**] a sign [𝄢] used in music to show that the notes are in the lower range

bassoon /bəˈsuːn/ NOUN [plural **bassoons**] a long wooden instrument that you play by blowing into it to make a low sound

bastion /ˈbæstɪən/ NOUN [plural **bastions**] a place or organization that supports traditional beliefs or ways of doing things 🕮 *The college was Oxford University's last bastion of female-only education.*

bat /bæt/ ▶ NOUN [plural **bats**]
1 a piece of wood used for hitting the ball in sports such as cricket and baseball
2 an animal that flies around at night, and looks like a mouse with wings
▶ VERB [bats, batting, batted] to use the bat in games such as cricket and rounders □ *It's Gary's turn to bat next.*

batch /bætʃ/ NOUN [plural **batches**] several people or things that are dealt with as a group □ *He stapled a batch of papers together.*

bated /ˈbeɪtɪd/ ADJECTIVE **with bated breath** feeling nervous or excited because you are waiting for something to happen □ *I waited with bated breath as they announced the winner.*

bath /bɑːθ/ ▶ NOUN [plural **baths**]
1 a long container that you fill with water and sit or lie in to wash yourself □ *Russell's in the bath.* 🕮 *She went upstairs and ran a bath* (= put water in it).
2 when you sit or lie in a long container filled with

water so that you can wash yourself 🔁 *I think I'll have a bath.*
▶ VERB [baths, bathing, bathed] to wash someone in a bath

bathe /beɪð/ VERB [bathes, bathing, bathed]
1 to wash your body □ *They are forced to bathe in polluted water.*
2 to swim in a lake, a river, or the sea
3 to wash a cut or wash a sore part of your body □ *I'm going to bathe my aching feet as soon as I get home.*

bathrobe /'bɑ:θrəʊb/ NOUN [plural bathrobes] a soft piece of clothing that looks like a coat, that you wear before or after having a bath

bathroom /'bɑ:θrʊm/ NOUN [plural bathrooms]
1 the room that you wash yourself in □ *The hotel rooms all have a private bathroom.* □ *a bathroom mirror*
2 go to the bathroom a US phrase meaning to go to the toilet

bathtub /'bɑ:θtʌb/ NOUN [plural bathtubs] the US word for **bath** (= container that you sit in to wash yourself)

bat mitzvah /ˌbæt 'mɪtsvə/ NOUN [plural bat mitzvahs] a religious ceremony for Jewish girls when they are 12. It marks the time when they start having religious responsibilities.

baton /'bætən/ NOUN [plural batons]
1 a stick, for example used by police to control crowds, or passed between runners in a race
2 a thin stick used by the person conducting (= moving their arms to control) an orchestra (= large group of musicians)

batsman /'bætsmən/ NOUN [plural batsmen] a man who is hitting the ball in cricket

battalion /bə'tæljən/ NOUN [plural battalions] a large group of soldiers

batten /'bætən/
◆ PHRASAL VERB [battens, battening, battened] **batten something down** to fix something with a long piece of wood to make sure it is tightly closed

batter /'bætə(r)/ ▶ VERB [batters, battering, battered] to hit someone or something very hard several times □ *He was battered to death with a hammer.* □ *Waves battered the shore.*
▶ NOUN, NO PLURAL a mixture of flour, milk and eggs, used for covering food before it is fried
● **battered** /'bætəd/ ADJECTIVE
1 damaged □ *a battered leather suitcase*
2 covered in batter □ *battered cod*

battering ram /'bætərɪŋ 'ræm/ NOUN [plural battering rams] a large heavy piece of wood or metal, used for breaking through a door

battery /'bætəri/ NOUN [plural batteries] a device used to supply electrical power to things like watches, cameras and car engines 🔁 *The car wouldn't start because the battery was flat* (= the battery did not work).

battle /'bætəl/ ▶ NOUN [plural battles]
1 a fight between two armies □ *the Battle of Hastings* □ *His father was killed in battle.*
2 a situation in which people compete or argue with each other 🔁 *She won a bitter legal battle to get custody of their child.* □ **+ for** *a battle for power* □ **with** *He was involved in a battle with his brother over some land.*
3 a determined effort to deal with a difficult situation □ **+ against** *the battle against crime* 🔁 *She lost her battle against cancer.*
▶ VERB [battles, battling, battled] to try very hard to do something difficult □ **+ to do something** *Surgeons battled to save her life.* □ **+ against** *Rescuers battled against strong winds and rough seas.* □ **+ for** *They are continuing to battle for compensation.*

battlefield /'bætəlfi:ld// NOUN [plural battlefields] a place where armies fight

battlements /'bætəlmənts/ PLURAL NOUN a wall around the top of a castle, with spaces for people to shoot weapons through

battleship /'bætəlʃɪp/ NOUN [plural battleships] a very large ship that has big guns

batty /'bæti/ ADJECTIVE [battier, battiest] an informal word meaning slightly silly and strange □ *a batty idea* □ *I can't remember where I put my keys. I must be going batty.*

bauble /'bɔ:bəl/ NOUN [plural baubles] a round shiny decoration that you hang on a tree at Christmas

baulk /bɔ:k/ VERB [baulks, baulking, baulked] to not want to do something because you think it is unpleasant or unreasonable □ *My father baulked at the cost of taking us all to Australia.*

bawdy /'bɔ:di/ ADJECTIVE [bawdier, bawdiest] referring to sex in a funny way □ *bawdy jokes*

bawl /bɔ:l/ VERB [bawls, bawling, bawled]
1 to shout loudly
2 an informal word meaning to cry

bay /beɪ/ NOUN [plural bays]
1 a piece of land on the coast that curves in □ *the Bay of Biscay*
2 an area that is used for a particular purpose 🔁 *The supermarket has promised to provide more disabled parking bays.* 🔁 *a loading bay* (= for taking goods on or off vehicles)
3 keep/hold something at bay to stop something bad from happening or affecting you □ *Treatment has kept the cancer at bay for the past five years.*

bayonet /'beɪənɪt/ NOUN [plural bayonets] a long knife fixed to the end of a gun

bay window /'beɪ 'wɪndəʊ/ NOUN [plural bay windows] a window that curves out from the wall of a house

bazaar /bə'zɑ:(r)/ NOUN [plural bazaars]
1 a market in Middle Eastern countries
2 an event where things are sold to make money for an organization

BBC /ˌbiːbiːˈsiː/ ABBREVIATION British Broadcasting Corporation; the television and radio company paid for by the public in the UK

BC /ˌbiːˈsiː/ ABBREVIATION before Christ; used after a date to show that it was before the birth of Jesus Christ, for example, *450 BC.*
➡ *go to* **AD**

be /biː/ ▶ VERB

1 used for giving information about someone or something □ *He's French.* □ *Are you hungry?* □ *Her brother's an accountant.*

2 there are/is/were, etc. used for saying that something exists or existed □ *There are a lot of people here.* □ *Is there anything else to eat?*

▶ AUXILIARY VERB

1 used with the present participle of another verb to talk about actions that were or are continuous □ *I am enjoying my course.* □ *What are you doing?* □ *He is not doing very well at school*

2 used with the present participle of another verb to talk about actions in the future □ *He is going to London next week.* □ *They are opening a new shop.* □ *I am coming back again later.*

3 used with the past participle of another verb to make passive sentences □ *She was taken to hospital.* □ *They have been warned before.* □ *The animals will be kept in a zoo.*

beach /biːtʃ/ NOUN [*plural* **beaches**] an area of sand or stones at the edge of the sea □ *We spent the day on the beach.* ☐ *The town has a beautiful sandy beach.*

beacon /ˈbiːkən/ NOUN [*plural* **beacons**] a bright light that is used as a warning of danger or as a sign of something

bead /biːd/ NOUN [*plural* **beads**]
1 a small round piece of glass, plastic or wood with a hole through it, used for making jewellery
2 a round drop of liquid □ *There were beads of sweat on his forehead.*

beagle /ˈbiːɡəl/ NOUN [*plural* **beagles**] a type of dog with long ears

beak /biːk/ NOUN [*plural* **beaks**] a bird's beak is its hard pointed mouth

beaker /ˈbiːkə(r)/ NOUN [*plural* **beakers**] a cup without a handle

beam /biːm/ ▶ NOUN [*plural* **beams**]
1 a line of light □ *the beam of the car's headlights*
2 a long thick piece of wood or metal that is used to support the weight of a building
3 a big smile
▶ VERB [**beams, beaming, beamed**]
1 to smile a big smile □ *Meg beamed at him gratefully.*
2 to send something using television or radio signals □ *The game was beamed around the world.*
3 if the sun beams, it shines brightly

bean /biːn/ NOUN [*plural* **beans**] a vegetable that is the large seed of some plants □ *kidney beans*

beanbag /ˈbiːnbæɡ/ NOUN [*plural* **beanbags**] a large bag that is filled with very small objects like beans, used for sitting on

bear /beə(r)/ ▶ VERB [**bears, bearing, bore, born** or **borne**]
1 to accept something unpleasant or painful ☐ *I can't bear the thought of him suffering.* □ *+ to do something Stephen just can't bear to part with his old toys.* □ *Can you bear to wait a bit longer for dinner?*
2 bear something in mind to remember that something is important □ *Please bear in mind that you only have an hour to write your essay.*
3 bear a resemblance to someone/something to be similar to someone or something □ *She bears a striking resemblance to her sister.* □ *The language bears little resemblance to English*
4 to carry something in your hand □ *Hassan appeared, bearing a cup of coffee.*
5 to have or show a particular name, picture, or design □ *The plaque on the wall bore his name.*
6 to give birth to a baby or young animal
▶ NOUN [*plural* **bears**] a large, strong animal with thick fur
● **bearable** /ˈbeərəbəl/ ADJECTIVE if something is bearable, you can accept it even though it is bad □ *The warmer weather made life a bit more bearable.*

beard /bɪəd/ NOUN [*plural* **beards**] the hair that grows on a man's chin ☐ *He wanted to grow a beard.* ☐ *Dieter shaved off his beard.*
● **bearded** /ˈbɪədɪd/ ADJECTIVE having a beard □ *a tall bearded man*

bearer /ˈbeərə(r)/ NOUN [*plural* **bearers**] someone who brings or carries something ☐ *I'm sorry to be the bearer of bad news.*

bearing /ˈbeərɪŋ/ NOUN [*plural* **bearings**]
1 have a bearing on something to affect a situation □ *His age will have a bearing on how quickly he recovers from his illness.*
2 get your bearings to find out where you are
3 lose your bearings to get confused and not know where you are

beast /biːst/ NOUN [*plural* **beasts**]
1 an animal, especially a large one
2 an old-fashioned word meaning a cruel person
● **beastly** /ˈbiːstlɪ/ ADJECTIVE [**beastlier, beastliest**] an old-fashioned word meaning cruel or unpleasant

beat /biːt/ ▶ VERB [**beats, beating, beat, beaten**]
1 to defeat someone in a game or competition □ *England were beaten 3-0 by Italy.* □ *+ at She beat me at squash.*
2 to hit someone or something many times □ *He was beaten and robbed by two men.*
3 to make a regular sound or movement □ *He could hear his heart beating.*
4 to deal successfully with a bad situation or illness

□ *Police are working with the community to try to beat crime.* □ *She beat cancer and went on to have a child.*
5 to mix food together very quickly □ *Beat the eggs.*
♦ IDIOM **off the beaten track** a long way from other people or houses
♦ PHRASAL VERB **beat someone up** to hit or kick someone until they are badly injured □ *He was beaten up by some boys in his class.*
▶ NOUN [*plural* **beats**]
1 a regular sound or movement like that made by your heart □ **+ of** *I could hear the rapid beat of her heart.*
2 a regular rhythm in music
3 an area that a police officer walks around regularly □ *We want more police officers on the beat.*

beautician /ˌbjuːˈtɪʃən/ NOUN [*plural* **beauticians**] someone whose job is to make people look better by doing things such as painting their nails or putting make-up on them

beautiful /ˈbjuːtɪful/ ADJECTIVE
1 very attractive □ *She was a very beautiful young woman.* ☐ *She looked beautiful in her long blue dress.* □ *beautiful countryside* □ *beautiful music*
2 very sunny and bright □ *It was a cold but beautiful day.*
• **beautifully** /ˈbjuːtəfəlɪ/ ADVERB
1 in a beautiful way □ *The card was beautifully decorated.*
2 with great care and skill □ *a beautifully made jacket*
• **beautify** /ˈbjuːtɪfaɪ/ VERB [**beautifies, beautifying, beautified**] to make a place or person more attractive

beauty /ˈbjuːtɪ/ NOUN [*plural* **beauties**]
1 *no plural* the quality of being very attractive ☐ *The area is noted for its natural beauty.* □ **+ of** *the beauty of her face*
2 **the beauty of something** a quality that makes something very good □ *The beauty of the software is that it is easy to use.*
3 a thing you think is very good □ *Just look at the fish he caught. Isn't it a beauty?*
4 a beautiful woman □ *She was a great beauty.*
5 beauty products/treatments, etc. things to make people more attractive

beauty salon /ˈbjuːtɪ ˈsælɒn/ NOUN [*plural* **beauty salons**] a place where people go for treatments to make them more attractive
beauty spot /ˈbjuːtɪ ˈspɒt/ NOUN [*plural* **beauty spots**] a beautiful place in the countryside that a lot of people go to
beaver /ˈbiːvə(r)/ NOUN [*plural* **beavers**] an animal with brown fur and a large flat tail that builds dams (= walls) made from sticks across rivers
♦ PHRASAL VERB [**beavers, beavering, beavered**] **beaver away** to work very hard □ *Sanjay's been beavering away at his homework.*

became /bɪˈkeɪm/ PAST TENSE OF **become**

because /bɪˈkɒz/ CONJUNCTION
1 used for giving the reason for something □ *We chose the hotel because it was easy for everyone to get*
to. □ *You can't borrow my bike because there's something wrong with the brakes.*
2 because of as a result of □ *Because of your rudeness, we've lost the job.* □ *We decided not to go because of the rain.*
3 just because used for saying that although one thing is true, something else may not be true □ *Just because I'm younger than you doesn't mean I don't know anything.*

beckon /ˈbekən/ VERB [**beckons, beckoning, beckoned**] to signal with your hand that you want someone to come closer to you □ *Alice beckoned to the waiter.*

become /bɪˈkʌm/ VERB [**becomes, becoming, became, become**]
1 to begin to be something □ *She'd become old and frail.* □ *He became prime minister in 1997.*
2 what became of someone/something used to ask what has happened to someone or something □ *Do you remember the woman with the pink coat? I wonder what became of her?*

becquerel /ˌbekəˈrel/ NOUN [*plural* **becquerels**] a unit used to measure radioactivity. A physics word.

bed /bed/ NOUN [*plural* **beds**]
1 a piece of furniture that you sleep on □ *He was ill and spent the day in bed.* ☐ *I got out of bed and went downstairs.* ☐ *What time do you usually go to bed?* ☐ *I need to make the bed (= put the sheets on it).* ☐ *The room had a double bed (= bed for two people) in it.*
2 the bottom of a river, a lake or the sea ☐ *the sea bed*
3 an area in a garden that contains flowers and other plants ☐ *He was weeding the flower bed.*

bed and breakfast /ˈbed ənd ˈbrekfəst/ NOUN [*plural* **bed and breakfasts**] a small hotel or someone's house where you can sleep and have breakfast
bedclothes /ˈbedkləʊðz/ PLURAL NOUN things such as sheets that you use for covering a bed
bedding /ˈbedɪŋ/ NOUN, NO PLURAL
1 things such as sheets that you use for covering a bed
2 something soft that animals sleep on, for example hay (= dried grass)
bedlam /ˈbedləm/ NOUN, NO PLURAL a situation or place in which there is a lot of noise and confusion □ *There was bedlam as everyone tried to get onto the train.*
bedlinen /ˈbedˌlɪnɪn/ NOUN, NO PLURAL things such as sheets that you use for covering a bed
bedraggled /bɪˈdrægəld/ ADJECTIVE untidy, wet and dirty
bedridden /ˈbedˌrɪdən/ ADJECTIVE unable to get out of bed because you are too ill
bedrock /ˈbedrɒk/ NOUN [*plural* **bedrocks**] the main ideas and beliefs that something is based on □ *Free speech is the bedrock of democracy.*

bedroom /'bedrʊm/ NOUN [plural **bedrooms**] a room that you sleep in ⌧ We have a spare bedroom so you can come and stay. □ bedroom furniture

bedside /'bedsaɪd/ NOUN, NO PLURAL the area next to a bed ⌧ a bedside table

bedsit /'bed,sɪt/ or **bedsitter** /'bed,sɪtə(r)// NOUN [plural **bedsits** or **bedsitters**] a room where you can live, usually with a bed and a small kitchen area

bedspread /'bedspred/ NOUN [plural **bedspreads**] a cover that you put over a bed

bedstead /'bedsted/ NOUN [plural **bedsteads**] the metal or wooden frame of a bed

bedtime /'bedtaɪm/ NOUN [plural **bedtimes**] the time when you usually go to bed ⌧ It's well past my bedtime. □ a bedtime story

bee /bi:/ NOUN [plural **bees**] a black and yellow insect that makes honey

beech /bi:tʃ/ NOUN [plural **beeches**] a tree with grey, smooth bark (= wood on the outside of a tree)

beef /bi:f/ NOUN, NO PLURAL meat from a cow ⌧ We had roast beef for dinner.

beefburger /'bi:f,bɜ:gə(r)/ NOUN [plural **beefburgers**] very small pieces of beef that have been pressed into a flat round shape and cooked

beefy /'bi:fɪ/ ADJECTIVE [**beefier, beefiest**] a beefy man is big and strong. An informal word.

beehive /'bi:haɪv/ NOUN [plural **beehives**] a box where you keep bees to make honey

beeline /'bi:laɪn/ NOUN □
♦ IDIOM **make a beeline for something** to move quickly towards something □ We made a beeline for the exit.

been /bi:n/ PAST PARTICIPLE OF be □ I have been thinking.

beep /bi:p/ ► VERB [**beeps, beeping, beeped**] if an electronic machine beeps, it makes a short, high sound □ The microwave started to beep.
► NOUN [plural **beeps**] when a machine beeps □ His watch gave a beep.

beer /bɪə(r)/ NOUN [plural **beers**]
1 no plural an alcoholic drink made from a type of grain ⌧ He had a pint of beer in his hand. ⌧ empty beer bottles
2 a glass of this drink □ I'll have a beer please.

beetle /'bi:təl/ NOUN [plural **beetles**] a black insect with a hard back

beetroot /'bi:tru:t/ NOUN [plural **beetroots**] a round, dark red vegetable that grows under the ground

befall /bɪ'fɔ:l/ VERB [**befalls, befalling, befell, befallen**] if something befalls you, it happens to you. A formal word.

befit /bɪ'fɪt/ VERB [**befits, befitting, befitted**] to be suitable for someone or something. A formal word. ⌧ They were elegantly dressed as befitted the occasion.

before /bɪ'fɔ:(r)/ ► PREPOSITION
1 earlier than something ⌧ He lost his job just before Christmas. □ I posted the letter the day before yesterday. □ + ing He tidied the house before going to bed.
2 if one place is before another place, you get to that place first □ Our house is just before the turning on the left.
3 before long soon □ Before long, we became good friends.
► ADVERB at an earlier time □ I don't think we've met before. ⌧ We had all been to the beach the day before.
► CONJUNCTION
1 earlier than the time when something will happen □ Wash your hands before you come to the table.
2 in order to prevent something bad from happening □ Stop fighting before someone gets hurt.
3 until □ It was a long time before I felt better.

beforehand /bɪ'fɔ:hænd/ ADVERB before the time when something else happens □ I decided ten days beforehand that I would go.

befriend /bɪ'frend/ VERB [**befriends, befriending, befriended**] to become someone's friend, especially because they need your help. A formal word.

beg /beg/ VERB [**begs, begging, begged**]
1 to ask someone for something in an eager or emotional way because you want it very much □ I begged him to come home.
2 to ask people for money in the street because you are very poor
3 I **beg your pardon** (a) a formal way of saying sorry when you have made a mistake □ Oh, I beg your pardon, I didn't realize this pen was yours. (b) a formal way of asking someone to repeat what they have just said because you did not hear it □ 'I'm going now.' 'I beg your pardon.' 'I said, I'm going now.'

began /bɪ'gæn/ PAST TENSE OF begin

beggar /'begə(r)/ NOUN [plural **beggars**] someone who asks people for money in the street

begin /bɪ'gɪn/ VERB [**begins, beginning, began, begun**]
1 to start □ The concert began at 7.30 and finished at 9.30. □ + to do something I was beginning to feel better. □ + ing She began walking towards the door. □ + by She began by apologizing. □ + with The year began with a big disappointment.
2 to begin with at the start of something □ Lorna didn't like her new school to begin with.
• **beginner** /bɪ'gɪnə(r)/ NOUN [plural **beginners**] someone who has just started to do or to learn something □ a guitar class for beginners
• **beginning** /bɪ'gɪnɪŋ/ NOUN [plural **beginnings**]
1 no plural the start of something or the first part of something ⌧ My birthday is at the beginning of July. ⌧ He led from the beginning of the race. ⌧ In the beginning, I didn't like her very much.
2 the beginnings of something the first signs or stages of something □ She had the beginnings of a bad headache.

begrudge /bɪˈɡrʌdʒ/ VERB [begrudges, begrudging, begrudged] to feel jealous because someone has something good and you do not think they deserve it ☺ *I don't begrudge him his success.*

beguiling /bɪˈɡaɪlɪŋ/ ADJECTIVE a formal word meaning attractive and interesting □ *a beguiling smile* □ *a beguiling place*

begun /bɪˈɡʌn/ PAST PARTICIPLE OF begin

behalf /bɪˈhɑːf/ NOUN on someone's behalf/on behalf of someone for someone else □ *Petra spoke on behalf of the other students.*

behave /bɪˈheɪv/ VERB [behaves, behaving, behaved]
1 to do things in a particular way ☺ *I'm sorry - I've behaved badly.* ☺ *He was behaving like a child!*
2 to be polite and not do anything that you should not do □ *Did the children behave?* ☺ *I hope Harry behaved himself.*

behavior /bɪˈheɪvjə(r)/ NOUN, NO PLURAL the US spelling of behaviour

behaviour /bɪˈheɪvjə(r)/ NOUN, NO PLURAL the way you behave ☺ *Children should be rewarded for good behaviour.* ☺ *I've never seen such bad behaviour.* □ + **towards** *His behaviour towards Sarah was appalling.*

➤ Remember that the noun **behaviour** is never used in the plural:
✓ *The children's behaviour was awful.*
✗ *The children's behaviours were awful.*

behead /bɪˈhed/ VERB [beheads, beheading, beheaded] to cut someone's head off

beheld /bɪˈheld/ PAST TENSE AND PAST PARTICIPLE OF behold

behind /bɪˈhaɪnd/ ▶ PREPOSITION
1 at the back of something or someone □ *Look behind the sofa.* □ *Rachel peeped out from behind the curtains.* □ *Shut the door behind you, please.*
2 making less progress than other people ☺ *Roberto's fallen behind the rest of the class*
3 supporting or encouraging someone or something ☺ *The crowd really got behind him and cheered as he ran to the finishing line.*
4 responsible for something □ *So who was behind the robbery?* □ *What were the reasons behind your decision?*
5 an experience is behind you when it happened in the past and does not affect you now □ *That's all behind him now.*
6 behind someone's back without someone knowing □ *I don't like people talking about me behind my back.*
▶ ADVERB
1 at the back ☺ *The car was hit from behind.*
2 late in doing something □ *I'm behind with my work.*
3 in the place where you were ☺ *I stayed behind after*

the class to talk to my teacher. ☺ *I left my bag behind.*
▶ NOUN [plural **behinds**] your bottom

behold /bɪˈhəʊld/ VERB [beholds, beholding, beheld] to see something. An old-fashioned word.

beige /beɪʒ/ ▶ ADJECTIVE having a light brown colour □ *They chose a beige carpet.*
▶ NOUN, NO PLURAL a light brown colour

being /ˈbiːɪŋ/ ▶ VERB the present participle of the verb be □ *Help! I'm being attacked!*
▶ NOUN [plural **beings**] a person or creature □ *a being from another planet*

belated /bɪˈleɪtɪd/ ADJECTIVE happening late or arriving late □ *a belated birthday present*

belch /beltʃ/ ▶ VERB [belches, belching, belched] to let air from your stomach come out of your mouth with a noise
▶ NOUN [plural **belches**] the noise made when you let air from your stomach come out of your mouth

beleaguered /bɪˈliːɡəd/ ADJECTIVE having a lot of problems. A formal word.

belfry /ˈbelfrɪ/ NOUN [plural **belfries**] a tower with a bell hanging in it

belie /bɪˈlaɪ/ VERB [belies, belying, belied] to give you the wrong idea about something. A formal word.
□ *Her obvious energy belies her age.*

belief /bɪˈliːf/ NOUN [plural **beliefs**] something you believe, especially something that you think is true or something that you think exists ☺ *religious beliefs* ☺ *It's a mistaken belief that men are better drivers than women.* □ + **that** *There is a widespread belief that the economy will improve.* □ + **in** *His belief in God remained with him all his life.*

believable /bɪˈliːvəbəl/ ADJECTIVE making you think that something is true or real □ *The story wasn't very believable.*

believe /bɪˈliːv/ VERB [believes, believing, believed]
1 to think that something is true □ *I believed his story.* □ *I found his excuses difficult to believe.* □ + **that** *I can't believe that you did that!*
2 to think that something is true although you are not completely sure. A formal word. □ + **that** *I believe that they're getting married.*
◆ PHRASAL VERB **believe in something**
1 to think that something exists □ *I don't believe in ghosts.* □
2 to think that something is important or acceptable □ *I don't believe in hitting children.*
● **believer** /bɪˈliːvə(r)/ NOUN [plural **believers**] someone who believes something, especially someone who believes in a particular religion

belittle /bɪˈlɪtəl/ VERB [belittles, belittling, belittled] to make someone or their achievements seem less important than they really are

bell /bel/ NOUN [plural **bells**]
1 a hollow metal object that makes a ringing sound when it moves ☺ *The church bells were ringing.*

2 a device that makes a ringing sound when you press it □ *a bicycle bell* ⊞ *She walked up to the front door and rang the bell.*

belligerent /bɪ'lɪdʒərənt/ ADJECTIVE wanting to argue or fight with people. A formal word.

bellow /'beləʊ/ ▶ VERB [**bellows, bellowing, bellowed**] to shout □ *He bellowed at us to stop what we were doing.*
▶ NOUN [*plural* **bellows**] a shout

belly /'belɪ/ NOUN [*plural* **bellies**]
1 an informal word for the stomach
2 an informal word for the front part of your body between your chest and your legs

belly-button /'belɪ ˈbʌtən/ NOUN [*plural* **belly-buttons**] an informal word for the small hollow mark on your stomach

belong /bɪ'lɒŋ/ VERB [**belongs, belonging, belonged**]
1 if something belongs in a particular place, that is where you usually keep it □ *That chair belongs in the kitchen.*
2 if you belong somewhere, you feel happy and comfortable there □ *She felt as if she didn't belong there.*
◆ PHRASAL VERBS **belong to someone** if something belongs to you, you own it □ *Who does this suitcase belong to?* **belong to something** to be a member of an organization □ *Peter belongs to the local tennis club.*
● **belongings** /bɪ'lɒŋɪŋz/ PLURAL NOUN the things you own ⊞ *They returned to the hotel to collect their belongings.* ⊞ *The bag contained a few personal belongings.*

beloved /bɪ'lʌvɪd/ ADJECTIVE loved very much □ *I lost my beloved old teddy bear.*

below /bɪ'ləʊ/ ▶ PREPOSITION
1 in a lower place or position □ *The plane was flying below the clouds.* □ *Simon was in the class below me in school.*
2 less than a particular amount or level □ *Audience numbers never fell below 1000.* ⊞ *The results were below average.*
▶ ADVERB at or to a lower place □ *We climbed to the top of the hill and looked down on the valley below.* □ *Write your name and address below.*

belt /belt/ ▶ NOUN [*plural* **belts**] a narrow piece of leather or cloth that you wear around your waist ⊞ *Karim undid his belt.*
▶ VERB [**belts, belting, belted**]
1 an informal word meaning to hit someone or something
2 **belt along/down, etc.** an informal word meaning to move very fast □ *They came belting down the road.*

bemoan /bɪ'məʊn/ VERB [**bemoans, bemoaning, bemoaned**] to say that you are not happy about something. A formal word.

bemused /bɪ'mjuːzd/ ADJECTIVE slightly confused □ *He was rather bemused by her attitude.*

bench /bentʃ/ NOUN [*plural* **benches**] a long seat ⊞ *a park bench*

benchmark /'bentʃmɑːk/ NOUN [*plural* **benchmarks**] something that acts as an agreed standard for comparing other things □ *These tests set the benchmark for educational achievement.*

bend /bend/ VERB [**bends, bending, bent**]
1 to move the top part of your body to a lower position □ *She bent down to pick up some paper she'd dropped.*
2 to move a part of your body so that it is no longer straight ⊞ *Bend your knees slightly.*
3 to curve □ *He bent the wire around the post.* □ *The road bends to the right up ahead.*
◆ IDIOMS **bend over backwards** to try very hard to do something □ *I've bent over backwards to be fair to you both.* **bend the rules** to allow something that is not usually allowed
▶ NOUN [*plural* **bends**] a curve ⊞ *There was a sharp bend in the road.*
◆ IDIOMS **be/go round the bend** to be/become mentally ill □ *I put my phone in the fridge - I must be going round the bend* **drive someone round the bend** to make someone very angry □ *Her constant chatter is driving me round the bend.*

beneath /bɪ'niːθ/ PREPOSITION, PREPOSITION
1 below or under something □ *He lay on the ground beneath the tree.* □ *I hadn't realized there was a second layer of chocolates beneath.*
2 if something is beneath you, you think you are too good for it □ *She thinks it's beneath her to do her own housework.*

benefactor /'benɪfæktə(r)/ NOUN [*plural* **benefactors**] someone who gives money to a person or organization to help them

beneficial /ˌbenɪ'fɪʃəl/ ADJECTIVE having a good effect on someone or something ⊞ *Improved diet had an extremely beneficial effect on patients.*

beneficiary /ˌbenɪ'fɪʃərɪ/ NOUN [*plural* **beneficiaries**] someone who gets money or an advantage from a situation □ *Schools in southern Africa will be the main beneficiaries of the charity.*

benefit /'benɪfɪt/ ▶ NOUN [*plural* **benefits**]
1 an advantage that you get from something ⊞ *Most patients get some benefit from the treatment.* ⊞ *The new system will bring enormous benefits.* ⊞ *The centre is run for the benefit of* (= in order to help) *the community.*
2 money that you get from the government if you are ill or do not have a job ⊞ *He was claiming unemployment benefit.* □ *The government wants to reduce the number of people who are on benefits.*
▶ VERB [**benefits, benefiting** *or* **benefitting, benefited** *or* **benefitted**] if you benefit from something, or if something benefits you, it helps you □ **+ from** *I think you'll benefit from the extra lessons.*

benevolent /bɪˈnevələnt/ ADJECTIVE a formal word meaning kind and generous

benign /bɪˈnaɪn/ ADJECTIVE
1 a benign tumour (= growth in your body) will not cause you any harm
2 a formal word meaning kind and gentle

bent /bent/ ▶ PAST TENSE AND PAST PARTICIPLE OF bend
▶ ADJECTIVE not straight □ a bent pin
♦ IDIOM be bent on doing something to be determined to do something

benzene /ˈbenziːn/ NOUN, NO PLURAL a colourless liquid used for making plastics and other chemical products. A chemistry word.

bequeath /bɪˈkwiːð/ VERB [bequeaths, bequeathing, bequeathed] to bequeath your money or property to someone is to arrange for them to get it after you die
● **bequest** /bɪˈkwest/ NOUN [plural bequests] money or property that is given by someone after their death

berate /bɪˈreɪt/ VERB [berates, berating, berated] to talk angrily to someone because they have done something wrong. A formal word.

bereaved /bɪˈriːvd/ ▶ ADJECTIVE having someone in your family who has died recently □ bereaved families
▶ NOUN the bereaved the family of someone who has died recently □ We had help from an organization offering counselling to the bereaved.
● **bereavement** /bɪˈriːvmənt/ NOUN [plural bereavements] when someone in your family dies

bereft /bɪˈreft/ ADJECTIVE
1 bereft of something completely without something. A formal word. □ The refugees were bereft of hope or comfort.
2 a formal word meaning extremely sad

beret /ˈbereɪ/ NOUN [plural berets] a flat round hat

berry /ˈberi/ NOUN [plural berries] a small soft fruit containing seeds □ Holly has red berries.

berserk /bəˈzɜːk/ ADJECTIVE go beserk to become very angry or violent. An informal phrase. □ Dad went berserk when he saw the damage to the car.

berth /bɜːθ/ ▶ NOUN [plural berths]
1 a bed on a boat or a train
2 a place in a port where a boat can stop
▶ VERB [berths, berthing, berthed] a ship berths when it stops and is tied up in a port

beseech /bɪˈsiːtʃ/ VERB or [beseeches, beseeching, besought or beseeched] to ask someone to do something in a very urgent way. A literary word.

beside /bɪˈsaɪd/ PREPOSITION
1 next to or at the side of someone or something □ There was a chair beside the bed. □ Go and stand beside Billy.
2 compared with □ Beside that tiny kitten the dog looks enormous.
3 beside the point having nothing to do with what you are talking about □ Yes, it was busy, but that's beside the point.
4 be beside yourself to be very upset or angry □ Her parents are beside themselves with grief.

besides /bɪˈsaɪdz/ ▶ PREPOSITION as well as □ Besides playing the piano, she sings in a choir.
▶ ADVERB also □ It's too wet to go out. Besides, I'm really tired.

besiege /bɪˈsiːdʒ/ VERB [besieges, besieging, besieged]
1 if a place or person is besieged by people, they are surrounded by them □ The headteacher was besieged by angry parents.
2 if you are beseiged with something such as questions or complaints, you get a lot of them
3 if an army besieges a place, they surround it

besotted /bɪˈsɒtɪd/ ADJECTIVE always thinking about someone because you love them so much

best /best/ ▶ ADJECTIVE better than everyone or everything else ▣ Mia is my best friend. ▣ What's the best way to cook this fish? □ It is probably best to arrive a little early.
▶ ADVERB
1 more than everything else ▣ What food do you like best? ▣ The area is best known for its wine.
2 in the most satisfactory way □ She performs best when she is slightly nervous.
3 as best you can as well as you can □ I know it's difficult but just do it as best you can.
▶ NOUN
1 the best the person or thing that is better than all others □ Which of these computers is the best?
2 do/try your best to do something as well as you can □ It doesn't matter if you don't win, just do your best.
3 at best in the most satisfactory situation □ At best, we can only hope to make £100 a week.
4 for the best if a decision or an action is for the best, it will be the best thing for the future, even though it may seem unpleasant now □ She's decided to get divorced. It's for the best really.
5 make the best of something to try to enjoy something or get an advantage from something even though the situation is not what you wanted
♦ IDIOMS the best of both worlds if you have the best of both worlds, you have the advantages of two different situations □ He wants the best of both worlds - to be a father, but still to have plenty of free time. make the best of something to accept a situation and try to deal with it as well as possible

best man /ˈbest ˈmæn/ NOUN, NO PLURAL the man at a wedding who helps the man who is getting married

bestow /bɪˈstəʊ/ VERB [bestows, bestowing, bestowed] a formal word meaning to give someone an important right or honour, or to give them something valuable

bestseller /ˈbest ˈselə(r)/ NOUN [plural bestsellers] a product that a lot of people buy
● **best-selling** /ˈbest ˈselɪŋ/ ADJECTIVE bought by a lot of people □ a best-selling novel

bet /bet/ ▶ VERB [bets, betting, bet or betted]
1 I bet (a) used for saying what you think will happen

or what you think is true □ *I bet he'll forget to come.* □ *I bet Jane wasn't pleased about that.* (b) used for saying that you understand why someone feels the way they do □ *'I was really upset when he told me.' 'I bet you were!'*
2 to try to win money by guessing the result of a competition, etc. □ *My uncle bets on horse races.* □ *I bet him 50p that I could climb the tree.*
▶ NOUN [*plural* **bets**] money that you risk by trying to guess the result of a competition 🖳 *I put a bet on the winning horse.*

betray /bɪ'treɪ/ VERB [**betrays, betraying, betrayed**]
1 to do something which harms someone who trusts you □ *He betrayed me by telling everyone my secret.*
2 if you betray your emotions, you show them □ *Her voice betrayed no nervousness.*
• **betrayal** /bɪ'treɪəl/ NOUN [*plural* **betrayals**] betraying someone

better /'betə(r)/ ▶ ADJECTIVE
1 of a higher standard or more suitable or enjoyable □ *I want to buy a better computer.* 🖳 *Is his work getting any better?* 🖳 *His French is much better than mine.* □ *It's better to buy spices from an Asian shop.*
2 not as ill 🖳 *I hope you get better soon.* 🖳 *Are you feeling better now?*
3 the bigger/faster, etc. the better the more big/fast, etc. something is, the more you will like it
▶ ADVERB
1 in a more enjoyable or suitable way or to a higher standard □ *Which do you like better, the green one or the blue one?* □ *Try to do better next time.* □ *I wish I could swim better.*
2 I/he, etc. had better used to say that someone ought to do something □ *I'd better hurry, or I'll be late.* □ *I think you had better apologize.*
3 better off (a) richer □ *We're better off now than we were ten years ago.* (b) in a better situation □ *You'd be better off hiring a car rather than buying one.*
4 know better to have enough experience to know that an action was not good □ *She should have known better than to try and trick him.* □ *I broke my leg jumping off a wall - I should have known better.*
▶ NOUN, NO PLURAL
1 something that is better □ *I had hoped for better.* □ *She deserved better from her colleagues.*
2 for the better if a situation changes for the better, it improves □ *My fitness level has changed for the better.*
3 get the better of someone to trick or defeat someone

between /bɪ'twi:n/ PREPOSITION, ADVERB
1 in the area that divides two people, things or places □ *What letter comes between Q and S in the alphabet?* □ *I had to stand between Dan and Shona.* □ *We were on the road between San Francisco and Los Angeles.*
2 in the period of time that separates two times □ *The shop is closed between 2 and 3.* □ *There was only a week between the wedding and their house move.*
3 used to show a range of amounts or measurements

□ *We usually have between 2 and 4 centimetres of rainfall in January.*
4 used to show the people or groups involved in something □ *There was an interesting discussion between Angela and Kim.* □ *The match between Leeds and Arsenal has been cancelled.* □ *Between us, we cleaned the whole house.*
5 used to show the differences of two things, people or groups □ *Can you see the difference between the real jewels and the fakes?*
6 if you have to choose or decide between two things, you have to choose one of them □ *I can't decide between the soup or the fish.*
7 used to show how something is divided □ *Russell and Colin divided the work between them.*

beverage /'bevərɪdʒ/ NOUN [*plural* **beverages**] a formal word meaning a drink
beware /bɪ'weə(r)/ VERB used for warning someone about something □ *The sign on the gate said 'Beware of the dog'.*

> ➤ The verb **beware** does not have different forms or tenses like other verbs, because it is only used when you are telling people what to do or giving them a warning.

bewilder /bɪ'wɪldə(r)/ VERB [**bewilders, bewildering, bewildered**] to confuse someone
• **bewildering** /bɪ'wɪldərɪŋ/ ADJECTIVE confusing 🖳 *a bewildering array/variety*
• **bewilderment** /bɪ'wɪldəmənt/ NOUN, NO PLURAL being bewildered □ *'What is this?' exclaimed Leo in bewilderment.*

bewitch /bɪ'wɪtʃ/ VERB [**bewitches, bewitching, bewitched**] to attract and interest someone so much that they cannot think about anything else

beyond /bɪ'jɒnd/ PREPOSITION, ADVERB
1 on the other side of something □ *Turn right just beyond the bridge.* □ *She had never travelled beyond Europe.* □ *I stared out of the window at the hills beyond.*
2 after a particular time □ *The strike is likely to continue beyond Christmas.*
3 more or greater than something □ *These prices are way beyond what we can afford.*
4 if something is beyond someone, it is too difficult for them to do or understand □ *This modern technology is beyond me.*
5 beyond belief/doubt/recognition, etc. unable to be believed, doubted, recognized, etc.

bi- /baɪ/ PREFIX bi- is added to the start of words to mean 'two' or 'twice' □ *bicycle* □ *bilingual*
bias /'baɪəs/ NOUN [*plural* **biases**] when someone supports one person or thing in a way that is unfair □ *She felt there was a bias against female employees.*
• **biased** /'baɪəst/ or **biassed** ADJECTIVE supporting one person or thing in an unfair way □ *He claimed that the report was biased.*

bib /bɪb/ NOUN [plural **bibs**] a piece of cloth that you put round a baby's neck to protect its clothes while it is eating

Bible /'baɪbəl/ NOUN [plural **Bibles**] the holy book of the Christian religion

• **biblical** /'bɪblɪkəl/ ADJECTIVE to do with the Bible, or in the Bible □ a biblical character

bibliography /ˌbɪblɪ'ɒgrəfɪ/ NOUN [plural **bibliographies**]
1 a list of books on a particular subject
2 a list of books that someone has used when writing something such as a book or an essay

bicentenary /ˌbaɪsen'tiːnərɪ/ NOUN [plural **bicentenaries**] the day or year that is 200 years after an important event □ 2009 is the bicentenary of Darwin's birth.

bicentennial /ˌbaɪsen'tenjəl/ NOUN [plural **bicentennials**] the US word for **bicentenary**

biceps /'baɪseps/ NOUN [plural **biceps**] the big muscles at the top of your arms

bicker /'bɪkə(r)/ VERB [bickers, bickering, bickered] to argue about something that is not important □ They were bickering about whether to go by train or bus.

bicycle /'baɪsɪkəl/ NOUN [plural **bicycles**] a vehicle you sit on and turn the wheels by pressing the pedals (= parts your feet go on) ⊞ I learned to ride a bicycle when I was six.

bid¹ /bɪd/ ▶ NOUN [plural **bids**]
1 an amount of money that you offer to pay for something that a lot of people want to buy ⊞ The highest bid for the house was £300,000.
2 an attempt to do something ⊞ They made a bid for freedom.
3 an offer to do a job for someone for an amount of money ⊞ We've put in a bid for the contract.
▶ VERB [bids, bidding, bid]
1 to offer to pay a particular amount of money for something ⊞ Will someone bid £5 for this beautiful old chair?
2 to offer to do a job for someone for an amount of money ⊞ Both companies have bid for the contract.

bid² /bɪd/ VERB [bids, bidding, bid or bade, bidden or bid] to say something such as 'good morning' or 'goodnight' to someone. An old-fashioned word. □ He bade me goodnight.

bide /baɪd/ VERB [bides, biding, bided] **bide your time** to be patient and wait for an opportunity to do something

bidet /'biːdeɪ/ NOUN [plural **bidets**] a low sink that you sit on to wash your bottom

biennial /ˌbaɪ'enɪəl/ ADJECTIVE happening every two years □ a biennial event

bifocals /ˌbaɪ'fəʊkəlz/ PLURAL NOUN glasses that help you to see things which are close to you and things which are a long way from you

big /bɪg/ ADJECTIVE [bigger, biggest]
1 large in size □ a big car □ It was the biggest fish he'd ever seen. ⊞ They live in a great big (= very big) house.

2 important and having a large effect □ a big decision □ a big mistake □ There's a big match on TV tonight.
3 **big brother/sister** a brother or sister who is older than you □ I've got a big sister and a little brother.
4 popular or famous □ He's big in the US.

bigamy /'bɪgəmɪ/ NOUN, NO PLURAL when someone is married to two people at the same time

big bang /'bɪg 'bæŋ/ NOUN **the big bang** the very large explosion that many scientists think created the universe

bighead /'bɪghed/ NOUN [plural **bigheads**] someone who thinks they are very clever and good at doing everything. An informal word.

• **bigheaded** /ˌbɪg'hedɪd/ ADJECTIVE thinking you are very clever and good at doing everything

bigot /'bɪgət/ NOUN [plural **bigots**] someone who has strong, unpleasant opinions about subjects such as politics and religion and who does not accept different opinions

• **bigoted** /'bɪgətɪd/ ADJECTIVE having strong, unpleasant opinions about subjects such as politics and religion and not accepting different opinions

• **bigotry** /'bɪgətrɪ/ NOUN, NO PLURAL when someone is bigoted

bike /baɪk/ NOUN [plural **bikes**] a bicycle
⊞ Can you ride a bike? ⊞ We went on a bike ride.
⊞ The road has a separate bike lane.

bikini /bɪ'kiːnɪ/ NOUN [plural **bikinis**] a piece of clothing in two parts that women wear for swimming

bile /baɪl/ NOUN, NO PLURAL a liquid made in your liver that helps you to digest food

bilingual /baɪ'lɪŋgwəl/ ADJECTIVE speaking or using two languages □ She's bilingual in French and German. □ a bilingual website

bilious /'bɪlɪəs/ ADJECTIVE feeling ill, as if you are going to vomit

bill /bɪl/ NOUN [plural **bills**]
1 a piece of paper showing how much you must pay for something ⊞ Have you paid the phone bill? □ a gas bill
2 a suggestion for a new law that people in a government vote for or against ⊞ The government have passed a bill (= made a law) which will restrict Internet gambling.
3 the US word for **note** (= piece of paper money) □ a $100 bill
4 a bird's beak

billboard /'bɪlbɔːd/ NOUN [plural **billboards**] a large board with advertisements on it

billiards /'bɪljədz/ NOUN, NO PLURAL a game in which you use long sticks to hit balls into pockets at the edge of a table

billion /'bɪljən/ NUMBER [billions] the number 1,000,000,000 □ The government gets billions of pounds a year from taxes.

billionaire /ˌbɪljəˈneə(r)/ NOUN [plural **billionaires**] someone who has a billion pounds or a billion dollars or more

billow /ˈbɪləʊ/ VERB [**billows, billowing, billowed**] to rise and be moved by the air □ *Smoke billowed from the chimney.*

bin /bɪn/ ▶ NOUN [plural **bins**] a container for putting rubbish in ⊞ *a rubbish bin* ⊞ *You should put paper in the recycling bin.*
▶ VERB [**bins, binning, binned**] to get rid of something by putting it in a bin. An informal word.

binary number /ˈbaɪnərɪ ˈnʌmbə(r)/ NOUN [plural **binary numbers**] a number that is made up of the numbers 0 and 1 only. Computers use these numbers to operate.

bind /baɪnd/ ▶ VERB [**binds, binding, bound**] to tie something together □ *The robbers bound his hands and feet with tape.*
▶ NOUN, NO PLURAL something you do that is boring or annoying □ *It was a bit of a bind having to take two buses to get to work.*

binder /ˈbaɪndə(r)/ NOUN [plural **binders**] a hard cover with metal rings inside, that you use for keeping pieces of paper in

binge /bɪndʒ/ ▶ VERB [**binges, bingeing** or **binging, binged**] to eat or drink too much in a short time
▶ NOUN [plural **binges**] a time when you eat or drink too much

bingo /ˈbɪŋgəʊ/ NOUN, NO PLURAL a game in which you mark numbers on a card when someone shouts those numbers. You win if you are the first person to mark all the numbers on your card.

binoculars /bɪˈnɒkjʊləz/ PLURAL NOUN a piece of equipment that you hold up to your eyes to help you see things that are a long way away □ *She was watching the birds with a pair of binoculars.*

bio- /ˈbaɪəʊ-/ PREFIX bio- is added to the beginning of words to mean 'to do with life or living things' □ *biology* □ *biochemistry*

biochemical /ˌbaɪəʊˈkemɪkəl/ ADJECTIVE to do with biochemistry

biochemistry /ˌbaɪəʊˈkemɪstrɪ/ NOUN, NO PLURAL the study of chemicals and chemical changes in living things

biodegradable /ˌbaɪəʊdɪˈgreɪdəbəl/ ADJECTIVE a biodegradable substance does not harm the environment because it decays quickly and naturally □ *biodegradable packaging*

biodiesel /ˈbaɪəʊˌdiːzəl/ NOUN, NO PLURAL diesel (= a type of fuel) that is made from plants

biodiversity /ˌbaɪəʊdaɪˈvɜːsɪtɪ/ NOUN, NO PLURAL all the different living things that exist in an area

biofuel /ˈbaɪəʊfjuəl/ NOUN, NO PLURAL a fuel made from plants

biogas /ˈbaɪəʊgæs/ NOUN, NO PLURAL a gas that is produced by dead plants

biographical /ˌbaɪəˈgræfɪkəl/ ADJECTIVE to do with a person's life □ *a biographical film*

biography /baɪˈɒgrəfɪ/ NOUN [plural **biographies**] a book about a real person's life □ + *of She wrote a biography of Napoleon.*

biological /ˌbaɪəˈlɒdʒɪkəl/ ADJECTIVE to do with living things and the way they grow and behave □ *a biological process*

biologist /baɪˈɒlədʒɪst/ NOUN [plural **biologists**] a person who studies biology

biology /baɪˈɒlədʒɪ/ NOUN, NO PLURAL the study of living things

biometric /ˌbaɪəʊˈmetrɪk/ ADJECTIVE biometric information is taken from the human body, for example the pattern of the eye, to make sure that people are who they say they are ⊞ *biometric data*

biopsy /ˈbaɪɒpsɪ/ NOUN [plural **biopsies**] a medical test in which some cells are removed from your body to see if they are healthy

biosphere /ˈbaɪəʊˌsfɪə(r)/ NOUN, NO PLURAL the biosphere the area on and above the Earth where living things exist

biotechnology /ˌbaɪəʊtekˈnɒlədʒɪ/ NOUN, NO PLURAL the use of living cells in science and industry

birch /bɜːtʃ/ NOUN [plural **birches**] a type of tree with thin smooth branches

bird /bɜːd/ NOUN [plural **birds**] a creature with wings and feathers that lays eggs □ *wild birds* □ *There was a bird's nest in the tree.*

bird of prey /ˈbɜːd əv ˈpreɪ/ NOUN [plural **birds of prey**] a bird that kills and eats small animals or birds

birdwatcher /ˈbɜːd ˈwɒtʃɪŋ/ NOUN [plural **birdwatchers**] someone whose hobby is birdwatching
• **birdwatching** /ˈbɜːd ˈwɒtʃə(r)/ NOUN, NO PLURAL the hobby of looking at birds

Biro /ˈbaɪrəʊ/ NOUN [plural **Biros**] a type of pen with a very small metal ball at the end where ink comes out. A trademark.

birth /bɜːθ/ NOUN [plural **births**]
1 the time when someone is born □ *He was there at the births of all his children.* ⊞ *What is your date of birth* (= the date when you were born)?
2 give birth if a woman gives birth, a baby comes out of her body □ *She gave birth to a healthy baby boy.*

birth control /ˈbɜːθ kənˈtrəʊl/ NOUN, NO PLURAL methods that are used to stop a woman becoming pregnant

birthday /ˈbɜːθdeɪ/ NOUN [plural **birthdays**] the date you were born which happens each year □ *It's my mother's 60th birthday next week.* ⊞ *Happy Birthday, John!* ⊞ *I'm going to his birthday party.* ⊞ *Did you get a lot of birthday presents?*

birthmark /ˈbɜːθmɑːk/ NOUN [plural **birthmarks**] a mark on someone's skin that they have had since they were born

birthplace /ˈbɜːθpleɪs/ NOUN [plural **birthplaces**] the place where someone was born

birthrate /'bɜːθreɪt/ NOUN [plural **birthrates**] the number of babies who are born in a place in a particular period of time

biscuit /'bɪskɪt/ NOUN [plural **biscuits**] a flat hard cake □ He was eating a chocolate biscuit. 🔁 a packet of biscuits

bisect /ˌbaɪ'sekt/ VERB [**bisects, bisecting, bisected**] a line bisects something when it divides it into two equal parts. A maths word.
• **bisector** /ˌbaɪ'sektə(r)/ NOUN [plural **bisectors**] a line that divides another line or angle into two equal parts. A maths word.

bishop /'bɪʃəp/ NOUN [plural **bishops**] an important priest in some Christian churches

bison /'baɪsən/ NOUN [plural **bison** or **bisons**] a large animal that looks like a cow but has long hair

bistro /'biːstrəʊ/ NOUN [plural **bistros**] a small informal restaurant or bar

bit[1] /bɪt/ NOUN [plural **bits**]
1 a bit (a) slightly □ I'm a bit tired today. 🔁 He looks a bit like David Beckham. (b) a short time □ We had to wait a bit for the bus. 🔁 I don't mind looking after her for a bit. (c) a small amount □ 'Would you like some more fish?' 'Yes, just a bit, please.' □ + of I need a bit of help with my homework.
2 a piece or part of something bigger □ + of There were some bits of the book that I enjoyed.
3 quite a bit a lot □ He's quite a bit taller than his wife.
4 the smallest unit of information in a computer. A computing word.

> ► The phrase **a bit** meaning 'slightly' is used a lot in spoken English but is too informal for formal written English. If you are writing an essay, it is better to use the words **slightly** or **a little**:
> ✔ Attitudes to this subject have changed slightly.
> ✘ Attitudes to this subject have changed a bit.

bit[2] /bɪt/ PAST TENSE OF **bite**

bitch /bɪtʃ/ NOUN [plural **bitches**] a female dog
• **bitchy** /'bɪtʃi/ ADJECTIVE [**bitchier, bitchiest**] saying unkind things about someone. An informal word. □ a bitchy remark

bite /baɪt/ ► VERB [**bites, biting, bit, bitten**]
1 to use your teeth to cut through something □ + into Guy bit into the apple. 🔁 A lot of people bite their nails.
2 if an animal bites, it injures someone with its teeth □ She was badly bitten by a dog.
♦ IDIOM **bite the bullet** to decide to do something that you do not really want to do □ In the end I had to bite the bullet and ask him for the money.
► NOUN [plural **bites**]
1 when you bite food with your teeth 🔁 Ali took a bite of the sausage.

2 an injury on your skin where an animal or insect has bitten you 🔁 an insect bite □ a mosquito bite
• **biting** /'baɪtɪŋ/ ADJECTIVE a biting wind is very cold

bitmap /'bɪtmæp/ NOUN [plural **bitmaps**] a computer image that is made up of a lot of small dots on the screen. A computing word.

bitten /'bɪtən/ PAST PARTICIPLE OF **bite**

bitter /'bɪtə(r)/ ADJECTIVE
1 angry because you feel someone has treated you badly □ He turned into a bitter old man.
2 describes an argument in which there are a lot of bad, angry feelings □ a bitter divorce battle
3 making you feel very disappointed 🔁 His career had been a bitter disappointment to him.
4 having a strong taste such as you find in strong coffee □ Dark chocolate is too bitter for me.
5 if the weather is bitter, it is extremely cold □ It's bitter out there!
• **bitterly** /'bɪtəli/ ADVERB
1 extremely, in a way that is bad 🔁 We were bitterly disappointed not to win.
2 bitterly cold extremely cold
• **bitterness** /'bɪtənɪs/ NOUN, NO PLURAL when something or someone is bitter

bitumen /'bɪtjʊmɪn/ NOUN, NO PLURAL a black substance used to make roads

bizarre /bɪ'zɑː(r)/ ADJECTIVE very strange □ bizarre behaviour

black /blæk/ ► ADJECTIVE
1 having the colour of coal or complete darkness □ I bought a black coat.
2 black people are of a race that have dark brown skin □ We need more black police officers.
3 black tea or coffee has no milk in it
► NOUN, NO PLURAL the colour of coal or complete darkness
♦ PHRASAL VERB [**blacks, blacking, blacked**] **black out** to become unconscious

blackberry /'blækbəri/ NOUN [plural **blackberries**]
1 a small black fruit that grows on a plant with sharp stems
2 Blackberry a very small computer that fits in your hand and does not have wires. A trademark.

blackbird /'blækbɜːd/ NOUN [plural **blackbirds**] a bird, the male having black feathers and a yellow beak

blackboard /'blækbɔːd/ NOUN [plural **blackboards**] a dark board that a teacher writes on in a classroom

blackcurrant /ˌblæk'kʌrənt/ NOUN [plural **blackcurrants**] a small, round, black fruit

blacken /'blækən/ VERB [**blackens, blackening, blackened**]
1 to become black or to make something black □ His face had been blackened by ash.
2 to make people think that someone is bad □ They had blackened her name, she claimed.

black eye /,blæk 'aɪ/ NOUN [*plural* **black eyes**] an injury which makes the skin around your eye look black

black hole /,blæk 'həʊl/ NOUN [*plural* **black holes**] an area in outer space that pulls everything into it. Nothing can escape from a black hole.

black ice /,blæk 'aɪs/ NOUN, NO PLURAL ice on a road that you cannot see and which is very dangerous

blacklist /'blæklɪst/ ▶ VERB [**blacklists, blacklisting, blacklisted**] to put someone on a list because they are bad or dangerous and not allow them to do something
▶ NOUN [*plural* **blacklists**] a list of people or things who are bad or dangerous

black magic /,blæk 'mædʒɪk/ NOUN, NO PLURAL magic which is used for bad purposes

blackmail /'blækmeɪl/ ▶ VERB [**blackmails, blackmailing, blackmailed**] to try to get money from someone by saying that you will tell people about their secrets
▶ NOUN, NO PLURAL the crime of blackmailing someone
• **blackmailer** /'blæk,meɪlə(r)/ NOUN [*plural* **blackmailers**] a criminal who blackmails someone

black market /,blæk 'mɑːkɪt/ NOUN, NO PLURAL if someone buys or sells something on the black market, they buy or sell it illegally

blackout /'blækaʊt/ NOUN [*plural* **blackouts**]
1 a time when there is complete darkness because there is no electricity
2 when someone becomes unconscious for a short time

black sheep /,blæk 'ʃiːp/ NOUN [*plural* **black sheep**] a person in a family who does bad things and causes their family to be ashamed

blacksmith /'blæk,smɪθ/ NOUN [*plural* **blacksmiths**] someone who makes and repairs things made of iron, especially shoes for horses

bladder /'blædə(r)/ NOUN [*plural* **bladders**] the organ in your body where urine is collected. A biology word.

blade /bleɪd/ NOUN [*plural* **blades**]
1 the sharp part of a knife or tool which cuts 🔁 *a razor blade*
2 a blade of grass a long thin piece of grass

blame /bleɪm/ ▶ VERB [**blames, blaming, blamed**]
1 to say that something is someone's fault □ *+ for He blamed me for the accident.*
2 be to blame to be responsible for something bad that has happened □ *Pilot error was to blame for the accident.*
♦ IDIOM **I don't blame you** used for saying that you can understand someone's reasons for doing something □ *I don't blame you for getting angry with him.*
▶ NOUN, NO PLURAL responsibility for something bad that has happened 🔁 *Why do I always get the blame for everything?* 🔁 *I'm not going to take the blame for someone else's mistake.*
• **blameless** /'bleɪmlɪs/ ADJECTIVE having done nothing wrong □ *The victim was entirely blameless.*

bland /blænd/ ADJECTIVE [**blander, blandest**]
1 not interesting or exciting □ *bland music*
2 bland food does not have a strong flavour

blank /blæŋk/ ▶ ADJECTIVE
1 with no writing on, or with no sound or pictures on 🔁 *a blank sheet of paper* □ *a blank CD*
2 showing no emotion or no understanding 🔁 *She gave me a blank stare.*
▶ NOUN [*plural* **blanks**] an empty space on a piece of paper

blank cheque /,blæŋk 'tʃek/ NOUN [*plural* **blank cheques**] a cheque that has been signed but without an amount of money written on it

blanket /'blæŋkɪt/ NOUN [*plural* **blankets**]
1 a cover for a bed, usually made of wool □ *a wool blanket*
2 a layer that covers everything □ *+ of A blanket of snow covered the roads.*

blankly /'blæŋklɪ/ ADVERB showing no emotion or understanding □ *They stared at me blankly.*

blare /bleə(r)/ ▶ VERB [**blares, blaring, blared**] to make a very loud and unpleasant sound □ *Music was blaring from the loudspeakers.*
▶ NOUN, NO PLURAL a loud unpleasant sound □ *the blare of a car's horn*

blasé /'blɑːzeɪ/ ADJECTIVE not excited or not worried about something because you have done it many times before □ *By the age of ten she was quite blasé about appearing on television.*

blaspheme /blæs'fiːm/ VERB [**blasphemes, blaspheming, blasphemed**] to say offensive things about God
• **blasphemous** /'blæsfəməs/ ADJECTIVE offensive about God or about people's religious beliefs
• **blasphemy** /'blæsfəmɪ/ NOUN [*plural* **blasphemies**] being blasphemous or a blasphemous word or phrase

blast /blɑːst/ ▶ NOUN [*plural* **blasts**]
1 an explosion 🔁 *They were killed in a bomb blast.* □ *Three people survived the blast.*
2 full blast as loud, strong, energetic, etc. as possible □ *They play their music full blast all night.*
3 a sudden strong movement of air □ *The door opened, letting in a blast of freezing air.*
4 a loud sound from something such as a horn □ *The lorry driver gave a couple of blasts on his horn.*
▶ VERB [**blasts, blasting, blasted**]
1 to make a lot of loud noise □ *Music was blasting out of the open windows.*
2 to use explosives to break up something such as rock
3 to criticize someone or something strongly □ *The mayor made a speech blasting his opponents.*
♦ PHRASAL VERB **blast off** if a rocket (= type of spacecraft) blasts off, it starts to go up into the air

blast-off /'blɑːst ,ɒf/ NOUN [*plural* **blast-offs**] the moment when a rocket (= type of spacecraft) goes up into the air

blatant /'bleɪtənt/ ADJECTIVE bad behaviour is blatant when it is very obvious and the person doing it does not seem to care 🖫 *It was a blatant lie.*

blaze /bleɪz/ ▶ NOUN [plural **blazes**] a big fire 🖫 *Firefighters put out the blaze.*
▶ VERB [**blazes, blazing, blazed**] to burn or shine brightly □ *Her eyes were blazing with anger.*

blazer /'bleɪzə(r)/ NOUN [plural **blazers**] a type of jacket, often worn as part of a uniform

blazing /'bleɪzɪŋ/ ADJECTIVE
1 burning very strongly □ *A blazing fire made the room very warm and cosy.*
2 very hot □ *We were sitting in the blazing sunshine.*
3 a blazing row a very angry argument

bleach /bliːtʃ/ ▶ NOUN, NO PLURAL a chemical used for cleaning things or making them more white
▶ VERB [**bleaches, bleaching, bleached**] to make something more white using bleach or because of being in the sun □ *Her hair was bleached blonde in the sun.*

bleak /bliːk/ ADJECTIVE [**bleaker, bleakest**]
1 without hope or happiness 🖫 *The book paints a bleak picture of life in Victorian times.* 🖫 *a bleak future/outlook*
2 a bleak place is cold, empty and not pleasant □ *a bleak winter landscape*

bleary /'blɪərɪ/ ADJECTIVE [**blearier, bleariest**] if your eyes are bleary, you cannot see very well because you are tired

bleat /bliːt/ ▶ VERB [**bleats, bleating, bleated**]
1 a sheep or goat bleats when it makes its usual sound
2 to complain in a weak or annoying way □ *She was bleating on about how unfair life was.*
▶ NOUN [plural **bleats**] the sound a sheep or goat makes

bleed /bliːd/ VERB [**bleeds, bleeding, bled**] when you bleed, blood comes out of a cut on your body □ *He was bleeding from a cut on his head.* 🖫 *My head was bleeding profusely* (= very much).
● **bleeding** /'bliːdɪŋ/ NOUN, NO PLURAL a flow of blood 🖫 *First try to stop the bleeding and then ring for an ambulance.*

bleep /bliːp/ ▶ NOUN [plural **bleeps**] a short sound made by an electronic device
▶ VERB [**bleeps, bleeping, bleeped**] if an electronic device bleeps, it makes a short sound
● **bleeper** /'bliːpə(r)/ NOUN [plural **bleepers**] an electronic device that makes a sound when someone wants to contact you

blemish /'blemɪʃ/ NOUN [plural **blemishes**]
1 a mark that spoils something □ *an apple covered with blemishes*
2 a bad action which damages someone's reputation □ *This is a serious blemish on his military record.*

blend /blend/ ▶ VERB [**blends, blending, blended**] to mix things together completely □ *Blend the butter and the sugar.*
◆ PHRASAL VERB **blend in** to look or seem the same as the other people or things that are around □ *The new houses blend in with the other houses in the area.*
▶ NOUN [plural **blends**] a mixture of two or more things □ *Banana milkshake is a blend of milk, banana and ice cream.*
● **blender** /'blendə(r)/ NOUN [plural **blenders**] a machine used for mixing food

bless /bles/ VERB [**blesses, blessing, blessed**]
1 be blessed with something to be lucky enough to have something □ *They've been blessed with two beautiful children.*
2 to ask God to protect someone or to make something holy □ *The priest blessed the bread and the wine.*
◆ IDIOM **Bless you!** something you say when someone sneezes

● **blessing** /'blesɪŋ/ NOUN [plural **blessings**]
1 something good that improves a situation □ *It was a blessing that he didn't suffer for long.*
2 your approval 🖫 *He gave his blessing to the plan.*
3 help and protection from God □ *They asked for God's blessing.*

blew /bluː/ PAST TENSE OF **blow**

blight /blaɪt/ ▶ NOUN, NO PLURAL something which spoils something □ *He thought the new houses were a blight on the village.*
▶ VERB [**blights, blighting, blighted**] to spoil something □ *His life was blighted by poor health.*

blind /blaɪnd/ ▶ ADJECTIVE
1 not able to see 🖫 *He went blind* (= became blind) *at the age of five.*
2 blind panic/rage, etc. an emotion that is so strong that you cannot think clearly
3 be blind to something to be unable to notice something □ *She loved him so much, she was blind to his faults.*
◆ IDIOMS **turn a blind eye to something** to pretend not to notice something □ *The company turned a blind eye to thefts from its warehouse.* **a blind spot** if someone has a blind spot about something, they do not notice it or they refuse to accept the truth about it □ *He has a real blind spot about money.*
▶ VERB [**blinds, blinding, blinded**] to make someone blind □ *He was blinded in the war.*
▶ NOUN [plural **blinds**]
1 the blind people who are blind
2 a covering that you pull down over a window

blind date /ˌblaɪnd 'deɪt/ NOUN [plural **blind dates**] a romantic meeting that is arranged for two people who do not know each other

blindfold /'blaɪndfəʊld/ ▶ NOUN [plural **blindfolds**] a cover put over someone's eyes to stop them seeing
▶ VERB [**blindfolds, blindfolding, blindfolded**] to put a blindfold on someone

blinding /'blaɪndɪŋ/ ADJECTIVE
1 a blinding light is very bright and stops you seeing for a short time
2 a blinding headache is very painful

- **blindingly** /'blaɪndɪŋlɪ/ ADVERB if something is blindingly clear, simple, etc., it is extremely clear, simple, etc.

blindly /'blaɪndlɪ/ ADVERB
1 without noticing what is around you □ *Claudia stared blindly out of the window.*
2 without considering all the facts or what might happen □ *You shouldn't blindly accept everything he says.*

blink /blɪŋk/ ▶ VERB [blinks, blinking, blinked] to close and open your eyes quickly □ *He was blinking in the strong sunlight.* □ *Emma tried to blink away the tears.*
▶ NOUN [plural blinks] when you close and open your eyes quickly

bliss /blɪs/ NOUN, NO PLURAL great happiness □ *The first few years of marriage were bliss.*
- **blissful** /'blɪsfʊl/ ADJECTIVE extremely happy □ *They spent a blissful week together.*
- **blissfully** /'blɪsfʊlɪ/ ADVERB happily 🕀 *Pete was blissfully unaware of the problems ahead.*

blister /'blɪstə(r)/ ▶ NOUN [plural blisters] a swollen area filled with liquid on your skin where it has been burned or rubbed
▶ VERB [blisters, blistering, blistered] to form blisters
- **blistering** /'blɪstərɪŋ/ ADJECTIVE
1 very hot 🕀 *blistering heat/sunshine*
2 criticizing someone or something very strongly 🕀 *a blistering attack*
3 very fast 🕀 *They set off at a blistering pace.*

blithe /blaɪð/ ADJECTIVE ignoring or not caring about possible dangers or bad results □ *He drove with a blithe disregard for the rules of the road.*
- **blithely** /'blaɪðlɪ/ ADVERB happily and without worrying or caring □ *Paul blithely imagines he can pass the exam without doing any work.*

blitz /blɪts/ ▶ NOUN [plural blitzes]
1 when you do a lot of something in a short time □ *The company has launched an advertising blitz.*
2 when a lot of bombs are dropped on a place
▶ VERB [blitzes, blitzing, blitzed]
1 to do a lot of something in a short time □ *We got together and blitzed the housework.*
2 to drop a lot of bombs on a place

blizzard /'blɪzəd/ NOUN [plural blizzards] a storm with strong winds and snow

bloated /'bləʊtɪd/ ADJECTIVE swollen and too full □ *His stomach felt bloated after the huge meal.*

blob /blɒb/ NOUN [plural blobs] a round lump of something soft □ *blobs of paint*

bloc /blɒk/ NOUN [plural blocs] a group of countries that work together and have similar political aims □ *the Soviet bloc*

block /blɒk/ ▶ NOUN [plural blocks]
1 a solid, usually square piece of something □ *Cut the wood into blocks.* □ *+ of a block of ice*
2 a large building with a lot of offices or homes in it 🕀 *a block of flats* 🕀 *a fifteen-storey office block*

3 a group of houses with roads on all four sides 🕀 *I went for a jog round the block.*
4 a US word for the distance from where one road crosses a street to the place where another road crosses it □ *He lives a few blocks from here.*
▶ VERB [blocks, blocking, blocked]
1 to stop people or things from getting through □ *The road was blocked by an overturned lorry.* 🕀 *A large police officer blocked our path/exit.* □ *+ up The channel was blocked up with sticks.*
2 to stop something from being done □ *The government threatened to block the deal.*
3 to be in front of someone so that they cannot see something or light cannot get to them 🕀 *A tall man in front was blocking my view.*
◆ PHRASAL VERBS **block something off** to close something such as a path or an entrance by placing something across it □ *The police had blocked off the road.* **block something out 1** to stop light or sound from reaching a place □ *Tall trees blocked out all the sunlight.* **2** if you block out thoughts or memories, you stop yourself thinking about them

blockade /blɒ'keɪd/ ▶ NOUN [plural blockades] when someone, usually soldiers, stops goods or people from getting in or out of a place 🕀 *The blockade was lifted in August.*
▶ VERB [blockades, blockading, blockaded] to surround a place to stop people and goods getting in and out

blockage /'blɒkɪdʒ/ NOUN [plural blockages] something that blocks a tube, flow of water, etc. □ *Dead leaves had caused a blockage in the drains.*

block capitals /ˌblɒk 'kæpɪtəlz/ PLURAL NOUN letters written as A, B, C, not a, b, c

blog /blɒg/ ▶ NOUN [plural blogs] a record of someone's activities and opinions that they put on the Internet for other people to read. A computing word.
▶ VERB [blogs, blogging, blogged] to write a blog. A computing word.
- **blogger** /'blɒgə(r)/ NOUN [plural bloggers] someone who writes a blog. A computing word.

bloke /bləʊk/ NOUN [plural blokes] an informal word meaning man □ *He's a nice bloke.*

blond or **blonde** /blɒnd/ ▶ ADJECTIVE [blonder, blondest]
1 blond hair is pale yellow □ *He had long blond hair.*
2 having pale yellow hair □ *There was a blonde woman sitting next to him.*
▶ NOUN [plural blonds or blondes] a person with pale yellow hair

blood /blʌd/ NOUN, NO PLURAL the red liquid that is inside your body □ *Your heart pumps blood around your body.* 🕀 *A blood test will show if you have an infection.*

bloodcurdling /'blʌdˌkɜːdlɪŋ/ ADJECTIVE very frightening 🕀 *a bloodcurdling scream*

blood donor /'blʌd ,dəʊnə(r)/ NOUN [plural **blood donors**] someone who has blood taken from their body so that an ill person can have it

blood group /'blʌd ˌgruːp/ NOUN [plural **blood groups**] one of the types of human blood. A biology word.

bloodhound /'blʌd,haʊnd/ NOUN [plural **bloodhounds**] a type of dog that finds things by smelling

blood pressure /'blʌd ,preʃə(r)/ NOUN, NO PLURAL the pressure at which blood flows around your body. A biology word ⊞ People with high blood pressure are more likely to have a heart attack.

bloodshed /'blʌdʃed/ NOUN, NO PLURAL violence in which many people are injured or killed

bloodshot /'blʌdʃɒt/ ADJECTIVE if your eyes are bloodshot, the white parts have red lines on them

bloodstream /'blʌdstriːm/ NOUN, NO PLURAL the blood moving round inside your body □ If the infection gets into the bloodstream, it is carried quickly round the body.

bloodthirsty /'blʌd,θɜːstɪ/ ADJECTIVE wanting to kill people or animals, or liking to see them being killed

blood transfusion /'blʌd træns,fjuːʒən/ NOUN [plural **blood transfusions**] when blood from someone else is put into the body of a person who is ill or injured

blood vessel /'blʌd ,vesəl/ NOUN [plural **blood vessels**] one of the tubes that carries blood around the body. A biology word.

bloody /'blʌdɪ/ ADJECTIVE [**bloodier, bloodiest**] covered in or full of blood □ a bloody nose

bloom /bluːm/ ▶ NOUN [plural **blooms**] a flower □ The stems are covered in large white blooms.
▶ VERB [**blooms, blooming, bloomed**] to produce flowers □ A lot of plants have bloomed early this year.

blossom /'blɒsəm/ ▶ NOUN [plural **blossoms**] the flowers that appear on a fruit tree before the fruit grows
▶ VERB [**blossoms, blossoming, blossomed**]
1 to produce blossom
2 a person blossoms when they become more successful or attractive □ She has blossomed into a lovely young woman.

blot /blɒt/ ▶ NOUN [plural **blots**]
1 a mark made by a small amount of ink □ an ink blot
2 a blot on something something that makes people have a bad opinion about someone □ It was a blot on his character.
▶ VERB [**blots, blotting, blotted**]
1 to make a mark with a little ink
2 to dry a wet surface by pressing something onto it
◆ PHRASAL VERB **blot something out** to make yourself stop thinking about something bad □ I had blotted out the memory completely.

blotch /blɒtʃ/ NOUN [plural **blotches**] a spot or mark of a different colour □ Maddy's skin was covered with red blotches.

• **blotchy** /'blɒtʃɪ/ ADJECTIVE covered with blotches ⊞ blotchy skin

blotting paper /'blɒtɪŋ ,peɪpə(r)/ NOUN, NO PLURAL soft thick paper that you use for drying ink marks

blouse /blaʊz/ NOUN [plural **blouses**] a woman's shirt □ a school blouse

blow /bləʊ/ ▶ VERB [**blows, blowing, blew, blown**]
1 wind blows when it moves around □ A cold wind was blowing from the east.
2 to push out air from your mouth onto something or into something □ Blow on your soup - it's hot.
3 to breathe into something such as a musical instrument in order to make a sound □ When I blow this whistle, I want you all to stop.
4 blow your nose to get the liquid out of your nose by forcing air through it
◆ PHRASAL VERBS **blow over** if an argument blows over, people forget about it **blow something up** to destroy something with an explosion □ He was planning to blow up the aeroplane and all its passengers.
▶ NOUN [plural **blows**]
1 a hard knock □ **+to** He suffered a blow to the face.
2 something disappointing that happens □ It was a blow not being able to go to the concert.

blow-dry /ˌbləʊ ˈdraɪ/ ▶ VERB [**blow-dries, blow-drying, blow-dried**] to dry your hair using a hairdryer (= piece of equipment that blows warm air at the hair)
▶ NOUN, NO PLURAL when someone blow-dries your hair ⊞ I made an appointment for a cut and blow-dry.

blowlamp /'bləʊlæmp/ NOUN [plural **blowlamps**] a tool that produces a very hot flame to heat things up or melt them

blown /bləʊn/ PAST PARTICIPLE OF blow

BLT /ˌbiːel'tiː/ ABBREVIATION bacon, lettuce and tomato; a type of sandwich

blubber /'blʌbə(r)/ NOUN, NO PLURAL the fat from whales (= large sea mammals) and other sea animals

bludgeon /'blʌdʒən/ VERB [**bludgeons, bludgeoning, bludgeoned**] to hit someone repeatedly with a heavy weapon □ He had been bludgeoned to death.

blue /bluː/ ▶ ADJECTIVE
1 having the colour of the sky ⊞ She was wearing a dark blue dress. ⊞ He has a pale blue shirt on.
2 an informal word that means sad
▶ NOUN [plural **blues**] the colour of the sky □ The sea was a deep blue.
◆ IDIOM **out of the blue** not expected at all □ Out of the blue, he announced that he was leaving.
➜ go to blues

bluebell /'bluːbel/ NOUN [plural **bluebells**] a plant with small flowers in the shape of bells

blueberry /'bluːbərɪ/ NOUN [plural **blueberries**] a dark blue berry (= small fruit) that you can eat

bluebottle /'bluːˌbɒtəl/ NOUN [plural **bluebottle**] a large flying insect with a shiny blue body

blue-collar /'blu:'kɒlə(r)/ ADJECTIVE blue-collar workers do jobs involving physical work, not jobs in offices

blueprint /'blu:prɪnt/ NOUN [plural **blueprints**] a plan of work that needs to be done, often of something that is going to be built

blues /blu:z/ PLURAL NOUN
1 slow, sad jazz music originally sung and played by Black Americans 🖻 a blues singer
2 the blues unhappy feelings □ I've just got the blues.

bluff /blʌf/ ► VERB [**bluffs, bluffing, bluffed**] to pretend that you know something that you do not, or that you are going to do something that you will not ► NOUN [plural **bluffs**] a time when you bluff

blunder /'blʌndə(r)/ ► NOUN [plural **blunders**] a bad or embarrassing mistake
► VERB [**blunders, blundering, blundered**]
1 to make a bad or embarrassing mistake
2 to move around in a heavy or awkward way □ We blundered around in the dark.

blunt /blʌnt/ ADJECTIVE [**blunter, bluntest**]
1 with an edge or point that is not sharp □ This knife is blunt.
2 saying what you think without trying to be polite □ He can be quite blunt.
• **bluntly** /'blʌntlɪ/ ADVERB without trying to be polite □ 'I hate it,' she said bluntly.

blur /blɜ:(r)/ NOUN, NO PLURAL
1 something that is difficult to see clearly 🖻 The cars raced past in a blur.
2 something that you cannot remember clearly 🖻 I don't know what happened next - it's all a blur.

blurt /blɜ:t/
♦ PHRASAL VERB [**blurts, blurting, blurted**] blurt **something out** to say something suddenly without thinking

blush /blʌʃ/ ► VERB [**blushes, blushing, blushed**] to start to have a red face because you are embarrassed □ Everyone turned to look at Philip, who blushed.
► NOUN [plural **blushes**] when your face turns red because you are embarrassed

bluster /'blʌstə(r)/ VERB [**blusters, blustering, blustered**] to talk in a loud, angry way, especially when you are frightened or nervous

blustery /'blʌstərɪ/ ADJECTIVE with strong winds □ It's quite blustery out there.

boa constrictor /'bəʊə kən'strɪktə(r)/ NOUN [plural **boa constrictors**] a large South American snake that kills animals by wrapping itself around them and pressing hard

boar /bɔ:(r)/ NOUN [plural **boars**]
1 a male pig
2 a wild pig

board /bɔ:d/ ► NOUN [plural **boards**]
1 a flat piece of wood 🖻 Please use a bread board for cutting on. 🖻 I lifted the carpets to look at the floor boards.
2 a flat piece of wood or cardboard with marks on it, used to play a game □ a chess board

3 a surface on the wall of a classroom where the teacher writes □ The answers are on the board.
4 a group of people who control a company or other organization 🖻 the board of directors 🖻 a board meeting
5 no plural meals that you get in a hotel when you are staying there 🖻 Do we want full board (= 2 meals a day)?
6 on board on a ship, aircraft or other vehicle □ There were 197 passengers on board.
► VERB [**boards, boarding, boarded**]
1 to get on a ship or an aeroplane □ Could all remaining passengers please board the plane.
2 if an aeroplane is boarding, people are getting onto it
• **boarder** /'bɔ:də(r)/ NOUN [plural **boarders**]
1 someone who pays in order to live in someone else's house with them
2 a student who lives at his or her school □ The school has day students and boarders.

boarding house /'bɔ:dɪŋ ˌhaʊs/ NOUN [plural **boarding houses**] a house which people can pay to live in for a short time

boarding pass /'bɔ:dɪŋ ˌpɑ:s/ or **boarding card** /'bɔ:dɪŋ ˌkɑ:d/ NOUN [plural **boarding passes** or **boarding cards**] a card that you need to show someone before you can get on an aeroplane or a ship □ Passengers are asked to have their boarding passes ready.

boarding school /'bɔ:dɪŋ ˌsku:l/ NOUN [plural **boarding schools**] a school in which students can live

boardroom /'bɔ:drʊm/ NOUN [plural **boardrooms**]
1 a room in which the managers of a company meet.
2 the people who control a company

boast /bəʊst/ ► VERB [**boasts, boasting, boasted**] to talk proudly about yourself in a way that other people find annoying □ He's always boasting about the famous people he knows.
► NOUN [plural **boasts**] something you say when you boast □ It was her proud boast that she never failed exams.
• **boastful** /'bəʊstfʊl/ ADJECTIVE often boasting about the good things you have done or the expensive things you own

boat /bəʊt/ NOUN [plural **boats**] a vehicle for travelling over water □ a fishing boat
♦ IDIOM in the same boat having the same problems as other people □ Don't worry, we're all in the same boat.

bob /bɒb/ VERB [**bobs, bobbing, bobbed**] to move up and down quickly □ She watched the little boats bobbing on the lake.

bobbin /'bɒbɪn/ NOUN [plural **bobbins**] a round object which thread goes around

bobble /'bɒbəl/ NOUN [plural **bobbles**] a small round piece of soft material, especially on top of a wool hat

bobsleigh /'bɒbsleɪ/ NOUN [plural **bobsleighs**] a small vehicle that is used for travelling fast down slopes in the snow

bode /bəʊd/ VERB [**bodes**]
1 bode well to show that something good will probably happen
2 bode ill to show that something bad will probably happen

bodice /'bɒdɪs/ NOUN [plural **bodices**] the part of a dress that fits tightly on the top part of the body

bodily /'bɒdɪlɪ/ ▶ ADJECTIVE to do with the body
🖫 The virus is found in bodily fluids such as blood.
▶ ADVERB in a way that involves your whole body □ He was carried bodily out of the room.

body /'bɒdɪ/ NOUN [plural **bodies**]
1 the whole physical form of a person or animal □ I had red spots all over my body.
2 a dead person □ His body was never found.

body-building /'bɒdɪ'bɪldɪŋ/ NOUN, NO PLURAL physical exercise such as lifting weights, that makes your muscles bigger and stronger.

bodyguard /'bɒdɪɡɑːd/ NOUN [plural **bodyguards**] someone whose job is to protect an important or famous person

bog /bɒɡ/ NOUN [plural **bogs**] an area of land that is very wet
♦ PHRASAL VERB [**bogs, bogging, bogged**] **bog someone down** if you get bogged down in something, you spend so much time on it that you cannot make any progress □ Try not to get bogged down in details.

boggle /'bɒɡəl/ VERB [**boggles, boggling, boggled**] **The mind boggles!** something you say when something is hard to imagine or understand. An informal phrase. □ Grandma's learning karate? The mind boggles!

boggy /'bɒɡɪ/ ADJECTIVE [**boggier, boggiest**] boggy ground is wet ground that you sink into when you step on it

bogus /'bəʊɡəs/ ADJECTIVE pretending to be real in order to trick people □ She was tricked by a bogus salesman. □ bogus documents

bohemian /bəʊˈhiːmɪən/ ▶ ADJECTIVE behaving and dressing in an informal way that is like artists, writers, etc.
▶ NOUN [plural **bohemians**] a person who lives in a bohemian way

boil /bɔɪl/ ▶ VERB [**boils, boiling, boiled**]
1 a liquid boils when it is heated until it produces bubbles and turns into gas □ Is the water boiling yet? □ Boil some water in a pan and add the pasta.
2 to cook food in boiling water □ I'm going to boil some eggs.
3 to heat a container of liquid until it is boiling □ Shall I boil the kettle?
♦ PHRASAL VERBS **boil down to something** to be the reason for something □ She'll never be a successful

pianist. It all boils down to lack of commitment. **boil over 1** if a liquid that is being heated boils over, it comes up and over the sides of its container **2** if a violent situation or emotion boils over, it becomes impossible to control
▶ NOUN [plural **boils**]
1 bring something to the boil to heat something until it boils □ Bring the water to the boil
2 a painful red swollen area on your skin caused by an infection

● **boiler** /'bɔɪlə(r)/ NOUN [plural **boilers**] a machine that heats water, especially for heating a building

● **boiling** /'bɔɪlɪŋ/ ADJECTIVE an informal word meaning very hot □ It's boiling in here!

boiling point /'bɔɪlɪŋ ,pɔɪnt/ NOUN [plural **boiling points**] the temperature at which a particular liquid boils □ The boiling point of water is 100 degrees Celsius.

boisterous /'bɔɪstərəs/ ADJECTIVE very active and full of energy □ a boisterous child

bold /bəʊld/ ADJECTIVE [**bolder, boldest**]
1 not afraid to take a risk 🖫 Calling an election was a bold move (= a brave thing to do) for the president. □ It was rather bold of him to ask that question.
2 with strong colours and shapes □ curtains with bold patterns
3 bold type or print is thick dark letters like this □ Her name is clearly written in bold type at the top of the page.

● **boldly** /'bəʊldlɪ/ ADJECTIVE in a brave, confident way □ Samuel walked boldly into the room, which was full of strangers.

bollard /'bɒlɑːd/ NOUN [plural **bollards**] a short post placed on a road to stop cars from driving somewhere

bolster /'bəʊlstə(r)/ VERB [**bolsters, bolstering, bolstered**] to make someone or something stronger or more confident □ We were bolstered up by the support of the crowds along the route.

bolt /bəʊlt/ ▶ NOUN [plural **bolts**]
1 a metal bar that you push across a door to lock it □ She slid back the bolts and opened the door.
2 a metal object with small, raised lines that you use with a nut (= metal object with a hole in the middle) to fasten pieces of wood or metal together
3 bolt of lightning a flash of light in the sky during a storm
▶ VERB [**bolts, bolting, bolted**]
1 to lock a door using a bolt □ We bolted all the doors before we went to bed.
2 to run away very fast □ Beth's pony bolted when it heard the noise.

bomb /bɒm/ ▶ NOUN [plural **bombs**] a weapon that explodes to cause serious damage to buildings, people, etc. 🖫 The bomb went off in a crowded market.
▶ VERB [**bombs, bombing, bombed**]
1 to attack a place using bombs □ Enemy aircraft bombed every town and village in the area.

2 bomb along/through, etc. an informal word meaning to move very fast □ *He came bombing down the road on his new bike.*

bombard /bɒmˈbɑːd/ VERB [bombards, bombarding, bombarded] to attack a place with bombs or guns
♦ PHRASAL VERB **bombard someone with something** to ask someone too many questions or to give them a large amount of something □ *They were bombarded with offers of cash.*

bomber /ˈbɒmə(r)/ NOUN [plural bombers]
1 an aeroplane that carries and drops bombs
2 a person who causes a bomb to explode somewhere □ *The police are still searching for last Friday's bombers.*

bombing /ˈbɒmɪŋ/ NOUN [plural bombings] an attack using bombs

bombshell /ˈbɒmʃel/ NOUN [plural bombshells] an informal word meaning a very surprising and usually bad piece of news ⊞ *Mark dropped a bombshell this morning - he's moving to Australia.*

bond /bɒnd/ ▶ NOUN [plural bonds]
1 something that makes people feel connected to each other □ *a bond of friendship*
2 a financial document from a government or a company that shows that you have given them money and they will pay it back with interest (= extra money)
3 the strong force that holds two atoms together. A chemistry word. □ *a chemical bond*
▶ VERB [bonds, bonding, bonded]
1 to make one thing stick firmly to another □ *Use glue to bond the two pieces together.*
2 if two people bond, they like each other and develop a strong relationship

bondage /ˈbɒndɪdʒ/ NOUN, NO PLURAL **in bondage** in a situation where you have no freedom, for example being a slave (= servant that is not paid)

bone /bəʊn/ NOUN [plural bones] one of the hard parts that form the frame inside the body of an animal or person □ *Brian broke a bone in his arm.*

bone marrow /ˈbəʊn ˌmærəʊ/ NOUN, NO PLURAL the soft substance inside bones. A biology word.

bonfire /ˈbɒnˌfaɪə(r)/ NOUN [plural bonfires] a large fire built outside

bonkers /ˈbɒŋkəz/ ADJECTIVE an informal word meaning mad ⊞ *His constant chattering is driving me bonkers!*

bonnet /ˈbɒnɪt/ NOUN [plural bonnets]
1 the part at the front of a car that covers the engine
2 a woman's or child's hat that you tie under the chin

bonus /ˈbəʊnəs/ NOUN [plural bonuses]
1 something good that you get in addition to something else good ⊞ *The food is great, and has the added bonus of being healthy too.*
2 extra money that people sometimes get in addition to their usual payment □ *a Christmas bonus*

bony /ˈbəʊni/ ADJECTIVE [bonier, boniest]
1 so thin that you can see the bones through the skin
2 full of bones □ *a bony piece of fish*

boo /buː/ ▶ VERB [boos, booing, booed] people in an audience boo when they make loud noises because they do not think the performance is good
▶ NOUN, EXCLAMATION [boos] a word that people in an audience shout when they do not think the performance is good

booby prize /ˈbuːbi ˌpraɪz/ NOUN [plural booby prizes] a prize that is given to the person who has come last in a competition

booby trap /ˈbuːbi ˌtræp/ NOUN [plural booby traps] a bomb that is hidden in order to kill or injure someone who does not know it is there

book /bʊk/ ▶ NOUN [plural books] a set of pages joined together inside a cover □ *a library book* □ *Have you read Dan Brown's new book?* □ *I'm reading a really interesting book about Mexico.*
➔ *go to* **books**
▶ VERB [books, booking, booked]
1 to buy tickets for something or to arrange to have or use something in the future □ *I'd like to book a table for four, please.* □ *We've booked a family holiday in Majorca.*
2 if the police book someone for something, they officially accuse them of that crime □ *She was booked for speeding.*

bookcase /ˈbʊkkeɪs/ NOUN [plural bookcases] a piece of furniture with shelves for books

booking /ˈbʊkɪŋ/ NOUN [plural bookings] an arrangement to buy something such as a ticket for a performance or a room in a hotel ⊞ *to make a booking* ⊞ *an advance booking*

bookkeeper /ˈbʊkˌkiːpə(r)/ NOUN [plural bookkeepers] a person whose job is to keep records of all the money a business earns and spends

● **bookkeeping** /ˈbʊkˌkiːpɪŋ/ NOUN, NO PLURAL keeping a record of all the money a business earns and spends

booklet /ˈbʊklɪt/ NOUN [plural booklets] a small book that gives information about something

bookmaker /ˈbʊkˌmeɪkə(r)/ NOUN [plural bookmakers]
1 someone whose job is to take money from people who bet (= risk money) on things like horse races, and then to pay money to the people who have bet on the winner
2 bookmaker's a shop where people can make bets (= risk money to try to get more back)

bookmark /ˈbʊkmɑːk/ ▶ NOUN [plural bookmarks]
1 something that you put between the pages of a book so that you can find the place where you stopped reading
2 a record on your computer of the address of a website that helps you find it again easily. A computing word.
▶ VERB [bookmarks, bookmarking, bookmarked] to make a record on your computer of the address of a website so that you can easily find it again. A computing word.

books /bʊks/ PLURAL NOUN the written financial records of a business or an organization

bookshelf /'bʊkʃelf/ NOUN [plural **bookshelves**] a shelf for holding books

bookshop /'bʊkʃɒp/ NOUN [plural **bookshops**] a shop that sells books

bookworm /'bʊkwɜːm/ NOUN [plural **bookworms**] someone who enjoys reading and reads a lot of books

boom /buːm/ ▶ NOUN [plural **booms**]
1 a situation in which a company or country sells a lot of products and makes a lot of money □ an economic boom
2 a time when something becomes very popular or successful □ the boom in organic foods
3 a loud noise like the sound of a big drum
▶ VERB [**booms, booming, boomed**]
1 if a business or the economy booms, it becomes very successful
2 to make a loud noise like the sound of a drum

boomerang /'buːməræŋ/ NOUN [plural **boomerangs**] a curved piece of wood that comes back towards you when you throw it

boon /buːn/ NOUN [plural **boons**] something that is very useful for you □ These tax cuts are a real boon for poor families.

boor /bʊə(r)/ NOUN [plural **boors**] a person, usually a man, who behaves in a rude way
• **boorish** /'bʊərɪʃ/ ADJECTIVE rude □ boorish behaviour

boost /buːst/ ▶ NOUN [plural **boosts**] something that makes something larger or more successful □ The school funds got a boost from the money raised at the summer fair.
▶ VERB [**boosts, boosting, boosted**] to make something larger or more successful □ Extra lessons will help to boost her confidence.

boot /buːt/ ▶ NOUN [plural **boots**]
1 a type of shoe that covers the ankle and often part of the leg
2 the covered place at the back of a car for storing bags, etc.
• IDIOM **get/be given the boot** to be told that you must leave your job. An informal phrase.
▶ VERB [**boots, booting, booted**]
1 an informal word meaning to kick □ She booted the ball over the fence.
2 to start the operating system (= program that controls all the other programs) of a computer. A computing word □ I've booted (up) the server.
• PHRASAL VERB **boot someone out** to force someone to leave a place. An informal word. □ Becky was booted out of the club for breaking the rules.

booth /buːð/ NOUN [plural **booths**] a small place with walls around it where you can do something privately, for example make a telephone call

booty /'buːtɪ/ NOUN, NO PLURAL
1 things that a thief has stolen

2 an informal word for a large amount of things you have bought or received

booze /buːz/ ▶ NOUN, NO PLURAL an informal word for alcoholic drink □ He smelt of booze.
▶ VERB [**boozes, boozing, boozed**] to drink a lot of alcoholic drinks. An informal word. □ He used to go out boozing every evening.

border /'bɔːdə(r)/ ▶ NOUN [plural **borders**]
1 the line which separates two countries or areas □ They settled near the Canadian border.
2 a strip around the edge of something, often for decoration □ a pillowcase with a pretty lace border
▶ VERB [**borders, bordering, bordered**]
1 to have a border with □ Germany borders France in the West.
2 to form a line around the edge of something □ The flowerbeds were bordered with small hedges.
• PHRASAL VERB **border on something** to almost be something □ His attention to detail borders on the ridiculous.

borderline /'bɔːdəlaɪn/ ▶ NOUN
1 the borderline the point at which one quality or state becomes another □ The borderline between humour and rudeness can be very thin.
2 on the borderline very close to being in a different group or having a different quality or state □ He passed the exam, but he was on the borderline (= he nearly failed).
▶ ADJECTIVE very close to being in a different group or having a different quality or state □ Your work is borderline. You might pass, but you might fail.

bore /bɔː(r)/ ▶ VERB [**bores, boring, bored**]
1 to make someone feel bored □ The speech bored him.
2 to make a hole in something with a sharp tool
▶ PAST TENSE OF **bear**
▶ NOUN [plural **bores**]
1 someone who makes you feel bored
2 a situation or a job that annoys you because it is difficult or boring □ It's a real bore having to look after her dog.
• **bored** /bɔːd/ ADJECTIVE feeling that something is not interesting or that you have nothing to do □ + **with** I'm really bored with my clothes. ⊞ The others enjoyed the show, but I was bored stiff (= extremely bored).
• **boredom** /'bɔːdəm/ NOUN, NO PLURAL the feeling of being bored
• **boring** /'bɔːrɪŋ/ ADJECTIVE not at all interesting □ My course is really boring.

➤ Remember the difference between the words **boring** and **bored. Boring** means 'not interesting'. **Bored** is how you feel when something is not interesting □ What a boring film! □ I was so bored during the film, I fell asleep.

born /bɔːn/ ▶ VERB **be born** (a) a person or animal is born when it comes out of its mother's body □ My sister was born in 1989. □ He was born with a heart *problem.* (b) something is born when it starts to exist □ *The idea for the film was born over dinner at Jack's house.*

> ► Remember that the verb is **be born** and not just **born:**
> ✓ *I was born in Germany.*
> ✗ *I born in Germany.*

► ADJECTIVE a born leader/performer, etc. is a very good leader/performer, etc. □ *Zoe's a born entertainer.*

borne /bɔːn/ PAST PARTICIPLE OF **bear**

borough /'bʌrə/ NOUN [*plural* **boroughs**] a town or part of a city

borrow /'bɒrəu/ VERB [**borrows, borrowing, borrowed**] to use something that belongs to someone else and give it back to them later □ *Can I borrow your pencil for a minute, please?* □ **+ from** *She borrowed £100 from her Dad.*

> ► Remember that when you **borrow** something, you use something that belongs to someone else. When you give something to someone else to use, the verb is **lend** □ *I borrowed Dan's mobile.* □ *Dan lent me his mobile.*

• **borrower** /'bɒrəuə(r)/ NOUN [*plural* **borrowers**] a person who borrows something, especially money from a bank

bosom /'buzəm/ ► NOUN [*plural* **bosoms**] a woman's chest
► ADJECTIVE a bosom friend is a very good friend

boss /bɒs/ NOUN [*plural* **bosses**] someone who is in charge of other people at work □ *I'm going to ask my boss for a pay rise.*
♦ PHRASAL VERB [**bosses, bossing, bossed**] **boss someone around/about** to tell other people what to do, in a way that annoys them □ *I wish Amy would stop bossing us all around.*
• **bossy** /'bɒsɪ/ ADJECTIVE always telling other people what to do □ *Stop being so bossy - you're not in charge here.*

botanic /bə'tænɪk/ or **botanical** /bə'tænɪkəl/ ADJECTIVE to do with plants or the study of plants ⌷ *We visited the city's botanic gardens.*
• **botanist** /'bɒtənɪst/ NOUN [*plural* **botanists**] someone who studies plants
• **botany** /'bɒtənɪ/ NOUN, NO PLURAL the study of plants
botch /bɒtʃ/ VERB [**botches, botching, botched**] to do something very badly □ *He botched his first attempt to score a goal.*

both /bəuθ/ PRONOUN, DETERMINER used for saying that the same thing is true for two people or things □ *She ate both cakes, and I didn't get one.* □ **+ of** *Both of the boys are good at tennis.* □ *Both the men wore black suits.* □ *We both like classical music.* □ *The book is both interesting and informative.*

bother /'bɒðə(r)/ ► VERB [**bothers, bothering, bothered**]
1 to do something that annoys or interrupts someone □ *Stop bothering me, I'm busy.*
2 can't be bothered if you can't be bothered to do something, you feel too lazy to do it □ *I can't be bothered to cook just for myself.*
3 to make you feel unhappy or worried □ *He said that losing the match didn't bother him.*
4 to take the time or make an effort to do something □ *Don't bother tidying up yet.*
► NOUN, NO PLURAL effort or difficulty □ *The address book saves you the bother of having to remember e-mail addresses.* □ *'I really appreciate your help.' 'It's no bother.'*

bottle /'bɒtəl/ NOUN [*plural* **bottles**]
1 a glass or plastic container used for holding liquids, often with a narrow part at the top □ **+ of** *a bottle of mineral water* □ *a wine bottle*
2 a plastic container used for feeding milk to a baby □ *Would you like to give the baby his bottle today?*
♦ PHRASAL VERB [**bottles, bottling, bottled**] **bottle something up** to avoid talking about unpleasant memories or feelings, even though it would make you feel better if you did

bottle bank /'bɒtəl ˌbæŋk/ NOUN [*plural* **bottle banks**] a large container in a public place where you can put empty glass bottles so that the glass can be used again

bottleneck /'bɒtəlnek/ NOUN [*plural* **bottlenecks**]
1 a problem in a process that causes the whole process to go more slowly □ *Strikes at the port are causing bottlenecks in delivery.*
2 a place where a road is narrow or blocked so that traffic has to move through it slowly

bottom /'bɒtəm/ ► NOUN [*plural* **bottoms**]
1 the lowest part of something □ **+ of** *He stood at the bottom of the stairs* □ *the bottom of the sea*
2 the surface on the lowest part of something □ *There were holes in the bottom of his shoes.*
3 the lowest level of success □ *My team is at the bottom of the league.*
4 the part of something that is furthest away □ *the bottom of the road/garden*
5 the part of your body that you sit on □ *Always keep your baby's bottom clean and dry.*
► ADJECTIVE
1 in the lowest position □ *Put the biggest books on the bottom shelf.*
2 at the lowest level of success ⌷ *She came bottom in the exam.*
• **bottomless** /'bɒtəmlɪs/ ADJECTIVE seeming to have no limits ⌷ *He seems to think there's a bottomless pit of money available.*

bottom line /ˈbɒtəm ˈlaɪn/ NOUN [plural **bottom lines**]

1 the amount of money that a business makes □ *Rises in oil prices will seriously affect our bottom line.*

2 the most important fact about something □ *The bottom line is that if you don't stop smoking, you could die.*

bough /baʊ/ NOUN [plural **boughs**] one of the bigger branches that grows from the trunk (= main part) of a tree

bought /bɔːt/ PAST TENSE AND PAST PARTICIPLE OF **buy**

boulder /ˈbəʊldə(r)/ NOUN [plural **boulders**] a very big stone

bounce /baʊns/ VERB [**bounces, bouncing, bounced**]

1 to hit a hard surface and move away again □ *The ball bounced high into the air.*

2 to jump up and down on a soft surface □ *The children were bouncing on the bed.*

♦ PHRASAL VERB **bounce back**

1 to feel better again soon after a failure or disappointment

2 if an e-mail bounces back, it does not reach the person it was sent to

bouncer /ˈbaʊnsə(r)/ NOUN [plural **bouncers**] someone whose job is to keep out people who are not wanted in a club, bar, etc.

bouncy /ˈbaʊnsɪ/ ADJECTIVE [**bouncier, bounciest**]

1 able to bounce easily □ *a bouncy ball*

2 a bouncy surface moves up and down when you move or jump on it

3 happy and lively □ *a bouncy child*

bound /baʊnd/ ▶ ADJECTIVE

1 if something is bound to happen, it is certain to happen □ *It's bound to rain if we don't take our coats.* □ *He's bound to notice the damage.*

2 be bound up with something to be closely connected with something □ *My feelings for the house are all bound up with memories of my childhood.*

3 having a formal duty to do something □ *I am bound by my contract not to talk to the press.*

4 going in a particular direction □ *The trucks were bound for Warsaw.* □ *At last we are homeward bound.*

▶ VERB [**bounds, bounding, bounded**]

1 to run with long jumping steps □ *The dogs bounded into the room, barking excitedly.*

2 if an area is bounded by something, that thing is along its edge □ *The farm is bounded by a forest to the east.*

▶ PAST TENSE AND PAST PARTICIPLE OF **bind**

▶ NOUN [plural **bounds**]

1 a jump □ *The deer was over the fence in a single bound.*

2 out of bounds if a place is out of bounds, you are not allowed to go there

boundary /ˈbaʊndərɪ/ NOUN [plural **boundaries**]

1 a line that divides two places □ *We live on the boundary between the city and the countryside.*

2 a limit □ *This research will push back the boundaries of science.*

boundless /ˈbaʊndlɪs/ ADJECTIVE without limits
🕮 *boundless energy*

bounty /ˈbaʊntɪ/ NOUN [plural **bounties**]

1 good things that are provided □ *The harvest festival is a celebration of nature's bounty.*

2 money paid as a reward, especially for catching or killing someone

bouquet /buˈkeɪ/ NOUN [plural **bouquets**] flowers that have been tied together in an attractive way

bourgeois /ˈbɔːʒwɑː/ ADJECTIVE typical of the middle class and their ideas

• **bourgeoisie** /ˌbɔːʒwɑːˈziː/ NOUN the bourgeoisie the middle class, especially people who are too interested in money or their social position

bout /baʊt/ NOUN [plural **bouts**] a period of something unpleasant, especially illness □ *a bout of flu*

boutique /buːˈtiːk/ NOUN [plural **boutiques**] a small shop that sells fashionable clothes

bow¹ /baʊ/ ▶ VERB [**bows, bowing, bowed**] to bend your head or the top part of your body forward to say hello to someone politely or to show them respect □ *Everyone bowed to the king and queen.*

♦ PHRASAL VERB **bow to something** to be forced to do what someone wants □ *In the end I had to bow to their demands for foreign holidays.*

▶ NOUN [plural **bows**]

1 when you bow 🕮 *The pianist came back on stage to take a bow.*

2 the pointed front part of a ship

bow² /bəʊ/ NOUN [plural **bows**]

1 a knot with two circular ends, used to tie shoes or for decoration □ *Tie the ribbon in a bow.*

2 a weapon made from a long piece of wood, used for shooting arrows

3 a long, straight piece of wood with horse hair stretched along it, used for playing a musical instrument such as a violin

bowel /ˈbaʊəl/ NOUN [plural **bowels**] the long tube inside the lower part of your body that food goes through after leaving your stomach

bowl /bəʊl/ ▶ NOUN [plural **bowls**]

1 a round, open container, used for holding food □ *a soup bowl* □ *a bowl of cornflakes*

2 in the US, used in the names of large areas where people go to watch sports such as baseball □ *Baker Bowl, Philadelphia*

➔ go to **bowls**

▶ VERB [**bowls, bowling, bowled**]

1 in sports such as cricket and baseball, to throw the ball towards a person who tries to hit it

2 to roll a large heavy ball along the ground in the game of bowls

♦ PHRASAL VERB **bowl someone over** to surprise someone very much with something good □ *Wendy was bowled over by their generosity.*

bow-legged /ˌbəʊˈlegɪd/ ADJECTIVE having legs that curve out at the knees.

bowler /'bəʊlə(r)/ NOUN [plural **bowlers**] the person who bowls in sports such as cricket and baseball

bowler hat /'bəʊlə(r) 'hæt/ NOUN [plural **bowler hats**] a black hat with a hard round top, that was worn by businessmen in the past

bowling /'bəʊlɪŋ/ NOUN, NO PLURAL a game in which players roll a large heavy ball along a track and try to knock over objects shaped like bottles

bowls /bəʊlz/ NOUN, NO PLURAL a game in which players roll heavy balls along a flat surface, and try to get them close to a smaller white ball

bow tie /ˌbəʊ 'taɪ/ NOUN [plural **bow ties**] a piece of cloth tied in a bow that men wear round their necks for formal events

box /bɒks/ ▶ NOUN [plural **boxes**]
1 a container, sometimes with a lid, used for holding or storing things
2 a small square on a page with information in it or with a space where you must write 🖫 *Tick the relevant box.*
▶ VERB [**boxes, boxing, boxed**] to take part in the sport of boxing
• **boxer** /'bɒksə(r)/ NOUN [plural **boxers**] someone who takes part in the sport of boxing

boxer shorts /'bɒksə(r) ˌʃɔːts/ PLURAL NOUN loose underwear for men that covers the bottom

boxing /'bɒksɪŋ/ NOUN, NO PLURAL a sport in which two people fight by hitting each other while wearing heavy gloves (= coverings for your hands)

Boxing Day /'bɒksɪŋ ˌdeɪ/ NOUN the day after Christmas Day

box office /'bɒks ˌɒfɪs/ NOUN [plural **box offices**] the place at a theatre or cinema where you buy tickets

boy /bɔɪ/ NOUN [plural **boys**] a male child
🞏 *a six-year-old boy* 🞏 *They've got two boys and a girl.*
🞏 *When I was a little boy I wanted to be a train driver.*

boycott /'bɔɪkɒt/ ▶ VERB [**boycotts, boycotting, boycotted**] to refuse to take part in an activity or to buy a particular product
▶ NOUN [plural **boycotts**] a situation in which someone boycotts an activity or product

boyfriend /'bɔɪˌfrend/ NOUN [plural **boyfriends**] a man or boy who you are having a romantic relationship with 🞏 *Emily has got a new boyfriend.*

boyhood /'bɔɪhʊd/ NOUN, NO PLURAL the period in your life when you are a boy

boyish /'bɔɪɪʃ/ ADJECTIVE looking or behaving like a boy, especially in a good way 🞏 *Even at forty, he still looks boyish.*

bra /brɑː/ NOUN [plural **bras**] a piece of underwear that women wear to support their breasts

brace /breɪs/ NOUN [plural **braces**]
1 a piece of wire that you have on your teeth to pull them into a straight position

2 a device that is used to hold part of the body in a straight position 🞏 *a neck brace*
➔ go to **braces**

bracelet /'breɪslɪt/ NOUN [plural **bracelets**] a piece of jewellery that you wear around your arm 🞏 *a diamond bracelet*

braces /'breɪsɪz/ PLURAL NOUN a piece of clothing that consists of two narrow pieces of material that you stretch over your shoulders to hold your trousers up

bracing /'breɪsɪŋ/ ADJECTIVE a bracing wind or a bracing walk is cold in a way that makes you feel healthy 🖫 *a bracing walk by the sea*

bracken /'brækən/ NOUN, NO PLURAL a wild plant with long, wide leaves that grows in forests and on hills

bracket /'brækɪt/ NOUN [plural **brackets**]
1 one of a pair of punctuation marks ( ) or [ ], used to separate information from the main text 🖫 *She added her own comments in brackets after each point.*
2 a group into which things are divided 🖫 *Holidays to the Caribbean are in a much higher price bracket than holidays to Spain.*
3 a piece of metal that is used to attach a shelf to a wall

brag /bræg/ VERB [**brags, bragging, bragged**] to talk about your achievements or possessions in a proud way that annoys people 🞏 *Kate's always bragging about the expensive gifts he gives her.*

braid /breɪd/ NOUN [plural **braids**]
1 a narrow woven (= made by twisting together) rope used for decorating military uniforms, furniture, etc.
2 the US word for **plait**

braille /breɪl/ NOUN, NO PLURAL a writing system for blind people which uses raised marks that they can read by touching them

brain /breɪn/ NOUN [plural **brains**]
1 the organ inside your head that controls all the other parts of your body, and that you think with 🞏 *the human brain*
2 **brains** intelligence 🞏 *Come on - use your brains!*

brainstorm /'breɪnstɔːm/ NOUN [plural **brainstorms**]
1 when you suddenly do something stupid that you cannot explain
2 the US word for **brainwave**

brainwash /'breɪnwɒʃ/ VERB [**brainwashes, brainwashing, brainwashed**] to make someone believe something by repeatedly telling them that it is true

brainwave /'breɪnweɪv/ NOUN **have a brainwave** to suddenly have a very good idea

brainy /'breɪni/ ADJECTIVE [**brainier, brainiest**] an informal word for clever 🞏 *Cathy is brainy enough to be a doctor.*

brake /breɪk/ ▶ NOUN [plural **brakes**] the part in a vehicle that you press to stop the vehicle or make it go slower 🞏 *Have you checked your brakes?* 🖫 *a brake pedal*
▶ VERB [**brakes, braking, braked**] to use a brake to stop

a vehicle or make it go slower □ *Dad braked suddenly and we were all thrown forward.*

bramble /'bræmbəl/ NOUN [plural **brambles**] a plant on which blackberries (= small, black fruit) grow

bran /bræn/ NOUN, NO PLURAL the brown part on the outside of grain

branch /brɑːntʃ/ ► NOUN [plural **branches**]
1 one of the smaller parts of a tree that grow out from the main straight part □ *Crows build their nests high in the branches of trees.*
2 one of the shops or businesses that belong to a larger organization 🖰 the local *branch* of the bank 🖰 *They're* opening a new *branch* in Livingston.
► VERB [**branches, branching, branched**] to separate into two or more parts like the branches of a tree □ *The road branches to the north and west.*
♦ PHRASAL VERBS **branch off** to leave the main part of something □ *We left the main street and branched off up a hill* **branch out** to develop in different ways □ *We're trying to branch out into selling on the Internet.*

brand /brænd/ NOUN [plural **brands**] a product that has a particular name, and that is made by a particular company □ *This isn't my usual brand of shampoo, but it's just as good.*

brandish /'brændɪʃ/ VERB [**brandishes, brandishing, brandished**] to hold up a weapon in your hand so that people can see it □ *Three robbers burst in brandishing guns.*

brand-new /ˌbrænd'njuː/ ADJECTIVE completely new □ *a brand-new car*

brandy /'brændɪ/ NOUN [plural **brandies**] a very strong alcoholic drink that people drink after a meal

brash /bræʃ/ ADJECTIVE speaking in a noisy, confident way that other people find annoying □ *I found her rather brash.*

brass /brɑːs/ ► NOUN, NO PLURAL
1 a yellow metal used for making things such as musical instruments
2 musical instruments that are made of the metal brass, such as the trumpet or the trombone
► ADJECTIVE made of brass □ *a brass candlestick*

brass band /ˌbrɑːs 'bænd/ NOUN [plural **brass bands**] a group of musicians who play brass instruments such as the trumpet or the trombone

brassy /'brɑːsɪ/ ADJECTIVE [**brassier, brassiest**] describes hair that is of a yellow colour that is not natural □ *a brassy blonde*

brat /bræt/ NOUN [plural **brats**] an informal word for a child who behaves badly

bravado /brə'vɑːdəʊ/ NOUN, NO PLURAL behaviour that you think will make people believe that you are brave and confident, even when you are not

brave /breɪv/ ► ADJECTIVE [**braver, bravest**] able to deal with danger without being afraid, or able to suffer pain without complaining □ *+ of* It was very brave of her to jump in the water and save the child. □ *This might hurt a little - just try to be brave.*

♦ IDIOM **put a brave face on something** to behave as if you are not afraid or worried, although you feel afraid or worried
► VERB [**braves, braving, braved**] to deal with a difficult situation so that you can do something □ *Over 8,000 people braved terrible weather conditions to see their team play.*
• **bravely** /'breɪvlɪ/ ADVERB in a brave way □ *She smiled bravely, even though she was in pain.*
• **bravery** /'breɪvərɪ/ NOUN, NO PLURAL being brave □ *an award for bravery*

bravo /ˌbrɑː'vəʊ/ EXCLAMATION a word used for saying that you liked a performance or that you think someone has done something well □ *There were calls of 'Bravo!' from the audience.*

brawl /brɔːl/ ► NOUN [plural **brawls**] a noisy fight, especially in a public place □ *He got involved in a brawl after the match.*
► VERB [**brawls, brawling, brawled**] to fight noisily, especially in a public place

brawn /brɔːn/ NOUN, NO PLURAL big, strong muscles
• **brawny** /'brɔːnɪ/ ADJECTIVE [**brawnier, brawniest**] having big, strong muscles □ *A brawny young man lifted the boxes out of the van.*

bray /breɪ/ ► NOUN [plural **brays**] the loud sound made by a donkey (= animal like a small horse)
► VERB [**brays, braying, brayed**] a donkey brays when it makes a loud sound

brazen /'breɪzən/ ► ADJECTIVE showing that you are not ashamed although you are doing something bad
► VERB [**brazens, brazening, brazened**] **brazen it out** to deal with a difficult or embarrassing situation by pretending that you are not worried or upset
• **brazenly** /'breɪzənlɪ/ ADVERB in a brazen way

brazier /'breɪzɪə(r)/ NOUN [plural **braziers**] a metal container in which people burn coal to keep themselves warm when they are standing outside for a long time in cold weather

breach /briːtʃ/ ► NOUN [plural **breaches**]
1 the breaking of an agreement or a relationship □ *a breach of the peace agreement*
2 a space or a hole in something solid like a wall □ *A breach in the dam caused flooding in the valley below.*
► VERB [**breaches, breaching, breached**] to break something or make a hole in it □ *The explosion breached the castle wall.*

bread /bred/ NOUN, NO PLURAL a basic food made with flour and water that is baked in an oven. It is often sold in a large piece and then cut into smaller pieces. 🖰 *a loaf of bread* 🖰 *a slice of bread* 🖰 *brown/white bread*

breadcrumbs /'bredkrʌmz/ PLURAL NOUN very small pieces of bread that can be used in cooking

breadline /'bredlaɪn/ NOUN **on the breadline** very poor

breadth /bredθ/ NOUN [plural **breadths**] the size of something measured from one side to the other □ *The* teacher told us to measure the length and breadth of the room.

breadwinner /'bred,wɪnə(r)/ NOUN [plural **breadwinners**] the person or people in a family who earn money 🔁 Janice is now the main breadwinner.

break /breɪk/ ▶ VERB [**breaks, breaking, broke, broken**]

1 to separate into pieces or to make something separate into pieces □ The vase fell to the floor and broke. □ + **off** I broke a piece off the biscuit. □ + **up** The company was broken up and sold in several parts.

2 to damage something or to become damaged □ My camera broke. □ I've broken my umbrella.

3 break your arm/leg, etc to damage a bone so that it cracks

4 break the rules/the law/your promise, etc. to not do what you should do, for example because it is a rule or you have made a promise

5 break the news to tell someone that something unpleasant has happened □ I didn't want to break the bad news to them.

6 break a record to do something better/faster, etc. than anyone has done it before

7 a boy's voice breaks when it gets deeper and becomes like a man's

♦ IDIOMS **break someone's heart** to make someone very unhappy □ It breaks my heart to see the children suffer. **break the ice** to make people who have only just met feel relaxed with each other □ We played a game to break the ice.

♦ PHRASAL VERBS **break down**
1 if a machine or vehicle breaks down, it stops working □ Sorry I'm late; the car broke down. **2** if a relationship or an agreement breaks down, it stops being successful □ Her marriage broke down under the strain. **3** to start to cry □ When I mentioned her brother, she broke down and sobbed. **break in** to get into a place by using force □ Thieves broke in using a hammer. **break off** to suddenly stop what you are doing or saying □ She broke off to answer the phone. **break something off** to end a relationship 🔁 She broke off their engagement. **break out** to start suddenly 🔁 Fighting broke out during a match against Liverpool. 🔁 Fire broke out in the warehouse. **break up**
1 if two people break up, they end their relationship □ She's broken up with her boyfriend.
2 a school breaks up when the term finishes and the holiday starts

▶ NOUN [plural **breaks**]
1 a short period of time in which someone stops an activity 🔁 Shall we have/take a break? 🔁 What time is your lunch break? □ + **from** I need a break from the children.
2 a time when something ends and something new begins □ + **with** The Queen's absence from this occasion marks a complete break with tradition.
3 an opening or crack in something □ + **in** a break in the clouds □ She suffered a nasty break in her leg.

4 a opportunity that gives you success □ She's always been a great singer; she was just waiting for a lucky break.

● **breakable** /'breɪkəbəl/ ADJECTIVE able to be broken easily

● **breakage** /'breɪkɪdʒ/ NOUN [plural **breakages**] when something is broken, or a thing that has been broken □ You will have to pay for any breakages.

breakdown /'breɪkdaʊn/ NOUN [plural **breakdowns**]
1 when a machine or vehicle stops working □ We had a breakdown on the motorway.
2 when something fails in a situation □ a breakdown in communication □ Stress contributed to the breakdown of his marriage.
3 a period of mental illness when someone is too upset or sad to deal with life 🔁 She suffered a breakdown after her divorce. 🔁 a nervous breakdown

breaker /'breɪkə(r)/ NOUN [plural **breakers**] a large wave that rolls onto the beach

breakfast /'brekfəst/ NOUN [plural **breakfasts**] the first meal that you eat in the morning □ What do you usually have for breakfast?

break-in /'breɪkɪn/ NOUN [plural **break-ins**] when someone enters a house or other building illegally, usually to steal things

breakneck /'breɪknek/ ADJECTIVE **at breakneck speed** very fast □ He ran down the street at breakneck speed.

breakthrough /'breɪkθruː/ NOUN [plural **breakthroughs**] a discovery or a success that you have after working for a long time □ This has been hailed as a breakthrough in the treatment of cancer.

break-up /'breɪkʌp/ NOUN [plural **break-ups**]
1 when a relationship or marriage fails □ He blamed me for the break-up of his marriage.
2 when a country or organization is divided into separate parts

breast /brest/ NOUN [plural **breasts**]
1 one of the two organs on the front of a woman's body that produce milk when she has a baby 🔁 breast milk 🔁 breast cancer
2 the front part of a bird's body, or the meat from this part 🔁 chicken breasts

breastbone /'brestbəʊn/ NOUN [plural **breastbones**] the main bone on the front of your chest

breastfeed /'brestfiːd/ VERB [**breastfeeds, breastfeeding, breastfed**] a woman breastfeeds a baby when she feeds it with milk from her breasts

breaststroke /'breststrəʊk/ NOUN, NO PLURAL a way of swimming in which you move your arms out to the sides and move your legs out to the sides while bending your knees

breath /breθ/ NOUN [plural **breaths**]
1 when you fill your lungs with air and then let the air out again 🔁 Take a deep breath.

2 the air that comes out of your mouth □ *We could see our breath in the freezing air.*

3 be out of breath to be breathing fast because you have been running or working hard □ *You shouldn't be out of breath after walking upstairs.*

4 get your breath back to wait until you can breathe normally again after a period of effort

5 hold your breath to breathe in but not breathe out again □ *They have to hold their breath for a long time under the water.*

6 under your breath if you say something under your breath, you say it very quietly

♦ IDIOMS a breath of fresh air someone or something that is new and interesting □ *She's a real breath of fresh air in the office.* take your breath away to surprise you very much □ *His generosity took my breath away.*

breathalyze *or* **breathalyse** /'breθəlaɪz/ VERB [breathalyzes, breathalyzing, breathalyzed] the police breathalyze drivers when they ask them to breathe into a special bag that shows if they have been drinking alcohol

• **breathalyzer** *or* **breathalyser** /'breθəlaɪzə(r)/ NOUN [plural breathalyzers] a piece of equipment used for breathalyzing drivers

breathe /briːð/ VERB [breathes, breathing, breathed] to take air into your lungs and let it out again □ *He was so quiet, I thought he had stopped breathing.* □ *It feels good to breathe some clean air again.*

♦ PHRASAL VERBS breathe in to take air into your lungs □ *Breathe in through your nose and count to ten.* breathe out to let air out of your lungs □ *Now breathe out through your mouth.*

➤ Remember that the verb **breathe** has an e at the end, while the noun **breath** does not. Be careful not to confuse the spellings of the verb **breathes** and the noun plural **breaths**.

breathless /'breθlɪs/ ADJECTIVE breathing fast because you have been running or working hard

breathtaking /'breθˌteɪkɪŋ/ ADJECTIVE very beautiful, surprising or exciting □ *The scenery was breathtaking.*

breed /briːd/ ▶ VERB [breeds, breeding, bred]

1 when animals breed they produce young animals □ *The birds breed across Europe and Asia.*

2 to produce young animals from dogs, cows, sheep, etc. □ *These dogs are bred for hunting.*

3 to cause people to have bad feelings □ *Lack of opportunity breeds despair in these young people.*

▶ NOUN [plural breeds] a particular type of animal □ *The Aberdeen Angus is a famous Scottish breed of cattle.*

• **breeder** /'briːdə(r)/ NOUN [plural breeders] someone who breeds animals □ *a dog breeder*

breeze /briːz/ NOUN [plural breezes] a light wind □ *a cool/gentle breeze*

• **breezy** /'briːzɪ/ ADJECTIVE [breezier, breeziest]

1 with a light wind blowing □ *a breezy day*

2 lively and confident ☐ *Shona's always bright and breezy in the mornings.*

brevity /'brevɪtɪ/ NOUN, NO PLURAL

1 when you use only a few words □ *Aim for brevity when you are e-mailing people.*

2 when something lasts for a short time only

brew /bruː/ VERB [brews, brewing, brewed]

1 to make beer

2 to make tea or coffee, or to leave tea or coffee in hot water to develop its flavour

3 if a storm or trouble is brewing, it will begin soon

• **brewer** /'bruːə(r)/ NOUN [plural brewers] a person or business that makes beer

• **brewery** /'bruːərɪ/ NOUN [plural breweries] a factory where beer is made

bribe /braɪb/ ▶ NOUN [plural bribes] money that is offered to someone so that they will do something dishonest ☐ *accept/take a bribe*

▶ VERB [bribes, bribing, bribed] to offer someone a bribe □ *You were a fool to try to bribe the policeman.*

• **bribery** /'braɪbərɪ/ NOUN, NO PLURAL offering bribes

bric-a-brac /'brɪkəˌbræk/ NOUN, NO PLURAL small, often decorative objects that are not worth very much

brick /brɪk/ NOUN [plural bricks] a block used for building walls □ *Someone had thrown a brick through the window.* ☐ *a brick wall*

bricklayer /'brɪkˌleɪə(r)/ NOUN [plural bricklayers] a person whose job is to build things with bricks

bridal /'braɪdəl/ ADJECTIVE belonging to or used by a bride □ *a white bridal car*

bride /braɪd/ NOUN [plural brides] a woman who is getting married

bridegroom /'braɪdgrum/ NOUN [plural bridegrooms] a man who is getting married

bridesmaid /'braɪdzmeɪd/ NOUN [plural bridesmaids] a girl or woman who helps a bride on her wedding day

bridge /brɪdʒ/ NOUN [plural bridges]

1 a structure that is built over a river or a road to allow people or vehicles to cross from one side to the other □ *We drove across the bridge.* ☐ *a railway bridge*

2 a card game for four people playing in pairs

bridle /'braɪdəl/ NOUN [plural bridles] the part of a horse's harness (= leather straps) that goes around its head

brie /briː/ NOUN, NO PLURAL a type of soft French cheese

brief /briːf/ ▶ ADJECTIVE [briefer, briefest] short □ *We had a brief telephone conversation.* □ *He wrote her a brief note.*

▶ VERB [briefs, briefing, briefed] to give someone information or instructions about something □ *Our football coach always briefs us before a match.*

▶ NOUN [plural briefs] the information or instructions that someone needs to do their work

➔ go to briefs

briefcase /'bri:fkeɪs/ NOUN [*plural* **briefcases**] a flat case for carrying business documents

briefing /'bri:fɪŋ/ NOUN [*plural* **briefings**] a meeting or a document that gives someone information or instructions □ *I give my boss regular briefings on our progress.*

briefly /'bri:flɪ/ ADVERB in or for a short amount of time □ *Tell us briefly what you want us to do.* □ *They stopped briefly to get some more petrol.*

briefs /bri:fz/ PLURAL NOUN underwear that you wear on your bottom

brigade /brɪ'geɪd/ NOUN [*plural* **brigades**] a group of soldiers that forms part of a group in the army
➔ *go to* fire brigade

brigadier /ˌbrɪgə'dɪə(r)/ NOUN [*plural* **brigadiers**] an army officer with a high rank

bright /braɪt/ ADJECTIVE [**brighter**, **brightest**]
1 producing a lot of light □ *We could see the bright lights of the city.*
2 full of light □ *This is a nice bright bedroom.*
3 a bright colour is strong and clear □ *His eyes were bright blue.*
4 happy and healthy □ *Grandad was a lot brighter this morning.*
5 clever □ *He was always the brightest child in our family.*
♦ IDIOM **a bright spot** a good part of a situation or event, usually one which is bad in general □ *His performance was the one bright spot of the evening.*
● **brighten** /'braɪtən/ VERB [**brightens**, **brightening**, **brightened**]
1 to become brighter or to make something brighter □ *The weather brightened up and we went out for a walk.* □ *A coat of paint would brighten the walls.*
2 to become happier and more energetic or to make someone happier and more energetic □ *Jack brightened up a bit when I suggested a game of cricket.*
● **brightly** /'braɪtlɪ/ ADVERB
1 with a lot of light □ *The sun shone brightly.*
2 happily and with energy □ *'Let's play,' she said brightly.*
● **brightness** /'braɪtnɪs/ NOUN, NO PLURAL the amount of light that something produces

brilliance /'brɪljəns/ NOUN, NO PLURAL
1 great skill □ *We had to admire the other team's brilliance.*
2 giving out strong light □ *the brilliance of the sunshine*
● **brilliant** /'brɪljənt/ ADJECTIVE
1 very clever, or showing great skill □ *Fiona gave a brilliant speech.*
2 very bright 🕮 *brilliant sunshine*
● **brilliantly** /'brɪljəntlɪ/ ADVERB
1 with great skill □ *Sanjay acted the bad-tempered king brilliantly.*
2 very brightly □ *The arena was brilliantly lit.*

brim /brɪm/ ▶ NOUN [*plural* **brims**]
1 the top edge of a container □ *His glass was filled right up to the brim.*
2 the lower part of a hat that sticks out □ *Val wore a big hat with a wide brim.*
▶ VERB [**brims**, **brimming**, **brimmed**] to be full to the top □ *The bin is brimming over with empty cans.* □ *Her eyes were brimming with tears.*

brine /braɪn/ NOUN, NO PLURAL water with salt in it, often used to keep food in

bring /brɪŋ/ VERB [**brings**, **bringing**, **brought**]
1 to take or carry a person or thing with you when you go somewhere □ + *to* *You can bring all your friends to the party.* □ *He brought a couple of jigsaws downstairs.* □ + *back* *He never brought back the book he borrowed.*
2 to cause a feeling or a situation □ + *to* *The new leaders brought peace to the area.* □ *Our grandchildren have brought us great happiness.*
3 cannot bring yourself to do something to not be able to do something because you find it unpleasant □ *I couldn't bring myself to be polite to her.*

➤ Use **bring** when you are talking about taking a person or thing towards you (the person speaking). Use **take** when you are talking about taking a person or thing away from you (the person speaking), or away from the place where you are now: □ *Could you bring my mobile when you come?* □ *I'll take some flowers to the hospital.*

♦ PHRASAL VERBS **bring something about** to cause something to happen □ *Motherhood had brought about enormous changes.* **bring something forward** to move the date or time of an event so that it happens earlier □ *They decided to bring forward their wedding.* **bring something in** to make people start using a new law or system □ *The government has brought in tax reforms.* **bring something off** to manage to do something successfully □ *They brought off the perfect crime.* **bring something on** to cause something bad, especially an illness □ *Doctors think his heart attack was brought on by stress.* **bring something out** when companies bring out a new product, they make it available to be bought □ *The band has brought out a new album.* **bring something up** **1** to mention a subject □ *Did anyone bring up the subject of payment?* **2** to make food come up from your stomach and out of your mouth **bring someone up** to look after a child until they are old enough to look after themselves □ *My parents brought me up to be polite and considerate.*

brink /brɪŋk/ NOUN on the brink of something if you are on the brink of something, it is going to happen very soon □ *Noreen was on the brink of tears.*

brisk /brɪsk/ ADJECTIVE [**brisker**, **briskest**] quick and energetic □ *We were walking at a brisk pace.*

• **briskly** /'brɪsklɪ/ ADVERB quickly and with energy □ *They walked briskly to keep warm.*

bristle /'brɪsəl/ NOUN [plural **bristles**] a short stiff hair on a man's face, or on a brush

• **bristly** /'brɪslɪ/ ADJECTIVE [bristlier, bristliest] covered with bristles

Brit /brɪt/ NOUN [plural **Brits**] a British person. An informal word □ *There are a lot of Brits in Majorca in the summer.*

Britain /'brɪtən/ NOUN England, Scotland and Wales

British /'brɪtɪʃ/ ► ADJECTIVE belonging to or coming from Britain □ *British industry*
► NOUN **the British** the people who come from Britain

Briton /'brɪtən/ NOUN [plural **Britons**] a person who comes from Britain □ *Several Britons were killed in the accident.*

brittle /'brɪtəl/ ADJECTIVE a brittle material or object is hard but can be easily broken □ *brittle bones*

broach /brəʊtʃ/ VERB [broaches, broaching, broached] to broach a subject or question is to begin to talk about it 🕮 *I haven't broached the subject of payment yet.*

broad /brɔːd/ ADJECTIVE [broader, broadest]
1 wide 🕮 *He was a tall man with broad shoulders.* 🕮 *She gave us a broad smile.*
2 including many different things 🕮 *We discussed a broad range of subjects.*
3 general 🕮 *The product has broad appeal across all ages.* 🕮 *She gave us a broad outline (= told us about the main parts) of her research.*
4 a broad accent is very strong
5 in broad daylight during the day, when people might be able to see □ *He was attacked in broad daylight.*

broadband /'brɔːdbænd/ NOUN, NO PLURAL an Internet connection that makes it possible to send and receive large amounts of information very quickly. A computing word. □ *We don't have broadband at home.*

broad bean /brɔːd 'biːn/ NOUN [plural **broad beans**] a large, pale green bean that is eaten as a vegetable

broadcast /'brɔːdkɑːst/ ► NOUN [plural **broadcasts**] a programme sent out on television or radio 🕮 *We watched a live broadcast of the World Cup Final.*
► VERB [broadcasts, broadcasting, broadcast] to send out information or programmes on television or radio □ *The interview was broadcast on Sunday.* □ *The BBC broadcast the event live.*

• **broadcaster** /'brɔːdkɑːstə(r)/ NOUN [plural **broadcasters**] someone whose job is to speak on television or radio programmes

• **broadcasting** /'brɔːdkɑːstɪŋ/ NOUN, NO PLURAL the work of television and radio companies

broaden /'brɔːdən/ VERB [broadens, broadening, broadened]

1 to become wider, or to make something wider □ *They've broadened the road.* □ *Her smile broadened.*
2 to include more things or people □ *The socialist party will have to broaden its appeal.*
♦ IDIOM **broaden your mind** to give you more knowledge about the world and make you accept different people more □ *They say that travel broadens the mind.*
➡ go to **broaden your** *horizons*

broadly /'brɔːdlɪ/ ADVERB
1 in most ways □ *Your answer is broadly right, but it isn't detailed enough.* 🕮 *Broadly speaking, we get on very well.*
2 if you smile broadly, you give a very wide smile □ *He came out of the room smiling broadly.*

broad-minded /ˌbrɔːd'maɪndɪd/ ADJECTIVE willing to accept other people's opinions or behaviour, and not easily shocked

broadsheet /'brɔːdʃiːt/ NOUN [plural **broadsheets**] a serious newspaper that that is printed on large pieces of paper

broccoli /'brɒkəlɪ/ NOUN, NO PLURAL a vegetable with a lot of very small green or purple flowers growing from a thick stem

brochure /'brəʊʃə(r)/ NOUN [plural **brochures**] a small book containing information about particular products or services, often with pictures □ *a holiday brochure*

broke /brəʊk/ ► PAST TENSE OF break
► ADJECTIVE having very little or no money. An informal word □ *I can't afford a holiday; I'm completely broke.*

broken /'brəʊkən/ ► PAST PARTICIPLE OF break
► ADJECTIVE
1 damaged, and often in several pieces 🕮 *broken glass* 🕮 *a broken bone*
2 if a machine is broken, it is not working □ *The washing machine is broken, I'm afraid.*
3 a broken home if a child comes from a broken home, its parents do not live together any more
4 if someone's heart is broken, they are very sad, especially because someone they loved has gone away or died 🕮 *They say she died of a broken heart.*

broken-hearted /ˌbrəʊkən'hɑːtɪd/ ADJECTIVE extremely sad, especially because someone you loved has gone away or died □ *I was broken-hearted when Robert left me.*

broker /'brəʊkə(r)/ NOUN [plural **brokers**] someone whose job is to buy or sell goods or services for other people □ *an insurance broker*

brolly /'brɒlɪ/ NOUN [plural **brollies**] an informal word for umbrella

bromine /'brəʊmiːn/ NOUN, NO PLURAL a dark red, usually liquid element. A chemistry word.

bronchitis /brɒŋ'kaɪtɪs/ NOUN, NO PLURAL a disease that affects the lungs, making it difficult to breathe

bronze /brɒnz/ ► NOUN [plural **bronzes**]
1 a metal that is formed from a mixture of copper and tin □ *The statue was cast in bronze.*
2 a bronze medal (= prize for coming third in a competition or race) □ *Williams came first, Miller came second, and Lewis got the bronze.*
3 a red-brown colour
► ADJECTIVE
1 made of bronze □ *a bronze medal*
2 having the colour of bronze
• **bronzed** /brɒnzd/ ADJECTIVE someone who is bronzed has dark skin because they have spent a lot of time in the sun

brooch /brəʊtʃ/ NOUN [plural **brooches**] a piece of jewellery with a pin on the back that you fasten to the front of a dress or jacket

brood /bru:d/ ► NOUN [plural **broods**]
1 a group of young birds that come out of their eggs at the same time □ *a brood of chicks*
2 a group of young children from the same family. A humorous word □ *Michael was the youngest of their brood of five.*
► VERB [**broods, brooding, brooded**] to think a lot about something unpleasant □ *Gerry's brooding over the goal he missed.*
• **broody** /'bru:dɪ/ ADJECTIVE
1 wanting to have a baby □ *I get all broody when I see other people's babies.*
2 thinking and worrying about something unpleasant

broom /bru:m/ NOUN [plural **brooms**] a brush with a long handle, used for cleaning the floor

broomstick /'bru:mstɪk/ NOUN [plural **broomsticks**]
1 a long stick with smaller sticks tied to one end that witches ride on in children's stories
2 a broom handle

broth /brɒθ/ NOUN, NO PLURAL thin soup often made with meat

brother /'brʌðə(r)/ NOUN [plural **brothers**]
1 a boy or man who has the same parents as you 🔊 *I share a bedroom with my little brother.* 🔊 *Do you have any brothers and sisters?*
2 a man who has the same opinions as you or is a member of the same organization as you □ *We call on our brothers abroad to end this dispute.*
• **brotherhood** /'brʌðəhʊd/ NOUN [plural **brotherhoods**]
1 a friendly feeling between boys and men
2 an organization for men

brother-in-law /'brʌðərɪnlɔ:/ NOUN [plural **brothers-in-law**] your sister's husband or the brother of your husband or wife

brotherly /'brʌðəlɪ/ ADJECTIVE to do with the feelings such as love and loyalty that brothers often have for each other 🔊 *brotherly love*

brought /brɔ:t/ PAST TENSE AND PAST PARTICIPLE OF bring

brow /braʊ/ NOUN [plural **brows**]
1 the part of your face above your eyes □ *She wrinkled her brow in confusion.*
2 your brows are your eyebrows (= lines of hair above your eyes)
3 the top of a hill □ *He tried to overtake a car on the brow of a hill.*

browbeat /'braʊbi:t/ VERB [**browbeats, browbeating, browbeat, browbeaten**] to force someone to do something by talking to them in a threatening way

brown /braʊn/ ► ADJECTIVE
1 having the colour of soil or wood 🔊 *She has light brown hair.* 🔊 *They painted the walls dark brown.*
2 having dark skin because of being in the sun 🔊 *I went quite brown when we were in Spain.*
► NOUN [plural **browns**] the colour of soil or wood □ *We chose a rich brown for the sofa.*

browse /braʊz/ VERB [**browses, browsing, browsed**]
1 to look at information on the Internet. A computing word. □ *This mobile phone lets you send emails and browse the Web.*
2 to look at things in a shop without buying them □ *'Can I help you?' 'I'm just browsing actually, thanks.'*
3 to read parts of a newspaper or magazine □ *She was browsing through the Times when Angela came in.*
• **browser** /'braʊzə(r)/ NOUN [plural **browsers**] a computer program that allows you to look at websites on the Internet. A computing word.

bruise /bru:z/ ► NOUN [plural **bruises**]
1 a dark mark that you get on your skin if it is hit □ *Joe's got a big black bruise just under his eye.*
2 a soft brown mark on a piece of fruit where it has been damaged
► VERB [**bruises, bruising, bruised**]
1 to make a bruise on someone's skin □ *Daniel bruised his knee when he fell.*
2 to damage a piece of fruit □ *Be careful not to bruise the peaches when you handle them.*

brunette /bru:'net/ ► NOUN [plural **brunettes**] a woman with brown hair
► ADJECTIVE having brown hair

brunt /brʌnt/ NOUN, NO PLURAL bear/take the brunt of something to take the worst part of something □ *The side of the bus bore the brunt of the impact.* □ *His wife bears the brunt of his bad temper.*

brush /brʌʃ/ ► VERB [**brushes, brushing, brushed**]
1 to make something tidy or clean using a brush 🔊 *Have you brushed your teeth?* 🔊 *Make sure you brush your hair before you go out.*
2 to remove something from a surface using your hand or a brush □ *+ off* *She brushed a hair off her skirt.*
3 to put liquid on to something using a brush □ *+ with* *Brush the fish with oil before cooking it.*
4 to touch something lightly □ *+ against* *She felt something brush against her shoulder.*
• PHRASAL VERBS **brush something aside/off** to refuse to accept what people say □ *The minister brushed aside suggestions that he was planning to*

resign. **brush up (on) something** to practise a skill □ *I need to brush up my French before I go on holiday.*
▶ NOUN [*plural* **brushes**]
1 an object with short hairs or thin pieces of plastic, wire, etc. fixed to a handle, used for tidying your hair, painting or cleaning □ *You'll need a stiff brush to get rid of the mud on those shoes.* □ *An artist needs a range of different brushes.*
2 give something a brush to clean or tidy something using a brush
3 a short experience of something unpleasant ⌗ *A brush with death convinced him to give up the sport.*

brusque /bruːsk/ ADJECTIVE not patient or polite towards people □ *I was shocked by her brusque manner.*
• **brusquely** /ˈbruːsklɪ/ ADVERB in a brusque way □ *'I'm sorry, I can't wait,' he said brusquely.*

Brussels sprout /ˈbrʌsəlz ˈspraʊt/ NOUN [*plural* **Brussels sprouts**] a green vegetable that looks like a very small cabbage

brutal /ˈbruːtəl/ ADJECTIVE very cruel □ *a brutal murder*
• **brutality** /bruːˈtælɪtɪ/ NOUN, NO PLURAL violent and cruel behaviour □ *We were shocked by the brutality of the attacks.*
• **brutally** /ˈbruːtəlɪ/ ADVERB
1 in a brutal way □ *She had been brutally murdered.*
2 brutally honest saying something that is true, even though you might upset people □ *I'm going to be brutally honest; I don't like your idea at all.*
• **brute** /bruːt/ ▶ ADJECTIVE **brute force/strength** great physical strength □ *Football is a game of skill - not just brute strength.*
▶ NOUN [*plural* **brutes**] a big, strong man who behaves in a cruel way

BSE /ˌbiːesˈiː/ NOUN, NO PLURAL a disease that affects cows' brains

BST /ˌbiːesˈtiː/ ABBREVIATION British Summer Time; a period in the summer when people in the UK put their clocks forward by one hour

BTW ABBREVIATION by the way; used in e-mails and text messages

bubble /ˈbʌbəl/ ▶ NOUN [*plural* **bubbles**] a very thin light ball of liquid filled with air ⌗ *soap bubbles* ⌗ *The children were blowing bubbles in the garden.*
▶ VERB [**bubbles, bubbling, bubbled**]
1 liquid bubbles when small balls of air form in it, usually because it is boiling □ *A big pot of soup was bubbling on the stove.*
2 to feel an emotion very strongly □ **+ over** *She was bubbling over with happiness in her new home.*

bubble gum /ˈbʌbəl ˌɡʌm/ NOUN, NO PLURAL a type of sweet that you chew, and that you can blow to form bubbles

bubbly /ˈbʌbəlɪ/ ▶ ADJECTIVE [**bubblier, bubbliest**]
1 happy and full of energy □ *We'll miss her sense of humour and bubbly personality.*
2 full of bubbles
▶ NOUN, NO PLURAL an informal word for champagne

(= pale wine with lots of bubbles) ⌗ *Let's open a bottle of bubbly.*

buck /bʌk/ NOUN [*plural* **bucks**]
1 an informal US word for an American dollar □ *It cost twenty bucks.*
2 make a fast/quick buck an informal phrase meaning to make money quickly
♦ IDIOMS **pass the buck** to blame someone for something or to give them responsibility for something you should be responsible for yourself **the buck stops here** used to say that you will take responsibility for something
♦ PHRASAL VERB [**bucks, bucking, bucked**] **buck (someone) up**
1 to become happier or to try to make someone happier □ *He bucked up a bit when the food arrived.*
2 buck your ideas up to start to try harder □ *We all need to get down to work and buck our ideas up.*

bucket /ˈbʌkɪt/ NOUN [*plural* **buckets**] a round open container with a handle, used for carrying water, or substances such as soil or sand ⌗ *a bucket of water* □ *You'll need about four buckets of soapy water to wash the car.*
• **bucketful** /ˈbʌkɪtfʊl/ NOUN [*plural* **bucketfuls**] the amount that a bucket will hold □ *We'll need a couple more bucketfuls of cement to finish the path.*

buckle /ˈbʌkəl/ ▶ NOUN [*plural* **buckles**] a metal object on the end of a belt or a strap, used for fastening it
▶ VERB [**buckles, buckling, buckled**]
1 to bend or break under pressure □ *His knees buckled and he fell and hit the road.* □ *The roof buckled under the weight of the snow.*
2 to fasten something with a buckle □ *She buckled her belt tightly around her waist.*
3 to become weak and to stop trying to succeed □ *The team lost two goals, but they refused to buckle.*
♦ PHRASAL VERB **buckle down** to start working hard or with determination □ *You'll have to buckle down to work when you go back to college.*

bud /bʌd/ NOUN [*plural* **buds**] the part of a plant from which a leaf or flower develops

Buddhism /ˈbʊdɪzəm/ NOUN, NO PLURAL a religion that is practised in many parts of the world, which follows the teaching of Buddha □ *He gave up politics, and went to Tibet to study Buddhism.*
• **Buddhist** /ˈbʊdɪst/ ▶ NOUN [*plural* **Buddhists**] someone who practises Buddhism
▶ ADJECTIVE to do with Buddhism or Buddhists ⌗ *a Buddhist monk*

budding /ˈbʌdɪŋ/ ADJECTIVE in the early stages of something □ *Henry's a budding scientist.*

buddy /ˈbʌdɪ/ NOUN [*plural* **buddies**] an informal word for a friend □ *They've been buddies since high school.*

budge /bʌdʒ/ VERB [**budges, budging, budged**]
1 if something will not budge, you cannot move it

□ *We tried to turn the key in the lock, but it wouldn't budge.*

2 to change your decision about something □ *The managers are unwilling to budge from their position.*

♦ PHRASAL VERB **budge up** to move along, so that there is space for someone to sit down. An informal word.

budgerigar /'bʌdʒərɪgɑː(r)/ NOUN [plural **budgerigars**] a small bird with brightly coloured feathers that is often kept as a pet

budget /'bʌdʒɪt/ ▶ NOUN [plural **budgets**]

1 an amount of money that a person, company or government has available to spend □ *We offer holidays to suit all budgets.* 🕭 *They were on a tight budget* (= did not have much money). □ *The company is cutting its marketing budget.* □ *the education budget*

2 the Budget a plan for how the government will spend money over a certain period of time □ *The Chancellor will submit the Budget to Parliament this afternoon.*

▶ VERB [budgets, budgeting, budgeted] to plan how you will spend a certain amount of money □ *You'll have to budget very carefully to make your money last a month.* □ *We've budgeted £1,000 for the website.*

▶ ADJECTIVE cheap □ *budget flights*

• **budgetary** /'bʌdʒɪtərɪ/ ADJECTIVE to do with a government's Budget. A formal word.

budgie /'bʌdʒɪ/ NOUN [plural **budgies**] a small bird with brightly coloured feathers that is often kept as a pet

buff /bʌf/ ▶ NOUN [plural **buffs**] someone who knows a lot about a particular subject □ *a film buff* □ *a computer buff*

▶ VERB [buffs, buffing, buffed] to rub a surface with a soft dry cloth to make it shiny

▶ ADJECTIVE [buffer, buffest] having a strong, attractive body. An informal word.

buffalo /'bʌfələu/ NOUN [plural **buffalos** or **buffaloes**] a large African animal like a cow, with curved horns

buffer /'bʌfə(r)/ NOUN [plural **buffers**]

1 something that protects a person or thing from harm □ *The grant money will provide us with a buffer for the first year.*

2 one of two round pieces of metal on the front of a train or at the end of a train track which reduce the force if the train hits the end of the track

3 an area in a computer's memory where information can be stored for a short time. A computing word.

buffet[1] /'bufeɪ/ NOUN [plural **buffets**] a meal where different types of food are put on a table from which people can choose what they want

buffet[2] /'bʌfɪt/ VERB [buffets, buffeting, buffeted] to knock someone or something about roughly □ *The little boat was buffeted by the storm.*

buffet car /'bufeɪ ˌkɑː(r)/ NOUN [plural **buffet cars**] the part of a train where you can buy food and drink

bug /bʌg/ ▶ NOUN [plural **bugs**]

1 an informal word for an infectious illness 🕭 *She's*

got a tummy bug. 🕭 *There's a nasty bug going round at the moment.*

2 a fault in a computer program 🕭 *She is trying to fix a bug in the program.*

3 a small insect

4 a small piece of electronic equipment used for secretly recording what people say

▶ VERB [bugs, bugging, bugged]

1 an informal word meaning to annoy someone □ *Stop bugging me!*

2 to put a bug in a place in order to record what people say □ *I think we're being bugged.*

buggy /'bʌgɪ/ NOUN [plural **buggies**] a folding seat on wheels, used for pushing a small child around

build /bɪld/ ▶ VERB [builds, building, built]

1 to make something by putting materials or parts together □ *He's planning to build his own house.* □ *The walls are built of wood.*

2 to increase □ *+ up* *Excitement is building up as the World Cup approaches.* □ *These exercises help to build upper body strength.*

3 to create and develop something □ *+ up* *She built up a chain of shoe shops.*

▶ NOUN, NO PLURAL the shape of your body □ *He had a strong, muscular build.*

♦ PHRASAL VERBS **build something in/into (something)** to make something part of something else □ *Make sure you build enough revision time into your schedule.* **build on something** to use an earlier success in order to develop further □ *We must build on our successes of the past three years.* **build up** to increase in amount □ *Resentment built up as she took more and more of the profits for herself.*

• **builder** /'bɪldə(r)/ [builders] someone whose job is to build and repair houses and other structures

• **building** /'bɪldɪŋ/ [buildings]

1 a structure with walls and a roof, for example a house or a church □ *What's the tallest building in the world?*

2 *no plural* the activity of building houses and other structures □ *There is a lot of building going on in this street.*

building site /'bɪldɪŋ ˌsaɪt/ NOUN [plural **building sites**] an area where something is being built

building society /'bɪldɪŋ səˈsaɪətɪ/ NOUN [plural **building societies**] an organization similar to a bank, from which people can borrow money to buy a house

build-up /'bɪldˌʌp/ NOUN [plural **build-ups**]

1 a gradual increase in something □ *Doctors found a build-up of fluid in his lungs.*

2 a time of increasing excitement before an event □ *the build-up to the football World Cup*

built /bɪlt/ PAST TENSE AND PAST PARTICIPLE OF build

bulb /bʌlb/ NOUN [plural **bulbs**]

1 a glass object that you put in an electric light to make it work □ *I need a new bulb for my bedside lamp.*

2 the round root of some plants □ *We planted some tulip bulbs at the weekend.*

bulbous /'bʌlbəs/ ADJECTIVE big and round

bulge /bʌldʒ/ ▶ VERB [bulges, bulging, bulged]
1 if someone's eyes or muscles bulge, they stick out □ *His eyes bulged in horror.*
2 if a container is bulging, it is very full □ *His sack was bulging with presents.*
▶ NOUN [plural **bulges**] a shape that curves out from a surface

bulimia /bʊ'lɪmɪə/ or **bulimia nervosa** /bʊ'lɪmɪə nɜː'vəʊsə/ NOUN, NO PLURAL an illness in which people make themselves vomit after eating in order to control their weight
● **bulimic** /bʊ'lɪmɪk/ ADJECTIVE suffering from bulimia

bulk /bʌlk/ ▶ NOUN
1 the bulk of something most of something □ *The bulk of his pocket money was spent on computer games.*
2 the large size of something □ *The massive bulk of Everest towered ahead.*
3 in bulk you buy in bulk when you buy something in large quantities □ *It's much cheaper to buy household goods in bulk.*
▶ ADJECTIVE to do with buying things in large quantities 🔁 *bulk buying*
◆ PHRASAL VERB [bulks, bulking, bulked] **bulk something out** to make something bigger by adding things to it □ *Bulk the soup out with some pasta.*
● **bulky** /'bʌlkɪ/ ADJECTIVE [bulkier, bulkiest] large or difficult to carry □ *a bulky package*

bull /bʊl/ NOUN [plural **bulls**]
1 an adult male cow
2 the male of some other animals, such as the elephant
◆ IDIOMS **like a bull in a china shop** not very careful and often breaking things or upsetting people **take the bull by the horns** to act in a firm way to deal with a difficult situation

bulldog /'bʊldɒg/ NOUN [plural **bulldogs**] a dog with short legs, a strong body and loose folds of skin on its face

bulldozer /'bʊldəʊzə(r)/ NOUN [plural **bulldozers**] a large vehicle with a heavy metal container at the front, used for moving large amounts of earth and stones

bullet /'bʊlɪt/ NOUN [plural **bullets**] a small piece of metal that is shot from a gun □ *a bullet wound* 🔁 *Several people were in the room when the bullets were fired.*
◆ go to **bite the bullet**

bulletin /'bʊlətɪn/ NOUN [plural **bulletins**] a television or radio report of the most recent things in the news □ *The next bulletin will be at 6 p.m.*

bulletproof /'bʊlɪt,pruːf/ ADJECTIVE made from a material that bullets cannot pass through 🔁 *a bulletproof vest*

bullfight /'bʊlfaɪt/ NOUN [plural **bullfights**] a type of entertainment that is traditionally performed in Spain, in which a man fights a bull
● **bullfighter** /'bʊl,faɪtə(r)/ NOUN [plural **bullfighters**] a person who fights a bull in a bullfight

bullion /'bʊljən/ NOUN, NO PLURAL bars of gold or silver

bull's-eye /'bʊlz,aɪ/ NOUN [plural **bull's-eyes**] the round red mark in the middle of a board that you aim at in sports like archery or darts

bully /'bʊlɪ/ ▶ NOUN [plural **bullies**] a person who frightens or hurts people who are smaller or weaker than they are
▶ VERB [bullies, bullying, bullied] to frighten or hurt smaller or weaker people
● **bullying** /'bʊlɪɪŋ/ NOUN, NO PLURAL when someone bullies another person

bumbag /'bʌmbæg/ NOUN [plural **bumbags**] a small bag attached to a belt. An informal word.

bumblebee /'bʌmbəlbiː/ NOUN [plural **bumblebees**] a large bee (= flying insect with yellow and black stripes on its body)

bump /bʌmp/ ▶ VERB [bumps, bumping, bumped] to knock against something by accident □ *The baby bumped her head on the table.* □ *I bumped into the wall.*
◆ PHRASAL VERB **bump into someone** to meet someone by chance □ *I bumped into Sarah in town today.*
▶ NOUN [plural **bumps**]
1 a raised part on a surface □ *He had a nasty bump on the back of his head.* □ *There were a lot of bumps in the road.*
2 a knock □ *I felt a gentle bump against my leg.*

bumper /'bʌmpə(r)/ ▶ NOUN [plural **bumpers**] a long bar fixed to the front and back of a car that protects it if it hits something
▶ ADJECTIVE bigger than usual 🔁 *We had a bumper crop of tomatoes this year.*

bumpy /'bʌmpɪ/ ADJECTIVE [bumpier, bumpiest]
1 covered in raised areas □ *a bumpy road*
2 a bumpy journey is uncomfortable because the surface of the road is rough
3 full of of problems 🔁 *Investors should prepare themselves for a a bumpy ride* (= a difficult time) *this year.* 🔁 *We got off to a bumpy start* (= started badly).

bun /bʌn/ NOUN [plural **buns**]
1 a small round sweet cake □ *a currant bun*
2 bread in the form of a round shape □ *a hamburger in a bun*
3 a hairstyle in which the hair is twisted into a tight ball and fixed at the back of the head

bunch /bʌntʃ/ ▶ NOUN [plural **bunches**]
1 a group of things tied or held together 🔁 *a bunch of flowers* □ *The caretaker has a big bunch of keys.*
2 a group of things that grow together □ *a bunch of grapes/bananas*
3 a bunch of something an informal US phrase

meaning a large number or amount of something □ *I've got a whole bunch of stuff to do.*
▶ VERB [**bunches, bunching, bunched**] to be close together or to move people or things close together □ *Bunch up a bit so I can get you all in the photo.* □ *The runners all bunched together at the beginning of the race.*

bundle /'bʌndəl/ ▶ NOUN [*plural* **bundles**] a group of things fastened together □ *a bundle of newspapers*
▶ VERB [**bundles, bundling, bundled**]
1 to push someone roughly into a place □ *He was bundled into a taxi before the photographers could see him.*
2 to include an extra product when you sell something □ *Their software is bundled with games and movie clips.*

bung /bʌŋ/ ▶ VERB [**bungs, bunging, bunged**] to put something somewhere quickly and without care. An informal word. □ *Bung it in the microwave.*
♦ PHRASAL VERB **bung something up** to cause something to become blocked. An informal word □ *The drains are bunged up with dead leaves.* □ *My nose is bunged up and I have a headache.*
▶ NOUN [*plural* **bungs**]
1 something used to block a hole so that liquid does not get in or out
2 an informal word for a bribe (= money paid illegally to make someone do what you want) □ *He told the BBC that he had never taken or received a bung.*

bungalow /'bʌŋgələʊ/ NOUN [*plural* **bungalows**] a house that is all on one level

bungee jumping /'bʌndʒiː 'dʒʌmpɪŋ/ NOUN, NO PLURAL a sport in which you jump from a high place with strong rubber ropes attached to your body

bungle /'bʌŋgəl/ VERB [**bungles, bungling, bungled**] to spoil something by doing it badly □ *The police have bungled this investigation from the beginning.*
● **bungler** /'bʌŋglə(r)/ NOUN [*plural* **bunglers**] someone who bungles something
● **bungling** /'bʌŋglɪŋ/ ADJECTIVE doing things badly □ *Bungling cops missed two chances to arrest a wanted man.*

bunk /bʌŋk/ NOUN [*plural* **bunks**] a narrow bed fixed to a wall
♦ IDIOM **do a bunk** an informal phrase meaning to escape from a place

bunk beds /'bʌŋk ˌbedz/ PLURAL NOUN two beds that are joined together with one above the other

bunker /'bʌŋkə(r)/ NOUN [*plural* **bunkers**]
1 a strong underground room used to protect people from bombs during a war □ *a nuclear bunker*
2 a hole filled with sand on a golf course
3 a large container for storing coal

bunny /'bʌnɪ/ NOUN [*plural* **bunnies**] a child's word for rabbit

Bunsen burner /ˌbʌnsən 'bɜːnə(r)/ NOUN [*plural* **Bunsen burners**] a piece of equipment that produces a flame, used by scientists to heat substances. A chemistry word.

bunting /'bʌntɪŋ/ NOUN, NO PLURAL a row of small triangular flags, used to decorate streets during celebrations

buoy /bɔɪ/ ▶ NOUN [*plural* **buoys**] a large object that floats in the sea, used to warn people or ships of danger
▶ VERB [**buoys, buoying, buoyed**]
1 if a company or other organization is buoyed by something, something has helped it to be more successful □ *The company was buoyed by strong profits last year.*
2 to make someone feel happier or more confident □ *The England players have been buoyed up by the return of their captain.*

● **buoyant** /'bɔɪənt/ ADJECTIVE
1 if a business or the economy is buoyant, it is successful
2 happy and confident □ *She was in a buoyant mood.*
3 able to float

burden /'bɜːdən/ ▶ NOUN [*plural* **burdens**]
1 something unpleasant or difficult that someone has to deal with 🕀 *The service will ease the burden on accident and emergency departments.* 🕀 *He offered to share the burden of the work.* □ *Running two homes is a big financial burden.*
2 if someone is a burden to you, you find it difficult to look after them or pay for their needs □ *I don't want to be a burden to you.*
3 something heavy that someone is carrying
▶ VERB [**burdens, burdening, burdened**] to give someone something difficult or unpleasant to deal with □ *The country is already burdened with debt.* □ *I don't want to burden you with all my problems.*

bureau /'bjʊərəʊ/ NOUN [*plural* **bureaux**]
1 an office or organization □ *the Graduate Recruitment Bureau*
2 a desk with drawers

● **bureaucracy** /bjʊə'rɒkrəsɪ/ NOUN, NO PLURAL all the rules that organizations have to follow, especially those that are annoying because they seem unnecessary □ *We are hoping to reduce unnecessary bureaucracy.*
● **bureaucrat** /'bjʊərəkræt/ NOUN [*plural* **bureaucrats**] an official person in an organization who seems to follow rules too exactly
● **bureaucratic** /ˌbjʊərə'krætɪk/ ADJECTIVE involving a lot of complicated rules □ *bureaucratic delays*

bureau de change /'bjʊərəʊ də 'tʃɔːndʒ/ NOUN [*plural* **bureaux de change** *or* **bureaus de change**] an office where you can buy foreign money

burette /bjʊ'ret/ NOUN [*plural* **burettes**] a glass tube with a hole at the bottom, used for adding measured amounts of liquid. A chemistry word.

burger /'bɜːgə(r)/ NOUN [*plural* **burgers**] a type of flat round food made from small pieces of meat that have been pressed together □ *I'll have a burger with fries and a coke, please.*

burglar /'bɜːɡlə(r)/ NOUN [plural **burglars**] someone who illegally enters a building in order to steal things □ *The burglars broke in through a downstairs window.*

burglar alarm /'bɜːɡlərə,lɑːm/ NOUN [plural **burglar alarms**] a piece of electronic equipment that makes a loud noise if someone tries to enter the building when it is switched on

burglary /'bɜːɡləri/ NOUN [plural **burglaries**] the crime of going into a building and stealing things □ *He called the police to report a burglary.*

burial /'beriəl/ NOUN [plural **burials**] when a dead person is put in the ground

burly /'bɜːli/ ADJECTIVE [**burlier, burliest**] a burly man is big, strong and heavy □ *a burly security guard*

burn /bɜːn/ ▶ VERB [**burns, burning, burnt** or **burned**]
1 to destroy something by setting fire to it, or to be destroyed in this way □ *We burn all our garden waste.* 🔁 *Both houses burnt to the ground.*
2 to be on fire □ *We could see the grass burning from miles away.*
3 to injure yourself by touching fire or heat □ *I burnt my hand on the cooker.*
4 to cook food for too long so that it becomes black □ *You've burnt the toast!*
5 to use fuel to make heat or energy
6 to put music, images or information on a CD-ROM
◆ PHRASAL VERBS **burn down** if a building burns down, it is completely destroyed in a fire □ *The old school burnt down.* **burn out** if a fire burns out, it stops burning **burn up** to be destroyed by fire
▶ NOUN [plural **burns**] an injury or mark left after touching fire or something very hot
● **burner** /'bɜːnə(r)/ NOUN [plural **burners**] an object that you use for burning things or for making heat □ *a wood burner*

burp /bɜːp/ ▶ VERB [**burps, burping, burped**] to make a sound by letting air come out of your stomach through your mouth
▶ NOUN [plural **burps**] the sound that you make when you burp

burrow /'bʌrəʊ/ ▶ VERB [**burrows, burrowing, burrowed**]
1 to make a hole or passage in the ground □ *They had managed to burrow deep into the hillside.*
2 to move into or under something heavy or thick □ *She burrowed deep into her duvet again.*
▶ NOUN [plural **burrows**] a hole or passage in the ground made by a small animal

bursary /'bɜːsəri/ NOUN [plural **bursaries**] an amount of money given to a student to allow them to study at college or university

burst /bɜːst/ ▶ VERB [**bursts, bursting, burst**]
1 to break or tear, especially from having too much pressure inside □ *The pipe had burst and water was running everywhere.* □ *He was bursting all the balloons with a pin.*
2 burst into flames to suddenly start to burn a lot

3 burst into tears to suddenly start to cry
◆ PHRASAL VERBS **burst in/into (somewhere)** to enter a room suddenly and violently □ *Both kids burst into our bedroom.* **burst out** to suddenly shout something □ *'Don't blame me!' he burst out.* **burst out crying/laughing** to suddenly start to cry or laugh
▶ NOUN [plural **bursts**] a sudden, short period of something □ *a burst of applause* □ *a burst of energy*

bury /'beri/ VERB [**buries, burying, buried**]
1 to put something in the ground, especially a dead person □ *She was buried in the village where she was born.* □ *They buried the treasure.*
2 bury your face/head in something to cover your face or head with something, often because you are upset □ *She buried her face in her hands.*
➡ go to bury the *hatchet*

bus /bʌs/ NOUN [plural **buses**] a large vehicle with a lot of seats for passengers 🔁 *I caught the bus into town.* 🔁 *Seven young men boarded the bus.* 🔁 *a school bus* 🔁 *a bus driver*

bus conductor /'bʌs kən'dʌktə(r)/ NOUN [plural **bus conductors**] a person whose job is to sell tickets to passengers on a bus

bush /bʊʃ/ NOUN [plural **bushes**]
1 a type of small tree □ *a rose bush*
2 the bush the wild part of some hot, dry countries where not many people live □ *the Australian bush*
● **bushy** /'bʊʃi/ ADJECTIVE [**bushier, bushiest**] growing in a thick mass □ *a long bushy tail* □ *a bushy beard*

busily /'bɪzɪli/ ADVERB in a busy way, with a lot of effort and concentration □ *They were all busily working on their computers.*

business /'bɪznɪs/ NOUN [plural **businesses**]
1 *no plural* buying and selling, and the work of producing things that people will buy 🔁 *He went into business* (= started buying and selling) *with his brother.* 🔁 *In 2004 her company went out of business* (= ended because they had no money). 🔁 *They do a lot of business with Asia* (= They sell a lot to Asia).
2 a company that makes and sells goods, or that sells services 🔁 *He runs the business with his wife.*
3 on business working □ *He travels a lot on business.*
4 a type of business □ *the music business* □ *the fashion business*

➤ Remember that you travel/go somewhere **on business**:
✓ *I was recently in Paris on business.*
✗ *I was recently in Paris for business.*

◆ IDIOM **Mind your own business!** used as a rude way of refusing to answer a personal question □ *'What's your boyfriend's name?' 'Mind your own business!'*
● **businesslike** /'bɪznɪslaɪk/ ADJECTIVE serious and effective □ *a businesslike manner*
● **businessman** /'bɪznɪsmæn/ NOUN [plural

businessmen] a man who works in business, usually in a high position

• **businesswoman** /ˈbɪznɪsˌwʊmən/ NOUN [plural **businesswomen**] a woman who works in business, usually in a high position

busker /ˈbʌskə(r)/ NOUN [plural **buskers**] a musician who performs in the street for money

bus stop /bʌs stɒp/ NOUN [plural **bus stops**] a place where a bus stops to let passengers get on or off □ *I saw Fiona standing at the bus stop.*

bust /bʌst/ ► NOUN [plural **busts**]
1 a woman's breasts
2 a model of a person's head and shoulders
► VERB [**busts, busting, bust** or **busted**]
1 an informal word that means to break something □ *I've gone and bust my zip.*
2 if a criminal is busted, they are arrested. An informal word.
► ADJECTIVE
1 go bust if a company goes bust, it has lost its money and cannot now operate
2 an informal word for broken

bustle /ˈbʌsəl/ NOUN, NO PLURAL noise and busy activity □ *She wanted to escape the bustle of the city.*
♦ PHRASAL VERB [**bustles, bustling, bustled**] bustle about/around to move around, doing a lot of different things □ *Melissa was bustling about in the kitchen.*
• **bustling** /ˈbʌsəlɪŋ/ ADJECTIVE full of noisy activity □ *They walked through the bustling market.*

busy /ˈbɪzɪ/ ADJECTIVE [**busier, busiest**]
1 doing a lot of things □ **+ with** *They're busy with wedding preparations.* □ **+ doing something** *I was busy getting dinner ready.* ⊞ *That report should keep him busy today.* ⊞ *I've had a very busy day.*
2 full of people or traffic ⊞ *We live on a busy street.* □ *Were the shops busy this morning?*
3 if someone's telephone is busy, it is being used when you try to call □ *Her phone's been busy for nearly an hour.*

but /bʌt/ ► CONJUNCTION
1 used for joining two parts of a sentence which say different or opposite things □ *She eats fish but not meat.* □ *He's not very attractive but he's a nice guy.* □ *I can cycle but I can't drive.* □ *I'd like to come but I haven't got time.*
2 used after you have said 'excuse me' or 'I'm sorry' before you ask for something or give an explanation □ *I'm sorry, but I don't have time to help at the moment.*
3 used for showing surprise when someone has just told you something □ *'I don't like Nicole.' 'But I thought you were friends.'*
► PREPOSITION except □ *No one knows but you.*
► NOUN [plural **buts**] no buts used for telling

someone that they must do what you have told them to do □ *'But I'm too tired.' 'No buts! we're going!'*

butane /ˈbjuːteɪn/ NOUN, NO PLURAL a type of gas in liquid form that is used as a fuel for cooking. A chemistry word.

butch /bʌtʃ/ ADJECTIVE a butch woman looks and behaves like a man

butcher /ˈbʊtʃə(r)/ NOUN [plural **butchers**]
1 someone whose job is to cut up and sell raw meat
2 butcher's a shop that sells raw meat

butler /ˈbʌtlə(r)/ NOUN [plural **butlers**] a male servant who looks after a rich person, or who is responsible for the other servants in a rich person's house

butt /bʌt/ ► NOUN [plural **butts**]
1 the part of a cigarette that remains when someone has finished smoking it ⊞ *a cigarette butt*
2 the wide end of the handle of a gun
♦ IDIOM be the butt of something if you are the butt of people's jokes, you are the person they make jokes about
► VERB [**butts, butting, butted**] to hit someone or something using your head □ *He walked back towards his opponent and butted his chest.*
♦ PHRASAL VERB butt in to interrupt someone while they are talking □ *Sorry to butt in, but can I ask a question?*

butter /ˈbʌtə(r)/ ► NOUN, NO PLURAL a yellow food made from milk, used for spreading on bread or for cooking ⊞ *a slice of bread and butter*
► VERB [**butters, buttering, buttered**] to spread butter on something such as bread □ *Butter the bread evenly.*
♦ PHRASAL VERB butter someone up to say nice things to someone so that they will do what you want them to do. An informal phrase.

buttercup /ˈbʌtəkʌp/ NOUN [plural **buttercups**] a common wild flower with yellow petals

butterfly /ˈbʌtəflaɪ/ NOUN [plural **butterflies**] a type of insect with large brightly coloured wings
♦ IDIOM get/have butterflies (in your stomach) to have an uncomfortable feeling in your stomach because you are nervous

buttocks /ˈbʌtəkz/ PLURAL NOUN your bottom

button /ˈbʌtən/ ► NOUN [plural **buttons**]
1 a small object that you press in order to make a machine work ⊞ *I pressed the button to call the lift.* □ *Press the start button.*
2 a small round object used for fastening clothes ⊞ *He did up/undid (= fastened/unfastened) his buttons.*
► VERB [**buttons, buttoning, buttoned**] to fasten something with buttons □ *Button up your coat; it's cold out there.* □ *The dress buttons at the back.*

buttonhole /ˈbʌtənhəʊl/ NOUN [plural **buttonholes**] a hole that you push a button through to fasten your clothes

buy /baɪ/ ► VERB [**buys, buying, bought**] to get something by giving money for it □ *I've bought the* tickets. □ *Have you bought him a present?* □ *+ from We buy most of our food from the supermarket.*

♦ PHRASAL VERBS **buy into something** to start believing in something □ *More consumers are buying into the idea of organic food.* **buy something up** to buy large amounts of something □ *We bought up almost all the flowers in the shop.*

▶ NOUN [*plural* **buys**] **a good buy** something that is not expensive and is of good quality □ *At £11,000, this car is a really good buy.*

• **buyer** /'baɪə(r)/ NOUN [*plural* **buyers**] is someone who buys something □ *Have they found a buyer for their house?*

buzz /bʌz/ ▶ NOUN, NO PLURAL

1 an informal word that means excitement 🔁 *I get a real buzz from performing in public.*

2 energy and interest that a group of people feel □ *There's a definite buzz about the office since Jane arrived.*

3 the continuous sound that a large flying insect makes □ *The constant buzz of insects disturbed his sleep.*

▶ VERB [**buzzes, buzzing, buzzed**]

1 to make a continuous sound like a large flying insect □ *Flies buzzed round our heads.*

2 to be full of noise and activity □ *The store was buzzing with activity.*

3 if your head or mind is buzzing, you have a lot of ideas and cannot relax □ *I left the meeting, my head buzzing with ideas.*

♦ PHRASAL VERB **buzz about/around** to move around, doing a lot of different things □ *Sylvie was buzzing about trying to organize everything.*

• **buzzer** /'bʌzə(r)/ NOUN [*plural* **buzzers**] a small piece of equipment that makes a continuous sound in order to get your attention □ *When the buzzer goes can you take the cake out of the oven?*

buzzword /'bʌzwɜːd/ NOUN [*plural* **buzzwords**] a word that has become very popular, especially in newspapers, and on the radio and television

by /baɪ/ ▶ PREPOSITION

1 shows who or what does something □ *a painting by Picasso* □ *The house was built by her grandfather.* □ *I was taught by nuns.*

2 near or next to something □ *There's a café by the station.*

3 using something □ *We came by train.* □ *All their*

clothes are made by hand. □ *Can I pay by credit card?* □ *+ doing something By buying food from local shops you are supporting your community.*

4 past □ *A tall boy ran by me.*

5 by accident/chance without intending to □ *We met by chance.* □ *I only discovered it by accident.*

6 by 20%/£500, etc. shows how much something has increased or decreased □ *Prices have risen by 20 percent.* □

7 by the arm/coat, etc. shows which part of someone you take in your hand □ *She grabbed me by the hand.*

8 before □ *I'll be home by 7.30.*

9 used when giving measurements of length and width □ *The room is 5 metres by 3 metres.*

▶ ADVERB past □ *A car went speeding by.*

♦ IDIOM **by the way** used before you say something that is not related to what you were saying before

bye /baɪ/ EXCLAMATION an informal word that means goodbye □ *Bye - see you later!*

bye-bye /baɪ baɪ/ EXCLAMATION a word used by children that means goodbye

by-election /'baɪˌɪ'lekʃən/ NOUN [*plural* **by-elections**] an election that takes place in a particular area in order to choose a new member of parliament

bygone /'baɪɡɒn/ ADJECTIVE in the past 🔁 *She seemed to belong to a bygone age/era.*

by-law /'baɪˌlɔː/ NOUN [*plural* **by-laws**] a law made by local government

bypass /'baɪpɑːs/ ▶ NOUN [*plural* **bypasses**] a road around a town or city

▶ VERB [**bypasses, bypassing, bypassed**] to avoid something □ *The thieves managed to bypass the security system.*

by-product /'baɪˌprɒdʌkt/ NOUN [*plural* **by-products**] something that is produced as a result of making something else

bystander /'baɪˌstændə(r)/ NOUN [*plural* **bystanders**] someone who sees an accident or crime happen, but who is not involved in it 🔁 *She was an innocent bystander.*

byte /baɪt/ NOUN [*plural* **bytes**] a unit for measuring the size of a computer file. A computing word.

byword /'baɪwɜːd/ NOUN [*plural* **bywords**] a **byword for something** something that is known for a particular thing □ *The area soon became a byword for violence.*

Cc

C or **c**[1] /si:/ the third letter of the alphabet

C[2] /si:/ ABBREVIATION
1 Celsius
2 centigrade

cab /kæb/ NOUN [plural **cabs**]
1 a taxi ⌂ We took a cab to the airport.
2 the part at the front of a truck or bus where the driver sits □ I climbed up into the cab next to Dad.

cabaret /'kæbəreɪ/ NOUN [plural **cabarets**] a performance, usually of dance, songs or comedy, at a restaurant or club

cabbage /'kæbɪdʒ/ NOUN [plural **cabbages**] a large round green vegetable formed of tight layers of leaves

cabin /'kæbɪn/ NOUN [plural **cabins**]
1 a simple wooden house ⌂ He built a log cabin in the forest.
2 a small room for sleeping in on a ship
3 the part of an aeroplane which the passengers sit in

cabin crew /'kæbɪn ˌkru:/ NOUN [plural **cabin crews**] the people whose job is to look after the passengers on an aeroplane

cabinet /'kæbɪnɪt/ NOUN [plural **cabinets**]
1 Cabinet a group of people with important government jobs who decide what the government will do □ She became a member of the Cabinet in 1990. □ a Cabinet meeting
2 a cupboard with shelves, used for storing things or for showing attractive objects □ a bathroom cabinet

cable /'keɪbəl/ NOUN [plural **cables**]
1 a tube containing wires that carry electricity or electronic signals □ a telephone cable
2 thick, strong metal rope □ Miles of cable were used to build the bridge.
3 no plural a television service in which programmes are sent along underground wires □ We can't get cable or satellite here.

cable car /'keɪbəl ˌkɑː(r)/ NOUN [plural **cable cars**] a vehicle that hangs from a cable and is used to carry people up mountains

cable television /ˌkeɪbəl 'telɪvɪʒən/ NOUN, NO PLURAL a television service in which programmes are sent along underground wires

cache /kæʃ/ NOUN [plural **caches**]
1 a supply of something that is hidden or stored somewhere □ Police discovered a huge cache of weapons.
2 a place in a computer's memory where data that is often used is stored temporarily. A computing word.

cackle /'kækəl/ ▶ NOUN [plural **cackles**] a loud and unpleasant laugh
▶ VERB [**cackles, cackling, cackled**] to laugh in a loud and unpleasant way

cacophony /kə'kɒfənɪ/ NOUN, NO PLURAL a loud and unpleasant mixture of sounds

cactus /'kæktəs/ NOUN [plural **cactuses** or **cacti**] a plant with thick leaves and sharp points which grows in very dry places

CAD /kæd/ ABBREVIATION computer-aided design; when computers are used to help draw plans for things like buildings or machines □ We used a new CAD program.

cadet /kə'det/ NOUN [plural **cadets**] a young person who is training to be in the police, army, etc.

cadge /kædʒ/ VERB [**cadges, cadging, cadged**] to ask other people for money, food, etc. □ He's always cadging drinks off people.

caesarean /sɪ'zeərɪən/ NOUN [plural **caesareans**] an operation in which a baby is taken out of its mother's body through a cut in her stomach

caesium /'si:zɪəm/ NOUN, NO PLURAL a soft, silver-white element. A chemistry word.

café /'kæfeɪ/ NOUN [plural **cafés**] a small restaurant that serves drinks and things to eat

cafeteria /ˌkæfɪ'tɪərɪə/ NOUN [plural **cafeterias**] a restaurant where the customers buy food and drink and take it to a table to eat it

cafetière /ˌkæfɪtɪ'eə(r)/ NOUN [plural **cafetières**] a container for making coffee with a part that you push down

caffeine /'kæfi:n/ NOUN, NO PLURAL a substance in coffee and tea that makes you feel more awake

caftan /'kæftæn/ NOUN [plural **caftans**] a loose, light piece of clothing with long sleeves

cage /keɪdʒ/ ▶ NOUN [plural **cages**] a box or an area with bars around it for keeping birds or animals in □ The pet shop sells bird cages and hamster cages.
▶ VERB [**cages, caging, caged**] to put an animal or bird in a cage
● **caged** /keɪdʒd/ ADJECTIVE kept in a cage □ caged birds

cagey /'keɪdʒɪ/ ADJECTIVE [**cagier, cagiest**] careful not to say much about something □ *She is very cagey about her family.*

cagoule /kə'gu:l/ NOUN [*plural* **cagoules**] a light coat with a hood (=covering for the head) that protects you from the rain

cahoots /kə'hu:ts/ NOUN **in cahoots** if two or more people are in cahoots, they are planning something dishonest □ *The shop manager was in cahoots with the thieves.*

cajole /kə'dʒəul/ VERB [**cajoles, cajoling, cajoled**] to persuade someone to do something by being nice to them or by making promises to them □ *He had been cajoled into going with them.*

cake /keɪk/ NOUN [*plural* **cakes**] a sweet food made from a baked mixture, usually of flour, sugar, butter and eggs 🖻 *a birthday cake* 🖻 *He made a cake for the school fair.* 🖻 *Would you like another slice of chocolate cake?*

♦ IDIOM **have your cake and eat it** to get all the advantages of a situation in a way that is unfair
➜ **go to** the **icing** on the cake, a **piece** of cake

• **caked** /keɪkt/ ADJECTIVE **caked in something** covered in a thick, dry layer of something □ *His shoes were caked in mud.*

calamity /kə'læmətɪ/ NOUN [*plural* **calamities**] something that causes a lot of damage or suffering

calcium /'kælsɪəm/ NOUN, NO PLURAL a white chemical element in chalk (=soft white rock) and in bones and teeth. A chemistry word.

calculate /'kælkjuleɪt/ VERB [**calculates, calculating, calculated**]
1 to find out an amount by using mathematics □ *One apple costs 13p. Calculate the cost of 174 apples.* □ *Do you understand how they calculate tax?*
2 to guess something using all the facts that you have □ **+ that** *The teenagers had calculated that no one would be home for another two hours.*

• **calculated** /'kælkjuleɪtɪd/ ADJECTIVE
1 made or done after considering all the facts that you have 🖻 *I decided to take a calculated risk.*
2 **calculated to do something** intended to do something □ *His words had been calculated to hurt her.*

• **calculating** /'kælkjuleɪtɪŋ/ ADJECTIVE carefully planning how to get what you want, without caring about other people

• **calculation** /ˌkælkju'leɪʃən/ NOUN [*plural* **calculations**]
1 when you use mathematics to find out an amount 🖻 *I did some quick calculations to work out the total cost.* □ *By my calculation, we should be finished by Tuesday.*
2 *no plural* when you plan carefully to get what you want, without caring about other people □ *an act of cold calculation*

• **calculator** /'kælkjuleɪtə(r)/ NOUN [*plural* **calculators**] an electronic machine that you use for doing mathematical calculations 🖻 *a pocket calculator*

calendar /'kælɪndə(r)/ NOUN [*plural* **calendars**]
1 something that shows all the days, weeks and months of the year □ *She looked on the calendar to see what date it would be on Monday.*
2 **the Christian/Islamic, etc. calendar** the way in which the days and special events of the year are arranged in the Christian/Islamic, etc. tradition
3 **the school/political/sporting, etc. calendar** the events which usually happen in a school, in politics, in a sport, etc. in a year □ *The race is one of the most exciting events in the sporting calendar.*

calf /kɑ:f/ NOUN [*plural* **calves**]
1 the back part of your leg below the knee
2 a young cow

caliber /'kælɪbə(r)/ NOUN [*plural* **calibers**] the US spelling of **calibre**

calibre /'kælɪbə(r)/ NOUN [*plural* **calibres**]
1 the quality or ability of something or someone □ *We need a manager of the highest calibre.*
2 the width of a gun's barrel (=tube the bullet goes through)

call /kɔ:l/ ► VERB [**calls, calling, called**]
1 if a person or thing is called something, that is their name □ *He's called Jonathan James.*
2 to describe someone in a particular way □ *How dare you call me a liar!*
3 to shout □ *I heard him calling my name.*
4 to ask someone to come to you □ *Call the children in from the garden.*
5 to telephone someone □ *Have you called your mother yet?*
6 to visit someone □ **+ in** *We called in to see Maria this morning.* □ **+ round** *My neighbour called round yesterday.*

➤ Remember that the verb **call** meaning 'telephone' is used without 'to':
✓ *I called my brother to wish him happy birthday.*
✗ *I called to my brother to wish him happy birthday.*

♦ PHRASAL VERBS **call for something** to demand that something happens □ *Campaigners have called for changes to the law.* **call for someone** to go to someone's house in order to go somewhere with them □ *I'll call for you at seven.* **call something off** to stop a plan or an activity □ *The search has been called off.* **call someone up** a US word meaning to telephone someone □ *He called me up in the middle of the night.* **call something up** to find information on your computer screen □ *He called up lots of information about horses.*

► NOUN [*plural* **calls**]
1 when you contact someone by telephone 🖻 *Give me a call tomorrow.* 🖻 *I'm sure I can find someone to fix you car – let me make a few calls.*

2 a call for something a demand for something to happen □ *The prime minister is facing calls for his resignation.*
3 a shout □ *They ignored his calls for help.*
4 a short visit 🔁 *I thought I might pay you a call tomorrow.*

call centre /'kɔːl ˌsentə(r)/ NOUN [*plural* **call centres**] a place where people work using the telephone to take orders or answer questions from customers

caller /'kɔːlə(r)/ NOUN [*plural* **callers**]
1 someone who makes a telephone call □ *Several callers complained about the show.*
2 someone who visits your house for a short time

caller ID /ˌkɔːlər aɪˈdiː/ NOUN, NO PLURAL a system on a telephone that shows who is calling

calling /'kɔːlɪŋ/ NOUN [*plural* **callings**] a strong feeling that you should do a particular type of job □ *He had felt a calling to become a teacher.*

callous /'kæləs/ ADJECTIVE cruel □ *a callous thief*

calm /kaːm/ ▶ ADJECTIVE [**calmer, calmest**]
1 not nervous, excited or upset □ *Try to stay calm.* □ *"Yes," he said in a calm voice.*
2 if the sea is calm, it is flat with no big waves
3 if the weather is calm, there are no storms
▶ NOUN, NO PLURAL
1 a peaceful situation in which there is no fighting □ *The President appealed for calm.*
2 a state in which you are not nervous, excited or upset □ *Impatience had replaced his usual calm.*
3 when there is not much wind □ *the calm of the early morning air*
▶ VERB [**calms, calming, calmed**] to make someone feel calm □ *They calmed the animal by stroking it gently.*
◆ PHRASAL VERB **calm (someone) down** to stop someone being angry, excited or upset, or to stop being angry, excited or upset □ *She took a couple of deep breaths to calm herself down.* □ *Just calm down! Nobody's going to hurt you.*
● **calmly** /'kaːmlɪ/ ADVERB without seeming nervous or excited □ *Grace walked calmly on to the stage.*
● **calmness** /'kaːmnɪs/ NOUN, NO PLURAL the quality of being calm □ *We were impressed by his calmness under pressure.*

calorie /'kælərɪ/ NOUN [*plural* **calories**] a unit used to measure how much energy food will produce

calves /kaːvz/ PLURAL OF **calf**

camcorder /'kæmkɔːdə(r)/ NOUN [*plural* **camcorders**] a type of camera that records moving pictures and sound

came /keɪm/ PAST TENSE OF **come**

camel /'kæməl/ NOUN [*plural* **camels**] a large animal that lives in the desert and has one or two humps (=tall rounded parts) on its back

cameo /'kæmɪəʊ/ NOUN [*plural* **cameos**] a small part which a famous person has in a film 🔁 *Tyson made a cameo appearance in the movie.*

camera /'kæmərə/ NOUN [*plural* **cameras**] a device for taking photographs, or for making television programmes or films 🔁 *I have a digital camera.* 🔁 *He's very confident in front of the television cameras.*

camera crew /'kæmərə ˌkruː/ NOUN [*plural* **camera crews**] the people who operate the cameras which are used for making a film or a television programme

cameraman /'kæmərəmæn/ NOUN [*plural* **cameramen**] someone whose job is to operate a television camera or film camera

camisole /'kæmɪsəʊl/ NOUN [*plural* **camisoles**] a piece of women's underwear that covers the top part of the body

camomile /'kæməmaɪl/ NOUN, NO PLURAL a plant with yellow flowers, used in drinks and medicines

camouflage /'kæməflɑːʒ/ ▶ NOUN, NO PLURAL a way of making something or someone difficult to see because they look similar to what is around them
▶ VERB [**camouflages, camouflaging, camouflaged**] to make something or someone difficult to see because they look similar to what is around them □ *With its speckled coat, the leopard is perfectly camouflaged in the branches of a tree.*

camp /kæmp/ ▶ NOUN [*plural* **camps**] a place where people live in tents or temporary shelters, usually for a short time 🔁 *a holiday camp* 🔁 *a refugee camp* 🔁 *The boys set up camp in our field.*
▶ VERB [**camps, camping, camped**] to stay somewhere for a short time in a tent or caravan (=vehicle for living in) □ *We camped next to the lake.*

campaign /kæmˈpeɪn/ ▶ NOUN [*plural* **campaigns**]
1 a series of activities designed to achieve something □ *an advertising campaign* □ *an election campaign*
2 a series of military attacks □ *Her dad fought in the Falklands campaign.*
▶ VERB [**campaigns, campaigning, campaigned**] to try to make something happen by organizing a series of activities □ *They've been campaigning for better street lighting.*
● **campaigner** /kæmˈpeɪnə(r)/ NOUN [*plural* **campaigners**] someone who campaigns for something

camper /'kæmpə(r)/ NOUN [*plural* **campers**] someone who is staying in tent for a holiday

camper van /'kæmpər ˌvæn/ NOUN [*plural* **camper vans**] a vehicle that you can live in while you are on holiday

camping /'kæmpɪŋ/ NOUN, NO PLURAL the activity of staying in a tent 🔁 *We went camping in France last summer.* 🔁 *The boys are on a camping trip.*

campsite /'kæmpsaɪt/ NOUN [*plural* **campsites**] a place where people stay in tents for a holiday □ *We found a good campsite near the river.*

campus /'kæmpəs/ NOUN [plural **campuses**] the land and buildings that form a university or college

can¹ /kæn/ MODAL VERB

1 to be able to do something □ Can you swim? Yes, I can. □ Can you see my keys anywhere?
2 to be allowed to □ Can I go swimming? Yes, you can.
3 used to ask someone to do something or give you something □ Can you open the window, please? □ Can you lend me some money?
4 used to talk about whether something is possible □ Can you buy tickets here? □ Tiredness can cause accidents.

➤ **Can** is the present tense form. Use **could** for the past tense.

➤ To ask for something politely, do not use **can** but instead use **could**: □ Could I use this chair, please?

can² /kæn/ ➤ NOUN [plural **cans**]

1 a closed metal container that keeps food or drink fresh 🕀 a beer can 🕀 Do you recycle your tin cans? 🕀 She opened a can of beans.
2 a container used for liquid or other substances □ a paint can
➤ VERB [**cans, canning, canned**] to pack food or drink in closed metal cans that keep it fresh

canal /kə'næl/ NOUN [plural **canals**]

1 a long passage filled with water, made for boats to travel along □ the Panama Canal
2 a tube in the body that something passes through. A biology word □ the spinal canal □ The baby passes down the birth canal.

canary /kə'neərɪ/ NOUN [plural **canaries**] a small yellow bird that is often kept as a pet

cancel /'kænsəl/ VERB [**cancels, cancelling/US canceling, cancelled/US canceled**]

1 to say that a planned event will not happen □ The match was cancelled because of the snow.
2 to stop something from being done or paid, etc. □ Please cancel my order. □ The cheque has been cancelled.
♦ PHRASAL VERB **cancel something out** when two things cancel each other out, they stop each other from having any effect □ What I saved in the price was cancelled out by the postage cost.
● **cancellation** /ˌkænsə'leɪʃən/ NOUN [plural **cancellations**] when something that was planned is now cancelled □ the cancellation of train services □ You might get a seat on the flight if there are any late cancellations.

cancer /'kænsə(r)/ NOUN, NO PLURAL a serious disease in which some cells in the body start to grow very quickly □ Smoking can cause lung cancer. 🕀 Use sun cream – you don't want to get skin cancer. 🕀 The drug is used to treat cancer patients.

● **cancerous** /'kænsərəs/ ADJECTIVE affected by cancer 🕀 cancerous cells

candid /'kændɪd/ ADJECTIVE honest □ Sheena was very candid about the mistakes she'd made.

candidacy /'kændɪdəsɪ/ NOUN, NO PLURAL the state of being a candidate for something □ She has announced her candidacy for mayor.

candidate /'kændɪdət/ NOUN [plural **candidates**]

1 someone who is trying to get a job □ **+ for** There are three candidates for the job. □ The Democratic candidate for the US presidency is Barack Obama.
2 someone who is taking an exam □ All our GCSE candidates were successful.

candidly /'kændɪdlɪ/ ADVERB in a way that tells the truth □ He spoke candidly about what had gone wrong.

candle /'kændəl/ NOUN [plural **candles**] a stick of wax with a piece of string through the middle which produces a flame when you burn it 🕀 I must light the candles on the dinner table. 🕀 Don't forget to blow out the candle.

candlelight /'kændəllaɪt/ NOUN, NO PLURAL the light produced by a candle □ They had to read by candlelight.
● **candlelit** /'kændəllɪt/ ADJECTIVE with light from candles 🕀 a candlelit dinner

candlestick /'kændəlstɪk/ NOUN [plural **candlesticks**] an object which holds a candle

candor /'kændə(r)/ NOUN, NO PLURAL the US spelling of candour

candour /'kændə(r)/ NOUN, NO PLURAL the quality of speaking honestly, especially about something which is embarrassing or unpleasant □ She spoke with surprising candour about her addiction.

candy /'kændɪ/ NOUN [plural **candies**] the US word for sweet (=small piece of sweet food)

cane /keɪn/ NOUN [plural **canes**]

1 the hollow, hard stem of some plants
2 a stick that someone uses to help them walk

canine /'keɪnaɪn/ ADJECTIVE

1 to do with dogs, or like a dog □ She is an expert in canine behaviour.
2 a canine tooth is sharp and pointed. A biology word.

canister /'kænɪstə(r)/ NOUN [plural **canisters**] a metal container for storing something 🕀 The gas canisters exploded.

cannibal /'kænɪbəl/ NOUN [plural **cannibals**] a person who eats other people
● **cannibalism** /'kænɪbəlɪzəm/ NOUN, NO PLURAL eating other people

cannon /'kænən/ NOUN [plural **cannons**] a large gun that fires cannonballs or other large explosives

cannonball /'kænənbɔːl/ NOUN [plural **cannonballs**] a metal or stone ball that is fired from a cannon

cannot /'kænɒt/ MODAL VERB the negative form of can □ I just cannot do it.

➤ In spoken English, **can't** is usually used instead of 'cannot'. □ *I can't come tonight.*

canoe /kə'nu:/ ▶ NOUN [*plural* **canoes**] a light boat with pointed ends which you move through the water using a paddle (=stick with wide flat ends)

▶ VERB [**canoes, canoeing, canoed**] to move on water in a canoe

• **canoeing** /kə'nu:ɪŋ/ NOUN, NO PLURAL the activity of using a canoe □ *a canoeing holiday*

can opener /'kæn ˌəʊpənə(r)/ NOUN [*plural* **can openers**] a device used in the kitchen for opening cans of food

canopy /'kænəpɪ/ NOUN [*plural* **canopies**]
1 a covering that is hung above something □ *a canopy over a bed*
2 a covering layer that is formed by leaves and branches ⊞ *the thick forest canopy*

can't /kɑːnt/ a short way to say and write cannot □ *I can't hear you.*

cantankerous /kæn'tæŋkərəs/ ADJECTIVE bad-tempered □ *He was a cantankerous old man.*

canteen /ˌkæn'tiːn/ NOUN [*plural* **canteens**] a restaurant in a school or work place □ *I had lunch with my friends in the school canteen.*

canter /'kæntə(r)/ ▶ VERB [**canters, cantering, cantered**] when a horse canters, it runs slowly
▶ NOUN, NO PLURAL the speed of a horse when it canters

canvas /'kænvəs/ NOUN [*plural* **canvases**]
1 a piece of strong cloth stretched on a frame for an artist to paint on
2 strong cloth used to make tents and sails

canvass /'kænvəs/ VERB [**canvasses, canvassing, canvassed**]
1 to try to persuade people to vote for you □ *He's canvassing for the Green Party.*
2 to ask a lot of people for their opinions about something

canyon /'kænjən/ NOUN [*plural* **canyons**] a deep valley with steep sides. A geography word. □ *the Grand Canyon*

cap /kæp/ ▶ NOUN [*plural* **caps**]
1 a soft hat, often with a flat part that sticks out at the front ⊞ *The officer wore a peaked cap.* □ *a baseball cap*
2 a small top for a bottle, tube or pen ⊞ *a bottle with a screw cap* □ *The pen will dry up if you leave the cap off.*

▶ VERB [**caps, capping, capped**]
1 to set a top level or amount for something which you must not go above □ *+ at* *The interest rate has been capped at 2%.*
2 if a player is capped, they are asked to play for the country's national team in an international game of football, rugby or cricket □ *He's been capped eight times now.*

3 be capped with something to have a layer of something on top □ *The mountains were capped with snow.*

♦ IDIOM **to cap it all** to be the worst thing that happens after a lot of other bad things have happened

capability /ˌkeɪpə'bɪlətɪ/ NOUN [*plural* **capabilities**] ability or power to do something ⊞ *The task is simply beyond his capabilities.* □ *The country wants to develop its nuclear capability.*

capable /'keɪpəbəl/ ADJECTIVE
1 if you are capable of something, you are able to do it □ *The old lady isn't capable of looking after herself any more.*
2 able to do things and deal with problems without help □ *She's a very capable person.*

➤ Note that the structure that comes after **capable** is **of doing something**:
✓ *She isn't capable of looking after a small child.*
✗ *She isn't capable to look after a small child.*

• **capably** /'keɪpəblɪ/ ADVERB in a capable way □ *Mary did the job very capably.*

capacitor /kə'pæsɪtə(r)/ NOUN [*plural* **capacitors**] a device used to store electrical charge. A physics word.

capacity /kə'pæsətɪ/ NOUN [*plural* **capacities**]
1 the total amount that a container or building will hold ⊞ *The hall has a seating capacity of 300.* □ *Each barrel has a capacity of 100 litres.*
2 someone's ability to do or experience something □ *Flynn has the capacity to be a great leader.* □ *He obviously has a capacity for leadership.*
3 in your capacity as something as part of your job □ *Mrs Jones came to the meeting in her capacity as head teacher.*

cape /keɪp/ NOUN [*plural* **capes**]
1 a coat without sleeves that is tied at the neck
2 an area of land that goes out into the sea □ *the Cape of Good Hope*

caper /'keɪpə(r)/ NOUN [*plural* **capers**] a silly activity that makes people laugh □ *He enjoyed the cartoon capers of Tom and Jerry.*

capillary /kə'pɪlərɪ/ NOUN [*plural* **capillaries**] a very narrow tube in the body that carries blood. A biology word.

capital /'kæpɪtəl/ ▶ NOUN [*plural* **capitals**]
1 the city where the government of a state or country is □ *+ of* *London is the capital of England.*
2 a large letter such as *B* that you write at the beginning of a sentence, or at the beginning of a name □ *Write your name in capitals at the top of the page.* ⊞ *The notice was typed in capital letters.*
3 *no plural* money that can be used to make more money ⊞ *My grandmother invested a lot of capital in the business.*

▶ ADJECTIVE a capital crime is one for which the punishment is death ⊞ *Murder is still a capital offence in some states.*

• **capitalism** /'kæpɪtəlɪzəm/ NOUN, NO PLURAL a system in which businesses are owned by business people and not by the government

• **capitalist** /'kæpɪtəlɪst/ ▶ NOUN [plural **capitalists**] someone who supports capitalism
▶ ADJECTIVE a capitalist country or society has a system of capitalism

• **capitalize** or **capitalise** /'kæpɪtəlaɪz/ VERB [**capitalizes, capitalizing, capitalized**] to write or print a letter of the alphabet in its large form, for example *B* and not *b*

♦ PHRASAL VERB **capitalize on something** to use something that happens to get an advantage for yourself □ *With our best player injured, the other team will be keen to capitalize on the situation.*

capital punishment /ˌkæpɪtəl 'pʌnɪʃmənt/ NOUN, NO PLURAL when someone is killed by the state as their punishment for a crime

capitulate /kə'pɪtjuleɪt/ VERB [**capitulates, capitulating, capitulated**] to agree to something than you were fighting against before. A formal word. □ *They eventually capitulated to international pressure to release the prisoners.*

cappuccino /ˌkæpu'tʃiːnəʊ/ NOUN [plural **cappuccinos**] coffee made with hot milk full of bubbles

capricious /kə'prɪʃəs/ ADJECTIVE often changing your opinions and behaviour suddenly

capsize /kæp'saɪz/ VERB [**capsizes, capsizing, capsized**] if a boat capsizes, it turns upside down

capsule /'kæpsjuːl/ NOUN [plural **capsules**]
1 a very small container with medicine inside
2 the part of a spacecraft in which the astronauts (=people who travel into space) live

captain /'kæptɪn/ ▶ NOUN [plural **captains**]
1 the person in charge of a ship or an aircraft □ *Everyone must obey the captain's orders.*
2 the person in charge of a sports team □ *He is the new England captain.*
3 a person of middle rank in the army, high rank in the navy or high rank in the US police □ *Captain Jones*
▶ VERB [**captains, captaining, captained**]
1 to be the captain of a team □ *Flintoff will captain the English cricket team.*
2 to be in charge of a ship or an aircraft

• **captaincy** /'kæptɪnsɪ/ NOUN [plural **captaincies**] the job of being captain or someone's time as a captain

caption /'kæpʃən/ NOUN [plural **captions**] words written near a picture to describe what is in it

captivate /'kæptɪveɪt/ VERB [**captivates, captivating, captivated**] to interest or attract someone very much □ *He was captivated by her strength and beauty.*

• **captivating** /'kæptɪveɪtɪŋ/ ADJECTIVE very attractive and interesting □ *a captivating smile*

captive /'kæptɪv/ ▶ ADJECTIVE
1 kept in a prison or in a place you are not allowed to leave □ *a captive bird* ▣ *He was held captive for five months.*
2 a captive audience/market people who have to watch something or buy something because they have no choice
▶ NOUN [plural **captives**] a prisoner

• **captivity** /kæp'tɪvətɪ/ NOUN, NO PLURAL when a person or animal is kept in a place which they are not allowed to leave □ *The bear spent its whole life in captivity.*

captor /'kæptə(r)/ NOUN [plural **captors**] a person who is keeping someone a prisoner

capture /'kæptʃə(r)/ ▶ VERB [**captures, capturing, captured**]
1 to catch an animal or person and not allow them to escape □ *Many soldiers were captured by the enemy.*
2 to succeed in getting something which other people are also competing for □ *They soon captured a large share of the toy market.*
3 to get control of a place or equipment by force □ *Armed soldiers have captured the airport.*
4 capture someone's imagination/attention, etc. to make someone feel very interested □ *Her stories captured the imagination of both parents and children.*
5 to express something in a way that seems true and real □ *The description captures the beauty of the place.*
▶ NOUN, NO PLURAL
1 when you catch someone or something ▣ *How long can the killer avoid capture?*
2 when you take or get control of a place or equipment □ *the capture of enemy tanks*

car /kɑː(r)/ NOUN [plural **cars**]
1 a vehicle with an engine and seats for a small number of passengers □ *Many children travel to school by car.* ▣ *You need a licence before you can drive a car.* ▣ *Where did you park the car?* ▣ *I've lost the car keys.*
2 the US word for a train carriage

carafe /kə'ræf/ NOUN [plural **carafes**] a glass container with a wide opening at the top, used for serving wine or water

caramel /'kærəmel/ NOUN [plural **caramels**]
1 a soft sweet made from sugar, butter and milk
2 *no plural* sugar that has been heated until it goes brown

carapace /'kærəpeɪs/ NOUN [plural **carapaces**] the hard shell on the back of animals such as turtles and crabs. A biology word.

carat /'kærət/ NOUN [plural **carats**] a measurement used for weighing valuable stones such as diamonds, and for describing how pure gold is □ *18 carat gold*

caravan /'kærəvæn/ NOUN [plural **caravans**] a vehicle for living in, especially on holiday, which can be pulled behind a car

carbohydrate /ˌkɑːbəʊ'haɪdreɪt/ NOUN [plural **carbohydrates**] a substance in foods such as potatoes and bread which gives your body energy

carbon /'ka:bən/ NOUN, NO PLURAL a chemical element which is in all living things and in substances such as coal and oil. A chemistry word.

carbonated /'ka:bəneɪtɪd/ ADJECTIVE a carbonated drink contains a lot of small bubbles

carbon copy /,ka:bən 'kɒpɪ/ NOUN [plural **carbon copies**] an exact copy of something or someone 🕮 Sarah is a carbon copy of her mother.

carbon cycle /'ka:bən ,saɪkəl/ NOUN the carbon cycle the way carbon moves between living things and the air. A chemistry and biology word.

carbon dioxide /,ka:bən daɪ'ɒksaɪd/ NOUN, NO PLURAL a gas that is produced when people and animals breathe out and when carbon is burned. A chemistry word.

carbon emissions /'ka:bən ɪ,mɪʃənz/ PLURAL NOUN the amount of carbon that is released into the atmosphere from fuels such as coal and oil □ Several countries agreed to reduce their carbon emissions.

carbon footprint /,ka:bən 'fʊtprɪnt/ NOUN [plural **carbon footprints**] the amount of carbon produced by the way a person lives

carbon monoxide /,ka:bən mɒ'nɒksaɪd/ NOUN, NO PLURAL a poisonous gas with no smell which is made when some types of fuel burn. A chemistry word.

carbon neutral /,ka:bən 'nju:trəl/ ADJECTIVE if an activity or an organization is carbon neutral, it saves as much carbon as it produces

carbon offsetting /,ka:bən 'ɒfsetɪŋ/ NOUN, NO PLURAL activities such as planting trees that are intended to reduce carbon

car boot sale /,ka: 'bu:t ,seɪl/ NOUN [plural **car boot sales**] an event where people sell things from the back of their cars

carburetor /,ka:bə'retə(r)/ NOUN [plural **carburetors**] the US spelling of carburettor

carburettor /,ka:bə'retə(r)/ NOUN [plural **carburettors**] the part of a car engine which mixes air and fuel so that it burns and provides power

carcass /'ka:kəs/ NOUN [plural **carcasses**] a dead body of an animal

carcinogen /ka:'sɪnədʒən/ NOUN [plural **carcinogens**] a substance that can cause cancer

• **carcinogenic** /,ka:sɪnə'dʒenɪk/ ADJECTIVE causing cancer □ carcinogenic chemicals

card /ka:d/ NOUN [plural **cards**]

1 a piece of stiff paper with a picture and a message 🕮 a birthday/Christmas card 🕮 I must send her a card.

2 no plural thick stiff paper □ coloured card

3 a small flat piece of plastic that you can use in shops and machines to pay for things □ Can I pay by card? 🕮 a bank card

4 a small piece of stiff paper or plastic with information on it □ a library card □ Here's my business card.

5 one of a set of rectangular pieces of card used for playing games 🕮 I bought a pack of cards.

6 cards games that are played with a set of cards

🕮 Do you like playing cards?

◆ IDIOMS **on the cards** if something is on the cards, it is probably going to happen **put/lay your cards on the table** to tell someone the truth about your situation or your plans

cardboard /'ka:dbɔ:d/ NOUN, NO PLURAL very stiff thick paper used to make boxes and packages for goods 🕮 a cardboard box

cardiac /'ka:dɪæk/ ADJECTIVE to do with the heart. A biology word. □ a cardiac surgeon

cardiac arrest /,ka:dɪæk ə'rest/ NOUN [plural **cardiac arrests**] when someone's heart suddenly stops working

cardigan /'ka:dɪgən/ NOUN [plural **cardigans**] a piece of clothing for your upper body that is made from wool and fastens with buttons down the front

cardinal¹ /'ka:dɪnəl/ NOUN [plural **cardinals**] a priest of high rank in the Roman Catholic Church

cardinal² /'ka:dɪnəl/ ADJECTIVE

1 cardinal numbers are numbers like one, two, three, not first, second, third. A maths word.

2 very important or basic 🕮 One of the cardinal rules of travel is to make sure you have your tickets.

cardiologist /,ka:dɪ'ɒlədʒɪst/ NOUN [plural **cardiologists**] a doctor who treats people with heart problems

• **cardiology** /,ka:dɪ'ɒlədʒɪ/ NOUN, NO PLURAL the area of medicine that deals with the heart

cardiovascular /,ka:dɪəʊ'væskjʊlə(r)/ ADJECTIVE to do with the heart and the tubes that carry blood around your body. A biology word.

care /keə(r)/ ► NOUN [plural **cares**]

1 no plural looking after someone 🕮 They need urgent medical care. 🕮 The care he received in hospital was excellent.

2 take care of someone/something to look after someone or something □ Their aunt took care of them after their parents died.

3 no plural when you give something a lot of attention or effort 🕮 Meg does her work with great care. 🕮 She took a lot of care over her appearance.

4 take care to be careful not to have an accident or make a mistake □ You must take care to lock all the doors. □ Take care – the roads are very icy!

5 something that makes you worried or unhappy 🕮 She was humming to herself as if she didn't have a care in the world.

6 in care children who are in care are being looked after by a local government department because their parents cannot look after them

► VERB [**cares, caring, cared**]

1 to think that something is interesting or important □ + *question word* He said he didn't care what happened. □ + *about* I don't care about your holiday plans – we've got work to do!

2 to feel love or affection for someone □ + *for* He really cares for his staff.

3 I/he/they, etc. **couldn't care less** an informal

phrase used to show that you do not think something is at all interesting or important □ *I couldn't care less what my Dad will say.*

4 Who cares? an informal phrase used to show that you do not think something is at all interesting or important

◆ PHRASAL VERB **care for someone/something** to look after a person or an animal □ *Sarah wants to be a vet so that she can care for sick animals.*

career /kə'rɪə(r)/ ► NOUN [plural **careers**] a job or type of work that you train for and continue doing for a long time □ + *in* *a career in the police force* □ *a teaching career* □ *We both chose law as a career.*

► VERB [**careers, careering, careered**] to move very quickly and without control □ *The car careered into a lamppost.*

carefree /'keəfriː/ ADJECTIVE having no worries □ *a carefree attitude* □ *a carefree life*

careful /'keəfʊl/ ADJECTIVE making sure that you do something correctly or safely 🖫 *Be careful when you cross the road.* □ + *to do something* *Dad is always careful to lock all the doors.*

● **carefully** /'keəfʊlɪ/ ADVERB without making mistakes or causing damage □ *Greta wrapped up the glass carefully in tissue paper.*

careless /'keəlɪs/ ADJECTIVE not being careful 🖫 *a careless mistake* □ *Alex is a bit careless with his money.*

● **carelessly** /'keəlɪslɪ/ ADVERB in a careless way □ *He threw the letter aside carelessly.*

● **carelessness** /'keəlɪsnɪs/ NOUN, NO PLURAL being careless

carer /'keərə(r)/ NOUN [plural **carers**] someone who looks after a child, an old person or an ill person

caress /kə'res/ ► VERB [**caresses, caressing, caressed**] to touch something or someone gently or with love □ *Her hand caressed the child's face.*

► NOUN [plural **caresses**] a gentle or loving touch

caretaker /'keəteɪkə(r)/ NOUN [plural **caretakers**] someone whose job is to look after a building □ *a school caretaker*

cargo /'kɑːgəʊ/ NOUN [plural **cargoes**] the things that a vehicle is carrying □ *The ship had a cargo of sugar and coffee.*

caricature /'kærɪkə,tʃʊə(r)/ ► NOUN [plural **caricatures**] a picture or a description of someone that makes their features stronger than they really are, often to make them seem funny

► VERB [**caricatures, caricaturing, caricatured**] to draw or describe someone in a way that makes their features stonger than they really are

caring /'keərɪŋ/ ADJECTIVE

1 kind and showing attention and affection □ *a caring father*

2 the caring professions jobs such as nursing that involve looking after people

carnage /'kɑːnɪdʒ/ NOUN, NO PLURAL when a lot of people are killed or injured □ *a scene of absolute carnage*

carnation /kɑː'neɪʃən/ NOUN [plural **carnations**] a pink or white flower with a long stem

carnival /'kɑːnɪvəl/ NOUN [plural **carnivals**] a celebration when people sing and dance outdoors wearing special clothes

carnivore /'kɑːnɪvɔː(r)/ NOUN [plural **carnivores**] an animal that eats meat. A biology word.

● **carnivorous** /kɑː'nɪvərəs/ ADJECTIVE eating meat. A biology word. □ *Tyrannosaurus rex was a huge carnivorous dinosaur.*

carol /'kærəl/ NOUN [plural **carols**] a song sung at Christmas □ *carol singing*

carotid artery /kə,rɒtɪd ,ɑːtərɪ/ NOUN [plural **carotid arteries**] either of the two tubes in your neck that take blood from your heart to your head. A biology word.

carousel /,kærə'sel/ NOUN [plural **carousels**] a moving surface from which you collect your bags in an airport

carp [1] /kɑːp/ NOUN [plural **carp**] a large fish that lives in lakes and rivers

carp [2] /kɑːp/ VERB [**carps, carping, carped**] to complain a lot in a way that is annoying □ *He was carping about the cost of everything.*

car park /kɑːr 'pɑːk/ NOUN [plural **car parks**] a building or place where cars can be left □ *The car park was full.*

carpel /'kɑːpəl/ NOUN [plural **carpels**] the female part of a flower. A biology word.

carpenter /'kɑːpəntə(r)/ NOUN [plural **carpenters**] someone whose job is to make things from wood

● **carpentry** /'kɑːpəntrɪ/ NOUN, NO PLURAL making things from wood

carpet /'kɑːpɪt/ ► NOUN [plural **carpets**]

1 a covering for a floor made of wool or a similar material □ *Don't get mud on the carpet.*

2 a carpet of something a soft layer of something covering the ground □ *a carpet of leaves*

► VERB [**carpets, carpeting, carpeted**] to cover an area with a carpet

carriage /'kærɪdʒ/ NOUN [plural **carriages**]

1 one of the long parts of a train where passengers si*

2 a vehicle with wheels that is pulled by horses

carriageway /'kærɪdʒweɪ/ NOUN [plural **carriageways**] one of the two sides of a big road or motorway, that are each used by traffic travelling in one direction □ *There's heavy traffic on the northbound carriageway.*

carrier /'kærɪə(r)/ NOUN [plural **carriers**]

1 a vehicle or company which moves people or thing* from one place to another □ *British Airways is one o*▶ *Britain's transatlantic carriers.*

2 someone who can pass a disease to another person but does not have it themselves

carrier bag /'kærɪə ˌbæg/ NOUN [plural **carrier bags**] a plastic or paper bag with handles

carrot /'kærət/ NOUN [plural **carrots**] a long orange vegetable that grows under the ground

carry /'kæri/ VERB [**carries, carrying, carried**]
1 to pick something up and take it somewhere □ This suitcase is too heavy for me to carry. □ You may only carry one bag onto the plane.
2 to have something with you in your hand, your pocket, etc. □ The robber was carrying a gun. □ Why were you carrying so much on you? □ **+ around** Do you have to carry that umbrella around with you?
3 to take something from one place to another □ The ship was carrying over 3,000 soldiers. □ Water is carried to the buildings in huge pipes.
4 when sound carries, it can be heard from a long way away □ His voice really carries.
5 to support the weight of something □ The bridge won't carry the weight of heavy lorries.
6 to have a particular result □ Credit card fraud can carry heavy penalties (=the punishment can be severe). □ Skiing carries the risk of injury.
7 to be responsible for something □ He had to carry the burden of his family's debts.
8 if a person or an animal carries a disease, they can pass it on to others □ These insects carry malaria.
◆ IDIOM **get carried away** to become too excited or enthusiastic □ I got carried away and bought three new pairs of shoes.
◆ PHRASAL VERBS **carry something off** to do something successfully □ The part of Lady Macbeth is a challenge, but she carried it off magnificently. **carry on 1** to continue □ **+ with** Carry on with your work while I go and see the headmaster. □ **+ ing** When the noise stopped, our guide was able to carry on speaking. **2** to go further in the same direction □ Carry on to the end of the road, then turn left. **3** to behave in a silly way □ Do stop carrying on like children, you two, please! **carry out something 1** to do a task □ carry out research/an experiment **2** to do something that you have said you will do 🕮 Will the terrorists manage to carry out their threat?

carrycot /'kærɪkɒt/ NOUN [plural **carrycots**] a small bed for a baby, with handles so that it can be carried

carry-on /ˌkærɪ'ɒn/ NOUN, NO PLURAL an informal word meaning a lot of unnecessary worry or excitement □ Really, what a carry-on! It's only her sister arriving, not the Queen.

cart /kɑːt/ ▶ NOUN [plural **carts**]
1 a vehicle for goods which is pulled by a horse 🕮 a horse and cart
2 the US word for trolley (=basket on wheels used in a supermarket)
▶ VERB [**carts, carting, carted**] an informal word meaning to take someone or something somewhere □ He fell and had to be carted off to hospital.

carte blanche /ˌkɑːt 'blɑ̃ʃ/ NOUN, NO PLURAL if you give someone carte blanche, you allow them to do what they want □ The new sales manager was given carte blanche to reorganize the whole sales team.

cartel /kɑː'tel/ NOUN [plural **cartels**] a group of businesses who agree to sell something at the same price so they all make a profit

cartilage /'kɑːtɪlɪdʒ/ NOUN, NO PLURAL a strong substance that bends, which is around bones in your knee, elbow, etc. A biology word.

carton /'kɑːtən/ NOUN [plural **cartons**] a box for food or drink that is made of cardboard □ a carton of milk

cartoon /kɑː'tuːn/ NOUN [plural **cartoons**]
1 a funny drawing or series of drawings in a newspaper or magazine
2 a film made from a long series of drawings 🕮 Mickey Mouse is a cartoon character.
● **cartoonist** /kɑː'tuːnɪst/ NOUN [plural **cartoonists**] someone who draws cartoons

cartridge /'kɑːtrɪdʒ/ NOUN [plural **cartridges**]
1 a small container that fits inside a piece of equipment and contains something such as film or ink 🕮 Do you know how to replace the ink cartridge in the printer?
2 a tube containing a bullet that goes inside a gun

cartwheel /'kɑːtwiːl/ NOUN [plural **cartwheels**] a movement in which you turn your body sideways onto your hands and your feet go up into the air, over your head

carve /kɑːv/ VERB [**carves, carving, carved**]
1 to make something by cutting wood, stone, etc. □ There are angels carved out of stone.
2 to cut meat into thin flat pieces using a sharp knife
3 to be successful in a particular job or activity □ She carved out a successful career as a literary agent.
◆ PHRASAL VERB **carve something up** to divide something in a way that seems wrong □ The countryside has been carved up for housing developers.
● **carving** /'kɑːvɪŋ/ NOUN [plural **carvings**]
1 an object made by cutting wood, stone, etc. 🕮 He does beautiful wood carvings.
2 the activity or skill of making objects by cutting wood, stone, etc.

carving knife /'kɑːvɪŋ ˌnaɪf/ NOUN [plural **carving knives**] a long, sharp knife used for cutting meat

cascade /kæ'skeɪd/ ▶ VERB [**cascades, cascading, cascaded**] to flow down or hang down in large amounts □ Water cascaded down the hillside.
▶ NOUN [plural **cascades**] a large amount of something which hangs or flows down

case /keɪs/ NOUN [plural **cases**]
1 a situation or an example of a particular situation □ Inspectors are examining several cases of cruelty to animals. 🕮 This is a classic case of failure to communicate. 🕮 You haven't got any money? In that case, you'd better get a job.
2 the case the true situation □ Is it the case that you

have never owned a passport? □ *If that's the case, you may as well sell it.*

3 (just) in case because of the possibility of something □ *I don't think it's going to rain, but I'll take my umbrella just in case.*

4 in my/his, etc. case according to someone's particular situation □ *Most people gave up the course through boredom, but in my case it was because I was too busy.*

5 in any case whatever happens or whatever a situation is □ *Hopefully the game will be exciting, but in any case it will be a new experience for me.*

6 a crime that the police are trying to solve □ *a murder case*

7 something that is being decided in a court 🖽*a court case* 🖽 *He won his case for unfair dismissal.*

8 when someone has a particular disease, or a person with that disease □ *Doctors are reporting an increase in the number of flu cases.*

9 a container for something □ *a violin case* □ *The crown jewels are in a glass case.*

10 a suitcase (=large container for carrying clothes on holiday) 🖽 *Have you packed your case yet?*

11 facts that prove an opinion or support one side in an argument 🖽 *He put the case for increased spending.* □ **+ for** *There is a strong case for allowing children more freedom.* □ **+ against** *She argued the case against building a new road.*

cash /kæʃ/ ▶ NOUN, NO PLURAL

1 money in the form of paper money and coins □ *The gardener likes to be paid in cash.*

2 money 🖽 *I'm rather short of cash* (=I haven't got much money).

▶ VERB [**cashes, cashing, cashed**] to cash a cheque is to change it for paper money or coins

♦ PHRASAL VERB **cash in on something** to make a profit from a situation, often in an unfair way □ *She quickly cashed in on her son's success by doing magazine articles and television interviews.*

cashback /'kæʃbæk/ NOUN, NO PLURAL if you get cashback when you buy things in a shop, you get money as well as your shopping □ *Do you want any cashback?*

cash card /'kæʃ ˌkɑːd/ NOUN [plural **cash cards**] a small plastic card that you use to buy things and to get money from machines

cash desk /'kæʃ ˌdesk/ NOUN [plural **cash desks**] a place where you go to pay for things in a shop

cashew /'kæʃuː/ NOUN [plural **cashews**] a curved nut that you can eat

cash flow /'kæʃ ˌfləʊ/ NOUN [plural **cash flows**] the rate at which money is received and spent by a business or organization

cashier /kæˈʃɪə(r)/ NOUN [plural **cashiers**] someone in a bank or shop whose job is to take and pay out money

cash machine /'kæʃ məˌʃiːn/ NOUN [plural **cash machines**] a machine, usually in the wall outside a bank, where you can get money using a small plastic card

cashmere /'kæʃmɪə(r)/ NOUN, NO PLURAL a very soft type of wool □ *a cashmere sweater.*

cashpoint /'kæʃpɔɪnt/ NOUN [plural **cashpoints**] a machine, usually in the wall outside a bank, where you can get money using a small plastic card

cash register /'kæʃ ˌredʒɪstə(r)/ NOUN [plural **cash registers**] a machine used in a shop to record and store the money paid by customers

casino /kəˈsiːnəʊ/ NOUN [plural **casinos**] a building where people play games in which they lose or win money

casket /'kɑːskɪt/ NOUN [plural **caskets**]
1 a small decorated box for keeping things in
2 the US word for **coffin**

casserole /'kæsərəʊl/ NOUN [plural **casseroles**]
1 a dish with a cover for cooking and serving food
2 a mixture of vegetables, meat, etc. cooked in a casserole □ *a beef casserole*

cassette /kəˈset/ NOUN [plural **cassettes**] a plastic case that contains music or pictures recorded on a long magnetic strip

cassette player /kəˈset ˌpleɪə(r)/ or **cassette recorder** /kəˌset rɪˈkɔːdə(r)/ NOUN [plural **cassette players** or **cassette recorders**] a machine for playing or recording sound using cassettes

cast /kɑːst/ ▶ VERB [**casts, casting, cast**]
1 to choose the actors who will be in a play or a film □ *He was cast as Shylock in The Merchant of Venice.*
2 if something casts light or a shadow somewhere, it makes it go there □ *The lamp cast light onto the desk.*
3 when you cast your vote, you vote for someone or something
4 cast doubt/suspicion on someone/something to make people think that someone or something cannot be trusted
5 cast a spell on someone/something to use magic on someone or something
6 a formal word meaning to throw □ *They were cast into prison.*

♦ IDIOM **cast a pall over something** to spoil an event or a situation □ *News of his death cast a pall over the celebrations.*

▶ NOUN [plural **casts**]
1 *no plural* the actors in a play or a film □ *a member of the cast*
2 a hard covering that is put on a broken arm or leg

castanets /ˌkæstəˈnets/ PLURAL NOUN a musical instrument made of two pieces of wood or plastic that you hold in your hand to make a clicking sound

castaway /'kɑːstəweɪ/ NOUN [plural **castaways**] someone who has been left alone on an island, usually after a ship sinks

caste /kɑːst/ NOUN [plural **castes**] a social class in Hindu society

caster sugar /'kɑːstə ˌʃʊgə(r)/ NOUN, NO PLURAL sugar with very small grains, used in cooking

castigate /'kæstɪgeɪt/ VERB [**castigates, castigating, castigated**] a formal word meaning to criticize someone severely □ *The minister responsible for the error was castigated by the prime minister.*

cast iron /ˌkɑːst ˈaɪən/ NOUN, NO PLURAL a type of very hard iron

• **cast-iron** ADJECTIVE

1 made of cast iron □ *There were cast-iron bars on the windows.*

2 very strong or impossible to doubt □ *This is not a cast-iron guarantee.*

castle /ˈkɑːsəl/ NOUN [plural **castles**]

1 a large building with high walls and towers, which was built to protect people from attack □ *Edinburgh Castle stands high above the city.* □ *We visited a ruined castle built by the Normans.*

2 a piece in the game of chess that looks like a castle

cast-offs /ˈkɑːstɒfs/ PLURAL NOUN clothes that people give away because they do not want them

castor sugar /ˈkɑːstə ˌʃʊɡə(r)/ NOUN, NO PLURAL another spelling of **caster sugar**

castrate /kæˈstreɪt/ VERB [castrates, castrating, castrated] to remove the sexual organs from a male animal

• **castration** /kæˈstreɪʃən/ NOUN, NO PLURAL the practice of castrating male animals

casual /ˈkæʒuəl/ ADJECTIVE

1 not formal □ *casual clothes* □ *She runs the hotel in quite a casual and relaxed style.*

2 not serious □ *He has had several casual relationships since his divorce.* □ *I worry about Sarita's casual attitude to her work.*

3 not planned, or with no particular meaning or importance □ *It was just a casual remark – I shouldn't have said anything.*

4 not permanent □ *casual work* 🔁 *The factory uses a lot of casual labour* (=temporary workers).

• **casually** /ˈkæʒuəlɪ/ ADVERB in a casual way □ *Most of the guests were casually dressed.*

casualty /ˈkæʒjuəltɪ/ NOUN [plural **casualties**]

1 someone who has been injured or killed □ *Ambulances rushed the casualties to hospital.*

2 the old name for **Accident and Emergency**; the hospital department that deals with people who have been injured or have suddenly become ill

3 something that has been damaged or no longer exists because of something else □ *Our local library was a casualty of the government spending cuts.*

cat /kæt/ NOUN [plural **cats**]

1 an animal which people keep as a pet, which catches mice and birds □ *I stroked the cat and it purred happily.*

2 a wild animals such as a lion, that belongs to the same family as the cat 🔁 *One of my favourite big cats is the snow leopard.*

➜ go to **let** the cat out of the bag

catalog /ˈkætəlɒɡ/ NOUN [plural **catalogs**], VERB [catalogs, cataloging, catalogued] the US spelling of **catalogue**

catalogue /ˈkætəlɒɡ/ ▶ NOUN [plural **catalogues**]

1 a book that shows the products you can buy from a company 🔁 *Mum got me some jeans from a mail order catalogue.*

2 a list of all the books or objects in a collection

3 a **catalogue of something** a series of bad things 🔁 *Their holiday seems to have been a catalogue of disasters.*

▶ VERB [catalogues, cataloguing, catalogued] to make a list of all the things in a collection

catalyst /ˈkætəlɪst/ NOUN [plural **catalysts**]

1 a substance which makes a chemical reaction happen more quickly but which does not change itself. A chemistry word.

2 something that makes a change happen □ *a catalyst for social change*

catalytic converter /ˌkætəlɪtɪk kənˈvɜːtə(r)/ NOUN [plural **catalytic converters**] a device that stops harmful gases from a car's engine being released into the air

catamaran /ˌkætəməˈræn/ NOUN [plural **catamarans**] a type of boat that looks like two boats joined together

catapult /ˈkætəpʌlt/ ▶ VERB [catapults, catapulting, catapulted]

1 to throw something or someone forward forcefully □ *The bike hit a rock and Tom was catapulted over the handlebars.*

2 to suddenly put someone into a new situation 🔁 *The TV show catapulted her to fame.*

▶ NOUN [plural **catapults**] a weapon for firing small stones, made from a stick and rubber which stretches

cataract /ˈkætərækt/ NOUN [plural **cataracts**] an eye condition in which someone gradually loses their ability to see

catarrh /kəˈtɑː(r)/ NOUN, NO PLURAL the thick substance in your nose and throat when you have a cold

catastrophe /kəˈtæstrəfɪ/ NOUN [plural **catastrophes**] an event that causes a lot of damage or suffering □ *The government has plans for dealing with floods and other natural catastrophes.*

• **catastrophic** /ˌkætəˈstrɒfɪk/ ADJECTIVE causing a lot of damage or suffering □ *The plane suffered catastrophic engine failure.*

catch /kætʃ/ ▶ VERB [catches, catching, caught]

1 to stop and hold something that is moving through the air □ *Throw the ball and I'll try to catch it.*

2 to stop a person or animal from escaping □ *James caught a huge fish.* □ *Police managed to catch the escaped prisoners.*

3 to get an illness □ *Most people catch between two and four colds a year.*

4 to get on a bus, train, etc. □ *I left early so that I could catch the 8.30 train.*

5 to discover someone doing something, especially something that they should not do □ *+ ing I caught*

him taking some money from my purse. □ *You wouldn't catch me wearing a silly hat like that.*
6 to become stuck on something, or to make something become stuck on something else □ *Sam caught his sleeve on the door handle.*
7 catch fire to start burning □ *The plane caught fire after its tyre burst on landing.*
8 catch sight of someone/something to see someone or something for a short time □ *I just managed to catch sight of the queen.*
9 not catch something used as a polite way of saying that you did not hear what someone said □ *I'm sorry, I didn't catch your name.*
➔ go to **catch someone's eye**
◆ PHRASAL VERBS **catch on** to become popular □ *The style never really caught on.* **catch someone out** to cause someone to make a mistake by tricking them
catch (someone/something) up
1 to reach someone or something that is in front of you by moving faster than them □ *We ran to catch the others up.*
2 to get to the same level as someone or something □ *When children miss a lot of school, it can be difficult for them to catch up with the others.*
▶ NOUN [*plural* **catches**]
1 when someone stops and holds something that was moving through the air □ *That was a brilliant catch!*
2 a problem that is not obvious immediately □ *The holiday was supposed to be free, but there was a catch, of course.*
3 the part on a door, chain, etc. that fastens it □ *The catch on my bracelet has broken.*
4 the number of fish someone has caught
● **catching** /ˈkætʃɪŋ/ ADJECTIVE if an illness is catching, other people can get it from you □ *I hope that sore throat you have isn't catching.*

catchment area /ˈkætʃmənt ˌeərɪə/ NOUN [*plural* **catchment areas**] an area from which a particular school gets its students

catchphrase /ˈkætʃfreɪz/ NOUN [*plural* **catchphrases**] a phrase that an entertainer uses repeatedly and that people remember

catchy /ˈkætʃɪ/ ADJECTIVE [**catchier, catchiest**] a catchy tune is one that you remember easily

categorical /ˌkætɪˈɡɒrɪkəl/ ADJECTIVE clear and emphasizing what you mean ⊞ *He gave a categorical assurance that no jobs would be lost.*
● **categorically** /ˌkætɪˈɡɒrɪkəlɪ/ ADVERB in a clear way which emphasizes what you mean ⊞ *He categorically denied any involvement in the crime.*

categorize or **categorise** /ˈkætəɡəraɪz/ VERB [**categorizes, categorizing, categorized**] to group people or things together by their type, size, age, etc. ⊞ *The plants are categorized according to their medical uses.*

category /ˈkætəɡərɪ/ NOUN [*plural* **categories**] a group of people or things of the same type ⊞ *Our members tend to fall into one of three categories.*

cater /ˈkeɪtə(r)/ VERB [**caters, catering, catered**] to prepare and supply food □ *We are catering for 100 guests.*
◆ PHRASAL VERB **cater for someone/something** to provide what is wanted or needed □ *We try to provide courses that cater for every age group.*
● **caterer** /ˈkeɪtərə(r)/ NOUN [*plural* **caterers**] a person or business whose job is to prepare and supply food at an event □ *We hired a caterer for the wedding.*
● **catering** /ˈkeɪtərɪŋ/ NOUN, NO PLURAL the job of preparing and supplying food ⊞ *We hired someone to do the catering.* □ *Marcus is doing a catering course.*

caterpillar /ˈkætəpɪlə(r)/ NOUN [*plural* **caterpillars**] a small soft animal that eats leaves and later becomes a butterfly (=insect with large colourful wings)

cat flap /ˈkæt ˌflæp/ NOUN [*plural* **cat flaps**] a small door for a cat to use

cathartic /kəˈθɑːtɪk/ ADJECTIVE helping you to express feelings and feel better □ *a cathartic experience*

cathedral /kəˈθiːdrəl/ NOUN [*plural* **cathedrals**] a large and important church □ *St Paul's Cathedral in London*

cathode /ˈkæθəʊd/ NOUN [*plural* **cathodes**] the positive electrode (=part where an electric current enters or leaves) in a battery. A physics word.

Catholic /ˈkæθlɪk/ ▶ ADJECTIVE to do with, or belonging to, the Roman Catholic Church □ *a Catholic priest*
▶ NOUN [*plural* **Catholics**] a member of the Roman Catholic Church
● **Catholicism** /kəˈθɒlɪsɪzəm/ NOUN, NO PLURAL the beliefs and practices of Catholics

Catseye /ˈkætsaɪ/ NOUN [*plural* **Catseyes**] a small object in the road surface which reflects light to help drivers at night. A trademark.

cattle /ˈkætəl/ PLURAL NOUN male and female cows on a farm □ *cattle farmers*

catty /ˈkætɪ/ ADJECTIVE [**cattier, cattiest**] an informal word meaning deliberately unkind □ *catty remarks*

catwalk /ˈkætwɔːk/ NOUN [*plural* **catwalks**] the path that models walk down at a fashion show

caught /kɔːt/ PAST TENSE AND PAST PARTICIPLE OF catch

cauldron /ˈkɔːldrən/ NOUN [*plural* **cauldrons**] a big old-fashioned container for cooking over a fire □ *a witch's cauldron*

cauliflower /ˈkɒlɪflaʊə(r)/ NOUN [*plural* **cauliflowers**] a round vegetable with green leaves around a hard white centre

cause /kɔːz/ ▶ VERB [**causes, causing, caused**] to make something happen □ *Do they know what caused the accident?* □ *Strong winds caused problems on the roads.* □ *+ to do something Unfortunately the delay caused me to miss my appointment.*
▶ NOUN [*plural* **causes**]
1 what makes something happen □ *There are many causes of poverty.* □ *The engineer can't find the cause of the problem.*
2 something that people support because they believe

it is good or useful ⊞ *She collects money for many good causes.*
3 a reason ⊞ *Her behaviour has never been a cause for concern before.*

causeway /'kɔːzweɪ/ NOUN [plural **causeways**] a raised road over shallow water or wet ground

caustic /'kɔːstɪk/ ADJECTIVE
1 a caustic remark is unkind
2 a caustic substance can burn things

caution /'kɔːʃən/ ▶ NOUN [plural **cautions**]
1 *no plural* when you take care to avoid danger or risk □ *Please drive with caution.*
2 an official warning from the police □ *The police let him off with a caution.*
▶ VERB [**cautions, cautioning, cautioned**]
1 a formal word meaning to warn someone □ *They cautioned us against swimming in the sea.*
2 if the police caution someone, they give them an official warning
• **cautionary** /'kɔːʃənərɪ/ ADJECTIVE giving a warning about something bad which can happen ⊞ *Her experience is a cautionary tale of the potential dangers of the Internet.*
• **cautious** /'kɔːʃəs/ ADJECTIVE very careful to avoid danger or risk □ *He's very cautious with his money.*
• **cautiously** /'kɔːʃəslɪ/ ADVERB in a cautious way □ *She stepped cautiously onto the ice.*

cavalier /ˌkævə'lɪə(r)/ ADJECTIVE if you have a cavalier attitude to something, you do not treat it carefully or seriously

cavalry /'kævəlrɪ/ NOUN, NO PLURAL soldiers who ride on horses

cave /keɪv/ NOUN [plural **caves**] a large hole in a mountain or under the ground □ *The cave was dark and damp.*
♦ PHRASAL VERB [**caves, caving, caved**] **cave in**
1 if a roof caves in, it falls down to the ground
2 to agree to something that you were against before □ *I've finally caved in to my daughter's pleas for a pet.*

caveman /'keɪvmæn/ NOUN [plural **cavemen**] someone who lived in a cave at the time when humans first existed

cavern /'kævən/ NOUN [plural **caverns**] a large cave
• **cavernous** /'kævənəs/ ADJECTIVE large and dark □ *a cavernous room*

caviar /'kævɪɑː(r)/ NOUN, NO PLURAL an expensive food that is the eggs of a large fish

caving /'keɪvɪŋ/ NOUN, NO PLURAL the sport of climbing through caves under the ground

cavity /'kævɪtɪ/ NOUN [plural **cavities**]
1 a space inside something □ *the chest cavity*
2 a hole in a tooth, caused by decay

cavort /kə'vɔːt/ VERB [**cavorts, cavorting, cavorted**] to jump or dance in a noisy or excited way □ *The children were cavorting about on the beach.*

cc /ˌsiː'siː/ ABBREVIATION cubic centimetre; a unit for measuring the volume of something

CCTV /ˌsiːsiːtiː'viː/ ABBREVIATION closed circuit television; a television system used in a building or area to prevent crime

CD /ˌsiː'diː/ ABBREVIATION compact disc; a disc with sound recorded on it □ *He bought a CD of Scottish folk songs.*

CD-ROM /ˌsiːdiː'rɒm/ ABBREVIATION compact disc read-only memory; a type of CD that stores a lot of information which you play on a computer □ *The dictionary is available on CD-ROM.*

cease /siːs/ VERB [**ceases, ceasing, ceased**] a formal word meaning to stop

ceasefire /'siːsfaɪə(r)/ NOUN [plural **ceasefires**] an agreement between two armies to stop fighting for a period of time

ceaseless /'siːslɪs/ ADJECTIVE a formal word meaning never stopping □ *the ceaseless noise of traffic*

cedar /'siːdə(r)/ NOUN [plural **cedars**] a large tree with red wood and small, thin leaves

ceiling /'siːlɪŋ/ NOUN [plural **ceilings**]
1 the surface at the top of a room □ *This house has very high ceilings.*
2 an upper limit □ *They set a ceiling of 7% on pay rises.*

celebrate /'selɪbreɪt/ VERB [**celebrates, celebrating, celebrated**] when you celebrate an event you have a party or do other special things because of it ⊞ *Dad took a day off work to celebrate his 50th birthday.* ⊞ *We like to celebrate Christmas in a traditional way.* □ *Mark passed his driving test, so we're going out to celebrate!*
• **celebrated** /'selɪbreɪtɪd/ ADJECTIVE famous □ *He is a celebrated artist.*
• **celebration** /ˌselɪ'breɪʃən/ NOUN [plural **celebrations**]
1 a party or something special that is done to celebrate an event □ *a wedding celebration*
2 *no plural* when you celebrate something ⊞ *They produced a book in celebration of his work.* □ *This ought to be a day of celebration.*
• **celebrity** /sɪ'lebrətɪ/ NOUN [plural **celebrities**] someone who is famous □ *Will there be any celebrities at the party?*

celery /'selərɪ/ NOUN, NO PLURAL a vegetable with long, pale green stems, usually eaten raw

cell /sel/ NOUN [plural **cells**]
1 the smallest part of a living thing □ *cancerous cells*
2 a small room that a prisoner is kept in or that a monk (=religious man) lives in

cellar /'selə(r)/ NOUN [plural **cellars**] an underground room used for storing things

cellist /'tʃelɪst/ NOUN [plural **cellists**] someone who plays the cello

cello /ˈtʃeləʊ/ NOUN [plural **cellos**] a musical instrument like a large violin that you hold between your knees

cellophane /ˈseləfeɪn/ NOUN, NO PLURAL a thin transparent material used to wrap things in. A trademark.

cellphone /ˈselfəʊn/ NOUN [plural **cellphones**] the US word for mobile phone

cellular /ˈseljʊlə(r)/ ADJECTIVE
1 to do with the cells of animals or plants. A biology word □ *cellular biology*
2 to do with mobile phones □ *a cellular network*

celluloid /ˈseljʊlɔɪd/ NOUN, NO PLURAL a type of plastic that film was made of in the past

cellulose /ˈseljʊləʊs/ NOUN, NO PLURAL a substance that forms the walls of plant cells. A biology word.

Celsius /ˈselsɪəs/ ADJECTIVE measured using the temperature measurement at which water freezes at 0 degrees and boils at 100 degrees □ *57 degrees Celsius*

cement /sɪˈment/ ▶ NOUN, NO PLURAL a grey powder that is mixed with sand and water for use in building
▶ VERB [**cements, cementing, cemented**]
1 to make a relationship stronger □ *It was a very special moment which cemented our friendship.*
2 to cover or stick things together with cement

cemetery /ˈsemɪtərɪ/ NOUN [plural **cemeteries**] a place where dead people are buried

censor /ˈsensə(r)/ ▶ VERB [**censors, censoring, censored**] to remove parts from books, films, etc. because they are offensive or not allowed ⊞ *Their letters were heavily censored.*
▶ NOUN [plural **censors**] someone whose job is to censor books, films, etc.

censure /ˈsenʃə(r)/ ▶ NOUN, NO PLURAL a formal word meaning severe criticism
▶ VERB [**censures, censuring, censured**] to criticize someone severely and in a formal way □ *The minister was censured for negligence.*

census /ˈsensəs/ NOUN [plural **censuses**] an official process of finding out how many people are living in a particular country and getting information about them

cent /sent/ NOUN [plural **cents**] a unit of money worth 1/100 of a dollar

cent- /sent/ PREFIX cent- is added to the beginning of words to mean a hundred □ *century* □ *centenary*

centenary /senˈtiːnərɪ/ NOUN [plural **centenaries**] a date when people celebrate an event that happened one hundred years earlier □ *It is a special exhibition to mark the centenary of the artist's birth.*

centennial /senˈtenɪəl/ NOUN [plural **centennials**] a US word for centenary

center /ˈsentə(r)/ NOUN [plural **centers**], VERB [**centers, centering, centered**] the US spelling of centre

centi- /ˈsentɪ/ PREFIX centi- is added to the beginning of words to mean a hundred or 1/100 of something □ *centimetre* □ *centigrade*

centigrade /ˈsentɪɡreɪd/ ADJECTIVE an old-fashioned word for Celsius□ *forty degrees centigrade*

centigram /ˈsentɪɡræm/ NOUN [plural **centigrams**] a unit for measuring weight. There are one hundred centigrams in a gram. This is often written **cg**.

centiliter /ˈsentɪliːtə(r)/ NOUN [plural **centiliters**] the US spelling of centilitre

centilitre /ˈsentɪliːtə(r)/ NOUN [plural **centilitres**] a unit for measuring liquid. There are one hundred centilitres in a litre. This is often written **cl**.

centimeter /ˈsentɪmiːtə(r)/ NOUN [plural **centimeters**] the US spelling of centimetre

centimetre /ˈsentɪmiːtə(r)/ NOUN [plural **centimetres**] a unit for measuring length, equal to 10 millimetres. This is often written **cm**. □ *The card measures eight centimetres across.* □ *These heels are 8cm high.*

centipede /ˈsentɪpiːd/ NOUN [plural **centipedes**] an insect with a long body and lots of pairs of legs

central /ˈsentrəl/ ADJECTIVE
1 near or in the centre of an object or a place □ *He works in central London.* □ *Our school has a central courtyard.*
2 being the main or most important part of an organization and controlling other parts of it □ *the central bank* □ *We have a system of central government.*
3 most important ⊞ *Love is the central theme of this film.* ⊞ *She played a central role/part in the campaign.* □ **+ to** *This point is central to our religion.*

central heating /ˌsentrəl ˈhiːtɪŋ/ NOUN, NO PLURAL a system used for heating houses where heated water goes through pipes to each room

centralization or **centralisation** /ˌsentrəlaɪˈzeɪʃən/ NOUN, NO PLURAL the process of centralizing something □ *We have seen increased centralization of our health services.*

centralize or **centralise** /ˈsentrəlaɪz/ VERB [**centralizes, centralizing, centralized**] to have the main and controlling part of an organization, system or country in one place □ *The company plans to centralize its accounting systems.*

central nervous system /ˌsentrəl ˈnɜːvəs ˌsɪstəm/ NOUN the central nervous system the brain and the spinal cord (=nerves in the spine that connect the body to the brain). A biology word.

centre /ˈsentə(r)/ ▶ NOUN [plural **centres**]
1 the middle or point of something □ *It is difficult to park in the city centre.* □ *These chocolates have soft centres.* □ **+ of** *He stood in the centre of the field.*
2 the most important part of something □ **+ of** *The woman at the centre of the dispute is refusing to speak to journalists.* □ *The idea is at the centre of an ambitious project.*
3 the centre of attention if something or someone

is the centre of attention, they are getting more attention than anything or anyone else

4 a place or a building used for a particular activity □ *a sports centre* □ *The centre carries out research into breast cancer.*

5 the political position that is not extreme □ *The prime minister has moved further to the centre.*

▶ VERB [**centres, centring, centred**] to put something in the centre □ *Centre the text underneath the image.*

◆ PHRASAL VERB **centre around/on something** to have something as its most important part □ *Talks centred on the need for international cooperation.*

century /ˈsentʃʊrɪ/ NOUN [*plural* **centuries**] a hundred years □ *She lived in the fifteenth century.* □ *a twentieth-century building*

ceramic /sɪˈræmɪk/ ADJECTIVE made of clay that is baked in a hot oven to make it hard □ *a ceramic dish*

● **ceramics** /sɪˈræmɪks/ NOUN
1 the art of making objects with clay
2 ceramic objects

cereal /ˈsɪərɪəl/ NOUN [*plural* **cereals**]
1 a plant such as wheat or rice, that is grown in order to use the grains for food
2 food made from cereal crops, especially one eaten for breakfast 🔁 *breakfast cereals*

cerebral /ˈserɪbrəl/ ADJECTIVE
1 to do with the brain. A biology word.
2 cerebral people think a lot, and cerebral books, etc. are difficult and need a lot of thought to understand them. A formal word.

ceremonial /ˌserɪˈməʊnɪəl/ ADJECTIVE to do with a ceremony □ *Opening Parliament is one of the monarch's ceremonial duties.*

● **ceremonious** /ˌserɪˈməʊnɪəs/ ADJECTIVE very formal and polite □ *He gave a ceremonious bow.*

● **ceremoniously** /ˌserɪˈməʊnɪəslɪ/ ADVERB in a grand and formal way □ *A huge cake was placed ceremoniously in the centre of the table.*

● **ceremony** /ˈserɪmənɪ/ NOUN [*plural* **ceremonies**]
1 a formal event where special or traditional words or actions are used 🔁 *a wedding ceremony* 🔁 *The graduation ceremony was held at the cathedral.* 🔁 *Who will be attending the award ceremony this year?*
2 *no plural* formal behaviour suitable for an important occasion □ *With great ceremony, the medals were brought forward.*

certain /ˈsɜːtən/ ADJECTIVE
1 with no doubts □ **+ about** *Dad wasn't certain about the time of the train.* □ **+ question word** *I'm not certain how it works.* □ **+ that** *I'm certain that I saw someone in the garden.*
2 sure to happen or be true □ **+ that** *It seems certain that he will get the job.* 🔁 *Make certain that the rope is tight.* □ **+ to do something** *She says you're certain to pass the exam.*

3 for certain without any doubt □ *I can't say for certain what will happen.*
4 used to talk about someone or something without saying exactly which person or thing you are talking about □ *There are certain rules which have to be obeyed.* □ *Certain people have been asked to leave.*
5 to a certain extent in some ways but not completely □ *I agree with you to a certain extent.*

● **certainly** /ˈsɜːtənlɪ/ ADVERB
1 used to show that there is no doubt about something □ *Joe certainly knows a lot about birds.* 🔁 *'Can I stay up until midnight?' 'Certainly not!'*
2 used to agree to something □ *'May I borrow your lawnmower?' 'Certainly.'*

● **certainty** /ˈsɜːtəntɪ/ NOUN [*plural* **certainties**]
1 *no plural* feeling or being certain □ *There is no certainty that the business will succeed.*
2 something that is sure to happen □ *Since my husband's death, I feel there are no certainties in life.*

certificate /səˈtɪfɪkət/ NOUN [*plural* **certificates**] an official document that shows something is true 🔁 *They asked to see my birth certificate.* □ *We each received a certificate for completing the course.*

● **certify** /ˈsɜːtɪfaɪ/ VERB [**certifies, certifying, certified**] to record in a formal way that something is true □ *Sign here to certify that this information is accurate.* □ *The product was certified as safe and non-toxic.*

cervical /səˈvaɪkəl, ˈsɜːvɪkəl/ ADJECTIVE to do with the cervix. A biology word. □ *cervical cancer*

cervix /ˈsɜːvɪks/ NOUN [*plural* **cervixes** or **cervices**] the small entrance to a woman's womb (=place where a baby grows). A biology word.

cesarean /sɪˈzeərɪən/ NOUN [*plural* **cesareans**] the US spelling of **caesarean**

cesium /ˈsiːzɪəm/ NOUN, NO PLURAL the US spelling of **caesium**

cessation /seˈseɪʃən/ NOUN, NO PLURAL when something bad stops. A formal word. □ *The government has called for a total cessation of terrorist activity.*

CFC /ˌsiːefˈsiː/ ABBREVIATION chlorofluorocarbon

cg /ˌsiːˈdʒiː/ ABBREVIATION centigram or centigrams

chafe /tʃeɪf/ VERB [**chafes, chafing, chafed**]
1 to rub your skin and make it sore □ *Toby's wellington boots were chafing his legs.*
2 to feel angry because you are not allowed to do what you want to do □ *He chafed against the rules of army life.*

chaffinch /ˈtʃæfɪntʃ/ NOUN [*plural* **chaffinches**] a small bird

chagrin /ˈʃægrɪn/ NOUN, NO PLURAL is a feeling of disappointment or anger when something does not happen the way you want it to □ *Much to his chagrin, he found that he had posted his application too late.*

chain /tʃeɪn/ ► NOUN [plural **chains**]
1 metal rings that are connected in a line □ *He wore a gold chain around his neck.* □ *The chain came off my bicycle.*
2 a group of similar shops, restaurants, etc. that have the same owner □ *+ of* *She owns a chain of restaurants.*
3 a chain of events several events that happen one after the other
► VERB [**chains, chaining, chained**] to fasten something or someone with a chain □ *often passive* *The bicycle was chained to the fence.*

chain mail /tʃeɪn ˌmeɪl/ NOUN, NO PLURAL a type of armour (=metal pieces that protect the body in a fight) worn in the past, made of many small metal rings

chain reaction /ˌtʃeɪn rɪˈækʃən/ NOUN [plural **chain reactions**]
1 a series of events where each event causes the next one
2 a chemical change that makes something that causes another change. A chemistry word.

chain saw /ˈtʃeɪn ˌsɔ:/ NOUN [plural **chain saws**] a powerful tool with a motor and a chain with sharp parts in it, used for cutting wood

chain store /ˈtʃeɪn ˌstɔ:(r)/ NOUN [plural **chain stores**] a shop that is part of a group of similar shops, all owned by the same company

chair /tʃeə(r)/ ► NOUN [plural **chairs**]
1 a piece of furniture that has a back and which one person sits on
2 the person who is in charge of a meeting, business or organization
► VERB [**chairs, chairing, chaired**] to be officially in charge of a meeting

chairlift /ˈtʃeəlɪft/ NOUN [plural **chairlifts**] a system of chairs hanging from thick wires, used for carrying people up mountains

chairman /ˈtʃeəmən/ NOUN [plural **chairmen**]
1 the person who is in charge of a company, group or organization □ *the chairman of the board*
2 the person who is in charge of a meeting

• **chairmanship** /ˈtʃeəmənʃɪp/ NOUN, NO PLURAL the job of being a chairman, or the time that someone is a chairman

chairperson /ˈtʃeəpɜ:sən/ NOUN [plural **chairpeople**] a male or female chairman

chairwoman /ˈtʃeəwʊmən/ NOUN [plural **chairwomen**] a female chairman

chalet /ˈʃæleɪ/ NOUN [plural **chalets**] a small wooden house, often on a mountain

chalk /tʃɔ:k/ NOUN, NO PLURAL
1 *no plural* a type of soft white stone □ *crumbling chalk cliffs*
2 pieces of this stone that you use to draw with □ *She wrote on the blackboard with chalk.*
♦ IDIOM as different as/like chalk and cheese completely different from each other

• **chalky** /ˈtʃɔ:kɪ/ ADJECTIVE [**chalkier, chalkiest**] tasting or feeling like chalk

challenge /ˈtʃælɪndʒ/ ► NOUN [plural **challenges**]
1 something that is difficult to do ℗ *The world faces a huge challenge in tackling climate change.* ℗ *We must ensure that these challenges are met* (=dealt with successfully). ℗ *Crime poses/presents a serious challenge to our community.*
2 when you try to change a rule, or do not accept a decision or someone's authority ℗ *There is likely to be a legal challenge to this ruling.* ℗ *We decided to mount a challenge against the president.*
3 when you ask someone to fight or compete with you □ *The approach of their army was a clear challenge.*
► VERB [**challenges, challenging, challenged**]
1 to try to change a rule, or to say that you do not accept a decision or someone's authority □ *We will challenge this decision in the courts.*
2 to ask someone to compete or fight □ *+ to* *He challenged his enemy to a duel.*
3 to ask someone if they have the right to be somewhere □ *The security guard challenged me and asked to see my identity card.*
4 if something challenges you, you find it difficult to do □ *This exam will challenge even our best pupils.*

• **challenger** /ˈtʃælɪndʒə(r)/ NOUN [plural **challengers**] someone who wants to try and beat another person in a game, election, etc.

• **challenging** /ˈtʃælɪndʒɪŋ/ ADJECTIVE difficult to do or understand □ *This book is very challenging for younger students.*

chamber /ˈtʃeɪmbə(r)/ NOUN [plural **chambers**]
1 a room for meetings or for a special purpose □ *the council chamber* □ *a burial chamber*
2 one of the parts of a parliament □ *the upper/lower chamber*
3 a space in a body, plant or machine □ *There was a blockage in one of the chambers of the heart.*
4 an old-fashioned word for a room or bedroom □ *the king's chamber*

chambermaid /ˈtʃeɪmbəmeɪd/ NOUN [plural **chambermaids**] a woman who cleans bedrooms in a hotel

chamber music /ˈtʃeɪmbə ˌmju:zɪk/ NOUN, NO PLURAL classical music for a small group of players

chameleon /kəˈmi:lɪən/ NOUN [plural **chameleons**] a small reptile that can change its colour to be the same as what is around it

champagne /ˌʃæmˈpeɪn/ NOUN, NO PLURAL a pale French wine with lots of bubbles, often drunk to celebrate something □ *Let's open a bottle of champagne.*

champion /ˈtʃæmpɪən/ ► NOUN [plural **champions**]
1 a person or team that has beaten all the others in a competition □ *He became world boxing champion at twenty-six.*

2 someone who strongly supports a particular belief or idea □ *Mrs Pankhurst was the champion of women's right to vote.*
▶ VERB [**champions, championing, championed**] to support a belief or idea strongly
• **championship** /ˈtʃæmpɪənʃɪp/ NOUN [*plural* **championships**] a competition to decide who is the champion

chance /tʃɑːns/ ▶ NOUN [*plural* **chances**]
1 a possibility that something will happen □ *+ that* *There is a good chance that she is still alive.* □ *+ of* *Our school has no chance of winning the match.* 🕀 *Our team doesn't stand a chance of winning.*
2 an opportunity □ *+ to do something* *I haven't had a chance to check yet.* 🕀 *You didn't give me a chance to answer.* 🕀 *This is your last chance to buy a ticket.*
3 by chance in a way that is not planned or expected □ *I saw him quite by chance at the supermarket.*
4 take a chance to take a risk □ *I took a chance on the weather staying dry and left my coat at home.*
5 *no plural* luck □ *Roulette is a game of chance.*

> ► Note that **chance** meaning 'a possibility that something will happen' is followed by **that** or **of** **doing something**: □ *What are the chances that they will win?* □ *What are the chances of them winning?*

▶ VERB [**chances, chancing, chanced**] to take a risk □ *The dog would probably have been fine at home, but I didn't want to chance it.*
▶ ADJECTIVE happening by accident □ *a chance meeting*

chancellor /ˈtʃɑːnsələ(r)/ NOUN [*plural* **chancellors**]
1 the British government official who is in charge of finance
2 the leader of the government of some European countries □ *the German chancellor*
3 the head of a university

Chancellor of the Exchequer /ˌtʃɑːnsələr əv ðɪ ɪksˈtʃekə(r)/ NOUN [*plural* **Chancellors of the Exchequer**] the British government official who is in charge of finance

chancy /ˈtʃɑːnsɪ/ ADJECTIVE [**chancier, chanciest**] involving a risk □ *It was a bit chancy taking a route we didn't know.*

chandelier /ˌʃændəˈlɪə(r)/ NOUN [*plural* **chandeliers**] a large light that hangs from the ceiling and is made from many small lights

change /tʃeɪndʒ/ ▶ VERB [**changes, changing, changed**]
1 to become different, or to make something different □ *+ into* *It has changed from a liquid into a gas.* □ *+ from* *The leaves changed from green to gold.*
2 to stop having or using one thing and start having or using another instead □ *We need to change the batteries.* □ *My daughter changed schools last term.* 🕀 *Don't try to change the subject* (=start talking about something else). □ *+ to* *I'm changing to a new dentist.*
3 to put on different clothes 🕀 *I must get changed*

(=change my clothes) *for work.* □ *+ into* *I will just change into my jeans.*
4 to get off a train, bus, etc. and get onto another one 🕀 *You have to change trains at York.* □ *Get a flight to Berlin and change there.*
5 to exchange one type of money for another □ *I need to change some dollars.*
6 change your mind to start to think or plan something different from before □ *I've changed my mind – I'll have soup not pasta, please.*
7 change the bed to put clean sheets on a bed
▶ NOUN [*plural* **changes**]
1 a difference 🕀 *I have made some changes to the timetable.* □ *+ in* *Let's wait until there is a change in the weather.*
2 a change something that is enjoyable because it is new and different 🕀 *It will make a change to go out to eat.* □ *I didn't hate my old job – I just fancied a change.*
3 for a change instead of the usual thing □ *Could you just stop complaining for a change?*
4 *no plural* money in the form of coins □ *Have you got any change?*
5 *no plural* the extra money that is given back to you when you have paid for something 🕀 *I told the taxi driver to keep the change.*
6 a change of clothes a different set of clothes to wear
• **changeable** /ˈtʃeɪndʒəbəl/ ADJECTIVE changing often □ *The weather is rather changeable.*

changing room /ˈtʃeɪndʒɪŋ ˌruːm/ NOUN [*plural* **changing rooms**]
1 a room where you can change your clothes before or after doing sport
2 a room in a clothes shop where you can try the clothes

channel /ˈtʃænəl/ ▶ NOUN [*plural* **channels**]
1 a television or radio station 🕀 *May I change channels, or are you watching this?* □ *Let's turn over to the other channel.*
2 channels the ways something is communicated, given or received 🕀 *You need to make your complaint through the proper channels.* □ *Our distribution channels have been affected by the war.*
3 a passage for water or ships to travel along □ *a shipping channel*
4 a narrow piece of sea □ *the English Channel*
▶ VERB [**channels, channelling/US channeling, channelled/US channeled**] to make water flow in a particular direction □ *This ditch channels water away from the campsite.*
♦ PHRASAL VERB **channel something into something** to use something for a particular purpose 🕀 *They should channel their energies into something more useful.*

chant /tʃɑːnt/ ▶ VERB [**chants, chanting, chanted**] to shout or sing something repeatedly
▶ NOUN [*plural* **chants**] something that people shout or sing repeatedly

Chanukah /ˈhɑːnəkə/ NOUN, NO PLURAL another spelling of Hanukkah

chaos /ˈkeɪɒs/ NOUN, NO PLURAL great confusion □ There was chaos in town when the traffic lights stopped working.

• **chaotic** /keɪˈɒtɪk/ ADJECTIVE completely confused, with no organization □ It was a chaotic scene with people running everywhere.

chap /tʃæp/ NOUN [plural **chaps**] an informal word for a man □ He's a nice chap.

chapel /ˈtʃæpəl/ NOUN [plural **chapels**] a small church, or a room used as a church □ the hospital chapel

chaplain /ˈtʃæplɪn/ NOUN [plural **chaplains**] a priest in the army or in a hospital, school or prison

chapped /tʃæpt/ ADJECTIVE chapped skin is dry, red and sore □ chapped lips

chapter /ˈtʃæptə(r)/ NOUN [plural **chapters**] one of the parts that a book is divided into □ Turn to Chapter 3 in your history books. □ Can I just finish (=finish reading) this chapter?

character /ˈkærəktə(r)/ NOUN [plural **characters**]
1 what someone or something is like and the qualities that they have □ Can you describe her character? Is she reliable? □ It isn't in his character to stay angry for long.
2 a person in a story, film or play □ Harry Potter is a fictional character. □ Who is your favourite character in the book?
3 an informal word for an unusual person □ Her dad's a bit of a character, isn't he?
4 a letter or symbol used in writing □ Chinese characters

• **characteristic** /ˌkærəktəˈrɪstɪk/ ▶ NOUN [plural **characteristics**] the features or qualities that make someone or something what they are □ Does he have any unusual characteristics?
▶ ADJECTIVE a characteristic feature or quality is typical of a particular person or thing □ Keith worked with his characteristic energy and enthusiasm.

• **characterization** or **characterisation** /ˌkærəktəraɪˈzeɪʃən/ NOUN, NO PLURAL the way a writer creates and develops characters in a story

• **characterize** or **characterise** /ˈkærəktəraɪz/ VERB [characterizes, characterizing, characterized]
1 to be a typical part of someone or something □ The disease is characterized by yellow skin and loss of appetite.
2 to describe someone in a particular way □ He'd been characterized as a villain.

charade /ʃəˈrɑːd/ NOUN [plural **charades**]
1 a situation that is false because people are not behaving sincerely □ Their marriage is just a charade – it will never last.
2 charades a game in which players have to act the title of a book, film or television programme

charcoal /ˈtʃɑːkəʊl/ NOUN, NO PLURAL wood that has been burnt until it is black and is used to draw with and as fuel

charge /tʃɑːdʒ/ ▶ VERB [**charges, charging, charged**]
1 to ask a particular amount of money for something □ + for How much do you charge for a haircut? □ The shopkeeper charged me $20 too much.
2 if the police charge someone with a crime, they accuse them officially □ + with He was charged with murder.
3 to move forward quickly and suddenly □ The boys came charging into the room. □ We charged down the hill towards them.
4 to attack someone or something by moving forward quickly □ Their officer gave the order to charge.
5 to fill a battery or piece of electrical equipment with electricity □ Where can I charge my phone?
▶ NOUN [plural **charges**]
1 the amount of money that you have to pay 🔁 You can have another cup of coffee free of charge (=without paying). □ There will be a small charge for postage and packing.
2 in charge controlling or managing something or someone □ I am in charge while the boss is away. □ Ms Handy is in charge of the sales department.
3 take charge to take control of something or someone □ Can you take charge of the food preparation?
4 when someone is accused of a crime 🔁 There was some evidence but not enough to bring charges against her. □ He was arrested on a charge of robbery.
5 a sudden forward attacking movement □ In the last minute of the match they made a charge for the line.
6 an amount of electricity in something

charge card /ˈtʃɑːdʒ ˌkɑːd/ NOUN [plural **charge cards**] a plastic card that you can use to buy things at a shop and pay for them later

charger /ˈtʃɑːdʒə(r)/ NOUN [plural **chargers**] an electrical device that you use to charge (=put electricity into) something such as a mobile phone

chariot /ˈtʃærɪət/ NOUN [plural **chariots**] an open vehicle with two wheels that is pulled by horses and was used in the past for racing and fighting

charisma /kəˈrɪzmə/ NOUN, NO PLURAL a personal quality that makes people attracted to you and interested in you □ He was a politician with lots of charisma.

• **charismatic** /ˌkærɪzˈmætɪk/ ADJECTIVE having charisma □ a charismatic leader

charitable /ˈtʃærətəbəl/ ADJECTIVE
1 a charitable organization, activity, etc. gives money or other help to people who need it
2 a charitable person is kind and does not criticize others

charity /ˈtʃærətɪ/ NOUN [plural **charities**]
1 an organization that gives money or other help to people who need it
2 no plural being kind and generous to other people

charm /tʃɑːm/ ▶ NOUN [plural **charms**]
1 no plural a quality that makes someone pleasant and attractive to other people
2 an object that is believed to be lucky

▶ VERB [**charms, charming, charmed**] to attract and please someone very much

• **charming** /'tʃɑːmɪŋ/ ADJECTIVE extremely pleasant □ *What a charming young man your son is.*

charred /tʃɑːd/ ADJECTIVE black from being burnt □ *We gazed at the charred remains of the hut.*

chart /tʃɑːt/ ▶ NOUN [*plural* **charts**]
1 a drawing that shows information □ *This chart shows the population growth over the last fifty years.*
2 the charts a list of the most popular music □ *Their new record went straight to the top of the charts.*
3 a map of the sea used by sailors
▶ VERB [**charts, charting, charted**]
1 to record the progress or development of something 🕮 *His book charts the progress of the reformers.*
2 to make a map of an area

charter /'tʃɑːtə(r)/ ▶ VERB [**charters, chartering, chartered**] to pay money to use a boat or an aeroplane
▶ NOUN [*plural* **charters**] a written statement of an organization's principles and duties

charter flight /'tʃɑːtə ˌflaɪt/ NOUN [*plural* **charter flights**] an aeroplane flight for which a travel company buys all the seats and sells them for a cheap price

chase /tʃeɪs/ ▶ VERB [**chases, chasing, chased**]
1 to run after someone or something to try to catch them □ *A police officer chased the thief down the High Street.* □ *Our dog was chasing a rabbit.*
2 chase someone/something away/off, etc. to run after someone or something quickly to make them go away □ *He angrily chased the children off his land.*
▶ NOUN [*plural* **chases**]
1 when someone or something is chased 🕮 *A man was arrested following a high-speed car chase.*
2 give chase to run after someone or something to try and catch them

chasm /'kæzəm/ NOUN [*plural* **chasms**]
1 a very big difference between people □ *There is a chasm between rich and poor.*
2 a deep narrow opening between rocks

chassis /'ʃæsi/ NOUN [*plural* **chassis**] the frame and wheels of a vehicle

chastise /tʃæ'staɪz/ VERB [**chastises, chastising, chastised**] to speak angrily to someone because they have done something wrong. A formal word.

chat /tʃæt/ ▶ VERB [**chats, chatting, chatted**] to talk to someone in a friendly way □ **+ to** *She was chatting to her friend on the phone.*
◆ PHRASAL VERB **chat someone up** to talk to someone in a friendly way because you want to start a romantic relationship with them. An informal phrase. □ *This guy at the bar started chatting me up.*
▶ NOUN [*plural* **chats**] a friendly talk 🕮 *Come round later and we can have a chat.*

chat room /'tʃæt ˌruːm/ NOUN [*plural* **chat rooms**] an area on the Internet where people can exchange messages. A computing word.

chatter /'tʃætə(r)/ VERB [**chatters, chattering, chattered**]
1 to talk about silly things that are not important □ *Stop chattering, you two, and get on with your work.*
2 if your teeth chatter, they knock together because you are cold or frightened

chatterbox /'tʃætəbɒks/ NOUN [*plural* **chatterboxes**] an informal word for someone who likes to talk a lot

chatty /'tʃæti/ ADJECTIVE [**chattier, chattiest**] a chatty person likes to talk to other people □ *At first she was shy, but now she's quite chatty.*

chauffeur /'ʃəʊfə(r)/ NOUN [*plural* **chauffeurs**] someone whose job is to drive a car for another person

chauvinism /'ʃəʊvɪnɪzəm/ NOUN, NO PLURAL
1 the belief of some men that men are better than women
2 the belief that your country is better than other countries

• **chauvinist** /'ʃəʊvɪnɪst/ NOUN [*plural* **chauvinists**]
1 a man who believes that men are better than women 🕮 *Clive is such a male chauvinist.*
2 someone who believes that their country is better than other countries

• **chauvinist** /'ʃəʊvɪnɪst/ or **chauvinistic** /ˌʃəʊvɪ'nɪstɪk/ ADJECTIVE showing chauvinism □ *I hate her chauvinist attitude.*

cheap /tʃiːp/ ▶ ADJECTIVE [**cheaper, cheapest**]
1 not costing a lot □ *a cheap air ticket* □ *It is cheaper to buy vegetables at the market.*
2 not charging high prices □ *a cheap restaurant*
3 not good in quality □ *The handbag looks very cheap.*
▶ ADVERB for a low price □ *I got these boots cheap in the sale.*

• **cheapen** /'tʃiːpən/ VERB [**cheapens, cheapening, cheapened**] to make someone or something seem less important or good □ *The dispute has cheapened their work.*

• **cheaply** /'tʃiːpli/ ADVERB for a low price □ *You can eat quite cheaply at these cafés.*

cheat /tʃiːt/ ▶ VERB [**cheats, cheating, cheated**] to behave dishonestly in order to succeed at something or get something □ *It's cheating to look at someone else's cards.* □ *Hey, you're cheating! That is against the rules.* □ **+ out of** *They cheated the old lady out of her savings.*
▶ NOUN [*plural* **cheats**] someone who cheats

check /tʃek/ VERB [**checks, checking, checked**]
1 to make sure that something is correct □ *Please check your work carefully before you hand it in.* □ *I think my appointment is at 10.30, but I'll just check in my diary.*
2 to find out □ **+ question word** *Could you check whether the post has arrived?* □ *He is just checking how many copies we need.*
3 to make sure that something is working correctly □ *The engineer came to check the fire alarm.*
4 to stop something something bad from continuing

□ *The ban on transporting cattle is intended to check the spread of the disease.*

◆ PHRASAL VERBS **check in** to tell the people at a hotel or airport that you have arrived □ *Please check in two hours before the flight.* **check out** to pay for your stay at a hotel and leave **check something/ someone out** an informal word meaning to find out what something or someone is like □ *Let's check out the clubs.* **check up on someone** to find out what someone is doing and how well they are doing it □ *Mum keeps coming in to check up on me.*

▶ NOUN [*plural* **checks**]

1 a test to see that something is correct or is working correctly ▣ *a health/safety check* ▣ *The police did fingerprint checks on the document.*

2 a pattern of squares □ *black-and-white check*

3 **hold/keep something in check** to control something and prevent it from increasing □ *I must keep my emotions in check.*

4 the US spelling of cheque

5 the US word for tick (sense 1)

6 the US word for a bill in a restaurant

checkbook /ˈtʃekbʊk/ NOUN [*plural* **checkbooks**] the US spelling of chequebook

checked /tʃekt/ ADJECTIVE having a pattern of squares □ *a checked shirt*

checkers /ˈtʃekəz/ PLURAL NOUN the US word for draughts

check-in /ˈtʃekɪn/ NOUN [*plural* **check-ins**]

1 a desk at an airport where passengers' tickets are checked

2 *no plural* the process that happens when you arrive at an airport

checkmate /ˈtʃekmeɪt/ NOUN [*plural* **checkmates**] a winning position in the game of chess

checkout /ˈtʃekaʊt/ NOUN [*plural* **checkouts**]

1 the place where you pay at a supermarket □ *There was a big queue at the checkout.*

2 the place on a website where you pay for things you have bought. A computing word.

checkpoint /ˈtʃekpɔɪnt/ NOUN [*plural* **checkpoints**] a place where soldiers or police stop vehicles or people

check-up /ˈtʃekʌp/ NOUN [*plural* **check-ups**] an examination by a doctor or a dentist to see if you are healthy □ *I have to go for regular check-ups.*

cheddar /ˈtʃedə(r)/ NOUN, NO PLURAL a type of hard British cheese

cheek /tʃiːk/ NOUN [*plural* **cheeks**]

1 one of the two areas on each side of your face below your eyes ▣ *She has lovely rosy cheeks.*

2 *no plural* rude behaviour that shows you do not respect someone ▣ *'He said I was the worst goalie he'd ever seen.' 'What a cheek!'* ▣ *She had the cheek to look in my bag.*

● **cheekily** /ˈtʃiːkɪlɪ/ ADVERB in a cheeky way □ *'Don't be stupid, sir,' he replied cheekily.*

● **cheeky** /ˈtʃiːkɪ/ ADJECTIVE [**cheekier, cheekiest**] a bit

rude, often in a funny way □ *You cheeky boy!* □ *a cheeky grin*

cheer /tʃɪə(r)/ VERB [**cheers, cheering, cheered**] to shout loudly to praise or encourage someone □ *We cheered loudly when he came onto the stage.*

□ *The spectators cheered each runner as they ran past.*

◆ PHRASAL VERBS **cheer someone on** to shout loudly to encourage someone in a competition or race □ *The crowd was cheering him on.* **cheer (someone) up** to feel happier, or to make someone feel happier □ *Cheer up! Don't look so miserable!* □ *I've got some news that will cheer you up.*

▶ NOUN [*plural* **cheers**]

1 a loud shout to show that you are pleased □ *When he caught the ball there was a big cheer from the crowd.*

2 *no plural* an old-fashioned word that means happiness □ *Christmas cheer*

● **cheerful** /ˈtʃɪəfʊl/ ADJECTIVE

1 happy □ *You're very cheerful this morning.*

2 bright and pleasant □ *That's a lovely cheerful colour!*

● **cheerfully** /ˈtʃɪəfʊlɪ/ ADVERB

1 in a happy way □ *He sang cheerfully as he worked.*

2 **I could cheerfully do something** used when you are annoyed with someone to joke that you would enjoy doing something bad to them □ *I could cheerfully strangle that boy sometimes, he is so lazy!*

● **cheering** /ˈtʃɪərɪŋ/ ADJECTIVE making you feel happier □ *There are some cheering signs of improvement in the weather.*

cheerio /ˌtʃɪərɪˈəʊ/ EXCLAMATION an informal word meaning goodbye □ *Cheerio, see you tomorrow.*

cheers /tʃɪəz/ EXCLAMATION

1 a word used to express your good wishes to other people when you are drinking alcohol together □ *Cheers, everyone. Happy New Year!*

2 an informal word meaning thank you □ *'Here's your book back.' 'Cheers.'*

cheery /ˈtʃɪərɪ/ ADJECTIVE [**cheerier, cheeriest**] happy □ *a cheery smile/wave*

cheese /tʃiːz/ NOUN [*plural* **cheeses**] a solid white or yellow food made from milk □ *cheese sauce* ▣ *Would you like some cheese and biscuits?* ▣ *Sprinkle some grated cheese on the top.*

➜ go to as different as/like *chalk* and cheese

cheesecake /ˈtʃiːzkeɪk/ NOUN [*plural* **cheesecakes**] a sweet food made with soft cheese on top of crushed biscuits

cheesy /ˈtʃiːzɪ/ ADJECTIVE [**cheesier, cheesiest**]

1 tasting or smelling of cheese

2 an informal word meaning of low quality or not fashionable □ *a cheesy song*

3 **a cheesy grin** a big smile

cheetah /ˈtʃiːtə/ NOUN [*plural* **cheetahs**] a large, wild cat which runs very fast

chef /ʃef/ NOUN [plural **chefs**] someone whose job is to cook in a restaurant or a hotel □ *Please tell the chef that was delicious.*

chemical /'kemɪkəl/ ► NOUN [plural **chemicals**] a substance that is formed by or used in chemistry 🔾 *The lorry contained dangerous chemicals.* □ *The hydrochloric acid and other chemicals are kept in the laboratory.*
► ADJECTIVE
1 involving or produced by chemistry 🔾 *a chemical reaction*
2 using or containing chemicals □ *a chemical solution*

chemical element /ˌkemɪkəl 'elɪmənt/ NOUN [plural **chemical elements**] a substance that cannot be divided into smaller chemical substances. A chemistry word.

chemist /'kemɪst/ NOUN [plural **chemists**]
1 someone who prepares medicines □ *Could you ask the chemist if my prescription is ready?*
2 chemist's a shop where medicines and products for washing, etc. are sold
3 someone who studies chemistry
• **chemistry** /'kemɪstrɪ/ NOUN, NO PLURAL
1 the study of chemical elements and how they react with each other □ *She studied physics and chemistry at A level.*
2 when two people feel attracted to each other □ *There seems to be a bit of chemistry between those two!*

chemotherapy /ˌkiːməʊ'θerəpɪ/ NOUN, NO PLURAL a treatment for cancer that uses powerful chemicals

cheque /tʃek/ NOUN [plural **cheques**] a piece of printed paper that you sign and use as a way of paying for things 🔾 *I wrote him a cheque for £50.* 🔾 *Our last customer paid by cheque.*

chequebook /'tʃekbʊk/ NOUN [plural **chequebooks**] a book of cheques for a particular person to use

cheque card /'tʃek ˌkɑːd/ NOUN [plural **cheque cards**] a small plastic card from your bank to show the person in a shop when you pay by cheque

cherish /'tʃerɪʃ/ VERB [**cherishes, cherishing, cherished**] to love and look after someone or something

cherry /'tʃerɪ/ NOUN [plural **cherries**] a small round red fruit with a hard seed inside

cherub /'tʃerəb/ NOUN [plural **cherubs** or **cherubim**] a type of angel (=creature with wings believed to live in heaven) that looks like an attractive fat baby

chess /tʃes/ NOUN, NO PLURAL a game where two players move pieces on a board with black and white squares 🔾 *a chess board* 🔾 *Tom plays chess almost every day.*

chest /tʃest/ NOUN [plural **chests**]
1 the front of your body between your neck and your stomach □ *a hairy chest* □ *chest pains*

2 a large box for storing things □ *a treasure chest*
♦ IDIOM get something off your chest to talk about something that has been worrying you or making you angry

chestnut /'tʃesnʌt/ ► NOUN [plural **chestnuts**] a shiny red-brown nut that has an outer shell covered with sharp points
► ADJECTIVE having a red-brown colour □ *chestnut hair*

chest of drawers /ˌtʃest əv 'drɔːz/ NOUN [plural **chests of drawers**] a piece of furniture with drawers for putting clothes in

chew /tʃuː/ VERB [**chews, chewing, chewed**]
1 to break up food inside your mouth with your teeth □ *My tooth is sore and it hurts to chew.* □ *He bit off a piece of bread and chewed it slowly.*
2 to bite something again and again without swallowing it □ + on *The dog was chewing on a bone.*
♦ PHRASAL VERB chew something over to think about something carefully, or to discuss it □ *I'll give you my answer later, after I've chewed it over.*

chewing gum /'tʃuːɪŋ ˌgʌm/ NOUN, NO PLURAL a sweet substance that you chew but do not swallow

chewy /'tʃuːɪ/ ADJECTIVE [**chewier, chewiest**] if food is chewy, you have to chew it a lot before you can swallow it

chick /tʃɪk/ NOUN [plural **chicks**] a baby bird

chicken /'tʃɪkɪn/ NOUN [plural **chickens**]
1 a bird that is kept on farms to produce eggs and to be eaten 🔾 *The farmer's wife keeps a few chickens.* 🔾 *This chicken has stopped laying* (=producing eggs).
2 no plural the meat from this bird □ *roast chicken*
3 an informal word meaning someone who is afraid □ *Jump! Don't be such a chicken.*
♦ PHRASAL VERB [**chickens, chickening, chickened**] chicken out an informal word meaning to decide not to do something because you are afraid □ *Pete chickened out of singing, though he had brought his guitar.*

chickenpox /'tʃɪkɪnpɒks/ NOUN, NO PLURAL an infectious disease which gives you spots on your skin that you want to scratch

chickpea /'tʃɪkpiː/ NOUN [plural **chickpeas**] a large light brown pea

chicory /'tʃɪkərɪ/ NOUN, NO PLURAL a green plant whose leaves are eaten in salads

chief /tʃiːf/ ► ADJECTIVE
1 biggest or most important □ *the chief city of the region* □ *My chief worry is the cost.*
2 chief adviser/correspondent, etc. the person who has the highest rank in a particular job
► NOUN [plural **chiefs**]
1 a person in charge of a group or organization □ *We heard a speech by the new police chief.* □ *Industry chiefs met today in London.*
2 a ruler of a tribe (=large group of related people) □ *an African tribal chief*

chief executive /ˌtʃiːf ɪgˈzekjutɪv/ NOUN [plural **chief executives**] the person who has the most important job in a company

chiefly /ˈtʃiːflɪ/ ADVERB mainly □ The programme is watched chiefly by women.

chiffon /ˈʃɪfɒn/ NOUN, NO PLURAL a thin transparent material

child /tʃaɪld/ NOUN [plural **children**]
1 a young human □ When my Dad was a child, he lived in New York. □ There are thirty children in my class.
2 a son or daughter ⊞ Sue never had (=gave birth to) any children. □ Our children are grown up now.

childbirth /ˈtʃaɪldbɜːθ/ NOUN, NO PLURAL the process of giving birth to a baby □ His mother died in childbirth.

childcare /ˈtʃaɪldkeə(r)/ NOUN, NO PLURAL when someone looks after children while their parents are working

childhood /ˈtʃaɪldhʊd/ NOUN, NO PLURAL the time in your life when you are a child □ My memories of childhood are very happy.

childish /ˈtʃaɪldɪʃ/ ADJECTIVE behaving in a silly way, like a child □ Don't be so childish!
• **childishly** /ˈtʃaɪldɪʃlɪ/ ADVERB in a childish way

childlike /ˈtʃaɪldlaɪk/ ADJECTIVE simple and trusting like a child □ childlike innocence

childminder /ˈtʃaɪldmaɪndə(r)/ NOUN [plural **childminders**] someone who looks after children when their parents are at work

childproof /ˈtʃaɪldpruːf/ ADJECTIVE if something is childproof, it is designed so that a child cannot open, use or damage it □ a childproof lock

children /ˈtʃɪldrən/ PLURAL OF child

chili /ˈtʃɪlɪ/ NOUN [plural **chilies**] the US spelling of chilli

chill /tʃɪl/ ▶ VERB [**chills, chilling, chilled**]
1 to make food or drink cold □ Chill the pudding in the fridge before serving.
2 an informal word meaning to relax □ I spent the afternoon chilling by the pool.
• PHRASAL VERB **chill out** an informal phrase meaning to relax □ We could just chill out with a couple of friends.
▶ NOUN, NO PLURAL
1 if there is a chill in the air, it feels cold
2 an illness that gives you a fever ⊞ She caught a chill out in the rain.

chilli /ˈtʃɪlɪ/ NOUN [plural **chillies**]
1 a small, red or green vegetable which is put in food to give it a hot taste
2 no plural spicy food containing red beans, tomatoes and usually meat

chilling /ˈtʃɪlɪŋ/ ADJECTIVE frightening □ a chilling story

chilly /ˈtʃɪlɪ/ ADJECTIVE [**chillier, chilliest**] cold □ It's a bit chilly in here.

chime /tʃaɪm/ ▶ NOUN [plural **chimes**] the sound of a bell or bells ringing
▶ VERB [**chimes, chiming, chimed**] to make a ringing sound

chimney /ˈtʃɪmnɪ/ NOUN [plural **chimneys**] a pipe above a fire that allows smoke to escape □ a factory chimney

chimpanzee /ˌtʃɪmpænˈziː/ NOUN [plural **chimpanzees**] a small African ape (=large monkey) with black fur, a flat face and large brown eyes

chin /tʃɪn/ NOUN [plural **chins**] the part of your face that is below your mouth □ The strap ties under your chin.

china /ˈtʃaɪnə/ NOUN, NO PLURAL
1 clay used for making things like cups and plates
2 cups, plates, etc. which are made from this clay

chink /tʃɪŋk/ NOUN [plural **chinks**]
1 a small opening □ A shaft of sunlight came through a chink in the curtains.
2 a sound made when coins or other small metal objects hit each other

chip /tʃɪp/ ▶ NOUN [plural **chips**]
1 a long thin piece of potato that is fried and eaten hot ⊞ fish and chips
2 the US word for **crisp** (=a very thin piece of potato cooked in oil and eaten cold) □ a bag of chips
3 a small piece broken off a hard object, or the place where a small piece has broken off □ The plate had a chip in it.
4 a very small part in a computer or other electronic equipment that contains a circuit (=system of wires) and stores information
◆ IDIOMS **a chip off the old block** someone who looks or behaves like one of their parents **have a chip on your shoulder** to have an angry attitude because you feel that you have not had advantages that other people have had □ She has a real chip on her shoulder about not going to university.
▶ VERB [**chips, chipping, chipped**] to break a small piece off something □ Roy chipped one of his teeth playing rugby.
◆ PHRASAL VERB **chip in** to say something in the middle of someone else's conversation □ She chipped in with a couple of suggestions.

chip and PIN /ˌtʃɪp ən ˈpɪn/ NOUN, NO PLURAL a system of paying for things in shops where you put a card into a machine and then press a secret combination of numbers into the machine

chipmunk /ˈtʃɪpmʌŋk/ NOUN [plural **chipmunks**] a small North American animal with a long thick tail and stripes on its back

chiropodist /kɪˈrɒpədɪst/ NOUN [plural **chiropodists**] someone whose job is to treat problems and diseases of people's feet
• **chiropody** /kɪˈrɒpədɪ/ NOUN, NO PLURAL the care and treatment of people's feet

chiropractor /ˈkaɪrəpræktə(r)/ NOUN [plural **chiropractors**] someone whose job is to reduce pain by pressing on joints (=places where bones meet) between bones in your body

chirp /tʃɜːp/ or **chirrup** /ˈtʃɪrəp/ ▶ VERB [**chirps, chirping, chirped** or **chirrups, chirruping, chirruped**]

to make a short high sound or sounds □ *birds chirping*
▶ NOUN [*plural* **chirps** or **chirrups**] a short high sound
□ *the chirp of baby birds*

• **chirpy** /'tʃɜːpɪ/ ADJECTIVE [**chirpier, chirpiest**] an
informal word meaning happy □ *You sound very chirpy
this morning!*

chisel /'tʃɪzəl/ ▶ NOUN [*plural* **chisels**] a very sharp
tool used for cutting pieces off wood, stone or metal
▶ VERB [**chisels, chiselling**/US **chiseling, chiselled**/US
chiseled] to cut something using a chisel □ *Josh
chiselled his name in the stone.*

chivalrous /'ʃɪvəlrəs/ ADJECTIVE a chivalrous man is
polite and shows respect towards women

chive /tʃaɪv/ NOUN [*plural* **chives**] a herb with long thin
leaves that taste slightly of onion

chlorinate /'klɔːrɪneɪt/ VERB [**chlorinates,
chlorinating, chlorinated**] to add chlorine to water in
swimming pools to kill any bacteria

chlorine /'klɔːriːn/ NOUN, NO PLURAL a gas with a
strong smell which is used to kill bacteria in water. A
chemistry word.

chlorofluorocarbon /ˌklɔːrəfluərəʊ'kɑːbən/ NOUN
[*plural* **chlorofluorocarbons**] a chemical that harms
the ozone layer (=layer of a type of oxygen that
protects the Earth from the sun). A chemistry word.

chlorophyll /'klɒrəfɪl/ NOUN, NO PLURAL a green
substance in the leaves of a plant that allows it to use
energy from the sun in a process called
photosynthesis. A biology word.

chock-a-block /ˌtʃɒkə'blɒk/ ADJECTIVE very full or
crowded. An informal word. □ *The city centre was
chock-a-block with tourists.*

chocolate /'tʃɒkələt/ NOUN [*plural* **chocolates**]
1 *no plural* a sweet brown food made from the seeds
of a tropical tree ▢ *milk/dark chocolate* ▢ *a bar of
chocolate*
2 one of many small sweets made with chocolate that
are sold together ▢ *a box of chocolates*
3 a sweet drink made with chocolate ▢ *a hot
chocolate*

choice /tʃɔɪs/ NOUN [*plural* **choices**]
1 when you can choose between different things ▢ *If I
had a choice, I'd work from home.* ▢ *I had to leave – I
had no choice.*
2 a decision to choose a person or thing ▢ *In the end I
had to make a choice.* ▢ *It was a hard choice to make.*
3 the different things you can choose from □ *+ of* *We
were given a choice of meat or fish.* ▢ *The bag is
available in a wide choice of colours.*
4 out of choice if you do something out of choice,
you do it because you want to do it □ *I wasn't there
out of choice. My mother had sent me.*

choir /'kwaɪə(r)/ NOUN [*plural* **choirs**] a group of
singers □ *She sings in the church choir.*

choke /tʃəʊk/ VERB [**chokes, choking, choked**] to not
be able to breathe because something is blocking your
throat □ *She choked on a fish bone.*

cholera /'kɒlərə/ NOUN, NO PLURAL a very infectious
disease that affects the stomach and can kill people

cholesterol /kə'lestərɒl/ NOUN, NO PLURAL a
substance in your body that can cause heart disease if
there is too much of it. A biology word □ *My Dad's got
high cholesterol.*

chomp /tʃɒmp/ VERB [**chomps, chomping, chomped**]
to chew noisily. An informal word. □ *She was
chomping on a carrot.*

choose /tʃuːz/ VERB [**chooses, choosing, chose,
chosen**] to take one particular thing or person from a
group of people or things □ *Can you help me choose a
present for grandma?* □ *Kitty chose a slice of chocolate
cake.* □ *+ between* *I can't choose between the red
one and the pink one.* □ *+ question word* *How do you
choose which charity to give money to?* □ *+ to do
something* *She chose to attend a university near home.*

• **choosy** /'tʃuːzɪ/ ADJECTIVE [**choosier, choosiest**]
wanting to find exactly the right thing. An informal
word.

chop /tʃɒp/ ▶ VERB [**chops, chopping, chopped**] to cut
something into pieces □ *Chop the onion into large
chunks.* □ *He was chopping wood for the fire.*
◆ PHRASAL VERBS **chop something down** to cut the
main part of a tree or big plant so that it falls down
chop something off to remove a part of
something by cutting it
◆ IDIOM **chop and change** to keep changing a situation
▶ NOUN [*plural* **chops**] a piece of meat, usually with a
bone □ *lamb chops*

• **chopper** /'tʃɒpə(r)/ NOUN [*plural* **choppers**] an
informal word for **helicopter** (=aircraft with blades on
top which turn round)

choppy /'tʃɒpɪ/ ADJECTIVE [**choppier, choppiest**] a
choppy sea has a lot of little waves caused by the wind

chopsticks /'tʃɒpstɪks/ PLURAL NOUN two thin sticks
used for eating with in places such as China and Japan

choral /'kɔːrəl/ ADJECTIVE sung by or written for a large
group of singers □ *choral music*

chord /kɔːd/ NOUN [*plural* **chords**] a musical sound
made by playing several notes together □ *Andy can
play a few chords on the guitar.*

chore /tʃɔː(r)/ NOUN [*plural* **chores**] something boring
that you have to do often in your home □ *I find ironing
a real chore.*

choreograph /'kɒrɪəɡrɑːf/ VERB [**choreographs,
choreographing, choreographed**]
1 to make a dance by deciding the movements the
dancers should make
2 to carefully organize an event or activity that has
many parts

• **choreographer** /ˌkɒrɪ'ɒɡrəfə(r)/ NOUN [*plural*
choreographers] someone whose job is to
choreograph dances

• **choreography** /ˌkɒrɪ'ɒɡrəfɪ/ NOUN, NO PLURAL the
work of planning dance movements for a performance

chortle /'tʃɔːtəl/ VERB [**chortles, chortling, chortled**]
to laugh

chorus /'kɔːrəs/ ► NOUN [plural **choruses**]
1 the part of a song that you repeat several times
□ *We all joined in with the chorus.*
2 the performers in a show who perform as a group and are not the main characters
3 a large group of people who regularly sing together
► VERB [**choruses, chorusing, chorused**] to speak or to sing together. A formal word. □ *'Happy birthday to you,' they chorused.*

chose /tʃəuz/ PAST TENSE OF choose

chosen /'tʃəuzən/ ► PAST PARTICIPLE OF choose
► ADJECTIVE being something that you have decided to do □ *Was that his chosen career?*

Christ /kraɪst/ NOUN Jesus Christ, the holy man that Christians believe is the Son of God

christen /'krɪsən/ VERB [**christens, christening, christened**] to give a baby a name in a ceremony and make him or her a member of the Christian religion
• **christening** /'krɪsənɪŋ/ NOUN [plural **christenings**] a ceremony at which a a baby is christened

Christian /'krɪstʃən/ ► NOUN [plural **Christians**]
someone who is a member of the religion that is based on the ideas of Jesus Christ and the Bible
► ADJECTIVE to do with Christianity or Christians
• **Christianity** /ˌkrɪstɪˈænətɪ/ NOUN, NO PLURAL the religion that is based on the ideas of Jesus Christ and the Bible

Christian name /'krɪstʃən ˌneɪm/ NOUN [plural **Christian names**] the first name of people from Western countries

Christmas /'krɪsməs/ ► NOUN, NO PLURAL 25 December, the day Christians celebrate the birth of Christ each year □ *Happy Christmas!*
► ADJECTIVE for or to do with Christmas 🖭 *Christmas decorations/presents*

Christmas Day /ˌkrɪsməs 'deɪ/ NOUN, NO PLURAL 25 December, the day on which Christmas is celebrated

Christmas Eve /ˌkrɪsməs 'iːv/ NOUN, NO PLURAL 24 December, the day before Christmas Day

Christmas tree /'krɪsməs ˌtriː/ NOUN [plural **Christmas trees**] a tree that you cover with decorations and lights and put in your house during the Christmas period

chromosome /'krəuməsəum/ NOUN [plural **chromosomes**] one of the very small parts in the centre of animal and plant cells that contain the genes (=parts that control what an animal or plant is like). A biology word.

chronic /'krɒnɪk/ ADJECTIVE
1 a chronic disease is one that continues for a long time
2 an informal way of saying that something is very bad □ *The smell from the lab was really chronic.*

chronicle /'krɒnɪkəl/ ► NOUN [plural **chronicles**] a record of things in the order that they happened
► VERB [**chronicles, chronicling, chronicled**] to write down a record of events in the order that they happen

chronological /ˌkrɒnəˈlɒdʒɪkəl/ ADJECTIVE in the order in which events happened □ *List your exam results in chronological order.*

chrysalis /'krɪsəlɪs/ NOUN [plural **chrysalises**] an insect such as a moth or butterfly at the stage when it develops inside a hard covering. A biology word.

chrysanthemum /krɪˈsænθəməm/ NOUN [plural **chrysanthemums**] a large, brightly coloured flower with a lot of petals

chubby /'tʃʌbɪ/ ADJECTIVE [**chubbier, chubbiest**] quite fat, but in an attractive way □ *the baby's chubby little legs*

chuck /tʃʌk/ VERB [**chucks, chucking, chucked**] an informal word meaning to throw something □ *He chucked a towel over to me.*
◆ PHRASAL VERB **chuck something away/out** an informal phrase meaning to throw something away
□ *I chucked out all the half-eaten food.*

chuckle /'tʃʌkəl/ ► VERB [**chuckles, chuckling, chuckled**] to laugh quietly □ *The story made me chuckle to myself.*
► NOUN [plural **chuckles**] a quiet laugh

chuffed /tʃʌft/ ADJECTIVE an informal word meaning very pleased □ *She's really chuffed about her exam results.*

chug /tʃʌg/ VERB [**chugs, chugging, chugged**] to make a noise like an engine moving slowly, or to move along slowly □ *The little steam train came chugging up the hill.*

chum /tʃʌm/ NOUN [plural **chums**] an informal word for friend □ *an old school chum*
• **chummy** /'tʃʌmɪ/ ADJECTIVE friendly □ *Try not to get too chummy with your staff.*

chunk /tʃʌŋk/ NOUN [plural **chunks**]
1 a thick piece of something □ *a chunk of cheese*
□ *pineapple chunks*
2 a large part of something □ *We had to use quite a chunk of our savings to pay for the damage to the car.*
• **chunky** /'tʃʌŋkɪ/ ADJECTIVE [**chunkier, chunkiest**]
1 thick and heavy □ *a warm chunky sweater*
2 a chunky person is short and heavy

church /tʃɜːtʃ/ NOUN [plural **churches**] a building where people, especially Christians, go to pray 🖭 *Do you go to church?*

churchyard /'tʃɜːtʃjɑːd/ NOUN [plural **churchyards**] the land around a church, where people are buried

churlish /'tʃɜːlɪʃ/ ADJECTIVE rude and not grateful □ *It would be churlish to refuse his generous offer.*

churn /tʃɜːn/ ► NOUN [plural **churns**] a machine for making butter from milk
► VERB [**churns, churning, churned**]
1 to mix something up so that the surface is rough
□ *The ground was churned up by all the car tyres.*
2 if your stomach is churning, it feels uncomfortable because you are nervous
3 to mix milk inside a churn to make it into butter
◆ PHRASAL VERB **churn something out** to produce large quantities of something quickly and without

much care □ *She manages to churn out a novel every six months.*

chute /ʃuːt/ NOUN [*plural* **chutes**] a long, thin sloping structure that water, objects or people slide down □ *a laundry chute*

chutney /ˈtʃʌtni/ NOUN [*plural* **chutneys**] a thick substance like jam, made from fruit or vegetables with vinegar (=sour brown liquid) and spices, which you eat with meat or cheese

CIA /ˌsiːaɪˈeɪ/ ABBREVIATION Central Intelligence Agency; the US organization that tries to get secret information about other countries

ciabatta /tʃəˈbɑːtə/ NOUN [*plural* **ciabattas**] a type of quite flat Italian bread

cider /ˈsaɪdə(r)/ NOUN, NO PLURAL an alcoholic drink made from apples

cigar /sɪˈɡɑː(r)/ NOUN [*plural* **cigars**] a thick tube made from dried tobacco leaves that people smoke

cigarette /ˌsɪɡəˈret/ NOUN [*plural* **cigarettes**] a thin tube of paper filled with tobacco that people smoke

cinder /ˈsɪndə(r)/ NOUN [*plural* **cinders**] a small piece of wood, paper, etc. that has been burned

cinema /ˈsɪnəmə/ NOUN [*plural* **cinemas**]
1 a place where you go to watch a film on a big screen □ *We went to the cinema last night.*
2 *no plural* the art or industry of making films □ *a career in cinema*

cinnamon /ˈsɪnəmən/ NOUN, NO PLURAL a brown spice used to give flavour to cakes and other food

circa /ˈsɜːkə/ PREPOSITION a word used before a date or a number to show that it is not exact □ *circa 1850*

circle /ˈsɜːkəl/ ▶ NOUN [*plural* **circles**]
1 a flat shape whose outside edge is a continuous curved line which is always the same distance away from a central point □ *Draw one circle for the head and another for the body.* □ *Form a circle in the centre of the room.*
2 a group of people who know each other or do a particular activity together □ *a sewing circle* □ *He's not part of my circle of friends.*
3 the circle the upper area of seats in a theatre or cinema
▶ VERB [**circles**, **circling**, **circled**]
1 to move in a circle □ *Vultures circled overhead.* □ *Several planes were circling the airport.*
2 to draw a circle around something □ *She circled the area on the map with a red pen.*

circuit /ˈsɜːkɪt/ NOUN [*plural* **circuits**]
1 a path, route or track that forms a circle □ *He drove five laps of the circuit.*
2 the path that electricity goes along between two points
3 a series of places or events regularly visited by people involved in a particular activity □ *the international golf circuit*

circular /ˈsɜːkjʊlə(r)/ ▶ ADJECTIVE
1 in the shape of a circle □ *a circular window*
2 a circular journey or route finishes in the same place that it started
▶ NOUN [*plural* **circulars**] a letter or advertisement that is sent to a lot of different people

circulate /ˈsɜːkjʊleɪt/ VERB [**circulates**, **circulating**, **circulated**]
1 to send something to all the members of a group □ *Details of the meeting will be circulated to all members of staff.*
2 if information, ideas, etc. circulate, they are passed to a lot of people ⊞ *Rumours are circulating that hundreds of jobs will be lost.*
3 to move around or through something □ *Water circulates in the central heating system.*

• **circulation** /ˌsɜːkjʊˈleɪʃən/ NOUN, NO PLURAL
1 the movement of blood around your body. A biology word □ *I have very poor circulation.*
2 movement around or through something □ *This system controls the circulation of air.*
3 in circulation being passed from one person to another □ *These fake banknotes are still in circulation.*
4 the number of copies of a particular newspaper or magazine that are regularly sold □ *a fall in circulation*

circumcise /ˈsɜːkəmsaɪz/ VERB [**circumcises**, **circumcising**, **circumcised**] to cut away the loose skin covering the end of the penis, either for medical or for religious reasons

• **circumcision** /ˌsɜːkəmˈsɪʒən/ NOUN [*plural* **circumcisions**] an operation to circumcise a man or a boy

circumference /səˈkʌmfərəns/ NOUN [*plural* **circumferences**] the outside edge of a circle, or the length of the outside edge of a circle. A maths word. □ *Mark a point on the circumference of the circle and draw a line through it.* □ *What's the circumference of this coin?*

circumflex /ˈsɜːkəmfleks/ NOUN [*plural* **circumflexes**] the symbol ^ that is put over some letters in some languages

circumspect /ˈsɜːkəmspekt/ ADJECTIVE a formal word meaning careful about what you do or say □ *She learnt to be more circumspect when talking to reporters.*

circumstances /ˈsɜːkəmstənsɪz/ PLURAL NOUN
1 the events or conditions that affect or cause a particular situation ⊞ *His reaction was understandable under the circumstances* (=when you consider the situation). ⊞ *Refunds of the fee are only allowed in exceptional circumstances.*
2 under no circumstances used for saying that something must not happen □ *Under no circumstances should you attempt to climb without a rope.*
3 the conditions you live in, especially how much money you have □ *You must notify the authorities of any change in your circumstances.*

• **circumstantial** /ˌsɜːkəmˈstænʃəl/ ADJECTIVE

circumstantial evidence makes you believe something is true but does not prove it

circumvent /ˌsɜːkəm'vent/ VERB [circumvents, circumventing, circumvented] a formal word meaning to find a way of avoiding a law or a difficulty □ *She was accused of using her fame to circumvent the country's adoption rules.*

circus /'sɜːkəs/ NOUN [plural circuses] a show performed in a big tent by people and often trained animals □ *We're taking the children to the circus tonight.*

cistern /'sɪstən/ NOUN [plural cisterns] a container for storing water, especially one connected to a toilet

citadel /'sɪtədəl/ NOUN [plural citadels] a strong castle inside a city where people went in the past if they were attacked

cite /saɪt/ VERB [cites, citing, cited] to mention something as an example or as proof □ *Try to cite some examples of good environmental schemes in your essay.*

citizen /'sɪtɪzən/ NOUN [plural citizens]
1 someone who lives in a particular town, state or country □ *citizens of Paris*
2 someone who has the right to live in a particular country permanently □ *He lives in Singapore but he's an Australian citizen.*
• **citizenship** /'sɪtɪzənʃɪp/ NOUN, NO PLURAL
1 the legal right to live in a particular country □ *She's applied for Canadian citizenship.*
2 the responsibilities and duties you have as a citizen □ *Children should be taught good citizenship.*

citrus fruit /'sɪtrəs ˌfruːt/ NOUN [plural citrus fruits] a fruit with a thick skin and a lot of juice, for example an orange or a lemon

city /'sɪti/ NOUN [plural cities] a large, important town 🔁 *Paris is the capital city of France.* □ *the city streets*

civic /'sɪvɪk/ ADJECTIVE to do with a city or the people who live in it □ *civic pride*

civil /'sɪvəl/ ADJECTIVE
1 to do with ordinary people, not people in military or religious organizations □ *civil life* □ *a civil marriage ceremony*
2 to do with private legal arguments, not criminal matters □ *a civil court*
3 talking or behaving in a polite way □ *He found it hard to be civil to his ex-boss.*
4 involving the people who live in a country □ *They started a campaign of civil disobedience.*

civil engineer /ˌsɪvəl endʒɪ'nɪə(r)/ NOUN [plural civil engineers] someone whose job is to plan and build public buildings and things like roads and bridges
• **civil engineering** /ˌsɪvəl endʒɪ'nɪərɪŋ/ NOUN, NO PLURAL the work of a civil engineer

civilian /sɪ'vɪljən/ NOUN [plural civilians] a person who is not a member of a military organization or the police

civilization or **civilisation** /ˌsɪvɪlaɪ'zeɪʃən/ NOUN [plural civilizations]
1 a society that has its own culture and organizations □ *ancient civilizations*
2 the process in which a society develops its own culture and organizations

civilize or **civilise** /'sɪvɪlaɪz/ VERB [civilizes, civilizing, civilized]
1 to help a society to develop its culture or organizations
2 to teach someone how to behave more politely
• **civilized** or **civilised** /'sɪvɪlaɪzd/ ADJECTIVE
1 a civilized society or country has an advanced culture and organizations
2 behaving politely and reasonably, without arguing □ *Let's try and have a civilized discussion instead of all shouting at once.*
3 pleasant and comfortable □ *'This is all very civilized,' he said, sipping his champagne.*

civil liberties /ˌsɪvəl 'lɪbətɪz/ PLURAL NOUN the basic rights you have to speak and behave in the way you want as long as you do not break the law

civil partnership /ˌsɪvəl 'pɑːtnəʃɪp/ NOUN [plural civil partnerships] an arrangement like a marriage between people of the same sex

civil rights /ˌsɪvəl 'raɪts/ PLURAL NOUN your basic rights to be treated fairly in society, to express yourself, and to practise your religion

civil servant /ˌsɪvəl 'sɜːvənt/ NOUN [plural civil servants] someone who works in the civil service of a country
• **civil service** /ˌsɪvəl 'sɜːvɪs/ NOUN the civil service all the departments of the government and the people who work in them

civil war /ˌsɪvəl 'wɔː(r)/ NOUN [plural civil wars] a war between different groups within the same country

CJD /ˌsiːdʒeɪ'diː/ ABBREVIATION Creutzfeldt-Jakob Disease; a serious illness that destroys your brain cells and can kill you

cl ABBREVIATION centilitre or centilitres

clad /klæd/ ADJECTIVE a formal word meaning dressed or covered □ *mountains clad in snow*

claim /kleɪm/ ▶ VERB [claims, claiming, claimed]
1 to say that something is true, even though there is no clear proof □ *Marco claims he saw a flying saucer.* □ *The group claims to represent over a million workers.*
2 to officially ask for something as your right or to say that it is yours □ *You'll need to fill in this form to claim unemployment benefit.* □ *If no one claims any of the lost items they will be sold for charity.*
3 claim responsibility/victory, etc. to say that you have done something or achieved something □ *Raj did all the cooking – I can't claim any credit.* □ *A left-wing group has claimed responsibility for the attack.*
▶ NOUN [plural claims]
1 a statement that something is true although it has not been proved 🔁 *The government has rejected claims that pensions will fall.* 🔁 *He denied claims of racism.*

2 when you ask for something that you have a right to or that you say is yours ᖰ *He was convicted of making false insurance claims.* ᖰ *compensation claims*

• **claimant** /ˈkleɪmənt/ NOUN [*plural* **claimants**] someone who makes a claim for money

clairvoyant /kleəˈvɔɪənt/ ▶ ADJECTIVE able to see what will happen in the future

▶ NOUN [*plural* **clairvoyants**] someone who says that they know what will happen in the future

clam /klæm/ NOUN [*plural* **clams**] a small sea creature with two shells that are joined at one side, which can be eaten

♦ PHRASAL VERB [**clams, clamming, clammed**] **clam up** to stop talking because you are embarrassed or want something to be a secret □ *When I asked him about his wife, he just clammed up.*

clamber /ˈklæmbə(r)/ VERB [**clambers, clambering, clambered**] to climb up or over things using your hands and feet ᴜ *They tried to clamber up the steep and slippery slope.*

clammy /ˈklæmɪ/ ADJECTIVE [**clammier, clammiest**] slightly wet, in an unpleasant, sticky way □ *His hands became clammy with fear.*

clamor /ˈklæmə(r)/ VERB [**clamors, clamoring, clamored**], NOUN, NO PLURAL the US spelling of **clamour**

clamour /ˈklæmə(r)/ ▶ VERB [**clamours, clamouring, clamoured**] to try to get something by asking for it loudly □ *All the children were clamouring to see what was in the box.*

▶ NOUN, NO PLURAL noisy shouts or demands

clamp /klæmp/ ▶ NOUN [*plural* **clamps**]
1 a tool for holding things together tightly
2 a piece of equipment attached tightly to something to stop it moving □ *a wheel clamp*

▶ VERB [**clamps, clamping, clamped**] to put a clamp on something □ *Clamp the two pieces of wood together until the glue dries.*

♦ PHRASAL VERB **clamp down** to try hard to stop something bad or illegal □ *We will have to clamp down on litter if we want to clean up the city.*

clampdown /ˈklæmpdaun/ NOUN [*plural* **clampdowns**] a strong effort to control or stop something bad or illegal □ *More police officers are being sent to the area as part of a clampdown on street crime.*

clan /klæn/ NOUN [*plural* **clans**] a group of families that are related to each other, especially in Scotland

clandestine /klænˈdestɪn/ ADJECTIVE a formal word meaning secret or hidden, especially because something is not allowed □ *a clandestine meeting*

clang /klæŋ/ ▶ VERB [**clangs, clanging, clanged**] to make a loud ringing sound, like a heavy piece of metal hitting against something hard □ *The prison gate clanged shut behind them.*

▶ NOUN [*plural* **clangs**] a loud ringing sound

clank /klæŋk/ ▶ VERB [**clanks, clanking, clanked**] to make a short loud sound, like metal hitting metal □ *Strange machines were clanking in the gloomy shed.*

▶ NOUN [*plural* **clanks**] a short loud sound like metal hitting metal

clap /klæp/ ▶ VERB [**claps, clapping, clapped**]
1 to hit your hands together, especially to show that you like or admire someone or something □ *The audience clapped and cheered.* □ *We all clapped in time to the music.*
2 to hit someone lightly on their shoulder or back to show you are pleased with them □ *He clapped his brother on the back.*

▶ NOUN [*plural* **claps**]
1 when you clap your hands ᖰ *Let's all give Adam a clap.*
2 a **clap of thunder** a sudden very loud sound made by thunder

clapped-out /ˌklæptˈaut/ ADJECTIVE an informal word meaning old and not working correctly □ *a clapped-out car*

claptrap /ˈklæptræp/ NOUN, NO PLURAL an informal word meaning nonsense □ *He described the report as utter claptrap.*

clarification /ˌklærɪfɪˈkeɪʃən/ NOUN [*plural* **clarifications**] when someone makes something clearer or easier to understand □ *Do the rules require any further clarification?*

clarify /ˈklærɪfaɪ/ VERB [**clarifies, clarifying, clarified**] to make something clearer or easier to understand □ *I asked her to clarify her remarks.*

clarinet /ˌklærəˈnet/ NOUN [*plural* **clarinets**] a musical instrument shaped like a long tube that you play by blowing through it and pressing its keys with your fingers

• **clarinettist** /ˌklærəˈnetɪst/ NOUN [*plural* **clarinettists**] someone who plays the clarinet

clarity /ˈklærətɪ/ NOUN, NO PLURAL how clear or easy to understand something is □ *the clarity of the image*

clash /klæʃ/ ▶ VERB [**clashes, clashing, clashed**]
1 if two people or groups clash, they fight or disagree angrily with each other □ *Protesters clashed with the police.*
2 if two events clash, they happen at the same time □ *Unfortunately the meeting clashes with my piano exam.*
3 if two colours clash, they do not look good together □ *The purple clashes with the red.*
4 if two metal objects clash, they make a loud sound as they hit each other

▶ NOUN [*plural* **clashes**]
1 an angry disagreement or fight □ *There were violent clashes between students and the police today.*
2 a sound made when two metal objects hit against each other

clasp /klɑːsp/ ▶ VERB [**clasps, clasping, clasped**] to hold something or someone tightly □ *Jenny was clasping a baby in her arms.*

▶ NOUN [*plural* **clasps**]
1 a small metal object used to fasten a bag, belt, or

piece of jewellery □ *The clasp's broken on this brooch.*
2 a way of holding something tightly

class /klɑːs/ ▶ NOUN [plural **classes**]
1 a group of students who are taught together, or a period of time during which a particular subject is taught □ *Hannah's in my class at school.* □ *I'm going to my aerobics class tonight.*
2 one of the social groups into which people can be divided according to their family, income, job, etc.
□ *the working class*
3 a division of things according to how good they are □ *Abby's a first class student.* □ *a second class degree*
4 a group of animals or plants that are related to each other or have similar qualities
▶ VERB [**classes, classing, classed**] to put people or things in a group with others that have similar qualities
□ **+ as** *Anyone under 16 is classed as a junior member.*

classic /ˈklæsɪk/ NOUN [plural **classics**] a great book or other work of art that is admired for a long time after it was written or made □ *great film classics*
➜ go to **classics**
▶ ADJECTIVE
1 very good and popular for a long time □ *classic children's stories*
2 a classic example of something is very typical □ *He made the classic mistake of thinking that he could do all his studying in the week before the exam.*
3 traditional in a way that is of high quality □ *classic clothes*
• **classical** /ˈklæsɪkəl/ ADJECTIVE
1 belonging to the style or culture of ancient Greece or Rome □ *classical architecture*
2 traditional □ *classical ballet*

classical music /ˌklæsɪkəl ˈmjuːzɪk/ NOUN, NO PLURAL traditional, serious music written by people like Beethoven and Verdi

classics /ˈklæsɪks/ NOUN, NO PLURAL the study of the literature, languages and culture of ancient Greece and Rome

classification /ˌklæsɪfɪˈkeɪʃən/ NOUN [plural **classifications**]
1 *no plural* the process of putting things into groups according to the qualities they have
2 a group that includes people or things with the same qualities

classified /ˈklæsɪfaɪd/ ADJECTIVE classified information is secret and known only by the government

classify /ˈklæsɪfaɪ/ VERB [**classifies, classifying, classified**] to put people or things into groups or classes according to what qualities they have □ *The books are classified by subject.*

classmate /ˈklɑːsmeɪt/ NOUN [plural **classmates**] someone in your school or college class

classroom /ˈklɑːsruːm/ NOUN [plural **classrooms**] a room where students have lessons

classy /ˈklɑːsɪ/ ADJECTIVE [**classier, classiest**] attractive, fashionable and expensive □ *a classy hotel*

clatter /ˈklætə(r)/ ▶ VERB [**clatters, clattering, clattered**] to make a loud noise like hard objects falling or hitting each other □ *He came clattering downstairs in his ski boots.*
▶ NOUN, NO PLURAL a sound made when hard objects fall or hit against each other ⊞ *The plates fell to the floor with a clatter.*

clause /klɔːz/ NOUN [plural **clauses**]
1 a group of words that makes up a sentence or part of a sentence □ *a relative clause*
2 a part of an official document or a law □ *clause 10 of the contract*

claustrophobia /ˌklɔːstrəˈfəʊbɪə/ NOUN, NO PLURAL a fear of small, crowded or closed spaces
• **claustrophobic** /ˌklɔːstrəˈfəʊbɪk/ ADJECTIVE afraid of small, crowded or closed spaces

claw /klɔː/ ▶ NOUN [plural **claws**]
1 one of the long pointed nails on the toes of some animals and birds
2 a long part at the end of the leg of some sea creatures and insects, that is used for holding things
▶ VERB [**claws, clawing, clawed**] to scratch something with claws or nails □ *The cat had been clawing at the sofa.*

clay /kleɪ/ NOUN, NO PLURAL a soft sticky substance in the ground that goes hard when it is baked and is used for making cups and bowls □ *clay pots*

clean /kliːn/ ADJECTIVE [**cleaner, cleanest**]
1 not dirty □ *clean hands* □ *a clean kitchen* □ *clean air* □ *clean drinking water* ⊞ *Everywhere looked clean and tidy.*
2 with no writing on □ *a clean sheet of paper*
3 showing that you have done nothing bad or illegal ⊞ *a clean driving licence* (=one that shows no driving crimes)
4 honest □ *a clean election*
♦ IDIOMS **come clean** to start to tell the truth about something **make a clean breast of something** to tell someone the truth about something you had been keeping secret
▶ VERB [**cleans, cleaning, cleaned**] to remove the dirt from something □ *I've just been cleaning the kitchen.* □ *Have you cleaned your teeth?*
♦ PHRASAL VERBS **clean something out** to remove things from a place and clean it very well □ *I've cleaned out the car.* **clean (something) up** to make a place clean and tidy, removing any rubbish □ *I'll start cleaning up this mess.* **clean up after someone** to clean a place after someone has made it dirty □ *I'm sick of cleaning up after you!*
▶ ADVERB completely □ *I clean forgot I was supposed to meet her.*
• **cleaner** /ˈkliːnə(r)/ NOUN [plural **cleaners**]
1 someone whose job is to clean places □ *The cleaner comes in once a week.*

2 a liquid for cleaning things □ *oven cleaner*

• **cleaning** /'kli:nɪŋ/ NOUN, NO PLURAL the activity of making a place clean ⊞ *My mother does all the cleaning.*

• **cleanliness** /'klenlɪnɪs/ NOUN, NO PLURAL the state of being clean or the process of keeping something clean

• **cleanly** /'kli:nlɪ/ ADVERB if something breaks cleanly, it breaks completely and in a tidy way □ *The log split cleanly in half.*

cleanse /klenz/ VERB [**cleanses, cleansing, cleansed**] to clean your skin or a cut □ *Cleanse the wound with antiseptic.*

• **cleanser** /'klenzə(r)/ NOUN [*plural* **cleansers**] a liquid or cream that cleanses your skin

clear /klɪə(r)/ ▶ ADJECTIVE [**clearer, clearest**]

1 easy to understand □ *I gave clear instructions.* □ *He drew a very clear map.*

2 obvious □ **+ that** *It was clear that she wasn't happy.* ⊞ *Sally made her feelings very clear.*

3 easy to see or hear □ *The recording wasn't very clear.* □ *The pictures were very clear.*

4 transparent □ *clear glass*

5 not blocked or covered by anything □ *a clear sky* □ *a clear view of the stage* □ **+ of** *The road was clear of traffic.*

▶ VERB [**clears, clearing, cleared**]

1 to remove people or things from a place □ *I'll just clear these dishes.* □ *Police cleared the streets around the car bomb.*

2 if the sky or the weather clears, it becomes brighter

3 if a judge or other person in authority clears someone of a crime, the judge decides that person is not guilty □ **+ of** *He was cleared of all charges.*

4 to jump over something without touching it □ *The pony cleared all the fences.*

✦ IDIOM **clear the air** to improve a problem that you have with someone by talking to them about it □ *Yesterday's meeting helped to clear the air.*

✦ PHRASAL VERBS **clear something away** to remove things that you have finished using in order to make a place tidy □ *I'll just clear away my papers.* **clear (something) up** to make a place tidy □ *I helped to clear up after the party.* **clear up** to get better □ *Her skin problem has cleared up.* □ *The weather has cleared up.*

▶ ADVERB not near something or not touching it ⊞ *Stand clear of the doors.*

▶ NOUN, NO PLURAL **in the clear** (a) not guilty of a crime or mistake (b) not in a bad situation any more □ *The goal put the team in the clear.*

• **clearance** /'klɪərəns/ NOUN [*plural* **clearances**]

1 *no plural* official permission to do something □ *The plane was given clearance to land.*

2 *no plural* the amount of space between one thing and another that is moving past it

3 the process of removing things that are not wanted

clear-cut /ˌklɪə(r)'kʌt/ ADJECTIVE obvious and not causing doubt □ *This was a clear-cut case of abuse.*

clearing /'klɪərɪŋ/ NOUN [*plural* **clearings**] an area in a forest where there are no trees

clearly /'klɪəlɪ/ ADVERB

1 in a way that is easy to see, hear, or understand □ *You can see it quite clearly in the photo.* □ *She explained it very clearly.*

2 obviously □ *Clearly, we can't do the job without enough people.*

cleaver /'kli:və(r)/ NOUN [*plural* **cleavers**] a knife with a large, square blade

clef /klef/ NOUN [*plural* **clefs**] a symbol used at the beginning of a piece of music to show how high or low the notes are

clemency /'klemənsɪ/ NOUN, NO PLURAL a decision that a king or leader makes not to punish someone severely. A formal word.

clementine /'kleməntaɪn/ NOUN [*plural* **clementines**] a fruit like a small orange.

clench /klentʃ/ VERB [**clenches, clenching, clenched**] to close part of your body tightly or press it tightly together □ *Clenching his teeth, he jumped out of the plane.*

clergy /'klɜ:dʒɪ/ PLURAL NOUN priests, especially in the Christian church

clergyman /'klɜ:dʒɪmən/ NOUN [*plural* **clergymen**] a man who is a priest

clergywoman /'klɜ:dʒɪwumən/ NOUN [*plural* **clergywomen**] a woman who is a priest

cleric /'klerɪk/ NOUN [*plural* **clerics**] a member of the clergy (=priests)

• **clerical** /'klerɪkəl/ ADJECTIVE

1 involved in office work □ *a clerical assistant*

2 used by or to do with the clergy (=priests) □ *a clerical collar*

clerk /klɑ:k/ NOUN [*plural* **clerks**]

1 an office worker whose job is to write letters, store documents, or keep financial records

2 the US word for shop assistant

clever /'klevə(r)/ ADJECTIVE [**cleverer, cleverest**]

1 good at learning and understanding things □ *He was a very clever boy.*

2 showing good understanding and intelligence □ *a clever idea*

3 skilful □ **+ with** *She's always been clever with her hands.*

cliché /'kli:ʃeɪ/ NOUN [*plural* **clichés**] a phrase that has been used so often it is not now interesting or original

click /klɪk/ ▶ VERB [**clicks, clicking, clicked**]

1 to press a button on a computer mouse in order to make the computer do something. A computing word. □ *Just type your message and click 'Send'.* □ **+ on** *Click on the icon to open the program.*

2 to make a short, sharp sound □ *We could hear her heels clicking on the stone floor.*

▶ NOUN [*plural* **clicks**]

1 a short, sharp sound □ *The box closed with a click.*
2 when you press a button on a computer mouse to make the computer do something. A computing word. □ *You can place your order with just one click.*

client /'klaɪənt/ NOUN [plural **clients**] someone who pays someone else for a service

cliff /klɪf/ NOUN [plural **cliffs**] the high, steep side of a piece of land, usually next to the sea

climactic /klaɪˈmæktɪk/ ADJECTIVE a climactic point or event is the most exciting or important one of a series

climate /'klaɪmɪt/ NOUN [plural **climates**]
1 the type of weather that a country or area usually gets □ *These plants only grow in hot climates.*
2 the situation and opinions that exist at a particular time □ *It's a risky decision in the current political climate.*

climate change /'klaɪmɪt ˌtʃeɪndʒ/ NOUN, NO PLURAL the way the weather is changing and the Earth is getting warmer □ *a conference on climate change*

climax /'klaɪmæks/ NOUN [plural **climaxes**] the most important, most exciting or most interesting point in a story or situation □ *The climax of the show was a dazzling firework display.*

climb /klaɪm/ ▶ VERB [**climbs, climbing, climbed**]
1 to go up or to go towards the top, often using your hands and feet □ *He likes to climb trees.* □ *It's a very difficult mountain to climb.*
2 to get into or out of something □ **+ into** *He climbed into his car and drove off.*
3 to increase in number □ *By last year, the number of people without a job had climbed to 2 million.*
♦ PHRASAL VERB **climb down** to admit that your opinion was wrong, especially after an argument
▶ NOUN [plural **climbs**] an act of climbing or the distance you climb □ *We had a steep climb to the top.*
• **climber** /'klaɪmə(r)/ NOUN [plural **climbers**]
1 someone who climbs, often as a hobby or sport □ *a very experienced climber*
2 a plant that grows upwards by attaching itself to things like walls and fences

clinch /klɪntʃ/ VERB [**clinches, clinching, clinched**] to do one last thing to win an agreement, argument or game ⊞ *That second goal has surely clinched it for United.*

cling /klɪŋ/ VERB [**clings, clinging, clung**]
1 to hold on to something tightly, usually because you are afraid □ *The child clung to her mother.*
2 to stick to or to fit something very tightly □ *His wet shirt clung to his body.*

clingfilm /'klɪŋfɪlm/ NOUN, NO PLURAL a very thin sheet of plastic that is used to cover food

clinic /'klɪnɪk/ NOUN [plural **clinics**] a place where people can see doctors to get treatment and advice □ *an eye clinic*

• **clinical** /'klɪnɪkəl/ ADJECTIVE
1 involving working with people who are ill instead of doing tests in a laboratory ⊞ *clinical trials*

2 not showing any emotion and not considering other people's feelings □ *a clinical approach*

clink /klɪŋk/ ▶ NOUN [plural **clinks**] a sharp ringing sound like the sound made when glasses or coins are hit together □ *the clink of glasses*
▶ VERB [**clinks, clinking, clinked**] to make a clink sound

clip /klɪp/ ▶ VERB [**clips, clipping, clipped**]
1 to cut small or short parts off something □ *He was busy clipping the hedge.*
2 to fasten something to something else with a pin □ *He had a badge clipped to his lapel.*
▶ NOUN [plural **clips**]
1 a small object that fastens something together or to something else ⊞ *a paper clip* ⊞ *a hair clip*
2 a short piece from a film or television programme □ *I've seen a clip from his new film.*

clip art /'klɪp ˌɑːt/ NOUN, NO PLURAL pictures that you can copy into your own computer documents. A computing word.

clipboard /'klɪpbɔːd/ NOUN [plural **clipboards**]
1 a place on a computer for storing information so that you can copy it into another document. A computing word.
2 a piece of strong card with a metal part at the top that you fasten paper to and write on as you move around

clippers /'klɪpəz/ PLURAL NOUN a tool used for cutting small bits from things □ *nail clippers*

clique /kliːk/ NOUN [plural **cliques**] a small group of people who are friendly to each other but keep other people out of the group
• **cliquey** /'kliːki/ ADJECTIVE [**cliquier, cliquiest**] behaving like a clique

cloak /kləʊk/ ▶ NOUN [plural **cloaks**]
1 a loose coat without sleeves that hangs down from the shoulders
2 a cloak of something something that hides the truth. A literary phrase. □ *His business dealings were hidden under a cloak of secrecy.*
▶ VERB [**cloaks, cloaking, cloaked**] to cover or hide something. A literary word. □ *The hills were cloaked in mist.*

cloakroom /'kləʊkruːm/ NOUN [plural **cloakrooms**] a room or area in a building where visitors can leave their coats, hats and bags

clobber /'klɒbə(r)/ VERB [**clobbers, clobbering, clobbered**]
1 to hit someone hard. An informal word.
2 to defeat someone. An informal word. □ *The home team got clobbered.*

clock /klɒk/ NOUN [plural **clocks**] an object which shows the time □ *an alarm clock* □ *There's a clock on the kitchen wall.*
♦ IDIOM **around/round the clock** during all of the day and all of the night □ *Emergency services have been working around the clock to find survivors.*
♦ PHRASAL VERB [**clocks, clocking, clocked**] **clock up**

something to get a particular number of something over a period of time □ *He clocked up over 100 goals for his country.*

clockwise /'klɒkwaɪz/ ADVERB, ADJECTIVE turning or moving in the same direction as the hands of a clock □ *a clockwise direction* □ *Turn the knob clockwise.*

clockwork /'klɒkwɜ:k/ NOUN, NO PLURAL **go/run like clockwork** to happen correctly, with no stops or problems

clog /klɒg/ ▶ VERB [**clogs, clogging, clogged**] to block something or be blocked □ *The drains are clogged up with leaves.*

▶ NOUN [*plural* **clogs**] a shoe with a wooden bottom

cloister /'klɔɪstə(r)/ NOUN [*plural* **cloisters**] a covered passage around the edge of a square garden in a religious building

clone /kləʊn/ ▶ NOUN [*plural* **clones**] an exact copy of a plant or animal, made by a scientist taking cells from that plant or animal

▶ VERB [**clones, cloning, cloned**] to make an exact copy of a plant or animal in this way □ *Scientists have successfully cloned a sheep.*

close¹ /kləʊz/ ▶ VERB [**closes, closing, closed**]
1 to shut □ *Could you close the door, please?* □ *The door closed behind him.* □ *Close your eyes and go to sleep.*
2 if a shop, restaurant, etc. closes, it stops serving people, for example at the end of a day □ *Supermarkets close around 8 o'clock.*
3 to stop operating as a business, permanently □ *A lot of shops in this area have closed.*
4 to finish something □ *I would like to close the meeting by thanking you all for coming.*
5 to finish using a computer program or document and make it go off your screen. A computing word.
♦ PHRASAL VERBS **close (something) down** to stop operating as a business, or make something stop operating as a business □ *A lot of small businesses are closing down.* **close in** to get nearer to someone so that you can catch or attack them □ *The troops are closing in on the rebels.* **close something off** to stop people from going into a place □ *Police closed off the streets around the theatre.*

▶ NOUN, NO PLURAL the end of something □ *The pound was weak at the close of trading.* ⊞ *She quickly brought the meeting to a close.*

close² /kləʊs/ ADJECTIVE [**closer, closest**]
1 near in distance or time □ **+ to** *The flat is close to the shops.* □ *It was close to midnight when he got back.*
2 if you are close to someone, you know and like them well □ **+ to** *I'm very close to my younger sister.* ⊞ *We invited a few close friends.*
3 a close relation is someone such as your mother, father, sister or brother
4 seeing or talking to someone often ⊞ *I'm still in close contact with my ex-colleagues.*
5 looking or listening carefully ⊞ *Pay close attention to what he says.* ⊞ *I kept a close eye on the time.*

6 a close game or competition is one in which people score almost the same number of points
7 warm and with no fresh air □ *It was very close inside the tent.*
♦ IDIOM **at close quarters** from very close to someone or something □ *I had never seen a lion at close quarters before.*
➡ go to a **close shave**
▶ ADVERB [**closer, closest**]
1 near □ *Her mother was standing close by.*
2 **be/come close to doing something** to almost do something □ *He came close to winning.*

close³ /kləʊs/ NOUN [*plural* **closes**] a street that cars can go into only at one end □ *They live at 16 Cathedral Close.*

closed /kləʊzd/ ADJECTIVE
1 not open □ *Laura kept her eyes closed.*
2 not open for business □ *The banks are closed on Sundays.*

close-knit /,kləʊs'nɪt/ ADJECTIVE a close-knit group of people shares similar ideas and supports each other

closely /'kləʊslɪ/ ADVERB
1 carefully □ *Police are examining the scene closely.*
2 with little distance between two things ⊞ *He entered, closely followed by his parents.*
3 if you work closely with someone, you work together, sharing information and ideas ⊞
4 if two things are closely connected, they are very similar or have a strong connection □ *Humans are very closely related to apes.*

closet /'klɒzɪt/ NOUN [*plural* **closets**] the US word for **cupboard**

close-up /'kləʊsʌp/ NOUN [*plural* **close-ups**] a photograph or part of a film that is taken from very close to something so that you can see all the details

closure /'kləʊʒə(r)/ NOUN [*plural* **closures**]
1 when a business, organization, etc. stops operating □ *school closures*
2 when you have finished dealing with a bad experience and your life is not now spoilt by it

clot /klɒt/ ▶ NOUN [*plural* **clots**] a solid mass that forms in liquids, especially in cream or blood
▶ VERB [**clots, clotting, clotted**] to form clots

cloth /klɒθ/ NOUN [*plural* **cloths**]
1 *no plural* material made of wool, cotton, etc., used for making clothes, etc. □ *cotton cloth* □ *a cloth bag*
2 a piece of cloth used for cleaning or drying □ *She wiped the table with a damp cloth.*

clothe /kləʊð/ VERB [**clothes, clothing, clothed**] to put clothes on someone or provide them with clothes □ *They need money to feed and clothe themselves.*
● **clothes** /kləʊðz/ PLURAL NOUN the things people wear to cover their bodies ⊞ *She wears very interesting clothes.* □ *baby clothes* □ *a clothes shop*

clothes peg /'kləʊz ,peg/ NOUN [plural **clothes pegs**] a small object that you use to fasten wet clothes to a line while they dry

clothing /'kləʊðɪŋ/ NOUN, NO PLURAL clothes, especially for a particular activity □ waterproof clothing □ Please bring a change of clothing. 🖾 a piece of clothing

cloud /klaʊd/ ▶ NOUN [plural **clouds**]
1 a white or grey mass of small water drops that is in the sky □ rain clouds □ dark clouds
2 a mass of smoke, dust, sand, etc. in the air □ a cloud of flies □ Clouds of smoke were billowing from the factory.
▶ VERB [**clouds, clouding, clouded**] to make something more difficult to see through □ His eyes clouded with tears.
♦ PHRASAL VERB **cloud over** if the weather or the sky clouds over, the sky becomes full of clouds

cloudburst /'klaʊdbɜːst/ NOUN [plural **cloudbursts**] when a lot of rain suddenly falls

cloudy /'klaʊdɪ/ ADJECTIVE [**cloudier, cloudiest**]
1 full of clouds 🖾 a cloudy sky
2 not transparent □ a cloudy liquid

clout /klaʊt/ ▶ NOUN [plural **clouts**]
1 influence and power □ These organizations have a lot of political clout.
2 a hard hit with the hand. An informal word.
▶ VERB [**clouts, clouting, clouted**] to hit someone with the hand. An informal word.

clove /kləʊv/ NOUN [plural **cloves**]
1 a small dried flower, used in cooking as a spice
2 one of the parts that makes up the root of some plants □ a clove of garlic

clover /'kləʊvə(r)/ NOUN, NO PLURAL a small plant with leaves that have three parts

clown /klaʊn/ NOUN [plural **clowns**] someone who wears funny clothes, has a painted face, and does silly things to make people laugh
♦ PHRASAL VERB [**clowns, clowning, clowned**] **clown around** to do silly things that make people laugh

club /klʌb/ ▶ NOUN [plural **clubs**]
1 an organization of people who meet regularly to do a particular activity, or the place where they meet
🖾 She belongs to a golf club. 🖾 I've joined a tennis club.
2 a place where people go at night to dance and drink
3 one of the sticks used in golf to hit the ball
4 a heavy piece of wood or metal used as a weapon
5 clubs one of the four types of playing card, which have the symbol (♣) printed on them □ the four of clubs
▶ VERB [**clubs, clubbing, clubbed**] go clubbing to go out dancing and drinking in clubs □ She goes clubbing on Saturday night.
♦ PHRASAL VERB **club together** to share the cost of something □ We all clubbed together to get her a present.

cluck /klʌk/ ▶ VERB [**clucks, clucking, clucked**] when a chicken clucks, it makes a repeated low sound.
▶ NOUN [plural **clucks**] the sound made by a chicken

clue /kluː/ NOUN [plural **clues**] a sign or piece of information that helps solve a problem, mystery or crime □ a crossword clue □ The police are looking for clues.
♦ IDIOM **not have a clue** an informal phrase meaning to know or understand nothing about something □ I didn't have a clue what she meant.

clump /klʌmp/ NOUN [plural **clumps**] a group of plants growing close together □ a clump of trees

clumsy /'klʌmzɪ/ ADJECTIVE [**clumsier, clumsiest**] a clumsy person is awkward in the way they move, often dropping things or knocking into things

clung /klʌŋ/ PAST TENSE AND PAST PARTICIPLE OF cling

cluster /'klʌstə(r)/ NOUN [plural **clusters**] a group of similar things that are near each other □ a cluster of cottages
♦ PHRASAL VERB [**clusters, clustering, clustered**] **cluster around (someone/something)** to form a group around someone or something □ The children clustered around the baby donkey.

clutch /klʌtʃ/ ▶ VERB [**clutches, clutching, clutched**] to hold something tightly in your hand or hands □ She clutched her mother's hand.
♦ PHRASAL VERB **clutch at something** to try to take hold of something □ I clutched at his arm as I fell.
▶ NOUN [plural **clutches**]
1 the part of a car's engine that you operate by pressing with your foot to change gears
2 clutches when someone controls someone else □ He fell into the clutches of a criminal gang.

clutter /'klʌtə(r)/ ▶ NOUN, NO PLURAL things that cover or fill a place so that it looks untidy □ I must get rid of some of this clutter.
▶ VERB [**clutters, cluttering, cluttered**] to fill a space with lots of things and make it untidy □ Books cluttered every surface.

cm ABBREVIATION centimetre or centimetres

Co ABBREVIATION Company, used in the name of a business □ Smith, Jenkins and Co.

co- /kəʊ/ PREFIX co- is added to the beginning of words to mean 'together with' or 'working with' □ co-star □ cooperate

coach /kəʊtʃ/ ▶ NOUN [plural **coaches**]
1 a comfortable bus for long journeys □ a coach station 🖾 a coach trip
2 someone who helps people to improve a skill, often a sport, or who gives extra teaching in a school subject □ a rugby coach □ a singing coach
3 in the past, a vehicle that was pulled by horses
▶ VERB [**coaches, coaching, coached**] to help someone to improve a skill, often a sport, or to give extra teaching to someone in a school subject □ He's being coached by an ex-Olympic champion.

• **coaching** /'kəʊtʃɪŋ/ NOUN, NO PLURAL teaching □ *She has extra coaching in French.*

coagulate /kəʊ'æɡjuleɪt/ VERB [coagulates, coagulating, coagulated] if a liquid, especially blood, coagulates, it becomes thick and sticky. A biology word.

coal /kəʊl/ NOUN, NO PLURAL a hard black substance that is dug out of the ground and burnt to give heat

coalition /ˌkəʊə'lɪʃən/ NOUN [plural coalitions] a government formed from two or more political parties working together 🔁 *a coalition government*

coal mine /'kəʊl ˌmaɪn/ NOUN [plural coal mines] a place where coal is dug out of the ground

coarse /kɔːs/ ADJECTIVE [coarser, coarsest]
1 rough □ *coarse cloth*
2 in large, irregular pieces □ *coarse sea salt*
3 rude □ *coarse language*

coast /kəʊst/ ► NOUN [plural coasts] the area of land next to the sea □ *It's a town on the west coast of Ireland.* □ *They've gone for a trip to the coast.*
♦ IDIOM **the coast is clear** if the coast is clear, there is no one around to see you or stop you doing something
► VERB [coasts, coasting, coasted]
1 to achieve something without making much effort □ + *to* United coasted to victory in the second half.
2 to travel in a vehicle without using any power □ *Jack coasted down the hill on his bike.*
• **coastal** /'kəʊstəl/ ADJECTIVE on or near a coast □ *a coastal town*

coastguard /'kəʊstɡɑːd/ NOUN [plural coastguards] someone whose job is to watch the sea near the coast to prevent illegal activities and to help ships in danger

coastline /'kəʊstlaɪn/ NOUN [plural coastlines] the edge of a coast □ *the beautiful Northumberland coastline*

coat /kəʊt/ ► NOUN [plural coats]
1 a piece of clothing with sleeves that you wear over your other clothes when you go out □ *He was wearing a thick winter coat.*
2 a layer of a substance 🔁 *a coat of paint*
3 the fur of an animal
► VERB [coats, coating, coated] to cover something with a thin layer of a substance □ *Their bodies were coated with mud.*

coat-hanger /'kəʊthæŋə(r)/ NOUN [plural coat-hangers] a piece of wood, plastic or metal with a curved part at the top, for hanging up clothes

coating /'kəʊtɪŋ/ NOUN [plural coatings] a layer of a substance covering something □ *There was a thin coating of snow on the ground.*

coax /kəʊks/ VERB [coaxes, coaxing, coaxed] to try to persuade someone to do something □ *He was finally coaxed into taking part in the game.*

cob /kɒb/ NOUN [plural cobs] a long round solid part of a maize plant that the seeds grow on

cobble /'kɒbəl/ NOUN [plural cobbles] a round stone used on the surface of a road

• **cobbled** /'kɒbəld/ ADJECTIVE covered with cobbles

cobbler /'kɒblə(r)/ NOUN [plural cobblers] someone whose job is making and repairing shoes

cobblestone /'kɒbəlstəʊn/ NOUN [plural cobblestones] a round stone used on the surface of a road

cobra /'kəʊbrə/ NOUN [plural cobras] a poisonous snake that makes its neck go flat before it attacks

cobweb /'kɒbweb/ NOUN [plural cobwebs] a pattern of thin crossing threads that a spider makes to catch insects

coccyx /'kɒksɪks/ NOUN [plural coccyxes or coccyges] a small bone shaped like a triangle at the bottom of your spine (=line of bones down your back). A biology word.

cock /kɒk/ ► NOUN [plural cocks] a male bird
► VERB [cocks, cocking, cocked]
1 to move a part of your body 🔁 *He cocked his head to one side.* □ *The dog suddenly cocked its ears.*
2 to make a gun ready to fire □ *The officer cocked his pistol.*
♦ PHRASAL VERB **cock (something) up** an informal word meaning to do something badly or wrong □ *I was supposed to book the hotel, but I cocked it up.*

cockerel /'kɒkərəl/ NOUN [plural cockerels] a male chicken

cockle /'kɒkəl/ NOUN [plural cockles] a type of sea creature with a small round shell, that you can eat

cockney /'kɒkni/ NOUN [plural cockneys]
1 someone who comes from East London
2 the way cockneys speak □ *a cockney accent*

cockpit /'kɒkpɪt/ NOUN [plural cockpits] the area in an aeroplane where the pilot sits

cockroach /'kɒkrəʊtʃ/ NOUN [plural cockroaches] a large brown or black insect usually found in dirty places

cocktail /'kɒkteɪl/ NOUN [plural cocktails]
1 an alcoholic drink made with two or more types of drink mixed together
2 a mixture of substances or characteristics □ *a cocktail of drugs*

cocky /'kɒki/ ADJECTIVE [cockier, cockiest] confident in an annoying way

cocoa /'kəʊkəʊ/ NOUN, NO PLURAL
1 a brown powder made from the seeds of a tropical tree, used to make chocolate
2 a hot drink made from cocoa powder mixed with milk

coconut /'kəʊkənʌt/ NOUN [plural coconuts] a large nut with a brown outer part with hair on, and white flesh and liquid inside 🔁 *coconut milk*

cocoon /kə'kuːn/ NOUN [plural cocoons] a case made by some insects inside which they change into their adult form

cod /kɒd/ NOUN [plural cod] a large sea fish that you can eat

coddle /'kɒdəl/ VERB [coddles, coddling, coddled] to protect someone too much

code /kəʊd/ ► NOUN [plural codes]

1 a set of signs or letters used instead of normal writing to send a secret message □ The letter was written in code. 🔁 They managed to break the code (=understand it).

2 a series of letters or numbers used to show what something is or to give information about it □ a tax code □ Please enter your security code.

3 the first part of a telephone number that tells you the area or the country □ What's the code for the UK?

4 a set of rules or laws 🔁 The company has its own code of conduct. 🔁 a strict dress code

5 a series of instructions used in computer software. A computing word.

► VERB [codes, coding, coded]

1 to give something a code to show what it is or to give information about it □ All the words are coded according to their subject area.

2 to put a message into code

3 to write instructions for a computer. A computing word.

• **coded** /'kəʊdɪd/ ADJECTIVE

1 written in code □ a coded message

2 expressed in way that is not direct □ The play contained coded criticism of the government.

coed /'kəʊed/ a short way to say and write coeducational

coeducation /ˌkəʊedʒʊ'keɪʃən/ NOUN, NO PLURAL the teaching of male and female students together

• **coeducational** /ˌkəʊedʒʊ'keɪʃənəl/ ADJECTIVE teaching both male and female students □ a coeducational school

coerce /kəʊ'ɜːs/ VERB [coerces, coercing, coerced] to force someone to do something that they do not want to do □ None of our employees will be coerced into retiring.

• **coercion** /kəʊ'ɜːʃən/ NOUN, NO PLURAL forcing someone to do something they do not want to do □ There were claims that they had used coercion.

coexist /ˌkəʊɪg'zɪst/ VERB [coexists, coexisting, coexisted] to live or exist together at the same time or in the same place □ The two religions coexist peacefully in the region.

• **coexistence** /ˌkəʊɪg'zɪstəns/ NOUN, NO PLURAL when two or more people or things coexist 🔁 They live in peaceful coexistence with their neighbours.

coffee /'kɒfɪ/ NOUN [plural coffees]

1 no plural a drink made from the beans of a tropical plant □ I don't drink coffee. 🔁 Let's have a cup of coffee. 🔁 black/white coffee (=coffee without/with milk)

2 a cup of this drink □ Two black coffees, please.

coffer /'kɒfə(r)/ NOUN [plural coffers]

1 coffers the money a company or organization has □ This money will swell the government's coffers.

2 a large strong box used to store valuable things

coffin /'kɒfɪn/ NOUN [plural coffins] a long wooden box that a dead body is put into to be buried

cog /kɒg/ NOUN [plural cogs] one of the pointed parts round the edge of a wheel in an engine or machine that helps it turn

cognac /'kɒnjæk/ NOUN, NO PLURAL a type of French brandy (=alcoholic drink)

cogwheel /'kɒgwiːl/ NOUN [plural cogwheels] a metal disc with points around its edge, used to turn other cogwheels or parts inside a machine

coherence /kəʊ'hɪərəns/ NOUN, NO PLURAL when something is coherent

• **coherent** /kəʊ'hɪərənt/ ADJECTIVE

1 clear and easy to understand □ He wasn't particularly coherent.

2 a coherent plan, argument, etc. is sensible and all the parts have been considered

• **coherently** /kəʊ'hɪərəntlɪ/ ADVERB in a clear and sensible way □ He argued forcibly and coherently against the changes.

coil /kɔɪl/ ► VERB [coils, coiling, coiled] to twist something long to form circles □ The huge snake coiled itself round the branch.

► NOUN [plural coils] a long piece of rope, wire, etc. twisted into circles □ a coil of thin wire

coin /kɔɪn/ ► NOUN [plural coins] a round, flat piece of metal money 🔁 a gold coin 🔁 a pound coin

► VERB [coins, coining, coined]

1 to use a new word or phrase for the first time

2 to coin a phrase something you say before using a phrase that is well known

coincide /ˌkəʊɪn'saɪd/ VERB [coincides, coinciding, coincided] when events coincide with each other, they happen at the same time □ The carnival will coincide with the beginning of the school holidays.

coincidence /kəʊ'ɪnsɪdəns/ NOUN [plural coincidences] when two things happen at the same time by chance 🔁 It was pure coincidence that I was on the train that day. □ By coincidence, his father also worked in China.

• **coincidental** /kəʊˌɪnsɪ'dentəl/ ADJECTIVE happening at the same time by chance □ It was completely coincidental that they arrived on the same day.

coke /kəʊk/ NOUN, NO PLURAL a type of fuel made from coal

cola /'kəʊlə/ NOUN [plural colas] a dark brown, sweet fizzy (=with bubbles) drink

colander /'kɒləndə(r)/ NOUN [plural colanders] a container with holes in the bottom used to remove water from food

cold /kəʊld/ ► ADJECTIVE [colder, coldest]

1 low in temperature □ a cold drink □ She hated cold weather. 🔁 It was a bitterly cold night. 🔁 It's freezing cold outside. □ His hands felt cold.

2 unfriendly or not showing emotion □ a cold stare □ She seemed so cold and uncaring.

♦ IDIOM **have/get cold feet** to suddenly feel afraid to do something that you had planned to do □ *He was due to sing at the concert, but he got cold feet at the last minute.*
▶ NOUN [*plural* **colds**]
1 a common illness that makes you cough and blocks your nose 🕮 *Hannah's got a cold.* 🕮 *I caught a cold while I was away.*
2 the cold cold weather or a low temperature □ *We waited around in the cold for an hour.*

cold-blooded /ˌkəʊld'blʌded/ ADJECTIVE
1 a cold-blooded person is cruel and shows no emotion □ *a cold-blooded killer*
2 a cold-blooded animal's temperature changes according to the temperature of the air or water around it. A biology word.

coldly /ˈkəʊldlɪ/ ADVERB in an unfriendly way □ *She treated them coldly.*

coldness /ˈkəʊldnɪs/ NOUN, NO PLURAL
1 being unfriendly and showing no emotion □ *Sarah heard the coldness in his voice.*
2 being cold □ *He was surprised by the coldness of the water.*

cold sore /ˈkəʊld ˌsɔː(r)/ NOUN [*plural* **cold sores**] a red, painful mark on your lip caused by a virus

cold war /ˌkəʊld 'wɔː(r)/ NOUN [*plural* **cold wars**] unfriendly political relations between countries, especially between the Soviet Union and the West after World War II

coleslaw /ˈkəʊlslɔː/ NOUN, NO PLURAL a salad made from raw cabbage (=vegetable with green leaves) and mayonnaise (=sauce made from eggs and oil)

colic /ˈkɒlɪk/ NOUN, NO PLURAL a sudden bad pain in the stomach, especially in babies

collaborate /kəˈlæbəreɪt/ VERB [**collaborates, collaborating, collaborated**]
1 to work together with someone else, sharing information and ideas □ *Dr Wallis collaborated with Japanese researchers on the study.*
2 to give information or help to an enemy □ *People who had collaborated with the former regime were imprisoned.*

• **collaboration** /kəˌlæbəˈreɪʃən/ NOUN, NO PLURAL
1 when people work together 🕮 *We work in close collaboration with local doctors.*
2 when someone helps an enemy

• **collaborator** /kəˈlæbəˌreɪtə(r)/ NOUN [*plural* **collaborators**]
1 someone who works with other people
2 someone who helps an enemy

collage /ˈkɒlɑːʒ/ NOUN [*plural* **collages**] a picture made by sticking different pieces of paper, fabric, etc. on a surface

collagen /ˈkɒlədʒən/ NOUN, NO PLURAL a substance found in the skin and bones. A biology word.

collapse /kəˈlæps/ ▶ VERB [**collapses, collapsing, collapsed**]
1 if a building or structure collapses, it falls down because it is too weak □ *The bridge collapsed under the lorry's weight.*

2 if a person collapses, they fall down because they are ill or very tired □ *He collapsed from exhaustion.* □ *I put down my bags and collapsed on the sofa.*
3 to fail suddenly and completely □ *Workers were left jobless after the company collapsed.*
4 to let your body fall onto a bed, chair, etc. because you are very tired
5 if furniture or equipment collapses, it can be folded up to make it smaller □ *The table collapses so that it can be stored under the seat.*
▶ NOUN [*plural* **collapses**]
1 when a building, structure or person falls down □ *After her collapse, she went to Switzerland to recover.*
2 when a business, government, plan, etc. fails □ *The country faces economic collapse.*

• **collapsible** /kəˈlæpsəbəl/ ADJECTIVE collapsible furniture or equipment can be folded so that it is smaller □ *a collapsible chair*

collar /ˈkɒlə(r)/ ▶ NOUN [*plural* **collars**]
1 the piece of material on a shirt or jacket that fits round your neck □ *I unbuttoned my shirt collar.*
2 a piece of leather or other material fastened round an animal's neck
▶ VERB [**collars, collaring, collared**]
1 an informal word meaning to stop someone to talk to them □ *A reporter collared him at a charity event.*
2 an informal word meaning to catch or arrest someone □ *He was collared by a security guard.*

collarbone /ˈkɒləbəʊn/ NOUN [*plural* **collarbones**] one of two bones that go from your shoulder to the front of your neck

collate /kəˈleɪt/ VERB [**collates, collating, collated**] to bring together pieces of information or documents and arrange them in order

colleague /ˈkɒliːg/ NOUN [*plural* **colleagues**] a person who you work with □ *A colleague of mine told me about it.*

collect /kəˈlekt/ VERB [**collects, collecting, collected**]
1 to get things from different places and put them together □ *The survey collected data from 500 people.* □ **+ up** *Could you collect up all the plates, please?*
2 to get and keep things of a particular type as a hobby □ *Ted collects unusual postcards.*
3 to go to a place to get someone or something □ *George collected me from the airport.* □ *The following items are collected for recycling.*
4 to receive money or a prize □ *She collected the award for Best Actress.*
5 to take money from people □ *I'm collecting donations for charity.*

• **collection** /kəˈlekʃən/ NOUN [*plural* **collections**]
1 things that have been collected together 🕮 *a private art collection* □ **+ of** *a collection of rare photographs* □ *The book is a collection of short stories.*
2 when you go to get something from a place □ *There*

were two parcels waiting for collection. □ *weekly rubbish collections*

3 a number of clothes or products for sale by a company at the same time □ *Louis Vuitton's autumn/ winter collection*

4 money collected from different people □ *We had a collection for Bob's retirement.*

● **collective** /kə'lektɪv/ ADJECTIVE involving or done by several people or groups, not just one □ *a collective decision*

collective farm /kə,lektɪv 'fɑːm/ NOUN [*plural* **collective farms**] a large farm owned by the government and worked on by a group of people

collective noun /kə,lektɪv 'naʊn/ NOUN [*plural* **collective nouns**] a word used to refer to a group of people or things. The words *family*, *team*, *staff*, *government*, *herd*, *luggage* and *furniture* are examples of collective nouns.

collectivize *or* **collectivise** /kə'lektɪvaɪz/ VERB [**collectivizes, collectivizing, collectivized**] to join several small farms or businesses and control them together

collector /kə'lektə(r)/ NOUN [*plural* **collectors**]
1 someone who finds and keeps things of the same type in a collection □ *an art collector*
2 someone who collects something as a job □ *a tax collector*

college /'kɒlɪdʒ/ NOUN [*plural* **colleges**]
1 in the UK, a place where people go to learn after they have left school ⊞ *She went to college to do catering.*
2 a US word for university
3 one of the parts that some universities are divided into □ *King's College, Cambridge*

collide /kə'laɪd/ VERB [**collides, colliding, collided**] when moving objects collide, they hit each other □ *The bus collided with a car.*

collie /'kɒlɪ/ NOUN [*plural* **collies**] a type of dog that is used to control sheep

colliery /'kɒljərɪ/ NOUN [*plural* **collieries**] a coal mine

collision /kə'lɪʒən/ NOUN [*plural* **collisions**] a crash between moving vehicles or objects □ *A collision between two lorries has closed the road.*

collocation /,kɒlə'keɪʃən/ NOUN [*plural* **collocations**] two or more words that are often used together. *Commit a crime*, *heavy rain* and *fall ill* are examples of collocations.

colloquial /kə'ləʊkwɪəl/ ADJECTIVE colloquial language is used in normal conversation but not in formal speaking or writing □ *a colloquial term*

collude /kə'luːd/ VERB [**colludes, colluding, colluded**] a formal word meaning to secretly do something dishonest with another person □ *He was accused of colluding with terrorists.*

● **collusion** /kə'luːʒən/ NOUN, NO PLURAL when people collude

cologne /kə'ləʊn/ NOUN, NO PLURAL light perfume (=pleasant-smelling liquid that you put on your skin)

colon /'kəʊlən/ NOUN [*plural* **colons**]
1 a punctuation mark (:) used to separate parts of a sentence or used before a list
2 part of your bowel. A biology word.

colonel /'kɜːnəl/ NOUN [*plural* **colonels**] an officer with a high rank in the army or air force

colonial /kə'ləʊnɪəl/ ADJECTIVE to do with a colony (=country controlled by another country) □ *colonial rule*

colonist /'kɒlənɪst/ NOUN [*plural* **colonists**] someone who goes to another country to start a colony (=country controlled by another country)

colonize *or* **colonise** /'kɒlənaɪz/ VERB [**colonizes, colonizing, colonized**]
1 to send people to start living in another country and to take control of it □ *The area was colonized by Dutch immigrants.*
2 to start living or growing in a new place □ *Golden eagles have colonized the island.*

colony /'kɒlənɪ/ NOUN [*plural* **colonies**]
1 a country or area that is controlled by another country ⊞ *The French established a colony there in the 19th century.*
2 a group of people, animals or plants of the same type living together □ *a colony of ants*
3 a group of people with similar ideas or jobs who live together □ *a hippy colony*

color /'kʌlə(r)/ NOUN [*plural* **colors**], ADJECTIVE, VERB [**colors, coloring, colored**] the US spelling of colour

color-blind /'kʌləblaɪnd/ ADJECTIVE the US spelling of colour-blind

colored /'kʌləd/ ADJECTIVE the US spelling of coloured

colorful /'kʌləfʊl/ ADJECTIVE the US spelling of colourful

● **colorfully** /'kʌləfʊlɪ/ ADVERB the US spelling of colourfully

coloring /'kʌlərɪŋ/ NOUN, NO PLURAL the US spelling of colouring

colorless /'kʌlələs/ ADJECTIVE the US spelling of colourless

colossal /kə'lɒsəl/ ADJECTIVE extremely large □ *a colossal amount of energy*

colour /'kʌlə(r)/ ▶ NOUN [*plural* **colours**]
1 red, blue, green, black, etc. □ **+ of** *Look at the colour of the sky.* □ *What colour are your eyes?* □ *The sea was a lovely blue colour.* ⊞ *There is a range of designs in bright colours.*
2 *no plural* using all colours, not just black and white □ *They printed the photos in colour.*
3 the colour of someone's skin, because of their race □ *We oppose all discrimination on the grounds of colour.*
4 *no plural* interest or excitement □ *We aim to bring some colour back into politics.*
5 off colour feeling slightly ill □ *I'm feeling a bit off colour today.*

► When you say the colour of something or ask about the colour of something, remember to use the verb **be** and not **have**:
✓ *Your jacket is a lovely colour.*
✗ *Your jacket has a lovely colour.*
✓ *What colour is your coat?*
✗ *What colour has your coat?*

► ADJECTIVE having or using colour □ *a colour TV* □ *a colour photograph*
► VERB [**colours, colouring, coloured**]
1 to make something a particular colour or to become a particular colour □ *Does she colour her hair?* □ *Jane's cheeks coloured and she looked away.*
2 to use pens, pencils, etc. to add colour to a picture □ *Colour the sun yellow.* □ *+ in Would you like to colour in your picture?*
3 to affect how you think or feel about something □ *Her view of the city is coloured by those early bad experiences.*

colour-blind /ˈkʌləblaɪnd/ ADJECTIVE not able to see the difference between some colours

coloured /ˈkʌləd/ ADJECTIVE having a colour or colours, not just black and white 卤 *a brightly coloured scarf* □ *Use different coloured pens.*

colourful /ˈkʌləful/ ADJECTIVE
1 having lots of bright colours □ *dancers in colourful costumes* □ *The garden was full of colourful flowers.*
2 interesting or exciting 卤 *Her uncle's a colourful character.*
• **colourfully** /ˈkʌləfulɪ/ ADVERB in a colourful way □ *colourfully dressed children*

colouring /ˈkʌlərɪŋ/ NOUN [plural **colourings**]
1 a substance used to give something a colour □ *red food colouring*
2 the colour of your skin and hair □ *That shade of green suits her dark colouring.*
3 no plural the activity of adding colour to a picture with pens, pencils, etc. □ *Would you like to do some colouring?*

colourless /ˈkʌlələs/ ADJECTIVE having no colour □ *Water is a colourless liquid.*

colt /kəult/ NOUN [plural **colts**] a young male horse

column /ˈkɒləm/ NOUN [plural **columns**]
1 a tall, thick post, usually made of stone □ *Huge marble columns support the roof.*
2 a piece of writing in a newspaper that appears regularly and is usually written by the same person 卤 *He writes a weekly newspaper column.*
3 numbers or words written one under the other on a page □ *+ of a column of figures* □ *Add up the numbers in the right-hand column.*
4 something with a long or tall narrow shape □ *+ of Columns of smoke and dust rose from the erupting volcano.*

5 a long line of people □ *+ of a column of marching soldiers*
• **columnist** /ˈkɒləmnɪst/ NOUN [plural **columnists**] a person who writes a regular column in a newspaper □ *a columnist for the New York Times*

coma /ˈkəumə/ NOUN [plural **comas**] when someone is unconscious for a long time □ *She was in a coma for ten days after the accident.*
• **comatose** /ˈkəumətəus/ ADJECTIVE in a coma or seeming to be in a coma

comb /kəum/ ► NOUN [plural **combs**]
1 an object with a row of very narrow parts along one side that you use to tidy your hair
2 a part that stands up on the top of some birds' heads
► VERB [**combs, combing, combed**]
1 to tidy your hair using a comb □ *She combed her hair.*
2 to search a place very carefully □ *Detectives were combing the area for clues.*

combat /ˈkɒmbæt/ ► NOUN, NO PLURAL fighting, especially in a war □ *The two soldiers died in combat.*
► VERB [**combats, combatting, combatted**] to try to stop something bad or harmful □ *The government brought in new measures to combat terrorism.* □ *He will receive treatment to combat the infection.*
• **combative** /ˈkɒmbətɪv/ ADJECTIVE always willing to argue or fight □ *This latest interview shows the minister in a rather combative mood.*

combination /ˌkɒmbɪˈneɪʃən/ NOUN [plural **combinations**]
1 several things that have been joined or mixed together □ *+ of The problem is due to a combination of factors.*
2 no plural the process of joining or mixing things 卤 *It's safe to use in combination with other drugs.*
3 a series of numbers used to open a lock □ *Who knows the combination to the safe?*

combination lock /ˌkɒmbɪˈneɪʃən ˌlɒk/ NOUN [plural **combination locks**] a lock that you open using a particular series of numbers

combine /kəmˈbaɪn/ VERB [**combines, combining, combined**]
1 to join or mix things together □ *Combine all the ingredients in a mixing bowl.* □ *+ with Carbon dioxide combines with water to form an acid.*
2 to do or use two or more things at the same time □ *+ with You need to take regular exercise, combined with a healthy diet.*

combine harvester /ˌkɒmbaɪn ˈhɑːvɪstə(r)/ NOUN [plural **combine harvesters**] a large farm machine that cuts crops and separates the grain from the stems

combustible /kəmˈbʌstəbəl/ ADJECTIVE a combustible substance will burn or catch fire □ *a highly combustible gas*

combustion /kəmˈbʌstʃən/ NOUN, NO PLURAL burning □ *the combustion of gases*

come /kʌm/ VERB [comes, coming, came, come]
1 to move towards someone or a place □ *Come here!* □ *Here comes Julia.* □ *He came back to see me later.* □ *She came in and said hello.*
2 to go with someone □ **+ with** *Are you coming with us or not?* □ *We're going swimming – do you want to come?*
3 to arrive □ *Has my parcel come yet?*
4 to move in a particular direction or to a particular level □ *Prices have come down.* □ *All the flowers have come up.* □ *We watched the sun come up.*
5 come second/last/before, etc. to have a particular position in a competition or a list □ *P comes before Q in the alphabet.* □ *Philippe came first in the English exam.*
6 come apart/off, etc. to become separated from something □ *I picked up the jug and the handle came off.*
7 How come ...? used to ask for an explanation □ *How come Penny isn't here?*

> ► Remember that the verb **come** means 'to move towards the speaker' or 'to move with the speaker'. For movements away from the speaker, use **go**: □ *Come here!* □ *Eva came to see us last night.* □ *Are you coming to the supermarket with me?*

♦ IDIOM **come clean** to tell the truth □ *I think it's time you came clean about your exam results.*
♦ PHRASAL VERBS **come about** to happen □ *How did the friendship come about?* **come along**
1 to arrive □ *Luckily a police officer came along at that moment.*
2 to go with someone □ *Do you mind if I come along?* **come from somewhere** to be born somewhere or to live somewhere □ *She comes from Brazil.* **Come on!** used to encourage someone or to make them go faster □ *Come on, we're going to be late for school!* **come out** to be available to buy or use □ *Their new CD comes out on Friday.* **come round** to become conscious again □ *When he came round, he could remember nothing about the accident.* **come to something** to be a particular amount of money □ *Six bananas and a bag of apples – that comes to £2.80, please.* **come up**
1 to happen □ *If the opportunity to travel comes up, you should take it.* □ *If any problems come up, just phone me.*
2 to be discussed □ *The subject of Midori's birthday party came up.* **come up with** to produce □ *She came up with several good ideas.*

comeback /ˈkʌmbæk/ NOUN [plural **comebacks**] when a performer starts to appear in public again after a period of not working 🔁 *She's made a comeback with a new album.*

comedian /kəˈmiːdɪən/ NOUN [plural **comedians**] a performer who tells jokes and funny stories

comedienne /kəˌmiːdɪˈen/ NOUN [plural **comediennes**] a female comedian

comedy /ˈkɒmədi/ NOUN [plural **comedies**] entertainment that makes you laugh □ *His latest movie is a comedy.* □ *a comedy sketch*

comet /ˈkɒmɪt/ NOUN [plural **comets**] a type of star that travels across the sky with a line of light behind it

comfort /ˈkʌmfət/ ► NOUN [plural **comforts**]
1 *no plural* a feeling of being relaxed and without pain or other unpleasant feelings □ *I prefer to travel in comfort, flying first class.* □ *When I buy shoes, I choose comfort before fashion.* 🔁 *People can now shop online in the comfort of their own home.*
2 *no plural* a feeling of being less sad or worried 🔁 *I took some comfort from her words.* 🔁 *We found comfort in the fact that we were not alone.*
3 something or someone that makes you feel less sad or worried □ *My children are a great comfort to me.*
4 *no plural* having enough money and other things to make your life easy and pleasant □ *They live in relative comfort.*
5 comforts things that make your life easier or more pleasant □ **+ of** *a hotel with all the comforts of home*
► VERB [comforts, comforting, comforted] to make someone feel happier by saying or doing nice things □ *Last night she was being comforted by relatives.*

● **comfortable** /ˈkʌmfətəbəl/ ADJECTIVE
1 relaxed and without pain □ *Are you comfortable there?* 🔁 *I was in a lot of pain and couldn't get comfortable.*
2 feeling pleasant and not causing any pain □ *a comfortable chair* □ *They're the most comfortable shoes I've got.*
3 not worried or nervous □ **+ with** *I'm not really comfortable with the idea of being filmed.* 🔁 *He immediately made me feel comfortable.*
4 having enough money for the things you need □ *a comfortable lifestyle* □ *She had saved for a comfortable retirement.*
5 a comfortable win is when you win something easily 🔁 *He started the tournament with a comfortable win over Murray.* 🔁 *a comfortable victory*

● **comfortably** /ˈkʌmfətəbli/ ADVERB
1 in a way that makes you feel pleasant and without pain □ *Are you all sitting comfortably?*
2 easily □ *They won comfortably.*

comfy /ˈkʌmfi/ ADJECTIVE [**comfier, comfiest**] an informal word for comfortable □ *a comfy chair*

comic /ˈkɒmɪk/ ► ADJECTIVE
1 to do with comedy 🔁 *a comic actor* □ *He has great comic timing.*
2 funny □ *His face had a really comic expression.*
► NOUN [plural **comics**]
1 a magazine, especially for children, that has picture stories
2 someone whose job is to tell jokes and make people laugh

• **comical** /'kɒmɪkəl/ ADJECTIVE funny □ *The situation was almost comical.*

comic strip /'kɒmɪk ˌstrɪp/ NOUN [*plural* **comic strips**] a series of pictures that tell a story

coming /'kʌmɪŋ/ ADJECTIVE that will happen soon □ *There will be changes in the coming months.*

comma /'kɒmə/ NOUN [*plural* **commas**] a punctuation mark (,) used to separate parts of a sentence

command /kə'mɑːnd/ ▶ VERB [**commands, commanding, commanded**]
1 to be in control of someone or something, especially in a military organization □ *He eventually rose to command the regiment.*
2 to order someone to do something □ *'Stand up straight!' he commanded.* □ + **to do something** *An officer commanded him to go back to his unit.*
3 to get respect, attention, etc. because you deserve it 🕮 *He commands great respect from his colleagues.*
4 to have a particular high price or value □ *Her paintings command huge prices.*
▶ NOUN [*plural* **commands**]
1 an order to do something 🕮 *You must obey commands.* 🕮 *He gave the command to shoot.*
2 no plural control of someone or something □ + **of** *He took command of the expedition.*
3 **in command** in control of a group of people □ *Who's the officer in command?*
4 an instruction that you give to a computer to make it do something. A computing word.
5 knowledge of a particular subject □ + **of** *She had a poor command of English.*

• **commandeer** /ˌkɒmən'dɪə(r)/ VERB [**commandeers, commandeering, commandeered**] to take something, especially for military use □ *The troops commandeered several buses.*

• **commander** /kə'mɑːndə(r)/ NOUN [*plural* **commanders**] someone who is in charge, especially in the police or a military organization

• **commanding** /kə'mɑːndɪŋ/ ADJECTIVE
1 in a position where you are likely to win or succeed 🕮 *He has a commanding lead over his rivals.*
2 powerful and getting respect and attention □ *He was a commanding figure.*

• **commandment** /kə'mɑːndmənt/ NOUN [*plural* **commandments**] one of the ten rules from God in the Bible

commando /kə'mɑːndəʊ/ NOUN [*plural* **commandos** *or* **commandoes**] a soldier who is specially trained to do difficult or dangerous tasks

commemorate /kə'meməreɪt/ VERB [**commemorates, commemorating, commemorated**] to do something to remember a special event or an important person, especially in a ceremony □ *There will be events to commemorate the 60th anniversary of independence.*

• **commemoration** /kəˌmemə'reɪʃən/ NOUN [*plural* **commemorations**] something that is done to remember and celebrate a person or an event □ *the annual commemoration of the end of the war*

commence /kə'mens/ VERB [**commences, commencing, commenced**] a formal word meaning to begin □ *The meeting will commence at 3 o'clock precisely.*

• **commencement** /kə'mensmənt/ NOUN, NO PLURAL a formal word for the beginning of something

commend /kə'mend/ VERB [**commends, commending, commended**] a formal word meaning to praise someone or something □ *Mr Brown commended the work of the police.*

• **commendable** /kə'mendəbəl/ ADJECTIVE deserving praise □ *commendable bravery*

• **commendation** /ˌkɒmən'deɪʃən/ NOUN [*plural* **commendations**] an honour or praise given to someone who has done something well 🕮 *He received a commendation for his actions.*

comment /'kɒment/ ▶ NOUN [*plural* **comments**]
1 something you say to give your opinion □ *I'd welcome any comments about the revised schedule.* 🕮 *He made the comments in a meeting.*
2 **no comment** something you say when you do not want to answer a formal question
▶ VERB [**comments, commenting, commented**] to give your opinion about something □ *'That was a waste of time,' Sally commented.* □ *A spokesman refused to comment on the reports.*

commentary /'kɒməntəri/ NOUN [*plural* **commentaries**] a description or explanation of an event as it happens □ *There will be live radio commentary of every match.*

• **commentate** /'kɒmənteɪt/ VERB [**commentates, commentating, commentated**] to describe an event as it happens, especially on radio or television □ *He was commentating on the match for the BBC.*

• **commentator** /'kɒmənteɪtə(r)/ NOUN [*plural* **commentators**] someone who gives a commentary □ *a football commentator*

commerce /'kɒmɜːs/ NOUN, NO PLURAL the buying and selling of goods and services □ *international commerce*

• **commercial** /kə'mɜːʃəl/ ▶ ADJECTIVE
1 to do with business and selling things □ *commercial and residential buildings* □ *a commercial airline*
2 to do with making a profit □ *The decision was made on purely commercial grounds.*
▶ NOUN [*plural* **commercials**] an advertisement for a product on television or radio

• **commercialized** *or* **commercialised** /kə'mɜːʃəlaɪzd/ ADJECTIVE only to do with making money □ *Christmas has become so commercialized.*

commiserate /kə'mɪzəreɪt/ VERB [**commiserates, commiserating, commiserated**] to show sympathy about something that is making someone unhappy

• **commiserations** /kəˌmɪzə'reɪʃənz/ PLURAL NOUN sympathy for a disappointment or an unhappy situation □ *He offered his commiserations.*

commission /kəˈmɪʃən/ ▸ NOUN [plural
commissions]
1 an official group of people who find out about and
make decisions about something □ the Commission for
Racial Equality □ an independent commission of experts
2 when you ask someone to produce a piece of work
for you □ He was given a commission to paint her
portrait.
3 money paid to someone according to how much
they sell □ He receives a commission of 5%.
▸ VERB [**commissions, commissioning,
commissioned**] to ask someone to produce a piece of
work □ He'd been commissioned to write a book.

commit /kəˈmɪt/ VERB [**commits, committing,
committed**]
1 to do something bad or illegal 🔂 He went on to
commit more serious crimes. 🔂 What makes people
commit murder? 🔂 to commit suicide
2 to promise or to decide to do something □ + to He
doesn't want to commit to a fixed timetable. 🔂 He has
committed himself to the club for next season.
3 to give money, time, etc. for a particular purpose
□ + to The government needs to commit more money
to redevelopment.
• **commitment** /kəˈmɪtmənt/ NOUN [plural
commitments]
1 a promise to do something 🔂 Viran made a definite
commitment to be there. 🔂 The government has made
a long-term commitment to the health service.
2 no plural strong support, effort and enthusiasm for
something 🔂 She has demonstrated great
commitment to the job.
3 something that you must do or are responsible for
🔂 She couldn't come because of work commitments.
🔂 I don't want to take on more financial commitments.
• **committed** /kəˈmɪtɪd/ ADJECTIVE having strong
beliefs or support for something □ a committed
Christian

committee /kəˈmɪti/ NOUN [plural **committees**] a
group of people chosen to do a particular job or to
make decisions about something □ I'm on the
committee for the summer fair.

commodious /kəˈməʊdiəs/ ADJECTIVE a formal word
meaning large, with a lot of space □ a commodious
hotel bedroom
commodity /kəˈmɒdəti/ NOUN [plural
commodities]
1 something that can be bought and sold □ There
were shortages of essential commodities.
2 something useful or necessary 🔂 Water is a precious
commodity.

common /ˈkɒmən/ ▸ ADJECTIVE [**commoner,
commonest**]
1 existing or happening often and in many places
🔂 Traffic jams are a common occurrence in cities. □ +
among The condition is common among older people.
□ Chickenpox is one of the commonest childhood
diseases.

2 shared by several people 🔂 Their common goal was
to make the event a success. 🔂 We share a common
language. 🔂 It's common knowledge (=everyone
knows) that Ann's leaving.
3 ordinary □ the common people
▸ NOUN [plural **commons**]
1 have something in common to share the same
idea, interest, characteristic, etc. as someone or
something else □ I didn't have anything in common
with him. □ The two countries have a great deal in
common.
2 in common with someone/something in the
same way as someone or something else □ In
common with other airlines, they have introduced
stricter safety measures.
3 a piece of land that belongs to and can be used by
everyone in an area □ Wimbledon Common
➡ go to **Commons**

common denominator /ˌkɒmən
dɪˈnɒmɪneɪtə(r)/ NOUN [plural **common
denominators**]
1 a number that can be divided exactly by all the
denominators (=numbers under the line) in a group of
fractions. A maths word.
2 something which is shared by everyone in a group
common factor /ˌkɒmən ˈfæktə(r)/ NOUN [plural
common factors] a number that two or more
numbers can be divided by exactly. A maths word.
common fraction /ˌkɒmən ˈfrækʃən/ NOUN [plural
common fractions] a fraction written with numbers
above and below a line. A maths word.
common ground /ˌkɒmən ˈɡraʊnd/ NOUN, NO
PLURAL interests or ideas which two or more people
share or agree on □ I believe we can find some
common ground between us.
common-law /ˌkɒmənˈlɔː/ ADJECTIVE your common-
law husband or wife is a man or woman that you have
lived with for a long time without being married
Common Market /ˌkɒmən ˈmɑːkɪt/ NOUN the
Common Market the old name for the European
Union (=political and economic organization of
European countries)
common multiple /ˌkɒmən ˈmʌltɪpəl/ NOUN
[plural **common multiples**] a number that can be
divided exactly by two or more other numbers. A
maths word.
commonplace /ˈkɒmənpleɪs/ ADJECTIVE not unusual
□ Wireless technology has become commonplace.
common room /ˈkɒmən ˌruːm/ NOUN [plural
common rooms] a room in a school or college where
students can relax between classes
Commons /ˈkɒmənz/ NOUN the **Commons** one of
the two parts of the British government, with elected
members
common sense /ˌkɒmən ˈsens/ NOUN, NO PLURAL
the ability to think and behave in a sensible, practical
way 🔂 Use your common sense. □ He tries to take a
common sense approach to his work.

commonwealth /'kɒmənwelθ/ NOUN [plural **commonwealths**]
1 a group of countries or states that share political and economic interests
2 the **Commonwealth** Britain and the countries that were ruled by Britain in the past
commotion /kə'məʊʃən/ NOUN [plural **commotions**] noisy and confused activity □ She heard a commotion outside.
communal /'kɒmjʊnəl/ ADJECTIVE shared by several people □ a communal garden
commune /'kɒmjuːn/ NOUN [plural **communes**] a group of people who live together sharing everything
communicable /kə'mjuːnɪkəbəl/ ADJECTIVE a communicable disease can be passed from one person to another

communicate /kə'mjuːnɪkeɪt/ VERB
[**communicates, communicating, communicated**] to share information, opinions, feelings, etc. with other people by speaking, writing, etc. □ + with We are looking for new ways to communicate with our customers. □ + by We communicate mainly by telephone and e-mail. □ He failed to communicate important information.
● **communication** /kə,mjuːnɪ'keɪʃən/ NOUN [plural **communications**]
1 no plural sharing of information ✸ Text messaging is a common form of communication. □ + with We want to improve communication with the public. □ + between There was poor communication between departments.
2 a formal word meaning a message □ We've received an urgent communication from head office.
● **communicative** /kə'mjuːnɪkətɪv/ ADJECTIVE willing to talk to others and give them information

Communion /kə'mjuːnjən/ NOUN, NO PLURAL in the Christian Church, the ceremony in which people eat bread and drink wine to represent Christ's body and blood
communism /'kɒmjʊnɪzəm/ NOUN, NO PLURAL a political system in which the government owns all industry and everyone is treated equally
● **communist** /'kɒmjʊnɪst/ ▶ NOUN [plural **communists**] someone who believes in communism
▶ ADJECTIVE believing in communism or to do with communists □ a communist country
community /kə'mjuːnətɪ/ NOUN [plural **communities**]
1 people living in a particular area ✸ The school serves the local community. □ He grew up in a small fishing community.
2 people who share the same interests, nationality, religion, job, etc. □ the Jewish community in the UK □ He is respected within the scientific community.
commute /kə'mjuːt/ VERB [**commutes, commuting, commuted**]
1 to travel regularly between home and work □ He commutes to London every day.

2 to officially change a punishment to a less severe one □ His death sentence was commuted to life in prison.
● **commuter** /kə'mjuːtə(r)/ NOUN [plural **commuters**] someone who commutes to work

compact /kəm'pækt/ ADJECTIVE small and taking up very little space □ a compact camera □ The equipment is very compact and easy to carry.

compact disc /,kɒmpækt 'dɪsk/ NOUN [plural **compact discs**] a disc with sound recorded on it
companion /kəm'pænjən/ NOUN [plural **companions**]
1 someone who is with you □ Who is her companion?
2 someone who spends a lot of time with someone □ She was his carer and devoted companion.
● **companionable** /kəm'pænjənəbəl/ ADJECTIVE friendly ✸ We ate our meal in companionable silence.
● **companionship** /kəm'pænjənʃɪp/ NOUN, NO PLURAL being with a friend or a group of friends and having a friendly relationship with them

company /'kʌmpənɪ/ NOUN [plural **companies**]
1 a business organization □ an insurance company □ He works for a small web design company.
2 no plural being with other people or the people you spend time with ✸ He's very good company (=fun to spend time with). □ She got into bad company and started going out late.
3 keep someone company to stay with someone or go somewhere with them □ Jon came along to keep me company.
4 part company to leave each other □ We parted company when we reached Paris.
5 a group of actors, dancers, singers, etc. □ the Royal Shakespeare Company

comparable /'kɒmpərəbəl/ ADJECTIVE similar in some way □ The two games are comparable in difficulty.

comparative /kəm'pærətɪv/ ▶ ADJECTIVE
1 in grammar, a comparative adjective or adverb usually ends with -er or is used with more. For example better, happier and more dangerous are comparative forms.
2 when compared with something else □ They reached the comparative safety of the camp.
3 comparing similar things □ a comparative analysis
▶ NOUN [plural **comparatives**] a comparative form of an adjective or adverb
● **comparatively** /kəm'pærətɪvlɪ/ ADVERB compared with something else □ The house was noisy, and the garden was comparatively quiet.

compare /kəm'peə(r)/ VERB [**compares, comparing, compared**]
1 to consider how two or more things are similar or different, or which is better □ + to The weather today is lovely compared to last week. □ + with The figure is slightly low compared with the national average. ✸ Their prices compare favourably with those of their

competitors. □ *Researchers compared the performance of the four groups.*
2 to describe someone or something as being like another person or thing □ **+ to** *She compared him to a mad dog.*

• **comparison** /kəm'pærɪsən/ NOUN [*plural* **comparisons**] when you compare things 🔁 *Many people have drawn a comparison between the two players.* □ **+ between** *Teachers were always making comparisons between me and my brother.* 🔁 *There's no comparison between shop cakes and home made cakes* (=home made cakes are much better). 🔁 *Taxes are low in comparison with other countries.*

compartment /kəm'pɑːtmənt/ NOUN [*plural* **compartments**]
1 a separate part within a container, piece of furniture, etc. □ *There was a secret compartment at the back of the desk.*
2 a separate area, especially in a train 🔁 *the first-class compartment*

compass /'kʌmpəs/ NOUN [*plural* **compasses**]
1 a piece of equipment that shows the direction of north, which you can use to find your way
2 **compasses** a piece of equipment used for drawing circles

compassion /kəm'pæʃən/ NOUN, NO PLURAL a feeling of sympathy for someone's suffering □ *He showed compassion for the poor.*

• **compassionate** /kəm'pæʃənət/ ADJECTIVE showing compassion

compatibility /kəm,pætə'bɪlɪtɪ/ NOUN, NO PLURAL the quality that allows people or things to work well together or have a good relationship

compatible /kəm'pætəbəl/ ADJECTIVE
1 compatible pieces of equipment can work together □ *Is the software compatible with your existing computer system?*
2 if people are compatible, they are able to have a good relationship □ *We just weren't really compatible.*
3 compatible ideas, beliefs or situations can exist together □ *Working such long hours isn't really compatible with family life.*

compatriot /kəm'pætrɪət/ NOUN [*plural* **compatriots**] a formal word for someone who comes from the same country as you

compel /kəm'pel/ VERB [**compels, compelling, compelled**] a formal word meaning to force someone to do something 🔁 *I felt compelled to get involved.*

• **compelling** /kəm'pelɪŋ/ ADJECTIVE
1 very interesting or exciting □ *It's a very dramatic and compelling story.*
2 compelling reasons or arguments are so strong that you cannot disagree with them 🔁 *There is compelling evidence of their guilt.* 🔁 *There was no compelling reason to stay.*

compensate /'kɒmpənseɪt/ VERB [**compensates, compensating, compensated**]
1 to pay someone money in exchange for something

they have lost or suffered □ *We were compensated for the extra hours we had to work.*
2 to make a bad result or situation seem better □ *His ability to get on with people compensates for his lack of experience.*

• **compensation** /,kɒmpən'seɪʃən/ NOUN, NO PLURAL
1 money given to someone for a loss or injury 🔁 *pay/receive compensation* □ *He received £5,000 in compensation.*
2 something which makes a bad situation seem better □ *A win today would be some compensation for recent disappointments.*

compère /'kɒmpeə(r)/ NOUN [*plural* **compères**] someone who introduces performers in a show

compete /kəm'piːt/ VERB [**competes, competing, competed**]
1 to take part in a race, competition, etc. □ **+ in** *I always dreamed of competing in the Olympics.* □ **+ against** *We'll be competing against some top teams.* □ **+ for** *Twenty-five players are competing for the title.* □ *He has the ability to compete at the highest level.*
2 to try to be more successful than someone else □ **+ with** *The company can't compete with larger rivals.* □ *UK business needs to compete internationally.*
3 to try to get something that other people also want □ **+ for** *Farmers and local people are competing for scarce water resources.* 🔁 *The three brothers were always competing for their mother's attention.*

competence /'kɒmpɪtəns/ NOUN, NO PLURAL the ability to do something well

• **competent** /'kɒmpɪtənt/ ADJECTIVE able to do something well □ *He's a very competent manager.*

• **competently** /'kɒmpɪtəntlɪ/ ADVERB effectively or skilfully □ *She handled the situation competently.*

competition /,kɒmpɪ'tɪʃən/ NOUN [*plural* **competitions**]
1 an event at which people try to win or to be better than the others 🔁 *She entered a competition to win a holiday.* 🔁 *He won a singing competition.*
2 *no plural* trying to win or to be more successful than other people or organizations 🔁 *There will be stiff competition for places.* 🔁 *There has always been fierce competition between Coca-Cola and Pepsi.* 🔁 *Newspapers now face competition from the Internet.*
3 **the competition** people or organizations you are competing against □ *We have to keep ahead of the competition.*

• **competitive** /kəm'petɪtɪv/ ADJECTIVE
1 to do with or involving competition 🔁 *a competitive sport*
2 liking to compete and win □ *I'm a very competitive person.*
3 if businesses are competitive, they are able to be successful □ *To remain competitive we have to cut costs.*
4 cheaper than other similar products or services

⌘ They offer high-quality products at competitive prices.

• **competitor** /kəmˈpetɪtə(r)/ NOUN [plural competitors]

1 someone taking part in a competition □ He's the oldest competitor in the race.

2 a company selling the same thing as another □ The company has two main competitors.

compilation /ˌkɒmpɪˈleɪʃən/ NOUN [plural compilations]

1 a collection of pieces of writing, music or information □ The album is a compilation of the band's greatest hits.

2 no plural the process of compiling something

compile /kəmˈpaɪl/ VERB [compiles, compiling, compiled] to collect information together to make a book, list, etc. ⌘ The firm has compiled a list of candidates. ⌘ The committee will compile a report on the event.

• **compiler** /kəmˈpaɪlə(r)/ NOUN [plural compilers] someone who compiles something

complacency /kəmˈpleɪsənsɪ/ NOUN, NO PLURAL the feeling that a situation is good enough, so you do not try very hard to improve it

• **complacent** /kəmˈpleɪsənt/ ADJECTIVE when you think a situation is good enough, so you do not try very hard to improve it ⌘ It's easy to become complacent about security.

complain /kəmˈpleɪn/ VERB [complains, complaining, complained] to say that you are not happy or satisfied about something □ + that He complained that it was too hot. □ + about Our neighbours complained about the noise.

♦ PHRASAL VERB **complain of something**

1 to say that you are ill □ She had complained of headaches.

2 to say that something bad has happened to you □ Several employees complained of discrimination.

• **complaint** /kəmˈpleɪnt/ NOUN [plural complaints]

1 when you complain about something □ + about We've received several complaints about his behaviour. ⌘ I wish to make a complaint. ⌘ They filed a formal complaint with the police.

2 an illness ⌘ The nurse treats patients with minor complaints.

complement ► NOUN /ˈkɒmplɪmənt/ [plural complements]

1 something that goes very well with another thing □ The sauce is a lovely complement to the meat.

2 something that is added something else □ The software is a complement to existing applications.

3 the total number or amount of something needed ⌘ The department is short of its full complement of 15 staff.

► VERB /ˈkɒmplɪment/ [complements, complementing, complemented] if two things complement each other, they go very well together

□ Our online resources complement the printed books.

• **complementary** /ˌkɒmplɪˈmentərɪ/ ADJECTIVE going well together □ These approaches are complementary and work well in combination.

complementary medicine /ˌkɒmplɪmentərɪ ˈmedsɪn/ NOUN, NO PLURAL types of medical treatment not used by most ordinary doctors

complete /kəmˈpliːt/ ► VERB [completes, completing, completed]

1 to finish something □ You must complete the test in 15 minutes. □ She completed a 10-week English course. □ The work should be completed by the end of March.

2 to make something whole by adding all the parts □ Complete the sentence using one word in each gap.

3 to write all the information needed on a form or document ⌘ Each participant completes a questionnaire. □ He had completed the necessary paperwork.

► ADJECTIVE

1 including all parts □ a complete set of golf clubs □ Here's the complete list of winners. □ + with It's a 5-star hotel complete with indoor pool and spa.

2 used to emphasize what you are saying □ I felt a complete fool. □ It was a complete surprise to me. ⌘ She received a letter from a complete stranger.

3 finished □ The building work is almost complete.

• **completely** /kəmˈpliːtlɪ/ ADVERB in every way or with every part finished □ I agree completely. □ The whole day was completely ruined. □ This job is completely different from what I did before. □ They had completely cleaned the whole house.

> ► Note that **completely** comes before adjectives that have strong meanings. Before adjectives that are less strong, use **very** or **extremely**: □ It's **completely** ridiculous. □ It's **very** silly. □ It's **completely** exhausting. □ It's **very** tiring.

• **completeness** /kəmˈpliːtnɪs/ NOUN, NO PLURAL the quality of being whole, with nothing missing □ We check the data for accuracy and completeness.

• **completion** /kəmˈpliːʃən/ NOUN, NO PLURAL when something is finished ⌘ The filming is nearing completion. □ Payment is due on completion of the work.

complex /ˈkɒmpleks/ ► ADJECTIVE with many different parts and difficult to understand □ These are complex issues. □ The situation has become increasingly complex.

► NOUN [plural complexes]

1 a group of buildings all with the same use □ a sports complex

2 a mental problem that makes someone very worried about something □ She has a real complex about her weight.

complexion /kəmˈplekʃən/ NOUN [plural **complexions**] the colour and condition of your skin □ She has blond hair and a fair complexion.

complexity /kəmˈpleksətɪ/ NOUN [plural **complexities**] the quality of being complicated or difficult

compliance /kəmˈplaɪəns/ NOUN, NO PLURAL obeying rules or someone else's wishes □ All the work is carried out in compliance with safety standards.

• **compliant** /kəmˈplaɪənt/ ADJECTIVE willing to do what another person wants

complicate /ˈkɒmplɪkeɪt/ VERB [**complicates, complicating, complicated**] to make something more difficult to understand or to deal with ⊞To complicate matters further, we could only film at night.

• **complicated** /ˈkɒmplɪkeɪtɪd/ ADJECTIVE difficult to understand or to deal with □ a complicated calculation □ The situation has become more complicated.

• **complication** /ˌkɒmplɪˈkeɪʃən/ NOUN [plural **complications**] something that creates a problem or difficulty ⊞The operation went well and there were no serious complications.

complicit /kəmˈplɪsət/ ADJECTIVE involved with or knowing about something wrong or illegal □ The company was complicit in the payment of bribes.

• **complicity** /kəmˈplɪsətɪ/ NOUN, NO PLURAL being complicit in something wrong or illegal

compliment ▶ NOUN /ˈkɒmplɪmənt/ [plural **compliments**]
1 something that you say that praises someone ⊞ Otto paid me a compliment for once.
2 compliments of someone used to say that something is from someone and you do not have to pay for it □ We finished with a brandy, compliments of the chef.
▶ VERB /ˈkɒmplɪment/ [**compliments, complimenting, complimented**] to praise someone □ Leo complimented her on her good taste.

• **complimentary** /ˌkɒmplɪˈmentərɪ/ ADJECTIVE
1 showing praise or admiration □ The article she wrote was very complimentary.
2 given free □ He sent us complimentary tickets for the show.

comply /kəmˈplaɪ/ VERB [**complies, complying, complied**] to obey a rule or to agree to do something □ It is impossible to comply with such demands. □ We have changed our procedures to comply with the new regulations.

component /kəmˈpəʊnənt/ NOUN [plural **components**] one of the parts of something □ The company manufactures electronic components. ⊞ Exercise is a key component of the treatment programme.

compose /kəmˈpəʊz/ VERB [**composes, composing, composed**]
1 to write a piece of music □ He has composed the music for a number of movies.
2 if something is composed of something, it is formed

of it □ The team is composed of three men and three women.
3 to write something that you have to think about a lot □ She sat down to compose a letter to Steven.
4 compose yourself to control your feelings and become calm □ She paused to compose herself.

• **composed** /kəmˈpəʊzd/ ADJECTIVE in control of your feelings □ He remained calm and composed.

• **composer** /kəmˈpəʊzə(r)/ NOUN [plural **composers**] someone who writes music

• **composite** /ˈkɒmpəzɪt/ ▶ ADJECTIVE made of several different parts or materials □ It is made of a lightweight composite material.
▶ NOUN [plural **composites**] something made of several different parts or materials □ The picture was a composite of several old photographs.

• **composition** /ˌkɒmpəˈzɪʃən/ NOUN [plural **compositions**]
1 no plural the parts that something is made of □ + of the chemical composition of the sample □ The culture reflects the city's ethnic composition.
2 a piece of music
3 no plural the process of writing music □ She studied composition.
4 an essay □ We had to write a composition on the nature of love.

compost /ˈkɒmpɒst/ NOUN, NO PLURAL a mixture of decayed plants and leaves that is spread on soil to improve its quality ⊞ a compost heap (=pile where compost is put)

composure /kəmˈpəʊzə(r)/ NOUN, NO PLURAL being in control of your feelings so that you are calm ⊞He took a moment to regain his composure.

compound ▶ NOUN /ˈkɒmpaʊnd/ [plural **compounds**]
1 a substance formed from two or more parts or substances. A chemistry word ⊞a chemical compound
2 an area surrounded by a fence or wall □ The troops were based in a walled compound.
3 a word made of two or more other words. The words airport and tape recorder are compounds.
▶ VERB /kəmˈpaʊnd/ [**compounds, compounding, compounded**] to make a problem worse by adding to it ⊞ Recent delays have compounded the problem.

compound eye /ˌkɒmpaʊnd ˈaɪ/ NOUN [plural **compound eyes**] an eye, for example of an insect, that is made of many small parts. A biology word

comprehend /ˌkɒmprɪˈhend/ VERB [**comprehends, comprehending, comprehended**] a formal word meaning to understand □ It's difficult to comprehend the scale of this disaster.

• **comprehensible** /ˌkɒmprɪˈhensəbəl/ ADJECTIVE able to be understood □ Her words were barely comprehensible beneath the sobs.

• **comprehension** /ˌkɒmprɪˈhenʃən/ NOUN, NO PLURAL understanding □ a test of reading comprehension

• **comprehensive** /ˌkɒmprɪˈhensɪv/ ▶ ADJECTIVE dealing with everything □ a comprehensive report

▶ NOUN [*plural* **comprehensives**] a comprehensive school

comprehensive school /ˌkɒmprɪˈhensɪv ˌskuːl/ NOUN [*plural* **comprehensive schools**] a secondary school (=school for children aged around 11–16) run by the state where pupils of all abilities are educated in all subjects

compress /kəmˈpres/ VERB [**compresses, compressing, compressed**]
1 to make something fit into a smaller space □ *A diesel engine works by compressing the fuel.*
2 to use a computer program to make a computer file smaller. A computing word.

comprise /kəmˈpraɪz/ VERB [**comprises, comprising, comprised**] a formal word meaning to contain or to be made of □ *The test will comprise two parts.* □ *The group was comprised of healthy individuals.*

compromise /ˈkɒmprəmaɪz/ ▶ VERB [**compromises, compromising, compromised**]
1 to give up some part of what you want so that an agreement can be made □ *I'm not willing to compromise on this issue.*
2 to risk harming or losing something ㊉ *Releasing this information could compromise national security.*
▶ NOUN [*plural* **compromises**] an agreement in which each person or side gives up something they want ㊉ *We've finally reached a compromise on where to go on holiday.*

compulsion /kəmˈpʌlʃən/ NOUN [*plural* **compulsions**]
1 a feeling that you must do something □ *She felt a sudden compulsion to leave the room.*
2 being forced to do something □ *There was no compulsion to take part.*
• **compulsive** /kəmˈpʌlsɪv/ ADJECTIVE
1 not able to control something or not able to stop doing something ㊉ *a compulsive liar/gambler*
2 so exciting or interesting that you cannot stop reading or watching ㊉ *The show has proved compulsive viewing.*
• **compulsory** /kəmˈpʌlsəri/ ADJECTIVE if something is compulsory, you must do it or have it □ *Subjects like Maths and English are compulsory.*

computer /kəmˈpjuːtə(r)/ NOUN [*plural* **computers**] an electronic machine that can store and deal with very large amounts of information ㊉ *a personal computer* ㊉ *I mostly use my computer to send emails.*
• **computerize** or **computerise** /kəmˈpjuːtəraɪz/ VERB [**computerizes, computerizing, computerized**] to use a computer to do something that was done in a different way before □ *There is a plan to computerize medical records.*
• **computerized** /kəmˈpjuːtəraɪzd/ ADJECTIVE stored in or dealt with by a computer □ *computerized records of fingerprints*
• **computing** /kəmˈpjuːtɪŋ/ NOUN, NO PLURAL the use of computers or the skill of working with computers □ *He studied computing.*

comrade /ˈkɒmreɪd/ NOUN [*plural* **comrades**] a friend, especially in the army

con /kɒn/ ▶ VERB [**cons, conning, conned**] an informal word meaning to trick someone into doing something or thinking that something is true □ *I think we've been conned.* □ *People are being conned into paying for unnecessary software.*
▶ NOUN [*plural* **cons**] an informal word for a trick □ *Ignore the email, it's just a con.*
➡ go to **pros** and **cons**

concave /ˈkɒnkeɪv/ ADJECTIVE curving in or down. A physics word. □ *a concave lens*

conceal /kənˈsiːl/ VERB [**conceals, concealing, concealed**] to hide something or to keep it secret □ *She concealed herself behind a bush.* □ *He couldn't conceal his disappointment.*
• **concealment** /kənˈsiːlmənt/ NOUN, NO PLURAL when something is concealed

concede /kənˈsiːd/ VERB [**concedes, conceding, conceded**]
1 to admit that something is true even though you do not want to □ *'It may be possible,' he conceded.*
2 to allow someone you are competing against to win a point, goal, game, etc. ㊉ *They conceded a goal in the 89th minute.*
3 concede defeat to accept that you have lost □ *He finally conceded defeat when it became clear his rival had more votes.*

conceit /kənˈsiːt/ NOUN, NO PLURAL the quality of having a very good opinion of yourself and what you can do □ *She was amazed at the actor's total lack of conceit.*
• **conceited** /kənˈsiːtɪd/ ADJECTIVE showing conceit □ *He's a conceited young man.*

conceivable /kənˈsiːvəbəl/ ADJECTIVE possible to imagine or believe □ *It's perfectly conceivable that it was lost in the post.* □ *She took photos from every conceivable angle.*
• **conceivably** /kənˈsiːvəbli/ ADVERB possibly □ *She could conceivably become the first woman president.*

conceive /kənˈsiːv/ VERB [**conceives, conceiving, conceived**]
1 to imagine something or to think of an idea □ *He couldn't conceive how he was going to do it.*
2 to think of an idea or a plan □ *He conceived a plan to take over the company.*
3 if a woman conceives, she becomes pregnant

concentrate /ˈkɒnsəntreɪt/ VERB [**concentrates, concentrating, concentrated**]
1 to give all your attention to something □ **+ on** *Try to concentrate on one thing at a time.* ㊉ *I had to concentrate hard to understand what he said.* ㊉ *The company is concentrating its efforts on the UK market.*
2 if things are concentrated in one place, they are all together in that place □ *Most hotels are concentrated in the south of the island.*
• **concentrated** /ˈkɒnsəntreɪtɪd/ ADJECTIVE
1 a concentrated liquid is stronger because some of

the water has been removed from it □ *concentrated orange juice*
2 using a lot of effort to achieve something ⏭ *We made a concentrated effort to finish the gardening.*
● **concentration** /ˌkɒnsənˈtreɪʃən/ NOUN [*plural* **concentrations**]
1 *no plural* when you give all your attention to something ⏭ *I lost concentration and started making mistakes.* □ *There was a look of concentration on her face.*
2 a large number or amount of something in one place ⏭ *We found a high concentration of pollen in the air.*

concentration camp /ˌkɒnsənˈtreɪʃən ˌkæmp/ NOUN [*plural* **concentration camps**] a prison where large numbers of people are kept, especially during a war

concentric /kənˈsentrɪk/ ADJECTIVE concentric circles are inside each other and have the same centre. A maths word.

concept /ˈkɒnsept/ NOUN [*plural* **concepts**]
1 an idea or principle □ *the concept of democracy* □ *We teach some of the basic concepts of web design.*
2 have no concept of something to not understand or be able to imagine something □ *He doesn't seem to have any concept of right and wrong.*
● **conception** /kənˈsepʃən/ NOUN [*plural* **conceptions**]
1 an understanding or belief about what something is like □ *He looked exactly like the popular conception of a scientist.*
2 when a woman becomes pregnant

concern /kənˈsɜːn/ ▶ VERB [**concerns, concerning, concerned**]
1 to worry someone □ *His disappearance was beginning to concern us.* □ *Which issue concerns you most right now?*
2 to affect or to be important to someone □ *Don't interfere in things that don't concern you.*
3 to be about something □ *The research concerns the long-term effects of poor diet.*
4 concern yourself with something to become involved in doing something or to pay attention to something □ *You mustn't concern yourself with the travel arrangements.*
▶ NOUN [*plural* **concerns**]
1 something that worries you or a feeling of worry □ *If you have any concerns about the exam, speak to your teacher.* ⏭ *He expressed concern about the safety of the vehicle.* ⏭ *There is widespread concern about fuel shortages.*
2 something that affects you or is important to you ⏭ *My main concern is getting a job.*
3 when you care about something □ *They showed no concern for the law.* □ *There was genuine concern for her welfare.*
● **concerned** /kənˈsɜːnd/ ADJECTIVE
1 worried or caring about someone or something □ *concerned parents* □ *Many people are concerned about the environmental impact of flying.*

2 involved in or affected by something □ *He thanked everyone concerned.*
3 as far as I'm/he's, etc. concerned used to show someone's opinion □ *As far as I'm concerned, he can go ahead.*
4 as far as something is concerned used to show what you are talking about □ *As far as food's concerned, I'll eat anything.*
● **concerning** /kənˈsɜːnɪŋ/ PREPOSITION about or involving someone or something □ *There are serious allegations concerning his behaviour.*

concert /ˈkɒnsət/ NOUN [*plural* **concerts**] a musical performance ⏭ *a rock concert*

concerted /kənˈsɜːtɪd/ ADJECTIVE done with a lot of effort by a group of people working together ⏭ *We must make a concerted effort to win this match.*

concertina /ˌkɒnsəˈtiːnə/ NOUN [*plural* **concertinas**] a musical instrument that you play by pushing the sides together while pressing buttons

concerto /kənˈtʃeətəʊ/ NOUN [*plural* **concertos**] a piece of music to be played by one instrument and an orchestra (=large group of musicians) ⏭ *a piano concerto*

concession /kənˈseʃən/ NOUN [*plural* **concessions**] something that you agree to in order to end a disagreement ⏭ *The company refused to make any concessions and the strike continued.*

conciliation /kənˌsɪliˈeɪʃən/ NOUN, NO PLURAL the process of reaching an agreement. A formal word. □ *Has there been any progress towards conciliation?*

concise /kənˈsaɪs/ ADJECTIVE short and containing all the information without unnecessary details □ *a concise summary*

conclude /kənˈkluːd/ VERB [**concludes, concluding, concluded**]
1 to decide something after thinking carefully about it □ *He concluded that she was lying.* □ *The researchers concluded that the risk is very low.*
2 a formal word meaning to end □ *The drama course concluded with a performance.*
3 to complete something such as an agreement □ *We hope to conclude the deal by Friday.*
● **concluding** /kənˈkluːdɪŋ/ ADJECTIVE last □ *the concluding chapter of the novel*
● **conclusion** /kənˈkluːʒən/ NOUN [*plural* **conclusions**]
1 a decision you make after thinking carefully about something □ *+ of* What was the main conclusion of the study? ⏭ *I've come to the conclusion that she just doesn't care.* ⏭ *You can reach your own conclusion about that.* ⏭ *It's difficult to draw any conclusions from one small survey.*
2 the last part of something □ *+ of* I just have to write the conclusion of my essay. □ *He spoke to reporters at the conclusion of the meeting.*
3 *no plural* when something is formally agreed or arranged □ *+ of* He was responsible for the conclusion of the peace treaty.

4 jump to conclusions to make a decision about something too quickly, without knowing all the facts

• **conclusive** /kən'kluːsɪv/ ADJECTIVE showing that something is certainly true ⊞ *There is no conclusive evidence to support this claim.*

• **conclusively** /kən'kluːsɪvli/ ADVERB without any doubt □ *The videotape proved conclusively that he was the person who had broken in.*

concoct /kən'kɒkt/ VERB [**concocts, concocting, concocted**]

1 to invent a story, plan, etc. which is not true ⊞ *She concocted a story to get out of the trip.*

2 to make something unusual by mixing different things, usually foods, together

• **concoction** /kən'kɒkʃən/ NOUN [*plural* **concoctions**] something made by mixing different things, usually foods, together □ *The drink is a concoction of fruit juices.*

concourse /'kɒŋkɔːs/ NOUN [*plural* **concourses**] a large room or area, for example at an airport or station □ *I'll meet you on the station concourse.*

concrete /'kɒŋkriːt/ ▶ NOUN, NO PLURAL a strong, hard building material made by mixing sand, cement (=grey powder), small stones and water □ *a slab of concrete*

➔ go to **set** in stone/concrete

▶ ADJECTIVE

1 made of concrete □ *a concrete floor*

2 certain or based on facts ⊞ *They found concrete evidence of fraud.* □ *There's a lack of concrete information.*

3 real or practical ⊞ *We are taking concrete steps to reduce crime.* □ *Do you have any concrete proposals to make?*

4 able to be seen or touched □ *A table is a concrete object.*

▶ VERB [**concretes, concreting, concreted**] to put concrete on something □ *Dan's going to concrete the driveway this weekend.*

concur /kən'kɜː(r)/ VERB [**concurs, concurring, concurred**] a formal word meaning to agree □ *The members concurred that a change of plan was needed.*

concurrent /kən'kʌrənt/ ADJECTIVE a formal word describing things which exist or happen at the same time □ *The system can support up to 5,000 concurrent users.*

• **concurrently** /kən'kʌrəntli/ ADVERB a formal word meaning happening at the same time □ *It was decided that the two races couldn't be run concurrently.*

concussion /kən'kʌʃən/ NOUN, NO PLURAL a slight injury to the brain caused by hitting your head

condemn /kən'dem/ VERB [**condemns, condemning, condemned**]

1 to say that someone or something is wrong or bad □ *The President has condemned the violence.*

2 if someone is condemned to a serious punishment, they are given it by a court ⊞ *He was condemned to death.*

3 to make someone experience a bad situation □ *His disability condemned him to a life of poverty.*

4 to say that a building must be destroyed because it is not safe

• **condemnation** /ˌkɒndem'neɪʃən/ NOUN [*plural* **condemnations**] saying that something is wrong or bad □ *The attack provoked international condemnation.*

condensation /ˌkɒnden'seɪʃən/ NOUN, NO PLURAL drops of water that form when hot air or steam touches a cold surface such as a window

condense /kən'dens/ VERB [**condenses, condensing, condensed**]

1 to make something shorter □ *The report condenses the results into just ten pages.*

2 if steam or gas condenses, it becomes a liquid as it gets cooler. A chemistry word.

condescending /ˌkɒndɪ'sendɪŋ/ ADJECTIVE showing that you think you are better than other people □ *a condescending attitude*

condiment /'kɒndɪmənt/ NOUN [*plural* **condiments**] things that you add to food to give it more flavour, for example salt and pepper

condition /kən'dɪʃən/ ▶ NOUN [*plural* **conditions**]

1 the state that someone or something is in □ **+ of** *There were concerns over the condition of the plane.* ⊞ *He was taken to hospital in a critical condition.* ⊞ *The house was in a poor condition.*

2 something that has to happen before something else does, especially as part of an agreement □ **+ of** *He broke the conditions of his licence.* ⊞ *I'll go on the condition that you come too.*

3 conditions the situation or things happening at a particular time or place ⊞ *The flight was cancelled due to bad weather conditions.* ⊞ *Our living conditions have improved.*

4 an illness ⊞ *She was diagnosed with a serious medical condition.* ⊞ *He had a heart condition.*

▶ VERB [**conditions, conditioning, conditioned**]

1 if you are conditioned to do something, you do it because you have been influenced by someone or something □ *Young troops are conditioned to obey orders.* □ *Our tastes are conditioned by fashion.*

2 to put conditioner on your hair

• **conditional** /kən'dɪʃənəl/ ADJECTIVE

1 depending on something else happening □ *She has a conditional offer of a place at university.* □ **+ on** *The deal is conditional on official approval.*

2 a conditional sentence usually starts with *if* and says that one thing must be true before another thing can be true

• **conditionally** /kən'dɪʃənəli/ ADVERB only if something else happens □ *They have conditionally approved the proposal.*

• **conditioner** /kən'dɪʃənə(r)/ NOUN [*plural* **conditioners**] a substance you put on your hair to make it softer

• **conditioning** /kən'dɪʃənɪŋ/ NOUN, NO PLURAL the

way people and animals are influenced by what they have experienced or have been told

condolences /kənˈdəʊlənsɪz/ PLURAL NOUN something you say to show your sympathy when someone has died 🔁 *He expressed his deepest condolences to the family.*

condone /kənˈdəʊn/ VERB [condones, condoning, condoned] to accept or allow something which is wrong □ *We don't condone violence in any form.*

conducive /kənˈdjuːsɪv/ ADJECTIVE if one thing is conducive to another, it encourages it or makes it easier □ *The noisy atmosphere was not conducive to a romantic evening.*

conduct ► VERB /kənˈdʌkt/ [conducts, conducting, conducted]
1 to organize or do something 🔁 *Doctors are conducting further tests.* □ *We are conducting a full investigation into the accident.*
2 conduct yourself to behave in a particular way □ *We expect you to conduct yourselves with dignity.*
3 to stand in front of an orchestra (=large group of musicians) to control their performance □ *Sarah Hobbs conducted the orchestra.*
4 if a material conducts electricity or heat, it allows electricity or heat to flow through it. A physics word.
5 a formal word meaning to take someone somewhere □ *The butler conducted us into the library.*
► NOUN, NO PLURAL /ˈkɒndʌkt/
1 the way someone behaves □ *Their reckless conduct was the cause of the accident.* 🔁 *There is a strict code of conduct.*
2 the way something is organized or done □ *An independent body is supervising the conduct of the election.*

• **conduction** /kənˈdʌkʃən/ NOUN, NO PLURAL the flow of electricity or heat through something. A physics word.

• **conductor** /kənˈdʌktə(r)/ NOUN [plural conductors]
1 someone who conducts an orchestra
2 an object that conducts electricity or heat. A physics word. □ *a lightning conductor*

cone /kəʊn/ NOUN [plural cones]
1 a solid shape with a round base and sides that slope up to a point at the top, or an object with this shape 🔁 *a traffic cone*
2 a fruit of a pine tree
3 a cone-shaped container used to hold ice cream

confectionery /kənˈfekʃənərɪ/ NOUN, NO PLURAL cakes and sweets

confederate /kənˈfedərət/ NOUN [plural confederates] someone who helps you, especially to do something illegal

• **confederation** /kənˌfedəˈreɪʃən/ NOUN [plural confederations] several groups or organizations that have joined together

confer /kənˈfɜː(r)/ VERB [confers, conferring, conferred]
1 to discuss something with other people in order to make a decision □ *He turned to confer with his lawyer.*

2 a formal word meaning to give someone something □ *A government job confers status and opportunity.*

• **conference** /ˈkɒnfərəns/ NOUN [plural conferences]
1 a large meeting of people to discuss a particular subject □ + **on** *a UN conference on climate change* 🔁 *The union is holding its annual conference this week.*
2 news/press conference a meeting at which someone gives information about something to newspapers, television, etc.

confess /kənˈfes/ VERB [confesses, confessing, confessed]
1 to admit to other people that you have done something wrong □ *He confessed to stealing the money.*
2 to admit something you feel embarrassed or guilty about □ *I don't mind confessing that I was terrified.* □ *'I'd forgotten his name,' she confessed.*

• **confession** /kənˈfeʃən/ NOUN [plural confessions]
1 when you confess that you are guilty of a crime or something wrong 🔁 *I've got a confession to make.* 🔁 *He made a full confession to the police.*
2 when you tell a priest all the things you have done wrong 🔁 *I haven't been to confession for years.*

confetti /kənˈfetɪ/ NOUN, NO PLURAL very small pieces of coloured paper that people throw in the air at weddings

confidant or **confidante** /ˈkɒnfɪdænt/ NOUN [plural confidants or confidantes] a friend who you discuss personal things with

confide /kənˈfaɪd/ VERB [confides, confiding, confided] to tell someone your secrets □ *She confided her secrets to her doctor.*

♦ PHRASAL VERB **confide in someone** to tell someone your secrets

confidence /ˈkɒnfɪdəns/ NOUN [plural confidences]
1 *no plural* being sure of yourself and your abilities □ + **to do something** *It gave me the confidence to try again.* 🔁 *We're growing in confidence.* 🔁 *I totally lost my confidence.*
2 *no plural* trusting someone's ability to do something □ + **in** *I have every confidence in your abilities.* □ + **of** *He has the confidence of investors.* 🔁 *We need to restore public confidence in the system.* 🔁 *They have lost confidence in their manager.*
3 *no plural* being sure about something □ *He expressed confidence that the project would go ahead*
4 a secret you tell someone □ *She's good at keeping confidences.*
5 in confidence if you tell someone something in confidence, you expect them not to tell anyone else □ *Can I talk to you in confidence?*

confidence trick /ˈkɒnfɪdəns ˌtrɪk/ NOUN [plural confidence tricks] a trick in which you persuade someone to trust you in order to get their money

confident /ˈkɒnfɪdənt/ ADJECTIVE
1 sure of yourself or your abilities □ + **in** *I'm confident in my own ability.* 🔁 *I'm feeling pretty confident.*

□ *She's a very confident swimmer.*
2 sure that something will happen or be successful □ **+ about** *We remain confident about the future.* □ **+ of** *We're still confident of victory.* □ **+ that** *I'm confident that we'll find the children safe and well.*

confidential /ˌkɒnfɪˈdenʃəl/ ADJECTIVE secret or private ⊞ *He had access to confidential information.* ⊞ *highly/strictly confidential*
• **confidentiality** /ˌkɒnfɪˌdenʃiˈæləti/ NOUN, NO PLURAL the state of being confidential □ *There has been a breach of confidentiality.*
• **confidentially** /ˌkɒnfɪˈdenʃəli/ ADVERB in a confidential way □ *The information will be treated confidentially.*
confidently /ˈkɒnfɪdəntli/ ADVERB
1 showing confidence in yourself □ *She walked confidently into the room.*
2 showing you are sure about something □ *He confidently predicted a home win.*

confine /kənˈfaɪn/ VERB [**confines, confining, confined**] to keep someone or something within limits or shut inside a place □ *The soldiers were confined to barracks.* □ *Please confine your remarks to the subject under discussion.*
• **confined** /kənˈfaɪnd/ ADJECTIVE a confined space is very small ⊞ *a confined area/space*
• **confinement** /kənˈfaɪnmənt/ NOUN, NO PLURAL being locked up or confined
• **confines** /ˈkɒnfaɪnz/ PLURAL NOUN the outside edges or limits of something □ *Prisoners are not allowed beyond the confines of the prison.*

confirm /kənˈfɜːm/ VERB [**confirms, confirming, confirmed**]
1 to say or to make sure that something is correct or true □ *Police would not confirm the identity of the woman.* □ **+ that** *A company spokesman confirmed that the director had resigned.* □ **+ question word** *She refused to confirm whether the rumour was true.* □ **+ as** *Robinson was confirmed as England captain yesterday.*
2 to say that something will happen as arranged □ **+ that** *Please confirm that you will be able to come to the meeting.* □ *I'm writing to confirm the booking.*
• **confirmation** /ˌkɒnfəˈmeɪʃən/ NOUN, NO PLURAL something that confirms an arrangement or the truth of something ⊞ *We have not yet received official confirmation of the report.*

confiscate /ˈkɒnfɪskeɪt/ VERB [**confiscates, confiscating, confiscated**] to take something away from someone as a punishment □ *Police confiscated a number of illegal weapons.* □ *Teachers can confiscate mobile phones.*
• **confiscation** /ˌkɒnfɪˈskeɪʃən/ NOUN, NO PLURAL when something is confiscated
conflagration /ˌkɒnfləˈɡreɪʃən/ NOUN [plural **conflagrations**] a formal word meaning a large fire that destroys a lot of things

conflict ▶ NOUN /ˈkɒnflɪkt/ [plural **conflicts**]
1 an argument or a disagreement ⊞ *We help to resolve conflicts between neighbours.* ⊞ *Money is often a source of conflict within families.*
2 fighting or a war ⊞ *There is an ongoing armed conflict in the region.*
3 if there is a conflict between two things, they cannot exist together □ *There's often a conflict between economic development and conservation.*
4 a conflict of interest a situation in which you cannot make a fair judgment because you will be affected by the result
▶ VERB /kənˈflɪkt/ [**conflicts, conflicting, conflicted**] if two things conflict, they cannot both exist or be true at the same time □ *The eyewitness reports conflicted.* □ *Some of their actions seem to conflict with their policies.*
• **conflicting** /kənˈflɪktɪŋ/ ADJECTIVE two conflicting things are opposite or compete with each other ⊞ *There were conflicting reports of what happened.*

conform /kənˈfɔːm/ VERB [**conforms, conforming, conformed**]
1 to behave in a way that most other people behave □ *We all face pressure to conform.*
2 if something conforms to a rule, it obeys it □ *All equipment has to conform to certain regulations.*
• **conformity** /kənˈfɔːməti/ NOUN, NO PLURAL
1 the quality of conforming □ *The study assessed men's conformity to traditional masculine roles.*
2 a formal word meaning conforming with a rule □ *Their religion demands conformity to a strict set of rules.*

confound /kənˈfaʊnd/ VERB [**confounds, confounding, confounded**] if something confounds you, you are very surprised because you find it difficult to understand □ *He confounded doctors by recovering completely.*

confront /kənˈfrʌnt/ VERB [**confronts, confronting, confronted**]
1 if you are confronted with a problem or a difficult situation, it appears and you have to deal with it □ *She was confronted with a difficult choice.* □ *How would you react if you were confronted by a real emergency situation?*
2 to try to do something about a problem or a difficult situation □ *We need to confront the challenge of climate change.*
3 to try to make someone admit something you think they have done wrong □ *You should confront her and ask her about the missing money.*
4 to stand in front of someone in a threatening way □ *He turned and confronted his attackers.* □ *He tried to jump out of a window when confronted by police.*
• **confrontation** /ˌkɒnfrʌnˈteɪʃən/ NOUN [plural **confrontations**] an angry argument or fight between two people or groups ⊞ *There was a violent confrontation between rival fans.* ⊞ *He's a man who avoids confrontation.*
• **confrontational** /ˌkɒnfrʌnˈteɪʃənəl/ ADJECTIVE

using strong methods that cause arguments or fights 🔁 *The government has taken a confrontational approach towards the strikers.*

confuse /kən'fju:z/ VERB [confuses, confusing, confused]

1 to make someone unable to think clearly or to understand something □ *I think it will confuse people if we make changes.*

2 to make something more difficult to understand 🔁 *To confuse matters further, they use two different systems.* □ *His comments have just confused the issue.*

3 to think one thing or person is something or someone else □ *I think you're confusing the two brothers.* □ **+ with** *A podcast should not be confused with a webcast.*

• **confused** /kən'fju:zd/ ADJECTIVE

1 unable to think clearly or understand something □ **+ about** *They seemed very confused about what was going on.* 🔁 *Angela looked confused.* □ *a confused expression*

2 not explained clearly or not easy to understand □ *We were getting confused messages.*

• **confusing** /kən'fju:zɪŋ/ ADJECTIVE difficult to understand □ *It was a very confusing situation.* 🔁 *Then things got very confusing.*

• **confusion** /kən'fju:ʒən/ NOUN

1 *no plural* a feeling of being confused 🔁 *The new rules caused confusion among tourists.* □ *I saw the look of confusion on her face.*

2 *no plural* a confusing situation □ *There was total confusion at the scene.* □ *The meeting ended in confusion.*

3 when two people or things are confused with each other 🔁 *We use different coloured text to avoid confusion.*

congeal /kən'dʒi:l/ VERB [congeals, congealing, congealed] if a liquid congeals, it becomes thick and almost solid

congenial /kən'dʒi:niəl/ ADJECTIVE a formal word meaning pleasant and friendly □ *We want to create a modern, congenial environment.*

congenital /kən'dʒenɪtəl/ ADJECTIVE congenital illnesses or problems are ones that a person is born with □ *congenital heart disease*

congested /kən'dʒestɪd/ ADJECTIVE crowded or blocked □ *The city's roads are badly congested.*

• **congestion** /kən'dʒestʃən/ NOUN, NO PLURAL when something is congested 🔁 *The scheme will ease traffic congestion in the city.* □ *Common symptoms are sneezing and nasal congestion.*

conglomerate /kən'glɒmərət/ NOUN [plural conglomerates] a large business formed from several smaller companies

congratulate /kən'grætʃuleɪt/ VERB [congratulates, congratulating, congratulated] to tell someone you are happy about their achievements or their good news □ *I congratulated her on her exam results.*

• **congratulations** /kən,grætʃu'leɪʃənz/ PLURAL

NOUN something you say to congratulate someone □ *Congratulations! That's great news.* □ **+ on** *Congratulations on passing your exams.* 🔁 *Simon called to offer his congratulations.*

➤ Remember that the preposition you use after the noun **congratulations** is on: □ *Congratulations on your marriage!*

congregate /'kɒŋgrɪgeɪt/ VERB [congregates, congregating, congregated] to come together somewhere in a group □ *Everyone had congregated around Ann's desk.*

• **congregation** /,kɒŋgrɪ'geɪʃən/ NOUN [plural congregations] all the people who are at a church service

congress /'kɒŋgres/ NOUN [plural congresses]

1 Congress the parliament of the United States, including the Senate and the House of Representatives

2 a meeting of many different people or organizations □ *the union's annual congress* □ *I attended an international congress to discuss refugees.*

congruent /'kɒŋgruənt/ ADJECTIVE congruent shapes are exactly the same size and shape. A maths word.

conical /'kɒnɪkəl/ ADJECTIVE shaped like a cone

conifer /'kɒnɪfə(r)/ NOUN [plural conifers] a type of tree with long thin leaves shaped like needles

• **coniferous** /kə'nɪfərəs/ ADJECTIVE coniferous trees grow cones (=hard, dry fruits). A biology word.

conjecture /kən'dʒektʃə(r)/ NOUN, NO PLURAL a formal word for the process of making opinions or judgments without having all the facts □ *The precise course of events remains a matter for conjecture.*

conjunction /kən'dʒʌŋkʃən/ NOUN [plural conjunctions]

1 in grammar, a word that connects other words or parts of a sentence. For example, *and*, *but* and *or* are conjunctions.

2 in conjunction with happening, working or done with something or someone else □ *The work is being done in conjunction with the Department of Transport.*

conjure /'kʌndʒə(r)/ VERB [conjures, conjuring, conjured] to make things appear or disappear as if by magic □ *She managed to conjure a meal out of nowhere.*

♦ PHRASAL VERB **conjure something up** to make you think of something □ *The smell of new hay conjured up a picture of the countryside.*

• **conjuror** /'kʌndʒərə(r)/ NOUN [plural conjurors] someone who does magic tricks

conker /'kɒŋkə(r)/ NOUN [plural conkers] a large brown seed of the horse chestnut tree

conman /'kɒnmæn/ NOUN [plural conmen] someone who tricks people, usually to get money

connect /kə'nekt/ VERB [connects, connecting, connected]

1 to join two things together □ *The Channel Tunnel connects Britain and France.* □ *The two parts of the building are connected by a corridor.*

2 to make it possible for people to communicate using

a telephone, computer, etc. □ + **to** *The number connects callers to voice mail.*

3 to see or understand how people or things are related to each other □ *The detective hadn't connected the two events in his mind.*

• **connected** /kə'nektɪd/ ADJECTIVE
1 related to or involved with someone or something □ *He loves everything connected with football.* ⌺ *I spoke to someone closely connected to the case.*
2 joined to something □ *There's a small camera connected to each car.*

• **connection** /kə'nekʃən/ NOUN [plural **connections**]
1 the relationship between two people, things or events □ + **between** *They researched the connection between diet and certain diseases.* □ + **with** *There is a possible connection with corruption.* □ + **to** *I have a personal connection to the town.*
2 something that connects telephones, computers, etc. □ *a high-speed broadband connection* □ *a wireless Internet connection*
3 something that joins two things together ⌺ *a loose electrical connection*
4 a train, bus or aeroplane that you need to catch to continue your journey ⌺ *We missed our connection to Stansted because our train was late.*
5 in connection with to do with □ *He is wanted by the police in connection with a theft.*

connive /kə'naɪv/ VERB [**connives, conniving, connived**]
1 to secretly plan something bad or illegal □ *Apparently, he connived in a plot to kill the prime minister.*
2 to ignore something bad or illegal and to allow it to continue □ *There were those who said he had known of the crime and had connived at it.*

connoisseur /ˌkɒnə'sɜː(r)/ NOUN [plural **connoisseurs**] someone who knows a lot about something such as food or art □ *When it comes to wine, she's something of a connoisseur.*

connotation /ˌkɒnə'teɪʃən/ NOUN [plural **connotations**] the feeling or extra meaning of a word or phrase in addition to its basic meaning ⌺ *The word carries negative connotations.*

conquer /'kɒŋkə(r)/ VERB [**conquers, conquering, conquered**]
1 to take control of a country or an area, especially in a war □ *Napoleon tried to conquer Egypt.*
2 to succeed in controlling a strong emotion, difficult situation, etc. □ *Claire seems to have finally conquered her shyness.* □ *It helped me to conquer my fear of heights.*

• **conqueror** /'kɒŋkərə(r)/ NOUN [plural **conquerors**] someone who conquers a country or an area

• **conquest** /'kɒŋkwest/ NOUN [plural **conquests**] when someone conquers a country or an area □ *the Spanish conquest of Mexico*

conscience /'kɒnʃəns/ NOUN [plural **consciences**]
1 your feeling of what is right and wrong □ *You should*

follow your conscience. ⌺ *Now I can relax with a clear conscience* (= without feeling guilty). ⌺ *He clearly had a guilty conscience.*
2 on your conscience if something is on your conscience, you feel guilty about it □ *I must help her – I don't want her death on my conscience.*

• **conscientious** /ˌkɒnʃɪ'enʃəs/ ADJECTIVE a conscientious person works hard and carefully to get things right □ *She was very conscientious about safety.*

• **conscientiously** /ˌkɒnʃɪ'enʃəslɪ/ ADVERB in a conscientious way □ *They carried out their duties conscientiously.*

conscientious objector /ˌkɒnʃɪenʃəs əb'dʒektə(r)/ NOUN [plural **conscientious objectors**] someone who refuses to fight in a war because they believe the war is wrong

conscious /'kɒnʃəs/ ADJECTIVE
1 aware of something □ + **of** *I'm conscious of the fact that we need to finish on time.* □ + **that** *I became increasingly conscious that people were watching me.*
2 awake and aware of what is around you ⌺ *He is now fully conscious following the operation.* □ *He had to fight to remain conscious.*
3 a conscious choice, decision, etc. is one that you have thought about ⌺ *He made a conscious decision to be more friendly towards them.* ⌺ *I've been making a conscious effort to eat more healthily.*

• **consciously** /'kɒnʃəslɪ/ ADVERB deliberately or being aware of what you are doing □ *They're consciously trying to change their image.*

• **consciousness** /'kɒnʃəsnɪs/ NOUN, NO PLURAL
1 the state of being awake and aware of what is around you ⌺ *She lost consciousness and woke up in hospital.* ⌺ *He never regained consciousness.*
2 being aware of or knowing about something ⌺ *We want to raise public consciousness about the issue.*

conscript ► VERB /kən'skrɪpt/ [**conscripts, conscripting, conscripted**] to force someone by law to join the armed forces □ *The government conscripted young men.*
► NOUN /'kɒnskrɪpt/ [plural **conscripts**] someone who is conscripted

• **conscription** /kən'skrɪpʃən/ NOUN, NO PLURAL the process of conscripting people

consecrate /'kɒnsɪkreɪt/ VERB [**consecrates, consecrating, consecrated**] to perform a ceremony to make something holy

• **consecration** /ˌkɒnsɪ'kreɪʃən/ NOUN, NO PLURAL the process of consecrating something

consecutive /kən'sekjutɪv/ ADJECTIVE one after the other □ *It snowed on three consecutive days.* □ *This is his fourth consecutive win.*

consensus /kən'sensəs/ NOUN, NO PLURAL agreement or a feeling shared by most people ⌺ *We couldn't reach a consensus on a name for the group.* ⌺ *The general consensus is that we should change the date.*

consent /kən'sent/ ► VERB [consents, consenting, consented] to agree to something □ He consented to be tested.

► NOUN, NO PLURAL when you agree to or allow something ⊞ Patients must give their consent for the treatment.

consequence /'kɒnsɪkwəns/ NOUN [plural consequences]

1 something that is the result of something else □ She didn't realize the consequences of her actions. ⊞ If you eat too much, you'll suffer the consequences. ⊞ They could face serious health consequences if they don't change their lifestyles.

2 a formal word meaning importance □ It was of no consequence. □ They achieved almost nothing of consequence.

● **consequent** /'kɒnsɪkwənt/ ADJECTIVE happening as a result □ He spoke about the problems in the fishing industry and the consequent loss of jobs.

● **consequently** /'kɒnsɪkwəntlɪ/ ADVERB as a result □ He injured his ankle and, consequently, he had to withdraw from the match.

conservation /ˌkɒnsə'veɪʃən/ NOUN, NO PLURAL

1 looking after something to prevent it being damaged or destroyed ⊞ nature conservation

2 being careful not to waste energy, water, etc. ⊞ We are encouraging energy conservation.

● **conservationist** /ˌkɒnsə'veɪʃənɪst/ NOUN [plural conservationists] someone who works to protect the environment

Conservative /kən'sɜːvətɪv/ NOUN [plural Conservatives] someone who supports the Conservative Party in the UK

conservative /kən'sɜːvətɪv/ ADJECTIVE

1 a conservative person does not like changes or new ideas □ He's a very conservative dresser.

2 a conservative estimate or guess is usually less than the real amount ⊞ Many people believe this is a conservative estimate.

conservatory /kən'sɜːvətərɪ/ NOUN [plural conservatories] a room or building which has walls and a roof made of glass

conserve /kən'sɜːv/ VERB [conserves, conserving, conserved]

1 to prevent something from being wasted or lost □ Close the windows to conserve heat.

2 to prevent something from being damaged or destroyed □ The country has to conserve its forests.

consider /kən'sɪdə(r)/ VERB [considers, considering, considered]

1 to think about something carefully □ I'll consider your idea. □ We're considering all the options. □ + **whether** I'm considering whether to go or not. □ + **ing** Have you considered hiring a car?

2 to have a particular opinion about someone or something □ I consider him to be a true friend. □ We will delete anything we consider inappropriate. □ I consider myself to be very lucky.

3 to think about what other people want or need □ He never considers other people's feelings.

► Note that when **consider** (meaning 'to think about something carefully') is followed by a verb, that verb is in the -ing form:
✓ She's considering leaving her job.
✗ She's considering to leave her job.

considerable /kən'sɪdərəbəl/ ADJECTIVE quite large or important □ a considerable distance □ We've spent a considerable amount of money already.

● **considerably** /kən'sɪdərəblɪ/ ADVERB quite a lot □ John earns considerably more than I do.

considerate /kən'sɪdərət/ ADJECTIVE thinking of other people and what they want □ It was considerate of you to help me.

consideration /kənˌsɪdə'reɪʃən/ NOUN [plural considerations]

1 thinking carefully about things ⊞ The idea deserves serious consideration. ⊞ We will give consideration to the request.

2 something that you have to think about when you are making a decision □ His health is the most important consideration. □ There are practical considerations, such as childcare.

3 take something into consideration to think about something while you are making a decision or a plan □ We will take all views into consideration.

4 thinking about other people and what they want □ We all want to be treated with consideration and respect. □ They showed little consideration for her privacy.

considering /kən'sɪdərɪŋ/ PREPOSITION, CONJUNCTION used to show how something is affected by something else □ Considering how clever you are, I think you should have done better. □ She played well considering she has been ill.

consign /kən'saɪn/

♦ PHRASAL VERB [consigns, consigning, consigned] **consign something to something** to put something somewhere as a way of getting rid of it. A formal phrase. □ That old sweater should be consigned to the bin!

● **consignment** /kən'saɪnmənt/ NOUN [plural consignments] several goods which are being sent together □ It was part of a consignment of medicines imported from France.

consist /kən'sɪst/

♦ PHRASAL VERB [consists, consisting, consisted] **consist of something** to be made of two or more things □ It was a simple meal, consisting of bread and cheese. ⊞ His diet consists mainly of meat and potatoes.

consistency /kən'sɪstənsɪ/ NOUN [plural consistencies]

1 when something is always the same in quality □ There is no consistency to his game.

2 how thick or smooth a substance is □ *The sauce should have the consistency of cream.*

• **consistent** /kən'sɪstənt/ ADJECTIVE always the same □ *The school has a consistent approach to dealing with bad behaviour.*

consolation /ˌkɒnsə'leɪʃən/ NOUN [*plural* **consolations**] something that makes a disappointment seem less bad □ *As a consolation for not getting the job, his girlfriend took him out to dinner.*

consolation prize /ˌkɒnsə'leɪʃən ˌpraɪz/ NOUN [*plural* **consolation prizes**] a prize given to someone who has come second in a competition

console[1] /kən'səʊl/ VERB [**consoles, consoling, consoled**] to make someone who is sad or disappointed feel better

console[2] /'kɒnsəʊl/ NOUN [*plural* **consoles**]
1 a piece of equipment that you connect to a television to play video games on 🕮 *a games console*
2 a board that has the controls for a machine on it

consolidate /kən'sɒlɪdeɪt/ VERB [**consolidates, consolidating, consolidated**] to make your power or success stronger □ *The team consolidated its lead with two more goals.*

consonant /'kɒnsənənt/ NOUN [*plural* **consonants**] any letter of the alphabet except *a, e, i, o,* or *u*

➡ *go to* vowel

consort /kɒn'sɔːt/
◆ PHRASAL VERB [**consorts, consorting, consorted**] **consort with someone** to spend time with someone that other people do not approve of. A formal phrase.

consortium /kən'sɔːtɪəm/ NOUN [*plural* **consortiums** *or* **consortia**] a group of companies who are working together □ *The jet was developed by a consortium of companies.*

conspicuous /kən'spɪkjʊəs/ ADJECTIVE very easy to see □ *Beth felt very conspicuous in her bright red dress.*

conspiracy /kən'spɪrəsɪ/ NOUN [*plural* **conspiracies**] a secret plan by a group of people to do something bad

• **conspirator** /kən'spɪrətə(r)/ NOUN [*plural* **conspirators**] one of a group of people who are planning to do something bad

• **conspire** /kən'spaɪə(r)/ VERB [**conspires, conspiring, conspired**]
1 to plan secretly with other people to do something bad □ *He had conspired to kill his business partner.*
2 conspire to do something if things that happen conspire to do something, they cause problems for you □ *Bad weather and injury had conspired to make him miss the game.*

constable /'kʌnstəbəl/ NOUN [*plural* **constables**] a police officer of low rank

constant /'kɒnstənt/ ADJECTIVE
1 never stopping □ *He was in constant pain.* □ *The city is under constant threat of attack.*

2 keeping at the same level □ *The thermostat keeps the house at a constant temperature.*

• **constantly** /'kɒnstəntlɪ/ ADVERB all the time □ *It rained constantly for a week.*

constellation /ˌkɒnstə'leɪʃən/ NOUN [*plural* **constellations**] a large group of stars

constipated /'kɒnstɪpeɪtɪd/ ADJECTIVE finding it difficult to get rid of solid waste from your body

• **constipation** /ˌkɒnstɪ'peɪʃən/ NOUN, NO PLURAL being constipated

constituency /kən'stɪtʃʊənsɪ/ NOUN [*plural* **constituencies**] a part of a country that elects someone to a parliament

• **constituent** /kən'stɪtʃʊənt/ NOUN [*plural* **constituents**]
1 something that is a part of a larger thing □ *The main constituent of the human body is water.*
2 a person who lives in a particular constituency

constitute /'kɒnstɪtjuːt/ VERB [**constitutes, constituting, constituted**] to be or to form something □ *Global warming constitutes a major threat to our planet.*

• **constitution** /ˌkɒnstɪ'tʃuːʃən/ NOUN [*plural* **constitutions**]
1 a set of rules or laws that a country or organization has
2 your health 🕮 *She has a very strong constitution.*

• **constitutional** /ˌkɒnstɪ'tʃuːʃənəl/ ADJECTIVE to do with a constitution

constrain /kən'streɪn/ VERB [**constrains, constraining, constrained**] to stop something from happening in the way someone wants it to □ *The research has been constrained by a lack of funding.*

• **constraint** /kən'streɪnt/ NOUN [*plural* **constraints**] something that stops something from happening in the way someone wants it to 🕮 *Financial constraints meant that staff were not given any training.*

constrict /kən'strɪkt/ VERB [**constricts, constricting, constricted**]
1 to become narrower or tighter, or to make something become narrower or tighter □ *Cold water makes your blood vessels constrict.*
2 to limit something □ *The new law constricts development along the coast.*

construct /kən'strʌkt/ VERB [**constructs, constructing, constructed**] to build something □ *The building was constructed in 1974.*

• **construction** /kən'strʌkʃən/ NOUN [*plural* **constructions**]
1 the process of building something □ *The substance is used in road construction.*
2 a formal word meaning something that has been built □ *metal constructions*

• **constructive** /kən'strʌktɪv/ ADJECTIVE helpful 🕮 *I offered her some constructive criticism.*

construe /kən'struː/ VERB [**construes, construing, construed**] to think that what someone says or does has a particular meaning □ *She didn't want to say anything that could be construed as an insult.*

consul /'kɒnsəl/ NOUN [plural **consuls**] a government official who works in a foreign city and helps visitors from his or her own country ☐ The British consul in Barcelona arranged for him to have a temporary passport.
• **consulate** /'kɒnsjulət/ NOUN [plural **consulates**] the office of a consul ☐ Protesters demonstrated outside the Mexican consulate in New York.

consult /kən'sʌlt/ VERB [**consults, consulting, consulted**]
1 to speak to someone or to look at something in order to get information or advice ☐ If symptoms persist, consult a doctor. ☐ Anna stopped to consult the map.
2 to speak to someone before you make a decision ☐ The staff weren't consulted about any of the changes.
• **consultancy** /kən'sʌltənsɪ/ NOUN [plural **consultancies**]
1 a business that offers advice and information about something ☐ He set up a management consultancy.
2 the job of offering advice and information about something ☐ The company offers consultancy services.
• **consultant** /kən'sʌltənt/ NOUN [plural **consultants**]
1 someone whose job is to give advice on a subject ☐ a marketing consultant
2 a hospital doctor who is an expert in a particular type of illness
• **consultation** /ˌkɒnsəl'teɪʃən/ NOUN [plural **consultations**] a meeting with an expert who can give you advice and information

consume /kən'sju:m/ VERB [**consumes, consuming, consumed**]
1 to use something such as energy or time ☐ Cities consume 75% of the world's energy.
2 a formal word meaning to eat or drink something ☐ Once opened, milk should be consumed within three days.
3 if you are consumed by a feeling or thought, you cannot think about anything else ☐ She was consumed by grief after the death of her daughter.
• **consumer** /kən'sju:mə(r)/ NOUN [plural **consumers**] someone who buys and uses things ☐ Consumers want choice and competitive prices.

consummate /'kɒnsəmət, kən'sʌmət/ ADJECTIVE a formal word meaning very skilful ☐ She is the consummate professional.

consumption /kən'sʌmpʃən/ NOUN, NO PLURAL
1 the use of things such as energy, fuel, water, etc. ☐ The newer model of car offers better fuel consumption. ☐ The leaflet suggests ways of reducing water consumption.
2 a formal word meaning eating or drinking something ☐ Most people need to increase their fruit and vegetable consumption.

contact /'kɒntækt/ ▶ NOUN [plural **contacts**]
1 no plural when you write to someone or speak to

them by telephone ☐ **+with** I've had no contact with my brother for over a year. ☐ I've lost contact with most of the people I went to school with. ☐ I keep in contact with all my ex-colleagues.
2 in contact if you are in contact with someone, you write to them or speak to them by telephone ☐ Have you been in contact with Adrian recently?
3 no plural when two things or people touch each other ☐ There was no physical contact between them. ☐ She became ill after coming into contact with infected chickens.
4 someone who you know who can help you ☐ He got the job through a business contact of his mother's.
▶ VERB [**contacts, contacting, contacted**] to write to someone or to speak to them on the telephone ☐ Anyone with information about the fire should contact police.

contact lens /'kɒntækt ˌlenz/ NOUN [plural **contact lenses**] a thin piece of plastic that you wear on your eye to help you see better

contagious /kən'teɪdʒəs/ ADJECTIVE a contagious disease can be spread between people if they touch each other

contain /kən'teɪn/ VERB [**contains, containing, contained**]
1 to include something or have it as a part ☐ The document contained important personal information. ☐ Oranges contain a lot of vitamin C.
2 to have something inside ☐ The bag contained some money.
3 to stop something bad from spreading ☐ Firefighters quickly managed to contain the fire.
4 to control a feeling ☐ Annie couldn't contain her excitement.

➤ Note that the verb **contain** (senses 1 + 2) is never used in the -ing form. It is always used in simple tenses:
✓ The bag contained my passport.
✗ The bag was containing my passport.

• **container** /kən'teɪnə(r)/ NOUN [plural **containers**] something for putting things in, for example a box ☐ She put the food in a plastic container. ☐ **+ of** a container of milk

contaminate /kən'tæmɪneɪt/ VERB [**contaminates, contaminating, contaminated**] to make something dirty or poisonous ☐ The water was contaminated with chemicals.
• **contamination** /kən,tæmɪ'neɪʃən/ NOUN, NO PLURAL making something dirty or poisonous

contemplate /'kɒntəmpleɪt/ VERB [**contemplates, contemplating, contemplated**] to think seriously about something ☐ We're contemplating moving to France.
• **contemplation** /ˌkɒntəm'pleɪʃən/ NOUN, NO PLURAL thinking in a quiet, serious way
• **contemplative** /kən'templətɪv/ ADJECTIVE

spending time thinking about something in a serious way

contemporary /kən'tempərərɪ/ ▶ ADJECTIVE
1 belonging to the time now 🔁 *an exhibition of contemporary art*
2 existing or done at the same time as something else □ *This is the only contemporary account of the event that we have.*
▶ NOUN [*plural* **contemporaries**] your contemporaries are people who are living at the same time as you

contempt /kən'tempt/ NOUN, NO PLURAL a strong feeling that someone or something is bad and that you do not respect them □ *She made no effort to hide her contempt for him.*
• **contemptible** /kən'temptəbəl/ ADJECTIVE bad and deserving no respect. A formal word. □ *a contemptible act of violence*
• **contemptuous** /kən'temptʃuəs/ ADJECTIVE showing that you think someone or something is bad and that you do not respect them □ *She was contemptuous of most politicians.*

contend /kən'tend/ VERB [**contends, contending, contended**]
1 to argue that something is true. A formal word. □ *Local people contend that new houses would mean an increase in traffic.*
2 to compete for something □ *He is contending for a place in the team.*
◆ PHRASAL VERB **contend with something** to deal with something difficult □ *Runners had to contend with rain and 52mph winds.*
• **contender** /kən'tendə(r)/ NOUN [*plural* **contenders**] someone who is taking part in a competition

content¹ /'kɒntent/ NOUN, NO PLURAL
1 the subject or ideas that a magazine, television programme, etc. deals with □ *The content is not suitable for children.*
2 the amount of a substance that something contains 🔁 *Pizzas have a very high fat content.*
➔ *go to* **contents**

content² /kən'tent/ ADJECTIVE happy □ *Tatsuya was quite content to let Mai help him.*
• **contented** /kən'tentɪd/ ADJECTIVE happy and satisfied □ *a contented smile* □ *Gemma was a contented baby.*

contention /kən'tenʃən/ NOUN [*plural* **contentions**]
1 an opinion that someone says during an argument. A formal word.
2 disagreement between people. A formal word.
• **contentious** /kən'tenʃəs/ ADJECTIVE a contentious subject is one that people disagree about 🔁 *a contentious issue*

contentment /kən'tentmənt/ NOUN, NO PLURAL being happy and satisfied

contents /'kɒntents/ PLURAL NOUN
1 the things that are inside something □ *She emptied the contents of her bag onto the table.*

2 the information and ideas that are in a piece of writing □ *The newspaper revealed the contents of the Prince's letter.*

contest /'kɒntest/ NOUN [*plural* **contests**] a competition 🔁 *She entered a singing contest.*
• **contestant** /kən'testənt/ NOUN [*plural* **contestants**] someone who is taking part in a contest

context /'kɒntekst/ NOUN [*plural* **contexts**]
1 the situation in which something happens and all the events that caused it 🔁 *These events need to be seen in the context of the decade in which they happened.*
2 the words before and after a word which help you to understand its meaning
3 **take something out of context** to repeat only a small part of what someone said so that the original meaning is changed

continent /'kɒntɪnənt/ NOUN [*plural* **continents**]
1 one of the large areas that the Earth's land is divided into. The continents are Africa, Antarctica, North America, South America, Asia, Australia and Europe
2 **the Continent** is a UK name for Europe but not including Britain □ *They drive on the right on the Continent.*
• **continental** /ˌkɒntɪ'nentəl/ ADJECTIVE
1 to do with Europe but not including Britain □ *Continental holidays have become more popular.*
2 to do with continents

continental crust /ˌkɒntɪnentəl 'krʌst/ NOUN, NO PLURAL the outer layer of the Earth including all the land and rocks. A geography word.
continental plate /ˌkɒntɪnentəl 'pleɪt/ NOUN [*plural* **continental plates**] one of the large pieces that the surface of the Earth is divided into. A geography word.

contingency /kən'tɪndʒənsɪ/ NOUN [*plural* **contingencies**]
1 something that might happen, especially something bad
2 something that is done to prepare for the possibility of something bad happening 🔁 *The government is making contingency plans for war.*

continual /kən'tɪnjuəl/ ADJECTIVE happening all the time without stopping □ *the continual noise of traffic*
• **continually** /kən'tɪnjuəlɪ/ ADVERB all the time □ *Language is continually changing.*
continuation /kən,tɪnju'eɪʃən/ NOUN [*plural* **continuations**]
1 when something continues to exist or happen □ *Extra funding has guaranteed the continuation of our work.*
2 when something starts again in order to continue from what happened before □ *We will meet next week for a continuation of these discussions.*

continue /kən'tɪnjuː/ VERB [**continues, continuing, continued**]
1 to keep happening, existing, or doing something without stopping □ + *for* *This disagreement has*

continued for many years. □ **+ to do something** Jake continued to do well at school. □ **+ ing** She continued working past retirement age. □ **+ with** He said he would continue with his campaign.
2 to start doing something again □ Police will continue the search in the morning.
3 to go further in the same direction □ **+ along** They continued along the road until they reached the village.

• **continuity** /ˌkɒntɪˈnjuːətɪ/ NOUN, NO PLURAL when something does not stop □ We try hard to ensure continuity of care for these patients.

• **continuous** /kənˈtɪnjuəs/ ADJECTIVE
1 existing or happening without stopping □ There has been a continuous improvement in exam results.
2 in grammar, the continuous form of a verb shows that something is continuing to happen □ The sentence 'They are playing football' is in the continuous form.

• **continuously** /kənˈtɪnjuəslɪ/ ADVERB without stopping □ Students are monitored continuously.

---

contorted /kənˈtɔːtɪd/ ADJECTIVE twisted in a way that is not natural □ His face was contorted with rage.

contour /ˈkɒntʊə(r)/ NOUN [plural **contours**]
1 the shape of the outside of something □ The car has very sleek contours.
2 a line on a map which joins places of the same height

contra- /ˈkɒntrə/ PREFIX contra- is added to the beginning of words to mean 'against' or 'opposite to' □ contradict □ contravene

contraception /ˌkɒntrəˈsepʃən/ NOUN, NO PLURAL preventing pregnancy □ various methods of contraception

• **contraceptive** /ˌkɒntrəˈseptɪv/ NOUN [plural **contraceptives**] something that is used to prevent a woman from becoming pregnant

contract[1] /ˈkɒntrækt/ NOUN [plural **contracts**] an official written agreement 🔁 She signed a contract to design clothes for a top store. 🔁 The company has won a contract to supply stationery to schools.

contract[2] /kənˈtrækt/ VERB [**contracts, contracting, contracted**]
1 to get a disease □ More than 400 people have contracted the virus.
2 to make an official agreement with someone to do something □ The company has been contracted to do the cleaning.
3 to become smaller □ Your stomach contracts if you don't eat for a long time.

• **contraction** /kənˈtrækʃən/ NOUN [plural **contractions**]
1 a painful movement of muscles in a woman's womb (=place where a baby grows) when she is having a baby
2 a word that is a short form of two other words □ 'I'm' is a contraction of 'I am'.

3 when something becomes smaller or less □ There was a contraction of economic activity.

• **contractor** /kənˈtræktə(r)/ NOUN [plural **contractors**] a company who provides goods or services for another company

• **contractual** /kənˈtræktʃuəl/ ADJECTIVE written in a contract □ a contractual agreement/obligation

contradict /ˌkɒntrəˈdɪkt/ VERB [**contradicts, contradicting, contradicted**]
1 to say that what someone has said is not correct □ Witnesses to the accident contradicted what the driver said.
2 if one statement contradicts another, they are so different that they cannot both be true □ The evidence seems to contradict the original report.

• **contradiction** /ˌkɒntrəˈdɪkʃən/ NOUN [plural **contradictions**]
1 something that makes a statement or fact seem not to be true because it shows the opposite
2 when someone says that what has been said is not correct

• **contradictory** /ˌkɒntrəˈdɪktərɪ/ ADJECTIVE a contradictory statement is one that states the opposite of what has just been said

contraption /kənˈtræpʃən/ NOUN [plural **contraptions**] a machine that looks strange

contrary /ˈkɒntrərɪ/ ▶ ADJECTIVE completely different from something else □ They have contrary views on the subject. 🔁 Contrary to popular belief (=although many people believe this), hair does not grow quicker if you cut it.
▶ NOUN, NO PLURAL
1 the contrary the opposite □ He's not a nervous person. Quite the contrary, in fact.
2 on the contrary used for emphasizing that the opposite is true □ The situation isn't depressing. On the contrary, there's a new feeling of hope.

contrast ▶ NOUN /ˈkɒntrɑːst/ [plural **contrasts**]
1 a big difference □ The contrast between the two men could not be greater.
2 in contrast to something used when comparing two things and saying that they are very different □ The team have played brilliantly this season which is in stark contrast to last season.
▶ VERB /kənˈtrɑːst/ [**contrasts, contrasting, contrasted**]
1 if two things contrast, they are very different from each other 🔁 His comments contrast sharply with those of his colleagues.
2 to compare two things and show the differences between them □ She contrasted her experiences of working in China with her time spent in India.

contravene /ˌkɒntrəˈviːn/ VERB [**contravenes, contravening, contravened**] to not obey a law or rule □ We believe the nuclear tests contravene international law.

• **contravention** /ˌkɒntrəˈvenʃən/ NOUN [plural **contraventions**] not obeying a law or rule, or something that does this □ *Their treatment of prisoners is in contravention of human rights laws.*

contribute /kən'trɪbjuːt, 'kɒntrɪbjuːt/ VERB [**contributes, contributing, contributed**]
1 to give something in order to buy or achieve something together with other people □ *We all contributed towards Paul's present.* □ *He contributed a lot to the discussion.*
2 to be one of the causes of something □ *Sunbathing has contributed significantly to the rise in skin cancer cases.*
• **contribution** /ˌkɒntrɪ'bjuːʃən/ NOUN [*plural* **contributions**] something that you give or do to help achieve something ⊞ *She has made a significant contribution to the project.*
• **contributor** /kən'trɪbjʊtə(r)/ NOUN [*plural* **contributors**]
1 someone who contributes something □ *He was a generous contributor to the party funds.*
2 one of the causes of something □ *Transport is one the biggest contributors to global emissions.*
• **contributory** /kən'trɪbjʊtəri/ ADJECTIVE helping to cause something ⊞ *Late payments were a contributory factor in the firm's failure.*

contrite /kən'traɪt/ ADJECTIVE very sorry about something bad you have done
• **contrition** /kən'trɪʃən/ NOUN, NO PLURAL being contrite

contrive /kən'traɪv/ VERB [**contrives, contriving, contrived**] a formal word meaning to succeed in doing something or making something happen in a clever way □ *She contrived never to be in the office at the same time as Tony.*
• **contrived** /kən'traɪvd/ ADJECTIVE false and not natural □ *The story seemed contrived.*

control /kən'trəul/ ▶ NOUN [*plural* **controls**]
1 *no plural* the power to make decisions for a country, organization, etc. □ *+ of The companies are competing for control of the airline.* ⊞ *The army has taken control of the city.*
2 in control having the power to make decisions in an organization, country etc. □ *He remains in control of the company.*
3 *no plural* the ability to make someone or something do what you want □ *+ over He has no control over his children.* ⊞ *Brock lost control of the car and it hit a tree.*
4 under control if something is under control, someone is dealing with it □ *The situation is under control.* □ *It took three hours to get the fire under control.*
5 a rule or law that limits something □ *Australia has tightened gun controls.* □ *+ on The government has introduced tighter controls on spending.*
6 out of control unable to be controlled □ *The situation is getting out of control.*
7 controls the handles, buttons etc. you use to make a vehicle or machine work
▶ VERB [**controls, controlling, controlled**]
1 to have the power to make decisions □ *Congress was controlled by the Democrats.*

2 to make someone or something do what you want □ *To be a good football player you must be able to control the ball.*
3 to limit something □ *They tried to control the spread of the disease.*
4 to behave calmly even if you feel angry or excited □ *He couldn't control his temper.*
• **controller** /kən'trəulə(r)/ NOUN [*plural* **controllers**] a person or thing that controls something

control tower /kən'trəul ˌtauə(r)/ NOUN [*plural* **control towers**] a tall building at an airport where people tell the pilots what to do

controversial /ˌkɒntrə'vɜːʃəl/ ADJECTIVE causing disagreement ⊞ *Nuclear power is a highly controversial issue.*
• **controversy** /kən'trɒvəsi/ NOUN [*plural* **controversies**] disagreement about something ⊞ *The decision has caused controversy in the UK.*

conundrum /kə'nʌndrəm/ NOUN [*plural* **conundrums**] a problem that is difficult to solve

conurbation /ˌkɒnɜː'beɪʃən/ NOUN [*plural* **conurbations**] a city that is formed when towns are joined by building on the land between them

convalesce /ˌkɒnvə'les/ VERB [**convalesces, convalescing, convalesced**] to rest after you have been ill so that your health improves
• **convalescence** /ˌkɒnvə'lesəns/ NOUN, NO PLURAL the time when someone is convalescing

convection /kən'vekʃən/ NOUN, NO PLURAL when heat moves through air or water as the hotter part rises. A physics word.
• **convector** /kən'vektə(r)/ NOUN [*plural* **convectors**] a device that heats a room by blowing out hot air

convene /kən'viːn/ VERB [**convenes, convening, convened**] to come together for a meeting, or to bring people together. A formal word. □ *He convened a meeting.* □ *We all convened in the school hall.*

convenience /kən'viːnjəns/ NOUN [*plural* **conveniences**]
1 *no plural* the state of being easy to use, reach or do □ *I like the convenience of living so close to the shops.* □ *For everyone's convenience, we will meet after school.*
2 something that makes people's lives easy or comfortable □ *The hotel has every modern convenience.*
• **convenient** /kən'viːnjənt/ ADJECTIVE
1 suitable and easy □ *Drinking fruit juice is a convenient way for children to get vitamin C.*
2 very close and easy to get to □ *+ for Our house is very convenient for the school.*
• **conveniently** /kən'viːnjəntli/ ADVERB in a convenient way

convent /'kɒnvənt/ NOUN [*plural* **convents**] a building where nuns (=religious women) live

convention /kən'venʃən/ NOUN [*plural* **conventions**]
1 a way of behaving that has become normal because people have been doing it for a long time

2 a meeting of people to discuss a particular subject □ *a science-fiction convention*
3 a formal agreement between governments

● **conventional** /kən'venʃənəl/ ADJECTIVE
1 traditional and not at all unusual ⊞ *Many people try homoeopathy if conventional medicine has not cured them.* □ *He uses conventional methods of teaching.*
2 conventional people are not willing to try new things

converge /kən'vɜːdʒ/ VERB [converges, converging, converged]
1 to come together at a particular place □ *The two roads converge just beyond the bridge.*
2 to come to a place and form a group there □ *Protesters converged on Trafalgar Square.*

conversant /kən'vɜːsənt/ ADJECTIVE **conversant with something** knowing about something or having experience of it. A formal word. □ *Young people are so conversant with technology.*

conversation /ˌkɒnvə'seɪʃən/ NOUN [plural conversations] a talk between people ⊞ *We had a long conversation about music.* □ *+ with I had a nice conversation with my Dad last night.* ⊞ *I overheard a conversation between my brother and his girlfriend.*

● **conversational** /ˌkɒnvə'seɪʃənəl/ ADJECTIVE to do with conversation

converse [1] /kən'vɜːs/ VERB [converses, conversing, conversed] when people converse, they talk to each other. A formal word.

converse [2] /'kɒnvɜːs/ NOUN, NO PLURAL **the converse** the opposite of a statement, fact etc.

● **conversely** /kən'vɜːsli/ ADVERB in the opposite way, or from the opposite point of view

conversion /kən'vɜːʃən/ NOUN [plural conversions]
1 when you change something from one thing to another □ *the conversion from analogue to digital television*
2 when someone changes to a different religion □ *her conversion from Christianity to Islam*

convert ▶ VERB /kən'vɜːt/ [converts, converting, converted]
1 to change something into something else □ *Convert this sum of money from pounds into dollars.*
2 to change from one religion to another one
▶ NOUN /'kɒnvɜːt/ [plural converts] someone who has changed to a different religion or opinion

● **convertible** /kən'vɜːtəbəl/ ▶ ADJECTIVE able to be changed from one thing to another
▶ NOUN [plural convertibles] a car with a soft roof that you can fold back

convex /kɒn'veks/ ADJECTIVE curving outwards

convey /kən'veɪ/ VERB [conveys, conveying, conveyed]
1 to communicate information, ideas or feelings □ *What are you trying to convey in this poem?*
2 a formal word meaning to take someone or something to a place □ *A bus conveyed us to the lecture theatre.*

conveyor belt /kən'veɪə ˌbelt/ NOUN [plural conveyor belts] a moving surface used to carry things from one place to another, especially in a factory

convict ▶ VERB /kən'vɪkt/ [convicts, convicting, convicted] to say in a court that someone is guilty of a crime □ *He was convicted of murder.*
▶ NOUN /'kɒnvɪkt/ [plural convicts] someone who has been found guilty of a crime and sent to prison

● **conviction** /kən'vɪkʃən/ NOUN [plural convictions]
1 a strong belief
2 when a judge says that someone is guilty of a crime □ *Greene has had many convictions for theft.*

convince /kən'vɪns/ VERB [convinces, convincing, convinced] to make someone believe that something is true □ *Vijay found it hard to convince his parents that he was too ill to go to school.*

● **convinced** /kən'vɪnst/ ADJECTIVE certain that something is true □ *David's convinced that he saw a ghost.*

● **convincing** /kən'vɪnsɪŋ/ ADJECTIVE
1 making you believe that something is true or right □ *He gave a fairly convincing argument against nuclear weapons.*
2 a convincing win is one in which someone wins by a large amount

convoluted /'kɒnvəluːtɪd/ ADJECTIVE complicated and difficult to understand □ *convoluted language*

convoy /'kɒnvɔɪ/ NOUN [plural convoys] a line of vehicles which are travelling together

convulsion /kən'vʌlʃən/ NOUN [plural convulsions] a sudden movement of your muscles, caused by illness

coo /kuː/ VERB [coos, cooing, cooed]
1 to make a soft gentle sound like that made by some birds such as a dove or pigeon
2 to speak in a soft voice, especially in order to show that you like something □ *They were all cooing over the baby.*

cook /kʊk/ ▶ VERB [cooks, cooking, cooked]
1 to prepare and heat food so that it is ready to eat ⊞ *I offered to cook a meal for her.* ⊞ *Ben was cooking dinner.* □ *Cook the pasta in a pan of boiling water.*
2 food cooks when it heats up and becomes ready to eat □ *While the potatoes are cooking, prepare the other vegetables.*
▶ NOUN [plural cooks] someone who prepares and cooks food ⊞ *Emma's really good cook.* □ *He works as a hospital cook.*

● **cooker** /'kʊkə(r)/ NOUN [plural cookers] a piece of kitchen equipment used for cooking food □ *a gas cooker*

> ► Note that a **cook** is someone who prepares and cooks food and a **cooker** is a piece of equipment used for cooking food.

● **cookery** /'kʊkəri/ NOUN, NO PLURAL the skill or activity of cooking food □ *She's doing a cookery course.*

cookie /'kʊkɪ/ NOUN [plural **cookies**]
1 a biscuit □ *a chocolate chip cookie*
2 a piece of computer information about which websites you have looked at. A computing word.

cooking /'kʊkɪŋ/ ▶ NOUN, NO PLURAL
1 when someone cooks food □ *Cooking is my main interest.*
2 the type of food that is cooked □ *I love my grandma's cooking.*
▶ ADJECTIVE for use in cooking □ *cooking oil*

cool /kuːl/ ▶ ADJECTIVE [**cooler, coolest**]
1 slightly cold 🔁 *There was a cool breeze.* 🔁 *I need a cool drink.*
2 an informal word meaning great □ *He has a really cool haircut.* □ *'I've got a new mobile.' 'Cool!'*
3 calm 🔁 *Try to stay cool in a dangerous situation.*
4 not friendly □ *He gave a cool reply.*
▶ VERB [**cools, cooling, cooled**] to become cooler or to make something cooler □ *Have a drink to help you cool down.*

coop /kuːp/ NOUN [plural **coops**] a building for keeping chickens in
♦ PHRASAL VERB [**coops, cooping, cooped**] **coop something/someone up** to keep a person or an animal in a small space □ *We've been cooped up indoors all day.*

cooperate /kəʊˈɒpəˌreɪt/ VERB [**cooperates, cooperating, cooperated**]
1 to work together with other people to achieve something □ *The two countries are cooperating with each other in the fight against terrorism.*
2 to help by doing something that someone wants you to □ *He refused to cooperate.*
● **cooperation** /kəʊˌɒpəˈreɪʃən/ NOUN, NO PLURAL
1 working with others so that something can be done or achieved
2 doing what someone asks or tells you to do
● **cooperative** /kəʊˈɒpərətɪv/ ADJECTIVE
1 willing to do what someone asks you to do
2 a cooperative business or organization is one that is managed or owned by everyone who works in it or uses it

coordinate /kəʊˈɔːdɪneɪt/ VERB [**coordinates, coordinating, coordinated**] to organize all the different parts of something □ *He is coordinating the research project.*

coordinates /kəʊˈɔːdɪnəts/ PLURAL NOUN the two sets of numbers or letters that show the exact position of something on a map or graph (=mathematical picture)

coordination /kəʊˌɔːdɪˈneɪʃən/ NOUN, NO PLURAL
1 the organization of people and activities so that they work well together
2 the ability to make different parts of your body work well together 🔁 *He has brilliant hand-eye coordination.*

cop /kɒp/ NOUN [plural **cops**] an informal word for a police officer □ *a New York cop*

cope /kəʊp/ VERB [**copes, coping, coped**] to be able to deal with something difficult □ *She said she couldn't cope with any more work.* □ *So many people came to the city that the transport system couldn't cope.*

co-pilot /'kəʊpaɪlət/ NOUN [plural **co-pilots**] the person who helps the main pilot on an aeroplane

copious /'kəʊpɪəs/ ADJECTIVE in large amounts
🔁 *They drank copious amounts of beer.* 🔁 *He made copious notes during the interview.*

copper /'kɒpə(r)/ ▶ NOUN [plural **coppers**]
1 *no plural* a red-brown metal
2 *no plural* a red-brown colour like this metal
3 a brown coin that has a low value
4 an informal word for police officer
▶ ADJECTIVE
1 made of copper □ *a copper kettle*
2 having the colour of copper □ *She had beautiful copper hair.*

copse /kɒps/ or **coppice** /'kɒpɪs/ NOUN [plural **copses** or **coppices**] a small group of bushes or trees

copy /'kɒpɪ/ ▶ NOUN [plural **copies**]
1 something that is made so that it looks exactly the same as something else 🔁 *Rick bought a CD and made a digital copy from that.* □ *+ of He sent a copy of her death certificate.*
2 one book, magazine, etc. from many the same that have been produced □ *+ of I bought a copy of her new book.*
▶ VERB [**copies, copying, copied**]
1 to make something that is exactly the same as something else □ *She copied the file onto a CD.*
2 to do the same things as someone else □ *Conrad copies everything his big brother does.* □ *He copied my idea.*
3 to write down words or information that you have found somewhere □ *I copied the train times into my notebook.* □ *She tried to copy my answers in the exam.*
♦ PHRASAL VERBS **copy something down** to write something that someone has told you or that is written somewhere □ *Copy down these questions and do them for homework.* **copy someone in** to send someone a copy of an email or a document □ *+ on Can you copy me in on your report?*

copyright /'kɒpɪraɪt/ NOUN, NO PLURAL the legal right to copy or use a book, film, etc. 🔁 *The company owns the copyright to thousands of songs.*

coral /'kɒrəl/ ▶ NOUN, NO PLURAL a hard pink or white substance formed from the bones of small sea creatures
▶ ADJECTIVE made of coral □ *a coral island* □ *a coral necklace*

coral reef /'kɒrəl ˌriːf/ NOUN [plural **coral reefs**] a large mass of coral under the sea

cord /kɔːd/ NOUN [plural **cords**]
1 a piece of thick string □ *The prisoner's hands were tied with cord.*

2 wire covered with plastic that connects a piece of equipment to an electrical supply

> ➤ Do not confuse the spellings of **cord** and **chord**, which have different meanings.

cordial /'kɔːdɪəl/ ➤ ADJECTIVE a formal word meaning friendly and polite □ *The two countries have a cordial relationship.*
➤ NOUN [plural **cordials**] a sweet fruit drink that you mix with water □ *lime cordial*

cordless /'kɔːdlɪs/ ADJECTIVE a cordless piece of electrical equipment does not have to be connected to an electricity supply all the time 🖪 *a cordless phone*

cordon /'kɔːdən/ NOUN [plural **cordons**] a line of police or soldiers standing around an area to stop people getting in 🖪 *Protesters broke through a police cordon.*
◆ PHRASAL VERB [cordons, cordoning, cordoned]
cordon something off
to put something around a place so that people cannot get in □ *Police cordoned off the crime scene.*

corduroy /'kɔːdərɔɪ/ NOUN, NO PLURAL cotton cloth with raised lines on it

core /kɔː(r)/ ➤ NOUN [plural **cores**]
1 the most important part of something 🖪 *This area is at the core of the Chinese manufacturing industry.*
2 the hard part with seeds in the middle of fruit like apples or pears □ *an apple core*
3 the centre of a planet
➤ ADJECTIVE most important 🖪 *core beliefs/values*
□ *Our core business was not affected by the strike.*

corgi /'kɔːgɪ/ NOUN [plural **corgis**] a type of dog with short legs

cork /kɔːk/ NOUN [plural **corks**]
1 no plural a light material from the outside part of a tree
2 a piece of cork, which is put inside the top of a wine bottle

corkscrew /'kɔːkskruː/ NOUN [plural **corkscrews**] a device used for pulling corks out of wine bottles

corn /kɔːn/ NOUN, NO PLURAL
1 a crop such as wheat that is grown for grain
2 the US word for **maize** or **sweetcorn**

cornea /'kɔːnɪə/ NOUN [plural **corneas**] the transparent layer that covers your eye. A biology word.

corner /'kɔːnə(r)/ ➤ NOUN [plural **corners**]
1 a point where two walls, edges or lines meet 🖪 *It was a large room with a table in the corner.* □ *+ of The corner of the page was creased.*
2 the point where two roads meet 🖪 *There's a hairdresser's on the corner.* 🖪 *The school is just round the corner.* □ *+ of I'll meet you at the corner of George Street and Alexander Road.*
3 a place away from the main area or far away □ *He's travelled to the far corners of the world.* □ *We put the statue in a shady corner of the garden.*
4 a kick or hit from the corner of a sports field in some games such as football

➤ VERB [corners, cornering, cornered] to get someone into a position that it is not easy to escape from □ *He had been cornered and attacked with a baseball bat.* □ *He cornered me at the office party and suggested we should go out for dinner.*

cornerstone /'kɔːnəstəʊn/ NOUN [plural **cornerstones**] the most important part of something, which everything else depends on □ *Voting is the cornerstone of democracy.*

cornet /'kɔːnɪt/ NOUN [plural **cornets**] a musical instrument that looks like a small trumpet

cornflakes /'kɔːnfleɪks/ PLURAL NOUN flat, baked pieces of corn (=grain) that you eat with milk for breakfast □ *a bowl of cornflakes*

cornflour /'kɔːnflaʊə(r)/ NOUN, NO PLURAL a white powder made from corn (=grain), used in cooking, for example to make a sauce thicker

cornflower /'kɔːnflaʊə(r)/ NOUN [plural **cornflowers**] a wild plant with bright blue flowers

corny /'kɔːnɪ/ ADJECTIVE [cornier, corniest] silly, or heard too many times before 🖪 *a corny joke*

coronary /'kɒrənərɪ/ ➤ ADJECTIVE to do with the heart. A biology word. □ *coronary disease*
➤ NOUN [plural **coronaries**] when someone's heart suddenly stops working correctly

coronation /ˌkɒrə'neɪʃən/ NOUN [plural **coronations**] a ceremony in which someone becomes a king or queen

coroner /'kɒrənə(r)/ NOUN [plural **coroners**] someone whose job is to find out the cause of someone's death

corporal /'kɔːpərəl/ NOUN [plural **corporals**] a soldier with a low rank

corporal punishment /ˌkɔːpərəl 'pʌnɪʃmənt/ NOUN, NO PLURAL punishment which involves hitting someone

corporate /'kɔːpərət/ ADJECTIVE to do with a large company □ *The corporate headquarters are in Vancouver.*

corporation /ˌkɔːpə'reɪʃən/ NOUN [plural **corporations**] a large company

corps /kɔː(r)/ NOUN [plural **corps**] a group in an army, especially one that does a special job □ *the Army Medical Corps*

corpse /kɔːps/ NOUN [plural **corpses**] a dead body

corpulent /'kɔːpjʊlənt/ ADJECTIVE a formal word meaning fat □ *a corpulent old man*

corpuscle /'kɔːpʌsəl/ NOUN [plural **corpuscles**] a red or white cell in the blood. A biology word.

correct /kə'rekt/ ➤ ADJECTIVE
1 right, not wrong 🖪 *The correct answer is 15.* □ *What is the correct pronunciation of that word?*
2 behaving in a way that is socially acceptable □ *My father was always very correct.*
➡ go to **politically correct**
➤ VERB [corrects, correcting, corrected]
1 to make something right □ *He had an operation on his ankle to correct the problem.*

2 to show someone the mistakes they have made in speaking or writing □ *He interrupted me to correct my grammar.*

• **correctly** /kə'rektlɪ/ ADVERB in a way that is correct □ *Make sure you enter your password correctly.*

• **correction** /kə'rekʃən/ NOUN [plural **corrections**] a change that makes something right ⊞ *They have made corrections to their earlier report.*

correlate /'kɒrəleɪt/ VERB [**correlates, correlating, correlated**] if two things correlate, one thing causes or influences the other thing. A formal word. □ *A mother's smoking in pregnancy correlates with low birth weight in her baby.*

• **correlation** /ˌkɒrə'leɪʃən/ NOUN, NO PLURAL when one thing causes or influences another thing. A formal word. ⊞ *Researchers found a strong correlation between poverty and ill health.*

correspond /ˌkɒrɪ'spɒnd/ VERB [**corresponds, corresponding, corresponded**]

1 if two things correspond, they are the same □ *Let's see if what he told you corresponds with what he told me.*

2 if people correspond, they write to each other. A formal word.

• **correspondence** /ˌkɒrɪ'spɒndəns/ NOUN, NO PLURAL

1 letters that people write to each other, or the activity of writing letters

2 a connection between two things

• **correspondent** /ˌkɒrɪ'spɒndənt/ NOUN [plural **correspondents**] someone who writes news reports about a particular subject □ *a political correspondent*

• **corresponding** /ˌkɒrɪ'spɒndɪŋ/ ADJECTIVE relating to or similar to something else □ *Prices have risen with no corresponding increase in wages.*

corridor /'kɒrɪdɔː(r)/ NOUN [plural **corridors**] a passage in a building with doors on one or both sides ⊞ *a long corridor* □ *I was chatting to her in the corridor.*

corroborate /kə'rɒbəreɪt/ VERB [**corroborates, corroborating, corroborated**] to give information that supports or proves what someone has said. A formal word. □ *Several witnesses corroborated her version of events.*

• **corroboration** /kəˌrɒbə'reɪʃən/ NOUN, NO PLURAL information that supports or proves what someone has said. A formal word.

corrode /kə'rəʊd/ VERB [**corrodes, corroding, corroded**] if metal corrodes, it is slowly destroyed by water or chemicals

• **corrosion** /kə'rəʊʒən/ NOUN, NO PLURAL when something corrodes

• **corrosive** /kə'rəʊsɪv/ ADJECTIVE able to gradually destroy metal □ *a corrosive acid*

corrugated /'kɒrəgeɪtɪd/ ADJECTIVE made in the shape of several folds ⊞ *a corrugated roof*

corrupt /kə'rʌpt/ ▶ ADJECTIVE

1 being dishonest in order to get money or power □ *corrupt officials*

2 corrupt information has been spoiled so that it is no longer correct □ *The data was corrupt.*

▶ VERB [**corrupts, corrupting, corrupted**]

1 to make someone behave dishonestly in order to get money or power □ *People are easily corrupted by power.*

2 to spoil information so that it is no longer correct □ *A virus corrupted all his data.*

• **corruption** /kə'rʌpʃən/ NOUN, NO PLURAL dishonest behaviour by people in powerful jobs □ *There was widespread corruption among the police.*

corset /'kɔːsɪt/ NOUN [plural **corsets**] a piece of tight underwear that women in the past wore around their waists to make their waists look smaller

cosh /kɒʃ/ NOUN [plural **coshes**] a short heavy stick used for hitting people

cosine /'kəʊsaɪn/ NOUN [plural **cosines**] in a triangle with one angle of 90°, the cosine is the length of the side next to an angle of less than 90° divided by the hypotenuse (=longest side). A maths word.

cosmetic /kɒz'metɪk / ADJECTIVE

1 designed to make you look more attractive □ *cosmetic products*

2 involving only small changes that are not important □ *The changes were merely cosmetic.*

• **cosmetics** /kɒz'metɪks/ PLURAL NOUN powders and creams that you put on your face to make you more attractive

cosmetic surgery /kɒzˌmetɪk 'sɜːdʒərɪ/ NOUN, NO PLURAL an operation that is done to make someone look more attractive ⊞ *She had cosmetic surgery to make her nose smaller.*

cosmic /'kɒzmɪk/ ADJECTIVE to do with the universe and outer space

cosmopolitan /ˌkɒzmə'pɒlɪtən/ ADJECTIVE including people or ideas from many parts of the world □ *cosmopolitan cities like London and New York*

cosmos /'kɒzmɒs/ NOUN, NO PLURAL the cosmos the universe

cosset /'kɒsɪt/ VERB [**cossets, cosseting, cosseted**] to give someone too much attention and care □ *It's not good to cosset your children.*

cost /kɒst/ ▶ VERB [**costs, costing, cost**]

1 to have a particular price □ *The ticket cost £35.* □ *How much does a litre of milk cost?* □ *This coat cost me a lot of money.* □ **+ to do something** *It cost £10,000 to fix the roof.*

2 to cost someone something is to make them lose that thing □ *His brave actions cost him his life.*

▶ NOUN [plural **costs**]

1 the amount of money that you need in order to buy or do something □ **+ of** *The average cost of a house in this area is £350,000.* ⊞ *the high cost of fuel* ⊞ *There has been an increase in the cost of living (=the price of food, clothes, etc.).*

2 damage that is done to someone or something □ **+ to** *There's a great cost to the environment when we burn carbon fuels.*

◆ IDIOM **at all costs** used for saying that you will do

something even if it is difficult or even if people suffer □ *Yushi was determined to succeed at all costs.*

• **costly** /ˈkɒstlɪ/ ADJECTIVE
1 expensive □ *The building was costly to repair.* ·
2 causing a lot of problems 🖭 *We made a few costly mistakes early in the game.*

co-star /ˈkəʊstɑː(r)/ ► VERB [co-stars, co-starring, co-starred] to be in a film or play with another famous actor
► NOUN [plural **co-stars**] one of two famous actors in a film or play

costume /ˈkɒstjuːm/ NOUN [plural **costumes**]
1 a set of clothes that you wear to make you look like a different person or like an animal or other creature □ *The costumes in the film were beautiful.* □ *He was in a vampire's costume at Amy's party.*
2 **in costume** wearing a costume □ *Everyone at the party was in costume.*
3 the traditional clothes from a country or from a time in the past 🖭 *The children were dressed in national costume for the parade.* □ *Elizabethan costumes*

cosy /ˈkəʊzɪ/ ADJECTIVE [cosier, cosiest] warm and comfortable □ *a cosy little bedroom* □ *I'm nice and cosy sitting here by the fire.*

cot /kɒt/ NOUN [plural **cots**] a bed with high sides that a baby sleeps in

cot death /ˈkɒt ˌdeθ/ NOUN [plural **cot deaths**] when a baby dies while it is sleeping and nobody knows why

cottage /ˈkɒtɪdʒ/ NOUN [plural **cottages**] a small house in the countryside or in a village □ *They've bought one of the cottages in the village.*

cotton /ˈkɒtən/ NOUN, NO PLURAL
1 a common type of cloth made from a plant □ *a white cotton shirt* □ *cotton sheets*
2 a plant that produces a soft white substance, used for making cloth □ *cotton farmers*

cotton wool /ˌkɒtən ˈwʊl/ NOUN, NO PLURAL a mass of soft cotton, used for cleaning cuts on your skin and for removing make-up

couch /kaʊtʃ/ NOUN [plural **couches**] a long, comfortable chair that two or more people can sit on

couch potato /ˈkaʊtʃ pəˌteɪtəʊ/ NOUN [plural **couch potatoes**] a lazy person, especially one who sits watching television a lot. An informal phrase.

cougar /ˈkuːɡə(r)/ NOUN [plural **cougars**] a large wild animal of the cat family that lives in America

cough /kɒf/ ► VERB [coughs, coughing, coughed] to make a loud rough sound in your throat as air comes out of your lungs □ *He was coughing and sneezing.*
► NOUN [plural **coughs**]
1 the noise you make when you cough 🖭 *She gave a little cough and looked up.*
2 an illness that causes you to cough 🖭 *I have got a bad cough.* 🖭 *You need some cough medicine.*

could /kʊd/ MODAL VERB
1 used as the past tense of **can** □ *We could see into the building.* □ *He could run very fast when he was young.* □ *He said we could go.*
2 used to ask for something or to ask someone to do something □ *Could I have a glass of water, please?* □ *Could you pass me the butter?*
3 used to make a suggestion □ *You could try texting her.* □ *We could go for a walk.*
4 used to say that something is possible □ *The weather could get better later.* □ *The disease could be prevented with good hygiene.*

couldn't /ˈkʊdənt/ a short way to say and write could not

could've /ˈkʊdəv/ a short way to say and write could have

council /ˈkaʊnsəl/ NOUN [plural **councils**]
1 a group of people who are elected to control a town or city 🖭 *Local councils are responsible for repairing roads.* □ *council leaders*
2 an official group of people who make decisions or give advice □ *a new business advisory council*

• **councillor** /ˈkaʊnsələ(r)/ NOUN [plural **councillors**] a member of a town or city council

► Be careful not to confuse the noun **council** with the noun and verb **counsel**.

council tax /ˈkaʊnsəl ˌtæks/ NOUN, NO PLURAL in Britain, a tax that you pay for local services such as schools and libraries, based on how much your house is worth

counsel /ˈkaʊnsəl/ ► VERB [counsels, counselling/US counseling, counselled/US counseled]
1 to give someone advice and help with their problems □ *Students were counselled following the death of their classmate.*
2 a formal word meaning to advise □ *He had been counselled by his lawyer to remain silent.*
► NOUN [plural **counsels**]
1 a lawyer who speaks in a court □ *the counsel for the defence*
2 a formal word meaning advice

• **counselling** /ˈkaʊnsəlɪŋ/ NOUN, NO PLURAL giving advice and help to people with problems □ *the student counselling service*

• **counsellor** /ˈkaʊnsələ(r)/ NOUN [plural **counsellors**] someone whose job is to give advice and help to people with problems

counseling /ˈkaʊnsəlɪŋ/ NOUN, NO PLURAL the US spelling of **counselling**

• **counselor** /ˈkaʊnsələ(r)/ NOUN [plural **counselors**] the US spelling of **counsellor**

count /kaʊnt/ ► VERB [counts, counting, counted]
1 to find out the total of something □ *He was busy counting his money.*
2 to say numbers in order □ *Can you count backwards from 10?*
3 to think of someone or something in a particular

way □ **+ as** *I counted him as one of my best friends.*
4 to be important □ *He played well when it counted.*
◆ PHRASAL VERBS **count against someone** to make it more difficult for someone to succeed □ *Lack of experience will count against him in the race.* **count on someone** to depend on someone □ *I was counting on him to help.* **count out something** to say the numbers aloud while you are counting something □ *He counted out £500.* **count towards something** to form part of a total □ *This essay will count towards your final grades.* **count up something** to find out the total of something □ *She counted up how many people there were.*
▶ NOUN [*plural* **counts**]
1 the process of counting, or the total you get ⊞ *She did a quick count of the people present.*
2 keep count to know how many of something there is
3 lose count to stop knowing how many of something there is
4 on all/both counts in all or both ways □ *The claim is wrong on all counts.*
5 a man of a high social rank

countable noun /ˌkaʊntəbəl ˈnaʊn/ NOUN [*plural* **countable nouns**] in grammar, a noun that can form a plural, e.g. *dog, table* or *car*
countdown /ˈkaʊntdaʊn/ NOUN, NO PLURAL
1 the time just before something important and exciting happens □ *The countdown to the World Cup has begun.*
2 when people count backwards to zero before something happens
counter /ˈkaʊntə(r)/ ▶ NOUN [*plural* **counters**]
1 the place where people are served in a shop or bank □ *She worked on the perfume counter.*
2 a small plastic disc used in some games that are played on a board □
3 the US word for **work surface**
▶ VERB [**counters, countering, countered**]
1 to reduce the bad effects that something has, or to prevent it from happening □ *We are doing everything we can to counter terrorism.*
2 to say something that disagrees with or criticizes what someone has said □ *'I can't do it,' she countered.*
counter- /ˈkaʊntə(r)/ PREFIX counter- is added to the beginning of words to mean 'the opposite of' □ *counteract*
counteract /ˌkaʊntərækt/ VERB [**counteracts, counteracting, counteracted**] to reduce or remove the bad effect of something ⊞ *Massage may be able to counteract the harmful effects of stress.*
counterattack /ˈkaʊntərətæk/ NOUN [*plural* **counterattacks**] an attack against someone who has attacked or criticized you first □ *The soldiers launched a counterattack.*
counterfeit /ˈkaʊntəfət/ ▶ ADJECTIVE not real, but made to look real □ *a counterfeit stamp*
▶ NOUN [*plural* **counterfeits**] a copy of something made to look as if it is real

counterfoil /ˈkaʊntəfɔɪl/ NOUN [*plural* **counterfoils**] the part of a ticket or cheque that is left when the main piece has been removed
counterpart /ˈkaʊntəpɑːt/ NOUN [*plural* **counterparts**] the person who does the same job as you but in a different place □ *The British Prime Minister will be meeting his European counterparts.*
countersign /ˈkaʊntəsaɪn/ VERB [**countersigns, countersigning, countersigned**] to sign a document that has already been signed by someone else
countess /ˈkaʊntɪs/ NOUN [*plural* **countesses**] a woman with a high social rank
countless /ˈkaʊntlɪs/ ADJECTIVE very many □ *I've done this countless times.*
count noun /ˈkaʊnt ˌnaʊn/ NOUN [*plural* **count nouns**] in grammar, a noun that can form a plural, e.g. *dog, table* or *car*

country /ˈkʌntrɪ/ ▶ NOUN [*plural* **countries**]
1 an area of land with its own government and national borders □ *We don't have the death penalty in this country.* ⊞ *Have you ever lived in a foreign country?*
2 the country (a) areas that are away from towns and cities □ *I prefer living in the country.* (b) all the people who live in a nation □ *The President has lost the support of the country.*
3 no plural a particular type of land □ *He ran for miles across open country.* □ *the mountainous country of southern China*
▶ ADJECTIVE in or from the countryside □ *country lanes* □ *The Prime Minister's country house is located on Lake Mousseau.*

countryman /ˈkʌntrɪmən/ NOUN [*plural* **countrymen**] someone who comes from the same country as you □ *He beat countryman Healey 6–2, 7–5.*
countryside /ˈkʌntrɪsaɪd/ NOUN, NO PLURAL land that is away from towns and cities ⊞ *The hotel is surrounded by open countryside.*

countrywoman /ˈkʌntrɪwʊmən/ NOUN [*plural* **countrywomen**] a woman who comes from the same country as you
county /ˈkaʊntɪ/ NOUN [*plural* **counties**] an area of a country or state that has its own local government □ *Yorkshire is a huge county.*
coup /kuː/ NOUN [*plural* **coups**]
1 when a group of people suddenly take control of a country without an election ⊞ *a military coup*
2 a great achievement □ *Signing Beckham was a real coup for the team.*

couple /ˈkʌpəl/ ▶ NOUN [*plural* **couples**]
1 two or approximately two □ **+ of** *I haven't seen him for a couple of months.* □ *She relaxed after the first couple of games.* □ *Who ate all the chocolates? I only had a couple.*
2 a husband and wife, or two people who have a similar close relationship ⊞ *Most people on the*

holiday were married couples. 🔄 Many young couples can't afford to buy a house.

► VERB [**couples, coupling, coupled**] **coupled with** combined with □ A high-fat diet coupled with a lack of exercise is causing many people to become obese.

coupon /'ku:pɒn/ NOUN [plural **coupons**] a piece of paper that you can use to get something free or at a cheaper price than usual

courage /'kʌrɪdʒ/ NOUN, NO PLURAL the ability to do difficult or frightening things 🔄 He didn't have the courage to tell her what he really thought. 🔄 John showed great courage throughout his ordeal. 🔄 I haven't plucked up the courage (=found the courage) to leave my job yet.

• **courageous** /kə'reɪdʒəs/ ADJECTIVE brave □ a courageous decision

courgette /kɔ:'ʒet/ NOUN [plural **courgettes**] a long green vegetable that you cook and eat

courier /'kʊrɪə(r)/ ► NOUN [plural **couriers**] someone who takes packages from one place to another □ a courier company

► VERB [**couriers, couriering, couriered**] to send something using a courier

course /kɔ:s/ NOUN [plural **courses**]
1 of course (a) used for saying yes □ 'Can I borrow your pen?' 'Of course you can.' (b) used for saying that what happened was what you expected □ We went on holiday and of course it rained the whole time.
2 of course not used for emphasizing the word no □ 'Did you leave the keys in the car?' 'No, of course not.'
3 a set of lessons on a particular subject 🔄 I'm doing a French course. 🔄 There was a four-year training course to become a teacher. □ **+ in** a part-time course in business studies
4 one of the parts of a meal 🔄 For the main course we had roast chicken.
5 the direction that a vehicle is travelling in 🔄 The pilot had to change course and land in Berlin.
6 the things that you do in a particular situation 🔄 He advised me on the best course of action.
7 a piece of land that a race is run on or a game of golf is played on □ a golf course
8 during/in the course of while something is happening □ During the course of the evening, I started to feel unwell.

► Remember that **course** (sense 3) is followed by the preposition in: □ She's doing a four-day course in travel writing.

court /kɔ:t/ ► NOUN [plural **courts**]
1 the room where legal trials take place 🔄 He will appear in court charged with murder.
2 the court the people who make a legal judgment about whether someone is guilty of a crime □ He told the court that he had never met the woman before.

3 an area where you play sports such as tennis or basketball □ an indoor tennis court
4 the home of a king or queen and the people who live with them

► VERB [**courts, courting, courted**]
1 to do things to try to get someone's support □ The party is attempting to court young voters.
2 to do something that brings a particular result □ He has courted controversy with offensive statements about the chairman.

courteous /'kɜ:tɪəs/ ADJECTIVE polite □ His manner was always courteous.

• **courtesy** /'kɜ:tɪsɪ/ NOUN [plural **courtesies**]
1 no plural polite behaviour 🔄 She didn't even have the courtesy to explain.
2 something polite that you do □ As a courtesy, she phoned before she visited him.
3 courtesy of (a) as a result of □ The team went into the lead courtesy of a brilliant goal from Miller. (b) used for saying who provided or paid for something □ Politicians travel all around the world courtesy of taxpayers.

courthouse /'kɔ:thaʊs/ NOUN [plural **courthouses**] a US word for a building with legal courts in it

courtier /'kɔ:tɪə(r)/ NOUN [plural **courtiers**] someone who works or spends a lot of time at a king or queen's home

court-martial /ˌkɔ:t'mɑ:ʃəl/ ► NOUN [plural **court-martials** or **courts-martial**] a military trial

► VERB [**court-martials, court-martialling, court-martialled**] to judge a soldier in a military court

courtroom /'kɔ:tru:m/ NOUN [plural **courtrooms**] the room where a trial takes place

courtship /'kɔ:tʃɪp/ NOUN [plural **courtships**] the time when you have a romantic relationship with someone before you get married

courtyard /'kɔ:tjɑ:d/ NOUN [plural **courtyards**] an open area that is surrounded by walls, usually next to a building

cousin /'kʌzən/ NOUN [plural **cousins**] the son or daughter of your aunt or uncle □ Clare and I are cousins.

cove /kəʊv/ NOUN [plural **coves**] a part of the coast where the sea is partly surrounded by land

covenant /'kʌvənənt/ NOUN [plural **covenants**] a formal written agreement

cover /'kʌvə(r)/ ► VERB [**covers, covering, covered**]
1 to put something over something else to hide or protect it □ **+ with** Mum had covered the table with a clean cloth. □ **+ up** We covered up the broken window with a board. □ Cover your mouth when you cough, please.
2 to form a layer on the surface of something □ The mountains were covered in snow. □ The carpets are covered in mud.
3 to deal with or to include a subject or some information □ The local newspaper covered the story.

◻ *The course covers every aspect of childcare.* ◻ *This law only covers UK residents.*

4 to travel a particular distance ◻ *We covered ten miles in three hours.*

5 to be a particular size ◻ *The farm covers an area of over a hundred square miles.*

6 to be enough to pay for something ◻ *£100 should cover our expenses.*

7 to provide protection from financial problems caused by a particular situation ◻ *Our insurance covers accidental damage.* ◻ *I'm covered for loss of earnings if I'm ill.*

◆ PHRASAL VERBS **cover for someone** to do someone's work while they are not there ◻ *I'm covering for Jenny while she's on holiday.* **cover something up** to stop people from discovering something bad you have done ◻ *He set fire to the house in an attempt to cover up his crime.*

▶ NOUN [*plural* **covers**]

1 something that you put on top of or around something to protect it ◻ *a duvet cover*

2 the outer part of a book or magazine 🔄 *There was a photograph of him on the front cover.*

3 *no plural* protection so that you get money if something bad happens ◻ *Make sure you have enough insurance cover if you are going on holiday.*

4 *no plural* protection from attack or bad weather 🔄 *We took cover in an old church.*

● **coverage** /'kʌvərɪdʒ/ NOUN, NO PLURAL when a newspaper or a television programme reports an event 🔄 *The channel showed live coverage of the game.*

● **covering** /'kʌvərɪŋ/ NOUN [*plural* **coverings**]

1 something that you use to cover something ◻ *The shop has a wide range of floor coverings.*

2 a layer which covers something ◻ *+ of There was a light covering of snow on the hills.*

covering letter /ˌkʌvərɪŋ 'letə(r)/ NOUN [*plural* **covering letters**] a letter that you include with something to give more information about it

covert /'kəʊvɜːt, 'kʌvət/ ADJECTIVE done secretly ◻ *a covert military operation*

covet /'kʌvɪt/ VERB [**covets, coveting, coveted**] to want something very much. A formal word.

● **covetous** /'kʌvɪtəs/ ADJECTIVE wanting something very much. A formal word.

COW /kaʊ/ NOUN [*plural* **cows**] a large animal kept on farms for its milk or meat 🔄 *The farmer had a large herd of cows.*

coward /'kaʊəd/ NOUN [*plural* **cowards**] someone who has no courage

● **cowardice** /'kaʊədɪs/ NOUN, NO PLURAL being a coward

● **cowardly** /'kaʊədlɪ/ ADJECTIVE behaving like a coward

cowboy /'kaʊbɔɪ/ NOUN [*plural* **cowboys**] a man who rides a horse and looks after cows in the US

cower /'kaʊə(r)/ VERB [**cowers, cowering, cowered**] to move your body away from someone because you are frightened

cowgirl /'kaʊgɜːl/ NOUN [*plural* **cowgirls**] a woman who rides a horse and looks after cows in the US

coy /kɔɪ/ ADJECTIVE [**coyer, coyest**]

1 pretending to be shy ◻ *a coy smile*

2 not willing to give information about something ◻ *She's very coy about her age.*

coyote /kɔɪ'əʊtɪ/ NOUN [*plural* **coyotes**] a wild dog that lives in North America

cozy /'kəʊzɪ/ ADJECTIVE [**cozier, coziest**] the US spelling of cosy

CPU /ˌsiːpiːˈjuː/ ABBREVIATION central processing unit; a part of a computer that controls what it does. A computing word.

crab /kræb/ NOUN [*plural* **crabs**] a sea creature with a round shell and ten legs, whose pink meat is eaten

crack /kræk/ ▶ VERB [**cracks, cracking, cracked**]

1 to break something so that a line appears on the surface, or to break in this way ◻ *I'm sorry, I've cracked this cup.* ◻ *The ice had started to crack.*

2 if you crack an egg or a nut, you break it open

3 to hit part of your body hard against something ◻ *He fell and cracked his head on the pavement.*

4 to solve something ◻ *We hope this will help us crack the mystery.*

5 crack a joke to make a joke

◆ PHRASAL VERBS **crack down** to start dealing with someone or something in a more severe way ◻ *The government is cracking down on illegal fishing.* **crack up** an informal word meaning to become mentally ill

▶ NOUN [*plural* **cracks**]

1 a narrow break ◻ *This mug has a crack in it.* ◻ *The ceiling had lots of cracks in it.*

2 a narrow space between two parts of something ◻ *The sun was coming in through a crack in the curtain.*

3 a sudden short sound ◻ *the crack of a whip*

◆ IDIOM **have a crack at something** to try to do something. An informal phrase.

crackdown /'krækdaʊn/ NOUN [*plural* **crackdowns**] when you start dealing with someone or something more severely ◻ *a crackdown on illegal street traders*

cracker /'krækə(r)/ NOUN [*plural* **crackers**]

1 a paper tube with a toy inside that you pull apart at Christmas

2 a plain, dry biscuit that you eat with cheese

crackle /'krækəl/ ▶ VERB [**crackles, crackling, crackled**] to make several short cracking noises ◻ *The fire crackled in the grate.*

▶ NOUN, NO PLURAL several short cracking noises ◻ *the crackle of twigs underfoot*

cradle /'kreɪdəl/ ▶ NOUN [*plural* **cradles**] a baby's bed that can move from side to side

▶ VERB [**cradles, cradling, cradled**] to hold someone or something carefully and gently ◻ *She cradled the baby in her arms.*

craft[1] /krɑːft/ ► NOUN [plural **crafts**] a skill in which you make something with your hands □ *They teach traditional crafts such as pottery and sewing.*
► VERB [**crafts, crafting, crafted**] to make something using skill □ *The statues were crafted from marble.*
craft[2] /krɑːft/ NOUN [plural **craft**] a boat
craftsman /'krɑːftsmən/ NOUN [plural **craftsmen**] a man who is skilled at making things with his hands
• **craftsmanship** /'krɑːftsmənʃɪp/ NOUN, NO PLURAL the skill of a craftsman or craftswoman
craftswoman /'krɑːftswumən/ NOUN [plural **craftswomen**] a woman who is skilled at making things with her hands
crafty /'krɑːftɪ/ ADJECTIVE [**craftier, craftiest**] good at getting what you want by tricking people
crag /kræg/ NOUN [plural **crags**] a high steep rock that sticks up from the area around it
• **craggy** /'krægɪ/ ADJECTIVE [**craggier, craggiest**]
1 with a lot of crags □ *We could see the craggy peaks of the island.*
2 a craggy face is strong with a lot of lines
cram /kræm/ VERB [**crams, cramming, crammed**]
1 to push people or things into a small space □ *Elizabeth tried to cram everything into her bags.* □ *We all crammed into the car.*
2 an informal word meaning to study a lot before an exam
• **crammed** /kræmd/ ADJECTIVE completely full □ *The shelves were absolutely crammed with books.*
cramp /kræmp/ NOUN [plural **cramps**] a sudden pain in a muscle that makes it feel tight
• **cramped** /kræmpt/ ADJECTIVE a cramped space is uncomfortable because it is too small
cranberry /'krænbərɪ/ NOUN [plural **cranberries**] a small red fruit with a sour taste □ *cranberry juice*
crane /kreɪn/ ► NOUN [plural **cranes**]
1 a tall machine used to lift and move heavy things
2 a large bird with a long neck and long thin legs
► VERB [**cranes, craning, craned**] to stretch your neck up to see something
cranium /'kreɪnɪəm/ NOUN [plural **crania** or **craniums**] your skull (=bone in your head). A biology word.
crank /kræŋk/ NOUN [plural **cranks**]
1 someone who has strange ideas or behaves in a strange way
2 a handle that you turn to make an engine or a piece of machinery start
• **cranky** /'kræŋkɪ/ ADJECTIVE [**crankier, crankiest**] bad-tempered □ *The baby was getting cranky.*
cranny /'krænɪ/ NOUN [plural **crannies**] a narrow opening, especially in a rock or wall
➔ go to every **nook** and **cranny**
crash /kræʃ/ ► VERB [**crashes, crashing, crashed**]
1 if a vehicle crashes, or you crash it, it hits something by accident □ *A plane had crashed into the mountain.* □ *Jane crashed her car last night.*
2 to make a loud noise, often by hitting something

□ *The crystal vase crashed to the floor.* □ *The waves were crashing against the rocks.*
3 if a computer crashes, it suddenly stops working. A computing word.
4 if the stock market (=the buying and selling of parts of businesses) crashes, it loses value suddenly
♦ PHRASAL VERB **crash out** an informal phrase meaning to go to sleep when you are very tired □ *We crashed out on Emma's floor.*
► NOUN [plural **crashes**]
1 an accident in which a vehicle hits something □ *Her parents were killed in a plane crash.*
2 a loud noise made when something breaks or falls □ *the crash of breaking glass*
3 when a computer suddenly stops working. A computing word.
4 when the value of a country's businesses suddenly falls □ *the stock market crash of 1987*
► ADJECTIVE done in a short time to get results quickly
🔁 *a crash diet* 🔁 *I took a crash course in French.*

crash helmet /'kræʃ ˌhelmɪt/ NOUN [plural **crash helmets**] a hard hat worn by motorcycle riders to protect their head
crash-land /ˌkræʃ'lænd/ VERB [**crash-lands, crash-landing, crash-landed**] to land an aeroplane suddenly in an emergency, sometimes causing damage or injuries
• **crash-landing** /ˌkræʃ'lændɪŋ/ NOUN [plural **crash-landings**] when you have to land an aeroplane in an emergency 🔁 *The pilot had to make a crash-landing in a field.*
crass /kræs/ ADJECTIVE stupid and not showing respect for other people's feelings □ *a crass remark*
crate /kreɪt/ NOUN [plural **crates**] a wooden or plastic box used for carrying or storing things, especially bottles
crater /'kreɪtə(r)/ NOUN [plural **craters**]
1 a large hole in the ground □ *The bomb left a crater 10 metres wide.*
2 the round hole at the top of a volcano (=mountain that explodes). A geography word.
cravat /krə'væt/ NOUN [plural **cravats**] a wide strip of thin cloth that is folded and tied under the collar of a man's shirt
crave /kreɪv/ VERB [**craves, craving, craved**] to want something very much 🔁 *Disruptive children often crave attention.*
• **craving** /'kreɪvɪŋ/ NOUN [plural **cravings**] a strong feeling that you need or want something □ *When she was pregnant she developed a craving for salty foods.*
crawl /krɔːl/ ► VERB [**crawls, crawling, crawled**]
1 to move on your hands and knees □ *The baby has just learnt to crawl.*
2 insects crawl when they move around on their legs □ *There's a spider crawling up the wall behind you.*
3 if vehicles crawl, they move very slowly □ *The traffic was crawling along at about 2 miles per hour.*
♦ PHRASAL VERB **crawl with something** or be **crawling with something** (a) to be too full of people

□ *The country was crawling with spies.* (b) to be covered with insects □ *The meat was crawling with flies.*

▶ NOUN, NO PLURAL

1 a very slow speed □ *We were moving forward at a crawl.*

2 a way of swimming in which you kick your legs and move one arm and then the other over your head

crayon /'kreɪɒn/ NOUN [*plural* **crayons**] a stick of coloured wax or a coloured pencil for drawing with

craze /kreɪz/ NOUN [*plural* **crazes**] something that is very popular for a short time □ *the craze for Japanese puzzles*

crazed /kreɪzd/ ADJECTIVE behaving in a wild, uncontrolled way □ *a crazed gunman*

crazy /'kreɪzɪ/ ADJECTIVE [**crazier, craziest**]

1 mad or stupid □ *a crazy idea* 🕮*Have you gone crazy?*

2 angry 🕮*Mum will go crazy when she finds out.* 🕮*His stupid questions drive me crazy.*

3 be crazy about someone/something to like someone or something very much □ *As a child, she was crazy about horses.*

creak /kri:k/ ▶ VERB [**creaks, creaking, creaked**] if a door or a piece of wood creaks, it makes a long low sound □ *The floorboards creaked as he crossed the room.*

▶ NOUN [*plural* **creaks**] a long low sound

• **creaky** /'kri:kɪ/ ADJECTIVE [**creakier, creakiest**] making long low sounds □ *a creaky gate*

cream /kri:m/ ▶ NOUN [*plural* **creams**]

1 *no plural* a thick yellow-white liquid that forms on top of milk □ *strawberries and cream*

2 a soft substance that you put on your skin or hair □ *suntan cream*

3 *no plural* a yellow-white colour

▶ ADJECTIVE having a yellow-white colour □ *a cream leather sofa*

♦ PHRASAL VERB [**creams, creaming, creamed**] cream something off to take the best part of something □ *He showed no interest in the business – he just creamed off all the profits.*

• **creamy** /'kri:mɪ/ ADJECTIVE [**creamier, creamiest**] containing cream or like cream □ *a creamy dessert*

crease /kri:s/ ▶ NOUN [*plural* **creases**] a line on cloth or paper where it has been folded or crushed □ *With this fabric you can shake out the creases.*

▶ VERB [**creases, creasing, creased**] to get creases or make something get creases □ *Linen creases very easily.*

create /kri:'eɪt/ VERB [**creates, creating, created**] to make something happen or exist □ *We are hoping to create an environmentally friendly building.* □ *Snow created problems for drivers today.* □ *He hoped to create a good impression by arriving on time.*

• **creation** /kri:'eɪʃən/ NOUN [*plural* **creations**]

1 *no plural* the act or process of creating something □ *He opposed the creation of a new department.*

2 something that has been made □ *This plastic dress is one of the designer's latest creations.*

3 the Creation the time when some people believe that God made the universe

• **creative** /kri:'eɪtɪv/ ADJECTIVE

1 good at imagining and making new things, especially works of art □ *She's a very creative artist.*

2 to do with creating things □ *the creative process*

• **creativity** /ˌkri:eɪ'tɪvətɪ/ NOUN, NO PLURAL the ability or imagination to make or invent things

• **creator** /kri:'eɪtə(r)/ NOUN [*plural* **creators**] someone who creates something □ *She was the creator of some of TV's most popular characters.*

creature /'kri:tʃə(r)/ NOUN [*plural* **creatures**] any living thing that is not a plant

crèche /kreʃ/ NOUN [*plural* **crèches**] a place where very young children are looked after while their parents are somewhere else

credentials /krɪ'denʃəlz/ PLURAL NOUN

1 the qualities and experience that make you suitable for a particular job or activity or make you seem good in a particular way □ *The company has worked hard to establish its green credentials.*

2 official documents that prove someone is who they say they are □ *Did you ask to see his credentials?*

credibility /ˌkredə'bɪlətɪ/ NOUN, NO PLURAL a quality that makes people believe and respect someone 🕮*The government has lost all credibility over the war.*

credible /'kredəbəl/ ADJECTIVE able to be believed □ *a credible story*

credit /'kredɪt/ ▶ NOUN [*plural* **credits**]

1 *no plural* a way of buying goods or services and paying for them later □ *I bought the car on credit.* 🕮*We offer interest-free credit on all goods over £200.*

2 *no plural* praise that people give you for something you have done 🕮*We all worked hard but Ben got most of the credit.* 🕮*I can't take all the credit for the success of the film.*

3 to someone's credit if behaviour is to someone's credit, they have done something good □ *To her credit, she never gave away Tammy's secret.*

4 be a credit to someone to do something that makes someone proud of you □ *Your children really are a credit to you.*

5 in credit your bank account is in credit when you have money in it

6 an amount paid into a bank account

➔ go to credits

▶ VERB [**credits, crediting, credited**]

1 to put some money into a bank account

2 to believe something 🕮*We could scarcely credit their cheek!*

♦ PHRASAL VERBS credit something to something to say that something was the reason for something good □ *They credited their success to a happy working environment.* credit someone with something

1 to say that someone is responsible for achieving something good □ *He was credited with saving many lives.*

2 to say that someone has a particular quality □ *Credit me with a bit of common sense!*

• **creditable** /ˈkredɪtəbəl/ ADJECTIVE good enough to deserve praise □ *a very creditable performance*

credit card /ˈkredɪt ˌkɑːd/ NOUN [plural **credit cards**] a small plastic card that allows you to buy things when you want them and to pay for them later □ *Can I pay by credit card?*

credit crunch /ˈkredɪt ˌkrʌntʃ/ NOUN [plural **credit crunches**] a time when it is difficult to borrow money, and people have less money to spend

credits /ˈkredɪts/ PLURAL NOUN the credits the list at the end of a film or television programme that shows who worked on it

creed /kriːd/ NOUN [plural **creeds**] something that you believe in, especially religious beliefs

creek /kriːk/ NOUN [plural **creeks**]
1 a small river
2 a narrow area of sea that flows into the land

creep /kriːp/ ▶ VERB [**creeps, creeping, crept**] to move slowly and quietly so that nobody hears you □ *He crept downstairs in the middle of the night.*

◆ PHRASAL VERB **creep up on someone**
1 to walk up very quietly behind someone to surprise them
2 if something creeps up on you, it happens gradually so you do not notice it happening □ *My retirement date just seemed to creep up on me.*

▶ NOUN [plural **creeps**]
1 someone who is nice to people only so that they will like them
2 someone who is unpleasant □ *What a creep!*

◆ IDIOM **give someone the creeps** to make someone feel frightened or disgusted □ *Her new boyfriend really gives me the creeps.*

• **creeper** /ˈkriːpə(r)/ NOUN [plural **creepers**] a plant that grows over the ground or up a wall

• **creepy** /ˈkriːpɪ/ ADJECTIVE [**creepier, creepiest**] making you feel nervous or frightened □ *a creepy old churchyard*

cremate /krɪˈmeɪt/ VERB [**cremates, cremating, cremated**] to burn a dead body instead of burying it

• **cremation** /krɪˈmeɪʃən/ NOUN [plural **cremations**] the burning of a dead body or dead bodies

• **crematorium** /ˌkreməˈtɔːrɪəm/ NOUN [plural **crematoriums** or **crematoria**] a building where cremations take place

creosote /ˈkriːəsəʊt/ NOUN, NO PLURAL a type of dark brown paint used to stop wood decaying

crept /krept/ PAST TENSE AND PAST PARTICIPLE OF creep

crescendo /krɪˈʃendəʊ/ NOUN [plural **crescendos**] when music or another sound gradually gets louder

crescent /ˈkresənt/ NOUN [plural **crescents**]
1 a curved shape that is pointed at each end and is wider in the middle □ *a crescent moon*
2 used in the names of some curved streets □ *21 Chestnut Crescent*

cress /kres/ NOUN, NO PLURAL a small plant with very small green leaves that are used in salads □ *an egg and cress sandwich*

crest /krest/ NOUN [plural **crests**]
1 the highest point of a hill or wave
2 the feathers that point upwards on the top of some birds' heads
3 a design that is used as the symbol of a family or organization

crestfallen /ˈkrestfɔːlən/ ADJECTIVE sad or disappointed

crevasse /krɪˈvæs/ NOUN [plural **crevasses**] a deep crack in rock or ice

crevice /ˈkrevɪs/ NOUN [plural **crevices**] a thin crack or opening in rock □ *a crevice between the rocks*

crew /kruː/ ▶ NOUN [plural **crews**]
1 a group of people who work together on a ship, aeroplane or train □ *The lifeboat has a crew of five.*
2 a team of skilled people who work together □ *The film crew were busy setting up lights and cameras.*
▶ VERB [**crews, crewing, crewed**] to crew a boat or ship is to work as a member of its crew
▶ PAST TENSE OF crow

crib /krɪb/ NOUN [plural **cribs**] the US word for cot

cricket /ˈkrɪkɪt/ NOUN [plural **crickets**]
1 no plural a game played outdoors between two teams of eleven players who score points by hitting a ball □ *a cricket bat*
2 a small insect that lives in grass and makes a noise by rubbing its wings together

• **cricketer** /ˈkrɪkɪtə(r)/ NOUN [plural **cricketers**] someone who plays cricket

cried /kraɪd/ PAST TENSE AND PAST PARTICIPLE OF cry

crime /kraɪm/ NOUN [plural **crimes**]
1 no plural illegal activities □ *a life of crime* 🔁 *The government is introducing new measures to fight crime.* 🔁 *Violent crime is increasing.*
2 an illegal activity □ *minor crimes like shoplifting* 🔁 *Have you ever committed a crime?* 🔁 *The police never managed to solve the crime* (=discover who did it).

▶ Note that a person **commits** a crime. A person does not **make** or **do** a crime.

• **criminal** /ˈkrɪmɪnəl/ ▶ NOUN [plural **criminals**] someone who has committed a crime □ *a dangerous criminal*
▶ ADJECTIVE
1 to do with crime or criminals 🔁 *He has a criminal record.*
2 illegal or very wrong □ *a criminal act*

crimson /ˈkrɪmzən/ ▶ ADJECTIVE having a dark red colour □ *She turned crimson with embarrassment.*
▶ NOUN, NO PLURAL a dark red colour

cringe /krɪndʒ/ VERB [cringes, cringing, cringed]
1 to move away from something because you are frightened □ *The young soldier was found cringing behind a wall.*
2 to feel very embarrassed □ *These old photos really make me cringe.*

crinkle /ˈkrɪŋkəl/ VERB [crinkles, crinkling, crinkled] to make something have a lot of small folds or lines □ *He crinkled his eyes against the sun.*
• **crinkly** /ˈkrɪŋklɪ/ ADJECTIVE [crinklier, crinkliest] having lots of crinkles □ *a crinkly skirt*

cripple /ˈkrɪpəl/ VERB [cripples, crippling, crippled]
1 to damage someone's body so that they cannot walk or move in a normal way □ *She was crippled by arthritis.*
2 to damage something badly so that it cannot work effectively □ *Rising oil prices are crippling the economy.*
• **crippling** /ˈkrɪplɪŋ/ ADJECTIVE
1 causing a lot of damage or having a very bad effect ☝ *crippling debts*
2 crippling pain is so bad that you cannot move

crisis /ˈkraɪsɪs/ NOUN [plural crises]
1 a very difficult or dangerous time or event □ *a financial crisis* □ *the growing crisis in the housing market*
2 in crisis in a very difficult or dangerous situation □ *The government is in crisis.*

crisp /krɪsp/ ▶ ADJECTIVE [crisper, crispest]
1 crisp food is pleasantly hard or fresh □ *crisp salad leaves* □ *crisp pastry*
2 clean and looking new □ *a crisp uniform*
3 crisp weather is cold and dry □ *a crisp spring morning*
4 a crisp image is very clear
▶ NOUN [plural crisps] a very thin piece of potato that is cooked in oil and eaten cold ☝ *a bag of crisps*
• **crispness** /ˈkrɪspnɪs/ NOUN, NO PLURAL the quality of being crisp □ *Chopped celery adds crispness to salads.*
• **crispy** /ˈkrɪspɪ/ ADJECTIVE [crispier, crispiest] pleasantly hard □ *cod in crispy batter*

criss-cross /ˈkrɪskrɒs/ VERB [criss-crosses, criss-crossing, criss-crossed] to cross an area several times in different directions □ *The park is criss-crossed with a network of footpaths.*

criterion /kraɪˈtɪərɪən/ NOUN [plural criteria] a standard you use when you have to make a choice or decision □ *He failed to meet the criteria for a university place.*

critic /ˈkrɪtɪk/ NOUN [plural critics]
1 someone who says that someone or something is bad □ *a critic of the government*
2 someone whose job is to give their opinion of new books, films, plays, etc. □ *He was the film critic for the Times.*
• **critical** /ˈkrɪtɪkəl/ ADJECTIVE
1 saying that you think something is bad or wrong

☝ *The report was highly critical of her work* □ *critical remarks/comments*
2 very important □ *The talks have reached a critical stage.* □ *Good hygiene is of critical importance.*
3 very serious ☝ *The patient is in a critical condition.*
• **critically** /ˈkrɪtɪkəlɪ/ ADVERB
1 in a way that shows disapproval □ *She looked critically at the children.*
2 very or seriously ☝ *critically ill* □ *a critically important decision*
• **criticism** /ˈkrɪtɪsɪzəm/ NOUN [plural criticisms]
1 *no plural* when you say what is bad about someone or something ☝ *Her actions drew criticism from colleagues.* ☝ *There has been widespread criticism of the new laws.* ☝ *The company has faced criticism from environmental campaigners.*
2 a statement about what you think is bad about someone or something □ *My only criticism is the story is too long.*
• **criticize** or **criticise** /ˈkrɪtɪsaɪz/ VERB [criticizes, criticizing, criticized] to say what you think is bad about someone or something □ *It always hurts when you criticize me.* □ **+ for** *They were criticized for leaving the children alone.*

croak /krəʊk/ ▶ VERB [croaks, croaking, croaked]
1 to speak in a rough voice because your throat is sore or dry
2 a frog (=small green animal that lives near water) croaks when it makes its deep sound
▶ NOUN [plural croaks]
1 the sound made by a frog
2 a low rough voice
• **croaky** /ˈkrəʊkɪ/ ADJECTIVE [croakier, croakiest] a croaky voice is deep and rough

crochet /ˈkrəʊʃeɪ/ VERB [crochets, crocheting, crocheted] to make clothes, etc. by using wool and a needle with a curved piece at the end

crockery /ˈkrɒkərɪ/ NOUN, NO PLURAL plates, bowls, cups, etc.

crocodile /ˈkrɒkədaɪl/ NOUN [plural crocodiles] a large reptile with a long tail and a big mouth that lives in rivers and lakes

crocus /ˈkrəʊkəs/ NOUN [plural crocuses] a small white, purple or yellow spring flower □ *a bowl of crocuses*

croissant /ˈkwæsɑ̃/ NOUN [plural croissants] a type of soft bread in a curved shape that you eat for breakfast

crony /ˈkrəʊnɪ/ NOUN [plural cronies] one of a group of friends who help each other, especially in a way that is not fair □ *The best jobs will go to his cronies.*

crook /krʊk/ NOUN [plural crooks]
1 an informal word for a criminal or someone who tricks people
2 the crook of your arm is the part on the inside where it bends
• **crooked** /ˈkrʊkɪd/ ADJECTIVE
1 not straight or even □ *crooked teeth* □ *That picture's crooked.*

2 an informal word meaning not honest □ *crooked cops*

crop /krɒp/ ▶ NOUN [*plural* **crops**]
1 a plant that is grown for food □ *They grow crops such as corn and maize.*
2 the amount of vegetables, fruit, etc. that is produced in a place at one time □ *Our apple trees produced a good crop this year.*
3 a group of things or people □ *This year's crop of novels is an extraordinary one.*
▶ VERB [**crops, cropping, cropped**]
1 to cut something very short □ *She cropped his hair very short.*
2 to cut the edges off a picture in order to make it fit somewhere, especially using a computer
♦ PHRASAL VERB **crop up** if something crops up, it happens when you are not expecting it □ *Something cropped up and I couldn't get to the meeting.*
● **cropped** /krɒpt/ ADJECTIVE cropped hair is cut very short

cropper /'krɒpə(r)/ NOUN, NO PLURAL
♦ IDIOM **come a cropper**
1 to fall over or have an accident □ *She came a cropper on some slippery steps.*
2 to fail or make a mistake □ *His team came a cropper in the first round.*

croquet /'krəʊkeɪ/ NOUN, NO PLURAL a game played on grass, in which you use long wooden hammers to hit balls through curved wires in the ground

cross /krɒs/ ▶ NOUN [*plural* **crosses**]
1 a shape made when two straight lines go over each other at a point in the middle
2 a symbol used in the Christian religion to represent the cross on which Christ died
3 the symbol 'x', used to show when an answer is wrong, or used to show someone where to write something on a document
4 a mixture of two different things □ + *between* *The film is a cross between Short Cuts and Love, Actually.*
5 a kick or hit of the ball across the field in sports such as football
▶ VERB [**crosses, crossing, crossed**]
1 to go from one side of something to the other
🔁 *Find a safe place to cross the road.* □ *A bridge crosses the river at that point.* □ *Troops crossed the border at dawn.*
2 if two things cross, they go across each other □ *The accident happened where the road and railway line cross.*
3 **cross your arms/fingers/legs** to put one arm/ finger/leg over the top of the other □ *She was sitting quietly, with her arms crossed.*
4 to make two different animals or plants breed together □ *They crossed this rose with a more disease-free variety.*
5 to kick or hit the ball across the field in sports such as football □ *He crossed the ball into the penalty box.*

♦ IDIOM **cross your mind** to come into your mind □ *It never crossed my mind that she'd believe me.*
➡ go to **cross paths (with someone)**
♦ PHRASAL VERBS **cross something off** to remove something from a list by drawing a line through it □ *Karen's crossed her name off the list for the quiz.*
cross something out to draw a line through something, usually because it is wrong □ *He crossed out his answer and started again.*
▶ ADJECTIVE [**crosser, crossest**] angry □ + *with* *I got very cross with him for not doing his homework.*

crossbar /'krɒsbɑː(r)/ NOUN [*plural* **crossbars**]
1 the piece of wood over the top of a goal in games such as football □ *Spurs have hit the crossbar again!*
2 the piece of metal that joins the front and back of a bicycle

cross-country /ˌkrɒs'kʌntrɪ/ ADJECTIVE across fields and countryside instead of a road or track □ *cross-country skiing*

cross-examination /'krɒsɪɡˌzæmɪ'neɪʃən/ NOUN [*plural* **cross-examinations**] a series of questions asked to check that what someone has said is true
● **cross-examine** /ˌkrɒsɪɡ'zæmɪn/ VERB [**cross-examines, cross-examining, cross-examined**] to ask someone a lot of questions to check that what they have said is true

cross-eyed /ˌkrɒs'aɪd/ ADJECTIVE a cross-eyed person has eyes that look towards their nose

crossfire /'krɒsfaɪə(r)/ NOUN, NO PLURAL a situation in which guns are being fired from different directions
🔁 *Two soldiers were caught in the crossfire.*

crossing /'krɒsɪŋ/ NOUN [*plural* **crossings**]
1 a place where you can cross a road or a river □ *Be sure to cross at the crossing.*
2 a journey from one side of an area of water to the other □ *It's a short ferry crossing from Mull to Iona.*

cross-legged /ˌkrɒs'leɡɪd/ ADJECTIVE, ADVERB sitting on the floor with your legs bent so that your knees are wide apart and one ankle is on top of the other □ *The children sat cross-legged in a circle.*

crossly /'krɒslɪ/ ADVERB angrily □ *'Leave me alone,' she said, crossly.*

cross purposes /ˌkrɒs 'pɜːpəsɪz/ PLURAL NOUN **at cross purposes** if two people are at cross purposes, they are talking about different things but they do not know this □ *We seem to be talking at cross purposes here.*

cross-reference /ˌkrɒs'refərəns/ NOUN [*plural* **cross-references**] a note in a book that tells you to look somewhere else for more information

crossroads /'krɒsrəʊdz/ NOUN [*plural* **crossroads**] a place where two roads meet and cross each other □ *Turn left at the crossroads up ahead.*

cross-section /'krɒssekʃən/ NOUN [*plural* **cross-sections**]
1 a small group of people or things that represents al

the different types in a large group □ *a cross-section of the public*

2 a cut made through a solid object so that you can see the structure inside, or a picture of this □ *a cross-section of the eye*

crosswalk /ˈkrɒswɔːk/ NOUN [*plural* **crosswalks**] the US word for **pedestrian crossing**

crossword /ˈkrɒswɜːd/ NOUN [*plural* **crosswords**] a game in which you write words that are the answers to questions into square spaces □ *Dad loves doing crosswords.*

crotch /krɒtʃ/ NOUN [*plural* **crotches**] the area of your body or of your trousers where your legs join your body

crouch /krautʃ/ VERB [**crouches, crouching, crouched**] to bend your legs and back so that your body is close to the ground □ *She crouched down to tie her shoe lace.*

crow /krəʊ/ ► NOUN [*plural* **crows**] a large black bird that makes a loud, rough sound

► VERB [**crows, crowing, crowed**]

1 if a cock (=male chicken) crows, it makes a loud sound, especially early in the morning

2 to talk a lot about something good that you have done in a way that annoys other people

crowbar /ˈkrəʊbɑː(r)/ NOUN [*plural* **crowbars**] a heavy metal bar with a curved end that is used for forcing things open

crowd /kraud/ ► NOUN [*plural* **crowds**] a large number of people or things together in one place □ *a football crowd* □ *crowds of shoppers* 🔊 *A crowd had gathered at the scene.*

► VERB [**crowds, crowding, crowded**] if a large number of people crowd somewhere, they fill that place □ *Onlookers crowded the streets.*

• **crowded** /ˈkraudɪd/ ADJECTIVE full of people □ *crowded shops*

crown /kraun/ ► NOUN [*plural* **crowns**]

1 a circle made of gold and valuable stones that a king or queen wears on their head at formal occasions

2 the top of something such as your head or a hill

► VERB [**crowns, crowning, crowned**] to make someone the king or queen of a country in a ceremony where a crown is put on their head

crucial /ˈkruːʃəl/ ADJECTIVE very important □ *The talks are now at a crucial stage.* □ *crucial information*

crucifix /ˈkruːsɪfɪks/ NOUN [*plural* **crucifixes**] a cross with a model of Christ on it, used as a symbol of the Christian religion

• **crucifixion** /ˌkruːsɪˈfɪkʃən/ NOUN [*plural* **crucifixions**] the punishment of fastening someone's hands and feet to a large wooden cross and leaving them there to die

• **crucify** /ˈkruːsɪfaɪ/ VERB [**crucifies, crucifying, crucified**] to punish someone by crucifixion

crude /kruːd/ ADJECTIVE [**cruder, crudest**]

1 made or done in a simple, rough way showing little

skill □ *I had a rather crude map that Josh had quickly drawn.*

2 rude □ *a crude joke*

cruel /ˈkruːəl/ ADJECTIVE [**crueller, cruellest**] causing pain or suffering to people or animals without caring □ **+ to do something** *It's cruel to keep an animal in such a small cage.* □ **+ to** *He was cruel to his children.*

• **cruelly** /ˈkruːəli/ ADVERB in a cruel way □ *The dog had been treated cruelly.*

• **cruelty** /ˈkruːəlti/ NOUN, NO PLURAL when someone is cruel □ *They were accused of cruelty to animals.*

cruise /kruːz/ ► VERB [**cruises, cruising, cruised**] to travel in a car, boat, etc. at the same speed

► NOUN [*plural* **cruises**] a holiday spent on a ship, travelling to a lot of different places

• **cruiser** /ˈkruːzə(r)/ NOUN [*plural* **cruisers**] a large, fast ship used in wars

crumb /krʌm/ NOUN [*plural* **crumbs**]

1 a very small piece of bread, cake, or biscuit

2 **a crumb of something** a very small amount of something □ *The late goal gave England a crumb of comfort.*

crumble /ˈkrʌmbəl/ VERB [**crumbles, crumbling, crumbled**] to break into very small pieces □ *The walls of the old house were crumbling.* □ *Crumble the biscuit on top of the fruit.*

• **crumbly** /ˈkrʌmbli/ ADJECTIVE [**crumblier, crumbliest**] breaking down easily into very small pieces □ *dry crumbly soil*

crumple /ˈkrʌmpəl/ VERB [**crumples, crumpling, crumpled**] to crush something so that it has a lot of folds in it, or to become crushed and folded in this way □ *He crumpled up the letter and threw it in the bin.* □ *a crumpled jacket*

crunch /krʌntʃ/ ► VERB [**crunches, crunching, crunched**]

1 to make a noise as you bite and eat something hard □ *She was crunching on a carrot stick.*

2 to make the sound of something being crushed □ *The snow crunched under our feet.*

► NOUN, NO PLURAL the sound of something being crushed □ *the crunch of feet on the gravel path*

♦ IDIOM **if/when it comes to the crunch** if or when you are in a difficult situation and you must make an important decision □ *When it came to the crunch, she knew she couldn't leave him.*

• **crunchy** /ˈkrʌntʃi/ ADJECTIVE [**crunchier, crunchiest**] crunchy food is pleasantly hard and makes a noise when you bite it □ *a crunchy biscuit*

crusade /kruːˈseɪd/ NOUN [*plural* **crusades**] a determined effort, over a period of time, to change or achieve something □ *a crusade for free health care*

• **crusader** /kruːˈseɪdə(r)/ NOUN [*plural* **crusaders**] someone who takes part in a crusade

crush /krʌʃ/ ► VERB [**crushes, crushing, crushed**] to press something so that it is broken or in small pieces

□ *His leg was crushed by a falling rock.* □ *Crush two cloves of garlic.*

▶ NOUN [plural **crushes**] a crowd of people forced to stand close together in a small space □ *Some fans were trampled in the crush.*

♦ IDIOM **have a crush on someone** to feel very attracted to someone, usually for a short time

• **crushed** /krʌʃt/ ADJECTIVE
1 broken up or made flat by a heavy weight □ *crushed peppercorns*
2 disappointed and sad □ *Maya felt crushed by their criticism.*

• **crushing** /'krʌʃɪŋ/ ADJECTIVE causing someone to be completely defeated ⊞ *a crushing defeat*

crust /krʌst/ NOUN [plural **crusts**]
1 the hard surface on the outside of bread or some other baked foods □ *Cut the crusts off two slices of bread.*
2 the Earth's crust is its outside layer

• **crusty** /'krʌstɪ/ ADJECTIVE [**crustier, crustiest**]
1 having a pleasantly hard crust ⊞ *crusty bread*
2 an informal word meaning bad-tempered and unfriendly □ *a crusty old professor*

crutch /krʌtʃ/ NOUN [plural **crutches**] a stick you put under your arm to help you walk if your leg or foot is hurt ⊞ *Poor Wayne came to watch the match on crutches.*

crux /krʌks/ NOUN, NO PLURAL **the crux of something** the most important or difficult part of a problem □ *The crux of the matter is lack of money.*

cry /kraɪ/ ▶ VERB [**cries, crying, cried**]
1 to produce liquid from your eyes because you are sad or in pain □ *I could hear a baby crying in the next room.*
2 to shout □ + *out* *She cried out in pain.*

♦ IDIOM **cry your eyes out** to cry a lot

♦ PHRASAL VERB **cry out for something** if something is crying out for something, it needs it very much □ *This kitchen is crying out for a coat of paint.*

▶ NOUN [plural **cries**]
1 *no plural* an act of crying ⊞ *She had a little cry on my shoulder.*
2 a shout □ + *for* *No one heard her cries for help.*

♦ IDIOM **be a far cry from something** to be very different from something □ *United's performance was a far cry from their usual magic.*

crypt /krɪpt/ NOUN [plural **crypts**] a room built under a church, where bodies were sometimes buried

cryptic /'krɪptɪk/ ADJECTIVE having a hidden meaning that is difficult to understand ⊞ *a cryptic remark*

crystal /'krɪstəl/ NOUN [plural **crystals**]
1 a small regular shape that some substances form when they become solid, for example salt, ice, or a mineral □ *sugar crystals*
2 *no plural* a type of high quality glass □ *crystal wine glasses*

cub /kʌb/ NOUN [plural **cubs**] a baby animal, for example a lion or bear

cube /kju:b/ NOUN [plural **cubes**]
1 a solid shape with six equal square sides □ *sugar cubes*
2 the number you get if you multiply a number by itself twice. A maths word. □ *The cube of 4 is 64.*

• **cubed** /kju:bd/ ADJECTIVE multiplied by itself twice. A maths word. □ *3 cubed is 27.*

cube root /ˌkju:b 'ru:t/ NOUN [plural **cube roots**] the cube root of a number is the number which equals it when it is multiplied by itself twice. A maths word. □ *The cube root of 125 is 5.*

cubic /'kju:bɪk/ ADJECTIVE a cubic measurement is one used to measure volume. For example, a cubic metre is a space one metre long, one metre wide and one metre high.

cubicle /'kju:bɪkəl/ NOUN [plural **cubicles**] a small space with walls around it that is separate from the rest of a room □ *Get changed in the cubicle.*

cuboid /'kju:bɔɪd/ NOUN [plural **cuboids**] a solid shape with six sides that are all rectangular. A maths word.

cuckoo /'kuku:/ NOUN [plural **cuckoos**] a bird that makes the sound 'cuckoo'

cucumber /'kju:kʌmbə(r)/ NOUN [plural **cucumbers**] a long vegetable with a green skin that you eat raw in salads

cuddle /'kʌdəl/ ▶ VERB [**cuddles, cuddling, cuddled**] to hold someone in your arms to show that you love them □ *They were kissing and cuddling on the sofa.*

♦ PHRASAL VERB **cuddle up** to sit or lie very close together □ *The baby panda cuddled up to its mother.*

▶ NOUN [plural **cuddles**] when you put your arms around someone and hold them closely ⊞ *Come and give me a cuddle.*

• **cuddly** /'kʌdlɪ/ ADJECTIVE [**cuddlier, cuddliest**] soft and pleasant to cuddle □ *a cuddly teddy bear*

cue /kju:/ NOUN [plural **cues**]
1 a signal to a performer to start doing something □ *He missed his cue to go on stage.*
2 something that lets you know it is time to do or say something □ *Charles yawned and said he was tired which was my cue to leave.*
3 **on cue** if something happens on cue, it happens at exactly the right moment □ *Right on cue, the telephone rang.*
4 a long thin stick used to hit the balls on the table in games like snooker and pool

cuff /kʌf/ NOUN [plural **cuffs**] the end part of a sleeve near your hand

♦ IDIOM **off the cuff** if you speak off the cuff, you speak without planning what you are going to say □ *I can't give you a precise answer off the cuff.*

cufflinks /'kʌflɪŋks/ PLURAL NOUN a pair of small objects used instead of buttons to fasten shirt cuffs

cuisine /kwɪ'zi:n/ NOUN [plural **cuisines**] a particular style of cooking □ *Mediterranean cuisine*

cul-de-sac /'kʌldəsæk/ NOUN [plural **cul-de-sacs**] a street that is blocked at one end

culinary /'kʌlɪnərɪ/ ADJECTIVE a formal word meaning to do with cooking □ *culinary skills*

cull /kʌl/ ▶ VERB [**culls, culling, culled**] to kill some of a particular animal so that there will not be too many animals of that type
▶ NOUN [*plural* **culls**] when animals are culled □ *a badger cull*

culminate /'kʌlmɪneɪt/ VERB [**culminates, culminating, culminated**]
♦ PHRASAL VERB **culminate in/with something** to finish with a particular event or result □ *The celebrations culminated in a fireworks display.*
● **culmination** /ˌkʌlmɪ'neɪʃən/ NOUN, NO PLURAL the final event or result of a series of events or actions □ *His promotion was the culmination of all his hard work.*

culpable /'kʌlpəbəl/ ADJECTIVE responsible for something bad. A formal word.

culprit /'kʌlprɪt/ NOUN [*plural* **culprits**] someone who has done something wrong

cult /kʌlt/ ▶ NOUN [*plural* **cults**]
1 a religion or a religious group, especially one with secret or strange beliefs
2 someone or something that becomes very popular or fashionable
▶ ADJECTIVE very popular or fashionable with a particular group of people ੴ *a cult hero*

cultivate /'kʌltɪveɪt/ VERB [**cultivates, cultivating, cultivated**]
1 to prepare land so that you can grow crops on it □ *Peasants used to cultivate the land.*
2 to grow a crop to eat or to sell □ *Rice is cultivated in India.*
3 to make something develop or improve □ *She has tried hard to cultivate her own style.*
● **cultivation** /ˌkʌltɪ'veɪʃən/ NOUN, NO PLURAL
1 the process of preparing land to grow crops
2 the process of growing crops
3 the process of developing or improving something

cultural /'kʌltʃərəl/ ADJECTIVE to do with culture, especially art, music and literature □ *cultural activities*

culture /'kʌltʃə(r)/ NOUN [*plural* **cultures**]
1 the customs and beliefs of a particular group or society that make it different from other people or societies □ *The school has students from many different cultures.*
2 *no plural* music, literature, art, etc.
● **cultured** /'kʌltʃəd/ ADJECTIVE well educated and knowing about things like art, music and literature

cumbersome /'kʌmbəsəm/ ADJECTIVE
1 large and awkward to carry or wear □ *a cumbersome diving suit*
2 slow and difficult to deal with □ *a cumbersome legal process*

cunning /'kʌnɪŋ/ ▶ ADJECTIVE clever in a dishonest way □ *I have a cunning plan.*
▶ NOUN, NO PLURAL the ability to get what you want by dishonest and clever planning

cup /kʌp/ ▶ NOUN [*plural* **cups**]
1 a small container with a handle that you drink from □ *cups and saucers* □ *Let's have a cup of tea.*
2 a metal cup given as a prize in a competition, or the competition itself □ *the World Cup*
♦ IDIOM **not be someone's cup of tea** if something is not your cup of tea, you do not like it or are not interested in it □ *Graphic novels aren't my cup of tea.*
▶ VERB [**cups, cupping, cupped**] to put your hands together and bend them to form the shape of a cup

cupboard /'kʌbəd/ NOUN [*plural* **cupboards**] a piece of furniture with shelves and a door, used to store things in □ *a kitchen cupboard* □ *The plates are in the cupboard.*

cupful /'kʌpful/ NOUN [*plural* **cupfuls**] the amount a cup will hold □ *Add a cupful of flour.*

curable /'kjuərəbəl/ ADJECTIVE a curable disease can be cured

curate /'kjuərət/ NOUN [*plural* **curates**] a priest in the Church of England whose job is to help a more important priest

curator /kjuə'reɪtə(r)/ NOUN [*plural* **curators**] someone whose job is to look after the things in a museum

curb /kɜːb/ ▶ VERB [**curbs, curbing, curbed**] to control something, especially something bad □ *He tried hard to curb his spending.*
▶ NOUN [*plural* **curbs**] the US spelling of kerb

curdle /'kɜːdəl/ VERB [**curdles, curdling, curdled**] if a liquid curdles it forms lumps, often because it has become sour □ *The milk has curdled.*

cure /kjuə(r)/ ▶ VERB [**cures, curing, cured**]
1 to make someone with an illness healthy again □ *+ of The treatment cured her of her insomnia.*
2 to make an illness end or go away □ *Nothing seemed to cure his migraines.*
3 to solve a problem □ *The government is determined to cure the problem of inflation.*
▶ NOUN [*plural* **cures**] something that makes an illness end or go away □ *+ for a cure for cancer*

curfew /'kɜːfjuː/ NOUN [*plural* **curfews**]
1 a law that says that people must stay in their houses after a particular time
2 a time when there is a curfew

curiosity /ˌkjuərɪ'ɒsətɪ/ NOUN [*plural* **curiosities**]
1 *no plural* the feeling of wanting to discover facts about something □ *Children have a natural curiosity about the world.*
2 a strange and interesting object

curious /'kjuərɪəs/ ADJECTIVE
1 wanting to know about something □ *+ about He was very curious about my past.* □ *+ to do something I was curious to hear her side of the story.*
2 strange or unusual □ *Her style is a curious mixture of jazz and country.*
● **curiously** /'kjuərɪəslɪ/ ADVERB
1 in a way that shows that you are curious □ *The*

children peered curiously in through the window.
2 in a strange or unusual way □ *curiously shaped rocks*

curl /kɜːl/ ▶ NOUN [plural **curls**] a piece of hair that forms a curved shape □ *blonde curls*
▶ VERB [**curls, curling, curled**]
1 to form curves or to make something form curves □ *Do you curl your hair or is it natural?*
2 to move in a curving shape □ *Smoke curled up from the chimneys.*
◆ PHRASAL VERB **curl up** to sit or lie with your arms and legs close to your body □ *Jenny curled up on the sofa and fell asleep.*
● **curly** /'kɜːlɪ/ ADJECTIVE [**curlier, curliest**] shaped like a curl or with a lot of curls 🕮 *curly hair* □ *a curly tail*

currant /'kʌrənt/ NOUN [plural **currants**] a small, black, dried soft fruit used especially in cakes

currency /'kʌrənsɪ/ NOUN [plural **currencies**] the money used in a particular country 🕮 *foreign currency* □ *The euro is the European currency.*

current /'kʌrənt/ ▶ ADJECTIVE existing or happening now □ *The current situation is not acceptable.*
▶ NOUN [plural **currents**]
1 a flow of water or air going in one direction 🕮 *Strong currents swept them out to sea.*
2 a flow of electricity through a wire

current account /ˌkʌrənt əˈkaʊnt/ NOUN [plural **current accounts**] a bank account that allows you to take money out at any time

current affairs /ˌkʌrənt əˈfeəz/ PLURAL NOUN important political events that are happening at the present time

currently /'kʌrəntlɪ/ ADVERB at the present time □ *We are currently experiencing problems with our website.*

curriculum /kəˈrɪkjʊləm/ NOUN [plural **curriculums** or **curricula**] a course of study or all the courses of study at a school or college

curry /'kʌrɪ/ NOUN [plural **curries**] a type of food cooked with spices □ *chicken curry*

curse /kɜːs/ ▶ NOUN [plural **curses**]
1 magic words which are intended to make someone have bad luck 🕮 *She put a curse on the family.*
2 a rude word
3 something that causes problems for a long time □ *Pollution is the curse of this city.*
▶ VERB [**curses, cursing, cursed**]
1 to use rude words
2 to say angry things about someone or something □ *I was cursing him for leaving the car so dirty.*

cursor /'kɜːsə(r)/ NOUN [plural **cursors**] a flashing mark on a computer screen that shows you where you are working. A computing word.

cursory /'kɜːsərɪ/ ADJECTIVE quick and short, without looking at the details 🕮 *The border guards gave our passports a cursory glance and waved us through.*

curt /kɜːt/ ADJECTIVE short and sounding unfriendly □ *a curt reply*

curtail /kɜːˈteɪl/ VERB [**curtails, curtailing, curtailed**] a formal word meaning to limit something or to make something shorter □ *Her tennis career was abruptly curtailed by a back injury.*

curtain /'kɜːtən/ NOUN [plural **curtains**] a long piece of material that can be pulled across a window 🕮 *Could you draw the curtains (=open or close the curtains), please?*

curtsy or **curtsey** /'kɜːtsɪ/ ▶ VERB [**curtsies, curtsying, curtsied** or **curtseys, curtseying, curtseyed**] a woman or girl curtsies when she bends her knees with one leg behind the other to show respect to a royal person □ *All the girls curtsied to the princess.*
▶ NOUN [plural **curtsies** or **curtseys**] the movement a girl or woman makes when she curtseys

curve /kɜːv/ ▶ NOUN [plural **curves** or **curtseys**] a line that bends
▶ VERB [**curves, curving, curved**] to form a curve or make something form a curve □ *The wall curves round the end of the garden.*

cushion /'kʊʃən/ ▶ NOUN [plural **cushions**]
1 a cloth bag filled with something soft that you sit on or rest against to be comfortable □ *There were some cushions on the sofa.*
2 something that protects something or keeps something off a hard surface □ *The hovercraft moves along on a cushion of air.*
▶ VERB [**cushions, cushioning, cushioned**]
1 to make something less unpleasant □ *A large divorce settlement cushioned the impact on his family.*
2 to provide a soft surface to protect something or someone if they fall or are hit □ *The snow cushioned her fall.*

cushy /'kʊʃɪ/ ADJECTIVE [**cushier, cushiest**] an informal word meaning very easy □ *a cushy job*

custard /'kʌstəd/ NOUN, NO PLURAL a thick, sweet sauce made from eggs, milk or cream, and sugar

custodial /kʌˈstəʊdɪəl/ ADJECTIVE a **custodial sentence** a punishment of being sent to prison

custody /'kʌstədɪ/ NOUN, NO PLURAL
1 when someone is kept in prison until their trial for a crime 🕮 *He was held in custody for several weeks.*
2 the legal right to have a child living with you, especially after parents separate 🕮 *She lost/won custody of the children.*

custom /'kʌstəm/ NOUN [plural **customs**]
1 something that people usually do or that is a tradition □ *Japanese customs* □ *It is my custom to walk to the station each morning.*
2 *no plural* you give a shop your custom when you buy things from it
● **customary** /'kʌstəmərɪ/ ADJECTIVE something that is customary is what usually happens □ *He tackled the job with his customary efficiency.*
● **customer** /'kʌstəmə(r)/ NOUN [plural **customers**] a

person who buys things or services from a shop or business □ *The business attracts customers from all over the country.* □ *This office handles customer complaints.*

• **customize** or **customise** /'kʌstəmaɪz/ VERB [**customizes, customizing, customized**] to make changes to something so that it is suitable for a particular person □ *The company customizes cars for disabled people.*

• **customs** /'kʌstəmz/ NOUN, NO PLURAL the place at an airport or port where officials check your bags to make sure they do not contain anything illegal □ *a customs officer*

---

cut /kʌt/ ▶ VERB [**cuts, cutting, cut**]

1 to use a knife or a sharp tool to divide something or remove a piece from something □ *Cut the cake into six pieces.* □ *Ben tried to cut the plank in two.* □ **+ off** *She's cut off all her hair.* □ **+ up** *Shall I help you cut up your food?*

2 to injure yourself by rubbing or hitting your skin with something sharp □ *I cut my finger on the can lid.*

3 to be able to cut □ *This knife doesn't cut very well.*

4 to reduce the amount or level of something □ *Mum and Dad have cut my allowance.*

5 to remove an amount of text from a computer document

◆ IDIOMS **cut someone short** to prevent someone from finishing what they were saying **cut something short** to stop something before it is finished □ *We had to cut short our visit to Zak's.*

◆ PHRASAL VERBS **cut across something** to go across a space instead of around the edge □ *We cut across the park to get home in time.* **cut back (something)** to reduce the amount of money spent on something □ *We need to cut back on our heating bills.* **cut down (on something)** to reduce the amount or number of something or to do something less □ *The doctor told her to cut down on red meat.* **cut someone off** if you are cut off on the telephone, the connection is broken before the call ends **cut someone/ something off**

1 to stop people from leaving a place □ *The whole town was cut off by the flooding.*

2 to stop the supply of something □ *If you don't pay your bill, the electricity will be cut off.* **cut something out**

1 to stop eating or drinking something □ *I feel much better since I cut meat out of my diet.*

2 **cut it out** an informal phrase used to tell someone that you want them to stop doing something

3 **not be cut out to do something** to not have the suitable qualities to do something □ *She decided she wasn't cut out to be a teacher.*

▶ NOUN [*plural* **cuts**]

1 an opening or injury made by something sharp □ *She's got a nasty cut on her forehead.* □ *He made two cuts in the fabric.*

2 a reduction in something □ *a price cut* □ *job cuts*

3 an informal word meaning a share of something □ *He's hoping for a cut of the profits.*

4 when someone's hair is cut, or the way hair looks when it has been cut □ *a cut and blow-dry*

cut-and-dried /ˌkʌtən'draɪd/ ADJECTIVE clearly decided, so there can be no change or argument

cutback /'kʌtbæk/ NOUN [*plural* **cutbacks**] a reduction in something, for example the amount of money an organization spends □ *The government announced cutbacks in defence spending.*

---

cute /kjuːt/ ADJECTIVE [**cuter, cutest**]

1 attractive or pretty □ *a cute little puppy*

2 clever in a way that does not show any respect □ *Don't try to be cute with me.*

---

cutlery /'kʌtləri/ NOUN, NO PLURAL knives, forks and spoons

cutlet /'kʌtlɪt/ NOUN [*plural* **cutlets**] a small piece of meat with a bone □ *lamb cutlets*

cut-price /'kʌtpraɪs/ ADJECTIVE cut-price goods are sold more cheaply than usual

cutting /'kʌtɪŋ/ ▶ NOUN [*plural* **cuttings**]

1 an article cut out of a newspaper or magazine

2 a piece cut off a plant that you use to grow a new plant

▶ ADJECTIVE meant to hurt someone's feelings □ *a cutting remark*

cutting-edge /ˌkʌtɪŋ'edʒ/ ADJECTIVE very modern and advanced □ *cutting-edge technology*

CV /ˌsiː'viː/ ABBREVIATION curriculum vitae; a list of your qualifications and the jobs you have done, that you show to someone you want to work for □ *She has an impressive CV.*

cwt ABBREVIATION hundredweight

cyanide /'saɪənaɪd/ NOUN, NO PLURAL a strong poison

cyber- /'saɪbə(r)/ PREFIX cyber- is added to the beginning of words to mean 'to do with electronic communication or the Internet'

cybercafé /'saɪbəkæfeɪ/ NOUN [*plural* **cybercafés**] a place where you can buy something to eat or drink and use the Internet

cyberspace /'saɪbəspeɪs/ NOUN, NO PLURAL the Internet, where electronic messages pass from one computer to another. A computing word.

---

cycle /'saɪkəl/ ▶ NOUN [*plural* **cycles**]

1 a series of things that happen one after the other and then start again □ *He seems to be trapped in a cycle of stealing and prison.*

2 a bicycle

▶ VERB [**cycles, cycling, cycled**] to ride a bicycle □ *I always cycle to school.*

• **cyclical** /'saɪklɪkəl/ ADJECTIVE happening in a cycle □ *We are experiencing a cyclical increase in prices.*

• **cyclist** /'saɪklɪst/ NOUN [*plural* **cyclists**] someone who rides a bicycle

cyclone /'saɪkləun/ NOUN [*plural* **cyclones**] a large storm that happens in tropical countries, with strong winds moving in a circle

cygnet /'sɪgnɪt/ NOUN [*plural* **cygnets**] a baby swan (=large white bird)

cylinder /'sɪlɪndə(r)/ NOUN [*plural* **cylinders**] a solid shape with a circular top and bottom and long straight sides

• **cylindrical** /sɪ'lɪndrɪkəl/ ADJECTIVE shaped like a cylinder

cymbals /'sɪmbəlz/ PLURAL NOUN a musical instrument made of two metal circles that you hit together

cynic /'sɪnɪk/ NOUN [*plural* **cynics**]
1 someone who believes that people are only interested in themselves and are not honest or sincere
2 someone who does not believe that something will be successful

• **cynical** /'sɪnɪkəl/ ADJECTIVE
1 behaving in a way that is not honest or kind in order to get an advantage □ *This was a cynical attempt to gain votes.*
2 believing that people are only interested in themselves and are not honest or sincere □ *He has such a cynical outlook on life.*
3 not believing that something will be successful □ *He was rather cynical about the new working system.*

• **cynicism** /'sɪnɪsɪzəm/ NOUN, NO PLURAL cynical beliefs

cyst /sɪst/ NOUN [*plural* **cysts**] a hard raised part filled with liquid in the body or under the skin

cytoplasm /'saɪtəuplæzəm/ NOUN, NO PLURAL the substance a cell is made of, except for the nucleus. A biology word.

czar /zɑ:(r)/ NOUN [*plural* **czars**] another spelling of tsar

D*d*

D or **d** /diː/ the fourth letter of the alphabet

dab /dæb/ ► VERB [**dabs, dabbing, dabbed**] to touch something lightly □ *She took out a tissue and dabbed her eyes.*

► NOUN [*plural* **dabs**] a light touch of something □ *She put a dab of face cream on each cheek.*

dabble /ˈdæbəl/ VERB [**dabbles, dabbling, dabbled**] to do an activity for a short time and not seriously □ *He dabbled in photography for a while.*

dachshund /ˈdækshʊnd/ NOUN [*plural* **dachshunds**] a dog with short legs and a long body

dad or **Dad** /dæd/ NOUN [*plural* **dads** or **Dads**] an informal word that means father and that you use for talking to your father □ *Hey Dad, I scored a goal today!* □ *It was really nice of your dad to help.*

daddy or **Daddy** /ˈdædɪ/ NOUN [*plural* **daddies** or **Daddies**] a word that children use for talking to or about their father □ *Read me another story, Daddy!* □ *I gave my daddy a big hug.*

daffodil /ˈdæfədɪl/ NOUN [*plural* **daffodils**] a yellow flower that appears in spring

daft /dɑːft/ ADJECTIVE [**dafter, daftest**] silly □ *What a daft thing to do.* □ *Don't be daft – you can't do that!*

dagger /ˈdægə(r)/ NOUN [*plural* **daggers**] a small knife that is used as a weapon

daily /ˈdeɪlɪ/ ► ADJECTIVE

1 happening or done every day ⊞ *Exercise is part of my daily routine.* □ *Two tablets is the correct daily dose.*
2 a daily newspaper is produced every day

► ADVERB every day □ *We have fresh bread delivered daily.*

dainty /ˈdeɪntɪ/ ADJECTIVE [**daintier, daintiest**] small and delicate □ *a dainty little girl*

dairy /ˈdeərɪ/ ► ADJECTIVE

1 to do with keeping cows to produce milk ⊞ *a dairy farmer*
2 dairy foods contain milk or are made from milk ⊞ *She can't eat dairy products.*

► NOUN [*plural* **dairies**] a place where foods such as butter and cheese are made from milk

dais /ˈdeɪɪs/ NOUN [*plural* **daises**] a raised area of floor at one end of a room □ *The speakers sat behind a table on the dais.*

daisy /ˈdeɪzɪ/ NOUN [*plural* **daisies**] a small white flower with a yellow centre

dale /deɪl/ NOUN [*plural* **dales**] a valley □ *I love the Yorkshire Dales.*

dally /ˈdælɪ/ VERB [**dallies, dallying, dallied**] to take too much time doing something □ *We really mustn't dally over lunch.*

♦ PHRASAL VERB **dally with something** to consider doing something but not seriously □ *I dallied with the idea of teaching abroad.*

Dalmatian /dælˈmeɪʃən/ NOUN [*plural* **Dalmatians**] a large dog that is white with dark spots

dam /dæm/ ► NOUN [*plural* **dams**] a wall across a river that holds a lot of the water back

► VERB [**dams, damming, dammed**] to build a dam across a river

damage /ˈdæmɪdʒ/ ► NOUN [*plural* **damages**]

1 *no plural* harm that is done by something ⊞ *The storm caused a lot of damage.* □ *+ to* *The storm did some damage to the roof.* □ *He suffered brain damage in the accident.*
2 **damages** money that a law court decides someone will get because they have been harmed ⊞ *She was awarded damages of £5000.*

> ► Note the verbs that are used with the noun **damage** (sense 1). Something **causes** damage or **does** damage:
> ✓ *The fire caused a lot of damage.*
> ✗ *The fire made a lot of damage.*

► VERB [**damages, damaging, damaged**] to spoil or break something □ *The book was damaged in the post.*

> ► Note that the verb **damage** is used for *things* and not *people*. For people, use **hurt** or **injure**: □ *The car was badly damaged in the accident.* □ *Both men were injured in the accident.*

• **damaging** /ˈdæmɪdʒɪŋ/ ADJECTIVE causing damage ⊞ *We all know about the damaging effects of the sun on our skin.*

dame /deɪm/ NOUN [*plural* **dames**] a title that is given to a woman because she has done some important work □ *Dame Judi Dench*

damn /dæm/ ► EXCLAMATION an informal word that people say when they are angry □ *Damn! I forgot my umbrella.* ⊞ *Damn it! Why isn't this machine working?*

► ADJECTIVE, ADVERB an informal word that people say

when they are angry □ *This damn machine won't work!* □ *You knew damn well I wasn't going!*
▶ NOUN **not give a damn (about something)** to not be interested in something. An informal phrase. □ *I don't give a damn what she thinks of me!*
▶ VERB [**damns, damning, damned**]
1 **Damn you/him, etc.!** used to show that you are angry with someone. An informal phrase. □ *Damn him! Why is he always late?*
2 to criticize someone very strongly
• **damned** /dæmd/ ADJECTIVE, ADVERB an informal word that people use when they are angry □ *Look what that damned cat has done!*
◆ IDIOM **I'm damned if I'll do something** used when you are angry to say that you will certainly not do something □ *Well I'm damned if I'll help him again!*
• **damning** /ˈdæmɪŋ/ ADJECTIVE
1 showing strong criticism of someone or something 🔁 *a damning report*
2 showing clearly that a person has done something wrong 🔁 *The police found some very damning evidence at the scene.*

damp /dæmp/ ▶ ADJECTIVE [**damper, dampest**] slightly wet □ *Wipe with a damp cloth.*

> ➤ Note that **damp** is usually used for objects and buildings and means 'slightly wet and unpleasant or cold'. When the air is slightly wet and warm, the word to use is **humid**: □ *The walls of the house were cold and damp.* □ *In summer it is hot and humid.*

▶ NOUN, NO PLURAL when something is damp □ *There is a patch of damp on the wall.*
• **dampen** /ˈdæmpən/ VERB [**dampens, dampening, dampened**] to make something slightly wet □ *Dampen the brush before using it.*

dance /dɑːns/ ▶ VERB [**dances, dancing, danced**] to move your feet and body to music □ *Let's dance!* □ *She danced with her boyfriend all evening.* □ *Will you teach me how to dance the tango?*
▶ NOUN [*plural* **dances**]
1 when you dance 🔁 *Why don't you have a dance with your dad?*
2 a particular set of steps that you do to music □ *The first dance we learnt was the waltz.*
3 *no plural* a type of dancing □ *Louise teaches modern dance.*
4 a party for dancing
• **dancer** /ˈdɑːnsə(r)/ NOUN [*plural* **dancers**] someone who dances
• **dancing** /ˈdɑːnsɪŋ/ NOUN, NO PLURAL the activity of moving your feet and body to music □ *I love dancing.*

dandelion /ˈdændɪlaɪən/ NOUN [*plural* **dandelions**] a common wild flower with lots of thin yellow petals
dandruff /ˈdændrʌf/ NOUN, NO PLURAL small dry pieces of dead skin in your hair □ *an anti-dandruff shampoo*

danger /ˈdeɪndʒə(r)/ NOUN [*plural* **dangers**]
1 a situation where something may harm you □ *Danger! Keep out!*
2 **in danger** in a situation where something could harm you □ *He wasn't in danger at any point.*
3 something or someone that may harm you □ *+ of the dangers of smoking* □ *+ to This man is a serious danger to the public.*
4 **danger of something** a chance that something bad might happen □ *Is there danger of flooding?* □ *We were in danger of missing our flight.*
• **dangerous** /ˈdeɪndʒərəs/ ADJECTIVE
1 likely to harm you □ *a dangerous substance*
2 likely to have a bad effect □ *It would be dangerous to ignore his opinions.*
• **dangerously** /ˈdeɪndʒərəslɪ/ ADVERB in a dangerous way □ *He was driving dangerously close to the edge.*

dangle /ˈdæŋɡəl/ VERB [**dangles, dangling, dangled**] to hang down loosely or to make something do this □ *We sat with our legs dangling in the water.* □ *He dangled the key on a string in front of me.*
dank /dæŋk/ ADJECTIVE [**danker, dankest**] a dank place is wet and cold
dapper /ˈdæpə(r)/ ADJECTIVE a dapper man is very tidy and wears good quality clothes
dappled /ˈdæpəld/ ADJECTIVE with light and dark areas □ *a dappled horse* □ *dappled sunlight through the trees*

dare /deə(r)/ VERB [**dares, daring, dared**]
1 **dare (to) do something** to be brave enough to do something □ *Rachel wouldn't dare argue with the boss.* □ *I never thought I'd dare to jump out of a plane.*
2 to ask someone to do something dangerous or frightening 🔁 *I dare you to climb to the top.*
3 **How dare you/he, etc. do something!** something you say when someone has done something that upsets you very much □ *How dare you speak to me like that!*
4 **Don't you dare!** used to tell someone that if they do something you will be very angry with them □ *Don't you dare throw that at me!*

daredevil /ˈdeədevəl/ ▶ NOUN [*plural* **daredevils**] someone who enjoys doing dangerous things
▶ ADJECTIVE dangerous □ *Eddie performed many daredevil stunts.*
daren't /deənt/ a short way to say and write dare not
daring /ˈdeərɪŋ/ ADJECTIVE
1 brave □ *a daring rescue attempt*
2 quite shocking □ *a daring outfit*

dark /dɑːk/ ▶ ADJECTIVE [**darker, darkest**]
1 without light 🔁 *When we looked outside it was getting dark.* 🔁 *All of a sudden it went dark.*
2 not light in colour and nearer to black than to white □ *dark blue* □ *Ruth has dark hair.*
3 a dark person has hair that is black or almost black □ *Both my children are dark.*

4 a formal word for sad □ *dark thoughts*
► NOUN, NO PLURAL
1 where there is no light □ *I'm not afraid of the dark.*
2 the time when it becomes dark outside ⌸ *Don't go out after dark without a torch.*

• **darken** /'dɑːkən/ VERB [**darkens, darkening, darkened**] to get darker, or to make something darker □ *The sky darkened and it began to rain.* □ *It helps if you darken the room a little.*

• **darkness** /'dɑːknɪs/ NOUN, NO PLURAL where there is no light

darkroom /'dɑːkruːm/ NOUN [plural **darkrooms**] a room that is kept dark and that people use when they develop photographs (=make photographs from film)

darling /'dɑːlɪŋ/ NOUN [plural **darlings**] a word used for talking to someone you love □ *What's the matter, darling?*

darn /dɑːn/ VERB [**darns, darning, darned**] to mend a hole in something made of wool using a needle ⌸ *She was darning his socks.*

dart /dɑːt/ ► NOUN [plural **darts**]
1 darts a game where you throw small arrows at a round board called a dartboard
2 a little arrow that can be used as a weapon or in the game of darts
► VERB [**darts, darting, darted**] to move somewhere fast □ *A child darted out of the door as I came in.*

dartboard /'dɑːtbɔːd/ NOUN [plural **dartboards**] a round board that you throw darts at in the game of darts

dash /dæʃ/ ► VERB [**dashes, dashing, dashed**]
1 to hurry somewhere □ *I've got to dash to the shops.* □ *Mary came in but then she dashed off again.*
2 a formal word that means to hit against something hard □ *The boat was dashed against the rocks.*
3 dash someone's hopes to take away what someone was hoping for □ *My hopes were dashed again when the examiner said I'd failed.*

♦ PHRASAL VERB **dash something off** to write something quickly □ *Mum dashed off two more letters while she was waiting.*
► NOUN [plural **dashes**]
1 a line '–' that is sometimes used in writing between parts of a sentence
2 a small amount of a liquid that you add to food or drink □ *Add a dash of vinegar.*
3 when you hurry to get somewhere ⌸ *The two boys made a dash for the door.* ⌸ *In our mad dash to catch the plane we forgot the presents.*

dashboard /'dæʃbɔːd/ NOUN [plural **dashboards**] the area in a car in front of the driver where you see information such as the speed and petrol level

dashing /'dæʃɪŋ/ ADJECTIVE an old-fashioned word that means attractive and dressed well □ *You look very dashing in that hat.*

data /'deɪtə/ NOUN, NO PLURAL information ⌸ *The hospital keeps a lot of personal data on its patients* □ *We collected data over a five year period.*

database /'deɪtəbeɪs/ NOUN [plural **databases**] information that is stored on a computer in an organized form □ *Details of known criminals are stored on a national computer database.*

data processing /ˌdeɪtə 'prəʊsesɪŋ/ NOUN, NO PLURAL the use of a computer to organize and store information. A computing word.

date /deɪt/ ► NOUN [plural **dates**]
1 the number of the day of the month, the month and the year □ *The date today is 30 July.*
2 a particular day of a particular month and year ⌸ *What is your date of birth?* ⌸ *Shall we fix/set a date for our next meeting?* ⌸ *We can decide all the details at a later date.*
3 an arrangement to meet someone that you are having a romantic relationship with or who you may start a romantic relationship with □ *Polly's got another date with Chris tonight.*
4 a small, brown, sticky fruit
► VERB [**dates, dating, dated**]
1 to write a date on a letter or other document □ *The letter was dated 3rd May.*
2 to decide how old something is □ *The ring's very old but I couldn't date it exactly.*
3 to become old-fashioned □ *Shoes always date very quickly.*
4 to have a romantic relationship with someone and meet them regularly □ *How long have you and Kelly been dating?*

♦ PHRASAL VERBS **date back to something** to have existed for a particular length of time or since a particular time □ *Our involvement with horses dates back to the sixteenth century.* **date from something** to have existed since a particular time □ *These silver items date from the 13th century.*

• **dated** /'deɪtɪd/ ADJECTIVE old-fashioned □ *My mobile phone looks rather dated now.*

daub /dɔːb/ VERB [**daubs, daubing, daubed**] to put a thick liquid such as paint roughly onto something □ *The car was daubed with red paint.*

daughter /'dɔːtə(r)/ NOUN [plural **daughters**] someone's female child □ *She was the daughter of a poet.* □ *Dave and Maria have a new baby daughter.*

daughter-in-law /'dɔːtərɪnˌlɔː/ NOUN [plural **daughters-in-law**] your son's wife □ *Have you met my daughter-in-law, Sandra?*

daunt /dɔːnt/ VERB [**daunts, daunting, daunted**] if you are daunted by something you are going to do, you are worried because it is difficult or a lot of work □ *I was a bit daunted by the size of the project.*

• **daunting** /'dɔːntɪŋ/ ADJECTIVE so difficult or needing so much work that you are worried ⌸ *Now we face the daunting task of playing against the champions.* ⌸ *Moving house is a daunting prospect (=makes you worry before you do it).*

dawdle /'dɔːdəl/ VERB [**dawdles, dawdling, dawdled**] to walk slowly □ *Ralph was dawdling along behind everyone else.*

dawn /dɔːn/ ▶ NOUN [*plural* **dawns**] the beginning of the day, when it gets light

▶ VERB [**dawns, dawning, dawned**] a formal word that means to start □ *A new age has dawned.*

♦ PHRASAL VERB **dawn on someone** if something dawns on you, you suddenly understand it □ *Then it dawned on me that she was his daughter.*

day /deɪ/ NOUN [*plural* **days**]

1 the twenty-four hours between one midnight (=12 am) and another □ *There are 365 days in a year.* □ *I do five hours' work a day.* 🔁 *I try to do some exercise every day.*

2 the time when there is light from the sun, or when you are awake □ *We spent the whole day on the beach.* □ *I spent all day cleaning the house.* □ *Did you have a good day at work?*

3 a time or period □ *in my grandfather's day* 🔁 *In those days we didn't have computers.*

4 one day used to talk about something that happened in the past or something that will happen in the future □ *One day I came home to discover my car had been stolen.* □ *I hope to have my own business one day.*

5 the other day a few days ago □ *I saw Julio the other day.*

6 these days used to talk about what things are like now □ *These days I don't play much tennis.*

daybreak /'deɪbreɪk/ NOUN, NO PLURAL when light first appears in the sky in the morning □ *He left before daybreak.*

daydream /'deɪdriːm/ ▶ VERB [**daydreams, daydreaming, daydreamed**] to think about things that you would like to happen □ *I used to daydream about being rich.*

▶ NOUN [*plural* **daydreams**] something pleasant that you daydream about

daylight /'deɪlaɪt/ NOUN, NO PLURAL

1 the light that comes from the sun during the day □ *In the daylight she looked pale.*

2 the part of the day when there is light □ *I'd like to get home in daylight.*

daytime /'deɪtaɪm/ NOUN, NO PLURAL the part of the day when there is light □ *Don't waste electricity by having the lights on in the daytime.* □ *daytime television*

day-to-day /ˌdeɪtə'deɪ/ ADJECTIVE happening or done regularly, every day 🔁 *These attacks now happen on a day-to-day basis* (=every day). 🔁 *Diane is in charge of the day-to-day running of the department.*

day trip /'deɪ ˌtrɪp/ NOUN [*plural* **day trips**] a visit to an interesting or attractive place that you go to and come back from in one day □ *We went on a day trip to the Pyramids.*

daze /deɪz/ ▶ NOUN **in a daze** confused or unable to think clearly □ *I stood there in a daze, not knowing what to do.*

▶ VERB [**dazes, dazing, dazed**] to shock and confuse someone □ *The knock on the head dazed him for a minute.*

● **dazed** /deɪzd/ ADJECTIVE shocked and confused □ *The survivors of the crash were dazed but unhurt.*

dazzle /'dæzəl/ VERB [**dazzles, dazzling, dazzled**]

1 if you are dazzled by a light, it is so bright that you cannot see well □ *I was dazzled by the car headlights.*

2 if you are dazzled by something or someone you think they are very exciting and special

● **dazzling** /'dæzlɪŋ/ ADJECTIVE

1 a dazzling light is so bright that you cannot see well

2 very exciting and special 🔁 *It was a truly dazzling performance.*

de- /diː/ PREFIX

1 de- is added to the beginning of words that are to do with removing something □ *decaffeinated* □ *defrost*

2 de- is added to the beginning of words to mean 'the opposite of' □ *decompose* □ *decode*

3 de- is found at the beginning of words that are to do with going down □ *descend* □ *decline*

dead /ded/ ▶ ADJECTIVE

1 not now living □ *I could see he was dead.* 🔁 *He dropped dead* (=died suddenly) *on the tennis court.* □ *a dead body*

2 no longer working 🔁 *My phone's gone dead.* □ *The batteries are dead.*

3 complete 🔁 *There was dead silence in the room.* □ *They came to a dead stop.*

▶ ADVERB

1 stop dead to stop suddenly and completely

2 exactly □ *They were standing dead in the centre of the circle.*

3 an informal word meaning very □ *dead boring/easy*

▶ NOUN, NO PLURAL

1 the dead people who have died

2 the dead of night the darkest and quietest part of the night

● **deaden** /'dedən/ VERB [**deadens, deadening, deadened**] to stop you feeling or hearing something so much □ *They gave him an injection to deaden the pain.*

dead end /ˌded 'end/ NOUN [*plural* **dead ends**] a road that does not lead to any other road □ *You'll have to turn around – this is a dead end.*

dead heat /ˌded 'hiːt/ NOUN [*plural* **dead heats**] when two people finish a race at exactly the same time

deadline /'dedlaɪn/ NOUN [*plural* **deadlines**] the time when something must be finished 🔁 *You'll miss the deadline if you delay.*

deadlock /'dedlɒk/ NOUN, NO PLURAL when people cannot agree and will not change what they think 🔁 *They talked all night in an effort to break* (=end) *the deadlock.*

deadly /'dedlɪ/ ADJECTIVE [deadlier, deadliest] able to kill 🖰 *a deadly weapon* 🖰 *a deadly poison*

deaf /def/ ▶ ADJECTIVE [deafer, deafest] not able to hear, or not able to hear well □ *Grandma is getting a bit deaf.*

▶ PLURAL NOUN **the deaf** people who are deaf

• **deafen** /'defən/ VERB [deafens, deafening, deafened] to make someone deaf for a short time □ *The explosion deafened us for a moment.*

• **deafening** /'defnɪŋ/ ADJECTIVE unpleasantly loud □ *The music was deafening and we had to leave.*

• **deafness** /'defnɪs/ NOUN, NO PLURAL being deaf

deal /diːl/ ▶ NOUN [plural deals]
1 an agreement, especially in business or politics 🖰 *make/strike a deal* 🖰 *We are about to sign a deal with a major record producer.* 🖰 *I got a good deal (=a cheap price) on my new car.*
2 the way someone is treated or the amount of something that they get 🖰 *Teachers always seem to get a raw/rough deal (=a bad deal) when it comes to pay.* □ *We are campaigning for a better deal for mental health patients.*
3 a great deal a large amount □ *We spent a great deal of money on solar panels.*
4 when cards are given to players in a game □ *It's your deal.*
▶ VERB [deals, dealing, dealt] to give cards to players in a game □ *You deal the cards this time.*
♦ PHRASAL VERBS **deal in something** to buy and sell something □ *They deal in luxury fabrics.* **deal with something/someone**
1 to take action, especially to solve a problem or to get something done □ *New houses were built to deal with the problem of homelessness.* □ *You take the boy to another room – I'll deal with his father.* □ *I need to deal with all these letters.*
2 to learn to accept a difficult situation □ *I'm finding it hard to deal with his death.*
3 to be about a particular subject □ *The programme deals with the true cost of cheap labour.*

• **dealer** /'diːlə(r)/ NOUN [plural dealers] someone who buys and sells things □ *an antiques dealer*

• **dealings** /'diːlɪŋz/ PLURAL NOUN contact with other people, especially to do business 🖰 *I have never had any dealings with his company.*

dear /dɪə(r)/ ▶ ADJECTIVE [dearer, dearest]
1 Dear the word you use with a name or title at the beginning of a letter □ *Dear Max* □ *Dear Sir*
2 loved 🖰 *a very dear friend*
3 expensive □ *The shoes were beautiful but very dear.*
▶ NOUN [plural dears] a word used for talking to someone that you like □ *Sorry, dear, what did you say?*
▶ EXCLAMATION **Oh dear!** something you say when something slightly bad has happened □ *Oh dear! I'm late again.*

• **dearly** /'dɪəlɪ/ ADVERB very much 🖰 *You know I love him dearly.*

dearth /dɜːθ/ NOUN, NO PLURAL when there is not enough of something. A formal word. □ *There's a dearth of good maths teachers.*

death /deθ/ NOUN [plural deaths]
1 the time when a person or animal stops living □ *He wrote this just before his death in 1875.* □ **+ from** *The number of deaths from cancer is decreasing all the time.* 🖰 *The cause of death was unknown.*
2 to death until you are dead □ *Most of these people starved to death.* □ *He choked to death.*
3 frightened, worried, etc. to death extremely frightened or worried, etc. □ *I was frightened to death when I saw the gun.*
♦ IDIOM **be at death's door** to be so ill that you are almost dead

deathbed /'deθbed/ NOUN **be on your deathbed** to be so ill that you are going to die soon

deathly /'deθlɪ/ ▶ ADJECTIVE extreme and unpleasant 🖰 *There was a deathly silence.*
▶ ADVERB in a way that is extreme and unpleasant 🖰 *She went deathly pale.*

death penalty /'deθ ˌpenəltɪ/ NOUN [plural death penalties] when someone is killed as a legal punishment for a crime

debacle /de'bɑːkəl/ NOUN [plural debacles] an embarrassing failure □ *The show was a complete debacle.*

debase /dɪ'beɪs/ VERB [debases, debasing, debased] to make something less valuable or respected □ *He criticized the debasing effect of mass culture.*

debatable /dɪ'beɪtəbəl/ ADJECTIVE if something is debatable, some people believe that it is true and some people do not □ *It's debatable whether animal fats are really bad for you.*

debate /dɪ'beɪt/ ▶ NOUN [plural debates] a big or formal discussion about something □ *a parliamentary debate*
▶ VERB [debates, debating, debated] to have a debate about something

debilitating /dɪ'bɪlɪteɪtɪŋ/ ADJECTIVE making someone weak. A formal word. 🖰 *He suffers from a debilitating illness.*

debit /'debɪt/ ▶ NOUN [plural debits] an amount of money that is taken out of a bank account
▶ VERB [debits, debiting, debited] to take money out of a bank account □ *The sum will be debited from your account on the first of every month.*

debit card /'debɪt ˌkɑːd/ NOUN [plural debit cards] a small plastic card for buying things by taking money immediately from your bank account

debonair /ˌdebə'neə(r)/ ADJECTIVE describes an attractive, confident man. An old-fashioned word.

debris /'deɪbriː/ NOUN, NO PLURAL the parts of something that has broken into pieces □ *Debris from the crashed aircraft lay all around.*

debt /det/ NOUN [plural debts]
1 an amount of money that one person owes to another 🖰 *I always pay off my debts.*

2 in debt owing someone money

• **debtor** /'detə(r)/ NOUN [plural **debtors**] a person who owes someone else money

debug /,di:'bʌg/ VERB [debugs, debugging, debugged] to remove mistakes from a computer program. A computing word.

• **debugger** /,di:'bʌgə(r)/ NOUN [plural **debuggers**] a computer program that debugs other programs. A computing word.

debunk /,di:'bʌŋk/ VERB [debunks, debunking, debunked] to prove that an idea or someone's opinion is wrong or silly

début /'deɪbju:/ NOUN [plural **débuts**] the first time an actor or performer performs in public 🖫 She made her début at the King's Theatre in 1999.

dec- /dek/ or **deca-** /'dekə/ PREFIX dec- or deca- is found at the beginning of words to do with the number ten □ decagon □ decimal

decade /'dekeɪd/ NOUN [plural **decades**] a period of ten years □ This is the first decade of the twenty-first century.

decadence /'dekədəns/ NOUN, NO PLURAL morally bad behaviour, especially when people only do things for pleasure

• **decadent** /'dekədənt/ ADJECTIVE when people are morally bad, only doing things for pleasure

decaff /'di:kæf/ NOUN, NO PLURAL an informal word for decaffeinated coffee □ Have you got any decaff?

decaffeinated /,di:'kæfɪneɪtɪd/ ADJECTIVE describes coffee which has no caffeine (=a substance that makes you feel more awake)

decagon /'dekəgɒn/ NOUN [plural **decagons**] a flat shape with ten straight sides

decapitate /dɪ'kæpɪteɪt/ VERB [decapitates, decapitating, decapitated] to cut off a person's head

decathlon /dɪ'kæθlɒn/ NOUN [plural **decathlons**] a sports competition in which you do ten different types of sports like running, jumping and throwing

decay /dɪ'keɪ/ ▶ NOUN, NO PLURAL when something becomes rotten or breaks into pieces 🖫 This toothpaste helps prevents gum disease and tooth decay.

▶ VERB [decays, decaying, decayed] to go rotten or break into pieces □ The bins were full of decaying food.

deceased /dɪ'si:st/ ▶ ADJECTIVE a formal word that means dead

▶ NOUN **the deceased** the particular person who has recently died □ We believe that the deceased knew his attacker.

deceit /dɪ'si:t/ NOUN, NO PLURAL when you lie or trick people

• **deceitful** /dɪ'si:tful/ ADJECTIVE lying or tricking people □ He is very deceitful.

deceive /dɪ'si:v/ VERB [deceives, deceiving, deceived] to make someone believe something that is not true □ + by Don't be deceived by his friendly manner. □ + into She was deceived into thinking she'd won a holiday. □ If she thinks Keith actually loves her, she's deceiving herself.

decelerate /,di:'seləreɪt/ VERB [decelerates, decelerating, decelerated] to become slower

December /dɪ'sembə(r)/ NOUN the twelfth month of the year, after November and before January □ Her birthday is in December.

decency /'di:sənsɪ/ NOUN, NO PLURAL behaviour that is good and of a high moral standard 🖫 She didn't even have the decency to tell me the news herself.

• **decent** /'di:sənt/ ADJECTIVE

1 acceptable or good enough □ Is there a decent butcher's near here? 🖫 After a decent interval (=an amount of time considered acceptable) he married again. 🖫 I think they have a decent chance of winning.

2 good, honest and of a high moral standard □ He's a very decent bloke.

decentralization or **decentralisation** /,di:sentrəlaɪ'zeɪʃən/ NOUN, NO PLURAL when something is decentralized

decentralize or **decentralise** /,di:'sentrəlaɪz/ VERB [decentralizes, decentralizing, decentralized] to change an organization so that the work is done in several places instead of one central place

deception /dɪ'sepʃən/ NOUN [plural **deceptions**] when you trick or lie to people □ an act of deliberate deception

• **deceptive** /dɪ'septɪv/ ADJECTIVE making you believe something that is not true □ That photo is quite deceptive – it makes me look a lot younger than I am.

• **deceptively** /dɪ'septɪvlɪ/ ADVERB in a way that is different from what you expect or think □ The apartment was deceptively spacious.

decibel /'desɪbel/ NOUN [plural **decibels**] a unit that is used for measuring how loud a sound is. A physics word.

decide /dɪ'saɪd/ VERB [decides, deciding, decided]

1 to choose what you are going to do □ + **to do something** Greg decided to buy a computer. □ + **that** She decided that she would go with him. □ I can't decide what to do.

2 to form an opinion after thinking about something □ + **that** I decided that the coat was too short for me.

3 to choose what to have or buy □ + **between** I can't decide between the blue one and the green one. □ + **on** I decided on the duck in the end.

4 to cause a result in a competition □ Amrish's goal decided the match.

• **decided** /dɪ'saɪdɪd/ ADJECTIVE certain or obvious 🖫 This essay is a decided improvement on your last effort.

• **decidedly** /dɪ'saɪdɪdlɪ/ ADVERB in a way that is certain and obvious □ He was looking decidedly unhappy.

deciduous /dɪ'sɪdjuəs/ ADJECTIVE a deciduous tree does not have leaves in the winter. A biology word.

decimal /'desɪməl/ ▶ ADJECTIVE

1 a decimal system is a way of counting based on the number ten

2 using or to do with a decimal system 🔂 *Britain changed to decimal currency* (=money in decimal units) *in 1971.* □ *a decimal number*

▶ NOUN [*plural* **decimals**] a fraction (=number that is less than a whole number) written as a decimal point followed by the number of tenths and hundredths. A maths word. □ *A half, written as a decimal, is 0.5.*

decimal place /ˌdesɪməl 'pleɪs/ NOUN [*plural* **decimal places**] a particular number or position after the decimal point in a decimal. A maths word. □ *3.846 rounded off* (=reduced) *to two decimal places is 3.85*

decimal point /ˌdesɪməl 'pɔɪnt/ NOUN [*plural* **decimal points**] a point (.) used in a decimal after the whole units and before the tenths. A maths word. □ *To multiply by ten, move the decimal point one place to the right.*

decimate /'desɪmeɪt/ VERB [**decimates, decimating, decimated**] to spoil or destroy a large part of something □ *Their crops have been decimated by the floods.*

• **decimation** /ˌdesɪ'meɪʃən/ NOUN, NO PLURAL when something is decimated

decipher /dɪ'saɪfə(r)/ VERB [**deciphers, deciphering, deciphered**] if you decipher something that is difficult to read, you discover what it says □ *Philip's handwriting is almost impossible to decipher.*

decision /dɪ'sɪʒən/ NOUN [*plural* **decisions**]

1 when you decide something 🔂 *I will let you know when I have made my decision.* 🔂 *Finally we took the difficult decision to sell the house.* 🔂 *Most of us think the directors came to the right decision.*

2 *no plural* the ability to decide about things □ *He acted with great decision.*

• **decisive** /dɪ'saɪsɪv/ ADJECTIVE

1 showing the ability to make decisions □ *I wish he'd be more decisive.*

2 completely certain and important 🔂 *Our college won a decisive victory over Queen's on Saturday.*

deck /dek/ NOUN [*plural* **decks**]

1 the flat part that you walk on on the outside of a boat □ *Let's take a walk up on deck.*

2 one of the levels of a boat or bus 🔂 *There are more seats on the upper deck.*

3 the US word for a **pack** of cards

✦ PHRASAL VERB [**decks, decking, decked**] **deck something out** if something is decked out with something, it has been decorated with it

deckchair /'dektʃeə(r)/ NOUN [*plural* **deckchairs**] a folding chair with a wooden frame that is used outdoors

declaration /ˌdeklə'reɪʃən/ NOUN [*plural* **declarations**] an announcement □ *a declaration of war*

declare /dɪ'kleə(r)/ VERB [**declares, declaring, declared**]

1 to announce something firmly or officially 🔂 *England declared war on Germany.* □ *She suddenly declared that she was leaving.*

2 **have something to declare** to have goods that you should pay tax on □ *Do you have anything to declare, Madam?*

3 to tell the tax authority about money you receive □ *Have you declared all your earnings?*

decline /dɪ'klaɪn/ VERB [**declines, declining, declined**]

1 to become weaker or smaller □ *His popularity has declined sharply.*

2 a formal word that means to refuse □ *I'm afraid I must decline your kind invitation.* □ *The minister declined to comment.*

decode /ˌdiː'kəʊd/ VERB [**decodes, decoding, decoded**] to find out the secret meaning of something

decompose /ˌdiːkəm'pəʊz/ VERB [**decomposes, decomposing, decomposed**] to decay

• **decomposition** /ˌdiːkɒmpə'zɪʃən/ NOUN, NO PLURAL the process of decaying

decor /'deɪkɔː(r)/ NOUN, NO PLURAL the style of decoration and furniture in a room □ *It's a lovely house, but I hate the decor.*

decorate /'dekəreɪt/ VERB [**decorates, decorating, decorated**]

1 to put things on or around something to make it look more attractive □ *We'll decorate the cake with sugar roses.*

2 to put paint or paper on the inside walls of a room □ *We've just decorated the dining room.*

3 if someone is decorated, they are given a medal (=metal disc) for doing something brave or good □ *He was decorated for bravery in the war.*

• **decoration** /ˌdekə'reɪʃən/ NOUN [*plural* **decorations**]

1 when you add something to make something more attractive, or the thing you add 🔂 *Christmas/party decorations*

2 *no plural* putting paint or paper on the inside walls of a room □ *The whole house is in need of decoration.*

• **decorative** /'dekərətɪv/ ADJECTIVE intended to make something look more attractive □ *The brass buttons are purely decorative* (=not for a real purpose).

• **decorator** /'dekəreɪtə(r)/ NOUN [*plural* **decorators**] someone whose job is to decorate rooms

decoy /'diːkɔɪ/ NOUN [*plural* **decoys**] a thing or person used to trick and catch someone

decrease ▶ VERB /dɪ'kriːs/ [**decreases, decreasing, decreased**] to make something less or to become less □ *A healthy diet helps to decrease the risk of heart disease.* □ *Josh's interest in football decreased as he got older.*

▶ NOUN /'diːkriːs/ [*plural* **decreases**] an amount by which something is smaller □ **+ in** *There was a decrease in violent crime in the area.* □ **+ of** *They saw a decrease of 5% in sales.*

decree /dɪˈkriː/ ► NOUN [plural **decrees**] an official order that something should happen
► VERB [**decrees, decreeing, decreed**] to announce publicly that something should happen. A formal word.

decrepit /dɪˈkrepɪt/ ADJECTIVE old and in bad condition

dedicate /ˈdedɪkeɪt/ VERB [**dedicates, dedicating, dedicated**] to spend a particular amount of time doing something □ *She dedicated her whole life to music.*
◆ PHRASAL VERB **dedicate something to someone** to say at the beginning of a book, song, etc. that it is for a person that you love or admire □ *This song is dedicated to my friends at home.*
● **dedicated** /ˈdedɪkeɪtɪd/ ADJECTIVE spending a lot of time and effort on what you do □ *She is a very dedicated nurse.*
● **dedication** /ˌdedɪˈkeɪʃən/ NOUN [plural **dedications**]
1 when you use a lot of time and effort to do something □ *He praised the dedication of the nurses.*
2 words used to dedicate a song, book, etc. to someone □ *The dedication read 'For Bill, for being so understanding.'*

deduce /dɪˈdjuːs/ VERB [**deduces, deducing, deduced**] to think that something is true from the information you have

deduct /dɪˈdʌkt/ VERB [**deducts, deducting, deducted**] to take an amount away from a larger number □ *Tax has already been deducted from your earnings.*
● **deduction** /dɪˈdʌkʃən/ NOUN [plural **deductions**]
1 an amount that you deduct
2 something that you deduce from the information you have

deed /diːd/ NOUN [plural **deeds**]
1 a formal word meaning something that someone has done
2 an official document that shows who owns something □ *Here are the deeds of the house.*

deem /diːm/ VERB [**deems, deeming, deemed**] a formal word meaning to have a particular opinion about something □ *I leave you to take whatever action you deem suitable.*

deep /diːp/ ► ADJECTIVE [**deeper, deepest**]
1 going a long way down from the top □ *Is the pond very deep?* □ *The sea was 30 metres deep at that point.*
2 deep feelings and emotions are very strong □ *I have a deep dislike of dogs.*
3 deep colours are strong and dark □ *I painted the walls deep blue.*
4 a deep sound is very low ▣ *a deep voice*
5 going a long way from the front to the back □ *a deep cupboard*
6 a deep sleep when someone is sleeping so much that it is difficult to wake them
7 a deep breath a big breath that fills your lungs □ *Take a deep breath then jump into the water.*
◆ IDIOM **in deep trouble** in a very bad situation □ *He'll*

be in deep trouble if his Dad finds out he's been stealing.
► ADVERB [**deeper, deepest**]
1 a long way from the top of something □ *They swam deep beneath the ocean.*
2 a long way from the edge of something □ *They travelled deep into the mountains.*
3 three/five, etc. deep in three/five, etc. rows □ *The soldiers were standing four deep.*
● **deepen** /ˈdiːpən/ VERB [**deepens, deepening, deepened**]
1 to become deeper or to make something deeper □ *The river deepens here to more than 2 metres.*
2 to become worse or to make something worse □ *A deepening gloom spread across the country.*

deep freeze /ˌdiːp ˈfriːz/ ► NOUN [plural **deep freezes**] a large container for storing frozen foods
► VERB [**deep-freezes, deep-freezing, deep-froze, deep-frozen**] to freeze food in order to store it

deep-fry /ˌdiːpˈfraɪ/ VERB [**deep-fries, deep-frying, deep-fried**] to cook food in hot oil that completely covers it □ *deep-fried fish*

deeply /ˈdiːplɪ/ ADVERB
1 very much □ *I deeply regret my actions.*
2 if you breathe deeply, you take a lot of air into your lungs

deep-seated /ˌdiːpˈsiːtɪd/ ADJECTIVE deep-seated feelings are strong and difficult to change

deer /dɪə(r)/ NOUN [plural **deer**] a large wild animal that has antlers (=parts like branches) on the head of the males

deface /dɪˈfeɪs/ VERB [**defaces, defacing, defaced**] to spoil the way something looks □ *Someone defaced the statue with paint.*

default /dɪˈfɔːlt/ NOUN [plural **defaults**]
1 the way that something is or will be if nothing is done to make it different □ *The default setting on my computer is for American English.*
2 by default if something happens by default it only happens because something else does not happen □ *She got the job by default as nobody else applied.*
◆ PHRASAL VERB [**defaults, defaulting, defaulted**] **default on something** to fail to pay or do something in the way that has been agreed □ *If you default on the rent you will have to leave.*

defeat /dɪˈfiːt/ ► VERB [**defeats, defeating, defeated**]
1 to beat someone in a war or competition ▣ *We shall defeat the enemy and restore peace.* □ *The visiting team were defeated 3–0.*
2 to prevent something from succeeding □ *The plan was defeated in a public vote.*
3 if something defeats you, you cannot do it or understand it □ *Do you know what this means? It defeats me.*
► NOUN [plural **defeats**]
1 a game, fight, war, etc. that you have lost ▣ *The king*

suffered a humiliating defeat by the rebel army.
🔁 *England had another heavy defeat in the cricket.*
2 *no plural* when you have been defeated 🔁 *After a long argument, I was forced to admit defeat.*

defect[1] /'di:fekt/ NOUN [*plural* **defects**] a fault that stops something from working correctly □ *He has a serious heart defect.*

defect[2] /dɪ'fekt/ VERB [**defects, defecting, defected**] to leave a country or organization and go to live or work in an enemy country or organization □ *The spy defected to the United States.*

● **defection** /dɪ'fekʃən/ NOUN [*plural* **defections**] when someone defects □ *There were three more defections when the athletes were in Canada.*

defective /dɪ'fektɪv/ ADJECTIVE not working well because of a fault

defector /dɪ'fektə(r)/ NOUN [*plural* **defectors**] someone who leaves their country or organization to live or work in an enemy country or organization

defence /dɪ'fens/ NOUN [*plural* **defences**]

1 *no plural* the act of protecting someone or something from attack, harm, criticism, etc. 🔁 *His bodyguards leaped to his defence.* 🔁 *The prime minister spoke out in defence of the chancellor.*
2 something that protects something or someone from attack, harm, criticism, etc. □ *They have built massive defences against the tide.* 🔁 *For him, humour is a defence mechanism (=way of protecting himself) that he uses when he feels criticized.*
3 *no plural* the military organizations that protect a country □ *There have been cuts in defence spending.*
4 the defence lawyers who are trying to prove in court that someone is not guilty
5 in sport, the members of a team who try to stop the other team from scoring

● **defenceless** /dɪ'fensləs/ ADJECTIVE defenceless people or animals are unable to protect themselves □ *a defenceless baby seal*

defend /dɪ'fend/ VERB [**defends, defending, defended**]

1 to protect someone or something from attack, harm, criticism, etc. □ **+ against** *Heavy armour on the tanks defends them against gunfire.* □ *Kim always defends his brother if people say he's too quiet.*
2 to try to prove to a court that someone is not guilty □ *He was defended by a top barrister.*
3 in sport, to try to stop the other team scoring □ *Leeds United defended well.*

● **defendant** /dɪ'fendənt/ NOUN [*plural* **defendants**] a person that is accused of committing a crime in a court

● **defensive** /dɪ'fensɪv/ ADJECTIVE

1 showing that you are angry if you think someone is criticizing you □ *He's very defensive about his work.*
2 designed to protect somewhere from an attack 🔁 *defensive weapons*

defense /dɪ'fens/ NOUN [*plural* **defenses**] the US spelling of defence

● **defenseless** /dɪ'fensləs/ ADJECTIVE the US spelling of defenceless

defer /dɪ'fɜ:(r)/ VERB [**defers, deferring, deferred**] to arrange to do something later than planned □ *The meeting was deferred until more people could come.*

deference /'defərəns/ NOUN, NO PLURAL a formal word meaning behaviour that shows that you respect someone and will obey them 🔁 *We were expected to show deference to our teachers.*

● **deferential** /ˌdefə'renʃəl/ ADJECTIVE showing deference 🔁 *Try to behave in a deferential manner towards customers.*

defiance /dɪ'faɪəns/ NOUN, NO PLURAL deliberately not obeying someone or something 🔁 *Pamela went out, in defiance of her parents' instructions.*

● **defiant** /dɪ'faɪənt/ ADJECTIVE showing defiance □ *a defiant child*

● **defiantly** /dɪ'faɪəntlɪ/ ADVERB in a defiant way

deficiency /dɪ'fɪʃənsɪ/ NOUN [*plural* **deficiencies**]
1 when your body does not have enough of something it needs □ *You have a vitamin B deficiency.*
2 a fault or a missing quality that means that something is not good enough □ *Her deficiencies as a mother were obvious to everyone.*

● **deficient** /dɪ'fɪʃənt/ ADJECTIVE
1 not having enough of something □ *Your diet is deficient in protein.*
2 a formal word meaning not good enough □ *The standard of care was seriously deficient.*

deficit /'defɪsɪt/ NOUN [*plural* **deficits**] how much less money you have than you need or expect □ *The accounts show a deficit of several hundred pounds.*

define /dɪ'faɪn/ VERB [**defines, defining, defined**]
1 to show or explain exactly what something is
□ *Researchers have defined three classes of offender.* □ *The scope of the project was poorly defined.*
2 to give the exact meaning of a word or phrase
3 to show the shape of something □ *The parking spaces are clearly defined by white lines.*

definite /'defɪnɪt/ ADJECTIVE certain □ *It's not definite, but the wedding will probably be in August.*
□ *I've noticed a definite improvement in his condition.*

definite article /ˌdefɪnɪt 'ɑ:tɪkəl/ NOUN [*plural* **definite articles**] the name used in grammar for the word the

➤ There are two kinds of article in English grammar: **the** is the *definite article* and **a** or **an** is the *indefinite article.*

definitely /'defɪnɪtlɪ/ ADVERB certainly □ *We'll definitely be back by 10 o'clock.* □ *'Do you think she'll pass the exam?' 'Oh yes, definitely.'* □ *I definitely want to go back there.*

definition /ˌdefɪˈnɪʃən/ NOUN [plural **definitions**]
1 an explanation of the meaning of a word or phrase
□ *Look up the definition of 'magic' in your dictionary.*
2 how clear an image is ⊞ *high definition television*
(=television that gives a very clear image)

definitive /dɪˈfɪnɪtɪv/ ADJECTIVE
1 very certain and not likely to change ⊞ *a definitive answer*
2 better than any others □ *You should read Sherwin's definitive book on this subject.*
• **definitively** /dɪˈfɪnɪtɪvlɪ/ ADVERB in a definitive way
□ *I can't say definitively that this treatment will work.*

deflate /dɪˈfleɪt/ VERB [**deflates, deflating, deflated**]
1 to let the air out of a tyre, balloon, etc.
2 to make someone feel less confident □ *He felt deflated after losing the match.*

deflect /dɪˈflekt/ VERB [**deflects, deflecting, deflected**]
1 deflect attention/blame, etc. to direct attention/blame, etc. away from yourself □ *The government is trying to deflect attention away from its recent failures.*
2 to change the direction that something is moving in
□ *Craig deflected the ball into the net.*

deforestation /diːˌfɒrɪˈsteɪʃən/ NOUN, NO PLURAL cutting down the trees in an area

deform /dɪˈfɔːm/ VERB [**deforms, deforming, deformed**] to spoil the shape of something □ *He had a disease that deforms your bones.*
• **deformed** /dɪˈfɔːmd/ ADJECTIVE not shaped in a normal way □ *He was born with a deformed arm.*
• **deformity** /dɪˈfɔːmətɪ/ NOUN [plural **deformities**] when something is deformed □ *a physical deformity*

defraud /dɪˈfrɔːd/ VERB [**defrauds, defrauding, defrauded**] to get money from a business or organization by dishonest actions □ *She defrauded the company of $40,000.*

defrost /ˌdiːˈfrɒst/ VERB [**defrosts, defrosting, defrosted**]
1 to make frozen food become no longer frozen
□ *Remember to defrost the chicken for tomorrow's lunch.*
2 to remove the ice from a fridge or freezer (=place where frozen food is kept)

deft /deft/ ADJECTIVE [**defter, deftest**] quick and skilful □ *With a few deft movements she created a paper flower.*
• **deftly** /ˈdeftlɪ/ ADVERB quickly and skilfully □ *Hannah deftly flicked the ball over the net.*

defunct /dɪˈfʌŋkt/ ADJECTIVE a formal word that means no longer existing or working □ *The company that made this product is now defunct.*

defuse /diːˈfjuːz/ VERB [**defuses, defusing, defused**]
1 if you defuse a bomb you remove part of it so that it cannot explode
2 if you defuse a difficult situation you make it more relaxed

defy /dɪˈfaɪ/ VERB [**defies, defying, defied**]
1 to refuse to obey someone or something □ *Defying his mother, he left the house.*

2 defy gravity to stay up in the air in a way that is not natural □ *These huge planes seem to defy gravity.*
3 defy belief/description, etc. to be impossible to believe/describe, etc. □ *It's a story that defies belief.*
4 defy someone to do something to say that you do not think it is possible for someone to do something □ *I defy you to do that again!*

degenerate ▶ VERB /dɪˈdʒenəreɪt/ [**degenerates, degenerating, degenerated**] to get worse □ *The situation soon degenerated into chaos.*
▶ ADJECTIVE /dɪˈdʒenərət/ morally bad □ *a degenerate lifestyle*
• **degenerative** /dɪˈdʒenərətɪv/ ADJECTIVE a degenerative disease is one that gradually makes you more and more ill

degradation /ˌdegrəˈdeɪʃən/ NOUN, NO PLURAL very bad conditions that make people feel ashamed

degrade /dɪˈgreɪd/ VERB [**degrades, degrading, degraded**]
1 to make someone feel that they are not respected □ *She felt dirty and degraded.*
2 to change something into a worse state
• **degrading** /dɪˈgreɪdɪŋ/ ADJECTIVE making a person feel degraded □ *a degrading job*

degree /dɪˈgriː/ NOUN [plural **degrees**]
1 a unit for measuring temperature, shown by the symbol ° □ *It's 30° (degrees) here today.*
2 a unit for measuring angles, shown by the symbol ° □ *An angle of 90° (degrees) is a right angle.*
3 an amount of something □ *You will have to accept a small degree of hardship.* ⊞ *I agree with her to some degree* (=in part). ⊞ *Their success depends to a large degree on the teenage market.*
4 a qualification that students can study for at a university or college □ *He's got a degree in German.* ⊞ *He did his degree at Cambridge.*

dehydrate /ˌdiːhaɪˈdreɪt/ VERB [**dehydrates, dehydrating, dehydrated**] to remove the water from something
• **dehydrated** /ˌdiːhaɪˈdreɪtɪd/ ADJECTIVE
1 weak and ill because you have not had enough water to drink □ *He was severely dehydrated.*
2 a dehydrated substance no longer contains water □ *dehydrated food*
• **dehydration** /ˌdiːhaɪˈdreɪʃən/ NOUN, NO PLURAL being dehydrated □ *He was suffering from dehydration.*

deign /deɪn/ VERB [**deigns, deigning, deigned**] if you deign to do something, you do it although you do not want to □ *He hardly ever deigned to come to my school concerts.*

deity /ˈdiːɪtɪ/ NOUN [plural **deities**] a formal word that means a god or goddess (=female god) □ *Jupiter and Juno are Roman deities.*

déjà vu /ˌdeʒɑːˈvuː/ NOUN, NO PLURAL the feeling that you have experienced exactly the same thing before

dejected /dɪˈdʒektɪd/ ADJECTIVE unhappy and disappointed

• **dejection** /dɪˈdʒekʃən/ NOUN, NO PLURAL when you are dejected

delay /dɪˈleɪ/ ► NOUN [plural **delays**] the extra time you have to wait if something happens later than expected □ *There was a delay of half an hour before take-off.* ✏ *Please return to your seats without delay.*
► VERB [**delays, delaying, delayed**]
1 to do something or make something happen later than was planned or expected □ *We delayed our holidays until after the strike.* □ *Buy now! Don't delay!*
2 to make someone or something late □ *I was delayed by the arrival of an unexpected visitor.*

delegate ► VERB /ˈdelɪgeɪt/ [**delegates, delegating, delegated**] to give a job to someone else to do for you
► NOUN /ˈdelɪgət/ [plural **delegates**] someone who goes to a meeting to represent someone else
• **delegation** /ˌdelɪˈgeɪʃən/ NOUN [plural **delegations**] a group of delegates

delete /dɪˈliːt/ VERB [**deletes, deleting, deleted**]
1 to remove something from a piece of writing □ *Someone has deleted your name from the list.* □ *I think we should delete the last paragraph.*
2 to remove something such as a file that is stored on a computer □ *I've accidentally deleted all their addresses.*
• **deletion** /dɪˈliːʃən/ NOUN [plural **deletions**] something that has been deleted or the act of deleting something

deli /ˈdelɪ/ NOUN [plural **delis**] a short way to say and write delicatessen

deliberate[1] /dɪˈlɪbərət/ ADJECTIVE done on purpose □ *He said it was an accident, but I'm sure it was deliberate.* ✏ *It was a deliberate attempt to confuse his opponent.*

deliberate[2] /dɪˈlɪbəreɪt/ VERB [**deliberates, deliberating, deliberated**] to think carefully about something □ *They deliberated for three hours over their decision.*

deliberately /dɪˈlɪbərətlɪ/ ADVERB on purpose □ *You deliberately dropped that so that you wouldn't have to eat it!*

delicacy /ˈdelɪkəsɪ/ NOUN [plural **delicacies**]
1 something to eat that is unusual or expensive □ *These eggs are regarded as a great delicacy here.*
2 *no plural* when something is easy to damage
3 *no plural* when a flavour, smell, etc. is not strong
4 *no plural* when a situation needs to be dealt with using great skill in order to avoid making people upset or angry

delicate /ˈdelɪkət/ ADJECTIVE
1 easily damaged □ *This china is very delicate.*
2 not strong ✏ *a delicate flavour* ✏ *a delicate fragrance*
3 needing to be treated or done very carefully ✏ *a delicate operation* ✏ *We must respect the delicate balance between humans and nature.* ✏ *After some delicate negotiations an agreement was reached.*
4 small and attractive □ *delicate fingers*
5 a delicate person is often ill

• **delicately** /ˈdelɪkətlɪ/ ADVERB
1 skilfully ✏ *She handled the situation very delicately.*
2 delicately balanced in a situation that could easily be damaged
3 carefully and politely □ *She sipped her tea delicately.*
4 not strongly □ *delicately flavoured*

delicatessen /ˌdelɪkəˈtesən/ NOUN [plural **delicatessens**] a shop that sells cooked meat, cheese, etc.

delicious /dɪˈlɪʃəs/ ADJECTIVE tasting very good ✏ *Mum's homemade soup tastes absolutely delicious.* □ *That was a delicious meal.*
• **deliciously** /dɪˈlɪʃəslɪ/ ADVERB in a delicious way □ *a deliciously creamy dessert*

delight /dɪˈlaɪt/ ► NOUN [plural **delights**] great pleasure □ *The baby squealed with delight when he saw his mother.* □ *It was such a delight to see her.*
► VERB [**delights, delighting, delighted**] to please someone very much
◆ PHRASAL VERB **delight in something** to get a lot of pleasure from something □ *He seems to delight in pointing out my mistakes.*
• **delighted** /dɪˈlaɪtɪd/ ADJECTIVE very pleased ✏ *That's great news – I'm absolutely delighted!* □ **+ to do something** *We'd be delighted to come to the party.*
• **delightful** /dɪˈlaɪtful/ ADJECTIVE very pleasant □ *What a delightful surprise!*
• **delightfully** /dɪˈlaɪtfulɪ/ ADVERB in a delightful way □ *a delightfully funny book*

delinquency /dɪˈlɪŋkwənsɪ/ NOUN, NO PLURAL bad and illegal behaviour ✏ *juvenile delinquency*

delinquent /dɪˈlɪŋkwənt/ ► NOUN [plural **delinquents**] someone who behaves badly and illegally
► ADJECTIVE behaving badly and illegally □ *a delinquent teenager*

delirious /dɪˈlɪrɪəs/ ADJECTIVE
1 thinking or speaking in a confused way because you are ill
2 extremely happy □ *When he scored the final goal the fans were delirious.*
• **deliriously** /dɪˈlɪrɪəslɪ/ ADVERB in an extremely happy way ✏ *We were deliriously happy.*

deliver /dɪˈlɪvə(r)/ VERB [**delivers, delivering, delivered**]
1 to take something, especially letters, packages or something you have bought, to a place □ *We're delivering leaflets to all the houses in this area.* □ *Our new washing machine is being delivered next week.*
2 to provide a service □ *Our company delivers training for managers.*
3 to do something that you have promised to do ✏ *The government has failed to deliver the tax cuts it promised.*
4 if someone delivers a baby, they help the baby to be born

• **delivery** /dɪˈlɪvəri/ NOUN [plural **deliveries**]
1 no plural when something is delivered 🔊 We took delivery of our new car on Friday. 🔊 The price includes free delivery.
2 something that has been delivered or will be delivered □ We are expecting a delivery of bricks.
3 no plural the process of providing a service □ They are responsible for the delivery of healthcare in the region.
4 when a baby is born □ It was a straightforward delivery.

delta /ˈdeltə/ NOUN [plural **deltas**] an area of land where a river divides into separate parts before it reaches the sea. A geography word.

delude /dɪˈluːd/ VERB [**deludes, deluding, deluded**] to make someone believe something that is not true □ If he thinks he looks good, he's deluding himself.
• **deluded** /dɪˈluːdɪd/ ADJECTIVE believing something that is not true □ Poor deluded fool!

deluge /ˈdeljuːdʒ/ ▶ NOUN [plural **deluges**]
1 a very large amount of something □ We've had a deluge of complaints.
2 a flood or a large amount of rain
▶ VERB [**deluges, deluging, deluged**] if you are deluged with things, you receive a very large number of them □ We were deluged with entries for our last competition.

delusion /dɪˈluːʒən/ NOUN [plural **delusions**] something that you believe that is not true 🔊 She's under the delusion (=believes wrongly) that I'm rich.

delve /delv/ VERB [**delves, delving, delved**]
1 to try to find information about something, or to study something carefully □ This book delves into the details of their business activities.
2 to put your hand in a container to try to find something □ Nan was delving into her handbag for her purse.

demand /dɪˈmɑːnd/ ▶ VERB [**demands, demanding, demanded**]
1 to ask for something in a forceful way that shows you do not expect to be refused □ They are demanding the release of all political prisoners. 🔊 He demanded an apology from the journalist. □ + to do something I demanded to see the manager. □ + that The group is demanding that the law should be changed.
2 to need something □ Her career demands total commitment. □ The sport demands a high level of fitness.
▶ NOUN [plural **demands**]
1 when someone asks for something in a very forceful way □ + for I gave in to his demands for a new computer. 🔊 Employers say they can't meet the union's demands.
2 no plural a need or wish for goods or services □ + for There is not much demand for sun cream at this time of year. 🔊 We do not have enough stock to meet the demand.
3 in demand wanted by a lot of people □ His legal skills are in demand all over the world.

4 make demands on someone/something to be difficult for someone, or to use up a lot of something □ Her charity work makes great demands on her time. □ The growing number of elderly people is making huge demands on the health service.
5 on demand when you want or need something □ She thinks the drug should be available on demand.
• **demanding** /dɪˈmɑːndɪŋ/ ADJECTIVE
1 needing a lot of time or effort □ a very demanding job 🔊 The sport is physically demanding.
2 wanting or needing a lot of attention □ She has a demanding job in the city. □ Toddlers can be extremely demanding.

demean /dɪˈmiːn/ VERB [**demeans, demeaning, demeaned**] **demean yourself** to behave in a way that makes people respect you less □ I would not demean myself by arguing about money.
• **demeaning** /dɪˈmiːnɪŋ/ ADJECTIVE making you feel that people do not respect you □ a demeaning job □ The new TV show is demeaning to women.

demeanor /dɪˈmiːnə(r)/ NOUN, NO PLURAL the US spelling of demeanour

demeanour /dɪˈmiːnə(r)/ NOUN, NO PLURAL the way someone looks and behaves □ Something in his demeanour made me suspicious.

demented /dɪˈmentɪd/ ADJECTIVE mad or mentally ill □ Her poor mother was demented with worry.

dementia /dɪˈmenʃə/ NOUN, NO PLURAL a medical condition, especially in old people, in which they gradually lose their memory and mental abilities □ She is suffering from dementia.

demise /dɪˈmaɪz/ NOUN, NO PLURAL the death of a person or the end of something □ Are we seeing the demise of the health service?

democracy /dɪˈmɒkrəsi/ NOUN [plural **democracies**]
1 no plural a form of government where people elect their leaders □ The allies plan to introduce democracy to the country.
2 a country that has this form of government □ We live in a democracy.
• **democrat** /ˈdeməkræt/ NOUN [plural **democrats**]
1 someone who believes in democracy
2 Democrat someone who supports the Democratic Party in the US
• **democratic** /ˌdeməˈkrætɪk/ ADJECTIVE
1 based on the system of democracy □ democratic elections
2 based on a system where everyone has an equal right to make a decision □ It was a democratic decision to move abroad.

demolish /dɪˈmɒlɪʃ/ VERB [**demolishes, demolishing, demolished**]
1 to destroy something, especially a building □ The flats will be demolished immediately.
2 to show that someone's opinions are wrong □ She demolished all their arguments.
3 to defeat someone completely □ They absolutely demolished their opponents.

- **demolition** /ˌdeməˈlɪʃən/ NOUN, NO PLURAL when something is demolished □ *We watched the demolition of the old sports centre.*

demon /ˈdiːmən/ NOUN [plural **demons**] an evil spirit

demonstrable /dɪˈmɒnstrəbəl/ ADJECTIVE that can be proved or shown □ *Sadly, Susan has made no demonstrable progress this year.*

- **demonstrably** /dɪˈmɒnstrəblɪ/ ADVERB in a way that can be shown or proved □ *The old teaching method is demonstrably better.*

demonstrate /ˈdemənstreɪt/ VERB [**demonstrates, demonstrating, demonstrated**]
1 to show that something exists or is true ⊞ *Katie's exam results clearly demonstrate the importance of good preparation.* □ *Her success demonstrates that women can do well in business.*
2 to show someone how to do something or how something works □ *Can you demonstrate how the ice cream maker works?*
3 to show that you have a particular feeling, quality or skill □ *Ben has demonstrated no interest in the project.* □ *She demonstrates a total lack of respect for authority.*
4 to march or stand with a group of other people to show that you support or disagree with something □ *They are demonstrating against the war.*

- **demonstration** /ˌdemənˈstreɪʃən/ NOUN [plural **demonstrations**]
1 an event where a group of people stand or march together to show that they support or disagree with something ⊞ *Supporters of the prisoners held a demonstration outside the court.* ⊞ *Over 5,000 people took part in the demonstration.* □ + **against** *They organized a peaceful demonstration against the war.*
2 when someone shows you how to do something or how something works □ *a cookery demonstration* ⊞ *The sales assistant gave us a demonstration of the phone's features.*
3 proof that something exists or is true □ *This attack is a clear demonstration of the need for stricter laws.*

- **demonstrative** /dɪˈmɒnstrətɪv/ ADJECTIVE a demonstrative person is happy to show and express their feelings

- **demonstrator** /ˈdemənstreɪtə(r)/ NOUN [plural **demonstrators**]
1 someone who takes part in a demonstration for or against something □ *Demonstrators marched through the city.*
2 someone who shows people how something works or how to do something □ *She works as a demonstrator in the kitchen department.*

demoralize or **demoralise** /dɪˈmɒrəlaɪz/ VERB [**demoralizes, demoralizing, demoralized**] to make someone feel less confident about doing something □ *The defeat had completely demoralized the team.*

demote /diːˈməʊt/ VERB [**demotes, demoting, demoted**] to give someone a less important and usually worse paid job

- **demotion** /dɪˈməʊʃən/ NOUN [plural **demotions**] when someone is demoted

demure /dɪˈmjʊə(r)/ ADJECTIVE quiet and shy

den /den/ NOUN [plural **dens**]
1 the home of a wild animal □ *a lion's den*
2 a place like a room that children make or find to play in □ *We've made a den in the woods.*

denial /dɪˈnaɪəl/ NOUN [plural **denials**]
1 when you say that something is not true □ *He repeated his denial of his guilt.*
2 **in denial** when you refuse to accept that something unpleasant has happened □ *He's still in denial about his wife's death.*
3 when someone is not allowed to do or have something □ *Keeping him in prison without trial is a denial of natural justice.*

denim /ˈdenɪm/ NOUN, NO PLURAL a strong cotton cloth, usually blue, that is used to make clothes □ *Joe was wearing a denim jacket.*

denominator /dɪˈnɒmɪneɪtə(r)/ NOUN [plural **denominators**] the number below the line in a fraction. A maths word.

denounce /dɪˈnaʊns/ VERB [**denounces, denouncing, denounced**] to say publicly that something is bad or that someone has done something bad □ *He was denounced as a liar.*

dense /dens/ ADJECTIVE [**denser, densest**]
1 containing a lot of people or things very close together □ *a dense forest*
2 thick and difficult to see through □ *Dense fog filled the valley.*
3 an informal word meaning stupid □ *Are you being deliberately dense?*

- **densely** /ˈdenslɪ/ ADVERB densely inhabited/ populated having a lot of people living there

- **density** /ˈdensɪtɪ/ NOUN [plural **densities**]
1 the number of people or things in a place □ *Population densities are low in this area.*
2 how thick something is
3 a measurement of a solid, gas or liquid which measures its mass compared to its volume. A physics word.

dent /dent/ ▶ NOUN [plural **dents**]
1 a hollow in a hard surface where it has been hit □ *There's a dent in the car bumper.*
2 a reduction in the amount of something □ *These wind farms could make a big dent in our carbon emissions.*
▶ VERB [**dents, denting, dented**]
1 to damage something or to reduce the amount of something □ *The injury has really dented her confidence.*
2 to make a dent in something □ *I'm sorry but I think I've dented your car.*

dental /ˈdentəl/ ADJECTIVE to do with teeth □ *Children get free dental care.*

dentist /ˈdentɪst/ NOUN [plural **dentists**] someone whose job is to look after people's teeth

- **dentistry** /ˈdentɪstrɪ/ NOUN, NO PLURAL

1 the work of a dentist
2 the study of teeth and the mouth □ *a degree in dentistry*

dentures /ˈdentʃəz/ PLURAL NOUN a set of artificial teeth

deny /dɪˈnaɪ/ VERB [denies, denying, denied]
1 to say that something is not true □ *+ that Nina denied that she had stolen the bag.* □ *+ ing He denies doing anything wrong.* □ *She denied any involvement in the crime.*
2 to not allow someone to have something or do something □ *She has been denied access to her children.*

deodorant /diːˈəudərənt/ NOUN [plural deodorants] a substance that you put on your body to stop unpleasant smells

depart /dɪˈpɑːt/ VERB [departs, departing, departed] to leave a place, especially to start a journey □ *Flight BA123 is now departing.* □ *+ from The Oxford train departs from platform 8.*

department /dɪˈpɑːtmənt/ NOUN [plural departments] a part of a school, shop, business or government that deals with a particular subject or area of work □ *the sales department* □ *The college has a very fine modern languages department.*
• **departmental** /ˌdiːpɑːˈtmentəl/ ADJECTIVE to do with a department □ *our departmental secretary*

department store /dɪˈpɑːtmənt ˌstɔː(r)/ NOUN [plural department stores] a large shop that has different departments which sell different types of product

departure /dɪˈpɑːtʃə(r)/ NOUN [plural departures]
1 when someone or something leaves a place □ *All departures are shown on the left of the timetable.* □ *We were shocked by her sudden departure from the school.*
2 a change from what is usual □ *This novel is a complete departure from his normal style.*

depend /dɪˈpend/ VERB [depends, depending, depended] it/that depends used to say that you are not certain because something else affects the situation □ *'Do you want to come to the film?' 'It depends how late it goes on.'* □ *'Are you going to invite Rick?' 'That depends. I think he's still angry with me.'*
♦ PHRASAL VERB **depend on someone/something**
1 to need the help of someone or something □ *Millions of children depend on charity for their education.* □ *The farm depends on government subsidies.*
2 if what happens depends on something else, it is affected by it and may change because of it □ *A lot will depend on how well you do in your exams.* □ *The outcome of the election depends on which party wins the voters' trust.*
3 to be able to trust someone to do what you want or need □ *I know I can depend on my family to help me.*

• **dependable** /dɪˈpendəbəl/ ADJECTIVE able to be trusted to do what you want or need □ *Our staff are very dependable.*

• **dependant** /dɪˈpendənt/ NOUN [plural dependants] someone whose food, clothes, house, etc. you have to pay for □ *Fill in the names of all your dependants.*

• **dependence** /dɪˈpendəns/ or **dependency** /dɪˈpendənsɪ/ NOUN, NO PLURAL when someone cannot live or manage without something □ *Our society needs to reduce its dependence on fossil fuels.* □ *alcohol dependency*

• **dependent** /dɪˈpendənt/ ▶ ADJECTIVE
1 needing something or someone to live or exist □ *She's totally dependent on her car to get around.*
2 dependent on something if something is dependent on something else, it is affected by it and may be changed by it □ *Getting into university is totally dependent on my exam results.*
▶ NOUN [plural dependents] the US spelling of **dependant**

depict /dɪˈpɪkt/ VERB [depicts, depicting, depicted] to show or describe something in a picture or story □ *The novel depicts the struggle to survive in Victorian London.*

deplete /dɪˈpliːt/ VERB [depletes, depleting, depleted] to reduce the amount of something, so that little is left □ *Our food stocks were being depleted.*

deplorable /dɪˈplɔːrəbəl/ ADJECTIVE very bad and shocking □ *Some families are still living in deplorable conditions.*

deplore /dɪˈplɔː(r)/ VERB [deplores, deploring, deplored] to say or think that something is very bad or shocking □ *The President said he deplored the use of violence.*

deploy /dɪˈplɔɪ/ VERB [deploys, deploying, deployed] if soldiers or weapons are deployed, they are sent to a place to be used □ *Troops have been deployed along the border.*
• **deployment** /dɪˈplɔɪmənt/ NOUN, NO PLURAL when soldiers or weapons are deployed

deport /dɪˈpɔːt/ VERB [deports, deporting, deported] to force a foreign person to leave a country □ *He will be deported when he finishes his prison sentence.*
• **deportation** /ˌdiːpɔːˈteɪʃən/ NOUN [plural deportations] when a foreign person is forced to leave a country □ *Several refugees now face deportation.*

depose /dɪˈpəuz/ VERB [deposes, deposing, deposed] to remove the leader of a country from their position □ *The president has been deposed.*

deposit /dɪˈpɒzɪt/ ▶ NOUN [plural deposits]
1 part of the price of something that you pay before you buy the thing, and that you will lose if you do not buy it ⊞ *We've put down a deposit on a flat.*
2 an amount of money that you pay into a bank account ⊞ *He made several large deposits.*
3 an amount of money that you pay when you rent

something, that you get back if you return the thing without any damage

4 a layer of a substance that has developed naturally or in a chemical process □ *coal deposits* □ *deposits of natural gas*

▶ VERB [deposits, depositing, deposited]

1 to put something down or to leave something or someone somewhere □ *They were fed up with people depositing rubbish in their garden.* □ *We deposited the children with my mother.*

2 to put money into a bank account □ *I'm hoping to deposit £50 a month into a savings account.*

3 to leave a layer of a substance behind □ *The overflowing river deposited a thick layer of mud in the village.*

deposit account /dɪ'pɒzɪt əˌkaʊnt/ NOUN [*plural* **deposit accounts**] a bank account that you use to save money in

depot /'depəʊ/ NOUN [*plural* **depots**]

1 a place where vehicles like buses or trains are kept when they are not being used

2 a building where goods are stored □ *a weapons depot*

3 a US word for a bus or train station

depraved /dɪ'preɪvd/ ADJECTIVE morally bad □ *The judge described the book as the work of a depraved mind.*

• **depravity** /dɪ'prævəti/ NOUN, NO PLURAL the state of being morally bad

depreciate /dɪ'priːʃieɪt/ VERB [depreciates, depreciating, depreciated] to become less valuable □ *New cars depreciate very quickly.*

• **depreciation** /dɪˌpriːʃi'eɪʃən/ NOUN, NO PLURAL when something depreciates

depress /dɪ'pres/ VERB [depresses, depressing, depressed]

1 to make someone feel unhappy □ *It depresses me to think of how much work we still have to do.*

2 to make a business or the economy less successful or prices lower □ *Poor sales have depressed the value of the company's shares.*

3 a formal word meaning to press something down □ *Depress the brake gently.*

• **depressed** /dɪ'prest/ ADJECTIVE

1 unhappy □ *I felt a bit depressed about how much weight I'd put on.*

2 suffering from depression □ *After my son was born I was depressed.*

3 a depressed area or economy does not have enough businesses or jobs □ *In recent months the housing market has become depressed.*

• **depressing** /dɪ'presɪŋ/ ADJECTIVE making a person feel unhappy □ *This dull weather is so depressing.*

• **depression** /dɪ'preʃən/ NOUN [*plural* **depressions**]

1 *no plural* an illness where you feel unhappy for a long time ⊞ *He was suffering from depression at the time.*

2 a period when the economy is in a bad state and a lot of people do not have a job □ *There is no hope of a quick end to the economic depression.*

3 a formal word for a hollow area of a surface □ *Water was collecting in the depressions in the path.*

deprivation /ˌdeprɪ'veɪʃən/ NOUN, NO PLURAL when someone does not have the basic things that they need □ *They live in conditions of extreme deprivation.*

deprive /dɪ'praɪv/ VERB [deprives, depriving, deprived] to take something important or necessary away from someone □ *She's been deprived of sleep for days.*

• **deprived** /dɪ'praɪvd/ ADJECTIVE not having all the things that are necessary for a normal life □ *They are working in the most deprived areas of the city*

depth /depθ/ NOUN [*plural* **depths**]

1 the distance from the top to the bottom of something □ *This instrument measures the depth of the water.* □ **+ of** *We dug down to a depth of around 2 metres.* □ *The swimming pool was only 2 metres in depth.*

2 the distance from the front to the back of something □ *We need to increase the depth of the shelves.*

3 *no plural* how much someone knows or feels about something □ *He surprised the examiners with the depth of his knowledge.*

4 in depth in a lot of detail □ *We discussed the situation in great depth.*

5 the depths of something (a) a position that is very deep or very far from the edge of something □ *Divers cannot explore the depths of the ocean.* (b) the worst part of an emotion ⊞ *He is in the depths of despair about his job.*

6 your depth the level of water that is not too deep for you to stand up in □ *Don't go out of your depth.*

♦ IDIOM **out of your depth** not having the knowledge or experience to understand or deal with a situation □ *He had looked after animals before, but he was out of his depth with lions.*

deputize *or* **deputise** /'depjutaɪz/ VERB [deputizes, deputizing, deputized] to do someone's job for a short time while they are away □ *Mrs Henderson was deputizing for the Principal that week.*

deputy /'depjuti/ NOUN [*plural* **deputies**] someone who has the job that is next in importance to another job □ *He is deputy sales manager.*

derail /dɪ'reɪl/ VERB [derails, derailing, derailed] if a train derails or is derailed, it comes off the track

• **derailment** /dɪ'reɪlmənt/ NOUN [*plural* **derailments**] when a train comes off the track

deranged /dɪ'reɪndʒd/ ADJECTIVE not normal in your behaviour, suggesting that you are mentally ill

derby /'dɑːbi/ NOUN [*plural* **derbies**] a sports match between two teams from the same town or area ⊞ *a local derby*

deregulate /ˌdiː'regjuleɪt/ VERB [deregulates, deregulating, deregulated] to remove rules, especially in business □ *The industry has been deregulated.*

• **deregulation** /ˌdiːregju'leɪʃən/ NOUN, NO PLURAL when something, especially a business, is deregulated

derelict /'derəlɪkt/ ADJECTIVE not now used and in bad condition □ *a derelict factory*

deride /dɪ'raɪd/ VERB [**derides, deriding, derided**] to show you think that someone or something is stupid and does not deserve respect. A formal word. □ *The film was derided by critics.*

• **derision** /dɪ'rɪʒən/ NOUN, NO PLURAL laughter or remarks which deride someone or something □ *At this comment there were shouts of derision from the crowd.*

derive /dɪ'raɪv/

♦ PHRASAL VERB [**derives, deriving, derived**] **derive something from something**

1 to get something, especially a good feeling, from something □ *He derives a lot of pleasure from his grandchildren.*

2 to be developed from something or made from a part of something □ *The substance is derived from corn.*

dermis /'dɜːmɪs/ NOUN, NO PLURAL the layer of skin that is just under the outer layer. A biology word.

derogatory /dɪ'rɒɡətəri/ ADJECTIVE saying something bad about someone or something 🔁 *a derogatory comment* 🔁 *a derogatory term*

derrick /'derɪk/ NOUN [*plural* **derricks**]

1 a crane (=machine for lifting heavy things), especially at a port

2 a tower over an oil well that lifts equipment

descend /dɪ'send/ VERB [**descends, descending, descended**]

1 a formal word meaning to go or climb down □ *They descended the stairs.* □ *The road descended steeply.*

2 a formal word meaning to start to exist or happen 🔁 *A silence descended on the room.* 🔁 *As darkness descended, it grew colder.*

♦ PHRASAL VERBS **descend from someone** if you are descended from someone, you come after them in the same family □ *He was descended from an Irish farming family.* **descend into something** to become worse and end in a bad state □ *The country is descending into civil war.*

• **descendant** /dɪ'sendənt/ NOUN [*plural* **descendants**] someone who is descended from a person who lived in the past □ *a direct descendant of Genghis Khan*

• **descending** /dɪ'sendɪŋ/ ADJECTIVE in order from the highest or most important to the lowest or least important 🔁 *They were arranged in descending order of height.*

• **descent** /dɪ'sent/ NOUN [*plural* **descents**]

1 a movement down □ *the descent of the mountain* □ *The plane started its descent.*

2 the origin of your family □ *a Frenchman of North African descent*

3 a slow change to a bad state or situation □ *the country's descent into anarchy*

describe /dɪ'skraɪb/ VERB [**describes, describing, described**] to say what happened or what someone or something is like □ *A reporter described the scene in detail.* □ + *question word Can you describe what you saw?* □ + *as He described his daughter as kind and caring.* 🔁 *She describes herself as a feminist.*

• **description** /dɪ'skrɪpʃən/ NOUN [*plural* **descriptions**]

1 when you describe someone or something □ + *of There's a description of the hotel.* 🔁 *She gave a detailed description of the man.* 🔁 *He fitted the general description of the attacker* (=his appearance was the same as what was described). 🔁 *a job description*

2 a type 🔁 *Goods of all descriptions can be bought there.*

• **descriptive** /dɪ'skrɪptɪv/ ADJECTIVE describing someone or something □ *a descriptive poem*

desert¹ /dɪ'zɜːt/ VERB [**deserts, deserting, deserted**] to go away and leave someone or something, especially the army □ *The soldier was shot for deserting.* □ *She deserted her young family.*

desert² /'dezət/ NOUN [*plural* **deserts**] an area of land where it rains very little so the ground is very dry □ *the Sahara desert*

desert island /,dezət 'aɪlənd/ NOUN [*plural* **desert islands**] a tropical island where nobody lives

deserve /dɪ'zɜːv/ VERB [**deserves, deserving, deserved**] if you deserve something, you should have it because of your behaviour □ *I'm pleased Molly won the prize – she deserves it.* □ + *to do something Samir deserves to be promoted.*

• **deservedly** /dɪ'zɜːvɪdli/ ADVERB in a way which is deserved □ *It has become very popular and deservedly so.*

• **deserving** /dɪ'zɜːvɪŋ/ ADJECTIVE worth supporting or helping 🔁 *a deserving cause*

desiccated /'desɪkeɪtɪd/ ADJECTIVE dried □ *desiccated coconut*

design /dɪ'zaɪn/ ▶ VERB [**designs, designing, designed**]

1 to plan something before it is built or made □ *The concert hall was designed by architect Frank Gehry.* □ *She designs clothes for a top fashion store.* □ *We design software to control robots.*

2 if something is designed for a particular purpose, it is made to do that thing □ + *to do something The paths are designed to encourage people to walk more.* □ + *for The equipment is designed for use in schools.*

▶ NOUN [*plural* **designs**]

1 the way in which something is planned before it is made □ + *of We have improved the design of the aircraft.* □ *She has won awards for her innovative designs.*

2 no plural the process of designing something new 🔁 *The company specializes in interior design.* 🔁 *She studied art and graphic design.*

3 a plan or drawing of something that could be made □ + *for a design for a new racing car*

4 a pattern □ *They wore dresses in bright floral designs.*

designate /'dezɪgneɪt/ VERB [designates, designating, designated] to choose someone or something for a particular purpose. A formal word. □ The area is designated as a wildlife reserve.

designer /dɪ'zaɪnə(r)/ ▶ NOUN [plural designers] someone whose job is to design things 🖫 a fashion designer □ a web designer
▶ ADJECTIVE expensive and fashionable and made by a famous company □ designer clothes □ designer sunglasses

desirable /dɪ'zaɪərəbəl/ ADJECTIVE very good or attractive and wanted by many people □ They live in a very desirable area.

desire /dɪ'zaɪə(r)/ ▶ NOUN [plural desires] a strong feeling of wanting something 🖫 He had a burning desire (=very much wanted) to become a doctor. □ We respect his desire for privacy.
▶ VERB [desires, desiring, desired]
1 a formal word meaning to want something very much □ You can have any model you desire.
2 if desired if you want □ Add more salt if desired.
• **desired** /dɪ'zaɪəd/ ADJECTIVE wanted or intended 🖫 His approach had the desired effect. □ Turn the water to the desired temperature.

desk /desk/ NOUN [plural desks]
1 a table for writing or working at 🖫 Andrew sat at his desk. □ There was a big pile of papers on her desk.
2 a place in a building where you can get information or a service 🖫 We went to the reception desk. 🖫 a check-in desk

desktop /'desktɒp/ NOUN [plural desktops] a computer screen that shows the icons (=small pictures) for programs you can use. A computing word.

desolate /'desələt/ ADJECTIVE
1 a desolate place has no people in it □ a desolate landscape
2 very unhappy □ She looked utterly desolate.
• **desolation** /ˌdesə'leɪʃən/ NOUN, NO PLURAL
1 a feeling of great sadness □ She felt a sense of grief and desolation.
2 the quality of being completely empty

despair /dɪ'speə(r)/ ▶ NOUN, NO PLURAL a feeling of having no hope 🖫 We were in deep despair. 🖫 There's a growing sense of despair among local people.
▶ VERB [despairs, despairing, despaired] to feel that you have no hope □ He despaired of ever seeing his son again.
• **despairing** /dɪ'speərɪŋ/ ADJECTIVE feeling despair □ She gave me a despairing look.

despatch /dɪ'spætʃ/ VERB [despatches, despatching, despatched] another spelling of dispatch

desperate /'despərət/ ADJECTIVE
1 feeling very worried and that you will do anything to improve your situation □ She was becoming increasingly desperate. 🖫 He made a last desperate attempt to escape.
2 needing something very much □ Farmers are desperate for workers. □ He was desperate to win.

3 extremely bad or serious 🖫 a desperate situation 🖫 They are in desperate need of financial assistance.
• **desperately** /'despərətlɪ/ ADVERB
1 extremely or very much □ a desperately difficult situation □ We're all desperately disappointed.
2 showing that you feel desperate □ She searched desperately for hours.
• **desperation** /ˌdespə'reɪʃən/ NOUN, NO PLURAL a feeling that you will do anything to improve your situation □ In desperation, she called the doctor.

despicable /dɪ'spɪkəbəl/ ADJECTIVE very bad or cruel □ a despicable crime □ His behaviour was absolutely despicable.

despise /dɪ'spaɪz/ VERB [despises, despising, despised] to hate someone or something very much □ The two men despised each other.

despite /dɪ'spaɪt/ PREPOSITION used to say that something happens or is true, even though something else makes it seem unlikely □ Despite the rain, we enjoyed the picnic. 🖫 I think that she'll be very good, despite the fact that she doesn't have much experience. □ + ing The team remained positive, despite losing their first two games.

despondency /dɪ'spɒndənsɪ/ NOUN, NO PLURAL a feeling of being unhappy and having no interest or enthusiasm □ There was an air of despondency at home.
• **despondent** /dɪ'spɒndənt/ ADJECTIVE feeling despondency □ He became despondent about the future.

despot /'despɒt/ NOUN [plural despots] a leader who keeps all the power for himself or herself and who behaves cruelly

dessert /dɪ'zɜ:t/ NOUN [plural desserts] sweet food eaten at the end of a meal □ We had ice cream for dessert.

dessertspoon /dɪ'zɜ:tspu:n/ NOUN [plural dessertspoons]
1 medium-sized spoon used for eating
2 the amount that a dessertspoon can hold □ Add three dessertspoons of sugar.

destination /ˌdestɪ'neɪʃən/ NOUN [plural destinations] the place someone is travelling to 🖫 We were very tired when we finally reached our destination. 🖫 The town is a popular tourist destination.

destined /'destɪnd/ ADJECTIVE if something is destined, it will certainly happen □ She is destined to become a star.
• **destiny** /'destɪnɪ/ NOUN [plural destinies]
1 what will happen to someone in the future □ I believe we can control our own destinies.
2 a power that some people believe controls what happens to you

destitute /'destɪtjuːt/ ADJECTIVE with no money, food or a place to live □ *The family were left destitute.*
• **destitution** /ˌdestɪ'tjuːʃən/ NOUN, NO PLURAL the state of being destitute

destroy /dɪ'strɔɪ/ VERB [**destroys, destroying, destroyed**]
1 to damage something so badly that it no longer exists or cannot be used □ *Thousands of homes were destroyed by the earthquake.* □ *A fire destroyed dozens of paintings at the museum.*
2 to kill an animal □ *Cattle on the infected farm had to be destroyed.*
• **destroyer** /dɪ'strɔɪə(r)/ NOUN [*plural* **destroyers**]
1 someone who destroys something
2 a fast military ship
• **destruction** /dɪ'strʌkʃən/ NOUN, NO PLURAL when something is destroyed □ + *of We need to stop the destruction of the rainforest.* □ *The storms caused widespread destruction.*
• **destructive** /dɪ'strʌktɪv/ ADJECTIVE doing a lot of damage or harm □ *The next storm was even more destructive.* □ *Jealousy can be very destructive within a marriage.*

detach /dɪ'tætʃ/ VERB [**detaches, detaching, detached**] to separate one thing from another □ *You can detach the hood from the jacket.*
• **detached** /dɪ'tætʃt/ ADJECTIVE
1 a detached house is not joined to another building
2 a detached person is not involved or interested in something □ *He felt a bit detached from what was going on.*
• **detachment** /dɪ'tætʃmənt/ NOUN [*plural* **detachments**]
1 a feeling that you are not involved in something
2 a group of soldiers doing a particular job □ *a small detachment of troops*

detail /'diːteɪl/ ▶ NOUN [*plural* **details**]
1 a small part, fact or piece of information about something □ + *of They provided details of the plans.* □ + *about We learnt more details about the incident.* 🔂 *For further details, see our website.* 🔂 *She didn't give any details.*
2 in detail including all the information or facts about something □ *She described in detail what had happened.* □ *We need to examine it in detail.*
3 go into detail to mention all the facts or information about something □ *I can't go into detail at the moment.*
▶ VERB [**details, detailing, detailed**] to list all the details of something □ *The invoice detailed everything he spent on materials.*
• **detailed** /'diːteɪld/ ADJECTIVE including all the facts or the smallest parts of something 🔂 *Can you send me detailed information about the trip?* 🔂 *a detailed description* □ *a detailed drawing*

detain /dɪ'teɪn/ VERB [**detains, detaining, detained**]
1 to make someone stay somewhere □ *He was detained by the police for 24 hours.*
2 a formal word meaning to delay someone □ *I'm sorry to have detained you.*

detect /dɪ'tekt/ VERB [**detects, detecting, detected**]
1 to discover something that is difficult to find □ *The dogs are trained to detect explosives.* □ *The test can detect cancer at an early stage.*
2 to notice something □ *I detected a hint of annoyance in his voice.*
• **detection** /dɪ'tekʃən/ NOUN, NO PLURAL finding or noticing things □ *Early detection of this illness is very important.*
• **detective** /dɪ'tektɪv/ NOUN [*plural* **detectives**] someone whose job is to try to find out information about a crime 🔂 *a private detective* 🔂 *a retired police detective* □ *She told detectives that she'd seen a man leaving the building.*
• **detector** /dɪ'tektə(r)/ NOUN [*plural* **detectors**] a piece of equipment that is used to detect something 🔂 *a smoke detector*

detention /dɪ'tenʃən/ NOUN [*plural* **detentions**]
1 when someone is kept in a place and not allowed to leave □ *He is being held in detention for questioning.*
2 when a student has to stay at school at the end of the day as a punishment

deter /dɪ'tɜː(r)/ VERB [**deters, deterring, deterred**] to make someone less likely to do something □ *Alcohol should be more expensive to deter youngsters from buying it.*

detergent /dɪ'tɜːdʒənt/ NOUN [*plural* **detergents**] a chemical used for cleaning things □ *washing detergent*

deteriorate /dɪ'tɪəriəreɪt/ VERB [**deteriorates, deteriorating, deteriorated**] to get worse □ *Joe's health is deteriorating rapidly.*
• **deterioration** /dɪˌtɪəriə'reɪʃən/ NOUN, NO PLURAL the process of deteriorating □ *There's been a deterioration in her condition.*

determination /dɪˌtɜːmɪ'neɪʃən/ NOUN, NO PLURAL a strong feeling that you want to do something, even when it is difficult □ *They showed great determination.* □ + *to do something He has a determination to win.*
• **determine** /dɪ'tɜːmɪn/ VERB [**determines, determining, determined**]
1 to discover the truth or facts about something □ *The police are still trying to determine exactly how she died.* □ *They are using a new method for determining the age of stars.*
2 to control or influence what happens □ *The weather will determine how long the event lasts.* □ *This issue could determine the outcome of the election.*
• **determined** /dɪ'tɜːmɪnd/ ADJECTIVE having or showing determination □ + *to do something The team was determined to finish first if they possibly could.* □ *She's a very determined young woman.* 🔂 *He's made a determined effort to lose weight.*

determiner /dɪˈtɜːmɪnə(r)/ NOUN [plural **determiners**] a word that is used before a noun to show how that noun is being used. For example, *the*, *this* and *some* are determiners.

deterrent /dɪˈterənt/ NOUN [plural **deterrents**] something that makes someone less likely to do something □ *Is prison an effective deterrent?*

detest /dɪˈtest/ VERB [**detests, detesting, detested**] to hate someone or something very much □ *He detests violence in any form.* □ *She detested him for what he had done.*

detonate /ˈdetəneɪt/ VERB [**detonates, detonating, detonated**] to explode or to make something explode □ *The bomb was detonated from across the street.*

• **detonator** /ˈdetəneɪtə(r)/ NOUN [plural **detonators**] the part of a bomb which makes it explode

detour /ˈdiːtʊə(r)/ NOUN [plural **detours**] a different and longer way of getting somewhere than usual 🖥 *I took a detour on the way home to visit my sister.*

detox /ˈdiːtɒks/ ▶ NOUN, NO PLURAL treatment to get rid of harmful substances such as drugs and alcohol from your body

▶ VERB [**detoxes, detoxing, detoxed**] to have treatment to remove harmful substances from your body

detract /dɪˈtrækt/

♦ PHRASAL VERB [**detracts, detracting, detracted**] **detract from something** to make something seem less good □ *The last-minute problems did not detract from the overall achievement.*

• **detractor** /dɪˈtræktə(r)/ NOUN [plural **detractors**] someone who criticizes something publicly

detrimental /ˌdetrɪˈmentəl/ ADJECTIVE damaging 🖥 *Large classes can have a detrimental effect on children's education.*

devalue /ˌdiːˈvæljuː/ VERB [**devalues, devaluing, devalued**]
1 to reduce the value of a country's money. An economics word.
2 to make something seem less important □ *His enemies have tried to devalue his achievements.*

devastate /ˈdevəsteɪt/ VERB [**devastates, devastating, devastated**]
1 to destroy something or damage it very badly □ *The storm devastated much of the city.*
2 to make someone very upset □ *His death has devastated our family.*

• **devastated** /ˈdevəsteɪtɪd/ ADJECTIVE
1 very shocked and upset □ *We were absolutely devastated by the news.*
2 completely destroyed □ *The minister visited the devastated area.*

• **devastating** /ˈdevəsteɪtɪŋ/ ADJECTIVE
1 making someone very shocked and upset □ *devastating news*
2 causing a lot of damage □ *devastating floods*

• **devastation** /ˌdevəˈsteɪʃən/ NOUN, NO PLURAL
1 when something has been destroyed or badly

damaged □ *There were scenes of devastation after the explosion.*
2 a feeling of being very shocked and upset

develop /dɪˈveləp/ VERB [**develops, developing, developed**]
1 to grow or change, or to make something grow bigger, better or more advanced □ *The young animals develop very quickly.* □ **+ into** *The eggs develop into adult insects.* □ *There are plans to develop tourism in the area.* □ *The process has developed over time.*
2 to design and create something new □ *Researchers are developing new technologies.* □ *We need to develop strategies to deal with this problem.*
3 to start to have an illness, problem, feeling, etc. □ *Smokers are more likely to develop cancer.* □ *He developed an interest in art.* □ *The equipment developed some technical problems.*
4 to start to happen or exist □ *The disease develops gradually.* □ *A close friendship developed between the two women.*
5 to make a photograph on a film into a picture
6 to build new buildings on land □ *This land is to be developed.*

• **developed** /dɪˈveləpt/ ADJECTIVE a developed country has an advanced economy, social structure, etc. 🖥 *Developed nations must cut carbon emissions.*

• **developer** /dɪˈveləpə(r)/ NOUN [plural **developers**]
1 a person whose job is to build new buildings on land
2 someone whose job is to design and create new products 🖥 *a software developer*

• **developing** /dɪˈveləpɪŋ/ ADJECTIVE
1 a developing country is quite poor and its economy is not very advanced
2 in the process of happening or growing □ *We're reporting on two developing news stories.*

• **development** /dɪˈveləpmənt/ NOUN [plural **developments**]
1 when something becomes bigger, better or more advanced 🖥 *There has been rapid economic development.* □ **+ of** *The condition affects the normal development of the brain.*
2 when something new is created □ **+ of** *This research may aid the development of new treatments.* □ *The project is still in the early stages of development.* 🖥 *New developments in mobile phone technology have made communication easier.*
3 when something begins to happen or exist □ **+ of** *Several factors affect the development of the disease.*
4 a new event in a story or situation 🖥 *They met to discuss the latest developments in the case.*
5 an area of land with new buildings on it □ *a housing development*

• **developmental** /dɪˌveləpˈmentəl/ ADJECTIVE to do with the development of a person □ *The centre is for children with developmental disabilities.*

deviate /ˈdiːvieɪt/ VERB [**deviates, deviating, deviated**] to do something different from what is normal or expected □ *We had to deviate from the original plan.*

• **deviation** /,di:vɪ'eɪʃən/ NOUN [*plural* **deviations**] something that is different from what is normal

device /dɪ'vaɪs/ NOUN [*plural* **devices**]

1 a tool or piece of equipment □ *a device for cleaning keyboards*

2 a bomb ⊞ *The police found an explosive device.*

♦ IDIOM **leave someone to their own devices** to leave someone to do what they want to do □ *Left to his own devices, he'd eat chips every day.*

devil /'devəl/ NOUN [*plural* **devils**]

1 **The Devil** the most powerful evil spirit in some religions

2 an evil spirit

3 an informal word for someone who behaves badly □ *The boys can be little devils sometimes.*

devil's advocate /,devəlz 'ædvəkət/

♦ IDIOM **play devil's advocate** to pretend to disagree with someone in order to test their argument

devious /'di:vɪəs/ ADJECTIVE clever in a way which is not honest □ *a devious plan*

devise /dɪ'vaɪz/ VERB [**devises, devising, devised**] to design a plan or way of doing something ⊞ *We need to devise a plan.* ⊞ *He devised a method of measuring earthquakes.*

devoid /dɪ'vɔɪd/ ADJECTIVE **devoid of something** a formal word meaning not having something □ *The village was completely devoid of life.*

devolution /,di:və'lu:ʃən/ NOUN, NO PLURAL the process of giving some government power to smaller areas

• **devolve** /dɪ'vɒlv/ VERB [**devolves, devolving, devolved**] to give some government power to a smaller area

devote /dɪ'vəʊt/

♦ PHRASAL VERB [**devotes, devoting, devoted**] **devote something to something/someone**

1 to give time, space, energy, etc. to something ⊞ *I want to devote more time to my family.* □ *We are devoting increased resources to training.*

2 **devote yourself to someone/something** to give all your time and interest to someone or something □ *She devoted herself to helping the poor.*

• **devoted** /dɪ'vəʊtɪd/ ADJECTIVE loving or caring about someone or something very much □ *He was a devoted husband and father.* □ *a devoted football fan*

• **devotee** /,devə'ti:/ NOUN [*plural* **devotees**]

1 someone who is very interested in something □ *She's a passionate devotee of the theatre.*

2 someone who follows a particular religion □ *a Hindu devotee*

• **devotion** /dɪ'vəʊʃən/ NOUN, NO PLURAL

1 great love or loyalty □ *I remember her devotion to her husband.*

2 a very strong belief in something □ *religious devotion*

devour /dɪ'vaʊə(r)/ VERB [**devours, devouring, devoured**]

1 to eat something very quickly □ *He devoured a huge breakfast.*

2 to read or listen to something with a lot of interest □ *As a child, I devoured books.*

devout /dɪ'vaʊt/ ADJECTIVE very religious □ *a devout Muslim*

dew /dju:/ NOUN, NO PLURAL very small drops of water that form on the ground at night

dexterity /dek'sterətɪ/ NOUN, NO PLURAL skill, especially using your hands □ *I admired her dexterity with a needle.*

• **dextrous** or **dexterous** /'dekstrəs/ ADJECTIVE skilful at using your hands

dhoti /'dəʊtɪ/ NOUN [*plural* **dhotis**] a long piece of cloth that Hindu men wear wrapped around the lower half of their bodies

di- /daɪ/ PREFIX di- is added to the beginning of words to mean 'two' □ *a dialogue*

diabetes /,daɪə'bi:ti:z/ NOUN, NO PLURAL a serious illness in which your body cannot control the amount of sugar in your blood

• **diabetic** /,daɪə'betɪk/ ▶ ADJECTIVE having diabetes or to do with diabetes □ *a diabetic patient*

▶ NOUN [*plural* **diabetics**] a person with diabetes

diabolical /,daɪə'bɒlɪkəl/ ADJECTIVE

1 an informal word meaning very bad □ *The service was absolutely diabolical.*

2 very evil

diagnose /'daɪəgnəʊz/ VERB [**diagnoses, diagnosing, diagnosed**] to decide what is wrong with a person or a piece of equipment □ *She was diagnosed with cancer last year.* □ *It's important to diagnose the disease early.* □ *An engineer diagnosed the problem and fixed it.*

• **diagnosis** /,daɪəg'nəʊsɪs/ NOUN [*plural* **diagnoses**] a decision about what is wrong with someone □ *The doctor made a diagnosis from one look at the patient.*

• **diagnostic** /,daɪəg'nɒstɪk/ ADJECTIVE to do with diagnosing an illness or problem ⊞ *a diagnostic test*

diagonal /daɪ'ægənəl/ ADJECTIVE going from one corner of something straight to the opposite corner ⊞ *a diagonal line*

• **diagonally** /daɪ'ægənəlɪ/ ADVERB in a diagonal direction □ *Cut it into slices diagonally.*

diagram /'daɪəgræm/ NOUN [*plural* **diagrams**] a drawing that explains something ⊞ *He drew a diagram of the building.*

dial /'daɪəl/ ▶ NOUN [*plural* **dials**]

1 the round part on a clock or a machine that shows the time or a measurement

2 a round control on a radio or other machine that you turn to operate it □ *I turned the radio dial.*

3 the round part of an old telephone that you turn to make a call

▶ VERB [**dials, dialling/US dialing, dialled/US dialed**] to call a telephone number ⊞ *She picked up the phone and dialled the number.* □ *In an emergency, dial 999*

dialect /'daɪəlekt/ NOUN [plural **dialects**] the form of a language that is used by people who live in a particular area and has some words that are not used by other speakers of the same language

dialog /'daɪəlɒg/ NOUN [plural **dialogs**] the US spelling of dialogue

dialog box /'daɪəlɒg ˌbɒks/ NOUN [plural **dialog boxes**] a box that appears on a computer screen to ask you what you want to do next

dialogue /'daɪəlɒg/ NOUN [plural **dialogues**]
1 formal discussion between two people or groups □ *We are hoping to open a dialogue with the government.*
2 the words or conversation of characters in a book, film, etc.

dial-up /'daɪəlʌp/ ADJECTIVE using a telephone connection. A computing word. □ *dial-up access*

dialysis /daɪ'ælɪsɪs/ NOUN, NO PLURAL treatment to remove harmful substances from the blood of a person whose kidneys do not work well enough

diameter /daɪ'æmɪtə(r)/ NOUN [plural **diameters**] a straight line from one side of a circle to the other through its centre, or this measurement. A maths word □ *the diameter of the pipe*

diamond /'daɪəmənd/ NOUN [plural **diamonds**]
1 a very hard, clear stone that is very valuable □ *a diamond ring*
2 a four-sided pointed shape (♦)
3 diamonds one of the four types of playing card, with a diamond symbol printed on them □ *the eight of diamonds*

diaper /'daɪəpə(r)/ NOUN [plural **diapers**] the US word for nappy

diaphragm /'daɪəfræm/ NOUN [plural **diaphragms**] a layer of muscle that separates your stomach from your chest. A biology word.

diarrhea /ˌdaɪə'rɪə/ NOUN, NO PLURAL the US spelling of diarrhoea

diarrhoea /ˌdaɪə'rɪə/ NOUN, NO PLURAL an illness which causes you go to the toilet very often and makes the solid waste from your body more liquid than usual

diary /'daɪərɪ/ NOUN [plural **diaries**]
1 a book with spaces for all the dates of the year where you can write things down □ *I've put the appointment in my diary.* □ *I'll check my diary.*
2 a book where you write down your experiences each day ☖ *He kept a diary.*

dice /daɪs/ ► NOUN [plural **dice**]
1 a small object with six square sides with different numbers of small round marks on each side that you use in games ☖ *Each player rolls the dice.*
2 small square pieces of food □ *Cut the tomato into small dice.*
► VERB [**dices, dicing, diced**] to cut food into dice □ *Finely dice the carrot.*
♦ IDIOM **dice with death** to do something very dangerous where you might be killed

dictate /dɪk'teɪt/ VERB [**dictates, dictating, dictated**]
1 to influence or control what happens □ *The timing will be dictated by the weather conditions.* □ *The market will dictate whether these airlines succeed.*
2 to tell someone exactly what to do □ *I will not be dictated to by head office.*
3 to say words for someone to write down □ *I have to type the letters that my boss dictates.*
● **dictation** /dɪk'teɪʃən/ NOUN [plural **dictations**] a piece of text that a teacher dictates for students to write down, or the process of doing this
● **dictator** /dɪk'teɪtə(r)/ NOUN [plural **dictators**] a person who has complete power over a country □ *a fascist dictator*
● **dictatorial** /ˌdɪktə'tɔːrɪəl/ ADJECTIVE to do with or behaving like a dictator □ *a dictatorial style of management*
● **dictatorship** /dɪk'teɪtəʃɪp/ NOUN [plural **dictatorships**]
1 government by a dictator
2 a country governed by a dictator □ *a military dictatorship*

dictionary /'dɪkʃənərɪ/ NOUN [plural **dictionaries**] a book that gives words in alphabetical order and their meanings □ *a French dictionary* □ **+ of** *a dictionary of medical terms*

did /dɪd/ PAST TENSE OF do

didn't /'dɪdənt/ a short way to say and write did not

die /daɪ/ VERB [**dies, dying, died**]
1 to stop living □ *Her father died suddenly at the age of 56.* □ *Six people died in the crash.* □ **+ of** *He died of heart failure.* □ **+ from** *He was taken to hospital, but died from his injuries.*
2 to disappear or stop existing □ *My love for him will never die.*
♦ IDIOM **be dying for something/to do something** an informal phrase meaning you want to have something or do something very much and you do not want to wait □ *I'm dying for a cold drink.* □ *The kids were dying to get outside.*
♦ PHRASAL VERBS **die away** to gradually become quieter or weaker and then stop □ *The noise of the siren gradually died away.* **die down** to gradually become quieter or less active □ *She waited until the applause had died down.* □ *All the attention seems to have died down now.* **die off** if a group dies off, the members die over a period of time until there are none left □ *The trees began to die off.* **die out** to gradually disappear or stop existing □ *More and more species of animal are dying out.* □ *The tradition died out decades ago.*

diesel /'diːzəl/ NOUN, NO PLURAL a heavy type of oil that is used as fuel

diet /'daɪət/ ► NOUN [plural **diets**]
1 the food that a person eats ☖ *Do you have a healthy diet?* ☖ *You need to eat a balanced diet.* □ **+ of** *They live on a basic diet of rice and beans.*

2 a limited amount or range of foods that someone eats, for example to lose weight ᴾ *Maybe you need to go on a diet.* ᴾ *She began to follow a strict diet.*
▶ VERB [**diets, dieting, dieted**] to eat less food in order to lose weight □ *I've never dieted, but I do do a lot of exercise.*

differ /ˈdɪfə(r)/ VERB [**differs, differing, differed**]
1 to not be the same as something else □ + *from* *His working methods differ from other TV producers.* □ + *in* *The males and females differ in size.* ᴾ *The eyewitness accounts differ.*
2 to disagree with someone about something □ + *over* *They differ over just about everything.* □ + *on* *Experts differ on how high the levels are.* ᴾ *Opinions differ widely over its real value.*

• **difference** /ˈdɪfrəns/ NOUN [*plural* **differences**]
1 the way in which two people or things are not the same □ + *between* *Is there a difference between male and female players?* □ + *in* *There was a noticeable difference in the children's behaviour.* ᴾ *There are big differences between the two cultures.* ᴾ *They don't know the difference between right and wrong.*
2 the amount by which one thing is different from another □ + *between* *The difference between 6 and 10 is 4.* ᴾ *The two sisters get on well, despite their age difference.*
3 a disagreement □ *Differences remain between the two sides.* ᴾ *I'm sure we can resolve our differences.* □ + *over* *They've had their differences over politics.* ᴾ *There were some serious differences of opinion.*
4 make a difference to have an effect on something □ + *to* *This will make a difference to people's lives.* □ *Working harder didn't make any difference – we still couldn't manage.*

• **different** /ˈdɪfrənt/ ADJECTIVE
1 not the same as someone or something else □ + *from* *He seems quite different from the rest of the boys.* □ + *in* *The two girls are very different in appearance and personality.* ᴾ *Each case is completely different.* □ *We listen to different types of music.*
2 used to talk about separate things of the same type □ *She teaches at several different schools.* □ *There are three different terminals at the airport.*

• **differently** /ˈdɪfrəntli/ ADVERB in a different way □ *Our new boss does everything differently.*

differentiate /ˌdɪfəˈrenʃɪeɪt/ VERB [**differentiates, differentiating, differentiated**]
1 to see or show the difference between two things □ *Many people don't differentiate between different types of fat.* □ *Children must be taught early to differentiate right from wrong.*
2 to be the quality or feature that makes something different from something else □ *What differentiates their product from their competitors'?*

• **differentiation** /ˌdɪfərenʃɪˈeɪʃən/ NOUN, NO PLURAL when people or things are different from each other, or

making them different □ *There is little differentiation between the rival candidates.*

difficult /ˈdɪfɪkəlt/ ADJECTIVE
1 not easy to do or understand □ *That's a very difficult question.* □ + *to do something* *It's becoming increasingly difficult to find a parking space.* □ + *for* *It's difficult for anyone to understand.* ᴾ *Many people are finding it difficult to get jobs.*
2 causing a lot of problems or unhappiness ᴾ *It's been a difficult time for us.* ᴾ *He was faced with a difficult situation.*
3 not friendly or easy to please □ *a difficult customer*

• **difficulty** /ˈdɪfɪkəlti/ NOUN [*plural* **difficulties**]
1 *no plural* when something is difficult to do or understand □ *You should be able to do this without difficulty.* □ + *ing* *She has difficulty sleeping.* □ + *in* *He was having difficulty in breathing.* □ + *with* *My grandmother now has difficulty with everyday tasks.* ᴾ *With great difficulty, he managed to pull himself out of the water.*
2 something that causes a problem ᴾ *We had a few difficulties at the beginning of the day.*

diffidence /ˈdɪfɪdəns/ NOUN, NO PLURAL the quality of being shy and nervous

• **diffident** /ˈdɪfɪdənt/ ADJECTIVE shy and nervous

diffraction /dɪˈfrækʃən/ NOUN, NO PLURAL when light or sound waves are broken up by being passed over something or through a small space. A physics word.

diffuse /dɪˈfjuːz/ VERB [**diffuses, diffusing, diffused**] to spread or make something spread over a wide area □ *The light diffused through the mist.*

• **diffusion** /dɪˈfjuːʒən/ NOUN, NO PLURAL
1 when light spreads over a wide area. A physics word.
2 when a substance gradually mixes with gas or liquid. A physics word.

dig /dɪg/ ▶ VERB [**digs, digging, dug**]
1 to make a hole, especially in the ground ᴾ *They dug a hole in the snow.* □ *They're digging a tunnel.*
2 to lift up and turn over soil with a spade (=tool with a flat, metal part that you push into the soil) □ *He's digging in the garden.*
◆ PHRASAL VERBS **dig (something) into something** to press or make something press hard into something □ *The cat dug its claws into the chair.* **dig something out** to find something that you have not seen for a long time □ *I dug out some old school photos.* **dig something up 1** to break or turn over the ground or a surface by digging □ *They were digging up the road.*
2 to remove something from under the ground by digging □ *We dug up some vegetables.*
3 to find information about someone or something □ *Journalists are trying to dig up stories from his past.*
◆ IDIOMS **dig the dirt** to discover bad information about a famous person that the person is trying to keep secret **dig your heels in** to refuse to do something or to change your opinion □ *I dug my heels in and insisted that we go back.*

► NOUN [*plural* **digs**]
1 a remark that you make to annoy someone deliberately □ *He couldn't resist a dig at his rival.*
2 a quick, hard push □ *She gave him a dig in the ribs.*
3 a place where people dig in the ground to look for ancient objects 🔁 *an archaeological dig*

digest /dar'dʒest/ VERB [**digests, digesting, digested**]
1 when the body digests food, it changes it into substances that it can use 🔁 *Bacteria in the stomach help to digest food.*
2 to read or hear new information and understand it □ *It took time to digest the news.*
• **digestion** /dar'dʒestʃən/ NOUN, NO PLURAL the process of digesting food
• **digestive** /dar'dʒestɪv/ ADJECTIVE to do with digesting food □ *It can cause digestive problems.*

digestive system /dar'dʒestɪv ˌsɪstəm/ NOUN [*plural* **digestive systems**] the system of body parts and processes that digest food. A biology word.

digger /'dɪɡə(r)/ NOUN [*plural* **diggers**] a machine that can move or break up large amounts of soil

digit /'dɪdʒɪt/ NOUN [*plural* **digits**]
1 a number from 0 to 9 □ *a six-digit number*
2 a formal word for finger or toe

digital /'dɪdʒɪtəl/ ADJECTIVE
1 storing information, sounds and pictures as sets of numbers or electronic signals 🔁 *a digital camera* 🔁 *a digital radio* 🔁 *There's been a growth in digital music sales.*
2 a digital clock or watch shows the time as numbers
• **digitally** /'dɪdʒɪtəlɪ/ ADVERB using digital equipment □ *The photos are digitally enhanced.*

digital television /ˌdɪdʒɪtəl 'telɪvɪʒən/ NOUN, NO PLURAL a method of broadcasting that uses electronic signals

digitize *or* **digitise** /'dɪdʒɪtaɪz/ VERB [**digitizes, digitizing, digitized**] to change data into a digital form (=as sets of numbers) so that it can be used by computers

dignified /'dɪɡnɪfaɪd/ ADJECTIVE behaving in a calm, controlled way that makes people respect you □ *I think she handled the situation in a very dignified way.* 🔁 *She kept a dignified silence throughout the trial.*

dignitary /'dɪɡnɪtərɪ/ NOUN [*plural* **dignitaries**] someone who has an important official job or position □ *The President is having lunch with foreign dignitaries.*

dignity /'dɪɡnətɪ/ NOUN, NO PLURAL
1 calm, controlled behaviour, especially in a difficult situation □ *She showed great dignity through a difficult period.* □ *I tried to maintain my dignity.*
2 respect for someone or for yourself 🔁 *This is a violation of human dignity.*

digress /dar'gres/ VERB [**digresses, digressing, digressed**] if you digress from the subject you are talking about, you start talking about something else □ *But I digress. Let me get back to the story.*
• **digression** /dar'greʃən/ NOUN [*plural* **digressions**]

when you digress □ *He told us tales of his travels, with frequent digressions.*

dike /dark/ NOUN [*plural* **dikes**] another spelling of **dyke**

dilapidated /dɪ'læpɪdeɪtɪd/ ADJECTIVE old and in bad condition □ *a dilapidated old car* □ *a dilapidated building*

dilate /dar'leɪt/ VERB [**dilates, dilating, dilated**] to become larger or wider, or to make something larger or wider □ *The pupils of your eyes dilate in the dark.*

dilemma /dɪ'lemə/ NOUN [*plural* **dilemmas**] when you have to decide which of two or more things to do and you are finding this decision difficult 🔁 *I'm in a dilemma over whether to go or not.* 🔁 *a moral dilemma*

dilettante /ˌdɪlɪ'tæntɪ/ NOUN [*plural* **dilettantes**] someone who is interested in subjects such as art or literature, but not in a very serious way

diligence /'dɪlɪdʒəns/ NOUN, NO PLURAL a serious and careful attitude to work □ *He has a reputation for honesty and diligence.*
• **diligent** /'dɪlɪdʒənt/ ADJECTIVE showing diligence □ *a diligent student*

dilute /dar'lu:t/ ► VERB [**dilutes, diluting, diluted**] to add water to a liquid so that it is weaker □ *Try diluting the juice with water.*
► ADJECTIVE a dilute liquid has been diluted. A chemistry word □ *a dilute solution*
• **dilution** /dar'lu:ʃən/ NOUN, NO PLURAL the process of diluting something

dim /dɪm/ ► ADJECTIVE [**dimmer, dimmest**]
1 not bright or clear 🔁 *We couldn't see much in the dim light.* □ *I made my way along the dim corridor.*
2 not clear or not well remembered 🔁 *I only have a dim memory of my great-grandfather.*
3 an informal word meaning not quick to understand things
◆ IDIOM **take a dim view of something** to not approve of something □ *We take a very dim view of such behaviour.*
► VERB [**dims, dimming, dimmed**] to become less bright, or to make something less bright 🔁 *The lights dimmed and the performance began.*

dime /daɪm/ NOUN [*plural* **dimes**] a US or Canadian coin worth ten cents
◆ IDIOM **a dime a dozen** very common

dimension /dɪ'menʃən/ NOUN [*plural* **dimensions**]
1 a part of a situation or subject 🔁 *There is a moral dimension to the work we do.* 🔁 *Ashley will add another dimension to the team.*
2 a measurement such as the length, width or area of something □ *Please give the dimensions of the doorway.*

diminish /dɪ'mɪnɪʃ/ VERB [**diminishes, diminishing, diminished**] to become less or smaller, or to make something less or smaller □ *I don't want to diminish the importance of this meeting.* □ *Recently, their power has diminished.*

diminutive /dɪ'mɪnjutɪv/ ▶ ADJECTIVE a formal word meaning very small □ *She appeared in the doorway, a diminutive figure.*
▶ NOUN [*plural* **diminutives**] a word formed with a suffix such as -*let* (e.g. *booklet*) or -*ette* (e.g. *statuette*), used to refer to a small type of something

dimly /'dɪmlɪ/ ADVERB
1 not clearly or brightly 🖪 *a dimly lit room* □ *It was only dimly visible through the smoke.*
2 not clearly understood or remembered □ *She dimly remembered someone telling her about it.*

dimple /'dɪmpəl/ NOUN [*plural* **dimples**] a small hollow place on the skin of your chin or cheek □ *Harry has dimples when he smiles.*

dim-witted /ˌdɪm'wɪtɪd/ ADJECTIVE stupid

din /dɪn/ NOUN, NO PLURAL a lot of very loud noise □ *The house was filled with the constant din of children.*

dine /daɪn/ VERB [**dines, dining, dined**] a formal word meaning to eat dinner (=main meal) □ *They regularly dine at the best restaurants.*
• **diner** /'daɪnə(r)/ NOUN [*plural* **diners**] someone who is eating dinner (=main meal), especially in a restaurant

dinghy /'dɪŋɡɪ/ NOUN [*plural* **dinghies**] a small boat for rowing or sailing

dingy /'dɪndʒɪ/ ADJECTIVE [**dingier, dingiest**] dark, unpleasant and often dirty □ *a small, dingy room*

dining room /'daɪnɪŋ ˌruːm/ NOUN [*plural* **dining rooms**] the room in a house or hotel where you have your meals

dinner /'dɪnə(r)/ NOUN [*plural* **dinners**]
1 a main meal in the evening or in the middle of the day □ *We had fish for dinner.* 🖪 *We sat down to eat dinner.* 🖪 *Alice is cooking dinner.*
2 a formal evening meal arranged for a lot of people □ *There's a dinner on the last night of the conference.*

dinner jacket /'dɪnə ˌdʒækɪt/ NOUN [*plural* **dinner jackets**] a formal jacket worn by a man, that is usually black or white

dinosaur /'daɪnəsɔː(r)/ NOUN [*plural* **dinosaurs**] a very large type of animal that lived millions of years ago and no longer exists

diode /'daɪəʊd/ NOUN [*plural* **diodes**] a piece of electronic equipment that allows electricity to move through it in one direction only. A physics word.

dip /dɪp/ ▶ VERB [**dips, dipping, dipped**]
1 to put something in and out of a liquid quickly □ *Dip the clothes in the dye.* □ *She dipped a toe into the water.*
2 to become lower in amount or level □ *At night temperatures dip below freezing.* □ *Sales dipped slightly last month.*
♦ PHRASAL VERB **dip into something**
1 to take a small amount of money from an amount saved □ *I had to dip into my savings.*
2 to read or watch small parts of something at different times
▶ NOUN [*plural* **dips**]

1 a fall in the level or amount of something □ *The company reported a 2% dip in profits.*
2 an informal word meaning a quick swim □ *Do you fancy a dip in the pool?*
3 a place in a surface or the ground that is lower than the part around it □ *There was a dip in the road.*
4 a soft food that you eat by dipping things in it □ *a cheese dip*

diploma /dɪ'pləʊmə/ NOUN [*plural* **diplomas**] a qualification that someone can study for in a particular subject □ **+ in** *She has a postgraduate diploma in Journalism Studies.*

diplomacy /dɪ'pləʊməsɪ/ NOUN, NO PLURAL
1 the job or skill of keeping friendly relationships between countries 🖪 *He is in New York for three days of international diplomacy at the UN.* □ *If diplomacy fails, we will have to consider other options.*
2 the ability to deal with people without offending them □ *The job requires enormous tact and diplomacy.*
• **diplomat** /'dɪpləmæt/ NOUN [*plural* **diplomats**] someone whose job is to keep good relationships and communications between countries □ *a British diplomat*
• **diplomatic** /ˌdɪplə'mætɪk/ ADJECTIVE
1 to do with the relationships between countries 🖪 *This could damage diplomatic relations between the two countries.* 🖪 *She led the diplomatic effort to end the crisis.*
2 showing diplomacy in dealing with people □ *You're being very diplomatic.*
• **diplomatically** /ˌdɪplə'mætɪkəlɪ/ ADVERB
1 in a way that does not offend anyone □ *'Both were very good,' she answered diplomatically.*
2 by using diplomacy □ *We want to resolve this issue diplomatically.*

dire /'daɪə(r)/ ADJECTIVE very bad, serious or extreme 🖪 *a dire warning* 🖪 *These people are in dire need of help.* 🖪 *If these spending cuts go ahead, they will have dire consequences.*

direct /dɪ'rekt/ ▶ ADJECTIVE
1 straight from one place to another 🖪 *It's the shortest, most direct route.* 🖪 *a direct flight between London and Beijing*
2 involving two people or things with nothing else between 🖪 *We had no direct contact with Mr Ellis.* 🖪 *They found a direct link between computer usage and back pain.*
3 honest and saying what you think □ *He's very direct in his approach.* □ *He asked some pretty direct questions.*
▶ ADVERB
1 going straight from one place to another □ *They fly daily direct from Glasgow to New York.*
2 in a way that involves two people or things only □ *We buy direct from the manufacturer.*
▶ VERB [**directs, directing, directed**]
1 to intend something for a particular person or

purpose □ *His remarks were directed at me.* □ *Many of the attacks are directed against civilians.*
2 to tell the actors in a film or play what to do 🔁 *The film was directed by Clint Eastwood.* □ *She directed the new Broadway production of the musical.*
3 to tell someone how to get somewhere □ *Could you direct me to the post office, please?*
4 to control or organize the way something is done □ *The police direct the traffic when it's busy.*

direct debit /dɪˌrekt ˈdebɪt/ NOUN [*plural* **direct debits**] an instruction to your bank to pay money regularly to a person or organization □ *We pay our bills by direct debit.*

direction /dɪˈrekʃən/ NOUN [*plural* **directions**]
1 the place or point a thing or person is going or facing towards □ *In which direction was she going – towards town or away?* □ **+ of** *He pointed in the direction of the kitchen.* 🔁 *The bus was travelling in the opposition direction.* 🔁 *They all headed off in different directions.* 🔁 *The wind has changed direction.*
2 **directions** instructions for getting somewhere or doing something 🔁 *I followed his directions as we headed out of town.* □ *Make sure you read the directions for use carefully.*
3 the way something develops or changes 🔁 *We are taking the company in a new direction.*
4 *no plural* controlling or organizing things □ *The dock was built under the direction of Brunel in the 1850s.*
5 *no plural* the feeling of having a clear purpose □ *I had no real direction in my life.*

directly /dɪˈrektlɪ/ ADVERB
1 with no other person or thing between or involved □ *It plugs directly into your computer.* □ *Did you talk directly to him?* 🔁 *He wasn't directly involved in the project.* 🔁 *She wasn't directly responsible for the error.*
2 straight from one place to another □ *We went directly to the station.*
3 exactly 🔁 *Chloe sat directly behind him.* 🔁 *He stood directly in front of me.*
4 saying exactly what you think in a clear, honest way □ *He didn't directly address the issue.*
5 immediately □ *We spoke directly after the meeting.*

direct object /dɪˌrekt ˈɒbdʒɪkt/ NOUN [*plural* **direct objects**] the noun or pronoun that is affected by the action of a verb. For example, in *He gave the boy a pound*, the direct object is *a pound*.

director /dɪˈrektə(r)/ NOUN [*plural* **directors**]
1 the manager of a business, organization or department □ **+ of** *the director of the CIA* 🔁 *the institute's executive director* 🔁 *the supermarket's finance director*
2 someone who makes a film or organizes a stage show 🔁 *a Hollywood film director* □ **+ of** *She's the artistic director of the Sydney Theatre Company.*

directory /dɪˈrektərɪ/ NOUN [*plural* **directories**]
1 a book containing an alphabetical list of names,

numbers or other information 🔁 *a telephone directory*
2 a computer file where other files, documents, etc. are stored. A computing word.

direct speech /dɪˌrekt ˈspiːtʃ/ NOUN, NO PLURAL in a story or report, the exact words that a person said

dirt /dɜːt/ ▶ NOUN, NO PLURAL
1 any substance that is not clean or that makes something become not clean □ *Rinse under water to remove any dirt.* □ *She brushed the dirt from the surface.*
2 soil □ *a mound of dirt* 🔁 *We drove up a dirt track to the farm.*
▶ ADVERB **dirt cheap/poor** extremely cheap or poor □ *I got it dirt cheap at the market.*

● **dirty** /ˈdɜːtɪ/ ADJECTIVE [**dirtier, dirtiest**]
1 not clean □ *dirty hands* □ *I cleared all the dirty dishes.* 🔁 *Try not to get your clothes dirty.* 🔁 *a pile of dirty laundry*
2 to do with sex in a way that is not polite 🔁 *a dirty joke*
3 not fair or not honest 🔁 *This is another of his dirty tricks.*
◆ IDIOM **do someone's dirty work** to do something unpleasant or dishonest for someone else □ *He pays other people to do his dirty work for him.*
▶ VERB [**dirties, dirtying, dirtied**] to make something dirty □ *I don't want to dirty my shoes.*

dis- /dɪs/ PREFIX
1 dis- is added to the beginning of words to mean 'not' □ *dislike*
2 dis- is added to the beginning of words to mean 'to do with separating and moving apart' □ *disjointed*

disability /ˌdɪsəˈbɪlətɪ/ NOUN [*plural* **disabilities**] a physical or mental problem that makes some parts of life difficult 🔁 *a physical disability* □ *Buildings should be accessible to people with disabilities.*

● **disable** /dɪsˈeɪbəl/ VERB [**disables, disabling, disabled**]
1 to stop a piece of equipment from working □ *The men disabled the security system.*
2 to cause someone to have a disability □ *She has been disabled by a back injury.*

● **disabled** /dɪsˈeɪbəld/ ▶ ADJECTIVE having a disability 🔁 *We provide support for disabled people.* 🔁 *Our son is severely disabled.*
▶ NOUN **the disabled** people who are disabled

disadvantage /ˌdɪsədˈvɑːntɪdʒ/ ▶ NOUN [*plural* **disadvantages**] something that makes something less attractive, less successful or more difficult □ **+ of** *The only disadvantage of the plan is that it could be too expensive.* □ *The advantages outweigh the disadvantages.*
▶ VERB [**disadvantages, disadvantaging, disadvantaged**] to cause someone to have a disadvantage □ *The schedule unfairly disadvantages players who have long matches.*
● **disadvantaged** /ˌdɪsədˈvɑːntɪdʒd/ ADJECTIVE poor

and without many opportunities 🔲 *He comes from a disadvantaged background.*

• **disadvantageous** /ˌdɪsædvɑːnˈteɪdʒəs/ ADJECTIVE causing a disadvantage □ *The new tax arrangements will be disadvantageous to people on low incomes.*

disaffected /ˌdɪsəˈfektɪd/ ADJECTIVE very disappointed and no longer supporting something □ *He hopes to win back disaffected voters.*

• **disaffection** /ˌdɪsəˈfekʃən/ NOUN, NO PLURAL being disaffected □ *There is growing disaffection with the President.*

disagree /ˌdɪsəˈgriː/ VERB [**disagrees, disagreeing, disagreed**] to have a different opinion from someone else about something □ **+ with** *I completely disagree with you about that.* □ **+ about** *Doctors disagree about how effective the treatment is.* □ **+ over** *Ministers disagree over who is to blame.* □ **+ on** *They disagree on almost everything.*

♦ PHRASAL VERBS **disagree with something** to not approve of something □ *Many people disagree with the death penalty.* **disagree with someone** an informal word meaning to make you feel ill □ *Something I ate disagreed with me.*

• **disagreeable** /ˌdɪsəˈgriːəbəl/ ADJECTIVE unpleasant □ *a disagreeable smell* □ *She's being very disagreeable this morning.*

• **disagreement** /ˌdɪsəˈgriːmənt/ NOUN [*plural* **disagreements**] when people have different opinions or argue 🔲 *We've had several disagreements on this subject.* □ *There are still some areas of disagreement.* □ **+ between** *There was some disagreement between John and Robert.* □ **+ over** *There are also disagreements over finances.*

disallow /ˌdɪsəˈlaʊ/ VERB [**disallows, disallowing, disallowed**] to officially say that something cannot be accepted □ *Our next shot was disallowed by the referee.*

disappear /ˌdɪsəˈpɪə(r)/ VERB [**disappears, disappearing, disappeared**]
1 if someone or something disappears, they go somewhere where they cannot be seen or found □ **+ from** *The woman disappeared from her home in April.* □ *He turned and disappeared into the crowd.* □ *The car disappeared down the street.*
2 to stop existing □ *The symptoms usually disappear within a couple of days.* □ *Finally the light disappeared altogether.*

• **disappearance** /ˌdɪsəˈpɪərəns/ NOUN [*plural* **disappearances**] when something or someone disappears □ *The police are investigating the disappearance of the businessman.*

disappoint /ˌdɪsəˈpɔɪnt/ VERB [**disappoints, disappointing, disappointed**] to make someone feel unhappy because something is not how they had hoped or expected □ *I'm sorry to disappoint you, but I can't come to your party.* □ *We don't want to disappoint our fans.*

• **disappointed** /ˌdɪsəˈpɔɪntɪd/ ADJECTIVE unhappy because something is not how you had hoped or expected □ **+ that** *I'm disappointed that he can't come.* □ **+ with** *I'm very disappointed with the result.* 🔲 *I feel bitterly disappointed.*

• **disappointing** /ˌdɪsəˈpɔɪntɪŋ/ ADJECTIVE not as good as you hoped or expected 🔲 *It was a disappointing performance by the team.* □ *It's extremely disappointing that we haven't made any progress.*

• **disappointingly** /ˌdɪsəˈpɔɪntɪŋlɪ/ ADVERB in a disappointing way □ *Progress is disappointingly slow.*

• **disappointment** /ˌdɪsəˈpɔɪntmənt/ NOUN [*plural* **disappointments**] a feeling of being disappointed or something that makes you disappointed □ *It was a disappointment to find that all the tickets had already been sold.* 🔲 *The hotel was a big disappointment.* 🔲 *She expressed her disappointment at the decision.*

disapproval /ˌdɪsəˈpruːvəl/ NOUN, NO PLURAL when you think something is bad, wrong or not suitable □ **+ of** *Her decision earned her the disapproval of her family.* 🔲 *His parents expressed their disapproval of the planned marriage.*

• **disapprove** /ˌdɪsəˈpruːv/ VERB [**disapproves, disapproving, disapproved**] to think that something or someone is bad, wrong or not suitable □ **+ of** *My parents definitely disapproved of my new friend.* □ *We were wearing short skirts and he clearly disapproved.*

• **disapproving** /ˌdɪsəˈpruːvɪŋ/ ADJECTIVE showing that you disapprove □ *a disapproving tone of voice*

disarm /dɪsˈɑːm/ VERB [**disarms, disarming, disarmed**]
1 to take a weapon away from someone □ *A security guard managed to disarm the intruder.*
2 to get rid of weapons that you have
3 to make someone feel less angry □ *His positive attitude disarmed many.*

• **disarmament** /dɪsˈɑːməmənt/ NOUN, NO PLURAL the process of getting rid of weapons 🔲 *He campaigned for nuclear disarmament.*

• **disarming** /dɪsˈɑːmɪŋ/ ADJECTIVE making people feel less angry or unfriendly by your behaviour □ *a disarming smile*

disarray /ˌdɪsəˈreɪ/ NOUN, NO PLURAL
1 in disarray very untidy □ *The kitchen was in complete disarray.*
2 a situation in which things are confused or not organized □ *The troops were thrown into disarray by the death of their leader.*

disaster /dɪˈzɑːstə(r)/ NOUN [*plural* **disasters**]
1 something that causes a lot of damage, injuries or deaths 🔲 *They help victims of natural disasters such as earthquakes.* 🔲 *The flight had just taken off when disaster struck.*
2 a very bad situation or failure □ *The whole day was an absolute disaster.* □ *This could be a disaster for the tourist industry.*

• **disastrous** /dɪˈzɑːstrəs/ ADJECTIVE extremely bad

⌨ *The plans could have disastrous consequences for wildlife.* □ *They made a disastrous start to the championship.*

disband /dɪsˈbænd/ VERB [**disbands, disbanding, disbanded**] a formal word meaning to stop working together as a group □ *The government has promised to disband the armed militias.*

disbelief /ˌdɪsbɪˈliːf/ NOUN, NO PLURAL not believing something □ *She shook her head in disbelief.* □ *He had an expression of complete disbelief.*

• **disbelieve** /ˌdɪsbɪˈliːv/ VERB [**disbelieves, disbelieving, disbelieved**] to think someone is lying or that something is not true □ *I have no reason to disbelieve him.*

• **disbelieving** /ˌdɪsbɪˈliːvɪŋ/ ADJECTIVE showing disbelief □ *He gave me a disbelieving look.*

disc /dɪsk/ NOUN [**plural discs**]

1 something flat and round □ *a small metal disc* □ *a disc of yellow plastic*

2 a record (=flat plastic object with music recorded on it) or CD (=small flat metal object with music or information recorded on it)

3 a round piece of cartilage (=strong substance in the body) between the bones in your back

discard /dɪˈskɑːd/ VERB [**discards, discarding, discarded**] to throw something away □ *a discarded wrapper* □ *Discard the herbs before serving.*

discern /dɪˈsɜːn/ VERB [**discerns, discerning, discerned**] a formal word meaning to see or recognize something □ *It is often difficult to discern the difference between the two.* □ *She could just discern shapes in the darkness.*

• **discernible** /dɪˈsɜːnəbəl/ ADJECTIVE able to be seen, heard or recognized ⌨ *There was no discernible difference.* □ *His voice was barely discernible above the noise.*

• **discerning** /dɪˈsɜːnɪŋ/ ADJECTIVE good at judging the quality of things □ *She was a discerning judge of character.*

discharge ▶ VERB /dɪsˈtʃɑːdʒ/ [**discharges, discharging, discharged**]

1 to allow someone to leave prison, a hospital or a military organization □ *She was discharged from hospital yesterday.*

2 if something discharges a substance, the substance comes out □ *The sewage is discharged into the river.*

3 a formal word meaning to do something you should ⌨ *He had failed to discharge his official duties.*

4 a formal word meaning to fire a weapon □ *Police say that no firearm was discharged.*

▶ NOUN /ˈdɪstʃɑːdʒ/ [**plural discharges**]

1 when someone is allowed to leave a hospital, prison or a military organization □ *He received an honourable discharge from the army.*

2 a substance that comes out of something □ *They were fined over illegal discharges of industrial waste.*

disciple /dɪˈsaɪpəl/ NOUN [**plural disciples**]

1 a person who follows and believes in someone else's ideas

2 one of the first people to follow Jesus Christ

disciplinarian /ˌdɪsɪplɪˈneərɪən/ NOUN [**plural disciplinarians**] someone who is very severe and punishes people who do not obey them □ *His father was a strict disciplinarian.*

disciplinary /ˈdɪsɪplɪnərɪ/ ADJECTIVE to do with punishment for breaking rules ⌨ *The investigation led to disciplinary action against several staff members.*

discipline /ˈdɪsɪplɪn/ ▶ NOUN [**plural disciplines**]

1 no plural when people are made to obey rules and behave in a particular way □ *We're concerned about the lack of discipline in the school.* ⌨ *He couldn't maintain discipline in the classroom.*

2 no plural the ability to control your own behaviour □ *Martial arts require concentration and physical discipline.*

3 a formal word meaning a subject of study ⌨ *an academic discipline*

▶ VERB [**disciplines, disciplining, disciplined**]

1 to punish someone □ *Parents were asked how they discipline their children.*

2 to teach someone to control their behaviour □ *I disciplined myself to train every day.*

• **disciplined** /ˈdɪsɪplɪnd/ ADJECTIVE behaving in a controlled and organized way □ *We need to take a more disciplined approach.*

disc jockey /ˈdɪsk ˌdʒɒkɪ/ NOUN [**plural disc jockeys**] someone who plays recorded music on the radio or at a club

disclaim /dɪsˈkleɪm/ VERB [**disclaims, disclaiming, disclaimed**] a formal word meaning to say that you are not responsible for something, or that you do not know about it □ *She disclaimed all responsibility for the mistake.*

• **disclaimer** /dɪsˈkleɪmə(r)/ NOUN [**plural disclaimers**] a written statement saying that someone does not accept responsibility for something

disclose /dɪsˈkləʊz/ VERB [**discloses, disclosing, disclosed**] to tell someone something new or secret ⌨ *I'm not authorized to disclose that information.* □ *She didn't want to disclose her name.*

• **disclosure** /dɪsˈkləʊʒə(r)/ NOUN [**plural disclosures**] when information is disclosed □ *Police are investigating an unauthorized disclosure of classified information.*

disco /ˈdɪskəʊ/ NOUN [**plural discos**] a place or party where people dance to recorded music

discolor /dɪsˈkʌlə(r)/ VERB [**discolors, discoloring, discolored**] the US spelling of discolour

• **discolored** /dɪsˈkʌləd/ ADJECTIVE the US spelling of discoloured

discolour /dɪsˈkʌlə(r)/ VERB [**discolours, discolouring, discoloured**] to become an unpleasant colour or to make something an unpleasant colour

• **discoloured** /dɪsˈkʌləd/ ADJECTIVE changed in

colour in a way that is not attractive □ *He had crooked, discoloured teeth.*

discomfort /dɪsˈkʌmfət/ NOUN, NO PLURAL
1 a feeling of being uncomfortable □ *The doctor asked if I had felt any discomfort.*
2 a feeling of being nervous or embarrassed □ *Some people have expressed discomfort with the decision.*

disconcert /ˌdɪskənˈsɜːt/ VERB [**disconcerts, disconcerting, disconcerted**] to make someone feel nervous or confused □ *Grace was clearly disconcerted by his unexpected arrival.*

• **disconcerting** /ˌdɪskənˈsɜːtɪŋ/ ADJECTIVE making you feel nervous or confused □ *I found his attitude a bit disconcerting.*

disconnect /ˌdɪskəˈnekt/ VERB [**disconnects, disconnecting, disconnected**]
1 to stop the supply of something such as gas or electricity □ *The phone has been disconnected.*
2 to separate things that were joined together □ *His harness became disconnected from the safety rope.*

disconsolate /dɪsˈkɒnsələt/ ADJECTIVE unhappy or disappointed

• **disconsolately** /dɪsˈkɒnsələtlɪ/ ADVERB in a disconsolate way □ *The golfers waited disconsolately as the rain poured down.*

discontent /ˌdɪskənˈtent/ NOUN, NO PLURAL a feeling of not being happy or satisfied with a situation ▣ *There is widespread discontent with the government.*

• **discontented** /ˌdɪskənˈtentɪd/ ADJECTIVE not happy or satisfied □ *They grew discontented with their work.*

discontinue /ˌdɪskənˈtɪnjuː/ VERB [**discontinues, discontinuing, discontinued**] to stop making or selling a product □ *That model has been discontinued.*

discord /ˈdɪskɔːd/ NOUN, NO PLURAL disagreement between people □ *The pay system in this office has always been a cause of discord.*

discount ▶ NOUN /ˈdɪskaʊnt/ [*plural* **discounts**] a reduction in the price of something □ *+ on There's a 10% discount on all goods.* ▣ *I got a £5 discount.* ▣ *The company offers discounts to students.*
▶ VERB /ˈdɪskaʊnt, dɪsˈkaʊnt/ [**discounts, discounting, discounted**]
1 to believe that something is not likely, possible or important □ *We can't discount the possibility of further legal action.*
2 to reduce the price of something □ *Many shops discount their prices just after Christmas.*

discourage /dɪsˈkʌrɪdʒ/ VERB [**discourages, discouraging, discouraged**]
1 to try to stop something happening or to persuade someone not to do something □ *They introduced new measures to discourage smoking.* □ *We want to discourage people from driving into the city centre.*
2 to make someone feel less confident or enthusiastic about something □ *Don't be discouraged by what he said.*

• **discouragement** /dɪsˈkʌrɪdʒmənt/ NOUN, NO PLURAL
1 the process of discouraging something or something that discourages □ *This shouldn't be a discouragement to other families.*
2 a feeling of disappointment that stops you continuing with something

• **discouraging** /dɪsˈkʌrɪdʒɪŋ/ ADJECTIVE making you feel less enthusiastic or confident about something □ *discouraging news*

discourteous /dɪsˈkɜːtɪəs/ ADJECTIVE rude and not showing respect

discover /dɪsˈkʌvə(r)/ VERB [**discovers, discovering, discovered**] to find information, a place or an object, especially for the first time □ *The settlers discovered gold in the mountains.* □ *The man's body was discovered yesterday.* □ *She finally discovered the truth.* □ *+ that We discovered that the paint wouldn't mix with water.* □ *+ question word Scientists hope to discover why numbers of the birds have dropped.*

• **discoverer** /dɪsˈkʌvərə(r)/ NOUN [*plural* **discoverers**] a person who finds something for the first time

• **discovery** /dɪsˈkʌvərɪ/ NOUN [*plural* **discoveries**] when someone discovers something, or the thing they discover □ *+ of the discovery of America* ▣ *He made a surprising discovery.*

discredit /dɪsˈkredɪt/ ▶ VERB [**discredits, discrediting, discredited**]
1 to prove that something is wrong or not true □ *As each slimming product is discredited a new one comes along.*
2 to damage someone's reputation so they lose respect □ *Her rivals have tried to discredit her.*
▶ NOUN, NO PLURAL loss of respect or damage to someone's reputation □ *Some pupils have brought discredit on the school by misbehaving on the buses.*

discreet /dɪˈskriːt/ ADJECTIVE careful not to say or do things that attract attention or that could cause trouble □ *I wish you'd be a little more discreet.*

• **discreetly** /dɪˈskriːtlɪ/ ADVERB in a discreet way □ *He left discreetly.*

discrepancy /dɪˈskrepənsɪ/ NOUN [*plural* **discrepancies**] a difference between things that should be the same □ *The auditors discovered discrepancies in the accounts.*

discretion /dɪˈskreʃən/ NOUN, NO PLURAL
1 the quality of being careful not to embarrass or cause trouble for others □ *Please behave with discretion in all matters concerning his financial affairs*
2 the right or skill to make judgments and decisions □ *Increases in salary are at the discretion of the Board*

• **discretionary** /dɪˈskreʃənərɪ/ ADJECTIVE (a) based on what someone decides, not on a rule or a right (b) *discretionary payments*

discriminate /dɪˈskrɪmɪneɪt/ VERB [**discriminates, discriminating, discriminated**]
1 to treat someone unfairly because of their colour,

religion, sex, etc. □ *Some employers were accused of discriminating against women.*
2 to recognize differences between things □ *They asked the children to discriminate between different shapes.*

• **discriminating** /dɪsˈkrɪmɪneɪtɪŋ/ ADJECTIVE able to make good judgments about the quality of something □ *Our more discriminating clients tend to choose the organic meat.*

• **discrimination** /dɪsˌkrɪmɪˈneɪʃən/ NOUN, NO PLURAL
1 treating people unfairly because of their colour, religion, sex, etc. ⊞ *racial discrimination* ⊞ *They have suffered discrimination.*
2 the ability to judge the quality of something

• **discriminatory** /dɪsˈkrɪmɪnətərɪ/ ADJECTIVE treating people unfairly because of their colour, religion, sex, etc. □ *These rules are discriminatory.*

discus /ˈdɪskəs/ NOUN [plural **discuses**] a heavy disc that is thrown as a sport

discuss /dɪsˈkʌs/ VERB [**discusses, discussing, discussed**] to talk about something □ *You should try to discuss these issues with your wife.* □ **+ question word** *We have been discussing whether or not to replace them.*

> ► Note that when you use the verb **discuss**, you must say what you are discussing:
> ✓ *I must discuss the problem with Angela.*
> ✗ *I must discuss with Angela.*

• **discussion** /dɪsˈkʌʃən/ NOUN [plural **discussions**] when people discuss something □ **+ about** *We got into a discussion about politics.* □ **+ between** *There have been weeks of discussion between US and Chinese officials.* ⊞ *The two sides have agreed to hold discussions next week.* □ *There are three options under discussion.*

disdain /dɪsˈdeɪn/ NOUN, NO PLURAL a feeling that you do not like or respect someone or something □ *He could not hide his disdain for Thomas.*

• **disdainful** /dɪsˈdeɪnful/ ADJECTIVE showing disdain □ *a disdainful expression*

disease /dɪˈziːz/ NOUN [plural **diseases**]
1 an illness □ **+ of** *Multiple sclerosis is a disease of the nervous system.* ⊞ *He developed heart disease.* ⊞ *The infection can cause liver disease.*
2 *no plural* illness generally □ *Poor hygiene leads to the spread of disease.* □ *Thousands died of disease and hunger.*

• **diseased** /dɪˈziːzd/ ADJECTIVE not healthy because of an illness □ *He had surgery to remove the diseased tissue.*

disembark /ˌdɪsemˈbɑːk/ VERB [**disembarks, disembarking, disembarked**] a formal word meaning to get off a boat or an aircraft

disenchanted /ˌdɪsɪnˈtʃɑːntɪd/ ADJECTIVE if you are disenchanted with something, you are no longer as enthusiastic about it as you were before

• **disenchantment** /ˌdɪsɪnˈtʃɑːntmənt/ NOUN, NO PLURAL when you become disenchanted with something □ *Life in Russia added to his disenchantment with communism.*

disfigure /dɪsˈfɪɡə(r)/ VERB [**disfigures, disfiguring, disfigured**] to spoil the look of something □ *Her face was disfigured by the attack.*

disgrace /dɪsˈɡreɪs/ ► NOUN, NO PLURAL
1 when someone loses respect because of something they have done □ *It's no disgrace to come last if you tried hard.* □ *You have brought disgrace to your family.*
2 in disgrace if you are in disgrace, other people are angry with you □ *Debbie's in disgrace for staying out all night.*
3 someone or something very bad or unacceptable ⊞ *I think it's an absolute disgrace that this has taken so long.* □ *He's a disgrace to his profession.*
► VERB [**disgraces, disgracing, disgraced**] to lose other people's respect because of your behaviour □ *I disgraced myself and my family.*

• **disgraceful** /dɪsˈɡreɪsful/ ADJECTIVE very bad or shocking ⊞ *I think their behaviour was absolutely disgraceful.* □ *There were disgraceful scenes at the end of the evening.*

• **disgracefully** /dɪsˈɡreɪsfulɪ/ ADVERB very badly □ *They treated him disgracefully.*

disgruntled /dɪsˈɡrʌntəld/ ADJECTIVE disappointed, unhappy or angry about something

disguise /dɪsˈɡaɪz/ ► NOUN [plural **disguises**] something you wear to change your appearance so that people do not recognize you □ *He left the hotel in disguise.*
► VERB [**disguises, disguising, disguised**]
1 to hide something such as your feelings or the truth □ *She couldn't disguise the fact that she was disappointed.*
2 to put a disguise on someone □ *She disguised herself as a tourist.*
3 to make something look, sound or seem like something else □ *He had an explosive device disguised as a laptop computer.*

disgust /dɪsˈɡʌst/ ► NOUN, NO PLURAL a strong feeling that you do not like or approve of something □ *The sight of the worms filled Luisa with disgust.*
► VERB [**disgusts, disgusting, disgusted**] to make someone feel disgust □ *They were disgusted by what they saw.* □ *It disgusts me that people can behave that way.*

• **disgusted** /dɪsˈɡʌstɪd/ ADJECTIVE feeling disgust □ *Alan gave her a disgusted look.*

• **disgusting** /dɪsˈɡʌstɪŋ/ ADJECTIVE
1 extremely unpleasant □ *a disgusting mess* ⊞ *It looked absolutely disgusting.*
2 very bad or shocking □ *disgusting behaviour*

dish /dɪʃ/ NOUN [plural **dishes**]
1 a plate or bowl for food □ *Cover the dish with a lid.* 🔁 *a pile of dirty dishes* 🔁 *I'll wash the dishes.*
2 food that has been prepared for eating □ *a fish dish* 🔁 *The restaurant serves traditional dishes.*
3 a round piece of equipment that receives television signals 🔁 *a satellite dish*
♦ PHRASAL VERBS [**dishes, dishing, dished**] **dish something out**
1 an informal word meaning to give or say things to people without much thought or care □ *My job's not just about dishing out pills.* □ *He's always dishing out advice.*
2 to serve food □ *I began dishing the rice out.* **dish something up** to serve food □ *She dished up some hot soup.*

dishcloth /'dɪʃklɒθ/ NOUN [plural **dishcloths**] a small cloth you use in the kitchen for washing dishes

disheartened /dɪs'hɑːtənd/ ADJECTIVE feeling less hope or confidence about something □ *Don't get disheartened.*
● **disheartening** /dɪs'hɑːtənɪŋ/ ADJECTIVE making you feel less hope or confidence □ *The results are disheartening.*

disheveled /dɪ'ʃevəld/ ADJECTIVE the US spelling of dishevelled

dishevelled /dɪ'ʃevəld/ ADJECTIVE with untidy hair and clothes □ *He looked slightly dishevelled.*

dishonest /dɪs'ɒnɪst/ ADJECTIVE not telling the truth, or doing things that are wrong or illegal □ *I didn't do anything dishonest.* □ *It would be dishonest to hide it from him.*
● **dishonestly** /dɪs'ɒnɪstlɪ/ ADVERB in a dishonest way □ *He obtained the money dishonestly.*
● **dishonesty** /dɪs'ɒnɪstɪ/ NOUN, NO PLURAL being dishonest □ *There were accusations of dishonesty and corruption.*

dishonor /dɪs'ɒnə(r)/ NOUN, NO PLURAL the US spelling of dishonour
● **dishonorable** /dɪs'ɒnərəbəl/ ADJECTIVE the US spelling of dishonourable
● **dishonorably** /dɪs'ɒnərəblɪ/ ADVERB the US spelling of dishonourably

dishonour /dɪs'ɒnə(r)/ NOUN, NO PLURAL when someone loses people's respect because of their bad behaviour □ *They brought dishonour on the whole army.*
● **dishonourable** /dɪs'ɒnərəbəl/ ADJECTIVE not honest and not deserving respect □ *He would do nothing dishonourable, even to save himself.*
● **dishonourably** /dɪs'ɒnərəblɪ/ ADVERB in a dishonourable way □ *You acted dishonourably.*

dishwasher /'dɪʃwɒʃə(r)/ NOUN [plural **dishwashers**] a machine for washing things such as plates, cups, etc. after a meal

disillusion /ˌdɪsɪ'luːʒən/ VERB [disillusions, disillusioning, disillusioned] to make you disappointed in something that you liked or approved of before □ *I'm sorry to disillusion you, but he's not really an actor.*
● **disillusioned** /ˌdɪsɪ'luːʒənd/ ADJECTIVE disappointed in something you liked or approved of before □ *I was feeling disillusioned with university and wondering whether to leave.*
● **disillusionment** /ˌdɪsɪ'luːʒənmənt/ NOUN, NO PLURAL the feeling of being disillusioned □ *He shared my disillusionment with the present government.*

disinfect /ˌdɪsɪn'fekt/ VERB [disinfects, disinfecting, disinfected] to clean something with a substance that destroys bacteria that might cause disease □ *All surfaces should be disinfected regularly.*
● **disinfectant** /ˌdɪsɪn'fektənt/ NOUN [plural **disinfectants**] a substance that kills bacteria

disintegrate /dɪs'ɪntɪgreɪt/ VERB [disintegrates, disintegrating, disintegrated]
1 to break into pieces □ *The plane disintegrated on impact.*
2 to become much worse or to fail □ *The country disintegrated into civil war.* □ *Her marriage had disintegrated.*
● **disintegration** /dɪsˌɪntɪ'greɪʃən/ NOUN, NO PLURAL the process of disintegrating

disinterested /dɪs'ɪntrəstɪd/ ADJECTIVE not being involved in something, and so able to make a fair judgment □ *A disinterested judge will make a fair decision.*

disjointed /dɪs'dʒɔɪntɪd/ ADJECTIVE confused and not in a clear order □ *She could only give a very disjointed account of what had happened.*

disk /dɪsk/ NOUN [plural **disks**]
1 a round flat object that computers use to store information on. A computing word □ *Insert a disk into drive D.* 🔁 *It requires at least 600MB of disk space.*
2 the US spelling of disc

disk drive /'dɪsk ˌdraɪv/ NOUN [plural **disk drives**] the part of a computer that reads information from disks. A computing word.

dislike /dɪs'laɪk/ ▶ VERB [dislikes, disliking, disliked] to not like someone or something □ *She disliked the idea of the children travelling alone.* □ *He disliked dentists intensely.* □ *+ ing I dislike having to get up early.*
▶ NOUN [plural **dislikes**] something you dislike or the feeling of disliking something or someone □ *He had a dislike of crowds.* 🔁 *They took an instant dislike to each other.*

dislocate /'dɪsləkeɪt/ VERB [dislocates, dislocating, dislocated] to move a bone in your body out of its correct position 🔁 *Tom dislocated his shoulder in a rugby match.*

dislodge /dɪs'lɒdʒ/ VERB [dislodges, dislodging, dislodged] to move something which was fixed in a position □ *The strong wind dislodged tiles from the roof.*

disloyal /dɪs'lɔɪəl/ ADJECTIVE not loyal to someone you should support □ *She felt it would be disloyal to her brother.*

• **disloyalty** /dɪs'lɔɪəltɪ/ NOUN, NO PLURAL when someone is disloyal

dismal /'dɪzməl/ ADJECTIVE
1 not bright or attractive, and making you feel unhappy □ *dismal weather*
2 very bad or disappointing □ *the team's dismal performance* □ *They have a dismal record on safety.*

dismantle /dɪs'mæntəl/ VERB [dismantles, dismantling, dismantled] to separate something into several pieces □ *They dismantled the equipment and packed it into the van.*

dismay /dɪs'meɪ/ NOUN, NO PLURAL an unpleasant feeling of surprise and worry □ *We watched in dismay as Ted fell into the water.* ⊞ *To her dismay, she found her foot was stuck.* ⊞ *Campaigners expressed dismay at the decision*

• **dismayed** /dɪs'meɪd/ ADJECTIVE feeling dismay □ *I was dismayed when I heard the news.*

dismiss /dɪs'mɪs/ VERB [dismisses, dismissing, dismissed]
1 to refuse to think about or accept an idea ⊞ *He dismissed suggestions that he was planning to leave.* □ *She dismissed the idea as too expensive.*
2 to make someone leave their job □ *She was dismissed for misconduct.* □ *He was dismissed from the army.*
3 to officially decide that a court case should not continue ⊞ *The judge dismissed the case because of lack of evidence.*
4 to send someone away □ *The class were dismissed by the teacher early today.*

• **dismissal** /dɪs'mɪsəl/ NOUN [plural dismissals]
1 when someone is dismissed from their job ⊞ *He is claiming unfair dismissal.*
2 when someone dismisses an idea

• **dismissive** /dɪs'mɪsɪv/ ADJECTIVE not treating something or someone as important □ *He made a dismissive gesture with his hand.*

• **dismissively** /dɪs'mɪsɪvlɪ/ ADVERB in a dismissive way □ *She spoke dismissively of her rival's work.*

dismount /ˌdɪs'maʊnt/ VERB [dismounts, dismounting, dismounted] to get off a bicycle or a horse

disobedience /ˌdɪsə'biːdɪəns/ NOUN, NO PLURAL when someone does not do what they are told to do

• **disobedient** /ˌdɪsə'biːdɪənt/ ADJECTIVE not doing what you are told to do □ *a disobedient dog* □ *He's rude and disobedient.*

• **disobey** /ˌdɪsə'beɪ/ VERB [disobeys, disobeying, disobeyed] to not do what you are told to do □ *How dare you disobey me!*

disorder /dɪs'ɔːdə(r)/ NOUN [plural disorders]
1 an illness □ *This could help to treat sleep disorders.*
2 when something is confused or badly organized □ *The meeting broke up in disorder.*
3 violent, uncontrolled behaviour by groups of people □ *There have been two nights of disorder in the city.*

• **disorderly** /dɪs'ɔːdəlɪ/ ADJECTIVE
1 behaving badly ⊞ *disorderly conduct*
2 untidy or badly organized □ *a disorderly house*

disorganized or **disorganised** /dɪs'ɔːgənaɪzd/ ADJECTIVE
1 not tidy or not well organized □ *Her clothes lay in a disorganized heap.*
2 bad at making plans or doing things in an efficient way □ *I found him a very disorganized person to work with.*

disorientated /dɪs'ɔːrɪənteɪtəd/ or **disoriented** /dɪs'ɔːrɪəntɪd/ ADJECTIVE confused about where you are or what is happening

• **disorientation** /dɪsˌɔːrɪən'teɪʃən/ NOUN, NO PLURAL when you are disorientated □ *She experienced feelings of panic and disorientation.*

disown /dɪs'əʊn/ VERB [disowns, disowning, disowned] to say that you do not want to have any connection with someone, especially your children □ *Her parents disowned her when she left the religion.*

disparage /dɪ'spærɪdʒ/ VERB [disparages, disparaging, disparaged] to say that someone or something is not very good □ *His comments were not intended to disparage the staff.*

• **disparagement** /dɪ'spærɪdʒmənt/ NOUN, NO PLURAL when someone disparages someone or something □ *There's so much disparagement of charitable work these days.*

• **disparaging** /dɪ'spærɪdʒɪŋ/ ADJECTIVE criticizing someone or something □ *We can do without your disparaging comments.*

• **disparagingly** /dɪ'spærɪdʒɪŋlɪ/ ADVERB in a disparaging way □ *He wrote disparagingly about modern poetry.*

disparity /dɪ'spærətɪ/ NOUN [plural disparities] a difference between two things, for example amounts of money □ *There is a huge disparity in their incomes.*

dispassionate /dɪ'spæʃənət/ ADJECTIVE able to form opinions and make judgments without becoming emotionally involved

dispatch /dɪ'spætʃ/ VERB [dispatches, dispatching, dispatched] a formal word meaning to send something or someone somewhere □ *The parcel was dispatched on the 29th.* □ *The navy dispatched a helicopter to help in the search.*

dispel /dɪ'spel/ VERB [dispels, dispelling, dispelled] to get rid of an idea or a feeling □ *He acted quickly to dispel investors' fears.*

dispensable /dɪ'spensəbəl/ ADJECTIVE not necessary □ *Some of these items can be regarded as dispensable extras.*

dispense /dɪ'spens/ VERB [dispenses, dispensing, dispensed]
1 to give something to people □ *The vending machines dispense cold drinks.*
2 to give people medicines □ *Only trained pharmacists can dispense the drug.*
♦ PHRASAL VERB **dispense with someone/**

something to stop using or to get rid of someone or something □ *He has dispensed with the services of his coach.*

• **dispenser** /dɪˈspensə(r)/ NOUN [plural **dispensers**] a machine that dispenses something □ *a cash dispenser* □ *a water dispenser*

dispersal /dɪˈspɜːsəl/ NOUN, NO PLURAL the action of dispersing people or things

disperse /dɪˈspɜːs/ VERB [**disperses, dispersing, dispersed**] to separate people or things and make them go in different directions, usually to get rid of them, or to separate in this way □ *The crowd is now beginning to disperse.*

displace /dɪsˈpleɪs/ VERB [**displaces, displacing, displaced**]
1 to make someone leave their home or country □ *Thousands of people were displaced during the war.*
2 to take the place of someone or something □ *Their party hopes to displace the military government.*
• **displacement** /dɪsˈpleɪsmənt/ NOUN, NO PLURAL when someone or something is displaced

display /dɪˈspleɪ/ ▶ NOUN [plural **displays**]
1 things which are arranged or presented for people to look at □ **+ of** *a display of the children's work* 🕮 *a fireworks display*
2 on display arranged for people to look at □ *The painting is on display at the National Gallery.*
3 when someone shows a particular feeling or quality □ **+ of** *It was a very public display of affection.* □ *They were impressed by her display of courage.*
4 the way you see things on a computer screen □ *You can change the display so that it's bigger.*
▶ VERB [**displays, displaying, displayed**]
1 to arrange things for people to look at □ *The treasure will be displayed in the museum for two months.* □ *All offices must display no smoking signs.*
2 to show a particular feeling or quality □ *The men displayed great courage.* □ *She displayed an early talent for driving.*
3 to show something on a computer screen □ *The pictures were displayed on a big screen.*

displease /dɪsˈpliːz/ VERB [**displeases, displeasing, displeased**] a formal word meaning to annoy someone □ *He was displeased with their performance.*
• **displeasure** /dɪsˈpleʒə(r)/ NOUN, NO PLURAL when someone is displeased

disposable /dɪˈspəʊzəbəl/ ADJECTIVE a disposable product is meant to be used and then thrown away □ *disposable nappies* □ *a disposable razor*

disposal /dɪˈspəʊzəl/ NOUN, NO PLURAL
1 getting rid of something 🕮 *We are using new methods of waste disposal.* □ *There are strict regulations about the disposal of chemicals.*
2 at your disposal available for you to use □ *There will be a car at your disposal.*

dispose /dɪˈspəʊz/
♦ PHRASAL VERB [**disposes, disposing, disposed**]

dispose of something to get rid of something □ *Where can I dispose of my old fridge?*

disposition /ˌdɪspəˈzɪʃən/ NOUN, NO PLURAL someone's character and the way they usually behave □ *This ride is not for those of a nervous disposition.*

disproportionate /ˌdɪsprəˈpɔːʃənət/ ADJECTIVE bigger or smaller than is right or reasonable when compared with something else □ *We feel we are paying a disproportionate share of the costs.*
• **disproportionately** /ˌdɪsprəˈpɔːʃənətli/ ADVERB in a disproportionate way □ *Poorer households will be disproportionately affected by the price rises.*

disprove /dɪsˈpruːv/ VERB [**disproves, disproving, disproved**] to prove that something is not true □ *This new evidence seems to disprove his theory.*

dispute /dɪˈspjuːt/ ▶ NOUN [plural **disputes**] a serious disagreement about something □ *They went on strike in a dispute over pay.* 🕮 *They are trying to resolve their dispute.*
▶ VERB [**disputes, disputing, disputed**] to say that something is not true or correct □ *They dispute that they have been treated fairly.*

disqualification /dɪsˌkwɒlɪfɪˈkeɪʃən/ NOUN, NO PLURAL when someone is stopped from doing something because they have done something wrong □ *Students could face disqualification if caught with mobile phones in exams.*

disqualify /dɪsˈkwɒlɪfaɪ/ VERB [**disqualifies, disqualifying, disqualified**] to stop someone from doing something because they have done something wrong □ *Two athletes were disqualified for a false start.*

disregard /ˌdɪsrɪˈɡɑːd/ VERB [**disregards, disregarding, disregarded**] to ignore or show no interest in something □ *They have completely disregarded my instructions.*

disrepair /ˌdɪsrɪˈpeə(r)/ NOUN, NO PLURAL a bad state or condition 🕮 *The building had fallen into disrepair.*

disreputable /dɪsˈrepjʊtəbəl/ ADJECTIVE not respected or not honest □ *I had heard of his disreputable business activities.*

• **disrepute** /ˌdɪsrɪˈpjuːt/ NOUN, NO PLURAL **bring something into disrepute** a formal phrase meaning to spoil the reputation of something □ *This sort of thing brings the club into disrepute.*

disrespect /ˌdɪsrɪˈspekt/ NOUN, NO PLURAL when someone behaves without respect towards someone or something □ *He showed complete disrespect for the local culture.*
• **disrespectful** /ˌdɪsrɪˈspektfʊl/ ADJECTIVE not showing respect towards someone or something □ *disrespectful behaviour*

disrupt /dɪsˈrʌpt/ VERB [**disrupts, disrupting, disrupted**] to stop something continuing as usual □ *Traffic was disrupted because of the march.*
• **disruption** /dɪsˈrʌpʃən/ NOUN [plural **disruptions**] when something is disrupted □ *There was disruption in the town centre caused by a burst water pipe.*

• **disruptive** /dɪsˈrʌptɪv/ ADJECTIVE causing disruption □ *Disruptive pupils will be excluded.*

dissatisfaction /ˌdɪssætɪsˈfækʃən/ NOUN, NO PLURAL when you are not pleased because something is not good enough □ *Public dissatisfaction with the government is growing.*

• **dissatisfied** /ˌdɪsˈsætɪsfaɪd/ ADJECTIVE not pleased because something is not good enough □ *She was becoming increasingly dissatisfied with her job.*

dissect /dɪˈsekt/ VERB [dissects, dissecting, dissected] to cut a dead body into pieces so that you can examine it

• **dissection** /dɪˈsekʃən/ NOUN, NO PLURAL when someone dissects something

dissent /dɪˈsent/ ▶ NOUN, NO PLURAL disagreement with an opinion or decision □ *Within the party there was dissent on some key issues.*

▶ VERB [dissents, dissenting, dissented] to disagree with an opinion or decision. A formal word.

• **dissenter** /dɪˈsentə(r)/ NOUN [plural dissenters] someone who disagrees with something □ *Political dissenters were imprisoned.*

dissertation /ˌdɪsəˈteɪʃən/ NOUN [plural dissertations] a long piece of writing on a particular subject, especially done for a university degree

disservice /dɪsˈsɜːvɪs/ NOUN, NO PLURAL **do someone a disservice** to do something that harms someone or to say something that makes other people's opinion of someone worse □ *By forbidding debate on the issue, he is doing a great disservice to the country.*

dissident /ˈdɪsɪdənt/ NOUN [plural dissidents] someone who publicly criticizes their country's government

dissimilar /dɪˈsɪmɪlə(r)/ ADJECTIVE different □ *These are two very dissimilar cultures.*

dissolve /dɪˈzɒlv/ VERB [dissolves, dissolving, dissolved]
1 to melt or be melted in liquid □ *Keep stirring until the sugar dissolves completely.* □ *Stir to dissolve the sugar.*
2 to officially end something such as a government, organization or legal arrangement □ *Parliament was dissolved in 2002.* □ *Their marriage was dissolved.*

dissuade /dɪˈsweɪd/ VERB [dissuades, dissuading, dissuaded] to persuade someone not to do something □ *She tried to dissuade her son from joining the army.*

distance /ˈdɪstəns/ NOUN [plural distances]
1 the space between things □ **+ between** *Measure the distance between the lines.* □ **+ from** *The hotel is only a short distance from the city centre.* 🔁 *He doesn't like driving long distances.*
2 in the distance if you see or hear something in the distance you see or hear it but it is a long way away □ *I could hear the sound of a train in the distance.*
3 at/from a distance at or from a place that is not close □ *I watched him from a distance.*
4 keep your distance (a) to not get too close to

something so that you are safe □ *They kept their distance from the bears.* (b) to not become involved with someone or something □ *He was advised to keep his distance from the media.*

• **distant** /ˈdɪstənt/ ADJECTIVE
1 far away in space or time □ *He heard distant voices which were getting closer.* 🔁 *The holiday seems like a distant memory now.* 🔁 *the distant past*
2 related to you but not closely 🔁 *She's a distant relative of my husband.*
3 not paying attention, and thinking about other things □ *He seemed a bit distant.*

• **distantly** /ˈdɪstəntlɪ/ ADVERB
1 from far away □ *lights glimmered distantly*
2 distantly related belonging to the same family, but not close relations
3 without showing much emotion or interest, often because you are thinking about something else □ *She smiled distantly.*

distaste /dɪsˈteɪst/ NOUN, NO PLURAL a feeling of dislike □ *He had a distaste for any kind of gossip.*

• **distasteful** /dɪsˈteɪstful/ ADJECTIVE unpleasant □ *She found the idea very distasteful.*

distil /dɪˈstɪl/ VERB [distils, distilling, distilled] to make a liquid pure by boiling it until it becomes a gas and then cooling it. A chemistry word. 🔁 *distilled water*

• **distillery** /dɪˈstɪlərɪ/ NOUN [plural distilleries] a factory that makes strong alcoholic drinks like whisky and brandy

distinct /dɪˈstɪŋkt/ ADJECTIVE
1 certain 🔁 *Winning the race remains a distinct possibility.* 🔁 *He had a distinct advantage over his rivals.*
2 easy to see, hear, smell etc. □ *Green tea has a distinct flavour.*
3 different □ *The two languages are quite distinct.*

• **distinction** /dɪˈstɪŋkʃən/ NOUN [plural distinctions]
1 a difference 🔁 *The terrorists made no distinction between military and civilian targets.*
2 something that makes someone or something different 🔁 *She had the distinction of being the first female airline pilot.*

• **distinctive** /dɪˈstɪŋktɪv/ ADJECTIVE different and easy to recognize □ *She has a very distinctive voice.*

distinguish /dɪˈstɪŋgwɪʃ/ VERB [distinguishes, distinguishing, distinguished]
1 to see a difference between things □ *If you're colour blind, you have difficulties distinguishing green from red.*
2 to be the quality that makes someone or something different □ *It's his intelligence as an actor that distinguishes him from other actors of his generation.*
3 to be able to hear or see something. A formal word. □ *In the dark I could just distinguish the shape of a man outside the window.*

• **distinguished** /dɪˈstɪŋgwɪʃt/ ADJECTIVE successful and respected □ *a distinguished professor* 🔁 *He had a long and distinguished career in the army.*

distort /dɪ'stɔːt/ VERB [distorts, distorting, distorted]
1 to change information so that it is not correct □ *He accused the government of distorting the facts.*
2 to change the shape or sound of something so that it seems strange □ *The microphone distorted his voice.*
• **distortion** /dɪ'stɔːʃən/ NOUN, NO PLURAL distorting something □ *This is a deliberate distortion of the truth.*

distract /dɪ'strækt/ VERB [distracts, distracting, distracted] to take someone's attention away from something □ *Advertisements at the side of the road can distract drivers.*
• **distracted** /dɪ'stræktɪd/ ADJECTIVE not able to think about something because you are thinking about something else □ *He looked distracted.*
• **distraction** /dɪ'strækʃən/ NOUN [plural distractions] something that takes your attention away from something □ *I can't work with all these distractions.*

distraught /dɪ'strɔːt/ ADJECTIVE extremely upset □ *They showed the distraught parents on television.*

distress /dɪ'stres/ ► NOUN, NO PLURAL when someone is upset □ *I didn't want to cause them any distress.*
► VERB [distresses, distressing, distressed] to upset someone
• **distressed** /dɪ'strest/ ADJECTIVE upset □ *He was too distressed to talk about it.*
• **distressing** /dɪ'stresɪŋ/ ADJECTIVE making someone feel very upset □ *It has been a very distressing time for me and my family.*

distribute /dɪ'strɪbjuːt/ VERB [distributes, distributing, distributed]
1 to give something to a lot of people □ *Please distribute the leaflets to your friends.*
2 to supply something to shops and companies □ *The company manufactures and distributes drinks.*
• **distribution** /ˌdɪstrɪ'bjuːʃən/ NOUN, NO PLURAL
1 the process of giving something to a group of people □ *He organized the distribution of food among the refugees.*
2 the way that something is shared or exists among a group of people □ *The distribution of wealth is not equal.*
3 the process of supplying things to shops and companies □ *He is involved in the marketing and distribution of new products.*
• **distributor** /dɪ'strɪbjutə(r)/ NOUN [plural distributors] a company that supplies goods to shops or companies

district /'dɪstrɪkt/ NOUN [plural districts] a part of a country or city □ *Shanghai's business district*

distrust /dɪs'trʌst/ ► NOUN, NO PLURAL a feeling that you cannot trust someone □ *Many people have a deep distrust of the government.*
► VERB [distrusts, distrusting, distrusted] to not trust someone or something

disturb /dɪ'stɜːb/ VERB [disturbs, disturbing, disturbed]
1 to interrupt what someone is doing □ *I'm sorry to disturb you, but I need to ask you a question.*
2 to upset or worry someone □ *The incident had disturbed him.*
3 to move something and change its position □ *I knew that someone had been at my desk because the papers had been disturbed.*
• **disturbance** /dɪ'stɜːbəns/ NOUN [plural disturbances]
1 an occasion when people fight or shout in a public place □ *There was a disturbance in the street last night.*
2 something that interrupts what you are doing □ *We hope that the event won't cause any disturbance to local residents.*
3 a change in the way your mind or a part of your body works □ *The drug can cause visual disturbances.*
• **disturbed** /dɪ'stɜːbd/ ADJECTIVE
1 upset or worried □ *He was deeply disturbed by the news.*
2 having serious mental or emotional problems □ *a disturbed child*
• **disturbing** /dɪ'stɜːbɪŋ/ ADJECTIVE making you feel upset or worried □ *She found the violence in the film disturbing.*

disused /ˌdɪs'juːzd/ ADJECTIVE not used any more □ *a disused railway station*

ditch /dɪtʃ/ ► NOUN [plural ditches] a long narrow hole at the side of a field or road
► VERB [ditches, ditching, ditched] an informal word meaning to get rid of something or someone

dither /'dɪðə(r)/ VERB [dithers, dithering, dithered] to be unable to make a decision □ *He was dithering over what to do.*

ditto /'dɪtəʊ/ ► ADVERB used for saying that something else is also true, to avoid repeating words □ *You can recycle empty cans and ditto bottles.*
► NOUN [plural dittos] the mark " that you write under a word in a list to show that you want to repeat that word

dive /daɪv/ ► VERB [dives, diving, dived]
1 to jump into water with your arms and head first □ **+ into** *Sasha dived into the pool.*
2 to swim under water using special equipment
3 to go down quickly through the air □ *She saw the plane suddenly dive.*
4 to quickly move somewhere □ *He dived behind the door when she came in.* □ *I went home and dived into the shower.*
► NOUN [plural dives]
1 a jump into water with your arms and head first
2 a time when you swim under water using special equipment
3 when something moves quickly down through the air ⊞ *The plane went into a steep dive.*
4 a sudden movement towards something ⊞ *The robbers made a dive for the open window.*
• **diver** /'daɪvə(r)/ NOUN [plural divers] someone who swims under water using special equipment

diverge /daɪˈvɜːdʒ/ VERB [diverges, diverging, diverged] to become different □ *Accounts of what happened after this point diverge dramatically.*
• **divergence** /daɪˈvɜːdʒəns/ NOUN [plural divergences] when two things become different □ *a divergence of opinion*

diverse /daɪˈvɜːs/ ADJECTIVE of very different types □ *He has appeared in a diverse range of films.*
• **diversify** /daɪˈvɜːsɪfaɪ/ VERB [diversifies, diversifying, diversified] to start to sell different products or offer different services □ *Many farms have diversified into holiday accommodation.*

diversion /daɪˈvɜːʃən/ NOUN [plural diversions]
1 something that is intended to take your attention away from something 🗣 *The younger boys created a diversion while the older ones stole the bike.*
2 a change in the way that something, especially money, is used □ *This has resulted in a diversion of funds to other projects.*
3 a different route for traffic because the usual one is closed
4 something you do so that you are not bored. A formal word. □ *Exploring the museum is a pleasant diversion for a rainy day.*

diversity /daɪˈvɜːsətɪ/ NOUN, NO PLURAL when there are many different types of people or things □ *Australia's cultural diversity*

divert /daɪˈvɜːt/ VERB [diverts, diverting, diverted]
1 to make something go in a different direction □ *Traffic was diverted because of an accident.*
2 to use something for a different purpose □ *The government should divert the money into education.*
3 **divert attention from** to take someone's attention away from something that you do not want them to notice □ *The country is keen to divert attention from its nuclear programme.*

divide /dɪˈvaɪd/ VERB [divides, dividing, divided]
1 to separate into parts, or to separate something into parts □ **+ into** *Divide the class into teams of five.* □ *The cell divides and becomes two cells.*
2 to separate something and give a part of it to several people □ **+ up** *They divided up the money.* □ **+ between** *She divided the cake between the children.*
3 to keep two areas separate □ **+ from** *A high wall divides our garden from theirs.*
4 to make a lot of people disagree □ *The decision has divided the community.*
5 to find how many times one number contains another number. A maths word. □ **+ by** *If you divide 12 by 3, you get 4.* □ *12 divided by 3 is 4.*
• **divided** /dɪˈvaɪdɪd/ ADJECTIVE if a group of people are divided, they do not agree about something □ *Experts are divided over the cause of the disease.* 🗣 *The country is deeply divided.*

dividend /ˈdɪvɪdend/ NOUN [plural dividends] an amount of money that you get regularly if you own shares in a company

divine /dɪˈvaɪn/ ADJECTIVE coming from God, or to do with God □ *divine punishment*

diving /ˈdaɪvɪŋ/ NOUN, NO PLURAL
1 the sport of swimming under water with special equipment
2 the sport of jumping into water with your arms and head first
➡ go to **scuba diving**

divisible /dɪˈvɪzəbəl/ ADJECTIVE able to be divided exactly □ *12 is divisible by 2, 3, 4 and 6.*

division /dɪˈvɪʒən/ NOUN [plural divisions]
1 *no plural* the process of separating people or things into groups or parts □ *cell division*
2 *no plural* the way something is shared between people □ **+ of** *We need a more equal division of power between governments.*
3 disagreement □ **+ between** *This created divisions between the police and the military.* 🗣 *There are deep divisions within the Democratic Party.*
4 *no plural* when you calculate how many times one number contains another number. A maths word.
5 a group within a large organization □ *He heads the company's sales and marketing division.*
6 one of several groups that sports teams or players are divided into 🗣 *The football team is in the top division.*

divisive /dɪˈvaɪsɪv/ ADJECTIVE causing disagreement 🗣 *a divisive issue*

divisor /dɪˈvaɪzə(r)/ NOUN [plural divisors] a number by which another number is divided. A maths word.

divorce /dɪˈvɔːs/ ▶ NOUN [plural divorces] the legal ending of a marriage 🗣 *We're getting a divorce.*
▶ VERB [divorces, divorcing, divorced] to legally end your marriage □ *His parents divorced when he was six.* □ *Julia is divorcing her husband.*
• **divorced** /dɪˈvɔːst/ ADJECTIVE
1 **get divorced** to legally end your marriage □ *My parents got divorced when I was six.*
2 having ended your marriage legally □ *Holmes is a divorced father of three.*
• **divorcee** /dɪvɔːˈsiː/ NOUN [plural divorcees] someone whose marriage has legally ended

divulge /daɪˈvʌldʒ/ VERB [divulges, divulging, divulged] to tell someone secret information □ *He refused to divulge any details of the agreement.*

DIY /ˌdiːaɪˈwaɪ/ ABBREVIATION do-it-yourself; when you make or repair things in the home yourself □ *DIY stores*

dizzy /ˈdɪzɪ/ ADJECTIVE [dizzier, dizziest] feeling as if everything around you is moving and you are going to fall 🗣 *You'll get dizzy if you spin round like that.* 🗣 *She's been suffering from dizzy spells.*

DJ /ˌdiːˈdʒeɪ/ ABBREVIATION disc jockey; someone who plays music in a club or on the radio

DNA /ˌdiːenˈeɪ/ ABBREVIATION deoxyribonucleic acid; the substance in the cells of living things that controls what they are like. A biology word.

do /duː/ ► AUXILIARY VERB [does, doing, did, done]
1 used with another verb to make questions and negative sentences □ *Do you want another drink?* □ *I don't (=do not) like her husband.* □ *She doesn't (=does not) play tennis.*
2 used to avoid repeating a verb □ *'I love chocolate.' 'So do I.'* □ *They spent a lot more money than I did.*
3 used to emphasize the main verb □ *I do love Paris.* □ *She does want to come, but she's very busy.*
4 used at the end of a sentence to make it into a question □ *Lucy goes to this school, doesn't she?*

► Notice that instead of **do not**, people often say or write the short form **don't** and instead of **does not**, people often say or write the short form **doesn't**.

► VERB [does, doing, did, done]
1 to perform an action □ *What are you doing?* □ *Make sure you do your homework.* □ *What does your mother do (=what is her job)?* □ **+ with** *What have you done with the map (=where is it)?*
2 to make something or to provide a service □ *Do you do picture framing?* □ *They do great cakes.*
3 to study a subject □ *I'm doing English and French.*
4 do badly/well to make bad/good progress □ *Oleg's doing well with his swimming.*
5 How are you doing? an informal way of asking someone about their health and situation □ *Hi Carlos – how are you doing?*
6 something will do something will be enough or be suitable □ *If you haven't got walking boots, trainers will do.*
7 to do with something connected with something □ *He's writing a book – something to do with astronomy.*
8 someone could do with something someone needs something. An informal phrase. □ *I could do with a hot drink.*
♦ PHRASAL VERBS do away with something to get rid of something □ *The school has done away with its uniform.* do something up **1** to fasten a piece of clothing □ *Do your jacket up.* **2** to repair or decorate a room or building do without (something) to manage without something
► NOUN [plural dos] an informal word for a party □ *The wedding's at three and there's an evening do afterwards.*

DOB ABBREVIATION date of birth
docile /ˈdəʊsaɪl/ ADJECTIVE a docile person or animal is quiet and easy to control
dock /dɒk/ ► NOUN [plural docks]
1 the place where ships stop so goods can be taken on and off
2 the dock the place in a court where the person who is accused of a crime sits
► VERB [docks, docking, docked]
1 a ship docks when it goes into a dock

2 a spacecraft docks when it joins another spacecraft during a flight
3 to reduce the amount of money, points, etc. that someone gets, as a punishment □ *They dock your wages if you're late.*
• **docker** /ˈdɒkə(r)/ NOUN [plural dockers] someone who works at a dock and takes goods onto and off a ship
dockyard /ˈdɒkjɑːd/ NOUN [plural dockyards] a place where ships are built or repaired

doctor /ˈdɒktə(r)/ ► NOUN [plural doctors]
1 someone whose job is to treat people who are ill 🕀 *You should see a doctor if your symptoms don't improve.* □ *Could I make an appointment with Doctor Kennedy, please?*
2 the doctor's the place where a doctor works □ *Go to the doctor's if your cough isn't any better.*
3 someone who has a university qualification of the highest level □ *Doctor Smith is the head of our physics department.*
► VERB [doctors, doctored, doctoring] to change something, especially in order to trick people □ *The photo had been doctored to make her look slimmer.*
• **doctorate** /ˈdɒktərət/ NOUN [plural doctorates] a university qualification of a very high level

---

doctrine /ˈdɒktrɪn/ NOUN [plural doctrines] a set of religious or political beliefs □ *Catholic doctrine*

document ► NOUN /ˈdɒkjumənt/ [plural documents]
1 a paper with official information on it □ *Make sure you have all your travel documents with you.* 🕀 *She had to sign some legal documents.*
2 something that you write and keep on a computer. A computing word. 🕀 *How do I open a new document?*
► VERB /ˈdɒkjument/ [documents, documenting, documented] to write about something or film it in order to record information about it □ *The events have been documented in many books.*
• **documentary** /ˌdɒkjuˈmentəri/ ► NOUN [plural documentaries] a film or television programme about real people or real events □ *They made a documentary on global warming.*
► ADJECTIVE
1 a documentary programme or film is about real people or real events 🕀 *It's a new documentary series set in a school.*
2 documentary evidence or proof is in the form of a document □ *You'll need to provide documentary proof of your age before you can buy alcohol.*
• **documentation** /ˌdɒkjumenˈteɪʃən/ NOUN, NO PLURAL
1 the documents you need to prove something □ *I bought the car legally, and I have all the documentation.*
2 instructions for how to make a computer or software work

doddle /ˈdɒdəl/ NOUN **be a doddle** an informal phrase meaning to be very easy □ *The exam was a doddle.*

dodge /dɒdʒ/ ▶ VERB [**dodges, dodging, dodged**]
1 to move quickly to avoid something □ *Graeme managed to dodge out of the way before the ball hit him.*
2 to avoid doing something or talking about something 🔁 *He dodged questions about his private life.*
▶ NOUN [*plural* **dodges**] a dishonest way of avoiding something. An informal word. 🔁 *a tax dodge*
● **dodgy** /ˈdɒdʒɪ/ ADJECTIVE [**dodgier, dodgiest**] an informal word meaning not honest or not of good quality □ *I've got a dodgy knee.* □ *He's known for his dodgy deals.*

doe /dəʊ/ NOUN [*plural* **does**] a female rabbit or deer

does /dʌz/ VERB the form of the verb do that is used with **he, she** and **it**

doesn't /ˈdʌzənt/ a short way to say and write does not

dog /dɒɡ/ ▶ NOUN [*plural* **dogs**] an animal with four legs that is kept as a pet, for hunting or for guarding buildings 🔁 *The dog barks whenever anyone comes to the house.* 🔁 *He walks the dog every evening.*
▶ VERB [**dogs, dogging, dogged**] if something dogs you, it causes problems for a long time □ *He was dogged by ill health throughout his life.*

dog-eared /ˈdɒɡɪəd/ ADJECTIVE a dog-eared book or page has been used so much that the corners are bent

dogged /ˈdɒɡɪd/ ADJECTIVE very determined 🔁 *Only her dogged determination kept her going.*

dogma /ˈdɒɡmə/ NOUN [*plural* **dogmas**] a belief or a set of beliefs that people are expected to believe without questioning them □ *religious dogma*
● **dogmatic** /dɒɡˈmætɪk/ ADJECTIVE certain that you are right and expecting other people to accept this without questioning you □ *He had dogmatic views about the game.*

dogsbody /ˈdɒɡzˌbɒdɪ/ NOUN [*plural* **dogsbodies**] someone who has to do all the small and boring jobs

doldrums /ˈdɒldrəmz/ PLURAL NOUN **the doldrums** a situation in which something is not very successful □ *The industry has been in the doldrums for the last five years.*

dole /dəʊl/ NOUN, NO PLURAL **be on the dole** to get money from the government because you do not have a job
◆ PHRASAL VERB [**doles, doling, doled**] **dole something out** to give something such as money or food to people □ *The company doled out free chocolates to angry customers.*

doll /dɒl/ NOUN [*plural* **dolls**] a toy in the shape of a person

dollar /ˈdɒlə(r)/ NOUN [*plural* **dollars**] the unit of money in many countries including the US, Canada, Australia and New Zealand. The written symbol is $. □ *They've spent millions of dollars on the project.*

dollop /ˈdɒləp/ NOUN [*plural* **dollops**] an amount of soft food that you have dropped from a spoon □ *Serve the cake with a dollop of cream.*

dolphin /ˈdɒlfɪn/ NOUN [*plural* **dolphins**] an intelligent sea mammal that has grey skin and a long pointed mouth

domain /dəˈmeɪn/ NOUN [*plural* **domains**] a particular subject or activity that someone is involved in or responsible for 🔁 *The information was already in the public domain.* □ *The kitchen is my husband's domain.*

domain name /dəˈmeɪn ˌneɪm/ NOUN [*plural* **domain names**] an address on the Internet. A computing word.

dome /dəʊm/ NOUN [*plural* **domes**] a raised round roof on a building

domestic /dəˈmestɪk/ ADJECTIVE
1 to do with your home, or happening in your home □ *I hate domestic tasks like cleaning and cooking.* 🔁 *She was the victim of domestic violence.*
2 to do with one particular country and not international □ *the government's domestic policies* 🔁 *At Boston, he hoped to take a domestic flight to Seattle.*
3 a domestic animal is kept as a pet or on a farm
● **domesticated** /dəˈmestɪkeɪtɪd/ ADJECTIVE
1 a domesticated animal is one that lives with people
2 a domesticated person likes looking after their home and family

dominance /ˈdɒmɪnəns/ NOUN, NO PLURAL when someone has more influence, power, and control than other people □ *The company's dominance of the home phone market is starting to wane.*
● **dominant** /ˈdɒmɪnənt/ ADJECTIVE
1 more important, powerful or noticeable than others □ *The issue of relationships is the dominant theme of the book.*
2 wanting to control other people □ *He had a very dominant father.*
3 a dominant gene gives a child a particular characteristic even if only one parent has it. A biology word.

dominate /ˈdɒmɪneɪt/ VERB [**dominates, dominating, dominated**]
1 to have more influence, power, or success than others □ *It's a company which has dominated the insurance market.*
2 to be the most important or most noticeable feature □ *The castle dominates the landscape.* □ *The plane crash dominated the news.*
● **domination** /ˌdɒmɪˈneɪʃən/ NOUN, NO PLURAL control or power over people or things □ *The country had ambitions of world domination.*

domineering /ˌdɒmɪˈnɪərɪŋ/ ADJECTIVE wanting to control people □ *She was very domineering.*

dominoes /'dɒmɪnəʊz/ NOUN, NO PLURAL a game played with small rectangular blocks that have spots on them

donate /də'neɪt/ VERB [**donates, donating, donated**] to give something, especially money, to someone who needs it □ *He donated money to a local charity.*

• **donation** /də'neɪʃən/ NOUN [plural **donations**] something, especially money, that you give to help a person or an organization 🕮 *She made generous donations to various charities.*

done /dʌn/ PAST PARTICIPLE OF do

donkey /'dɒŋkɪ/ NOUN [plural **donkeys**] an animal that looks like a small horse with long ears

donor /'dəʊnə(r)/ NOUN [plural **donors**]
1 someone who gives part of their body for someone else to use 🕮 *Blood donors are urgently needed.*
2 someone who gives money to help a person or organization 🕮 *An anonymous donor has offered £5,000 to help find the girl's killer.*

don't /dəʊnt/ a short way to say and write do not

doodle /'du:dəl/ ► NOUN [plural **doodles**] a drawing that you do while you are thinking about something else
► VERB [**doodles, doodling, doodled**] to draw a doodle

doom /du:m/ ► NOUN, NO PLURAL when something bad is certain to happen 🕮 *I felt a sense of doom.*
► VERB if someone or something is doomed to something unpleasant, that thing is certain to happen 🕮 *The project was doomed to failure.*

• **doomed** /du:md/ ADJECTIVE certain to have a bad end □ *Investigators say the doomed flight may have been on the wrong runway.*

door /dɔ:(r)/ NOUN [plural **doors**]
1 the thing you open to get into a building, room, cupboard or vehicle 🕮 *Janie opened the door and went in.* 🕮 *She quickly closed the door.* 🕮 *There was a bell by the front door.* 🕮 *Just go and knock on the door.* □ *She closed the car door.*
2 the space in a wall where you go into a building or room □ *He was so fat he could barely get through the door.*
3 at the door if there is someone at the door, someone is waiting for you to open the door so they can come inside □ *Mum, there's someone at the door.*

doorbell /'dɔ:bel/ NOUN [plural **doorbells**] a button on the door of a building that you press to ring a bell to tell the people inside that you are there

doorknob /'dɔ:nɒb/ NOUN [plural **doorknobs**] a round handle that you use to open or close a door

doormat /'dɔ:mæt/ NOUN [plural **doormats**]
1 a piece of rough material by a door, which you clean your shoes on
2 someone who allows other people to treat them badly. An informal word.

doorstep /'dɔ:step/ NOUN [plural **doorsteps**]
1 the step in front of the door of a house □ *There was a parcel on the doorstep when I got home.*
2 on someone's doorstep very close to someone's

house □ *There are some great parks right on your doorstep.*

doorway /'dɔ:weɪ/ NOUN [plural **doorways**] the entrance to a room or building □ *He was standing in the doorway.*

dormant /'dɔ:mənt/ ADJECTIVE not active now but possibly active later □ *a dormant volcano* 🕮 *The virus can lie dormant for several years.*

dormitory /'dɔ:mətərɪ/ NOUN [plural **dormitories**] a bedroom for several people, especially in a school

DOS /dɒs/ ABBREVIATION disk operating system; the software that makes all the different parts of a computer work together. A computing word.

dosage /'dəʊsɪdʒ/ NOUN [plural **dosages**] the amount of a medicine that you should take 🕮 *Doctors put him on a high dosage of the drug.*

dose /dəʊs/ NOUN [plural **doses**]
1 an amount of medicine that you take at one time 🕮 *You get side effects if you take a high dose of the drug.*
2 a dose of something an amount of a quality □ *The debate badly needs a dose of realism.*

dossier /'dɒsɪeɪ/ NOUN [plural **dossiers**] a set of papers with information about someone or something 🕮 *The police have compiled a dossier on key gang members.*

dot /dɒt/ ► NOUN [plural **dots**]
1 a small round mark
2 the symbol . in an Internet or email address □ *Is it 'al dot wood?'* (=Is it 'al.wood?')
3 on the dot at exactly the time mentioned. An informal phrase. □ *Matilda arrived at three o'clock on the dot.*
► VERB [**dots, dotting, dotted**] if a large area is dotted with things, there are a lot of them with spaces between each thing □ *The hillside was dotted with sheep.*

dote /dəʊt/
♦ PHRASAL VERB [**dotes, doting, doted**] **dote on someone** to love someone very much □ *She dotes on her grandchildren.*

• **doting** /'dəʊtɪŋ/ ADJECTIVE loving someone very much □ *doting parents*

double /'dʌbəl/ ► ADJECTIVE
1 twice as much or twice as many □ *He was given a double dose of medicine.*
2 having or involving two parts or things which are the same □ *double doors* □ *She's a double Olympic medallist.*
3 suitable for two people 🕮 *It costs £100 a night for a double room.*
4 used when you are saying that a particular number or letter is repeated □ *You spell 'marry' m-a-double r-y.*
► NOUN [plural **doubles**]
1 twice as much □ *She gets paid double for doing the same job.*
2 a room for two people in a hotel □ *I've booked a double and two singles.*

3 doubles a tennis game played between two pairs of players
4 your double someone who looks like you very much □ *I saw your double in the street yesterday.*
▶ VERB [**doubles, doubling, doubled**] to become twice as big, or to make something become twice as big □ **+ in** *The shares have doubled in value.* □ *The drug doubles your risk of having a heart attack.*
♦ PHRASAL VERBS **double as something/someone** to have another use or job □ *The hall doubles as a dining room.* **double over/up** to bend at your waist because you are in pain or laughing a lot □ *He doubled up in pain.* DETERMINER twice as big or twice as much □ *She earns double the amount I do.*

double bass /ˌdʌbəl ˈbeɪs/ NOUN [*plural* **double basses**] a musical instrument that looks like a very large violin which you play standing up
double bed /ˌdʌbəl ˈbed/ NOUN [*plural* **double beds**] a big bed for two people
double-check /ˌdʌbəlˈtʃek/ VERB [**double-checks, double-checking, double-checked**] to check something again so that you are completely sure □ *He called the airport to double-check what time the flight leaves.*
double-click /ˌdʌbəlˈklɪk/ VERB [**double-clicks, double-clicking, double-clicked**] to click twice with a computer mouse. A computing word.
double-decker /ˌdʌbəlˈdekə(r)/ NOUN [*plural* **double-deckers**] a bus with two levels
double figures /ˌdʌbəl ˈfɪɡəz/ PLURAL NOUN numbers which are between 10 and 99 □ *Their score didn't even reach double figures.*
double glazing /ˌdʌbəl ˈɡleɪzɪŋ/ NOUN, NO PLURAL windows with two layers of glass in them
double helix /ˌdʌbəl ˈhiːlɪks/ NOUN [*plural* **double helixes**] the shape of a DNA molecule. A biology word.
double standard /ˌdʌbəl ˈstændəd/ NOUN [*plural* **double standards**] a way of treating people which is unfair
doubly /ˈdʌblɪ/ ADVERB extra □ *He went back to make doubly sure that the door was locked.*

doubt /daʊt/ ▶ NOUN [*plural* **doubts**]
1 a feeling of not being certain about something 🔁*Leo had serious doubts about the plan.* 🔁*I have no doubt that you will succeed.* 🔁*This raises doubts about* (=makes me not certain about) *his reliability.*
2 without (a) doubt certainly □ *She was without doubt the best singer of her generation.*
3 be in doubt if something is in doubt, it is not certain whether it will succeed or continue to exist □ *His future at the club is in doubt.*
4 no doubt used for emphasizing that something seems very certain □ *No doubt he'll be late as usual.*
▶ VERB [**doubts, doubting, doubted**] to think that something is probably not true or will probably not happen □ **+ that** *I doubt that he will agree.* 🔁*'Do you think Rebecca will come?' 'I doubt it.'*
● **doubtful** /ˈdaʊtful/ ADJECTIVE

1 probably not true, or probably not going to happen 🔁*It's doubtful whether she'll take the job.*
2 not certain about something □ *I asked Jim whether he would be here but he seemed doubtful.*

dough /dəʊ/ NOUN, NO PLURAL a mixture of flour and water for making bread
doughnut /ˈdəʊnʌt/ NOUN [*plural* **doughnuts**] a small round cake, often with a hole in the middle
dour /dʊə(r)/ ADJECTIVE [**dourer, dourest**] serious and not friendly □ *a dour expression*
dove /dʌv/ NOUN [*plural* **doves**] a white bird, used as a sign of peace
dowdy /ˈdaʊdɪ/ ADJECTIVE [**dowdier, dowdiest**] not attractive and not fashionable □ *a dowdy woman*

down /daʊn/ ▶ ADVERB
1 towards or in a lower position □ *He was sitting down.* □ *She bent down to speak to the child.* □ *I'll put the box down here.*
2 to a smaller size, amount or level □ *He cut the picture down to fit the frame.* □ *Can you turn the television down, please?*
3 along □ *I'm just going down to the post office.*
4 in or towards the south □ *We're driving down from Edinburgh tonight.*
▶ PREPOSITION
1 towards or in a lower part □ *There were tears running down his face.*
2 along □ *Rachel was walking down the road.*
▶ ADJECTIVE
1 an informal word meaning unhappy □ *You seem a bit down.*
2 if a computer or website is down, it is not working. A computing word □ *I can't book the tickets because the website's down.*
▶ VERB [**downs, downing, downed**] to drink something very quickly. An informal word. □ *He downed a whole litre of milk.*
▶ NOUN, NO PLURAL soft feathers

downcast /ˈdaʊnkɑːst/ ADJECTIVE
1 sad
2 if your eyes are downcast, you are looking down
downfall /ˈdaʊnfɔːl/ NOUN, NO PLURAL when someone suddenly loses their power and stops being successful □ *The scandal eventually led to the president's downfall.*
downhearted /ˌdaʊnˈhɑːtɪd/ ADJECTIVE feeling sad because you have not achieved something
downhill /ˌdaʊnˈhɪl/ ▶ ADVERB
1 down a slope □ *The car rolled downhill.*
2 go downhill to become worse □ *The school's gone downhill since I was there.*
▶ ADJECTIVE going down a slope □ *a downhill skiing race*
download /ˈdaʊnləʊd/ ▶ VERB [**downloads, downloading, downloaded**] to copy information, such as pictures or music, onto your computer from the Internet or another computer. A computing word.

□ *You can download music for free.* □ *The file is downloading now.*

▶ NOUN [plural **downloads**] something that you have downloaded. A computing word.

• downloadable /ˌdaʊnˈləʊdəbəl/ ADJECTIVE able to be downloaded. A computing word. □ *downloadable games*

downmarket /ˌdaʊnˈmɑːkɪt/ ADJECTIVE low in quality and price □ *downmarket shops*

downpour /ˈdaʊnpɔː(r)/ NOUN [plural **downpours**] a lot of rain that falls in a short period of time

downright /ˈdaʊnraɪt/ ADJECTIVE, ADVERB used for emphasizing something bad □ *Some of the ideas were downright silly.*

downstairs ▶ ADVERB /ˌdaʊnˈsteəz/ to or on a lower level of a building 🔁 *He went downstairs to get breakfast.* □ *The kids were all downstairs.*

▶ ADJECTIVE /ˈdaʊnsteəz/ on a lower level in a building □ *a downstairs bathroom*

downstream /ˌdaʊnˈstriːm/ ADVERB further down a river in the direction it is flowing in

downtime /ˈdaʊntaɪm/ NOUN, NO PLURAL time when a computer is not working. A computing word.

down-to-earth /ˌdaʊntəˈɜːθ/ ADJECTIVE someone who is down-to-earth accepts the true facts of their situation and does not pretend to be something that they are not

downturn /ˈdaʊntɜːn/ NOUN [plural **downturns**] a time when there is less business than usual □ *There has been a downturn in the housing market.*

downward /ˈdaʊnwəd/ ADJECTIVE towards a lower place or position □ *a downward slope*

• downwards /ˈdaʊnwədz/ or downward /ˈdaʊnwəd/ ADVERB towards a lower place or position □ *The path winds downwards to the lake.*

dowry /ˈdaʊəri/ NOUN [plural **dowries**] money and property that a woman's family gives to her husband's family when they marry

doze /dəʊz/ ▶ VERB [**dozes, dozing, dozed**] to sleep lightly for a short time

◆ PHRASAL VERB doze off to start to sleep □ *He dozed off in his armchair.*

▶ NOUN [plural **dozes**] a short sleep 🔁 *I had a doze after lunch.*

dozen /ˈdʌzən/ NOUN [plural **dozens**]
1 twelve □ *a dozen eggs* 🔁 *There were about two dozen* (=24) *people at the party.* 🔁 *I read half a dozen* (=6) *pages.*
2 dozens of something an informal phrase meaning a lot of something □ *He's been in dozens of films.*

dozy /ˈdəʊzi/ ADJECTIVE [**dozier, doziest**]
1 feeling as if you want to sleep □ *The heat was making me dozy.*
2 an informal word meaning stupid

Dr ABBREVIATION doctor. The abbreviation is used in writing. □ *Dr Smith*

drab /dræb/ ADJECTIVE [**drabber, drabbest**] not interesting and not bright in colour □ *She was wearing a drab grey cardigan.*

draft /drɑːft/ ▶ NOUN [plural **drafts**]
1 a piece of writing that is not in its final form 🔁 *This is just the first draft of my essay.*
2 the US spelling of draught

▶ VERB [**drafts, drafting, drafted**] to write something that you will change before you finish it □ *He was drafting a letter to his boss.*

draftsman /ˈdrɑːftsmən/ NOUN [plural **draftsmen**] another spelling of draughtsman

drag /dræg/ ▶ VERB [**drags, dragging, dragged**]
1 to pull something along the ground □ *Thomas came out of school, dragging his school bag behind him.*
2 to pull someone or something strongly or violently □ *The police dragged him out of the car.*
3 to make someone go somewhere when they do not want to □ *Mum dragged me round the shops all morning.*
4 if time or an event drags, it seems to pass very slowly because you are bored
5 to move words or pictures on a computer screen by pulling them with a mouse. A computing word.

◆ PHRASAL VERBS drag someone into something to make someone become involved in an unpleasant situation □ *I wish you two wouldn't drag me into your arguments.* drag on to continue for too long □ *The play seemed to drag on for hours.*

▶ NOUN, NO PLURAL an informal word for something that is annoying or boring □ *Choir practice was always such a drag.*

drag and drop /ˌdræg ən ˈdrɒp/ VERB [**drags and drops, dragging and dropping, dragged and dropped**] to move words or pictures on a computer screen by pulling them with a mouse. A computing word.

dragon /ˈdrægən/ NOUN [plural **dragons**] a big imaginary animal with wings, that breathes fire from its mouth

dragonfly /ˈdrægənflaɪ/ NOUN [plural **dragonflies**] an insect with a thin colourful body and long wings

drain /dreɪn/ ▶ VERB [**drains, draining, drained**]
1 to make the liquid in something flow away □ *They had to drain the tank* □ *Drain the pasta and serve with the sauce.*
2 if a liquid drains, it flows away □ *She watched the water drain down the sink.*
3 if you drain a cup or a glass, you drink all the liquid in it
4 to make someone feel very tired □ *The work had drained him.*

▶ NOUN [plural **drains**]
1 a pipe or hole that allows waste water to flow away □ *The drain was blocked.*
2 a drain on something something that uses a lot of your money □ *Childcare is a big drain on our finances.*

◆ IDIOM down the drain an informal phrase meaning wasted □ *If I quit the course, that's six hundred pounds down the drain.*

• **drainage** /'dreɪnɪdʒ/ NOUN, NO PLURAL removing waste water by systems of pipes and rivers

• **drained** /dreɪnd/ ADJECTIVE extremely tired □ *After being in court all day, I felt completely drained.*

draining board /'dreɪnɪŋ ˌbɔːd/ NOUN [plural **draining boards**] a surface next to a kitchen sink where you put wet dishes when you have washed them

drainpipe /'dreɪnpaɪp/ NOUN [plural **drainpipes**] a pipe on the outside of a building, that takes waste water down into the ground

drama /'drɑːmə/ NOUN [plural **dramas**]
1 a play at the theatre or on television ⊞ *a TV drama* ⊞ *an Australian drama series*
2 no plural plays and acting in general □ *Dan studied drama at Birmingham University.* ⊞ *She went to drama school.*
3 something exciting which happens ⊞ *They watched the drama unfold (=happen) from her bedroom window.*

• **dramatic** /drə'mætɪk/ ADJECTIVE
1 sudden and unexpected ⊞ *There has been a dramatic increase in the number of exam passes.* ⊞ *Computers have led to dramatic changes in work habits.*
2 exciting and involving activity and danger □ *He described his dramatic rescue from the sinking boat.*
3 to do with plays and the theatre □ *the dramatic works of an author*
4 dramatic behaviour is done to make other people notice you □ *Anna spread her hands in a dramatic gesture.*

• **dramatically** /drə'mætɪkəli/ ADVERB in a dramatic way □ *Prices rose dramatically last month.*

• **dramatist** /'dræmətɪst/ NOUN [plural **dramatists**] someone who writes plays

• **dramatization** or **dramatisation** /ˌdræmətaɪ'zeɪʃən/ NOUN [plural **dramatizations**] a play which is based on a book or real event □ *She won a prize for her dramatization of Edith Wharton's novel.*

• **dramatize** or **dramatise** /'dræmətaɪz/ VERB [**dramatizes, dramatizing, dramatized**]
1 to make a theatre or television play from a book or real event
2 to make a story or report more exciting than the real event

drank /dræŋk/ PAST TENSE OF **drink**

drape /dreɪp/ VERB [**drapes, draping, draped**]
1 to put cloth loosely over or around something □ *Sue draped the shawl around her shoulders.*
2 if something is draped in or with a piece of cloth, it is covered by it □ *The coffin was draped in the Australian flag.*

drapes /dreɪps/ PLURAL NOUN a US word for **curtains**

drastic /'dræstɪk/ ADJECTIVE having a very big effect ⊞ *Drastic action is needed to reduce pollution levels.*

• **drastically** /'dræstɪkəli/ ADVERB in an extreme and sudden way □ *The place has changed drastically since I was last there.*

draught /drɑːft/ NOUN [plural **draughts**]
1 a movement of air in a room which feels cold

2 draughts a game for two people who move flat, round pieces on a board that has black and white squares on it

draughtsman /'drɑːftsmən/ NOUN [plural **draughtsmen**] someone whose job is to draw plans for something such as a machine or building

draughty /'drɑːfti/ ADJECTIVE [**draughtier, draughtiest**] a draughty building or room is cold because cold air blows into it

draw /drɔː/ ▶ VERB [**draws, drawing, drew, drawn**]
1 to make a picture with a pencil or pen □ *Ellie was drawing.* ⊞ *She drew a lovely picture of a horse.*
2 to attract people □ *The programme drew 13 million viewers.* ⊞ *The festival draws crowds of up to 30,000 people.* □ **+ to** *He was drawn to Australia because of the weather.*
3 draw (someone's) attention to someone/something to make someone notice someone or something □ *I was trying not to draw attention to myself.*
4 to get a particular reaction ⊞ *The policy drew criticism from many people.*
5 to score the same number of points as someone else in a game □ *We drew 2-2.*
6 draw closer/near to move closer in time or distance □ *As they drew closer she saw a path.* □ *Election day is drawing near.*
7 draw the curtains to pull curtains so that they cover a window or do not cover a window
8 to pull something from somewhere or pull something in a particular direction. A literary word. □ *He drew a small piece of paper from his pocket.*
♦ IDIOM draw the line to not do something because you think it is wrong or too much □ *I love sweet food, but even I draw the line at her chocolate cake.*
➡ go to **draw lots**
♦ PHRASAL VERBS **draw someone into something** to involve someone in a conversation or argument □ *I won't be drawn into their dispute.* **draw on something** to use your knowledge for a particular purpose □ *He had a lot of experience to draw on.* **draw something up** to write something such as a plan or document ⊞ *They've drawn up a list of the best candidates.* **draw up** if a vehicle draws up, it stops □ *A taxi drew up outside the house.*
▶ NOUN [plural **draws**]
1 a game that ends with both players or teams having the same score ⊞ *The game ended in a draw.*
2 when a winner or two teams who will play each other in a competition are chosen by chance ⊞ *They won a car in a prize draw.*

drawback /'drɔːbæk/ NOUN [plural **drawbacks**] a disadvantage ⊞ *The only drawback is the cost.*

drawer /'drɔː(r)/ NOUN [plural **drawers**] a part of a piece of furniture that you pull out and keep things in ⊞ *He opened the drawer and got out some paper.* ⊞ *The pens are in the top drawer.*

drawing /'drɔːɪŋ/ NOUN [plural **drawings**]
1 a picture done with a pencil or pen ⊞ She did a few drawings. □ + **of** a drawing of a house
2 no plural making pictures using a pencil or pen □ Most children like drawing.

drawing pin /'drɔːɪŋ ˌpɪn/ NOUN [plural **drawing pins**] a short pin with a wide, round top that you use for fixing paper to a wall

drawl /drɔːl/ ▶ VERB [**drawls, drawling, drawled**] to speak slowly with long vowel sounds □ 'I don't know,' he drawled.
▶ NOUN, NO PLURAL a slow way of speaking with long vowel sounds

drawn /drɔːn/ PAST PARTICIPLE OF draw

dread /dred/ ▶ VERB [**dreads, dreading, dreaded**]
1 to feel worried or frightened about something that is going to happen □ We're all dreading the exams.
2 I dread to think used for saying that something that might happen is too unpleasant to think about □ If children had found the tablets, I dread to think what might have happened.
▶ NOUN, NO PLURAL a feeling of fear □ The thought of flying fills me with dread.

dreadful /'dredfʊl/ ADJECTIVE very bad □ dreadful news □ a dreadful film
● **dreadfully** /'dredfʊlɪ/ ADVERB
1 very badly □ I thought he behaved dreadfully towards her.
2 very □ I'm dreadfully sorry.

dreadlocks /'dredlɒks/ PLURAL NOUN hair that is in long twisted pieces

dream /driːm/ ▶ NOUN [plural **dreams**]
1 the things you think and see in your mind while you sleep ⊞ I had a very strange dream last night. □ + **about** I had a dream about you. ⊞ a bad dream
2 something you hope will happen □ It was always her dream to go to Hollywood.
3 in a dream not noticing what is happening around you because you are thinking of other things
4 of your dreams that is perfect for you □ She met the man of her dreams while working in New York.
▶ VERB [**dreams, dreaming, dreamt** or **dreamed**]
1 to think about and see something in your mind while you sleep □ + **that** Last night I dreamt that I was lying on a beach. □ + **about** I often dream about flying.
2 to imagine something that you would like to happen □ + **of** I've always dreamt of moving to the coast.
3 wouldn't dream of doing something used for saying that you would never do something because you think it is bad □ I would never dream of telling your secrets to anyone.

> ► Note that sense 2 of the verb **dream** is followed by **of** + the ing-form of the verb:
> ✓ I've always dreamt of owning a restaurant.
> ✗ I've always dreamt to own a restaurant.

◆ PHRASAL VERB **dream something up** to think of

something, especially something clever or unusual □ Eliza dreamt up the scheme.
▶ ADJECTIVE a dream house, wedding etc. is one that is perfect or exactly what you want □ Working in a chocolate factory would be my dream job.
● **dreamy** /'driːmɪ/ ADJECTIVE [**dreamier, dreamiest**] thinking about pleasant things and not what is happening around you □ She was a dreamy child.

dreary /'drɪərɪ/ ADJECTIVE [**drearier, dreariest**] boring □ He'd had a dreary day at the office.

dredge /dredʒ/ VERB [**dredges, dredging, dredged**] to remove mud and sand from the bottom of a lake or river
◆ PHRASAL VERB **dredge something up** to talk about something bad that happened in the past

dregs /dregz/ PLURAL NOUN the bits that are sometimes left in the bottom of a cup or glass after you have finished drinking something

drench /drentʃ/ VERB [**drenches, drenching, drenched**] if you are drenched in something, you are completely wet □ Ben was drenched in sweat.

dress /dres/ ▶ NOUN [plural **dresses**]
1 a piece of clothing for girls or women like a top and skirt joined together □ She was wearing a black dress. ⊞ a wedding dress
2 no plural clothes of a particular type ⊞ The dancers were wearing traditional Highland dress.
▶ VERB [**dresses, dressing, dressed**]
1 to put clothes on yourself or someone else ⊞ She got dressed and had breakfast. □ I'll dress the children.
2 to wear a particular style of clothes □ She always dresses smartly.
3 if you dress a cut or injury, you cover it

> ► Note that when you put clothes on yourself, you **get dressed**:
> ✓ I get dressed in the dark.
> ✗ I dress myself in the dark.

◆ PHRASAL VERB **dress up**
1 to put on clothes that make you look like someone else □ Oliver is going to dress up as a pirate.
2 to wear clothes that are more formal than the clothes you usually wear □ Can I go in jeans, or do I need to dress up?
● **dressed** /drest/ ADJECTIVE
1 wearing clothes □ Are you dressed yet?
2 wearing a particular type of clothes □ + **in** Ali was dressed in jeans and a T-shirt. □ He's always well dressed.
● **dresser** /'dresə(r)/ NOUN [plural **dressers**] a piece of furniture with a cupboard at the bottom and shelves above for keeping plates on

- **dressing** /'dresɪŋ/ NOUN [plural **dressings**]
  1 a sauce for a salad 🔁 a salad dressing.
  2 something you use to cover a cut or injury on your skin

dressing-gown /'dresɪŋgaʊn/ NOUN [plural **dressing-gowns**] a piece of clothing that looks like a long coat, which you wear in your house when you are not dressed

dress rehearsal /,dres rɪ'hɜːsəl/ NOUN [plural **dress rehearsals**] the final practice for a play or show, using all the clothes

drew /druː/ PAST TENSE OF **draw**

dribble /'drɪbəl/ VERB [dribbles, dribbling, dribbled]
  1 to let liquid come out of your mouth □ The baby was dribbling.
  2 if a liquid dribbles somewhere, it flows slowly □ Blood was dribbling from a cut on his neck.
  3 to move a ball along in front of you as you run □ He dribbled past a couple of players.

dried /draɪd/ ▶ PAST TENSE AND PAST PARTICIPLE OF **dry** □ Jill dried the glasses with a soft cloth.
  ▶ ADJECTIVE dried food or flowers have had the water taken out of them 🔁 dried fruit □ dried herbs

drier /'draɪə(r)/ NOUN [plural **driers**] another spelling of **dryer**

drift /drɪft/ ▶ VERB [drifts, drifting, drifted]
  1 to move with a current of water or air □ Smoke drifted over the city.
  2 to slowly move somewhere □ It was late and people were starting to drift away.
  3 to start to do something without having planned it □ I just drifted into teaching.
  ◆ PHRASAL VERBS **drift apart** if two people drift apart, they gradually stop being friends **drift off** to gradually start to sleep 🔁 Tom drifted off to sleep.
  ▶ NOUN [plural **drifts**]
  1 a slow and gradual change or movement □ There has been a drift away from religion, particularly among young people.
  2 a pile of snow or sand that has been blown by the wind 🔁 a snow drift
  3 get/catch someone's drift to understand the general meaning of what someone says □ I think I get your drift.

drill /drɪl/ ▶ NOUN [plural **drills**]
  1 a tool for making holes in something hard, such as stone □ an electric drill
  2 a practice so that people know what to do in a particular situation 🔁 We have a fire drill every month at school. □ a military training drill
  3 a way of teaching something by making students repeat something several times
  ▶ VERB [drills, drilling, drilled]
  1 to make a hole in something hard 🔁 She drilled a hole in the wall. □ They had to drill through rock.
  2 to teach someone something by making them do it

several times □ All staff are drilled in emergency procedures.

drink /drɪŋk/ ▶ VERB [drinks, drinking, drank, drunk]
  1 to swallow a liquid □ I drink a lot of coffee. 🔁 I'll get you something to drink.
  2 to drink alcohol □ Mark doesn't drink.
  ◆ PHRASAL VERB **drink to someone/something** to hold your glass up before you drink something, in order to wish someone good health, success etc □ Let's drink to your good health!
  ▶ NOUN [plural **drinks**]
  1 a liquid that you swallow 🔁 Can I have a drink, please? □ + of Would you like a drink of water?
  2 no plural drinks in general □ We hadn't had any food or drink all day.
  3 an alcoholic drink □ They went out for a few drinks to celebrate.
  4 no plural alcoholic drinks □ Please do not bring drink into the hostel.
- **drinker** /'drɪŋkə(r)/ NOUN [plural **drinkers**]
  1 someone who regularly drinks alcohol 🔁 He used to be a heavy drinker (=someone who regularly drinks a lot of alcohol).
  2 someone who drinks a particular type of drink □ coffee drinkers
- **drinking** /'drɪŋkɪŋ/ NOUN, NO PLURAL when someone drinks alcohol □ His drinking was becoming a problem.

drip /drɪp/ ▶ NOUN [plural **drips**]
  1 a drop of liquid □ We're trying to catch the drips in a bucket.
  2 a series of falling drops of liquid □ I could hear the drip of the bathroom tap all night.
  3 a piece of hospital equipment for putting liquids into someone's body □ He was on a drip for a week.
  ▶ VERB [drips, dripping, dripped]
  1 if a liquid drips, it falls in drops □ Water was dripping from the trees.
  2 to produce drops of liquid □ I can hear a tap dripping somewhere.

drive /draɪv/ ▶ VERB [drives, driving, drove, driven]
  1 to make a car, bus, etc. move and control where it goes and how fast it moves □ Can you drive? □ I had to drive my mother's car. □ We drove to Spain. □ She drove me to the airport.
  2 drive someone mad/crazy to annoy someone very much □ He was driving me mad with all his questions.
  3 to make someone leave a place □ + away/out of Police fired tear gas to drive away the crowd.
  4 to strongly influence someone or something □ The big banks are driving the market. □ He was driven by greed.
  ➡ go to **drive someone round the** bend, **drive someone up the** wall
  ▶ NOUN [plural **drives**]
  1 a journey in a car 🔁 We went for a drive in the country. 🔁 He began the long drive home. □ It's a two-hour drive to the coast.

2 an area in front of a house where you can put your car □ *There were two cars on the drive.*

3 a part of a computer that stores information. A computing word. □ *The PC has a standard DVD drive.*

4 an effort by a government or organization to do something □ *It's part of a recruitment drive for new nurses.*

5 no plural the wish to achieve things that makes you try hard

6 Drive used in the names of some roads □ *My address is 13 Bishop's Drive.*

drive-by /'draɪvbaɪ/ ADJECTIVE a drive-by shooting is done by someone driving past in a car

drivel /'drɪvəl/ NOUN, NO PLURAL nonsense □ *He's talking drivel.*

driven /'drɪvən/ PAST PARTICIPLE OF **drive**

driver /'draɪvə(r)/ NOUN [plural **drivers**] a person who drives a car, etc. □ *a taxi driver* □ *She's a good driver.*

driveway /'draɪvweɪ/ NOUN [plural **driveways**] an area in front of a house where you can put your car □ *There was a car parked in the driveway.*

driving /'draɪvɪŋ/ NOUN, NO PLURAL when you drive a car, etc. or the way that you drive 🗗 *Jane's having driving lessons.* □ *He was arrested for dangerous driving.*

driving licence /'draɪvɪŋ ˌlaɪsəns/ NOUN [plural **driving licences**] an official document that shows you are allowed to drive □ *He didn't have a driving licence.* 🗗 *A clean driving licence (=showing that you have never done anything wrong while driving) is essential for the job.*

drizzle /'drɪzəl/ ► NOUN, NO PLURAL very light rain ► VERB [**drizzles, drizzling, drizzled**] to rain very lightly
• **drizzly** /'drɪzli/ ADJECTIVE drizzly weather is when it is raining very lightly

drone /drəʊn/ ► VERB [**drones, droning, droned**] to make a continuous low sound □ *Helicopters droned above us.*
♦ PHRASAL VERB **drone on** to talk a lot about something boring □ *I had to listen to Nate droning on about work.*
► NOUN, NO PLURAL a continuous low sound □ *She could hear the drone of traffic outside.*

drool /druːl/ ► VERB [**drools, drooling, drooled**] to let liquid come out of your mouth □ *The dog was drooling.*
♦ PHRASAL VERB **drool over someone/something** to admire someone or something too much, in a way that is silly □ *We stood drooling over the dresses in the window.*

droop /druːp/ VERB [**droops, drooping, drooped**] to hang down □ *The flowers were starting to droop.* □ *Her head drooped slightly forwards.*

drop /drɒp/ ► VERB [**drops, dropping, dropped**]
1 to fall to the ground, or to let something fall to the ground □ *She tripped and dropped her glass.* □ *The ball dropped into the hole.*

2 to change to a lower level or amount □ *The*

temperature drops at night. □ **+ from** *The exam pass rate has dropped from 75% to 60%.*

3 to stop doing something or stop continuing with something 🗗 *He dropped everything and went to help his mother in France.* □ *They've had to drop their plans.*

4 to decide not to include someone in a team □ **+ from** *Davis was dropped from the team.*

5 if you drop someone somewhere, you take them there in your car, and then drive somewhere else yourself □ *I'll drop you at the doctor's on my way to the supermarket.*

♦ PHRASAL VERBS **drop by/in/round** to visit someone for a short time □ *Why don't you drop round for a coffee later?* **drop off** to start sleeping. An informal phrase. □ *Jim dropped off in front of the TV.* **drop someone/something off** to take someone or something to a place □ *I've got to drop this bag off at my Mum's house.* **drop out** to stop doing something before you have finished □ *She dropped out of school at the age of fifteen.*

► NOUN [plural **drops**]

1 a very small amount of a liquid □ **+ of** *Was that a drop of rain?* □ *There were some drops of blood on the floor.*

2 no plural a decrease 🗗 *There has been a sharp drop (=big drop) in profits.* □ **+ in** *There was a small drop in the number of tourists last year.*

3 no plural the distance down from a high place to the ground 🗗 *She leant over the wall, gazing down at the steep drop below.*

4 no plural a small amount of drink □ *Would you like a drop more tea?*

drop-down menu /'drɒpdaʊn ˌmenjuː/ NOUN [plural **drop-down menus**] a list of things to choose from on a computer screen that appears when you click on it

drought /draʊt/ NOUN [plural **droughts**] a time when very little rain falls 🗗 *The country is currently suffering from a severe drought.*

drove /drəʊv/ PAST TENSE OF **drive**

drown /draʊn/ VERB [**drowns, drowning, drowned**]
1 to die because of being under water and not able to breathe □ *Three soldiers drowned when their truck fell into a river.*

2 to kill someone by holding them under water
♦ PHRASAL VERB **drown out something** to stop something from being heard by making a louder sound □ *Her voice was drowned out by the sound of the music.*

drowsy /'draʊzi/ ADJECTIVE [**drowsier, drowsiest**] tired and almost asleep □ *The heat was making me drowsy.*

drudgery /'drʌdʒəri/ NOUN, NO PLURAL boring, hard work

drug /drʌg/ ► NOUN [plural **drugs**]
1 a medicine 🗗 *Doctors usually prescribe the drug for children.*

2 an illegal substance that people take to change the

way they feel 🔁 *He was on drugs* (=regularly taking drugs) 🔁 *I've never taken drugs.* 🔁 *a drug addict*
▶ VERB [**drugs, drugging, drugged**] to give someone a drug that will make them unconscious

drugstore /'drʌgstɔ:(r)/ NOUN [*plural* **drugstores**]
the US word for chemist's

drum /drʌm/ ▶ NOUN [*plural* **drums**]
1 an instrument that is round and has a skin stretched over it that you hit to make a rhythm 🔁 *He plays the drums in a band.* 🔁 *a drum kit* (=a set of drums)
2 a tall round container for liquids 🔁 *an oil drum*
▶ VERB [**drums, drumming, drummed**]
1 to hit something in a regular rhythm □ *Rain was drumming on the roof.*
2 to hit your fingers against something several times □ *He was drumming impatiently on the steering wheel.*
♦ PHRASAL VERBS **drum something into someone** to make someone understand that something is important by saying it to them many times □ *My parents drummed it into me that I had to be brave.* **drum something up** to try to get people to support you or buy things from you □ *He went to China to try to drum up new business.*
• **drummer** /'drʌmə(r)/ NOUN [*plural* **drummers**] someone who plays the drums

drunk /drʌŋk/ ▶ PAST PARTICIPLE OF **drink**
▶ ADJECTIVE having drunk too much alcohol 🔁 *He got drunk at the party.*
• **drunken** /'drʌŋkən/ ADJECTIVE having drunk too much alcohol, or involving people who have drunk too much alcohol □ *a drunken brawl*

dry /draɪ/ ▶ ADJECTIVE [**drier, driest**]
1 not wet □ *Are the clothes dry yet?*
2 with little rain 🔁 *dry weather* □ *a hot, dry summer*
3 dry hair or skin does not have enough natural oils in it □ *a shampoo for dry hair* □ *My skin gets very dry in the winter.*
4 boring to read or listen to □ *I find her writing rather dry.*
5 dry humour is funny in a way that is not obvious
6 dry wine is not sweet
▶ VERB [**dries, drying, dried**] to make something dry, or to become dry □ *He dried his hands on the towel.* □ *She hung the clothes out to dry.*
♦ PHRASAL VERBS **dry (someone/something) off** to become dry, or to make someone or something dry □ *He went swimming and then dried off in the sun.* **dry up**
1 if something dries up, there is no more available □ *Work often dries up for models when they reach 35.*
2 if a river or lake dries up, there is no water in it **dry (something) up** to dry plates, bowls, etc. after someone has washed them

dry-clean /ˌdraɪ'kli:n/ VERB [**dry-cleans, dry-cleaning, dry-cleaned**] to clean clothes with chemicals instead of water

• **dry cleaner's** /ˌdraɪ 'kli:nəz/ NOUN, NO PLURAL a shop where clothes are dry-cleaned
• **dry cleaning** /ˌdraɪ 'kli:nɪŋ/ NOUN, NO PLURAL
1 clothes that are dry-cleaned
2 cleaning clothes using a chemical instead of water
dryer /'draɪə(r)/ NOUN [*plural* **dryers**] a machine that dries wet clothes or hair
dual /'dju:əl/ ADJECTIVE having two parts 🔁 *Hening has dual Belgian/French nationality.*
dual carriageway /ˌdju:əl 'kærɪdʒweɪ/ NOUN [*plural* **dual carriageways**] a road with two lines of traffic going in each direction
dub /dʌb/ VERB [**dubs, dubbing, dubbed**]
1 to give someone or something a different name that describes them in some way □ *The ceremony was dubbed 'The invisible wedding' by Italian newspapers.*
2 to change the language in a film or television programme into a different language □ *The film has been dubbed into Russian.*
dubious /'dju:bɪəs/ ADJECTIVE
1 not sure about something □ *I'm a bit dubious about his ability to do the job.*
2 probably dishonest or not true □ *He knows some very dubious people.*
duchess /'dʌtʃɪs/ NOUN [*plural* **duchesses**] the title of a woman who has a very high social rank

duck /dʌk/ ▶ NOUN [*plural* **ducks**]
1 a water bird with short legs and a wide, flat beak □ *wild ducks*
2 *no plural* the meat from a duck □ *roast duck*
▶ VERB [**ducks, ducking, ducked**]
1 to lower your head or body so that you are not hit or seen 🔁 *Hamish ducked his head to get through the low doorway.* □ **+ behind** *He ducked behind a car when the shooting began.*
2 to avoid something difficult such as a question, subject or responsibility 🔁 *The Prime Minister ducked questions on whether taxes would be increased.*

duckling /'dʌklɪŋ/ NOUN [*plural* **ducklings**] a baby duck
duct /dʌkt/ NOUN [*plural* **ducts**]
1 a tube in your body that carries liquid □ *The tear duct is in the corner of the eye.*
2 a pipe in a building □ *heating ducts*
dud /dʌd/ ▶ NOUN [*plural* **duds**] someone or something that is not good. An informal word. □ *His next film was a dud.*
▶ ADJECTIVE not working correctly □ *a dud light bulb*

due /dju:/ ▶ ADJECTIVE
1 expected to arrive or happen □ **+ at** *The train is due at 10:15.* □ **+ in** *Their baby is due in March.* □ **+ to do something** *The project is due to start next month.*
2 needing to be paid □ *The rent is due at the beginning of the month.*
3 **due to something** because of something □ *The plane was delayed due to bad weather.*
4 if something is due to you, you deserve it or

someone owes it to you □ *He paid the money that was due to her.*

5 be due for something if you are due for something, it is time for you to have that thing □ *I'm due for a pay rise.*

6 a formal word meaning suitable and correct □ *He gave the matter due consideration.*

▶ ADVERB directly □ *London is due south of here.*

duel /'dju:əl/ NOUN [plural **duels**] in the past, a fight using weapons between two men who have argued

duet /dju:'et/ NOUN [plural **duets**] a piece of music sung or played by two people

dug /dʌg/ PAST TENSE AND PAST PARTICIPLE OF **dig**

duke /dju:k/ NOUN [plural **dukes**] a title for a man with a very high social rank

dull /dʌl/ ▶ ADJECTIVE [**duller, dullest**]

1 boring □ *It was the dullest job you could imagine.* □ *Life is never dull when John's around.*

2 not bright □ *It was a dull, grey day.*

3 a dull sound is low and not clear □ *His head hit the door with a dull thud.*

4 a dull pain is not strong but continues for a long time ▣ *She felt a dull ache in her stomach.*

▶ VERB [**dulls, dulling, dulled**] to make a feeling or sound less strong □ *He took a tablet to dull the pain.*

duly /'dju:lɪ/ ADVERB a formal word meaning at the correct time, in the correct way, or as expected □ *The new car was duly admired by friends and colleagues.*

dumb /dʌm/ ADJECTIVE [**dumber, dumbest**]

1 an informal word meaning stupid □ *He kept asking me dumb questions.*

2 not able to speak

♦ PHRASAL VERB [**dumbs, dumbing, dumbed**] **dumb (something) down** to make something so simple or easy to understand that it makes it less good □ *Television companies have been accused of dumbing down programmes.*

dumbfounded /dʌm'faʊndɪd/ ADJECTIVE extremely surprised

dummy /'dʌmɪ/ ▶ NOUN [plural **dummies**]

1 a model of a person □ *The cars are tested for crashes with dummies in them.*

2 a rubber object that a baby sucks for comfort

3 something that is made to look like something real, but is not real □ *There were two pills but one of them was a dummy.*

▶ ADJECTIVE made to look real, but not real □ *a dummy bomb*

dump /dʌmp/ ▶ VERB [**dumps, dumping, dumped**]

1 to put something somewhere quickly □ *He dumped his bag in the hall and ran upstairs.*

2 to leave something somewhere because you do not want it □ *It is not acceptable to dump toxic waste in the sea.*

3 an informal word meaning to end a relationship with your boyfriend or girlfriend □ *Dan's upset because his girlfriend's dumped him.*

▶ NOUN [plural **dumps**]

1 a place where people can leave things they do not want □ *I'm going to take the old sofa to the dump.*

2 an informal word for a dirty or untidy place □ *This flat is such a dump.*

dumpling /'dʌmplɪŋ/ NOUN [plural **dumplings**] a mixture of fat and flour in the shape of a ball, that you cook in a boiling liquid

dumpy /'dʌmpɪ/ ADJECTIVE [**dumpier, dumpiest**] an informal word meaning short and fat

dune /dju:n/ NOUN [plural **dunes**] a hill of sand

dung /dʌŋ/ NOUN, NO PLURAL the solid waste of animals

dungarees /ˌdʌŋgə'ri:z/ PLURAL NOUN trousers with a square part attached that covers your chest and pieces that go over your shoulders

dungeon /'dʌndʒən/ NOUN [plural **dungeons**] a dark underground room, used as a prison in the past

duo /'dju:əʊ/ NOUN [plural **duos**] two people who perform together ▣ *a comedy duo*

duodecimal /ˌdju:əʊ'desɪməl/ ADJECTIVE using units of 12 as the base for a system of counting. A maths word.

duodenum /ˌdju:əʊ'di:nəm/ NOUN [plural **duodenums** or **duodena**] the first part of the small intestine (=tube that food goes into to be digested), just below the stomach. A biology word.

dupe /dju:p/ VERB [**dupes, duping, duped**] to trick someone □ *The tourists were duped into handing over their money.*

duplex /'dju:pleks/ NOUN [plural **duplexes**] the US word for **semi**

duplicate¹ /'dju:plɪkeɪt/ VERB [**duplicates, duplicating, duplicated**]

1 to make a copy of something □ *Many entries in the database have been duplicated.*

2 to repeat something in exactly the same way □ *He is hoping to duplicate that success at the Olympic Games.*

duplicate² /'dju:plɪkət/ ▶ NOUN [plural **duplicates**] an exact copy □ *She sent a duplicate of the photo.*

▶ ADJECTIVE exactly the same □ *a duplicate key*

duplication /ˌdju:plɪ'keɪʃən/ NOUN, NO PLURAL

1 when something has the same purpose or effect as another thing so it is not necessary □ *To avoid duplication, each team will be assigned a particular task.*

2 copying something exactly □ *the duplication of images*

durability /ˌdjʊərə'bɪlətɪ/ NOUN, NO PLURAL the ability to stay in a good condition for a long time □ *The material is known for its durability.*

durable /'djʊərəbəl/ ADJECTIVE staying in a good condition for a long time □ *durable building materials*

duration /djʊ'reɪʃən/ NOUN, NO PLURAL the length of time that something continues. A formal word. ▣ *Hotel guests are offered a car for the duration of their stay.*

duress /dju'res/ NOUN, NO PLURAL **under duress** if you do something under duress, you do it because someone forces you to, and not because you want to.

A formal phrase. □ *The contract was signed under duress.*

during /ˈdjuərɪŋ/ PREPOSITION
1 at one point in a period of time □ *My great grandfather was killed during the war.*
2 through the whole of a period of time □ *The garden looks beautiful during the summer.*

➤ Remember that **during** is not used to talk about how long something happens. Use **for** for this:
✓ I studied English **for** three years.
✗ I studied English **during** three years.

dusk /dʌsk/ NOUN, NO PLURAL the time in the evening when it starts to get dark 🔁 *Dusk was falling.*

dust /dʌst/ ► NOUN, NO PLURAL a powder of dirt on a surface or in the air 🔁 *A thin layer of dust covered the desk.* 🔁 *The horses kicked up a cloud of dust.* 🔁 *The books were gathering dust in his attic.*
► VERB [**dusts, dusting, dusted**] to clean dust from something using a cloth □ *I've dusted the shelves.*
♦ PHRASAL VERB **dust something off** to get something ready to use when you have not used it for a long time □ *She dusted off her dancing shoes in preparation for the ball.*

dustbin /ˈdʌstbɪn/ NOUN [*plural* **dustbins**] a container for rubbish, which is outside your house □ *She threw the empty boxes in the dustbin.*

duster /ˈdʌstə(r)/ NOUN [*plural* **dusters**] a cloth for removing dust from surfaces

dustman /ˈdʌstmən/ NOUN [*plural* **dustmen**] someone whose job is to collect rubbish from people's houses

dustpan /ˈdʌstpæn/ NOUN [*plural* **dustpans**] a flat container with a handle, that you brush dust and waste into 🔁 *a dustpan and brush*

dusty /ˈdʌstɪ/ ADJECTIVE [**dustier, dustiest**] covered with dust □ *a dusty floor* □ *Children played in the dusty streets.*

dutiful /ˈdjuːtɪfʊl/ ADJECTIVE a dutiful person does what other people think they should do. A formal word. □ *Amir tried to be a dutiful son.*

duty /ˈdjuːtɪ/ NOUN [*plural* **duties**]
1 something that you do because other people expect you to do it or because it is morally right to do it 🔁 *He felt he had a moral duty to help her.* □ **+ to do something** *Society has a duty to protect children.*
2 duties the things that you have to do in your job 🔁 *The President has a number of official duties next week.* □ *My duties include producing reports.*
3 on/off duty if someone such as a doctor, police officer etc. is on duty, they are working, and if they are off duty, they are not working □ *Which doctor is on duty tonight?*
4 a tax □ **+ on** *The government will raise the duty on imports.*

duty-free /ˌdjuːtɪˈfriː/ ADJECTIVE duty-free products are cheaper because you can bring them into a country without paying tax □ *duty-free perfume* 🔁 *We went to the duty-free shop at the airport.*

duvet /ˈduːveɪ/ NOUN [*plural* **duvets**] a thick warm cover for your bed □ *He pulled the duvet over his head.* 🔁 *a duvet cover*

DVD /ˌdiːviːˈdiː/ ABBREVIATION digital versatile disk; a type of disk with pictures and sound recorded on it □ *The movie is available on DVD.* 🔁 *a DVD player* 🔁 *The children were watching a DVD.*

dwarf /dwɔːf/ ► NOUN [*plural* **dwarfs** *or* **dwarves**] an imaginary creature in children's stories, which looks like a very small man
► ADJECTIVE dwarf plants are much smaller than the usual type □ *dwarf apple trees*
► VERB [**dwarfs, dwarfing, dwarfed**] to make something else look small in comparison □ *The new hotel dwarfs the buildings around it.*

dwell /dwel/ VERB [**dwells, dwelling, dwelt**] a literary word meaning to live somewhere
♦ PHRASAL VERB **dwell on something** to think or talk for too long about something unpleasant □ *There's no point in dwelling on your mistakes now.*
● **dwelling** /ˈdwelɪŋ/ NOUN [*plural* **dwellings**] a formal word for home □ *The region will have 2,000 new dwellings in the next 10 years.*

dwindle /ˈdwɪndəl/ VERB [**dwindles, dwindling, dwindled**] to become less □ *Church membership has dwindled.*
● **dwindling** /ˈdwɪndlɪŋ/ ADJECTIVE becoming less □ *Australia is facing dwindling water supplies.*

dye /daɪ/ ► NOUN [*plural* **dyes**] a substance used for changing the colour of cloth or hair
► VERB [**dyes, dyeing, dyed**] to use a substance to change the colour of cloth or hair □ *Emma dyed her hair red.*

dyke /daɪk/ NOUN [*plural* **dykes**]
1 a wall that stops water from flooding the land
2 a narrow passage in the ground, that takes water away from fields

dynamic /daɪˈnæmɪk/ ADJECTIVE
1 full of energy and new ideas □ *a dynamic young manager*
2 changing continuously □ *a dynamic situation*
3 to do with movement. A physics word.
● **dynamics** /daɪˈnæmɪks/ NOUN, NO PLURAL
1 the way in which things and people affect each other □ *Serious illness can change the dynamics of a family.*
2 the part of physics that is to do with movement. A physics word.

dynamite /ˈdaɪnəmaɪt/ NOUN, NO PLURAL
1 a powerful explosive
2 something which could cause a lot of excitement or arguments □ *The immigration issue is political dynamite.*

dynasty /ˈdɪnəstɪ/ NOUN [*plural* **dynasties**] a family whose members rule a company, are in charge of a business, etc. for a long time

dyslexia /dɪsˈleksɪə/ NOUN, NO PLURAL a brain problem which makes it difficult for someone to read and spell

• **dyslexic** /dɪsˈleksɪk/ ADJECTIVE having dyslexia

E*e*

e- /i:/ PREFIX e- is added to the beginning of words to mean 'electronic' or to do with the Internet □ *e-commerce*

E[1] *or* **e** /i:/ the fifth letter of the alphabet

E[2] /i:/ ABBREVIATION east

each /i:tʃ/ DETERMINER, PRONOUN

1 every separate person or thing □ *We had to pay £5 each.* □ *+ of Each of the soldiers was given a gun.* □ *He had a heavy suitcase in each hand.*

2 each other used to show that each person or thing in a group of two or more does something to the others □ *The team all hugged each other.* □ *The cat and dog don't like each other much.*

➤ Remember that **each** is followed by a singular noun: □ *Each person starts the game with five cards.*

eager /'i:gə(r)/ ADJECTIVE wanting very much to do or have something □ *+ to do something Imran seems eager to learn.*

● **eagerly** /'i:gəlɪ/ ADVERB in an eager way ⊞ *This is the eagerly awaited new film from the Spanish director.*

● **eagerness** /'i:gənɪs/ NOUN, NO PLURAL being eager □ *In his eagerness to get there, he fell over.*

eagle /'i:gəl/ NOUN [*plural* **eagles**] a large bird with a curved beak that hunts small birds and animals

ear /ɪə(r)/ NOUN [*plural* **ears**]

1 one of the two parts on each side of your head that you hear with □ *He whispered something in my ear.*

2 the part at the top of the stem of some plants where the grains grow □ *an ear of corn*

◆ IDIOMS **couldn't believe their ears** used to say that someone was very surprised when they were told something □ *I couldn't believe my ears when she said she was going to marry Ben.* **fall on deaf ears** to be ignored □ *Her pleas for help fell on deaf ears.* **have an ear for something** to be able to recognize and repeat sounds □ *Ann has an ear for languages.* **keep your ears open** to try to get information about something by listening to what people say **play it by ear** to decide how to act as a situation develops instead of having a plan at the beginning □ *We don't have any firm instructions, so you'll have to just play it by ear.* **play something by ear** to play a piece of music without reading the notes

earache /'ɪəreɪk/ NOUN, NO PLURAL pain inside your ear

eardrum /'ɪədrʌm/ NOUN [*plural* **eardrums**] a thin, tight skin inside your ear that allows you to hear sounds

earl /ɜːl/ NOUN [*plural* **earls**] a British man with a high social rank □ *Earl Spencer* □ *the Earl of Warwick*

earlobe /'ɪələʊb/ NOUN [*plural* **earlobes**] the soft round part that hangs down at the bottom of your ear

early /'ɜːlɪ/ ADJECTIVE, ADVERB [**earlier, earliest**]

1 happening or arriving before others or before the expected or normal time □ *Nick had taken an earlier train.* □ *I'm tired so I'm going to bed early tonight.*

2 near the beginning of something □ *It's so quiet here in the early morning.* □ *She showed musical talent early in life.* ⊞ *The police were in the early stages of the investigation.*

3 early on in the first part of something □ *He defended really well early on in the match.*

4 at the earliest used to say that something will not happen or be done before a particular time □ *The new house won't be ready until August at the earliest.*

5 the early hours the time between 12 o'clock at night and the beginning of the morning □ *The robbery must have taken place in the early hours.*

earmark /'ɪəmɑːk/ VERB [**earmarks, earmarking, earmarked**] to decide to use something, especially money, for a particular purpose □ *That money's been earmarked for a new car.*

earn /ɜːn/ VERB [**earns, earning, earned**]

1 to get money for work that you do □ *He earns about £45,000 a year.* ⊞ *Does she earn her living (= get all the money she needs to live) as an artist?*

2 to get something good, such as praise, because you have done something well □ *He worked hard and earned the respect of his colleagues.*

3 to get money as interest on an amount you have in a bank or have lent to someone □ *Your savings can earn 5.5% in our high-interest account.*

➤ Remember that you **earn** money for work that you do. You **win** money in a competition □ *He earns a very good salary.* □ *He won a million pounds on the lottery.*

earnest /'ɜːnɪst/ ▶ ADJECTIVE serious and honest □ The three men were in earnest conversation.
▶ NOUN, NO PLURAL **in earnest** (a) speaking honestly about what you want to do □ Was he in earnest when he said he wanted to leave? (b) if something happens in earnest, it happens more seriously than before □ The war began in earnest that May.

earnings /'ɜːnɪŋz/ PLURAL NOUN money that you get from working

earphones /'ɪəfəʊnz/ PLURAL NOUN a piece of electronic equipment that you wear in or on your ears so that you can listen to music, radio, etc.

earplugs /'ɪəplʌgz/ PLURAL NOUN small pieces of a soft material that you put in your ears to keep out noise

earring /'ɪərɪŋ/ NOUN [plural **earrings**] a piece of jewellery for the ear □ a pair of earrings □ diamond earrings

earshot /'ɪəʃɒt/ NOUN, NO PLURAL
1 out of earshot too far away to hear
2 in/within earshot close enough to hear

ear-splitting /'ɪəˌsplɪtɪŋ/ ADJECTIVE extremely loud □ An ear-splitting scream came from the attic.

earth /ɜːθ/ NOUN [plural **earths**]
1 Earth the planet we live on 🖻 life on Earth □ The Earth rotates around the sun.
2 no plural soil □ a pile of earth
3 no plural the surface of our planet □ The earth shook with the explosion.
4 a wire that makes electrical equipment safer by taking the electric current into the ground
♦ IDIOMS **cost the earth** to cost a lot of money. An informal phrase. □ Their new house must have cost the earth. **how/what/where/why on earth?** used to emphasize a question, usually when you are very surprised □ How on earth did that happen? □ What on earth was he wearing?
● **earthly** /'ɜːθli/ ADJECTIVE
1 used to emphasize a question or a negative statement 🖻 There is no earthly reason why you shouldn't go.
2 to do with life on Earth and not life in heaven. A literary word.

earthquake /'ɜːθkweɪk/ NOUN [plural **earthquakes**] when the ground suddenly moves, often causing serious damage to buildings

earthworm /'ɜːθwɜːm/ NOUN [plural **earthworms**] a small, long, thin animal that lives in the soil

ease /iːz/ ▶ NOUN, NO PLURAL
1 with ease easily □ She won the race with ease.
2 at ease relaxed □ He's never completely at ease talking to strangers.
▶ VERB [**eases, easing, eased**]
1 to become less difficult or painful, or to make something less difficult or painful 🖻 These tablets should ease the pain. □ Tensions in the area have gradually eased.
2 to move something somewhere gradually □ They eased the last big block into position.

♦ PHRASAL VERB **ease off** to gradually stop □ The rain seems to be easing off now.

easel /'iːzəl/ NOUN [plural **easels**] a frame used to hold a picture while someone is painting it

easily /'iːzɪli/ ADVERB
1 with no effort or difficulty □ Chelsea won easily.
2 certainly □ She's easily the most successful female pop singer today.
3 very possibly □ It could easily be two weeks before you get a replacement.

east /iːst/ ▶ NOUN, NO PLURAL
1 the direction that you look towards to see the sun rise □ Which way is east? □ York is to the east of Harrogate.
2 the countries in Asia □ We do a lot of business in the East.
3 the part of a country that is in the east □ There has been heavy rain in the east today.
▶ ADJECTIVE, ADVERB in or towards the east □ the east coast □ East London □ We headed east.

Easter /'iːstə(r)/ NOUN, NO PLURAL a Christian holiday in March or April to celebrate when Christ came back to life from the dead □ the Easter holidays □ Easter Sunday

Easter egg /'iːstə(r) ˌeg/ NOUN [plural **Easter eggs**] a chocolate egg, given as a present at Easter.

easterly /'iːstəli/ ADJECTIVE
1 towards the east □ They set off in an easterly direction.
2 coming from the east □ an easterly breeze

eastern /'iːstən/ ADJECTIVE
1 in or from the east part of a country or area □ the eastern coast of America □ Eastern England
2 to do with the countries of Asia □ She's studying eastern philosophy.

eastward /'iːstwəd/ or **eastwards** /'iːstwədz/ ADVERB to or towards the east □ We were sailing eastwards.

easy /'iːzi/ ▶ ADJECTIVE [**easier, easiest**]
1 not difficult to do □ an easy exam paper
2 I'm easy said when someone offers you a choice and you are happy to have or do any of the things offered □ 'Shall we order a pizza or a curry?' 'I'm easy, you choose.'
▶ ADVERB [**easier, easiest**] **take it easy** to relax and not work hard □ Grandad's taking it easy in the garden.
♦ IDIOMS **Easier said than done.** used to say that something is difficult to do □ I know I should get the kids to help but that's easier said than done. **go easy on someone** to treat someone more gently □ Go easy on Matt, he's having a hard time at the moment. **go easy on something** to eat or use only a little of something □ My doctor said I should go easy on the red meat.

easy-going /ˌiːzɪˈɡəʊɪŋ/ ADJECTIVE relaxed and not often upset or angry

eat /iːt/ VERB [eats, eating, ate, eaten]
1 to put food in your mouth and swallow it □ We've eaten all the bread. □ He ate a huge meal. 🔊 Do you fancy something to eat?
2 to have a meal □ What time would you like to eat?
◆ PHRASAL VERBS **eat away at someone** if a bad memory or feeling eats away at you, you cannot forget it and it makes you feel bad **eat away at something** to gradually destroy something □ The acid eats away at the tooth enamel. **eat into something** to use more of your money, time, etc., than you had planned □ The journey to work really eats into my day. **eat out** to have a meal in a restaurant □ We eat out about twice a month. **eat something up 1** to eat all of an amount of food □ Eat up your vegetables, Maisie. **2** to use all of something valuable □ The repairs had eaten up all of their savings.
● **eater** /ˈiːtə(r)/ NOUN [plural eaters]
1 someone who eats in a particular way □ She's not a big eater. □ a fussy eater
2 a person or animal that eats a particular thing □ It's a good restaurant for meat eaters.

eaves /iːvz/ PLURAL NOUN the edges of a roof that stick out over the walls

eavesdrop /ˈiːvzdrɒp/ VERB [eavesdrops, eavesdropping, eavesdropped] to listen to other people's conversations without them knowing □ I think Tony was eavesdropping on our conversation.

eBay /ˈiːbeɪ/ NOUN, NO PLURAL a website where you can buy and sell things. A trademark. 🔊 She buys a lot of clothes on eBay.

ebb /eb/ ▶ VERB [ebbs, ebbing, ebbed]
1 to gradually get less and less □ Her enthusiasm for the project has slowly ebbed away.
2 when the tide ebbs, the sea flows away from the land
▶ NOUN, NO PLURAL **be at a low ebb** if a good feeling is at a low ebb, there is very little of it at a particular time □ Morale was at a low ebb after the strike.

ebony /ˈebənɪ/ NOUN, NO PLURAL a very hard black wood from an African tree

eccentric /ɪkˈsentrɪk/ ADJECTIVE behaving in a way that is strange or different from most people □ an eccentric millionaire
● **eccentricity** /ˌeksenˈtrɪsətɪ/ NOUN [plural eccentricities] eccentric behaviour

ECG /ˌiːsiːˈdʒiː/ ABBREVIATION electrocardiogram or electrocardiograph; a medical test in which you are connected to a machine that measures how well your heart is beating

echo /ˈekəʊ/ ▶ VERB [echoes, echoing, echoed]
1 a sound echoes when it comes back and you hear it again □ Their laughter echoed in the empty concert hall.
2 to repeat what someone has said or thought □ The minister echoed the Foreign Secretary's view.

▶ NOUN [plural echoes] a sound that you hear again after it is sent back off a surface such as a wall

eclectic /ɪˈklektɪk/ ADJECTIVE including a lot of different styles or types of things 🔊 There's an eclectic mix of musical instruments.

eclipse /ɪˈklɪps/ NOUN [plural eclipses] when the sun disappears behind the moon or the moon is covered by the Earth's shadow □ a total eclipse of the sun

eco- /ˈiːkəʊ/ PREFIX eco- is added to the beginning of words to mean 'to do with the environment' □ eco-friendly

eco-friendly /ˈiːkəʊˌfrendlɪ/ ADJECTIVE not harmful to the environment □ eco-friendly detergents

ecological /ˌiːkəˈlɒdʒɪkəl/ ADJECTIVE to do with ecology □ an ecological disaster

ecology /ɪˈkɒlədʒɪ/ NOUN, NO PLURAL the study of how plants and animals exist together and how their environment affects them

e-commerce /ˈiːkɒmɜːs/ NOUN, NO PLURAL the business of buying and selling goods on the Internet

economic /ˌiːkəˈnɒmɪk/ ADJECTIVE
1 to do with money, business and industry 🔊 More economic growth is predicted. 🔊 economic development □ an economic forecast
2 making a profit □ The business was no longer economic and closed down.
● **economical** /ˌiːkəˈnɒmɪkəl/ ADJECTIVE costing only a little money □ It's a very economical car to run.
● **economics** /ˌiːkəˈnɒmɪks/ NOUN, NO PLURAL the study of how money, business and industry are organized □ a degree in economics
● **economist** /ɪˈkɒnəmɪst/ NOUN [plural economists] someone who studies economics
● **economize** or **economise** /ɪˈkɒnəmaɪz/ VERB [economizes, economizing, economized] to save money by using less of something or buying something cheaper

economy /ɪˈkɒnəmɪ/ NOUN [plural economies]
1 all the money a country or area creates through producing and selling goods and services, and the way that money is used □ Canada's economy grew fast. □ Tourism benefits the local economy.
2 when someone is careful not to waste something such as money, time or fuel □ We're looking for a car that offers both performance and economy. 🔊 The company will have to make economies to survive.

ecosystem /ˈiːkəʊˌsɪstəm/ NOUN [plural ecosystems] all the plants and animals in an area and the way they depend on each other and on their environment to live

ecotourism /ˈiːkəʊˌtʊərɪzəm/ NOUN, NO PLURAL holidays that are organized so that they help local people and do not damage the environment
● **ecotourist** /ˈiːkəʊˌtʊərɪst/ NOUN [plural ecotourists] someone who takes a holiday like this

ecstasy /'ekstəsɪ/ NOUN, NO PLURAL a feeling of great happiness or pleasure
• **ecstatic** /ek'stætɪk/ ADJECTIVE extremely happy
eczema /'eksɪmə/ NOUN, NO PLURAL a disease in which your skin develops dry, red areas

edge /edʒ/ ► NOUN [plural **edges**]
1 the outer part or end of something □ We stood on the edge of the cliff. □ I live on the outer edge of the city. □ Trim off all the rough edges.
2 a side of something that is sharp enough to cut
3 an advantage that makes someone or something more successful than others □ **+ over** This technology gives us a competitive edge over our rivals.
4 **on edge** nervous and slightly bad-tempered
♦ IDIOM **take the edge off something** to make a pain, bad emotion, etc. slightly less strong
► VERB [**edges, edging, edged**]
1 to move slowly and carefully □ Harry edged along the narrow ledge.
2 to put something round the edge of something, usually as decoration □ The pillowcases were edged with lace.

edgeways /'edʒweɪz/ ADVERB
♦ IDIOM **not get a word in edgeways** to not have the chance to speak because other people are talking too much □ You can't get a word in edgeways once he starts.

edging /'edʒɪŋ/ NOUN [plural **edgings**] something that goes round the edge of something else, usually as decoration

edgy /'edʒɪ/ ADJECTIVE [**edgier, edgiest**]
1 nervous and slightly bad-tempered
2 fashionable in an unusual and exciting way

edible /'edɪbəl/ ADJECTIVE
1 safe to eat □ edible mushrooms
2 good enough to eat □ Her chocolate cake was barely edible.

edifice /'edɪfɪs/ NOUN [plural **edifices**] a very large building □ The town hall is an imposing edifice.

edit /'edɪt/ VERB [**edits, editing, edited**]
1 to prepare a book, document, film, etc. by correcting mistakes and making any changes that are needed
2 to be the editor of a newspaper, magazine, etc.
• **edition** /ɪ'dɪʃən/ NOUN [plural **editions**]
1 the copies of a book, newspaper, etc. that are printed at the same time □ The story was in the early editions of the newspaper. □ I bought the hardback edition of her first novel.
2 one of a series of television or radio programmes □ I saw her on Saturday's edition of the talk show.
• **editor** /'edɪtə(r)/ NOUN [plural **editors**]
1 someone whose job is to prepare a book, document, newspaper, etc. to be published by correcting mistakes and making any changes that are needed □ He thanked his editor for all her help.
2 someone who is in charge of a newspaper, magazine, etc. or someone who writes or talks about a particular

subject for a newspaper, television show, etc. □ He is the arts editor of The Guardian.
• **editorial** /ˌedɪ'tɔːrɪəl/ ► ADJECTIVE to do with editing or editors □ the editorial staff □ She questioned my editorial judgement.
► NOUN [plural **editorials**] an article in a newspaper or magazine that expresses the opinion of the editor or the owner

educate /'edjʊkeɪt/ VERB [**educates, educating, educated**]
1 to teach someone □ He was educated at the local school.
2 to give people information about something so that they understand it more □ **+ about** We need to educate people about the importance of exercise.
• **educated** /'edjʊkeɪtɪd/ ADJECTIVE an educated person knows a lot because they have had a good education □ a highly educated workforce
• **education** /ˌedjʊ'keɪʃən/ NOUN, NO PLURAL the process of teaching, especially in schools or colleges □ Our students receive a good standard of education. □ secondary education
• **educational** /ˌedjʊ'keɪʃənəl/ ADJECTIVE to do with teaching and learning ⊞ She organized an educational visit to the museum. □ He works for a company manufacturing educational toys.

-ee /iː/ SUFFIX
1 -ee is added to the end of words to mean 'someone who is having something done to them' □ interviewee □ employee
2 -ee is added to the end of words to mean 'someone who has done a particular thing' □ escapee (= someone who has escaped)

eel /iːl/ NOUN [plural **eels**] a type of fish that has a long thin body like a snake

eerie /'ɪərɪ/ ADJECTIVE [**eerier, eeriest**] strange in a frightening way □ a dark and eerie old house
• **eerily** /'ɪərɪlɪ/ ADVERB in an eerie way □ The forest suddenly became eerily silent.

effect /ɪ'fekt/ NOUN [plural **effects**]
1 if one thing has an effect on another, it influences it or causes something to happen to it □ **+ on** His asthma has no effect on his ability as a footballer. □ She was suffering from the effects of a long plane journey.
2 **come into effect** to start to be used □ The law came into effect in July.
3 **bring/put something into effect** to start to use knowledge, a plan, a law, etc. □ We will put our training into effect as soon as we get back to work.
4 **take effect** to start to have results or to produce changes □ It will be a few minutes before the drugs take effect.
5 the way something has been made to look or sound, or the reaction that people have to it □ Soft lighting creates a romantic effect in this room. ⊞ They added the sound effects later.

6 in effect used to explain in a short way what the true situation is □ *In effect, they were unable to work again.*

> ► Be careful not to confuse **effect**, which is a noun, with **affect**, which is a verb: □ *One thing has an effect on another.* □ *One thing affects another.*

• **effective** /ɪˈfektɪv/ ADJECTIVE
1 working well or producing the results you want □ *This claims to be an effective treatment for the common cold.* □ *Do you know of an effective way of removing chewing gum from a carpet?*
2 if a law, plan, etc. is effective from a particular time, that is when it starts to be used □ **+ from** *The new system will be effective from January 1st.*
3 used to talk about what the real situation is □ *Troops have taken effective control of the region.*
• **effectively** /ɪˈfektɪvlɪ/ ADVERB
1 in a successful way □ *He dealt with the problem very effectively.*
2 used to talk about what the real situation is □ *We were effectively without food or water.*

effeminate /ɪˈfemɪnət/ ADJECTIVE an effeminate man behaves like a woman
effervescent /ˌefəˈvesənt/ ADJECTIVE
1 an effervescent liquid is full of bubbles of gas
2 someone with an effervescent personality has a lot of enthusiasm and energy
efficiency /ɪˈfɪʃənsɪ/ NOUN, NO PLURAL when someone or something works well and does not waste time or energy □ *Increased efficiency has cut their costs.*

efficient /ɪˈfɪʃənt/ ADJECTIVE working well and not wasting any time or energy □ *The questionnaire was an efficient method of collecting information.* □ *This is not an efficient use of resources.*
• **efficiently** /ɪˈfɪʃəntlɪ/ ADVERB in an efficient way □ *She organised the show very efficiently.*

effort /ˈefət/ NOUN [plural **efforts**]
1 the physical or mental energy that you need to do something 🔊 *She made a real effort to be friendly.* 🔊 *You must put some more effort into your school work.* □ **+ to do something** *It takes a lot of effort to be an athlete.*
2 an attempt □ *That was a really good effort, Sonia.*
• **effortless** /ˈefətlɪs/ ADJECTIVE not needing a lot of effort □ *A good ballet dancer makes it look effortless.*
• **effortlessly** /ˈefətlɪslɪ/ ADVERB in an effortless way

eg or **e.g.** /ˌiːˈdʒiː/ ABBREVIATION for example□ *The zoo specializes in African animals, eg the lion and the giraffe.*
egalitarian /ɪˌɡælɪˈteərɪən/ ADJECTIVE giving everyone the same rights and opportunities. A formal word □ *an egalitarian society*
egestion /iːˈdʒestʃən/ NOUN, NO PLURAL the way waste food comes out of the body. A biology word.

egg /eg/ NOUN [plural **eggs**]
1 an oval object with a shell or case, in which a baby bird, reptile or fish develops 🔊 *The cuckoo lays its eggs in another bird's nest.*
2 an oval object with a shell produced by a chicken or similar bird that we eat as food 🔊 *a boiled/fried egg* 🔊 *Beat two egg yolks with a little milk.*
3 a special cell stored inside the body of a female mammal which can grow into a baby
♦ IDIOMS **have egg on your face** to be very embarrassed because of something silly you have done **put all your eggs in one basket** to put all your money or effort into one thing, so that if it fails you lose everything
♦ PHRASAL VERB [**eggs, egging, egged**] **egg someone on** to encourage someone to do something, usually something bad □ *He hit the man again, as his friends egged him on.*

eggplant /ˈegplɑːnt/ NOUN [plural **eggplants**] the US word for aubergine
eggshell /ˈegʃel/ NOUN [plural **eggshells**] the hard thin shell covering an egg
ego /ˈiːgəʊ/ NOUN [plural **egos**] the opinion you have of yourself □ *All the attention and praise was good for her ego.*
Eid /iːd/ NOUN, NO PLURAL either of two Muslim celebrations, especially Eid-ul-Fitr which is held each year to celebrate the end of Ramadan, when there is a big meal and people give each other presents
eiderdown /ˈaɪdədaʊn/ NOUN [plural **eiderdowns**] a warm covering for a bed, filled with feathers or some other light material

eight /eɪt/ NUMBER [plural **eights**] the number 8

eighteen /ˌeɪˈtiːn/ NUMBER the number 18
eighteenth /ˌeɪˈtiːnθ/ NUMBER 18th written as a word

eighth /eɪtθ/ ► NUMBER 8th written as a word □ *the eighth book in the series* □ *Our team finished eighth.*
► NOUN [plural **eighths**] 1/8 ; one of eight equal parts of something

eightieth /ˈeɪtɪəθ/ NUMBER 80th written as a word
eighty /ˈeɪtɪ/ NUMBER [plural **eighties**]
1 the number 80
2 the eighties the years between 1980 and 1989

either /ˈaɪðə(r)/ ► ADVERB used in negative sentences to mean 'as well' □ *If you don't go, I won't go either.* □ *Dan doesn't like cheese either.*
► CONJUNCTION **either ... or** used to show a choice □ *You can have either a video game or a CD.*
► DETERMINER, PRONOUN
1 one or the other □ *She can write with either hand.* □ **+ of** *I can't afford either of them.*
2 both 🔊 *They stood on either side of the Queen.*

eject /ɪˈdʒekt/ VERB [**ejects, ejecting, ejected**]
1 to push or throw someone or something out of a place □ *He was ejected from the nightclub.*
2 to remove something from a machine, usually by pressing a button □ *How do you eject the CD?*

3 to escape from an aircraft in an emergency by operating a special seat which is thrown out of the plane

eke /iːk/
◆ PHRASAL VERB [**ekes, eking, eked**] **eke something out** to not use much of something that you have a small amount of, in order to make it last longer □ *We had to eke out our supplies of water for ten days.*

elaborate ▶ ADJECTIVE /ɪˈlæbərət/ involving complicated detail or decoration □ *an elaborate plan* □ *elaborate costumes*

▶ VERB /ɪˈlæbəreɪt/ [**elaborates, elaborating, elaborated**] to explain something in more detail □ *Would you like to elaborate on that statement?*

elapse /ɪˈlæps/ VERB [**elapses, elapsing, elapsed**] when time elapses, it passes □ *Three years elapsed before I saw her again.*

elastic /ɪˈlæstɪk/ ▶ ADJECTIVE able to stretch and then go back to its original size

▶ NOUN, NO PLURAL a type of material with rubber or a similar substance in it to make it stretch

elastic band /ɪˌlæstɪk ˈbænd/ NOUN [*plural* **elastic bands**] a small thin circle of rubber used for holding things together

elated /ɪˈleɪtɪd/ ADJECTIVE very pleased and excited □ *They were elated after winning the cup.*
● **elation** /ɪˈleɪʃən/ NOUN, NO PLURAL the state of being elated

elbow /ˈelbəʊ/ ▶ NOUN [*plural* **elbows**] the part in the middle of your arm where it bends

▶ VERB [**elbows, elbowing, elbowed**] to push someone with your elbow, especially to get past them 🔁 *She managed to elbow her way to the front of the queue.*

elder /ˈeldə(r)/ ▶ ADJECTIVE older □ *She has an elder brother.*

▶ NOUN [*plural* **elders**]
1 the elder the older of two people □ *She's the elder of two sisters.*
2 your elders people who are older than you □ *We were taught to respect our elders.*
● **elderly** /ˈeldəlɪ/ ▶ ADJECTIVE old □ *an elderly lady*
▶ NOUN **the elderly** people who are old □ *Sarah works in a care home for the elderly.*

eldest /ˈeldɪst/ ▶ ADJECTIVE oldest □ *Alex is my eldest child.*

▶ NOUN **the eldest** the person who is the oldest □ *Fiona is the eldest of three sisters.*

elect /ɪˈlekt/ VERB [**elects, electing, elected**] to choose someone for a particular job or position in an organization by voting □ *The committee has to elect a chairperson.* □ *The president was elected in 2004.*
● **election** /ɪˈlekʃən/ NOUN [*plural* **elections**] when people choose someone by voting 🔁 *Nobody knows when he will decide to hold the election.* 🔁 *Her party won the election.*
● **elector** /ɪˈlektə(r)/ NOUN [*plural* **electors**] someone who votes in an election

● **electoral** /ɪˈlektərəl/ ADJECTIVE to do with elections or electors 🔁 *electoral reform*
● **electorate** /ɪˈlektərət/ NOUN [*plural* **electorates**] all the people who can vote in an election □ *His policies are popular with the electorate.*

electric /ɪˈlektrɪk/ ADJECTIVE
1 made or worked by electricity □ *an electric spark* □ *an electric light* □ *electric current*
2 very exciting □ *In the hall, the atmosphere was electric.*
● **electrical** /ɪˈlektrɪkəl/ ADJECTIVE to do with electricity □ *She's studying electrical engineering.* □ *The shop sells small electrical appliances like kettles and irons.*

electrician /ˌɪlekˈtrɪʃən/ NOUN [*plural* **electricians**] someone whose job is to put in or repair electrical equipment

electricity /ˌɪlekˈtrɪsətɪ/ NOUN, NO PLURAL a type of energy used to make light and heat and to make machines work □ *We're trying to save electricity by turning off our computers at night.*

electrify /ɪˈlektrɪfaɪ/ VERB [**electrifies, electrifying, electrified**]
1 to make people very excited □ *His performance in Othello has been electrifying audiences.*
2 to supply electricity to machines or equipment to make them work

electro- /ɪˈlektrəʊ/ PREFIX electro- is added to the beginning of words to mean 'to do with electricity' □ *electromagnet*

electrocute /ɪˈlektrəkjuːt/ VERB [**electrocutes, electrocuting, electrocuted**] if someone is electrocuted, they are killed by a strong electric current which passes through their body □ *He was electrocuted while he was trying to fix the lights.*
● **electrocution** /ɪˌlektrəˈkjuːʃən/ NOUN, NO PLURAL when someone is electrocuted

electrode /ɪˈlektrəʊd/ NOUN [*plural* **electrodes**] a small metal device that allows electricity to pass from a source of power, such as a battery, to a piece of equipment. A physics and chemistry word.

electrolysis /ˌɪlekˈtrɒləsɪs/ NOUN, NO PLURAL when electricity is passed through a substance to cause chemical change. A physics and chemistry word.

electromagnet /ɪˌlektrəʊˈmægnɪt/ NOUN [*plural* **electromagnets**] a magnet that works when electricity passes through it. A physics word.
● **electromagnetic** /ɪˌlektrəʊmæɡˈnetɪk/ ADJECTIVE using an electric current to make something magnetic. A physics word.

electron /ɪˈlektrɒn/ NOUN [*plural* **electrons**] one of the parts of an atom that move around the nucleus and have a negative electrical charge. A chemistry and physics word.

electronic /ˌɪlekˈtrɒnɪk/ ADJECTIVE

1 using electricity and very small electrical parts to work 🔲 *an electronic device* 🔲 *They sell computers and other electronic equipment.*

2 using electronic equipment □ *electronic communications* □ *electronic music*

3 to do with electronics □ *electronic engineering*

• **electronics** /ˌɪlekˈtrɒnɪks/ NOUN, NO PLURAL the study of how electricity flows and how it can be used in machinery

elegance /ˈelɪgəns/ NOUN, NO PLURAL the quality of being attractive and having good style □ *The city has an air of elegance about it.*

• **elegant** /ˈelɪgənt/ ADJECTIVE attractive and having good style □ *an elegant lady* □ *an elegant house*

• **elegantly** /ˈelɪgəntlɪ/ ADVERB in an elegant way □ *She dances very elegantly.* □ *an elegantly dressed woman*

element /ˈelɪmənt/ NOUN [*plural* **elements**]

1 a part of something □ *They are unhappy about some elements of the course.* □ *His work has a political element.* 🔲 *There is an element of truth in her accusations.*

2 a substance that cannot be divided into smaller chemical substances, for example hydrogen, oxygen and carbon. A chemistry word.

3 the part of a piece of electrical equipment that produces heat. A physics word.

4 **the elements** the weather □ *They were stuck on a bare hillside, completely exposed to the elements.*

5 **in your element** doing the things that you are best at or that you enjoy the most □ *She was in her element bossing all the soldiers around.*

• **elementary** /ˌelɪˈmentərɪ/ ADJECTIVE

1 basic □ *You have forgotten the elementary principles of journalism.* □ *He is making too many elementary mistakes.*

2 to do with the first stages of studying a subject □ *elementary maths* □ *elementary classes/students*

3 to do with the education that very young children receive □ *elementary education/teachers*

elementary particle /ˌelɪmentərɪ ˈpɑːtɪkəl/ NOUN [*plural* **elementary particles**] one of the very small pieces of matter that make up a subatomic particle. A physics word.

elementary school /ˌelɪˈmentərɪ ˌskuːl/ NOUN [*plural* **elementary schools**] the US word for primary school

elephant /ˈelɪfənt/ NOUN [*plural* **elephants**] a very large animal with a long nose, large ears and thick grey skin

elevate /ˈelɪveɪt/ VERB [**elevates, elevating, elevated**]

1 a formal word meaning to move something to a higher position or level □ *Elevate the patient's feet slightly.*

2 a formal word meaning to give something a more important position □ *These roles have elevated her international status.*

• **elevation** /ˌelɪˈveɪʃən/ NOUN, NO PLURAL

1 the height of something above sea level

2 when something is elevated

• **elevator** /ˈelɪveɪtə(r)/ NOUN [*plural* **elevators**] the US word for lift (= for carrying people up and down in a tall building)

eleven /ɪˈlevən/ NUMBER [*plural* **elevens**] the number 11

eleventh /ɪˈlevənθ/ NUMBER 11th written as a word

elf /elf/ NOUN [*plural* **elves**] an imaginary creature like a very small person which often causes trouble in stories

• **elfin** /ˈelfɪn/ ADJECTIVE like an elf, especially with small, attractive features □ *an elfin face*

elicit /ɪˈlɪsɪt/ VERB [**elicits, eliciting, elicited**] a formal word meaning to get information, an answer or a reaction from someone 🔲 *The suggestions elicited a positive response.* □ *He tried to elicit a bit more detailed information.*

eligible /ˈelɪdʒəbəl/ ADJECTIVE

1 suitable for or allowed to do something □ *Am I eligible for a payment?* □ *There are 6 million eligible voters in the country.*

2 an eligible man is someone who would be suitable to marry

eliminate /ɪˈlɪmɪneɪt/ VERB [**eliminates, eliminating, eliminated**]

1 to get rid of something completely □ *We aim to eliminate poverty.* 🔲 *The new technology eliminates the need for ID cards and passwords.*

2 to remove someone from a competition, for example by beating them □ *The team was eliminated from the World Cup in the quarter finals.*

3 to decide that someone or something is not involved in something, so you can ignore them □ *The man has been eliminated from police enquiries.*

• **elimination** /ɪˌlɪmɪˈneɪʃən/ NOUN, NO PLURAL

1 when someone or something is eliminated

2 a process of elimination when you decide an answer by getting rid of all possible answers until only one is left

elite /ɪˈliːt/ ► NOUN [*plural* **elites**] the best, most important or most powerful people in a society or group □ *the country's ruling elite* □ *the sporting elite* ► ADJECTIVE of very high quality □ *an elite athlete*

• **elitism** /ɪˈliːtɪzəm/ NOUN, NO PLURAL when rich, powerful or well educated people have more power or advantages than everyone else □ *There is still some elitism in the world of classical music.*

• **elitist** /ɪˈliːtɪst/ ADJECTIVE to do with elitism □ *The university still has a rather elitist image.*

elk /elk/ NOUN [*plural* **elk** *or* **elks**] a type of very large deer that is found in northern Europe and Asia

ellipse /ɪˈlɪps/ NOUN [*plural* **ellipses**] an oval shape. A maths word.

• **elliptical** /ɪˈlɪptɪkəl/ ADJECTIVE shaped like an oval. A maths word.

elm /elm/ NOUN [*plural* **elms**] a type of tall tree with wide round leaves

elocution /ˌelə'kjuːʃən/ NOUN, NO PLURAL the skill of speaking correctly and clearly

elongate /'iːlɒŋgeɪt/ VERB [elongates, elongating, elongated] to get longer or to make something longer

• **elongated** /'iːlɒŋgeɪtɪd/ ADJECTIVE long and narrow, especially more than usual □ It has an elongated neck, like a giraffe.

elope /ɪ'ləʊp/ VERB [elopes, eloping, eloped] to run away secretly with someone to get married □ He eloped with the Earl's daughter.

• **elopement** /ɪ'ləʊpmənt/ NOUN, NO PLURAL when someone elopes

eloquence /'eləkwəns/ NOUN, NO PLURAL the ability to talk and express yourself well □ She spoke with such eloquence.

• **eloquent** /'eləkwənt/ ADJECTIVE able to talk and express yourself well □ an eloquent speech

• **eloquently** /'eləkwəntlɪ/ ADVERB in an eloquent way □ He spoke eloquently.

else /els/ ADVERB

1 as well as the thing or person that has been talked about ▣ Promise not to tell anyone else. ▣ You must wait in the queue, the same as everybody else. ▣ There's something else I need to tell you.

2 different from something or someone ▣ I had to leave. What else could I have done? ▣ I hate swimming. Can't we do something else instead? ▣ He must have been angry. Why else would he have reacted like that?

3 or else (a) used to say that a bad thing will happen if another thing does not happen □ Put on a jumper or else you'll get cold. (b) used to talk about two different situations, actions or possibilities □ Our students are usually young adults, or else older people wanting a change of career. (c) used to say that something must be true because something different would have happened if it was not □ She must have been ill, or else I'm sure she would have come.

elsewhere /els'weə(r)/ ADVERB in or to another place □ It's too expensive here, we'll have to look elsewhere.

elude /ɪ'luːd/ VERB [eludes, eluding, eluded]

1 to avoid being caught □ He managed to elude the police for weeks.

2 if something eludes you, you are not able to achieve it □ An effective treatment has long eluded scientists.

3 if a word or an idea eludes you, you cannot remember it □ The phrase he wanted eluded him.

• **elusive** /ɪ'luːsɪv/ ADJECTIVE difficult to see or find □ They are searching for the rare and elusive snow leopard.

elves /elvz/ PLURAL OF elf

emaciated /ɪ'meɪʃieɪtɪd/ ADJECTIVE very thin and weak because of illness or not eating enough

e-mail or email /'iːmeɪl/ ▶ NOUN [plural e-mails or emails]

1 no plural the system for sending messages between computers □ They keep in touch by e-mail. □ Are you on e-mail? ▣ What's your e-mail address?

2 a written message sent between computers ▣ He sends me an e-mail every day.

▶ VERB [e-mails, e-mailing, e-mailed or emails, emailing, emailed] to send someone an e-mail □ I'll e-mail you the address.

emanate /'eməneɪt/ VERB [emanates, emanating, emanated] a formal word meaning to come from something or somewhere □ Loud music emanated from the upstairs flat.

emancipate /ɪ'mænsɪpeɪt/ VERB [emancipates, emancipating, emancipated] a formal word meaning to give someone freedom and political rights □ Emancipating the working classes no longer seems to be the party's principal aim.

• **emancipation** /ɪˌmænsɪ'peɪʃən/ NOUN, NO PLURAL when a group of people are emancipated □ the emancipation of women

embankment /ɪm'bæŋkmənt/ NOUN [plural embankments] a slope of soil built along the sides of a railway, river or road

embargo /em'bɑːgəʊ/ NOUN [plural embargoes] an official order stopping trade with another country ▣ There are no signs that the arms embargo will be lifted.

embark /ɪm'bɑːk/ VERB [embarks, embarking, embarked] to get on a ship or an aircraft at the beginning of a journey

♦ PHRASAL VERB **embark on something** to start doing something new □ We're about to embark on an exciting new project.

embarrass /ɪm'bærəs/ VERB [embarrasses, embarrassing, embarrassed] to make someone feel ashamed or stupid □ Stop it! You're embarrassing me! □ The information could embarrass the president if it gets out.

• **embarrassed** /ɪm'bærəst/ ADJECTIVE looking or feeling ashamed or stupid □ an embarrassed silence ▣ Quinn felt embarrassed. □ + about They're very embarrassed about what's happened. □ + by She looked a little embarrassed by all the attention.

• **embarrassing** /ɪm'bærəsɪŋ/ ADJECTIVE making you feel embarrassed □ It was one of those embarrassing moments. ▣ a highly embarrassing photo □ + for The incident was very embarrassing for the government.

• **embarrassingly** /ɪm'bærəsɪŋlɪ/ ADVERB in an embarrassing way □ Things have gone embarrassingly wrong.

• **embarrassment** /ɪm'bærəsmənt/ NOUN, NO PLURAL

1 a feeling of being embarrassed ▣ Check the price in advance to avoid embarrassment. ▣ I don't want to cause her any embarrassment.

2 someone or something that makes you feel embarrassed □ The case is a huge embarrassment for the authorities.

embassy /'embəsɪ/ NOUN [plural embassies] a group of officials who represent their government in a foreign country, or the building where they work □ the Australian embassy in Washington

embedded /ɪmˈbedɪd/ ADJECTIVE
1 fixed firmly in the surface of something □ *The boat had become embedded in the mud.*
2 being a very important part of something and difficult to change □ *Hunting is deeply embedded in their culture.*

embellish /ɪmˈbelɪʃ/ VERB [**embellishes, embellishing, embellished**] to add details to something to make it more interesting or more decorated □ *He had embellished the story a bit.* □ *The boxes are embellished with gold and silver.*
• **embellishment** /ɪmˈbelɪʃmənt/ NOUN [*plural* **embellishments**] something added to embellish something □ *The story is so amazing, it needs no embellishment.*

embers /ˈembəz/ PLURAL NOUN the small hot pieces left when coal or wood is burnt in a fire

embezzle /ɪmˈbezəl/ [**embezzles, embezzling, embezzled**] to steal money that belongs to someone you work for □ *He embezzled money from his clients.*
• **embezzlement** /ɪmˈbezəlmənt/ NOUN, NO PLURAL the crime of embezzling money

emblem /ˈembləm/ NOUN [*plural* **emblems**] an object or image that is used as a symbol to represent something □ *The thistle is the emblem of Scotland.*

embodiment /ɪmˈbɒdɪmənt/ NOUN, NO PLURAL the embodiment of something when someone embodies something □ *She is the embodiment of good health.*

embody /ɪmˈbɒdɪ/ [**embodies, embodying, embodied**] to represent or to be a good example of an idea or a quality □ *She embodies the spirit of the Olympic games.*

embrace /ɪmˈbreɪs/ ▶ VERB [**embraces, embracing, embraced**]
1 to put your arms around someone and hold them as a sign of love or being friends □ *The two friends embraced warmly.*
2 to accept an idea or activity with enthusiasm ⌕ *They've embraced the idea of distance learning.* □ *Small businesses have embraced the new technology.*
3 a formal word meaning to include something □ *The subject embraces both maths and science.*
▶ NOUN [*plural* **embraces**] when you put your arms round someone □ *They parted with an embrace.*

embroider /ɪmˈbrɔɪdə(r)/ VERB [**embroiders, embroidering, embroidered**] to sew patterns or pictures with coloured threads on a piece of cloth □ *a silk scarf embroidered with flowers*
• **embroidery** /ɪmˈbrɔɪdərɪ/ NOUN [*plural* **embroideries**]
1 the activity of embroidering
2 a piece of cloth that has been embroidered

embryo /ˈembrɪəʊ/ NOUN [*plural* **embryos**] a baby or animal when it starts growing inside its mother's womb. A biology word.

emerald /ˈemərəld/ ▶ NOUN [*plural* **emeralds**] a valuable green stone used in jewellery □ *an emerald ring*
▶ ADJECTIVE having a bright green colour like an emerald

emerge /ɪˈmɜːdʒ/ VERB [**emerges, emerging, emerged**]
1 to come out of something or from behind something □ *The baby crocodiles emerge from the eggs.* □ *Al emerged from the tent.*
2 to become known or recognized □ *More details have emerged about the accident.*
• **emergence** /ɪˈmɜːdʒəns/ NOUN, NO PLURAL when something appears or becomes recognized □ *the emergence of a new virus* □ *China's emergence as a world power*

emergency /ɪˈmɜːdʒənsɪ/ ▶ NOUN [*plural* **emergencies**] a sudden, unexpected and usually dangerous event that needs immediate action ⌕ *In an emergency, call my husband's number.* ⌕ *I always take my mobile with me in case of emergencies.* ⌕ *a medical emergency*
▶ ADJECTIVE to do with an emergency □ *emergency surgery* □ *The plane made an emergency landing.*

emergency services /ɪˈmɜːdʒənsɪ ˌsɜːˈvɪsɪz/ PLURAL NOUN organizations that deal with accidents, fire, crime, etc. such as the police and fire service

emigrant /ˈemɪgrənt/ NOUN [*plural* **emigrants**] someone who leaves the country where they were born to live in a different country
• **emigrate** /ˈemɪgreɪt/ VERB [**emigrates, emigrating, emigrated**] to leave the country where you were born in order to live in a different country □ *The family emigrated to Australia in 1954.*

eminent /ˈemɪnənt/ ADJECTIVE famous and respected □ *an eminent lawyer*

emission /ɪˈmɪʃən/ NOUN [*plural* **emissions**]
1 something that goes out into the air, such as smoke from a factory ⌕ *We must reduce carbon emissions.* □ *emissions of greenhouse gases*
2 the process of going out into the air

emit /ɪˈmɪt/ VERB [**emits, emitting, emitted**] to send light, heat, gas or a sound out into the air. A formal word. □ *The substance emits light.* □ *The machine emitted a high-pitched screech.*

emoticon /ɪˈməʊtɪkɒn/ NOUN [*plural* **emoticons**] a sideways image of a face made with keyboard symbols. People put emoticons in e-mails to show that they are joking, or pleased, etc. A computing word.

emotion /ɪˈməʊʃən/ NOUN [*plural* **emotions**] a feeling, such as love, hate, fear or anger ⌕ *He showed no emotion throughout the trial.* □ *Anya struggled to control her emotions.* ⌕ *I've got mixed emotions* (= good and bad feelings) *about the place.*
• **emotional** /ɪˈməʊʃənəl/ ADJECTIVE showing or having strong feelings □ *an emotional speech* ⌕ *I get emotional just talking about it.* □ *He was in a highly emotional state.*

• **emotionally** /ɪ'məʊʃənəlɪ/ ADVERB
1 in a way that is to do with someone's emotions
□ *He is still emotionally fragile.*
2 in an emotional way □ *He spoke very emotionally.*

empathize *or* **empathise** /'empəθaɪz/ VERB
[**empathizes, empathizing, empathized**] to
understand how someone feels because you have
experienced the same things they have □ *I can
empathize with the family's situation.*
• **empathy** /'empəθɪ/ NOUN, NO PLURAL the ability to
understand how someone feels

emperor /'empərə(r)/ NOUN [*plural* **emperors**] the
ruler of an empire

emphasis /'emfəsɪs/ NOUN [*plural* **emphases**]
1 special importance or attention you give to
something 🔁 *Schools put too much emphasis on
exams.* 🔁 *We need a greater emphasis on English skills.*
2 extra force or strength you give to a word or sound
when you are speaking □ **+ on** *You say it with the
emphasis on the second syllable.*
• **emphasize** *or* **emphasise** /'emfəsaɪz/ VERB
[**emphasizes, emphasizing, emphasized**] to give
special importance or attention to something 🔁 *I want
to emphasize the importance of road safety.* □ *She
emphasized that she had been treated very well.*
• **emphatic** /ɪm'fætɪk/ ADJECTIVE strong and clear
□ *The answer is an emphatic yes.* □ *an emphatic
victory*
• **emphatically** /ɪm'fætɪkəlɪ/ ADVERB in a strong,
clear way □ *He emphatically denied any connection.*

empire /'empaɪə(r)/ NOUN [*plural* **empires**]
1 a group of countries governed by one leader or
government □ *the Roman empire*
2 a group of companies controlled by one person or
organization □ *a global media empire*

employ /ɪm'plɔɪ/ VERB [**employs, employing,
employed**]
1 to pay someone to work for you □ *The company
employs skilled workers.* □ **+ as** *He was employed as a
design consultant.* □ **+ to do something** *We
employed a local builder to do the work.*
2 a formal word meaning to use something □ *Police
employed DNA techniques to solve the crime.*
• **employee** /ɪm'plɔɪi:/ NOUN [*plural* **employees**]
someone who works for a company or another person
🔁 *The company has 16 full-time employees.* □ **+ of**
We spoke to a former employee of the firm.
• **employer** /ɪm'plɔɪə(r)/ NOUN [*plural* **employers**] a
company or person who employs people □ *It's a
chance for students to meet potential employers.*
□ *The factory is the area's largest employer.*
• **employment** /ɪm'plɔɪmənt/ NOUN, NO PLURAL
1 paid work for a company or person 🔁 *Are you in full-
time employment?* 🔁 *He found employment as a
security guard.*
2 a formal word meaning the use of something

empower /ɪm'paʊə(r)/ VERB [**empowers,
empowering, empowered**]
1 to give someone the skills, confidence, etc. to
control their life □ *We aim to empower people with
disabilities.*
2 be empowered to do something to have the
power or authority to do something □ *The police are
not empowered to break up peaceful demonstrations.*
empress /'emprɪs/ NOUN [*plural* **empresses**] a
female ruler of an empire

emptiness /'emptɪnɪs/ NOUN, NO PLURAL
1 a feeling of having no meaning, emotion or purpose
□ *There was an emptiness in his eyes.*
2 the state of being empty □ *the emptiness of outer
space*

empty /'emptɪ/ ► ADJECTIVE [**emptier, emptiest**]
1 containing nothing or no one □ *an empty box*
🔁 *There was an empty space between the two
buildings.* □ *The restaurant was almost empty.* □ **+ of**
The streets were empty of traffic.
2 with no emotion or purpose □ *Without Tom her life
felt empty.*
3 not sincere or likely to be effective 🔁 *This is just
another empty promise.*
► VERB [**empties, emptying, emptied**] to become
empty, or to make something empty □ *Empty your
pockets.* □ *The theatre slowly emptied.*

emu /'i:mju:/ NOUN [*plural* **emus**] a very large
Australian bird that cannot fly
emulate /'emjuleɪt/ VERB [**emulates, emulating,
emulated**] a formal word meaning to copy someone
or something because you admire them □ *We hope to
emulate the success of such schemes in other
countries.*
emulsion /ɪ'mʌlʃən/ NOUN [*plural* **emulsions**]
1 a type of paint that produces a surface that is not
shiny
2 a smooth mixture of two or more liquids. A
chemistry word.

en- /en-/ PREFIX en- is added to the beginning of words
to mean 'into' □ *enclose* (= put something into
something)
enable /ɪ'neɪbəl/ VERB [**enables, enabling, enabled**]
to make it possible for someone to do something
□ *The software enables users to download music.*
-enabled /-ɪ'neɪbəld/ SUFFIX -enabled is added to the
end of words to mean 'having the technology or
equipment to do a particular thing' □ *a WiFi-enabled
phone*
enact /ɪ'nækt/ VERB [**enacts, enacting, enacted**]
1 a formal word meaning to make something law
□ *They have little chance of enacting this bill.*
2 to perform a story as a play □ *Children from the
Sunday school enacted Jesus's life.*
• **enactment** /ɪ'næktmənt/ NOUN, NO PLURAL when
something is enacted. A formal word. □ *the
enactment of new legislation*

enamel /ɪˈnæməl/ ► NOUN, NO PLURAL
1 a hard shiny substance used to cover metal to protect or decorate it
2 the hard white substance that covers teeth
► ADJECTIVE made of or covered with enamel □ *an enamel plate*

encapsulate /ɪnˈkæpsjʊleɪt/ VERB [**encapsulates, encapsulating, encapsulated**] to say the main facts about something in a short, clear way. A formal word. □ *It's difficult to encapsulate a lifetime's work in a single lecture.*

enchanted /ɪnˈtʃɑːntɪd/ ADJECTIVE
1 finding someone or something very attractive and interesting. A formal word. □ *I was enchanted by the children.*
2 affected by magic □ *an enchanted forest*
● **enchanting** /ɪnˈtʃɑːntɪŋ/ ADJECTIVE very attractive. A formal word. □ *an enchanting smile*

enclose /ɪnˈkləʊz/ VERB [**encloses, enclosing, enclosed**]
1 to put something in an envelope with a letter □ *I'm enclosing a copy of the certificate.*
2 to be all around something □ *The children's play area is enclosed by a wooden fence.*
● **enclosed** /ɪnˈkləʊzd/ ADJECTIVE surrounded by something 🔄 *an enclosed space*
● **enclosure** /ɪnˈkləʊʒə(r)/ NOUN [*plural* **enclosures**]
1 an area of land with a wall or fence around it □ *the penguin enclosure at the zoo*
2 something you put in an envelope with a letter. A formal word.

encompass /ɪnˈkʌmpəs/ VERB [**encompasses, encompassing, encompassed**] to include many things, ideas, etc. A formal word. □ *The course encompasses all aspects of painting.*

encore /ˈɒŋkɔː(r)/ NOUN [*plural* **encores**] an extra song etc. at the end of a performance because the audience wants more

encounter /ɪnˈkaʊntə(r)/ ► VERB [**encounters, encountering, encountered**]
1 to experience something bad 🔄 *We didn't encounter any problems.* □ *The troops encountered fierce resistance.*
2 a formal word meaning to meet someone by chance
► NOUN [*plural* **encounters**] a meeting that happens by chance □ *I had a chance encounter with a ski instructor from the same resort.*

encourage /ɪnˈkʌrɪdʒ/ VERB [**encourages, encouraging, encouraged**]
1 to support someone and make them feel confident about doing something □ **+ to do something** *We encourage students to work together.* □ *My parents encouraged me to write.* □ *We have been encouraged by recent successes.*
2 to make something more likely to happen □ *The school aims to encourage healthy eating.*
  encouragement /ɪnˈkʌrɪdʒmənt/ NOUN, NO PLURAL when you encourage someone or something □ *The crowd shouted encouragement to the team.*

🔄 *They offered her words of encouragement.* □ **+ to do something** *She needed no encouragement to dive into the pool.*
● **encouraging** /ɪnˈkʌrɪdʒɪŋ/ ADJECTIVE giving you confidence or hope 🔄 *an encouraging sign* □ *The results are highly encouraging.*
● **encouragingly** /ɪnˈkʌrɪdʒɪŋlɪ/ ADVERB in an encouraging way □ *He smiled encouragingly at her.*

encroach /ɪnˈkrəʊtʃ/ VERB [**encroaches, encroaching, encroached**] to take away or use up something. A formal word. □ *The job began to encroach on my family life.*

encyclopedia *or* **encyclopaedia** /ɪnˌsaɪkləʊˈpiːdɪə/ NOUN [*plural* **encyclopedias** *or* **encyclopaedias**] a book with information about many subjects, or on a particular subject □ *an encyclopedia of art*
● **encyclopedic** *or* **encyclopaedic** /ɪnˌsaɪkləʊˈpiːdɪk/ ADJECTIVE giving or having a lot of facts and information about many things

end /end/ ► NOUN [*plural* **ends**]
1 the last part of something □ *The end of the book is very sad.* □ *I'll come back at the end of the week.*
2 the part of something that is furthest away from the middle □ *He poked me with the end of a stick.* 🔄 *There is a church at the other end of this street.* 🔄 *We sat at opposite ends of the table.*
3 when something does not exist any more 🔄 *We were sad when our holiday came to an end.* 🔄 *I hope this agreement will put an end to the fighting.*
4 in the end after a long period of time □ *The train was delayed, but we got there in the end.*
5 an aim or purpose □ *They used their power for their own private ends.*
6 for days/weeks, etc. on end for many days/ weeks, etc. □ *In the hospital, they kept us waiting for hours on end.*
► VERB [**ends, ending, ended**] to finish □ *Our holiday ends tomorrow.* □ **+ with** *He ended his speech with a joke.* □ *The word cough ends with a 'f' sound.*
♦ PHRASAL VERB **end up somewhere/doing something** to have to do something or to finish in a bad situation □ *I knew he'd end up in prison.* □ *I ended up catching a later train.*

endanger /ɪnˈdeɪndʒə(r)/ VERB [**endangers, endangering, endangered**] to cause someone to be in a dangerous situation 🔄 *His actions could have endangered the lives of people nearby.* □ *These chemicals could endanger public health.*
● **endangered** /ɪnˈdeɪndʒəd/ ADJECTIVE an endangered type of animal or plant may soon stop existing because there are very few still alive □ *an endangered species* □ *a list of endangered animals*

endear /ɪnˈdɪə(r)/ VERB [**endears, endearing, endeared**] to make someone like you □ *He also endeared himself to staff with his sense of humour.*
● **endearing** /ɪnˈdɪərɪŋ/ ADJECTIVE making people like you □ *Her honesty is very endearing.*

endeavour /ɪnˈdevə(r)/ ▶ VERB [**endeavours, endeavouring, endeavoured**] a formal word meaning to try hard □ *We endeavour to meet the highest possible standards.*
▶ NOUN [*plural* **endeavours**]
1 a formal word meaning the effort or energy people put into doing things □ *human endeavour*
2 a formal word meaning an attempt to do something □ *I wish you luck in all your endeavours.*

ending /ˈendɪŋ/ NOUN [*plural* **endings**]
1 the last part of a story ⌑ *The story had a happy ending.* □ *+ of* *I don't want to spoil the ending of the film.*
2 no plural when something ends □ *+ of* *This contributed to the ending of the Cold War.*
3 letters added to the end of a word □ *an irregular past tense ending*

endless /ˈendlɪs/ ADJECTIVE seeming to never finish □ *The task seemed endless.* ⌑ *There's an endless supply of cheap workers.*
• **endlessly** /ˈendlɪslɪ/ ADVERB in a way that continues for a long time or distance □ *They argued endlessly about it.*

endocrine gland /ˈendəʊkraɪn ˌɡlænd/ NOUN [*plural* **endocrine glands**] an organ in the body that produces hormones (= chemicals that control how the body grows). A biology word.

endorse /ɪnˈdɔːs/ VERB [**endorses, endorsing, endorsed**] to give your support to something or someone publicly □ *The UN has endorsed the plan.* □ *He refused to endorse any of the candidates.*
• **endorsement** /ɪnˈdɔːsmənt/ NOUN [*plural* **endorsements**] public support for someone or something □ *He welcomed the union's endorsement of the new plan.* ⌑ *This was a ringing endorsement* (= very enthusiastic support).

endow /ɪnˈdaʊ/ VERB [**endows, endowing, endowed**]
1 be endowed with something to have a particular quality or ability. A formal phrase. □ *She was endowed with a beauty that most women dream of.*
2 to give a large amount of money to a hospital, college, etc.
• **endowment** /ɪnˈdaʊmənt/ NOUN [*plural* **endowments**]
1 money given to an organization □ *The college receives several endowments from private individuals.*
2 a natural quality or ability that someone has. A formal word.

endurance /ɪnˈdjʊərəns/ NOUN, NO PLURAL the ability to do something physically difficult for a long time □ *a test of endurance* □ *We do fitness work to improve endurance.*

endure /ɪnˈdjʊə(r)/ VERB [**endures, enduring, endured**]
1 to suffer something unpleasant, especially for a long time □ *He endured long periods of loneliness.* □ *She endured terrible pain.*

2 to last for a long time □ *Our friendship endured until his death.*
• **enduring** /ɪnˈdjʊərɪŋ/ ADJECTIVE continuing to exist ⌑ *How can you explain the enduring appeal of this film?*

enemy /ˈenɪmɪ/ ▶ NOUN [*plural* **enemies**]
1 someone who is against you and wants to harm you ⌑ *He made a few enemies while he was there.* □ *+ of* *They are viewed as enemies of the regime.*
2 the enemy in a war, the people or country you are fighting against □ *We will defend ourselves and defeat the enemy.*
♦ IDIOM be your own worst enemy to do things which harm you more than other people □ *Sometimes he's his own worst enemy.*
▶ ADJECTIVE to do with the enemy □ *enemy troops*

energetic /ˌenəˈdʒetɪk/ ADJECTIVE very active and full of energy □ *an energetic dance* □ *I feel a lot more energetic.*

energy /ˈenədʒɪ/ NOUN [*plural* **energies**]
1 the strength or power you have to work or to be active □ *Young children have loads of energy.* □ *My boss has tremendous energy and enthusiasm.* □ *+ to do something* *I didn't have the energy to walk home.*
2 a form of power, such as heat or electricity ⌑ *Turn off lights to save energy.* ⌑ *nuclear energy* ⌑ *renewable sources of energy* □ *energy efficiency*

enforce /ɪnˈfɔːs/ VERB [**enforces, enforcing, enforced**]
1 to make sure people obey a law or rule ⌑ *It is the job of the police to enforce the law.* □ *Airlines must ensure the rules are enforced.*
2 to make sure that something happens □ *He tried to enforce discipline in the team.*
• **enforcement** /ɪnˈfɔːsmənt/ NOUN, NO PLURAL when something is enforced ⌑ *law enforcement* □ *the enforcement of public health rules*

engage /ɪnˈɡeɪdʒ/ VERB [**engages, engaging, engaged**]
1 to make someone interested and get their attention □ *A good speaker will engage their audience.*
2 a formal word meaning to start to employ someone □ *She engaged a top lawyer to represent her.*
3 engage someone in conversation to start a conversation with someone
♦ PHRASAL VERB engage in something to take part in an activity. A formal phrase. □ *Are they willing to engage in discussions?*
• **engaged** /ɪnˈɡeɪdʒd/ ADJECTIVE
1 if two people are engaged, they have promised to marry each other □ *+ to* *She's engaged to actor Alec Donovan.* ⌑ *The couple got engaged last month.*
2 if a telephone or toilet is engaged, it is being used
• **engagement** /ɪnˈɡeɪdʒmənt/ NOUN [*plural* **engagements**]
1 a promise to marry someone ⌑ *They announced their engagement in September.*

2 an arrangement to meet someone or to do something ▣ *He has a lot of social engagements.* □ *The prince was forced to cancel several official engagements.*

engine /'endʒɪn/ NOUN [plural **engines**]
1 a part of a machine that uses energy to produce movement □ *a car with a diesel engine* ▣ *He closed the door and started the engine.*
2 the part at the front of a train that pulls it along □ *a steam engine*

engineer /ˌendʒɪ'nɪə(r)/ ► NOUN [plural **engineers**]
1 someone who designs and makes things like bridges, roads or machines
2 someone who works with and repairs engines and machines □ *a telephone engineer*
► VERB [**engineers, engineering, engineered**] to make something happen by clever planning □ *He tried to engineer a meeting between the two sides.*
• **engineering** /ˌendʒɪ'nɪərɪŋ/ NOUN, NO PLURAL the study or work of designing and making machines, roads, bridges, etc. ▣ *He graduated in mechanical engineering.*

English /'ɪŋglɪʃ/ ► ADJECTIVE
1 belonging to or from England □ *the English countryside*
2 to do with the English language □ *an English translation*
► NOUN
1 *no plural* the main language of Britain, North America and Australia, and an official language in some other countries □ *She speaks English very well.*
2 the English people from England

Englishman /'ɪŋglɪʃmən/ NOUN [plural **Englishmen**] a man who comes from England, or who has English parents

engrave /ɪn'greɪv/ VERB [**engraves, engraving, engraved**] to cut a pattern or letters into a hard surface □ *The trophy is engraved with the names of previous winners.*
• **engraving** /ɪn'greɪvɪŋ/ NOUN [plural **engravings**]
1 a picture made by engraving
2 the process or skill of engraving

engrossed /ɪn'grəʊst/ ADJECTIVE if you are engrossed in something, it takes all your attention or interest □ *I sat engrossed in a book.*

engulf /ɪn'gʌlf/ VERB [**engulfs, engulfing, engulfed**]
1 to surround something and cover it completely □ *Fire engulfed the building.*
2 if fighting or violence engulfs a place, it affects all of it □ *Violence is threatening to engulf the entire city.*

enhance /ɪn'hɑːns/ VERB [**enhances, enhancing, enhanced**] to improve something □ *The swimmer claims he has never used drugs to enhance his performance.*
• **enhancement** /ɪn'hɑːnsmənt/ NOUN [plural **enhancements**] when something is improved, or the

improvement itself □ *There were a number of security enhancements put in place at the airport.*

enigma /ɪ'nɪgmə/ NOUN [plural **enigmas**] someone or something mysterious that no one understands □ *Their sudden disappearance remains an enigma.*
• **enigmatic** /ˌenɪg'mætɪk/ ADJECTIVE mysterious and impossible to understand □ *an enigmatic smile*

enjoy /ɪn'dʒɔɪ/ VERB [**enjoys, enjoying, enjoyed**]
1 to like doing something □ *They seemed to enjoy the concert.* □ *Enjoy your meal!* □ *+ ing I enjoy playing tennis.*
2 **enjoy yourself** to have a good time doing something □ *We enjoyed ourselves at the party.* □ *He was clearly enjoying himself.*
3 to experience something good or an advantage. A formal word. □ *He has enjoyed some success as an author.*
• **enjoyable** /ɪn'dʒɔɪəbəl/ ADJECTIVE fun and giving you pleasure □ *The whole trip was a really enjoyable experience.*
• **enjoyment** /ɪn'dʒɔɪmənt/ NOUN, NO PLURAL when you enjoy something ▣ *I get tremendous enjoyment out of the sport.* □ *+ of I don't let the illness affect my enjoyment of life.*

enlarge /ɪn'lɑːdʒ/ VERB [**enlarges, enlarging, enlarged**] to make something bigger □ *Click here to enlarge the image.*
♦ PHRASAL VERB **enlarge on/upon something** a formal word meaning to give more information about something
• **enlargement** /ɪn'lɑːdʒmənt/ NOUN [plural **enlargements**]
1 when something is enlarged □ *the enlargement of the European Union*
2 a larger photograph made from a smaller one

enlighten /ɪn'laɪtn/ VERB [**enlightens, enlightening, enlightened**] a formal word meaning to explain something to someone
• **enlightened** /ɪn'laɪtənd/ ADJECTIVE having good, modern ideas and beliefs about something ▣ *We now have a more enlightened attitude towards disability.*
• **enlightening** /ɪn'laɪtənɪŋ/ ADJECTIVE giving you new information about something □ *an enlightening conversation*

enlist /ɪn'lɪst/ VERB [**enlists, enlisting, enlisted**]
1 to join the army, navy or air force □ *He enlisted in the Marines.*
2 to ask someone to help or support you ▣ *He enlisted the help of his brother.*

enmity /'enmətɪ/ NOUN, NO PLURAL a feeling of strong dislike towards someone. A formal word.

enormity /ɪ'nɔːmətɪ/ NOUN, NO PLURAL how large or important something is □ *We are aware of the enormity of the problem.*

enormous /ɪ'nɔːməs/ ADJECTIVE very big or great □ *an enormous tree* ▣ *It cost an enormous amount of money.* □ *The staff were under enormous pressure.*
• **enormously** /ɪ'nɔːməslɪ/ ADVERB very much or

extremely □ *They all enjoyed themselves enormously.* □ *We are enormously grateful.*

enough /ɪ'nʌf/ ► DETERMINER, PRONOUN

1 as much or as many as you need or want □ *Have you all had enough to eat?* □ *We need some more oil – there isn't enough here.* □ *I've got enough problems without this!*

2 have had enough of something if you have had enough of something, you do not want to have it or do it any more □ *I've had enough of cooking every day!* ► ADVERB as much as is needed or wanted □ *She's not pretty enough to be a model.* □ *Stop when you think you've written enough.*

enquire /en'kwaɪə(r)/ VERB [enquires, enquiring, enquired] another spelling of inquire

• **enquiry** /en'kwaɪərɪ/ NOUN [plural enquiries] another spelling of inquiry

enrage /ɪn'reɪdʒ/ VERB [enrages, enraging, enraged] to make someone very angry □ *The referee's decision enraged Chelsea fans.*

enrich /ɪn'rɪtʃ/ VERB [enriches, enriching, enriched] to improve something by adding something to it □ *Art enriches people's lives.* □ *The nutrients enrich the soil.*

enrol /ɪn'rəʊl/ VERB [enrols, enrolling, enrolled] to put your name or someone else's name on a list to become a member of a course, club, college, etc. □ *Jackie's just enrolled at a stage school.* □ *It costs £50 to enrol a child in the activities programme.*

• **enrolment** /ɪn'rəʊlmənt/ NOUN [plural enrolments] the process of enrolling or the number of people enrolled □ *There's been an increase in international student enrolments.*

enroll /ɪn'rəʊl/ VERB [enrolls, enrolling, enrolled] the US spelling of enrol

• **enrollment** /ɪn'rəʊlmənt/ NOUN [plural enrollments] the US spelling of enrolment

ensue /ɪn'sjuː/ VERB [ensues, ensuing, ensued] a formal word meaning to happen after something, often caused by that thing □ *Hundreds of people came into the shop and chaos ensued.*

• **ensuing** /ɪn'sjuːɪŋ/ ADJECTIVE happening after something, often caused by that thing □ *Police shot one of the protesters and 12 more people were injured in the ensuing battle.*

ensure /ɪn'ʃʊə(r)/ VERB [ensures, ensuring, ensured] to make certain of something. A formal word. □ *Please ensure you have all your belongings with you when you leave the train.*

entail /ɪn'teɪl/ VERB [entails, entailing, entailed] to involve something or to make it necessary □ *Can you tell me what the job will entail?*

entangled /ɪn'tæŋgəld/ ADJECTIVE

1 twisted together and difficult to separate □ *The animals get entangled in the fishing nets.*

2 involved in a difficult situation that you cannot escape from □ *The company has become entangled in a legal battle.*

enter /'entə(r)/ VERB [enters, entering, entered]

1 to go into a place □ *A tall man entered the room.* □ *He entered hospital at 3pm.* □ *The bullet entered his skull.* □ *They entered the country illegally.*

2 to put information in a book, document, computer, etc. □ *Enter your name here.* □ *The data is entered in a special computerized system.*

3 to get to a particular period of time □ *We are entering a new era of prosperity.* □ *Talks have entered their fourth week.*

4 to start to take part in a job or an activity □ *He entered parliament at the age of forty.* □ *Our company entered the Chinese market in 1996.*

5 to take part in a competition or an exam □ *My mum agreed to enter the mother's race.*

6 enter a plea to tell a court that you are guilty or not guilty □ *She entered a plea of not guilty.*

♦ PHRASAL VERB **enter into something** to become involved with something □ *France has agreed to enter into discussions with other countries.*

enterprise /'entəpraɪz/ NOUN [plural enterprises]

1 a business or organization □ *a large commercial enterprise*

2 a large or difficult plan or activity □ *The research project is a joint enterprise between UCLA and the University of California.*

3 the ability to think of new ideas and to make them happen

• **enterprising** /'entəpraɪzɪŋ/ ADJECTIVE able to think of new ideas and not frightened of taking risks □ *Some enterprising individuals are already using the technology to create their own TV channels.*

entertain /,entə'teɪn/ VERB [entertains, entertaining, entertained]

1 to do something which people find interesting and enjoyable □ *Emily entertained us by telling a few jokes.* □ *A band entertained the crowd.*

2 to invite people as your guests for a meal or a drink □ *Tom tends to cook when we're entertaining.*

3 a formal word meaning to consider an idea 🕮 *He had entertained thoughts of leaving his job.*

• **entertainer** /,entə'teɪnə(r)/ NOUN [plural entertainers] someone who performs to entertain people □ *He's one of Britain's most popular entertainers.*

• **entertaining** /,entə'teɪnɪŋ/ ADJECTIVE interesting and enjoyable □ *She gave an entertaining account of her trip.* □ *It was a highly entertaining match.*

• **entertainment** /,entə'teɪnmənt/ NOUN [plural entertainments] something that entertains people □ *There's live entertainment every night.* 🕮 *Traditional dancers provided the entertainment.* 🕮 *There are new forms of entertainment developing on the Internet.*

enthral /ɪn'θrɔːl/ VERB [enthrals, enthralling, enthralled] to interest you and hold your attention completely

• **enthralled** /ɪn'θrɔːld/ ADJECTIVE very interested by

something and giving it all your attention □ *an enthralled audience*

• **enthralling** /ɪnˈθrɔːlɪŋ/ ADJECTIVE very interesting and taking all your attention □ *an enthralling contest*

enthuse /ɪnˈθjuːz/ VERB [**enthuses, enthusing, enthused**] to speak or write about how much you like something in an excited way □ *'Great dance!' she enthused, smiling at him.*

enthusiasm /ɪnˈθjuːzɪæzəm/ NOUN, NO PLURAL when you are very interested in something or want to do it very much □ **+ for** *Her enthusiasm for her subject remains as strong.* ⊞ *There was a general lack of enthusiasm for the project.*

• **enthusiast** /ɪnˈθjuːzɪæst/ NOUN [*plural* **enthusiasts**] someone who is very interested or involved in a particular thing □ *a cycling enthusiast*

• **enthusiastic** /ɪnˌθjuːzɪˈæstɪk/ ADJECTIVE showing enthusiasm □ **+ about** *Not everyone is enthusiastic about the idea.* □ *You don't sound very enthusiastic.*

• **enthusiastically** /ɪnˌθjuːzɪˈæstɪkəlɪ/ ADVERB in an enthusiastic way

entice /ɪnˈtaɪs/ VERB [**entices, enticed, enticing**] to persuade someone to do something by promising them something good □ *Companies offer bonuses to entice young mothers back to work.*

entire /ɪnˈtaɪə(r)/ ADJECTIVE all of something □ *He lived his entire life in the same town.*

• **entirely** /ɪnˈtaɪəlɪ/ ADVERB completely □ *It was my fault entirely.* □ *The two things are entirely different.*

• **entirety** /ɪnˈtaɪərətɪ/ NOUN, NO PLURAL the whole of something □ *I haven't seen the finished film in its entirety.*

entitle /ɪnˈtaɪtəl/ VERB [**entitles, entitling, entitled**] **1** to give someone the right to have or to do something □ *You are entitled to five weeks' holiday per year.* **2** to give something a title □ *The book is entitled 'A Soldier's Tale'.*

• **entitlement** /ɪnˈtaɪtəlmənt/ NOUN [*plural* **entitlements**] something you are entitled to □ *holiday entitlement*

entity /ˈentətɪ/ NOUN [*plural* **entities**] a formal word for a complete, separate thing ⊞ *The two companies have the same owner but they operate as separate entities.*

entrance /ˈentrəns/ NOUN [*plural* **entrances**] **1** the part of a building where you go into it ⊞ *I'll meet you outside the main entrance.* □ **+ of** *There are security staff at the entrance of the building.* □ **+ to** *There were clear signs at the entrance to the tunnel.* **2** when you go into a place ⊞ *Everyone looked round as the singer made her entrance.* **3** the right to go into a place or to become a member of an organization □ *a university entrance exam* ⊞ *There's an entrance fee of £8.*

• **entrant** /ˈentrənt/ NOUN [*plural* **entrants**] someone who enters a competition or exam □ *Competition entrants must be 16 or over.*

entreat /ɪnˈtriːt/ VERB [**entreats, entreating, entreated**] to ask someone for something in an eager or emotional way because you want it very much. A formal word. □ *She entreated him to leave the gun behind.*

• **entreaty** /ɪnˈtriːtɪ/ NOUN [*plural* **entreaties**] when you entreat someone to do something. A formal word. □ *He left that day, despite Anna's passionate entreaties.*

entrepreneur /ˌɒntrəprəˈnɜː(r)/ NOUN [*plural* **entrepreneurs**] a person who starts a business using their own ideas and usually their own money □ *China's young entrepreneurs*

• **entrepreneurial** /ˌɒntrəprəˈnɜːrɪəl/ ADJECTIVE to do with entrepreneurs ⊞ *an entrepreneurial spirit*

entrust /ɪnˈtrʌst/ VERB [**entrusts, entrusting, entrusted**] to give someone the responsibility of dealing with or looking after something □ *I wouldn't entrust my child's education to these people.*

entry /ˈentrɪ/ NOUN [*plural* **entries**] **1** when you go into a place ⊞ *They were refused entry into the country.* ⊞ *We gained entry (= got in) through an open window.* □ **+ to** *This card gives you free entry to most museums.* □ **+ into** *They were allowed entry into the area.* **2** no entry a phrase used on signs to show that you must not go into a place. **3** a piece of information that is written in a book, document, computer system, etc. □ *I checked my diary entry for that day.* **4** something that you have done to try to win a competition ⊞ *The winning entries will be announced next week.* □ *The competition attracted thousands of entries.* **5** when you become a member of an organization or start to take part in a job or activity □ **+ into** *The year 2001 saw their entry into the European Union.* □ *Many people opposed their entry into the war.*

envelop /ɪnˈveləp/ VERB [**envelops, enveloping, enveloped**] to surround and cover something completely □ *A thick fog enveloped the hills.*

envelope /ˈenvələup/ NOUN [*plural* **envelopes**] a folded paper cover for a letter, especially one that is sent by post □ *a brown A4 envelope* ⊞ *You haven't opened the envelope.*

envious /ˈenvɪəs/ ADJECTIVE wanting something that someone else has □ *He was rather envious of his brother's success.*

environment /ɪnˈvaɪərənmənt/ NOUN [*plural* **environments**] **1** the environment all the things, such as air, land, sea, animals and plants, that make up the natural world around us ⊞ *Our main aim is to protect the environment.*

2 the things that surround you where you live, work or do something ⊞ *We want to create a positive working environment.* □ *It provides a safe environment for young children to play.*

• **environmental** /ɪnˌvaɪərənˈmentəl/ ADJECTIVE to do with the environment □ *an environmental group* □ *environmental concerns*

• **environmentalist** /ɪnˌvaɪərənˈmentəlɪst/ NOUN [plural **environmentalists**] someone who tries to protect the environment from damage

• **environmentally** /ɪnˌvaɪərənˈmentəlɪ/ ADVERB in a way that is to do with the environment □ *These chemicals are environmentally damaging.*

environmentally friendly /ɪnˌvaɪərənˌmentəlɪ ˈfrendlɪ/ ADJECTIVE not harmful to the environment

envisage /ɪnˈvɪzɪdʒ/ VERB [envisages, envisaging, envisaged] to imagine something or to think it is likely to happen in the future □ *I tried to envisage a life without Lily.* □ *We don't envisage taking on more staff.*

envoy /ˈenvɔɪ/ NOUN [plural **envoys**] a government official sent to another country to meet with a foreign government □ *the United Nations envoy to Bosnia*

envy /ˈenvɪ/ ▶ NOUN, NO PLURAL
1 a feeling of wanting what someone else has □ *I felt a little envy at her success.*
2 be the envy of someone to be something that other people would very much like to have □ *Our health system was once the envy of the world.*
▶ VERB [envies, envying, envied] to want what someone else has □ *We envied him because he didn't have to go to school.*

enzyme /ˈenzaɪm/ NOUN [plural **enzymes**] a chemical substance made in both animals and plants, which causes chemical changes. A biology word.

ephemeral /ɪˈfemərəl/ ADJECTIVE lasting only for a short time. A formal word.

epic /ˈepɪk/ ▶ NOUN [plural **epics**] a long story, poem or film about great events or exciting adventures □ *His new film is a historical epic.*
▶ ADJECTIVE like an epic □ *an epic journey*

epicenter /ˈepɪsentə(r)/ NOUN [plural **epicenters**] the US spelling of epicentre

epicentre /ˈepɪsentə(r)/ NOUN [plural **epicentres**] the point on the ground just above the strongest part of an earthquake (= when the earth shakes)

epidemic /ˌepɪˈdemɪk/ NOUN [plural **epidemics**] a situation in which a disease spreads quickly and many people become ill at the same time □ *a flu epidemic*

epidermis /ˌepɪˈdɜːmɪs/ NOUN, NO PLURAL the outer layer of skin. A biology word.

epidural /ˌepɪˈdjʊərəl/ NOUN [plural **epidurals**] a medical treatment in which a drug is put into the lower part of your back in order to stop you feeling pain

epiglottis /ˌepɪˈglɒtɪs/ NOUN [plural **epiglottises**] a small part at the back of your tongue which stops food from going into the pipe that is for air. A biology word.

epilepsy /ˈepɪlepsɪ/ NOUN, NO PLURAL an illness that affects the brain, making someone shake in an

uncontrolled way, or become unconscious for short periods

• **epileptic** /ˌepɪˈleptɪk/ ▶ ADJECTIVE
1 caused by epilepsy □ *an epileptic fit*
2 affected by epilepsy □ *She's epileptic.*
▶ NOUN [plural **epileptics**] someone who suffers from epilepsy

episode /ˈepɪsəʊd/ NOUN [plural **episodes**]
1 one separate part of a story that is broadcast on the radio or television over a period of time
2 an event □ *It was one of the most embarrassing episodes of his life.*

epitaph /ˈepɪtɑːf/ NOUN [plural **epitaphs**] a short piece of writing on a dead person's grave

epitome /ɪˈpɪtəmɪ/ NOUN, NO PLURAL the epitome of something a typical example of something □ *Slim and dressed all in black, she is the epitome of elegance.*

• **epitomize** or **epitomise** /ɪˈpɪtəmaɪz/ VERB [epitomizes, epitomizing, epitomized] to be a typical example of something. A formal word. □ *His lack of skill epitomizes everything that is wrong with the team.*

epoch /ˈiːpɒk/ NOUN [plural **epochs**] a period of time in history

equal /ˈiːkwəl/ ▶ ADJECTIVE
1 of the same size, value or amount □ *Cut the cake into four roughly equal slices.*
2 having or deserving the same rights as other people □ *Men and women were finally regarded as equal.* ⊞ *equal rights for all*
▶ VERB [equals, equalling/US equaling, equalled/US equaled]
1 to be the same in size, value or amount □ *Two plus two equals four.*
2 to achieve as much as someone else □ *She equalled the world record in training.*
▶ NOUN [plural **equals**] someone who has the same rights or importance as another person □ *The women quite rightly expect to be treated by the men as equals.*

• **equality** /iːˈkwɒlətɪ/ NOUN, NO PLURAL when everyone has the same rights and importance ⊞ *racial equality* ⊞ *sexual equality*

• **equalize** or **equalise** /ˈiːkwəlaɪz/ VERB [equalizes, equalizing, equalized]
1 to win a point that gives you the same score as a team you are playing against □ *Rooney equalized just before half-time.*
2 to make two or more things equal □ *When you swallow, it equalizes the pressure in your ears.*

• **equalizer** or **equaliser** /ˈiːkwəlaɪzə(r)/ NOUN [plural **equalizers**] a goal that makes two teams' scores the same

• **equally** /ˈiːkwəlɪ/ ADVERB
1 to the same level □ *The two drivers were equally to blame for the accident.* □ *He works hard but Tom works equally hard.*
2 in amounts or parts that are the same □ *Share the sweets out equally.*
3 in a way that gives the same rights and importance to everyone □ *I try to treat the children equally.*

equal opportunities /ˈiːkwəl ˌɒpəˈtjuːnətɪz/ PLURAL NOUN the set of ideas which states that people of all races, sexes, ages, etc. must have the same chances to do things, especially at work □ *They have been fighting for an equal opportunities policy.*

equation /ɪˈkweɪʒən/ NOUN [plural **equations**] a mathematical statement that shows that two sets of numbers are equal

equator /ɪˈkweɪtə(r)/ NOUN, NO PLURAL the equator the line drawn on maps that goes around the middle of the Earth □ *Kampala is just north of the equator.*

equilateral /ˌiːkwɪˈlætərəl, ˌekwɪˈlætərəl/ ADJECTIVE an equilateral triangle has three equal sides. A maths word.

equilibrium /ˌiːkwɪˈlɪbrɪəm, ˌekwɪˈlɪbrɪəm/ NOUN, NO PLURAL equal balance between two things

equip /ɪˈkwɪp/ VERB [equips, equipping, equipped]
1 to provide something or someone with all the machines, furniture, etc. that are needed for a particular purpose □ *a fully equipped hospital*
2 to provide someone with the skills they need in order to do something □ *The aim of the course is to equip young people for the business world.*

• **equipment** /ɪˈkwɪpmənt/ NOUN, NO PLURAL the machines, furniture, etc. that you need in order to do a particular activity or job □ *camping equipment* □ *office equipment* 🖫 *a piece of equipment*

➤ Remember that **equipment** is never used in the plural:
✓ We need more equipment.
✗ We need more equipments.

equivalent /ɪˈkwɪvələnt/ ➤ NOUN [plural **equivalents**] something that has the same value, use, meaning or effect as something else □ *The Internet has become the modern equivalent of a telephone or a daily newspaper.* □ *Children eat the equivalent of almost twelve bags of sugar every year.*
➤ ADJECTIVE having the same value, use, meaning or effect □ *The average temperature of Mars is roughly equivalent to the temperature in Antarctica.*

-er /-ər/ SUFFIX
1 -er is added to the end of words to mean 'a person or thing that does something' □ *teacher*
2 -er is added to the end of some adjectives to make a comparative form □ *brighter*

era /ˈɪərə/ NOUN [plural **eras**] a period of time 🖫 *The country is entering a new era of peace and prosperity.*

eradicate /ɪˈrædɪkeɪt/ VERB [eradicates, eradicating, eradicated] to get rid of something bad completely. A formal word. □ *The government aims to eradicate poverty by 2015.*

• **eradication** /ɪˌrædɪˈkeɪʃən/ NOUN, NO PLURAL when you eradicate something. A formal word.

erase /ɪˈreɪz/ VERB [erases, erasing, erased]
1 to remove information or files from a computer □ *The file had somehow been erased.*
2 to get rid of something completely. A formal word. □ *She had erased the memory.*

• **eraser** /ɪˈreɪzə(r)/ NOUN [plural **erasers**] a small piece of rubber used to remove pencil marks from paper

erect /ɪˈrekt/ ➤ VERB [erects, erecting, erected]
1 to build something. A formal word. □ *They erected a monument to their leader.* □ *A barrier was erected around the area.*
2 to put the parts of a tent together. A formal word. □ *We had to erect the tent in the dark.*
➤ ADJECTIVE standing up straight □ *an erect posture*

• **erection** /ɪˈrekʃən/ NOUN, NO PLURAL the act of erecting something. A formal word.

erode /ɪˈrəʊd/ VERB [erodes, eroding, eroded]
1 if something erodes or is eroded, its surface is gradually removed by wind or water, for example □ *Houses are falling into the sea as the coastline erodes.*
2 to gradually make a quality less strong. A formal word. □ *The recent scandal has eroded public confidence in the government.*

• **erosion** /ɪˈrəʊʒən/ NOUN, NO PLURAL when something is eroded □ *soil erosion*

erotic /ɪˈrɒtɪk/ ADJECTIVE to do with sex □ *an erotic painting*

errand /ˈerənd/ NOUN [plural **errands**] run an errand to do a small job that involves going somewhere

erratic /ɪˈrætɪk/ ADJECTIVE changing often and when you do not expect it □ *Her increasingly erratic behaviour is causing concern.*

• **erratically** /ɪˈrætɪkəlɪ/ ADVERB in an erratic way □ *Police said he had been driving erratically.*

error /ˈerə(r)/ NOUN [plural **errors**] a mistake 🖫 *He admits making some errors.* 🖫 *The report blamed human error for the air crash.*

error message /ˈerə ˌmesɪdʒ/ NOUN [plural **error messages**] a message that appears on a computer screen when there is a problem. A computing word.

erupt /ɪˈrʌpt/ VERB [erupts, erupting, erupted]
1 violence or fighting erupts when it starts suddenly □ *Violence erupted at the demonstration.*
2 a volcano erupts when hot rocks, flames and dust suddenly come out of it

• **eruption** /ɪˈrʌpʃən/ NOUN [plural **eruptions**] when something erupts □ *a volcanic eruption*

escalate /ˈeskəleɪt/ VERB [escalates, escalating, escalated] to make or become worse or more serious □ *The violence has escalated in recent weeks.*

• **escalator** /ˈeskəleɪtə(r)/ NOUN [plural **escalators**] a set of moving stairs for carrying people between the levels of a building 🖫 *Shall we take the escalator?*

escapade /ˌeskəˈpeɪd/ NOUN [plural **escapades**] an exciting and dangerous adventure

escape /ɪˈskeɪp/ ➤ VERB [escapes, escaping, escaped]
1 to get away from a place where you are being kept □ **+ from** *The lion had escaped from its cage.*
2 to get away from a dangerous place or situation □ **+ from** *He escaped from the country hidden in a lorry.*

□ *When fire broke out, we managed to escape through the window.*

3 to avoid something unpleasant 🔁 *You're lucky to have escaped punishment.* 🔁 *They escaped injury by wrapping themselves in blankets.*

4 if something escapes attention, notice, etc. nobody notices it 🔁 *It has not escaped my attention that you have been late every day this week.* □ *This software uses advanced technology to escape detection.*

5 if something escapes you, you cannot remember it □ *I've met her before, but her name escapes me.*

6 if a substance escapes from a container, it comes out of it

▶ NOUN [*plural* **escapes**]

1 when someone gets away from a place or a bad situation □ **+ from** *He wrote a book about his daring escape from prison.*

2 when someone avoids something unpleasant 🔁 *Our car was balanced on the edge of the mountain – we had a very lucky escape.* 🔁 *The family had a narrow escape* (= could have been killed) *when their house was bombed.*

3 something that makes you forget about the problems of your life □ *Dancing is a means of escape for me.*

• **escaped** /ɪˈskeɪpt/ ADJECTIVE an escaped prisoner or animal has got away from the place where they were being kept

• **escapee** /ɪˌskeɪˈpiː/ NOUN [*plural* **escapees**] someone who has escaped, for example from prison

escape key /ɪˈskeɪp ˌkiː/ NOUN [*plural* **escape keys**] the key on a computer keyboard with 'Esc' on it, which allows you to leave a screen. A computing word.

escort ▶ VERB /ɪˈskɔːt/ [**escorts, escorting, escorted**] to go somewhere with someone in order to look after them □ *Airport staff will escort your child to the boarding gate.*

▶ NOUN /ˈeskɔːt/ [*plural* **escorts**] someone who escorts another person 🔁 *The players needed a police escort to get to the bus.*

esophagus /iːˈsɒfəgəs/ NOUN [*plural* **esophaguses**] the US spelling of **oesophagus**

especially /ɪˈspeʃəli/ ADVERB

1 very, more than anything or anyone else □ *I was especially impressed by the food.* □ *He wasn't especially clever.* □ *The children, especially the younger ones, were tired.*

2 for one person or purpose only □ **+ for** *I bought it especially for you.* □ **+ to do something** *I came here especially to see you.*

espionage /ˈespiənɑːʒ/ NOUN, NO PLURAL the activity of trying to find out another country's or company's secrets

espresso /eˈspresəʊ/ NOUN [*plural* **espressos**] a strong black coffee that you drink in small amounts

-ess /es/ SUFFIX -ess is added to the end of words to make a female form □ *lioness*

essay /ˈeseɪ/ NOUN [*plural* **essays**] a piece of writing by a student about a particular subject □ **plus_on** *Students are required to write a 4,000-word essay on a topic of their choice.*

essence /ˈesəns/ NOUN, NO PLURAL

1 the essence of something the most important part of something, or its true character □ *The film captures the essence of life in 18th-century Paris.*

2 a liquid that contains the very strong taste of the plant it has come from □ *vanilla essence*

essential /ɪˈsenʃəl/ ADJECTIVE if something is essential, you must do it or have it □ **+ that** *It is essential that we all stay together.* 🔁 *Fat is an essential part of our diet.* □ *A car is useful, but not essential.*

• **essentially** /ɪˈsenʃəli/ ADVERB

1 used for saying that something is mostly true □ *He looked a little older, but essentially the same.*

2 used for emphasizing the most important part of what you are saying □ *Essentially, he's her father, and that is what matters.*

• **essentials** /ɪˈsenʃəlz/ PLURAL NOUN things that you must have 🔁 *Just bring the bare essentials; your wallet, your passport and your ticket.*

-est /-ɪst/ SUFFIX -est is added to the end of some adjectives to make a superlative form □ *neatest*

establish /ɪˈstæblɪʃ/ VERB [**establishes, establishing, established**]

1 to start an organization or business □ *He established a small bakery.*

2 to make something start to exist □ *Police have established a good relationship with the community.* □ *We are trying to establish trade links with the area.*

3 to discover the truth about something □ *We managed to establish that he was born in Cambridge.* □ *Police have not established the cause of death.*

4 to become successful at something □ *He established himself as the leading expert on Mozart.* 🔁 *She established her reputation as an international artist.*

• **established** /ɪˈstæblɪʃt/ ADJECTIVE having existed successfully for a long time □ *an established business*

• **establishment** /ɪˈstæblɪʃmənt/ NOUN [*plural* **establishments**]

1 when something is started □ *The report recommends the establishment of a new committee.*

2 the educational/medical/scientific, etc. **establishment** the people who control a particular activity or job

3 the establishment the most important and powerful people in a country □ *She uses her art to challenge the establishment.*

4 an organization or business □ *a research establishment*

estate /ɪˈsteɪt/ NOUN [*plural* **estates**]

1 a large area with a lot of buildings on it 🔁 *an industrial estate* 🔁 *a housing estate*

2 a large area of land that belongs to one person or family

3 all the things that a person owns, especially when they die

4 a large type of car with a lot of space behind the seats for carrying things □ *a Volvo estate*

estate agent /ɪˈsteɪt ˌeɪdʒənt/ NOUN [plural **estate agents**] someone whose job is to help people to buy and sell houses and apartments

estate car /ɪˈsteɪt ˌkɑː(r)/ NOUN [plural **estate cars**] a large type of car with a lot of space behind the seats for carrying things

esteem /ɪˈstiːm/ NOUN, NO PLURAL respect and admiration for someone. A formal word.
➡ *go to self-esteem*

● **esteemed** /ɪˈstiːmd/ ADJECTIVE respected and admired by a lot of people □ *an esteemed author*

esthetic /iːsˈθetɪk/ ADJECTIVE the US spelling of aesthetic

● **esthetically** /iːˈsˈθetɪkəlɪ/ ADVERB the US spelling of aesthetically

estimate ▶ VERB /ˈestɪmeɪt/ [**estimates, estimating, estimated**] to try to judge the size, amount or value of something, using the information that you have □ *The government estimated the cost at over £5 million.* □ *Experts estimate that thousands of deaths every year are caused by unhealthy diets.*
▶ NOUN /ˈestɪmət/ [plural **estimates**]
1 when you estimate something
2 a statement telling a customer how much a service will cost

● **estimated** /ˈestɪmeɪtɪd/ ADJECTIVE approximate □ *An estimated 650,000 people have died as a result of the war.*

● **estimation** /ˌestɪˈmeɪʃən/ NOUN **in my estimation** in my opinion or judgment □ *She's really gone up in my estimation* (= I admire her more now than I did before).

estranged /ɪˈstreɪndʒd/ ADJECTIVE
1 no longer living with your husband or wife ⊞ *his estranged wife* ⊞ *her estranged husband*
2 no longer seeing or speaking to your family or friends □ *In the 1990s, he became estranged from his family.*

estrogen /ˈiːstrədʒən/ NOUN, NO PLURAL the US spelling of oestrogen

estuary /ˈestjuərɪ/ NOUN [plural **estuaries**] the wide part of a river where it flows into the sea. A geography word.

etc or **etc.** /ɪtˈsetərə/ ABBREVIATION used after a list to show that there are other similar things that you have not mentioned □ *The art shop sells paints, canvases, brushes, etc.*

etch /etʃ/ VERB [**etches, etching, etched**] to cut writing or images into a hard surface such as stone or metal
➡ IDIOM **be etched on your memory/mind** if something bad is etched on your memory or mind, you cannot forget it

etching /ˈetʃɪŋ/ NOUN [plural **etchings**] a picture

made using a print from a piece of metal that has the picture cut into it

eternal /ɪˈtɜːnəl/ ADJECTIVE
1 lasting forever, or seeming to last forever □ *the eternal cycle of the seasons* ⊞ *the secret of eternal youth*
2 always being a particular type of person □ *Max is the eternal optimist.*

● **eternally** /ɪˈtɜːnəlɪ/ ADVERB forever ⊞ *I'm eternally grateful to you for all your help.*

● **eternity** /ɪˈtɜːnətɪ/ NOUN, NO PLURAL
1 all of time, that never ends
2 a very long time □ *After what seemed an eternity, she spoke.*

ethic /ˈeθɪk/ NOUN [plural **ethics**]
1 **ethics** rules about what is right and wrong □ *Journalists must follow a code of ethics.*
2 a belief or principle that affects the way someone behaves ⊞ *I admire her work ethic.*

● **ethical** /ˈeθɪkəl/ ADJECTIVE
1 involving rules about what is right and wrong □ *ethical standards*
2 morally right □ *ethical consumers*

ethnic /ˈeθnɪk/ ADJECTIVE to do with a group of people who have the same race and culture ⊞ *The Pashtuns form the main ethnic group of Afghanistan.*

ethnic minority /ˌeθnɪk maɪˈnɒrətɪ/ NOUN [plural **ethnic minorities**] a group of people who all have the same race or culture, living in a place where most people have a different race or culture

etiquette /ˈetɪket/ NOUN, NO PLURAL a set of rules to do with polite behaviour

EU /ˌiːˈjuː/ ABBREVIATION **the EU** the European Union; a political and economic organization of European countries

eucalyptus /ˌjuːkəˈlɪptəs/ NOUN [plural **eucalyptuses** or **eucalypti**] a tree with leaves containing oil that has a strong smell, used in medicines

euphemism /ˈjuːfəmɪzəm/ NOUN [plural **euphemisms**] a polite word or phrase that you use instead of a more direct one, to talk about something unpleasant □ *He never talked about dying, preferring the euphemism 'pass away'.*

euphoria /juːˈfɔːrɪə/ NOUN, NO PLURAL a feeling of great excitement and happiness

● **euphoric** /juːˈfɒrɪk/ ADJECTIVE feeling very excited and happy

euro /ˈjuərəʊ/ NOUN [plural **euros**] the main unit of money in many European countries □ *There are 100 cents in a euro.*

European /ˌjuərəˈpiːən/ ▶ ADJECTIVE belonging to or from Europe
▶ NOUN [plural **Europeans**] a person from Europe

European Union /ˌjuərəˌpiːən ˈjuːnjən/ NOUN, NO PLURAL **the European Union** a political and economic organization of European countries

euthanasia /ˌjuːθəˈneɪzɪə/ NOUN, NO PLURAL when someone helps a very old or ill person to die, so that they will not suffer any longer

evacuate /ɪˈvækjueɪt/ VERB [**evacuates, evacuating, evacuated**] to leave a place because it is dangerous, or to make people leave a place because it is dangerous □ *Hundreds of people had to evacuate their homes during the floods.* □ *Residents were evacuated from the areas affected by the fires.*

• **evacuation** /ɪˌvækjuˈeɪʃən/ NOUN [*plural* **evacuations**] the act of evacuating people or a place

• **evacuee** /ɪˌvækjuˈiː/ NOUN [*plural* **evacuees**] someone who has been evacuated from a place, especially during a war

evade /ɪˈveɪd/ VERB [**evades, evading, evaded**]
1 to avoid being caught or noticed. A formal word. □ *He managed to evade capture for 13 months before the police found him.*
2 to avoid dealing with something that you should deal with. A formal word. □ *The opposition have accused him of evading responsibility.*

evaluate /ɪˈvæljueɪt/ VERB [**evaluates, evaluating, evaluated**] to decide how good or useful something is. A formal word. □ *Studies will evaluate the performance of the new drug.*

evaporate /ɪˈvæpəreɪt/ VERB [**evaporates, evaporating, evaporated**] if liquid evaporates, it turns into gas or steam. A chemistry word.

• **evaporation** /ɪˌvæpəˈreɪʃən/ NOUN, NO PLURAL when liquid evaporates. A chemistry word.

evasion /ɪˈveɪʒən/ NOUN [*plural* **evasions**] when someone tries to avoid dealing with something, or being caught 🔁 *He was charged with tax evasion.*

• **evasive** /ɪˈveɪsɪv/ ADJECTIVE not answering questions directly or honestly □ *She became evasive when I asked her why she had left the job.* 🔁 *He gave a rather evasive answer.*

• **evasively** /ɪˈveɪsɪvlɪ/ ADVERB in an evasive way □ *I can't remember,' said Phil evasively.*

eve /iːv/ NOUN [*plural* **eves**]
1 the day or evening before a particular day □ *He died on the eve of his 80th birthday.*
2 Eve used in the names of some days that come before an important day □ *Christmas Eve* □ *New Year's Eve*

even /ˈiːvən/ ▶ ADVERB
1 used to emphasize another word □ *It was even colder the next morning.* □ *Max is even better than Adam at football.* □ *Even Pia seemed to be enjoying herself.*
2 even though although □ *She still tried to help him, even though he was so rude to her.*
3 even if used to say that what you are going to say next would not change anything □ *Grandad wouldn't go on holiday even if we paid for it.*
▶ ADJECTIVE
1 an even surface is level and smooth
2 equal □ *The scores were even.*

3 regular and not changing □ *The wine must be stored at an even temperature.*
4 an even number is one that can be divided by 2

◆ PHRASAL VERB [**evens, evening, evened**] **even (something) out**
1 to become level □ *The track evened out once we got over the hill.*
2 to become equal □ *Sometimes she works more and sometimes I do – it evens out in the end.*

evening /ˈiːvnɪŋ/ NOUN [*plural* **evenings**] the last part of the day, before the night begins 🔁 *What are you doing this evening?* 🔁 *We're going to the cinema on Friday evening.* 🔁 *They usually watch TV in the evening.* 🔁 *What time do you usually have your evening meal?*

evenly /ˈiːvənlɪ/ ADVERB
1 in an even or smooth way □ *Spread the icing evenly over the top of the cake.*
2 in a way that is equal □ *The two teams were evenly matched.*

event /ɪˈvent/ NOUN [*plural* **events**]
1 something that happens 🔁 *These events occurred in the 19th century.* 🔁 *Recent events have made it necessary to introduce new rules.* 🔁 *Millions of people watched the events unfold (= happen) on TV.*
2 something such as sport or entertainment that is organized □ *The next event is the men's relay.* 🔁 *This is the biggest event ever staged in the city.* 🔁 *The main event this evening is a display of horse riding.*
3 in the event of a formal phrase meaning if something happens □ *In the event of an emergency, follow these instructions.*
4 in any event whatever happens □ *The train was late, but in any event we'd never have got there on time.*

• **eventful** /ɪˈventful/ ADJECTIVE full of interesting events □ *She's led an eventful life.*

eventual /ɪˈventʃuəl/ ADJECTIVE happening at the end of a period of time or as a result of a process □ *They lost the match to the eventual winners, Liverpool.*

• **eventuality** /ɪˌventʃuˈælətɪ/ NOUN [*plural* **eventualities**] something bad that might happen. A formal word. □ *We need to be prepared for every eventuality.*

• **eventually** /ɪˈventʃuəlɪ/ ADVERB at the end of a period of time or as a result of a process □ *The bus eventually arrived, half an hour late.*

ever /ˈevə(r)/ ADVERB
1 at any time or at all □ *Have you ever been to France?* □ *Nobody ever offers to help me.* □ *It was the most delicious meal ever.* □ *If you are ever in Edinburgh, do come and see me.*
2 bigger/happier, etc. than ever bigger/happier, etc. than at any time before □ *The music was louder than ever.*
3 ever since since the time when □ *He's been unhappy ever since he started at his new school.*

4 ever so/ever such a very □ *It's ever so hot in here.* □ *He's ever such a nice boy.*
5 for ever for all future time □ *I'm sure we'll be friends for ever.*

evergreen /ˈevəɡriːn/ ▶ ADJECTIVE evergreen plants and trees do not lose their leaves in the winter. A biology word.
▶ NOUN [plural **evergreens**] an evergreen plant or tree

everlasting /ˌevəˈlɑːstɪŋ/ ADJECTIVE lasting for ever □ *everlasting love*

every /ˈevrɪ/ DETERMINER
1 all the people or things □ *Every runner will get a medal for taking part.* □ *There were eight cakes on the plate, and she ate every one.*
2 every day/week/three hours, etc. used to show how often something happens □ *He does 200 press-ups every day.*
3 every so often/every now and then sometimes □ *He comes to visit us every now and then.*
4 every other day/evening, etc. on one of each two days/evenings, etc. □ *I only have to work every other day.*

> ➤ Remember that **every** is followed by a singular noun: □ *Every student in the group owns a mobile phone.*

everybody /ˈevrɪˌbɒdɪ/ PRONOUN everyone
□ *I thought everybody liked ice cream.* □ *Could everybody listen, please?*

everyday /ˈevrɪdeɪ/ ADJECTIVE normal and happening often ₲ *Acts of violence are an everyday occurrence for these people.* ₲ *Mobile phones have become part of everyday life for many children.*

everyone /ˈevrɪwʌn/ PRONOUN
1 every person □ *Everyone likes Jonathan.* □ *I knew everyone at the party.* ₲ *Everyone else* (= all other people) *had left by this point.*
2 people generally □ *Surely everyone likes chocolate.* □ *Everyone wants to be liked.*

everything /ˈevrɪθɪŋ/ PRONOUN
1 all the things in a place or situation □ *Everything in the room was covered in dust.* ₲ *We kept the books, and threw everything else in the bin.*
2 life in general □ *Is everything okay?* □ *Everything seems worse when you're tired.*

everywhere /ˈevrɪweə(r)/ ADVERB in or to every place □ *We looked everywhere but couldn't find it.* □ *They go everywhere together.*

evict /ɪˈvɪkt/ VERB [**evicts, evicting, evicted**] to force someone to leave a home or an area of land □ *Fourteen families were evicted from land they had farmed for generations.*
• **eviction** /ɪˈvɪkʃən/ NOUN [plural **evictions**] when someone is evicted from their home or land

evidence /ˈevɪdəns/ NOUN, NO PLURAL
1 facts or objects that help to prove something □ *His body was examined and no evidence of the disease found.*
2 facts or statements that help someone in a court of law to decide if someone has committed a crime or not □ *Mr Gleeson was the only witness to give evidence yesterday.*
• **evident** /ˈevɪdənt/ ADJECTIVE obvious or easy to understand □ *It was evident that she was unhappy.*
• **evidently** /ˈevɪdəntlɪ/ ADVERB
1 obviously □ *Howard was evidently confused by her answer.*
2 used for saying that something is probably true, based on the information that you have □ *Evidently, there had been some sort of argument.*

evil /ˈiːvəl/ ▶ ADJECTIVE morally very bad and cruel □ *an evil man* □ *This was an evil act.*
▶ NOUN, NO PLURAL evil actions generally □ *So are we all capable of evil?*

evoke /ɪˈvəʊk/ VERB [**evokes, evoking, evoked**] to make a particular memory or feeling come into your mind. A formal word. ₲ *This place evokes so many memories.*

evolution /ˌiːvəˈluːʃən/ NOUN, NO PLURAL the process by which animals and plants change over many thousands of years in order to suit their environment
• **evolve** /ɪˈvɒlv/ VERB [**evolves, evolving, evolved**]
1 animals and plants evolve when they change very gradually over many thousands of years
2 if something evolves, it gradually changes over time

ewe /juː/ NOUN [plural **ewes**] an adult female sheep

ex- /eks/ PREFIX
1 ex- is added to the beginning of words to mean 'outside' □ *exterior*
2 ex- is added to the beginning of words to mean 'former' □ *an ex-president* □ *his ex-girlfriend*

exacerbate /ɪɡˈzæsəbeɪt/ VERB [**exacerbates, exacerbating, exacerbated**] to make something worse. A formal word. □ *Bad weather only exacerbated the problem.*

exact /ɪɡˈzækt/ ADJECTIVE accurate in every way □ *Those were his exact words.* □ *I don't recall the exact date.* □ *The exact amount of money was never stated.* □ *This is an exact copy of the document.*
• **exactly** /ɪɡˈzæktlɪ/ ADVERB
1 used when saying prices, amounts, the time, etc. that are completely accurate □ *That comes to £10 exactly.* □ *It's five o'clock exactly.*
2 in every way □ *That's exactly what I was thinking.* □ *He looks exactly like his father.* ₲ *The coats look exactly the same to me.*
3 used for agreeing strongly with what someone has said □ *'She should be pleased she's got a job.' 'Exactly.'*
4 not exactly used for saying that what someone says is not completely right □ *'You're a nurse, aren't you?' 'Well, not exactly; I work in an old people's home.'*

exaggerate /ɪgˈzædʒəreɪt/ VERB [exaggerates, exaggerating, exaggerated] to say that something is more extreme than it really is □ *He's not that fat – you're exaggerating!* □ *The media have exaggerated the scale of the problem.*

• **exaggeration** /ɪgˌzædʒəˈreɪʃən/ NOUN [plural exaggerations] when you exaggerate □ *It's a slight exaggeration to call them enemies – they just don't especially like each other.*

exam /ɪgˈzæm/ NOUN [plural exams] an important test of someone's knowledge or ability 🖪 *I'm taking my final exams in June* 🖪 *She passed her exams.* 🖪 *What if he fails his exams?*

• **examination** /ɪgˌzæmɪˈneɪʃən/ NOUN [plural examinations]
1 a formal word that means exam
2 when a doctor looks carefully at your body to see if there is anything wrong
3 *no plural* when someone looks carefully at something □ *On closer examination, the painting turned out to be a copy.*

• **examine** /ɪgˈzæmɪn/ VERB [examines, examining, examined]
1 to look at something carefully □ *The sample was examined under a microscope.*
2 if a doctor examines you, he or she looks carefully at your body to see if there is anything wrong □ *The doctor examined her throat and ears.*
3 to consider something carefully □ *Police are examining the possibility that the driver may have fallen asleep.*

• **examiner** /ɪgˈzæmɪnə(r)/ NOUN [plural examiners] someone whose job is to test people's knowledge or ability

example /ɪgˈzɑːmpəl/ NOUN [plural examples]
1 something which has all the features or qualities of the type of thing that you are talking about □ *This is a typical example of a building from this period.* 🖪 *Let me give you an example of what I mean.*
2 for example used for giving an example of something □ *People drive unnecessarily. Jo, for example, drives to her friend's house which is 10 minutes' walk away.*
3 good behaviour that other people should copy 🖪 *You should set an example to the younger children* (= behave in a good way that they can copy).

exasperate /ɪgˈzɑːspəreɪt/ VERB [exasperates, exasperating, exasperated] to make you feel annoyed because you cannot do what you want to do

• **exasperated** /ɪgˈzɑːspəreɪtəd/ ADJECTIVE annoyed because you cannot do what you want to do □ *She gave an exasperated sigh.*

• **exasperating** /ɪgˈzɑːspəreɪtɪŋ/ ADJECTIVE making you feel exasperated □ *It's so exasperating when she won't listen to you.*

• **exasperation** /ɪgˌzɑːspəˈreɪʃən/ NOUN, NO PLURAL when you feel exasperated

excavate /ˈekskəveɪt/ VERB [excavates, excavating, excavated] to dig in the ground in order to find things from the past □ *They are currently excavating the site.*

• **excavation** /ˌekskəˈveɪʃən/ NOUN [plural excavations] when people excavate in order to find things from the past

exceed /ɪkˈsiːd/ VERB [exceeds, exceeding, exceeded]
1 to be greater than a particular limit or amount □ *He exceeded the speed limit by 30 kilometres per hour.*
2 exceed your expectations to be better than you expected □ *This year's profit exceeded our expectations.*

• **exceedingly** /ɪkˈsiːdɪŋlɪ/ ADVERB a formal word that means extremely □ *Both men played exceedingly well.*

excel /ɪkˈsel/ VERB [excels, excelling, excelled] to be extremely good at something. A formal word. □ *He excels in sport and music.*

• **excellence** /ˈeksələns/ NOUN, NO PLURAL the quality of being excellent □ *educational excellence*

• **excellent** /ˈeksələnt/ ADJECTIVE
1 extremely good or of a very high standard □ *Her work is excellent.*
2 used for showing that you are pleased about something □ *'I've finished writing the report.' 'Excellent!'*

except /ɪkˈsept/ PREPOSITION, CONJUNCTION not including something □ *He works every day except Sunday.* □ *+ that* *I feel better now, except that my head still hurts a bit.* □ *+ for* *Everyone stayed, except for the children.*

• **exception** /ɪkˈsepʃən/ NOUN [plural exceptions]
1 something that is not the same as the others in a group, and so cannot be included in a statement about them □ *With a few exceptions, the people were very friendly.* □ *There is one exception to this rule.*
2 make an exception to say that one person does not have to follow a particular rule □ *You're not really supposed to leave the room during the lesson, but I'll make an exception for you.*

• **exceptional** /ɪkˈsepʃənəl/ ADJECTIVE
1 very good or special □ *She showed exceptional courage.*
2 not likely to happen often □ *Surgery can be considered only in exceptional circumstances.*

• **exceptionally** /ɪkˈsepʃənəlɪ/ ADVERB extremely or in a way that is unusual □ *You've all done exceptionally well.*

excerpt /ˈeksɜːpt/ NOUN [plural excerpts] a short piece that has been taken from a book, film, piece of music etc.

excess ▶ NOUN /ɪkˈses/ [plural excesses]
1 too much of something □ *There was an excess of fat in his blood.*

2 in excess of more than a particular amount □ *The football club has debts in excess of £10 million.*
3 to excess if you do something to excess, you do it too much □ *Chips and ice cream were top of the list of items which children eat to excess.*
4 excesses bad or harmful things which someone does too much □ *She was trying to lose weight after the excesses of the holiday.*
▶ ADJECTIVE /'ekses/ more than you want, or more than is allowed 🔁 *Many airlines charge you for excess baggage.*
• **excessive** /ɪk'sesɪv/ ADJECTIVE too much or too great □ *Police officers are not allowed to use excessive force when arresting someone.*

exchange /ɪks'tʃeɪndʒ/ ▶ VERB [exchanges, exchanging, exchanged]
1 to give someone something and take something from them □ *We exchanged rings as a sign of our friendship.* □ *They exchanged phone numbers.* □ *We only exchanged a few words* (= spoke for a short time). □ *This website enables us to exchange information.*
2 to take something back to a shop and get something else instead □ **+ for** *I'd like to exchange these trousers for a smaller size.*
3 to do something to someone who does the same to you □ *They exchanged amused glances.* □ *During the argument, blows were exchanged* (= they hit each other).
4 to change money to the money of another country □ *I want to exchange these dollars for euros.*
▶ NOUN [plural exchanges]
1 in exchange for something if you do something or give something in exchange for something, you do it or give it to get that thing □ *He took bribes in exchange for passing on information.*
2 when you give something to someone and take something from them □ **+ of** *The exchange of food is a symbol of our community.*
3 a conversation, often an angry one 🔁 *He had a heated exchange* (= angry conversation) *with his boss.*

excite /ɪk'saɪt/ VERB [excites, exciting, excited] to make someone feel excited
• **excited** /ɪk'saɪtɪd/ ADJECTIVE feeling very happy and not calm because something good is going to happen 🔁 *He was getting excited about the party.* □ **+ about** *It was my first trip to the US and I was really excited about it.* □ **+ to do something** *I'm excited to be part of the team.*
• **excitedly** /ɪk'saɪtɪdli/ ADVERB in an excited way □ *The dog jumped around excitedly.*
• **excitement** /ɪk'saɪtmənt/ NOUN, NO PLURAL the feeling of being excited 🔁 *The news caused great excitement.* □ *In her excitement, she had forgotten something important.* □ **+ of** *I still remember the excitement of winning the competition.*
• **exciting** /ɪk'saɪtɪŋ/ ADJECTIVE making you feel excited □ *an exciting opportunity* □ **+ to do something** *The game was exciting to watch.*

► Remember the difference between the words **excited** and **exciting**. If you are **excited**, you are very happy because something good is going to happen. Something that is **exciting** makes you feel excited: □ *I was so* **excited** *during that game.* □ *It was such an* **exciting** *game.*

exclaim /ɪk'skleɪm/ VERB [exclaims, exclaiming, exclaimed] to say something suddenly and loudly because you are surprised, angry, etc. □ *'What a wonderful surprise!' she exclaimed.*
• **exclamation** /ˌeksklə'meɪʃən/ NOUN [plural exclamations] something you say suddenly or loudly because you are surprised, angry, etc. □ *Vicky gave an exclamation of delight.*
exclamation mark /ˌeksklə'meɪʃən ˌmɑːk/ NOUN [plural exclamation marks] a punctuation mark (!) that you write after an exclamation
exclude /ɪk'skluːd/ VERB [excludes, excluding, excluded]
1 to not allow someone to take part in something or go into a place □ *Paul was excluded from school for a week as a punishment.*
2 to deliberately not include something □ *The figures exclude children under the age of twelve.*
3 to decide that something cannot be possible 🔁 *He had blood tests to exclude the possibility of an infection.*
• **excluding** /ɪk'skluːdɪŋ/ PREPOSITION not including someone or something □ *The hotel costs £70 a night excluding meals.*
• **exclusion** /ɪk'skluːʒən/ NOUN [plural exclusions]
1 when someone is not allowed to take part in something or go into a place □ *If found guilty, he risks exclusion from the team.*
2 something that is deliberately not included □ *Insurance policies usually contain some exclusions.*
3 to the exclusion of if you do something to the exclusion of something else, you do it so much that you do not have time for the other thing. A formal phrase. □ *His obsession with golf to the exclusion of his family was the reason his wife divorced him.*
• **exclusive** /ɪk'skluːsɪv/ ADJECTIVE
1 available only for one person or for one group of people □ *On Wednesdays, women are given exclusive access to the spa.*
2 expensive, and designed for people who have a lot of money □ *an exclusive restaurant*
3 published in only one newspaper, or shown on only one television station 🔁 *Kewell did an exclusive interview with Channel Nine.*
4 exclusive of not including something □ *It costs £20, exclusive of postage.*
▶ NOUN [plural exclusives] a story that is published by only one newspaper or magazine, or reported by only one television station
• **exclusively** /ɪk'skluːsɪvli/ ADVERB only □ *The stadium is used exclusively for big international events.*
excrement /'ekskrɪmənt/ NOUN, NO PLURAL a formal word meaning the solid waste from a person's or animal's body

excrete /ɛk'skriːt/ VERB [excretes, excreting, excreted] to get rid of waste from your body. A biology word. □ *The drug causes the kidneys to excrete water and salt.*

• **excretion** /ɛk'skriːʃən/ NOUN [*plural* excretions] excreting something, or something that is excreted. A biology word.

excruciating /ɪk'skruːʃieɪtɪŋ/ ADJECTIVE
1 extremely painful
2 used for emphasizing how bad something is □ *He told us about his holiday in excruciating detail.*

excursion /ɪk'skɜːʃən/ NOUN [*plural* excursions] a short visit to a place □ *They were on a school excursion to the theatre.*

excusable /ɪk'skjuːzəbəl/ ADJECTIVE if something bad is excusable, you can understand why someone did it, and forgive them □ *His behaviour was excusable because he was tired.*

excuse ▶ NOUN /ɪk'skjuːs/ [*plural* excuses]
1 a reason you give to explain why you did something wrong or did not do something 🖼 *I'm sick of you making excuses about your work.* 🖼 *He's late again – he'd better have a good excuse this time!* □ *+ for There's no excuse for this sort of behaviour.*
2 a reason to do or have something that you want 🖼 *She was just looking for an excuse to stop working.* □ *His promotion was a good excuse for a party.*
▶ VERB /ɪk'skjuːz/ [excuses, excusing, excused]
1 excuse me (a) something that you say to get someone's attention □ *Excuse me, could you tell me the way to the library?* □ *Excuse me, Susan, there's someone on the phone for you.* (b) used to say sorry □ *Oh, excuse me, I didn't realize this seat was taken.*
2 to forgive someone for doing something, especially something that is not serious □ *Please excuse the mess in here.* □ *I hope you'll excuse us being late.*
3 to be a reason why someone does something bad □ *Having a headache doesn't excuse her rudeness.*
4 if you are excused something, you are allowed not to do it □ *+ from Could I be excused from tennis today, as I don't feel well?*

execute /'eksɪkjuːt/ VERB [executes, executing, executed]
1 to kill someone as an official punishment □ *Many of the prisoners were executed.*
2 a formal word meaning to do something that has been ordered or planned □ *We continue to execute our business plan.*

• **execution** /ˌeksɪ'kjuːʃən/ NOUN [*plural* executions]
1 killing someone as an official punishment □ *He is facing execution for his role in the terrorist bombings.*
2 when someone does something that has been ordered or planned. A formal word. □ *They tried to block the execution of a High Court order.*

• **executioner** /ˌeksɪ'kjuːʃənə(r)/ NOUN [*plural* executioners] someone whose job is to kill criminals as an official punishment

executive /ɪg'zekjʊtɪv/ ▶ NOUN [*plural* executives] someone who has an important job in a company □ *senior executives of British Airways*
▶ ADJECTIVE
1 to do with making important decisions in a company □ *the executive committee*
2 designed for rich people who have important jobs □ *an executive jet*

exemplary /ɪg'zempləri/ ADJECTIVE a formal word which describes something that is so good that other people should copy it □ *Ralf carried out his duties in an exemplary manner.*

exemplify /ɪg'zemplɪfaɪ/ VERB [exemplifies, exemplifying, exemplified] to be a typical example of something. A formal word. □ *He exemplified many qualities which people admire.*

exempt /ɪg'zempt/ ▶ ADJECTIVE allowed not to do something such as obey a law or pay for something □ *Non-UK residents are exempt from the tax.*
▶ VERB [exempts, exempting, exempted] to give someone permission not to do something that other people must do □ *Teachers were exempted from military service.*

• **exemption** /ɪg'zempʃən/ NOUN [*plural* exemptions] being exempt from something □ *tax exemptions*

exercise /'eksəsaɪz/ ▶ NOUN [*plural* exercises]
1 *no plural* physical activities done to keep your body strong and healthy 🖼 *We should all take more exercise.* 🖼 *Regular exercise will help to control your weight.*
2 a particular movement done to make your body strong and healthy □ *We did some stretching exercises.* □ *This exercise works the stomach muscles.*
3 a piece of written work you do when you are studying □ *Please do exercise 4 in your grammar book.* □ *This exercise deals with prepositions.*
4 an activity that is intended to achieve something 🖼 *The object of the exercise was to impress his boss.* □ *Our staff see this as an exercise in cutting costs.*
5 an activity done by a military organization to prepare for war 🖼 *Their forces have been conducting (= doing) joint exercises for about ten years.*
▶ VERB [exercises, exercising, exercised]
1 to do exercises to make you strong and healthy 🖼 *I try to exercise regularly.* □ *You should try to exercise the damaged joints.*
2 to use something 🖼 *Travellers have been told to exercise caution (= be careful) in the region.* 🖼 *I intend to exercise my right to vote in the election.*

exert /ɪg'zɜːt/ VERB [exerts, exerting, exerted]
1 to use your influence or power to make something happen □ *Government leaders are exerting pressure on the country to stop its military operations.*
2 exert yourself to use a lot of effort and energy

• **exertion** /ɪg'zɜːʃən/ NOUN [*plural* exertions] when you use a lot of physical or mental energy □ *I stood there, breathless with exertion.*

exhale /eks'heɪl/ VERB [exhales, exhaling, exhaled] a formal word meaning to breathe air out through your nose or mouth

exhaust /ɪg'zɔ:st/ ▶ VERB [exhausts, exhausting, exhausted]
1 to make someone very tired □ *Normally that jog would have exhausted me.*
2 to use all of something □ *They have exhausted all their legal options.* □ *The city is exhausting its supply of water.*
▶ NOUN [plural **exhausts**]
1 the pipe on a vehicle which waste gas come out of
2 the waste gas that comes out of a vehicle 🔁 *exhaust fumes*

• **exhausted** /ɪg'zɔ:stɪd/ ADJECTIVE extremely tired □ *She was completely exhausted by the time she got home.*

• **exhausting** /ɪg'zɔ:stɪŋ/ ADJECTIVE making you feel extremely tired □ *It was an exhausting climb.*

• **exhaustion** /ɪg'zɔ:stʃən/ NOUN, NO PLURAL a feeling of extreme tiredness □ *The singer cancelled his tour because of stress and exhaustion.*

• **exhaustive** /ɪg'zɔ:stɪv/ ADJECTIVE done very carefully and completely □ *Police made an exhaustive search of the area.*

exhibit /ɪg'zɪbɪt/ ▶ NOUN [plural **exhibits**] something that people go to see in a place such as a museum □ *The sculpture is the newest exhibit at London's National Gallery.*
▶ VERB [exhibits, exhibiting, exhibited]
1 a formal word meaning to show a quality or feeling □ *She began to exhibit symptoms of poisoning.*
2 to show something in a place such as a museum □ *Julia exhibits her paintings at a small local gallery.*

• **exhibition** /ˌeksɪ'bɪʃən/ NOUN [plural **exhibitions**]
1 a show where people go to see paintings, photographs, etc. 🔁 *an art exhibition* □ **+ of** *The museum will be holding an exhibition of works by Monet.*
2 on exhibition if things such as paintings or photographs are on exhibition, people can go to see them □ *This remarkable jewellery was recently on exhibition in Paris.*
3 an exhibition of sth when someone or something shows a particular skill, feeling, etc. □ *The rescue had been an exhibition of pure courage.*

• **exhibitor** /ɪg'zɪbɪtə(r)/ NOUN [plural **exhibitors**] someone who exhibits their work

exhilarated /ɪg'zɪləreɪtɪd/ ADJECTIVE feeling excited and full of energy □ *You could see the experience had left him exhilarated.*

• **exhilarating** /ɪg'zɪləreɪtɪŋ/ ADJECTIVE making you feel exhilarated □ *We had an exhilarating ride across the fields.*

• **exhilaration** /ɪgˌzɪlə'reɪʃən/ NOUN, NO PLURAL a feeling of excitement and energy

exile /'eksaɪl/ ▶ NOUN [plural **exiles**]
1 someone who has been forced to leave their country, usually for political reasons

2 in exile if someone is in exile, they have been forced to live in a country that is not their own, for political reasons □ *The former leader is now living in exile in Japan.*
▶ VERB [exiles, exiling, exiled] if you are exiled, you are forced to leave your own country and live somewhere else, for political reasons

exist /ɪg'zɪst/ VERB [exists, existing, existed]
1 to be real, or to happen □ *Does God really exist?* □ *Similar problems exist in Britain.*
2 to stay alive, especially in difficult conditions □ *It's possible to exist without food for a few days.* □ **+ on** *He seems to exist on a diet of burgers and chips.*

• **existence** /ɪg'zɪstəns/ NOUN, NO PLURAL
1 when someone or something exists □ *The rule was in existence for almost 40 years.* □ **+ of** *We can no longer deny the existence of global warming.*
2 the type of life that someone has □ *She had a lonely and miserable existence.*

• **existing** /ɪg'zɪstɪŋ/ ADJECTIVE happening or present now □ *The existing rules apply to anyone over 18.* □ *Existing customers are being offered a discount.*

exit /'eksɪt/ ▶ NOUN [plural **exits**]
1 a door you go through to leave a public building or vehicle 🔁 *The bus has an emergency exit at the back.*
2 when someone leaves a place 🔁 *He made a quick exit.*
3 a road you use to leave a motorway or roundabout (= circle that vehicles drive around) 🔁 *Take the next exit.*
4 when someone leaves something such as a competition or type of work □ **+ from** *The team had a shock early exit from the tournament.* □ *The defeat marked his exit from politics.*
▶ VERB [exits, exiting, exited]
1 a formal word meaning to leave a place □ *They exited the stadium by the west gate.*
2 a formal word meaning to leave something such as a competition or business □ *She exited the competition after losing to Lindsay Davenport.*
3 to stop using a computer program □ *How do I exit?*

exodus /'eksədəs/ NOUN, NO PLURAL when a lot of people leave a place at the same time 🔁 *The lack of jobs has led to a mass exodus of young people from the area.*

exonerate /ɪg'zɒnəreɪt/ VERB [exonerates, exonerating, exonerated] to officially say that someone should not be blamed for something □ *The investigation into the accident exonerated him entirely.*

exorbitant /ɪg'zɔ:bɪtənt/ ADJECTIVE unreasonably expensive □ *Exorbitant house prices are preventing many young people from buying a house.*

exotic /ɪg'zɒtɪk/ ADJECTIVE interesting and unusual, and often to do with a foreign country □ *exotic animals* □ *exotic holidays*

expand /ɪk'spænd/ VERB [expands, expanding, expanded] to become bigger, or to make something become bigger □ *Many cities are expanding very* *rapidly.* □ *The company plans to expand its range of products.*

➜ go to **expand your horizons**

expanse /ɪk'spæns/ NOUN [*plural* **expanses**] a large area of land, sea or sky 🔁 *She looked out of the window at the vast expanse of sky.*

expansion /ɪk'spænʃən/ NOUN, NO PLURAL when something increases in size or amount □ *The rapid expansion of the airline industry has led to cheap flights.*

expect /ɪk'spekt/ VERB [**expects, expecting, expected**]
1 to think that something will happen or be true □ *We're expecting an announcement soon.* □ *I expect he's forgotten the meeting.* □ *I didn't expect anything like this to happen.* □ **+ to do something** *Sales are expected to fall next month.* □ **+ that** *I expect that it will be hot in Portugal.*
2 to think that something or someone will arrive □ *I'm expecting a phone call from Mary.*
3 to think that something ought to happen or that you have a right to it □ **+ to do something** *I expect you to behave better than this.* □ *Our customers expect a first class service.*
4 if you are expected to do something, you have to do it □ *We are expected to do 3 hours homework a day.*
5 a woman who is expecting a baby is pregnant
• **expectant** /ɪk'spektənt/ ADJECTIVE
1 thinking that something good will happen
2 an expectant mother is a pregnant woman
• **expectation** /ˌekspek'teɪʃən/ NOUN [*plural* **expectations**]
1 how you think something will be, especially when you think it will be good 🔁 *We had very high/low expectations of our builders.* 🔁 *The job didn't really live up to my expectations.* 🔁 *It will be impossible to meet their expectations.* 🔁 *The company's profits exceeded expectations.*
2 when you expect something to happen or to be true □ *My expectation was that I would be paid for the work.* □ *He had no expectation of winning.*

expedition /ˌekspɪ'dɪʃən/ NOUN [*plural* **expeditions**] a long journey, especially to a dangerous place or to a place that has not been visited before □ *The group went on an expedition to the South Pole.*

expel /ɪk'spel/ VERB [**expels, expelling, expelled**]
1 to make someone leave a school, country or organization because they have done something wrong □ *John was expelled from school for hitting a teacher.*
2 a formal word meaning to force a liquid or gas out of something

expend /ɪk'spend/ VERB [**expends, expending, expended**] a formal word meaning to use time, energy or money □ *He didn't want to expend any more energy on the problem.*
• **expendable** /ɪk'spendəbəl/ ADJECTIVE not

necessary, and possible to get rid of □ *The company had decided that 20 of its employees were expendable.*

expenditure /ɪk'spendɪtʃə(r)/ NOUN, NO PLURAL
1 a formal word meaning the amount of money that a government, organization or person spends □ *Government expenditure on education has risen.*
2 a formal word meaning the use of money, energy or time □ *The process has improved and there's now less expenditure of fuel.*

expense /ɪk'spens/ NOUN [*plural* **expenses**]
1 the money that you pay for something 🔁 *medical/legal expenses* 🔁 *The money he gave me will cover the expense of the transport.* 🔁 *We have to pay our own travelling expenses.*
2 the high cost of something 🔁 *I didn't want to go to the expense of hiring a car.* 🔁 *They repaired the painting at great expense.* 🔁 *No expense was spared* (= a lot of money was spent) *to make the palace perfect.*
3 expenses money that you spend while you are doing your job, that your employer will pay back to you 🔁 *I can put the meal on my expenses.*
4 at the expense of something if one thing happens or exists at the expense of another, the second thing is damaged or destroyed by it □ *Academic achievement came at the expense of her health.*
• **expensive** /ɪk'spensɪv/ ADJECTIVE costing a lot of money □ *These clothes are too expensive for me.* □ *expensive gifts/equipment*
• **expensively** /ɪk'pensɪvlɪ/ ADVERB in an expensive way □ *expensively dressed*

experience /ɪk'spɪərɪəns/ ▶ NOUN [*plural* **experiences**]
1 *no plural* knowledge and skill that you get by doing something or by something happening to you 🔁 *The players have been gaining experience over the last four years.* 🔁 *She had no experience of looking after children.* □ **+ of** *The company is looking for someone with experience of managing budgets.*
2 in my experience used for saying what you think is true because of what life has taught you □ *In my experience, most children enjoy watching television.*
3 something that happens to you 🔁 *We had a bad experience on holiday.* 🔁 *The whole experience was terrifying.* □ *Watching a baby being born was an amazing experience.*
▶ VERB [**experiences, experiencing, experienced**] if you experience something, it happens to you or you feel it □ *Many customers were experiencing problems with Internet access.* □ *He had never experienced such pain.*
• **experienced** /ɪk'spɪərɪənst/ ADJECTIVE having skill and knowledge because you have done something for a long time □ *an experienced teacher*

experiment /ɪk'sperɪmənt/ ▶ NOUN [*plural* **experiments**]
1 a scientific test to discover or prove something 🔁 *Two experiments were conducted, using children*

suffering from heart problems. 🔁 *The experiment shows that lack of sleep affects people's performance of basic tasks.*

2 something new which you try, to discover whether it is successful □ *This soup is a bit of an experiment.*

▶ VERB [experiments, experimenting, experimented]

1 to try different things to find out what they are like □ **+ with** *He experimented with various ingredients until he came up with the perfect recipe.*

2 to do scientific tests to discover or prove something □ **+ on** *The team had experimented on rats.*

• **experimental** /ɪkˌsperɪ'mentəl/ ADJECTIVE

1 using new ideas and methods that have not been tested yet □ *an experimental school*

2 to do with scientific tests □ *experimental data*

expert /'ekspɜːt/ ▶ NOUN [plural **experts**] someone who knows a lot about something □ *legal/health experts* □ **+ on/in** *She's an expert on Middle East politics.*

▶ ADJECTIVE

1 very good at something, or knowing a lot about something □ *expert skiers*

2 expert help or advice is given by someone who knows a lot about something 🔁 *We took expert advice.*

• **expertise** /ˌekspɜː'tiːz/ NOUN, NO PLURAL special skill or knowledge □ *technical expertise*

expire /ɪk'spaɪə(r)/ VERB [expires, expiring, expired] if an official document or agreement expires, the time when you can use it ends □ *Your passport expired last month.*

• **expiry** /ɪk'spaɪəri/ NOUN, NO PLURAL the end of the time in which you can use something 🔁 *The contract's expiry date is 2012.*

explain /ɪk'spleɪn/ VERB [explains, explaining, explained]

1 to give someone more or simpler information so that they can understand something □ **+ question word** *Could you explain what you mean?* □ **+ to** *She explained the rules of the game to me.*

2 to give or to be a reason for something □ *He was asked to explain his absence.* □ *Having a bad childhood can explain the behaviour of some criminals.* □ **+ that** *She explained that she had lost her keys.*

▶ Note that you cannot *explain someone something*. You must *explain something to someone*:
✓ *She explained the rules to me.*
✗ *She explained me the rules.*

• **explanation** /ˌeksplə'neɪʃən/ NOUN [plural explanations]

1 something you say or write to make something easy to understand 🔁 *She gave an explanation of how to do it.* □ **+ of** *The teacher started with an explanation of why plants are green.*

2 a reason for something 🔁 *The research offers several explanations for this behaviour.* □ **+ for** *Is there a scientific explanation for this?*

• **explanatory** /ɪk'splænətəri/ ADJECTIVE explaining something □ *an explanatory note*

explicit /ɪk'splɪsɪt/ ADJECTIVE clear and exact □ *Michael gave me explicit instructions about how to do it.*

explode /ɪk'spləʊd/ VERB [explodes, exploding, exploded]

1 to burst (= break suddenly so the parts fly out) and make a very loud noise 🔁 *A bomb exploded in the centre of the city.* □ *The car exploded, killing two police officers.* □ *Fireworks exploded in every direction.*

2 to suddenly start shouting because you are very angry □ *He exploded with rage.*

▶ Note that a bomb **explodes**. When people make a bomb explode in a building, aeroplane, etc. they **blow up** that building, aeroplane, etc: □ *The bomb exploded in the centre of the building.* □ *They blew up the building.*

exploit ▶ VERB /ɪk'splɔɪt/ [exploits, exploiting, exploited]

1 to use someone unfairly to help you get what you want □ *These people are often exploited as they will work for very little money.*

2 to use something so that you get as much advantage as possible □ *He was keen to exploit new opportunities.*

▶ NOUN /'eksplɔɪt/ [plural **exploits**] a brave or exciting thing that someone has done □ *He told us about his wartime exploits.*

• **exploitation** /ˌeksplɔɪ'teɪʃən/ NOUN, NO PLURAL exploiting someone or something □ *the exploitation of foreign workers*

exploration /ˌeksplə'reɪʃən/ NOUN [plural explorations]

1 going to a place to find out about it □ *space exploration*

2 a careful study or discussion of a subject □ *The report provides a thorough exploration of how the new law will affect schools.*

explore /ɪk'splɔː(r)/ VERB [explores, exploring, explored]

1 to travel around a place and find out what it is like □ *The hotel is a good base for exploring the region.* □ *Radar technology will help us to explore the planet Mars.*

2 to think about and discuss something 🔁 *I'm exploring the possibility of working abroad.* 🔁 *The charity is exploring new ways of raising money.*

• **explorer** /ɪk'splɔːrə(r)/ NOUN [plural **explorers**] someone who travels to places that people have not been to before □ *a Polar explorer*

explosion /ɪkˈspləʊʒən/ NOUN [plural **explosions**]
1 when something such as a bomb explodes □ The explosion happened inside the building. 🕮 Two soldiers were killed in a roadside bomb explosion. 🕮 He was seriously injured in a gas explosion.
2 a sudden large increase in something 🕮 The population explosion was caused by immigration. □ + of There has been an explosion of interest in American football.
• **explosive** /ɪkˈspləʊsɪv/ ▶ ADJECTIVE
1 able to cause an explosion □ a highly explosive gas 🕮 an explosive device
2 possibly making people become angry or violent 🕮 a potentially explosive situation
▶ NOUN [plural **explosives**] a substance that can cause an explosion

exponent /ɪkˈspəʊnənt/ NOUN [plural **exponents**]
1 someone who tries to persuade other people that a principle or idea is right. A formal word. □ He was an early exponent of women's rights.
2 a small, raised number that shows how many times an amount must be multiplied by itself. A maths word.
• **exponential** /ˌekspəˈnenʃəl/ ADJECTIVE
1 an exponential increase is a very large increase. A formal word.
2 connected to a number's exponent. A maths word.

export ▶ VERB /ɪkˈspɔːt/ [**exports, exporting, exported**]
1 to sell goods to another country □ India exports rice and wheat to many countries.
2 if you export computer information, you copy it to another place. A computing word.
▶ NOUN /ˈekspɔːt/ [plural **exports**]
1 a product that a country sells to another country □ Syria's main export is oil.
2 the process of selling goods to another country □ The country relies on the export of wool.
• **exporter** /ekˈspɔːtə(r)/ NOUN [plural **exporters**] a country or company which exports goods □ They are the world's biggest exporter of coal.

expose /ɪkˈspəʊz/ VERB [**exposes, exposing, exposed**]
1 to show something that was covered or hidden □ He pulled up his shirt to expose his stomach.
2 to tell the public about bad or dishonest things that someone important has done □ Journalists exposed widespread corruption in the government.
3 if someone is exposed to something harmful, they are in a place or situation where they experience it □ He had been exposed to the virus.
4 to let someone experience something □ The idea was to expose the students to modern art.
• **exposure** /ɪkˈspəʊʒə(r)/ NOUN [plural **exposures**]
1 being in a situation in which you experience something □ He'd had little exposure to foreign cultures. □ Too much exposure to the sun is bad for the skin.
2 when something bad that someone important has done is reported in a newspaper or on television □ He was forced to resign after the exposure of his affair.
3 a medical problem that is caused by being outside in

cold weather for too long □ The climbers were found suffering from exposure.

express /ɪkˈspres/ ▶ VERB [**expresses, expressing, expressed**] to show or tell people what you are thinking or feeling 🕮 He expressed his concerns about the safety of the equipment. 🕮 She expressed strong views about education. 🕮 Amy expressed surprise at his comments. □ He was unable to express himself clearly.
▶ ADJECTIVE
1 travelling fast from one place to another 🕮 an express train □ The package arrived express delivery.
2 an express wish or purpose is one that is very clear and certain. A formal word. □ The plan cannot be carried out without the express approval of the President.
▶ NOUN [plural **expresses**] a train or bus that is fast because it does not stop at many places □ We caught the express to Leeds.
• **expression** /ɪkˈspreʃən/ NOUN [plural **expressions**]
1 a look on your face that shows what you are thinking or feeling 🕮 I could tell by the expression on his face that he didn't believe me. 🕮 I couldn't read her facial expression. □ + of Bindi put on an expression of great surprise.
2 a word or phrase 🕮 Dieter always uses very old-fashioned expressions.
3 something that you do or say as a way of showing what you feel or think □ + of He wore the clothes as an expression of his faith.
• **expressive** /ɪkˈspresɪv/ ADJECTIVE clearly showing what someone's feelings are □ Kate has one of those expressive faces.
• **expressly** /ɪkˈspreslɪ/ ADVERB
1 a formal word meaning clearly and certainly 🕮 Doctors had expressly forbidden him from flying.
2 a formal word meaning for one particular purpose □ I went to school expressly to talk to his teacher.

expulsion /ɪkˈspʌlʃən/ NOUN [plural **expulsions**] being ordered to leave a place □ He was depressed following his expulsion from university.

exquisite /ɪkˈskwɪzɪt/ ADJECTIVE very beautiful and delicate □ exquisite pink roses

extend /ɪkˈstend/ VERB [**extends, extending, extended**]
1 to make something bigger □ We're having our kitchen extended. □ The airport has plans to extend the runway.
2 to make something continue for longer □ The contract was extended by three months.
3 to make something include or affect more people □ The ban has been extended to schools.
4 to cover a distance or area □ The wall extended for about a mile.
5 a formal word meaning to stretch out your arm, hand or leg □ She extended a hand towards me.
• **extended** /ɪkˈstendɪd/ ADJECTIVE a formal word meaning continuing for a long time 🕮 He often missed school for extended periods because of ill health.

• **extension** /ɪk'stenʃən/ NOUN [plural **extensions**]
1 a part added to a building □ They're building an extension at the side of the house.
2 the process of making something bigger □ the extension of the rail network
3 the process of making something include more people or things □ Ministers have called for an extension of anti-terror laws.
4 extra time that is added to something □ Can I have an extension to finish my project? □ a two-year contract extension
5 a telephone line to a particular person in an office □ Can I have extension 4321, please?

• **extensive** /ɪk'stensɪv/ ADJECTIVE large in size or amount ⊕ The fire caused extensive damage. ⊕ He has an extensive collection of rare books.

• **extent** /ɪk'stent/ NOUN, NO PLURAL
1 the size or degree of something □ What's the extent of the damage?
2 to some extent/to a certain extent in some ways □ The situation has improved to some extent.

exterior /ɪk'stɪərɪə(r)/ ▶ NOUN [plural **exteriors**]
1 the outside of something □ The house had a very impressive exterior.
2 someone's behaviour which hides their real character □ Behind that tough exterior is a very shy girl.
▶ ADJECTIVE on or for the outside of something □ exterior walls
➡ go to interior

exterminate /ɪk'stɜːmɪneɪt/ VERB [**exterminates**, **exterminating**, **exterminated**] to kill all of a particular group of animals or people

external /ɪk'stɜːnəl/ ADJECTIVE
1 on the outside of a person or thing □ The building has external lighting.
2 from outside a particular country, organization etc. □ The university applied for external funding.

extinct /ɪk'stɪŋkt/ ADJECTIVE
1 a type of animal or plant which is extinct no longer exists □ Many types of frog have already become extinct.
2 an extinct volcano (= mountain that explodes) no longer erupts (= sends out smoke and hot rocks)

• **extinction** /ɪk'stɪŋkʃən/ NOUN, NO PLURAL being extinct ⊕ A lot of mammals are facing extinction.

extinguish /ɪk'stɪŋgwɪʃ/ VERB [**extinguishes**, **extinguishing**, **extinguished**] a formal word meaning to make a fire stop burning or to make a light stop shining □ Firefighters tried to extinguish the flames.

• **extinguisher** /ɪk'stɪŋgwɪʃə(r)/ NOUN [plural **extinguishers**] a piece of equipment for stopping small fires ⊕ Public buildings have fire extinguishers.

extortionate /ɪk'stɔːʃənət/ ADJECTIVE very expensive □ Fans complain about extortionate ticket prices.

extra /'ekstrə/ ▶ ADJECTIVE more or more than usual □ The extra money will be used to buy books. □ The teacher gives Raj extra help with maths. □ The room is £70 but meals are extra (= meals are not included in the price).

▶ ADVERB more than usual □ I get paid extra for working at weekends. □ I bought an extra large box of chocolates.
▶ NOUN [plural **extras**]
1 something you can choose to have that is not included in the price of something ⊕ Optional extras on the car include air conditioning and heated seats.
2 an actor in a film or television programme who does not say anything but is one of a crowd of people

extra- /'ekstrə/ PREFIX extra- is added to the beginning of words to mean 'more' or 'further away than' □ extraordinary □ extraterrestrial

extract ▶ VERB /ɪk'strækt/ [**extracts**, **extracting**, **extracted**]
1 a formal word meaning to remove something from a place □ No dentist will extract a tooth that could be saved.
2 to get something such as information or money from someone who does not want to give it to you. A formal word □ Police tried to extract a confession from him.
▶ NOUN /'ekstrækt/ [plural **extracts**]
1 a short piece from a book or film □ He read an extract from the book.
2 a substance that has been removed from a plant □ vanilla extract

• **extraction** /ɪk'strækʃən/ NOUN [plural **extractions**]
1 when something is extracted □ oil extraction
2 of Irish/European/Jewish etc. extraction having parents or grandparents etc. who were Irish, European etc.

extraneous /ɪk'streɪnɪəs/ ADJECTIVE a formal word meaning not directly related to something □ extraneous details

extraordinarily /ɪk'strɔːdənrəlɪ/ ADVERB extremely and in a surprising way □ She was extraordinarily beautiful.

extraordinary /ɪk'strɔːdənrɪ/ ADJECTIVE very special, unusual or surprising □ Ann told me the most extraordinary story. ⊕ He knew he had seen something quite extraordinary (= very extraordinary). □ + that It's extraordinary that he survived the accident.

extraterrestrial /ˌekstrətə'restrɪəl/ ▶ ADJECTIVE from a planet or place that is not Earth
▶ NOUN [plural **extraterrestrials**] a creature from another planet

extravagance /ɪk'strævəgəns/ NOUN [plural **extravagances**]
1 spending a lot of money or using a lot of something
2 something that you spend too much money on □ My only extravagance was handbags.

extravagant /ɪk'strævəgənt/ ADJECTIVE
1 spending or costing too much money, or using too much of something □ an extravagant lifestyle □ Don't be too extravagant with the paper – we haven't much left.
2 extreme and probably unreasonable □ The advertisement makes some extravagant claims.

extravaganza /ɪkˌstrævəˈɡænzə/ NOUN [plural **extravaganzas**] a big and exciting show or event which has cost a lot of money □ a Hollywood wedding extravaganza

extravert /ˈekstrəvɜːt/ NOUN [plural **extraverts**] another spelling of extrovert

extreme /ɪkˈstriːm/ ▶ ADJECTIVE

1 very great 🔁 The roads are icy, and motorists should drive with extreme caution. □ We were working under extreme pressure.

2 very unusual or severe 🔁 Planes cannot take off or land in extreme weather conditions. 🔁 In extreme cases, the illness can cause death.

3 extreme opinions, beliefs etc. are very strong and unreasonable 🔁 She was often ridiculed for her extreme views.

4 at the furthest edge of something □ My mother is on the extreme right of the picture.

▶ NOUN [plural **extremes**]

1 something that is much greater, much more severe etc. than usual □ + of The crops cannot survive extremes of temperature.

2 the other/opposite extreme used when comparing two things that are as different as possible □ Some of the holidays on offer cost just £99 per person. At the other extreme, they have world cruises costing £20,000.

3 go to extremes to do something much more than is usual or reasonable □ She went to extremes to change her image, even having cosmetic surgery.

• **extremely** /ɪkˈstriːmlɪ/ ADVERB very □ He found it extremely difficult to relax. □ Education is extremely important. □ Ben did extremely well in the test.

> ➤ **Extremely** is not used before adjectives which have a strong meaning:
> ✓ It was extremely difficult to hear.
> ✗ It was extremely impossible to hear.
> ➤ If you are using an adjective with a strong meaning, put an adverb such as **completely** or **absolutely** before it: □ It was absolutely impossible to hear.

extricate /ˈekstrɪkeɪt/ VERB [**extricates, extricating, extricated**] extricate yourself a formal word meaning to manage to stop being involved in a difficult situation □ He was trying to extricate himself from this embarrassing situation.

extrovert /ˈekstrəvɜːt/ NOUN [plural **extroverts**] a confident person who enjoys being with other people

exuberant /ɪɡˈzjuːbərənt/ ADJECTIVE happy, excited and full of energy □ He was young and exuberant.

eye /aɪ/ ▶ NOUN [plural **eyes**]

1 one of the two things on your face which you see with □ I have blonde hair and blue eyes. 🔁 John closed his eyes and tried to sleep. 🔁 When she opened her eyes again, he'd gone.

2 the hole in a needle that you put the thread through ➡ go to black eye

♦ IDIOMS catch someone's eye (a) if something catches your eye, you notice it □ A sudden movement caught my eye. (b) if you catch someone's eye, you look at them to get their attention □ I tried to catch Penny's eye. have your eye on something to want something and think that you will get it □ I've got my eye on a velvet coat. keep an eye on someone/something to look after someone or something to make sure they are safe □ Could you keep an eye on the children for me? keep an eye out for something/someone to watch so that you see something or someone □ Keep an eye out for any mistakes. keep your eyes open to watch carefully for something □ Keep your eyes open for signs of the illness. lay/set eyes on something/someone to see something or someone for the first time □ As soon as I laid eyes on the house, I knew I wanted to live there. not see eye to eye to disagree with someone about something □ We don't see eye to eye about religion. take your eye/eyes off someone/something to stop looking at something or someone □ I only took my eye off her for a minute and she'd gone. □ She can't take her eyes off him! be up to your eyes in something to have too much of something □ I'm up to my eyes in work at the moment.

▶ VERB [**eyes, eyeing, eyed**] to look at someone or something □ They eyed our bags suspiciously.

♦ PHRASAL VERB **eye someone/something up** to look at someone or something in a way that shows that you like them or want them □ I could see him eyeing up my CD collection.

eyeball /ˈaɪbɔːl/ NOUN [plural **eyeballs**] the round part that makes up your whole eye

eyebrow /ˈaɪbraʊ/ NOUN [plural **eyebrows**] one of the two lines of hair above your eyes

eye-catching /ˈaɪˌkætʃɪŋ/ ADJECTIVE if something is eye-catching, it looks unusual and attractive so you notice it □ an eye-catching display

eyelash /ˈaɪlæʃ/ NOUN [plural **eyelashes**] one of the many hairs round the edges of your eyes

eyelid /ˈaɪlɪd/ NOUN [plural **eyelids**] one of the pieces of skin that cover your eyes when your eyes are closed

eyeliner /ˈaɪˌlaɪnə(r)/ NOUN [plural **eyeliners**] make-up that you use to draw a line around your eyes

eye-opener /ˈaɪˌəʊpənə(r)/ NOUN [plural **eye-openers**] something which shows you what someone or something is really like and surprises you □ The film of his life is quite an eye-opener.

eyeshadow /ˈaɪˌʃædəʊ/ NOUN [plural **eyeshadows**] coloured make-up that you put on your eyelids (= skin over your eyes)

eyesight /ˈaɪsaɪt/ NOUN, NO PLURAL the ability to see □ Her eyesight is poor so she wears contact lenses.

eyesore /ˈaɪsɔː(r)/ NOUN [plural **eyesores**] something ugly that spoils a view □ The new building is an eyesore.

eyewitness /ˌaɪˈwɪtnɪs/ NOUN [plural **eyewitnesses**] someone who has seen a crime or accident happen □ Police are appealing for eyewitnesses.

F or **f** /ef/ the sixth letter of the alphabet

F² /ef/ ABBREVIATION **Fahrenheit**

fable /'feɪbəl/ NOUN [plural **fables**] a story that teaches a lesson about how people should behave

fabric /'fæbrɪk/ NOUN [plural **fabrics**] cloth □ They are made of natural fabrics such as cotton or linen.

fabricate /'fæbrɪkeɪt/ VERB [**fabricates, fabricating, fabricated**] to invent information to trick people □ It was later proved that the police had fabricated evidence.

• **fabrication** /ˌfæbrɪ'keɪʃən/ NOUN [plural **fabrications**] an invented story or piece of information □ Her explanations were pure fabrication.

fabulous /'fæbjʊləs/ ADJECTIVE extremely good □ The weather was fabulous. □ You look fabulous in that dress.

façade /fə'sɑːd/ NOUN [plural **façades**]
1 the front of a building □ The library has a glass façade.
2 a false appearance which hides what someone or something is really like □ His happiness was just a façade.

face /feɪs/ ▶ NOUN [plural **faces**]
1 the front of your head where your eyes, nose, and mouth are □ She had a huge smile on her face.
2 pull/make a face to twist your face into a strange expression
3 the part of a clock or watch where the numbers are
4 the vertical side of a mountain or cliff (= steep side of high land next to the sea)
➡ go to **keep a straight face**
▶ VERB [**faces, facing, faced**]
1 to be in a particular direction □ My house faces the park. □ She turned to face him.
2 to have to deal with a difficult situation □ She has faced many difficulties in her life.
3 can't face doing something if you can't face doing something, it is too unpleasant for you to do □ I just can't face cooking this evening.
◆ PHRASAL VERB **face up to something** to accept and deal with a problem □ You must face up to your responsibilities.

facecloth /'feɪsklɒθ/ NOUN [plural **facecloths**] a small square cloth for washing yourself

facelift /'feɪslɪft/ NOUN [plural **facelifts**]
1 a medical operation to make someone's face look younger by making the skin tighter
2 work to make a building or place look more attractive □ The building has had a £2 million facelift.

facet /'fæsɪt/ NOUN [plural **facets**] a part or a feature of a situation or of a person's character □ I had not known about this facet of her personality before.

facetious /fə'siːʃəs/ ADJECTIVE trying to say something funny in a way that is annoying or not suitable □ Let's have no more facetious suggestions.

• **facetiously** /fə'siːʃəslɪ/ ADVERB in a facetious way □ I didn't mean that facetiously.

facial /'feɪʃəl/ ▶ ADJECTIVE to do with your face 🕮 a facial expression
▶ NOUN [plural **facials**] a beauty treatment for your face

facilitate /fə'sɪlɪteɪt/ VERB [**facilitates, facilitating, facilitated**] a formal word meaning to make a task or process easier □ Nowadays students have access to all sorts of visual aids that facilitate the learning process.

facility /fə'sɪlətɪ/ NOUN [plural **facilities**]
1 facilities buildings, rooms or equipment that you can use for doing something 🕮 The university has excellent sports facilities. □ The company provides childcare facilities for employees.
2 a feature of a machine, system, etc. that makes it able to do something □ I want a mobile phone with an Internet facility.
3 a building used for a particular purpose 🕮 The injured were taken to the nearest medical facility.
4 an ability □ + **for** He has a great facility for solving problems.

fact /fækt/ NOUN [plural **facts**]
1 something that you know is true □ + **about** We don't yet know all the facts about the accident. 🕮 You need to face facts (= accept the truth) - you'll never be a successful ballet dancer. 🕮 You should get your facts straight (= be sure you know the truth) before you make accusations like that. 🕮 I know for a fact (= I'm certain) that he was in London last week. 🕮 The fact is, I'm too scared to talk to him. 🕮 The fact that she's ill means she can't work full-time.
2 in fact/as a matter of fact used to give more information about something □ They know each other well; in fact they went to school together.
3 in fact used to say what is really true □ He said he was ill, when in fact he was at the football match.
4 no plural real things, not things that are imagined

□ *The movie is based on fact.* □ *She doesn't seem able to separate fact from fiction.*
5 the facts of life information about sex and how babies are born

faction /ˈfækʃən/ NOUN [*plural* **factions**] a group that is part of a larger group but has different opinions from others in that group

factor /ˈfæktə(r)/ NOUN [*plural* **factors**]
1 something that causes or influences a situation □ *The weather is often one of the main factors in choosing where to go for a holiday.* 🔁 *Price is an important factor for many people.* 🔁 *Blood pressure is a key risk factor for heart disease.*
2 a number that a larger number can be divided by exactly. A maths word.

factory /ˈfæktərɪ/ NOUN [*plural* **factories**] a building where something is made in large quantities □ *a chocolate factory*

factual /ˈfæktʃuəl/ ADJECTIVE based on facts □ *factual information* □ *The report contains factual errors.*

faculty /ˈfækəltɪ/ NOUN [*plural* **faculties**]
1 a natural ability that someone has, especially to see, hear, speak, think, etc. □ *the faculty of speech* □ *He's 95 but he still has all his faculties.*
2 a department of a university □ *the Faculty of Law*

fad /fæd/ NOUN [*plural* **fads**] something that is popular or fashionable for a short time □ *a passing fad for skateboarding*

fade /feɪd/ VERB [**fades, fading, faded**]
1 to disappear or become less strong gradually □ *Hopes of finding him were starting to fade.* □ *His smile faded.* □ *Their voices faded into the background.*
2 to lose colour and become less bright □ *These jeans have faded.* □ *The light was fading.*

faeces /ˈfiːsiːz/ PLURAL NOUN a formal word for solid waste from people's or animal's bodies

Fahrenheit /ˈfærənˌhaɪt/ NOUN, NO PLURAL a system for measuring temperature in which water freezes at 32 degrees and boils at 212 degrees

fail /feɪl/ ► VERB [**fails, failing, failed**]
1 to not be successful □ + *in* *They failed in their attempt to sail round the world.* □ + *to do something* *The business failed to attract enough customers.* □ *After four years, the marriage failed.* 🔁 *We failed miserably in our efforts to cheer him up.*
2 if you fail an exam or test, you do not pass it □ *My brother failed his driving test.*
3 to not do something that is expected or needed □ + *to do something* *The parcel failed to arrive.* □ *Yesterday's announcement failed to address the main problems.* □ *They failed to provide adequate food for the animals.*
4 if a part of a machine or part of your body fails, it stops working □ *The brakes failed.* □ *My eyesight is beginning to fail.*
5 to not help someone □ *Our society is failing the poor.*

6 never fail to do something to always do something □ *His rudeness never fails to amaze me.*
► NOUN [*plural* **fails**]
1 a result in a test or an exam that is not successful
2 without fail (a) used to show that something always happens in a particular way or at a particular time □ *He visits me every day, without fail* (b) used to emphasize that something must be done □ *I want your homework in tomorrow, without fail!*

• **failed** /feɪld/ ADJECTIVE not successful 🔁 *He had two failed attempts at climbing Everest.* □ *a failed marriage*

• **failing** /ˈfeɪlɪŋ/ ► NOUN [*plural* **failings**] a bad quality or fault □ *Her worst failing is being late all the time.*
► PREPOSITION **failing that** if that is not possible □ *We can get a lift from my Dad, or failing that, there's always the bus.*

• **failure** /ˈfeɪljə(r)/ NOUN [*plural* **failures**]
1 when something is not successful 🔁 *Their first attempt ended in failure.* □ + *of* *After the failure of his business, he went to live abroad.*
2 when you do not do something that is wanted or needed □ + *to do something* *The hospital's failure to give her the correct drugs contributed to her death.*
3 someone or something that is not successful □ *She felt like a failure.* □ *The party was a complete failure.*
4 when something stops working □ *a power failure* 🔁 *He died of heart failure.*

faint /feɪnt/ ► ADJECTIVE [**fainter, faintest**]
1 difficult to see, hear or smell □ *There's a faint mark on the carpet.* □ *the faint sound of footsteps* □ *He gave a faint smile.*
2 if you feel faint, you feel as though you might become unconscious 🔁 *I suddenly felt faint.*
3 very slight 🔁 *She still holds out a faint hope of finding it.*
4 not have the faintest idea used to emphasize that you do not know something □ *I don't have the faintest idea where it is.*
5 the faintest used to emphasize that something is very slight □ *There wasn't the faintest chance he'd be chosen.* □ *He only has the faintest hint of an accent.*
► VERB [**faints, fainting, fainted**] to suddenly become unconscious and fall to the ground □ *Richard fainted when he saw the blood.*

• **faintly** /ˈfeɪntlɪ/ ADVERB
1 in a way that is difficult to see, hear or smell □ *'Yes,' she said faintly.* □ *The room smelled faintly of smoke.*
2 slightly □ *He looked faintly ridiculous.*

fair /feə(r)/ ► ADJECTIVE [**fairer, fairest**]
1 treating everyone in the same, reasonable way 🔁 *It's not fair! Ella got more cake than me.* 🔁 *a fair trial/election* 🔁 *Make sure Patsy does her fair share of the work.*
2 acceptable and reasonable □ + *on* *It's not fair on my family to go away so often.* 🔁 *Make sure you get a fair price for the jewellery.* 🔁 *To be fair, Mohon has been working very hard recently.*

3 fair skin or hair is light in colour

4 quite large 🔁 *There's a fair amount of food left.* 🔁 *We have a fair bit of work still to do* 🔁 *There's a fair chance that they will win.*

5 fair weather is pleasant, with no rain

6 quite good but not very good □ *Joe's work is only fair.*

7 fair enough used to say that you accept what has been said □ *'I couldn't help because I had to visit my grandma.' 'Oh, fair enough then.'*

◆ IDIOM **be fair game** to be something or someone that people feel they can criticize or use in a bad way □ *For journalists, the private lives of politicians are fair game.*

▶ NOUN [*plural* **fairs**] an event held outdoors, where you can ride on machines, play games, etc.

• **fairly** /'feəlɪ/ ADVERB

1 quite a lot, but not extremely □ *He is fairly well paid.* □ *It's fairly obvious that she is lying.*

2 in a fair way □ *They treat their staff fairly.* □ *The money was divided fairly between them.*

• **fairness** /'feənɪs/ NOUN, NO PLURAL being fair □ *They treated us with fairness.*

---

fairy /'feərɪ/ NOUN [*plural* **fairies**] an imaginary creature which looks like a small person with wings

fairy lights /'feərɪ ˌlaɪts/ PLURAL NOUN coloured lights for decoration, especially on a Christmas tree

fairy story /'feərɪ ˌstɔːrɪ/ *or* **fairy tale** /'feərɪ ˌteɪl/ NOUN [*plural* **fairy stories** *or* **fairy tales**] a traditional story in which magic things happen

faith /feɪθ/ NOUN [*plural* **faiths**]

1 great trust and belief in someone or something 🔁 *I have a lot of faith in him.* 🔁 *I've lost faith in the whole system.*

2 a religion □ *the Christian faith* □ *people of different faiths*

3 religious belief generally □ *He was a man of deep faith.*

4 good faith a belief that what you are doing is good, honest or legal □ *He acted in good faith.*

• **faithful** /'feɪθfʊl/ ADJECTIVE loyal and keeping your promises □ *a faithful friend* □ *He was faithful to his wife.*

• **faithfully** /'feɪθfʊlɪ/ ADVERB

1 in a loyal, honest way □ *She promised faithfully to come.*

2 Yours faithfully something you write at the end of a formal letter that begins with 'Dear Sir' or 'Dear Madam'

fake /feɪk/ ▶ ADJECTIVE not real, but copying something else □ *fake fur* □ *He was travelling on a fake passport.*

▶ NOUN [*plural* **fakes**] a copy of something instead of the real thing □ *It's hard to spot a fake.*

▶ VERB [**fakes, faking, faked**]

1 to make a copy of something and pretend it is real □ *Roberts admitted he had faked the documents.*

2 to pretend something in order to trick someone □ *He faked an injury to avoid playing.*

---

falcon /'fɔːlkən/ NOUN [*plural* **falcons**] a bird that kills other animals for food

---

fall /fɔːl/ VERB [**falls, falling, fell, fallen**]

1 to drop down to the ground □ *The apples fell from the tree.* □ *Snow fell all morning.*

2 to suddenly go down to the ground by accident □ *Ben fell downstairs.* □ *+ off He fell off a fence and broke his arm.*

3 fall apart/off/out, etc. to become separated □ *The doll's arms fell off.* □ *All his hair fell out.*

4 if an amount, price or temperature falls, it goes down □ *+ by The temperature has fallen by several degrees.* □ *+ to Prices fell to their lowest levels since June.*

5 to start being in a particular state 🔁 *They fell in love.* 🔁 *I often fall asleep at the cinema.* 🔁 *He fell ill on holiday.*

➡ go to **fall on deaf ears**

◆ PHRASAL VERBS **fall for someone** to start to love someone **fall for something** to be tricked by something □ *I told her I'd give her the money later and she fell for it!* **fall over** to fall to the ground or onto one side □ *I fell over and cut my knee.* **fall out** to stop being friends □ *Carlos and Sergei have fallen out.* **fall through** to fail or not happen □ *Their plans for a holiday have fallen through.*

▶ NOUN [*plural* **falls**]

1 when someone falls by accident □ *My grandmother had a serious fall last week.*

2 a decrease in a price, amount or temperature □ *+ in There has been a fall in unemployment.*

3 the US word for **autumn**

---

fallacy /'fæləsɪ/ NOUN [*plural* **fallacies**] an idea that is not true although many people think it is □ *It's a fallacy that cutting your hair makes it grow faster.*

fallible /'fæləbəl/ ADJECTIVE not perfect and likely to be wrong or to make mistakes □ *Even teachers are fallible.*

fallopian tube /fəˌləʊpɪən 'tjuːb/ NOUN [*plural* **fallopian tubes**] one of the two tubes that carry a woman's eggs to the womb (= place where the baby grows). A biology word.

fallout /'fɔːlaʊt/ NOUN, NO PLURAL

1 radioactive dust from a nuclear explosion

2 the bad results of something that has happened □ *We are still dealing with the fallout of last year's financial crisis.*

---

false /fɔːls/ ADJECTIVE

1 not true or based on information that is not correct □ *He made a false statement to the police.* □ *These claims are completely false.* 🔁 *We had a false sense of security.* 🔁 *We don't want to give people false hope.*

2 not real or natural 🔁 *false teeth* □ *a false passport*

3 not showing your real feelings □ *a false smile*

◆ IDIOM **under false pretences** if you do something under false pretences, you do it by tricking someone □ *He admitted he had married her under false pretences.*

false alarm /ˌfɔːls əˈlɑːm/ NOUN [plural **false alarms**] when you believe something bad or dangerous is going to happen, but it does not □ *Someone thought there was a fire, but it was a false alarm.*

falsely /ˈfɔːlslɪ/ ADVERB not correctly □ *I was falsely accused of theft.*

● **falseness** /ˈfɔːlsnɪs/ NOUN, NO PLURAL being false

falsification /ˌfɔːlsɪfɪˈkeɪʃən/ NOUN, NO PLURAL when someone falsifies something □ *the falsification of documents*

falsify /ˈfɔːlsɪfaɪ/ VERB [**falsifies, falsifying, falsified**] to change information in order to trick people □ *He had falsified the firm's accounts.*

falter /ˈfɔːltə(r)/ VERB [**falters, faltering, faltered**]
1 to pause or have difficulty when you are moving or speaking □ *He walked steadily beside me and only faltered occasionally.* □ *His voice faltered slightly.*
2 to become less confident, strong or effective □ *Once we were sure of what we were doing we never faltered.*

fame /feɪm/ NOUN, NO PLURAL the state of being known by a lot of people 🖫 *She found fame in a hit TV series.* 🖫 *He achieved international fame as a novelist.* 🖫 *Young actors go to Hollywood seeking fame and fortune* (= fame and money).

familiar /fəˈmɪljə(r)/ ADJECTIVE
1 known to you □ *His voice sounded familiar.* 🖫 *It looked vaguely familiar.* 🖫 *There were a few familiar faces* (= people you know) *at the party.*
2 be familiar with something to have seen or used something before □ *I'm not familiar with this software.* □ *If you're familiar with the area, it's just next to the big park.*
3 common and happening often 🖫 *Electric cars are becoming a more familiar sight.* □ *This is a sadly familiar story.*
4 behaving in a friendly and informal way □ *I thought he was too familiar.*

● **familiarize** or **familiarise** /fəˈmɪljəraɪz/ VERB [**familiarizes, familiarizing, familiarized**] **familiarize yourself with something** to make sure you know something □ *Try to familiarize yourself with the rules.*

family /ˈfæmlɪ/ NOUN [plural **families**]
1 a group of people who are related to each other 🖫 *I invited my whole family to the wedding.* 🖫 *I met her parents and several other family members.* 🖫 *She discussed the decision with family and friends.* □ *The minister met the families of the victims.*
2 the children in a family □ *I have a wife and family at home.* 🖫 *He wants to marry and start a family* (= have children).
3 a group of animals, plants or languages that are related to each other

➤ **Family** can be used with a singular or plural verb in British English: □ *The family next door has a dog.* □ *The family next door have a dog.*

family tree /ˌfæmlɪ ˈtriː/ NOUN [plural **family trees**] a picture which shows the relationships within a family

famine /ˈfæmɪn/ NOUN [plural **famines**] a situation in which many people in an area do not have enough food and may die □ *The country was hit by a severe drought and famine.*

famished /ˈfæmɪʃt/ ADJECTIVE very hungry

famous /ˈfeɪməs/ ADJECTIVE known by a lot of people □ *a famous actor* □ *a famous painting* □ **+ for** *She is most famous for her role in Star Wars.* □ **+ as** *He later became famous as a children's writer.*

fan /fæn/ ▶ NOUN [plural **fans**]
1 someone who likes or admires a person or thing very much □ *football fans* □ *She's a big fan of Madonna.*
2 a machine with thin blades that turn round and make the air cooler □ *There was a ceiling fan in our room.*
3 something that you move in front of your face to make you feel cooler
▶ VERB [**fans, fanning, fanned**]
1 to move something in front of your face to make you feel cooler □ *He fanned himself with his cap.*
2 to make a fire burn more strongly □ *Strong winds fanned the flames.*
◆ PHRASAL VERB **fan out** to spread in different directions □ *Rescue teams fanned out across the area.*

fanatic /fəˈnætɪk/ NOUN [plural **fanatics**]
1 someone who has very extreme political or religious beliefs 🖫 *a religious fanatic*
2 someone who likes something very much and spends a lot of time doing it □ *a cycling fanatic*
● **fanatical** /fəˈnætɪkəl/ ADJECTIVE
1 having very extreme political or religious beliefs □ *a fanatical preacher*
2 liking something very much and spending a lot of time doing it □ *He's fanatical about football.*
● **fanaticism** /fəˈnætɪˌsɪzəm/ NOUN, NO PLURAL very strong religious or political beliefs that can make people behave unreasonably

fancy /ˈfænsɪ/ ▶ VERB [**fancies, fancying, fancied**]
1 an informal word meaning to want to have or do something □ *Do you fancy going to the cinema?* □ *I really fancy a curry.*
2 an informal word meaning to be attracted to someone □ *My friend fancies you.*
3 to think that something or someone will be successful 🖫 *They fancy their chances of winning tomorrow.* □ *Whitaker is strongly fancied for the best actor award.*
4 fancy yourself (as something) to think you are or could be a particular type of person, often wrongly □ *He fancies himself as a poet.*
▶ ADJECTIVE [**fancier, fanciest**]
1 fashionable or expensive □ *fancy clothes* □ *We went for a meal at a fancy restaurant.*
2 clever or complicated □ *We don't use any fancy equipment.*
3 decorated and not plain □ *fancy cakes*

▶ NOUN, NO PLURAL

1 take your fancy to make you want to have or do something □ *Do any of these dresses take your fancy?*
2 take a fancy to someone an informal phrase meaning to be attracted to someone □ *I think he's taken a fancy to you.*

fancy dress /ˌfænsɪ 'dres/ NOUN, NO PLURAL clothes that you wear to a party to make you look like someone or something else 🔁 *a fancy dress party* □ *Are you going in fancy dress?*

fanfare /'fænfeə(r)/ NOUN [plural **fanfares**] a short, loud piece of music played on a trumpet

fang /fæŋ/ NOUN [plural **fangs**] a long, pointed tooth of an animal or a snake

fantasize or **fantasise** /'fæntəsaɪz/ VERB [**fantasizes, fantasizing, fantasized**] to imagine something good happening to you that is not likely □ *He used to fantasize about being a famous actor.*

fantastic /fæn'tæstɪk/ ADJECTIVE
1 an informal word meaning extremely good □ *We had a fantastic time in Rome.* □ *This is a fantastic opportunity for us.* 🔁 *You look fantastic!*
2 an informal word meaning very large 🔁 *They've spent a fantastic amount of money.*
3 not real or not true □ *a fantastic tale*

fantasy /'fæntəsɪ/ NOUN [plural **fantasies**]
1 something good that you imagine but that probably will not happen □ *I often think about going to live somewhere warm and sunny but it's just a fantasy.*
2 a story about imaginary things □ *The film is a futuristic fantasy.*

FAQ /ˌefeɪˈkjuː/ ABBREVIATION frequently asked questions; a list of questions about a particular subject

far /fɑː(r)/ ▶ ADVERB [**farther** or **further, farthest** or **furthest**]
1 a long distance □ *Don't go too far.* □ **+ away** *Is the hotel very far away?* □ **+ to** *It's not far to Paris.* □ **+ from** *He lives not far from the church.*
2 a long time in the past or the future □ *Records go as far back as the 16th century.* □ *We can't tell you the exact number of guests this far in advance.*
3 an amount of progress 🔁 *I haven't got very far with my homework.*
4 much □ *She's a far better swimmer than I am.* □ *He's far more interested in football.* 🔁 *These trousers are far too small for me.*
5 as far as I know/can remember, etc. used to say what you think is true □ *As far as I can remember, there aren't any very steep hills.*
6 as far as something is concerned used to talk about a particular thing □ *As far as food is concerned, I'm happy with a sandwich.*
7 as far as I'm/he's, etc. concerned used to talk about someone's opinion □ *As far as I'm concerned, you can take all the money.*
8 as far as possible as much as possible □ *I try to avoid sugar as far as possible.*
9 by far used to emphasize the quality you are talking

about □ *He's by far the most talented of our dancers.*
10 far from not at all □ *The problem is still far from being sorted out.*
11 so far until now □ *So far, there haven't been any accidents.*

➤ Note that **far**, meaning 'a long distance', is mainly used in questions and in negative sentences: □ *How far is it to the town centre?* □ *It's not far from the town centre.*
➤ In positive sentences, we usually say **a long way**: □ *It's a long way from the town centre.*

▶ ADJECTIVE
1 the far part of something is the part that is the greatest distance from you 🔁 *The house is on the far side of the lake.*
2 the far left/right the people with the most extreme political opinions

farce /fɑːs/ NOUN [plural **farces**]
1 a situation that is silly because it is so confused or badly organized □ *The trial has become a complete farce.*
2 a theatre play in which funny and unlikely things happen

fare /feə(r)/ ▶ NOUN [plural **fares**]
1 the price of a journey by bus, train, aeroplane, etc. 🔁 *The train fare to London is £33.* 🔁 *Cheap air fares make travel much easier.*
2 a formal word for a type of food □ *They serve hearty German fare.*
▶ VERB [**fares, faring, fared**] used to say how well or badly someone does in a situation 🔁 *Companies are faring better than they did last year.* 🔁 *The party fared poorly in the elections.*

Far East /ˌfɑːr 'iːst/ NOUN, NO PLURAL the countries of East and Southeast Asia, including Japan and China

farewell /ˌfeəˈwel/ ▶ EXCLAMATION an old-fashioned word for goodbye.
▶ NOUN [plural **farewells**] an old-fashioned word for a goodbye □ *We said our farewells.* □ *a farewell speech*

far-fetched /ˌfɑːˈfetʃt/ ADJECTIVE very unlikely to be true □ *a far-fetched story* □ *That's not such a far-fetched idea.*

farm /fɑːm/ ▶ NOUN [plural **farms**] an area of land where crops are grown and animals are kept 🔁 *a dairy farm* (= which keeps cows for milk) 🔁 *a farm animal* □ *He works on a farm.*
▶ VERB [**farms, farming, farmed**] to use land for growing crops or keeping animals for meat □ *They have farmed the land here for generations.*
• **farmer** /'fɑːmə(r)/ NOUN [plural **farmers**] someone who owns and works on a farm □ *a local sheep farmer*

farmhouse /'fɑːmhaʊs/ NOUN [plural **farmhouses**] a house on a farm where the farmer lives

farming /'fɑːmɪŋ/ NOUN, NO PLURAL the activity or business of working on and managing a farm □ *The* *organization promotes organic farming.* 🔲 *He grew up in a small farming community.*

farmland /'fɑːmlænd/ NOUN, NO PLURAL land that is used for farming

farmyard /'fɑːmjaːd/ NOUN [plural **farmyards**] an area surrounded by buildings on a farm

far-reaching /ˌfɑːˈriːtʃɪŋ/ ADJECTIVE having an important effect or affecting many people 🔲 *The new rules are bound to have far-reaching consequences for schools.*

fascinate /'fæsɪneɪt/ VERB [**fascinates, fascinating, fascinated**] to interest and attract someone very much □ *The story of Tutankhamun has fascinated people for many years.* □ *The thing that fascinates me is the variety of shapes and colours.*

• **fascinated** /'fæsɪneɪtɪd/ ADJECTIVE very interested and attracted by something □ *As a kid I was fascinated by the stars.* □ *She watched the fascinated expressions of the children.*

• **fascinating** /'fæsɪneɪtɪŋ/ ADJECTIVE very interesting 🔲 *a fascinating story* □ *It's the island's wildlife that I find fascinating.*

• **fascination** /ˌfæsɪˈneɪʃən/ NOUN, NO PLURAL a great interest in something □ *I've always had a fascination for unusual animals.* □ *the public's fascination with celebrities* □ *She watched in fascination.*

fascism /'fæʃɪzəm/ NOUN, NO PLURAL a political system in which the state has strong control over all areas of society

• **fascist** /'fæʃɪst/ ► NOUN [plural **fascists**]
1 someone who supports fascism
2 someone who tries to control other people and ignores their opinions
► ADJECTIVE to do with fascism 🔲 *a fascist regime* 🔲 *The country was ruled by a fascist dictator.*

fashion /'fæʃən/ NOUN [plural **fashions**]
1 something, especially a piece of clothing, that is very popular at a particular time □ + **for** *There was a fashion for tight jeans.* □ *Short skirts were in fashion then.* 🔲 *She wears all the latest fashions.*
2 *no plural* the business of making and selling clothes 🔲 *a fashion designer* 🔲 *a fashion magazine*
3 the way someone does something □ *The second half began in a similar fashion.*

• **fashionable** /'fæʃənəbəl/ ADJECTIVE popular with many people at a particular time □ *a fashionable restaurant* 🔲 *The area has become fashionable with students.* □ + **to do something** *It's fashionable to play team sports again.*

fast¹ /fɑːst/ ► ADJECTIVE [**faster, fastest**]
1 quick □ *a fast car* □ *He was the fastest runner.*
2 if a clock or watch is fast, it shows a time that is later than the correct time
► ADVERB [**faster, fastest**]
1 quickly □ *She can run very fast.* □ *We're working as fast as we can.* □ *The population has grown faster than in any other region.*

2 fast asleep completely asleep □ *The boys are fast asleep.*
3 firmly or tightly 🔲 *The door was stuck fast.*

fast² /fɑːst/ ► VERB [**fasts, fasting, fasted**] to not eat any food for a period of time, often for religious reasons □ *I am fasting because it is Ramadan.*
► NOUN [plural **fasts**] a time when you fast

fasten /'fɑːsən/ VERB [**fastens, fastening, fastened**] to join or fix two things or parts together 🔲 *Please fasten your seat belts.* □ + **to** *The phone was fastened to the wall.* □ *She fastened the papers together with a stapler.* □ *The dress fastens at the back.*

• **fastener** /'fɑːsənə(r)/ NOUN [plural **fasteners**] something that is used to join two things together

fast food /ˌfɑːst ˈfuːd/ NOUN, NO PLURAL food that is prepared and served quickly in a restaurant, such as a hamburger

fastidious /fəˈstɪdɪəs/ ADJECTIVE wanting everything to be tidy, clean and perfect

fat /fæt/ ► ADJECTIVE [**fatter, fattest**]
1 a fat person has too much flesh, usually because they eat too much 🔲 *George is getting fat, isn't he?* 🔲 *Do these jeans make me look fat?* □ *Fat children are often teased.*
2 thick or large □ *a big, fat book*

> ► It is not polite to describe someone as **fat**. To sound less rude, use the words **big** or **overweight**: □ *She's quite big at the moment and unhappy about it.*

♦ IDIOM **fat chance** used to mean you think something is very unlikely. An informal phrase. □ *Will he tidy up? Fat chance!*
► NOUN [plural **fats**]
1 a soft white substance that forms a layer under your skin 🔲 *Can exercise reduce body fat?*
2 a substance like oil that is in food or used in cooking □ *Limit the amount of fat you eat.* 🔲 *Hard cheese has a higher fat content.*

fatal /'feɪtəl/ ADJECTIVE
1 causing someone's death 🔲 *a fatal accident* 🔲 *The disease is potentially fatal.*
2 causing serious problems □ *a fatal mistake*

• **fatality** /fəˈtælətɪ/ NOUN [plural **fatalities**] a death in an accident □ *We want to reduce the number of fatalities and injuries in road accidents.*

• **fatally** /'feɪtəlɪ/ ADVERB in a way which causes someone's death □ *He was fatally wounded.*

fate /feɪt/ NOUN, NO PLURAL
1 the things that happen to someone, especially bad things 🔲 *I hope that the others don't suffer the same fate.* 🔲 *The High Court will decide the fate of the three men.*
2 a power that seems to control what happens □ *She believes that fate brought them together.*

- **fated** /ˈfeɪtɪd/ ADJECTIVE likely to happen because of fate □ *We were fated to meet.*
- **fateful** /ˈfeɪtfʊl/ ADJECTIVE having an important, usually bad, effect on future events 🕮 *It turned out to be a fateful decision.* 🕮 *We look back on that fateful day in 2001.*

father /ˈfɑːðə(r)/ ▶ NOUN [*plural* **fathers**]
1 your male parent □ *I'll speak to my father.*
2 Father the title of some priests □ *Father Anthony*
3 the father of something the man who first started something □ *Sigmund Freud is known as the father of psychoanalysis.*

▶ **Father** is a formal way of speaking or referring to your male parent. Most young people use the word **Dad** instead and young children often use the word **Daddy**.

▶ VERB [**fathers, fathering, fathered**] a formal word meaning to be the father of a child □ *He had four wives and fathered many children.*

Father Christmas /ˌfɑːðə ˈkrɪsməs/ NOUN an imaginary old man with a white beard and a red coat who children believe brings presents on Christmas Eve
fatherhood /ˈfɑːðəˌhʊd/ NOUN, NO PLURAL being a father □ *the joys of fatherhood*
father-in-law /ˈfɑːðərɪnˌlɔː/ NOUN [*plural* **fathers-in-law**] the father of your wife or husband
fatherly /ˈfɑːðəli/ ADJECTIVE like a kind father □ *a fatherly hug*
fathom /ˈfæðəm/ VERB [**fathoms, fathoming, fathomed**] to understand something after thinking about it □ *I still can't fathom why he didn't tell me.*
fatigue /fəˈtiːg/ NOUN, NO PLURAL extreme tiredness □ *The condition can cause fatigue and shortness of breath.*
fatten /ˈfætən/ VERB [**fattens, fattening, fattened**] to make an animal fatter so it can be eaten □ *The pigs are being fattened up for sale.*
- **fattening** /ˈfætənɪŋ/ ADJECTIVE making you fatter 🕮 *fattening foods* □ *Chocolate is very fattening.*
fatty /ˈfæti/ ADJECTIVE [**fattier, fattiest**] containing a lot of fat 🕮 *Try to avoid fatty foods.*
faucet /ˈfɔːsɪt/ NOUN [*plural* **faucets**] the US word for a water tap

fault /fɔːlt/ ▶ NOUN [*plural* **faults**]
1 the fact of being responsible for something bad or wrong □ *Sorry, that's my fault – I left it unlocked.* □ *+ of This is not the fault of the teachers.* □ *The driver was not at fault.* 🕮 *I believe the fault lies with the government.*
2 a mistake, problem or bad feature □ *The plane developed a technical fault.* □ *+ with There was a fault with the design.* □ *For all his faults, he's always been good to me.*
3 find fault (with someone/something) to criticize someone or something □ *He always seems to find fault with her work.*
4 a long crack in the Earth's surface which causes earthquakes (= when the earth shakes) 🕮 *a fault line*

▶ VERB [**faults, faulting, faulted**] to criticize someone or something □ *I can't fault his effort.*
- **faultless** /ˈfɔːltlɪs/ ADJECTIVE perfect □ *a faultless performance*
- **faulty** /ˈfɔːlti/ ADJECTIVE not working correctly □ *a faulty computer*

fauna /ˈfɔːnə/ NOUN, NO PLURAL the animals, birds and insects that live in an area. A biology word.

favor /ˈfeɪvə(r)/ NOUN [*plural* **favors**], VERB [**favors, favoring, favored**] the US spelling of favour
- **favorable** /ˈfeɪvrəbəl/ ADJECTIVE the US spelling of favourable
- **favorably** /ˈfeɪvrəbli/ ADVERB the US spelling of favourably
favorite /ˈfeɪvrɪt/ ADJECTIVE, NOUN [*plural* **favorites**] the US spelling of favourite
- **favoritism** /ˈfeɪvrɪˌtɪzəm/ NOUN, NO PLURAL the US spelling of favouritism

favour /ˈfeɪvə(r)/ ▶ NOUN [*plural* **favours**]
1 something you do for someone to help them 🕮 *Could you do me a favour and check my homework?* 🕮 *I need to ask you a favour.* 🕮 *As a special favour, Bill's fixing my car.*
2 in favour of something supporting something as a good idea □ *I'm in favour of higher pay for nurses.* □ *Workers have voted in favour of strike action.*
3 in someone's favour giving someone an advantage □ *The exchange rate is in our favour at the moment.*
4 in/out of favour popular/not popular □ *This sort of music has gone out of favour.*
5 no plural a formal word meaning when people like or approve of something 🕮 *These reforms have found favour with the public.*

▶ VERB [**favours, favouring, favoured**]
1 to treat one person or group better than others □ *The legal system seems to favour the wealthy.*
2 to use, like or support something □ *Many people favour the death penalty.* □ *She favoured tight-fitting dresses.*
- **favourable** /ˈfeɪvrəbəl/ ADJECTIVE
1 making someone like and approve of someone or something, or showing that you like and approve of someone or something 🕮 *The tidy room created a favourable impression.* □ *Inspectors wrote a very favourable report.*
2 good and suitable □ *We're hoping for favourable weather conditions.*
3 giving agreement □ *We're hoping for a favourable reply.*
4 giving someone an unfair advantage □ *They were accused of giving some people favourable treatment.*
- **favourably** /ˈfeɪvrəbli/ ADVERB in a favourable way 🕮 *Her exam results compare favourably with (= are better than) those of her friends.* 🕮 *We were favourably impressed by (= liked) their work.*

favourite /ˈfeɪvrɪt/ ► ADJECTIVE your favourite person or thing is the one you like best □ *My favourite colour is purple.* □ *Who's your favourite player?* ► NOUN [plural **favourites**]
1 the person or thing you like best □ *I love all cheese, but brie is my favourite.*
2 someone who is treated better than others by a teacher, parent, etc.
3 the person or animal that most people think will win a competition ⊞ *Jones is firm/hot favourite to win the 100m.*
• **favouritism** /ˈfeɪvrɪtɪzəm/ NOUN, NO PLURAL when someone is treated better than others in a way that is not fair.

fawn /fɔːn/ ► NOUN [plural **fawns**] a young deer
► ADJECTIVE having a pale brown colour
◆ PHRASAL VERB [**fawns, fawning, fawned**] **fawn over someone** to praise someone too much to try to make them like you

fax /fæks/ ► NOUN [plural **faxes**]
1 a written message that is sent by a machine over a telephone line ⊞ *I sent a fax to the bank.*
2 a machine used for sending a fax message
► VERB [**faxes, faxing, faxed**] to send someone a fax

FBI /ˌefbiːˈaɪ/ ABBREVIATION Federal Bureau of Investigation; the national police of the US

fear /fɪə(r)/ ► NOUN [plural **fears**]
1 *no plural* the feeling of being very frightened □ *She was shaking with fear.* ⊞ *They live in constant fear of attack.*
2 a feeling of being frightened or worried about a particular thing □ **+ of** *John has a fear of spiders.* □ **+ about** *He has raised fears about the future of the company.* □ **+ for** *She expressed fears for their safety.* ⊞ *The news confirmed her worst fears.*
3 for fear of something because you are worried about something bad happening □ *She didn't complain for fear of losing her job.*
► VERB [**fears, fearing, feared**]
1 to be afraid of or worried about someone or something □ *Experts fear the virus could spread.* □ **+ that** *She feared that she was already too late.* □ **+ for** *He feared for his safety.* ⊞ *She feared for her life* (= thought she might die).
2 fear the worst to be worried that something very bad has happened or will happen
• **fearful** /ˈfɪəful/ ADJECTIVE
1 feeling frightened or worried about something □ *The villagers are fearful of another attack.*
2 very bad □ *He woke up with a fearful headache.*
• **fearfully** /ˈfɪəfuli/ ADVERB
1 showing fear □ *She looked up fearfully.*
2 a formal word that means extremely □ *It was fearfully hot.*
• **fearless** /ˈfɪələs/ ADJECTIVE not frightened by anything □ *a fearless fighter*
• **fearlessly** /ˈfɪələsli/ ADVERB not showing

any fear □ *He spoke out fearlessly against the regime.*
• **fearsome** /ˈfɪəsəm/ ADJECTIVE very frightening □ *The gang have a fearsome reputation.*

feasibility /ˌfiːzəˈbɪləti/ NOUN, NO PLURAL the state of being feasible □ *We're investigating the feasibility of the project.*
feasible /ˈfiːzəbəl/ ADJECTIVE possible to be done or achieved □ *Cycling to work isn't feasible for many people.*
feast /fiːst/ NOUN [plural **feasts**] a large meal for a special occasion
feat /fiːt/ NOUN [plural **feats**]
1 something someone does that needs a lot of skill, strength or courage □ *a feat of strength and endurance* ⊞ *He achieved the remarkable feat of staying on the bestseller list for 237 weeks.*
2 be no mean feat to be difficult to achieve □ *Getting four young children ready for school is no mean feat.*

feather /ˈfeðə(r)/ NOUN [plural **feathers**] one of the long light things that cover a bird's body
• **feathery** /ˈfeðəri/ ADJECTIVE soft and light like a feather

feature /ˈfiːtʃə(r)/ ► NOUN [plural **features**]
1 a part or quality of something □ **+ of** *One of the key features of the system is its flexibility.* ⊞ *The phone's other features include a camera, radio and MP3 player.* ⊞ *The school buses have special safety features.*
2 a part of your face, such as your eyes, nose or mouth ⊞ *She described the man's hair colour and facial features.*
3 a special article in a newspaper or magazine about something □ *The magazine ran a feature on highly paid women.*
► VERB [**features, featuring, featured**] to have someone or something as an important part □ *The film features some exotic locations.* □ **+ in** *The same woman features in several of his paintings.*

February /ˈfebruəri/ NOUN the second month of the year, after January and before March □ *I started my new job in February.*
fed /fed/ PAST TENSE AND PAST PARTICIPLE OF **feed**
federal /ˈfedərəl/ ADJECTIVE
1 to do with a group of states which make some of their own laws but also have a national government □ *a federal system*
2 to do with the national government of a country made up of states, like the US □ *a federal court*
• **federation** /ˌfedəˈreɪʃən/ NOUN [plural **federations**] a group of states or organizations which have joined together □ *the Italian football federation*
fed up /ˌfed ˈʌp/ ADJECTIVE annoyed or bored with something that has been happening for a long time □ *I've been peeling potatoes all morning and I'm fed up now.* □ *We're fed up with your moaning.*

fee /fiː/ NOUN [plural **fees**] an amount of money that you pay for a service □ **+ for** *They charge a monthly* *fee for unlimited Internet access.* 🖳 *Companies pay a fee to advertise on the site.*

feeble /'fi:bəl/ ADJECTIVE [**feebler, feeblest**]
1 very weak □ *He looked feeble and ill.* □ *a feeble voice*
2 not good or effective 🖳 *a feeble excuse* 🖳 *He made a feeble attempt to protest.*
• **feebly** /'fi:bli/ ADVERB in a feeble way □ *She struggled feebly.*

feed /fi:d/ ► VERB [**feeds, feeding, fed**]
1 to give food to a person or an animal □ *Dad was feeding the baby.* □ *I don't earn enough money to feed my family.* □ *Can you feed my cat while I'm on holiday?*
2 to eat food □ **+ on** *Rabbits feed on grass.* □ **+ off** *The caterpillars feed off the leaves.*
3 to provide something to a person or a machine, often continuously □ **+ into** *The information is fed into a computer.*
► NOUN [*plural* **feeds**]
1 food for animals or babies □ *cattle feed*
2 the fast movement of information, pictures, etc. to a computer or other equipment □ *You can watch a live feed of the debate on the website.*

feedback /'fi:dbæk/ NOUN, NO PLURAL opinions from people about work you are doing or have done, intended to help you do it better 🖳 *It's always good to get feedback from customers.*

feel /fi:l/ ► VERB [**feels, feeling, felt**]
1 to have an emotion or to be in a particular state □ *I feel tired.* □ *Do you feel better today?* □ *How are you feeling?* □ *I don't feel any anger towards them.*
2 to experience something touching you or happening to you □ *Suddenly, she felt a hand on her shoulder.* □ *He could feel himself falling.* □ *I felt a pain in my leg.*
3 if something feels a certain way, that is how it seems to you □ *Your forehead feels hot.* □ *It feels strange to be back here.* □ *It feels as though nobody is interested.*
4 to touch something with your fingers to see what it is like □ *Feel how soft her fur is!*
5 to think or believe something □ *I feel he should have asked my opinion first.*
6 **feel like something** to want something or want to do something □ **+ ing** *Do you feel like going for a swim?*
► NOUN, NO PLURAL the way something is when you touch it □ *I love the feel of these silk sheets.*
• **feeler** /'fi:lə(r)/ NOUN [*plural* **feelers**] one of the two long parts on an insect's head
• **feeling** /'fi:lɪŋ/ NOUN [*plural* **feelings**]
1 an emotion □ *There was a feeling of excitement amongst the children.*
2 something that you experience physically, or the ability to experience it □ *I don't like the feeling of being under water.* 🖳 *I lost the feeling in my toes.*
3 a belief that something is true 🖳 *I have the feeling that she's avoiding me.*

4 opinion □ *My feeling is that they should pay for the damage.*
➡ *go to* **hurt** someone's feelings

feet /fi:t/ PLURAL OF **foot**
feign /feɪn/ VERB [**feigns, feigning, feigned**] to pretend to be experiencing a feeling, an illness, etc. □ *She feigned illness to avoid going to school.*
feline /'fi:laɪn/ ADJECTIVE to do with cats
fell[1] /fel/ PAST TENSE OF **fall**
fell[2] /fel/ VERB [**fells, felling, felled**] if you fell a tree, you cut it down
fellow /'feləʊ/ ► NOUN [*plural* **fellows**]
1 an old-fashioned word for a boy or man □ *He's an unusual fellow.*
2 a person whose job is to teach or study at a university □ *He's a fellow of Trinity College, Cambridge.*
► ADJECTIVE used to refer to a person who is similar to you in some way □ *He chatted with fellow passengers.*
• **fellowship** /'feləʊʃɪp/ NOUN [*plural* **fellowships**]
1 the position of being a fellow at a university
2 a feeling of being friends between people who have similar interests
3 a club or organization
felony /'feləni/ NOUN [*plural* **felonies**] a US word meaning a serious crime such as murder □ *He could face felony charges.*
felt[1] /felt/ NOUN, NO PLURAL a type of cloth made of rolled and pressed wool
felt[2] /felt/ PAST TENSE AND PAST PARTICIPLE OF **feel**
felt-tip pen /ˌfeltˌtɪp 'pen/ NOUN [*plural* **felt-tip pens**] a pen with a writing point made of soft material
female /'fi:meɪl/ ► ADJECTIVE belonging to the sex which can give birth or lay eggs □ *a female athlete* □ *She won the award for best female artist.* □ *A female lion is called a lioness.*
► NOUN [*plural* **females**] a female animal or person □ *We saw an adult female with three cubs.*

feminine /'femɪnɪn/ ADJECTIVE
1 to do with women, or having qualities that are typical of a woman □ *a feminine voice* □ *This outfit feels more feminine.*
2 in English grammar, feminine forms of words refer to females. For example, *she* is a feminine pronoun.
• **femininity** /ˌfemɪ'nɪnəti/ NOUN, NO PLURAL being like a woman
• **feminism** /'femɪnɪzəm/ NOUN, NO PLURAL the belief that women should have the same rights and opportunities as men
• **feminist** /'femɪnɪst/ NOUN [*plural* **feminists**] someone who supports feminism

fence /fens/ ► NOUN [*plural* **fences**] a wooden or metal structure that goes around or separates land □ *He put up a fence around the garden.*
► VERB [**fences, fencing, fenced**] to put a fence around or across an area □ *They fenced off the end of their garden.*

◆ IDIOM **be/sit on the fence** to not make a choice between two possibilities or opinions □ *I'm sitting on the fence on this and waiting to find out a bit more.*

fencing /ˈfensɪŋ/ NOUN, NO PLURAL
1 a sport in which people fight with thin swords (= long metal blades)
2 fences or the wood or metal that is used to make them

fend /fend/ VERB [**fends, fending, fended**] **fend for yourself** to look after yourself without help from other people □ *She was left to fend for herself in a strange city.*

◆ PHRASAL VERB **fend someone/something off** to defend yourself against an attack or criticism □ *The minister tried to fend off the accusations.*

fender /ˈfendə(r)/ NOUN [*plural* **fenders**] the US word for bumper

ferment /fəˈment/ VERB [**ferments, fermenting, fermented**] when beer or wine ferments, the sugar becomes alcohol

● **fermentation** /ˌfɜːmənˈteɪʃən/ NOUN, NO PLURAL the process of fermenting

fern /fɜːn/ NOUN [*plural* **ferns**] a plant with long leaves like feathers

ferocious /fəˈrəʊʃəs/ ADJECTIVE extremely violent, strong or dangerous □ *a ferocious dog* □ *a ferocious storm*

● **ferociously** /fəˈrəʊʃəsli/ ADVERB in a ferocious way □ *They fought ferociously.*

● **ferocity** /fəˈrɒsəti/ NOUN, NO PLURAL being ferocious □ *She was shocked by the ferocity of his anger.*

ferret /ˈferɪt/ ▶ NOUN [*plural* **ferrets**] a small animal with a long body, used to hunt rabbits
▶ VERB [**ferrets, ferreting, ferreted**] to look for something somewhere □ *She was ferreting around in her bag for her keys.*

◆ PHRASAL VERB **ferret something out** to look for something that is difficult to find □ *Reporters are trying to ferret out the names of those involved.*

ferry /ˈferi/ ▶ NOUN [*plural* **ferries**] a boat that carries people and vehicles 🖫 *a passenger ferry* 🖫 *We took a ferry to a smaller island.*
▶ VERB [**ferries, ferrying, ferried**] to take people regularly from one place to another □ *A shuttle bus ferries tourists between the hotel and the airport.*

fertile /ˈfɜːtaɪl/ ADJECTIVE
1 fertile land is good for growing crops on □ *fertile soil*
2 a fertile person or animal is able to produce children or young animals
3 producing a lot of new ideas □ *You have a fertile imagination.*
4 fertile ground a situation which encourages something □ *Spying is fertile ground for authors and film-makers.*

● **fertility** /fɜːˈtɪləti/ NOUN, NO PLURAL being fertile □ *She is having fertility treatment.*

● **fertilization** *or* **fertilisation** /ˌfɜːtɪlaɪˈzeɪʃən/ NOUN, NO PLURAL the act of fertilizing something

● **fertilize** *or* **fertilise** /ˈfɜːtɪlaɪz/ VERB [**fertilizes, fertilizing, fertilized**]
1 to add a substance to soil so that plants grow better
2 to put male and female cells together to produce a baby or a young plant or animal

● **fertilizer** *or* **fertiliser** /ˈfɜːtɪlaɪzə(r)/ NOUN [*plural* **fertilizers**] a substance you put on soil to make plants grow better

fervent /ˈfɜːvənt/ ADJECTIVE very enthusiastic and sincere □ *He was a fervent admirer of Picasso.*

● **fervour** /ˈfɜːvə(r)/ NOUN, NO PLURAL a strong enthusiasm for or belief in something □ *A wave of religious fervour swept the country.* □ *He spoke with fervour about the need for reform.*

fervor /ˈfɜːvə(r)/ NOUN, NO PLURAL the US spelling of fervour

festival /ˈfestɪvəl/ NOUN [*plural* **festivals**]
1 a series of special events of a particular type 🖫 *a film festival* 🖫 *a five-day music festival* □ **+ of** *an annual festival of traditional music*
2 a special time or day when people celebrate something 🖫 *a religious festival* □ **+ of** *the Muslim festival of Eid*

● **festive** /ˈfestɪv/ ADJECTIVE to do with happy celebrations □ *a festive occasion* □ *a festive atmosphere* 🖫 *We spent the festive season* (= Christmas) *with my family.*

● **festivities** /feˈstɪvətiz/ PLURAL NOUN the things you do to celebrate a special event □ *the Independence Day festivities*

festoon /feˈstuːn/ VERB [**festoons, festooning, festooned**] to decorate a place with colourful decorations □ *The city was festooned with flags.*

fetch /fetʃ/ VERB [**fetches, fetching, fetched**]
1 to go somewhere and bring something or someone back with you □ *Could you fetch the newspaper for me, please?* □ *I'll come and fetch you.* □ *The women fetch water from the river.*
2 to be sold for a particular amount of money 🖫 *The painting fetched a record price.* □ *It is expected to fetch £100,000 at auction.*

fête /feɪt, fet/ NOUN [*plural* **fêtes**] a special event held outside with games and things for sale □ *a school fête*

fetus /ˈfiːtəs/ NOUN [*plural* **fetuses**] the US spelling of foetus

feud /fjuːd/ ▶ NOUN [*plural* **feuds**] a serious argument between two people or groups that continues for a long time
▶ VERB [**feuds, feuding, feuded**] to have a feud with someone

fever /ˈfiːvə(r)/ NOUN [*plural* **fevers**] if you have a fever, your body temperature is higher than normal because you are ill 🖫 *He had a high fever.*

● **feverish** /ˈfiːvərɪʃ/ ADJECTIVE feeling very hot because you are ill

few /fjuː/ DETERMINER, PRONOUN [**fewer, fewest**]
1 a small number □ *I packed a few apples and some bread.* □ *A few people tried to help him.* □ *I visit her every few days.* □ *The past few weeks have been very difficult.*
2 some but not many □ *We only had a few replies to our advert.* □ *Few of the children had seen a cow before.* 🕮 *Very few people know her real name.*
3 quite a few quite a lot □ *There were quite a few mistakes in his work.*

fiancé /fɪˈɒnseɪ/ NOUN [*plural* **fiancés**] a woman's fiancé is the man she has promised to marry □ *She will marry her fiancé in April.*

fiancée /fɪˈɒnseɪ/ NOUN [*plural* **fiancées**] a man's fiancée is the woman he has promised to marry □ *Tom's fiancée is a teacher.*

fiasco /fɪˈæskəʊ/ NOUN [*plural* **fiascos**] a situation that is a complete and embarrassing failure

fib /fɪb/ ▶ NOUN [*plural* **fibs**] an informal word meaning a lie about something which is not important 🕮 *Many young children tell fibs.*
▶ VERB [**fibs, fibbing, fibbed**] to tell a lie about something that is not important

fibre /ˈfaɪbə(r)/ NOUN [*plural* **fibres**]
1 a substance in food which your body cannot digest, and which helps your bowels work well □ *Brown bread is high in fibre.*
2 a cloth made up of threads 🕮 *Try to wear clothes made from natural fibres, such as cotton.*
3 a thin thread of something □ *Fibres from the girl's clothing were found in his car.*

fibreglass /ˈfaɪbəɡlɑːs/ NOUN, NO PLURAL a strong, light material made from very small pieces of glass or plastic

fibre optics /ˌfaɪbər ˈɒptɪks/ NOUN, NO PLURAL the use of small threads of glass to send information in the form of light. A physics word.

fickle /ˈfɪkəl/ ADJECTIVE always changing your opinion about people or things

fiction /ˈfɪkʃən/ NOUN, NO PLURAL
1 books about imaginary people and situations 🕮 *He enjoys reading crime fiction.* 🕮 *JK Rowling is one of the most famous children's fiction writers.*
2 something that is not true or real 🕮 *Her excuses were pure fiction.*
• **fictional** /ˈfɪkʃənəl/ ADJECTIVE from a book or story, and not real 🕮 *Harry Potter is a well-known fictional character.*
• **fictitious** /fɪkˈtɪʃəs/ ADJECTIVE not true, or not real □ *a fictitious name*

fiddle /ˈfɪdəl/ ▶ VERB [**fiddles, fiddling, fiddled**]
1 to touch something repeatedly with small movements □ *She was fiddling with her hair.*
2 to move something slightly in order to improve it or make it work □ *He was fiddling with the wires at the back of the computer.*
3 to change something in a way that is not honest in order to get money or an advantage □ *He fiddles his taxes.*
▶ NOUN [*plural* **fiddles**]
1 an informal word for a violin (= musical instrument)
2 an informal word meaning a dishonest way of getting money
• **fiddly** /ˈfɪdli/ ADJECTIVE difficult to do or use because very small parts are involved □ *Changing the battery in a watch can be quite fiddly.*

fidget /ˈfɪdʒɪt/ VERB [**fidgets, fidgeting, fidgeted**] to keep moving because you are nervous or bored

field /fiːld/ ▶ NOUN [*plural* **fields**]
1 an area of land used for growing crops or keeping animals on □ *There were lots of cows in the field.* □ + *of We saw a lovely field of poppies.*
2 an area of grass used for playing sport on 🕮 *a football field*
3 a subject that people study, or the type of work they do □ *These charts are widely used by experts in the medical field.* □ *This is a new and exciting field of research.*
▶ VERB [**fields, fielding, fielded**]
1 to be the team that throws and catches the ball instead of hitting it, in games such as cricket or baseball
2 to send a team of people to take part in a game or election □ *They fielded a very strong team.*
3 to deal with a lot of something such as questions or telephone calls □ *The Prime Minister fielded questions on a range of subjects.*
• **fielder** /ˈfiːldə(r)/ NOUN [*plural* **fielders**] someone who is in the sports team that is fielding

fiend /fiːnd/ NOUN [*plural* **fiends**] an evil person

fierce /fɪəs/ ADJECTIVE [**fiercer, fiercest**]
1 violent and angry □ *a fierce animal* □ *fierce fighting*
2 very powerful or strong 🕮 *The company faces fierce competition.* □ *Fierce winds brought down power lines.*
• **fiercely** /ˈfɪəsli/ ADVERB in a fierce way □ *She defended her cubs fiercely.* □ *He is fiercely opposed to the new airport.*

fiery /ˈfaɪəri/ ADJECTIVE
1 full of strong or angry feelings □ *He has a fiery temper.* □ *a fiery speech*
2 like fire □ *a fiery orange light*

fifteen /ˌfɪfˈtiːn/ NUMBER the number 15

fifteenth /ˌfɪfˈtiːnθ/ NUMBER 15th written as a word

fifth /fɪfθ/ ▶ NUMBER 5th written as a word □ *Today is their fifth wedding anniversary.*
▶ NOUN [*plural* **fifths**] 1/5 ; one of five equal parts of something □ *A fifth of the money is mine.*

fiftieth /ˈfɪftiəθ/ NUMBER 50th written as a word

fifty /'fɪftɪ/ NUMBER [plural **fifties**]
1 the number 50
2 the fifties the years between 1950 and 1959

fig /fɪg/ NOUN [plural **figs**] a fruit with a lot of seeds in it, which is often eaten dried

fight /faɪt/ ▶ VERB [**fights, fighting, fought**]
1 to use your body or weapons to try to defeat someone □ They started fighting. □ My great-grandfather fought in the second world war. □ Troops fought a fierce battle in the desert.
2 to argue with someone □ **+ about** They're fighting about who should do the washing up. □ **+ over** They're fighting over her money (= arguing about who should have it).
3 to try to stop something 🄐 fight crime/infection. □ **+ against** We are fighting against plans for a new airport.
4 to try to achieve something □ **+ for** They were fighting for the right to vote. □ **+ to do something** He is fighting to get his job back.
♦ PHRASAL VERB **fight back**
1 to fight against someone who has attacked you
2 to argue against or try to stop someone who has criticized you or harmed you □ After years of poor treatment, the workers are starting to fight back.
3 fight back tears to try not to cry
▶ NOUN [plural **fights**]
1 when people use physical force to hurt each other □ **+ between** There was a fight between local gangs.
2 when people argue with each other □ I had a fight with my Mum about staying out late. 🄐 Josh is always trying to pick a fight (= start an argument).
3 when people try to stop something □ **+ against** We need everyone to help in the fight against racism.
4 when people try hard to achieve something □ **+ for** His book describes the long fight for justice.
5 a boxing (= sport where people hit each other) competition
● **fighter** /'faɪtə(r)/ NOUN [plural **fighters**]
1 someone who is fighting
2 a fast military aeroplane used for attacking
● **fighting** /'faɪtɪŋ/ NOUN, NO PLURAL when people are fighting, especially in a war 🄐 fierce/heavy fighting

figment /'fɪgmənt/ NOUN [plural **figments**] a **figment of someone's imagination** something that someone imagines is real, but that does not really exist

figurative /'fɪgərətɪv/ ADJECTIVE a figurative use of a word has a meaning that has developed from its main meaning. For example, 'She was glued to the television all day' is a figurative use of 'glued'.

figure /'fɪgə(r)/ ▶ NOUN [plural **figures**]
1 a number that tells you an amount, especially in official documents 🄐 official/government figures 🄐 The latest unemployment figures were released (= told to the public) today. 🄐 Figures show that obesity has increased.
2 a number □ He paid a four figure sum (= over

£1,000). 🄐 The number of deaths has reached double figures (= is at least 10).
3 the shape of your body □ She's got a lovely figure.
4 a person of a particular type 🄐 He is a leading/senior figure in the government. □ Privacy is difficult for public figures.
5 a person that you do not know or cannot see clearly □ There was a shadowy figure in the doorway.
6 a shape. A maths word. □ a three-sided figure
▶ VERB [**figures, figuring, figured**]
1 to be part of something □ **+ in** Babies don't figure in her plans for the future.
2 to think that something is true □ **+ that** I figured that we could manage without him.
3 it/that figures used to say that you are not surprised about something bad □ Casey's given up college? That figures.
♦ PHRASAL VERBS **figure something out** to understand something complicated □ I can't figure out how to open this cupboard. **figure someone out** to understand someone's character or behaviour □ She says she wants to be alone, then complains that nobody visits her – I just can't figure her out.

figure of speech /ˌfɪgər əv 'spiːtʃ/ NOUN [plural **figures of speech**] a word or phrase used in a different way from usual to create a particular idea. For example, if you say someone is a lion, you mean that they are as brave or fierce as a lion.

file /faɪl/ ▶ NOUN [plural **files**]
1 a place for storing information on a computer. A computing word. □ I've created a new file for the accounts. □ I downloaded some image files.
2 a collection of information about something or someone 🄐 We keep files on all our employees.
3 on file if information is on file, it is recorded and kept somewhere □ We'll keep your details on file.
4 a piece of folded card for keeping documents in
5 a tool with a rough edge for making things smooth
6 in single file if people walk in single file, they walk with one person behind another
▶ VERB [**files, filing, filed**]
1 to put documents into a file □ Please file these application forms under 'rejects'.
2 to take official, especially legal action 🄐 She decided to file for divorce.
3 to walk somewhere, one person behind another □ The children filed into the hall.
4 to make something smooth using a file

file extension /'faɪl ɪkˌstenʃən/ NOUN [plural **file extensions**] three letters at the end of a computer document's name that show the type of document

filename /'faɪlneɪm/ NOUN [plural **filenames**] the name that you give to a computer file. A computing word.

filing cabinet /'faɪlɪŋ ˌkæbɪnɪt/ NOUN [plural **filing cabinets**] a piece of furniture for an office, which has big drawers for keeping papers in.

filings /'faɪlɪŋz/ PLURAL NOUN very small pieces of metal that have been cut from a larger piece □ *iron filings*

fill /fɪl/ VERB [fills, filling, filled]

1 to make a container or space full □ + *with* *The waiter filled our glasses with wine.* □ *The room was filled with smoke* □ + *up* *She filled up the pan with water.*

2 to become full □ + *with* *The concert hall quickly filled with people.* □ + *up* *The room had filled up by the time we got back.*

3 if a sound, smell, etc. fills a place, you easily notice it 🔁 *The sound of laughter filled the air.*

4 to make someone have a feeling very strongly □ + *with* *The idea filled her with excitement.* □ *He was filled with hate.*

5 to provide something that people need or want 🔁 *The service will fill a gap in healthcare provision.*

6 to do a job, or find someone to do a job 🔁 *Many positions are filled by doctors from overseas.*

♦ PHRASAL VERB **fill something in/out** to write information in the spaces on an official document 🔁 *To apply for a place on the course, you need to fill in this form.*

fillet /'fɪlɪt/ ▶ NOUN [plural **fillets**] a piece of meat or fish with no bones in it

▶ VERB [**fillets, filleting, filleted**] to remove the bones from meat or fish

filling /'fɪlɪŋ/ ▶ NOUN [plural **fillings**]

1 a substance used to fill a hole in your tooth □ *Ben hasn't got any fillings.*

2 food that is put inside things such as cakes or sandwiches (= pieces of bread with food between) □ *pancakes with a chocolate filling*

▶ ADJECTIVE food that is filling makes your stomach feel full

filling station /'fɪlɪŋ ˌsteɪʃən/ NOUN [plural **filling stations**] a place where you buy petrol

film /fɪlm/ ▶ NOUN [plural **films**]

1 a story that you watch in a cinema or on television 🔁 *Have you seen this James Bond film?* 🔁 *He was watching a film on television.* 🔁 *They made a film about his life.* 🔁 *a film star* (= a famous actor who has been in many films)

2 something you put inside a camera so you can take photographs 🔁 *I need a new roll of film.*

3 a film of something a thin layer of something on a surface □ *The glass was covered with a film of dirt.*

▶ VERB [**films, filming, filmed**] to make a film of something □ *They were filming scenes for her new movie.* □ *'Brokeback Mountain' was filmed in Canada.*

filter /'fɪltə(r)/ ▶ NOUN [plural **filters**] a device that you put a liquid or gas through in order to remove solid substances □ *a water filter*

▶ VERB [**filters, filtered, filtering**]

1 to put something through a filter

2 if light or sound filters into a place, small amounts of it reach there □ *Light was filtering into the bedroom through a gap in the curtains.*

3 if news or information filters somewhere, people gradually hear about it □ *News of his resignation filtered through the college.*

filth /fɪlθ/ NOUN, NO PLURAL

1 dirt

2 rude words or pictures

● **filthy** /'fɪlθɪ/ ADJECTIVE [**filthier, filthiest**]

1 very dirty □ *His clothes were filthy.*

2 very rude □ *filthy language*

fin /fɪn/ NOUN [plural **fins**] one of the two parts on a fish that help it to balance and swim

final /'faɪnəl/ ▶ ADJECTIVE

1 coming at the end □ *I'm reading the final chapter of the book.* □ *On the final day of his tour, the Prime Minister visited a school.*

2 a final decision, offer, agreement etc. cannot be changed 🔁 *We haven't made a final decision yet.* □ *They're waiting for final approval of the plans.*

▶ NOUN [plural **finals**] the last game in a competition, which decides who will win □ *Federer will play Henman in the final.* □ *The team are through to the finals.*

finale /fɪ'nɑːlɪ/ NOUN [plural **finales**] the last part of a show or piece of music

finalist /'faɪnəlɪst/ NOUN [plural **finalists**] a person or team who is in the last part of a competition

finalize or **finalise** /'faɪnəlaɪz/ VERB [**finalizes, finalizing, finalized**] to decide the last details of something, such as a plan or journey □ *The deal was finalized on Monday.*

finally /'faɪnəlɪ/ ADVERB

1 after a long time □ *When he finally arrived, it was after midnight.*

2 used to introduce the last in a list of things □ *Finally, I would like to thank everyone who has helped.*

finance ▶ NOUN /'faɪnæns/ [plural **finances**]

1 *no plural* things that are to do with money, especially in a government or company □ *John is an expert in finance.* 🔁 *She's the company's finance director.*

2 *no plural* the money needed for something in business □ *They're struggling to raise the finance for a new theatre.*

3 finances the money that an organization or person has □ *Our finances are in a healthy state.* 🔁 *He handles the finances of several charities.*

▶ VERB /faɪ'næns/ [**finances, financing, financed**] to provide the money for something, especially in business □ *They took out a loan to finance the project.*

● **financial** /faɪ'nænʃəl/ ADJECTIVE to do with money 🔁 *banks and other financial institutions* 🔁 *Many companies are facing financial difficulties.*

● **financially** /faɪ'nænʃəlɪ/ ADVERB in a way that is to do with money □ *He is financially secure.*

finch /fɪntʃ/ NOUN [plural **finches**] a small bird with a short beak

find /faɪnd/ ▶ VERB [**finds, finding, found**]
1 to discover or see something or someone you have been looking for □ *I can't find my pencil case.* □ *The murderer was never found.*
2 to discover something by chance □ *A jogger found the body by the river last night.* □ *I found a beetle in my soup.*
3 to discover that something has happened or that something is true □ *The survey found a link between birth weight and intelligence.* □ *+ that* *I find that it is best to call her in the mornings.* □ *I found I had forgotten my phone.*
4 to discover an answer, a reason or a way of doing something 🔁 *We found a way to stop the leak.* 🔁 *We are trying to find a solution to the problem of litter.*
5 to have a particular experience of someone or something □ *I found him very rude.* □ *I found it difficult to lift the rocks.*
6 to get something 🔁 *She found work in a local hospital.* □ *I managed to find somewhere to live.*
7 to manage to have enough of something 🔁 *I don't know how she finds the time to go running every day.* □ *Somehow, he found the courage to speak his mind.*
8 find yourself doing something to become aware that you are doing something without intending to □ *I found myself feeling sorry for her.*
9 find your way to get to a place □ *Can you find your way to the station?*
10 find someone guilty/not guilty to say that someone is guilty/not guilty in a court □ *He was found guilty of murder and sentenced to life in prison.*
◆ PHRASAL VERB **find out (something)** to discover information or the truth about something □ *+ that* *We found out that they had been stealing from us.* □ *+ about* *She used the Internet to find out about bees.* □ *I need to find out how to set up a website.*
▶ NOUN [plural **finds**] something or someone useful, good or valuable that has been found □ *The baker's in Hope Street was a real find!*
● **finding** /ˈfaɪndɪŋ/ NOUN [plural **findings**] information that is got by studying a subject 🔁 *The scientists published their findings in the journal 'Nature'.*

fine /faɪn/ ADJECTIVE [**finer, finest**]
1 good or acceptable □ *'Let's meet at seven.' 'OK, that sounds fine.'* □ *'Is the water hot enough?' 'Yes, it's fine, thanks.'*
2 healthy or happy □ *'How are you?' 'I'm fine, thanks.'* 🔁 *Don't worry, I'm absolutely fine.*
3 of a very good quality □ *The museum has many fine examples of Japanese art.* □ *It was a fine performance.*
4 very thin, or made of very small pieces □ *a fine needle* □ *fine powder*
5 sunny, with no rain 🔁 *The fine weather brought many people to the coast.*

► Note that the adjective **fine**, meaning 'healthy or happy' never has the word 'very' before it:
✓ *'How are you, Lilia?' 'I'm fine, thanks.'*
✗ *'How are you, Lilia?' 'I'm very fine, thanks.'*

▶ ADVERB an informal word meaning well □ *I get on fine with my parents.* □ *The system works fine.* 🔁 *Leaving a bit later suits me just fine.*
▶ NOUN [plural **fines**] money that someone must pay as a punishment 🔁 *He was given a parking fine.* 🔁 *She was ordered to pay a fine of £60 for speeding.*
▶ VERB [**fines, fining, fined**] to make someone pay a fine □ *He was fined for dropping litter.*
● **finely** /ˈfaɪnli/ ADVERB
1 into very thin small pieces 🔁 *Chop the onion finely.*
2 in a beautiful way that impresses people □ *The palace was finely decorated.*
3 very exactly □ *a finely tuned machine*

finesse /fɪˈnes/ NOUN, NO PLURAL if you do something with finesse, you do it with skill and style

finger /ˈfɪŋɡə(r)/ ▶ NOUN [plural **fingers**] one of the five long parts at the end of your hand 🔁 *Sam had a cut on his little finger* (= smallest finger).
➜ *go to* **index finger**
◆ IDIOMS **(keep your) fingers crossed** used for saying that you hope something will happen □ *We're keeping our fingers crossed that he passes the exam.* □ *Fingers crossed the train arrives on time.* **put your finger on something** to understand exactly what is wrong, different etc. □ *Something wasn't right but I couldn't put my finger on it.*
▶ VERB [**fingers, fingering, fingered**] to touch something with your fingers □ *She fingered the necklace she was wearing.*

fingernail /ˈfɪŋɡəneɪl/ NOUN [plural **fingernails**] the hard part at the top of each finger □ *He bites his fingernails.*
fingerprint /ˈfɪŋɡəprɪnt/ NOUN [plural **fingerprints**] the mark that your finger leaves when you touch something □ *The police took his fingerprints.*
fingertip /ˈfɪŋɡətɪp/ NOUN [plural **fingertips**]
1 the top end of each finger
2 have something at your fingertips to have something easily available and ready to use □ *He had all the latest facts at his fingertips.*

finish /ˈfɪnɪʃ/ ▶ VERB [**finishes, finishing, finished**]
1 to complete something □ *Have you finished your homework?* □ *+ ing* *I've finished cleaning the bathroom.*
2 to come to an end □ *What time did the film finish?*
3 to use, eat or drink all of something □ *I've finished the last of the bread.*
4 to have a particular position at the end of a race, competition, etc. □ *He finished third in the long jump.* □ *They finished five points ahead of their nearest rivals.*
◆ PHRASAL VERBS **finish something off**

1 to complete the last part of something □ *I just need to finish off the housework.*
2 to eat, drink or use the last part of something □ *The children finished off all the sausages.* **finish with something** to stop using or needing something □ *Have you finished with the bread knife?* **finish up** to end by being in a particular place or situation □ *We finished up having to apologize to our neighbours.*
▶ NOUN [*plural* **finishes**]
1 the end of a race ⌗ *It was a close finish.*
2 the last part of something ⌗ *The course was badly planned from start to finish.*
• **finished** /ˈfɪnɪʃt/ ADJECTIVE
1 completed ⌗ *the finished product*
2 if you are finished, you have completed what you are doing □ *I'll be finished in a moment.*

finite /ˈfaɪnaɪt/ ADJECTIVE having a limit or an end ⌗ *Oil and coal are finite resources.*

fir /fɜː(r)/ NOUN [*plural* **firs**] a type of tree with very thin, sharp leaves that keeps those leaves in winter

fire /ˈfaɪə(r)/ ▶ NOUN [*plural* **fires**]
1 *no plural* flames and heat that are caused by something burning □ *The building was destroyed by fire.*
2 when something burns in a way that is not intended ⌗ *Fire broke out* (= started) *in the warehouse.* ⌗ *We used buckets of water to put out the fire.* ⌗ *The curtains caught fire* (= started to burn).
3 on fire burning □ *Soon the whole building was on fire.*
4 set fire to something to make something burn
5 a pile of wood, coal, etc. that is burned to provide heat ⌗ *I lit a fire in the bedroom.*
6 a device that heats a room using gas or electricity □ *Put the fire on if you're cold.*
7 when guns are shot ⌗ *The troops came under heavy fire.*
• IDIOM **come under fire** to be criticized □ *Company bosses have come under fire for giving themselves huge salaries.*
▶ VERB [**fires, firing, fired**]
1 to fire a gun is to shoot a bullet from it
2 an informal word meaning to tell someone that they must leave their job □ *She was fired for bullying her colleagues.*
• PHRASAL VERBS **fire something off** to quickly send a letter, message or instructions to do something □ *He fired off a letter to the editor.* **fire someone up** to make someone enthusiastic or angry □ *We were all fired up and ready for the match.*

fire alarm /ˈfaɪər əˌlɑːm/ NOUN [*plural* **fire alarms**] a bell that rings to warn you of a fire in a building

firearm /ˈfaɪərɑːm/ NOUN [*plural* **firearms**] a formal word meaning a gun

fire brigade /ˈfaɪə brɪˌɡeɪd/ NOUN [*plural* **fire brigades**] the group of people whose job is to stop fires burning

fire engine /ˈfaɪər ˌendʒɪn/ NOUN [*plural* **fire engines**] a vehicle that carries firefighters and their equipment

fire escape /ˈfaɪər ɪˌskeɪp/ NOUN [*plural* **fire escapes**] stairs on the outside of a building, which people use if there is a fire

firefighter /ˈfaɪəˌfaɪtə(r)/ NOUN [*plural* **firefighters**] someone whose job is to stop fires burning □ *Firefighters battled for two hours to get the blaze under control.*

fireman /ˈfaɪəmən/ NOUN [*plural* **firemen**] a man whose job is to stop fires burning

fireplace /ˈfaɪəpleɪs/ NOUN [*plural* **fireplaces**] the space for a fire in the wall of a room, or the frame around this space

fire station /ˈfaɪə ˌsteɪʃən/ NOUN [*plural* **fire stations**] a building where firefighters and their vehicles and equipment wait until they are needed

firewall /ˈfaɪəwɔːl/ NOUN [*plural* **firewalls**] software that protects your computer when you are on the Internet. A computing word.

firewood /ˈfaɪəwʊd/ NOUN, NO PLURAL wood for burning

firework /ˈfaɪəwɜːk/ NOUN [*plural* **fireworks**] something which explodes and makes bright lights in the sky for entertainment ⌗ *The festival ended with a spectacular fireworks display.*

firing squad /ˈfaɪərɪŋ ˌskwɒd/ NOUN [*plural* **firing squads**] a group of soldiers whose job is to shoot and kill a prisoner

firm /fɜːm/ ▶ ADJECTIVE [**firmer, firmest**]
1 not soft □ *a firm bed*
2 certain and not changing □ *He has very firm views on education.* □ *There was no firm evidence linking him to the crime.*
3 showing that you are in control and that you mean what you say □ *She spoke in a quiet but firm voice.* □ *She is a very firm leader.* □ + **with** *You should be more firm with the children.*
4 tight, strong and not going to move □ *Betsy took a firm hold on the tray.*
▶ NOUN [*plural* **firms**] a company □ *Sally works for a law firm.* □ *a software firm*
• **firmly** /ˈfɜːmlɪ/ ADVERB in a firm way ⌗ *I firmly believe he's innocent.* □ *'No I won't,' he said firmly.* □ *Raj pressed the lid down firmly.*

first /fɜːst/ ▶ DETERMINER, NUMBER
1 coming before everyone or everything else □ *His was the first name on the list.* □ *The first time I went skiing, I hated it.* □ *Take the first road on the left.*
2 1st written as a word
3 best in a competition, exam, etc □ *first place/prize*
4 at the beginning of something □ *The first few months of college were tough.*
▶ ADVERB
1 before anyone or anything else □ *You can phone Josh, but eat your dinner first.* □ *First you need to dig the foundations.*
2 for the first time □ *We first met at university.* □ *I first became aware of the problem last week.*
3 doing better than everyone else in a competition,

exam, etc. ⊞ *Philip came first in the cookery competition.*

4 at first at the beginning □ *At first I couldn't speak French at all.*

5 more important than anything or anyone else ⊞ *I have to put my children's happiness first.* ⊞ *It's obvious that money comes first for her.*

▶ PRONOUN, NOUN, NO PLURAL

1 the person or thing that comes before all others □ *She was the first to realise how the drug could be used.* □ *This is the first in a series of Beethoven concerts.* □ *The doctor's ready now. Who's first?*

2 a first something that has never happened before □ *Everyone's here on time today – I think that must be a first.*

3 the best result in a UK university exam ⊞ *He got a first in economics.*

first aid /ˌfɜːst ˈeɪd/ NOUN, NO PLURAL simple medical treatment that you give to an injured or ill person as soon as you can ⊞ *a first aid course*

first-class /ˌfɜːstˈklɑːs / ▶ ADJECTIVE

1 used about travel when you pay more for a better seat etc., and about post when you pay more for a quicker service □ *a first-class train ticket* □ *a first-class stamp*

2 extremely good □ *It was a first-class game of football.*

▶ ADVERB using the best or most expensive type □ *Len always travels first-class.*

first-hand /ˌfɜːstˈhænd / ADJECTIVE learned because you have done something yourself and not because someone else has told you ⊞ *I know from first-hand experience how difficult skiing is.*

firstly /ˈfɜːstlɪ/ ADVERB used for introducing the first of several things □ *Firstly, I'd like to welcome everybody.*

first name /ˌfɜːst ˈneɪm/ NOUN [plural **first names**] the name that comes before your family name □ *Her first name's 'Jane' and her surname is 'Smith'.*

first person /ˌfɜːst ˈpɜːsən/ NOUN, NO PLURAL in grammar, the form of words used when people are talking or writing about themselves □ *'I' and 'we' are first person pronouns.*

first-rate /ˌfɜːstˈreɪt / ADJECTIVE excellent □ *a first-rate doctor*

fish /fɪʃ/ ▶ NOUN [plural **fish** or **fishes**]

1 an animal that lives and swims in water ⊞ *They were trying to catch fish in the stream.*

2 *no plural* the meat from this animal eaten as food □ *We had fish for dinner.*

> ➤ Note that the plural form of **fish** is usually **fish**. **Fishes** is not common but is sometimes used when talking about different types of fish:
> ✓ *We caught a lot of fish.*
> ✗ *We caught a lot of fishes.*

▶ VERB [fishes, fishing, fished]

1 to try to catch fish □ + *for* *The men were fishing for salmon.*

2 to look for something in a bag, drawer, etc. □ *Amy was fishing in her bag for her key.*

◆ PHRASAL VERB **fish something out** to pull something out from somewhere. An informal phrase. □ *She fished the papers out of the bin.*

fisherman /ˈfɪʃəmən/ NOUN [plural **fishermen**] someone who catches fish as a job or sport

fishing /ˈfɪʃɪŋ/ NOUN, NO PLURAL the sport or job of catching fish ⊞ *We're going fishing at the weekend.* ⊞ *the fishing industry*

fishing rod /ˈfɪʃɪŋ ˌrɒd/ NOUN [plural **fishing rods**] a long stick used for catching fish

fishmonger /ˈfɪʃˌmʌŋɡə(r)/ NOUN [plural **fishmongers**]

1 someone who sells fish

2 fishmonger's a shop that sells fish

fission /ˈfɪʃən/ NOUN, NO PLURAL dividing an atom so that energy is given out. A physics word.

fist /fɪst/ NOUN [plural **fists**] your hand when it is closed tightly □ *Don't shake your fist at me!*

fit /fɪt/ VERB [fits, fitting, fitted]

1 to be the right shape or size for someone or something □ *The dress fits you perfectly.* □ *The cupboard will fit in the corner.*

2 to have enough room to put something or someone somewhere, or to be small enough to go somewhere □ *I can't fit any more documents in this file.* □ *We tried to get the piano up the stairs, but it wouldn't fit.*

3 to fix something in a place □ *We're having new kitchen units fitted next week.* □ + *with* *He was fitted with a pacemaker.*

4 to be what someone describes or asks for ⊞ *He certainly fits the description issued by the police.*

5 to be suitable for something □ *Bright colours don't really fit our image.* □ *The services on offer don't fit the needs of our clients.*

◆ PHRASAL VERBS **fit in**

1 to become accepted by a group of people □ *They were all very sporty, and I didn't really fit in.*

2 to be a part of something □ *We need to update our online business, and that's where your skills fit in.* **fit someone/something in** to have time to see someone or do something □ *We can fit you in to see the doctor at ten.*

▶ ADJECTIVE [fitter, fittest]

1 healthy, especially because of doing exercise ⊞ *I'm trying to get fit.*

2 suitable or good enough □ + *to do something* *This food isn't fit to eat.* ⊞ *I wasn't in a fit state to work.*

▶ NOUN [plural **fits**]

1 whether or not something is the right size and shape for something or someone □ *The jacket was a perfect fit.*

2 a sudden period of doing something or feeling a particular way □ *I cleaned the whole house in a fit of enthusiasm.* □ *He collapsed in a fit of laughter.*

3 a period of illness where someone's body makes sudden movements they cannot control

◆ IDIOM **have a fit** to become very angry. An informal phrase.

● **fitness** /ˈfɪtnɪs/ NOUN, NO PLURAL
1 how healthy someone is □ *I'm hoping to improve my fitness.* 🖰 *physical fitness*
2 how suitable someone or something is □ *Many people doubt his fitness to govern.*

● **fitting** /ˈfɪtɪŋ/ ADJECTIVE suitable 🖰 *The award is a fitting tribute to a great actor.*

five /faɪv/ NUMBER [*plural* **fives**] the number 5

fix /fɪks/ ▶ VERB [**fixes, fixing, fixed**]
1 to attach something to something else □ + *to* *She fixed the shelves to the wall.*
2 to repair something □ *He's trying to fix the roof.* 🖰 *I need to get the car fixed.*
3 to solve a problem 🖰 *All our staff are working to fix the problem.*
4 to decide something 🖰 *Have you fixed a date for the wedding?*

◆ PHRASAL VERB **fix something up**
1 to arrange something such as a meeting or visit □ *They fixed up a meeting for the following week.*
2 to repair and improve something such as a building □ *Taxpayers money was used to fix up the Opera House.*

▶ NOUN [*plural* **fixes**] something which solves a problem 🖰 *The problem is a long-term one and there are no quick fixes.*

● **fixation** /fɪkˈseɪʃən/ NOUN [*plural* **fixations**] a very strong interest in something, which other people think is not normal □ *He had a fixation with knives.*

● **fixed** /fɪkst/ ADJECTIVE not changing □ *He had a fixed smile on his face.* □ *He works for a fixed number of hours each week.*

fizz /fɪz/ VERB [**fizzes, fizzing, fizzed**] if liquid fizzes, it makes the noise of bubbles breaking

● **fizzy** /ˈfɪzi/ ADJECTIVE [**fizzier, fizziest**] a fizzy drink has bubbles in it

flabbergasted /ˈflæbəˌgɑːstɪd/ ADJECTIVE an informal word meaning extremely surprised

flabby /ˈflæbi/ ADJECTIVE [**flabbier, flabbiest**] fat, and having skin that is not tight □ *flabby arms*

flag /flæg/ ▶ NOUN [*plural* **flags**] a piece of cloth with a pattern on it, used as the symbol of a country or organization □ *The American flag has stars and stripes on it.* 🖰 *Hundreds of people were waving flags as the Queen arrived.* 🖰 *Flags across the country were flying at half-mast when the President died.*

▶ VERB [**flags, flagging, flagged**] to become tired or weak

◆ PHRASAL VERB **flag someone/something down** to wave at the driver of a car to make them stop □ *I tried to flag down a taxi.*

flagpole /ˈflægpəʊl/ NOUN [*plural* **flagpoles**] a pole that you hang a flag from

flagrant /ˈfleɪgrənt/ ADJECTIVE obvious, and showing that you do not care that you are doing something bad □ *He showed a flagrant disregard of the speed limit.*

flagstone /ˈflægstəʊn/ NOUN [*plural* **flagstones**] a flat piece of stone used for making a path or floor

flail /fleɪl/ VERB [**flails, flailing, flailed**] to move your arms or legs in a violent and uncontrolled way □ *She flailed around in the water, and screamed for help.*

flair /fleə(r)/ NOUN, NO PLURAL
1 a natural ability to do something well □ *He has a flair for cooking.*
2 when you do something in an interesting and skilful way □ *We need a designer with plenty of flair.*

flake /fleɪk/ ▶ NOUN [*plural* **flakes**] a small thin piece of something □ *A few flakes of snow began to fall.*
▶ VERB [**flakes, flaking, flaked**] to come off in small flat pieces □ *Paint was flaking off the door.*

● **flaky** /ˈfleɪki/ ADJECTIVE [**flakier, flakiest**] breaking up easily into small thin pieces □ *flaky pastry*

flamboyant /flæmˈbɔɪənt/ ADJECTIVE
1 very confident and behaving in a way that attracts attention □ *a flamboyant actor*
2 bright and colourful □ *flamboyant clothes*

flame /fleɪm/ ▶ NOUN [*plural* **flames**]
1 the hot orange gas you see in a fire 🖰 *Flames leapt from the roof.* 🖰 *Firefighters tried to put out the flames.*
2 in flames burning □ *The building was in flames.*
3 burst into flames/go up in flames to suddenly start burning □ *The plane skidded off the runway and burst into flames.*
4 an angry or rude e-mail. A computing word.
▶ VERB [**flames, flaming, flamed**] to send someone an angry or rude e-mail. A computing word.

● **flaming** /ˈfleɪmɪŋ/ ADJECTIVE burning □ *Flaming debris fell from the plane before it crashed.*

flamenco /fləˈmeŋkəʊ/ NOUN [*plural* **flamencos**] an energetic Spanish dance

flamingo /fləˈmɪŋgəʊ/ NOUN [*plural* **flamingoes** or **flamingos**] a large pink bird with long legs

flammable /ˈflæməbəl/ ADJECTIVE something that is flammable burns easily 🖰 *The gas is highly flammable.*

➤ **Inflammable** means the same as **flammable**.

flan /flæn/ NOUN [*plural* **flans**] a circle of pastry that has something inside it □ *a lemon flan*

flank /flæŋk/ ▶ VERB [**flanks, flanking, flanked**] if you are flanked by two people, you have one of them on each side of you □ *She left the courtroom flanked by police officers.*
▶ NOUN [*plural* **flanks**] the side of an animal's body, especially a horse's

flannel /ˈflænəl/ NOUN [*plural* **flannels**]
1 a piece of cloth used for washing yourself
2 a type of soft, warm cloth, used especially for night clothes

flap /flæp/ ▶ VERB [**flaps, flapping, flapped**]
1 if a bird flaps its wings, it moves them up and down

2 if a piece of cloth flaps, it moves backwards and forwards □ *The flags were flapping in the wind.*

▶ NOUN [*plural* **flaps**]

1 a piece of something that hangs down over an opening □ *He closed the tent flaps.*

2 a movement up and down, like that of a bird's wings

flare /fleə(r)/ ▶ VERB [**flares, flaring, flared**]

1 to suddenly start to burn or shine brightly □ *The fire had flared up again overnight.*

2 if something such as anger or violence flares, it suddenly starts or becomes worse □ *Violence flared in several towns.*

3 if an illness or injury flares, it comes back again or becomes worse □ *His knee injury flared up after the game.*

▶ NOUN [*plural* **flares**] something that produces a bright light to show that you need help

flash /flæʃ/ ▶ VERB [**flashes, flashing, flashed**]

1 if a light flashes, it goes on and off quickly □ *The warning light was flashing.* ⊞ *a flashing light*

2 to make a light go on and off quickly □ *He flashed his car lights to warn other drivers of the danger.*

3 to appear for a short time and then disappear □ *Some important news suddenly flashed up on the screen.*

4 to move very quickly □ + *by* *The cars flashed by.* ⊞ *A bullet flashed past his head.*

5 to show something to someone quickly □ *Mary flashed her card to the man on the door.*

6 if you flash a smile or look at someone, you smile at them or look at them for a short time □ *He flashed a cheeky grin for the camera.*

▶ NOUN [*plural* **flashes**]

1 a sudden bright light ⊞ *a flash of lightning*

2 a light on a camera that you use when you are taking photographs indoors

3 a sudden feeling □ + *of* *He had a flash of guilt.*

4 **in a flash** an informal phrase meaning very quickly □ *She was out of the door in a flash.*

▶ ADJECTIVE

1 happening very suddenly ⊞ *a flash flood*

2 expensive and designed to make people notice you. An informal word. □ *Rick drives around in a really flash car.*

flashback /'flæʃbæk/ NOUN [*plural* **flashbacks**]

1 part of a film or book which shows you what happened earlier

2 a sudden clear memory of something that happened to you in the past □ *She experienced flashbacks and nightmares after the accident.*

flashlight /'flæʃlaɪt/ NOUN [*plural* **flashlights**] the US word for **torch** (= small electric light)

flashy /'flæʃɪ/ ADJECTIVE [**flashier, flashiest**] expensive, and designed to make people notice you □ *a flashy car*

flask /flɑːsk/ NOUN [*plural* **flasks**]

1 a container for keeping drinks hot or cold

2 a glass bottle with a wide base, used in science for holding liquids

flat /flæt/ ▶ ADJECTIVE [**flatter, flattest**]

1 level, smooth and not sloping □ *a flat roof* □ *Place the box on a flat surface.* □ *I'd like to have a flatter stomach.*

2 lying on a surface □ *She lay flat on the floor.*

3 a flat tyre does not have enough air in it

4 a flat battery has no more power in it

5 a flat drink does not have enough bubbles in it

6 without emotion or enthusiasm □ *She spoke in a flat voice.*

7 a flat rate or amount is always the same ⊞ *He charges a flat fee of £50 per hour.*

8 in music, lower by half a note

9 flat shoes do not have high heels (= parts at the back)

▶ ADVERB

1 in a way that is level, smooth and not sloping □ *I spread the carpet flat on the floor.*

2 stretched out on a surface □ *Omar was lying flat on his back.*

3 **in 10 minutes/2 seconds, etc. flat** in only 10 minutes/2 seconds, etc. □ *I did my homework in five minutes flat.*

4 **flat out** as fast or with as much effort as possible □ *We worked flat out to get it finished.*

▶ NOUN [*plural* **flats**]

1 a set of rooms that someone lives in, which are part of a larger building

2 in written music, a sign (♭) that makes a note lower by half a note

• **flatly** /'flætlɪ/ ADVERB

1 in a determined way ⊞ *He flatly refused to do it.* ⊞ *She flatly denied taking the money.*

2 without emotion or enthusiasm

• **flatten** /'flætən/ VERB [**flattens, flattening, flattened**]

1 to destroy something completely □ *A tornado flattened the village.*

2 to make something become flat

flatter /'flætə(r)/ VERB [**flatters, flattering, flattered**]

1 to say nice things to someone because you want to please them, especially when you are not being sincere □ *I'm sure he's just flattering me when he said he enjoyed reading my article.*

2 if clothes flatter you, they make you look attractive when you wear them □ *That dress really flatters you.*

3 **flatter yourself** to believe that your abilities or achievements are better than they are □ *Don't flatter yourself. He talks to everyone.*

• **flattered** /'flætəd/ ADJECTIVE feeling pleased because someone has shown that they like you □ *I was really flattered that they invited me to the wedding.*

• **flattering** /'flætərɪŋ/ ADJECTIVE

1 making you look attractive □ *a flattering photo* □ *a flattering skirt*

2 making you feel special or important □ *It was very flattering to be asked to join the school council.*

3 praising someone and making them feel pleased □ *He made some flattering remarks about my work.*

- **flattery** /'flætərɪ/ NOUN, NO PLURAL nice things you say to someone because you want to please them, especially when you are not being sincere

flavor /'fleɪvə(r)/ NOUN [plural **flavors**], VERB [**flavors, flavoring, flavored**] the US spelling of flavour

- **flavored** /'fleɪvəd/ ADJECTIVE the US spelling of flavoured

- **-flavored** /'fleɪvəd/ SUFFIX the US spelling of -flavoured

- **flavoring** /'fleɪvərɪŋ/ NOUN [plural **flavorings**] the US spelling of flavouring

flavour /'fleɪvə(r)/ ▶ NOUN [plural **flavours**]
1 the taste that something has □ Chocolate is my favourite ice cream flavour. □ Brown rice has a wonderful nutty flavour.
2 no plural a good or strong taste 🖫 The herbs add flavour to the salad.
3 no plural a special quality that something has □ The big cities have a much more international flavour.
▶ VERB [**flavours, flavouring, flavoured**] if food is flavoured with something, that thing has been added to give the food a particular taste □ pasta flavoured with garlic

- **flavoured** /'fleɪvəd/ ADJECTIVE with something added to give a particular taste □ flavoured water

- **-flavoured** /'fleɪvəd/ SUFFIX added to the end of a word to show what something tastes of □ chocolate-flavoured milk

- **flavouring** /'fleɪvərɪŋ/ NOUN [plural **flavourings**] something added to food to give it a particular taste

flaw /flɔ:/ NOUN [plural **flaws**] a fault in someone or something □ The building is prone to leaks because of design flaws.

- **flawed** /flɔ:d/ ADJECTIVE having faults or mistakes □ The system is seriously flawed.

- **flawless** /'flɔ:ləs/ ADJECTIVE perfect, with no faults □ a flawless performance

flea /fli:/ NOUN [plural **fleas**] a very small insect that jumps and bites people or animals

fleck /flek/ NOUN [plural **flecks**] a very small mark or spot of a colour or a substance □ Her black hair had flecks of grey in it.

- **flecked** /flekt/ ADJECTIVE marked with flecks □ green eyes flecked with gold

fled /fled/ PAST TENSE AND PAST PARTICIPLE OF flee

fledgling /'fledʒlɪŋ/ ADJECTIVE new and still developing □ Her fledgling career in fashion was going well.

flee /fli:/ VERB [**flees, fleeing, fled**] a formal word meaning to run away or to escape □ Nina turned and fled.

fleece /fli:s/ NOUN [plural **fleeces**]
1 the wool on a sheep
2 a type of soft, warm, artificial material
3 a jacket made from fleece

fleet /fli:t/ NOUN [plural **fleets**] a group of ships or vehicles □ a fleet of boats

fleeting /'fli:tɪŋ/ ADJECTIVE lasting for only a short time □ a fleeting smile

flesh /fleʃ/ NOUN, NO PLURAL
1 the part of a person's or animal's body between the skin and the bones □ The salmon's flesh should be pink and firm.
2 a person's skin □ her pale flesh
3 the soft inside part of fruit and vegetables □ Cut the avocado in half and scoop out the flesh.

flew /flu:/ PAST TENSE OF fly

flex /fleks/ ▶ NOUN [plural **flexes**] a piece of wire covered in plastic, which carries electricity to a piece of equipment
▶ VERB [**flexes, flexing, flexed**] to bend part of your body so that the muscle becomes tight

flexibility /ˌfleksə'bɪlətɪ/ NOUN, NO PLURAL the quality of being flexible

flexible /'fleksəbəl/ ADJECTIVE
1 able to change to suit different people or situations □ flexible arrangements
2 easy to bend □ flexible wires

flick /flɪk/ ▶ VERB [**flicks, flicking, flicked**]
1 to send something through the air quickly and suddenly, often with your fingers □ She flicked the fly off her coat. □ He flicked the ball back to me.
2 to move quickly and suddenly, or to make something move quickly and suddenly □ Leah flicked her hair back confidently.
3 if you flick a switch, you press it to make something start working
◆ PHRASAL VERB **flick through something** to look quickly at each page in a magazine, book, etc.
▶ NOUN [plural **flicks**] a sudden quick movement □ He passed the ball with a deft flick.

flicker /'flɪkə(r)/ ▶ VERB [**flickers, flickering, flickered**]
1 if a light or flame flickers, it changes several times from bright to weak □ The light flickered and went out.
2 to last for a very short time and then disappear □ A faint smile flickered across my father's face.
3 to make a sudden small movement □ Her eyelids flickered.
▶ NOUN [plural **flickers**]
1 when a light or flame is sometimes bright and sometimes weak □ The kitchen was dark apart from the flicker of a candle.
2 a flicker of something a feeling or expression that lasts for a very short time □ He felt a flicker of hope.

flight /flaɪt/ NOUN [plural **flights**]
1 a journey in an aircraft □ + from a direct flight from Heathrow to Singapore 🖫 He boarded a flight to Tokyo.
2 a set of stairs 🖫 We walked up several flights of stairs. 🖫 a flight of steps □ She climbed the five flights to her apartment.
3 no plural the action of flying □ a flock of birds in flight
◆ IDIOM **a flight of fancy/imagination** something you imagine which is fun or exciting, but very unlikely □ He dismissed the idea as a flight of fancy.

flight attendant /'flaɪt ə,tendənt/ NOUN [plural **flight attendants**] a person whose job is to look after passengers while they are on an aeroplane

flimsy /'flɪmzɪ/ ADJECTIVE [**flimsier, flimsiest**]
1 thin or light and likely to break or tear □ We sat on flimsy plastic chairs. □ a flimsy summer dress
2 difficult to believe and not able to be trusted □ He was arrested on flimsy evidence.

flinch /flɪntʃ/ VERB [**flinches, flinching, flinched**] to move part of your body suddenly, because you are frightened or in pain □ The boys flinched at the sound of gunfire.
♦ PHRASAL VERB **flinch from something** to avoid doing something difficult □ She didn't flinch from asking tough questions.

fling /flɪŋ/ VERB [**flings, flinging, flung**] to throw or move something using a lot of force □ He flung his racket down. □ She flung her arms round him. □ She flung herself down in the chair, completely exhausted.

flint /flɪnt/ NOUN [plural **flints**] a hard, grey stone that can produce a flame and was used in the past to make tools

flip /flɪp/ VERB [**flips, flipping, flipped**]
1 to turn over quickly or to make something turn over quickly □ The car ran off the road and flipped over. □ After a couple of minutes, flip the fish over to cook the other side.
2 to change the position of something with a quick movement □ Someone flipped the light switch. □ She took the box and flipped the lid open.
♦ PHRASAL VERB **flip through something** to look quickly at the pages of a book or magazine □ She sat in the waiting room flipping through a magazine.

flippant /'flɪpənt/ ADJECTIVE not serious and not suitable for the situation □ a flippant remark
● **flippantly** /'flɪpəntlɪ/ ADVERB in a flippant way □ He replied rather flippantly.

flipper /'flɪpə(r)/ NOUN [plural **flippers**]
1 one of the large flat feet that some sea animals have to help them swim
2 a wide, long, flat shoe that you wear to help you swim under water

flirt /flɜːt/ ► VERB [**flirts, flirting, flirted**] to behave as though you think someone is attractive □ Emma was flirting with her sister's boyfriend.
♦ PHRASAL VERB **flirt with something**
1 to think about doing something, but not in a serious way □ He's flirting with the idea of becoming a monk.
2 flirt with danger/disaster, etc. to take a serious risk
► NOUN [plural **flirts**] someone who often flirts with people
● **flirtation** /flɜː'teɪʃən/ NOUN, NO PLURAL
1 when you flirt with someone
2 when you become interested in something for a short time □ He had a brief flirtation with politics.
● **flirtatious** /flɜː'teɪʃəs/ ADJECTIVE flirting a lot

flit /flɪt/ VERB [**flits, flitting, flitted**] to move quickly and lightly from one place to another □ His eyes flitted round the room. □ The butterfly flitted from flower to flower.

float /fləʊt/ ► VERB [**floats, floating, floated**]
1 to move slowly or to stay on the surface of a liquid and not sink □ Leaves were floating on the surface of the lake. □ The boat floated slowly down the river.
2 to stay in the air or to move slowly through the air □ He let go of the balloon and it floated away. □ Voices floated down the stairs.
3 to start selling shares (= parts of a company that people buy and sell) in a company □ + **on** The company was floated on the stock exchange last year.
4 to suggest an idea for people to think about ⊞ I floated the idea at yesterday's meeting. □ They floated plans to build new offices.
► NOUN [plural **floats**] an object that is designed to float on water, for example to help someone swim

flock /flɒk/ ► NOUN [plural **flocks**] a group of sheep or birds
► VERB [**flocks, flocking, flocked**] to move or come together in large numbers □ Thousands of tourists flock to the town every summer. □ Fans have flocked to see him.

flog /flɒg/ VERB [**flogs, flogging, flogged**]
1 to hit someone repeatedly with something as a punishment
2 an informal word meaning to sell something

flood /flʌd/ ► NOUN [plural **floods**]
1 a lot of water covering a place that is usually dry □ Two days of heavy rain caused floods.
2 a large number of people or things that appear suddenly in a place □ + **of** They received a flood of complaints.
3 a floods of tears a lot of crying □ The little boy was in floods of tears.
► VERB [**floods, flooding, flooded**]
1 if water floods a place or if a place floods, it becomes covered in a lot of water □ Large parts of the town were flooded. □ The river has flooded its banks.
2 to arrive somewhere in large numbers □ Demonstrators flooded the streets. □ The newspaper has been flooded with complaints.

floodgates /'flʌdgeɪts/ PLURAL NOUN open the floodgates to suddenly let a lot of people do something □ If we give one person permission, we'll open the floodgates to hundreds of similar requests.

flooding /'flʌdɪŋ/ NOUN, NO PLURAL when an area that is usually dry is covered with water □ The storms caused severe flooding.

floodlight /'flʌdlaɪt/ NOUN [plural **floodlights**] a bright light used at night for lighting outside areas □ The match was played under floodlights.
● **floodlit** /'flʌdlɪt/ ADJECTIVE lit by floodlights

floor /flɔː(r)/ ► NOUN [plural **floors**]
1 the surface that you stand on in a room □ There were toys all over the kitchen floor. □ The hall has a wooden floor.

2 one of the levels in a building □ *Which floor is your apartment on?* □ *Our office is on the top floor of the building.*

3 the ground at the bottom of a particular area □ *the forest/ocean floor*

▶ VERB [**floors, flooring, floored**]

1 to hit someone so hard that they fall down □ *He floored his opponent in the sixth round.*

2 to surprise someone so much that they do not know how to react □ *I was slightly floored by the question.*

floorboard /'flɔːbɔːd/ NOUN [plural **floorboards**] one of the long narrow boards which form a wooden floor

flop /flɒp/ ▶ VERB [**flops, flopping, flopped**]

1 to fall or sit down suddenly in a heavy way □ *She flopped into the nearest armchair.* □ *I flopped down on the bed.*

2 to hang or fall loosely □ *His hair flopped over his eyes.*

3 if an event, product, etc. flops, it is not successful. An informal word □ *His last few films have flopped.*

▶ NOUN [plural **flops**]

1 an informal word for something that is not successful □ *The film was a box office flop.*

2 a sudden, heavy movement

• **floppy** /'flɒpɪ/ ADJECTIVE [**floppier, floppiest**] soft and hanging down loosely □ *She wore a big, floppy summer hat.* □ *a dog with floppy ears*

floppy disk /ˌflɒpɪ 'dɪsk/ NOUN [plural **floppy disks**] a disk inside a flat piece of plastic that is used for copying information from a computer. A computing word.

flora /'flɔːrə/ NOUN, NO PLURAL the trees and plants that grow in an area. A biology word. 🔁 *He's an expert on the local flora and fauna (= plants and animals).*

floral /'flɔːrəl/ ADJECTIVE

1 made of flowers □ *a floral arrangement*

2 decorated with pictures of flowers □ *floral wallpaper*

florid /'flɒrɪd/ ADJECTIVE

1 a florid face is red or pink □ *florid cheeks.*

2 too decorated or complicated □ *a florid description*

florist /'flɒrɪst/ NOUN [plural **florists**]

1 someone who sells flowers

2 florist's a shop that sells flowers

floss /flɒs/ ▶ NOUN, NO PLURAL thread you use for cleaning between your teeth 🔁 *dental floss*

▶ VERB [**flosses, flossing, flossed**] to clean your teeth using floss

flotation /fləʊ'teɪʃən/ NOUN [plural **flotations**] when a company sells shares on the stock market □ *the successful flotation of the company*

flounce /flaʊns/ VERB [**flounces, flouncing, flounced**] to walk away suddenly, because you are angry or upset □ *Kat flounced out of the room and slammed the door.*

flounder /'flaʊndə(r)/ VERB [**flounders, floundering, floundered**]

1 to fail or experience difficulties □ *The economy continued to flounder.*

2 to not know what to say or do in a situation □ *I felt I was floundering in the interview.*

3 to move in an awkward way, especially because you are trying not to sink in water

flour /'flaʊə(r)/ NOUN, NO PLURAL powder made from wheat (= grain), used for making bread and cakes

flourish /'flʌrɪʃ/ ▶ VERB [**flourishes, flourishing, flourished**]

1 to develop quickly and well □ *Her new business is flourishing.* □ *Wildlife is once again flourishing in the area.*

2 to wave something in the air □ *The tour guide flourished her umbrella.*

▶ NOUN [plural **flourishes**] a special, skilful or large movement □ *He removed his hat with a flourish.*

flout /flaʊt/ VERB [**flouts, flouting, flouted**] if you flout a law or rule, you intentionally do not obey it □ *Drivers who flout the rule face a fine.*

flow /fləʊ/ ▶ VERB [**flows, flowing, flowed**]

1 if a liquid flows, it moves along □ **+ through** *The River Thames flows through London.* □ **+ into** *The water flows into the sea.* □ *Tears flowed down her face.*

2 to move continuously and easily without stopping 🔁 *The traffic was flowing freely.* □ *Foreign investment flowed into the country.*

3 if ideas, conversation, etc. flow, they continue in an easy, relaxed way □ *His words flowed easily.* □ *The conversation flowed smoothly.*

▶ NOUN [plural **flows**] a continuous movement of something □ **+ of** *We used bandages to stop the flow of blood.* □ 🔁 *a steady flow of tourists*

flow chart /'fləʊ tʃɑːt/ NOUN [plural **flow charts**] a picture showing the different stages in a process

flower /'flaʊə(r)/ ▶ NOUN [plural **flowers**] the coloured part of a plant □ *Tulips are my favourite flower.* 🔁 *We picked some wild flowers.* 🔁 *They gave her a bunch of flowers.*

▶ VERB [**flowers, flowering, flowered**] to produce flowers □ *Bluebells usually flower in May.*

flowerbed /'flaʊəbed/ NOUN [plural **flowerbeds**] a piece of ground in a garden, park, etc. where flowers are grown

flowerpot /'flaʊəpɒt/ NOUN [plural **flowerpots**] a round clay or plastic container for growing plants in

flown /fləʊn/ PAST PARTICIPLE OF **fly**

fl oz ABBREVIATION **fluid ounce** or **fluid ounces**

flu /fluː/ NOUN, NO PLURAL an illness like a very bad cold which makes you feel hot and tired 🔁 *Last month she caught flu.* □ *I had a bad bout of flu.*

fluctuate /'flʌktʃʊeɪt/ VERB [**fluctuates, fluctuating, fluctuated**] to keep changing in amount, level or character 🔁 *House prices fluctuated wildly over the next few months.*

• **fluctuating** /'flʌktʃʊeɪtɪŋ/ ADJECTIVE often changing □ *fluctuating temperatures*

• **fluctuation** /ˌflʌktʃʊ'eɪʃən/ NOUN [plural

fluctuations] when something fluctuates □ *There are daily fluctuations in oil prices.*

flue /flu:/ NOUN [plural **flues**] a metal tube that takes air or smoke away from a fire

fluent /'flu:ənt/ ADJECTIVE able to speak a language easily and well □ *She speaks fluent German.*

• **fluently** /'flu:əntlɪ/ ADVERB easily and well □ *Hannah speaks Italian fluently.*

fluff /flʌf/ ▶ NOUN, NO PLURAL small, soft pieces from wool or other material □ *You've got a bit of fluff on your sleeve.*

▶ VERB [**fluffs, fluffing, fluffed**]

1 an informal word meaning to do something badly or to make a mistake □ *She was so nervous, she fluffed her lines.*

2 to shake something to make it bigger, softer and more full of air □ *Polly fluffed up her hair.*

• **fluffy** /'flʌfɪ/ ADJECTIVE [**fluffier, fluffiest**] very soft or covered in fur or soft material □ *a fluffy toy* □ *a pile of fluffy towels*

fluid /'flu:ɪd/ ▶ NOUN [plural **fluids**] a liquid □ *Runners should drink plenty of fluids.*

▶ ADJECTIVE

1 able to flow like a liquid □ *Blood is a fluid substance.*

2 changing often □ *It's a very fluid situation.*

3 moving in a smooth and easy way □ *Their moves were fluid and well-rehearsed.*

fluid ounce /ˌflu:ɪd 'aʊns/ NOUN [plural **fluid ounces**] a unit for measuring liquid, equal to 1/20 pint. This is often written **fl oz**.

fluke /flu:k/ NOUN [plural **flukes**] a lucky or unusual thing that happens by chance □ *It was just a complete fluke that I won.*

flume /flu:m/ NOUN [plural **flumes**] a tube with water in the bottom that you can slide down into a swimming pool

flung /flʌŋ/ PAST TENSE AND PAST PARTICIPLE OF **fling**

fluorescent /flʊə'resənt/ ADJECTIVE

1 a fluorescent light is an electric light in the shape of a tube that produces a very bright light

2 very brightly coloured and easy to see □ *fluorescent yellow socks* □ *Workers wear fluorescent jackets.*

fluoride /'flʊəraɪd/ NOUN, NO PLURAL a chemical added to toothpaste (= substance for cleaning your teeth) or water to protect your teeth. A chemistry word.

flurry /'flʌrɪ/ NOUN [plural **flurries**]

1 a short period of activity or emotion □ *There's been a recent flurry of interest in the sport.*

2 a small amount of snow or rain □ *snow flurries*

flush /flʌʃ/ ▶ VERB [**flushes, flushing, flushed**]

1 to press or pull a handle to make water go down a toilet 🔁 *I can't flush the toilet.*

2 to get rid of something by moving it somewhere with a strong flow of water □ *Plastic objects shouldn't be flushed down the toilet.* □ *The chemicals are flushed into the canal.*

3 to become red in the face □ *He flushed with embarrassment.*

▶ NOUN [plural **flushes**]

1 when your face becomes red and sometimes hot □ *Side effects may include hot flushes.*

2 a sudden feeling or emotion for a short time □ *a flush of pride*

3 when you flush a toilet

▶ ADJECTIVE

1 if two surfaces are flush, they are exactly level with each other □ *The edge of the pool is flush with the ground.*

2 an informal word meaning having more money than usual

fluster /'flʌstə(r)/ VERB [**flusters, flustering, flustered**] to make someone feel nervous and confused □ *Nothing seemed to fluster her.*

• **flustered** /'flʌstəd/ ADJECTIVE feeling nervous and confused □ *I got a bit flustered.*

flute /flu:t/ NOUN [plural **flutes**] a musical instrument you play by holding it sideways against your mouth and blowing into it

flutter /'flʌtə(r)/ ▶ VERB [**flutters, fluttering, fluttered**]

1 to move quickly up and down or from side to side □ *Her eyelids fluttered.* □ *The flags fluttered in the breeze.*

2 to move lightly and quickly through the air □ *Leaves fluttered down and covered the ground.*

▶ NOUN [plural **flutters**]

1 a short, quick, gentle movement □ *a flutter of wings*

2 a sudden, short feeling or emotion □ *I felt a little flutter of excitement.*

flux /flʌks/ NOUN, NO PLURAL a state of continuous change 🔁 *Our plans are in a state of flux.*

fly /flaɪ/ ▶ VERB [**flies, flying, flew, flown**]

1 to travel in an aircraft □ **+ to** *He flew to Miami.* □ *She flew in by helicopter.*

2 to move through the air using wings □ *A robin flew across the garden.* □ *A plane flew overhead.*

3 to take someone or something somewhere in an aircraft □ *His body was flown back to Australia.*

4 to control an aircraft □ *She learned to fly a helicopter.*

5 to move very quickly □ *A bullet flew past my head.* 🔁 *The door flew open.*

6 send someone/something flying to knock someone or something and make them fall □ *He stood up quickly and the chess pieces went flying.*

7 if time flies, it goes by quickly

8 fly into a temper/rage to suddenly become very angry

◆ IDIOMS **with flying colours** if you pass an exam with flying colours, you get a very high mark **fly off the handle** to suddenly become very angry □ *I only asked when he would be ready and he flew off the handle.*

▶ NOUN [plural **flies**] a small insect that flies

flyer /'flaɪə(r)/ NOUN [plural **flyers**] a small piece of paper that advertises something

flying saucer /ˌflaɪɪŋ ˈsɔːsə(r)/ NOUN [plural **flying saucers**] a round object in the sky, which some people believe is a spacecraft from another planet

flyover /ˈflaɪˌəʊvə(r)/ NOUN [plural **flyovers**] a road that crosses over another road like a bridge

flywheel /ˈflaɪwiːl/ NOUN [plural **flywheels**] a heavy wheel in a machine or engine that moves a part of it

foal /fəʊl/ NOUN [plural **foals**] a young horse

foam /fəʊm/ ▶ NOUN, NO PLURAL
1 a mass of small bubbles on top of a liquid □ *I like to eat the foam off my coffee with a spoon.*
2 a thick substance containing lots of small bubbles 🔂 *shaving foam*
3 a soft material that is full of small holes, often used in furniture □ *a foam mattress*
▶ VERB [**foams, foaming, foamed**] to produce foam □ *The horse was foaming at the mouth.*

fob /fɒb/
◆ PHRASAL VERB [**fobs, fobbing, fobbed**] **fob someone off** to try to stop someone asking questions or complaining by telling them something that is not true □ *She fobbed him off with excuses.*

focus /ˈfəʊkəs/ ▶ VERB [**focuses, focusing, focused**]
1 to concentrate on one particular thing □ *The report focused on the need to improve standards.* 🔂 *She wants to focus attention on the problem.*
2 if your eyes focus, they change to let you see something clearly □ *It took a while for my eyes to focus.*
3 to make small changes to equipment such as a camera so that you get a clear picture
▶ NOUN, NO PLURAL
1 when you focus on one thing, or the thing you focus on 🔂 *My main focus is to play well.* 🔂 *She soon became the focus of media attention.*
2 in focus if an image is in focus, it can be seen clearly □ *Make sure the faces are in focus.*
3 out of focus if an image is out of focus, it cannot be seen clearly □ *Some of the photos were out of focus.*

fodder /ˈfɒdə(r)/ NOUN, NO PLURAL food for horses or farm animals

foe /fəʊ/ NOUN [plural **foes**] a formal word for an enemy □ *The two men are old foes.*

foetus /ˈfiːtəs/ NOUN [plural **foetuses**] a baby before it is born. A biology word.

fog /fɒg/ NOUN, NO PLURAL thick, low cloud that makes it difficult to see 🔂 *The flight was delayed due to thick fog.* □ *The fog had lifted slightly.*
● **foggy** /ˈfɒgi/ ADJECTIVE [**foggier, foggiest**] having a lot of fog □ *a foggy day* □ *foggy weather*
◆ IDIOM **not have the foggiest (idea)** used to emphasize that you do not know anything about something □ *I haven't got the foggiest idea where he is.*

foghorn /ˈfɒghɔːn/ NOUN [plural **foghorns**] equipment that makes a loud noise to warn ships when it is foggy

foil /fɔɪl/ NOUN, NO PLURAL metal in very thin sheets, used for wrapping food

foist /fɔɪst/
◆ PHRASAL VERB [**foists, foisting, foisted**] **foist something on/onto/upon someone** to force someone to take, accept or deal with something they do not want to □ *The extra work was just foisted upon us.*

fold /fəʊld/ ▶ VERB [**folds, folding, folded**]
1 to bend one part of something so that it covers another part □ *Dan folded the letter and put it in the envelope.* □ *He folded the clothes neatly.*
2 to make something smaller by bending parts of it □ **+ up** *He folded up his laptop and put it in his bag.* □ *The back seats fold down to give more luggage space.*
3 fold your arms to cross your arms over your chest
4 if a business folds, it stops because it is not successful
▶ NOUN [plural **folds**]
1 a line or mark where something is folded
2 a thick piece of cloth, skin, etc. that hangs in a loose way □ *He reached inside the folds of his coat.*

folder /ˈfəʊldə(r)/ NOUN [plural **folders**]
1 a cardboard or plastic cover for holding papers
2 a place where you keep documents on a computer. A computing word.

foliage /ˈfəʊliɪdʒ/ NOUN, NO PLURAL the leaves on a tree or plant

folk /fəʊk/ ▶ PLURAL NOUN people □ *He has more money than most folk around here.* 🔂 *Babies and old folk are most at risk.*
▶ ADJECTIVE to do with the traditions and culture of the people of a country or area 🔂 *an Irish folk song* 🔂 *Russian folk tales*

folklore /ˈfəʊklɔː(r)/ NOUN, NO PLURAL the customs, beliefs, stories and traditions of a particular country or group of people □ *The story has become part of the folklore of the area.*

folk music /fəʊk ˌmjuːzɪk/ NOUN, NO PLURAL traditional music from a particular country or area

follicle /ˈfɒlɪkəl/ NOUN [plural **follicles**] a small hole in the skin where a hair grows. A biology word.

follow /ˈfɒləʊ/ VERB [**follows, following, followed**]
1 to go behind someone or something and go where they go □ *He followed her down the street.*
2 to happen after something □ *The meal was followed by a dance.*
3 to be next in size, quality, importance, etc. 🔂 *Our team won, followed closely by the London team.*
4 to be interested in something and continue to get information about it 🔂 *We have been following the baby elephant's progress.*
5 to do what a person or a rule, law, etc. says you should do 🔂 *We decided to follow his advice and catch the train.* 🔂 *Just open the letter and follow the instructions in it.*

6 follow someone's example to act in the same way as someone else □ *I'm going to follow my brother's example and get up earlier.*

7 if you follow a road, you go along it □ *Follow the path to the end and turn right.*

8 to understand what someone is saying □ *Do you follow me?*

◆ PHRASAL VERB **follow something up** to take further action or to get more information about something □ *Detectives are following up reports that the child has been seen in France.*

● **follower** /ˈfɒləʊə(r)/ NOUN [plural **followers**] someone who supports or admires a person or particular ideas

● **following** /ˈfɒləʊɪŋ/ ADJECTIVE

1 the following day, week, year, etc. is the next one □ *I finished work on Friday and we went on holiday the following Wednesday.*

2 used to introduce what you are going to say or write about next □ *The following people should come with me.*

▶ PREPOSITION after something has happened □ *Following his arrest, police made a thorough search of his office.*

▶ NOUN, NO PLURAL a group of people who support or admire someone or something □ *The band has a large following in Germany.*

folly /ˈfɒlɪ/ NOUN [plural **follies**] something you think is silly or dangerous □ *It's absolute folly to drive as fast as that in the fog.*

fond /fɒnd/ ADJECTIVE [**fonder, fondest**]

1 fond of someone/something liking someone or something □ **+ ing** *We're very fond of walking in the countryside.* □ *He is particularly fond of chocolate.* 🔁 *I've grown very fond of the children.*

2 causing or expressing happy or friendly feelings 🔁 *I have fond memories of my time at university.*

fondle /ˈfɒndəl/ VERB [**fondles, fondling, fondled**] to touch a person or animal in a way which shows affection □ *He fondled the dog's ears.*

fondly /ˈfɒndlɪ/ ADVERB in a way that shows you like someone or something □ *Miss Price is fondly remembered at the school.*

fondness /ˈfɒndnɪs/ NOUN, NO PLURAL when you like someone or something □ *She has a fondness for designer shoes.*

font /fɒnt/ NOUN [plural **fonts**]

1 a style of letters used in printing or computer documents

2 a large stone bowl in a church for holding water during a baptism (= when someone becomes a member of the Christian religion) ceremony

food /fuːd/ NOUN [plural **foods**]

1 *no plural* things that people and animals eat □ *They didn't have enough food.* □ *We often eat Chinese food.* 🔁 *pet food*

2 a particular type of food □ *Try to avoid processed foods.*

➤ Note that **food** is not usually used in the plural. **Foods** is sometimes used when talking about different types of food but is not common:
✓ *I buy most of our food at the supermarket.*
✗ *I buy most of our foods at the supermarket.*

food chain /ˈfuːd tʃeɪn/ NOUN **the food chain** a series of living things where each thing is eaten by the next thing in the series. A biology word.

foodie /ˈfuːdɪ/ NOUN [plural **foodies**] a person who loves food and eats only the best food

food miles /ˈfuːd maɪlz/ PLURAL NOUN how far food travels from the place where it is grown to the place where people eat it

food processor /ˈfuːd ˈprəʊsesə(r)/ NOUN [plural **food processors**] an electric machine for cutting or mixing food

foodstuff /ˈfuːdstʌf/ NOUN [plural **foodstuffs**] any substance used as food □ *They lack basic foodstuffs such as bread and cheese.*

fool /fuːl/ ▶ NOUN [plural **fools**]

1 a stupid or silly person □ *I'm not a complete fool.* □ *I didn't want to look a fool.*

2 make a fool of yourself to do something that makes people think you are silly □ *They're going to make fools of themselves.*

3 make a fool (out) of someone to try to make someone look silly

▶ VERB [**fools, fooling, fooled**] to trick someone □ *His story didn't fool anyone.* □ *Don't be fooled by cheap copies.*

◆ PHRASAL VERB **fool about/around** to behave in a silly way or to have fun □ *He was fooling around on his bike.*

foolhardy /ˈfuːlˌhɑːdɪ/ ADJECTIVE taking silly and unnecessary risks □ *It would be foolhardy to sell now.*

foolish /ˈfuːlɪʃ/ ADJECTIVE silly or stupid □ *a foolish mistake* □ *He didn't want to appear foolish.*

foolproof /ˈfuːlpruːf/ ADJECTIVE a foolproof plan, method, etc. is one that cannot go wrong □ *I've got a foolproof recipe for bread.*

foot /fʊt/ NOUN [plural **feet**]

1 one of the parts of your body that you stand on □ *He has a broken foot.* 🔁 *We got to our feet* (= stood up) *when she came in.* 🔁 *I've been on my feet* (= standing up) *all day.*

2 a unit for measuring length, equal to 12 inches. This is often written **ft**.

3 the foot of the bottom of something □ *We camped at the foot of the mountain.*

4 on foot if you travel on foot, you walk

5 set foot in/on somewhere to go to a place □ *She'd never set foot in a casino.*

◆ IDIOMS **put your feet up** to rest and relax **put your foot down** to say in a forceful way what you want or what you want to happen **put your foot in it** to say something by accident that upsets or annoys someone. An informal phrase.

➡ go to **get cold feet, sweep someone off their feet**

footage /'futɪdʒ/ NOUN, NO PLURAL a filmed record of an event □ *We bring you live footage of the ceremony.*

football /'futbɔːl/ NOUN [plural **footballs**]
1 *no plural* a sport played by two teams who try to kick a ball into a goal ⏣ *The boys are playing football outside.* ⏣ *a football match* ⏣ *a game of football* ⏣ *a football team*
2 the ball used for playing football □ *Some kids were kicking a football about.*
• **footballer** /'futbɔːlə(r)/ NOUN [plural **footballers**] someone who plays football, especially as their job

footbridge /'futbrɪdʒ/ NOUN [plural **footbridges**] a narrow bridge for people to walk across

foothills /'futhɪlz/ PLURAL NOUN hills at the bottom of a high mountain

foothold /'futhəuld/ NOUN [plural **footholds**]
1 a place where you can put your foot when you are climbing
2 a strong position from which you can make progress ⏣ *The company has gained a foothold in the Asian market.*

footing /'futɪŋ/ NOUN, NO PLURAL
1 when you are standing in a firm position ⏣ *I lost my footing and fell.*
2 someone's position or situation ⏣ *We're on a sound financial footing.*
3 the relationship between two people or groups ⏣ *The two groups are on an equal footing.*

footnote /'futnəut/ NOUN [plural **footnotes**] a note at the bottom of a page, which adds information about something in the text above

footpath /'futpɑːθ/ NOUN [plural **footpaths**] a path you can walk on, especially in the countryside

footprint /'futprɪnt/ NOUN [plural **footprints**]
1 a mark that your foot leaves on the ground □ *footprints in the snow*
2 the amount of the Earth's energy that each person or business uses □ *I'm trying to reduce my footprint by using the car less.*

footstep /'futstep/ NOUN [plural **footsteps**] the sound of someone walking □ *I could hear footsteps.*

footwear /'futweə(r)/ NOUN, NO PLURAL things such as shoes and boots that you wear on your feet □ *Wear sensible footwear.*

for /fɔː(r)/ PREPOSITION
1 to be received or used by someone, or to help someone □ *There's a letter for you.* □ *She made a cake for her Mum.* □ *I did all the ironing for Peter.*
2 in order to do something or to get something □ *He asked me for money.* □ *Let's go for a walk.* □ *I went to the supermarket for some eggs.*
3 used to show a reason or what something is intended to do □ *What's this switch for?* □ *He was*

arrested for shoplifting. □ *I gave her a necklace for her birthday.*
4 used to show an amount of time, distance, money, etc. □ *I've lived here for eight years.* □ *We walked for two miles.* □ *I got these trainers for £30.*
5 meaning something □ *What's the word for 'girl' in French?*
6 supporting or agreeing with someone or something □ *I voted for her.* □ *Are you for or against the new airport?*

➤ When you are explaining why someone does something, remember to use the infinitive **to do** something. Do not use **for**:
✓ *I went home to see my mother.*
✗ *I went home for seeing my mother.*

forbid /fə'bɪd/ VERB [**forbids, forbidding, forbade, forbidden**] to tell someone that they must not do something □ **+ to do something** *They forbade their daughter to see Henry any more.* □ **+ from** *He is forbidden from discussing the case.* □ *The school rules forbid the use of mobile phones in class.*
• **forbidden** /fə'bɪdən/ ADJECTIVE not allowed □ *Smoking is forbidden throughout the hospital.* ⏣ *Alcohol is strictly forbidden.*
• **forbidding** /fə'bɪdɪŋ/ ADJECTIVE looking frightening or unfriendly □ *She gave me a forbidding stare.*

force /fɔːs/ ➤ NOUN [plural **forces**]
1 *no plural* power or physical strength □ *The force of the explosion damaged many buildings.*
2 **by force** by violent physical action □ *They took the land by force.*
3 a group of people, such as police or soldiers, who are trained to work together ⏣ *the armed forces* □ *A defence force was sent into the region.*
4 something or someone with power or influence ⏣ *market forces* □ *Their new leader is felt to be a force for good.*
5 **come into force** if a rule or law comes into force, it starts being used
6 **in force** (a) if a law or rule is in force, it is being used and must be obeyed (b) if people do something in force, a lot of them are involved □ *Police arrived in force to stop the demonstration.*
➤ VERB [**forces, forcing, forced**]
1 to make someone do something □ **+ to do something** *He forced me to give him money.* □ **often passive** *She was forced to move house.*
2 to make something move by using your strength □ *The police had to force the door open.*
• **forced** /fɔːst/ ADJECTIVE a forced smile or laugh is not sincere
• **forceful** /'fɔːsful/ ADJECTIVE forceful opinions are very strong, and forceful people express their opinions in a strong way ⏣ *She has a forceful personality.* ⏣ *a forceful argument*

• **forcefully** /'fɔːsfʊlɪ/ ADVERB in a forceful way □ *He insisted forcefully that he was innocent.*

forceps /'fɔːseps/ PLURAL NOUN a piece of medical equipment with two narrow parts, used for holding things firmly

forcible /'fɔːsəbəl/ ADJECTIVE done using physical force □ *He protested about the forcible removal of the children from their families.*

• **forcibly** /'fɔːsəblɪ/ ADVERB using physical force □ *I was forcibly detained for three hours at the police station.*

ford /fɔːd/ NOUN [plural **fords**] a part of a river that is not deep where you can drive across

fore- /fɔː(r)/ PREFIX fore- is added to the beginning of words to mean 'before' or 'at the front of' □ *forename* (= the name before your family name)

forearm /'fɔːr,ɑːm/ NOUN [plural **forearms**] the part of your arm that is below your elbow

foreboding /fɔː'bəʊdɪŋ/ NOUN, NO PLURAL a feeling that something bad is going to happen 🔁 *As he entered the house, he had a sense of foreboding.*

forecast /'fɔːkɑːst/ ► NOUN [plural **forecasts**] a statement about what is likely to happen in the future, based on information 🔁 *a weather forecast* □ + *of We had a forecast of heavy rain.*

► VERB [**forecasts, forecasting, forecast**] to make a forecast □ *Rain is forecast for the weekend.* □ *The company has forecast record profits.*

• **forecaster** /'fɔː,kɑːstə(r)/ NOUN [plural **forecasters**] someone whose job is to forecast something 🔁 *a weather forecaster* □ *Forecasters say that prices are likely to rise.*

forecourt /'fɔːkɔːt/ NOUN [plural **forecourts**] an open area with a hard surface in front of a building □ *a garage forecourt*

forefather /'fɔː,fɑːðə(r)/ NOUN [plural **forefathers**] someone in your family who lived a long time ago

forefinger /'fɔː,fɪŋɡə(r)/ NOUN [plural **forefingers**] the finger that is next to your thumb

forefront /'fɔːfrʌnt/ NOUN, NO PLURAL the forefront an important or leading position □ *His team of scientists was at the forefront of research into breast cancer.*

forego /fɔː'ɡəʊ/ VERB [**foregoes, foregoing, forewent, foregone**] another spelling of forgo

foregone conclusion /ˌfɔːɡɒn kən'kluːʒən/ NOUN, NO PLURAL a result that is certain before it happens □ *The election seemed like a foregone conclusion.*

foreground /'fɔːɡraʊnd/ NOUN, NO PLURAL the foreground the part of a view or a picture that is nearest to you □ *There's a group of children in the foreground, with the sea behind them.*

forehand /'fɔːhænd/ NOUN [plural **forehands**] in games such as tennis, a way of hitting the ball with your arm out on the side that you hold the racket (= thing you hit the ball with)

forehead /'fɔːhed/ NOUN [plural **foreheads**] the top part of your face above your eyes

foreign /'fɒrən/ ADJECTIVE

1 from a country that is not your country 🔁 *a foreign language* □ *a group of foreign tourists*
2 to do with other countries 🔁 *foreign policy* □ *the foreign minister*
3 strange and not familiar □ + *to The whole situation was completely foreign to me.*

• **foreigner** /'fɒrənə(r)/ NOUN [plural **foreigners**] someone who comes from a country that is not your country

foreleg /'fɔːleɡ/ NOUN [plural **forelegs**] one of the front legs of an animal that has four legs

foreman /'fɔːmən/ NOUN [plural **foremen**] someone who is in charge of a group of workers

foremost /'fɔːməʊst/ ADJECTIVE the most famous or important □ *He is one of the country's foremost experts on the disease.*

forename /'fɔːneɪm/ NOUN [plural **forenames**] a formal word for the name or names that come before your family name

forensic /fə'rensɪk/ ADJECTIVE to do with using science to solve crimes □ *forensic medicine* 🔁 *There was no forensic evidence.*

• **forensics** /fə'rensɪks/ PLURAL NOUN the use of science to solve crimes

foresee /fɔː'siː/ VERB [**foresees, foreseeing, foresaw, foreseen**] to expect that something will happen □ *We didn't foresee this problem.*

• **foreseeable** /fɔː'siːəbəl/ ADJECTIVE the foreseeable future as far in the future as you can reasonably know about □ *The situation will remain as it is for the foreseeable future.*

• **foresight** /'fɔːsaɪt/ NOUN, NO PLURAL when you know or guess what will happen in the future □ *There was a lack of foresight by the company.*

forest /'fɒrɪst/ NOUN [plural **forests**] a place where a lot of trees are growing together □ *We stayed at a camp deep in the forest.*

• **forested** /'fɒrɪstɪd/ ADJECTIVE covered in forest □ *a thickly forested area*

• **forestry** /'fɒrɪstrɪ/ NOUN, NO PLURAL planting and looking after trees and forests

forever /fə'revə(r)/ ADVERB

1 for all future time □ *You can't stay in your room forever.* □ *Their lives have been changed forever.*
2 an informal word meaning 'for a very long time' □ *It took forever to get there.*
3 used to mean that something happens often □ + *ing They're forever arguing.*

foreword /'fɔːwɜːd/ NOUN [plural **forewords**] an introduction at the start of a book

forfeit /'fɔːfɪt/ VERB [**forfeits, forfeiting, forfeited**] to have something taken away from you because of something you have done □ *If someone commits a serious crime, they forfeit their right to vote.*

forgave /fə'ɡeɪv/ PAST TENSE OF forgive

forge /fɔːdʒ/ ▶ VERB [**forges, forging, forged**]
1 to make an illegal copy of something □ *He was sent to prison for forging passports.*
2 to develop a good relationship with someone or something □ *The Chinese have forged trade links around the world.*
◆ PHRASAL VERB **forge ahead** to make good progress with something □ *She's forging ahead with her acting career.*
▶ NOUN [*plural* **forges**] a place where metal is heated and shaped to make things

● **forgery** /'fɔːdʒəri/ NOUN [*plural* **forgeries**]
1 the crime of making an illegal copy of something □ *He faces charges of forgery.*
2 an illegal copy of something □ *The painting turned out to be a forgery.*

forget /fə'get/ VERB [**forgets, forgetting, forgot, forgotten**]
1 to be unable to remember something □ *I've forgotten his name.* □ *+ that I forgot that you had been there before.* □ *+ about I had forgotten about the heat here.*
2 to not remember to do something or that something is happening □ *+ to do something I forgot to feed the dog.* □ *+ that He forgot that Milo was coming.* 🔁 *Don't forget to lock the door.* 🔁 *I completely forgot her birthday.*
3 to not remember to bring something □ *Val's forgotten her umbrella.*
4 to stop thinking or caring about something □ *Forget about your exams and come to the party.*
● **forgetful** /fə'getful/ ADJECTIVE often forgetting things

forgivable /fə'gɪvəbəl/ ADJECTIVE if something is forgivable, you can understand it and so forgive it □ *It was a forgivable error.*

forgive /fə'gɪv/ VERB [**forgives, forgiving, forgave, forgiven**] to stop being angry with someone for something they have done □ *+ for Have you forgiven him for breaking the window?* □ *His family can never forgive the killers.* □ *If anything happens to her, I'll never forgive myself.*
● **forgiveness** /fə'gɪvnɪs/ NOUN, NO PLURAL when you forgive someone 🔁 *I want to ask your forgiveness.*
● **forgiving** /fə'gɪvɪŋ/ ADJECTIVE willing to forgive □ *Others might not be quite so forgiving.*

forgo /fɔː'gəʊ/ VERB [**forgoes, forgoing, forwent, forgone**] a formal word meaning to decide not to have or do something you would like □ *We might have to forgo a holiday this year.*

forgot /fə'gɒt/ PAST TENSE OF forget

forgotten /fə'gɒtən/ ▶ PAST PARTICIPLE OF forget
▶ ADJECTIVE not remembered by anyone □ *forgotten heroes*

fork /fɔːk/ ▶ NOUN [*plural* **forks**]
1 an object with a handle and points that you use for lifting food to your mouth 🔁 *a knife and fork*
2 a place where a road or river divides and goes in two different directions □ *We came to a fork in the road.*

3 a tool with a long handle and points that you use for digging
▶ VERB [**forks, forking, forked**] if a road or a river forks, it divides into two parts going in different directions □ *Just after the bridge, the road forks.*
◆ PHRASAL VERB **fork out** an informal word meaning to pay for something, especially when you do not want to □ *Students have to fork out £3,000 a year in tuition fees.*
● **forked** /fɔːkt/ ADJECTIVE divided into two parts at one end 🔁 *a forked tongue*

fork-lift truck /ˌfɔːklɪft 'trʌk/ NOUN [*plural* **fork-lift trucks**] a vehicle with two flat parts on the front for lifting and moving heavy things

forlorn /fə'lɔːn/ ADJECTIVE looking lonely and unhappy □ *He looked so forlorn.* □ *a forlorn figure*

form /fɔːm/ ▶ NOUN [*plural* **forms**]
1 a type of something □ *What form of transport do you use?* □ *I have tried various forms of exercise.* □ *You need to use some form of wrist support.*
2 a document with questions and spaces to write your answers 🔁 *You have to fill in a form to get a passport.* □ *Can you sign this form, please?*
3 the way that something is □ *He gets most of his calories in the form of sugar.* 🔁 *In its current form, the organization is not effective.* 🔁 *My stress takes the form of frequent headaches.*
4 the shape of someone or something □ *I saw his lifeless form on the floor.*
5 a class at school □ *Which form are you in?*
6 how well or badly someone is doing 🔁 *Our team was on top form (= very good) today.*
▶ VERB [**forms, forming, formed**]
1 to start to exist or to make something start to exist □ *How was the Earth formed?* □ *An idea formed in his mind.* □ *I formed a good impression of his work.* □ *His party is likely to form the next government.*
2 to be something or the thing that something is made of □ *This article could form the basis of a book.* □ *The area forms part of a safari park.*
3 to make a particular shape □ *The children held hands and formed a circle.*

formal /'fɔːməl/ ADJECTIVE
1 following rules about what is polite and correct, not friendly and relaxed □ *a formal dinner party* □ *The atmosphere was very formal.*
2 public or official, or following official rules or methods 🔁 *A formal announcement is expected tomorrow.* 🔁 *I wish to make a formal complaint.*
3 formal education or training involves study at a school or college 🔁 *She received little formal education.* 🔁 *He has no formal qualifications.*
● **formality** /fɔː'mælətɪ/ NOUN [*plural* **formalities**]
1 something that must be done because of rules or the law □ *There are certain legal formalities to go through.*
2 formal, polite behaviour □ *There's a lack of formality that I really like.*

• **formally** /'fɔ:məlɪ/ ADVERB
1 officially □ *They have formally announced their engagement.*
2 in a way that follows rules about what is polite and correct □ *They were formally dressed for the occasion.*

format /'fɔ:mæt/ ▶ NOUN [plural **formats**] the way something is designed or arranged □ *Please send two photographs in digital format.* □ *There are plans to change the format of the tournament.*
▶ VERB [**formats, formatting, formatted**]
1 to prepare a computer disk so that you can store information on it. A computing word.
2 to arrange the design of information on a page or document

formation /fɔ:'meɪʃən/ NOUN [plural **formations**]
1 when something is formed □ *the formation of a new government* □ *They believe it is a new planet in the process of formation.*
2 a shape made by the way people or things are arranged □ *a huge rock formation*

former /'fɔ:mə(r)/ ▶ ADJECTIVE existing or true in the past but not now □ *the former President* □ *In former times, people did not travel so much.*
▶ NOUN, NO PLURAL **the former** the first of two people or things you mention □ *We visited America and Canada but stayed longer in the former.*
• **formerly** /'fɔ:məlɪ/ ADVERB in the past but not now □ *Their house was formerly a shop.*

formidable /'fɔ:mɪdəbəl/ ADJECTIVE difficult to deal with or frightening □ *a formidable task* □ *He proved a formidable opponent.*

formula /'fɔ:mjʊlə/ NOUN [plural **formulas** or **formulae**]
1 in maths or chemistry, a set of letters, numbers or symbols that represent a rule, structure, etc. □ *What's the formula for calculating the area of a circle?* ⊞ *a mathematical formula*
2 a method or plan for achieving something ⊞ *There is no magic formula* (= simple, easy method) *to solve the problem.*
3 the combination of substances used to make something
• **formulate** /'fɔ:mjʊleɪt/ VERB [**formulates, formulating, formulated**] to invent and develop a plan or idea □ *We didn't have much time to formulate a plan.*
• **formulation** /ˌfɔ:mjʊ'leɪʃən/ NOUN [plural **formulations**]
1 the process of formulating something □ *the formulation of government policy*
2 the combination of substances used to make something

fort /fɔ:t/ NOUN [plural **forts**] a strong building used by soldiers to to defend a place from attack

forth /fɔ:θ/ ADVERB
1 **back and forth** in one direction then in the opposite direction □ *They threw the ball back and*
forth. □ *He goes back and forth between Canada and the US.*
2 a formal word meaning forwards, out of or away from a place □ *They went forth into the desert.*

forthcoming /ˌfɔ:θ'kʌmɪŋ/ ADJECTIVE happening soon □ *forthcoming events* □ *They played some tracks from their forthcoming album.*

forthright /'fɔ:θraɪt/ ADJECTIVE very honest and saying what you think □ *John was forthright in his criticism.*

fortieth /'fɔ:tɪɪθ/ NUMBER 40th written as a word

fortifications /ˌfɔ:tɪfɪ'keɪʃənz/ PLURAL NOUN strong walls or buildings that are built to defend a place from attack

fortify /'fɔ:tɪfaɪ/ VERB [**fortifies, fortifying, fortified**]
1 to make someone or something stronger □ *I had a big breakfast to fortify myself for the journey.*
2 to build strong walls, etc. around a place to protect it against attack □ *a fortified compound*

fortnight /'fɔ:tnaɪt/ NOUN [plural **fortnights**] a period of two weeks □ *We're going to Greece for a fortnight.* □ *I've been very busy over the past fortnight.* □ *He visits her once a fortnight.*
• **fortnightly** /'fɔ:tnaɪtlɪ/ ADVERB, ADJECTIVE happening every two weeks □ *They're paid fortnightly.* □ *a fortnightly magazine*

fortress /'fɔ:trɪs/ NOUN [plural **fortresses**] a strong building used to defend a place from attack

fortunate /'fɔ:tʃənət/ ADJECTIVE lucky □ *We were fortunate to catch our train, we were so late.* □ *It's extremely fortunate that no one was hurt.* □ *We should help people who are less fortunate than ourselves.*
• **fortunately** /'fɔ:tʃənətlɪ/ ADVERB used to say that something lucky has happened □ *Fortunately, nobody was injured.*

fortune /'fɔ:tʃu:n/ NOUN [plural **fortunes**]
1 a very large amount of money □ *His uncle died and left him a fortune.* ⊞ *He made his fortune in the oil industry.*
2 an informal word used to mean a lot of money ⊞ *They spent a fortune on it.*
3 **fortunes** the good and bad things which happen to someone □ *It was a year of mixed fortunes for the party.*
4 good luck ⊞ *Sue had the good fortune to win first prize.*

fortune-teller /'fɔ:tʃu:nˌtelə(r)/ NOUN [plural **fortune-tellers**] a person who says they can tell people what is going to happen to them in the future

forty /'fɔ:tɪ/ NUMBER [plural **forties**]
1 the number 40
2 **the forties** the years between 1940 and 1949

forum /'fɔ:rəm/ NOUN [plural **forums**] a place or situation in which people can discuss things and express their opinions □ *an online forum* □ *The programme is intended to be a forum for public debate.*

forward /'fɔ:wəd/ ▶ ADJECTIVE
1 in the direction that is in front of you □ *a forward movement*
2 thinking about or planning for the future ⌷ *It just takes a little forward planning.*
▶ VERB [**forwards, forwarding, forwarded**] to send a letter or e-mail you have received to someone else □ *He forwarded the e-mail to several colleagues.*
▶ NOUN [*plural* **forwards**] a player in some team sports whose main job is to attack and to try to score
• **forward** /'fɔ:wəd/ *or* **forwards** /'fɔ:wədz/ ADVERB
1 in the direction that is in front of you □ *The car moved slowly forwards.* □ *Amy leaned forward.* ⌷ *He rocked backwards and forwards.*
2 towards a better or more developed state or situation ⌷ *This is a big step forward.* □ *We hope the political process can move forward.*
3 towards the future □ *We want to look forwards, not backwards.*

forward slash /'fɔ:wəd ˌslæʃ/ NOUN [*plural* **forward slashes**] the symbol '/', often used in Internet addresses
fossil /'fɒsəl/ NOUN [*plural* **fossils**] a dead animal or plant that has been kept in a piece of rock for thousands of years
fossil fuel /'fɒsəl ˌfjuəl/ NOUN [*plural* **fossil fuels**] a fuel such as coal or oil that is formed from animals and plants that lived thousands of years ago
fossilize *or* **fossilise** /'fɒsəlaɪz/ VERB [**fossilizes, fossilizing, fossilized**] to become a fossil
foster /'fɒstə(r)/ VERB [**fosters, fostering, fostered**]
1 to look after a child as part of your family for a period of time while their parents cannot look after them
2 to encourage an idea or a feeling to develop □ *Sports can foster teamwork.*
foster child /'fɒstə(r) ˌtʃaɪld/ NOUN [*plural* **foster children**] a child who is looked after by another family for a period of time when its parents cannot look after them
foster parent /'fɒstə(r) ˌpeərənt/ NOUN [*plural* **foster parents**] someone who looks after children that are not their own
fought /fɔ:t/ PAST TENSE AND PAST PARTICIPLE OF fight
foul /faʊl/ ADJECTIVE [**fouler, foulest**]
1 very dirty or with a bad smell or taste □ *The tea tasted foul.*
2 very unpleasant ⌷ *foul weather* ⌷ *He's in a foul mood.*
3 against the rules of a sport or game □ *a foul shot*
➡ IDIOMS **fall foul of someone/something** to have problems because you have not obeyed a rule or someone in authority □ *She soon fell foul of the law.*
foul play dishonest behaviour, especially causing someone's death □ *Police said there were no signs of foul play.*
▶ NOUN [*plural* **fouls**] an action that is against the rules of a sport □ *He was sent off for a foul on another player.*

▶ VERB [**fouls, fouling, fouled**]
1 a formal word meaning to make something dirty □ *Do not allow your dogs to foul the play area.*
2 to do something that is against the rules of a sport
found[1] /faʊnd/ VERB [**founds, founding, founded**] to start an organization □ *The college was founded in 1950.*
found[2] /faʊnd/ PAST TENSE AND PAST PARTICIPLE OF find
foundation /faʊn'deɪʃən/ NOUN [*plural* **foundations**]
1 an idea or principle that something is based on □ *Literacy is one of the basic foundations of education.* □ *This new technology forms the foundation of all our products.* □ *Her accusations have no foundation in truth.*
2 a situation from which something else can develop □ *Jealousy and suspicion are not a good foundation for a happy marriage.* ⌷ *His government laid the foundations for better human rights.*
3 when an organization, business or country is started □ *She has worked here since the company's foundation in 1997.*
4 an organization that provides money for a particular purpose □ *a scientific/educational foundation*
5 **foundations** the part of a building that is under the ground and which supports it ⌷ *They have dug the foundations for our new home.*
founder /'faʊndə(r)/ NOUN [*plural* **founders**] someone who starts an organization
foundry /'faʊndrɪ/ NOUN [*plural* **foundries**] a factory where metal or glass is melted and made into things
fountain /'faʊntɪn/ NOUN [*plural* **fountains**] a structure that pushes water up into the air for decoration in a garden or park

fountain pen /'faʊntɪn ˌpen/ NOUN [*plural* **fountain pens**] a pen that you fill with ink
four /fɔ:(r)/ NUMBER [*plural* **fours**] the number 4

fourteen /ˌfɔ:'ti:n/ NUMBER the number 14
fourteenth /ˌfɔ:'ti:nθ/ NUMBER 14th written as a word
fourth /fɔ:θ/ ▶ NUMBER 4th written as a word □ *You are fourth on the list.* □ *Mario finished fourth in the race.*
▶ NOUN [*plural* **fourths**] a US word for quarter

fowl /faʊl/ NOUN [*plural* **fowl** *or* **fowls**] a bird that is kept for its meat and eggs, for example a chicken
fox /fɒks/ NOUN [*plural* **foxes**] a wild animal that looks like a dog, with red fur and a thick tail
foxglove /'fɒksglʌv/ NOUN [*plural* **foxgloves**] a tall plant with purple flowers shaped like bells
foyer /'fɔɪeɪ/ NOUN [*plural* **foyers**] the area inside the entrance to a large building such as a theatre or a hotel
fracas /'fræka:/ NOUN, NO PLURAL a noisy argument or fight □ *He got involved in a fracas outside a nightclub.*
fraction /'frækʃən/ NOUN [*plural* **fractions**]
1 an amount, such as 1/2 or 3/8 , that is part of a whole number

2 a small amount or part of something □ *It lasted only a fraction of a second.* □ *This is a tiny fraction of total government spending.*

• **fractionally** /ˈfrækʃənəlɪ/ ADVERB by a very small amount □ *This one is fractionally higher.*

fracture /ˈfræktʃə(r)/ ▶ VERB [**fractures, fracturing, fractured**] to crack or break something, especially a bone in your body □ *Emma's fractured her arm.*
▶ NOUN [*plural* **fractures**] a crack or break in something, especially a bone in your body

fragile /ˈfrædʒaɪl/ ADJECTIVE
1 not very strong and likely to be broken, damaged or destroyed □ *The bones become fragile and more likely to break.* □ *a fragile peace*
2 thin and weak □ *Her mother looked so fragile.*
• **fragility** /frəˈdʒɪlətɪ/ NOUN, NO PLURAL the state of being fragile

fragment ▶ NOUN /ˈfrægmənt/ [*plural* **fragments**] a small piece that has broken off something □ *There were fragments of glass on the floor.*
▶ VERB /frægˈment/ [**fragments, fragmenting, fragmented**] to break into small pieces or parts
• **fragmentary** /ˈfrægməntərɪ/ ADJECTIVE consisting of small pieces or parts which are not well connected □ *The accounts we have are fragmentary and inconclusive.*

fragrance /ˈfreɪgrəns/ NOUN [*plural* **fragrances**]
1 a pleasant smell □ *the sweet fragrance of jasmine flowers*
2 a pleasant-smelling liquid which people put on their bodies
• **fragrant** /ˈfreɪgrənt/ ADJECTIVE smelling pleasant □ *fragrant flowers*

frail /freɪl/ ADJECTIVE [**frailer, frailest**] thin and weak □ *a frail old man*
• **frailty** /ˈfreɪltɪ/ NOUN [*plural* **frailties**] physical, mental or moral weakness □ *He's still very active despite his frailty.* 🕮 *We are all subject to human frailties.*

frame /freɪm/ ▶ NOUN [*plural* **frames**]
1 a structure that fits around the edge of something, for example a picture or a window
2 a structure that supports something, and around which the thing is built □ *My bike has a lightweight frame.*
3 frames the part that holds the glass parts in a pair of glasses
4 the shape of someone's body □ *a muscular frame*
5 frame of mind the way someone is feeling □ *He's in a very positive frame of mind.*
▶ VERB [**frames, framing, framed**]
1 to put something such as a picture in a frame □ *I'm going to get this photo framed.*
2 to form an edge around something □ *Her face was framed with golden curls.*
3 to develop a plan or a law □ *New legislation is being framed.*
4 a formal word meaning to express or show

something in a particular way □ *They have framed their argument in legal terms.*
5 to make it look as though someone who is not guilty has committed a crime □ *He claims he was framed.*

framework /ˈfreɪmwɜːk/ NOUN [*plural* **frameworks**]
1 the basic ideas or principles that something is based on □ *We operate within a legal framework.* □ *This provides a framework for sustainable development.*
2 the structure that supports something such as a building □ *the framework of the building*

franchise /ˈfræntʃaɪz/ NOUN [*plural* **franchises**] the right to sell the goods or services of a particular company using the company's name □ *He's the manager of a fast food franchise.*

frank /fræŋk/ ADJECTIVE [**franker, frankest**] honest and saying what you think 🕮 *We had a fairly frank discussion.* 🕮 *To be quite frank, I don't think it'll work.*
• **frankly** /ˈfræŋklɪ/ ADVERB
1 used to give an honest opinion □ *Frankly, I don't think he's good enough for the job.*
2 in a direct, honest way □ *She spoke frankly about her experiences.*
• **frankness** /ˈfræŋknɪs/ NOUN, NO PLURAL the quality of being frank □ *She was surprised at the General's frankness.*

frantic /ˈfræntɪk/ ADJECTIVE
1 done with a lot of energy and activity, by people who are very worried □ *They joined in the frantic search for survivors.*
2 extremely worried □ *His mother was frantic with worry.*
• **frantically** /ˈfræntɪkəlɪ/ ADVERB in a frantic way □ *We've been working frantically to get finished in time.*

fraternal /frəˈtɜːnəl/ ADJECTIVE to do with brothers □ *fraternal loyalty*
• **fraternity** /frəˈtɜːnətɪ/ NOUN [*plural* **fraternities**]
1 a feeling of being friends and having shared interests
2 in the US, a club or group for male students at a college

fraternization *or* **fraternisation** /ˌfrætənaɪˈzeɪʃən/ NOUN, NO PLURAL when people fraternize. A formal word.

fraternize *or* **fraternise** /ˈfrætənaɪz/ VERB [**fraternizes, fraternizing, fraternized**] a formal word meaning to meet with people as friends, especially people from a different group □ *Muslims and Christians fraternized with each other without apparent tension.*

fraud /frɔːd/ NOUN [*plural* **frauds**]
1 the crime of tricking people to get money □ *He was found guilty of credit card fraud.*
2 someone who tricks other people by pretending to be something they are not
• **fraudulent** /ˈfrɔːdjʊlənt/ ADJECTIVE deliberately dishonest or intended to trick people. A formal word □ *Her claims were fraudulent.*
• **fraudulently** /ˈfrɔːdjʊləntlɪ/ ADVERB in a fraudulent way. A formal word. □ *He obtained the money fraudulently.*

fraught /frɔːt/ ADJECTIVE
  1 nervous and worried, or making you feel nervous and worried □ *She looked fraught.* □ *The preparations were fraught.*
  2 fraught with something full of danger or problems □ *The journey was fraught with danger.* □ *The strategy is fraught with risk.*

fray /freɪ/ VERB [frays, fraying, frayed]
  1 if cloth frays, the threads along the edge become loose
  2 if your temper or nerves fray, you gradually become more angry or less calm 🔁 *Tempers were fraying on both sides.*
  • **frayed** /freɪd/ ADJECTIVE with loose threads along the edge □ *frayed jeans*

freak /friːk/ ► NOUN [plural freaks]
  1 a very strange person or a person who looks very strange
  2 an informal word for someone who is very interested in something □ *a health freak*
  ► ADJECTIVE extremely unusual 🔁 *a freak accident* 🔁 *a freak storm*
  ► VERB [freaks, freaking, freaked] an informal word meaning to suddenly become very angry or upset about something □ *She'll freak when she sees what they've done to her car.*

freckle /'frekəl/ NOUN [plural freckles] a small brown mark on your skin, especially your face
  • **freckled** /'frekəld/ ADJECTIVE covered in freckles □ *She has pale, freckled skin.*

free /friː/ ► ADJECTIVE
  1 not costing any money □ *It's free to get into the museum.* □ *I've got two free tickets for the show.*
  2 not controlled by people or laws □ *We were given free access to all the files.* □ *The country needs to hold free and fair elections.* □ **+ to do something** *You are free to leave whenever you wish.*
  3 not a prisoner □ *He is once more a free man.* 🔁 *They broke into the compound and set the prisoners free.*
  4 available to be used □ *Is this seat free?*
  5 not busy □ *Are you free this evening?*
  6 free time time when you are not busy and can do what you want
  7 free from/of something not containing or having a particular unpleasant thing □ *All our cakes are free from additives.*
  8 feel free something you say when you are saying that someone can do something or have something □ *Feel free to help yourself from the drinks machine.*
  ► ADVERB
  1 without any payment □ *Children under 5 travel free.*
  2 out of a place where a person or animal is being kept or tied up □ *They struggled to get free.* 🔁 *They managed to break free of their chains.*
  3 without being controlled □ *All their children were allowed to roam free.*
  ► VERB [frees, freeing, freed]

  1 to let a person or animal out of a prison or place where they were being kept □ *The remaining hostages were freed this morning.*
  2 to manage to get someone out of a place □ *A man was freed from the burning wreckage.*
  3 to take away something, for example work or problems, that makes someone's life difficult □ *The inheritance has freed her from the strain of supporting five children.*
  4 to make something available to be used □ **+ up** *Having the motorbike will free up the car for my wife to use.*
  • **-free** /friː/ SUFFIX -free is added to the end of words to mean 'without' □ *fat-free*
  • **freedom** /'friːdəm/ NOUN, NO PLURAL
  1 the right to do what you want 🔁 *freedom of speech/ movement*
  2 the state of not being a prisoner
  3 freedom from something not having something unpleasant □ *freedom from fear*

free enterprise /ˌfriː ˈentəpraɪz/ NOUN, NO PLURAL a system where businesses operate with little government control. An economics word.

freehand /'friːhænd/ ADJECTIVE, ADVERB a freehand drawing is done without the help of things such as a ruler

free kick /ˌfriː ˈkɪk/ NOUN [plural free kicks] when a football player is allowed to kick the ball without anyone from the other team trying to stop them

freelance /'friːlɑːns/ ADJECTIVE, ADVERB working for yourself and not working as a part of a company or organization □ *a freelance journalist* □ *Sally works freelance as a writer.*

freely /'friːli/ ADVERB
  1 without being limited or controlled 🔁 *The information is freely available.* □ *You can speak freely to me.*
  2 in a willing way 🔁 *I freely admit I was wrong.*

free market /ˌfriː ˈmɑːkɪt/ NOUN [plural free markets] a system where the price of goods depends on how much there is of something and how many people want it. An economics word.

free-range /ˌfriːˈreɪndʒ/ ADJECTIVE to do with animals that are allowed to move around a farm 🔁 *free-range eggs*

free speech /ˌfriː ˈspiːtʃ/ NOUN, NO PLURAL the right to express your opinions without being punished

freeway /'friːweɪ/ NOUN [plural freeways] the US word for motorway

freewheel /ˌfriːˈwiːl/ VERB [freewheels, freewheeling, freewheeled] to ride a bicycle without turning the pedals (= parts you push with your feet)

freeze /friːz/ ► VERB [freezes, freezing, froze, frozen]
  1 to become very cold and hard, or to turn into ice □ *The lake freezes in winter.* □ **+ over** *The river froze over* (= became covered in ice).
  2 to store food at a very cold temperature so it keeps for a long time □ *We'll eat some and freeze the rest.*

3 if someone freezes they become very cold □ *You'll freeze if you go out without a coat!*

4 to stop moving suddenly, usually because you are afraid □ *He froze when he saw the dog.*

5 to stop the level or amount of something increasing □ *University tuition fees have been frozen for the next two years.*

▶ NOUN [*plural* **freezes**]

1 when the level of something is fixed 🔄 *Doctors have accepted a pay freeze for this year.*

2 when a process is suddenly stopped □ *We need a freeze on all new airport expansion.*

3 a period of very cold weather

• **freezer** /'fri:zə(r)/ NOUN [*plural* **freezers**] a machine for keeping food very cold

• **freezing** /'fri:zɪŋ/ ADJECTIVE very cold □ *It's freezing in here!* 🔄 *It was freezing cold outside.*

freezing point /'fri:zɪŋ ,pɔɪnt/ NOUN [*plural* **freezing points**] the temperature at which a liquid becomes solid. A chemistry word.

freight /freɪt/ NOUN, NO PLURAL goods that are being carried by a truck, ship or plane

• **freighter** /'freɪtə(r)/ NOUN [*plural* **freighters**] a large ship or plane for carrying goods

French fries /,frentʃ 'fraɪz/ PLURAL NOUN long thin pieces of potato, fried in oil □ *a burger with French fries*

French horn /,frentʃ 'hɔ:n/ NOUN [*plural* **French horns**] a large musical instrument made of a curved metal tube which is wide at one end, played by blowing into it

French window /,frentʃ 'wɪndəu/ NOUN [*plural* **French windows**] a tall glass door that opens onto a garden

frenetic /frə'netɪk/ ADJECTIVE involving a lot of excitement and quick activity 🔄 *They work at such a frenetic pace.* 🔄 *The announcement was followed by a week of frenetic activity.*

frenzied /'frenzɪd/ ADJECTIVE very excited and uncontrolled 🔄 *a frenzied attack* 🔄 *frenzied activity*

frenzy /'frenzɪ/ NOUN, NO PLURAL a state or period of great excitement, activity and emotion 🔄 *a frenzy of activity* 🔄 *Their engagement has generated a media frenzy.*

frequency /'fri:kwənsɪ/ NOUN [*plural* **frequencies**]

1 how often something happens □ *Global warming may increase the frequency of severe hurricanes.*

2 the number of times sound or radio waves pass the same point in one second. A physics word. 🔄 *Many animals can hear higher frequencies than we can.*

• **frequent** /'fri:kwənt/ ADJECTIVE happening often □ *Dave makes frequent visits to his grandmother.* □ *His e-mails are becoming more frequent.*

• **frequently** /'fri:kwəntlɪ/ ADVERB often □ *Lee is frequently late for work.* □ *She frequently appears in women's magazines.*

fresh /freʃ/ ADJECTIVE [**fresher, freshest**]

1 fresh food is not old, and has not been dried, frozen, etc. 🔄 *fresh fruit/vegetables* □ *This salad will stay fresh for a day or two.*

2 new and different 🔄 *They hope to make a fresh start in Australia.* □ *I'll put some fresh sheets on the bed.*

3 fresh air is clean air in outside areas 🔄 *I'm going for a walk to get some fresh air.*

4 fresh water does not contain salt

5 made or done recently □ *A layer of fresh snow lay on the ground.*

6 having a pleasant, clean smell □ *a fresh, floral fragrance*

• **freshen** /'freʃən/ VERB [**freshens, freshening, freshened**] to make something fresher □ *I use a mouthwash to freshen my breath.*

• **freshly** /'freʃlɪ/ ADVERB only just made or done 🔄 *freshly baked bread*

• **freshness** /'freʃnɪs/ NOUN, NO PLURAL the quality of being fresh

freshwater /'freʃ,wɔ:tə(r)/ ADJECTIVE a freshwater fish lives in rivers and lakes, not in the sea

fret /fret/ VERB [**frets, fretting, fretted**] to feel worried and unable to relax □ *If he's late coming home she starts to fret.*

friction /'frɪkʃən/ NOUN, NO PLURAL

1 when one surface rubs against another surface, making movement more difficult. A physics word. □ *Oil is used to reduce friction.*

2 disagreement or arguing □ *The rumours have caused friction within the band.* 🔄 *Housework is a common source of friction between couples.*

Friday /'fraɪdɪ/ NOUN [*plural* **Fridays**] the day of the week after Thursday and before Saturday □ *It's my birthday on Friday.*

fridge /frɪdʒ/ NOUN [*plural* **fridges**] a machine that you store food or drink in to keep it cold and fresh □ *He opened the fridge to get some milk.* □ *There's some chocolate in the fridge.*

fried /fraɪd/ ▶ PAST TENSE AND PAST PARTICIPLE OF fry □ *She fried the fish in butter.*

▶ ADJECTIVE cooked in hot oil or fat □ *a fried egg*

friend /frend/ NOUN [*plural* **friends**]

1 someone who you know well and like □ *+ of She's a friend of mine.* 🔄 *Lindsay is my best friend.* 🔄 *They only told their family and close friends.*

2 friends if two people are friends, they know and like each other □ *+ with I'm friends with her sister.* 🔄 *They remained good friends after university.* 🔄 *The boys soon became friends.*

3 make friends (with someone) to meet and become friends with someone □ *She soon made friends.* □ *I made friends with Alex at college.*

• **friendliness** /'frendlɪnɪs/ NOUN, NO PLURAL

1 being friendly towards people

2 the quality of not harming something □ *They rate products in terms of their environmental friendliness.*

- **friendly** /ˈfrendlɪ/ ▶ ADJECTIVE [**friendlier, friendliest**]
1 kind and pleasant towards someone □ **+ to** *She's friendly to everyone.* □ *a friendly smile* □ *The staff are friendly and helpful.*
2 being friends with someone □ **+ with** *I've been friendly with the family for years.* 🔁 *He became friendly with Richard.*
3 to do with a game that is played for fun, not as part of a competition □ *a friendly match*
▶ NOUN [*plural* **friendlies**] a game played for fun, not as part of a competition □ *He's in the team for tomorrow's friendly against Spain.*

- **-friendly** /ˈfrendlɪ/ SUFFIX -friendly is added to the end of words to mean 'not harming something' or 'welcoming a particular type of people' □ *eco-friendly* (= not harming the environment) *packaging* □ *a child-friendly restaurant*

- **friendship** /ˈfrendʃɪp/ NOUN [*plural* **friendships**] the relationship you have with a friend 🔁 *We have a close friendship.* 🔁 *She formed a lifelong friendship with Ellis.*

---

frieze /friːz/ NOUN [*plural* **friezes**] a long narrow strip of decorated paper that you put on a wall

frigate /ˈfrɪɡət/ NOUN [*plural* **frigates**] a small military ship

fright /fraɪt/ NOUN [*plural* **frights**] a sudden feeling of fear 🔁 *You gave me a fright, jumping out like that!* 🔁 *I got a fright when I saw it.* 🔁 *She took fright* (= felt suddenly afraid) *and ran off.*

- **frighten** /ˈfraɪtən/ VERB [**frightens, frightening, frightened**] to make someone feel afraid or worried □ *A sudden noise frightened the horses.* □ *You'll frighten the baby!*

◆ PHRASAL VERB **frighten someone away/off** to make a person or animal so nervous that they move or run away □ *We lit a fire to frighten away wild animals.* □ *Too much technology might frighten customers off.*

- **frightened** /ˈfraɪtənd/ ADJECTIVE afraid or very worried □ **+ of** *He's frightened of dogs.* □ **+ to do something** *He was too frightened to tell his parents.* 🔁 *I felt very frightened.* □ *a frightened expression*

- **frightening** /ˈfraɪtənɪŋ/ ADJECTIVE making you feel afraid or very worried □ *a frightening experience* □ *They look very frightening.* □ *That's a frightening thought!*

- **frighteningly** /ˈfraɪtənɪŋlɪ/ ADVERB in a way that frightens or worries you □ *He's frighteningly fast.*

frill /frɪl/ NOUN [*plural* **frills**]
1 a narrow strip of cloth pulled into folds that is attached to something as a decoration
2 frills extra things which are added to something to make it more attractive, special, etc. 🔁 *It's a basic hotel with no frills.*

- **frilly** /ˈfrɪlɪ/ ADJECTIVE decorated with frills □ *a frilly skirt*

fringe /frɪndʒ/ ▶ NOUN [*plural* **fringes**]
1 hair that hangs down over the top part of your face

2 the outside edge of something □ *There's a lot of poor housing on the fringes of the city.*
3 loose threads that hang down from the edge of something as decoration
▶ ADJECTIVE not belonging to the main part, group or activity 🔁 *They're a fringe group and don't represent the views of the main party.*
▶ VERB [**fringes, fringing, fringed**] if a place or thing is fringed with something, it has that thing along its edge □ *The lake is fringed by trees.*

frisky /ˈfrɪskɪ/ ADJECTIVE [**friskier, friskiest**] lively and full of energy □ *a frisky puppy*

fritter /ˈfrɪtə(r)/
◆ PHRASAL VERB [**fritters, frittering, frittered**] fritter **something away** to waste time or money on silly things

frivolous /ˈfrɪvələs/ ADJECTIVE fun and not serious or necessary

frizzy /ˈfrɪzɪ/ ADJECTIVE [**frizzier, frizziest**] frizzy hair has very small tight curls

fro /frəʊ/ ADVERB to and fro backwards and forwards □ *The mast swayed to and fro.*

frog /frɒɡ/ NOUN [*plural* **frogs**] a small brown or green animal that can jump and swim and lives near water

frogman /ˈfrɒɡmən/ NOUN [*plural* **frogmen**] someone whose job is to swim under water wearing special clothes and using breathing equipment □ *police frogmen*

frogmarch /ˈfrɒɡmɑːtʃ/ VERB [**frogmarches, frogmarching, frogmarched**] if two people frogmarch someone somewhere, they force the person to walk there by holding each arm firmly

frolic /ˈfrɒlɪk/ VERB [**frolics, frolicking, frolicked**] to play in a lively and happy way □ *Lambs were frolicking in the fields.*

from /frəm/ PREPOSITION
1 used to show where or when something started or where it was before □ *She's driving up from London.* □ *The shops are open from nine to five.* □ *He took a photograph from the drawer.* □ *You can get batteries from the shop over the road.* □ *He stole some money from his parents.*
2 used to show who gave or sent something □ *I had a lovely card from Julie.*
3 used to show where someone was born or lives □ *I'm from Taiwan.*
4 used to show what something is made of or what has caused something □ *Yogurt is made from milk.* □ *He was shivering from the cold.*
5 used to show how far something is □ *Do you live far from here?* □ *We are 15 miles from the nearest supermarket.*
6 from now on starting now and continuing into the future □ *From now on I'll be much more careful about locking the house.*

front /frʌnt/ ▶ NOUN [*plural* **fronts**]
1 the part of something that faces forwards, or the part that is furthest forwards □ *The house has a red front.* □ *The front of the car was badly damaged.*

2 in front of someone/something (a) next to the front part of something □ *Please don't park in front of the gates.* □ *He stood right in front of me.* □ *She jumped in front of the moving train.* (b) where someone can see or hear you □ *He hit the children in front of their parents.* □ *She loves performing in front of a large audience.*

3 in front further forward than someone or something □ *I was driving along when the car in front suddenly stopped.*

4 an area where fighting takes place during a war
▶ ADJECTIVE at the front of something 🔁 *I knocked on the front door.* 🔁 *We sat in the front row.*

frontier /ˈfrʌntɪə(r)/ NOUN [*plural* **frontiers**]
1 a dividing line between two countries □ *Pakistan's western frontier* □ **+ of** *He extended the frontiers of his empire.* □ **+ with** *The mountains mark Nepal's frontier with India.*
2 the newest or most advanced ideas or the limits of our knowledge □ *We aim to advance the frontiers of biotechnology.*

frost /frɒst/ NOUN [*plural* **frosts**]
1 *no plural* a very thin layer of white ice that forms on surfaces outside when the weather is cold □ *There's frost on the ground.*
2 a time when frost forms 🔁 *There was a hard frost last night.*

frostbite /ˈfrɒstbaɪt/ NOUN, NO PLURAL an injury to parts of the body, especially the fingers and toes, caused by extreme cold

frosted /ˈfrɒstɪd/ ADJECTIVE frosted glass has a surface that you cannot see through

frosty /ˈfrɒstɪ/ ADJECTIVE [**frostier, frostiest**]
1 when it is frosty, everything is covered in frost (= a thin, white layer of ice) □ *a frosty morning*
2 not friendly □ *Relations between the two countries have been frosty for some time.*

froth /frɒθ/ ▶ NOUN, NO PLURAL a lot of small bubbles on top of a liquid □ *She stirred the thick froth on her cappuccino.*
▶ VERB [**froths, frothing, frothed**] to form froth
● **frothy** /ˈfrɒθɪ/ ADJECTIVE [**frothier, frothiest**] with froth on the top □ *a frothy milkshake*

frown /fraʊn/ ▶ VERB [**frowns, frowning, frowned**] to look as if you are angry, worried or thinking a lot by moving your eyebrows (= lines of hair above your eyes) down □ *She frowned when I suggested it.*
◆ PHRASAL VERB **frown on/upon something/ someone** to disapprove of something or someone □ *Smoking is frowned on.*
▶ NOUN [*plural* **frowns**] when you frown

froze /frəʊz/ PAST TENSE OF freeze □ *The milk froze in the fridge.*

frozen /ˈfrəʊzən/ ▶ PAST PARTICIPLE OF freeze □ *It was so cold that the lake had frozen.*
▶ ADJECTIVE frozen food is stored at a very cold temperature to make it last for a long time □ *a packet of frozen peas*

fructose /ˈfrʌktəʊs/ NOUN, NO PLURAL a type of sugar found in some types of fruit. A biology word.

frugal /ˈfruːgəl/ ADJECTIVE careful with your money and saving it instead of spending a lot

fruit /fruːt/ NOUN
1 *no plural* a food such as an apple or a banana which grows on a plant and contains the seeds of the plant 🔁 *fruit and vegetables* 🔁 *We eat plenty of fresh fruit.* 🔁 *I usually have a piece of fruit for breakfast.*
2 **the fruits of something** the good results of something, especially work □ *We're now seeing the fruits of our labour.*

> ➤ Note that **fruit** is not usually used in the plural. Sometimes the plural **fruits** is used, meaning 'types of fruit' but it is not common:
> ✓ You should eat more fruit.
> ✗ You should eat more fruits.

fruitcake /ˈfruːtkeɪk/ NOUN [*plural* **fruitcakes**] a cake containing dried fruits

fruitful /ˈfruːtfʊl/ ADJECTIVE having good results □ *a fruitful meeting*

fruition /fruːˈɪʃən/ NOUN, NO PLURAL a formal word for the result you have been trying to achieve □ *This is the fruition of five years' work.* 🔁 *The plan never came to fruition.*

fruitless /ˈfruːtlɪs/ ADJECTIVE not producing the result you wanted □ *a fruitless search*

fruit salad /ˌfruːtˈsæləd/ NOUN [*plural* **fruit salads**] a dish of small pieces of different fruit

frumpy /ˈfrʌmpɪ/ ADJECTIVE [**frumpier, frumpiest**] wearing old-fashioned clothes that do not make you look attractive

frustrate /frʌˈstreɪt/ VERB [**frustrates, frustrating, frustrated**]
1 to make you feel annoyed because you cannot do or achieve what you want □ *It frustrates me that we can't get started sooner.* □ *Call centres often frustrate customers.*
2 to prevent someone from doing something □ *Bad weather frustrated efforts to rescue the men.*
● **frustrated** /frʌˈstreɪtɪd/ ADJECTIVE annoyed because you cannot do or achieve what you want □ *He became increasingly frustrated at the lack of progress.* □ *frustrated passengers*
● **frustrating** /frʌˈstreɪtɪŋ/ ADJECTIVE making you feel frustrated □ *frustrating delays* □ *It's very frustrating for everyone concerned.*
● **frustration** /frʌˈstreɪʃən/ NOUN [*plural* **frustrations**] a feeling of being frustrated or something that causes this feeling □ *She expressed frustration at the authorities.* □ *We all moan about the frustrations of office life.*

fry /fraɪ/ VERB [**fries, frying, fried**] to cook something in hot oil or fat □ *Fry the onions in a little olive oil.*

frying pan /ˈfraɪɪŋ ˌpæn/ NOUN [*plural* **frying pans**] a flat pan with a long handle for frying food □ *Heat the* oil in a large frying pan. ◆ IDIOM out of the frying pan into the fire used for saying that someone has left one bad situation but is now in a different and much worse situation

ft /ˌefˈtiː/ ABBREVIATION foot (= measurement) or feet

fudge /fʌdʒ/ ▶ NOUN, NO PLURAL a soft sweet made from butter and sugar
▶ VERB [fudges, fudging, fudged] to avoid giving a clear answer or details □ The final report fudged the issue.

fuel /fjuəl/ ▶ NOUN [plural fuels] a substance such as gas, wood or coal that burns to give heat, light or power □ The trains run on diesel fuel. 🔒 fuel consumption
▶ VERB [fuels, fuelling/US fueling, fuelled/US fueled]
1 to make something stronger, worse, etc. □ His comments have fuelled speculation that he might resign. □ The riots were fuelled by anger and frustration.
2 to use or to put fuel into a vehicle, machine, etc. □ The power station is fuelled by coal.

fugitive /ˈfjuːdʒətɪv/ NOUN [plural fugitives] someone who has escaped from the police

-ful /fʊl/ SUFFIX
1 -ful is added to the end of words to mean 'full of' □ joyful
2 -ful is added to the end of words to mean 'the amount that something holds' □ spoonful

fulfil /fʊlˈfɪl/ VERB [fulfils, fulfilling, fulfilled]
1 to do a particular job or something you are expected to do 🔒 He fulfils a vital role within the team. 🔒 He failed to fulfil his financial obligations.
2 to achieve something you wanted to do 🔒 It was a chance to fulfil a childhood dream.
3 to have the qualities or standard needed for something 🔒 Only those who fulfil very strict criteria are accepted.
• **fulfilling** /fʊlˈfɪlɪŋ/ ADJECTIVE making you feel that you have achieved something good □ Being a youth worker is a fulfilling job.
• **fulfilment** /fʊlˈfɪlmənt/ NOUN, NO PLURAL
1 a feeling of having achieved something good □ It gives you a sense of fulfilment.
2 when you do something that you have always wanted to do or have promised to do □ This is the fulfilment of a dream for me. □ the fulfilment of their duties
fulfill /fʊlˈfɪl/ VERB [fulfills, fulfilling, fulfilled] the US spelling of fulfil
• **fulfillment** /fʊlˈfɪlmənt/ NOUN, NO PLURAL the US spelling of fulfilment

full /fʊl/ ADJECTIVE [fuller, fullest]
1 containing as much as possible □ The train was full. □ He gave me a full bottle of milk. □ The jug was only half full.
2 containing a lot of something □ Your work is full of mistakes. □ My socks are full of holes.

3 complete 🔒 He told me the full story. 🔒 She made a full recovery.
4 having eaten enough □ + up No more cake for me, thanks - I'm full up.
5 full speed/volume,etc. as fast/loud, etc. as possible
6 in full in a complete form □ The interview was published in full.
➡ go to give full rein to something

full moon /ˌfʊl ˈmuːn/ NOUN [plural full moons] the moon when it is a complete circle

full stop /ˌfʊl ˈstɒp/ NOUN [plural full stops] the mark (.) used for showing where a sentence ends

full-time /ˌfʊlˈtaɪm/ ADJECTIVE, ADVERB working for all the hours of a normal job, not part of the time 🔒 a full-time job 🔒 a full-time employee 🔒 We both work full-time.

fully /ˈfʊli/ ADVERB completely □ He hasn't fully recovered from the accident. □ We are fully aware of the problem. □ The hotel is fully booked.

fumble /ˈfʌmbəl/ VERB [fumbles, fumbling, fumbled] to use your hands in an awkward way, often to try to find something □ Raj fumbled in his pocket for the key.

fume /fjuːm/ VERB [fumes, fuming, fumed] to be very angry about something □ She's absolutely fuming over the decision.
• **fumes** /fjuːmz/ PLURAL NOUN smoke or gas that is unpleasant to breathe in 🔒 the smell of exhaust fumes □ He was overcome by the fumes from the fire.

fun /fʌn/ NOUN, NO PLURAL
1 enjoyment and pleasure 🔒 Skateboarding is really good fun. 🔒 It was great fun! 🔒 We had a lot of fun at the party. □ That sounds like fun.
2 make fun of someone/something to make jokes about someone or something, in a way that is not kind □ They're always making fun of my accent.

function /ˈfʌŋkʃən/ ▶ NOUN [plural functions]
1 the purpose of someone or something 🔒 Proteins perform different functions in the body. 🔒 The operating system controls the basic functions of a computer.
2 a large social event 🔒 a social function 🔒 The hotel often hosts private functions such as weddings.
▶ VERB [functions, functioning, functioned] to work in the correct way 🔒 In some patients these cells don't function properly. □ The system seems to be functioning normally.
• **functional** /ˈfʌŋkʃənəl/ ADJECTIVE
1 practical and useful □ a functional design
2 working correctly □ The ship has been repaired and is now fully functional.

function key /ˈfʌŋkʃən ˌkiː/ NOUN [plural function keys] one of the keys at the top of a computer keyboard that has an F and a number on it. A computing word.

fund /fʌnd/ ► NOUN [plural **funds**]
1 an amount of money for a particular purpose □ *a pension fund* □ *We set up a fund for victims of the earthquake.*
2 funds money available to spend ▣ *Should we spend public funds on such projects?* ▣ *The event was to raise funds for charity.*
► VERB [**funds, funding, funded**] to provide money for a particular purpose □ *The research was funded by the Medical Research Council.*

fundamental /ˌfʌndə'mentəl/ ADJECTIVE basic and important □ *the fundamental rules of management* □ *This raises some fundamental questions.*
• **fundamentalism** /ˌfʌndə'mentəˌlɪzəm/ NOUN, NO PLURAL a belief that traditional religious rules should be followed exactly
• **fundamentalist** /ˌfʌndə'mentəlɪst/ NOUN [plural **fundamentalists**] someone who believes that traditional religious rules should be followed exactly □ *religious fundamentalists*
• **fundamentally** /ˌfʌndə'mentəlɪ/ ADVERB in a basic and important way □ *I fundamentally disagree.* □ *They have fundamentally different views of the world.*
• **fundamentals** /ˌfʌndə'mentəlz/ PLURAL NOUN the basic parts, rules, etc. of something □ *They learn the fundamentals of website design.*

funding /'fʌndɪŋ/ NOUN, NO PLURAL money for a particular purpose, especially from a government ▣ *public funding* ▣ *The council provides funding for the homeless shelter.*

funeral /'fju:nərəl/ NOUN [plural **funerals**] a ceremony for a person who has recently died in which the body of the dead person is buried or burned ▣ *I didn't go to her funeral.*

funfair /'fʌnfeə(r)/ NOUN [plural **funfairs**] an event at which people can enjoy themselves going on rides (= large machines you ride on for fun) and playing games

fungus /'fʌngəs/ NOUN [plural **fungi**] a plant with no leaves or flowers, for example a mushroom

funnel /'fʌnəl/ NOUN [plural **funnels**]
1 a tube that is wide at the top and narrow at the bottom, used for pouring liquid into a container
2 a large tube through which smoke leaves a ship

funnily /'fʌnɪlɪ/ ADVERB in a way that seems strange or surprising ▣ *Funnily enough, we were born on exactly the same day.*

funny /'fʌnɪ/ ADJECTIVE [**funnier, funniest**]
1 making you laugh □ *a funny story* □ *I don't find him very funny.* □ *They looked so funny that she had to smile.* ▣ *Luckily, he saw the funny side of the situation.*
2 strange, surprising or unusual □ *There was a funny noise coming from the engine.* ▣ *The funny thing is, I was just about to call him when he called me.*

➤ Do not confuse the adjective **funny** with the noun **fun**. Something that is **funny** makes you laugh. Something that you describe as **fun** is very enjoyable although it may not make you laugh:
□ *That was such a funny film – I laughed all the way through.* □ *Skating is fun.*

funny bone /'fʌnɪ ˌbəʊn/ NOUN [plural **funny bones**] a part of your elbow that hurts when you hit it against something

fur /fɜ:(r)/ NOUN, NO PLURAL
1 the soft hair on some animals □ *a rabbit with soft, brown fur*
2 the skin and fur of an animal when it is removed or material made to look like this □ *a fur hat*

furious /'fjʊərɪəs/ ADJECTIVE
1 extremely angry □ *We're absolutely furious about this.* □ *I had a furious row with Charlotte.*
2 done with a lot of energy, activity or speed □ *He set off at a furious pace.*
• **furiously** /'fjʊərɪəslɪ/ ADVERB
1 in a way that shows you are very angry □ *Clive reacted furiously.*
2 very fast or with a lot of energy □ *They worked furiously to get everything clean.*

furnace /'fɜ:nɪs/ NOUN [plural **furnaces**] a large, very hot oven used in some industrial processes

furnish /'fɜ:nɪʃ/ VERB [**furnishes, furnishing, furnished**] to put furniture in a house or room □ *The six large rooms are furnished with antiques.*
• PHRASAL VERB **furnish someone with something** to give something to someone, especially information. A formal phrase.
• **furnishings** /'fɜ:nɪʃɪŋz/ PLURAL NOUN the furniture, carpets and curtains in a house or room

furniture /'fɜ:nɪtʃə(r)/ NOUN, NO PLURAL objects such as beds, tables and chairs that you put in a room ▣ *A small bed and an old wardrobe were the only pieces of furniture in the room.*

➤ Remember that **furniture** is an uncountable noun:
✓ *We don't have any furniture.*
✗ *We don't have any furnitures.*

furor /'fjʊrɔ:r/ NOUN, NO PLURAL the US spelling of furore

furore /fjʊ'rɔ:rɪ/ NOUN, NO PLURAL general excitement or anger in reaction to something ▣ *Her appointment caused a furore.*

furrow /'fʌrəʊ/ ► NOUN [plural **furrows**]
1 a long narrow cut made in the ground by a plough (= farm equipment)
2 a deep line in the skin of your face, especially above your eyes □ *He gazed out of the window with a slight furrow of his brow.*
► VERB [**furrows, furrowing, furrowed**] to make a furrow in your skin when you are worried,

concentrating etc. □ *His brow furrowed in concentration.*

furry /ˈfɜːrɪ/ ADJECTIVE [**furrier, furriest**] covered in fur □ *a small furry animal*

further /ˈfɜːðə(r)/ ▶ ADJECTIVE, ADVERB

1 at or to a greater distance away □ **+ from** *Which is further from here, London or Aberdeen?* □ **+ up** *Santa Monica is a few miles further up the coast.* □ *I walked further than I needed.* □ *We travelled further north.*

2 more or extra 🕮 *If you need further information, please ask.* □ *He refused to comment further* (= say more). 🕮 *Prices may rise even further.*

▶ VERB [**furthers, furthering, furthered**] to help something be successful □ *These qualifications will help further your career.*

further education /ˈfɜːðə ˌedjuˈkeɪʃən/ NOUN, NO PLURAL education or training for people who have left school but do not go to university

furthermore /ˌfɜːðəˈmɔː(r)/ ADVERB a formal word used when you are adding something to what you have already said □ *His plans will be very expensive. Furthermore, they will cause a lot of disruption.*

furthest /ˈfɜːðəst/ ADVERB, ADJECTIVE at or to the greatest distance or amount □ *Who can throw the ball the furthest?* □ **+ from** *They sat in the corner furthest from the door.* □ *We reached the furthest point south.*

furtive /ˈfɜːtɪv/ ADJECTIVE done secretly to avoid being seen □ *a furtive glance*
• **furtively** /ˈfɜːtɪvlɪ/ ADVERB in a furtive way □ *He whispered furtively.*

fury /ˈfjʊərɪ/ NOUN, NO PLURAL a very strong feeling of anger □ *The announcement sparked fury from unions.*

fuse /fjuːz/ ▶ NOUN [*plural* **fuses**]

1 a wire inside a piece of electrical equipment that makes it stop working if too much electricity passes through it 🕮 *I think the fuse has blown.*

2 the part of a bomb or firework that starts the explosion 🕮 *Light the fuse and stand well back.*

◆ IDIOM **a short fuse** if someone has a short fuse, they become angry very easily □ *Tom has a very short fuse.*

▶ VERB [**fuses, fusing, fused**]

1 if two things fuse or are fused, they join together to form one thing □ *The broken bones will eventually fuse back together.*

2 if a piece of electrical equipment fuses, the fuse stops it working

fuselage /ˈfjuːzəlɑːʒ/ NOUN [*plural* **fuselages**] the main part of an aeroplane

fusion /ˈfjuːʒən/ NOUN, NO PLURAL

1 when two or more things are combined □ *He experimented with a fusion of styles, mixing flamenco with jazz.*

2 when the nuclei (= centre parts) of atoms are combined to produce nuclear energy. A physics word. 🕮 *nuclear fusion*

fuss /fʌs/ ▶ NOUN, NO PLURAL

1 unnecessary worry, excitement or anger about something □ *I don't know what all the fuss is about.* 🕮 *I don't want to make a fuss about it.*

2 **make a fuss of someone** to give someone a lot of attention □ *He made a great fuss of her when she visited.*

▶ VERB [**fusses, fussing, fussed**] to worry too much about something or give it too much attention □ *She fusses over her pet dog.*

• **fussy** /ˈfʌsɪ/ ADJECTIVE [**fussier, fussiest**]

1 worrying too much about small details that are not important

2 only liking particular things □ *Children can be so fussy about food.* 🕮 *a fussy eater*

futile /ˈfjuːtaɪl/ ADJECTIVE having no effect or result 🕮 *He made a futile attempt to escape.* □ *Their efforts proved futile.*

• **futility** /fjuːˈtɪlətɪ/ NOUN, NO PLURAL when something is not likely to have any effect or result □ *the futility of war*

futon /ˈfuːtɒn/ NOUN [*plural* **futons**] a simple bed on a wooden frame or on the floor that can also be folded to use as a seat

future /ˈfjuːtʃə(r)/ ▶ NOUN [*plural* **futures**]

1 **the future** the time to come after now □ *You can't know what will happen to you in the future.* 🕮 *We expect a decision in the near future.* 🕮 *We won't be moving, at least for the foreseeable future.*

2 what will happen to someone or something in the future □ **+ of** *Digital technology is threatening the future of the music industry.* 🕮 *He has a bright future in management.*

3 **in future** in the time from now on □ *In future, please be more careful.*

▶ ADJECTIVE happening or existing in a time after now □ *future plans* □ *We need to preserve the planet for future generations.*

future tense /ˌfjuːtʃə ˈtens/ NOUN [*plural* **future tenses**] the form of a verb that you use when you are talking about what will happen in the future

futuristic /ˌfjuːtʃəˈrɪstɪk/ ADJECTIVE seeming to belong in the future, or about events in the future □ *futuristic buildings*

fuzz /fʌz/ NOUN, NO PLURAL thin, light hair or feathers
• **fuzzy** /ˈfʌzɪ/ ADJECTIVE [**fuzzier, fuzziest**]

1 not clear □ *a fuzzy image*

2 covered in soft short hair

Gg

G *or* **g** /dʒiː/ the seventh letter of the alphabet

g /dʒiː/ ABBREVIATION gram or grams

gab /gæb/ NOUN, NO PLURAL
- ◆ IDIOM **have the gift of the gab** to be good at talking □ *A salesman needs to have the gift of the gab.*

gabble /ˈgæbəl/ VERB [**gabbles, gabbling, gabbled**] to talk so quickly that it is difficult for other people to understand what you are saying

gable /ˈgeɪbəl/ NOUN [*plural* **gables**] a side of a building where the wall and the roof form a triangular shape

gadget /ˈgædʒɪt/ NOUN [*plural* **gadgets**] a tool or small piece of equipment □ *I've got a gadget to unblock the sink.*

gaffe /gæf/ NOUN [*plural* **gaffes**] when someone says or does something that upsets or embarrasses people, often without meaning to □ *His first gaffe was asking my mother her age.*

gag /gæg/ ▶ NOUN [*plural* **gags**]
1 something put over someone's mouth to stop them speaking
2 an informal word meaning a joke
▶ VERB [**gags, gagging, gagged**]
1 to put a gag over someone's mouth to stop them speaking 🔁 *The bank manager was found, bound and gagged, in an office.*
2 to stop someone talking about something □ *The government took steps to gag the media.*
3 to feel as if you are going to vomit □ *The smell of raw meat made her gag.*

gaggle /ˈgægəl/ NOUN [*plural* **gaggles**] a group of noisy people □ *a gaggle of young girls*

gaily /ˈgeɪli/ ADVERB
1 in a happy way □ *She laughed gaily.*
2 with bright colours □ *gaily coloured banners*

gain /geɪn/ ▶ VERB [**gains, gaining, gained**]
1 to get or achieve something □ *You gain twenty extra points for that move.* 🔁 *We could not gain access* (= get in) *to the building.* 🔁 *Rebel soldiers have fought to gain control of the area.*
2 to increase in amount, speed, weight, etc. □ *I gained over 20 kilos when I was pregnant.*
3 to get something good from a situation □ *It's wrong that criminals should gain from their crimes by writing books.* 🔁 *There's nothing to be gained by waiting any longer.*
- ◆ IDIOM **gain ground** to become more successful when compared to someone or something else □ *They are gaining ground on the larger companies.*

- ◆ PHRASAL VERB **gain on someone** to get closer to someone in a race or competition
▶ NOUN [*plural* **gains**]
1 something that you get or achieve that is more than you had before □ *Her loss was my gain.* □ *The party made big gains in the local elections.*
2 money or advantages that someone gets □ *personal/political gain*

gait /geɪt/ NOUN, NO PLURAL the way someone walks □ *His gait was unsteady, and he seemed confused.*

gala /ˈgɑːlə/ NOUN [*plural* **galas**] a special public event or entertainment □ *a swimming gala* □ *a gala dinner*

galaxy /ˈgæləksi/ NOUN [*plural* **galaxies**] a very large group of stars in the universe □ *Our galaxy is the Milky Way.*

gale /geɪl/ NOUN [*plural* **gales**] a very strong wind □ *The old apple tree blew down in a gale.*

gall /gɔːl/ ▶ VERB [**galls, galling, galled**] if something galls you, it annoys you □ *What really galls me is that she never apologized.*
▶ NOUN, NO PLURAL **have the gall to do something** to be rude enough to do something □ *He wouldn't have the gall to say something like that.*

gallant /ˈgælənt/ ADJECTIVE
1 brave □ *It was a gallant effort to win the title.*
2 very polite and showing respect, especially to women □ *a gallant young man*
- • **gallantry** /ˈgæləntri/ NOUN, NO PLURAL being gallant □ *He won an award for gallantry in battle.*

gall bladder /ˈgɔːl ˌblædə(r)/ NOUN [*plural* **gall bladders**] an organ near your liver where a substance that helps you digest food is stored. A biology word.

galleon /ˈgæliən/ NOUN [*plural* **galleons**] a large Spanish sailing ship used in the sixteenth and seventeenth centuries

gallery /ˈgæləri/ NOUN [*plural* **galleries**]
1 a large building or a shop where works of art are shown to the public
2 an open floor high up at the back or side of a large room, for example a theatre □ *Seats in the gallery are usually much cheaper.*

galley /ˈgæli/ NOUN [*plural* **galleys**]
1 a kitchen on a boat or aeroplane
2 a type of ship used by the Ancient Greeks and Romans

gallon /ˈgælən/ NOUN [*plural* **gallons**] a unit for measuring liquids, equal to 8 pints

gallop /'gæləp/ ► VERB [gallops, galloping, galloped] a horse gallops when it runs at its fastest speed with all four feet off the ground at the same time
♦ PHRASAL VERB **gallop through something** to do something very quickly □ *We seem to be galloping through the work today.*
► NOUN [plural **gallops**]
1 a fast run □ *She set off at a gallop.*
2 a ride on a horse going at this speed

gallows /'gæləʊz/ NOUN [plural **gallows**] a high wooden frame where criminals were killed in the past by hanging them □ *He was sent to the gallows for murder.*

galore /gə'lɔ:(r)/ ADJECTIVE used after a noun to emphasize that there is a large number of that thing □ *There were goals galore in this afternoon's match.*

galvanize or **galvanise** /'gælvə,naɪz/ VERB [galvanizes, galvanizing, galvanized]
1 to shock someone and make them suddenly decide to do something 🔄 *His father's death galvanized him into action.*
2 to cover metal with a layer of zinc (= blue-white metal) to stop it being damaged by water

gamble /'gæmbəl/ ► VERB [gambles, gambling, gambled] to risk money on the result of a game, race or competition □ *He enjoyed gambling on horse races.*
♦ PHRASAL VERB **gamble on something** to take a risk that something will happen □ *We've decided to gamble on the rain stopping before we have our barbecue.*
► NOUN [plural **gambles**] something you decide to do that is a risk 🔄 *We took a gamble on the weather.* 🔄 *Their gamble paid off (= was successful).*
• **gambler** /'gæmblə(r)/ NOUN [plural **gamblers**] someone who gambles money on the result of a race or game
• **gambling** /'gæmblɪŋ/ NOUN, NO PLURAL the activity of risking money on the result of a game, race or competition

game /geɪm/ NOUN [plural **games**]
1 an activity that people do for enjoyment, that has rules, often needs skill, and is usually won or lost □ *a computer game* 🔄 *After dinner, we all played games.* □ *a game of tennis/chess*
2 in some sports, a game is one of the parts of a complete match □ *He won the first set 7 games to 5.*
3 games when people do sport at school or at an organized event □ *the Olympic Games*
4 no plural wild animals and birds that are hunted for their meat
5 something that someone is not serious about □ *Running a business is just a game to her.*
♦ IDIOM **give the game away** to let someone know something that spoils a surprise or a secret

gamekeeper /'geɪm,ki:pə(r)/ NOUN [plural **gamekeepers**] someone whose job is to look after wild animals and birds on private land where they are going to be hunted

gamer /'geɪmə(r)/ NOUN [plural **gamers**] someone who plays a lot of computer games

game show /'geɪm ,ʃəʊ/ NOUN [plural **game shows**] a television programme where people play games

gamete /'gæmi:t/ NOUN [plural **gametes**] a cell that joins with a cell of the opposite sex to form a cell that grows into a person, animal or plant. A biology word.

gamma globulin /,gæmə 'glɒbjʊlɪn/ NOUN, NO PLURAL a substance in the blood that gives protection against some diseases. A biology word.

gamma radiation /'gæmə ,reɪdɪ'eɪʃən/ NOUN, NO PLURAL rays that are produced by some radioactive substances. A physics word.

gander /'gændə(r)/ NOUN [plural **ganders**] a male goose

gang /gæŋ/ NOUN [plural **gangs**]
1 a group of young people who spend time together and often cause trouble □ *Her son's got involved in a gang in town.*
2 an organized group of criminals □ *Police have arrested a gang of bank robbers.*
3 an informal word meaning a group of friends who meet regularly □ *I'm meeting up with the gang tonight.*
♦ PHRASAL VERB [gangs, ganging, ganged] **gang up on someone** to form a group to attack or criticize someone □ *She felt that the other girls were ganging up on her.*

gangling /'gæŋglɪŋ/ or **gangly** /'gæŋglɪ/ ADJECTIVE tall and thin □ *a gangling youth*

gangrene /'gæŋgri:n/ NOUN, NO PLURAL a medical condition where a part of the body dies because blood is not flowing through it

gangster /'gæŋstə(r)/ NOUN [plural **gangsters**] a member of a group of criminals

gangway /'gæŋweɪ/ NOUN [plural **gangways**]
1 a narrow passage where people can walk between rows of seats, for example on an aeroplane or in a cinema
2 a narrow bridge used to get on and off a ship

gaol /dʒeɪl/ NOUN [plural **gaols**] another spelling of jail
• **gaoler** /'dʒeɪlə(r)/ NOUN [plural **gaolers**] another spelling of jailer

gap /gæp/ NOUN [plural **gaps**]
1 an opening or space in the middle of something or between things □ *The fox got through a gap in the wall.* □ *He has a gap between his front teeth.*
2 a difference between two things □ *The gap between rich and poor is widening.* 🔄 *There's a big age gap between her two children.*
3 something missing □ *There's a gap in his memory around the time of the accident.*
4 a period of time when something stops □ *He's going back to university after a three-year gap.*

gape /geɪp/ VERB [gapes, gaping, gaped]
1 to look at someone or something with your mouth open, usually because you are very surprised or impressed □ *We all gaped at her in amazement.*
2 to be wide open □ *Her dressing gown was gaping open.*

• **gaping** /'geɪpɪŋ/ ADJECTIVE wide open 💬 *a gaping hole/wound*

gap year /'gæp jɪə(r)/ NOUN [plural **gap years**] a year between school and university that some students spend working or travelling □ *She took a gap year and went to Australia.*

garage /'gærɑːʒ, 'gærɪdʒ/ NOUN [plural **garages**]
1 a small building that you keep your car in
2 a place where vehicles are repaired, or a shop selling petrol

garbage /'gɑːbɪdʒ/ NOUN, NO PLURAL the US word for rubbish

garbled /'gɑːbəld/ ADJECTIVE not clear and not correct □ *I heard a garbled version of what happened.*

garden /'gɑːdən/ NOUN [plural **gardens**]
1 a piece of land next to a house where flowers, trees and vegetables are grown 💬 *The front garden is mainly lawn.*
2 gardens a large area of grass, trees, flowers, etc. for the public to use or around a big house

• **gardener** /'gɑːdnə(r)/ NOUN [plural **gardeners**] someone who works in a garden

• **gardening** /'gɑːdnɪŋ/ NOUN, NO PLURAL the activity of working in and taking care of a garden

gargle /'gɑːgəl/ VERB [gargles, gargling, gargled] to move a liquid around in your mouth without swallowing in order to clean your mouth

garish /'geərɪʃ/ ADJECTIVE garish colours or patterns are too bright □ *He was wearing a hideous jacket in garish green stripes.*

garland /'gɑːlənd/ NOUN [plural **garlands**] flowers or leaves twisted together into a circle □ *Christmas garlands of holly and ivy*

garlic /'gɑːlɪk/ NOUN, NO PLURAL a plant like a small onion with a strong taste and smell used in cooking to add flavour 💬 *Crush two cloves of garlic with the spices.*

garment /'gɑːmənt/ NOUN [plural **garments**] a formal word meaning a piece of clothing

garnish /'gɑːnɪʃ/ ▶ VERB [garnishes, garnishing, garnished] to decorate food with something such as herbs or pieces of fruit or vegetables □ *Garnish the fish with slices of cucumber.*
▶ NOUN [plural **garnishes**] something used to garnish food □ *The chicken was served with a garnish of parsley.*

garrison /'gærɪsən/ NOUN [plural **garrisons**] a group of soldiers living in and guarding a town or building

garrulous /'gærələs/ ADJECTIVE garrulous people talk too much

gas /gæs/ ▶ NOUN [plural **gases** or **gasses**]
1 a substance that is not liquid or solid and that moves about like air □ *Oxygen and carbon dioxide are two of the gases that make up air.*
2 no plural a gas or mixture of gases that burns easily and is used for cooking or heating □ *a gas fire*
3 no plural the US word for petrol

▶ VERB [gasses, gassing, gassed] to kill a person or animal using poisonous gas

gaseous /'gæsɪəs, 'geɪsɪəs/ ADJECTIVE to do with gas or in the form of gas. A chemistry and physics word.

gash /gæʃ/ ▶ NOUN [plural **gashes**] a deep open cut □ *She had a gash in her leg.*
▶ VERB [gashes, gashing, gashed] to make a long deep cut in something

gas mask /'gæs ˌmɑːsk/ NOUN [plural **gas masks**] a cover for your nose and mouth that protects you from poisonous gas

gasoline /'gæsəliːn/ NOUN, NO PLURAL the US word for petrol

gasp /gɑːsp/ ▶ VERB [gasps, gasping, gasped]
1 to take a short sudden breath in through your open mouth because you are shocked or surprised □ *They all gasped in horror.*
2 to find it hard to breathe 💬 *He slumped to the floor, gasping for breath.*
▶ NOUN [plural **gasps**] the sound of a sudden short breath

gastric /'gæstrɪk/ ADJECTIVE to do with the stomach □ *a gastric ulcer*

gastroenteritis /ˌgæstrəʊˌentəˈraɪtɪs/ NOUN, NO PLURAL a painful stomach illness caused by a virus or by bacteria in food

gastropod /'gæstrəpɒd/ NOUN [plural **gastropods**] an animal with a soft body and often a shell, for example a snail. A biology word.

gastropub /'gæstrəʊpʌb/ NOUN [plural **gastropubs**] a pub which sells good quality food

gate /geɪt/ NOUN [plural **gates**]
1 the part of a fence, wall etc. that opens and closes like a door □ *Please close the gate.*
2 the place where passengers get on or off a plane at an airport □ *Flight BA123 to Rome is now boarding at Gate 12.*

gateau /'gætəʊ/ NOUN [plural **gateaus** or **gateaux**] a large cake made in layers, usually decorated with cream, chocolate or fruit □ *a chocolate gateau*

gatecrash /'geɪtkræʃ/ VERB [gatecrashes, gatecrashing, gatecrashed] to go to a party or other private event without being invited □ *A gang of youths had gatecrashed the party.*

• **gatecrasher** /'geɪtkræʃə(r)/ NOUN [plural **gatecrashers**] someone who goes to a party without being invited

gateway /'geɪtweɪ/ NOUN [plural **gateways**]
1 an opening in a fence or wall with a gate in it
2 the way to get somewhere or to achieve something □ *This invention is the gateway to the future.*
3 a connection between two computer systems that allows information to be passed between them. A computing word.

gather /'gæðə(r)/ VERB [gathers, gathering, gathered]
1 if people gather or are gathered, they come together or are brought together in a group 💬 *A crowd gathered*

at the airport. □ *The teachers gathered all the children together in the dining hall.*
2 to collect things or bring them together □ *Police are gathering as much information as they can about the attacker.* □ *The lecturer gathered together all her papers.*
3 to understand something because you hear or read about it □ *From what I can gather, she lives with her parents.* □ *'He's a keen gardener.' 'So I gathered.'*
4 gather speed/support, etc. to gradually get faster/get more support, etc.
• **gathering** /'gæðərɪŋ/ NOUN [*plural* **gatherings**] a party or occasion where a lot of people get together ⏹ *We usually have a big family gathering at Christmas.*

gaudy /'gɔ:dɪ/ ADJECTIVE [**gaudier, gaudiest**] having very bright colours □ *gaudy Hawaiian shirts*

gauge /geɪdʒ/ ▶ NOUN [*plural* **gauges**]
1 a piece of equipment for measuring things such as temperature or amounts □ *a fuel gauge*
2 a fact or method that you can use to judge a situation □ *Exports are an important gauge of economic activity.*
▶ VERB [**gauges, gauging, gauged**]
1 to make a judgment about a situation □ *I can never gauge what his reaction will be.*
2 to measure something such as a temperature or amount

gaunt /gɔ:nt/ ADJECTIVE a gaunt person is very thin, often because they are ill

gauntlet /'gɔ:ntlɪt/ NOUN [*plural* **gauntlets**] a thick glove that protects your hand and lower arm
• IDIOM **throw down the gauntlet** to invite someone to fight or compete with you

gauze /gɔ:z/ NOUN, NO PLURAL a very thin cloth that is used to cover injuries

gave /geɪv/ PAST TENSE OF **give**

gawky /'gɔ:kɪ/ ADJECTIVE [**gawkier, gawkiest**] tall and awkward □ *a gawky teenage boy*

gawp /gɔ:p/ VERB [**gawps, gawping, gawped**] to look at something with your mouth open because you are shocked or surprised □ *I was carried out on a stretcher with everybody gawping at me.*

gay /geɪ/ ▶ ADJECTIVE [**gayer, gayest**]
1 homosexual or to do with homosexuals □ *a gay bar* □ *a gay marriage*
2 an old-fashioned word meaning happy and excited
3 an old-fashioned word meaning brightly coloured □ *gay banners*
▶ NOUN [*plural* **gays**] someone who is homosexual

gaze /geɪz/ ▶ VERB [**gazes, gazing, gazed**] to look at something or someone for a long time, especially because they are interesting or attractive □ *The children gazed longingly at the toys in the window.*
▶ NOUN, NO PLURAL a long look

gazelle /gə'zel/ NOUN [*plural* **gazelles**] a type of African or Asian animal that looks like a small deer with long, delicate legs

GB /,dʒi:'bi:/ ABBREVIATION Great Britain

GCSE /,dʒi:si:es'i:/ ABBREVIATION General Certificate of Secondary Education; an exam taken by students in England and Wales at around the age of 16 □ *He's doing GCSE maths.*

gear /gɪə(r)/ NOUN [*plural* **gears**]
1 the set of parts in a car or bicycle that controls how fast the wheels turn □ *Our new car has five gears.*
2 a particular position of the gears on a vehicle ⏹ *She still finds it hard to change gear.* ⏹ *Put the car into first gear and move off.*
3 the clothes and equipment you use for a particular sport or job □ *tennis gear*
◆ PHRASAL VERBS [**gears, gearing, geared**] **gear something to/towards someone/something** to arrange something so that it is suitable for a particular group, situation or purpose □ *The course is geared to more advanced students.* **gear (someone/ something) up for something** to get ready or make someone or something ready for something □ *Everything's geared up for the exams at the moment.*

gearbox /'gɪəbɒks/ NOUN [*plural* **gearboxes**] the part of a motor vehicle that contains a set of gears

geek /gi:k/ NOUN [*plural* **geeks**] a person who is very interested in a particular hobby, for example computers, but is not good at making friends. An informal word.

geese /gi:s/ PLURAL OF **goose**

gel /dʒel/ ▶ NOUN [*plural* **gels**] a thick clear substance that is between a liquid and a solid ⏹ *shower gel* ⏹ *Do you use hair gel?*
▶ VERB [**gels, gelling, gelled**]
1 if an idea gels, it becomes clearer
2 if a group of people gels, the people begin to form a good relationship

gelatine /'dʒeləti:n/ NOUN, NO PLURAL a clear substance used in cooking to make liquids thick or firm

gem /dʒem/ NOUN [*plural* **gems**]
1 a valuable stone that is used in jewellery
2 someone or something that you like or admire very much □ *This is an absolute gem of a museum.*

gender /'dʒendə(r)/ NOUN [*plural* **genders**]
1 the state of being male or female
2 the form of a noun, pronoun or adjective, which can be masculine, feminine or neuter

gene /dʒi:n/ NOUN [*plural* **genes**] a part of a living cell that is passed on from parents to children and that controls things like hair or skin colour. A biology word.

genealogy /,dʒi:nɪ'ælədʒɪ/ NOUN [*plural* **genealogies**] the history of how past and present members of a family are related

genera /'dʒenərə/ PLURAL OF **genus**

general /'dʒenərəl/ ▶ ADJECTIVE
1 involving or affecting most people or things □ *There was a general feeling of gloom.* ⏹ *Sales to the general public* (= ordinary people) *will begin on July 11.*
2 not detailed or exact, but giving the most important information □ *Can you give me a general idea of what it will cost?* ⏹ *I understand the principles of economics*

in general terms. 🔁 *As a general rule* (= in most situations) *I use two eggs for every 125g flour.*

3 in general (a) considering the whole of something or someone □ *Schools are achieving better results in general.* □ *There is agreement among the population in general.* **(b)** in most situations □ *In general, I think it's better to travel by train.*

4 dealing with a lot of activities, subjects or parts of a subject □ *He does general household repairs.* □ *I'm looking for a general introduction to Western art.*

▶ NOUN [*plural* **generals**] an important army officer

general anaesthetic /ˈdʒenərəl ˌænɪsˈθetɪk/ NOUN [*plural* **general anaesthetics**] a drug that makes you not conscious while you have a medical operation

general election /ˌdʒenərəl ɪˈlekʃən/ NOUN [*plural* **general elections**] an election in which all the people in a country vote to choose the people who will be in the next government

generalization *or* **generalisation** /ˌdʒenərəlaɪˈzeɪʃən/ NOUN [*plural* **generalizations**] a general statement based on a few facts that is usually but not always true 🔁 *I shouldn't make generalizations but Italians are very creative.*

generalize *or* **generalise** /ˈdʒenərəlaɪz/ VERB [**generalizes, generalizing, generalized**] to state an opinion about a group of people or things that is true for most of them but may not be true for all □ *It's impossible to generalize about marriage.*

general knowledge /ˌdʒenərəl ˈnɒlɪdʒ/ NOUN, NO PLURAL what someone knows about a lot of different things in the world, instead of about one particular subject

generally /ˈdʒenərəli/ ADVERB

1 by most people or in most cases □ *She's generally considered Britain's greatest actor.* □ *They were generally well dressed.*

2 usually □ *Children generally start school at about the age of five.*

3 in a way that states basic facts but not details □ *She spoke very generally about life in the UK.*

general practitioner /ˌdʒenərəl prækˈtɪʃənə(r)/ NOUN [*plural* **general practitioners**] a doctor who looks after people from a particular area and treats them for a lot of different illnesses

generate /ˈdʒenəreɪt/ VERB [**generates, generating, generated**]

1 to create something □ *His work generated a lot of interest.* □ *We generate more profit from the training side of our business.*

2 to produce energy □ *The house uses solar power to generate electricity.*

• **generation** /ˌdʒenəˈreɪʃən/ NOUN [*plural* **generations**]

1 all the people in a family or society who were born at about the same time 🔁 *the younger generation* □ *There were four generations of the family at the wedding.*

2 the average time it takes for a child to become an

adult, usually considered to be about 25 years □ *His family have been farmers for generations.*

3 the production of something, especially energy □ *the generation of electricity*

4 a product that is produced at a particular time, usually more developed than it was before □ *A new generation of environmentally friendly vehicles is available.*

• **generator** /ˈdʒenəreɪtə(r)/ NOUN [*plural* **generators**] a machine that produces electricity

generosity /ˌdʒenəˈrɒsəti/ NOUN, NO PLURAL the quality of being generous

generous /ˈdʒenərəs/ ADJECTIVE

1 giving a lot of money, presents or time to others □ *The locals are kind and generous people.*

2 bigger or more than usual or expected □ *He made a generous donation to the appeal fund.* □ *She took a generous helping of pasta.*

• **generously** /ˈdʒenərəsli/ ADVERB in a generous way □ *Please give generously.*

genetic /dʒɪˈnetɪk/ ADJECTIVE to do with genes or genetics. A biology word □ *a genetic defect*

genetically modified /dʒɪˌnetɪkəli ˈmɒdɪfaɪd/ ADJECTIVE genetically modified plants or animals have had one or more of their genes changed so that their natural characteristics are improved □ *genetically modified crops*

genetic engineering /dʒɪˈnetɪk ˌendʒɪˈnɪərɪŋ/ NOUN, NO PLURAL the science of changing how living things develop by changing the information in their genes

genetics /dʒɪˈnetɪks/ NOUN, NO PLURAL the scientific study of how living things develop as a result of the qualities children take from their parents in their genes

genial /ˈdʒiːniəl/ ADJECTIVE pleasant and friendly □ *a genial man*

• **geniality** /ˌdʒiːniˈæləti/ NOUN, NO PLURAL the quality of being genial

• **genially** /ˈdʒiːniəli/ ADVERB in a genial way

genie /ˈdʒiːni/ NOUN [*plural* **genies** *or* **genii**] in magical stories, a spirit who can give someone what they wish for □ *The genie granted Aladdin three wishes.*

genitals /ˈdʒenɪtəlz/ PLURAL NOUN the sexual organs. A biology word.

genius /ˈdʒiːniəs/ NOUN [*plural* **geniuses**]

1 someone who is extremely clever or skilful

2 the quality of being extremely clever or skilful □ *the genius of Shakespeare*

genocide /ˈdʒenəsaɪd/ NOUN, NO PLURAL when a lot of people from one race, religion or country are intentionally killed

genome /ˈdʒiːnəʊm/ NOUN [*plural* **genomes**] the set of genes that make up a cell or living thing. A biology word □ *the human genome*

genre /ˈʒɒrə/ NOUN [*plural* **genres**] a particular type or style of literature, music, etc. □ *Hitchcock was a master of the horror genre.*

genteel /dʒen'tiːl/ ADJECTIVE behaving very politely, like people from a high social class □ *She was drinking her tea in genteel sips.*

gentle /'dʒentəl/ ADJECTIVE [**gentler, gentlest**]
1 careful not to hurt or upset anyone or anything □ *He was a gentle man.* □ *She gave him a gentle tap on his shoulder.*
2 not strong, severe or violent □ *a gentle breeze*
3 a gentle slope is not steep

gentleman /'dʒentəlmən/ NOUN [*plural* **gentlemen**]
1 a word used to refer politely to a man □ *Good morning, gentlemen.* 🔁 *Ladies and gentlemen, welcome to the show.*
2 a man who is polite and treats people with respect □ *Her husband's a real gentleman.*
• **gentlemanly** /'dʒentəlmənlɪ/ ADJECTIVE polite

gentleness /'dʒentəlnɪs/ NOUN, NO PLURAL the quality or state of being gentle □ *I was surprised at the gentleness of his touch.*

gently /'dʒentlɪ/ ADVERB in a gentle way □ *He picked the injured bird up gently.*

gentry /'dʒentrɪ/ NOUN, NO PLURAL the gentry an old-fashioned word for people from a high social class

gents /dʒents/ NOUN, NO PLURAL the gents a public toilet for boys and men □ *Where is the gents, please?*

genuine /'dʒenjuɪn/ ADJECTIVE
1 real or true □ *a genuine work of art*
2 honest and not pretending □ *Her sympathy was genuine.*
• **genuinely** /'dʒenjuɪnlɪ/ ADVERB really or honestly □ *I was genuinely impressed.*

genus /'dʒenəs/ NOUN [*plural* **genera**] a group of animals or plants which have the same characteristics. A biology word.

geo- /'dʒiːəʊ/ PREFIX geo- is added to the beginning of words to mean 'to do with the Earth' □ *geology*

geographic /dʒɪə'græfɪk/ or geographical /dʒɪə'græfɪkəl/ ADJECTIVE to do with geography and where things are on the Earth's surface

geography /dʒɪ'ɒgrəfɪ/ NOUN, NO PLURAL the study of the Earth's surface and the countries, weather and people of the world □ *human geography*

geological /dʒɪə'lɒdʒɪkəl/ ADJECTIVE to do with geology or the surface of the earth

geologist /dʒɪ'ɒlədʒɪst/ NOUN [*plural* **geologists**] someone who studies geology

geology /dʒɪ'ɒlədʒɪ/ NOUN, NO PLURAL the study of the Earth's rocks and soil

geometric /dʒɪə'metrɪk/ or geometrical /dʒɪə'metrɪkəl/ ADJECTIVE
1 made up of straight lines and angles □ *a geometric pattern*
2 to do with geometry

geometry /dʒɪ'ɒmɪtrɪ/ NOUN, NO PLURAL a type of maths in which you study angles, lines and shapes

geranium /dʒɪ'reɪnɪəm/ NOUN [*plural* **geraniums**] a garden plant that has a lot of red, pink or white flowers

gerbil /'dʒɜːbɪl/ NOUN [*plural* **gerbils**] a small animal similar to a large mouse that is often kept as a pet

geriatric /,dʒerɪ'ætrɪk/ ADJECTIVE to do with old people and the illnesses they suffer from □ *a geriatric care unit*
• **geriatrics** /,dʒerɪ'ætrɪks/ NOUN, NO PLURAL the medical care and treatment of old people

germ /dʒɜːm/ NOUN [*plural* **germs**] a very small living thing that can cause disease □ *This disinfectant kills most germs.*

German measles /,dʒɜːmən 'miːzəlz/ NOUN, NO PLURAL a disease children sometimes get which causes red spots on the skin

germinate /'dʒɜːmɪneɪt/ VERB [**germinates, germinating, germinated**] a seed germinates or is germinated when it begins to grow. A biology word.
• **germination** /,dʒɜːmɪ'neɪʃən/ NOUN, NO PLURAL the process of germinating. A biology word.

gestation /dʒe'steɪʃən/ NOUN, NO PLURAL the time when a baby human or animal is growing inside its mother. A biology word.

gesticulate /dʒe'stɪkjuleɪt/ VERB [**gesticulates, gesticulating, gesticulated**] to wave your hands or arms to express something □ *The officer shouted and gesticulated towards the car.*

gesture /'dʒestʃə(r)/ ► NOUN [*plural* **gestures**]
1 a movement made with your hand, arm or head to express what you think or feel 🔁 *The driver made a rude gesture out of the car window.*
2 something you do to show how you feel about someone or something 🔁 *It was a nice gesture to send the flowers.*
► VERB [**gestures, gesturing, gestured**] to point at something or express something by moving your hand, arm or head □ *She gestured towards the garden.*

get /get/ VERB [**gets, getting, got**]
1 to take, receive or buy something □ *Isabel got lots of birthday presents.* □ *Did you get my letter?* □ *I got a new dress today.*
2 to go somewhere and then bring something back □ *Could you get me a drink?* □ *I'll go and get the money.*
3 get away/in/out, etc. to move in a particular direction □ *We managed to get over the wall.* □ *All the chickens have got out.* □ *Catch a bus, and get off near the cathedral.*
4 to become □ *The baby's getting bigger every day.* □ *I got wet in the rain.* □ *If I mention money, he always gets angry.* □ *The wine glasses got broken.*
5 if you get somewhere, you arrive there □ *We got to New York at 5 o'clock in the morning.* □ *What time will you get home?* □ *The train gets in at three thirty.*
6 if you get a bus, train, etc., that is how you travel. □ *I usually get the train to work.*
7 to become ill with a particular illness □ *They had an injection to stop them getting measles.*
8 if you get something done, you make sure it is done

□ *We got our house painted.* □ *I need to get the washing done.*

◆ PHRASAL VERBS **get something across** to explain something □ **+ to** *The government is struggling to get its message across.* **get along** if two people get along, they are friendly □ **+ with** *She gets along really well with her cousins.* **get around to doing something** to do something that you have been intending to do □ *We finally got around to decorating the bathroom.* **get at someone** to criticize someone □ *I felt that the teacher was getting at me.* **get at something** if someone is getting at something, they are trying to express it □ *He kept mentioning the past, but I wasn't sure what he was getting at.* **get away with something** to avoid being punished or criticized □ *I'm hoping to miss the next meeting, if I can get away with it.* **get on 1** to make progress □ **+ with** *I need to get on with my work.* □ *How are you getting on in your new job?* **2** to be friendly □ *Pierre and Alex don't really get on.* **get out of something** to avoid doing something □ *He'll do anything to get out of the washing up.* **get over something** to feel better after being ill or unhappy □ *He never really got over his wife's death.* **get round to doing something** to do something that you have been intending to do □ *I'd like to do more exercise, but I never seem to get round to it.* **get through** to manage to talk to someone on the telephone □ *I tried to ring her, but I couldn't get through.* **get through something** to reach the end of a difficult situation □ *It was a terrible illness, but his determination helped to get him through it.* **get (someone) up** to wake up and get out of bed □ *I always get up early.* □ *My Dad gets me up in the morning.* **get up to something** to do something, often something wrong □ *Sent to the head teacher? What's she been getting up to now?*

geyser /ˈgiːzə(r)/ NOUN [plural **geysers**] a strong stream of hot water that comes up out of the ground

ghastly /ˈgɑːstlɪ/ ADJECTIVE [**ghastlier, ghastliest**] very unpleasant or ugly □ *a ghastly smell* □ *There's been a ghastly accident.*

ghetto /ˈgetəʊ/ NOUN [plural **ghettos**] a poor area in a town where a lot of people of the same race, religion, etc. live

ghost /gəʊst/ NOUN [plural **ghosts**] the spirit of a dead person which some people think they can see □ *Do you believe in ghosts?*

● **ghostly** /ˈgəʊstlɪ/ ADJECTIVE [**ghostlier, ghostliest**] making you think of ghosts □ *a ghostly light*

ghoul /guːl/ NOUN [plural **ghouls**]
1 in stories, an evil spirit that steals and eats dead bodies
2 someone who is too interested in death, accidents, etc.

● **ghoulish** /ˈguːlɪʃ/ ADJECTIVE too interested in death, accidents etc. □ *A crowd of ghoulish onlookers stood round the ambulance.*

giant /ˈdʒaɪənt/ ▶ NOUN [plural **giants**]
1 in stories, a man who is extremely tall and strong
2 a very large company or organization □ *the software giant, Microsoft*
▶ ADJECTIVE much bigger than usual □ *a giant crane* □ *a giant tortoise*

gibberish /ˈdʒɪbərɪʃ/ NOUN, NO PLURAL language that has no meaning, or language that you cannot understand □ *He was talking absolute gibberish.*

giddy /ˈgɪdɪ/ ADJECTIVE [**giddier, giddiest**] if you feel giddy, you feel as if everything around you is moving and you cannot stay standing

gift /gɪft/ NOUN [plural **gifts**]
1 a present 🔁 *a wedding gift* 🔁 *Many children give gifts to their teacher at the end of term.* 🔁 *a gift shop* □ **+ from** *The necklace had been a gift from her boyfriend.*
2 a natural ability □ **+ for** *Adam has a gift for languages.*

● **gifted** /ˈgɪftɪd/ ADJECTIVE having a natural ability to do something extremely well □ *a gifted child* □ *a gifted writer*

gig /gɪg/ NOUN [plural **gigs**] an informal word for a pop music concert

gigabyte /ˈgɪgəbaɪt/ NOUN [plural **gigabytes**] a unit used to measure computer information, equal to approximately a thousand megabytes. A computing word.

gigantic /dʒaɪˈgæntɪk/ ADJECTIVE extremely big □ *a gigantic statue*

giggle /ˈgɪgəl/ ▶ VERB [**giggles, giggling, giggled**] to laugh in a silly or nervous way
▶ NOUN [plural **giggles**] a silly or nervous laugh

gills /gɪlz/ PLURAL NOUN a fish's gills are the openings at each side of its body, which it breathes through

gilt /gɪlt/ ADJECTIVE decorated with a thin layer of gold □ *a gilt frame*

gimmick /ˈgɪmɪk/ NOUN [plural **gimmicks**] something that is done to get people's attention, but is not useful □ *The policy is just a political gimmick.*

gin /dʒɪn/ NOUN, NO PLURAL a strong alcoholic drink

ginger /ˈdʒɪndʒə(r)/ ▶ NOUN, NO PLURAL a root that has a spicy taste and is used in cooking
▶ ADJECTIVE ginger hair is a reddish-brown colour

● **gingerly** /ˈdʒɪndʒəlɪ/ ADVERB if you do something gingerly, you do it slowly and carefully because you are nervous about what will happen □ *She stepped gingerly onto the wobbly bridge.*

giraffe /dʒɪˈrɑːf/ NOUN [plural **giraffes**] an African animal with a very long neck and long legs

girder /ˈgɜːdə(r)/ NOUN [plural **girders**] a long piece of metal used for supporting a bridge or building

girl /gɜːl/ NOUN [plural **girls**] a female child or young woman □ *Police are searching for a missing 10-year-old girl.* 🔁 *a teenage girl* 🔁 *There were two little girls* (= very young girls) *playing in the garden.*

girlfriend /'gɜːlfrend/ NOUN [plural **girlfriends**]
1 a girl or woman that you are having a romantic relationship with □ *Dan has a new girlfriend.*
2 a female friend that a girl or woman has □ *I go out with my girlfriends once a week.*

gist /dʒɪst/ NOUN, NO PLURAL **the gist** the main points of something that someone says or writes □ *Pam told me the gist of their conversation.*

give /ɡɪv/ VERB [gives, giving, gave, given]
1 to let someone have something □ *Give your bags to the porter.* □ *Make sure you give back all the books you borrowed.* □ *Let me give you some advice.* □ *This news gives us hope.* □ *He gave us permission to visit the temple.* □ *Could you give us some information about hotels?*
2 to make someone have something □ *They were given a severe punishment.* □ *Our boss gives us too much work.* □ *The sudden noise gave me a fright.*
3 give evidence/a performance/a speech, etc. to say something or to perform in public □ *She gave evidence at his trial.* □ *He gave a wonderful performance of Beethoven's Moonlight Sonata.*
4 to make a sound or a movement □ *He gave a shout of joy.* □ *She gave her brother a kick.*
5 if something gives, it bends or breaks when too much weight is put on top of it □ *The rotten floorboard gave under him.*
6 give way if you give way to another vehicle, you stop to allow it to drive before you
♦ PHRASAL VERBS **give something away** **1** to let someone have something without paying for it □ *I gave away all my old toys.* **2** to tell a secret □ *The party was meant to be a surprise, but Billy gave it away.* **give in** to agree to something you did not want to agree to □ *I kept asking for the new computer game, and eventually Dad gave in and bought it for me.* **give something out** to give something to a group of people □ *Can you give out the reading books please, Kazuo?* **give up** to stop trying to guess an answer □ *'How many beans are there in this jar?' 'Three hundred? A thousand? I give up.'* **give up (something)** **1** if you give up a habit, you stop doing it □ *She's managed to give up smoking.* **2** to stop doing something before it is finished, because it is too difficult □ *I've given up trying to keep this room tidy.* □ *Don't give up – only another mile to go!*
● **given** /'ɡɪvən/ ► ADJECTIVE decided or agreed □ *You have a given time to complete each question.* □ *On any given day, there are several dozen accidents.*
► PREPOSITION considering the fact that □ *Given that they don't have much money, their offer is extremely generous.*
► PAST PARTICIPLE OF **give**

glaciation /ˌɡleɪsɪ'eɪʃən/ NOUN, NO PLURAL when land becomes covered in glaciers. A geography word.

glacier /'ɡlæsɪə(r)/ NOUN [plural **glaciers**] a large mass of ice that moves slowly down a mountain valley

glad /ɡlæd/ ADJECTIVE [gladder, gladdest]
1 pleased and happy because of something □ + *that* *I'm just glad that the exams are over.* □ + *to do something* *I'm so glad to see you.*
2 willing and happy □ + *to do something* *I'd be glad to help if you need me.*
3 be glad of something a formal phrase meaning to be grateful for something □ *He was glad of an excuse to leave.*

gladiator /'ɡlædɪˌeɪtə(r)/ NOUN [plural **gladiators**] in ancient Rome, a man who fought other men or animals to entertain people

gladly /'ɡlædli/ ADVERB happily or with pleasure □ *She offered him some coffee which he gladly accepted.*

glamorous /'ɡlæmərəs/ ADJECTIVE attractive, fashionable and exciting □ *She was looking very glamorous in a black dress.* □ *a glamorous lifestyle*

glamour /'ɡlæmə(r)/ NOUN, NO PLURAL a special quality that makes someone or something seem attractive, fashionable and exciting □ *She will add some glamour to the show.*

glance /ɡlɑːns/ ► VERB [glances, glancing, glanced]
1 to look at something or someone for a very short time □ + *at* *Anselm glanced nervously at his watch.* □ + *around* *He glanced around to see if anyone was looking.*
2 glance at/over something to read something very quickly □ *He glanced at his notes before he spoke.*
► NOUN [plural **glances**]
1 a quick look 🔁 *He cast a nervous glance at Yvonne.* 🔁 *Richard and I exchanged glances* (= we looked at each other for a short time).
2 at a glance if you see or understand something at a glance, you see or understand it immediately □ *She could tell at a glance that her father was upset.*

gland /ɡlænd/ NOUN [plural **glands**] an organ in your body that produces a substance that your body needs. A biology word.
● **glandular** /'ɡlændjʊlə(r)/ ADJECTIVE to do with a gland or glands. A biology word.

glandular fever /ˌɡlændjʊlə(r) 'fiːvə(r)/ NOUN, NO PLURAL an infectious illness which makes you feel tired and weak for a very long time

glare /ɡleə(r)/ ► VERB [glares, glaring, glared]
1 to look at someone in a way that shows you are very angry □ *Mia glared at him.*
2 if a light glares, it is bright and makes your eyes hurt □ *The setting sun glared in her eyes.*
► NOUN [plural **glares**]
1 *no plural* very strong bright light that makes your eyes hurt □ *He stood in the harsh glare of the car's headlights.*
2 *no plural* when someone gets a lot of attention from newspapers, television, etc., especially when they

do not want it □ *The singer even changed hotels to avoid the media glare.*
3 an angry look
• **glaring** /'gleərɪŋ/ ADJECTIVE
1 very obvious 🔄 *a glaring mistake*
2 very bright, and making your eyes hurt □ *the glaring sun*

glass /glɑːs/ ► NOUN [plural **glasses**]
1 *no plural* a hard transparent material, used for making bottles, windows, etc. 🔄 *There was broken glass all over the pavement.* 🔄 *She stepped on a piece of glass and cut her foot.*
2 a container made of glass, which you drink from □ *a tall glass* 🔄 *a wine glass* □ *+ of* She drank three glasses of milk. 🔄 *Betsy poured a glass of juice.*
3 **glasses** something you wear to help you see better, which consists of two pieces of plastic or glass in a frame 🔄 *I need a new pair of glasses.* 🔄 *My Dad wears glasses.*
► ADJECTIVE made of glass □ *a glass bowl*
• **glassy** /'glɑːsɪ/ ADJECTIVE [**glassier, glassiest**]
1 shiny like glass, or transparent like glass □ *the glassy surface of the water*
2 if someone's eyes are glassy, they show no feeling, usually because the person is ill

glaze /gleɪz/ ► VERB [**glazes, glazing, glazed**]
1 if your eyes glaze, you start to look bored or tired □ *Riley's eyes glazed over.*
2 to cover clay objects with a substance that makes them shiny
3 to put glass into the frame of a window
► NOUN [plural **glazes**] a liquid you put on something to make it look shiny
• **glazier** /'gleɪzɪə(r)/ NOUN [plural **glaziers**] someone whose job is to put glass in the frame of a window

gleam /gliːm/ ► VERB [**gleams, gleaming, gleamed**]
1 to shine □ *A light gleamed in the distance.*
2 if your eyes or face gleam, they show a good feeling very strongly □ *Her eyes were gleaming with pride.*
► NOUN [plural **gleams**]
1 a light □ *He saw the first gleam of sunrise on the horizon.*
2 a good feeling that someone shows in their eyes or face □ *There was a gleam of satisfaction in her eyes.*
• **gleaming** /'gliːmɪŋ/ ADJECTIVE clean and shiny □ *a gleaming black sports car*

glean /gliːn/ VERB [**gleans, gleaning, gleaned**] to find out information by asking questions and listening carefully □ *I tried to glean as much information as I could from him.*

glee /gliː/ NOUN, NO PLURAL a feeling of pleasure because something good has happened to you or because something bad has happened to someone else □ *Ray told them about my accident with a certain amount of glee.*
• **gleeful** /'gliːfʊl/ ADJECTIVE showing glee □ *a gleeful smile*

glib /glɪb/ ADJECTIVE [**glibber, glibbest**] said with little thought, and having little meaning □ *a glib answer*

glide /glaɪd/ VERB [**glides, gliding, glided**] to move smoothly and quietly □ *The waiters glide effortlessly between the tables.*
• **glider** /'glaɪdə(r)/ NOUN [plural **gliders**] an aeroplane with no engine which moves on air currents
• **gliding** /'glaɪdɪŋ/ NOUN, NO PLURAL the activity of flying a glider

glimmer /'glɪmə(r)/ ► NOUN [plural **glimmers**]
1 a glimmer of hope/interest etc. a small amount of something good, especially hope or interest
2 a weak light □ *We could see the glimmer of torches inside the tent.*
► VERB [**glimmers, glimmering, glimmered**] to shine with a weak light □ *Something glimmered in the dark.*

glimpse /glɪmps/ ► NOUN [plural **glimpses**] when you see someone or something only for a very short time 🔄 *People climbed on fences, hoping to catch a glimpse of (= see) the princess.*
► VERB [**glimpses, glimpsing, glimpsed**] to see someone or something only for a very short time, or to see only part of them □ *Through the trees he glimpsed a woman on the path.*

glint /glɪnt/ ► VERB [**glints, glinting, glinted**]
1 to shine brightly with flashes of light □ *The knife was glinting in the sun.*
2 if someone's eyes glint, they seem to shine, often because someone is excited about something, especially something bad
► NOUN [plural **glints**]
1 a flash of very bright light
2 a light that seems to shine in someone's eyes when they are excited, especially about something bad □ *There was a wicked glint in his eye as he said it.*

glisten /'glɪsən/ VERB [**glistens, glistening, glistened**] to shine because of being wet or covered in something such as oil □ *Her eyes glistened with tears.*

glitter /'glɪtə(r)/ ► VERB [**glitters, glittering, glittered**] to shine with small flashes of light □ *His eyes glittered in the light.*
► NOUN, NO PLURAL
1 when something shines with small flashes of light □ *the glitter of the jewels*
2 very small shiny pieces of metal, used for decorating things
3 an exciting and attractive quality that something has □ *the glitter of Hollywood*
• **glittering** /'glɪtərɪŋ/ ADJECTIVE
1 very exciting and successful 🔄 *a glittering career*
2 shining with small flashes of light □ *glittering silver trophies*

gloat /gləʊt/ VERB [**gloats, gloating, gloated**] to show too much pleasure at your own success or at someone else's failure □ *He always beat me at tennis but he never gloated over his victories.*

global /'gləʊbəl/ ADJECTIVE
1 to do with or involving the whole world □ *Global sales rose by 20%.* □ *global climate change*

2 involving everyone or everything □ *a global increase in pay*

• **globalization** *or* **globalisation** /ˌgləʊbəlaɪ
'zeɪʃən/ NOUN, NO PLURAL the way that all the countries of the world are becoming similar, especially because of big companies selling the same thing in many countries

• **globally** /'gləʊbəlɪ/ ADVERB around the whole world □ *The company operates globally.* □ *Globally, 2.6 billion people lack access to clean water supplies.*

global warming /ˌgləʊbəl 'wɔːmɪŋ/ NOUN, NO PLURAL the gradual increase in the Earth's temperature caused by pollution

globe /gləʊb/ NOUN [*plural* **globes**]
1 a large ball with a map of the Earth printed on it
2 the globe the world □ *The company has offices around the globe.*

gloom /gluːm/ NOUN, NO PLURAL
1 a feeling of sadness and no hope □ *News of the accident added to her gloom.*
2 darkness □ *A man appeared out of the gloom.*

• **gloomy** /'gluːmɪ/ ADJECTIVE [**gloomier, gloomiest**]
1 suggesting that a situation is bad and will get worse □ *There were gloomy predictions of a rise in unemployment.*
2 sad and without hope □ *He was in a gloomy mood.*
3 unpleasantly dark □ *a gloomy passageway*

glorify /'glɔːrɪfaɪ/ VERB [**glorifies, glorifying, glorified**]
1 to make something bad seem to have good qualities □ *It was said that the films glorified violence.*
2 to praise someone, especially God

glorious /'glɔːrɪəs/ ADJECTIVE
1 extremely beautiful or good □ *glorious sunshine* □ *The hotel is surrounded by glorious countryside.*
2 deserving or receiving praise □ *a glorious victory*

glory /'glɔːrɪ/ NOUN [*plural* **glories**]
1 praise and admiration □ *His moment of glory came when he won the championship.*
2 great beauty 🖪 *The house has been restored to its former glory.*
◆ PHRASAL VERB [**glories, glorying, gloried**] **glory in something** to enjoy something and be proud of it □ *They gloried in their unexpected victory.*

gloss /glɒs/ NOUN, NO PLURAL
1 a type of paint that produces a shiny surface □ *a tin of gloss*
2 shine on a surface
◆ PHRASAL VERB [**glosses, glossing, glossed**] **gloss over something** to say little about a problem because you do not want to make it seem important

glossary /'glɒsərɪ/ NOUN [*plural* **glossaries**] a list of words and their meanings, at the end of a book

glossy /'glɒsɪ/ ADJECTIVE [**glossier, glossiest**]
1 smooth and shiny 🖪 *glossy hair* □ *a glossy surface*
2 glossy magazines are printed on shiny paper and have a lot of pictures in them

glove /glʌv/ NOUN [*plural* **gloves**] something you wear to cover your hand 🖪 *a pair of gloves* 🖪 *I wear gloves in the winter.* 🖪 *It's a good idea to wear rubber gloves when you're cleaning.*

glow /gləʊ/ ▶ NOUN, NO PLURAL
1 warm or soft light □ *the glow of the fire*
2 a healthy colour that someone's face has □ *Her skin still has a youthful glow.*
3 a glow of satisfaction/pride etc. a good feeling of being satisfied, proud, etc. □ *He felt a glow of satisfaction when he looked at his work.*
▶ VERB [**glows, glowing, glowed**]
1 to burn or shine with a soft light □ *A fire glowed in the corner of the room.*
2 to look warm and healthy □ *Her cheeks were glowing.*
3 glow with pride/satisfaction/confidence, etc. to show that you are very proud, satisfied, etc. □ *She was glowing with pride as she watched her son accept the award.*

glower /'glaʊə(r)/ VERB [**glowers, glowering, glowered**] to look at someone in an angry way

glowing /'gləʊɪŋ/ ADJECTIVE
1 burning or shining with a soft light □ *the glowing lights of the village*
2 praising someone a lot 🖪 *He got a glowing report from his teachers.*

glucose /'gluːkəʊs/ NOUN, NO PLURAL a type of sugar

glue /gluː/ ▶ NOUN [*plural* **glues**] a substance used for sticking things together □ *Use glue to stick the fabric onto the paper.*
▶ VERB [**glues, gluing** *or* **glueing, glued**]
1 to stick something using glue 🖪 *He glued the two pieces of wood together.*
2 if you are glued to a television or computer screen, you are looking at it all the time. An informal phrase. □ *The kids are just glued to the TV all day.*

• **gluey** /'gluːɪ/ ADJECTIVE covered with glue, or sticky like glue

glum /glʌm/ ADJECTIVE [**glummer, glummest**] unhappy

gluten /'gluːtən/ NOUN, NO PLURAL a sticky substance in wheat and some other grains

glutton /'glʌtən/ NOUN [*plural* **gluttons**]
1 someone who eats too much
2 a glutton for punishment someone who seems to enjoy doing things that are unpleasant or difficult

• **gluttony** /'glʌtənɪ/ NOUN, NO PLURAL eating too much

GM /ˌdʒiː'em/ ABBREVIATION genetically modified

GMT /ˌdʒiːem'tiː/ ABBREVIATION Greenwich Mean Time; the time in Greenwich, England that is used to calculate the time in other parts of the world

gnarled /nɑːld/ ADJECTIVE twisted and rough □ *gnarled trees*

gnat /næt/ NOUN [*plural* **gnats**] a small flying insect that bites

gnaw /nɔː/ VERB [**gnaws, gnawing, gnawed**] to keep biting a hard object □ *The dog was gnawing at a bone.*

gnome /nəum/ NOUN [plural **gnomes**]
1 in stories, a little man with a pointed hat who can do magic
2 a model of a little man with a pointed hat, used as a garden decoration

go /gəu/ ► VERB [**goes, going, went, gone**]
1 to travel or move somewhere □ I'm going home now. □ + **to** We're going to France for our holiday. □ He went into the other room. □ I wish she'd go away. □ He left home at 18 and never went back.
2 to travel or move somewhere so that you can do something □ + **to** She goes to school in the next village. □ + **for** Shall we go for a swim? □ We all went cycling.
3 to leave or disappear □ It's six o'clock, so I'll have to go soon. □ I'm sure I left my coat here, but it's gone. □ The food all went very quickly.
4 if a road or path goes somewhere, it leads there □ Does this road go to Edinburgh?
5 the place where something goes is where it fits or is kept □ That piece of the jigsaw goes at the top. □ The cups go on the top shelf.
6 to become □ Her face went pale. □ Your soup's gone cold.
7 to happen in a particular way □ The concert went well. □ How's your new job going?
8 be going to do something (a) to intend to do something □ I'm going to write to Molly. □ What were you going to say? (b) to be expected to happen □ I think it's going to rain.
◆ go to go to great lengths to do something
◆ PHRASAL VERBS **go about something** to do something in a particular way □ I'm not sure how to go about slicing this chicken. **go ahead** to start to do something □ + **with** They're going ahead with the new airport. **go around 1** to be enough for everyone □ Are there enough books to go around? **2** if someone goes around doing something, they often do something that upsets other people □ You can't go around telling lies about him. **go by** if time goes by, it passes **go down** to become lower in level □ His temperature has gone down a bit. **go down with something** to get an illness □ She's gone down with a tummy bug. **go for something** to choose something □ I'm going to go for the curry. **go into something 1** to talk about something in detail □ She told me a lot about her marriage, though I won't go into that now. **2** to start working in a particular type of job □ After university, he went into banking. **go off 1** if food goes off, it becomes rotten **2** to explode □ A bomb has gone off in a busy London street. **go off someone/something** to stop liking someone or something □ I've gone off spicy food. **go on 1** to continue for a period of time □ His speech went on for hours. **2** to continue doing something □ + **ing** He went on singing, despite the noise. □ + **with** Go on with your work. **3** if something is going on, it is happening □ What's going on? **go out** to leave your

house, especially for a social activity □ Are you going out tonight? **go round 1** to be enough for everyone □ Is there enough bread to go round? **2** if someone goes round doing something, they often do something that upsets other people □ She goes round complaining to anyone who'll listen. **go through something** to experience something □ She went through agony during the illness. **go through with something** to do something even though it is difficult □ They persuaded her to go through with the operation. **go up** to become higher in level □ Prices have gone up again.
► NOUN [plural **goes**]
1 an attempt ⊞ It doesn't matter if you can't climb to the top - just have a go. ⊞ She asked me if I'd go to dancing lessons with her, so I decided to give it a go.
2 when it is your turn to do something, especially in a game □ Pick up a card, Adam – it's your go.
◆ IDIOMS **have a go at someone** to criticize someone □ He had a go at me for not doing my homework. **on the go** active or busy □ I'm on the go from the moment I wake up.

goad /gəud/ VERB [**goads, goading, goaded**] to make someone do something by annoying them until they do it □ He had tried to goad them into fighting.
go-ahead /'gəuə,hed/ NOUN, NO PLURAL **get/give the go-ahead** to get or give permission to do something □ The government has given the go-ahead for a new power station.

goal /gəul/ NOUN [plural **goals**]
1 something that you want to achieve ⊞ If she works hard, she should achieve her goal. ⊞ The government's long-term goal is to reduce the number of people in prison.
2 a point scored when a ball goes into the net in a game such as football or hockey ⊞ Cahill scored the first goal. ⊞ Giggs scored the winning goal.
3 the area where the ball must go to score a point in a game such as football or hockey □ He was standing in front of the goal.

goalie /'gəulɪ/ NOUN [plural **goalies**] an informal word for a goalkeeper
goalkeeper /'gəul,ki:pə(r)/ NOUN [plural **goalkeepers**] the player who stands in front of the net in a game such as football and who tries to stop the ball going into the net

goat /gəut/ NOUN [plural **goats**] an animal with horns and long hair under its chin □ The cheese is made from goat's milk.

gobble /'gɒbəl/ VERB [**gobbles, gobbling, gobbled**] to eat something very quickly □ He gobbled down the burger in three bites.
go-between /'gəubɪ,twi:n/ NOUN [plural **go-betweens**] someone who takes messages between people who cannot meet or who do not want to meet

goblin /'gɒblɪn/ NOUN [plural **goblins**] in stories, a small ugly creature who tricks people

god /gɒd/ NOUN [plural **gods**]

1 God *no plural* the spirit that Christians, Muslims and Jews pray to ⊞ *Do you believe in God?*
2 a spirit that some people believe controls nature or represents a particular quality □ *Greek and Roman gods* □ *+ of* Thor was the Viking god of thunder.

godchild /'gɒdtʃaɪld/ NOUN [plural **godchildren**] your godchild is a child whose parents have asked you to support their child and make sure that the child learns about Christianity

god-daughter /'gɒddɔːtə(r)/ NOUN [plural **god-daughters**] a female godchild

goddess /'gɒdɪs/ NOUN [plural **goddesses**] a female god

godfather /'gɒdfɑːðə(r)/ NOUN [plural **godfathers**] a child's godfather is a man who has agreed to make sure that the child learns about Christianity

godmother /'gɒdmʌðə(r)/ NOUN [plural **godmothers**] a child's godmother is a woman who has agreed to make sure that the child learns about Christianity

godparent /'gɒdpeərənt/ NOUN [plural **godparents**] a godfather or godmother

godsend /'gɒdsend/ NOUN, NO PLURAL someone or something that is very helpful when you are having problems

goes /gəʊz/ VERB the present tense of the verb go when it is used with 'he', 'she', or 'it' □ *He goes to work at eight o'clock.*

goggles /'gɒgəlz/ PLURAL NOUN something you wear to protect your eyes when you are swimming or working with things that might damage your eyes □ *a pair of swimming goggles*

going /'gəʊɪŋ/ ▶ NOUN, NO PLURAL
1 how easy, difficult or slow something is ⊞ *She found the course very hard going* (= difficult).
2 when someone leaves □ *What were the reasons for his going?*
▶ ADJECTIVE **the going rate/price** the amount you usually have to pay for a particular thing □ *£150 is about the going rate for a hotel room round here.*

go-kart /'gəʊkɑːt/ NOUN [plural **go-karts**] a small low car with no roof, used for racing

gold /gəʊld/ ▶ NOUN [plural **golds**]
1 *no plural* a valuable pale yellow metal, used to make jewellery □ *bars of gold*
2 a gold medal (= prize for coming first in a competition or race) □ *He won gold in the long jump.*
▶ ADJECTIVE
1 made of gold □ *a gold ring*
2 having the colour of gold □ *a gold leather handbag*
• **golden** /'gəʊldən/ ADJECTIVE
1 made of gold □ *a golden crown*
2 having the colour of gold □ *golden hair*

golden wedding /ˌgəʊldən 'wedɪŋ/ NOUN [plural **golden weddings**] the day that is exactly fifty years after someone's wedding

goldfish /'gəʊldfɪʃ/ NOUN [plural **goldfish**] a small orange fish that people keep as a pet

golf /gɒlf/ NOUN, NO PLURAL a game in which you have to hit a small ball into holes in the ground ⊞ *a golf ball* ⊞ *My Dad plays golf.* ⊞ *an 18-hole golf course* ⊞ *Professional golfers have someone to carry their golf clubs* (= sticks used for hitting the ball).
• **golfer** /'gɒlfə(r)/ NOUN [plural **golfers**] someone who plays golf

gone /gɒn/ PAST PARTICIPLE OF go

gong /gɒŋ/ NOUN [plural **gongs**] a large round piece of metal that you hit with a stick to make a loud sound

good /gʊd/ ▶ ADJECTIVE [**better, best**]
1 suitable or of a high standard □ *That's a good idea.* □ *I've got some good news for you.* □ *She has been a good friend to me.* □ *I know a good way to cook rice.*
2 enjoyable or pleasant □ *Did you have a good holiday?* □ *We had a good time in Moscow.*
3 able to do something well □ *+ at* Mark's very good at fixing cars. □ *Ben's a pretty good cook.*
4 something you say to show you are pleased □ *Oh, good – Harry's arrived.*
5 **good for you** something that is good for you makes you healthy or makes your life better □ *Eat your vegetables – they're good for you.*
6 kind and helpful □ *My grandparents are very good to me.*
7 a good child or animal behaves well □ *The children have been very good.*
♦ IDIOMS **it's a good job** it is lucky □ *It's a good job you had an umbrella with you.*
➡ go to **have a good *mind* to do something**

➤ Remember that **good** is an adjective and not an adverb. Use the adverb **well** to say that someone does something in a way that is good: □ *She is a good cook.*
✓ She cooks very well.
✗ She cooks very **good**.

▶ NOUN, NO PLURAL
1 something that produces an advantage ⊞ *Cleaning it with water won't do any good – you need soap.* ⊞ *I know this medicine tastes bad, but it's for your own good.*
2 **no good/not any good** not of good quality, or not helpful □ *These gloves are no good – they're too thin.* □ *It's no good phoning her – she never has her phone switched on.*
3 **do someone good** to make someone feel better or to make their life better □ *Have a day off work – it will do you good.*

4 what is morally right □ *We recognize the difference between good and evil.* **for good forever** □ *I left home for good when I was 18.*

good afternoon /gʊd ˌɑːftəˈnuːn/ EXCLAMATION something that you say when you meet someone in the afternoon

goodbye /gʊdˈbaɪ/ EXCLAMATION something you say when you are leaving or when other people are leaving □ *Goodbye, Anna. See you next week.* 吾 *I felt sad when it was time to say goodbye.*

good evening /gʊd ˈiːvnɪŋ/ EXCLAMATION a formal way of saying 'hello' when you see someone in the evening □ *Good evening ladies and gentlemen, and welcome to the show.*

good-looking /ˈgʊdlʊkɪŋ/ ADJECTIVE someone who is good-looking has an attractive face □ *Amy's new boyfriend is really good-looking.*

good morning /gʊd ˈmɔːnɪŋ/ EXCLAMATION a formal way of saying 'hello' when you see someone in the morning □ *Good morning, everyone.*

goodness /ˈgʊdnɪs/ NOUN, NO PLURAL
1 being good and kind
2 things in food that will make you healthy when you eat it □ *Tomatoes are full of goodness.*
♦ IDIOMS **for goodness' sake** something you say when you are annoyed □ *For goodness sake, Dave, just open the door!* **Goodness (me)!** something you say when you are surprised □ *Goodness me, it's five o'clock already.* **goodness (only) knows** used for emphasizing that you do not know something □ *Goodness knows how long it will take us to get there.*

good night /gʊd ˈnaɪt/ EXCLAMATION
1 something you say to someone just before you go to sleep at night □ *Good night, Mum.* 吾 *He's upstairs saying good night to the children.*
2 a formal way of saying 'goodbye' to people late in the evening □ *Good night. Thanks for coming.*

goods /gʊdz/ PLURAL NOUN things that have been made to sell □ *electrical goods* □ *cars, jewellery and other luxury goods* 吾 *Sales of household goods have fallen.*

goodwill /ˌgʊdˈwɪl/ NOUN, NO PLURAL good feelings towards someone, especially kindness and wanting to help 吾 *As a gesture of goodwill he offered to pay for my coat which he'd ruined.*

gooey /ˈguːi/ ADJECTIVE [**gooier, gooiest**] an informal word meaning soft and sticky □ *a lovely gooey chocolate cake*

google /ˈguːgəl/ VERB [**googles, googling, googled**] to look for something on the Internet using the Google *(trademark)* search engine (= program which looks for words that you have typed). A computing word. □ *I googled the company and found out all about them.*

goose /guːs/ NOUN [*plural* **geese**] a large white or grey bird

gooseberry /ˈgʊzbəri/ NOUN [*plural* **gooseberries**] a small round green fruit which is sour

goosebumps /ˈguːsbʌmps/ *or* **goosepimples** /ˈguːsˈpɪmpəlz/ PLURAL NOUN very small lumps on your skin that you get when you are cold

gore /gɔː(r)/ ▶ NOUN, NO PLURAL lots of blood □ *The film contains a lot of gore.*
▶ VERB [**gores, goring, gored**] if an animal gores someone, it injures them with its horns

gorge /gɔːdʒ/ NOUN [*plural* **gorges**] a deep narrow valley
♦ PHRASAL VERB [**gorges, gorging, gorged**] **gorge (yourself) on something** to eat too much of something □ *They gorged themselves on chocolate cake.*

gorgeous /ˈgɔːdʒəs/ ADJECTIVE very beautiful or pleasant □ *The baby's absolutely gorgeous.* □ *gorgeous weather*

gorilla /gəˈrɪlə/ NOUN [*plural* **gorillas**] an animal that looks like a very large monkey

gory /ˈgɔːri/ ADJECTIVE [**gorier, goriest**] with a lot of blood and often violence □ *a gory film*

gosling /ˈgɒzlɪŋ/ NOUN [*plural* **goslings**] a baby goose

gospel /ˈgɒspəl/ NOUN [*plural* **gospels**]
1 the gospel the life of Jesus Christ and the things he taught
2 one of the four parts in the Bible that describe Jesus Christ's life

gossip /ˈgɒsɪp/ ▶ NOUN [*plural* **gossips**]
1 informal talk about other people, often about their private lives □ *She told me all the latest gossip.* □ *Tim loves a good gossip.*
2 someone who enjoys talking about other people's lives, in a way that you disapprove of
▶ VERB [**gossips, gossiping, gossiped**] to talk about other people, often about their private lives

got /gɒt/ PAST TENSE AND PAST PARTICIPLE OF get

➤ In North America the past participle of 'get' is **gotten** and not 'got'. □ *She'd gotten mad at him.*

gouge /gaʊdʒ/ VERB [**gouges, gouging, gouged**] to make a deep hole or cut in something □ *The explosion had gouged a huge hole in the ground.*
♦ PHRASAL VERB **gouge something out** to remove something by digging or cutting it out of something □ *Be careful, you almost gouged my eye out with that pen!*

gourmet /ˈgʊəmeɪ/ ▶ ADJECTIVE involving very good food □ *a gourmet meal* □ *a gourmet restaurant*
▶ NOUN [*plural* **gourmets**] someone who likes good food

govern /ˈgʌvən/ VERB [**governs, governing, governed**]
1 to officially control a country or area □ *The country was governed by the Republicans.* □ *the governing party*
2 to control the way that something happens or is done □ *The gene governs cell division.* □ *There are laws governing the disposal of toxic waste.*

- **governess** /'gʌvənɪs/ NOUN [plural **governesses**] a woman who taught children in their home in the past
- **government** /'gʌvənmənt/ NOUN [plural **governments**]

1 the group of people who control a country or area ▣ The party will form the next government. □ The government has announced an increase in taxes. ▣ government officials ▣ a government department ▣ He criticized government policies.

2 no plural the process or way of controlling a country or area □ We need a new style of government.

3 in government controlling a country □ The Labour Party has been in government for more than ten years.

- **governor** /'gʌvənə(r)/ NOUN [plural **governors**] someone who is in charge of a place or organization □ the governor of Arkansas □ a school governor

gown /gaʊn/ NOUN [plural **gowns**]

1 a long formal dress that women wear on special occasions

2 a loose piece of clothing worn in hospital □ a hospital gown

GP /ˌdʒiːˈpiː/ ABBREVIATION general practitioner; a doctor who looks after people from a particular area and treats them for a lot of different illnesses

grab /græb/ VERB [**grabs, grabbing, grabbed**]

1 to take something suddenly or violently □ He grabbed my bag and ran away. □ She grabbed my arm as I fell.

2 grab someone's attention to get someone's attention □ It was his unusual tie which grabbed my attention.

3 an informal word meaning to get some food or sleep quickly because you are busy □ Let's stop and grab a sandwich.

4 if you grab a chance or opportunity, you take it in an eager way ▣ Tom grabbed the chance to join the team.

grace /greɪs/ ▶ NOUN, NO PLURAL

1 a smooth and attractive way of moving □ He kicks the ball with effortless grace.

2 polite and pleasant behaviour □ She dealt with the situation with grace and humour.

3 with good grace in a willing way, and without complaining □ Ben accepted the decision with good grace.

4 a prayer that some people say before a meal □ Dad said grace.

▶ VERB [**graces, gracing, graced**] to be somewhere and make it more attractive □ Her photo has graced the cover of many magazines.

- **graceful** /'greɪsfʊl/ ADJECTIVE

1 smooth and attractive in shape or in the way you move □ He watched her graceful movements. □ the graceful curve of the dome

2 polite and pleasant

- **gracefully** /'greɪsfʊlɪ/ ADVERB in a graceful way

gracious /'greɪʃəs/ ADJECTIVE polite and kind □ It was very gracious of you to apologize.

grade /greɪd/ ▶ NOUN [plural **grades**]

1 a number or letter that shows how good a student's work is ▣ She got a grade A in her English exam. ▣ He achieved top grades in his exams.

2 a level of quality or importance □ The jewellery is made from a lower grade of gold. □ He had been promoted to a higher grade at work.

3 the US word for form (= school class)

4 make the grade to be successful, or to achieve the necessary standard □ She was a singer who failed to make the grade.

▶ VERB [**grades, grading, graded**]

1 to separate things into groups of similar size or quality □ Hotels are graded according to the facilities they offer and their cleanliness. □ a grading system

2 to judge the quality of a student's work by giving it a particular letter or number □ Students' work is graded from A–E.

gradient /'greɪdɪənt/ NOUN [plural **gradients**] a measure of how steep a slope is

gradual /'grædʒʊəl/ ADJECTIVE happening slowly over a long period □ There has been a gradual improvement in his work. □ Recovery will be a very gradual process.

- **gradually** /'grædʒʊəlɪ/ ADVERB slowly over a long period □ His health has gradually improved. □ Gradually, her life began to return to normal.

graduate ▶ NOUN /'grædʒʊət/ [plural **graduates**] someone who has a degree (= qualification) from a university or college □ George is a graduate of Edinburgh University.

▶ VERB /'grædʒʊeɪt/ [**graduates, graduating, graduated**] to get a degree (= qualification) from a university or college

- **graduation** /ˌgrædʒʊˈeɪʃən/ NOUN, NO PLURAL when you finish a university course and get a degree (= qualification) □ a graduation ceremony

graffiti /grəˈfiːtɪ/ NOUN, NO PLURAL writing or pictures which people have written or drawn illegally on walls, trains, etc.

graft /grɑːft/ ▶ VERB [**grafts, grafting, grafted**] to take something such as skin or bone from a healthy part of someone's body and use it to repair a damaged part □ He had skin grafted from his leg onto his arm.

▶ NOUN [plural **grafts**] a piece of skin or bone taken from a healthy part of someone's body and used to repair a damaged part ▣ The burns were so bad that she needed a skin graft.

grain /greɪn/ NOUN [plural **grains**]

1 no plural the seeds of crops such as wheat or rice □ They export grain to Russia.

2 a seed from a crop such as wheat or rice □ + of a grain of rice

3 one of the very small pieces of something such as sugar, salt, etc. □ + of grains of sand

4 the pattern of lines on the surface of wood

gram /græm/ NOUN [plural **grams**] a unit for measuring weight, equal to one thousandth of a kilogram. This is often written **g**.

grammar /ˈgræmə(r)/ NOUN [plural **grammars**]
1 no plural the rules of a particular language, for example how words are formed and how words are put together in a sentence □ French grammar
2 a book of grammar rules

grammar school /ˈgræmə(r) ˌskuːl/ NOUN [plural **grammar schools**] in Britain, a school for children from 11–18 who have passed a special exam

grammatical /grəˈmætɪkəl/ ADJECTIVE
1 to do with grammar □ grammatical rules □ a grammatical error
2 correct according to the rules of grammar □ That sentence isn't grammatical, is it?
• **grammatically** /grəˈmætɪkəlɪ/ ADVERB according to the rules of grammar ⌨ Is that grammatically correct?

gramme /græm/ NOUN [plural **grammes**] another spelling of gram

gran /græn/ NOUN [plural **grans**] an informal word for grandmother

grand /grænd/ ADJECTIVE [**grander, grandest**] very large, expensive or special, making you feel admiration □ The house itself was very grand.

grandad /ˈgrændæd/ NOUN [plural **grandads**] an informal word for grandfather

grandchild /ˈgrændtʃaɪld/ NOUN [plural **grandchildren**] a child of your son or daughter □ We've got three grown-up children and five grandchildren.

granddaughter /ˈgrændɔːtə(r)/ NOUN [plural **granddaughters**] the daughter of your son or daughter

grandfather /ˈgrændfɑːðə(r)/ NOUN [plural **grandfathers**] the father of your mother or father ⌨ my paternal grandfather (= father's father) ⌨ my maternal grandfather (= mother's father) □ He recently became a grandfather.

grandly /ˈgrændlɪ/ ADVERB in a way that looks or sounds important, or tries to do this □ 'I'm the senior consultant,' he said rather grandly.

grandma /ˈgrænmɑː/ NOUN [plural **grandmas**] an informal word for grandmother □ At the weekend I usually visit my grandma.

grandmother /ˈgrænmʌðə(r)/ NOUN [plural **grandmothers**] the mother of your mother or father ⌨ my maternal grandmother (= mother's mother) ⌨ my paternal grandmother (= father's mother) □ We called in to see my grandmother.

grandpa /ˈgrænpɑː/ NOUN [plural **grandpas**] an informal word for grandfather □ My grandpa loved singing.

grandparent /ˈgrænpeərənt/ NOUN [plural **grandparents**] a parent of your father or your mother □ I went to stay with my elderly grandparents.

grandson /ˈgrænsʌn/ NOUN [plural **grandsons**] the son of your son or daughter

grandstand /ˈgrændstænd/ NOUN [plural **grandstands**] a large structure for people watching a sports event with rows of seats

granite /ˈgrænɪt/ NOUN, NO PLURAL a very hard grey or red rock

granny /ˈgrænɪ/ NOUN [plural **grannies**] an informal word for grandmother

grant /grɑːnt/ ▶ VERB [**grants, granting, granted**]
1 to officially allow someone to have or to do something they have asked for ⌨ The judge granted him permission to appeal. □ His request was granted.
2 take something/someone for granted to expect something or someone to be there as usual and to forget that you are lucky to have them □ We take our health for granted.
3 take something for granted to expect something to happen without checking or thinking much about it □ You can't take anything for granted. ⌨ She took it for granted that I would agree.
4 a formal word meaning to admit that something is true □ It's very difficult, I grant you.
▶ NOUN [plural **grants**] an amount of money that has been given to you for a special purpose ⌨ The college received a grant of £20,000 to improve computer facilities. □ She applied for a research grant.

granule /ˈgrænjuːl/ NOUN [plural **granules**] a very small grain or part □ sugar granules

grape /greɪp/ NOUN [plural **grapes**] a small, pale green or dark red fruit that grows in groups and is used to make wine ⌨ a bunch of grapes

grapefruit /ˈgreɪpfruːt/ NOUN [plural **grapefruit** or **grapefruits**] a round fruit with thick yellow skin and yellow or pink flesh and a sour taste

grapevine /ˈgreɪpvaɪn/ NOUN [plural **grapevines**]
1 a plant that grapes grow on
2 the grapevine an informal word used to talk about how information spreads quickly in conversations between people ⌨ I heard on the grapevine that she's planning to leave.

graph /grɑːf/ NOUN [plural **graphs**] a picture with lines drawn between different points, used to show how things compare to each other or how something changes

graphic /ˈgræfɪk/ ADJECTIVE
1 showing or giving a lot of detail, often in a way which is shocking ⌨ He went into graphic detail about the operation. □ a graphic description of the attack

2 to do with drawing, painting or text and its design 🖳 *graphic design*

• **graphically** /ˈɡræfɪkəlɪ/ ADVERB including a lot of detail, so very clear and sometimes shocking □ *The film graphically demonstrates the horrors of war.*

• **graphics** /ˈɡræfɪks/ PLURAL NOUN pictures, drawings and text, especially those on a computer screen □ *The game has very realistic graphics.*

graphics card /ˈɡræfɪks ˌkɑːd/ NOUN [plural **graphics cards**] a part inside a computer that allows the computer to show pictures and video. A computing word.

graphite /ˈɡræfaɪt/ NOUN, NO PLURAL a black soft form of the mineral carbon, used in pencils

graph paper /ˈɡrɑːf ˌpeɪpə(r)/ NOUN, NO PLURAL paper covered in very small squares

grapple /ˈɡræpəl/ VERB [**grapples, grappling, grappled**] to hold someone and fight with them □ *The bodyguard tried to grapple him to the floor.*
♦ PHRASAL VERB **grapple with something** to try hard to understand or to deal with something difficult

grasp /ɡrɑːsp/ ▶ VERB [**grasps, grasping, grasped**]
1 to take hold of something tightly □ *She saw the dog and grasped my hand.* □ *He grasped the rope and began to climb.*
2 to understand an idea □ *I still couldn't grasp what he was trying to tell me.* 🖳 *It might be difficult for children to grasp this concept.*
3 to take advantage of an opportunity 🖳 *She grasped the opportunity to speak to Dr Williams alone.*
♦ IDIOM **grasp the nettle** to deal directly with something difficult or unpleasant □ *We've got to grasp the nettle and get rid of polluting cars.*
▶ NOUN, NO PLURAL
1 when you understand or know about something □ *He has a fairly good grasp of the language.* □ *I have to get a grasp on what's happening here.*
2 when you take hold of something firmly □ *He held her wrist in a firm grasp.*
3 the ability to achieve something □ *A deal was within our grasp.*

grass /ɡrɑːs/ NOUN, NO PLURAL a plant with very thin green leaves which covers gardens and fields □ *I cut the grass at the weekend.* 🖳 *a blade of grass* (= one leaf)
♦ IDIOM **the grass is (always) greener on the other side** the situation somewhere else or for someone else always seems better than your own

grasshopper /ˈɡrɑːshɒpə(r)/ NOUN [plural **grasshoppers**] a brown or green insect with long back legs that can jump

grass roots /ˌɡrɑːs ˈruːts/ PLURAL NOUN the ordinary people in a society or organization, not its leaders □ *He's lost touch with the grass roots of the party.*

grassy /ˈɡrɑːsɪ/ ADJECTIVE [**grassier, grassiest**] covered with grass □ *a grassy field*

grate [1] /ɡreɪt/ VERB [**grates, grating, grated**]
1 to cut food into small, thin pieces by rubbing it against a grater (= kitchen tool) □ *grated cheese*

2 to make an unpleasant noise by rubbing against something □ *The two surfaces grated against each other.*
3 to annoy someone □ *His attitude has started to grate.*

grate [2] /ɡreɪt/ NOUN [plural **grates**] a frame of metal bars which holds the wood, coal, etc. in a fireplace (= space for a fire in the wall of a room)

grateful /ˈɡreɪtfʊl/ ADJECTIVE pleased with someone and wanting to thank them because they have done something for you □ + *for* *I'm very grateful for all your kindness.* □ + *to* *I felt so grateful to him for stopping to help.* □ *She gave me a grateful smile.*

• **gratefully** /ˈɡreɪtfʊlɪ/ ADVERB in a grateful way □ *We gratefully accepted the offer.*

grater /ˈɡreɪtə(r)/ NOUN [plural **graters**] a kitchen tool with a lot of small holes with sharp edges on its surface, used for cutting food into small bits

grating /ˈɡreɪtɪŋ/ NOUN [plural **gratings**] a cover for something with holes in it so that water or air can pass through

gratitude /ˈɡrætɪtjuːd/ NOUN, NO PLURAL a feeling of being grateful to someone □ *She expressed her gratitude to the hospital.* 🖳 *I owe a debt of gratitude to my parents for their support.*

grave [1] /ɡreɪv/ NOUN [plural **graves**] a place where a dead body is buried

grave [2] /ɡreɪv/ ADJECTIVE [**graver, gravest**]
1 very serious □ *a grave mistake* 🖳 *You are in grave danger.* 🖳 *He expressed grave concern about the situation.*
2 looking serious □ *She looked grave for a moment.*

gravel /ˈɡrævəl/ NOUN, NO PLURAL small stones used to cover roads, paths, etc.

gravestone /ˈɡreɪvstəʊn/ NOUN [plural **gravestones**] a piece of stone with writing on it which says who is buried in a grave

graveyard /ˈɡreɪvjɑːd/ NOUN [plural **graveyards**] a place where dead bodies are buried

gravitate /ˈɡrævɪteɪt/ VERB [**gravitates, gravitating, gravitated**] to be attracted to someone or something, or to gradually move towards something □ *People tend to gravitate towards her at a party because she's such good fun.*

gravity /ˈɡrævətɪ/ NOUN, NO PLURAL
1 the force that pulls things towards the earth and makes them fall to the ground
2 a formal word meaning how serious something is □ *We appreciate the gravity of the situation.*

gravy /ˈɡreɪvɪ/ NOUN, NO PLURAL a hot sauce made from the juices that come out of meat while it is cooking

gray /ɡreɪ/ ADJECTIVE, NOUN [plural **grays**] the US spelling of grey

graze /ɡreɪz/ ▶ VERB [**grazes, grazing, grazed**]
1 if animals graze, they move around eating grass and other plants

2 to hurt your skin by rubbing it against something hard and rough □ *I fell and grazed my knees.*
3 to touch the surface of something lightly □ *His hand grazed mine as he held the door open.*
▶ NOUN [*plural* **grazes**] a mark on your skin where it has been grazed

grease /griːs/ ▶ NOUN, NO PLURAL
1 a substance such as fat or thick oil □ *a grease stain*
2 a substance like thick oil used to make parts of machines move smoothly
▶ VERB [**greases, greasing, greased**] to rub grease on something □ *Grease the pan well.*
• **greasy** /ˈgriːsɪ/ ADJECTIVE [**greasier, greasiest**]
1 covered in or containing grease □ *greasy food* □ *He wiped his greasy fingers on his jeans.*
2 containing a lot of natural oil □ *greasy hair*

great /greɪt/ ADJECTIVE [**greater, greatest**]
1 very good □ *This is a great opportunity for you to travel.* □ *Our builders have done a great job.* □ *Your hair looks great like that.* □ *I've had a great idea!*
2 very large in size, amount or level □ *The elephant lifted one of its great feet.* ⧉ *We had a great deal of* (= a lot of) *trouble getting the information we needed.* ⧉ *His dinner party was a great success.* □ *They were in great danger.*
3 very good and skilled □ *He was one of the greatest scientists of all time.* □ *She's a great player.*
4 important and powerful □ *great armies* □ *a great nation*
5 a slightly informal word meaning very enjoyable □ *It was a great film.* □ *We had a great time in Venice.*
6 a slightly informal way of expressing pleasure or agreement □ *'We'll meet you at seven.' 'Great – see you then!'*

Great Britain /ˌgreɪt ˈbrɪtən/ NOUN England, Scotland and Wales

great-grandchild /ˌgreɪtˈgrændtʃaɪld/ NOUN [*plural* **great-grandchildren**] your grandson's or granddaughter's child

great-grand-daughter /ˌgreɪtˈgrændɔːtə(r)/ NOUN [*plural* **great-grand-daughters**] your grandson's or granddaughter's daughter

great-grandfather /ˌgreɪtˈgrændfɑːðə(r)/ NOUN [*plural* **great-grandfathers**] your grandmother's or grandfather's father

great-grandmother /ˌgreɪtˈgrænmʌðə(r)/ NOUN [*plural* **great-grandmothers**] your grandmother's or grandfather's mother

great-grandparent /ˌgreɪtˈgrænpeərənt/ NOUN [*plural* **great-grandparents**] a parent of your grandmother or grandfather

great-grandson /ˌgreɪtˈgrænsʌn/ NOUN [*plural* **great-grandsons**] your grandson's or grand-daughter's son

greatly /ˈgreɪtlɪ/ ADVERB very much □ *The effects can vary greatly.* □ *I greatly admire what he's done.* □ *Your help is greatly appreciated.* □ *Smoking greatly increases your risk of developing cancer.*

greatness /ˈgreɪtnɪs/ NOUN, NO PLURAL when someone is very important, respected or skilled □ *He has achieved greatness as a player.*

greed /griːd/ NOUN, NO PLURAL when you want more of something than you need, especially food or money □ *Big businesses are often accused of greed and selfishness.*
• **greedily** /ˈgriːdɪlɪ/ ADVERB in a greedy way
• **greediness** /ˈgriːdɪnɪs/ NOUN, NO PLURAL the quality of being greedy
• **greedy** /ˈgriːdɪ/ ADJECTIVE [**greedier, greediest**] wanting more of something than you need □ *You greedy pig! You've eaten it all.*

green /griːn/ ▶ ADJECTIVE
1 having the colour of leaves or grass □ *He's wearing a green coat.* □ *The curtains were dark green.*
2 to do with protecting the environment □ *She's involved in green politics.* □ *We're trying to be green by cycling to work.*
3 **green spaces** places with grass and plants
▶ NOUN [*plural* **greens**]
1 the colour of leaves and grass
2 an area of short grass on a golf course

green belt /ˈgriːn ˌbelt/ NOUN, NO PLURAL an area of green fields around a city where you are not allowed to build

greenery /ˈgriːnərɪ/ NOUN, NO PLURAL plants with green leaves

green fingers /ˌgriːn ˈfɪŋgəz/ PLURAL NOUN someone who has green fingers is good at making plants grow

greengrocer /ˈgriːnˌgrəʊsə(r)/ NOUN [*plural* **greengrocers**]
1 someone who sells fruit and vegetables
2 **greengrocer's** a shop selling fruit and vegetables

greenhouse /ˈgriːnhaʊs/ NOUN [*plural* **greenhouses**] a building with glass walls and a glass roof that stays warm and is used for growing plants in

greenhouse effect /ˈgriːnhaʊs ɪˌfekt/ NOUN, NO PLURAL the heating of the Earth's surface caused by pollution which stops heat from leaving the atmosphere

greenhouse gas /ˈgriːnhaʊs ˌgæs/ NOUN [*plural* **greenhouse gases**] a gas that stops heat from leaving the atmosphere, causing the temperature of Earth to increase □ *Greenhouse gases include carbon dioxide and methane.*

greens /griːnz/ PLURAL NOUN green vegetables such as cabbage □ *Be sure to eat all your greens.*

greet /griːt/ VERB [**greets, greeting, greeted**]
1 to say something to someone when they arrive or when you meet them □ *She went outside to greet her visitors.* □ *He was greeted by a crowd of fans at the airport.*
2 to react to something in a particular way □ ***+ with*** *The announcement was greeted with enthusiasm.*
• **greeting** /ˈgriːtɪŋ/ NOUN [*plural* **greetings**]

something polite or friendly that you say when you meet someone or send a message to someone □ They exchanged friendly greetings. □ John sends his warmest greetings.

grenade /grə'neɪd/ NOUN [plural **grenades**] a small bomb that explodes a few seconds after someone throws it

grew /gru:/ PAST TENSE OF **grow**

grey /greɪ/ ► ADJECTIVE

1 having the colour you get when you mix black and white □ The sheets were grey with dirt.

2 grey hair has become grey or white as someone gets older ⊞ At what age did you go grey?

3 if the weather is grey, there are lots of clouds and it seems as though it will rain

♦ IDIOM **a grey area** a subject or situation which people are not sure about because there are no clear rules □ We are not allowed to accept money, but other gifts are a bit of a grey area.

► NOUN [plural **greys**] the colour you get when you mix black and white

greyhound /'greɪhaʊnd/ NOUN [plural **greyhounds**] a type of dog with a thin body and narrow head which can run very fast

grid /grɪd/ NOUN [plural **grids**]

1 a pattern of lines that cross each other to form squares

2 a system of wires which carry electricity to a large area □ the Australian electricity grid

3 a map with a set of numbered lines to help you find places

4 metal bars that cross each other to form squares

grid reference /'grɪd ˌrefrəns/ NOUN [plural **grid references**] a set of numbers or letters used to show a place on a map

grief /gri:f/ NOUN, NO PLURAL a feeling of great sadness, especially when someone has died □ He expressed his grief at his baby daughter's death. □ His death prompted an outpouring of grief.

♦ IDIOM **come to grief** to fail or to have an accident □ Drivers often come to grief on the mountain roads.

grievance /'gri:vəns/ NOUN [plural **grievances**] something you complain about because you think it is wrong or unfair ⊞ People will get a chance to air their grievances (= say what is making them angry) at the meeting.

grieve /gri:v/ VERB [grieves, grieving, grieved] to feel very sad, especially because someone has died □ She was still grieving for her dead son.

grievous /'gri:vəs/ ADJECTIVE a formal word meaning very serious □ He suffered grievous injuries. □ a grievous error

• **grievously** /'gri:vəslɪ/ ADVERB in a very serious way □ He was grievously wounded.

grill /grɪl/ ► VERB [grills, grilling, grilled]

1 to cook food by putting it close to direct heat □ Grill the fish for a couple of minutes on each side.

2 to ask someone a lot of questions □ Detectives

grilled him about his recent movements.

► NOUN [plural **grills**]

1 a piece of kitchen equipment which cooks food under a direct heat

2 metal bars which food can be cooked on over a fire

grille /grɪl/ NOUN [plural **grilles**] a cover for a door, window, etc. made of wire or metal bars

grilling /'grɪlɪŋ/ NOUN [plural **grillings**] when someone asks you a lot of difficult questions □ The minister faced a grilling by journalists about the new plans.

grim /grɪm/ ADJECTIVE [grimmer, grimmest]

1 very unpleasant, worrying or shocking □ The situation looked pretty grim. ⊞ The pictures illustrate the grim reality of life in the refugee camps.

2 serious and unfriendly □ The men wore grim expressions.

grimace /'grɪmɪs/ ► VERB [grimaces, grimacing, grimaced] to twist your face into an expression of pain, dislike, etc. □ She tried to get up and grimaced in pain. □ He grimaced at the memory.

► NOUN [plural **grimaces**] when you grimace

grime /graɪm/ NOUN, NO PLURAL dirt that has been on a surface for a long time □ He wiped away a thick layer of grime.

grimly /'grɪmlɪ/ ADVERB

1 in a serious, unfriendly way □ He nodded grimly.

2 showing determination □ In the second half, the team hung on grimly.

grimy /'graɪmɪ/ ADJECTIVE [grimier, grimiest] covered with dirt □ a grimy window

grin /grɪn/ ► VERB [grins, grinning, grinned] to give a big smile □ Ben was grinning broadly as he came out.

♦ IDIOM **grin and bear it** to accept a difficult situation without complaining □ You'll just have to grin and bear it.

► NOUN [plural **grins**] a big smile □ His face broke into a broad grin.

grind /graɪnd/ ► VERB [grinds, grinding, ground]

1 to crush something solid into a powder □ ground pepper □ The rocks are ground into dust.

2 grind your teeth to make a noise when you rub your teeth together

3 grind to a halt to gradually become slower and stop moving or working □ The traffic ground to a halt.

4 to make something smooth or sharp by rubbing it against a hard surface

♦ PHRASAL VERB **grind someone down** to make someone lose their confidence and energy □ He was ground down by weeks of illness.

► NOUN, NO PLURAL something that is difficult and boring to do ⊞ the daily grind of work

• **grinder** /'graɪndə(r)/ NOUN [plural **grinders**] a machine that grinds things such as coffee beans

• **grinding** /'graɪndɪŋ/ ADJECTIVE

1 used to emphasize that something is very bad and continues without stopping ⊞ These people live in grinding poverty.

2 a grinding halt when something stops moving or

working completely □ *The whole city came to a grinding halt.*

grindstone /ˈgraɪndstəʊn/ NOUN [plural **grindstones**] a circular stone that turns on top of another stone and is used to grind corn

♦ IDIOM **have/keep your nose to the grindstone** to be working very hard, especially for a long time □ *He kept his nose to the grindstone.*

grip /grɪp/ ▶ VERB [**grips, gripping, gripped**]
1 to hold something tightly □ *Martha gripped his arm.* □ *I gripped the steering wheel tighter.*
2 to hold your attention completely □ *The story has gripped the public imagination.*
3 to feel an emotion very strongly and suddenly □ *Panic gripped him suddenly.* □ *The small community was gripped by fear.*
▶ NOUN [plural **grips**]
1 when someone holds something tightly ⊞ *He tightened his grip on her shoulder.*
2 control over something ⊞ *He has further tightened his grip on power.* □ *They have a firm grip on the market.*
3 in the grip of something in a difficult situation □ *The south is in the grip of a severe drought.*
4 get a grip (on something) to try to control your emotions □ *You need to calm down and get a grip.*
5 a small U-shaped piece of wire used to keep hair in place
♦ IDIOM **come/get to grips with something** to understand and to start to deal with something □ *I had to get to grips with the fact that I couldn't walk.*
● **gripping** /ˈgrɪpɪŋ/ ADJECTIVE holding your attention completely □ *a gripping film*

grisly /ˈgrɪzli/ ADJECTIVE unpleasant and frightening, often involving blood or death □ *a grisly story*

gristle /ˈgrɪsəl/ NOUN, NO PLURAL a hard substance that is sometimes found in meat
● **gristly** /ˈgrɪsli/ ADJECTIVE containing pieces of gristle

grit /grɪt/ ▶ NOUN, NO PLURAL
1 very small sharp pieces of stone or sand □ *He brushed the grit off his trousers.*
2 bravery and determination □ *She showed true grit to hang on and win the second set.*
▶ VERB [**grits, gritting, gritted**] to put grit onto a road to stop vehicles sliding on ice
♦ IDIOM **grit your teeth**
1 to hold your teeth tightly together, for example when you are angry or in pain □ *She gritted her teeth against the pain.* □ *He replied through gritted teeth.*
2 to show bravery and determination □ *I gritted my teeth and plunged into the water.*
● **gritty** /ˈgrɪti/ ADJECTIVE [**grittier, grittiest**]
1 feeling rough like grit
2 brave and determined □ *He had a gritty determination to succeed.*
3 showing unpleasant details about life □ *a gritty television drama*

grizzly /ˈgrɪzli/ NOUN [plural **grizzlies**] a grizzly bear

grizzly bear /ˈgrɪzli ˌbeə(r)/ NOUN [plural **grizzly bears**] a type of large brown bear found in parts of the United States and Canada

groan /grəʊn/ ▶ VERB [**groans, groaning, groaned**]
1 to make a long deep sound to express pain, unhappiness, etc. □ *He groaned in pain.*
2 to say something in a way that shows you are unhappy □ *'Not again!' Matt groaned.*
3 to make a sound like a groan □ *The trees creaked and groaned.*
▶ NOUN [plural **groans**]
1 when you groan □ *She got slowly to her feet with a groan.*
2 a complaint ⊞ *There are always a few moans and groans.*

grocer /ˈgrəʊsə(r)/ NOUN [plural **grocers**]
1 grocer's a shop selling food and things for the house
2 someone who runs a shop selling food and things for the house
● **groceries** /ˈgrəʊsəriz/ PLURAL NOUN food and things for the house that you buy regularly □ *a bag of groceries* □ *More people now buy their groceries online.*
● **grocery** /ˈgrəʊsəri/ ADJECTIVE to do with groceries or a grocer's □ *grocery shopping* □ *a grocery list*

groggy /ˈgrɒgi/ ADJECTIVE [**groggier, groggiest**] slightly weak, tired and not able to think clearly □ *They were still groggy from their long flight.*

groin /grɔɪn/ NOUN [plural **groins**] the place where your legs join your body

groom /gruːm/ ▶ VERB [**grooms, grooming, groomed**]
1 to look after an animal, especially by brushing its fur □ *She groomed and exercised the horses.*
2 to prepare someone for a particular position or job □ *She's being groomed for an important role.*
3 to make yourself look clean and tidy □ *He has carefully groomed hair.*
4 when animals groom each other, they clean each other's fur
▶ NOUN [plural **grooms**]
1 someone whose job is to look after horses
2 a bridegroom (= man who is getting married)
● **grooming** /ˈgruːmɪŋ/ NOUN, NO PLURAL the things that people do to keep clean and make themselves look good □ *They sell men's grooming products.*

groove /gruːv/ NOUN [plural **grooves**] a long narrow line cut into a surface □ *Deep grooves had been cut into the stone.*

grope /grəʊp/ VERB [**gropes, groping, groped**]
1 to feel with your hand to try to find something you cannot see □ *I groped around for my glasses.* □ *She groped in her pocket for her ticket.*
2 to try to think of a word or an answer □ *I groped for an answer.*

gross /grəʊs/ ▶ ADJECTIVE [**grosser, grossest**]
1 a gross amount is the total amount without

anything being taken away, especially tax 🔁 *monthly gross income*

2 very bad or serious 🔁 *He was dismissed for gross misconduct* (= very bad behaviour). 🔁 *His death was a result of gross negligence by his employer.*

3 an informal word meaning very unpleasant or offensive □ *It tastes pretty gross.*

▶ VERB [**grosses, grossing, grossed**] to earn a particular amount of money before tax, etc. is taken away □ *The film has grossed £13.5 million.*

• **grossly** /ˈɡrəʊslɪ/ ADVERB to a great level □ *The claim is grossly exaggerated.*

grotesque /ɡrəʊˈtesk/ ADJECTIVE very ugly or unpleasant □ *grotesque masks*

• **grotesquely** /ɡrəʊˈtesklɪ/ ADVERB in a grotesque way □ *His face was grotesquely distorted.*

grotty /ˈɡrɒtɪ/ ADJECTIVE [**grottier, grottiest**] an informal word meaning unpleasant or of bad quality □ *He lived in a grotty little apartment.*

ground[1] /ɡraʊnd/ ▶ NOUN [*plural* **grounds**]

1 the Earth's surface □ *The damaged satellite is expected to fall to the ground next week.* □ *These plants thrive on higher ground.*

2 earth or soil □ *The ground is frozen.* □ *fertile ground*

3 an area where a particular sport is played □ *a football ground*

4 an area of information 🔁 *We have covered a lot of ground in this lesson.* 🔁 *Every time we talk, we go over the same ground* (= talk about the same things).

➔ *go to* **grounds**

◆ IDIOMS **get (something) off the ground** to start something successfully □ *I tried to set up a football club, but it never really got off the ground.* **gain/lose ground** to become more/less popular or successful **stand your ground** to refuse to change your opinion about something

➔ *go to* **suit** **someone down to the ground**

▶ VERB [**grounds, grounding, grounded**] to stop an aircraft from leaving the ground

ground[2] /ɡraʊnd/ PAST TENSE AND PAST PARTICIPLE OF **grind**

grounded /ˈɡraʊndɪd/ ADJECTIVE

1 sensible and not too emotional □ *She has remained grounded despite her fame.*

2 **be grounded in/on something** to be based on something □ *Their work is grounded in street culture.*

ground floor /ˌɡraʊnd ˈflɔː(r)/ NOUN, NO PLURAL the floor of a building at the level of the ground outside □ *The electrical department is on the ground floor.*

grounding /ˈɡraʊndɪŋ/ NOUN, NO PLURAL knowledge of the basic facts or skills relating to something 🔁 *The job should give her a good grounding in management technique.*

grounds /ɡraʊndz/ PLURAL NOUN

1 the area of land that surrounds and belongs to a large house or building □ *They attended a party in the grounds of the castle.*

2 reasons for doing something □ *There are some*

grounds for optimism. □ *He had to retire on health grounds.*

group /ɡruːp/ ▶ NOUN [*plural* **groups**]

1 a number of people or things that are together or that belong together □ **+ of** *There was a small group of people waiting outside.* □ *We split the samples into three different groups.* □ *Environmental groups have opposed the plans.*

2 a number of people who perform music together 🔁 *a pop group*

▶ VERB [**groups, grouping, grouped**] to put people or things together in a group or groups □ *The children were grouped according to age.*

grouse[1] /ɡraʊs/ NOUN [*plural* **grouse**] a type of fat bird that lives on open land and is hunted for sport

grouse[2] /ɡraʊs/ ▶ VERB [**grouses, grousing, groused**] to complain about something □ *People always grouse about ticket prices.*

▶ NOUN [*plural* **grouses**] a complaint

grove /ɡrəʊv/ NOUN [*plural* **groves**] a small group of trees growing close together □ *an olive grove*

grovel /ˈɡrɒvəl/ VERB [**grovels, grovelling**/US **groveling, grovelled**/US **groveled**]

1 to show someone too much respect in order to try to make them like you or forgive you □ *I wish he wouldn't grovel to the boss like that.*

2 to move close to the ground on your hands and knees, usually in order to look for something

grow /ɡrəʊ/ VERB [**grows, growing, grew, grown**]

1 if a person, animal or plant grows, it becomes bigger or taller □ *He's grown as tall as his father.* □ *The grass has grown a lot this week.*

2 if you grow plants, you put seeds in the ground and look after them □ *We grow vegetables in our garden.* □ *organically grown produce*

3 if your hair or nails grow, they become longer

4 to increase in amount or size □ *The world's population is growing rapidly.* □ *Since he changed schools, his confidence has grown.*

5 to become □ *It was growing dark.* □ *The sound grew louder.*

◆ PHRASAL VERBS **grow on someone** if something grows on you, you start to like it □ *I must admit that the yellow walls are growing on me.* **grow out of something** **1** if a child grows out of clothes, they become too big for them **2** to stop liking or doing something as you become older □ *I used to take a doll to bed, but I grew out of it in the end.* **grow up 1** to become older or to become an adult

2 to stop behaving like a child □ *I wish you'd grow up and take some responsibility!*

3 to develop □ *An unpleasant atmosphere grew up in the office.*

• **grower** /ˈɡrəʊə(r)/ NOUN [*plural* **growers**] someone who grows crops to sell

• **growing** /ˈɡrəʊɪŋ/ ADJECTIVE increasing 🔁 *Growing*

numbers of nurses are leaving their jobs. □ *There are growing fears for his safety.*

growl /graʊl/ ▶ VERB [**growls, growling, growled**]
1 if an animal such as a dog growls, it makes a deep threatening noise in its throat □ *Two black guard dogs growled.*
2 if a person growls, they talk in a deep voice, often because they are angry
▶ NOUN [*plural* **growls**] a deep threatening sound □ *The dog let out a low growl.*

grown /grəʊn/ PAST PARTICIPLE OF grow

grown-up /ˈgrəʊnʌp/ ▶ NOUN [*plural* **grown-ups**] an adult □ *The grown-ups enjoyed themselves as much as the children.*
▶ ADJECTIVE adult □ *We have three grown-up children.*

growth /grəʊθ/ NOUN [*plural* **growths**]
1 *no plural* when something grows, develops or gets bigger □ + *of the rapid growth of computer technology* □ + *in The company reported a growth in sales.* □ *economic growth* □ *Warmth brings about growth in the garden.*
2 a lump that grows on the body □ *A growth developed on his hand.*

grub /grʌb/ NOUN [*plural* **grubs**]
1 a form of an insect with a soft body because it has just come out of an egg
2 an informal word for food

grubby /ˈgrʌbi/ ADJECTIVE [**grubbier, grubbiest**] slightly dirty □ *Go and wash those grubby hands!*

grudge /grʌdʒ/ ▶ VERB [**grudges, grudging, grudged**]
1 to feel that someone does not deserve something □ *We did not grudge them their good fortune, after all their problems.*
2 to give your time, money, etc. unwillingly □ *I grudged the months I had spent with them.*
▶ NOUN [*plural* **grudges**] a feeling of anger or dislike for someone because of something they have done in the past 🔲 *I don't* bear *a grudge against them.*
● **grudging** /ˈgrʌdʒɪŋ/ ADJECTIVE given unwillingly □ *In spite of his bad temper, his courage had earned him the grudging respect of his men.*
● **grudgingly** /ˈgrʌdʒɪŋli/ ADVERB in a grudging way □ *'I suppose she could stay with us,' Tina offered, grudgingly.*

grueling /ˈgruːəlɪŋ/ ADJECTIVE the US spelling of gruelling

gruelling /ˈgruːəlɪŋ/ ADJECTIVE very difficult and making you very tired □ *It was a gruelling climb to the summit of the mountain.*

gruesome /ˈgruːsəm/ ADJECTIVE very unpleasant, violent and upsetting □ *a gruesome murder*

gruff /grʌf/ ADJECTIVE [**gruffer, gruffest**] a gruff voice is deep and sounds unfriendly

grumble /ˈgrʌmbəl/ ▶ VERB [**grumbles, grumbling, grumbled**] to complain in an unhappy way, especially about small things □ *She was grumbling about the food.*

▶ NOUN [*plural* **grumbles**] a complaint □ *There were some grumbles about scheduling.*

grumpily /ˈgrʌmpɪli/ ADVERB in a grumpy way □ *'Oh, all right then.' he said, grumpily.*

grumpy /ˈgrʌmpi/ ADJECTIVE [**grumpier, grumpiest**] bad-tempered □ *He's grumpy in the morning.*

grunt /grʌnt/ ▶ VERB [**grunts, grunting, grunted**] to make a deep noise like a pig □ *He only grunted in response.*
▶ NOUN [*plural* **grunts**] a deep noise like a pig

guarantee /ˌgærənˈtiː/ ▶ NOUN [*plural* **guarantees**]
1 a promise that something will certainly be done or will happen 🔲 *I give a guarantee that we will do everything we can.* □ *Simply having talent is no guarantee of success.*
2 a promise that a product will be repaired or replaced if there is something wrong with it □ *a money-back guarantee* □ *The equipment has a one-year guarantee.*
▶ VERB [**guarantees, guaranteeing, guaranteed**]
1 to make a promise that something will happen or be done □ *We couldn't guarantee his safety.*
2 to give a guarantee for a product that is sold

guard /gɑːd/ ▶ NOUN [*plural* **guards**]
1 someone whose job is to protect a person or place, or to make sure that prisoners do not escape
2 under guard being protected or prevented from escaping □ *He was taken to the prison under armed guard.*
3 keep/stand guard to protect a person or place, or to make sure that prisoners do not escape □ *I stood guard over the money.*
4 a group of soldiers or police who are protecting a person or place □ *the presidential guard*
5 an object that protects or covers something □ *a mouth guard* □ *a fire guard*
6 on guard (a) responsible for protecting a person or place □ *There were no soldiers on guard that night.* (b) ready to deal with a difficult situation □ *You need to be on guard for suspicious phone calls.*
7 off guard not ready to deal with a difficult situation □ *She caught me off guard and I agreed to help her.*
8 drop/lower you guard to stop being careful □ *If you lower your guard for a minute, he'll start asking you personal questions.*
▶ VERB [**guards, guarding, guarded**]
1 to make sure that someone does not escape □ *You guard the back entrance.*
2 to protect someone or something □ *I guarded the children while he went for help.*
◆ PHRASAL VERB **guard against something** to try to make sure that something does not happen □ *I take regular breaks to guard against tiredness.*
● **guarded** /ˈgɑːdɪd/ ADJECTIVE careful not to show your emotions or give too much information 🔲 *a guarded response*
● **guardian** /ˈgɑːdɪən/ NOUN [*plural* **guardians**]
1 someone who is legally responsible for a child when its parents have died

2 someone who protects something □ *We see ourselves as guardians of democracy.*

guerrilla /gə'rɪlə/ NOUN [*plural* **guerrillas**] a fighter who is a member of a small or unofficial army fighting for political reasons

guess /ges/ ▶ VERB [**guesses, guessing, guessed**]
1 to give an answer or opinion without knowing all the facts □ **+ question word** *Guess how old she is.*
2 to give a correct answer or correct information without knowing all the facts □ **+ that** *He guessed that we were hiding something from him.* ▣ *You'll never guess what I've done!*
3 I guess a slightly informal phrase used to say that you think something is true □ *I guess we'll have to sell the car.*
▶ NOUN [*plural* **guesses**] an answer or opinion made by guessing ▣ *At a rough guess, I'd say he's forty.*

guest /gest/ NOUN [*plural* **guests**]
1 someone you invite to your house or to a party □ *a wedding guest* □ *She was one of 200 guests at the party.*
2 someone staying in a hotel □ *Hotel guests can use the gym for free.*
3 a famous person who appears on a television or radio show ▣ *Let me introduce our special guest.*

guesthouse /'gesthaʊs/ NOUN [*plural* **guesthouses**] a small hotel

guffaw /gʌ'fɔ:/ ▶ VERB [**guffaws, guffawing, guffawed**] to laugh loudly
▶ NOUN [*plural* **guffaws**] a loud laugh

GUI /,dʒi: ju: 'aɪ/ ABBREVIATION Graphical User Interface; a way of showing information on a computer screen using pictures and symbols. A computing word.

guidance /'gaɪdəns/ NOUN, NO PLURAL advice about how you should do something □ *We provide guidance on environmental management.*

guide /gaɪd/ ▶ NOUN [*plural* **guides**]
1 someone whose job is to show places to people who are visiting □ *A guide showed us around the cathedral.*
2 something that helps you make a correct judgment about something ▣ *As a rough guide, I cook 50g rice for each person.* □ *If house prices are any guide, this area is becoming more popular.*
3 a book that gives information about a place or tells you how to do something
▶ VERB [**guides, guiding, guided**]
1 to go with someone to show them where to go or tell them about a place
2 to help someone or something move in the right direction □ *Metal tracks guide the missiles into place.*
3 to show someone how to behave or how to do something □ **+ through** *My parents helped to guide me through a difficult time in my life.* □ *His religion is the guiding principle of his life.*

guidebook /'gaɪdbʊk/ NOUN [*plural* **guidebooks**] a book which contains information for people visiting a particular place

guide dog /'gaɪd ,dɒg/ NOUN [*plural* **guide dogs**] a specially trained dog used by a blind person to help them get around

guidelines /'gaɪdlaɪnz/ PLURAL NOUN advice or rules about how to do something □ *Our company has strict guidelines on safety at work.*

guild /gɪld/ NOUN [*plural* **guilds**] an organization for people with the same job, especially a skilled job □ *the writer's guild*

guile /gaɪl/ NOUN, NO PLURAL the quality of being clever, often in a dishonest way

guillotine /'gɪlə,ti:n/ NOUN [*plural* **guillotines**]
1 a piece of equipment with a blade that falls very quickly, which was used in the past to cut off criminals' heads
2 a machine with a very sharp blade used for cutting paper

guilt /gɪlt/ NOUN, NO PLURAL
1 an unpleasant feeling you get when you know you have done something wrong □ *a sense of guilt* □ *She felt no guilt at what she had done.*
2 the fact that you have done something wrong □ *He admitted his guilt and accepted the punishment.*
• **guiltily** /'gɪltɪlɪ/ ADVERB in a way that shows you feel guilty □ *We looked at each other guiltily.*
• **guilty** /'gɪltɪ/ ADJECTIVE [**guiltier, guiltiest**]
1 ashamed because you have done something wrong ▣ *I felt guilty about lying to them.* □ *I had a guilty conscience.*
2 having committed a crime □ **+ of** *They are guilty of war crimes.* ▣ *He pleaded guilty to manslaughter.* ▣ *He was found guilty of drug smuggling.*
3 responsible for doing something wrong □ **+ of** *She's guilty of neglecting her duties as a mother.*

guinea pig /'gɪnɪ ,pɪg/ NOUN [*plural* **guinea pigs**]
1 a small animal with fur and no tail that children often keep as a pet
2 an informal word for someone who is used as part of an experiment, for example to test a new medicine

guitar /gɪ'tɑ:(r)/ NOUN [*plural* **guitars**] an instrument with strings that you play with your fingers or a small piece of plastic ▣ *an electric guitar*
• **guitarist** /gɪ'tɑ:rɪst/ NOUN [*plural* **guitarists**] someone who plays the guitar, especially as their job

gulf /gʌlf/ NOUN [*plural* **gulfs**]
1 a large area of sea almost surrounded by land □ *the Gulf of Taranto*
2 a very big difference between two situations or between the way two groups of people live ▣ *The gulf between the rich and the poor is widening.*

gull /gʌl/ NOUN [*plural* **gulls**] a white or grey sea bird

gullible /'gʌləbəl/ ADJECTIVE a gullible person believes what they are told and is easily tricked □ *Gullible pensioners were paying far too much to handymen.*

gully /'gʌlɪ/ NOUN [plural **gullies**] a deep narrow valley that was made by rain or a fast stream

gulp /gʌlp/ ▶ VERB [**gulps, gulping, gulped**]
1 to eat or drink something quickly □ *He gulped down his tea.*
2 to swallow loudly because you are nervous, afraid or surprised □ *Mum gulped when she saw the bill.*
▶ NOUN [plural **gulps**]
1 the sound made when you gulp □ *'Don't leave me', she said with a gulp.*
2 an amount of food or drink that is being eaten or drunk quickly □ *He finished the beer in two gulps.*

gum /gʌm/ ▶ NOUN [plural **gums**]
1 the hard pink part in your mouth that your teeth grow from ⊞ *gum disease*
2 *no plural* a soft sweet substance that you chew but do not swallow □ *a stick of gum*
3 a type of fruit sweet that you can chew □ *fruit gums*
4 *no plural* a type of glue used to stick paper or card
▶ VERB [**gums, gumming, gummed**] to stick something with gum
• **gummy** /'gʌmɪ/ ADJECTIVE [**gummier, gummiest**] sticky like gum □ *The baby's hands were gummy with jam.*

gun /gʌn/ NOUN [plural **guns**] a weapon that fires bullets from a metal tube ⊞ *The soldier quickly loaded his gun.*
➡ *go to* **jump** the gun, **stick** to your guns
◆ PHRASAL VERB [**guns, gunning, gunned**] **gun someone down** to shoot someone

gunfire /'gʌnfaɪə(r)/ NOUN, NO PLURAL when guns are fired or the sound that this makes □ *They suddenly heard gunfire in the distance.*

gunge /gʌndʒ/ NOUN, NO PLURAL any unpleasant sticky substance □ *There was a layer of black gunge on the inside of the oven.*

gunman /'gʌnmən/ NOUN [plural **gunmen**] a man who uses a gun to steal from people or kill them □ *Two masked gunmen attacked him in his own home.*

gunpoint /'gʌnpɔɪnt/ NOUN, NO PLURAL at gunpoint when someone is pointing a gun at you □ *Customers were held at gunpoint while the men emptied the tills.*

gunpowder /'gʌn,paʊdə(r)/ NOUN, NO PLURAL an explosive powder, used in bombs and fireworks (= objects that explode in the sky with bright colours)

gunshot /'gʌnʃɒt/ NOUN [plural **gunshots**] when a gun is fired, or the noise this makes ⊞ *We're seeing more gunshot wounds in the hospital nowadays.*

gurgle /'gɜːgəl/ ▶ VERB [**gurgles, gurgling, gurgled**]
1 to make a sound like water flowing through a narrow space
2 if a baby gurgles, it makes quiet, happy sounds
▶ NOUN [plural **gurgles**] a gurgling sound □ *We could hear the gurgle of water in the pipes.*

guru /'gʊruː/ NOUN [plural **gurus**]
1 a Hindu or Sikh religious leader and teacher
2 a teacher or leader whose ideas or opinions you respect □ *a tennis guru*

gush /gʌʃ/ ▶ VERB [**gushes, gushing, gushed**]
1 if liquid gushes, it flows out suddenly and in large amounts □ *Blood was gushing from a wound on her forehead.*
2 to praise someone or something so much that it does not seem sincere □ *'What an absolutely fabulous meal,' she gushed.*
▶ NOUN [plural **gushes**] a large amount of a liquid that suddenly flows □ *Suddenly a gush of water poured out of the tap.*

gust /gʌst/ NOUN [plural **gusts**] a sudden strong wind □ *A gust of wind blew her hat off.*

gusto /'gʌstəʊ/ NOUN, NO PLURAL **with gusto** with great enthusiasm and enjoyment □ *He ate his spaghetti with gusto.*

gusty /'gʌstɪ/ ADJECTIVE [**gustier, gustiest**] gusty weather has sudden strong winds

gut /gʌt/ ▶ NOUN [plural **guts**]
1 the tube that takes food from your stomach to be passed out of your body as waste
2 **guts** (a) courage and determination ⊞ *It took guts to stand up to his father.* □ *He didn't have the guts to tell me he was leaving.* (b) the organs inside an animal's body
3 a fat stomach □ *His gut was hanging over his trousers.*
◆ IDIOM **hate someone's guts** to hate someone very muc
▶ VERB [**guts, gutting, gutted**]
1 to destroy or remove everything inside a place □ *The building was gutted by fire.*
2 to remove the organs from inside the body of a dead fish or animal
▶ ADJECTIVE based on your feelings and emotions ⊞ *My gut reaction was to run away.* ⊞ *I just had a gut feeling that she was lying.*

gutter /'gʌtə(r)/ NOUN [plural **gutters**]
1 a long, curved piece of plastic or metal that is fastened to the edge of a roof to carry away the water when it rains
2 the curved edge of a road where water can flow away

guy /gaɪ/ NOUN [plural **guys**]
1 an informal word for a man
2 **guys** used in informal situations to talk to or about two or more people □ *Do any of you guys want some chips?*

guzzle /'gʌzəl/ VERB [**guzzles, guzzling, guzzled**] to eat or drink something quickly □ *Did you guzzle all the chocolate?*

gym /dʒɪm/ NOUN [plural **gyms**]
1 a room or building with equipment for doing exercises □ *I go to the gym three times a week.*
2 exercises that you do inside, especially at school □ *We have gym on Wednesday.*

gymnasium /dʒɪm'neɪzɪəm/ NOUN [plural **gymnasiums** or **gymnasia**] a large room or building with equipment for doing exercises

gymnast /'dʒɪmnæst/ NOUN [plural **gymnasts**] someone trained to do gymnastics
• **gymnastics** /dʒɪm'næstɪks/ NOUN, NO PLURAL a

sport in which people use their bodies to bend, jump, etc. in a beautiful way

gynaecologist /ˌgaɪnɪˈkɒlədʒɪst/ NOUN [*plural* **gynaecologists**] a doctor who treats medical problems that only affect women

• **gynaecology** /ˌgaɪnɪˈkɒlədʒɪ/ NOUN, NO PLURAL

the study and treatment of medical problems that only affect women

gynecologist /ˌgaɪnɪˈkɒlədʒɪst/ NOUN [*plural* **gynecologists**] the US spelling of gynaecologist

• **gynecology** /ˌgaɪnɪˈkɒlədʒɪ/ NOUN, NO PLURAL the US spelling of gynaecology

H*h*

H or **h** /eɪtʃ/ the eighth letter of the alphabet

ha /hɑː/ ABBREVIATION hectare or hectares

habit /'hæbɪt/ NOUN [plural habits]

1 something that you do regularly, especially without thinking about it □ **+ of** *We want to get kids into the habit of regular exercise.* ⊞ *Tommy has a bad habit of grinding his teeth.* ⊞ *We asked people about their eating habits.*

2 a long, simple dress worn by some religious people □ *a nun's habit*

♦ IDIOMS **change/break the habit(s) of a lifetime** to change the way you have always done something **old habits die hard** used to mean that it is difficult to change your behaviour

habitable /'hæbɪtəbəl/ ADJECTIVE in good enough condition for people to live in □ *Some of the flats were barely habitable.*

habitat /'hæbɪtæt/ NOUN [plural habitats] the place where an animal or a plant lives or grows ⊞ *We wanted to study the otters in their natural habitat.*

habitual /hə'bɪtʃuəl/ ADJECTIVE

1 usual or done regularly, as a habit □ *She had her habitual morning cup of coffee.*

2 used to describe a particular habit or activity □ *a habitual criminal* □ *a habitual liar*

● **habitually** /hə'bɪtʃuəlɪ/ ADVERB regularly or usually □ *She looked in the old handbag that she habitually carried.*

hack /hæk/ ► VERB [hacks, hacking, hacked]

1 to cut something roughly □ *They hacked their way through the thick jungle.* □ *She hacked off chunks of hair.*

2 to get into someone's computer illegally to look at information stored there. A computing word □ *He hacked into military computer systems.*

► NOUN [plural hacks] an informal word for someone who writes for money, often poor quality writing □ *a newspaper hack*

● **hacker** /'hækə(r)/ NOUN [plural hackers] someone who illegally hacks into other people's computers. A computing word.

hacksaw /'hæksɔː/ NOUN [plural hacksaws] a tool with a thin blade (= cutting part), used to cut metal

had /hæd/ PAST TENSE AND PAST PARTICIPLE OF have

haddock /'hædək/ NOUN [plural haddock or haddocks] a type of sea fish with firm, white flesh that is eaten as food

hadn't /'hædənt/ a short way to say and write had not□ *Laura hadn't expected to win.*

haemoglobin /ˌhiːmə'ɡləʊbɪn/ NOUN, NO PLURAL a red substance in blood that carries oxygen around the body. A biology word.

haemorrhage /'hemərɪdʒ/ ► NOUN [plural haemorrhages] when someone suddenly loses a lot of blood

► VERB [haemorrhages, haemorrhaging, haemorrhaged] to suddenly lose a lot of blood

hag /hæg/ NOUN [plural hags] an ugly old woman

haggard /'hægəd/ ADJECTIVE a haggard person looks thin and tired, worried or ill □ *Cho looked haggard.*

haggis /'hægɪs/ NOUN [plural haggises] a Scottish food made from the organs of a sheep that are cut into small pieces and mixed with grains and herbs

haggle /'hægəl/ VERB [haggles, haggling, haggled] to argue about the details of something, especially to try to get a lower price for something you want to buy □ *He haggled with the taxi driver over a fare to the temple.*

● **haggling** /'hæglɪŋ/ NOUN, NO PLURAL when you haggle with someone

haiku /'haɪkuː/ NOUN [plural haikus] a poem in a Japanese style with three lines and 17 syllables (= parts of words)

hail /heɪl/ ► VERB [hails, hailing, hailed]

1 to say publicly that someone or something is good or important □ *The pilot was hailed as a hero.* □ *Scientists around the world hailed the breakthrough.*

2 to shout or to wave to someone to get their attention □ *I hailed a taxi on the main road.*

3 if it hails, small white balls of frozen ice fall from the sky

♦ PHRASAL VERB **hail from somewhere** to come from a particular place □ *He hailed from a small village in the mountains.*

► NOUN, NO PLURAL

1 small white balls of frozen ice that fall from the sky □ *a hail storm*

2 a hail of something a large number of things that are fired or thrown □ *He was gunned down in a hail of bullets.*

hailstones /'heɪlstəʊnz/ PLURAL NOUN small white balls of frozen water that fall from the sky

hair /heə(r)/ NOUN [plural hairs]

1 *no plural* all the thin threads that grow on your head ⊞ *long/short hair* ⊞ *straight/curly hair* ⊞ *She's*

tall with shoulder-length blonde *hair.* 🔊 *I need to get my hair cut.*
2 one of the thin threads that grow on the surface of the skin of animals and humans □ *It made the hairs on my arms stand up.*

> ➤ Remember that 'hair' meaning 'all the hair on your head' is never used in the plural:
> ✓ *She has short hair.*
> ✗ *She has short hairs.*

◆ IDIOMS **Keep your hair on!** a slightly rude phrase used to tell someone to stop being so angry □ *Keep your hair on! I'll pay for the damage.* **make someone's hair stand on end** to make someone very frightened or shocked □ *The thought of finding a snake makes my hair stand on end.*

➔ go to **split hairs**, **let** your hair down, not **turn** a hair

hairbrush /ˈheəbrʌʃ/ NOUN [*plural* **hairbrushes**] a brush for brushing your hair

haircut /ˈheəkʌt/ NOUN [*plural* **haircuts**]
1 when someone cuts your hair □ *You need a haircut.*
2 the style in which your hair is cut □ *She's got a new haircut.*

hairdo /ˈheəduː/ NOUN [*plural* **hairdos**] the style in which your hair has been cut and arranged

hairdresser /ˈheədresə(r)/ NOUN [*plural* **hairdressers**]
1 someone whose job is to cut, arrange and colour people's hair
2 hairdresser's a place where a hairdresser works
• **hairdressing** /ˈheədresɪŋ/ NOUN, NO PLURAL the skill or work of a hairdresser

hairdryer *or* **hairdrier** /ˈheədraɪə(r)/ NOUN [*plural* **hairdryers** *or* **hairdriers**] a piece of electrical equipment that dries your hair by blowing hot air over it

hairgrip /ˈheəgrɪp/ NOUN [*plural* **hairgrips**] a narrow piece of bent metal that you can push into your hair to keep it in place

hairline /ˈheəlaɪn/ NOUN [*plural* **hairlines**] the line along the top of your face where your hair starts to grow

hair-raising /ˈheəˈreɪzɪŋ/ ADJECTIVE very frightening or dangerous □ *It was a hair-raising ride.*

hairstyle /ˈheəstaɪl/ NOUN [*plural* **hairstyles**] the style in which your hair has been cut and arranged □ *She showed off her new hairstyle.*

hairy /ˈheərɪ/ ADJECTIVE [**hairier**, **hairiest**]
1 covered with hair □ *a hairy chest*
2 an informal word meaning very frightening or dangerous □ *If it is stormy, the ferry crossing can get a bit hairy.*

halal /həˈlɑːl/ ADJECTIVE halal meat is from animals killed and prepared according to the laws of Islam

half /hɑːf/ ► NOUN, DETERMINER [*plural* **halves**]
1 1/2; one of two equal parts of something □ *He ate half and I ate the other half.* □ *You have an hour and a half to play.* 🔊 *Meet us here in half an hour.*
2 in half if you break, cut, etc. something in half, you divide it into two equal parts □ *We cut the cake in half.*
3 half past one/two, etc. 30 minutes after one o'clock/two o'clock, etc. □ *He left at half past six.*
► ADVERB
1 to the amount of a half □ *This glass is only half full.* □ *She is half Spanish* (= one of her parents is Spanish).
2 partly, but not completely □ *I was half asleep.*

half-baked /ˌhɑːfˈbeɪkt/ ADJECTIVE not well considered or planned □ *He's full of half-baked ideas.*

half board /ˌhɑːf ˈbɔːd/ NOUN, NO PLURAL when a hotel provides breakfast and an evening meal, but not a meal in the middle of the day □ *The cost is £250 per night, half board.*

half-brother /ˈhɑːfbrʌðə(r)/ NOUN [*plural* **half-brothers**] a male relation with either the same father or the same mother as you

half day /ˌhɑːf ˈdeɪ/ NOUN [*plural* **half days**] a day when people work for only the morning or the afternoon

half-hearted /ˌhɑːfˈhɑːtɪd/ ADJECTIVE without much enthusiasm or effort 🔊 *He made a rather half-hearted attempt to apologize.*
• **half-heartedly** /ˌhɑːfˈhɑːtɪdlɪ/ ADVERB in a half-hearted way

half-life /ˈhɑːflaɪf/ NOUN [*plural* **half-lives**] the time it takes for a substance to become half as radioactive as it was at the beginning. A physics word

half-mast /ˌhɑːfˈmɑːst/ NOUN, NO PLURAL if a flag is at half-mast, it is in a position halfway up the pole, usually because someone has died

half moon /ˌhɑːf ˈmuːn/ NOUN [*plural* **half moons**] the moon when it looks like half a circle

half-price /ˌhɑːfˈpraɪs/ ADJECTIVE, ADVERB costing only half the usual price □ *half-price goods* □ *We bought the furniture half-price in a sale.*

half-sister /ˈhɑːfsɪstə(r)/ NOUN [*plural* **half-sisters**] a female relation with either the same father or the same mother as you

half-term /ˌhɑːfˈtɜːm/ NOUN [*plural* **half-terms**] a short holiday from school about halfway through the school term

half-time /ˌhɑːf ˈtaɪm/ NOUN, NO PLURAL in some sports, a break from play in the middle of the game □ *They led 2–0 at half-time.*

halfway /ˌhɑːfˈweɪ/ ADVERB, ADJECTIVE in the middle between two places, or in the middle of a period of time □ *At the halfway point of my journey, I stopped for a break.* □ *I had to leave halfway through the lesson.*

hall /hɔːl/ NOUN [*plural* **halls**]
1 an area just inside the entrance to a house that you go through to get to other rooms or to the stairs □ *She*

checked her hair in the mirror in the hall. 🗗 The front door opens into a small entrance hall.

2 a large building or room where meetings, concerts and other events are held 🗗 a concert hall 🗗 a meeting at the village hall

hallelujah /ˌhælɪˈluːjə/ EXCLAMATION a shout or exclamation of praise to God

hallmark /ˈhɔːlmɑːk/ NOUN [plural **hallmarks**]
1 a mark on things made of gold or silver to show their quality
2 a quality that is typical of something □ The hallmark of a good writer is the ability to hold the reader's attention.

hallo /həˈləʊ/ EXCLAMATION another spelling of hello

Hallowe'en /ˌhæləʊˈiːn/ NOUN, NO PLURAL the night of October 31st, when children dress to look like ghosts, witches, etc.

hallucinate /həˈluːsɪneɪt/ VERB [**hallucinates**, **hallucinating**, **hallucinated**] to see things that are not really there □ The fever made him hallucinate.
● **hallucination** /həˌluːsɪˈneɪʃən/ NOUN [plural **hallucinations**] something you see that is not really there

hallway /ˈhɔːlweɪ/ NOUN [plural **hallways**] a small room inside the entrance of a house or building with doors going into other rooms □ She walked down the long, narrow hallway.

halo /ˈheɪləʊ/ NOUN [plural **haloes**] a circle of light round the head of a holy person in religious pictures

halogen /ˈhælədʒən/ NOUN [plural **halogens**] any of five chemical elements that combine with hydrogen to form salts. A chemistry word.

halt /hɔːlt/ ▶ VERB [**halts**, **halting**, **halted**]
1 to stop happening or developing or to stop something happening or developing □ The government is taking measures to halt the spread of the disease. □ These attacks should halt immediately.
2 to stop moving or to make something stop moving □ Traffic suddenly halted.
▶ NOUN [plural **halts**]
1 when something stops happening or developing 🗗 He called a halt to the press conference and walked out.
2 when something stops moving 🗗 The car came to an abrupt halt.

halter /ˈhɔːltə(r)/ NOUN [plural **halters**] a rope you put over a horse's head, so that you can hold it or lead it

halting /ˈhɔːltɪŋ/ ADJECTIVE pausing often when you are speaking because you are nervous or not certain □ She addressed us in a shy, rather halting voice.
● **haltingly** /ˈhɔːltɪŋlɪ/ ADVERB in a halting way □ He spoke haltingly as he described his experience.

halve /hɑːv/ VERB [**halves**, **halving**, **halved**]
1 to divide or cut something into two equal parts □ Halve the mushrooms.
2 to reduce something to half its original size or amount □ We aim to halve the number of deaths in

road accidents. □ The investment has almost halved in value.
● **halves** /hɑːvz/ PLURAL OF **half**

ham /hæm/ NOUN, NO PLURAL meat from the leg of a pig which has been cooked using salt or smoke

hamburger /ˈhæmbɜːɡə(r)/ NOUN [plural **hamburgers**] a round flat shape made from very small pieces of meat that is fried and usually eaten between pieces of bread

hamlet /ˈhæmlɪt/ NOUN [plural **hamlets**] a small village

hammer /ˈhæmə(r)/ ▶ NOUN [plural **hammers**] a tool with a heavy metal or wooden part at the end of a handle, used for hitting nails, etc.
▶ VERB [**hammers**, **hammering**, **hammered**]
1 to hit something with a hammer □ Hammer the nails in one by one.
2 to hit something hard □ **+ on** He was hammering on the door with his fists. □ The region was hammered by powerful storms.
3 an informal word meaning to beat someone completely or easily □ We hammered the other team 10–0.
◆ IDIOM **hammer something home** to tell someone something forcefully so that they understand it □ We really need to hammer this message home.
◆ PHRASAL VERB **hammer something out** to discuss or argue about something until everyone agrees □ The two sides tried to hammer out a deal.

hammock /ˈhæmək/ NOUN [plural **hammocks**] a bed made of a long piece of material hung from ropes at either end

hamper[1] /ˈhæmpə(r)/ VERB [**hampers**, **hampering**, **hampered**] to make it difficult for someone or something to make progress □ Rescue efforts were hampered by rain.

hamper[2] /ˈhæmpə(r)/ NOUN [plural **hampers**] a large basket (= container made from very thin pieces of wood) with a lid, often used for carrying food

hamster /ˈhæmstə(r)/ NOUN [plural **hamsters**] a small animal with soft fur and a short tail, often kept as a pet

hand /hænd/ ▶ NOUN [plural **hands**]
1 the part of your body at the end of your arm □ I took her by the hand. □ They walked hand in hand (= with their hands joined together). 🗗 Hold hands with me while we cross the road. 🗗 He refused to shake hands with my father.
2 by hand (a) if something is made or done by hand, it is made or done by a person, not a machine (b) if a letter is delivered by hand, someone brings it to you without posting it
3 help 🗗 Can I give you a hand with those bags? 🗗 Do you need a hand with the washing up?
4 at/on/to hand near and ready to be used □ Make sure you keep plenty of clean water to hand.

5 in hand being dealt with □ *The party arrangements are all in hand.*

6 at someone's hands if you are harmed at someone's hands, they harm you □ *He died at the hands of terrorists.*

7 be **in someone's hands** if something is in someone's hands, they are responsible for it □ *The matter is in the hands of my legal team.*

8 the part of a watch or clock that points to the time

◆ IDIOMS **get/lay your hands on something** to be able to get something □ *I've managed to lay my hands on a lovely piece of velvet.* **have your hands full** to be very busy □ *With four small children, she's really got her hands full.* **on the one hand ... on the other hand** used to compare the advantages and disadvantages of something □ *On the one hand, working at home saves me a lot of time, on the other hand it can be rather lonely.*

▶ VERB [**hands, handing, handed**] to give something to someone □ *Could you hand me a plate?*

◆ PHRASAL VERBS **hand something back** to give something back to the person who gave it to you □ *I handed back the keys.* **hand something down** to give something to someone younger than you □ *These traditions have been handed down over the centuries.* **hand something in** to give something to someone, for example a teacher □ *Have you handed in your homework?* **hand something out** to give something to everyone in a group □ *Can you hand out the textbooks?* **hand something over** to give something to someone □ *Hand over all your money.*

handbag /'hændbæg/ NOUN [*plural* **handbags**] a woman's bag for carrying things like money and keys □ *a black leather handbag*

handbook /'hændbʊk/ NOUN [*plural* **handbooks**] a book of instructions on how to do something □ *I bought an illustrated handbook on first aid.*

handbrake /'hændbreɪk/ NOUN [*plural* **handbrakes**] a brake (= part that makes a vehicle stop) in a vehicle that you operate using your hand

handcuffs /'hændkʌfs/ PLURAL NOUN a pair of metal rings joined by a chain which police use to lock around a prisoner's wrists (= parts of the arms next to the hands)

handful /'hændfʊl/ NOUN [*plural* **handfuls**]
1 an amount that you can hold in your hand □ *a handful of rice*
2 a handful of something a small number of something □ *Only a handful of people turned up.*
3 a handful an informal word for a child or an animal whose behaviour makes them difficult to deal with □ *Greta can be quite a handful.*

hand-held /'hændheld/ ADJECTIVE small enough to hold in your hand during use □ *It was filmed using a hand-held video camera.*

handicap /'hændɪkæp/ ▶ NOUN [*plural* **handicaps**]
1 an old-fashioned word for a physical or mental injury or disability that prevents someone from living

normally □ *A school for children with mental and physical handicaps.*
2 a disadvantage that prevents you doing something easily or as well as other people □ *Lack of qualifications can be a major handicap.*
▶ VERB [**handicaps, handicapping, handicapped**] to cause someone to have a disability or a disadvantage
● **handicapped** /'hændɪkæpt/ ADJECTIVE an old-fashioned word meaning having a disability

handicraft /'hændɪkrɑːft/ NOUN [*plural* **handicrafts**] an activity such as sewing or working with wood that involves making something using your hands, using artistic skill

handiwork /'hændɪwɜːk/ NOUN, NO PLURAL something that you have made or done yourself □ *He put down the paintbrush and stepped back to admire his handiwork.*

handkerchief /'hæŋkətʃɪf/ NOUN [*plural* **handkerchiefs**] a small piece of cloth or thin, soft paper used for drying your nose or eyes

handle /'hændəl/ ▶ NOUN [*plural* **handles**]
1 the part of an object that you use to pick it up and hold it □ *a brush with a long handle*
2 the part of a door that you hold when you open and close it 🖰 *a door handle*
◆ IDIOM **get/have a handle on something** to start to understand or to control something □ *We need to get a better handle on the problem.*
➔ go to **fly off the handle**
▶ VERB [**handles, handling, handled**]
1 to deal with something □ *Mr Peters is handling all the arrangements for the trip.* 🖰 *I would have* handled *the situation differently.*
2 to touch something or to hold it with your hands □ *Try not to handle the fruit too much.*
3 to buy or sell something, often illegally 🖰 *He was arrested on suspicion of* handling *stolen goods.*

handlebars /'hændəlbɑːz/ PLURAL NOUN the curved part at the front of a bicycle that you hold with your hands

handler /'hændlə(r)/ NOUN [*plural* **handlers**] someone who trains or controls an animal □ *Several police dogs arrived with their handlers.*

handmade /ˌhænd'meɪd/ ADJECTIVE made by a person, not a machine □ *handmade silk scarves*

handout /'hændaʊt/ NOUN [*plural* **handouts**]
1 money, food or clothing that is given free to poor people
2 a document containing information that is given to people at a class, a talk, etc.

handrail /'hændreɪl/ NOUN [*plural* **handrails**] a long, narrow bar that people can hold on to, for example when going up and down stairs

handset /'hændset/ NOUN [*plural* **handsets**] the part of a telephone that you hold in your hand and talk or listen through □ *Lift the handset and dial the number you want.*

handshake /'hændʃeɪk/ NOUN [plural **handshakes**] the action of taking someone's right hand in yours and moving it up and down when you meet them or leave them, or to make an agreement with them □ *He greeted me with a handshake.*

handsome /'hænsəm/ ADJECTIVE [**handsomer, handsomest**]
1 attractive, especially used about a man □ *a handsome young actor* □ *He looked so handsome in his uniform.*
2 large in size or amount □ *They made a handsome profit.*

hands-on /ˌhændz'ɒn/ ADJECTIVE involving doing something yourself instead of reading about it or watching others do it 🕮 *I want to get more hands-on experience.*

handstand /'hændstænd/ NOUN [plural **handstands**] a movement in which you balance on your hands, holding your body and legs straight up in the air

handwriting /'hændraɪtɪŋ/ NOUN, NO PLURAL
1 writing done with a pen or a pencil, not printed □ *The speech is written in a notebook in Dr King's own handwriting.*
2 the way someone's writing looks □ *He has neat handwriting.*
• **handwritten** /ˌhænd'rɪtən/ ADJECTIVE written with a pen or pencil, not printed □ *a handwritten note*

handy /'hændɪ/ ADJECTIVE [**handier, handiest**]
1 useful and easy to use □ *It's a handy size for carrying in your pocket.*
2 **come in handy** an informal phrase meaning to be useful □ *Bring the torch, it might come in handy.*
3 near and easy to reach □ *The house is handy for the station.*

handyman /'hændɪmæn/ NOUN [plural **handymen**] someone who does small building and repair jobs

hang /hæŋ/ VERB [**hangs, hanging, hung**]
1 to attach something so that the top part is fixed and the lower part is able to move □ *Hang your jackets on the pegs.* □ *Joe was hanging upside down by his feet.* □ *The branches hung down to the ground.*
2 to kill someone by tying a rope around their neck and making them drop so that the rope is tight □ *He hanged himself in his prison cell.*
♦ PHRASAL VERBS **hang about/around** to stay in a place, doing nothing □ *There was a group of boys hanging round outside our house.* **hang back** to stay behind other people because you are shy or do not want to do something **hang on** 1 to hold something tightly □ *Hang on tight and we'll pull you up.* 2 an informal word meaning to wait □ *Hang on a minute!* **hang onto/on to something** an informal word meaning to keep something □ *You should hang onto those records – they might be worth something one*

day. **hang something up** to put something such as clothing in a place where it can hang □ *We hung up our coats in the hall.*
▶ NOUN, NO PLURAL
♦ IDIOM **get the hang of something** to learn how to do something or use something □ *I can't get the hang of this camera.*

hangar /'hæŋə(r)/ NOUN [plural **hangars**] a large building where aeroplanes are kept

hangdog /'hæŋdɒg/ ADJECTIVE looking sad or ashamed 🕮 *He wore a hangdog expression.*

hanger /'hæŋə(r)/ NOUN [plural **hangers**] a shaped piece of metal, wood or plastic used to hang clothes on

hang-glider /'hæŋglaɪdə(r)/ NOUN [plural **hang-gliders**] a large frame covered in cloth which a person hangs from to fly through the air
• **hang-gliding** /'hæŋglaɪdɪŋ/ NOUN, NO PLURAL the sport of flying in hang-gliders

hangman /'hæŋmən/ NOUN [plural **hangmen**] someone whose job is to kill criminals by hanging them

hangover /'hæŋəʊvə(r)/ NOUN [plural **hangovers**]
1 a feeling of being ill, especially having a headache, that people sometimes get after they have drunk too much alcohol
2 something that remains after an event or period of time is over □ *The system is a hangover from the Soviet era.*

hang-up /'hæŋʌp/ NOUN [plural **hang-ups**] something about your body, behaviour, etc. that makes you feel worried or embarrassed □ *She's always had a hang-up about her nose.*

hanker /'hæŋkə(r)/
♦ PHRASAL VERB [**hankers, hankering, hankered**] **hanker after/for something** to want something very much □ *He was soon hankering for a career in Hollywood.*
• **hankering** /'hæŋkərɪŋ/ NOUN, NO PLURAL a feeling of wanting something very much □ *I've got a hankering for a chicken sandwich.*

hankie or **hanky** /'hæŋkɪ/ NOUN [plural **hankies**] an informal word meaning handkerchief (= piece of cloth or paper used for drying the nose or eyes)

Hanukkah /'hɑːnəkə/ NOUN, NO PLURAL a Jewish celebration lasting for eight days in November or December

haphazard /ˌhæp'hæzəd/ ADJECTIVE with no organization or planning □ *The market stalls are set up in a rather haphazard way.*

happen /'hæpən/ VERB [**happens, happening, happened**]
1 if something happens, it takes place, usually without being planned □ *The accident happened last week.* □ *I pressed the button but nothing happened.* 🕮 *He'll be pleased, whatever happens.*
2 to be the result of something □ **+ to** *Do you know what's happened to the front door key?* □ *Whatever happened to your coat? It's covered in paint.* □ *What happens if you forget to log off?*

3 happen to do something to do something by chance □ *She just happened to be there and saw the whole thing.*

• **happening** /'hæpənɪŋ/ NOUN [plural **happenings**] a strange or unusual event

happily /'hæpɪlɪ/ ADVERB

1 feeling, showing or expressing happiness □ *The girls were smiling happily.* 🕮 *They're happily married.*
2 in a willing way □ *She happily agreed to help.*
3 with a lucky result □ *Happily, it all turned out well.*

happiness /'hæpɪnɪs/ NOUN, NO PLURAL the state of being happy 🕮 *He has finally found happiness in his personal life.* □ *My children are my greatest source of happiness.*

happy /'hæpɪ/ ADJECTIVE [**happier, happiest**]

1 pleased and feeling that a situation is good □ *It was the happiest day of her life.* □ *He looked really happy.* 🕮 *More money won't make her happy.*
2 making you feel happy □ *I had a very happy childhood.* □ *The story has a happy ending.*
3 satisfied □ **+ with** *My teacher wasn't happy with my performance.* □ *I'm more than happy with our progress so far.*
4 happy to do something very willing to do something □ *I'd be happy to drive you there.*
5 Happy Birthday/Christmas, etc. used to say that you hope someone will be happy on a special day

happy-go-lucky /ˌhæpɪ-gəʊ-'lʌkɪ/ ADJECTIVE happy and enjoying life, and not worrying about the future □ *He's a happy-go-lucky youngster.*

harangue /hə'ræŋ/ ► VERB [**harangues, haranguing, harangued**] to express your opinion or to criticize someone strongly and loudly □ *Several players harangued the referee.*
► NOUN [plural **harangues**] when you harangue someone

harass /'hærəs, hə'ræs/ VERB [**harasses, harassing, harassed**] to repeatedly annoy or upset someone □ *She was constantly harassed by journalists and photographers.*

• **harassed** /'hærəst, hə'ræst/ ADJECTIVE feeling worried, often because you have too much to do □ *She looked tired and harassed.*

• **harassment** /'hærəsmənt, hə'ræsmənt/ NOUN, NO PLURAL harassing someone or being harassed

harbor /'hɑːbə(r)/ VERB [**harbors, harboring, harbored**], NOUN [plural **harbors**] the US spelling of harbour

harbour /'hɑːbə(r)/ ► NOUN [plural **harbours**] a safe area of water near the coast, usually protected by big walls, where ships come so that people can go onto the land □ *The ship sailed into Sydney harbour.*
► VERB [**harbours, harbouring, harboured**]
1 to keep a feeling in your mind for a long time □ *She'd harboured a grudge against them for years.* □ *He harboured ambitions to become an actor.*
2 to protect a criminal from being found by the police

hard /hɑːd/ ► ADJECTIVE [**harder, hardest**]

1 firm and solid and not easy to bend or break □ *This bread is a bit hard.* □ *The ball will only bounce on a hard surface.*
2 difficult to do □ **+ to do something** *It was hard to concentrate with all the noise.* □ *The exam was really hard.*
3 needing a lot of effort 🕮 *hard work*
4 unpleasant or full of problems 🕮 *They had a hard life.* 🕮 *He had a hard time in the army.*
5 be hard on someone (a) to criticize someone or to be unkind to someone □ *You shouldn't be so hard on your children – they are trying their best.* **(b)** to be a difficult situation for someone □ *It's hard on her family when she's ill.*
♦ IDIOM **a hard line** a very forceful and severe way of dealing with something □ *The club has taken a hard line against racism.*
► ADVERB [**harder, hardest**]
1 with a lot effort 🕮 *They always work hard.* 🕮 *You need to try harder.*
2 with a lot of force □ *It was raining hard when we got there.*

hardback /'hɑːdbæk/ NOUN [plural **hardbacks**] a book that has a hard cover

hardboard /'hɑːdbɔːd/ NOUN, NO PLURAL thin strong board made from small pieces of wood pressed together

hard-boiled /ˌhɑːd'bɔɪld/ ADJECTIVE a hard-boiled egg has been boiled in its shell until the inside is solid

hard copy /ˌhɑːd 'kɒpɪ/ NOUN [plural **hard copies**] information printed from a computer onto paper

hardcover /'hɑːdkʌvə(r)/ NOUN [plural **hardcovers**] an especially US word for a book that has a hard cover

hard disk /'hɑːd ˌdɪsk/ or **hard drive** /'hɑːd ˌdraɪv/ NOUN [plural **hard disks** or **hard drives**] a part inside a computer where information is stored. A computing word.

harden /'hɑːdən/ VERB [**hardens, hardening, hardened**]
1 to become hard or solid □ *The mixture hardens into a solid gel.*
2 to become less gentle, kind or willing to change □ *Both sides have hardened their positions.*

hard-fought /ˌhɑːd'fɔːt/ ADJECTIVE using a lot of effort against someone who is determined to win □ *a hard-fought election*

hard-hearted /ˌhɑːd'hɑːtɪd/ ADJECTIVE not caring about other people's feelings or problems

hardline /'hɑːdlaɪn/ ADJECTIVE having strong or extreme opinions and refusing to change them □ *He's known for his hardline stance on immigration.*

hardly /'hɑːdlɪ/ ADVERB

1 only just or almost not □ *I hardly know him.* □ *He hardly spoke a word of English.* 🕮 *There were hardly any people there.* 🕮 *We hardly ever saw her.* □ *He'd hardly put the key in the door when down came the rain.*
2 used for emphasis to mean not at all □ *She's hardly*

likely to want him at the party after the way he insulted her. □ *She could hardly be described as beautiful!*

> ➤ Notice that the word **hardly** does not mean 'with a lot of effort' or 'with a lot of force'. For these two meanings, use the word **hard**:
> ✓ *She works so hard.*
> ✗ She works so hardly.
> ✓ *It's raining hard.*
> ✗ It's raining hardly.

hardship /'hɑːdʃɪp/ NOUN [plural **hardships**] something that makes your life difficult, especially not having enough money or comfort 🕮 *They are in severe financial hardship.* □ *Rising prices are causing widespread hardship.*

hard shoulder /ˌhɑːd 'ʃəʊldə(r)/ NOUN, NO PLURAL the strip of road at either side of a motorway for use in an emergency

hard up /ˌhɑːd 'ʌp/ ADJECTIVE an informal word meaning poor □ *His family is too hard up to be able to afford the fees.*

hardware /'hɑːdweə(r)/ NOUN, NO PLURAL
1 the machines and equipment that make up a computer system. A computing word □ *We need to update our computer hardware and software.*
2 tools and equipment used in the house and garden 🕮 *a hardware store*
3 equipment, machines, vehicles, etc. especially used by the military 🕮 *They are a leading supplier of military hardware.*

hard-wearing /ˌhɑːd'weərɪŋ/ ADJECTIVE well made and able to last a long time □ *The fabric is hard-wearing and waterproof.*

hardy /'hɑːdɪ/ ADJECTIVE [**hardier, hardiest**] strong and able to deal with difficult conditions □ *a hardy plant* 🕮 *A few hardy souls* (= people) *jumped into the icy cold water.*

hare /heə(r)/ ▶ NOUN [plural **hares**] an animal similar to a rabbit that has very large ears and runs very quickly
▶ VERB [**hares, haring, hared**] to run somewhere very quickly □ *She hared off to get a ladder.*

hare-brained /'heəbreɪnd/ ADJECTIVE silly and not likely to be successful 🕮 *a hare-brained scheme*

hark /hɑːk/ VERB [**harks, harking, harked**] an old-fashioned or literary word meaning to listen □ *Hark, the nightingale is singing.*
◆ PHRASAL VERB **hark back to something** to remember or to return to something that happened in the past □ *The style harks back to the 1960s.*

harm /hɑːm/ ▶ VERB [**harms, harming, harmed**] to hurt, damage or cause problems for someone or something □ *You might harm your eyes if you sit too close to the TV.* □ *She believes that violent video games can harm children.* □ *We know that air travel harms the environment.*
▶ NOUN, NO PLURAL
1 damage, injury or problems 🕮 *The knife wasn't sharp enough to cause much harm.* 🕮 *If you stay with me,*

you won't come to any harm. 🕮 *It wouldn't do any harm to ask for advice.*
2 there's no harm in doing something used to say that an action will not cause problems and may help a situation □ *I don't think you'll be able to persuade him to come, but there's no harm in trying.*

● **harmful** /'hɑːmfʊl/ ADJECTIVE causing damage, injury or problems □ *Use a cream to protect your skin from the sun's harmful rays.*

● **harmless** /'hɑːmlɪs/ ADJECTIVE
1 not causing any damage, injury or problems □ *This substance is harmless to animals.*
2 not intended to offend or upset people □ *harmless fun*

harmonica /hɑː'mɒnɪkə/ NOUN [plural **harmonicas**] a small musical instrument that you hold to your mouth and play by blowing air through it

harmonious /hɑː'məʊnɪəs/ ADJECTIVE
1 having a friendly relationship without disagreements □ *The atmosphere at work was generally harmonious.*
2 fitting well together in an attractive way □ *The architecture is varied, but the overall effect is harmonious.*
3 pleasant to listen to

● **harmoniously** /hɑː'məʊnɪəslɪ/ ADVERB in a harmonious way □ *People of different faiths live together harmoniously in this area.*

harmonize or **harmonise** /'hɑːmənaɪz/ VERB [**harmonizes, harmonizing, harmonized**]
1 to look attractive together □ *The buildings harmonize with their surroundings.*
2 to make systems, rules, etc. more similar so that they work well together □ *We want to harmonize the regulations in different European countries.*
3 to sing or play music in harmony, or to provide a harmony for a main tune □ *He harmonized the melody with violins and cellos.*

harmony /'hɑːmənɪ/ NOUN [plural **harmonies**]
1 when people live in a peaceful and friendly way □ *We live in harmony with our neighbours.*
2 a combination of musical notes that sound pleasant together □ *complex vocal harmonies*
3 when things look attractive together □ *The building is in complete harmony with its surroundings.*

harness /'hɑːnɪs/ ▶ NOUN [plural **harnesses**]
1 a set of leather straps that attach a horse to something it is pulling
2 a set of straps for attaching someone to something 🕮 *He climbs without a safety harness.*
▶ VERB [**harnesses, harnessing, harnessed**]
1 to control something in order to use it for a particular purpose 🕮 *We need to harness the power of the sea to provide energy.*
2 to put a harness on a horse or a person □ *The dancers are harnessed to wires.*

harp /hɑːp/ NOUN [plural **harps**] a musical instrument with strings stretched across an open triangular frame
◆ PHRASAL VERB [**harps, harping, harped**] **harp on**

(about something) to keep talking about something in an annoying way □ *Will you stop harping on about dinner?*

• **harpist** /ˈhɑːpɪst/ NOUN [*plural* **harpists**] someone who plays the harp

harpoon /hɑːˈpuːn/ NOUN [*plural* **harpoons**] a spear (= long, sharp weapon) with a rope attached that is used for hunting large fish

harpsichord /ˈhɑːpsɪkɔːd/ NOUN [*plural* **harpsichords**] a musical instrument similar to a small piano, often used in old music

harrowing /ˈhærəʊɪŋ/ ADJECTIVE very upsetting or unpleasant □ *a harrowing experience* □ *There were harrowing scenes of badly injured children.*

harsh /hɑːʃ/ ADJECTIVE [**harsher, harshest**]
1 very cold, uncomfortable or difficult, etc. □ *a harsh climate* □ *a harsh winter* □ *The poor lived in very harsh conditions.*
2 cruel, severe and often unfair □ *a harsh punishment* ⊞ *harsh criticism* ⊞ *He had harsh words for his teammate.*
3 unpleasantly strong or loud □ *harsh light* □ *the harsh cry of a bird*

• **harshly** /ˈhɑːʃlɪ/ ADVERB in a harsh way □ *'Stand up,' he said harshly.* □ *The report was harshly critical.* □ *They were treated harshly.*

• **harshness** /ˈhɑːʃnɪs/ NOUN, NO PLURAL the quality of being harsh □ *She was surprised by the harshness of his tone.*

harvest /ˈhɑːvɪst/ ▶ NOUN [*plural* **harvests**]
1 the activity of collecting crops □ *Heavy rains delayed the harvest.*
2 the amount of a crop that is collected □ *The price rise is due to poor wheat harvests.*
▶ VERB [**harvests, harvesting, harvested**] to collect a crop □ *The apples are harvested in late summer.*

has /hæz/ VERB the present tense of the verb have when it is used with **he**, **she** and **it** □ *He has brown eyes.*

has-been /ˈhæzbiːn/ NOUN [*plural* **has-beens**] an informal word for someone who was famous or successful in the past, but who is no longer important or interesting

hash /hæʃ/ NOUN [*plural* **hashes**] the sign '#' that is used on telephones
♦ IDIOM **make a hash of something** an informal phrase meaning to spoil something by doing it badly

hasn't /ˈhæzənt/ a short way to say and write has not □ *Anne hasn't arrived yet.*

hassle /ˈhæsəl/ ▶ NOUN [*plural* **hassles**] something that annoys you or causes problems for you. An informal word. □ *Avoid the hassle of finding a parking space: take the bus.*
▶ VERB [**hassles, hassling, hassled**] to repeatedly ask someone something in a way that annoys them □ *We were continually hassled by journalists.*

haste /heɪst/ NOUN, NO PLURAL when someone hurries, especially when this causes them to make mistakes □ *In her haste she almost dropped the basket.* □ *He has criticized the government for acting in haste.*

• **hasten** /ˈheɪsən/ VERB [**hastens, hastening, hastened**]
1 to cause something to happen sooner □ *The shock hastened his death.*
2 I **hasten to add** used when you want to explain something quickly to avoid someone getting the wrong opinion about what you have just said □ *I couldn't believe it. Not, I hasten to add, that I thought he was lying.*

• **hastily** /ˈheɪstɪlɪ/ ADVERB very quickly, often without enough planning □ *We hastily packed our bags and caught the next plane home.*

• **hasty** /ˈheɪstɪ/ ADJECTIVE [**hastier, hastiest**] done quickly, often without enough planning □ *I scribbled a hasty note.* □ *You shouldn't make any hasty decisions about something so important.*

hat /hæt/ NOUN [*plural* **hats**] a covering you wear on your head □ *a straw hat* □ *a fur hat*

hatch¹ /hætʃ/ VERB [**hatches, hatching, hatched**]
1 to make a plan, especially in secret □ *They're hatching a plot to give Fiona a surprise birthday party.*
2 an egg hatches when a baby bird or reptile breaks out of it □ *The eggs hatch after about ten days.*
3 baby birds or reptiles hatch when they break out of their eggs □ *We watched the chicks hatch.*

hatch² /hætʃ/ NOUN [*plural* **hatches**]
1 an opening in a wall, especially one through which food can be passed
2 an opening or a door in a ship or an aircraft □ *an escape hatch*

hatchback /ˈhætʃbæk/ NOUN [*plural* **hatchbacks**] a type of car with a large door at the back that opens upwards

hatchet /ˈhætʃɪt/ NOUN [*plural* **hatchets**] a small axe (= tool for cutting wood)
♦ IDIOM **bury the hatchet** to become friends again after an argument

hate /heɪt/ ▶ VERB [**hates, hating, hated**]
1 to dislike someone or something very much □ **+ ing** *I hate being late.* □ *I hate the idea of wasting all that money.*
2 I **hate to do something** used to say sorry when you are going to say or do something that someone will not like □ *I hate to say this, but I think you're going to miss your plane.*
▶ NOUN [*plural* **hates**]
1 *no plural* a very strong feeling that you do not like someone or something □ *There was a look of real hate in his eyes.*
2 something that you hate ⊞ *Lateness is one of his pet hates.*

• **hateful** /ˈheɪtful/ ADJECTIVE very unkind or unpleasant □ *What a hateful thing to say!*

• **hatred** /ˈheɪtrɪd/ NOUN, NO PLURAL a very strong feeling that you do not like someone or something □ *I have a hatred of dogs.* ⊞ *He was accused of promoting racial hatred.*

hat-trick /ˈhætˌtrɪk/ NOUN [plural **hat-tricks**] when a team or a player is successful three times in a game, for example by scoring three goals

haughty /ˈhɔːtɪ/ ADJECTIVE [**haughtier, haughtiest**] behaving as though you think you are better or more important than other people □ She gave him a haughty look.

haul /hɔːl/ ▶ VERB [**hauls, hauling, hauled**]
1 to pull someone or something using a lot of effort □ He managed to haul himself up on to a narrow ledge.
2 to force someone to go somewhere □ He was hauled off the train by a security guard.
▶ NOUN [plural **hauls**] an amount of something that someone manages to get, often something illegal □ Police claimed that the thieves' total haul was worth about $155,000. □ He returned home with his haul of fish.
• **haulage** /ˈhɔːlɪdʒ/ NOUN, NO PLURAL the business of carrying goods from one place to another □ a haulage company

haunt /hɔːnt/ ▶ VERB [**haunts, haunting, haunted**]
1 if a ghost (= dead person's spirit) haunts a place, people think it appears there □ People claim that the castle is haunted by the ghost of the young prince.
2 if a bad feeling or memory haunts you, you often think about it □ The image of that face haunted his dreams.
▶ NOUN [plural **haunts**] a place where you often go □ This club is one of my old haunts.
• **haunted** /ˈhɔːntɪd/ ADJECTIVE
1 visited by ghosts (= spirits of dead people) □ Some people believe that this room is haunted. □ a haunted castle
2 looking very frightened or worried □ She always seemed to have a haunted look.
• **haunting** /ˈhɔːntɪŋ/ ADJECTIVE sad and beautiful in a way that you cannot forget □ a haunting melody

haute couture /ˌəʊt kuːˈtʊə(r)/ NOUN, NO PLURAL very expensive and fashionable clothes

haute cuisine /ˌəʊt kwɪˈziːn/ NOUN, NO PLURAL cooking of a very high standard

have /hæv/ ▶ AUXILIARY VERB used with the past participle of another verb to form the present perfect tense or the past perfect tense □ I have bought a new car. □ Have you fed the rabbit? □ She has been feeling tired recently. □ They had opened a restaurant in Athens.
▶ VERB [**has, having, had**]
1 used for describing someone or something □ He has got black hair. □ The room had patches of damp on the walls. □ The soup had a delicious flavour.
2 to own something □ He has a house in Spain. □ I have got three brothers. □ She has the determination to win.
3 used for saying that someone has something with them □ Do you have a towel I could use? □ He had a large dog with him.

4 to have an illness is to suffer from it □ She has cancer. □ I had a terrible headache.
5 have a look/shower/walk, etc. to do a particular thing
6 to have food or drink is to eat it or drink it □ You'll have lunch with us, won't you? □ I had a huge curry last night.
7 to experience something □ We've had a lot of problems. □ I hope you have a great time in Mexico.
➡ go to have your cake and eat it

> ► Notice (sense 2) that **have** and **have got** are both used to mean 'to own something'. It is normal, especially in spoken English, to use the short forms of **have got** and **has got**: □ I've got a dog. (= I have got a dog). □ She's got a dog. (= She has got a dog).

▶ MODAL VERB
1 have to do something if you have to do something, you must do it □ I have to go away for a few days. □ You'll have to give him the money. 🔊 I don't have to go to work tomorrow.
2 used for telling someone how to do something □ You have to press the green button.

> ► Notice that when **have to** (sense 1) is negative, the negative form is usually made with **do**: □ I don't have to go. □ He doesn't have to work.
> ► The question form of **have to** is also made with **do**: □ Do you have to tell him? □ Do we have to come?

haven /ˈheɪvən/ NOUN [plural **havens**] a place where people or animals can be safe 🔊 The families were moved to a safe haven in the mountains.

haven't /ˈhævənt/ a short way to say and write have not □ I haven't seen the film yet.

havoc /ˈhævək/ NOUN, NO PLURAL a state of damage, destruction or confusion 🔊 Heavy rain has caused havoc on the roads. 🔊 Spicy food plays havoc with my digestion.

hawk /hɔːk/ NOUN [plural **hawks**] a bird that can see very well and hunts small animals for food

hawthorn /ˈhɔːθɔːn/ NOUN [plural **hawthorns**] a small tree with thorns (= sharp points), pink or white flowers and red berries (= small fruits)

hay /heɪ/ NOUN, NO PLURAL grass that has been cut and dried, used to feed animals

hay fever /ˌheɪ ˈfiːvə(r)/ NOUN, NO PLURAL a medical condition caused by pollen (= powder produced by flowers) which makes you feel as if you have a cold

haystack /ˈheɪstæk/ NOUN [plural **haystacks**] a large pile of hay that is left in a field until it is needed

haywire /ˈheɪwaɪə(r)/ ADJECTIVE go haywire to stop working correctly and to start behaving in an uncontrolled way □ The virus causes the human body to go haywire.

hazard /ˈhæzəd/ ▶ NOUN [plural **hazards**] something that could cause harm or damage ⊞ *Undercooked food is a potential health hazard.* ⊞ *a fire hazard* ⊞ *Industrial waste poses a hazard to the environment.*
▶ VERB [**hazards, hazarding, hazarded**] hazard a guess to risk making a guess about something □ *'How many people were there?' 'I don't know, but I'd hazard a guess at about two thousand.'*
• **hazardous** /ˈhæzədəs/ ADJECTIVE dangerous □ *Hazardous driving conditions led to several accidents this afternoon.*

haze /heɪz/ NOUN [plural **hazes**] air that is difficult to see through because of heat, smoke, dust, etc.

hazel /ˈheɪzəl/ ▶ NOUN [plural **hazels**] a small tree on which nuts grow
▶ ADJECTIVE having a light green-brown colour □ *hazel eyes*

hazelnut /ˈheɪzəlnʌt/ NOUN [plural **hazelnuts**] a nut that you can eat, that grows on a hazel tree

hazy /ˈheɪzɪ/ ADJECTIVE [**hazier, haziest**]
1 not clear because of heat, smoke, dust, etc. in the air □ *The sea was blue under a hazy sky.*
2 hazy memories are not clear □ *He has only hazy memories of his father.*

he /hiː/ PRONOUN used to talk or write about a man, boy or male animal that has already been mentioned □ *Everyone likes Ted because he is so funny.* □ *Don't worry – he won't bite.*

head /hed/ ▶ NOUN [plural **heads**]
1 the part of the body that contains the brain, eyes, mouth, etc. □ *She suffered serious head injuries.* □ *He turned his head to look at the clock.* ⊞ *nod/shake your head* ⊞ *She was dressed in black from head to toe.*
2 your mind □ *The idea just popped into my head.*
3 the person who is in charge of an organization or a group of people □ *He is the former head of the prison service.*
4 the top or front of something □ *Put your name at the head of each page.* □ *I went straight to the head of the queue.*
➡ go to **heads**
♦ IDIOMS **be over someone's head** to be too difficult for someone to understand □ *The stuff about economics was right over my head* **can't make head nor tail of something** to not be able to understand what something means or how something works □ *I can't make head nor tail of these instructions.* **come to a head** if a situation comes to a head, it becomes so much worse that it must be dealt with **go to someone's head** if success, praise, etc. goes to someone's head, they become too proud **head over heels 1** if you fall head over heels, you fall in a sudden and forceful way □ *He slipped on the ice and went head over heels.* **2** if you are head over heels in love, you love someone very much **keep your head** to stay calm □ *She kept her head in a crisis.* **laugh/scream, etc. your head off** an informal phrase meaning to laugh/shout, etc. a lot **lose your head** to become very

frightened or excited and behave in a way that is not calm
➡ go to **off the top of your head**
▶ VERB [**heads, heading, headed**]
1 to go towards a particular place □ *It's time for us to head home.* □ *We were heading north along the motorway.*
2 to be in charge of an organization or a group of people □ *She heads the development team.*
3 to hit a ball with your head

headache /ˈhedeɪk/ NOUN [plural **headaches**]
1 a pain in your head ⊞ *I've got a splitting headache.* ⊞ *That noise is giving me a headache.*
2 something that gives you a lot of problems ⊞ *The new rule has created a major headache for airport security staff.*

header /ˈhedə(r)/ NOUN [plural **headers**] when you hit the ball with your head in a game of football □ *Doyle sent a powerful header towards the goal.*

headfirst /ˌhedˈfɜːst/ ADVERB moving forwards with your head in front of the rest of your body □ *I fell headfirst down the stairs.*

heading /ˈhedɪŋ/ NOUN [plural **headings**] a title at the beginning of a piece of writing

headland /ˈhedlənd/ NOUN [plural **headlands**] a piece of land that sticks out into the sea

headlight /ˈhedlaɪt/ NOUN [plural **headlights**] one of the two big lights at the front of a vehicle

headline /ˈhedlaɪn/ NOUN [plural **headlines**]
1 the words that are printed in large letters at the top of a newspaper article
2 headlines the most important news stories that are reported at the beginning of a news programme on the television or radio □ *Here is Charlotte Green with today's headlines.*

headlong /ˈhedlɒŋ/ ADVERB
1 with your head in front of the rest of your body □ *She plunged headlong down the stairs.*
2 rush/plunge headlong into something to start to do something too quickly, before you have had enough time to think carefully about it □ *We must not rush headlong into this war.*

headmaster /ˌhedˈmɑːstə(r)/ NOUN [plural **headmasters**] a male teacher who is in charge of a school

headmistress /ˌhedˈmɪstrɪs/ NOUN [plural **headmistresses**] a female teacher who is in charge of a school

head-on /ˌhedˈɒn/ ▶ ADVERB
1 if two cars hit each other head-on, the front parts of both cars hit each other
2 without trying to avoid unpleasant things □ *We need to tackle these problems head-on.*
▶ ADJECTIVE describes a car accident in which two cars moving towards each other hit each other ⊞ *a head-on collision*

headphones /'hedfəunz/ PLURAL NOUN a piece of equipment with two parts that you wear over your ears, so that you can listen to music, etc. and other people do not hear it

headquarters /ˌhed'kwɔːtəz/ PLURAL NOUN
1 the central office from which a large business or organization is controlled □ *Our company headquarters are in London.*
2 a place from which an army or police force is controlled

headroom /'hedrum/ NOUN, NO PLURAL
1 the space between someone's head and a ceiling □ *For a small car, the Micra gives you plenty of headroom.*
2 used on road signs to show how much space there is under a bridge □ *Maximum headroom 2.3 metres.*

heads /hedz/ PLURAL NOUN the side of a coin that has a picture of a head on it □ *Heads or tails?*

headscarf /'hedskɑːf/ NOUN [plural **headscarves**] a woman's thin scarf (= piece of cloth), worn over the head

headset /'hedset/ NOUN [plural **headsets**] a piece of equipment with two parts that you wear over your ears for listening, and a part near your mouth that you speak into

headstand /'hedstænd/ NOUN [plural **headstands**] a position in which your body is upside down, with your head and hands on the ground and your feet pointing upwards

head start /ˌhed 'stɑːt/ NOUN, NO PLURAL an advantage that you have over other people, especially by starting before them ⊞ *Nursery French classes give your children a great head start in their schooling.*

headstone /'hedstəun/ NOUN [plural **headstones**] a piece of stone with writing on it which says who is buried in a grave

headstrong /'hedstrɒŋ/ ADJECTIVE determined to do what you want to do, and unwilling to take advice from other people

heads-up /ˌhedz'ʌp/ NOUN, NO PLURAL a warning that something will happen, usually so that someone can prepare ⊞ *Dan gave me a heads-up that Judy would be there.*

headteacher /ˌhed'tiːtʃə(r)/ NOUN [plural **headteachers**] a teacher who is in charge of a school

headway /'hedweɪ/ NOUN, NO PLURAL **make headway** to make progress □ *The discussions continued for hours, but we made little headway.*

headwind /'hedwɪnd/ NOUN [plural **headwinds**] a wind that blows towards you and slows you down

heady /'hedɪ/ ADJECTIVE [**headier, headiest**]
1 making you feel excited and confident □ *We thought we could do everything back in those heady days of the 1960s.*
2 having a pleasant and strong effect on you □ *The room was filled with the heady aroma of spices.*

heal /hiːl/ VERB [**heals, healing, healed**] to become healthy again, or to make a person or part of the body healthy again □ *The wound needs time to heal.* □ *The*

substance is used for healing cuts and injuries generally. □ *With time, the body will heal itself.*
• **healer** /'hiːlə(r)/ NOUN [plural **healers**] someone who makes ill people better, especially a person who does not use modern medical methods □ *She went to a spiritual healer for help.*

health /helθ/ NOUN, NO PLURAL
1 how well your body is □ *Her health has been very poor recently.* ⊞ *Too much red meat is bad for your health.* ⊞ *He appeared to be in good health.* ⊞ *She was forced to leave due to ill health.*
2 the work of looking after ill people and of preventing illness generally □ *The government spends a huge amount on health.* ⊞ *The country lacks trained health workers.*
3 how successful a business, industry or economy is □ *The growth of tourism has been good for the health of the economy.*

health care /'helθ ˌkeə(r)/ NOUN, NO PLURAL the organizations that look after people's health □ *private health care*

health centre /'helθ ˌsentə(r)/ NOUN [plural **health centres**] a place where people from a particular area can go to see a doctor or a nurse

health club /'helθ ˌklʌb/ NOUN [plural **health clubs**] a place where people who are members can go to do activities such as swimming and exercise classes

health food /'helθ ˌfuːd/ NOUN [plural **health foods**] food that is believed to be good for your health

healthily /'helθɪlɪ/ ADVERB in a way that is good for your health □ *I eat healthily.*

healthiness /'helθɪnɪs/ NOUN, NO PLURAL being healthy

health service /'helθ ˌsɜːvɪs/ NOUN [plural **health services**] an organization that provides medical care for everyone

health visitor /'helθ ˌvɪzɪtə(r)/ NOUN [plural **health visitors**] a nurse who visits people in their homes

healthy /'helθɪ/ ADJECTIVE [**healthier, healthiest**]
1 physically well and not ill in any way □ *Exercise and a good diet can help you stay healthy.* □ *She seems perfectly healthy.*
2 having a good effect on your health ⊞ *healthy eating* ⊞ *She has a very healthy lifestyle.*
3 showing a good attitude and likely to have a good result □ *A certain level of competition between companies is healthy.*
4 something that is healthy is successful and likely to stay successful ⊞ *a healthy economy*
5 a healthy amount of money is a large amount □ *She now has a good career and a healthy bank balance.*

heap /hiːp/ ▶ NOUN [plural **heaps**]
1 an untidy pile of things □ *I found a heap of dirty clothes at the top of the stairs.* ⊞ *His clothes were in a heap in the bottom of the wardrobe.*
2 heaps of something a lot of something. An

informal phrase. □ *There's heaps of time before the match starts.*

▶ VERB [**heaps, heaping, heaped**]

1 to make a big untidy pile of things □ *His plate was heaped with food.*

2 heap praise/criticism on someone to praise or criticize someone a lot

hear /hɪə(r)/ VERB [**hears, hearing, heard**]

1 to be aware of sounds through your ears □ *Can you hear that clicking noise?* □ *I heard the sound of an explosion.* □ *She screamed, but nobody heard her.*

2 to be told something □ *+ that I heard that she was unhappy in her job.* □ *The court heard that the men both used false passports.* □ *+ about Did you hear about Rob's accident?*

3 I hear used to talk about something you have been told □ *I hear you're getting married.*

4 have heard of someone/something to know that someone or something exists □ *I'd never heard of him before.*

♦ PHRASAL VERB **hear from someone** to receive a letter, email, telephone call, etc. from someone □ *Have you heard from Joss recently?*

● **hearing** /ˈhɪərɪŋ/ NOUN [*plural* **hearings**]

1 your ability to hear □ *My hearing was affected by the constant noise.*

2 in your hearing if something is said in your hearing, you hear it

3 an official meeting where a judge or a group of people hear the facts about something □ *a court hearing*

4 a chance to give your explanation or opinions ⊞ *I don't feel that I had a fair hearing.*

hearing aid /ˈhɪərɪŋ ˌeɪd/ NOUN [*plural* **hearing aids**] a small piece of equipment that is fitted onto a person's ear in order to help them hear better

hearsay /ˈhɪəseɪ/ NOUN, NO PLURAL things other people have told you for which you have no proof □ *His evidence was nothing more than hearsay.*

hearse /hɜːs/ NOUN [*plural* **hearses**] a large black car used for carrying the dead body to a funeral

heart /hɑːt/ NOUN [*plural* **hearts**]

1 the organ that sends blood around your body ⊞ *My heart was beating very fast.* ⊞ *He suffers from heart disease.*

2 the centre of something □ *+ of She lives in the heart of the city.*

3 the most important part of something □ *+ of Jealousy is at the heart of their problems.* ⊞ *I really tried to get to the heart of what was upsetting her.*

4 at heart used to say what someone's real character is □ *He's a conventional man at heart.*

5 someone's feelings or character □ *She captured the hearts of the audience.* □ *Ken has a kind heart.*

6 a shape (♥) that represents the human heart and human love

7 hearts one of the four types of playing card, which have the symbol (♥) printed on them

♦ IDIOMS **know/learn something (off) by heart** to know or learn something so well that you do not have to read it □ *I learned the whole poem off by heart.* **not have the heart to do something** to be too kind to do something □ *I didn't have the heart to tell him his story was rubbish.* **someone's heart sinks** if someone's heart sinks, they are disappointed or expect that something bad will happen □ *My heart sank when I saw how dirty the holiday cottage was.*

➡ *go to* **break** someone's heart

heartache /ˈhɑːteɪk/ NOUN, NO PLURAL great sadness

heart attack /ˈhɑːt əˌtæk/ NOUN [*plural* **heart attacks**] when someone's heart suddenly stops working □ *He died of a heart attack .*

heartbeat /ˈhɑːtbiːt/ NOUN [*plural* **heartbeats**] the regular sound or movement that your heart makes

heartbreak /ˈhɑːtbreɪk/ NOUN, NO PLURAL great sadness

● **heartbreaking** /ˈhɑːtbreɪkɪŋ/ ADJECTIVE making you feel extremely sad □ *a heartbreaking story*

● **heartbroken** /ˈhɑːtbrəʊkən/ ADJECTIVE feeling extremely sad because something very bad has happened □ *Kay was heartbroken when he left her.*

hearten /ˈhɑːtən/ VERB [**heartens, heartening, heartened**] to make someone feel happier about a situation □ *I was heartened to see so many people at the meeting.*

● **heartening** /ˈhɑːtənɪŋ/ ADJECTIVE making you feel happier about a situation

heartfelt /ˈhɑːtfelt/ ADJECTIVE completely sincere ⊞ *a heartfelt apology*

hearth /hɑːθ/ NOUN [*plural* **hearths**] the area in front of a fireplace (= the space for a fire in the wall of a room)

heartily /ˈhɑːtɪlɪ/ ADVERB

1 loudly and with enthusiasm □ *They all laughed heartily at all his jokes.*

2 sincerely or completely ⊞ *I'm heartily sick of their constant complaints.*

heartless /ˈhɑːtlɪs/ ADJECTIVE unkind and cruel

heart-rending /ˈhɑːtrendɪŋ/ ADJECTIVE making you feel great sympathy and sadness for someone □ *heart-rending scenes of poverty*

heart-throb /ˈhɑːtθrɒb/ NOUN [*plural* **heart-throbs**] an informal word for a very attractive man, especially one who is famous

heart-to-heart /ˌhɑːttəˈhɑːt/ NOUN [*plural* **heart-to-hearts**] a conversation between two people in which they talk about their private feelings

hearty /ˈhɑːtɪ/ ADJECTIVE [**heartier, heartiest**]

1 loud, enthusiastic and friendly □ *He gave a hearty laugh.*

2 a hearty meal is a large meal □ *a hearty breakfast*

heat /hiːt/ ▶ NOUN [*plural* **heats**]

1 *no plural* the quality of being hot or how hot something is □ *The panels use heat from the sun.* □ *Turn up the heat until the soup is boiling.*

2 the heat very hot weather □ *I can't stand the heat in summer.*

3 no plural anger or strong feelings □ *She tried to calm them down and take the heat out of the situation.*

4 a game or a race to decide who goes on to the next stage of a competition □ *Ian won his heat and went through to the semi-final.*

♦ IDIOM **in the heat of the moment** when you are very angry or excited and not controlling your words or behaviour □ *Some very nasty things were said in the heat of the moment.*

▶ VERB [**heats, heating, heated**] to make something hot or hotter □ *We use solar energy to heat our water.* □ *Heat the oven to medium.*

♦ PHRASAL VERB **heat (something) up** to become hotter or to make something hotter □ *We heated up the soup over the fire.*

• **heated** /'hi:tɪd/ ADJECTIVE full of anger or strong feelings ⊞ *a heated debate*

• **heater** /'hi:tə(r)/ NOUN [plural **heaters**] a piece of equipment that heats water or a place □ *I'll turn this heater on.*

heath /hi:θ/ NOUN [plural **heaths**] an area of wild land covered with grass and low bushes. A geography word.

heather /'heðə(r)/ NOUN, NO PLURAL a plant with small purple or white flowers, that grows close to the ground on hills and mountains

heating /'hi:tɪŋ/ NOUN, NO PLURAL the system or machinery used to heat a building

heatwave /'hi:tweɪv/ NOUN [plural **heatwaves**] a period of time when the weather is much hotter than usual

heave /hi:v/ VERB [**heaves, heaving, heaved**] to lift, pull or throw something heavy using a lot of effort □ *We spent the morning heaving boxes of books into the van.* □ *Both teams heaved on the rope.*

♦ IDIOM **heave a sigh of relief** to feel happy because something unpleasant or worrying has not happened or has ended □ *We'll all heave a sigh of relief when the project is finished.*

heaven /'hevən/ NOUN [plural **heavens**]

1 no plural in some religions, the place where God lives and where good people go when they die

2 no plural something that is very pleasant □ *I had no work and no children for three whole days – it was heaven.*

3 **the heavens** the sky □ *The heavens opened and the rain came lashing down.*

• **heavenly** /'hevənlɪ/ ADJECTIVE

1 to do with heaven □ *a heavenly choir of angels*

2 very pleasant □ *It was heavenly just lying in the sunshine.*

heavily /'hevɪlɪ/ ADVERB

1 a lot or to a large degree □ *The soldiers were heavily armed.* □ *His wife is heavily pregnant.*

2 with a lot of force or weight □ *It was snowing heavily when we left.* □ *She fell heavily, twisting her ankle.*

heaviness /'hevɪnɪs/ NOUN, NO PLURAL when something is heavy

heavy /'hevɪ/ ADJECTIVE [**heavier, heaviest**]

1 something that is heavy weighs a lot □ *The bags were too heavy for me to carry.*

2 if you say how heavy something is, you say how much it weighs □ *How heavy are these bricks?*

3 large in amount or degree ⊞ *heavy traffic* ⊞ *heavy rain/snow* ⊞ *There was heavy fighting in the region.*

4 **a heavy smoker/drinker** someone who smokes a lot/drinks a lot of alcohol

5 **a heavy burden/load/responsibility**, etc. something that is difficult for someone to manage to deal with

6 using a lot of force □ *a heavy blow*

heavy-handed /ˌhevɪ'hændɪd/ ADJECTIVE using more force than is necessary when dealing with a situation □ *I think the police response was a bit heavy-handed.*

heavy industry /ˌhevɪ 'ɪndʌstrɪ/ NOUN [plural **heavy industries**] an industry or industries that use large machinery to produce coal, metal, ships etc.

heckle /'hekəl/ VERB [**heckles, heckling, heckled**] to interrupt a speaker or performer with loud remarks or questions □ *Someone started to heckle from the back of the hall.*

• **heckler** /'heklə(r)/ NOUN [plural **hecklers**] someone who heckles a speaker or performer

hectare /'hekteə(r)/ NOUN [plural **hectares**] a unit for measuring area equal to 10,000 square metres. This is often written **ha**.

hectic /'hektɪk/ ADJECTIVE very busy, with a lot of activity □ *We've had a rather hectic week.*

he'd /hi:d/ a short way to say and write he had or he would □ *He'd never been there before.* □ *He'd do it for me if I asked him.*

hedge /hedʒ/ ▶ NOUN [plural **hedges**] a line of bushes or trees growing close together that separates one piece of land from another □ *A thick hedge surrounds the garden.*

▶ VERB [**hedges, hedging, hedged**] to avoid answering a question

hedgehog /'hedʒhɒg/ NOUN [plural **hedgehogs**] a small wild animal with sharp points all over its body

hedgerow /'hedʒrəʊ/ NOUN [plural **hedgerows**] a line of bushes and small trees growing close together along the side of a road or field

heed /hi:d/ ▶ VERB [**heeds, heeding, heeded**] to pay attention to advice or a warning ⊞ *He didn't heed the warning.*

▶ NOUN, NO PLURAL **pay/take heed** to pay attention to something □ *Drivers are taking heed of anti-drinking advice.*

• **heedless** /'hi:dlɪs/ ADJECTIVE paying no attention to possible danger or difficulty □ *He dived in and saved her, heedless of the risk to himself.*

heel /hi:l/ NOUN [plural **heels**]

1 the back part of your foot □ *She was getting a blister on her heel.*

2 the part of a shoe under the back of your foot 🔛 *She was wearing high heels.*

3 the part of a sock that covers your heel

hefty /'heftɪ/ ADJECTIVE [**heftier, heftiest**]
1 large and strong or fat □ *She's a fairly hefty woman.*
2 large in amount 🔛 *I got a hefty fine for driving in a bus lane.*

height /haɪt/ NOUN [*plural* **heights**]
1 how tall or high someone or something is □ *He's of average height.* □ *I'd say the wall's about six feet in height.*
2 *no plural* the fact of being tall □ *I remarked on his height.*
3 how far above the ground something is □ *We are now flying at a height of 11,000 metres.*
4 *no plural* the strongest or most extreme point that something reaches or can reach □ *He was at the height of his fame.* □ *It is the height of stupidity to throw a lit firework.*
5 heights high places □ *I'm afraid of heights.* □ *A coach took us up to the heights of Machu Picchu.*
• **heighten** /'haɪtən/ VERB [**heightens, heightening, heightened**] to increase or be increased □ *The film's music heightens the tension.* □ *Passive smoking heightens the risk of lung cancer.*

heinous /'heɪnəs/ ADJECTIVE very bad and shocking. A formal word. 🔛 *He has been accused of a heinous crime.*

heir /eə(r)/ NOUN [*plural* **heirs**] the person who has a legal right to someone's money or property when they die □ *He is the heir to a large fortune.*

heiress /'eərɪs/ NOUN [*plural* **heiresses**] a girl or woman who has a legal right to someone's money or property when they die

heirloom /'eəluːm/ NOUN [*plural* **heirlooms**] something valuable that is given by parents or grandparents to their children or grandchildren 🔛 *That clock was a family heirloom.*

held /held/ PAST TENSE AND PAST PARTICIPLE OF hold □ *She held my hand* □ *We had held the meeting in David's office.*

helicopter /'helɪkɒptə(r)/ NOUN [*plural* **helicopters**] a small aircraft without wings that is lifted into the air by long thin parts on top which turn round very fast

helium /'hiːliəm/ NOUN, NO PLURAL a gas that is lighter than air. A chemistry word.

he'll /hiːl/ a short way to say and write he will□ *He'll be here soon.*

hell /hel/ NOUN, NO PLURAL
1 in some religions, the place where bad people go when they die
2 a very unpleasant experience □ *The last few months of the relationship were hell.*

hello /həˈləʊ/ EXCLAMATION something you say when you meet someone or begin talking to someone on the telephone □ *Hello, Sophie. How are you?* □ *Hello, it's Mark.*

helm /helm/ NOUN [*plural* **helms**]
1 the wheel or handle used to change direction on a ship or boat
2 the helm used for saying that someone is in charge of a company or organization □ *He took over the helm 14 months ago.*

helmet /'helmɪt/ NOUN [*plural* **helmets**] a hard hat worn to protect your head □ *a cycling helmet* □ *a fireman's helmet*

help /help/ ▶ VERB [**helps, helping, helped**]
1 to do something to make a situation or activity easier for someone □ **+ to do something** *I helped him to find somewhere to stay.* □ *I find a warm bath helps to relax me.* □ **+ with** *My Mum helped me with my homework.*
2 to make a situation better or easier □ *If you've got a cold, eating oranges might help.* □ *It helps if you put the heavier items at the bottom.* □ *I took some painkillers, but they didn't help much.*
3 can't help (doing) something if you can't help something, you cannot stop yourself from doing it or stop it happening □ *She couldn't help laughing when she saw his face.*
4 help yourself to take something without waiting for someone to give it to you □ *Help yourself to some food.*
♦ PHRASAL VERB **help (someone) out** to help someone by doing work for them or giving them money □ *My parents help out with the rent.*
▶ NOUN [*plural* **helps**]
1 *no plural* when someone does something to make a situation or an activity easier for someone 🔛 *He needs help with his garden.* 🔛 *I was in debt, but I didn't know where to get help.* 🔛 *He tried to seek help for his depression.* 🔛 *These children get extra help with their reading.*
2 someone or something that helps someone 🔛 *Thanks for the advice. It was a great help.* □ *I couldn't work out how to use the system, and the instructions weren't much help.*
3 part of a computer system that tells you how to deal with problems or questions. A computing word.
▶ EXCLAMATION **Help!** used to shout for help in a serious situation

help desk /'help ˌdesk/ NOUN [*plural* **help desks**] a person or people who give advice to people who are having problems with a computer system. A computing word.

helper /'helpə(r)/ NOUN [*plural* **helpers**] someone who helps another person

helpful /'helpfʊl/ ADJECTIVE
1 useful □ *helpful advice*
2 willing to help □ *There was a lot of tidying up, but the children were very helpful.*
• **helpfully** /'helpfʊlɪ/ ADVERB in a helpful way □ *She helpfully suggested that I might get information at the library.*

helping /'helpɪŋ/ NOUN [plural **helpings**] an amount of food put on a plate for one person □ Who'd like a second helping?

helpless /'helplɪs/ ADJECTIVE not able to do anything for yourself, or to help other people in trouble □ How could anyone rob a helpless old man?
• **helplessly** /'helplɪslɪ/ ADVERB in a helpless way □ We had to watch helplessly while our daughter died.

helpline /'helplaɪn/ NOUN [plural **helplines**] a telephone number that you can call for advice on a particular subject □ Ring our 24-hour free helpline.

hem /hem/ ► NOUN [plural **hems**] the edge of a piece of cloth that has been folded over and sewn down □ I could let down the hem on that skirt for you.
► VERB [**hems, hemming, hemmed**] to sew a hem on the edge of a piece of cloth
♦ PHRASAL VERB **hem someone in** to surround someone and stop them moving in any direction □ A line of policemen hemmed the marchers in.

hemisphere /'hemɪsfɪə(r)/ NOUN [plural **hemispheres**]
1 one half of the Earth □ the northern hemisphere
2 a shape which is like half of a ball. A maths word.

hemoglobin /ˌhiːmə'gləʊbɪn/ NOUN, NO PLURAL the US spelling of haemoglobin

hemorrhage /'hemərɪdʒ/ NOUN [plural **hemorrhages**], VERB [**hemorrhages, hemorrhaging, hemorrhaged**] the US spelling of haemorrhage

hemp /hemp/ NOUN, NO PLURAL a plant that is used to make ropes and rough cloth

hen /hen/ NOUN [plural **hens**] a female chicken

hence /hens/ ADVERB
1 for this reason □ He's just had some bad news, hence his gloomy expression.
2 from this time or from this place □ five years hence

henna /'henə/ NOUN, NO PLURAL a reddish-brown dye (= substance that adds colour) that you can use to colour your hair or decorate your body

hen party /'hen ˌpɑːtɪ/ or **hen night** /'hen ˌnaɪt/ NOUN [plural **hen parties** or **hen nights**] a party for a group of women, especially one held just before a woman gets married

hepatitis /ˌhepə'taɪtɪs/ NOUN, NO PLURAL a disease of the liver that can be very serious

her /hɜː(r)/ ► PRONOUN used as the object of a sentence to talk or write about a woman, girl or female animal that has already been mentioned □ I'm looking for Mrs Peters. Have you seen her? □ I gave the letter to her.
► DETERMINER belonging to or to do with a woman, girl or female animal □ Her hair is blonde. □ That's her problem, not mine.

herald /'herəld/ ► VERB [**heralds, heralding, heralded**] to be a sign that something is going to happen or come soon □ The treaty heralded the birth of a new Europe.
► NOUN [plural **heralds**] a sign that something is going to happen or come soon □ Snowdrops are a herald of spring.

herb /hɜːb/ NOUN [plural **herbs**] a plant that is used for giving flavour to food and for making medicines □ herbs and spices □ a herb garden
• **herbal** /'hɜːbəl/ ADJECTIVE made with herbs □ herbal medicines □ herbal tea

herbivore /'hɜːbɪvɔː(r)/ NOUN [plural **herbivores**] an animal that eats only grass and plants. A biology word.
• **herbivorous** /hɜː'bɪvərəs/ ADJECTIVE eating only grass and plants. A biology word □ Deer are herbivorous.

herd /hɜːd/ ► NOUN [plural **herds**] a large group of animals of one type that live as a group □ a herd of cattle
► VERB [**herds, herding, herded**] to make animals or people come together and go somewhere in a group □ We were herded into a small room at the back.

here /hɪə(r)/ ADVERB
1 in or to this place □ I like it here. □ Come here! □ You can leave your shoes here. □ He's American, but he's lived over here for years.
2 used to say that someone or something has arrived or has been found □ Here's Tom at last. □ Here's the house we are looking for.
3 used when you give someone something □ Here, put on this jacket. □ Here you are – we saved some food for you.
4 at a particular place in a talk or a piece of writing □ There were so many people involved, I can't list them all here.
5 in the present time, or at the present point in an activity □ How shall we proceed from here? □ Wait until summer is here.
6 here and there in a few different places □ There were a few mistakes here and there.

hereafter /ˌhɪər'ɑːftə(r)/ ► ADVERB used in legal documents to mean after this or from this time on. A formal word.
► NOUN, NO PLURAL the hereafter life after death

hereby /ˌhɪə'baɪ/ ADVERB used in legal documents to say what you are going to do and how it will be done. A formal word. □ We hereby promise to abide by this agreement.

hereditary /hɪ'redɪtərɪ/ ADJECTIVE passed on from parent to child □ a hereditary disease
• **heredity** /hɪ'redɪtɪ/ NOUN, NO PLURAL the way in which qualities and features are passed from a parent to a child before the child is born

heresy /'herəsɪ/ NOUN [plural **heresies**] an opinion or belief, especially a religious one, that is different from what most people in a group or society believe and is considered wrong □ Galileo was charged with heresy for his beliefs.

heritage /'herɪtɪdʒ/ NOUN, NO PLURAL the buildings, customs, culture, etc. of a country that are important because they have existed for a long time □ *Spain's cultural heritage*

hermaphrodite /hɜ:'mæfrədaɪt/ NOUN [plural **hermaphrodites**] an animal or a plant with both male and female sex organs. A biology word.

hermit /'hɜ:mɪt/ NOUN [plural **hermits**] someone who lives alone and does not see other people

• **hermitage** /'hɜ:mɪtɪdʒ/ NOUN [plural **hermitages**] a place where a hermit lives

hero /'hɪərəʊ/ NOUN [plural **heroes**]

1 someone who people admire because of the brave or difficult things they have done □ *Nelson Mandela is a hero to many of us.*

2 the most important male character in a story or film □ *The hero of the book is a New York detective.*

• **heroic** /hɪ'rəʊɪk/ ADJECTIVE very brave □ *He threw himself in front of her in a heroic attempt to save her.*

• **heroine** /'herəʊɪn/ NOUN [plural **heroines**]

1 a woman or girl who people admire because of the brave or difficult things she has done

2 the most important female character in a story or film

• **heroism** /'herəʊɪzəm/ NOUN, NO PLURAL very brave behaviour □ *He won a medal for his heroism in battle.*

heron /'herən/ NOUN [plural **herons**] a bird with long legs and a long neck that lives near water and catches fish in its long sharp beak

herring /'herɪŋ/ NOUN [plural **herring** or **herrings**] a small, silver, sea fish that is eaten as food

hers /hɜ:z/ PRONOUN used to talk or write about things belonging to or to do with a woman or girl that has already been mentioned □ *I gave Sandra my phone number and she gave me hers.* □ *'Was it your idea, or Ann's?' 'It was hers.'*

► Notice that there is no apostrophe between the r and the s in **hers**.

herself /hɜ:'self/ PRONOUN

1 the reflexive form of her □ *Did Barbara hurt herself when she fell down?* □ *She sang to herself as she worked.*

2 used to show that she does something without any help from other people □ *She always answers every fan letter herself.* 🕮 *She's only 3 but she can get dressed all by herself.*

3 used to emphasize the pronoun she □ *I wanted to speak to Gina herself.*

4 by herself not with or near other people □ *She always sits by herself.*

5 to herself without having to share with anyone else □ *She had the whole flat to herself.*

he's /hi:z/ a short way to say and write he is or he has □ *He's my brother.* □ *He's done all the work.*

hesitant /'hezɪtənt/ ADJECTIVE slow to do something and showing that you are are nervous or not sure that you should do it □ *She gave a rather hesitant answer.*

• **hesitate** /'hezɪ,teɪt/ VERB [**hesitates, hesitating, hesitated**]

1 to pause before you say or do something because you are not sure you should say or do it □ *She hesitated before answering his question.*

2 not hesitate to do something to do something immediately because you know you should □ *If you need any help, don't hesitate to call me.*

• **hesitation** /,hezɪ'teɪʃən/ NOUN [plural **hesitations**] when you pause before saying or doing something because you are not sure you should say or do it □ *He accepted without hesitation.* □ *There was a brief hesitation before she answered.*

hexagon /'heksəgən/ NOUN [plural **hexagons**] a shape with six sides. A maths word.

• **hexagonal** /hek'sægənəl/ ADJECTIVE in the shape of a hexagon. A maths word.

hey /heɪ/ EXCLAMATION an exclamation used to get someone's attention or show you are surprised □ *Hey, stop that!* □ *Hey, look at this!*

heyday /'heɪdeɪ/ NOUN, NO PLURAL the time when someone or something was most famous or successful 🕮 *In her heyday she was the highest paid star on Broadway*

HGV /,eɪtʃdʒi:'vi:/ ABBREVIATION heavy goods vehicle; a large vehicle such as a truck

hi /haɪ/ EXCLAMATION hello □ *Hi, Charlotte!* □ *Hi, how are you?*

hiatus /haɪ'eɪtəs/ NOUN [plural **hiatuses**] a period of time in which nothing happens. A formal word. □ *After a two-year hiatus the band are back on tour.*

hibernate /'haɪbəneɪt/ VERB [**hibernates, hibernating, hibernated**] if an animal hibernates, it sleeps all winter □ *Her tortoise was hibernating in a box in the shed.*

• **hibernation** /,haɪbə'neɪʃən/ NOUN, NO PLURAL when an animal hibernates 🕮 *Bears go into hibernation in the winter.*

hiccup /'hɪkʌp/ ► NOUN [plural **hiccups**]

1 a sudden repeated noise in your throat that you cannot control 🕮 *Fizzy drinks often give me hiccups.* 🕮 *She laughed so much she got the hiccups.*

2 a small problem that causes a delay □ *There were a few hiccups at the start of the project..*

► VERB [**hiccups, hiccupping, hiccupped**] to make repeated noises in your throat that you cannot control

hide¹ /haɪd/ VERB [**hides, hiding, hid, hidden**]

1 to put or keep something or someone in a place where people cannot see or find them easily □ *I hid her presents under my bed.* □ *He kept his money hidden from his wife.*

2 to go to a place where people cannot see you □ *Eva was hiding and the other children were looking for her.* □ *He hid behind a tree.*

3 to not let other people know about your feelings or some information □ *Sarah didn't try to hide her disappointment at losing.* □ *I've got nothing to hide.*

hide² /haɪd/ NOUN [plural **hides**] the skin of an animal

hide-and-seek /ˌhaɪdən'siːk/ NOUN, NO PLURAL a game in which one child hides and the other players look for him or her

hideous /'hɪdɪəs/ ADJECTIVE extremely ugly □ *I thought the dress was hideous.*

hideout /'haɪdaʊt/ NOUN [*plural* **hideouts**] a place where someone hides, especially from the police □ *The gang had a secret hideout in the mountains.*

hiding /'haɪdɪŋ/ NOUN, NO PLURAL when someone stays in a secret place or changes their appearance so that no one will find them ⬚ *The ex-spy is believed to be in hiding in London.* ⬚ *He knew he would be arrested so he went into hiding.*

hierarchy /'haɪəˌrɑːkɪ/ NOUN [*plural* **hierarchies**] a system or organization in which people are arranged according to their rank or importance □ *It is mostly men at the top of the political hierarchy.*

hieroglyphics /ˌhaɪərə'glɪfɪks/ PLURAL NOUN a system of writing used in Ancient Egypt in which little pictures represent letters and words

hi-fi /'haɪˌfaɪ/ NOUN [*plural* **hi-fis**] a piece of electronic equipment for playing music

high /haɪ/ ▶ ADJECTIVE [**higher, highest**]

1 a large distance above the ground □ *The apples were too high to reach.* □ *It's best to keep medicines on a high shelf.*

2 a long distance from the bottom to the top □ *It is a very high building.* □ *They built a high wall around the house.*

3 having a particular height □ *The fence is 4 metres high.* □ *How high is Snowdon?*

4 large in amount or level ⬚ *The temperature was unusually high.* ⬚ *We drove at high speed through the town.* ⬚ *We were shocked at the high cost of housing.* ⬚ *They found high levels of radiation in the area.*

5 very good ⬚ *high quality* ⬚ *We expect a very high standard of work.*

6 important □ *He had a high rank in the army.*

7 a high sound or musical note is near the top of the range of sounds □ *We could hear the children's high voices.*

◆ IDIOM **it's high time** used to emphasize that something should happen or be done very soon □ *It's high time Leo got a job.*

> ▶ Remember that people who are big in height are described as **tall** and not **high**:
> ✓ *Her father is very tall.*
> ✗ *Her father is very high.*

▶ ADVERB [**higher, highest**]

1 at or to a large distance above the ground □ *She threw the ball high in the air.* □ *Dirty clothes were piled high in her bedroom.* □ *The village is perched high above the sea.*

2 at or to a large amount or level □ *The temperature rose higher and higher.* □ *Prices remain high.*

▶ NOUN [*plural* **highs**]

1 the largest amount or level that something reaches

□ *Confidence was at an all-time high.* ⬚ *Temperatures reached a high of 25 degrees.*

2 a feeling of happiness □ *We were all on a high after winning the match.*

highbrow /'haɪbraʊ/ ADJECTIVE highbrow books, programmes, discussions, etc. are serious and enjoyed by intelligent, well educated people □ *They have very highbrow conversations over dinner.*

high chair /'haɪ ˌtʃeə(r)/ NOUN [*plural* **high chairs**] a chair with long legs for a baby or young child to sit in while they are eating

higher education /'haɪə(r) ˌedjuː'keɪʃən/ NOUN, NO PLURAL education at a university or college □ *They have two children, both now in higher education.*

high jump /'haɪ ˌdʒʌmp/ NOUN, NO PLURAL a sport in which people try to jump over a horizontal bar that gets higher as the competition continues

highland /'haɪlənd/ ADJECTIVE to do with an area that has a lot of mountains □ *a highland cottage*

● **highlands** /'haɪləndz/ PLURAL NOUN an area of a country that has a lot of mountains □ *the Scottish Highlands*

highlight /'haɪlaɪt/ ▶ VERB [**highlights, highlighting, highlighted**]

1 to emphasize something □ *These figures highlight a growing problem.*

2 to mark words on a page with a different colour so that people give them more attention □ *I've highlighted the important quotations in green.*

▶ NOUN [*plural* **highlights**]

1 the best part of an event or period of time □ *His singing was the highlight of the concert.*

2 highlights lines of a lighter colour that are put in your hair

● **highlighter** /'haɪlaɪtə(r)/ NOUN [*plural* **highlighters**] a pen with brightly coloured transparent ink that you use to mark words in a piece of writing

highly /'haɪlɪ/ ADVERB

1 very □ *highly qualified teachers* □ *This seems highly unlikely.*

2 highly paid paid a lot of money □ *highly paid executives*

3 highly regarded/respected admired by a lot of people □ *a very highly regarded politician*

4 speak/think highly of someone to admire someone □ *Martin's always spoken very highly of you*

highly-strung /ˌhaɪlɪ'strʌŋ/ ADJECTIVE very nervous and easily made upset

high-maintenance /ˌhaɪ'meɪntənəns/ ADJECTIVE needing a lot of effort and attention □ *a high-maintenance hairstyle*

Highness /'haɪnɪs/ NOUN [*plural* **Highnesses**] Your/Her/His Highness a title you use when you are speaking about or to a member of a royal family

high-pitched /ˌhaɪ'pɪtʃt/ ADJECTIVE a high-pitched voice or sound is high and sometimes unpleasant

high-powered /ˌhaɪ'paʊəd/ ADJECTIVE very powerful and responsible □ *high-powered jobs in industry* □ *a high-powered executive*

high-rise /ˈhaɪraɪz/ ► ADJECTIVE high-rise buildings are tall and narrow with a lot of levels
► NOUN [plural **high-rises**] a very tall building

high school /ˈhaɪ ˌskuːl/ NOUN [plural **high schools**] in the US, a school for children aged between 14 and 18

high street /ˈhaɪ ˌstriːt/ NOUN [plural **high streets**] the main street of a town, where the shops and banks are □ Most of the high street banks will be raising their interest rates.

high-tech /ˌhaɪˈtek/ ADJECTIVE using the most modern technology □ high-tech security equipment □ high-tech computer graphics

highway /ˈhaɪweɪ/ NOUN [plural **highways**] a US word for a road between towns and cities

Highway Code /ˌhaɪweɪ ˈkəʊd/ NOUN, NO PLURAL the Highway Code a set of official rules that tells you how to use the roads

hijack /ˈhaɪdʒæk/ VERB [**hijacks, hijacking, hijacked**] to take control of an aeroplane by force □ Two students hijacked the plane in Thailand.

• **hijacker** /ˈhaɪdʒækə(r)/ NOUN [plural **hijackers**] someone who hijacks an aeroplane □ The hijackers were arrested by Australian police.

• **hijacking** /ˈhaɪdʒækɪŋ/ NOUN [plural **hijackings**] the crime of taking control of an aeroplane by force

hike /haɪk/ ► NOUN [plural **hikes**]
1 a long walk in the countryside
2 a sudden increase in the level of something □ a hike in interest rates
► VERB [**hikes, hiking, hiked**]
1 to go for a long walk in the countryside
2 to increase the level of something □ Retailers have hiked up the price of many household goods.

• **hiker** /ˈhaɪkə(r)/ NOUN [plural **hikers**] someone who goes for long walks in the countryside

• **hiking** /ˈhaɪkɪŋ/ NOUN, NO PLURAL the activity of taking long walks in the countryside

hilarious /hɪˈleərɪəs/ ADJECTIVE very funny □ The film was hilarious.

• **hilarity** /hɪˈlærəti/ NOUN, NO PLURAL when people think something is very funny and laugh loudly □ His comments caused great hilarity.

hill /hɪl/ NOUN [plural **hills**] a raised or high area of land, smaller than a mountain □ We went walking in the Tuscan hills.

♦ IDIOM **over the hill** if someone is over the hill, they are too old to do something

hillside /ˈhɪlsaɪd/ NOUN [plural **hillsides**] the side of a hill

hilly /ˈhɪli/ ADJECTIVE [**hillier, hilliest**] a hilly area has a lot of hills

hilt /hɪlt/ NOUN [plural **hilts**] the handle of a knife or sword

♦ IDIOM **to the hilt** very much or as much as you possibly can □ I'd defend his character to the hilt.

him /hɪm/ PRONOUN used as the object of a sentence to talk or write about a man, boy or male animal that has already been mentioned □ I'm looking for Mr Peters. Have you seen him anywhere? □ She threw the book at him.

himself /hɪmˈself/ PRONOUN
1 the reflexive form of him□ He poked himself in the eye by mistake. □ The old man was muttering to himself.
2 used to show that he does something without any help from other people □ I was surprised he did all the cooking himself. 🔁 Jack can tie his shoelaces all by himself already.
3 used to emphasize the pronoun him□ He's never been to London himself.
4 **by himself** not with or near other people □ He stood by himself in a corner.
5 **to himself** without having to share with anyone else □ He enjoyed having his mother to himself.

hind /haɪnd/ ADJECTIVE **hind leg/foot** the back leg or foot of an animal □ The horse reared up on its hind legs.

hinder /ˈhɪndə(r)/ VERB [**hinders, hindering, hindered**] to make it more difficult to do something □ Lack of money has hindered research into the disease.

• **hindrance** /ˈhɪndrəns/ NOUN [plural **hindrances**] something that makes it difficult to do something

hindsight /ˈhaɪndsaɪt/ NOUN, NO PLURAL understanding of an event or situation that you have after it has happened 🔁 With hindsight I can see I was a fool to trust him.

Hindu /ˈhɪnduː/ ► NOUN [plural **Hindus**] a person whose religion is Hinduism
► ADJECTIVE to do with Hinduism □ The main Hindu gods are Brahma, Vishnu and Shiva.

• **Hinduism** /ˈhɪnduːɪzəm/ NOUN, NO PLURAL a religion of India and parts of South East Asia, which has many gods and teaches that after people die they will return to life in another body

hinge /hɪndʒ/ NOUN [plural **hinges**] a piece of metal or plastic which attaches a door to its frame, and allows the door to open and close

♦ PHRASAL VERB [**hinges, hinging, hinged**] **hinge on something** if one thing hinges on another, it depends on it □ Whether he gets into university hinges on his A level results.

hint /hɪnt/ ► NOUN [plural **hints**]
1 something that suggests what you think or want but not in a direct way 🔁 She dropped a hint that something exciting was about to happen. 🔁 He kept yawning but no one took the hint and went home.
2 a helpful piece of advice □ Can you give me any hints on how to learn vocabulary?
3 a small amount of something □ fizzy water with a hint of lemon
► VERB [**hints, hinting, hinted**] to suggest something in a way that is not clear or direct □ Laura hinted that she might be leaving.

hip /hɪp/ NOUN [plural **hips**] each of the two parts at the side of your body, below your waist and above your leg □ *Gran fell and broke her hip.*

hip-hop /'hɪphɒp/ NOUN, NO PLURAL a type of pop music in which the words are about social problems and are spoken not sung □ *hip-hop groups*

hippie /'hɪpɪ/ NOUN [plural **hippies**] a long-haired person in the 1960s who believed in peace and love and was against war and tradition

hippo /'hɪpəʊ/ NOUN [plural **hippos**] an informal word for a hippopotamus

hippopotamus /ˌhɪpə'pɒtəməs/ NOUN [plural **hippopotamuses** or **hippopotami**] a large African animal with a heavy body, small ears and short legs, that lives near or in rivers

hippy /'hɪpɪ/ NOUN [plural **hippies**] another spelling of hippie

hire /'haɪə(r)/ ► VERB [hires, hiring, hired]
1 to pay to use something for a period of time, especially a short period, and then return it □ *We hired bikes while we were on holiday.*
2 to begin to employ someone □ *I've decided to hire a cleaner.*

► Notice that in British English you **hire** things usually for a short time, only paying once to use them. You **rent**, usually for a longer period, a house or an office, etc., paying every month or many times. In American English you always **rent** things. The verb **hire** is not used.

► NOUN, NO PLURAL when you pay to use something for a period of time □ *The holiday price includes the hire of a car.* ⊞ *There are boats for hire on the lake.*

his /hɪz/ ► DETERMINER belonging to or to do with to him □ *Julian has left his coat behind.* □ *Blame Harry. It was his idea.*
► PRONOUN used to talk or write about things belonging to or to do with to a man, boy or male animal that has already been mentioned □ *I didn't have an umbrella so Grandad lent me his.*

hiss /hɪs/ ► VERB [hisses, hissing, hissed]
1 to make a noise like a long 's' sound □ *a hissing snake*
2 to say something quietly and angrily □ *'I said be quiet!' he hissed.*
► NOUN [plural **hisses**] a sound like that made by a snake □ *We could hear the hiss of gas escaping from the pipe.*

histogram /'hɪstəgræm/ NOUN [plural **histograms**] a diagram in which amounts are shown using thick lines of different heights. A maths word.

historian /hɪ'stɔːrɪən/ NOUN [plural **historians**] someone who studies history □ *a local historian*

• **historic** /hɪ'stɒrɪk/ ADJECTIVE important and likely to be remembered for a long time □ *a historic victory*

• **historical** /hɪ'stɒrɪkəl/ ADJECTIVE to do with history □ *historical records*

► Notice the difference between **historic** and **historical**. **Historic** means 'important in history'. **Historical** means 'to do with history': □ *This was a historic moment.* □ *She writes historical novels.*

• **history** /'hɪstərɪ/ NOUN [plural **histories**]
1 no plural all the things that happened in the past, or the study of things that happened in the past □ *local history* □ *modern European history* □ *He studied history at university.* □ *history books*
2 the series of events or things that happened or relate to someone or something in the past ⊞ *We didn't know the patient's medical history.* □ *+ of He has a history of mental illness.*

hit /hɪt/ ► VERB [hits, hitting, hit]
1 to touch against someone or something with force □ *Stop hitting your brother!* □ *The plane hit the ground and burst into flames.* □ *I hit my head on the cupboard door.* □ *She hit him with a baseball bat.* □ *Storms hit the west coast last night.*
2 to have a bad effect on someone □ *The business was hit by big rent rises.* ⊞ *The area was hard hit by unemployment.*
3 to reach a particular level □ *Temperatures hit record levels today.* ⊞ *The sales team managed to hit their target.*
4 if the truth about something hits you, you suddenly become aware of it □ *It suddenly hit me that we could die.*
♦ IDIOM **hit it off** to like each other quickly □ *We met in Spain, and hit it off straight away.*
♦ PHRASAL VERBS **hit back** to attack or criticize someone who has attacked or criticized you □ *The singer hit back at critics who accused her of being too sentimental.* **hit on/upon something** to have a good idea about something □ *He'd hit on the perfect solution to the problem.*
► NOUN [plural **hits**]
1 something or someone that is very popular □ *The show was an instant hit.* □ *He's a big hit with the old ladies.*
2 when you touch against something with force □ *I got a hit on my arm.*
3 a record of someone looking at a document on the Internet. A computing word. □ *Our website gets over three thousand hits a week.*
► ADJECTIVE popular and successful □ *a hit song*

hit-and-miss /ˌhɪtən'mɪs/ or **hit-or-miss** /ˌhɪtə'mɪs/ ADJECTIVE not planned or organized well, so sometimes successful and sometimes not □ *Their methods are pretty hit-and-miss.*

hit-and-run /ˌhɪtən'rʌn/ ► ADJECTIVE to do with an accident in which a driver hits someone but does not stop to help the injured person □ *a hit-and-run drive*
► NOUN [plural **hit-and-runs**] a hit-and-run acciden

hitch /hɪtʃ/ ▶ VERB [hitches, hitching, hitched]
1 to get a free ride in a vehicle by standing at the side of the road and waiting for someone to stop and take you with them □ *We couldn't afford the train ticket so we decided to hitch.* 🔲 *I hitched a lift out of town.*
2 to fasten one thing to another □ *He hitched the caravan to the back of the car.*
◆ PHRASAL VERB **hitch something up** to pull up a piece of your clothing □ *She hitched her skirt up and climbed over the wall.*
▶ NOUN [plural **hitches**] a small difficulty 🔲 *The school show went off without a hitch.*

hitchhike /'hɪtʃhaɪk/ VERB [hitchhikes, hitchhiking, hitchhiked] to get a free ride in a vehicle by standing at the side of the road and waiting for someone to stop and take you with them □ *We hitchhiked around Europe.*
● **hitchhiker** /'hɪtʃhaɪkə(r)/ NOUN [plural **hitchhikers**] someone who hitchhikes

hi-tech /ˌhaɪ'tek/ ADJECTIVE another spelling of high-tech

hitherto /ˌhɪðə'tuː/ ADVERB until now. A formal word. □ *Hitherto the librarian had always been in charge of the keys.*

HIV /ˌeɪtʃaɪ'viː/ ABBREVIATION human immunodeficiency virus; the virus that causes the disease AIDS

hive /haɪv/ NOUN [plural **hives**] a container that bees live in and where they store their honey
◆ IDIOM **a hive of activity** a place where everyone is busy doing something

HMS /ˌeɪtʃem'es/ ABBREVIATION His or Her Majesty's Ship; used in the names of British Royal Navy ships □ *HMS Victory*

hoard /hɔːd/ ▶ VERB [hoards, hoarding, hoarded] to collect things and store them away in large quantities □ *He started hoarding food because he thought there was going to be a war.*
▶ NOUN [plural **hoards**] a large store of things that you have collected and kept □ *a hoard of Roman coins*
● **hoarder** /'hɔːdə/ NOUN [plural **hoarders**] someone who likes saving and keeping a lot of things

hoarding /'hɔːdɪŋ/ NOUN [plural **hoardings**] a large board in the street where advertisements are put up

hoarse /hɔːs/ ADJECTIVE [hoarser, hoarsest] if you are hoarse, your voice sounds rough, often because your throat is sore □ *He was hoarse from cheering on the team.*

hoax /həʊks/ NOUN [plural **hoaxes**] a trick in which someone tells people something bad that is not true, for example by saying that there is a bomb somewhere 🔲 *He was accused of making hoax calls to the fire brigade.*

hob /hɒb/ NOUN [plural **hobs**] the top surface of a cooker where you heat food in pans

hobble /'hɒbəl/ VERB [hobbles, hobbling, hobbled] to walk with difficulty because your foot or leg hurts □ *He was hobbling around the pitch.*

hobby /'hɒbɪ/ NOUN [plural **hobbies**] something you like doing in your free time 🔲 *My Dad's favourite hobby is birdwatching.* 🔲 *It's my new hobby.* 🔲 *She didn't really have any hobbies.*

hockey /'hɒkɪ/ NOUN, NO PLURAL a game in which two teams use curved sticks to hit a ball into a net 🔲 *We play hockey at school.* 🔲 *a hockey stick* □ *a hockey team*

hoe /həʊ/ ▶ NOUN [plural **hoes**] a garden tool used for turning soil
▶ VERB [hoes, hoeing, hoed] to use a hoe to turn soil in a garden

hog /hɒg/ ▶ VERB [hogs, hogging, hogged] to use something yourself which stops other people from using it. An informal word. □ *He had parked badly and was hogging two parking spaces.*
▶ NOUN [plural **hogs**] a pig

hoist /hɔɪst/ ▶ VERB [hoists, hoisting, hoisted] to lift something □ *He hoisted his bag over his shoulder.*
▶ NOUN [plural **hoists**] a piece of equipment for lifting heavy things

hold /həʊld/ ▶ VERB [holds, holding, held]
1 to have something in your hand or hands □ *He was holding a big wooden box.* 🔲 *Hold tight – we're going over some rough ground.*
2 to support something or to stop something moving □ *The pieces of wood are held together with nails.* 🔲 *Use glue to hold the cardboard in place.*
3 to keep a part of your body in a particular position □ *Hold your hands in the air.*
4 to organize an event □ *We held the meeting in our office.* 🔲 *The government will never hold talks with terrorists.* 🔲 *The general has promised to hold an election.*
5 to have space for something □ *The room holds 300 people.*
6 to contain something □ *This rack holds my wine collection.*
7 to keep someone as a prisoner □ *He is being held in a Russian jail.* 🔲 *The three women were held hostage for over an hour.*
8 to keep information or documents □ *All his papers are held at the bank.* □ *The police hold records on all the suspects.*
9 to have a particular job or position in an organization □ *She holds the post of director.*
10 to have a particular opinion □ *He holds the view that women should stay at home.*
11 hold your breath to deliberately not breathe
12 hold hands to curve your hand around someone else's hand
13 hold a record to be the person or thing that is the best, biggest, fastest, etc. □ *He holds the world record for the 400m.*
➡ go to **hold your own**
◆ PHRASAL VERBS **hold something against someone** to continue to feel angry with someone about something they did in the past □ *I got the job he*

wanted and he's always held it against me. **hold
something/someone back** to stop someone or
something making progress □ *A lack of formal
education did not hold her back.* **hold something
down** **1** to keep prices, amounts, etc. at a low level
□ *The company has tried to hold down wages.*
2 if you hold down a job, you manage to continue
doing it □ *He's held down a steady job for two years
now.* **hold off** to wait for a period of time before
doing something □ *He decided to hold off contacting
her.* **hold on** **1** to hold something tightly □ *Hold on
tight! We're coming to get you.* **2** to wait □ *Hold on a
minute – I just need to check my email.* **hold out** **1** to
continue to be enough □ *I don't know how long our
supplies will hold out.* **2** to continue to manage in a
difficult situation □ *The soldiers started firing at us, but
we held out until our comrades arrived.* **hold
someone/something up** to make something or
someone slow or late □ *We got held up by the
traffic.* □ *All these regulations are holding up
progress.*

▶ NOUN [*plural* **holds**]

1 when you hold something, or the way something is
held ⌾*I got hold of the handle and pulled it hard.*
⌾*Try to catch hold of the rope.* ⌾*My hands were so
wet, I couldn't keep hold of the rail.*

2 **get hold of something** to manage to get
something □ *Do you know where I can get hold of
some cheap bricks?*

3 **get hold of someone** to manage to speak to
someone □ *I've been trying to get hold of her all
morning.*

4 **on hold** (a) if an activity is on hold, it has been
stopped until a later time (b) if someone puts you on
hold on the telephone, they leave you waiting to speak
to someone

5 power that someone can use to control someone
□ **+ over** *He had a strong hold over all his pupils.*

6 the place in a ship or an aeroplane where goods or
bags are stored

holdall /ˈhəʊldɔːl/ NOUN [*plural* **holdalls**] a large soft
bag

holder /ˈhəʊldə(r)/ NOUN [*plural* **holders**]

1 someone who has something ⌾*Ticket holders are
entitled to a refund if the concert is cancelled.* ⌾*He's
the world record holder for the 100m.*

2 something used for holding something else □ *a
toothbrush holder*

hold-up /ˈhəʊldʌp/ NOUN [*plural* **hold-ups**]

1 a delay □ *The train conductor apologized for the
hold-up.*

2 when someone uses a gun to try to steal money
from a shop or bank

hole /həʊl/ NOUN [*plural* **holes**]

1 a space in the surface of something □ **+ in** *He had a
hole in his sock.* □ *She drilled a hole in the wall.*

2 a space dug in the ground ⌾*They dug a deep hole in
the ground to plant the rose bush in.* □ *a rabbit hole*

3 in golf, one of the places in the ground that you try
to hit the ball into

holiday /ˈhɒlɪdeɪ/ NOUN [*plural* **holidays**]

1 a time when you do not have to work or go to school
⌾*What are you doing in the summer holidays?* ⌾*The
museum is very busy during school holidays.*

2 **on holiday** if you are on holiday, you are not
working or not at school for a period □ *I'm on holiday
next week.*

3 a period of time when you stay in a different place to
enjoy yourself ⌾*We're going on holiday next week.*
□ *a skiing holiday* ⌾*Spain is a popular holiday
destination for British travellers.*

4 an official day when many people in a country do
not have to go to work ⌾*1st August is a national
holiday in Switzerland.*

▶ The word **holiday** is used by British speakers of
English. North American speakers of English use
the word **vacation**.

holiness /ˈhəʊlɪnɪs/ NOUN, NO PLURAL

1 being holy

2 **His/Your Holiness** a title used for the Pope, and
some other religious leaders

hollow /ˈhɒləʊ/ ▶ ADJECTIVE [**hollower, hollowest**]

1 having an empty space inside □ *hollow chocolate
eggs* □ *a hollow tube*

2 having no real meaning or emotion □ *a hollow
promise* □ *a hollow victory*

3 hollow cheeks and eyes have a surface that curves in

▶ NOUN [*plural* **hollows**] an empty space in something
or an area that is lower than the area around it □ *There
were cracks and hollows in the rock.*

holly /ˈhɒlɪ/ NOUN, NO PLURAL a tree with sharp leaves
and red berries (= small fruit)

holocaust /ˈhɒləkɔːst/ NOUN [*plural* **holocausts**]

1 **the Holocaust** the murder of many Jewish people
by the Nazis in the 1930s and 1940s

2 an event in which many people are killed and many
things are damaged □ *a nuclear holocaust*

hologram /ˈhɒləɡræm/ NOUN [*plural* **holograms**] a
type of picture that does not look as if it is flat,
especially when you move it

holster /ˈhəʊlstə(r)/ NOUN [*plural* **holsters**] a
container for a gun that someone wears on a belt

holy /ˈhəʊlɪ/ ADJECTIVE [**holier, holiest**]

1 to do with God or religion □ *The Koran is the Muslim
holy book.* □ *The Golden Temple is a holy site in
Punjab.*

2 having strong religious feelings □ *a holy man*

homage /ˈhɒmɪdʒ/ NOUN, NO PLURAL **pay homage to
something/someone** to do or say something to
show your respect for someone or their achievements
□ *He paid homage to the artist by writing a book about
her.*

home /həʊm/ ▶ NOUN [plural **homes**]
1 the place where you live or where you lived when you were a child □ *I left my watch at home.* 🔁 *He left home at the age of twenty.* 🔁 *Cambridge is my home town.*
2 a building that people live in □ *We can't afford to buy our own home.* □ *Hundreds of new homes will be built in the city.*
3 the place where something started or where a lot of something exists or is done □ *Mumbai is the home of the Indian film industry.*
4 a place where people or animals who need care live □ *a children's home* □ *an old people's home*
5 the place where a sports team is based □ *The home side is favourite to win.*
◆ IDIOMS **be/feel at home** to be very relaxed and confident in a place **make yourself at home** to be relaxed in a place as if it was where you live
▶ ADVERB **1** to the place where you live 🔁 *It's time to go home.* 🔁 *Thousands of soldiers are returning home this week.* □ *I met Freddie on my way home.*
2 at the place where you live □ *Will you be home tomorrow?*

> ▶ Notice that you **go home** or **get home**. You do not say 'go to home' or 'get to home':
> ✓ *I usually get home later.*
> ✗ *I usually get to home later.*

◆ PHRASAL VERB [**homes, homing, homed**] **home in on something** to give a lot of attention to a particular part of something □ *He homed in on the sales figures.*

homeless /ˈhəʊmlɪs/ ▶ ADJECTIVE having nowhere to live □ *Thousands of people have been made homeless by the earthquake.*
▶ NOUN **the homeless** people who have nowhere to live □ *The charity provides meals for the homeless.*
● **homelessness** /ˈhəʊmlɪsnɪs/ NOUN, NO PLURAL when people have nowhere to live □ *Homelessness is a problem in many big cities.*

homely /ˈhəʊmli/ ADJECTIVE [**homelier, homeliest**] pleasant and comfortable □ *The hotel is quiet and homely.*

homemade /ˌhəʊmˈmeɪd/ ADJECTIVE made in someone's home and not in a factory □ *homemade cakes*

homeopath /ˈhəʊmɪəˌpæθ/ NOUN [plural **homeopaths**] someone who uses homeopathy to treat people
● **homeopathic** //ˌhəʊmɪəʊˈpæθɪk/ ADJECTIVE to do with homeopathy □ *homeopathic remedies*
● **homeopathy** /ˌhəʊmɪˈɒpəθi/ NOUN, NO PLURAL treating diseases by giving someone a very small amount of a substance that in large amounts would cause the illness

home page /ˈhəʊm ˌpeɪdʒ/ NOUN [plural **home pages**] the first page on a website. A computing word.

homesick /ˈhəʊmsɪk/ ADJECTIVE feeling unhappy because you are away from home and your family □ *A lot of children feel homesick when they first spend time away from their parents.*
● **homesickness** /ˈhəʊmsɪknɪs/ NOUN, NO PLURAL the feeling of being homesick

homeward /ˈhəʊmwəd/ ADJECTIVE, ADVERB towards home □ *his homeward journey*

homework /ˈhəʊmwɜːk/ NOUN, NO PLURAL school work that you have to do at home 🔁 *Have you done your maths homework yet?* 🔁 *The teacher gives us too much homework.*

homicidal /ˌhɒmɪˈsaɪdəl/ ADJECTIVE wanting to murder someone

homicide /ˈhɒmɪsaɪd/ NOUN [plural **homicides**] a US or legal word for murder (= the crime of killing someone)

homoeopath /ˈhəʊmɪəʊˌpæθ/ NOUN [plural **homoeopaths**] another spelling of homeopath
● **homoeopathic** /ˌhəʊmɪəʊˈpæθɪk/ ADJECTIVE another spelling of homeopathic
● **homoeopathy** /ˌhəʊmɪˈɒpəθi/ NOUN, NO PLURAL another spelling of homeopathy

homograph /ˈhɒməɡrɑːf/ NOUN [plural **homographs**] a word that has the same spelling as another word but has a different meaning and often a different pronunciation □ *'Lead' meaning 'guide', and 'lead' meaning 'a type of metal' are homographs.*

homonym /ˈhɒmənɪm/ NOUN [plural **homonyms**] a word that has the same spelling or pronunciation as another word, but has a different meaning

homophone /ˈhɒməfəʊn/ NOUN [plural **homophones**] a word that has the same pronunciation as another word but has a different spelling and meaning □ *'See' and 'sea' are homophones.*

homosexual /ˌhɒməˈsekʃʊəl/ ▶ ADJECTIVE attracted to people of the same sex
▶ NOUN [plural **homosexuals**] someone who is attracted to people of the same sex
● **homosexuality** /ˌhɒməˌsekʃuˈælɪti/ NOUN, NO PLURAL being attracted to people of the same sex

hone /həʊn/ VERB [**hones, honing, honed**] to improve a skill that you already have

honest /ˈɒnɪst/ ADJECTIVE
1 an honest person can be trusted and does not lie, cheat or steal □ *You can trust her – she's very honest.*
2 sincere and telling the truth 🔁 *The honest answer is I'm not sure what I'm going to do.* □ *If you want my honest opinion, I don't like him very much.* □ **+ about** *You need to be honest about your own abilities.* □ **+ with** *I'm afraid I haven't been completely honest with you.*
3 **to be honest** used before you say what you really think □ *To be honest, I don't really want to go.*
● **honestly** /ˈɒnɪstli/ ADVERB
1 in an honest way □ *Martin told me honestly what he thought.* □ *He behaved very honestly and handed the money in to the police.*

2 used for emphasizing that what you are saying is true even though it is surprising □ *I honestly didn't realize you were all waiting for me.*

3 something you say to show that you are annoyed □ *Honestly, I wish you'd listen to what I tell you.*

• **honesty** /ˈɒnɪstɪ/ NOUN, NO PLURAL

1 being honest □ *Thanks for telling me. I appreciate your honesty.*

2 in all honesty used for saying what you really think □ *In all honesty, it's been quite a difficult experience.*

honey /ˈhʌnɪ/ NOUN, NO PLURAL

1 a sweet food that bees make

2 a word you use when talking to someone you love □ *Are you OK, honey?*

honeycomb /ˈhʌnɪkəʊm/ NOUN [*plural* **honeycombs**] a structure with many small holes where bees store honey

honeymoon /ˈhʌnɪmuːn/ NOUN [*plural* **honeymoons**] a holiday that a man and woman go on just after their wedding □ *Rob and Sarah went to Mexico for their honeymoon.*

honk /hɒŋk/ ► VERB [**honks, honking, honked**] to make a loud, short sound with a car horn

► NOUN [*plural* **honks**] a loud, short sound made by a car horn

honor /ˈɒnə(r)/ VERB [**honors, honoring, honored**], NOUN [*plural* **honors**] the US spelling of honour

• **honorable** /ˈɒnərəbəl/ ADJECTIVE the US spelling of honourable

• **honorably** /ˈɒnərəblɪ/ ADVERB the US spelling of honourably

honorary /ˈɒnərərɪ/ ADJECTIVE given to show respect and admiration for someone □ *The footballer was given an honorary degree from Edinburgh University.*

honour /ˈɒnə(r)/ ► NOUN [*plural* **honours**]

1 *no plural* when someone behaves in a way that is honest and good □ *I felt that he was questioning my honour.*

2 *no plural* the respect that people have for someone who has behaved well or achieved something that people admire □ *I am fighting for my family's honour.*

3 in someone's honour/in honour of someone in order to show respect to someone □ *I wrote the book in honour of my father.*

4 something that makes you proud □ *It was an honour to meet him.* □ *It is a great honour to be here today.*

5 a reward that someone is given in public because they have achieved something □ *She received an honour from the Queen.*

6 guest of honour the most important guest at an event

► VERB [**honours, honouring, honoured**]

1 to show respect to someone who has behaved in a good way or achieved something that people admire □ *They built a monument to honour the dead.*

2 to behave in a way that does not go against an

agreement, principle, someone's wish, etc. □ *All the countries have honoured the treaty.*

• **honourable** /ˈɒnərəbəl/ ADJECTIVE honest and morally good □ *He is an honourable man.*

• **honourably** /ˈɒnərəblɪ/ ADVERB in an honourable way □ *I have no doubt she behaved honourably.*

hood /hʊd/ NOUN [*plural* **hoods**]

1 the part of a coat, etc. which you can pull up to cover the back of your head

2 the US word for bonnet (= part of a car)

• **hooded** /ˈhʊdɪd/ ADJECTIVE having or wearing a hood □ *a hooded sweatshirt* □ *a hooded gunman*

-hood /hʊd/ SUFFIX -hood is added to the end of words to mean 'the state of being something' or 'the time when someone is something' □ *childhood*

hoody /ˈhʊdɪ/ NOUN [*plural* **hoodies**] a piece of clothing for the top half of the body with a hood (= part that covers the back of the head)

hoof /huːf/ NOUN [*plural* **hooves**] the hard foot on an animal such as a horse or a cow

hook /hʊk/ ► NOUN [*plural* **hooks**]

1 a bent piece of metal or plastic that you hang things on □ *Hang your coats on the hook.*

2 a bent piece of metal used for catching fish

3 off the hook if a telephone is off the hook, the part you speak into has not been put back correctly, so nobody can call you

♦ IDIOM let/get someone off the hook to allow someone to avoid a duty or avoid an unpleasant situation □ *I'm not going to let you off the hook just yet.*

► VERB [**hooks, hooking, hooked**] to hang or catch something using a hook

♦ PHRASAL VERB hook someone/something up to connect someone or something to a piece of equipment □ *He was hooked up to a heart monitor.*

hook and eye /ˌhʊk ən ˈaɪ/ NOUN [*plural* **hooks and eyes**] a small metal hook (= curved metal part) and ring, used for fastening clothes

hooked /hʊkt/ ADJECTIVE

1 liking something very much and wanting to do it a lot ⊞*I played the game with Ian a couple of times and got hooked.*

2 curved □ *a hooked nose*

hooligan /ˈhuːlɪgən/ NOUN [*plural* **hooligans**] someone who is violent and noisy in a public place

• **hooliganism** /ˈhuːlɪgənɪzəm/ NOUN, NO PLURAL the behaviour of hooligans

hoop /huːp/ NOUN [*plural* **hoops**] a ring of metal, plastic or wood

hooray /hʊˈreɪ/ EXCLAMATION used for showing that you are pleased when something good has happened □ *We've won! Hooray!*

hoot /huːt/ ► NOUN [*plural* **hoots**]

1 the sound made by an owl (= bird) or a car horn

2 a sound you make when you think something is funny or stupid □ *His comments were met with hoots from the audience.*

3 someone or something that that makes you laugh. An informal word. □ *Maria's an absolute hoot.*

▶ VERB [**hoots, hooting, hooted**]
1 to make a sound that shows you think something is funny or stupid □ *The crowd whistled and hooted.*
2 to make a sound with a car horn □ *Another driver hooted at him.*
3 if an owl (= bird) hoots, it makes a noise
• **hooter** /ˈhuːtə(r)/ NOUN [plural **hooters**] a device that makes a loud sound, for example as a warning □ *the ship's hooter*

Hoover /ˈhuːvə(r)/ NOUN [plural **Hoovers**] a machine that cleans floors by sucking up small bits. A trademark.
• **hoover** VERB [**hoovers, hoovering, hoovered**] to clean a floor using a machine that sucks up small bits □ *He hoovered up the salt he'd spilt.*

hooves /huːvz/ PLURAL OF hoof

hop /hɒp/ ▶ VERB [**hops, hopping, hopped**]
1 to jump on one leg
2 if a bird or animal hops, it moves by jumping □ *A little bird hopped onto the arm of the chair.*
3 an informal word meaning to move somewhere quickly, especially to get in or out of a vehicle quickly □ *Hop in and I'll take you to the station.*
▶ NOUN [plural **hops**] a jump, especially on one leg
➡ go to **hops**

hope /həʊp/ ▶ VERB [**hopes, hoping, hoped**] to think that something is possible and to wish for it to happen or be true □ **+ that** *I hope that David manages to get home for Christmas.* □ **+ to do something** *I hope to set up my own business next year.* □ **+ for** *I'm hoping for a new bike for my birthday.* 🔁 *'Will the bank still be open?' 'I hope so!'* 🔁 *'Is he coming with us?' 'I hope not.'*
▶ NOUN [plural **hopes**]
1 *no plural* a feeling that the future will be good or that something good will happen 🔁 *We're not giving up hope of finding her.* 🔁 *The new centre offers hope to people with cancer.* 🔁 *We knew it would be difficult to succeed, but we never lost hope.*
2 something that you wish will happen or be true □ *My hope is that he will agree to lend us the money.* 🔁 *News of the president's interest really raised our hopes.*
3 something that gives you a chance of success 🔁 *Going to court is our only hope of getting justice.* 🔁 *There is little hope of finishing the work on time.*
4 in the hope of something in order to try to get something or make something happen □ *I left work early in the hope of meeting Tom.*

• **hopeful** /ˈhəʊpfʊl/ ▶ ADJECTIVE
1 feeling that the future will be good or that something good will happen □ *I'm very hopeful that we can find a suitable house.*
2 making you feel that something good will happen □ *The fact that he's contacted you is a very hopeful sign.*
▶ NOUN [plural **hopefuls**] someone who is hoping to be successful, especially in entertainment □ *Hundreds of young hopefuls queued all night for the chance of a part in the musical.*

• **hopefully** /ˈhəʊpfʊli/ ADVERB
1 used to say that you hope something will happen □ *Hopefully she'll have forgotten about our homework.*
2 showing hope □ *'Is there any more?' she asked hopefully.*

• **hopeless** /ˈhəʊpləs/ ADJECTIVE
1 without any hope of succeeding □ *We tried to put out the flames, but it was hopeless.*
2 an informal word meaning very bad □ *Chris was hopeless in goal.*

• **hopelessly** /ˈhəʊpləsli/ ADVERB extremely 🔁 *We got hopelessly lost.*

hops /hɒps/ PLURAL NOUN the flowers used for making beer

horde /hɔːd/ NOUN [plural **hordes**] a large crowd □ *Hordes of tourists wandered around the town.*

horizon /həˈraɪzən/ NOUN
1 the horizon the line where the land and sky seem to meet
2 on the horizon probably going to happen soon □ *There are more changes on the horizon.*
◆ IDIOM broaden/expand your horizons to increase the experiences that you have had □ *The job gave him the opportunity to broaden his horizons.*

horizontal /ˌhɒrɪˈzɒntəl/ ADJECTIVE straight and parallel to the ground 🔁 *a horizontal line* □ *She was wearing a T-shirt with horizontal stripes.*

hormonal /hɔːˈməʊnəl/ ADJECTIVE to do with or caused by hormones □ *a hormonal problem*

hormone /ˈhɔːməʊn/ NOUN [plural **hormones**] a chemical that your body makes, which controls things such as how the body grows. A biology word.

horn /hɔːn/ NOUN [plural **horns**]
1 one of the two pointed things made of bone on the heads of some animals, such as a goat □ *a bull's horns*
2 a device in a vehicle that you press to make a loud noise 🔁 *He heard a car horn outside.* 🔁 *Drivers sounded their horns as the men ran into the road.*
3 a musical instrument made of metal that you blow into □ *the French horn*
• **horned** /hɔːnd/ ADJECTIVE with horns on the head □ *horned animals*

horoscope /ˈhɒrəskəʊp/ NOUN [plural **horoscopes**] a description of what might happen to you, which is based on the position of stars when you were born

horrendous /hɒˈrendəs/ ADJECTIVE extremely bad or shocking □ *a horrendous crime*

horrible /ˈhɒrəbəl/ ADJECTIVE very unpleasant □ *It was a horrible feeling to think I wouldn't see him again.* □ *a horrible situation* □ *Why are you being so horrible to everyone?*
• **horribly** /ˈhɒrəbli/ ADVERB in a horrible way 🔁 *The plan went horribly wrong.* □ *He had been horribly injured in the accident.*

horrid /ˈhɒrɪd/ ADJECTIVE an old-fashioned word meaning very unpleasant □ *a horrid place* □ *a horrid man*

horrific /hɒˈrɪfɪk/ ADJECTIVE extremely bad, often involving death or injuries □ *a horrific car crash* □ *horrific scenes of violence*

horrified /ˈhɒrɪfaɪd/ ADJECTIVE extremely shocked and upset □ *He was horrified at the suggestion that he had cheated.*

horrify /ˈhɒrɪfaɪ/ VERB [**horrifies, horrifying, horrified**] to shock and upset someone □ *It's a story that will horrify any parent.*

• **horrifying** /ˈhɒrɪfaɪɪŋ/ ADJECTIVE shocking and upsetting □ *horrifying pictures of starving children*

horror /ˈhɒrə(r)/ ▶ NOUN [*plural* **horrors**]
1 a strong feeling of shock and upset □ *I watched in horror as the car went up in flames.*
2 something that is extremely shocking and upsetting □ *He had witnessed such horrors while fighting.*
3 to someone's horror used when saying that something makes you feel shocked and upset □ *To my horror, I realized it was a dead body.*
▶ ADJECTIVE a horror film or story is very frightening and often unpleasant

horse /hɔːs/ NOUN [*plural* **horses**] a large animal which people ride or use for pulling things 🕮 *Have you ever ridden a horse?* 🕮 *The horse galloped (= ran) across the field.*

horseback /ˈhɔːsbæk/ NOUN, NO PLURAL on horseback riding a horse

horse-chestnut /ˌhɔːsˈtʃesnʌt/ NOUN [*plural* **horse-chestnuts**] a tree which has smooth brown nuts that children play with

horsepower /ˈhɔːspaʊə(r)/ NOUN, NO PLURAL a unit for measuring the power of engines

horseriding /ˈhɔːsraɪdɪŋ/ NOUN, NO PLURAL the activity of riding on a horse □ *My hobbies are reading and horseriding.*

horseshoe /ˈhɔːsʃuː/ NOUN [*plural* **horseshoes**] a curved piece metal fastened to a horse's foot

horticulture /ˈhɔːtɪkʌltʃə(r)/ NOUN, NO PLURAL the science or activity of growing plants

hose /həʊz/ NOUN [*plural* **hoses**] a long tube used for putting water on fires or gardens

hosiery /ˈhəʊzɪəri/ NOUN, NO PLURAL a formal word for socks and tights (= thin coverings for legs)

hospice /ˈhɒspɪs/ NOUN [*plural* **hospices**] a hospital for people who are dying

hospitable /hɒˈspɪtəbəl/ ADJECTIVE friendly to visitors, liking to provide food and a pleasant place to stay □ *It's a beautiful country and the people are very hospitable.*

hospital /ˈhɒspɪtəl/ NOUN [*plural* **hospitals**] a building where people go for medical treatment when they are ill or injured □ *Jane is in hospital having an operation.* 🕮 *She was taken to hospital after being stabbed.* 🕮 *He's recovered and is coming out of hospital tomorrow.* □ *a psychiatric hospital* 🕮 *Many*

hospital wards (= rooms where people stay) have been closed.

hospitality /ˌhɒspɪˈtæləti/ NOUN, NO PLURAL
1 being friendly to visitors, liking to provide food and a pleasant place to stay □ *The hotel is known for its warm hospitality.*
2 food, drink and entertainment that a company gives to people □ *the hospitality industry*

hospitalize or **hospitalise** /ˈhɒspɪtəlaɪz/ VERB [**hospitalizes, hospitalizing, hospitalized**] if someone is hospitalized, they are in a hospital for treatment □ *He was hospitalized for two months following his accident.*

host /həʊst/ ▶ NOUN [*plural* **hosts**]
1 someone who introduces the guests on a television show □ *He's a well-known game show host.*
2 a place that provides the equipment and space for a big event 🕮 *London will play host to the Olympic Games in 2012.* □ *the host nation*
3 the person at a party or meal who has invited you and arranged everything
4 a host of something a lot of people or things □ *The player has struggled with a host of injuries.*
▶ VERB [**hosts, hosting, hosted**]
1 to be the host of a big event □ *The city of Athens hosted the Olympics in 2004.*
2 to provide the systems that allow a website to operate. A computing word.

hostage /ˈhɒstɪdʒ/ NOUN [*plural* **hostages**] someone who is kept as a prisoner until the people holding them get what they want 🕮 *He was taken hostage by a group of militants.*

hostel /ˈhɒstəl/ NOUN [*plural* **hostels**] a cheap place for people to stay □ *a youth hostel* □ *He was staying in a hostel for homeless people.*

hostess /ˈhəʊstes/ NOUN [*plural* **hostesses**]
1 the woman at a party or meal who has invited you and arranged everything
2 a woman who introduces the guests on a television show

hostile /ˈhɒstaɪl/ ADJECTIVE
1 unfriendly or showing strong dislike □ *a hostile reaction* □ *Hostile crowds booed and jeered at the Prime Minister.*
2 difficult to live in □ *Not many plants can survive in the hostile mountain conditions.*
3 to do with an enemy in a war □ *hostile territory*

• **hostility** /hɒˈstɪləti/ NOUN, NO PLURAL
1 unfriendly behaviour □ *Immigrants have faced a lot of hostility.*
2 when people show that they disagree with something very strongly □ *There was widespread hostility to the plan.*
3 hostilities a formal word that means fighting in a war □ *We hope the deal will end the hostilities.*

hot /hɒt/ ADJECTIVE [**hotter, hottest**]
1 having a high temperature □ *Don't touch the oven*

It's very hot. □ *Is there any hot water left?* □ *It was a very hot summer.* ⊞ *It was a boiling hot day.*

2 spicy □ *hot curries*

3 if someone has a hot temper, they get angry very easily

4 a hot topic a subject that people are very interested in at the moment

♦ PHRASAL VERB **[hots, hotting, hotted]** hot up if a situation hots up, it becomes more exciting □ *Things hotted up a bit when the band arrived.*

hot chocolate /ˌhɒt ˈtʃɒkələt/ NOUN, NO PLURAL a drink made from hot milk mixed with chocolate powder

hotdog /ˈhɒtdɒg/ NOUN [plural **hotdogs**] a sausage in a long piece of bread

hotel /həʊˈtel/ NOUN [plural **hotels**] a building that you pay to stay in when you are travelling or on holiday ⊞ *We stayed in a five-star hotel.* ⊞ *Our hotel room didn't even have a television.* ⊞ *Hotel guests have free use of the swimming pool.*

hotline /ˈhɒtlaɪn/ NOUN [plural **hotlines**] a special telephone number that you can call to get information ⊞ *Call our hotline for more information about special offers.*

hotly /ˈhɒtli/ ADVERB

1 in an angry way ⊞ *He hotly denied that he'd cheated.*

2 hotly contested if a competition is hotly contested, people are competing very strongly against each other

hot spot /ˈhɒt ˌspɒt/ NOUN [plural **hot spots**]

1 a place where a lot of bad activity happens □ *Police have published a list of crime hot spots.*

2 a place where there is a lot of fighting and violence □ *He has reported from many of the world's hot spots.*

3 a very popular place □ *This is a hot spot for fine dining.*

hot-water bottle /ˌhɒtˈwɔːtə ˌbɒtəl/ NOUN [plural **hot-water bottles**] a rubber container that you fill with hot water and use for making your bed warm

hound /haʊnd/ ▶ NOUN [plural **hounds**] a dog used for hunting

▶ VERB **[hounds, hounding, hounded]** to follow someone everywhere they go, asking them a lot of questions or taking a lot of photographs of them □ *Many celebrities are hounded by the press.*

hour /ˈaʊə(r)/ NOUN [plural **hours**]

1 a period of time that lasts 60 minutes. There are 24 hours in one day □ *Each lesson lasts an hour.* □ *An hour later, they had all gone.* □ *I do an hour's exercise every day.* ⊞ *I'll be about half an hour.*

2 the period of time when something happens □ *What hours do you work?* ⊞ *Our opening hours are 9–5.* ⊞ *Shall we meet up in the lunch hour?*

3 hours an informal word meaning a long time ⊞ *We spent hours talking on the phone.*

hourly /ˈaʊəli/ ADJECTIVE, ADVERB

1 happening every hour □ *The trains run hourly from here.*

2 for each hour ⊞ *an hourly rate/wage*

house /haʊs/ ▶ NOUN [plural **houses**]

1 a building in which people, especially one family, live □ *Our house is the one with the yellow door.* ⊞ *We moved house last year.*

2 the people who live in a house □ *Their party kept the whole house awake.*

3 the place where a particular activity or business happens □ *an opera house* □ *a software house*

♦ IDIOMS get on like a house on fire to like each other very much □ *I introduced her to my mother, and they got on like a house on fire.* on the house if you are given food or drinks on the house in a restaurant, bar, etc., you do not have to pay for them

▶ VERB /haʊz/ **[houses, housing, housed]**

1 to provide someone with a place to live □ *They were housed in old army barracks.*

2 to keep something in a particular place □ *The collection is housed in a pleasant old building.*

houseboat /ˈhaʊsbəʊt/ NOUN [plural **houseboats**] a boat on a river that you can live in

housebound /ˈhaʊsbaʊnd/ ADJECTIVE unable to leave your house because you are too ill or old

household /ˈhaʊshəʊld/ ▶ NOUN [plural **households**] all the people who live in the same house □ *Most UK households have access to the Internet.*

▶ ADJECTIVE to do with your home □ *household chores* □ *household bills*

● **householder** /ˈhaʊsˌhəʊldə(r)/ NOUN [plural **householders**] someone who owns or rents a house

household name /ˌhaʊshəʊld ˈneɪm/ NOUN [plural **household names**] someone or something that is very famous

housekeeper /ˈhaʊskiːpə(r)/ NOUN [plural **housekeepers**] someone whose job is to cook and clean in someone else's house

houseplant /ˈhaʊsplɑːnt/ NOUN [plural **houseplants**] a plant that you grow in your house

house-trained /ˈhaʊstreɪnd/ ADJECTIVE a house-trained pet has learnt to be clean inside the house

housewarming /ˈhaʊswɔːmɪŋ/ NOUN [plural **housewarmings**] a party in your new house to celebrate moving into it □ *We're having a housewarming next week.*

housewife /ˈhaʊswaɪf/ NOUN [plural **housewives**] a woman who stays at home to look after her family and house, and does not have a paid job □ *She tried to be the perfect housewife.*

housework /ˈhaʊswɜːk/ NOUN, NO PLURAL the work you do to keep your house clean and tidy ⊞ *She hated doing the housework.*

➤ Remember that **housework** is not used in the plural:
✓ Who does most of the housework?
✗ Who does most of the houseworks?

housing /ˈhaʊzɪŋ/ ➤ NOUN, NO PLURAL homes for people to live in □ There is a shortage of affordable housing.
➤ ADJECTIVE to do with houses □ a housing project
🔄 The housing market (= buying and selling houses) has slowed down.

hovel /ˈhɒvəl/ NOUN [plural hovels] a small, dirty and untidy place that someone lives in □ The family lived in a two-room hovel.

hover /ˈhɒvə(r)/ VERB [hovers, hovering, hovered]
1 to stay still in the air □ Police helicopters hovered overhead.
2 to stand somewhere because you are waiting to do something □ The waiter hovered, ready to take our order.

hovercraft /ˈhɒvəkrɑːft/ NOUN [plural hovercrafts] a vehicle that travels across water or land, and has a cushion (= soft bag) of air under it

how /haʊ/ ADVERB
1 used for asking or talking about the way something is done □ + to do something I'll show you how to tie a reef knot. □ How will we get there? □ Do you know how to turn the oven on?
2 used for asking or talking about size, amount, level or age □ I don't know how old Maurice is exactly. □ How strong do you like your tea? □ How much is that DVD player? 🔄 How many brothers and sisters have you got?
3 used for asking or talking about what something is like or what form or condition it is in □ How do you want this money – cash or cheque? □ How's work? □ How's the new extension coming on?
4 used for asking or talking about someone's health 🔄 Hello, how are you today? □ How's your leg now?
5 How about ...? used for making a suggestion □ How about asking the children to help?
6 used to emphasize an adjective or an adverb □ How odd that she didn't phone. □ He died? Oh, how sad.

➤ Remember that **how** is not used with **like** to ask someone to describe someone or something. The correct phrase for this is **what is someone/ something like?**:
✓ What is your new teacher like?
✗ How is your new teacher like?

however /haʊˈevə(r)/ CONJUNCTION, ADVERB
1 used for saying that something does not affect a situation □ However hard he tried, he couldn't do it. 🔄 She wanted to travel to Australia however much it cost. □ Your donation, however small, will make an important difference.
2 despite what has just been said □ The business had been successful. Over the past few years, however, sales had started to fall. □ People were saying that the

school was going to close. However, the school denied the rumours.
3 used for asking how something is done when you are surprised. A formal word □ However did you find this place?
4 in any way □ Do it however you want to.

howl /haʊl/ ➤ VERB [howls, howling, howled]
1 if a dog or wolf howls, it makes a long, high noise
2 to shout or cry loudly □ He was howling with pain.
3 if the wind howls, it makes a lot of noise □ The wind howled in off the sea.
➤ NOUN [plural howls]
1 a long, loud sound made by a wolf or dog
2 a loud shout of pain or laughter

how's /haʊz/ a short way to say or write how is or how has □ How's your mother?

HQ /ˌeɪtʃˈkjuː/ ABBREVIATION headquarters

HTML /ˌeɪtʃtiːemˈel/ ABBREVIATION hypertext markup language; a system used for writing things on the Internet. A computing word.

hub /hʌb/ NOUN [plural hubs]
1 the most important place where something happens □ Mumbai is the financial hub of India.
2 the central part of a wheel

hubbub /ˈhʌbʌb/ NOUN, NO PLURAL the noise made by a lot of people talking at the same time

huddle /ˈhʌdəl/ ➤ VERB [huddles, huddling, huddled] if people or animals huddle, they stay very close to each other, for example because they are cold or frightened □ The children huddled together under the blanket.
➤ NOUN [plural huddles] a group of people standing or sitting very close to each other □ They stood in a huddle on the pavement.

hue /hjuː/ NOUN [plural hues] a literary word meaning colour

huff /hʌf/ ➤ NOUN, NO PLURAL in a huff annoyed with someone and showing this by your behaviour. An informal phrase. □ He walked off in a huff.
➤ VERB [huffs, huffing, huffed]
1 to say something in a way that shows you are annoyed □ 'I'm not coming here again,' he huffed.
2 huff and puff (a) to breathe noisily, for example because you have been running □ He ran past huffing and puffing. (b) to behave in a way that shows you are annoyed □ He was in a terrible mood, huffing and puffing about how he had lost all his work.

hug /hʌg/ ➤ VERB [hugs, hugging, hugged] to put your arms around someone and hold them □ My mother was always hugging and kissing us. □ Everyone was crying and hugging each other.
➤ NOUN [plural hugs] the action of putting your arm around someone and holding them 🔄 I could see she was upset so I gave her a hug.

huge /hjuːdʒ/ ADJECTIVE very big □ The school has spent a huge amount of money on the project. □ The film was a huge success. □ I'm a huge fan of his music. □ The house was huge.

- **hugely** /ˈhjuːdʒlɪ/ ADVERB very or very much □ *hugely popular*

hulk /hʌlk/ NOUN [plural **hulks**]
1 a very large and heavy person or thing □ *the towering hulk of the new building*
2 an old ship, car, etc. that is not used any more □ *She saw the rusting hulk of an old bus.*
- **hulking** /ˈhʌlkɪŋ/ ADJECTIVE very large and heavy □ *He noticed a hulking figure in the doorway.*

hull /hʌl/ NOUN [plural **hulls**] the bottom part of a boat that goes into the water

hullabaloo /ˌhʌləbəˈluː/ NOUN, NO PLURAL an informal word for a lot of excitement or anger about something □ *There was a big hullabaloo when three members of staff were fired.*

hullo /həˈləʊ/ EXCLAMATION another spelling of hello

hum /hʌm/ ▶ VERB [**hums, humming, hummed**]
1 to sing with your mouth closed □ *She hummed quietly to herself as she worked.*
2 to make a low continuous noise like someone humming □ *He turned the key and the engine hummed into life.*
▶ NOUN, NO PLURAL a low continuous sound □ *We could hear the hum of conversation.*

human /ˈhjuːmən/ ADJECTIVE
1 to do with people and the way that people behave ⊞ *They appeared to have no respect for human life.* ⊞ *Everyone wants to win: it's human nature.*
2 to do with people's bodies ⊞ *The human brain can process huge amounts of information.* ⊞ *The human body is designed for physical activity.*
3 be only human if you say that someone is only human, you mean that it is not reasonable to expect them to be better, stronger, etc. □ *You can't do everything; you're only human.*
- **human** or **human being** /ˌhjuːmən ˈbiːɪŋ/ NOUN [plural **humans** or **human beings**] a person □ *Is there a vaccine to protect humans from the disease?* □ *Technology has enabled human beings to survive longer.*

humane /hjuːˈmeɪn/ ADJECTIVE kind to people and animals and causing as little suffering as possible □ *Ministers called for the humane treatment of war prisoners.*
- **humanely** /hjuːˈmeɪnlɪ/ ADVERB in a humane way □ *The animals are killed quickly and humanely.*
humanitarian /hjuːˌmænɪˈteərɪən/ ADJECTIVE
1 to do with reducing the suffering of people who have been affected by problems such as floods or war ⊞ *The trucks were carrying humanitarian aid like food and cooking fuel.*
2 to do with a situation, such as war, that causes great suffering to many people □ *The government was accused of creating a humanitarian crisis.*
humanities /hjuːˈmænɪtɪz/ PLURAL NOUN the humanities subjects that are not sciences, for example history and languages

humanity /hjuːˈmænɪtɪ/ NOUN, NO PLURAL
1 all the people in the world □ *We must act now to save humanity.*
2 kindness towards other people □ *He always showed humanity to his students.*
humankind /ˌhjuːmənˈkaɪnd/ NOUN, NO PLURAL people in general □ *He has committed some of the worst crimes in the history of humankind.*
humanly /ˈhjuːmənlɪ/ ADVERB humanly possible possible for a person to do □ *They did all that was humanly possible to save his life.*
human resources /ˌhjuːmən rɪˈsɔːsɪz/ NOUN, NO PLURAL the department in a company that is responsible for looking after the people who work there
human rights /ˌhjuːmən ˈraɪts/ PLURAL NOUN basic rights such as freedom and fair treatment, especially by a government □ *The organization promotes human rights for all.*
humble /ˈhʌmbəl/ ▶ ADJECTIVE [**humbler, humblest**]
1 not believing that you are important
2 having a low social position □ *He comes from a humble background.*
3 in my humble opinion used humorously when you are giving your opinion about something
▶ VERB [**humbles, humbling, humbled**] to make someone feel humble □ *I was humbled by their generosity.*
humdrum /ˈhʌmdrʌm/ ADJECTIVE boring and ordinary □ *a humdrum existence*
humid /ˈhjuːmɪd/ ADJECTIVE humid air or weather is hot and slightly wet
- **humidity** /hjuːˈmɪdətɪ/ NOUN, NO PLURAL how humid the air is □ *Humidity levels were high.*
humiliate /hjuːˈmɪlɪeɪt/ VERB [**humiliates, humiliating, humiliated**] to make someone feel stupid or ashamed □ *His wife accused him of humiliating her in public.*
- **humiliating** /hjuːˈmɪlɪeɪtɪŋ/ ADJECTIVE making you feel stupid or ashamed □ *The team has suffered yet another humiliating defeat.*
- **humiliation** /hjuːˌmɪlɪˈeɪʃən/ NOUN, NO PLURAL when you feel humiliated □ *She has tried, unsuccessfully, to avoid more public humiliation.*
humility /hjuːˈmɪlətɪ/ NOUN, NO PLURAL a way of behaving that shows that you do not believe that you are better or more important than other people □ *She should show a bit of humility and admit that she was wrong.*
humor /ˈhjuːmə(r)/ NOUN, NO PLURAL, VERB [**humors, humoring, humored**] the US spelling of humour
- **humorless** /ˈhjuːmələs/ ADJECTIVE the US spelling of humourless
humorous /ˈhjuːmərəs/ ADJECTIVE funny ⊞ *He told us a humorous story about a man on his wedding day.* ⊞ *The President made a humorous remark.*
humour /ˈhjuːmə(r)/ ▶ NOUN, NO PLURAL
1 the quality that makes something funny □ *She*

suddenly saw the humour in the situation and laughed loudly.

2 the ability to know when something is funny, or to say things that make people laugh □ *He loved her for her humour and her quiet determination.* ⓺ *We share the same sense of humour.*

3 your mood □ *There was a lot of ill humour in the office.*

▶ VERB [**humours, humouring, humoured**] to pretend to agree with someone in order to please them

● **humourless** /'hju:mələs/ ADJECTIVE not funny, or not showing that you think things are funny □ *He was a small, humourless man in his fifties.*

hump /hʌmp/ NOUN [*plural* **humps**]

1 a rounded part that sticks out from a surface, especially the ground □ *They have installed speed humps in our street.*

2 a rounded lump on the back of a camel (= desert animal)

3 a rounded lump at the top of someone's back

hunch /hʌntʃ/ ▶ NOUN [*plural* **hunches**] a feeling you have that something might be true ⓺ *She had a hunch that something was wrong.*

▶ VERB [**hunches, hunching, hunched**] to sit or stand with the top part of your body bent forward □ *He hunched over his books.*

hundred /'hʌndrəd/ NUMBER [**hundreds**]

1 the number 100

2 hundreds a large number. An informal word □ *+ of There were hundreds of people queuing for tickets.*

hundredth /'hʌndrədθ/ ▶ NUMBER 100th written as a word

▶ NOUN [*plural* **hundredths**] 1/100; one of a hundred equal parts of something□ *He lost the race by two hundredths of a second.*

hundredweight /'hʌndrədweɪt/ NOUN [*plural* **hundredweight**] a unit for measuring weight, equal to 8 stone

hung /hʌŋ/ PAST TENSE AND PAST PARTICIPLE OF hang

hunger /'hʌŋɡə(r)/ ▶ NOUN, NO PLURAL

1 a feeling that you want to eat □ *It seemed that nothing would satisfy his hunger.*

2 not having enough food □ *These children are dying of hunger.*

3 a very strong feeling of wanting something □ *+ for He has a real hunger for success.*

▶ VERB [**hungers, hungering, hungered**] to want something very much □ *+ for He hungered for excitement in his life.*

● **hungrily** /'hʌŋɡrɪli/ ADVERB in a way that shows you are hungry □ *She took a slice of the cake and ate it hungrily.*

● **hungry** /'hʌŋɡri/ ADJECTIVE [**hungrier, hungriest**]

1 having a feeling of wanting to eat □ *The children were starting to get hungry.*

2 go hungry to not have enough to eat □ *If you don't eat your fish, you'll have to go hungry.*

3 wanting something very much □ *+ for The team is hungry for success this season.*

hunk /hʌŋk/ NOUN [*plural* **hunks**] a big, rough piece of something such as bread or cheese □ *Jake tore a hunk of bread from the loaf.*

hunt /hʌnt/ ▶ VERB [**hunts, hunting, hunted**]

1 to chase and kill animals for food or for sport □ *The men hunt seals and the women fish.* □ *+ for They were out hunting for rabbits.*

2 to try to find someone or something □ *+ for More than 40 officers are hunting for the killer.*

□ *Investigators are hunting for more clues.*

◆ PHRASAL VERB **hunt someone/something down** to look for someone or something until you find them □ *Police are determined to hunt the killer down.*

▶ NOUN [*plural* **hunts**]

1 when people search for someone or something ⓺ *Police launched a hunt for the child when she failed to return home.*

2 when people chase and kill animals for food or for sport ⓺ *People attended fox hunts across the country today.*

● **hunter** /'hʌntə(r)/ NOUN [*plural* **hunters**] a person or animal that hunts

● **hunting** /'hʌntɪŋ/ NOUN, NO PLURAL the activity of chasing and killing animals for food or for sport □ *She wants a ban on hunting.*

hurdle /'hɜːdəl/ ▶ NOUN [*plural* **hurdles**]

1 a problem that needs to be solved in order to make progress ⓺ *Finding enough money was a major hurdle for our business.* ⓺ *He had to face many hurdles on the road to recovery.*

2 a bar or frame that people or horses jump over in a race □ *She won the 400-metre hurdles in the Olympic Games.*

▶ VERB [**hurdles, hurdling, hurdled**] to jump over something such as a fence □ *The police officer hurdled the wooden gate, and went after the man.*

● **hurdler** /'hɜːdlə(r)/ NOUN [*plural* **hurdlers**] a competitor in a hurdles race

hurl /hɜːl/ VERB [**hurls, hurling, hurled**]

1 to throw something with great force □ *A brick was hurled through her window.*

2 hurl abuse/insults, etc. to shout rude things at someone

hurrah /hu'rɑː/ EXCLAMATION used for showing that you are pleased when something good has happened □ *Hurrah! We've won!*

hurricane /'hʌrɪkən/ NOUN [*plural* **hurricanes**] a storm with very strong winds

hurried /'hʌrɪd/ ADJECTIVE done quickly □ *We ate a hurried breakfast, and left the house.*

● **hurriedly** /'hʌrɪdli/ ADVERB quickly □ *The boy hurriedly hid something under his jacket.*

hurry /'hʌri/ ▶ VERB [**hurries, hurrying, hurried**]

1 to go somewhere quickly □ *She turned and hurried*

back along the path. □ *The streets were full of people hurrying home to their families.*
2 to do something more quickly □ *You'll have to hurry if you want to leave at six.*

◆ PHRASAL VERB **hurry up** to start moving somewhere or doing something more quickly □ *Hurry up! We're going to be late.* □ *I wish he'd hurry up in the bathroom.*

▶ NOUN, NO PLURAL

1 in a hurry doing something or going somewhere quickly, because you do not have much time □ *We had to finish the job in a hurry.* □ *I can't talk now – I'm in a hurry.*
2 there's no hurry used for telling someone that they do not need to do something quickly because you have a lot of time □ *Call me back when you're ready; there's no hurry.*
3 not be in a hurry to do something to not need to do something quickly or to not want to do it soon □ *I'm in no hurry to get married.*
4 the need to do something quickly □ *What's the hurry? She won't be back for hours.*

hurt /hɜːt/ VERB [hurts, hurting, hurt]
1 to cause pain or injury to someone □ *She fell and hurt her ankle.* □ *Will the injection hurt?*
2 to be painful □ *My shoulder hurts.*
3 to make someone feel upset □ *The truth can hurt sometimes.* □ *His criticism really hurt her.*
4 to harm something □ *This publicity won't hurt her chances of being elected.* □ *This political crisis could well hurt the economy.*

◆ IDIOM **hurt someone's feelings** to make someone feel upset □ *If you don't visit her, you'll hurt her feelings.*

▶ ADJECTIVE

1 injured ⊞ *Be careful – someone could get hurt.*
2 upset ⊞ *I was deeply hurt by his lack of appreciation.*
▶ NOUN, NO PLURAL when someone is upset □ *Her remarks have caused a lot of hurt.*

◆ **hurtful** /ˈhɜːtfʊl/ ADJECTIVE making someone feel upset □ *His comments were very hurtful.*

hurtle /ˈhɜːtəl/ VERB [hurtles, hurtling, hurtled] to move very fast, often in a dangerous or uncontrolled way □ *The car hurtled down a slope and crashed into a tree.*

husband /ˈhʌzbənd/ NOUN [plural husbands] the man that a woman is married to □ *Her husband died five years ago.*

hush /hʌʃ/ ▶ VERB [hushes, hushing, hushed] to tell someone to be quiet □ *She hushed the children.*

◆ PHRASAL VERB **hush something up** to stop people from knowing something □ *There were several accidents at the hospital, but it was all hushed up.*
▶ NOUN, NO PLURAL a sudden silence □ *A sudden hush fell over the crowd.*

hushed /hʌʃt/ ADJECTIVE very quiet □ *'I must speak with you,' he said in a hushed voice.*

husky[1] /ˈhʌskɪ/ ADJECTIVE a husky voice is deep and rough

husky[2] /ˈhʌskɪ/ NOUN [plural huskies] a type of large dog that is used to pull heavy things over snow

hustle /ˈhʌsəl/ ▶ VERB [hustles, hustling, hustled] to make someone go somewhere quickly, often by pushing them □ *The protesters were hustled out of the hotel by ten police officers.*

▶ NOUN, NO PLURAL **hustle and bustle** busy and noisy activity □ *The hotel is ideal for those who like the hustle and bustle of the city.*

hut /hʌt/ NOUN [plural huts] a small, simple building made of wood, mud or metal

hutch /hʌtʃ/ NOUN [plural hutches] a wooden box with a wire front and a door, in which small pets such as rabbits are kept

hyacinth /ˈhaɪəsɪnθ/ NOUN [plural hyacinths] a plant with a lot of small, sweet-smelling flowers growing on one stem

hybrid /ˈhaɪbrɪd/ NOUN [plural hybrids]
1 an animal or plant that has been produced from two different types of animal or plant
2 a mixture of different types of things □ *This is an unusual hybrid of classical and jazz styles.*
3 a type of car that uses both petrol and another type of energy, especially electricity

hydrant /ˈhaɪdrənt/ NOUN [plural hydrants] a pipe in the street that is connected to the main water supply, used for getting water to put out fires

hydraulic /haɪˈdrɔːlɪk/ ADJECTIVE operated by liquid moving with pressure □ *hydraulic brakes*

hydro- /ˈhaɪdrəʊ/ PREFIX hydro- is added to the beginning of words to mean 'water' □ *hydrogen* □ *hydroelectric*

hydrocarbon /ˌhaɪdrəˈkɑːbən/ NOUN [plural hydrocarbons] one of several chemical substances found in coal and oil. A chemistry word.

hydrochloric acid /ˌhaɪdrəˈklɒrɪk ˈæsɪd/ NOUN, NO PLURAL a type of acid used in a strong form in industry and found in a weak form in the stomach for digesting food. A chemistry word.

hydroelectric /ˌhaɪdrəʊɪˈlektrɪk/ ADJECTIVE to do with electricity produced using the power of water

◆ **hydroelectricity** /ˌhaɪdrəʊɪlekˈtrɪsəti/ NOUN, NO PLURAL electricity produced using the power of water

hydrofoil /ˈhaɪdrəfɔɪl/ NOUN [plural hydrofoils] a type of boat that rises slightly above the surface of the water when it is moving fast

hydrogen /ˈhaɪdrədʒən/ NOUN, NO PLURAL the lightest gas that exists, which combines with oxygen to make water. A chemistry word.

hydrogenated /haɪˈdrɒdʒɪneɪtɪd/ ADJECTIVE hydrogenated fats and oils have hydrogen added, usually to make them more solid. A chemistry word.

hyena /haɪˈiːnə/ NOUN [plural hyenas] a wild animal similar to a dog, that lives in Asia and Africa, and makes a noise that sounds like laughter

hygiene /'haɪdʒiːn/ NOUN, NO PLURAL keeping yourself and the things around you clean, so that you stay healthy □ *The best way to avoid infection is to practise good hygiene.* 🖰 *Poor food hygiene can cause disease.*

• **hygienic** /haɪ'dʒiːnɪk/ ADJECTIVE without any dirt or bacteria □ *Viruses can spread even in the most hygienic situations.*

hymn /hɪm/ NOUN [plural **hymns**] a song sung by Christians to praise God

hype /haɪp/ ► NOUN, NO PLURAL when something is talked about a lot, especially on television or in newspapers, to make it seem good or interesting □ *There has been a lot of media hype surrounding the movie.*
► VERB [**hypes, hyping, hyped**] to talk about or advertise something a lot in order to make people interested in it □ *They were hyped as the best Brazilian team of all time.*

hyped up /ˌhaɪpt ˈʌp/ ADJECTIVE behaving in a very excited way. An informal word. □ *The children were all hyped up after the party.*

hyper /'haɪpə(r)/ ADJECTIVE behaving in an excited and uncontrolled way. An informal word. □ *The kids always go hyper just before bedtime.*

hyper- /'haɪpə(r)-/ PREFIX hyper- is added to the beginning of words to mean 'more than normal' or 'bigger than normal' □ *hyperactive* □ *hypermarket*

hyperactive /ˌhaɪpər'æktɪv/ ADJECTIVE much more active than most people, and often finding it difficult to concentrate

hyperlink /'haɪpəlɪŋk/ NOUN [plural **hyperlinks**] a connection on a website or other computer document that you can click on in order to move to another website or document. A computing word.

hypermarket /'haɪpəˌmɑːkɪt/ NOUN [plural **hypermarkets**] a very large supermarket

hypertext /'haɪpətekst/ NOUN, NO PLURAL computer text containing words and images that you can click on in order to move to a related document, image or piece of text. A computing word.

hyphen /'haɪfən/ NOUN [plural **hyphens**] the short line (-) used for joining two words together, or for showing that a word has been divided and part of it is on the next line

• **hyphenate** /'haɪfəneɪt/ VERB [**hyphenates, hyphenating, hyphenated**] to use a hyphen to join two words, or to divide a word at the end of a line

hypnosis /hɪp'nəʊsɪs/ NOUN, NO PLURAL a state in which you seem to be in a deep sleep, but in which you can be influenced, or a treatment using this state □ *I tried hypnosis to give up smoking.* □ *Under hypnosis, she was able to remember more about the incident.*

• **hypnotic** /hɪp'nɒtɪk/ ADJECTIVE making you feel as if you have been hypnotized □ *They danced to the hypnotic beat of the African drums.*

• **hypnotism** /'hɪpnətɪzəm/ NOUN, NO PLURAL the practice of hypnotizing people

• **hypnotist** /'hɪpnətɪst/ NOUN [plural **hypnotists**] someone who hypnotizes people

• **hypnotize** or **hypnotise** /'hɪpnətaɪz/ VERB [**hypnotizes, hypnotizing, hypnotized**] to put someone into a state of hypnosis

hypochondriac /ˌhaɪpə'kɒndriæk/ NOUN [plural **hypochondriacs**] someone who worries a lot about their health, and often thinks that they are ill

hypocrisy /hɪ'pɒkrəsɪ/ NOUN, NO PLURAL when someone pretends to have strong moral beliefs, but does not behave according to these beliefs

• **hypocrite** /'hɪpəkrɪt/ NOUN [plural **hypocrites**] someone who pretends to have strong moral beliefs, but does not behave according to those beliefs

• **hypocritical** /ˌhɪpə'krɪtɪkəl/ ADJECTIVE showing hypocrisy □ *It's a bit hypocritical to accuse him of greed when you've just eaten a whole chocolate cake.*

hypodermic needle /ˌhaɪpəˌdɜːmɪk 'niːdəl/ or **hypodermic syringe** /ˌhaɪpəˌdɜːmɪk sɪ'rɪndʒ/ NOUN [plural **hypodermic needles** or **hypodermic syringes**] a medical instrument with a sharp, hollow needle, used for putting drugs into someone's body through their skin

hypotenuse /haɪ'pɒtənjuːz/ NOUN [plural **hypotenuses**] in a triangle with one angle of 90°, the hypotenuse is the longest side, which is opposite that angle. A maths word.

hypothermia /ˌhaɪpəʊ'θɜːmɪə/ NOUN, NO PLURAL a medical condition in which someone's body temperature becomes dangerously low because they are very cold

hypothesis /haɪ'pɒθɪsɪs/ NOUN [plural **hypotheses**] a theory or idea that is suggested as a possible explanation for something, but that has not yet been proved □ *They carried out a series of experiments to test their hypothesis.*

• **hypothesize** or **hypothesise** /haɪ'pɒθɪsaɪz/ VERB [**hypothesizes, hypothesizing, hypothesized**] to form a hypothesis about something □ *Scientists have hypothesized that this type of activity may have health benefits.*

• **hypothetical** /ˌhaɪpə'θetɪkəl/ ADJECTIVE based on what can be imagined, instead of on facts □ *Imagine a hypothetical situation in which you're rich and famous*

hysterectomy /ˌhɪstə'rektəmɪ/ NOUN [plural **hysterectomies**] a medical operation to remove a woman's womb (= part where a baby grows)

hysteria /hɪs'tɪərɪə/ NOUN, NO PLURAL when people cannot control their actions because of extreme fear, excitement, etc. □ *The media were accused of arousing public hysteria over the incident.*

• **hysterical** /hɪs'terɪkəl/ ADJECTIVE
1 reacting to something in an uncontrolled way, because of extreme fear, excitement, etc. □ *She burst into hysterical tears.* □ *He was absolutely hysterical with excitement.*
2 very funny. An informal word. □ *Have you seen his new film? It's absolutely hysterical.*

• **hysterically** /hɪs'terɪkəlɪ/ ADVERB
1 in a hysterical way □ *She screamed hysterically, tearing at her hair.*

2 something that is hysterically funny is extremely funny

• **hysterics** /hɪsˈterɪks/ PLURAL NOUN

1 behaviour that is extremely emotional and uncontrolled □ *He was in hysterics, screaming and shouting at everyone.*

2 uncontrolled laughter □ *The audience was in hysterics.*

I i

I¹ *or* **i** /aɪ/ the ninth letter of the alphabet

I² /aɪ/ PRONOUN used to talk or write about yourself □ *I live near Edinburgh.* □ *I didn't forget your birthday, did I?*

-ible /-əbəl/ SUFFIX -ible is added to the end of words to mean 'able to be' □ *accessible* □ *visible*

-ic /-ɪk/ *or* **-ical** /-ɪkəl/ SUFFIX -ic or -ical is added to the end of words to mean 'to do with a particular thing' □ *historic* □ *political*

ice /aɪs/ ▶ NOUN, NO PLURAL frozen water □ *The ice melted and the water began to rise.* 🖫 *Her hand felt like a block of ice.*
➡ **go to break** the ice
▶ VERB [**ices, icing, iced**] to cover a cake with icing (= sweet substance) □ *Finally, ice the cake and decorate it with sweets.*
◆ PHRASAL VERB **ice over/up** to become covered in ice □ *The lake iced over in January this year.*

Ice Age /aɪs ˌeɪdʒ/ NOUN **the Ice Age** a period of time in the past when a large part of the Earth was covered with ice

iceberg /ˈaɪsbɜːɡ/ NOUN [*plural* **icebergs**] a large mass of ice floating in the sea

ice cap /ˈaɪs ˌkæp/ NOUN [*plural* **ice caps**] a layer of ice that permanently covers the land and the sea at the North and South Pole

ice cream /ˌaɪs ˈkriːm/ NOUN [*plural* **ice creams**]
1 *no plural* a sweet frozen food made from milk or cream □ *I'll have some strawberry ice cream, please.*
2 an amount of ice cream for one person □ *Would you like an ice cream?*

ice cube /ˈaɪs ˌkjuːb/ NOUN [*plural* **ice cubes**] a small block of ice that you put in a drink to make it cold

ice hockey /ˈaɪs ˌhɒki/ NOUN, NO PLURAL a sport played on ice in which two teams use curved sticks to try to hit a small round object into a net

ice lolly /ˌaɪs ˈlɒli/ NOUN [*plural* **ice lollies**] a piece of sweet, fruit-flavoured ice on a stick

ice rink /ˈaɪs ˌrɪŋk/ NOUN [*plural* **ice rinks**] a large area of ice, often in a building, where you can skate (= move over ice wearing special boots with blades on the bottom)

ice skate /ˈaɪs ˌskeɪt/ NOUN [*plural* **ice skates**] a boot with a metal blade on the bottom, that you wear for moving over ice

• **ice-skating** /ˈaɪsˌskeɪtɪŋ/ NOUN, NO PLURAL the activity of moving over ice wearing ice skates □ *We go ice-skating every Sunday.*

icicle /ˈaɪsɪkəl/ NOUN [*plural* **icicles**] a long thin piece of ice that hangs from something

icing /ˈaɪsɪŋ/ NOUN, NO PLURAL a substance made from sugar and water that you use for decorating cakes
◆ IDIOM **the icing on the cake** something that makes a good situation even better □ *It was great to get the job, but being able to work with Renate is the icing on the cake.*

icing sugar /ˈaɪsɪŋ ˌʃʊɡə(r)/ NOUN, NO PLURAL sugar in the form of a powder, used for making icing

icon /ˈaɪkɒn/ NOUN [*plural* **icons**]
1 a person or thing that is famous or that represents a particular idea 🖫 *a fashion icon* □ *The Eiffel Tower is Paris's most famous icon.*
2 a small symbol on a computer screen that represents a program or a file. A computing word □ *Click on the browser icon on your desktop.*
• **iconic** /aɪˈkɒnɪk/ ADJECTIVE very famous and representing a particular idea □ *She was an iconic figure in the pop world.*

ICT /ˌaɪsiːˈtiː/ ABBREVIATION information and communication technology; a school subject to do with computers and electronic forms of communication

icy /ˈaɪsi/ ADJECTIVE [**icier, iciest**]
1 covered with ice □ *Drivers lost control of their cars on the icy roads.*
2 extremely cold □ *An icy wind was blowing.* □ *She threw off her jacket and jumped into the icy water.*
3 extremely unfriendly □ *She gave him an icy look.*

ID /ˌaɪˈdiː/ ABBREVIATION identification; an official document that proves who you are □ *We'll need some form of ID.*

I'd /aɪd/ a short way to say and write I would or I had □ *I'd like another drink, please.* □ *I'd just gone to bed when the phone rang.*

idea /aɪˈdɪə/ NOUN [*plural* **ideas**]
1 a thought or plan about something you could do 🖫 *It was a good/brilliant idea to look online.* 🖫 *Taking six children swimming was a bad idea.* 🖫 *I've had an idea about how to fix the fence.* □ **+ to do something** *It was Kate's idea to buy a van.*
2 *no plural* knowledge about something 🖫 *I had no idea what was happening.* □ *Can you give us some idea of how many people are coming?* □ *Do you have any idea how to switch the heating on?*

3 a belief □ + *about* He has some strange ideas about food. 🔄 I don't want you to get the wrong idea about our relationship.

4 no plural a plan or purpose □ + *of* What's the idea of keeping the rabbits in separate hutches? □ The idea is to see if we like camping before we buy a tent.

5 no plural the way you think something is or would be □ + *of* The idea of giving a speech in front of all those people terrifies me. □ Rock climbing isn't my idea of fun.

ideal /aɪˈdɪəl/ ▶ ADJECTIVE

1 exactly right for a particular purpose □ It's an ideal house for a family. 🔄 The meeting was an ideal opportunity to make my announcement.

2 in an ideal world used for talking about what you would like, even if this is not possible □ In an ideal world, all the costs would be shared.

3 not ideal used for saying that an arrangement or plan is not very convenient for you □ 'Can you come on Thursday evening?' 'Well, it's not ideal, but I'll try.'
▶ NOUN [plural ideals]

1 an idea about what is good and right that you try to follow in the way that you behave □ He seems to have trouble living up to his ideals.

2 someone or something that you believe is a perfect example of something □ Garbo was everyone's ideal of beauty.

• **idealism** /aɪˈdɪəlɪzəm/ NOUN, NO PLURAL the belief that it is possible to achieve something good or perfect, even if this is unlikely

• **idealist** /aɪˈdɪəlɪst/ NOUN [plural idealists] someone who believes that something good or perfect can be achieved, even if this is unlikely

• **idealize** or **idealise** /aɪˈdɪəlaɪz/ VERB [idealizes, idealizing, idealized] to believe that someone or something is perfect, or better than they really are □ We often idealize our parents when we are children.

• **ideally** /aɪˈdɪəli/ ADVERB

1 used for talking about what you would like to do or have, even if this is not possible □ Ideally, I'd like to finish this by tomorrow.

2 in a way that is exactly right, or just what you want □ The hotel is ideally situated for the beach.

identical /aɪˈdentɪkəl/ ADJECTIVE exactly the same 🔄 She gave birth to identical twins. □ The room was identical to his own.

identification /aɪˌdentɪfɪˈkeɪʃən/ NOUN, NO PLURAL

1 an official document that gives details such as your name and your date of birth, sometimes with a photograph of you on it, to prove who you are □ The men wore their uniforms and carried official identification.

2 the process of finding out who someone is or what something is

identify /aɪˈdentɪfaɪ/ VERB [identifies, identifying, identified]

1 to recognize someone or something and to say who or what they are □ She had to identify the body. □ Maps helped them identify the buildings. □ We were taught how to identify the signs of mental illness.

2 to find something □ Scientists have identified the gene that is responsible for the disease. □ We are trying to identify suitable buildings to rent.

3 to be a sign that shows what someone or something is □ Her uniform identified her as a member of the armed forces.

♦ PHRASAL VERBS **identify with someone** to understand someone and to share their feelings □ The author does not intend us to identify with the main character. **be identified with someone/something** to be considered to be connected to or involved with someone or something □ She is identified with left-wing politics.

identity /aɪˈdentəti/ NOUN [plural identities]

1 who someone is □ Police are trying to discover the identity of the thief. 🔄 Can you confirm your identity?

2 the qualities that make a person or an organization what they are, and different from others □ We are losing our sense of national identity.

identity card /aɪˈdentəti ˌkɑːd/ NOUN [plural identity cards] an official document showing details of who someone is

identity theft /aɪˈdentəti ˌθeft/ NOUN, NO PLURAL stealing information about someone in order to pretend to be them, for example to get money from their bank account

idiocy /ˈɪdiəsi/ NOUN, NO PLURAL being stupid □ I couldn't believe the idiocy of his suggestion.

idiom /ˈɪdiəm/ NOUN [plural idioms] a phrase that has a meaning that you cannot understand simply by knowing the meaning of the separate words □ The idiom 'once in a blue moon' means 'very rarely'.

• **idiomatic** /ˌɪdiəˈmætɪk/ ADJECTIVE

1 expressed in a natural way □ He speaks fluent, idiomatic French.

2 containing idioms □ idiomatic language

idiot /ˈɪdiət/ NOUN [plural idiots] a stupid person □ I felt like a complete idiot.

• **idiotic** /ˌɪdiˈɒtɪk/ ADJECTIVE extremely stupid □ That's an idiotic idea.

idle /ˈaɪdəl/ ADJECTIVE

1 without a particular purpose 🔄 Let's not waste time in idle chatter.

2 lazy 🔄 Those children are just bone idle (= very lazy).

3 if a machine is idle, it is not being used

• **idly** /ˈaɪdli/ ADVERB not doing anything, or without a particular purpose □ She sat, idly looking through a magazine.

idol /ˈaɪdəl/ NOUN [plural idols]

1 someone you admire very much, or someone very famous and admired by many people □ The show is hosted by former pop idol, Donny Osmond.

2 a picture or object that people pray to

• **idolize** or **idolise** /ˈaɪdəlaɪz/ VERB [idolizes, idolizing, idolized] to admire someone or something very much □ He idolizes David Beckham.

idyllic /ɪˈdɪlɪk, aɪˈdɪlɪk/ ADJECTIVE extremely pleasant or beautiful □ *It sounds like you had an idyllic childhood.* □ *The cottage is in an idyllic spot.*

if /ɪf/ CONJUNCTION

1 used to say that something must happen before something else can happen or be true □ *If we leave now, we should catch the train.* □ *If you do your homework now, you can go out later.*

2 used to say that something will be the result of something that might happen or be true □ *He will have to go into hospital if his condition gets worse.* 🖽 *I hope the bricks will arrive tomorrow. If not, the builders won't be able to work.* 🖽 *Will you be at home tomorrow? If so* (= if you are), *would you mind taking in a parcel for me?*

3 whether □ *I don't know if I can come on Thursday.* □ *He asked me if I minded him smoking.*

4 used for talking about a situation you are imagining □ *You wouldn't behave like that if your father were still alive.*

5 every time □ *I always call in at his house if I'm passing.*

6 if only used to talk about something you wish would happen or be true □ *If only he'd listen to your advice!*

7 What if ...? used to ask what will happen if something else happens or is true □ *What if I miss the phone call?*

i.e. /ˌaɪˈiː/ ABBREVIATION used for giving more information to show what you mean □ *The whole trip, i.e. food, travel and hotel, cost £500.*

igloo /ˈɪɡluː/ NOUN [plural **igloos**] a round house made from blocks of snow

igneous /ˈɪɡnɪəs/ ADJECTIVE igneous rock is formed from hot liquid rock from a volcano (= mountain that explodes). A geography word.

ignite /ɪɡˈnaɪt/ VERB [ignites, igniting, ignited]

1 to start to burn or to make something start to burn □ *The fuel ignited, causing a massive blaze.* □ *Lightning and high winds ignited the dry wood.*

2 to cause strong feelings such as anger □ *The attack has ignited fury throughout the country.*

• **ignition** /ɪɡˈnɪʃən/ NOUN, NO PLURAL the place where you put your key to start a vehicle's engine

ignorance /ˈɪɡnərəns/ NOUN, NO PLURAL not knowing about a subject or a situation □ *The report suggests that there is widespread ignorance about the disease.* 🖽 *They were living in blissful ignorance of the outside world.*

• **ignorant** /ˈɪɡnərənt/ ADJECTIVE

1 not knowing about something □ *Many people are ignorant of the dangers.* 🖽 *Ministers still appear to be blissfully ignorant of this fact.*

2 stupid and rude □ *What an ignorant thing to say!*

ignore /ɪɡˈnɔː(r)/ VERB [ignores, ignoring, ignored]

1 to not pay attention to someone or something □ *He ignored all my advice.* □ *The sport has been generally ignored by the media.*

2 to pretend not to notice someone □ *I said hello, but she just ignored me.*

iguana /ɪˈɡwɑːnə/ NOUN [plural **iguanas**] a large reptile with sharp points on its back, that lives mainly in South America

il- /ɪl/ PREFIX il- is added to the beginning of words to mean 'not' □ *illogical* □ *illegal*

ileum /ˈɪlɪəm/ NOUN [plural **ilea**] the last part of the small intestine. A biology word.

I'll /aɪl/ a short way to say and write I will□ *I'll be back next week.* □ *I'll carry these things for you.*

ill /ɪl/ ADJECTIVE

1 suffering from an illness 🖽 *Do you feel ill?* 🖽 *She fell ill after eating chicken that was not cooked properly.* 🖽 *He is seriously ill with cancer.*

2 bad or harmful 🖽 *He seemed to be suffering no ill effects from his accident.* 🖽 *We have no ill feelings towards her.*

➤ Notice that you use **seriously ill** and not 'badly ill' to describe someone with a very bad illness.

ill- /ɪl/ ADVERB bad or badly □ *ill-treat* □ *ill-tempered*

illegal /ɪˈliːɡəl/ ADJECTIVE not allowed by the law □ *It is illegal to sell alcohol to children.* □ *They are involved in illegal activitites.*

• **illegality** /ˌɪlɪˈɡælətɪ/ NOUN, NO PLURAL being illegal

• **illegally** /ɪˈliːɡəlɪ/ ADVERB in an illegal way □ *Your car is parked illegally.* □ *He was found guilty of illegally possessing a firearm.*

illegible /ɪˈledʒɪbəl/ ADJECTIVE impossible to read □ *His handwriting is almost illegible.*

illegitimate /ˌɪlɪˈdʒɪtɪmət/ ADJECTIVE having parents who are not married to each other □ *He believes he is the illegitimate child of a princess.*

illicit /ɪˈlɪsɪt/ ADJECTIVE

1 not allowed by law □ *They were involved in forgery and other illicit activities.*

2 disapproved of by most people

illiterate /ɪˈlɪtərət/ ADJECTIVE unable to read or write

ill-mannered /ˌɪlˈmænəd/ ADJECTIVE not polite □ *She felt that she had been ill-mannered, and was ashamed of herself.*

illness /ˈɪlnɪs/ NOUN [plural **illnesses**]

1 a disease 🖽 *He is suffering from a serious illness.* 🖽 *Measles was once a common childhood illness.* □ *The illness is caused by a virus.*

2 no plural bad health □ *Illness prevented him from competing in the championship.*

illogical /ɪˈlɒdʒɪkəl/ ADJECTIVE not based on clear or sensible thought □ *Offering plastic bags to online shoppers is totally illogical.*

ill-tempered /ˌɪlˈtempəd/ ADJECTIVE speaking or behaving angrily or rudely □ *ill-tempered remarks*

ill-treat /ˌɪlˈtriːt/ VERB [ill-treats, ill-treating, ill-treated] to treat a person or an animal in a cruel way □ *Some of the older residents had been ill-treated.*

• **ill-treatment** /ˌɪlˈtriːtmənt/ NOUN, NO PLURAL when

a person or an animal is treated in a cruel way □ *There was clear evidence of abuse and ill-treatment by staff.*

illuminate /ɪˈluːmɪneɪt/ VERB [illuminates, illuminating, illuminated]
1 to make a dark place brighter with light, or to shine lights on something □ *Fires illuminated the night sky.*
2 to make something easier to understand.

• **illuminated** /ɪˈluːmɪneɪtɪd/ ADJECTIVE made bright using lights □ *An illuminated sign informed us that there were traffic queues ahead.*

• **illuminating** /ɪˈluːmɪneɪtɪŋ/ ADJECTIVE giving information that makes something easier to understand □ *Well, that was a very illuminating discussion.*

• **illumination** /ɪˌluːmɪˈneɪʃən/ NOUN, NO PLURAL the use of light to make something brighter □ *The light from behind the door provided the only illumination.*

illusion /ɪˈluːʒən/ NOUN [plural illusions]
1 a false idea or belief 🕮 *He's under the illusion that it's easy to get a job.* 🕮 *She had no illusions about her son's abilities.*
2 something that is not really what it seems to be 🕮 *Try using mirrors to create an illusion of space.*

illustrate /ˈɪləstreɪt/ VERB [illustrates, illustrating, illustrated]
1 to give an example or to be an example that explains something 🕮 *He told us a story to illustrate his point.* □ *Her case illustrates the importance of using a good lawyer.*
2 to draw pictures to go in books, magazines, etc. □ *She illustrated several books for children.*

• **illustration** /ˌɪləˈstreɪʃən/ NOUN [plural illustrations]
1 a picture in a book, magazine, etc.
2 an example that shows that something is true or what something is like □ *That was a perfect illustration of why the safety harness is essential.* □ *To give you an illustration: if you invest £3,000 a year, you could end up with a sum of £50,000 at the end of the period.*

• **illustrator** /ˈɪləstreɪtə(r)/ NOUN [plural illustrators] someone who draws pictures for books, magazines, etc.

illustrious /ɪˈlʌstrɪəs/ ADJECTIVE admired and respected by many people. A formal word □ *The book charts Churchill's illustrious political career.*

ill-will /ˌɪlˈwɪl/ NOUN, NO PLURAL bad feelings towards someone because of something that has happened in the past 🕮 *We bear them no ill-will, and wish them the best of luck.*

I'm /aɪm/ a short way to say and write I am□ *I'm hungry.* □ *I'm going to New York tomorrow.*

im- /ɪm/ PREFIX im- is added to the beginning of words to mean 'not' □ *immature* □ *immoral*

image /ˈɪmɪdʒ/ NOUN [plural images]
1 an idea or opinion that people have about someone or something 🕮 *She likes to project an image of confidence.* 🕮 *The agency is aiming to create an image of a dynamic, modern city.*
2 a picture, especially one on television, film or on a

computer □ *We have new images of accident.* 🕮 *A special camera was used to capture images of the child in its mother's womb.*
3 a picture that you have in your mind □ *Disturbing images filled his head.*
4 be the image of someone to look exactly like someone □ *Jessica is the image of her mother.*

• **imagery** /ˈɪmɪdʒərɪ/ NOUN, NO PLURAL
1 pictures or objects that represent an idea □ *The movie is full of striking visual imagery.*
2 pictures □ *Satellite imagery shows us the effects of global warming.*
3 in literature, words that produce pictures in your mind □ *We discussed Shakespeare's use of imagery in 'Hamlet'.*

imaginary /ɪˈmædʒɪnərɪ/ ADJECTIVE existing in your mind but not real □ *It is perfectly normal for children to have imaginary friends.*

• **imagination** /ɪˌmædʒɪˈneɪʃən/ NOUN, NO PLURAL
1 your ability to think of new ideas or to form interesting pictures and stories in your mind. 🕮 *Rory has a very vivid imagination.* 🕮 *Reading encourages children to use their imagination.*
2 when someone believes something that is not true or real □ *She thinks people hate her, but it's all in her imagination.*

• **imaginative** /ɪˈmædʒɪnətɪv/ ADJECTIVE
1 using new and interesting ideas □ *That's an imaginative design.*
2 using the imagination □ *Imaginative play is important for children.*

• **imagine** /ɪˈmædʒɪn/ VERB [imagines, imagining, imagined]
1 to form a picture of someone or something in your mind □ **+ question word** *I tried to imagine what he would look like.* □ **+ that** *Imagine that you're the manager of a large company.* □ **+ ing** *Imagine having your own aeroplane!*
2 to think that something is probably true □ *I imagine he'll want some food.*
3 to think that something exists or is true when it does not or is not □ *I keep imagining I can hear voices.*

imam /ɪˈmɑːm/ NOUN [plural imams] a Muslim priest or leader

imbalance /ɪmˈbæləns/ NOUN [plural imbalances] when things are not arranged fairly or equally □ *There is an imbalance between the amount they eat and the amount of calories they use up.*

imbecile /ˈɪmbɪsiːl/ NOUN [plural imbeciles] a stupid person □ *I felt like a complete imbecile!*

imitate /ˈɪmɪteɪt/ VERB [imitates, imitating, imitated]
1 to copy someone or something because you like them or it □ *He tries to imitate the style of famous artists.*
2 to copy the way someone speaks or behaves as a joke □ *He's always imitating my friend's voice.*

• **imitation** /ˌɪmɪˈteɪʃən/ NOUN [plural imitations]

1 when you copy the way someone speaks or behaves as a joke □ *He does a good imitation of his English teacher.*
2 a copy of something □ *He threatened them with an imitation gun.* 🕮 *Their records are a pale imitation (= not as good) of their live performances.*

• **imitator** /ˈɪmɪteɪtə(r)/ NOUN [plural **imitators**] someone who copies someone or something else □ *As a successful politician, he has many imitators.*

immaculate /ɪˈmækjʊlət/ ADJECTIVE
1 extremely clean and tidy □ *The house looked immaculate.*
2 completely perfect □ *With immaculate timing, he arrived just as we were starting.*

immature /ˌɪməˈtjʊə(r)/ ADJECTIVE
1 behaving in a silly way that is typical of a younger person □ *I was too immature to be a father.*
2 not yet completely developed □ *Her immature lungs struggled for oxygen.*

• **immaturity** /ˌɪməˈtjʊərətɪ/ NOUN, NO PLURAL being immature or behaving in an immature way

immediate /ɪˈmiːdɪət/ ▶ ADJECTIVE
1 happening now, and without delay 🕮 *I can't give you an immediate response.* □ *They demanded the immediate withdrawal of troops.*
2 existing now 🕮 *We are in no immediate danger.* 🕮 *Her immediate concern is for her children.*
3 closest to someone or something 🕮 *Police evacuated the immediate area.* 🕮 *I'm only inviting my immediate family.*
4 the immediate future the next period of time □ *I certainly don't plan to change jobs in the immediate future.*

• **immediately** /ɪˈmiːdɪətlɪ/ ▶ ADVERB
1 now or without delay □ *Come here immediately!* □ *I rang the doctor immediately.*
2 immediately before/after something in the period just before/after something □ *Immediately before the bomb went off, they were talking on the balcony.*
3 with no space between □ *Immediately in front of the church you will see a signpost.*
▶ CONJUNCTION as soon as □ *Immediately I got the message, I ran to tell father.*

immense /ɪˈmens/ ADJECTIVE extremely large in size, amount or degree □ *Some children are under immense pressure to succeed.* □ *He used his immense wealth to help a lot of people.*

• **immensely** /ɪˈmenslɪ/ ADVERB extremely □ *He's immensely popular.*

immerse /ɪˈmɜːs/ VERB [**immerses, immersing, immersed**]
1 to put something in a liquid so that it is completely covered □ *The cloth is then immersed in dye.*
2 immerse yourself in something/be immersed in something to give all of your attention to something □ *After the divorce, Brian immersed himself*

in his work. □ *She was too immersed in her magazine article to notice me.*

• **immersion** /ɪˈmɜːʃən/ NOUN, NO PLURAL
1 when you put something into a liquid
2 when you spend most of your time doing something or in a particular situation □ *His immersion in Spanish culture influenced his art deeply.*

immigrant /ˈɪmɪɡrənt/ NOUN [plural **immigrants**] someone who has come to live in a country from another country

immigration /ˌɪmɪˈɡreɪʃən/ NOUN, NO PLURAL
1 when people come to live in a foreign country □ *Immigration rose sharply in 2007.* 🕮 *The government has announced new immigration laws.*
2 the place where a person's documents are checked when they come into a country □ *She was stopped at immigration and questioned for hours.*

imminent /ˈɪmɪnənt/ ADJECTIVE something that is imminent is going to happen very soon 🕮 *Her life is in imminent danger.* 🕮 *There is no imminent threat to health.*

immobile /ɪˈməʊbaɪl/ ADJECTIVE not moving or not able to move □ *He lay immobile on the floor.*

• **immobilize** or **immobilise** /ɪˈməʊbɪlaɪz/ VERB [**immobilizes, immobilizing, immobilized**] to prevent someone or something from moving □ *The ankle needs to be immobilized to give it a chance to heal.*

immoral /ɪˈmɒrəl/ ADJECTIVE morally wrong □ *He accused her of immoral conduct.*

• **immorality** /ˌɪməˈrælətɪ/ NOUN, NO PLURAL immoral behaviour

immortal /ɪˈmɔːtəl/ ADJECTIVE
1 living for ever □ *This type of accident makes you realize you're not immortal.*
2 very famous, and likely to be remembered for a long time □ *Who said the immortal words 'You ain't seen nothing yet'?*

• **immortality** /ˌɪmɔːˈtælətɪ/ NOUN, NO PLURAL being immortal □ *He wants to achieve immortality through his work.*

• **immortalize** or **immortalise** /ɪˈmɔːtəˌlaɪz/ VERB [**immortalizes, immortalizing, immortalized**] to make someone or something famous for a long time □ *She was immortalized in Betjeman's poem.*

immune /ɪˈmjuːn/ ADJECTIVE
1 not affected by something □ *I am not immune to criticism.*
2 unable to be infected by a particular disease. A biology word □ *Some people are naturally immune to the virus.*
3 not affected by a law □ *Diplomats are immune from prosecution.*

immune system /ɪˈmjuːn ˌsɪstəm/ NOUN [plural **immune systems**] the system in your body that protects it from disease. A biology word.

immunity /ɪˈmjuːnətɪ/ NOUN, NO PLURAL
1 your ability to avoid getting a particular disease. A biology word □ *Catching chickenpox gives lifelong immunity against the virus.*

2 when you cannot be punished for something □ *As President, he enjoys immunity from prosecution.* 🕮 *She has diplomatic immunity.*

immunization *or* **immunisation** /ˌɪmjuːnaɪ'zeɪʃən/ NOUN [*plural* **immunizations**] when a substance is put into someone's body, usually through their skin, to prevent them from getting a particular disease in the future □ *Has your daughter had all her immunizations?*

• **immunize** *or* **immunise** /'ɪmjuːnaɪz/ VERB [**immunizes, immunizing, immunized**] to put a substance into someone's skin, usually through their skin, to prevent them from getting a particular disease in the future □ *Has he been immunized against measles?*

imp /ɪmp/ NOUN [*plural* **imps**]
1 an imaginary creature that looks like a small man and behaves badly
2 a child who behaves badly in a way that is not very serious

impact ► NOUN /'ɪmpækt/ [*plural* **impacts**]
1 the effect that something has □ *The changes will have a significant impact on schools.*
2 the force of one thing hitting another thing □ *The car is designed to absorb the impact of a crash.*
► VERB /ɪm'pækt/ [**impacts, impacting, impacted**] to have an effect on something □ *A long journey could impact on the team's performance.*

impair /ɪm'peə(r)/ VERB [**impairs, impairing, impaired**] to make something less good, especially by damaging it □ *Even a small amount of alcohol can impair your ability to drive.*

• **impairment** /ɪm'peəmənt/ NOUN [*plural* **impairments**] when part of your body does not work correctly □ *His stroke caused some visual impairment.*

impale /ɪm'peɪl/ VERB [**impales, impaling, impaled**] to push a sharp object through something □ *His leg was impaled on a piece of broken railing.*

impart /ɪm'pɑːt/ VERB [**imparts, imparting, imparted**]
1 to give someone information or your opinions □ *She was desperate to impart the great news.*
2 to give a particular quality to something □ *The leaves impart a spicy flavour to the dish.*

impartial /ɪm'pɑːʃəl/ ADJECTIVE not influenced by one particular person or group □ *Phone this number for free and impartial advice.*

• **impartiality** /ɪmˌpɑːʃɪ'ælətɪ/ NOUN, NO PLURAL being impartial

impassable /ɪm'pɑːsəbəl/ ADJECTIVE if a road or path is impassable, you cannot travel along it

impasse /æm'pɑːs/ NOUN, NO PLURAL a situation in which no more progress is possible 🕮 *Our discussion seems to have reached an impasse.*

impassive /ɪm'pæsɪv/ ADJECTIVE not showing any emotion □ *Her face was totally impassive.*

• **impassively** /ɪm'pæsɪvlɪ/ ADVERB in an impassive way □ *He listened impassively to my story of childhood hardship.*

impatience /ɪm'peɪʃəns/ NOUN, NO PLURAL being impatient □ *He never showed any sign of impatience.*

• **impatient** /ɪm'peɪʃənt/ ADJECTIVE
1 wanting something to happen soon □ *She was impatient to get started on the job.*
2 annoyed because you have to wait or because someone is making mistakes □ *Flights were delayed and passengers were becoming impatient.*

• **impatiently** /ɪm'peɪʃəntlɪ/ ADVERB in a way that shows you are impatient □ *'Hurry up!' she said impatiently.*

impeccable /ɪm'pekəbəl/ ADJECTIVE perfect □ *The car is still in impeccable condition.* □ *The children's behaviour was impeccable.*

• **impeccably** /ɪm'pekəblɪ/ ADVERB perfectly □ *The dogs were impeccably groomed.*

impede /ɪm'piːd/ VERB [**impedes, impeding, impeded**] to delay the progress of someone or something □ *Snow impeded their progress.*

• **impediment** /ɪm'pedɪmənt/ NOUN [*plural* **impediments**]
1 something that delays progress or prevents something from happening □ *Lack of time is a major impediment to getting exercise.*
2 a speech impediment a problem that affects someone's ability to speak

impel /ɪm'pel/ VERB [**impels, impelling, impelled**] to force someone to do something. A formal word. □ *Curiosity impelled me to visit her one more time.* □ *I felt impelled to protest.*

impending /ɪm'pendɪŋ/ ADJECTIVE an impending event is going to happen very soon □ *They failed to warn us of the impending disaster.*

imperative /ɪm'perətɪv/ ► ADJECTIVE extremely important or necessary □ *It is absolutely imperative that we take this opportunity now.*
► NOUN, NO PLURAL the imperative a verb form that you use to tell someone to do something

imperceptible /ˌɪmpə'septəbəl/ ADJECTIVE too small or quiet to be noticed □ *His nod was almost imperceptible.*

imperfect /ɪm'pɜːfɪkt/ ADJECTIVE having some faults □ *We live in an imperfect world.*

• **imperfection** /ˌɪmpə'fekʃən/ NOUN [*plural* **imperfections**] a fault □ *Avoid jokes that relate to people's physical imperfections.*

imperial /ɪm'pɪərɪəl/ ADJECTIVE
1 to do with an empire (= a number of countries governed by one ruler) □ *It's a book about Britain's imperial past.*
2 to do with a system of measuring or weighing that uses units such as feet for measuring length and pounds for measuring weight

• **imperialism** /ɪm'pɪərɪəlɪzəm/ NOUN, NO PLURAL
1 when one country rules several other countries
2 when one country has a lot of influence over other countries □ *American cultural imperialism*

• **imperialist** /ɪm'pɪərɪəlɪst/ ADJECTIVE to do with imperialism

imperious /ɪmˈpɪərɪəs/ ADJECTIVE showing that you think people should obey you. A formal word. □ *'Bring me a clean glass,' she said in an imperious voice.*

impermeable /ɪmˈpɜːmɪəbəl/ ADJECTIVE impermeable substances do not allow liquid or gas to pass through them. A biology or physics word.

impersonal /ɪmˈpɜːsənəl/ ADJECTIVE intended for people generally but not showing interest in separate people and not friendly □ *Big hotels can be a bit impersonal.*

impersonate /ɪmˈpɜːsəneɪt/ VERB [impersonates, impersonating, impersonated] to copy the way someone talks and behaves, especially to entertain people

• **impersonation** /ɪmˌpɜːsəˈneɪʃən/ NOUN [plural impersonations] an attempt to impersonate someone □ *Ben can do a brilliant impersonation of the Prime Minister.*

• **impersonator** /ɪmˈpɜːsəneɪtə(r)/ NOUN [plural impersonators] someone who impersonates people

impertinence /ɪmˈpɜːtɪnəns/ NOUN, NO PLURAL a formal word meaning rude behaviour that shows you do not respect someone

• **impertinent** /ɪmˈpɜːtɪnənt/ ADJECTIVE a formal word meaning behaving in a rude way and not showing respect □ *an impertinent child*

impervious /ɪmˈpɜːvɪəs/ ADJECTIVE
1 a formal word meaning not affected by something □ *He seems impervious to the cold.*
2 an impervious material does not let water pass through it □ *impervious surfaces*

impetuous /ɪmˈpetʃʊəs/ ADJECTIVE doing things without thinking about what might happen as a result □ *He was young and impetuous.*

impetus /ˈɪmpɪtəs/ NOUN, NO PLURAL
1 an influence which helps something to happen □ *Sometimes it takes a tragedy to provide the impetus for change.*
2 the force which makes something move. A physics word.

impinge /ɪmˈpɪndʒ/
♦ PHRASAL VERB [impinges, impinging, impinged]
impinge on someone/something to affect someone or something, especially in a bad way □ *Having a bad neighbour can really impinge on your life.*

implant ▶ VERB /ɪmˈplɑːnt/ [implants, implanting, implanted] to put something into someone's body to make it work or look better □ *A device is implanted in the heart which regulates the heartbeat.*
▶ NOUN /ˈɪmplɑːnt/ [plural implants] something that is implanted in someone's body to make it work or look better □ *dental implants*

implausible /ɪmˈplɔːzəbəl/ ADJECTIVE difficult to accept as true or real □ *It seemed an implausible excuse.*

implement ▶ VERB /ˈɪmplɪment/ [implements, implementing, implemented] to start using a new

plan, law, system, etc. □ *The new rules will be implemented next year.*
▶ NOUN /ˈɪmplɪmənt/ [plural implements] a formal word for a tool □ *sharp implements*

• **implementation** /ˌɪmplɪmenˈteɪʃən/ NOUN, NO PLURAL implementing something □ *the implementation of new laws*

implicate /ˈɪmplɪkeɪt/ VERB [implicates, implicating, implicated] to suggest that someone is involved in something bad such as a crime □ *He was implicated in the murder of his neighbour.*

• **implication** /ˌɪmplɪˈkeɪʃən/ NOUN [plural implications]
1 a possible effect or result □ *What are the implications of the President's announcement?*
2 something that is suggested and not said directly □ *He rejected the implication that the project was a waste of money.*

implicit /ɪmˈplɪsɪt/ ADJECTIVE
1 suggested or shown but not said directly □ *implicit criticism*
2 complete, without any doubts □ *I have implicit faith in her abilities.*

implore /ɪmˈplɔː(r)/ VERB [implores, imploring, implored] a formal word meaning to ask someone in a strong and emotional way to do something □ *He tearfully implored her not to leave.*

imply /ɪmˈplaɪ/ VERB [implies, implying, implied] to suggest that something is true without saying it directly □ *Are you implying that he lied?*

impolite /ˌɪmpəˈlaɪt/ ADJECTIVE a formal word meaning rude □ *It seemed impolite to ask how old she was.*

import ▶ VERB /ɪmˈpɔːt/ [imports, importing, imported]
1 to bring a product from another country into your country in order to sell it □ + *into* *The cars had been imported into the UK.* □ + *from* *Many electrical goods are imported from Japan.*
2 to copy computer information from another place. A computing word.
▶ NOUN /ˈɪmpɔːt/ [plural imports]
1 a product that is brought from another country into your country in order to sell □ *The country is dependent on oil imports.*
2 *no plural* the process of bringing a product into a country to sell □ + *of* *There's a ban on the import of wild birds.* □ *import restrictions*
➜ *go to* **export**

importance /ɪmˈpɔːtəns/ NOUN, NO PLURAL
1 when something is important □ + *of* *This just shows the importance of education.* ⯗ *She stressed the importance of eating healthily.*
2 **of great/utmost/vital importance** extremely important □ *The industry is of vital importance to the UK economy.*

• **important** /ɪmˈpɔːtənt/ ADJECTIVE
1 necessary or having a big effect on something □ *Books are an important part of our culture.* + *to do*

something ⌑ *It's important to listen to what the teacher is saying.* □ **+ that** *It's important that people are given this information.* □ **+ to** *Amy's career is very important to her.* ⌑ *For me, the most important thing is to be happy.*

2 an important person has a lot of power or influence □ *The Prime Minister is the most important person in government.*

► Remember that something is **important to** someone and not **important for** someone:
✓ *My family is very important to me.*
✗ *My family is very important for me.*

• **importantly** /ɪmˈpɔːtəntlɪ/ ADVERB more/most importantly used before saying something that is more important or the most important thing □ *I love it here in Hong Kong and more importantly, the children love it too.*

---

impose /ɪmˈpəʊz/ VERB [**imposes, imposing, imposed**]
1 to force someone to accept something new such as a rule or punishment □ *The government imposed a new tax.*
2 to make someone do something for you in a way that is not convenient for them □ *They said I could stay with them but I didn't like to impose on them.*
• **imposing** /ɪmˈpəʊzɪŋ/ ADJECTIVE an imposing person or thing is big in a way that makes you admire them □ *an imposing building*

impossibility /ɪmˌpɒsəˈbɪlətɪ/ NOUN [*plural* **impossibilities**] something that is not possible ⌑ *Searching every home for the missing girl would be a physical impossibility.*

impossible /ɪmˈpɒsəbəl/ ► ADJECTIVE
1 not possible ⌑ *an impossible task* **+ to do something** ⌑ *It's impossible to explain.* ⌑ *Ink stains are almost impossible to get rid of.* ⌑ *Rain made it impossible for the game to continue.*
2 an impossible situation is very difficult ⌑ *The new rules have put teachers in an impossible position.*
3 someone who is impossible is unreasonable and annoying
► NOUN, NO PLURAL the impossible something that is not possible □ *You're asking me to do the impossible.*
• **impossibly** /ɪmˈpɒsəblɪ/ ADVERB extremely □ *She was impossibly beautiful.*

impostor /ɪmˈpɒstə(r)/ NOUN [*plural* **impostors**] someone who pretends to be someone else in order to trick people

impoverished /ɪmˈpɒvərɪʃt/ ADJECTIVE very poor □ *impoverished countries*

impractical /ɪmˈpræktɪkəl/ ADJECTIVE
1 not sensible or able to be done or used easily □ *an impractical suggestion* □ *Their clothes are very pretty but rather impractical.*

2 an impractical person is not good at doing normal, useful things, such as planning or repairing things

imprecise /ˌɪmprɪˈsaɪs/ ADJECTIVE not exact or not correct □ *imprecise measurements*

impress /ɪmˈpres/ VERB [**impresses, impressing, impressed**] to make someone feel admiration □ *He was trying to impress his friends in his new car.* □ *Her attitude impressed me.*
• **impressed** /ɪmˈprest/ ADJECTIVE admiring someone or something very much □ *The teacher didn't look very impressed when she saw my work.* □ *I was impressed at how quickly they dealt with the problem.*
• **impression** /ɪmˈpreʃən/ NOUN [*plural* **impressions**]
1 an idea or feeling that you get about someone or something ⌑ *I got the impression that he wasn't happy.* ⌑ *She gives the impression of not really caring.*
2 the effect that someone or something has on you ⌑ *The film made a big impression on me*
3 when someone copies the way someone else talks and behaves in order to entertain people ⌑ *She does a great impression of Juan.*
• **impressive** /ɪmˈpresɪv/ ADJECTIVE making you feel admiration □ *an impressive performance* □ *She's a very impressive woman.*

imprison /ɪmˈprɪzən/ VERB [**imprisons, imprisoning, imprisoned**] to put someone in prison or in a place they cannot escape from □ *He was imprisoned for fraud.*
• **imprisonment** /ɪmˈprɪzənmənt/ NOUN, NO PLURAL when someone is imprisoned □ *She was sentenced to 20 years' imprisonment.*

improbable /ɪmˈprɒbəbəl/ ADJECTIVE unlikely to happen or unlikely to be true □ *a highly improbable story*

impromptu /ɪmˈprɒmptjuː/ ADJECTIVE not planned □ *an impromptu speech*

improper /ɪmˈprɒpə(r)/ ADJECTIVE a formal word meaning not suitable, not right or not honest □ *It would be improper for me to comment before the court case.*

improper fraction /ɪmˌprɒpə(r) ˈfrækʃən/ NOUN [*plural* **improper fractions**] a fraction where the number above the line is bigger than the number below the line. A maths word.

improve /ɪmˈpruːv/ VERB [**improves, improving, improved**]
1 to become better □ *I hope the weather improves soon.* □ *The situation has slowly improved.*
2 to make something better □ *Exercise can improve your health.* □ *The new law is intended to improve road safety.* □ *This treatment will improve the quality of life for many cancer sufferers.*
• **improvement** /ɪmˈpruːvmənt/ NOUN [*plural* **improvements**]
1 *no plural* the process of becoming better or of making something better ⌑ *His test results have shown a great improvement.* ⌑ *We have seen no improvement in the health service.* ⌑ *There has been a*

significant improvement in living standards. □ + *in an improvement in behaviour*
2 a change that makes something better □ *improvements to the home*

improvise /ˈɪmprəˌvaɪz/ VERB [**improvises, improvising, improvised**]
1 to decide what to say or do at the time when you are saying or doing it and not before □ *I had forgotten the notes for my talk so I had to improvise.*
2 to make something using the things that are available because you do not have the correct equipment □ *We improvised a shelter from some old blankets.*

impudence /ˈɪmpjʊdəns/ NOUN, NO PLURAL a formal word meaning rude behaviour or remarks
● **impudent** /ˈɪmpjʊdənt/ ADJECTIVE a formal word meaning rude and showing no respect

impulse /ˈɪmpʌls/ NOUN [*plural* **impulses**]
1 a sudden feeling that makes you want to do something □ *He resisted the impulse to hit the man.*
2 on impulse without thinking first □ *On impulse, he put his arm around her.*
● **impulsive** /ɪmˈpʌlsɪv/ ADJECTIVE doing things suddenly without thinking first □ *Jane is very impulsive.*

impunity /ɪmˈpjuːnətɪ/ NOUN, NO PLURAL **with impunity** without any risk of being punished. A formal phrase. □ *Some companies ignore the rules with impunity.*

impure /ɪmˈpjʊə(r)/ ADJECTIVE not pure □ *impure hydrogen*
● **impurity** /ɪmˈpjʊərətɪ/ NOUN [*plural* **impurities**] something in a substance that makes it dirty or not pure □ *impurities in water*

in- /ɪn/ PREFIX
1 in- is added to the beginning of words to mean 'not' □ *inaccurate* □ *informal*
2 in- is added to the beginning of words to mean 'in', 'into' or 'towards' □ *inland*

in¹ /ɪn/ ▶ PREPOSITION
1 inside something □ *He keeps his keys in the drawer.* □ *The books are in my bedroom.*
2 at a place □ *They live in Nottingham.*
3 being part of something □ *There's a hole in my trousers.* □ *There was a strange smell in the air.*
4 at a particular time □ *It's my birthday in May.*
5 after a period of time □ *I'll be back in a few minutes.*
6 wearing particular clothes □ *Who's the woman in the red dress?*
7 shown as part of something □ *I looked in the dictionary to find the spelling of 'weird'.*
8 using a particular thing □ *They were speaking in Japanese.* □ *The letter was written in purple ink.*
▶ ADVERB
1 into a place or towards the inside of something □ *Come in and sit down.* □ *Push the needle in.* □ *A wide belt will hold your tummy in.*

2 at your home or place of work □ *I'm sorry, Dad's not in. Can I take a message?* 🕮 *I usually get in at around eight.*
3 having arrived 🕮 *What time does your train get in?*
▶ ADJECTIVE fashionable □ *Pilates seems to be the in thing to do these days.*

in² /ɪn/ ABBREVIATION inch or inches

inability /ˌɪnəˈbɪlətɪ/ NOUN, NO PLURAL the fact of not being able to do something □ *He criticized the government's inability to deal with the problem.*

inaccessible /ˌɪnəkˈsesəbəl/ ADJECTIVE impossible to reach □ *The forest is inaccessible by road.*

inaccuracy /ɪnˈækjʊrəsɪ/ NOUN [*plural* **inaccuracies**] when a statement or detail is not correct or exact □ *The report was full of inaccuracies.* □ *He criticized the book for its inaccuracy.*
● **inaccurate** /ɪnˈækjʊrət/ ADJECTIVE not exact or correct □ *inaccurate information*

inaction /ɪnˈækʃən/ NOUN, NO PLURAL when someone is not doing anything to solve a problem □ *He blamed the government's inaction for the increasing crime rate.*
● **inactive** /ɪnˈæktɪv/ ADJECTIVE not doing anything □ *Being overweight and inactive has a bad effect on your health.*
● **inactivity** /ˌɪnækˈtɪvətɪ/ NOUN, NO PLURAL when someone or something is not doing anything □ *physical inactivity*

inadequacy /ɪnˈædɪkwəsɪ/ NOUN [*plural* **inadequacies**] not being good enough or not being enough □ *She suffered from feelings of inadequacy.*
● **inadequate** /ɪnˈædɪkwət/ ADJECTIVE not enough, or not good enough □ *inadequate water supplies*

inadvertent /ˌɪnədˈvɜːtənt/ ADJECTIVE a formal word meaning done by accident □ *inadvertent damage*
● **inadvertently** /ˌɪnədˈvɜːtəntlɪ/ ADVERB a formal word meaning by accident □ *I had inadvertently left the door unlocked.*

inadvisable /ˌɪnədˈvaɪzəbəl/ ADJECTIVE not sensible and likely to have bad results □ *It is highly inadvisable for children to watch television all day.*

inane /ɪˈneɪn/ ADJECTIVE stupid and annoying □ *inane questions*

inanimate /ɪnˈænɪmət/ ADJECTIVE not alive
🕮 *inanimate objects such as chairs and books*

inapplicable /ˌɪnəˈplɪkəbəl/ ADJECTIVE a formal word meaning not able to be used or not suitable for a particular situation □ *Old laws often seem inapplicable to the modern world.*

inappropriate /ˌɪnəˈprəʊprɪət/ ADJECTIVE not suitable for a particular situation or occasion □ *inappropriate behaviour*

inarticulate /ˌɪnɑːˈtɪkjʊlət/ ADJECTIVE not able to express clearly what you want to say

inaudible /ɪˈnɔːdɪbəl/ ADJECTIVE not loud enough to hear □ *His reply was inaudible.*

inaugural /ɪˈnɔːgjʊrəl/ ADJECTIVE first, and marking the beginning of something important □ *the President's inaugural speech* □ *the airline's inaugural flight*

• **inaugurate** /ɪˈnɔːgjureɪt/ VERB [inaugurates, inaugurating, inaugurated] to mark the beginning or opening of something important with a ceremony □ *The research centre was inaugurated in 1998.*

• **inauguration** /ɪˌnɔːgjuˈreɪʃən/ NOUN [plural inaugurations] a ceremony to mark the beginning or opening of something important □ *Bush's inauguration as president*

in-box /ˈɪnbɒks/ NOUN [plural in-boxes] the place on a computer which stores email messages that people have sent to you. A computing word. □ *I was looking through my in-box for Bret's email.*

incapable /ɪnˈkeɪpəbəl/ ADJECTIVE not able to do something □ *He seems incapable of making any kind of decision.*

incapacitate /ˌɪnkəˈpæsɪteɪt/ VERB [incapacitates, incapacitating, incapacitated] if you are incapacitated by something, it makes you too ill or weak to live in a normal way. A formal word □ *He was incapacitated by ill health.*

• **incapacity** /ˌɪnkəˈpæsəti/ NOUN, NO PLURAL
1 when you are not able to do something. A formal word. □ *The problem is his incapacity to recognize the truth.*
2 when you cannot live in a normal way because you are ill or weak. A formal word.

incendiary /ɪnˈsendɪəri/ ADJECTIVE an incendiary bomb is designed to start a fire when it explodes ⓗ *Police discovered several incendiary devices.*

incense /ˈɪnsens/ NOUN, NO PLURAL a substance that smells nice when you burn it, often used in religious ceremonies

incentive /ɪnˈsentɪv/ NOUN [plural incentives] something that encourages you to do something □ *Praise gives students an incentive to work harder.*

incessant /ɪnˈsesənt/ ADJECTIVE continuous, in a way that is annoying □ *incessant rain*

inch /ɪntʃ/ NOUN [plural inches] a unit for measuring length, equal to about 2.5 centimetres □ *The ruler was 12 inches long.*

incidence /ˈɪnsɪdəns/ NOUN [plural incidences] how often something happens, especially something bad, such as illness or crime □ *This country has one of the highest incidences of breast cancer.*

• **incident** /ˈɪnsɪdənt/ NOUN [plural incidents] something that happens, especially something bad such as a crime. A formal word. □ *a violent incident* □ *She reported the incident to the police.*

• **incidental** /ˌɪnsɪˈdentəl/ ADJECTIVE happening in connection with something else but less important than it □ *These details are incidental to the story.*

• **incidentally** /ˌɪnsɪˈdentəli/ ADVERB something you say when you are going to talk about a new subject or add some more information □ *Incidentally, did you know Jack was getting married?*

incinerate /ɪnˈsɪnəreɪt/ VERB [incinerates, incinerating, incinerated] to burn waste

• **incinerator** /ɪnˈsɪnəreɪtə(r)/ NOUN [plural incinerators] a container for burning waste

incision /ɪnˈsɪʒən/ NOUN [plural incisions] a cut made in something, especially during a medical operation. A formal word.

incisive /ɪnˈsaɪsɪv/ ADJECTIVE showing that you are intelligent and understand something very well □ *incisive comments*

incisor /ɪnˈsaɪzə(r)/ NOUN [plural incisors] one of the teeth at the front of your mouth that you use to cut food. A biology word.

incite /ɪnˈsaɪt/ VERB [incites, inciting, incited] to encourage people to be violent or do something bad □ *He denied that his speech had incited violence.*

inclination /ˌɪnklɪˈneɪʃən/ NOUN [plural inclinations] a feeling that makes you want to do something ⓗ *He showed no inclination to help.*

incline ▶ VERB /ɪnˈklaɪn/ [inclines, inclining, inclined] if you incline your head, you move it down. A formal word.
▶ NOUN /ˈɪnklaɪn/ [plural inclines] a slope

• **inclined** /ɪnˈklaɪnd/ ADJECTIVE
1 be inclined to agree/think something to have an opinion although you are not completely certain □ *I must say I'm inclined to agree with her.*
2 be inclined to do something (a) to want to do something, although you are not completely certain □ *I'm inclined to tell him the truth.* (b) to often do something □ *He's inclined to make silly mistakes.*

include /ɪnˈkluːd/ VERB [includes, including, included]
1 if one thing includes another thing, the second thing is part of the first thing □ *The price of the ticket includes dinner.* □ *The guest list included many famous people.* □ *Ryan's films include 'Sleepless in Seattle' and 'Against the Ropes'.*
2 to allow someone to be part of a group □ **+ in** *Students are included in making decisions.*

• **including** /ɪnˈkluːdɪŋ/ PREPOSITION a word used to show that a person or thing is part of a larger group □ *We went to all the museums, including the new one.* □ *Seven people, including two young girls, died in the accident.*

• **inclusion** /ɪnˈkluːʒən/ NOUN, NO PLURAL when you include someone or something as part of a larger group □ *His inclusion in the team was a surprise.*

• **inclusive** /ɪnˈkluːsɪv/ ADJECTIVE
1 an inclusive price includes everything □ *A three-day course costs £700, fully inclusive.*
2 used for saying that the first and last thing you mention is included □ *From Tuesday to Thursday inclusive is three days.*
3 including all types of people □ *We need a more inclusive government.*

incoherent /ˌɪnkəʊˈhɪərənt/ ADJECTIVE not clear, and difficult to understand □ *He had left an incoherent message on my answerphone.*

income /ˈɪnkʌm/ NOUN [plural incomes]
1 the amount of money you earn ⓗ *He had an annual income of £35,000.* ⓗ *The average household income*

has increased. □ **+from** *She has had income from the sale of two houses.*

2 on a high/low income earning a lot/not much money □ *There aren't enough houses for people on low incomes.*

income tax /'ɪŋkʌm ˌtæks/ NOUN, NO PLURAL tax that you have to pay on the money you earn

incoming /'ɪnkʌmɪŋ/ ADJECTIVE

1 just starting an important job □ *the incoming director*

2 coming into a place □ *The airport was shut and incoming flights were diverted.*

incompatible /ˌɪnkəm'pætɪbəl/ ADJECTIVE

1 if people are incompatible, they are so different that they cannot have a good relationship

2 too different to exist or be used together □ *The software is incompatible with the operating system.*

incompetence /ɪn'kɒmpɪtəns/ NOUN, NO PLURAL when someone is incompetent

● **incompetent** /ɪn'kɒmpɪtənt/ ADJECTIVE not doing your job well □ *an incompetent government*

incomplete /ˌɪnkəm'pliːt/ ADJECTIVE not finished, or not having all the necessary parts □ *an incomplete jigsaw puzzle*

incomprehensible /ˌɪnkɒmprɪ'hensəbəl/ ADJECTIVE impossible to understand □ *The article was completely incomprehensible.*

inconceivable /ˌɪnkən'siːvəbəl/ ADJECTIVE extremely surprising and so impossible to imagine □ *In the past, it was inconceivable that a woman would ever become Prime Minister.*

inconclusive /ˌɪnkən'kluːsɪv/ ADJECTIVE not giving you certain proof of something □ *The test results were inconclusive.*

incongruous /ɪn'kɒŋgruəs/ ADJECTIVE a formal word meaning different from the things or people in a particular situation and so not suitable □ *He looked rather incongruous in his suit when everyone else was wearing jeans.*

inconsiderate /ˌɪnkən'sɪdərət/ ADJECTIVE not thinking about other people's feelings □ *It was very inconsiderate of him not to tell you he was going to be late.*

inconsistency /ˌɪnkən'sɪstənsɪ/ NOUN [plural **inconsistencies**]

1 something that cannot be true if something else is also true □ *The report contained several inconsistencies.*

2 failing to behave in the same way each time in the same situation □ *The government has been accused of inconsistency in the way it treats refugees.*

● **inconsistent** /ˌɪnkən'sɪstənt/ ADJECTIVE

1 if two reports, statements, etc. are inconsistent, they cannot both be true □ *inconsistent statements*

2 sometimes of good quality and sometimes of bad quality □ *Her work is very inconsistent.*

3 not showing the same principles as something else □ *His behaviour was inconsistent with his religious beliefs.*

inconsolable /ˌɪnkən'səuləbəl/ ADJECTIVE too upset for anyone to comfort you

inconspicuous /ˌɪnkən'spɪkjuəs/ ADJECTIVE not easy to see □ *I'm too tall to be inconspicuous.*

inconvenience /ˌɪnkən'viːnjəns/ ▶ NOUN [plural **inconveniences**] problems that something or someone causes you □ *We apologize for the delay and for any inconvenience caused.*

▶ VERB [**inconveniences, inconveniencing, inconvenienced**] to cause problems for someone

● **inconvenient** /ˌɪnkən'viːnjənt/ ADJECTIVE causing problems □ *Have I called at an inconvenient time?*

incorporate /ɪn'kɔːpəreɪt/ VERB [**incorporates, incorporating, incorporated**] to include something □ *The television incorporates all the latest technology.*

incorrect /ˌɪnkə'rekt/ ADJECTIVE wrong □ *The answer to number three is incorrect.* □ *He'd been given incorrect information.*

● **incorrectly** /ˌɪnkə'rektlɪ/ ADVERB in a way that is wrong □ *The packets were incorrectly labelled.*

increase ▶ VERB /ɪn'kriːs/ [**increases, increasing, increased**]

1 to become bigger in size or amount ▣ *The number of students has increased dramatically over the last ten years.* □ **+ in** *The house has increased in value.* □ **+ by** *Their wages will increase by 4%.*

2 to make something become bigger in size or amount ▣ *Being overweight increases the risk of heart disease.* ▣ *The government plans to increase the number of police officers.*

▶ NOUN /'ɪnkriːs/ [plural **increases**]

1 a rise in amount or size □ *price increases* □ **+ in** *There's been a big increase in sales.*

2 on the increase happening more often than before, or becoming bigger in amount □ *Violent crime is on the increase.* □ *House prices are on the increase.*

● **increasing** /ɪn'kriːsɪŋ/ ADJECTIVE becoming bigger in amount or size □ *An increasing number of people have a computer in their house.*

● **increasingly** /ɪn'kriːsɪŋlɪ/ ADVERB more and more □ *The need to reduce car use is becoming increasingly important.*

incredible /ɪn'kredəbəl/ ADJECTIVE

1 extremely good or great □ *To reach the finals is an incredible achievement.* □ *He showed incredible strength.*

2 difficult to believe □ *It's incredible that he didn't realize he was so ill.*

● **incredibly** /ɪn'kredəblɪ/ ADVERB

1 used for saying that something is difficult to believe □ *Incredibly, no one was injured in the accident.*

2 extremely □ *She's incredibly beautiful.*

incredulous /ɪn'kredjuləs/ ADJECTIVE unable to believe something □ *Don't sound so incredulous*

increment /'ɪnkrɪmənt/ NOUN [plural **increments**] one of a series of increases, especially in the money you earn for doing a job

incriminate /ɪnˈkrɪmɪneɪt/ VERB [**incriminates, incriminating, incriminated**] to show that someone has taken part in a crime □ *All the evidence incriminated her.*

incubator /ˈɪnkjubeɪtə(r)/ NOUN [plural **incubators**]
1 a piece of hospital equipment that a premature (= born too early) or ill baby lives in while it has medical treatment
2 a piece of equipment that keeps eggs warm until a baby bird comes out

incur /ɪnˈkɜː(r)/ VERB [**incurs, incurring, incurred**] to get something unpleasant because of what you have done. A formal word. □ *Any member of the team who breaks the rules will incur a penalty.*

incurable /ɪnˈkjʊərəbəl/ ADJECTIVE an incurable illness cannot be cured

indecency /ɪnˈdiːsənsɪ/ NOUN, NO PLURAL behaviour that shocks and offends people
• **indecent** /ɪnˈdiːsənt/ ADJECTIVE shocking and offensive □ *indecent pictures*

indeed /ɪnˈdiːd/ ADVERB
1 used to emphasize what you are saying □ *He was driving very fast indeed.* □ *It was indeed a mistake.*
2 a formal word used to add something which supports what you have just said □ *The Internet has become very popular. Indeed most people now have Internet access at home.*
3 used when someone has said something annoying or surprising □ *'Mum, James said he wasn't going to do his homework.' 'Did he, indeed?'*

indefensible /ˌɪndɪˈfensəbəl/ ADJECTIVE too bad to be excused □ *His behaviour was completely indefensible.*

indefinite /ɪnˈdefɪnɪt/ ADJECTIVE not having a fixed limit □ *He was jailed for an indefinite period.*

indefinite article /ɪnˌdefɪnɪt ˈɑːtɪkəl/ NOUN [plural **indefinite articles**] the word *a* or the word *an*

> ➤ There are two types of article in English grammar: **a** or **an** is the *indefinite article* and **the** is the *definite article.*

indefinitely /ɪnˈdefɪnɪtlɪ/ ADVERB for a period of time with no fixed limits □ *The game was postponed indefinitely.*

indelible /ɪnˈdeləbəl/ ADJECTIVE impossible to remove or forget □ *indelible ink* □ *indelible memories*

independence /ˌɪndɪˈpendəns/ NOUN, NO PLURAL
1 when a country is not controlled by another country ⌨ *East Timor gained independence in 2002.*
2 when someone does not depend on other people for help □ *financial independence*
• **independent** /ˌɪndɪˈpendənt/ ADJECTIVE
1 not controlled by another government or organization □ *independent companies* □ *+ from Mozambique became independent from Portugal in 1975.* □ *+ of The council will be independent of the government.*

2 fair because of not being influenced by anyone or anything ⌨ *The business was valued by an independent expert.* ⌨ *An independent inquiry was launched after a man died while being arrested.*
3 not depending on other people for help □ *My great-grandmother's 90 but she's very independent.* ⌨ *Some students are financially independent.*

indestructible /ˌɪndɪˈstrʌktəbəl/ ADJECTIVE too strong to be destroyed

index /ˈɪndeks/ NOUN [plural **indexes** or **indices**]
1 an alphabetical list in a book that tells you what page you can find information on □ *Look up 'wild flowers' in the index.*
2 a system that is used to compare things, especially prices, and to record changes □ *The Nikkei stock market index has risen by 40%.*

index finger /ˈɪndeks ˌfɪŋgə(r)/ NOUN [plural **index fingers**] the finger that is next to your thumb

indicate /ˈɪndɪkeɪt/ VERB [**indicates, indicating, indicated**]
1 to show that something is true or that something exists □ *The study indicates that 70% of road accidents happen on country roads.*
2 to show an intention or opinion, though not directly □ *He has indicated a willingness to help.*
3 to show someone what they should look at or where they should go □ *There was an arrow indicating where to go.*
4 to show which way you are going to turn in a vehicle □ *Always indicate before turning.*
• **indication** /ˌɪndɪˈkeɪʃən/ NOUN [plural **indications**] a sign of something □ *This comment was an indication of his state of mind at the time.* ⌨ *Did he give you any indication when it would be finished?*
• **indicative** /ɪnˈdɪkətɪv/ ADJECTIVE indicative of something showing that something is true or that something exists. A formal phrase. □ *These symptoms could be indicative of a more serious illness.*
• **indicator** /ˈɪndɪkeɪtə(r)/ NOUN [plural **indicators**]
1 something which shows you how successful or healthy something is ⌨ *Your resting heart rate is a good indicator of your general fitness.*
2 a flashing light on a car that shows which way the car is going to turn

indifference /ɪnˈdɪfərəns/ NOUN, NO PLURAL when someone shows no interest in someone or something and does not care about them □ *He showed complete indifference to their suffering.*
• **indifferent** /ɪnˈdɪfərənt/ ADJECTIVE
1 not interested in something or someone and not caring about them □ *Clare was indifferent to his feelings.*
2 not good but not bad □ *The hotel was nice but the food was fairly indifferent.*

indigenous /ɪnˈdɪdʒɪnəs/ ADJECTIVE having always existed in a place and not coming to it from somewhere else □ *The domestic cat isn't actually indigenous to Europe.*

indigestion /ˌɪndɪ'dʒestʃən/ NOUN, NO PLURAL an uncomfortable feeling in your stomach after you have eaten

indignant /ɪn'dɪgnənt/ ADJECTIVE angry because you think you have been treated unfairly □ *The company received letters of complaint from indignant customers.*
• **indignation** /ˌɪndɪg'neɪʃən/ NOUN, NO PLURAL being indignant

indignity /ɪn'dɪgnətɪ/ NOUN [plural **indignities**] a situation that makes you feel ashamed, usually in front of other people 🔁 *They suffered the indignity of a 6-0 defeat.*

indigo /'ɪndɪgəʊ/ ► ADJECTIVE having a dark, purple-blue colour □ *an indigo sweater*
► NOUN, NO PLURAL a dark, purple-blue colour

indirect /ˌɪndɪ'rekt/ ADJECTIVE
1 not directly caused by something, or not directly related to something □ *indirect effects*
2 not saying something in an obvious and clear way □ *She made an indirect reference to her father.*
3 not going the shortest way □ *an indirect route*

indirect object /ˌɪndɪrekt 'ɒbdʒɪkt/ NOUN [plural **indirect objects**] in grammar, the person that something is given to, done to, etc. □ *In the sentence 'I bought my mother a watch.', 'mother' is the indirect object.*

indirect speech /ˌɪndɪrekt 'spiːtʃ/ NOUN, NO PLURAL reporting what someone said without repeating their exact words □ *'He said he would come with me' is an example of indirect speech.*

indiscreet /ˌɪndɪ'skriːt/ ADJECTIVE talking about subjects which should be private, often when the subject relates to other people □ *She can be very indiscreet.*

indiscriminate /ˌɪndɪ'skrɪmɪnət/ ADJECTIVE done to everyone or everything, without thinking about who or what will be harmed □ *indiscriminate attacks*

indispensable /ˌɪndɪ'spensəbəl/ ADJECTIVE someone or something that is indispensable is so useful that you cannot manage without them □ *The Internet is an indispensable tool for businesses.*

indistinct /ˌɪndɪ'stɪŋkt/ ADJECTIVE not easy to see, hear or remember □ *indistinct images*

individual /ˌɪndɪ'vɪdʒuəl/ ► ADJECTIVE
1 for or relating to one person only □ *The choice you make depends on your individual circumstances.*
2 considered separately from other things or people 🔁 *We do not comment on individual cases.* □ *Each individual school has its own rules.*
3 unusual and different in a way that is interesting □ *She is known for her highly individual designs.*
► NOUN [plural **individuals**] one person rather than a group □ *The medical study included 100 healthy individuals.*
• **individuality** /'ɪndɪˌvɪdʒu'æləti/ NOUN, NO PLURAL a quality that makes someone or something different from others

• **individually** /ˌɪndɪ'vɪdʒuəli/ ADVERB separately from other things or people □ *Wrap each glass individually.* □ *He talked to each student individually.*

indoctrinate /ɪn'dɒktrɪneɪt/ VERB [**indoctrinates, indoctrinating, indoctrinated**] to try to make someone have particular beliefs and not consider any others □ *Some religious groups were accused of indoctrinating children.*

indoor /'ɪndɔː(r)/ ADJECTIVE inside a building □ *an indoor swimming pool* □ *indoor activities* □ *indoor plants*
• **indoors** /ˌɪn'dɔːz/ ADVERB into or inside a building □ *It was cooler indoors.* 🔁 *Police warned people to stay indoors.* 🔁 *We went indoors because it started to rain.*

induce /ɪn'djuːs/ VERB [**induces, inducing, induced**]
1 a formal word meaning to persuade someone to do something □ *Nothing would induce him to move back to the city.*
2 a formal word meaning to cause a particular feeling or state □ *The drug is used to induce sleep.*
• **inducement** /ɪn'djuːsmənt/ NOUN [plural **inducements**] something that is offered to someone as a way of persuading them to do something □ *financial inducements*

induction course /ɪn'dʌkʃən ˌkɔːs/ NOUN [plural **induction courses**] a training course for a company's new employees

indulge /ɪn'dʌldʒ/ VERB [**indulges, indulging, indulged**]
1 to allow yourself to do or have something because you enjoy it □ *He regularly indulged in his favourite breakfast of pancakes and syrup.*
2 to allow someone to do or have anything they want □ *Indulging children by buying them everything they want is not good.*
• **indulgence** /ɪn'dʌldʒəns/ NOUN [plural **indulgences**]
1 indulging yourself or someone else □ *He led a life of indulgence.*
2 something expensive or special that you have because you want it and not because you need it □ *I didn't need a new bike - it was a complete in dulgence.*
• **indulgent** /ɪn'dʌldʒənt/ ADJECTIVE allowing someone to do or have everything they want □ *indulgent parents*

industrial /ɪn'dʌstrɪəl/ ADJECTIVE
1 relating to industry and factories □ *industrial laws* □ *Industrial production fell last month.* □ *Pollution is caused by industrial processes.*
2 an industrial place has a lot of industries in it □ *industrial towns*
• **industrialization** or **industrialisation** /ɪnˌdʌstrɪəlaɪ'zeɪʃən/ NOUN, NO PLURAL the process of developing industries in a country □ *China's rapid industrialization*

• **industrialized** or **industrialised** /ɪn'dʌstrɪəlaɪzd/ ADJECTIVE an industrialized country or area has a lot of industries in it

industrious /ɪn'dʌstrɪəs/ ADJECTIVE working very hard □ *an industrious student*

industry /'ɪndəstrɪ/ ▶ NOUN [plural **industries**]
1 no plural the production of goods, especially in a factory □ *The chemical is widely used in industry.*
🕮 *Heavy industry* (= production of large goods) *has almost disappeared from the area.*
2 all the companies involved in one particular type of trade or service □ *She had a successful career in the music industry.* □ *The violence has damaged the country's tourism industry.* □ *Electricity and gas industries are facing rising costs.*
▶ ADJECTIVE to do with industry or a particular industry
🕮 *Industry experts have predicted an increase in online fraud.* 🕮 *Industry leaders met to discuss the new proposals.*

inedible /ɪn'edɪbəl/ ADJECTIVE too bad to eat □ *The meal was completely inedible.*

ineffective /ˌɪnɪ'fektɪv/ ADJECTIVE not achieving the result you want □ *The drug is ineffective against this form of the disease.*

ineffectual /ˌɪnɪ'fektʃuəl/ ADJECTIVE
1 achieving very little □ *The government's response to the disaster was largely ineffectual.*
2 not able to do something well □ *an ineffectual leader*

inefficiency /ˌɪnɪ'fɪʃənsɪ/ NOUN [plural **inefficiencies**] being inefficient, or something that is inefficient □ *the inefficiency of the government*

• **inefficient** /ˌɪnɪ'fɪʃənt/ ADJECTIVE not using energy, time, money, etc. in the most effective way □ *an inefficient heating system* □ *The project is an inefficient use of taxpayers' money.*

ineligible /ɪn'elɪdʒəbəl/ ADJECTIVE not allowed to have or do something because of a rule or law □ *You are ineligible to vote until you are 18.*

inept /ɪ'nept/ ADJECTIVE having or showing no skill □ *an inept performance*

inequality /ˌɪnɪ'kwɒlətɪ/ NOUN [plural **inequalities**] when some people have more power, money, opportunities, etc. than other people □ *We need to tackle social inequality.*

inert /ɪ'nɜːt/ ADJECTIVE
1 not moving □ *He lay inert on the floor.*
2 inert substances do not produce a reaction with other substances. A chemistry word.

inertia /ɪ'nɜːʃə/ NOUN, NO PLURAL
1 when nobody does anything and nothing changes
2 the force that keeps something in the same position, or makes something continue moving until something else stops it. A physics word.

inevitable /ɪn'evɪtəbəl/ ▶ ADJECTIVE certain to happen and not possible to avoid □ *Further conflict in the region is inevitable.*
▶ NOUN, NO PLURAL the inevitable something which is certain to happen □ *Then one day, the inevitable*

happened, and he was called to the headteacher's office.

inexcusable /ˌɪnɪk'skjuːzəbəl/ ADJECTIVE too bad to be excused □ *inexcusable behaviour*

inexpensive /ˌɪnɪk'spensɪv/ ADJECTIVE cheap □ *The shop has a wide selection of inexpensive kitchen equipment.*

inexperience /ˌɪnɪk'spɪərɪəns/ NOUN, NO PLURAL not having much experience of something □ *His mistake was put down to youthful inexperience.*

• **inexperienced** /ˌɪnɪk'spɪərɪənst/ ADJECTIVE not having much experience or knowledge of something □ *Insurance premiums are high for inexperienced young drivers.*

inexplicable /ˌɪnɪk'splɪkəbəl/ ADJECTIVE impossible to explain □ *Daisy felt an inexplicable urge to scream.*

inextricably /ˌɪnɪk'strɪkəblɪ/ ADVERB if things are inextricably connected, you cannot separate them □ *In the book, fact and fiction are inextricably linked.*

infallible /ɪn'fæləbəl/ ADJECTIVE
1 never making a mistake □ *Like most of my friends, I assumed our teachers were infallible.*
2 certain to work or be successful □ *I have an infallible method for making jam.*

infamous /'ɪnfəməs/ ADJECTIVE famous for doing something bad

• **infamy** /'ɪnfəmɪ/ NOUN, NO PLURAL being famous for doing something bad

infancy /'ɪnfənsɪ/ NOUN, NO PLURAL
1 the time when someone is a baby or a very young child
2 in its infancy only just beginning to exist or develop □ *This technology is still in its infancy.*

• **infant** /'ɪnfənt/ NOUN [plural **infants**] a baby or a very young child

• **infantile** /'ɪnfəntaɪl/ ADJECTIVE behaving in a silly way, like a young child □ *I'm sick of his infantile jokes.*

infantry /'ɪnfəntrɪ/ NOUN, NO PLURAL soldiers who fight on foot

infatuated /ɪn'fætʃueɪtɪd/ ADJECTIVE loving someone very much in a way that seems silly because you do not know them very well □ *She's completely infatuated with him.*

infect /ɪn'fekt/ VERB [infects, infecting, infected]
1 to give someone an illness □ **+ with** *Several patients were infected with the virus.*
2 if a computer is infected with a virus (= harmful program), it is damaged because of it. A computing word.
3 if a place, cut or substance is infected, it contains bacteria that cause disease □ *The wound had become infected.*
4 to make other people have the same feeling as you □ *She infected us all with her enthusiasm.*

• **infection** /ɪn'fekʃən/ NOUN [plural **infections**]
1 a disease that is caused by bacteria, a virus, etc. □ *an ear infection*
2 no plural the process of becoming infected □ *The hospital has taken steps to prevent infection.*

- **infectious** /ɪnˈfekʃəs/ ADJECTIVE
1 an infectious disease can be passed from one person to another ⊞ *The virus is highly infectious.*
2 infectious feelings or laughter quickly spread to other people □ *You have such an infectious laugh.* □ *His enthusiasm was infectious.*

infer /ɪnˈfɜː(r)/ VERB [**infers, inferring, inferred**] to form an opinion from information you already know □ *I inferred from our conversation that she was unhappy at home.*

- **inference** /ˈɪnfərəns/ NOUN [plural **inferences**] something that you think is true because of information you already know

inferior /ɪnˈfɪərɪə(r)/ ▶ ADJECTIVE not as good as someone or something else □ *Amy often felt inferior to the other women in the office.* □ *This cake was made with inferior ingredients.*
▶ NOUN [plural **inferiors**] someone who is less important or not as good as someone else □ *She treated him like a social inferior.*

- **inferiority** /ɪnˌfɪərɪˈɒrətɪ/ NOUN, NO PLURAL being or feeling inferior to someone or something else □ *Charles commented on the inferiority of the wine.*

inferno /ɪnˈfɜːnəʊ/ NOUN [plural **infernos**] a large and dangerous fire

infertile /ɪnˈfɜːtaɪl/ ADJECTIVE
1 infertile land does not produce good crops
2 an infertile person or animal cannot have babies

- **infertility** /ˌɪnfəˈtɪlətɪ/ NOUN, NO PLURAL when a person, animal or piece of land is infertile ⊞ *Doctors have suggested infertility treatment* (= medical treatment to help a woman become pregnant).

infest /ɪnˈfest/ VERB [**infests, infesting, infested**] if animals, insects or plants that you do not want infest a place, there are a lot of them there □ *The whole house was infested with mice.*

infiltrate /ˈɪnfɪltreɪt/ VERB [**infiltrates, infiltrating, infiltrated**] to join an organization or group secretly in order to get information about it □ *The journalist had infiltrated the gang to get a story.*

infinite /ˈɪnfɪnət/ ADJECTIVE
1 without any limits or end □ *The universe is infinite.*
2 very great □ *My maths teacher had infinite patience with me.*

- **infinitely** /ˈɪnfɪnətlɪ/ ADVERB very much □ *This computer is infinitely better than the last one.*

infinitive /ɪnˈfɪnɪtɪv/ NOUN [plural **infinitives**] the basic form of a verb that can be used to make all the other forms, for example *to play* or *to eat*

infinity /ɪnˈfɪnətɪ/ NOUN, NO PLURAL
1 space or time that has no end or limit
2 the largest possible number. A maths word.

infirm /ɪnˈfɜːm/ ADJECTIVE weak, especially because of being old or ill

- **infirmary** /ɪnˈfɜːmərɪ/ NOUN [plural **infirmaries**] used in the name of some hospitals □ *Sunderland Eye Infirmary*

- **infirmity** /ɪnˈfɜːmətɪ/ NOUN [plural **infirmities**] an

illness, or when someone is weak because of being old or ill

inflamed /ɪnˈfleɪmd/ ADJECTIVE red and swollen because of an infection □ *Her eyes were inflamed and sore.*

inflammable /ɪnˈflæməbəl/ ADJECTIVE inflammable substances burn very easily □ *Paper is highly inflammable.*

inflammation /ˌɪnfləˈmeɪʃən/ NOUN [plural **inflammations**] swelling, pain and sometimes red skin in part of your body □ *The drug will reduce the inflammation in your joints.*

inflatable /ɪnˈfleɪtəbəl/ ADJECTIVE an inflatable object must be filled with air before you use it □ *They crossed the river in an inflatable dinghy.*

inflate /ɪnˈfleɪt/ VERB [**inflates, inflating, inflated**] to fill something with air □ *The tyres need to be inflated.*

- **inflation** /ɪnˈfleɪʃən/ NOUN, NO PLURAL
1 when prices increase or the rate at which they increase □ *The priority is to keep inflation low.*
2 when something is filled with air

inflect /ɪnˈflekt/ VERB [**inflects, inflecting, inflected**]
1 when a word inflects, it changes its ending to show number, tense etc. so that it is suitable for the words it is with
2 to change the way your voice sounds, for example to show you are asking a question

- **inflection** /ɪnˈflekʃən/ NOUN [plural **inflections**]
1 a change in the form of a word to show its tense, number, etc. so that it is suitable for the words it is with
2 a word that has been changed in this way. For example, *finds, finding* and *found* are inflections of the verb *find*
3 when you change the way your voice sounds, for example to show you are asking a question

inflexible /ɪnˈfleksəbəl/ ADJECTIVE
1 unwilling to change or impossible for someone to change □ *an inflexible attitude* □ *inflexible rules*
2 stiff and unable to bend □ *inflexible plastic*

inflict /ɪnˈflɪkt/ VERB [**inflicts, inflicting, inflicted**] to make someone suffer something unpleasant or painful □ *The home team inflicted a heavy defeat on the visitors.*

in-flight /ˈɪnˌflaɪt/ ADJECTIVE happening or provided during a flight □ *The standard of in-flight meals has improved greatly.*

influence /ˈɪnfluəns/ ▶ NOUN [plural **influences**]
1 the power to affect other people or things □ *+ over He has considerable influence over his colleagues.* □ *+ on Exchange rates have a big influence on our business.* ⊞ *He was found guilty of driving under the influence of alcohol.*
2 someone or something that has an effect on other people or things □ *Ann is a good influence on you.* □ *Her films reflect her diverse cultural influences.*
▶ VERB [**influences, influencing, influenced**] to have an effect on someone or something □ *His advice*

influenced my decision. □ *My early work was influenced by Samuel Beckett.*

• **influential** /ˌɪnfluˈenʃəl/ ADJECTIVE having a lot of influence 🕮 *He was one of the most influential figures in Hollywood at that time.*

influenza /ˌɪnfluˈenzə/ NOUN, NO PLURAL a formal word for flu (= illness like a very bad cold)

influx /ˈɪnflʌks/ NOUN [plural **influxes**] when a lot of people or things come to a place □ *There has been an influx of tourists from the mainland.*

info /ˈɪnfəʊ/ NOUN, NO PLURAL an informal word for information

inform /ɪnˈfɔːm/ VERB [**informs, informing, informed**] to tell someone about something, especially officially □ *If you trespass again I'll inform the police.* □ **+ that** *We were informed that our luggage had been lost.* □ **+ of** *I'll inform you of my decision.* 🕮 *Please keep me informed of your whereabouts.*

informal /ɪnˈfɔːməl/ ADJECTIVE
1 relaxed and friendly, or suitable for relaxed occasions □ *The meeting was an informal affair.* □ *We can wear informal clothes to the office at weekends.*
2 informal language and words can be used when you are speaking to your friends, but they are not as suitable for writing

informant /ɪnˈfɔːmənt/ NOUN [plural **informants**] someone who gives information to someone else

information /ˌɪnfəˈmeɪʃən/ NOUN, NO PLURAL facts about someone or something □ **+ on** *Have you got any information on things to do in the area?* □ **+ about** *I gave him some information about our services.* 🕮 *The report provides a lot of information about medical errors.* 🕮 *For further information visit our website.* 🕮 *That is a very interesting piece of information.*

► Remember that **information** cannot be used in the plural:
  ✓ *I got some* **information** *off the Internet.*
  ✗ *I got some informations off the Internet.*
► To talk about one fact about a subject and not many facts, use the phrase **piece of information**:
  □ *Here's a useful* **piece of information.**

---

information technology /ˈɪnfəˌmeɪʃən tekˈnɒlədʒɪ/ NOUN, NO PLURAL the study or use of computers to store, send or use information

---

► You will often see the abbreviation for information technology, which is **IT**.

---

informative /ɪnˈfɔːmətɪv/ ADJECTIVE giving you a lot of useful information □ *I found her article very informative.*

informed /ɪnˈfɔːmd/ ADJECTIVE having enough information or knowledge about something 🕮 *Parents should be able to make an informed decision about their children's education.*

informer /ɪnˈfɔːmə(r)/ NOUN [plural **informers**] someone who secretly gives information about a crime to the police

infrared /ˌɪnfrəˈred/ ADJECTIVE infrared light cannot be seen but gives out heat

infrastructure /ˈɪnfrəˌstrʌktʃə(r)/ NOUN, NO PLURAL the basic systems and services, such as transport, communications, water and power, that a country or organization needs to operate

infrequent /ɪnˈfriːkwənt/ ADJECTIVE not happening very often □ *an infrequent bus service*

• **infrequently** /ɪnˈfriːkwəntlɪ/ ADVERB not often

infringe /ɪnˈfrɪndʒ/ VERB [**infringes, infringing, infringed**]
1 to limit someone's rights or freedom □ *People see the introduction of identity cards as infringing on their civil liberties.*
2 to break a law or rule □ *Their policies may infringe EU law.*

• **infringement** /ɪnˈfrɪndʒmənt/ NOUN [plural **infringements**]
1 when someone's rights or freedom are limited □ *This is a serious infringement on public freedom.*
2 the act of breaking a law or rule □ *an infringement of building regulations*

infuriate /ɪnˈfjʊərɪeɪt/ VERB [**infuriates, infuriating, infuriated**] to make someone very angry

• **infuriated** /ɪnˈfjʊərɪeɪtɪd/ ADJECTIVE extremely angry

• **infuriating** /ɪnˈfjʊərɪeɪtɪŋ/ ADJECTIVE making you extremely angry □ *I find his behaviour absolutely infuriating.*

ingenious /ɪnˈdʒiːnɪəs/ ADJECTIVE clever and involving new ideas □ *He came up with an ingenious scheme to make money.*

• **ingenuity** /ˌɪndʒɪˈnjuːətɪ/ NOUN, NO PLURAL skill at inventing things or solving problems □ *The size of the building was a challenge to the architects' ingenuity.*

ingot /ˈɪŋɡət/ NOUN [plural **ingots**] a block of metal, especially gold or silver

ingrained /ɪnˈɡreɪnd/ ADJECTIVE
1 if behaviour or opinions are ingrained, they have existed for a long time and are difficult to change □ *Texting has become ingrained in our culture.*
2 ingrained dirt has been rubbed in and is difficult to get out

ingratitude /ɪnˈɡrætɪtjuːd/ NOUN, NO PLURAL when someone is not grateful

ingredient /ɪnˈɡriːdɪənt/ NOUN [plural **ingredients**]
1 one of the things you use to make a particular food □ *Mix the dry ingredients in a bowl.*
2 one of the qualities something needs to be successful □ *Music is an essential ingredient of most teenagers' lives.*

inhabit /ɪnˈhæbɪt/ VERB [**inhabits, inhabiting, inhabited**] to live in a particular place □ *The series looks at the creatures that inhabit our planet.*

• **inhabitant** /ɪnˈhæbɪtənt/ NOUN [plural **inhabitants**] someone who lives in a place □ *There are* differences between the inhabitants of the two islands.

• **inhabited** /ɪnˈhæbɪtɪd/ ADJECTIVE with people living there □ The south-east is the most densely inhabited area of England.

inhale /ɪnˈheɪl/ VERB [inhales, inhaling, inhaled] to breathe air, smoke, etc. into your lungs □ She inhaled deeply.

• **inhaler** /ɪnˈheɪlə(r)/ NOUN [plural inhalers] a small tube which contains medicine to help you breathe more easily if you have asthma (= an illness that makes it difficult to breathe)

inherent /ɪnˈhɪərənt, ɪnˈherənt/ ADJECTIVE being a basic and permanent part of something □ We cannot ignore the risks inherent in gambling.

• **inherently** /ɪnˈhɪərəntlɪ, ɪnˈherəntlɪ/ ADVERB in a basic and permanent way □ The scheme is inherently flawed.

inherit /ɪnˈherɪt/ VERB [inherits, inheriting, inherited]
1 to receive money or other possessions from someone who has died □ Imogen inherited the house from her father.
2 to get a particular characteristic from one of your parents □ I inherited my fair hair from my mother.
3 to be left with a particular situation or problem by someone who has been in your position before you □ The new government has inherited a failing transport system.

• **inheritance** /ɪnˈherɪtəns/ NOUN [plural inheritances]
1 money or possessions that you receive from someone who has died □ She lived on a small inheritance from her grandmother.
2 when you receive a characteristic from one of your parents □ They are carrying out research into the inheritance of certain diseases.

inhibit /ɪnˈhɪbɪt/ VERB [inhibits, inhibiting, inhibited]
1 to prevent something from happening or to make it happen more slowly □ The drug may inhibit the growth of bacteria.
2 to make someone feel nervous or embarrassed so that they do not behave in a natural way □ He was inhibited by the presence of TV cameras.

• **inhibited** /ɪnˈhɪbɪtɪd/ ADJECTIVE not feeling relaxed or confident enough to do or say what you want □ Teenagers often feel inhibited in adult company.

• **inhibition** /ˌɪnhɪˈbɪʃən/ NOUN [plural inhibitions] a feeling of being nervous or embarrassed that stops you doing or saying what you want ⊞ The children soon lost their inhibitions and joined in the dancing.

inhospitable /ˌɪnhɒˈspɪtəbəl/ ADJECTIVE
1 an inhospitable place is not pleasant to live in because it is too hot, cold, dangerous, etc. □ The jungles of South America are the most inhospitable places on earth.
2 not friendly and welcoming □ When we arrived, Guy was most inhospitable.

inhuman /ˌɪnˈhjuːmən/ ADJECTIVE extremely cruel □ His treatment of the prisoners was inhuman.

inhumane /ˌɪnhjuːˈmeɪn/ ADJECTIVE treating people or animals in an extremely cruel way □ They campaigned against inhumane methods of rearing chickens.

inhumanity /ˌɪnhjuːˈmænətɪ/ NOUN, NO PLURAL extremely cruel behaviour □ They were shocked by the inhumanity of prison life.

initial /ɪˈnɪʃəl/ ▶ ADJECTIVE at the beginning ⊞ Initial reports suggest the crash was caused by engine failure. ⊞ My initial reaction was horror.
▶ NOUN [plural initials] the first letter of a word, especially someone's name □ His initials are J.C.

• **initially** /ɪˈnɪʃəlɪ/ ADVERB in the beginning □ Initially, things were very difficult.

initiate /ɪˈnɪʃɪeɪt/ VERB [initiates, initiating, initiated]
1 to start something □ Max initiated the conversation.
2 to accept someone into a group or organization with a special ceremony □ He was initiated into the priesthood at the age of 25.
3 to teach someone about something they know nothing about □ I was initiated into the art of making jam.

• **initiation** /ɪˌnɪʃɪˈeɪʃən/ NOUN [plural initiations]
1 when something is started by someone □ He is responsible for the initiation and design of new wind farms.
2 when someone is accepted into a group or organization □ an initiation ceremony
3 when someone is taught something new □ That was my initiation into the world of drug companies.

• **initiative** /ɪˈnɪʃətɪv/ NOUN [plural initiatives]
1 a new plan or process to solve a problem or improve a situation □ The government has introduced an initiative to keep teenagers in school
2 the ability to do something without waiting for someone else to tell you what to do □ He showed great initiative when dealing with customers' complaints. ⊞ Eventually Mia took the initiative (= decided what should be done) and called a taxi.

inject /ɪnˈdʒekt/ VERB [injects, injecting, injected]
1 to put a substance into someone's body using a needle □ She has to inject herself with insulin every day.
2 to add a particular quality to a situation □ Leah tried to inject some enthusiasm into her voice.
3 to provide money for something □ Local businesses have agreed to inject cash into the club.

• **injection** /ɪnˈdʒekʃən/ NOUN [plural injections]
1 when a substance is injected into someone's body □ insulin injections
2 when money is provided □ They need a huge injection of funds.
3 when a quality is added to a situation □ These people need an injection of reality.

injure /ˈɪndʒə(r)/ VERB [injures, injuring, injured]
1 to hurt someone or something □ Matt injured his knee in a skiing accident.
2 to harm something □ The fall injured her pride.

• **injured** /'ɪndʒəd/ ▶ ADJECTIVE hurt □ *Fiona was badly injured in a road accident.*
▶ NOUN, NO PLURAL the injured people who are injured □ *The injured were rushed to hospital.*
• **injury** /'ɪndʒəri/ NOUN [plural **injuries**] damage to part of your body ⊞ *a serious head injury* ⊞ *He was lucky to suffer only minor injuries in the crash.*

injustice /ɪn'dʒʌstɪs/ NOUN [plural **injustices**] when people are treated unfairly or an action that is unfair □ *I was hurt by the injustice of her criticism.*

ink /ɪŋk/ NOUN [plural **inks**] a coloured liquid used for writing or printing

inkling /'ɪŋklɪŋ/ NOUN, NO PLURAL a slight idea that something might happen or be true □ *Sheila had no inkling of what awaited her.*

inland ▶ ADJECTIVE /'ɪnlənd/ not by the sea □ *Britain's inland waterways*
▶ ADVERB /ɪn'lænd/ in a direction away from the sea □ *The people fled inland to escape the tsunami.*

in-laws /'ɪnlɔːz/ PLURAL NOUN the relations of your husband or wife □ *I'm spending Christmas with my in-laws.*

inlet /'ɪnlet/ NOUN [plural **inlets**] a narrow area of water that flows into the land from the sea

inmate /'ɪnmeɪt/ NOUN [plural **inmates**] someone who is being kept in a prison

inn /ɪn/ NOUN [plural **inns**] a small hotel or pub, especially in the countryside

innate /ɪ'neɪt/ ADJECTIVE innate qualities and abilities are ones that you are born with, or ones that are very natural for you □ *He had an innate sense of justice.*

inner /'ɪnə(r)/ ADJECTIVE
1 on the inside or close to the centre of something □ *She kept her purse in the inner pocket of her bag.*
2 near the centre of a city □ *inner London*
3 inner feelings or thoughts are private and secret

inner city /ˌɪnə 'sɪti/ NOUN [plural **inner cities**] an area in the centre of a large city, often with social problems □ *We are failing the children in our inner cities.*
• **inner-city** ADJECTIVE from or to do with an inner city □ *inner-city schools/neighbourhoods*

innermost /'ɪnəməʊst/ ADJECTIVE your innermost thoughts and feelings are private and secret

innings /'ɪnɪŋz/ NOUN [plural **innings**] the period of time when one player or team is hitting the ball in cricket

innocence /'ɪnəsəns/ NOUN, NO PLURAL
1 when someone is not guilty of a crime □ *New evidence proved his innocence.*
2 when someone does not have much experience of life □ *The bully took advantage of Billy's innocence.*
• **innocent** /'ɪnəsənt/ ADJECTIVE
1 not guilty of a crime □ *An innocent man had been hanged in error.* □ *She claims she is innocent of the crime.*

2 used to emphasize that someone who is hurt, injured or killed had done nothing wrong □ *Several innocent bystanders were caught in the crossfire.*
3 not intended to hurt or upset someone □ *It was a perfectly innocent remark but he was furious about it.*
4 not having much experience of life □ *The film is not suitable for innocent children.*
• **innocently** /'ɪnəsəntli/ ADVERB
1 in a way that is not intended to hurt or upset anyone □ *He acted quite innocently.*
2 in a way that is intended to make people think you are not guilty □ *I smiled innocently at her.*

innovation /ˌɪnə'veɪʃən/ NOUN [plural **innovations**] something completely new, especially a new method of doing something □ *He keeps up with all the latest innovations in medicine.*
• **innovative** /'ɪnəvətɪv/ ADJECTIVE using new and original ideas □ *His book is an innovative approach to reducing stress.*

innuendo /ˌɪnju'endəʊ/ NOUN [plural **innuendos** or **innuendoes**] a remark that is intended to express something rude or unpleasant in a way that is not direct

inoculate /ɪ'nɒkjʊleɪt/ VERB [inoculates, inoculating, inoculated] to protect someone from a disease by injecting (= putting a substance into the body with a needle) them with a substance containing a very small amount of the disease □ *Babies are inoculated against measles.*
• **inoculation** /ɪˌnɒkjʊ'leɪʃən/ NOUN [plural **inoculations**] when someone is inoculated

inoffensive /ˌɪnə'fensɪv/ ADJECTIVE not likely to offend or upset anyone □ *His type of humour is very inoffensive.*

inordinate /ɪn'ɔːdɪnət/ ADJECTIVE much greater than is usual or reasonable □ *She spends an inordinate length of time in the bathroom every morning.*
• **inordinately** /ɪn'ɔːdɪnətli/ ADVERB much more than is usual or reasonable □ *Their goods are inordinately expensive.*

inorganic /ˌɪnɔː'gænɪk/ ADJECTIVE not a living thing or not made from living things. A chemistry word. □ *inorganic materials*

in-patient /'ɪnpeɪʃənt/ NOUN [plural **in-patients**] someone who is staying in a hospital for treatment

input /'ɪnpʊt/ ▶ NOUN, NO PLURAL
1 energy, ideas or money that you put into something to make it succeed □ *I had very little input in the project.*
2 information that is put into a computer. A computing word.
▶ VERB [inputs, inputting, input or inputted] to put information into a computer. A computing word □ *We paid someone to input all the names and addresses.*

inquest /'ɪnkwest/ NOUN [plural **inquests**] a legal process to find out how someone died ⊞ *An inquest will be held to establish the cause of death.*

inquire /ɪn'kwaɪə(r)/ VERB [inquires, inquiring, inquired] to ask for information about something

□ *He inquired how to get to the library.* □ *I'm inquiring about the job advertised in the paper.*

♦ PHRASAL VERB **inquire after someone** to ask how someone is or what they are doing, to be polite □ *Kevin inquired after your father.*

• **inquiry** /ɪnˈkwaɪərɪ/ NOUN [plural **inquiries**]
1 a question you ask in order to get information □ *We've had a number of inquiries about hybrid cars.*
2 an official process to find out why something happened □ *There was an inquiry into the children's deaths.* □ *He's helping police with their inquiries.*

inquisitive /ɪnˈkwɪzətɪv/ ADJECTIVE wanting to know about a lot of different things, and often asking a lot of questions □ *an inquisitive child*

• **inquisitively** /ɪnˈkwɪzətɪvlɪ/ ADVERB in an inquisitive way □ *She could see several neighbours peering inquisitively out of their windows.*

insane /ɪnˈseɪn/ ADJECTIVE
1 having a serious mental illness
2 very silly □ *Her work schedule is just insane.*

• **insanity** /ɪnˈsænətɪ/ NOUN, NO PLURAL
1 when someone has a serious mental illness
2 when something is very silly □ *Deciding to build our own house was just insanity.*

insatiable /ɪnˈseɪʃəbəl/ ADJECTIVE always wanting more of something 🔁 *She seems to have an insatiable appetite for celebrity gossip.*

inscribe /ɪnˈskraɪb/ VERB [inscribes, inscribing, inscribed] to cut or write words on the surface of something □ *We had her name inscribed on the back of the bracelet.*

• **inscription** /ɪnˈskrɪpʃən/ NOUN [plural inscriptions] words that are cut or written on something □ *We could not read the inscription on the medal.*

insect /ˈɪnsekt/ NOUN [plural **insects**] a small creature with six legs and often wings, for example a bee or a fly

insecure /ˌɪnsɪˈkjʊə(r)/ ADJECTIVE
1 not feeling confident □ *After her mother's death she became increasingly insecure.*
2 not safe or protected □ *Many jobs in banking are now insecure.*

• **insecurity** /ˌɪnsɪˈkjʊərətɪ/ NOUN [plural insecurities]
1 when someone is not confident □ *He suffers all the usual teenage insecurities*
2 when something is not safe or protected □ *They were concerned about the insecurity of the building.*

insensitive /ɪnˈsensətɪv/ ADJECTIVE
1 not noticing other people's feelings □ *She was always making insensitive remarks about her sister.*
2 not affected by physical things such as pain or cold □ *He seemed to be insensitive to the noise around him.*

• **insensitively** /ɪnˈsensətɪvlɪ/ ADVERB in an insensitive way

• **insensitivity** /ɪnˌsensəˈtɪvətɪ/ NOUN, NO PLURAL the state of being insensitive

inseparable /ɪnˈsepərəbəl/ ADJECTIVE not able to be separated or kept apart □ *At school we were inseparable.*

insert /ɪnˈsɜːt/ VERB [inserts, inserting, inserted] to put something into something else □ *He inserted some coins into the meter.* □ *You need to insert a few more examples.*

• **insertion** /ɪnˈsɜːʃən/ NOUN [plural insertions] when something is inserted into something else, or the thing that is inserted □ *He made several insertions in my text.*

inside ▶ PREPOSITION /ɪnˈsaɪd/
1 in or into a building, container or area □ *She put the book inside her bag.* □ *Draw a cross inside the box.*
2 in an organization, group of people, etc. □ *People inside the company know the truth.*
3 in less than a particular amount of time □ *We'll be there inside an hour.*

▶ ADVERB /ɪnˈsaɪd/
1 in or into a building □ *Come inside - you'll get cold.*
2 in or into a container or an area □ *Has that tin got anything inside?*
3 in someone's mind □ *I may have looked confident, but I was terrified inside.*

▶ ADJECTIVE /ˈɪnsaɪd/
1 in or facing the middle of something □ *Keep it in an inside pocket.*
2 provided by someone who is a member of an organization, group, etc. and knows about it 🔁 *She gave us some inside information about how the company works.*

▶ NOUN /ɪnˈsaɪd/ [plural insides]
1 the inside the part that is in the middle and not on the outside □ *The inside of his jacket was torn.*
2 inside out if clothes are inside out, the part that should be on the inside is on the outside □ *You've got your socks on inside out.*

insight /ˈɪnsaɪt/ NOUN [plural insights]
1 the ability to understand something clearly □ *Her book on depression showed great insight into the illness.*
2 the chance to understand something clearly □ *The book offers an insight into the mind of a killer.*

insignificant /ˌɪnsɪɡˈnɪfɪkənt/ ADJECTIVE not at all important □ *He spends too much time describing insignificant details.*

insincere /ˌɪnsɪnˈsɪə(r)/ ADJECTIVE pretending to feel something that you do not really feel □ *an insincere compliment*

• **insincerely** /ˌɪnsɪnˈsɪəlɪ/ ADVERB in an insincere way □ *The waiter smiled insincerely at us.*

• **insincerity** /ˌɪnsɪnˈserətɪ/ NOUN, NO PLURAL when someone is insincere

insipid /ɪnˈsɪpɪd/ ADJECTIVE boring, not strong or bright, or without much flavour □ *She served up a rather insipid lamb stew.*

insist /ɪnˈsɪst/ VERB [insists, insisting, insisted]
1 to say firmly that something must happen or be

done □ **+ on** *I always insist on a single room.* □ **+ on** *Fay insisted on paying.* □ **+ that** *The school insists that all students must wear full uniform.*
2 to keep saying firmly that something is true □ **+ that** *Mark insists that he hasn't done anything wrong.*
• **insistence** /ɪnˈsɪstəns/ NOUN, NO PLURAL
1 when you insist that something must happen or be done □ *At the chairman's insistence, another meeting was arranged.* □ *He soon rebelled against his mother's insistence on good manners.* □ *Some schools ignored the government's insistence that all children should learn a foreign language.*
2 when you insist that something is true □ *Despite his insistence that he was innocent, he was charged with murder.*
• **insistent** /ɪnˈsɪstənt/ ADJECTIVE insisting that something must happen or be done □ *Sarah was insistent that we should visit her.*

insolence /ˈɪnsələns/ NOUN, NO PLURAL behaviour that shows no respect or politeness
• **insolent** /ˈɪnsələnt/ ADJECTIVE rude and not showing respect □ *The headmaster will not tolerate insolent behaviour.*

insoluble /ɪnˈsɒljʊbəl/ ADJECTIVE
1 an insoluble substance cannot be dissolved
2 an insoluble problem, mystery, etc. is impossible to solve

insomnia /ɪnˈsɒmnɪə/ NOUN, NO PLURAL when you are not able to sleep □ *He has suffered from insomnia since he was a child.*
• **insomniac** /ɪnˈsɒmnɪæk/ NOUN [plural **insomniacs**] someone who regularly suffers from insomnia

inspect /ɪnˈspɛkt/ VERB [**inspects, inspecting, inspected**]
1 to look very carefully at someone or something □ *He inspected our documents closely.*
2 to officially visit a place to make sure that everything there is the way it should be □ *The school is to be inspected next week.*
• **inspection** /ɪnˈspɛkʃən/ NOUN [plural **inspections**]
1 when you look very carefully at someone or something ⊞ *On close inspection, I realized the note wasn't in Josh's handwriting.*
2 an official visit to inspect a place ⊞ *Public health officers carry out regular inspections of restaurants.*
• **inspector** /ɪnˈspɛktə(r)/ NOUN [plural **inspectors**]
1 someone whose job is to inspect a place such as a school or restaurant
2 a police officer with quite a high rank
3 someone whose job is to check tickets on a bus or train

inspiration /ˌɪnspəˈreɪʃən/ NOUN [plural **inspirations**]
1 someone or something that encourages you and gives you new ideas □ *I use the countryside as inspiration for my paintings.*
2 a sudden good idea ⊞ *Newton had a flash of inspiration when he saw the apple fall from the tree.*

3 be an inspiration to someone to be someone or something that everyone admires and would like to copy □ *Her courage is an inspiration to us all.*
• **inspirational** /ˌɪnspəˈreɪʃənəl/ ADJECTIVE giving you ideas and enthusiasm □ *She is an inspirational teacher.*

inspire /ɪnˈspaɪə(r)/ VERB [**inspires, inspiring, inspired**] to give someone ideas and enthusiasm □ *My mother inspired me to write stories.*
• **inspired** /ɪnˈspaɪəd/ ADJECTIVE showing a lot of ability and special qualities □ *He gave an inspired performance of the Schubert.*

instability /ˌɪnstəˈbɪlətɪ/ NOUN, NO PLURAL
1 when a situation keeps changing □ *The country went through a long period of economic instability.*
2 when someone's mental state keeps changing

install or **instal** /ɪnˈstɔːl/ VERB [**installs** or **instals, installing, installed**]
1 to put a piece of equipment in place and make it ready to use □ *We have installed central heating.*
2 to put software on to a computer to be used. A computing word □ *I installed the software and began the work.*
3 to give someone an important job or position □ *She was installed as Prime Minister in May.*
• **installation** /ˌɪnstəˈleɪʃən/ NOUN [plural **installations**]
1 when equipment or software is installed □ *They paid for the installation of a new kitchen.*
2 when someone is installed in a job or position
3 a building with equipment for a particular purpose, for example for the army or a large business □ *a military installation*

installment /ɪnˈstɔːlmənt/ NOUN [plural **installments**] the US spelling of instalment

instalment /ɪnˈstɔːlmənt/ NOUN [plural **instalments**]
1 one of a number of payments that you make for something □ *I paid the last instalment on the car today.*
2 one of several parts of a story in a magazine, on television, etc. □ *Don't miss next week's thrilling instalment!*

instance /ˈɪnstəns/ NOUN [plural **instances**]
1 for instance for example □ *Some birds, penguins for instance, cannot fly at all.*
2 an example of something □ *In some instances, legal action was taken.*

instant /ˈɪnstənt/ ▶ ADJECTIVE
1 happening immediately □ *The film was an instant success.*
2 able to be prepared very quickly □ *instant coffee*
▶ NOUN [plural **instants**]
1 a very short time □ *The doctor will be with you in an instant.*
2 a particular moment in time □ *At that very instant, the phone rang.*
• **instantaneous** /ˌɪnstənˈteɪnɪəs/ ADJECTIVE done or

happening immediately or very quickly □ *The search results are almost instantaneous.*

● **instantly** /'ɪnstəntlɪ/ ADVERB immediately □ *I recognized him instantly.*

instant messaging /ˌɪnstənt 'mesɪdʒɪŋ/ NOUN, NO PLURAL communicating by using the Internet in a way where you can reply to someone immediately when they send you a message. A computing word.

instead /ɪn'sted/ ADVERB in place of someone or something else □ *Bob was ill so Joe went instead.* □ **+ of** *You could use a pencil instead of a pen.* □ *Instead of moaning you could actually help.*

> ► Notice that when you put a verb after **instead**, you need the preposition **of** before the verb. Also, the verb must be in the *-ing* form: □ **Instead of** *lying in bed all day, you could work.*

instep /'ɪnstep/ NOUN [plural **insteps**] the raised top part of your foot

instigate /'ɪnstɪɡeɪt/ VERB [instigates, instigating, instigated] to make something happen, especially an official process □ *The committee has instigated an inquiry into the affair.*

● **instigation** /ˌɪnstɪ'ɡeɪʃən/ NOUN, NO PLURAL when something is instigated □ *A thorough investigation of the claims is being carried out at the instigation of the local MP.*

● **instigator** /'ɪnstɪɡeɪtə(r)/ NOUN [plural **instigators**] the person who instigates something

instil /ɪn'stɪl/ VERB [instils, instilling, instilled] to make someone think or feel something □ *We are trying to instil some confidence in these youngsters.*

instill /ɪn'stɪl/ VERB [instills, instilling, instilled] the US spelling of instil

instinct /'ɪnstɪŋkt/ NOUN [plural **instincts**] the natural way you react or behave without thinking or being taught □ *These animals have a strong survival instinct.* □ *My first instinct was to run away.*

● **instinctive** /ɪn'stɪŋktɪv/ ADJECTIVE behaving or reacting by instinct □ *Parents have an instinctive urge to protect their children.*

● **instinctively** /ɪn'stɪŋktɪvlɪ/ ADVERB in an instinctive way □ *I knew instinctively that something was wrong.*

institute /'ɪnstɪtjuːt/ ► NOUN [plural **institutes**] an organization where people study a particular subject □ *We have a training institute in Florida.*

► VERB [institutes, instituting, instituted] to start a new system, process, rule, etc. □ *The company has instituted a smoking ban.*

institution /ˌɪnstɪ'tjuːʃən/ NOUN [plural **institutions**]
1 a large organization □ *I have worked for several banks and other financial institutions.*
2 the act of starting a system, process, rule, etc. □ *We have seen the institution of new rules governing social work.*
3 a place where people are sent to be looked after, for example a prison or a hospital □ *Her aunt had spent years in a mental institution.*

4 a tradition or social custom that has lasted for a long time □ *the institution of marriage*

instruct /ɪn'strʌkt/ VERB [instructs, instructing, instructed]
1 to tell someone to do something □ *I instructed her to go straight home.*
2 to teach someone □ *Staff will be instructed in the correct use of the machinery.*

● **instruction** /ɪn'strʌkʃən/ NOUN [plural instructions]
1 instructions printed information about how to do something □ *Read the instructions before you begin.* 🖰 *Make sure you follow the instructions.*
2 something you are told to do □ *She stood there shouting instructions at us.*
3 *no plural* when you are taught something □ *I had a day's golf instruction.*

● **instructive** /ɪn'strʌktɪv/ ADJECTIVE providing a lot of useful information □ *It was a very instructive talk.*

● **instructor** /ɪn'strʌktə(r)/ NOUN [plural **instructors**] someone who teaches a sport or a skill □ *a driving instructor*

instrument /'ɪnstrʊmənt/ NOUN [plural instruments]
1 something used for making music, for example a violin or a piano 🖰 *She plays several musical instruments.*
2 a tool for doing a particular task □ *surgical instruments*
3 a piece of equipment that is used for measuring speed, fuel, height, etc. □ *He showed us the plane's instrument panel.*

● **instrumental** /ˌɪnstrʊ'mentəl/ ADJECTIVE
1 instrumental music is written for musical instruments and not singers
2 helpful in making something happen □ *His wife was instrumental in his success.*

insufficient /ˌɪnsə'fɪʃənt/ ADJECTIVE not enough □ *There was insufficient evidence to make an arrest.*

● **insufficiently** /ˌɪnsə'fɪʃəntlɪ/ ADVERB not enough □ *We were insufficiently prepared for the climate.*

insulate /'ɪnsjʊleɪt/ VERB [insulates, insulating, insulated] to cover something with a material that does not let electricity, heat or sound through □ *Make sure your loft is adequately insulated.*

● **insulation** /ˌɪnsjʊ'leɪʃən/ NOUN, NO PLURAL the process of insulating something, or the material used to do this

insulin /'ɪnsjʊlɪn/ NOUN, NO PLURAL a chemical produced in your body that controls the amount of sugar in your blood. A biology word.

insult ► VERB /ɪn'sʌlt/ [insults, insulting, insulted] to say or do something rude that offends someone □ *He was fired for insulting his line manager.*

► NOUN /'ɪnsʌlt/ [plural **insults**] a remark or action that is rude and offends someone □ *The crowd were hurling insults at the referee.* □ *To sell the jewellery is an insult to her memory.*

• **insulting** /ɪnˈsʌltɪŋ/ ADJECTIVE rude and offensive □ *I found her patronizing attitude insulting.*

insurance /ɪnˈʃɔːrəns/ NOUN, NO PLURAL an arrangement in which you pay a company money and they pay the costs if you have an accident or are ill, or if something you own is damaged or stolen □ *car insurance* 🔁 *I've taken out health insurance.*

insure /ɪnˈʃɔː(r)/ VERB [**insures, insuring, insured**] to pay money to a company who will pay the costs if you have an accident or are ill, or if something you own is damaged or stolen □ + *for She insured her jewellery for £50,000.* □ + *against Are you insured against loss of earnings?*

insurgent /ɪnˈsɜːdʒənt/ NOUN [*plural* **insurgents**] someone who is fighting against the government or army of their country

intact /ɪnˈtækt/ ADJECTIVE not broken or damaged □ *One of the mosaic floors has been preserved intact.*

intake /ˈɪnteɪk/ NOUN [*plural* **intakes**]
1 the amount of something that you eat, drink or take into your body □ *Doctors advise cutting down our daily intake of salt.*
2 an intake of breath a sudden breath in, often caused by shock □ *There was a sharp intake of breath when the result was announced.*
3 the group of people who start at a school, university, company, etc. at the same time

integer /ˈɪntɪdʒə(r)/ NOUN [*plural* **integers**] a whole number. A maths word.

integral /ˈɪntɪɡrəl/ ADJECTIVE forming a necessary and important part of something □ *Sport is an integral part of my life.*

integrate /ˈɪntɪɡreɪt/ VERB [**integrates, integrating, integrated**]
1 to become part of a group of people □ *Women have been fully integrated into the regiment.*
2 to combine two or more things so that they work well together □ *Transport planning should be integrated with energy policy.*

integrated circuit /ˈɪntɪˌɡreɪtɪd ˈsɜːkɪt/ NOUN [*plural* **integrated circuits**] a microchip (= small computer part) with a large number of electronic parts instead of several separate parts. A computing word.

integration /ˌɪntɪˈɡreɪʃən/ NOUN, NO PLURAL when people or things are integrated □ *She is studying the integration of minority groups into society.*

integrity /ɪnˈteɡrəti/ NOUN, NO PLURAL the quality of being honest and having high moral standards □ *Colleagues praised his integrity and devotion to his patients.*

intellect /ˈɪntəlekt/ NOUN [*plural* **intellects**]
1 your ability to think about things and understand them
2 a very intelligent person □ *He was one of the great intellects of the 20th century.*

intellectual /ˌɪntəˈlektjuəl/ ▶ ADJECTIVE
1 to do with the ability to think about things and understand them □ *intellectual development*

2 intellectual activities involve using your brain to understand complicated ideas
3 intelligent and interested in complicated ideas □ *He's very intellectual.*
▶ NOUN [*plural* **intellectuals**] someone who is intelligent and likes thinking about complicated ideas

intelligence /ɪnˈtelɪdʒəns/ NOUN, NO PLURAL
1 your ability to learn and understand things □ *No one is questioning your son's intelligence.*
2 secret information about other countries □ *During the war she worked in military intelligence.*
• **intelligent** /ɪnˈtelɪdʒənt/ ADJECTIVE
1 clever and able to understand things quickly 🔁 *These students are highly intelligent.*
2 showing intelligence □ *The report was an intelligent analysis of the prison system.*
• **intelligently** /ɪnˈtelɪdʒəntli/ ADVERB in an intelligent way □ *He spoke intelligently about politics.*

intelligible /ɪnˈtelɪdʒəbəl/ ADJECTIVE clear enough to understand □ *His handwriting was barely intelligible.* □ *This kind of explanation is simply not intelligible to a young child.*

intend /ɪnˈtend/ VERB [**intends, intending, intended**]
1 to plan to do something □ + *to do something I intend to visit Will when I'm in Seattle.* □ + *ing They intended staying longer but their money ran out.*
2 be intended for someone/something to be designed or made for a particular person or purpose □ *This course is intended for people who already have a basic knowledge of Spanish.* □ *This furniture is intended for outdoor use.*

intense /ɪnˈtens/ ADJECTIVE very great or strong □ *intense heat* □ *He came under intense pressure to resign.*
• **intensely** /ɪnˈtensli/ ADVERB very much □ *She is intensely interested in Chinese politics.*
• **intensify** /ɪnˈtensɪfaɪ/ VERB [**intensifies, intensifying, intensified**] to become greater or stronger, or to make something greater or stronger □ *Fighting has intensified since the elections.* □ *We intensified our efforts to find new staff.*
• **intensity** /ɪnˈtensəti/ NOUN, NO PLURAL the strength of something □ *The battle went on with new intensity.* □ *The heat increased in intensity.*
• **intensive** /ɪnˈtensɪv/ ADJECTIVE
1 involving a lot of effort or activity in a short time □ *an intensive language course*
2 intensive farming tries to produce as much as possible from the land

intensive care /ɪnˌtensɪv ˈkeə(r)/ NOUN, NO PLURAL a part of a hospital that looks after people who are very ill or badly injured □ *One of the victims was still in intensive care last night.*

intent /ɪnˈtent/ ▶ ADJECTIVE
1 if you are intent on doing something, you are

determined to do it □ *Lorna was intent on winning the athletics' trophy.*
2 giving a lot of concentration to something □ *The inspector looked at him with intent curiosity.* □ *Gary didn't hear her, intent on his gardening magazine.*
▶ NOUN, NO PLURAL when you intend to do something □ *It was not my intent to offend him.*

• **intention** /ɪnˈtenʃən/ NOUN [*plural* **intentions**] the thing you plan to do □ **+ to do something** *It is my intention to finish before 5 o'clock.* 🔁 *He had no intention of obeying his father.*

• **intentional** /ɪnˈtenʃənəl/ ADJECTIVE done deliberately □ *Do you think his rudeness was intentional?*

• **intentionally** /ɪnˈtenʃənəlɪ/ ADVERB deliberately □ *Did he intentionally deceive the police?*

• **intently** /ɪnˈtentlɪ/ ADVERB with a lot of concentration □ *She examined the document intently.*

inter- /ˈɪntə(r)/ PREFIX inter- is added to the beginning of words to mean 'between' or 'among' a group of people or things □ *international* □ *interfaith*

interact /ˌɪntərˈækt/ VERB [**interacts, interacting, interacted**]
1 to talk to other people and do things with them □ *Joe always interacted well with other children.*
2 if two things interact, they have an effect on each other □ *The drug is thought to interact with chemicals in the brain.*

• **interaction** /ˌɪntərˈækʃən/ NOUN [*plural* **interactions**]
1 when people interact with each other □ *We looked at the interaction between doctor and patient.*
2 when two or more things have an effect on each other □ *There is a possibility of interaction between the medicines.*

• **interactive** /ˌɪntərˈæktɪv/ ADJECTIVE
1 involving communication between two people □ *interactive teaching methods*
2 interactive computer programs, electronic games, etc. react to the instructions that you give them

intercept /ˌɪntəˈsept/ VERB [**intercepts, intercepting, intercepted**] to stop and take something that is going from one place to another □ *The police intercepted the parcel before it arrived at its destination.*

interchangeable /ˌɪntəˈtʃeɪndʒəbəl/ ADJECTIVE when two things are interchangeable, you can use either of them in the same situations with the same result □ *The strap and the handle are interchangeable.*

intercom /ˈɪntəkɒm/ NOUN [*plural* **intercoms**] a system that allows you to talk to people who are in a different part of a building or vehicle 🔁 *The pilot spoke to us over the intercom.*

interest /ˈɪntrəst/ ▶ NOUN [*plural* **interests**]
1 *no plural* the feeling of wanting to know about something or give your attention to something □ **+ in** *I have no interest in cricket.* 🔁 *I try to take an interest in my husband's work.* 🔁 *He expressed an interest in learning Chinese.* 🔁 *In the end, I lost interest in my studies.*

2 something that you enjoy doing or learning about □ *My main interests are sport and reading.*
3 *no plural* extra money that you have to pay back when you have borrowed money, or that a bank pays you for having your money □ **+ on** *The interest on the car payments was huge.* 🔁 *I had to pay interest on the loan.* 🔁 *They charge 10% interest.*
4 **interests** the things that give someone an advantage or make their life good 🔁 *I have to protect the interests of my family.* □ *We look after the interests of our members.*
5 **be in someone's interest(s)** to be something that will give someone an advantage or make their life better □ *It's not in my interests to give you the information.* □ *It is in the national interest to publish these documents.*
6 **in the interest(s) of something** in order to achieve or protect something □ *In the interests of peace, I gave all the children a bar of chocolate.*
▶ VERB [**interests, interesting, interested**] to make someone want to know about something or do an activity □ **+ in** *I'm trying to interest him in ancient music.* □ *Can I interest you in a boat ride?*

• **interested** /ˈɪntrəstɪd/ ADJECTIVE
1 having or showing interest □ **+ in** *Dan is very interested in old cars.* □ **+ to do something** *I'd be interested to hear her side of the story.*
2 wanting to do something □ **+ in** *I'm not interested in making money.* □ *I'm interested in buying a bike.*

• **interesting** /ˈɪntrəstɪŋ/ ADJECTIVE making you feel interested □ *It was a very interesting story.* □ *It is interesting to note that he had never been to Egypt.*

> ➤ Remember the difference between the words **interesting** and **interested**. **Interesting** means 'making you feel interested'. **Interested** is how you feel when something is interesting: □ *It's a very interesting subject.* □ *I'm very interested in the subject.*

interest rate /ˈɪntrəst ˌreɪt/ NOUN [*plural* **interest rates**] the amount of extra money that you have to pay back when you borrow money, or that a bank pays you for having your money 🔁 *Interest rates rose by 1.5% last month.* □ *Banks announced a cut in interest rates.*

interface /ˈɪntəfeɪs/ NOUN [*plural* **interfaces**] the place in a computer system where information goes from one part to another, or the way the person using the computer sees the information on it. A computing word.

interfaith /ˈɪntəfeɪθ/ ADJECTIVE involving people from different religions □ *an interfaith service*

interfere /ˌɪntəˈfɪə(r)/ VERB [**interferes, interfering, interfered**] to get involved in a situation where you are not wanted □ *Many teenagers feel their parents interfere too much in their lives.*

♦ PHRASAL VERB **interfere with something** to affect something in a bad way □ *The illness doesn't interfere with my ability to do the job.*

- **interference** /ˌɪntəˈfɪərəns/ NOUN, NO PLURAL
1 when someone interferes in something □ *political interference*
2 electronic signals that spoil the sound or picture on a television or radio

interim /ˈɪntərɪm/ ▶ ADJECTIVE temporary □ *an interim government*
▶ NOUN, NO PLURAL **in the interim** in the time between two events

interior /ɪnˈtɪərɪə(r)/ ▶ NOUN [plural **interiors**] the inside of something □ *The interior of the house was perfectly maintained.*
▶ ADJECTIVE on or for the inside of something □ *an interior wall*
➔ go to **exterior**

interjection /ˌɪntəˈdʒekʃən/ NOUN [plural **interjections**] a word or phrase used to express a strong feeling like surprise, shock or anger. For example, *Oh!* and *Hooray!* are interjections.

interlude /ˈɪntəluːd/ NOUN [plural **interludes**] a short period of time between two events or situations □ *He lived in London all his life except for a brief interlude in New York.*

intermediate /ˌɪntəˈmiːdɪət/ ADJECTIVE
1 between a basic and advanced level in a subject □ *an intermediate English course* 🕮 *The book is for students studying maths at an intermediate level.*
2 between two stages, places, levels, etc. □ *It's an intermediate step in the process.*

intermission /ˌɪntəˈmɪʃən/ NOUN [plural **intermissions**] a short pause in the middle of a play or concert

intermittent /ˌɪntəˈmɪtənt/ ADJECTIVE happening some of the time but not continuously □ *intermittent rain*

internal /ɪnˈtɜːnəl/ ADJECTIVE
1 inside your body □ *internal injuries* □ *internal organs*
2 within an organization or country □ *an internal investigation* □ *internal flights*

international /ˌɪntəˈnæʃənəl/ ADJECTIVE involving several countries □ *international law* □ *an international conference* □ *international trade*
- **internationally** /ˌɪntəˈnæʃənəlɪ/ ADVERB in many parts of the world □ *the internationally acclaimed author*

Internet /ˈɪntənet/ ▶ NOUN, NO PLURAL **the Internet** a computer system that allows people around the world to share information □ *I found this hotel on the Internet.*
▶ ADJECTIVE to do with the Internet 🕮 *Most homes now have Internet access.* 🕮 *Internet users*

interpret /ɪnˈtɜːprɪt/ VERB [interprets, interpreting, interpreted]
1 to understand something in a particular way □ **+ as** *I interpreted his silence as shyness.* □ *Legal experts are divided over how to interpret the law.*
2 to change what someone has said into a different

language □ *If you don't speak French, we can provide someone to interpret for you.*
- **interpretation** /ɪnˌtɜːprɪˈteɪʃən/ NOUN [plural **interpretations**]
1 a way of explaining or understanding something □ *a literal interpretation of the text*
2 the way someone performs a piece of music, a play, etc. □ *He was famous for his interpretations of Mozart's music.*
- **interpreter** /ɪnˈtɜːprɪtə(r)/ NOUN [plural **interpreters**] someone whose job is to change what someone says into a different language

interrogate /ɪnˈterəgeɪt/ VERB [interrogates, interrogating, interrogated] to ask someone a lot of questions in order to get information, especially in a forceful or threatening way □ *The terrorist suspects were interrogated.*
- **interrogation** /ɪnˌterəˈgeɪʃən/ NOUN, NO PLURAL when someone is interrogated □ *the interrogation of prisoners*
- **interrogator** /ɪnˈterəgeɪtə(r)/ NOUN [plural **interrogators**] someone who interrogates another person

interrupt /ˌɪntəˈrʌpt/ VERB [interrupts, interrupting, interrupted]
1 to stop someone when they are in the middle of saying or doing something □ *I'm sorry to interrupt, but what time do we have to leave?* □ *Could I just interrupt you for a moment?*
2 to stop a process or activity for a short time □ *She interrupted the meeting to make a phone call.* □ *His career was interrupted by World War II.*
- **interruption** /ˌɪntəˈrʌpʃən/ NOUN [plural **interruptions**]
1 something that stops you doing or saying something □ *I can't work with all these interruptions.*
2 when something stops for a period of time □ **+ in** *an interruption in oil supplies*

intersect /ˌɪntəˈsekt/ VERB [intersects, intersecting, intersected] if lines or roads intersect, they cross each other
- **intersection** /ˌɪntəˈsekʃən/ NOUN [plural **intersections**] a place where lines or roads cross each other

intersperse /ˌɪntəˈspɜːs/ VERB [intersperses, interspersing, interspersed] to put one type of thing among another type of thing, in various different places □ *Fruit trees were interspersed with shrubs.*

interval /ˈɪntəvəl/ NOUN [plural **intervals**]
1 a period of time between two things □ *Her husband died in 1990, and after a decent interval, she married again.* 🕮 *After a short interval the police arrived.* □ **+ of** *an interval of two weeks*
2 **at weekly/monthly etc. intervals** used for saying how often something happens □ *Meetings are held at regular intervals.* □ *You should have a dental check-up at six month-intervals.*

3 at 5m/3m etc. intervals used to describe the distance between objects □ *There were bins placed at regular intervals along the road.*
4 a short pause in the middle of a concert or play □ *I bought an ice cream during the interval.*

intervene /ˌɪntəˈviːn/ VERB [intervenes, intervening, intervened]
1 to do something to try to stop an argument, fight or problem □ *The government intervened in the dispute.*
2 if something intervenes, it happens, and stops or delays something else □ *He was the favourite to win the game until injury intervened.*
3 to say something which interrupts someone □ *'Shut up both of you!' she intervened swiftly.*
• intervening /ˌɪntəˈviːnɪŋ/ ADJECTIVE the intervening period/years/months etc. the time, years, months, etc. between two events
• intervention /ˌɪntəˈvenʃən/ NOUN [plural interventions] when someone intervenes in something □ *military intervention*

interview /ˈɪntəvjuː/ ► NOUN [plural interviews]
1 a meeting in which someone asks you a lot of questions to find out if you are suitable for a job or a place on a course ⌨ *I have got an interview this afternoon.* ⌨ *I wear this suit for job interviews.* □ *+ for I didn't even get an interview for the job.*
2 a meeting in which someone asks a famous person questions ⌨ *Most reporters are nervous if they do an interview with the Queen.* ⌨ *The singer doesn't give interviews very often.* ⌨ *In an exclusive interview with this paper, she talks openly about her marriage.*
3 a meeting in which the police ask someone questions ⌨ *A tape of the police interview was played in court.*
► VERB [interviews, interviewing, interviewed] to ask someone questions at an interview □ *The driver was interviewed by police.*
• interviewer /ˈɪntəvjuːə(r)/ NOUN [plural interviewers] the person who asks the questions at an interview

intestines /ɪnˈtestɪnz/ PLURAL NOUN the tubes that take food from your stomach. A biology word.
intimate /ˈɪntɪmət/ ADJECTIVE
1 having a very close relationship with someone ⌨ *intimate friends*
2 relating to private and personal things ⌨ *intimate details of their relationship*
3 an intimate place is friendly and relaxed and usually small □ *We found a nice, intimate restaurant where we could chat.*
4 an intimate knowledge of something is a very good and detailed knowledge ⌨ *I don't have an intimate knowledge of the area.*
intimidate /ɪnˈtɪmɪdeɪt/ VERB [intimidates, intimidating, intimidated] to frighten someone, especially by threatening them □ *He won't let his attackers intimidate him into moving away from the area.*

• intimidated /ɪnˈtɪmɪdeɪtɪd/ ADJECTIVE frightened or not confident □ *Try not to feel intimidated by a large audience.*
• intimidating /ɪnˈtɪmɪdeɪtɪŋ/ ADJECTIVE making you feel frightened or less confident □ *He can be quite intimidating.*
• intimidation /ɪnˌtɪmɪˈdeɪʃən/ NOUN, NO PLURAL when someone is intimidated

into /ˈɪntʊ/ PREPOSITION
1 towards the inside of a room, container, area, etc. □ *We went into the house.* □ *I got into bed.* □ *He shovelled earth into the hole.*
2 towards the lower part of a substance □ *Our feet sank into the soft sand.* □ *He fell into the water.*
3 hitting against something □ *I drove into a wall.*
4 used for saying how something or someone changes □ *She cut the pizza into four pieces.* □ *The caterpillar changed into a butterfly.*
5 towards a particular thing □ *He looked into my eyes.* □ *She gazed into the mirror.*
6 to do with a particular subject or situation □ *How did we get into this mess?* □ *We are holding an investigation into child poverty.*
7 used when talking about dividing one number by another □ *2 into 4 goes twice.*

intolerable /ɪnˈtɒlərəbəl/ ADJECTIVE so bad that you cannot continue □ *The situation became intolerable.*
intolerance /ɪnˈtɒlərəns/ NOUN, NO PLURAL being intolerant
• intolerant /ɪnˈtɒlərənt/ ADJECTIVE refusing to accept behaviour and ideas that are different from your own
intonation /ˌɪntəˈneɪʃən/ NOUN, NO PLURAL the way that your voice goes up and down, showing your feelings and intentions, when you speak
Intranet /ˈɪntrənet/ NOUN [plural Intranets] a system of connected computers in an organization which allows the people in that organization to read the same information. A computing word. □ *You'll find the sales figures on the Intranet.*
intransitive /ɪnˈtrænsətɪv/ ADJECTIVE an intransitive verb does not have an object □ *In the sentence 'He fell.', the verb 'fall' is intransitive.*
intravenous /ˌɪntrəˈviːnəs/ ADJECTIVE into a vein (= tube that carries blood) □ *an intravenous injection*
intrepid /ɪnˈtrepɪd/ ADJECTIVE showing no fear and willing to do dangerous things □ *Our intrepid reporter is at the scene of the crime.*
intricate /ˈɪntrɪkət/ ADJECTIVE having a lot of small parts or details □ *an intricate pattern*
intrigue ► VERB /ɪnˈtriːg/ [intrigues, intriguing, intrigued] to interest someone and make them want to know more □ *The whole subject has always intrigued me.*
► NOUN /ˈɪntriːg/ [plural intrigues] secret plans to do something bad □ *It was a fascinating story of intrigue*
• intriguing /ɪnˈtriːgɪŋ/ ADJECTIVE very interesting and unusual □ *The house was an intriguing mixture of old and new.*

intrinsic /ɪnˈtrɪnsɪk/ ADJECTIVE part of the basic features of something or someone 🔁 *Computers are an intrinsic part of modern life.*

---

introduce /ˌɪntrəˈdjuːs/ VERB [introduces, introducing, introduced]
1 if you introduce two people who do not know each other, you tell each of them the other person's name □ **+ to** *He introduced me to his sister.* □ *Have you two been introduced?*
2 to make something start to happen or be used □ *The new law was introduced in 1999.*
3 to tell an audience the name of someone who is going to speak or perform to them □ *It gives me great pleasure to introduce tonight's speaker.*
♦ PHRASAL VERB **introduce someone to something** to give someone the chance to experience something new □ *She introduced me to tap dancing.*
● **introduction** /ˌɪntrəˈdʌkʃən/ NOUN [plural introductions]
1 *no plural* when something is started or begins to be used □ *They opposed the introduction of identity cards.*
2 the first part of a book, speech or piece of music
3 a book, course, etc. that teaches you the basic facts about a subject □ *She wrote an introduction to Chinese painting.*
4 when two people are introduced □ *After the introductions, we all sat down.*
● **introductory** /ˌɪntrəˈdʌktəri/ ADJECTIVE
1 intended to explain what will come later or give the basic facts about a subject □ *I attended his introductory lectures on Greek philosophy.*
2 given when a product or service begins in order to encourage people to buy it 🔁 *an introductory offer*

---

introvert /ˈɪntrəvɜːt/ NOUN [plural introverts] someone who is quiet and shy

intrude /ɪnˈtruːd/ VERB [intrudes, intruding, intruded] to become involved in a situation where you are not wanted □ *She had no wish to intrude on his life.*
● **intruder** /ɪnˈtruːdə(r)/ NOUN [plural intruders] someone who goes into a place where they should not be, especially to steal something □ *Intruders stole all her jewellery.*
● **intrusion** /ɪnˈtruːʒən/ NOUN [plural intrusions] someone or something that is not wanted in a situation 🔁 *Stella's arrival was an unwelcome intrusion.*
● **intrusive** /ɪnˈtruːsɪv/ ADJECTIVE becoming involved in a situation that should be private, in a way that is wrong □ *He found the media's interest in his private life intrusive.*

intuition /ˌɪntjuːˈɪʃən/ NOUN [plural intuitions] an idea that something is true, based on your feelings instead of knowledge □ *Intuition can tell a mother that her child is ill.*
● **intuitive** /ɪnˈtjuːɪtɪv/ ADJECTIVE based on intuition □ *intuitive judgements*

inundate /ˈɪnʌndeɪt/ VERB [inundates, inundating, inundated] if you are inundated with something, you receive so much of it that you cannot deal with it all □ *The office has been inundated with offers of help.*

invade /ɪnˈveɪd/ VERB [invades, invading, invaded]
1 to enter a country with an army, and try to take control of it □ *7000 troops invaded the country.*
2 invade someone's privacy to become involved in someone's private life when they do not want this
3 if a lot of people invade a place, they go there □ *Every summer, the island is invaded by tourists.*
● **invader** /ɪnˈveɪdə(r)/ NOUN [plural invaders] someone who invades another country

invalid¹ /ɪnˈvælɪd/ ADJECTIVE
1 not acceptable because of a law or rule □ *an invalid bus pass*
2 not correct or not based on facts □ *an invalid excuse*
invalid² /ˈɪnvəlɪd/ NOUN [plural invalids] someone who is ill or unable to look after themselves

invaluable /ɪnˈvæljuəbəl/ ADJECTIVE extremely useful □ *an invaluable piece of advice*

invariably /ɪnˈveəriəbli/ ADVERB always □ *Dean is invariably late for everything.*

invasion /ɪnˈveɪʒən/ NOUN [plural invasions]
1 an attack on a country by an army entering it □ **+ of** *The government decided to launch an invasion of the country.*
2 when a lot of people go to a place □ *The town is preparing for its biggest invasion of the year - the annual pop festival.*
3 an invasion of privacy involvement in someone's private life which is not wanted □ *Publishing the photos was an invasion of privacy.*

invent /ɪnˈvent/ VERB [invents, inventing, invented]
1 to design or create a new type of thing □ *Thomas Edison invented the electric light bulb.* □ *There was a lot of argument about who had invented the word.*
2 to think of a story or excuse that is not true 🔁 *She invented an excuse not to go to his house.*
● **invention** /ɪnˈvenʃən/ NOUN [plural inventions]
1 a new type of thing which someone has designed or created □ *The washing machine was a brilliant invention.*
2 *no plural* when someone designs or creates a new type of thing □ **+ of** *The invention of the computer would change the world forever.*
3 a story or excuse that is not true □ *Is crime increasing, or is it just an invention of the media?*
● **inventive** /ɪnˈventɪv/ ADJECTIVE using new and interesting ideas □ *He has an inventive mind.* □ *an inventive solution*
● **inventor** /ɪnˈventə(r)/ NOUN [plural inventors] someone who has invented something new

---

inverse /ɪnˈvɜːs/ ADJECTIVE an inverse relationship between two amounts is one in which one amount becomes bigger at the same rate as the other one becomes smaller

invert /ɪn'vɜːt/ VERB [inverts, inverting, inverted] a formal word meaning to turn something upside-down

invertebrate /ɪn'vɜːtɪbrət/ NOUN [plural invertebrates] an animal that does not have a bone in its back, for example an insect or worm. A biology word.

inverted /ɪn'vɜːtɪd/ ADJECTIVE turned upside-down

inverted commas /ɪnˌvɜːtɪd 'kɒməz/ PLURAL NOUN the symbols ' ' or " ", used in writing to show what someone says

invest /ɪn'vest/ VERB [invests, investing, invested] to put money in a bank or business in order to make more money □ My Dad has invested some money in the business.
♦ PHRASAL VERB **invest in something** to buy something expensive that will be useful □ I think we need to invest in a new printer.

investigate /ɪn'vestɪgeɪt/ VERB [investigates, investigating, investigated] to try to find out about something such as an accident or crime □ Police are investigating his death.
● **investigation** /ɪnˌvestɪ'geɪʃən/ NOUN [plural investigations] an attempt to find out about something such as an accident or a crime ⊞ Officials have launched an investigation into allegations of corruption.
● **investigator** /ɪn'vestɪgeɪtə(r)/ NOUN [plural investigators] someone who is investigating something

investment /ɪn'vestmənt/ NOUN [plural investments]
1 when you use money to get a profit or to make a business successful □ The country hopes to attract foreign investment in its telephone network.
2 something you spend a lot of money on because it will be very useful ⊞ A warm coat is a good investment.

investor /ɪn'vestə(r)/ NOUN [plural investors] someone who gives money to a bank or business in order to get a profit

invigorating /ɪn'vɪgəreɪtɪŋ/ ADJECTIVE making you feel full of energy □ We went for an invigorating walk by the sea.

invincible /ɪn'vɪnsəbəl/ ADJECTIVE impossible to defeat or destroy □ Young people often feel invincible.

invisibility /ɪnˌvɪzə'bɪləti/ NOUN, NO PLURAL being impossible to see

invisible /ɪn'vɪzəbəl/ ADJECTIVE impossible to see □ The star is almost invisible.

invitation /ˌɪnvɪ'teɪʃən/ NOUN [plural invitations]
1 when someone asks you if you would like to go somewhere or do something □ + to We've had an invitation to William and Charlotte's wedding. □ + to do something He accepted an invitation to meet the President.
2 a card or piece of paper that you use for inviting someone to something ⊞ I've bought some party invitations. ⊞ Those are pretty wedding invitations.
3 something that encourages something bad to

happen □ + to Leaving your car door open is an invitation to thieves.

invite ▶ VERB /ɪn'vaɪt/ [invites, inviting, invited]
1 to ask someone if they would like to do something or go somewhere □ + for We've invited some friends round for dinner. □ + to Raj has invited me to his birthday party. □ + to do something Beth was invited to speak at the conference.
2 to encourage something bad to happen □ Using those words is likely to invite criticism.
♦ PHRASAL VERBS **invite someone in** to ask someone to come into your house □ When we got to her house, she invited me in. **invite someone over/round** to ask someone to come to your house, for example to have a meal with you □ I've invited Ann round tonight.
▶ NOUN /'ɪnvaɪt/ [plural invites] an informal word meaning an invitation □ Have you had an invite to the wedding?
● **inviting** /ɪn'vaɪtɪŋ/ ADJECTIVE attractive and pleasant, making you want something or want to go somewhere □ an inviting smell □ an inviting restaurant

invoice /'ɪnvɔɪs/ ▶ NOUN [plural invoices] a piece of paper showing you the goods or services that you have bought and how much you must pay for them
▶ VERB [invoices, invoicing, invoiced] to send someone an invoice

involuntary /ɪn'vɒləntəri/ ADJECTIVE an involuntary movement or action is one you cannot control □ Sneezing is an involuntary action.

involve /ɪn'vɒlv/ VERB [involves, involving, involved]
1 if an activity or situation involves something, that thing is a part of it □ The treatment involves a slight risk. □ + ing The job involves selling Internet space to companies.
2 to affect someone or something □ Crimes involving children are very rare. □ Five vehicles were involved in the accident.
3 to allow someone to take part in something □ + in The school tries to involve students in decision-making.
● **involved** /ɪn'vɒlvd/ ADJECTIVE
1 get/be involved to take part in something □ I don't want to get involved in an argument. □ He's been involved in politics for 30 years.
2 an involved story or explanation is long and complicated
3 be/get involved with someone to have a relationship with someone □ He's not the sort of man you want to get involved with.
● **involvement** /ɪn'vɒlvmənt/ NOUN, NO PLURAL when someone takes part in something ⊞ He doesn't have any direct involvement in the company. □ + in He denies any involvement in the killing. □ + of The project was carried out with the full involvement of local people.

inward /'ɪnwəd/ ADJECTIVE
1 in your mind and not shown to other people □ inward satisfaction □ an inward smile

2 towards the inside or middle of something □ *the natural inward curve of your lower back*

• **inwardly** /'ɪnwədlɪ/ ADVERB in your own mind but not shown to other people □ *Inwardly, she felt very scared.*

• **inwards** /'ɪnwədz/ ADVERB towards the inside of something □ *The door swung inwards.*

iodine /'aɪədi:n/ NOUN, NO PLURAL a chemical element, sometimes used to clean cuts on the body. A chemistry word.

ion /'aɪən/ NOUN [plural **ions**] an atom with an electrical force. A chemistry and physics word.

iota /aɪ'əʊtə/ NOUN, NO PLURAL a very small amount □ *Anyone with an iota of intelligence could see he was lying.*

IOU /ˌaɪəʊ'ju:/ ABBREVIATION I owe you; a note that you sign to say that you owe someone money

IQ /ˌaɪ'kju:/ ABBREVIATION intelligence quotient; how intelligent someone is, is measured by a special test 🖰 *She has a very high IQ.*

ir- /ɪr/ PREFIX ir- is added to the beginning of words to mean 'not' □ *irreversible* □ *irresponsible*

irascible /ɪ'ræsəbəl/ ADJECTIVE often becoming angry. A formal word.

irate /aɪ'reɪt/ ADJECTIVE extremely angry □ *Hundreds of irate customers have complained about the company.*

iris /'aɪrɪs/ NOUN [plural **irises**]
1 the coloured circle in your eye. A biology word.
2 a tall plant with purple, white or yellow flowers

Irish /'aɪrɪʃ/ ► ADJECTIVE belonging to or from Ireland
► NOUN, NO PLURAL the Irish people from Ireland

irk /ɜ:k/ VERB [**irks, irking, irked**] to annoy someone □ *It irks me that she never thanked us.*

iron /'aɪən/ ► NOUN [plural **irons**]
1 *no plural* a hard strong metal that is used to make steel and is also found in small amounts in your blood and some food □ *The railings were made from iron.* □ *Spinach contains vitamin C and iron.*
2 a piece of electrical equipment that you press on clothes to make them smooth □ *Have you switched the iron off?*
► ADJECTIVE made from iron □ *iron gates*
► VERB [**irons, ironing, ironed**] to make clothes smooth using an iron □ *Ben was ironing some shirts.*

ironic /aɪ'rɒnɪk/ ADJECTIVE
1 an ironic situation is surprising, often because it is the opposite of what you expected □ *It's ironic that a man who spent his life treating heart disease should die of a heart attack.*
2 saying the opposite of what you really mean □ *Were you being ironic when you described her as 'lovely'?*

ironing /'aɪənɪŋ/ NOUN, NO PLURAL
1 the activity of making clothes smooth by pressing them with a piece of electrical equipment 🖰 *Mum always watches television while she's doing the ironing.*
2 clothes which you are going to iron, or which you

have just ironed □ *There was a pile of ironing on the chair.*

ironing board /'aɪənɪŋ ˌbɔ:d/ NOUN [plural **ironing boards**] a flat board that you iron clothes on

irony /'aɪrənɪ/ NOUN [plural **ironies**]
1 a situation that is surprising because it is the opposite of what you expected 🖰 *The irony is that the man who cooks all this marvellous food can no longer taste it.*
2 using words that are the opposite of what you really mean in order to be funny

irregular /ɪ'regjʊlə(r)/ ADJECTIVE
1 having a different amount of time or space between separate things 🖰 *an irregular heartbeat* □ *The trees had been planted at irregular intervals.*
2 not smooth or even □ *irregular shapes*
3 not following the usual rules of grammar □ *irregular verbs*
4 a formal word meaning not following the usual moral or legal rules

• **irregularity** /ɪˌregjʊ'lærətɪ/ NOUN [plural **irregularities**]
1 a situation in which the usual moral or legal rules have not been followed 🖰 *The company was investigated for financial irregularities.*
2 when things have a different amount of time or space between each one □ *heartbeat irregularity*
3 when something is not smooth or even

irrelevance /ɪ'reləvəns/ NOUN [plural **irrelevances**] something that is not related to a particular situation or subject and is not important □ *It's a mistake to view the local media as an irrelevance.*

• **irrelevant** /ɪ'reləvənt/ ADJECTIVE not related to a particular situation or subject so not important □ *His comments were completely irrelevant to the discussion.*

irreplaceable /ˌɪrɪ'pleɪsəbəl/ ADJECTIVE too special or valuable to be replaced □ *irreplaceable documents*

irresistible /ˌɪrɪ'zɪstəbəl/ ADJECTIVE
1 if something is irresistible, it is so attractive that you want it □ *The offer of a cool swim on a hot day was irresistible.*
2 too strong to ignore or control □ *She had an irresistible urge to scream.*

irrespective /ˌɪrɪ'spektɪv/ ADJECTIVE irrespective of something not influenced by a particular fact □ *Workers should be treated the same, irrespective of their sex or age.*

irresponsible /ˌɪrɪ'spɒnsəbəl/ ADJECTIVE behaving in a silly way without thinking about the bad things that might happen □ *It was completely irresponsible to leave a six-year-old at home alone.*

irreversible /ˌɪrɪ'vɜ:səbəl/ ADJECTIVE lasting forever 🖰 *Pollution has caused irreversible damage to the environment.*

irrigate /'ɪrɪgeɪt/ VERB [**irrigates, irrigating, irrigated**] to supply land or crops with water

- **irrigation** /ˌɪrɪ'ɡeɪʃən/ NOUN, NO PLURAL supplying land or crops with water

irritable /'ɪrɪtəbəl/ ADJECTIVE becoming annoyed very easily □ *Jamal is irritable if he doesn't get enough sleep.*

irritate /'ɪrɪteɪt/ VERB [**irritates, irritating, irritated**]
1 to make someone feel annoyed □ *It irritates me that he never helps with the washing up.*
2 to make something such as your skin or eyes sore □ *Some sun creams can irritate your skin.*

- **irritated** /'ɪrɪteɪtɪd/ ADJECTIVE annoyed 🖫 *I was starting to get irritated.*

- **irritating** /'ɪrɪteɪtɪŋ/ ADJECTIVE making you feel annoyed □ *He had an irritating habit of repeating everything I said.*

- **irritation** /ˌɪrɪ'teɪʃən/ NOUN [*plural* **irritations**]
1 feeling annoyed about something □ *She couldn't hide her irritation.*
2 something that annoys you □ *His constant complaints are an irritation.*
3 a sore feeling on your skin or in your eyes □ *Smoke causes eye irritation.*

is /ɪz/ VERB the present tense of the verb be when it is used with **he, she,** or **it** □ *He is tall.* □ *It is too hot.*

> ➤ Note that instead of **he is, she is** and **it is**, people often say and write the short forms, **he's, she's** and **it's:** □ *He's here.* □ *She's tall.* □ *It's great.*

-ise /aɪz/ SUFFIX another way of spelling -ize

-ish /ɪʃ/ SUFFIX -ish is added to the end of words to mean 'slightly' □ *reddish* (= slightly red)

Islam /'ɪzlɑːm/ NOUN, NO PLURAL the Muslim religion that was started by Mohammed

- **Islamic** /ɪz'læmɪk/ ADJECTIVE to do with Islam □ *Islamic law* □ *the Islamic faith*

island /'aɪlənd/ NOUN [*plural* **islands**] an area of land surrounded by sea □ *There are lots of unusual plants on the island.* □ *the Caribbean island of Trinidad* 🖫 *a remote island in the Pacific Ocean* □ *the Channel Islands*

isle /aɪl/ NOUN [*plural* **isles**] a word meaning 'island', used in poems or in the name of an island □ *the Isles of Scilly*

-ism /-ɪzəm/ SUFFIX -ism is added to the end of words to make nouns to do with beliefs or qualities □ *communism* □ *heroism*

isn't /'ɪzənt/ a short way to say and write is not □ *It isn't fair.*

isobar /'aɪsəbɑː(r)/ NOUN [*plural* **isobars**] a line on a weather map that joins places with the same air pressure. A geography word.

isolate /'aɪsəleɪt/ VERB [**isolates, isolating, isolated**] to separate someone or something from other people or things □ *The infected animals were isolated in a field.*

- **isolated** /'aɪsəleɪtɪd/ ADJECTIVE
1 feeling alone and sad that you do not meet other people □ *Old people often feel isolated.*
2 far away from other places □ *an isolated farmhouse*
3 happening only once and not related to other events 🖫 *This theft was an isolated incident.*

- **isolation** /ˌaɪsə'leɪʃən/ NOUN, NO PLURAL
1 when a person, place or thing is separate from others □ *The deal should end the country's economic isolation.*
2 a feeling of being alone and sad because you do not meet other people □ *Working from home can lead to isolation.*
3 in isolation separately from other people or things □ *Each incident must be considered in isolation.*

isosceles /aɪ'sɒsəliːz/ ADJECTIVE an isosceles triangle has two sides of the same length. A maths word.

isotope /'aɪsətəup/ NOUN [*plural* **isotopes**] one of the forms of a chemical element with the same number of protons but a different number of neutrons. A chemistry word.

ISP /ˌaɪes'piː/ ABBREVIATION Internet Service Provider; a company that sells you a connection to the Internet. A computing word.

issue /'ɪʃuː/ ▶ NOUN [*plural* **issues**]
1 a subject that people discuss or that causes problems □ **+ of** *We discussed the issue of funding.* 🖫 *Polly raised the issue of transport.* 🖫 *We are trying to address the issue* (= deal with the issue) *of truancy.* 🖫 *The environment is a key issue in this election campaign.* 🖫 *The issue arose because one of the children made a complaint.*
2 at issue being discussed or causing arguments □ *The matter at issue is whether the centre should open at the weekend.*
3 a newspaper or magazine that is one of a number printed and sold at the same time □ *Have you seen this week's issue of the magazine?*
4 *no plural* the act of supplying someone with something □ *She organized the issue of warm bedding.*
▶ VERB [**issues, issuing, issued**]
1 to say something to the public in an official way 🖫 *issue a statement/warning*
2 to supply someone with something □ **+ with** *We were all issued with pens.*

-ist /ɪst/ SUFFIX
1 -ist is added to the end of words to make nouns to do with people who do a particular thing □ *artist*
2 -ist is added to the end of words to make nouns to do with people who have particular beliefs □ *communist*

isthmus /'ɪsməs/ NOUN [*plural* **isthmuses**] a narrow piece of land with water on each side that goes between two larger pieces of land. A geography word.

IT /ˌaɪ'tiː/ ABBREVIATION information technology

it /ɪt/ PRONOUN
1 used to talk or write about something that has already been mentioned □ *I've lost my book. Have you seen it?* □ *It was a great day.*
2 used to talk about a fact or opinion □ *It's expensive*

to travel by train. □ *It's very quiet here, isn't it?*
□ *What's it like in Spain?*
3 used to talk about the weather, time and dates □ *It rained yesterday.* □ *What time is it?* □ *It's 3 o'clock.*
4 used to talk about distance □ *It's a long way to the coast.* □ *How far is it to your house?*
5 used to tell someone who is there, on the telephone, etc. □ *Hello, it's Pat here.* □ *It's your brother at the door.*
6 used as the object of a sentence □ *I liked it when he sang that song.* □ *I considered it to be rude.*
7 used as the subject of a sentence □ *It made me happy to see him laugh.* □ *It seems as though he's forgotten us.*

talics /ɪ'tælɪks/ PLURAL NOUN a style of writing in which the letters slope to the right. The examples given in this book are in *italics*.

tch /ɪtʃ/ ▶ VERB [**itches, itching, itched**] if part of your body itches, it feels uncomfortable and makes you want to scratch it
▸ IDIOM **be itching to do something** an informal phrase meaning to want to do something very much □ *I was itching to play football again.*
▶ NOUN [*plural* **itches**] an uncomfortable feeling on part of your body that makes you want to scratch it
□ *I've got an itch on my back.*

itchy /'ɪtʃɪ/ ADJECTIVE an itchy part of your body feels uncomfortable and makes you want to scratch it

'd /'ɪtəd/ a short way to say and write it would or it had□ *It'd be good if you could come.* □ *It'd been raining all day.*

tem /'aɪtəm/ NOUN [*plural* **items**]
1 one thing which is part of a group or is on a list
□ *There were several items on the list.* 🔁 *He left his mobile phone and other personal items in the car.*
🔁 *She had some very expensive items of clothing in her wardrobe.*
2 a piece of news in a newspaper, magazine or on television 🔁 *I saw an interesting news item.* □ **+ on/about** *There was an item on famous painters.*

itemize or **itemise** /'aɪtəmaɪz/ VERB [**itemizes, itemizing, itemized**] to give things separately in a list,

with details about each thing □ *Phone companies usually itemize your calls.*

itinerary /aɪ'tɪnərərɪ/ NOUN [*plural* **itineraries**] a list of the places you will visit when you are travelling □ *France, Germany and Italy are on the President's itinerary.*

it'll /ɪtəl/ a short way to say and write it will□ *It'll be nice to see you.*

it's /ɪts/ a short way to say and write it is or it has□ *It's snowing.* □ *It's been a long time since I saw you.*

> ► Try not to confuse the spellings of **its** and **it's**. **Its** is the possessive form of **it**, and tells you something belongs to **it**: *The bird built its nest.* **It's** is a short form of two words put together: *I think it's going to rain.*

its /ɪts/ ADJECTIVE belonging to or to do with it □ *Keep the hat in its box.* 🔁 *The school has its own tennis courts.*

itself /ɪt'self/ PRONOUN
1 the reflexive form of it□ *The school has transformed itself.* □ *Australia has found itself in a difficult position.*
2 used to show that a thing or animal does something without any help from anyone or anything else □ *The cut soon healed itself.* 🔁 *The dog managed to get free all by itself.*
3 used to emphasize the pronoun it□ *I don't dislike the building itself.*
4 **by itself** not with or near other things □ *The cottage stood by itself on a hillside.* □ *Talent by itself is not enough to make you successful.*

I've /aɪv/ a short way to say and write I have□ *I've finished my homework.* □ *I've got six cats.*

ivory /'aɪvərɪ/ NOUN, NO PLURAL the hard white substance that an elephant's tusks (= long teeth) are made of

ivy /'aɪvɪ/ NOUN, NO PLURAL a plant with dark green leaves which grows up walls

-ize or **-ise** /-aɪz/ SUFFIX -ize or -ise is added to the end of words to make verbs to do with making something become a particular way □ *computerize*

J or **j** /dʒeɪ/ the tenth letter of the alphabet

jab /dʒæb/ ▶ VERB [**jabs, jabbing, jabbed**] to push something sharp quickly and hard into something □ *He jabbed me in the arm with his pen.*
▶ NOUN [*plural* **jabs**]
1 when you quickly push something sharp into or towards something □ *She gave him a jab in the ribs with her elbow.*
2 when you put a substance into someone's body with a needle, in order to stop them getting a disease ⊞ *a flu jab*

jack /dʒæk/ NOUN [*plural* **jacks**]
1 a playing card with a picture of a young man, that comes between the ten and the Queen in value □ *the jack of hearts*
2 a tool used to raise something heavy off the ground, especially a car

jackal /ˈdʒækəl/ NOUN [*plural* **jackals**] a wild animal that looks like a dog and hunts in groups

jacket /ˈdʒækɪt/ NOUN [*plural* **jackets**] a short coat, usually with long sleeves □ *a leather jacket* □ *a denim jacket*

jacket potato /ˌdʒækɪt pəˈteɪtəʊ/ NOUN [*plural* **jacket potatoes**] a potato baked in the oven in its skin

jack-knife /ˈdʒæknaɪf/ VERB [**jack-knifes, jack-knifing, jack-knifed**] if a truck jack-knifes, it loses control and bends so that the back moves round towards the front

jackpot /ˈdʒækpɒt/ NOUN [*plural* **jackpots**] the largest prize in a game or competition
♦ IDIOM **hit the jackpot** to be very successful, usually winning a lot of money

Jacuzzi /dʒəˈkuːzɪ/ NOUN [*plural* **Jacuzzis**] a warm bath or pool with a lot of bubbles in the water. A trademark.

jade /dʒeɪd/ NOUN, NO PLURAL a green stone used in jewellery

jaded /ˈdʒeɪdɪd/ ADJECTIVE feeling tired and bored, especially because you have been doing the same thing for a long time

jagged /ˈdʒægɪd/ ADJECTIVE with sharp, edges or points □ *a jagged rock* □ *a jagged edge*

jaguar /ˈdʒægjʊə(r)/ NOUN [*plural* **jaguars**] a large wild cat with black spots, that comes from South and Central America

jail /dʒeɪl/ ▶ NOUN [*plural* **jails**] a building where criminals are kept □ *She was sentenced to 12 month in jail.* ⊞ *He's just been released from jail.*
▶ VERB [**jails, jailing, jailed**] to put someone in a jail □ *Peters was jailed for 30 months for assaulting a neighbour.*
● **jailer** /ˈdʒeɪlə(r)/ NOUN [*plural* **jailers**] someone wh guards people while they are in prison

jam /dʒæm/ ▶ NOUN [*plural* **jams**]
1 a sweet, sticky food made of fruit and sugar that yo spread on bread □ *strawberry jam*
2 a line of vehicles that are not moving or are movir very slowly ⊞ *I got stuck in a traffic jam.*
▶ VERB [**jams, jamming, jammed**]
1 to push something into a space so that it fits very tightly □ *She jammed the clothes into her suitcase.*
2 to become or to make something become unable to mov or work □ *I tried to open the door but it was jamme*
3 to fill a place completely with people or things □ **with** *The M6 was jammed with traffic after an accident.* ⊞ *All the cupboards were jammed full of clothes.*
4 to send out a signal that stops a radio from being hea

jammy /ˈdʒæmɪ/ ADJECTIVE [**jammier, jammiest**]
1 filled or covered with jam (= sweet food made w fruit) □ *jammy doughnuts*
2 an informal word meaning lucky

jangle /ˈdʒæŋgəl/ ▶ VERB [**jangles, jangling, jangle** to make the ringing sound of metal hitting against metal □ *He walked up the path, jangling his keys.*
▶ NOUN [*plural* **jangles**] the ringing sound of meta hitting against metal □ *She could hear the jangle c coins in his pocket.*

janitor /ˈdʒænɪtə(r)/ NOUN [*plural* **janitors**] the U word for **caretaker**

January /ˈdʒænjʊərɪ/ NOUN the first month of the year, after December and before February □ *My birthday is in January.*

jar /dʒɑː(r)/ ▶ NOUN [*plural* **jars**] a glass containe with a wide neck and a lid, used for storing food □ *jam jar* □ *a jar of coffee*
▶ VERB [**jars, jarring, jarred**]
1 to hurt or damage something from a sudden hit movement □ *He fell awkwardly, jarring his spine.*
2 to make you feel slightly annoyed □ *Her voice j starts to jar after a while.*

jargon /ˈdʒɑːgən/ NOUN, NO PLURAL special words and phrases used by people working in a particular job, which are difficult for other people to understand □ *computer jargon*

jasmine /ˈdʒæzmɪn/ NOUN [*plural* **jasmines**] a bush or climbing plant with white or yellow flowers with a sweet smell

jaundice /ˈdʒɔːndɪs/ NOUN, NO PLURAL an illness that makes your skin and the whites of your eyes become yellow, usually caused by your liver not working correctly

• **jaundiced** /ˈdʒɔːndɪst/ ADJECTIVE
1 not expecting good things to happen because of your bad experiences in the past □ *Her mother had a very jaundiced view of men.*
2 suffering from jaundice □ *The baby was slightly jaundiced.*

jaunt /dʒɔːnt/ NOUN [*plural* **jaunts**] a short journey made for pleasure □ *a jaunt to the seaside*

• **jaunty** /ˈdʒɔːntɪ/ ADJECTIVE [**jauntier**, **jauntiest**] happy and confident

javelin /ˈdʒævəlɪn/ NOUN [*plural* **javelins**]
1 a long light stick with a pointed end that you throw in a sports event
2 the javelin the sports event in which you throw a javelin as far as you can

jaw /dʒɔː/ NOUN [*plural* **jaws**] the lower part of your face made up of two bones that your teeth grow in
▸ IDIOM **someone's jaw drops** if someone's jaw drops, they show with their face that they are extremely surprised □ *She told us what she earned and our jaws dropped.*

jazz /dʒæz/ NOUN, NO PLURAL a type of music with a strong beat that is often changed or added to as it is played □ *modern jazz*
▸ PHRASAL VERB [**jazzes**, **jazzing**, **jazzed**] **jazz something up** to make something brighter and more colourful. An informal phrase. □ *You can jazz up an old sofa with some bright cushions.*

jazzy /ˈdʒæzɪ/ ADJECTIVE [**jazzier**, **jazziest**] an informal word meaning bright and colourful □ *That's a very jazzy tie you have on.*

JCB /ˌdʒeɪsiːˈbiː/ NOUN [*plural* **JCBs**] a large machine used for digging and moving earth and stones. A trademark.

jealous /ˈdʒeləs/ ADJECTIVE
1 feeling angry and unhappy because someone has something you want or because you want to be like someone else □ + *of* *He's jealous of his brother's success.* ⊞ *She made me jealous by going out with her other friends.*
2 feeling upset and angry because you think someone you love is in love with someone else □ *a jealous wife*

jealousy /ˈdʒeləsɪ/ NOUN, NO PLURAL jealous feelings

jeans /dʒiːnz/ PLURAL NOUN trousers made of denim (= thick, usually blue, cotton)

Jeep /dʒiːp/ NOUN [*plural* **Jeeps**] a small, strong vehicle that can travel over rough ground. A trademark

jeer /dʒɪə(r)/ ▸ VERB [**jeers**, **jeering**, **jeered**] to shout rude remarks at someone and laugh at them □ *The crowd jeered as the team left the pitch.*
▸ NOUN [*plural* **jeers**] an angry shout or laugh □ *The speaker was greeted with jeers from the gallery.*

Jell-o /ˈdʒeləʊ/ NOUN, NO PLURAL the US word for jelly. A trademark.

jelly /ˈdʒelɪ/ NOUN [*plural* **jellies**]
1 a soft, sweet food with a fruit flavour that shakes when you move it and is eaten cold □ *a bowl of jelly and ice cream*
2 a US word for jam

jellyfish /ˈdʒelɪfɪʃ/ NOUN [*plural* **jellyfish** or **jellyfishes**] a sea animal with a soft transparent body that can sting you (= hurt you by putting poison into your skin)

jeopardize or **jeopardise** /ˈdʒepədaɪz/ VERB [**jeopardizes**, **jeopardizing**, **jeopardized**] to harm something or put something in danger □ *The injury could jeopardize her chances of winning a medal.*
• **jeopardy** /ˈdʒepədɪ/ NOUN, NO PLURAL **in jeopardy** in a situation where something risks being lost or damaged □ *Her life is in jeopardy.*

jerk /dʒɜːk/ ▸ VERB [**jerks**, **jerking**, **jerked**]
1 to make a short sudden movement □ *The driver started the engine and the old bus jerked forward.*
2 to pull something with a sudden rough movement □ *He jerked his hand away.*
▸ NOUN [*plural* **jerks**]
1 a short sudden movement
2 an informal word for a stupid person
• **jerky** /ˈdʒɜːkɪ/ ADJECTIVE jerky movements are short and quick

jersey /ˈdʒɜːzɪ/ NOUN [*plural* **jerseys**]
1 a warm piece of clothing with sleeves that you pull on over your head and wear on the top half of your body
2 a soft cotton or wool cloth used for making clothes □ *a black dress in soft jersey*

Jesus /ˈdʒiːzəs/ or **Jesus Christ** /ˌdʒiːzəs ˈkraɪst/ NOUN the man who Christians believe to be the son of God and on whose teachings Christianity is based

jet /dʒet/ ▸ NOUN [*plural* **jets**]
1 a fast plane with powerful engines □ *a passenger jet*
2 a strong fast flow of liquid or gas forced through a small hole □ *The printer releases jets of coloured ink.*
▸ VERB [**jets**, **jetting**, **jetted**] to fly somewhere □ *Dan's jetting off to New York this Saturday.*

jet-black /ˌdʒetˈblæk/ ADJECTIVE very dark black □ *jet-black hair*

jet lag /ˈdʒet ˌlæg/ NOUN, NO PLURAL a tired feeling that you get after a long journey by plane to a place where the time is different

Jet Ski /ˈdʒet ˌskiː/ NOUN [plural **Jet Skis**] a small vehicle like a motorcycle for one or two people to ride on water. A trademark.

• **jet-skiing** /ˈdʒetˌskiːɪŋ/ NOUN, NO PLURAL the sport of riding on jet skis

jetty /ˈdʒetɪ/ NOUN [plural **jetties**] a wooden structure at the edge of a lake or the sea where small boats can stop

Jew /dʒuː/ NOUN [plural **Jews**] someone whose religion is Judaism or whose family originally came from the ancient Hebrew people of Israel

jewel /ˈdʒuːəl/ NOUN [plural **jewels**] a valuable stone, used to make jewellery □ a ring set with precious jewels

• **jeweler** /ˈdʒuːələ(r)/ NOUN [plural **jewelers**] the US spelling of jeweller

• **jeweller** /ˈdʒuːələ(r)/ NOUN [plural **jewellers**] someone whose job is making or selling jewellery

• **jewellery** /ˈdʒuːəlrɪ/ NOUN, NO PLURAL things that you wear to decorate your body and clothes, often made of metal and valuable stones □ She wears a lot of gold jewellery. 🖰 a beautiful piece of jewellery

• **jewelry** /ˈdʒuːəlrɪ/ NOUN, NO PLURAL the US spelling of jewellery

Jewish /ˈdʒuːɪʃ/ ADJECTIVE to do with Jews or Judaism □ a Jewish religious festival □ Jewish history

jibe /dʒaɪb/ NOUN [plural **jibes**] a rude or insulting remark □ I'm sick of her jibes about my age.

jig /dʒɪg/ NOUN [plural **jigs**] a lively dance in which people jump about □ an Irish jig

jiggle /ˈdʒɪgəl/ VERB [**jiggles, jiggling, jiggled**] to quickly move from side to side, or up and down many times, or to make something do this □ I tried jiggling the key in the lock.

jigsaw /ˈdʒɪgsɔː/ NOUN [plural **jigsaws**] a picture cut up into a lot of pieces that you have to fit together again 🖰 The children were doing a jigsaw on the floor

jingle /ˈdʒɪŋgəl/ ► VERB [**jingles, jingling, jingled**] to make the ringing sound of light pieces of metal hitting against each other □ Bells were jingling in the background.

► NOUN [plural **jingles**]

1 a short song used to advertise a product on the television or radio

2 a ringing sound made when light pieces of metal hit against each other □ She heard the jingle of keys as he walked up the path.

jinx /dʒɪŋks/ NOUN [plural **jinxes**] bad luck, or a person or thing that brings bad luck

• **jinxed** /dʒɪŋkst/ ADJECTIVE having bad luck and not able to stop it □ I was beginning to think the whole project was jinxed.

jittery /ˈdʒɪtərɪ/ ADJECTIVE nervous □ Katie was very jittery before her driving test.

job /dʒɒb/ NOUN [plural **jobs**]

1 the work someone does regularly for money 🖰 He needs to get a job. 🖰 They offered me a job in the shop. 🖰 He lost his job because of the illness. □ + as She got a job as a chef. 🖰 a part-time/full-time job

2 a piece of work □ There are plenty of jobs to do about the house.

3 a good/bad, etc. job the standard of work someone has done □ You've made a good job of that painting. □ The builders did a great job.

4 something that is your responsibility □ It's my job to make sure there's enough food.

5 have a job an informal phrase meaning to find something difficult □ I had a job finding her house.

➤ If you want to ask someone what type of job they do, the usual question is **What do you do?** or **What do you do for a living?** People do not usually ask 'What is your job?'

➔ go to it's a good job

• **jobless** /ˈdʒɒblɪs/ ► ADJECTIVE not having a job, or to do with people who do not have jobs □ The jobless rate has fallen.

► PLURAL NOUN **the jobless** people who do not have a job

jobshare /ˈdʒɒbʃeə(r)/ VERB [**jobshares, jobsharing, jobshared**] to divide the duties and pay of one job between two people who work at different times □ I've jobshared with Anna for 5 years now.

• **jobsharing** /ˈdʒɒbʃeərɪŋ/ NOUN, NO PLURAL when two or more people jobshare

jockey /ˈdʒɒkɪ/ NOUN [plural **jockeys**] someone who rides a horse in races □ a champion jockey

jocular /ˈdʒɒkjʊlə(r)/ ADJECTIVE intended to be funny □ a jocular remark

jodhpurs /ˈdʒɒdpəz/ PLURAL NOUN trousers that you wear for riding a horse

jog /dʒɒg/ ► VERB [**jogs, jogging, jogged**]

1 to run slowly, especially for exercise □ She jogs around the park every morning.

2 to push or knock something gently by mistake □ You jogged my elbow and made me spill my tea!

◆ IDIOM **jog someone's memory** to make someone remember something □ Police reconstructions are designed to jog people's memories about crimes.

► NOUN [plural **jogs**] a slow run for exercise □ They've gone for a jog along the beach.

• **jogger** /ˈdʒɒgə(r)/ NOUN [plural **joggers**] someone who jogs for exercise

• **jogging** /ˈdʒɒgɪŋ/ NOUN, NO PLURAL running slowly for exercise

join /dʒɔɪn/ VERB [**joins, joining, joined**]

1 to become a member of a group or organization □ I've joined a rowing club. □ He joined the army last year. □ I joined the company in 1999.

2 to connect things together □ + to You have to join the metal part to the wood.

3 to come together at a particular point □ The track joins the main road just around this corner.

4 to come together with other people □ Please welcome Jill Smith, who joins us from London. □ Would you like to join us for lunch?

5 join hands to hold someone's hand with your hand

♦ IDIOM **join forces with someone** to work together with someone to achieve something □ *Our school joined forces with the girls' school to put on a play.*

♦ PHRASAL VERB **join in** to take part in an activity with other people □ *He didn't join in with the singing.* NOUN [*plural* **joins**] a place where two things are joined together

joint /dʒɔɪnt/ ▶ NOUN [*plural* **joints**]
1 a place in your body where two bones meet □ *painful hip joints*
2 a large piece of meat that is cooked whole □ *a joint of beef*
3 a place where two or more things join □ *Water was leaking from a joint in the pipe.*
▶ ADJECTIVE done or owned together 🔄 *The project was a joint effort between Tom and Sue.* 🔄 *Some married couples have a joint account.*

● **jointly** /dʒɔɪntlɪ/ ADVERB together □ *They're applying jointly for a mortgage.*

joke /dʒəʊk/ ▶ NOUN [*plural* **jokes**]
1 something that someone says or does to make people laugh 🔄 *Matt is always telling jokes.*
2 something that you cannot respect or be serious about because it is so bad □ *The whole company has become a bit of a joke.*

♦ IDIOMS **be no joke** to be difficult and to need a lot of work or effort □ *It's no joke managing a team that size.* **go beyond a joke** if a bad situation goes beyond a joke, it becomes very serious
▶ VERB [**jokes, joking, joked**]
1 to make a joke □ *The kids were laughing and joking about him missing the goal.*
2 Just/Only joking! something you say meaning that what you have just said is not true and was intended to be funny □ *There's a big rip in your trousers. Only joking!*
3 You're joking! something you say when someone says something extremely surprising □ *'She's only twenty.' 'You're joking! I thought she was nearer forty!'*
joker /dʒəʊkə(r)/ NOUN [*plural* **jokers**]
1 someone who likes telling jokes or making people laugh
2 one of two cards in a set of playing cards that can be used as any card in some games

jolly /dʒɒlɪ/ ADJECTIVE [**jollier, jolliest**] happy □ *a man with a jolly face*

jolt /dʒəʊlt/ ▶ NOUN [*plural* **jolts**]
1 a sudden, forceful movement □ *The train stopped with a jolt.*
2 an unpleasant shock □ *The news gave Liam a bit of a jolt.*
▶ VERB [**jolts, jolting, jolted**] to make a sudden, forceful movement □ *The roller coaster jolted to a top.*

jostle /dʒɒsəl/ VERB [**jostles, jostling, jostled**] to push roughly against someone in a crowd □ *The prime minister was jostled by an angry mob.*

jot /dʒɒt/
♦ PHRASAL VERB [**jots, jotting, jotted**] **jot something down** to write a small amount quickly □ *He quickly jotted down the car number plate.*

joule /dʒuːl/ NOUN [*plural* **joules**] a unit of measurement of work or energy. A physics word.

journal /dʒɜːnəl/ NOUN [*plural* **journals**]
1 a magazine about a particular subject □ *He subscribes to several political journals.*
2 a book in which someone writes what they have done each day

● **journalism** /dʒɜːnəlɪzəm/ NOUN, NO PLURAL the work of writing articles for newspapers, magazines, television or radio □ *a career in journalism*

● **journalist** /dʒɜːnəlɪst/ NOUN [*plural* **journalists**] someone who works in journalism

journey /dʒɜːnɪ/ NOUN [*plural* **journeys**] when you travel from one place to another, especially a long distance □ *He has a two-hour journey to work each day.* □ *The train journey was very pleasant.*

➤ Note that when you visit a place and come back again, you usually call this a **trip** and not a journey: □ *Dan has just come back from a trip to Paris.*

jovial /dʒəʊvɪəl/ ADJECTIVE happy and friendly □ *David was in a very jovial mood.*

joy /dʒɔɪ/ NOUN [*plural* **joys**]
1 a feeling of being very happy □ *She finally experienced the joy of holding her child.*
2 something that makes you very happy □ *The new model is a joy to drive.*

joyful /dʒɔɪful/ or **joyous** /dʒɔɪəs/ ADJECTIVE very happy □ *the joyful occasion of their wedding*

joypad /dʒɔɪpæd/ NOUN [*plural* **joypads**] the thing with buttons on that you hold in your hand and press when you play a computer game

joyride /dʒɔɪraɪd/ NOUN [*plural* **joyrides**] a fast drive for pleasure in a stolen car

● **joyrider** /dʒɔɪraɪdə(r)/ NOUN [*plural* **joyriders**] someone who steals a car and drives it for pleasure

● **joyriding** /dʒɔɪraɪdɪŋ/ NOUN, NO PLURAL the crime of stealing a car and driving it fast for pleasure

joystick /dʒɔɪstɪk/ NOUN [*plural* **joysticks**] a vertical handle used to control movement in an aircraft or used when playing a computer game

JP /ˌdʒeɪˈpiː/ ABBREVIATION Justice of the Peace; a judge in a local law court

JPEG /dʒeɪpeg/ NOUN [*plural* **JPEGs**] a type of computer file that contains pictures. A computing word.

Jr ABBREVIATION Junior; used after someone's name to show they are the younger of two men in a family with the same name □ *John Willis Jr*

jubilant /'dʒu:bɪlənt/ ADJECTIVE very happy, usually because of achieving a success □ *Jubilant supporters surrounded their team.*

• **jubilation** /,dʒu:bɪ'leɪʃən/ NOUN, NO PLURAL great happiness because of achieving a success

jubilee /'dʒu:bɪli:/ NOUN [plural **jubilees**] a celebration of an important event that happened on a particular day many years ago □ *The Queen celebrated her golden jubilee in 2002.*

Judaism /'dʒu:deɪ,ɪzəm/ NOUN, NO PLURAL the Jewish religion which is based on the Old Testament of the Bible

judge /dʒʌdʒ/ ► VERB [judges, judging, judged]
1 to form an opinion about someone or something □ **+ on** *I tend to judge books on their story rather than their use of language.* □ **+ by** *It's wrong to judge people by what clothes they wear.* □ *They judged it necessary to hire a bodyguard.* □ *The event was judged a success.*
2 to decide who or what is the winner of a competition □ *I was asked to judge the jam making competition.*
3 to try to guess the amount, size, etc. of something □ *I failed to judge the distance correctly and drove into a wall.*
4 to have a bad opinion of a person or their behaviour □ *I try not to judge other people.*
► NOUN [plural **judges**]
1 someone who is in charge of a trial in court and decides what punishments should be given
2 someone who judges a competition
3 a good/bad, etc. judge of something someone who is good/bad, etc. at forming the correct opinion of something □ *He is a poor judge of character.*

• **judgement** or **judgment** /'dʒʌdʒmənt/ NOUN [plural **judgements** or **judgments**]
1 the ability to make good decisions or form correct opinions 🔁 *When it comes to education, I trust her judgement.* 🔁 *I can't tell you exactly how much salt to add – just use your judgement.*
2 an opinion about someone or something 🔁 *In my judgement, it wouldn't be a very sensible thing to do.* 🔁 *You will have to make a judgement about whether or not to trust her.*
3 the decision made by a judge in a court 🔁 *He is due to pass judgment on Wednesday.*

• **judgemental** or **judgmental** /dʒʌdʒ'mentəl/ ADJECTIVE quick to form a bad opinion of a person or someone's behaviour

judicial /dʒu:'dɪʃəl/ ADJECTIVE to do with judges or a court of law □ *a judicial review*

judiciary /dʒu:'dɪʃərɪ/ NOUN [plural **judiciaries**] the judiciary the part of a country's government that is responsible for its legal system and is made up of all its judges

judicious /dʒu:'dɪʃəs/ ADJECTIVE sensible and showing good judgment □ *Many dishes are improved by a judicious use of spices.*

judo /'dʒu:dəu/ NOUN, NO PLURAL a sport from Japan in which two people fight and try to throw each other to the ground

jug /dʒʌg/ NOUN [plural **jugs**] a container with a handle used for pouring liquids □ *a milk jug* □ *a jug of cream*

juggernaut /'dʒʌgənɔ:t/ NOUN [plural **juggernauts**] a very long truck

juggle /'dʒʌgəl/ VERB [juggles, juggling, juggled]
1 to keep several balls, etc. in the air by repeatedly throwing them up and catching them
2 to deal with several jobs or activities at the same time □ *A lot of women juggle a job with looking after their home and their family.*

• **juggler** /'dʒʌglə(r)/ NOUN [plural **jugglers**] someone who juggles to entertain people

juice /dʒu:s/ NOUN [plural **juices**]
1 the liquid in fruit or vegetables, often used as a drink □ *a glass of orange juice*
2 the liquid that comes out of a piece of meat while it is being cooked

• **juicy** /'dʒu:sɪ/ ADJECTIVE [juicier, juiciest]
1 full of juice □ *a nice juicy peach*
2 describes information about another person's private life that is interesting and slightly shocking □ *a juicy bit of gossip*

jukebox /'dʒu:kbɒks/ NOUN [plural **jukeboxes**] a machine that plays music when you put money in it and press buttons

July /dʒu:'laɪ/ NOUN the seventh month of the year, after June and before August □ *Clara will be 11 in July.*

jumble /'dʒʌmbəl/ ► VERB [jumbles, jumbling, jumbled] to mix things up so that they are untidy □ *His clothes are all jumbled up in his drawers.*
► NOUN, NO PLURAL a lot of things that have been mixed up in an untidy way □ *It's hard to find anything in the jumble on Pam's desk.*

jumble sale /'dʒʌmbəl ,seɪl/ NOUN [plural **jumble sales**] a sale where old things or things you do not want are sold to get money for an organization

jumbo /'dʒʌmbəu/ ► ADJECTIVE very big □ *a jumbo crossword*
► NOUN [plural **jumbos**] a jumbo jet

jumbo jet /,dʒʌmbəu 'dʒet/ NOUN [plural **jumbo jets**] a very big plane that can carry hundreds of passengers

jump /dʒʌmp/ ► VERB [jumps, jumping, jumped]
1 to push yourself off the ground or other surface with your legs □ *We jumped up and down in excitement* □ **+ over** *The dog jumped over the wall.* □ *He jumped down from the tree.*
2 to go over something by pushing yourself into the air with your legs □ *The horse jumped the fence.*
3 to move or go somewhere quickly □ *As soon as I heard the news, I jumped on a train to Scotland.* □ *He jumped to his feet when she came in.*
4 to increase suddenly in amount or value □ *Share*

jumped more than 20%. □ *Property prices have jumped dramatically.*

5 to make a movement because you are suddenly afraid 🔁 *The noise of the bell made me jump.*

6 jump the queue to go to the front of a queue (= line of people waiting)

♦ IDIOM **jump the gun** to start doing something too soon □ *Asking her to marry you after 3 weeks was jumping the gun a bit, wasn't it?*

♦ PHRASAL VERB **jump at something** to accept an opportunity in a very eager way 🔁 *He jumped at the chance to work in Africa.*

▶ NOUN [*plural* **jumps**]

1 when you push yourself off the ground with your legs □ *Do three more jumps.*

2 something to be jumped over, or a distance that must be jumped

3 a sudden increase □ *+ in* *There has been a jump in the unemployment numbers.*

jumper /ˈdʒʌmpə(r)/ NOUN [*plural* **jumpers**] a warm piece of clothing with sleeves that you pull on over your head and wear on the top half of your body

jumpy /ˈdʒʌmpɪ/ ADJECTIVE [**jumpier, jumpiest**] an informal word for nervous □ *Adam was getting jumpy about his exam results.*

junction /ˈdʒʌŋkʃən/ NOUN [*plural* **junctions**] a place where roads or railway lines meet and cross □ *Turn right at the junction ahead.*

juncture /ˈdʒʌŋktʃə(r)/ NOUN [*plural* **junctures**] a particular point in a series of events. A formal word. □ *We can't possibly give up at this juncture.*

June /dʒuːn/ NOUN the sixth month of the year, after May and before July □ *We're moving house in June.*

jungle /ˈdʒʌŋɡəl/ NOUN [*plural* **jungles**] a thick forest in a hot country □ *the Peruvian jungle*

junior /ˈdʒuːnjə(r)/ ▶ ADJECTIVE

1 having a lower position in an organization □ *junior staff* □ *She's a junior minister at the Foreign Office.*

2 of or for younger people □ *junior members of the tennis club* □ *junior classes*

▶ NOUN [*plural* **juniors**]

1 be 5/10 etc. years someone's junior to be 5/10 etc years younger than someone □ *His brother is 3 years his junior.*

2 someone who has a low position in an organization □ *an office junior*

3 a child in a junior school

junior high school /ˌdʒuːnjə ˈhaɪ ˌskuːl/ NOUN [*plural* **junior high schools**] a school in the US for young people between 12 and 14 years old

junior school /ˈdʒuːnjə ˌskuːl/ NOUN [*plural* **junior schools**] a school in Britain for children between 7 and 11 years old

junk /dʒʌŋk/ NOUN, NO PLURAL old things with little use or value □ *Most of this is junk and we can just get rid of it.*

junk food /ˈdʒʌŋk ˌfuːd/ NOUN, NO PLURAL food that is not good for your health but that you can eat and prepare quickly

junk mail /ˈdʒʌŋk ˌmeɪl/ NOUN, NO PLURAL advertisements that are sent to you by post although you did not ask for them

jurisdiction /ˌdʒʊərɪsˈdɪkʃən/ NOUN, NO PLURAL the power of an official organization to make legal decisions □ *Libraries come under the jurisdiction of the local authority.*

juror /ˈdʒʊərə(r)/ NOUN [*plural* **jurors**] one of the members of a jury

♦ **jury** /ˈdʒʊərɪ/ NOUN [*plural* **juries**]

1 a group of people in a court of law who listen to the facts and decide whether someone is guilty of a crime or not

2 a group of people who decide who will win a competition

♦ IDIOM **the jury is (still) out** used for saying that no one has yet decided for sure whether something is a good thing or not □ *The jury is still out on whether these vitamins help prevent the disease.*

just /dʒʌst/ ▶ ADVERB

1 at this time, or at a particular time in the past □ *I'm just getting dressed.* □ *We were just sitting down to dinner.* 🔁 *Just then, a man came in.* 🔁 *I can't talk to you just now.*

2 a very short time ago □ *I've just finished work.* □ *The clock's just struck five.*

3 only □ *I'll just have a sandwich.* □ *It was just a joke.* □ *I just want to go home.*

4 almost not 🔁 *I could only just see him.* □ *We just managed to swim to the shore.* □ *She was just ahead of me.*

5 used to emphasize what you are saying □ *I was just devastated by the news.* □ *A cold drink was just what I needed.*

6 just about almost □ *I've just about finished here.*

7 be just about to do something to be going to do something very soon □ *I was just about to phone you.*

8 just as at the same time as □ *Just as we got there, the fire alarm went off.*

▶ ADJECTIVE

1 fair □ *a just decision*

2 deserved □ *a just reward*

justice /ˈdʒʌstɪs/ NOUN [*plural* **justices**]

1 *no plural* fair treatment of people by the law □ *The group is fighting for justice for all.*

2 *no plural* the quality of being fair when dealing with people and their problems

3 *no plural* the system of laws which judges and punishes people □ *the criminal justice system*

4 a US word for **judge**

justifiable /ˈdʒʌstɪˌfaɪəbəl/ ADJECTIVE acceptable because of having a good reason □ *His reaction was completely justifiable in the circumstances.*

♦ **justifiably** /ˈdʒʌstɪˌfaɪəblɪ/ ADVERB in a justifiable way □ *She was justifiably annoyed.*

♦ **justification** /ˌdʒʌstɪfɪˈkeɪʃən/ NOUN [*plural* **justifications**] a good reason for doing something □ *There is no justification for that sort of behaviour.*

• **justify** /'dʒʌstɪfaɪ/ VERB [**justifies, justifying, justified**] to be a good reason for something or to give a good reason for something □ *I couldn't justify spending all that money on myself.*

justly /'dʒʌstlɪ/ ADVERB
1 in a way that is right or reasonable □ *She is justly proud of her son's achievements.*
2 fairly □ *The headmaster dealt with the matter justly in my opinion.*

jut /dʒʌt/ VERB [**juts, jutting, jutted**] to stick out from the surrounding surface or edge □ *The peninsula juts out into the Irish Sea.*

juvenile /'dʒuːvənaɪl/ ▶ ADJECTIVE
1 for or to do with young people □ *a juvenile court*

2 behaving in a silly way like a child □ *a juvenile sense of humour*
▶ NOUN [*plural* **juveniles**] a young person

juvenile delinquent /ˌdʒuːvənaɪl dɪ'lɪŋkwənt/ NOUN [*plural* **juvenile delinquents**] a young person who commits a crime

juxtapose /ˌdʒʌkstə'pəʊz/ VERB [**juxtaposes, juxtaposing, juxtaposed**] to put two people or things together, often to show how different they are. A formal word.
• **juxtaposition** /ˌdʒʌkstəpə'zɪʃən/ NOUN [*plural* **juxtapositions**] when people or things are juxtaposed. A formal word. □ *The artist uses fascinating juxtapositions of colours and textures.*

K*k*

K[1] *or* **k** /keɪ/ the 11th letter of the alphabet

K[2] /keɪ/ ABBREVIATION

1 one thousand □ *She earns £30K a year.*

2 kilobyte

kaleidoscope /kə'laɪdəskəup/ NOUN [*plural* **kaleidoscopes**] a tube that you look into, with small pieces of coloured glass that make different patterns when you turn the tube

kangaroo /ˌkæŋgə'ru:/ NOUN [*plural* **kangaroos**] an Australian animal that moves by jumping, and carries its baby in a pouch (= a pocket at the front of its body)

karaoke /ˌkærɪ'əukɪ/ NOUN, NO PLURAL a type of entertainment in which members of the audience sing popular songs while recorded music is played

karate /kə'ra:tɪ/ NOUN, NO PLURAL a type of Japanese fighting in which you use your hands and feet

kayak /'kaɪæk/ NOUN [*plural* **kayaks**] a type of long narrow boat for one person that you move using a paddle (= long piece of wood) with two flat ends

Kb *or* **KB** /ˌkeɪ'bi:/ ABBREVIATION kilobyte

kebab /kɪ'bæb/ NOUN [*plural* **kebabs**] pieces of meat cooked on a long thin stick

keel /ki:l/ NOUN [*plural* **keels**] a long piece of wood or metal attached under a ship, used for balancing it

➤ IDIOM **on an even keel** continuing calmly, without problems or sudden changes □ *The company has had a difficult few months but we're back on an even keel now.*

➤ PHRASAL VERB [**keels, keeling, keeled**] **keel over** to fall because you are ill or tired □ *He suddenly just keeled over.*

keen /ki:n/ ADJECTIVE [**keener, keenest**]

1 interested in or enjoying a particular activity very much □ *Jim's a keen swimmer.* □ **+ on** *She's very keen on riding.* 🔁 *She has a keen interest in art.*

2 wanting to do something □ **+ to do something** *Everyone seemed very keen to help.*

3 a keen sense of smell or hearing is a very good sense of smell or hearing □ *Mice have a keen sense of smell.*

keenly /'ki:nlɪ/ ADVERB strongly □ *The government is keenly aware of the problem.*

keenness /'ki:nnɪs/ NOUN, NO PLURAL when someone is keen

keep /ki:p/ ► VERB [**keeps, keeping, kept**]

1 to make someone or something stay in a particular state □ *Keep the door closed.* □ *The noise kept me awake.* □ *Keep still!* □ *Keep your mouth shut!*

2 to prevent someone or something going to a particular place □ *Keep the children away from the fire.* □ *I tried to keep the sun off my face.* □ *A high fence kept out strangers.*

3 **keep doing something** to continue to do something, or to do something repeatedly □ *It's hard to keep going when you're so tired.* □ *I keep forgetting to lock the door.*

4 to continue to have or own something □ *You can keep the book.* □ *The company has promised that they will keep their jobs.*

5 to put something in a particular place when you are not using it □ *I keep my diary in a drawer.* 🔁 *This ring is valuable - make sure you keep it in a safe place.*

6 to make someone stay in a particular place □ *They're keeping him in hospital for a few more days.* □ *She was kept in after school.*

7 to have a written record of something 🔁 *to keep notes/records* □ *I kept a diary for years.*

8 **keep a promise** to do what you have promised to do

9 **keep a secret** to not tell anyone a secret

➡ *go to* **keep an eye on someone/something, keep an eye out for someone/something, keep your eyes open, keep your ears open, keep a straight face, keep your hair on**

♦ PHRASAL VERBS **keep something down**

1 to make an amount or level of something stay low □ *We have managed to keep our prices down.*

2 to eat something without vomiting □ *He hasn't kept anything down today.* **keep on doing something** to continue to do something, or to do something repeatedly □ *He ignored the cries and kept on walking.* □ *They keep on waking me up.* **keep to something**

1 to stay in an area □ *Keep to the marked path.*

2 to do what you have said you will do □ *We decided to keep to our original plan.* **keep up**

1 to move at the same speed as someone else □ *She walks so fast I can hardly keep up.*

2 to make the same amount of progress as someone or something else □ *Their rivals invested in new technology, and they failed to keep up.*

3 to know and understand something □ *We need to keep up with all the latest research.* **keep up something** to continue to do something □ *I've been keeping up my exercise programme.*

► NOUN, NO PLURAL the money that you need in order to live 🔁 *I earn my keep by doing housework.*

- **keeper** /'ki:pə(r)/ NOUN [plural **keepers**] a person who looks after something, especially animals in a zoo
- **keeping** /'ki:pɪŋ/ NOUN, NO PLURAL
1 in keeping with something in the same style as something, and suitable to be with or near it □ *The new building is not in keeping with its surroundings.*
2 in someone's keeping being kept by someone

kennel /'kenəl/ NOUN [plural **kennels**] a small shelter for a dog

kept /kept/ PAST TENSE AND PAST PARTICIPLE OF **keep**

kerb /kɜ:b/ NOUN [plural **kerbs**] the edge of a pavement (= the path along the side of a road)

kernel /'kɜ:nəl/ NOUN [plural **kernels**] the soft part in the shell of a nut or inside the stone of a fruit

kerosene *or* **kerosine** /'kerəsi:n/ NOUN, NO PLURAL the US word for **paraffin**

ketchup /'ketʃəp/ NOUN, NO PLURAL a thick red sauce made from tomatoes

kettle /'ketəl/ NOUN [plural **kettles**] a container with a lid and a handle, used for boiling water ⌨ *I've put the kettle on* (= I am heating water in a kettle) *for a cup of tea*

kettledrum /'ketəldrʌm/ NOUN [plural **kettledrums**] a large metal drum in the shape of a bowl

key /ki:/ ► NOUN [plural **keys**]
1 a small metal object used for locking something such as a door or window, or for starting the engine of a vehicle ⌨ *I switched the light off and turned the key in the lock.* ⌨ *Have you seen my car keys?* ⌨ *a bunch of keys*
2 a button on a computer keyboard or a telephone ⌨ *Use the arrow keys to move from one image to the next.* □ *Press any key to continue.*
3 the main thing that helps you to achieve something □ **+ to** *Confidence is the key to success in this business.*
4 one of the white or black parts you press on a piano or a similar instrument to make a sound
5 a set of musical notes □ **+ of** *This piece is played in the key of D minor.*
6 a list of signs with their meanings □ *The key is printed on the back of the map.*
7 a list of answers to questions in an exercise or test
► ADJECTIVE most important ⌨ *He played a key role in the campaign.* ⌨ *Dean is one of the team's key players.* □ **+ to** *Their support is key to the success of the project.*
► VERB [**keys, keying, keyed**] to put data into a computer or other piece of electronic equipment using a keyboard □ **+ in** *Please key in your personal number.*

keyboard /'ki:bɔ:d/ NOUN [plural **keyboards**]
1 a piece of computer equipment with keys (= buttons) on it that you press to put information into the computer
2 the set of keys on a musical instrument such as a piano □ *a piano keyboard*

3 an electronic musical instrument that is similar to a piano
- **keyboarder** /'ki:bɔ:də(r)/ NOUN [plural **keyboarders**] someone whose job is to enter information on a computer

keyhole /'ki:həʊl/ NOUN [plural **keyholes**] the part of a lock that you put a key into

keypad /'ki:pæd/ NOUN [plural **keypads**] a small keyboard on a telephone, for example

key ring /ki: rɪŋ/ NOUN [plural **key rings**] a metal ring for keeping keys on

kg /ˌkeɪˈdʒi:/ ABBREVIATION **kilogram** or **kilograms**

khaki /'kɑ:kɪ/ ► ADJECTIVE having a green-brown colour □ *a khaki uniform*
► NOUN, NO PLURAL a green-brown colour

kHz ABBREVIATION **kilohertz**

kick /kɪk/ ► VERB [**kicks, kicking, kicked**]
1 to hit someone or something with your foot □ *Jane kicked the ball over the fence.* □ *He kicked me in the leg.*
2 to move your legs quickly and with force □ *She was carried, kicking and screaming, to the car.*
♦ PHRASAL VERBS **kick in** to start to have an effect □ *You'll feel better when the painkillers kick in.* **kick (something) off** to start something □ *We kicked off the session with a discussion about love.* **kick someone out** to make someone leave a place □ *He was kicked out of the army for laziness.*
► NOUN [plural **kicks**]
1 when you kick, or kick something □ *I gave him a kick in the shins.*
2 an informal word meaning a feeling of pleasure or excitement ⌨ *He gets a kick out of driving fast.*

kick-off /kɪk-ɒf/ NOUN [plural **kick-offs**] the start of a football game

kick-start /kɪk-stɑ:t/ VERB [**kick-starts, kick-starting, kick-started**] to make something start working or start being successful, especially after a less successful period □ *That television appearance kick-started her career.*

kid /kɪd/ ► NOUN [plural **kids**]
1 an informal word meaning child □ *Have they got any kids?* □ *You can't expect him to look after the baby – he's just a kid.*
2 a young goat
► VERB [**kids, kidding, kidded**]
1 to say something that is not true, as a joke. An informal word. □ *Don't worry; I'm only kidding.*
2 kid yourself to try to believe something that is not true □ *She says she's happy but I think she's just kidding herself.*
3 Are you kidding? an informal way of saying that you think something someone has said is not true or not sensible □ *'She's 40.' 'Are you kidding? She looks about 60!'*

kidnap /'kɪdnæp/ VERB [**kidnaps, kidnapping, kidnapped**] to take someone away using force, and ask their family or the government for something such as money in exchange for their safe return □ *The journalist was kidnapped three weeks ago.*

● **kidnapper** /'kɪdnæpə(r)/ NOUN [*plural* **kidnappers**] a person who kidnaps someone □ *The kidnappers have demanded a ransom of £2 million.*

● **kidnapping** /'kɪdnæpɪŋ/ NOUN [*plural* **kidnappings**] when someone is kidnapped □ *There have been several kidnappings in this part of the world recently.*

kidney /'kɪdnɪ/ NOUN [*plural* **kidneys**] one of the two organs in your body that clean your blood and remove waste from it. A biology word.

kill /kɪl/ VERB [**kills, killing, killed**]
1 to make a person or animal die □ *Two people were killed in the crash.* □ *The explosion killed six people.* □ *He tried to kill himself.*
2 if part of your body is killing you, it hurts a lot □ *My feet are killing me.*

● **killer** /'kɪlə(r)/ NOUN [*plural* **killers**] a person who kills someone □ *Police have appealed for more information to help catch the killer.*

● **killing** /'kɪlɪŋ/ NOUN [*plural* **killings**] when someone is killed □ *Police are investigating the killing.*
➡ IDIOM **make a killing** to make a lot of money

kiln /kɪln/ NOUN [*plural* **kilns**] a large oven for baking clay things such as bricks

kilo /'kiːləʊ/ NOUN [*plural* **kilos**] a short way to say and write **kilogram**

kilo- /'kɪləʊ/ PREFIX kilo- is added to the beginning of words to mean 'one thousand' □ *kilogram* □ *kilometre*

kilobyte /'kɪləbaɪt/ NOUN [*plural* **kilobytes**] a unit for measuring computer memory or data, equal to 1024 bytes. This is often written **Kb**. A computing word.

kilogram *or* **kilogramme** /'kɪləˌgræm/ NOUN [*plural* **kilograms** *or* **kilogrammes**] a unit for measuring weight, equal to 1000 grams. This is often written **kg**. □ *Katherine weighs 60 kilograms.*

kilohertz /'kɪləˌhɜːts/ NOUN [*plural* **kilohertz**] a unit for measuring radio waves. This is often written **kHz**. A physics word.

kilometre /'kɪləˌmiːtə(r), kɪˈlɒmɪtə(r)/ NOUN [*plural* **kilometres**] a unit for measuring distance, equal to 1000 metres. This is often written **km**. □ *We live 20 kilometres from the coast.*

kilowatt /'kɪləˌwɒt/ NOUN [*plural* **kilowatts**] a unit for measuring electrical power, equal to 1000 watts. This is often shortened to **kW**.

kilt /kɪlt/ NOUN [*plural* **kilts**] a traditional Scottish piece of clothing that looks like a skirt and is worn especially by men

kimono /kɪˈməʊnəʊ/ NOUN [*plural* **kimonos**] a traditional Japanese piece of clothing that looks like a long coat, and is tied round the waist

kin /kɪn/ NOUN, NO PLURAL a formal word that means all your family
➡ go to next of kin

kind /kaɪnd/ ▶ NOUN [*plural* **kinds**]
1 a type of person or thing □ *+ of* What kind of dog have you got? ⊞ *Encourage children to try different kinds of fruit.* ⊞ *There are all kinds of styles to choose from.*
2 **kind of** an informal phrase that means slightly □ *It's kind of like Sara's dress.*
▶ ADJECTIVE [**kinder, kindest**] behaving in a way that shows you care about people and want to make them happy □ *She's the kindest person I know.* □ *+ to* You've all been very kind to me. □ *+ of* It was kind of you to help us. □ *Thank you for your kind offer.*

kindergarten /'kɪndəˌgɑːtən/ NOUN [*plural* **kindergartens**]
1 in the UK, a school for children under five
2 in the US, the first year of school education for children aged five or six

kind-hearted /ˌkaɪndˈhɑːtɪd/ ADJECTIVE kind towards other people

kindly /'kaɪndlɪ/ ▶ ADVERB
1 in a kind way □ *Charlotte has very kindly offered to help.*
2 used for politely asking someone to do something when you are angry □ *Would you kindly be quiet!*
3 **not take kindly to something** to be annoyed by something □ *I do not take kindly to being called a liar.*
▶ ADJECTIVE [**kindlier, kindliest**] an old-fashioned word that means kind □ *a kindly old lady*

kindness /'kaɪndnɪs/ NOUN, NO PLURAL when someone is kind □ *What I like most about him is his kindness.* ⊞ *This small act of kindness made a great impression on her.*

kinetic /kɪˈnetɪk, kaɪˈnetɪk/ ADJECTIVE to do with movement. A physics word.

king /kɪŋ/ NOUN [*plural* **kings**]
1 a man who rules a country, being the most important male member of its royal family □ *He's the future king of Great Britain.*
2 a man who is considered to be the best at a particular thing □ *+ of* Elvis, the king of rock.
3 a playing card with a picture of a king on it
4 in the game of chess, the most important piece that each player has one of and that can move in any direction

● **kingdom** /'kɪŋdəm/ NOUN [*plural* **kingdoms**] a country ruled by a king or queen □ *the United Kingdom* □ *the kingdom of Denmark*

kingfisher /'kɪŋˌfɪʃə(r)/ NOUN [*plural* **kingfishers**] a bird that eats fish and has an area of bright blue on it

king-size /'kɪŋˌsaɪz/ *or* **king-sized** /'kɪŋˌsaɪzd/ ADJECTIVE larger than the usual size □ *We've bought a king-size bed.*

kink /kɪŋk/ NOUN [plural **kinks**] a curve or twist in something, often something that should be straight □ *The water won't flow if there's a kink in the tube.*

kiosk /ˈkiːɒsk/ NOUN [plural **kiosks**] a small shop that sells things such as newspapers, drinks and sweets

kipper /ˈkɪpə(r)/ NOUN [plural **kippers**] a herring (= type of fish) that has been treated with smoke

kiss /kɪs/ ▶ VERB [**kisses, kissing, kissed**] to touch someone with your lips, especially on their mouth or face, to show that you feel love or affection for them 🔁 *He kissed her goodbye and got into the car.* □ *She leaned towards him and kissed his cheek.*
▶ NOUN [plural **kisses**] when you kiss someone 🔁 *He gave her a kiss.* □ *+ on a kiss on the lips*

kit /kɪt/ NOUN [plural **kits**]
1 the clothes that you need for a particular activity 🔁 *I brought my football kit home for washing.*
2 a set of tools or equipment that you need for a particular activity □ *a first aid kit* □ *a bicycle repair kit*
3 a set of parts that you can put together to make something □ *I got a model boat kit for my birthday.*

kitchen /ˈkɪtʃɪn/ NOUN [plural **kitchens**] a room where you prepare and cook food, and sometimes eat food □ *John is in the kitchen.* 🔁 *I sat at the kitchen table and drank my coffee.*

kite /kaɪt/ NOUN [plural **kites**] a toy made of a light material with a long string attached to it that you hold while it flies in the air

kitten /ˈkɪtən/ NOUN [plural **kittens**] a young cat

kitty /ˈkɪti/ NOUN [plural **kitties**] an amount of money that is collected by a group of people and used for a particular purpose

kiwi /ˈkiːwiː/ NOUN [plural **kiwis**] a bird from New Zealand that cannot fly

kiwi fruit /ˈkiːwiː fruːt/ NOUN [plural **kiwi fruit**] a small fruit with bright green flesh, black seeds and skin with small hairs

km ABBREVIATION kilometre or kilometres

knack /næk/ NOUN, NO PLURAL a skill □ *Gina has a knack for making people do what she wants.* 🔁 *They seem to have lost the knack of winning.*

knead /niːd/ VERB [**kneads, kneading, kneaded**] to press dough (= the soft substance that you cook to make bread) repeatedly with your hands before you cook it

knee /niː/ NOUN [plural **knees**]
1 the part in the middle of your leg where the leg bends □ *a knee injury*
2 the part of a pair of trousers that covers your knee

kneecap /ˈniːkæp/ NOUN [plural **kneecaps**] the bone at the front of your knee

kneel /niːl/ VERB [**kneels, kneeling, knelt**] to move into a position in which your knees and lower legs are on the ground, or to be in this position □ *+ down She*

knelt down beside me and stroked my hair. □ *He was kneeling by the bed, praying.*

knelt /nelt/ PAST TENSE AND PAST PARTICIPLE OF kneel

knew /njuː/ PAST TENSE OF know

knickers /ˈnɪkəz/ PLURAL NOUN a piece of underwear for women or girls, which covers the bottom

knick-knack /ˈnɪknæk/ NOUN [plural **knick-knacks**] a small decorative object that is usually not expensive

knife /naɪf/ ▶ NOUN [plural **knives**]
1 a tool with a blade and a handle, used especially for cutting food 🔁 *Have we got enough knives and forks?* □ *a sharp knife*
2 a similar tool with a sharp blade, used as a weapon 🔁 *She was injured in a knife attack.*
▶ VERB [**knifes, knifing, knifed**] to attack someone using a knife □ *He was knifed in the back.*

knight /naɪt/ NOUN [plural **knights**]
1 in the past, a soldier of a high social class who rode a horse
2 a man who has been given an honour by a British king or queen that allows him to use the title 'Sir'
3 in the game of chess, a piece which looks like a horse's head
• **knighthood** /ˈnaɪthʊd/ NOUN [plural **knighthoods**] an honour given by a British king or queen that allows a man to use the title 'Sir'

knit /nɪt/ VERB [**knits, knitting, knitted**] to make something, for example a piece of clothing, using two long knitting needles (= pointed metal or wooden sticks) and wool □ *I'm knitting a scarf.*
• **knitting** /ˈnɪtɪŋ/ NOUN, NO PLURAL the activity of making things using wool and long needles □ *a knitting pattern*

knives /naɪvz/ PLURAL OF knife

knob /nɒb/ NOUN [plural **knobs**]
1 a round handle on a door or a drawer 🔁 *a door knob*
2 a round button used for controlling a piece of equipment such as a radio □ *Keep turning the knob until the sound is clear.*
3 a small lump of something □ *a knob of butter*

knock /nɒk/ ▶ VERB [**knocks, knocking, knocked**]
1 to hit someone or something so that it moves or falls □ *+ over The cat knocked over the vase.* □ *The blast knocked us off our feet.* □ *I fell and knocked my tooth out.*
2 to hit a hard surface, especially a door, with your hand in order to get attention □ *Knock before you come in.* □ *+ on I knocked on the door but nobody answered.*
3 if someone's confidence is knocked, they become less confident
4 an informal word meaning to criticize someone or something □ *It's a very generous offer, so don't knock it.*
♦ PHRASAL VERBS **knock off something** to take an amount away from a price □ *She knocked off £5*

because there was a button missing. **knock someone out 1** to make someone become unconscious **2** to defeat a person or a team in a competition □ **+ of** *Liverpool have been knocked out of the cup.*
▶ NOUN [*plural* **knocks**]
1 a hit □ *He's had a nasty knock on the head.*
2 the sound of someone or something knocking on a hard surface □ *There was a knock at the door.*
3 when someone or something is criticized or damaged 🔊 *The economy has taken a knock.*

• **knocker** /'nɒkə(r)/ NOUN [*plural* **knockers**] a metal object on a door, which you knock with

knockout /'nɒkaʊt/ ▶ NOUN [*plural* **knockouts**] a competition in which a player or team stops being in the competition if they lose a game □ *They went out in the third round of the knockout.*
▶ ADJECTIVE a **knockout blow/punch** a hit in a boxing match that makes someone unconscious

knot /nɒt/ ▶ NOUN [*plural* **knots**]
1 a join made by tying two ends of string, rope or cloth together 🔊 *to tie a knot*
2 a mass of untidy, twisted threads of hair, string, etc. that are difficult to separate □ *Let's comb these knots out of your hair.*
3 a unit for measuring how fast a ship is travelling
▶ VERB [**knots, knotting, knotted**] to tie something with a knot □ *A scarf was knotted around his neck.*

know /nəʊ/ VERB [**knows, knowing, knew, known**]
1 to have information or knowledge about something □ *I didn't know the answer to her questions.* 🔊 *'What's the capital of Hungary?' 'I don't know.'* □ **+ question word** *Do you know where he lives?* □ *She knows how to make me happy.* □ **+ about** *I didn't know about the course.*
2 to be familiar with a person □ *I didn't know anyone at the party.* 🔊 *I got to know her when I was a student.* 🔊 *I don't know him very well.*
3 to be familiar with a place or a thing because you have been there, seen it, used it, etc. □ *Do you know Berlin well?* □ *I know his work.*
4 let someone know to tell someone something

□ *I'm going to be late - could you let John know, please?*
5 be known as something to be called something □ *Cromwell's supporters were known as Roundheads.*

➤ Remember that to **know** something means to *have* knowledge about something. To **find out** something is to *get* knowledge about something:
✓ *I called Annie to find out when she was leaving.*
✗ *I called Annie to know when she was leaving.*

• **knowing** /'nəʊɪŋ/ ADJECTIVE showing that you know something that is supposed to be secret □ *He gave me a knowing look.*

knowledge /'nɒlɪdʒ/ NOUN, NO PLURAL the information that you know about something 🔊 *Candidates need to show that they have a basic knowledge of English.* 🔊 *It's common knowledge* (= everyone knows) *that he has health problems.* □ **+ of** *She has a good knowledge of sport.*

• **knowledgeable** /'nɒlɪdʒəbəl/ ADJECTIVE knowing a lot about something □ *She's very knowledgeable about Greek history.*

known /nəʊn/ ▶ PAST PARTICIPLE OF **know**
▶ ADJECTIVE
1 that people know about □ *There is no known cure for the disease.*
2 famous □ *She is known for her performance in the film 'The Red Shoes'.*

knuckle /'nʌkəl/ NOUN [*plural* **knuckles**] one of the parts of your fingers where they bend or where they join your hand

koala /kəʊˈɑːlə/ NOUN [*plural* **koalas**] an Australian animal that looks like a small bear, climbs trees and eats leaves from the eucalyptus tree

Koran /kəˈrɑːn/ NOUN **the Koran** the holy book of the Islamic religion

kosher /'kəʊʃə(r)/ ADJECTIVE describes food which is prepared according to Jewish law

kung-fu /ˌkʌŋˈfuː/ NOUN, NO PLURAL a type of Chinese fighting using the hands and feet

kW ABBREVIATION **kilowatt** or **kilowatts**

L*l*

L or **l**[1] /el/ the 12th letter of the alphabet

l[2] /el/ ABBREVIATION litre

lab /læb/ NOUN [plural **labs**] a short way to say and write laboratory

label /'leɪbəl/ ► NOUN [plural **labels**]
1 a small piece of paper or cloth that is fixed to something and gives information about it □ *The washing instructions are on the label.* □ *I looked at the ingredients on the label.*
2 a company that records and sells music ⊞ *a record label*
3 a company that makes fashionable clothes, or the clothes they make ⊞ *Her wardrobe is full of designer labels.*
4 a word or phrase that is used to describe someone or something □ *With his next novel, he shed the label of science fiction writer.*
► VERB [**labels, labelling**/US **labeling, labelled**/US **labeled**]
1 to fix a label to something □ *All the boxes have been carefully labelled.* □ *Manufacturers should label their products more clearly.*
2 to describe someone or something using a particular word or phrase □ *Take care not to label a child a troublemaker.*

labor /'leɪbə(r)/ ► NOUN, NO PLURAL the US spelling of labour
► VERB [**labors, laboring, labored**] the US spelling of labour
● **laborer** /'leɪbərə(r)/ NOUN [plural **laborers**] the US spelling of labourer

laboratory /lə'bɒrətrɪ/ NOUN [plural **laboratories**] a room containing equipment for scientific work □ *a laboratory experiment* □ *Further tests were carried out at a laboratory.*

laborious /lə'bɔːrɪəs/ ADJECTIVE difficult, boring and taking a lot of hard work □ *a laborious task* □ *We had to go through a long, laborious process.*
● **laboriously** /lə'bɔːrɪəslɪ/ ADVERB in a laborious way □ *He laboriously copied it all by hand.*

labour /'leɪbə(r)/ ► NOUN, NO PLURAL
1 workers, especially in a particular country or type of work ⊞ *There is a shortage of skilled labour.* □ *the rising cost of labour* ⊞ *the labour market*
2 work, especially hard, physical work ⊞ *He was used to hard, manual labour.*
3 the process of giving birth to a baby ⊞ *She went into labour this morning.*

4 a **labour of love** work you do because you want to not for money
► VERB [**labours, labouring, laboured**] to work hard, especially doing physical work □ *Farm workers were labouring in the fields.*
● **labourer** /'leɪbərə(r)/ NOUN [plural **labourers**] a person who does hard physical work □ *a farm labourer.*

Labour Party /'leɪbə(r) 'pɑːtɪ/ NOUN, NO PLURAL in the UK, one of the main political parties

labrador /'læbrədɔː(r)/ NOUN [plural **labradors**] a large black or cream-coloured dog with short fur

labyrinth /'læbərɪnθ/ NOUN [plural **labyrinths**] a complicated system of paths that is difficult to find your way through □ *an underground labyrinth of tunnels*

lace /leɪs/ ► NOUN [plural **laces**]
1 a decorative cloth with delicate patterns of many holes □ *a collar trimmed with lace*
2 a piece of string for tying up shoes or other clothing ⊞ *He bent down to tie his shoe laces.*
► VERB [**laces, lacing, laced**] to put laces in something or to tie laces □ *He laced up his boots.*

lace-ups /'leɪsʌps/ PLURAL NOUN shoes that are tied with laces

lack /læk/ ► VERB [**lacks, lacking, lacked**] to be without something or not to not have enough of something □ *Audrey lacks a sense of humour.* □ *We lack the resources to deal with all the requests.*
► NOUN, NO PLURAL when you do not have something or you do not have enough of something □ *+ of H was suffering from lack of sleep.* ⊞ *He shows a complete lack of understanding.*
● **lacking** /'lækɪŋ/ ADJECTIVE if something is lacking, there is not enough of it □ *He is lacking in confidence* ⊞ *Support for the leader has been sadly lacking in recent months.*

lackluster /'læk,lʌstə(r)/ ADJECTIVE the US spelling of lacklustre

lacklustre /'læk,lʌstə(r)/ ADJECTIVE not exciting or energetic □ *a lacklustre performance*

lacquer /'lækə(r)/ ► NOUN [plural **lacquers**] a clear liquid which is put on a surface to make it hard and shiny
► VERB [**lacquers, lacquering, lacquered**] to cover something with lacquer

lactate /læk'teɪt/ VERB [**lactates, lactating, lactate**] to produce milk from the breasts. A biology word.

• **lactation** /ˌlækˈteɪʃən/ NOUN, NO PLURAL when milk is produced from the breasts

lactose /ˈlæktəus/ NOUN, NO PLURAL a type of sugar that is found in milk. A biology word.

lacy /ˈleɪsɪ/ ADJECTIVE
1 made of or containing lace (= cloth with a delicate pattern of holes) □ *a lacy blouse*
2 like lace

lad /læd/ NOUN [plural **lads**] an informal word for a boy or young man □ *He's a nice lad.*

ladder /ˈlædə(r)/ NOUN [plural **ladders**]
1 a set of steps that you use for climbing up to high places and can move around to different places □ *He had to climb a ladder to reach the top cupboard.*
2 a situation in which there are different levels of importance and people repeatedly try to reach a higher level, especially by working 🔁 *She hopes to make her way up the career ladder.*
3 a long hole in someone's tights (= underwear that covers a woman's legs) □ *There's a ladder in your tights.*

laden /ˈleɪdən/ ADJECTIVE carrying or holding a lot of something □ *He was laden with bags of shopping.* □ *The tree is laden with fruit.*

ladies /ˈleɪdɪz/ PLURAL NOUN a public toilet for women and girls □ *Where is the ladies, please?*

ladle /ˈleɪdəl/ ▶ NOUN [plural **ladles**] a large spoon for serving liquids, especially soup
▶ VERB [**ladles, ladling, ladled**] to serve something with a ladle □ *Mrs Moore was busy ladling soup into bowls.*

lady /ˈleɪdɪ/ NOUN [plural **ladies**]
1 a polite word for a woman □ *Ask that lady if the seat by her is free.* 🔁 *Good evening ladies and gentlemen.*
2 in the UK, a title for a woman with a high social rank

ladybird /ˈleɪdɪbɜːd/ NOUN [plural **ladybirds**] a small insect that is usually red with black spots

ladylike /ˈleɪdɪlaɪk/ ADJECTIVE behaving in a polite, controlled way that some people think is suitable for a woman

ladyship /ˈleɪdɪʃɪp/ NOUN [plural **ladyships**] a title you use when you are speaking about or to a woman of high social rank who has the title of 'Lady'

lag /læg/ ▶ VERB [**lags, lagging, lagged**]
1 to make progress more slowly than something else □ *The company is lagging a long way behind its rivals.*
2 to move more slowly than someone or something else □ *One child lagged behind the rest of the group.*
▶ NOUN [plural **lags**] the period of time or delay between two things happening 🔁 *There's a slight time lag between receiving the request and sending it to the warehouse.*

lager /ˈlɑːgə(r)/ NOUN [plural **lagers**] a light-coloured beer

lagoon /ləˈguːn/ NOUN [plural **lagoons**] an area of water separated from the sea by sand or rocks. A geography word.

laid /leɪd/ PAST TENSE AND PAST PARTICIPLE OF **lay** □ *She laid the baby on the blanket.*

laid-back /ˌleɪdˈbæk/ ADJECTIVE relaxed and not worrying about things □ *He's pretty laid-back.*

lain /leɪn/ PAST PARTICIPLE OF **lie**[2] (= put your body in a flat position) □ *I had lain down for a moment and fallen fast asleep.*

lake /leɪk/ NOUN [plural **lakes**] a large area of water with land all around it □ *Lake Como*

lamb /læm/ NOUN [plural **lambs**]
1 a young sheep
2 *no plural* meat from a young sheep □ *roast lamb* □ *lamb chops*

lame /leɪm/ ADJECTIVE [**lamer, lamest**]
1 not able to walk well because of an injury □ *a lame horse*
2 difficult to believe or respect 🔁 *He made up some lame excuse.*
♦ IDIOM **lame duck** someone who is weak and not likely to succeed □ *The minister is looking increasingly like a lame duck.*

• **lamely** /ˈleɪmlɪ/ ADVERB in a way that is difficult to believe □ *'My bus was late,' she said lamely.*

lament /ləˈment/ ▶ NOUN [plural **laments**] a sad song or poem, especially about someone's death
▶ VERB [**laments, lamenting, lamented**] a formal word meaning to feel or to express sadness about something □ *He was lamenting the passing of the old days.*

• **lamentable** /ˈlæməntəbəl/ ADJECTIVE extremely bad, in a way that makes you feel upset □ *a lamentable waste of money*

laminated /ˈlæmɪneɪtɪd/ ADJECTIVE
1 covered with thin, clear plastic
2 made by sticking layers together □ *laminated flooring*

lamp /læmp/ NOUN [plural **lamps**] a light, especially one which stands on a table □ *a table lamp* □ *a bedside lamp* □ *an old oil lamp*

lamppost /ˈlæmppəust/ NOUN [plural **lampposts**] a tall pole in the street with a light at the top

lampshade /ˈlæmpʃeɪd/ NOUN [plural **lampshades**] a cover placed over a light

LAN /læn/ ABBREVIATION local area network; a system connecting the computers of people who are in the same building. A computing word.

land /lænd/ ▶ NOUN [plural **lands**]
1 *no plural* an area of ground □ *an acre of land* 🔁 *agricultural land*
2 *no plural* the part of the Earth not covered by water 🔁 *It's good to be back on dry land.*
3 a word for a country used especially in stories 🔁 *He talked of his adventures in foreign lands.*
▶ VERB [**lands, landing, landed**]
1 when an aircraft lands, it arrives on the ground after

a flight □ *The plane landed around 3pm.* □ *The flight landed safely at Glasgow airport.*
2 to stop somewhere after flying or falling □ *The bird landed on a branch.* □ *The book fell off the table and landed heavily on the floor.* □ *I slipped but managed to land on my feet.*
3 to get something you want, especially a job □ *He landed a job with the local paper.*
4 to cause someone to be in a difficult situation or to have problems □ *He's always landing me in trouble.* □ *I found myself landed with a huge phone bill.*
• **landing** /ˈlændɪŋ/ NOUN [*plural* **landings**]
1 the process of moving a plane down to the ground ⊞ *The helicopter made an emergency landing.*
2 when someone or something reaches the ground after flying or falling □ *He had a soft landing in some leaves.*
3 the floor at the top of some stairs or the floor between two sets of stairs □ *She reached the second-floor landing.*

landfill /ˈlændfɪl/ NOUN [*plural* **landfills**] a large hole in the ground where waste is put ⊞ *a landfill site*

landlady /ˈlændˌleɪdɪ/ NOUN [*plural* **landladies**]
1 a woman who owns a house that someone else pays to live in
2 a woman who runs a pub or a small hotel

landline /ˈlændlaɪn/ NOUN [*plural* **landlines**] a phone with wires which is not a mobile phone □ *Have you tried his landline?*

landlord /ˈlændlɔːd/ NOUN [*plural* **landlords**]
1 a man who owns a house that someone else pays to live in □ *Her landlord raised the rent.*
2 a man who runs a pub or a small hotel ⊞ *a pub landlord*

landmark /ˈlændmɑːk/ NOUN [*plural* **landmarks**]
1 a place, especially a building, that helps you know where you are because you can easily recognize it □ *The tower is one of the city's most famous landmarks.* □ *He spotted a familiar landmark.*
2 an important event or achievement □ *The speech is viewed as a landmark in American history.*

landmine /ˈlændmaɪn/ NOUN [*plural* **landmines**] a bomb that is put under the ground and explodes if someone walks or drives over it

landscape /ˈlændskeɪp/ NOUN [*plural* **landscapes**]
1 a view of a large area of land □ *He looked out at the beautiful landscape.* □ *a snowy landscape*
2 when a piece of paper is arranged so that it is wider than it is tall

landslide /ˈlændslaɪd/ NOUN [*plural* **landslides**]
1 when a large amount of the ground slides down the side of a hill □ *Heavy rain triggered landslides.*
2 when one person or political party wins very easily in an election ⊞ *He won a landslide victory in 2000.*

lane /leɪn/ NOUN [*plural* **lanes**]
1 a narrow road □ *We drove along narrow country lanes.*
2 a strip of a road separated by painted lines ⊞ *She pulled out into the fast lane.* □ *The northbound lane of the motorway was closed after an accident.*
3 a route that ships or aircraft use in the sea or air ⊞ *a busy shipping lane*

language /ˈlæŋgwɪdʒ/ NOUN [*plural* **languages**]
1 *no plural* communication using speech and writing □ *formal language* ⊞ *He was warned for using foul language* (= offensive words). ⊞ *He used some interesting language to describe the scene.* □ *+ of the language of diplomacy*
2 the words used by a particular group, especially the people that live in one country □ *the English language* ⊞ *All children should learn a foreign language.* ⊞ *Do you speak any other languages?*
3 a system of symbols that represent instructions, used to program computers □ *a programming language*

languid /ˈlæŋgwɪd/ ADJECTIVE doing things slowly and without energy □ *a languid voice*
languish /ˈlæŋgwɪʃ/ VERB [**languishes**, **languishing**, **languished**] to stay in an unhappy or difficult situation □ *Political activists languished in prison for years.*
lanky /ˈlæŋkɪ/ ADJECTIVE [**lankier**, **lankiest**] tall and thin, sometimes in a way that is not attractive □ *a lanky 15-year-old boy*
lantern /ˈlæntən/ NOUN [*plural* **lanterns**] a light inside a clear container that you can carry
lap /læp/ ▶ NOUN [*plural* **laps**]
1 the top part of a person's legs when they are in a sitting position □ *Jessie sat on her mother's lap.*
2 one complete journey around a race track □ *He crashed out on the first lap of the race.*
♦ IDIOM **in the lap of luxury** in a very comfortable situation, with expensive things around you
▶ VERB [**laps**, **lapping**, **lapped**]
1 to drink something with the tongue sticking out □ *The cat was lapping milk from a saucer.*
2 if water laps, it moves gently against rocks or onto beach □ *The waves were lapping at our feet.*
3 to pass someone more than once as you go round race track
♦ PHRASAL VERB **lap something up** to enjoy experiencing or hearing something very much □ *She lapped up the compliments about her new dress.*
lapel /ləˈpel/ NOUN [*plural* **lapels**] the front part of the collar of a coat or jacket □ *He had a flower pinned t his lapel.*
lapse /læps/ ▶ NOUN [*plural* **lapses**]
1 a failure to work or to happen for a short period o time □ *a lapse of concentration* □ *There was a seriou lapse in security.*
2 a period of time between two things happening □ *After a lapse of ten years, he started to play footba again.*

▶ VERB [lapses, lapsing, lapsed] if an agreement or an arrangement lapses, it finishes after a period of time □ *His insurance policy had lapsed.*

♦ PHRASAL VERB **lapse into something** to gradually become quieter or less active □ *They both lapsed into silence.*

laptop /ˈlæptɒp/ NOUN [plural **laptops**] a small computer that can be carried easily. A computing word.

lard /lɑːd/ NOUN, NO PLURAL a hard, white fat that is used in cooking and that comes from a pig

larder /ˈlɑːdə(r)/ NOUN [plural **larders**] a large cupboard where food is kept □ *a well-stocked larder*

large /lɑːdʒ/ ADJECTIVE [**larger, largest**] big or bigger than normal in size or amount □ *a large house* □ *A large number of people were waiting.* □ *Large parts of the country are without power.*

♦ IDIOMS **at large 1** generally □ *This is a problem, not just for parents, but for the community at large.* **2** if a dangerous animal or a criminal is at large, they are free and have not been caught □ *The suspects may still be at large.* **by and large** mostly or in most situations □ *The situation was by and large peaceful.* □ *Americans, by and large, support the policy.*

large intestine /lɑːdʒ ɪnˈtestɪn/ NOUN [plural **large intestines**] the lower part of the body's system for digesting food, where food that is not digested is made into solid waste. A biology word.

largely /ˈlɑːdʒlɪ/ ADVERB mainly or mostly □ *The church has been largely rebuilt.* □ *The report was largely positive.*

lark /lɑːk/ NOUN [plural **larks**]
1 a singing bird that flies high in the sky
2 something you do for fun. An informal word. □ *We were just having a lark.*
PHRASAL VERB [larks, larking, larked] **lark about/around** to do something for fun or as a joke. An informal phrase. □ *We were larking about at the back of the class.*

larva /ˈlɑːvə/ NOUN [plural **larvae** /ˈlɑːviː/] an insect in its first stage after coming out of the egg. A biology word.

laryngitis /ˌlærɪnˈdʒaɪtɪs/ NOUN, NO PLURAL an illness that makes your throat sore and makes it difficult for you to talk

larynx /ˈlærɪŋks/ NOUN [plural **larynxes**] the part at the top of the throat that contains the vocal cords (= the parts that make your voice). A biology word.

lasagne or **lasagna** /ləˈzænjə/ NOUN [plural **lasagnes** or **lasagnas**] an Italian food made up of layers of pasta, and layers of meat or vegetables with a white sauce and cheese

laser /ˈleɪzə(r)/ NOUN [plural **lasers**] a very narrow, powerful beam of light ⏺*a laser beam* □ *The surgery uses lasers.*

laser printer /ˈleɪzə(r) prɪnt(r)/ NOUN [plural **laser printers**] a fast printer for a computer, that uses light from a laser

lash /læʃ/ ▶ NOUN [plural **lashes**]
1 when someone is hit with a whip (= a long thin piece of leather) as a punishment □ *ten lashes of the whip*
2 an eyelash (= one of the many hairs round the edges of your eyes)
▶ VERB [lashes, lashing, lashed]
1 to hit someone or something with force □ *Rain lashed against the tent.*
2 to tie something up with rope or string □ *The banners were lashed to the walls of the buildings.*
3 to hit someone with a whip
♦ PHRASAL VERB **lash out**
1 to suddenly hit or attack someone □ *He suddenly lashed out, knocking me to the ground.*
2 to criticize someone very strongly □ *Yesterday he lashed out at his critics.*

lass /læs/ NOUN [plural **lasses**] a girl or a young woman

lasso /læˈsuː/ ▶ NOUN [plural **lassoes** or **lassos**] a long rope with a circle that gets tighter when the rope is pulled, used especially for catching wild horses
▶ VERB [lassoes, lassoing, lassoed] to throw a lasso around something to catch it

last /lɑːst/ ▶ ADJECTIVE, DETERMINER
1 most recent □ *We moved house last October.* □ *In the last few months we have been very busy.* □ *On my last birthday, he gave me a necklace.* □ *The last time I ate fish, I was ill.* □ *Their last album was a huge success.*
2 coming after all the others □ *We caught the last train to Cambridge.* □ *This is the last time I will ever help you.* □ *That was her last public appearance.*
3 **the last moment/minute** the latest possible time before something □ *Our flight was cancelled at the last moment.* □ *Don't leave it to the last minute to book a hotel.*
4 the final one remaining □ *She ate my last toffee.*
5 used to emphasize that someone or something is not wanted or not suitable □ *She's the last person I'd ask for help.* □ *The last thing he needs is more work.*
➡ *go to* **be on its last legs**
▶ ADVERB
1 after all the others □ *She arrived last.* □ *Make sure you add the sugar last.* ⏺*I came last in the swimming race.*
2 most recently □ *When did you last see Anna?*
▶ VERB [lasts, lasting, lasted]
1 to continue for a period of time □ *The lesson seemed to last for ever.* □ *The film lasted over three hours.*
2 to remain in good condition □ *These boots have lasted well.*
3 to manage to stay safe, stay alive, or stay in a job □ *Without shelter, I wasn't sure we'd last the night.* ⏺*She won't last long in a job like that.*
4 to be enough □ *The food lasted for three days.*
▶ NOUN, PRONOUN

1 the person or thing that comes after all the others □ *You are always the last to finish.* □ *Am I the last?*
2 the final person or thing remaining □ **+ of** *I've eaten the last of the apples.*
3 **at last** after a long period of time □ *I've found a job at last.*

• **lasting** /ˈlɑːstɪŋ/ ADJECTIVE continuing to exist for a long time □ *They hope to achieve a lasting peace.* □ *His book made a lasting impression on me.*

• **lastly** /ˈlɑːstlɪ/ ADVERB after all other people or things □ *Lastly, I just want to thank my wife.*

latch /lætʃ/ NOUN [*plural* **latches**]
1 a piece of wood or metal that you lift or lower to open or fasten a door
2 a type of lock that needs a key to be opened from the outside

◆ PHRASAL VERBS [**latches, latching, latched**] **latch on** to start to understand or to be interested in something **latch onto something/someone** to hold tightly onto someone or something or to follow them closely

late /leɪt/ ADJECTIVE, ADVERB [**later, latest**]
1 after the time that is expected or necessary □ *The bus was late.* □ **+ for** *If you don't hurry, you'll be late for work.* □ *I was too late to help him.* □ *I'm coming to the meeting, but I might be a bit late.*
2 near the end of the day 🔁 *The children stayed up late to watch a movie.* 🔁 *Will the party go on late?* 🔁 *It's getting late - we should leave.*
3 near the end of a period of time □ *the late 18th century* □ *It was late afternoon by the time we arrived.*
4 recent, or happening or produced towards the end of a period of time □ *Her late work was more experimental.* □ *The late editions all had the news.*
5 a formal word meaning dead □ *This house belonged to the late Mrs Edwards.*

• **lately** /ˈleɪtlɪ/ ADVERB recently □ *I haven't been to many parties lately.*

• **lateness** /ˈleɪtnɪs/ NOUN, NO PLURAL being late □ *She apologized for her lateness.*

• **later** /ˈleɪtə(r)/ ADJECTIVE, ADVERB
1 after the time you have been talking about □ *Later, he married an artist.* □ *She rang me later to apologize.* □ *Two years later I received a letter from him.* □ *Is there a later train?*
2 more recent, or happening or produced towards the end of a period □ *Later versions of the software include that feature.* □ *I am a great admirer of his later novels.* 🔁 *In later life, he became very deaf.*

• **latest** /ˈleɪtɪst/ ▶ ADJECTIVE most recent □ *I regularly check the Internet for the latest news.* □ *We stock all the latest fashions.*
▶ NOUN
1 **the latest** the most recent example of something □ *This is the latest in a series of mistakes.*
2 **at the latest** used to emphasize that something must happen or be done before a particular time □ *You must be home by seven at the latest.*

latecomer /ˈleɪtˌkʌmə(r)/ NOUN [*plural* **latecomers**] someone who is late for an event

lather /ˈlɑːðə(r)/ NOUN, NO PLURAL small bubbles that you get when you mix soap in water □ *Rinse off the lather.*
◆ IDIOM **in a lather** very upset or worried about something

Latin /ˈlætɪn/ NOUN, NO PLURAL the language of the ancient Romans

latitude /ˈlætɪtjuːd/ NOUN [*plural* **latitudes**] the position of a place along imaginary lines around the Earth north and south of the equator (= line around the middle of the Earth). It is measured in degrees north and south.

latte /ˈlæteɪ/ NOUN [*plural* **lattes**] a drink made with strong coffee and hot milk

latter /ˈlætə(r)/ ▶ ADJECTIVE nearer the end of a period of time than the beginning 🔁 *the latter part of the 19th century*
▶ NOUN, NO PLURAL **the latter** the second one of two people or things mentioned □ *If I'm offered tea or coffee, I'll always take the latter.*

• **latterly** /ˈlætəlɪ/ ADVERB a formal word that means recently

laudable /ˈlɔːdəbəl/ ADJECTIVE deserving praise. A formal word □ *This is a laudable first attempt at portrait painting.*

laugh /lɑːf/ ▶ VERB [**laughs, laughing, laughed**] to make a sound of enjoyment when you think something is funny □ **+ at** *She laughed at my jokes* □ **+ about** *We can laugh about the whole thing now* 🔁 *It really made me laugh.* 🔁 *They burst out laughing* (= suddenly laughed loudly).
◆ PHRASAL VERBS **laugh at someone/something** to laugh or say something rude because you think someone or something is stupid □ *Wallis just laughed at the suggestion.* **laugh something off** to make a joke about something to show that it is not important to you □ *She laughed off the criticisms.*
▶ NOUN [*plural* **laughs**]
1 when you laugh, or the sound that you make when you laugh 🔁 *He gave a nervous laugh.* □ *He has a very loud laugh.*
2 **a (good) laugh** an informal phrase that means a person or an activity that is fun □ *John's a good laugh.*
3 **have a laugh** an informal phrase that means to have fun and enjoy yourself □ *We all have such a laugh together.*
4 **for a laugh** an informal phrase that means for fun or as a joke □ *I only did it for a laugh.*

• **laughable** /ˈlɑːfəbəl/ ADJECTIVE very bad and deserving to be laughed at □ *a laughable suggestion*

laughing stock /ˈlɑːfɪŋ ˌstɒk/ NOUN [*plural* **laughing stocks**] someone or something that everyone thinks is silly and does not deserve respect

laughter /ˈlɑːftə(r)/ NOUN, NO PLURAL when someone laughs or the sound that they make when they laugh □ *I could hear laughter in the next room.* 🔁 *We were in fits of laughter.*

launch /lɔ:ntʃ/ ► VERB [**launches, launching, launched**]
1 to start an important piece of work ⓖ *We are launching an investigation into the incident.*
2 to start to sell a new product □ *The latest model will be launched next month.*
3 to send a rocket or a spacecraft into the sky □ *The first Sputnik satellite was launched into space in 1957.*
4 to put a boat or ship in the water for the first time
♦ PHRASAL VERB **launch into something** to start saying something with enthusiasm or anger □ *He then launched into a great long speech on the subject.*
► NOUN [*plural* **launches**]
1 when a spacecraft, ship, etc. is launched □ *a shuttle launch*
2 when an important piece of work is started □ *the campaign launch*
3 when a new product starts to be sold □ *This month sees the launch of the latest version.*

launch pad /'lɔ:ntʃ ˌpæd/ NOUN [*plural* **launch pads**] a place that a spacecraft is launched from

launder /'lɔ:ndə(r)/ VERB [**launders, laundering, laundered**]
1 to put money into legal businesses to hide the fact that it was made illegally
2 to wash or clean clothes so that they are ready to wear again. A formal word.

launderette /ˌlɔ:ndə'ret/ NOUN [*plural* **launderettes**] a shop full of washing machines that you can pay to use

laundry /'lɔ:ndrɪ/ NOUN, NO PLURAL clothes that are going to be washed, or have just been washed □ *a pile of dirty laundry* □ *a laundry basket* ⓖ *I've done the laundry.*

laundry detergent /'lɔ:ndrɪ dɪ'tɜ:dʒənt/ NOUN, NO PLURAL the US phrase for washing powder (= a powder used for washing clothes)

lava /'lɑ:və/ NOUN, NO PLURAL the hot liquid rock that comes out of a volcano (= mountain that explodes) and becomes solid as it cools down. A geography word.

lavatory /'lævətrɪ/ NOUN [*plural* **lavatories**] a formal word for toilet □ *a public lavatory*

lavender /'lævəndə(r)/ ► NOUN [*plural* **lavenders**] a plant with small purple flowers with a strong, sweet smell
► ADJECTIVE having a pale purple colour

lavish /'lævɪʃ/ ► VERB [**lavishes, lavishing, lavished**] to give someone a lot, or too much of something □ *Her parents had always lavished gifts on her.*
► ADJECTIVE very generous, with more than enough of everything □ *a lavish dinner* □ *a lavish lifestyle*

lavishly /'lævɪʃlɪ/ ADVERB in a lavish way □ *a lavishly decorated room*

law /lɔ:/ NOUN [*plural* **laws**]
1 the law an official set of rules that everyone in a country or state must obey ⓖ *They have broken the law.*

2 be against the law to not be allowed by law □ *Driving at the age of 13 is against the law.*
3 an official rule in a country or state that everyone must obey □ + *against* *laws against discrimination*
4 the law as a subject for studying or a job □ *He studied law at university.*
5 by law if you have to do something by law, there is an official rule which says that you must do it □ *You are required by law to provide this information.*
6 a scientific rule that explains why something always happens in the same way □ + *of* *the laws of gravity*
● **lawful** /'lɔ:fʊl/ ADJECTIVE allowed by the law □ *The strike was not lawful.*

lawn /lɔ:n/ NOUN [*plural* **lawns**] an area of short grass in a garden ⓖ *I need to mow the lawn* (= cut the grass with a machine).

lawnmower /'lɔ:nˌməʊə(r)/ NOUN [*plural* **lawnmowers**] a machine for cutting grass

lawsuit /'lɔ:su:t/ NOUN [*plural* **lawsuits**] a disagreement between two people that a court of law is asked to make a decision about

lawyer /'lɔ:jə(r)/ NOUN [*plural* **lawyers**] someone whose job is to advise people about the law and to act for other people in legal situations ⓖ *a defence lawyer* □ *His lawyer said he would appeal against the sentence.*

lax /læks/ ADJECTIVE [**laxer, laxest**] not carefully controlled □ *Lax security at the airport was to blame.*

laxative /'læksətɪv/ NOUN [*plural* **laxatives**] a drug or food that makes you pass solid waste from your body

lay /leɪ/ VERB [**lays, laying, laid**]
1 to put something down carefully □ + *on* *She laid the book on the table.* □ + *down* *Slowly, he laid down the gun.* □ *I went to lay flowers on his grave.*
2 to put something into its correct position □ *to lay bricks* □ *A railway track was laid between the cities.*
3 if a bird lays an egg, it produces it
4 lay the table to put knives, forks, etc. on a table to prepare for a meal
5 lay the blame/responsibility (for something) on someone to say that it is someone's fault that something has happened
6 lay the foundations to do what is necessary for something to develop □ *They are trying to lay the foundations for a lasting peace.*
➜ go to lay eyes on something/someone
♦ PHRASAL VERBS **lay something down** to say officially how something should be done □ *lay down rules/standards* **lay into someone** to attack or criticize someone **lay someone off** to stop employing someone **lay something on** to provide something, for example food or a service □ *They laid on buses to take all the guests to the hotel.* **lay something out** to explain something □ *The article lays out her vision for the future.*

► Try not to confuse the verbs **lay** and **lie**. To **lay** something somewhere is to put something down. To **lie** somewhere is to be in a flat position: □ *She looked for a place to lay the baby.* □ *Why don't you lie on the sofa and watch TV?*

► ADJECTIVE

1 involved in religious activities but not an official employee of the church □ *a lay preacher*

2 not having a detailed knowledge of a particular subject □ *I was speaking to a lay audience.*

► PAST TENSE OF **lie**²

lay-by /'leɪbaɪ/ NOUN [plural **lay-bys**] an area at the side of a road where drivers can stop for a short time

layer /'leɪə(r)/ ► NOUN [plural **layers**]

1 an amount of a substance that covers something or is between other things □ + **of** *The grass was covered with a layer of snow.* ⊞ *Remove the outer layers of the onion.* □ *Wear several layers of clothing.* □ *Dust had settled in a thin layer over everything.*

2 a level of an organization or system □ *This just adds another layer of bureaucracy.*

► VERB [**layers, layering, layered**] to arrange something in layers □ *The dessert is made by layering fruit and ice cream.*

layman /'leɪmən/ NOUN [plural **laymen**] a person who has no special knowledge or training in a subject ⊞ *Can you explain that in layman's terms?*

layoff /'leɪɒf/ NOUN [plural **layoffs**] when a company stops employing people because there is no work for them to do □ *The company blamed the layoffs on the recession.*

layout /'leɪaʊt/ NOUN [plural **layouts**] the way things are arranged □ *The diagram shows the layout of the rooms.*

laze /leɪz/ VERB [**lazes, lazing, lazed**] to be lazy and to do very little □ *I just like to laze around in the holidays.*

• **laziness** /'leɪzɪnɪs/ NOUN, NO PLURAL when someone is lazy

• **lazy** /'leɪzi/ ADJECTIVE [**lazier, laziest**]

1 not liking to work hard or to exercise □ *At school they say he's very lazy.* □ *She's far too lazy to walk to work.*

2 relaxing, involving little effort □ *I've had a very lazy morning in bed with the papers.*

lb ABBREVIATION pound (= weight)

lead¹ /liːd/ ► VERB [**leads, leading, led**]

1 to show someone where to go by going first or going with them □ *You lead and I'll follow on my bike.* □ *She led me into a large room.*

2 if a road, path, etc. leads somewhere, that is where it goes □ + **to** *This road leads to London.*

3 to be winning in a race or competition, or to be the most successful at something □ *Liverpool were leading 2-0 at the end of the first half.* □ + **by** *They are leading by three goals to nil.* ⊞ *Our company leads the world in aviation technology.*

4 to direct or control an activity or a group of people □ *The team should be led by someone with a lot of experience.* □ *A new officer has been brought in to lead the investigation.*

5 to cause someone to do something □ + **to do something** *His expression led me to think he was lying.* ⊞ *I was led to believe that he was a doctor.* □ *The long hours led me to give up my career in law.*

6 **lead a comfortable/full/normal, etc. life** to live in a particular way

7 **lead the way** to be the first to do something □ *This university led the way in introducing schemes to attract poorer students.*

♦ PHRASAL VERBS **lead to something** to cause something to happen or exist □ *Long hours at work led to the breakdown of his marriage.* □ *Using the mouse too much can lead to wrist problems.* **lead up to something** to happen before something □ *He took part in the talks that led up to the deal.* □ *We were very busy in the weeks leading up to the election.*

► NOUN [plural **leads**]

1 the position in a race or competition where you are winning □ *Jenkins has been in the lead for most of the race.* ⊞ *Juventus took the lead after 23 minutes.*

2 when you show someone where to go or what to do ⊞ *I didn't know what to do, so I just followed Ted's lead.*

3 a wire that connects a piece of electrical equipment to an electricity supply

4 a long, narrow piece of leather attached to a dog's collar in order to hold it. ⊞ *All dogs must be kept on a lead.*

5 a piece of information that may help police solve a crime □ *The police are following up several new leads.*

6 the main actor in a play, film, etc. ⊞ *He plays the lead in Miller's new production.*

lead² /led/ NOUN [plural **leads**]

1 a soft, dark grey metal

2 the dark grey inside part of a pencil

leader /'liːdə(r)/ NOUN [plural **leaders**]

1 a person who is in charge of a group of people □ + **of** *the leader of the expedition* ⊞ *a religious leader* ⊞ *the country's political leaders* □ *the Republican Party leader*

2 the person, team, etc. that is winning a race or competition at a particular time □ *He's now just three points behind the leader.*

3 the company that sells most of a particular type of product, or the best-selling product itself □ *a brand leader*

• **leadership** /'liːdəʃɪp/ NOUN, NO PLURAL

1 being a leader □ *The club has done well under Will's leadership.*

2 the ability to be a good leader □ *He's a good worker but he lacks leadership.*

leading /'liːdɪŋ/ ADJECTIVE

1 most important or most successful □ *He is one of Scotland's leading playwrights.* □ *the team's leading scorer*

2 in first position in a race or competition at a particular time □ *She was in the leading group with three miles to go.*

leaf /li:f/ NOUN [*plural* **leaves**]
1 a flat green part of a plant or tree that grows out from a stem or a branch □ *The sun shone through the leaves.* □ *a plate of salad leaves*
2 a page of a book
♦ IDIOMS **take a leaf out of someone's book** to copy someone's behaviour because it is good or successful **turn over a new leaf** to change your life by starting to behave in a better way
♦ PHRASAL VERB [**leafs, leafing, leafed**] **leaf through something** to look quickly through the pages of a book, a magazine, etc. □ *She sat in the waiting room, leafing through a magazine.*

leaflet /'li:flɪt/ NOUN [*plural* **leaflets**] a piece of paper that gives printed information about something □ *a leaflet about recycling*

leafy /'li:fɪ/ ADJECTIVE [**leafier, leafiest**]
1 with a lot of leaves □ *green leafy vegetables*
2 with a lot of plants or trees □ *a leafy suburb*

league /li:g/ NOUN [*plural* **leagues**]
1 a group of teams that play sports matches against each other □ *the professional basketball league* 🔢 *I'm still hoping we can win the league this season.* 🔢 *They're top of the league table.*
2 a group of people or things of the same quality 🔢 *She's a good enough actress, but not in the same league as* (= definitely not as good as) *Katherine Hepburn.* 🔢 *The car's in a league of its own* (= better than any other) *when it comes to fuel economy.*
3 a group of people or countries who agree to work together
4 **be in league with someone** to work or plan with someone else, especially to do something bad

leak /li:k/ ▶ NOUN [*plural* **leaks**]
1 a hole that liquid or gas can escape or enter through, or the gas or liquid that escapes □ *There could be a leak in the pipe.* 🔢 *a gas leak*
2 when someone tells people secret information □ *There have been too many leaks of classified information.*
▶ VERB [**leaks, leaking, leaked**]
1 if gas or liquid leaks, it escapes from or enters something and if an object leaks, gas or liquid escapes from or enters it through a hole □ *Gas was leaking from somewhere under the floor.* □ *My boots leak.*
2 to tell people secret information □ *This news was leaked to a newspaper yesterday.*
PHRASAL VERB **leak out** if secret information leaks out, it becomes known publicly

leakage /'li:kɪdʒ/ NOUN [*plural* **leakages**] when gas, a liquid or information leaks □ *We lost a lot of oil through leakage.* □ *the leakage of private memos*

leaky /'li:kɪ/ ADJECTIVE [**leakier, leakiest**] having small holes or cracks which a gas or liquid can leak out of □ *a leaky roof*

lean /li:n/ ▶ VERB [**leans, leaning, leant** *or* **leaned**]
1 to move your body in a particular direction by bending at the waist □ **+ forward** *He leaned forward to kiss her.* □ **+ back** *She leaned back in her chair.* □ **+ over** *Could you lean over and get the salt for me?* □ **+ out** *She leaned out of the window.*
2 to put something against something so that it is supported by it, or to be in this position □ **+ on** *She leaned her head on his shoulder.* □ **+ against** *A bike was leaning against the wall.*
3 to be in a position that is not exactly vertical □ *The tree leans slightly to one side.*
▶ ADJECTIVE [**leaner, leanest**] with no fat or little fat □ *I only buy lean meat.*

leap /li:p/ ▶ VERB [**leaps, leaping, leapt** *or* **leaped**]
1 to move suddenly and quickly □ *She leapt up and ran to the door.* □ *I leapt out of bed.*
2 to jump high or a long distance □ *We saw dolphins leaping out of the water.* □ *The dancer leapt into the air.*
♦ PHRASAL VERB **leap at something** to accept an offer or to take an opportunity with enthusiasm □ *I leapt at the chance to meet them.*
▶ NOUN [*plural* **leaps**]
1 a big and sudden increase or improvement □ *This is a huge leap forward for us.* □ *a 45% leap in profits*
2 a big jump □ *He took an impressive leap over the fence.*
♦ IDIOM **in/by leaps and bounds** used to say that someone or something is making progress quickly □ *The team's coming along in leaps and bounds.*

leap year /li:p jɪə(r)/ NOUN [*plural* **leap years**] a year that happens every four years and has 366 days. The extra day is February 29.

learn /lɜ:n/ VERB [**learns, learning, learnt** *or* **learned**]
1 to get to know about something or get to know how to do something □ **+ to do something** *He's learning to drive.* □ *She wanted to learn English.* □ **+ question word** *I learned how to cook from my mother.* □ **+ about** *We learnt about the local culture.* □ **+ from** *I've learnt from my mistakes.*
2 to find out some news or information □ **+ that** *I was surprised to learn that she'd already left.* □ **+ of** *I was saddened to learn of his death.* □ **+ whether** *Today he will learn whether he needs surgery.*
3 **learn your lesson** to not do something wrong or silly again because of your past experiences
● **learned** / 'lɜ:nɪd/ ADJECTIVE a formal word meaning having a lot of knowledge about academic subjects □ *a learned man*
● **learner** /'lɜ:nə(r)/ NOUN [*plural* **learners**] a person who is learning something □ *It's a book for young language learners.* 🔢 *He was a quick learner.*
● **learning** /'lɜ:nɪŋ/ NOUN, NO PLURAL
1 the process of learning something □ *He had no aptitude for language learning.*
2 knowledge, especially from studying □ *a man of great learning*

lease /li:s/ ▶ NOUN [*plural* **leases**] an agreement to rent a flat or a house to someone 🔢 *He signed a lease on a two-bedroom apartment.*

♦ IDIOM **a new lease of life** a new feeling of enthusiasm, happiness or health □ *Since the move he's had a new lease of life.*

▶ VERB [**leases, leasing, leased**] to rent something to someone □ *They lease the land from the local council.*

leash /li:ʃ/ NOUN [*plural* **leashes**] a long piece of leather, etc. attached to a dog's collar to control or to lead it

least /li:st/ ▶ ADVERB

1 less than anyone or anything else in size, amount or degree □ *She chose the least expensive trousers.* □ *He always turns up when you least expect him.* □ *These price rises will affect those who are least able to afford them.*

2 at least (a) not less than □ *She must be at least 50.* □ *It will take at least two hours to get there.* (b) used before you add a positive statement after talking about something bad □ *She was very late, but at least she phoned to let us know.* (c) used to correct what you have just said or to make it less certain □ *I saw her in the library - at least, I think it was her.*

3 not least used to emphasize the importance of something □ *I try to avoid her - not least because she's always asking me for money.*

▶ DETERMINER, PRONOUN

1 the smallest amount, size or degree □ *The person who had the least difficulty was the tallest.* □ *Of everyone here, I know least about the subject.* □ *He is the richest, but he gave the least.*

2 at the (very) least used to show that this is the smallest amount or degree possible □ *At the very least, you could have offered to help.*

3 not in the least (bit)/not the least bit not at all □ *He wasn't the least bit sorry for all the trouble he caused.*

leather /'leðə(r)/ NOUN, NO PLURAL a strong material for making shoes, bags and clothes that is made from the skin of an animal □ *a leather jacket* □ *a pair of black leather boots*

leave /li:v/ ▶ VERB [**leaves, leaving, left**]

1 to go away from a place □ *I left the office early.* □ *The train leaves at two.* □ *I left work at four thirty.* 🕮 *I left home when I was 18.*

2 to not take something with you when you go away □ *Maria left her umbrella on the bus.* □ **+ behind** *I left all my books behind.*

3 to put something or someone somewhere □ *Leave your shoes by the back door.* □ *I left the children with a neighbour.*

4 to allow something to be in a particular position or state □ *Leave the conditioner in your hair for five minutes.* □ *She left the door unlocked.*

5 to end a relationship with someone you live with □ *His wife left him.*

6 to cause a situation or an emotion □ *The illness left me without a job.* □ *High crime rates have left people afraid to go out after dark.*

7 to not use all of something □ *Is there any milk left?*

8 to not do something but do it later or let someone else do it □ *I'll leave the washing up and do it in the morning.* □ **+ to** *I left all the driving to her.*

9 to give something to someone after your death □ *Her grandmother left Joy all her jewellery.*

10 leave someone/something alone to stop touching something or talking to someone □ *Journalists wouldn't leave her alone.* □ *Leave my clothes alone.*

➔ go to **leave someone to their own** *devices*, **leave a bad/bitter/nasty**, etc. *taste* in your mouth

♦ PHRASAL VERBS **leave someone/something out** to not include someone or something □ *I told him what she said, but I left out the rude bits.* 🕮 *Some of our members felt left out because they could not do the activities.* **leave something over** if something is left over, it is what remains when the rest of something has been used □ *There was a lot of food left over from the party.*

▶ NOUN, NO PLURAL a period of holiday from work □ *I had a week's leave.* □ *He committed the crime while he was on leave from the army.*

leaves /li:vz/ PLURAL OF **leaf**

lecture /'lektʃə(r)/ ▶ NOUN [*plural* **lectures**]

1 a talk by someone to a group of people to teach them about something □ **+ on** *a lecture on economics* 🕮 *He was due to give a lecture at Leeds University.* 🕮 *He attended a lecture by Carl Jung.*

2 a long, serious talk that criticizes someone for their behaviour □ *He got a lecture from the coach about punctuality.*

▶ VERB [**lectures, lecturing, lectured**]

1 to give a lecture or lectures about a particular subject □ *He lectured on history at Cambridge University.*

2 to give someone a long serious talk about their behaviour □ *She's always lecturing me about my diet.*

• **lecturer** /'lektʃərə(r)/ NOUN [*plural* **lecturers**] a person who gives lectures, especially to college and university students

led /led/ PAST TENSE AND PAST PARTICIPLE OF **lead**[1] □ *Connor led a wild life for many years.* □ *Where have you led us?*

ledge /ledʒ/ NOUN [*plural* **ledges**] a narrow shelf under a window, or a part of a vertical surface that sticks ou 🕮 *a window ledge* □ *Both birds were perched on a ledge halfway up the cliff.*

leek /li:k/ NOUN [*plural* **leeks**] a long green and whit vegetable that tastes like an onion

leeway /'li:weɪ/ NOUN, NO PLURAL freedom to do wh you want or to change your plans □ *Individual schoo now have greater leeway to plan spending.*

left[1] /left/ ▶ ADJECTIVE, ADVERB on or towards the sid of your body that is to the west if you are facing nor 🕮 *Can you write with your left hand?* 🕮 *You stand o the left side of him.* 🕮 *Now turn left.* □ *Click on th link in the top left corner of the screen.*

▶ NOUN, NO PLURAL

1 the left side or direction □ *Stop just here on the left.* □ *Diana is standing to the left of Robert.*
2 the left people or groups with political opinions that support ideas about sharing money and power equally

left² /left/ PAST TENSE AND PAST PARTICIPLE OF **leave** □ *She left early.* □ *I've left my book at home.*

left click /'left ˌklɪk/ VERB [**left clicks, left clicking, left clicked**] to press the left button on a computer mouse so that the computer will do something. A computing word.

left-hand /'lefthænd/ ADJECTIVE on the left side of something 🔁 *Look at the numbers on the left-hand side of the page.* 🔁 *The ball flew into the bottom left-hand corner of the net.*

left-handed /ˌleft'hændɪd/ ADJECTIVE using your left hand to do things, especially to write □ *Are you left handed?* □ *a left-handed batsman*

leftovers /'leftəʊvəz/ PLURAL NOUN food that has not been eaten at a meal □ *Shall I put the leftovers in the fridge?*

left wing /ˌleft 'wɪŋ/ NOUN the left wing the members of a political party that believe most strongly in ideas about sharing money and power equally □ *the left wing of the Labour Party*

left-wing /'left ˌwɪŋ/ ADJECTIVE supporting the ideas of the political left □ *left-wing politicians*

leg /leg/ NOUN [*plural* **legs**]
1 one of the parts of the body that animals and humans stand and walk on □ *I broke my leg skiing.* □ *How many legs do spiders have?* □ *Try standing on one leg.*
2 the part of a pair of trousers that covers one leg
3 one of the pieces that support a table, chair, etc.
4 one part in a journey or a competition □ *This is the second leg of the race across Europe.*

▸ IDIOMS **not have a leg to stand on** to not have any proof that you are right in an argument □ *He'll never win his claim for compensation - he doesn't have a leg to stand on.* **be on its last legs** if something is on its last legs, it is in such a bad condition that it will soon stop working or continuing to exist □ *My washing machine's on its last legs.* **pull someone's leg** to trick someone as a joke □ *He didn't really grow the bananas - he's only pulling your leg.*

legacy /'legəsɪ/ NOUN [*plural* **legacies**]
1 something that still exists as a result of things that happened in the past □ *Hatred and mistrust are the legacies of war.* 🔁 *As a writer he has left a lasting legacy.*
2 something that you receive from someone after their death

legal /'li:gəl/ ADJECTIVE
1 allowed by the law □ *Is it legal to ride your bike on the pavement?*
2 to do with the law □ *the legal profession* □ *Consult your legal advisor.*

legalize *or* **legalise** /'li:gəlaɪz/ VERB [**legalizes, legalizing, legalized**] to make something allowed by law

legally /'li:gəlɪ/ ADVERB in a way that is legal □ *He acquired the business legally.*

legend /'ledʒənd/ NOUN [*plural* **legends**]
1 an old traditional story that is usually not true □ *the legend of St George and the dragon*
2 a very famous person □ *Formula One legend, Ayrton Senna*

legendary /'ledʒəndrɪ/ ADJECTIVE
1 to do with old stories □ *legendary knights*
2 very famous □ *His goal-scoring skills were legendary.*

leggings /'legɪnz/ PLURAL NOUN thin, tight women's trousers made of a material that stretches

legible /'ledʒəbəl/ ADJECTIVE legible writing can be read

legion /'li:dʒən/ NOUN [*plural* **legions**]
1 a very big number □ *He still has legions of fans.*
2 in the past, a group of many thousand Roman soldiers

legislate /'ledʒɪsleɪt/ VERB [**legislates, legislating, legislated**] to make a new law or laws □ *The government has legislated against smoking in public places.*

legislation /ˌledʒɪs'leɪʃən/ NOUN, NO PLURAL
1 a set of laws □ *The government brought in legislation to improve food labelling.*
2 the process of making laws

legitimate /lɪ'dʒɪtɪmət/ ADJECTIVE
1 allowed by law □ *the legitimate government*
2 having a good reason and so able to be accepted or understood □ *In my opinion she has a legitimate complaint.*

legitimately /lɪ'dʒɪtɪmətlɪ/ ADVERB according to the law □ *a legitimately elected government*

leisure /'leʒə(r)/ NOUN, NO PLURAL time when you do not have to work □ *Families are spending more on leisure.* 🔁 *What do you do in your leisure time?*

◆ IDIOM **at your leisure** when you have time □ *Take the brochure home and read it at your leisure.*

leisure centre /ˈleʒə(r) ˌsentə(r)/ NOUN [*plural* **leisure centres**] a public building where you can swim and play sports

leisurely /'leʒəlɪ/ ADVERB without hurrying □ *We walked at a leisurely pace.*

lemon /'lemən/ NOUN [*plural* **lemons**] an oval fruit with a hard, yellow skin and very sour juice □ *tea with a slice of lemon* □ *Add the juice of a lemon.*

lemonade /ˌlemə'neɪd/ NOUN [*plural* **lemonades**]
1 a cold drink with a lemon flavour and a lot of bubbles □ *a bottle of lemonade*
2 a cold drink made from fresh lemon juice, water and sugar □ *a glass of homemade lemonade*

lend /lend/ VERB [**lends, lending, lent**] to let someone use something or have some money for a short time □ *Could you lend me £5, Mum?* □ *+ to Adam has lent his MP3 player to Andy.* □ *The bank no longer lends to first-time buyers.*
♦ IDIOM **lend a hand** to help someone

➤ Remember that when you **lend** something, you give something to someone else to use. When you use something that belongs to someone else, the verb is **borrow** □ *Dan lent me his mobile.* □ *I borrowed Dan's mobile.*

length /leŋθ/ NOUN [*plural* **lengths**]
1 how long something is from one end to the other end □ *Measure the table's length.* □ *The pieces of wood were all different lengths.*
2 how long something is in time □ *The average length of a stay in hospital is four days.*
3 how long a speech or piece of writing is □ *Quotes from other authors added to the length of the essay.*
4 at length if you talk at length, you talk for a long time □ *The doctor explained the different treatments at length.*
5 a piece of something long and thin such as a rope or pipe □ *I need a length of plastic piping.*
♦ IDIOM go to great lengths to do something to make a lot of effort and do a lot of things in order to try to achieve something □ *They went to great lengths to ensure his safety.*
● **lengthen** /leŋθən/ VERB [**lengthens, lengthening, lengthened**] to become longer or to make something longer □ *I think you should lengthen that skirt.* □ *Shadows lengthened as the sun went down.*

lengthways /leŋθweɪz/ *or* **lengthwise** /leŋθwaɪz/ ADVERB in the direction along the length of something □ *Fold the sheet of paper lengthways.*

lengthy /leŋθɪ/ ADJECTIVE [**lengthier, lengthiest**] taking a long time □ *Getting a passport was a lengthy process.*

lenient /liːnjənt/ ADJECTIVE
1 not giving severe punishments □ *The judge was too lenient.*
2 describes a punishment that is not severe □ *a lenient sentence*

lens /lenz/ NOUN [*plural* **lenses**]
1 a curved piece of glass that you look through in glasses, cameras and scientific instruments □ *a zoom lens* □ *Adjust the lens in the telescope.*
2 a part of your eye behind your pupil (= black hole at the front) that helps you see clearly

Lent /lent/ NOUN, NO PLURAL the forty days before Easter when some Christians do not eat something that they like □ *Anna's given up chocolate for Lent.*

lent /lent/ PAST TENSE AND PAST PARTICIPLE OF lend □ *I lent him a book.* □ *I've lent her some money.*

lentil /lentɪl/ NOUN [*plural* **lentils**] a small orange, brown or green seed that is dried and cooked □ *lentil soup*

leopard /lepəd/ NOUN [*plural* **leopards**] a large animal of the cat family with yellow fur and dark spots

leotard /liːətɑːd/ NOUN [*plural* **leotards**] a tight piece of clothing covering your body from the neck to the top of the legs that you wear for doing exercises or dancing

leper /lepə(r)/ NOUN [*plural* **lepers**] someone who suffers from leprosy
● **leprosy** /leprəsɪ/ NOUN, NO PLURAL a serious infectious disease that affects the skin and nerves and can damage parts of the body

less /les/ ▶ DETERMINER, PRONOUN a smaller amount of □ *We'll have to spend less money.* □ *I have less time than Patrick.* □ *I had less on my plate than you.* □ *+ of He spends less of his time with his children.*

➤ Notice that **less** is used with uncountable nouns, for example *time* and *money*. With the plural form of countable nouns, for example *cars* and *people*, use **fewer**: □ *I have less money than I used to.* □ *I have fewer problems than I used to.*

▶ ADVERB
1 used to make comparative forms of adjectives and adverbs, with the meaning 'not as much' □ *My clothes are less expensive.* 🔊 *I'm less patient than you.* 🔊 *These instructions are a lot less complicated.* 🔊 *I'm less and less interested in TV.*
2 to a smaller degree □ *I exercise less these days.* 🔊 *I eat less than I used to.* 🔊 *I see her less and less.*
▶ PREPOSITION taking away a particular amount □ *The cost will be £100 less the discount.*
● **lessen** /lesən/ VERB [**lessens, lessening, lessened**] to become less or to make something less □ *The drug should lessen the pain.*

-less /lɪs/ SUFFIX –less is added to the end of words to mean 'without' □ *hopeless* □ *thoughtless*

lesser /lesə(r)/ ADJECTIVE not so large or important as other things you are considering □ *Auden, Eliot and few lesser poets* □ *He had been involved in burglary and other lesser crimes.* 🔊 *Bill is also guilty but to a lesser extent* (= not as much).
♦ IDIOM the lesser of two evils the less bad or harmful of two bad or harmful things □ *He regarded the Nationalist party as the lesser of two evils.*

lesson /lesən/ NOUN [*plural* **lessons**]
1 a period of time in which you learn something or teach someone something □ *When's your next lesson* □ *a driving lesson* 🔊 *I'm taking swimming lessons.*
2 something that you learn from life and experience □ *The war has taught us some valuable lessons.*
♦ IDIOM teach someone a lesson to punish someone that they will not do something again

let /let/ VERB [**lets, letting, let**]
1 to allow someone to do something or something

happen □ *He won't let anyone use his tools.* □ *This card lets me travel free.*

2 to allow someone or something to go somewhere □ **+ in** *They won't let him in the building.* □ *She won't let the children out of her sight.* □ *These windows let in the rain.*

3 **let's** used to make a suggestion about what to do □ *Let's go swimming.* □ *Let's get out of here.*

4 **let go** to stop holding something □ *He grasped my hand and wouldn't let go.* □ *Now you can let go of the rope.*

5 **let someone know** to tell someone something □ *Could you let Mick know I'll be late?* □ *I want to let everyone know why I acted the way I did.*

6 **Let's see/Let me see** used when you are thinking about something or trying to remember something □ *I've worked here for - let me see - over twenty years.*

7 **let alone** used to emphasize that one thing is even more impossible than another □ *I can't even run for the bus, let alone run a marathon!*

8 to rent a room, building, etc. to someone

♦ IDIOMS **let the cat out of the bag** to tell someone something secret, often by mistake □ *We were planning a surprise party, but Alex let the cat out of the bag.* **let your hair down** to relax and have a good time □ *Come to the party with us - let your hair down for once!*

➡ *go to* **let something** *slip*

♦ PHRASAL VERBS **let someone down** to upset someone by behaving badly or not doing something they expected you to do □ *Our suppliers have let us down.* □ *You've let yourself down and you've let your family down.* **let someone off** to not punish someone for something bad they have done **let on** to tell someone something secret

let /lɛt/ SUFFIX **-let** is added to the end of words to mean 'very small' □ *piglet*

lethal /ˈliːθəl/ ADJECTIVE causing or able to cause death □ *a lethal weapon* □ *a lethal dose of the drug*

lethargic /ləˈθɑːdʒɪk/ ADJECTIVE having no energy and feeling that you do not want to do anything □ *After my big lunch I felt very lethargic.*

lethargy /ˈlɛθədʒɪ/ NOUN, NO PLURAL a feeling of being lethargic

letter /ˈlɛtə(r)/ NOUN [*plural* **letters**]

1 a message that you write and send by post to another person 🔁 *Why don't you write a letter?* 🔁 *I got a letter from Laura this morning.*

2 one of the written shapes that you combine to write words, like *a*, *b* or *c* □ *the letters of the alphabet*

letterbox /ˈlɛtəbɒks/ NOUN [*plural* **letterboxes**]

1 a thin hole in a door or wall through which letters are delivered to a building

2 a large metal container with a hole in the front, where people can post letters

lettuce /ˈlɛtɪs/ NOUN [*plural* **lettuces**] a vegetable with large green leaves that are used in salads

leukaemia /luːˈkiːmɪə/ NOUN, NO PLURAL a type of cancer that affects the body's white blood cells

leukemia /luːˈkiːmɪə/ NOUN, NO PLURAL the US spelling of leukaemia

level /ˈlɛvəl/ ▶ ADJECTIVE

1 flat or horizontal □ *a piece of level ground* □ *Add a level tablespoonful of flour.*

2 at the same height as something else □ **+ with** *The picture needs to be level with the mirror next to it.*

3 having the same score as someone else □ *The two teams were level at half-time.*

▶ NOUN [*plural* **levels**]

1 the amount, size or number of something 🔁 *Sudoku puzzles need a high level of concentration.* 🔁 *Low levels of contamination were recorded.*

□ *Unemployment has stayed at the same level for over three years.*

2 a particular height or distance above or below the ground □ *She hung the pictures at eye level.* □ *The water level was rising.*

3 the particular ability or standard of someone or something □ *It's best to start at beginners' level.* □ *He played squash at international level.*

4 one of the floors that a building has

▶ VERB [**levels, levelling/**US **leveling, levelled/**US **leveled**]

1 to make something flat, smooth or horizontal □ *The ground will have to be levelled before they can build on it.*

2 to make things equal □ *Gray scored again to level the scores.*

♦ PHRASAL VERBS **level something at someone**

1 to accuse someone of something □ *Charges of corruption have been levelled at the government.*

2 to point a gun at someone or something **level off/out** to become flat, equal or level □ *House prices have begun to level off.* □ *The plane levelled out at 2000 feet.*

level crossing /ˈlɛvəl ˈkrɒsɪŋ/ NOUN [*plural* **level crossings**] a place where a road crosses a railway line

lever /ˈliːvə(r)/ ▶ NOUN [*plural* **levers**]

1 a handle that operates a machine or an engine □ *Push the lever up to start the engine.* □ *a gear lever*

2 a strong bar that you press on in order to move something heavy

▶ VERB [**levers, levering, levered**] to move something by forcing a bar under or behind it □ *He tried to lever the lid off with a knife.*

levy /ˈlɛvɪ/ ▶ VERB [**levies, levying, levied**] to officially take money as a tax □ *VAT is levied on all goods sold.*

▶ NOUN [*plural* **levies**] an amount of money that must be paid, especially a tax □ *The government plan to introduce an extra levy on fuel.*

liability /ˌlaɪəˈbɪlətɪ/ NOUN [*plural* **liabilities**]

1 legal responsibility for something □ *The driver of the other car has admitted liability for the crash.*

2 a person or thing that causes serious problems for you

liable /ˈlaɪəbəl/ ADJECTIVE
1 liable to do something often doing something, especially something bad □ *She's liable to lose her temper.*
2 legally responsible for something □ *You are liable for any damage you cause.*

liaise /lɪˈeɪz/ VERB [liaises, liaising, liaised] to exchange information regularly with other people so that you can work together effectively □ *You will need to liaise with staff in other departments.*

• **liaison** /lɪˈeɪzɒn/ NOUN, NO PLURAL communication between different groups or organizations that work together □ *We need better liaison between the departments.*

liar /ˈlaɪə(r)/ NOUN [plural liars] someone who tells lies

libel /ˈlaɪbəl/ NOUN [plural libels] the printing of a statement about someone that is not true and that damages people's opinion of them □ *He sued the newspaper for libel.*

liberal /ˈlɪbərəl/ ADJECTIVE
1 accepting different ideas and types of behaviour □ *It's a very liberal society.*
2 liberal political parties believe in greater personal freedom and a more equal society

liberally /ˈlɪbərəlɪ/ ADVERB in large amounts or generously □ *Pour the sauce liberally over the dish.*

liberate /ˈlɪbəreɪt/ VERB [liberates, liberating, liberated] to set someone free □ *The hostages were eventually liberated by the army.*

• **liberation** /ˌlɪbəˈreɪʃən/ NOUN, NO PLURAL being set free from someone else's control □ *the liberation of France in 1945*

liberty /ˈlɪbətɪ/ NOUN [plural liberties] freedom to do or say what you want, or go where you want □ *Prisoners are deprived of their liberty.*

librarian /laɪˈbreərɪən/ NOUN [plural librarians] someone who works in a library □ *the school librarian*

• **library** /ˈlaɪbrərɪ/ NOUN [plural libraries] a building or room that has a lot of books, CDs or DVDs that you can borrow 🕮 *library books*

lice /laɪs/ PLURAL OF louse

licence /ˈlaɪsəns/ NOUN [plural licences] an official document that gives someone permission to do or have something □ *a driving licence* □ *a licence to sell alcohol*

license /ˈlaɪsəns/ ▶ VERB [licenses, licensing, licensed] to give someone official permission to do something □ *The restaurant is licensed to serve alcohol.*
▶ NOUN the US spelling of licence

lichen /ˈlaɪkən, ˈlɪtʃən/ NOUN [plural lichens] a type of very small plant that grows on surfaces like rocks and trees

lick /lɪk/ ▶ VERB [licks, licking, licked] to move your tongue over something □ *The cat was licking its paws.* □ *She licked her lips nervously.*
▶ NOUN [plural licks]

1 a movement of your tongue over something □ *Can I have a lick of your lolly?*
2 a lick of paint a layer of paint □ *A lick of paint and this room will be fine.*

licorice /ˈlɪkərɪs/ NOUN, NO PLURAL the US spelling of liquorice

lid /lɪd/ NOUN [plural lids] a cover that fits the top of a container □ *Can you get the lid off this jar?*

lie¹ /laɪ/ ▶ VERB [lies, lying, lied] to say something that you know is not true □ *+ about* *He lied about his age.* □ *+ to* *Did you lie to me?*
▶ NOUN [plural lies] something that you say that is not true when you know that it is not true 🕮 *He's always telling lies.*

> ► Notice that people **tell lies**. They do not 'say lies':
> ✓ *Don't tell lies, Oliver.*
> ✗ *Don't say lies, Oliver.*

lie² /laɪ/ VERB [lies, lying, lay, lain]
1 to be in a flat position, for example on the floor or on a bed, or to put your body in this position □ *She's been lying on a beach all day.* □ *Lie flat on your back.* □ *Go and lie on the couch.*
2 to be on a surface □ *There were clothes lying all over the floor.* □ *Snow lay on the hills.*
3 to be in a particular position □ *The town lies to the east of Geneva.*
♦ PHRASAL VERBS **lie down** to put your body into a flat position, especially to rest □ *I don't feel well – I'm going to lie down for a while.* **lie in** to stay in bed in the morning later than usual □ *I usually lie in on Sundays.*

> ► Notice that the past tense of **lie** when it means 'to say something that you know is not true' is **lied**. The past tense of **lie** when it means 'to be in a flat position' is **lay**.

lieutenant /lefˈtenənt/ NOUN [plural lieutenants] an officer in the army or navy

life /laɪf/ NOUN [plural lives]
1 the time between being born and dying 🕮 *He spent his life helping others.* 🕮 *I've had these problems my whole life.* 🕮 *He lived in Glasgow all his life.* □ *Our lives have been ruined by this disease.*
2 the way someone lives 🕮 *They live a simple life.* 🕮 *We lead a quiet life.* 🕮 *This course will change your life.*
3 the existence of a person 🕮 *I'm not prepared to risk my life to save your dog.* 🕮 *He saved my life.* 🕮 *Hundreds of soldiers have lost their lives in this conflict.*
4 no plural the state of being alive □ *I kept feeling his pulse for any sign of life.*
5 real life the way things are in the real world □ *You see all these rich people on TV, but real life isn't like that.*
6 someone's personal/professional/social, etc life a particular part of someone's existence

7 *no plural* living things □ *Is there human life anywhere else in the universe?* □ *plant life*
8 the period of time that something exists or works 🔁 *This table started life as part of a railway track.* □ *Using this feature will extend the life of your batteries.*
9 energy and enthusiasm □ *Try to put a bit more life into your singing.* 🔁 *He's always full of life.*

lifeboat /'laɪfbəʊt/ NOUN [plural **lifeboats**] a boat used for saving people from dangerous situations at sea □ *the lifeboat crew*

life coach /'laɪf ˌkəʊtʃ/ NOUN [plural **life coaches**] someone who is employed to give someone advice about how to get what they want in life

life-cycle /'laɪf ˌsaɪkəl/ NOUN [plural **life-cycles**] the different forms that a living thing changes into during its life

life expectancy /'laɪf ɪk'spektənsɪ/ NOUN [plural **life expectancies**] how long someone is likely to live

lifeguard /'laɪfɡɑːd/ NOUN [plural **lifeguards**] someone who works at a swimming pool or on a beach, helping people who are in dangerous situations in the water

life jacket /'laɪf ˌdʒækɪt/ NOUN [plural **life jackets**] a jacket filled with air that will float and stop someone from sinking in water

lifeless /'laɪflɪs/ ADJECTIVE
1 dead or seeming dead □ *Her brother lay lifeless in the corner.*
2 with no energy or emotion □ *a lifeless performance*

lifelike /'laɪflaɪk/ ADJECTIVE looking like a real thing or person □ *a lifelike doll*

lifeline /'laɪflaɪn/ NOUN [plural **lifelines**] something that you depend on, usually because it is your only way of communicating when you need help □ *The telephone is her lifeline.*

lifelong /'laɪflɒŋ/ ADJECTIVE lasting the whole of your life 🔁 *They were lifelong friends.*

life-size /'laɪf ˌsaɪz/ ADJECTIVE being the same size as the real person or thing □ *a life-size model of James Bond*

lifespan /'laɪfspæn/ NOUN [plural **lifespans**] the length of time someone lives or something lasts □ *A lot of modern appliances have a short lifespan.*

lifestyle /'laɪfstaɪl/ NOUN [plural **lifestyles**] the way that someone lives □ *We try to have a healthy lifestyle.*

lifetime /'laɪftaɪm/ NOUN [plural **lifetimes**] the length of time that a particular person is alive □ *These children will see such technological advances in their lifetime.*

lift /lɪft/ ▶ VERB [lifts, lifting, lifted]
1 to move something upwards or raise it □ *She lifted the baby out of his cot.* □ *He was so weak that he couldn't lift his head.*
2 to move upwards and disappear □ *The fog seems to be lifting.*
3 to officially end a rule that says something is not allowed □ *The ban on imports was lifted last month.*

▶ NOUN [plural **lifts**]
1 a machine like a large box that carries people or things between floors in a tall building 🔁 *Take the lift to the sixth floor.*
2 a ride in someone's car 🔁 *Could you give me a lift home?*
3 when you move something or someone upwards □ *Try to do ten lifts with each leg.*

lift-off /'lɪftɒf/ NOUN [plural **lift-offs**] the time when a spacecraft leaves the ground

ligament /'lɪɡəmənt/ NOUN [plural **ligaments**] a band of strong tissue in the body that joins bones together. A biology word □ *He has torn a ligament in his thigh.*

light /laɪt/ ▶ NOUN [plural **lights**]
1 *no plural* brightness from something such as the sun or a piece of electrical equipment □ *There isn't enough light to read.* 🔁 *A ray of light shone through the curtains.* 🔁 *The room was filled with bright light.*
2 a piece of equipment that produces light 🔁 *Don't forget to switch off the light.* 🔁 *I turned on the light.* 🔁 *Where is the light switch?*
3 set light to something to make something burn
4 a flame that you use to make a cigarette burn 🔁 *Have you got a light?*

◆ IDIOMS **bring something to light** if facts are brought to light, they are discovered □ *Investigation of the company's accounts brought to light the scale of the fraud.* **come to light** if facts come to light, people discover them □ *The mistake only came to light a year later.* **shed/throw light on something** to provide information that helps people understand something □ *I was wondering if you could shed any light on the matter of the missing documents.*

▶ ADJECTIVE [**lighter, lightest**]
1 bright or not dark □ *It's still light enough to read.* 🔁 *Mike got up as soon as it began to get light.*
2 pale in colour □ *light blue* □ *You can make colours lighter by adding white to them.*
3 not heavy □ *My bike has a very light frame.* □ *This bag feels light.*
4 not strong or in large amounts 🔁 *Light winds reduced the temperature.* 🔁 *Traffic is light around London tonight.* □ *I felt a light touch on my arm.*
5 not serious or difficult □ *I did a little light housework.* □ *I want some light reading for my holiday.*

◆ IDIOM **make light of something** to act or talk as if something is not serious □ *She makes light of her problems.*

▶ VERB [**lights, lighting, lit**]
1 to make something start to burn 🔁 *Let's light the fire.*
2 to start burning □ *Why won't the cooker light?*
3 to light a place is to make it brighter □ *The stage was lit with candles.*

◆ PHRASAL VERB **light up** if your face or eyes light up, you suddenly look happy

light bulb /laɪt bʌlb/ NOUN [plural **light bulbs**] a hollow glass object that contains a wire which produces light when electricity passes through it □ *energy-saving light bulbs*

lighten /'laɪtən/ VERB [**lightens, lightening, lightened**]

1 if a situation lightens or is lightened, it becomes less serious ⊞ *He tried to lighten the mood by making a few jokes.*

2 to make something brighter □ *The white walls certainly lighten the room.*

3 to reduce the amount of work that must be done □ *Having an assistant has lightened my workload.*

♦ PHRASAL VERB **lighten up** to become less serious. An informal phrase. □ *You've got to learn to lighten up a bit.*

lighter /'laɪtə(r)/ NOUN [plural **lighters**] a small object that produces a flame to make a cigarette start burning □ *Do you have a lighter I could use?*

light-hearted /ˌlaɪt'hɑːtɪd/ ADJECTIVE for fun and not serious □ *a light-hearted remark*

lighthouse /'laɪthaʊs/ NOUN [plural **lighthouses**] a tall, narrow building next to the sea with a flashing light at the top to tell ships of danger or to show them where to go

light industry /laɪt 'ɪndəstrɪ/ NOUN, NO PLURAL factories that produce small goods such as electrical parts for machines in the home

lighting /'laɪtɪŋ/ NOUN, NO PLURAL the lights used in a room □ *soft lighting*

lightly /'laɪtlɪ/ ADVERB

1 gently □ *She touched me lightly on the arm and smiled.*

2 not much □ *a lightly boiled egg* □ *She was lightly tanned.*

3 not in a serious way □ *I did not take this decision lightly* (= I thought about it very seriously).

♦ IDIOM **get off lightly** to be punished less than you expected or have less trouble than you expected □ *Brown got off lightly with a yellow card for the foul.*

lightning /'laɪtnɪŋ/ ► NOUN, NO PLURAL a bright flash of electricity in the sky that sometimes happens in a storm □ *a flash of lightning* ⊞ *thunder and lightning* ⊞ *The church steeple was struck by lightning in the storm.*

► ADJECTIVE very fast or sudden ⊞ *The firemen called a lightning strike.*

lightweight /'laɪtweɪt/ ADJECTIVE

1 not heavy □ *a lightweight raincoat*

2 not important or serious □ *a lightweight comedy*

light year /laɪt jɪə(r)/ NOUN [plural **light years**] the distance that light travels in a year, which is 6 billion miles

likable /'laɪkəbəl/ ADJECTIVE another spelling of likeable

like¹ /laɪk/ ► PREPOSITION

1 similar to □ *Geraldine looks just like her mother.*

2 in a similar way to □ *She dances like a professional.*

3 if you ask what someone or something is like, you want someone to describe them □ *What's your new teacher like?*

4 typical of □ *It's not like you to be late.*

5 used to give examples □ *I love sports like tennis and badminton.*

♦ IDIOM **look/feel like death warmed up** to look or feel very ill

► CONJUNCTION

1 as if □ *You look like you've seen a ghost.*

2 in the same way as. An informal word □ *Tie the knot like I showed you.*

like² /laɪk/ VERB [**likes, liking, liked**]

1 to think that something or someone is pleasant or enjoyable □ *I like pizza.* □ *I don't like football.* ⊞ *I like this house better than our old house.* ⊞ *I don't like the idea of eating raw fish.* ⊞ *He liked the way she talked.* □ **+ ing** *I don't like coming home after dark.* □ **+ to do something** *I like to get up early.*

2 Would you like ...? used to offer someone something □ *Would you like a biscuit?* □ *Would you like to come with us?*

3 would like if you would like something, you want it □ *I'd like a cup of tea.*

4 would like to do something if you would like to do something, you want to do it □ *I'd like to go home now.*

5 if you like (a) used when you make an offer □ *I'll come with you if you like.* (b) used to say yes when someone suggests doing something □ *'Shall I bring some food?' 'Yes, if you like.'*

► Notice that **would like** meaning 'want to do something' *(sense 4)* is followed by the verb form **to do something**:
✓ *I would like to go home.*
✗ *I would like that I go home.*

likeable /'laɪkəbəl/ ADJECTIVE a likeable person is nice and easy to like

likelihood /'laɪklɪhʊd/ NOUN, NO PLURAL how likely it is that something will happen □ *There's a strong likelihood of rain today.*

likely /'laɪklɪ/ ADJECTIVE

1 expected to happen □ **+ to do something** *People are more likely to come if the weather is good.* □ **+ that** *It's very likely that nobody will come.*

2 probably true □ *That seems the most likely explanation.*

like-minded /ˌlaɪk'maɪndɪd/ ADJECTIVE having similar opinions and enjoying the same things □ *She set up the film club with a group of like-minded friends.*

liken /'laɪkən/ VERB [**likens, likening, likened**] to say that two people or things are like each other □ *Her writing has been likened to J. K. Rowling's.*

likeness /'laɪknɪs/ NOUN [plural **likenesses**]
1 when two people or things are similar in appearance 🔃 *There is a strong likeness between the girls.*
2 something that looks very similar to the real thing or person □ *It's a good likeness of your father.*

likewise /'laɪkwaɪz/ ADVERB in the same way. A formal word. 🔃 *Peter has left and I suggest we do likewise.*

liking /'laɪkɪŋ/ NOUN, NO PLURAL
1 when you enjoy something 🔃 *Most children have a liking for chocolate.*
2 for your liking if something is too big/bright etc. for your liking, it is bigger/brighter, etc. than you want it to be □ *The bed was too soft for my liking.*
3 take a liking to someone to start to like someone that you have just met
4 to be to someone's liking if something is to someone's liking, it is how they like it. A formal phrase. □ *Is the room to your liking, Madam?*

lilac /'laɪlək/ ▶ NOUN [plural **lilacs**]
1 a bush or tree with groups of white or purple flowers that hang down
2 a pale purple colour
▶ ADJECTIVE pale purple

lily /'lɪlɪ/ NOUN [plural **lilies**] a tall plant with large white or coloured flowers that smell very sweet

limb /lɪm/ NOUN [plural **limbs**]
1 a leg or an arm
2 a large branch of a tree

lime /laɪm/ ▶ NOUN [plural **limes**]
1 a small, sour fruit that looks like a green lemon □ *Add the juice of two limes.*
2 a large tree with yellow flowers
3 *no plural* a white substance that is used to help plants grow and to make cement (= substance used in building)
4 *no plural* a bright green colour
▶ ADJECTIVE having a bright green colour □ *a lime green shirt*

limelight /'laɪmlaɪt/ NOUN, NO PLURAL the limelight attention that famous people get from the public □ *She liked being in the limelight.*

limerick /'lɪmərɪk/ NOUN [plural **limericks**] a funny poem with five lines

limestone /'laɪmstəʊn/ NOUN, NO PLURAL a type of rock that is used in building and in making cement (= grey powder mixed with water and used for building)

limit /'lɪmɪt/ ▶ NOUN [plural **limits**]
1 the largest or smallest amount or level that is allowed 🔃 *There's a time limit for this test* 🔃 *She had above the legal limit of alcohol in her blood.* 🔃 *Each person is allowed 10kg of luggage, and you are over the limit.*
2 the largest amount or level of something that is possible □ *+ to There's a limit to how much I can help her.*
3 the outside edge of an area □ *the city limits*
▶ VERB [**limits, limiting, limited**]
1 to keep someone or something below a particular

amount or level □ *Places on the course are limited, so book early.* □ *People covered their windows to limit damage from the storm.* □ *+ to I shall have to limit you to one cake each.*
2 if something is limited to a particular place or group of people, it only happens or exists in that place or group □ *+ to These beliefs are not limited to rural communities.*

• **limitation** /ˌlɪmɪ'teɪʃən/ NOUN [plural **limitations**]
1 something that stops something from reaching the highest possible amount or level □ *We have to work within the limitations of the law.* □ *The government has placed limitations on their freedom to demonstrate.*
2 an area in which someone or something is not good □ *Life in the country has its limitations.*

• **limited** /'lɪmɪtɪd/ ADJECTIVE small in amount or number □ *a limited choice*

limousine /'lɪməziːn/ NOUN [plural **limousines**] a large expensive car with a driver □ *a chauffeur-driven limousine*

limp /lɪmp/ ▶ VERB [**limps, limping, limped**] to walk with difficulty because your leg or foot hurts □ *Beckham limped off the pitch.*
▶ NOUN, NO PLURAL a way of walking that is not even and shows that someone's leg or foot hurts □ *He walked with a limp.*
▶ ADJECTIVE [**limper, limpest**] not stiff or firm □ *This lettuce has gone a bit limp.* 🔃 *a limp handshake*

limpet /'lɪmpɪt/ NOUN [plural **limpets**] a small sea creature with a shell shaped like a cone that fastens itself to rocks

line /laɪn/ ▶ NOUN [plural **lines**]
1 a long thin mark □ *There are white lines in the middle of the road.* 🔃 *Draw a straight line from A to B.* 🔃 *Sign on the dotted line.* 🔃 *The first runners have already crossed the finishing line.*
2 a row of things or people □ *The children formed an orderly line.* □ *There is a line of fine oak trees by the road.*
3 a border between two areas or two situations □ *They crossed the state line that morning.* 🔃 *There can be a fine line (= a very small difference) between humour and rudeness.*
4 a row of words on a page □ *Look at the first line of the poem.*
5 a piece of rope, wire, etc. used for a particular purpose □ *I was hanging the washing on the line.*
6 a telephone connection □ *There's a strange noise on this line.*
7 a mark on an older person's face
8 a part of a railway □ *Flooding has closed the line between Edinburgh and Glasgow.*
9 an opinion or a way of thinking about something □ *+ on What's your company's line on flexible working hours?* 🔃 *Her line of argument was that more families should receive financial help.*
10 the US word for queue

11 along the lines of something similar to something □ *I wrote a letter along the lines of the one I sent to Bob.*

➔ go to **draw the line**, **read between the lines**
▶ VERB **[lines, lining, lined]**
1 to be in a row along the sides of something □ *Police officers will line the route of the procession.*
2 to cover the inside of a piece of clothing or a container with something □ *The cloak is lined with fur.*
◆ PHRASAL VERB **line (someone/something) up** to stand in a row or to put people or things in a row □ *Line up by the door.* □ *All the spice jars were lined up on the shelf.*

linear /'lɪnɪə(r)/ ADJECTIVE
1 connected with or using lines or length □ *linear measurements*
2 able to be represented by a straight line. A maths word. □ *a linear equation*

lined /laɪnd/ ADJECTIVE
1 a lined piece of clothing has material sewn on the inside □ *a lined jacket*
2 lined skin has a lot of marks because of age
3 lined paper has lines on it to write on

linen /'lɪnɪn/ NOUN, NO PLURAL
1 a type of cloth like a heavy, slightly rough, cotton that is made from a plant □ *a linen jacket*
2 things made of cloth used to cover beds or tables □ *table linen*

liner /'laɪnə(r)/ NOUN [plural **liners**]
1 a large ship that carries passengers
2 something that is put inside a container to keep it clean □ *a bin liner*

linesman /'laɪnzmən/ NOUN [plural **linesmen**] a man whose job is to decide whether a ball has crossed a line during a game such as tennis or football

linger /'lɪŋgə(r)/ VERB [lingers, lingering, lingered] to stay somewhere for a long time □ *Fans were still lingering at the stage door.* □ *The smell of fish seemed to linger for days.*

lingerie /'lænʒərɪ/ NOUN, NO PLURAL women's underwear □ *expensive silk lingerie*

linguist /'lɪŋgwɪst/ NOUN [plural **linguists**] someone who speaks a lot of languages, or someone who teaches linguistics
● **linguistic** /lɪŋ'gwɪstɪk/ ADJECTIVE to do with language or linguistics
● **linguistics** /lɪŋ'gwɪstɪks/ NOUN, NO PLURAL the scientific study of language

lining /'laɪnɪŋ/ NOUN [plural **linings**] a covering on the inside of a piece of clothing or a container □ *a jacket lining* □ *a silver box with a velvet lining*

link /lɪŋk/ ▶ NOUN [plural **links**]
1 a relationship between two people or things □ **+ between** *Research soon proved the link between smoking and lung cancer.* □ **+ with** *It is thought that the group has links with terrorist organizations.*
2 a way of travelling between two places □ *There's a new rail link between the airport and the city centre.*

3 a connection between two files, especially on a website. A computing word. □ *Click on the link to reserve your tickets.*
4 one of the rings of a chain
▶ VERB **[links, linking, linked]**
1 if two people or things are linked, they are connected to each other in some way □ *The two murders are not thought to be linked.* □ *Were these two events linked in any way?* 🖰 *Diet and health are closely linked.*
2 to provide a way of travelling between two places □ *A walkway links the two buildings.*
◆ PHRASAL VERB **link (something/someone) up** to form a connection □ *Other stores have linked up with designers to produce more collections.*

lint /lɪnt/ NOUN, NO PLURAL a soft type of cloth for covering cuts or small injuries

lion /'laɪən/ NOUN [plural **lions**] a large, wild animal of the cat family, the male of which has thick hair around its head

lioness /'laɪənes/ NOUN [plural **lionesses**] a female lion

lip /lɪp/ NOUN [plural **lips**]
1 either the upper or the lower outside edge of your mouth □ *He kissed her lightly on the lips.*
2 the edge of a container that liquid is poured out of

liposuction /'lɪpəʊˌsʌkʃən/ NOUN, NO PLURAL a medical treatment in which fat is sucked out of someone's body to make them look thinner

lip-read /'lɪpˌriːd/ VERB [lip-reads, lip-reading, lip-read] to watch the way someone's lips move in order to understand what they are saying because you cannot hear them
● **lip-reading** /'lɪpˌriːdɪŋ/ NOUN, NO PLURAL when someone lip-reads

lipstick /'lɪpstɪk/ NOUN [plural **lipsticks**] make-up that women put on their lips to make the lips a different colour □ *She was wearing bright red lipstick*

liqueur /lɪ'kjʊə(r)/ NOUN [plural **liqueurs**] a strong, sweet alcoholic drink, usually drunk at the end of a meal □ *an orange liqueur*

liquid /'lɪkwɪd/ ▶ NOUN [plural **liquids**] a substance that can flow, such as water or oil □ *In hot weather make sure you drink plenty of liquids.*
▶ ADJECTIVE in the form of a liquid □ *a liquid detergent*
● **liquidize** or **liquidise** /'lɪkwɪdaɪz/ VERB [liquidizes, liquidizing, liquidized] to make something into a liquid □ *Add 300 ml of water and liquidize the ingredients.*
● **liquidizer** or **liquidiser** /'lɪkwɪdaɪzə(r)/ NOUN [plural **liquidizers**] a machine for making solid food into a smooth liquid

liquor /'lɪkə(r)/ NOUN, NO PLURAL a US word for alcoholic drink

liquorice /'lɪkərɪs/ NOUN, NO PLURAL a black sweet made using the root of a plant

lisp /lɪsp/ ▶ NOUN [plural **lisps**] a way of speaking in which 's' sounds like 'th' 🔁 *Al has a slight lisp.*
▶ VERB [**lisps, lisping, lisped**] to speak with a lisp

list /lɪst/ ▶ NOUN [plural **lists**] a group of things such as names, numbers or prices, written one below the other □ *His name is on the list.* 🔁 *a shopping list* 🔁 *I've added your name to the list.* 🔁 *You should make a list of things to do.*

> ➤ Notice the preposition. Something is **on** a list and not 'in' a list:
> ✓ *I'll put your name on the list.*
> ✗ *I'll put your name in the list.*

▶ VERB [**lists, listing, listed**] to write a list, or to give information in the form of a list □ *The players are listed alphabetically.*

listen /'lɪsən/ VERB [**listens, listening, listened**]
1 to pay attention to a sound so that you can hear it □ **+ to** *Listen to me when I'm talking!* □ *Do you ever listen to classical music?* □ *I often listen to the radio.*
2 to pay attention to someone's advice and do what they suggest □ *I told you to wear a coat but you wouldn't listen!*
◆ PHRASAL VERBS **listen (out) for something** to try to hear something □ *Will you listen out for the baby while I'm in the shower?* **listen in (on something)** to secretly listen to other people speaking □ *The police had been listening in on his calls.*
◆ **listener** /'lɪsənə(r)/ NOUN [plural **listeners**]
1 someone who listens to a radio show □ *listeners to the breakfast show*
2 a good listener someone who listens when people speak to them and concentrates on what they are saying

listless /'lɪstlɪs/ ADJECTIVE tired and without energy □ *She had felt listless all day.*

lit /lɪt/ PAST TENSE AND PAST PARTICIPLE OF **light** □ *She lit the fire.* □ *I haven't lit the candles yet.*

liter /'liːtə(r)/ NOUN [plural **liters**] the US spelling of **litre**

literacy /'lɪtərəsɪ/ NOUN, NO PLURAL the ability to read and write □ *There are concerns over levels of literacy and numeracy.*

literal /'lɪtərəl/ ADJECTIVE meaning exactly what the word says 🔁 *That's the literal translation.* 🔁 *The hole in the ozone layer isn't a hole in the literal sense.*

literally /'lɪtərəlɪ/ ADVERB
1 used to emphasize that something surprising is true □ *One side was literally two centimetres lower than the other.*
2 in a literal way □ *The word literally translates as chief or leader.*

literary /'lɪtərərɪ/ ADJECTIVE to do with books, writers and literature 🔁 *a literary critic* □ *a literary magazine*

literate /'lɪtərət/ ADJECTIVE able to read and write □ *He had no education and was barely literate.*

literature /'lɪtrətʃə(r)/ NOUN, NO PLURAL
1 stories, poetry and plays □ *He's studying English literature.* □ *20th-century children's literature*
2 all the written information about a subject □ *Most scientific literature supports the theory.*

litigation /ˌlɪtɪ'geɪʃən/ NOUN, NO PLURAL a formal word meaning the use of the legal system to make a decision about a disagreement □ *We hope to avoid litigation.*

litmus /'lɪtməs/ NOUN, NO PLURAL a substance that shows whether something is acid or alkaline. A chemistry word.

litmus paper /'lɪtməs 'peɪpə(r)/ NOUN, NO PLURAL a type of paper containing litmus, used to show whether something is acid or alkaline. A chemistry word.

litre /'liːtə(r)/ NOUN [plural **litres**] a unit for measuring liquid, equal to 100 centilitres □ **+ of** *a litre of water* □ *Petrol now costs more than £1 per litre.*

litter /'lɪtə(r)/ ▶ NOUN [plural **litters**]
1 paper and other rubbish that people have thrown on the ground in a public place 🔁 *You can be fined for dropping litter.*
2 a group of animals born to the same mother at the same time □ *a litter of puppies*
▶ VERB [**litters, littering, littered**]
1 to be spread around a place in an untidy way □ *Children's toys littered the floor.*
2 be littered with something to include a lot of something bad □ *The article was littered with errors.*

little /'lɪtəl/ ▶ DETERMINER, PRONOUN, ADVERB [**less, least**]
1 not much □ *There is little hope of finding them alive.* □ *She cares so little for other people's opinions.* □ *It costs very little to go on a camping holiday.* □ **+ of** *I remember very little of what he said.*
2 a little a small amount or to a small degree □ *I added a little salt.* □ *'Would you like milk?' 'Just a little, please.'* □ *Jump up and down a little to keep warm.* □ *I'm feeling a little cold.*
▶ ADJECTIVE [**littler, littlest**]
1 small □ *They stuck little pieces of cardboard all over it.* □ *He's got his own little bicycle.* 🔁 *Can I have a little bit of butter?*
2 short in time or distance 🔁 *It's only a little way to the hotel.* 🔁 *He'll be here in a little while.*
3 young 🔁 *a little boy/girl* 🔁 *my little brother/sister*
4 not important or serious 🔁 *She worries about every little thing.*

live¹ /lɪv/ VERB [**lives, living, lived**]
1 to be alive □ *Cats don't usually live for much more than twenty years.* □ *People are living longer these days.*
2 to have your home in a certain place □ *How long have you lived in Madrid?* □ *I live next door to Sam.*
3 to pass your life in a certain way □ *She's used to living alone.*

◆ PHRASAL VERBS **live something down** to make people forget something embarrassing that you did □ *Fancy forgetting my own birthday - I'll never live it down!* **live on something 1** to eat a particular type of food □ *They live on nuts and insects.* **2** money you live on is money you use for the things you need □ *We managed to live on our savings for two years.* **live up to something** to be as good as you hoped or expected □ *The restaurant didn't really live up to my expectations.*

live² /laɪv/ ▶ ADJECTIVE
1 not dead □ *We bought some live oysters.*
2 connected to an electricity supply □ *a live socket*
3 a live broadcast is happening as you watch or hear it ▶ ADVERB if something is broadcast live, it is happening as you watch or hear it □ *We are going live to our correspondent in Berlin.*

livelihood /ˈlaɪvlihʊd/ NOUN [plural **livelihoods**] the way you earn enough money to live □ *Many families lost their homes and their livelihoods as a result of the floods.*

lively /ˈlaɪvli/ ADJECTIVE [**livelier, liveliest**] full of activity, interest or energy □ *a group of lively children* ♫ *There was a lively debate on the issue.* □ *The café has great food and a lively atmosphere.*

liver /ˈlɪvə(r)/ NOUN [plural **livers**] a large organ in your body that is very important for cleaning your blood. A biology word.

livestock /ˈlaɪvstɒk/ NOUN, NO PLURAL farm animals

livid /ˈlɪvɪd/ ADJECTIVE extremely angry □ *I told Ian and he was livid.*

living /ˈlɪvɪŋ/ ▶ NOUN [plural **livings**]
1 the money you earn from working and that you live on ♫ *I make my living as a professional actor.* ♫ *He earns a living by teaching the piano.* ♫ *I make a decent living* (= enough money). ♫ *What do you do for a living?* (= What is your job?)
2 the way you live □ *We want to encourage healthy living.*
▶ ADJECTIVE
1 alive □ *a living organism* □ *She has no living relatives.*
2 to do with the way people live ♫ *Living standards have improved.*

living room /ˈlɪvɪŋ ruːm/ NOUN [plural **living rooms**] a room in a house for sitting and relaxing in □ *I was in the living room, watching television.*

lizard /ˈlɪzəd/ NOUN [plural **lizards**] a reptile with four legs, a long body and a tail

llama /ˈlɑːmə/ NOUN [plural **llamas**] a large South American animal with a long neck, that is kept for its wool and to carry things

load /ləʊd/ ▶ VERB [**loads, loading, loaded**]
1 to put something into a vehicle, especially a ship or a truck □ + **up** *We loaded up the van with furniture.* □ +

onto *The boxes are loaded onto a truck.* □ + **with** *A tanker loaded with oil has sunk off the coast.*
2 to put something into a machine or piece of equipment □ *Have you loaded the dishwasher?*
3 to put a program into a computer's memory so you can use it □ *The laptop comes loaded with anti-virus software.*
4 to put bullets in a gun
▶ NOUN [plural **loads**]
1 the things that a vehicle or person is carrying or can carry ♫ *The ship was carrying a load of new cars.* □ *There were two lorry loads of rubbish.* □ *Take another load upstairs.*
2 loads/a load an informal word meaning a large amount □ *We have loads to talk about.* □ + **of** *He brought a load of food with him.*
3 the amount of work that someone has to do ♫ *We can't handle the current work load.*
4 the amount of something that a machine can deal with at one time □ *We had to do several loads of laundry.*
5 a load of something an informal phrase used to emphasize that something is completely stupid, wrong, etc. □ *What a load of rubbish!*

● **loaded** /ˈləʊdɪd/ ADJECTIVE
1 if a gun is loaded, it has bullets in it ♫ *a loaded gun*
2 carrying a load □ *a fully loaded plane*
3 with a second or hidden meaning ♫ *That's a loaded question, isn't it?* □ *a loaded term*
4 an informal word meaning very rich □ *He's absolutely loaded.*

loaf /ləʊf/ NOUN [plural **loaves**] a large piece of bread for cutting into smaller pieces □ + **of** *a loaf of bread* □ *a brown sliced loaf*
◆ PHRASAL VERB [**loafs, loafing, loafed**] **loaf about/around** to spend time doing very little

loan /ləʊn/ ▶ NOUN [plural **loans**]
1 money that you borrow ♫ *He wasn't able to repay the loan.* ♫ *They took out a loan* (= arranged to borrow money) *to extend the house.* ♫ *a bank loan*
2 on loan borrowed from someone □ *The painting is on loan from the National Gallery.*
▶ VERB [**loans, loaning, loaned**] to lend something to someone □ *My brother loaned me the money to buy a new car.*

loathe /ləʊð/ VERB [**loathes, loathing, loathed**] to hate someone or something □ *I loathe shopping.*
● **loathing** /ˈləʊðɪŋ/ NOUN, NO PLURAL a feeling of great dislike

loaves /ləʊvz/ PLURAL OF **loaf**

lob /lɒb/ ▶ VERB [**lobs, lobbing, lobbed**] to throw or hit something high into the air □ *The men lobbed grenades into the building.*
▶ NOUN [plural **lobs**] when you lob something

lobby /ˈlɒbi/ ▶ NOUN [plural **lobbies**]
1 a room inside the entrance to a building ♫ *I'll meet you in the hotel lobby.*
2 a group of people who try to persuade politicians

about something 🔁 *an environmental lobby group*
□ *America's powerful gun lobby*
▶ VERB [**lobbies, lobbying, lobbied**] to try to persuade
politicians about a particular subject □ *Small
businesses are lobbying for a change in the rules.*

lobe /ləʊb/ NOUN [*plural* **lobes**]
1 the soft round part at the bottom of your ear
2 one part of a body organ that has several parts, like
the brain. A biology word.

lobster /'lɒbstə(r)/ NOUN [*plural* **lobsters**] a sea
animal with a hard shell, two large claws (= hard
curved parts) and eight legs

local /'ləʊkəl/ ▶ ADJECTIVE to do with the area near to
you □ *our local library* □ *a local newspaper* 🔁 *local
government* 🔁 *Local residents are unhappy about the
plans.*
▶ NOUN [*plural* **locals**]
1 someone who lives in a particular area □ *If you want
to know the way, you'd better ask a local.*
2 an informal word meaning the pub nearest to your
home

local anaesthetic /'ləʊkəl ˌænɪs'θetɪk/ NOUN
[*plural* **local anaesthetics**] a drug that makes part of
your body lose feeling before you have medical
treatment

locality /lə'kælətɪ/ NOUN [*plural* **localities**] a formal
word meaning a particular place and the area around it
□ *There are higher rates of crime in rural localities.*

locally /'ləʊkəlɪ/ ADVERB in or from the area near to
you □ *Most of our vegetables are grown locally.* □ *The
hill is known locally as Old Misty.*

locate /ləʊ'keɪt/ VERB [**locates, locating, located**]
1 to find out exactly where something or someone is
□ *He was trying to locate the school on the map.*
□ *Police have now located the girl's mother.*
2 be located by/in/near, etc. to be in a particular
place □ *Their headquarters are located in Paris.* □ *The
camps are mostly located near the border.*

location /ləʊ'keɪʃən/ NOUN [*plural* **locations**]
1 a place or position □ *+ of Nobody knows the exact
location of the meeting.* □ *We have over 200 staff at
40 locations across the country.*
2 on location if a film is made on location, it is filmed
in a real place and not in a studio (= special building
where films are recorded)

loch /lɒχ/ NOUN [*plural* **lochs**] a lake in Scotland

lock /lɒk/ ▶ NOUN [*plural* **locks**]
1 a device that fastens things such as doors and
drawers, usually opened and closed using a key
□ *There was no lock on the door.* □ *We had to change
the lock on the front door.*
2 under lock and key in a place which is locked
□ *The weapons are kept safely under lock and key.*
3 a small part of a river or canal (= artificial river) with
gates that allows boats to move to a higher or lower
level
4 a piece of someone's hair □ *a lock of blonde hair*
▶ VERB [**locks, locking, locked**]

1 to fasten something such as a door with a key, or to
be fastened this way 🔁 *Lock the door when you leave.*
□ *This door doesn't lock.*
2 to put something or someone in a place that is
locked □ *+ up He's a dangerous criminal who should
be locked up.* □ *+ away I locked all my jewellery away
in a box.* □ *+ in The medicines are locked in a
cupboard.*
3 to become fixed in a position □ *The wheels locked
and the car skidded off the road.*

locker /'lɒkə(r)/ NOUN [*plural* **lockers**] a small
cupboard, especially one that can be locked □ *I left my
suitcase in a luggage locker at the station.*

locomotion /ˌləʊkə'məʊʃən/ NOUN, NO PLURAL a
formal word meaning the power to move or the way
something moves

• **locomotive** /ˌləʊkə'məʊtɪv/ NOUN [*plural*
locomotives] a railway engine that pulls trains

locust /'ləʊkəst/ NOUN [*plural* **locusts**] a large insect
that flies in large groups that eat and destroy plants

lodge /lɒdʒ/ ▶ VERB [**lodges, lodging, lodged**]
1 to officially make a complaint, say that you should
be given something, etc. 🔁 *The team lodged a
complaint with the FIA.* □ *We have lodged a planning
application with the council.*
2 to become fixed somewhere, often when this is not
wanted □ *A piece of apple had lodged between his
front teeth.* □ *He has a bullet lodged in his brain.*
3 to live in a room in someone else's house and pay
them rent
▶ NOUN [*plural* **lodges**] a small house in the
countryside □ *a hunting lodge* □ *a ski lodge*

• **lodger** /'lɒdʒə(r)/ NOUN [*plural* **lodgers**] a person
who lives in rooms that they rent in someone else's
house

• **lodging** /'lɒdʒɪŋ/ NOUN [*plural* **lodgings**] a place to
stay, especially for a short time

loft /lɒft/ NOUN [*plural* **lofts**] the space between the
roof of a house and the rooms □ *Our suitcases are
stored in the loft.*

log /lɒg/ ▶ NOUN [*plural* **logs**]
1 a part of a branch or tree that has been cut up
2 an official written record of what happens, especially
on a journey
▶ VERB [**logs, logging, logged**] to make an official
written record of something
♦ PHRASAL VERBS log in/on to start using a computer,
website, etc. by typing in a word or code (= series of
letters or numbers) log off/out to stop using a
computer, website, etc. by clicking on something on
the screen

logarithm /'lɒgərɪðəm/ NOUN [*plural* **logarithms**]
one of a series of numbers in lists that are used to
make multiplying and dividing easier. A maths word.

loggerheads /'lɒgəhedz/ PLURAL NOUN be at
loggerheads if you are at loggerheads with someone,
you argue or disagree with them strongly □ *They are
at loggerheads over plans to cut down the trees.*

logic /'lɒdʒɪk/ NOUN, NO PLURAL a way of thinking using facts and reason □ *I could see the logic of his argument.* ⊞ *This decision just defies logic* (= does not seem reasonable).

● **logical** /'lɒdʒɪkəl/ ADJECTIVE based on or using logic □ *What's the logical thing to do next?* ⊞ *There is only one logical conclusion.*

● **logically** /'lɒdʒɪkəlɪ/ ADVERB in a logical way □ *Logically, there was no other alternative.* □ *We need to think logically about this.*

login /'lɒgɪn/ NOUN [*plural* **logins**] the letters or numbers that you type into a box on the computer screen in order to to start using a system. A computing word.

logo /'ləʊgəʊ/ NOUN [*plural* **logos**] a design that is the symbol of a company or a product □ *The company has launched a new logo.*

loiter /'lɔɪtə(r)/ VERB [**loiters, loitering, loitered**] to stand or wait in a place doing nothing □ *Her friends loitered at the door.*

loll /lɒl/ VERB [**lolls, lolling, lolled**]
1 to lie or sit in a lazy, relaxed way □ *Pete's been lolling about watching football all afternoon.*
2 if your head or your tongue lolls, it hangs loosely □ *Her head lolled to one side.*

lollipop /'lɒlɪpɒp/ NOUN [*plural* **lollipops**] a hard sweet on a stick

lolly /'lɒlɪ/ NOUN [*plural* **lollies**]
1 a lollipop
2 an ice lolly

lone /ləʊn/ ADJECTIVE alone, single or only □ *He was killed by a lone gunman.* ⊞ *She's a lone parent with two young children.*

loneliness /'ləʊnlɪnɪs/ NOUN, NO PLURAL
1 when you are unhappy because you are alone □ *He felt a growing sense of loneliness.*
2 the state of being a long way from anything or anyone else

lonely /'ləʊnlɪ/ ADJECTIVE [**lonelier, loneliest**]
1 unhappy because you are alone, with no friends around you ⊞ *She suddenly felt very lonely.* ⊞ *I get lonely at the weekends.*
2 far from other places and with very few people □ *He lived in a lonely cottage on the hillside.*

loner /'ləʊnə(r)/ NOUN [*plural* **loners**] a person who prefers to be alone and who avoids close relationships □ *Steve's always been a loner.*

long[1] /lɒŋ/ ► ADJECTIVE [**longer, longest**]
1 lasting a lot of time ⊞ *It took a long time to persuade her to come.* □ *There were long delays on the trains.*
2 measuring a long distance from one end to the other □ *She has very long hair.* □ *We went on a long journey.* □ *How long is the rope?* ⊞ *It's a long way home from here.*
3 a long book or document has a lot of pages or words
4 having a certain length □ *The garden is 50m long.* □ *The film was three hours long.*

→ go to in the long/short *run*
► ADVERB [**longer, longest**]
1 for a long time □ *Have you been waiting long?* □ *It won't be long till she starts school.* □ *The concert didn't last long.*
2 much earlier or later than the time you are talking about ⊞ *The house was knocked down long ago.* ⊞ *He was a vegetarian long before I met him.*
3 as long as used for saying that something must happen or be true before something else can happen or be true □ *You can borrow my jacket as long as you bring it back tomorrow.*
4 before long soon □ *Before long, we were all singing songs.*
5 no longer not now □ *I no longer wish to see her.*

long[2] /lɒŋ/ VERB [**longs, longing, longed**] to want something very much □ *I was longing to sit down.* □ *They were longing for a chance to rest.*

long division /'lɒŋ dɪ'vɪʒən/ NOUN, NO PLURAL a method of dividing one number, usually a long one, by another, in which all the calculations are written down. A maths word.

longevity /lɒn'dʒevətɪ/ NOUN, NO PLURAL when someone lives for a long time. A formal word □ *Improvements in diet have led to an increase in longevity.*

longing /'lɒŋɪŋ/ NOUN, NO PLURAL a feeling of wanting something very much □ *They were looking at the food with longing.*

● **longingly** /'lɒŋɪŋlɪ/ ADVERB in a way that shows that you want something very much

longitude /'lɒndʒɪtjuːd/ NOUN [*plural* **longitudes**] the position of a place east or west of an imaginary line that passes from north to south through Greenwich, London. A geography word.

long jump /'lɒŋ ˌdʒʌmp/ NOUN, NO PLURAL a sports event where you run up to a line and then jump forward as far as possible

long-life /'lɒŋ ˌlaɪf/ ADJECTIVE made or designed to last longer than usual ⊞ *long-life batteries* ⊞ *a carton of long-life milk*

long-range /'lɒŋ ˌreɪndʒ/ ADJECTIVE
1 able to reach a great distance ⊞ *long-range missile*
2 looking a long way into the future ⊞ *a long-range weather forecast*

long-sighted /'lɒŋ'saɪtɪd/ ADJECTIVE able to see objects that are far away more clearly than things closer to you

long-standing /'lɒŋ'stændɪŋ/ ADJECTIVE having existed for a long time □ *She is in a long-standing relationship.*

long-suffering /'lɒŋ'sʌfərɪŋ/ ADJECTIVE accepting the trouble and problems that someone has caused in a patient way over a long period time □ *She played the part of his long-suffering wife.*

long-term /'lɒŋˌtɜːm/ ADJECTIVE
1 continuing to exist or have an effect a long time into the future □ *We know nothing about the long-term*

effects of this medicine. □ What are your long-term plans?

2 having existed for a long time □ She was in a long-term relationship.

long-winded /ˌlɒŋˈwɪndɪd/ ADJECTIVE if a piece of writing or speech is long-winded, it is much longer than necessary □ a long-winded explanation

loo /luː/ NOUN [plural **loos**] an informal word for a toilet □ I need to go to the loo.

look /lʊk/ VERB [**looks, looking, looked**]
1 to turn your eyes to see something □ + at She was looking at the view. □ Look behind you. □ Oh look, there's a deer over there! □ Look where you're going!
2 to try to find something or someone □ + for I'm looking for my passport.
3 to have a particular appearance □ You look a bit tired. □ Kate looked fine when I saw her yesterday.
4 to seem □ It looks as if Joe won't be coming. □ His job prospects are looking good.
♦ IDIOM **look on the bright side** to think about the good parts of a situation that is mostly bad □ 'The power's been cut off again.' 'Oh well, look on the bright side - you'll be saving on your electricity bills!'

> ➤ Notice the prepositions that are used with **look**. When you turn your eyes to see something (sense 1), you look **at** something:
> ✓ I looked at the clock.
> ✗ I looked the clock.

➡ go to **look down your** nose at someone/something, **look** the part
♦ PHRASAL VERBS **look after someone** to take care of someone or something □ Her husband looks after the baby during the day. **look at something** to think about something in order to make a decision about it □ We're looking at ways of making the road safer. **look down on someone/something** to think that you are better than someone or too good for something □ She never looked down on poor people. **look forward to something** to feel pleased and excited about something that is going to happen □ I'm really looking forward to meeting his family.

> ➤ When look forward to is followed by a verb, the verb is in the -ing form:
> ✓ We're looking forward to seeing you!
> ✗ We're looking forward to see you.

look into something to try to find information about something □ I'm looking into the possibility of having solar panels. **look out** to be careful because something might be dangerous □ Look out! The path is very slippery. **look something up** to look in a book, on a computer, etc. to find information about something □ I looked up the word 'digest' in the dictionary. **look up** if things are looking up, a situation is getting better **look up to someone** to

admire someone □ I always looked up to my older brother.
▶ NOUN [plural **looks**]
1 when you look at something or someone 🕮 May I have a look at your watch? 🕮 Take a look at these documents. 🕮 I had a good look round their house.
2 when you try to find something or someone 🕮 I had a look outside, but I couldn't see her.
3 an expression on someone's face □ She gave me a warning look. □ There was a look of disgust on his face.
4 the appearance of someone or something 🕮 I don't like the look of those black clouds. □ The house had a neglected look about it.
5 someone's **looks** how attractive someone is □ She is worried that she is losing her looks.

look-alike /ˈlʊkəˌlaɪk/ NOUN [plural **look-alikes**] a person who looks very like someone else □ a Prince Charles look-alike

lookout /ˈlʊkaʊt/ NOUN [plural **lookouts**]
1 a person who watches for danger □ The lookout spotted a boat on the horizon.
2 a place where someone can watch from, especially for danger □ a lookout tower
3 **keep a lookout/be on the lookout** to watch carefully for something □ I'll keep a lookout for the missing books. □ We're always on the lookout for opportunities to expand.
4 your (own) **lookout** your problem or worry and nobody else's. An informal phrase □ If you do not study for the exam, that's your own lookout.

loom¹ /luːm/ NOUN [plural **looms**] a machine for making cloth

loom² /luːm/ VERB [**looms, looming, loomed**]
1 to appear over or in front of you, especially in a frightening way □ A shadowy figure loomed towards us.
2 if an unpleasant or difficult event or situation looms, it is likely to happen soon □ A big decision is looming before us.

loop /luːp/ NOUN [plural **loops**] a circle of something such as a thread, a piece of string or a narrow piece of cloth □ Make a loop and pull one end through it.
▶ VERB [**loops, looping, looped**] to form a loop □ She had a scarf looped around her neck.

loophole /ˈluːphəʊl/ NOUN [plural **loopholes**] something that allows people to avoid doing what they should do without breaking a rule or the law □ She found a loophole in her contract.

loose /luːs/ ▶ ADJECTIVE [**looser, loosest**]
1 not tight or firmly fixed □ a loose knot □ Wear loose, comfortable clothing. 🕮 One of the screws had come loose.
2 not tied up or shut in □ Her hair was hanging loose. □ Let the dogs run around loose.
3 not exact or detailed □ a loose translation □ The descriptions were very loose.
4 not carefully organized or official □ The organization was a loose alliance of political groups.

♦ IDIOMS **at a loose end** having free time but nothing to do □ *I found myself at a loose end.* **loose ends** the last details or parts of something that need to be dealt with □ *There are still a few loose ends to tie up.*
▶ NOUN, NO PLURAL **on the loose** if a criminal or a wild animal is on the loose, they have escaped and are free □ *A dangerous killer is on the loose.*

● **loosely** /ˈluːslɪ/ ADVERB
1 not firmly or tightly □ *She had a silk scarf tied loosely around her neck.* □ *His arms hung loosely at his sides.*
2 not exactly or in detail □ *The book is loosely based on a true story.* □ *I'm using the term loosely.*
3 not in an organized or official way □ *They are loosely connected to the Conservative Party.*

● **loosen** /ˈluːsən/ VERB [**loosens, loosening, loosened**] to make something less firm, fixed or tight □ *I had to loosen my belt.* □ *She loosened her grip on Frank's arm.*

loot /luːt/ ▶ NOUN stolen goods or money
▶ VERB [**loots, looting, looted**] to steal things from shops or houses, especially during times of violence □ *Shops were looted during the riot.*

● **looter** /ˈluːtə(r)/ NOUN [*plural* **looters**] a person who loots from shops or houses

● **looting** /ˈluːtɪŋ/ NOUN, NO PLURAL when people loot from shops or houses □ *There were reports of widespread looting in the city.*

lopsided /ˌlɒpˈsaɪdɪd/ ADJECTIVE with one side higher or lower than the other □ *a lopsided smile*

lord /lɔːd/ NOUN [*plural* **lords**]
1 used as the title of a man with a high social rank in the UK, or a man with this title □ *Lord Asquith* □ *the Lord Mayor of London*
2 Lord used in prayers as a way of addressing God
3 the Lords one of the two parts of the British government, with members who are not elected

lordship /ˈlɔːdʃɪp/ NOUN [*plural* **lordships**] your lordship used to address or refer to some men with a high social rank in the UK □ *May we express our gratitude to your lordship?*

lore /lɔː(r)/ NOUN, NO PLURAL the traditional knowledge, stories and beliefs of a group of people

lorry /ˈlɒrɪ/ NOUN [*plural* **lorries**] a large vehicle for carrying heavy goods by road 🖽 *a lorry driver*

lose /luːz/ VERB [**loses, losing, lost**]
1 to not be able to find someone or something □ *I've lost my keys.*
2 to have something taken away from you 🖽 *Fifty people have lost their jobs.* 🖽 *He was willing to lose his life for his beliefs.*
3 to have less of something than you had before 🖽 *She has lost weight recently.* 🖽 *The children soon lost interest in the animals.* 🖽 *The business is losing money.*
4 to not have something you had before 🖽 *I was so angry, I lost control and started shouting.* 🖽 *I would*

hate to lose contact with my friends. 🖽 *I lost sight (= stopped being able to see) of the train.*
5 to be beaten in a competition, election, etc. □ **+ by** *I lost by 4 games to 6.* 🖽 *We narrowly lost (= only just lost) the match.*
6 a clock or watch loses time when it goes too slowly □ *My watch is losing about a minute a day.*

♦ IDIOMS **lose count of something** used for emphasizing that something has happened many times □ *I've lost count of the number of times I've been in hospital.* **lose the plot** to start behaving strangely. An informal phrase. □ *I keep forgetting things - I think I'm losing the plot!* **lose sight of something** to forget about an important fact or aim because you are thinking about other things □ *We must not lose sight of the fact that the club is supposed to be fun.*
➔ go to **lose** the *thread*, **lose** *sleep* over something

♦ PHRASAL VERB **lose out** to not get something that other people get □ *Bill lost out when his father gave the business to his brothers.*

● **loser** /ˈluːzə(r)/ NOUN [*plural* **losers**]
1 the person who does not win a competition, election, etc. □ *Even the loser will win a huge amount of money.*
2 an informal word meaning someone who never seems to succeed at anything

loss /lɒs/ NOUN [*plural* **losses**]
1 when you lose something □ *She was sacked over the loss of confidential documents.* □ **+ of** *He spoke about the loss of his home in a fire.* 🖽 *There will be some job losses.*
2 when you have less of something than you had before 🖽 *She gives advice about weight loss.* 🖽 *He seemed to suffer a loss of confidence.* □ *Many older people are affected by hearing loss.*
3 when a business spends more money than it earns, or this amount of money □ **+ of** *The company announced a pre-tax loss of £2 million.*
4 the death of someone 🖽 *I was still mourning the loss of my brother.* 🖽 *It's surprising that there wasn't a greater loss of life.*
5 be at a loss (to do something) when you do not know what to do or to say in a situation □ *They're still at a loss to explain what went wrong.*
6 a disadvantage □ *It'll be your loss if you do not buy this wonderful car.*
7 when you lose a race, competition etc. □ *This is the team's sixth loss in a row.*

lost /lɒst/ ▶ ADJECTIVE
1 if something is lost, nobody knows where it is □ *The painting has been lost for centuries.*
2 someone who is lost does not know where they are 🖽 *How did you get lost when you had a map?* 🖽 *We were hopelessly lost.*
3 confused and not able to understand something □ *I'm lost – can you explain that last bit again?*
4 no longer existing or available □ *a lost opportunit*

🖰 *I never travelled when I was younger, but now I'm making up for lost time.*
5 be lost without someone/something to be unable to manage without someone or something □ *I'd be lost without my mobile phone.*
▶ PAST TENSE OF lose

lot /lɒt/ NOUN [*plural* **lots**]
1 a lot/lots a large number or amount □ **+ of** *There were a lot of people there.* □ *I bought lots of food.* □ *She doesn't eat a lot.* □ *We've got a lot to talk about.*
2 a lot better/happier/quicker, etc. much better/happier/quicker, etc. □ *You'd keep a lot warmer if you wore a hat.*
3 a group of things or people □ *Another lot of visitors will arrive tomorrow.*
4 the lot everything □ *He had fifteen paintings and sold the lot.*

> ➤ Notice (*sense 1*) that **a** only goes before **lot** and not before **lots** □ *She has a lot of friends.* □ *She has lots of friends.*

◆ IDIOM **draw lots** to make a decision by pulling out one of several pieces of paper □ *They drew lots to decide who would jump first.*

lotion /ˈləʊʃən/ NOUN [*plural* **lotions**] a thick liquid for putting on your skin or hair 🖰 *a bottle of suntan lotion* □ *a moisturizing lotion*

lottery /ˈlɒtəri/ NOUN [*plural* **lotteries**]
1 a game where people win money or prizes when their number or ticket is chosen by chance from many others 🖰 *He looked like he'd won the lottery.*
2 a situation where something depends on chance, usually in an unfair way

loud /laʊd/ ▶ ADJECTIVE [**louder, loudest**]
1 making a lot of sound 🖰 *a loud noise* 🖰 *She asked again in a louder voice.* □ *The music was too loud for me.*
2 a loud colour is very bright
▶ ADVERB [**louder, loudest**]
1 making a lot of sound □ *Could you speak a little louder please?* □ *I screamed as loud as I could.*
2 out loud so that other people can hear you □ *I read the letter out loud.* □ *She laughed out loud.*
◆ IDIOM **loud and clear** in a way that is clear and easy to understand □ *The message came across loud and clear.*

loudhailer /ˌlaʊdˈheɪlə(r)/ NOUN [*plural* **loudhailers**] a device that you hold and speak into to make your voice much louder

loudly /ˈlaʊdli/ ADVERB making a lot of sound □ *The crowds cheered loudly.* □ *I knocked again more loudly.*

loudspeaker /ˌlaʊdˈspiːkə(r)/ NOUN [*plural* **loudspeakers**] a piece of electrical equipment that makes voices and sounds louder

lounge /laʊndʒ/ ▶ NOUN [*plural* **lounges**]
1 a room in a house where you sit and relax □ *I was watching TV in the lounge.*
2 a room in a public building where people can sit to relax or to wait □ *a hotel lounge* 🖰 *an airport lounge*
▶ VERB [**lounges, lounging, lounged**] to sit or to lie somewhere in a lazy way □ *The students were lounging around the common room.*

louse /laʊs/ NOUN [*plural* **lice**] a small insect that lives on a person or an animal

lousy /ˈlaʊzi/ ADJECTIVE [**lousier, lousiest**] an informal word that means very bad □ *lousy weather* □ *I've had a lousy day.* □ *I'm feeling lousy.*

lout /laʊt/ NOUN [*plural* **louts**] a young man who behaves in a rude and unpleasant way
• **loutish** /ˈlaʊtɪʃ/ ADJECTIVE rude, unpleasant and violent □ *loutish behaviour*

lovable /ˈlʌvəbəl/ ADJECTIVE easy to love or to like a lot □ *a lovable child* □ *She's such a lovable character.*

love /lʌv/ ▶ VERB [**loves, loving, loved**]
1 to have a strong romantic feeling for someone □ *I love you.*
2 to have a strong emotional feeling for a friend or family member who you like and care about □ *I loved my mother very much.*
3 to like or enjoy something very much □ *I love Chinese food.* □ **+ ing** *He loves teasing the children.* □ **+ to do something** *I'd love to be able to play the piano.*
▶ NOUN [*plural* **loves**]
1 *no plural* a strong romantic feeling for someone 🖰 *She fell in love with him at university.* 🖰 *Within days, they were madly in love* (= loved each other very much). □ **+ for** *My love for him did not survive.*
2 *no plural* a strong emotional feeling for a friend or family member who you like and care about □ **+ for** *Her love for her children kept her going.*
3 *no plural* a feeling of liking or enjoying something very much □ **+ of** *I did not share her love of opera.*
4 something or someone that you love □ *Her great love was music.* □ *Robert was her first love.*
5 *no plural* used at the end of a letter □ *Hope to see you soon. Love, Emma.* □ *Have a great birthday. Lots of love, Mum.*
6 give/send someone your love to ask someone to pass on a message of affection to someone □ *'I'm going to see Fiona next week.' 'Really? Do give her my love.'*
• **loveless** /ˈlʌvlɪs/ ADJECTIVE without love 🖰 *He felt trapped in a loveless marriage.*

loveliness /ˈlʌvlinɪs/ NOUN, NO PLURAL the quality of being attractive or pleasant

lovely /ˈlʌvli/ ADJECTIVE [**lovelier, loveliest**]
1 beautiful or attractive □ *She has lovely eyes.* 🖰 *You look lovely in that dress.*

2 enjoyable or pleasant □ *It was lovely to see you again.* □ *It was a lovely evening.*
3 kind and friendly □ *She's a really lovely woman.*

lover /ˈlʌvə(r)/ NOUN [*plural* **lovers**]
1 a person who is having a romantic relationship with someone else
2 someone who is very interested in or enthusiastic about something □ *an art lover* □ *a music lover* □ *I've always been an animal lover.*

loving /ˈlʌvɪŋ/ ADJECTIVE
1 showing or expressing love □ *a loving look* □ *She has a very loving family.*
2 **in loving memory** used to remember someone who has died □ *In loving memory of my father, John.*
• **lovingly** /ˈlʌvɪŋlɪ/ ADVERB in a loving way □ *He gazed lovingly at her.*

low /ləʊ/ ▶ ADJECTIVE, ADVERB [**lower, lowest**]
1 near to the ground or short in height □ *a low hedge* □ *I can reach the lowest branches.*
2 less than usual in amount or level □ *We are experiencing very low temperatures.* □ *I try to look for the lowest prices.* □ *The risk of frost is very low now.* □ **+ in** *Skimmed milk is low in fat.*
3 a low sound or musical note is near the bottom of the range of sounds
4 quiet □ *He spoke in a low voice.*
5 not bright □ *low lighting*
6 unhappy 🔒 *He was feeling low.*
▶ ADVERB [**lower, lowest**] in or to a low position or level □ *Their supplies began to run low.* □ *They flew low over the desert.*
▶ NOUN [*plural* **lows**] a very low level 🔒 *Unemployment is at an all-time low.*

low-cost /ˈləʊˌkɒst/ ADJECTIVE charging a low price for something □ *low-cost airlines*

lowdown /ˈləʊdaʊn/ NOUN, NO PLURAL **the lowdown** the most important or interesting facts about someone or something 🔒 *Daniel gave me the lowdown on the market research project.*

lower /ˈləʊə(r)/ ▶ VERB [**lowers, lowering, lowered**]
1 to move something to a position nearer the bottom of something or nearer the ground □ **+ into** *They lowered the boat into the water.* □ *She lowered her head slightly.*
2 to reduce something in amount or degree □ *They have lowered their prices.* 🔒 *A good diet can lower your risk of heart disease.* 🔒 *She lowered her voice to a whisper.*
▶ ADJECTIVE below something else or nearer the bottom of something □ *the lower jaw* □ *a lower back problem*

lower class /ˈləʊə(r) ˈklɑːs/ NOUN [*plural* **lower classes**] people with the lowest position in a society, with the least money □ *The lower classes have a poorer standard of living.* □ *lower class families*

low-key /ˈləʊˌkiː/ ADJECTIVE quiet and with little activity or attention □ *We had a low-key wedding with only six guests.*

lowly /ˈləʊlɪ/ ADJECTIVE [**lowlier, lowliest**] having a job or position that is not important □ *Don't ask me, I'm just a lowly assistant.*

loyal /ˈlɔɪəl/ ADJECTIVE always supporting or being a friend to someone 🔒 *a loyal fan* 🔒 *We want to reward loyal customers.* 🔒 *He remained loyal to the party.*
• **loyally** /ˈlɔɪəlɪ/ ADVERB in a loyal way □ *She has stood loyally by her husband throughout the troubles.*
• **loyalty** /ˈlɔɪəltɪ/ NOUN, NO PLURAL being loyal to someone 🔒 *You always have a sense of loyalty to your home town.* □ **+ to** *The fans have demonstrated their loyalty to the team.*

lozenge /ˈlɒzɪndʒ/ NOUN [*plural* **lozenges**]
1 a sweet that you suck to help a sore throat
2 a diamond shape

LP /ˌelˈpiː/ NOUN [*plural* **LPs**] a record which plays for 20 to 30 minutes on each side

L-plate /ˈelpleɪt/ NOUN [*plural* **L-plates**] a small white sign with a red letter *L* on it, put on a car that is driven by someone learning to drive

Ltd ABBREVIATION Limited; used in the names of companies □ *Joe Bloggs Shoes Ltd*

lubricate /ˈluːbrɪkeɪt/ VERB [**lubricates, lubricating, lubricated**] to put oil or another substance on a machine to make it run smoothly
• **lubrication** /ˌluːbrɪˈkeɪʃən/ NOUN, NO PLURAL when you lubricate something, or a substance used to lubricate

lucid /ˈluːsɪd/ ADJECTIVE
1 clear and easily understood □ *She gave a lucid explanation of the differences.*
2 thinking and speaking clearly □ *There are only short periods when she is lucid.*
• **lucidity** /luːˈsɪdətɪ/ NOUN, NO PLURAL the quality of being lucid
• **lucidly** /ˈluːsɪdlɪ/ ADVERB in a lucid way

luck /lʌk/ NOUN, NO PLURAL
1 when something good happens by chance 🔒 *With a bit of luck, we'll be there by lunch time.* 🔒 *Meeting Tim was a real piece of luck.* 🔒 *When I heard I had won, I couldn't believe my luck.* 🔒 *I wished him luck with his exam.*
2 the way things happen by chance 🔒 *bad/good luck* □ *Whether or not you'll get on the course depends on your luck.*
3 when you are successful at something 🔒 *Have you had any luck selling your house?* □ *I've been trying to buy a wedding dress, but without any luck so far.*
4 **Good luck!** used to tell someone that you hope they will succeed □ *Good luck with your exams.*
5 **Bad luck!** used to say that you are sorry about something bad that has happened to someone □ *You broke your arm? Oh, bad luck!*
6 **Hard/Tough luck!** used to say that you do not have any sympathy for someone □ *She missed the*

train? Well that's tough luck - she should have got up earlier.

♦ IDIOM **try your luck** to see if you will be successful at something □ She went to Hollywood to try her luck in the movies.

➜ *go to push your luck*

• **luckily** /'lʌkɪlɪ/ ADVERB because of good luck □ The car hit us, but luckily nobody was badly hurt. □ Luckily for me, the door was unlocked.

• **lucky** /'lʌkɪ/ ADJECTIVE [**luckier, luckiest**]
1 a lucky person has good luck □ **+ to do something** You're lucky to live so near the school. □ **+ that** It's lucky that they didn't discover the truth.
2 bringing good luck □ a lucky charm
3 You'll be lucky! used to say that you do not think someone has a chance of success □ Get the children to wash up? You'll be lucky! □ You'll be lucky if you manage to see her - she's off to Paris in ten minutes.

lucrative /'lu:krətɪv/ ADJECTIVE making a lot of money □ a lucrative business

ludicrous /'lu:dɪkrəs/ ADJECTIVE completely silly or unreasonable □ It's a ludicrous idea!

lug /lʌg/ VERB [**lugs, lugging, lugged**] to pull or to carry something with difficulty. An informal word. □ He lugged the suitcases up the stairs.

luggage /'lʌgɪdʒ/ NOUN, NO PLURAL a traveller's bags and cases 🕮 I was only travelling with hand luggage. 🕮 Each passenger can check in two pieces of luggage. 🕮 a luggage rack

> ➤ Remember that the noun **luggage** is not used in the plural:
> ✓ I had so much luggage .
> ✗ I had so many luggages.

lukewarm /'lu:kwɔ:m/ ADJECTIVE
1 describes liquid that is slightly warm □ The water in the shower was only lukewarm.
2 only slightly interested or enthusiastic □ We got a fairly lukewarm welcome.

lull /lʌl/ ► VERB [**lulls, lulling, lulled**]
1 to make someone feel calm and relaxed □ She rocked the pram gently, lulling the baby to sleep.
2 to make someone feel relaxed and confident, often when they should not □ We were lulled into a false sense of security.
► NOUN [*plural* **lulls**] a time when something noisy, busy or violent stops for a while □ There was a lull in the fighting.

lullaby /'lʌləbaɪ/ NOUN [*plural* **lullabies**] a gentle song to help a child to sleep

lumber /'lʌmbə(r)/ VERB [**lumbers, lumbering, lumbered**] to move in a slow, heavy and awkward way □ We saw a bear lumbering through the forest.
➜ PHRASAL VERB **lumber someone with something** to give someone something they do not want, especially a task □ I got lumbered with the clearing up.

lumberjack /'lʌmbədʒæk/ NOUN [*plural* **lumberjacks**] someone whose job is cutting down trees for wood

luminous /'lu:mɪnəs/ ADJECTIVE bright enough to be seen in the dark □ a luminous jacket

lump /lʌmp/ NOUN [*plural* **lumps**]
1 a small piece of something without a clear shape □ **+ of** a lump of coal □ a bowl of sugar lumps
2 a hard piece of tissue growing on or in your body □ She found a lump in her breast.

♦ IDIOM **a lump in your throat** a feeling in your throat when you are going to cry □ There was a lump in my throat as I waved goodbye.

♦ PHRASAL VERB [**lumps, lumping, lumped**] **lump something together** to think about or to deal with a number of different people or things all in the same way □ You can't just lump all old people together.

lump sum /'lʌmp 'sʌm/ NOUN [*plural* **lump sums**] a large amount of money all paid at one time □ He got a lump sum when he retired.

lumpy /'lʌmpɪ/ ADJECTIVE [**lumpier, lumpiest**] full of lumps □ a lumpy sauce

lunacy /'lu:nəsɪ/ NOUN, NO PLURAL stupid and possibly dangerous behaviour □ It would be lunacy to travel in this weather.

lunar /'lu:nə(r)/ ADJECTIVE to do with the moon □ a lunar eclipse

lunatic /'lu:nətɪk/ NOUN [*plural* **lunatics**] someone who behaves in a stupid or dangerous way □ He was driving like a lunatic.

lunch /lʌntʃ/ NOUN [*plural* **lunches**] the meal that you eat in the middle of the day 🕮 I had a sandwich for lunch. 🕮 I had lunch with a friend. 🕮 We ate lunch in a small café. 🕮 We took a packed lunch. 🕮 I'll call you during my lunch break.

lunchtime /'lʌntʃtaɪm/ NOUN [*plural* **lunchtimes**] the time in the middle of the day when you have lunch □ I'll meet you at lunchtime. □ They arrived yesterday lunchtime.

lung /lʌŋ/ NOUN [*plural* **lungs**] one of the two organs inside your chest like bags that you use for breathing. A biology word.

lunge /lʌndʒ/ ► VERB [**lunges, lunging, lunged**] to make a sudden strong or violent movement forwards □ He suddenly lunged forward and grabbed the bag from her.
► NOUN [*plural* **lunges**] a sudden violent movement forwards 🕮 An angry customer made a lunge at the manager.

lurch /lɜ:tʃ/ ► VERB [**lurches, lurching, lurched**]
1 to move along in an uncontrolled way □ The boat lurched and we fell over. □ The van lurched forward, then stopped again.
2 if your heart or your stomach lurches, you have a sudden, uncomfortable feeling of surprise, excitement, fear etc.

▶ NOUN [plural **lurches**] a sudden, uncontrolled movement □ The bus stopped with a lurch.

lure /ljʊə(r)/ ▶ VERB [**lures, luring, lured**] to persuade a person or an animal to do something using a reward □ Scraps of food are used to lure the animals out of their burrows. □ They're offering special deals to lure customers back.

▶ NOUN [plural **lures**] something that lures an animal or person to do something □ Few people can resist the lure of a big salary.

lurk /lɜːk/ VERB [**lurks, lurking, lurked**] to wait secretly where you cannot be seen, especially because you are going to do something bad □ Someone was lurking in the bushes.

luscious /'lʌʃəs/ ADJECTIVE looking, smelling or tasting very good □ a luscious peach

lush /lʌʃ/ ADJECTIVE [**lusher, lushest**] lush plants are green, healthy and growing well □ Cows graze on the lush farmland.

luster /'lʌstə(r)/ NOUN, NO PLURAL the US spelling of lustre

lustre /'lʌstə(r)/ NOUN, NO PLURAL

1 a shiny appearance □ the dazzling lustre of white marble

2 the quality which makes something special ⊞ The brand has lost its lustre in recent years.

• **lustrous** /'lʌstrəs/ ADJECTIVE shiny and healthy looking □ her long, lustrous hair

luxuriant /lʌg'ʒʊərɪənt/ ADJECTIVE growing in a thick and healthy way □ luxuriant forest

luxurious /lʌg'ʒʊərɪəs/ ADJECTIVE very comfortable and expensive □ The hotel room was very luxurious. □ She enjoyed a luxurious lifestyle.

• **luxury** /'lʌkʃərɪ/ NOUN [plural **luxuries**]

1 a situation in which you are very comfortable, with expensive or beautiful things □ They live in luxury. □ We stayed in five-star luxury. □ a luxury hotel □ luxury goods

2 something that is pleasant, and often expensive, but not necessary □ We couldn't afford luxuries such as chocolate.

3 something that is very special because you cannot do it often □ A day on my own is such a luxury.

-ly /lɪ/ SUFFIX

1 -ly is added to the end of words to make adverbs describing the way that something is or is done □ carefully

2 -ly is added to the end of words to mean 'happening every particular amount of time' □ weekly

lymph /lɪmf/ NOUN, NO PLURAL a clear liquid containing white blood cells that helps keep the blood healthy. A biology word.

• **lymphatic** /lɪm'fætɪk/ ADJECTIVE connected to the system that produces lymph. A biology word. □ the lymphatic system

lymph gland /lɪmf ˌglænd/ or **lymph node** /lɪmf 'nəʊd/ NOUN [plural **lymph glands** or **lymph nodes**] one of many small organs in the body that help to fight infection. A biology word.

lyric /'lɪrɪk/ NOUN [plural **lyrics**]

1 lyrics the words of a song □ He wrote the lyrics for most of their songs.

2 a short poem about feelings and emotions

• **lyrical** /'lɪrɪkəl/ ADJECTIVE sounding like poetry or music □ a lyrical description of the scenery

M*m*

M *or* **m** /em/ the 13th letter of the alphabet

m /em/ ABBREVIATION metre or metres, or million

mac /mæk/ NOUN [*plural* **macs**] a coat you wear when it is raining

macabre /məˈkɑːbrə/ ADJECTIVE strange and unpleasant, often to do with death □ *a macabre painting of skulls and bones*

macaroni /ˌmækəˈrəʊnɪ/ NOUN, NO PLURAL pasta in the shape of short tubes

machine /məˈʃiːn/ NOUN [*plural* **machines**] a piece of equipment that uses power to do a particular job □ *a washing machine* □ *a coffee machine* ⊞ *He used a fax machine in the office.* □ *Cows are usually milked by machine.*

machine gun /məˈʃiːn ˌɡʌn/ NOUN [*plural* **machine guns**] an automatic gun that fires a lot of bullets very quickly

machinery /məˈʃiːnərɪ/ NOUN, NO PLURAL big machines □ *farm machinery* ⊞ *Cranes and other heavy machinery were used to remove the debris.*

macho /ˈmætʃəʊ/ ADJECTIVE describes a man who behaves in a typically male way, for example by being strong and not showing his feelings

mackerel /ˈmækərəl/ NOUN [*plural* **mackerels** *or* **mackerel**] a small sea fish which you can eat

mad /mæd/ ADJECTIVE [**madder**, **maddest**]
1 an informal word meaning stupid □ *Swimming where you know there are sharks is a mad thing to do.* □ *I thought he was mad wanting to climb Everest.*
2 mentally ill ⊞ *The poor woman went mad with grief.*
3 a mainly US word meaning very angry □ *I got mad at him for lying to me.*
4 go mad an informal phrase meaning to become very angry or behave in a way that is not controlled □ *She'll go mad if she finds out you tricked her.*
5 be mad about/on someone/something to like someone or something very much □ *He's mad about football.*
6 like mad (a) as quickly as possible and using a lot of energy □ *She was pedalling like mad to keep up with the others.* (b) a lot □ *My arms were hurting like mad.*

madam /ˈmædəm/ NOUN [*plural* **madams**]
1 no plural a formal and polite word used for talking to a woman, for example when serving her in a shop or restaurant □ *Can I help you, madam?*

2 Dear Madam a way of beginning a formal letter to a woman when you do not know her name □ *Dear Madam, I'm writing to enquire about the job which was advertised in the newspaper.*

mad cow disease /ˌmæd ˈkaʊ dɪˌziːz/ NOUN, NO PLURAL an informal phrase for BSE

madden /ˈmædən/ VERB [**maddens**, **maddening**, **maddened**] to make someone feel very annoyed
● **maddening** /ˈmædənɪŋ/ ADJECTIVE very annoying □ *a maddening attitude*

made /meɪd/ ▶ PAST TENSE AND PAST PARTICIPLE OF make
▶ ADJECTIVE
1 be made from/of something to consist of something, or to be built from something □ *a necklace made of shells* □ *The carpet is made from recycled materials.*
2 be made for someone/something to be perfect for a person or situation □ *The role was just made for him.*

madly /ˈmædlɪ/ ADVERB
1 using a lot of energy or enthusiasm □ *We were rushing about madly trying to get ready in time.*
2 extremely □ *He was madly jealous.* ⊞ *They're madly in love.*

madness /ˈmædnɪs/ NOUN, NO PLURAL stupid or dangerous behaviour ⊞ *In a moment of madness he hit the other man.*

magazine /ˌmæɡəˈziːn/ NOUN [*plural* **magazines**] a thin book with pictures in it which is usually published every week or every month ⊞ *Amy was reading a magazine.* □ *a fashion magazine* □ *a magazine article*

maggot /ˈmæɡət/ NOUN [*plural* **maggots**] an insect with a soft body, which becomes a fly

magic /ˈmædʒɪk/ ▶ NOUN, NO PLURAL
1 a strange power that some people believe exists, causing strange things to happen that you cannot explain ⊞ *Wizards use magic.*
2 tricks, such as making things disappear, which are done to entertain people □ *Children love watching magic.*
3 a beautiful and attractive quality which makes something or someone seem special □ *The island's special magic attracts thousands of tourists each year.* □ **+ of** *the magic of Christmas*
4 as if by magic in a surprising way that you cannot explain □ *Helen saw a bird fly up, and then, as if by magic, disappear.*

▶ ADJECTIVE
1 involving tricks such as making things disappear
🔲 *magic tricks* □ *a magic show*
2 able to make impossible things happen 🔲 *a magic
wand* □ *a magic potion*
• **magical** /ˈmædʒɪkəl/ ADJECTIVE
1 special and exciting or attractive □ *a magical
atmosphere* □ *a magical place*
2 done using magic, or having magic powers
□ *magical powers* □ *magical healing*
• **magically** /ˈmædʒɪkəlɪ/ ADVERB using magic, or in a
way that seems to be magic □ *The next morning, the
missing books had magically reappeared on the shelf.*
• **magician** /məˈdʒɪʃən/ NOUN [plural **magicians**]
1 someone who does magic tricks to entertain people
2 someone who has magic powers, especially in
stories

magistrate /ˈmædʒɪstreɪt/ NOUN [plural
magistrates] a judge who deals with crimes which are
not of the most serious type
magma /ˈmægmə/ NOUN, NO PLURAL hot, liquid rock
inside the Earth. A geography word.
magnanimous /ˌmægˈnænɪməs/ ADJECTIVE kind or
generous in a situation in which you could be angry,
jealous, etc. A formal word. □ *In a magnanimous
gesture, he congratulated his opponent.*
magnesium /mægˈniːzɪəm/ NOUN, NO PLURAL a light,
silver-white metal element that burns with a very
bright flame. A chemistry word.
magnet /ˈmægnɪt/ NOUN [plural **magnets**]
1 a piece of iron which makes other metal objects
move towards it
2 be a magnet for someone to be a person or place
which attracts a lot of people □ *Paris is a magnet for
artists.*
• **magnetic** /mægˈnetɪk/ ADJECTIVE
1 having the power of a magnet □ *Iron has magnetic
properties.* □ *The satellite will measure the sun's
magnetic field.*
2 able to attract people □ *Sara had a magnetic
personality.*
• **magnetism** /ˈmægnɪtɪzəm/ NOUN, NO PLURAL
1 the power that a magnet has to attract metals. A
physics word.
2 the power some people have to attract or influence
other people
magnification /ˌmægnɪfɪˈkeɪʃən/ NOUN [plural
magnifications]
1 *no plural* making things seem bigger or closer than
they really are
2 the amount, shown by a number, by which an
instrument like a microscope or a telescope makes
things seem bigger
magnificence /mægˈnɪfɪsəns/ NOUN, NO PLURAL
being magnificent □ *the magnificence of a cathedral*
• **magnificent** /mægˈnɪfɪsənt/ ADJECTIVE extremely
beautiful or skilful, making you feel great admiration
□ *The apartment has magnificent views of the lake.*
□ *It was a truly magnificent performance by this team.*

• **magnificently** /mægˈnɪfɪsəntlɪ/ ADVERB in a
magnificent way □ *The team played magnificently.*
magnify /ˈmægnɪfaɪ/ VERB [**magnifies, magnifying,
magnified**]
1 to make something seem more important or serious
than it really is □ *The problems are magnified because
of his age.*
2 to make something seem bigger or closer than it
really is □ *The lens magnifies the image.*
magnifying glass /ˈmægnɪfaɪɪŋ ˌglɑːs/ NOUN
[plural **magnifying glasses**] a piece of glass that you
hold in your hand which makes small writing and small
objects look bigger
magnitude /ˈmægnɪtjuːd/ NOUN, NO PLURAL the great
size or degree of something □ *The government has
failed to understand the magnitude of the problem.*
magnolia /mægˈnəʊlɪə/ NOUN [plural **magnolias**] a
bush with large white or pink flowers that smell sweet
magpie /ˈmægpaɪ/ NOUN [plural **magpies**] a large
black and white bird
mahogany /məˈhɒgənɪ/ NOUN, NO PLURAL a hard dark
wood used for making furniture
maid /meɪd/ NOUN [plural **maids**] a woman whose job
is to keep the rooms clean and tidy in a hotel or house
maiden /ˈmeɪdən/ ▶ NOUN [plural **maidens**] an old-
fashioned word for a young woman who is not married
▶ ADJECTIVE **maiden voyage/flight** the first journey
that a ship or plane makes
maiden name /ˈmeɪdən ˌneɪm/ NOUN [plural
maiden names] the family name that a married
woman had when she was born

mail /meɪl/ ▶ NOUN, NO PLURAL
1 letters and packages which are sent by post □ *Mail
was being delivered to the wrong address.*
2 the system of sending and delivering letters and
packages □ *His passport had been sent in the mail.*

> ➤ Remember that the noun **mail** is not used in the
> plural:
> ✔ We get a lot of mail.
> ✘ We get a lot of mails.

▶ VERB [**mails, mailing, mailed**]
1 to send a letter or package in the post
2 to e-mail someone □ *I'll mail you some photos.*

mailbox /ˈmeɪlbɒks/ NOUN [plural **mailboxes**]
1 the place on a computer where e-mails are stored. A
computing word □ *I had eight messages in my
mailbox.*
2 especially in the US, a box outside someone's house
where their letters are delivered
3 the US word for postbox
mailing list /ˈmeɪlɪŋ ˌlɪst/ NOUN [plural **mailing lists**]
a list of people that an organization or business
regularly sends information to
mail order /ˌmeɪl ˈɔːdə(r)/ NOUN, NO PLURAL a system
of buying things, in which you choose something at
home and it is delivered to you

maim /meɪm/ VERB [**maims, maiming, maimed**] to injure someone badly and permanently □ *Many soldiers were maimed or killed in the war.*

main /meɪn/ ▶ ADJECTIVE
1 biggest or most important □ *The main reason I do sport is to improve my health.* □ *a main road* □ *Police guarded the main entrance of the building.*
2 the main thing the most important part of a situation □ *The baby is healthy and that's the main thing.*

main course /ˌmeɪn 'kɔːs/ NOUN [*plural* **main courses**] the main part of a meal □ *For my main course I had fish.*

mainframe /'meɪnfreɪm/ NOUN [*plural* **mainframes**] a large, powerful computer that is used by many people. A computing word.

mainland /'meɪnlənd/ ▶ NOUN, NO PLURAL **the mainland** the main part of a country and not the islands around it □ *The island is 25 miles off the Scottish mainland.*
▶ ADJECTIVE used for describing the main part of a country and not the islands around it □ *mainland China*

mainly /'meɪnlɪ/ ADVERB mostly or in most cases □ *Her job mainly involves organizing conferences.* □ *We chose Spain mainly because of the weather.* □ *The spice is used mainly in Indian cooking.*

mains /meɪnz/ PLURAL NOUN
1 the pipes or wires that carry water or electricity into a building □ *Some of the houses don't have mains electricity.*
2 the mains the place inside a building where you connect something to the electricity supply □ *Plug this into the mains.*

mainstream /'meɪnstriːm/ ▶ ADJECTIVE involving or using ordinary ideas or methods which most people accept □ *the mainstream media* □ *a mainstream school*
▶ NOUN, NO PLURAL **the mainstream** the most ordinary ideas or methods which most people accept □ *The party is not in the political mainstream.*

maintain /meɪn'teɪn/ VERB [**maintains, maintaining, maintained**]
1 to make something continue at the same level or in the same way as before □ *Players need to maintain their fitness levels.* □ *The Republican Party has maintained control of the country.*
2 to keep a house or piece of equipment in good condition □ *The car hadn't been maintained properly.*
3 a formal word meaning to keep saying that something is true even if other people do not believe you 🕀 *Robinson maintained his innocence* (=said he was innocent) *throughout the trial.* □ *Geddings maintained that he had not intended to mislead anyone.*

• maintenance /'meɪntənəns/ NOUN, NO PLURAL
1 regular cleaning or repairs done to keep something in good condition 🕀 *The bridge has been closed for routine maintenance work.*
2 making something continue at the same level or in the same way as before □ *Our school is committed to the maintenance of high standards.*
3 money that someone pays regularly to their former wife or husband

maisonette /ˌmeɪzə'net/ NOUN [*plural* **maisonettes**] an apartment which has stairs in it

maize /meɪz/ NOUN, NO PLURAL a tall plant with yellow seeds that you eat as a vegetable

majestic /mə'dʒestɪk/ ADJECTIVE very big and beautiful, making you feel great admiration □ *majestic mountains* □ *a majestic cathedral*

majesty /'mædʒəstɪ/ NOUN [*plural* **majesties**]
1 His/Her/Your Majesty a title used when speaking to or about a king or queen □ *Her Majesty will be attending a Thanksgiving service next week.*
2 *no plural* a formal word meaning the quality of being great and beautiful □ *the majesty of the mountains*

major /'meɪdʒə(r)/ ▶ ADJECTIVE very big, serious or important □ *a major problem* □ *major changes* □ *The company has offices in all major cities.*
▶ NOUN [*plural* **majors**] an army officer above the rank of captain

majority /mə'dʒɒrətɪ/ ▶ NOUN [*plural* **majorities**]
1 *no plural* most of the people or things in a group □ **+ of** *The study showed that a majority of people have access to the Internet.* □ *The illness is linked to diet in the majority of cases.* 🕀 *The vast majority of students agreed with the proposal.*
2 be in the majority to form the largest group □ *In the nursing profession, women are in the majority.*
3 the number of votes by which one person or group wins an election 🕀 *Harper won a comfortable majority.* □ **+ of** *He won by a majority of 120.*
▶ ADJECTIVE to do with most people in a group □ *a majority decision*

make /meɪk/ ▶ VERB [**makes, making, made**]
1 to create something □ *I'll make dinner.* □ *She makes all the children's clothes.* □ *They've made a film of the book.*
2 to cause someone to feel a particular emotion □ *It made me so angry.* □ *That film makes me cry.*
3 to force someone to do something □ *My parents made me do my homework.* □ *No one is going to make you go if you don't want to.*
4 make an appointment/date to arrange to see someone at a particular time □ *I've made a doctor's appointment.*
5 used with some nouns to do with speech □ *May I make a suggestion?* □ *He made a very strange comment.* □ *I've made a complaint.* □ *He made an interesting point.*
6 make a decision to decide something □ *Have you made a decision yet?*

7 make a mistake to do something wrong □ *Everyone makes mistakes.*

8 make progress to develop or improve □ *The children are all making progress.*

9 make a noise/sound to cause there to be a noise or sound □ *The children were making so much noise.*

10 to earn money □ *He makes about $90,000 a year.* □ *You can make a lot of money in banking.*

11 to be the total amount of two or more numbers added together □ *Six and six makes twelve.*

12 to manage to go somewhere or manage to arrive somewhere in time to do something □ *I don't think I'm going to make the party tonight.* □ *If we hurry, we might just make the earlier train.*

13 make do to accept or use something although it is not exactly what you wanted □ *If we can't borrow Andrew's van we'll have to make do with the car.*

14 make it to manage to go somewhere or manage to arrive somewhere in time to do something □ *If we run we might just make it before the train leaves.*

➡ *go to* make the *best* of something, make a *clean* breast of something

♦ PHRASAL VERBS **make something into something** to change something so that it becomes something else □ *We've made the back room into an office.* **make something of someone/something** to think of someone or something in a particular way □ *What do you make of his girlfriend?* **make something/someone out** to be able to see or hear something or someone although with difficulty □ *His voice was very low but I could just make out what he said.* **make out something** to pretend something is true □ *He made out that he was rich.* **make it up to someone** to do something nice for someone so that they will forgive you □ *I know I haven't been home much this week but I'll make it up to you – I'll take you out for dinner.* **make up** to become friendly again after an argument **make up something** to give an explanation that is not true □ *He made up some excuse about the train being late.* **make up for something** to make someone feel less upset or angry about something you have done by doing something nice □ *He was late but made up for it by bringing me a present.*

▶ NOUN [*plural* **makes**] the name of a company that produces a particular product □ *What make is your washing machine?*

make-believe /'meɪk bɪ,liːv/ NOUN, NO PLURAL things that someone pretends are real

makeover /'meɪkəʊvə(r)/ NOUN [*plural* **makeovers**] a number of changes that are made to someone or something in order to improve their appearance 🕮 *She looks like she's had a makeover.*

maker /'meɪkə(r)/ NOUN [*plural* **makers**] a person, business or machine that makes a particular type of thing □ *a film maker* □ *a coffee maker*

makeshift /'meɪkʃɪft/ ADJECTIVE temporary and made from whatever is available □ *a makeshift refugee camp*

make-up /'meɪkʌp/ NOUN, NO PLURAL

1 coloured substances that you put on your face to improve or change your appearance 🕮 *A lot of women wear make-up.* 🕮 *She was putting on her make-up.*

2 the combination of characteristics or qualities that form a person or their character 🕮 *You can't change your genetic make-up.*

3 the people or things that form a group □ *+ of There has been a change in the make-up of the audience.*

making /'meɪkɪŋ/ NOUN, NO PLURAL

1 the process or business of producing something □ *decision making* □ *He was involved in the making of the film.*

2 have the makings of something to have all the qualities needed to become something □ *Olivia has the makings of a very good singer.*

3 of your own making done or caused by yourself □ *The problems are all of his own making.*

malaria /mə'leərɪə/ NOUN, NO PLURAL a serious tropical disease which people can get if they are bitten by a mosquito (=type of insect)

male /meɪl/ ▶ ADJECTIVE

1 belonging to the sex that does not have babies □ *male students* □ *a male swan* □ *The group's members are mostly male.*

2 to do with men or boys □ *He heard a male voice in the next room.* □ *male hormones*

▶ NOUN [*plural* **males**] a male person or animal □ *Thirty thousand adult males disappear every year.*

malevolent /mə'levələnt/ ADJECTIVE a formal word meaning wanting to harm someone □ *his malevolent influence*

malfunction /,mæl'fʌŋkʃən/ ▶ NOUN [*plural* **malfunctions**] a fault that causes something to stop working correctly □ *a technical malfunction*

▶ VERB [**malfunctions, malfunctioning, malfunctioned**] to not work correctly □ *The automatic gates were malfunctioning.*

malice /'mælɪs/ NOUN, NO PLURAL a feeling of wanting to harm or upset someone □ *I have no malice towards her.*

• **malicious** /mə'lɪʃəs/ ADJECTIVE

1 deliberately trying to harm or upset someone □ *malicious rumours*

2 designed to cause damage to someone's computer □ *malicious software*

malignant /mə'lɪɡnənt/ ADJECTIVE a malignant lump in the body is caused by cancer

mall /mɔːl, mæl/ NOUN [*plural* **malls**] a shopping centre that is indoors

mallet /'mælɪt/ NOUN [*plural* **mallets**] a wooden hammer

malnutrition /,mælnjuː'trɪʃən/ NOUN, NO PLURAL a medical condition in which someone is ill because they have not eaten enough healthy food for a long time

malt /mɔːlt/ NOUN, NO PLURAL grain that is used in making beer and whisky (=strong alcoholic drink)

maltreat /ˌmælˈtriːt/ VERB [**maltreats, maltreating, maltreated**] to treat a person or animal cruelly
• **maltreatment** /ˌmælˈtriːtmənt/ NOUN, NO PLURAL cruel treatment of a person or animal □ *the maltreatment of prisoners*

mammal /ˈmæməl/ NOUN [*plural* **mammals**] an animal that feeds its babies on milk from its own body □ *Humans, cows and dogs are mammals.*

mammoth /ˈmæməθ/ ▶ ADJECTIVE very large □ *a mammoth task*
▶ NOUN [*plural* **mammoths**] a type of elephant with hair on its skin that lived a very long time ago

man /mæn/ ▶ NOUN [*plural* **men**]
1 an adult male human □ *a young man* □ *an old man* □ *a married man* □ *I work mainly with men.*
2 *no plural* humans considered as a group □ *Man is closely related to the ape.*
▶ VERB [**mans, manning, manned**] to be the person who is in charge of a particular machine or a particular place at work □ *Bernhard was manning the information desk.*

manage /ˈmænɪdʒ/ VERB [**manages, managing, managed**]
1 to succeed in doing something □ + *to do something The prisoners managed to escape.* □ *We couldn't manage without your help.* □ *Emma managed a smile even though she didn't feel very happy.*
2 to be in charge of a business, team, etc. □ *Who manages the business for you?* □ *Alan is managing the new project.*
3 to live on very little money □ *I don't know how he manages on his student grant.*
4 to use money, time, etc. in a sensible way □ *The scheme helps families to manage their finances.*
• **manageable** /ˈmænɪdʒəbəl/ ADJECTIVE easy to control or deal with □ *With more staff, the workload will be more manageable.* □ *manageable hair*
• **management** /ˈmænɪdʒmənt/ NOUN, NO PLURAL
1 the job of controlling a business or activity □ *a job in management* 🔁 *The report criticized his management style.* 🔁 *management skills*
2 the people who control a company □ *The management has agreed to further talks.* □ *The restaurant is under new management.* 🔁 *senior management*
3 the way that something is controlled □ + *of The government's successful management of the economy continues.*
• **manager** /ˈmænɪdʒə(r)/ NOUN [*plural* **managers**] someone who is in charge of a company, team, etc. □ *a project manager* □ *a football manager* 🔁 *She's a senior manager for a law firm.* □ + *of Can I speak to the manager of the hotel, please?*
• **manageress** /ˌmænɪdʒəˈres/ NOUN [*plural* **manageresses**] a woman who is in charge of a restaurant, shop, etc.
• **managerial** /ˌmænɪˈdʒɪəriəl/ ADJECTIVE to do with managing a company □ *He doesn't have much managerial experience.*

managing director /ˌmænɪdʒɪŋ dɪˈrektə(r)/ NOUN [*plural* **managing directors**] someone who is in charge of a big company

mandarin /ˈmændərɪn/ NOUN [*plural* **mandarins**] a type of small orange

mandatory /ˈmændətəri/ ADJECTIVE a formal word meaning necessary because of a rule or law □ *The mandatory retirement age for judges was 70.*

mane /meɪn/ NOUN [*plural* **manes**] the long hair on a horse's or lion's neck

maneuver /məˈnuːvə(r)/ NOUN [*plural* **maneuvers**], VERB [**maneuvers, maneuvering, maneuvered**] the US spelling of manoeuvre

mangled /ˈmæŋɡəld/ ADJECTIVE crushed and twisted □ *Rescuers searched through the mangled wreckage of the train.*

mango /ˈmæŋɡəʊ/ NOUN [*plural* **mangos** *or* **mangoes**] a tropical fruit with a green skin and yellow flesh

manhandle /ˈmænhændəl/ VERB [**manhandles, manhandling, manhandled**] to move someone or something roughly □ *He had been manhandled by security guards.*

manhole /ˈmænhəʊl/ NOUN [*plural* **manholes**] a covered hole in a road which someone goes down to examine pipes

manhood /ˈmænhʊd/ NOUN, NO PLURAL
1 the period of time when someone is a man □ *A ceremony is held when a boy reaches manhood.*
2 qualities which are typical of a man

manhunt /ˈmænhʌnt/ NOUN [*plural* **manhunts**] a search for a criminal 🔁 *Police have launched a massive manhunt for the killer.*

mania /ˈmeɪniə/ NOUN [*plural* **manias**]
1 a very strong enthusiasm for something □ *World Cup mania was sweeping the country.*
2 a type of mental illness
• **maniac** /ˈmeɪniæk/ NOUN [*plural* **maniacs**] someone who behaves in a dangerous or stupid way □ *Slow down, you maniac!*
• **manic** /ˈmænɪk/ ADJECTIVE
1 extremely excited and active and not able to relax □ *He sounded slightly manic when we spoke.*
2 involving a lot of uncontrolled activity □ *Children's parties are always a bit manic.*
3 suffering from mania

manicure /ˈmænɪkjʊə(r)/ ▶ NOUN [*plural* **manicures**] a treatment in which someone makes your hands and nails look attractive, for example by cutting the nails
▶ VERB [**manicures, manicuring, manicured**] to give someone a manicure

manifesto /ˌmænɪˈfestəʊ/ NOUN [*plural* **manifestos** *or* **manifestoes**] a written statement of what a political party intends to do

manipulate /məˈnɪpjʊleɪt/ VERB [**manipulates, manipulating, manipulated**]

1 to control someone or something so that they do what you want, often in a dishonest way □ *He knew how to manipulate the media.*
2 to move or use something in a skilful way □ *The software allows you to manipulate information and images.*
• **manipulation** /mə,nɪpju'leɪʃən/ NOUN, NO PLURAL manipulating something or someone
• **manipulative** /mə'nɪpjulətɪv/ ADJECTIVE controlling people so that they do what you want, in a dishonest way

mankind /mæn'kaɪnd/ NOUN, NO PLURAL all humans □ *This is one of the most deadly diseases in the history of mankind.*

manly /'mænlɪ/ ADJECTIVE [**manlier, manliest**] having typical male qualities, such as strength

man-made /,mæn 'meɪd/ ADJECTIVE made or caused by people and not natural □ *a man-made lake* □ *man-made disasters*

manner /'mænə(r)/ NOUN [*plural* **manners**]
1 the way in which a person behaves towards other people □ *He had a very aggressive manner.*
2 the way in which something happens or is done □ *The boys behaved in a very responsible manner.* □ **+ of** *The manner of his death was extremely shocking.*
3 manners polite ways of behaving in a social situation ❑ *His parents had taught him good manners.* ❑ *It's bad manners* (=it is not polite) *to talk when your mouth is full of food.* ❑ *She needs to learn some manners.*
4 all manner of many different types of person or thing □ *The shop stocks all manner of things.*
• **mannerism** /'mænərɪzəm/ NOUN [*plural* **mannerisms**] the way in which a particular person speaks or behaves □ *John's mannerisms are very much like his father's.*

manoeuvre /mə'nu:və(r)/ ▶ NOUN [*plural* **manoeuvres**]
1 a difficult movement that needs skill and attention □ *The ice skaters performed a perfect manoeuvre.*
2 something clever which you do to get something you want □ *political manoeuvres*
3 a movement of a lot of soldiers and military equipment
▶ VERB [**manoeuvres, manoeuvring, manoeuvred**] to move something somewhere carefully or skilfully □ *She manoeuvred the car into a very small space.*

manpower /'mænpauə(r)/ NOUN, NO PLURAL the workers who are needed for a particular job □ *We don't have the manpower to cope with such a heavy workload.*

mansion /'mænʃən/ NOUN [*plural* **mansions**] a very large, expensive house

manslaughter /'mænslɔ:tə(r)/ NOUN, NO PLURAL the crime of killing someone but not intentionally

mantelpiece /'mæntəlpi:s/ NOUN [*plural* **mantelpieces**] the shelf above a fireplace (=a space for a fire in the wall of a room)

manual /'mænjuəl/ ▶ ADJECTIVE
1 involving your hands or physical strength ❑ *manual work* ❑ *manual labour*
2 done by a person and not automatic □ *The car has a manual gearbox.*
▶ NOUN [*plural* **manuals**] a book that tells you how to do something such as use a machine

manufacture /,mænju'fæktʃə(r)/ ▶ VERB [**manufactures, manufacturing, manufactured**] to make something in a factory □ *The company manufactures car parts*
▶ NOUN, NO PLURAL the process of making something in a factory □ *These chemicals are used in the manufacture of explosives.*
• **manufacturer** /,mænju'fæktʃərə(r)/ NOUN [*plural* **manufacturers**] a company that makes something in a factory □ *food manufacturers*
• **manufacturing** /,mænju'fæktʃərɪŋ/ NOUN, NO PLURAL the business of making things in factories □ *More than 30,000 manufacturing jobs have been lost.*

manure /mə'njuə(r)/ NOUN, NO PLURAL solid waste from animals that you put on soil to make plants grow better

manuscript /'mænjuskrɪpt/ NOUN [*plural* **manuscripts**]
1 the original copy of a book or document, written or typed by the writer
2 a very old book or document that someone wrote before printing was invented

many /'menɪ/ DETERMINER, PRONOUN [*plural* **more, most**]
1 a lot or a large number □ *Were there many people at the party?* □ *We've had so many problems.* □ *There are too many people here.* □ *She doesn't have many friends.*
2 how many used to ask about the number of something □ *How many chairs will you need?*

> ➤ Remember that **many** is used with the plural forms of *countable* nouns. It is not used with *uncountable* nouns:
> ✓ *How **many** plates do we need?*
> ✗ *How many food do we need?*
> ➤ With uncountable nouns, the word **much** is used:
> □ *How **much** food do we need?*

map /mæp/ ▶ NOUN [*plural* **maps**] a drawing of an area which shows things such as roads, rivers and hills □ *Where's Tokyo on this map?* ❑ *Emma stopped the car and looked at the map.* ❑ *She drew a little map to show where her house was.* ❑ *a road map* □ **+ of** *Have you got a map of France?*
▶ VERB [**maps, mapping, mapped**] to make a map of an area
♦ PHRASAL VERB **map something out** to plan exactly how something will happen □ *His parents had mapped out his life for him.*

maple /'meɪpəl/ NOUN [plural **maples**] a tree that produces a sweet substance

mar /mɑː(r)/ VERB [**mars, marring, marred**] to spoil something □ *The argument had marred the evening for her.*

marathon /'mærəθən/ ► NOUN [plural **marathons**]
1 a race in which people run approximately 26 miles or 42 kilometres ⧉ *She ran her first marathon last year.*
2 a long and difficult activity □ *He defeated Federer after a five-set marathon.*
► ADJECTIVE very long and difficult □ *The agreement was reached after marathon talks.*

marble /'mɑː.bəl/ NOUN [plural **marbles**]
1 *no plural* a type of smooth stone used for making things □ *a marble statue*
2 a small glass ball that children play with

March /mɑːtʃ/ NOUN the third month of the year, after February and before April □ *I'm going to Chile in March.*

march /mɑːtʃ/ ► VERB [**marches, marching, marched**]
1 to walk with many other people in order to protest (=show that you disagree) about something □ **+ through** *Anti-war protesters marched through the streets.* □ **+ on** *Around 1,000 workers marched on (=marched towards) Parliament.*
2 if soldiers march, they walk together with the same, regular steps
3 to walk somewhere quickly in an angry, confident or determined way □ **+ into/out of** *He marched into the office and demanded to speak to the manager.*
► NOUN [plural **marches**]
1 an event in which a large group of people walk somewhere to protest (=show that they disagree) about something □ **+ against** *2,000 people took part in a march against the new employment laws.*
2 a walk with regular steps done by soldiers □ *a slow march*
● **marcher** /'mɑː.tʃə(r)/ NOUN [plural **marchers**] a person who is marching in order to show that they disagree about something

mare /meə(r)/ NOUN [plural **mares**] a female horse

margarine /ˌmɑːdʒəˈriːn, ˌmɑːɡəˈriːn/ NOUN, NO PLURAL a soft yellow food that you spread on bread and use in cooking

margin /'mɑːdʒɪn/ NOUN [plural **margins**]
1 the amount by which someone wins an election or competition ⧉ *Republicans won the election by a wide margin (=by a lot of votes).*
2 the empty space at the side of a page □ *The teacher had written some comments in the margin.*
3 an extra amount of something that you include to be sure that you will be safe or successful ⧉ *There is very little margin for error in these calculations.*
● **marginal** /'mɑːdʒɪnəl/ ADJECTIVE small and not important □ *a marginal improvement*
● **marginally** /'mɑːdʒɪnəlɪ/ ADVERB slightly □ *This product is marginally better.*

marina /məˈriːnə/ NOUN [plural **marinas**] an area of water where small boats are kept

marine /məˈriːn/ ► ADJECTIVE
1 to do with the sea and the animals that live there □ *marine animals* □ *the marine environment*
2 to do with ships □ *marine engineers*
► NOUN [plural **marines**] a soldier who fights on land and at sea

marital /'mærɪtəl/ ADJECTIVE to do with marriage □ *They were having marital problems.* ⧉ *Are employers allowed to ask about your marital status (=whether you are married or not)?*

mark /mɑːk/ ► NOUN [plural **marks**]
1 an area of something that is a different colour from the thing it is on □ *There's a dirty mark on the sofa.* □ *The rabbit's fur is brown, with black marks.* □ *The bite marks have faded now.*
2 a number or letter that says how well you have done a piece of school work, exam, etc. ⧉ *a high/low mark* ⧉ *He got top marks (=the best possible marks) in all his exams.*
3 the halfway/high-water/100-point, etc. mark used to show the level or amount of something
4 a mark of something a sign that something exists or is true □ *They were silent for a minute as a mark of respect.*
5 leave a mark on something to have a continuing effect on someone or something □ *He really left his mark on the Australian community.*
► VERB [**marks, marking, marked**]
1 to happen in order to celebrate something □ *A concert was held to mark the anniversary of his birth.*
2 to show that something is happening or true □ *The protest marked the beginning of a campaign for democracy.* □ *This film marks his return to adventure stories.*
3 to judge the quality of and correct a student's work, exam, etc.
4 to make a mark on the surface of something □ *Shoes with black soles may mark this floor.*
5 to write words or a symbol on something □ *I've marked on the list the people I want to see.* □ *Go along the path marked 'exit'.*
● **marked** /mɑːkt/ ADJECTIVE obvious ⧉ *There has been a marked improvement in her work.*
● **marker** /'mɑː.kə(r)/ NOUN [plural **markers**]
1 something used to mark the position of something
2 a pen with a thick point that is used to write on several surfaces

market /'mɑːkɪt/ ► NOUN [plural **markets**]
1 a building or outside area where people sell things □ *a street market* □ *an outdoor market* □ *a fish market* ⧉ *a market stall*
2 the buying and selling of a particular thing ⧉ *The housing market is not as strong as it was.* ⧉ *The company has increased its market share.*
3 the market the business of buying and selling stocks and shares (=parts of companies that can be

bought and sold) □ *The New York market closed higher yesterday.*
4 the number of people who want to buy something □ *There is a huge market for mobile phones.*
5 the typical place or group of people that a product is sold to □ *The magazine is aimed at the teenage market.* □ *Our main market is in Europe.*
6 on the market available for people to buy □ *The house has been on the market for six months.*
▶ VERB [**markets, marketing, marketed**] to advertise something in order to persuade people to buy it □ *The company markets the drug in the US.* □ *+ as It was marketed as a sugar-free drink.*
• **marketing** /'maːkɪtɪŋ/ NOUN, NO PLURAL the job of deciding how to advertise a product and what price to sell it for ⊞ *a marketing campaign* □ *Paul's the marketing manager for an electronics company.*

marketplace /'maːkɪtpleɪs/ NOUN [*plural* **marketplaces**]
1 the marketplace the business of buying and selling products □ *Companies need to be able to compete in the global marketplace.*
2 an area outdoors where there is a market

market research /ˌmaːkɪt rɪ'sɜːtʃ/ NOUN, NO PLURAL the work of finding out what products people buy and what they like about them

markings /'maːkɪŋz/ PLURAL NOUN
1 the colours and patterns on an animal or bird □ *The bird has beautiful yellow and white markings on its wings.*
2 things which are painted or written on something □ *The road markings were very unclear.*

marmalade /'maːməleɪd/ NOUN, NO PLURAL jam made from oranges or lemons

maroon /mə'ruːn/ ▶ ADJECTIVE having a dark, purple-red colour □ *a maroon T-shirt*
▶ NOUN, NO PLURAL a dark purple-red colour

marooned /mə'ruːnd/ ADJECTIVE left in a place that you cannot escape from □ *He was marooned on a desert island.*

marquee /maː'kiː/ NOUN [*plural* **marquees**] a very large tent used for parties, weddings or shows □ *They've hired a marquee for their wedding reception.*

marriage /'mærɪdʒ/ NOUN [*plural* **marriages**]
1 the legal relationship of being husband and wife □ *My parents had a long and happy marriage.*
2 the ceremony in which a man and woman become husband and wife □ *The marriage took place in St Paul's Cathedral.*

> ➤ Notice that a **marriage** is a ceremony in which a man and woman become husband and wife. The occasion when two people become husband and wife, when friends and family dance and eat, etc. is called a **wedding**:
> ✓ *I was invited to the wedding.*
> ✗ *I was invited to the marriage.*

married /'mærɪd/ ADJECTIVE
1 having a husband or wife □ *a married man* □ *a married couple* □ *+ to Miranda is married to John.* ⊞ *They are getting married in June.*
2 to do with marriage □ *married life*

marrow /'mærəʊ/ NOUN [*plural* **marrows**]
1 the soft substance inside long bones such as the ones in your leg. A biology word.
2 a large vegetable that has a thick green skin and is white inside

marry /'mæri/ VERB [**marries, marrying, married**]
1 to make someone your husband or wife in a special ceremony □ *Andrew has asked me to marry him.* □ *Her brother never married.*
2 to officially perform the ceremony that makes two people become husband and wife □ *They were married by the bishop.*

marsh /maːʃ/ NOUN [*plural* **marshes**] an area of land that is soft and wet all the time

marshal /'maːʃəl/ ▶ NOUN [*plural* **marshals**]
1 an official who controls the crowds at big public events such as pop concerts □ *The marshals at football matches usually wear yellow jackets.*
2 in the US, a police officer or fire officer with a high rank
▶ VERB [**marshals, marshalling/**US **marshaling, marshalled/**US **marshaled**] to bring together or organize people or things in order to achieve a particular aim □ *The rebels were marshalling their forces for an attack.*

marshmallow /ˌmaːʃ'mæləʊ/ NOUN [*plural* **marshmallows**] a very soft pink or white sweet

marshy /'maːʃi/ ADJECTIVE marshy ground is very wet and soft

marsupial /maː'suːpiəl/ NOUN [*plural* **marsupials**] an animal such as the kangaroo whose babies are carried in a pouch (=pocket) on the mother's front. A biology word.

martial /'maːʃəl/ ADJECTIVE to do with military organizations or war ⊞ *The city is now under martial law* (=being controlled by the army).

martial art /ˌmaːʃəl 'aːt/ NOUN [*plural* **martial arts**] a fighting sport such as karate or judo in which you use your hands and feet

Martian /'maːʃən/ NOUN [*plural* **Martians**] in stories, a creature from the planet Mars

martyr /'maːtə(r)/ ▶ NOUN [*plural* **martyrs**] someone who is killed because of their beliefs
▶ VERB [**martyrs, martyring, martyred**] to kill someone because of their beliefs □ *Hundreds were brutally martyred for their faith.*
• **martyrdom** /'maːtədəm/ NOUN, NO PLURAL when someone is martyred

marvel /'maːvəl/ ▶ NOUN [*plural* **marvels**] someone or something that is extremely effective and surprising □ *the marvels of modern medicine*
▶ VERB [**marvels, marvelling/**US **marveling,**

marvelled/*US* marveled] to admire something very much □ *We could only marvel at Ronaldo's skills.*

• **marvellous** /'mɑːvələs/ ADJECTIVE extremely good □ *That's marvellous news!*

marvelous /'mɑːvələs/ ADJECTIVE the US spelling of marvellous

mascara /mæs'kɑːrə/ NOUN, NO PLURAL make-up that you put on your eyelashes (=hairs around your eyes) to make them look darker and longer

mascot /'mæskət/ NOUN [plural **mascots**] a person or object that a person or team thinks brings them good luck

masculine /'mæskjʊlɪn/ ADJECTIVE
1 to do with men, or having qualities that are typical of a man □ *a deep, masculine voice*
2 in English grammar, masculine forms of words refer to males. For example, *he* is a masculine pronoun.
• **masculinity** /,mæskjʊ'lɪnəti/ NOUN, NO PLURAL being like a man

mash /mæʃ/ VERB [mashes, mashing, mashed] to crush something, especially food, until it is soft □ *I'll mash the potatoes.*

mask /mɑːsk/ ▶ NOUN [plural **masks**] something that you wear over your face in order to protect it, to hide or for decoration □ *a carnival mask* □ *The surgeon removed his mask to speak to her.*
▶ VERB [masks, masking, masked] to prevent something such as a feeling or smell from being noticed □ *She sprayed air freshener to mask the cooking smells.*

mason /'meɪsən/ NOUN [plural **masons**] someone whose job is to make things from stone
• **masonry** /'meɪsənri/ NOUN, NO PLURAL the parts of a building that are made of stone □ *He was hit by a piece of falling masonry.*

mass /mæs/ ▶ NOUN [plural **masses**]
1 a large lump or quantity of something with no clear shape □ **+ of** *The car was reduced to a mass of tangled metal.* □ *The little girl had a mass of blonde curls.*
2 masses a lot of something. An informal word. □ *He's got masses of toys.*
3 no plural in science, a measure of the quantity of material in something
4 the masses the ordinary people in a society and not the rich, powerful people
5 Mass a ceremony in some Christian churches in which people eat bread and drink wine
▶ ADJECTIVE involving a very large number of people □ *a mass meeting* 🕀 *mass unemployment*
▶ VERB [masses, massing, massed] to come together or bring people together in large numbers □ *Soldiers are massing on the border.*

massacre /'mæsəkə(r)/ ▶ NOUN [plural **massacres**] the killing of a large number of people
▶ VERB [massacres, massacring, massacred] to kill a large number of people □ *Hundreds of villagers were massacred in the attack.*

massage /'mæsɑːʒ/ ▶ VERB [massages, massaging, massaged] to rub parts of a person's body in order to make them relax or to make the muscles less painful □ *Could you massage my shoulders?*
▶ NOUN [plural **massages**] when someone massages you 🕀 *I gave her a foot massage.*

massive /'mæsɪv/ ADJECTIVE very big □ *She earns a massive amount of money.*
• **massively** /'mæsɪvli/ ADVERB extremely □ *She was massively overweight.*

mass media /,mæs 'miːdɪə/ PLURAL NOUN newspapers, radio, television and the Internet

mass-produce /,mæs prə'djuːs/ VERB [mass-produces, mass-producing, mass-produced] to make large numbers of things cheaply in a factory □ *mass-produced goods*
• **mass production** /,mæs prə'dʌkʃən/ NOUN, NO PLURAL when things are mass-produced

mast /mɑːst/ NOUN [plural **masts**]
1 a tall pole used for sending out radio, television and mobile phone signals
2 a tall pole for holding the sails of a boat or ship

master /'mɑːstə(r)/ ▶ NOUN [plural **masters**]
1 a man who has control over something □ *a dog and its master*
2 someone who is very good at a particular activity □ *a master of disguise*
3 an original document, film or recording from which you can make copies □ *the master file*
4 Master a formal title for a boy, used before his name □ *Master Teddy Smith*
5 Master's (degree) a university qualification that you can study for after you have got a degree (=first university qualification) □ *a Master's in law*
▶ ADJECTIVE very skilled in a particular job or activity □ *a master craftsman*
▶ VERB [masters, mastering, mastered]
1 to learn how to do something well □ *Juggling needs quite a lot of practice before you master it.*
2 to control a feeling □ *I've never managed to master my fear of heights.*
• **masterful** /'mɑːstəfʊl/ ADJECTIVE very skilful □ *a masterful performance*

mastermind /'mɑːstəmaɪnd/ ▶ NOUN [plural **masterminds**] the person who plans and organizes a complicated activity □ *Waterman was the musical mastermind behind her career.*
▶ VERB [masterminds, masterminding, masterminded] to plan and organize all the details of a complicated activity □ *It is thought that he also masterminded the bomb attack on the Metro last year.*

masterpiece /'mɑːstəpiːs/ NOUN [plural **masterpieces**] a book, painting, piece of music or other work of art that is one of the greatest of its type

mastery /'mɑːstəri/ NOUN, NO PLURAL
1 great skill at something □ *her mastery of the language*
2 control over something □ *mastery of the seas*

mat /mæt/ NOUN [*plural* **mats**]
1 a flat piece of material for covering or protecting part of a floor □ *a door mat*
2 a small piece of material for putting under something to protect a table's surface □ *a table mat*

match /mætʃ/ ▶ NOUN [*plural* **matches**]
1 a sports competition between two players or two teams 🖭 *a football match* 🖭 *Who won the match?*
2 a short, thin piece of wood with a substance on the end that produces fire when it is rubbed on a rough surface 🖭 *He struck a match to light a candle.*
3 something that is similar to another thing or suitable to be with another thing, especially in its colour or pattern □ *This isn't the same make of paint but it's a very good match.*
4 a person or animal who is as good as another 🖭 *I could beat him over a mile, but I was no match for him when it came to the 100 metres.*
▶ VERB [**matches, matching, matched**]
1 to be the same colour or style □ *Her handbag matched her shoes.* □ *His handwriting matched that on the letter.*
2 to be as good as or as large as someone or something else □ *I can't match Joe's strength.* □ *The company will match* (=give the same amount) *any sum of money you donate.*
3 to put two people or things together because they are suitable for each other □ **+ to** *Match the word on the left to its meaning on the right.*
♦ PHRASAL VERBS **match up** if two pieces of information match up, they are the same □ *The police found that their stories didn't match up.* **match up to something** to be as good as someone or something else □ *The holiday didn't match up to our expectations.*

matchbox /'mætʃbɒks/ NOUN [*plural* **matchboxes**] a small cardboard box that contains matches
matching /'mætʃɪŋ/ ADJECTIVE the same in colour or design □ *She wore a dress with a matching jacket.*

mate /meɪt/ ▶ NOUN [*plural* **mates**]
1 an informal word for a friend □ *He's a good mate of mine.* 🖭 *She's my best mate.*
2 an informal, friendly word used for talking to someone □ *You all right, mate?* □ *Thanks, mate.*
3 the male or female that an animal breeds with
▶ VERB [**mates, mating, mated**] animals and birds mate when they have sex to produce babies □ *Swans mate for life.*

material /mə'tɪərɪəl/ NOUN [*plural* **materials**]
1 cloth □ *The jacket was made of a very thick material.*
2 a substance used for making something else □ *building materials* □ *raw materials for the steel industry*
3 information and ideas in a piece of writing □ *She used her experiences as material for her new book.* □ *publicity material*

materialistic /mə,tɪərɪə'lɪstɪk/ ADJECTIVE believing that money and possessions are the most important things in life □ *We live in a materialistic society.*
materialize *or* **materialise** /mə'tɪərɪəlaɪz/ VERB [**materializes, materializing, materialized**] to happen □ *Did the promised pay rise ever materialize?*
maternal /mə'tɜːnəl/ ADJECTIVE
1 to do with, or typical of, a mother □ *maternal feelings* 🖭 *a maternal instinct*
2 related through your mother's side of your family □ *your maternal grandmother*
maternity /mə'tɜːnɪti/ ADJECTIVE to do with pregnancy and giving birth 🖭 *maternity clothes* □ *a maternity hospital*
math /mæθ/ NOUN, NO PLURAL the US word for maths

mathematical /,mæθə'mætɪkəl/ ADJECTIVE to do with or using mathematics □ *a mathematical genius* □ *a mathematical calculation*

mathematician /,mæθəmə'tɪʃən/ NOUN [*plural* **mathematicians**] someone who studies mathematics or is an expert in mathematics

mathematics /,mæθə'mætɪks/ NOUN, NO PLURAL the study of measurements, numbers, quantities and shapes. A formal word.

maths /mæθs/ NOUN, NO PLURAL a short way to say and write mathematics

matinée /'mætɪneɪ/ NOUN [*plural* **matinées**] a performance at a theatre or cinema in the afternoon

matrices /'meɪtrɪsiːz/ PLURAL OF matrix
matrimony /'mætrɪməni/ NOUN, NO PLURAL the state of being married. A formal word.
matrix /'meɪtrɪks/ NOUN [*plural* **matrixes** *or* **matrices**] an arrangement of numbers or symbols in lines that go up and down, used in maths. A maths word.
matron /'meɪtrən/ NOUN [*plural* **matrons**] an old-fashioned word for an important nurse in a hospital
matt *or* **matte** /mæt/ ADJECTIVE not shiny □ *photos with a matt finish* □ *matt paint*
matted /'mætɪd/ ADJECTIVE in a thick mass because of being wet or dirty □ *matted hair*

matter /'mætə(r)/ ▶ NOUN [*plural* **matters**]
1 a subject or situation □ *He wants to see you to discuss a personal matter.* □ *We need to think about all the practical matters.* □ **+ for** *This is a matter for the police.* 🖭 *To make matters worse, I had forgotten my phone.*
2 the matter used to talk about something that is wrong with something or causing a problem 🖭 *What's the matter with Rachel? She's very quiet.* 🖭 *I know something's the matter with Eve.* □ *What's the matter with these tomatoes? They look brown.*
3 *no plural* any substance that takes up space and is part of the physical universe
4 *no plural* a particular type of substance □ *We added plenty of organic matter to the soil*

5 as a matter of fact used to add information or to say that something that has just been said is wrong □ *As a matter of fact, he's one of the richest men in the country.*

6 a matter of something used to talk about what is needed for something to happen □ *He'll be fine in the exam – it's just a matter of confidence.* □ *It's a matter of making sure the foundations are deep enough.*

7 a matter of days/hours, etc. used to say that something will happen in a short time □ *The symptoms should improve in a matter of days.*

▶ VERB [**matters, mattering, mattered**] to be important 🔁 *It doesn't matter if you're late – we can save you some food.* □ *Does it matter if the door isn't completely closed?* □ *Winning matters to him more than it should.*

• **matter-of-fact** /ˌmætər əv ˈfækt/ ADJECTIVE dealing with or talking about an unusual or upsetting situation in a calm way, as if it was normal □ *She tried hard to be matter-of-fact about it all.*

mattress /ˈmætrɪs/ NOUN [*plural* **mattresses**] the thick, soft part of a bed, that you lie on

mature /məˈtjʊə(r)/ ▶ ADJECTIVE
1 completely grown or developed □ *a mature male elephant* □ *mature trees*
2 behaving in a sensible way, like an adult □ *He's a very mature 13-year-old.*
▶ VERB [**matures, maturing, matured**]
1 to become completely grown or developed
2 to start to behave in a sensible way, like an adult

• **maturity** /məˈtjʊərəti/ NOUN, NO PLURAL
1 when someone behaves in a sensible way, like an adult □ *I've never known such maturity in a child of her age.*
2 when someone or something is completely grown or developed □ *These animals reach maturity after two years.*

maul /mɔːl/ VERB [**mauls, mauling, mauled**] if you are mauled by a wild animal, it attacks you and badly injures you □ *The zoo keeper was mauled by one of the lions.*

mauve /məʊv/ ▶ ADJECTIVE having a pale purple colour
▶ NOUN, NO PLURAL a pale purple colour

maximum /ˈmæksɪməm/ ▶ NOUN, NO PLURAL the greatest amount or degree that is possible or allowed □ *The maximum I'm prepared to pay is £200.* □ *The car will hold a maximum of five people.*
▶ ADJECTIVE being the greatest amount or degree that is possible or allowed □ *The maximum speed limit is 40 mph on this road.* □ *The crime carries a maximum penalty of five years' imprisonment.*

May /meɪ/ NOUN the fifth month of the year, after April and before June □ *The weather was awful in May.*

may /meɪ/ MODAL VERB
1 used to talk about the possibility that something is true or something will happen □ *I may apply for the job, but I'm not sure yet.* □ *He thinks she may be lying.*

2 a formal word used for asking for or giving permission □ *May I ask what you're doing in my room?* □ *You may leave the table now.*

3 may ... but used to show that although one thing is true, there is another thing that is more important □ *You may not enjoy studying, but qualifications are important.*

4 may as well used to say that you should probably do something because there is nothing better to do □ *We may as well wait inside.*

maybe /ˈmeɪbi/ ADVERB
1 possibly □ *Maybe she called earlier.* □ *Maybe they're not coming.* □ *It'll take two, maybe three, days to paint the room.*
2 used for suggesting something that you are not sure about □ *Maybe we should tell him.*

mayhem /ˈmeɪhem/ NOUN, NO PLURAL a confused or noisy situation in which no one is in control □ *The accident caused mayhem on the motorway.*

mayonnaise /ˌmeɪəˈneɪz/ NOUN, NO PLURAL a thick white sauce made with oil and eggs □ *prawn mayonnaise sandwiches*

mayor /meə(r)/ NOUN [*plural* **mayors**] a man or woman elected as the official leader of a town or city

maze /meɪz/ NOUN [*plural* **mazes**] a complicated system of paths that you have to try to find your way out of

MB /ˌem ˈbiː/ ABBREVIATION megabyte

MD /ˌem ˈdiː/ ABBREVIATION managing director

me /miː/ PRONOUN used as the object in a sentence to talk or write about yourself □ *Would you make me a cup of tea, please?* □ *Are there any letters for me?* □ *Hi, it's me. Sorry, but I'm going to be late.*

▶ Remember that **me** is used after a verb or preposition. In a sentence in which you are doing the action, use **I** before the verb: □ *I gave her some flowers.* □ *He gave me some flowers.*

meadow /ˈmedəʊ/ NOUN [*plural* **meadows**] a field of grass

meager /ˈmiːɡə(r)/ ADJECTIVE the US spelling of meagre

meagre /ˈmiːɡə(r)/ ADJECTIVE very small in amount □ *How can you survive on such a meagre diet?*

meal /miːl/ NOUN [*plural* **meals**] food that you eat at one time, for example, breakfast, lunch or dinner 🔁 *We're going out for a meal on Saturday night.* 🔁 *I have my main meal in the evening.*

mean[1] /miːn/ VERB [**means, meaning, meant**]
1 to have a particular meaning □ *What does 'intrepid' mean?* □ *Her name means 'lucky' in Arabic.*
2 to try to express an opinion or a fact □ *I didn't know what she meant when she told me to speak like a lady.* □ *What did she mean by 'too academic'?* 🔁 *I see what you mean about his bad temper.*

3 to intend to do something □ **+ to do something** I'm sorry. I didn't mean to upset you. □ Did you mean to take this turning?

4 to be a sign that something will happen, or to have a particular result □ **+ that** Higher wages meant that more people could afford cars. □ Dark clouds usually mean rain. □ The right equipment can mean the difference between life and death.

5 to be serious about what you have said 🖢 If you don't tidy your room, you won't have dinner, and I mean it this time! □ She keeps threatening to leave, but she doesn't really mean it.

6 to be important to someone □ **+ to** That puppy means such a lot to her. □ Fame meant nothing to him.

7 to be intended for someone or something □ The sweets were meant for the children.

8 be meant to do something if you are meant to do something, someone has said that you must do it □ I'm meant to do my homework before I watch TV.

9 I mean used to correct something you have said □ He was born in 1948 – I mean 1958.

mean² /miːn/ ▶ ADJECTIVE [**meaner, meanest**]

1 a mean person does not like spending money or giving things to other people □ She's too mean to pay to have her hair cut.

2 unkind □ Mum, Adam's being mean to me!

3 a US word meaning violent and frightening □ a mean dog

4 average. A maths word. □ The mean income was £400 per week.

▶ NOUN [*plural* **means**] the average. A maths word.

➡ go to means

meander /mɪˈændə(r)/ VERB [**meanders, meandering, meandered**]

1 if a river or road meanders, it turns many times

2 to walk or move slowly in no particular direction □ We spent the day meandering around the village.

meaning /ˈmiːnɪŋ/ NOUN [*plural* **meanings**]

1 what a word or action expresses □ The music conveys the meaning of the text. □ I didn't understand the meaning of his words. □ We searched for a hidden meaning in his letter.

2 importance or purpose □ We all want to understand the meaning of life. □ He helped me understand the meaning of these events.

● **meaningful** /ˈmiːnɪŋfʊl/ ADJECTIVE

1 useful or important □ meaningful discussions

2 intended to express something □ a meaningful look

3 showing a meaning that can be understood □ a meaningful comparison

● **meaningless** /ˈmiːnɪŋlɪs/ ADJECTIVE

1 having no purpose or importance □ He felt as if his life was meaningless.

2 having no meaning □ It's a fairly meaningless phrase.

meanness /ˈmiːnnɪs/ NOUN, NO PLURAL

1 when someone does not like spending money or giving things to other people

2 unpleasant or unkind behaviour

means /miːnz/ NOUN [*plural* **means**]

1 a way or method of doing something □ a means of transport □ a means of payment

2 money □ Does he have the means to buy a car?

3 by all means used to politely give someone permission to do something □ 'Can I have a look at your magazine?' 'By all means.'

4 by no means not at all or in no way □ It was by no means the worst talk I'd heard.

meant /ment/ PAST TENSE AND PAST PARTICIPLE OF mean □ I meant every word I said. □ She had meant to tell him but had forgotten.

meantime /ˈmiːntaɪm/ NOUN, NO PLURAL in the meantime in the time before something happens □ We're having the car repaired but in the meantime we're borrowing my sister's.

meanwhile /ˈmiːnwaɪl/ ADVERB

1 in the time before something happens □ I'll start the report once the sales figures are in. Meanwhile I've got plenty of work to be getting on with.

2 at the same time □ Tom was enjoying himself with his friends. Meanwhile, I was working like crazy back here.

measles /ˈmiːzəlz/ NOUN, NO PLURAL an infectious disease, especially among children, in which you feel very hot and your skin is covered in red spots

measly /ˈmiːzlɪ/ ADJECTIVE [**measlier, measliest**] too small in amount. An informal word. □ All I had to eat was one measly little biscuit.

measurable /ˈmeʒərəbəl/ ADJECTIVE big enough to be measured or noticed □ There's no measurable difference between them.

measure /ˈmeʒə(r)/ ▶ VERB [**measures, measuring, measured**]

1 to find how tall, long, wide, fast, etc. something is □ She was measuring the window for some new curtains.

2 to judge how good or bad something is □ How do you measure success? □ This is the only way we know of measuring the performance of such schemes.

3 to be a particular size □ The room measures 3.5 metres from the door to the window.

▶ NOUN [*plural* **measures**]

1 an official action done to achieve something or deal with something 🖢 The school is being closed as a temporary measure. 🖢 The government is introducing new measures to combat obesity.

2 a unit used in measuring □ A kilogram is a measure of weight, while a kilometre is a measure of distance or length.

● **measurement** /ˈmeʒəmənt/ NOUN [*plural* **measurements**]

1 a size or amount found by measuring □ Can you write down the exact measurements of the floor?

2 no plural the act of measuring something

meat /miːt/ NOUN [*plural* **meats**] the flesh of animals eaten as food 🖢 red meat such as beef 🖢 white meat such as chicken

• **meaty** /'mi:tɪ/ ADJECTIVE [**meatier, meatiest**] containing a lot of meat □ *The food tends to be quite meaty.*

mechanic /mɪ'kænɪk/ NOUN [*plural* **mechanics**] someone whose job is to repair vehicles and machines 🔁 *a car mechanic*
• **mechanical** /mɪ'kænɪkəl/ ADJECTIVE
1 to do with machines □ *There must have been a mechanical failure.* □ *a mechanical device*
2 done without thinking or without showing emotion □ *He moved his hands in an almost mechanical way.*
• **mechanics** /mɪ'kænɪks/ PLURAL NOUN
1 the study of how machines work and how physical forces act on objects
2 the mechanics of something the way something is done □ *I don't understand the mechanics of their financial arrangements.*
• **mechanism** /'mekənɪzəm/ NOUN [*plural* **mechanisms**] a working part of a machine, or its system of working parts □ *The cogs and springs are part of the clock's mechanism.*

medal /'medəl/ NOUN [*plural* **medals**] a metal disk given as a prize in a competition or for brave actions 🔁 *an Olympic medal* 🔁 *a gold/silver/bronze medal* 🔁 *He was awarded a medal for bravery.*
• **medallist** /'medəlɪst/ NOUN [*plural* **medallists**] someone who has won a medal in a competition 🔁 *an Olympic gold medallist*

meddle /'medəl/ VERB [**meddles, meddling, meddled**] to become involved in things that are not your responsibility, in an annoying way □ *They should stop meddling in other countries' affairs.*

media /'mi:dɪə/ ▶ PLURAL NOUN the media newspapers, television and radio or other means of communicating information to the public □ *There was nothing in the media about his speech.* 🔁 *The event received a lot of media coverage.*
▶ PLURAL OF **medium**

mediaeval /ˌmedɪ'i:vəl/ ADJECTIVE another spelling of medieval

median /'mi:dɪən/ ▶ NOUN [*plural* **medians**] the middle number or amount in a series of numbers or amounts. A maths word.
▶ ADJECTIVE being the median. A maths word □ *the median price/age*

mediate /'mi:dɪeɪt/ VERB [**mediates, mediating, mediated**] to try to find an agreement between two people or groups who are arguing about something □ *An independent committee has been set up to mediate between the two companies.*
• **mediation** /ˌmi:dɪ'eɪʃən/ NOUN, NO PLURAL when you mediate between people or groups □ *All attempts at mediation have so far failed.*
• **mediator** /'mi:dɪeɪtə(r)/ NOUN [*plural* **mediators**] someone who mediates between people or groups □ *United Nations mediators are trying to secure a lasting peace.*

medic /'medɪk/ NOUN [*plural* **medics**] an informal word for a doctor or a medical student

medical /'medɪkəl/ ▶ ADJECTIVE to do with medicine or doctors and their work 🔁 *He did not need further medical treatment.* 🔁 *She's receiving the best medical care.* 🔁 *the medical staff* 🔁 *a serious medical condition*
▶ NOUN [*plural* **medicals**] a general examination by a doctor to find out about a person's health □ *The new player passed a medical yesterday.*

medical certificate /'medɪkəl səˌtɪfɪkət/ NOUN [*plural* **medical certificates**] a document from a doctor that gives information about your health, for example if you are too ill to work

medically /'medɪkəlɪ/ ADVERB by or to do with medicine □ *The illness can be treated medically.* □ *She is not medically qualified.*

medication /ˌmedɪ'keɪʃən/ NOUN, NO PLURAL medicine □ *He is on medication for his epilepsy.*

medicinal /mə'dɪsɪnəl/ ADJECTIVE to do with medicine or having an effect like medicine □ *medicinal plants*

medicine /'medɪsɪn/ NOUN [*plural* **medicines**]
1 a substance used to treat or prevent illnesses □ *cough medicine* 🔁 *Have you taken your medicine?*
2 *no plural* the science of treating and preventing illnesses 🔁 *He studied medicine at the University of Melbourne.* □ *traditional Chinese medicine*

medieval /ˌmedɪ'i:vəl/ ADJECTIVE to do with the period of history from about AD 1000 to AD 1500 □ *a medieval castle*

mediocre /ˌmi:dɪ'əʊkə(r)/ ADJECTIVE not of very good quality □ *a mediocre performance*
• **mediocrity** /ˌmi:dɪ'ɒkrətɪ/ NOUN, NO PLURAL the state of being mediocre

meditate /'medɪteɪt/ VERB [**meditates, meditating, meditated**]
1 to try to empty your mind or to concentrate on only one thing in order to relax or for religious reasons □ *He was sitting cross-legged, meditating.*
2 to think about something carefully □ *She was meditating on her future.*
• **meditation** /ˌmedɪ'teɪʃən/ NOUN, NO PLURAL when you meditate

medium /'mi:dɪəm/ ▶ ADJECTIVE in the middle of a group of amounts or sizes □ *He is dark and of medium height.* □ *Heat a large pan over a medium heat.* 🔁 *Small and medium sized businesses will be affected.*
▶ NOUN [*plural* **mediums** or **media**]
1 a way of expressing or communicating information □ + *for* *The Internet is a popular medium for advertising.* □ + *of* *SMS is a cheap medium of communication.*
2 something that is used for a particular purpose □ *Memory Sticks are now a popular storage medium.*
▶ NOUN [*plural* **mediums**] someone who believes they can communicate with the dead

medley /'medlɪ/ NOUN [plural **medleys**]
1 a piece of music combining several other pieces of music □ *He played a medley of Scottish tunes.*
2 a mixture of different things □ *a medley of exotic fruit*

meek /mi:k/ ADJECTIVE [**meeker, meekest**] gentle and not likely to complain or argue with other people □ *He's portrayed as being very meek and mild.*
• **meekly** /'mi:klɪ/ ADVERB without complaining or arguing □ *'Sorry,' said Lily meekly.*
• **meekness** /'mi:knɪs/ NOUN, NO PLURAL the quality of being meek

meet /mi:t/ VERB [**meets, meeting, met**]
1 to come to the same place as someone else by chance □ *Guess who I met in town?*
2 to come to the same place as someone else because you have arranged to see them □ *Let's meet for a coffee next week.* □ *Is there anywhere we can meet privately?* □ *The committee meets once a month.*
3 to wait for someone at a particular place where they will arrive □ *We'll meet her at the airport.*
4 to be with and speak to someone for the first time □ *Have you met my big sister, Jane?* 🔁 *I'm very pleased to meet you at last.*
5 two things meet when they come together or touch □ *Turn right where the road meets a track.*
6 to achieve something or to be big enough, good enough, etc. to do something 🔁 *There is no play area to meet the needs of children.* □ *Extra funding will help us meet the challenge.*
7 to experience something □ *We met a lot of resistance to our plans for a new airport.*
8 to meet the cost of something is to pay for it
♦ PHRASAL VERBS **meet up** to come together with other people in order to do something □ *We meet up about once a week for a chat.* **meet with something** to get a particular reaction □ *My suggestion that we go for a walk met with groans from the others.*
• **meeting** /'mi:tɪŋ/ NOUN [plural **meetings**] a time when people come together, especially to discuss something □ *We need to arrange a meeting to discuss this matter.* □ *Anne's in a meeting at the moment.*

mega- /'megə/ PREFIX
1 mega- is added to the beginning of words to mean 'a million' □ *megabyte*
2 mega- is added to the beginning of words to mean 'very large or great' □ *a Hollywood megastar* (=extremely famous person)

megabyte /'megəbaɪt/ NOUN [plural **megabytes**] a unit used to measure computer memory or data, equal to approximately a million bytes. This is often written **Mb**. A computing word.

megahertz /'megəhɜ:ts/ NOUN [plural **megahertz**] a unit of measurement of radio waves and the speed of a computer. A physics and computing word.

megaphone /'megəfəun/ NOUN [plural **megaphones**] a device shaped like a cone that

someone speaks through to make their voice sound louder

meiosis /maɪ'əusɪs/ NOUN, NO PLURAL when a cell divides twice to make four cells, each with half the number of chromosomes of the original cell. A biology word.

melancholy /'melənkəlɪ/ ▶ ADJECTIVE sad, or making you feel sad □ *The dog gave a melancholy howl.*
▶ NOUN, NO PLURAL a feeling of sadness

mellow /'meləu/ ▶ ADJECTIVE [**mellower, mellowest**]
1 soft and pleasant in sound, colour, taste, etc. □ *We listened to the mellow sound of the clarinet.*
2 calm and relaxed □ *He was in a mellow mood.*
▶ VERB [**mellows, mellowing, mellowed**] to become more gentle and relaxed, especially as you get older □ *I think he's mellowed with age.*

melodic /mɪ'lɒdɪk/ ADJECTIVE having a pleasant tune or pleasant to listen to □ *a simple, melodic tune* □ *a melodic voice*

melodious /mɪ'ləudɪəs/ ADJECTIVE pleasant to listen to □ *He had a deep, melodious voice.*

melodrama /'melə,drɑ:mə/ NOUN [plural **melodramas**] a story, play, etc. with a lot of exciting action that is more extreme than in real life
• **melodramatic** /,melədrə'mætɪk/ ADJECTIVE making things seem more shocking or exciting than they really are □ *Stop being so melodramatic.*

melody /'melədɪ/ NOUN [plural **melodies**] a tune, especially one that is pleasant to listen to □ *The song had a catchy melody.*

melon /'melən/ NOUN [plural **melons**] a large round fruit with a thick green or yellow skin and sweet, yellow or orange flesh

melt /melt/ VERB [**melts, melting, melted**]
1 to become soft or liquid when heated □ *By mid-afternoon the snow had melted.* □ *Salt is used to melt ice on roads.* □ *Stir in the melted butter.*
2 to make someone feel kindness, affection or sympathy 🔁 *He's got a smile that will melt your heart.*
♦ PHRASAL VERBS **melt away** to disappear □ *The tension soon melted away.* **melt something down** to heat metal until it becomes liquid **melt into something** to become part of something so that people cannot see you any more □ *He got past the guards and melted into the crowd.*

melting point /'meltɪŋ ,pɔɪnt/ NOUN [plural **melting points**] the temperature at which a particular substance melts when it is heated

member /'membə(r)/ NOUN [plural **members**] a person who belongs to a group or organization □ *+ of He's the youngest member of the team.* 🔁 *They celebrated with friends and family members.* 🔁 *It was reported by a member of the public.* 🔁 *The restaurant is open to members of staff.*
• **membership** /'membəʃɪp/ NOUN [plural **memberships**]
1 no plural being a member □ *+ of Membership of the gym costs £600 a year.*

2 all the people who are members of a group or club □ *The union membership voted to reject the offer.*

membrane /'membreɪn/ NOUN [plural **membranes**] a thin layer that covers or separates some parts of the body. A biology word.

memento /mɪ'mentəʊ/ NOUN [plural **mementos**] something that you keep to help you remember something you have done or a place you have visited □ *Take this as a memento of your visit.*

memo /'meməʊ/ NOUN [plural **memos**] a short note that you send to someone who works in the same company or organization as you

memoirs /'memwɑːz/ PLURAL NOUN someone's memoirs are a book that they write about their life

memorable /'memərəbəl/ ADJECTIVE a memorable event is one that you remember because it is special or important □ *Their kiss was the most memorable moment of the film.*

• **memorably** /'memərəblɪ/ ADVERB in a way that will not be forgotten

memorial /mɪ'mɔːrɪəl/ NOUN [plural **memorials**] a statue (=stone object) or other structure built to remember a person or an event □ *a war memorial*

memorize or **memorise** /'meməraɪz/ VERB [**memorizes, memorizing, memorized**] to learn something so that you are able to remember it □ *Memorize your password, don't write it down.*

memory /'memərɪ/ NOUN [plural **memories**]
1 the ability to remember things □ *There are several ways to improve your memory.* □ **+ for** *I've got an awful memory for names* (=I don't remember them). 🔁 *He suffers from short-term memory loss.*
2 something you remember □ **+ of** *He has happy memories of his school days.* 🔁 *The pictures brought back painful memories.*
3 *no plural* the part of a computer where information is stored. A computing word □ *6GB of memory*
4 in living memory from a time that people who are alive now can still remember □ *Last month's storm was the worst in living memory.*
5 in memory of someone as a way of remembering someone who has died □ *There will be a minute's silence in memory of the accident victims.*

Memory Stick /'memərɪ ˌstɪk/ NOUN [plural **Memory Sticks**] a small piece of electronic equipment that you use for storing information which you can then copy onto a computer. A trademark.

men /men/ PLURAL OF **man**

menace /'menəs/ ▶ NOUN [plural **menaces**]
1 something that causes or might cause trouble or danger □ *These biting flies are a real menace.*
2 when something seems threatening □ *His voice was full of menace.*
▶ VERB [**menaces, menacing, menaced**] to threaten someone or something □ *They were menaced by gangs of young men as they walked home.*
• **menacing** /'menəsɪŋ/ ADJECTIVE threatening or frightening □ *a menacing look*

mend /mend/ ▶ VERB [**mends, mending, mended**]
1 to repair something that is broken or damaged □ *We need to mend the hole in the tent.* □ *I took my watch to be mended.*
2 to end an argument or disagreement between people □ *They tried to mend relations with their neighbours.*
♦ IDIOMS **mend fences** to improve a relationship with someone after an argument or disagreement **mend your ways** to improve your behaviour that has been bad in the past □ *He promised he would mend his ways.*
▶ NOUN, NO PLURAL **be on the mend** to be getting better or improving after an illness or problems

menial /'miːnɪəl/ ADJECTIVE menial jobs need little skill or training and are boring to do 🔁 *She had a series of menial jobs.*

meningitis /ˌmenɪn'dʒaɪtɪs/ NOUN, NO PLURAL a serious illness which affects the brain

menopause /'menəpɔːz/ NOUN, NO PLURAL the time in a woman's life when her loss of blood each month stops and she can no longer get pregnant

menstrual /'menstruəl/ ADJECTIVE to do with menstruation. A biology word.

menstruation /ˌmenstru'eɪʃən/ NOUN, NO PLURAL the regular flow of blood that a woman has from her womb (=place where baby grows) each month. A biology word.

-ment /mənt/ SUFFIX -ment is added to the end of verbs to make nouns relating to the results of the actions or processes of the verb □ *accomplishment*

mental /'mentəl/ ADJECTIVE to do with the mind or thinking □ *mental arithmetic* □ *Does she have the mental strength to be a top player?* 🔁 *mental illness* 🔁 *mental health services*
• **mentality** /men'tælətɪ/ NOUN [plural **mentalities**] the attitudes and opinions that someone has □ *I don't understand the mentality of people who do these things.*
• **mentally** /'mentəlɪ/ ADVERB in or with the mind □ *You must commit yourself mentally and physically when you practise yoga.*

mention /'menʃən/ ▶ VERB [**mentions, mentioning, mentioned**]
1 to talk or to write about something, but not in detail □ *Nobody mentioned it before.* □ **+ in** *His name was mentioned in the report.* □ **+ to** *Don't mention it to Jonathan.* □ **+ that** *You mentioned that he's got a new car.* 🔁 *As I mentioned earlier, I hadn't met him before.*
2 not to mention used to add and to emphasize something extra □ *It means more demand on energy and water, not to mention the extra waste and pollution.*
3 don't mention it something you say to be polite when someone thanks you for something
▶ NOUN [plural **mentions**] when you mention something 🔁 *He made no mention of marriage.* 🔁 *She got a special mention in the front of the book.*

menu /'menju:/ NOUN [plural **menus**]

1 a list of the food available in a restaurant □ *Would you like to look at the menu?* □ *We have a three-course set menu.*
2 on a computer, a list of choices on the screen that you can choose from. A computing word. 🖳 *a drop-down menu*

menu bar / 'menju: ˌbɑ:(r)/ NOUN [plural **menu bars**] the part at the top of a computer screen that has instructions such as 'file' and 'edit'. A computing word.

menu option / 'menju: ˌɒpʃən/ NOUN [plural **menu options**] one of the instructions such as 'file' or 'edit' at the top of a computer screen. A computing word.

MEP /ˌemi:'pi:/ ABBREVIATION Member of the European Parliament; someone who has been elected to represent people in the European Parliament

mercenary /'mɜ:sɪnərɪ/ ▶ NOUN [plural **mercenaries**] a soldier who fights for any army or country that will pay him
▶ ADJECTIVE interested only in getting money for yourself □ *He's become very mercenary.*

merchandise /'mɜ:tʃəndaɪs/ NOUN, NO PLURAL goods that are bought and sold □ *They sell sports merchandise.*
• **merchandising** /'mɜ:tʃənˌdaɪzɪŋ/ NOUN, NO PLURAL selling products related to a film, book, sports team, etc. □ *The team earns millions from merchandising and sponsorship.*

merchant /'mɜ:tʃənt/ ▶ NOUN [plural **merchants**] someone who has a business buying and selling goods □ *a wine merchant*
▶ ADJECTIVE to do with buying, selling and transporting goods □ *a merchant ship*

merchant bank /ˌmɜ:tʃənt 'bæŋk/ NOUN [plural **merchant banks**] a bank that provides services to companies
• **merchant banker** /ˌmɜ:tʃənt 'bæŋkə(r)/ NOUN [plural **merchant bankers**] someone who works for a merchant bank

merchant navy /ˌmɜ:tʃənt 'neɪvɪ/ NOUN [plural **merchant navies**] ships that are used to transport goods, not for military purposes

merciful /'mɜ:sɪful/ ADJECTIVE
1 willing to forgive and show kindness □ *They begged the king to be merciful.*
2 something that is merciful is lucky for you because it ends a bad situation □ *For him, death was a merciful release.*
• **mercifully** /'mɜ:sɪfulɪ/ ADVERB
1 used to say you are pleased or grateful for something □ *After the heat outside, the room was mercifully cool.*
2 in a merciful way □ *He was treated mercifully.*

merciless /'mɜ:sɪlɪs/ ADJECTIVE cruel and not willing to forgive or be kind □ *a merciless attack*
• **mercilessly** /'mɜ:sɪlɪslɪ/ ADVERB in a merciless way □ *They mocked her mercilessly.*

mercury /'mɜ:kjʊrɪ/ NOUN, NO PLURAL a silver chemical element, used in liquid form in thermometers (=devices to measure temperature). A chemistry word.

mercy /'mɜ:sɪ/ NOUN [plural **mercies**]
1 the quality of being kind and willing to forgive someone, especially someone you have power over 🖳 *The judge showed no mercy to the killers.* □ *He ignored their pleas for mercy.*
2 at the mercy of someone/something in a situation that is controlled by someone or something else that could harm you □ *The little fishing boat was at the mercy of the weather.*
3 something you are grateful for 🖳 *It was a small mercy at the end of a terrible day.*

mere /mɪə(r)/ ADJECTIVE [**merest**]
1 used to emphasize that something is small or not important □ *The flight from London to Madrid cost a mere £25.* □ *A mere handful of people turned up.* □ *There was the merest hint of a smile on his face.*
2 used to emphasize that something is important even though it seems small 🖳 *The mere fact that I could walk was amazing after all my injuries.*
• **merely** /'mɪəlɪ/ ADVERB only or simply □ *I asked him again but he merely shrugged his shoulders.*

merge /mɜ:dʒ/ VERB [**merges, merging, merged**] if two things or organizations merge, they combine or join with each other □ *Her work life seemed to be increasingly merging with her home life.* □ *The two companies merged in 1999.*
• **merger** /'mɜ:dʒə(r)/ NOUN [plural **mergers**] when two or more businesses join to form a single company

meridian /mə'rɪdɪən/ NOUN [plural **meridians**] an imaginary line around the Earth passing through the North Pole and the South Pole

meringue /mə'ræŋ/ NOUN [plural **meringues**] a sweet food made from a mixture of egg whites and sugar and baked

merit /'merɪt/ ▶ NOUN [plural **merits**] a quality that makes something or someone valuable or important □ *The film lacks artistic merit.* □ *Players are picked for the team on merit.*
▶ VERB [**merits, meriting, merited**] to deserve something □ *His idea merits serious consideration.*

mermaid /'mɜ:meɪd/ NOUN [plural **mermaids**] in stories, a beautiful creature who lives in the sea and is half a woman and half a fish

merrily /'merɪlɪ/ ADVERB
1 in a happy way □ *They laughed and chattered merrily.*
2 without thinking enough about what you are doing □ *He was merrily helping himself to all our food.*

merry /'merɪ/ ADJECTIVE [**merrier, merriest**] happy and showing that you are enjoying yourself □ *He whistled a merry tune.*

Merry Christmas /ˌmerɪ 'krɪsməs/ EXCLAMATION something that people say or write to wish people a happy time at Christmas

merry-go-round /ˈmerɪɡəuraund/ NOUN [plural **merry-go-rounds**] a large machine with models of animals and vehicles that children sit on as it goes round and round

mesh /meʃ/ ▶ NOUN [plural **meshes**] wire or thread formed into a net □ a fine wire mesh

▶ VERB [**meshes, meshing, meshed**] to fit or to work together well □ This new theory meshes well with existing evidence.

mesmerize or **mesmerise** /ˈmezməraɪz/ VERB [**mesmerizes, mesmerizing, mesmerized**] to be very attractive or interesting and take all your attention □ Audiences all over the country have been mesmerized by their performance.

mess /mes/ NOUN [plural **messes**]
1 an untidy or dirty state □ The kitchen's in a mess.
2 someone or something that is dirty or untidy □ I'd been gardening and I looked a right mess. □ Your room's a complete mess.
3 something that is in a confused state or that involves a lot of problems □ His whole life was in a mess. 🖬 He made a complete mess of the accounts.
◆ PHRASAL VERBS [**messes, messing, messed**] **mess about/around 1** to waste time with silly behaviour □ Stop messing about and get on with your work!
2 to spend time in a relaxed way doing something that does not need much effort □ I've just been messing around in the garden. **mess someone about/around** to treat someone badly by not doing something you said you would do or by changing your plans. An informal word. □ I'm really sorry to mess you around, but I won't be able to meet you today after all.
mess something up 1 to do something badly or to spoil something □ I messed up my French exam.
2 to make something untidy □ She messed up all my carefully arranged papers.

message /ˈmesɪdʒ/ ▶ NOUN [plural **messages**]
1 a piece of written or spoken information sent from one person to another 🖬 I sent a message wishing him luck. 🖬 I left a message on her phone. 🖬 a text message □ **+ from** She's received thousands of messages from well-wishers. □ **+ of** messages of support
2 the most important idea that you want people to understand from a book, speech, action, etc. 🖬 This sends a clear message that this behaviour is not acceptable.
▶ VERB [**messages, messaging, messaged**] to send someone a message using a mobile phone or computer

message board /ˈmesɪdʒ ˌbɔːd/ NOUN [plural **message boards**] a place on a website where you can read messages from other people and write messages to other people. A computing word.

messaging /ˈmesɪdʒɪŋ/ NOUN, NO PLURAL sending and receiving messages using mobile phones or computers

messenger /ˈmesɪndʒə(r)/ NOUN [plural **messengers**] someone who carries messages from one person to another

messiah /mɪˈsaɪə/ NOUN [plural **messiahs**]
1 someone who comes to save people from unhappiness or evil
2 the Messiah in the Christian religion, Jesus Christ

Messrs /ˈmesəz/ PLURAL OF Mr; often used in the name of a company or business □ Messrs Stein and Goldsmith, jewellers to the rich and famous.

messy /ˈmesi/ ADJECTIVE [**messier, messiest**]
1 untidy or dirty □ a messy room □ He had long, messy hair.
2 complicated and unpleasant to deal with □ a messy divorce

met /met/ PAST TENSE AND PAST PARTICIPLE OF **meet**

metabolism /mɪˈtæbəlɪzəm/ NOUN, NO PLURAL the process that changes food in your body into energy. A biology word.

metal /ˈmetəl/ NOUN [plural **metals**] a hard shiny material such as iron, steel, gold or silver □ The car was now a heap of twisted metal. 🖬 precious metals 🖬 The car was sold for scrap metal.
● **metallic** /məˈtælɪk/ ADJECTIVE
1 looking, sounding or tasting like metal □ It shut with a metallic click. □ I had a horrible metallic taste in my mouth.
2 made of or to do with metal □ a small metallic object
3 shiny like metal □ metallic paint

metallurgy /məˈtælədʒɪ/ NOUN, NO PLURAL the study of metals

metamorphose /ˌmetəˈmɔːfəuz/ VERB [**metamorphoses, metamorphosing, metamorphosed**] a formal word meaning to change completely in appearance or form
● **metamorphosis** /ˌmetəˈmɔːfəsɪs, ˌmetəmɔːˈfəusɪs/ NOUN [plural **metamorphoses**]
1 a complete change in the appearance of something
2 when some animals and insects change from one form to another as they develop. A biology word.

metaphor /ˈmetəfə(r)/ NOUN [plural **metaphors**] a way of describing something by comparing it to something else □ To use a boxing metaphor, the minister got knocked out in the first round.
● **metaphorical** /ˌmetəˈfɒrɪkəl/ ADJECTIVE using a metaphor

meteor /ˈmiːtɪə(r)/ NOUN [plural **meteors**] a piece of rock travelling through space very fast
● **meteoric** /ˌmiːtɪˈɒrɪk/ ADJECTIVE
1 happening or developing very fast, in a surprising way 🖬 He enjoyed a meteoric rise to fame in the 1980s.
2 to do with meteors

• **meteorite** /'miːtɪəraɪt/ NOUN [*plural* **meteorites**] a meteor that has fallen to Earth

meteorologist /ˌmiːtɪəˈrɒlədʒɪst/ NOUN [*plural* **meteorologists**] someone who studies the weather and says whether it will rain, be sunny, etc. in the near future

• **meteorology** /ˌmiːtɪəˈrɒlədʒɪ/ NOUN, NO PLURAL the study of weather

meter /'miːtə(r)/ NOUN [*plural* **meters**]
1 a device that measures and records the amount of something 🔁 *a gas meter* ☐ *Take a meter reading on the day you move in.*
2 the US spelling of metre

methane /'miːθeɪn/ NOUN, NO PLURAL a gas that is produced when plant material decays. A biology and chemistry word.

method /'meθəd/ NOUN [*plural* **methods**] a way of doing something, especially a planned or organized way ☐ + *of* *methods of disease prevention* ☐ + *for* *We need to develop new methods for dealing with the problem.* 🔁 *Artists here use traditional methods.* ☐ *teaching methods* ☐ *farming methods*

• **methodical** /məˈθɒdɪkəl/ ADJECTIVE well-organized and using a system for doing something ☐ *a methodical approach*

• **methodically** /məˈθɒdɪkəlɪ/ ADVERB in a methodical way

meths /meθs/ NOUN, NO PLURAL a short way to say and write methylated spirits

methylated spirits /ˌmeθɪleɪtɪd ˈspɪrɪts/ NOUN, NO PLURAL a type of alcohol which is used as a fuel and not drunk

meticulous /məˈtɪkjʊləs/ ADJECTIVE paying careful attention to every detail ☐ *It took weeks of meticulous planning.*

• **meticulously** /məˈtɪkjʊləslɪ/ ADVERB very carefully ☐ *The event was meticulously planned.*

metre /'miːtə(r)/ NOUN [*plural* **metres**]
1 a unit for measuring length, equal to 100 centimetres. ☐ + *of* *Almost two metres of snow had fallen.* ☐ *It's suitable for boats up to three metres in length.* ☐ *He fell just ten metres from the finish line.* ☐ *a 400 metre runner* 🔁 *2500 square metres of office space*
2 the regular rhythm of poetry or music

• **metric** /'metrɪk/ ADJECTIVE to do with a system of measuring that uses units such as litres and grams, based on tens

metro /'metrəʊ/ NOUN [*plural* **metros**] an underground train system ☐ *the Moscow metro* 🔁 *Where's the nearest metro station?*

metropolis /məˈtrɒpəlɪs/ NOUN [*plural* **metropolises**] a large city, especially a capital city

• **metropolitan** /ˌmetrəˈpɒlɪtən/ ADJECTIVE to do with a large city 🔁 *a metropolitan area* ☐ *the Metropolitan Police Force*

mettle /'metəl/ NOUN, NO PLURAL a formal word meaning courage and determination 🔁 *It was a hard match but the team showed their mettle.*

mg /ˌem ˈdʒiː/ ABBREVIATION milligram

miaow /miːˈaʊ/ ▶ NOUN [*plural* **miaows**] the sound that a cat makes
▶ VERB [**miaows, miaowing, miaowed**] a cat miaows when it makes this sound

mice /maɪs/ PLURAL OF mouse

micro- /'maɪkrəʊ/ PREFIX micro- is added to the beginning of words to mean 'very small' ☐ *microchip* ☐ *microorganism*

microbe /'maɪkrəʊb/ NOUN [*plural* **microbes**] an extremely small living thing, such as a virus or bacterium. A biology word.

microbiology /ˌmaɪkrəʊbaɪˈɒlədʒɪ/ NOUN, NO PLURAL the study of very small living things

microchip /'maɪkrəʊtʃɪp/ NOUN [*plural* **microchips**] a very small part in a computer or other electronic equipment that contains a circuit (=system of wires) and stores information

microclimate /'maɪkrəʊˌklaɪmət/ NOUN [*plural* **microclimates**] the weather in a particular area that is different from the area around it

microcosm /'maɪkrəʊkɒzəm/ NOUN [*plural* **microcosms**] something small that has all the features or qualities of something larger that it is part of. A formal word. ☐ *The city is sometimes seen as a microcosm of US society.*

microorganism /ˌmaɪkrəʊˈɔːgənɪzəm/ NOUN [*plural* **microorganisms**] an extremely small living thing, such as a virus or bacterium. A biology word.

microphone /'maɪkrəfəʊn/ NOUN [*plural* **microphones**] an electronic device used for recording sound or making sound louder ☐ *Speak into the microphone.* ☐ *She took the microphone to address the crowd.*

microprocessor /ˌmaɪkrəʊˈprəʊsesə(r)/ NOUN [*plural* **microprocessors**] the part inside a computer that makes it work. A computing word.

microscope /'maɪkrəskəʊp/ NOUN [*plural* **microscopes**] a piece of equipment with lenses (=curved pieces of glass) that makes very small objects look much larger so that you can study them closely

• **microscopic** /ˌmaɪkrəˈskɒpɪk/ ADJECTIVE microscopic objects are so small they can only be seen using a microscope

microwave /'maɪkrəweɪv/ NOUN [*plural* **microwaves**]
1 a very short radio wave. A physics word.
2 a microwave oven

microwave oven /ˌmaɪkrəweɪv ˈʌvən/ NOUN [*plural* **microwave ovens**] an oven that cooks food very quickly using electrical and magnetic waves instead of heat

mid- /mɪd/ PREFIX mid- is added to the beginning words to mean 'to do with the middle of something' ☐ *midsummer* (=in the middle of summer)

midday /ˌmɪd'deɪ/ NOUN, NO PLURAL twelve o'clock in the middle of the day, or around this time □ *She arrived at midday yesterday.* ◫ *We waited in the hot midday sun.* ◫ *They had bread and cheese for their midday meal.*

middle /'mɪdəl/ ▶ NOUN [plural **middles**]
1 the middle the point, position or part furthest from the sides or edges of something □ *Let me sit in the middle.* □ *+ of They live on an island in the middle of the ocean.*
2 the point in a period of time that is half way through that period of time □ *+ of I woke up in the middle of the night.* □ *He stood up and asked a question in the middle of the meeting.*
3 be in the middle of doing something to be busy doing something □ *I can't come to the phone – I'm in the middle of bathing the children.*
4 your stomach
♦ IDIOM **the middle of nowhere** somewhere that is far away from houses, towns, etc □ *She has a little cottage in the middle of nowhere.*
▶ ADJECTIVE
1 in the central point or position of something □ *I liked the middle section of the book.* □ *I was driving in the middle lane.* □ *He's the middle child of a family of five boys.*
2 at a level that is in the centre of a range of levels □ *They are a middle income family.* □ *a soldier of middle rank*

middle-aged /ˌmɪdəl'eɪdʒd/ ADJECTIVE approximately between the ages of 45 and 60 □ *a middle-aged man*

Middle Ages /ˌmɪdəl 'eɪdʒɪz/ NOUN, NO PLURAL **the Middle Ages** the period of history, especially European history, approximately between the years 1100 and 1450 □ *The monastery was built in the Middle Ages.*

middle class /ˌmɪdəl 'klɑːs/ ▶ NOUN [plural **middle classes**] the social class that consists mainly of educated people who have a good standard of living ▶ ADJECTIVE to do with the middle class □ *a middle class family*

Middle East /ˌmɪdəl 'iːst/ NOUN, NO PLURAL **the Middle East** all the countries in the area where Europe, Asia and Africa meet, including Egypt, Israel, Jordan, Lebanon, Syria, Iran and Iraq
• **Middle-Eastern** /ˌmɪdəl 'iːstən/ ADJECTIVE in or to do with the Middle East □ *Middle-Eastern countries*

midget /'mɪdʒɪt/ NOUN [plural **midgets**] a very small person

Midlands /'mɪdləndz/ PLURAL NOUN **the Midlands** the area in the middle of England

midnight /'mɪdnaɪt/ NOUN, NO PLURAL twelve o'clock at night □ *The competition closes at midnight tonight.* □ *It was past midnight when we finally got home.*

midriff /'mɪdrɪf/ NOUN [plural **midriffs**] the area around the middle of your body, above your waist

midst /mɪdst/ NOUN, NO PLURAL
1 in the midst of something in the middle of a situation □ *The whole country is in the midst of an economic crisis.*
2 in your midst among a group of people □ *They didn't realize there was a celebrity in their midst.*

midsummer /ˌmɪd'sʌmə(r)/ NOUN, NO PLURAL the period in the middle of the summer

midway /ˌmɪd'weɪ/ ADVERB, ADJECTIVE
1 in the middle point between two times □ *He scored midway through the second half.* ◫ *He has reached the midway point of his four-year term.*
2 at the middle point between two places □ *It's a small town midway between Glasgow and Edinburgh.*

midweek /ˌmɪd'wiːk/ ADJECTIVE, ADVERB in the middle of the week, on or around Wednesday □ *We tend to do the shopping midweek.* □ *The midweek match has been cancelled.*

midwife /'mɪdwaɪf/ NOUN [plural **midwives**] a nurse who is specially trained to help women when they are having babies

might¹ /maɪt/ MODAL VERB
1 used to talk about the possibility that something is true or something will happen □ *He might stay.* □ *It might rain.*
2 you might like/want to do something used to make polite suggestions □ *You might want to take some extra food with you.*
3 used to ask permission in a polite and slightly formal way □ *Might I borrow your dictionary?*
4 might as well used to say that you should probably do something because there is nothing better to do □ *If you can't be bothered to practise, you might as well give up the piano.*

might² /maɪt/ NOUN, NO PLURAL a formal word meaning power or strength ◫ *He pulled with all his might.*

might've /'maɪtəv/ a short way to say and write might have

mighty /'maɪti/ ADJECTIVE [**mightier, mightiest**] a formal word meaning big and powerful □ *the mighty Mississippi River*

migraine /'miːgreɪn, 'maɪgreɪn/ NOUN [plural **migraines**] a very bad headache that lasts a long time

migrant /'maɪgrənt/ NOUN [plural **migrants**] someone who goes to live in a different country to find work □ *skilled migrants*

migrate /maɪ'greɪt/ VERB [**migrates, migrating, migrated**]
1 if birds or animals migrate, they travel to a different part of the world at the same time each year □ *The birds migrate northwards in spring.*
2 to move to a different country to find work □ *His family migrated to Australia in 1918.*
• **migration** /maɪ'greɪʃən/ NOUN, NO PLURAL when birds, animals or people migrate

mike /maɪk/ NOUN [plural **mikes**] an informal word for microphone

mild /maɪld/ ADJECTIVE [milder, mildest]
1 mild weather is quite warm □ *The weather was unusually mild for November.* ☜ *The mild winter had prevented ice from forming on the lake.*
2 not severe or not serious □ *The virus causes a relatively mild illness.* □ *She looked at him with mild annoyance.*
3 having a flavour that is not strong □ *mild cheese* □ *Chicken has a mild flavour.*
4 a mild person is gentle and quiet

mildew /'mɪldju:/ NOUN, NO PLURAL a substance that grows on plants and walls if they are slightly wet
mildly /'maɪldlɪ/ ADVERB
1 slightly □ *Eric looked mildly surprised at my comments.*
2 to put it mildly said after you have said something which you could have expressed in a much stronger way □ *It was a bit of a shock, to put it mildly.*

mile /maɪl/ NOUN [plural miles]
1 a unit for measuring distance, equal to 1760 yards □ *The ship was 20 miles off the coast.* ☜ *His car was travelling at a speed of 110 miles per hour.* ☜ *The traffic jam was six miles long.*
2 miles an informal word meaning a long way □ *They live miles away.* □ *We walked for miles.*
• **mileage** /'maɪlɪdʒ/ NOUN, NO PLURAL the number of miles that a vehicle has travelled since it was new ☜ *high/low mileage*

mileometer /maɪ'lɒmɪtə(r)/ NOUN [plural mileometers] an instrument in a car that shows how many miles the car has travelled
milestone /'maɪlstəʊn/ NOUN [plural milestones] an important event in someone's life or in the development of something □ *The game was a milestone in British sporting history.*
militant /'mɪlɪtənt/ ▶ ADJECTIVE willing to do extreme or violent things to achieve political or social changes
▶ NOUN [plural militants] someone who is militant
military /'mɪlɪtərɪ/ ▶ ADJECTIVE to do with the army, navy or air force ☜ *Military forces invaded the country.* ☜ *Many soldiers were injured in military operations.* ☜ *a military base* □ *a military commander*
▶ NOUN, NO PLURAL the military a country's army, navy and air force □ *the US military* □ *All men have to serve two years in the military.*

militia /mɪ'lɪʃə/ NOUN [plural militias] a group of people who are not soldiers for their job, but who are trained to fight if necessary
milk /mɪlk/ ▶ NOUN, NO PLURAL a white liquid produced by female animals, which people drink or which is used to feed babies □ *Would you like a glass of milk?* □ *Breast milk contains important nutrients for babies.*
▶ VERB [milks, milking, milked]
1 to take milk from a cow or goat □ *The cows are milked by machine.*

2 to get every advantage you can from someone or something □ *He claimed she was milking the tragedy for publicity.*

milkman /'mɪlkmən/ NOUN [plural milkmen] a man whose job is delivering milk to people's houses
milkshake /'mɪlkʃeɪk/ NOUN [plural milkshakes] a sweet drink made of milk mixed with a flavoured liquid □ *a banana milkshake*
milk tooth /'mɪlk ˌtu:θ/ NOUN [plural milk teeth] one of the first set of teeth that grow in a child's mouth
milky /'mɪlkɪ/ ADJECTIVE [milkier, milkiest]
1 containing a lot of milk □ *a hot milky drink*
2 looking like milk □ *a milky liquid*
mill /mɪl/ ▶ NOUN [plural mills]
1 a building with machinery for crushing corn and other grain
2 a factory that produces a particular material such as cotton, paper or wool □ *a paper mill*
3 a machine in your kitchen for crushing pepper (=black spice) or coffee □ *a pepper mill*
▶ VERB [mills, milling, milled] to crush grain, pepper, etc. in a mill
♦ PHRASAL VERB **mill around/about (something)** if people are milling around, they are moving around a place □ *Crowds of people were milling around St Mark's Square.*
millennium /mɪ'lenɪəm/ NOUN [plural millennia] a period of a thousand years
milligram or milligramme /'mɪlɪgræm/ NOUN [plural milligrams or milligrammes] a unit for measuring weight, equal to one thousandth of a gram. This is often written **mg**.
milliliter /'mɪlɪli:tə(r)/ NOUN [plural milliliters] the US spelling of millilitre
millilitre /'mɪlɪli:tə(r)/ NOUN [plural millilitres] a unit for measuring liquid, equal to one thousandth of a litre. This is often written **ml**.
millimeter /'mɪlɪmi:tə(r)/ NOUN [plural millimeters] the US spelling of millimetre
millimetre /'mɪlɪmi:tə(r)/ NOUN [plural millimetres] a unit for measuring length, equal to one thousandth of a metre. This is often written **mm**
million /'mɪljən/ NUMBER [plural millions]
1 the number 1,000,000
2 millions a very large number. An informal word □ *of There were millions of flies crawling on the food.*

millionaire /ˌmɪljə'neə(r)/ NOUN [plural millionaires] someone who has a million pounds or a million dollars or more
millionth /'mɪljənθ/ ▶ NUMBER 1,000,000[th] written as a word
▶ NOUN [plural millionths] 1/1,000,000; one of a million equal parts of something
millipede /'mɪlɪpi:d/ NOUN [plural millipedes] a small insect with a long body and a lot of legs
mime /maɪm/ ▶ VERB [mimes, miming, mimed]
1 to tell a story or show an action using only

movements and not words or real objects □ *Ella mimed chopping vegetables.*

2 to pretend to sing or play a musical instrument while a piece of recorded music is played □ *The band were accused of miming during their concert.*

▶ NOUN, NO PLURAL the use of movements only and not words or real objects to tell a story or show an action □ *a mime artist*

mimic /'mɪmɪk/ ▶ VERB [mimics, mimicking, mimicked]

1 to copy the way someone speaks or behaves as a joke

2 to behave or react in the same way as someone or something else □ *Scientists are working on a drug that will mimic the effects of exercise.*

▶ NOUN [plural **mimics**] someone who copies the way people talk or behave □ *Joe's a good mimic.*

• **mimicry** /'mɪmɪkri/ NOUN, NO PLURAL the action of mimicking someone

min /mɪn/ ABBREVIATION

1 minute, used in writing

2 minimum, used in writing

mince /mɪns/ ▶ NOUN, NO PLURAL meat that has been cut into very small pieces using a machine

▶ VERB [minces, mincing, minced] to cut food into very small pieces using a machine □ *minced beef*

mind /maɪnd/ ▶ NOUN [plural **minds**]

1 your brain, or your ability to think, understand, remember, etc. □ *All sorts of thoughts went through my mind.*

2 bear/keep something in mind to remember something □ *Bear in mind that the shops shut at 6:00.*

3 make up your mind to decide □ *I couldn't make up my mind whether to go to Paris or not.*

4 on your mind if something is on your mind, you are thinking about it a lot and usually worrying about it □ *I've got a lot on my mind at the moment.*

5 come/spring to mind to be something that you think of □ *He wants the name of a good restaurant, but nothing springs to mind.*

6 have someone/something in mind to be thinking of a particular person or thing □ *Do you have any particular colour in mind for the curtains?*

7 all in the mind if something is all in the mind, you are imagining it □ *He thinks people are laughing at him, but it's all in the mind.*

◆ IDIOMS be/go out of your mind to become extremely worried or upset □ *We were out of our minds with worry for them.* have a good mind to do something to want to do something because you are angry □ *I've a good mind to complain to his boss!* put your mind to something to try very hard to achieve something by thinking hard and giving it all your attention □ *I could probably do this crossword if I put my mind to it.* put/set someone's mind at rest to make someone stop being worried □ *I'm going to go back to check that the door's locked – just to put my mind at rest.* take your mind off something to stop you thinking about something bad by making you think about something

else □ *I'm in a lot of pain, but going dancing takes my mind off it.*

➡ go to cross your mind, be in two minds, speak your mind, slip your mind

▶ VERB [minds, minding, minded]

1 to be upset or annoyed by something □ *Do you mind if I smoke? □ I'm sure Sue wouldn't mind you borrowing her car.*

2 would you mind doing something used to ask someone politely to do something □ *Would you mind opening the window?*

3 to look after someone or something □ *She was at home, minding the children.*

4 used to tell someone to be careful not to get hurt □ *Mind your head on that branch.*

5 never mind used to say that something is not important □ *'I haven't finished my homework.' 'Never mind, you can hand it in tomorrow.'*

6 mind you used to start part of a sentence that is the opposite to what you said before □ *I'm shocked to hear that Mick's in prison. Mind you, he was always in trouble at school.*

◆ PHRASAL VERB **mind out** used to tell someone to be careful not to get hurt □ *Mind out – there's a car coming!*

• **minder** /'maɪndə(r)/ NOUN [plural **minders**] someone who looks after another person and protects them from harm

• **mindless** /'maɪndlɪs/ ADJECTIVE

1 a mindless job is boring and does not need any thought or imagination

2 mindless violence, damage, etc. is done for no reason

mine¹ /maɪn/ PRONOUN used to talk or write about things belonging to or to do with you □ *Is this book yours or mine? □ Jan is a friend of mine.*

mine² /maɪn/ ▶ NOUN [plural **mines**]

1 a place where people dig something such as coal or gold from the ground □ *a coal mine*

2 a bomb that is hidden in the ground or in water, which explodes when someone touches it

▶ VERB [mines, mining, mined]

1 to dig into the ground in order to get something such as coal or gold □ *Diamonds are mined from the rocks.*

2 to put bombs under the ground or in water

minefield /'maɪnfiːld/ NOUN [plural **minefields**]

1 a situation that has many possible problems □ *This is a political minefield for the government.*

2 an area of land with explosive mines in it

miner /'maɪnə(r)/ NOUN [plural **miners**] someone who works in a mine

mineral /'mɪnərəl/ NOUN [plural **minerals**]

1 a natural substance in the earth, such as coal, salt or gold □ *Our mineral resources are not infinite.*

2 a natural substance such as iron or zinc that your body needs to stay healthy ⊞ *Some vegetables contain a lot of vitamins and minerals.*

mineral water / ˈmɪnərəl ˌwɔːtə(r/ NOUN [*plural* **mineral waters**] water that you buy in bottles, which comes from under the ground □ *a bottle of mineral water*

mingle /ˈmɪŋgəl/ VERB [**mingles, mingling, mingled**]
1 to meet and talk to a lot of people, moving from one person to another □ *The players mingled with the crowd and posed for photographs.*
2 if substances, smells, feelings, etc. mingle, they mix □ *The smoke mingled with the mist.*

mini- /ˈmɪni/ PREFIX mini- is added to the beginning of words to mean 'small' or 'short' □ *minibus* □ *miniskirt*

miniature /ˈmɪnətʃə(r)/ ▶ ADJECTIVE very much smaller than normal □ *a miniature camera*
▶ NOUN [*plural* **miniatures**]
1 a very small model of something bigger
2 a very small painting of someone

mini-break / ˈmɪnibreɪk/ NOUN [*plural* **mini-breaks**] a short holiday □ *We've just booked a two-night mini-break in Amsterdam.*

minibus /ˈmɪnibʌs/ NOUN [*plural* **minibuses**] a small bus for about 12 people

minimal /ˈmɪnɪməl/ ADJECTIVE very small in amount or degree □ *The fire caused minimal damage.*

• **minimize** or **minimise** /ˈmɪnɪmaɪz/ VERB [**minimizes, minimizing, minimized**] to reduce something to the smallest amount or degree possible □ *Good hygiene minimizes the risk of infection.*

• **minimum** /ˈmɪnɪməm/ ▶ ADJECTIVE being the smallest amount or degree that is possible or allowed 🗗 *The minimum age for driving in the UK is 17.* □ *£250 was the minimum amount needed to open a bank account.*
▶ NOUN, NO PLURAL the smallest amount or degree that is possible or allowed 🗗 *At college he did the bare minimum of work.* 🗗 *We need to keep costs to a minimum.* □ **+ of** *He did his duties with the minimum of fuss.* □ *The hotel costs a minimum of £200 a night.*

mining /ˈmaɪnɪŋ/ NOUN, NO PLURAL the job of digging something such as coal or gold from the ground □ *the mining industry*

miniskirt /ˈmɪniskɜːt/ NOUN [*plural* **miniskirts**] a very short skirt

minister /ˈmɪnɪstə(r)/ NOUN [*plural* **ministers**]
1 a politician who is in charge of a government department 🗗 *Government ministers will visit China next week.* □ *the health minister* □ **+ of/for** *the Minister for Education*
2 a priest in some Christian churches □ *a Methodist minister*
♦ PHRASAL VERB [**ministers, ministering, ministered**]
minister to someone a formal word meaning to help someone, especially someone who is ill, old or poor □ *Houk has ministered to the sick and needy for over 20 years.*

• **ministerial** /ˌmɪnɪˈstɪəriəl/ ADJECTIVE to do with government ministers □ *a ministerial meeting*

• **ministry** /ˈmɪnɪstri/ NOUN [*plural* **ministries**]

1 a government department □ *the Ministry of Defence* □ *ministry officials*
2 the job of a church minister

mink /mɪŋk/ NOUN [*plural* **mink**]
1 a small animal with very valuable fur
2 *no plural* the dark brown fur of a mink □ *a mink coat*

minor /ˈmaɪnə(r)/ ▶ ADJECTIVE not serious or important 🗗 *He suffered minor injuries in the accident.* □ *I've made a few minor changes to the report.* 🗗 *The problems were relatively minor.*
▶ NOUN [*plural* **minors**] someone who is legally a child

minority /maɪˈnɒrəti/ ▶ NOUN [*plural* **minorities**]
1 a small group of people which is part of a much larger group 🗗 *A small minority of our students are from Africa.*
2 **be in the minority** to form less than half of a group □ *In this country, people without Internet access are in the minority.*
3 a group of people of a different race or religion than most people in a country 🗗 *ethnic minorities*
▶ ADJECTIVE
1 to do with less than half of a group of people □ *This is very much a minority view.*
2 to do with groups that are of a different race or religion from most people in a country □ *minority communities* □ *minority faiths*

mint /mɪnt/ NOUN [*plural* **mints**]
1 *no plural* a plant with strong-smelling leaves, used in cooking
2 a type of sweet with a strong flavour
3 a factory which makes coins

minus /ˈmaɪnəs/ ▶ PREPOSITION
1 used for showing that one number is taken away from another number □ *8 minus 2 is 6*
2 without □ *He came home covered in mud and minus one shoe.*
▶ ADJECTIVE
1 less than zero □ *minus ten degrees*
2 used after a letter to show that a score for a piece of work is slightly less than the score represented by the letter alone □ *I got an A minus for my essay.*
▶ NOUN [*plural* **minuses**]
1 a sign (−) used in maths to show that you should take one number away from another number, or that a number is less than zero
2 something bad about a situation 🗗 *There are pluses and minuses* (=advantages and disadvantages) *to having brothers and sisters.*

minuscule /ˈmɪnəskjuːl/ ADJECTIVE extremely small □ *minuscule differences*

minute[1] /ˈmɪnɪt/ NOUN [*plural* **minutes**]
1 a period of sixty seconds □ *The journey only lasted a few minutes.* □ *I loved every minute of my visit.* □ *Rendell scored in the eighth minute.*
2 a short time □ *Wait a minute while I look for my keys.* □ *Just a minute – I need to phone Clara.*
3 the exact time □ *I knew something was wrong the minute I saw him.* □ *At that very minute there was a loud explosion.*

4 any minute very soon □ *Paul will be here any minute now.* □ *The bomb could explode at any minute.*

5 this minute immediately □ *Come here this minute!*

➔ *go to* **minutes**

minute² /maɪˈnjuːt/ ADJECTIVE

1 extremely small □ *Minute traces of blood were found on his clothes.*

2 in minute detail considering or giving all the details □ *The report examines the event in minute detail.*

minute³ /ˈmɪnɪt/ VERB [**minutes, minuting, minuted**] to make an written record of something that was said in a meeting □ *I'd like it minuted that I oppose the plan.*

minutes /ˈmɪnɪts/ PLURAL NOUN a written record of a meeting 🖫 *Who is going to take the minutes?*

miracle /ˈmɪrəkəl/ NOUN [*plural* **miracles**]

1 something extremely lucky that happens and that no one would expect □ *It's a miracle that no one was killed in the accident.* □ *a miracle cure*

2 something that happens which seems impossible and that people think God has done

● **miraculous** /mɪˈrækjʊləs/ ADJECTIVE extremely lucky and not expected 🖫 *He made a miraculous recovery.*

● **miraculously** /mɪˈrækjʊləslɪ/ ADVERB in a lucky way which you did not expect □ *Miraculously, he survived the accident.*

mirage /mɪˈrɑːʒ/ NOUN [*plural* **mirages**] an image of water which does not exist, caused by very hot air

mirror /ˈmɪrə(r)/ ▶ NOUN [*plural* **mirrors**] a piece of special glass that you look at to see an image of yourself □ *Ben was looking at himself in the mirror.* 🖫 *There was a full-length mirror in the bedroom.*

▶ VERB [**mirrors, mirroring, mirrored**] to be the same as something else or show what something else is like □ *The film mirrors his life very closely.*

mirth /mɜːθ/ NOUN, NO PLURAL a literary word meaning laughter

mis- /mɪs/ PREFIX mis- is added to the beginning of words to mean 'bad' or 'badly', or 'wrong' or 'wrongly' □ *misbehave* □ *misunderstand*

misadventure /ˌmɪsədˈventʃə(r)/ NOUN [*plural* **misadventures**]

1 a formal word meaning something bad that happens to you □ *After a series of misadventures, he was glad to be at home.*

2 no plural a word used in British law when someone dies because of an accident 🖫 *The verdict was death by misadventure.*

misapprehension /ˌmɪsæprɪˈhenʃən/ NOUN [*plural* **misapprehensions**] a formal word meaning a belief that is wrong □ *Police shot him under the misapprehension that he was a terrorist.*

misbehave /ˌmɪsbɪˈheɪv/ VERB [**misbehaves, misbehaving, misbehaved**] to behave badly □ *Players who misbehave are fined.*

● **misbehavior** /ˌmɪsbɪˈheɪvjə(r)/ NOUN, NO PLURAL the US spelling of **misbehaviour**

● **misbehaviour** /ˌmɪsbɪˈheɪvjə(r)/ NOUN, NO PLURAL bad behaviour

miscalculate /ˌmɪsˈkælkjʊleɪt/ VERB [**miscalculates, miscalculating, miscalculated**]

1 to judge a situation wrongly □ *The government miscalculated the public reaction.*

2 to calculate an amount wrongly □ *The doctor had miscalculated how much of the drug to give him.*

● **miscalculation** /ˌmɪskælkjuˈleɪʃən/ NOUN [*plural* **miscalculations**] when someone miscalculates something □ *It was a serious miscalculation.*

miscarriage /mɪsˈkærɪdʒ/ NOUN [*plural* **miscarriages**]

1 when a baby comes out of its mother's body so early that it is not developed and dies

2 a miscarriage of justice when someone is punished for a crime they did not commit

miscellaneous /ˌmɪsəˈleɪnɪəs/ ADJECTIVE of many different types □ *There was a box containing miscellaneous items.*

mischief /ˈmɪstʃɪf/ NOUN, NO PLURAL slightly bad behaviour that does not cause serious harm □ *I hope you children haven't been getting up to mischief.*

● **mischievous** /ˈmɪstʃɪvəs/ ADJECTIVE enjoying causing trouble, but in a way that does not cause serious harm □ *a mischievous boy* □ *a mischievous smile*

misconception /ˌmɪskənˈsepʃən/ NOUN [*plural* **misconceptions**] a belief that is wrong, showing that you do not understand something 🖫 *It's a common misconception that cancer only affects older people.*

misconduct /mɪsˈkɒndʌkt/ NOUN, NO PLURAL a formal word meaning bad or unacceptable behaviour 🖫 *The doctor was found guilty of professional misconduct.*

misconstrue /ˌmɪskənˈstruː/ VERB [**misconstrues, misconstruing, misconstrued**] to understand something in the wrong way □ *His shyness had been misconstrued as rudeness.*

misdemeanor /ˌmɪsdɪˈmiːnə(r)/ NOUN [*plural* **misdemeanors**] the US spelling of **misdemeanour**

misdemeanour /ˌmɪsdɪˈmiːnə(r)/ NOUN [*plural* **misdemeanours**] a formal word meaning something bad that someone has done □ *He has learned from his past misdemeanours.*

miser /ˈmaɪzə(r)/ NOUN [*plural* **misers**] someone who keeps all their money because they hate spending it

miserable /ˈmɪzərəbəl/ ADJECTIVE

1 very unhappy □ *She's miserable because all her friends are away.* □ *Dan looked pretty miserable.*

2 making you feel unhappy □ *What miserable weather!* □ *She'd had a miserable childhood.*

3 in a bad mood □ *Smile! Don't be so miserable!*

4 small in amount, and not enough □ *I got a miserable £5.50 for three hours' work!*

● **miserably** /ˈmɪzərəblɪ/ ADVERB

1 in an unhappy way □ *Alyssa nodded miserably.*

2 completely and in a disappointing way 🖫 *His attempt to win had failed miserably.*

miserly /'maɪzəlɪ/ ADJECTIVE very unwilling to spend money

misery /'mɪzərɪ/ NOUN [plural **miseries**]
1 no plural great unhappiness or suffering □ Bad weather has caused misery for thousands of air travellers.
2 someone who is in a bad mood □ Come and join us, you misery!
3 put someone out of their misery to make someone stop worrying by telling them something they are waiting to hear □ Come on, put me out of my misery. Did you pass your driving test or not?

misfit /'mɪsfɪt/ NOUN [plural **misfits**] someone who is very different from other people in a group and is not accepted by them □ I felt like a social misfit.

misfortune /mɪs'fɔ:tʃu:n/ NOUN [plural **misfortunes**] bad luck 🕮 I had the misfortune of sitting next to a very noisy group of people.

misgivings /mɪs'gɪvɪŋz/ PLURAL NOUN doubts or worries 🕮 I have serious misgivings about some of the decisions he has made.

misguided /ˌmɪs'gaɪdɪd/ ADJECTIVE based on beliefs or ideas that are not correct □ The scheme was a misguided attempt to help students.

mishandle /ˌmɪs'hændəl/ VERB [mishandles, mishandling, mishandled] to deal with a situation badly, causing problems □ The government has mishandled the crisis.

mishap /'mɪshæp/ NOUN [plural **mishaps**] a slight accident or mistake

misinterpret /ˌmɪsɪn'tɜ:prɪt/ VERB [misinterpret, misinterpreting, misinterpreted] to understand something wrongly □ They misinterpreted the results of the study.

misjudge /mɪs'dʒʌdʒ/ VERB [misjudges, misjudging, misjudged]
1 to have the wrong opinion about a person or situation □ I realize now that I had misjudged him.
2 to judge an amount or distance wrongly □ They misjudged the amount of time needed to get to the airport.

mislay /mɪs'leɪ/ VERB [mislays, mislaying, mislaid] to lose something for a short time □ Em had mislaid her keys.

mislead /mɪs'li:d/ VERB [misleads, misleading, misled] to make someone believe something that is not true □ The government deliberately misled the public about the state of the economy.
• **misleading** /mɪs'li:dɪŋ/ ADJECTIVE making someone believe something that is not true □ misleading information

misprint /'mɪsprɪnt/ NOUN [plural **misprints**] a mistake made in printing □ That's definitely a misprint. It should be 10, not 100.

Miss /mɪs/ NOUN [plural **Misses**]
1 a word used before the name of a girl or a woman who is not married □ Miss Smith □ Miss Zoe Arnison
2 a word children use for talking to a female teacher □ I haven't done my homework, Miss.

miss /mɪs/ ► VERB [misses, missing, missed]
1 to fail to hit or catch something you are aiming at 🕮 A bullet narrowly missed (=only just missed) his spine. □ He missed the penalty.
2 to not go to something or experience something □ I had to miss my daughter's school concert. □ Don't miss their new show!
3 to miss a train, bus, plane, etc. is to not arrive in time to catch it
4 to feel sad because of someone you can no longer be with or something you can no longer have or do 🕮 I missed my family terribly when I lived abroad. □ + ing I miss being able to walk on the beach.
5 to be too late for something □ I missed the first few minutes of the concert. □ Kate? You've just missed her, I'm afraid.
6 to not notice something 🕮 Our house has a pink front door – you can't miss it! □ Why is he so angry? Did I miss something?
7 to not take an opportunity □ If you don't take this job, you'll be missing the best chance of your life.
8 to not achieve something □ He always misses his sales targets.
9 to discover that you have lost something or someone □ When did you first miss your purse?
♦ PHRASAL VERBS **miss someone/something out** to not include someone or something □ He read us the book, but he missed out all the rude words. **miss out** to not get something that other people get □ I was away at school, so I missed out on all the fun.
► NOUN [plural **misses**] when you do not hit something you are aiming at □ His miss cost his team the match.
♦ IDIOM **give something a miss** to decide not to do something □ I was feeling tired, so I decided to give the party a miss.

missile /'mɪsaɪl/ NOUN [plural **missiles**]
1 a weapon that travels long distances and explodes when it hits something □ long-range missiles
2 an object that someone throws to hit someone or something □ Police were hit by bottles, stones and other missiles.

missing /'mɪsɪŋ/ ADJECTIVE
1 if someone or something is missing, they are not where you expect them to be and you do not know where they are 🕮 Some important documents had gone missing. □ Rescue teams are looking for three missing climbers.
2 not included in something □ Kewell was missing from the team because of injury.

mission /'mɪʃən/ NOUN [plural **missions**]
1 an important job that someone has been sent to do by a government or organization □ He visited Baghdad on a fact-finding mission.
2 a military operation □ He had been killed during a combat mission.
3 a space flight □ The astronauts were on a mission to Mars.

4 a group of people who are sent to do something by their government □ *members of the diplomatic mission*
5 something that you very much want to achieve ⌻ *It was my father's mission in life to protect these birds.*
• **missionary** /ˈmɪʃənərɪ/ NOUN [*plural* **missionaries**] someone who goes to another country to teach people about Christianity

misspell /ˌmɪsˈspel/ VERB [**misspells, misspelling, misspelt** *or* **misspelled**] to spell something in the wrong way □ *You've misspelt my name. It should be 'Jayne' not 'Jane'.*
• **misspelling** /ˌmɪsˈspelɪŋ/ NOUN [*plural* **misspellings**] a word that is spelt the wrong way

mist /mɪst/ ▶ NOUN [*plural* **mists**] very small drops of water in the air that make it difficult for you to see ⌻ *A fine mist hung over the city.* ⌻ *The morning mist had lifted.*
▶ VERB [**mists, misting, misted**] if your eyes mist, they fill with tears □ *Chrissy's eyes misted as she thought about her mother.*
◆ PHRASAL VERB **mist up/over** to become covered with small drops of water □ *The windows misted up while she was cooking.*

mistake /mɪˈsteɪk/ ▶ NOUN [*plural* **mistakes**]
1 something wrong that you do ⌻ *We've all made mistakes.* ⌻ *She knew that inviting him would be a big mistake.* ⌻ *There were lots of spelling mistakes in his writing.* □ *+ to do something* *It was a mistake to come here.*
2 by mistake by accident □ *He deleted the file by mistake.* □ *The letter had been delivered to the wrong house by mistake.*
▶ VERB [**mistakes, mistaking, mistook, mistaken**]
1 to understand something in the wrong way □ *No one could mistake his meaning.*
2 there is no mistaking something used for saying that something is very obvious □ *There was no mistaking the pride in his voice.*
◆ PHRASAL VERB **mistake someone/something for someone/something** to think wrongly that a person or thing is someone or something else □ *People often mistake Clare for her sister.*
mistaken /mɪˈsteɪkən/ ADJECTIVE if you are mistaken, you are wrong about something □ *If they thought that was the end of their problems, they were mistaken.* ⌻ *He was shot in the mistaken belief that he was a terrorist.*
mistakenly /mɪˈsteɪkənlɪ/ ADVERB wrongly □ *She mistakenly believed that their love would last.*

mistletoe /ˈmɪsəltəʊ/ NOUN, NO PLURAL a plant with white berries which is used as a decoration inside houses at Christmas
mistook /mɪsˈtʊk/ PAST TENSE OF **mistake**
mistreat /ˌmɪsˈtriːt/ VERB [**mistreats, mistreating, mistreated**] to treat a person or animal cruelly □ *The prisoners had been mistreated.*

• **mistreatment** /ˌmɪsˈtriːtmənt/ NOUN, NO PLURAL cruel treatment □ *the mistreatment of animals*
mistrust /ˌmɪsˈtrʌst/ ▶ NOUN, NO PLURAL a feeling that you cannot trust someone or something □ *The public has a deep mistrust of this government.*
▶ VERB [**mistrusts, mistrusting, mistrusted**] to not trust someone or something
misty /ˈmɪstɪ/ ADJECTIVE [**mistier, mistiest**] with a lot of small drops of water in the air □ *a misty morning*
misunderstand /ˌmɪsʌndəˈstænd/ VERB [**misunderstands, misunderstanding, misunderstood**] to understand something in the wrong way □ *I'm sorry, I misunderstood your question.*
• **misunderstanding** /ˌmɪsʌndəˈstændɪŋ/ NOUN [*plural* **misunderstandings**]
1 a problem caused by not understanding something correctly □ *I think there's been a misunderstanding.*
2 a slight disagreement or argument
misuse ▶ VERB /ˌmɪsˈjuːz/ [**misuses, misusing, misused**] to use something in the wrong way □ *He is accused of misusing public money.*
▶ NOUN, NO PLURAL /ˌmɪsˈjuːs/ when you use something in the wrong way □ *the misuse of power*
mite /maɪt/ NOUN [*plural* **mites**]
1 a very small insect
2 an informal word for a child who you feel sorry for □ *The poor little mite looked terrified.*
3 a mite an informal phrase meaning slightly □ *She looked a mite annoyed.*
mitigating /ˈmɪtɪgeɪtɪŋ/ ADJECTIVE making a crime or mistake seem less serious ⌻ *His age was a mitigating factor in the crime.*
mitosis /maɪˈtəʊsɪs/ NOUN, NO PLURAL when a cell divides into two cells, each with the same number of chromosomes as the original cell. A biology word.
mitten /ˈmɪtən/ NOUN [*plural* **mittens**] a glove (=something you wear on your hand) without separate parts for each finger

mix /mɪks/ ▶ VERB [**mixes, mixing, mixed**]
1 to combine two or more substances □ *If you mix black paint and white paint, you get grey.* ⌻ *In a small bowl, mix together the garlic and butter.* □ *+ with* *Mix the powder with water.*
2 to combine □ *Oil and water don't mix.*
3 to combine two or more styles, activities, feelings, etc. □ *The President believed it was wrong to mix religion and politics.* □ *+ with* *The villa successfully mixes modern architecture with antique-style furniture.*
4 to talk to people and spend time with them socially □ *Marija was very shy and found it difficult to mix.* □ *+ with* *My Mum doesn't like the people I mix with.*
◆ PHRASAL VERBS **mix someone/something up** to think that a person or thing is someone or something else □ *The twins are very alike and the teacher often mixes them up.* **mix something up** to put a group of things in the wrong order □ *Somehow the pages have all got mixed up.*
▶ NOUN [*plural* **mixes**]

1 a combination of people or things □ + *of The film was an odd mix of comedy and horror.*
2 a powder that you combine with liquid to make a particular food □ *a cake mix*

• **mixed** /mɪkst/ ADJECTIVE
1 involving many different types □ *We live in a racially mixed society.* □ *a mixed salad*
2 partly good and partly bad □ *The film has had mixed reviews.* □ *The strategy produced mixed results.*
3 for both girls and boys, or men and women □ *a mixed school*
4 mixed feelings when you are happy and unhappy about something at the same time □ *I have mixed feelings about going back to work.*

mixed-race /ˌmɪkst ˈreɪs/ ADJECTIVE having one parent from one race (=group of people with the same skin colour, type of hair, etc.) and the other parent from a different race

mixed up /ˌmɪkst ˈʌp/ ADJECTIVE
1 confused 🕀 *I got mixed up and thought the meeting was on Thursday rather than Friday.*
2 be mixed up in something if you are mixed up in something illegal or bad, you are involved in it □ *He had been mixed up in a credit card fraud.*
3 having a lot of emotional problems. An informal word □ *He's a very mixed up little boy.*

mixer /ˈmɪksə(r)/ NOUN [plural **mixers**] a machine used for mixing something □ *a cement mixer*

mixture /ˈmɪkstʃə(r)/ NOUN [plural **mixtures**]
1 a combination of different things 🕀 *The city is a strange mixture of old and new buildings.* □ + *of I felt a mixture of anger and sadness.*
2 a substance that you get by combining two or more things □ *Stir the mixture until the sugar dissolves.*

mix-up /ˈmɪksʌp/ NOUN [plural **mix-ups**] a mistake that happens because someone is confused about something

ml /ˌem ˈel/ ABBREVIATION millilitre or millilitres

mm /ˌem ˈem/ ABBREVIATION millimetre or millimetres

mnemonic /nɪˈmɒnɪk/ NOUN [plural **mnemonics**] a word, phrase or poem that helps you remember something

moan /məʊn/ ▶ VERB [**moans, moaning, moaned**]
1 to complain about something, often in a way that annoys other people □ *Oh stop moaning!* □ *Tim was moaning about the weather.*
2 to make a long, low sound, usually because you are in pain □ *I could hear the injured passengers moaning in pain.*
▶ NOUN [plural **moans**]
1 when you complain about something, often in a way that annoys other people 🕀 *She was having a moan about the cost of everything.*
2 a long, low sound you make, usually when you are in pain

moat /məʊt/ NOUN [plural **moats**] a deep hole around a castle, designed to prevent attacks

mob /mɒb/ ▶ NOUN [plural **mobs**] an angry crowd □ *A mob attacked his house with petrol bombs.*
▶ VERB [**mobs, mobbing, mobbed**] if a crowd of people mobs someone, they surround them □ *The singer was mobbed by fans.*

mobile /ˈməʊbaɪl/ ▶ ADJECTIVE
1 able to move or be moved □ *He was older and less mobile than his wife.* □ *a mobile home*
2 socially mobile able to move from a lower social class to a higher one
▶ NOUN [plural **mobiles**]
1 a telephone that you carry with you □ *Is your mobile switched on?* 🕀 *Have you got my mobile number?*
2 a decoration that you hang from a ceiling

mobile phone /ˌməʊbaɪl ˈfəʊn/ NOUN [plural **mobile phones**] a telephone that you carry with you

mobility /məˈbɪləti/ NOUN, NO PLURAL
1 being able to move around □ *These exercises will help improve mobility.*
2 social mobility the ability to move from a lower social class to a higher one

mobilize or **mobilise** /ˈməʊbɪlaɪz/ VERB [**mobilizes, mobilizing, mobilized**]
1 to organize a group of people to support something □ *The party were trying to mobilize voters.*
2 to prepare to fight a war, or prepare soldiers to fight a war □ *Troops were quickly mobilized.*

moccasin /ˈmɒkəsɪn/ NOUN [plural **moccasins**] a soft leather shoe

mock /mɒk/ ▶ VERB [**mocks, mocking, mocked**] to be unkind to someone by making jokes about them or by copying what they say or do □ *Other people might mock David's voice, but I love it.*
▶ ADJECTIVE not real but made to look real □ *a mock leather sofa*

• **mockery** /ˈmɒkəri/ NOUN, NO PLURAL
1 make a mockery of something to make something seem stupid or not useful □ *This judgment makes a mockery of the whole legal system.*
2 when someone mocks someone or something

modal verb /ˌməʊdəl ˈvɜːb/ NOUN [plural **modal verbs**] a verb such as 'ought' or 'might' that is used to show ideas such as being possible, necessary, certain, etc.

mode /məʊd/ NOUN [plural **modes**]
1 a formal word meaning a method of doing something □ *a mode of transport*
2 the value that appears most often in a series of numbers. A maths word.

model /ˈmɒdəl/ ▶ NOUN [plural **models**]
1 a small copy of something bigger □ + *of On display was a model of the ship.* 🕀 *He enjoys making models of aeroplanes.*
2 a person whose job is to wear clothes at fashion shows and for magazine photographs 🕀 *a fashion model* □ *a male model*
3 a particular type of car, machine, etc. that a company makes 🕀 *The latest model allows you to download video podcasts.*

4 a way of doing something, for example a way of operating a business 🔄 *They have developed a very successful business model.*

▶ VERB [models, modelling/US modeling, modelled/US modeled]

1 to work as a model, wearing clothes at fashion shows and for magazine photographs

2 if something is modelled on something else, it copies it □ *The programme is modelled on a popular US game show.*

◆ PHRASAL VERB **model yourself on someone** to try to be like someone else □ *He has modelled himself on the former president.*

▶ ADJECTIVE

1 a model car, building, etc. is a small copy of a real one □ *He enjoys making model planes.*

2 behaving perfectly □ *She was a model student.*

• **modelling** /'mɒdəlɪŋ/ NOUN, NO PLURAL the job of working as a model, wearing clothes at fashion shows and for magazine photographs □ *She had a very successful modelling career.*

modem /'məʊdɛm/ NOUN [plural **modems**] a device that connects a computer to a telephone line. A computing word.

moderate ▶ ADJECTIVE /'mɒdərət/

1 not extreme □ *He was recommended to take moderate exercise.* □ *moderate heat*

2 having political or religious beliefs that are not extreme

▶ NOUN /'mɒdərət/ [plural **moderates**] someone whose political or religious beliefs are not extreme

▶ VERB /'mɒdəreɪt/ [moderates, moderating, moderated] to make something less extreme □ *The organization has moderated its position.*

• **moderately** /'mɒdərətlɪ/ ADVERB quite but not very □ *The campaign was moderately successful.*

moderation /mɒdə'reɪʃən/ NOUN, NO PLURAL

1 in moderation if you do something in moderation, you do it only a little □ *It's fine to eat sugar in moderation.*

2 when beliefs or actions are not extreme

modern /'mɒdən/ ADJECTIVE

1 to do with the present time and not the past 🔄 *In the modern world, most women go out to work.* 🔄 *Modern life is very busy.*

2 using the most recent ideas, styles, etc. 🔄 *modern art* 🔄 *modern technology*

modernity /mɒ'dɜːnətɪ/ NOUN, NO PLURAL being modern □ *There was a conflict between modernity and tradition.*

modernization *or* **modernisation** /ˌmɒdənaɪ'zeɪʃən/ NOUN, NO PLURAL making something more modern □ *economic modernization*

modernize *or* **modernise** /'mɒdənaɪz/ VERB [modernizes, modernizing, modernized] to become more modern, or to make something more modern

modern languages /ˌmɒdən 'læŋgwɪdʒɪz/ PLURAL NOUN languages that are spoken now, such as German or Spanish, which you study at school or university

modest /'mɒdɪst/ ADJECTIVE

1 quite small □ *a modest increase* □ *a modest apartment*

2 not talking about your skills and achievements even when you have been successful □ *Paul is very modest.*

• **modesty** /'mɒdɪstɪ/ NOUN, NO PLURAL the quality of not being too proud of your abilities and achievements □ *With characteristic modesty, he never spoke about his work.*

modicum /'mɒdɪkəm/ NOUN, NO PLURAL **a modicum of something** a formal phrase meaning a little of something □ *Anyone with a modicum of intelligence could see that he would fail.*

modification /ˌmɒdɪfɪ'keɪʃən/ NOUN [plural modifications] a small change, or the process of changing something 🔄 *They've made some modifications to the boat.*

• **modify** /'mɒdɪfaɪ/ VERB [modifies, modifying, modified] to change something slightly □ *We've had to modify our plans.*

module /'mɒdjuːl/ NOUN [plural modules]

1 a separate part of a college or university course □ *We're doing a module on English grammar.*

2 a separate unit that is part of something larger □ *the space station's escape module*

mohair /'məʊheə(r)/ NOUN, NO PLURAL soft wool that comes from a type of goat

Mohammed /mə'hæmɪd/ NOUN the Arab holy man on whose ideas the religion of Islam is based

moist /mɔɪst/ ADJECTIVE [moister, moistest] slightly wet □ *moist air*

• **moisten** /'mɔɪsən/ VERB [moistens, moistening, moistened] to make something slightly wet □ *He licked his lips to moisten them.*

• **moisture** /'mɔɪstʃə(r)/ NOUN, NO PLURAL a small amount of liquid in or on something □ *This helps keep the moisture in the soil.*

• **moisturize** *or* **moisturise** /'mɔɪstʃəraɪz/ VERB [moisturizes, moisturizing, moisturized] to put cream on your skin to make it soft and not dry

• **moisturizer** *or* **moisturiser** /'mɔɪstʃəraɪzə(r)/ NOUN [plural moisturizers] a cream you put on your skin to make it soft and not dry

molar /'məʊlə(r)/ NOUN [plural molars] one of the large teeth that you chew with at the back of your mouth. A biology word.

mole /məʊl/ NOUN [plural moles]

1 a small brown spot on your skin which is permanent

2 a small animal which lives underground and is almost blind

3 someone who works for an organization and gives secret information to its competitors

molecular /mə'lekjʊlə(r)/ ADJECTIVE to do with molecules □ *molecular structure*

molecule /'mɒlɪkjuːl/ NOUN [plural molecules] the smallest unit that a chemical element or compound can be divided into. Molecules are made up of two or more atoms. A chemistry or physics word.

molehill /'məʊlhɪl/ NOUN [plural **molehills**] a pile of earth that a mole pushes up while it is digging underground

mollycoddle /'mɒlɪkɒdəl/ VERB [**mollycoddles, mollycoddling, mollycoddled**] to treat someone too kindly and protect them from unpleasant things too much

molten /'məʊltən/ ADJECTIVE molten rock or metal is liquid because it is very hot

mom /mɒm/ NOUN [plural **moms**] the US word for mum

moment /'məʊmənt/ NOUN [plural **moments**]
1 a short period of time □ Stop what you're doing for a moment. ⊞ Wait a moment – I'm not ready. ⊞ Please take a moment (=use a short period of time) to read this information.
2 a particular point in time □ Just at that moment, she heard a door slam. □ Winning this competition has been the proudest moment in my athletics career.
3 at the moment now □ The house is empty at the moment.
4 at any moment at any time soon □ Doctors have said he could die at any moment.
5 in a moment very soon □ I'll explain what I mean in a moment. □ I'll be back in a moment.
6 the moment (that) as soon as □ The moment I met him I knew we'd be friends.
● **momentarily** /'məʊməntərɪlɪ/ ADVERB for a short period of time □ He was momentarily suspended in the air.
● **momentary** /'məʊməntərɪ/ ADJECTIVE continuing for only a very short time □ There was a momentary pause, and then everyone started talking.

momentous /mə'mentəs/ ADJECTIVE very important, causing big changes □ a momentous occasion □ a momentous decision

momentum /mə'mentəm/ NOUN, NO PLURAL
1 when something continues to develop, increase or become more successful ⊞ The idea is gaining political momentum.
2 the force that makes a moving object continue to move. A physics word.

monarch /'mɒnək/ NOUN [plural **monarchs**] a king or queen
● **monarchy** /'mɒnəkɪ/ NOUN [plural **monarchies**]
1 a system in which a country has a king or queen □ The Greek monarchy was abolished in 1973.
2 a country that has a king or queen □ Britain is a monarchy.

monastery /'mɒnəstərɪ/ NOUN [plural **monasteries**] a building where monks (=religious men) live
● **monastic** /mə'næstɪk/ ADJECTIVE to do with monasteries or monks (=religious men)

Monday /'mʌndɪ/ NOUN [plural **Mondays**] the day of the week after Sunday and before Tuesday □ On Monday, I went to London. □ See you next Monday.

monetary /'mʌnɪtərɪ/ ADJECTIVE to do with money, especially the money in a country's economy □ The government is tightening its monetary policy.

money /'mʌnɪ/ NOUN, NO PLURAL
1 coins and paper notes that you use for buying things □ We don't have the money for a new car. ⊞ Dan spends most of his money on computer games. ⊞ I'm trying to save some money. ⊞ She earns a lot of money.
2 make money to earn money or to make a profit □ He had never made much money from writing.
□ She made a lot of money from the sale of the house.

mongrel /'mʌngrəl/ NOUN [plural **mongrels**] a dog that is a mixture of different breeds

monitor /'mɒnɪtə(r)/ ▶ VERB [**monitors, monitoring, monitored**] to check something regularly to see how it changes □ The school monitors the progress of all its students.
▶ NOUN [plural **monitors**]
1 a screen that is attached to a computer. A computing word □ a computer monitor
2 a piece of equipment which measures something continuously □ a heart monitor

monk /mʌnk/ NOUN [plural **monks**] one of a group of religious men who live together

monkey /'mʌnkɪ/ NOUN [plural **monkeys**] an animal with a long tail that lives in trees in hot countries □ The monkeys were trained to perform simple tasks.

mono- /'mɒnəʊ/ PREFIX mono- is added to the beginning of words to mean 'one' or 'single' □ monologue □ monorail

monologue /'mɒnəlɒg/ NOUN [plural **monologues**] a long speech by one person, especially in a play

monopolize or **monopolise** /mə'nɒpəlaɪz/ VERB [**monopolizes, monopolizing, monopolized**] to control something completely so that other people or organizations cannot take part in it or share it □ He monopolized the conversation and no one had the chance to speak. □ The company had for a long time monopolized the software business.
● **monopoly** /mə'nɒpəlɪ/ NOUN [plural **monopolies**]
1 when a company or government controls a particular business or industry so that other companies cannot compete □ The law ended the state's monopoly on broadcasting.
2 a big company that controls a particular industry or business □ He was the manager of an electricity monopoly.

monorail /'mɒnəreɪl/ NOUN [plural **monorails**] a railway on which the trains run on one rail (=long piece of metal), instead of two rails

monotone /'mɒnətəʊn/ NOUN, NO PLURAL a way of speaking in which your voice never changes □ He spoke in a low monotone.
● **monotonous** /mə'nɒtənəs/ ADJECTIVE boring because of never changing □ monotonous work
● **monotony** /mə'nɒtənɪ/ NOUN, NO PLURAL when

something is boring because it never changes □ *the monotony of the task*

monsoon /mɒn'su:n/ NOUN [*plural* **monsoons**] the season when it rains a lot in some hot countries

monster /'mɒnstə(r)/ ▶ NOUN [*plural* **monsters**]
1 in stories, a very big and frightening creature □ *My little boy thinks there are monsters under his bed.*
2 a cruel and evil person
▶ ADJECTIVE an informal word meaning extremely big □ *a monster truck*

monstrosity /mɒn'strɒsəti/ NOUN [*plural* **monstrosities**] something that is big and very ugly □ *The building was a monstrosity.*

monstrous /'mɒnstrəs/ ADJECTIVE
1 morally very bad □ *a monstrous crime*
2 big and very ugly

month /mʌnθ/ NOUN [*plural* **months**]
1 one of twelve periods that a year is divided into □ *the month of May* □ *the winter months* ⊞ *I went to France last month.* ⊞ *It's my birthday next month.*
2 any period of approximately four weeks or 30 days □ *We spent a few months in Melbourne.* □ *People often wait several months for an appointment.*
3 a long time □ *Police spent months investigating the case.*

● **monthly** /'mʌnθli/ ADJECTIVE, ADVERB happening once a month □ *a monthly meeting* □ *He is paid monthly.*

monument /'mɒnjumənt/ NOUN [*plural* **monuments**]
1 something that has been built in memory of a person or event □ *They built a monument to Sir Walter Scott.*
2 a building or structure that is important in history □ *The Parthenon is one of Greece's ancient monuments.*

● **monumental** /ˌmɒnju'mentəl/ ADJECTIVE extremely big or important □ *a monumental task*

moo /mu:/ ▶ VERB [**moos, mooing, mooed**] a cow moos when it makes a long low sound
▶ NOUN [*plural* **moos**] the long low sound a cow makes

mood /mu:d/ NOUN [*plural* **moods**]
1 someone's feelings at a particular time ⊞ *I woke up in a bad mood this morning.* ⊞ *You're in a good mood today!* ⊞ *The government has misjudged the public mood.* □ **+ of** *There was a mood of optimism in Europe at the time.*
2 **be in a mood** to feel angry or unhappy □ *He was still in a mood after their argument that morning.*
3 **be/feel in the mood** to feel as if you want to do something □ *I didn't feel in the mood for going out.*

moodiness /'mu:dɪnɪs/ NOUN, NO PLURAL when someone is moody

moody /'mu:di/ ADJECTIVE [**moodier, moodiest**] often becoming angry or unhappy □ *moody teenagers*

moon /mu:n/ NOUN
1 **the moon** the round object that you see in the sky at night and which moves around the Earth ⊞ *The*

moon shone brightly. ⊞ *Neil Armstrong made the first moon landing.*
2 **full/half/crescent/new moon** used for talking about the shape of the moon at a particular time □ *There was a full moon* (=the moon looked like a complete circle) *that night.* □ *He watched the new moon* (=a moon that looks like a thin curve) *rising.*
3 a similar object that moves around another planet □ *Saturn's moons*
◆ IDIOM **be over the moon** an informal phrase meaning to be very happy about something that has happened □ *He was over the moon when he passed his driving test.*

moonlight /'mu:nlaɪt/ NOUN, NO PLURAL light that comes from the moon □ *His eyes shone in the moonlight.*
● **moonlit** /'mu:nlɪt/ ADJECTIVE lit by the moon □ *a clear moonlit night*

moor¹ /mɔ:(r)/ NOUN [*plural* **moors**] a large high area of land that is covered with grass and bushes. A geography word.

moor² /mɔ:(r)/ VERB [**moors, mooring, moored**] to fasten a boat to something

moorland /'mɔ:lənd/ NOUN [*plural* **moorlands**] a large high area of land that is covered with grass and bushes. A geography word.

moose /mu:s/ NOUN [*plural* **moose**] a large deer with big, flat horns which lives in North America

mop /mɒp/ ▶ NOUN [*plural* **mops**]
1 something with a long handle that you use for washing floors
2 a lot of thick, often untidy, hair □ *He had a mop of black hair.*
▶ VERB [**mops, mopping, mopped**]
1 to clean a floor with a mop
2 to remove a liquid from something using a cloth □ *He mopped his sweaty face with a handkerchief.*
◆ PHRASAL VERB **mop something up** to clean a liquid from a surface using a cloth or mop □ *The waiter mopped up the spilled tea.*

mope /məʊp/ VERB [**mopes, moping, moped**] to spend time feeling bored or unhappy and doing little □ *Ben spent most of the day moping around in his pyjamas.*

moped /'məʊped/ NOUN [*plural* **mopeds**] a light motorcycle with a small engine

moraine /mɒ'reɪn/ NOUN, NO PLURAL earth and stones that have been carried along by glaciers (=large masses of ice). A geography word.

moral /'mɒrəl/ ▶ ADJECTIVE
1 to do with right and wrong and the way people should behave ⊞ *She had high moral standards.* □ *He objected to the war for moral reasons.*
2 behaving in a way that is right and good
▶ NOUN [*plural* **morals**] something that a story or experience teaches you about how to behave ⊞ *The moral of the story is never give up.*
➔ *go to* **morals**

morale /mə'rɑ:l/ NOUN, NO PLURAL how confident or happy a person or group of people feel □ *Morale in the office is fairly low.* ⌕ *Pay rises usually improve morale.*

morality /mə'rælətɪ/ NOUN, NO PLURAL beliefs about what is right or wrong behaviour

moralize *or* **moralise** /'mɒrəlaɪz/ VERB [**moralizes, moralizing, moralized**] to say what is the right way to behave, especially in a way that criticizes other people's behaviour

morally /'mɒrəlɪ/ ADVERB to do with what is right or wrong behaviour □ *Not paying your taxes is morally wrong.*

morals /'mɒrəlz/ PLURAL NOUN the beliefs someone has about what is right and wrong behaviour □ *His remarks have started a public debate on the nation's morals.*

morbid /'mɔ:bɪd/ ADJECTIVE too interested in death or other subjects that most people think are sad or unpleasant ⌕ *He had developed a morbid fascination with the murders.*

more /mɔ:(r)/ ▶ DETERMINER, PRONOUN
1 a larger number or amount □ *He has more friends than anyone else I know.* ⌕ *The bill was more than £10,000.* □ *He knows more about elephants than anyone else in the UK.* ⌕ *More and more people are buying organic food.*
2 something in addition to what you have, what is there, or what you have talked about ⌕ *Is there any more cake?* ⌕ *Would you like some more coffee?* □ *You need to do more to help.* □ *8 people died, and at least twenty more were injured.*
▶ ADVERB
1 used to make comparative forms of adjectives and adverbs, especially ones with 2 or more syllables ⌕ *He's more patient than I am.* □ *More recently, I have begun to enjoy crime novels.* ⌕ *Harry's a lot more emotional than his sister.*
2 to a greater degree ⌕ *I exercise more than I used to.* ⌕ *I like her more and more.*
3 more or less almost, but not exactly □ *We've more or less finished decorating the kitchen.* □ *She more or less said she didn't trust us.*
4 the more ... the more/less used to say that if one thing increases, another thing will increase or decrease □ *The more I read about Cuba, the more I want to go there.*
● **moreish** /'mɔ:rɪʃ/ ADJECTIVE moreish food makes you want to eat more of it. An informal word.

moreover /mɔ:'rəʊvə(r)/ ADVERB a formal word for also □ *We do not have the facilities for this project. Moreover, we do not have enough staff.*

morgue /mɔ:g/ NOUN [*plural* **morgues**] a place where dead bodies are kept until they are buried or burned

morning /'mɔ:nɪŋ/ NOUN [*plural* **mornings**]
1 the early part of the day from when the sun rises to the middle of the day □ *He takes the dog for a walk every morning.* ⌕ *He was late this morning.*
2 the period from the middle of the night to the middle of the day □ *Adam didn't get to bed till 3 o'clock in the morning.*
3 in the morning (a) in the early part of the day □ *I'm usually quite tired in the morning.* (b) tomorrow morning □ *See you in the morning.*
4 Good morning! used to say 'hello' when you meet someone in the morning

moron /'mɔ:rɒn/ NOUN [*plural* **morons**] an informal word for a very stupid person □ *Some moron left the fridge door open all night.*
● **moronic** /mə'rɒnɪk/ ADJECTIVE an informal word that means very stupid

morose /mə'rəʊs/ ADJECTIVE bad-tempered and speaking little

morphine /'mɔ:fi:n/ NOUN, NO PLURAL a powerful drug used to make pain less strong

morsel /'mɔ:səl/ NOUN [*plural* **morsels**] a small piece of food □ *Joe finished off every morsel of the pie.*

mortal /'mɔ:təl/ ▶ ADJECTIVE
1 unable to live forever and sure to die one day □ *We are all mortal.*
2 very great or extreme ⌕ *She lived in mortal fear of being discovered.* ⌕ *The two men became mortal enemies.*
3 causing someone to die ⌕ *He was dealt a mortal blow* (=He was injured so badly that he died).
▶ NOUN [*plural* **mortals**] a human being. A literary word.
● **mortality** /mɔ:'tælətɪ/ NOUN, NO PLURAL
1 the fact that you will not live forever □ *He was well aware of his own mortality.*
2 the number of deaths in a particular group or at a particular time ⌕ *Infant mortality is still very high in the region.* ⌕ *The mortality rate from the war continues to rise.*
● **mortally** /'mɔ:təlɪ/ ADVERB causing death ⌕ *The soldier was mortally wounded.*

mortar /'mɔ:tə(r)/ NOUN [*plural* **mortars**]
1 a type of large gun that fires explosives up into the air □ *a mortar attack*
2 a substance that is put between bricks in order to hold the bricks in place

mortgage /'mɔ:gɪdʒ/ NOUN [*plural* **mortgages**] money that you borrow from a bank or financial organization in order to buy a house or land ⌕ *They've taken out a huge mortgage on the flat.*

mortified /'mɔ:tɪfaɪd/ ADJECTIVE extremely embarrassed □ *She was mortified when she realized her mistake.*

mortuary /'mɔ:tʃʊərɪ/ NOUN [*plural* **mortuaries**] a place where dead bodies are kept until they are buried or burned

mosaic /məʊ'zeɪɪk/ NOUN [*plural* **mosaics**] a picture made by fitting together many small pieces of coloured glass or stone □ *Roman mosaics*

Moslem /'mɒzləm/ NOUN [plural **Moslems**], ADJECTIVE another spelling of **Muslim**

mosque /mɒsk/ NOUN [plural **mosques**] a place where Muslims meet and pray

mosquito /mə'ski:təʊ/ NOUN [plural **mosquitoes** or **mosquitos**] an insect which feeds by biting people or animals and sucking their blood

moss /mɒs/ NOUN [plural **mosses**] a small green plant that grows on rocks, trees, or the ground, in slightly wet places

• **mossy** /'mɒsɪ/ ADJECTIVE [**mossier, mossiest**] covered with moss □ a mossy bank by the river

most /məʊst/ ▶ DETERMINER, PRONOUN

1 the largest number or amount □ Most people support the policy. □ Which club has spent most money on new players this season? □ All three children eat a lot but Tom eats the most.

2 almost all □ Most of my friends are people I know from work. □ I like most types of fruit.

3 at the most and not more □ The trip should cost £500 at the most.

4 make the most of something to get as much advantage as possible from something that may not continue □ Make the most of the good weather while it lasts.

▶ ADVERB

1 used to make superlative forms of adjectives and adverbs, especially ones with two or more syllables □ Paul was the most intelligent boy in the class. □ Most importantly, he has learned to pay more attention in class.

2 more than anyone or anything else □ What kind of music do you like most?

• **mostly** /'məʊstlɪ/ ADVERB in most cases or most of the time □ They mostly play indoors. □ The band plays mostly '70s music.

MOT /ˌeməʊ'ti:/ NOUN [plural **MOTs**] in Britain, a test done on cars more than three years old to make sure they are safe to drive

motel /məʊ'tel/ NOUN [plural **motels**] a hotel near a main road for people who are travelling by car

moth /mɒθ/ NOUN [plural **moths**] an insect with large wings that flies at night

mother /'mʌðə(r)/ ▶ NOUN [plural **mothers**]

1 the female parent of a person or animal □ My mother was very tall. □ The cubs learn to hunt from their mother.

2 Mother the title of some nuns (=religious women who live together) □ Mother Teresa

▶ VERB [**mothers, mothering, mothered**] to be kind to someone and look after them □ Zoe has always mothered her little brother.

motherhood /'mʌðəhʊd/ NOUN, NO PLURAL the state of being a mother

mother-in-law /'mʌðərɪnˌlɔ:/ NOUN [plural **mothers-in-law**] the mother of your husband or wife

motherly /'mʌðəlɪ/ ADJECTIVE kind and often looking after other people

Mother's Day /'mʌðəz ˌdeɪ/ NOUN, NO PLURAL a Sunday in the spring when children give their mothers cards and presents □ a Mother's Day card

mother tongue /ˌmʌðə 'tʌŋ/ NOUN [plural **mother tongues**] the first language you learn to speak as a child □ English is not her mother tongue.

motif /məʊ'ti:f/ NOUN [plural **motifs**] a shape or design that is repeated in a pattern

motion /'məʊʃən/ ▶ NOUN [plural **motions**]

1 movement or how something moves □ The motion of the waves made him sleepy. 🔁 Do not attempt to get off while the ride is in motion.

2 one movement that you make □ He flicked the fly away with a quick motion of his wrist.

3 a suggestion that is voted on at a formal meeting or in a court of law 🔁 The motion was passed unanimously.

♦ IDIOM **go through the motions** to do something because you have to, but with little effort or enthusiasm

▶ VERB [**motions, motioning, motioned**] to make a movement with your hand in order to show someone that you want them to do something □ He motioned for her to come forward.

• **motionless** /'məʊʃənlɪs/ ADJECTIVE not moving at all

motivate /'məʊtɪveɪt/ VERB [**motivates, motivating, motivated**]

1 to make someone feel interested and enthusiastic so that they want to do something □ A good coach knows how to motivate his team.

2 to cause someone to act in a particular way □ He had been motivated by greed.

• **motivation** /ˌməʊtɪ'veɪʃən/ NOUN [plural **motivations**]

1 no plural enthusiasm and interest in doing something □ At university, he lacked motivation.

2 something that makes you want to do something □ Pregnancy was her motivation to stop smoking.

motive /'məʊtɪv/ NOUN [plural **motives**] the reason someone has for doing something □ There seemed to be no motive for the attack.

motor /'məʊtə(r)/ ▶ NOUN [plural **motors**] the part of a machine that uses petrol, electricity, etc. to produce movement and make the machine work □ an electric motor

▶ ADJECTIVE

1 to do with vehicles that have engines □ motor racing □ the motor industry

2 using the power of an engine □ a motor mower

motorbike /'məʊtəbaɪk/ NOUN [plural **motorbikes**] a vehicle with two wheels and an engine. You sit on it like a bicycle.

motor car /'məʊtə ˌkɑ:/ NOUN [plural **motor cars**] a car. An old-fashioned phrase.

motorcycle /'məʊtəˌsaɪkəl/ NOUN [plural **motorcycles**] a motorbike or moped

• **motorcyclist** /'məʊtə,saɪklɪst/ NOUN [plural **motorcyclists**] someone who rides a motorbike or moped

motorist /'məʊtərɪst/ NOUN [plural **motorists**] someone who drives a car

motor racing /'məʊtə ,reɪsɪŋ/ NOUN, NO PLURAL the sport of driving cars very fast around a track

motorway /'məʊtəweɪ/ NOUN [plural **motorways**] a wide road for vehicles travelling fast over long distances

mottled /'mɒtəld/ ADJECTIVE covered with small areas of different colour and different shapes

motto /'mɒtəʊ/ NOUN [plural **mottoes** or **mottos**] a short sentence or phrase that states the beliefs or purpose of a person or organization □ The motto of the Scouts is 'Be prepared'.

mould /məʊld/ ▶ NOUN [plural **moulds**]
1 a hollow container which a liquid is poured into so that the liquid has the same shape as the container when it is cool and firm □ a jelly mould
2 a soft green or black substance that grows on old food or in wet conditions □ The bathroom ceiling was covered in mould.
▶ VERB [**moulds, moulding, moulded**] to shape something with your hands or in a mould □ She moulded the icing into pretty flower shapes.

• **mouldy** /'məʊldɪ/ ADJECTIVE [**mouldier, mouldiest**] covered with mould □ The bread has gone mouldy.

moult /məʊlt/ VERB [**moults, moulting, moulted**] birds and animals moult when they lose their feathers or hair

mound /maʊnd/ NOUN [plural **mounds**]
1 a pile or large amount of something □ a mound of ironing
2 a small hill or pile of earth or stones □ a burial mound

Mount /maʊnt/ NOUN [plural **Mounts**] used before the names of mountains □ the top of Mount Everest

mount /maʊnt/ VERB [**mounts, mounting, mounted**]
1 to organize something in order to achieve a particular aim ▣ Local residents are mounting a protest against the plans.
2 if a feeling among a group of people mounts, it increases in level □ Fears are mounting for the safety of the young climbers.
3 to fix an object onto something □ They've mounted the speakers on the wall.
4 to go up steps or get onto something □ The audience applauded as she mounted the stage.
5 to get on a horse or bicycle
♦ PHRASAL VERB **mount up** to gradually increase □ The cost soon mounts up.

mountain /'maʊntɪn/ NOUN [plural **mountains**] a very high hill □ the Rocky Mountains □ We spent our holiday walking in the mountains. □ a mountain range

mountain bike /'maʊntɪn ,baɪk/ NOUN [plural **mountain bikes**] a bicycle with thick tyres and a strong frame, for riding on rough ground

• **mountain biking** / 'maʊntɪn ,baɪkɪŋ/ NOUN, NO PLURAL the sport or activity of riding a mountain bike

mountaineer /,maʊntɪ'nɪə(r)/ NOUN [plural **mountaineers**] someone who climbs mountains

• **mountaineering** /,maʊntɪ'nɪərɪŋ/ NOUN, NO PLURAL the sport or activity of climbing mountains

mountainous /'maʊntɪnəs/ ADJECTIVE having a lot of mountains □ mountainous countries like Nepal

mounted /'maʊntɪd/ ADJECTIVE riding a horse □ mounted policemen

mourn /mɔːn/ VERB [**mourns, mourning, mourned**] to be very sad because someone you love has died □ She was still mourning for her husband.

• **mourner** /'mɔːnə(r)/ NOUN [plural **mourners**] someone who is at a funeral □ The church was packed with mourners.

• **mournful** /'mɔːnfʊl/ ADJECTIVE full of sadness □ mournful music

• **mourning** /'mɔːnɪŋ/ NOUN, NO PLURAL when someone mourns for someone who has died ▣ a period of mourning

mouse /maʊs/ NOUN [plural **mice**]
1 a small animal with grey or brown fur and a long tail
2 a small device that you move with your hand in order to make a computer do things. A computing word.

mouse mat /'maʊs ,mæt/ NOUN [plural **mouse mats**] a small piece of material that you move a computer mouse on

mousse /muːs/ NOUN [plural **mousses**]
1 a soft, cold, sweet food that is made with cream and eggs □ chocolate mousse
2 a substance that you put in your hair to keep it in a particular style □ a styling mousse

moustache /mə'stɑːʃ/ NOUN [plural **moustaches**] a line of hair that some men grow above their top lip

mousy /'maʊsɪ/ ADJECTIVE [**mousier, mousiest**]
1 a mousy person is shy and nervous
2 mousy hair is light brown

mouth /maʊθ/ ▶ NOUN [plural **mouths**]
1 the part of your face that you use for speaking and eating and which contains your tongue and teeth
2 the place where a river flows into the sea
3 the entrance to a cave, tunnel (=passage through the earth), etc.
▶ VERB [**mouths, mouthing, mouthed**] to make the shapes of words with your mouth without making the sounds □ She mouthed something at me but I didn't understand.

• **mouthful** /'maʊθfʊl/ NOUN [plural **mouthfuls**]
1 an amount of food or drink that you put in your mouth at one time □ She ate a few mouthfuls of soup

2 a word or phrase that is difficult to say □ *Her surname's a bit of a mouthful.*

mouthpiece /'mauθpi:s/ NOUN [plural **mouthpieces**]
1 the part of a musical instrument or telephone that you put in or close to your mouth
2 a person, newspaper, etc. that states the opinions of a particular group □ *a mouthpiece of the government*

mouthwash /'mauθwɒʃ/ NOUN, NO PLURAL a liquid that you use for cleaning your mouth and teeth

mouth-watering /'mauθ,wɔ:tərɪŋ/ ADJECTIVE mouth-watering food looks or smells very good and makes you want to eat it

movable /'mu:vəbəl/ ADJECTIVE able to be moved

move /mu:v/ ► VERB [**moves, moving, moved**]
1 to change position, or to change the position of something □ *Please move your bag off the kitchen table.* □ *He moved forwards to kick the ball.* □ *Nobody moved as the clock struck.* □ *I'm sure I saw the curtain move.*
2 if a person or an organization moves, they go to live or work in a different place □ *+ to We moved to London in 2003.* ⊞ *We moved house over ten times while I was a child.* □ *Our office is moving to Bristol.*
3 to change the time of something □ *The meeting has been moved to next Monday.*
4 to make you feel a strong, usually sad, emotion ⊞ *I was moved to tears by her story.*
5 to make progress □ *The building work is moving ahead well.* □ *Now we've got the money, we can get moving with the project.*
6 to take action to do something □ *+ to do something Police moved quickly to control the riot.*
♦ PHRASAL VERBS **move in** to begin to live in a new home or work in a new place □ *We moved in last year.*
move on
1 to leave the place where you have been and go somewhere else □ *We stayed in Venice for 2 weeks before moving on.*
2 to start to do something different or to talk about something different □ *The job was getting boring, so I decided it was time to move on.* □ *+ to I think we've made a decision about the hall – shall we move on to the playing fields?* **move out** to leave the place where you have been living or working □ *I moved out of my parents' house when I was 18.* **move over/up** to change your position in order to make space for someone or something □ *Can you move up a bit so we can get the door closed?*
► NOUN [plural **moves**]
1 an action that achieves something ⊞ *Buying a house turned out to be a good move.* ⊞ *They made no move to help her.* ⊞ *I've given him my phone number – it's up to him to make the next move.*
2 a move towards/away from something a change in a situation or in people's opinions which makes something more/less common or popular □ *There has been a move towards providing more care for patients at home.*

3 when you go to live or work in another place □ *I've packed all my files ready for the office move.* □ *They split up after her move to London.*
4 a change of position □ *The slightest move was painful.*
5 when you move a piece in a game such as chess □ *Come on, it's your move.*
♦ IDIOMS **get a move on** an informal phrase meaning to hurry □ *Get a move on – we're going to be late!* **make a move** an informal word meaning to leave a place, especially where you have been a guest □ *We'd better make a move – our train leaves at six.*

● **movement** /'mu:vmənt/ NOUN [plural **movements**]
1 a change of position or place □ *I saw a slight movement of the curtain.* □ *Aim for slow, graceful movements of the arms.* □ *The police tracked the movements of all the suspects.*
2 a group of people with the same interests or aims □ *the anti-war movement*
3 movement towards/away from something a change in a situation or in people's opinions that makes something more/less common or popular □ *There has been some movement towards accepting the peace proposals.*
4 a part of a long piece of classical music

movie /'mu:vi/ NOUN [plural **movies**]
1 a film □ *Do you have a favourite movie?* □ *a movie star* □ *a horror movie*
2 the movies a cinema □ *Let's go to the movies.*

moving /'mu:vɪŋ/ ADJECTIVE making you feel emotional □ *She made a moving speech about her son.*

● **movingly** /'mu:vɪŋli/ ADVERB in a moving way

mow /məʊ/ VERB [**mows, mowing, mowed, mown** or **mowed**] to cut grass with a machine ⊞ *Simon's mowing the lawn.*

● **mower** /'məʊə(r)/ NOUN [plural **mowers**] a machine for cutting grass

MP /,em'pi:/ ABBREVIATION Member of Parliament; someone who has been elected to the British parliament

MP3 /,empi:'θri:/ NOUN [plural **MP3s**] a computer file that stores music and recorded speech

MP3 player /,empi:'θri: ,pleɪə(r)/ NOUN [plural **MP3 players**] a small piece of computer equipment for storing and playing music and recorded speech

mph /,empi:'eɪtʃ/ ABBREVIATION miles per hour; a unit for measuring speed □ *The maximum speed on this road is 30 mph.*

MPV /,empi:'vi:/ ABBREVIATION multi-purpose vehicle; a large car that carries more people than a normal car

Mr /'mɪstə(r)/ NOUN a title used before a man's name □ *My art teacher is called Mr Jackson.* □ *Hello, Mr Rose.*

MRI /,emɑ:'raɪ/ ABBREVIATION magnetic resonance imaging; a system that produces images of the organs inside the body □ *an MRI scan*

Mrs /ˈmɪsɪz/ NOUN a title used before a married woman's name □ *That's my neighbour, Mrs Baker.* □ *Good morning, Mrs Clarke.*

MRSA /ˌemɑːresˈeɪ/ ABBREVIATION methicillin resistant straphylococcus aureus; a type of bacteria that is found in hospitals and that makes people seriously ill

MS /ˌem ˈes/ ABBREVIATION multiple sclerosis

Ms /mɪz, məz/ NOUN a title sometimes used before a woman's name, whether she is married or not □ *Ms Duggan*

much /mʌtʃ/ ► DETERMINER, PRONOUN

1 how much used in questions about amounts □ *How much fruit do you eat each day?* □ *The pay depends on how much responsibility you take on.* □ *How much are* (=what is the price) *of these apples?*
2 used in negative sentences to say that there is not a large amount of something □ *A few more days won't make much difference.* □ *She doesn't say much.* □ *There isn't much to laugh about.* □ *'Do you have any money?' 'Not much.'*
3 too much (a) more than is wanted, needed or acceptable □ *We bought far too much food.* □ *She has missed too much of the course to do the exam.* □ *We've got too much work.* (b) too difficult, upsetting, etc. for someone to accept or deal with □ *Her rudeness was too much for me, and I burst into tears.*
4 so much used to emphasize the large amount of something □ *I have so much work to do.* □ *Why did you give me so much food?*
5 as much used to talk about amounts that are as large as something else □ *I hope I can give you as much support as you've given me.*
6 a lot or a lot of □ *Much of what was said was irrelevant.* □ *There was much laughter coming from the girls' room.*
7 not much of a used to say that something or someone is not good in quality □ *It's not much of a home – more like a shed really.* □ *I'm not much of a musician.*

> ► Remember that **much** is only used with nouns that are not used in the plural:
> ✓ *I've eaten too much food.*
> ✗ *There are too much cars on the road.*
> ► With nouns that are in the plural, the word **many** is used: □ *How many dogs do they have?*

► ADVERB

1 often or a lot □ *Do you miss your old school much?* ⊞ *Thanks very much – you've been a great help.* ⊞ *He doesn't love her as much as she loves him.* ⊞ *I had to work away from home too much in my last job.*
2 used to emphasize comparative adjectives □ *He's much taller than his brother.* □ *She's much more beautiful now she's older.*

muck /mʌk/ NOUN

1 an informal word that means dirt □ *You've trodden muck all over the carpet.*

2 waste from farm animals □ *The farmer was spreading muck on the fields.*
♦ PHRASAL VERBS [mucks, mucking, mucked] muck about/around to behave in a silly way or to waste time. An informal phrase. □ *We haven't time to muck about.* muck something up to do something badly. An informal phrase. □ *I mucked up the last paper of the exam.*

● **mucky** /ˈmʌkɪ/ ADJECTIVE [muckier, muckiest] an informal word that means dirty □ *Get your mucky feet off the sofa!*

mucus /ˈmjuːkəs/ NOUN, NO PLURAL a thick sticky liquid that is produced by some parts of your body, for example, your nose

mud /mʌd/ NOUN, NO PLURAL soft wet soil □ *His football boots were covered in mud.*

muddle /ˈmʌdəl/ ► NOUN [plural muddles] a confused situation or state □ *He is in such a muddle financially.*
► VERB [muddles, muddling, muddled] to put things in the wrong order □ *She'd muddled all the papers.*
♦ PHRASAL VERBS muddle something up to put things in the wrong order □ *Please don't muddle up my revision notes.* muddle someone/something up to confuse two things or people with each other □ *I often get Klaus muddled up with his brother.*

muddy /ˈmʌdɪ/ ADJECTIVE [muddier, muddiest] covered or filled with mud □ *The track through the woods was very muddy.* □ *Take off your muddy boots.*

mudguard /ˈmʌdɡɑːd/ NOUN [plural mudguards] a curved piece of plastic or metal over the wheel of a bicycle or motorcycle, which stops mud and water from hitting the rider

muesli /ˈmjuːzlɪ/ NOUN, NO PLURAL a mixture of grains, nuts and dried fruit eaten with milk for breakfast □ *a bowl of muesli*

muffin /ˈmʌfɪn/ NOUN [plural muffins]
1 a small cake for one person □ *a blueberry muffin*
2 a small round piece of bread that is cut in two and eaten hot with butter □ *toasted muffins*

muffle /ˈmʌfəl/ VERB [muffles, muffling, muffled] to make a sound quieter
● **muffled** /ˈmʌfəld/ ADJECTIVE a muffled sound is not loud or clear □ *A muffled scream came from the garden.*
● **muffler** /ˈmʌflə(r)/ NOUN [plural mufflers] the US word for silencer

mug /mʌɡ/ ► NOUN [plural mugs] a cup with straight sides and a handle □ *a mug of hot chocolate*
► VERB [mugs, mugging, mugged] to attack someone in a public place and steal their money or something they are carrying □ *John was mugged just outside the station.*
● **mugger** /ˈmʌɡə(r)/ NOUN [plural muggers] someone who mugs people

• **mugging** /'mʌgɪŋ/ NOUN [plural **muggings**] when someone is mugged

muggy /'mʌgɪ/ ADJECTIVE [**muggier, muggiest**] in muggy weather, the air is hot and slightly wet in a way that is unpleasant

mule /mjuːl/ NOUN [plural **mules**]
1 an animal that is used to carry heavy things and whose parents are a male donkey and a female horse
2 a type of woman's shoe with no part to cover the back of your foot

mull /mʌl/
♦ PHRASAL VERB [**mulls, mulling, mulled**] **mull something over** to spend time thinking about something carefully □ *I sat down to mull over what she had said.*

multi- /'mʌltɪ/ PREFIX multi- is added to the beginning of words to mean 'many' □ *multicultural studies* □ *a multinational company*

multicultural /ˌmʌltɪˈkʌltʃərəl/ ADJECTIVE involving or including people from many races and religions □ *a multicultural society*

multilateral /ˌmʌltɪˈlætərəl/ ADJECTIVE involving more than two countries or groups □ *Both countries have agreed to take part in multilateral talks on the crisis.*

multimedia /ˌmʌltɪˈmiːdɪə/ ADJECTIVE using sound, images and film in computers □ *multimedia content*

multinational /ˌmʌltɪˈnæʃənəl/ ► ADJECTIVE
1 operating in many different countries □ *a multinational company*
2 with people from many different countries □ *a multinational force*
► NOUN [plural **multinationals**] a big company that operates in many different countries □ *He works for one of the big multinationals.*

multiple /'mʌltɪpəl/ ► ADJECTIVE many □ *She suffered multiple injuries in the crash.*
► NOUN [plural **multiples**] a number that contains another number an exact number of times. A maths word □ *9 and 12 are multiples of 3.*

multiple-choice /ˌmʌltɪpəl 'tʃɔɪs/ ADJECTIVE a multiple-choice exam or question gives you different answers from which you choose the answer that you think is correct

multiple sclerosis /ˌmʌltɪpəl skləˈrəʊsɪs/ NOUN, NO PLURAL a serious illness that gradually stops a person from being able to walk and speak

multiplex /'mʌltɪpleks/ NOUN [plural **multiplexes**] a large cinema with many rooms for showing different films at the same time

multiplication /ˌmʌltɪplɪˈkeɪʃən/ NOUN, NO PLURAL the process of multiplying one number by another. A maths word.

multiply /'mʌltɪplaɪ/ VERB [**multiplies, multiplying, multiplied**]
1 to increase a number by adding it to itself a particular number of times. A maths word □ *13 multiplied by 3 is 39.*
2 to increase or make something increase by a large

amount □ *The number of coffee bars on our high streets has multiplied in recent years.*

multiracial /ˌmʌltɪˈreɪʃəl/ ADJECTIVE involving or including people from many races □ *Britain is a multiracial society.*

multi-storey /ˌmʌltɪˈstɔːrɪ/ ADJECTIVE a multi-storey building has a lot of floors □ *a multi-storey car park*

multitasking /ˈmʌltɪˌtɑːskɪŋ/ NOUN, NO PLURAL when you do many things at the same time □ *Multitasking is a normal feature of office life.*

multitude /'mʌltɪtjuːd/ NOUN **a multitude of something** a very large number of something. A formal phrase. □ *The new system has introduced a whole multitude of problems.*

mum /mʌm/ NOUN [plural **mums**] an informal word for mother □ *Can I have another cake, Mum?* □ *How's your mum?*

mumble /'mʌmbəl/ VERB [**mumbles, mumbling, mumbled**] to speak quietly or without opening your mouth enough, so that people cannot understand you □ *He mumbled something about not having enough money.*

mummy /'mʌmɪ/ NOUN [plural **mummies**]
1 a child's word for mother □ *Mummy, can we go now?* □ *Where's your mummy, Jake?*
2 a dead body that is rubbed with special substances and covered with cloth to stop it decaying □ *an Egyptian mummy*

mumps /mʌmps/ NOUN, NO PLURAL an infectious disease that children get, in which the neck becomes swollen and sore

munch /mʌntʃ/ VERB [**munches, munching, munched**] to eat something, especially noisily □ *Claire was happily munching her chocolate bar.*

mundane /mʌnˈdeɪn/ ADJECTIVE ordinary, happening often, and not exciting □ *mundane tasks*

municipal /mjuːˈnɪsɪpəl/ ADJECTIVE to do with a city or town and its local government □ *the municipal elections*

munitions /mjuːˈnɪʃənz/ PLURAL NOUN weapons and military equipment □ *a munitions factory*

mural /'mjʊərəl/ NOUN [plural **murals**] a picture that is painted directly onto a wall

murder /'mɜːdə(r)/ ► NOUN [plural **murders**] the crime of killing someone deliberately ⧆ *He admitted committing the murder.* ⧆ *He was charged with attempted murder (=trying to kill someone).*
► VERB [**murders, murdering, murdered**] to kill someone deliberately □ *She denies murdering her husband.*

• **murderer** /'mɜːdərə(r)/ NOUN [plural **murderers**] someone who has murdered another person

• **murderous** /'mɜːdərəs/ ADJECTIVE likely or intended to kill someone □ *a murderous attack*

murky /'mɜːkɪ/ ADJECTIVE [murkier, murkiest]
1 dark or dirty and difficult to see through □ *murky pond water*
2 dishonest and secret □ *the murky world of arms dealing*

murmur /'mɜːmə(r)/ ▶ VERB [murmurs, murmuring, murmured] to speak very quietly □ *He murmured something in her ear.*
▶ NOUN [*plural* murmurs]
1 something that is said very quietly
2 a low, continuous noise made by voices or sounds far away □ *We could hear the murmur of traffic in the distance.*

muscle /'mʌsəl/ NOUN [*plural* muscles] one of the parts in the body that are connected to bones and that cause the body to move by becoming shorter or longer □ *stomach muscles* ⚅ *Joe has pulled a muscle (=injured the muscle) in his leg.*
◆ PHRASAL VERB [muscles, muscling, muscled] muscle in to get involved in an activity that the people doing it do not want you to be involved in □ *Jane's trying to muscle in on the book club now.*
● **muscular** /'mʌskjʊlə(r)/ ADJECTIVE
1 having big, strong muscles □ *muscular arms*
2 to do with the muscles □ *muscular pain*

museum /mju:'zi:əm/ NOUN [*plural* museums] a building where collections of interesting things are arranged for people to see □ *the Natural History Museum*

mush /mʌʃ/ NOUN, NO PLURAL food that is soft and wet □ *Don't overcook the vegetables or they'll turn to mush.*

mushroom /'mʌʃrʊm/ ▶ NOUN [*plural* mushrooms] a type of fungus (=plant with no leaves or flowers) that you can eat, with a stem and a flat or round top □ *mushroom risotto*
▶ VERB [mushrooms, mushrooming, mushroomed] to increase in size or number very quickly □ *The use of mobile phones has mushroomed over the past decade.*

mushy /'mʌʃɪ/ ADJECTIVE [mushier, mushiest]
1 soft and wet
2 too romantic or emotional in a way that seems silly □ *mushy love songs*

music /'mju:zɪk/ NOUN, NO PLURAL
1 sounds arranged in patterns, sung or played by instruments ⚅ *Do you like classical music?* ⚅ *I've been listening to a lot of dance music recently.* □ *a music teacher*
2 the written sounds that represent a piece of music ⚅ *I wish I could read music.*

> ► Remember that the noun **music** is not used in the plural:
> ✓ *He listens to a lot of music.*
> ✗ *He listens to a lot of musics.*

● **musical** /'mju:zɪkəl/ ▶ ADJECTIVE

1 to do with music □ *She has no musical training.*
⚅ *Do you play a musical instrument?*
2 good at playing or singing music □ *The whole family is very musical.*
3 having a sound that is pleasant to listen to □ *a musical voice*
▶ NOUN [*plural* musicals] a play or film in which there is a lot of singing and dancing □ *He loves all the old Hollywood musicals.*
● **musician** /mju:'zɪʃən/ NOUN [*plural* musicians] someone who plays a musical instrument □ *She's one of our most talented young musicians.*

Muslim /'mʊzlɪm/ *or* **Moslem** /'mɒzləm/ ▶ NOUN [*plural* Muslims *or* Moslems] someone who believes in Islam
▶ ADJECTIVE to do with Islam □ *Friday is the Muslim holy day.*

muslin /'mʌzlɪn/ NOUN, NO PLURAL a thin cotton cloth

mussel /'mʌsəl/ NOUN [*plural* mussels] a small sea creature that has two joined black oval shells and can be eaten

must /məs, məst, *stressed* mʌst/ MODAL VERB
1 used to say that something is necessary □ *You must arrive for your interview on time.* □ *We mustn't be late.*
2 used to say that you think something is true □ *You must be very tired after such a long journey.* □ *They must have known about the money.*
3 used to make an offer or a suggestion □ *You must come over for dinner.* □ *We must meet up soon.*
4 used to say that you intend to do something □ *I must phone my mother this evening.*

mustache /'mʌstæʃ/ NOUN [*plural* mustaches] an American spelling of moustache

mustard /'mʌstəd/ NOUN, NO PLURAL a cold yellow or brown sauce used to give food a hot taste

muster /'mʌstə(r)/ VERB [musters, mustering, mustered] to feel or make other people feel enough courage, enthusiasm or energy to do something □ *I'm trying to muster up the energy to go out.*

mustn't /'mʌsənt/ a short way to say and write must not □ *I mustn't forget.*

> ► Note that **mustn't** means it is *necessary not to do something.* To say that it is *not necessary to do something,* use **don't need/have to:**
> ✓ *Come if you like but you don't need to.*
> ✗ *Come if you like but you mustn't to.*

musty /'mʌstɪ/ ADJECTIVE [mustier, mustiest] having a slightly wet, unpleasant smell □ *a musty old library*

mutate /mju:'teɪt/ VERB [mutates. mutating, mutated] when living things mutate, their genes (=parts that control characteristics) change so they develop a different form. A biology word.
● **mutation** /mju:'teɪʃən/ NOUN [*plural* mutations] when a living thing mutates. A biology word.

mute /mju:t/ ADJECTIVE not speaking or not able to speak
• **muted** /'mju:tɪd/ ADJECTIVE
1 not bright or loud □ *The room was tastefully decorated in muted colours.* □ *We could hear muted voices outside.*
2 not showing strong feelings □ *He gave a cautious and slightly muted response.*

mutilate /'mju:tɪleɪt/ VERB [mutilates, mutilating, mutilated] to damage someone's body badly, especially by cutting off a part of it □ *a mutilated body*
• **mutilation** /ˌmju:tɪ'leɪʃən/ NOUN, NO PLURAL when a body is mutilated

mutiny /'mju:tɪni/ ▶ NOUN [plural **mutinies**] when a group of people refuses to obey someone in authority, especially when sailors on a ship refuse to obey orders
▶ VERB [mutinies, mutinying, mutinied] to refuse to obey the orders of someone in authority □ *The crew mutinied against the captain.*

mutter /'mʌtə(r)/ VERB [mutters, muttering, muttered] to speak quietly, often when you are complaining □ *He muttered something about people never listening to him.*

mutton /'mʌtən/ NOUN, NO PLURAL meat from an adult sheep

mutual /'mju:tʃuəl/ ADJECTIVE
1 a mutual feeling is one that two or more people feel for each other □ *mutual admiration* □ *It's a relationship based on mutual respect.* □ *I don't like Maria and I'm sure the feeling's mutual.*
2 shared by two people □ *Peter and Ahmed have a mutual friend who works at the library.*
• **mutually** /'mju:tʃuəli/ ADVERB relating to both sides in a situation □ *We hope to come to a mutually acceptable agreement.*

muzzle /'mʌzəl/ ▶ NOUN [plural **muzzles**]
1 the nose and mouth of an animal such as a dog
2 a cover put over a dog's nose and mouth to stop it biting people
3 the open end of a gun, where the bullet comes out
▶ VERB [muzzles, muzzling, muzzled]
1 to put a muzzle on a dog
2 to stop someone from saying what they want to say

my /maɪ/ DETERMINER belonging to or to do with me □ *There's my son.* □ *Have you seen my boots anywhere?*

myriad /'mɪrɪəd/ ▶ NOUN **a myriad of something** a formal word meaning a very large number of things □ *We have a myriad of options now at the supermarket.*
▶ ADJECTIVE a formal word meaning very many □ *society's myriad problems*

myself /maɪ'self/ PRONOUN
1 the reflexive form of *I* □ *I was washing myself.* □ *I cut myself on the glass.* □ *I felt really proud of myself.*
2 used to show that you do something without any help from other people □ *I suppose I'll have to do it myself if no one else can be bothered.* ᵫ *I can't take care of him all by myself.*
3 used to emphasize the pronoun *I* □ *I have not seen the film myself.*
4 by myself not with or near other people □ *I live by myself.*
5 to myself without having to share with anyone else □ *I had the whole swimming pool to myself.*

mysterious /mɪ'stɪərɪəs/ ADJECTIVE
1 strange and difficult to understand or explain ᵫ *He died in mysterious circumstances.* □ *No one knows why she left – it's very mysterious.*
2 keeping something secret □ *Why are you being so mysterious about where you went last night?*
• **mysteriously** /mɪ'stɪərɪəsli/ ADVERB in a mysterious way □ *Both documents disappeared mysteriously one evening.*
• **mystery** /'mɪstəri/ NOUN [plural **mysteries**]
1 something strange which you do not understand and which cannot be explained ᵫ *She set out to solve the mystery of his disappearance.* ᵫ *What happened to her remains a mystery.*
2 *no plural* the quality of being strange, interesting and not completely understood ᵫ *She has an air of mystery about her.*
3 a film, book etc. with a story in which strange events are not explained until the end ᵫ *a murder mystery*

mystic /'mɪstɪk/ NOUN [plural **mystics**] someone who tries to understand things to do with religion or the spirit by praying or meditating (=removing all thoughts from the mind)
• **mystical** /'mɪstɪkəl/ ADJECTIVE
1 to do with mystics
2 involving magical or religious powers

mystify /'mɪstɪfaɪ/ VERB [mystifies, mystifying, mystified] if you are mystified by something, you do not understand or cannot explain it □ *Doctors were mystified by her symptoms.* □ *Helena looked mystified.*

myth /mɪθ/ NOUN [plural **myths**]
1 a story about ancient gods, heroes (=brave people) and monsters (=frightening creatures) □ *Greek and Roman myths*
2 something that many people believe, but which is not true ᵫ *The study dispels the myth* (=proves the myth wrong) *that late-night eating causes weight gain.*
• **mythical** /'mɪθɪkəl/ ADJECTIVE existing only in myths □ *mythical creatures like dragons and unicorns*
• **mythological** /ˌmɪθə'lɒdʒɪkəl/ ADJECTIVE to do with myth or mythology
• **mythology** /mɪ'θɒlədʒɪ/ NOUN, NO PLURAL stories about ancient gods and heroes (=brave people)

N*n*

N¹ *or* **n** /en/ the 14th letter of the alphabet

N² /en/ ABBREVIATION **north**

n/a /ˌen ˈeɪ/ ABBREVIATION not applicable; something you write on a form when it asks a question that you do not need to answer

nab /næb/ VERB [**nabs, nabbing, nabbed**]
1 an informal word meaning to take something quickly □ *The best seats had all been nabbed when we arrived.*
2 an informal word meaning to catch someone who has done something wrong □ *The police nabbed me parking on a yellow line.*

naff /næf/ ADJECTIVE [**naffer, naffest**] an informal word meaning not good or not fashionable □ *a rather naff website*

nag /næg/ VERB [**nags, nagging, nagged**]
1 to keep criticizing someone or complaining because they have not done something □ *I keep nagging him to go to the dentist's.*
2 if worry or doubts nag you, you cannot stop thinking about them □ *The thought that he might not contact me has been nagging at the back of my mind.*
● **nagging** /ˈnægɪŋ/ ADJECTIVE causing you worry or pain for a long time □ *I had nagging doubts about the safety of the expedition.*

nail /neɪl/ ▶ NOUN [*plural* **nails**]
1 the hard covering on top of the ends of your fingers and toes 🔁 *You need to cut your nails.* 🔁 *a pair of nail scissors*
2 a thin pointed piece of metal, used to join things together, especially pieces of wood
▶ VERB [**nails, nailing, nailed**] to attach or join something with a nail or nails □ *Nail the number on the door.*

naïve /naɪˈiːv/ ADJECTIVE too ready to trust other people because of not having much experience of life □ *He had taken advantage of her naïve belief in his honesty.*
● **naïvely** /naɪˈiːvlɪ/ ADVERB in a naïve way □ *I naïvely thought that he really loved me.*

naked /ˈneɪkɪd/ ADJECTIVE
1 not wearing any clothes □ *He stripped naked to the waist to cut the grass.* 🔁 *The children were running around stark naked in the sun.*
2 not covered or protected □ *a naked flame* □ *a naked light bulb*

3 a naked feeling or emotion is not hidden although it may be shocking □ *There was naked hostility in his eyes.*
4 the naked eye if you can see something with the naked eye, you can see it without the help of any special equipment □ *House mites are too small to be seen with the naked eye.*

name /neɪm/ ▶ NOUN [*plural* **names**]
1 the word or words that you use to refer to a person, animal, place or thing □ *What's your name?* 🔁 *Write your name and address here.* □ *I can't remember the name of the street.* □ *She changed her name when she got married.*
2 by name using your name □ *He asked for you by name.*
3 the reputation that a person or an organization has □ *The company has a name for quality.* 🔁 *He made his name as an international footballer .* 🔁 *This kind of behaviour gives football fans a bad name.* 🔁 *He is going to court to try to clear his name (=prove that bad things that have been said about him are not true).*
4 in the name of something if something is done in the name of something, it is done to help that thing be successful □ *Many wars have been fought in the name of religion.* □ *He led 15 Arctic expeditions in the name of science.*
▶ VERB [**names, naming, named**]
1 to give someone or something a name □ *They've named their son Samuel.* □ *The ship has not been named yet.*
2 to say what the name of someone or something is □ *The dead men will not be named until their families have been informed.*
3 to choose someone for a job or a position in an organization □ **+ as** *She was named as the next chief executive.*

> ➤ Note that to **name** someone is to give someone (often a baby) or something a name. To say the name of someone or something, use **be called**:
> ✓ *She is called Justina.*
> ✗ *She is named Justina.*

◆ PHRASAL VERB **name someone after someone** to give someone the same name as someone else to show respect or love for that person □ *She was named after her grandmother.*

• **nameless** /'neɪmlɪs/ ADJECTIVE
1 with no name, or with a name that is not known □ *a nameless soldier*
2 with a name that is not given ⊞ *A person who shall remain nameless has eaten all the chocolate.*

namely /'neɪmlɪ/ ADVERB used to give more detail about what you have just mentioned □ *Two of our members, namely the Grimes brothers, have won medals this term.*

namesake /'neɪmseɪk/ NOUN [plural **namesakes**] someone who has the same name as you

nanny /'nænɪ/ NOUN [plural **nannies**] a person whose job is to look after someone's child or children, usually in their own home

nano- /'nænəʊ/ PREFIX nano- is added to the beginning of words to mean 'extremely small' □ *nano-technology*

nap /næp/ NOUN [plural **naps**] a short sleep during the day ⊞ *The baby usually has a nap in the afternoon.*
▶ VERB [**naps, napping, napped**] to have a nap

nape /neɪp/ NOUN [plural **napes**] the back of your neck

napkin /'næpkɪn/ NOUN [plural **napkins**] a piece of cloth or paper that you can use during a meal to protect your clothes or clean your mouth or fingers □ *white linen napkins*

nappy /'næpɪ/ NOUN [plural **nappies**] a thick piece of soft cloth or paper that you fasten around a baby's bottom ⊞ *Could you change the baby's nappy?*

narcotic /nɑːˈkɒtɪk/ ▶ NOUN [plural **narcotics**]
1 any illegal drug
2 a drug that makes you want to sleep or stops you feeling pain
▶ ADJECTIVE making you want to sleep or feel less pain □ *Alcohol can have a narcotic effect.*

narrate /nəˈreɪt/ VERB [**narrates, narrating, narrated**] to speak the words of a story □ *The story was narrated by Stephen Fry.*

• **narration** /nəˈreɪʃən/ NOUN [plural **narrations**] the process of speaking the words of a story

• **narrative** /'nærətɪv/ NOUN [plural **narratives**] a story or a description of events □ *Too much description slows down the narrative.*

• **narrator** /nəˈreɪtə(r)/ NOUN [plural **narrators**] the person who speaks the words of a story

narrow /'nærəʊ/ ▶ ADJECTIVE [**narrower, narrowest**]
1 not very wide □ *She found a narrow door in the garden wall.* □ *The road was too narrow for overtaking.*
2 only just achieved □ *The Democrats won by a narrow margin.* ⊞ *We had a narrow escape when our car went off the road.*
3 limited in range □ *We have a narrow range of options.*
▶ VERB [**narrows, narrowing, narrowed**] to become narrower or to make something narrower □ *The road narrows as you leave the village.*
PHRASAL VERB **narrow something down** to reduce the number of possibilities □ *We've narrowed the candidates down to three.*

• **narrowly** /'nærəʊlɪ/ ADVERB by a small amount
□ *United were narrowly defeated by 6 goals to 5.*
□ *The bullet narrowly missed his heart.*

narrow-minded /ˌnærəʊˈmaɪndɪd/ ADJECTIVE not willing to accept new ideas or other people's opinions

nasal /'neɪzəl/ ADJECTIVE to do with the nose □ *a nasal spray*

nastiness /'nɑːstɪnɪs/ NOUN, NO PLURAL being nasty

nasty /'nɑːstɪ/ ADJECTIVE [**nastier, nastiest**]
1 very unpleasant or unkind □ *The drug left a nasty taste in my mouth.* □ *He's always saying nasty things about everybody.*
2 serious □ *a nasty accident*

nation /'neɪʃən/ NOUN [plural **nations**]
1 a country with its own government □ *the African nations*
2 the people of a country □ *Today the nation is voting for a new government.*

• **national** /'næʃənəl/ ▶ ADJECTIVE
1 to do with the whole of a country □ *They report local, national and international news.* ⊞ *National security is a priority.* ⊞ *House prices in the south-east are well above the national average.*
2 typical of a particular country □ *Paella is the national dish of Spain.* □ *Dancers in national costume greeted the president.*
▶ NOUN [plural **nationals**] someone who officially lives in a particular country □ *UK nationals require a visa to visit China.*

national anthem /ˌnæʃənəl ˈænθəm/ NOUN [plural **national anthems**] the official song of a country

nationalism /'næʃənəlɪzəm/ NOUN, NO PLURAL
1 the belief that the people of a country should have their own government □ *Irish nationalism*
2 a great love for your own country

• **nationalist** /'næʃənəlɪst/ ▶ NOUN [plural **nationalists**]
1 someone who wants their country to have its own government □ *Scottish nationalists*
2 someone with a great love for your own country
▶ ADJECTIVE wanting your country to have its own government □ *nationalist beliefs*

nationality /ˌnæʃəˈnælətɪ/ NOUN [plural **nationalities**] the state of being a legal member of a particular country □ *Omar has British nationality.* ⊞ *Louis has dual nationality because his mother is French and his father is American.*

nationalize or **nationalise** /'næʃənəlaɪz/ VERB [**nationalizes, nationalizing, nationalized**] if an industry or company is nationalized, the government takes control of it □ *In Britain the railways were nationalized for years.*

national park /ˌnæʃənəl ˈpɑːk/ NOUN [plural **national parks**] an area of countryside that the government protects so that the public can enjoy it

national service /ˌnæʃənəl ˈsɜːvɪs/ NOUN, NO PLURAL a period of time that young people have to spend in the army in some countries □ He did his national service in Northern Greece.

nationwide /ˌneɪʃənˈwaɪd/ ADJECTIVE, ADVERB in every part of a country □ The party is planning a nationwide drive to crack down on crime. □ The scheme will be launched nationwide next year.

native /ˈneɪtɪv/ ▶ ADJECTIVE
1 to do with the place you were born in □ His native language is French. □ In 1965 he left his native Austria.
2 to do with the first people who lived in a place □ the native inhabitants of New Zealand □ native art
3 native animals and plants live or grow naturally in a place and were not brought there from another place □ These plants are native to the west coast.
▶ NOUN [plural natives] someone who was born in a particular place □ She's a native of New South Wales.

Native American /ˌneɪtɪv əˈmerɪkən/ NOUN [plural Native Americans] a person from the race of people who lived in North or South America before the Europeans arrived there

NATO /ˈneɪtəʊ/ ABBREVIATION North Atlantic Treaty Organization; an organization of North American and European countries that give each other military support

natter /ˈnætə(r)/ ▶ VERB [natters, nattering, nattered] an informal word meaning to talk with someone about things that are not important □ We left them nattering about the wedding.
▶ NOUN, NO PLURAL an informal word meaning a conversation about things that are not important ⊞ They were having a natter about last night's match.

natural /ˈnætʃərəl/ ADJECTIVE
1 to do with or made by nature, not by people or machines □ the natural world □ an area of outstanding natural beauty ⊞ An earthquake is an example of a natural disaster. ⊞ The old man had died of natural causes.
2 normal or to be expected □ It's only natural to be a little nervous before a test.
3 a natural characteristic or ability is something you have from when you are born □ She has a natural flair for languages. □ His hair has a natural curl.

natural gas /ˌnætʃərəl ˈɡæs/ NOUN, NO PLURAL gas that comes from under the ground and can be used for heating and cooking

natural history /ˌnætʃərəl ˈhɪstəri/ NOUN, NO PLURAL the study of plants and animals

naturalist /ˈnætʃərəlɪst/ NOUN [plural naturalists] someone who studies plants and animals

naturalize or **naturalise** /ˈnætʃərəlaɪz/ VERB [naturalizes, naturalizing, naturalized] be naturalized to become an official member of a country you were not born in

naturally /ˈnætʃərəli/ ADVERB
1 as would be expected □ Naturally, we were annoyed not to win.

2 in a way that is normal □ Joe began to relax and act a bit more naturally.
3 having been born with a particular characteristic □ She has a naturally bubbly personality.
4 without help from anything artificial □ Let the skin heal naturally.

natural resources /ˌnætʃərəl rɪˈsɔːsɪz/ PLURAL NOUN substances that people use and that exist naturally, like wood, oil and water

natural selection /ˌnætʃərəl sɪˈlekʃən/ NOUN, NO PLURAL the way that plants and animals that are strong and suitable for the place where they live have more young and live longer than others. A biology word.

nature /ˈneɪtʃə(r)/ NOUN [plural natures]
1 no plural everything in the world that was not made or changed by people, such as animals, trees, the sea, etc. □ I love watching programmes about nature. □ the forces of nature
2 a person's character or qualities ⊞ It's human nature to protect one's family. ⊞ It's not in her nature to be unkind.
3 the type of a particular thing □ What is the nature of your complaint? ⊞ I like crime novels and books of that nature.

▶ Note that **nature** (sense 1) is never used with **the**:
✓ I've always loved nature.
✗ I've always loved the nature.

nature reserve /ˈneɪtʃə rɪˌzɜːv/ NOUN [plural nature reserves] an area of land where plants and animals are protected

naughtiness /ˈnɔːtɪnɪs/ NOUN, NO PLURAL bad behaviour or not doing what you are told to do

naughty /ˈnɔːti/ ADJECTIVE [naughtier, naughtiest] behaving badly or not doing what you are told to do □ You've been a very naughty little boy.

nausea /ˈnɔːzɪə/ NOUN, NO PLURAL the feeling that you are going to vomit □ The drug may cause nausea in some patients.
● **nauseating** /ˈnɔːzɪeɪtɪŋ/ ADJECTIVE making you feel as if you are going to vomit □ a nauseating smell
● **nauseous** /ˈnɔːzɪəs/ ADJECTIVE feeling as if you are going to vomit

nautical /ˈnɔːtɪkəl/ ADJECTIVE to do with ships, sailors and the sea □ The pub has a nautical theme.

naval /ˈneɪvəl/ ADJECTIVE to do with the navy □ an important naval base

navel /ˈneɪvəl/ NOUN [plural navels] the small hollow in the centre of your stomach where you were connected to your mother before you were born

navigate /ˈnævɪɡeɪt/ VERB [navigates, navigating, navigated]
1 to use a map or other equipment to find your way somewhere in a vehicle □ My mother always drove and my father had to navigate.
2 to find your way around or through a difficult place □ There were several flights of stairs to navigate with our luggage.

3 to deal with a complicated system or situation □ *We had to navigate the legal system.*
• **navigation** /ˌnævɪˈɡeɪʃən/ NOUN, NO PLURAL
1 the process of using maps or other equipment to find your way somewhere
2 when ships or aircraft travel on a journey
3 a way to understand and use a complicated system □ *The website has clear navigation tools.*
• **navigator** /ˈnævɪɡeɪtə(r)/ NOUN [*plural* **navigators**] someone who navigates in a vehicle

navy /ˈneɪvi/ NOUN [*plural* **navies**]
1 the navy military ships and the soldiers that work on them ▣ *Matt is hoping to join the navy.*
2 a very dark blue colour
• **navy** /ˈneɪvi/ ADJECTIVE of a very dark blue colour □ *a navy jacket*

navy blue /ˌneɪvi ˈbluː/ ▶ NOUN, NO PLURAL a very dark blue colour
▶ ADJECTIVE of a very dark blue colour □ *navy blue trousers*

NB /ˌen ˈbiː/ ABBREVIATION written at the start of a sentence to make someone pay particular attention to it □ *NB Latecomers will not be admitted.*

near /nɪə(r)/ ▶ PREPOSITION, ADVERB [**nearer, nearest**]
1 a short distance away □ *I live quite near Tom.* □ **+ to** *We rented a house near to the beach.* □ *Stand a little nearer and you'll be able to see better.* □ *They took him to the nearest hospital.*
2 a short time in the future □ *I don't want to take on extra work so near my exams.* ▣ *It's a bit early to plan the food – let's talk about it nearer the time.*
3 nowhere near not at all close in distance, time or a quality □ *The station is nowhere near here.* □ *He's nowhere near as handsome as his brother.*
4 near to something close to having achieved something or finished something □ *We're near to completing the plans for our journey.*
5 close to an amount or level □ *Their estimate was near our budget of £2 million.* □ *Temperatures were near freezing point.*
6 almost □ *It's near impossible to see that it's a fake.* □ *Her performance was near perfect.*
7 almost in a particular state □ *Sarah was near tears.*
▶ ADJECTIVE [**nearer, nearest**] not far away in distance or time ▣ *Will you be seeing Kate in the near future?* □ *He is a near neighbour of mine.* □ *The ball struck the near post.*
▶ VERB [**nears, nearing, neared**] to come close to something in distance or time □ *As we neared the building, the faces at the window became clearer.* □ *The building work is nearing completion.* □ *She is nearing the end of her time as president.*

nearby /ˌnɪəˈbaɪ/ ADJECTIVE, ADVERB quite close to where you are or the place you are talking about □ *We went to a nearby restaurant for dinner.* □ *Is there a bank nearby?*

➤ Note that **nearby** is not a preposition. The preposition with the same meaning is **near**:
✓ *Their apartment is very near the office.*
✗ *Their apartment is very nearby the office.*

nearly /ˈnɪəli/ ADVERB almost but not completely □ *We're nearly there.* □ *Nearly everyone had a good time.* □ *They've lived there for nearly three years.*

neat /niːt/ ADJECTIVE [**neater, neatest**]
1 tidy and arranged carefully □ *Your handwriting's very neat.* ▣ *Anna always keeps her room neat and tidy.*
2 done in a clever or skilful way □ *Rooney scored with a neat shot into the corner of the goal.*
3 a neat alcoholic drink is not mixed with another liquid □ *She was drinking neat whisky.*
4 a US word for good or nice □ *What a neat car!*
• **neatly** /ˈniːtli/ ADVERB in a tidy way □ *The papers were stacked neatly in the corner.*

necessarily /ˌnesəˈserɪli/ ADVERB not necessarily not in every case □ *Men aren't necessarily stronger than women.*

necessary /ˈnesəsəri/ ADJECTIVE needed in order to do something, get something or make something happen □ *The website lists the necessary skills for each job.* ▣ *I can work late if necessary.* □ **+ to do something** *Is it necessary to come early?* □ **+ for** *Good English is necessary for this job.*

necessitate /nɪˈsesɪteɪt/ VERB [**necessitates, necessitating, necessitated**] a formal word meaning to make something necessary □ *A manufacturer's fault necessitated the recall of the toys.*

necessity /nɪˈsesəti/ NOUN [*plural* **necessities**]
1 the need for something □ *There's absolutely no necessity for you to stay.* ▣ *She went back to work out of necessity.*
2 something that is needed □ *A warm coat is a necessity in this weather.*

neck /nek/ NOUN [*plural* **necks**]
1 the part of your body between your head and your shoulders □ *She had her headphones slung around her neck.*
2 the opening in a piece of clothing that you put your head through □ *This T-shirt is too baggy around the neck.*
3 the narrow part of a bottle near its opening
♦ IDIOMS **be up to your neck (in something)** to be very busy □ *Sue's up to her neck in work this week.* **neck and neck** if two people in a race or competition are neck and neck they are level with each other and either of them could win
➡ go to **stick** your neck out

necklace /ˈnekləs/ NOUN [*plural* **necklaces**] a piece of jewellery you wear around your neck □ *a diamond necklace*

nectar /'nektə(r)/ NOUN, NO PLURAL the sweet liquid that bees collect from flowers to make honey. A biology word.

nectarine /'nektərɪn/ NOUN [plural **nectarines**] a soft round fruit with a smooth red and yellow skin and yellow flesh with a lot of juice

née /neɪ/ ADJECTIVE a word used in front of the family name that a woman had before she got married □ *Mrs Janet Carter, née Tindale*

need /niːd/ ► VERB [**needs, needing, needed**]
1 if you need something, you must have it in order to exist or to do something □ *I need a sharp knife.* □ *I need your advice.* □ *Do you need any help?* □ *This provides the energy needed to heat the building.*
2 if you need to do something, you must do it, and if you need to have a particular quality, you must have it □ **+ to do something** *We all need to eat and drink.* □ *You need to make more effort with your studies.* □ *You need to be tough to be a doctor.*
3 someone doesn't need to do something/ needn't do something it is not necessary for someone to do something □ *She doesn't need to pay me.* □ *You needn't hurry.*
4 if something needs to be done, someone should do it □ **+ ing** *The dogs need feeding.* □ *These clothes need a wash.*
► NOUN [plural **needs**]
1 something that it is necessary to have □ **+ for** *There is an urgent need for more nurses.* 🔁 *These new buses meet the needs of wheelchair users.*
2 something that it is necessary to do □ **+ to do something** *He recognizes the need to invest more money.* 🔁 *There is no need to wait for me.*
3 be in need of something to need something □ *This house is in need of a thorough clean.*
4 no plural the state of not having enough food, money, etc. □ *We were shocked at the levels of need in the area.*

► Remember that the noun **need** takes the preposition **for**:
✓ *There is a need for more housing.*
✗ *There is a need of more housing.*

---

needle /'niːdəl/ NOUN [plural **needles**]
1 a small, pointed piece of metal used for sewing 🔁 *a needle and thread* 🔁 *Can you thread this needle for me?*
2 the thin, sharp metal part of a medical instrument for putting a drug into someone's body or taking blood out
3 a thin part on a piece of equipment that moves to point to a measurement □ *The needle on the dial was showing 80 mph.*
4 a long thin piece of wood, metal or plastic that is used for knitting (=making something with wool and two long sticks) 🔁 *a pair of knitting needles*

needless /'niːdlɪs/ ADJECTIVE not necessary □ *a needless waste of money* 🔁 *Needless to say, we never saw him again.*

needn't /'niːdənt/ a short way to say and write need not

needy /'niːdɪ/ ► ADJECTIVE [**needier, neediest**] not having enough money □ *We hope to provide help for needy families who have lost their homes.*
► NOUN **the needy** people who do not have enough money □ *The charity does a lot of work to help the needy.*

negative /'negətɪv/ ► ADJECTIVE
1 not feeling hope or enthusiasm □ *Since his illness he's been feeling very negative.* 🔁 *You'll never win until you lose that negative attitude.*
2 bad or harmful □ *The drug has a number of negative effects.*
3 if the result of a test is negative, it shows that something has not happened or been found □ *The result of the pregnancy test was negative.*
4 a negative word or phrase expresses the meaning 'not' or 'no' □ *a negative sentence* □ *We got a negative reply to our request.*
5 a negative number is less than zero, for example −5. A maths word.
► NOUN [plural **negatives**]
1 a film before it is printed, where light objects appear dark and dark objects appear light
2 a word or phrase that expresses the meaning 'not' or 'no'

---

negative equity /ˌnegətɪv 'ekwətɪ/ NOUN, NO PLURAL the situation when your house is worth less than the amount you owe to the organization that lent you the money for it

neglect /nɪ'glekt/ ► VERB [**neglects, neglecting, neglected**]
1 to not give someone or something enough care and attention □ *I've been neglecting the housework because I've been so busy.* □ *The couple are accused of neglecting their children.*
2 neglect to do something to not do something, often deliberately □ *She neglected to mention she had been sacked from her previous job.*
► NOUN, NO PLURAL when someone or something does not get enough care or attention □ *The poor garden has suffered years of neglect.*

negligence /'neglɪdʒəns/ NOUN, NO PLURAL when someone does not take enough care with something, especially if it harms someone □ *They sued their GP for medical negligence.*
● **negligent** /'neglɪdʒənt/ ADJECTIVE not careful enough in a job or activity that affects someone else □ *The court decided the train company had not been negligent.*

negligible /'neglɪdʒəbəl/ ADJECTIVE very small and not important □ *The extra money has had a negligible effect so far.*

negotiable /nɪˈɡəʊʃəbəl/ ADJECTIVE a negotiable price, offer, etc. can be discussed and changed □ *The price of the house was not negotiable.*

negotiate /nɪˈɡəʊʃɪeɪt/ VERB [**negotiates, negotiating, negotiated**]

1 to try to make an agreement with someone by having discussions with them □ *Employees are currently negotiating with managers over a pay rise.* □ *The two parties are hoping to negotiate a settlement to the conflict.*

2 to successfully move over, along or through something □ *He had trouble negotiating the last fence and came in third.*

• **negotiation** /nɪˌɡəʊʃɪˈeɪʃən/ NOUN [*plural* **negotiations**] when people discuss a subject in order to come to an agreement on it □ *Negotiations had reached a difficult stage.* 🕮 *We will not enter into negotiations with terrorists.*

• **negotiator** /nɪˈɡəʊʃɪeɪtə(r)/ NOUN [*plural* **negotiators**] someone who tries to make people come to an agreement by having discussions □ *a peace negotiator*

Negro /ˈniːɡrəʊ/ NOUN [*plural* **Negroes**] an old-fashioned word for a black person, that many people now think is offensive

neigh /neɪ/ ▶ VERB [**neighs, neighing, neighed**] to make the long high noise that a horse makes
▶ NOUN [*plural* **neighs**] the noise that a horse makes

neighbor /ˈneɪbə(r)/ NOUN [*plural* **neighbors**] the US spelling of **neighbour**

• **neighborhood** /ˈneɪbəhʊd/ NOUN [*plural* **neighborhoods**] the US spelling of **neighbourhood**

• **neighboring** /ˈneɪbərɪŋ/ ADJECTIVE the US spelling of **neighbouring**

neighbour /ˈneɪbə(r)/ NOUN [*plural* **neighbours**]

1 someone who lives near you or in the next house to you □ *We asked a neighbour to feed the cat.* 🕮 *Cecilia was our next-door neighbour for twelve years.*

2 a person or country that is near another person or country □ *Britain's nearest neighbour is France.*

• **neighbourhood** /ˈneɪbəhʊd/ NOUN [*plural* **neighbourhoods**] an area of a town or city □ *This is a pretty neighbourhood with a lot of trees and parks.*

• **neighbouring** /ˈneɪbərɪŋ/ ADJECTIVE next to or near □ *We spent the afternoon shopping in a neighbouring town.*

neither /ˈnaɪðə(r)/ ▶ DETERMINER, PRONOUN not either of two people or things □ *Neither woman seemed to understand English.* □ *Neither of us can go.*
▶ CONJUNCTION **neither ... nor** used when something negative is true of two people or things □ *Neither Peter nor Michael turned up.* □ *I neither know, nor care, where he is.*
▶ ADVERB used to say that a negative statement is also true about someone or something else □ *I can't go and neither can Fay.* □ *'I don't like garlic.' 'Neither does Richard.'* 🕮 *'I'm not working today.' 'Me neither, let's go out.'*

neon /ˈniːɒn/ NOUN, NO PLURAL a gas that shines very brightly when electricity passes through it. A chemistry word 🕮 *the neon lights of the city*

nephew /ˈnefjuː/ NOUN [*plural* **nephews**] the son of your brother or sister, or the son of your wife's or husband's brother or sister

nerve /nɜːv/ NOUN [*plural* **nerves**]

1 one of the connections like threads that carry messages between your brain and other parts of your body. A biology word □ *the optic nerve* □ *nerve endings*

2 the courage you need to do something difficult or dangerous □ **+ to do something** *I didn't have the nerve to jump.*

3 a way of behaving that is rude or likely to annoy people 🕮 *You've got a nerve talking to me like that!* □ **+ to do something** *I don't know how she had the nerve to criticize my driving.*

4 nerves nervous feelings 🕮 *She went for a walk to calm her nerves.*

♦ IDIOM **get on someone's nerves** to annoy someone, especially by doing the same thing many times □ *His constant complaints were getting on my nerves.*

nerve-racking /ˈnɜːvˌrækɪŋ/ ADJECTIVE making you feel very nervous □ *Driving in Rome was nerve-racking, to say the least.*

nervous /ˈnɜːvəs/ ADJECTIVE

1 worried or frightened □ *I get terribly nervous just before I go on stage.* □ *a nervous laugh* □ **+ about** *She was very nervous about her interview.*

2 to do with the nerves in your body. A biology word □ *nervous disorders*

nervous breakdown /ˌnɜːvəs ˈbreɪkdaʊn/ NOUN [*plural* **nervous breakdowns**] a mental illness in which someone is so worried, unhappy and tired that they cannot deal with their normal life □ *He had a nervous breakdown when he was only 17.*

nervously /ˈnɜːvəsli/ ADVERB in a worried, slightly frightened, way □ *She giggled nervously.*

nervousness /ˈnɜːvəsnɪs/ NOUN, NO PLURAL a worried, slightly frightened feeling □ *He struggled to hide his nervousness.*

nervous system /ˈnɜːvəs ˌsɪstəm/ NOUN [*plural* **nervous systems**] all the nerves in your body and the way they connect to your brain to send messages about feeling and movement. A biology word.

-ness /nɪs/ SUFFIX -ness is added to the end of adjectives to make nouns relating to the qualities or states of the adjectives □ *sadness*

nest /nest/ ▶ NOUN [*plural* **nests**] a place where birds or some kinds of insects and animals live and have their babies □ *We found a wasps' nest in a tree.*
▶ VERB [**nests, nesting, nested**] to build a nest

nestle /'nesəl/ VERB [nestles, nestling, nestled]
1 to press yourself into a warm and comfortable place or position □ *She nestled her head against his chest.*
2 to be in a protected, partly hidden place □ *We rented a cottage that nestled at the foot of the hill.*

net /net/ ► NOUN [plural **nets**]
1 a material made of crossed string or rope with holes between, or something made from this and used for a particular purpose ⌘ *a fishing net* ⌘ *a mosquito net* ⌘ *The trapeze artists performed without a safety net.*
2 a thin material made of crossed threads with holes between □ *net curtains*
3 the Net the Internet ⌘ *She spends hours surfing the Net.*
► VERB [nets, netting, netted]
1 to get something, especially a profit □ *The sale of his company netted him over $4 million.*
2 to kick or throw a ball into a net in a sport □ *Roberto netted his fifth goal in three matches.*
► ADJECTIVE
1 a net amount of money has had all the costs such as tax taken off it ⌘ *We made a net profit of over £3,000.*
2 the net result or effect of something is its result or effect when you consider all the parts of it
3 the net weight of something is its weight without its container

netball /'netbɔːl/ NOUN, NO PLURAL a game where two teams of players throw a ball to each other and try to score goals by throwing the ball through a high net

netting /'netɪŋ/ NOUN, NO PLURAL material made of crossed threads, ropes or wires with holes between. ⌘ *Wire netting surrounds the old church.*

nettle /'netəl/ NOUN [plural **nettles**] a wild plant that has leaves which hurt you if you touch them
➜ *go to* grasp the nettle

network /'netwɜːk/ NOUN [plural **networks**]
1 a system of roads, railways lines, etc. that cross and connect with one another □ *A strike has shut down the railway network.*
2 a group of people or companies that work together or help each other □ *She is lucky to have the support of a wide network of friends.* □ *The company has a network of dealers throughout the country.*
3 a system of computers that are all connected together so that they can share information
4 a group of television or radio companies that broadcast the same programmes □ *The show went out on a big cable network.*
● **networking** /'netwɜːkɪŋ/ NOUN, NO PLURAL
1 when someone uses social events to meet people who might help their job or business
2 when computers are connected together. A computing word.

neural /'njʊərəl/ ADJECTIVE to do with your nerves. A biology word.

neurologist /njʊə'rɒlədʒɪst/ NOUN [plural **neurologists**] a doctor who treats diseases which affect the nerves in your body
● **neurology** /njʊə'rɒlədʒɪ/ NOUN, NO PLURAL the study of the nerves in your body and the way they send messages to your brain, and of the diseases that affect them

neuron /'njʊərɒn/ or **neurone** /'njʊərəʊn/ NOUN [plural **neurons** or neurones] a nerve cell that sends messages between the brain and the body. A biology word.

neurotic /ˌnjʊə'rɒtɪk/ ADJECTIVE worrying about things too much □ *She is becoming neurotic about what she eats.*

neuter /'njuːtə(r)/ ► VERB [neuters, neutering, neutered] to do a medical operation on an animal so that it cannot have babies
► ADJECTIVE in the grammar of some languages, words that are neuter are not masculine or feminine and may have special pronouns, different endings for their adjectives, etc.

neutral /'njuːtrəl/ ► ADJECTIVE
1 not supporting either side in an argument, war or competition □ *The referee must remain neutral.*
2 a neutral colour is not strong or bright
► NOUN, NO PLURAL when the gears in a vehicle are not connecting the power of the engine to the wheels
□ *She put the car in neutral and put the handbrake on.*
● **neutrality** /njuː'trælɪtɪ/ NOUN, NO PLURAL the state of being neutral in an argument, war or competition
● **neutralize** or **neutralise** /'njuːtrəlaɪz/ VERB [neutralizes, neutralizing, neutralized] to prevent something from having an effect □ *Extra soldiers are intended to neutralize the threat of attack.*

neutron /'njuːtrɒn/ NOUN [plural **neutrons**] a part of the nucleus of an atom with no electrical charge. A physics word.

never /'nevə(r)/ ADVERB
1 not ever □ *I've never been abroad.* □ *It's never too late to learn.* □ *I promise never to say that again.* □ *I would never do anything to hurt you.*
2 used to express surprise □ *'Chris is getting married.' 'Never! I don't believe it.'*

> ► Note that **never** usually goes before a 'to infinitive'. It does not go between 'to' and the verb:
> ✓ I promise never to do it again.
> ✗ I promise to never do it again.

never-ending /ˌnevər'endɪŋ/ ADJECTIVE continuing for a long time or for ever □ *There was a never-ending stream of traffic outside our window.*

nevertheless /ˌnevəðə'les/ ADVERB despite that □ *The car isn't perfect, but it's very good nevertheless.*

new /njuː/ ADJECTIVE [newer, newest]
1 not existing before, or only recently made, found, invented, etc. □ *A new hospital is being built in the city.*

□ We are creating entirely new online materials.
□ These accusations are not new. ⊞ New technology has improved international communications.
2 only recently bought or received □ He bought a new jacket. □ I got a new bike for my birthday.
3 different □ I met my new boss today. □ He showed me a new way to make cheese sauce.
4 not familiar □ Working in a team is a new experience for me. □ **+ to** The business world is still new to her.
5 new to something if you are new to an area or an activity, you have only recently come there or started to do it □ She's still quite new to the job.

newborn /'nju:bɔːn/ ADJECTIVE a newborn baby has just been born

newcomer /'nju:kʌmə(r)/ NOUN [plural **newcomers**] a person who has recently arrived □ Catriona's family are newcomers to the village.

newfangled /ˌnju:'fæŋgəld/ ADJECTIVE new and complicated in a way that annoys you □ I can't get used to this newfangled mobile phone.

newly /'nju:lɪ/ ADVERB recently □ the newly appointed London Mayor

news /nju:z/ NOUN, NO PLURAL
1 new information □ **+ about** Have you heard the news about Raj? □ **+ of** News of her safe return was greeted with joy. □ **+ on** Is there any news on the completion date yet? ⊞ We've had some good news; Beth is pregnant. ⊞ I'm afraid I've got some bad news.
2 the news information about important events on the radio or television, or in newspapers, etc. ⊞ the local/national news □ They always watch the news at 10 o'clock.

➤ Remember that **news** is used with a singular verb:
✓ The news is so bad at the moment.
✗ The news are so bad at the moment.

---

newsagent /'nju:zeɪdʒənt/ NOUN [plural **newsagents**]
1 someone who sells newspapers and magazines
2 newsagent's a shop that sells newspapers and magazines and usually other things like sweets and cigarettes

newsgroup /'nju:zgru:p/ NOUN [plural **newsgroups**] a place on the Internet where people who are interested in a particular subject can leave messages. A computing word.

newsletter /'nju:zletə(r)/ NOUN [plural **newsletters**] a short report about a club or organization that is regularly sent to its members □ the monthly newsletter

newspaper /'nju:zpeɪpə(r)/ NOUN [plural **newspapers**]
1 large folded pieces of paper printed with reports and pictures about recent events and sold every day or every week □ I saw your picture in the newspaper. ⊞ He started out on the local newspaper.

2 no plural the paper that newspapers are printed on □ Wrap the glasses in newspaper and pack them carefully.

New Testament /ˌnju: 'testəmənt/ NOUN, NO PLURAL **the New Testament** the second part of the Christian Bible, written after Jesus Christ was born

New Year /ˌnju: 'jɪə(r)/ NOUN, NO PLURAL the first few days of January, when people often celebrate □ They're having a New Year's party. □ Happy New Year!

New Year's Day /ˌnju: jɪəz 'deɪ/ NOUN, NO PLURAL 1 January, the first day of the year

New Year's Eve /ˌnju: jɪəz 'iːv/ NOUN, NO PLURAL 31 December, the last day of the year

next /nekst/ ▶ ADJECTIVE
1 following or happening immediately after □ What's the next name on the list? □ I need to phone him in the next hour or so. □ The next morning he felt much better. □ Next time I see Sally, I'll ask her.
2 next week/Saturday/year, etc. the week/Saturday/year, etc. after this one □ Do you want to come round next weekend?
3 nearest to the place where you are now □ Take the next left. □ The next town is five miles away.
▶ ADVERB
1 immediately after something else □ What will happen next? □ Next we need to paint the walls.
2 the next best/most important, etc. the second best/most important, etc. □ Cycling was the next most popular form of exercise.
3 the time when you next do something is the first time you do it again □ When are you likely to next see Julie?
4 Whatever next? something you say when you are surprised about something that exists or has happened □ Blue roses? Whatever next?
▶ PREPOSITION
1 next to (a) in a position at the side of someone or something □ I put the book down next to her.
⊞ Nobody wants to live right next to a motorway. (b) in the second position of importance, quality, etc.
□ Next to France, Ireland is my favourite place for a holiday.
2 next to nothing almost nothing □ I earn next to nothing from my writing.
▶ PRONOUN
1 the person or thing that follows or happens immediately after someone or something else
□ Who's next to see the doctor? □ They've already sacked 20 staff – who's going to be next?
2 the week/Saturday/year, etc. after next two weeks/Saturdays/years, etc. from the present □ I'm going to New York the week after next.

next door /ˌnekst 'dɔ:(r)/ ADJECTIVE, ADVERB in the next house, building or room ⊞ We have very nice next door neighbours. □ Our office is next door to the station. □ We get on well with the people next door.

next of kin /ˌnekst əv ˈkɪn/ NOUN [plural **next of kin**] your closest relation □ *The army will inform his next of kin of his death.*

NHS /ˌenɪtʃes/ ABBREVIATION **the NHS** the National Health Service; the system which provides free medical treatment for people in the UK □ *He had the operation done on the NHS.*

nib /nɪb/ NOUN [plural **nibs**] the point of a pen where the ink comes out

nibble /ˈnɪbəl/ VERB [**nibbles, nibbling, nibbled**] to eat something with little bites □ *A mouse had nibbled right through the wires.*

nice /naɪs/ ADJECTIVE [**nicer, nicest**]
1 pleasant, good or attractive □ *If the weather's nice, we can go for a walk.* □ *She took me to a really nice restaurant.* 🕮 *Have a nice time in Germany!*
2 kind or friendly □ *That wasn't a very nice thing to do.* □ + **to** *She's always nice to the children.* □ + **of** *It was very nice of Rob to give me a lift.* □ + **about** *My tutor was really nice about my work.*
3 nice and... used to emphasize a positive quality □ *It was nice and warm in the kitchen.*
• **nicely** /ˈnaɪslɪ/ ADVERB
1 well □ *My carrots are coming along nicely this year.* □ *She played the piano very nicely.*
2 in a polite way 🕮 *Ask the lady nicely.*
• **niceness** /ˈnaɪsnɪs/ NOUN, NO PLURAL being pleasant or attractive

niche /niːʃ/ NOUN [plural **niches**]
1 a situation or job that you feel very comfortable and happy in 🕮 *She seems to have found her niche in life.*
2 a hollow space in a wall where objects can be put
3 an opportunity for a business or a product □ *We realized that there was a niche for a women-only decorating service.*

niche market /ˌniːʃ ˈmɑːkɪt/ NOUN [plural **niche markets**] when a product or a service is produced for only a small number of people who want it

nick /nɪk/ ▶ NOUN [plural **nicks**]
1 a small cut □ *He had a nick on his chin.*
2 the nick an informal word for a prison or a police station
3 in good/bad nick an informal phrase meaning in good or bad condition □ *My car's six years old but in pretty good nick.*
♦ IDIOM **in the nick of time** just before it is too late □ *We got out of the burning house in the nick of time.*
▶ VERB [**nicks, nicking, nicked**]
1 an informal word meaning to steal something □ *Who's nicked my pen?*
2 an informal word meaning to arrest someone □ *Connor got nicked for speeding last night.*
3 to make a very small cut in something □ *I nicked my finger on a tin can.*

nickel /ˈnɪkəl/ NOUN [plural **nickels**]
1 a white metal that is often mixed with other metals. A chemistry word.
2 an American or Canadian coin worth five cents

nickname /ˈnɪkneɪm/ ▶ NOUN [plural **nicknames**] a name that you use for someone that is not their real name □ *His nickname at school was 'President' because his real name's Kennedy.*
▶ VERB [**nicknames, nicknaming, nicknamed**] to call someone by a nickname □ *They nicknamed him 'Scottie'.*

nicotine /ˈnɪkətiːn/ NOUN, NO PLURAL the poisonous substance in tobacco

niece /niːs/ NOUN [plural **nieces**] the daughter of your brother or sister, or the daughter of your wife's or husband's brother or sister

nifty /ˈnɪftɪ/ ADJECTIVE [**niftier, niftiest**] an informal word meaning effective and designed in a clever way □ *a nifty little gadget*

niggle /ˈnɪgəl/ VERB [**niggles, niggling, niggled**] to worry or annoy you slightly but for a long time □ *The question was niggling at the back of her mind.*
• **niggling** /ˈnɪglɪŋ/ ADJECTIVE not very serious but not going away □ *a niggling back injury* □ *She still had some niggling doubts about his suitability for the job.*

night /naɪt/ NOUN [plural **nights**]
1 the time when it is dark and when people usually sleep 🕮 *I hardly slept last night.* 🕮 *I spent the night at my sister's.* 🕮 *The dog woke me up in the middle of the night.* 🕮 *He's been having sleepless nights worrying about work.*
2 at night during the time when it is dark □ *I don't walk the streets on my own at night.*
3 the part of the evening before you go to bed 🕮 *I went out with David last night.* □ *Are you doing anything on Saturday night?* □ *I'm having a night out with my friends on Friday.*
4 Good night. something you say when you leave someone in the evening, or when you or they go to bed
5 have an early/a late night to go to bed early/late

> ➤ Notice that we usually say **at night** to mean 'during the time when it is dark':
> ✓ *I never drive at night.*
> ✗ *I never drive in the night.*

nightclub /ˈnaɪtklʌb/ NOUN [plural **nightclubs**] a place where people can dance and drink late at night

nightdress /ˈnaɪtdres/ NOUN [plural **nightdresses**] a loose dress that a woman or girl sleeps in

nightfall /ˈnaɪtfɔːl/ NOUN, NO PLURAL the time when it starts to get dark in the evening □ *They set off at nightfall.*

nightingale /ˈnaɪtɪŋgeɪl/ NOUN [plural **nightingales**] a small bird that sings beautifully

nightly /ˈnaɪtlɪ/ ADJECTIVE, ADVERB every night □ *He makes nightly visits to the park with the dog.* □ *Episodes of the show are broadcast nightly.*

nightmare /ˈnaɪtmeə(r)/ NOUN [plural **nightmares**]
1 a frightening dream □ *Older children often have nightmares.*

2 a very unpleasant experience □ *The drive home was a complete nightmare.*

night shift /ˈnaɪt ˌʃɪft/ NOUN [plural **night shifts**]
1 a period of time when people work during the night □ *I'm doing night shifts this week.*
2 the group of people who work in a place at night

nightshirt /ˈnaɪtʃɜːt/ NOUN [plural **nightshirts**] a long loose shirt for sleeping in

nil /nɪl/ NOUN, NO PLURAL
1 a score of zero in a game or sport □ *The score was eight-nil.*
2 used to mean that something does not exist □ *Their chances of survival are virtually nil.*

nimble /ˈnɪmbəl/ ADJECTIVE [**nimbler, nimblest**]
1 able to move quickly and easily □ *She darted around with nimble movements.*
2 able to react quickly to a situation □ *The more nimble companies have been able to make big profits.*
• **nimbly** /ˈnɪmblɪ/ ADVERB in a nimble way □ *He jumped nimbly aside to let the bike pass.*

nine /naɪn/ NUMBER [plural **nines**] the number 9

nineteen /ˌnaɪnˈtiːn/ NUMBER [plural **nineteens**] the number 19

nineteenth /ˌnaɪnˈtiːnθ/ NUMBER 19th written as a word

ninetieth /ˈnaɪntiəθ/ NUMBER 90th written as a word

ninety /ˈnaɪntɪ/ NUMBER [plural **nineties**]
1 the number 90
2 the nineties the years between 1990 and 1999

ninth /naɪnθ/ ▶ NUMBER 9th written as a word
▶ NOUN [plural **ninths**] 1/9 ; one of nine equal parts of something

nip /nɪp/ ▶ VERB [**nips, nipping, nipped**]
1 an informal word meaning to go somewhere quickly or for a short time □ *I must just nip to the shops.*
2 to bite someone or to press someone's skin in a quick, sharp way □ *The dog was nipping at his ankles.*
• IDIOM **nip something in the bud** to stop something before it can develop or grow □ *These problems should be nipped in the bud.*
▶ NOUN [plural **nips**]
1 a small bite or sharp pressing movement □ *The insects can give you a nasty nip.*
2 a cold feeling ⊞ *There's a nip in the air today.*

nipple /ˈnɪpəl/ NOUN [plural **nipples**] the darker, pointed part on a woman's breasts or a man's chest

nippy /ˈnɪpɪ/ ADJECTIVE [**nippier, nippiest**]
1 an informal word meaning cold □ *It's a bit nippy out today.*
2 an informal word meaning able to move quickly □ *a nippy little car*

nitrate /ˈnaɪtreɪt/ NOUN [plural **nitrates**] a chemical that is used to make crops grow better. A chemistry word.

nitrogen /ˈnaɪtrədʒən/ NOUN, NO PLURAL a colourless gas that is found in air. A chemistry word.

no /nəʊ/ ▶ EXCLAMATION
1 used to refuse, disagree or give a negative answer

□ *'Can you give me a lift to the station?' 'No, sorry, I need to get straight home.'* □ *'Tim's really stupid.' 'No he isn't!'* □ *'Can I have some more cake?' 'No, you've had more than enough already.'* □ *'Are you all right?' 'No, I've got my foot stuck.'*
2 used to agree with a negative statement □ *'The weather's not very good today.' 'No, it's a bit cold.'*
3 used to express shock or surprise ⊞ *Oh no! I've left my passport at home!* □ *'Chris and Alice are getting married.' 'No! They've only known each other a few weeks!'*
• IDIOM **not take no for an answer** to refuse to accept that someone will not do something or does not want something
▶ DETERMINER
1 not any □ *They have no money.* □ *There is no need to bring a coat.* □ *It is no secret that he hates his job.* □ *No decisions have been taken yet.*
2 used to say that something is not allowed □ *No smoking.*
▶ ADVERB not any □ *She's no better this morning.*
⊞ *No fewer than four players were sent off during the match.* □ *Payment is due no later than the 15th.*

No. *or* **no.** /nəʊ/ ABBREVIATION number

nobility /nəˈbɪlətɪ/ NOUN, NO PLURAL
1 the nobility people in the highest social groups of society □ *the Italian nobility*
2 the quality of being noble □ *There was a certain nobility about him.*

noble /ˈnəʊbəl/ ADJECTIVE [**nobler, noblest**]
1 brave and honest, or helping other people in a way that people admire □ *We are doing important work for a noble cause.*
2 belonging to a high social class □ *He comes from a noble family.*

nobleman /ˈnəʊbəlmən/ NOUN [plural **noblemen**] a man who belongs to one of the highest social groups in a society

noblewoman /ˈnəʊbəlwʊmən/ NOUN [plural **noblewomen**] a woman who belongs to one of the highest social groups in a society

nobly /ˈnəʊblɪ/ ADVERB in a way that is brave and honest or helps other people in a way that people admire □ *He went nobly into battle.*

nobody /ˈnəʊbədɪ/ ▶ PRONOUN not any person □ *Nobody tells me what to do!* □ *There was nobody at home.* ⊞ *Nobody else noticed it.*

▶ Note that **nobody** is always followed by a singular verb:
✓ *Nobody has said anything.*
✗ *Nobody have said anything.*

▶ NOUN [plural **nobodies**] a person who is not at all important □ *He's just a nobody.*

nocturnal /nɒkˈtɜːnəl/ ADJECTIVE
1 nocturnal animals are active at night. A biology word □ *Lemurs are nocturnal animals.*
2 happening at night

nod /nɒd/ ▶ VERB [**nods, nodding, nodded**]
1 to move your head up and down, especially to agree or to say 'yes' 🔁 *He nodded his head enthusiastically.* 🔁 *His wife nodded in agreement.*
2 to move your head in a particular direction to point to something □ *She nodded towards the door.*
◆ PHRASAL VERB **nod off** an informal word meaning to start sleeping □ *Grandma nodded off in her chair.*
▶ NOUN [*plural* **nods**] when you nod your head 🔁 *He gave a small nod.*

noise /nɔɪz/ NOUN [*plural* **noises**]
1 a sound 🔁 *Did you hear a noise outside?* 🔁 *The bird was making screeching noises.* 🔁 *There was a sudden, loud noise.*
2 *no plural* sound that is loud or unpleasant □ *+ of* *He shouted over the noise of the engine.* 🔁 *Could you please make a little less noise?* 🔁 *The background noise made it difficult to hear.*
● **noisily** /ˈnɔɪzɪlɪ/ ADVERB in a way that makes a lot of noise □ *A helicopter circled noisily overhead.*
● **noisy** /ˈnɔɪzɪ/ ADJECTIVE [**noisier, noisiest**] making a lot of noise □ *a noisy party* □ *Some people complain about noisy neighbours.* □ *The fridge seems very noisy – is there something wrong with it?*

nomad /ˈnəʊmæd/ NOUN [*plural* **nomads**] a member of a group of people, usually with animals, who move from place to place instead of living in the same place all the time
● **nomadic** /nəʊˈmædɪk/ ADJECTIVE to do with or like a nomad □ *nomadic tribes*

nominate /ˈnɒmɪneɪt/ VERB [**nominates, nominating, nominated**] to suggest someone for a job, position or prize □ *Charles nominated Peter as leader of the group.* □ *She was nominated for an Oscar.*
● **nomination** /ˌnɒmɪˈneɪʃən/ NOUN [*plural* **nominations**] when someone or something is nominated for something 🔁 *He's seeking the Republican nomination for governor.* 🔁 *She received a Grammy nomination for her debut album.*
● **nominee** /ˌnɒmɪˈniː/ NOUN [*plural* **nominees**] a person who has been nominated for a job, position or prize □ *a presidential nominee*

non- /nɒn/ PREFIX non- is added to the beginning of words to mean 'not' □ *a non-smoker* (=someone who does not smoke)

nonchalance /ˈnɒnʃələns/ NOUN, NO PLURAL the quality of being nonchalant □ *We were impressed by his nonchalance.*

nonchalant /ˈnɒnʃələnt/ ADJECTIVE calm and not worried or excited □ *He tried to sound nonchalant.*

non-committal /ˌnɒnkəˈmɪtəl/ ADJECTIVE avoiding giving a clear opinion or decision □ *The minister gave a typically non-committal reply.*

nondescript /ˈnɒndɪskrɪpt/ ADJECTIVE very ordinary and boring, with no noticeable qualities □ *They live in a rather nondescript bungalow.*

none /nʌn/ ▶ PRONOUN not any □ *+ of* *None of them are going to admit to being wrong.* □ *We looked for more biscuits but there were none left.* 🔁 *Most people there ate little food, or none at all.*
▶ ADVERB
1 **none the less** nonetheless
2 not at all or not very 🔁 *I heard the answer but I'm none the wiser* (=I still do not understand). 🔁 *His feet were none too clean.*

nonentity /nɒnˈentɪtɪ/ NOUN [*plural* **nonentities**] someone who is not important or interesting □ *Most of the other candidates are political nonentities.*

nonetheless /ˌnʌnðəˈles/ ADVERB despite that □ *It would not be easy; nonetheless, he intended to try his best.* □ *There have been one or two delays; the road will open on time, nonetheless.*

non-existent /ˌnɒnɪgˈzɪstənt/ ADJECTIVE not existing □ *Medical facilities are almost non-existent in this area.*

non-fiction /ˌnɒnˈfɪkʃən/ NOUN, NO PLURAL writing that is about real facts, not invented stories

nonplussed /ˌnɒnˈplʌst/ ADJECTIVE surprised and confused □ *For a moment, Sylvia looked nonplussed.*

nonsense /ˈnɒnsəns/ NOUN, NO PLURAL
1 something that is not true or sensible 🔁 *His theory is a load of nonsense.* 🔁 *You're talking nonsense.* 🔁 *These reports are absolute nonsense.*
2 silly behaviour □ *Stop your nonsense now please.*
3 **make a nonsense of something** to make something seem stupid or unreasonable □ *It made a complete nonsense of all my plans.*
● **nonsensical** /nɒnˈsensɪkəl/ ADJECTIVE not true or reasonable □ *It would be nonsensical to pay someone to do the work and then do it yourself.*

non-stop /ˌnɒnˈstɒp/ ADJECTIVE, ADVERB without a rest or a pause □ *There was non-stop hammering from the room above.* □ *It's rained non-stop for three days.*

non-toxic /ˌnɒnˈtɒksɪk/ ADJECTIVE not poisonous □ *We only use non-toxic plastics.*

noodle /ˈnuːdəl/ NOUN [*plural* **noodles**] a long thin piece of pasta

nook /nʊk/ NOUN [*plural* **nooks**] a small corner or space, especially where something can be hidden
◆ IDIOM **every nook and cranny/all the nooks and crannies** every part of a place □ *I've cleaned every nook and cranny of the flat.*

noon /nuːn/ NOUN, NO PLURAL twelve o'clock in the middle of the day □ *We'll have our lunch at noon.* □ *It was a few minutes past noon.*

no one *or* **no-one** /ˈnəʊwʌn/ PRONOUN not any person □ *No one's in at the moment.* □ *No one knows what happened.* □ *There was no one to ask.* 🔁 *There was no one else in the building.*

> ➤ Note that **no one** is always followed by a singular verb:
> ✓ *No one tells me anything.*
> ✗ *No one tell me anything.*

noose /nu:s/ NOUN [*plural* **nooses**] a circle of rope that becomes tighter when the end is pulled, used to kill people or catch animals

nor /nɔː(r)/ CONJUNCTION
1 neither ... nor used when something negative is true of two people or things □ *Neither Jack nor Jenny is at home.* □ *Neither the teachers nor the parents are happy with the situation.*
2 used after a negative statement to say that the same is true for someone else □ *He didn't see anything unusual, and nor did any of his friends.* □ *I'm sure Jack wouldn't like that and nor would I.*

norm /nɔːm/ NOUN [*plural* **norms**] what people usually do or what usually happens 🔁 *It has become the norm to send young children to nursery school.* □ *He wrote about changing social norms.*

normal /'nɔːməl/ ADJECTIVE
1 usual and expected □ + *to do something It's normal to feel hungry at lunchtime.* □ + *for This temperature is normal for August.* □ *He just wants to live a normal life.* 🔁 *There's been a lot of building work, but we should be back to normal soon.*
2 as normal in the usual and expected way □ *Conditions were tough, but we just carried on as normal.*
• **normality** /nɔː'mælətɪ/ NOUN, NO PLURAL when things are normal □ *After all the excitement it was good to return to normality.*
• **normally** /'nɔːməlɪ/ ADVERB
1 usually □ *We normally go to bed pretty early.* □ *Normally, I drive to work.* □ *I don't normally do this kind of thing.*
2 in the usual and expected way □ *This plant has developed normally, but the other one is diseased.*

north /nɔːθ/ ▶ NOUN, NO PLURAL
1 the direction that is to your left when you are facing the rising sun
2 the part of a country or the world that is in the north □ *He lives in the north of England.*
▶ ADJECTIVE, ADVERB in or towards the north □ *the cold north wind* □ *We were travelling north on the motorway.*
• **northbound** /'nɔːθbaʊnd/ ADJECTIVE moving or going towards the north 🔁 *northbound traffic*

north-east /ˌnɔːθ'iːst/ ▶ NOUN, NO PLURAL
1 the direction between north and east
2 the part of a country between the north and the east □ *the north-east of Scotland*
▶ ADJECTIVE, ADVERB in or towards the north-east □ *The north-east region of Spain.*

northerly /'nɔːðəlɪ/ ADJECTIVE coming from, or going towards, the north □ *a northerly breeze* □ *going in a northerly direction* □ *the island's most northerly point*

northern /'nɔːðən/ ADJECTIVE in or from the north □ *the cold northern climate* □ *Northern districts will have some rain.*
• **northerner** /'nɔːðənə(r)/ NOUN [*plural* **northerners**] a person from the north

North Pole /ˌnɔːθ 'pəʊl/ NOUN, NO PLURAL the North Pole the point on the Earth that is furthest north

northward /ˌnɔːθwəd/ *or* **northwards** /'nɔːθwədz/ ADVERB to or towards the north □ *We cycled northwards for several miles.*

north-west /ˌnɔːθ'west/ ▶ NOUN, NO PLURAL
1 the direction between north and west
2 the part of a country between the north and the west □ *the north-west of England*
▶ ADJECTIVE, ADVERB in or towards the north-west

nose /nəʊz/ NOUN [*plural* **noses**]
1 the part of your face that you breathe and smell through 🔁 *I need to blow my nose.* 🔁 *I had sore eyes and a runny nose.*
2 the front part of something that sticks out, for example, the front of an aircraft
♦ IDIOMS get up someone's nose an informal phrase meaning to annoy someone □ *He really gets up my nose with his constant boasting.* look down your nose at someone/something to act as if you think that someone or something is not good enough □ *I saw the way she looked down her nose at our staff.* poke/stick your nose in/into something an informal phrase meaning to be too interested in something that does not involve you □ *I don't want him poking his nose into my business.* put someone's nose out of joint to offend someone □ *He talked to Ally all evening, and I could see that Anna had her nose put out of joint.* turn your nose up at something to refuse to accept something because you do not think it is good enough for you □ *She turned her nose up at my soup.* under someone's nose if something happens under someone's nose, they are there when it happens, but they do not notice □ *He was rescued from under the noses of his guards.*
➡ go to have/keep your nose to the *grindstone*
♦ PHRASAL VERB [**noses, nosing, nosed**] nose about/around (somewhere) to look around a place, often in order to find information □ *I found him nosing around in my office.*

nosedive /'nəʊzdaɪv/ ▶ VERB [**nosedives, nosediving, nosedived**]
1 to fall very quickly in value or quality □ *His career nosedived.*
2 to fall very quickly towards the ground □ *The two-seater plane nosedived into a field.*
▶ NOUN [*plural* **nosedives**]
1 a sudden loss of value or quality 🔁 *The company's shares took a nosedive.*

2 when an aircraft falls very quickly towards the ground ⌾ *The plane went into a nosedive.*

nosey /'nəʊzɪ/ ADJECTIVE another spelling of **nosy**

nostalgia /nɒ'stældʒə/ NOUN, NO PLURAL a feeling of mixed happiness and sadness when you remember times in the past □ *The programme prompted a wave of nostalgia for his youth.*

• **nostalgic** /nɒ'stældʒɪk/ ADJECTIVE thinking of or making you remember happy times in the past □ *We enjoyed a nostalgic evening of black and white movies.*

nostril /'nɒstrɪl/ NOUN [plural **nostrils**] one of the two openings in your nose that you breathe and smell through

nosy /'nəʊzɪ/ ADJECTIVE [**nosier, nosiest**] always wanting to find out about other people and what they are doing □ *I shut the garage door because of the nosy neighbours.* □ *I'm sorry for being so nosy.*

not /nɒt/ ADVERB

1 used after verbs like *be* and *do* and modal verbs to make negative sentences. It often becomes **n't** when it is added to verbs □ *I'm not going.* □ *They have not made a decision yet.* □ *It isn't fair.* □ *I can't hear you.*
2 used to give the next words or phrase a negative meaning □ *I told her not to look.* □ *Not everyone was happy with the decision.* □ *'Are you ready?' 'Not yet.'* □ *'Did it upset you?' 'Not at all.'* □ *Let's not go there again.*
3 used with verbs like *hope* and *suspect* or adverbs like *certainly* or *definitely* to make a negative reply □ *'Will you be much longer?' 'I hope not.'* □ *'Can I borrow £5?' 'Certainly not.'*
4 *or not* used to express a negative possibility □ *I don't know if he'll be there or not.*
5 *not only ... but* used to say that more than one thing has happened or is true □ *Not only was he rude, but he left without paying the bill.*
6 *not a/one* used to emphasize that there is or was no thing or person □ *Not one of his students passed the exam.* □ *There was not a drop of water to drink.*

► Note that **not** usually goes before a 'to infinitive'. It does not go between 'to' and the verb:
✓ He told me **not to** be late
✗ He told me to **not** be late.

notable /'nəʊtəbəl/ ADJECTIVE important and worth remembering □ *The most notable part of the evening was the music.* ⌾ *The whole family were there, with one notable exception.*

• **notably** /'nəʊtəblɪ/ ADVERB especially □ *I loved the old buildings, notably the palace.*

notch /nɒtʃ/ NOUN [plural **notches**]
1 a small, V-shaped cut in something □ *We cut notches in a stick as the days passed.*
2 a level of quality or amount □ *He'll have to raise his game a few notches.*

♦ PHRASAL VERB [**notches, notching, notched**] **notch something up** to achieve something □ *He notched up the 85th win of his career.*

note /nəʊt/ ► NOUN [plural **notes**]
1 a short piece of writing to help you remember something ⌾ *I made a note of his phone number.* □ *I've got a note of all their names.*
2 a short letter ⌾ *I wrote her a note to say how sorry I was.* ⌾ *He scribbled a note to his wife.*
3 notes information that you write down when you are reading a book, in a lesson, etc. ⌾ *There is a handout, so you don't need to take notes.*
4 take note to notice something or to pay attention to something □ *We failed to take note of the speed regulations.* □ *Cyclists take note: a helmet could save your life.*
5 a short explanation of something in a book □ *There are notes at the end of each chapter.*
6 a feeling or quality ⌾ *His speech struck just the right note of optimism.* □ *On a happier note, I am pleased to welcome our new assistant.*
7 a piece of paper money □ *a five pound note*
8 a single musical sound or the written sign for it □ *I can't reach the high notes.*

► VERB [**notes, noting, noted**]
1 to notice something or to pay attention to something □ *+ that* *I noted that she always wore red, and wondered why.* □ *We noted the absence of the prince.*
2 to say or write something □ *+ that* *He also noted that the building seemed in need of repair.* □ *She noted sadly that most of the trees have been cut down.*
♦ PHRASAL VERB **note something down** to write something down so that you will not forget it □ *I noted down the train times.*

notebook /'nəʊtbʊk/ NOUN [plural **notebooks**]
1 a small book that you use to write things down in
2 a very small computer that you can carry around. A computing word.

notepad /'nəʊtpæd/ NOUN [plural **notepads**]
1 several pieces of paper joined together at one end, used for writing
2 a small computer that you can carry around. A computing word.

notepaper /'nəʊtpeɪpə(r)/ NOUN, NO PLURAL plain paper that you use for writing letters on □ *a sheet of headed notepaper*

nothing /'nʌθɪŋ/ PRONOUN
1 not anything □ *There's nothing to eat.* □ *There's nothing wrong with me.* □ *He carried on as if nothing had happened.* ⌾ *There was nothing else we could do.* ⌾ *I've heard nothing but* (=only) *praise for her work.*
2 not something important or valuable □ *'What are you writing?' 'Oh, it's nothing – just a little poem.'*
3 be/have nothing to do with someone if something is nothing to do with you, there is no reason for you to know about it or be involved with it □ *It's nothing to do with you what I spend my money on.*

4 for nothing (a) without being paid □ *He mended my car for nothing.* (b) with no successful result □ *You mean we did all that work for nothing?*

5 have nothing to do with something to not be involved in something □ *I had nothing to do with the decision.*

6 have nothing to lose to be in a situation where it is worth taking a risk because even if you fail, it will not be worse □ *I had nothing to lose, so I told him exactly what I thought.*

7 nothing like (a) not at all similar □ *He's nothing like his brother.* (b) not almost □ *The water's nothing like hot enough yet.*

8 nothing much not a lot or nothing important □ *'What did you have for lunch?' 'Nothing much.'*

9 there's nothing like used to say that something is the best thing □ *There's nothing like a bit of sunshine to cheer you up.*

10 There's nothing to it. used to say that something is easy to do □ *Just slip the rope over the hook – there's nothing to it.*

11 stop at nothing if someone would stop at nothing to achieve something, they would do anything, even something bad, to achieve it

➤ Remember that **nothing** is not used with other negative words, such as 'not' and 'never':
✓ She said nothing.
✗ She didn't say nothing. □ *She didn't say anything.*

● **nothingness** /ˈnʌθɪŋnɪs/ NOUN, NO PLURAL a state where nothing exists

notice /ˈnəʊtɪs/ ➤ VERB [**notices, noticing, noticed**] to become aware of something because you see, hear, feel, smell or taste it □ *I noticed a funny smell in the hall.* □ *Did you notice the way George was looking at Emily?* □ **+ that** *I noticed that the kitchen window was open.* □ **+ question word** *He noticed how she kept checking her mobile.*

➤ Note that the verb **notice** is *not* used with the verbs 'can' and 'could':
✓ I noticed that she was thinner.
✗ I could notice that she was thinner.

➤ NOUN [*plural* **notices**]

1 a written sign □ *a notice pinned on the board* □ *A handwritten notice on the door said 'Closed'.* □ *The council has put up warning notices next to the river.*

2 *no plural* attention 🕮 *No one took any notice of* (=paid attention to) *her.* 🕮 *It's come to our notice that you are always late.* 🕮 *It didn't escape my notice that Jo left early.*

3 *no plural* a warning about something that is going to happen 🕮 *Please give me notice if you plan to visit.* 🕮 *We have to be ready to leave at a moment's notice.* 🕮 *The schedule was changed at short notice.*

4 your notice when you officially tell your employer that you are going to leave your job, or the time you work after this 🕮 *Cathy's handed in her notice.*

5 until further notice until someone says that the situation has changed □ *The museum is closed until further notice.*

noticeable /ˈnəʊtɪsəbəl/ ADJECTIVE obvious or easy to see □ *There was a noticeable difference in his appearance.* □ *The most noticeable feature was the smell.*

● **noticeably** /ˈnəʊtɪsəblɪ/ ADVERB in a way that is obvious □ *We were all noticeably more relaxed after dinner.*

notification /ˌnəʊtɪfɪˈkeɪʃən/ NOUN [*plural* **notifications**] when someone officially tells you something 🕮 *You will receive notification of any changes to the payments.*

notify /ˈnəʊtɪfaɪ/ VERB [**notifies, notifying, notified**] to officially tell someone about something □ *You will be notified of the date.*

notion /ˈnəʊʃən/ NOUN [*plural* **notions**] an idea or a belief □ *This goes against the whole notion of free speech.*

notoriety /ˌnəʊtəˈraɪətɪ/ NOUN, NO PLURAL the quality of being notorious 🕮 *They had gained notoriety as one of the most violent gangs in Chicago.*

notorious /nəʊˈtɔːrɪəs/ ADJECTIVE famous for something bad □ *a notorious criminal*

● **notoriously** /nəʊˈtɔːrɪəslɪ/ ADVERB well known in a bad way □ *That model is notoriously unreliable.*

nought /nɔːt/ NOUN [*plural* **noughts**]

1 the number 0 □ *The code is a series of ones and noughts.* □ *It's nought point five centimetres long.* □ *The car can go from nought to sixty in four seconds.*

2 nothing 🕮 *All their efforts had come to nought* (=produced nothing).

noun /naʊn/ NOUN [*plural* **nouns**] a word that refers to a person, a thing, or a quality. For example, *tree, Sue, air* and *happiness* are nouns.

nourish /ˈnʌrɪʃ/ VERB [**nourishes, nourishing, nourished**] to provide people, animals or plants with the food they need to grow or stay healthy

● **nourishing** /ˈnʌrɪʃɪŋ/ ADJECTIVE containing the substances you need to stay healthy □ *a nourishing meal*

● **nourishment** /ˈnʌrɪʃmənt/ NOUN, NO PLURAL the food you need to stay healthy □ *Eggs provide a vital source of nourishment.*

novel /ˈnɒvəl/ ➤ NOUN [*plural* **novels**] a book that tells an invented story □ *a historical/romantic novel* ➤ ADJECTIVE completely new and different from anything else □ *What a novel idea!* 🕮 *They take a novel approach to education.*

● **novelist** /ˈnɒvəlɪst/ NOUN [*plural* **novelists**] a person who writes novels

● **novelty** /ˈnɒvəltɪ/ NOUN [*plural* **novelties**]

1 the quality of being novel 🔁 *At first I enjoyed living abroad, but the novelty soon wore off.*
2 something that is novel or that you have not experienced before □ *In this part of the world, mothers who work full-time are still a bit of a novelty.*
3 a small cheap toy or other object with no practical use

November /nəʊ'vembə(r)/ NOUN, NO PLURAL the eleventh month of the year, after October and before December □ *What's the weather like in November?*

novice /'nɒvɪs/ NOUN [plural **novices**] someone who is only just learning how to do something □ *a novice rider*

now /naʊ/ ▶ ADVERB
1 at the present time □ *It is now five o'clock.* □ *I'm working as a teacher now.* 🔁 *He has refused to speak until now.*
2 from this moment, though not before □ *Now I can see him.* □ *You can look at the answers now.* 🔁 *From now on, I'll be giving you homework every day.*
3 from this moment, as a result of something □ *Now I can afford to go on holiday.* □ *Now will you try to be more careful?*
4 immediately □ *I'll do it now.* 🔁 *I want to see you in my office right now!*
5 used to start a sentence □ *Now, can anyone tell me the last two kings of England?* 🔁 *Now then, I gather there has been some bad behaviour in class.*
6 any day/moment/time, etc. now used to say that something will happen very soon □ *The weather should change any day now.*
7 (every) now and then sometimes, but not often □ *Every now and then I treat myself to a really hot curry.*
8 for now for the present time, though the situation might change □ *She's working part time for now.*
9 just now a very short time ago □ *I saw Jim outside just now.*
▶ CONJUNCTION as a result of something or after something has happened □ *Now that I've thought about it more, I've decided not to go.* □ *It's very quiet now Jon has gone.*

nowadays /'naʊədeɪz/ ADVERB at the present time, usually when compared to the past □ *Nowadays, women usually have their babies in hospital.* □ *There's much more for youngsters to do nowadays than there was 20 years ago.*

nowhere /'nəʊweə(r)/ ADVERB
1 not anywhere □ *We've got nowhere to go.* 🔁 *These birds are found nowhere else in the world.*
2 get/go nowhere to not make any progress or be successful □ *This is useless – we're getting nowhere.* □ *The talks have been going nowhere.*
3 nowhere to be found/seen impossible to see or find anywhere □ *Her son was nowhere to be found.* □ *The cat was nowhere to be seen.*

4 from/out of nowhere appearing or happening suddenly or in a way that is not expected □ *The storm had appeared from nowhere.* □ *The car just came out of nowhere.*
5 nowhere near not at all close in distance, time or a quality □ *Paris is nowhere near Marseilles.* □ *The stadium was nowhere near full.*

noxious /'nɒkʃəs/ ADJECTIVE harmful or poisonous □ *noxious gases*

nozzle /'nɒzəl/ NOUN [plural **nozzles**] a part at the end of a pipe that controls a liquid or gas that comes out of it

nuance /'njuːɒns/ NOUN [plural **nuances**] a slight difference in meaning, appearance, etc. □ *They don't understand the nuances of the language.*

nuclear /'njuːklɪə(r)/ ADJECTIVE
1 to do with the reaction that happens when atoms are divided or forced together 🔁 *nuclear power* 🔁 *a nuclear bomb*
2 to do with the central part of an atom. A physics word.

nucleus /'njuːklɪəs/ NOUN [plural **nuclei**]
1 the central part of an atom. A physics word.
2 the central part of a living cell. A biology word.
3 the central or most important part of something □ *The nucleus of the team hasn't changed.*

nude /njuːd/ ▶ ADJECTIVE not wearing any clothes □ *a nude woman*
▶ NOUN [plural **nudes**] a picture of someone without clothes on

nudge /nʌdʒ/ ▶ VERB [**nudges, nudging, nudged**]
1 to push someone or something gently, especially with your elbow □ *I nudged him and he began to speak.*
2 to move or to change gradually by small amounts □ *The unemployment rate nudged up to 4.8%.*
▶ NOUN [plural **nudges**] a gentle push, especially with your elbow 🔁 *Give him a nudge or he'll fall asleep.*

nudity /'njuːdəti/ NOUN, NO PLURAL not having any clothes on □ *The state has laws against public nudity.*

nugget /'nʌgɪt/ NOUN [plural **nuggets**]
1 a small lump of something □ *a gold nugget*
2 a piece of information or advice □ *He gave me some useful nuggets of information.*

nuisance /'njuːsəns/ NOUN [plural **nuisances**] a person, thing or situation that annoys you or causes problems for you □ *The rabbits have become a nuisance to local gardeners.* 🔁 *'I've locked myself out. 'Oh, what a nuisance!'* 🔁 *He was making a nuisance of himself, shouting and singing loudly.*

numb /nʌm/ ▶ ADJECTIVE [**number, numbest**]
1 if a part of your body is numb, you cannot feel it 🔁 *was so cold my hands had gone completely numb.*
2 so shocked that you cannot think clearly or show any emotion □ *I was numb with grief.*
▶ VERB [**numbs, numbing, numbed**]
1 to cause a pain to become less or to stop someone feeling strong emotions □ *They took drugs to numb their feelings.*

2 to cause a part of the body to lose feeling □ *The cold numbed our fingers.*

number /'nʌmbə(r)/ ► NOUN [*plural* **numbers**]
1 a word or a symbol showing how many of something there are or in what position something is in a series □ *the number four* □ *Please write down any three figure number.* □ *I was number eight on the list.*
2 a quantity of things or people □ **+ of** *We hope to increase the number of customers.* 🗗 *He keeps a large number of animals.* □ *A number of* (=several) *people have complained.*
3 a number that represents something or someone, for example to show what they are or who they belong to □ *a membership number* □ *What is your account number?*
4 a telephone number □ *I'll give you my number.* 🗗 *I must have dialled the wrong number.*
5 a song or a piece of music □ *a catchy number*
► VERB [**numbers, numbering, numbered**]
1 to give a thing or a person a number as part of a series □ *The boxes are all clearly numbered.* □ *Have you numbered the pages?*
2 to be a particular quantity □ *The crowd numbered many thousands.*
3 *someone's/something's days are numbered* someone or something will not exist or be in a particular situation for much longer □ *His days as chief of the organization are numbered.*

number plate /'nʌmbəpleɪt/ NOUN [*plural* **number plates**] a metal sign on the front and the back of a vehicle, showing the letters and numbers that represent that vehicle

numbness /'nʌmnɪs/ NOUN, NO PLURAL when you lose feeling in a part of your body □ *Their sting can cause slight numbness.*

numeracy /'nju:mərəsɪ/ NOUN, NO PLURAL the ability to use numbers and to do basic mathematics □ *Some school-leavers lack basic literacy and numeracy skills.*

numeral /'nju:mərəl/ NOUN [*plural* **numerals**] a symbol that represents a number □ *a Roman numeral*

numerate /'nju:mərət/ ADJECTIVE able to use numbers and to do basic mathematics

numerator /'nju:məreɪtə(r)/ NOUN [*plural* **numerators**] the number above the line in a fraction. A maths word.

numerical /nju:'merɪkəl/ ADJECTIVE to do with numbers or using numbers □ *Put the cards into numerical order.*

numerous /'nju:mərəs/ ADJECTIVE many □ *Numerous people have had the same experience.* 🗗 *I've met him on numerous occasions.*

nun /nʌn/ NOUN [*plural* **nuns**] a member of a religious group of women who live away from other people

nurse /nɜːs/ ► NOUN [*plural* **nurses**] a person whose job is to look after people when they are ill or injured, especially in a hospital □ *She works as a nurse at the hospital.*

► VERB [**nurses, nursing, nursed**] to look after someone when they are ill or injured □ *He had nursed her back to health over several weeks.*

nursery /'nɜːsərɪ/ NOUN [*plural* **nurseries**]
1 a place where babies and young children are looked after while their parents are at work □ *Lizzie goes to a local nursery three days a week.*
2 a place where plants are grown and sold
3 a room in a house for young children

nursery rhyme /'nɜːsərɪ ˌraɪm/ NOUN [*plural* **nursery rhymes**] a short simple traditional poem or song for children

nursery school /'nɜːsərɪ ˌskuːl/ NOUN [*plural* **nursery schools**] a school for children between about three and five years old

nursing /'nɜːsɪŋ/ NOUN, NO PLURAL the job of being a nurse

nursing home /'nɜːsɪŋ həʊm/ NOUN [*plural* **nursing homes**] a place where people live when they are too old or ill to look after themselves

nurture /'nɜːtʃə(r)/ VERB [**nurtures, nurturing, nurtured**]
1 to look after a person, animal or plant so that they grow in a healthy way □ *After birth, all mammals nurture their offspring.*
2 to help and encourage someone or something to develop □ *The scholarship was set up to nurture young talent.*

nut /nʌt/ NOUN [*plural* **nuts**]
1 the fruit of some trees that has a hard shell and an inside part that can often be eaten □ *a cashew nut* □ *a bag of mixed nuts*
2 a small piece of metal with a hole in the middle which fits onto the end of a bolt (=thin piece of metal) to hold things together □ *a wheel nut*
3 an informal word for someone who is very interested in or enthusiastic about something □ *He's a bit of a fitness nut.*
♦ IDIOM **the nuts and bolts** the basic parts or details of a job or an activity □ *I knew nothing about the nuts and bolts of running a business.*

nutmeg /'nʌtmeg/ NOUN [*plural* **nutmegs**] a hard brown seed that is made into a powder and used as a spice to flavour food

nutrient /'nju:trɪənt/ NOUN [*plural* **nutrients**]
1 any substance in food that gives you energy and makes you healthy □ *Iron is an essential nutrient for many animals.*
2 any substance in soil that helps plants to grow

nutrition /nju:'trɪʃən/ NOUN, NO PLURAL
1 food and the way it affects your health □ *Good nutrition is necessary for a quick recovery.* □ *information about nutrition*
2 the study of food and how it affects health □ *a nutrition expert*

● **nutritional** /nju:'trɪʃənəl/ ADJECTIVE to do with nutrition 🗗 *These drinks offer no nutritional value.* □ *a nutritional supplement*

• **nutritious** /njuˈtrɪʃəs/ ADJECTIVE healthy for you to eat or drink □ *a nutritious meal*

nutshell /ˈnʌtʃəl/ NOUN [plural **nutshells**] the hard shell around a nut

♦ IDIOM **in a nutshell** expressed in as few words as possible □ *To put it in a nutshell, we must stop spending so much money.*

nutty /ˈnʌtɪ/ ADJECTIVE [**nuttier, nuttiest**]

1 containing nuts or tasting of nuts □ *a nutty flavour*

2 an informal word meaning silly or very strange □ *a nutty idea*

nuzzle /ˈnʌzəl/ VERB [**nuzzles, nuzzling, nuzzled**] to rub your face or nose gently against something □ *The dog nuzzled his face.*

nylon /ˈnaɪlɒn/ NOUN, NO PLURAL a strong, light artificial material used for example to make clothes and rope □ *a black nylon bag*

Oo

O *or* **o** /əʊ/ the 15th letter of the alphabet

oak /əʊk/ NOUN [*plural* **oaks**] a large tree with seeds called acorns, or the wood from this tree

OAP /ˌəʊeɪ'piː/ ABBREVIATION old age pensioner

oar /ɔː(r)/ NOUN [*plural* **oars**] a long piece of wood with a flat end, used for making a boat move

oasis /əʊ'eɪsɪs/ NOUN [*plural* **oases**]
1 a place in a desert where there are plants and water
2 a calm, pleasant place that is surrounded by noise and activity □ *The hotel is an oasis of calm in a busy city.*

oath /əʊθ/ NOUN [*plural* **oaths**] a formal promise
🕮 *Members swear an oath of secrecy about the group.*

oats /əʊts/ PLURAL NOUN a type of grain that people and animals eat

obedience /ə'biːdɪəns/ NOUN, NO PLURAL the quality of being willing to do what a person or rule tells you to do □ *Teachers expect obedience from their pupils.*

• **obedient** /ə'biːdɪənt/ ADJECTIVE doing what a person or rule tells you to do □ *an obedient child*

obese /əʊ'biːs/ ADJECTIVE extremely fat

• **obesity** /əʊ'biːsəti/ NOUN, NO PLURAL when someone is obese □ *childhood obesity*

obey /ə'beɪ/ VERB [**obeys, obeying, obeyed**] to do what a person or rule tells you to do □ *He was taught to obey his parents.* 🕮 *Drivers must obey the law.* 🕮 *He refused to obey a court order.*

obituary /ə'bɪtʃuəri/ NOUN [*plural* **obituaries**] an announcement in a newspaper that someone has died, with a short description of their life

object¹ /'ɒbdʒɪkt/ NOUN [*plural* **objects**]
1 a thing that you can see or touch but not a person or animal □ *There were various objects on the table.* □ *Keep sharp objects away from children.*
2 an aim or purpose □ *His main object in life was to become rich.* □ **+ of** *The object of the exercise is to improve teaching standards.*
3 object of something someone or something that people have a particular feeling about □ *The Prime Minister became an object of ridicule.*
4 in grammar, the person or thing that a verb affects □ *In the sentence 'I ate the apple', 'apple' is the object.*

object² /əb'dʒekt/ VERB [**objects, objecting, objected**] to say that you do not want something to happen □ *Nobody objected to the original proposal.*

• **objection** /əb'dʒekʃən/ NOUN [*plural* **objections**] a reason you do not want something to happen □ *My only objection is that he is too young.* 🕮 *I have no objections to the changes.*

• **objectionable** /əb'dʒekʃənəbəl/ ADJECTIVE offensive □ *I find his attitude thoroughly objectionable.*

objective /əb'dʒektɪv/ ► NOUN [*plural* **objectives**] an aim or purpose 🕮 *They achieved their main objective of raising money for the hospital.*
► ADJECTIVE telling facts which are not influenced by opinions or feelings □ *We make an objective assessment of each student's progress.*

obligation /ˌɒblɪ'geɪʃən/ NOUN [*plural* **obligations**] a duty to do something 🕮 *Schools have a legal obligation to take good care of students.*

• **obligatory** /ə'blɪgətəri/ ADJECTIVE
1 something that is obligatory must be done because of a law or rule □ *Voting is obligatory in Peru.*
2 if something is obligatory in a particular situation, it is done so often that people expect it □ *After the wedding ceremony there were the obligatory photographs.*

• **oblige** /ə'blaɪdʒ/ VERB [**obliges, obliging, obliged**]
1 if you are obliged to do something, you must do it □ *Banks are obliged to list the names of their directors.*
2 to help someone by doing something they have asked you to do 🕮 *He asked me to speak at the conference and I was happy to oblige.*

• **obliged** /ə'blaɪdʒd/ ADJECTIVE **feel obliged to do something** to feel that you must do something for someone □ *I felt obliged to ask her to the party as she had invited me to hers.*

• **obliging** /ə'blaɪdʒɪŋ/ ADJECTIVE willing to help □ *He's very obliging.*

oblique /ə'bliːk/ ADJECTIVE saying something in a way that is not direct. A formal word □ *He made an oblique reference to the problem.*

obliterate /ə'blɪtəreɪt/ VERB [**obliterates, obliterating, obliterated**] to destroy something completely □ *The house was obliterated by an earthquake.*

oblivion /ə'blɪvɪən/ NOUN, NO PLURAL
1 when someone or something has been completely forgotten □ *Many television presenters slide into oblivion.*
2 a state in which you are not aware of what is happening around you □ *The sleeping pill brings almost instant oblivion.*

• **oblivious** /ə'blɪvɪəs/ ADJECTIVE not aware of what is

happening □ *He seemed oblivious to the chaos around him.*

oblong /'ɒblɒŋ/ ► NOUN [*plural* **oblongs**] a rectangle ► ADJECTIVE in the shape of a rectangle □ *an oblong table*

obnoxious /əb'nɒkʃəs/ ADJECTIVE rude and unpleasant □ *obnoxious behaviour*

oboe /'əubəu/ NOUN [*plural* **oboes**] a musical instrument shaped like a long tube that you play by blowing through it

obscene /əb'siːn/ ADJECTIVE
1 unpleasant and shocking □ *obscene language*
2 too large and morally wrong □ *He earns an obscene amount of money.*

• **obscenity** /əb'senətɪ/ NOUN [*plural* **obscenities**]
1 a word that is very rude □ *The youths shouted obscenities at the police.*
2 behaviour or language that is unpleasant or shocking

obscure /əb'skjuə(r)/ ► ADJECTIVE only known by a few people □ *an obscure artist*
► VERB [**obscures, obscuring, obscured**]
1 to cover something so that you cannot see it □ *Thick clouds obscured the sun.*
2 to hide a fact or make it difficult to understand □ *The article deliberately obscures some vital facts.*

• **obscurity** /əb'skjuərətɪ/ NOUN, NO PLURAL the state when people do not know about or do not remember someone or something □ *After years of obscurity, he suddenly found himself famous.*

obsequious /əb'siːkwɪəs/ ADJECTIVE a formal word meaning too eager to agree with someone or do things for them □ *an obsequious manner*

observant /əb'zɜːvənt/ ADJECTIVE good at noticing things

observation /ˌɒbzə'veɪʃən/ NOUN [*plural* **observations**]
1 a remark 🕮 *She made some interesting observations about their relationship.*
2 *no plural* when you watch someone or something very carefully □ *He has been kept in hospital for observation.*

observatory /əb'zɜːvətərɪ/ NOUN [*plural* **observatories**] a building with equipment for people to look at the stars and planets

observe /əb'zɜːv/ VERB [**observes, observing, observed**]
1 to watch someone or something very carefully □ *Police continued to observe his actions with interest.*
2 a formal word meaning to notice someone or something □ *Scientists observed no serious side effects of the drug.*
3 to obey a rule, agreement or religious tradition □ *The older members of the community still observe this tradition.*
4 a formal word meaning to say something that you notice □ *'You're very smartly dressed,' he observed.*

• **observer** /əb'zɜːvə(r)/ NOUN [*plural* **observers**]
1 someone who sees something 🕮 *A casual observer* (=someone who sees something but does not pay close attention to it) *would not have realized that anything was wrong.*
2 someone who watches something as a job □ *political observers*

obsess /əb'ses/ VERB [**obsesses, obsessing, obsessed**] to think about someone or something too much of the time □ *I don't have time to obsess about eating and fitness any more.*

• **obsessed** /əb'sest/ ADJECTIVE thinking about someone or something too much of the time □ *He became obsessed with football.*

• **obsession** /əb'seʃən/ NOUN [*plural* **obsessions**]
1 a person or thing that you cannot stop thinking about □ *Horse-racing had become an obsession for him.*
2 *no plural* when you cannot stop thinking about something □ *David's tidiness borders on obsession.*

• **obsessive** /əb'sesɪv/ ADJECTIVE unable to stop thinking about something or behaving in a particular way □ *obsessive jealousy*

obsolescent /ˌɒbsə'lesənt/ ADJECTIVE being replaced by something newer and better. A formal word □ *obsolescent technology*

obsolete /'ɒbsəliːt/ ADJECTIVE no longer used because there is now something newer and better □ *Much of this technology is now obsolete.*

obstacle /'ɒbstəkəl/ NOUN [*plural* **obstacles**]
1 something that stops you from doing what you want to do □ *He had overcome a lot of obstacles in his life.*
2 an object that is in front of you and that you must move or go around in order to go forward

obstetrician /ˌɒbstə'trɪʃən/ NOUN [*plural* **obstetricians**] a doctor who deals with pregnant women and the birth of babies

• **obstetrics** /ɒb'stetrɪks/ NOUN, NO PLURAL the area of medicine to do with pregnant women and the birth of babies

obstinacy /'ɒbstɪnəsɪ/ NOUN, NO PLURAL when someone is obstinate

• **obstinate** /'ɒbstənət/ ADJECTIVE refusing to change your ideas or behaviour □ *an obstinate child*

obstruct /əb'strʌkt/ VERB [**obstructs, obstructing, obstructed**]
1 to block somewhere such as a road, door or path, so that people cannot move along or through it □ *The road was obstructed by a fallen tree.*
2 to stop someone from seeing something □ *Her hat was obstructing his vision.*
3 to try to prevent something from happening □ *He was arrested for obstructing the police investigation.*

• **obstruction** /əb'strʌkʃən/ NOUN [*plural* **obstructions**]
1 when something blocks somewhere such as a road, door or path, so that people cannot move along or through it □ *A badly parked car was causing an obstruction.*
2 when something prevents something else from happening □ *the obstruction of justice*

obtain /əb'teɪn/ VERB [obtains, obtaining, obtained] a formal word meaning to get something □ *Clients can obtain information from our website.*

> ➤ Note that the word **obtain** is used mainly in formal situations and is not common. The usual word is **get**:
> ✓ *Where did you get your jacket?*
> ✗ *Where did you obtain your jacket?*

obtuse /əb'tjuːs/ ADJECTIVE
1 a formal word meaning stupid
2 an obtuse angle is more than 90°. A maths word.

obvious /'ɒbvɪəs/ ADJECTIVE easy to see or understand □ **+ that** *It was obvious that she was unhappy.* 🕮 *It was blindingly obvious* (=very obvious) *that the project would fail* 🕮 *He started crying for no obvious reason.* □ **+ to** *It was obvious to anyone in the room that he was lying.*

• **obviously** /'ɒbvɪəslɪ/ ADVERB
1 used for giving information that you expect other people will already know or will agree with □ *Obviously, I'll need some help.* □ *Obviously we're not happy with this situation.*
2 in a way that is easy to see or understand □ *Lara was so obviously disappointed.*

occasion /ə'keɪʒən/ NOUN [plural **occasions**]
1 a particular time when something happens □ *I've met him on several occasions.* 🕮 *He has run in the race on three previous occasions.*
2 an important event 🕮 *She only wore the shoes for special occasions.* 🕮 *The shop has been trading for 50 years and is offering free drinks to mark the occasion.*
3 **on occasion(s)** sometimes □ *We've had arguments on occasion.*

• **occasional** /ə'keɪʒənəl/ ADJECTIVE happening sometimes but not often □ *They made occasional visits to Scotland.* 🕮 *Eating the occasional ice cream won't make you fat.*

• **occasionally** /ə'keɪʒənəlɪ/ ADVERB sometimes but not often □ *I occasionally go to the theatre.* 🕮 *Very occasionally I've felt lonely.*

occult /ɒ'kʌlt/ NOUN, NO PLURAL **the occult** things which are to do with magic or mysterious powers that cannot be explained

occupant /'ɒkjupənt/ NOUN [plural **occupants**] a formal word meaning someone who is in a building or vehicle □ *the occupants of the flat*

occupation /ˌɒkjuˈpeɪʃən/ NOUN [plural **occupations**]
1 a formal word meaning job □ *Firefighting is a dangerous occupation.* □ *professional occupations*
2 *no plural* when an army enters a country or area and takes control of it □ **+ of** *the Roman occupation of Britain*
3 a formal word meaning something you like doing in your free time □ *Reading is his favourite occupation.*

• **occupational** /ˌɒkjuˈpeɪʃənəl/ ADJECTIVE to do with your job 🕮 *For bank workers, robbery is an occupational hazard* (=something bad that sometimes happens in a particular job). □ *occupational pensions*

occupied /'ɒkjupaɪd/ ADJECTIVE
1 already being used by someone □ *Are these buildings occupied?*
2 busy doing something 🕮 *This book should keep you occupied for a while.*
3 controlled by the army of another country □ *occupied territories*

occupier /'ɒkjupaɪə(r)/ NOUN [plural **occupiers**] a formal word meaning the person who lives in a particular house or flat

occupy /'ɒkjupaɪ/ VERB [occupies, occupying, occupied]
1 to occupy a space is to fill it □ *A table occupied the centre of the room.*
2 if someone occupies a building, they live or work there □ *The building is occupied by several small companies.*
3 to keep someone busy □ *She has more than enough to occupy her.* □ *He occupied himself with the garden.*
4 to enter a country or area and take control of it with an army □ *Soldiers were occupying the town.*
5 a formal word meaning to have a particular job or position □ *It was the first time a woman had occupied the position of Prime Minister.*

occur /ə'kɜː(r)/ VERB [occurs, occurring, occurred]
1 a formal word meaning to happen □ *The accident occurred last night.*
2 to exist or be present □ *Dragons only occur in fairy tales.*
♦ PHRASAL VERB **occur to someone** if something occurs to you, you suddenly think it □ *It never occurred to me that I should see a doctor about it.*

• **occurrence** /ə'kʌrəns/ NOUN [plural **occurrences**] something that happens □ *Shark attacks are a very rare occurrence.*

ocean /'əʊʃən/ NOUN [plural **oceans**]
1 one of the 5 large areas of sea in the world □ *the Atlantic Ocean*
2 **the ocean** the salt water that covers most of the Earth's surface □ *ocean currents*

o'clock /ə'klɒk/ ADVERB used after the numbers one to twelve to say what time of day it is □ *School starts at nine o'clock.* □ *'What time is it?' 'It's nearly 12 o'clock.'*

octagon /'ɒktəgən/ NOUN [plural **octagons**] a shape with eight sides. A maths word.

• **octagonal** /ɒk'tægənəl/ ADJECTIVE in the shape of an octagon. A maths word.

octave /'ɒktɪv/ NOUN [plural **octaves**] a range of eight musical notes, for example from one C to the next C above or below it

October /ɒkˈtəʊbə(r)/ NOUN, NO PLURAL the tenth month of the year, after September and before November □ *He retired in October.*

octopus /ˈɒktəpəs/ NOUN [plural **octopuses**] a sea animal with eight long arms

odd /ɒd/ ADJECTIVE [**odder, oddest**]
1 strange □ *It seems an odd choice.* □ *He's very odd.*
2 happening sometimes but not often □ *There has been the odd occasion when we've disagreed.*
3 without the other one of a pair □ *an odd shoe*
4 of different types, sizes, shapes, etc. □ *Have you got any odd bits of wood I could use?*
5 an odd number is a number that you cannot divide exactly by two □ *5 and 7 are odd numbers.*
6 20 odd/50 odd, etc. approximately 20, 50, etc. □ *He's lived here 30 odd years.*

● **oddity** /ˈɒdəti/ NOUN [plural **oddities**] a strange or unusual person or thing □ *He's always been a bit of an oddity.*

● **oddly** /ˈɒdli/ ADVERB
1 strangely □ *He's behaving very oddly.*
2 oddly enough used for saying that something seems surprising or strange □ *Oddly enough, he didn't seem disappointed that he'd lost.*

odds /ɒdz/ PLURAL NOUN
1 the chances of something happening □ *The odds are that he will win.*
2 against all odds if something happens against all odds, it happens even though it did not seem possible □ *Against all odds, she made a full recovery.*
3 at odds with someone/something disagreeing with someone or something □ *The countries are at odds with each other on many issues.*
◆ IDIOM it makes no odds an informal way of saying that it is not important to you what happens □ *It makes no odds to me whether he comes or not.*

odds and ends /ˌɒdz ən ˈendz/ PLURAL NOUN different small objects which are not valuable □ *I keep various odds and ends in that drawer.*

odious /ˈəʊdiəs/ ADJECTIVE a formal word meaning extremely unpleasant □ *an odious man*

odor /ˈəʊdə(r)/ NOUN [plural **odors**] the US spelling of odour

odour /ˈəʊdə(r)/ NOUN [plural **odours**] a smell, especially a bad one □ *There was a strong odour of rotting fish.*

oesophagus /iːˈsɒfəgəs/ NOUN [plural **oesophaguses** or oesophagi] the tube that takes food from the mouth to the stomach. A biology word.

oestrogen /ˈiːstrədʒən/ NOUN, NO PLURAL a chemical substance that causes female characteristics to develop. A biology word.

of /əv/ PREPOSITION
1 used to show an amount or measurement □ *hundreds of people* □ *a pint of milk* □ *an increase of 13%* □ *I'm part of a team.* □ *I left home at the age of 16.*
2 used to show which members of a group are affected or being talked about □ *I have some bananas,* but none of them are ripe. □ *Many of our members are over 60.* □ *All of the children will receive a present.*
3 used to talk about the characteristics or qualities that someone or something has □ *Did you notice the size of their offices?*
4 used after a noun to show a particular example of that thing □ *There have been several cases of cholera.* □ *I grew up in the town of Aylesbury.* □ *We worked together for a short period of time.*
5 made from or caused by something □ *They constructed a building of ice.* □ *There was a large pile of newspapers in the corner.* □ *The whole house smelled of garlic.* □ *We could hear their shouts of joy.* □ *He died of hunger.*
6 about something, showing something or to do with something □ *He told us stories of his adventures in India.* □ *I need a map of Berlin.* □ *I always carry a photograph of my children.* □ *You remind me of my sister.* □ *He was frightened of bees.*
7 containing something □ *I gave her a box of chocolates.* □ *Would you like a glass of water?* □ *I read a book of his poems.*
8 belonging to or experienced by someone or something □ *The furniture is the property of the school.* □ *I lost the lid of the box.* □ *We must consider the needs of the patients.*
9 used to show the position of something or someone □ *We live just south of Edinburgh.* □ *I sat at the side of the bed.* □ *There is a large garden to the rear of the property.*

off /ɒf/ ▶ ADVERB, PREPOSITION
1 away from the top or surface of something □ *I took the book off the shelf.* □ *Keep off the grass.* □ *I'm trying to get the mud off my shoes.* □ *Make sure you don't fall off!*
2 no longer attached to something □ *The petals have all dropped off.* □ *Some tiles have come off the roof.*
3 away from a place □ *He walked off and left me.*
4 if you take clothes off, you stop wearing them □ *I took off my jacket.* □ *He had his shoes off.*
5 out of a public vehicle □ *I got off the train in Padua.* □ *Take the number 7 bus and get off at the station.*
6 not operating □ *I switched the heating off.* □ *Make sure your phones are off.*
7 if a price has a particular amount off, it is reduced by that amount □ *All computer games are 20% off this week.*
8 not at work or at school □ *Why don't you take the day off?* □ *She's off work today.*
9 away in distance or time □ *We were drifting a few miles off the coast.* □ *The holiday seems a long way off.*
10 near to something, and usually connected to it □ *My office is off the main corridor.* □ *Our road is just off the main road.*
▶ ADJECTIVE
1 if food is off, it is rotten and cannot be eaten □ *This milk is off.*
2 not at work or school □ *Lulu is off on Fridays.*

3 not going to happen now □ *The holiday is off.*
4 not correct □ *The figures were off by a large amount.*
5 if a particular food is off in a restaurant, they have sold it all and you cannot now have it □ *The salmon is off.*
➜ *go to* **badly-off, well-off**

offal /ˈɒfəl/ NOUN, NO PLURAL animal organs such as the liver, heart, etc. which people eat

off-chance /ˈɒftʃɑːns/ NOUN, NO PLURAL **on the off-chance** if you do something on the off-chance, you do it because you hope something good might happen even though it does not seem likely □ *I don't suppose they'll have any tickets left, but I'll ring up on the off-chance.*

offence /əˈfens/ NOUN [plural **offences**]
1 a crime □ *The police charged him with three offences.* ▯ *He has committed several violent offences.* ▯ *Burning the flag is a criminal offence in some countries.*
2 no plural when you upset someone by saying or doing something ▯ *His comments certainly caused offence.* ▯ *Philip took offence* (=felt offended) *at the suggestion.*

offend /əˈfend/ VERB [**offends, offending, offended**]
1 to make someone feel upset or angry by something you say or do □ *I hope I didn't offend anyone.*
2 a formal word meaning to commit a crime □ *Prisons are full of people who have offended more than once.*
offended /əˈfendɪd/ ADJECTIVE angry or upset because of something that someone has said or done □ *I felt very offended that he hadn't invited me to the wedding.*
offender /əˈfendə(r)/ NOUN [plural **offenders**] a person who has committed a crime □ *young offenders*
offense /əˈfens/ NOUN [plural **offenses**] the US spelling of **offence**

offensive /əˈfensɪv/ ▶ ADJECTIVE
1 rude and insulting □ *offensive remarks* ▯ *He found the question deeply offensive.*
2 very unpleasant □ *an offensive smell*
3 used for or to do with attacking ▯ *offensive weapons*
▶ NOUN [plural **offensives**] a military attack ▯ *The army launched a major offensive against the rebels.*

offer /ˈɒfə(r)/ ▶ VERB [**offers, offering, offered**]
1 to ask someone if they want something □ *She offered me another drink.* □ *+ to He offered the sweets to all the children in the class.*
2 to say that you will do something for someone □ *+ to do something She offered to carry my bag for me.*
3 to provide something □ *The college offers a wide variety of courses.* □ *An accountant might be able to offer you some advice.*
4 to say that you will pay a particular amount of money for something □ *I'll offer you £50 for the picture.*

▶ NOUN [plural **offers**]
1 when you ask someone if they want something or if you can do something for them ▯ *It was a very generous offer.* ▯ *I've had several job offers.* ▯ *She accepted his offer to drive her home.* □ *+ of an offer of help*
2 an amount of money offered ▯ *They made an offer of £300,000 for the house.*
3 when something is being sold at a lower price than usual ▯ *Check the company's website for special offers.*
4 **on offer** (a) available □ *There's a free lunch on offer for anyone who helps.* (b) being sold at a lower price than usual □ *These chocolates were on offer.*
• **offering** /ˈɒfərɪŋ/ NOUN [plural **offerings**] something that you give to someone □ *This is the television channel's latest offering.*

offhand /ˌɒfˈhænd/ ▶ ADJECTIVE slightly rude and unfriendly □ *You were a bit offhand with her at the meeting.*
▶ ADVERB now and without thinking about something □ *Can you tell me offhand how much it might cost?*

office /ˈɒfɪs/ NOUN [plural **offices**]
1 a building where people work for a company ▯ *Our head office* (=main office) *is in London.* ▯ *an office building* ▯ *office workers*
2 the room in which a particular person works □ *The manager is in her office.*
3 a room or building used for a particular purpose □ *the tourist information office* □ *The ticket office opens at 8 o'clock.*
4 an important job or position □ *He's only been in office for a year.* ▯ *She held office for several years.* □ *+ of the office of President*

officer /ˈɒfɪsə(r)/ NOUN [plural **officers**]
1 a person in the army, navy or air force who is in charge of ordinary soldiers □ *senior army officers*
2 someone who has a particular job in a government or organization □ *a prison officer* □ *immigration officers* □ *He's the chief executive officer of the company.*
3 a police officer □ *Armed officers shot the man.*

official /əˈfɪʃəl/ ▶ ADJECTIVE
1 done or approved by a government or someone in authority □ *an official announcement* □ *Canada has two official languages.* □ *Official figures show that crime has risen by 10%.*
2 to do with an important job □ *The Queen has cancelled her official engagements due to illness.* □ *The President will make an official visit to Moscow.*
3 an official reason, explanation, etc. is one that people are told, but it may not be true □ *The official explanation was that he was ill.*
▶ NOUN [plural **officials**] someone who has an important job in an organization, especially a government ▯ *government officials*
• **officially** /əˈfɪʃəli/ ADVERB

1 publicly and formally □ *The new library is now officially open.* □ *He will officially retire next week.*
2 according to the information that people have been given, although it may not be true □ *Officially the company is saying that he chose to resign.*

officious /ə'fɪʃəs/ ADJECTIVE too eager to tell other people what to do □ *An officious little man told us to move our bicycles.*

offing /'ɒfɪŋ/ NOUN, NO PLURAL **be in the offing** to be going to happen soon □ *Apparently there's a deal in the offing.*

off-licence /'ɒflaɪsəns/ NOUN [plural **off-licences**] a shop that sells alcohol

offline /ˌɒf'laɪn/ ADJECTIVE a computer which is offline is not connected to the Internet. A computing word.

offload /ɒf'ləʊd/ VERB [**offloads, offloading, offloaded**] to sell or give something that you do not want to someone else □ *The company is trying to offload its troubled restaurant business.*

off-peak /ˌɒf'piːk/ ADJECTIVE, ADVERB at the cheapest, least popular times □ *I always travel off-peak.*

off-putting /'ɒfpʊtɪŋ/ ADJECTIVE making you not want to go somewhere, have something, etc. □ *His description of the hotel was a bit off-putting.*

offset /'ɒfset/ VERB [**offsets, offsetting, offset**] one thing offsets another thing when it has the opposite effect and creates a balance □ *The price rises will be offset by tax cuts.*

● **offsetting** /'ɒfsetɪŋ/ NOUN, NO PLURAL when you do something that reduces the amount of carbon dioxide in the air, such as paying for someone to plant trees, because you are doing something that puts more carbon dioxide in the air, such as flying by aeroplane

offshoot /'ɒfʃuːt/ NOUN [plural **offshoots**] a company or group that has developed from a larger one □ *The company is an offshoot of a large American multinational.*

offshore /ˌɒf'ʃɔː(r)/ ADJECTIVE
1 in the sea, not far from the land □ *offshore oil rigs*
2 an offshore wind is blowing away from the land towards the sea □ *offshore breezes*

offside /ˌɒf'saɪd/ ADJECTIVE in a position that is not allowed by the rules of a game such as football □ *The goal was disallowed because Rodriguez was offside.*

offspring /'ɒfsprɪŋ/ NOUN [plural **offspring**] a formal word for the child of a person or animal □ *Parents are responsible for their offspring.*

off-white /ˌɒf'waɪt/ ► NOUN, NO PLURAL a white colour that is slightly yellow or slightly grey
► ADJECTIVE having a white colour that is slightly yellow or slightly grey □ *an off-white wedding dress*

often /'ɒfən, 'ɒftən/ ADVERB
1 many times □ *I often go to the cinema.* □ *I don't play tennis very often now.* 🔁 *How often do you see Jess?* 🔁 *I wish I could travel more often.* 🔁 *He visits the area quite often.*
2 in many situations or cases □ *Jokes are often*

difficult to translate. □ *Often, schools are unable to deal with problem students.*

ogre /'əʊgə(r)/ NOUN [plural **ogres**]
1 a frightening person □ *Her father was a bit of an ogre.*
2 a big, ugly and frightening man in children's stories

oh /əʊ/ EXCLAMATION
1 used when you have just understood something □ *Oh, I see.* □ *Oh, so that's why she isn't here.*
2 used when you are disappointed or annoyed □ *Oh, that's a shame!* □ *Oh no, the computer has just crashed!*
3 used when you are very pleased or surprised □ *Oh, that's very kind!* □ *Oh, that's fantastic!*

oil /ɔɪl/ ► NOUN, NO PLURAL
1 a thick, dark liquid under the ground that is used for making petrol □ *Oil prices have increased.* □ *the oil industry* □ *US oil production*
2 a thick liquid from plants or animals, used in cooking □ *olive oil* □ *vegetable oil* □ *Heat the oil in a pan and fry the onions until soft.*
► VERB [**oils, oiling, oiled**] to put oil on something

oilfield /'ɔɪlfiːld/ NOUN [plural **oilfields**] a place where there is oil under the ground or under the sea

oil paint /'ɔɪl ˌpeɪnt/ NOUN [plural **oil paints**] paint made with oil

● **oil painting** /'ɔɪl ˌpeɪntɪŋ/ NOUN [plural **oil paintings**] a picture painted with oil paints

oil rig /'ɔɪl ˌrɪg/ NOUN [plural **oil rigs**] a large structure with equipment for getting oil from under the ground or under the sea

oil well /'ɔɪl ˌwel/ NOUN [plural **oil wells**] a hole that is made to get oil from under the ground or under the sea

oily /'ɔɪli/ ADJECTIVE [**oilier, oiliest**] like oil, or covered with oil □ *an oily liquid* □ *an oily cloth*

oink /ɔɪŋk/ NOUN [plural **oinks**] the sound that a pig makes

ointment /'ɔɪntmənt/ NOUN [plural **ointments**] a substance that you rub onto your skin as a medical treatment

OK or **okay** /ˌəʊ'keɪ/ ► EXCLAMATION
1 an informal way of agreeing or asking someone if they agree □ *'I'll come over after work.' 'OK'.* □ *OK! I'll do it!* □ *You need to do your homework before Friday, OK?*
2 used before you start talking, especially to many people □ *OK, first of all I'd like to welcome you all to the school.*
► ADJECTIVE, ADVERB
1 an informal word meaning allowed or acceptable 🔁 *Is it OK if I get there a bit later?* 🔁 *'I'm really sorry I forgot your birthday.' 'That's OK.'* □ **+ to do something** *Is it OK to open the window?*
2 an informal word meaning good enough □ *Do I look OK in this dress?* □ *I think I did OK in the exam.*
3 an informal word meaning healthy and happy

□ 'How are you?' 'I'm OK, thanks.' □ Are you feeling OK now?

old /əʊld/ ADJECTIVE [**older, oldest**]

1 used to talk about someone's age 🔁 How old are you? □ He's nine years old.

2 having lived or existed for a long time 🔁 an old man/ woman □ an old church □ She's not old enough to vote. □ I'm too old to go out partying all night. □ My older brother (=older than me) is a builder.

3 having been owned or used for a long time □ I wore a pair of old shoes.

4 used to talk about something or someone from a time before now □ My old car didn't have air conditioning. □ The old road went through the town centre. □ I saw one of my old teachers yesterday.

5 an old friend someone who has been your friend for a long time

6 the old days a period in history, or earlier in your life □ In the old days, we never locked our doors.

old age /ˌəʊld 'eɪdʒ/ NOUN, NO PLURAL the time when someone is old □ He wrote poems in his old age.

old age pensioner /ˌəʊld eɪdʒ 'penʃənə(r)/ NOUN [**plural old age pensioners**] an old person who has stopped working

old-fashioned /ˌəʊld'fæʃənd/ ADJECTIVE not modern or fashionable □ old-fashioned clothes □ His ideas are very old-fashioned. □ He contacted her in the old-fashioned way, by writing a letter.

Old Testament /ˌəʊld 'testəmənt/ NOUN, NO PLURAL the Old Testament the first part of the Christian Bible, which deals with the time before Christ was born

O level /'əʊˌlevəl/ NOUN [**plural O levels**] an exam in a particular subject that students in England, Wales and Northern Ireland took in the past at about age 16. The exam has been replaced by GCSEs □ She's got (=has been successful in) an O level in French.

olive /'ɒlɪv/ ▶ NOUN [**plural olives**]

1 a small black or green fruit that is not sweet. It is eaten and is used to make oil for cooking.

2 a dark yellow-green colour

▶ ADJECTIVE having a dark yellow-green colour □ an olive carpet

olive oil /ˌɒlɪv 'ɔɪl/ NOUN, NO PLURAL oil from olives, used in cooking

Olympic /ə'lɪmpɪk/ ADJECTIVE to do with the Olympic Games □ an Olympic athlete □ an Olympic medal

Olympic Games /əˌlɪmpɪk 'ɡeɪmz/ or **Olympics** ə'lɪmpɪks/ PLURAL NOUN the Olympic Games/the Olympics the international sports competition that takes place every four years in a different country

ombudsman /'ɒmbʊdzmən/ NOUN [**plural ombudsmen**] a person who deals with complaints that people make about a government or other official organization

omelet /'ɒmlɪt/ NOUN [**plural omelets**] the US spelling of omelete

omelette /'ɒmlɪt/ NOUN [**plural omelettes**] a food made by mixing eggs and frying them, often with other food inside □ a cheese omelette

omen /'əʊmen/ NOUN [**plural omens**] a sign showing you that something good or bad is going to happen 🔁 It was a sunny day, which he took as a good omen.

ominous /'ɒmɪnəs/ ADJECTIVE giving a warning that something bad is going to happen □ There are ominous signs that the Earth's weather pattern is changing dramatically.

omission /ə'mɪʃən/ NOUN [**plural omissions**]

1 something that has not been included but should have been 🔁 There are some glaring omissions (=very obvious things missing) in his report.

2 when something is not included □ the omission of his name from the list

omit /ə'mɪt/ VERB [**omits, omitting, omitted**]

1 to not include something □ This detail was omitted from the documents.

2 omit to do something a formal phrase meaning to not do something, often because you forget □ I omitted to tell him about the meeting.

omni- /'ɒmnɪ/ PREFIX omni- is added to the beginning of words to mean 'all', 'every' or 'everywhere' □ omnivore

omnivore /'ɒmnɪvɔː(r)/ NOUN [**plural omnivores**] an animal that eats meat and plants. A biology word.

● **omnivorous** /ɒm'nɪvərəs/ ADJECTIVE eating meat and plants. A biology word □ Humans are omnivorous.

on /ɒn/ ▶ PREPOSITION

1 touching or supported by the top surface of something □ The books are on the table. □ We built our house on a hill. □ I was standing on one leg.

2 onto something □ Rain was falling on the crowd. □ I jumped on the bike.

3 sticking to or hanging from something □ There were lots of pictures on the walls. □ Put your coat on the peg.

4 used to say what day or date something happens □ He's coming to see us on Friday.

5 about □ He gave me a book on Scottish history. □ I can't comment on her views.

6 using a particular form of transport □ I came on the bus.

7 being performed or broadcast □ The programme will be on TV next week.

8 used to say how much time or money you use for a particular thing □ We spent £300 on flowers.

9 as a result of touching or hitting something □ I tripped on a loose stone. □ She hit her head on the shelf.

10 using a particular machine or piece of equipment □ He's on the phone at the moment. □ The letter was written on a typewriter.

11 affecting someone or something □ This is an attack on our freedom. □ I don't have any influence on their decisions.

12 have something on you to be carrying something □ *Have you got a pen on you?*
▶ ADVERB
1 if you have a piece of clothing on, you are wearing it □ *Put your coat on.*
2 if a machine or a piece of equipment is on, it is working or being used □ *Switch the light on.* □ *Shall we have the heating on?*
3 used to show that an action continues □ *We worked on into the night.* □ *We all became bored as he droned on about football.*
4 onto a vehicle □ *I got on at Cambridge station.*
5 being performed or broadcast □ *What's on at the cinema?*
6 going to take place □ *Is the party still on?*
7 forward □ *They moved on.* □ *We went on until we came to a river.*
8 happening or planned □ *I've got a lot on at the moment.* □ *Have you got anything on this weekend?*
9 on and on continuing for a long time □ *The speeches went on and on.*
10 on and off sometimes □ *I've been going to the gym on and off for months.*
♦ IDIOMS **be/go on about someone/something** to talk a lot about someone or something □ *He's always going on about his dogs.* **go on at someone** to complain to someone repeatedly, or to repeatedly ask someone to do something □ *She's always going on at me to get my hair coloured.*

once /wʌns/ ▶ ADVERB
1 one time only □ *He only did it once.* □ *It's the kind of opportunity you get once in your life.* □ *I only met him once.*
2 once a/every one time in every period of time □ *I wash my car once a week.* □ *We meet about once every four or five months.*
3 at a time in the past □ *People once lived in caves.* □ *They once owned the whole town.* □ *I was a communist once.*
4 once again/more again, or one more time □ *I found myself alone once more.* □ *He is once again in prison.* □ *Basic errors have once again cost lives.*
5 at once (a) immediately □ *Miss Peters wants to see you at once.* (b) at the same time □ *I can't do two things at once.*
6 all at once (a) suddenly □ *All at once, the crowd started to move.* (b) at the same time □ *The movie was funny and inspiring all at once.*
7 once in a while sometimes, but not often □ *I like to go to the opera once in a while.*
8 once or twice a few times □ *I've met him once or twice.*
▶ CONJUNCTION as soon as □ *Once you've finished, you can go.* □ *Once I started getting into debt, I was always anxious.*

oncoming /ˈɒnkʌmɪŋ/ ADJECTIVE oncoming vehicles are moving towards you □ *the oncoming traffic*

one /wʌn/ ▶ NUMBER [*plural* ones] the number 1
▶ PRONOUN [*plural* ones]
1 used to avoid repeating a word □ *These plums are delicious – would you like one?* □ *My fridge broke and I had to buy a new one.* □ *Our house is one of the ones with a yellow door.*
2 a formal word meaning anyone or you □ *One can see the sea from here.*
3 one another each other □ *They embraced one another.* □ *They have great respect for one another.*
4 one at a time separately □ *I spoke to the children one at a time.*
5 one by one one after the other □ *One by one, people began to get up and leave.*
▶ DETERMINER
1 used to talk about one particular person or thing □ *We've only had one reply.* □ **+ of** *One of my friends came round.* 🄑 *One or two of the apples were rotten.*
2 one day/evening, etc. on a day/evening, etc. in the future that has not been decided □ *We must meet up for lunch one day.*

one-off /ˌwʌnˈɒf/ ▶ ADJECTIVE happening only once □ *a one-off payment*
▶ NOUN [*plural* one-offs] something that happens only once □ *The meeting was just a one-off.*
onerous /ˈəʊnərəs/ ADJECTIVE a formal word meaning difficult to do and needing a lot of effort □ *an onerous task*

oneself /wʌnˈself/ PRONOUN the reflexive form of 'one' used for talking about yourself or people in general. A formal word □ *One can lie to oneself as well as to other people.*

one-sided /ˌwʌnˈsaɪdɪd/ ADJECTIVE
1 with one person or team having a lot more skill than the other □ *a one-sided game*
2 showing or considering only one opinion, in a way that is unfair □ *It was a very one-sided account of what happened.*
one-to-one /ˌwʌntəˈwʌn/ ADJECTIVE between only two people □ *Seriously ill patients need one-to-one care.*

one-way /ˌwʌnˈweɪ/ ADJECTIVE
1 allowing cars to travel in one direction only 🄑 *It was a narrow one-way street.* 🄑 *The town had a very complicated one-way system.*
2 a one-way ticket, price, etc. is for travelling to a place but not coming back □ *The airline is offering one-way fares to Paris for £25.*

ongoing /ˌɒnˈɡəʊɪŋ/ ADJECTIVE continuing now □ *an ongoing investigation*

onion /ˈʌnjən/ NOUN [*plural* onions] a round vegetable with many layers that makes your eyes hurt when you cut it □ *Fry the onions until they are soft.* □ *onion soup*

online /ˌɒnˈlaɪn/ ADJECTIVE, ADVERB using the Internet □ *online advertising* □ *online videos* 🄑 *Younger*

people are more likely to go online for the news.
🖭 *Many people now shop online.*

onlooker /'ɒn,lʊkə(r)/ NOUN [plural **onlookers**]
someone who watches something happening □ *A crowd of onlookers had gathered.*

only /'əʊnlɪ/ ► ADVERB
1 used to emphasize how small an amount, number, etc. is □ *There are only two weeks left.* □ *Only one of us can win.* □ *She left the job after only a week.* □ *This is only the beginning.*
2 nobody or nothing else □ *Only you can do it.* □ *I only use the best quality ingredients.* □ *She would only say that she was disappointed.*
3 used to say that something is not important or not intended to be harmful □ *'What's that noise?' 'Oh, it's only the children.'* □ *I was only trying to help.*
4 only just (a) a very short time ago □ *I've only just finished my essay.* (b) by a very small amount □ *He only just beat me.*
5 not only used to say that one thing is true and another, often surprising, thing is true too □ *Not only did he apologise, he bought everyone a present.* □ *We will not only save money, but we'll get the job done quicker.*
► ADJECTIVE without any others of the same type □ *It was the only book on keeping goats that I could find.* □ *His only son was killed in the war.* 🖭 *She was an only child* (=had no brothers or sisters).
► CONJUNCTION used to say that something cannot happen or is not true □ *I'd like to come, only I have to work.*

onomatopoeia /,ɒnəmætə'piːə/ NOUN, NO PLURAL
when words sound like the thing they describe, for example 'splash'

onset /'ɒnset/ NOUN, NO PLURAL **the onset of something** the start of something □ *The onset of symptoms occurs 48 hours after infection.*

onslaught /'ɒnslɔːt/ NOUN [plural **onslaughts**] an attack □ *a verbal onslaught*

onto /'ɒntə/ PREPOSITION
1 used for showing movement into a position in or on something □ *I climbed onto the roof.* □ *Jim got onto the bus.* □ *The dog rolled onto its side.*
2 if you are onto someone, you know who has done something bad. An informal word □ *It looks like the police are onto him.*
3 be onto something to have discovered something useful or important □ *The scientists soon realized that they were onto something.*

onus /'əʊnəs/ NOUN, NO PLURAL **the onus is on someone to do something** it is someone's responsibility to do something □ *The onus is on schools to ensure that bullying is dealt with properly.*

onward /'ɒnwəd/ ADJECTIVE going forward, or continuing □ *Train passengers transferred to buses for their onward journey.*

● **onwards** /'ɒnwədz/ or **onward** /'ɒnwəd/ ADVERB
1 from ... onwards from a particular time and continuing □ *The rule will apply from 2010 onwards.*
2 a formal word meaning forwards □ *They rode onwards.*

ooze /uːz/ VERB [oozes, oozing, oozed]
1 to flow slowly □ *The glue oozed out of the tube.*
2 an informal word meaning to have a lot of a quality □ *He oozes confidence.*

opal /'əʊpəl/ NOUN [plural **opals**] a white stone used in jewellery

opaque /əʊ'peɪk/ ADJECTIVE difficult to see through □ *opaque glass*

open /'əʊpən/ ► ADJECTIVE
1 not shut or fastened 🖭 *The window was wide open.* □ *An open book lay on the table.* □ *The door burst open and Lila ran in.* □ *His eyes were open and he was still breathing.*
2 if a shop or a business is open, people can go there and use it □ *We are open from 9–5.* □ *Is the restaurant open on Mondays?*
3 not covered, surrounded or blocked 🖭 *She had a love of open spaces.* □ *I like to walk in the open countryside.* □ *He had an open wound on his leg.* □ *The Oxford road is open again.*
4 if a computer program or document is open, it is ready to be used. A computing word.
5 available to be visited or used 🖭 *The meeting is open to the public.* □ *She declared the hospital officially open.* □ *The new road will be open in June.*
6 honest and not keeping secrets □ *He was very open with me about his work.* □ *We would like to see a more open style of government.* □ *We need open debate on the subject.*
7 open emotions are not hidden □ *They showed open hostility to the strangers.*
8 not yet decided □ *The matter is still open for discussion.*
9 if you are open to something, you are willing to consider it 🖭 *I've got some ideas about the new building, but I'm open to suggestions.* □ *We are open to the challenge that a new business brings.*
10 if something or someone is open to problems or difficulties, there is a risk that they will get them □ *You must not leave yourself open to criticism.*
♦ IDIOM **have/keep an open mind** to not form an opinion until you know all the facts about something □ *He hasn't been here long, so I'm keeping an open mind about the quality of his work.*
► VERB [opens, opening, opened]
1 to move to a position that is not shut or fastened, or to make something do this □ *He opened the door.* □ *I opened my eyes.* □ *Open your books on page 34.*
2 to remove the cover from a package, letter, etc. □ *I opened my birthday presents this morning.* □ *Have you opened the letter from the bank yet?*
3 if a shop or business opens, you can start to go there and use it □ *What time does the surgery open?* □ *We don't open on Sundays.*

4 to become available to be visited or used, or to make something available to be visited or used □ *The new supermarket opened last week.* □ *They will be opening the new road in December.*

5 to make a computer program or document ready to use. A computing word □ *Open the spreadsheet and click at the top of the column.*

6 to begin something □ *He opened the meeting with a speech of welcome.* □ *Police have opened an enquiry into the shooting.*

7 if you open a bank account, you make an arrangement with a bank to keep your money there

8 open fire to start to shoot □ *Gunmen opened fire on the building.*

♦ PHRASAL VERBS open something up to create new opportunities □ *My qualifications opened up the chance to travel.* open up to start to be willing to talk about yourself and your feelings □ *He opened up to the nurse and confessed his fears.*

▶ NOUN, NO PLURAL

1 in the open outside □ *We slept in the open.*

2 in/into the open not secret □ *It's time their financial affairs were brought into the open.*

• opener /ˈəʊpənə(r)/ NOUN [plural openers] something that opens a container such as a bottle or a can □ *a tin opener*

• opening /ˈəʊpənɪŋ/ NOUN [plural openings]

1 a hole or space □ *There was an opening in the fence.*

2 the beginning of something □ *The opening of the film was very violent.*

3 an opportunity, especially to get a job □ *There is an opening in the sales team.*

4 an event to mark the start of a place, building, etc. being available to visit or use □ *We all went to the opening of the new museum.*

▶ ADJECTIVE happening at the beginning of something 🔁 *I'd like to make a few opening remarks.* □ *The opening chapter is rather technical.*

• openly /ˈəʊpənlɪ/ ADVERB without trying to hide anything 🔁 *She talked openly about her illness.*

open-minded /ˌəʊpənˈmaɪndɪd/ ADJECTIVE willing to consider new and different ideas □ *My doctor's quite open-minded about alternative therapies.*

openness /ˈəʊpənnɪs/ NOUN, NO PLURAL when someone is willing to tell people things □ *We need more openness in government.*

open-plan /ˌəʊpənˈplæn/ ADJECTIVE open-plan rooms or buildings are not divided into smaller areas by walls □ *an open-plan office*

opera /ˈɒpərə/ NOUN [plural operas] a musical play in which the words are sung □ *an opera singer*

operate /ˈɒpəreɪt/ VERB [operates, operating, operated]

1 if machinery or equipment operates, it works, and if you operate it, you make it work □ *The radio operates on batteries.* □ *My job was to operate the switchboard.*

2 if a system or service operates, it exists and can be used, and if you operate a system or service, you

organize it and make it work □ *The train service only operates in the summer months.* □ *The organization operates a complaints procedure.*

3 if a business or an organization operates, it does its work, and if someone operates a business or organization, they manage it □ *Some prisons are operated by private security firms.*

4 to cut into someone's body to repair or remove a part when someone is ill □ **+ on** *They operated on the boy to save his sight.*

operating system /ˈɒpəreɪtɪŋ ˌsɪstəm/ NOUN [plural operating systems] a set of programs that control how a computer works. A computing word.

operating theater /ˈɒpəreɪtɪŋ ˌθɪətə(r)/ NOUN [plural operating theaters] the US spelling of operating theatre

operating theatre /ˈɒpəreɪtɪŋ ˌθɪətə(r)/ NOUN [plural operating theatres] a room in a hospital where doctors do operations

operation /ˌɒpəˈreɪʃən/ NOUN [plural operations]

1 when a doctor cuts into someone's body in order to repair or remove part of it 🔁 *He has to have an operation on his heart.* 🔁 *a minor operation*

2 a carefully planned and organized action □ *a rescue operation* □ *It was a joint operation between British and Spanish troops.*

3 a business or organization □ *The company is combining two of its existing operations.*

4 no plural when something is working or being used □ *The operation of the machine is controlled by computer.* □ *The hotel has just completed its first year of operation.*

5 in/into operation when something is in operation it is working or being used, and when something comes into operation, it starts working or being used □ *The new tax scheme is now in operation.* □ *When will the new trains be coming into operation?*

• operational /ˌɒpəˈreɪʃənəl/ ADJECTIVE

1 working or able to be used □ *The new terminal is now fully operational.*

2 to do with how a system, machine or business work □ *operational costs*

operator /ˈɒpəreɪtə(r)/ NOUN [plural operators]

1 someone whose job is to work a machine □ *a lift operator*

2 someone whose job is to connect telephone calls □ *Ask the operator to put you through to his extension*

3 a person or company that does a particular type of business □ *a tour operator*

ophthalmic /ɒfˈθælmɪk/ ADJECTIVE to do with the eye □ *an ophthalmic optician*

opinion /əˈpɪnjən/ NOUN [plural opinions]

1 what you think or believe □ **+ of** *What's your opinion of the new arts centre?* □ **+ about** *My opinions about education have changed.* 🔁 *She has strong opinions about the war.* 🔁 *In my opinion, yo did the right thing.* 🔁 *She didn't give (=say) her opinio*

of the film. 🖩 *I have a very high/low* (=good/bad) *opinion of most of my colleagues.*
2 public opinion what most people think or believe □ *Public opinion has turned against the party.*

➤ Note that you **give** (or **express**) an opinion. You do not 'say' an opinion:
✔ *Did she give her opinion of Claudia's work?*
✘ *Did she say her opinion of Claudia's work?*

• **opinionated** /ə'pɪnjəneɪtɪd/ ADJECTIVE having very strong opinions, and often refusing to accept that you are wrong □ *I found him arrogant and opinionated.*

opinion poll /ə'pɪnjən ˌpəʊl/ NOUN [*plural* **opinion polls**] when a number of people are asked questions to find out what they think about a particular subject □ *The latest opinion polls show the president's popularity is falling.*

opponent /ə'pəʊnənt/ NOUN [*plural* **opponents**]
1 someone you compete against in a game or a competition □ *He beat his opponent by four points.*
2 someone who disagrees with an idea, action, etc. and tries to stop or change it □ *She is a fierce opponent of the war.* □ *He threw his political opponents in jail.*

opportune /'ɒpətjuːn/ ADJECTIVE happening at a useful or lucky time 🖩 *He chose an opportune moment to make the announcement.*

opportunity /ˌɒpə'tjuːnətɪ/ NOUN [*plural* **opportunities**]
1 a chance to do something or a situation when you can do something □ *She saw the trip as the opportunity of a lifetime.* □ + **for** *There will be an opportunity for questions later.* □ + **to do something** *I had the opportunity to travel a lot in Europe.* 🖩 *I took the opportunity to speak to the senator in private.*
2 a job or something that is worth doing □ *We can give you information about employment opportunities.* □ *There are a lot of opportunities in the army.*

oppose /ə'pəʊz/ VERB [**opposes, opposing, opposed**] to disagree with someone's ideas, plans or actions and try to change or stop them □ *Local people opposed the plan to expand the airport.*
opposed /ə'pəʊzd/ ADJECTIVE
1 opposed to something disagreeing with someone's ideas, plans or actions □ *He's always been opposed to battery farming.*
2 as opposed to used to emphasize the difference between two things □ *I'm interested in European cinema, as opposed to the Hollywood variety.*
opposing /ə'pəʊzɪŋ/ ADJECTIVE
1 playing or fighting against each other □ *The two brothers fought on opposing sides in the war.* □ *A penalty was awarded to the opposing team.*
2 opposing ideas or beliefs are completely different □ *My husband and I have opposing views on education.*

opposite /'ɒpəzɪt/ ➤ ADJECTIVE
1 facing something or on the other side of something □ *The answers are on the opposite page.* □ *She lives on the opposite side of town.*
2 completely different □ *Her remarks had the opposite effect to what she intended.* □ *They walked off in opposite directions.*
➤ PREPOSITION, ADVERB facing something or on the other side of something □ *The house opposite mine is up for sale.* □ *Who lives in the house opposite?* □ *I was sitting opposite my brother at the table.*
➤ NOUN [*plural* **opposites**] someone or something that is completely different from someone or something else □ *Hot is the opposite of cold.* □ *My sister and I are complete opposites.*

opposition /ˌɒpə'zɪʃən/ NOUN, NO PLURAL
1 strong disagreement with something and efforts to change it □ *The plan has met with opposition from the medical profession.*
2 the people you are fighting or competing against □ *United come up against tough opposition this afternoon.*
3 the Opposition the main political party that opposes the party in government □ *the leader of the Opposition*

oppress /ə'pres/ VERB [**oppresses, oppressing, oppressed**]
1 to treat a group of people cruelly or unfairly, often by limiting what they can do □ *These laws oppress women.*
2 to make someone feel worried or unhappy □ *The silence in the room oppressed her.*

• **oppression** /ə'preʃən/ NOUN, NO PLURAL cruel or unfair treatment, often limiting what people can do □ *They fought against the oppression of the working classes.*

• **oppressive** /ə'presɪv/ ADJECTIVE
1 cruel and unfair, often limiting what people can do □ *an oppressive regime*
2 making you feel worried and uncomfortable □ *Her husband's presence was oppressive.*
3 oppressive weather is hot and uncomfortable, with no wind □ *the oppressive heat of the desert*

opt /ɒpt/ VERB [**opts, opting, opted**] to make a choice or a decision to do something □ *I opted for the strawberry gateau.* □ *She opted to stay on at college.*
◆ PHRASAL VERB **opt out** to decide not to do something □ *I opted out of the trip.*

optic /'ɒptɪk/ ADJECTIVE to do with the eye. A biology word □ *the optic nerve*

optical /'ɒptɪkəl/ ADJECTIVE to do with the eyes, sight or light □ *an optical instrument*

optical illusion /ˌɒptɪkəl ɪ'luːʒən/ NOUN [*plural* **optical illusions**] something which tricks your eyes, making you think you can see something that is not really there

optician /ɒpˈtɪʃən/ NOUN [plural **opticians**] someone whose job is to test your eyes and make and sell glasses

optimism /ˈɒptɪmɪzəm/ NOUN, NO PLURAL when you believe that good things will happen □ *She was full of optimism about her new job.*

• **optimist** /ˈɒptɪmɪst/ NOUN [plural **optimists**] someone who usually believes that good things will happen

• **optimistic** /ˌɒptɪˈmɪstɪk/ ADJECTIVE hoping or believing that good things will happen □ *I'm not feeling very optimistic about this exam.*

• **optimistically** /ˌɒptɪˈmɪstɪkəlɪ/ ADVERB in an optimistic way □ *'She might still come,' he said optimistically.*

optimum /ˈɒptɪməm/ ADJECTIVE the best or most suitable □ *The flat is small but optimum use is made of the space.*

option /ˈɒpʃən/ NOUN [plural **options**]
1 something that you can choose or decide to do □ *There are several options open to me.* □ *Is there a vegetarian option on the menu?* □ *Our only option was to accept his offer.* □ **+ of doing something** *We have the option of buying or leasing a car.*
2 keep/leave your options open to arrange a situation so that you still have choices about it in the future □ *They're pressing me to accept the job, but I want to keep my options open a bit longer.*

• **optional** /ˈɒpʃənəl/ ADJECTIVE if something is optional, you can have it or do it if you want to, but you do not have to □ *Music was an optional subject at my school.* ▢ *The car has a lot of optional extras.*

or /ɔː(r)/ CONJUNCTION
1 used to show possibilities or choices □ *Would you prefer tea or coffee?* □ *We could see a film or go for a walk.* □ *Their little girl must be seven or eight.* □ *Shall we have pizza, pasta or risotto?*
2 used after a negative verb to say not any of a list of things or people □ *I don't like him or his sister.*
3 used for saying what will happen if something is not done □ *I'd better go or I'll miss the last bus.*
4 used to explain or correct something you have just said □ *30% of the population, or three out of ten people, voted.* □ *There were ten of us, or rather nine.*

-or /-ə(r)/ SUFFIX another way of spelling -er
oral /ˈɔːrəl/ ▶ ADJECTIVE
1 spoken, not written □ *an oral examination*
2 to do with the mouth □ *oral hygiene*
▶ NOUN [plural **orals**] an examination where you have to speak □ *I've got my Spanish oral tomorrow.*

• **orally** /ˈɔːrəlɪ/ ADVERB
1 by speaking □ *I prefer to communicate orally rather than by e-mail.*
2 by swallowing □ *This medicine must be taken orally.*

orange /ˈɒrɪndʒ/ ▶ ADJECTIVE having the colour you get if you mix red and yellow □ *This bush has tiny orange flowers in summer.*
▶ NOUN [plural **oranges**]
1 a round fruit with orange skin and a lot of juice □ *orange juice*
2 *no plural* the colour you get if you mix red and yellow

orang-utan /ɒˈræŋətæn/ NOUN [plural **orang-utans**] an animal like a monkey with long arms and orange or brown hair

orator /ˈɒrətə(r)/ NOUN [plural **orators**] a person who is good at making public speeches □ *a great orator*

orbit /ˈɔːbɪt/ ▶ NOUN [plural **orbits**] the circular path along which something moves around a sun, moon or planet □ *The spaceship is in orbit round the moon.*
▶ VERB [**orbits**, **orbiting**, **orbited**] to go round a sun, moon or planet □ *The spacecraft is orbiting Earth.*

orchard /ˈɔːtʃəd/ NOUN [plural **orchards**] an area of land where fruit trees are grown □ *a cherry orchard*

orchestra /ˈɔːkɪstrə/ NOUN [plural **orchestras**] a large group of musicians playing together □ *a symphony orchestra*

• **orchestral** /ɔːˈkestrəl/ ADJECTIVE written for or played by an orchestra □ *orchestral music*

orchestrate /ˈɔːkɪstreɪt/ VERB [**orchestrates**, **orchestrating**, **orchestrated**] to organize or arrange a complicated event or activity so that you get the result you want □ *He was responsible for orchestrating the whole presidential campaign.*

orchid /ˈɔːkɪd/ NOUN [plural **orchids**] a flower with an unusual shape

ordain /ɔːˈdeɪn/ VERB [**ordains**, **ordaining**, **ordained**] to make someone a priest in a special ceremony □ *Some Christian churches have decided to ordain women.*

ordeal /ɔːˈdiːl/ NOUN [plural **ordeals**] a very unpleasant experience □ *He spent ten years in prison, but survived the ordeal with great courage.*

order /ˈɔːdə(r)/ ▶ NOUN [plural **orders**]
1 an instruction to do something ▢ *The soldier was given the order to shoot.* ▢ *I refuse to take orders from that man.* ▢ *They obeyed the order to retreat.*
2 under orders if you are under orders, you have been told to do something or to behave in a particular way □ *We were under orders not to speak to anyone.*
3 when you ask for food or goods that you will pay for ▢ *The waiter came to take our order.* ▢ *The government has placed an order for ten new helicopters.*
4 the way things are arranged ▢ *The books are in alphabetical order of their authors.* □ *List the options in your order of preference.*
5 when people are calm and obeying the law ▢ *Troops were called in to restore order to the region.*
6 a state where everything is tidy or in its correct state □ *I need to get my accounts in order.*
7 in order to do something so that something can happen or be done □ *She took the money in order to buy food.* □ *I phoned him in order to arrange a meeting.*
8 out of order not working correctly □ *The toilets are out of order today.*

▶ VERB [orders, ordering, ordered]
1 to tell someone to do something □ **+ to do something** *The doctor ordered her to rest for a few days.*
2 to say that something must happen or be done □ *The government has ordered an enquiry into the incident.* □ *I can prove that he ordered the killing.*
3 to ask for food or goods that you will pay for □ *I ordered some magazines from the newsagent.* □ *I ordered the pizza.*
4 to arrange things in a particular way □ *I ordered the CDs according to the type of music.*
• **orderly** /ˈɔːdəlɪ/ ADJECTIVE
1 controlled and behaving well □ *Please form an orderly queue.*
2 in a tidy or correct arrangement □ *He kept orderly records of all his expenses.*

ordinal /ˈɔːdɪnəl/ ADJECTIVE ordinal numbers are numbers like first, second, third. A maths word.

ordinarily /ˈɔːdənərəlɪ/ ADVERB usually □ *I don't ordinarily drink wine.*
• **ordinary** /ˈɔːdənərɪ/ ADJECTIVE
1 normal and not unusual or different □ *It was just an ordinary Monday morning.* □ *Ordinary people don't buy designer clothes.*
2 **out of the ordinary** unusual or different from normal □ *Your tests show nothing out of the ordinary.*

ordination /ˌɔːdɪˈneɪʃən/ NOUN [plural ordinations] the act or ceremony of making someone a priest □ *His parents attended his ordination.*

ore /ɔː(r)/ NOUN [plural ores] rock or earth which contains a metal □ *iron ore*

organ /ˈɔːgən/ NOUN [plural organs]
1 a part of your body that has a special purpose □ *an organ donor* (=someone who lets their organs be used after they die)
2 a large musical instrument with keys like a piano and several long pipes that air is pushed through, often found in churches □ *She played the organ at our wedding.*

organic /ɔːˈgænɪk/ ADJECTIVE
1 organic food is produced without using chemicals □ *I only buy organic vegetables.*
2 found in or made by living things □ *organic fertilizers*
3 containing carbon. A chemistry word □ *organic compounds*
• **organically** /ɔːˈgænɪkəlɪ/ ADVERB without using chemicals □ *Organically grown vegetables are often more expensive.*

organism /ˈɔːgənɪzəm/ NOUN [plural organisms] any living thing, especially one that is very small. A biology word □ *Samples of marine organisms were collected from the sea bed.*

organist /ˈɔːgənɪst/ NOUN [plural organists] someone who plays the organ (=large instrument like a piano that is played in a church)

organization *or* **organisation** /ˌɔːgənaɪˈzeɪʃən/ NOUN [plural organizations]
1 a group of people who work together for a purpose □ *He's working for a voluntary organization that helps ex-prisoners.*
2 *no plural* the activity of arranging or preparing for an event or an activity □ *The festival took months of organization.*
3 *no plural* the way in which something is arranged or organized □ *Paul's essays show a lack of organization.*
• **organize** *or* **organise** /ˈɔːgənaɪz/ VERB [organizes, organizing, organized]
1 to arrange and prepare an event or an activity □ *We've organized a surprise party for his birthday.*
2 to make something tidy or to put something in order □ *He organized all the papers into neat piles.*
• **organized** *or* **organised** /ˈɔːgənaɪzd/ ADJECTIVE
1 involving a group of people who plan and do something together □ *We went on an organized tour of the vineyard.* □ *organized crime*
2 an organized person is good at planning and arranging things □ *I'm just not very organized.*
• **organizer** *or* **organiser** /ˈɔːgənaɪzə(r)/ NOUN [plural organizers] someone who organizes an event or an activity □ *a conference organizer*

Orient /ˈɔːrɪənt/ NOUN, NO PLURAL the Orient an old-fashioned word for the countries in eastern Asia such as China and Japan □ *spices from the Orient*

oriental /ˌɔːrɪˈentəl/ ADJECTIVE from or to do with the countries of eastern Asia such as China and Japan □ *oriental cuisine*

orienteering /ˌɔːrɪənˈtɪərɪŋ/ NOUN, NO PLURAL a sport in which you run across countryside, finding your way with a map

origin /ˈɒrɪdʒɪn/ NOUN [plural origins]
1 the cause of something or place where something starts □ *There are many theories about the origin of our solar system.* □ *The English language contains many words of Anglo-Saxon origin.*
2 the country, race, class etc. that someone comes from □ *Her family are Italian in origin.* ⊞ *Please state your ethnic origin on the form.*
• **original** /əˈrɪdʒɪnəl/ ▶ ADJECTIVE
1 existing from the beginning, or not having been changed □ *The original story had been changed over the centuries.* □ *Our house still has the original fireplaces.*
2 new and interesting, and not like others of its type □ *a novel full of original ideas* ⊞ *Her paintings are highly original.*
3 done by the artist himself or herself □ *He own an original drawing by Picasso.*
▶ NOUN [plural originals] a piece of art that is in the form in which it was first created and is not a copy □ *The original of this painting is in Florence.*
• **originality** /əˌrɪdʒɪˈnælətɪ/ NOUN, NO PLURAL the quality of being new and interesting and not like others of its type □ *I admire the originality of his paintings.*
• **originally** /əˈrɪdʒɪnəlɪ/ ADVERB

1 in the beginning □ *His family comes from Scotland originally.*
2 before something changed or was changed □ *The building was originally used as a store.*
• **originate** /əˈrɪdʒɪneɪt/ VERB [**originates, originating, originated**] to start to happen or exist □ *This style of painting originated in China.*

ornament ▶ NOUN /ˈɔːnəmənt/ [*plural* **ornaments**] an object used to decorate a room, building or place □ *Every surface was covered with china ornaments.*
▶ VERB /ˈɔːnəmənt/ [**ornaments, ornamenting, ornamented**] to decorate something □ *The ceiling was richly ornamented.*
• **ornamental** /ˌɔːnəˈmentəl/ ADJECTIVE having no purpose except decoration □ *an ornamental pond*

ornate /ɔːˈneɪt/ ADJECTIVE decorated with a complicated design □ *A huge mirror with an ornate surround hung over the fire.*

ornithologist /ˌɔːnɪˈθɒlədʒɪst/ NOUN [*plural* **ornithologists**] someone who studies or is an expert on birds
• **ornithology** /ˌɔːnɪˈθɒlədʒɪ/ NOUN, NO PLURAL the study of birds

orphan /ˈɔːfən/ ▶ NOUN [*plural* **orphans**] a child whose parents are both dead
▶ VERB [**orphans, orphaning, orphaned**] if you are orphaned, you become an orphan □ *Sadie was orphaned at the age of six.*
• **orphanage** /ˈɔːfənɪdʒ/ NOUN [*plural* **orphanages**] a home for orphans

orthodox /ˈɔːθədɒks/ ADJECTIVE
1 having ideas that most people accept and think are correct □ *orthodox medical treatment*
2 keeping the traditional customs and beliefs of Judaism or some types of Christianity □ *orthodox Jews*

orthopaedic /ˌɔːθəˈpiːdɪk/ ADJECTIVE to do with the treatment or study of bones and muscles

orthopedic /ˌɔːθəˈpiːdɪk/ ADJECTIVE the US spelling of orthopaedic

oscillate /ˈɒsɪleɪt/ VERB [**oscillates, oscillating, oscillated**]
1 to keep changing between two feelings, opinions or types of behaviour □ *His mood oscillated between elation and depression.*
2 to move between one position and another regularly and repeatedly □ *The magnetic field oscillates to create magnetic waves.*

osmosis /ɒzˈməʊsɪs/ NOUN, NO PLURAL when a liquid goes through a thin layer, for example water into the roots of a plant. A biology word.

ostensible /ɒˈstensəbəl/ ADJECTIVE an ostensible reason for something is one that people state but that may not be true □ *The ostensible purpose of the meeting was to promote good community relations.*
• **ostensibly** /ɒˈstensəblɪ/ ADVERB if something is ostensibly the reason for something, people say it is the reason but it may not be □ *His arrest was ostensibly for theft but was really for political reasons.*

ostentatious /ˌɒstənˈteɪʃəs/ ADJECTIVE intended to attract attention or admiration, often by showing how rich or powerful someone is □ *Martins was wearing the ostentatious jewellery of a hip-hop singer.*
• **ostentatiously** /ˌɒstənˈteɪʃəslɪ/ ADVERB in a very ostentatious or obvious way □ *She ostentatiously ignored his comments.*

osteopath /ˈɒstɪəpæθ/ NOUN [*plural* **osteopaths**] someone whose job is to treat pain in the bones and muscles by moving and rubbing them with their hands
• **osteopathy** /ˌɒstɪˈɒpəθɪ/ NOUN, NO PLURAL a form of treatment for pain in the bones and muscles in which an osteopath moves and rubs them with their hands

osteoporosis /ˌɒstɪəʊpəˈrəʊsɪs/ NOUN, NO PLURAL a disease in which the bones become weak and break easily

ostracize *or* **ostracise** /ˈɒstrəsaɪz/ VERB [**ostracizes, ostracizing, ostracized**] to deliberately leave someone out of a group by refusing to speak to them or be friendly with them □ *He was ostracized by his former workmates for refusing to join the strike.*

ostrich /ˈɒstrɪtʃ/ NOUN [*plural* **ostriches**] a large bird which cannot fly but runs very fast

other /ˈʌðə(r)/ ▶ ADJECTIVE
1 used to talk about something or someone else of a similar type □ *Do you have any other news to tell me?* □ *I have lots of other questions.* ▣ *I prefer living with other people.* ▣ *There were lots of other things to do.*
2 different from the thing or person you have been talking about □ *There must be some other reason.* □ *Does this dress come in any other colours?* ▣ *I thought Kate would be taller than Jo, but it was the other way round* (=the opposite).
3 used to talk about the second of two things or people, when the first has already been mentioned □ *Where is my other glove?* □ *I live on the other side of town.* ▣ *This vase is Chinese, and the other one is Japanese.*
4 used to talk about the remaining people or things □ *The other team members will arrive tomorrow.*
5 the other day/week, etc. a few days/weeks, etc ago □ *I saw Adam a few days ago.*
6 every other day/Sunday/ on one of each two days/Sundays, etc. □ *I try to run every other day.*
7 other than except □ *I had no food other than a bar of chocolate I found in my bag.* □ *Other than Charlie nobody was interested in my news.*
8 somewhere/someone, etc. or other used to say somewhere/someone, etc. when it is not important exactly where or who □ *I ought to give him something or other for his birthday.*
▶ PRONOUN
1 the second of two □ *Here's one sock, but where is the other?*
2 others things or people of a similar type □ *I really enjoyed that book. Do you have any others by her?*
3 the others the remaining people or things □ *I've found some of her letters, but where are the others?* □ *Wait for the others to arrive.*

4 others other people □ *I find her amusing. Others might disagree.*

otherwise /ˈʌðəwaɪz/ ADVERB

1 used to say what will happen if something is not done or is not true □ *You need to get up, otherwise you'll be late.* □ *I hope it won't be cold. Otherwise we'll need to take coats.*

2 if the thing that has just been mentioned is not true □ *He must have seen the letter, otherwise how could he have known the truth?*

3 except for the thing that has just been mentioned □ *I've got a cold, but I'm fine otherwise.* □ *One person raised his hand. Otherwise, nobody moved.*

4 different from what has been said □ *Unless I hear otherwise, I'll be there at ten.* □ *I thought the food was fine, but Des thought otherwise.*

otter /ˈɒtə(r)/ NOUN [*plural* **otters**] a small animal with brown fur that lives by rivers, swims well and eats fish

ouch /aʊtʃ/ EXCLAMATION a word that people say when they feel a sudden pain

ought /ɔːt/ MODAL VERB

1 ought to do something (a) used to say what is the best or right thing to do □ *I think we ought to call the police.* □ *He ought to wear glasses.* (b) used to say that you expect something to be true □ *They ought to reach Berlin by tomorrow.* □ *Three loaves ought to be enough.*

2 ought to have used to say what would have been the right thing to do when you have done something different □ *They ought to have travelled by train.* □ *He ought to have had more sense.*

oughtn't /ˈɔːtənt/ a short way to say and write ought not □ *You really oughtn't to see him again.*

ounce /aʊns/ NOUN [*plural* **ounces**] a unit for measuring weight, equal to 1/16 of a pound. This is often written **oz.**

our /ˈaʊə(r)/ ADJECTIVE belonging to or to do with us □ *That is our car.*

ours /ˈaʊəz/ PRONOUN used to talk or write about things belonging to or to do with us □ *That car is ours.* □ *These books are ours.*

ourselves /aʊəˈselvz/ PRONOUN

1 the reflexive form of *we* □ *We saw ourselves in the mirror.* □ *We should keep some of the money for ourselves.*

2 used to show that we do something without any help from other people □ *We painted the room ourselves.* 🔊 *We built the house all by ourselves.*

3 used to emphasize the pronoun *we* □ *We ourselves played no part in this.*

4 by ourselves not with or near other people □ *They left us by ourselves in a cold room.*

5 to ourselves without having to share with anyone else □ *We had the whole hotel to ourselves.*

-ous /-əs/ SUFFIX -ous is added to the end of words to mean 'having a particular quality' □ *adventurous*

oust /aʊst/ VERB [**ousts, ousting, ousted**] to force someone out of their position or job □ *She was ousted from her position on the board.*

out /aʊt/ ADVERB, PREPOSITION

1 from inside a container, hole, vehicle, etc. □ *She opened her bag and took out an umbrella.* □ **+ of** *He got out of the car.* 🔊 *I opened the cupboard and a bag of rice fell out.*

2 away from your home or work for a social activity 🔊 *Are you going out tonight?* □ *I was out with Gerry last night.*

3 away from your home or work □ *I phoned, but you were out.*

4 away from a building or place □ *I stood out in the garden.* □ **+ of** *She was dragged out of the room by armed guards.* □ *He is not allowed to go out of the country.*

5 out of used to say what something is made from □ *The shelter was made out of sticks.*

6 used to talk about places that are far away □ *My brother lives in Florida. I'd love to spend some time out there with him.*

7 if a fire or light is out, it is not shining □ *When we reached the house, all the lights were out.*

8 no longer in a game or competition because you have lost □ *The batsman is out.* □ **+ of** *England are out of the World Cup.*

9 available to be bought or seen □ *His latest film will be out next week.*

10 out of because of □ *I only went to see her out of curiosity.*

11 out of something with no more of something remaining □ *The printer's out of ink.*

12 two/six, etc. out of ten/a hundred, etc. used to say how many people or things in a group are involved in or affected by something

13 not accurate □ *I think my measurements were a bit out.* □ **+ by** *His estimate was out by over £1,000.*

out-and-out /ˌaʊtənˈaʊt/ ADJECTIVE in every way □ *an out-and-out liar*

outback /ˈaʊtbæk/ NOUN, NO PLURAL **the outback** the areas in Australia that are far away from towns and cities

out-box /ˈaʊtbɒks/ NOUN [*plural* **out-boxes**] the place on a computer which stores e-mail messages that you are going to send. A computing word.

outbreak /ˈaʊtbreɪk/ NOUN [*plural* **outbreaks**] when something such as war or a disease starts □ *There's been a fresh outbreak of measles in the area.*

outbuilding /ˈaʊtbɪldɪŋ/ NOUN [*plural* **outbuildings**] a building that is separate from but near to a main building, for example for keeping tools, animals or vehicles in

outburst /ˈaʊtbɜːst/ NOUN [*plural* **outbursts**] when someone suddenly says something that shows strong emotion, especially anger □ *Her outburst shocked her colleagues.*

outcast /'aʊtkɑːst/ NOUN [plural **outcasts**] someone who is not accepted by society or by other members of a group ⊞ *The defendant was described as a social outcast with a history of drug abuse.*

outcome /'aʊtkʌm/ NOUN [plural **outcomes**] the final result of something □ *What was the outcome of your discussion?*

outcrop /'aʊtkrɒp/ NOUN [plural **outcrops**] a rock or group of rocks that sticks out above the surface of the ground

outcry /'aʊtkraɪ/ NOUN [plural **outcries**] a strong reaction of anger or disapproval by a large number of people □ *The decision caused a public outcry.*

outdated /ˌaʊt'deɪtɪd/ ADJECTIVE old-fashioned and no longer suitable □ *They are using terribly outdated systems for their customer records.*

outdo /ˌaʊt'duː/ VERB [**outdoes, outdoing, outdid, outdone**] to do something better than someone else □ *The girls tried to outdo each other in their kindness.*

outdoor /ˌaʊt'dɔː(r)/ ADJECTIVE happening or done outside or for use outside □ *an outdoor swimming pool* □ *outdoor shoes*

• **outdoors** /ˌaʊt'dɔːz/ ADVERB outside □ *She sat outdoors in the sun.* □ *Don't go outdoors if it's raining.*

outer /'aʊtə(r)/ ADJECTIVE
1 on or near the outside of something □ *Peel off the outer layers of the onion.*
2 furthest away from the centre □ *the outer suburbs of Paris*

outer space /ˌaʊtə 'speɪs/ NOUN, NO PLURAL the area outside the Earth's atmosphere where the other planets and stars are □ *Many people long to meet visitors from outer space.*

outfit /'aʊtfɪt/ NOUN [plural **outfits**]
1 a set of clothes that are worn together □ *I've bought myself a new outfit for the wedding.* □ *Jake got a cowboy outfit for his birthday.*
2 an organization or business □ *He runs a small transport outfit.*

outgoing /ˌaʊt'gəʊɪŋ/ ADJECTIVE
1 friendly and liking to talk to other people □ *Sally's quite a confident, outgoing girl.*
2 leaving a position of authority □ *The outgoing president gave his final speech.*
3 going out of or away from a place □ *We can't make outgoing calls from this phone.*

• **outgoings** /'aʊtgəʊɪŋz/ PLURAL NOUN money that you have to spend on regular costs like rent, food, travelling etc. □ *I'm trying to cut down on my monthly outgoings.*

outgrow /ˌaʊt'grəʊ/ VERB [**outgrows, outgrowing, outgrew, outgrown**]
1 to become too big for something □ *She has outgrown all her clothes.*
2 to lose your interest in something as you get older □ *I think I might be outgrowing my obsession with fantasy novels.*

outing /'aʊtɪŋ/ NOUN [plural **outings**] a short journey made for pleasure □ *I took the kids on an outing to the seaside.*

outlandish /ˌaʊt'lændɪʃ/ ADJECTIVE very strange and unusual □ *As a student, he wore the most outlandish clothes.*

outlast /ˌaʊt'lɑːst/ VERB [**outlasts, outlasting, outlasted**] to last or live longer than someone or something else □ *I think these shoes will outlast us all.*

outlaw /'aʊtlɔː/ ▶ VERB [**outlaws, outlawing, outlawed**] to make something illegal □ *Should computer hacking be outlawed completely?*
▶ NOUN [plural **outlaws**] a criminal, especially one who moves from place to place to avoid being caught

outlay /'aʊtleɪ/ NOUN [plural **outlays**] an amount of money that is spent, especially in order to start a business or something that you want to do □ *The scheme required an initial outlay of £50,000.*

outlet /'aʊtlet/ NOUN [plural **outlets**]
1 a way of expressing or using strong feelings or ideas □ *Sports like boxing are seen as an outlet for male aggression.* □ *What Becky needs is an outlet for her creativity.*
2 a shop or business that sells goods made by a particular company or of a particular type □ *The number of fast food outlets in the town has rocketed.*
3 a place where a gas or liquid can flow out of something

outline /'aʊtlaɪn/ ▶ VERB [**outlines, outlining, outlined**]
1 to explain the main ideas and facts about something □ *The headmaster outlined the planned changes to the school.*
2 to draw or make a line around the outside of something □ *She drew a red square, outlined in blue.*
▶ NOUN [plural **outlines**]
1 a line that shows the shape of something □ *First he drew the outline of a church seen against the sky.*
2 a short description of the main parts of something □ *Just give me an outline of the facts.*

outlive /ˌaʊt'lɪv/ VERB [**outlives, outliving, outlived**] to live or exist longer than someone or something else □ *He outlived his older brother by fifteen years.*

outlook /'aʊtlʊk/ NOUN [plural **outlooks**]
1 someone's attitude to life □ *He has a strange outlook on life.*
2 what is likely to happen in the future □ *The outlook for the economy is poor.*
3 a view □ *From the top there is a wonderful outlook over the valley.*

outlying /'aʊtˌlaɪɪŋ/ ADJECTIVE at the edges of or a short distance away from a particular place □ *They moved to the town from one of the outlying villages*

outmoded /ˌaʊt'məʊdəd/ ADJECTIVE not modern or fashionable □ *The doctor has some outmoded ideas about bringing up children.*

outnumber /ˌaʊt'nʌmbə(r)/ VERB [**outnumbers, outnumbering, outnumbered**] to be more in number than another group of people or things □ *The boys outnumber the girls by three to two.*

out-of-date /ˌaʊtəv'deɪt/ ADJECTIVE old and often no longer useful or suitable □ *Our computer systems are becoming rather out-of-date.* □ *I have an out-of-date list of addresses.*

outpatient /'aʊtpeɪʃənt/ NOUN [*plural* **outpatients**] someone who comes to a hospital for treatment but does not sleep there at night

outpost /'aʊtpəʊst/ NOUN [*plural* **outposts**]
1 part of a business or organization that is far away from its main part □ *His restaurant empire includes outposts in Dubai , Tokyo and New York.*
2 a small military camp (=place where people live in tents) far away from the main army, built especially to protect it from a surprise attack

outpouring /'aʊtˌpɔːrɪŋ/ NOUN [*plural* **outpourings**] a public expression of a strong emotion □ *There was an outpouring of grief at her death.*

output /'aʊtpʊt/ ▶ NOUN [*plural* **outputs**]
1 a quantity of goods produced or an amount of work done □ *The output of this factory increased last year.*
2 the information produced by a computer
3 the power produced by an engine or a piece of equipment
▶ VERB [**outputs, outputting, output**] to produce information from a computer □ *The data is output in the form of a spreadsheet.*

outrage /'aʊtreɪdʒ/ ▶ NOUN [*plural* **outrages**]
1 a strong feeling of anger or shock □ *Her remarks caused outrage among animal lovers.*
2 a shocking or cruel action □ *The decision to close the hospital is an outrage.*
▶ VERB [**outrages, outraging, outraged**] to make someone feel shocked and angry □ *Fay was outraged by his behaviour.*

outrageous /aʊt'reɪdʒəs/ ADJECTIVE shocking or very unreasonable □ *His behaviour was absolutely outrageous.* □ *This restaurant charges outrageous prices.*

outrageously /aʊt'reɪdʒəslɪ/ ADVERB in an outrageous way □ *It's outrageously expensive to go to the opera.*

outright ▶ ADVERB /ˌaʊt'raɪt/ in a clear and complete way □ *We won outright.* 🔁 *When the bomb exploded, they were killed outright* (=immediately).
▶ ADJECTIVE /'aʊtraɪt/ clear and complete □ *Many people want an outright ban on public smoking.*

outset /'aʊtset/ NOUN **at/from the outset** at or from the beginning □ *The project was in difficulty from the outset.*

outshine /aʊt'ʃaɪn/ VERB [**outshines, outshining, outshone**] to do something much better than someone else □ *Jo easily outshone the other candidates.*

outside ▶ ADVERB /ˌaʊt'saɪd/ not inside a building □ *Let's eat outside.* □ *He went outside for a cigarette.*
▶ PREPOSITION
not inside a building, room or area, but near it □ *He*

was standing outside our house. □ *I come from a small village just outside York.*
2 not part of something □ *Nursery schools are outside our area of responsibility.* □ *Catering for large weddings is outside my experience.*
▶ ADJECTIVE /'aʊtsaɪd/
1 not inside a building □ *We painted the outside walls of the shed.* □ *Gran's old house used to have an outside toilet.* 🔁 *He wanted the outside world* (=people in other places) *to know of his suffering.*
2 not belonging to a group or organization □ *We've had to get in some outside support to help with the conference.*
3 an outside chance a very small possibility □ *City still have an outside chance of winning the trophy.*
▶ NOUN /ˌaʊt'saɪd, 'aʊtsaɪd/ [*plural* **outsides**] the **outside** the outer surface or part of something □ *The outside of the house was painted white.* □ *The cake was burnt on the outside.*

● **outsider** /ˌaʊt'saɪdə(r)/ NOUN [*plural* **outsiders**]
1 someone who does not belong to a particular group or place □ *I have lived here for ten years, but I still feel like an outsider.*
2 a horse or person that is not expected to win a race or competition

outsize /'aʊtsaɪz/ ADJECTIVE bigger than the largest usual size □ *outsize clothing*

outskirts /'aʊtskɜːts/ PLURAL NOUN **the outskirts** the outer parts of a town or city □ *He lives on the outskirts of Edinburgh.*

outspoken /ˌaʊt'spəʊkən/ ADJECTIVE saying exactly what you mean, even if it upsets people □ *She is an outspoken critic of the government.*

outstanding /ˌaʊt'stændɪŋ/ ADJECTIVE
1 excellent □ *an outstanding student*
2 not yet paid or done □ *You must complete all your outstanding assignments.* □ *This bill for your mobile phone is still outstanding.*

outstretched /ˌaʊt'stretʃt/ ADJECTIVE if part of your body is outstretched, it is stretched out as far as possible, usually in order to reach something □ *She stood with outstretched arms waiting to welcome them.*

out-tray /'aʊttreɪ/ NOUN [*plural* **out-trays**] the container in your office where you put letters or papers ready for posting or passing to someone else

outward /'aʊtwəd/ ADJECTIVE
1 to do with how things appear □ *She shows no outward sign of unhappiness.*
2 away from a place □ *The outward flight was severely delayed.*

● **outward** /'aʊtwəd/ *or* **outwards** /'aʊtwədz/ ADVERB towards the outside □ *Most windows open outward.*

● **outwardly** /'aʊtwədlɪ/ ADVERB in the way that something seems, which may not be the truth □ *Outwardly they were cheerful.*

outweigh /ˌaʊt'weɪ/ VERB [**outweighs, outweighing, outweighed**] to be more important than something else □ *The advantages outweigh the disadvantages.*

outwit /ˌaʊtˈwɪt/ VERB [outwits, outwitting, outwitted] to get an advantage over someone by doing something clever, often to trick them □ *She outwitted the police and managed to escape.*

oval /ˈəʊvəl/ ▶ ADJECTIVE shaped like a circle with the edges pressed slightly together □ *an oval table* ▶ NOUN [*plural* **ovals**] an oval shape □ *He drew an oval.*

ovary /ˈəʊvərɪ/ NOUN [*plural* **ovaries**]
1 the part of a woman's body where eggs are formed. A biology word.
2 the part of a flower where seeds are formed. A biology word.

oven /ˈʌvən/ NOUN [*plural* **ovens**] the part of a cooker that is shaped like a box with a door and is used for cooking and heating food □ *Bake the cake in the centre of the oven for 30 minutes.*

oven glove /ˈʌvən ˌɡlʌv/ NOUN [*plural* **oven gloves**] a special glove (=covering for your hand) made of a thick material that you use when you take hot food out of an oven

ovenproof /ˈʌvənpruːf/ ADJECTIVE ovenproof dishes do not break when they are put into a hot oven

over /ˈəʊvə(r)/ ▶ PREPOSITION
1 above someone or something, or moving across the place above someone or something □ *His photograph hung over the fireplace.* □ *An eagle flew right over our heads.*
2 about a particular subject □ *They quarrelled over the children.* □ *He was in court over a dispute with a neighbour.*
3 more than □ *He's over 90 years old.* □ *She left school just over three years ago.*
4 across □ *We ran over the bridge.*
5 covering something or someone □ *I put a blanket over her legs.* □ *There was snow over the hills.*
🕮 *You've got mud all over your clothes.*
6 on the other side of something □ *There is a house just over that hill.* □ *The sun set over the horizon.* □ *My house is just over the road.*
7 be/get over something to feel better after being ill or unhappy □ *He never got over the disappointment.* □ *I had the flu, but I'm over it now.*
8 used to talk about controlling or defeating someone or something □ *Chelsea celebrated their win over Leeds.* □ *He ruled over the entire country.*
▶ ADVERB
1 moving across the place above someone or something □ *An aeroplane flew over.*
2 from one side to the other □ *That bridge isn't safe – I'm not going over.*
3 higher in number or amount □ *Children aged seven and over may swim alone.*
4 onto the other side □ *The dog rolled over in the mud.* □ *Turn your papers over.*
5 to a particular place □ *He walked over to speak to them.* □ *Would you like to come over for lunch?*

6 towards the side □ *Could you stand a bit further over to the right?* □ *I moved over to make room for him.*
7 remaining □ *There were two cakes left over.*
8 all over again again, from the beginning □ *My computer crashed, and I had to do my essay all over again.*
9 over and over again and again □ *I told her over and over not to talk to strangers.*
▶ ADJECTIVE
1 finished □ *The match is already over.*
2 over and done with if you get an unpleasant task over and done with, you complete it so that you do not have to worry about it any more

over- /ˈəʊvə(r)/ PREFIX over- is added to the beginning of words to mean 'too' or 'too much' □ *Be careful not to get overconfident.* □ *an overcrowded train*

overall ▶ ADJECTIVE /ˈəʊvərɔːl/ including everything □ *The overall cost of the holiday has gone up.*
▶ ADVERB /ˌəʊvərˈɔːl/ considering or including everything or everyone □ *Overall, I'm very pleased with the film.*
▶ NOUN /ˈəʊvərɔːl/ [*plural* **overalls**]
1 a piece of clothing like a thin coat worn over ordinary clothes to protect them □ *She wears an overall when cleaning the house.*
2 overalls a piece of clothing that covers the legs and body, worn to protect clothing during dirty work

overawed /ˌəʊvərˈɔːd/ ADJECTIVE frightened or nervous because something is so big or powerful, or because you admire it so much □ *He was completely overawed by the splendid surroundings of the palace*

overbearing /ˌəʊvəˈbeərɪŋ/ ADJECTIVE trying to control other people without thinking about their feelings □ *I can't stand his overbearing manner.*

overboard /ˈəʊvəbɔːd/ ADVERB over the side of a ship or boat and into the water □ *He jumped overboard to save the drowning man.* □ *Man overboard!*
♦ IDIOM go overboard to do something too much, often because you are excited about something □ *I think you've gone a bit overboard with the decorations.*

overcame /ˌəʊvəˈkeɪm/ PAST TENSE OF overcome

overcast /ˌəʊvəˈkɑːst/ ADJECTIVE dark and with a lot of clouds □ *The sky was overcast but it didn't rain.*

overcharge /ˌəʊvəˈtʃɑːdʒ/ VERB [**overcharges, overcharging, overcharged**] to charge someone too much money for something □ *I think you've overcharged me for the wine.*

overcoat /ˈəʊvəkəʊt/ NOUN [*plural* **overcoats**] a long warm coat □ *a cashmere overcoat*

overcome /ˌəʊvəˈkʌm/ VERB [**overcomes, overcoming, overcame, overcome**]
1 to manage to deal successfully with a problem □ *She has struggled to overcome her depression.*
2 if you are overcome by an emotion, it has a very strong effect on you and you cannot control it □ *He shut himself away, overcome with grief.*
3 if you are overcome by an illness, or by smoke, heat

etc., it makes you very ill, weak or unconscious □ *One fireman was overcome by the fumes.*

overcook /ˌəʊvəˈkʊk/ VERB [**overcooks, overcooking, overcooked**] to cook food for too long □ *overcooked vegetables*

overcrowded /ˌəʊvəˈkraʊdɪd/ ADJECTIVE an overcrowded place has too many people or things in it □ *our overcrowded prisons*

• **overcrowding** /ˌəʊvəˈkraʊdɪŋ/ NOUN, NO PLURAL when there are too many people or things in one place □ *There is severe overcrowding on our rail network.*

overdo /ˌəʊvəˈduː/ VERB [**overdoes, overdoing, overdid, overdone**] to do something too much or to use too much of something ⊞ *It's good to work hard, but don't overdo it.*

• **overdone** /ˌəʊvəˈdʌn/ ADJECTIVE cooked too much □ *He gave us an overdone steak.*

overdose ► NOUN /ˈəʊvədəʊs/ [*plural* **overdoses**] more of a drug or medicine than is safe □ *an overdose of sleeping pills*
► VERB /ˌəʊvəˈdəʊs/ [**overdoses, overdosing, overdosed**] to take too much of a drug or medicine

overdraft /ˈəʊvədrɑːft/ NOUN [*plural* **overdrafts**] when a bank allows you to take more money out of your account than you have put in □ *I have a £500 overdraft limit.*

overdrawn /ˌəʊvəˈdrɔːn/ ADJECTIVE when you have taken more money out of your bank account than you have put in ⊞ *I don't want to go overdrawn.*

overdrive /ˈəʊvədraɪv/ NOUN, NO PLURAL an extra gear in some motor vehicles for travelling fast □ *She put the car into overdrive.*

IDIOM go/move into overdrive to become very active or to start making a lot of effort □ *As soon as I asked her to help with the wedding, Mum went into overdrive.*

overdue /ˌəʊvəˈdjuː/ ADJECTIVE if something is overdue, it should have happened, been done, been paid, etc. before now □ *Our library books are overdue.* □ *He received a long overdue promotion.*

overestimate /ˌəʊvərˈestɪmeɪt/ VERB [**overestimates, overestimating, overestimated**] to think that something is larger or better than it really is □ *Geologists overestimated the amount of gold to be found in the rock.*

overflow /ˌəʊvəˈfləʊ/ VERB [**overflows, overflowing, overflowed**]
1 if a container overflows, liquid flows over its edges, and if a liquid overflows, it flows over the edges of a container □ *The sink overflowed and flooded the bathroom.*
2 if a river or a lake overflows, it becomes too full and water flows out of it
3 if a place is overflowing with people or things, there are too many of them to fit there □ *There were boxes overflowing with toys.* □ *The crowd overflowed into the street.*

overgrown /ˌəʊvəˈɡrəʊn/ ADJECTIVE full of plants that have grown too large and thick □ *The back garden is completely overgrown with weeds.*

overhang /ˌəʊvəˈhæŋ/ VERB [**overhangs, overhanging, overhung**] to hang over something □ *The stream was overhung by the branches of a tree.*

overhaul ► VERB /ˌəʊvəˈhɔːl/ [**overhauls, overhauling, overhauled**]
1 to examine a machine and repair any damage □ *He had his car overhauled at the garage.*
2 to change a system a lot in order to make it more effective □ *There are plans to overhaul the tax system.*
► NOUN /ˈəʊvəhɔːl/ [*plural* **overhauls**] when you overhaul something □ *The mechanic gave the car a complete overhaul.*

overhead /ˌəʊvəˈhed/ ADVERB, ADJECTIVE above your head or high above the ground □ *A plane was flying overhead.* □ *overhead cables*

overheads /ˈəʊvəhedz/ PLURAL NOUN the money that a business has to spend regularly on things like rent and electricity

overhear /ˌəʊvəˈhɪə(r)/ VERB [**overhears, overhearing, overheard**] to hear what someone says when they are not talking to you □ *I overheard them talking about me.*

overjoyed /ˌəʊvəˈdʒɔɪd/ ADJECTIVE very happy □ *We were overjoyed to hear that he was safe.*

overland /ˈəʊvəlænd/ ADVERB, ADJECTIVE across land, instead of by sea or air □ *They travelled overland across America.* □ *an overland safari*

overlap ► VERB /ˌəʊvəˈlæp/ [**overlaps, overlapping, overlapped**]
1 if objects overlap, part of each one is covered by part of another one □ *Each roof tile overlaps the one below it.* □ *The curtains should be wide enough to overlap.*
2 if two things overlap, they include some of the same parts, ideas, etc. □ *The categories often overlap.*
► NOUN /ˈəʊvəlæp/ [*plural* **overlaps**]
1 when two things overlap □ *There's some overlap between the two company's markets.*
2 the amount by which something overlaps □ *There's an overlap of half an hour between the two programmes.*

overload /ˌəʊvəˈləʊd/ VERB [**overloads, overloading, overloaded**]
1 when something is overloaded, it has too many people or things in it or on it □ *The car was overloaded and dangerously close to the ground.*
2 if you are overloaded with work or problems, you have more than you can deal with □ *Many social workers are overloaded with cases.*
3 to give a machine or system more information, work, etc. than it can deal with □ *The mobile phone network was overloaded.*
4 to cause too much electricity to pass through an electrical system

overlook /ˌəʊvəˈlʊk/ VERB [**overlooks, overlooking, overlooked**]

1 to fail to notice or consider something □ *You have overlooked one important detail.*
2 to ignore a fault or mistake □ *I shall overlook your lateness this time.*
3 to have a view over a place □ *The house overlooks the river.*

overly /ˈəʊvəlɪ/ ADVERB too much or very much □ *The figures were overly optimistic.* □ *He didn't seem overly concerned.*

overnight /ˌəʊvəˈnaɪt/ ADJECTIVE, ADVERB
1 for or during the night □ *an overnight train* □ *The centre provides overnight accommodation.* 🖥 *We stayed overnight in London.*
2 sudden or suddenly 🖥 *an overnight success* □ *He became a hero overnight.*

overpower /ˌəʊvəˈpaʊə(r)/ VERB [overpowers, overpowering, overpowered]
1 to defeat someone because you are stronger than them □ *He was overpowered by two policemen.*
2 to affect you so strongly that you cannot think or behave normally □ *They were overpowered by the smell.*
• **overpowering** /ˌəʊvəˈpaʊərɪŋ/ ADJECTIVE very strong □ *an overpowering smell*

overran /ˌəʊvəˈræn/ PAST TENSE OF overrun

overrated /ˌəʊvəˈreɪtɪd/ ADJECTIVE not as good or as important as people believe □ *His new film is overrated.*

overreact /ˌəʊvərɪˈækt/ VERB [overreacts, overreacting, overreacted] to react in a way that is too extreme to be reasonable □ *When I burst into tears, he accused me of overreacting.*

overriding /ˌəʊvəˈraɪdɪŋ/ ADJECTIVE more important than anything else □ *a matter of overriding importance* □ *Their overriding consideration is the need to maintain peace in the area.*

overrule /ˌəʊvəˈruːl/ VERB [overrules, overruling, overruled] to officially change a decision □ *The President has the power to overrule parliament in certain circumstances.*

overrun /ˌəʊvəˈrʌn/ VERB [overruns, overrunning, overran, overrun]
1 if a place is overrun with something, there are very large numbers of that thing there □ *The house is overrun with mice.*
2 to continue for longer than planned or to cost more than planned □ *The concert overran by half an hour.*

oversaw /ˌəʊvəˈsɔː/ PAST TENSE OF oversee

overseas /ˌəʊvəˈsiːz/ ADJECTIVE, ADVERB in, to or from another country □ *an overseas job* □ *overseas students* □ *They went overseas.*

oversee /ˌəʊvəˈsiː/ VERB [oversees, overseeing, oversaw, overseen] to watch something being done to check that it is done correctly □ *His job is to oversee the factory workers.*

overshadow /ˌəʊvəˈʃædəʊ/ VERB [overshadows, overshadowing, overshadowed]
1 if an unpleasant thing overshadows an event, it

makes it less enjoyable □ *The race was overshadowed by the death of a competitor.*
2 to seem much more successful or important than someone or something else □ *Clare was always overshadowed by her brilliant sister.*

oversight /ˈəʊvəsaɪt/ NOUN [plural oversights] a mistake that you make because you have not noticed something □ *It was a serious oversight on his part.*

oversleep /ˌəʊvəˈsliːp/ VERB [oversleeps, oversleeping, overslept] to sleep for longer than you planned to □ *I was late for the lecture because I overslept.*

overt /ˈəʊvɜːt, əʊˈvɜːt/ ADJECTIVE not secret or hidden □ *He was taken aback by the overt hostility of the locals.*

overtake /ˌəʊvəˈteɪk/ VERB [overtakes, overtaking, overtook, overtaken]
1 to move past a vehicle that is travelling in the same direction □ *He overtook a police car.*
2 to become more successful than someone or something else □ *China has overtaken Germany as the world's biggest exporter.*

overthrow /ˌəʊvəˈθrəʊ/ ▶ VERB [overthrows, overthrowing, overthrew, overthrown] to take power away from a leader or a government by force □ *They are plotting to overthrow the current regime.*
▶ NOUN, NO PLURAL /ˈəʊvəθrəʊ/ when a leader or a government is overthrown

overtime /ˈəʊvətaɪm/ NOUN, NO PLURAL extra time spent working in addition to your normal working hours 🖥 *We had to work overtime to get everything finished.*

overtly /əʊˈvɜːtlɪ/ ADVERB in an overt way □ *The newspaper article was overtly critical of the regime.*

overtook /ˌəʊvəˈtʊk/ PAST TENSE OF overtake

overture /ˈəʊvətjʊə(r)/ NOUN [plural overtures]
1 a piece of music played at the start of an opera or ballet
2 a friendly attempt to start a discussion or a relationship 🖥 *They have started to make overtures to neighbouring governments.*

overturn /ˌəʊvəˈtɜːn/ VERB [overturns, overturning, overturned]
1 to officially change a decision □ *The ruling was overturned by the court of appeal.*
2 to turn something upside down or to turn upside down □ *Chairs were overturned and glasses were broken.* □ *The bus overturned in wet conditions.*

overweight /ˌəʊvəˈweɪt/ ADJECTIVE an overweight person is too heavy □ *I'm about four kilos overweight.*

overwhelm /ˌəʊvəˈwelm/ VERB [overwhelms, overwhelming, overwhelmed]
1 to have a very strong and sudden effect on someone □ *We were overwhelmed with joy.*
2 to be too much for someone or something to deal with □ *I'm overwhelmed with work at the moment.* □ *Heavy rain overwhelmed the drainage system.*

3 to defeat someone completely □ *Our soldiers were overwhelmed by the enemy.*

• **overwhelming** /ˌəʊvəˈwelmɪŋ/ ADJECTIVE
1 very large or important □ *They won an overwhelming victory over their rivals.* 🖺 *An overwhelming majority of workers voted to strike.*
2 overwhelming emotions and feelings are very strong □ *There's an overwhelming feeling of relief.* □ *The temptation was almost overwhelming.*

• **overwhelmingly** /ˌəʊvəˈwelmɪŋli/ ADVERB used to emphasize that something is very strong or very large □ *They voted overwhelmingly in favour of the reform.*

overwork ▶ VERB /ˌəʊvəˈwɜːk/ [overworks, overworking, overworked] to work too hard or to make someone work too hard
▶ NOUN, NO PLURAL /ˈəʊvəwɜːk/ when you work too hard □ *Overwork made him ill.*

• **overworked** /ˌəʊvəˈwɜːkt/ ADJECTIVE made to work too hard □ *The staff are overworked.*

overwrite /ˌəʊvəˈraɪt/ VERB [overwrites, overwriting, overwrote, overwritten] to replace information in a computer file with different information. A computing word.

ovulate /ˈɒvjuleɪt/ VERB [ovulates, ovulating, ovulated] when a woman or female animal ovulates, she produces eggs. A biology word.

• **ovulation** /ˌɒvjuˈleɪʃən/ NOUN, NO PLURAL the process of ovulating. A biology word.

owe /əʊ/ VERB [owes, owing, owed]
1 to have to pay money to someone □ *I owe Val £10.* □ **+ to** *He owes money to suppliers.*
2 used to say that someone deserves something from someone 🖺 *I think you owe Simon an apology.* □ *We owe it to future generations to protect the planet.*
3 to have something only because of someone or something □ **+ to** *He owes his success to his family.* □ *The college owes its existence to a small group of wealthy individuals.*

owing to /ˈəʊɪŋ tə/ PREPOSITION because of □ *He withdrew from the competition owing to a back injury.* □ *The club closed down owing to lack of funding.*

owl /aʊl/ NOUN [plural owls] a large bird that hunts at night

own /əʊn/ ▶ ADJECTIVE belonging to or done by the person mentioned □ *I need to spend more time with my own family.* □ *The rules are for your own safety.* □ *Is this all your own work?* 🖺 *I'd love to have a horse of my very own.*
▶ PRONOUN
1 used to show that something belongs to someone or something □ *I lent him a pencil, because he forgot to bring his own.* □ *There are plenty of showers – each bedroom has its own.*
2 on your own (a) without help from anyone else

□ *He managed to finish the work on his own.* □ *Did you do this all on your own?* (b) alone □ *I live on my own in a small flat.*
3 of your own if someone or something has something of its own, it belongs only to them □ *I'd love a bedroom of my own.* □ *Each apartment has a small garden of its own.*

◆ IDIOMS **get your own back** to do something unpleasant to someone who has done something unpleasant to you **get/have your own way** to make things happen in the way you want them to, often when other people disagree □ *We all wanted to go to Greece, but Maria got her own way as usual, so we're going to Florida.* **hold your own** to be as confident or successful as other people in a situation □ *She did well to hold her own with all those experienced politicians.*
▶ VERB [owns, owning, owned] you own something if it belongs to you, especially if you have bought it □ *I own a car.* □ *He doesn't own a single book.*

◆ PHRASAL VERB **own up** to admit that you did something wrong □ *Nobody owned up to breaking the chair.*

• **owner** /ˈəʊnə(r)/ NOUN [plural owners] a person who owns something

• **ownership** /ˈəʊnəʃɪp/ NOUN, NO PLURAL when someone owns something □ *He retained ownership of the firm.* 🖺 *Home ownership has risen.*

own goal /ˌəʊn ˈɡəʊl/ NOUN [plural own goals]
1 a goal that someone scores by mistake against their own team
2 something you do that harms yourself

ox /ɒks/ NOUN [plural oxen] a large, male cow used for pulling farm machines

oxbow lake /ˌɒksbəʊ ˈleɪk/ NOUN [plural oxbow lakes] a lake that is formed when part of a river curves so much that it separates from the rest of the river. A geography word.

oxide /ˈɒksaɪd/ NOUN [plural oxides] a chemical that is made of oxygen and another substance. A chemistry word.

oxygen /ˈɒksɪdʒən/ NOUN, NO PLURAL a gas that has no taste, colour or smell, and forms part of the air. A chemistry word.

oxymoron /ˌɒksɪˈmɔːrɒn/ NOUN [plural oxymorons] when two words that seem to be opposites are used together, for example 'deafening silence'

oyster /ˈɔɪstə(r)/ NOUN [plural oysters] a type of sea creature in a shell that can be eaten

oz ABBREVIATION ounce

ozone /ˈəʊzəʊn/ NOUN, NO PLURAL a form of oxygen with a strong smell. A chemistry word.

ozone layer /ˈəʊzəʊn ˌleɪə(r)/ NOUN, NO PLURAL the layer of ozone that is around the Earth and that protects the planet from the harmful effects of the sun

Pp

P *or* **p** /piː/ the 16th letter of the alphabet

p /piː/ ABBREVIATION page or pence

p & p /ˌpiːənˈpiː/ ABBREVIATION postage and packing; the price that you must pay for someone to send something to you by post

PA /ˌpiːˈeɪ/ ABBREVIATION personal assistant

pace /peɪs/ ▶ NOUN [*plural* **paces**]
1 the speed at which something happens or at which someone does something □ *the pace of change* □ *He was walking at a very slow pace.*
2 a step ⊞ *Take four paces forward.*
3 keep pace with someone/something to move at the same speed as someone or change at the same speed as someone or something □ *Manufacturers are struggling to keep pace with demand for the product.*
▶ VERB [**paces, pacing, paced**]
1 to walk backwards and forwards because you are worried □ *She was pacing up and down, waiting for the phone to ring.*
2 pace yourself to do something at a sensible speed so that you are not too tired □ *You need to pace yourself because there are a lot of things to see in New York.*

pacemaker /ˈpeɪsmeɪkə(r)/ NOUN [*plural* **pacemakers**] a small device that is put in someone's body to keep their heart beating correctly

pachyderm /ˈpækɪdɜːm/ NOUN [*plural* **pachyderms**] an animal with very thick skin, for example a rhinoceros or an elephant. A biology word.

pacifism /ˈpæsɪfɪzəm/ NOUN, NO PLURAL the belief that all wars are wrong

• **pacifist** /ˈpæsɪfɪst/ NOUN [*plural* **pacifists**] someone who believes that all wars are wrong

• **pacify** /ˈpæsɪfaɪ/ VERB [**pacifies, pacifying, pacified**] to make someone calm after they have been upset or angry □ *'That's a pretty dress,' he said in an attempt to pacify her.*

pack /pæk/ ▶ VERB [**packs, packing, packed**]
1 to put things in a bag or case ready for a journey □ *She packed hurriedly and caught the next train.* □ *Ben packed his bag for the holiday.* □ *Make sure you pack your swimming costume.*
2 to put something into a box so it can be moved, sold or stored □ *She has a job packing chocolates in a factory.* □ **+ in** *The food was packed in brown paper bags.* □ **+ up** *They packed up all their furniture ready for the house move.*
3 if people pack a place, a lot of them go there and fill

it □ *Reporters packed the courtroom.* □ **+ into** *More then 15,000 fans packed into the sports stadium.*
♦ PHRASAL VERBS **pack something in**
1 an informal phrase meaning to stop doing something □ *She had been forced to pack her job in because of illness.*
2 an informal phrase meaning to do a lot of things in a short time □ *I managed to pack in three trips to the cinema this week.* **pack someone off** an informal word meaning to send someone away suddenly □ *He was packed off to boarding school at the age of eight.* **pack up** an informal word meaning to stop working □ *My printer has packed up again.* **pack (something) up** to put things into bags or boxes so that they can be moved □ *He packed up his belongings and left.* □ *We decided to pack up and go home.*
▶ NOUN [*plural* **packs**]
1 a set of documents that have been put together ⊞ *All new students will receive an information pack.* □ *If you are interested in the job, you can download an application pack.*
2 a set of products that are sold together □ *I bought a pack of 6 cakes.*
3 a small container that something is sold in □ **+ of** *pack of chewing gum*
4 a set of 52 cards that you play games with □ **+ of** *pack of cards*
5 a group of animals that live and hunt together □ **+ of** *a pack of wolves*
6 a group of similar people, especially people you do not like □ **+ of** *There was a pack of kids standing outside the shop.*

package /ˈpækɪdʒ/ ▶ NOUN [*plural* **packages**]
1 something that has been wrapped in paper or put in a box, especially so it can be sent by post □ *He sent th package to his brother.* □ *Police will destroy any suspicious packages.*
2 a group of products or services that are sold togeth □ *The company has launched a new broadband package.* □ *The hotel offers a wedding package.*
3 a set of plans that are designed to deal with something □ *The government announced a new aid package for some of the world's poorest countries.*
4 a US word for a container or a box that a product sold in
▶ VERB [**packages, packaging, packaged**]

1 to put something in a box or bag or to wrap them up in order to be sold □ *The sweets are packaged in pretty boxes.*

2 to sell a product or service together with other products or services □ *A small instruction book is packaged with the DVD.*

3 to try to make someone or something appear to have particular qualities □ *The cosmetic surgery is packaged as a holiday.*

• **packaged** /ˈpækɪdʒd/ ADJECTIVE sold in a container or bag □ *packaged fruit and vegetables*

package holiday /ˈpækɪdʒ ˌhɒlɪdeɪ/ NOUN [plural **package holidays**] a holiday in which a company arranges everything such as your travel and your hotel

packaging /ˈpækɪdʒɪŋ/ NOUN, NO PLURAL the material that a product is sold in □ *Supermarkets are asking suppliers to reduce packaging.*

packed /pækt/ ADJECTIVE

1 very crowded □ *The train was packed.*

2 containing a lot of something □ *Bananas are packed with vitamins and minerals.*

packed lunch /ˌpækt ˈlʌntʃ/ NOUN [plural **packed lunches**] food in a container that you take to eat at school, work, etc.

packet /ˈpækɪt/ NOUN [plural **packets**] a box or bag containing several of the same things □ *There were a lot of seeds in the packet.* ⊞ *He opened the packet and offered me some peanuts.* □ + **of** *a packet of biscuits* □ *a packet of crisps*

packing /ˈpækɪŋ/ NOUN, NO PLURAL

1 the process of putting things into bags or boxes so that you can take them somewhere ⊞ *Have you done your packing for the holiday?*

2 the material you use for wrapping and protecting objects, especially when you send them somewhere ⊞ *There will be a small extra charge for postage and packing.*

pact /pækt/ NOUN [plural **pacts**] an agreement between two people, groups or countries ⊞ *We made a pact never to tell anyone what happened.*

pad /pæd/ ► NOUN [plural **pads**]

1 a thick piece of soft material, used for protecting something or for making it more comfortable □ *I always wear knee pads and elbow pads when I'm roller skating.*

2 a book of pieces of paper, used for drawing or writing on □ *a sketch pad*

3 a special place where helicopters (=type of aircraft) can fly from or land, or where a spacecraft leaves the ground ⊞ *They sent a satellite into space from the launch pad.*

► VERB [**pads, padding, padded**]

1 to walk somewhere very quietly □ *He padded into the kitchen in his pyjamas.*

2 to fill or wrap something with a soft material □ *The horses' hooves had been padded with cloth to muffle the sound.*

PHRASAL VERB **pad something out** to add

information to a speech or piece of writing in order to make it longer, often when this is not necessary □ *The book had been padded out with old material.*

• **padded** /ˈpædɪd/ ADJECTIVE filled or covered with a soft material □ *a padded envelope* □ *a padded jacket*

• **padding** /ˈpædɪŋ/ NOUN, NO PLURAL

1 soft material used for filling something

2 unnecessary information that has been added to a speech or piece of writing, in order to make it longer

paddle /ˈpædəl/ ► VERB [**paddles, paddling, paddled**]

1 to move a boat through water using a paddle □ *She paddled the canoe down the river.*

2 to walk in water that is not deep □ *The children were paddling in the sea.*

► NOUN [plural **paddles**] a short piece of wood with a flat end, used for rowing a boat

paddock /ˈpædək/ NOUN [plural **paddocks**] a field where someone keeps horses

paddy field /ˈpædɪ ˌfiːld/ NOUN [plural **paddy fields**] a field where rice is grown

padlock /ˈpædlɒk/ ► NOUN [plural **padlocks**] a lock with a curved metal part on top and a key that goes in the bottom, used for locking things such as bicycles or gates

► VERB [**padlocks, padlocking, padlocked**] to fasten something using a padlock □ *I padlocked my bike to the railings.*

paediatric /ˌpiːdɪˈætrɪk/ ADJECTIVE to do with the medical treatment of children □ *a paediatric nurse*

• **paediatrician** /ˌpiːdɪəˈtrɪʃən/ NOUN [plural **paediatricians**] a doctor who treats children

• **paediatrics** /ˌpiːdɪˈætrɪks/ NOUN, NO PLURAL the area of medicine to do with children

pagan /ˈpeɪɡən/ ► NOUN [plural **pagans**] someone who believes in a religion that is not one of the world's main religions

► ADJECTIVE to do with pagans or paganism □ *a pagan festival*

• **paganism** /ˈpeɪɡənɪzəm/ NOUN, NO PLURAL pagan beliefs and customs

page /peɪdʒ/ ► NOUN [plural **pages**]

1 a piece of paper in a book, newspaper or magazine, or one side of it □ *The information can be found on page 135.* ⊞ *His picture was on the front page of the newspaper.* ⊞ *She turned the pages very slowly.*

2 the writing or pictures that you see on a computer screen, especially as part of a website □ *You need to refresh the page to see the information.* ⊞ *Visit our information page to find out more.*

► VERB [**pages, paging, paged**] to call someone by sending a message to their pager (=small piece of electronic equipment) □ *Nurses paged the doctor.*

pageant /ˈpædʒənt/ NOUN [plural **pageants**] a show outdoors, especially one that tells a historical or religious story

• **pageantry** /ˈpædʒəntrɪ/ NOUN, NO PLURAL special clothes, music, decorations, etc. which are used in formal ceremonies □ *He loved the colour and pageantry of the festival.*

pager /'peɪdʒə(r)/ NOUN [plural **pagers**] a small electronic device that makes a noise to tell you to telephone someone or go somewhere

paid /peɪd/ ► PAST TENSE AND PAST PARTICIPLE OF pay
► ADJECTIVE
1 paid work is work for which you get money 🕮 *Have you had any paid employment in the last six months?* 🕮 *She has a highly paid job.*
2 paid holiday or paid leave is time when your employer pays you although you are not working □ *I have six weeks paid leave a year.*

pail /peɪl/ NOUN [plural **pails**] an open container with a handle, used for carrying liquids

pain /peɪn/ ► NOUN [plural **pains**]
1 the unpleasant feeling you have when part of your body hurts □ *stomach pains* 🕮 *He felt a stinging pain.* 🕮 *Aspirin is used to relieve pain* (=make pain less bad). 🕮 *Ann felt a sharp pain in her leg.* □ *+ in He had pains in his chest.*
2 be in pain to have an unpleasant feeling because part of your body hurts □ *Amy was in constant pain from a broken shoulder.* □ *He was obviously in great pain.*
3 *no plural* sadness 🕮 *She felt that seeing him would cause her too much pain.* 🕮 *Nothing I can say will ease the pain* (=make it less bad). □ *+ of The pain of leaving his wife behind was almost too much to bear.*
4 an informal word meaning someone or something that is annoying □ *Sometimes she can be a real pain.*
♦ IDIOM be at/take pains to do something to make a lot of effort to do something □ *He took great pains to be fair to everyone.*
► VERB [**pains, paining, pained**] to make someone feel sad or upset □ *It pained him to see food wasted.*
● **pained** /peɪnd/ ADJECTIVE showing that you feel sad, upset or angry 🕮 *He stared at the damage with a pained expression.*
● **painful** /'peɪnfʊl/ ADJECTIVE
1 making you feel unhappy or ashamed 🕮 *painful memories* □ *His time in prison had been a very painful experience.* □ *+ for It is painful for parents to see their child so unhappy.* □ *+ to do something It was too painful to think about his failed marriage.*
2 causing physical pain □ *Is your knee still painful?* □ *She had a painful lump on her arm.*
● **painfully** /'peɪnfʊli/ ADVERB
1 used to emphasize that something is bad □ *It was a painfully slow process.* □ *She was painfully thin.*
2 in a painful way □ *This type of poison would kill an animal slowly and painfully.*

painkiller /'peɪnkɪlə(r)/ NOUN [plural **painkillers**] a drug that reduces pain

painless /'peɪnləs/ ADJECTIVE
1 causing no physical pain □ *a painless death*
2 not unpleasant or difficult □ *Checking in at the airport was relatively painless.*

painstaking /'peɪnzteɪkɪŋ/ ADJECTIVE done very carefully and slowly □ *painstaking research*

paint /peɪnt/ ► NOUN [plural **paints**] a coloured substance that you put on a surface to change its colour or to make a picture □ *a tin of red paint* 🕮 *The ceiling needs a new coat of paint.* □ *a box of oil paints*
► VERB [**paints, painting, painted**]
1 to put paint on a surface □ *Dan was painting the front door.* □ *The dining room was painted red.*
2 to make a picture using paint □ *He painted a portrait of the queen.*

paintbrush /'peɪntbrʌʃ/ NOUN [plural **paintbrushes**] a brush you use for painting

painter /'peɪntə(r)/ NOUN [plural **painters**]
1 an artist who makes pictures using paint
2 someone whose job is to paint buildings and rooms 🕮 *My Dad is a painter and decorator.*

painting /'peɪntɪŋ/ NOUN [plural **paintings**]
1 a picture that someone has made using paint □ *They sold a painting by Monet.*
2 *no plural* the activity of painting walls or pictures □ *I enjoy painting.*

pair /peə(r)/ ► NOUN [plural **pairs**]
1 two things of the same kind that you use or keep together □ *+ of a pair of socks* □ *a pair of shoes* □ *a pair of china dogs*
2 a single thing made up of two parts □ *I bought a pair of jeans.* □ *a pair of glasses* □ *a pair of scissors*
3 two people who do something together, or who are friends □ *The Australian pair won the game.* □ *The teacher asked us to work in pairs.*
► VERB [**pairs, pairing, paired**] to put two people or things together □ *+ with The T-shirt looks great paired with jeans*
♦ PHRASAL VERB pair up if two people pair up, they join together to do something □ *The two singers will pair up again for a new album.*

pajamas /pə'dʒɑːməz/ PLURAL NOUN the US spelling of pyjamas

pal /pæl/ NOUN [plural **pals**] an informal word meaning friend □ *My Mum met one of her old school pals.*

palace /'pælɪs/ NOUN [plural **palaces**] a big, grand house where a king, queen or president lives □ *the presidential palace* □ *Crowds of people stood outside the palace gates.*

palatable /'pælətəbəl/ ADJECTIVE
1 acceptable □ *The policy was changed to make it more palatable to voters.*
2 having a pleasant flavour □ *The cheese is very palatable.*

palate /'pælət/ NOUN [plural **palates**]
1 the top part of the inside of your mouth. A biology word.
2 your ability to taste and judge flavours □ *The restaurant serves dishes to suit every palate.*

palaver /pə'lɑːvə(r)/ NOUN, NO PLURAL an informal word meaning a situation that causes a lot of work worry □ *He'd had to go through the palaver of applying for a new passport.*

pale /peɪl/ ▶ ADJECTIVE [**paler, palest**]
1 light in colour □ *She was wearing a pale blue T-shirt.* □ *the pale light of dawn*
2 having very white skin, especially because you are ill or because you have had a shock □ *She looked very pale and thin.* 🖬 *He suddenly went very pale.*
3 less important, less good etc. when compared with something else 🖬 *After the illness, he was a pale imitation of his former self.*
▶ VERB [**pales, paling, paled**] to seem less important, less good, etc. when compared with something else □ *The amount she earns pales in comparison with the £500,000 a year that her sister earns.*

palette /ˈpælət/ NOUN [*plural* **palettes**] a board that artists mix paints on

pall /pɔːl/ ▶ VERB [**palls, palling, palled**] to become less interesting or less enjoyable □ *Life as a manager was beginning to pall.*
▶ NOUN [*plural* **palls**] **a pall of smoke/dust** a thick cloud of smoke or dust
➡ *go to* **cast a pall over something**

pallet /ˈpælɪt/ NOUN [*plural* **pallets**] a wooden base used for moving or storing heavy things

pallid /ˈpælɪd/ ADJECTIVE pale and unhealthy □ *There were tears running down his pallid cheeks.*

pallor /ˈpælə(r)/ NOUN, NO PLURAL the pale colour that someone's skin has when they are unhealthy or afraid

palm /pɑːm/ NOUN [*plural* **palms**]
1 the inside surface of your hand 🖬 *She kept wiping the palms of her hands on her skirt.*
2 a tree that grows in hot, dry places
PHRASAL VERB [**palms, palming, palmed**] **palm something off** to get rid of something that you do not want by persuading someone else to take it or buy it □ *She palms all her old clothes off on me.*

palpable /ˈpælpəbəl/ ADJECTIVE easy to notice □ *There was a palpable sense of relief when the boy was found.*

palpitations /ˌpælpɪˈteɪʃənz/ PLURAL NOUN if you have palpitations, your heart beats quickly and with an irregular rhythm

paltry /ˈpɔːltri/ ADJECTIVE a paltry amount is very small and often not enough □ *a paltry sum of money*

pamper /ˈpæmpə(r)/ VERB [**pampers, pampering, pampered**] to look after someone very well and do nice things for them □ *We spent the day being pampered at a spa.*

pampered /ˈpæmpəd/ ADJECTIVE getting a lot of care and attention, often too much, which makes you unpleasant □ *The report describes pampered teenagers who never have to do any chores.*

pamphlet /ˈpæmflɪt/ NOUN [*plural* **pamphlets**] a thin book with a paper cover, which has information in it

pan /pæn/ ▶ NOUN [*plural* **pans**] a metal container with a handle, used for cooking food □ *Cover the pan with a lid.*

▶ VERB [**pans, panning, panned**]
1 an informal word meaning to criticize something a lot □ *Critics panned the film.*
2 if a television or film camera pans somewhere, it moves in that direction □ *The camera panned around the room.*
♦ PHRASAL VERB **pan out** to develop in a particular way □ *He had no regrets about the way his career had panned out.*

panache /pəˈnæʃ/ NOUN, NO PLURAL confidence and skill □ *They danced with great panache.*

pancake /ˈpænkeɪk/ NOUN [*plural* **pancakes**] a thin food made by frying a mixture of milk, flour and eggs

pancreas /ˈpæŋkriəs/ NOUN [*plural* **pancreases**] a small organ in the body which produces substances that help you digest food. A biology word.

panda /ˈpændə/ NOUN [*plural* **pandas**] a large animal from China which is black and white, and looks like a bear

pandemonium /ˌpændɪˈməʊniəm/ NOUN, NO PLURAL a lot of noise and confusion □ *There was pandemonium on the street after the explosion.*

pander /ˈpændə(r)/
♦ PHRASAL VERB [**panders, pandering, pandered**] **pander to someone** to do everything that someone wants, even if it is wrong, in order to please them □ *The government was accused of pandering to large companies.*

pane /peɪn/ NOUN [*plural* **panes**] a piece of glass used in a window or door □ *a pane of glass*

panel /ˈpænəl/ NOUN [*plural* **panels**]
1 a usually rectangular piece of wood, glass, etc. that is part of a door, wall, etc.
2 a group of people who are chosen to discuss or judge something, or to answer questions □ *A panel of judges will decide on the winner.*
3 the part of a machine where the switches are □ *a control panel*

● **paneling** /ˈpænəlɪŋ/ NOUN, NO PLURAL the US spelling of **panelling**

● **panelist** /ˈpænəlɪst/ NOUN [*plural* **panelists**] the US spelling of **panellist**

● **panelling** /ˈpænəlɪŋ/ NOUN, NO PLURAL wood or other material used for panels in walls, doors, etc.

● **panellist** /ˈpænəlɪst/ NOUN [*plural* **panellists**] one of the members of a panel

pang /pæŋ/ NOUN [*plural* **pangs**] a sudden strong feeling □ *a pang of guilt*

panic /ˈpænɪk/ ▶ NOUN, NO PLURAL a sudden strong feeling of fear or worry that makes you unable to think calmly 🖬 *The fire caused panic.* □ *People ran into the streets in panic when the earthquake struck.*
▶ VERB [**panics, panicking, panicked**] to be so frightened or worried that you cannot think calmly □ *There's no need to panic. We've got plenty of time.*

● **panicky** /ˈpænɪki/ ADJECTIVE frightened, worried and unable to think calmly

panic-stricken /ˈpænɪkstrɪkən/ ADJECTIVE extremely frightened

pannier /'pænɪə(r)/ NOUN [plural **panniers**] a bag on the side of a bicycle or an animal such as a horse

panorama /ˌpænə'rɑːmə/ NOUN [plural **panoramas**] a view of a wide area of land

pansy /'pænzɪ/ NOUN [plural **pansies**] a garden plant with bright flowers

pant /pænt/ VERB [**pants, panting, panted**]
1 to breathe quickly and noisily, especially because you have been using a lot of physical effort □ He was sweating and panting.
2 to say something while breathing quickly and noisily □ 'I've just run two miles to catch this train,' he panted.

panther /'pænθə(r)/ NOUN [plural **panthers**] a large, wild, black cat

panties /'pæntɪz/ PLURAL NOUN underwear that a woman or girl wears to cover her bottom □ a pair of panties

pantihose /'pæntɪhəʊz/ NOUN another spelling of pantyhose

pantomime /'pæntəmaɪm/ NOUN [plural **pantomimes**] a Christmas play for children, based on a traditional story with jokes and singing

pantry /'pæntrɪ/ NOUN [plural **pantries**] a small room near a kitchen, used for storing food

pants /pænts/ PLURAL NOUN
1 a piece of underwear that covers your bottom 🔁 a clean pair of pants
2 the US word for trousers

pantyhose /'pæntɪhəʊz/ PLURAL NOUN the US word for tights

papal /'peɪpəl/ ADJECTIVE to do with the Pope (=leader of the Catholic Church) □ a papal visit

paper /'peɪpə(r)/ ▶ NOUN [plural **papers**]
1 no plural the thin material that you write on or draw on, or that you wrap things in 🔁 I wrote his address on a piece of paper. □ The present was wrapped in pretty pink paper.
2 a newspaper 🔁 Have you read today's paper? 🔁 I saw the article in the local paper.
3 a piece of writing or a talk on a subject that you have studied 🔁 He has written many influential papers. □ + on She published a research paper on the disease.
4 an exam □ an exam paper □ He showed me last year's maths paper.
5 on paper (a) used when you are judging something from written information but the real situation may be different □ The deal had seemed good on paper. (b) if you put information or ideas on paper, you write them down □ It sometimes helps to put your feelings down on paper.
➡ go to papers
▶ ADJECTIVE made from paper or cardboard □ a paper bag □ paper cups
▶ VERB [**papers, papering, papered**] to cover the walls of a room with paper

paperback /'peɪpəbæk/ NOUN [plural **paperbacks**] a book with a cover made from thick paper

paper clip /'peɪpə ˌklɪp/ NOUN [plural **paper clips**] a piece of bent wire, used for holding pieces of paper together

papers /'peɪpəz/ PLURAL NOUN official documents □ legal papers □ He's signed the divorce papers.

paperweight /'peɪpəweɪt/ NOUN [plural **paperweights**] a heavy object that you put on top of pieces of paper to stop them moving

paperwork /'peɪpəwɜːk/ NOUN, NO PLURAL work such as writing letters or reports, or keeping records □ The job involves a lot of paperwork.

par /pɑː(r)/ NOUN, NO PLURAL
1 be on a par (with something) to be the same size, standard, etc. as something else □ The city is on a par with London in terms of size.
2 below par not as good as usual, or not the expected standard □ The team are performing below par.

parable /'pærəbəl/ NOUN [plural **parables**] a story, especially from the Bible, that teaches people a moral or religious lesson

parabola /pə'ræbələ/ NOUN [plural **parabolas**] a curve like the one made by an object being thrown up and dropping down again. A maths word.

paracetamol /ˌpærə'siːtəmɒl/ NOUN [plural **paracetamols**] a drug that reduces pain

parachute /'pærəʃuːt/ ▶ NOUN [plural **parachutes**] a large piece of cloth attached to a person's body by strings that they use to help them fall safely if they jump from an aircraft
▶ VERB [**parachutes, parachuting, parachuted**] to jump from an aircraft using a parachute
• **parachutist** /'pærəʃuːtɪst/ NOUN [plural **parachutists**] someone who parachutes

parade /pə'reɪd/ ▶ NOUN [plural **parades**]
1 an event in which people or vehicles move through an area to celebrate something, often with music, decorations, etc. □ Hundreds of people took part in the carnival parade.
2 on parade if soldiers are on parade, they march together
▶ VERB [**parades, parading, paraded**]
1 to walk with a lot of other people in order to celebrate something or to complain about something □ Demonstrators paraded through the streets of the city.
2 to walk somewhere so that people will admire you □ She was parading round the room in her new dress.
3 to show people something such as a skill or your possessions, in order to make them admire you □ He enjoyed parading his wealth and power.

paradise /'pærədaɪs/ NOUN, NO PLURAL
1 in some religions, the place good people go when they die
2 a perfect place or situation □ The island is a paradise for birdwatchers.

paradox /'pærədɒks/ NOUN [plural **paradoxes**] a person, thing or situation that is strange because it has features which seem impossible to have together

□ *It's a paradox of western society that rising wealth seems to come together with rising unhappiness.*
• **paradoxical** /ˌpærəˈdɒksɪkəl/ ADJECTIVE combining two qualities or ideas that seem to be the opposite of each other □ *He finds himself in a paradoxical situation – a pacifist arguing for war.*

paraffin /ˈpærəfɪn/ NOUN, NO PLURAL a type of oil used for heating, and in lights

paragon /ˈpærəgən/ NOUN [plural **paragons**] someone who is perfect ⊞ *She has always been a paragon of virtue* (=very good, honest, etc.).

paragraph /ˈpærəgrɑːf/ NOUN [plural **paragraphs**] a part of a piece of writing that starts on a new line and contains one or more sentences □ *I read the first paragraph of the article.*

parallel /ˈpærəlel/ ▶ ADJECTIVE
1 parallel lines have the same distance between them all the way along ⊞ *She drew two parallel lines.* ⊞ *Lockwood Road runs parallel to Hollies Road.*
2 happening at the same time and in a similar way □ *Parallel studies have been carried out in Japan and the US.*
▶ NOUN [plural **parallels**] a way in which things, people or situations are similar ⊞ *The author drew parallels between the situation now and the situation in the 1980s* (=showed how the two situations are similar). □ **+ between** *There are striking parallels between the two bridges.*
▶ VERB [**parallels, paralleling, paralleled**] a formal word meaning to be similar to something else, or to happen at the same time as something else □ *Their findings parallel work done by scientists in the US.*

parallelogram /ˌpærəˈleləgræm/ NOUN [plural **parallelograms**] a shape with four straight sides, with the opposite sides parallel. A maths word.

paralyse /ˈpærəlaɪz/ VERB [**paralyses, paralysing, paralysed**]
1 if someone is paralysed by something, they are unable to move their body, or are unable to move part of their body □ *He was paralysed by a skiing accident in which he broke his neck.*
2 to make something unable to work or continue normally □ *Heavy snow falls paralysed the road and rail network.*

paralysed /ˈpærəlaɪzd/ ADJECTIVE unable to move your body or unable to move part of your body □ *The accident left him paralysed.*

paralysis /pəˈrælɪsɪs/ NOUN, NO PLURAL when someone cannot move their body or cannot move a part of their body

paralyze /ˈpærəlaɪz/ VERB [**paralyzes, paralyzing, paralyzed**] the US spelling of paralyse

paralyzed /ˈpærəlaɪzd/ ADJECTIVE the US spelling of paralysed

paramedic /ˌpærəˈmedɪk/ NOUN [plural **paramedics**] someone who works in an ambulance (=medical emergency vehicle) and is trained to help ill or injured people

paramilitaries /ˌpærəˈmɪlɪtəriz/ PLURAL NOUN soldiers who are part of a paramilitary group
• **paramilitary** /ˌpærəˈmɪlɪtəri/ ADJECTIVE operating like an army but not an official army □ *a paramilitary organization*

paramount /ˈpærəmaʊnt/ ADJECTIVE more important than anything else □ *The children's safety is paramount.*

paranoia /ˌpærəˈnɔɪə/ NOUN, NO PLURAL when someone believes that people are trying to harm them or that people do not like them although there is no proof of this
• **paranoid** /ˈpærənɔɪd/ ADJECTIVE believing that people do not like you and are trying to harm you although there is no proof of this □ *He was paranoid about someone stealing his money.*

parapet /ˈpærəpet/ NOUN [plural **parapets**] a low wall along the edge of a bridge or roof

paraphernalia /ˌpærəfəˈneɪliə/ NOUN, NO PLURAL all the different objects that you need for doing something □ *Kevin packed all his fishing paraphernalia into the back of the car.*

paraphrase /ˈpærəfreɪz/ ▶ VERB [**paraphrases, paraphrasing, paraphrased**] to say or write something in a different way, usually in order to explain it more clearly
▶ NOUN [plural **paraphrases**] a different and usually clearer way of saying or writing something

parasite /ˈpærəsaɪt/ NOUN [plural **parasites**]
1 an animal or plant that lives on or in another animal or plant in order to get food from it. A biology word.
2 someone who gets the things they need to live from other people's effort □ *He's just a parasite – he should go and get a job.*
• **parasitic** /ˌpærəˈsɪtɪk/ ADJECTIVE
1 a parasitic animal or plant is a parasite. A biology word □ *a parasitic worm*
2 a parasitic disease is caused by a parasite. A biology word.

paratrooper /ˈpærətruːpə(r)/ NOUN [plural **paratroopers**] a soldier who jumps out of aircraft using a parachute (=large piece of cloth attached to the body by strings)
• **paratroops** /ˈpærətruːps/ PLURAL NOUN a group of paratroopers

parcel /ˈpɑːsəl/ NOUN [plural **parcels**] something wrapped in paper and sent somewhere □ *A parcel arrived for you this morning.* ⊞ *She opened the parcel and there were three books inside.*

parched /pɑːtʃt/ ADJECTIVE
1 an informal word meaning very thirsty
2 parched land is extremely dry

parchment /ˈpɑːtʃmənt/ NOUN [plural **parchments**] a material made from animal skin and used for writing on in the past, or a document written on this

pardon /ˈpɑːdən/ ▶ EXCLAMATION
1 used to ask someone to repeat what they have just

said because you did not hear it □ *'We're going to be late.' 'Pardon?' 'I said, we're going to be late.'*

2 pardon me used when you have just made a rude noise with your body

▶ VERB [**pardons, pardoning, pardoned**] to officially forgive someone who has committed a crime □ *He was pardoned by President Clinton in 2001.*

▶ NOUN [*plural* **pardons**]

1 an official order to forgive someone for a crime □ *Although he died in 1998, his family are still campaigning for a full pardon.*

2 I beg your pardon (a) a formal way of saying sorry when you have made a mistake □ *Oh, I beg your pardon – I thought you meant I should sit here.* (b) a formal way of asking someone to repeat what they have just said because you did not hear it

parent /ˈpeərənt/ NOUN [*plural* **parents**] your mother or father □ *My parents divorced last year.* □ *Her proud parents watched as she received the award.*

• **parentage** /ˈpeərəntɪdʒ/ NOUN, NO PLURAL used for talking about who your parents are, where they come from, what their religion is, etc. □ *He was born in Vienna of Jewish parentage.*

• **parental** /pəˈrentəl/ ADJECTIVE to do with a parent or parents □ *parental responsibilities*

parenthesis /pəˈrenθɪsɪs/ NOUN [*plural* **parentheses**] one of the two signs ( ) which you use in writing □ *The children's ages are in parentheses after their names.*

parenthood /ˈpeərənthʊd/ NOUN, NO PLURAL being a parent □ *the joys of parenthood*

parenting /ˈpeərəntɪŋ/ NOUN, NO PLURAL the activity of looking after your own children 🔁 *parenting skills*

parish /ˈpærɪʃ/ NOUN [*plural* **parishes**] an area that has its own church □ *a parish priest*

• **parishioner** /pəˈrɪʃənə(r)/ NOUN [*plural* **parishioners**] someone who lives in a parish, especially someone who goes to the church

park /pɑːk/ ▶ NOUN [*plural* **parks**] an area of grass and trees in a town where people can go to relax □ *I went for a walk in the park.* 🔁 *They were sitting on a park bench.*

▶ VERB [**parks, parking, parked**] to leave a vehicle in a place, for example by the side of the road or in a car park 🔁 *She parked the car outside the house.* □ *Dad drove into town but couldn't find anywhere to park.*

• **parking** /ˈpɑːkɪŋ/ NOUN, NO PLURAL

1 space where you can park your vehicle □ *There is free parking for museum visitors.* 🔁 *She drove round, looking for a parking space.*

2 the process of putting a vehicle into a space and leaving it there □ *Many learner drivers find parking very difficult.*

parking lot /ˈpɑːkɪŋ ˌlɒt/ NOUN [*plural* **parking lots**] the US word for car park

parking meter /ˈpɑːkɪŋ ˌmiːtə(r)/ NOUN [*plural* **parking meters**] a piece of equipment at the side of a road that you put money in so you can park your car near to it

parking ticket /ˈpɑːkɪŋ ˌtɪkɪt/ NOUN [*plural* **parking tickets**] a piece of paper telling you that you must pay money because you have parked your vehicle illegally

parliament /ˈpɑːləmənt/ NOUN [*plural* **parliaments**] a group of people who make the laws for a country □ *the Scottish parliament* 🔁 *He entered parliament* (=was elected to a parliament) *in 1981.*

• **parliamentary** /ˌpɑːləˈmentərɪ/ ADJECTIVE to do with a parliament □ *a parliamentary debate*

parlor /ˈpɑːlə(r)/ NOUN [*plural* **parlors**] the US spelling of parlour

parlour /ˈpɑːlə(r)/ NOUN [*plural* **parlours**] a shop selling a particular product or service □ *an ice cream parlour* □ *a beauty parlour*

parmesan /ˌpɑːmɪˈzæn/ NOUN, NO PLURAL a type of hard Italian cheese

parochial /pəˈrəʊkɪəl/ ADJECTIVE interested only in things which affect the area where you live □ *a parochial attitude*

parody /ˈpærədɪ/ ▶ NOUN [*plural* **parodies**] a piece of music, a book, etc. that copies the style of another one in a funny way □ *Their act contained parodies of TV advertisements.*

▶ VERB [**parodies, parodying, parodied**] to copy the style of another writer, musician, etc. in a funny way

parole /pəˈrəʊl/ NOUN, NO PLURAL an arrangement in which someone is allowed to leave prison early but must go back to prison if they do not behave well 🔁 *Roberts was released on parole in 2005.*

parrot /ˈpærət/ NOUN [*plural* **parrots**] a tropical bird with brightly coloured feathers that can copy what people say

parsley /ˈpɑːslɪ/ NOUN, NO PLURAL a herb with green leaves, used in cooking

parsnip /ˈpɑːsnɪp/ NOUN [*plural* **parsnips**] a long, pale yellow vegetable that grows under the ground

part /pɑːt/ ▶ NOUN [*plural* **parts**]

1 one of the pieces, areas, amounts, etc. that together make something □ *The pizza is cut into six equal parts.* □ *She lives in a remote part of Scotland.* □ *I spent part of the day working in the garden.* □ *They made me feel part of the family.*

2 take part to be involved in an activity with other people □ *Everyone can take part in the competition.* □ *She took part in a run for charity.*

3 some, but not all of something □ **+ of** *Part of the problem is that he works such long hours.* □ *Part of me thinks we should just forget about her.*

4 in part to some degree □ *I still feel that he's in part to blame.*

5 the way in which someone is involved in a situation or an activity 🔁 *He played an important part in postwar politics.* □ *I had no part in the arrangements.*

6 a character in a play, film, etc. or the words or

actions that the character has to say or do 🔂 *He's playing the part of Othello.* ▢ *I need to learn my part.*
7 a piece of a machine or a piece of equipment 🔂 *We took plenty of spare parts for the van.*

◆ IDIOM **look the part** to look the way someone is expected to look in a particular situation or for a particular activity ▢ *In her neat blouse and glasses, she really looked the part of a strict headmistress.*

▶ ADVERB to some degree 🔂 *The creature is part man, part beast.* ▢ *She is part German.*

▶ VERB [**parts, parting, parted**]
1 when people part, they go away from each other ▢ *We parted at the end of the street.* 🔂 *They parted company in Toronto.* ▢ *After ten years of marriage, they agreed to part.*
2 when two things part, they move away from each other to leave a space, and if you part two things, you make a space between them ⊓ *Suddenly, the clouds parted and we had a wonderful view.* ▢ *We parted the curtains slightly.*
3 if you part your hair, you make a line in it and brush the hair away from that line on both sides

◆ PHRASAL VERB **part with something** to give something away, often when you do not want to ▢ *I couldn't bear to part with my books.*

partial /ˈpɑːʃəl/ ADJECTIVE
1 not complete ▢ *a partial success*
2 **be partial to something** to like something ▢ *She's very partial to chocolate.*
● **partially** /ˈpɑːʃəlɪ/ ADVERB not completely ▢ *a partially eaten biscuit*

participant /pɑːˈtɪsɪpənt/ NOUN [plural **participants**] someone who takes part in an event or activity with other people ▢ *She was an active participant in the debate.*

participate /pɑːˈtɪsɪpeɪt/ VERB [**participates, participating, participated**] to take part in an event or activity ▢ *The programme aims to encourage more children to participate in sport.*
● **participation** /pɑːˌtɪsɪˈpeɪʃən/ NOUN, NO PLURAL taking part in an event or activity ▢ *In the 19th century, participation in politics was very rare for women.*

participle /ˈpɑːtɪsɪpəl/ NOUN [plural **participles**] a word formed from a verb and used as an adjective, or to form different tenses of the verb. The present participle usually ends in '-ing' and the past participle usually ends in '-ed'.

particle /ˈpɑːtɪkəl/ NOUN [plural **particles**] a very small piece of something ▢ *a particle of dust* ▢ *tiny carbon particles*

particular /pəˈtɪkjʊlə(r)/ ▶ ADJECTIVE
1 used to show that you are talking about one person or thing and not others ▢ *On that particular day I was early.* ▢ *Is there a particular person I should speak to about this?*
2 especially great ▢ *He took particular care when*

writing the letter. ▢ *Aircraft safety is an area of particular concern.*
3 if a person is particular, they have strong opinions about what they like and dislike and are not easy to please ▢ **+ about** *She's very particular about what she eats.*

▶ NOUN [plural **particulars**]
1 **in particular** (a) especially ▢ *I enjoy reading novels, romantic fiction in particular.* ▢ *There's a lot of pressure on young women in particular.* (b) special or important 🔂 *We just chatted about nothing in particular.* 🔂 *Did you notice anything in particular?*
2 **particulars** details about a person or situation ▢ **+ of** *I don't know all the particulars of the case.*

● **particularly** /pəˈtɪkjʊləlɪ/ ADVERB
1 very, or more than usual ▢ *The noise was particularly loud.* ▢ *Young babies are particularly vulnerable.* 🔂 *They were not particularly helpful.*
2 used to show that something is true for one person or thing more than others ▢ *Temperatures were very high this summer, particularly in July.* ▢ *The changes will affect those on low incomes, particularly the elderly.*

parting /ˈpɑːtɪŋ/ NOUN [plural **partings**]
1 when you leave someone or say goodbye
2 a line in your hair where you brush the hair in opposite directions

partition /pɑːˈtɪʃən/ ▶ NOUN [plural **partitions**]
1 a thin wall that divides a room into parts ▢ *The bank clerk sits behind a glass partition.*
2 when you divide a country into separate areas or countries ▢ *Pakistan was formed at the partition of India in 1947.*

▶ VERB [**partitions, partitioning, partitioned**]
1 to divide a country into areas or countries ▢ *The only solution was to partition the country into two separate states.*
2 to divide a room using a partition

partly /ˈpɑːtlɪ/ ADVERB in some ways or to some degree, but not completely ▢ *I was partly to blame for the mix-up.* ▢ *He had to leave his job, partly because of his health.* ▢ *That's only partly true.*

partner /ˈpɑːtnə(r)/ NOUN [plural **partners**]
1 one of two people who do something together, such as dancing or playing a game 🔂 *a dance partner* ▢ *a tennis partner*
2 one of two or more people who own a business together 🔂 *She's a senior partner in a law firm.* 🔂 *his former business partner*
3 someone you are married to or have a sexual relationship with ▢ *She lives with her long-term partner and their two children.*
4 a country or an organization that works with or has an agreement with another 🔂 *Brazil is one of our largest trading partners.*
● **partnership** /ˈpɑːtnəʃɪp/ NOUN [plural **partnerships**]
1 a relationship between two or more people or

groups working together 🔄 *The company has formed partnerships with several universities.*
2 a business owned by two or more partners

part of speech /ˌpɑːt əv ˈspiːtʃ/ NOUN [plural **parts of speech**] in grammar, one of the groups that words belong to depending on the job they do, such as noun, verb, adjective or adverb

partridge /ˈpɑːtrɪdʒ/ NOUN [plural **partridges**] a small round grey and brown wild bird that is hunted for sport and food

part-time /ˌpɑːtˈtaɪm/ ADJECTIVE, ADVERB working for only part of a full working day or week 🔄 *a part-time job* 🔄 *She works part-time for the local newspaper.*

party /ˈpɑːtɪ/ ► NOUN [plural **parties**]
1 an event where people celebrate something or enjoy themselves together eating, drinking, dancing, etc. 🔄 *a birthday party* 🔄 *We're having a party next week.* 🔄 *He threw a huge party to celebrate.*
2 an organized group of people who share the same political beliefs and try to get elected to the government 🔄 *a political party* 🔄 *the party leader* ☐ *He joined the Labour Party in 1936.*
3 a group of people travelling or doing something together ☐ + *of The museum was busy with several parties of schoolchildren.*
4 a formal word for a person or group involved in a legal agreement or disagreement ☐ *Interested parties have been asked to submit proposals.* ☐ *He isn't the only guilty party.*
► VERB [**parties, partying, partied**] to enjoy yourself at a party ☐ *He was out partying with friends at a nightclub.*

➤ Note that you **have** or **throw** a party (noun, sense 1): You do not 'make' a party:
✓ *We're having a party for Celia's 21st birthday.*
✗ *We're making a party for Celia's 21st birthday.*

pass /pɑːs/ ► VERB [**passes, passing, passed**]
1 to go past something ☐ *The lorry passed us on a bend.* ☐ *I pass her house every morning.*
2 to move in a particular direction or to a particular place ☐ *The procession passed in front of the town hall.* ☐ *The road passes through a forest.*
3 to be successful in an exam ☐ *She passed her entrance exams.* ☐ *I've got my driving test tomorrow, but I don't think I'll pass.*
4 to give someone something with your hand ☐ *Pass me the butter, please.* ☐ + *to He passed a note to his colleague.*
5 if time passes, it goes by ☐ *A whole year passed and she did not receive a letter from him.* ☐ *The morning passed slowly.*
6 **pass the time** to do something to use a period of time ☐ *I passed the time reading a book.*
7 to kick, hit or throw the ball to someone else on your team in a sport ☐ *He passed the ball to Edwards.*
8 to go higher than a particular level or amount ☐ *Donations have passed the £1 million mark.*

9 to officially accept a law 🔄 *The government has passed new legislation to deal with Internet fraud.*
10 to come to an end or go away ☐ *The storm passed and the sun came out again.* ☐ *The pain soon passed.*
11 **pass sentence** when judges pass sentence, they say what someone's punishment will be

➤ Remember that you **spend** a period of time somewhere. You do not 'pass' a period of time: ☐ *I spent the summer in Barcelona.* ☐ *I've spent all morning cleaning.* ☐ *We spent the holidays at my grandparents.*

➜ **go to pass the** *buck*
◆ PHRASAL VERBS **pass something around/round** to offer something to everyone in a group ☐ *She passed round the biscuits.* **pass away/on** to die **pass something down** to give something or teach something to someone younger than you ☐ *The stories were passed down from generation to generation.* **pass for someone/something** to look enough like someone or something that people could believe that you were that person or thing ☐ *She's nearly fifty, but she could pass for a thirty-year-old.*
pass something on
1 to give someone something that has been given to you ☐ *Can you pass on a message for me?* ☐ *When you've finished with the book, could you pass it on to Paola?*
2 to give someone an illness ☐ *I don't want to pass on my cold to anyone.* **pass out** to become unconscious ☐ *When I saw the blood, I passed out.*
► NOUN [plural **passes**]
1 a successful result in an exam or on a course
2 a ticket or document that allows you to go into a place or to travel on a vehicle 🔄 *Have you got your bus pass?*
3 when you kick, hit or throw the ball to someone else on your team in a sport
4 a narrow path between mountains

passable /ˈpɑːsəbəl/ ADJECTIVE
1 of quite a good standard but not the best ☐ *He does a passable imitation of Elvis.*
2 if a road is passable, it is not blocked and can be travelled along

passage /ˈpæsɪdʒ/ NOUN [plural **passages**]
1 a long narrow room or area that connects rooms or places ☐ *He ran down a narrow passage between buildings.* ☐ *a secret underground passage*
2 a part of a piece of writing or music ☐ *Read the next passage aloud.* ☐ + *from He quoted a passage from the Bible.*
3 a tube in the body that air or liquid passes through 🔄 *Your nasal passages are connected to your nose.*
4 a journey or a route through a place ☐ *Huge icebergs blocked our passage.*

5 when something or someone makes progress from one stage to another □ *We are watching the passage of this legislation through parliament.*
6 the passage of time when time passes

passageway /ˈpæsɪdʒweɪ/ NOUN [plural **passageways**] a passage between rooms or places □ *She led us through a long narrow passageway.*

passenger /ˈpæsɪndʒə(r)/ NOUN [plural **passengers**] someone travelling in a vehicle who is not the driver or someone who works on it ⊞ *an airline passenger* ⊞ *I sat in the passenger seat.*

passer-by /ˌpɑːsəˈbaɪ/ NOUN [plural **passers-by**] someone who is passing a place when something happens □ *Several passers-by were injured in the explosion.*

passing /ˈpɑːsɪŋ/ ▶ ADJECTIVE
1 lasting only for a short time and not important or serious □ *For many children, it's just a passing phase.*
2 moving, walking, driving, etc. past somewhere □ *A passing motorist stopped to help.*
▶ NOUN, NO PLURAL
1 when something ends or no longer exists □ *They regret the passing of old traditions.*
2 when time passes □ *With each passing day, their hopes faded.*
3 in passing if you say something in passing, you mention it quickly while you are talking about something else □ *He only mentioned Foster in passing.*

passion /ˈpæʃən/ NOUN [plural **passions**]
1 very strong beliefs and opinions about something □ *He spoke with real passion.* ⊞ *Passions are running high* (=people are very angry and upset) *in the city.*
2 *no plural* a very strong feeling of love □ *He kissed her in a moment of passion.*
3 something you are very interested in and enthusiastic about □ *They share a passion for the countryside.*

passionate /ˈpæʃənɪt/ ADJECTIVE
1 showing strong emotions or beliefs □ *She's a passionate advocate of animal rights.* □ *I feel very passionate about this issue.*
2 having a strong feeling of love □ *They had a very passionate relationship.*

passionately /ˈpæʃənɪtlɪ/ ADVERB in a passionate way □ *He spoke passionately about the need for action.*

passive /ˈpæsɪv/ ADJECTIVE
1 allowing things to happen to you without reacting or doing anything to change them □ *These people are not just passive victims.* □ *He had a largely passive role.*
2 a passive verb is used when the person or thing that is the subject of the verb does not do the action but has something done to them, for example in the sentence *The leaves are being eaten by caterpillars.*

passively /ˈpæsɪvlɪ/ ADVERB in a passive way □ *He just sat passively and listened.*

passive smoking /ˌpæsɪv ˈsməʊkɪŋ/ NOUN, NO PLURAL when you breathe in the smoke from other people's cigarettes

Passover /ˈpɑːsəʊvə(r)/ NOUN, NO PLURAL a Jewish celebration in March or April, remembering the escape of the ancient Jews from Egypt

passport /ˈpɑːspɔːt/ NOUN [plural **passports**]
1 an official document with your photograph and personal details that you carry when you travel to a foreign country □ *a British passport* ⊞ *You have to show your passport.* □ *passport control*
2 something that makes it possible to do or achieve something □ *She saw education as a passport to a better life.*

password /ˈpɑːswɜːd/ NOUN [plural **passwords**] a secret word that you have to know before you are allowed into a place, or before you can use a computer or system ⊞ *Please enter your password.*

past /pɑːst/ ▶ PREPOSITION, ADVERB
1 up to and further than □ *She dashed past me, gasping as she ran.* □ *He just walked past without saying hello.* □ *Bullets flew past my head.* □ *Follow the road past a cottage.*
2 further than □ *Turn right just past the bridge.* □ *A few miles past the farm, we came to a turning.*
3 used for saying the time up to 30 minutes after an hour □ *It's ten past three.* □ *I'll meet you at half past ten.*
4 later than □ *It's past eight o'clock.* □ *It's well past my bedtime.*
5 after a particular stage or level □ *This bread is past its best.*
6 used for talking about a period of time passing □ *Days went past and still there was no news.*
7 past it an informal phrase meaning too old to do the things you used to do □ *He thinks anyone over 30 is past it.*
8 wouldn't put something past someone used to say that you think it is possible that someone has done something, especially something bad □ *I wouldn't put it past her to leave without paying back the money.*
▶ NOUN, NO PLURAL
1 the past the time before the present □ *I have met him a few times in the past.* □ *When we meet, we never talk about the past.*
2 someone's past is their life and experiences until now, and a country's past is what has happened there and what its people have done □ *I don't know much about her past.* □ *The country is trying to forget its military past.*
3 the past the form of a verb that is used for talking about things that happened before the present
▶ ADJECTIVE
1 having happened or existed in the time before the present □ *I have admitted my past mistakes.* ⊞ *They know from past experience that free food will attract a crowd.*
2 used to talk about a period of time just before the

present □ *The past few days have been very difficult for all of us.*

3 having had a particular position in a country or an organization □ *Paintings of past presidents hang on the walls.*

4 finished □ *I used to mix with movie stars, but that's all past now.*

pasta /'pæstə/ NOUN, NO PLURAL a food made from flour, water and eggs and formed into different shapes □ *pasta with tomato sauce*

paste /peɪst/ ▶ NOUN [plural **pastes**]
1 a soft, slightly wet mixture, often of food □ *tomato paste* □ *Mix until you have a smooth, thick paste.*
2 *no plural* a type of glue for sticking paper
▶ VERB [**pastes, pasting, pasted**]
1 to stick something onto a surface with glue □ *There were posters pasted all over the wall.*
2 to move words or a picture from one place on a computer screen to another. A computing word 🖥 *You can cut and paste the text into your own document.*

pastel /'pæstəl/ ▶ ADJECTIVE pastel colours are pale and contain a lot of white □ *pastel blue*
▶ NOUN [plural **pastels**]
1 a soft stick used to draw with
2 a pale colour

pasteurization *or* **pasteurisation** /ˌpɑːstʃəraɪ'zeɪʃən/ NOUN, NO PLURAL the process of heating milk to kill all the bacteria in it
● **pasteurize** *or* **pasteurise** /'pɑːstʃəraɪz/ VERB [**pasteurizes, pasteurizing, pasteurized**] to heat milk so that all the bacteria in it are killed

pastime /'pɑːstaɪm/ NOUN [plural **pastimes**] something you enjoy doing for fun □ *Reading is one of my favourite pastimes.*

pastor /'pɑːstə(r)/ NOUN [plural **pastors**] a priest in some churches

pastoral /'pɑːstərəl/ ADJECTIVE
1 to do with giving people help or advice about personal problems, especially by a teacher or a priest 🖥 *The college provides excellent pastoral care.*
2 to do with the countryside or country life □ *a pastoral scene*

past participle /ˌpɑːst 'pɑːtɪsɪpəl/ NOUN [plural **past participles**] the form of a verb that usually ends with '-ed' and is used to form the perfect tense, passive forms and sometimes adjectives

pastry /'peɪstrɪ/ NOUN [plural **pastries**]
1 *no plural* a mixture of flour and fat made into a flat piece and baked with food inside
2 a cake made with pastry

past tense /ˌpɑːst 'tens/ NOUN [plural **past tenses**] a form of a verb that you use when you are talking about what has happened in the past. For example, *relaxed* in *I relaxed after the race* is a past tense.

pasture /'pɑːstʃə(r)/ NOUN [plural **pastures**] a field with grass for cows and other animals to eat

pasty[1] /'peɪstɪ/ ADJECTIVE [**pastier, pastiest**] having skin that is pale and looks unhealthy

pasty[2] /'pæstɪ/ NOUN [plural **pasties**] a piece of pastry folded around food such as meat and vegetables

pat /pæt/ ▶ VERB [**pats, patting, patted**] to touch or to hit someone or something gently with your flat hand in a friendly way □ *Celia patted his shoulder kindly.* □ *He patted the horse's neck.*
◆ IDIOMS **pat someone on the back** to praise someone for something they have done □ *I patted myself on the back for a job well done.*
▶ NOUN [plural **pats**] when you pat someone or something □ *He gave the dog a pat on the head.*
◆ IDIOMS **a pat on the back** praise for doing something □ *She deserves a pat on the back.*

patch /pætʃ/ ▶ NOUN [plural **patches**]
1 a small area of something, especially that is different from what is around it □ *a patch of grass* 🖥 *a vegetable patch* (=area of ground where you grow vegetables) □ *There's a damp patch on the wall.*
2 a piece of material used to cover a hole □ *a jacket with patches on the elbows*
3 a period of time with a particular quality 🖥 *He's been going through a rough patch in his career.*
4 a piece of material used to cover a damaged eye □ *She had to wear a patch over her right eye.*
5 a piece of software used to fix a computer problem. A computing word. □ *You can download a patch from the website.*
◆ IDIOM **not a patch on someone/something** much less good than someone or something else □ *He's a good player, but not a patch on Gordon.*
▶ VERB [**patches, patching, patched**] to repair a hole using a patch □ *We patched the hole in the roof.*
◆ PHRASAL VERBS **patch something up**
1 to become friendly with someone again after an argument □ *The two men have patched things up now.*
2 to repair something, often not very carefully □ *We tried to patch up the wall.* **patch someone up** to give someone who is injured basic medical treatment □ *The nurse patched them up and sent them home.*

patchwork /'pætʃwɜːk/ NOUN, NO PLURAL
1 small pieces of cloth sewn together in a decorative pattern 🖥 *a patchwork quilt*
2 something that is made up of different pieces □ *a green patchwork of fields*

patchy /'pætʃɪ/ ADJECTIVE [**patchier, patchiest**]
1 existing in some places but not in others 🖥 *patchy fog*
2 good sometimes but not always □ *The standard of cooking can be a bit patchy.*

paté /'pæteɪ/ NOUN [plural **patés**] a smooth mixture of meat, fish or vegetables that you eat on bread

patent /'peɪtənt/ ▶ NOUN [plural **patents**] an official document that gives one person or company the right to make and sell a product and stops others from copying it

▶ VERB [patents, patenting, patented] to get a patent for something □ *She patented her design.*

▶ ADJECTIVE obvious □ *His patent lack of enthusiasm annoyed his colleagues.*

• **patently** /'peɪtəntlɪ/ ADVERB very clearly 🔊 *It's patently obvious he had no intention of doing it.*

paternal /pə'tɜːnəl/ ADJECTIVE

1 to do with being a father □ *He showed off his daughter's trophy with paternal pride.*

2 from your father's side of the family □ *my paternal grandparents*

• **paternity** /pə'tɜːnətɪ/ ▶ NOUN, NO PLURAL the state of being a father □ *There were some doubts over the baby's paternity.*

▶ ADJECTIVE to do with being or becoming a father □ *paternity leave*

path /pɑːθ/ NOUN [plural **paths**]

1 a narrow route across a piece of ground that people walk or ride a bicycle along □ *We walked along a narrow path through the woods.* □ *Dad was coming up the garden path.* 🔊 *There's a cycle path beside the canal.*

2 the direction in which something travels or moves □ **+ of** *People living in the path of the storm were evacuated.*

3 a particular way of doing or achieving something 🔊 *She took an unusual career path.*

▶ IDIOM **cross paths (with someone)** if you cross paths with someone or your paths cross, you meet each other by chance □ *I'd crossed paths with Stevens before.*

pathetic /pə'θetɪk/ ADJECTIVE

1 an informal word meaning not at all useful, skilful or effective □ *This knife is pathetic. It won't cut anything!* 🔊 *She made a pathetic attempt to deny it.*

2 causing you to feel sympathy or sadness □ *She's a rather pathetic figure these days.*

pathetic fallacy /pə,θetɪk 'fæləsɪ/ NOUN, NO PLURAL when animals or objects are described as having human feelings

pathogen /'pæθədʒən/ NOUN [plural **pathogens**] a microorganism that causes disease. A biology word.

pathologist /pə'θɒlədʒɪst/ NOUN [plural **pathologists**] an expert in diseases, especially one who examines people who have died to discover the reason for their deaths

pathology /pə'θɒlədʒɪ/ NOUN, NO PLURAL the study of diseases

pathway /'pɑːθweɪ/ NOUN [plural **pathways**]

1 a path that you can walk along □ *Paved pathways lead through the garden.*

2 a route from one place to another that things such as electricity or signals move along □ *pathways to the brain*

3 a way that something can be done or achieved □ *There is no established pathway for women to enter this profession.*

patience /'peɪʃəns/ NOUN, NO PLURAL

1 the ability to stay calm, especially when waiting for something, doing something for a long time or dealing with something or someone annoying □ *You need to have a lot of patience when dealing with young children.* 🔊 *I'm losing my patience with her silly behaviour.*

2 a card game played by one person

• **patient** /'peɪʃənt/ ▶ ADJECTIVE showing patience □ **+ with** *I'm a slow learner and he's been very patient with me.* □ *I'm not a very patient person.*

▶ NOUN [plural **patients**] someone who is being treated by a doctor or a nurse 🔊 *The clinic treats patients with eye problems.* □ *Every patient receives advice about healthy eating.*

• **patiently** /'peɪʃəntlɪ/ ADVERB in a patient way 🔊 *We waited patiently for a bus.*

patio /'pætɪəʊ/ NOUN [plural **patios**] a flat area covered in stone at the back of a house, where people can sit

patriot /'pætrɪət/ NOUN [plural **patriots**] someone who loves and is loyal to his or her country

• **patriotic** /,pætrɪ'ɒtɪk/ ADJECTIVE showing love and loyalty to your country □ *a patriotic song* □ *He's very patriotic.*

• **patriotism** /'pætrɪətɪzəm/ NOUN, NO PLURAL the quality of being patriotic

patrol /pə'trəʊl/ ▶ VERB [patrols, patrolling/US patroling, patrolled/US patroled] to go around an area or building watching for any trouble or problems □ *Troops patrol the border.*

▶ NOUN [plural **patrols**]

1 a group of soldiers or police officers who patrol an area 🔊 *a police patrol*

2 when someone patrols an area 🔊 *The soldiers were on a routine patrol when they were attacked.*

patron /'peɪtrən/ NOUN [plural **patrons**]

1 someone who supports the work of an artist, musician, etc. □ *He was a great patron of the arts.*

2 a famous person who gives their public support to an organization □ *She became patron of the Multiple Sclerosis Society.*

3 a customer of a shop, restaurant or business □ *The restaurant offers discounts to regular patrons.*

• **patronage** /'pætrənɪdʒ/ NOUN, NO PLURAL support or money given by a patron to a person or an organization □ *He was known for his patronage of the arts.*

patronize or **patronise** /'pætrənaɪz/ VERB [patronizes, patronizing, patronized]

1 to treat someone in a way that shows you think you are better than them or think that they are stupid □ *Since his promotion, he thinks he can patronize all the junior clerks.* □ *Don't patronize me!*

2 a formal word meaning to be a customer in a shop, restaurant, etc. □ *He and his family have patronized our shop for as long as we can remember.*

• **patronizing** /'pætrənaɪzɪŋ/ ADJECTIVE behaving in a way that shows you think you are better than someone or think that they are stupid □ *I hate his patronizing manner.* □ *a patronizing tone of voice*

• **patronizingly** /'pætrənaɪzɪŋlɪ/ ADVERB in a patronizing way □ *She remarked patronizingly that the work was very good for a beginner.*

patron saint /ˌpeɪtrən 'seɪnt/ NOUN [plural **patron saints**] a saint (=very holy person in the Christian religion) who is believed to protect a place, activity or trade □ *St Andrew is the patron saint of Scotland.*

patter /'pætə(r)/ ▶ VERB [**patters, pattering, pattered**] to make quick, light sounds by hitting or falling on something □ *The rain was pattering on the windows.*

▶ NOUN, NO PLURAL

1 a series of quick, light sounds of something hitting something □ *I heard the patter of feet in the room above.*

2 fast, confident speech, especially by someone selling something □ *He started on his usual sales patter.*

pattern /'pætən/ NOUN [plural **patterns**]

1 the way in which something normally happens or is organized □ **+ of** *the pattern of the seasons* ▣ *The game followed a familiar pattern.* ▣ *When we analyzed the data, a clear pattern emerged.* ▣ *annual weather patterns*

2 a design of shapes, colours, etc. repeated on a surface □ *The room was decorated in floral patterns.* □ *The boxes are carved with intricate patterns.*

3 a set of instructions and shapes used for making something □ *a sewing pattern*

• **patterned** /'pætənd/ ADJECTIVE having a design of shapes, colours, etc. □ *a patterned dress*

paunch /pɔːntʃ/ NOUN [plural **paunches**] a fat stomach □ *You're getting a bit of a paunch.*

pauper /'pɔːpə(r)/ NOUN [plural **paupers**] an old-fashioned word for a very poor person □ *He was buried in a pauper's grave.*

pause /pɔːz/ ▶ VERB [**pauses, pausing, paused**]

1 to stop what you are doing for a short time □ **+ to do something** *The actor paused to speak to fans.* □ *He paused for a moment before replying.*

2 to stop a CD, DVD, etc. for a short time by pressing a button

▶ NOUN [plural **pauses**]

1 a short stop or rest ▣ *There was a long pause before anyone spoke.* □ **+ for** *He kept going with hardly a pause for breath.*

2 a button that you press to pause a CD, DVD, etc. □ *Press pause.*

pave /peɪv/ VERB [**paves, paving, paved**] to make a layer of stones, bricks etc. on an area of ground □ *The courtyard is paved with local stone.*

• IDIOM **pave the way for something** to do something that makes it possible for something else to happen □ *This decision could pave the way for other legal cases.*

pavement /'peɪvmənt/ NOUN [plural **pavements**] a path next to a road which people walk along □ *He waited on the pavement in front of the shop.*

pavilion /pə'vɪljən/ NOUN [plural **pavilions**]

1 a building at a sports ground where players change their clothes

2 a large building or tent, especially at an event

paving stone /'peɪvɪŋ ˌstəʊn/ NOUN [plural **paving stones**] a piece of flat stone used to cover a path or an outside area

paw /pɔː/ ▶ NOUN [plural **paws**] the foot of some animals, such as cats and dogs

▶ VERB [**paws, pawing, pawed**] to touch something with a paw □ *The horse pawed the ground.*

pawn /pɔːn/ NOUN [plural **pawns**]

1 one of the small, least important pieces in the game of chess

2 someone who is used and controlled by someone more powerful □ *These people are being used as political pawns.*

pay /peɪ/ ▶ VERB [**pays, paying, paid**]

1 to give money in order to buy something or because you owe someone □ **+ for** *I'll pay for the meal.* ▣ *He offered to pay the bill.* □ *I don't pay tax in this country.* □ **+ by** *Can I pay by credit card?*

2 to give someone money for work that they do □ *I need the money to pay the builder.* □ *I get paid on the 15th of each month.*

3 to give you an advantage □ **+ to do something** *It pays to book in advance.* □ *Crime does not pay.*

4 to suffer because of something you have done ▣ *She paid dearly (=suffered a lot) for her carelessness.* □ **+ for** *I'll make you pay for what you did.*

5 **pay attention** to concentrate on something □ *She paid great attention to his words.*

6 **pay someone a compliment** to say something nice about someone

7 **pay tribute to someone** to say or do something to show your respect and admiration for someone

8 **pay someone/something a visit** to visit someone or something

---

➤ Note that you pay **for** the thing that you are buying: □ *Camille paid for the watch.*
✓ *Camille paid £120* **for** *the watch.*
✗ *Camille paid the watch.*

♦ PHRASAL VERBS **pay someone back** to do something bad to someone because of something bad they have done to you **pay off** if an action pays off, it gives you an advantage □ *Giving up my job was a risk, but it really paid off.* **pay off something** to pay all of the money that you owe for something □ *In a couple of years, we'll have paid off the mortgage.* **pay up** to pay money that you owe, especially when you do not want to

▶ NOUN, NO PLURAL someone's **pay** is the amount of money they are paid by their employer □ *The job's* boring, but the pay's good. 🔁 I asked him for a pay rise. 🔁 Many workers are facing pay cuts.

• **payable** /ˈpeɪəbəl/ ADJECTIVE
1 that must be paid □ The second instalment is payable on or before 1 July.
2 a cheque that is payable to someone has their name written on it 🔁 Cheques should be made payable to 'Smith Mills Limited'.

pay-as-you-go /ˌpeɪ əzjuˈgəʊ/ ADJECTIVE paying for a service just before you use it, not after you have used it □ pay-as-you-go mobile phones

payee /ˌpeɪˈiː/ NOUN [plural payees] someone who money or a cheque is paid to

payment /ˈpeɪmənt/ NOUN [plural payments]
1 money paid for something 🔁 We make monthly payments. □ All payments will be made to your bank account. 🔁 He received a cash payment of £200.
2 no plural when you pay for something □ + of He was involved with the payment of bribes.

payout /ˈpeɪaʊt/ NOUN [plural payouts] a large amount of money that is paid to someone

pay-per-view /ˌpeɪpəˈvjuː/ NOUN, NO PLURAL a system in which you pay an amount of money to watch a particular television programme

payroll /ˈpeɪrəʊl/ NOUN [plural payrolls] a list of all the people that a company employs and the money that they earn □ The company has 500 people on the payroll.

payslip /ˈpeɪslɪp/ NOUN [plural payslips] a piece of paper from your employer that shows details of money you have earned, tax you have paid, etc.

PC /ˌpiːˈsiː/ ABBREVIATION
1 personal computer
2 police constable; used before a police officer's name □ PC Evans

PDA /ˌpiːdiːˈeɪ/ ABBREVIATION personal digital assistant; a small computer that you can hold in your hand. A computing word.

PDF /ˌpiːdiːˈef/ ABBREVIATION portable document format; a type of computer file that you can send from one computer to another. A computing word.

PE /ˌpiːˈiː/ ABBREVIATION physical education; a school subject in which children learn sports, games and exercises

pea /piː/ NOUN [plural peas] a small round green vegetable

peace /piːs/ NOUN, NO PLURAL
1 a situation in which there is no war or violence □ The two countries have been at peace for 50 years. 🔁 We are seeking to bring peace to the region. 🔁 The police were at the demonstration to keep the peace. 🔁 peace talks 🔁 a peace deal
2 a situation which is quiet and calm □ I want a little peace to get on with my homework. 🔁 She goes to the library for a bit of peace and quiet.

peaceful /ˈpiːsfʊl/ ADJECTIVE

1 not involving war or violence □ a peaceful protest 🔁 It says its nuclear programme is for peaceful purposes.
2 quiet and calm □ She felt more peaceful than she had all day. □ a peaceful seaside town
3 not wanting to be involved in war or violence □ a peaceful nation

• **peacefully** /ˈpiːsfʊli/ ADVERB
1 quietly and calmly 🔁 She died peacefully in her sleep. □ The baby was sleeping peacefully.
2 without any violence □ The demonstration began peacefully. □ The two groups live peacefully together.

peacetime /ˈpiːstaɪm/ NOUN, NO PLURAL a period of time when there is no war

peach /piːtʃ/ ► NOUN [plural peaches] a round fruit with a soft skin, pale orange flesh and a large stone inside
► ADJECTIVE having a pale orange colour like a peach

peacock /ˈpiːkɒk/ NOUN [plural peacocks] a large, male bird with a long tail with colourful feathers

peak /piːk/ ► NOUN [plural peaks]
1 the highest, greatest or most successful level □ the peak of the holiday season 🔁 She reached the peak of her career in the 1990s. 🔁 The trains are packed at peak times.
2 the pointed top of a mountain or hill 🔁 snow-covered mountain peaks
3 the flat part at the front of a cap (=soft hat) that sticks out
► VERB [peaks, peaking, peaked] to reach the highest, greatest or most successful level □ Traffic usually peaks about 5 or 6 o'clock.
► ADJECTIVE when the largest number of people are using or doing something □ I try to travel outside peak periods.

peal /piːl/ ► NOUN [plural peals]
1 a sound made by one or more large bells ringing together
2 a loud sound of laughter 🔁 They burst into peals of laughter.
3 a loud sound of thunder
► VERB [peals, pealing, pealed] if bells peal, they ring loudly together

peanut /ˈpiːnʌt/ NOUN [plural peanuts] a type of nut that grows underground in a shell and can be eaten

peanut butter /ˌpiːnʌt ˈbʌtə(r)/ NOUN, NO PLURAL a thick, soft mixture made with crushed peanuts that you spread on bread

pear /peə(r)/ NOUN [plural pears] a fruit with green, yellow or brown skin and white flesh which is round at the bottom and narrower at the top

pearl /pɜːl/ NOUN [plural pearls]
1 a round, white object, formed inside the shell of an oyster (=sea creature), and used for making jewellery □ a pearl necklace
2 a pearl of wisdom a useful piece of information

peasant /'pezənt/ NOUN [plural **peasants**] a poor person who works on the land in a poor country □ *a peasant farmer*

peat /piːt/ NOUN, NO PLURAL a substance formed in the ground over many years from decayed plants, used for growing plants or as a fuel for burning

pebble /'pebəl/ NOUN [plural **pebbles**] a small stone that has been made smooth by water

peck /pek/ ▶ VERB [**pecks, pecking, pecked**] if a bird pecks, it hits something or picks something up with its beak □ *Birds pecked at the crumbs.*

♦ IDIOM **pecking order** the order of power or importance of people or animals within a group □ *He dropped down the pecking order under the new coach.*
▶ NOUN [plural **pecks**]
1 when a bird pecks
2 a quick, light kiss □ *He gave me a peck on the cheek.*

peckish /'pekɪʃ/ ADJECTIVE an informal word meaning slightly hungry □ *I'm a bit peckish.*

peculiar /pɪ'kjuːliə(r)/ ADJECTIVE
1 strange or not expected, sometimes in an unpleasant way □ *a very peculiar smell* □ *It seems peculiar that no one noticed.* □ *That would explain his peculiar behaviour recently.*
2 **peculiar to someone/something** typical of a particular person, place or thing □ *It's a phenomenon peculiar to this region.*

● **peculiarity** /pɪ,kjuː'lɪ'ærətɪ/ NOUN [plural **peculiarities**]
1 a peculiar thing, habit or quality □ *She put up with her grandmother's peculiarities.*
2 a feature or characteristic typical of one person, thing or place □ *We have to respond to the peculiarities of the market.*

● **peculiarly** /pɪ'kjuː'lɪəlɪ/ ADVERB
1 in a strange way □ *He's been behaving very peculiarly.*
2 in way that is typical of a particular person, thing or place □ *a peculiarly British habit*

pedal /'pedəl/ ▶ NOUN [plural **pedals**] a part that you push with your foot, such as on a bicycle, in a car or on a machine 🖻 *the brake pedal*
▶ VERB [**pedals, pedalling**/US**pedaling, pedalled**/US**pedaled**] to push the pedals on a bicycle or to ride a bicycle □ *We hired bikes and pedalled along the coast road.*

pedantic /pɪ'dæntɪk/ ADJECTIVE thinking too much about correct details or rules □ *Oh, don't be so pedantic; you know what I meant!*

peddle /'pedəl/ VERB [**peddles, peddling, peddled**]
1 to sell something illegal or of bad quality □ *They peddle cigarettes to kids.*
2 to try to persuade people to believe a story, idea, etc., especially one that is not true □ *Don't believe the propaganda peddled by the industry.*

pedestal /'pedɪstəl/ NOUN [plural **pedestals**] a base that something stands on, especially a statue (=stone model of a person)

♦ IDIOM **put/place someone on a pedestal** to admire

someone so much that you think they are perfect □ *We tend to put sportsmen on a pedestal.*

pedestrian /pɪ'destrɪən/ ▶ NOUN [plural **pedestrians**] someone who is walking and not travelling in a vehicle □ *Pedestrians and cyclists are given priority in the city centre.*
▶ ADJECTIVE a formal word meaning ordinary and boring □ *The main dishes were rather pedestrian.*

pedestrian crossing /pɪ,destrɪən 'krɒsɪŋ/ NOUN [plural **pedestrian crossings**] a place marked on a road where vehicles must stop to allow people to cross

pediatric /,piːdɪ'ætrɪk/ ADJECTIVE the US spelling of paediatric

● **pediatrician** /,piːdɪə'trɪʃən/ NOUN [plural **pediatricians**] the US spelling of paediatrician

● **pediatrics** /,piːdɪ'ætrɪks/ NOUN, NO PLURAL the US spelling of paediatrics

pedigree /'pedɪgriː/ ▶ NOUN [plural **pedigrees**]
1 a record of the family history of an animal, especially with all members of the same breed
2 the past experiences or achievements of a person or an organization □ *He has an impressive pedigree as a manager.*
3 your family history
▶ ADJECTIVE a pedigree animal has a family history with all members of the same breed □ *a pedigree dog*

pedlar /'pedlə(r)/ NOUN [plural **pedlars**] a person who travels around selling small things

peek /piːk/ ▶ VERB [**peeks, peeking, peeked**]
1 to look at something quickly, especially when you should not be looking □ *He peeked inside the box.*
2 to be just seen behind something □ *A blue book was peeking out of her bag.*
▶ NOUN [plural **peeks**] a quick look 🖻 *He took a peek inside the room.*

peel /piːl/ ▶ VERB [**peels, peeling, peeled**]
1 to remove the skin of a vegetable or a piece of fruit □ *She was peeling potatoes.* □ **+ off** *Let the peppers cool then peel off the skin.*
2 to remove something from a surface by pulling it carefully □ **+ off** *He carefully peeled off the label.* □ **+ away** *I opened the box and peeled away the layers of tissue paper.*
3 if paint or skin peels, it comes off in small pieces □ *The paint was peeling off the walls.*

♦ PHRASAL VERB **peel something off** to remove clothes that are tight or wet □ *We peeled off our wet suits.*
▶ NOUN, NO PLURAL the skin of some fruit and vegetables □ *orange peel*

● **peeler** /'piːlə(r)/ NOUN [plural **peelers**] a kitchen tool used to peel vegetables □ *a potato peeler*

peep /piːp/ ▶ VERB [**peeps, peeping, peeped**]
1 to be just seen from behind something □ *The sun peeped out from behind the clouds.*
2 to look at something quickly and usually secretly, especially through or from behind something □ *He peeped over the top of the wall.*

▶ NOUN [*plural* **peeps**]
1 a slight sound ⊞ *You won't hear a peep out of us.*
2 a quick look at something ⊞ *I had a peep into next door's garden.*

peer /pɪə(r)/ ▶ VERB [**peers, peering, peered**] to look at something carefully, usually because it is difficult to see ☐ *He peered through a downstairs window.*
▶ NOUN [*plural* **peers**]
1 people of a similar age or social position to you ☐ *She was popular with her peers and teachers.*
2 in the UK, someone who has a high social position and a special title, for example 'Lord'

peer group /pɪə ˌgruːp/ NOUN [*plural* **peer groups**] all the people of a similar age or social position to you ☐ *Children are greatly influenced by their peer groups.*

peer pressure /pɪə ˌpreʃə(r)/ NOUN, NO PLURAL the influence that people of a similar age or social position have on you ☐ *There's a lot of peer pressure on teenagers to wear the latest fashions.*

peeved /piːvd/ ADJECTIVE annoyed ☐ *I was a bit peeved because she was late.*

peg /peg/ NOUN [*plural* **pegs**]
1 a small object used for fastening wet clothes to a string to dry
2 a bent piece of metal or plastic for hanging coats, hats or jackets on ⊞ *a coat peg*
3 a piece of wood or metal used to fix something in place ⊞ *a tent peg*

pejorative /pɪˈdʒɒrətɪv/ ADJECTIVE a pejorative word or phrase is offensive or expresses criticism ☐ *a pejorative term*
• **pejoratively** /pɪˈdʒɒrətɪvlɪ/ ADVERB in a pejorative way ☐ *The word is used pejoratively.*

pelican /ˈpelɪkən/ NOUN [*plural* **pelicans**] a large white bird with a large part that hangs down under its beak where it stores fish

pelican crossing /ˌpelɪkən ˈkrɒsɪŋ/ NOUN [*plural* **pelican crossings**] a place where people can cross the road with lights that you use by pressing a button to make the traffic stop

pellet /ˈpelɪt/ NOUN [*plural* **pellets**]
1 a small hard round piece of a substance ☐ *pet food pellets*
2 a small round piece of metal used in some guns ☐ *a shotgun pellet*

pelt /pelt/ ▶ VERB [**pelts, pelting, pelted**]
1 to throw things at someone or something with force ☐ *The minister's car was pelted with eggs.*
2 if rain pelts down, it falls with force ☐ *Rain pelted down outside.*
3 to run or to move very fast ☐ *He came pelting down the road on his bike.*
▶ NOUN [*plural* **pelts**]
1 the skin from an animal ☐ *beaver pelts*
2 (at) full pelt moving very fast ☐ *He was running at full pelt.*

pelvic /ˈpelvɪk/ ADJECTIVE to do with the pelvis. A biology word ☐ *the pelvic bone*

pelvis /ˈpelvɪs/ NOUN [*plural* **pelvises**] the large round bones that connect the bottom of your back to your legs. A biology word.

pen /pen/ ▶ NOUN [*plural* **pens**]
1 an object used for writing with ink ⊞ *a ballpoint pen* ☐ *Have you got a pen and paper?*
2 a small area surrounded by a fence and used for keeping animals in
▶ VERB [**pens, penning, penned**]
1 to put an animal in a pen
2 to write something ☐ *Tom Martin will pen the script for the new film.*
♦ PHRASAL VERB **pen someone in** to prevent someone from moving or escaping ☐ *Supporters were penned in behind barriers.*

penal /ˈpiːnəl/ ADJECTIVE to do with the punishment of criminals ☐ *penal reform* ☐ *a penal code*

penalize *or* **penalise** /ˈpiːnəlaɪz/ VERB [**penalizes, penalizing, penalized**]
1 to punish someone for breaking a rule or law ☐ *Players can be penalized for swearing.*
2 to give someone a disadvantage ☐ *Rises in fuel prices penalize families with big cars.*
• **penalty** /ˈpenəltɪ/ NOUN [*plural* **penalties**]
1 a punishment for breaking a rule or law ⊞ *He faces a maximum penalty of 10 years in jail.* ⊞ *The regulator has imposed a penalty of £20,000 on the bank.*
2 a free shot at the goal in some sports, given because a player in the other team has broken a rule ⊞ *Henry scored a penalty.* ⊞ *Rooney will take the penalty.*

penance /ˈpenəns/ NOUN, NO PLURAL punishment that you accept to show you are sorry for doing something wrong

pence /pens/ PLURAL OF **penny** ☐ *a ten pence coin*

penchant /ˈpɑ̃ʃɑ̃/ NOUN, NO PLURAL have a penchant for something to like something very much

pencil /ˈpensəl/ NOUN [*plural* **pencils**] a long thin wooden object for writing or drawing, with a black or coloured substance in the centre ☐ *coloured pencils* ☐ *a pencil drawing*
♦ PHRASAL VERB [**pencils, pencilling/US penciling, pencilled/US penciled**] **pencil something in** to plan or to arrange something which may be changed later ☐ *The meeting is pencilled in for 10 March.*

pencil sharpener /ˈpensəl ˌʃɑːpənə(r)/ NOUN [*plural* **pencil sharpeners**] a device for making the point of a pencil sharp

pendant /ˈpendənt/ NOUN [*plural* **pendants**] a piece of jewellery that hangs from a long chain around your neck

pending /ˈpendɪŋ/ ▶ PREPOSITION a formal word meaning waiting for something else to happen first ☐ *He was held in prison pending trial.*
▶ ADJECTIVE a formal word meaning waiting to be decided or dealt with ☐ *The court's decision is still pending.*

pendulum /'pendjʊləm/ NOUN [plural **pendulums**] a weight at the end of a long bar that moves from side to side, especially inside a large clock

penetrate /'penɪtreɪt/ VERB [**penetrates, penetrating, penetrated**]
1 to get into or through something □ Rain could not penetrate those thick trees. □ The knife penetrated his heart.
2 to successfully join a group or to be successful in a particular area □ Our company has begun to penetrate new markets in South America.
• **penetrating** /'penɪtreɪtɪŋ/ ADJECTIVE
1 a penetrating look seems to be reading your thoughts □ a penetrating gaze/stare
2 a penetrating sound is loud and can be heard through other sounds
3 intelligent and understanding something very well □ a penetrating analysis
• **penetration** /ˌpenɪ'treɪʃən/ NOUN, NO PLURAL when something penetrates something else

pen friend /'pen ˌfrend/ NOUN [plural **pen friends**] a friend you write letters to, but do not meet

penguin /'peŋgwɪn/ NOUN [plural **penguins**] a black and white bird that cannot fly but uses its wings to swim under water

penicillin /ˌpenɪ'sɪlɪn/ NOUN, NO PLURAL a drug used for treating infections caused by bacteria

peninsula /pə'nɪnsjʊlə/ NOUN [plural **peninsulas**] a long area of land that sticks out from a larger area of land, and has water around most of it. A geography word.

penis /'piːnɪs/ NOUN [plural **penises**] the male organ for urinating and producing babies. A biology word.

penknife /'pennaɪf/ NOUN [plural **penknives**] a small knife with blades that fold into the handle

pennant /'penənt/ NOUN [plural **pennants**] a long flag with a point at one end

penniless /'penɪlɪs/ ADJECTIVE having no money □ penniless refugees

penny /'penɪ/ NOUN [plural **pence** or pennies or p]
1 a small British coin worth one hundredth of £1 □ Crisps cost 40 pence.
2 every penny all of someone's money □ He spends every penny he earns on computer games.
3 not pay/not cost a penny to not pay or not cost any money at all □ The great thing about this food is that it doesn't cost a penny.

➤ Note that when you are saying how much something costs, the plural **pence** is used. When you are talking about the coins themselves, use the plural **pennies**: □ It cost me fifty pence. □ I only had a few pennies left in my purse.

pension /'penʃən/ NOUN [plural **pensions**] an amount of money that a government or company regularly gives someone when they are too old to work 🔃 My grandma gets a state pension (=a pension that a government gives people). 🔃 a company pension (=a pension that a company gives to former employees) 🔃 The company has a good pension scheme.
• **pensioner** /'penʃənə(r)/ NOUN [plural **pensioners**] someone who gets a pension

pensive /'pensɪv/ ADJECTIVE thinking about something in a serious way □ He was in a pensive mood.

pentagon /'pentəgən/ NOUN [plural **pentagons**] a solid shape with five sides. A maths word.

pentathlon /pen'tæθlən/ NOUN [plural **pentathlons**] a sports competition in which you must do five different sports

pent-up /ˌpent'ʌp/ ADJECTIVE a pent-up feeling is one which you feel strongly but have not expressed □ pent-up frustration

penultimate /pə'nʌltɪmət/ ADJECTIVE coming not last in a series of things but next to last □ the penultimate game of the competition

people /'piːpəl/ ► PLURAL NOUN
1 men, women and children □ young people □ How many people have you invited to your party? □ People don't like being criticized.
2 the people the ordinary people in a country who do not have important positions □ The Prime Minister must listen to the people if he wants to get re-elected.
3 plural **peoples** a formal word meaning a race or group of people in a particular country □ + of all the peoples of the world □ the Russian people
► VERB [**peoples, peopling, peopled**] if a place is peopled by a particular type of person, they live there. A formal word □ It's an area that's peopled by very poor families

➤ Remember that the noun **people** always takes a plural verb: □ People are generally happy with the government.

➤ Remember also that you do not say 'all people' or 'every people'. Instead you say **everyone** or **everybody**:
✓ Everyone feels sad sometimes.
✗ All people feel sad sometimes.

people carrier /'piːpəl ˌkærɪə(r)/ NOUN [plural **people carriers**] a large, high car which carries up to eight people

pepper /'pepə(r)/ ► NOUN [plural **peppers**]
1 no plural a powder with a strong taste which is added to food 🔃 He sprinkled salt and pepper on his food. 🔃 freshly ground black pepper
2 a hollow red, green or yellow vegetable which is eaten raw or cooked □ a sliced red pepper
► VERB [**peppers, peppering, peppered**] if something is peppered with things, it includes a lot of them □ The article was peppered with references to the attack.

peppercorn /'pepəkɔːn/ NOUN [plural **peppercorns**]
a very small dried fruit that is crushed to make pepper
pepper mill /'pepə ˌmɪl/ NOUN [plural **pepper mills**]
a piece of kitchen equipment used for crushing
peppercorns
peppermint /'pepəmɪnt/ NOUN [plural
peppermints]
1 a strong, fresh taste that comes from a herb and is
used in food
2 a sweet that tastes of peppermint
peppery /'pepəri/ ADJECTIVE tasting of pepper □ *a
peppery sauce*
pep talk /'pep ˌtɔːk/ NOUN [plural **pep talks**] a talk
that is intended to encourage someone to work harder
□ *The players were given a pep talk by their manager
before the game.*

per /pɜː(r)/ PREPOSITION for each □ *The meal will cost
£20 per person.* □ *He was driving at 65 miles per hour
when the crash happened.* □ *How much are the apples
per kilo?*

perceive /pə'siːv/ VERB [perceives, perceiving,
perceived]
1 to understand or think about something in a particular
way □ *He was perceived as a threat to the state.*
2 a formal word meaning to notice something □ *I
perceived that something was not right.*

percent /pə'sent/ or **per cent** /pə 'sent/ ADVERB,
ADJECTIVE, NOUN in or for every 100, shown by the
symbol % □ *Sales have increased by ten percent.*
□ *There has been a five percent fall in the number of
people who are unemployed.* □ *Sixty percent of
schoolchildren felt that they got too much homework.*
percentage /pə'sentɪdʒ/ NOUN [plural
percentages] a number that is expressed as a number
in 100 ⊞ *A high percentage of students got top grades.*
□ *What percentage of children have a television in
their bedrooms?*

perceptible /pə'septəbəl/ ADJECTIVE a formal word
meaning able to be noticed □ *The change was barely
perceptible.*
perception /pə'sepʃən/ NOUN [plural **perceptions**]
1 the way you see or understand something □ *The
visit changed my perception of the city.*
2 the ability to see, hear or feel something □ *Anxiety
can affect a person's perception of pain.*
perceptive /pə'septɪv/ ADJECTIVE good at noticing
and understanding things □ *She's very perceptive for a
child.*
perch /pɜːtʃ/ ▶ VERB [perches, perching, perched]
1 if something is perched somewhere, it is on the top
or edge of something □ *The house is perched on a
hillside overlooking the lake.*
2 to sit on the edge of something □ *She perched on a
stool next to me.*
▶ NOUN [plural **perches**] something that a bird sits on
ercussion /pə'kʌʃən/ NOUN, NO PLURAL musical
instruments that you hit or shake, such as drums

• **percussionist** /pə'kʌʃənɪst/ NOUN [plural
percussionists] someone who plays percussion
instruments
perennial /pə'reniəl/ ▶ ADJECTIVE never ending
□ *Then there is the perennial problem of how to
dispose of toxic waste.*
▶ NOUN [plural **perennials**] a plant that lives for more
than one year

perfect ▶ ADJECTIVE /'pɜːfɪkt/
1 without any mistakes or faults □ *Emma has perfect
teeth.* □ *Your English is perfect.*
2 exactly right for something □ *Jones was the perfect
choice for the role.* □ *South Beach is the perfect place
for a holiday.*
3 very good □ *The shoes were a perfect fit.* □ *This
building is a perfect example of 1930s architecture.*
4 complete □ *a perfect stranger* □ *Ed's idea made
perfect sense to me.*
▶ VERB /pə'fekt/ [perfects, perfecting, perfected] to
make something perfect □ *The hills are ideal for skiers
determined to perfect their technique.*
▶ NOUN, NO PLURAL /'pɜːfɪkt/ the perfect the tense of
a verb that in English is formed with has/have/had and
the past participle □ *'He has played tennis for years' is
in the perfect.*
• **perfection** /pə'fekʃən/ NOUN, NO PLURAL the state of
being perfect □ *Some people try to achieve physical
perfection.* □ *The meat was cooked to perfection* (=it
was cooked perfectly).
• **perfectionist** /pə'fekʃənɪst/ NOUN [plural
perfectionists] someone who tries to do everything
perfectly
• **perfectly** /'pɜːfɪktli/ ADVERB
1 in an extremely good way □ *The children behaved
perfectly.* □ *His arrival was perfectly timed because the
meal was just ready.*
2 completely □ *It was perfectly obvious that he was
lying.* □ *The equipment is old but it's perfectly safe.*

perforate /'pɜːfəreɪt/ VERB [perforates, perforating,
perforated] to make a small hole in something
• **perforated** /'pɜːfəreɪtɪd/ ADJECTIVE having a small
hole, or many small holes □ *a perforated eardrum*
• **perforation** /ˌpɜːfə'reɪʃən/ NOUN [plural
perforations] a small hole in something, especially
many small holes in paper that help you to tear it

perform /pə'fɔːm/ VERB [performs, performing,
performed]
1 to do a task □ *Surgeons perform operations.* □ *He
found it difficult to perform simple tasks after the
accident.*
2 to act in a play, sing a song, etc. with people
watching you □ *It was the first time we'd performed
the song.* □ *I love performing in front of a live
audience.*
3 perform well/poorly/badly etc. to do something
well or badly □ *His team performed poorly in both
games.* □ *The business has performed well* (=it has
been successful) *in difficult circumstances.*

• **performance** /pə'fɔ:məns/ NOUN [plural **performances**]
1 an occasion when someone acts in a play, sings a song, etc. with people watching them 🔁 The show included a live performance by several bands. 🔁 Kylie gave an impromptu performance. □ + of We went to a performance of Mozart's 'Magic Flute'.
2 the level of success that someone or something has 🔁 The team needs to improve its performance. 🔁 Her poor performance in the exams was very disappointing.

• **performer** /pə'fɔ:mə(r)/ NOUN [plural **performers**]
1 a singer, actor, etc. who performs □ She's a great performer. □ a circus performer
2 someone or something who does something with a particular level of success 🔁 He is one of the team's top performers. □ The school has been rated as a poor performer.

perfume /'pɜ:fju:m/ NOUN [plural **perfumes**] a liquid that women put on their skin to make them smell nice 🔁 She always wears perfume. □ I could smell her perfume.

• **perfumed** /'pɜ:fju:md/ ADJECTIVE containing perfume □ a perfumed body lotion

perhaps /pə'hæps/ ADVERB
1 possibly □ I can't find Leo. Perhaps he's left. □ Perhaps I shouldn't have told him.
2 used when you are suggesting something □ Perhaps we should invite Lisa. What do you think?

peril /'perɪl/ NOUN [plural **perils**] a formal word meaning danger □ He describes the perils of the open sea. □ The business's future was in peril.

• **perilous** /'perɪləs/ ADJECTIVE a formal word meaning dangerous □ It was a perilous journey across miles of desert.

perimeter /pə'rɪmɪtə(r)/ NOUN [plural **perimeters**] the edge of an area □ Guards patrol the perimeter of the military camp. □ a perimeter fence

period /'pɪərɪəd/ ▶ NOUN [plural **periods**]
1 an amount of time □ The work was done over a two-year period. 🔁 Rachel has learned a lot in a short period of time. 🔁 He had spent long periods in prison. □ + of He lived there for a period of several years.
2 a time in history □ the Regency period □ one of the earliest geological periods
3 one of the parts that a day at school is divided into □ We had history first period.
4 the flow of blood each month from a woman's body
5 the US word for full stop
▶ ADJECTIVE in the style of a time in history □ period costumes

• **periodic** /,pɪərɪ'ɒdɪk/ ADJECTIVE happening sometimes but not often □ periodic attacks

• **periodical** /,pɪərɪ'ɒdɪkəl/ NOUN [plural **periodicals**] a magazine about a particular subject that is published regularly

periodic table /,pɪərɪɒdɪk 'teɪbəl/ NOUN, NO PLURAL the periodic table a list of all the chemical elements,

arranged by the structure of their atoms. A chemistry word.

peripheral /pə'rɪfərəl/ ADJECTIVE
1 not as important as other things □ a peripheral role
2 to do with the outer edge of something □ peripheral nerves

• **periphery** /pə'rɪfərɪ/ NOUN [plural **peripheries**] the outer edge of something □ Land on the periphery of the city is very expensive now.

perish /'perɪʃ/ VERB [perishes, perishing, perished] a formal word meaning to die □ Four children perished in the fire.

• **perishable** /'perɪʃəbəl/ ADJECTIVE perishable food does not stay fresh for long □ Fresh meat, milk and other perishable foods should be kept in a refrigerator.

perjury /'pɜ:dʒərɪ/ NOUN, NO PLURAL the crime of telling a lie in a court

perk /pɜ:k/ NOUN [plural **perks**] something extra that someone's employer gives them such as free meals or a free car □ Free train travel is one of the perks of working for a railway company.
◆ PHRASAL VERB [perks, perking, perked] perk (someone) up to feel happier, or to make someone feel happier □ The children perked up when I mentioned getting an ice cream.

• **perky** /'pɜ:kɪ/ ADJECTIVE [perkier, perkiest] happy and full of energy □ He seemed perky enough.

perm /pɜ:m/ ▶ NOUN [plural **perms**] a chemical treatment that makes your hair curly for a long time 🔁 My grandmother had a perm.
▶ VERB [perms, perming, permed] to make someone's hair curly for a long time by putting chemicals on it

permanence /'pɜ:mənəns/ NOUN, NO PLURAL the state of lasting forever or for a very long time

• **permanent** /'pɜ:mənənt/ ADJECTIVE lasting forever or for a very long time □ The accident left him with permanent brain damage. □ Ella has been offered a permanent job. □ We need a permanent solution to the problem.

• **permanently** /'pɜ:mənəntlɪ/ ADVERB in a way that lasts forever or for a very long time □ Her sight had been permanently damaged. □ Many new mothers feel permanently tired.

permeable /'pɜ:mɪəbəl/ ADJECTIVE permeable substances allow liquid or gas to pass through them. A biology or physics word.

permissible /pə'mɪsəbəl/ ADJECTIVE a formal word meaning allowed by a rule □ Some cities have pollution levels that are higher than the permissible limits.

permission /pə'mɪʃən/ NOUN, NO PLURAL if you have permission to do something, someone says you can do it 🔁 A doctor can't operate on you unless you give permission. 🔁 You need to get permission from your teacher if you want to leave the class early. 🔁 Rob has taken his Dad's car without permission. □ + to do **something** I asked her permission to use the phone

> Remember that you **get permission** or **give permission** to do something. You do not 'get/ give a permission':
> ✓ I **got permission** from my teacher to leave early.
> ✗ I got a permission from my teacher to leave early.

permit ▶ VERB /pə'mɪt/ [**permits, permitting, permitted**] a formal word meaning to allow something □ *Smoking is not permitted anywhere in the building.*
▶ NOUN /'pɜːmɪt/ [*plural* **permits**] an official document that allows you to do something □ *a work permit*
perpendicular /ˌpɜːpən'dɪkjʊlə(r)/ ADJECTIVE at an angle of 90° to something. A maths word □ *a perpendicular line*
perpetrate /'pɜːpɪtreɪt/ VERB [**perpetrates, perpetrating, perpetrated**] a formal word meaning to do something bad or illegal □ *They perpetrated one of the largest frauds in legal history.*
• **perpetrator** /'pɜːpɪtreɪtə(r)/ NOUN [*plural* **perpetrators**] a formal word meaning someone who has done something bad or illegal
perpetual /pə'petʃuəl/ ADJECTIVE never ending or happening too often □ *They live in perpetual fear of attacks.*
• **perpetuate** /pə'petʃueɪt/ VERB [**perpetuates, perpetuating, perpetuated**] to make something continue for a long time, especially something that is bad or wrong. A formal word □ *Stories like this perpetuate the myth that women are bad drivers.*
perplex /pə'pleks/ VERB [**perplexes, perplexing, perplexed**] to confuse someone
• **perplexed** /pə'plekst/ ADJECTIVE confused because you do not understand something □ *a perplexed expression*
persecute /'pɜːsɪkjuːt/ VERB [**persecutes, persecuting, persecuted**] to treat someone badly and unfairly, especially because of their religion, race or beliefs □ *Christians were persecuted in the Roman Empire.*
persecution /ˌpɜːsɪ'kjuːʃən/ NOUN, NO PLURAL when someone is persecuted
persecutor /'pɜːsɪkjuːtə(r)/ NOUN [*plural* **persecutors**] someone who persecutes other people
perseverance /ˌpɜːsɪ'vɪərəns/ NOUN, NO PLURAL determination to continue with something although it is difficult
persevere /ˌpɜːsɪ'vɪə(r)/ VERB [**perseveres, persevering, persevered**] to continue doing something although it is difficult □ *It's not an easy task but she perseveres.*
persist /pə'sɪst/ VERB [**persists, persisting, persisted**] 1 if something bad persists, it continues □ *If the problem persists, talk to your doctor.* 2 to continue to do or say something □ *'Why can't I go, Mum?' he persisted.*

• **persistence** /pə'sɪstəns/ NOUN, NO PLURAL when someone continues to do something in a determined way □ *I admire your persistence.*
• **persistent** /pə'sɪstənt/ ADJECTIVE 1 continuing to do something even when it is difficult or when someone tells you to stop □ *I said I wasn't interested but the salesman was quite persistent.* 2 if something unpleasant is persistent, it continues for a long time □ *persistent rain*

person /'pɜːsən/ NOUN [*plural* **people**] 1 a man, woman or child □ *Heather's a really nice person.* □ *Tatsuya was the first person in his family to go to university.* □ *How many people were at the party?* 🕮 *Jeremy is the kind of person who knows everything.* 2 **in person** if you do something in person, you do it by going somewhere instead of by writing or by sending someone else to do it □ *He apologized to her in person.*

> Note that the plural of person is usually **people**. The plural 'persons' is sometimes used in formal writing but it is not used generally:
> ✓ Most **people** here own a car.
> ✗ Most **persons** here own a car.

personal /'pɜːsənəl/ ADJECTIVE 1 belonging to, or to do with one particular person □ *a personal opinion* □ *personal belongings* 🕮*I know from personal experience that the exam is very difficult.* 2 private and to do with your health, relationships, etc. 🕮 *The singer's personal life has been quite troubled.* □ *Never give out personal information to a company on the phone.* 3 done by someone and not by a person representing them □ *The Prime Minister wrote a personal reply to her letter.*

personal assistant /ˌpɜːsənəl ə'sɪstənt/ NOUN [*plural* **personal assistants**] someone whose job is to help another person, for example by writing e-mails and letters, organizing meetings, etc.
personal computer /ˌpɜːsənəl kəm'pjuːtə(r)/ NOUN [*plural* **personal computers**] a small computer that is designed to be used by one person

personality /ˌpɜːsə'nælətɪ/ NOUN [*plural* **personalities**] 1 someone's character and the qualities they have 🕮 *Artie has a very outgoing personality.* □ *The accident had changed his personality.* 2 a famous person 🕮 *He's one of America's best-known TV personalities.* 3 *no plural* qualities that make people notice you and want to be with you □ *He's got a lot of personality.*

personalized /'pɜːsənəlaɪzd/ ADJECTIVE 1 marked with your name or with a particular decoration to show that it is yours □ *personalized notepaper* 2 done or made in a way that is suitable for a particular person □ *We offer personalized treatment.*

personally /ˈpɜːsənəlɪ/ ADVERB
1 used when stating your own opinion □ *Personally, I don't like him.*
2 done by you and not by anyone else □ *He wrote to everyone personally.*
3 take something personally to think that someone is saying something bad about you and feel upset □ *He was criticizing the organization and not you – I wouldn't take it personally.*

personal pronoun /ˌpɜːsənəl ˈprəʊnaʊn/ NOUN [*plural* **personal pronouns**] one of the pronouns such as 'I', 'she', 'they', or 'him' that refers to a particular person, thing or group of people or things

personnel /ˌpɜːsəˈnel/ NOUN, NO PLURAL
1 the people who work for a particular company or organization □ *army personnel*
2 the department in a company that finds new people to work for the company and keeps records of employees □ *Mel works in personnel.*

perspective /pəˈspektɪv/ NOUN [*plural* **perspectives**]
1 a way of thinking about or judging something □ *Try thinking about the problem from a different perspective.*
2 put/keep something in perspective to think about something in a sensible way and not think it is more important than it really is

perspiration /ˌpɜːspəˈreɪʃən/ NOUN, NO PLURAL a formal word meaning sweat

perspire /pəˈspaɪə(r)/ VERB [**perspires, perspiring, perspired**] a formal word meaning to sweat

persuade /pəˈsweɪd/ VERB [**persuades, persuading, persuaded**]
1 to make someone agree to do something by telling them why they should do it □ + *to do something* I *tried to persuade Tanya to come with us.*
2 to make someone believe something □ + *that* I *managed to persuade her that I was telling the truth.* □ + *of* He *tried to persuade the jury of his innocence.*

• **persuasion** /pəˈsweɪʒən/ NOUN [*plural* **persuasions**]
1 no plural when you persuade someone ⊞ *After a little gentle persuasion, he agreed to come with us.*
2 a formal word meaning a political or religious belief □ *The course is intended for people of all religious persuasions.*

• **persuasive** /pəˈsweɪsɪv/ ADJECTIVE able to make people do what you want, or able to make people change their opinions □ *She can be very persuasive.* □ *a persuasive argument*

pertain /pəˈteɪn/
♦ PHRASAL VERB [**pertains, pertaining, pertained**]
pertain to something if one thing pertains to another thing, it is to do with it. A formal word. □ *Documents pertaining to the case have been stolen.*

perturb /pəˈtɜːb/ VERB [**perturbs, perturbing, perturbed**] a formal word meaning to make someone feel worried

• **perturbed** /pəˈtɜːbd/ ADJECTIVE a formal word meaning worried □ *She didn't seem at all perturbed by the news.*

peruse /pəˈruːz/ VERB [**peruses, perusing, perused**] a formal word meaning to read or look at something □ *His lawyer perused the documents.*

pervade /pəˈveɪd/ VERB [**pervades, pervading, pervaded**] a formal word meaning to be in every part of a place □ *The smell of sweat pervaded the room.*

• **pervasive** /pəˈveɪsɪv/ ADJECTIVE a formal word meaning existing everywhere □ *a pervasive feeling of despair*

perverse /pəˈvɜːs/ ADJECTIVE strange and the opposite of what you expect or consider reasonable □ *He takes a perverse pleasure in upsetting his mother.*

pessimism /ˈpesɪmɪzəm/ NOUN, NO PLURAL the belief that the future will be bad □ *There is general pessimism about the state of the economy.*

• **pessimist** /ˈpesɪmɪst/ NOUN [*plural* **pessimists**] someone who usually expects bad things to happen

• **pessimistic** /ˌpesɪˈmɪstɪk/ ADJECTIVE expecting that bad things will happen □ *a pessimistic outlook*

pest /pest/ NOUN [*plural* **pests**]
1 an animal or insect that destroys crops
2 an informal word for an annoying person, often a child

pester /ˈpestə(r)/ VERB [**pesters, pestering, pestered**] to annoy someone by asking them for something many times □ *The children were pestering me to buy them ice creams.*

pesticide /ˈpestɪsaɪd/ NOUN [*plural* **pesticides**] a chemical used for killing insects which destroy crops

pet /pet/ ▶ NOUN [*plural* **pets**] an animal that you keep in your home ⊞ *Do you have any pets?* □ *Dogs and cats are very popular pets.* □ *Adam has a pet rabbit.*
▶ VERB [**pets, petting, petted**] to touch and move your hand along an animal's fur

petal /ˈpetəl/ NOUN [*plural* **petals**] one of the coloured parts of a flower □ *rose petals*

peter /ˈpiːtə(r)/
♦ PHRASAL VERB [**peters, petering, petered**] peter out to gradually end □ *Her voice petered out.*

petite /pəˈtiːt/ ADJECTIVE a girl or woman who is petite is attractively small and thin

petition /pɪˈtɪʃən/ ▶ NOUN [*plural* **petitions**] a piece of paper that a lot of people sign to try to get a government or someone in authority to do something ⊞ *We signed a petition against the closure of the post office.*
▶ VERB [**petitions, petitioning, petitioned**] to officially ask a government or someone in authority to do something by giving them a petition □ *They're petitioning the local council for better street lighting*

Petri dish /ˈpiːtrɪ ˌdɪʃ/ NOUN [*plural* **Petri dishes**] a flat dish used by scientists for growing bacteria or other cells. A chemistry word.

petrified /ˈpetrɪfaɪd/ ADJECTIVE extremely frightened

petrol /'petrəl/ NOUN, NO PLURAL a fuel for cars, made from oil □ I've just filled the car up with petrol. □ petrol prices

petrol cap /'petrəl ˌkæp/ NOUN [plural **petrol caps**] the small part of a car that you take off to put petrol in

petroleum /pɪ'trəʊlɪəm/ NOUN, NO PLURAL oil from under the ground, used for making petrol

petrol station /'petrəl ˌsteɪʃən/ NOUN [plural **petrol stations**] a place where you buy petrol for a car

petticoat /'petɪkəʊt/ NOUN [plural **petticoats**] a piece of clothing like a thin skirt or dress that a woman wears under her skirt or dress

petty /'petɪ/ ADJECTIVE [**pettier, pettiest**]
1 not serious, or not important □ petty details
🖏 petty crimes
2 unpleasant to other people because of something that is not important

petulance /'petjʊləns/ NOUN, NO PLURAL the quality of being petulant

• **petulant** /'petjʊlənt/ ADJECTIVE bad-tempered because you cannot do or have what you want

pew /pju:/ NOUN [plural **pews**] a long wooden seat in a church

pewter /'pju:tə(r)/ NOUN, NO PLURAL a grey metal that is a mixture of the metals lead and tin

pH /ˌpi:'eɪtʃ/ NOUN, NO PLURAL a number that says how acid or alkaline a substance is. A chemistry word.

phantom /'fæntəm/ ▶ NOUN [plural **phantoms**] the spirit of a dead person which some people think they can see
▶ ADJECTIVE imagined and not existing □ phantom pains

pharaoh /'feərəʊ/ NOUN [plural **pharaohs**] a king in ancient Egypt

pharmaceutical /ˌfɑ:mə'sju:tɪkəl/ ADJECTIVE to do with the making and selling of medicines 🖏 the pharmaceutical industry

pharmacist /'fɑ:məsɪst/ NOUN [plural **pharmacists**] someone who prepares and sells medicines

• **pharmacy** /'fɑ:məsɪ/ NOUN [plural **pharmacies**]
1 a shop where medicines are prepared and sold □ You can get most medicines at your local pharmacy.
2 no plural the study of medicines and how they work

phase /feɪz/ NOUN [plural **phases**] a stage in the development of a thing or person □ The first phase of the project was to interview 100 students. □ Children go through so many phases.

• PHRASAL VERBS [**phases, phasing, phased**] **phase something in** to gradually start using a new law, system, etc. □ The changes will be phased in over two years. **phase something out** to gradually stop using something □ The one-cent coins were phased out a few years ago.

PhD /ˌpi:eɪtʃ'di:/ ABBREVIATION Doctor of Philosophy; the highest university degree □ He's doing a PhD in applied mathematics.

pheasant /'fezənt/ NOUN [plural **pheasants**] a large bird with a long tail, that is hunted for sport and eaten

phenomenal /fɪ'nɒmɪnəl/ ADJECTIVE very great □ The show was a phenomenal success.

• **phenomenon** /fɪ'nɒmɪnən/ NOUN [plural **phenomena**] something that happens or exists, especially something that is unusual and difficult to explain □ The researchers are studying natural phenomena such as storms and tornadoes.

phew /fju:/ EXCLAMATION a way of writing the sound that people make when they are hot or tired, or when they are happy because they have avoided an unpleasant situation □ 'Phew, it's hot in there!' □ Phew, what a relief!

philosopher /fɪ'lɒsəfə(r)/ NOUN [plural **philosophers**] someone who studies philosophy

• **philosophical** /ˌfɪlə'sɒfɪkəl/ ADJECTIVE
1 to do with philosophy □ a philosophical debate
2 calmly accepting a bad situation because you cannot change it □ He was very philosophical about not getting the job.

• **philosophy** /fɪ'lɒsəfɪ/ NOUN [plural **philosophies**]
1 no plural the study of ideas about life □ She did philosophy at university.
2 a set of beliefs about how you should live □ My philosophy is to work hard and play hard.

phlegm /flem/ NOUN, NO PLURAL the thick yellow substance produced in your nose and throat when you have a cold

phobia /'fəʊbɪə/ NOUN [plural **phobias**] a very strong fear of something that you cannot explain or control □ Maria's got a phobia about spiders.

phone /fəʊn/ ▶ NOUN [plural **phones**]
1 a telephone 🖏 Here's my phone number. 🖏 The phone was ringing. 🖏 Can you answer the phone please? □ You can order a pizza by phone.
2 on the phone using the telephone □ Mum's on the phone at the moment. □ I talk to my cousins on the phone every week.
▶ VERB [**phones, phoning, phoned**] to speak to someone using a telephone □ I phoned my grandma last night. □ + up I'll phone up and find out when the library opens.

> ➤ Note that you **phone** a person or place. You do not 'phone to' a person or place:
> ✓ I'll phone Javier.
> ✗ I'll phone to Javier.
> ✓ I'll phone the hospital.
> ✗ I'll phone to the hospital.

• PHRASAL VERB **phone (someone) back** to call someone again using a telephone, because you could not talk to them the first time □ I'm busy just now. I'll phone you back later.

phone box /'fəʊn ˌbɒks/ NOUN [plural **phone boxes**] a small structure in a public place containing a telephone which you can pay to use □ There's a phone box outside the station.

phone call /ˈfəʊn ˌkɔːl/ NOUN [*plural* **phone calls**] when you speak to someone using a telephone ☐ *I'm just going to make a quick phone call.*

phone-in /ˈfəʊnɪn/ NOUN [*plural* **phone-ins**] a television or radio programme in which people can telephone to give their opinions or to ask questions

phone number /ˈfəʊn ˌnʌmbə(r)/ NOUN [*plural* **phone numbers**] the series of numbers that you use to call a particular telephone ☐ *What's your phone number?*

phonetic /fəˈnetɪk/ ADJECTIVE to do with the sounds people make when they talk

• **phonetics** /fəˈnetɪks/ NOUN, NO PLURAL the study of the sounds that people make when they talk

phoney /ˈfəʊni/ *or* **phony** /ˈfəʊni/ ADJECTIVE [**phonier, phoniest**]
1 not real ☐ *He'd given us a phony address.*
2 not sincere ☐ *phoney laughter*

phosphorus /ˈfɒsfərəs/ NOUN, NO PLURAL a chemical element that burns if air touches it. A chemistry word.

photo /ˈfəʊtəʊ/ NOUN [*plural* **photos**] a photograph ☐ *digital photos* ☐ *Who's that woman in the photo?* ☐ *She took a photo of Clare and me on the beach.* ☐ *They showed us their wedding photos.* ☐ *+ of There were photos of the children all over the house.*

photo- /ˈfəʊtəʊ/ PREFIX photo- is added to the beginning of words to mean 'to do with light' or 'to do with photographs' ☐ *photosynthesis* ☐ *photocopier*

photocopier /ˈfəʊtəʊkɒpɪə(r)/ NOUN [*plural* **photocopiers**] a machine that copies a document by taking a photograph of it

• **photocopy** /ˈfəʊtəʊkɒpɪ/ ▶ NOUN [*plural* **photocopies**] a copy of a document that you make using a photocopier ☐ *He made a photocopy of the instructions.*
▶ VERB [**photocopies, photocopying, photocopied**] to make a copy of a document using a photocopier ☐ *Why don't you photocopy the map?*

photogenic /ˈfəʊtəʊˈdʒenɪk/ ADJECTIVE always looking attractive in photographs ☐ *Suki is very photogenic.*

photograph /ˈfəʊtəɡrɑːf/ ▶ NOUN [*plural* **photographs**] a picture made with a camera ☐ *I took a photograph using my new camera.* ☐ *+ of a photograph of Lake Geneva*
▶ VERB [**photographs, photographing, photographed**] to make a picture of something using a camera ☐ *She photographed me in the school play.*

• **photographic** /ˌfəʊtəʊˈɡræfɪk/ ADJECTIVE to do with photographs or photography ☐ *We have photographic evidence of the damage.*

• **photographer** /fəˈtɒɡrəfə(r)/ NOUN [*plural* **photographers**] someone who takes photographs, especially as their job ☐ *He's a professional photographer.* ☐ *a press photographer* (= photographer for a newspaper) ☐ *a fashion photographer*

• **photography** /fəˈtɒɡrəfi/ NOUN, NO PLURAL the art of taking photographs ☐ *digital photography* ☐ *John teaches photography at the college.*

Photostat /ˈfəʊtəʊstæt/ NOUN [*plural* **Photostats**] a copy of a document made on a particular type of machine. A trademark.

photosynthesis /ˌfəʊtəʊˈsɪnθəsɪs/ NOUN, NO PLURAL the process by which plants make their food from the sun. A biology word.

phrasal verb /ˌfreɪzəl ˈvɜːb/ NOUN [*plural* **phrasal verbs**] a verb that you use with an adverb or preposition, which has a different meaning from the verb used alone ☐ *'Give up' and 'get on' are examples of phrasal verbs.*

phrase /freɪz/ ▶ NOUN [*plural* **phrases**] a group of words that have a particular meaning ☐ *She used the phrase 'unwelcome attention' several times.*
▶ VERB [**phrases, phrasing, phrased**] to express something using particular words ☐ *He phrased the question very carefully to avoid upsetting her.*

phrase book /ˈfreɪz ˌbʊk/ NOUN [*plural* **phrase books**] a book that shows you useful words and phrases in a foreign language, which you use when you are travelling ☐ *an Italian phrase book*

physical /ˈfɪzɪkəl/ ADJECTIVE
1 to do with the body ☐ *These children have low levels of physical activity.*
2 to do with real things that you can see or touch, and not things that exist only in your mind ☐ *There was no physical evidence to link him to the crime.*

• **physically** /ˈfɪzɪkəli/ ADVERB
1 in a way that is to do with the body ☐ *I'm trying to get physically fit.*
2 in the real world, according to the laws of physics ☐ *It's physically impossible to get this work done by Friday.*

physicist /ˈfɪzɪsɪst/ NOUN [*plural* **physicists**] someone who studies physics, usually as their job

physics /ˈfɪzɪks/ NOUN, NO PLURAL the scientific study of natural forces, for example, heat, light, sound and electricity

physiological /ˌfɪzɪəˈlɒdʒɪkəl/ ADJECTIVE to do with the way the bodies of living things work ☐ *They are attempting to study the physiological effects of vitamins.*

physiology /ˌfɪzɪˈɒlədʒɪ/ NOUN, NO PLURAL
1 the scientific study of the bodies of living things
2 the way in which the body of a particular animal or plant works ☐ *He is studying the physiology of sharks*

physiotherapist /ˌfɪzɪəʊˈθerəpɪst/ NOUN [*plural* **physiotherapists**] someone whose job is to give people physiotherapy

• **physiotherapy** /ˌfɪzɪəʊˈθerəpɪ/ NOUN, NO PLURAL the treatment of injuries and diseases by moving part of the body

physique /fɪˈziːk/ NOUN [plural **physiques**] the shape and size of someone's body ◻ He has a slim physique.

pi /paɪ/ NOUN, NO PLURAL a number that is used to show the relationship between the distance around a circle and the distance across it. A maths word.

pianist /ˈpɪənɪst/ NOUN [plural **pianists**] someone who plays the piano ◻ a concert pianist

piano /pɪˈænəʊ/ NOUN [plural **pianos**] a musical instrument that you play by pressing the black and white keys on a long keyboard

piccolo /ˈpɪkələʊ/ NOUN [plural **piccolos**] a type of small flute (=a musical instrument that you blow into) with a high sound

pick /pɪk/ ▶ VERB [**picks, picking, picked**]
1 to choose a person or thing from a group ◻ Jones has been picked for the England team. ◻ Pick any card from the pack.
2 to take fruit, flowers or vegetables from the plant or tree they are growing on ◻ The children picked a bunch of wild flowers for their mum. ◻ I picked a few strawberries for tea.
3 to remove a small piece of something, using your finger and thumb ◻ She carefully picked the fluff off her jacket.
4 pick an argument/a fight to deliberately start an argument or a fight with someone
5 pick someone's pocket to steal something from someone's pocket
6 pick a lock to use a piece of wire to open a lock
▶ PHRASAL VERBS **pick on someone** to treat one particular person unkindly or unfairly ◻ Please stop picking on your brother. **pick up** to increase or improve ◻ Sales have picked up since summer. **pick someone/something up** to go and collect someone or something from somewhere ◻ Could you pick me up at the airport tomorrow? ◻ I need to pick up my dry cleaning. **pick something up 1** to lift something ◻ She picked up the phone and started to dial. ◻ They asked us to pick up the litter. **2** to learn something by watching or listening instead of having lessons ◻ I just picked the language up while I was living in Mexico. **3** to find or get something ◻ We're hoping to pick up some bargains in the sales. ◻ I picked up a tummy bug on holiday.
▶ NOUN [plural **picks**]
1 have/take your pick to choose what you want from a group ◻ You can take your pick from a wide range of cheeses.
2 the pick of something the best in a group ◻ See page 29 for the pick of this season's new styles.
3 a tool with a wooden handle and curved metal end for breaking hard ground

picket /ˈpɪkɪt/ ▶ VERB [**pickets, picketing, picketed**] to stand outside a place, usually a place of work, to try to stop other people going in, as a way of showing your

anger about something ◻ Striking postmen picketed outside the sorting office.
▶ NOUN [plural **pickets**] a group of people who are picketing ◻ Unions organized a picket in front of the factory.

pickle /ˈpɪkəl/ ▶ NOUN [plural **pickles**] food made from fruit or vegetables that are put in vinegar (=liquid with a sour taste) or water with salt so that they can be kept for a long time ◻ We had a cheese and pickle sandwich.
▶ VERB [**pickles, pickling, pickled**] to put fruit, vegetables or meat in vinegar or water with salt to make them last for a long time ◻ We use these onions for pickling.
• **pickled** /ˈpɪkəld/ ADJECTIVE kept in vinegar or water with salt ◻ pickled herrings

pickpocket /ˈpɪkpɒkɪt/ NOUN [plural **pickpockets**] a criminal who steals things from people's pockets or bags

picky /ˈpɪki/ ADJECTIVE [**pickier, pickiest**] difficult to please and only liking a few things. An informal word ⊞ Our first child was a really picky eater.

picnic /ˈpɪknɪk/ ▶ NOUN [plural **picnics**] a meal that you take with you to eat outdoors ⊞ We had a picnic on the beach. ⊞ There's a beautiful picnic area in the forest.

> ▶ Note that you **have** a picnic. You do not 'make' a picnic:
> ✓ We had a picnic in the park.
> ✗ We made a picnic in the park.

▶ VERB [**picnics, picnicking, picnicked**] to have a picnic
• **picnicker** /ˈpɪknɪkə(r)/ NOUN [plural **picnickers**] someone who is having a picnic

pictogram /ˈpɪktəɡræm/ NOUN [plural **pictograms**] a diagram where amounts are represented by simple pictures. A maths word.

pictorial /pɪkˈtɔːrɪəl/ ADJECTIVE to do with pictures or using pictures to show something ◻ a pictorial encyclopaedia

picture /ˈpɪktʃə(r)/ ▶ NOUN [plural **pictures**]
1 a painting, drawing or photograph ◻ The walls were covered with pictures of her family. ⊞ Draw a picture of your house. ⊞ Can I take a picture (=take a photograph) of your garden?
2 an idea or description of what something or someone is like ◻ Police psychologists have built up a picture of a likely suspect. ◻ He had a picture in his mind of what he wanted to do. ◻ The report provides an accurate picture of services for the disabled.
3 the big/bigger/wider picture the whole situation, not just one part of it ◻ I know that job losses are hard to accept, but we have to look at the bigger picture.
4 an image on a screen ◻ The picture is rather poor on TVs in this area.
5 the pictures an old-fashioned word for the cinema ◻ We went to the pictures last night.
6 a film ◻ 'Titanic' won the award for best picture.

♦ IDIOM keep/put someone in the picture to make sure someone knows what is happening □ *There have been lots of changes in the organization – I'll put you in the picture over lunch.*

▶ VERB [**pictures, picturing, pictured**]
1 to form an image of something in your mind □ *I just couldn't picture my mother as a young girl.*
2 to show someone in a picture □ *Angelina is pictured here with her father.*

picture messaging /'pɪktʃə ˌmesɪdʒɪŋ/ NOUN, NO PLURAL when you send and receive pictures on a mobile phone

picturesque /ˌpɪktʃə'resk/ ADJECTIVE a picturesque place is attractive to look at □ *a picturesque old castle*

pie /paɪ/ NOUN [*plural* **pies**] food such as meat, vegetables or fruit, baked in a covering of pastry □ *apple pie and custard* □ *chicken and mushroom pie*

piece /piːs/ NOUN [*plural* **pieces**]
1 an amount or example of something of a particular type □ *a piece of wood* □ *Use a fresh piece of paper for each answer.* □ *Let me give you a piece of advice.*
2 one of the parts that join together to make a particular thing □ *a jigsaw with 300 pieces* □ *Cut the pizza into eight pieces.* 🖉 *He took the clock to pieces to repair it.* 🖉 *I just touched the stool and it fell to pieces.*
3 a single story, report, piece of music etc. □ *There's a short piece in the paper about our company.* □ *They played one of Schubert's pieces for violin and piano.*
4 one of the objects you move in games like chess
5 a coin of a particular value □ *a 50p piece*
♦ IDIOMS a piece of cake something that is a piece of cake is very easy to do □ *The driving test should be a piece of cake for you.* give someone a piece of your mind to speak angrily to someone because of something they have done go to pieces to be unable to work normally or think clearly because you are in a very difficult situation □ *I just went to pieces after my husband left me.*
♦ PHRASAL VERB [**pieces, piecing, pieced**] **piece something together** to discover the truth about something by putting together all the separate pieces of information you have □ *Forensic experts have pieced together the last moments of her life.*

piecemeal /'piːsmiːl/ ADJECTIVE done a little at a time and in no particular order □ *The party was criticized for having a piecemeal approach to policy making.*

pier /pɪə(r)/ NOUN [*plural* **piers**] a long wooden or metal structure built out over the sea that people can walk along

pierce /pɪəs/ VERB [**pierces, piercing, pierced**]
1 if a sharp object pierces something, it makes a hole in it 🖉 *I've just had my ears pierced.*
2 if light or sound pierces something, it can be seen or heard through it □ *A shaft of sunlight managed to pierce the clouds.*
♦ **piercing** /'pɪəsɪŋ/ ADJECTIVE

1 very strong, loud or unpleasant □ *A piercing wind was blowing off the sea.* □ *a piercing scream*
2 seeming to know what you are thinking □ *The detective gave her a piercing look.*

pig /pɪg/ NOUN [*plural* **pigs**] a farm animal with a fat body, small eyes and a curly tail, kept for meat

pigeon /'pɪdʒɪn/ NOUN [*plural* **pigeons**] a grey bird that is often seen in towns or kept for racing

pigeon-hole /'pɪdʒɪnhəʊl/ ▶ NOUN [*plural* **pigeon-holes**] one of a series of open boxes attached to a wall, used to put people's letters in
▶ VERB [**pigeon-holes, pigeon-holing, pigeon-holed**] to judge what type of person someone is without knowing much about them

piggyback /'pɪgɪbæk/ NOUN [*plural* **piggybacks**] a way of carrying someone on your back with your arms supporting their legs 🖉 *I gave Katie a piggyback home.*

pig-headed /ˌpɪg'hedɪd/ ADJECTIVE unwilling to change your opinions even if it is obvious that you are wrong

piglet /'pɪglɪt/ NOUN [*plural* **piglets**] a baby pig

pigment /'pɪgmənt/ NOUN [*plural* **pigments**] a substance that gives something a colour □ *He used natural pigments in his paints.*

pigsty /'pɪgstaɪ/ NOUN [*plural* **pigsties**]
1 a small building where pigs are kept
2 an informal word for a dirty or very untidy place □ *Your room's a complete pigsty.*

pigtail /'pɪgteɪl/ NOUN [*plural* **pigtails**] a piece of hair that has been plaited (=had three pieces twisted together)

pike /paɪk/ NOUN [*plural* **pike** *or* **pikes**] a large fish that lives in lakes or rivers and can be eaten

Pilates /pɪ'lɑːteɪz/ NOUN, NO PLURAL a way of exercising in which you stretch your body and make your muscles stronger

pile /paɪl/ ▶ NOUN [*plural* **piles**]
1 a number of things one on top of the other □ *a pile of leaves* □ *Dirty dishes were stacked in piles around the room.*
2 piles of something an informal phrase meaning lot of something □ *I've got piles of work to do.*
▶ VERB [**piles, piling, piled**] to put things on top of each other in a pile □ *They piled all the chairs against the wall.*
♦ PHRASAL VERB **pile up** to increase in amount □ *Work has started to pile up in the office.*

pile-up /'paɪlʌp/ NOUN [*plural* **pile-ups**] when several vehicles crash into each other □ *Two people were killed in a pile-up involving six vehicles.*

pilfer /'pɪlfə(r)/ VERB [**pilfers, pilfering, pilfered**] to steal things which are not worth much money □ *Everyone pilfers the occasional envelope from work.*

pilgrim /'pɪlgrɪm/ NOUN [*plural* **pilgrims**] a person who is travelling to a holy place
♦ **pilgrimage** /'pɪlgrɪmɪdʒ/ NOUN [*plural* **pilgrimages**] a journey to a holy place □ *They went on a pilgrimage to Mecca.*

pill /pɪl/ NOUN [*plural* **pills**] a small piece of solid medicine that you swallow □ *antihistamine pills*

pillage /'pɪlɪdʒ/ ▶ VERB [**pillages, pillaging, pillaged**] to steal things from a place during a war
▶ NOUN, NO PLURAL stealing things from a place during a war

pillar /'pɪlə(r)/ NOUN [*plural* **pillars**] a tall, strong structure, usually made of stone, used to support something □ *The statue is on top of a stone pillar.*

pillow /'pɪləʊ/ NOUN [*plural* **pillows**] a bag full of feathers or other soft material that you rest your head on when you are in bed

pillowcase /'pɪləʊkeɪs/ *or* **pillowslip** /'pɪləʊslɪp/ NOUN [*plural* **pillowcases** *or* **pillowslips**] a cover for a pillow

pilot /'paɪlət/ ▶ NOUN [*plural* **pilots**]
1 someone who flies a plane or other aircraft □ *an airline pilot* □ *a pilot's licence*
2 a single television programme that is made and shown to find out if people would watch a whole series
▶ VERB [**pilots, piloting, piloted**]
1 to fly a plane or other aircraft
2 to arrange for a small group of people to try a new product in order to find out if it will be successful
□ *The software is being piloted in a major supermarket.*

pimple /'pɪmpəl/ NOUN [*plural* **pimples**] a small pink lump on your skin

PIN /pɪn/ ABBREVIATION personal identification number; a secret number that you press on a machine in order to use a bank card □ *I forgot my PIN.*

pin /pɪn/ ▶ NOUN [*plural* **pins**]
1 a very thin, pointed piece of metal used for holding together pieces of cloth when you are sewing
2 a thin piece of metal or wood, used for holding things together □ *He's had a pin in his leg since the accident.*
▶ VERB [**pins, pinning, pinned**]
1 to fasten something in place with a pin □ *She pinned the flower to her dress.*
2 to hold someone somewhere firmly so that they cannot move □ *The policemen pinned him against the wall.*
PHRASAL VERB **pin someone down**
1 to make someone decide about something □ *I need to pin her down about a date for the meeting.*
2 to hold someone on the ground so that they cannot move

pinafore /'pɪnəfɔː(r)/ NOUN [*plural* **pinafores**] a loose dress with no sleeves that you wear over a shirt

pincer /'pɪnsə(r)/ NOUN [*plural* **pincers**] one of the strong front legs of some sea animals, used for holding things

pinch /pɪntʃ/ ▶ VERB [**pinches, pinching, pinched**]
1 to press someone's skin or flesh tightly between your thumb and finger, especially in order to hurt them

□ *Tom pinched me, Mum!*
2 if a shoe or piece of clothing pinches, it hurts you because it is too small or tight □ *This jacket pinches a little under the arms.*
3 an informal word that means to steal something □ *Have you pinched my magazine?*
▶ NOUN [*plural* **pinches**]
1 a small amount of something that you pick up between your finger and thumb 🏶 *Add a pinch of salt.*
2 when you pinch someone □ *She gave him a pinch on the arm.*
♦ IDIOM **feel the pinch** to not have enough money □ *Consumers are beginning to feel the pinch as prices rise.*

• **pinched** /pɪntʃt/ ADJECTIVE if someone's face is pinched, it looks thin and pale because they are ill or cold

pine¹ /paɪn/ NOUN [*plural* **pines**]
1 a tall tree with needles (=thin pointed leaves)
2 *no plural* the light coloured wood of a pine tree

pine² /paɪn/ VERB [**pines, pining, pined**] to feel sad, usually because you are not with a person that you love

pineapple /'paɪnæpəl/ NOUN [*plural* **pineapples**] a large fruit with sweet yellow flesh and a thick brown skin with sharp points on it □ *pineapple juice*

ping /pɪŋ/ ▶ VERB [**pings, pinging, pinged**] to make a short high noise like a small hard object hitting against metal □ *Did you hear the microwave ping?*
▶ NOUN [*plural* **pings**] a pinging noise □ *an electronic ping*

pink /pɪŋk/ ▶ ADJECTIVE having the colour you get if you mix red and white □ *She wore a pink dress.* □ *His cheeks were pink from running.*
▶ NOUN, NO PLURAL the colour you get if you mix red and white

pinnacle /'pɪnəkəl/ NOUN [*plural* **pinnacles**]
1 the time in someone's life when they are most successful □ *Playing King Lear was the pinnacle of his acting career.*
2 a high pointed rock or mountain

pinpoint /'pɪnpɔɪnt/ VERB [**pinpoints, pinpointing, pinpointed**]
1 to find out exactly what something is □ *Doctors were unable to pinpoint the cause of death.*
2 to find out exactly where something is □ *With this system police can instantly pinpoint the location of a mobile phone.*

pins and needles /ˌpɪnz ən 'niːdəlz/ NOUN, NO PLURAL a feeling of sharp little pains in a part of your body after you have been in the same position for too long

pint /paɪnt/ NOUN [*plural* **pints**] a unit for measuring liquid, equal to 20 fluid ounces 🏶 *a pint of milk/beer*

pioneer /ˌpaɪə'nɪə(r)/ ▶ NOUN [*plural* **pioneers**]
1 one of the first people to develop a new idea, skill or method □ *Charles Babbage was one of the pioneers of computer technology.*

2 one of the first people to go to a new country to live and work there □ *the American pioneers*
▶ VERB [**pioneers, pioneering, pioneered**] to be one of the first people to do or make something □ *The hospital is pioneering new surgical techniques.*

pious /'paɪəs/ ADJECTIVE following religious rules very carefully in your life

pip /pɪp/ NOUN [*plural* **pips**] a small seed in a fruit such as an apple or lemon

pipe /paɪp/ ▶ NOUN [*plural* **pipes**]
1 a metal or plastic tube through which water or gas can flow ⊞ *A pipe had burst and there was water everywhere.*
2 a tube with a hollow bowl at one end used for smoking tobacco ⊞ *Grandpa used to smoke a pipe.*
3 a musical instrument which is a tube or many tubes stuck together that you play by blowing through
▶ VERB [**pipes, piping, piped**] to carry liquid or gas from one place to another through pipes □ *Water is piped from the reservoir to the nearby cities.*
♦ PHRASAL VERB **pipe up** to suddenly say something after you have been quiet for a time

pipeline /'paɪplaɪn/ NOUN [*plural* **pipelines**] a long pipe that crosses the land or sea and carries oil or gas
♦ IDIOM **in the pipeline** being planned or organized, or about to happen □ *Further job losses are in the pipeline.*

pipette /pɪ'pet/ NOUN [*plural* **pipettes**] a small, glass tube used by scientists for sucking up small amounts of liquid. A chemistry word.

piping hot /ˌpaɪpɪŋ 'hɒt/ ADJECTIVE food or drink that is piping hot is very hot □ *She brought me a bowl of piping hot soup.*

piracy /'paɪrəsɪ/ NOUN, NO PLURAL
1 the illegal copying and selling of things such as DVDs, books and computer software
2 stealing things from ships while they are at sea
♦ **pirate** /'paɪrət/ ▶ NOUN [*plural* **pirates**]
1 someone who steals things from ships while they are at sea □ *As a boy, he loved stories about pirates and smugglers.*
2 someone who makes and sells illegal copies of things such as DVDs, books and computer software
▶ ADJECTIVE illegally copied □ *pirate DVDs*

pistol /'pɪstl/ NOUN [*plural* **pistols**] a small gun that is held in one hand

piston /'pɪstən/ NOUN [*plural* **pistons**] a round piece of metal that fits inside a tube in an engine and moves up and down to produce power

pit /pɪt/ NOUN [*plural* **pits**]
1 a large, deep hole dug in the ground □ *The dead animals were buried in a pit.*
2 a deep mine, especially a coal mine □ *His father and grandfather had both worked at the pit.*
3 **the pits** the place at the side of a race track where the cars stop to get fuel or have their tyres changed
♦ PHRASAL VERB [**pits, pitting, pitted**] **pit someone against someone** to make two people or teams

fight or compete with each other □ *The semi-final pits Wigan against Hull.*
➔ **go to** **pit your wits** against someone

pitch /pɪtʃ/ ▶ NOUN [*plural* **pitches**]
1 an area of ground, often with lines marked on it, where people play games like football, rugby or cricket □ *a football pitch*
2 the level of activity or excitement ⊞ *The excitement reached fever pitch in the last five minutes of the game.*
3 when you try to persuade someone to buy something ⊞ *It was the usual sales pitch.*
4 how high or low a sound is
▶ VERB [**pitches, pitching, pitched**]
1 to create something for people of a particular age, level of understanding, etc. □ *The talk was pitched just right for the audience.*
2 to make a sound at a particular level □ *The next song was pitched very high.*
3 to throw or fall suddenly in a particular direction □ *The boat rocked violently and Joe pitched forward into the lake.*
4 **pitch a tent** to put up a tent so that it is ready to use
5 in baseball, to be the player who throws the ball at the person with the stick
♦ PHRASAL VERB **pitch in** to work with other people on something □ *We can get the job done if we all pitch in.*

pitch-black /ˌpɪtʃ'blæk/ *or* **pitch-dark** /ˌpɪtʃ'dɑːk/ ADJECTIVE very dark □ *It was pitch-dark in the forest.*

pitcher /'pɪtʃə(r)/ NOUN [*plural* **pitchers**]
1 in baseball, the player who throws the ball at the person with the stick
2 the US word for jug

pitfall /'pɪtfɔːl/ NOUN [*plural* **pitfalls**] a difficulty or danger that a particular action might cause □ *You should be aware of the pitfalls of buying a second-hand car.*

pitiful /'pɪtɪful/ ADJECTIVE
1 very bad □ *It was a pitiful performance by the national team.*
2 making you feel sad □ *The dog – thin and dirty after weeks of neglect – was a pitiful sight.*

pitta bread /'pɪtə ˌbred/ NOUN [*plural* **pitta breads**] a type of flat bread originally from the Middle East

pittance /'pɪtəns/ NOUN, NO PLURAL a very small amount of money □ *She works so hard and gets paid pittance.*

pity /'pɪtɪ/ ▶ NOUN, NO PLURAL
1 sadness you feel for other people who are suffering or in trouble □ *She felt a wave of pity for the poor old man, abandoned by his family.*
2 **it's a pity...** used for saying that you feel sorry or disappointed about a situation □ *It's a pity that John couldn't come.*
3 **take pity on someone** to feel so sorry for someone that you help them □ *Mark took pity on me and gave me a lift home.*
▶ VERB [**pities, pitying, pitied**] to feel pity for someone □ *I really pity her, having a mother like that*

pivot /'pɪvət/ ▶ NOUN [plural **pivots**]
1 a pin or central point on which something balances and turns
2 the most important part of something on which everything else is based □ These policies are the pivot of the government's strategy.
▶ VERB [**pivots, pivoting, pivoted**] to turn while balancing on a central point

pixel /'pɪksəl/ NOUN [plural **pixels**] one of the very small parts that form pictures on a computer or television screen

pixie /'pɪksɪ/ NOUN [plural **pixies**] in stories, a creature like a small man with pointed ears who can do magic

pizza /'piːtsə/ NOUN [plural **pizzas**] a flat round piece of bread with cheese, vegetables or meat on top that is baked in an oven □ a mushroom pizza 🕮 Would you like another slice of pizza?

placard /'plækɑːd/ NOUN [plural **placards**] a large sign with a message on it that someone carries in a public place, often to show that they disagree with something □ Students holding placards marched through the town.

placate /plə'keɪt/ VERB [**placates, placating, placated**] to say or do things to make someone less angry or offended

place /pleɪs/ ▶ NOUN [plural **places**]
1 a particular area, position, town, building, etc. □ We rented a place by the sea. □ I imagine Beijing is a very interesting place. □ She broke her arm in three places. 🕮 Make sure you keep the money in a safe place. 🕮 Smoking is not allowed in public places.
2 the position where something should be, or where something or someone usually is □ Put the books back in their proper place on the shelf.
3 take place to happen □ The election is due to take place next month. □ The wedding took place in secret.
4 all over the place (a) in or to many different places □ You see lovely buildings all over the place. □ We travelled all over the place. (b) in an untidy state □ She left her books all over the place.
5 the opportunity to be in a team, go on a course, take part in a competition, etc. □ She has a place to study English at Cambridge University. 🕮 That win has secured Liverpool a place in the final.
6 a seat on a public vehicle or in a public building □ Please go back to your places and sit down. 🕮 Would you save my place while I get a coffee?
7 a position in a queue (=line of people waiting) 🕮 Now I've lost my place in the queue.
8 in first/third/last, etc. place used to show someone's position at the end of a race or competition
9 in place (a) in the correct position □ Make sure the safety harness is in place. (b) if rules, systems, etc. are in place, they exist and can be used □ They have put measures in place to combat theft.
10 in place of someone/something instead of someone/something □ Pat is here today, in place of Marc, who is ill.

11 out of place (a) not suitable for or comfortable in a particular situation □ I felt a bit out of place wearing jeans at such a glamorous party. (b) not in the correct position □ She never has a hair out of place.
♦ IDIOMS fall/fit into place
1 if things fall into place, you suddenly understand them □ When I learned that Zoe was his daughter, things fell into place.
2 to start to happen in a successful way □ After months of trying to organize the trip, everything is starting to fall into place. put someone in their place to make someone aware that they are not as important or clever as they think they are
▶ VERB [**places, placing, placed**]
1 to put something somewhere, usually with care □ He placed his hand on her shoulder. □ She placed a flower on the grave.
2 to cause someone or something to be in a particular situation or state □ He had placed me in a very awkward spot by promising that I would go to the party. □ Money worries placed a great strain on their marriage. □ The government has placed restrictions on public pay rises.
3 to have a particular opinion about something or someone □ He placed a lot of faith in his staff. □ She placed great importance on personal morality.
4 if you place an advertisement somewhere, you arrange for it to be shown there
5 place a call to make a telephone call □ At 6.15 he placed a call to the emergency services.

placebo /plə'siːbəʊ/ NOUN [plural **placebos**] a substance with no effect on the body, used in testing medicines or given to people who think they need medicine but do not

placement /'pleɪsmənt/ NOUN [plural **placements**] a temporary job that allows someone to get experience of working □ I got a work placement in a school last summer.

placenta /plə'sentə/ NOUN [plural **placentas**] the organ inside the mother that provides food for a growing baby. A biology word.

place value /'pleɪs ˌvæljuː/ NOUN, NO PLURAL the value of a number decided by its position, for example if it is a one, a ten, a hundred, etc. A maths word.

placid /'plæsɪd/ ADJECTIVE gentle and calm □ a placid baby

plague /pleɪg/ ▶ NOUN [plural **plagues**]
1 a serious disease that spreads very quickly and causes many people to die □ The plague struck London in the 17th century.
2 a large number of insects or other animals that suddenly appear and cause damage or problems □ a plague of red ants
▶ VERB [**plagues, plaguing, plagued**] to cause someone a lot of pain or trouble for a long time □ The squad has been plagued by injuries this season.

plaice /pleɪs/ NOUN [plural **plaice**] a type of flat sea fish that people eat

plain /pleɪn/ ► ADJECTIVE [plainer, plainest]
1 obvious ⊞ She made it quite plain that she didn't like me.
2 in one colour or without any decoration or pattern □ a plain white tablecloth
3 simple or ordinary □ He likes fairly plain cooking.
4 a plain person is not attractive
► NOUN [plural plains] a large flat area of land
► ADVERB completely □ Leaving her kids alone in the house was just plain wrong.

plait /plæt/ ► NOUN [plural plaits] a piece of hair that is formed by twisting three thinner pieces of hair over and under each other □ She wears her hair in plaits.
► VERB [plaits, plaiting, plaited] to make a plait

plan /plæn/ ► VERB [plans, planning, planned]
1 to decide what you are going to do and how you are going to do it □ We spent months planning the wedding. □ Always plan your essay before you start writing.
2 to hope and expect to do something in the future □ + to do something Natasha is planning to go to university next year. □ + on doing something They're planning on taking a year off to travel.
3 to draw a design of something such as a building □ We got a designer in to plan the garden.
► NOUN [plural plans]
1 an idea or arrangement for something you hope to do in the future □ What are your plans for the future? □ + to do something We have no plans to move house at the moment. ⊞ There's been a change of plan. We're going out on Friday instead. ⊞ If everything goes according to plan, she'll arrive at 11.
2 a drawing that shows how a building, town, machine, etc. will be built ⊞ The council is drawing up plans to redevelop the town centre.

plane /pleɪn/ ► NOUN [plural planes]
1 an aeroplane
2 a flat or level surface □ A cube has six planes.
3 a tool with a sharp blade in the bottom, used for making a wooden surface smooth
► VERB [planes, planing, planed] to make wood smooth and level using a plane

planet /'plænɪt/ NOUN [plural planets] any of the large objects in space that move around a sun or star □ the planet Venus

planetarium /ˌplænɪ'teərɪəm/ NOUN [plural planetariums] a building with a curved ceiling where you can look at lights that represent the positions of the stars and planets

plank /plæŋk/ NOUN [plural planks] a long flat piece of wood

planning /'plænɪŋ/ NOUN, NO PLURAL
1 the process of deciding what you are going to do and how you are going to do it □ The festival has taken weeks of planning.
2 control over what people build in towns and other areas □ town planning

plant /plɑːnt/ ► NOUN [plural plants]
1 any living thing that grows from the ground and has a stem, roots and leaves □ Young plants must be protected from frost. □ a tobacco plant
2 a factory or industrial building □ a power plant
► VERB [plants, planting, planted]
1 to put seeds or plants in soil so that they grow □ They're planting trees along the roadside.
2 to secretly put something illegal or stolen in a place that will make someone appear guilty of a crime □ Pete claims the drugs were planted on him.
3 plant a bomb to hide a bomb somewhere
4 to put something firmly in a place or position □ He planted his feet on either side of the rope and pulled.
• **plantation** /plæn'teɪʃən/ NOUN [plural plantations]
1 a large area of land where tea, cotton, coffee, etc. is grown □ a sugar plantation
2 an area of land where trees are grown to be used as wood

plaque /plɑːk/ NOUN [plural plaques]
1 a metal plate with writing on it, fixed to a wall in memory of a famous person or event
2 no plural a substance that forms on teeth and can cause tooth decay

plasma /'plæzmə/ NOUN, NO PLURAL the clear liquid part of blood. A biology word.

plasma screen /'plæzmə ˌskriːn/ NOUN [plural plasma screens] a television screen that is made up of two sheets of glass with special gases between them and produces very clear pictures

plaster /'plɑːstə(r)/ ► NOUN [plural plasters]
1 a piece of soft sticky cloth that you put over a cut to keep it clean
2 no plural a substance that is put on walls and dries to form a hard, smooth surface
3 in plaster if your arm, leg etc. is in plaster, it has a hard cover around it to protect a broken bone
► VERB [plasters, plastering, plastered]
1 to cover a lot of a surface with one thing or many things □ We plastered ourselves in sun cream before going out. □ Her bedroom walls are plastered with posters.
2 to put plaster on walls

plaster cast /'plɑːstə ˌkɑːst/ NOUN [plural plaster casts] a hard cover put around a broken arm or leg to protect it while it gets better

plastic /'plæstɪk/ ► NOUN [plural plastics] a light, strong substance made from chemicals and used to make many different things □ toys made of plastic
► ADJECTIVE made of plastic □ plastic bags

Plasticine /'plæstɪsiːn/ NOUN, NO PLURAL a soft substance that children use for making small model and shapes. A trademark.

plastic surgery /ˌplæstɪk 'sɜːdʒəri/ NOUN, NO PLURAL medical operations to improve someone's appearance or to repair damage to skin

plate 509 **playwright** P

plate /pleɪt/ NOUN [plural **plates**]
1 a flat dish for eating or serving food from □ *a paper/ plastic plate* □ *Pass your plates.*
2 a thin flat piece of metal or another hard substance □ *a steel plate*
3 one of the large areas of rock that make up the Earth's surface. A geography word.
4 a large picture or photograph in a book □ *a colour plate*

plateau /ˈplætəʊ/ NOUN [plural **plateaus** or plateaux]
1 a wide, flat area of high land. A geography word.
2 a period when the level of something does not change ⊞ *Sales of computers have reached a plateau.*

platelet /ˈpleɪtlɪt/ NOUN [plural **platelets**] a small part of a cell in the blood that makes it go thick if you have a cut. A biology word.

platform /ˈplætfɔːm/ NOUN [plural **platforms**]
1 the area next to the tracks at a railway station, where passengers get on and off trains □ *The 9:45 service to Leeds will leave from platform 4.*
2 a raised area of floor where performers and speakers stand so that the audience can see them
3 the main changes a political party promises to make if it is elected □ *He campaigned on a platform of low taxation.*

platinum /ˈplætɪnəm/ NOUN, NO PLURAL a very valuable silver metal that is used to make jewellery

platoon /pləˈtuːn/ NOUN [plural **platoons**] a small group of soldiers

platter /ˈplætə(r)/ NOUN [plural **platters**] a large plate used for serving food

plausible /ˈplɔːzəbəl/ ADJECTIVE seeming to be reasonable and true □ *It was a plausible excuse.*

play /pleɪ/ ▶ VERB [**plays, playing, played**]
1 to spend time enjoying yourself with games or toys □ *The children were playing in the garden.*
2 to take part in a sport or game □ *He plays cricket on Saturdays.* □ *Luke played well in the last match.* □ **+ for** *He used to play for the national team.*
3 to make music with a musical instrument, or to perform a piece of music □ *Do you play the piano?* □ *He played all the Beethoven sonatas.*
4 if you play a CD, DVD, etc., you put it in a machine to make it produce sound or images
5 to act as a character in a film, play, etc. ⊞ *She plays the part of Harry's daughter.*
6 **play a part in something** to be involved in something □ *Money played no part in her decision.*
7 **play a joke/trick on someone** to do something to trick someone or make them laugh
IDIOM **play safe** to not take any risks □ *I decided to play safe and cook something I'd done before.*
➔ go to **play it by ear, play devil's advocate**
PHRASAL VERBS **play about/around** to behave in a silly way □ *Stop playing about and get on with your work!* **play along** to pretend to agree with someone, or to pretend that something is true □ *She likes to*

imagine she's a princess, and the rest of us just play along with her. **play (around) with something** to think of ideas and ways of doing things □ *We are playing around with the idea of charging entrance fees.* **play at something** to do something in a way that is not serious □ *She only has four cows – she's just playing at farming.* **play something down** to try to make something seem less important □ *He always plays down his health problems.* **play up**
1 if children play up, they behave in a silly way
2 if a machine or a piece of equipment plays up, it does not work correctly □ *Sorry, I can't hear you – my phone's playing up.*
3 if a part of your body is playing up, you are having problems with it □ *My ears are playing up again.* **play with something** to touch or move something repeatedly, usually because you are bored or nervous □ *Stop playing with your food!*
▶ NOUN [plural **plays**]
1 a story that is performed by actors in a theatre ⊞ *Our school is putting on a play.*
2 *no plural* the activity of taking part in a sport or game □ *Play was stopped because of the rain.*
3 *no plural* the activity of enjoying yourself with games and toys □ *Young children learn best through play.*

playdate /ˈpleɪdeɪt/ NOUN [plural **playdates**] an arrangement made by parents for children to play together □ *Emily and Molly have a playdate on Saturday.*

player /ˈpleɪə(r)/ NOUN [plural **players**]
1 someone who plays a sport or game
2 someone who plays a musical instrument
3 a machine for playing DVDs, CDs, etc.

playful /ˈpleɪfʊl/ ADJECTIVE
1 full of fun or wanting to play □ *a playful puppy*
2 not intended to be serious □ *a playful remark*

playground /ˈpleɪgraʊnd/ NOUN [plural **playgrounds**] an area, often next to a school or in a public park, where children play □ *Harry fell and hurt his knee in the playground.*

playgroup /ˈpleɪgruːp/ NOUN [plural **playgroups**] an organized group where very young children can go to play and learn together

playing card /ˈpleɪɪŋ ˌkɑːd/ NOUN [plural **playing cards**] one of a set of 52 rectangular pieces of card used for playing games

playing field /ˈpleɪɪŋ ˌfiːld/ NOUN [plural **playing fields**] an area of land used for playing sports such as football □ *the school playing fields*

playmate /ˈpleɪmeɪt/ NOUN [plural **playmates**] a child who plays with another child

play-off /ˈpleɪɒf/ NOUN [plural **play-offs**] an extra game played to decide the winner from two players or teams with equal points in a competition

playschool /ˈpleɪskuːl/ NOUN [plural **playschools**] another word for playgroup

playwright /ˈpleɪraɪt/ NOUN [plural **playwrights**] someone who writes plays

plc /ˌpiːelˈsiː/ ABBREVIATION public limited company; a company in the UK with shares that people can buy

plea /pliː/ NOUN [plural **pleas**]
1 a statement that someone makes in a law court to say if they have committed a crime or not □ a plea of guilty/not guilty
2 when someone asks for something in a serious and emotional way □ I couldn't ignore this plea for help.

plead /pliːd/ VERB [**pleads, pleading, pleaded**]
1 to ask for something in a serious, emotional way because you want it very much □ She pleaded with her boss to give her one last chance.
2 to say whether you are guilty or not guilty of a crime in a law court ⊞ He pleaded guilty to all three charges.
3 plead ignorance to pretend that you did not know about something

pleasant /ˈplezənt/ ADJECTIVE
1 nice or enjoyable □ We had a very pleasant evening at Sarah's. □ It was very pleasant, sitting out in the garden.
2 friendly and easy to talk to □ Our new neighbours seem very pleasant.
• **pleasantly** /ˈplezəntlɪ/ ADVERB in a pleasant way □ She smiled very pleasantly at us. ⊞ I was pleasantly surprised by his attitude.

please /pliːz/ ► EXCLAMATION
1 used as a polite way of asking for something □ Could I have a glass of water, please? □ Please could you turn the music down? □ Would you please leave?
2 yes, please used as a polite way of accepting an offer □ 'Would you like another biscuit?' 'Yes, please.'
► VERB [**pleases, pleasing, pleased**]
1 to make someone happy by doing what they want □ You can't please everyone. □ My mother is quite hard to please.
2 as/anything/whatever, etc. you please in any way or at any time you want □ You can come and go as you please. □ You can do whatever you please in your own home.
3 please yourself used to tell someone you do not care what they do
• **pleased** /pliːzd/ ADJECTIVE
1 happy or satisfied with something □ + with He was pleased with the way the garden looked. □ + at We were all pleased at the result. □ + to do something She looked pleased to see him. □ She wasn't pleased when he told her he'd lost the tickets.
2 pleased with yourself proud of what you have done, often in an annoying way
3 (I'm) pleased to meet you. something you say to be polite when you meet someone for the first time
• **pleasing** /ˈpliːzɪŋ/ ADJECTIVE
1 making you feel happy or satisfied □ a pleasing result
2 enjoyable □ a visually pleasing design
• **pleasingly** /ˈpliːzɪŋlɪ/ ADVERB in an enjoyable way □ a pleasingly rich chocolate cake

pleasurable /ˈpleʒərəbəl/ ADJECTIVE giving pleasure or enjoyment □ a pleasurable sensation

pleasure /ˈpleʒə(r)/ NOUN [plural **pleasures**]
1 no plural a feeling of enjoyment or satisfaction ⊞ She took pleasure in cooking. ⊞ It gives me great pleasure to be here today.
2 something that you enjoy □ He enjoys the simple pleasures of life. ⊞ It's a great pleasure to welcome you back.
3 no plural time spent enjoying yourself and not working □ Is your trip business or pleasure? □ We encourage students to read for pleasure.
4 it's my pleasure used when someone thanks you. A formal phrase. □ 'Thank you so much for all your help.' 'It's my pleasure.'

pleat /pliːt/ NOUN [plural **pleats**] a fold made or sewn in a piece of cloth
• **pleated** /ˈpliːtɪd/ ADJECTIVE having folds or folded lines □ a pleated skirt

plectrum /ˈplektrəm/ NOUN [plural **plectrums**] a small piece of plastic or metal used to play the strings of a guitar

pledge /pledʒ/ ► NOUN [plural **pledges**] a serious promise ⊞ The government has made a pledge to improve school food. □ He has received pledges of support from all over the world.
► VERB [**pledges, pledging, pledged**] to promise seriously to do or to give something □ The prime minister pledged to increase spending. □ The US has pledged $6 million in aid.

plentiful /ˈplentɪfʊl/ ADJECTIVE existing or available in large amounts ⊞ There was a plentiful supply of fresh fish. □ Food was cheap and plentiful.

plenty /ˈplentɪ/ PRONOUN, ADVERB
1 a lot of something, as much as you need or more than you need □ + of You'll have plenty of time to complete the test. □ Remember to drink plenty of water. ⊞ There's plenty more bread in the freezer if we run out.
2 plenty big/long, etc. enough easily big/long, etc. enough □ The dress is plenty big enough for you.

pliable /ˈplaɪəbəl/ ADJECTIVE easy to bend without breaking □ The material is strong and pliable.

pliers /ˈplaɪəz/ PLURAL NOUN a tool used for holding and pulling small things or for cutting wire

plight /plaɪt/ NOUN, NO PLURAL a very bad or difficult situation □ She talked about the plight of refugees.

plinth /plɪnθ/ NOUN [plural **plinths**] a block of stone on which a statue (=model made from stone or metal) stands

plod /plɒd/ VERB [**plods, plodding, plodded**]
1 to walk slowly with heavy steps □ He plodded back up the hill.
2 to work slowly, especially doing a job that you find boring □ I'm still plodding along with the project.

plonk /plɒŋk/ VERB [**plonks, plonking, plonked**] an informal word meaning to put something down in a careless or noisy way □ *She plonked a couple of glasses on the table.*

♦ PHRASAL VERB **plonk yourself down** an informal phrase meaning to sit down somewhere in a careless way □ *He plonked himself down on the sofa and turned on the TV.*

plop /plɒp/ ► NOUN [*plural* **plops**] the sound of a small object dropping into water □ *The frog jumped back into the pond with a plop.*

► VERB [**plops, plopping, plopped**]
1 to fall or to drop making this sound
2 an informal word meaning to drop something or to sit somewhere carelessly □ *Jenny plopped down on an armchair.*

plot /plɒt/ ► NOUN [*plural* **plots**]
1 the story of a play, book or film □ *the plot of a novel* □ *The film's plot is based on a true story.*
2 a secret plan, especially to do something bad □ *an alleged plot to kidnap a soldier*
3 a piece of land to be used for a particular purpose □ *a vegetable plot* □ *a plot of land*
➜ go to **lose the plot**

► VERB [**plots, plotting, plotted**]
1 to plan to do something bad or illegal □ *The group are thought to be plotting more attacks.*
2 to mark points on a map or a graph (=mathematical picture showing changes or comparing things) □ *He used a map to plot his route across the mountains.*

plough /plaʊ/ ► NOUN [*plural* **ploughs**] a farm tool with a heavy blade which is pulled through the soil to turn the soil over

► VERB [**ploughs, ploughing, ploughed**] to turn over soil with a plough

♦ PHRASAL VERBS **plough into something** to hit something with force □ *The car lost control and ploughed into a group of people.* **plough something into something** to spend a lot of money on something in order to improve it □ *They are ploughing more money into education.* **plough through something**
1 to work slowly and with difficulty until you finish something □ *We ploughed through hundreds of documents searching for information.*
2 to hit something with force and go through it □ *The car ploughed through a wall and into a garden.*

plover /ˈplʌvə(r)/ NOUN [*plural* **plovers**] a small bird that finds food in water

ploy /plɔɪ/ NOUN [*plural* **ploys**] a clever plan or method to achieve something, often by tricking people □ *This is just a marketing ploy.*

pluck /plʌk/ VERB [**plucks, plucking, plucked**]
1 to quickly take something or someone from a place □ *Five survivors were plucked from the sea.*
2 to remove the feathers from a dead bird before cooking it
3 to take hold of something and to pull it firmly so that it comes out or off □ *He plucked a leaf from the tree.*

♦ IDIOM **pluck up (the) courage (to do something)** to find the courage to do something difficult □ *It took me ages to pluck up the courage to talk to her.*

plug /plʌg/ ► NOUN [*plural* **plugs**]
1 an object attached to a piece of electrical equipment by a wire which connects it to an electricity supply
2 an object that you use for blocking a hole, especially in a bath or sink □ *a bath plug*
3 when someone talks about a new book, film, etc. in public to make people interested in it □ *The interview was just a plug for his new book.*

♦ IDIOMS **pull the plug (on something)** to stop an activity from continuing □ *The channel announced that it is pulling the plug on the programme.*

► VERB [**plugs, plugging, plugged**]
1 to push something into a hole to block it □ *We need to plug the leak in the boat.*
2 to talk about a new film, book, etc. to make people interested in it □ *The author plugged his new book during the interview.* **plug a gap/hole** to provide something that is missing and needed □ *They need new players to plug the gaps left by those who went in the summer.*

♦ PHRASAL VERBS **plug away** to keep working or doing something for a long time. An informal phrase. □ *He plugs away in his studio every day.* **plug something in** to connect a piece of electrical equipment to the electricity supply □ *I plugged in my laptop.* **plug something into something**
1 to connect one piece of electrical equipment to another □ *Plug the camera into your computer to download pictures.*
2 to connect a piece of electrical equipment to the electricity supply □ *Don't leave your phone charger plugged into a socket when you're not using it.*

plughole /ˈplʌɡhəʊl/ NOUN [*plural* **plugholes**] the hole in a sink or a bath that water flows out of

plum /plʌm/ NOUN [*plural* **plums**] a soft red, purple or yellow fruit with a smooth skin and a large seed in the middle

plumage /ˈpluːmɪdʒ/ NOUN, NO PLURAL a bird's feathers □ *exotic birds with bright plumage*

plumb /plʌm/ VERB [**plumbs, plumbing, plumbed**] **plumb the depths/ plumb new depths** to reach the worst point in something □ *Relations between the countries have plumbed new depths.*

♦ PHRASAL VERB **plumb in something** to connect something such as a washing machine to a water supply

● **plumber** /ˈplʌmə(r)/ NOUN [*plural* **plumbers**] someone whose job is to connect and repair water and gas pipes

● **plumbing** /ˈplʌmɪŋ/ NOUN, NO PLURAL
1 the system of pipes that carry water and gas in a building
2 the work of a plumber

plume /pluːm/ NOUN [*plural* **plumes**]
1 a long feather □ *ostrich plumes*

2 a tall cloud of dust or smoke moving up in the air 🖭 *a plume of smoke*

plummet /'plʌmɪt/ VERB [**plummets, plummeting, plummeted**]
1 to quickly become much lower in value or amount □ *Temperatures plummeted to minus five degrees.*
2 to fall straight down very fast □ *They plummeted to the ground.*

plump /plʌmp/ ADJECTIVE [**plumper, plumpest**] fat or round in a pleasant way □ *She squeezed the baby's plump little legs.*
♦ PHRASAL VERB [**plumps, plumping, plumped**] **plump for something** an informal phrase meaning to choose something □ *I finally plumped for the green dress.*

plunder /'plʌndə(r)/ ▶ VERB [**plunders, plundering, plundered**] to steal everything valuable from a place, often causing a lot of damage □ *Buildings were set on fire and shops were plundered.*
▶ NOUN, NO PLURAL
1 when someone plunders a place
2 things stolen in this way

plunge /plʌndʒ/ ▶ VERB [**plunges, plunging, plunged**]
1 to fall suddenly and with force □ *The bus plunged off a mountain road.*
2 to quickly become much lower in value or amount □ *The share price has plunged.* □ *Temperatures plunged below freezing.*
3 to jump, especially into water □ *They plunged into the cool water.*
4 to push something, such as a knife, violently into something □ *He plunged a knife into her stomach.*
♦ PHRASAL VERB **plunge something into something** to cause something to be suddenly in a particular, often bad, state □ *The violence threatens to plunge the country into civil war.* □ *The building was plunged into darkness.*
▶ NOUN [*plural* **plunges**]
1 a fall □ *He survived a 20-metre plunge.*
2 a sudden fall in value or amount □ *a plunge in oil prices*
♦ IDIOM **take the plunge** to do something important or difficult after considering it for a long time □ *He took the plunge and quit his job.*

pluperfect /ˌpluːˈpɜːfɪkt/ NOUN, NO PLURAL the tense of a verb that shows that an action finished before a particular time or event in the past, formed using *had* and a past participle

plural /'plʊərəl/ ▶ NOUN [*plural* **plurals**] the form of a noun, pronoun or verb that you use when there is more than one of something
▶ ADJECTIVE in the plural form □ *a plural noun*

plus /plʌs/ ▶ PREPOSITION
1 added to □ *8 plus 2 is 10.* □ *He charges $50 an hour, plus travel expenses.*
2 as well as □ *There are six children, plus two adults.*
▶ ADJECTIVE
1 used to describe a measurement or temperature

that is greater than zero □ *plus ten degrees centigrade*
2 used after a number to show that the real amount may be more than that number □ *You have to be 60 plus to join the club.*
▶ NOUN [*plural* **pluses**]
1 a mathematical symbol (+) showing that a number is to be added to another
2 an advantage 🖭 *Being near to the beach is a big plus.*

plush /plʌʃ/ ADJECTIVE [**plusher, plushest**] expensive and comfortable □ *a plush hotel* □ *plush carpets*

plutonium /pluːˈtəʊnɪəm/ NOUN, NO PLURAL a very poisonous radioactive element. A chemistry word.

ply /plaɪ/ VERB [**plies, plying, plied**]
1 a formal word meaning to travel along a particular route □ *The liners plied between England and South Africa.*
2 ply your trade to work, especially in a particular place □ *He's now plying his trade in New York.*
♦ PHRASAL VERB **ply someone with something** to keep giving someone a lot of something □ *They plied me with coffee and cake.*

plywood /'plaɪwʊd/ NOUN, NO PLURAL thick board made up of thin layers of wood glued together

PM /ˌpiːˈem/ ABBREVIATION prime minister

pm or **p.m.** /ˌpiːˈem/ ABBREVIATION added after the time to show that it is in the afternoon or the evening

pneumatic /njuːˈmætɪk/ ADJECTIVE
1 filled with air □ *pneumatic tyres*
2 worked using air pressure □ *a pneumatic drill*

pneumonia /njuːˈməʊnɪə/ NOUN, NO PLURAL a serious infection of the lungs which makes breathing difficult and painful

poach /pəʊtʃ/ VERB [**poaches, poaching, poached**]
1 to cook food by heating it gently in water or another liquid □ *poached eggs*
2 to hunt and kill fish, birds or animals on someone else's land without permission
3 to persuade someone to leave one job or organization to join another □ *He was poached by a private company.*
● **poacher** /'pəʊtʃə(r)/ NOUN [*plural* **poachers**] someone who poaches animals, birds or fish

PO box /ˌpiːˈəʊ ˌbɒks/ NOUN [*plural* **PO boxes**] post office box; a numbered box at a post office where letters can be sent for you to collect

pocket /'pɒkɪt/ ▶ NOUN [*plural* **pockets**]
1 an extra piece of cloth sewn into a piece of clothing or a bag, used for keeping small things in □ *It was in my jeans pocket.* □ *He pulled his wallet from his back pocket.*
2 the amount of money you are able to spend on something □ *There are presents to suit every pocket.*
3 a small area or group which is separate and different from others □ *+ of pockets of mist* □ *There are small pockets of resistance in the south.*
4 out of pocket having lost money as the result of something □ *Nobody will be left out of pocket.*
▶ VERB [**pockets, pocketing, pocketed**]

1 to steal money □ *It was said that she pocketed the proceeds.*
2 to put something in your pocket □ *He pocketed his keys.*
3 to earn or to win money □ *Senior managers will pocket huge bonuses.*
▶ ADJECTIVE small enough to fit in a pocket □ *a pocket calculator*

pocketbook /'pɒkɪtbʊk/ NOUN [*plural* **pocketbooks**]
1 a US word for wallet
2 a US word for handbag

pocket money /'pɒkɪt ˌmʌnɪ/ NOUN, NO PLURAL
money that parents regularly give their children to buy small things □ *They spent all their pocket money on sweets.*

pod /pɒd/ NOUN [*plural* **pods**] a long narrow part that grows on plants and has seeds inside

podcast /'pɒdkɑːst/ NOUN [*plural* **podcasts**] a recording that you get from a website and then listen to on a computer or MP3 player (=small piece of computer equipment)

podgy /'pɒdʒɪ/ ADJECTIVE [**podgier, podgiest**] an informal word meaning slightly fat □ *podgy little hands*

podium /'pəʊdɪəm/ NOUN [*plural* **podiums**] a small raised area that someone stands on, often to speak to a lot of people 🖫 *The chairman took the podium (=stood on the podium) to open the conference.*

poem /'pəʊɪm/ NOUN [*plural* **poems**] a piece of writing using interesting language, arranged in short lines, often using words with the same sounds □ *a love poem* 🖫 *He wrote a poem for her.*

poet /'pəʊɪt/ NOUN [*plural* **poets**] someone who writes poems □ *He was a poet and novelist.*

poetic /pəʊ'etɪk/ ADJECTIVE
1 expressing ideas with beauty and imagination □ *a poetic account of his childhood*
2 to do with poems □ *poetic language*

poetry /'pəʊɪtrɪ/ NOUN, NO PLURAL poems in general □ *a book of poetry*

poignant /'pɔɪnjənt/ ADJECTIVE making you feel sadness or sympathy 🖫 *There is that poignant moment in the film when the mother sees her son for the last time.*

point /pɔɪnt/ ▶ NOUN [*plural* **points**]
1 an idea, opinion, or thing you want to say 🖫 *He made the point that some people wouldn't be able to afford the service.* 🖫 *I do take your point (=understand your opinion) about the high fence.* 🖫 *'Meg says it's not fair for the girls to do all the work.' 'Well, she does have a point (=her opinion is worth considering).*
2 the reason for something or the purpose of something 🖫 *What's the point of going home if you just have to go straight back out again?* 🖫 *I can't really see the point of exercising.* 🖫 *There's no point in asking her – she won't come.*

3 the most important thing about what has been said 🖫 *The point is, we can't afford a holiday.* 🖫 *She talked for so long, I thought she'd never get to the point.* 🖫 *He missed the point entirely – it's about fun, not making money.*
4 a particular time in an event or process 🖫 *At that point, we decided to leave.* 🖫 *I've reached the point with my studies where I'd like to specialize more.* 🖫 *At some point today, I need to phone Miriam.*
5 a particular place □ *Drinks are available at several points along the route.* □ *This is the highest point in England.*
6 a feature or characteristic 🖫 *I know you don't like Mike, but he does have some good points.*
7 the sharp end of something □ *Make a small hole with the point of a needle.*
8 the mark '.' that is used in decimal numbers that have a part less than one, e.g. 5.34
9 a unit for showing the score in a game or a competition □ *Who got the highest number of points?* 🖫 *You score 2 points for each correct answer.*
10 be at the point of doing something to be going to do something very soon □ *We were at the point of signing the contract when the buyers pulled out.*
11 up to a point in part □ *I agree with you up to a point.*
▶ VERB [**points, pointing, pointed**]
1 to show someone something by holding your finger or a thin object towards it □ + *at He pointed at a man in black.* □ *She pointed towards the exit with her umbrella.*
2 to face in a particular direction, or to make something face a particular direction □ + *at He pointed the gun at the target.* □ *The sign pointed north.* □ *What time is it when the little hand points to the three?*
◆ PHRASAL VERBS **point something/someone out** to show someone a person or thing □ *I pointed out his mother, sitting in the crowd.* □ *He pointed out the damage to the wood.* **point something out** to make someone aware of a fact □ *He pointed out that he had been waiting for over an hour.* **point to something** to show that something is probably true □ *All the evidence points to his guilt.*

point-blank /ˌpɔɪnt'blæŋk/ ADJECTIVE, ADVERB
1 in a direct or rude way □ *She refused point-blank to come.*
2 very close 🖫 *The gun was fired at point-blank range.*

pointed /'pɔɪntɪd/ ADJECTIVE
1 with a sharp end □ *a pointed stick*
2 direct and showing that you disagree □ *He made a few pointed comments.* □ *pointed criticism*

pointer /'pɔɪntə(r)/ NOUN [*plural* **pointers**]
1 an informal word for a piece of advice 🖫 *She gave me a few pointers on how to dress.*
2 something which tells you about a situation or how

something is developing □ *This result is an important pointer to future success.*

3 a long stick you use to point to things

pointless /'pɔɪntlɪs/ ADJECTIVE having no purpose or meaning □ *a pointless argument* □ *It's pointless asking him – he'll never come.*

point of view /ˌpɔɪnt əv 'vjuː/ NOUN [*plural* **points of view**]

1 a way of considering or judging a situation □ *From an ethical point of view, I see nothing wrong.*

2 an opinion about something □ *They have different points of view.*

poise /pɔɪz/ NOUN, NO PLURAL

1 a calm, confident way of behaving □ *He recovered his poise to win the second game.*

2 a controlled and attractive way of standing or moving □ *She had the poise of a dancer.*

• **poised** /pɔɪzd/ ADJECTIVE

1 waiting and ready to do something □ *She looks poised to be the first female winner of the award.* □ *He stood poised on the edge of the diving board.*

2 calm, confident and controlled

poison /'pɔɪzən/ ► NOUN [*plural* **poisons**] a substance that causes death or illness when you eat, drink or breathe it □ *a deadly poison* □ *rat poison*

► VERB [**poisons, poisoning, poisoned**]

1 to kill or harm someone with poison □ *They were poisoned by carbon monoxide fumes.*

2 to add poison or another dangerous substance to something □ *These chemicals are poisoning the water.*

• **poisoning** /'pɔɪzənɪŋ/ NOUN, NO PLURAL an illness caused by a poison or other harmful substance ⌹ *She had mild food poisoning.*

• **poisonous** /'pɔɪzənəs/ ADJECTIVE

1 containing poison □ *This cleaning liquid is poisonous.*

2 a poisonous animal can produce poison □ *a poisonous snake*

poke /pəʊk/ ► VERB [**pokes, poking, poked**]

1 to quickly push something or someone with your finger or with something sharp □ *He poked me in the ribs.*

2 to appear through a hole or from behind something □ *She poked her head through the curtains.* □ *His hair was poking out from under his hat.*

♦ PHRASAL VERB **poke around** to look for something, especially by moving things □ *He was poking around in my drawers, looking for the photo.*

♦ IDIOM **poke fun at someone** to make jokes about someone or something in an unkind way □ *He was poking fun at my hat.*

➔ *go to* **poke your** *nose* **in/into something**

► NOUN [*plural* **pokes**] when you poke someone or something □ *She gave me another poke in the arm.*

• **poker** /'pəʊkə(r)/ NOUN [*plural* **pokers**]

1 a heavy metal stick used for moving wood or coal in a fire

2 *no plural* a card game played for money

poky /'pəʊkɪ/ ADJECTIVE [**pokier, pokiest**] a poky place is too small □ *a poky little kitchen*

polar /'pəʊlə(r)/ ADJECTIVE to do with the north or south pole (=areas at the top and bottom of the Earth) □ *a polar region* □ *polar ice*

polar bear /'pəʊlə ˌbeə(r)/ NOUN [*plural* **polar bears**] a large white bear that lives near the North Pole

pole /pəʊl/ NOUN [*plural* **poles**]

1 a long thin stick made of metal or wood, often used for supporting something □ *an aluminium tent pole*

2 one of the two areas at the most northern and southern points of the Earth

3 one of the two ends of a magnet (=piece of iron that makes metal objects move towards it). A physics word.

4 the front position at the start of a motor race ⌹ *pole position* □ *The Ferrari is in on pole for tomorrow's race.*

♦ IDIOM **poles apart** completely different or opposite □ *Their styles are poles apart.*

polecat /'pəʊlkæt/ NOUN [*plural* **polecats**] a small wild animal with a long body

pole vault /'pəʊl ˌvɔːlt/ NOUN, NO PLURAL a sports event in which you get yourself over a high bar using a long pole

• **pole vaulter** NOUN [*plural* **pole vaulters**] someone who takes part in a pole vault competition

police /pə'liːs/ ► NOUN, NO PLURAL the people whose job is to make people obey the law and to catch people who break the law ⌹ *One of his neighbours called the police.* □ *Last night police were questioning four men.* ⌹ *the police force* ⌹ *a police investigation*

► VERB [**polices, policing, policed**]

1 to make sure an event or area is safe by using police officers □ *It was a huge operation to police the demonstration.*

2 to make people obey laws or rules □ *But how do we police the Internet?*

policeman /pə'liːsmən/ NOUN [*plural* **policemen**] male police officer

police officer /pə'liːs ˌɒfɪsə(r)/ NOUN [*plural* **police officers**] a member of the police □ *an armed police officer*

police station /pə'liːs ˌsteɪʃən/ NOUN [*plural* **police stations**] a building where the police have their offices

policewoman /pə'liːswʊmən/ NOUN [*plural* **policewomen**] a female police officer

policy /'pɒləsɪ/ NOUN [*plural* **policies**]

1 a plan about how to deal with something by a government, political party, business, etc. □ *government policies* ⌹ *US foreign policy* □ *the party's policy on immigration*

2 an arrangement you have with an insurance company (=company that gives you money if you damage something, etc.) ⌹ *a home insurance policy*

polio /'pəʊlɪəʊ/ NOUN, NO PLURAL a serious disease that affects the nerves and muscles

polish /'pɒlɪʃ/ ▶ VERB [**polishes, polishing, polished**]
1 to rub something until it shines □ *Remember to polish your shoes.*
2 to improve a skill by doing something many times □ *I've had plenty of opportunities to polish my public speaking skills.*
♦ PHRASAL VERB **polish something off** to eat or to drink all of something □ *She polished off the chocolate cake.*
▶ NOUN [*plural* **polishes**]
1 a substance used to polish something 🔁 *shoe polish* □ *furniture polish*
2 when you polish something □ *He gave the car a good polish.*
♦ **polished** /'pɒlɪʃt/ ADJECTIVE
1 clean and shiny □ *a polished wooden floor*
2 showing great skill □ *He's a polished performer.*

polite /pə'laɪt/ ADJECTIVE [**politer, politest**] behaving in a pleasant way towards other people, for example, saying 'thank you' and 'please' □ *Her children are very polite.* □ **+ to** *She was polite to hospital staff.* □ **+ to do something** *He was too polite to interrupt.*
♦ **politely** /pə'laɪtli/ ADVERB in a polite way □ *'Would you like a seat?' he asked her politely.* □ *She politely declined the invitation.*
♦ **politeness** /pə'laɪtnɪs/ NOUN, NO PLURAL the quality of being polite □ *I agreed to go out of politeness.*

political /pə'lɪtɪkəl/ ADJECTIVE to do with politics, politicians or government 🔁 *a political party* 🔁 *a political leader* □ *a political and economic crisis*
♦ **politically** /pə'lɪtɪkli/ ADVERB in a way that is to do with politics □ *Politically, she was very naive.*

politically correct /pə'lɪtɪkəli kə'rekt/ ADJECTIVE said or done so that no one is offended, especially so that women and people of a different race are not offended

politician /ˌpɒlə'tɪʃən/ NOUN [*plural* **politicians**] someone whose job is politics, especially someone who has been elected to a parliament □ *People don't seem to trust politicians.*

politics /'pɒlətɪks/ NOUN, NO PLURAL
1 ideas or activities to do with governing a country □ *He's very interested in politics.*
2 the job of being a politician 🔁 *He entered politics after leaving university.*
3 the things that people in a group do in order to get more power than other members of the group 🔁 *I'm fed up with office politics.*
4 someone's beliefs about politics □ *I don't know about his politics.*

polka /'pɒlkə/ NOUN [*plural* **polkas**] a fast traditional dance, or music for this dance

poll /pəʊl/ ▶ NOUN [*plural* **polls**]
1 when a number of people are asked their opinion on a particular subject 🔁 *The poll showed that about 55% of people are against the war.* 🔁 *The poll was conducted for a local newspaper.*
2 a political election in which people vote 🔁 *Voters go to the polls* (=vote) *on 24 November.*
▶ VERB [**polls, polling, polled**] to ask a number of people their opinion on a particular subject □ *Over half the people polled said they were unhappy with the government.*

pollen /'pɒlən/ NOUN, NO PLURAL the powder that a flower releases and which can make new seeds. A biology word.

pollinate /'pɒlɪneɪt/ VERB [**pollinates, pollinating, pollinated**] to put the pollen from one plant on another plant, causing seeds to start to form. A biology word.
♦ **pollination** /ˌpɒlɪ'neɪʃən/ NOUN, NO PLURAL the process of pollinating plants. A biology word.

polling station /'pəʊlɪŋ ˌsteɪʃən/ NOUN [*plural* **polling stations**] the building where you vote in an election

pollutant /pə'luːtənt/ NOUN [*plural* **pollutants**] a substance that causes harm to the air, soil or water □ *pollutants from vehicle exhausts*

pollute /pə'luːt/ VERB [**pollutes, polluting, polluted**] to let harmful substances go into the air, soil or water □ *We need to find energy sources which don't pollute the environment.*
♦ **pollution** /pə'luːʃən/ NOUN, NO PLURAL
1 substances which pollute 🔁 *the health effects of air pollution* 🔁 *a major source of pollution* □ **+ from** *We need to reduce pollution from traffic.*
2 when harmful substances pollute a place □ **+ of** *We need to take action against the pollution of the oceans.*

polo /'pəʊləʊ/ NOUN, NO PLURAL a game played by two teams of players on horses who hit a ball along the ground using hammers with long handles

polo neck /'pəʊləʊ ˌnek/ NOUN [*plural* **polo necks**] a sweater (=top made from wool) with a high round neck

poly- /'pɒli/ PREFIX poly- is added to the beginning of words to mean 'many'

polyester /ˌpɒli'estə(r)/ NOUN, NO PLURAL a light, artificial cloth used for making clothes

polygon /'pɒlɪgɒn/ NOUN [*plural* **polygons**] a shape with three or more sides. A maths word.

polymer /'pɒlɪmə(r)/ NOUN [*plural* **polymers**] a chemical compound made of small molecules of the same type joined together to form large molecules. A chemistry word.

polystyrene /ˌpɒlɪ'staɪriːn/ NOUN, NO PLURAL a very light plastic material used for making containers and for protecting delicate objects

polythene /'pɒlɪθiːn/ NOUN, NO PLURAL a very thin plastic material used for making bags, etc.

pomegranate /'pɒmɪˌgrænɪt/ NOUN [*plural* **pomegranates**] a round fruit with a thick brown skin and a lot of small red parts inside containing seeds

pomp /pɒmp/ NOUN, NO PLURAL formal, traditional ceremony with special clothes, music, etc. □ *the traditional pomp and ceremony of the state opening of Parliament*

pompous /'pɒmpəs/ ADJECTIVE too serious and thinking you are very important □ *That sounds terribly pompous.*

poncho /'pɒntʃəʊ/ NOUN [plural **ponchos**] a loose piece of clothing covering the shoulders and top half of the body which has a hole for your head to go through

pond /pɒnd/ NOUN [plural **ponds**] a small area of water, smaller than a lake □ *a garden pond* □ *a fish pond*

ponder /'pɒndə(r)/ VERB [**ponders, pondering, pondered**] to think about something carefully and for a long time □ *He'd pondered the question all day.*

pong /pɒŋ/ ▶ NOUN, NO PLURAL an informal word meaning a strong unpleasant smell □ *There's a bit of a pong coming from the bin.*

▶ VERB [**pongs, ponging, ponged**] an informal word meaning to have a strong unpleasant smell □ *The changing room pongs of stale sweat.*

pony /'pəʊni/ NOUN [plural **ponies**] a small horse

ponytail /'pəʊniteɪl/ NOUN [plural **ponytails**] a hairstyle with your hair tied at the back of your head and hanging down

pony-trekking /'pəʊniˌtrekɪŋ/ NOUN, NO PLURAL the activity of riding ponies over long distances in the countryside

poodle /'puːdəl/ NOUN [plural **poodles**] a type of dog with curly hair

pool /puːl/ ▶ NOUN [plural **pools**]
1 an area of water made for swimming in □ *The hotel has an indoor pool.* □ *a heated pool*
2 a small area of liquid □ *There was a small pool of blood on the floor.*
3 *no plural* a game in which two players try to hit coloured balls into holes around the edge of a table using a long, wooden stick
4 a group of people or things that are available or are shared by several people □ *There's a growing pool of candidates for the leadership role.* □ *a car pool*
▶ VERB [**pools, pooling, pooled**] to put things together so that everyone can use them ▣ *We should all work together and pool our resources.*

poor /pʊə(r)/ ADJECTIVE [**poorer, poorest**]
1 having little money and owning few things □ *a poor country* □ *His family were very poor.*
2 of a low standard □ *The paper was of poor quality.* ▣ *He's in very poor health.* □ *It was a poor performance by the team generally.*
3 used to show that someone or something deserves sympathy □ *Poor you! You sound so ill.* □ *The poor little thing is all wet.*
● **poorly** /'pʊəli/ ▶ ADVERB badly or not well enough □ *a poorly paid job* □ *He performed fairly poorly in both matches.*
▶ ADJECTIVE [**poorlier, poorliest**] an informal word meaning ill □ *Grant's feeling a bit poorly today.*

pop /pɒp/ ▶ NOUN [plural **pops**]
1 *no plural* modern music with short, simple songs and a strong beat ▣ *pop music* ▣ *a pop star* ▣ *a catchy pop song*

2 a short sound like something exploding □ *They heard a loud pop.* □ *The bottle opened with a pop.*
3 *no plural* a sweet drink with bubbles
▶ VERB [**pops, popping, popped**]
1 to go somewhere quickly, for a short time □ *+ out* I *just popped out for a few minutes.* □ *+ into* I *need to pop into the office.*
2 to put something somewhere quickly □ *I'll just pop the pizza in the oven.* □ *Karen popped her head around the door.*
3 to make a short sound like something exploding □ *The fire crackled and popped.* ▣ *I could hear the sound of corks popping.*
4 to suddenly tear, making a loud noise, or to make something do this □ ▣ *I could hear balloons popping in the background.*
◆ IDIOM **pop the question** to ask someone to marry you. An informal phrase.
◆ PHRASAL VERB **pop up** to suddenly appear □ *Bars and cafés are popping up all over the place.*

popcorn /'pɒpkɔːn/ NOUN, NO PLURAL a food made from seeds of grain which break open when they are heated

Pope /pəʊp/ NOUN [plural **Popes**] the leader of the Catholic Church

poplar /'pɒplə(r)/ NOUN [plural **poplars**] a type of tall, thin tree

poppy /'pɒpi/ NOUN [plural **poppies**] a tall, red flower that grows in fields

popular /'pɒpjʊlə(r)/ ADJECTIVE
1 liked by a lot of people □ *a popular tourist destination* □ *She was a very popular student.* □ *+ with* *The beach is popular with tourists.* ▣ *Podcasts are becoming increasingly popular.* ▣ *The new resort has proved hugely popular.*
2 believed or felt by many people ▣ *According to popular belief, cutting your hair will help it to grow.* ▣ *You can't change popular opinion overnight.* □ *As a leader he has enormous popular support.*
3 to do with ordinary people, not experts ▣ *popular culture* □ *a popular science book*
● **popularity** /ˌpɒpjʊˈlærəti/ NOUN, NO PLURAL when a lot of people like something or someone □ *The popularity of the sport has increased in recent years.*
● **popularize** or **popularise** /'pɒpjʊləraɪz/ VERB [**popularizes, popularizing, popularized**] to make something popular □ *YouTube has popularized the idea of sharing videos.*
● **popularly** /'pɒpjʊləli/ ADVERB by many or most people □ *The Academy Awards are popularly known as the Oscars.*

populate /'pɒpjʊleɪt/ VERB [**populates, populating, populated**] if people or animals populate an area, they live there □ *The area is mostly populated by recent immigrants.*
● **populated** /'pɒpjʊleɪtɪd/ ADJECTIVE a populated area has people living there ▣ *a populated area* ▣ *Polluti...*

is worse in *densely populated* (=with many people) urban areas.

• **population** /ˌpɒpjuˈleɪʃən/ NOUN [plural **populations**]

1 all the people who live in an area, country, etc. ⊕ *The troops are there to protect the local population.* □ *More than half the world's population live in cities.*

2 the number of people who live in an area, country, etc. □ **+ of** *The city has a population of around two million.*

3 the people or animals of a particular type who live in an area □ **+ of** *a large population of seabirds* □ *the elderly population*

pop-up /ˈpɒpʌp/ ADJECTIVE

1 a pop-up book has pictures which stick up when you open the book

2 describes something on a computer screen which suddenly appears when you click the mouse or press a key. A computing word □ *a pop up menu*

porcelain /ˈpɔːsəlɪn/ ▶ NOUN, NO PLURAL a hard, white substance used to make good quality plates, cups, etc.

▶ ADJECTIVE made from porcelain □ *a porcelain doll*

porch /pɔːtʃ/ NOUN [plural **porches**] a small covered entrance to a house

porcupine /ˈpɔːkjupaɪn/ NOUN [plural **porcupines**] a small animal that has long sharp needles on its back

pore /pɔː(r)/ NOUN [plural **pores**] one of the very small holes in your skin that sweat comes out of. A biology word.

♦ PHRASAL VERB [**pores, poring, pored**] **pore over something** to read things very carefully, examining them in detail □ *We spent the day poring over papers.*

pork /pɔːk/ NOUN, NO PLURAL meat from a pig □ *a pork chop*

porous /ˈpɔːrəs/ ADJECTIVE allowing liquids and gases to pass through □ *porous soil*

porpoise /ˈpɔːpəs/ NOUN [plural **porpoises**] a large sea mammal, similar to a dolphin

porridge /ˈpɒrɪdʒ/ NOUN, NO PLURAL a food made by cooking oats (=a type of grain) in water or milk, often eaten for breakfast

port /pɔːt/ NOUN [plural **ports**]

1 a place where ships can stop on the coast, and the town or city around it □ *the Israeli port of Haifa* □ *a major shipping port* □ *It's a small fishing port on the south coast.*

2 a hole in a computer which another piece of equipment can be connected to. A computing word □ *a USB port*

3 *no plural* a strong, sweet type of red wine

4 *no plural* the left side of a ship or aircraft when you are facing the front

portable /ˈpɔːtəbəl/ ADJECTIVE small enough to be carried easily □ *a portable television* □ *a portable DVD player*

porter /ˈpɔːtə(r)/ NOUN [plural **porters**]

1 someone whose job is to carry bags for people at a station, hotel, etc. □ *The porter will take your bags up to your room.*

2 someone whose job is to look after a building □ *the night porter at the hotel*

3 someone whose job is to move people and things around in a hospital □ *a hospital porter*

portfolio /ˌpɔːtˈfəʊlɪəʊ/ NOUN [plural **portfolios**]

1 a collection of pictures, photographs, etc. that you show to people so they can see what your work is like

2 a flat case for carrying large drawings, paintings, etc.

porthole /ˈpɔːthəʊl/ NOUN [plural **portholes**] a round window in the side of a ship or plane

portion /ˈpɔːʃən/ NOUN [plural **portions**]

1 a part of a total amount □ *She spends a large portion of her income on clothes.*

2 how much food one person eats at a meal □ *Try eating smaller portions.*

portly /ˈpɔːtlɪ/ ADJECTIVE [**portlier, portliest**] quite fat

portrait /ˈpɔːtreɪt/ NOUN [plural **portraits**]

1 a painting or photograph of a person, especially of their face □ *a portrait of the prince* ⊕ *a portrait painter*

2 a description of something □ *The novels provide a vivid portrait of India during this period.*

portray /pɔːˈtreɪ/ VERB [**portrays, portraying, portrayed**]

1 to make someone or something seem a particular way by writing things about them or by showing particular pictures of them □ *He was portrayed in the media as a hero.*

2 to act the part of a character or to show an emotion in a film or play □ *He is portrayed in the film by actor, Guy Pearce.*

• **portrayal** /pɔːˈtreɪəl/ NOUN [plural **portrayals**] when you portray someone or something □ *She won an Oscar for her portrayal of Queen Elizabeth II.*

pose /pəʊz/ ▶ VERB [**poses, posing, posed**]

1 to cause a danger or a problem ⊕ *Air pollution poses a serious threat to health.* ⊕ *Discarded plastic bottles pose an environmental risk.*

2 to sit or stand still while someone takes a photograph or paints a picture of you □ *They posed for pictures with their arms around each other.*

3 to ask a question ⊕ *The report poses more questions than it answers.*

♦ PHRASAL VERB **pose as something** to pretend to be someone you are not □ *The thief posed as a gas repair man.*

▶ NOUN [plural **poses**]

1 a position you put your body in, especially for a picture

2 when someone behaves in a way that is not natural or sincere so that other people will admire them □ *He's not intellectual at all. It's just a pose.*

• **poser** /ˈpəʊzə(r)/ NOUN [plural **posers**]

1 someone who behaves in a way to make people admire them

2 a question that is difficult to answer

posh /pɒʃ/ ADJECTIVE [**posher, poshest**]

1 an informal word meaning expensive and

comfortable □ *a posh hotel* □ *a posh London restaurant*
2 an informal word meaning from a high social class □ *a posh accent*

position /pə'zɪʃən/ ► NOUN [plural **positions**]
1 a way of standing, sitting or lying □ *I must have been sleeping in an awkward position.*
2 the place where something is, or the way in which it has been put there □ *His pipe was in its usual position, beside his chair.* □ *Push the lever to the 'on' position.*
3 the situation that someone is in ⍟ *Our team is in a strong position to win the championship.* ⍟ *Her demands put me in a very difficult position.* □ *Unfortunately, I am not in a position* (=I am not able) *to help you.* □ *In her position, I'd hire a really good lawyer.*
4 an opinion □ **+ on** *This statement explains the government's position on immigration.* □ *He thinks organic farming is stupid, and he'll never change his position.*
5 a person or organization's level of power, importance, or influence ⍟ *This new office will strengthen the position of our business in the area.* ⍟ *She is struggling to maintain her position as a leading expert on Renaissance art.*
6 a job or post ⍟ *What is the percentage of women holding senior positions here?* ⍟ *Our marketing manager left, and we have not yet filled his position.* □ *He applied for a teaching position.*
► VERB [**positions, positioning, positioned**]
1 to put someone or something in a particular place, often to be ready to do something □ *A camera was positioned above the door.* □ *Masked gunmen positioned themselves around the grounds.*
2 to try to make people think about a person or an organization in a particular way □ *He positioned the party as the true champion of family values.*
3 to put a person or an organization in a particular situation, in order to achieve something □ *The company is well positioned for growth.*

positive /'pɒzɪtɪv/ ADJECTIVE
1 completely certain □ **+ that** *Are you absolutely positive that he's German?* □ **+ about** *Jack has seen the letter. I'm positive about that.*
2 feeling happy about a situation and believing that the future will be good ⍟ *He has a very positive attitude to life.* ⍟ *It can be difficult to remain positive when you have so many problems.*
3 if an experience or the result of an action is positive, you get a good result from it □ *I have had a very positive experience with acupuncture.* ⍟ *The currency rate had a positive effect on our business.*
4 if someone's reaction to something is positive, they like it or agree to it ⍟ *I am not expecting a positive response to my request for more money.* ⍟ *Feedback from the show's audiences has been overwhelmingly positive.*
5 if you take positive action, you do something to try

to achieve something ⍟ *He took positive steps to improve his education.*
6 if the result of a test is positive, it shows that something has happened or been found ⍟ *The athlete tested positive for banned substances.*
7 a positive number is one that is greater than zero. A maths word.
● **positively** /'pɒzɪtɪvlɪ/ ADVERB
1 in a positive way □ *People usually respond positively to encouragement.* □ *She talks positively about her childhood experiences.*
2 used to emphasize your description of someone or something □ *He was positively furious.*

posse /'pɒsɪ/ NOUN [plural **posses**] a group of people who are standing together, doing the same thing □ *There was a posse of journalists waiting outside the house.*

possess /pə'zes/ VERB [**possesses, possessing, possessed**] a formal word meaning to have something □ *He was charged with possessing an illegal weapon.* □ *Candidates should possess strong communication skills.*
● **possessed** /pə'zest/ ADJECTIVE controlled by an evil spirit
● **possession** /pə'zeʃən/ NOUN [plural **possessions**]
1 something you possess ⍟ *They packed up their personal possessions.* ⍟ *The ring was her most prized possession.*
2 *no plural* when you possess something □ **+ of** *He was charged with possession of a firearm.* □ *Illegal drugs were found in his possession.* ⍟ *The bank took possession of the apartment.*
● **possessive** /pə'zesɪv/ ► ADJECTIVE
1 wanting someone to give only you their love and attention □ *He's very jealous and possessive.*
2 not wanting to share your things with other people □ *Children are very possessive with their toys.*
3 in grammar, showing who or what a person or thing belongs to □ *a possessive pronoun such as 'mine'*
► NOUN [plural **possessives**] in grammar, a word that shows who or what a person or thing belongs to

possibility /ˌpɒsə'bɪlətɪ/ NOUN [plural **possibilities**]
1 the chance that something might happen □ **+ of** *We were warned about the possibility of flooding.* □ **+ that** *There's a strong possibility that the tour will be cancelled.* ⍟ *The minister raised the possibility of military action.*
2 something that might happen ⍟ *Civil war is now a real possibility.* ⍟ *Storms are a distinct possibility.*
3 one choice from things which are all possible □ **+ of** *We discussed the possibility of moving abroad.* ⍟ *Have you considered other possibilities?*

possible /'pɒsəbəl/ ADJECTIVE
1 something that is possible can happen or be done □ **+ to do something** *It isn't possible to see the doctor today.* ⍟ *Try to avoid the area if possible.* ⍟ *Several advances have been made possible by new technology.*

2 something that is possible may be true □ **+ that** *It's possible that I made a mistake.* □ *That doesn't seem possible.* 🖰 *There are several possible explanations.*
3 **as soon/quickly, etc. as possible** as soon, quickly, etc. as you can □ *We need the work doing as quickly as possible.*
4 **the best/highest, etc. possible** used to say that something is the best, highest, etc. that exists □ *He's receiving the best possible care.* □ *I'll speak to him at the earliest possible opportunity.*
• **possibly** /ˈpɒsəblɪ/ ADVERB
1 perhaps □ *It could take about 5 days, possibly longer.*
2 used with *can* and *could* for emphasis □ *It was worse than we could possibly imagine.* □ *He can't possibly need more money!*
3 used when you ask someone politely to do something that might cause problems for them □ *Could you possibly get there a little earlier?*

post /pəʊst/ ▶ NOUN [*plural* **posts**]
1 *no plural* the service which collects and delivers letters and packages, or the letters and packages sent □ *I sent it by post.* □ *Has the post arrived yet?*
2 a job □ *the post of finance director* □ *a teaching post* 🖰 *He held a senior post at the bank.*
3 a long piece of wood fixed into the ground 🖰*a fence post* 🖰*a goal post*
4 a message which has been put on a website. A computing word □ *a blog post* □ *She announced the tour in a post on her website.*
5 a place where a soldier or guard stands □ *a police border post*
▶ VERB [**posts, posting, posted**]
1 to send a letter or package by post 🖰 *I posted the letter yesterday.*
2 to put a message, video, picture, etc. on a website. A computing word □ *He posted a message to fans on his website.* □ *A video of the interview was posted on the internet.*
3 to send someone to another place to work for a while □ *He was posted to the BBC's New York office.*
IDIOM **keep someone posted** to tell someone if a situation changes, especially someone in a different place □ *Keep me posted if there are any developments.*

post- /pəʊst/ PREFIX post- is added to the beginning of words to mean 'after' □ *postwar* (=after a war)

postage /ˈpəʊstɪdʒ/ NOUN, NO PLURAL the cost of sending a letter or package 🖰 *That's £35 plus £4 postage and packing.*

postage stamp /ˈpəʊstɪdʒ ˌstæmp/ NOUN [*plural* **postage stamps**] a formal word for a stamp (=a printed piece of paper that you buy and stick on letters before you post them)

postal /ˈpəʊstəl/ ADJECTIVE to do with the service that collects and delivers letters and packages □ *a postal worker*

postal order /ˈpəʊstəl ˌɔːdə(r)/ NOUN [*plural* **postal orders**] a document you buy at a post office as a safe way of sending money by post

postbox /ˈpəʊstbɒks/ NOUN [*plural* **postboxes**] a container in a public place where letters can be posted

postcard /ˈpəʊstkɑːd/ NOUN [*plural* **postcards**] a card with a picture on one side. You write on the other side and send the card by post without an envelope □ *a picture postcard* □ *I'll send you a postcard from Tokyo.*

post code /ˈpəʊst ˌkəʊd/ NOUN [*plural* **post codes**] a series of letters and numbers at the end of an address

postdate /ˌpəʊstˈdeɪt/ VERB [**postdates, postdating, postdated**] to write a date on something such as a cheque or document, which is later than the date when you are writing it

poster /ˈpəʊstə(r)/ NOUN [*plural* **posters**] a large notice or picture used for advertising, for decorating a wall, or for giving information □ *She has posters of movie stars all over her bedroom walls.*

posterior /pɒˈstɪərɪə(r)/ ▶ ADJECTIVE a formal word meaning at the back □ *the posterior area of the brain*
▶ NOUN [*plural* **posteriors**] a formal word meaning the back of something

posterity /pɒˈsterətɪ/ NOUN, NO PLURAL the people who will live in the future □ *These works of art should be preserved for posterity.*

postgraduate /ˌpəʊstˈgrædʒuət/ ▶ NOUN [*plural* **postgraduates**] a person who already has a university qualification and who is studying for an advanced qualification
▶ ADJECTIVE to do with postgraduates □ *postgraduate students* □ *a postgraduate course*

posthumous /ˈpɒstʃʊməs/ ADJECTIVE to do with something that happens after a person's death □ *He received a posthumous award for bravery.*
• **posthumously** /ˈpɒstʃʊməslɪ/ ADVERB after someone's death □ *Butler's novel was published posthumously in 1903.*

postman /ˈpəʊstmən/ NOUN [*plural* **postmen**] someone whose job is to deliver letters and packages to houses or offices □ *Has the postman been yet?*

postmark /ˈpəʊstmɑːk/ NOUN [*plural* **postmarks**] an official mark put on a letter showing the date and place it was posted

postmaster /ˈpəʊstmɑːstə(r)/ NOUN [*plural* **postmasters**] someone whose job is managing a post office

postmistress /ˈpəʊstmɪstrɪs/ NOUN [*plural* **postmistresses**] a woman whose job is managing a post office

post mortem /ˌpəʊst ˈmɔːtəm/ NOUN [*plural* **post mortems**] a medical examination of a dead body to find out the cause of death

postnatal /ˌpəʊstˈneɪtəl/ ADJECTIVE to do with the time just after a woman has given birth to a baby □ *postnatal depression*

post office /ˈpəʊst ˌɒfɪs/ NOUN [*plural* **post offices**] a shop where you can post letters and packages, and buy stamps

postpone /ˌpəʊstˈpəʊn/ VERB [**postpones, postponing, postponed**] to decide to do something at a later time than planned □ *We had to postpone our trip to Paris.*

• **postponement** /ˌpəʊstˈpəʊnmənt/ NOUN [*plural* **postponements**] when you postpone something □ *the postponement of the elections*

postscript /ˈpəʊstskrɪpt/ NOUN [*plural* **postscripts**] an extra message written at the end of a letter, usually after the abbreviation *PS*

posture /ˈpɒstʃə(r)/ NOUN [*plural* **postures**] the position of your body when you stand, sit or walk, especially the position of your back and shoulders □ *Back pain can be caused by poor posture.*

postwar /ˌpəʊstˈwɔː(r)/ ADJECTIVE to do with the period after a war, especially the Second World War □ *postwar rebuilding* □ *the postwar period*

posy /ˈpəʊzɪ/ NOUN [*plural* **posies**] a few small flowers which have been tied together

pot /pɒt/ ▶ NOUN [*plural* **pots**] a round container used for cooking, for storing things in, or for growing plants in □ **+ of** *a pot of paint* ⊞ *a pile of dirty pots and pans* (=containers used for cooking) ⊞ *a flower pot* (=container for growing plants)
▶ VERB [**pots, potting, potted**]
1 to put a plant into a pot
2 to hit a ball into a hole in a game of pool, snooker or billiards

potassium /pəˈtæsɪəm/ NOUN, NO PLURAL a soft, white metal. A chemistry word.

potato /pəˈteɪtəʊ/ NOUN [*plural* **potatoes**] a very common white, round vegetable that grows underground with a brown or yellow skin □ *mashed potato* □ *roast potatoes*

potato chip /pəˈteɪtəʊ ˌtʃɪp/ NOUN [*plural* **potato chips**] the US phrase for crisp (=very thin piece of potato cooked in oil)

potency /ˈpəʊtənsɪ/ NOUN, NO PLURAL how strong something is □ *the potency of the drug*

• **potent** /ˈpəʊtənt/ ADJECTIVE powerful, strong or effective □ *a potent poison* □ *a potent mix of frustration and resentment*

potential /pəˈtenʃəl/ ▶ ADJECTIVE able to become something in the future □ *a potential customer* □ *a potential risk* □ *This technology has many other potential uses.*
▶ NOUN, NO PLURAL
1 qualities that could be developed successfully in the future □ *She's a player with great potential.* ⊞ *He hasn't reached his full potential yet.*

2 the possibility that something may happen or develop □ *There's a lot of potential for economic growth.*

• **potentially** /pəˈtenʃəlɪ/ ADVERB possibly true in the future □ *potentially dangerous side effects* □ *This is potentially bad news for workers.*

pothole /ˈpɒthəʊl/ NOUN [*plural* **potholes**] a hole in a road

potion /ˈpəʊʃən/ NOUN [*plural* **potions**] a drink containing medicine or poison, or one that people believe has a magical effect

pot plant /ˈpɒt ˌplɑːnt/ NOUN [*plural* **pot plants**] a plant grown inside the house in a container

potter /ˈpɒtə(r)/ ▶ VERB [**potters, pottering, pottered**] to move about in a relaxed way, especially at home, doing small jobs □ *Jenny pottered around in the kitchen.*
▶ NOUN [*plural* **potters**] someone who makes things from clay

pottery /ˈpɒtərɪ/ NOUN [*plural* **potteries**]
1 *no plural* objects such as bowls and cups made from clay
2 *no plural* the job or activity of making things from clay
3 a place where things are made from clay

potty /ˈpɒtɪ/ ▶ NOUN [*plural* **potties**] a container that a small child sits on to go to the toilet
▶ ADJECTIVE [**pottier, pottiest**] an informal word meaning stupid or strange □ *He has some fairly potty ideas.*

pouch /paʊtʃ/ NOUN [*plural* **pouches**]
1 a small soft bag
2 the fold of skin that some female animals carry their babies in

pouffe /puːf/ NOUN [*plural* **pouffes**] a low soft seat with no back or arms

poultry /ˈpəʊltrɪ/ NOUN, NO PLURAL
1 birds such as chickens and turkeys that are kept for people to eat
2 the meat from these birds

pounce /paʊns/ VERB [**pounces, pouncing, pounced**] to jump or move forward suddenly to attack or catch someone or something □ *The cat pounced on the mouse.*

♦ PHRASAL VERB **pounce on something** to criticize someone for something very quickly □ *Critics pounced on the Senator's comments.*

pound /paʊnd/ ▶ NOUN [*plural* **pounds**]
1 the main unit of money in Britain. The written symbol is £. □ *They cost just a few pounds each.* □ *multi-million pound contract*
2 a coin worth one pound
3 a unit for measuring weight, equal to 16 ounces. This is often written *lb*.
▶ VERB [**pounds, pounding, pounded**]
1 to hit something hard repeatedly □ *Someone was pounding at the door, trying to get in.*
2 if your heart pounds, it beats quickly, usually because you are afraid □ *My heart was pounding before the interview.*

3 to walk or run with heavy steps □ *He came pounding up behind me.*

pour /pɔː(r)/ VERB [pours, pouring, poured]
1 to make a liquid flow out of a container □ **+ into** *She poured the orange juice into a glass.* □ **+ out** *She poured out the tea.* □ **+ over** *Pour the sauce over the chicken.*
2 to rain very hard ⊞ *It's pouring with rain outside.* □ *The rain was pouring down.*
3 to flow out of something fast and in large quantities □ *Water was pouring through the ceiling.* □ *The sweat poured down his face.*
4 to go into or leave somewhere in large numbers □ *Crowds of people poured out of the stadium.*
♦ PHRASAL VERB **pour something out** to talk about your feelings suddenly and with emotion □ *He poured out his troubles to me.*

pout /paʊt/ ▶ VERB [pouts, pouting, pouted] to push your lips out because you are angry or in order to look attractive
▶ NOUN [plural **pouts**] when someone pouts

poverty /ˈpɒvəti/ NOUN, NO PLURAL the state of being poor □ *Many families are living in poverty.* □ *a campaign to reduce global poverty*

powder /ˈpaʊdə(r)/ NOUN [plural **powders**] a substance in the form of very small dry pieces, like dust □ *chilli powder* □ *washing powder* □ *She sprinkled some cocoa powder on the top.*
powdered /ˈpaʊdəd/ ADJECTIVE dried and made into a powder □ *powdered milk*
powdery /ˈpaʊdəri/ ADJECTIVE made of very small pieces, like powder □ *powdery snow*

power /ˈpaʊə(r)/ ▶ NOUN [plural **powers**]
1 the ability to control or influence people or things □ *economic/military power* □ **+ over** *The big factory owners had a lot of power over local people.* □ *They really understand the power of the media.*
2 energy used for working machines, or the supply of this energy ⊞ *nuclear power* ⊞ *We are looking at new ways to generate power.* ⊞ *Electricity companies are working day and night to restore power to the area.*
3 political control □ *His government was in power (=ruling the country) for over 10 years.* ⊞ *The army seized power last year.* ⊞ *Tony Blair came to power in 1997.*
4 a country with a lot of influence in the world □ *He says that Western powers are failing to deal with climate change.*
5 strength or force □ *The power of the blast knocked me over.*
6 the official right to do something □ **+ to do something** *We don't have the power to issue visas.* □ *The committee's powers are limited.*
7 do everything in your power to do everything that you can to achieve something □ *Doctors did everything in their power to save her.*
8 the number of times a number has to be multiplied by itself. For example, '10 to the power of 4' is 10 x 10 x 10 x 10. A maths word.
▶ VERB [powers, powering, powered]
1 to provide something with the energy to work □ *Batteries are used to power the telescope.*
2 to move very quickly and with force, or to make something move very quickly and with force □ *He powered the ball into the net.*

power cut /ˈpaʊə ˌkʌt/ NOUN [plural **power cuts**] a period when there is no electricity because of a problem with the supply

powerful /ˈpaʊəful/ ADJECTIVE
1 having the ability to control or influence people or things □ *a powerful politician* □ *a powerful nation*
2 having a lot of physical force □ *a powerful earthquake* □ *a powerful backhand*
3 very effective, being able to do a lot □ *Computers have become more powerful.*
4 having a very strong effect on the body or mind □ *a powerful drug*
5 a person's body is powerful if it has big, strong muscles
• **powerfully** /ˈpaʊəfuli/ ADVERB in a powerful way □ *a tall, powerfully built man*

powerless /ˈpaʊələs/ ADJECTIVE not able to control or to affect things ⊞ *She felt powerless to stop him.*
power outage /ˈpaʊər ˌaʊtɪdʒ/ NOUN [plural **power outages**] the US phrase for power cut
power station /ˈpaʊə ˌsteɪʃən/ NOUN [plural **power stations**] a building where electricity is produced □ *a nuclear power station*
PR /ˌpiːˈɑː(r)/ ABBREVIATION public relations

practical /ˈpræktɪkəl/ ▶ ADJECTIVE
1 to do with real situations, not ideas ⊞ *This research has no practical applications.* ⊞ *They provide practical advice.*
2 useful and suitable ⊞ *It's the most practical solution to the problem.* □ *It's not practical to cycle in a long skirt.*
3 good at repairing things and doing things with your hands □ *He's not a very practical person.*
4 able to make sensible decisions □ *She's much more practical than her sister.*
▶ NOUN [plural **practicals**] a lesson or an examination in which students learn or use practical skills

practical joke /ˌpræktɪkəl ˈdʒəʊk/ NOUN [plural **practical jokes**] a trick that makes someone look silly and makes other people laugh
practically /ˈpræktɪkəli/ ADVERB
1 almost □ *It was practically full.* □ *Practically everything was destroyed.*
2 in a way that is to do with real situations ⊞ *Practically speaking, it won't have much effect.*

practice /ˈpræktɪs/ ▶ NOUN [plural **practices**]
1 *no plural* when you do something often so that you get better at it □ *He'll soon learn to play the violin with*

a bit more practice. □ He goes to choir practice on Mondays.

2 an activity, especially one that people have been doing for a long time □ They campaigned to end the practice of torture. □ She studied their religious practices.

3 put something into practice to do something which was an idea or a plan □ We formed a community to put our ideas about society into practice.

4 in practice used for saying what really happens when it is different from what you think will happen □ Making bicycles freely available seemed a good idea, but in practice they just got stolen.

5 be out of practice to not have done something for a long time □ I'd love to play in your hockey team, but I'm a bit out of practice.

6 good/best practice a good/the best way to do something □ It's good practice to consult with patients' relatives.

7 the place where a doctor, lawyer, etc. works □ She set up a medical practice in the town.
▶ VERB [practices, practicing, practiced] the US spelling of practise

• **practiced** /ˈpræktɪst/ ADJECTIVE the US spelling of practised

• **practicing** /ˈpræktɪsɪŋ/ ADJECTIVE the US spelling of practising

practise /ˈpræktɪs/ VERB [practises, practising, practised]

1 to do something again and again so that you get better at it □ + ing Practise breathing through your nose. □ To become a good musician, you must practise regularly.

2 to do something, especially as part of a tradition or a religion □ He practises yoga. □ They are free to practise their religion.

3 to work as a doctor, lawyer, etc. □ to practise medicine/law

• **practised** /ˈpræktɪst/ ADJECTIVE skilful because of having a lot of experience □ He stretched the pizza dough with practised ease.

• **practising** /ˈpræktɪsɪŋ/ ADJECTIVE
1 a practising member of a religion believes in that religion and follows its rules □ He is a practising Catholic.
2 working in a particular job □ She is a practising lawyer.

➤ Remember that in British English, **practise** with an s is a verb. **Practice** with a c is a noun: □ This gave me a chance to practise my language skills. □ I have football practice tonight.

pragmatic /præɡˈmætɪk/ ADJECTIVE sensible and possible in a particular situation ⧉ He has a pragmatic approach to politics. □ a pragmatic solution

• **pragmatically** /præɡˈmætɪkəli/ ADVERB in a pragmatic way

• **pragmatism** /ˈpræɡmətɪzəm/ NOUN, NO PLURAL a pragmatic way of dealing with things

• **pragmatist** /ˈpræɡmətɪst/ NOUN [plural pragmatists] a person who is pragmatic

prairie /ˈpreəri/ NOUN [plural prairies] a large area of flat land covered with grass in North America. A geography word.

praise /preɪz/ ▶ VERB [praises, praising, praised]
1 to say how well someone has done and how you admire them □ + for He was widely praised for his work. □ The prime minister praised the rescue effort.
2 to express thanks to God □ Praise the Lord!
▶ NOUN, NO PLURAL when you praise someone □ + for She received praise for her handling of the incident. ⧉ He won praise from the team coach.

praiseworthy /ˈpreɪzwɜːði/ ADJECTIVE good and deserving praise □ a praiseworthy effort

pram /præm/ NOUN [plural prams] a small vehicle with wheels that a baby lies in and which you push

prance /prɑːns/ VERB [prances, prancing, pranced] to dance or to jump about, especially because you want people to look at you □ The singer pranced around the stage.

prank /præŋk/ NOUN [plural pranks] a trick you play on someone as a joke

prawn /prɔːn/ NOUN [plural prawns] a small sea animal you can eat that has a curved shaped and is pink when cooked

pray /preɪ/ VERB [prays, praying, prayed]
1 to speak to a god □ + for She knelt down and prayed for forgiveness. □ + to He prayed to Allah.
2 to hope very much that something will happen □ + for We were praying for a nice sunny day. □ + that They prayed that someone would find them.

• **prayer** /preə(r)/ NOUN [plural prayers]
1 the words that you use when you pray to a god □ the Lord's prayer ⧉ He said a prayer of thanks. □ They went to the mosque for Friday prayers.
2 no plural when you pray to a god □ They knelt in prayer.

pre- /priː/ PREFIX pre- is added to the beginning of words to mean 'before' □ prehistoric (=before the time when history was written down) □ pre-dinner drinks

preach /priːtʃ/ VERB [preaches, preaching, preached]
1 to talk to a group of people about a religious subject usually as part of a church service ⧉ Father Andrew w preach the sermon.
2 to speak about something to persuade people to accept it □ He preached patience and understandin
3 to give someone advice in an annoying way □ He always preaching to me about studying hard.

• **preacher** /ˈpriːtʃə(r)/ NOUN [plural preachers] someone who preaches at a religious service

precarious /prɪˈkeəriəs/ ADJECTIVE
1 dangerous or full of risks ⧉ With the manager no against him, he's in a very precarious position.
2 likely to fall □ The tree was leaning over at a precarious angle.

• **precariously** /prɪˈkeərɪəslɪ/ ADVERB in a precarious way □ *He was standing precariously close to the edge.*

precaution /prɪˈkɔːʃən/ NOUN [plural **precautions**] something you do to avoid an accident or a problem happening 🖭 *We're taking all necessary precautions.* 🖭 *They stopped work on the site as a safety precaution.*

• **precautionary** /prɪˈkɔːʃənərɪ/ ADJECTIVE done as a precaution 🖭 *He was taken to hospital as a precautionary measure.*

precede /prɪˈsiːd/ VERB [**precedes, preceding, preceded**] to come or to happen before something else □ *They were involved in the protests that preceded last week's election.*

• **precedence** /ˈpresɪdəns/ NOUN, NO PLURAL when one person or thing is more important than another 🖭 *Public health must take precedence over economic considerations.*

• **precedent** /ˈpresɪdənt/ NOUN [plural **precedents**]
1 something that happened in the past and now provides a rule for what should happen in future 🖭 *a legal precedent* 🖭 *This decision sets a precedent.*
2 something that happened in the past that is similar to something now 🖭 *The scale of the book's success is without precedent.*

• **preceding** /prɪˈsiːdɪŋ/ ADJECTIVE coming or happening before □ *He hadn't seen his family during the preceding year.*

precinct /ˈpriːsɪŋkt/ NOUN [plural **precincts**]
1 an area of shops in the centre of a town where cars are not allowed 🖭 *a shopping precinct*
2 precincts the area around a large building □ *the cathedral precincts*

precious /ˈpreʃəs/ ▶ ADJECTIVE
1 very valuable and rare □ *precious stones* □ *In many parts of the world, water is a precious resource.*
2 very important to someone □ *His books are very precious to him.*
▶ ADVERB precious little/few used to emphasize there is very little or very few of something □ *There's precious little evidence.*

precipice /ˈpresɪpɪs/ NOUN [plural **precipices**] a high, steep side of a piece of land

precise /prɪˈsaɪs/ ADJECTIVE
1 exact □ *the precise location* □ *He didn't give any precise details.* 🖭 *At that precise moment, the bell rang.*
2 careful and accurate □ *Her work is very precise.*

precisely /prɪˈsaɪslɪ/ ADVERB
1 exactly or accurately □ *We need to find out precisely what happened.* □ *It arrived at precisely 12.34.*
2 used to emphasize the reason for something 🖭 *He explained that his books are strange precisely because his own life is so ordinary.*
3 used to strongly agree with someone's opinion

precision /prɪˈsɪʒən/ NOUN, NO PLURAL the quality of being exact and accurate □ *He hit the target again and again with precision.*

precocious /prɪˈkəʊʃəs/ ADJECTIVE a precocious child is more advanced than is usual for his or her age

pre-date /ˌpriːˈdeɪt/ VERB [**pre-dates, pre-dating, pre-dated**] to have existed or been built before something else □ *Balloons pre-date aircraft.*

predator /ˈpredətə(r)/ NOUN [plural **predators**] an animal that hunts and eats other animals

• **predatory** /ˈpredətərɪ/ ADJECTIVE hunting and eating other animals □ *predatory birds*

predecessor /ˈpriːdɪsesə(r)/ NOUN [plural **predecessors**]
1 the person who did a particular job before someone else got that job □ *My predecessor was in this job for twenty years.*
2 something that existed before something else and was replaced by the new thing □ *The European Economic Community was a predecessor of the European Union.*

predicament /prɪˈdɪkəmənt/ NOUN [plural **predicaments**] a difficult situation in which you do not know what to do □ *I found myself in a predicament.*

predict /prɪˈdɪkt/ VERB [**predicts, predicting, predicted**] to say that you think something will happen in the future □ *They're predicting snow for next week.*

• **predictable** /prɪˈdɪktəbəl/ ADJECTIVE expected or easy to predict □ *The ending of the film was entirely predictable.*

• **predictably** /prɪˈdɪktəblɪ/ ADVERB in a way that is easy to predict □ *Predictably, Josh arrived late.*

• **prediction** /prɪˈdɪkʃən/ NOUN [plural **predictions**] when you predict something, or something that is predicted 🖭 *I don't want to make any predictions yet.*

predictive texting /prɪˌdɪktɪv ˈtekstɪŋ/ NOUN, NO PLURAL the way that words appear on a mobile phone when you type in the first letter of the words in a text message

predominant /prɪˈdɒmɪnənt/ ADJECTIVE main or most common □ *The predominant colour in his paintings is blue.*

• **predominantly** /prɪˈdɒmɪnəntlɪ/ ADVERB mostly or mainly □ *The trains are predominantly old, out-of-date models.*

pre-empt /prɪˈempt/ VERB [**pre-empts, pre-empting, pre-empted**]
1 to do something in order to prevent something else happening □ *We must take action to pre-empt any potential terrorist attacks.*
2 to do or to say something before someone else is able to □ *I don't want to pre-empt anything the Minister is going to say.*

• **pre-emptive** /prɪˈemptɪv/ ADJECTIVE done in order to prevent something 🖭 *The actor launched a pre-emptive strike against film critics yesterday.*

preen /priːn/ VERB [**preens, preening, preened**]
1 if a bird preens, it cleans its feathers
2 to spend a lot of time improving your appearance □ *Sasha was preening herself in front of the mirror.*

preface /ˈprefɪs/ ▶ NOUN [plural **prefaces**] a short introduction at the start of a book

▶ VERB [**prefaces, prefacing, prefaced**] to say or to write something before the main thing you want to say or write

prefect /'pri:fekt/ NOUN [plural **prefects**] an older student in a school who has some responsibilities over younger students

prefer /prɪ'fɜ:(r)/ VERB [**prefers, preferring, preferred**] to like or to want one thing more than something else □ I prefer the red dress to the black one. □ + **to do something** We'd prefer to stay near the beach. □ He prefers not to talk about his family in public. □ + **ing** I prefer working from home. □ You can bring your own food if you prefer.

• **preferable** /'prefərəbəl/ ADJECTIVE better than something else □ A sandwich would be preferable to any of the food in that café.

• **preferably** /'prefərəblɪ/ ADVERB used to show what you would prefer □ We're looking for a two-bedroom flat, preferably near the town centre.

• **preference** /'prefərəns/ NOUN [plural **preferences**] when you prefer one thing to another, or something that you like or prefer ⊞ The choice is down to personal preference. □ The children showed a preference for sweet foods.

prefix /'pri:fɪks/ NOUN [plural **prefixes**] a group of letters that is added to the beginning of a word to make another word

pregnancy /'pregnənsɪ/ NOUN [plural **pregnancies**] the period when a woman or a female animal carries a developing baby inside her □ Smoking during pregnancy can harm the baby.

• **pregnant** /'pregnənt/ ADJECTIVE if a woman or a female animal is pregnant, she is carrying a developing baby inside her ⊞ a pregnant woman □ + **with** She was pregnant with twins. ⊞ She got pregnant again quite quickly.

preheat /,pri:'hi:t/ VERB [**preheats, preheating, preheated**] to turn an oven on so it reaches a particular temperature before you put the food in it □ Preheat the oven to 180°.

prehistoric /,pri:hɪ'stɒrɪk/ ADJECTIVE to do with the time in the past before history was written down □ prehistoric times □ prehistoric animals

prejudice /'predʒudɪs/ ▶ NOUN [plural **prejudices**] when someone has an unfair opinion or dislike of someone or something without knowing or understanding them ⊞ racial prejudice □ There is still prejudice against people with mental disabilities.

▶ VERB [**prejudices, prejudicing, prejudiced**]
1 to cause someone to have an unfair opinion about someone or something □ She said the publicity could prejudice the jury against her client.
2 a formal word meaning to have a harmful effect on something □ I don't want to say anything that might prejudice the investigation.

• **prejudiced** /'predʒudɪst/ ADJECTIVE having a

prejudice against someone or something □ prejudiced attitudes □ He's prejudiced against female writers.

preliminary /prɪ'lɪmɪnərɪ/ ▶ ADJECTIVE done or said before the main event or activity ⊞ The preliminary results are promising, but more work is needed. □ This process is at a very preliminary stage.

▶ NOUN [plural **preliminaries**] something said or done to prepare for a main event

premature /'premətjuə(r)/ ADJECTIVE
1 a premature baby is born before the time it should have been born
2 happening or done too early or before the usual time □ It's a bit premature to talk about wedding plans. □ premature deaths from cancer

• **prematurely** /'premətjuəlɪ/ ADVERB early or before the usual time □ His playing career ended prematurely.

premier /'premɪə(r)/ ▶ ADJECTIVE best, most successful or most important □ France's premier resort □ one of the world's premier sports events

▶ NOUN [plural **premiers**] the political leader of a country □ the Chinese premier

premiere /'premɪeə(r)/ ▶ NOUN [plural **premieres**] the first public showing or performance of a film, play etc. ⊞ the world premiere of the new James Bond film

▶ VERB [**premieres, premiering, premiered**] to be shown or performed in public for the first time □ The film will premiere at the Cannes Film Festival.

premise /'premɪs/ NOUN [plural **premises**]
1 a formal word meaning an idea or a theory that something is based on □ The basic premise of the programme is to encourage exercise.
2 premises the buildings and land owned and used by an organization □ The fire affected several shops and other business premises.

premium /'pri:mɪəm/ ▶ NOUN [plural **premiums**]
1 a regular amount of money that you pay for insurance (=arrangement in which a company gives you money if you have an accident or are ill) ⊞ an insurance premium
2 an extra amount that you have to pay for something ⊞ Companies will pay a premium for advertising during popular shows.
3 at a premium difficult to get and so often expensive □ Hotel space is at a premium during the festival.
4 put/place a premium on something to think that something is very important or valuable □ We put a premium on fresh, local ingredients.

▶ ADJECTIVE of the highest quality and often expensive □ premium food products ⊞ a premium rate call

premonition /,premə'nɪʃən/ NOUN [plural **premonitions**] a feeling you have that something is going to happen ⊞ She had a premonition that her sister was going to have an accident.

preoccupation /pri:,ɒkju'peɪʃən/ NOUN [plural **preoccupations**] something that you think about too much of the time □ She has an unhealthy preoccupation with food.

• **preoccupied** /pri:'ɒkjupaɪd/ ADJECTIVE thinking s

much about one thing that you do not pay enough attention to other things □ He had become preoccupied with work.

• **preoccupy** /pri:'ɒkjupaɪ/ VERB [**preoccupies, preoccupying, preoccupied**] if something preoccupies you, you think about it a lot

prepaid /ˌpri:'peɪd/ ADJECTIVE paid for before you need or use it □ prepaid postage

preparation /ˌprepə'reɪʃən/ NOUN [plural **preparations**]

1 no plural when you get ready for something □ **+ for** This is ideal preparation for next week's tournament. ⯑ We did some shopping in preparation for the trip. □ Make sure the food preparation area is clean.

2 something you do to get ready for something □ How are the wedding preparations going? ⯑ We're making the final preparations for the opening.

preparatory /prɪ'pærətəri/ ADJECTIVE preparing for something □ Some preparatory work is needed before building can start.

prepare /prɪ'peə(r)/ VERB [**prepares, preparing, prepared**]

1 to get ready for something or to make something ready □ **+ for** We need to prepare for the long journey. □ **+ to do something** They are preparing to open a new shop. □ He prepared a report on the company. □ We have to prepare students for working life. ⯑ Prepare yourself for a shock when you see him.

2 to make food ready for eating □ Mum was in the kitchen, preparing dinner.

prepared /prɪ'peəd/ ADJECTIVE

1 ready to do something ⯑ We're much better prepared this year.

2 made before you need or use it ⯑ His lawyer read a prepared statement. □ They sell ready prepared meals.

3 prepared to do something willing to do something □ How much are you prepared to pay?

preposition /ˌprepə'zɪʃən/ NOUN [plural **prepositions**] a word or phrase used before a noun or a pronoun to show things like position, time or method. For example, in, by and out of are prepositions.

prepossessing /ˌpri:pə'zesɪŋ/ ADJECTIVE a formal word meaning attractive □ It's not a very prepossessing building.

preposterous /prɪ'pɒstərəs/ ADJECTIVE stupid and unreasonable □ That's a preposterous suggestion!

prescribe /prɪ'skraɪb/ VERB [**prescribes, prescribing, prescribed**]

to tell a patient to take a particular medicine Doctors often prescribe antibiotics for infections. a formal word meaning to say officially that something must be done

prescription /prɪ'skrɪpʃən/ NOUN [plural **prescriptions**]

a written instruction from a doctor saying that someone needs a particular medicine □ **+ for** a

prescription for sleeping pills ⯑ a prescription drug (=medicine that must be prescribed by a doctor)

2 on prescription if a medicine is on prescription, you can only get it if you have a written instruction from a doctor saying that you need it

• **prescriptive** /prɪ'skrɪptɪv/ ADJECTIVE a formal word meaning telling people exactly what to do □ There is a very prescriptive approach to teaching reading.

presence /'prezəns/ NOUN, NO PLURAL

1 the fact of someone or something being somewhere □ Tests indicated the presence of the disease. ⯑ He was questioned in the presence of a lawyer.

2 a group of soldiers or police officers who are in a place for a particular reason ⯑ the US military presence in the region ⯑ There was a heavy police presence outside the stadium.

3 make your presence felt to make people notice you and listen to you □ The protesters really made their presence felt.

4 presence of mind the ability to think and act in a calm and sensible way □ She had the presence of mind to call an ambulance.

present¹ /'prezənt/ ▶ NOUN [plural **presents**]

1 something you give to someone, for example for their birthday □ I've got a present for you. ⯑ a birthday present ⯑ The children opened their Christmas presents.

2 the present the time now

3 at present now □ He doesn't have a job at present.

▶ ADJECTIVE

1 being in a particular place □ Both men were present at the meeting. □ Vitamin D is present in small quantities in food.

2 to do with the time now □ The present system isn't working. ⯑ We'll look at fashion from the 50s to the present day.

present² /prɪ'zent/ VERB [**presents, presenting, presented**]

1 to give something to someone formally, often at a ceremony □ She presented the best actor award. □ The captain was presented with the trophy.

2 to tell facts to people, especially in a formal way □ They presented new evidence in court.

3 to cause something ⯑ This will present problems for some schools.

4 to show someone or something in a particular way □ We want to present a more modern image.

5 to introduce a radio or television show □ She presents the news on the BBC.

6 to introduce one person to another in a formal way

• **presentable** /prɪ'zentəbəl/ ADJECTIVE clean or tidy enough to be seen in public □ He got up, washed, and made himself as presentable as possible.

• **presentation** /ˌprezən'teɪʃən/ NOUN [plural **presentations**]

1 a talk to a group of people explaining or describing something ⯑ She gave a presentation on her research.

2 when you show something to people or the way in

which it is shown or arranged □ *The presentation of food is very important.*

3 when something, such as a prize, is formally given to someone □ *a presentation ceremony*

• **presenter** /prɪˈzentə(r)/ NOUN [*plural* **presenters**]
1 someone who introduces the parts of a radio or television programme □ *the presenter of Radio 4's Today Programme*
2 someone who gives a presentation

presently /ˈprezntlɪ/ ADVERB
1 a formal word meaning now □ *Are you employed presently?*
2 an old-fashioned word meaning 'soon' □ *The bus should be here presently.*

present participle /ˌprezənt ˈpɑːtɪsɪpəl/ NOUN [*plural* **present participles**] the form of a verb ending in -ing, usually used after the verb *be*. For example, *going* in *I was going.*

present tense /ˌprezənt ˈtens/ NOUN [*plural* **present tenses**] a form of a verb used to show that the action is happening now

preservation /ˌprezəˈveɪʃən/ NOUN, NO PLURAL when you preserve something □ *The preservation of the rainforests is extremely important.*

preservative /prɪˈzɜːvətɪv/ NOUN [*plural* **preservatives**] a substance that is put in food or on wood to stop it decaying □ *The drink contains no artificial colourings or preservatives.*

preserve /prɪˈzɜːv/ ▶ VERB [**preserves, preserving, preserved**] to keep something the same, stopping it from being lost or destroyed □ *We try to preserve our traditions and culture.* □ *ancient fossils preserved in rocks*
▶ NOUN [*plural* **preserves**]
1 a food such as jam that is made by cooking fruit with sugar □ *strawberry preserve*
2 an activity that is thought to be suitable only for a particular type of person □ *Sailing should not be the preserve of the rich.*
3 a safe area for plants and animals

preside /prɪˈzaɪd/ VERB [**presides, presiding, presided**] to be in charge of a meeting or a formal event □ *Reverend Williams presided over the ceremony.* □ *the presiding judge*

presidency /ˈprezɪdənsɪ/ NOUN [*plural* **presidencies**] the position of being a president or the time when someone is a president □ *He won the presidency again in 1980.* □ *It was the most serious crisis of Mr Chirac's presidency.*

president /ˈprezɪdənt/ NOUN [*plural* **presidents**]
1 the elected leader of a country that has no king or queen □ *the Russian president* □ *+ of the president of Pakistan* □ *President Bush*
2 the person with the highest position in a company or an organization □ *+ of He became president of General Motors in 1920.*

• **presidential** /ˌprezɪˈdenʃəl/ ADJECTIVE to do with

the president of a country 🕭 *the presidential election* 🕭 *a presidential candidate*

press /pres/ ▶ VERB [**presses, pressing, pressed**]
1 to push something, or to push something firmly against something else □ *Press the red button.* □ *Orla pressed her lips together.* □ *Nothing's happening – try pressing harder.*
2 to try to persuade someone to do something or agree to something □ *+ to do something They pressed us to decide a date for the meeting.* □ *+ on tried to press him on his promise to visit.* □ *+ for We are pressing for an official enquiry into the accident.* 🕭 *She is taking legal advice in order to press her claim for compensation.*
3 press a point to repeat what you have said in order to try to make someone accept your opinion □ *I suggested she might pay for the damage, but she was so upset, I didn't press the point.*
4 press charges to make someone be officially accused of a crime in a court □ *Having looked at the evidence, the police decided not to press charges against her.*
5 to make clothes flat by ironing them
6 to move in a particular direction in a close group □ *The crowd pressed forward to see the princess.*
♦ PHRASAL VERB **press ahead/on** to continue with something, even if there are difficulties □ *We were all tired, but we decided to press ahead and finish the job.*
▶ NOUN [*plural* **presses**]
1 the press newspapers and magazines, and the people who write for them □ *He issued a statement t the press.* □ *Press reports suggested that he was sacked from the post.* □ *She was mocked in the pres*
2 a bad/good press criticism/praise from newspapers, magazines, television, etc. □ *Their new family car received a very bad press.*
3 a push against something □ *I gave the panel a pre and it opened.*
4 a machine that prints books, newspapers, etc.
5 a company that makes and prints books □ *He published his book with one of the academic presse*

press conference /ˈpres ˌkɒnfərəns/ NOUN [*plu* **press conferences**] an official meeting at which someone gives information to people who work in television and on newspapers and answers their questions 🕭 *The police are holding a press conferen this afternoon.*

pressing /ˈpresɪŋ/ ADJECTIVE important and needing be dealt with now □ *There is a pressing need for m judges in our courts.*

press office /ˈpres ˌɒfɪs/ NOUN [*plural* **press offic** a department of an organization that deals with th people who work on newspapers

press-up /ˈpresʌp/ NOUN [*plural* **press-ups**] an exercise in which you lie on your front and use yo hands to push the top half of your body up off the fl □ *He does 20 press-ups every morning.*

pressure /'preʃə(r)/ NOUN [plural **pressures**]
1 no plural when someone tries to persuade or force someone to do something □ **+ to do something** The government are under pressure to change the law. ⊞ Her father put pressure on her to study medicine. ⊞ I don't want to put you under pressure.
2 no plural the force on or against a surface from something pressing on it □ Applying pressure to the wound will stop the bleeding.
3 the force that a liquid or gas has when it is inside something □ air pressure □ high blood pressure
4 difficulties and problems that cause you to worry □ the pressures of work
• **pressurize** or **pressurise** /'preʃəraɪz/ VERB [pressurizes, pressurizing, pressurized]
1 to persuade or force someone to do something □ I felt I had been pressurized into leaving.
2 to control the air pressure inside something
• **pressurized** or **pressurised** /'preʃəraɪzd/ ADJECTIVE with a high air pressure inside □ a pressurized container

prestige /pre'sti:ʒ/ NOUN, NO PLURAL respect and admiration □ There's a certain prestige attached to working for such a company.
• **prestigious** /pre'stɪdʒəs/ ADJECTIVE generally admired and respected □ She teaches at one of the most prestigious universities in Canada.

presumably /prɪ'zju:məblɪ/ ADVERB used for saying something that you think is probably true □ Presumably the picnic will be cancelled if it rains.

presume /prɪ'zju:m/ VERB [presumes, presuming, presumed] to believe that something is true without having any proof □ I presume you've invited Sophie to the party? ⊞ Six soldiers are missing, presumed dead.
presumption /prɪ'zʌmpʃən/ NOUN [plural **presumptions**] when you presume something, or something that is presumed □ The presumption is that you are innocent until you are proved guilty.
presumptuous /prɪ'zʌmptʃuəs/ ADJECTIVE being too confident with someone in a way that does not show respect for them □ It's a bit presumptuous giving advice to your teacher!
pre-tax /ˌpri:'tæks/ ADJECTIVE before tax has been paid ⊞ pre-tax profits

pretence /prɪ'tens/ NOUN, NO PLURAL when you behave in a way that makes people believe something that is not true ⊞ She was struggling to keep up the pretence that she still loved her husband.
• go to under false pretences

pretend /prɪ'tend/ VERB [pretends, pretending, pretended]
1 to try to make someone believe something that is not true □ **+ that** She closed her eyes and pretended that she was asleep. □ **+ to do something** Chris was sitting at the table, pretending to do his homework.
2 to imagine that something is true as part of a game □ **+ to do something** The children were pretending to be robots.

pretense /prɪ'tens/ NOUN [plural **pretenses**] the US spelling of pretence
pretentious /prɪ'tenʃəs/ ADJECTIVE trying to sound more clever or interesting than you really are in order to make people admire you □ Jim found her pretentious.
pretext /'pri:tekst/ NOUN [plural **pretexts**]
1 a false reason that you give for doing something
2 on the pretext of If you do something on the pretext of doing something else, you pretend that you are doing the first thing in order to do the second thing □ He stayed at home on the pretext of tidying his bedroom.
prettiness /'prɪtɪnɪs/ NOUN, NO PLURAL being pretty □ the prettiness of the garden

pretty /'prɪtɪ/ ▶ ADJECTIVE [**prettier, prettiest**]
1 a pretty woman or girl is attractive □ His girlfriend is very pretty.
2 things that are pretty are attractive, often in a delicate way □ She was wearing a pretty white dress. □ What pretty flowers!
▶ ADVERB
1 quite □ Eight out of ten is a pretty good mark.
2 very ⊞ That's a pretty good salary, if you ask me!
3 pretty much/well almost □ The building work is pretty much finished.

prevail /prɪ'veɪl/ VERB [prevails, prevailing, prevailed] to be the main quality or influence in a situation. A formal word. □ Let's hope that common sense will prevail. □ He was brought up in an area where violence prevailed.
• **prevailing** /prɪ'veɪlɪŋ/ ADJECTIVE
1 most common at a particular time or among a particular group of people □ That is the prevailing attitude among young people.
2 most common in a particular area □ The prevailing winds blow from the south.
prevalence /'prevələns/ NOUN, NO PLURAL how prevalent something is
• **prevalent** /'prevələnt/ ADJECTIVE common in a particular place or among a particular group of people □ The disease is becoming increasingly prevalent in some parts of the UK.

prevent /prɪ'vent/ VERB [prevents, preventing, prevented] to stop something happening or someone doing something □ Police are working hard to prevent gun crime. □ **+ from** They were prevented from leaving the building.
• **preventable** /prɪ'ventəbəl/ ADJECTIVE able to be prevented □ preventable illnesses
• **prevention** /prɪ'venʃən/ NOUN, NO PLURAL when you prevent something ⊞ crime prevention □ the prevention of infection
• **preventive** /prɪ'ventɪv/ ADJECTIVE done in order to make sure that something bad, such as illness or crime, does not start □ preventive medicine □ preventive measures

preview /'pri:vju:/ NOUN [plural **previews**]
1 a showing or performance of a film, play, etc. to a small group of people before it is shown to everyone □ *Previews of the musical start this week.*
2 a short piece of a film, programme, etc. used to advertise it

previous /'pri:vɪəs/ ADJECTIVE happening or existing before □ *Please write down your previous address.* □ *I have some previous experience of working with children.*
• **previously** /'pri:vɪəslɪ/ ADVERB before □ *I'd met Sven a few months previously.* □ *He previously worked in a bank.*

prey /preɪ/ NOUN, NO PLURAL an animal or bird that another animal hunts, kills and eats
♦ PHRASAL VERBS [**preys, preying, preyed**] **prey on something** to hunt something and kill it □ *Wolves prey on small mammals.* **prey on someone** to use someone who is weak or easy to trick in order to get what you want, for example money □ *These people prey on the elderly.*
♦ IDIOM **prey on someone's mind** if something preys on your mind, you cannot stop thinking or worrying about it □ *Her comments were preying on my mind.*

price /praɪs/ ▶ NOUN [plural **prices**]
1 the amount of money that something costs ✍ *Food prices continue to rise.* ✍ *House prices are falling.*
2 a disadvantage that you experience as a result of doing something bad or trying to achieve something ✍ *He committed a crime and he paid the price.* □ *the price of fame*
▶ VERB [**prices, pricing, priced**]
1 to set a price for something □ *The new flats are priced at £250,000.*
2 to mark a price on something
• **priceless** /'praɪslɪs/ ADJECTIVE
1 extremely valuable □ *priceless works of art*
2 an informal word meaning very funny □ *The look on his face was priceless.*
• **pricey** /'praɪsɪ/ ADJECTIVE [**pricier, priciest**] an informal word for expensive □ *It's a nice club but the drinks are a bit pricey.*

prick /prɪk/ ▶ VERB [**pricks, pricking, pricked**] to make a very small hole in something with a sharp object □ *Diane pricked her finger on a rose bush.*
▶ NOUN [plural **pricks**] a sudden short pain you feel when something pricks your skin □ *I felt a slight prick as the nurse gave me the injection.*
prickle /'prɪkəl/ ▶ NOUN [plural **prickles**] one of the many thin sharp points on some animals and plants □ *Be careful of the prickles.*
▶ VERB [**prickles, prickling, prickled**] to feel something unpleasant on your skin as if many sharp points are pressing against it, or to cause this feeling □ *She felt her skin prickle in the heat.*
• **prickly** /'prɪklɪ/ ADJECTIVE [**pricklier, prickliest**]
1 covered in prickles or feeling like many sharp points

□ *a prickly bush* □ *I find wool next to my skin very prickly.*
2 becoming annoyed easily □ *She's rather prickly.*
pride /praɪd/ NOUN, NO PLURAL
1 a feeling of pleasure because you have achieved something or because someone such as your child has achieved something □ *There was such pride in his face as he looked at his baby daughter.*
2 respect for yourself ✍ *Jenny always took pride in her appearance.*
3 a feeling of being better or more important than other people
4 **someone's pride and joy** something or someone that makes you very happy □ *That garden is her pride and joy.*

priest /pri:st/ NOUN [plural **priests**] someone who performs religious services in some religions □ *a Roman Catholic priest*
• **priestess** /ˌpri:st'es/ NOUN [plural **priestesses**] a female priest in some ancient or non-Christian religions
• **priesthood** /'pri:sthʊd/ NOUN, NO PLURAL the job and responsibilities of being a priest, or priests as a group

prim /prɪm/ ADJECTIVE [**primmer, primmest**] shocked by anything rude
primarily /'praɪmərɪlɪ/ ADVERB mainly □ *These free newspapers are targeted primarily at young people.*

primary /'praɪmərɪ/ ▶ ADJECTIVE main □ *Heart disease is still one of the primary causes of early death.*
▶ NOUN [plural **primaries**] in the US, a vote in each state in which a political party chooses who will represent them in a general election □ *the New Hampshire primary*

primary colour /ˌpraɪmərɪ 'kʌlə(r)/ NOUN [plural **primary colours**] one of the colours red, blue and yellow which make other colours when they are mixed together
primary school /'praɪmərɪ ˌsku:l/ NOUN [plural **primary schools**] a school for children between the ages of four and eleven
primate /'praɪmeɪt/ NOUN [plural **primates**] an animal that belongs to the group that includes monkeys and humans
prime /praɪm/ ▶ ADJECTIVE
1 main □ *Good health care is a matter of prime importance.* ✍ *He is the prime suspect in the investigation.*
2 best □ *a prime cut of beef* ✍ *houses in a prime location*
▶ NOUN, NO PLURAL the time of someone's life when they are at their best and most successful ✍ *In his prime, Muhammad Ali was the most famous man in the world.*
▶ VERB [**primes, priming, primed**]
1 to prepare someone with the information they ne

for an event such as a meeting □ *We were all primed with questions to ask the guest speaker.*
2 to prime a bomb is to make it ready to explode

prime minister /ˌpraɪm ˈmɪnɪstə(r)/ NOUN [*plural* **prime ministers**] the leader of the government in Britain and in many other countries of the world □ *the Irish prime minister*

prime number /ˌpraɪm ˈnʌmbə(r)/ NOUN [*plural* **prime numbers**] a number that can only be divided exactly by 1 or itself. A maths word.

primitive /ˈprɪmɪtɪv/ ADJECTIVE
1 belonging to the earliest stages of development □ *primitive man* □ *a primitive computer*
2 simple and not modern or comfortable □ *The accommodation was fairly primitive.*

primrose /ˈprɪmrəʊz/ NOUN [*plural* **primroses**] a wild plant with small pale yellow flowers

prince /prɪns/ NOUN [*plural* **princes**] the son or grandson of a king or queen, or the male ruler of a small state or country □ *Prince Charles*

princess /ˌprɪnˈses/ NOUN [*plural* **princesses**] the daughter or granddaughter of a king or queen, or the wife of a prince □ *Princess Caroline of Monaco*

principal /ˈprɪnsɪpəl/ ▶ ADJECTIVE main
□ *Steel-making was the principal industry in the area.*
▶ NOUN [*plural* **principals**] the person in charge of a school, college or university
  principally /ˈprɪnsɪpəlɪ/ ADVERB mainly or mostly □ *She collects old toys, principally dolls.*

principle /ˈprɪnsɪpəl/ NOUN [*plural* **principles**]
1 a general rule or idea about how something is done □ *We follow the principle of first come, first served.* □ *The government has drawn up principles of good practice for landlords.*
2 a general rule that you base your behaviour on because you think it is morally right 🔄 *It was against his principles to borrow money.*
3 in principle in general although not in all the details □ *The president has agreed in principle to hold democratic elections.*
4 on principle if you do something on principle, you do it because you believe it is morally right □ *He doesn't eat meat on principle.*

print /prɪnt/ ▶ VERB [**prints, printing, printed**]
to produce words, pictures, etc. on paper or another surface using a machine □ *We printed 500 copies of the letter.* □ *Cooking instructions are printed on the back of the label.* □ *All our reference books are printed in Italy.* □ *Is this document ready to print?*
to publish writing in a newspaper, magazine, etc. □ *They did not print my letter.*
to write words without joining the letters together □ *Print your name at the top of the form.*
PHRASAL VERB **print something out** to make a printed copy of a document or image from a computer □ *I printed out the map.*

▶ NOUN [*plural* **prints**]
1 words, pictures, etc. that are produced on paper or another surface using a machine □ *She can only read books with large print.* □ *I was so excited to see my name in print.*
2 in/out of print still/not still published □ *His novels went out of print years ago.*
3 a mark that is left when something has pressed on a surface □ *Prints from his boots could still be seen in the mud.*
4 a fingerprint (=mark left when someone has touched something)
5 a copy of an original picture by an artist □ *He has a print of the Mona Lisa on his wall.*
6 a type of picture made by pressing a raised image into ink and then onto paper
7 a pattern on a piece of paper or material □ *Floral prints are popular for summer dresses.*
• **printer** /ˈprɪntə(r)/ NOUN [*plural* **printers**]
1 a machine that prints words and pictures from a computer
2 a person or company whose business is printing books, newspapers, etc.

printout /ˈprɪntaʊt/ NOUN [*plural* **printouts**]
information from a computer that is printed on paper

prior /ˈpraɪə(r)/ ADJECTIVE
1 happening or existing before □ *I couldn't go because I had a prior engagement.*
2 prior to something before something □ *Little is known about the days prior to his death.*

prioritize or **prioritise** /praɪˈɒrɪtaɪz/ VERB
[**prioritizes, prioritizing, prioritized**] to decide which task is most important and must be done first □ *He's not very good at prioritizing his work.*
• **priority** /praɪˈɒrətɪ/ NOUN [*plural* **priorities**]
1 the most important thing, which has to be dealt with before other things 🔄 *The environment is a top priority for the government.* 🔄 *The football club has made it a priority to wipe out racism at matches.*
2 the quality of being more important than anything else 🔄 *The university aims to give priority to students from state schools.* 🔄 *Families who are homeless must take priority on housing lists.*

prise /praɪz/ VERB [**prises, prising, prised**] to force something open, off or out, often using a flat tool □ *He prised open the lid with a screwdriver.*

prism /ˈprɪzəm/ NOUN [*plural* **prisms**]
1 an object made of clear glass that separates a beam of white light into seven colours
2 a solid shape with sides that are parallel and ends that are the same shape, e.g. a triangle. A maths word

prison /ˈprɪzən/ NOUN [*plural* **prisons**] a building where criminals are kept □ *Her father is in prison.* 🔄 *If he commits another crime he will be sent to prison.* 🔄 *He was released from prison last month.*
• **prisoner** /ˈprɪzənə(r)/ NOUN [*plural* **prisoners**]
1 someone who is kept in prison as a punishment □ *Four prisoners share each cell.*

2 someone who is kept in a place and cannot get out 🖻 *Her father had kept her prisoner in the cellar for over 20 years.*

pristine /'prɪstiːn/ ADJECTIVE in perfect condition, like new □ *Charlie was wearing a pair of pristine white trainers.*

privacy /'prɪvəsɪ, 'praɪvəsɪ/ NOUN, NO PLURAL being alone where people cannot see or hear you □ *A higher fence will give us a bit more privacy.*

private /'praɪvɪt/ ▶ ADJECTIVE

1 belonging to or used by only one person, or a small group of people □ *a private beach* □ *The prince flew in on his private plane.*

2 where other people cannot see or hear you □ *Can we find somewhere more private?*

3 owned and managed by people or companies, not by the government □ *private industry* □ *a private hospital*

4 to do with relationships, family and the things that people do when they are not working 🖻 *He never discusses his private life in interviews* □ *I never make private calls from the office.*

5 if someone is private, they talk very little about their feelings □ *He was a very private man.*

▶ NOUN [*plural* **privates**]

1 an ordinary soldier in the army

2 **in private** with no one else present □ *Could I speak to you in private for a moment?*

• **privately** /'praɪvɪtlɪ/ ADVERB

1 away from other people □ *Can we talk privately?*

2 a privately owned company is owned by a person or business and not by the government

3 secretly □ *Privately, he thought they were all fools.*

private school /ˌpraɪvɪt 'skuːl/ NOUN [*plural* **private schools**] a school which parents must pay to send their children to

privatization or **privatisation** /ˌpraɪvɪtaɪ'zeɪʃən/ NOUN, NO PLURAL the process by which a business or industry that is owned and controlled by the government is sold to private companies □ *the privatization of the rail network*

• **privatize** or **privatise** /'praɪvɪtaɪz/ VERB [**privatizes, privatizing, privatized**] to sell a business or industry that is owned by the government to private companies

privet /'prɪvɪt/ NOUN, NO PLURAL a plant that is often used to make hedges (=lines of bushes that separate areas of land)

privilege /'prɪvɪlɪdʒ/ NOUN [*plural* **privileges**]

1 a special right or advantage given to only one person, or to only a few people □ *The directors have special privileges such as their own dining room.*

2 a special experience that makes you feel very lucky □ *It's been a great privilege to work with you all.*

• **privileged** /'prɪvɪlɪdʒd/ ADJECTIVE having advantages that most people do not have □ *She comes from a very privileged background.* □ *I felt privileged to work with such a great director.*

prize /praɪz/ ▶ NOUN [*plural* **prizes**] something won in a competition or given as a reward for good work 🖻 *The first prize was a trip to France.* 🖻 *Adam won a prize in the raffle.*

▶ ADJECTIVE a prize animal, vegetable or flower is good enough to win a prize

▶ VERB [**prizes, prizing, prized**] to consider something to be very valuable or important □ *Gold has always been prized for its beauty and rarity.*

pro /prəʊ/ NOUN [*plural* **pros**] someone who is paid for playing a sport □ *a golf pro*

✦ IDIOM **pros and cons** the advantages and disadvantages of something □ *We discussed the pros and cons of moving abroad.*

pro- /prəʊ/ PREFIX

1 pro- is added to the beginning of words to mean something to do with 'beginning' or 'forward' □ *prologue* □ *proceed*

2 pro- is also added to the beginning of words to mean 'supporting someone or something' □ *Henry's always been pro-Europe.*

probability /ˌprɒbə'bɪlətɪ/ NOUN [*plural* **probabilities**]

1 how probable it is that something will happen □ *Thi has a 40 per cent probability of success.*

2 something that will probably happen □ *Redundancies are now a probability.*

probable /'prɒbəbəl/ ADJECTIVE likely to be true or t happen □ *A lit cigarette was the probable cause of th fire.* □ *It now seems probable that we will go to wa*

• **probably** /'prɒbəblɪ/ ADVERB used for saying that something is likely to happen or be true □ *I'll probabl be late.* □ *He'll probably lose it anyway.*

probation /prə'beɪʃən/ NOUN, NO PLURAL

1 a period of time during which someone who committed a crime must not do anything wrong or they will go to prison □ *He was put on probation for s months.*

2 a period of time when someone in a new job is watched to make sure they can do the job well

• **probationary** /prə'beɪʃənərɪ/ ADJECTIVE to do wi probation □ *I have to work a probationary period o three months.*

probation officer /prə'beɪʃən 'ɒfɪsə(r)/ NOUN [*plural* **probation officers**] someone whose job is t help criminals who are on probation and check tha they are doing nothing wrong

probe /prəʊb/ ▶ VERB [**probes, probing, probed**] t ask questions in order to find out information abou someone or something 🖻 *She asked some very probing questions.*

▶ NOUN [*plural* **probes**]

1 when someone asks questions in order to find ou facts about someone or something

2 a long thin medical tool that is used for looking things inside the body

3 a spacecraft with no people that is sent into space collect information

probiotic /ˌprəʊbaɪˈɒtɪk/ ► NOUN [plural **probiotics**] a food or pill that contains bacteria of the type that some people think makes you healthy
► ADJECTIVE containing probiotics □ *probiotic yoghurt*

problem /ˈprɒbləm/ NOUN [plural **problems**]
1 a situation that is causing difficulties □ *financial problems* □ **+ with** *There's a problem with the car.* ⌑ *He's having problems with someone at work.* ⌑ *I don't want to cause any problems for you.* □ *We had problems finding a hotel.*
2 no problem (a) used for agreeing to do something for someone □ *'Could you get some milk on the way home, please?' 'Sure, no problem.'* (b) used when someone thanks you for something □ *'Thanks for lending me your bike.' 'No problem.'*
3 have a problem with something/someone to not like something or someone or to not approve of them
4 a question that you have to answer or solve □ *maths problems*

► Note that you 'have problems **doing** something'. You do not have problems 'to do something':
✓ *We had problems finding the house.*
✗ *We had problems to find the house.*

► A very bad problem is a **serious** problem and not an 'important' problem:
✓ *Debt is a very serious problem.*
✗ *Debt is a very important problem.*

problematic /ˌprɒbləˈmætɪk/ ADJECTIVE causing problems □ *The arrangements were problematic.*

proboscis /prəʊˈbɒsɪs/ NOUN [plural **proboscises** or **proboscises**] a long, thin tube that some insects have for sucking. A biology word.

procedure /prəˈsiːdʒə(r)/ NOUN [plural **procedures**] a way of doing something or the order in which things are done ⌑ *There are standard procedures for customers making complaints.*

proceed /prəˈsiːd/ VERB [proceeds, proceeding, proceeded]
1 to continue something. A formal word. □ *She has decided not to proceed with her application.*
2 proceed to do something to do something next, especially something annoying □ *He said he wasn't hungry and proceeded to eat two slices of cake.*
3 to go somewhere. A formal word. □ *Passengers for flight 394 to Madrid should proceed to gate 21.*

proceedings /prəˈsiːdɪŋz/ PLURAL NOUN
1 things that are done or said, especially in a formal situation □ *A power cut interrupted the proceedings.*
2 legal action □ *She has started proceedings against the company.*

proceeds /ˈprəʊsiːdz/ PLURAL NOUN the money made from a sale or other event □ *All the proceeds from the concert will go to famine relief.*

process /ˈprəʊsɪz/ ► NOUN [plural **processes**]
1 a series of actions or events that have a particular result □ *the production process* □ *Getting a visa is a lengthy process.*
2 a series of changes □ *the ageing process*
3 in the process while doing something □ *He won the cup, breaking the course record in the process.*
4 in the process of (doing) sth in the middle of doing something □ *We're in the process of buying a house in France.*
► VERB [processes, processing, processed]
1 to deal with information in several official stages or on a computer □ *We will process your order as quickly as possible.*
2 to treat something with chemicals to make it last longer □ *processed food* □ *Cocoa butter is processed to remove the fat.*
● **procession** /prəˈseʃən/ NOUN [plural **processions**] a line of people or vehicles moving along slowly, one behind the other □ *a funeral procession*

proclaim /prəˈkleɪm/ VERB [proclaims, proclaiming, proclaimed] to state something publicly or officially □ *He proclaimed his innocence.*
● **proclamation** /ˌprɒkləˈmeɪʃən/ NOUN [plural **proclamations**] a public announcement of something important □ *the proclamation of independence*

procure /prəˈkjʊə(r)/ VERB [procures, procuring, procured] a formal word meaning to succeed in getting something □ *It was impossible to procure funding for the project.*

prod /prɒd/ ► VERB [prods, prodding, prodded]
1 to press something with a finger or pointed object □ *She prodded him in the back.*
2 to encourage someone to do something, especially something they have agreed to do □ *He'll get the information for you but you have to prod him.*
► NOUN [plural **prods**]
1 when you press something with a finger or pointed object
2 when you encourage someone to do something, especially something they have agreed to do ⌑ *Give her a prod if she forgets.*

prodigious /prəˈdɪdʒəs/ ADJECTIVE very great □ *prodigious talent* □ *prodigious wealth*
● **prodigiously** /prəˈdɪdʒəslɪ/ ADVERB extremely □ *She is prodigiously talented.*

prodigy /ˈprɒdɪdʒɪ/ NOUN [plural **prodigies**] a young person who is extremely clever or extremely good at something ⌑ *a child prodigy*

produce ► VERB /prəˈdjuːs/ [produces, producing, produced]
1 to make, grow or create something □ *The new factory will produce goods for export.* □ *The plum tree didn't produce much fruit last year.* □ *The sun produces both light and heat.*
2 to have a particular effect □ *This style of teaching produces better results.*
3 to show something so that people can see it □ *The conjuror produced a rabbit from a hat.* □ *The diary was produced as evidence at the trial.*

4 to organize the actors, equipment and money, etc. that are needed for a film, programme, play or musical recording □ *a film produced by George Lucas*
▶ NOUN, NO PLURAL /ˈprɒdjuːs/ things that are grown or produced on farms, especially food 🔁 *The village shop sells local produce.*

• **producer** /prəˈdjuːsə(r)/ NOUN [plural **producers**]
1 someone who organizes the actors, equipment and money, etc. that are needed for a film, programme or musical recording □ *an independent producer*
2 someone who makes products or grows produce to be sold □ *a major wine producer*

product /ˈprɒdʌkt/ NOUN [plural **products**]
1 something that is produced in large numbers for selling 🔁 *dairy products* □ *household cleaning products*
2 the result of something □ *We are all the products of our environment.*

• **production** /prəˈdʌkʃən/ NOUN [plural **productions**]
1 no plural making, growing or producing something, or the amount that is produced □ *the production of organic food* □ *We now have two of these types of car in production.* □ *We have increased production by 30%.*
2 a performance or number of performances of a play or show □ *He played the lead in the school production of 'Grease'.*
3 no plural the process of organizing the actors, equipment and money, etc. needed for a film, programme or musical recording □ *a TV production company*

• **productive** /prəˈdʌktɪv/ ADJECTIVE
1 having useful results □ *I had a very productive day at work.* □ *a productive meeting*
2 producing a lot of something □ *This was the most productive period of his writing career.*

• **productivity** /ˌprɒdʌkˈtɪvətɪ/ NOUN, NO PLURAL the rate at which goods are produced, or the rate at which one person works to produce something □ *The company introduced measures designed to increase productivity.*

prof /prɒf/ ABBREVIATION professor □ *Prof Cale*

profession /prəˈfeʃən/ NOUN [plural **professions**]
1 a type of job that needs special qualifications and training, for example, medicine, law and teaching □ *He is considering going into the legal profession.*
2 all the people who work in a particular profession □ *The medical profession has been angered by her remarks.*

• **professional** /prəˈfeʃənəl/ ADJECTIVE
1 to do with a profession □ *professional training*
2 doing something for money instead of as a hobby or for pleasure □ *a professional footballer*
3 doing a job with great skill and care □ *She is always very calm and professional.*

• **professionalism** /prəˈfeʃənəlɪzəm/ NOUN, NO PLURAL a way of doing something that shows great skill and care

• **professionally** /prəˈfeʃənəlɪ/ ADVERB
1 with the special qualifications and training needed for a particular job □ *a professionally qualified accountant*
2 in a way that shows great skill or care □ *He managed a difficult situation very professionally.*
3 for money and not as a hobby □ *He never played football professionally.*
4 in a way that is to do with your work □ *I've known him professionally for ten years or more.*

professor /prəˈfesə(r)/ NOUN [plural **professors**]
1 in the UK, the most important teacher in a university department
2 in the US, a teacher in a university or college

proficiency /prəˈfɪʃənsɪ/ NOUN, NO PLURAL the level of skill you have achieved in doing something □ *proficiency in a second language*

• **proficient** /prəˈfɪʃənt/ ADJECTIVE good at something that needs skill or practice □ *a proficient diver*

profile /ˈprəʊfaɪl/ NOUN [plural **profiles**]
1 a short description of someone or something □ *We have drawn up a profile of our ideal candidate.*
2 the idea or opinion that most people have about someone or something □ *The company's profile has changed over the years.* 🔁 *The case has had a very high profile* (=has had a lot of attention) *in the British press.*
3 the shape of someone's face seen from the side □ *The photo shows Jessica in profile.*

profit /ˈprɒfɪt/ ▶ NOUN [plural **profits**] money you make by selling something for more than you paid for it □ *The company is looking for ways to increase its profits.* 🔁 *We made a profit when we sold the house.* 🔁 *Many farmers find it hard to sell their meat at a profit.*

➤ Note that you **make** a profit. You do not 'gain' a profit:
✓ *We made a big profit on the sale.*
✗ *We gained a big profit on the sale.*

▶ VERB [**profits, profiting, profited**] to get an advantage from something □ *Convicted criminals are not allowed to profit from their crimes.*

• **profitable** /ˈprɒfɪtəbəl/ ADJECTIVE
1 making a profit □ *a profitable business*
2 useful and valuable □ *This might be a more profitable use of your time.*

profound /prəˈfaʊnd/ ADJECTIVE
1 very great □ *profound changes* 🔁 *Losing her mother as a child had a profound effect on Anna.*
2 profound feelings are very strong □ *He had a profound sense of guilt about his past.*
3 showing a lot of knowledge and understanding □ *profound comments*

- **profoundly** /prə'faʊndlɪ/ ADVERB in a profound way □ *I was profoundly shocked by what she said.*

profuse /prə'fju:s/ ADJECTIVE produced or given in large amounts □ *profuse bleeding.* □ *profuse apologies*

- **profusely** /prə'fju:slɪ/ ADVERB very much 🔁 *He apologized profusely.* □ *The wound was bleeding profusely.*

progesterone /prə'dʒestərəʊn/ NOUN, NO PLURAL a substance produced in the bodies of women and female animals which makes the womb (=organ where the baby grows) ready for pregnancy. A biology word.

program /'prəʊgræm/ ▶ NOUN [plural **programs**]
1 a set of instructions put into a computer to make it perform a task. A computing word. □ *a word processing program*
2 the US spelling of programme
▶ VERB [**programs, programming, programmed**]
1 to put a set of instructions into a computer or piece of electronic equipment to make it do something. A computing word.
2 the US spelling of programme

programme /'prəʊgræm/ NOUN [plural **programmes**]
1 a television or radio show □ *an arts programme*
2 a list of planned events or activities □ *the government's education programme* □ *a programme of reform*
3 a thin book that gives information about an event or performance

- **programmer** /'prəʊgræmə(r)/ NOUN [plural **programmers**] someone whose job is to write computer programs

programming /'prəʊgræmɪŋ/ NOUN, NO PLURAL the work of writing computer programs

progress ▶ NOUN, NO PLURAL /'prəʊgres/
1 improvement of skills or knowledge 🔁 *Freya has made a lot of progress in the last year.*
2 in progress happening or being done now □ *Work is currently in progress to develop the site.*
3 movement forward or towards something □ *The bus made very slow progress through the crowds.*
▶ VERB /prə'gres/ [**progresses, progressing, progressed**]
1 to develop □ *The work is progressing well.* □ *As the disease progresses, the patient requires more care.*
2 if a period of time progresses, it continues □ *As the evening progressed, I felt more and more tired.*
3 to go forward □ *They progressed slowly up the icy ridge.*

progression /prə'greʃən/ NOUN, NO PLURAL
1 development from one stage to the next □ *the progression of a disease*
2 movement forward

progressive /prə'gresɪv/ ADJECTIVE
1 using very modern ideas □ *a progressive school*
2 happening gradually □ *The disease causes progressive damage to the immune system.*

- **progressively** /prə'gresɪvlɪ/ ADVERB gradually □ *Dad's sight is getting progressively worse.*

prohibit /prə'hɪbɪt/ VERB [**prohibits, prohibiting, prohibited**] to not allow people officially to do something □ *Smoking is prohibited in most public places.*

- **prohibition** /ˌprəʊɪ'bɪʃən/ NOUN [plural **prohibitions**] an official order that people are not allowed to do something □ *a prohibition on drinking outside*

- **prohibitive** /prə'hɪbətɪv/ ADJECTIVE so expensive that you cannot buy something □ *Property prices in the south-east are prohibitive.*

project ▶ NOUN /'prɒdʒekt/ [plural **projects**]
1 a piece of work that is planned with a particular aim □ *a research project* □ *a major construction project*
2 a piece of work done by a student, often involving collecting information on a subject and writing about it 🔁 *Hannah's doing a project on Henry VIII.*
▶ VERB /prə'dʒekt/ [**projects, projecting, projected**]
1 to calculate an amount in the future, using information that you have now □ *Sales are projected to rise in the spring.*
2 to make light or an image from a film fall onto a flat surface or screen □ *The concert was projected live onto a big screen in the square.*
3 if you project a particular quality, you make everyone believe that you have that quality □ *He's trying to project himself as a caring politician.*
4 to make your voice loud enough to be heard a long way away
5 to stick out from a surface

- **projection** /prə'dʒekʃən/ NOUN [plural **projections**]
1 a calculation about an amount in the future, using information that you have now □ *Economists have to make projections about future sales.*
2 when light or an image from a film falls onto a flat surface or screen
3 something that sticks out

- **projectionist** /prə'dʒekʃənɪst/ NOUN [plural **projectionists**] someone who operates a film projector, especially in a cinema

- **projector** /prə'dʒektə(r)/ NOUN [plural **projectors**] a machine used to project films on to a screen □ *an overhead projector*

proletariat /ˌprəʊlɪ'teərɪət/ NOUN, NO PLURAL the proletariat the workers in a society, who do not own property

proliferate /prə'lɪfəreɪt/ VERB [**proliferates, proliferating, proliferated**] to quickly increase in number □ *Companies such as these have proliferated in the last few years.*

- **proliferation** /prəˌlɪfə'reɪʃən/ NOUN, NO PLURAL when something increases quickly □ *Recent years have seen the proliferation of leisure facilities in the town.*

prolific /prə'lɪfɪk/ ADJECTIVE a prolific writer, artist, etc. produces a lot of work □ *a prolific composer*

prologue /'prəʊlɒg/ NOUN [plural **prologues**] a short introduction at the beginning of a play, story or poem

prolong /prə'lɒŋ/ VERB [prolongs, prolonging, prolonged] to make something continue for longer □ drugs to prolong life

• **prolonged** /prə'lɒŋd/ ADJECTIVE continuing for a long time or for longer than expected □ a prolonged absence from school

prom /prɒm/ NOUN [plural **proms**] in the US, a formal party for students at a high school (=school for children between 14 and 18) at the end of a school year

promenade /ˌprɒmə'nɑ:d/ NOUN [plural **promenades**] a wide path for people to walk along by the sea

prominence /'prɒmɪnəns/ NOUN, NO PLURAL being prominent

• **prominent** /'prɒmɪnənt/ ADJECTIVE
1 important and known by a lot of people □ a prominent member of the government
2 sticking out or easily seen □ a prominent landmark

• **prominently** /'prɒmɪnəntlɪ/ ADVERB in a prominent way □ Long skirts feature prominently in all the fashion shows.

promise /'prɒmɪs/ ► VERB [promises, promising, promised]
1 to tell someone that you will certainly do something □ **+ to do something** I've promised to help Rebecca with the food. □ **+ that** I promise that I'll pay you back. □ But you promised me you'd come!
2 to say that you will certainly give something to someone □ I've promised my copy of the book to Mila.
3 promise to be to show signs of being good or successful □ It promises to be another lovely day tomorrow.
► NOUN [plural **promises**]
1 something that someone promises to do 🕮 I'm not making any promises . 🕮 I try to keep my promises (=do what I have said I will do). 🕮 The unions accused the government of breaking its promise to them (=not doing what it said it would).
2 no plural signs that someone or something will be good or successful in the future 🕮 She shows great promise as a gymnast.

• **promising** /'prɒmɪsɪŋ/ ADJECTIVE showing signs of being good or successful in the future □ She's one of our most promising young tennis players.

promontory /'prɒməntərɪ/ NOUN [plural **promontories**] an area of land that sticks out into the sea. A geography word.

promote /prə'məʊt/ VERB [promotes, promoting, promoted]
1 to help something to happen more □ Our aim is to promote peace amongst nations. □ We must do more to promote recycling.
2 to give someone a more important job or a job that earns more money in the same organization □ Jack's been promoted to store manager.

3 to tell people about something in order to persuade them to buy it or use it □ The book stores are all promoting her latest novel.

• **promotion** /prə'məʊʃən/ NOUN [plural **promotions**]
1 a move to a more important job or a job that earns more money in the same organization 🕮 Let's hope she gets her promotion.
2 when you help something to happen more □ the promotion of green issues
3 activities and materials which tell people about something in order to persuade them to buy it or use it

prompt /prɒmpt/ ► ADJECTIVE doing something or happening without delay or at exactly the right time □ Thank you for your prompt reply to my letter.
► VERB [prompts, prompting, prompted]
1 to cause someone to do something □ The scandal in the newspapers prompted his resignation. □ What prompted you to tell him?
2 to tell someone, especially an actor, what they should say next

• **promptly** /'prɒmptlɪ/ ADVERB without delay or at exactly the right time □ All complaints must be dealt with promptly. □ The concert started promptly at 7.30.

• **promptness** /'prɒmptnɪs/ NOUN, NO PLURAL being prompt

prone /prəʊn/ ADJECTIVE
1 often suffering from something □ He's always been prone to headaches. □ an injury-prone football player
2 lying flat, especially with your face down. A formal word.

prong /prɒŋ/ NOUN [plural **prongs**] one of the points of a fork

pronoun /'prəʊnaʊn/ NOUN [plural **pronouns**] a word that can be used in place of a noun. For example, in the sentence Sara ate the ice cream, Sara and the ice cream could be changed to pronouns and the sentence would be She ate it.

pronounce /prə'naʊns/ VERB [pronounces, pronouncing, pronounced]
1 to say the sound of a word or letter □ The two 'z's in pizza are pronounced 'tz'. □ How do you pronounce your surname?
2 to state something formally and publicly □ He was pronounced dead at the scene of the accident. □ I now pronounce you man and wife.

• **pronounced** /prə'naʊnst/ ADJECTIVE noticeable □ He walks with a very pronounced limp.

pronto /'prɒntəʊ/ ADVERB an informal word that means quickly or soon □ Could you do it pronto?

pronunciation /prəˌnʌnsɪ'eɪʃən/ NOUN [plural **pronunciations**] the way that a word is pronounced □ The pronunciation of some Arabic words is very difficult for English speakers.

proof /pru:f/ NOUN, NO PLURAL facts or objects which prove that something is true □ **+ that** Do we have any proof that she was actually there? 🕮 I was asked to provide proof of identity.

-proof /pruːf/ SUFFIX -proof is added to the end of words to mean 'protected against' □ *waterproof*

prop /prɒp/ ▶ NOUN [*plural* **props**]

1 something such as a piece of wood used to hold a structure up

2 a piece of furniture or other object used in a play or film □ *the props department*

▶ VERB [**props, propping, propped**] if you prop something against a wall or other surface you let it rest against it □ *He propped his bicycle against the wall and came in.*

◆ PHRASAL VERBS **prop something up** to use a prop or props to stop something falling down □ *The roof had been propped up with metal posts.* **prop yourself up** to support yourself with your arms or with an object □ *She propped herself up with a pillow.*

propaganda /ˌprɒpəˈgændə/ NOUN, NO PLURAL ideas, information or opinions that are spread by a political group or by one side in a war, in order to influence people

propel /prəˈpel/ VERB [**propels, propelling, propelled**] to push something forward, often using an engine or some other form of power □ *a jet-propelled engine*

● **propeller** /prəˈpelə(r)/ NOUN [*plural* **propellers**] an object with blades that turn and make a ship or aeroplane move forward

proper /ˈprɒpə(r)/ ADJECTIVE

1 correct and suitable □ *The staff hadn't received proper training.* □ *The proper procedures were followed.*

2 real or good enough □ *This is my first proper meal for days.*

3 behaving in a way that is socially accepted □ *She wanted to know the proper way to address him.*

● **properly** /ˈprɒpəli/ ADVERB correctly or suitably □ *You're not properly dressed for the cold.* □ *Come on, children, sit up properly.*

proper fraction /ˌprɒpə ˈfrækʃən/ NOUN [*plural* **proper fractions**] a fraction where the number below the line is bigger than the number above the line. A maths word.

proper noun /ˌprɒpə ˈnaʊn/ NOUN [*plural* **proper nouns**] a noun that is the name of a particular person, place or thing and begins with a capital letter

property /ˈprɒpəti/ NOUN [*plural* **properties**]

1 a house and the land it is on 🗗 *Private property – keep off!* □ *property prices*

2 *no plural* the things that belong to you 🗗 *Customers must look after their personal property.*

3 a quality or ability to do something □ *The substance is said to have unique properties.*

► Remember that **property** meaning 'the things that belong to you' is not used in the plural:
✓ *Stolen* **property** *is returned to the rightful owners.*
✗ *Stolen properties are returned to the rightful owners.*

prophecy /ˈprɒfɪsi/ NOUN [*plural* **prophecies**] a statement that something will happen in the future

● **prophesy** /ˈprɒfɪsaɪ/ VERB [**prophesies, prophesying, prophesied**] to say that something will happen in the future

prophet /ˈprɒfɪt/ NOUN [*plural* **prophets**] in some religions, a man chosen by God to teach people and give them his messages □ *the Prophet Isaiah*

proportion /prəˈpɔːʃən/ NOUN [*plural* **proportions**]

1 a part of a whole amount or total □ *A small proportion of old people live in care homes.*

2 the number or amount of two groups or things when compared with each other □ *The proportion of women to men in the company has risen.*

3 **in proportion** at the right size compared with other parts □ *Her legs are short but they're in proportion.*

4 **out of proportion** (a) at the wrong size compared with something else □ *The cat is surely out of proportion with the people in the picture.* (b) seeming too important or serious □ *You've been thinking about the problem for too long and got it out of proportion.*

5 **in proportion to** something at the same rate or by the same amount as something 🗗 *Salaries should rise in proportion to experience.*

6 **proportions** (a) the size of something □ *a house of generous proportions* (=a large house) (b) the level of something □ *The problem has now reached alarming proportions.*

● **proportional** /prəˈpɔːʃənəl/ ADJECTIVE of the correct size, amount or level in relation to something else □ *Tax is proportional to income.*

proposal /prəˈpəʊzəl/ NOUN [*plural* **proposals**]

1 a plan or suggestion □ *The council has come up with a proposal to ease traffic congestion.*

2 when someone asks another person to marry them

● **propose** /prəˈpəʊz/ VERB [**proposes, proposing, proposed**]

1 to suggest a plan or idea □ *I propose that we hold the meeting at a later date.*

2 to intend to do something. A formal word. □ *I don't propose to tell him about the matter.*

3 to ask someone to marry you

► Note that **propose** meaning 'to suggest a plan or idea' is followed by **that** and not 'to do something':
✓ *I propose that we discuss this with Maria tomorrow.*
✗ *I propose to discuss this with Maria tomorrow.*

● **proposition** /ˌprɒpəˈzɪʃən/ NOUN [*plural* **propositions**]

1 an offer or suggestion □ *an interesting proposition*

2 a statement expressing an opinion or judgment □ *We have no evidence to support the proposition that he is lying.*

proprietor /prəˈpraɪətə(r)/ NOUN [*plural* **proprietors**] the owner of a shop or business

prose /prəʊz/ NOUN, NO PLURAL writing that is not a poem

prosecute /'prɒsɪkju:t/ VERB [prosecutes, prosecuting, prosecuted] to accuse someone of a crime and take them to court □ *She is being prosecuted for fraud.*
• **prosecution** /ˌprɒsɪ'kju:ʃən/ NOUN [plural prosecutions]
1 the lawyer or team of lawyers who try to prove that someone is guilty in a court of law □ *She was called as a witness for the prosecution.*
2 the process of prosecuting someone □ *He faces prosecution for assault.*

prospect /'prɒspekt/ ► NOUN [plural prospects]
1 the possibility of something happening □ *And is there no prospect of promotion?*
2 the thought or idea of something that will happen in the future □ *The prospect of a three-hour exam filled him with dread.*
3 prospects chances of success in the future □ *Employment prospects are not good at present.*
► VERB /prə'spekt/ [prospects, prospecting, prospected] to search for gold or other valuable metals in the earth
• **prospective** /prə'spektɪv/ ADJECTIVE likely to be or become something □ *We've found a prospective buyer for the house.* □ *The college had applications from nearly 200 prospective students.*

prospectus /prə'spektəs/ NOUN [plural prospectuses] a small book that gives you information about a school, college or university and the courses it offers

prosper /'prɒspə(r)/ VERB [prospers, prospering, prospered] to succeed, especially by making a lot of money
• **prosperity** /prɒs'perəti/ NOUN, NO PLURAL success, especially having a lot of money
• **prosperous** /'prɒspərəs/ ADJECTIVE successful, especially by making a lot of money

prostrate /'prɒstreɪt/ ADJECTIVE lying flat with your face down. A formal word

protagonist /prə'tægənɪst/ NOUN [plural protagonists] the main person in a play, film or story

protect /prə'tekt/ VERB [protects, protecting, protected] to keep someone or something safe from harm or danger □ *A mother will always protect her children.* □ **+ from** *Protect the young plants from frost.*
• **protection** /prə'tekʃən/ NOUN, NO PLURAL when someone or something is protected □ **+ against** *A good diet provides protection against some diseases.*
• **protective** /prə'tektɪv/ ADJECTIVE
1 providing protection □ *protective equipment*
2 wanting to protect someone □ *She is very protective of her children.*
• **protector** /prə'tektə(r)/ NOUN [plural protectors] someone who protects another person

protégé or **protégée** /'prɒteʒeɪ/ NOUN [plural protégés or protégées] someone who is helped and advised by an older, more experienced person

► This word is spelt **protégée** when the person helped or advised is a woman.

protein /'prəuti:n/ NOUN [plural proteins] a substance in foods such as eggs, meat and milk that is necessary for strength and growth

protest ► VERB /prə'test/ [protests, protesting, protested] to march or stand with a group of other people to show that you disagree with something □ *Thousands took to the streets to protest about the war.*
► NOUN /'prəutest/ [plural protests] a strong statement saying that something is wrong, or an organized action against something □ *Several MPs resigned in protest at the cuts.* □ *Students organized a peaceful protest against the regime.*

Protestant /'prɒtɪstənt/ ► NOUN [plural Protestants] a member of one of the Christian churches that separated from the Catholic Church in the 1500s
► ADJECTIVE to do with Protestants or their church

protester /prə'testə(r)/ NOUN [plural protesters] someone who does something to show that they do not agree with something □ *Anti-airport protesters blocked the roads.*

proton /'prəutɒn/ NOUN [plural protons] one of the parts of a nucleus of an atom which has a positive electrical charge. A physics word.

protoplasm /'prəutəuplæzəm/ NOUN, NO PLURAL the transparent liquid inside living cells. A biology word.

prototype /'prəutətaɪp/ NOUN [plural prototypes] the first model of a new design, for example of a car used to test how well it works before it is produced in large numbers

protractor /prə'træktə(r)/ NOUN [plural protractors] an object like half a circle, used for measuring angles. A maths word.

protrude /prə'tru:d/ VERB [protrudes, protruding, protruded] to stick out from something □ *A pen was protruding from his pocket.*
• **protrusion** /prə'tru:ʒən/ NOUN [plural protrusions] something that sticks out from something

proud /praud/ ADJECTIVE [prouder, proudest]
1 feeling pleased about your achievements or about the achievements of someone such as your child □ *She felt very proud when her son got the award.* □ *Holding the winner's trophy was a really proud moment for me.* □ **+ of** *I'm proud of the fact that I carried on and didn't give up.* □ **+ to do something** *He was very proud to play for the national team.*
2 not wanting to ask for help although you need it □ *She's too proud to let anyone pay her bills.*
3 thinking that you are better than other people, in a way that annoys people
• **proudly** /'praudli/ ADVERB in a proud way □ *She proudly showed me her medal.*

prove /pruːv/ VERB [proves, proving, proved]
1 to show that something is true 🔁 *Carter was determined to prove his innocence.* □ **+ that** *DNA tests proved that he was guilty.*
2 if something proves useful, impossible, etc., you find that it is useful, etc. □ *The business proved to be so successful that we had to take on more staff.*
3 prove yourself to show people that you can do something well □ *When you start a new job you feel you have to prove yourself.*
• **proven** /ˈpruːvən/ ADJECTIVE shown to be true or good □ *There is no scientifically proven cure for colds.*

proverb /ˈprɒvɜːb/ NOUN [plural **proverbs**] an old phrase that most people know which gives you advice about life □ *There is a legendary Chinese proverb which states 'A journey of a thousand miles starts with a single step'.*
• **proverbial** /prəˈvɜːbɪəl/ ADJECTIVE used when you are using all or part of a proverb □ *The last few days have been like the proverbial calm before the storm.*

provide /prəˈvaɪd/ VERB [provides, providing, provided] to give or supply something □ *The hospital provides information on the treatments available.* □ *School provides an opportunity for children to learn and develop.* □ **+ with** *The refugees were provided with food and shelter.*
→ PHRASAL VERB **provide for someone** to give someone the money, food, etc. that they need □ *She worked all hours to provide for her family.*

provided /prəˈvaɪdɪd/ *or* **providing** /prəˈvaɪdɪŋ/ CONJUNCTION used when saying that one thing will happen only if another thing happens □ *Providing you have no objection, I'd like you to work next Sunday.* □ *You'll do well in the test, provided that you work hard.*

province /ˈprɒvɪns/ NOUN [plural **provinces**]
1 one of the parts that some countries are divided into □ *Sichuan province in China*
2 the provinces the parts of a country that are not near the capital city
provincial /prəˈvɪnʃəl/ ADJECTIVE
1 to do with a province or the provinces □ *a provincial government*
2 old-fashioned and not typical of people in a capital city □ *provincial attitudes*

provision /prəˈvɪʒən/ NOUN, NO PLURAL
1 when someone provides something □ *the provision of healthcare*
2 make provision for someone/something to make arrangements for something that you will need □ *Many people aren't making sufficient provision for their retirement.*
provisional /prəˈvɪʒənəl/ ADJECTIVE not certain, and possibly going to change 🔁 *They've set a provisional date for the meeting.*
provisions /prəˈvɪʒənz/ PLURAL NOUN supplies of food

provocation /ˌprɒvəˈkeɪʃən/ NOUN [plural **provocations**] something that makes you feel angry □ *He used to hit people at the slightest provocation.*
provocative /prəˈvɒkətɪv/ ADJECTIVE intended to make someone angry □ *provocative questions*
provoke /prəˈvəʊk/ VERB [provokes, provoking, provoked]
1 to cause a particular reaction or feeling, often an angry one □ *His remarks have provoked a lot of criticism.*
2 to make someone angry deliberately □ *The children are always provoking each other.*

prowl /praʊl/ VERB [prowls, prowling, prowled] to walk around somewhere slowly and secretly □ *The murderer prowled the streets looking for his next victim.*
• **prowler** /ˈpraʊlə(r)/ NOUN [plural **prowlers**] someone who walks around secretly somewhere, intending to do something bad

proximity /prɒkˈsɪmətɪ/ NOUN, NO PLURAL the quality of being near to something or someone 🔁 *People living in close proximity to the factory have complained about the noise.*

proxy /ˈprɒksɪ/ NOUN [plural **proxies**] someone who has the authority to do something for you, especially to vote

prude /pruːd/ NOUN [plural **prudes**] someone who is too easily shocked

prudence /ˈpruːdəns/ NOUN, NO PLURAL a formal word meaning the quality of being prudent
• **prudent** /ˈpruːdənt/ ADJECTIVE a formal word meaning careful and sensible □ *prudent advice*

prudish /ˈpruːdɪʃ/ ADJECTIVE too easily shocked □ *My parents are very prudish.*

prune /pruːn/ ► VERB [prunes, pruning, pruned] to cut bits off a plant
► NOUN [plural **prunes**] a dried plum (=fruit with a smooth skin and a big seed in the middle)

pry /praɪ/ VERB [pries, prying, pried] to try to find out things that people do not want you to know □ *She didn't want to answer questions from prying journalists.*

PS /ˌpiːˈes/ ABBREVIATION postscript. You write PS when you want to add something to the end of a letter □ *PS Say hi to David from me.*

psalm /sɑːm/ NOUN [plural **psalms**] a song in the Bible

pseudo- /ˈsjuːdəʊ/ PREFIX pseudo- is added to the beginning of words to mean 'pretending to be something' □ *pseudonym* □ *pseudo-scientific language*

pseudonym /ˈsjuːdəʊnɪm/ NOUN [plural **pseudonyms**] a name that someone, especially a writer, uses instead of their real name

psyche /ˈsaɪkɪ/ NOUN [plural **psyches**] your mind and feelings □ *the female psyche*

psychiatric /ˌsaɪkɪˈætrɪk/ ADJECTIVE to do with mental illness □ *a psychiatric hospital*
• **psychiatrist** /saɪˈkaɪətrɪst/ NOUN [plural **psychiatrists**] a doctor who treats mentally ill people

- **psychiatry** /saɪˈkaɪətrɪ/ NOUN, NO PLURAL the study and treatment of mental illness

psychic /ˈsaɪkɪk/ ► ADJECTIVE having special powers such as knowing what people are thinking, and what will happen in the future
► NOUN [plural **psychics**] someone who is psychic

psychoanalysis /ˌsaɪkəʊəˈnæləsɪs/ NOUN, NO PLURAL a form of treatment for people with mental problems where the patient talks about their life to help them understand their feelings

- **psychoanalyst** /ˌsaɪkəʊˈænəlɪst/ NOUN [plural **psychoanalysts**] someone who is trained to do psychoanalysis

- **psychoanalyze** or **psychoanalyse** /ˌsaɪkəʊˈænəlaɪz/ VERB [**psychoanalyzes, psychoanalyzing, psychoanalyzed**] to treat someone or study someone by using psychoanalysis

psychological /ˌsaɪkəˈlɒdʒɪkəl/ ADJECTIVE to do with the mind □ psychological damage

- **psychologist** /saɪˈkɒlədʒɪst/ NOUN [plural **psychologists**] someone who has studied psychology and human behaviour

- **psychology** /saɪˈkɒlədʒɪ/ NOUN, NO PLURAL the study of the mind and how it affects the way we behave

psychopath /ˈsaɪkəʊpæθ/ NOUN [plural **psychopaths**] someone who is very violent and dangerous

- **psychopathic** /ˌsaɪkəʊˈpæθɪk/ ADJECTIVE to do with a psychopath □ psychopathic behaviour

PTO /ˌpiːtiːˈəʊ/ ABBREVIATION please turn over; written at the bottom of a page to show that someone should turn the page and read the other side

pub /pʌb/ NOUN [plural **pubs**] a place where people buy and drink alcoholic drinks, especially in the UK

puberty /ˈpjuːbətɪ/ NOUN, NO PLURAL the time when a child's body changes into an adult's body 🕮 Girls usually reach puberty earlier than boys.

public /ˈpʌblɪk/ ► ADJECTIVE
1 to do with the people generally of a country 🕮 There has been a change in public opinion on this issue. 🕮 There is a lot of public support for the idea.
2 available for everyone □ a public park □ public libraries □ public events
3 to do with the government and not private companies □ public funding □ public employees
4 known by everyone 🕮 It's public knowledge that they're getting married. 🕮 They refused to make the investigation's findings public.
► NOUN, NO PLURAL
1 the public people generally 🕮 A member of the public called the police 🕮 The product will go on sale to the general public tomorrow.
2 in public in a place where anyone can see □ He was embarrassed when his parents kissed in public.

- **publicly** /ˈpʌblɪklɪ/ ADVERB

1 in a way that the public can hear or see □ He has said publicly that he supports communism.
2 by the public □ publicly owned companies

publication /ˌpʌblɪˈkeɪʃən/ NOUN [plural **publications**]
1 no plural the process of printing and selling a book, magazine, etc. □ The publication of the images provoked a strong reaction.
2 something such as a magazine or newspaper that is printed and sold

publicity /pʌbˈlɪsɪtɪ/ NOUN, NO PLURAL
1 attention that something gets from newspapers, television, etc. 🕮 The affair attracted a lot of publicity.
2 the activity of making people aware of a new product, film, etc. 🕮 He took part in a publicity campaign for the new film.

publicize or **publicise** /ˈpʌblɪsaɪz/ VERB [**publicizes, publicizing, publicized**] to tell people about a new book, film, etc., or about an event that is going to happen □ The event was well publicized.

public relations /ˌpʌblɪk rɪˈleɪʃənz/ NOUN, NO PLURAL the job of making a company, famous person, product, etc. seem good to the public

public school /ˌpʌblɪk ˈskuːl/ NOUN [plural **public schools**]
1 in the UK, a school that you pay to go to, often where you stay as well as study
2 in the US, a school that the government pays for

public transport /ˌpʌblɪk ˈtrænspɔːt/ NOUN, NO PLURAL trains and buses that people can use □ We need to encourage more people to use public transport.

public transportation /ˈpʌblɪk trænspɔːˈteɪʃən/ NOUN, NO PLURAL the US phrase for **public transport**

publish /ˈpʌblɪʃ/ VERB [**publishes, publishing, published**]
1 to print a book, magazine, etc. so that people can buy it □ The book was published in September.
2 if a newspaper or magazine publishes an article, photograph, etc., it prints it □ The newspaper published her letter. □ The magazine published photos of the Princess on the beach.
3 to make information available to people generally □ The company does not publish sales information.

- **publisher** /ˈpʌblɪʃə(r)/ NOUN [plural **publishers**] a person or company that publishes books, newspapers or magazines

- **publishing** /ˈpʌblɪʃɪŋ/ NOUN, NO PLURAL the work business of producing books, newspapers and magazines so people can buy them □ Isabella works publishing. □ a publishing company

puck /pʌk/ NOUN [plural **pucks**] the hard flat object that players hit in the game of ice hockey

pudding /ˈpʊdɪŋ/ NOUN [plural **puddings**] sweet food eaten at the end of a meal □ We've got ice cream and pudding.

puddle /ˈpʌdəl/ NOUN [plural **puddles**] a small pool of rain on the ground □ Young children love splashing in puddles.

puerile /'pjʊəraɪl/ ADJECTIVE a formal word meaning silly and like a young child □ *a puerile sense of humour*

puff /pʌf/ ► VERB [**puffs, puffing, puffed**] to breathe quickly because you have been exercising 🔄 *John was puffing and panting as he came up the hill.*

◆ PHRASAL VERBS **puff something out** if you puff out your cheeks or your chest, you make them bigger by filling them with air **puff up** if part of your body puffs up, it swells, because you are ill or injured □ *His face had puffed up where he'd been hit.*

► NOUN [plural **puffs**] a small amount of breath, wind, air or smoke □ *a puff of air*

puffin /'pʌfɪn/ NOUN [plural **puffins**] a big, black and white sea bird with a brightly coloured beak

puffy /'pʌfɪ/ ADJECTIVE [**puffier, puffiest**] swollen □ *His eyes were puffy because he'd been crying.*

pull /pʊl/ ► VERB [**pulls, pulling, pulled**]

1 to hold something and move it towards you □ *He pulled the door open.* 🔄 *Stop pulling my hair!* 🔄 *He pointed the gun at her and pulled the trigger.* □ *+ at He kept pulling at my sleeve.*

2 if a machine, vehicle, etc. pulls something, it is attached to it and moves it □ *We had to get a tractor to pull our car out of the mud.* □ *The gliders are pulled up into the air by a winch.*

3 to separate the pieces of something or to damage something □ *+ apart We pulled apart the curtains and looked inside.* □ *+ down The old houses will be pulled down.* □ *+ off He pulled off the insect's wings.*

4 if you pull a muscle you hurt it by stretching it too much

5 to suddenly produce a weapon and threaten someone with it □ *Then he pulled a gun on us.*

6 pull a face to twist your face into an ugly or funny shape

7 pull yourself together to manage to become calm after having been upset □ *I managed to pull myself together enough to call the police.*

◆ go to **pull someone's** *leg*, **pull your** *socks* **up, pull** *strings*, **pull the** *wool* **over someone's eyes, pull the** *plug* **(on something)**

PHRASAL VERBS **pull ahead**

1 to get in front of someone by moving faster than them □ *The other runners started to pull ahead.*

2 to make more progress than someone else □ *The Democrats seem to be pulling ahead in the polls.* **pull something apart** to criticize something in detail □ *He just pulled my argument apart.* **pull away**

1 if a vehicle pulls away, it moves away

2 to move away from someone who is trying to hold you or touch you □ *She pulled away when he tried to kiss her.* **pull back** to decide not to do something, often because of the risk □ *They have pulled back from investing any more money in the company.* **pull in/into somewhere**

1 if a vehicle pulls in, it stops at the side of the road or goes into a place □ *We'll pull in at the next lay-by.*

2 if train pulls in, it arrives at a station **pull something off** to be successful at doing something,

often something that was a risk □ *Providing food for a thousand guests was a huge challenge, but we pulled it off.* **pull something on** if you pull on clothes, you put them on quickly □ *I pulled on an old pair of jeans.* **pull out**

1 to stop being involved in an event or an activity □ *She had to pull out of the race because of injury.*

2 if a car or truck pulls out, it moves onto a road or moves in front of something □ *A huge lorry pulled out right in front of me.*

3 if a train pulls out, it leaves a station **pull (something) out** if an army pulls out of an area, it leaves it □ *They have pulled their forces out of the region.* **pull over** if a vehicle pulls over, it moves to the side of the road and often stops **pull through** to stay alive after a serious illness or injury □ *He has major head injuries, and doctors don't know if he will pull through.* **pull together** to work hard together to achieve something □ *The whole team pulled together to win the cup.* **pull up** if a vehicle pulls up, it stops

► NOUN [plural **pulls**]

1 when you hold something and move it towards you □ *give the handle a pull*

2 no plural the force that causes something to move in a particular direction □ *the pull of gravity*

pull-down menu /'pʊldaʊn ˌmenjuː/ NOUN [plural **pull-down menus**] a list of instructions on a computer screen which only appears when you click on a button. A computing word.

pulley /'pʊlɪ/ NOUN [plural **pulleys**] a piece of equipment for lifting heavy things which consists of a rope and a wheel

pullover /'pʊlˌəʊvə(r)/ NOUN [plural **pullovers**] a piece of clothing for the top part of your body made of wool that you pull over your head

pulmonary /'pʌlmənərɪ/ ADJECTIVE to do with the lungs. A biology word.

pulp /pʌlp/ NOUN, NO PLURAL

1 a soft wet substance that you make by crushing something □ *paper made from wood pulp*

2 the soft flesh of some fruits and vegetables

pulpit /'pʊlpɪt/ NOUN [plural **pulpits**] the high place in a church where a priest stands to talk to people

pulsate /pʌl'seɪt/ VERB [**pulsates, pulsating, pulsated**] to move or make sounds with a strong regular rhythm

pulse /pʌls/ ► NOUN [plural **pulses**]

1 your pulse is the regular movement that you feel on your lower arm or neck, caused by your heart pushing blood through your body 🔄 *The nurse took my pulse* (=counted the number of movements in one minute).

2 pulses seeds that you can eat, for example peas and beans

► VERB [**pulses, pulsing, pulsed**] to move or change with a regular rhythm □ *The lights were pulsing from blue to pink.*

pulverize or **pulverise** /'pʌlvəraɪz/ VERB [**pulverizes, pulverizing, pulverized**] to crush something into many small pieces or into a powder □ *The rock had been pulverized.*

puma /'pju:mə/ NOUN [*plural* **pumas**] a large, wild cat that lives in America

pummel /'pʌməl/ VERB [**pummels, pummelling, pummelled**] to hit something or someone several times with your closed hand □ *He started pummelling on the door.*

pump /pʌmp/ ▶ NOUN [*plural* **pumps**] a piece of equipment that makes a gas or liquid move into or out of something □ *She got a bicycle pump and put some air in the tyres.* ⊞ *a petrol pump* (=for putting petrol into a car) □ *a water pump*
▶ VERB [**pumps, pumping, pumped**] to force liquid or gas to move somewhere □ *Your heart pumps blood around your body.* □ *Water is pumped from the well.*
◆ PHRASAL VERBS **pump something into something** to spend a lot of money on a business or piece of work □ *They have pumped millions of pounds into the business.* **pump something up** to put air into something using a pump □ *Ellie was pumping her bike tyres up.*

pumpkin /'pʌmpkɪn/ NOUN [*plural* **pumpkins**] a large, round, orange vegetable with a thick skin

pun /pʌn/ NOUN [*plural* **puns**] a joke using words that sound the same but have different meanings

punch /pʌntʃ/ ▶ VERB [**punches, punching, punched**]
1 to hit someone or something with your closed hand □ *He punched the man in the face.*
2 to make a small hole in something using a special tool ⊞ *The tool is used for punching holes in metal.*
▶ NOUN [*plural* **punches**]
1 a hit using your closed hand
2 a tool for making a hole in something

punchline /'pʌntʃlaɪn/ NOUN [*plural* **punchlines**] the last line of a joke which is the funny part

punch-up /'pʌntʃʌp/ NOUN [*plural* **punch-ups**] a fight in which people punch each other. An informal word.

punchy /'pʌntʃi/ ADJECTIVE [**punchier, punchiest**] powerful and effective □ *a punchy performance*

punctual /'pʌŋktʃuəl/ ADJECTIVE arriving at exactly the arranged time and not late □ *Robert was always very punctual.* □ *Switzerland has punctual and reliable trains.*
● **punctuality** /ˌpʌŋktʃuˈæləti/ NOUN, NO PLURAL the quality of being punctual
● **punctually** /'pʌŋktʃuəli/ ADVERB at exactly the right time □ *They arrived punctually*

punctuate /'pʌŋktʃueɪt/ VERB [**punctuates, punctuating, punctuated**]
1 to put marks such as , . ! in a piece of writing
2 if something is punctuated with things, these things happen several times in it □ *Her story was punctuated by little squeaks and giggles.*
● **punctuation** /ˌpʌŋktʃuˈeɪʃən/ NOUN, NO PLURAL the use of marks such as , . ! in writing □ *Children find punctuation difficult.*

punctuation mark /ˌpʌŋktʃuˈeɪʃən ˌmɑːk/ NOUN [*plural* **punctuation marks**] one of the marks such as , . ! which are used in writing

puncture /'pʌŋktʃə(r)/ ▶ NOUN [*plural* **punctures**] a small hole made by something sharp, especially in a tyre
▶ VERB [**punctures, puncturing, punctured**] to make a small hole in something □ *A bullet had punctured the fuel tank.*

pungent /'pʌndʒənt/ ADJECTIVE a pungent smell is very strong and sometimes not pleasant □ *the pungent smell of fish*

punish /'pʌnɪʃ/ VERB [**punishes, punishing, punished**] to make someone suffer because they have done something wrong □ **+for** *He was punished for his crimes.* □ **+ by/with** *People who drop litter will be punished with fines.*
● **punishable** /'pʌnɪʃəbəl/ ADJECTIVE having a particular punishment □ *The crime of murder is punishable by death in many countries.*
● **punishing** /'pʌnɪʃɪŋ/ ADJECTIVE involving a lot of work or activity and making you feel extremely tired ⊞ *The Prime Minister has had a punishing schedule in recent weeks.*
● **punishment** /'pʌnɪʃmənt/ NOUN [*plural* **punishments**] something that is done to punish someone ⊞ *He had to stay behind after school as a punishment.* □ **+ for** *The maximum punishment for murder was life sentence in prison.* ⊞ *The old man escaped punishment after promising never to drive again.*

punk /pʌŋk/ NOUN [*plural* **punks**]
1 *no plural* a type of loud music that was especially popular in the 1970s and 1980s
2 someone who likes punk music and often has brightly coloured hair

punnet /'pʌnɪt/ NOUN [*plural* **punnets**] a small box that fruit is sold in

punt /pʌnt/ ▶ NOUN [*plural* **punts**] a boat with a flat bottom that you move by pushing a pole against the bottom of a river
▶ VERB [**punts, punting, punted**] to travel on a river a punt

punter /'pʌntə(r)/ NOUN [*plural* **punters**] an informal word meaning customer □ *He's one of our regular punters.*

puny /'pju:ni/ ADJECTIVE [**punier, puniest**] small and weak □ *a puny boy*

pup /pʌp/ NOUN [*plural* **pups**] a young dog or a young seal (=large animal that lives on land and in the sea

pupa /'pju:pə/ NOUN [*plural* **pupae**] an insect in the stage of development before it becomes an adult. A biology word.

pupil /'pju:pəl/ NOUN [*plural* **pupils**]
1 a student in a school □ *primary school pupils* □ *former pupils of the school*
2 the small black circle in the middle of your eye ⊞ *Pupils dilate to let in more light.*

puppet /ˈpʌpɪt/ NOUN [plural **puppets**] a toy in the shape of an animal or person that you move by pulling strings or by putting it on your hand □ The children enjoyed the puppet show.

puppy /ˈpʌpɪ/ NOUN [plural **puppies**] a young dog

purchase /ˈpɜːtʃəs/ ▶ VERB [**purchases, purchasing, purchased**] a formal word meaning to buy something □ Tickets may be purchased in advance.
▶ NOUN [plural **purchases**]
1 a formal word meaning something you have bought □ I was admiring your purchases.
2 no plural a formal word meaning the act of buying something □ There has been an increase in the purchase of household goods.
• **purchaser** /ˈpɜːtʃəsə(r)/ NOUN [plural **purchasers**] a formal word meaning someone who buys something

pure /pjʊə(r)/ ADJECTIVE [**purer, purest**]
1 not mixed with anything else □ pure gold □ pure oxygen
2 complete □ There was a look of pure joy on his face. ⟐ It was pure chance that we met.
3 clean □ pure water

puree /ˈpjʊəreɪ/ NOUN, NO PLURAL a thick substance made by crushing fruit or vegetables □ tomato puree

purely /ˈpjʊəlɪ/ ADVERB only or simply □ She is criticized purely because of her appearance.

purge /pɜːdʒ/ ▶ VERB [**purges, purging, purged**] to get rid of people or things that are not wanted □ He had tried to purge his political opponents.
▶ NOUN [plural **purges**] the act of getting rid of people or things that are not wanted

purify /ˈpjʊərɪfaɪ/ VERB [**purifies, purifying, purified**] to make something pure by taking out the bad or dirty substances □ The water is then purified.

purity /ˈpjʊərətɪ/ NOUN, NO PLURAL the quality of being pure

purple /ˈpɜːpəl/ ▶ ADJECTIVE having the colour you get if you mix red and blue □ The carpet was dark purple. □ His face was purple with rage.
▶ NOUN, NO PLURAL the colour you get if you mix red and blue

purpose /ˈpɜːpəs/ NOUN [plural **purposes**]
1 what you intend to achieve when you do something □ + of The main purpose of the trip was to improve students' French. ⟐ He had entered the building with the sole purpose of stealing something. □ The website can be used for educational purposes too.
2 on purpose deliberately □ He broke the vase on purpose to annoy me.
3 no plural a feeling of knowing what you want to achieve ⟐ I lack a sense of purpose.

purposeful /ˈpɜːpəsfʊl/ ADJECTIVE showing that you know what you want to achieve □ He walked into the office with a purposeful stride.

purposely /ˈpɜːpəslɪ/ ADVERB deliberately □ She had purposely embarrassed him.

purr /pɜː(r)/ ▶ VERB [**purrs, purring, purred**] a cat purrs when it makes a long, low noise because it is happy
▶ NOUN [plural **purrs**] the long, low noise that a cat makes when it is happy

purse /pɜːs/ ▶ NOUN [plural **purses**]
1 a small container that women carry money in □ She had a lot of money in her purse. □ Mary opened her purse and got out some coins.
2 the US word for handbag
▶ VERB [**purses, pursing, pursed**] purse your lips to bring your lips together tightly in a round shape □ Billy pursed his lips thoughtfully.

pursue /pəˈsjuː/ VERB [**pursues, pursuing, pursued**]
1 to do something or try to achieve something over a period of time □ She wanted to pursue a career in the media.
2 to continue discussing something or trying to find out about something ⟐ She looked a bit embarrassed so I didn't pursue the matter.
3 to chase someone or something in order to catch them □ Should the police pursue stolen cars at high speed?
• **pursuer** /pəˈsjuːə(r)/ NOUN [plural **pursuers**] someone who is chasing someone or something in order to catch them
• **pursuit** /pəˈsjuːt/ NOUN [plural **pursuits**]
1 no plural the act of chasing someone or something ⟐ The dogs were in pursuit of a hare.
2 no plural when you try to achieve something, usually over a period of time □ the pursuit of happiness
3 pursuits a formal word meaning hobbies ⟐ She enjoys walking, climbing and other outdoor pursuits.

pus /pʌs/ NOUN, NO PLURAL a thick yellow substance that forms in an infected part of your body

push /pʊʃ/ ▶ VERB [**pushes, pushing, pushed**]
1 to press against someone or something with your hands or body, so that they move □ I had to push him up the hill in his wheelchair. □ The new tooth is pushing the old one out. □ She pushed the door open. □ He pushed back his chair.
2 to go in a particular direction, moving people out of your way □ He pushed to the front of the queue. □ I tried to push closer to the stage.
3 to try to make someone do something they do not want to do □ + into He was pushed into accepting the job. □ + to do something They pushed me to agree to the plan.
4 to make someone work very hard □ Our teachers pushed us to the limit. □ In this sport, you really have to push yourself.
5 to make something reach a particular level, value, etc. □ Inflation is pushing prices up.
♦ IDIOM push your luck to take a big risk that may result in failure or trouble □ They offered us a bed for the night, but we thought that asking for a car as well would be pushing our luck.
♦ PHRASAL VERBS push someone about/around to force someone to do what you want them to do □ I'm

fed up with letting my family push me around. **push ahead/forward** to continue with something, even if there are difficulties □ *The government is pushing ahead with tax reforms.* **push for something** to try to achieve something or get something □ *We are pushing for better working conditions.* **push in** to join a queue (=line of people waiting) in front of people who were there before you **push on**

1 to make an effort to make progress with something □ *We need to push on and finish the digging.*

2 to continue a journey □ *We decided to push on to Tokyo.* **push someone/something over** to push someone or something so that they fall □ *He pushed his friend over in the playground.* **push something through** to get a law, plan, etc. accepted □ *The government is pushing through new legislation on hunting.*

▶ NOUN [*plural* **pushes**]

1 when you press against someone or something with your hands or body, so that it moves □ *The door's a bit stiff – give it a good push.*

2 an effort to achieve something □ **+ for** *He is stepping up his training in a final push for a gold medal.*

3 if you give someone a push, you encourage them to do something □ *He's capable of passing his exams, but he'll need a push.*

4 the push if you get the push, you have to leave your job. An informal phrase.

5 at a push if you say that something is possible at a push, it is possible but not easy □ *I can get five people in my car, or six at a push.*

pushchair /ˈpʊʃtʃeə(r)/ NOUN [*plural* **pushchairs**] a chair on wheels used for pushing a young child around

pushy /ˈpʊʃi/ ADJECTIVE [**pushier, pushiest**] behaving in an unpleasant way because you are determined to get what you want or determined to make someone do something □ *The school often has to deal with pushy parents.*

pussy /ˈpʊsi/ *or* **pussycat** /ˈpʊsikæt/ NOUN [*plural* **pussies** *or* **pussycats**] an informal word meaning cat, which is often used by children

put /pʊt/ VERB [**puts, putting, put**]

1 to move something to a place or position □ *Put the shopping on the table.* □ *He put his hands in the air.* □ *She put her arms around me.*

2 to cause someone or something to be in a particular situation or state □ *Your actions put lives at risk.* □ *He put pressure on me to agree to the proposal.* □ *He was put to death.* □ *Plans for the office move have been put in place.*

3 put something into effect/practice, etc. to make something start to work or be used □ *We learned some new exercise techniques, which I'll be putting into practice next week.*

4 put a stop/end to something to make something stop □ *We must put a stop to this bad behaviour in class.*

5 to say or write something in a particular way □ *She*

described him as 'unusual', which is a polite way of putting it.

6 to write something □ *Where do I put my address?* □ *I need to leave her a message, but I'm not sure what to put.*

➔ go to put your *feet* up, put your *foot* down, put your *foot* in it, put your *mind* to something, put your *mind* at rest, put someone in their *place*, put *two* and two together

◆ PHRASAL VERBS **put something across/over** to explain something □ *They used computer graphics to help put across their ideas.* **put something aside**

1 to keep something so that it can be used later □ *We put aside a bit of money each month to use for birthdays.*

2 to not allow yourself to be affected by an emotion, opinion or problem □ *In a disaster situation, governments must put aside politics and work together.* **put something away**

1 to put something in the place where it is kept □ *He never puts his clothes away.*

2 if you put money away, you save it, usually in a bank **put something back** to put something in the place where it came from □ *Could you put the milk back in the fridge?* **put someone/something down** to put someone or something onto a surface □ *He put down the gun.* **put someone down** to criticize someone and make them feel stupid or not important **put something down** if a protest (=when people complain publicly about something) or an attempt to take control of a country or area is put down, it is stopped with force □ *Troops were sent in to put down the uprising.* **put someone down for something** to put someone's name on a list to do something or to become a member of an organization □ *We've put James down to do karate.* **put something down to something** to think that something is the reason for a situation □ *He puts his poor performance down to a knee injury.* **put forward something** to state an idea, opinion, etc. for other people to consider □ *They put forward a proposal to get the club out of debt.* **put in something/put something into something** to spend money, time or energy doing something □ *They put a lot of effort into the play.* **put off something** to delay doing something □ *I know I'll need an operation on my shoulder, but I'm trying to put it off as long as possible.* **put someone off** to prevent someone from concentrating **put someone off (something)** to make someone not want to do something or not want to have something □ *That fall put me off climbing for ever.* **put something on**

1 to start wearing something □ *You'd better put on a coat.*

2 to make a machine or piece of equipment start working □ *Shall we put the heating on?*

3 put on weight to become fatter **put something out**

1 to make a fire stop burning □ *Firefighters were called to put out the blaze.*

2 to turn a light off **put someone through** to connect someone to the person they want to speak to on the telephone □ *Just a moment, I'll put you through to the accounts department.* **put someone through something** to make someone experience something unpleasant □ *The job would have meant moving house every six months, and I couldn't put my family through that.* **put something to someone** to suggest something to someone □ *I'll put your offer to him and see what he thinks.* **put something up**
1 to build something such as a wall or fence □ *They put up a barrier between the two areas.*
2 to fasten something to a wall □ *We put up signs advertising the concert.*
3 put up the price/cost of something to increase the price of something **put someone up** to let someone stay in your home for a few days □ *I put her up while she looked for a job.* **put up with someone/something** to accept a situation or someone's behaviour although you do not like it □ *I can't put up with his laziness any longer!*

---

putrid /ˈpjuːtrɪd/ ADJECTIVE rotten and smelling bad □ *putrid meat*

putt /pʌt/ ▶ VERB [**putts, putting, putted**] in golf, to hit a ball gently so that it rolls towards the hole ▶ NOUN [*plural* **putts**] in golf, a gentle hit of the ball that you make so that it will go into the hole

putty /ˈpʌti/ NOUN, NO PLURAL a soft substance used for fixing glass in window frames

puzzle /ˈpʌzəl/ ▶ NOUN [*plural* **puzzles**]
1 a game or toy that gives you a problem to solve 🕮 *Ben was doing a jigsaw puzzle.*
2 something that is difficult to understand

🕮 *Researchers hope to solve the puzzle of why some children develop the disease.*
▶ VERB [**puzzles, puzzling, puzzled**] if something puzzles you, you feel confused because you do not understand it □ *Their unexplained deaths puzzled police for years.*
◆ PHRASAL VERB **puzzle over something** to think about something carefully and for a long time in order to understand it □ *Doctors have puzzled over why women are more likely to suffer from the disease.*
● **puzzled** /ˈpʌzəld/ ADJECTIVE confused and not understanding something □ *She had a puzzled look on her face.*
● **puzzling** /ˈpʌzlɪŋ/ ADJECTIVE difficult to understand □ *puzzling behaviour*

PVC /ˌpiːviːˈsiː/ ABBREVIATION polyvinyl chloride; a type of plastic

pyjamas /pəˈdʒɑːməz/ PLURAL NOUN loose trousers and a shirt that you wear in bed 🕮 *He was wearing a pair of pyjamas.* □ *silk pyjamas*

pylon /ˈpaɪlən/ NOUN [*plural* **pylons**] a tall metal structure that supports electric wires

pyramid /ˈpɪrəmɪd/ NOUN [*plural* **pyramids**] a solid shape with a square base and triangular sides which form a point at the top

pyre /ˈpaɪə(r)/ NOUN [*plural* **pyres**] a pile of wood for burning dead bodies on

Pyrex /ˈpaɪəreks/ NOUN, NO PLURAL a type of glass used for making dishes that can be used in an oven. A trademark. □ *a Pyrex bowl*

python /ˈpaɪθən/ NOUN [*plural* **pythons**] a large snake that kills animals by winding itself around them

Qq

Q *or* **q** /kjuː/ the 17th letter of the alphabet

quack /kwæk/ ▶ NOUN [*plural* **quacks**] the sound made by a duck (=a common water bird)
▶ VERB [**quacks, quacking, quacked**] to make the sound of a duck

quadrant /ˈkwɒdrənt/ NOUN [*plural* **quadrants**] a shape that is a quarter of a circle. A maths word.

quadrilateral /ˌkwɒdrɪˈlætərəl/ NOUN [*plural* **quadrilaterals**] any shape with four sides. A maths word.

quadruped /ˈkwɒdrʊped/ NOUN [*plural* **quadrupeds**] an animal that has four feet. A biology word.

quadruple /kwɒˈdruːpəl/ ▶ VERB [**quadruples, quadrupling, quadrupled**] to become four times bigger or to make something four times bigger □ *The shopkeeper had quadrupled the price.*
▶ ADJECTIVE made up of four parts or events, or four times more than usual □ *a quadruple murder*

quadruplet /ˈkwɒdrʊplɪt/ NOUN [*plural* **quadruplets**] one of four children born at one time to the same mother

quagmire /ˈkwæɡmaɪə(r)/ NOUN [*plural* **quagmires**]
1 an area of soft, very wet ground □ *Heavy rain had turned the garden into a quagmire.*
2 a difficult and complicated situation □ *He has become bogged down in a political quagmire.*

quail /kweɪl/ NOUN [*plural* **quail** *or* **quails**] a small brown bird that is hunted for food

quaint /kweɪnt/ ADJECTIVE [**quainter, quaintest**] old-fashioned in a pleasant or attractive way □ *a quaint little fishing village*

quake /kweɪk/ ▶ VERB [**quakes, quaking, quaked**]
1 to be very frightened or nervous so that your body shakes □ *She was quaking in fear.*
2 to shake violently □ *The ground quaked under their feet.*
▶ NOUN [*plural* **quakes**] a short way to say and write earthquake

qualification /ˌkwɒlɪfɪˈkeɪʃən/ NOUN [*plural* **qualifications**]
1 an exam you have passed or a course you have completed ▣ *He lacks formal academic qualifications.* ▣ *She gained her teaching qualification at Leeds University.*
2 a skill or quality you have that makes you suitable for a job or position □ + *for* *His only qualification for the job was some experience in journalism.*
3 *no plural* when you do what is needed to get

something such as a place in a competition □ + *for* *They missed out on qualification for the World Cup.*
4 something you add to what you say to make it less strong or less certain □ *He welcomed the proposals, but with one qualification.*

● **qualified** /ˈkwɒlɪfaɪd/ ADJECTIVE
1 having the qualifications needed for a job □ *a qualified teacher.* □ *He was the most qualified candidate.*
2 having the skills or knowledge needed to do something □ *Alison would be better qualified to comment on that.*
3 not completely certain or positive because of some doubts or limits □ *Unions gave their qualified backing to the proposals.*

● **qualifier** /ˈkwɒlɪfaɪə(r)/ NOUN [*plural* **qualifiers**]
1 a game that someone must win to enter the main part of a sports competition □ *His next game will be the European Championship qualifier against Italy.*
2 a person or a team that has won a game to enter the main part of a competition

● **qualify** /ˈkwɒlɪfaɪ/ VERB [**qualifies, qualifying, qualified**]
1 to have the qualities that make you suitable for something or give you the right to something □ + *for* *They qualify for free legal advice.* □ + *as* *The family do not qualify as refugees.*
2 to pass an exam or to complete a course needed to do a job □ + *as* *He qualified as a lawyer.* □ + *in* *She qualified in medicine in London.*
3 to do what is needed to enter a competition or the next stage of a competition □ + *for* *Australia qualified for the finals.*
4 to add something to what you have said to make it less strong or less certain □ *He qualified his comment by adding that he didn't expect much progress this year.*

quality /ˈkwɒlɪtɪ/ ▶ NOUN [*plural* **qualities**]
1 how good or bad something is ▣ *All our courses are of a very high quality.* □ + *of* *The quality of her work is much better now.* ▣ *Your health affects your quality of life.* ▣ *We are taking measures to improve air quality.*
2 *no plural* when something is of a very good standard □ *The company has a reputation for quality.*
3 a part of someone's character □ *Her best qualities are her kindness and honesty.*
4 a feature of something □ + *of* *The unique qualities of the soil here produce excellent grapes.*

▶ ADJECTIVE of a high standard □ *a quality brand*
□ *There's a need for more quality childcare facilities.*

qualms /kwɑ:mz/ NOUN, NO PLURAL doubts about whether something is right, especially morally ⓖ *He has no qualms about dismissing staff who can't do the job.*

quandary /ˈkwɒndərɪ/ NOUN [plural **quandaries**] a situation in which it is very difficult to make a decision □ *Ann was in a quandary over whether to move to Australia.*

quantity /ˈkwɒntətɪ/ NOUN [plural **quantities**] the amount or number of something □ + *of* We only need a small quantity of paper. □ *People throw away huge quantities of food.* ⓖ *It can be produced cheaply and in large quantities.* ⓖ *We need to improve both the quantity and quality of facilities.*

quarantine /ˈkwɒrəntiːn/ ▶ NOUN, NO PLURAL when a person or an animal is kept away from other people or animals because they have or might have a disease □ *The animals were being held in quarantine.*
▶ VERB [**quarantines, quarantining, quarantined**] to put a person or an animal in quarantine

quarrel /ˈkwɒrəl/ ▶ VERB [**quarrels, quarrelling**/US **quarreling, quarrelled**/US **quarreled**] to argue about something, usually with someone you know well □ *I've quarrelled with my brother.*
▶ NOUN [plural **quarrels**] an argument, usually with someone you know well □ *I've had a quarrel with the manager.*

quarry /ˈkwɒrɪ/ ▶ NOUN [plural **quarries**]
1 a place where stone is dug out of the ground □ *a limestone quarry*
2 an animal that is being hunted □ *He caught sight of his quarry a few metres away.*
▶ VERB [**quarries, quarrying, quarried**] to dig stone out of the ground

quart /kwɔ:t/ NOUN [plural **quarts**] a unit for measuring liquids, equal to 2 pints

quarter /ˈkwɔ:tə(r)/ ▶ NOUN [plural **quarters**]
1 1/4 ; one of four equal parts of something □ *We cut the cake into quarters.*
2 **quarter past/to** 15 minutes after/before the hour □ *He arrived at quarter past three.*
3 **quarter after/of** the US phrase for 15 minutes after/before the hour
4 one of four equal parts of a year □ *In the first quarter, the company made a profit.*
5 a coin with the value of 25 cents
▶ VERB [**quarters, quartering, quartered**] to divide something into four equal parts □ *She quartered the melon.*

quarter-final /ˌkwɔ:təˈfaɪnəl/ NOUN [plural **quarter-finals**] the part of a competition involving the last eight teams or players □ *She reached the quarter-finals of the French Open.*

quarterly /ˈkwɔ:təlɪ/ ADJECTIVE, ADVERB happening, done or produced every three months □ *quarterly payments*

quarters /ˈkwɔ:təz/ PLURAL NOUN rooms to stay in, especially for soldiers ⓖ *He showed them to their sleeping quarters.*

quartet /kwɔ:ˈtet/ NOUN [plural **quartets**]
1 a group of four musicians or singers □ *a string quartet*
2 a piece of music written for four musicians or singers

quartz /kwɔ:ts/ NOUN, NO PLURAL a hard substance found in rocks that can be used in clocks and watches

quash /kwɒʃ/ VERB [**quashes, quashing, quashed**]
1 to stop something you do not like from continuing ⓖ *He was keen to quash the rumours.*
2 to officially change a legal decision ⓖ *An appeal court quashed his conviction.*

quasi- /ˈkweɪzaɪ/ PREFIX quasi- is added to the beginning of words to mean 'almost, but not quite' □ *She has a quasi-official role.*

quaver /ˈkweɪvə(r)/ ▶ VERB [**quavers, quavering, quavered**] if your voice quavers, it shakes slightly □ *Her voice quavered with fright as she spoke.*
▶ NOUN [plural **quavers**] when your voice quavers

quay /ki:/ NOUN [plural **quays**] a hard area built next to the water where things are put onto and taken off ships

queasy /ˈkwi:zɪ/ ADJECTIVE [**queasier, queasiest**] feeling like you might vomit □ *The motion of the boat made her queasy.*

queen /kwi:n/ NOUN [plural **queens**]
1 a woman who rules a country which has a royal family □ *Queen Elizabeth II* □ + *of* the Queen of Denmark
2 the wife of a king
3 a woman who is the most successful or most important in a particular area □ + *of* Madonna, the queen of pop
4 a playing card with a picture of a queen on it □ *the queen of hearts*
5 in the game of chess, the piece that has a crown and can move in any direction
6 the largest female insect in a group, that produces eggs □ *a queen bee*

queer /kwɪə(r)/ ADJECTIVE [**queerer, queerest**] strange or unusual □ *queer behaviour*

quench /kwentʃ/ VERB [**quenches, quenching, quenched**] **quench your thirst** to drink until you no longer feel thirsty

query /ˈkwɪərɪ/ ▶ NOUN [plural **queries**] a question □ *Please phone me if you have any queries.*
▶ VERB [**queries, querying, queried**] to question whether something is correct or true □ *I rang the gas company to query my bill.*

quest /kwest/ NOUN [plural **quests**] a search for something or an attempt to do something, especially a long and difficult one □ *He vowed to continue his quest for justice.*

question /'kwestʃən/ ▶ NOUN [plural questions]
1 the words you say or write when you want to ask something 🖫 After the talk, some people asked questions. 🖫 He refused to answer my question. 🖫 She faced some tough questions about how the money was spent.
2 a situation or problem that needs to be discussed or solved □ There is the question of how much to pay him. 🖫 We need to address the question of funding. 🖫 Toni raised the question of transport.
3 a doubt about something □ + over There is still a question over ownership of the building. 🖫 Staffing difficulties have called into question their ability to do the work. 🖫 This incident has raised questions about airport security.
4 no question of something no possibility that something will happen or be agreed to □ There's no question of him leaving.
5 be a question of something used to talk about the most important fact in a situation □ It's a question of cost.
6 in question the person or thing in question is the person or thing being talked about □ The patient in question has a history of mental illness.
7 out of the question if you say that something is out of the question, you are emphasizing that it is not possible □ A pay rise is out of the question at the moment.
▶ VERB [questions, questioning, questioned]
1 to ask someone questions, often officially □ She was questioned by the military police. □ He questioned me about where I had found the jewels. □ He questioned why I had decided to leave my job.
2 to express doubts about something □ They questioned the truth of his statement. 🖫 I would question the wisdom of buying a house at the moment.
● **questionable** /'kwestʃənəbəl/ ADJECTIVE
1 possibly not true or completely correct □ The official government statistics look questionable to me.
2 possibly not honest or legal □ They were involved in some highly questionable deals.
● **questioning** /'kwestʃənɪŋ/ NOUN, NO PLURAL when someone is asked questions, especially by the police □ He was brought in for questioning over the robbery.

question mark /'kwestʃən ˌmɑːk/ NOUN [plural question marks] the mark (?) that you write after a sentence which is a question

questionnaire /ˌkwestʃə'neə(r)/ NOUN [plural questionnaires] a list of questions to be answered by several people to get information 🖫 The students were asked to complete a short questionnaire.

queue /kjuː/ ▶ NOUN [plural queues] a line of people waiting for something □ + of There was a long queue of people waiting for taxis. 🖫 We joined the queue for tickets.
▶ VERB [queues, queuing, queued] to stand in a queue □ We had to queue for three hours to get the tickets.

quibble /'kwɪbəl/ ▶ VERB [quibbles, quibbling, quibbled] to argue or to complain about details that are not important □ They were quibbling over who should pay for what.
▶ NOUN [plural quibbles] a complaint or criticism about a detail that is not important

quiche /kiːʃ/ NOUN [plural quiches] an open pastry case filled with eggs and cheese, often with vegetables or meat

quick /kwɪk/ ▶ ADJECTIVE [quicker, quickest]
1 taking a short time □ Can we take a quick break? □ I had a quick look at the website.
2 fast □ He's very quick on his feet.
3 quick to do something doing something immediately or very soon □ She's always quick to help. □ He was quick to see the business opportunity.
▶ ADVERB an informal word meaning quickly □ Come quick! □ It all happened so quick.
● **quickly** /'kwɪklɪ/ ADVERB
1 in a short time or immediately □ I get bored quickly. □ He quickly realized his mistake. 🖫 I need to sort this out as quickly as possible.
2 fast □ He had to move quickly. □ The fire quickly spread.
● **quickness** /'kwɪknɪs/ NOUN, NO PLURAL the quality of being quick □ I was surprised by the quickness of his reply.

quicksand /'kwɪksænd/ NOUN, NO PLURAL loose wet sand that things sink into

quick-tempered /ˌkwɪk'tempəd/ ADJECTIVE getting angry easily □ He was unfriendly and quick-tempered.

quid /kwɪd/ NOUN [plural quid] an informal word for a pound (£1) □ He paid fifty quid for the jacket.

quiet /'kwaɪət/ ▶ ADJECTIVE [quieter, quietest]
1 making little noise or no noise □ a quiet voice 🖫 He asked everyone to be quiet. 🖫 He kept quiet, not wanting to disturb her.
2 calm and without much activity □ It was a quiet street with little traffic. □ It had been a relatively quiet week.
3 not saying very much □ He was quite quiet and shy
4 felt, but not expressed □ There was a quiet confidence about him.
5 keep (something) quiet to not speak about something because it is a secret □ He was told to keep quiet about the payments.
▶ NOUN, NO PLURAL a quiet situation or time □ She returned to the quiet of her room. 🖫 All he wanted was a bit of peace and quiet.
▶ VERB [quiets, quieting, quieted] to make someone calm and quiet □ He raised a hand to quiet the crowd
● **quieten** /'kwaɪətən/ VERB [quietens, quietening, quietened] to become quiet and calm or to make someone or something quiet and calm □ Things seem to have quietened down. □ Her mother was trying to quieten her.
● **quietly** /'kwaɪətlɪ/ ADVERB

1 with little or no noise □ *She slipped quietly from the room.* □ *'It's okay,' she said quietly.*
2 in a calm way that is not obvious □ *He was quietly confident.*
• **quietness** /'kwaɪətnɪs/ NOUN, NO PLURAL the state or quality of being quiet □ *I like the quietness of early morning.*

quill /kwɪl/ NOUN [*plural* **quills**] a large feather made into a pen

quilt /kwɪlt/ NOUN [*plural* **quilts**] a warm cover for a bed, filled with feathers or another soft material
• **quilted** /'kwɪltɪd/ ADJECTIVE made of two layers of cloth with a soft material between them □ *a quilted jacket*

quintet /ˌkwɪn'tet/ NOUN [*plural* **quintets**]
1 a group of five musicians or singers
2 a piece of music written for five musicians or singers

quintuplet /ˌkwɪn'tju:plɪt/ NOUN [*plural* **quintuplets**] one of five children born at one time to the same mother

quip /kwɪp/ ▶ NOUN [*plural* **quips**] a clever and funny remark or reply
▶ VERB [**quips, quipping, quipped**] to make a quip
□ *'Flattery will get you everywhere,' she quipped.*

quirk /kwɜ:k/ NOUN [*plural* **quirks**]
1 something strange or unusual in a person's behaviour □ *Wearing odd socks is just one of his little quirks.*
2 something strange or unexpected that happens 🗗 *By a quirk of fate, they met again years later.*
• **quirky** /'kwɜ:kɪ/ ADJECTIVE [**quirkier, quirkiest**] strange and unusual □ *a quirky sense of humour*

quit /kwɪt/ VERB [**quits, quitting, quit**]
1 to leave a job, school, etc. □ *He's quit his job.* □ *She quit university to become a singer.*
2 to stop doing something □ *I'm going to quit smoking.*

quite /kwaɪt/ ADVERB
1 to some degree but not very or completely □ *I'm quite hungry but I don't mind waiting.* □ *I'm quite nervous about it.* □ *They're quite likely to win.*
2 completely □ *I'm afraid I'm not quite ready.* □ *She made her position quite clear.* □ *It had quite the opposite effect.*
3 quite a bit/a few/a while, etc. a large amount, a long time, etc. compared to what is normal or expected □ *He lost quite a bit of money.* □ *It took us quite a while.*
4 used for emphasis □ *It was really quite amazing.* □ *It was quite an experience.*

5 used to agree with something someone has just said □ *'If he's twenty, he shouldn't expect his mother to cook for him.' 'Quite.'*

quits /kwɪts/ ADJECTIVE if two people are quits, they do not owe each other anything, especially money □ *I've paid for the damage to your car – now we're quits.*

quitter /'kwɪtə(r)/ NOUN [*plural* **quitters**] an informal word meaning someone who stops trying to do something too easily

quiver /'kwɪvə(r)/ ▶ VERB [**quivers, quivering, quivered**] to shake slightly □ *Her lip quivered and her eyes filled with tears.*
▶ NOUN [*plural* **quivers**] when something quivers □ *There was a slight quiver in his voice.*

quiz /kwɪz/ ▶ NOUN [*plural* **quizzes**] a competition in which you have to answer questions □ *a general knowledge quiz*
▶ VERB [**quizzes, quizzing, quizzed**] to ask someone a lot of questions □ *He was quizzed by police.*

quizzical /'kwɪzɪkəl/ ADJECTIVE showing that you do not understand or believe something 🗗 *She gave him a quizzical look.*

quota /'kwəʊtə/ NOUN [*plural* **quotas**] an amount that someone is allowed to have or has to do □ *EU fishing quotas* □ *We all have to achieve our quota of sales.*

quotation /kwəʊ'teɪʃən/ NOUN [*plural* **quotations**]
1 a set of words taken from a speech or piece of writing □ *a quotation from Shakespeare*
2 a price which someone gives you for doing a job □ *I'd like a quotation for replacing these missing roof tiles.*

quotation marks /kwəʊ'teɪʃən ˌmɑ:ks/ PLURAL NOUN the symbols ' ' or " " used in writing to show that someone's words are being repeated exactly

quote /kwəʊt/ ▶ VERB [**quotes, quoting, quoted**]
1 to repeat someone's words exactly as they said or wrote them □ *He quoted a passage from the Bible.* □ *One newspaper quoted him as saying: 'People are only interested in price.'*
2 to say how much money you will charge for doing something □ *He quoted a price for repairing the bicycle.*
▶ NOUN [*plural* **quotes**]
1 words which are quoted □ *a famous quote from Adam Smith*
2 a price quoted for a job 🗗 *He gave me a quote for the repairs.*

Qur'an /kə'rɑ:n/ NOUN another spelling of Koran

R *or* **r** /ɑː(r)/ the 18th letter of the alphabet

rabbi /ˈræbaɪ/ NOUN [*plural* **rabbis**] a Jewish religious leader

rabbit /ˈræbɪt/ NOUN [*plural* **rabbits**] a small animal with long ears and soft fur, which people keep as a pet, or which lives in holes in the ground □ *She let me stroke her pet rabbit.*

rabble /ˈræbəl/ NOUN, NO PLURAL a noisy group of people who are behaving badly

rabid /ˈræbɪd, ˈreɪbɪd/ ADJECTIVE
1 having extremely strong opinions, or behaving in an angry and often unpleasant way □ *My brother is a rabid fan of rap music.*
2 suffering from rabies □ *a rabid dog*

rabies /ˈreɪbiːz/ NOUN, NO PLURAL a serious disease caused by being bitten by an infected animal

race /reɪs/ ▶ NOUN [*plural* **races**]
1 a competition to see who can get somewhere fastest or do something fastest □ *I'm running in a race this weekend.* ⊞ *Lewis won the race.*
2 one of the groups that people can be divided into according to their skin colour and physical characteristics □ *It's our hope that people of all races can live together in peace.*
3 a competition to get a position of power ⊞ *Kerry was defeated in the US presidential race of 2004.*
□ + **for** *Johnson won the race for mayor of London.*
4 *no plural* a situation in which a person or group tries to be the first to do something □ + **to do something** *Scientists were involved in the race to find a cure for AIDS.*
5 a race against time/the clock a situation in which something must be done in a very short time
□ *Paterson is facing a race against time to be fit for Friday's game.*
▶ VERB [**races, racing, raced**]
1 to compete against someone in a race □ *I'll race you to the postbox.* □ + **against** *His horse will be racing against some of the best horses in the country.*
2 to go somewhere very quickly, or to move someone or something very quickly □ + **to** *Ambulances raced to the scene of the accident.* □ *Emma raced down the stairs to answer the door.* □ *He was raced to hospital with a suspected heart attack.*
3 if your heart or mind races, it works at a faster speed than normal □ *I could feel my heart racing with*

excitement. □ *My mind was racing after such a busy and eventful day.*
4 to use an animal or a vehicle to compete in races □ *My Grandad raced horses for more than 40 years.*

racecourse /ˈreɪskɔːs/ NOUN [*plural* **racecourses**] the track that horses race on

racehorse /ˈreɪshɔːs/ NOUN [*plural* **racehorses**] a horse that competes in races

racial /ˈreɪʃəl/ ADJECTIVE to do with a person's race
□ *racial discrimination*
● **racially** /ˈreɪʃəli/ ADVERB in a way that is to do with someone's race □ *They consider themselves racially distinct from their neighbours.*

racing /ˈreɪsɪŋ/ NOUN, NO PLURAL the sport of racing animals or vehicles ⊞ *Dad watches horse racing on the television.* ⊞ *He's one of the most famous people in motor racing.* ⊞ *a racing driver*

racism /ˈreɪsɪzəm/ ▶ NOUN, NO PLURAL unfair treatment of someone or dislike of someone because they belong to a different race □ *The scheme aims to tackle racism in schools.* □ *He was a victim of racism.*
● **racist** /ˈreɪsɪst/ ADJECTIVE to do with racism □ *racist remarks*
▶ NOUN [*plural* **racists**] someone who dislikes people or treats them unfairly because they belong to a different race

rack /ræk/ ▶ NOUN [*plural* **racks**] a place where things are kept, usually made of narrow pieces of wood or metal □ *I put my bag in the luggage rack.*
▶ VERB [**racks, racking, racked**]
1 if you are racked with pain or with a feeling, you suffer a lot because of it □ *She was racked with guilt that she hadn't done more to save his life.*
2 rack your brains an informal phrase meaning to think very hard to think of something □ *I've racked my brains but I can't think of an answer to the problem.*

racket /ˈrækɪt/ NOUN [*plural* **rackets**]
1 a piece of equipment that you use for hitting the ball in games such as tennis □ *a tennis racket*
2 an informal word meaning a loud and unpleasant noise ⊞ *They were making a terrible racket.*
3 an informal word meaning an illegal way of making money □ *He had been involved in a smuggling racket.*

radar /'reɪdɑː(r)/ NOUN [plural **radars**] a system or piece of equipment that uses radio waves to find the position of aeroplanes, ships, etc.

radiance /'reɪdɪəns/ NOUN, NO PLURAL
1 happiness that shows on your face
2 how bright something is
• **radiant** /'reɪdɪənt/ ADJECTIVE
1 showing that you are very happy □ *a radiant smile*
2 bright □ *radiant sunshine*

radiate /'reɪdɪeɪt/ VERB [**radiates, radiating, radiated**]
1 to show an emotion or quality in your face or behaviour □ *Wendi radiated confidence.*
2 to send out heat or light □ *She was enjoying the warmth radiating from the log fire.*
3 to spread out in different directions from a central point □ *Secret alleyways radiate from the harbour.*
• **radiation** /,reɪdɪ'eɪʃən/ NOUN, NO PLURAL
1 energy from a nuclear reaction which can harm or kill people. A physics word □ *radiation sickness* □ *They were exposed to high levels of radiation.*
2 heat or light in the form of waves which you cannot see. A physics word □ *solar radiation*
• **radiator** /'reɪdɪeɪtə(r)/ NOUN [plural **radiators**]
1 a metal object that is filled with hot water to heat a room
2 part of an engine that keeps it cool

radical /'rædɪkəl/ ▶ ADJECTIVE
1 believing that there should be big political and social changes □ *radical views*
2 big and important □ *radical changes*
▶ NOUN [plural **radicals**] someone who believes that there should be big political and social changes
• **radically** /'rædɪkəli/ ADVERB in a big and important way 🔁 *The new system is radically different from what we had before.*

radio /'reɪdɪəʊ/ ▶ NOUN [plural **radios**]
1 a piece of equipment that you use for listening to programmes which are broadcast 🔁 *Raj switched the radio on to hear the news.* □ *He bought a digital radio.*
2 *no plural* programmes that you listen to using a radio 🔁 *I enjoy listening to the radio.* 🔁 *The local radio station broadcasts travel news.* 🔁 *a radio show* □ *James is a radio presenter.*
3 *no plural* a system of broadcasting that uses sound waves to send messages □ *He gave orders by radio.* 🔁 *They lost radio contact with the crew.*
4 a piece of electrical equipment, for example on a ship or plane, that receives or sends messages as sound waves
▶ VERB [**radios, radioing, radioed**] to communicate with someone by radio □ *The captain of the ship radioed for help.*

radioactive /,reɪdɪəʊ'æktɪv/ ADJECTIVE sending out harmful radiation (=energy from a nuclear reaction). A physics word □ *radioactive substances*
radioactivity /,reɪdɪəʊæk'tɪvəti/ NOUN, NO PLURAL

harmful energy that is produced by a radioactive substance. A physics word.
radiographer /,reɪdɪ'ɒɡrəfə(r)/ NOUN [plural **radiographers**] someone whose job is to do X-rays (=pictures of the inside of someone's body) in a hospital
• **radiography** /,reɪdɪ'ɒɡrəfi/ NOUN, NO PLURAL the job or science of doing X-rays

radiotherapy /,reɪdɪəʊ'θerəpi/ NOUN, NO PLURAL the use of radiation (=energy from a nuclear reaction) to treat diseases such as cancer

radish /'rædɪʃ/ NOUN [plural **radishes**] a small round vegetable with a red skin and strong taste that is eaten raw in salads

radius /'reɪdɪəs/ NOUN [plural **radii**]
1 within a 15 mile/10 km, etc. radius less than 15 miles/10 kilometres, etc. from a particular place □ *We deliver anywhere within a ten-mile radius of the store.*
2 the distance from the centre of a circle to the edge. A maths word.

raffle /'ræfəl/ ▶ NOUN [plural **raffles**] a competition in which people buy a ticket with a number on, and win a prize if their number is chosen 🔁 *Would you like to buy a raffle ticket?*
▶ VERB [**raffles, raffling, raffled**] to offer something as a prize in a raffle

raft /rɑːft/ NOUN [plural **rafts**]
1 a flat boat made from long pieces of wood tied together
2 a raft of something a lot of things □ *They have a raft of issues to deal with.*

rafter /'rɑːftə(r)/ NOUN [plural **rafters**] one of the sloping pieces of wood that form the frame of a roof

rag /ræɡ/ NOUN [plural **rags**] an old piece of cloth □ *an oily rag*
➔ *go to* **rags**

rage /reɪdʒ/ ▶ NOUN, NO PLURAL
1 extreme anger that you cannot control □ *He killed his wife in a fit of jealous rage.* 🔁 *I've never seen him fly into a rage (=become extremely angry) like that before.*
2 all the rage an informal phrase meaning fashionable or popular □ *These tiny bags are all the rage.*
▶ VERB [**rages, raging, raged**]
1 to continue with a lot of force, violence or anger □ *The fire raged for almost a week.* □ *Debate is still raging over whether he should be prosecuted.*
2 to speak in an angry way □ *'Don't you touch her!' John raged.*

ragged /'ræɡɪd/ ADJECTIVE
1 torn and untidy □ *ragged clothes*
2 having a rough edge □ *a ragged hole*

rags /ræɡz/ PLURAL NOUN
1 clothes which are old and torn □ *The children were dressed in rags.*
2 rags to riches used for describing a situation in which someone who is very poor becomes very rich □ *Her life had been a rags to riches story.*

raid /reɪd/ ▶ NOUN [plural **raids**]
1 a sudden military attack □ *a bombing raid*
2 a sudden unexpected visit from the police, who enter a building and search it □ *Guns were found during a police raid on the house.*
3 a violent attack on a bank, shop, etc. to steal things □ *He was arrested for a £250,000 raid on a jeweller's shop.*
▶ VERB [**raids, raiding, raided**]
1 to attack a place using weapons □ *Troops raided villages.*
2 to use force to enter a place in order to search it □ *Police raided the premises and questioned staff.*
3 to attack a place in order to steal things □ *Armed robbers raided her home.*
• **raider** /'reɪdə(r)/ NOUN [plural **raiders**] someone who attacks a place, especially to steal something

rail /reɪl/ NOUN [plural **rails**]
1 no plural the railway system □ *Travelling by rail is more relaxing than driving.* 🔁 *Rail fares have increased again.*
2 a bar for hanging things on 🔁 *a towel rail*
3 a bar that you hold to stop you falling □ *Hold onto the rail.*
4 one of the two long metal bars that form a track for trains
• **railing** /'reɪlɪŋ/ NOUN [plural **railings**] a fence made of vertical metal bars, or the bar that goes along the top of a fence like this □ *He was leaning on the railings.*

railroad /'reɪlrəʊd/ NOUN [plural **railroads**] the US word for **railway**

railway /'reɪlweɪ/ ▶ NOUN [plural **railways**]
1 a track for trains to travel on □ *Glasgow has Scotland's only underground railway.*
2 the railway the system and organizations to do with trains □ *We need to encourage more people to use the railway.*
▶ ADJECTIVE to do with trains and the tracks they use 🔁 *I'll meet you at the railway station.* 🔁 *Children should be told about the danger of playing on railway lines.* □ *a railway bridge*

rain /reɪn/ ▶ NOUN, NO PLURAL water that falls from the sky □ *The children didn't want to go out in the rain.* 🔁 *Heavy rain (=a large amount of rain) has caused flooding in the area.* 🔁 *500mm of rain fell last month.* 🔁 *It was pouring with rain (=a lot of rain was falling) outside.*
▶ VERB [**rains, raining, rained**] when it rains, water falls from the sky 🔁 *It's raining so take an umbrella.* 🔁 *It rained heavily (=a lot of rain fell) all night.*
♦ PHRASAL VERB **be rained off** if an event is rained off, it has to stop because there is too much rain □ *The game was rained off.*

rainbow /'reɪnbəʊ/ NOUN [plural **rainbows**] a curved line of colours that you see in the sky when it is raining and sunny at the same time

raincoat /'reɪnkəʊt/ NOUN [plural **raincoats**] a light coat that you wear when it rains □ *She was wearing a blue raincoat.*

rainfall /'reɪnfɔːl/ NOUN, NO PLURAL the amount of rain that falls in a particular place over a particular period of time 🔁 *Heavy rainfall lead to widespread flooding.*

rainforest /'reɪnfɒrɪst/ NOUN [plural **rainforests**] a tropical forest with very tall trees which are close together, in an area where it rains a lot. A geography word □ *the Amazon rainforest*

rainy /'reɪnɪ/ ADJECTIVE [**rainier, rainiest**] raining a lot □ *a rainy day*

raise /reɪz/ ▶ VERB [**raises, raising, raised**]
1 to lift something to a higher position □ *Raise your hand if you know the answer.* □ *The wreck was slowly raised from the sea bed.* □ *She raised her eyebrows in surprise.*
2 to increase the amount or level of something □ *They've raised the rent again.* □ *We are trying to raise standards in the school.* □ *This case has raised awareness of the disease.*
3 to mention a new subject in a discussion □ *I want to raise a matter that we all care very much about.* 🔁 *His teachers have raised concerns about his health.*
4 to cause a particular emotion or reaction 🔁 *The accident raised questions over safety standards.* 🔁 *The drop in oil prices has raised fears of a recession.*
5 to collect money for a particular purpose □ *We're raising money for charity.*
6 if you raise children, you look after them until they are adults □ *My wages are not enough to raise a family.*
7 **raise your voice** to speak more loudly than normal
8 if you raise crops, you grow them, and if you raise animals, you keep them

> ▶ Note that **raise** is always followed by an object:
> □ *She raised her hand.* □ *They have raised taxes.*
> ▶ The verb **rise** has the same meaning but is used without an object:
> ✓ *Taxes have risen.*
> ✗ *Taxes have raised.*

▶ NOUN [plural **raises**] the US word for **rise** (=increase in the amount of money you earn)

raisin /'reɪzən/ NOUN [plural **raisins**] a dried grape (=small round fruit)

rake /reɪk/ ▶ NOUN [plural **rakes**] a garden tool with a long handle and thin metal pieces on the end, used for making the soil level and smooth, or for collecting up dead leaves, etc.
▶ VERB [**rakes, raking, raked**] to use a rake to collect dead leaves or to make soil smooth
♦ PHRASAL VERB **rake something in** to earn a large amount of money. An informal phrase 🔁 *His book has sold really well – he must be raking it in.*

rally /'rælɪ/ ▶ NOUN [plural **rallies**]
1 a large public meeting to support something or to complain about something □ *Over 1000 people attended an anti-war rally.*
2 a car race on public roads □ *a rally driver*
▶ VERB [**rallies, rallying, rallied**]
1 to join other people in order to support someone or something, especially when they are having problems □ *Parents rallied behind the headteacher.*
2 to improve or to become higher or stronger again □ *The team rallied and went on to win the game.*
◆ PHRASAL VERB **rally round (someone)** if people rally round, they try to help someone who is having problems □ *Friends rallied round and offered to do the shopping and drive me to hospital appointments.*

RAM /ræm/ ABBREVIATION Random Access Memory; a type of computer memory. A computing word.

ram /ræm/ ▶ VERB [**rams, ramming, rammed**]
1 to hit something with a lot of force □ *The boat was clearly going to ram the pier.*
2 to push something somewhere using a lot of force □ *Boyd rammed the ball into the net.*
▶ NOUN [plural **rams**] a male sheep

Ramadan /ˌræmə'dæn/ NOUN, NO PLURAL the ninth month of the Islamic year, when Muslims do not eat anything during the day

ramble /'ræmbəl/ ▶ VERB [**rambles, rambling, rambled**]
1 to talk for a long time in a confusing or boring way □ *He rambled on about his horses.*
2 to walk in the countryside for pleasure
▶ NOUN [plural **rambles**] a long walk in the countryside
rambler /'ræmblə(r)/ NOUN [plural **ramblers**] someone who walks in the countryside
rambling /'ræmblɪŋ/ ADJECTIVE
1 a rambling building or garden is big and has an irregular shape □ *a rambling house*
2 long and confusing □ *a rambling speech*

ramp /ræmp/ NOUN [plural **ramps**]
1 a sloping surface that joins two places that are at different levels □ *We should be able to get the wheelchair up the ramp quite easily.*
2 the US word for slip road

rampage /ræm'peɪdʒ/ ▶ VERB [**rampages, rampaging, rampaged**] to run around a place, causing a lot of damage □ *Protestors rampaged through the streets, attacking shops and government buildings.*
▶ NOUN **go on the rampage** if a group of people go on the rampage, they run around an area, behaving violently and causing damage □ *English football fans went on the rampage after their team lost.*

rampant /'ræmpənt/ ADJECTIVE increasing or spreading very fast □ *rampant inflation*

rampart /'ræmpɑːt/ NOUN [plural **ramparts**] a pile of earth or a wall that was built around a castle or city to protect it in the past

ramshackle /'ræmʃækəl/ ADJECTIVE a ramshackle building is in very bad condition

ran /ræn/ PAST TENSE OF **run**

ranch /rɑːntʃ/ NOUN [plural **ranches**] a large farm where cows or horses are kept

rancid /'rænsɪd/ ADJECTIVE rancid food tastes or smells unpleasant because the fat in it is no longer fresh □ *rancid butter*

random /'rændəm/ ADJECTIVE
1 done without a plan or a system □ *a random selection*
2 at random without a plan or system □ *The killer had chosen his victims at random.*
● **randomly** /'rændəmlɪ/ ADVERB in a random way □ *Numbers are chosen randomly.*

rang /ræŋ/ PAST TENSE OF **ring**

range /reɪndʒ/ ▶ NOUN [plural **ranges**]
1 a group of things of a similar type □ **+ of** *The shop stocks a huge range of toys and games.* 🔁 *There is a wide range of courses to choose from.*
2 all the ages, numbers, etc. that are included within fixed limits 🔁 *Most of the sofas we sell are in the £500–£1,000 price range.* 🔁 *The programme is aimed at children in the 10–13 age range.*
3 the distance from which something can be seen, heard or reached 🔁 *Spectators have to stand well out of range of the arrows.* 🔁 *He shot the man at close range* (=from a position that is very close).
4 an area where you can practise hitting golf balls or shooting □ *a firing range*
5 a group of hills or mountains 🔁 *a mountain range*
▶ VERB [**ranges, ranging, ranged**]
1 to include both things that are mentioned, and other things between them □ **+ from** *The company has accommodation ranging from hostels to luxury hotels.* □ *Prices range from £70–£150 per night.*
□ **+ between** *The dancers' ages ranged between 16 and 40.*
2 to deal with a lot of different subjects □ **+ over** *The articles range over many topics.*
● **ranger** /'reɪndʒə(r)/ NOUN [plural **rangers**] someone whose job is to look after a forest or an area of countryside

rank /ræŋk/ ▶ NOUN [plural **ranks**]
1 someone's level in an organization or in society 🔁 *A private is the lowest rank in the British army.* 🔁 *A duchess has a very high social rank.* □ **+ of** *He held the rank of colonel.* □ *There are now more women in the senior ranks of the profession.*
2 ranks the people who belong to a particular group □ *He has now joined the ranks of the world's richest people.* □ *There is corruption within the party's own ranks.*
3 break ranks to show publicly that you disagree with a group that you belong to □ *He broke ranks with party leaders on the issue.*
▶ VERB [**ranks, ranking, ranked**] to have a certain position that shows how good, bad, important, etc someone or something is □ **+ as** *He ranks as one of the world's best actors.* □ **+ among** *The country ranks among the world's poorest.*
● **ranking** /'ræŋkɪŋ/ NOUN [plural **rankings**] a position

on a list that shows how good or bad someone or something is □ *The player is 44th in the official world tennis rankings.*

ransack /ˈrænsæk/ VERB [ransacks, ransacking, ransacked] to search a place in an untidy way and steal things □ *The house had been ransacked.*

ransom /ˈrænsəm/ NOUN [plural ransoms] an amount of money that is paid to a criminal so that they will give back a person they have taken as a prisoner ⊞ *They paid a ransom of over $1million.*

rant /rænt/ ▶ VERB [rants, ranting, ranted] to talk or write a lot in an angry way □ *He was ranting about the disgusting state of the country.*
▶ NOUN [plural rants] a long, angry speech or piece of writing □ *He phoned me up to have a rant about the legal system.*

rap /ræp/ ▶ VERB [raps, rapping, rapped] to hit something quickly and hard □ *Lisa rapped on the door.*
▶ NOUN [plural raps]
1 a quick hard hit □ *There was a rap on the window.*
2 a type of pop music with words that are spoken in rhythm

rapid /ˈræpɪd/ ADJECTIVE done, happening or moving quickly □ *There has been a rapid growth in air travel.*
● **rapidly** /ˈræpɪdli/ ADVERB quickly □ *The town is expanding rapidly.*
● **rapids** /ˈræpɪdz/ PLURAL NOUN parts of a river where the water flows very quickly, usually over dangerous rocks

rapport /ræˈpɔː(r)/ NOUN, NO PLURAL a feeling of understanding someone and liking them ⊞ *The teachers at the school have a very good rapport with the students.*

rapture /ˈræptʃə(r)/ NOUN, NO PLURAL
1 great happiness □ *There was an expression of rapture on his face.*
2 in rapture(s) in a state of great happiness and enthusiasm □ *The audience was in raptures over her singing.*
● **rapturous** /ˈræptʃərəs/ ADJECTIVE showing happiness and enthusiasm ⊞ *There was rapturous applause at the end of the performance.*

rare /reə(r)/ ADJECTIVE [rarer, rarest]
1 not happening or existing often □ *This type of attack is extremely rare.* □ *This is a rare example of a blue diamond.* □ *On rare occasions, errors are made.* □ + **to do something** *It's rare to find a vase like this in perfect condition.*
2 rare meat is cooked for a short time and often still has blood in it □ *I like my steak rare.*
● **rarely** /ˈreəli/ ADVERB not often □ *I rarely see him.* □ *He's a keen football fan and rarely misses a game.*

rarity /ˈreərəti/ NOUN [plural rarities]
1 something that is not common or does not happen very often □ *Rain is a rarity in that part of the world.*
2 the quality of being rare □ *The jewel is very expensive because of its rarity.*

rascal /ˈrɑːskəl/ NOUN [plural rascals] a child who behaves badly but who you still feel affection for

rash /ræʃ/ ▶ NOUN [plural rashes]
1 an area of red spots on your skin, often caused by an illness ⊞ *I came out in a rash* (=developed a rash).
2 a rash of something several unpleasant things that suddenly start happening □ *There has been a rash of kidnappings recently.*
▶ ADJECTIVE [rasher, rashest] done without careful thought □ *It was a rash promise.*

rasher /ˈræʃə(r)/ NOUN [plural rashers] a thin piece of bacon (=meat from a pig)

raspberry /ˈrɑːzbəri/ NOUN [plural raspberries] a small soft red fruit that grows on bushes

rat /ræt/ NOUN [plural rats] an animal that looks like a large mouse with a long tail

rate /reɪt/ ▶ NOUN [plural rates]
1 how often something happens, or the number of people or things it happens to □ *Unemployment rates have fallen.* □ *We need to lower crime rates.* □ *The birth rate has risen.*
2 the speed at which something happens □ *The rate of progress has been very slow.* □ *The disease is spreading at a tremendous rate.* ⊞ *At this rate, we'll have eaten all the food before lunch time.*
3 an amount of money that is paid for something □ *They charge very high rates for their services.* □ *Rates of pay have risen.* □ *The exchange rate is in our favour at the moment.* □ *The banks have raised interest rates.*
4 at any rate used to say that at least one part of what you have said is certain □ *He's gone to see his cousin or someone – a relative at any rate.*
➡ go to first-rate, second-rate, third-rate
▶ VERB [rates, rating, rated]
1 to judge the quality or level of someone or something □ *How do you rate him as a tennis player?* □ *Patients were asked to rate their pain on a scale of 1 – 5.*
2 to deserve something □ *The incident rated a mention in the national news.*

rather /ˈrɑːðə(r)/ ADVERB
1 slightly □ *It's rather cold in here, isn't it?* □ *He felt rather tired after such a long journey.*
2 rather than instead of □ *Many people choose to rent rather than buy houses.* □ *Rather than punishment, some children need support to improve their behaviour.*
3 would rather used when saying what you would prefer to do □ *I would rather talk about this later if you don't mind.* □ *I'd rather go swimming.*
4 or rather used when giving more accurate information about what you have said □ *I've already agreed; or rather, I haven't said 'no'.*

ratio /ˈreɪʃɪəʊ/ NOUN [plural ratios] the relationship between two numbers or amounts that shows how much bigger one is than the other □ *Our nursery has a ratio of one member of staff to three children.*

ration /ˈræʃən/ ▶ NOUN [plural **rations**] a limited amount of something that you are allowed to have □ *I ate my ration of biscuits for the day before lunchtime.*
▶ VERB [**rations, rationing, rationed**] to limit the amount of something that people are allowed to have because there is not a lot available □ *Sugar was rationed during the war.*

rational /ˈræʃənəl/ ADJECTIVE reasonable and sensible □ *a rational decision*

• **rationale** /ˌræʃəˈnɑːl/ NOUN, NO PLURAL the reasons for a decision or belief □ *He challenged the government's rationale for going to war.*

• **rationalize** or **rationalise** /ˈræʃənəlaɪz/ VERB [**rationalizes, rationalizing, rationalized**] to think of reasons to explain your behaviour □ *People often try to rationalize their bad habits.*

rat race /ˈræt ˌreɪs/ NOUN, NO PLURAL the rat race the unpleasant situation in life when people have to work too much and compete with each other

rattle /ˈrætəl/ ▶ VERB [**rattles, rattling, rattled**]
1 if something rattles, it makes a noise by hitting against something else repeatedly □ *The windows were rattling in the wind.*
2 to shake something so that it makes a noise □ *She rattled the door but it was locked.*
3 an informal word meaning to make someone feel worried or less confident □ *A police warning had rattled the gang.*
▸ PHRASAL VERB **rattle something off** to quickly say something you have learned, especially a list □ *He rattled off the names of all the US presidents.*
▶ NOUN [plural **rattles**]
1 the noise that something hard and loose makes when it is shaken □ *There's a bad rattle coming from the engine.*
2 a baby's toy that makes a noise when you shake it

rattlesnake /ˈrætəlsneɪk/ NOUN [plural **rattlesnakes**] a poisonous snake that makes a noise with its tail

ratty /ˈrætɪ/ ADJECTIVE [**rattier, rattiest**] an informal word meaning bad-tempered □ *By the end of the day the children are ratty.*

raucous /ˈrɔːkəs/ ADJECTIVE loud and unpleasant □ *raucous laughter*

ravage /ˈrævɪdʒ/ VERB [**ravages, ravaging, ravaged**] to damage something very badly □ *The area has been ravaged by drought.*

ravages /ˈrævɪdʒɪz/ PLURAL NOUN the ravages of something the bad effects of something □ *Some people have cosmetic surgery to stop the ravages of old age.*

rave /reɪv/ ▶ VERB [**raves, raving, raved**]
1 to talk about something very enthusiastically □ *He's been raving about a new computer game he's bought.*
2 to talk in an angry and confused way
▶ NOUN [plural **raves**] a very large party where people dance to loud music

raven /ˈreɪvən/ NOUN [plural **ravens**] a large black bird

ravenous /ˈrævənəs/ ADJECTIVE very hungry

ravine /rəˈviːn/ NOUN [plural **ravines**] a deep narrow valley with steep sides. A geography word.

ravioli /ˌrævɪˈəʊlɪ/ NOUN, NO PLURAL a type of pasta in the shape of squares with meat, cheese or vegetables inside

ravishing /ˈrævɪʃɪŋ/ ADJECTIVE extremely beautiful

raw /rɔː/ ADJECTIVE [**rawer, rawest**]
1 raw food is not cooked □ *raw vegetables* □ *raw meat*
2 a raw substance is still in its natural state 喦 *raw materials* 喦 *Raw sewage had been pumped into the river.*
3 a raw feeling or quality is strong and natural 喦 *raw emotions* □ *Her grief at her father's death was still raw.*
4 having no experience or training 喦 *He was only 16 and a raw recruit in the army.*
5 raw skin is red and sore
♦ IDIOM **hit/touch a raw nerve** to upset or offend someone by something that you say □ *Powell's comments hit a raw nerve.*

ray /reɪ/ NOUN [plural **rays**]
1 a beam of light □ *a ray of sunlight*
2 **a ray of hope** a small amount of hope □ *This research offers a ray of hope for asthma sufferers.*

razor /ˈreɪzə(r)/ NOUN [plural **razors**] a sharp tool that you use for shaving hair from your face and body □ *He uses an electric razor.* 喦 *a razor blade*

Rd /rəʊd/ ABBREVIATION Road

re- /riː/ PREFIX re- is added to the beginning of words to mean 'again' □ *reappear* □ *rearrange*

reach /riːtʃ/ ▶ VERB [**reaches, reaching, reached**]
1 to arrive somewhere □ *We didn't reach the cottage till long after dark.* □ *The train reached London at 10.34.* □ *My letter never reached him.*
2 to be able to touch or hold something □ *I can't reach the top shelf.*
3 to stretch out your arm to touch or hold something □ *He reached over me to get some bread.* □ **+ for** *As I reached for the fruit, I fell off the ladder.*
4 to be long enough to touch something □ *The ladder didn't reach to the top window.* □ *Charlotte's hair reaches right down her back.*
5 to get to a particular amount, level or situation □ *Temperatures have reached 35°.* 喦 *We have nearly reached our target of £1,000.* 喦 *I've reached a point where I don't care what happens to him any more.*
6 **reach an agreement/a decision, etc.** to agree/ decide, etc. about something □ *The jury failed to reach a verdict.*
7 to contact someone, especially by telephone □ *I've been trying to reach you all day.*

➤ Note that **reach** meaning 'to arrive somewhere' is never followed by 'to':
✓ *It was midnight by the time we reached London.*
✗ It was midnight by the time we reached to London.

▶ NOUN, NO PLURAL

1 beyond/out of (someone's) reach (a) too far away to touch or hold □ *Keep all medicines out of reach.* (b) not possible for someone to have or achieve □ *They feel that a university education is beyond their reach.*

2 within (someone's) reach (a) close enough for someone to touch or hold □ *I made sure all his equipment was within reach.* (b) possible for someone to get or achieve □ *Suddenly, the gold medal seems within her reach.*

3 within reach of something close enough to get to a place □ *The house is within easy reach of the beach.*

react /rɪˈækt/ VERB [reacts, reacting, reacted]

1 to behave or feel a particular way because of something that has happened or something someone has said □ *How did Helen react when she heard the news?* □ **+ to** *He reacted angrily to their criticism.* □ **+ by** *He reacted by sacking 10 workers.*
2 if a substance reacts with another substance, it changes when they are put together. A chemistry word.
3 to experience unpleasant effects because of something you have eaten or put on your skin □ **+ to** *My eyes reacted to the chlorine in the pool.*

• **reaction** /rɪˈækʃən/ NOUN [plural **reactions**]
1 behaviour or feelings that are a result of something that has happened or something someone has said □ *Did you see his reaction when he found out?* □ **+ to** *There has been a huge reaction to his death.* □ *The news provoked angry reactions from members of the public.*
2 the change that happens when two substances are put together. A chemistry word. □ *a chemical reaction*
3 an unpleasant effect caused by something you have eaten or put on your skin □ *He had an allergic reaction to the drug.*
4 reactions the ability to move quickly when something happens □ *You need very fast reactions to play tennis well.*

read /riːd/ ▶ VERB [reads, reading, read]

1 to look at words and understand them □ *He was reading a novel.* □ **+ about** *I read about the court case in the papers.* □ **+ that** *I read that they were going to open a new store.*
2 to look at words and say them aloud □ *I always read a story to the children at bedtime.*
3 to understand the meaning of symbols, numbers, etc. ⏃ *Can you read music?* □ *The man came to read the electricity meter.*
4 to show an amount or level on a piece of equipment □ *The thermometer reads 31 degrees.*

5 if a computer or a piece of equipment reads something, it understands and uses the information on it □ *A scanner reads the bar codes.*

♦ IDIOM **read between the lines** to guess a meaning that is not expressed in a direct way □ *He wrote saying he understood our decision, but reading between the lines, I could tell he was upset.*

♦ PHRASAL VERBS **read something into something** to think that an action or someone's words have a particular extra meaning, often when they do not □ *She only said that she was feeling tired – you shouldn't read too much into that.* **read something out** to read something aloud □ *He read out the list of names.* **read something through** to read the whole of something, often to check for mistakes □ *Make sure you read through your essay and correct your spelling.* **read up about/on something** to read about a subject or to get more information about it □ *I need to read up on the Romans before my next class.*
▶ NOUN [plural **reads**]
1 a good/difficult, etc. read something that is good/difficult, etc. to read
2 an act of reading □ *Have a read and see what you think.*

• **readable** /ˈriːdəbəl/ ADJECTIVE easy or enjoyable to read

• **reader** /ˈriːdə(r)/ NOUN [plural **readers**] a person who reads □ *Regular readers will recognize this name.*

readily /ˈredɪlɪ/ ADVERB

1 quickly and easily ⏃ *The fruit is readily available in most supermarkets.*
2 in a willing way □ *The whole family readily agreed to help.*

readiness /ˈredɪnɪs/ NOUN, NO PLURAL

1 being ready and prepared for something □ *The car had been filled with petrol in readiness for the journey.*
2 being willing to do something □ *The country has signalled its readiness to negotiate.*

reading /ˈriːdɪŋ/ NOUN [plural **readings**]

1 *no plural* the activity of looking at and understanding written words □ *How does the school teach reading?* □ *The course will help you improve your reading skills.*
2 *no plural* something that you read □ *This book is essential reading for anyone who is interested in Spanish history.*
3 a measurement made by an instrument □ *The instrument provides you with an accurate blood sugar reading.*
4 an event at which someone reads something to people, or the thing they read □ *We went to a poetry reading.* □ *a reading from Shakespeare*
5 the way that someone understands a particular situation or event □ **+ of** *His reading of the situation was more optimistic.*

ready /ˈredɪ/ ADJECTIVE

1 prepared for something ⏃ *He was getting ready to leave.* □ **+ for** *Are the children ready for bed?*

2 prepared and available to use, eat, etc. □ *Dinner's ready.* □ *The report should be ready by the end of the year.*
3 willing □ + *to do something He was always ready to help.*

ready meal /'redɪ ˌmiːl/ NOUN [*plural* **ready meals**] a complete meal which you buy already cooked from a shop and heat and eat at home

real /rɪəl/ ADJECTIVE
1 existing, and not invented or imaginary ⊞ *In real life the actor is a quiet family man.* □ *The story is based on real events.*
2 true and not pretended □ *Everyone calls her 'Sunny' but her real name is Barbara.* □ *The real reason he missed the class was that he had forgotten to bring his homework.*
3 not artificial □ *The seats are made of real leather.* □ *The diamond looked real.*
4 used for emphasizing something □ *The death of my mother was a real shock.*
5 get real an informal way of of telling someone that they are being silly and unreasonable about something □ *It's time to get real and do something to stop the damage to the environment.*

real estate /'rɪəl ɪˌsteɪt/ NOUN, NO PLURAL buildings and land □ *real estate investors*

realism /'rɪəlɪzəm/ NOUN, NO PLURAL
1 the ability to accept the real situation and deal with it in a sensible way
2 a style of art or writing which shows things as they really are
realist /'rɪəlɪst/ NOUN [*plural* **realists**] someone who accepts situations as they really are, instead of pretending that they are different
realistic /ˌrɪə'lɪstɪk/ ADJECTIVE
1 accepting or based on the true facts of a situation ⊞ *The team has a realistic chance of winning the competition.* □ + *about Navarez seems realistic about his future.*
2 looking or sounding real □ *The fight scenes were very realistic.* □ *In the film, they used a doll for the baby but it looked very realistic.*
realistically /ˌrɪə'lɪstɪkəlɪ/ ADVERB
1 considering the true facts of a situation □ *Realistically, there was no chance of success.*
2 in a way that looks real □ *The grapes were realistically painted.*

reality /rɪ'ælətɪ/ NOUN [*plural* **realities**]
1 the true facts of a situation □ *We must face reality.*
2 in reality used when saying what the true situation is, especially when it seems different □ *Everyone thought she was very successful, but in reality she was almost bankrupt.*
3 become a reality to start to exist or happen □ *I dreamt of playing in the world championship, but never thought it would become a reality.*

reality TV /rɪˌælətɪ tiː'viː/ NOUN, NO PLURAL television programmes with real people in real situations, not actors pretending to do things

realization *or* **realisation** /ˌrɪəlaɪ'zeɪʃən/ NOUN, NO PLURAL when you suddenly realize something □ *The realization that they were sinking caused instant panic.*

realize *or* **realise** /'rɪəlaɪz/ VERB [**realizes, realizing, realized**]
1 to know and understand something that you did not know or understand before ⊞ *I suddenly realized that he wasn't joking.* □ *I didn't realize he was so ill.*
2 to achieve something □ *He never realized his ambition to become a professional footballer.*

really /'rɪəlɪ/ ADVERB
1 very or very much □ *I really like Dan.* □ *I'm really excited about the holiday.* □ *I don't really like fish.*
2 used for saying what the true situation is □ *Did you really mean what you said?* □ *He doesn't really have much choice.*
3 not really no or not completely □ *'Are you ready for your trip?' 'Not really, there's still a lot of things I need to do.'*
4 Really? used when you are surprised or interested by what someone has just said □ *'Mrs Robinson is leaving the school in July.' 'Really?'*

realm /relm/ NOUN [*plural* **realms**]
1 an area of knowledge or activity □ *Within the realms of political commentators, he is considered highly.*
2 a literary word for a country that has a king or queen
real-time /'rɪəltaɪm/ ADJECTIVE describes computer systems that deal with new information exactly at the time when the information arrives. A computing word.

reap /riːp/ VERB [**reaps, reaping, reaped**]
1 to get something good as a result of something you have done ⊞ *He passed the exam so he's reaped the benefits of all that hard work.*
2 to cut and collect a crop

reappear /ˌriːə'pɪə(r)/ VERB [**reappears, reappearing, reappeared**] to appear again after not being seen for a period of time □ *Weeds keep reappearing if they are not removed at the root.*
● **reappearance** /ˌriːə'pɪərəns/ NOUN [*plural* **reappearances**] when someone or something reappears □ *His sudden reappearance surprised everyone.*

rear /rɪə(r)/ ▶ NOUN, NO PLURAL **the rear** the back part of something □ *They were sitting at the rear of the plane.*
▶ ADJECTIVE at the back of something □ *The rear wheels of the car were stuck in mud.*
▶ VERB [**rears, rearing, reared**]
1 if you rear children or animals, you look after them as they grow
2 if a horse or other animal rears, it lifts its front legs into the air

rearrange /ˌriːə'reɪndʒ/ VERB [**rearranges, rearranging, rearranged**]

1 to change the position of things □ *They had rearranged the furniture in the room.*
2 to change the time when something will happen □ *The president has rearranged his schedule so he can attend the service.*

reason /ˈriːzən/ ▶ NOUN [*plural* **reasons**]
1 the reason for something is why it happened, exists or is true **+ for** *No one knows the reason for his disappearance.* □ **+ that** *The reason that I phoned was to see if you want to meet for lunch.* ⚐ *There are many good reasons for taking up a sport.* ⚐ *He did not give any reason for his lateness.* ⚐ *That is the reason why I moved to Paris.*
2 *no plural* a good cause for something □ **+ to do something** *We have reason to suspect he is guilty.* ⚐ *He has good reason to be happy.* ⚐ *There is no reason to be afraid.* ⚐ *She could see no reason to apologize.*
3 *no plural* the ability to think clearly and behave in a sensible way □ *Will you please listen to reason?* ⚐ *We all tried to make him see reason.* ⚐ *Order whatever food you'd like, within reason.*
▶ VERB [**reasons, reasoning, reasoned**] to consider the facts about something and decide what you think is true □ *I reasoned that he might have missed the train.*
◆ PHRASAL VERB **reason with someone** to try to persuade someone to change their actions or beliefs by telling them what is true or sensible □ *He waved a gun around as police tried to reason with him.*
● **reasonable** /ˈriːzənəbəl/ ADJECTIVE
1 sensible and fair □ *I suppose it's a reasonable decision.* □ *Any reasonable person would agree with that.* ⚐ *We proved beyond reasonable doubt that she was guilty.*
2 if something is reasonable, there are good reasons why you think it is true or correct □ *They made the reasonable assumption that we would be late.* □ *These figures seem reasonable to me.*
3 quite large but not very large ⚐ *We have a reasonable chance of winning the competition.* ⚐ *I eat a reasonable amount of vegetables.*
4 of quite high quality but not very high quality □ *He's a reasonable swimmer.*
5 not very expensive □ *Their clothes are very reasonable.*
● **reasonably** /ˈriːzənəblɪ/ ADVERB
1 in a sensible and fair way □ *He has behaved very reasonably towards us.*
2 to quite a high level or standard □ *I'm reasonably good at the piano.* □ *He is in a reasonably paid job.*
● **reasoned** /ˈriːzənd/ ADJECTIVE having been considered carefully □ *a reasoned argument/decision*
● **reasoning** /ˈriːzənɪŋ/ NOUN, NO PLURAL the process of thinking about the facts about something and making a judgment about it □ *He tried to explain the reasoning behind his decision.*

reassurance /ˌriːəˈʃɔːrəns/ NOUN [*plural* **reassurances**] something that stops someone from

feeling worried □ *Young children need reassurance from their parents.*
reassure /ˌriːəˈʃɔː(r)/ VERB [**reassures, reassuring, reassured**] to say or do something to make someone feel less worried □ *He tried to reassure me that everything would be all right.*
● **reassuring** /ˌriːəˈʃɔːrɪŋ/ ADJECTIVE making you feel less worried □ *a reassuring look*
rebate /ˈriːbeɪt/ NOUN [*plural* **rebates**] an amount of money that is paid back to someone because they have paid too much ⚐ *a tax rebate*
rebel ▶ NOUN [*plural* **rebels**]
1 someone who fights against a government □ *Rebels have clashed with government troops.*
2 someone who refuses to obey rules or people in authority □ *He was always a bit of a rebel at school.*
▶ VERB /rɪˈbel/ [**rebels, rebelling, rebelled**]
1 to fight against a government
2 to refuse to obey rules or someone in authority □ *It's not unusual for teenagers to rebel against their parents.*
● **rebellion** /rɪˈbeljən/ NOUN [*plural* **rebellions**]
1 when people refuse to obey their leader or people in authority □ *teenage rebellion*
2 the use of violence to try to change a government □ *The government tried to crush the rebellion.*
● **rebellious** /rɪˈbeljəs/ ADJECTIVE difficult to control and not wanting to obey rules or people in authority □ *rebellious teenagers*
reboot /ˌriːˈbuːt/ VERB [**reboots, rebooting, rebooted**] to start a computer again. A computing word □ *You'll have to reboot to save these changes.*
rebound /rɪˈbaʊnd/ VERB [**rebounds, rebounding, rebounded**] to move back after hitting a surface □ *The ball rebounded off the edge of the goal.*
◆ PHRASAL VERB **rebound on someone** if something you have done rebounds on you, it has a bad effect on you □ *His comments may rebound on him.*
rebuild /ˌriːˈbɪld/ VERB [**rebuilds, rebuilding, rebuilt**]
1 to build something again when it has been destroyed □ *Engineers have been called in to rebuild the bridge.*
2 to make something strong and successful again after it has been damaged □ *It will take a long time to rebuild trust between them.* ⚐ *Charities are helping these people to rebuild their lives after the flood.*
rebuke /rɪˈbjuːk/ ▶ VERB [**rebukes, rebuking, rebuked**] to speak angrily to someone because they have done something wrong
▶ NOUN [*plural* **rebukes**] something that is said in an angry way to someone who has done something wrong ⚐ *The President's comments earned him a sharp rebuke from environmentalists.*
recall /rɪˈkɔːl/ VERB [**recalls, recalling, recalled**]
1 to remember □ *Do you recall how we used to play here as children?*
2 to order someone to come back □ *The government has recalled all its diplomats.*
3 if a store or company recalls a product, they ask

people to return it because there is something wrong with it

recap /'ri:kæp/ ▶ VERB [**recaps, recapping, recapped**] to repeat the most important points of what has been said □ *To recap, this button switches it on, and this one controls volume.*

▶ NOUN [*plural* **recaps**] when you recap something □ *Could you give us a brief recap, please?*

recapture /ˌri:ˈkæptʃə(r)/ VERB [**recaptures, recapturing, recaptured**]
1 to bring back a feeling or experience from the past □ *The film perfectly recaptures the atmosphere of 1940s Hollywood.*
2 to catch a person or animal that has escaped

recede /ri:ˈsi:d/ VERB [**recedes, receding, receded**]
1 to move backwards □ *The flood water is starting to recede.*
2 to become less □ *His fear had receded a little.*
3 if a man's hair is receding, he is starting to lose hair at the front of his head

receipt /rɪˈsi:t/ NOUN [*plural* **receipts**]
1 a piece of paper you get when you buy something or when you have paid money to someone □ *Make sure you keep the receipt.* □ *a credit card receipt* □ *+ for* *The receipt for the clothes was still in the bag.*
2 *no plural* a formal word meaning the fact that you have received something ᵍ *On receipt of the debit card, you must sign it.* □ *+ of* *He confirmed receipt of the letter.*

receive /rɪˈsi:v/ VERB [**receives, receiving, received**]
1 to get or be given something □ *+ from* *She received a letter from her aunt.* □ *She has been receiving treatment for cancer.* □ *The story received a lot of attention.* □ *He received an award for his work.*
2 if something is received in a particular way, that is how people react to it ᵍ *The idea was well received* (=people liked it). □ *The new policy was received badly.*
3 to welcome guests at a formal occasion □ *The mayor stood near the door and received his guests personally.*
4 be on/at the receiving end of something to be the person who is affected by something, especially something unpleasant □ *He had been on the receiving end of her bad temper.*

receiver /rɪˈsi:və(r)/ NOUN [*plural* **receivers**]
1 the part of a telephone that you hear and speak through □ *'Goodbye,' he said, and replaced the receiver.*
2 a piece of equipment that receives electronic, radio or television signals □ *All new televisions have a digital receiver.*

recent /'ri:sənt/ ADJECTIVE
1 happening only a short time ago □ *recent events* □ *The most recent figures show that violent crimes are increasing.* □ *These changes are relatively recent.*
2 in recent years/months/weeks, etc. in the years,

months, etc. just before now □ *They've won the competition twice in recent years.*

• **recently** /'ri:səntlɪ/ ADVERB a short time ago □ *I saw Ann quite recently.* □ *He recently bought a new car.* □ *Recently, the situation became worse.*

receptacle /rɪˈseptəkəl/ NOUN [*plural* **receptacles**] a formal word meaning container

reception /rɪˈsepʃən/ NOUN [*plural* **receptions**]
1 a big, formal party ᵍ *The wedding reception was at a hotel.* ᵍ *Government leaders will attend a reception hosted by the Queen.* □ *+ for* *a reception for the French president*
2 *no plural* the place where people go when they arrive at a hotel, office building, etc. □ *He was checking in at reception.* ᵍ *She walked up to the reception desk.* ᵍ *The hotel has a large reception area.*
3 the way someone reacts to something ᵍ *The Prime Minister got a very friendly reception when he visited the factory.*
4 *no plural* the quality of the sound or pictures that you get on a radio, television, mobile phone, etc. □ *There's poor mobile phone reception in some rural areas.*

• **receptionist** /rɪˈsepʃənɪst/ NOUN [*plural* **receptionists**] someone whose job is to welcome and help people who arrive at a hotel, office building, etc.

receptive /rɪˈseptɪv/ ADJECTIVE willing to accept suggestions and new ideas □ *They've become more receptive to change.*

recess /rɪˈses/ NOUN [*plural* **recesses**]
1 a space where a wall is further back than the rest of the wall □ *The vase was placed in a small recess.*
2 a time when parliament or law courts do not work

recession /rɪˈseʃən/ NOUN [*plural* **recessions**] a time when a country's economy is not successful □ *The rise in oil prices could trigger a recession.*

recessive /rɪˈsesɪv/ ADJECTIVE a recessive gene is only passed on to a child if both parents have it. A biology word.

recipe /'resɪpɪ/ NOUN [*plural* **recipes**]
1 a set of instructions for how to cook something ᵍ *a recipe book* □ *+ for* *This is a delicious recipe for chocolate cake.*
2 a recipe for disaster/success, etc. something that will probably have a very bad/good, etc. result □ *Exercising on a hot day and not drinking anything is a recipe for disaster.*

recipient /rɪˈsɪpɪənt/ NOUN [*plural* **recipients**] a formal word meaning a person who receives something □ *He has been the recipient of several awards.*

reciprocal /rɪˈsɪprəkəl/ ADJECTIVE involving two people or groups who each do the same for each other □ *a reciprocal arrangement*

• **reciprocate** /rɪˈsɪprəkeɪt/ VERB [**reciprocates, reciprocating, reciprocated**] to do the same thing for someone as they have done for you, or to have the same feelings for someone that they have for you □ *His affection was not reciprocated.*

recital /rɪˈsaɪtəl/ NOUN [plural **recitals**] a performance of music, songs or poetry, usually by one person □ *an organ recital*

recite /rɪˈsaɪt/ VERB [**recites, reciting, recited**] to say something that you have learned, such as a poem

reckless /ˈrekləs/ ADJECTIVE doing something without caring or thinking about the results of your actions □ *reckless driving*

• **recklessly** /ˈrekləsli/ ADVERB in a reckless way □ *He was accused of recklessly endangering the life of others.*

reckon /ˈrekən/ VERB [**reckons, reckoning, reckoned**]
1 to think that something is true □ *I reckon we'll win.*
2 to calculate □ *The cost of restoring the painting is reckoned at £8,000.*

♦ IDIOM a force/power to be reckoned with someone or something that can have a strong effect on a situation □ *The new party is a force to be reckoned with.*

♦ PHRASAL VERBS **reckon on something** to expect something to happen, and to base your plans on it □ *I hadn't reckoned on getting stuck in traffic.* **reckon with something/someone** to consider the possible effect of something or someone □ *They hadn't reckoned with the anger of his fans.*

reclaim /rɪˈkleɪm/ VERB [**reclaims, reclaiming, reclaimed**]
1 to get back something that you have lost or that has been taken from you □ *Luggage that is not reclaimed by passengers at the airport is sold.*
2 to improve an area of land so that it can be used

recline /rɪˈklaɪn/ VERB [**reclines, reclining, reclined**]
1 to lie in a relaxed way □ *Ginny was reclining on the sofa.*
2 if a chair reclines, you can move the back to a lower position

recluse /rɪˈkluːs/ NOUN [plural **recluses**] a person who lives alone and does not like being with other people

• **reclusive** /rɪˈkluːsɪv/ ADJECTIVE living alone and not wanting to be with other people

recognition /ˌrekəgˈnɪʃən/ NOUN, NO PLURAL
1 the fact of knowing someone or something because you have seen them before □ *a smile of recognition*
2 respect and admiration □ *She has earned international recognition for her work.*
3 agreement that something is true or important □ *There is a growing recognition that play is important in children's development.*

recognizable *or* **recognisable** /ˈrekəgnaɪzəbəl/ ADJECTIVE easy to recognize □ *He is barely recognizable since he shaved off his beard.*

• **recognize** *or* **recognise** /ˈrekəgnaɪz/ VERB [**recognizes, recognizing, recognized**]
1 to know who or what someone or something is because you have seen them before □ *I recognized his face but couldn't remember his name* □ *Emma hadn't seen him for 50 years, but recognized him immediately.*

2 to accept that something is true □ *We recognize the importance of research.* □ *+ that* *Most people recognize that there is no easy solution to the problem of global warming.*
3 to officially accept that something is legal □ *Other countries have refused to recognize the new state.*
4 to show that you respect and admire what someone has done □ *His scientific achievements were recognized when he was awarded the Nobel Prize.*

recoil /rɪˈkɔɪl/ VERB [**recoils, recoiling, recoiled**]
1 to move back suddenly from someone or something that frightens you or that you do not like □ *She recoiled from his touch.*
2 to feel that something is unpleasant or morally wrong □ *Most people recoil from the idea of torture.*

recollect /ˌrekəˈlekt/ VERB [**recollects, recollecting, recollected**] a formal word meaning to remember □ *He could clearly recollect events of 35 years ago.*

• **recollection** /ˌrekəˈlekʃən/ NOUN [plural **recollections**] something that you remember 🖷 *I have absolutely no recollection of what happened.*

recommend /ˌrekəˈmend/ VERB [**recommends, recommending, recommended**]
1 to advise someone to do something □ *+ that* *Health experts recommend that you eat at least five portions of fruit or vegetables every day.* □ *We don't recommend the use of this drug.*
2 to suggest to someone that they would like something □ *+ to* *My sister recommended this book to me.*

► Note that **recommend**, meaning 'to advise' is followed by a noun or is followed by that.... It is not followed by 'to do something': □ *She recommended new glasses.*
✓ *She recommended that I buy new glasses.*
✗ *She recommended me to buy new glasses.*

• **recommendation** /ˌrekəmenˈdeɪʃən/ NOUN [plural **recommendations**]
1 something that someone advises you to do □ *The school will implement the inspector's recommendations.*
2 something that a person suggests you would like □ *bought the game on my friend's recommendation.*

reconcile /ˈrekənsaɪl/ VERB [**reconciles, reconciling, reconciled**]
1 to find a way in which two very different situations beliefs, etc. can both exist together □ *She couldn't reconcile her religious faith with the feelings of hatre she had for her attackers.*
2 if you are reconciled with someone, you are friend with them again after an argument

♦ PHRASAL VERB **reconcile yourself to something** to accept that you will have to do or deal with something unpleasant □ *He has reconciled himself the idea of spending six weeks in hospital.*

• **reconciliation** /ˌrekənsɪlɪ'eɪʃən/ NOUN, NO PLURAL
1 when two people or groups form a friendly relationship again after an argument □ *There is no prospect of a reconciliation.*
2 a way in which two very different situations, beliefs, etc. can both exist together

reconsider /ˌriːkən'sɪdə(r)/ VERB [reconsiders, reconsidering, reconsidered] to think again about a decision, to decide if you should change it □ *We have agreed to reconsider the policy.*

reconstruct /ˌriːkən'strʌkt/ VERB [reconstructs, reconstructing, reconstructed]
1 to build something again □ *Many of the buildings had to be reconstructed following the earthquake.*
2 to be able to describe or copy a situation or event by using information that you have □ *Police used computer technology to reconstruct the crash scene.*

• **reconstruction** /ˌriːkən'strʌkʃən/ NOUN [plural reconstructions]
1 when you describe or copy a situation or an event using information that you have □ *The film shows a reconstruction of the battle.*
2 the act of building something again □ *The reconstruction of the city is still not complete.*

---

record ▶ NOUN /'rekɔːd/ [plural records]
1 a piece of information that has been stored in a document or on a computer 🖥 *They keep records of all overseas sales.* 🖥 *Records show that crime has risen.* 🖥 *medical/dental records* 🖥 *She now has a criminal record .*
2 the things that a person or an organization has achieved or done □ *She has an excellent record on motivating staff.* 🖥 *The company has a very poor safety record.*
3 the best achievement ever in a particular activity, especially a sport 🖥 *He holds the record for the high jump.* 🖥 *She broke the previous record by 2 seconds.* 🖥 *He has set a new record for sailing the Atlantic.*
4 the highest/lowest/most expensive, etc. on record the highest/lowest/most expensive, etc. thing that has ever happened or existed and been recorded □ *It was the hottest summer on record.*
5 off the record if you say something off the record, you do not say it in public □ *Several MPs have told me off the record that they think the prime minister should resign.*
6 on (the) record if you say something on the record, you say it officially and publicly □ *He went on the record as a supporter of independence.*
7 a round flat piece of plastic that music and speech can be stored on □ *I found a pile of old jazz records.*
IDIOM put/set the record straight to make sure that people know the truth about something □ *People are accusing me of disloyalty, and I want to set the record straight.*

▶ VERB /rɪ'kɔːd/ [records, recording, recorded]
1 to put sounds or images on a CD, video, etc. 🖥 *I phoned her, but all I got was a recorded message. The band recorded their first album in 1982.*
2 to keep information about something in a document or on a computer □ *All their addresses are recorded in a central database.*
3 to measure the amount or level of something □ *The meter records how much electricity is being produced.*
4 to achieve something □ *Liverpool recorded another victory today.*

▶ ADJECTIVE /'rekɔːd/ bigger, better, faster, etc. than has ever happened or existed before □ *Record temperatures have led to water shortages.* 🖥 *I finished my meal in record time.*

• **recorder** /rɪ'kɔːdə(r)/ NOUN [plural recorders]
1 a machine that copies and stores sounds or images
2 a simple musical instrument made from a wooden pipe with holes that you cover with your fingers as you blow

• **recording** /rɪ'kɔːdɪŋ/ NOUN [plural recordings]
1 sounds or images that have been recorded □ *I have a recording of the poet's own voice.*
2 no plural the process of recording sounds or images □ *They argued a lot during recording.*

---

recoup /rɪ'kuːp/ VERB [recoups, recouping, recouped] to get back money that you have spent or lost □ *The initial investment of £50,000 is unlikely to be recouped.*

---

recover /rɪ'kʌvə(r)/ VERB [recovers, recovering, recovered]
1 to get better after being ill, injured or upset □ *The doctor says I am recovering very well.* □ **+ from** *He is recovering from a stress-related illness.* □ *Most parents never recover from the death of a child.*
2 to return to a normal condition after problems or damage □ *The sea can take years to recover after an oil spillage.* □ *There are signs that the economy is recovering.*
3 to get something back that has been lost, stolen, etc. □ **+ from** *They recovered several bodies from the wreckage of the plane.* □ *Police recovered several weapons from the apartment.*
4 to get back control over something □ *I paused for a moment to recover my breath.* □ *Dudley recovered his composure and apologized.*

• **recovery** /rɪ'kʌvərɪ/ NOUN [plural recoveries]
1 the process of getting better after being ill, injured or upset 🖥 *He made a miraculous recovery.* 🖥 *She is expected to make a full recovery from her injuries.*
2 the process of returning to a normal condition after problems or damage □ *economic recovery*
3 when someone gets something back that has been stolen or lost □ *the recovery of stolen goods*

---

recreate /ˌriːkrɪ'eɪt/ VERB [recreates, recreating, recreated] to make something so that it is the same as it was in the past or the same as it is in another place □ *The play successfully recreates the atmosphere of wartime London.*

recreation /ˌrekrɪ'eɪʃən/ NOUN, NO PLURAL a formal word meaning enjoyable things that you do in your free time □ *outdoor recreation*

• **recreational** /ˌrekrɪˈeɪʃənəl/ ADJECTIVE to do with recreation □ *recreational activities*

recreation ground /ˌrekrɪˈeɪʃən ˌɡraʊnd/ NOUN [*plural* **recreation grounds**] an area of land where people can play sports and games

recrimination /rɪˌkrɪmɪˈneɪʃən/ NOUN [*plural* **recriminations**] when two people criticize and blame each other 🔃 *The talks broke up with bitter recriminations on both sides.*

recruit /rɪˈkruːt/ ▶ VERB [**recruits, recruiting, recruited**] to find new people to work for a company or join an organization □ *The company recruits a few school-leavers each year.*
▶ NOUN [*plural* **recruits**] someone who has recently joined a company or organization 🔃 *New recruits are given a tour of the building.*

• **recruitment** /rɪˈkruːtmənt/ NOUN, NO PLURAL the process of recruiting people □ *We'd like to see the recruitment of more women.*

rectangle /ˈrektæŋɡəl/ NOUN [*plural* **rectangles**] a shape with four straight sides and four angles of 90 degrees. The opposite sides are of the same length, but two sides are longer than the other two.

• **rectangular** /rekˈtæŋɡjʊlə(r)/ ADJECTIVE having the shape of a rectangle □ *a rectangular table*

rectify /ˈrektɪfaɪ/ VERB [**rectifies, rectifying, rectified**] a formal word meaning to correct something such as a mistake or problem □ *The mistake was soon rectified.*

recuperate /rɪˈkuːpəreɪt/ VERB [**recuperates, recuperating, recuperated**] to spend time getting better after an illness or injury □ *He is at home recuperating from a knee injury.*

• **recuperation** /rɪˌkuːpəˈreɪʃən/ NOUN, NO PLURAL the process of getting better after an illness or injury

recur /rɪˈkɜː(r)/ VERB [**recurs, recurring, recurred**] to happen again □ *There is a possibility that the situation will recur.*

• **recurrence** /rɪˈkʌrəns/ NOUN [*plural* **recurrences**] when something happens again □ *There has been a recurrence of the same problem.*

• **recurrent** /rɪˈkʌrənt/ or **recurring** /rɪˈkɜːrɪŋ/ ADJECTIVE happening several times □ *Bad weather was a recurrent problem.*

recycle /ˌriːˈsaɪkəl/ VERB [**recycles, recycling, recycled**] to save something so that it can be used again or to do something to a substance so that it can be used again □ *I keep the bags in this drawer and recycle them.* □ *Most plastics can be recycled.*

• **recycled** /ˌriːˈsaɪkəld/ ADJECTIVE made from something which has been used before □ *recycled paper*

• **recycling** /ˌriːˈsaɪklɪŋ/ NOUN, NO PLURAL the process of dealing with things which have been used so that they can be used again □ *We need to encourage recycling.*

red /red/ ▶ ADJECTIVE

1 having the colour of blood □ *She drives a red car.* 🔃 *He was wearing a bright red shirt.* 🔃 *The carpet was dark red.*

2 go red if you go red, your cheeks become red because you are embarrassed □ *He went bright red when he saw me.*

3 red hair is an orange colour
▶ NOUN [*plural* **reds**] the colour of blood □ *The walls were painted a deep red.*

red blood cell /ˌred ˈblʌd ˌsel/ NOUN [*plural* **red blood cells**] Red blood cells have no nucleus and they give the blood its red colour. A biology word.

redeem /rɪˈdiːm/ VERB [**redeems, redeeming, redeemed**]

1 to make something seem less bad □ *The show was partly redeemed by the excellent music.*

2 redeem yourself to do something which makes people have a better opinion of you after you have done something bad □ *He had been given a chance to redeem himself.*

3 to exchange something for something else □ *The voucher can be redeemed for a free swimming lesson at any local pool.*

• **redemption** /rɪˈdempʃən/ NOUN, NO PLURAL

1 beyond redemption too badly damaged to be saved or improved □ *The cake was burned beyond redemption.*

2 when a person is saved from the power of evil, especially according to the Christian religion

redevelop /ˌriːdɪˈveləp/ VERB [**redevelops, redeveloping, redeveloped**] to improve an area by repairing buildings or building new ones □ *The area by the river has been redeveloped.*

• **redevelopment** /ˌriːdɪˈveləpmənt/ NOUN, NO PLURAL when an area is redeveloped □ *The city centre is due for redevelopment next year.*

red-handed /ˌredˈhændɪd/ ADVERB

◆ IDIOM **catch someone red-handed** an informal phrase meaning to see someone at the moment when they are doing something bad

red herring /ˌred ˈherɪŋ/ NOUN [*plural* **red herrings**] a fact that is not important but which takes your attention from something that is important

red tape /ˌred ˈteɪp/ NOUN, NO PLURAL official rules and processes which seem unnecessary and which make things happen very slowly □ *There is a lot of red tape involved in adopting children.*

reduce /rɪˈdjuːs/ VERB [**reduces, reducing, reduced**]

1 to make something smaller or less □ *Eating a healthy diet significantly reduces your risk of heart disease.* □ *We need to reduce pollution.* □ **+ to** *We have reduced the number of classes from six to four.*

2 reduce someone to tears to make someone start crying □ *His comments had reduced her to tears.*

◆ PHRASAL VERB **reduce someone to doing something** to make someone do something which is worse than they did before □ *He was a famous act-*

who had been reduced to doing television
advertisements for toilet paper.

• **reduction** /rɪ'dʌkʃən/ NOUN [*plural* **reductions**] a
decrease in the size, number, or amount of something
🖭 *We're offering massive price reductions.* □ *+ in
There has been a significant reduction in the number of
deaths on our roads.*

---

redundancy /rɪ'dʌndənsɪ/ NOUN [*plural*
redundancies]
1 when someone must leave their job because there is
not enough work □ *There have been a lot of
redundancies in the company.*
2 the fact of being no longer needed or used because
better, newer or similar things already exist

• **redundant** /rɪ'dʌndənt/ ADJECTIVE
1 redundant workers no longer have a job because
their company does not have enough work for them
🖭 *820 people were made redundant when the factory
closed.*
2 not needed or used because there are better, newer
or similar things □ *Floppy disks have become virtually
redundant.*

reed /ri:d/ NOUN [*plural* **reeds**] a tall plant which looks
like grass and grows in water

reef /ri:f/ NOUN [*plural* **reefs**] a line of rocks, sand or
coral (=hard substance made from small sea creatures)
near the surface of the sea. A geography word.

reek /ri:k/ VERB [**reeks, reeking, reeked**] to smell very
unpleasant □ *His clothes reeked of fish.*

reel /ri:l/ ▶ NOUN [*plural* **reels**] an object that you
wind something such as film, thread, etc. around
▶ VERB [**reels, reeling, reeled**]
1 be reeling from something to feel very shocked
by something □ *The area is still reeling from a tropical
storm which killed over 600 people.*
2 to walk in a way that looks as if you might fall over
PHRASAL VERB **reel something off** to say a long list
of things very quickly □ *She reeled off the names of
everyone she had invited to the party.*

re-elect /ˌriːɪ'lekt/ VERB [**re-elects, re-electing,
re-elected**] to elect someone again □ *He hopes to be
re-elected next year.*

re-election /ˌriːɪ'lekʃən/ NOUN, NO PLURAL when
someone is re-elected □ *I will not be standing for
re-election.*

ref /ref/ NOUN [*plural* **refs**] a short way to say and write
referee

refer /rɪ'fɜː(r)/
PHRASAL VERBS [**refers, referring, referred**] **refer to
someone/something** to mention someone or
something □ *She referred to the wedding several
times.* □ *+ as He referred to the man as 'Robert'.* **refer
to something**
a formal word meaning to look at something in
order to get information □ *Please refer to the
catalogue for more details.*
to be about something □ *The figures refer to the
period between 1990 and 2000.* **refer someone/**

something to someone/something to send
someone or something to another place to be dealt
with □ *My doctor referred me to the hospital to get an
X-ray.* □ *The matter has been referred to the police.*

• **referee** /ˌrefə'riː/ ▶ NOUN [*plural* **referees**] the
person in a game such as football, who makes sure the
players obey the rules □ *The referee blew his whistle to
end the game.*
▶ VERB [**referees, refereeing, refereed**] to be a referee
during a game □ *Dixon refereed the match.*

• **reference** /'refrəns/ NOUN [*plural* **references**]
1 a remark that mentions someone or something
🖭 *She made no reference to what had happened the
day before.*
2 the process of looking at something to get
information, or the thing you look at 🖭 *He filed the
documents away for future reference.*
3 a written report on your character that someone
reads before offering you a job □ *You'll need a
reference from your previous employer.*
4 with/in reference to something a formal phrase,
used to show what a remark, letter, etc. is referring to
□ *With reference to your letter of June 4th, I am
pleased to inform you that your application has been
successful.*

---

reference book / 'refrəns bʊk/ NOUN [*plural*
reference books] a book that you look in for
information

referendum /ˌrefə'rendəm/ NOUN [*plural* **referenda**
or **referendums**] when the people of a country vote on
a political question 🖭 *We promise to hold a
referendum on the issue.*

referral /rɪ'fɜːrəl/ NOUN [*plural* **referrals**] when
someone sends you to another person for help or
information □ *The doctor can make a referral to a
cancer specialist.*

refill ▶ VERB /ˌriː'fɪl/ [**refills, refilling, refilled**] to fill
something again □ *We'll need to refill the tank before
we go much further.*
▶ NOUN /'riːfɪl/ [*plural* **refills**] something used to refill
an empty container □ *Can you buy refills for that kind
of pen?*

refine /rɪ'faɪn/ VERB [**refines, refining, refined**]
1 to make a substance pure □ *Oil is refined into petrol.*
2 to improve something gradually □ *We are refining
the technique.*

• **refined** /rɪ'faɪnd/ ADJECTIVE
1 a refined substance has been made pure by removing
material that is not wanted from it □ *refined sugar*
2 polite and understanding style and culture □ *a
refined gentleman*

• **refinement** /rɪ'faɪnmənt/ NOUN [*plural*
refinements]
1 a small change you make to improve something, or
the process used to do this □ *The system needs further
refinement.*
2 polite behaviour and knowledge of style and culture
□ *She was a woman of great refinement.*

• **refinery** /rɪ'faɪnərɪ/ NOUN [*plural* **refineries**] a factory where substances such as oil or foods are refined 🔁 *an oil refinery*

refit ▶ VERB /ˌriːˈfɪt/ [**refits, refitting, refitted**] to repair and put new equipment, furniture, etc. into a vehicle, a room or a building □ *The ship has been refitted.*
▶ NOUN /ˈriːfɪt/ [*plural* **refits**] when something is refitted □ *The stadium has undergone a major refit.*

reflect /rɪˈflekt/ VERB [**reflects, reflecting, reflected**]
1 if something is reflected, you can see an image of it in a surface like a mirror □ **+ in** *She caught sight of herself reflected in a shop window.*
2 to be a sign of something □ **+ question word** *Her face reflected how she felt inside.* 🔁 *The price reflects the fact that the house is in a very popular area.*
3 to send back heat, light etc. from a surface □ *The surface reflects light.* □ *The sunlight reflected off the pond.*
4 to think carefully about something, especially something that has happened □ **+ on** *I need time to reflect on my experiences.*
5 reflect well/badly, etc. on someone/ something to cause people to have a good/bad, etc. opinion of someone or something □ *This sort of behaviour reflects badly on the school.*
• **reflection** /rɪˈflekʃən/ NOUN [*plural* **reflections**]
1 an image that you can see in a surface like a mirror □ *He stared at his own reflection in the mirror.*
2 a sign that shows what something is like □ *The match wasn't an accurate reflection of his ability.*
3 a reflection on someone/something when something creates a good or bad opinion of someone or something □ *His bad manners are a reflection on his parents.*
4 your thoughts about things that have happened or the process of thinking like this □ *We all need some time for quiet reflection.*
• **reflective** /rɪˈflektɪv/ ADJECTIVE
1 thinking carefully about things □ *He was in a reflective mood.*
2 a reflective surface sends back light and can be seen easily when light shines on it □ *They wear reflective jackets.*
• **reflector** /rɪˈflektə(r)/ NOUN [*plural* **reflectors**] a piece of metal or plastic which reflects light, especially on a vehicle or a bicycle

reflex /ˈriːfleks/ ▶ NOUN [*plural* **reflexes**] a physical movement that is an automatic reaction to something □ *He had quick reflexes* (=reacted very quickly).
▶ ADJECTIVE a reflex action is one that is done automatically and without thinking

reflexive /rɪˈfleksɪv/ ADJECTIVE
1 to do with words that show that the subject of a verb is the same as its object □ *'Hurt yourself' is a reflexive verb.* □ *'Himself' is a reflexive pronoun.*
2 done automatically and without thinking □ *a reflexive action*

reflexologist /ˌriːflekˈsɒlədʒɪst/ NOUN [*plural* **reflexologists**] someone who treats medical conditions by pressing on particular places on the bottom of your feet
• **reflexology** /ˌriːflekˈsɒlədʒɪ/ NOUN, NO PLURAL the work of a reflexologist

reform /rɪˈfɔːm/ ▶ VERB [**reforms, reforming, reformed**]
1 to make changes to something in order to improve it □ *There are plans to reform the exams system.*
2 to improve your behaviour or to help someone do this □ *a reformed smoker*
▶ NOUN [*plural* **reforms**] changes that are made to improve something, or the process of making these changes □ *There were calls for reform of the tax system.*
• **reformer** /rɪˈfɔːmə(r)/ NOUN [*plural* **reformers**] someone who tries to achieve changes to improve something □ *a social reformer*

refract /rɪˈfrækt/ VERB [**refracts, refracting, refracted**] if light is refracted, it changes direction when it hits the surface of something like water or glass. A physics word.
• **refraction** /rɪˈfrækʃən/ NOUN, NO PLURAL when light refracts. A physics word.

refrain /rɪˈfreɪn/ ▶ VERB [**refrains, refraining, refrained**] a formal word meaning to stop yourself from doing something □ *Please refrain from talking in the library.*
▶ NOUN [*plural* **refrains**]
1 a part of a song that is repeated
2 a remark or a complaint that is often repeated □ *'No more roads' has become a common refrain.*

refresh /rɪˈfreʃ/ VERB [**refreshes, refreshing, refreshed**]
1 to make you feel cooler or less tired □ *The cool air refreshed him a bit.* □ *She woke up feeling refreshed and rested.*
2 refresh someone's memory to make someone remember something □ *Maybe this photo will refresh your memory.*
3 to change what is on a computer screen so that you can see the latest information. A computing word.
• **refreshing** /rɪˈfreʃɪŋ/ ADJECTIVE
1 making you feel cooler or less tired □ *a refreshing drink*
2 new and different in a pleasant way 🔁 *The series made a refreshing change from the usual crime show*
• **refreshments** /rɪˈfreʃmənts/ PLURAL NOUN food and drink □ *Are refreshments available inside the park?* 🔁 *Light refreshments will be provided.*

refrigerate /rɪˈfrɪdʒəreɪt/ VERB [**refrigerates, refrigerating, refrigerated**] to put food or drink in a fridge to keep it cold □ *Cover the mixture and refrigerate overnight.*
• **refrigeration** /rɪˌfrɪdʒəˈreɪʃən/ NOUN, NO PLURAL when you refrigerate things □ *It will keep for several days without refrigeration.*
• **refrigerator** /rɪˈfrɪdʒəreɪtə(r)/ NOUN [*plural* **refrigerators**] a machine that you can store food or drink in to keep it cold and fresh

refuel /ˌriːˈfjʊəl/ VERB [refuels, refuelling/US refueling, refuelled/US refueled] to fill a vehicle with fuel again □ We stopped to refuel at a petrol station.

refuge /ˈrefjuːdʒ/ NOUN [plural refuges]
1 protection from danger ⌘ The family took refuge from the fighting in a church.
2 a place where someone can go to be safe from danger □ They run a refuge for homeless people.
• **refugee** /ˌrefjʊˈdʒiː/ NOUN [plural refugees] a person who goes to another country because they are not safe in their own country ⌘ a refugee camp

refund ▶ VERB /rɪˈfʌnd/ [refunds, refunding, refunded] to give someone back some money that they have paid ⌘ We'll refund your money if you're not completely satisfied.
▶ NOUN /ˈriːfʌnd/ [plural refunds] money that is refunded ⌘ He got a refund from the airline

refusal /rɪˈfjuːzəl/ NOUN [plural refusals] when you refuse to accept or to do something □ His refusal to discuss the problem led to more bad feeling.

refuse[1] /rɪˈfjuːz/ VERB [refuses, refusing, refused]
1 to say that you will not do something □ He refused to help me. □ She refused a request for an interview.
2 to say that you will not accept something you are offered □ Gerry refused a cup of tea but took a glass of water.

refuse[2] /ˈrefjuːs/ NOUN, NO PLURAL a formal word for rubbish that people throw away □ household refuse

regain /rɪˈɡeɪn/ VERB [regains, regaining, regained] to get something back that you had before □ Boston regained the lead in the second half. ⌘ He regained consciousness in hospital.

regal /ˈriːɡəl/ ADJECTIVE like or suitable for a king or queen

regard /rɪˈɡɑːd/ ▶ VERB [regards, regarding, regarded]
1 to think about someone or something in a particular way □ My mother still regards me as a child. □ He was regarded with suspicion by many.
2 a formal word meaning to look at someone or something □ He regarded me thoughtfully.
▶ NOUN, NO PLURAL
1 respect or care for someone or something ⌘ They went ahead without regard for our opinion. ⌘ The professor's work is held in high regard.
2 in/with regard to something a formal phrase meaning to do with something □ I am writing in regard to your recent advertisement. □ Where do they stand with regard to the law?
3 in that/this regard in the way already mentioned □ No one was injured, so we're lucky in that regard.

regarding /rɪˈɡɑːdɪŋ/ PREPOSITION about □ I'd like to talk to you regarding next weekend. □ Police have appealed for information regarding the incident.

regardless /rɪˈɡɑːdlɪs/ ADVERB without paying any attention to something □ Regardless of the cost, I'm determined to take this holiday. □ We warned them, but they carried on regardless.

• **regards** /rɪˈɡɑːdz/ PLURAL NOUN
1 used when sending good wishes to someone ⌘ Give my regards to Fiona when you see her.
2 used at the end of a friendly but polite letter or e-mail

regatta /rɪˈɡætə/ NOUN [plural regattas] an event with several boat races

regenerate /rɪˈdʒenəreɪt/ VERB [regenerates, regenerating, regenerated] to improve something so that it returns to its original good state □ The council is regenerating old housing.
• **regeneration** /rɪˌdʒenəˈreɪʃən/ NOUN, NO PLURAL when something is regenerated □ urban regeneration projects

reggae /ˈreɡeɪ/ NOUN, NO PLURAL a style of music that has strong rhythms, originally from Jamaica

regime /reɪˈʒiːm/ NOUN [plural regimes]
1 a system of government, especially one you disapprove of □ There have been attempts to topple the repressive regime.
2 a system of rules □ The hospital has a strict regime of hygiene.

regiment /ˈredʒɪmənt/ NOUN [plural regiments] a large group of soldiers in an army
• **regimental** /ˌredʒɪˈmentəl/ ADJECTIVE to do with an army regiment
• **regimented** /ˈredʒɪmentɪd/ ADJECTIVE organized in a very controlled way □ She runs the school in a very regimented manner.

region /ˈriːdʒən/ NOUN [plural regions]
1 a large area of land such as a part of a country with a particular characteristic □ We visited some of the wine-making regions of Spain. □ The region's economy is growing steadily.
2 a part of the body □ He had a pain in the chest region. □ The injury affected the region of her brain responsible for language.
3 in the region of approximately □ Repairs will cost in the region of £500.
• **regional** /ˈriːdʒənəl/ ADJECTIVE to do with a particular region of a country □ a regional accent □ a regional newspaper

register /ˈredʒɪstə(r)/ ▶ VERB [registers, registering, registered]
1 to put your name on an official list □ + for We registered for the new term's swimming class. □ + with Make sure you register with the embassy. □ You must register your son's birth in the next week.
2 to express an opinion or to show a feeling □ The fans registered their protest by staying away. □ Her face registered her disappointment.
3 if a device registers a measurement, it shows it □ The earthquake registered 8.6 on the Richter scale.
4 to notice and understand something □ She certainly heard the news but I don't know if it really registered.
▶ NOUN [plural registers]
1 an official list of names □ Our teacher takes the register every morning. □ a register of births and deaths

2 a style of language used in a particular situation, for example whether it is formal or informal

• **registrar** /ˌredʒɪˈstrɑ:(r)/ NOUN [plural **registrars**] a person whose job is to keep official records, especially of births, marriages and deaths

• **registration** /ˌredʒɪˈstreɪʃən/ NOUN [plural **registrations**] when you put your name on an official list □ **+ for** Registration for next term's classes starts on the 20th. 🔁 a registration fee 🔁 You need to complete a registration form.

• **registry** /ˈredʒɪstrɪ/ NOUN [plural **registries**] an office or building where official records are kept

registration number /ˌredʒɪˈstreɪʃən ˌnʌmbə(r)/ NOUN [plural **registration numbers**] the set of numbers and letters on the front and back of a vehicle

registry office /ˈredʒɪstrɪ ˌɒfɪs/ or **register office** /ˈredʒɪstə(r) ˌɒfɪs/ NOUN [plural **registry offices** or **register offices**] the place where you go to register a birth, marriage or death, or to have a marriage ceremony

regret /rɪˈɡret/ ▶ VERB [**regrets, regretting, regretted**]

1 to wish that something had not happened and to feel sorry about it □ He regretted his decision bitterly. □ **+ ing** Yes I'm sorry, I regret saying that. □ I regret not working harder at school. □ **+ that** He now regrets that he didn't do more.

2 a formal word used to say politely that you are sorry about something □ **+ that** We regret that the rest of the tour will be cancelled. □ **+ to do something** We regret to inform you that the flight has been delayed.
▶ NOUN [plural **regrets**] a sad feeling about something that has happened 🔁 Marion had no regrets about leaving home. 🔁 He expressed regret for his actions. 🔁 It is with great regret that I am leaving the club.

• **regretful** /rɪˈɡretfʊl/ ADJECTIVE feeling regret about something that has happened □ He sounded regretful.

• **regretfully** /rɪˈɡretfʊlɪ/ ADVERB in a way that shows regret □ She shook her head regretfully.

• **regrettable** /rɪˈɡretəbəl/ ADJECTIVE if something is regrettable, you wish it had not happened □ a regrettable accident □ It's very regrettable that things turned out this way.

• **regrettably** /rɪˈɡretəblɪ/ ADVERB used to show that you wish something had not happened □ Regrettably, a number of mistakes were made.

regular /ˈreɡjʊlə(r)/ ▶ ADJECTIVE

1 happening often or doing something often 🔁 We all know the benefits of regular exercise. 🔁 I keep in regular contact with my family. 🔁 He writes to me on a regular basis. □ She was a regular visitor to the museum.

2 having the same amount of time or space between each thing □ He has a regular heartbeat. 🔁 I still see the doctor at regular intervals.

3 of a standard size or quality □ I'll have a regular coffee, please.

4 following the usual rules of grammar □ 'Cat' has a regular plural. 🔁 'Pick' is a regular verb.

5 a US word meaning usual □ My regular doctor was away.
▶ NOUN [plural **regulars**] someone who often goes to the same bar, shop, etc. □ He's a regular in our restaurant.

• **regularity** /ˌreɡjʊˈlærətɪ/ NOUN, NO PLURAL

1 when something often happens or is often done □ She began to get lost with alarming regularity.

2 the state of having the same amount of time or space between each thing □ The trees are arranged with a pleasing regularity.

• **regularly** /ˈreɡjʊləlɪ/ ADVERB

1 often □ We regularly have to call the police on a Saturday night. □ Patients are regularly denied medical care.

2 with the same amount of time or space between each thing □ The flowers were planted regularly along the border. □ All the equipment is regularly checked.

regulate /ˈreɡjʊleɪt/ VERB [**regulates, regulating, regulated**]

1 to control an organization, a process, an activity, etc, using rules □ These companies are regulated by the Financial Services Authority.

2 to control a machine so that it works how you want it to □ You can regulate the temperature of the heating.

3 to control a process within the body □ Hormones regulate appetite.

• **regulation** /ˌreɡjʊˈleɪʃən/ NOUN [plural **regulations**]

1 a rule or a law □ We can't allow that – it's against the regulations. 🔁 There are strict safety regulations.

2 the process of regulating something □ the regulation of greenhouse emissions

• **regulator** /ˈreɡjʊleɪtə(r)/ NOUN [plural **regulators**] person whose job is to regulate something □ There were complaints to the media regulator.

• **regulatory** /ˈreɡjʊlətərɪ/ ADJECTIVE to do with regulating organizations, processes or activities □ The industry has its own regulatory authority.

rehabilitate /ˌri:əˈbɪlɪteɪt/ VERB [**rehabilitates, rehabilitating, rehabilitated**] to help someone to have a normal life after they have had serious problems □ We want to rehabilitate young criminals

• **rehabilitation** /ˈri:əˌbɪlɪˈteɪʃən/ NOUN, NO PLURAL the process of rehabilitating someone □ a drug rehabilitation centre □ He's continuing his rehabilitation from a knee injury.

rehearsal /rɪˈhɜ:səl/ NOUN [plural **rehearsals**] a practice for a performance □ We are starting rehearsals for the new show.

rehearse /rɪˈhɜ:s/ VERB [**rehearses, rehearsing, rehearsed**] to practise performing something □ Can we rehearse that last bit again?

reheat /ˌri:ˈhi:t/ VERB [**reheats, reheating, reheated**] to make food or drink hot again □ Once cooked, do not reheat.

rehouse /ˌri:ˈhaʊz/ VERB [**rehouses, rehousing, rehoused**] to provide someone with somewhere els to live ◻ *Hundreds of people need to be rehoused following the flood.*

reign /reɪn/ ▶ VERB [**reigns, reigning, reigned**]
1 to rule over a country as a king or queen ◻ *Queen Victoria reigned for over sixty years.*
2 to be very important, successful etc. at a particular time 🖪 *It's clear that the actress still reigns supreme in Hollywood.*
3 to be the main feature or feeling of a situation ◻ *Confusion reigns over when he is due to arrive.*
▶ NOUN [*plural* **reigns**]
1 the time when someone is the king or queen of a country ◻ *in the reign of King John*
2 a time when someone is important, successful or powerful ◻ *The defeat ended his reign as world champion.*

reimburse /ˌriːɪmˈbɜːs/ VERB [**reimburses, reimbursing, reimbursed**] to give someone back the money they have paid for something ◻ *The theatre will reimburse everyone who had tickets for the cancelled performance.*

rein /reɪn/ NOUN [*plural* **reins**]
1 a long piece of leather which goes around a horse's neck and is used to control it ◻ *He held the horse's reins tightly.*
2 the reins control of something 🖪 *He took the reins of the bank last July.*
3 free rein freedom to do what you want ◻ *They are given free rein to read what they want.*
◆ IDIOMS give full rein to something to allow something to happen or develop in a way that is not controlled ◻ *We want you to give full rein to your artistic powers.* keep a tight rein on something to control something a lot ◻ *She keeps a tight rein on her feelings.*
◆ PHRASAL VERB [**reins, reining, reined**] rein someone/ something in to start to control something that has got out of control ◻ *The party leader must try to rein in his more extreme supporters.*

reincarnation /ˌriːɪnkɑːˈneɪʃən/ NOUN, NO PLURAL the idea that the spirit of a dead person is born again in a new body ◻ *Do they believe in reincarnation?*

reindeer /ˈreɪndɪə(r)/ NOUN [*plural* **reindeer**] a type of large deer with large horns that lives in northern areas

reinforce /ˌriːɪnˈfɔːs/ VERB [**reinforces, reinforcing, reinforced**]
1 to make an idea, a feeling, etc. stronger ◻ *Parents need to reinforce these healthy eating messages.*
◻ *Magazines reinforce the idea that girls have to be very thin.*
2 to make something stronger ◻ *reinforced glass* ◻ *The concrete walls have been reinforced with steel.*

reinforcement /ˌriːɪnˈfɔːsmənt/ NOUN [*plural* **reinforcements**]
1 when something is reinforced ◻ *Teachers use positive reinforcement to encourage good behaviour.*
2 reinforcements extra soldiers, police officers, etc. sent somewhere ◻ *The army has sent reinforcements to the area.*

reinstate /ˌriːɪnˈsteɪt/ VERB [**reinstates, reinstating, reinstated**]
1 to give someone back the job or position they had before ◻ *His supporters want him reinstated as Chairman.*
2 to bring back something that existed before ◻ *The ban has been reinstated.*

reiterate /riːˈɪtəreɪt/ VERB [**reiterates, reiterating, reiterated**] a formal word meaning to say something again to make people understand it ◻ *In answer to your question, I can only reiterate my organization's position on the matter.*

reject ▶ VERB /rɪˈdʒekt/ [**rejects, rejecting, rejected**]
1 to refuse to accept something ◻ *The machine rejected my coin.* ◻ *Unions rejected the offer.*
🖪 *Graham rejected the idea out of hand* (=without considering it).
2 to decide not to accept someone for a job, a course, etc. ◻ *He was rejected for the job.* ◻ *Her application was rejected.*
3 to not give someone enough love or attention ◻ *He felt rejected by his family.*
4 if the body rejects an organ that has been put into it from another person, it does not accept it
▶ NOUN /ˈriːdʒekt/ [*plural* **rejects**] someone or something that has been rejected because they are not good enough
● **rejection** /rɪˈdʒekʃən/ NOUN [*plural* **rejections**]
1 when someone or something is not accepted ◻ *They are challenging the rejection of their building application in court.* ◻ *I received a rejection letter.*
2 the feeling of not being loved or wanted ◻ *She struggled with feelings of rejection.*
3 when the body rejects a new organ

rejoice /rɪˈdʒɔɪs/ VERB [**rejoices, rejoicing, rejoiced**] to feel or to show great happiness ◻ *His family rejoiced at the news.*

relapse /rɪˈlæps/ ▶ NOUN [*plural* **relapses**]
1 when someone becomes ill again after a period of improvement 🖪 *She suffered a relapse.*
2 when a situation or someone's behaviour becomes worse again after a period of improvement ◻ *At home, there was a relapse into arguments and bitterness.*
▶ VERB [**relapses, relapsing, relapsed**]
1 to become worse again after a period of improvement ◻ *By that time, the whole country had relapsed into chaos.*
2 to go back to the state you were in before ◻ *He relapsed into silence.*
3 to become ill again after a period of improvement ◻ *She relapsed after the holiday, and died soon after.*

relate /rɪˈleɪt/ VERB [**relates, relating, related**]
1 to show a connection between two things ◻ *The study attempted to relate mobile phone use to headaches.*
2 to tell a story or to say what happened ◻ *They related their strange experience to their friends.*
◆ PHRASAL VERB relate to someone/something
1 to be connected with someone or something ◻ *The charges relate to the death of a man last November.*

☐ *The figures relate to the period 2004-2005.*
2 to understand or to feel sympathy for someone or something ☐ *I couldn't relate to any of the characters.*
• **related** /rɪ'leɪtɪd/ ADJECTIVE
1 connected ☐ *Is violent crime related to violence on TV?* ☐ *They published a series of related articles.*
2 belonging to the same family as someone else ☐ *We have the same surname, but we're not related.*

➤ Remember that one thing is **related to** another thing. It is not 'related with' another thing:
✓ *Health is very much related to diet.*
✗ *Health is very much related with diet.*

• **relation** /rɪ'leɪʃən/ NOUN [plural **relations**]
1 a connection between things ☐ **+ between** *Scientists established the relation between smoking and lung cancer.* ⊞ *Most movies bear no relation to (=are nothing like) reality.*
2 relations the way in which people, groups or countries deal with each other ⊞ *international relations* ☐ **+ between** *Relations between the two organizations are friendly.* ☐ **+ with** *They have good relations with their neighbours.*
3 someone in your family ⊞ *All our friends and relations were there.* ☐ **+ of** *He's a distant relation of Tolstoy.*
4 in relation to (a) a formal phrase meaning to do with ☐ *They might have important information in relation to this incident.* (b) when compared to something else ☐ *It's a measure of your weight in relation to your height.*
• **relationship** /rɪ'leɪʃənʃɪp/ NOUN [plural **relationships**]
1 the way people or groups feel about each other and deal with each other ☐ **+ with** *Anne felt she had a good relationship with her brother.* ☐ **+ between** *There's a close relationship between our two countries.* ⊞ *They had a father-son relationship.*
2 the connection between things ☐ **+ between** *What's the relationship between these numbers?* ☐ *There seems to be little relationship between how hard I work and how much I achieve.*
3 the situation when people spend time together and have romantic feelings for each other ☐ *He's having a relationship with a younger woman.*

/'relətɪv/ ► NOUN [plural **relatives**] a member of your family ⊞ *We invited all our friends and relatives.* ⊞ *She has no close relatives.* ⊞ *He's a distant relative of the prime minister.*
► ADJECTIVE
1 compared with similar people or things ☐ *We are in a period of relative calm.* ☐ *It compares the relative merits of the two education systems.*
2 relative to compared with ☐ *Housing costs are low relative to those of London.* ☐ *The situation has improved relative to 12 months ago.*
• **relatively** /'relətɪvlɪ/ ADVERB quite, compared with similar people or things ☐ *It's a relatively easy journey.*

/rɪ'læks/ VERB [**relaxes, relaxing, relaxed**]
1 to rest and become calmer and less worried ☐ *We spent the afternoon relaxing by the pool* ☐ *Relax - the children are quite safe.* ☐ *A holiday will help to relax you.*
2 to let your muscles become less tight ☐ *Feel your shoulders relax.*
3 to make a rule less severe ☐ *The government has relaxed the immigration rules.*
• **relaxation** /ˌriːlæk'seɪʃən/ NOUN, NO PLURAL
1 when you relax or relax a part of your body ☐ *We practised relaxation techniques.* ⊞ *I need a little rest and relaxation.*
2 when a rule is relaxed ☐ *a relaxation of security restrictions*
• **relaxed** /rɪ'lækst/ ADJECTIVE
1 feeling calm, comfortable and not worried ☐ *People are relaxed and enjoying themselves.* ☐ *a relaxed atmosphere*
2 not worrying much about rules, details, etc. ☐ *We take a relaxed approach to discipline.*
• **relaxing** /rɪ'læksɪŋ/ ADJECTIVE making you feel relaxed ☐ *We had a relaxing break in the country.* ☐ *a relaxing massage*

---

relay /'riːleɪ/ ► VERB [**relays, relaying, relayed**]
1 to pass a message from one person to another ☐ *She relayed the information to the others.*
2 to broadcast something on television or radio ☐ *His speech was relayed across the world.*
► NOUN [plural **relays**] a relay race
relay race /'riːleɪ ˌreɪs/ NOUN [plural **relay races**] a race for teams in which each person in the team does part of the race, one after the other

/rɪ'liːs/ ► VERB [**releases, releasing, released**]
1 to let a person or an animal go free ☐ *Three more prisoners have been released.* ☐ **+ from** *He was released from prison in 2004.*
2 to stop holding something ☐ *Release the handbrake slowly.* ☐ *We released the balloons and they floated into the air.*
3 to let a substance spread into an area ☐ **+ into** *Carbon dioxide is released into the atmosphere.*
4 to make something available to the public ☐ *The film is released in cinemas on December 1.* ☐ *She released her first album last year.* ☐ *The company released a statement yesterday.*
► NOUN [plural **releases**]
1 when someone or something is allowed to go free ☐ **+ of** *The government demanded the release of the hostages.* ☐ **+ from** *I met him just after his release from prison.*
2 when something is made available to the public ☐ **+ of** *The tour follows the release of her latest album.* ⊞ *a news release*
3 when a substance is allowed to spread into an area

relegate /'relɪgeɪt/ VERB [relegates, relegating, relegated] to move someone or something down to a less important or successful position or level □ *My team has been relegated to the third division.*
• **relegation** /ˌrelɪ'geɪʃən/ NOUN, NO PLURAL when someone is relegated

relent /rɪ'lent/ VERB [relents, relenting, relented]
1 to agree to something or allow something after refusing before □ *She is hoping they might relent and allow her to visit her son.*
2 to become less strong or severe □ *The rain relented slightly.*
• **relentless** /rɪ'lentlɪs/ ADJECTIVE never stopping or becoming less strong □ *We stood all day in the relentless heat.* 🔁 *He was under relentless pressure at work.*
• **relentlessly** /rɪ'lentlɪsli/ ADVERB in a relentless way □ *Her comments were relentlessly critical.*

relevance /'reləvəns/ NOUN, NO PLURAL the way that something is connected to or important for something else □ *What possible relevance can this have to me?* □ *He explained the relevance of the findings.*
• **relevant** /'reləvənt/ ADJECTIVE connected to or important for a subject, situation, etc. □ *Is this answer relevant to the question?* 🔁 *They sent us all the relevant information.*

reliability /rɪˌlaɪə'bɪlɪti/ NOUN, NO PLURAL how much you can trust or believe someone or something □ *This will improve the reliability of the system.* □ *He questioned the reliability of the witness.*

reliable /rɪ'laɪəbəl/ ADJECTIVE
1 a reliable person can be trusted to do what they say they will do or to do something well □ *We need to find a reliable supplier of spare parts.* □ *He's one of the team's most reliable players.*
2 a reliable system, piece of equipment, vehicle, etc. works well and does not often stop working □ *I need a reliable car to get me to work.* □ *The trains aren't very reliable.*
3 reliable information can be believed and is probably true or correct □ *Her letters are a reliable source of information.* □ *There are no reliable estimates of the number of people affected.*
• **reliably** /rɪ'laɪəbli/ ADVERB in a way that can be trusted or believed □ *The service operates reliably and efficiently.* 🔁 *I'm reliably informed that she's planning to leave.*

reliance /rɪ'laɪəns/ NOUN, NO PLURAL when you need someone or something and cannot manage without them □ *We need to reduce our reliance on cars.*
• **reliant** /rɪ'laɪənt/ ADJECTIVE reliant on someone/something needing someone or something and not able to manage without them □ *The charity is totally reliant on donations from the public.*

relic /'relɪk/ NOUN [plural relics] an important object from the past □ *a religious relic*

relief /rɪ'liːf/ NOUN, NO PLURAL
1 a good feeling because something bad or unpleasant stops or does not happen 🔁 *He gave a sigh of relief.* □ *It was a relief to be outside in the fresh air again.* □ *To my relief, no one was hurt.*
2 food, medicine, etc. to help a large group of people in need □ *The agency provides relief for flood victims.* 🔁 *You can help the disaster relief effort.*
3 when you stop pain or suffering or make it less 🔁 *Talk to your doctor about pain relief.* □ *This cream can provide relief from the symptoms of eczema.*
• **relieve** /rɪ'liːv/ VERB [relieves, relieving, relieved]
1 to stop pain, suffering or a problem or to make it less □ *The drug is used to relieve pain.* □ *The new clinic will relieve pressure on the hospital.* □ *He read magazines to relieve the boredom.*
2 to replace someone who is working so they can stop working □ *Wallis came up to relieve him for his lunch break.*
◆ PHRASAL VERB **relieve someone of something**
1 a formal word meaning to take a problem or something heavy from someone □ *Let me relieve you of that heavy suitcase.*
2 a formal word meaning to tell someone to leave a job □ *He was relieved of his duties.*
• **relieved** /rɪ'liːvd/ ADJECTIVE feeling relief □ *I'm so relieved that you're home safely.* □ *She looked relieved.*

religion /rɪ'lɪdʒən/ NOUN [plural religions] belief in a god or gods, and the activities and traditions to do with this belief □ *What is the role of religion in our society?* □ *We teach respect for different religions and cultures.*
• **religious** /rɪ'lɪdʒəs/ ADJECTIVE
1 to do with religion □ *a religious service* 🔁 *a religious leader* 🔁 *religious beliefs*
2 having strong beliefs about a god or gods 🔁 *He was a deeply religious man.* □ *I'm not particularly religious.*

relinquish /rɪ'lɪŋkwɪʃ/ VERB [relinquishes, relinquishing, relinquished] a formal word meaning to give up something or your right to something □ *She relinquished the chairmanship to let a younger person take over.*

relish /'relɪʃ/ ▶ VERB [relishes, relishing, relished] to enjoy something very much □ *He relished the prospect of living alone.*
▶ NOUN [plural relishes]
1 *no plural* great enjoyment □ *He told them about his experiences with great relish.*
2 a cold, thick sauce eaten with other food to add flavour □ *onion relish*

relive /ˌriː'lɪv/ VERB [relives, reliving, relived] to remember an experience very clearly □ *She was forced to relive her ordeal in court.*

relocate /ˌriːləu'keɪt/ VERB [relocates, relocating, relocated] to move to another place □ *My firm relocated to Edinburgh.*

reluctance /rɪˈlʌktəns/ NOUN, NO PLURAL when someone is unwilling to do something □ She was disappointed by their reluctance to help.

• **reluctant** /rɪˈlʌktənt/ ADJECTIVE unwilling to do something □ She seemed reluctant to talk about it. □ He was a rather reluctant participant.

• **reluctantly** /rɪˈlʌktəntlɪ/ ADVERB in a way that shows that you are unwilling □ Nick reluctantly agreed.

rely /rɪˈlaɪ/
◆ PHRASAL VERB [relies, relying, relied] **rely on someone/something**

1 to need someone or something in order to exist or be successful □ We rely on the help of parents and friends. 呂 The system relies heavily on computer technology.

2 to trust someone or something to do what they say they will do or what they should do □ You can rely on our support. □ We can rely on Alan to sort it out. □ You can't rely on the trains in this country.

remain /rɪˈmeɪn/ VERB [remains, remaining, remained]

1 to continue to be in the same state or condition □ He remained silent on the issue. □ His location remains a mystery. □ I won't vote for them while he remains leader.

2 to stay in the same place or position □ She is expected to remain in hospital for another week.

3 to be left when everything or everyone else has gone □ All that remains in the fireplace is a pile of ash. □ The chemotherapy kills the cancer cells that remain after surgery.

4 to continue to exist 呂 Several questions remain about the details of the plan. 呂 The fact remains that she shouldn't have been there.

5 **it remains to be seen** it is not yet known, but will be known in the future □ It remains to be seen whether he'll be able to persuade his parents.

• **remainder** /rɪˈmeɪndə(r)/ NOUN, NO PLURAL **the remainder** what is left of something after some of it has gone □ He spent the remainder of his life in London. □ I tipped the remainder of the liquid away.

• **remaining** /rɪˈmeɪnɪŋ/ ADJECTIVE continuing to be there after other people or things have gone, been used, etc. □ The remaining contestants will perform tonight. □ We can use the remaining time to tidy up.

• **remains** /rɪˈmeɪnz/ PLURAL NOUN

1 parts of something that are left after the main part has gone □ People returned to the remains of their burnt homes. □ the remains of a Roman temple

2 the body of a dead person □ Her remains will be flown back to this country for burial. 呂 Human remains were found.

remake /ˈriːmeɪk/ NOUN [plural remakes] a new film that has the same story and title as an earlier film □ a remake of the classic 1950s horror movie

remark /rɪˈmɑːk/ ▶ VERB [remarks, remarking, remarked] to express an opinion or a thought □ +

that Tim remarked that he liked Di's hat. □ + **on** She didn't remark on the new painting.
▶ NOUN [plural remarks] something you say when expressing an opinion or a thought □ + **about** He made a nasty remark about my writing. □ + **on** The President's remarks on immigration caused controversy. 呂 He made a racist remark.

• **remarkable** /rɪˈmɑːkəbəl/ ADJECTIVE surprising or noticeable, usually in a way that you admire □ It's a remarkable story. □ It's remarkable how quickly she recovered.

• **remarkably** /rɪˈmɑːkəblɪ/ ADVERB in a very surprising or noticeable way □ Remarkably, there were no injuries. □ They looked remarkably similar.

remaster /ˌriːˈmɑːstə(r)/ VERB [remasters, remastering, remastered] to make a new and better recording of an old recording 呂 The record has recently been digitally remastered.

remedial /rɪˈmiːdɪəl/ ADJECTIVE

1 intended to improve something that is in a bad state 呂 Urgent remedial action is needed to save the business.

2 intended to help people who have difficulty learning skills such as reading and writing □ She attends a remedial maths class.

remedy /ˈremədɪ/ ▶ NOUN [plural remedies]

1 something that treats an illness 呂 a herbal remedy □ Cloves are a traditional remedy for toothache.

2 something that solves a problem □ Their policies are seen as a remedy for the country's economic crisis.
▶ VERB [remedies, remedying, remedied] to deal with a problem or a bad situation 呂 People are without homes and nothing has been done to remedy the situation.

remember /rɪˈmembə(r)/ VERB [remembers, remembering, remembered]

1 to have something from the past in your mind or to bring something back to your mind □ I couldn't remember her name. □ + **question word** I don't remember why we chose it. □ + **that** She suddenly remembered that she'd left the window open. □ + in He remembered seeing a young girl outside. □ + **as** He will be remembered as a great player.

2 not to forget to do something □ + **to do something** Remember to take your key with you.

• **remembrance** /rɪˈmembrəns/ NOUN, NO PLURAL when you show that you have not forgotten someone who has died □ a service of remembrance 呂 There was a minute's silence in remembrance of the victims.

remind /rɪˈmaɪnd/ VERB [reminds, reminding, reminded] to make someone remember something □ + **to do something** Remind me to close the window before I go out. □ She reminded herself why she was there. □ + **that** I want to remind everybody that the bus will leave at four o'clock. □ + **of** She sent an email reminding students of the new timetable.
◆ PHRASAL VERB **remind someone of someone/ something**

1 to make you think about someone or something from the past □ *That picture reminds me of our holiday last year.*

2 to make you think about someone or something because of being similar to them □ *Thomas reminded her of her father.*

➤ Note that if someone or something makes you think about someone or something from the past, they **remind** you of them. Remind in this sense is always followed by **to**:
✓ *She reminds me of my sister.*
✗ *She reminds me my sister.*

• **reminder** /rɪˈmaɪndə(r)/ NOUN [plural **reminders**]
1 something that makes you remember someone or something □ *His scars are a constant reminder of the accident.* □ *This serves as a reminder of why we need to be careful.*
2 something that helps someone remember to do something □ *She received a reminder from the gas company that the bill was due.*

reminisce /ˌremɪˈnɪs/ VERB [**reminisces, reminiscing, reminisced**] to think, talk or write about things you remember from the past, usually happy times □ *Most of the meal was spent reminiscing about our school days.*

reminiscence /ˌremɪˈnɪsəns/ NOUN [plural **reminiscences**] when you remember things from the past or the things you remember □ *The speech was mostly reminiscences about his childhood.*

reminiscent /ˌremɪˈnɪsənt/ ADJECTIVE **reminiscent of someone/something** similar to something else and making you think of it □ *Her paintings use colours and shapes reminiscent of children's TV programmes.*

remission /rɪˈmɪʃən/ NOUN, NO PLURAL a period of time when a serious illness does not affect you □ *His cancer is in remission.*

remittance /rɪˈmɪtəns/ NOUN [plural **remittances**] a formal word meaning money that you send to pay for something

remnant /ˈremnənt/ NOUN [plural **remnants**] a small piece of something that is left after the rest has been used, lost or destroyed □ *Police found remnants of fireworks in the building.*

remorse /rɪˈmɔːs/ NOUN, NO PLURAL a strong guilty feeling about something bad or wrong that you have done □ *She was full of remorse for her actions.*

remorseful /rɪˈmɔːsful/ ADJECTIVE feeling very guilty and sorry □ *She was genuinely remorseful.*

remorsefully /rɪˈmɔːsfulɪ/ ADVERB in a way that shows remorse

remorseless /rɪˈmɔːsləs/ ADJECTIVE
not feeling guilty or sorry for what you have done □ *a remorseless killer*
never stopping □ *the remorseless heat*

remorselessly /rɪˈmɔːsləslɪ/ ADVERB in a way that never stops

remote /rɪˈməʊt/ ▶ ADJECTIVE [**remoter, remotest**]
1 a remote place is very far away from other places □ *a remote village*
2 a remote chance is very slight □ *There's not even a remote possibility that we'll win.*
3 able to be used from a distance □ *The system allows remote access to staff working from home.*
▶ NOUN [plural **remotes**] a remote control

remote control /rɪˌməʊt kənˈtrəʊl/ NOUN [plural **remote controls**]
1 a device for operating equipment such as a television from a distance
2 a system for operating something from a distance □ *The bomb was detonated by remote control.*

remotely /rɪˈməʊtlɪ/ ADVERB
1 slightly □ *I'm not even remotely interested.* □ *We weren't doing anything remotely dangerous.*
2 from a distance □ *a remotely operated vehicle*

removal /rɪˈmuːvəl/ NOUN [plural **removals**] when something is removed □ *He called for the removal of foreign troops.* □ *Doctors advised the removal of the tumour.*

remove /rɪˈmuːv/ VERB [**removes, removing, removed**]
1 to take something away or to get rid of something □ *The police have removed the car.* □ *Doctors removed the tumour.* □ **+ from** *Remove the pan from the heat and stir in the cream.*
2 to take clothes off □ *Please remove your shoes at the door.*
3 to make someone leave a job or position □ **+ from** *He was removed from office after corruption charges.*
4 be removed from something to be completely different from something □ *The dream is very far removed from reality.*

renal /ˈriːnəl/ ADJECTIVE to do with the kidneys. A biology word.

rename /ˌriːˈneɪm/ VERB [**renames, renaming, renamed**] to give something or someone a new name □ *I renamed all the files in that folder.*

render /ˈrendə(r)/ VERB [**renders, rendering, rendered**]
1 a formal word meaning to put someone or something into a particular state or condition □ *His rudeness rendered me speechless.* □ *Snow had rendered the road impassable.*
2 a formal word meaning to do something for someone □ *They attempted to render medical assistance.*

rendezvous /ˈrɒndɪvuː/ NOUN [plural **rendezvous**] an arranged meeting, especially a secret one

rendition /renˈdɪʃən/ NOUN [plural **renditions**] a performance of something such as a song □ *We had to listen to my uncle's rendition of 'White Christmas'.*

renew /rɪˈnjuː/ VERB [**renews, renewing, renewed**]
1 to start doing something again after a break, often with more energy □ *We'll renew our attempt to get the rules changed.*
2 to make or to pay for something to continue for

another period of time □ *You can renew your bus pass at the office.*

renewable /rɪ'njuːəbəl/ ADJECTIVE describes a type of natural energy such as power from the sun which can be replaced quickly and which will not end
• **renewables** /rɪ'njuːəblz/ PLURAL NOUN types of energy which are renewable

renewal /rɪ'njuːəl/ NOUN [plural **renewals**]
1 when something starts again or you start something again after a break □ *There has been a renewal of interest in his novels.*
2 when you make or pay for something to continue for another period of time □ *My contract is due for renewal in August.*

renewed /rɪ'njuːd/ ADJECTIVE starting again after a break, sometimes with more energy □ *Renewed fighting has broken out.* □ *There have been renewed efforts to find the killer.*

renounce /rɪ'naʊns/ VERB [renounces, renouncing, renounced]
1 a formal word meaning to say publicly that you no longer agree with or believe in something □ *They are trying to persuade the rebels to renounce violence.*
2 a formal word meaning to officially give up a right to something □ *He renounced his claim to the land.*

renovate /'renəveɪt/ VERB [renovates, renovating, renovated] to repair and improve an old building so that it can be used again □ *We've completely renovated the house.*
• **renovation** /ˌrenə'veɪʃən/ NOUN [plural **renovations**] when you renovate a building □ *The museum is undergoing renovation.*

renown /rɪ'naʊn/ NOUN, NO PLURAL a formal word meaning when someone is known and respected by many people □ *a man of great renown*
• **renowned** /rɪ'naʊnd/ ADJECTIVE famous and respected □ *She was renowned for her stirring political speeches.*

rent /rent/ ▶ VERB [rents, renting, rented]
1 to pay someone money so that you can use a house or other building □ *We rented a villa near the beach.*
2 a mainly US word meaning to pay someone money to use something such as a car or tools for a short time □ *She rented a car for the week.*
3 to let other people pay to use something you own □ **+ out** *They rent out the building for weddings.* □ **+ to** *We'll rent the house to students while we're away.*

► Note that in British English, **rent** is mainly used for houses and other buildings. The verb **hire** means 'to pay someone money to use something such as a car or tools for a short time'.

▶ NOUN [plural **rents**] money you pay to the owner of a house or other building to use it 🔊 *He's struggling to pay the rent.*
• **rental** /'rentəl/ NOUN [plural **rentals**]

1 when you rent something □ *a car rental business*
2 the amount of rent you pay

reorganization or **reorganisation** /riːˌɔːgənaɪ'zeɪʃən/ NOUN, NO PLURAL when something is reorganized □ *He was moved to a new department as part of the company's reorganization.*

reorganize or **reorganise** /riː'ɔːgənaɪz/ VERB [reorganizes, reorganizing, reorganized] to organize something again in a different way in order to make it better □ *We have reorganized our adult classes.*

rep /rep/ NOUN [plural **reps**] an informal word for someone who sells the products and services of a company 🔊 *She's a sales rep for a computer firm.*

repaid /rɪ'peɪd/ PAST TENSE AND PAST PARTICIPLE OF repay

repair /rɪ'peə(r)/ ▶ VERB [repairs, repairing, repaired]
1 to fix something that is damaged or not working □ *Can the washing machine be repaired?* 🔊 *It will cost millions to repair the damage done by the storms.*
2 to try to improve a bad situation □ *It will take time to repair the damage caused by the scandal.*
▶ NOUN [plural **repairs**]
1 something you do to repair something □ *The ship needed extensive repairs.*
2 in good/bad repair in good or bad condition □ *The car is in remarkably good repair for its age.*

reparations /ˌrepə'reɪʃənz/ PLURAL NOUN money paid by a country that has lost a war

repartee /ˌrepɑː'tiː/ NOUN, NO PLURAL conversation in which people make clever or humorous remarks

repay /rɪ'peɪ/ VERB [repays, repaying, repaid]
1 to pay back money that you have borrowed □ *They are struggling to repay the loans.*
2 to do something for someone because they did something kind for you □ *How can we ever repay the kindness?*
• **repayment** /rɪ'peɪmənt/ NOUN [plural **repayments**] money you repay □ *monthly mortgage repayments*

repeat /rɪ'piːt/ ▶ VERB [repeats, repeating, repeated]
1 to say something again □ *Could you repeat your name please?* □ *She repeated her request.* □ *I don't want to repeat myself* (=say the same thing again).
2 to do something again or to happen again □ *I hope this mistake will never be repeated.* □ *The programme is repeated on Friday at 10pm.*
3 to tell someone something you were told by someone else □ *Don't you dare repeat this to your friends.*
▶ NOUN [plural **repeats**]
1 something that happens again □ *She wants to avoid a repeat of what happened last year.* 🔊 *He's hoping for a repeat performance of last month's win.*
2 a television or radio programme that is broadcast again □ *They were watching repeats of old comedy shows.*
• **repeated** /rɪ'piːtɪd/ ADJECTIVE done or happening

several times □ *After repeated attempts to phone him, I finally went round to his office.*

● **repeatedly** /rɪˈpiːtɪdlɪ/ ADVERB again and again □ *The victim had been stabbed repeatedly.*

repel /rɪˈpel/ VERB [repels, repelling, repelled]
1 to keep someone or something away □ *This material repels water.* □ *Use a spray to repel mosquitoes.*
2 to force someone who is attacking you to move back □ *Soldiers were ready to repel any attack.*
3 if something repels you, you find it very unpleasant □ *People are both fascinated and repelled by the terrible images.*

● **repellent** /rɪˈpelənt/ ► ADJECTIVE very unpleasant □ *a repellent sight*
► NOUN [plural **repellents**] a substance that you use to keep something away □ *an insect repellent*

● **repent** /rɪˈpent/ VERB [repents, repenting, repented] to be sorry for something that you have done □ *He repented of his crimes.*

● **repentance** /rɪˈpentəns/ NOUN, NO PLURAL when you repent

● **repentant** /rɪˈpentənt/ ADJECTIVE sorry for something you have done □ *She looked ashamed and repentant.*

● **repercussions** /ˌriːpəˈkʌʃənz/ PLURAL NOUN the bad effects of an action or an event that follow later □ *This attack could have serious repercussions for the tourist industry.*

● **repertoire** /ˈrepətwɑː(r)/ NOUN [plural **repertoires**] all the music, songs, etc. that a performer knows and can perform

● **repetition** /ˌrepɪˈtɪʃən/ NOUN [plural **repetitions**] when something is repeated □ *We don't want a repetition of yesterday's argument.* □ *learning by repetition*

● **repetitive** /rɪˈpetɪtɪv/ ADJECTIVE boring because the same thing is repeated many times □ *They have to do lots of simple, repetitive tasks.*

replace /rɪˈpleɪs/ VERB [replaces, replacing, replaced]
1 to take the place of another thing or person □ *The company bought new computers to replace the old ones.* □ *The cinema was demolished and replaced by a supermarket.* □ + **with** *The phone has been replaced with a newer version.* □ + **as** *He was replaced as chairman last year.*
2 to put something back where it was before or in its correct position □ *Make sure you replace the books in exactly the right order.*

● **replacement** /rɪˈpleɪsmənt/ NOUN [plural **replacements**] a person or thing that replaces another one □ *This is broken so I'd like a replacement, please.* □ *They will have to find a replacement for the injured goalkeeper.*

● **replay** ► NOUN /ˈriːpleɪ/ [plural **replays**]
1 a sports match that is played again because nobody won the first time □ *He scored in the second-round replay.*

2 an important moment in a sports match that is shown again on television
► VERB /ˌriːˈpleɪ/ [replays, replaying, replayed] to play a sports match again because there was no winner the first time

replenish /rɪˈplenɪʃ/ VERB [replenishes, replenishing, replenished] to get more of something to replace what has been used □ *Health officials are appealing for blood donors to help replenish supplies.*

● **replenishment** /rɪˈplenɪʃmənt/ NOUN, NO PLURAL when you replenish something

replica /ˈreplɪkə/ NOUN [plural **replicas**] an accurate copy of something □ *a replica football shirt*

replicate /ˈreplɪkeɪt/ VERB [replicates, replicating, replicated] to do something or make something again so that it is exactly the same □ *The company is hoping to replicate the success it had in Japan*

reply /rɪˈplaɪ/ ► VERB [replies, replying, replied] to answer □ *'No, I don't!' he replied angrily.* □ + **that** *He replied that he was planning to stay another week.* □ + **to** *You haven't replied to my question yet.*
► NOUN [plural **replies**] an answer □ + **to** *We've had a number of replies to our advertisement.* □ *In reply, Phoebe gave a nod.* 🔁 *He received no reply to his letters.*

report /rɪˈpɔːt/ ► NOUN [plural **reports**]
1 a description of something that has happened □ + **of** *Reports of an accident are just coming in.* 🔁 *a television news report*
2 a written description of a situation or the results of a study □ + **on** *a UN report on climate change* □ + **into** *the police report into the accident* 🔁 *The organization will publish its annual report tomorrow.*
3 a teacher's written description of a student's progress 🔁 *a school report*
► VERB [reports, reporting, reported]
1 to tell people about an event or situation on television, on radio, in newspapers, etc. □ *The whole story was reported in the papers.* □ + **on** *Tonight we'll be reporting on religious education.*
2 to give information about a situation or an event □ + **ing** *Witnesses reported seeing the bus lose control.* □ + **on** *There were regular meetings to report on progress.* □ *The company reported a record annual profit.*
3 to tell someone officially that something has happened □ + **to** *Did you report the incident to the police?*
4 to make a complaint about someone's behaviour □ *I reported the bus driver for not stopping.*
5 to go to a place and tell them that you have arrived □ + **to** *Please report to reception when you enter the building.* □ + **for** *He didn't report for work yesterday.*

● **reportedly** /rɪˈpɔːtɪdlɪ/ ADVERB used to show that you have heard information but cannot be sure it is true □ *She reportedly threatened to resign.*

reported speech /rɪˌpɔːtɪd 'spiːtʃ/ NOUN, NO PLURAL the words you use when you say what someone has said without using their exact words

reporter /rɪ'pɔːtə(r)/ NOUN [plural **reporters**] a person whose job is to describe events for newspapers, television or radio news programmes, etc. ⊞ *a newspaper reporter*

repossess /ˌriːpə'zes/ VERB [**repossesses, repossessing, repossessed**] to take back something that someone has bought, for example a car or a house, because they cannot finish paying for it □ *He lost his job and his house was repossessed.*
• **repossession** /ˌriːpə'zeʃən/ NOUN [plural **repossessions**] when something is repossessed

represent /ˌreprɪ'zent/ VERB [**represents, representing, represented**]
1 to speak or to act officially for someone else □ *Our MPs represent us in the government.* □ *He was represented by a lawyer.*
2 to be something or to be equal to something □ *The virus represents a major threat to public health.* □ *This figure represents an increase of 8%.*
3 to be a symbol or an example of something □ *The crown represents the king or queen.*
4 to take part in a competition for your country, school, etc. □ *She has represented her country at the highest level.*
5 to show or to describe something in a particular way □ **+ as** *The children in the picture were all represented as angels.*
• **representation** /ˌreprɪzen'teɪʃən/ NOUN [plural **representations**]
1 when someone is represented by someone else ⊞ *You are entitled to legal representation.*
2 when someone or something is shown in a particular way □ *It was not an accurate representation of his views.*
3 representations a formal word for something you officially ask for or complain about ⊞ *He made representations to the Foreign Office.*
• **representative** /ˌreprɪ'zentətɪv/ ► NOUN [plural **representatives**]
1 someone who represents someone else □ *a union representative* □ *There were representatives of several international organizations at the meeting.*
2 someone whose job is to sell the products of the company they work for ⊞ *a sales representative*
► ADJECTIVE typical of a group of people or things □ *a representative sample* □ *These statistics are representative of the overall population.*

repress /rɪ'pres/ VERB [**represses, repressing, repressed**]
1 to try not to show or to express a feeling □ *She repressed a smile.*
2 to control people by force □ *The regime represses any dissent.*
• **repressed** /rɪ'prest/ ADJECTIVE

1 not able or willing to show your feelings □ *She plays a repressed housewife.*
2 if a feeling is repressed, you do not show it □ *repressed emotions*
• **repression** /rɪ'preʃən/ NOUN, NO PLURAL when someone or something is repressed □ *There have been allegations of political repression.*
• **repressive** /rɪ'presɪv/ ADJECTIVE controlling people by force □ *a repressive regime*

reprieve /rɪ'priːv/ ► NOUN [plural **reprieves**] when a punishment or an unpleasant event is stopped or delayed □ *She won a last-minute reprieve from being deported.*
► VERB [**reprieves, reprieving, reprieved**] to stop or to delay a punishment or an unpleasant event

reprimand /'reprɪmɑːnd/ ► VERB [**reprimands, reprimanding, reprimanded**] to officially criticize someone for doing something wrong □ *She was reprimanded for unprofessional conduct.*
► NOUN [plural **reprimands**] when someone is reprimanded □ *He received a written reprimand.*

reprint ► VERB /ˌriː'prɪnt/ [**reprints, reprinting, reprinted**]
1 to print more copies of a book
2 to print a copy of a piece of writing, a photograph, etc.
► NOUN /'riːprɪnt/ [plural **reprints**] a new copy of a book

reprisal /rɪ'praɪzəl/ NOUN [plural **reprisals**] something unpleasant you do to someone because o something bad they have done to you □ *The countr will suffer reprisals for their attacks.*

reproach /rɪ'prəʊtʃ/ ► NOUN [plural **reproaches**]
1 an expression of criticism or disappointment abou someone's behaviour □ *He gave her a look of reproach.*
2 above/beyond reproach very good and not able to be criticized □ *His behaviour was beyond reproach*
► VERB [**reproaches, reproaching, reproached**] to criticize someone for their behaviour □ *The teacher reproached the pupils for being noisy.*
• **reproachful** /rɪ'prəʊtʃfʊl/ ADJECTIVE showing criticism □ *reproachful words*

reproduce /ˌriːprə'djuːs/ VERB [**reproduces, reproducing, reproduced**]
1 to make something again or to copy something □ *The child had reproduced his father's signature.* □ *Other scientists failed to reproduce the same result*
2 to produce babies, young animals or plants. A biology word. □ *The virus reproduces quickly.*
• **reproduction** /ˌriːprə'dʌkʃən/ NOUN [plural **reproductions**]
1 a copy of something □ *a reproduction of the painting*
2 the process of producing babies or young animals plants. A biology word. □ *human reproduction*
• **reproductive** /ˌriːprə'dʌktɪv/ ADJECTIVE to do wit the process of reproduction. A biology word. □ *the reproductive organs*

reptile /ˈreptaɪl/ NOUN [plural **reptiles**] an animal with cold blood that lays eggs, such as a snake or lizard. A biology word.

republic /rɪˈpʌblɪk/ NOUN [plural **republics**] a country with no king or queen, but with an elected government and usually a president (=elected leader)
• **republican** /rɪˈpʌblɪkən/ ADJECTIVE
1 belonging to a republic or wanting your country to be a republic
2 Republican someone who supports the Republican Party in the US

repulsive /rɪˈpʌlsɪv/ ADJECTIVE very unpleasant □ She found the images repulsive.

reputable /ˈrepjʊtəbəl/ ADJECTIVE considered to be of good quality, honest, etc. □ a reputable company

reputation /ˌrepjʊˈteɪʃən/ NOUN [plural **reputations**] the opinion that most people have of someone or something based on experience □ The restaurant has a very good reputation □ + for He has a reputation for being a very tough player. □ + as The country has built a reputation as a tourist destination. 🕮 He gained an international reputation.

reputed /rɪˈpjuːtɪd/ ADJECTIVE used to say that people in general consider something to be true □ She is reputed to be earning over £500,000 a year.

reputedly /rɪˈpjuːtɪdli/ ADVERB according to what most people believe □ She is reputedly the most talented member of the government.

request /rɪˈkwest/ ▶ NOUN [plural **requests**]
1 when someone politely asks for something 🕮 I've got a request to make. □ + for There were hundreds of requests for information. □ + to do something The man refused repeated requests to leave.
on request if something is available on request, it is available to people who ask for it
▶ VERB [**requests, requesting, requested**] to ask politely for something □ The committee requested additional information. □ The pilot requested permission to land. □ + that She requested that the case be delayed.

> Note that you **request** something. You do not 'request for' something:
> ✓ He requested an invitation.
> ✗ He requested for an invitation.

requiem /ˈrekwɪəm/ NOUN [plural **requiems**] a religious piece of music that is played at a Christian service for someone who has died

require /rɪˈkwaɪə(r)/ VERB [**requires, requiring, required**]
to need something □ Do you require any further information? □ He required treatment for an ankle injury.
be required to do something to officially have to do something □ All staff are required to dress appropriately. 🕮 All passengers are required by law to wear seat belts.

requirement /rɪˈkwaɪəmənt/ NOUN [plural **requirements**]
1 something you have to have or to do in order to do something else 🕮 There is no legal requirement to notify the parents. 🕮 It meets the safety requirements.
2 something that you need or want 🕮 Each kitchen is designed to meet customer requirements.

rerun /ˈriːrʌn/ NOUN [plural **reruns**] a television programme that is repeated

resat /ˌriːˈsæt/ PAST TENSE AND PAST PARTICIPLE OF resit

reschedule /ˌriːˈʃedjuːl/ VERB [**reschedules, rescheduling, rescheduled**] to arrange for something to happen at a different time □ My meeting has been rescheduled.

rescue /ˈreskjuː/ ▶ VERB [**rescues, rescuing, rescued**] to save someone from danger □ + from Firefighters rescued the people from the burning house.
▶ NOUN [plural **rescues**] when someone is rescued □ They were stranded with no hope of rescue. 🕮 Fire fighters made several rescue attempts. 🕮 A passing driver came to her rescue.
• **rescuer** /ˈreskjuːə(r)/ NOUN [plural **rescuers**] a person who rescues someone

research /rɪˈsɜːtʃ, ˈriːsɜːtʃ/ ▶ NOUN [plural **researches**] when you study a subject carefully to find new information □ + into They fund research into causes of cancer. 🕮 The research was carried out in 2005. 🕮 The research shows little educational benefit to homework.
▶ VERB [**researches, researching, researched**] to study a subject carefully to find new information □ She is researching her family history. □ I was researching a book about Einstein.
• **researcher** /rɪˈsɜːtʃə(r)/ NOUN [plural **researchers**] a person who researches something

resemblance /rɪˈzembləns/ NOUN [plural **resemblances**] when things or people look or seem similar in some way □ Can you see the resemblance between the brothers? 🕮 The film bears little resemblance to (=is quite different from) the original book.
• **resemble** /rɪˈzembəl/ VERB [**resembles, resembling, resembled**] to look similar or to seem similar in some way □ Tom resembles his father. □ The website resembles the front page of a newspaper.

resent /rɪˈzent/ VERB [**resents, resenting, resented**] to feel angry or unhappy about something you think is unfair □ She resented being interrupted. □ He resented his sister because of the attention she received.
• **resentful** /rɪˈzentfʊl/ ADJECTIVE feeling angry and unhappy about something you think is unfair □ a resentful look
• **resentment** /rɪˈzentmənt/ NOUN, NO PLURAL the feeling of resenting something 🕮 There is deep resentment towards the authorities.

reservation /ˌrezəˈveɪʃən/ NOUN [plural reservations]
1 an arrangement to keep a place for you in a restaurant, hotel, plane, etc. □ + *for* We have a reservation for dinner. ⊞ I'd like to make a reservation for two double rooms, please.
2 a feeling of doubt about something □ + *about* Some people expressed reservations about the plans. ⊞ Peter had reservations about moving abroad.
• **reserve** /rɪˈzɜːv/ ▶ VERB [reserves, reserving, reserved]
1 to ask a hotel, restaurant, etc. to keep a place for you □ I'd like to reserve a table for dinner tonight, please. □ We reserved seats in a no-smoking section.
2 to keep something for a particular use or person □ + *for* Some seats are reserved for elderly or disabled passengers. □ Mix in half the sugar, reserving the rest for the icing.
3 to wait before expressing your opinion about something ⊞ I'll reserve judgment until I see it for myself.
4 reserve the right to do something a formal phrase meaning to keep the right to do something in the future □ The management reserves the right to refuse entry.
▶ NOUN [plural reserves]
1 an amount of something you have available to use in the future □ the world's oil reserves □ She seems to have amazing reserves of energy and patience.
2 someone or something available to be used if another person or thing is not available □ He was a reserve in the England team. □ He managed to open his reserve parachute.
3 in reserve available to be used if needed □ It's always wise to keep some money in reserve.
4 an area of land where plants or animals are protected ⊞ a nature reserve
5 no plural the quality of being quiet and not showing your feelings □ Despite his initial reserve, he soon started to make friends.
• **reserved** /rɪˈzɜːvd/ ADJECTIVE quiet and not showing your feelings □ He's a reserved man.

reservoir /ˈrezəvwɑː(r)/ NOUN [plural reservoirs] a large lake where water is collected and stored in order to be used by people in an area
reset button /ˈriːset ˌbʌtən/ NOUN [plural reset buttons] a switch on a computer that lets you turn the computer off and then on again if the computer is not working
reshuffle /ˈriːʃʌfəl/ NOUN [plural reshuffles] when people within a group are given different jobs, especially in the government ⊞ There's been another cabinet reshuffle by the Prime Minister.
reside /rɪˈzaɪd/ VERB [resides, residing, resided] a formal word meaning to live in a place
• **residence** /ˈrezɪdəns/ NOUN [plural residences] a formal word meaning where someone lives □ Buckingham Palace is one of the queen's official residences. □ What is your country of residence?

• **resident** /ˈrezɪdənt/ ▶ NOUN [plural residents] someone who lives in a place ⊞ Local residents are opposed to the plans.
▶ ADJECTIVE living in a place □ How long have you been resident in this country?
• **residential** /ˌrezɪˈdenʃəl/ ADJECTIVE
1 a residential area has mostly houses, not offices or factories
2 a residential activity is one where you stay at the place where you are working or studying □ a residential course for teachers
residue /ˈrezɪdjuː/ NOUN [plural residues] an amount left after the rest of a substance has gone or been used □ It left a sticky residue.
resign /rɪˈzaɪn/ VERB [resigns, resigning, resigned] to officially say that you are leaving your job □ She resigned from her post as finance director.
♦ PHRASAL VERB **resign yourself to something** to accept something unpleasant that you cannot change □ He had resigned himself to defeat. □ They're resigned to losing the house.
• **resignation** /ˌrezɪgˈneɪʃən/ NOUN [plural resignations]
1 when you resign from your job □ a letter of resignation □ There have been calls for the minister's resignation. ⊞ He's handed in his resignation.
2 a feeling of accepting something unpleasant that you cannot change □ a look of resignation
• **resigned** /rɪˈzaɪnd/ ADJECTIVE accepting a bad situation that you cannot change □ a resigned sigh □ I'm resigned to the fact that I will never be rich.
resilience /rɪˈzɪliəns/ NOUN, NO PLURAL the quality of being able to deal with hard treatment or difficult situations without being badly affected □ She showed great resilience in coming back to win the match.
• **resilient** /rɪˈzɪliənt/ ADJECTIVE able to deal with hard treatment or difficult situations without being badly affected □ She's a strong and resilient woman.
resin /ˈrezɪn/ NOUN, NO PLURAL a sticky substance produced by some trees
resist /rɪˈzɪst/ VERB [resists, resisting, resisted]
1 to try to stop something from happening or to refuse to accept something □ The bank resisted pressure to cut interest rates.
2 to stop yourself from doing or having something you want ⊞ She resisted the temptation to take a look. □ The opportunity was too good to resist.
3 to fight against someone or something, especially when they are attacking you. □ They couldn't resist attackers. ⊞ He resisted arrest.
• **resistance** /rɪˈzɪstəns/ NOUN, NO PLURAL
1 when you refuse to accept something ⊞ The plans have met stiff resistance.
2 when you fight against someone or something □ armed resistance ⊞ The rebels put up fierce resistance.
3 the ability to not be affected by something □ the body's resistance to disease

4 the amount by which a substance can stop or slow down an electric current. A physics word.

• **resistant** /rɪˈzɪstənt/ ADJECTIVE
1 not harmed or affected by something □ *a water-resistant watch* □ *The bacteria have become resistant to antibiotics.*
2 not accepting something □ *They are stubbornly resistant to change.*

resit /ˌriːˈsɪt/ ▶ VERB [resits, resitting, resat] to take an exam again
▶ NOUN /ˈriːsɪt/ [plural resits] when you take an exam again

resolute /ˈrezəluːt/ ADJECTIVE very determined not change your opinions or decisions □ *Jim remained resolute in his refusal to sing.*

• **resolutely** /ˈrezəluːtlɪ/ ADVERB in a determined way □ *We have resolutely refused to do extra work.*

• **resolution** /ˌrezəˈluːʃən/ NOUN [plural resolutions]
1 an official decision which a group of people vote for ☐ *The UN passed a resolution imposing sanctions.*
2 a firm decision to do something ☐ *I made several New Year's resolutions.*
3 when you solve a problem or a disagreement □ *We are hoping for a diplomatic resolution of the dispute.*
4 the quality of being determined

• **resolve** /rɪˈzɒlv/ ▶ VERB [resolves, resolving, resolved]
1 to solve or successfully deal with a problem or a disagreement □ *He tried to resolve the dispute peacefully.*
2 to make a firm decision to do something □ *We have resolved to try harder next time.*
▶ NOUN, NO PLURAL determination □ *I have always admired his resolve.*

resort /rɪˈzɔːt/
PHRASAL VERB [resorts, resorting, resorted] **resort to something** to do something you do not want to do in order to solve a problem □ *The worst thing would be to resort to violence.*
▶ NOUN [plural resorts]
1 a place where people go on holiday □ *a popular seaside resort* □ *a ski resort*
2 a **last resort** something you do only when everything else has failed □ *I suppose we could borrow the money as a last resort.*

resound /rɪˈzaʊnd/ VERB [resounds, resounding, resounded] to make a loud sound that fills a place, or to be filled with a loud sound □ *The scream resounded through the building.*

• **resounding** /rɪˈzaʊndɪŋ/ ADJECTIVE
1 complete or very great ☐ *a resounding victory* ☐ *The tour has been a resounding success.*
2 loud and filling a place with sound □ *It hit the floor with a resounding crash.*

resource /rɪˈzɔːs/ NOUN [plural resources] something that you have and are able to use ☐ *the country's natural resources* □ *He blamed a lack of resources for the delays.*

• **resourceful** /rɪˈzɔːsfʊl/ ADJECTIVE good at finding ways of doing things and solving problems □ *We had little to work with so we had to be resourceful.*

• **resourcefulness** /rɪˈzɔːsfʊlnəs/ NOUN, NO PLURAL the quality of being resourceful

respect /rɪˈspekt/ ▶ NOUN [plural respects]
1 the feeling of admiring someone or something because of their behaviour or their achievements □ **+ of** *She earned the respect of her colleagues.* □ **+ for** *I have the utmost respect for Mr Williams.*
2 polite behaviour towards someone □ **+ for** *Their behaviour shows a lack of respect for others.* ☐ *He treats everyone with respect.*
3 a feeling that something is important or powerful and should be treated carefully ☐ *The sea can be very dangerous - you must treat it with respect.*
4 a part of something or a way of thinking about it ☐ *In many respects, the two boys are very similar.* □ *The plan was good in every respect.*
5 with respect to someone/something a formal phrase meaning to do with someone or something □ *No decision has yet been made with respect to the new stadium.*
▶ VERB [respects, respecting, respected]
1 to admire someone or something because of their behaviour or achievements □ *I respect her enormously.* ☐ *He was highly respected in the local community.*
2 to treat someone politely and show care for their beliefs, rights, etc. □ *We ask the media to respect her privacy.* □ *They have failed to respect the human rights of the refugees.*
3 to agree to obey a rule, a decision, etc. □ *We will respect their decision.*

• **respectability** /rɪˌspektəˈbɪlɪtɪ/ NOUN, NO PLURAL the quality of being accepted by society as good, correct, honest, etc. □ *His writing has only recently achieved mainstream respectability.*

• **respectable** /rɪˈspektəbəl/ ADJECTIVE
1 accepted by society as good, correct, honest, etc. □ *Simon comes from a respectable family.*
2 quite good □ *a perfectly respectable score*

• **respectably** /rɪˈspektəblɪ/ ADVERB
1 in a socially acceptable way □ *She was respectably dressed.*
2 quite well □ *He played very respectably.*

• **respected** /rɪˈspektɪd/ ADJECTIVE admired by many people □ *She was a respected lawyer.*

• **respectful** /rɪˈspektfʊl/ ADJECTIVE showing respect for someone or something □ *a respectful attitude* □ *I stayed a respectful distance away.*

• **respectfully** /rɪˈspektfʊlɪ/ ADVERB in a way that shows respect □ *Everyone respectfully bowed their heads as the coffin went past.*

respective /rɪˈspektɪv/ ADJECTIVE to do with each person or thing that has been mentioned separately □ *David and Diane are each good at their respective jobs.*

• **respectively** /rɪˈspektɪvlɪ/ ADVERB in the same order as the things already mentioned □ *Colin, Jane and Ian were given £5, £3 and £1 respectively.*

respiration /ˌrespəˈreɪʃən/ NOUN, NO PLURAL
1 a formal word for breathing
2 when living things make energy from food. A biology word.
• **respirator** /ˈrespəreɪtə(r)/ NOUN [plural **respirators**] a machine that helps someone to breathe when they are too ill to do it naturally
• **respiratory** /rɪˈspɪrətəri/ ADJECTIVE to do with breathing ⊞ the respiratory system

respite /ˈrespaɪt/ NOUN, NO PLURAL a period of rest from something unpleasant or difficult □ The pain continued without respite for about two hours.

resplendent /rɪˈsplendənt/ ADJECTIVE very bright and attractive in a grand way □ She was resplendent in a red satin dress.

respond /rɪˈspɒnd/ VERB [responds, responding, responded]
1 to answer or to react □ If someone hits you, you tend to respond by hitting back. □ 'That's not my problem,' Gina responded. □ Police responded quickly to the call.
2 to improve as a result of treatment □ She is responding well to treatment.
• **response** /rɪˈspɒns/ NOUN [plural **responses**] an answer or a reaction □ His response was a shake of his head. □ What was the response of his colleagues to his announcement?

responsibility /rɪˌspɒnsəˈbɪlɪti/ NOUN [plural **responsibilities**]
1 something that you must do or deal with □ + for The manager has responsibility for all the business. □ + of The first responsibility of a government is to protect its citizens. □ + to do something It's my responsibility to make sure all the doors are locked.' □ They share the childcare responsibilities.
2 blame for doing something, usually something bad ⊞ I take full responsibility for the mistake. ⊞ No one has yet claimed responsibility for the bombing.
• **responsible** /rɪˈspɒnsəbəl/ ADJECTIVE
1 if you are responsible for something, you are the person who must do it or deal with it □ + for Who is responsible for keeping the money? □ the minister responsible for transport
2 if you are responsible for something which happens, you are to blame for it □ + for Is human activity directly responsible for global warming? ⊞ He felt partly responsible for the mess. ⊞ We hold the company responsible for her death.
3 sensible and able to be trusted □ I'm looking for a responsible teenager to babysit.
4 involving important jobs or decisions □ He holds a responsible position within the company.
• **responsibly** /rɪˈspɒnsɪbli/ ADVERB in a sensible way, showing good judgment □ Drivers must act responsibly. □ He called on industry to behave more responsibly.

responsive /rɪˈspɒnsɪv/ ADJECTIVE
1 reacting in a quick and positive way □ The disease

was much more responsive to the second drug. □ The steering on this car is much more responsive.
2 willing to talk or answer questions □ I tried to make conversation, but he wasn't very responsive.

rest /rest/ ▶ NOUN [plural **rests**]
1 the **rest** the part of something that is left, or the people or things that are left □ I don't want to spend the rest of my life here. □ The rest of the country will have showers. □ I want half of you in this room and the rest outside.
2 a time when you relax or sleep ⊞ Why don't you have a rest before dinner?
3 come to rest to stop moving □ The coin rolled off the table and came to rest under his feet. □ Her eyes came to rest on the letter.
▶ VERB [rests, resting, rested]
1 to relax or sleep after an activity □ You should rest every few minutes when you're lifting such heavy weights.
2 if you rest part of your body, you stop using it so that it becomes less tired □ Let's stop and rest our legs for a minute.
3 to be supported by something, or to put something on something else for support □ He left his spade resting against a wall. □ Mo rested her hands on the piano keys for a moment.
♦ PHRASAL VERB **rest on something** to depend on something □ The success of the business rests on one product.

restart /ˌriːˈstɑːt/ VERB [restarts, restarting, restarted]
1 to turn a computer off and then on again □ Have you tried restarting your computer?
2 to start again or to start something again □ The course restarts in September.

restaurant /ˈrestərɒnt/ NOUN [plural **restaurants**] a place where you can buy and eat a meal □ a Chinese restaurant

restful /ˈrestful/ ADJECTIVE making you feel calm and relaxed □ restful music

restless /ˈrestlɪs/ ADJECTIVE not able to stay still or quiet because you are nervous, worried or bored □ The audience began to get restless after about an hour.
• **restlessly** /ˈrestlɪsli/ ADVERB in a restless way □ The horses stamped restlessly.
• **restlessness** /ˈrestlɪsnɪs/ NOUN, NO PLURAL a feeling of being restless

restoration /ˌrestəˈreɪʃən/ NOUN, NO PLURAL when you make something the way it was before □ After the fire, the restoration of the church took three years. □ the restoration of democracy
• **restore** /rɪˈstɔː(r)/ VERB [restores, restoring, restored]
1 to bring something back that existed before ⊞ Police struggled to restore order. □ He's trying to restore public confidence in the government.
2 to repair something so it is like it was before □ The house had been restored to its former glory.

3 a formal word meaning to give something back to the person it belongs to □ *The necklace has now been restored to its grateful owner.*

restrain /rɪˈstreɪn/ VERB [**restrains, restraining, restrained**]
1 to stop someone from doing something, often using force □ *He attacked the man as friends tried to restrain him.*
2 to control your emotions or behaviour □ *We had to restrain ourselves from laughing.*
3 a formal word meaning to stop something increasing □ *The government needs to restrain spending.*
● **restrained** /rɪˈstreɪnd/ ADJECTIVE calm and not showing much emotion □ *I expected him to be furious, but he was very restrained.*
● **restraint** /rɪˈstreɪnt/ NOUN [*plural* **restraints**]
1 *no plural* when you control your emotions or behaviour □ *She behaved with amazing restraint.* 🕮 *He urged both sides in the dispute to show restraint.*
2 something that prevents you from doing something or stops something from increasing □ *Wage restraints have angered unions.*
3 something that limits someone's physical movement □ *Police used restraints to keep him on the bed.*

restrict /rɪˈstrɪkt/ VERB [**restricts, restricting, restricted**] to limit something □ *We are restricting people to one ticket each.* □ *Parents can restrict children's access to certain websites.*
● **restriction** /rɪˈstrɪkʃən/ NOUN [*plural* **restrictions**] a limit on something □ *Are there any parking restrictions on this road?* 🕮 *Airlines imposed restrictions on hand luggage.*
● **restrictive** /rɪˈstrɪktɪv/ ADJECTIVE limiting something, often too much □ *restrictive laws*

restroom /ˈrestrʊm/ NOUN [*plural* **restrooms**] a US word for a room with a toilet, especially for public use

restructure /ˌriːˈstrʌktʃə(r)/ VERB [**restructures, restructuring, restructured**] to change the way a company, system, etc. is organized □ *They have radically restructured the business.*
● **restructuring** /ˌriːˈstrʌktʃərɪŋ/ NOUN, NO PLURAL when you restructure something

result /rɪˈzʌlt/ ▶ NOUN [*plural* **results**]
1 what happens because of something else □ *+ of This could be another result of global warming.* 🕮 *He died as a result of the accident.* 🕮 *He tried to play again too quickly, with the result that he made the injury worse.*
2 the score or the winner at the end of a competition, an election, etc. □ *the election result* □ *+ of Do you know the result of yesterday's match?*
3 the information you get at the end of a study or an experiment □ *+ of the results of the survey* 🕮 *the test results*
4 the score that you get in an exam 🕮 *She got good exam results.*
5 **get results** success in something you do 🕮 *His methods get results.*

▶ VERB [**results, resulting, resulted**] to happen because of something else □ *The fire apparently resulted from a dropped cigarette.*
◆ PHRASAL VERB **result in something** to cause something □ *The changes will result in the loss of 300 jobs.*

resume /rɪˈzjuːm/ VERB [**resumes, resuming, resumed**] a formal word meaning to start again □ *Normal services will resume next week.*

résumé /ˈrezjuːmeɪ/ NOUN [*plural* **résumés**]
1 a mainly US word for a list of your qualifications and the jobs you have done, that you show to someone you want to work for
2 a short explanation or description of something □ *I gave them a brief résumé of what had been discussed.*

resumption /rɪˈzʌmpʃən/ NOUN, NO PLURAL a formal word meaning when something resumes (=starts again) □ *the resumption of peace talks*

resurgence /rɪˈsɜːdʒəns/ NOUN, NO PLURAL when something begins to happen again, often in a stronger way than before □ *There was a resurgence of violence in the area.*

resurrect /ˌrezəˈrekt/ VERB [**resurrects, resurrecting, resurrected**] to bring something back into use after a long time □ *They've resurrected plans for a tram system.*
● **resurrection** /ˌrezəˈrekʃən/ NOUN, NO PLURAL
1 when you resurrect something
2 **the Resurrection** the Christian belief that Jesus Christ came back to life after his death

resuscitate /rɪˈsʌsɪteɪt/ VERB [**resuscitates, resuscitating, resuscitated**] to make someone start breathing again when they have stopped □ *Doctors were unable to resuscitate him.*
● **resuscitation** /rɪˌsʌsɪˈteɪʃən/ NOUN, NO PLURAL when you resuscitate someone 🕮 *Someone gave him mouth-to-mouth resuscitation.*

retail /ˈriːteɪl/ ▶ NOUN, NO PLURAL the selling of goods to the public, usually in shops □ *I work in retail.*
▶ VERB [**retails, retailing, retailed**] to be sold at a particular price □ *The device will retail at £48.*
● **retailer** /ˈriːteɪlə(r)/ NOUN [*plural* **retailers**] a person or company that sells goods to the public, usually in a shop □ *a clothing retailer*
● **retailing** /ˈriːteɪlɪŋ/ NOUN, NO PLURAL the business of selling goods to the public

retain /rɪˈteɪn/ VERB [**retains, retaining, retained**] to keep something □ *A smaller house would retain heat better in the winter.*

retaliate /rɪˈtælɪeɪt/ VERB [**retaliates, retaliating, retaliated**] to do something bad to someone because they have done something bad to you □ *He retaliated by pushing the other player in the chest.*
● **retaliation** /rɪˌtælɪˈeɪʃən/ NOUN, NO PLURAL when someone retaliates 🕮 *The bombing was in retaliation for recent killings of rebel fighters.*

retch /retʃ/ VERB [**retches, retching, retched**] to almost vomit □ *The smell made me retch.*

retention /rɪ'tenʃən/ NOUN, NO PLURAL when something is kept or not allowed to leave or escape □ *Pay is a key factor in the recruitment and retention of staff.*

rethink /ri:'θɪŋk/ ▶ VERB [**rethinks, rethinking, rethought**] to think about something again and decide what changes to make □ *We urge the government to rethink its policy on immigration.*
▶ NOUN, NO PLURAL /'ri:θɪŋk/ the act of rethinking something □ *The policy needs a complete rethink.*

reticence /'retɪsəns/ NOUN, NO PLURAL the quality of being reticent

reticent /'retɪsənt/ ADJECTIVE giving little information □ *He was very reticent about his plans.*

retina /'retɪnə/ NOUN [*plural* **retinas** or **retinae**] the area at the back of your eye that receives light and sends signals to your brain. A biology word.

retinue /'retɪnju:/ NOUN [*plural* **retinues**] a group of people who travel with an important or famous person

retire /rɪ'taɪə(r)/ VERB [**retires, retiring, retired**]
1 to stop working because you are old □ *Many people retire at 65.* □ *+ from She had just retired from a career in nursing.* □ *+ as He retired as director in 2005.*
2 a formal word meaning to go to a quiet place □ *+ to He retired to his bedroom.*
• **retired** /rɪ'taɪəd/ ADJECTIVE no longer working because you are old □ *a retired teacher*
• **retirement** /rɪ'taɪəmənt/ ▶ NOUN [*plural* **retirements**] **1** the period of time after you stop working because you are old □ *I hope you enjoy your retirement.*
2 the act of stopping work because you are old □ *He announced his retirement from politics.* 🕮 *Tom had taken early retirement* (=stopped working before the usual age).
▶ ADJECTIVE to do with the time when you stop working because you are old 🕮 *He is close to retirement age.* □ *a retirement party*
• **retiring** /rɪ'taɪərɪŋ/ ADJECTIVE shy and talking little

retort /rɪ'tɔ:t/ ▶ VERB [**retorts, retorting, retorted**] to answer quickly in an angry or humorous way □ *'You don't scare me,' she retorted.*
▶ NOUN [*plural* **retorts**] a quick and angry or humorous answer □ *an angry retort*

retrace /rɪ'treɪs/ VERB [**retraces, retracing, retraced**] retrace your steps to walk back exactly the same way that you came □ *I retraced my steps but there was no sign of my wallet.*

retrain /,ri:'treɪn/ VERB [**retrains, retraining, retrained**] to learn new skills for a different job □ *He retrained as a plumber.*
• **retraining** /,ri:'treɪnɪŋ/ NOUN, NO PLURAL learning new skills so that you can get a different job

retreat /rɪ'tri:t/ ▶ NOUN [*plural* **retreats**]
1 when you go to a place which is safer or quieter 🕮 *When they had gone, I beat a hasty retreat* (=went very quickly) *back into the house.*
2 a quiet place where people go to rest and relax □ *He*
spent the weekend at the presidential retreat at Camp David.*
3 when an army moves back because it does not want to fight □ *a strategic retreat*
▶ VERB [**retreats, retreating, retreated**]
1 to go somewhere safer or quieter □ *He retreated to the car and phoned the police.*
2 if an army retreats, it moves back because it does not want to fight

retrieve /rɪ'tri:v/ VERB [**retrieves, retrieving, retrieved**]
1 to find something and bring it back □ *He retrieved his pen from under the sofa.*
2 to get information that is stored on a computer
• **retriever** /rɪ'tri:və(r)/ NOUN [*plural* **retrievers**] a type of dog

return /rɪ'tɜ:n/ ▶ VERB [**returns, returning, returned**]
1 to go or come back to a place □ *We fly out on Friday and return the following Wednesday.* □ *+ to We all returned to our classrooms.* □ *+ from He returned from his skiing holiday with a broken leg.* 🕮 *All the air crew have returned safely.*
2 to start to happen or exist again □ *When we reache the town, our fears returned.* □ *Her cancer has returned.*
3 to take, put or send something back □ *Please retur your books by Friday.* □ *+ to All sports equipment should be returned to the gym.*
4 to do something to someone that they have done t you 🕮 *She never returns my calls* (=telephones me back). 🕮 *The soldiers immediately returned fire* (=sho at the people who were shooting them). □ *He returned my smile.*
5 return a verdict to say whether someone is guilt of a crime or not
◆ PHRASAL VERB **return to something**
1 to go back to the condition or situation that someone or something was in before 🕮 *Life in the ca is beginning to return to normal.*
2 to start doing something again 🕮 *The miners we forced to return to work.* □ *He turned away and returned to his gardening.*
3 to start talking again about a subject that has already been discussed □ *Can we return to the issue safety?*
▶ NOUN [*plural* **returns**]
1 when someone comes or goes back to a place □ *to On my return to the house, I found the door w open.* □ *+ from After his return from Africa, he sett in London.* 🕮 *They celebrated the safe return of th climbers.*
2 when something starts to happen or exist again □ *Police ensured the return of order to the area.* □ *+ The opposition has demanded a return to democra*
3 when something is taken, put or sent back □ *+ We are delighted at the safe return of the stolen painti*
4 in return in exchange for something □ *When w away, she walks our dog, and in return I water her*

plants. □ *He gave me some CDs in return for the book.*
5 when someone starts doing something again □ *+ to We are expecting her return to work next week.*
6 a key on a computer keyboard that starts a new line or makes the computer do something ⊞ *Type your password and press return.*
7 a ticket that allows you to travel to a place and back again □ *I'd like a return to Glasgow, please.*
8 something that has been taken back, especially to a shop □ *All the tickets have been sold, but there may be some returns later.*
9 a profit □ *+ of The shares generated a return of over 20%.* □ *+ on We were hoping for a higher return on our investment.*
10 an official form that you have to complete, especially to do with tax ⊞ *I haven't filled in my tax return yet.*
▶ ADJECTIVE
1 to do with a journey to and from a place ⊞ *a return ticket/trip*
2 to do with the part of a journey when you are coming back ⊞ *The return journey took over 4 hours.* □ *Our return flight was delayed.*
3 a return match or game is the second one of two between the same people

reunion /riːˈjuːnjən/ NOUN [plural **reunions**] a meeting of people such as friends or family members who have not seen each other for a long time □ *a family reunion*

reunite /ˌriːjuːˈnaɪt/ VERB [**reunites**, **reuniting**, **reunited**] people are reunited when they meet again after not seeing each other for a long time □ *The injured soldiers were flown home and were reunited with their families.*

Rev /rev/ ABBREVIATION **Reverend**, used in writing □ *Rev Pat Green*

rev /rev/ VERB [**revs**, **revving**, **revved**] to make an engine go faster

reveal /rɪˈviːl/ VERB [**reveals**, **revealing**, **revealed**]
to tell someone something that is secret or surprising □ *He refused to reveal details of the project.*
to show something that you could not see before □ *The mobile phone has a screen which slides back to reveal the keyboard.*

revealing /rɪˈviːlɪŋ/ ADJECTIVE
telling you something that you did not know □ *a revealing interview*
revealing clothes show a part of the body that is usually covered □ *a revealing dress*

revel /ˈrevəl/
PHRASAL VERB [**revels**, **revelling/US reveling**, **revelled/US reveled**] **revel in something** to enjoy a situation very much □ *Maxine revelled in all the attention she got.*

revelation /ˌrevəˈleɪʃən/ NOUN [plural **revelations**]
a surprising fact which was secret □ *The article was full of revelations about his private life.*
a good experience which surprises you very much □ *Seeing them in concert was a revelation.*

reveler /ˈrevələ(r)/ NOUN [plural **revelers**] the US spelling of **reveller**

reveller /ˈrevələ(r)/ NOUN [plural **revellers**] someone who is having fun in a noisy way at a party

revenge /rɪˈvendʒ/ NOUN, NO PLURAL when you hurt or upset someone because they have hurt or upset you or someone that you love ⊞ *Ben had ruined her life and she was determined to get revenge.* ⊞ *a revenge attack*

revenue /ˈrevənjuː/ NOUN, NO PLURAL money that a business or government gets □ *Most of the government's revenue comes from taxes.*

reverberate /rɪˈvɜːbəreɪt/ VERB [**reverberates**, **reverberating**, **reverberated**] if a sound reverberates, it comes back and you hear it again □ *The sound of gunfire reverberated along the valley.*
• **reverberation** /rɪˌvɜːbəˈreɪʃən/ NOUN [plural **reverberations**] when a sound reverberates

revere /rɪˈvɪə(r)/ VERB [**reveres**, **revering**, **revered**] a formal word meaning to respect and admire someone or something very much □ *It's a holy site revered by Jews and Muslims.*
• **reverence** /ˈrevərəns/ NOUN, NO PLURAL great respect and admiration
• **Reverend** /ˈrevərənd/ NOUN [plural **Reverends**] a title used before the name of some Christian priests □ *Reverend Ian Black*

reversal /rɪˈvɜːsəl/ NOUN [plural **reversals**] a change so that something becomes the opposite of what it was before □ *The win was a dramatic reversal of fortune for the team.*

reverse /rɪˈvɜːs/ ▶ VERB [**reverses**, **reversing**, **reversed**]
1 if a vehicle reverses, it moves backwards □ *A car was reversing.*
2 to make a vehicle move backwards □ *She reversed the car into the parking space.*
3 to change something so that it is the opposite of what it was before ⊞ *The government has reversed its decision.*
▶ NOUN, NO PLURAL
1 **the reverse** the opposite □ *It's not bad news - in fact, the reverse.*
2 **in reverse** in the opposite order □ *We visited the same places as them but in reverse.*
3 the position which you put a car's controls in to make it move backwards □ *I put the car in reverse.*
▶ ADJECTIVE opposite to what you expect □ *The policy had the reverse effect.*
• **reversible** /rɪˈvɜːsəbəl/ ADJECTIVE
1 able to be changed back □ *This is not a reversible process.*
2 reversible clothes can be worn with the inside part on the outside □ *a reversible jacket*

revert /rɪˈvɜːt/ VERB [**reverts**, **reverting**, **reverted**] to go back to the way something was before □ *Many ex-prisoners revert to a life of crime.*

review /rɪˈvjuː/ ▶ VERB [**reviews**, **reviewing**, **reviewed**]
1 to examine something again, often in order to

decide if changes should be made □ *The company is reviewing its safety procedures following the accident.* □ *Lawyers are reviewing the case.*
2 to write your opinion of a new book, play, etc. □ *She reviewed the book for the New York Times.*
3 the US word for revise (=study)
▶ NOUN [plural **reviews**]
1 when something is examined again, often in order to decide if changes need to be made □ + *of* *The government is conducting a review of the policy.*
2 under review being examined again □ *All our contracts are under review.*
3 an article which gives someone's opinion of a new book, play, etc. □ *a film review* 🖫 *The play got some good reviews.* □ + *of* *He wrote a review of the book.*
• **reviewer** /rɪ'vjuːə(r)/ NOUN [plural **reviewers**] someone who writes their opinion of new books, plays, etc.

revise /rɪ'vaɪz/ VERB [**revises, revising, revised**]
1 to change something, often in order to improve it □ *The revised edition of the dictionary has hundreds of new words in it.* □ *We've had to revise our plans.*
2 to study for an exam by looking again at the work you have done □ + *for* *Guy was busy revising for his Chinese exam.*
• **revision** /rɪ'vɪʒən/ NOUN [plural **revisions**]
1 change made in order to improve something □ *The law needs revision.*
2 work that you do before an exam, by looking at work you have already done 🖫 *I need to do some revision for my history test.*

revival /rɪ'vaɪvəl/ NOUN [plural **revivals**]
1 a performance of something that has not been performed for many years □ *a revival of an old musical*
2 an increase in how popular or successful something is □ *There has been a revival of interest in his music.*

revive /rɪ'vaɪv/ VERB [**revives, reviving, revived**]
1 to make someone conscious again □ *Doctors were unable to revive him.*
2 to make something popular or successful again □ *He was trying to revive his career.*
3 to make someone feel better and less tired □ *A cool shower should revive you.*

revolt /rɪ'vəʊlt/ ▶ NOUN [plural **revolts**]
1 when a group of people use violence in order to change a government
2 when people refuse to accept the authority of a leader □ *The leader is facing a revolt by members of his party.*
▶ VERB [**revolts, revolting, revolted**]
1 to use violence in order to change a government
2 to refuse to accept the authority of a leader
3 if you are revolted by something, it shocks you or makes you feel ill □ *I was revolted by the thought of eating worms.*
• **revolting** /rɪ'vəʊltɪŋ/ ADJECTIVE extremely unpleasant □ *a revolting smell*

revolution /ˌrevə'luːʃən/ NOUN [plural **revolutions**]
1 a time when people use violence to change a government □ *the French Revolution of 1789*
2 a complete change in something such as an industry or society □ *Computers have led to a revolution in the way we work.*
3 a complete turn of something such as a wheel
• **revolutionary** /ˌrevə'luːʃənərɪ/ ▶ ADJECTIVE
1 completely new and different □ *revolutionary technology*
2 to do with a political revolution □ *Castro's revolutionary movement*
▶ NOUN [plural **revolutionaries**] someone who is involved in a political revolution
• **revolutionize** or **revolutionise** /ˌrevə'luːʃənaɪz/ VERB [**revolutionizes, revolutionizing, revolutionized**] to completely change something and make it better □ *The drug could revolutionize the way that cancer is treated.*

revolve /rɪ'vɒlv/ VERB [**revolves, revolving, revolved**] to move in a circle around something □ *The Earth revolves around the sun.*
♦ PHRASAL VERB **revolve around someone/ something** to have something as the main part □ *The film revolves around two teenage criminals.*
• **revolver** /rɪ'vɒlvə(r)/ NOUN [plural **revolvers**] a type of small gun
• **revolving** /rɪ'vɒlvɪŋ/ ADJECTIVE moving in a circle □ *a revolving door*

reward /rɪ'wɔːd/ ▶ NOUN [plural **rewards**] something you get for doing something good or useful □ *financial rewards* □ + *for* *The victim's family are offering a £5,000 reward for any information that helps catch the killer.* □ *He got his reward for all his hard work when the team scored a goal.*
▶ VERB [**rewards, rewarding, rewarded**] to give someone something good for something they have done □ + *for* *He was rewarded for all his hard work* □ + *with* *The baby rewarded me with a smile as I picked her up.*
• **rewarding** /rɪ'wɔːdɪŋ/ ADJECTIVE giving you a feeling of satisfaction □ *Nursing can be a very rewarding job*

rewind /riː'waɪnd/ VERB [**rewinds, rewinding, rewound**] to make a tape (=long strip on which pictures and sound are recorded) move back towards the beginning

rewrite /riː'raɪt/ ▶ VERB [**rewrites, rewriting, rewrote, rewritten**] to write something again, make changes to it □ *You'll have to rewrite this because full of mistakes.*
▶ NOUN /'riːraɪt/ [plural **rewrites**] something which has been written again

rhetoric /'retərɪk/ NOUN, NO PLURAL words that are intended to make people believe or admire you, but which are not sincere □ *political rhetoric*
• **rhetorical** /rɪ'tɒrɪkəl/ ADJECTIVE a rhetorical question is one that is not a real question because you do not intend anyone to answer it

rheumatism /ˈruːmətɪzəm/ NOUN, NO PLURAL a disease that makes your knees, hips, etc. and muscles painful

rhino /ˈraɪnəʊ/ NOUN [plural **rhinos**] an informal word for rhinoceros

rhinoceros /raɪˈnɒsərəs/ NOUN [plural **rhinoceroses**] a large, grey animal from Africa and Asia that has thick skin and a horn on its nose

rhizome /ˈraɪzəʊm/ NOUN [plural **rhizomes**] a thick stem of a plant that grows along or under the ground. A biology word.

rhododendron /ˌrəʊdəˈdendrən/ NOUN [plural **rhododendrons**] a large bush with big flowers

rhombus /ˈrɒmbəs/ NOUN [plural **rhombuses or rhombi**] a shape with four straight sides and four angles that are not 90°. A maths word.

rhubarb /ˈruːbɑːb/ NOUN a plant that has red stems which you cook and eat as fruit

rhyme /raɪm/ ► VERB [**rhymes, rhyming, rhymed**] if words rhyme, they end with the same sound □ 'Ghost' rhymes with 'toast'.
► NOUN [plural **rhymes**]
1 a word that sounds like another, or a pair of words that have a similar sound □ I don't think there is a rhyme for 'orange'.
2 a short poem or song using words which rhyme □ a book of children's rhymes
3 poetry that uses words which sound similar at the end of each line □ The story was written in rhyme.

rhythm /ˈrɪðəm/ NOUN [plural **rhythms**] a repeated pattern of sounds or movements □ He had an irregular heart rhythm. □ + **of** Amy's foot was tapping to the rhythm of the music. 🕮 She has a good sense of rhythm.

rhythmic /ˈrɪðmɪk/ ADJECTIVE a rhythmic sound or movement has a repeated pattern

rib /rɪb/ NOUN [plural **ribs**] one of the curved bones in your chest, around your heart and lungs

ribbon /ˈrɪbən/ NOUN [plural **ribbons**] a long, narrow piece of cloth, used for example to tie your hair up, or as a decoration on a present

rib cage /ˈrɪb ˌkeɪdʒ/ NOUN [plural **rib cages**] the set of bones that form your chest

rice /raɪs/ NOUN, NO PLURAL brown or white grains that you cook and eat as food □ boiled rice 🕮 a grain of rice □ brown rice □ rice fields

rich /rɪtʃ/ ► ADJECTIVE [**richer, richest**]
1 having a lot of money □ Her Dad's very rich. □ rich countries 🕮 He was looking for ways to get rich (=become rich).
2 full of something good 🕮 Nuts and seeds are a particularly rich source of iron. □ + **in** Oranges are rich in vitamin C.
3 full of interesting events, ideas, etc. □ The city has a very rich history. □ The area is home to a rich variety of wildlife.
4 rich food contains a lot of butter or cream □ The cake was very rich so I only managed a small piece.
5 rich colours are strong and bright □ The carpet was a rich red.
► NOUN, NO PLURAL the rich people who have a lot of money □ She enjoyed reading about the lifestyles of the rich and famous.

• **riches** /ˈrɪtʃɪz/ PLURAL NOUN a literary word meaning a lot of money and expensive things

• **richly** /ˈrɪtʃlɪ/ ADVERB
1 in a beautiful way, often using expensive and brightly coloured materials □ The rooms were richly decorated.
2 if something is richly deserved, you deserve it very much
3 with a lot of money □ She was richly rewarded.

Richter scale /ˈrɪktə ˌskeɪl/ NOUN, NO PLURAL the Richter scale a way of measuring how strong earthquakes (=the ground suddenly moving) are. A geography word.

rickshaw /ˈrɪkʃɔː/ NOUN [plural **rickshaws**] a type of vehicle used in East Asia, in which passengers are pulled by someone who is walking or riding a bicycle

ricochet /ˈrɪkəʃeɪ/ VERB [**ricochets, ricocheting, ricocheted**] if a bullet or stone ricochets off something, it hits it and moves away from it

rid /rɪd/ ADJECTIVE
1 get rid of something (a) to throw something away or give it to someone else □ My parents got rid of the old sofa and bought a new one. (b) to make something go away that you do not want □ I opened the window to get rid of the smell. □ I can't seem to get rid of this cold.
2 get rid of someone to make someone go away □ He arrived at 7 o'clock and we couldn't get rid of him.
♦ PHRASAL VERB [**rids, ridding, rid**] rid someone/ something of something to get rid of something bad □ Scientists are working to rid the world of this virus.

• **riddance** /ˈrɪdəns/ NOUN, NO PLURAL Good riddance! said when you are pleased that someone or something has gone

ridden /ˈrɪdən/ PAST PARTICIPLE OF ride

riddle /ˈrɪdəl/ NOUN [plural **riddles**]
1 a strange or confusing question with a clever answer that you have to work out
2 a mystery that is difficult to solve □ How the burglar got into the house is a bit of a riddle.

riddled /ˈrɪdəld/ ADJECTIVE riddled with something (a) full of something bad □ The letter was riddled with errors. (b) full of a lot of small holes □ The glass was riddled with holes where the bullets had hit it.

ride /raɪd/ ► VERB [**rides, riding, rode, ridden**]
1 to travel on a bicycle, motorcycle or horse □ I learned to ride a bike when I was six. □ Do you ride (=ride a horse)? □ He turned and rode off.
2 to travel in or on a vehicle □ She had been riding around in the car all day.

◆ PHRASAL VERBS **ride on something** if one thing rides on something else, it depends on it in order to be successful □ *The whole future of the team is riding on this game.* **ride something out** to get to the end of a difficult situation without being harmed □ *The business is confident it can ride out the economic recession.*

▶ NOUN [*plural* **rides**]
1 a journey in or on a vehicle □ *It was a short bus ride from the airport to the hotel.* ⊞ *We went for a bike ride.* □ *+ in* *I had a ride in her new car.* □ *+ on* *Can I have a ride on your bike?*
2 a machine that people ride on for fun which moves them up and down or moves them very fast, etc. ⊞ *We went on all the rides at the fair.*
3 a bumpy/rough, etc. ride used for talking about how difficult a situation is □ *It's likely to be a fairly rough ride for the school over the next few months.*
● **rider** /ˈraɪdə(r)/ NOUN [*plural* **riders**] someone sitting on and controlling a bicycle, motorcycle or horse □ *horse riders*

ridge /rɪdʒ/ NOUN [*plural* **ridges**]
1 a long narrow piece of high land □ *mountain ridges*
2 a narrow raised line on the surface of something

ridicule /ˈrɪdɪkjuːl/ ▶ VERB [**ridicules, ridiculing, ridiculed**] to say unkind things about someone or something in order to make them seem silly □ *His accent was ridiculed by the other children.*
▶ NOUN, NO PLURAL unkind remarks that people make in order to make someone or something seem silly □ *The minister faced public ridicule over his comments.*
● **ridiculous** /rɪˈdɪkjʊləs/ ADJECTIVE very silly □ *It's a ridiculous idea!*

riding /ˈraɪdɪŋ/ NOUN, NO PLURAL the activity or sport of riding horses ⊞ *Mia goes riding every week.* □ *riding lessons*

rife /raɪf/ ADJECTIVE if something bad is rife, it exists or happens often □ *Crime is rife in this area.*

rifle /ˈraɪfəl/ NOUN [*plural* **rifles**] a type of long gun
◆ PHRASAL VERB [**rifles, rifling, rifled**] **rifle through something** to search a lot of things quickly, especially in order to steal something □ *I caught him rifling through the papers on my desk.*

rift /rɪft/ NOUN [*plural* **rifts**]
1 a situation in which two people or groups have argued with each other ⊞ *The talks were an attempt to heal the rift between the two countries.*
2 a large long crack in the land

rift valley /ˌrɪft ˈvælɪ/ NOUN [*plural* **rift valleys**] a valley with steep sides that is formed when the ground moves. A geography word.

rig /rɪg/ ▶ VERB [**rigs, rigging, rigged**] to do something dishonest so that a competition or election has the result that you want □ *The election must have been rigged.*
◆ PHRASAL VERB **rig something up** to make something quickly using things that you have □ *We rigged up a new aerial using a wire coat hanger.*

▶ NOUN [*plural* **rigs**] a large structure, used for getting oil or gas from under the sea □ *an oil rig*
● **rigging** /ˈrɪgɪŋ/ NOUN, NO PLURAL the ropes that support a ship's sails

right /raɪt/ ▶ ADJECTIVE
1 correct □ *+ about* *He was right about the train being late.* □ *Make sure you sign in the right place.* □ *Are we going in the right direction?* ⊞ *I got most of the answers right.* ⊞ *'I hear you're leaving.' 'That's right, I've got a new job.'*
2 suitable or in the condition that you want or expect □ *+ for* *He is not the right person for the job.* □ *We didn't have the right clothes for the weather.* ⊞ *I need a new table, and this one looks just right.* □ *As soon as I saw her, I knew that something wasn't right.*
3 fair or acceptable □ *It doesn't seem right that so many people in the world are hungry.* □ *+ to do something* *It's not right to tax the poor.*
4 on or to the side that is towards the east when you are facing north □ *I write with my right hand.* □ *We sat on the right side of the church.*
▶ ADVERB
1 towards the direction that is to the east when you are facing north □ *Now turn right.*
2 exactly □ *Don't move - stay right there.* □ *We were right in the middle of dinner.* □ *Stay right behind me.*
3 immediately □ *I'll come right after lunch.* ⊞ *I want the work done right now.*
4 all the way □ *This road goes right round the outside of the park.* □ *I watched the film right to the end.*
5 correctly □ *Can't you do anything right?*
6 used to get someone's attention before you speak or start to do something □ *Right, shall we go outside?*
▶ NOUN [*plural* **rights**]
1 something that you are allowed to do or have, either officially or because it is acceptable □ *+ to* *Everyone has a right to a decent education.* □ *These laws protect their religious rights.* ⊞ *You have no right to speak to me like that.* ⊞ *What gives her the right to tell us what to do?*
2 no plural the side or direction that is on or towards the right side of your body □ *There's a chemist over there on the right.*
3 no plural behaviour that is morally good □ *These children do not know right from wrong.*
4 the right people or groups with political opinions that support ideas such as having private owners of companies and people taking responsibility for their own lives

▶ Note (*noun, sense 1*) that you have a **right to** something or the **right to do** something. You do not have the 'right of' something:
✓ *Everybody has a right to healthcare.*
✗ *Everybody has a right of healthcare.*

▶ VERB [**rights, righting, righted**]
1 to put something back in a vertical position □ *I righted the glass and filled it again.*

2 to do something to make a bad or unfair situation better □ *We cannot right the mistakes of the past.*

right angle /'raɪt ˌæŋgəl/ NOUN [*plural* **right angles**] an angle of 90°, like the corner of a square. A maths word.

right click /ˌraɪt 'klɪk/ VERB [**right clicks, right clicking, right clicked**] to press the right button on a computer mouse so that the computer will do something. A computing word.

righteous /'raɪtʃəs/ ADJECTIVE
1 morally good □ *a righteous man*
2 righteous indignation/anger strong angry feelings when you think that something is not fair or not morally right

rightful /'raɪtfʊl/ ADJECTIVE considered as legally or morally correct ⊞ *The stolen goods were returned to their rightful owners.*

right-hand /ˌraɪt'hænd/ ADJECTIVE
1 on the right side of something □ *Take the right-hand turn.* ⊞ *The post office is on the right-hand side of the road.*
2 someone's **right-hand man** or **woman** is the person they depend on to work with and help them

right-handed /ˌraɪt'hændɪd/ ADJECTIVE using your right hand to do things, especially to write □ *Are you right-handed?* □ *a right-handed tennis player*

rightly /'raɪtlɪ/ ADVERB
1 correctly or fairly □ *Phil has rightly pointed out that Monday 12th is a bank holiday.*
2 in a way that is reasonable in a situation □ *People are rightly concerned about this decision.*

right of way /ˌraɪt əv 'weɪ/ NOUN [*plural* **rights of way**]
1 the right to drive onto a road or across a road before other vehicles □ *Who has right of way at the roundabout?*
2 a path that people can walk on which crosses land that someone owns

right wing /ˌraɪt 'wɪŋ/ NOUN **the right wing** the members of a political party who do not like change □ *the right wing of the Conservative Party*

right-wing /ˌraɪt'wɪŋ/ ADJECTIVE supporting the ideas of the political right □ *right-wing politicians*

rigid /'rɪdʒɪd/ ADJECTIVE
1 unwilling to change or impossible for someone to change □ *a rigid schedule* □ *The rules are very rigid.*
2 stiff and impossible to bend □ *a rigid frame*

rigmarole /'rɪgmərəʊl/ NOUN, NO PLURAL a process that is annoying because it is so long and complicated □ *I had to go through the whole rigmarole of re-applying for the licence.*

rigorous /'rɪgərəs/ ADJECTIVE very careful and dealing with every detail □ *We make rigorous safety checks on all the equipment.*

rim /rɪm/ NOUN [*plural* **rims**]
the top edge of a container such as a cup or bowl
the outside edge of something like a wheel

rind /raɪnd/ NOUN [*plural* **rinds**] the thick skin on some foods such as lemons, cheese or bacon

ring[1] /rɪŋ/ ▶ NOUN [*plural* **rings**]
1 a round piece of jewellery that you wear on your finger ⊞ *a wedding ring* □ *I was wearing a diamond ring.*
2 something in the shape of a circle □ *The children sat in a ring around the story-teller.* □ *The house was surrounded by a ring of fire.*
3 a group of people involved in an illegal activity □ *a spy ring*
4 an area where people do the sport of boxing
5 an area where people perform in a circus (=show where people and animals perform)
▶ VERB [**rings, ringing, ringed**]
1 to surround someone or something □ *The area is ringed with trees.*
2 to draw a circle around something □ *Ring any items that you are interested in.*

ring[2] /rɪŋ/ ▶ VERB [**rings, ringing, rang, rung**]
1 if a bell rings, it produces a sound, and if you ring a bell, you make it produce a sound □ *I think I heard the doorbell ring.*
2 to telephone someone □ *I'm ringing about the car you have for sale.*
3 if the telephone rings, it makes a sound so that you know someone is telephoning you

> ▶ Note that you **ring** (= telephone) a person or place. You do not 'ring to' a person or place:
> ✓ *I'll just ring my sister.*
> ✗ *I'll just ring to my sister.*

♦ PHRASAL VERBS **ring (someone) back** to telephone someone after they have telephoned you □ *I'm a bit busy - can I ring you back later?* **ring out** to make a loud, clear noise □ *Suddenly, shots rang out.* **ring someone up** to telephone someone □ *She rang me up in the middle of the night.*
▶ NOUN [*plural* **rings**]
1 give someone a ring to telephone someone □ *I'll give you a ring tomorrow.*
2 the sound a bell makes □ *Did I hear a ring at the door?*

ringleader /'rɪŋliːdə(r)/ NOUN [*plural* **ringleaders**] the leader of a group of people who are doing something bad

ringlet /'rɪŋlɪt/ NOUN [*plural* **ringlets**] a long curl of hair

ring road /'rɪŋ ˌrəʊd/ NOUN [*plural* **ring roads**] a road that goes around a town or city

ringtone /'rɪŋtəʊn/ NOUN [*plural* **ringtones**] the sound that a mobile phone makes when you call it

rink /rɪŋk/ NOUN [*plural* **rinks**] a large area of ice where people skate (=move wearing boots with metal blades on the bottom)

rinse /rɪns/ ▶ VERB [**rinses, rinsing, rinsed**] to remove dirt or soap from something by putting it in clean water □ *Rinse your hair well after shampooing it.*
▶ NOUN [*plural* **rinses**] a wash with clean water □ *He gave the cup a rinse.*

riot /ˈraɪət/ ▶ NOUN [plural **riots**]
1 a time when a large crowd of people behave violently in a public place 🔁 *His election sparked riots in the capital.* 🔁 *Riot police were brought in to control the crowd.*
2 run riot (a) to become impossible to control □ *Her emotions were running riot.* (b) to behave in a noisy and uncontrolled way □ *Too many parents allow their children to run riot.*
▶ VERB [**riots, rioting, rioted**] if a crowd of people riot, they behave violently in a public place
• **rioter** /ˈraɪətə(r)/ NOUN [plural **rioters**] someone who takes part in a riot □ *Rioters threw stones and bottles at police.*
• **rioting** /ˈraɪətɪŋ/ NOUN, NO PLURAL violent behaviour in a public place by a crowd of people 🔁 *Rioting broke out in the streets of the city.*
• **riotous** /ˈraɪətəs/ ADJECTIVE
1 involving a lot of noise and excitement □ *a riotous celebration*
2 noisy and violent □ *riotous behaviour*

rip /rɪp/ ▶ VERB [**rips, ripping, ripped**]
1 to tear something roughly □ *She ripped sheets into strips and used them as bandages.* □ *Steve had ripped his trousers on the barbed wire.*
2 to remove something quickly and forcefully □ *The storm ripped the roof off their house.*
♦ PHRASAL VERBS **rip someone off** to charge someone too much money for something. An informal phrase. □ *Some of the taxi drivers rip tourists off.* **rip something up** to tear something into small pieces □ *I ripped the letter up and put it in the bin.*
▶ NOUN [plural **rips**] a rough tear □ *There was a rip in my sleeve where the handlebars had caught it.*

ripe /raɪp/ ADJECTIVE [**riper, ripest**]
1 ripe fruit is ready to be picked or eaten □ *The plums were ripe and juicy.* □ *ripe tomatoes*
2 be ripe for something to be ready for something to happen, especially when it should have happened sooner □ *The company is ripe for a takeover.*
3 ripe old age an old age □ *He lived to the ripe old age of 98.*
• **ripen** /ˈraɪpən/ VERB [**ripens, ripening, ripened**] when fruit ripens, it becomes ready to pick or eat □ *The apples are ripening quickly this year.*

rip-off /ˈrɪpɒf/ NOUN [plural **rip-offs**] something that is much too expensive. An informal word. □ *At £100 a ticket, the show is a complete rip-off.*

ripple /ˈrɪpəl/ ▶ NOUN [plural **ripples**]
1 a small movement on the surface of water □ *Tiny fish were causing ripples in the water.*
2 a feeling or sound that spreads gradually through a place □ *A ripple of nervous laughter followed his comments.*
▶ VERB [**ripples, rippling, rippled**] to move like waves □ *The curtains rippled in the breeze.*

rise /raɪz/ ▶ VERB [**rises, rising, rose, risen**]
1 to go up □ *A column of smoke rose above the village.* □ **+ up** *The balloon rose up into the air.* □ *The sun rises in the east.* □ *Ahead, the ground rose steeply.*
2 to increase in level □ *Prices have risen this year.* 🔁 *Profits rose sharply in the second half of the year.* □ *The government has tried to calm rising panic about fuel costs.*
3 to become successful or powerful □ **+ to** *She rose to the position of chief executive.* 🔁 *He is a rising star in the government.*
4 rise to the challenge/occasion to manage to deal with a difficult situation successfully
5 to stand up □ *We all rose when the judge entered.*
6 to get out of bed □ *His habit was to rise early for breakfast.*
7 to fight against a government or someone in power □ **+ up** *The people rose up to protest about food shortages.*

> ► Note that **rise** has no object after it. If you want to say 'to make something go up' or 'to make something increase in level', use the verb **raise**. Raise is always followed by an object:
> ✔ *She raised her hand.*
> ✗ *She rose her hand.*
> ✔ *They raised prices.*
> ✗ *They rose prices.*

♦ PHRASAL VERB **rise above something** to not let an unpleasant situation affect you □ *The group is constantly arguing, but he manages to rise above all that.*
▶ NOUN [plural **rises**]
1 an increase in level □ *There has been a rise in the number of homeless people.*
2 when a person or a business becomes successful or powerful □ *The firm's rise from a small operation in Mick's bedroom to a multinational company shows that anyone can be successful.* 🔁 *The programme looks at her sudden rise to fame.*
3 give rise to something to cause something to happen or exist □ *The accident has given rise to worries about safety.*
4 an increase in pay □ *I'm going to ask my boss for a rise.*

risk /rɪsk/ ▶ NOUN [plural **risks**]
1 a possibility that something bad will happen □ **+ of** *We face the risk of losing our homes.* □ **+ that** *There is a risk that the whole project might be called off.* 🔁 *If you give up your job, you will be taking a big risk.* 🔁 *Without advertising, they run the risk of being ignored.*
2 something that could cause problems or danger in the future □ **+ to** *These laws are a risk to free speech.* □ *Smoking is a well known health risk.*
3 at risk in a situation where something bad might happen □ *Their traditional way of life is at risk.* □ *The children are at risk of violence.*
4 at your own risk if you do something at your own

risk, you take responsibility for anything bad that might happen to you □ *Bags can be left here at the customer's own risk.*

▶ VERB [**risks, risking, risked**]

1 to do something although you know there is a possibility that something bad will happen □ *I risked a glance at the document.* □ + *ing* *She couldn't risk phoning him.*

2 to put yourself in a situation where something bad could happen to you □ *He risked punishment by entering the room.* □ + *ing* *She risked failing her exams.*

3 to take the chance of damaging or losing something 🕀 *Soldiers are risking their lives every day.* □ *We have risked a lot of money on this business.*

▶ Note that the verb **risk** is followed by **doing something** and never by 'to do something':
✓ *I wouldn't risk telling him.*
✗ *I wouldn't risk to tell him.*

• **risky** /'rɪskɪ/ ADJECTIVE [**riskier, riskiest**] dangerous □ *It's too risky to wait any longer.*

isotto /rɪ'zɒtəʊ/ NOUN [*plural* **risottos**] an Italian dish of rice, often with meat or fish

isqué /'riːskeɪ/ ADJECTIVE risqué jokes, stories, remarks, etc. are slightly rude

ite /raɪt/ NOUN [*plural* **rites**] a ceremony, especially one to do with a religion □ *funeral rites*

itual /'rɪtʃʊəl/ ▶ NOUN [*plural* **rituals**]

1 a series of formal actions that are part of a ceremony □ *religious rituals*

2 something that you often do at the same time or in the same way □ *Reading stories to your child should be part of the bedtime ritual.*

▶ ADJECTIVE to do with a ritual □ *ritual dances*

val /'raɪvəl/ ▶ NOUN [*plural* **rivals**] a person or organization that competes against another □ *The two teams are bitter rivals.*

▶ ADJECTIVE competing against each other □ *rival gangs* □ *rival political parties*

▶ VERB [**rivals, rivalling/US rivaling, rivalled/US rivaled**] to be as good, as something or someone else □ *Shop-bought vegetables can't rival the ones you grow yourself.*

ivalry /'raɪvəlrɪ/ NOUN, NO PLURAL when people or organizations compete against each other □ *There's a lot of rivalry between the twins.*

ver /'rɪvə(r)/ NOUN [*plural* **rivers**] a large stream of water that flows across land □ *There were several boats on the river.* 🕀 *He crossed the river using the main bridge.* □ *the River Nile*

et /'rɪvɪt/ ▶ VERB [**rivets, riveting, riveted**] if you are riveted by something, you find it very interesting and cannot stop looking at it

NOUN [*plural* **rivets**] a type of large pin used for holding pieces of metal together

• **riveting** /'rɪvɪtɪŋ/ ADJECTIVE extremely interesting, keeping all your attention □ *It's a riveting story.*

road /rəʊd/ NOUN [*plural* **roads**]

1 a hard, level surface for vehicles to travel along □ *There were a lot of cars parked in the road.*
🕀 *Children need to learn how to cross the road safely.*
🕀 *The accident happened on the main road between Pula and Porec.* 🕀 *We live on a very busy road.* 🕀 *He died in a road accident.*

2 **over/across the road** on the opposite side of a road □ *Mark and Carrie live across the road from us.*

3 **down/along the road** further on the same road □ *My school is just down the road.*

4 **by road** in a vehicle that travels on the road □ *The journey to London is three hours by road.*

5 **Road** used in the name of some roads □ *They live at 12 Lockwood Road.*

road rage /'rəʊd ˌreɪdʒ/ NOUN, NO PLURAL angry or violent behaviour between drivers on the road □ *He was arrested following a road rage incident.*

roadside /'rəʊdsaɪd/ ADJECTIVE happening or placed by the side of a road □ *roadside bombings*

roadworks /'rəʊdwɜːks/ PLURAL NOUN the work of repairing a road surface □ *Roadworks are causing delays on the motorway.*

roadworthy /'rəʊdˌwɜːðɪ/ ADJECTIVE if a vehicle is roadworthy, it is in good enough condition to drive on the roads

roam /rəʊm/ VERB [**roams, roaming, roamed**] to walk or travel around a place without a particular aim 🕀 *You see youths roaming the streets at night.*

roar /rɔː(r)/ ▶ VERB [**roars, roaring, roared**]

1 to make a continuous loud sound □ *Planes roared overhead.*

2 if a vehicle roars somewhere, it moves there quickly, making a loud sound □ *Cars roared past as we sat at the roadside.*

3 to say something in a loud, angry voice □ *'Get out!' he roared.*

4 when a lion roars, it makes a loud sound

▶ NOUN [*plural* **roars**]

1 a loud deep sound □ *the roar of the engine*

2 the call or sound that a lion makes

roast /rəʊst/ ▶ VERB [**roasts, roasting, roasted**]

1 to cook meat or vegetables in an oven or over a fire □ *Roast the potatoes at the same time as the turkey.*

2 meat or vegetables roast when they cook in an oven or over a fire □ *The sauce can be made while the vegetables are roasting.*

▶ ADJECTIVE cooked in the oven □ *roast potatoes* □ *roast beef*

▶ NOUN [*plural* **roasts**] a piece of meat that has been cooked in the oven □ *We're having a roast tonight.*

• **roasting** /'rəʊstɪŋ/ ADJECTIVE an informal word meaning very hot □ *It was roasting outside today.*

rob /rɒb/ VERB [robs, robbing, robbed]
1 to steal something from a place or person 🔄 *They robbed a bank.* □ + *of The family were robbed of jewellery worth at least £1 million.*
2 **rob someone of something** to take something important from someone □ *He was robbed of the chance to compete by an injury.*

> ➤ Remember that thieves **rob** people and places. They **steal** money and objects: □ *My parents were robbed in the street.* □ *They had robbed a bank.* □ *They stole my father's wallet.* □ *They stole five hundred pounds from her.*

• **robber** /ˈrɒbə(r)/ NOUN [plural **robbers**] a person who steals 🔄 *Armed robbers broke into his house.* 🔄 *a bank robber*
• **robbery** /ˈrɒbərɪ/ NOUN [plural **robberies**] the crime of stealing something from a person or place 🔄 *He committed several robberies.* 🔄 *a bank robbery* 🔄 *He was in prison for armed robbery.* 🔄 *Parvez was shot during an attempted robbery.*

robe /rəʊb/ NOUN [plural **robes**] a long loose piece of clothing □ *a priest's robes*
robin /ˈrɒbɪn/ NOUN [plural **robins**] a small brown bird with a red chest
robot /ˈrəʊbɒt/ NOUN [plural **robots**] a machine that can do things like a person
• **robotic** /rəʊˈbɒtɪk/ ADJECTIVE to do with or similar to a robot □ *Robotic devices are used in performing some types of surgery.*
robust /rəʊˈbʌst/ ADJECTIVE strong □ *a robust economy* □ *He was in robust health.*

rock /rɒk/ ► NOUN [plural **rocks**]
1 the hard stone substance that the Earth is made of □ *volcanic rock* □ *The team were digging a tunnel through solid rock.*
2 a large stone □ *Protesters threw rocks at the police.*
3 a type of music with a strong beat that is played on electric guitars and drums □ *He played in a rock band.*
► VERB [rocks, rocking, rocked]
1 to move or move something gently backwards and forwards or from side to side □ *She was rocking the baby in her arms.* □ *The boats rocked gently in the harbour.*
2 to make a place shake □ *Three bombs rocked the capital, killing at least 20 people.*
3 to shock a lot of people □ *Several corruption scandals have rocked the government.*
4 if something or someone rocks, they are extremely good. An informal word. □ *This place rocks!*
♦ IDIOM **rock the boat** to cause problems by criticizing something or by trying to change something which other people are satisfied with. An informal phrase □ *I don't want to rock the boat.*

rock and roll *or* **rock 'n' roll** /ˌrɒk ən ˈrəʊl/ NOUN, NO PLURAL a type of pop music with a strong beat that was popular in the 1950s

rocket /ˈrɒkɪt/ ► NOUN [plural **rockets**]
1 a long thin weapon with a bomb in it which is fired from a plane or ship □ *Rockets were fired across the border.* □ *a rocket attack*
2 a long thin spacecraft □ *The Ariane rocket was launched from the EU space centre.*
3 something which explodes high in the sky and makes bright lights for entertainment
► VERB [rockets, rocketing, rocketed] to increase very quickly □ *Oil prices have rocketed.*
rocking chair /ˈrɒkɪŋ ˌtʃeə(r)/ NOUN [plural **rocking chairs**] a chair which moves backwards and forwards when you sit on it
rocking horse /ˈrɒkɪŋ ˌhɔːs/ NOUN [plural **rocking horses**] a child's toy horse that they can sit on and rock backwards and forwards
rock music /ˈrɒk ˌmjuːzɪk/ NOUN, NO PLURAL a type of music with a strong beat that is played on electric guitars and drums
rocky /ˈrɒkɪ/ ADJECTIVE [rockier, rockiest]
1 made of rock, or covered with rocks □ *the rocky slopes of the mountains*
2 a relationship or situation that is rocky is difficult and may not be successful □ *Their marriage has been going through a rocky patch.*
rod /rɒd/ NOUN [plural **rods**] a long thin pole 🔄 *a fishing rod*
rode /rəʊd/ PAST TENSE OF **ride**
rodent /ˈrəʊdənt/ NOUN [plural **rodents**] a small animal with long sharp front teeth, such as a rabbit or mouse
rodeo /ˈrəʊdɪəʊ/ NOUN [plural **rodeos**] a show of riding and other skills by cowboys (=men who ride horses and look after cows in the US)
roe /rəʊ/ NOUN, NO PLURAL the eggs of a fish, eaten as food
rogue /rəʊg/ ► NOUN [plural **rogues**] a dishonest or badly behaved man or boy 🔄 *He's a lovable rogue* (=someone who behaves badly but you still like them).
► ADJECTIVE not behaving in the same way as other people or things, and likely to cause problems □ *rogue nations*

role /rəʊl/ NOUN [plural **roles**]
1 the character that an actor is in a play or film 🔄 *Daniel Radcliffe played the role of Harry Potter in the film.* 🔄 *It was his first starring role* (=important role) *a Hollywood movie.*
2 the job or purpose that someone or something has 🔄 *Diet plays an important role in maintaining good health.* □ + *of The role of women has changed greatly over the last century.*

roll /rəʊl/ ► VERB [rolls, rolling, rolled]
1 to move along like a ball, or to make something move in this way □ + *down/along, etc. Rocks sometimes rolled down the hills.* □ *She rolled the ball along the ground.*
2 to move on wheels, or to make something on wheels move □ *Take the brake off and let the car*

forwards. □ **+ into** *The train rolled into the station.* □ *I rolled the bike into the yard.*

3 to turn your body when you are lying down, or to turn someone else's body when they are lying down □ **+ over** *My back hurts every time I roll over in bed.* □ *She rolled the baby onto his tummy.*

4 if a small amount of liquid rolls, it moves smoothly down a surface □ **+ down** *Tears were rolling down her cheeks.*

5 to fold something so that it forms the shape of a ball or a tube □ *She rolled her clothes in tissue paper before packing them.* □ **+ up** *Roll the sleeping bag up tightly and tie the string around it.*

6 roll your eyes to move your eyes upwards, especially to show that you are annoyed □ *He just rolled his eyes when I told him what had happened.*

◆ IDIOM **be rolling in it** an informal phrase meaning to be very rich

◆ PHRASAL VERBS **roll something up**

1 to make a piece of clothing shorter by folding it □ *She rolled her sleeves up so they didn't get wet.*

2 to fold something so that it forms the shape of a ball or tube □ *The carpet had been rolled up.* **roll up** an informal word meaning to arrive, especially late □ *John rolled up just as the others were leaving.*

◆ NOUN [*plural* **rolls**]

1 a small loaf of bread for one person, often with something such as meat or cheese in it □ *I had a cheese roll for lunch.*

2 something that has been rolled into the shape of a tube □ **+ of** *a roll of toilet paper* □ *We'll need 12 rolls of wallpaper for this room.*

3 an official list of names, for example the names of students at a school or the people who can vote in an election 🔁 *He's not on the electoral roll.*

4 a long deep sound □ *a drum roll* □ *a roll of thunder*

5 be on a roll an informal phrase meaning to be in a period in which you are having a lot of success □ *The team are on a roll at the moment having won the last five games.*

roll call /'rəʊl ˌkɔ:l/ NOUN [*plural* **roll calls**] when someone calls out the names from a list

roller /'rəʊlə(r)/ NOUN [*plural* **rollers**] something in the shape of a tube, used for spreading something or for making something flat □ *She was painting the room with a roller.*

rollerblades /'rəʊləbleɪdz/ PLURAL NOUN boots with a row of wheels on the bottom, used for skating. A trademark.

roller coaster /'rəʊlə ˌkəʊstə(r)/ NOUN [*plural* **roller coasters**]

1 a steep track on which people ride for fun in a very fast train

2 a situation which changes often and suddenly, causing strong emotions □ *Pregnancy had been an emotional roller coaster.*

roller skate /'rəʊlə ˌskeɪt/ ◆ NOUN [*plural* **roller skates**] a boot with two pairs of wheels on the bottom, used for skating

◆ VERB [**roller skates, roller skating, roller skated**] to move using roller skates

● **roller skating** /'rəʊlə ˌskeɪtɪŋ/ NOUN, NO PLURAL the activity of moving on roller skates

rolling pin /'rəʊlɪŋ ˌpɪn/ NOUN [*plural* **rolling pins**] a thick stick that you roll over pastry to make it flat

ROM /rɒm/ ABBREVIATION Read Only Memory; a type of memory in a computer that allows you to see information, but not change it. A computing word.

Roman Catholic /ˌrəʊmən 'kæθlɪk/ ◆ NOUN [*plural* **Roman Catholics**] a member of the part of the Christian church that has the Pope for a leader

◆ ADJECTIVE to do with, or belonging to, the Roman Catholic Church

romance /rəʊ'mæns/ NOUN [*plural* **romances**]

1 *no plural* the feelings connected with being in love □ *They met at college and romance soon blossomed.*

2 a short relationship between people who are in love 🔁 *The couple had a whirlwind romance* (=short and exciting relationship).

3 *no plural* a feeling of excitement and mystery connected with something □ *He loved the romance of long-distance train travel.*

4 a love story □ *She read mainly romances.*

Roman numeral /ˌrəʊmən 'nju:mərəl/ NOUN [*plural* **Roman numerals**] one of the letters used to represent numbers in the system used by the ancient Romans, in which, for example I = 1 and V = 5

romantic /rəʊ'mæntɪk/ ADJECTIVE

1 to do with feelings of love 🔁 *a romantic relationship* 🔁 *His latest film is a romantic comedy.* □ *a romantic dinner for two*

2 thinking of or showing things as better and more exciting than they are in real situations □ *I had this romantic idea of life as an actor.*

● **romantically** /rəʊ'mæntɪkəli/ ADVERB in a way that is to do with love □ *She's not romantically involved with anyone just now.*

● **romanticize** or **romanticise** /rəʊ'mæntɪsaɪz/ VERB [**romanticizes, romanticizing, romanticized**] to think of or show something as better and more exciting than it really is, ignoring all the bad things □ *It was said that the film romanticized all crime.*

romp /rɒmp/ VERB [**romps, romping, romped**]

1 to play with a lot of energy and movement □ *The children can romp around outside in the sun.*

2 an informal word meaning to win a game or a race very easily 🔁 *His horse romped home in the Gold Cup.* □ *They romped to a 6-1 win.*

roof /ru:f/ NOUN [*plural* **roofs**]

1 the part that covers the top of a building or vehicle □ *The house has a red tiled roof.* □ **+ of** *He climbed onto the roof of the building.*

2 the roof of your mouth the top inside surface of your mouth

◆ IDIOMS **go through the roof** an informal phrase meaning to reach an extremely high level □ *Prices have gone through the roof.* **hit the roof** an informal phrase meaning to become very angry a roof over your head a house, flat, etc. to live in □ *At least we have food and a roof over our heads.*

roof rack /'ruːf ˌræk/ NOUN [plural **roof racks**] a metal frame that you can fix to the roof of a car, for carrying things

rook /rʊk/ NOUN [plural **rooks**]
1 a large black bird
2 in the game of chess, a piece which is shaped like a castle

room /ruːm, rʊm/ NOUN [plural **rooms**]
1 one of the areas a building is divided into inside □ *We have three rooms downstairs and four upstairs.* □ *She got up and left the room.* 🔁 *He went back to his hotel room.*
2 no plural space for something □ + **for** *Is there room for another chair?* □ *There wasn't enough room in the car for everyone.* □ + **to do something** *They had no room to move.*
3 no plural an opportunity or possibility that something can happen □ + **for** *I feel there's still a lot of room for improvement.*

roommate /'ruːmmeɪt/ NOUN [plural **roommates**]
1 in the UK, a person you share a room with, for example as a student
2 in the US, a person you share a house or flat with

roomy /'ruːmɪ/ ADJECTIVE [**roomier, roomiest**] having a lot of space □ *a roomy cabin*

roost /ruːst/ ▶ NOUN [plural **roosts**] the place where a bird rests at night
▶ VERB [**roosts, roosting, roosted**] if a bird roosts somewhere, it sits or sleeps there at night
• **rooster** /'ruːstə(r)/ NOUN [plural **roosters**] a male chicken

root /ruːt/ ▶ NOUN [plural **roots**]
1 the part of a plant that grows underground □ + **of** *the roots of the tree*
2 the basic cause of a problem □ + **of** *The root of all our troubles is that we don't have enough money.* 🔁 *We must address the root causes of the violence.*
3 the part of a tooth or hair that holds it to your body
4 roots the origin of someone or something □ *his working class roots* □ *The company traces its roots back to 1830.*
• IDIOMS **take root**
1 to start to be believed or to develop □ *His ideas now seem to have taken root in the UK.*
2 to start growing roots
▶ VERB [**roots, rooting, rooted**]
1 to grow roots □ *The plants root very easily in compost.*
2 **be rooted in something** to come from or to be caused by something □ *His art is rooted in the folk tradition.* **rooted to the spot** an informal phrase meaning not able to move because you are surprised or afraid
• PHRASAL VERBS **root around** to search for something,

especially in an untidy way □ *Who's been rooting around in my desk?* **root for someone** to support someone and want them to win □ *I'll be rooting for the local team.* **root something out** to find something and get rid of it □ *He promised to root out corruption.*

rope /rəʊp/ ▶ NOUN [plural **ropes**]
1 very thick strong string
2 **the ropes** the things someone needs to know to do a job 🔁 *She's still learning the ropes.* 🔁 *Matthew will show you the ropes.*
• IDIOM **on the ropes** having problems and likely to lose or fail □ *After last week's defeat in parliament, the party are on the ropes.*
▶ VERB [**ropes, roping, roped**] to tie something with rope □ *The climbers are roped together.*
• PHRASAL VERBS **rope someone in/into something** to persuade someone to do something, especially when they do not want to □ *I got roped into playing* **rope something off** to separate part of an area using rope, especially to stop people going there

ropy or **ropey** /'rəʊpɪ/ ADJECTIVE [**ropier, ropiest**] an informal word meaning of fairly bad quality □ *a ropy performance*

rosary /'rəʊzərɪ/ NOUN [plural **rosaries**] a string with beads (=small balls) on it that people in some religions use to count prayers as they say them

rose¹ /rəʊz/ ▶ NOUN [plural **roses**] a garden plant with sharp points on the stems and flowers that smell sweet
▶ ADJECTIVE having a pale pink colour

rose² /rəʊz/ PAST TENSE OF **rise** □ *The temperature rose steadily as the day wore on.*

rosemary /'rəʊzmərɪ/ NOUN, NO PLURAL a plant with thin leaves that are used in cooking

rosette /rəʊ'zet/ NOUN [plural **rosettes**] a round decoration made of ribbon (=long, narrow piece of cloth), often given as a prize for winning something

roster /'rɒstə(r)/ NOUN [plural **rosters**] the US word for rota

rostrum /'rɒstrəm/ NOUN [plural **rostrums**] a small raised area that someone stands on to make a speech

rosy /'rəʊzɪ/ ADJECTIVE [**rosier, rosiest**]
1 pink in colour □ *rosy cheeks*
2 positive or likely that good things will happen □ *The future certainly looks rosy for Hugh.*

rot /rɒt/ ▶ VERB [**rots, rotting, rotted**] to decay or make something decay □ *The leaves fall on the forest floor and gradually rot into the soil.* □ *Sugar rots the teeth.*
▶ NOUN, NO PLURAL decay □ *They've discovered some rot in the roof timbers.*
• IDIOM **stop the rot** to stop a bad situation from becoming worse

rota /'rəʊtə/ NOUN [plural **rotas**] a list of jobs to be done that shows who must do them and when they must be done □ *a cleaning rota*

rotary /'rəʊtərɪ/ ADJECTIVE moving round and round like a wheel

rotate /rəʊ'teɪt/ VERB [rotates, rotating, rotated]
1 to turn around like a wheel, or to make something turn around like a wheel □ *Each wheel rotates on its own axle.*
2 to replace one person or thing with another in a particular order □ *Rotating the different kinds of vegetables we grow keeps the soil healthy.*
• **rotation** /rəʊ'teɪʃən/ NOUN [plural **rotations**]
1 a rotating movement □ *The rotation of the blades keeps the air moving.*
2 when people or things rotate

rotor /'rəʊtə(r)/ NOUN [plural **rotors**] a part of a machine that turns round a point □ *a helicopter rotor blade*

rotten /'rɒtən/ ADJECTIVE
1 decayed or decaying □ *rotten eggs* □ *a rotten floorboard*
2 an informal word meaning very bad or unpleasant □ *We had a rotten meal there.* □ *I felt rotten when I woke up.*

rough /rʌf/ ▶ ADJECTIVE [rougher, roughest]
1 not smooth □ *We drove along a rough track.* □ *I get very rough skin on my feet.*
2 not gentle □ *Rugby is a rough game.*
3 a rough sea has a lot of big waves because the wind is strong □ *The sea was too rough for swimming in.*
4 not exact □ *a rough guess/estimate*
5 full of problems and causing unhappiness 🔊 *She had quite a rough time in her first job.*
6 ill 🔊 *I felt rough the next day.*
7 a rough place or area is unpleasant and often dangerous
8 done quickly and not completely finished □ *a rough sketch*
▶ ADVERB if people live rough or sleep rough, they sleep outside because they do not have homes

roughage /'rʌfɪdʒ/ NOUN, NO PLURAL a substance in food which your body cannot digest, and which helps your bowels work well

roughen /'rʌfən/ VERB [roughens, roughening, roughened] to make something less smooth

roughly /'rʌflɪ/ ADVERB
1 approximately □ *There were roughly ten thousand people in the stadium.* 🔊 *They're roughly the same size.* □ *Her name roughly translates as 'white flower'.*
2 in a quick way, without being careful or gentle □ *If you handle the flowers roughly, you'll damage them.*
3 *roughly chopped onions*

roughness /'rʌfnɪs/ NOUN, NO PLURAL
1 the quality of not being smooth □ *the roughness of his skin*
2 when someone or something is not gentle

roulette /ruː'let/ NOUN, NO PLURAL a game in which a ball is dropped onto a turning wheel marked with numbers and people guess where the ball will stop

round /raʊnd/ ▶ ADVERB, PREPOSITION
1 on all sides □ *We sat round the table.* □ *We tied a rope round the tree.*
2 moving in a circle or along the edges of something □ *The Moon goes round the Earth.* 🔊 *We drove round and round in circles.*
3 to face the opposite direction □ *If you look round, you can see the clock.* 🔊 *He turned round and waved.*
4 to the other side of something □ *We were allowed to go round the back of the theatre.* 🔊 *I saw Jo coming round the corner.*
5 in or to different parts of a place □ *We travelled all round Spain.*
6 to someone's home 🔊 *Why don't you come round for supper?* 🔊 *I'm going round to Fred's after school.*
7 near 🔊 *Do you live round here?*
8 from one person or place to another □ *The news got round pretty quickly.* □ *Please pass the books round to everyone.*
9 round about approximately □ *They pay round about £10 per hour.*
➡ go to be/go round the **bend**, drive someone round the **bend**
▶ ADJECTIVE [rounder, roundest]
1 having the shape of a circle or a ball □ *a round table* □ *The Earth is round.*
2 a round number is shown as the nearest unit, for example 1, 10, 100, 1,000
▶ NOUN [plural **rounds**]
1 a part of a competition □ *They lost in the second round of the cup.* □ *The Swedish team is through to the next round.*
2 when someone goes to several people or houses as part of their job □ *Our postman usually finishes his round by midday.*
3 a group of events □ *We're doing the next round of interviews tomorrow.* □ *His life is just one long round of parties.*
4 drinks that you buy for several people □ *It's my round - what would you like?*
5 a single bullet or similar object fired from a weapon
6 a round of applause when people clap
7 a round of golf a game of golf
▶ VERB [rounds, rounding, rounded] to go around something □ *As I rounded the corner, I came face to face with Sharon.*
◆ PHRASAL VERBS **round something down** to reduce a number to the nearest suitable unit. A maths word. **round something off** to end an event or an activity in a suitable way □ *We rounded off the evening with some dancing.* **round on someone** to suddenly speak angrily to someone or about someone □ *The minister rounded on his critics, accusing them of lying.* **round someone/something up** to bring a group of animals or people together □ *Farmers are rounding the animals up for the winter.* □ *Police are trying to round up all the suspects.* **round something up** to increase a number to the nearest suitable unit. A

maths word. □ *The fare was £4.50, so I rounded it up to £5.*

roundabout /ˈraʊndəbaʊt/ NOUN [*plural* **roundabouts**]
1 a place where several roads meet and the traffic must go around a circle in the same direction before turning onto the next road □ *Turn left at the roundabout.*
2 a round structure that children sit on while it turns round

rounders /ˈraʊndəz/ PLURAL NOUN a team game in which players try to hit a ball then run around four sides of a square

roundly /ˈraʊndlɪ/ ADVERB clearly and completely or by many people ⊞ *We were roundly criticized for failing to finish.* □ *He was roundly defeated.*

round-the-clock /ˌraʊndðəˈklɒk/ ADJECTIVE during all the day and all the night

round trip /ˈraʊnd ˌtrɪp/ NOUN [*plural* **round trips**] when you go to a place and come back again □ *It's a round trip of nearly five hundred miles.*

round-up /ˈraʊndʌp/ NOUN [*plural* **round-ups**] a short description of information or events □ *Let's go back to the studio for the latest news round-up.*

rouse /raʊz/ VERB [**rouses, rousing, roused**]
1 to cause an emotion □ *It's a topic that always rouses passions.*
2 a formal word meaning to wake someone up
• **rousing** /ˈraʊzɪŋ/ ADJECTIVE exciting and making people feel enthusiastic □ *rousing music* □ *a rousing speech*

rout /raʊt/ ▶ NOUN [*plural* **routs**] a complete defeat
▶ VERB [**routs, routing, routed**] to defeat someone completely

route /ruːt/ NOUN [*plural* **routes**]
1 a way of getting from one place to another ⊞ *Which route do you take to work?* □ *a bus route* □ *+ of There were police all along the route of the march.* □ *It's the main route between London and Bristol.*
2 a way of achieving something □ *He went down a fairly traditional career route.*

routine /ruːˈtiːn/ ▶ NOUN [*plural* **routines**]
1 the usual things that you do and they way you do them ⊞ *Exercise should be part of your daily routine.* □ *They settled into a routine of family life.*
2 a performance that someone does in the same way many times ⊞ *a dance routine*
▶ ADJECTIVE normal and done regularly □ *a routine inspection*

rove /raʊv/ VERB [**roves, roving, roved**] to move or to travel around from one place to another □ *His eyes roved around the room.*
• **roving** /ˈraʊvɪŋ/ ADJECTIVE moving or travelling from place to place □ *a roving reporter*

row¹ /raʊ/ NOUN [*plural* **rows**]
1 a number of people or things arranged next to each

other in a line □ *the front row of seats* □ *Sow the seeds in a straight row.* □ *a row of figures*
2 in a row happening one after another □ *They've lost five matches in a row.*

row² /rəʊ/ VERB [**rows, rowing, rowed**] to pull a boat through water using oars (=long wooden poles)
row³ /raʊ/ ▶ NOUN [*plural* **rows**]
1 a noisy argument or strong disagreement ⊞ *Tom had a row with his girlfriend.* □ *The incident caused a political row.* □ *They went on strike in a row over pay.*
2 a loud unpleasant noise □ *Why are the children making such a row?*
▶ VERB [**rows, rowing, rowed**] to argue noisily □ *They were always rowing and falling out.*

➤ Notice the different pronunciations. **row¹** and **row²** are pronounced the same and rhyme with **low**. **row³** is pronounced differently and rhymes with **how**.

rowboat /ˈrəʊbəʊt/ NOUN [*plural* **rowboats**] the US word for **rowing boat**

rowdy /ˈraʊdɪ/ ADJECTIVE [**rowdier, rowdiest**] noisy and likely to cause trouble □ *a rowdy party*

rowing boat /ˈrəʊɪŋ ˌbəʊt/ NOUN [*plural* **rowing boats**] a small boat that you pull through the water using oars (=long wooden poles)

royal /ˈrɔɪəl/ ADJECTIVE to do with a king or queen or their family ⊞ *the Danish royal family* □ *a royal wedding*
• **royalty** /ˈrɔɪəltɪ/ NOUN, NO PLURAL all the members of the king or queen's family

RSVP /ˌɑːresviːˈpiː/ ABBREVIATION written on an invitation in order to ask for a reply

rub /rʌb/ ▶ VERB [**rubs, rubbing, rubbed**]
1 to move your hand or an object backwards and forwards over a surface □ *He was rubbing his eyes.* □ *She rubbed her cheek against the velvet.*
2 to spread a substance on something and move it backwards and forwards with your fingers so that it covers it or goes into its surface □ *She rubbed cream onto the red skin.*
3 to press and move against something, often causing pain or damage □ *My shoes are rubbing and giving me blisters.*
♦ IDIOM rub it in to say something which makes someone feel even worse about something which has embarrassed or upset them. An informal phrase □ *OK, he knows he did badly in the exam - there's no need to rub it in.*
♦ PHRASAL VERBS rub off if a characteristic or feeling rubs off on someone, they get it from someone else □ *I wish some of her enthusiasm would rub off on her sisters.* rub something out to remove words or pictures by rubbing them with a piece of rubber or cloth □ *Copy these words off the board before I rub them out.*
▶ NOUN [*plural* **rubs**] a movement of your hand or

object over a surface □ *Let me give your neck a rub where it's aching.*

rubber /ˈrʌbə(r)/ NOUN [plural **rubbers**]
1 *no plural* a strong substance that stretches and bends easily, made from tree juices □ *shoes with rubber soles* □ *a pair of rubber gloves*
2 a small block that you rub on paper in order to remove pencil marks

rubber band /ˌrʌbə ˈbænd/ NOUN [plural **rubber bands**] a small thin circle of rubber you put around things to hold them together

rubber stamp /ˌrʌbə ˈstæmp/ NOUN [plural **rubber stamps**] a small tool for printing numbers or short words on paper
• **rubber-stamp** VERB [rubber-stamps, rubber-stamping, rubber-stamped] to officially agree to a plan or a decision without giving it attention □ *The minister rubber stamped the decision.*

rubbish /ˈrʌbɪʃ/ ► NOUN, NO PLURAL
1 things that have been thrown away because they are no longer wanted □ *Put the rubbish in the bin.* □ *More household rubbish could be recycled.* 🔁 *a rubbish bin*
2 an informal word for something someone says that is not true or is stupid 🔁 *He's talking rubbish.*
3 an informal word for something of very bad quality □ *Her new chat show is absolute rubbish.*
► ADJECTIVE an informal word meaning of very bad quality or stupid □ *That was a rubbish suggestion!*

rubble /ˈrʌbəl/ NOUN, NO PLURAL the broken pieces that are left when a building falls down □ *a pile of rubble*

ruby /ˈruːbɪ/ NOUN [plural **rubies**] a dark red stone that is used in jewellery

rucksack /ˈrʌksæk/ NOUN [plural **rucksacks**] a bag that you carry on your back

rudder /ˈrʌdə(r)/ NOUN [plural **rudders**] the flat piece at the back of a boat or an aeroplane that moves to control its direction

ruddy /ˈrʌdɪ/ ADJECTIVE [**ruddier, ruddiest**] pink and healthy looking □ *a ruddy complexion*

rude /ruːd/ ADJECTIVE [**ruder, rudest**]
1 insulting and not polite □ **+ to** *She was very rude to hotel staff.* □ *I don't mean to be rude, but isn't it a bit old?* □ **+ to do something** *It would be rude to ignore them.*
2 embarrassing or offensive and not acceptable in a polite situation □ *rude jokes* □ *a rude word*
3 rude awakening something shocking that happens suddenly

► Note that someone is **rude to** someone else and not 'rude with' someone else:
✓ He was very rude to my mother.
✗ He was very rude with my mother.

rudely /ˈruːdlɪ/ ADVERB in a way that is rude 🔁 *She was rudely interrupted in the middle of her speech.*

• **rudeness** /ˈruːdnɪs/ NOUN, NO PLURAL when someone is rude □ *I apologize for my friend's rudeness.*

rueful /ˈruːfʊl/ ADJECTIVE showing that you are slightly sorry or sad about something □ *She gave a rueful smile.*
• **ruefully** /ˈruːfʊlɪ/ ADVERB in a rueful way □ *He shrugged ruefully.*

ruff /rʌf/ NOUN [plural **ruffs**] a piece of cloth in many folds that was worn around the neck in the past

ruffle /ˈrʌfəl/ VERB [**ruffles, ruffling, ruffled**]
1 to rub something, usually hair, so that it is not smooth □ *She ruffled the child's hair.*
2 to annoy or upset someone □ *She never seems to get ruffled.*

rug /rʌg/ NOUN [plural **rugs**] a cover for the floor which is not fixed □ *a sheepskin rug*

rugby /ˈrʌgbɪ/ NOUN, NO PLURAL a sport played by two teams in which the players throw and run with an oval ball 🔁 *a rugby player* 🔁 *He plays rugby.*

rugged /ˈrʌgɪd/ ADJECTIVE
1 rough with a lot of rocks □ *a rugged coastline*
2 with strong but attractive features □ *He has rugged good looks.*

ruin /ˈruːɪn/ ► VERB [**ruins, ruining, ruined**]
1 to spoil something completely □ *The rain had ruined my hairstyle.* □ *The injury threatens to ruin her athletics career.*
2 to cause someone to lose all their money
► NOUN [plural **ruins**]
1 something such as an old building that has fallen down □ *a Roman ruin* □ *the ancient Inca ruins of Machu Picchu*
2 when someone loses everything they have 🔁 *He faced financial ruin.*
3 in ruins destroyed or completely spoilt □ *The city was in ruins after the earthquake.*
• **ruined** /ˈruːɪnd/ ADJECTIVE destroyed □ *a ruined castle*

rule /ruːl/ ► NOUN [plural **rules**]
1 an instruction about what is allowed or what is not allowed □ *It's against the rules to move your feet when you're holding the ball.* 🔁 *She was disqualified from the competition for breaking the rules.* 🔁 *You must follow* (=obey) *all the rules carefully.* 🔁 *There are strict rules about employing staff.*
2 the person or group that controls a country or an area 🔁 *The country is under military rule.*
3 a principle that shows how something happens, especially in language or science □ *The rule for forming plurals is fairly simple.* □ *What you described would not follow the rules of physics.*
4 as a rule usually □ *I have my hair cut every six weeks as a rule.*
➜ go to a **rule of** *thumb*
► VERB [**rules, ruling, ruled**]
1 to control a country or an area □ *He ruled France in the 18th century.* □ *She is a minister in the ruling socialist party.*

2 to make an official decision □ + *that* *The judge has ruled that the prisoner can go free.*

♦ PHRASAL VERB **rule something/someone out** to decide that something is not possible or that something or someone cannot be used or chosen □ *The police have ruled out murder.* □ *His injury rules him out of the next match.*

• **ruler** /'ru:lə(r)/ NOUN [plural **rulers**]
1 a person who controls a country or an area □ *Gandhi never became ruler of India.*
2 a flat strip of wood, plastic or metal, used to draw straight lines or for measuring short lengths

• **ruling** /'ru:lɪŋ/ NOUN [plural **rulings**] an official decision, often by a judge □ *They plan to challenge the judge's ruling in the European Court.*

rum /rʌm/ NOUN, NO PLURAL a strong alcoholic drink made from sugar

rumble /'rʌmbəl/ ▶ VERB [**rumbles, rumbling, rumbled**]
1 to make a low continuous sound □ *Thunder rumbled in the distance.*
2 to move along making a long, low sound □ *A truck rumbled down the street.*
▶ NOUN [plural **rumbles**] a long low sound □ *the distant rumble of traffic*

rummage /'rʌmɪdʒ/ VERB [**rummages, rummaging, rummaged**] to search for something by moving things in an untidy way □ *She rummaged in her handbag for a pen.*

rummy /'rʌmi/ NOUN, NO PLURAL a card game where each player has seven cards and tries to collect sets of similar cards

rumor /'ru:mə(r)/ ▶ NOUN [plural **rumors**] the US spelling of rumour
▶ VERB [**rumors, rumoring, rumored**] the US spelling of rumour

rumour /'ru:mə(r)/ ▶ NOUN [plural **rumours**] information that people tell each other, although it may not be true □ *I heard a rumour that Jen was leaving.* 🔁 *Someone has been spreading rumours.*
▶ VERB [**rumours, rumouring, rumoured**] if something is rumoured, people say it is true, although it may not be □ *The player is rumoured to be joining Chelsea.*

rump /rʌmp/ NOUN [plural **rumps**] the area around an animal's tail or above its back legs

rumpus /'rʌmpəs/ NOUN, NO PLURAL a noisy situation where people are arguing or complaining □ *His comments caused a rumpus outside the courtroom.*

run /rʌn/ ▶ VERB [**runs, running, ran, run**]
1 to move with very fast steps □ *We had to run for the bus.* □ *They ran down the street screaming.*
2 to run in a race or as a sport □ *I'm hoping to run a marathon.* □ *He runs every morning.*
3 to control or organize an organization, event or activity □ *She runs a successful transport business.* □ *The college runs part-time courses.* □ *The party is not ready to run the country.*
4 if an activity or event runs for a particular time, that

is when or how long it takes place □ *The course runs over the summer.* □ *The movie ran for over four hours.*
5 if a machine or a piece of equipment is running, it is being used □ *I left the engine running while I ran into the house.* □ + *on* *The heating runs on solar energy.*
6 to use a computer program □ *We run Windows in the office.* □ *I ran a grammar check on the document.*
7 if a liquid runs somewhere, it flows in that direction □ *I had tears running down my face.* □ *Water ran over the side of the bath.*
8 if your nose is running, liquid is coming out of it
9 if buses and trains are running, they are travelling and people can use them □ *The number 5 bus runs every 10 minutes.* 🔁 *The trains never run on time.*
10 to take someone somewhere in a car □ *I run the children to school if it's raining.*
11 to move something through or across something □ *Grace ran her finger down the list.* □ *He ran his fingers through his hair.*
12 if something runs in a particular direction or position, that is where it is □ *A path ran behind the house.* □ *Wires ran overhead.*
13 to be at a particular level □ + *at* *Sales are running at around 150 per month.* 🔁 *Food supplies were running low.*

♦ PHRASAL VERBS **run across someone/something** to meet someone or find something by chance □ *I ran across Kelly in the library the other day.* **run around** to be busy doing things □ *I've been running around preparing for his visit.* **run around after someone** to be busy doing things for someone □ *I've been running around after the children.* **run away**
1 to leave a place secretly 🔁 *I ran away from home several times.*
2 to try to get away from an unpleasant situation □ *You can't just run away from your responsibilities.* **run someone/something down**
1 to knock someone or something over with a vehicle □ *The lorry driver simply ran him down.*
2 to criticize someone or something repeatedly □ *He is constantly trying to run down his colleagues.* **run for something** to try to be elected for a position □ *She is running for president.* **run into someone** to meet someone by chance □ *I ran into Jake at the supermarket.* **run into something**
1 to drive a vehicle into an object □ *I lost control and ran into a wall.*
2 to reach a particular level □ *His legal costs ran into thousands of dollars.*
3 to begin to experience problems □ *The project ran into financial difficulties.* **run off** to suddenly leave a place or a person □ *My father ran off when I was 3.* **run out**
1 to use the whole amount of something □ *We have run out of money.*
2 to be completely used □ *The milk has run out.* **run someone/something over** to drive over someone or something in a vehicle □ *I reversed and ran over his bike.* **run through something**

1 to quickly read something or tell someone about something □ *Let me run through the rules again.*
2 to quickly practise something □ *Can we run through the last act?* **run something up** if you run up debts or bills (=money you owe for things you have bought), you owe that amount □ *I ran up huge debts at college.*
run up against something if you run up against a problem or a difficult situation, you experience it □ *We ran up against a lot of prejudice against women.*
▶ NOUN [*plural* **runs**]
1 when you run in a race or as a sport 🔁 *I always go for a run before breakfast.* □ *That run was fast enough to give him a place in the Olympic team.*
2 when you move with very fast steps 🔁 *When she saw Terry, she broke into a run* (=started running).
3 make a run for it to try to escape by running away □ *He spotted the open door and made a run for it.*
4 on the run trying to escape, especially from the police □ *While he was on the run, he had contact with his sister.*
5 a series of similar events □ *a run of bad luck*
6 the length of time a show, television programme, etc, continues □ *The musical had a long Broadway run.*
7 a journey in a vehicle □ *We chatted on the run down to Devon.*
8 a point that a player wins in a game like cricket or baseball 🔁 *He scored 58 runs.*
9 an area with a fence where animals are kept □ *a chicken run*
10 a practice/trial run when you do something in order to practise it, before doing it in a real situation
▸ IDIOM in the long/short run at or during the time that is far away/near □ *In the short run, you can expect some financial losses.*

runaway /ˈrʌnəweɪ/ ▶ NOUN [*plural* **runaways**] someone who has left their home secretly □ *a teenage runaway*
▶ ADJECTIVE
1 happening or succeeding very quickly and easily 🔁 *Their latest product has been a runaway success.* 🔁 *Ellis was the runaway winner.*
2 having left your home secretly □ *a runaway schoolgirl*
3 a runaway vehicle is out of control and moving very fast

run-down /ˌrʌnˈdaʊn/ ADJECTIVE
1 not kept in good condition □ *a run-down neighbourhood*
2 tired and not healthy

rung[1] /rʌŋ/ NOUN [*plural* **rungs**] a step on a ladder (=a piece of equipment with steps you climb up to reach a high place)

rung[2] /rʌŋ/ PAST PARTICIPLE OF **ring**[2] □ *Have you rung your mother?*

run-in /ˈrʌnɪn/ NOUN [*plural* **run-ins**] an informal word for an argument or a fight 🔁 *I had a bit of a run-in with one of the directors.*

runner /ˈrʌnə(r)/ NOUN [*plural* **runners**]
1 a person or animal that runs □ *He's a very fast runner.* □ *a marathon runner*
2 someone who carries something illegally from one place to another □ *a drug runner*
3 a blade on the bottom of something that it slides along on

runner-up /ˌrʌnərˈʌp/ NOUN [*plural* **runners-up**] the person who finishes in second place in a competition 🔁 *She finished runner-up in last year's race.*

running /ˈrʌnɪŋ/ ▶ NOUN, NO PLURAL
1 the sport or activity of moving with very fast steps 🔁 *She gets up early to go running.* □ *He took up marathon running.*
2 the organization and management of something □ + *of You'll be responsible for the running of the shop.* 🔁 *She's still involved with the day-to-day running of the company.*
3 in/out of the running an informal phrase meaning having/not having a chance of winning something □ *He's still in the running for the championship.*
▶ ADJECTIVE
1 used to say that something happens a number of times, one directly after another □ *The album is at number one for the third week running.*
2 continuing without stopping □ *a running commentary on the events*
3 running water water which comes through pipes from a water supply □ *The cottage has no running water or electricity.*

runny /ˈrʌnɪ/ ADJECTIVE [**runnier, runniest**]
1 in a liquid state □ *runny honey*
2 if you have a runny nose or eyes, they are producing a lot of liquid 🔁 *I had a cough and a runny nose.*

run-of-the-mill /ˌrʌnəvðəˈmɪl/ ADJECTIVE ordinary or average, not special in any way □ *They offer a fairly run-of-the-mill range of pub food.*

run-up /ˈrʌnʌp/ NOUN, NO PLURAL the period of time or events immediately before an important event □ *the run-up to the competition*

runway /ˈrʌnweɪ/ NOUN [*plural* **runways**] the long, wide road at an airport that aeroplanes take off from and land on

rupture /ˈrʌptʃə(r)/ ▶ VERB [**ruptures, rupturing, ruptured**] to tear or to break open, or to cause this □ *He ruptured a knee ligament.* □ *A gas pipeline ruptured.*
▶ NOUN [*plural* **ruptures**] a break or tear, especially in a muscle or an organ

rural /ˈrʊərəl/ ADJECTIVE to do with the countryside 🔁 *She grew up in a rural area.* □ *a rural community*

rush /rʌʃ/ ▶ NOUN [*plural* **rushes**]
1 a sudden, strong movement or feeling □ *a rush of cold air* 🔁 *She felt a rush of excitement.* 🔁 *an adrenaline rush*
2 a hurry □ *It was a bit of a rush but we got there in time.*

3 be in a rush to be hurrying □ *I was in a rush to get to the airport on time.*

4 when a large number of people try to go somewhere or do something at the same time □ *There was a sudden rush for the door.* □ *a rush for tickets*

▶ VERB [rushes, rushing, rushed]

1 to move or to do something quickly and suddenly □ *Firefighters rushed to the scene.* □ *Several colleagues rushed to help the woman.*

2 to take someone or something somewhere very quickly ⊞ *I was rushed to hospital in an ambulance.*

3 to do something too quickly and without enough care □ *I don't want to rush things.*

rush hour /'rʌʃ ˌauə(r)/ NOUN [*plural* **rush hours**] the time when there is most traffic because people are travelling to or from work ⊞ *the morning rush hour* ⊞ *Trains are packed during the evening rush hour.*

rusk /rʌsk/ NOUN [*plural* **rusks**] a hard dry biscuit that babies eat

russet /'rʌsɪt/ NOUN, NO PLURAL a red-brown colour

rust /rʌst/ ▶ NOUN, NO PLURAL a brown substance that forms on iron and other metals if they are in air and water

▶ VERB [rusts, rusting, rusted] to become covered in rust □ *The equipment was just left to rust.*

rustic /'rʌstɪk/ ADJECTIVE simple, in a way that is typical of the countryside □ *The house had a certain rustic charm.*

rustle /'rʌsəl/ ▶ VERB [rustles, rustling, rustled] to make a soft dry sound when moving, or to make something do this □ *Trees rustled in the breeze.* □ *They rustled their papers.*

♦ PHRASAL VERB **rustle something up** to make something quickly from what you have available □ *I could rustle up an omelette.*

▶ NOUN [*plural* **rustles**] when something rustles □ *the rustle of a silk dress*

rusty /'rʌstɪ/ ADJECTIVE [rustier, rustiest]

1 covered in rust (=a reddish-brown substance that forms on metal) □ *rusty nails*

2 if a skill is rusty, it is not as good as it was before □ *My Spanish is a bit rusty these days.*

rut /rʌt/ NOUN [*plural* **ruts**]

1 a boring situation where nothing changes ⊞ *I was getting stuck in a rut and I needed a change.*

2 a deep track made by a wheel □ *There were deep ruts in the road.*

ruthless /'ru:θlɪs/ ADJECTIVE cruel and trying to achieve what you want without caring how your behaviour affects others □ *a ruthless dictator*

● **ruthlessly** /'ru:θlɪslɪ/ ADVERB in a ruthless way □ *ruthlessly ambitious*

● **ruthlessness** /'ru:θlɪsnɪs/ NOUN, NO PLURAL the quality of being ruthless

rye /raɪ/ NOUN, NO PLURAL a type of grain that is used for making flour

Ss

S¹ *or* **s** /es/ the 19th letter of the alphabet

S² /es/ ABBREVIATION south

Sabbath /'sæbəθ/ NOUN **the Sabbath** the day of the week for rest and prayer in some religions

sabbatical /sə'bætɪkəl/ NOUN [*plural* **sabbaticals**] a period when a university teacher does not teach because they are studying away from the university

sabotage /'sæbətɑːʒ/ ► NOUN, NO PLURAL
1 deliberate damage that someone does to an enemy's property or equipment □ *an act of sabotage*
2 secret action that is intended to stop someone or something from succeeding

► VERB [**sabotages, sabotaging, sabotaged**]
1 to deliberately damage an enemy's property or equipment □ *Rebels had sabotaged the electricity supply lines.*
2 to do something to stop someone or something from being successful

sac /sæk/ NOUN [*plural* **sacs**] any part of a plant or animal that is like a bag, especially one that contains liquid. A biology word.

saccharin /'sækərɪn/ NOUN, NO PLURAL a very sweet chemical that is used instead of sugar

saccharine /'sækərɪn/ ADJECTIVE too romantic, in a way that is annoying □ *a saccharine romantic comedy*

sachet /'sæʃeɪ/ NOUN [*plural* **sachets**] a small flat bag that contains a little of a liquid or powder □ *a sachet of shampoo*

sack /sæk/ ► NOUN [*plural* **sacks**]
1 a large bag made of strong material used for carrying or storing things □ *a sack of potatoes*
2 the sack when you lose your job ⊞ *He got the sack for being late all the time.* ⊞ *They'll give her the sack if she doesn't work harder.*
► VERB [**sacks, sacking, sacked**] to tell someone they can no longer have their job □ *He was sacked for stealing.*

sacrament /'sækrəmənt/ NOUN [*plural* **sacraments**] any of several important Christian ceremonies such as marriage or baptism (= naming a child)

sacred /'seɪkrɪd/ ADJECTIVE
holy, or to do with God □ *a sacred shrine*
to do with religion □ *sacred music*
very important and not to be changed □ *I'm standing on the sacred turf of this world-famous football ground.*

sacrifice /'sækrɪfaɪs/ ► NOUN [*plural* **sacrifices**]
1 giving up something important to you in order to achieve something that is more important, or the thing that you give up in this way ⊞ *We had to make sacrifices in order to be able to buy a house.*
2 the act of killing someone or something and offering them to a god, or the person or animal that is killed in this way

► VERB [**sacrifices, sacrificing, sacrificed**]
1 to give up something that is important to you in order to achieve something that is more important □ *He sacrificed his life to save his fellow soldiers.*
2 to kill someone or something and offer them to a god

sacrilege /'sækrɪlɪdʒ/ NOUN, NO PLURAL treating something that is holy or admired without respect

• **sacrilegious** /ˌsækrɪ'lɪdʒəs/ ADJECTIVE not showing respect for something that is holy or admired

sad /sæd/ ADJECTIVE [**sadder, saddest**]
1 unhappy ⊞ *I felt sad saying goodbye to them.* □ **+ to do something** *I'll be sad to leave the company after so many years.*
2 making you feel unhappy □ *a sad film* □ *a sad story*
3 if something is sad, it is bad and you wish it was different ⊞ *It's a sad fact that some people think there is nothing wrong with violence.*
4 boring and not fashionable □ *I'm so sad, I spent my holiday working.*

• **sadden** /'sædən/ VERB [**saddens, saddening, saddened**] to make someone feel unhappy □ *We were greatly saddened by the news.*

saddle /'sædəl/ ► NOUN [*plural* **saddles**]
1 a leather seat for putting on a horse's back
2 a seat on a bicycle or motorcycle
► VERB [**saddles, saddling, saddled**] to put a saddle on a horse so that you can ride it
♦ PHRASAL VERB **saddle someone with something** to give someone a difficult job or responsibility

sadism /'seɪdɪzəm/ NOUN, NO PLURAL when someone enjoys being cruel and hurting other people

• **sadist** /'seɪdɪst/ NOUN [*plural* **sadists**] someone who enjoys being cruel and hurting other people

• **sadistic** /sə'dɪstɪk/ ADJECTIVE enjoying being cruel and hurting other people □ *a sadistic attack*

sadly /'sædlɪ/ ADVERB
1 used for saying that you wish something was not true □ *Sadly, she can't be here with us today.*
2 in an unhappy way □ *She waved sadly.*

sadness /'sædnɪs/ NOUN, NO PLURAL a feeling of unhappiness □ *It is with great sadness that we announce the death of our mother, Nancy.*

sae /'es eɪ 'i:/ ABBREVIATION stamped addressed envelope; an envelope with your name, address and a stamp on it

safari /sə'fɑːrɪ/ NOUN [plural **safaris**] a journey to watch wild animals living in their natural home, especially in Africa

safari park /sə'fɑːrɪ pɑːk/ NOUN [plural **safari parks**] a large area of land where wild animals are kept for visitors to see

safe /seɪf/ ▶ ADJECTIVE [**safer, safest**]
1 not likely to cause harm or damage □ *That ladder doesn't look very safe to me.* □ **+ to do something** *Is it safe to drink the water?* ⸙ *We need a safe place to rest.*
2 not in danger of being harmed, damaged, lost, etc. □ *You must keep these documents safe.* □ **+ from** *Nobody is safe from the disease.*
3 not damaged, harmed, stolen, etc □ *Thank goodness you're safe!* ⸙ *They are celebrating the safe return of the paintings.*
▶ NOUN [plural **safes**] a strong box with a lock, where money or valuable objects are kept

safeguard /'seɪfgɑːd/ ▶ NOUN [plural **safeguards**] something that protects against danger or harm □ *The double lock is a safeguard against theft.*
▶ VERB [**safeguards, safeguarding, safeguarded**] to protect someone or something from danger or harm □ *These vaccinations safeguard our children against deadly diseases.*

safekeeping /ˌseɪf'kiːpɪŋ/ NOUN, NO PLURAL for safekeeping in order to stop something being lost or damaged □ *The documents are in the file for safekeeping.*

safely /'seɪflɪ/ ADVERB without risk or danger □ *Drive safely.* □ *We got everyone home safely.* □ *The children were safely tucked up in bed.*

safety /'seɪftɪ/ NOUN, NO PLURAL
1 being safe, not being in danger or dangerous □ *The safety of passengers is our first concern.* □ *Tests will ensure the safety of the drugs.*
2 a safe place □ *Everyone dived for safety.*

safety belt /'seɪftɪ belt/ NOUN [plural **safety belts**] a strong belt in a car or plane that goes across your body ⸙ *Fasten your safety belt.*

safety pin /'seɪftɪ pɪn / NOUN [plural **safety pins**] a pin with a cover that fits over the sharp point when it is closed

safety valve /'seɪftɪ vælv/ NOUN [plural **safety valves**] a device on a piece of equipment that lets gas or liquid escape if the pressure is too high

saffron /'sæfrən/ NOUN, NO PLURAL thin yellow threads from a plant that are used to add colour and flavour to food

sag /sæg/ VERB [**sags, sagging, sagged**] to hang down or not be firm □ *The mattress has begun to sag in the middle.*

saga /'sɑːgə/ NOUN [plural **sagas**]
1 a long story, especially one about a group of people over many years □ *a family saga*
2 a series of events that take a long time to tell someone about □ *We were delayed coming home - actually it's a bit of a saga.*

sage /seɪdʒ/ NOUN [plural **sages**]
1 a herb that is used in cooking to add flavour
2 a literary word for a wise man

said /sed/ PAST TENSE AND PAST PARTICIPLE OF say □ *She said she was coming.* □ *They have said I can come back any time.*

sail /seɪl/ ▶ VERB [**sails, sailing, sailed**]
1 to travel somewhere in a ship or a boat □ *They're sailing off the coast of Sweden.*
2 to start a journey in a ship □ *The ferry sails at noon.*
♦ PHRASAL VERB **sail through something** to do something quickly and easily □ *Amy sailed through her exams with no bother.*
▶ NOUN [plural **sails**]
1 a sheet of strong cloth attached to a boat, which catches the wind and carries the boat along
2 a wide flat blade that turns on a windmill (=a building where flour is made)
● **sailing** /'seɪlɪŋ/ NOUN, NO PLURAL the sport or activity of sailing small boats

sailing boat /'seɪlɪŋ bəʊt/ NOUN [plural **sailing boats**] a small boat with sails

sailor /'seɪlə(r)/ NOUN [plural **sailors**]
1 someone who works on a ship □ *a merchant sailo*
2 someone who goes sailing □ *Joe's a keen sailor.*

saint /seɪnt/ NOUN [plural **saints**]
1 a dead person that the Christian church believes wa especially holy □ *Saint Francis*
2 a very good and kind person □ *She's an absolute saint, looking after her mother like that.*
● **saintly** /'seɪntlɪ/ ADJECTIVE very good or very holy

sake /seɪk/ NOUN [plural **sakes**]
1 for someone's sake in order to help someone □ *For his mother's sake, he wanted to be there.* □ *Please don't go to any trouble just for my sake.*
2 for the sake of something in order to get or achieve something □ *I gave in for the sake of peac*

salad /'sæləd/ NOUN [plural **salads**] a mixture of usually raw vegetables that sometimes includes oth food, such as fish or cheese □ *a mixed salad* □ *rice salad*

salami /sə'lɑːmɪ/ NOUN [plural **salamis**] a type of sausage made from cooked meat and usually eate cold

salary /'sælərɪ/ NOUN [plural **salaries**] an amount money that a person is paid for doing their job ea month or year □ *The job offers an annual salary of £35,000.*

sale /seɪl/ NOUN [plural **sales**]
1 no plural the process of selling things for money □ *the sale of houses*
2 the act of selling one thing ⊞ *Have you made any sales yet?*
3 an event at which things are sold for money □ *a sale of antique furniture*
4 for sale available for someone to buy □ *Are these paintings for sale?* ⊞ *They've just put their house up for sale.*
5 a time when goods are sold at cheaper prices than usual □ *the January sales*
6 on sale (a) offered for sale □ *The DVD is on sale now.* (b) available to buy for less than the usual price □ *Designer dresses now on sale on the 5th floor.*
7 sales (n) how many things a company sells □ *Sales are down for last month.* ⊞ *sales figures* (b) the department of a company whose work is selling things □ *She works in sales.*

sales assistant /ˈseɪlz əˈsɪstənt/ NOUN [plural **sales assistants**] someone whose job is to sell things in a shop

sales clerk /ˈseɪlz klɜːrk/ NOUN [plural **sales clerks**] the US phrase for sales assistant

salesman /ˈseɪlzmən/ NOUN [plural **salesmen**] a man whose job is to sell goods or services to customers

sales rep /ˈseɪlz rep/ NOUN [plural **sales reps**] someone who travels to different places, selling things for a company

saleswoman /ˈseɪlzˌwʊmən/ NOUN [plural **saleswomen**] a woman whose job is to sell goods or services to customers

salient /ˈseɪlɪənt/ ADJECTIVE being the most important or noticeable. A formal word. □ *These are the salient features of the proposed legislation.*

saline /ˈseɪlaɪn/ ADJECTIVE containing salt □ *a saline solution*

saliva /səˈlaɪvə/ NOUN, NO PLURAL the liquid that your mouth produces

sallow /ˈsæləʊ/ ADJECTIVE [**sallower, sallowest**] sallow skin is pale, slightly yellow, and does not look healthy □ *a sallow complexion*

salmon /ˈsæmən/ NOUN [plural **salmon**]
1 a large silver fish that swims up rivers to produce its eggs
2 the orange-pink flesh from this fish eaten as food
3 an orange-pink colour

salmonella /ˌsælməˈnelə/ NOUN, NO PLURAL a type of bacteria found in food that can make you very ill

salon /ˈsælɒn/ NOUN [plural **salons**] a shop where people will cut your hair or improve the appearance of part of your body

saloon /səˈluːn/ NOUN [plural **saloons**] a car with front and back seats and a separate space for carrying things

salsa /ˈsælsə/ NOUN [plural **salsas**]
1 a type of Latin-American music, or a dance for this music
2 a cold sauce with tomatoes and spices in it

salt /sɔːlt, sɒlt/ ▶ NOUN, NO PLURAL a white substance that comes from the ground or the sea and is used often for giving flavour to food ⊞ *salt and pepper* ⊞ *Add a pinch of salt.*
▶ VERB [**salts, salting, salted**] to add salt to food
• **salted** /ˈsɔːltɪd/ ADJECTIVE with salt added □ *salted peanuts*
• **salty** /ˈsɔːltɪ/ ADJECTIVE [**saltier, saltiest**] containing salt or tasting very strongly of salt □ *I thought the soup was too salty.*

salubrious /səˈluːbrɪəs/ ADJECTIVE a salubrious place is pleasant, clean and crime does not happen often ⊞ *This is not the most salubrious part of London.*

salutary /ˈsæljʊtərɪ/ ADJECTIVE a salutary experience is difficult but has a good effect on your future behaviour. A formal word. □ *Criticism is often salutary.*

salute /səˈluːt/ ▶ VERB [**salutes, saluting, saluted**]
1 to show respect to someone, especially a military officer, by touching your head with your right hand
2 to praise someone or something that someone has done, often publicly □ *The newspapers all salute her efforts to restore peace.*
▶ NOUN [plural **salutes**]
1 a movement that shows respect to someone you meet, especially a military officer □ *The Queen returned the salute.*
2 an event, speech etc. that shows respect for someone □ *His first words were a salute to the people of South Africa.*

salvage /ˈsælvɪdʒ/ ▶ VERB [**salvages, salvaging, salvaged**]
1 to save what you can after a building or ship has been damaged or destroyed □ *We managed to salvage a few belongings after the fire.*
2 to succeed in achieving one good thing in a situation where you have failed generally
▶ NOUN, NO PLURAL when things are salvaged or the things that are salvaged □ *a salvage operation*

salvation /sælˈveɪʃən/ NOUN, NO PLURAL
1 in the Christian religion, when God saves you from evil
2 someone or something that saves you in a bad situation □ *Once again, Rooney was England's salvation, scoring in the final minute of the game.*

same /seɪm/ ▶ ADJECTIVE, PRONOUN
1 the same (a) the person or thing mentioned, not a different one □ *He won the lottery and left his job on the same day.* ⊞ *We both started speaking at the same time.* (b) exactly like someone or something else ⊞ *I was wearing the same jacket as Barbara.* ⊞ *He broke his own mobile phone and now he's done the same thing to mine!* *You know I'd do the same for you.* (c) not changed □ *I thought she might have grown up a bit since leaving home, but she's just the same.*

2 same here used to say that something is also true for you. An informal phrase. □ *'I'm always late for work.' 'Same here - my boss gets really angry!'*
3 at the same time used to say that another thing is also true □ *He needs to keep active, but at the same time he should be careful of his knees.*
▶ ADVERB in the same way □ *We tend to dress the same.* □ *We treat all our children the same.*

sample /'sɑːmpəl/ ▶ NOUN [*plural* **samples**] a small amount or number of something that shows what the rest is like ⊞ *The magazine came with a free sample of chocolate.* ⊞ *This was a random sample of consumers.*
▶ VERB [**samples, sampling, sampled**] to try a small amount of food or drink to find out what it is like □ *Would you like to sample our new yoghurt?*

sanatorium /ˌsænə'tɔːrɪəm/ NOUN [*plural* **sanatoriums** *or* **sanatoria**] a hospital that cares for people who need treatment or rest for a long time

sanction /'sæŋkʃən/ ▶ NOUN [*plural* **sanctions**]
1 an official order to stop speaking with or doing trade with a country that has broken international law ⊞ *international sanctions* ⊞ *trade sanctions*
2 official permission or approval for an action □ *The proposed changes to the Act will require the sanction of Parliament.*
3 a punishment for breaking a rule or law
▶ VERB [**sanctions, sanctioning, sanctioned**] to give official permission for something

sanctity /'sæŋktɪtɪ/ NOUN, NO PLURAL the quality or condition of being holy or of deserving respect □ *the sanctity of marriage*

sanctuary /'sæŋktʃʊərɪ/ NOUN [*plural* **sanctuaries**]
1 a place that officially protects someone ⊞ *Many refugees seek sanctuary in these countries.*
2 a safe place where animals can live in a natural environment and not be hunted □ *a bird sanctuary*

sand /sænd/ ▶ NOUN, NO PLURAL very small grains of rock that are found on beaches and in deserts
▶ VERB [**sands, sanding, sanded**] to make a surface, especially wood, smooth by rubbing it with something rough

sandal /'sændəl/ NOUN [*plural* **sandals**] a light open shoe for wearing when the weather is warm

sandbag /'sændbæg/ NOUN [*plural* **sandbags**] a strong bag filled with sand that is used to build walls in order to keep out flood water or bullets

sandcastle /'sænd‚kɑːsəl/ NOUN [*plural* **sandcastles**] a pile of sand made to look like a castle, usually built by children playing on a beach

sand dune /'sænd djuːn/ NOUN [*plural* **sand dunes**] a hill of sand near a beach or in the desert

sandpaper /'sænd‚peɪpə(r)/ NOUN, NO PLURAL strong paper with a layer of sand stuck to one side, used for making wood smooth

sandstone /'sændstəun/ NOUN, NO PLURAL a type of light-coloured stone that is used in building

sandwich /'sænwɪdʒ/ ▶ NOUN [*plural* **sandwiches**] two pieces of bread with food between them □ *a ham sandwich* □ *a toasted sandwich*
▶ VERB **be sandwiched between someone/ something** to be in a small space between two bigger things or people □ *I was sandwiched between two huge men on the Metro.*

sandy /'sændɪ/ ADJECTIVE [**sandier, sandiest**]
1 covered with sand, or with sand inside □ *a sandy beach* □ *sandy shoes*
2 sandy hair is a light red-brown colour

sane /seɪn/ ADJECTIVE [**saner, sanest**]
1 not mad or mentally ill □ *The judge was told that Foster was sane at the time of the murder.*
2 sensible and showing good judgment □ *Reducing the stress in your life seems like a very sane thing to do.*

sang /sæŋ/ PAST TENSE OF **sing**

sanitary /'sænɪtərɪ/ ADJECTIVE to do with keeping clean and healthy □ *Diseases spread quickly where sanitary conditions are poor.*

sanitation /ˌsænɪ'teɪʃən/ NOUN, NO PLURAL ways of protecting people's health by providing clean water and taking dirty water and waste away from buildings

sanity /'sænɪtɪ/ NOUN, NO PLURAL not being mad or mentally ill

sank /sæŋk/ PAST TENSE OF **sink** □ *The ship sank in rough waters.*

Santa Claus *or* **Santa** /'sæntə/ NOUN an imaginary old man with a white beard in a red coat who children believe brings presents on Christmas Eve □ *What did Santa bring you?*

sap /sæp/ ▶ NOUN, NO PLURAL the liquid inside plants and trees
▶ VERB [**saps, sapping, sapped**] to make someone feel weak and tired ⊞ *The heat saps my energy .*

sapling /'sæplɪŋ/ NOUN [*plural* **saplings**] a young tree

sapphire /'sæfaɪə(r)/ NOUN [*plural* **sapphires**] a dark blue stone that is used in jewellery

sarcasm /'sɑːkæzəm/ NOUN, NO PLURAL saying one thing when you mean the opposite, in order to criticize someone or make them feel stupid □ *'Nice jacket,' said Max, with heavy sarcasm.*
● **sarcastic** /sɑː'kæstɪk/ ADJECTIVE using sarcasm □ *didn't know if he really liked it or if he was being sarcastic.*

sardine /sɑː'diːn/ NOUN [*plural* **sardines**] a type of small sea fish that people eat

sardonic /sɑː'dɒnɪk/ ADJECTIVE showing no respect for what someone has said □ *a sardonic smile*
● **sardonically** /sɑː'dɒnɪkəlɪ/ ADVERB in a sardonic way □ *He laughed sardonically.*

sari /'sɑːrɪ/ NOUN [*plural* **saris**] a long piece of cloth that is wrapped round the body and worn as a dress, especially by women in South Asia

sarong /sə'rɒŋ/ NOUN [*plural* **sarongs**] a wide piece of cloth that is wrapped round the lower part of the body and worn as a skirt

sash /sæʃ/ NOUN [plural **sashes**] a strip of cloth worn around the waist or over one shoulder, usually as part of a uniform

sat /sæt/ PAST TENSE AND PAST PARTICIPLE OF **sit** □ *He sat down.* □ *I've sat here for an hour waiting for you!*

Satan /'seɪtən/ NOUN another name for the Devil (=the most powerful evil spirit in some religions)

satchel /'sætʃəl/ NOUN [plural **satchels**] a bag that you wear over your shoulder, used by children for carrying books to school

satellite /'sætəlaɪt/ NOUN [plural **satellites**]
1 a piece of equipment that is put in space to travel around the Earth in order to send and receive information □ *a satellite link* □ *a weather/communications satellite*
2 a natural object in space, such as the moon, that moves around a planet or star

satellite dish /'sætəlaɪt dɪʃ/ NOUN [plural **satellite dishes**] a circular piece of equipment that is attached to the side of a building to receive signals for satellite television

satellite television /'sætəlaɪt 'telɪ,vɪʒən/ NOUN, NO PLURAL television programmes that are sent to people's televisions using satellites

satin /'sætɪn/ NOUN, NO PLURAL a type of cloth with a shiny surface

satire /'sætaɪə(r)/ NOUN [plural **satires**]
1 the use of humour to criticize stupid or bad behaviour
2 any book, film, play or television programme using this type of humour □ *a political satire*

satirical /sə'tɪrɪkəl/ ADJECTIVE using satire □ *He writes for a satirical magazine.* □ *a satirical cartoon*

satirize or **satirise** /'sætəraɪz/ VERB [**satirizes, satirizing, satirized**] to criticize someone or something using satire □ *Her first play satirized the political system.*

satisfaction /,sætɪs'fækʃən/ NOUN, NO PLURAL a feeling of pleasure at having achieved something or got something good □ *She looked at the finished work with satisfaction.* □ *+ from doing something I get a lot of satisfaction from cooking.* 🖫 *Job satisfaction is extremely important.*

satisfactory /,sætɪs'fæktərɪ/ ADJECTIVE of a good enough standard □ *Her progress in maths was described as satisfactory.* □ *We are still waiting for a satisfactory outcome to the situation.*

satisfied /'sætɪsfaɪd/ ADJECTIVE
pleased because you have achieved something or got something good □ *+ with Are you satisfied with the progress on the project?* □ *You're never satisfied - that's your problem.* □ *a satisfied customer*
if you are satisfied that something is true, you are certain that it is true □ *+ that I am satisfied that they did all they could to help her.*

satisfy /'sætɪsfaɪ/ VERB [**satisfies, satisfying, satisfied**]
to make someone pleased by giving them what they want or need □ *The resort should satisfy even the most experienced skiers.* □ *This proposal is unlikely to satisfy campaigners.*
2 if something satisfies a rule or condition, it has or does what is necessary for it 🖫 *Are you sure you satisfy the entry requirements for law school?*
3 to provide proof that something is true □ *+ that The defendant was unable to satisfy the police that his dog was not dangerous.*
● **satisfying** /'sætɪs,faɪɪŋ/ ADJECTIVE
1 making you feel pleased because you have achieved something or got something good □ *I find my work as a doctor very satisfying.* □ *It's very satisfying to see the results of your cooking.*
2 a satisfying meal is one in which there is enough food to make you feel full

SATNAV /'sæt'næv/ ABBREVIATION satellite navigation; a piece of equipment especially used in cars to tell the driver how to get to a place

satsuma /,sæt'su:mə/ NOUN [plural **satsumas**] a fruit like a small orange

saturate /'sætʃəreɪt/ VERB [**saturates, saturating, saturated**] to make something extremely wet □ *His shirt was saturated with sweat.*

Saturday /'sætədɪ/ NOUN [plural **Saturdays**] the day of the week after Friday and before Sunday □ *On Saturday, we went shopping.* □ *What are you doing next Saturday?*

sauce /sɔ:s/ NOUN [plural **sauces**] a liquid food with a particular flavour that you put on other food □ *She had spaghetti with tomato sauce.* □ *ice cream with chocolate sauce*

saucepan /'sɔ:spən/ NOUN [plural **saucepans**] a round metal container with a handle, used for cooking food on top of an oven

saucer /'sɔ:sə(r)/ NOUN [plural **saucers**] a small plate that goes under a cup □ *a cup and saucer*

sauna /'sɔ:nə/ NOUN [plural **saunas**]
1 a hot room where you sit and sweat
2 a period of time inside a sauna 🖫 *I had a sauna at the health club.*

saunter /'sɔ:ntə(r)/ ▶ VERB [**saunters, sauntering, sauntered**] to walk slowly for pleasure □ *We were just sauntering round the park.*
▶ NOUN [plural **saunters**] a slow walk for pleasure □ *We went for a saunter along the seafront.*

sausage /'sɒsɪdʒ/ NOUN [plural **sausages**] a long tube of meat mixed with spices

sausage roll /'sɒsɪdʒ 'rəʊl/ NOUN [plural **sausage rolls**] a small amount of meat mixed with spices inside a tube of pastry

sauté /'səʊteɪ/ ▶ VERB [**sautés, sautéing, sautéed** or **sautéd**] to fry food quickly in a little butter or oil □ *Lightly sauté the mushrooms.*

▶ ADJECTIVE fried quickly in a little butter or oil □ *sauté potatoes*

savage /'sævɪdʒ/ ▶ ADJECTIVE
1 very violent and cruel □ *savage beatings*
2 criticizing someone or something very strongly
🕮 *He launched a savage attack on his former employer.*

▶ VERB [**savages, savaging, savaged**]
1 to attack and badly injure someone □ *A young child had been savaged by a dog.*
2 to criticize something or someone very strongly
□ *The film was savaged by the critics.*
● **savagely** /'sævɪdʒlɪ/ ADVERB in a violent and cruel way □ *The 78-year-old woman was savagely attacked on her way home.*
● **savagery** /'sævɪdʒrɪ/ NOUN, NO PLURAL extreme violence □ *Police were shocked by the savagery of the attack.*

savanna *or* **savannah** /sə'vænə/ NOUN, NO PLURAL a large area in a hot country, with grass and not many trees. A geography word.

save /seɪv/ ▶ VERB [**saves, saving, saved**]
1 to stop someone or something being harmed, killed or destroyed □ *The firefighters saved everyone in the building.* □ *Switch off lights and help save the planet.*
□ **+ from** *A shelter of branches and leaves saved them from freezing.* 🕮 *The correct equipment could save your life.*
2 to avoid using something, or to use less of it than usual □ *You can save 40 minutes by taking the motorway.*
3 to keep something so that you can use it later
□ *Save any food that's left over and heat it up later.*
□ *We're saving our energy for tomorrow's walk.*
4 to keep money, usually in a bank, so that you can use it later □ *We have saved regularly all our lives.*
5 to make it possible to avoid doing something
□ *Plastic window frames will save you a lot of work in the future.* □ **+ ing** *If you all write your names on a piece of card, it will save me having to ask every time.*
6 to make a computer store information. A computing word □ *Make sure you save your work regularly.*
7 to not let the ball go in the net in sports such as football □ *He saved a penalty.*
◆ PHRASAL VERBS **save on something** to not spend the money that something would cost if you bought it or used it □ *With better insulation you can save on your heating bills.* **save up** to keep money so that you can use it in the future □ **+ for** *I'm saving up for a new car.*
▶ NOUN [*plural* **saves**] when someone stops the ball going into the net in a sport such as football 🕮 *He made two brilliant saves.*
● **saver** /'seɪvə(r)/ NOUN [*plural* **savers**] someone who is saving money, usually in a bank
● **saving** /'seɪvɪŋ/ NOUN [*plural* **savings**]
1 an amount that you have avoided spending □ *There are big savings to be made in the summer sales.* □ *That is a saving of £35 on the normal price.*
2 **savings** money that you have saved in a bank

□ *Joe's going to spend all his savings on a drum kit.*
● **saviour** /'seɪvjə(r)/ NOUN [*plural* **saviours**]
1 someone who saves something from harm or danger
2 **Saviour** in Christian religions, Jesus Christ

savior /'seɪvjə(r)/ NOUN [*plural* **saviors**] the US spelling of saviour
savour /'seɪvə(r)/ VERB [**savours, savouring, savoured**] to eat or drink something slowly in order to enjoy it for longer □ *We ate the cake slowly, savouring every mouthful.*
● **savoury** /'seɪvərɪ/ ADJECTIVE not sweet or not containing sugar □ *I much prefer savoury snacks to sweets.*

saw[1] /sɔː/ ▶ NOUN [*plural* **saws**] a tool with a thin blade used for cutting through wood or metal
▶ VERB [**saws, sawing, sawed, sawn**] to cut through wood or metal using a saw
saw[2] /sɔː/ PAST TENSE OF see □ *I saw Paolo last week.*
sawdust /'sɔːdʌst/ NOUN, NO PLURAL the thick dust that is produced when wood is cut with a saw
sawn /sɔːn/ PAST PARTICIPLE of saw
sax /sæks/ NOUN [*plural* **saxes**] a saxophone □ *a tenor sax*
saxophone /'sæksəfəʊn/ NOUN [*plural* **saxophones**] a long curved musical instrument made of metal that you play by blowing into it and pressing different keys
● **saxophonist** /ˌsæk'sɒfənɪst/ NOUN [*plural* **saxophonists**] someone who plays the saxophone

say /seɪ/ ▶ VERB [**says, saying, said**]
1 to express something in words □ *I asked her about the rumours, but she wouldn't say anything.* □ *I asked for more money, but my boss said no.* □ **+ that** *Officials say that the death toll has reached 30.* □ **+ about** *Did she say anything about the wedding?*
2 to give information in words or signs □ *What does the notice say?* □ *My watch said six.*
3 to mean something □ *They seem to be saying that the building is not suitable.* □ *I'm not saying she's mean - it's just that she never shares her things.*
4 to show what something or someone is like □ **+ about** *The state of the offices said a lot about the company.* □ *What do your clothes say about you?*
5 used to give a possibility □ *Say we were to print the book in India - could we be sure of getting it on time?* □ *We only need a few more people - 20 say - to get the job done.*

> ► Remember that you **say** something but you do not 'say someone something':
> ✓ She said she was leaving.
> ✗ She said me she was leaving.

▶ NOUN, NO PLURAL
1 when you are involved in making a decision 🕮 *I had no say in how the money was spent.*
2 **have your say** to be allowed to give your opinion

about something □ *Let Mark finish speaking, then you can have your say.*

• **saying** /'seɪɪŋ/ NOUN [*plural* **sayings**] a phrase or sentence that people often use, giving advice or saying something that many people believe is true □ *Gran's favourite saying was 'an apple a day keeps the doctor away'.*

scab /skæb/ NOUN [*plural* **scabs**] a hard covering of dried blood that forms over a cut

• **scabby** /'skæbɪ/ ADJECTIVE [**scabbier, scabbiest**] covered in scabs □ *a scabby knee*

scaffold /'skæfəʊld/ NOUN [*plural* **scaffolds**] in the past, a structure where criminals were killed by hanging them by the neck or cutting off their head

• **scaffolding** /'skæfəldɪŋ/ NOUN, NO PLURAL a structure of long metal poles and wooden boards for people to stand on when they are working on the outside of a building

scald /skɔːld/ ▶ VERB [**scalds, scalding, scalded**] to burn someone with very hot liquid or steam
▶ NOUN [*plural* **scalds**] a burn caused by hot liquid or steam

scale /skeɪl/ ▶ NOUN [*plural* **scales**]
1 the general size or level of something □ *The cyclone has caused destruction on a huge scale.* □ *Experts warn that the scale of the problem is increasing.*
2 a series of numbers or marks used for measuring the level of something □ *The earthquake measured 3.2 on the Richter scale.* □ *Patients are asked to grade the pain they feel on a scale of one to ten.*
3 the size of something such as a model or a map, compared to the real size of the thing it represents □ *What's the scale of the map?*
4 scales an instrument for weighing things 🖪 *a set of kitchen scales* 🖪 *I weighed myself on the bathroom scales.*
5 a series of musical notes that goes up in order □ *the scale of G major* 🖪 *I try to practise my scales each day.*
6 one of the small thin pieces covering the skin of a fish or snake
▶ VERB [**scales, scaling, scaled**] to climb up something □ *People were scaling the wall, singing and shouting.*
PHRASAL VERB **scale something up/down** to increase/lower the size, level or importance of something □ *The massive police operation is slowly being scaled down.*

scallion /'skælɪən/ NOUN [*plural* **scallions**] the US word for spring onion

scallop /'skɒləp/ NOUN [*plural* **scallops**] a sea animal that lives in a shell and that you can eat

scalp /skælp/ NOUN [*plural* **scalps**] the skin on the part of the head where the hair grows

scalpel /'skælpəl/ NOUN [*plural* **scalpels**] a small sharp knife, used especially by doctors who do medical operations

scaly /'skeɪlɪ/ ADJECTIVE [**scalier, scaliest**] scaly skin has small pieces falling off it because it is very dry

scam /skæm/ NOUN [*plural* **scams**] an illegal way of making money. An informal word. □ *Don't fall for it - it's a scam.*

scamper /'skæmpə(r)/ VERB [**scampers, scampering, scampered**] to run quickly and lightly, taking short steps □ *The puppy scampered around the garden.*

scampi /'skæmpɪ/ NOUN, NO PLURAL large prawns (=small sea animals) that are fried

scan /skæn/ ▶ VERB [**scans, scanning, scanned**]
1 to use a piece of equipment to copy a picture of something onto a computer □ *Scan the photo and then e-mail it to me.*
2 to use a piece of equipment to produce an image of inside someone's body or inside a piece of luggage □ *All bags are scanned at the airport.*
3 to read something very quickly □ *Lou scanned the jobs section of the paper, looking for anything suitable.*
4 to look all around an area from one position □ *The police were scanning the crowd for signs of trouble.*
▶ NOUN [*plural* **scans**] a medical process in which a special machine produces an image of the inside of your body □ *a brain scan*

scandal /'skændəl/ NOUN [*plural* **scandals**]
1 a situation in which important people behave in a way that is morally very wrong □ *a political/financial scandal*
2 talk or writing in the newspapers, etc. about behaviour that shocks people

• **scandalize** or **scandalise** /'skændəlaɪz/ VERB [**scandalizes, scandalizing, scandalized**] to make people feel extremely shocked or offended □ *The family was scandalized by the marriage.*

• **scandalous** /'skændələs/ ADJECTIVE shocking or wrong □ *It's a scandalous waste of public money.*

scanner /'skænə(r)/ NOUN [*plural* **scanners**]
1 a machine that copies a picture or document into a computer. A computing word.
2 a machine that produces a picture of the inside of a part of someone's body as part of a medical test □ *an MRI scanner*
3 a machine that can read information using light □ *a bar code scanner*

scant /skænt/ ADJECTIVE [**scanter, scantest**] very little or not enough □ *There is scant evidence for any of these claims.* 🖪 *She paid scant attention to the teacher's words.*

• **scanty** /'skæntɪ/ ADJECTIVE [**scantier, scantiest**] very small □ *a scanty nightshirt*

scapegoat /'skeɪpgəʊt/ NOUN [*plural* **scapegoats**] someone who is blamed for something that they did not do so that someone else will not be blamed 🖪 *The manager was made a scapegoat for the team's poor performance.*

scar /skɑː(r)/ ▶ NOUN [*plural* **scars**]
1 a mark that is left on skin from an injury 🖪 *The surgery left a small scar.*
2 a bad feeling that you have for a long time after a bad experience 🖪 *The accident also left some*

psychological scars. 🔲 *He still bears the mental scars of the ordeal.*

▶ VERB [**scars, scarring, scarred**] to cause a scar □ *He was badly scarred by the fire.*

scarce /'skeəs/ ADJECTIVE [**scarcer, scarcest**] only available in small amounts □ *Food was scarce in wartime.* □ *scarce resources*

● **scarcely** /'skeəsli/ ADVERB almost not at all □ *The place had scarcely changed.* □ *I could scarcely believe it.*

● **scarcity** /'skeəsɪti/ NOUN [plural **scarcities**] when something is scarce □ *There was a scarcity of clean water.*

scare /skeə(r)/ ▶ VERB [**scares, scaring, scared**]

1 to frighten or to worry someone □ *We don't want to scare people.* □ *The reports are intended to scare us into driving more carefully.*

2 scare the daylights/life, etc. out of someone to frighten someone very much. An informal phrase.

◆ PHRASAL VERB scare someone away/off

1 to make someone worried so that they decide not to do something □ *Recent attacks in the region have scared away the tourists.*

2 to frighten someone so that they leave □ *He scared the thieves off.*

▶ NOUN [plural **scares**]

1 a situation in which a lot of people are frightened or worried about something □ *a public health scare* 🔲 *There was a bomb scare at the airport.*

2 when something frightens or worries you for a short time 🔲 *It gave us all a bit of a scare when Maria fainted.*

scarecrow /'skeəkrəʊ/ NOUN [plural **scarecrows**] a simple model of a person in a field intended to frighten birds away

scared /'skeəd/ ADJECTIVE frightened □ *I'm scared of spiders.* □ *She's scared of her teacher.* □ *She lay in bed, too scared to move.* 🔲 *I'm scared stiff (=very frightened) of heights.* 🔲 *I was scared to death (=very frightened) of messing it up.*

scarf /skɑ:f/ NOUN [plural **scarves**] a piece of cloth that you wear around your neck or head to keep warm or to look attractive □ *a silk scarf* □ *a thick woollen scarf*

scarlet /'skɑ:lət/ NOUN, NO PLURAL a bright red colour

scarper /'skɑ:pə(r)/ VERB [**scarpers, scarpering, scarpered**] an informal word meaning to run away □ *They scarpered without paying the bill.*

scarves /skɑ:vz/ PLURAL OF scarf

scary /'skeəri/ ADJECTIVE [**scarier, scariest**] making you feel frightened or very worried □ *a scary film* □ *The scary thing is how quickly the disease spreads.*

scathing /'skeɪðɪŋ/ ADJECTIVE criticizing severely □ *a scathing comment* □ *He was scathing about the government's economic policy.*

● **scathingly** /'skeɪðɪŋli/ ADVERB in a scathing way

scatter /'skætə(r)/ VERB [**scatters, scattering, scattered**]

1 to spread something in a lot of places over a wide area □ *Scatter the seeds evenly over the prepared soil.*

2 if people or animals scatter, they suddenly run away in different directions □ *The crowd scattered with the arrival of the police.*

scatterbrain /'skætəbreɪn/ NOUN [plural **scatterbrains**] an informal word for someone who often forgets things

● **scatterbrained** /'skætəbreɪnd/ ADJECTIVE often forgetting things. An informal word.

scattered /'skætəd/ ADJECTIVE in a lot of places over a wide area or over a period of time 🔲 *Some scattered showers are expected later.* □ *About 20 people were killed in scattered violence across the country.*

● **scattering** /'skætərɪŋ/ NOUN [plural **scatterings**] a small number or quantity, spread over a wide area □ *There was a thin scattering of snow.*

scavenge /'skævɪndʒ/ VERB [**scavenges, scavenging, scavenged**]

1 to search in rubbish for things that can be used or eaten □ *Stray dogs scavenged for food from the dustbins.*

2 if a wild bird or animal scavenges, they eat dead animals that have already been killed by something else □ *scavenging vultures*

● **scavenger** /'skævɪndʒə(r)/ NOUN [plural **scavengers**] a person or an animal that scavenges

scenario /sɪ'nɑ:rɪəʊ/ NOUN [plural **scenarios**] a situation that might happen □ *We're prepared for a possible scenarios.* 🔲 *The worst-case scenario (=worst possible situation) is that we get no money for the project.*

scene /si:n/ NOUN [plural **scenes**]

1 the place where an event happens □ *+ of the scene of the accident* 🔲 *a crime scene* □ *An ambulance was very quickly on the scene.*

2 part of a play, a book or a film that happens in one place □ *We'll have to film the scene on the beach next* 🔲 *the opening scene of Othello* □ *+ from It was like a scene from a Hollywood movie.*

3 a place or situation as someone sees it □ *+ of Before me was a scene of celebration.* □ *Rescuers described a scene of utter devastation.* □ *There were chaotic scenes as fights broke out.*

4 a loud and embarrassing argument in a public place 🔲 *There's no need to make a scene.*

5 the people and things to do with a particular activity or way of living 🔲 *They burst onto the music scene in 2004.* 🔲 *The city's arts scene is flourishing.*

6 behind the scenes not seen by the public □ *He prefers to work behind the scenes.*

7 set the scene (for something) (a) to create a situation which shows what might happen next or makes something likely □ *His speech set the scene for a hard-fought election campaign.* (b) to describe a general situation before talking about a particular event □ *First, let me set the scene.*

● **scenery** /'si:nəri/ NOUN, NO PLURAL

1 what you see around you, especially the countryside □ *You get to see some wonderful scenery from the train.* □ *We stopped to take in the stunning scenery.*

🖼 He needed a change of scenery (=to go somewhere different).

2 the large pictures used in the theatre behind the actors

• **scenic** /ˈsiːnɪk/ ADJECTIVE with attractive things to look at, especially the countryside □ a scenic route □ a scenic area

scent /sent/ ► NOUN [plural **scents**]

1 a good smell □ The scent of lilies can fill a whole room.

2 a liquid that women put on their skin to make them smell nice

3 the smell of an animal that other animals can follow

► VERB [**scents, scenting, scented**]

1 to find something by smell □ A hungry animal will scent food long before it sees it.

2 to have a feeling that something exists or might happen □ Two guards, scenting trouble, hurried over.

• **scented** /ˈsentɪd/ ADJECTIVE with a pleasant smell □ a scented candle □ scented oils

sceptic /ˈskeptɪk/ NOUN [plural **sceptics**] a person who doubts whether something is true or as good as other people believe □ Where alternative medicine is concerned, I'm a sceptic.

sceptical /ˈskeptɪkəl/ ADJECTIVE doubting that something is true □ Yuko thinks it will work, but I'm still sceptical. □ She's sceptical about the benefits the Olympics will bring.

sceptre /ˈseptə(r)/ NOUN [plural **sceptres**] a pole that a king or queen carries at official ceremonies

schedule /ˈʃedjuːl/ ► NOUN [plural **schedules**] a plan that shows when things should happen or be done □ a flight schedule □ He has a very busy work schedule. □ The building work finished on schedule (=when planned). □ The project is already six months behind schedule.

► VERB [**schedules, scheduling, scheduled**] to plan that something will happen at a particular time □ The meeting has been scheduled for next Wednesday.

scheme /skiːm/ ► NOUN [plural **schemes**]

1 a plan or system for doing something □ a national training scheme □ a pension scheme

2 a plan to get money, usually by tricking people □ a fraudulent tax scheme

3 in the scheme of things as part of the general situation or the way things are organized □ In the scheme of things, it's a small amount of money.

► VERB [**schemes, scheming, schemed**] to make secret plans, especially to cause harm or damage □ He was scheming to push Willis out of his job.

scheming /ˈskiːmɪŋ/ ADJECTIVE clever at getting what you want in a dishonest way □ She plays a scheming politician.

schizophrenia /ˌskɪtsəˈfriːnɪə/ NOUN, NO PLURAL a severe mental illness in which someone cannot always understand what is real and what is not

schizophrenic /ˌskɪtsəˈfrenɪk/ ► ADJECTIVE to do with schizophrenia

► NOUN [plural **schizophrenics**] someone who is suffering from schizophrenia

scholar /ˈskɒlə(r)/ NOUN [plural **scholars**] a person who studies a particular subject and has a lot of knowledge of it □ a scholar of Greek

• **scholarly** /ˈskɒləlɪ/ ADJECTIVE showing a deep knowledge of a subject 🖼 a scholarly work about Victorian art

• **scholarship** /ˈskɒləʃɪp/ NOUN [plural **scholarships**]

1 money given to a student to pay for their studies at a school or university □ There are several scholarships available for very bright students.

2 serious study of a subject

• **scholastic** /skəˈlæstɪk/ ADJECTIVE a formal word meaning to do with schools and education □ scholastic achievements

school /skuːl/ ► NOUN [plural **schools**]

1 a place where children go to learn 🖼 You'll go to school when you're five years old. □ We walked home from school together.

2 no plural the time when you are at school □ He plays football after school on a Wednesday. 🖼 She left school at sixteen.

3 no plural all the students and teachers in a school □ The whole school was in the playground.

4 in the US, a college or university □ Where did you go to school?

5 a part of a college or a university □ + of the Stanford University school of medicine

6 a place where people go to learn a particular skill 🖼 a language school

7 a large number of fish or dolphins (=sea mammals) that swim together in a group □ a large school of fish

8 school of thought a particular opinion or way of thinking about something □ There are two schools of thought regarding its origin.

► VERB [**schools, schooling, schooled**] a formal word meaning to educate a child □ The brothers are being schooled at home.

school age /ˈskuːl eɪdʒ/ NOUN, NO PLURAL the age when a child must go to school □ children of school age

schoolboy /ˈskuːlbɔɪ/ NOUN [plural **schoolboys**] a boy who goes to school

schoolchild /ˈskuːltʃaɪld/ NOUN [plural **schoolchildren**] a child who goes to school □ a large party of schoolchildren

schooldays /ˈskuːldeɪz/ PLURAL NOUN the time in your life when you go to school □ His schooldays were the happiest days of his life.

schoolgirl /ˈskuːlɡɜːl/ NOUN [plural **schoolgirls**] a girl who goes to school

schooling /ˈskuːlɪŋ/ NOUN, NO PLURAL education, especially at school □ He had no formal schooling.

school-leaver /ˈskuːlˈliːvə(r)/ NOUN [plural **school-leavers**] a young person who is leaving or has recently left school □ a training scheme for unemployed school-leavers

schoolteacher /'sku:l‚ti:tʃə(r)/ NOUN [*plural* **schoolteachers**] a teacher in a school

schoolwork /'sku:lwɜ:k/ NOUN, NO PLURAL the work that a child does at school or for school

science /'saɪəns/ NOUN [*plural* **sciences**]

1 *no plural* the study and knowledge of the physical world and the way things happen in it ⊞ *He studied science and mathematics.* □ *Few now question the science behind climate change.*

2 a particular part of science, especially chemistry, physics or biology □ *biological science* □ *environmental science* □ **+ of** *the science of genetics*

3 the organized study of something □ *a degree in political science* □ *the School of Social Sciences*

science fiction /ˌsaɪəns 'fɪkʃən/ NOUN, NO PLURAL stories and films that take place in an imagined future or in other parts of the universe □ *a science fiction novel*

scientific /ˌsaɪən'tɪfɪk/ ADJECTIVE

1 to do with science ⊞ *scientific research* ⊞ *a paper in a scientific journal*

2 based on an organized system of rules, methods or tests □ *The survey wasn't very scientific, but it gives a rough picture.*

• **scientifically** /ˌsaɪən'tɪfɪkəlɪ/ ADVERB according to the rules of science □ *a scientifically proven law*

scientist /'saɪəntɪst/ NOUN [*plural* **scientists**] someone who studies science or who works in science □ *Scientists believe the condition is genetic.* □ *a team of forensic scientists*

scissors /'sɪzəz/ PLURAL NOUN a cutting tool that you hold in one hand that has two blades joined in the middle ⊞ *a pair of scissors* □ *She cut them up using kitchen scissors.*

> ► Remember that **scissors** is a plural noun:
> ✓ You'll need **some** scissors.
> ✗ You'll need **a** scissors.

scoff /skɒf/ VERB [**scoffs, scoffing, scoffed**]

1 to show you think that someone or something is stupid and does not deserve respect, sometimes by laughing □ *Many MPs scoffed at the idea.*

2 an informal word meaning to eat something very fast □ *If you leave those crisps near Nick he'll scoff the lot.*

scold /skəʊld/ VERB [**scolds, scolding, scolded**] to criticize someone angrily for doing something wrong. An old-fashioned word.

• **scolding** /'skəʊldɪŋ/ NOUN [*plural* **scoldings**] when someone is scolded. An old-fashioned word.

scone /skɒn, skəʊn/ NOUN [*plural* **scones**] a small, round, plain cake that is often eaten with butter and jam

scoop /sku:p/ ► VERB [**scoops, scooping, scooped**]

1 to lift or to remove something in your curved hands or with a large spoon or similar tool □ *She scooped up*

a handful of water. □ *Scoop out the seeds with a teaspoon.*

2 an informal word meaning to win something such as money or a prize □ *He scooped the Best Actor award for the role.*

► NOUN [*plural* **scoops**]

1 a tool like a large spoon for lifting liquid or soft substances, or the amount that this tool holds □ *an ice cream scoop* □ *Serve chilled with a scoop of cream.*

2 a news story that a newspaper prints before other newspapers do

scooter /'sku:tə(r)/ NOUN [*plural* **scooters**]

1 a smaller and less powerful motorcycle ⊞ *Young men ride by on motor scooters.*

2 a child's toy with two wheels at either end of a board and a tall handle, which you stand on and push yourself along

scope /skəʊp/ NOUN, NO PLURAL

1 the whole range of matters that something deals with □ *That whole question falls outside the scope of this meeting.*

2 an opportunity or possibility that something can happen □ *There's plenty of scope for improving these plans.* □ *There's a lot of scope for growth.*

scorch /skɔːtʃ/ VERB [**scorches, scorching, scorched**] to burn the surface of something □ *The flames had scorched his clothes.*

• **scorched** /skɔːtʃd/ ADJECTIVE dried by heat or slightly burnt □ *an area of scorched grass*

• **scorching** /'skɔːtʃɪŋ/ ADJECTIVE very hot □ *It was a scorching day.* ⊞ *The game was played in scorching heat.*

score /skɔː(r)/ ► VERB [**scores, scoring, scored**]

1 to get a point in a game, test or competition ⊞ *Ronaldo scored the winning goal.* ⊞ *Drivers score ? points for a win.* □ **+ for** *Hamilton has scored again fc the Rovers.* □ **+ against** *He scored against Brazil in th World Cup.*

2 to keep a record of the points that are won in a gam or competition □ *Who's scoring?*

3 to scratch a surface with something sharp

► NOUN [*plural* **scores**]

1 the number of points that you get in a game, test competition ⊞ *What was the final score?* ⊞ *What's t highest score you can get?* ⊞ *Katie's test scores weren't very good.*

2 scores of something a lot of something □ *We' received scores of e-mails about this.*

3 on this/that score to do with the subject or thi mentioned □ *We have plenty of food so we'll have worries on that score.*

4 a piece of written music ⊞ *a musical score* ⊞ *St wrote the score for the film.*

scoreboard /'skɔːbɔːd/ NOUN [*plural* **scoreboards** board on which the score in a game is shown

scorer /'skɔːrə(r)/ NOUN [plural **scorers**] someone who scores points in a game or competition 🔄 *He was the team's top scorer last season.*

scorn /skɔːn/ ▶ VERB [**scorns, scorning, scorned**] a formal word meaning to refuse to accept something because you think it is stupid or nor worth your attention □ *He initially scorned the idea.*
▶ NOUN, NO PLURAL a formal word for a feeling that someone or something is stupid or not worth your attention 🔄 *She poured scorn on the suggestion* (=said it was stupid).
• **scornful** /'skɔːnfʊl/ ADJECTIVE showing scorn □ *He was scornful of the minister's claims.*
• **scornfully** /'skɔːnfʊlɪ/ ADVERB in a way that shows scorn

scorpion /'skɔːpɪən/ NOUN [plural **scorpions**] an animal that looks like a large insect and has a curved, poisonous tail

scoundrel /'skaʊndrəl/ NOUN [plural **scoundrels**] an old-fashioned word that means a man who behaves badly and dishonestly

scour /'skaʊə(r)/ VERB [**scours, scouring, scoured**]
1 to search a large area carefully □ *Teams of villagers scoured the hillside for the missing climber.*
2 to clean a surface by rubbing hard with something rough □ *The saucepans needed scouring.*

scourge /skɜːdʒ/ NOUN [plural **scourges**] a cause of great suffering or harm to many people or to a particular group of people □ *Cancer is the scourge of Western society.*

scout /skaʊt/ ▶ NOUN [plural **scouts**]
1 the Scouts an organization for young people that encourages activities outdoors and practical skills
2 a member of the Scouts 🔄 *a boy scout*
3 someone whose job is going to different places, looking for people who are very good at particular things, for example sport 🔄 *The young player was spotted by a talent scout last year.*
▶ VERB [**scouts, scouting, scouted**] to search for something, especially in many places □ *I'll scout around for a chair that matches the others.*

scowl /skaʊl/ ▶ VERB [**scowls, scowling, scowled**] to look at someone or something in an angry way
▶ NOUN [plural **scowls**] an angry look

scrabble /'skræbəl/ VERB [**scrabbles, scrabbling, scrabbled**] to try to find or to get hold of something with your fingers □ *He was on his knees, scrabbling about in the sand trying to find his glasses.*

scramble /'skræmbəl/ ▶ VERB [**scrambles, scrambling, scrambled**]
1 to climb or to move using your hands and feet, especially with difficulty □ *We scrambled up the side of the hill.*
2 to push other people out of the way to get to something □ *People were scrambling to get to the bargains before anyone else.*
3 to mix eggs together and cook them
4 to change a message or broadcast so that it can only be understood using special equipment

▶ NOUN [plural **scrambles**]
1 a difficult climb over rough ground
2 when you push other people out of the way to get to something first
3 a race on motorcycles over rough ground

scrambled egg /'skræmbəld 'eg/ NOUN [plural **scrambled eggs**] eggs mixed together and cooked in a pan

scrap /skræp/ ▶ NOUN [plural **scraps**]
1 a small piece or amount of something 🔄 *I have his address written on a scrap of paper.* □ *There isn't a scrap of evidence against us.*
2 old or broken vehicles and machines that can be taken apart and their parts used again 🔄 *scrap metal*
3 an informal word for a fight
▶ VERB [**scraps, scrapping, scrapped**]
1 to decide not to use something or to stop using it □ *Let's just scrap the whole idea now.* 🔄 *The plan has been scrapped.*
2 to get rid of a machine, vehicle, etc.
3 an informal word meaning to fight with someone

scrapbook /'skræpbʊk/ NOUN [plural **scrapbooks**] an empty book you can fill with pictures, articles, etc.

scrape /skreɪp/ ▶ VERB [**scrapes, scraping, scraped**]
1 to get something off a surface by using something sharp or rough □ *Scrape the mud off your shoes before you come in.*
2 to damage something slightly by rubbing it against something rough □ *Eva fell off her bike and scraped her knee.*
3 to manage to achieve something with difficulty □ *They scraped a win in the last few minutes of the game.*
4 scrape a living to manage to live on a small amount of money
♦ PHRASAL VERBS **scrape by** to manage to live on a small amount of money □ *Millions of people scrape by on less than a dollar a day.* **scrape through (something)** to only just achieve something □ *They scraped through to the semi-finals.* **scrape something together** to manage to collect enough of something, especially money, with difficulty □ *We scraped together enough money for a deposit.*
▶ NOUN [plural **scrapes**]
1 a mark or injury caused by scraping something □ *They suffered only minor scrapes and bruises.*
2 a difficult situation 🔄 *I got into a few scrapes when I was travelling.*

scrap heap /'skræp hiːp/ NOUN [plural **scrap heaps**]
1 a place where objects, machines and vehicles that have been thrown away are left in a pile
2 on the scrap heap not wanted or considered useful any longer

scrappy /'skræpɪ/ ADJECTIVE [**scrappier, scrappiest**] performed or organized badly □ *a scrappy game*

scratch /skrætʃ/ ▶ VERB [**scratches, scratching, scratched**]
1 to make a mark on a surface with something sharp or pointed □ *The car was quite badly scratched.*

□ *Students had scratched their names on the desks.*
2 to rub your nails on your skin, usually because it feels uncomfortable □ *She scratched her nose.* □ *Try not to scratch the spots.*

♦ IDIOMS **scratch your head** to not be able to understand or think of something **scratch the surface (of something) 1** to only understand or deal with a small part of something much larger □ *These changes barely scratch the surface of the problem.*
2 to start looking at something more carefully □ *But scratch the surface and you find the situation is more complicated.*

▶ NOUN [*plural* **scratches**]
1 a mark left on a surface or your skin by something sharp □ *He looked for scratches on the car.* □ *They escaped with minor scratches.*
2 when you rub your nails on your skin
3 from scratch from the beginning □ *They learn to cook simple, healthy meals from scratch.*
4 up to scratch good enough □ *The work wasn't up to scratch.*

scrawl /skrɔːl/ ▶ VERB [**scrawls, scrawling, scrawled**] to write in a very untidy way □ *People had scrawled messages on the wall.*

▶ NOUN, NO PLURAL very untidy writing

scrawny /'skrɔːnɪ/ ADJECTIVE [**scrawnier, scrawniest**] very thin, in an unhealthy way □ *a few scrawny chickens*

scream /skriːm/ ▶ VERB [**screams, screaming, screamed**]
1 to make a high, loud sound because you are frightened, excited or in pain □ **+ out** *The woman screamed out and the man ran off.* □ **+ in** *The children screamed in terror.* □ **+ with** *He was screaming with pain.* ☖ *She screamed at the top of her voice.*
2 to shout words in a high voice because you are frightened, angry or in pain □ **+ at** *Fans screamed abuse at the referee.* □ *'Run!' he screamed.* ☖ *They heard someone screaming for help.*

▶ NOUN [*plural* **screams**] a loud, high noise or shout □ **+ of** *a scream of agony* □ *She let out a high-pitched scream.*

♦ IDIOM **be a scream** to be very funny. An informal phrase.

scree /skriː/ NOUN, NO PLURAL small pieces of broken rock, for example on the side of a mountain. A geography word.

screech /skriːtʃ/ ▶ NOUN [*plural* **screeches**] a sudden, unpleasant, high sound □ *the screech of an owl* □ *There was a screech of tyres as the car sped away.*

▶ VERB [**screeches, screeching, screeched**] to make a screech ☖ *The car screeched to a halt* (=stopped while making a loud, high sound).

screen /skriːn/ ▶ NOUN [*plural* **screens**]
1 the part of a computer, television or cinema that you watch images on ☖ *a computer screen* □ *a 17-inch screen* ☖ *Fans watched on giant TV screens.*

2 no plural cinema films in general □ *the screen adaptation of the novel* ☖ *She made her big screen* (=cinema and not television) *début last year.*
3 a piece of wood, cloth, metal, etc. that divides one area from another or prevents something from being seen □ *We were separated by a glass screen.*

▶ VERB [**screens, screening, screened**]
1 to test a lot of people for a particular illness □ *All the workers here are screened for the virus.*
2 to check someone to make sure they are suitable for something □ *They screen applicants for any criminal convictions.* □ *All passengers are screened for weapons.*
3 to show a television programme or film □ *They are screening the whole series for the third time.*
4 to hide something □ *This part of the garden is screened by a high fence.*

screen dump /'skriːn dʌmp/ NOUN [*plural* **screen dumps**] an image of what you can see on a computer screen at a particular time. A computing word.

screenplay /'skriːnpleɪ/ NOUN [*plural* **screenplays**] the written text for a film, including the actors' words and directions

screen saver /'skriːn ˌseɪvə(r)/ NOUN [*plural* **screen savers**] a picture that appears on a computer screen when the computer has not been used for some time. A computing word.

screw /skruː/ ▶ NOUN [*plural* **screws**] a small, pointed, metal object used to fix things together by turning it around into a hole

▶ VERB [**screws, screwing, screwed**]
1 to fix a screw into something □ *Screw the bits of wood together.*
2 to attach or to fasten something with a turning movement □ *Screw the lid on tightly.*

♦ PHRASAL VERBS **screw (something) up** an informal word meaning to make a mistake or to do something badly **screw something up 1** to crush something especially paper □ *He screwed up her letter and dropped it in the bin.* **2 screw up your eyes/face** to twist your face because you are in pain, concentrating, etc.

screwdriver /'skruːˌdraɪvə(r)/ NOUN [*plural* **screwdrivers**] a tool with a long, thin metal part used for turning screws

scribble /'skrɪbəl/ ▶ VERB [**scribbles, scribbling, scribbled**]
1 to write very quickly and in an untidy way □ *I scribbled his name down before I forgot it.*
2 to draw untidy lines and shapes □ *The baby had pen and was scribbling on the wall.*

▶ NOUN [*plural* **scribbles**]
1 writing that is very untidy
2 untidy lines and shapes that someone has drawn

scrimp /skrɪmp/ VERB [**scrimps, scrimping, scrimped**] to spend as little money as possible by living cheaply ☖ *After scrimping and saving for a year, we had enough money for a short holiday.*

script /skrɪpt/ ▶ NOUN [plural **scripts**]
1 the words of a film, play, speech, etc. ▣ *a film script* □ *She writes scripts for TV series.*
2 the type of letters used to write a language □ *Cyrillic script*
▶ VERB [**scripts, scripting, scripted**] to write a script for a performance or speech □ *The film version was scripted by Bob Goldberg.*

scripture /'skrɪptʃə(r)/ NOUN [plural **scriptures**] the holy writings of a religion, for example the Bible

scriptwriter /'skrɪptˌraɪtə(r)/ NOUN [plural **scriptwriters**] a person who writes scripts for films

scroll /skrəʊl/ ▶ NOUN [plural **scrolls**] a long roll of paper with writing on it
▶ VERB [**scrolls, scrolling, scrolled**] to move text up or down on a computer screen so that you can see different parts of it. A computing word □ *Scroll down to the bottom of the page.*

scroll bar /'skrəʊl ˌbɑː(r)/ NOUN [plural **scroll bars**] a long, thin area on the side or bottom of a computer screen that allows you to move text so that you can see different parts of it. A computing word.

scrounge /skraʊndʒ/ VERB [**scrounges, scrounging, scrounged**] an informal word meaning to get something from someone else and not buy it yourself □ *He was trying to scrounge a drink off me.*

scrounger /'skraʊndʒə(r)/ NOUN [plural **scroungers**] an informal word for someone who scrounges things

scrub /skrʌb/ ▶ VERB [**scrubs, scrubbing, scrubbed**] to rub something hard to get it clean □ *We'll need to scrub these stains off the floor.*
▶ NOUN, NO PLURAL
1 a dry area of land with small trees and bushes
2 when you scrub something

scruff /skrʌf/ NOUN [plural **scruffs**]
1 someone who looks very untidy
2 by the scruff of the neck by holding the collar or the back of a person's or an animal's neck □ *The mother cat lifts her kittens in her mouth by the scruff of the neck.*

scruffy /'skrʌfɪ/ ADJECTIVE [**scruffier, scruffiest**] untidy and dirty □ *scruffy clothes* □ *She was looking scruffy.*

scrum /skrʌm/ NOUN [plural **scrums**] a time in the game of rugby when players from both teams form a circle by joining arms with their heads down and try to win the ball

scrumptious /'skrʌmpʃəs/ ADJECTIVE tasting very good □ *a scrumptious dessert*

scrunch /skrʌntʃ/ ▶ VERB [**scrunches, scrunching, scrunched**]
1 to crush or press something □ *She scrunched up the empty packet in her hand.*
2 to make the noise of something hard being crushed □ *The gravel scrunched under our feet.*
▶ NOUN, NO PLURAL the noise of something hard being crushed

scrunchie /'skrʌntʃɪ/ NOUN [plural **scrunchies**] a circular piece of cloth with rubber inside which girls and women use to hold their hair together at the back of their head

scruples /'skruːpəlz/ PLURAL NOUN moral beliefs which make you unwilling to do something that you believe is wrong □ *He had no scruples about taking money from his elderly mother.*

scrupulous /'skruːpjʊləs/ ADJECTIVE
1 careful not to do anything that is unfair, dishonest or morally wrong □ *A less scrupulous individual would have kept the money.*
2 paying careful attention to even the smallest details □ *He's scrupulous about keeping accurate accounts.*
● **scrupulously** /'skruːpjʊləslɪ/ ADVERB in a scrupulous way □ *scrupulously honest* □ *The room was scrupulously clean.*

scrutinize or **scrutinise** /'skruːtɪnaɪz/ VERB [**scrutinizes, scrutinizing, scrutinized**] to examine or look at something carefully □ *She scrutinized his face for any sign of emotion.*
● **scrutiny** /'skruːtɪnɪ/ NOUN, NO PLURAL close and careful examination □ *The president's personal life came under close public scrutiny.*

scuba diving /'skuːbə ˌdaɪvɪŋ/ NOUN, NO PLURAL the sport of swimming under the surface of water using special equipment to help you breathe

scuff /skʌf/ VERB [**scuffs, scuffing, scuffed**] to make marks on something by rubbing it against something rough □ *I've scuffed my new boots already.*

scuffle /'skʌfəl/ NOUN [plural **scuffles**] a short fight involving a small number of people □ *There was a scuffle outside the club.*

sculpt /skʌlpt/ VERB [**sculpts, sculpting, sculpted**] to make an object using a material such as clay, stone or wood
● **sculptor** /'skʌlptə(r)/ NOUN [plural **sculptors**] an artist who makes sculptures
● **sculpture** /'skʌlptʃə(r)/ NOUN [plural **sculptures**]
1 an object that an artist makes using a material like clay, stone or wood □ *'The Kiss' is a famous sculpture by Rodin.*
2 no plural the art of making objects using materials like clay, stone or wood

scum /skʌm/ NOUN, NO PLURAL a layer of dirt or an unpleasant substance on the surface of a liquid

scurry /'skʌrɪ/ VERB [**scurries, scurrying, scurried**] to move quickly □ *The mouse scurried back into its hole.*

scuttle /'skʌtəl/ VERB [**scuttles, scuttling, scuttled**] to move quickly with short, fast steps

scuzzy /'skʌzɪ/ ADJECTIVE [**scuzzier, scuzziest**] dirty and unpleasant. An informal word.

scythe /saɪð/ NOUN [plural **scythes**] a tool with a long curved blade that is used for cutting long grass or crops

sea /siː/ NOUN [plural **seas**]
1 no plural the salt water that covers most of the Earth's surface □ *They live by the sea.* □ *I love swimming in the sea.* □ *Australia is completely surrounded by sea.*
2 a large area of salt water □ *the Dead Sea*

seabed /'si:bed/ NOUN, NO PLURAL the ground under the sea

seabird /'si:b3:d/ NOUN [plural **seabirds**] any bird that lives on or near the sea and finds its food in it

seafood /'si:fu:d/ NOUN, NO PLURAL fish and sea animals that you can eat, especially animals in shells

seafront /'si:frʌnt/ NOUN, NO PLURAL the area of a town next to the sea □ *We walked down by the seafront.*

seagull /'si:gʌl/ NOUN [plural **seagulls**] a large bird that lives near the sea and has grey and white feathers

seahorse /'si:hɔ:s/ NOUN [plural **seahorses**] a type of small fish that swims vertically and has a head and neck that look like a horse's

seal /si:l/ ▶ NOUN [plural **seals**]
1 a large animal with shiny fur that spends its time both in the sea and on land
2 a piece of plastic or paper, etc. around part of a container that you must break in order to open the container
3 something that keeps something firmly closed so that air or water cannot get in or out □ *The washing machine needs a new seal.*
4 an official mark printed on or pressed into a document to show that it is legal □ *the presidential seal*
▶ VERB [**seals, sealing, sealed**]
1 to stick the top part of an envelope down so that it is closed
2 to close a container or an area by covering it completely with something so that air or liquid cannot get into it or get out of it
◆ PHRASAL VERB **seal off something** to prevent people from entering or leaving a place □ *After the bomb scare, police sealed off the city centre.*

sea level /'si: 'levəl/ NOUN, NO PLURAL the average level of the sea's surface, used as the point from which the height of land is measured □ *The summit is 4000 feet above sea level.*

sea lion /'si: 'laɪən/ NOUN [plural **sea lions**] a type of large seal (=animal with shiny fur that lives in the sea and on land)

seam /si:m/ NOUN [plural **seams**]
1 a line of sewing that joins two pieces of cloth □ *The seam has split.*
2 a layer of coal in the ground

seaman /'si:mən/ NOUN [plural **seamen**] a sailor

seaplane /'si:pleɪn/ NOUN [plural **seaplanes**] a type of aircraft that is designed to take off from and land on water

sear /sɪə(r)/ VERB [**sears, searing, seared**] to burn the surface of something

search /s3:tʃ/ ▶ VERB [**searches, searching, searched**]
1 to look carefully for something or someone □ **+ for** *I'm still searching for my keys.* □ **+ through** *Firefighters searched through the wreckage for survivors.*
2 if police search someone or something, they examine them in order to find something such as drugs or weapons □ *Both men were arrested and searched.* □ *Police searched his flat.*
3 to look for information on the Internet. A computing word □ *Have you tried searching the Net?*
▶ NOUN [plural **searches**]
1 an attempt to find someone or something 🖻 *The police made a thorough search for the missing child.* □ **+ for** *We will stop at nothing in our search for her.*
2 **in search of** in order to find □ *They went off in search of somewhere to eat.*
3 an attempt to achieve something □ *the search for happiness*
4 an attempt to find information on the Internet. A computing word 🖻 *Have you done a search on his name?*

● **searchable** /'s3:tʃəbəl/ ADJECTIVE searchable computer files are organized in a way that allows you to look for particular information, words, etc. A computing word.

search engine /'s3:tʃ 'endʒɪn/ NOUN [plural **search engines**] a computer program that helps you to search for something on the Internet. A computing word.

searching /'s3:tʃɪŋ/ ADJECTIVE showing that you want to find out the truth □ *a searching question*

searchlight /'s3:tʃlaɪt/ NOUN [plural **searchlights**] a strong light that can be turned in different direction

search party /'s3:tʃ 'pɑ:tɪ/ NOUN [plural **search parties**] a group of people who make an organized search for someone who is missing

search warrant /'s3:tʃ 'wɒrənt/ NOUN [plural **search warrants**] an official document giving the police permission to search a building

seashell /'si:ʃel/ NOUN [plural **seashells**] an empty shell that a sea creature used to live in

seashore /'si:ʃɔ:(r)/ NOUN, NO PLURAL the area of land next to the sea

seasick /'si:sɪk/ ADJECTIVE feeling like you will vomit when you are on a boat, because of its movement

● **seasickness** /'si:sɪknɪs/ NOUN, NO PLURAL the feeling of being seasick

seaside /'si:saɪd/ NOUN, NO PLURAL a place near the sea where people go on holiday □ *Let's have a day at the seaside.* 🖻 *a seaside resort*

season /'si:zən/ ▶ NOUN [plural **seasons**]
1 one of the four main periods that the year is divided into, each having different weather □ *Spring is my favourite season.*
2 a period of the year when a particular thing happens □ *the football season* □ *This hotel will be packed in the holiday season.*
3 **in season** growing now and available in large quantities □ *Strawberries are in season for most of the summer.*
4 **out of season** (a) not growing now so not available in large quantities □ *I try not to buy vegetables that are out of season.* (b) at the time of year when most people do not visit a place □ *Holidays are much cheaper out of season.*

▶ VERB [**seasons, seasoning, seasoned**] to add flavour to food by putting salt, herbs or spices into it
● **seasonal** /'si:zənəl/ ADJECTIVE
1 happening only at particular times of the year □ *The farm offers seasonal employment to fruit-pickers.*
2 growing now so fresh and full of flavour □ *Our main courses are served with a selection of seasonal vegetables.*
● **seasoning** /'si:zənɪŋ/ NOUN [*plural* **seasonings**] salt, herbs and spices that you use to add flavour to food

season ticket /'si:zən 'tɪkɪt/ NOUN [*plural* **season tickets**] a ticket that you can use as often as you like for a particular period of time

seat /si:t/ ▶ NOUN [*plural* **seats**]
1 a piece of furniture for sitting on □ *a garden seat* □ *He was in the passenger seat of the car.*
2 a chair that you pay to sit on in a vehicle or in a theatre □ *I've booked three seats for the theatre.* □ *I prefer window seats in aeroplanes.*
3 the part of a chair that you sit on
4 a position in a parliament or committee (=group of people chosen to make decisions about something) ⚑ *The party lost three seats in the election.*
▶ VERB [**seats, seating, seated**]
1 to have enough room for a particular number of people to sit down □ *The new theatre seats 600 people.*
2 to give someone a place to sit. A formal word.
3 **be seated** to be sitting down

seat belt /'si:t 'belt/ NOUN [*plural* **seat belts**] a strong belt in a car or plane that goes across your body □ *Please fasten your seat belts now.*

seating /'si:tɪŋ/ NOUN, NO PLURAL the type or number of seats available in a place, or the way that they are arranged □ *The hotel dining room has seating for 70 guests.*

seaweed /'si:wi:d/ NOUN, NO PLURAL a type of plant that grows in the sea

seaworthy /'si:,wɜ:ðɪ/ ADJECTIVE a boat that is seaworthy is in good enough condition to be sailed on the sea

sec /sek/ NOUN [*plural* **secs**] an informal word meaning a very short time □ *I'll be back in a sec.*

secateurs /,sekə'tɜ:z/ PLURAL NOUN a tool used for cutting plants

secluded /sɪ'klu:dɪd/ ADJECTIVE a secluded place is quiet and private □ *a secluded beach*

seclusion /sɪ'klu:ʒən/ NOUN, NO PLURAL when you are alone, away from other people □ *He has spent much of the last two years in seclusion.*

second¹ /'sekənd/ ▶ NUMBER 2nd written as a word □ *Julia is their second daughter.* □ *Marta came second in the race.* □ *This programme is the second in a series of three.*
▶ VERB [**seconds, seconding, seconded**] to second an idea or plan is to support it when someone suggests it

second² /'sekənd/ NOUN [*plural* **seconds**]
1 one of 60 parts that a minute is divided into □ *He ran the race in 57 seconds.*
2 a very short time □ *Just wait a second.*

secondary /'sekəndərɪ/ ADJECTIVE
1 secondary education is for students between the age of 11 and 18
2 less important than something else □ *Your health comes first. Money is secondary.*
3 being something that develops from something else □ *a secondary infection*

secondary school /'sekəndərɪ 'sku:l/ NOUN [*plural* **secondary schools**] a school for students between the ages of 11 and 18

second best /'sekənd 'best/ ▶ NOUN, NO PLURAL
1 the person or thing that is next after the best □ *He was the second best in his class at maths*
2 something that is not as good as you would like it to be □ *I'm not going to settle for second best.*
▶ ADJECTIVE not best but next best □ *She's the team's second best scorer.*

second-class /'sekənd'klɑːs/ ▶ ADJECTIVE
1 describes the less expensive way of travelling that most people choose and the less expensive way of sending post that is slower □ *a second-class compartment* □ *a second-class stamp*
2 not as good or not as important as other people or things ⚑ *Some of the immigrants were treated like second-class citizens.*
▶ ADVERB using the cheapest type □ *I sent the letter second-class.*

second cousin /'sekənd 'kʌzən/ NOUN [*plural* **second cousins**] the son or daughter of one of your parent's cousins

second-hand /'sekənd'hænd/ ADJECTIVE, ADVERB
1 used for describing things which someone else has owned before you □ *a second-hand car* □ *Kathryn buys all her clothes second-hand.*
2 told to you by someone who got the information from another person □ *I only heard the news second-hand.*

secondly /'sekəndlɪ/ ADVERB used for introducing the second thing you want to mention □ *And secondly, I'd like to thank Mrs Ambrose for all her help.*

second nature /'sekənd 'neɪtʃə(r)/ NOUN, NO PLURAL something that you do without thinking because it seems so normal or natural □ *Texting is second nature to young people now.*

second person /'sekənd 'pɜːsən/ NOUN, NO PLURAL in grammar, the form of a word that is used for the person you are talking or writing to □ *'You' is a second person pronoun.*

second-rate /'sekənd'reɪt/ ADJECTIVE not of good quality □ *a second-rate hotel*

second thoughts /'sekənd 'θɔːts/ PLURAL NOUN
1 **have second thoughts** to start to have doubts about a decision you have made □ *She seems to be having second thoughts about getting married.*
2 **on second thoughts** used for saying that you have

changed your mind about something □ *You can come with me. On second thoughts, it might be best if you wait here.*

secrecy /'si:krəsɪ/ NOUN, NO PLURAL the quality of being secret

secret /'si:krɪt/ ► NOUN [*plural* **secrets**]

1 a piece of information that must not be told to other people 🔁 *I'll tell you a little secret.* 🔁 *She can't keep a secret* (=not tell someone a secret). 🔁 *The birthday party was a well-kept secret.*

2 *no plural* a way of achieving something □ *Her hair always looks so good. I wish I knew her secret.* □ *+ of The secret of success is hard work.*

3 **in secret** without other people knowing □ *They began to meet in secret.*

4 **make no secret of something** to make your feelings clear to other people □ *She made no secret of her desire to have a child.*

5 **the secrets of something** the things that people do not yet understand or know about □ *These images could help reveal the secrets of the universe.*

► ADJECTIVE not told or shown to other people □ *secret information* 🔁 *The facts of the case were kept secret.* □ *The talks were held at a secret location.*

secretarial /ˌsekrə'teərɪəl/ ADJECTIVE to do with the job of a secretary □ *secretarial skills*

secretary /'sekrətərɪ/ NOUN [*plural* **secretaries**]

1 someone whose job is to type letters, arrange meetings and take notes at business meetings, etc. □ *Please leave a message with my secretary if I'm out.*

2 someone who is in charge of a government department □ *the education secretary* □ *He's the former British foreign secretary.*

Secretary of State /'sekrətərɪ əv 'steɪt/ NOUN [*plural* **Secretaries of State**]

1 in the UK, someone who is in charge of one of the main government departments such as education, health or defence

2 in the US, the person who is in charge of the government department which deals with matters that involve other countries

secrete /sɪ'kri:t/ VERB [**secretes, secreting, secreted**] if a plant or animal secretes a substance, it produces it. A biology word. □ *The plant secretes a sticky liquid that attracts flies.*

• **secretion** /sɪ'kri:ʃən/ NOUN [*plural* **secretions**] a substance that a plant or animal produces. A biology word.

secretive /'si:krətɪv/ ADJECTIVE not wanting to tell people about something □ *Logan was very secretive about his past.*

secretly /'si:krɪtlɪ/ ADVERB in a secret way □ *They met secretly.*

secret service /'si:krɪt 'sɜ:vɪs/ NOUN [*plural* **secret services**]

1 a government department that tries to discover information about other countries □ *a secret service agent*

2 in the US, the government department that protects the President

sect /sekt/ NOUN [*plural* **sects**] a group of people who have different beliefs from a larger group, especially in a religion

• **sectarian** /sek'teərɪən/ ADJECTIVE to do with religious differences between groups □ *sectarian violence*

section /'sekʃən/ NOUN [*plural* **sections**] one of the parts that together make up something □ *The table has three sections that fit together.* □ *the fiction section of the library* □ *the arts section of the newspaper*

sector /'sektə(r)/ NOUN [*plural* **sectors**]

1 one of the parts that an area is divided into □ *the American sector of the city*

2 one of the parts that a country's economy is divided into □ *the retail sector*

secular /'sekjʊlə(r)/ ADJECTIVE not religious or not to do with religion 🔁 *a secular state* □ *secular music*

secure /sɪ'kjʊə(r)/ ► ADJECTIVE

1 not likely to fail or change □ *a secure job* □ *They are financially secure.*

2 safe, confident and not worried □ *Children need to feel secure.*

3 safe against attack or harm □ *You can make your home more secure by installing a burglar alarm.*

4 a secure place is guarded so that only particular people can go into it or leave it □ *Police have taken the family to a secure location.* □ *a secure area of the airport*

5 firmly fixed or fastened □ *Check that the ropes are secure.*

► VERB [**secures, securing, secured**]

1 to get something important □ *She has secured a place at the best college in the country.*

2 to fix or fasten something firmly □ *The tent was secured with ropes and pegs.*

3 to make something safe from being attacked or harmed □ *Soldiers were brought in to secure the border.*

• **security** /sɪ'kjʊərətɪ/ ► NOUN, NO PLURAL

1 safety from danger or crime and the things that are done to achieve this 🔁 *We need to tighten airport security.* 🔁 *The policy was a threat to national security.*

2 the people in an organization whose job is to protect the buildings and workers □ *Call security if you see anything suspicious.*

3 a feeling of safety and confidence or a situation that provides this 🔁 *A stable family background can give children a sense of security.*

4 the situation when something is not likely to fail or change 🔁 *Job security is very important for most people.* 🔁 *A lot of people are worried about financial security.*

5 property or goods that you legally promise to give someone if you cannot pay back the money you have

borrowed from them □ *He used his house as security on the loan.*

▶ ADJECTIVE to do with the safety of someone or something ⊞ *a security guard* ⊞ *The airport needs to improve security measures.* □ *a security risk*

sedate /sɪ'deɪt/ ▶ VERB [**sedates, sedating, sedated**] to give someone a drug to make them feel calmer
▶ ADJECTIVE calm and slow □ *Pedro walked at a more sedate pace.*

• **sedation** /sɪ'deɪʃən/ NOUN, NO PLURAL when someone is sedated

• **sedative** /'sedətɪv/ NOUN [*plural* **sedatives**] a drug that someone is given to sedate them

sedentary /'sedəntəri/ ADJECTIVE a sedentary job or way of life is one in which you sit down most of the time and do very little exercise

sediment /'sedɪmənt/ NOUN, NO PLURAL a solid substance that forms at the bottom of a liquid

• **sedimentary** /,sedɪ'mentəri/ ADJECTIVE sedimentary rock is formed from the sand and stones at the bottom of rivers or the sea. A geography word.

seduce /sɪ'dju:s/ VERB [**seduces, seducing, seduced**] to cause someone to do something that they would not usually do □ *The prospect of making a quick profit seduced him into buying the shares.*

• **seductive** /sɪ'dʌktɪv/ ADJECTIVE attractive and making you want to do something □ *a seductive idea*

see /si:/ VERB [**sees, seeing, saw, seen**]
1 to look at someone or something and notice them □ *The dog goes mad whenever he sees a cat.* □ *I saw you coming.* □ *Can you see where the switch is?*
2 to meet someone or spend time with them □ *Have you seen Peter much lately?* □ *I'm seeing Billie at the weekend.*
3 to watch a film, television programme, etc. □ *Did you see 'Pride and Prejudice'?*
4 to understand something ⊞ *Now I see what you mean.* ⊞ *I don't see why I should tidy up your mess.* ⊞ *'He couldn't come because he didn't have a ticket.' 'Oh, I see.'*
5 to find out something by waiting for something to happen □ *I'll see what she says.* □ *Let's see how today's lesson goes.* □ *See if you can arrange a taxi.*
6 to find out information about something □ *Can you see what time the bank opens?* □ *As we have seen, Cromwell was hated by the Irish.*
7 to imagine something or to believe that something will happen □ *I can't see him as a father.* □ *I can't see the building being ready by June.*
8 if you see someone somewhere, you go there with them □ *I'll see you to the door.*
9 if you see that something happens, you make sure that it happens □ **+ that** *I'll see that he's back before eight.*
10 if a place or a period of time sees something, that is where or when it happens □ *The town saw mass unemployment in the eighties.*
11 I'll see/We'll see used to say that you will consider agreeing to what someone has asked, but will

not decide immediately □ *'Can I have a new bike for my birthday?' 'We'll see.'*
12 let me see used when you are trying to remember something □ *It must have been - let me see - at least fifteen years ago.*
13 See you. an informal way of saying goodbye
14 you see used when you are explaining something □ *We didn't have a car then, you see.*
➡ go to not see eye to eye

◆ PHRASAL VERBS see about something to deal with something or to organize something □ *We need to see about the lighting.* see something in someone/ something to believe that someone or something has particular, usually good, qualities □ *She's always hanging round with Rob - I don't know what she sees in him.* see someone off to go with someone to say goodbye to them see someone/something off to defeat or get rid of someone or something that is threatening you □ *He saw off over twenty other artists to win the prize.* see someone out to go to the door with someone who is leaving see out something to finish spending a period of time in a particular place or doing a particular thing □ *He saw out the decade in London.* see through someone/something to understand that someone or something is trying to trick you □ *I knew they only wanted my money - I could see through their flattery.* see something through to finish doing something, even if it is difficult □ *We're determined to see this job through.* see to something to deal with something □ *Don't worry about the travel arrangements - I'll see to all that.*

seed /si:d/ NOUN [*plural* **seeds**]
1 a thing that a plant produces and that new plants grow from ⊞ *Sow the seeds about two inches deep in the soil.* □ *sunflower seeds*
2 the seeds of something something that makes a new situation start to develop

• **seedless** /'si:dlɪs/ ADJECTIVE seedless fruit has no seeds in it □ *seedless grapes*

• **seedling** /'si:dlɪŋ/ NOUN [*plural* **seedlings**] a very young plant

seeing /'si:ɪŋ/ CONJUNCTION seeing as/that used for saying a reason □ *We thought we'd visit you, seeing as we were in the area.*

seek /si:k/ VERB [**seeks, seeking, sought**]
1 a formal word meaning to try to find or achieve something □ *They were seeking a long-term solution.*
2 a formal word meaning to ask for something □ *You should seek the advice of a doctor.*

> ► Note that **seek**, meaning 'to try to find' is only
> used in formal English. The usual phrase for this
> meaning is **look for**:
> ✓ *I'm looking for a good hairdresser.*
> ✗ *I'm seeking a good hairdresser.*

seem /si:m/ VERB [**seems, seeming, seemed**] to appear to be something □ *He seemed very pleased to see you.* ⊞ *She seemed like a very nice young woman.*

🔁 *It seems likely that he will be in hospital for several weeks.* ☐ *It seems strange we haven't heard from him.* ☐ **+ to do something** *Nothing seems to worry him.*

• **seemingly** /ˈsiːmɪŋlɪ/ ADVERB used for saying what seems true although it is probably not true ☐ *The queue to get in was seemingly endless.*

seen /siːn/ PAST PARTICIPLE OF see

seep /siːp/ VERB [**seeps, seeping, seeped**] to flow through something in small amounts ☐ *Blood was seeping through his shirt.*

seesaw /ˈsiːsɔː/ NOUN [*plural* **seesaws**] a long board that two children sit on, one at each end, and when one child moves high into the air, the other child moves down towards the ground

seethe /siːð/ VERB [**seethes, seething, seethed**] to be extremely angry, often without shouting or showing your anger

see-through /ˈsiːθruː/ ADJECTIVE made of plastic or cloth that you can see through ☐ *a see-through dress*

segment /ˈsegmənt/ NOUN [*plural* **segments**] one of several parts of something ☐ *Divide the orange into segments.* ☐ *The policy will affect many segments of society.*

segregate /ˈsegrɪgeɪt/ VERB [**segregates, segregating, segregated**] to separate different groups of people ☐ *Police segregated the fans from rival football teams.*

• **segregation** /ˌsegrɪˈgeɪʃən/ NOUN, NO PLURAL the act of separating groups of people

seismic /ˈsaɪzmɪk/ ADJECTIVE to do with earthquakes (=sudden movements of the Earth's surface). A geography word.

• **seismograph** /ˈsaɪzməgrɑːf/ NOUN [*plural* **seismographs**] a piece of equipment for measuring earthquakes (=sudden movements of the Earth's surface). A geography word.

seize /siːz/ VERB [**seizes, seizing, seized**]
1 to take something into your hand quickly and firmly ☐ *Joel seized my hand and shook it.*
2 to use an opportunity enthusiastically and effectively 🔁 *He seized the opportunity to join the team.* ☐ *She seized her chance to escape.*
3 to take control of a place, especially using force 🔁 *Rebels seized control of the city.*
4 if the police or government officers seize something, they take it away from someone ☐ *Police raided his home and seized several computers.*

♦ PHRASAL VERBS **seize on something** to use something quickly and enthusiastically in order to get an advantage for yourself ☐ *He seized on the figures as evidence that the government is failing.* **seize up** to stop moving or working correctly ☐ *My back seized up and I couldn't move.* ☐ *The car's engine seized up.*

• **seizure** /ˈsiːʒə(r)/ NOUN [*plural* **seizures**]
1 when police or government officers take something away from someone ☐ *the seizure of illegal weapons*
2 a sudden attack of an illness, which makes your brain not work correctly for a short time ☐ *A few hours after birth, he suffered a seizure.*

3 the act of taking control of a place, especially using force ☐ *the seizure of power*

seldom /ˈseldəm/ ADVERB not often ☐ *He seldom travelled abroad.* ☐ *A teacher's job is seldom an easy one.*

select /sɪˈlekt/ ▶ VERB [**selects, selecting, selected**] to choose someone or something ☐ *She selected some items and went to pay for them.* ☐ **+ for** *Hawthorne has been selected for the Olympic hockey team.*

▶ ADJECTIVE
1 a select group is a small group of people who have been chosen carefully ☐ *He agreed to speak to a select group of journalists.*
2 of very good quality, or expensive ☐ *select wines*

• **selection** /sɪˈlekʃən/ NOUN [*plural* **selections**]
1 a range of things that you can choose from 🔁 *The shop has a wide selection of boots and shoes.*
2 something that you have chosen ☐ *Bring your selection to the cash desk at the door.*
3 the process of choosing someone or something ☐ *Jury selection for the trial began yesterday.*

• **selective** /sɪˈlektɪv/ ADJECTIVE
1 careful about who or what you choose ☐ *The club i very selective about its members.*
2 involving only the people or things which have bee chosen ☐ *The marketing campaign is aimed at a selective group of donors.*

self /self/ NOUN [*plural* **selves**] your character 🔁 *He was worried about revealing his true self to her.*

self- /self/ PREFIX self- is added to the beginning of words to mean 'relating to or done by yourself or b itself' ☐ *self-control* ☐ *self-imposed* ☐ *self-raising flour*

self-appointed /ˌselfəˈpɔɪntɪd/ ADJECTIVE giving yourself a responsibility or job without getting othe people's agreement ☐ *self-appointed community leaders*

self-assurance /ˌselfəˈʃʊərəns/ NOUN, NO PLURAL t quality of being confident about your own abilities

• **self-assured** /ˌselfəˈʃʊərd/ ADJECTIVE confident about your own abilities

self-catering /ˌselfˈkeɪtərɪŋ/ ADJECTIVE cooking yc own meals on a holiday, or allowing someone to d this ☐ *a self-catering holiday/apartment*

self-centred /ˌselfˈsentə(r)d/ ADJECTIVE thinking o about yourself and not about other people

self-confessed /ˌselfkənˈfest/ ADJECTIVE admittin that you have a bad habit or that you are a particu type of bad person ☐ *a self-confessed chocolate addict* ☐ *a self-confessed thief*

self-confidence /ˌselfˈkɒnfɪdəns/ NOUN, NO PLU being sure of yourself and your own abilities

• **self-confident** /ˌselfˈkɒnfɪdənt/ ADJECTIVE sure yourself and your own abilities

self-conscious /ˌselfˈkɒnʃəs/ ADJECTIVE nervous because you think other people are looking at you criticizing you □ *She felt very self-conscious dancing in public.*

self-contained /ˈselfkənˈteɪnd/ ADJECTIVE
1 a self-contained flat has its own kitchen and bathroom
2 not needing help from other people □ *She's very self-contained.*

self-control /ˈselfkənˈtrəʊl/ NOUN, NO PLURAL your ability to control your behaviour when you are angry, excited, etc. □ *I lost my self-control, and hit him.*

self-defence /ˈselfdɪˈfens/ NOUN, NO PLURAL the process of trying to defend yourself when someone is attacking you □ *classes in self-defence* □ *He said he fired the gun in self-defence.*

self-defense /ˈselfdɪˈfens/ NOUN, NO PLURAL the US spelling of self-defence

self-destructive /ˈselfdɪˈstrʌktɪv/ ADJECTIVE often doing things that harm you

self-discipline /ˈselfˈdɪsɪplɪn/ NOUN, NO PLURAL the ability to keep making yourself do difficult or hard things in order to achieve something □ *She lacks self-discipline.*

● **self-disciplined** /ˈselfˈdɪsɪplɪnd/ ADJECTIVE having self-discipline

self-drive /ˈselfˈdraɪv/ ADJECTIVE a self-drive holiday is one in which you drive to the place you are going

self-employed /ˈselfɪmˈplɔɪd/ ADJECTIVE having your own business instead of being employed by someone else □ *a self-employed painter and decorator*

self-employment /ˈselfɪmˈplɔɪmənt/ NOUN, NO PLURAL the situation when you have your own business and are not employed by someone else

self-esteem /ˈselfɪˈstiːm/ NOUN, NO PLURAL the belief that you are a nice and successful person ⊞ *She's always had low self-esteem.*

self-evident /ˈselfˈevɪdənt/ ADJECTIVE obvious □ *It is self-evident that the world's resources cannot cope with an increasing population.*

self-explanatory /ˈselfɪkˈsplænətrɪ/ ADJECTIVE easy to understand, and needing no more explanation □ *The title is self-explanatory.*

self-help /ˈselfˈhelp/ NOUN, NO PLURAL ways of dealing with your own problems instead of depending on other people □ *a self-help manual*

self-importance /ˈselfɪmˈpɔːtəns/ NOUN, NO PLURAL behaviour that shows that you think you are more important than other people

self-important /ˈselfɪmˈpɔːtənt/ ADJECTIVE behaving as if you are more important than other people

self-imposed /ˈselfɪmˈpəʊzd/ ADJECTIVE a self-imposed rule, punishment, etc. is one you have chosen yourself □ *The school has a self-imposed deadline of August 24 for completion of the project.*

self-indulgent /ˈselfɪnˈdʌldʒənt/ ADJECTIVE doing too many things for your own pleasure or interest

self-inflicted /ˈselfɪnˈflɪktɪd/ ADJECTIVE caused by yourself □ *self-inflicted wounds*

self-interest /ˈselfˈɪntrəst/ NOUN, NO PLURAL interest only in what will help you □ *He acted purely out of self-interest.*

● **self-interested** /ˈselfˈɪntrestɪd/ ADJECTIVE interested only in what will help you

selfish /ˈselfɪʃ/ ADJECTIVE thinking only about yourself and not about what other people might want or need □ *He's a very selfish person.* □ *I decided to stay for purely selfish reasons.*

● **selfishly** /ˈselfɪʃlɪ/ ADVERB in a selfish way □ *He acted very selfishly.*

● **selfishness** /ˈselfɪʃnɪs/ NOUN, NO PLURAL the state of being selfish

selfless /ˈselflɪs/ ADJECTIVE thinking about other people and not about yourself □ *Her selfless acts saved a young man's life.*

self-made /ˈselfˈmeɪd/ ADJECTIVE rich because you have worked hard □ *a self-made woman* □ *a self-made millionaire*

self-pity /ˈselfˈpɪtɪ/ NOUN, NO PLURAL the feeling that your situation is worse than other people's and that you deserve sympathy

self-portrait /ˈselfˈpɔːtreɪt/ NOUN [plural **self-portraits**] a drawing or painting of you that you have done yourself

self-raising flour /ˈselfˈreɪzɪŋ flaʊə(r)/ NOUN, NO PLURAL flour that makes cakes rise when you cook them

self-reliance /ˈselfrɪˈlaɪəns/ NOUN, NO PLURAL the ability to do things by yourself without help

● **self-reliant** /ˈselfrɪˈlaɪənt/ ADJECTIVE able to do things by yourself without help

self-respect /ˈselfrɪˈspekt/ NOUN, NO PLURAL the feeling that you are as good as anyone else and should treat yourself and other people well

● **self-respecting** /ˈselfrɪˈspektɪŋ/ ADJECTIVE feeling self-respect □ *No self-respecting teenager would want their parents to come with them on a night out.*

self-righteous /ˈselfˈraɪtʃəs/ ADJECTIVE believing that you are morally a very good person, in a way that annoys another people

self-sacrifice /ˈselfˈsækrɪfaɪs/ NOUN, NO PLURAL when you choose not to do or have something that you want, in order to help someone else □ *It was an act of courage and self-sacrifice.*

self-satisfied /ˈselfˈsætɪsfaɪd/ ADJECTIVE too pleased with yourself and your achievements □ *a self-satisfied grin*

self-service /ˈselfˈsɜːvɪs/ ADJECTIVE involving customers getting or doing something themselves □ *a self-service restaurant* □ *The airline provides a self-service check-in.*

self-sufficient /ˈselfsəˈfɪʃənt/ ADJECTIVE able to provide everything you need for yourself

sell /sel/ VERB [**sells, selling, sold**]
1 to give someone something in exchange for money □ **+ for** *They sold the house for £450,000.* □ **+ to** *She sold the business to a Chinese company.* □ *He sold me his bike.*

2 to have something available for people to buy □ *The shop sells handmade chocolates.* □ *Do you sell batteries?*
3 if something sells, people buy it □ *Tickets sold quickly for both shows.* ℗ *T-shirts sell well* (=a lot of people buy T-shirts) *at this time of year.* □ *The album sold 350,000 copies in Australia.*
4 sell for/at £300/£60, etc. used for saying what price someone pays for something □ *Apartments in this area sell for around £200,000.*
5 if you sell an idea, you try to make people accept it □ *You'll need to sell the idea to your employer.*
♦ PHRASAL VERBS **sell something off** to sell something quickly for a low price □ *The company has sold off eight of its stores.* **sell out 1** if a shop sells out of something, there is none of it left for people to buy □ *I'm sorry, we've sold out of milk.* **2** if something sells out, there is none left for people to buy □ *When I got there, all the tickets had sold out.* **sell up** to sell your house or business □ *We sold up and moved to France.*

sell-by date /'selbaɪ ˌdeɪt/ NOUN [plural **sell-by dates**] a date on a food package, which shows when shops should stop selling the food ℗ *The sausages were past their sell-by date.*
seller /'selə(r)/ NOUN [plural **sellers**]
1 someone who is selling something □ *ticket sellers*
2 top/big seller a product that a lot of people buy □ *The toy was a top seller last Christmas.*
Sellotape /'seləteɪp/ NOUN, NO PLURAL a long, narrow piece of sticky plastic that you use for sticking paper together. A trademark.
sellout /'selaʊt/ NOUN [plural **sellouts**] an event for which all the tickets have been sold □ *The concert was a sellout.*
semblance /'sembləns/ NOUN, NO PLURAL **a/some semblance of something** when something seems to have a particular quality □ *He tried to bring some semblance of order to the proceedings.*
semen /'siːmən/ NOUN, NO PLURAL the liquid produced by the male sex organs. A biology word.
semester /sɪ'mestə(r)/ NOUN [plural **semesters**] the US word for **term** (=period that a school or college year is divided into)
semi /'semi/ NOUN [plural **semis**] a house that is joined to another house on one side
semi- /'semi/ PREFIX semi- is added to the beginning of words to mean 'half' or 'partly' □ *semicircle* □ *semi-precious*
semicircle /'semiˌsɜːkəl/ NOUN [plural **semicircles**] half a circle
semicolon /ˌsemɪ'kəʊlən/ NOUN [plural **semicolons**] a punctuation mark (;) used to separate different parts of a sentence or list
semiconductor /ˌsemɪkən'dʌktə(r)/ NOUN [plural **semiconductors**] a substance that allows some electricity to go through it. A physics word.
semi-detached /ˌsemɪdɪ'tætʃt/ ADJECTIVE a semi-detached house is joined to another house on one side

semi-final /ˌsemɪ'faɪnəl/ NOUN [plural **semi-finals**] one of the two games in a competition which are played just before the last game ℗ *Sweden reached the semi-final of the 1994 World Cup.*
seminar /'semɪnɑː(r)/ NOUN [plural **seminars**] a meeting to discuss and learn about a particular subject □ *a marketing seminar*
semi-precious /ˌsemɪ'preʃəs/ ADJECTIVE a semi-precious stone is used for making jewellery but is not as valuable as some other stones
senate /'senɪt/ NOUN [plural **senates**] the smaller but more powerful part of a government which has two parts, for example in countries such as the US and France □ *The French senate approved the bill.* □ *a senate committee*
● **senator** /'senətə(r)/ NOUN [plural **senators**] a member of a senate □ *Democratic senator, Hillary Clinton*

send /send/ VERB [**sends, sending, sent**]
1 to arrange for something to go somewhere □ *He sent me an e-mail.* □ *Sophia sent him a birthday card.* □ **+ to** *I sent a text message to my Dad.*
2 to make someone go somewhere ℗ *He was sent home from school because he was sick.* □ **+ to** *The doctor took one look and sent me straight to hospital* □ *The government sent a team of rescue workers to the area.*
3 to cause someone to be in a particular state □ *The loneliness was sending me crazy.* □ *The warmth sent me to sleep.*
♦ PHRASAL VERBS **send something back** to return something to the person who sent it to you □ *He filled in the questionnaire and sent it back.* **send for someone** to ask for someone to come to you □ *They sent for a doctor.* **send someone in** to send a large group of soldiers or police officers to deal with a situation □ *The government has sent in troops to restore calm.* **send something in** to send something to an organization □ *Hundreds of readers have sent in stories of their own experiences.* **send off for something** to write to an organization and ask them to send you something □ *I sent off for a catalogue.* **send someone off** to make a player leave a sports game because they have done something wrong □ *He was sent off for swearing at the referee.* **send something out** to send something to a lot of people □ *Have you sent out the party invitations yet?*
● **sender** /'sendə(r)/ NOUN [plural **senders**] the person who sent a letter, e-mail, etc. □ *If this letter is not delivered, please return it to the sender.*

senile /'siːnaɪl/ ADJECTIVE very confused and often forgetting things because of old age
● **senility** /sɪ'nɪləti/ NOUN, NO PLURAL the state of being senile
senior /'siːnɪə(r)/ ▶ ADJECTIVE
1 having a higher position in an organization □ *sen*

government officials □ She has a very senior position in the company.
2 older □ senior members of the family □ senior players
▶ NOUN [plural **seniors**]
1 be 5/10 etc. years someone's senior to be 5/10 etc. years older than someone □ My brother is six years my senior.
2 a US word for **senior citizen**

senior citizen /'si:nɪə 'sɪtɪzən/ NOUN [plural **senior citizens**] an older person who does not work any more

seniority /ˌsi:nɪ'ɒrətɪ/ NOUN, NO PLURAL how old or powerful a person is □ We sat along the table in order of seniority.

sensation /sen'seɪʃən/ NOUN [plural **sensations**]
1 a physical feeling, or the ability to have physical feelings □ He had a burning sensation in his chest. □ She lost all sensation in the right side of her face.
2 a feeling that you cannot explain □ I had a strange sensation that I had been there before.
3 a state of excitement or shock □ The announcement caused quite a sensation.

sensational /sen'seɪʃənəl/ ADJECTIVE
1 extremely good or exciting □ Kate looked sensational in her new dress.
2 causing a lot of excitement or shock □ sensational news

sense /sens/ ▶ NOUN [plural **senses**]
1 no plural a feeling or belief about someone or something □ People need work that gives them a sense of achievement. □ They have created a sense of calm in the building. □ I got the sense that he was worried about something.
2 one of the five abilities of sight, touch, taste, hearing and smell □ Janet lost her sense of smell after an illness.
3 no plural a natural quality □ I don't think he has much of a sense of humour. □ She has a great sense of style.
4 no plural the ability to understand things and make sensible decisions □ Someone had the sense to call an ambulance. □ We were grateful for her good sense.
5 no plural a good reason □ + in I can't see the sense in buying another computer.
6 the meaning of a word or of speech or writing □ A single English word can have lots of different senses. □ You only have to understand the general sense of the passage.
make sense (a) to have a clear meaning □ Her explanations didn't make sense. (b) to be a sensible thing to do □ It makes sense to switch to low energy light bulbs.
make sense of something to understand something that is difficult to understand □ I couldn't make sense of all the different types of pension schemes.
▶ VERB [senses, sensing, sensed] to become aware of something without being told □ + that I sensed that not many people agreed with what I was saying.

● **senseless** /'senslɪs/ ADJECTIVE
1 stupid and with no purpose □ senseless violence
2 unconscious □ A firemen was knocked senseless by a falling lamppost.
● **senselessness** /'senslɪsnɪs/ NOUN, NO PLURAL when something is stupid and has no purpose □ the senselessness of war

sense of humour /'sens əv 'hju:mə(r)/ NOUN, NO PLURAL your ability to understand things that are funny and to say funny things yourself □ She's got a good sense of humour.

sensible /'sensɪbəl/ ADJECTIVE
1 showing good judgment and the ability to make good decisions □ Lizzie's a very sensible girl. 🖭 a sensible decision 🖭 He did the sensible thing and called the police. 🖭 It's sensible to have insurance when you travel.
2 sensible shoes and clothes are comfortable instead of fashionable □ a good sensible pair of walking shoes

> ➤ Note that **sensible** when used to describe a person does not mean 'very easily offended or upset'. For this, use the word **sensitive**.

● **sensibly** /'sensɪblɪ/ ADVERB in a way that shows good judgment □ Jeff very sensibly kept the receipt.

sensitive /'sensɪtɪv/ ADJECTIVE
1 a sensitive situation or subject needs to be dealt with or spoken about carefully in order to avoid offending people □ Mental health is a sensitive issue.
2 very quickly and easily affected by something □ Fair skin is usually very sensitive to the sun.
3 being aware of other people's feelings and careful not to upset them □ He's a very sensitive, caring young man.
4 very easily offended or upset □ Jamie's very sensitive about being bald. □ She was very sensitive to criticism.
5 a sensitive piece of equipment can measure very small changes □ The alarm is very sensitive and is sometimes set off by birds or cats.
● **sensitively** /'sensɪtɪvlɪ/ ADJECTIVE in a way that carefully considers how people are feeling □ The matter has been dealt with very sensitively.
● **sensitivity** /ˌsensɪ'tɪvɪtɪ/ NOUN, NO PLURAL
1 the quality of always being aware of other people's feelings and careful not to upset them
2 when something is very quickly and easily affected by something □ This increases the skin's sensitivity to sunlight.

sensor /'sensə(r)/ NOUN [plural **sensors**] a device that notices things such as heat, light or movement □ A sensor on the front of the camera measures how much light is available.
● **sensory** /'sensərɪ/ ADJECTIVE to do with sight, hearing, smell, taste and touch □ sensory nerves

sensual /'sensjuəl/ ADJECTIVE to do with physical feelings □ sensual experiences
● **sensuous** /'sensjuəs/ ADJECTIVE giving you physical

pleasure □ *She loved the sensuous feeling of silk against her skin.*

sent /sent/ PAST TENSE AND PAST PARTICIPLE OF send

sentence /'sentəns/ ▶ NOUN [plural **sentences**]
1 a group of words that usually includes a verb and expresses a statement or question □ *He hadn't finished his sentence before she interrupted him.*
2 the punishment that a judge gives to someone who has committed a crime ⍟ *Floyd received a five year prison sentence.* ⍟ *He is serving a life sentence* (=in prison for the rest of his life) *for killing a police officer.* ⍟ *Two of the killers were given a death sentence* (=a punishment of death).
▶ VERB [**sentences, sentencing, sentenced**] when a judge sentences a criminal, he or she tells them what their punishment will be □ *+ to The whole gang was sentenced to life imprisonment.*

sentiment /'sentɪmənt/ NOUN [plural **sentiments**]
1 a formal word meaning opinion or feeling □ *Several other people share these sentiments.*
2 feelings such as sympathy or love □ *There's no place for sentiment in professional sport.*
• **sentimental** /ˌsentɪ'mentəl/ ADJECTIVE
1 showing too many emotions such as sympathy or love □ *a sentimental love story*
2 to do with emotions ⍟ *The necklace is not worth much but it has a lot of sentimental value because it was my mother's.*

sentry /'sentrɪ/ NOUN [plural **sentries**] a soldier who guards an entrance

separable /'sepərəbəl/ ADJECTIVE able to be separated from each other or from the main part of something □ *a coat with a separable hood*

separate ▶ ADJECTIVE /'sepərət/
1 different and not the same ⍟ *This is a completely separate matter.* □ *The children have separate bedrooms.*
2 not touching something else or not joined to it □ *+ from Cycle paths keep bikes separate from traffic.*
▶ VERB /'sepəreɪt/ [**separates, separating, separated**]
1 to divide something into different parts □ *+ into The class was separated into two teams.* □ *+ from This article about his life separates fact from fiction.*
2 to be between two things so that they do not touch each other □ *The north and the south are separated by a range of high mountains.* □ *+ from Only a thin camping mat separated me from the hard ground.*
3 to keep people apart from each other □ *A teacher had to separate the boys who were fighting.*
4 to stop living with your husband or wife □ *My parents separated last year.* □ *+ from He had recently separated from his wife.*
• **separately** /'sepərətlɪ/ ADVERB not together □ *Each of the suspects was interviewed separately by the police.*
• **separation** /ˌsepə'reɪʃən/ NOUN [plural **separations**]
1 when people are apart from each other □ *+ from*

Lily found the long separation from her family very difficult while she was working abroad.
2 keeping things apart □ *+ of They wanted a strict separation of church and state.* □ *I firmly believe in the separation of work from family life.*
3 when a husband and wife decide to stop living with each other □ *The couple announced their separation in May.*

September /sep'tembə(r)/ NOUN the ninth month of the year, after August and before October □ *School starts again in September.*

septic /'septɪk/ ADJECTIVE infected with bacteria □ *a septic wound*

sequel /'siːkwəl/ NOUN [plural **sequels**] a book, play or film that continues an earlier story

sequence /'siːkwəns/ NOUN [plural **sequences**]
1 a series of things that happen one after the other ⍟ *It was a remarkable sequence of events.*
2 the order in which something happens or exists □ *Put these numbers in the correct sequence.*
3 a part of a film □ *The film's opening sequence was filmed in Geneva.* □ *She choreographed the film's dance sequences.*

sequin /'siːkwɪn/ NOUN [plural **sequins**] a small shiny circle that you sew onto clothes as a decoration

serenade /ˌserə'neɪd/ ▶ NOUN [plural **serenades**] song that someone sings for someone they love
▶ VERB [**serenades, serenading, serenaded**] to sing or play music for someone you love

serene /sɪ'riːn/ ADJECTIVE calm and peaceful □ *a serene smile*
• **serenely** /sɪ'riːnlɪ/ ADVERB in a calm and peaceful way
• **serenity** /sɪ'renətɪ/ NOUN, NO PLURAL the quality of being calm and peaceful

sergeant /'saːdʒənt/ NOUN [plural **sergeants**]
1 an officer of middle rank in the police □ *Sergeant Adam Cragg was the officer in charge.*
2 an officer of middle rank in the army

sergeant-major /'saːdʒənt'meɪdʒə(r)/ NOUN [plural **sergeant-majors**] an army rank above sergeant

serial /'sɪərɪəl/ ▶ NOUN [plural **serials**] a story that's printed or broadcast in several parts □ *'Cranford Chronicles' is a five-part television drama serial.*
▶ ADJECTIVE serial killer/murderer/offender, etc. someone who commits the same type of crime many times

serial number /'sɪərɪəl 'nʌmbə(r)/ NOUN [plural **serial numbers**] a different number that is printed on each product or on paper money

series /'sɪəriːz/ NOUN [plural **series**]
1 a series of something several similar things that happen or are done one after the other □ *a series of accidents* □ *They held a series of meetings.*
2 a set of television or radio programmes with the same subject or the same characters ⍟ *They're filming a new TV series.* □ *a comedy series* □ *+ of an old series of 'Cheers'*

serious /ˈsɪərɪəs/ ADJECTIVE
1 important and needing attention ⌻ *The report raises serious questions about the quality of education.* ⌻ *Obesity is becoming a serious health issue.*
2 very bad ⌻ *a serious accident* ⌻ *serious injuries* ⌻ *Noy was involved in several killings and other serious crimes.*
3 meaning what you are saying and not joking or pretending □ *I can never tell when he's joking and when he's being serious.* □ *+ about Are you serious about becoming a teacher?*
4 a serious person is sensible, quiet, and does not laugh much □ *William was a very serious little boy.*

seriously /ˈsɪərɪəslɪ/ ADVERB
1 very badly ⌻ *Her father is seriously ill.* ⌻ *Jan was seriously injured in the accident.*
2 in a way that shows you think something is important ⌻ *We're taking these threats very seriously* ⌻ *We're seriously considering moving to Japan.*
3 used to emphasize that you are not joking, or to ask someone whether they are joking □ *Seriously, I didn't sleep for three nights because I was so worried.* □ *'John said he would pay.' 'Seriously?'*
4 an informal word meaning very □ *They sell seriously expensive clothes.*

sermon /ˈsɜːmən/ NOUN [plural **sermons**] a speech that a priest makes in a church

serpent /ˈsɜːpənt/ NOUN [plural **serpents**] an old word for a snake

serrated /sɪˈreɪtɪd/ ADJECTIVE having an edge with sharp points in the shape of Vs □ *a serrated knife*

servant /ˈsɜːvənt/ NOUN [plural **servants**] someone who works in a big house and does jobs such as cooking and cleaning for the person who owns the house

serve /sɜːv/ ▶ VERB [serves, serving, served]
to give someone food or drink □ *I'll serve the soup and you can give out the spoons.* □ *Serve the cheese with crusty bread.*
to sell things to customers in a shop □ *Are you being served?*
to work for a person or an organization □ *Brown had served the family for fifty years.* □ *As a soldier, he served in Egypt.* □ *+ as He served as treasurer for three years.*
to be used for a particular purpose □ *+ as The cave served as a shelter for the night.* □ *+ to do something This news serves to remind us of all we owe to our soldiers.* ⌻ *These new regulations serve no useful purpose.*
to provide something for people or an area □ *This hospital serves nearly a million local people.* □ *There is a bus network serving these villages.*
to be in prison for a period of time □ *She's serving 6 months for fraud.* ⌻ *After he has served his sentence, he hopes to become an actor.*
to start playing by throwing the ball up and hitting it in sports such as tennis

8 if an amount of food serves a certain number of people, it is enough for that number □ *The recipe says the pie serves six.*
9 serve someone right if a bad situation or result serves you right, you deserve it □ *If you're sick, it serves you right for eating too much chocolate.*
▶ NOUN [plural **serves**] throwing the ball up and hitting it to start playing a point in tennis ⌻ *a very fast serve*

• **server** /ˈsɜːvə(r)/ NOUN [plural **servers**]
1 a computer that stores information or does work for other computers that are connected to it. A computing word.
2 the person who serves in sports such as tennis

service /ˈsɜːvɪs/ ▶ NOUN [plural **services**]
1 a system to provide something that people need, or an organization that provides it □ *There have been cuts in mental health services.* □ *The firm has promised to improve the bus service.* ⌻ *The charity provides basic services to homeless people.* ⌻ *We are offering a free e-mail service.*
2 *no plural* the help that someone gives you in a place such as a hotel or shop □ *I love the things they sell, but the service is awful.*
3 *no plural* the period of time that you work for a business or organization □ *She resigned after 25 years' service in the company.* ⌻ *He has 30 years of military service.*
4 something that you do to help someone □ *Can I be of any service to you?* □ *He was given an award for services to the community.*
5 when a car or machine is checked and repaired □ *I'm taking my car in for a service.*
6 the services a country's military organizations
7 a religious ceremony ⌻ *The queen attended a service to remember the dead.*
8 when you throw the ball up and hit it to start playing a point in tennis □ *a terrible first service*
9 in service/out of service being used/no longer being used □ *These aircraft have now been taken out of service.*
▶ VERB [services, servicing, serviced] to check and repair a car or a machine □ *We need to get the boiler serviced.*

service charge /ˈsɜːvɪs ˌtʃɑːdʒ/ NOUN [plural **service charges**] in a restaurant, an amount of money that is added to the bill (=piece of paper showing what you must pay) and given to the person who brought the food and drink to your table

service industry /ˈsɜːvɪs ˌɪndʌstrɪ/ NOUN [plural **service industries**] an industry that provides a service but does not make products

service station /ˈsɜːvɪs ˌsteɪʃən/ NOUN [plural **service stations**] a place where you can buy petrol, especially a place on a motorway where you can also buy food

serviette /ˌsɜːvɪˈet/ NOUN [plural **serviettes**] a piece of cloth or paper that you use during a meal to protect your clothes or clean your mouth or fingers

servile /'sɜːvaɪl/ ADJECTIVE too eager to obey and please someone

serving /'sɜːvɪŋ/ NOUN [plural **servings**] an amount of food enough for one person □ *The packet says it contains four servings.*

sesame /'sesəmi/ NOUN, NO PLURAL a plant whose seeds and oil are used in cooking □ *sesame seeds*

session /'seʃən/ NOUN [plural **sessions**]
1 a period of time that is used for doing something □ *He missed last night's training session.*
2 a meeting or a series of meetings of a court or parliament □ *He called a special session of parliament to deal with the crisis.*

set /set/ ▶ VERB [**sets, setting, set**]
1 to decide on a level for something □ *Prices were set too high.* 🖻 *We need to set a limit on what we will spend.* 🖻 *The company has set new targets for growth.*
2 to decide the time or date of something 🖻 *Have they set a date for the meeting?* □ *The government has set a timetable for change.*
3 to put something somewhere □ *Set the tray down on the table.*
4 to be in a particular position □ *The house is set well back from the road.*
5 to cause something or someone to happen or to do something □ + *ing Her remarks set me thinking.* 🖻 *My accident set in motion a whole chain of events.*
6 to make a piece of equipment ready to work at a particular time □ *Don't forget to set the DVD to record.* 🖻 *Did you set the alarm?*
7 if a substance sets, it becomes solid □ *Wait an hour or so for the jelly to set.*
8 if a book, film, etc. is set somewhere, that is where the story happens □ *Her first novel is set in Berlin.*
9 the sun sets when it goes down
10 if a teacher sets work or sets an exam, they tell the students to do it □ *The teacher doesn't set my children enough homework.*
11 set an example to behave in a way that other people may copy □ *I try to set the children a good example by wearing my cycle helmet.*
12 set a record to achieve the best result ever in an activity, especially a sport □ *She set a new world record for the 100m.*
13 set someone/something free to let a person or an animal out of the place where they are being kept
➜ *go to* set eyes on something/someone, set your mind at rest, put/set the record straight, set your sights on something, set the stage for something

♦ PHRASAL VERBS **set about something** to start doing something □ *They set about the cooking with enthusiasm.* □ + *ing He set about cleaning the car.*
set something aside 1 to save something for a particular purpose □ *I set aside part of my wages each week.* □ *We set aside a whole evening to talk.* **2** to not consider something or not be affected by something □ *We tried to set aside our differences and work together.* □ *She set aside her usual caution.* **set**

something down 1 to write something down □ *He set down his evidence in a 50 page document.*
2 to officially decide rules, systems, etc. □ *They have set down new guidelines on dealing with challenging behaviour.* **set in** if something, usually something bad, sets in, it starts to exist □ *Tiredness had begun to set in.* **set off** to start a journey □ *We need to set off early tomorrow.* **set something off** to make something start working or happening □ *The smoke set off the fire alarm.* **set someone/something on someone** to make a person or animal attack someone □ *I'll set my dogs on you!* **set out 1** + *to do something* to intend to do something □ *I set out to prove him wrong.* **2** to start a journey □ *We set out after breakfast.* **set something out** to explain something to someone □ *He set out his plans for future development.* **set something up 1** to start a business, organization or group □ *A tribunal was set up to hear the case.* □ *He set up his firm in 2003.* **2** to make something ready to be used □ *I set up a bank account for my son.* □ *We have set up a new website.* □ *I need to set up my equipment.* **3** to arrange for something to happen □ *We need to set up a meeting.* **set upon someone/something** to attack someone or something □ *He was set upon and robbed.*

▶ NOUN [plural **sets**]
1 a group of people or things that belong together or are used together □ *a set of chairs* □ *a chess set*
2 a radio or television □ *We have a technical problem, please do not adjust your set.* **3** the place where actors perform in a play, film, etc. □ *He had to wear the wig all the time on set.*
4 a series of games that form part of a tennis match
5 a group of people with similar interests □ *He is part of a very sporty set.*
6 a group of numbers. A maths word.
▶ ADJECTIVE
1 fixed □ *We meet at set times each week.*
2 set menu a menu with a limited choice of food for a fixed price
3 ready or prepared □ + *to do something Are we set to go?*
4 not willing to change your opinions or behaviour 🖻 *She has very set ideas about how to cook fish.*
♦ IDIOM **set in stone/concrete** if a decision or a plan is set in stone/concrete, it cannot be changed □ *We're thinking of selling the house, but nothing's set in stone yet.*

setback /'setbæk/ NOUN [plural **setbacks**] a problem that stops you making progress 🖻 *The project suffered a major setback when the manager resigned.*

set square /'set ˌskweə(r)/ NOUN [plural **set squares**] a plastic object shaped like a triangle, used for measuring angles. A maths word.

settee /se'tiː/ NOUN [plural **settees**] a comfortable chair for two or more people □ *Guy and Anna were sitting on the settee.*

setting /'setɪŋ/ NOUN [plural **settings**]
1 the place where something is or where something happens □ *The hotel is the perfect setting for a wedding reception.*
2 the place or period of time in which the events in a film, book, story etc. happen □ *She chose Los Angeles as the setting for her novels.*
3 the position of the controls on a piece of equipment □ *What setting did you have the oven on?*

settle /'setəl/ VERB [**settles, settling, settled**]
1 if you settle an argument, you end it by agreeing something □ *I wish they would settle their differences.* □ *The case was settled out of court.*
2 to decide on something or to arrange something □ *Have you settled on a date for the wedding?* ▢ *That settles it - I'm leaving!* ▢ *That's settled - we'll all meet next Tuesday.*
3 to pay money that you owe □ *The bill can be settled in cash or with a cheque.* ▢ *This money helped us settle our debts.*
4 to become relaxed and comfortable in a situation □ *Harry settled into his armchair and fell asleep.* □ *Settle back and enjoy the show!*
5 to make someone feel calm and relaxed □ *I need to settle the kids before they go to bed.* □ *I need something to settle my nerves.*
6 to go somewhere and make your home there □ *The family settled in New South Wales.* □ *They may not settle permanently in the UK.*
7 to land on a surface or on the bottom of something and stay there □ *A fly settled on the picture frame for a moment.* □ *The snow's too wet to settle.*
PHRASAL VERBS **settle down** to start to live a life with less change, for example by staying somewhere for a long time or staying in a relationship □ *I'm not ready to settle down and have kids yet.* **settle (someone) down** to become calm or make someone calm after being nervous or excited □ *Settle down now, it's time to do some work.* **settle for something** to accept something that is not exactly what you wanted □ *I was hoping for £1,000, but in the end I settled for £800.* **settle in** to start to feel happy and confident in a new situation □ *She's finding it difficult to settle in at her new school.* **settle up** to pay someone the money that you owe them □ *I'll settle up with you at the end of the evening.*

settled /'setəld/ ADJECTIVE
happy and confident in a situation, and not wanting to change □ *Now I've got a flat, I feel much more settled.*
good, and not likely to change □ *The weather is quite settled at the moment.*

settlement /'setəlmənt/ NOUN [plural **settlements**]
an agreement that ends an argument ▢ *The two sides have failed to reach a settlement.* ▢ *a divorce settlement*
a place where people have come and built homes

□ *New settlements have grown up in the desert.*
3 the payment of an amount of money that is owed □ *Please accept this cheque as settlement of the bill.*
• **settler** /'setlə(r)/ NOUN [plural **settlers**] someone who goes with other people to a place and builds a home there

seven /'sevən/ NUMBER [plural **sevens**] the number 7

seventeen /ˌsevən'tiːn/ NUMBER the number 17
seventeenth /ˌsevən'tiːnθ/ NUMBER 17th written as a word

seventh /'sevənθ/ ▶ NUMBER 7th written as a word
□ *the seventh day of the week*
▶ NOUN [plural **sevenths**] $\frac{1}{7}$; one of seven equal parts of something

seventieth /'sevəntɪəθ/ NUMBER 70th written as a word
seventy /'sevəntɪ/ NUMBER [plural **seventies**]
1 the number 70
2 the seventies the years between 1970 and 1979
sever /'sevə(r)/ VERB [**severs, severing, severed**]
1 to cut through something □ *He bled to death after a piece of glass severed an artery in his neck.*
2 to end a relationship or connection □ *She had severed all links with her parents several years ago.*

several /'sevərəl/ DETERMINER, PRONOUN more than a few but not a lot □ *I met him several years ago.* □ *Several people admired her dress.* □ *+ of Several of my friends have dogs.* □ *Would you like one of these leaflets? I've got several.*

➤ If you want to say 'a very small number' do not use the word **several**. Instead, use the phrase **a few**:
✓ *I've got a lot of friends but only a few close friends.*
✗ *I've got a lot of friends but only several close friends.*

severe /sɪ'vɪə(r)/ ADJECTIVE
1 very bad □ *severe weather conditions* □ *He suffered severe head injuries in the accident.* □ *She has severe health problems.*
2 extreme □ *severe punishments* □ *There were severe restrictions on the sale of weapons.* □ *severe criticism*
3 not friendly or kind □ *a severe expression*
• **severely** /sɪ'vɪəlɪ/ ADVERB in a way that is extreme □ *Two of the passengers were severely injured.*
• **severity** /sɪ'verɪtɪ/ NOUN, NO PLURAL the quality of being severe □ *I don't think you understand the severity of the situation.*

sew /səʊ/ VERB [**sews, sewing, sewed, sewn**] to use a needle and thread to join things together □ *He sewed the button back on his shirt.*

sewage /'suːɪdʒ/ NOUN, NO PLURAL the waste from people's bodies that is taken away from houses in underground pipes □ *the sewage system*

sewer /'suːə(r)/ NOUN [plural **sewers**] an underground pipe for taking sewage away from buildings

sewing /'səʊɪŋ/ NOUN, NO PLURAL
1 the skill or activity of making or repairing things using a needle and thread □ *I'm not very good at sewing.*
2 something that you are making using a needle and thread □ *She put down her sewing and looked at him over her glasses.*

sewing machine /'səʊɪŋ məˈʃiːn/ NOUN [plural **sewing machines**] a machine that you use for sewing cloth together

sewn /səʊn/ PAST PARTICIPLE OF sew

sex /seks/ NOUN [plural **sexes**]
1 no plural the act in which a man puts his penis into a woman's vagina □ *sex education*
2 no plural the fact of being male or female □ *It is now technically possible for couples to choose the sex of their baby.* □ *There are laws against sex discrimination.*
3 the group that includes girls and women, or the group that includes boys and men ⊞ *Some teenagers feel very embarrassed about talking to members of the opposite sex.* □ *The classes are intended for both sexes.*
• **sexism** /'seksɪzəm/ NOUN, NO PLURAL unfair treatment of someone because they are a woman or because they are a man □ *The scheme aims to tackle sexism in the workplace.*
• **sexist** /'seksɪst/ ADJECTIVE to do with sexism □ *sexist attitudes* □ *sexist remarks*
▶ NOUN [plural **sexists**] someone who treats another person unfairly because they are a woman or because they are a man
• **sexual** /'sekʃʊəl/ ADJECTIVE
1 to do with or involving the activity of sex □ *a sexual relationship* □ *sexual behaviour*
2 to do with the differences between men and women □ *sexual equality*
• **sexy** /'seksɪ/ ADJECTIVE sexually attractive

sh /ʃ/ EXCLAMATION used to show that you want someone to be quiet □ *Sh! You'll wake the baby.*

shabby /'ʃæbɪ/ ADJECTIVE [**shabbier, shabbiest**]
1 old and slightly damaged □ *shabby clothes*
2 bad and not fair □ *He complained about the shabby treatment he had received.*

shack /ʃæk/ NOUN [plural **shacks**] a small building made of wood or metal

shackle /'ʃækəl/ VERB [**shackles, shackling, shackled**]
1 to put metal rings around a prisoner's hands or feet to stop them from moving
2 if you are shackled by something, it prevents you from doing what you want □ *I was shackled by my guilt.*
• **shackles** /'ʃækəlz/ PLURAL NOUN

1 chains that are used to fasten a prisoner's hands or feet together
2 things which limit your freedom □ *He wanted to throw off the shackles of anxiety and self-doubt.*

shade /ʃeɪd/ ▶ NOUN [plural **shades**]
1 no plural an area which is cooler and darker because there is no light from the sun □ *He was lying in the shade of a tree.* □ *On hot days I prefer sitting in the shade.* □ *This plant prefers shade.*
2 an object that goes around a light and prevents the light being too bright □ *a lamp with a purple shade*
3 a particular type of a colour □ + of *The wall was painted in a deep shade of green.*
4 a shade slightly □ *Can you make it a shade looser?* □ *He was a shade under 1.80m tall.*
5 shades an informal word for sunglasses
▶ VERB [**shades, shading, shaded**] to protect something from the sun □ *A row of trees shaded the path.*

shadow /'ʃædəʊ/ ▶ NOUN [plural **shadows**]
1 a dark shape on a surface caused when an object is between the surface and a bright light □ *There was a shadow on the wall.* ⊞ *The candle cast shadows around the room.*
2 no plural an area that is dark because light cannot reach it □ *I couldn't see his face because it was in shadow* ⊞ *The candle cast shadows*
3 a bad effect or influence ⊞ *Many people are living under the shadow of war.* ⊞ *Her son's death cast a shadow over* (=had a bad effect on) *the rest of her life.*
4 beyond/without a shadow of doubt used for emphasizing that you are certain about something □ *Without a shadow of doubt, that man saved my life.*
▶ VERB [**shadows, shadowing, shadowed**] to follow someone and watch what they are doing □ *She noticed the bodyguard shadowing him.*
▶ ADJECTIVE having a particular job in the main political party which competes against the party that rules the country □ *the shadow education minister*
• **shadowy** /'ʃædəʊɪ/ ADJECTIVE
1 like a shadow and not easy to see clearly □ *Shadowy figures moved in and out of the trees.*
2 mysterious and secret □ *a shadowy organization*

shady /'ʃeɪdɪ/ ADJECTIVE [**shadier, shadiest**]
1 a shady place has little light because it is covered by something □ *The plant will grow best in a shady spot.*
2 slightly illegal or dishonest □ *shady business deals*

shaft /ʃɑːft/ NOUN [plural **shafts**]
1 a long hole down into the ground or down a building □ *a lift shaft* □ *a mine shaft*
2 a long handle of a tool or weapon
3 a shaft of light a line of light

shaggy /'ʃægɪ/ ADJECTIVE [**shaggier, shaggiest**] shaggy hair or fur is long and untidy

shake /ʃeɪk/ ▶ VERB [**shakes, shaking, shook, shaken**]
1 to make many quick small movements from side to side or up and down □ *The whole area shook when the bomb landed.* □ *Mina was shaking with fear.* □ *His hands were shaking as he tried to sign his name.*

2 to make something move quickly from side to side or up and down several times □ *The wind was shaking the trees and rattling the windows.* □ *A huge explosion shook the building.* □ *Shake the bottle before opening.*

3 to shock or upset someone □ *It was an event that shook the world.* □ *He was still very shaken by the news.*

4 shake your head to move your head from side to side as a way of saying 'no' □ *I asked if she was coming and he just shook his head.*

5 shake hands to hold someone's hand and move it up and down when you meet them for the first time or when making an agreement □ *He shook hands with the Prime Minister.* □ *We shook hands and the deal was done.*

6 if your voice shakes, you sound nervous □ *'What shall I do?' she said, her voice shaking slightly.*

PHRASAL VERBS **shake something off** to get rid of an illness, injury or problem □ *I can't seem to shake off this cold.* **shake something out** to shake something so that any dust or dirt comes out of it □ *He shook out the rug and folded it up.* **shake someone up** to shock or upset someone □ *The accident shook me up a bit.* **shake something up** to make big changes in an organization □ *The new leader was serious about shaking up the party.*

▶ NOUN [plural **shakes**]

a quick movement from side to side or backwards and forwards 🕮 *Give the bottle a quick shake.*

an informal word for milkshake

shake-up /ˈʃeɪkʌp/ NOUN [plural **shake-ups**] a big change in an organization or system □ *The report led to a shake-up in security procedures.*

shaky /ˈʃeɪkɪ/ ADJECTIVE [**shakier, shakiest**]

not very good or certain 🕮 *The team recovered after a slightly shaky start.* □ *The future of the project looks very shaky.*

making small quick movements from side to side or up and down □ *shaky hands*

physically weak □ *My legs felt a little shaky when I got out of bed.*

shall /ʃəl/ MODAL VERB

used to make a suggestion or an offer □ *Shall we play chess?* □ *Shall I open the window?*

how/what/when, etc. shall used to ask someone what to do □ *What shall I cook for dinner?* □ *When shall we phone him?*

used as a formal way of saying what you will do in the future □ *I shall make an official complaint.* □ *I shall never forget this moment.*

shallow /ˈʃæləʊ/ ADJECTIVE [**shallower, shallowest**]

not deep 🕮 *shallow water* 🕮 *The children were playing in the shallow end of the pool.* □ *The lake was quite shallow.* □ *a shallow dish*

never thinking about things which are important or serious □ *I found her very shallow.*

sham /ʃæm/ NOUN, NO PLURAL something that is done to make people believe something that is not true □ *The trial was a sham.*

shamble /ˈʃæmbəl/ VERB [**shambles, shambling, shambled**] to walk slowly and awkwardly without lifting your feet very much □ *The old man shambled along, leaning on his stick.*

shambles /ˈʃæmbəlz/ NOUN, NO PLURAL a shambles something that is organized very badly or is very untidy □ *The education system is a shambles.*

shame /ʃeɪm/ ▶ NOUN

1 it's/what a shame used when saying that you are disappointed about something □ *What a shame that you can't come to the party.* □ *It's a shame we can't stay longer.* □ *It would be a great shame if you had to give up playing the violin.*

2 no plural the embarrassing feeling you have when you know you have done something wrong 🕮 *Emma felt a sense of shame about the things she had done.* 🕮 *His crimes had brought shame on his whole family.* □ + of *He had suffered the shame of being arrested in front of his friends.*

3 have no shame to not feel embarrassed or guilty although you have done something bad □ *These young criminals have no shame.*

4 put someone to shame to be much better than someone or something □ *Their results put ours to shame.*

▶ VERB [**shames, shaming, shamed**] to make someone feel ashamed

♦ PHRASAL VERB **shame someone into (doing) something** to make someone feel so ashamed that they do something □ *The government has been shamed into action.*

● **shameful** /ˈʃeɪmfʊl/ ADJECTIVE so bad that you should be ashamed □ *shameful behaviour*

● **shameless** /ˈʃeɪmlɪs/ ADJECTIVE not feeling embarrassed or guilty although you should do □ *It was a shameless attempt to win votes.*

shampoo /ʃæmˈpuː/ ▶ NOUN [plural **shampoos**] liquid soap used especially for washing your hair □ *a bottle of shampoo*

▶ VERB [**shampoos, shampooing, shampooed**] to wash something using shampoo

shan't /ʃɑːnt/ a short way to say and write shall not □ *I shan't be late.*

shanty town /ˈʃæntɪ taʊn/ NOUN [plural **shanty towns**] an area where poor people live in small, basic houses built from pieces of wood or metal

shape /ʃeɪp/ ▶ NOUN [plural **shapes**]

1 the form that is made by the outer edge of something □ *She made a cake in the shape of a piano.* □ *His body has changed shape dramatically.* □ *The children stuck coloured shapes onto the card.* □ *What shape is the window?*

2 the health or condition of someone or something 🕮 *The team is in good shape for Saturday's match.*

🔁 *He leaves the company in better shape than he found it.* 🔁 *I'm getting a bit out of shape* (=not strong and healthy). 🔁 *He runs every day to keep in shape* (=stay strong and healthy).

3 take shape to develop so that you can see what the end result will be □ *Gradually, the novel started to take shape in my mind.*

▶ VERB [**shapes, shaping, shaped**]

1 to influence the development of something or someone □ *Her views were shaped by her experiences in China.* □ *He wants to use his power to shape the future.*

2 to make something a particular shape □ *He shapes the clay pots on the potter's wheel.*

♦ PHRASAL VERB **shape up**

1 to develop, usually in a satisfactory way □ *This is shaping up to be a really exciting match.*

2 an informal word meaning to improve your work or your behaviour □ *We'll have to sack him if he doesn't shape up.*

• **shapeless** /'ʃeɪplɪs/ ADJECTIVE having no particular shape □ *a shapeless old cardigan*

• **shapely** /'ʃeɪplɪ/ ADJECTIVE a shapely body or part of a body has an attractive shape □ *shapely legs*

share /ʃeə(r)/ ▶ VERB [**shares, sharing, shared**]

1 to divide something between two or more people □ + *between We had two pizzas to share between 7 people.* □ + *among I shared the sweets among the children.*

2 to have or use something at the same time as someone else □ *There aren't enough books to go round so some of you will have to share.* □ *She shares a home with her elderly mother.* □ *We must all share the blame for the accident.*

3 to allow someone to have part of something that is yours or to use something that is yours □ *She kindly shared her lunch with me.* □ *William wouldn't share his toys.*

4 to have the same feelings, opinions or experiences as someone else □ *They shared her interest in antique furniture.* □ *I share your concerns about the level of debt.*

5 to tell someone something □ *She shared her tips on growing roses.*

♦ PHRASAL VERB **share something out** to divide something between each person in a group □ *We shared out the food between us.*

▶ NOUN [*plural* **shares**]

1 a part of a total number or amount of something that is divided between people □ *I took my share of the cake.* 🔁 *We hope to increase our share of the market.* 🔁 *She wants a larger share of the profits.*

2 a reasonable amount of something, often something unpleasant □ *I've done my share of hard work.* 🔁 *He's had more than his fair share of tragedy.*

3 one of the equal parts of the value of a company that you can buy or sell □ + *in She has shares in the bank.* 🔁 *I bought shares in his business.* 🔁 *Shares rose/ fell* (=increased/lost value) *at the news.*

shareholder /'ʃeə,həʊldə(r)/ NOUN [*plural* **shareholders**] someone who owns shares in a company

shark /ʃɑːk/ NOUN [*plural* **sharks**] a large sea fish with very sharp teeth

sharp /ʃɑːp/ ▶ ADJECTIVE [**sharper, sharpest**]

1 having a thin edge or a pointed end that can cut things easily □ *a sharp knife* □ *sharp teeth*

2 a sharp decrease or increase is sudden and large 🔁 *There has been a sharp rise in crime.*

3 a sharp contrast/difference, etc. a very big difference □ *There is a sharp contrast in their lifestyles.*

4 a sharp pain is sudden, short and painful

5 a sharp bend or turn is one that changes direction suddenly

6 a sharp image is clear □ *I can get a really sharp focus with this camera.*

7 clever and quick to notice things

8 if your hearing or eyesight (=how well you can see) is sharp, you can hear or see very well

9 showing anger □ *She received a sharp rebuke from her mother.*

10 a sharp taste is quite sour or bitter

11 in music, higher by half a note

▶ ADVERB

1 5 o'clock, 6.15, etc. sharp at exactly 5 o'clock, 6.15, etc.

2 with a sudden change of direction □ *Turn sharp left at the next set of traffic lights.*

▶ NOUN [*plural* **sharps**] in written music, a sign (♯) that makes a note higher by half a note

• **sharpen** /'ʃɑːpən/ VERB [**sharpens, sharpening, sharpened**]

1 to make something sharp or sharper □ *The leopard was sharpening its claws on a tree.* □ *I need to sharpen this pencil.*

2 to make an image clearer □ *How do you sharpen focus?*

• **sharpener** /'ʃɑːpənə(r)/ NOUN [*plural* **sharpeners**] device that you use to sharpen pencils or knives

• **sharply** /'ʃɑːplɪ/ ADVERB

1 suddenly and by a large amount 🔁 *Temperatures fall sharply at night.*

2 in a strong and angry way □ *The report sharply criticized his handling of the affair.*

3 if you turn sharply, you turn suddenly in a completely different direction

shatter /'ʃætə(r)/ VERB [**shatters, shattering, shattered**]

1 to break into lots of very small pieces or to break something into lots of very small pieces □ *He dropped the glass and it shattered.* □ *The explosion shattered windows.*

2 to completely destroy a feeling, a belief or a state □ *His confidence was shattered.* □ *The early morning calm was shattered by the sound of gunfire.*

• **shattered** /'ʃætəd/ ADJECTIVE
1 very shocked or upset by something that has happened □ *He was completely shattered when his brother died.*
2 an informal word meaning very tired □ *I must get some sleep - I'm shattered.*

shave /ʃeɪv/ ▶ VERB [shaves, shaving, shaved]
1 to use a razor (=thin, sharp piece of metal) to cut away hair that is growing on your face or body □ *He shaved and showered, then got dressed.* □ **+ off** *He shaved off his beard.*
2 to cut very thin layers from something with a sharp blade □ *Shave off thin slices of cheese.*
▶ NOUN [plural shaves] when you shave □ *You need a shave and a haircut.*
• IDIOM **a close shave** a situation in which you only just avoid something bad or dangerous □ *The crew had a close shave when the boat's engine caught fire.*

• **shaven** /'ʃeɪvən/ ADJECTIVE if part of someone's body is shaven, it has been shaved □ *We saw monks with shaven heads.*

• **shaver** /'ʃeɪvə(r)/ NOUN [plural shavers] an electrical tool for shaving hair

shavings /'ʃeɪvɪŋz/ PLURAL NOUN very thin strips of wood or metal that have been cut off a surface with a sharp tool

shawl /ʃɔːl/ NOUN [plural shawls] a large piece of cloth for covering a woman's shoulders

she /ʃiː/ PRONOUN used to talk or write about a woman, girl or female animal that has already been mentioned □ *Madeleine is funny. She really makes me laugh.*

sheaf /ʃiːf/ NOUN [plural sheaves]
1 many pieces of paper that are tied or held together □ *He carried a thick sheaf of papers.*
2 pieces of a crop such as wheat which have been cut and tied together

shear /ʃɪə(r)/ VERB [shears, shearing, sheared, sheared or shorn]
1 to cut wool from a sheep
2 if a piece of metal shears, it breaks off □ *The bolt had sheared off.*

shears /ʃɪəz/ PLURAL NOUN a cutting tool with two large sharp blades

sheath /ʃiːθ/ NOUN [plural sheaths] a long narrow case for a knife

sheathe /ʃiːð/ VERB [sheathes, sheathing, sheathed] to cover something in order to protect it

shed /ʃed/ ▶ NOUN [plural sheds] a simple wooden or metal building used for working in or for storing things □ *a garden shed*
▶ VERB [sheds, shedding, shed]
1 to get rid of something that you do not need □ *I've managed to shed a few pounds (=lose some weight). The company is trying to shed its traditional image.*
2 to let clothes, skin, leaves etc. fall or drop off □ *Snakes shed their skin.*

3 shed tears to cry
4 shed blood used to mean that someone is injured or killed □ *The army is ready to shed its blood to defend the country.*
➜ go to **shed light** on something

she'd /ʃiːd/ a short way to say and write she had or she would □ *She'd forgotten her umbrella.* □ *She'd rather not say.*

shedload /'ʃedləʊd/ NOUN [plural shedloads] an informal word that means a lot of something □ *They've made shedloads of money.*

sheen /ʃiːn/ NOUN a soft shine on a surface □ *a grey silk suit with a metallic sheen*

sheep /ʃiːp/ NOUN [plural sheep] a farm animal with a thick wool coat ▣ *a flock of sheep*

► Remember that the plural form of **sheep** is the same as the singular form □ *He has a lot of sheep.*

sheepdog /'ʃiːpdɒg/ NOUN [plural sheepdogs] a dog trained to control sheep

sheepish /'ʃiːpɪʃ/ ADJECTIVE if someone looks sheepish, they look slightly embarrassed □ *a sheepish grin*
• **sheepishly** /'ʃiːpɪʃlɪ/ ADVERB in a way that shows you are slightly embarrassed □ *He smiled sheepishly.*

sheepskin /'ʃiːpskɪn/ NOUN, NO PLURAL leather made from the skin of a sheep, usually with the wool left on it □ *a sheepskin rug*

sheer /ʃɪə(r)/ ADJECTIVE
1 used to emphasize the degree, size, strength, etc. of something □ *The sheer scale of the building is breathtaking.* □ *The first problem is the sheer size of the city.*
2 complete or only □ *It was sheer luck that no one was hurt.* □ *He ate four bags of crisps. It was just sheer greed.*
3 very steep or vertical □ *There were sheer cliffs on either side.*
4 sheer cloth is so thin you can see through it

sheet /ʃiːt/ NOUN [plural sheets]
1 a large, flat piece of cloth used to cover a bed □ *I'll just change the sheets on your bed.*
2 a single piece of paper or a document on a single piece of paper □ **+ of** *an A4 sheet of paper* □ *She gave him a fact sheet about diabetes.*
3 a large thin flat piece of metal, plastic, glass, etc. □ **+ of** *a sheet of aluminium foil* □ *They covered it with a plastic sheet.*

sheikh /ʃeɪk/ NOUN [plural sheikhs] a leader in an Arab country

shelf /ʃelf/ NOUN [plural shelves]
1 a flat piece of wood, metal, etc. fixed horizontally to a wall or as part of a cupboard, used for putting things on □ *She stood on a chair to reach the top shelf of the kitchen cupboard.* ▣ *He got a job stacking supermarket shelves.*
2 an area of land or the bottom of the sea that is like a

shelf, with a flat top. A geography word. □ *the coastal shelf*

shell /ʃel/ ► NOUN [plural **shells**]

1 a hard covering on an egg or a nut □ *Remove the hard outer shell of the nut.*

2 a hard covering that protects the body of some sea creatures or other animals □ *a snail shell*

3 a metal case filled with explosives which is fired from a large gun □ *The building was hit by a mortar shell.* □ *Tanks fired shells.*

4 the outer parts of a building, vehicle or other structure

► VERB [**shells, shelling, shelled**]

1 to fire an explosive shell □ *The enemy were shelling the area.*

2 to remove nuts, eggs or vegetables from their shells □ *freshly shelled peas*

◆ PHRASAL VERB **shell out** an informal word meaning to pay a lot of money to buy something □ *They shelled out £120 each for tickets.*

she'll /ʃiːl/ a short way to say and write she will □ *She'll be back in a minute.*

shellfish /ˈʃelfɪʃ/ NOUN [plural **shellfish**] animals with a hard outer shell that live in the sea, rivers or lakes

shelter /ˈʃeltə(r)/ ► NOUN [plural **shelters**]

1 a building or other structure that provides protection from harm or bad weather □ *an underground bomb shelter* □ *Earthquake victims are living in makeshift shelters.*

2 no plural protection from danger or bad weather 🔁 *It was pouring with rain, so we took shelter in a shop doorway.* □ *The explosion sent people running for shelter.*

► VERB [**shelters, sheltering, sheltered**]

1 to stay in a place where you are protected from harm or bad weather □ *We sheltered from the rain under a tree.* □ *Thirty people sheltered in the basement.*

2 to protect someone from harm □ *The family were accused of sheltering criminals.*

● **sheltered** /ˈʃeltəd/ ADJECTIVE

1 protected from wind and rain □ *We found a sheltered spot to stop for a picnic.*

2 protected from the difficult or unpleasant things in life 🔁 *She had a very sheltered upbringing.*

3 sheltered **accommodation/housing** places where old or ill people live alone but there is someone to help them if they need it

shelve /ʃelv/ VERB [**shelves, shelving, shelved**] to decide not to do something that had been planned □ *The company shelved plans to expand into Asia.*

shelves /ʃelvz/ PLURAL OF shelf

shepherd /ˈʃepəd/ ► NOUN [plural **shepherds**] someone whose job is to look after sheep

► VERB [**shepherds, shepherding, shepherded**] to control the direction of a group of people □ *She shepherded the children into a side room.*

sherbet /ˈʃɜːbət/ NOUN [plural **sherbets**] a powder with a fruit flavour and a sharp taste

sheriff /ˈʃerɪf/ NOUN [plural **sheriffs**]

1 in the US, the person who is in charge of the police in a particular area

2 in England and Wales, the person who represents the king or queen in a particular area

3 in Scotland, a judge

sherry /ˈʃeri/ NOUN, NO PLURAL a type of strong Spanish wine

she's /ʃiːz/ a short way to say and write she is or she has □ *She's my friend.* □ *She's always been my friend.*

shield /ʃiːld/ ► NOUN [plural **shields**]

1 a large, flat object that is carried to protect someone's body from an attack □ *They were faced by police carrying riot shields.*

2 a prize for winning a competition in the shape of a shield

3 something that protects someone or something from harm or danger □ *a heat shield*

► VERB [**shields, shielding, shielded**] to protect someone or something from harm or danger □ *He had his hand over his eyes, shielding them from the strong sun.*

shift /ʃɪft/ ► VERB [**shifts, shifting, shifted**]

1 to move something or to change position □ *Tom shifted uncomfortably in his seat.* □ *She shifted her weight from foot to foot.*

2 to change something from one state, subject, etc. to another □ *Aid workers are shifting their attention from emergency help to long-term planning.*

► NOUN [plural **shifts**]

1 a change from one thing to another □ *This represents a major shift in policy.*

2 the period of time when one group of people work 🔁 *The miners worked 12-hour shifts.* 🔁 *Who's on the night shift this week?*

3 a simple, loose dress

shift key /ˈʃɪft kiː/ NOUN [plural **shift keys**] the key on a computer that lets you write capital letters (=large letters, for example at the beginning of sentences). A computing word.

shifty /ˈʃɪfti/ ADJECTIVE [**shiftier, shiftiest**] looking or behaving in a way that seems dishonest □ *The younger man looked a little shifty.*

shilling /ˈʃɪlɪŋ/ NOUN [plural **shillings**] an old British coin worth five pence

shimmer /ˈʃɪmə(r)/ VERB [**shimmers, shimmering, shimmered**] to shine with a moving light □ *The sea shimmered in the afternoon sun.*

shin /ʃɪn/ NOUN [plural **shins**] the front part of your leg below your knee

shine /ʃaɪn/ ► VERB [**shines, shining, shone**]

1 to send out or reflect light 🔁 *The sun's shining - let's eat outside.* □ *We could see the lights of the city shining below us.*

2 to point a light on something □ *Don't shine your torch in my face.*

3 to be bright and shiny □ *She had polished the copper pans until they shone.*
4 to be very good at something □ *Lorna really shone in the gymnastics competition.*
▶ NOUN, NO PLURAL
1 a bright and shiny appearance □ *Julie's hair had a beautiful shine.*
2 the act of rubbing something until it is shiny □ *Do you want me to give your shoes a shine?*

shingle /ˈʃɪŋɡəl/ NOUN, NO PLURAL a lot of small stones on a beach or near a river

shingles /ˈʃɪŋɡəlz/ NOUN, NO PLURAL a disease that causes painful red spots on an area of your skin

shining /ˈʃaɪnɪŋ/ ADJECTIVE a shining example of something someone or something that is very good at something □ *She's a shining example of growing old gracefully.*

shiny /ˈʃaɪnɪ/ ADJECTIVE [shinier, shiniest] with a smooth surface that reflects light □ *shiny hair* □ *a shiny new bicycle*

ship /ʃɪp/ ▶ NOUN [plural ships] a large boat that carries passengers or goods on sea journeys □ *Her ship sails from Southampton tomorrow.* □ *They travelled from South Africa by ship.*
▶ VERB [ships, shipping, shipped] to carry something somewhere on a ship or in another vehicle □ *The waste is shipped abroad for disposal.* □ *You order was shipped this morning.*

shipment /ˈʃɪpmənt/ NOUN [plural shipments]
a quantity of goods sent by ship □ *We're expecting another shipment of the consoles next week.*
the sending of goods from one place to another □ *I'll organize shipment of your order.*

shipping /ˈʃɪpɪŋ/ NOUN, NO PLURAL
the business of sending goods from one place to another □ *a shipping company*
ships and boats considered as a group □ *The rocks are a danger to shipping.*

-ship /ʃɪp/ SUFFIX -ship is added to the end of words to make nouns relating to the relationships between people □ *friendship*

shipshape /ˈʃɪpʃeɪp/ ADJECTIVE tidy and in order

shipwreck /ˈʃɪprek/ NOUN [plural shipwrecks] a ship that has been destroyed or sunk, especially by hitting rocks

shipwrecked /ˈʃɪprekt/ ADJECTIVE involved in a shipwreck □ *shipwrecked sailors* □ *a shipwrecked tanker*

shipyard /ˈʃɪpjɑːd/ NOUN [plural shipyards] a place where ships are built and repaired

shirk /ʃɜːk/ VERB [shirks, shirking, shirked] to avoid doing something that you should do □ *Bill never shirked his responsibilities as a father.*

shirker /ˈʃɜːkə(r)/ NOUN [plural shirkers] someone who avoids work, a responsibility or a duty

shirt /ʃɜːt/ NOUN [plural shirts] a piece of clothing for the top half of your body, often made from cotton, with long or short sleeves, a collar, and buttons down the front

shiver /ˈʃɪvə(r)/ ▶ VERB [shivers, shivering, shivered] to shake slightly because you are cold or frightened □ *She shivered in her flimsy cotton dress.*
▶ NOUN [plural shivers] a shake that goes through your body when you are cold or frightened □ *A shiver of terror went down his spine.*
• **shivery** /ˈʃɪvəri/ ADJECTIVE shivering, because you are cold or ill □ *Daisy's hot and shivery and has a nasty cough.*

shoal /ʃəʊl/ NOUN [plural shoals] a large group of fish swimming together

shock /ʃɒk/ ▶ NOUN [plural shocks]
1 no plural a strong and unpleasant reaction you have when something bad happens that you do not expect □ *The whole town is in shock at the news of the closures.* ⊞ *You gave me such a shock bursting in like that!* ⊞ *I got quite a shock when I saw the bill.*
2 something that happens and makes you very surprised and upset □ *The news of his arrest was a terrible shock to his family.*
3 no plural a serious medical condition when you feel very weak because of an injury to your body ⊞ *He had lost so much blood that he went into shock.*
4 a sudden violent shake or movement, for example caused by a crash or an explosion □ *The shock of the impact threw us all forward.*
5 a current of electricity that passes through your body ⊞ *I got an electric shock when I unplugged the iron.*
▶ VERB [shocks, shocking, shocked]
1 to surprise and upset someone very much □ *I was shocked to see how ill he looked.*
2 to say or do something to embarrass or disgust someone □ *Some young artists deliberately set out to shock the public.*

shock absorber /ˈʃɒk əbˈsɔːbə(r)/ NOUN [plural shock absorbers] a device fitted to a car's wheels to make travelling over rough ground more comfortable

shocking /ˈʃɒkɪŋ/ ADJECTIVE
1 making you feel surprised and upset □ *The news report contained some shocking scenes of the war.*
2 very bad □ *The weather's been shocking this summer.*

shoddy /ˈʃɒdi/ ADJECTIVE [shoddier, shoddiest] not very well made or made with poor quality materials □ *shoddy workmanship*

shoe /ʃuː/ NOUN [plural shoes] something made of leather or a similar material that you wear on your foot □ *high-heeled shoes* ⊞ *a pair of shoes* □ *a shoe shop*

shoelace /'ʃu:leɪs/ NOUN [plural **shoelaces**] a thin piece of material or leather tied through holes in a shoe to fasten it □ *He bent down to fasten his shoelace.*

shoestring /'ʃu:strɪŋ/ NOUN **on a shoestring** spending or having very little money □ *They manage to run the youth club on a shoestring.*

shone /ʃɒn/ PAST TENSE AND PAST PARTICIPLE OF **shine**

shoo /ʃu:/ EXCLAMATION used when you want to chase a person or animal away

shook /ʃʊk/ PAST TENSE OF **shake**

shoot /ʃu:t/ ► VERB [**shoots, shooting, shot**]
1 to fire a gun or other weapon □ *I shot an arrow in the air.* □ *Stop or I'll shoot!*
2 to kill or injure a person or animal with a gun □ *He had been shot three times in the chest.* ⊞ *A passer-by was shot dead in the incident.*
3 to go somewhere very quickly □ *The rocket shot up into the air.* □ *Pain shot through his body.*
4 in games like football, basketball, etc., to kick, hit or throw the ball to try to score a point or points □ *He shot at goal but the ball went wide.* □ *'Shoot!' the crowd shouted.*
5 to make a film or video, or take a photograph □ *They're shooting some scenes at Alnwick Castle.*
♦ PHRASAL VERB **shoot up** if a price, rate or amount shoots up, it increases a lot very quickly □ *Food prices have shot up in the last six months.*
► NOUN [plural **shoots**]
1 a new part of a plant or a very young plant □ *bamboo shoots*
2 when someone takes photographs or makes a film □ *a fashion shoot*
● **shooting** /'ʃu:tɪŋ/ NOUN [plural **shootings**]
1 a situation when someone is shot with a gun □ *There's been a fatal shooting in South London.*
2 the sport of hunting animals or birds with a gun □ *grouse shooting*

shooting star /'ʃu:tɪŋ 'stɑ:(r)/ NOUN [plural **shooting star**] a piece of rock that burns in the Earth's atmosphere, making a line of bright light in the night sky

shop /ʃɒp/ ► NOUN [plural **shops**] a place where goods are sold or a particular service is provided □ *a flower shop* □ *We spent the afternoon going around the shops at the mall.*
► VERB [**shops, shopping, shopped**] to buy things in shops □ *I hate shopping for clothes.*

shopaholic /ʃɒpə'hɒlɪk/ NOUN [plural **shopaholics**] someone who loves shopping and spends too much time and money on it

shop assistant /'ʃɒp ə'sɪstənt/ NOUN [plural **shop assistants**] someone who sells things and looks after customers in a shop

shopkeeper /'ʃɒp,ki:pə(r)/ NOUN [plural **shopkeepers**] someone who owns or manages a shop

shoplifter /'ʃɒp,lɪftə(r)/ NOUN [plural **shoplifters**] someone who steals things from shops
● **shoplifting** /'ʃɒp,lɪftɪŋ/ NOUN, NO PLURAL the crime of stealing things from shops

shopper /'ʃɒpə(r)/ NOUN [plural **shoppers**] someone who goes to shops or is shopping □ *We had to push through crowds of Saturday shoppers.*

shopping /'ʃɒpɪŋ/ NOUN, NO PLURAL
1 the activity of going around shops to buy things ⊞ *Let's go shopping tomorrow.*
2 the things you buy at the shops □ *Can you get the shopping out of the boot?*

shopping center /'ʃɒpɪŋ 'sentə(r)/ NOUN [plural **shopping centers**] the US phrase for **shopping centre**

shopping centre /'ʃɒpɪŋ 'sentə(r)/ NOUN [plural **shopping centres**] an area or large building with a lot of different shops

shore /ʃɔ:(r)/ NOUN [plural **shores**] the area of land next to the sea or next to a lake

shorn /ʃɔ:n/ PAST PARTICIPLE OF **shear**

short /ʃɔ:t/ ► ADJECTIVE [**shorter, shortest**]
1 small in height, length or distance □ *a short skirt* □ *The school is a short walk from here.* □ *She has short hair.* □ *My brother is very short.*
2 continuing for a small period of time □ *We watched a short film about whales.* □ *We'll take a short break now.*
3 not having many words or pages □ *Can you give us a short description of the house?* □ *It's quite a short book.*
4 not having enough of something □ **+ of** *The troops are short of equipment.* ⊞ *Water was in short supply.*
5 if someone is short with you, they speak in a rude, angry way, not using many words
6 be short for something to be a shorter way of saying or writing something □ *'Jon' is short for 'Jonathan'.*
➡ go to a short **fuse**, in the **long/short run**
► ADVERB
1 not having enough of something □ *We are three players short.* ⊞ *I won't let my children go short.* ⊞ *Our supplies were beginning to run short.*
2 not reaching a particular level, quality or position ⊞ *My ball stopped slightly short of the last hole.* ⊞ *behaviour fell short of the standards required.*
3 short of something without doing something □ *Short of locking him in his room, I don't know how to stop him staying out late.*
4 cut something short to end something before it's finished □ *We cut short our holiday to go and help.*
➡ go to **stop short of something**
► NOUN
1 in short something you say before you say the main fact or facts about something you have been talking about □ *In short, the whole holiday was a disaster.*
2 for short being a short form of a word □ *I'm Alistair, but you can call me Al for short.*
● **shortage** /'ʃɔ:tɪdʒ/ NOUN [plural **shortages**] when

there is not enough of something □ *People in the region face severe food shortages.*

● **shortness** /'ʃɔ:tnɪs/ NOUN, NO PLURAL **shortness of breath** when you feel that you cannot breathe in enough air

shortbread /'ʃɔ:tbred/ NOUN, NO PLURAL a rich sweet biscuit made from flour, sugar and butter

short circuit /ʃɔ:t 'sɜ:kɪt/ NOUN [plural **short circuits**] when a bad connection in a piece of electrical equipment stops it from working

short-circuit VERB [**short-circuits, short-circuiting, short-circuited**] to have a short circuit

shortcoming /'ʃɔ:t,kʌmɪŋ/ NOUN [plural **shortcomings**] a fault in someone or something □ *Whatever her shortcomings as a teacher, the children love her.*

short cut /ʃɔ:t 'kʌt/ NOUN [plural **short cuts**]
1 a quicker way of travelling between two places □ *I took a short cut home across the fields.*
2 a way of doing something that saves time and effort □ *I'm afraid it must be done this way; there are no short cuts.*
3 a picture or a group of keys on a computer that allow you to do something quickly. A computing word.

shorten /'ʃɔ:tən/ VERB [**shortens, shortening, shortened**] to make something shorter or to become shorter □ *We're working hard to shorten the waiting list for the operation.* □ *The days are shortening.*

shortfall /'ʃɔ:tfɔ:l/ NOUN [plural **shortfalls**]
1 a failure to reach the level or amount expected or needed □ *A shortfall in the grain harvest has caused prices to rise.*
2 the amount by which something is less than you expected or needed it to be □ *There's a shortfall of £3 million which can't be accounted for.*

short form /ʃɔ:t 'fɔ:m/ NOUN [plural **short forms**] a word made from two words that have been joined together and some letters missed out. An apostrophe places the missing letters. For example, *don't* is a short form of 'do not'.

shorthand /'ʃɔ:thænd/ NOUN, NO PLURAL a fast way of writing what someone is saying by using symbols □ *He's taking a shorthand and typing course.*

shortlist /'ʃɔ:tlɪst/ ► NOUN [plural **shortlists**] a list of people or things that are being considered for a job, prize, etc., chosen from a much larger number □ *He made the shortlist but didn't get the job.*
► VERB [**shortlists, shortlisting, shortlisted**] to put someone on a shortlist □ *He has been shortlisted for the post of chief executive.*

short-lived /ʃɔ:t'lɪvd/ ADJECTIVE lasting only for a short time □ *Their joy was short-lived.*

shortly /'ʃɔ:tlɪ/ ADVERB
1 soon □ *We'll shortly be arriving at Waverley Station.*
2 shortly before/after within a short period of time before or after something □ *The bomb exploded shortly before midday.*
3 in a rude, angry way □ *'I can't help you,' the manager said shortly.*

shorts /ʃɔ:ts/ PLURAL NOUN
1 short trousers that stop above your knees □ *a pair of shorts*
2 a mainly US word for underwear for men

short-sighted /ʃɔ:t'saɪtɪd/ ADJECTIVE
1 unable to see things clearly unless they are very close to you □ *The clinic offers laser treatment to short-sighted patients.*
2 not thinking about what is likely to happen in the future □ *The company was criticized for its short-sighted planning.*

short-tempered /ʃɔ:t'tempəd/ ADJECTIVE a short-tempered person gets angry very easily

short-term /ʃɔ:t'tɜ:m/ ADJECTIVE lasting for only a short time □ *Dad's short-term memory is poor.* □ *Borrowing a striker from another club provided a short-term solution to the problem.*

shot /ʃɒt/ ► NOUN [plural **shots**]
1 the act of firing a gun or the sound of it being fired □ *I heard a shot out in the alley.* 🔊 *Someone took a shot at me!*
2 an informal word meaning a chance or attempt to do something □ *It's Murray's first shot at the Wimbledon title.* 🔊 *I didn't think I'd get the job, but I gave it a shot anyway.*
3 a kick, hit or throw of the ball to try to score a point or points □ *It was an excellent shot that just missed the goal.*
4 a photograph or an image in a film □ *I managed to get some good shots of the mountains.*
5 a small amount of medicine that is put into your body through a needle □ *a shot of morphine*
6 a heavy metal ball that is thrown in a sports event
7 like a shot very quickly □ *If they offered me the right price, I'd sell the house like a shot.*
► PAST TENSE AND PAST PARTICIPLE OF **shoot**

shotgun /'ʃɒtgʌn/ NOUN [plural **shotguns**] a type of long gun used for hunting animals and birds

shot put /ʃɒt ,pʊt/ NOUN, NO PLURAL **the shot put** a sports event in which people throw a heavy metal ball as far as possible

● **shot putter** /ʃɒt ,pʊtə(r)/ NOUN [plural **shot putters**] someone who puts the shot

should /ʃʊd/ MODAL VERB
1 used to say what is the best or right thing to do □ *He said that we should all go home.* □ *Should I write her a letter?* □ *You shouldn't eat too much chocolate.*
2 should have used to say what would have been the right thing to do when you have done something different □ *I should have helped him.* □ *I'm late - I should have taken a taxi.*
3 used to say that you expect something to be true □ *The train should be arriving in a couple of minutes.* □ *The children should be asleep by eight.*
4 why should/shouldn't someone do something used to ask in an angry way for a reason □ *Why should I be the one to apologize?*

shoulder /ˈʃəʊldə(r)/ ▶ NOUN [plural **shoulders**]
1 one of the two parts of your body between your neck and your arms
2 a piece of meat that includes the top of the animal's front leg □ *a shoulder of lamb*
▶ VERB [**shoulders, shouldering, shouldered**] to take responsibility for something □ *Kath had to shoulder the burden of caring for her mother.*

shoulder bag /ˈʃəʊldə ˈbæg/ NOUN [plural **shoulder bags**] a bag that you can put over your shoulder

shoulder blade /ˈʃəʊldə ˈbleɪd/ NOUN [plural **shoulder blades**] either of the two flat bones at the top of your back below each shoulder

shoulder strap /ˈʃəʊldə ˈstræp/ NOUN [plural **shoulder straps**]
1 a thin piece of cloth that goes over your shoulder to hold up clothes such as a dress □ *Katie was wearing a black dress with thin shoulder straps.*
2 a thin piece of leather or cloth attached to a bag, that you can carry over your shoulder

shouldn't /ˈʃʊdənt/ a short way to say and write should not □ *You shouldn't have waited out in the rain.*

should've /ˈʃʊdəv/ a short way to say and write should have □ *You should've seen him!*

shout /ʃaʊt/ ▶ VERB [**shouts, shouting, shouted**] to say something very loudly or to make a loud noise with your voice □ *Someone was shouting my name.* □ *There's no need to shout.* □ *+ at* *She's always shouting at the children.*
◆ PHRASAL VERB **shout something out** to say something loudly □ *Don't all shout out the answers at once!*
▶ NOUN [plural **shouts**] a loud cry or call □ *There were shouts of approval from the crowd.*

shove /ʃʌv/ ▶ VERB [**shoves, shoving, shoved**]
1 to push someone or something hard or roughly □ *Someone shoved me in the back.*
2 to put something somewhere quickly and without care □ *I shoved a few clothes in a suitcase and left.*
▶ NOUN [plural **shoves**] a hard or rough push ⊞ *I gave him a shove and he fell into the pool.*

shovel /ˈʃʌvəl/ ▶ NOUN [plural **shovels**] a tool for digging or moving earth, sand, snow, etc. □ *a garden shovel*
▶ VERB [**shovels, shovelling** or US **shoveling, shovelled** or US **shoveled**] to move earth, sand, snow, etc. using a shovel □ *I helped Dad shovel the snow off the drive.*

show /ʃəʊ/ ▶ VERB [**shows, showing, showed, shown**]
1 to prove that something exists or is true □ *+ that* *The evidence shows that he could not have committed the crime.* □ *Polls show an increase in support for the president.* ⊞ *This incident shows why it is important to follow safety regulations.*
2 to allow someone to see something or to cause them to see it □ *Show me your new bike.* □ *Young*
people were shown images of knife wounds. □ *His website shows pictures of him with his family.*
3 to allow someone to watch you doing something so that they learn how to do it □ *Can you show me how to work the DVD player?*
4 to tell someone where to go or where someone is, by explaining, pointing or taking them there □ *I showed her where to put her coat.* □ *+ to* *I'll show you to your room*
5 to give information about something □ *This timetable shows all the trains to London.*
6 to express your feelings □ *I try to show an interest in his work.* □ *The man showed no emotion as the judge read his sentence.*
7 to be able to be noticed □ *The scar hardly shows.* □ *I tried not to let my disappointment show.*
◆ PHRASAL VERBS **show someone around/round (something)** to take someone to all the parts of a place so that they can see it for the first time □ *The children showed me around the gardens.* **show someone in** to bring someone into a room, usually to meet people **show off** to behave in a way that makes people notice you, or to talk a lot about something that you own, because you want people to admire you □ *He's always showing off about his car* **show something/someone off** to show something or someone to other people because you are proud of them □ *She likes to show off her legs in short skirts.* **show someone out** to take someone to the door when they are going to leave **show up** to arrive □ *She showed up an hour late.* **show someone up** to do something that embarrasses someone □ *Dad always shows me up in front of my friends.*
▶ NOUN [plural **shows**]
1 a performance in the theatre or on radio or television □ *He is starring in a new comedy show on the BBC*
2 an event where people or businesses can show things to the public □ *We went to a boat show.* □ *a fashion show*
3 when people express their feelings or opinions □ *the workers walked out in a show of support for the sacked colleagues.* □ *Six ships were sent to the region in a show of force.*
4 on show able to be seen □ *Some of her statues are on show in New York.*
5 for show (a) in order for people to look at, not use □ *The antique glasses are just for show.* (b) in order to create a particular, often false, appearance □ *All that sports gear is just for show - she never does any exercise.*

showbiz /ˈʃəʊbɪz/ NOUN, NO PLURAL an informal way of saying or writing show business □ *a showbiz magazine*

show business /ˈʃəʊ ˈbɪznɪs/ NOUN, NO PLURAL the entertainment business, including films, theatre, radio and television □ *Thousands of kids dream of a career in show business.*

showcase /ˈʃəʊkeɪs/ ▶ NOUN [plural **showcases**] a situation or event that shows the qualities and skills of a person or thing □ *The fair is a showcase for local* and crafts. □ *The competition offers a showcase of British talent.*

▶ VERB [**showcases, showcasing, showcased**] to be designed to show the qualities and skills of a person or thing □ *The concert will showcase new local bands.*

showdown /ˈʃəʊdaʊn/ NOUN [*plural* **showdowns**] a big argument or meeting to end a disagreement □ *Management and unions seem to be heading for a showdown.*

shower /ˈʃaʊə(r)/ ▶ NOUN [*plural* **showers**]
1 a piece of bathroom equipment that produces a flow of water that you stand under to wash yourself □ *Adam's in the shower.*
2 an act of washing yourself under a shower 🕀 *I had a shower to cool off.*
3 a short period of rain □ *We got caught in a shower.*
4 a lot of small things falling through the air □ *The fire sent out a shower of sparks.*

▶ VERB [**showers, showering, showered**]
1 to wash your body under a shower □ *Alex quickly showered and got ready for the party.*
2 to give someone a large number or amount of things □ *He showered her with expensive gifts.*
3 to cover someone or something with a lot of falling pieces □ *The square was showered with debris after the blast.*

showery /ˈʃaʊəri/ ADJECTIVE with short periods of rain □ *Tomorrow it will be showery in the south.*

showjumping /ˈʃəʊdʒʌmpɪŋ/ NOUN, NO PLURAL a competitive sport in which people go over series of jumps on horses

shown /ʃəʊn/ PAST PARTICIPLE OF show

show-off /ˈʃəʊɒf/ NOUN [*plural* **show-offs**] someone who behaves in a way that makes people notice them, or talks a lot about something that they own, because they want people to admire them □ *I can't stand her. She's such a show-off.*

showroom /ˈʃəʊruːm/ NOUN [*plural* **showrooms**] a place where people can look at the things that are on sale □ *a car showroom*

showy /ˈʃəʊi/ ADJECTIVE [**showier, showiest**] attracting attention, for example by being big and bright, often in a way that people disapprove of

shrank /ʃræŋk/ PAST TENSE OF shrink

shrapnel /ˈʃræpnəl/ NOUN, NO PLURAL pieces of metal that fly out in all directions when a bomb explodes □ *A piece of shrapnel hit him in the thigh.*

shred /ʃred/ ▶ NOUN [*plural* **shreds**]
1 a small, thin piece that has been cut or torn from something □ *shreds of paper* 🕀 *His shirt was torn to shreds.*
2 a very small amount of something □ *They didn't have a shred of evidence to link him to the crime.*
• **in shreds** badly damaged or completely destroyed □ *By this time her marriage was in shreds.*

▶ VERB [**shreds, shredding, shredded**] to tear or cut something into very small, thin pieces □ *Shred the lettuce finely.*

shrewd /ʃruːd/ ADJECTIVE [**shrewder, shrewdest**] clever and showing good judgment □ *a shrewd guess* □ *He was a shrewd politician.*

shriek /ʃriːk/ ▶ VERB [**shrieks, shrieking, shrieked**] to make a loud high noise or speak in a loud high voice because you are afraid, excited, etc. □ *She shrieked when she saw the mouse.* □ *'Watch out!' he shrieked.*

▶ NOUN [*plural* **shrieks**] the noise of a person or animal shrieking □ *Shrieks of laughter came from the games room.*

shrill /ʃrɪl/ ADJECTIVE a shrill sound is high, loud and unpleasant □ *a shrill voice*

shrimp /ʃrɪmp/ NOUN [*plural* **shrimps** or **shrimp**] a small sea creature with a shell that turns pink when it is cooked

shrine /ʃraɪn/ NOUN [*plural* **shrines**] a religious place where people go to pray, often because it has something to do with a holy person □ *a shrine to the Virgin Mary*

shrink /ʃrɪŋk/ VERB [**shrinks, shrinking, shrank, shrunk**]
1 to get smaller or to make something smaller in size, amount or value □ *My sweater shrank in the wash.* □ *The number of honey bees has shrunk dramatically.*
2 to move away from something because you are shocked or frightened □ *She shrank back, terrified of the snarling animal.*
♦ PHRASAL VERB **shrink from something** to avoid doing something because you find it unpleasant □ *He did not shrink from his duty.*

shrivel /ˈʃrɪvəl/ VERB [**shrivels, shrivelling** or US **shriveling, shrivelled** or US **shriveled**] to become smaller and drier □ *The leaves of the plant will shrivel in strong sunlight.*

shroud /ʃraʊd/ ▶ NOUN [*plural* **shrouds**] a cloth wrapped around a dead body □ *the Turin shroud*
▶ VERB [**shrouds, shrouding, shrouded**] to cover something completely □ *The hills were shrouded in mist.*

shrub /ʃrʌb/ NOUN [*plural* **shrubs**] a small bush
• **shrubbery** /ˈʃrʌbəri/ NOUN [*plural* **shrubberies**] an area in a garden where shrubs are grown

shrug /ʃrʌg/ ▶ VERB [**shrugs, shrugging, shrugged**] to raise and lower your shoulders in a movement that shows you do not know something or that you do not care about it 🕀 *She shrugged her shoulders and said, 'I don't know.'*
♦ PHRASAL VERB **shrug something off**
1 to show that something does not worry you □ *He shrugged off claims that he had lost the support of the party.*
2 to deal with something easily □ *He soon managed to shrug off his injury.*

▶ NOUN [*plural* **shrugs**] a quick up and down movement of your shoulders □ *'If you like,' she said with a shrug.*

shrunk /ʃrʌŋk/ PAST PARTICIPLE OF shrink

shrunken /ˈʃrʌŋkən/ ADJECTIVE smaller than before or than normal □ *a shrunken old man*

shudder /'ʃʌdə(r)/ ▶ VERB [shudders, shuddering, shuddered]
1 to shake suddenly, usually because of shock or disgust □ *She shuddered when she thought of his injuries.*
2 to shake violently □ *The whole house shuddered as the lorry passed.*
▶ NOUN [plural shudders] a sudden shaking movement □ *'Don't remind me!' she said with a shudder.*

shuffle /'ʃʌfəl/ VERB [shuffles, shuffling, shuffled]
1 to walk slowly, sliding your feet along the ground without lifting them □ *The old woman shuffled slowly into the hall.*
2 to move your body because you feel nervous, bored or uncomfortable □ *The audience were beginning to shuffle around in their seats.*
3 to mix up a set of playing cards before playing a game □ *Whose turn is it to shuffle?*

shun /ʃʌn/ VERB [shuns, shunning, shunned] to deliberately ignore or avoid someone or something □ *He's a great actor but has always shunned the limelight.*

shunt /ʃʌnt/ VERB [shunts, shunting, shunted]
1 to move people or things to another place, especially to avoid having to deal with them □ *Toxic waste was shunted all around Europe.*
2 to move a train from one track to another

shush /ʃʊʃ/ EXCLAMATION used to tell someone to be quiet □ *'Shush! There's someone coming!'*

shut /ʃʌt/ ▶ VERB [shuts, shutting, shut]
1 to close something or to become closed □ *Could you please shut the window?* □ *I heard the door shut as he left.* □ *She shut her eyes and tried to remember his face.*
2 to close a business for the day or for a short period of time □ *The shop shuts at 6 every evening.*
3 to put someone or something in a place so that they cannot go anywhere else □ *Can you shut the dogs outside?*
◆ PHRASAL VERBS **shut someone/something away** to put someone or something in a place they cannot get out of □ *He should be shut away in prison.* **shut (something) down 1** if a business, factory, shop etc. shuts down, or if someone shuts it down, it closes □ *The factory shut down several years ago.* **2** to stop a machine from working **shut someone/something in (something)** to put a person or an animal in a place they cannot get out of □ *We shut the rabbit in its cage.* **shut something off** to stop a machine from working or power or water from flowing □ *Shut off the electricity at the mains.* **shut someone/something out** to close a door, gate, etc. to stop a person or animal entering a place □ *I had to close the window to shut out the flies.* **shut (someone) up** an informal word meaning to stop talking or make someone stop talking □ *I wish he'd shut up for once.* □ *Once she gets on to the old days, nothing will shut her up.* **shut someone/something up** to keep a person or

animal in a place □ *I've been shut up in the house all day.*
▶ ADJECTIVE
1 closed □ *All the windows were shut.*
2 if a business is shut, it has closed for the day or for a short period of time □ *The swimming pool is shut for repairs.*

shutter /'ʃʌtə(r)/ NOUN [plural shutters]
1 a wooden or metal cover for a window that can be opened or closed
2 the moving part inside a camera, which opens for a moment when a photograph is taken

shuttle /'ʃʌtəl/ ▶ NOUN [plural shuttles] an air, train or other transport service that goes backwards and forwards between two places □ *There's a shuttle bus to the airport.*
▶ VERB [shuttles, shuttling, shuttled] to go backward and forwards between two places

shuttlecock /'ʃʌtəlkɒk/ NOUN [plural shuttlecocks] the object that is hit in the sport of badminton

shy /ʃaɪ/ ▶ ADJECTIVE [shyer, shyest]
1 nervous and not confident when meeting and speaking to people 🖲 *My brother is painfully shy.*
2 embarrassed or nervous about doing something **of/about doing something** *Oliver's never been shy of saying what he thinks.*
▶ VERB [shies, shying, shied] if a horse shies, it turns to the side suddenly because it has been frightened
◆ PHRASAL VERB **shy away from something** to avoid something or avoid doing something because you are frightened or nervous □ *She had always shied away from talking about her childhood.*
● **shyly** /'ʃaɪli/ ADVERB in a shy way □ *She smiled shyly*
● **shyness** /'ʃaɪnɪs/ NOUN, NO PLURAL the state of being shy

SI /ˌes'aɪ/ ABBREVIATION an abbreviation used to describe units of measurement. A maths and physics word. □ *SI units*

sibling /'sɪblɪŋ/ NOUN [plural siblings] a brother or sister □ *Most younger children tend to copy their older siblings.*

sick /sɪk/ ▶ ADJECTIVE [sicker, sickest]
1 feel sick to feel as if you are going to vomit □ *smell made me feel physically sick.*
2 be sick to vomit 🖲 *He was violently sick.*
3 sick people or animals are ill □ *He looks after his mother.* 🖲 *I got sick on holiday.*
4 off sick not at work because you are ill
5 to do with time when you are not at work because you are ill □ *sick leave* □ *sick pay*
6 sick of something/someone an informal phrase meaning angry about something/someone or bored with something/someone □ *I'm sick of having to do his work for him.* □ *I'm sick of salad - can't we have a hot meal?*
7 make someone sick (a) to make someone angry

and upset □ *It makes me sick the way she expects everyone to do what she wants all the time.* (b) to make someone very jealous □ *She does everything well - it makes me sick!*

8 very unpleasant and cruel □ *a sick joke*

▶ NOUN **the sick** people who are ill □ *The sick were taken to hospital.*

• **sicken** /'sɪkən/ VERB [**sickens, sickening, sickened**]
1 to make someone feel upset and shocked □ *I was sickened by their cruelty.*
2 to become ill □ *The child began to sicken.*

• **sickening** /'sɪkənɪŋ/ ADJECTIVE very unpleasant and shocking □ *sickening violence*

sick leave /'sɪk 'liːv/ NOUN, NO PLURAL a period when you do not go to work because you are ill □ *Natasha's on sick leave at the moment.*

sickly /'sɪklɪ/ ADJECTIVE [**sicklier, sickliest**]
1 If food is sickly, it makes you feel ill because it contains too much sugar, cream, etc. □ *The cake was a bit sickly.*
2 someone who is sickly is often ill or gets ill easily □ *a sickly child*

sickness /'sɪknɪs/ NOUN, NO PLURAL
1 when someone is ill □ *He had a lot of time off work due to sickness.*
2 an illness in which you vomit □ *These tablets may cause sickness.*

side /saɪd/ NOUN [**plural sides**]
1 the outer surface or edge of something, especially one that is not the top, bottom, front or back □ *He built a house by the side of the river.* □ *Go round the side of the building.* □ *Write on both sides of the paper.* □ *We sat on opposite sides of the table.* ⊞ *The two soldiers stood on either side of (=both sides of) the ring.*
2 one of the parts or areas of something when it is divided □ *In the UK, people drive on the left hand side of the road.* □ *We live in the north side of town.* ⊞ *Australia is on the other side of the world.*
3 the area of something that is near the edge □ *Could you move to the side, please?* □ *He put the pasta to one side and started making the sauce.*
4 an edge or flat surface of a shape □ *How many sides does a hexagon have?*
5 the left or right part of someone's body □ *She stood by his side all day.* □ *Could you lie on your side, please?* **side by side** next to each other □ *They sat side by side on the sofa.*
6 one of the people or groups who are arguing □ *Both sides agree that discussions are needed.*
7 if you are on someone's side, you support them in an argument ⊞ *Why do you always take Mum's side?*
8 one of the teams in a competition □ *He was chosen as captain of the England side.*
9 a quality, characteristic or part of a situation □ *I look after the legal side of the business.* □ *There's a nasty side to him.* □ *We could see the funny side of the situation.*

♦ PHRASAL VERB [**sides, siding, sided**] **side with someone** to support someone in an argument □ *Dad always sides with my sister when we argue.*

sideboard /'saɪdbɔːd/ NOUN [**plural sideboards**] a piece of furniture with cupboards and drawers, used for storing plates and glasses

sideburns /'saɪdbɜːnz/ PLURAL NOUN hair that grows on a man's face, in front of his ears

sidecar /'saɪdkɑː(r)/ NOUN [**plural sidecars**] a small vehicle that is attached to the side of a motorcycle for a passenger

side effect /'saɪd ɪ'fekt/ NOUN [**plural side effects**]
1 an unpleasant effect of a drug ⊞ *The drug can have serious side effects.*
2 an extra result of a situation □ *Traffic jams, noise and pollution are the worst side effects of increasing the number of tourists.*

sidekick /'saɪdkɪk/ NOUN [**plural sidekicks**] someone who helps or spends time with a more powerful or important person. An informal word. □ *I couldn't speak to the boss, but I spoke to one of his sidekicks.*

sidelight /'saɪdlaɪt/ NOUN [**plural sidelights**] one of the small lights on the front of a car, next to the main lights

sideline /'saɪdlaɪn/ ▶ NOUN [**plural sidelines**]
1 an extra job in addition to your main job □ *She's a hairdresser with a sideline as a children's entertainer.*
2 the line along each side of a sports field which marks the edge of the playing area
3 the sidelines (a) the area behind the line marking the edge of a playing field □ *The coach was frantically shouting instructions from the sidelines.* (b) a situation where you are not involved in what is happening and do not try to influence it □ *The government were accused of sitting on the sidelines and watching people die of starvation.*

▶ VERB [**sidelines, sidelining, sidelined**]
1 to stop someone talking part in something or being involved in something, often in an unfair way.
□ *Employers were accused of sidelining the unions.*
2 to stop someone being able to play in a sport □ *For the last three months she has been sidelined by a knee injury.*

sidelong /'saɪdlɒŋ/ ADJECTIVE **a sidelong look/ glance** a quick look from the corner of your eye □ *He started to speak, after a sidelong glance at his mother.*

sideshow /'saɪdʃəʊ/ NOUN [**plural sideshows**] a small show or entertainment that is part of a larger, more important show

sidestep /'saɪdstep/ VERB [**sidesteps, sidestepping, sidestepped**]
1 to avoid dealing with something difficult or unpleasant □ *The minister deftly sidestepped the journalist's question.*
2 to avoid someone or something by moving to one side □ *Ronaldo sidestepped the defender and sent a perfect cross to Rooney.*

sidetrack /'saɪdtræk/ VERB [**sidetracks, sidetracking, sidetracked**] to make someone forget what they were talking about or doing and start talking about or doing something else □ *Sorry, I got sidetracked by all this talk of food.*

sidewalk /'saɪdwɔːk/ NOUN [*plural* **sidewalks**] the US word for pavement

sideways /'saɪdweɪz/ ADJECTIVE, ADVERB

1 to, towards or from the side □ *The train lurched and I fell sideways onto the man in the next seat.* □ *I saw him cast a sideways glance at the clock.*

2 with one side facing forward □ *I think the table will go through the door sideways.*

siding /'saɪdɪŋ/ NOUN [*plural* **sidings**] a short length of railway track where trains are kept when they are not being used

sidle /'saɪdəl/ VERB [**sidles, sidling, sidled**] to move somewhere quietly because you do not want to be noticed □ *He sidled up to her and handed her a drink.*

SIDS /sɪdz/ ABBREVIATION sudden infant death syndrome; when a baby suddenly dies in its sleep and the reason is not known

siege /siːdʒ/ NOUN [*plural* **sieges**]

1 a situation in which an army surrounds a place and stops supplies from getting in or people from getting out □ *The port was under siege.*

2 a situation in which people surround a building to complain about something or to force the people inside to come out □ *Police shot the gunman after a 12-hour armed siege of the property.*

siesta /sɪ'estə/ NOUN [*plural* **siestas**] a short sleep in the afternoon, especially in hot countries 🔄 *I decided to take a siesta in my room.*

sieve /sɪv/ ► NOUN [*plural* **sieves**] a round kitchen tool with a bottom made of a wire or plastic net, used to separate larger pieces of a substance, especially food, from liquids or powders

► VERB [**sieves, sieving, sieved**] to put something through a sieve □ *Sieve the stock carefully.*

sift /sɪft/ VERB [**sifts, sifting, sifted**]

1 to pass a substance such as flour or sugar through a sieve to remove larger pieces □ *Sifting the flour will help make a lighter cake.*

2 to look at every part of a place or in every part of documents, etc. in order to find something
□ *Investigators are sifting through the rubble to find the cause of the fire.*

sigh /saɪ/ ► VERB [**sighs, sighing, sighed**] to breathe out noisily, because you feel tired, disappointed, unhappy, etc. □ *She sighed wearily as she looked at the pile of ironing she had to do.*

► NOUN [*plural* **sighs**] a long noisy breath out, often because you are tired, disappointed, unhappy, etc.
□ *'I'm afraid there's still no news,' he said with a sigh.* 🔄 *When Phil finally got home we all breathed a huge sigh of relief.*

sight /saɪt/ NOUN [*plural* **sights**]

1 *no plural* the ability to see □ *He lost his sight in an explosion.*

2 *no plural* when you see something □ *He fainted at*

the sight of blood. 🔄 *I caught sight of him, hurrying round a corner.*

3 *no plural* the place or area you are able to see □ *We watched the ship until it disappeared from sight.* 🔄 *We were soon within sight of land.* 🔄 *We waved until their car was out of sight.*

4 something that you see □ *Foxes are a familiar sight round here.* □ *I'll never forget the sight of all those people waving flags.* □ *Joe and Ben can't stand the sight of each other.*

5 **the sights** interesting places to visit in a country or area □ *He offered to show me the sights of Hong Kong.*

6 an informal word for a person or thing that looks ugly, shocking, silly, untidy, etc. □ *What a sight she is with that bright blue hair!*

♦ IDIOM **set your sights on something** to try to achieve something □ *She has set her sights on Olympic gold.*

➨ go to **lose sight of something**

● **sighted** /'saɪtɪd/ ADJECTIVE sighted people can see □ *the partially sighted*

● **sighting** /'saɪtɪŋ/ NOUN [*plural* **sightings**] when someone sees something, especially something that is hard to find □ *There have been several sightings of the bear.*

sight-read /'saɪtˌriːd/ VERB [**sight-reads, sight-reading, sight-read**] to play or sing music by reading the notes, without having heard or seen the music before

sightseeing /'saɪtˌsiːɪŋ/ NOUN, NO PLURAL travelling around looking at interesting things and places □ *The hotel organized a sightseeing trip to the Roman amphitheatre.*

● **sightseer** /'saɪtˌsiːə(r)/ NOUN [*plural* **sightseers**] someone who goes sightseeing □ *In August the city is full of sightseers.*

sign /saɪn/ ► NOUN [*plural* **signs**]

1 something that shows that something is happening or will happen or that something exists □ **+ of** *There's no sign of spring arriving yet.* □ **+ that** *There are signs that the economy is recovering.* 🔄 *My boss is showing signs of stress.* 🔄 *I can't see much sign of progress.* 🔄 *The fact that he is eating well is a good sign.*

2 an object in a public place with words, symbols or pictures that give information □ *The sign said 'No smoking'.* □ *Follow the signs to the car park.*

3 a movement or a sound that tells someone something, or tells them to do something □ *A glance towards the door was our sign to leave.*

4 a symbol with a particular meaning □ *a dollar sign*

► VERB [**signs, signing, signed**]

1 to write your name on something, for example to agree officially to something, or to prove that something was done by you □ *Please sign the contract and return it to us.* □ *The letter was not signed.* □ *painting is a signed original.*

2 if a sports team signs a player, they make an official agreement that that person to play for them

♦ PHRASAL VERB **sign up** to agree to join an activity

course, etc. □ *I've signed up for a week's rock climbing course.*

signal /ˈsɪgnəl/ ▶ NOUN [*plural* **signals**]
1 a sign, action or sound that sends a message to someone ⊞ *When I give the signal, turn on the music.* □ **+ to do something** *The troops waited for the signal to attack.*
2 a fact, event or action that shows what someone is going to do or what is probably going to happen □ **+ of** *The government is accused of ignoring the signals of a recession.*
3 a piece of equipment that gives information to the driver of a vehicle, especially to tell them whether to stop or go □ *traffic signals*
4 a series of waves of sound or light received by a radio or television □ *We picked up a strong signal from another ship.*
▶ VERB [**signals, signalling** or US **signaling, signalled** or US **signaled**]
1 to make a sign, sound or movement to tell someone something □ *You must signal well before the junction.* □ **+ to** *Jo was signalling to us from across the room.*
2 to show that you are ready or willing to do something □ *The unions have signalled that they will accept the new offer.*
3 to mark or show something that is happening or will happen □ *The birth of her first child signalled a complete change in her life.*

signature /ˈsɪgnətʃə(r)/ NOUN [*plural* **signatures**]
your name, written by you, for example on the bottom of a letter or on a document □ *Someone had forged my signature on the form.*

signature tune /ˈsɪgnətʃə(r) ˈtjuːn/ NOUN [*plural* **signature tunes**] a piece of music that is always played before and after a particular television or radio programme

significance /sɪgˈnɪfɪkəns/ NOUN, NO PLURAL the meaning or importance of something □ *I didn't appreciate the significance of what he said at the time.*
significant /sɪgˈnɪfɪkənt/ ADJECTIVE
1 large or important □ *A significant number of children are failing to reach the required standard.* *She is now recognized as one of the most significant novelists of the 20th century.*
2 having a particular meaning □ *Do you think it's significant that he left no note for his wife?*
significantly /sɪgˈnɪfɪkəntli/ ADVERB
1 by a large amount or in a way that is noticeable *Standards of health are significantly better nowadays.*
2 in a way that has a particular meaning *Significantly, the company has not denied the reports.*
signify /ˈsɪgnɪfaɪ/ VERB [**signifies, signifying, signified**] to have a particular meaning □ *A symbol of a skull and crossbones signifies a poison.*

sign language /ˈsaɪn ˈlæŋgwɪdʒ/ NOUN, NO PLURAL a set of movements made with the hands that is used to communicate with deaf people

signpost /ˈsaɪnpəʊst/ NOUN [*plural* **signposts**] a sign by a road showing which direction to go to get to a particular place
• **signposted** /ˈsaɪnpəʊstɪd/ ADJECTIVE shown with signposts □ *The route is clearly signposted.*

Sikh /siːk/ ▶ NOUN [*plural* **Sikhs**] someone whose religion is Sikhism
▶ ADJECTIVE to do with Sikhs or Sikhism □ *We visited the Sikh temple at Amritsar.*
• **Sikhism** /ˈsiːkɪzəm/ NOUN, NO PLURAL a religion in which people believe in one God, started by Guru Nanak in Punjab in North India

silence /ˈsaɪləns/ ▶ NOUN [*plural* **silences**]
1 *no plural* when it is completely quiet and no sound can be heard □ *For a moment there was absolute silence in the theatre.*
2 a period when there is no sound or no one speaks □ *The players observed two minutes' silence for their former teammate.*
3 when someone refuses to talk about something □ *At last she has broken her silence about her divorce.*
▶ VERB [**silences, silencing, silenced**]
1 to stop someone speaking or something making a noise □ *Her father silenced her with a glare.*
2 to prevent someone from giving their opinion or criticizing you □ *The regime has failed to silence all of its opponents.*
• **silencer** /ˈsaɪlənsə(r)/ NOUN [*plural* **silencers**]
1 an object put on a gun to reduce the noise it makes when it is fired
2 an object fitted to a car to reduce the noise of the engine
• **silent** /ˈsaɪlənt/ ADJECTIVE
1 not speaking or making any noise ⊞ *The crowd fell silent.* □ *They sat in silent contemplation.*
2 completely quiet □ *the silent churchyard*
3 not giving any information about something ⊞ *'You have the right to remain silent,' said the police officer.*
4 a silent letter is one that is written as part of a word, but has no sound when the word is spoken, for example the 'b' in 'lamb'
• **silently** /ˈsaɪləntli/ ADVERB without speaking or making any noise □ *He put the phone down silently.*

silhouette /ˌsɪluːˈet/ NOUN [*plural* **silhouettes**] the dark shape of something seen when there is something light behind it □ *Robert drew the city in silhouette.*
• **silhouetted** /ˌsɪluːˈetɪd/ ADJECTIVE seen in the form of a silhouette □ *I saw a figure approaching, silhouetted against the setting sun.*

silicon /ˈsɪlɪkən/ NOUN, NO PLURAL a chemical element used in electronic devices and for making glass. A chemistry word.

silicon chip /ˈsɪlɪkən ˈtʃɪp/ NOUN [*plural* **silicon chips**] a very small piece of silicon used in computers and other electronic devices

silicone /ˈsɪlɪkəʊn/ NOUN, NO PLURAL a substance formed from silicon and other substances, used in many things such as paints and rubbers. A chemistry word.

silk /sɪlk/ NOUN [*plural* **silks**] a soft smooth cloth made from the very soft thin threads produced by a silkworm □ *The dress was made of ivory silk.* □ *a silk kimono*

• **silken** /ˈsɪlkən/ ADJECTIVE like silk or made from silk □ *silken thread*

silkworm /ˈsɪlkwɜːm/ NOUN [*plural* **silkworms**] a type of caterpillar (=small soft creature) which produces threads that are used to make silk

silky /ˈsɪlki/ ADJECTIVE [**silkier, silkiest**] soft and smooth, like silk □ *silky hair*

sill /sɪl/ NOUN [*plural* **sills**] a horizontal shelf made of wood or stone at the bottom of the opening for a window

silliness /ˈsɪlɪnɪs/ NOUN, NO PLURAL silly behaviour

• **silly** /ˈsɪli/ ADJECTIVE [**sillier, silliest**]
1 showing that you are not intelligent or not thinking about something carefully or seriously □ *a silly mistake* □ *How could you be so silly?*
2 not important or serious □ *She gets so upset over silly little things.*
3 making you look stupid or funny □ *a silly hat*

silt /sɪlt/ NOUN, NO PLURAL sand and mud that are carried along and left behind by flowing water

silver /ˈsɪlvə(r)/ ▶ NOUN [*plural* **silvers**]
1 *no plural* a valuable shiny grey metal, used to make jewellery, etc. □ *This tray is made of solid silver.*
2 a silver medal (=prize for coming second in a competition or race)
▶ ADJECTIVE
1 made of silver □ *a pair of silver earrings*
2 having the colour of silver □ *silver paint*

silver lining /ˈsɪlvə ˈlaɪnɪŋ/ NOUN, NO PLURAL a positive or good part of a bad or unpleasant situation □ *She's very good at finding the silver lining to any setback.*

silver wedding /ˈsɪlvə ˈwedɪŋ/ NOUN [*plural* **silver weddings**] a celebration of 25 years of marriage

silvery /ˈsɪlvəri/ ADJECTIVE looking like silver or silver in colour □ *Birch trees have silvery bark.*

SIM card /ˈsɪm ˈkɑːd/ NOUN [*plural* **SIM cards**] a plastic card inside a mobile phone that stores information such as names and telephone numbers

similar /ˈsɪmɪlə(r)/ ADJECTIVE two things are similar when they are like each other but not exactly the same □ + *to* *An alligator is similar to a crocodile, but smaller.*

• **similarity** /ˌsɪmɪˈlærəti/ NOUN [*plural* **similarities**]
1 the degree to which one thing is like another □ + *to* *Her similarity to her sister is uncanny.* ⏏ *This painting bears no similarity to Waldorf's other work.*

2 a characteristic that two people or things share □ *There are several similarities between the two novels.*

• **similarly** /ˈsɪmɪləli/ ADVERB in the same or a similar way □ *The report makes a comparison of similarly priced MP3 players.*

simile /ˈsɪmɪli/ NOUN [*plural* **similes**] a sentence or phrase in which one thing is described by being compared with another, using *as* or *like*. For example, *Its fleece was white as snow* and *He ran like a hare* are similes

simmer /ˈsɪmə(r)/ VERB [**simmers, simmering, simmered**] to cook food slowly by boiling it very gently

◆ PHRASAL VERB **simmer down** to become calm after being angry or excited □ *It's best to leave him alone until he simmers down.*

simper /ˈsɪmpə(r)/ VERB [**simpers, simpering, simpered**] to smile in a way that looks silly and is not natural

simple /ˈsɪmpəl/ ADJECTIVE [**simpler, simplest**]
1 easy to do, solve or understand □ *a simple sum* □ *The dishwasher came with a set of simple instructions.* □ *This mobile phone is very simple to use.*
2 plain or without any decoration □ *a simple design* □ *I like simple home cooking.*
3 basic or not complicated □ *Stone Age men could make simple tools.* □ *The simple truth is he's too old for the job.*

• **simplicity** /sɪmˈplɪsəti/ NOUN, NO PLURAL
1 being plain, natural or not complicated □ *His work reflects the simplicity of Japanese painting.*
2 being easy to do, solve or understand

simplification /ˌsɪmplɪfɪˈkeɪʃən/ NOUN, NO PLURAL the act of simplifying something

• **simplify** /ˈsɪmplɪfaɪ/ VERB [**simplifies, simplifying, simplified**] to make something easier to do or understand □ *We have tried to simplify the testing process.*

simplistic /sɪmˈplɪstɪk/ ADJECTIVE making a problem or situation seem less complicated or difficult than really is □ *a simplistic argument*

• **simplistically** /sɪmˈplɪstɪkəli/ ADVERB in a simplistic way □ *I think the play has been interpreted too simplistically.*

simply /ˈsɪmpli/ ADVERB
1 only □ *Now, it's simply a question of waiting until something happens.*
2 used to emphasize what you are saying □ *I simply don't understand him!*
3 in a way that is not difficult or complicated □ *I explain it simply so that you all understand.*
4 with no decorations or extra details □ *a simply furnished apartment*

simulate /ˈsɪmjuleɪt/ VERB [**simulates, simulating, simulated**]

1 to make something that seems real but is not □ *The emergency services simulated a major disaster.*
2 to pretend to feel a particular emotion □ *He simulated disgust.*

• **simulation** /ˌsɪmjuˈleɪʃən/ NOUN [*plural* **simulations**]
1 the process of simulating something
2 something that simulates something □ *computer simulations*

• **simulator** /ˈsɪmjuleɪtə(r)/ NOUN [*plural* **simulators**] a machine that simulates how computers operate, used especially to train people to operate aircraft □ *a flight simulator*

simultaneous /ˌsɪməlˈteɪnɪəs/ ADJECTIVE happening or done at exactly the same time □ *a simultaneous translation*

simultaneously /ˌsɪməlˈteɪnɪəslɪ/ ADVERB at exactly the same time □ *The commentary was broadcast simultaneously on the radio.*

sin /sɪn/ NOUN [*plural* **sins**] a very bad thing to do, especially one that breaks a religious law □ *the sin of pride* 🕮 *He felt that he had committed a sin.*

since /sɪns/ ▶ CONJUNCTION

1 from a particular time or event in the past until the present □ *Ann's been a lot happier since she changed jobs.* □ *He's put on weight since I saw him last.*
2 because □ *I decided to go shopping, since I had some free time.*

▶ PREPOSITION

from a particular time in the past until the present □ *The little girl has been missing since Christmas.* □ *We've been living here since 1986.* □ *I haven't spoken to Gretta since last week.*

since when? used to show that you are surprised or annoyed about something □ *Since when did he have the right to tell us what to do?*

▶ ADVERB

from the time that has already been mentioned until the present □ *She joined the choir last month and has been going to practice regularly since.* 🕮 *I came to London in 1995, and I've lived here ever since.*
at a later time than the time first mentioned □ *They met last year and have since become friends.*

sincere /sɪnˈsɪə(r)/ ADJECTIVE

1 honest and saying what you really think □ *I'm never sure he's being sincere with me.*
2 used to emphasize that the feeling you are expressing is real □ *We'd like to offer our sincere thanks to our hosts.*

• **sincerely** /sɪnˈsɪəlɪ/ ADVERB

in a way that is sincere □ *I sincerely hope you're right about this.*

Yours sincerely used at the end of a letter when you have used the name of the person you are writing to

• **sincerity** /sɪnˈserətɪ/ NOUN, NO PLURAL being sincere □ *Nobody could doubt his sincerity.*

sine /saɪn/ NOUN [*plural* **sines**] in a triangle with one angle of 90°, the sine is the length of the side opposite one of the angles of less than 90° divided by the hypotenuse (=longest side). A maths word.

sinew /ˈsɪnjuː/ NOUN [*plural* **sinews**] a type of strong body tissue that joins your muscles to your bones

• **sinewy** /ˈsɪnjuːɪ/ ADJECTIVE a sinewy body is thin with strong muscles

sinful /ˈsɪnful/ ADJECTIVE morally wrong or breaking a religious law □ *It's sinful to throw so much food away.*

• **sinfulness** /ˈsɪnfulnɪs/ NOUN, NO PLURAL being sinful

sing /sɪŋ/ VERB [**sings, singing, sang, sung**]

1 to make musical sounds with your voice □ *She sings in a Gospel choir.* □ *I asked him to sing my favourite song.*
2 birds sing when they make musical sounds

singe /sɪndʒ/ VERB [**singes, singeing, singed**] to burn the surface or edge of something slightly by touching it with something hot □ *I singed the tablecloth with the iron.*

singer /ˈsɪŋə(r)/ NOUN [*plural* **singers**] a person who sings, especially as their job □ *a folk singer*

singing /ˈsɪŋɪŋ/ NOUN, NO PLURAL the activity of making musical sounds with your voice □ *a singing teacher*

single /ˈsɪŋɡəl/ ▶ ADJECTIVE

1 only one □ *I didn't get a single card on my birthday.* □ *A single shelf held all her belongings.*
2 talking about each thing in a group separately 🕮 *He rang me every single day while he was away.*
3 not married □ *a club for single women*
4 for use by one person □ *a single room* □ *a pair of single sheets*
5 a single ticket is used for a journey in one direction
6 a single parent looks after their children on their own □ *a single mother*

▶ NOUN [*plural* **singles**]

1 a ticket for a journey you make in one direction but not back again □ *How much is a single to York?* □ *Two singles to Kings Cross.*
2 a musical CD or record with only one or two songs on it 🕮 *a hit single* (=very popular song)
3 singles in sports like tennis and badminton, a game when one player plays against another □ *The men's singles final is this afternoon.*

◆ PHRASAL VERB [**singles, singling, singled**] **single someone/something out** to choose one person or thing from a group to say good or bad things about □ *Jamie felt he had been singled out for criticism.*

single bed /ˈsɪŋɡəl ˈbed/ NOUN [*plural* **single beds**] a bed for one person

single file /ˈsɪŋɡəl ˈfaɪl/ ▶ NOUN, NO PLURAL a line of people or vehicles one behind the other □ *The soldiers marched in single file.*

▶ ADVERB in one line □ *They walked single file along the narrow ridge.*

single-handed /ˈsɪŋɡəlˈhændɪd/ ADJECTIVE, ADVERB without anyone else's help □ *He carried out the rescue single-handed.*

• **single-handedly** /ˈsɪŋɡəlˈhændɪdli/ ADVERB without anyone else's help □ *He transformed the organization single-handedly.*

single-minded /ˈsɪŋɡəlˈmaɪndɪd/ ADJECTIVE being determined to achieve something

singly /ˈsɪŋɡli/ ADVERB one at a time or separately □ *The flowers grow singly or in clusters.*

singsong /ˈsɪŋsɒŋ/ ADJECTIVE a singsong voice goes up and down like someone singing

singular /ˈsɪŋɡjʊlə(r)/ ▶ ADJECTIVE

1 in grammar, a singular form of a word is the form used to talk about one person, thing or group □ *'Child' is the singular form of 'children'.*
2 very noticeable or unusual □ *He has produced a poem of singular beauty.*
▶ NOUN the singular the form of a noun, pronoun, adjective or verb that you use to talk about one person, thing or group □ *The singular is 'sheep' and the plural is also 'sheep'.*

• **singularly** /ˈsɪŋɡjʊləli/ ADVERB extremely or in a noticeable way □ *He was singularly unprepared for life in the outback.*

sinister /ˈsɪnɪstə(r)/ ADJECTIVE making you feel that something harmful or evil will happen □ *a sinister black figure*

sink /sɪŋk/ ▶ VERB [sinks, sinking, sank, sunk]

1 to drop below the surface of water and move down to the bottom, or to make something do this □ *The boat sank in a storm.* □ *She fell in and sank below the surface of the water.*
2 to move to a lower position or level □ *The sun was sinking towards the horizon.* □ + **into** *He sank to his knees.*
3 to go into or to push something into the surface of something soft □ + **into** *Our feet sank deep into the mud.* □ *The dog sank its teeth into the postman's leg.*
4 if your heart sinks, you feel sad or disappointed
♦ PHRASAL VERBS **sink in** if a fact sinks in, you understand it completely □ *It took a moment for the news to sink in.* **sink something into something** to spend a large amount of money on an activity or a business □ *All her cash was sunk into the company.*
▶ NOUN [plural sinks] a bowl fixed to the wall in a kitchen or bathroom, used for washing in ▣ *She put the dirty cups in the kitchen sink.*

sinner /ˈsɪnə(r)/ NOUN [plural sinners] someone who has committed a sin

sinuous /ˈsɪnjuəs/ ADJECTIVE with a lot of curves □ *the sinuous movement of a snake*

sinus /ˈsaɪnəs/ NOUN [plural sinuses] one of the hollow spaces in the bones in your head that are connected to your nose

• **sinusitis** /ˌsaɪnəˈsaɪtɪs/ NOUN, NO PLURAL an illness in which your sinuses become very painful

sip /sɪp/ ▶ VERB [sips, sipping, sipped] to drink something slowly taking only a small amount at a time □ *Russell sipped his coffee.*
▶ NOUN [plural sips] when you sip a drink ▣ *She took a sip of water.*

siphon /ˈsaɪfən/ ▶ NOUN [plural siphons] a tube used to move a liquid from one container into another
▶ VERB [siphons, siphoning, siphoned]
1 to take something, especially money, from somewhere dishonestly, a small amount at a time □ *They siphoned cash from victims' bank accounts.* □ *They allegedly siphoned off $10 million from aid funds.*
2 to move liquid using a siphon □ *Two men were caught siphoning diesel from a lorry.*

sir /sɜː(r)/ NOUN [plural sirs]

1 a polite way of speaking or writing to a man, especially one you do not know □ *Excuse me, sir. Can I help you?*
2 Dear Sir a way of beginning a formal letter to a man when you do not know his name
3 a title used before the name of a knight (=a man with a high social rank) □ *Sir Paul McCartney*

siren /ˈsaɪərən/ NOUN [plural sirens] a device that makes a very loud noise to warn people of something □ *I heard police sirens outside.*

sirloin /ˈsɜːlɔɪn/ NOUN [plural sirloins] a piece of beef (=meat from a cow) cut from the top of the back of

sister /ˈsɪstə(r)/ NOUN [plural sisters]

1 a girl or a woman who has the same parents as you ▣ *He had two older sisters.* ▣ *She was walking to school with her younger sister.*
2 a female nurse who is in charge of part of a hospital □ *a ward sister*
3 a nun (=a member of a female religious group), often used as a title □ *Sister Dorothy*

• **sisterhood** /ˈsɪstəhʊd/ NOUN [plural sisterhoods]
1 a friendly feeling among women and girls
2 a group of women, especially nuns

sister-in-law /ˈsɪstərɪnlɔː/ NOUN [plural sisters-in-law] your brother's wife, or your husband or wife's sister

sit /sɪt/ VERB [sits, sitting, sat]

1 to be in a position where your weight is supported on your bottom, not your legs □ *I sat next to my friend.* ▣ *Would you please sit still while I get the books out.* □ + **on** *He was sitting on the sofa.* □ + **down** *They were sitting down waiting for me.*
2 to move your body into a position where your weight is supported by your bottom □ *He came in and sat on the floor.* □ + **down** *Sit down now, and get on with your work, please.*
3 to make someone sit somewhere □ *We sat the children on extra cushions.*
4 to be in a particular place without moving or being used □ *There was a big parcel sitting on the kitchen table.* □ *This jam's been sitting on the shelf for months.*

5 if you sit an exam, you do an exam □ *She's sitting her GCSEs next term.*
6 if an official group of people sits, it has a meeting □ *The committee sits on the second Tuesday of each month.*

✦ PHRASAL VERBS **sit about/around** to spend time sitting down and not doing much □ *We've been sitting about chatting all morning.* **sit back** to relax and wait for something to happen □ *Just sit back and enjoy the show.* **sit up 1** to move from a lying position to a sitting position □ *Can you manage to sit up?* **2** to sit with your back straight 🖻 *Sit up straight and pay attention!*

sitcom /'sɪtkɒm/ NOUN [plural **sitcoms**] a television comedy programme that is always in the same place and has the same characters

site /saɪt/ ► NOUN [plural **sites**]
1 a place where something happens or happened, or a place used for a certain purpose □ + *of* *the site of a battle* 🖻 *He works on a construction site.* □ *It is one of the most visited archaeological sites in Europe.* □ *The minister visited the crash site.*
2 a website. A computing word 🖻 *an Internet site* □ *The footage is posted on video sharing sites like YouTube.*
3 **on site** available or happening in an office, factory, etc., not in another place □ *He was treated by the company doctor on site.* □ *There's a small shop on site.*
► VERB [**sites, siting, sited**] to build something in a particular place □ *The factory is sited next to a large housing development.*

sitting room /'sɪtɪŋrum / NOUN [plural **sitting rooms**] a room, usually in a house, for sitting and relaxing in

situate /'sɪtjueɪt/ VERB [**situates, situating, situated**] something is situated somewhere, it is in that place or position □ *The university is situated on the outskirts of Dallas.* □ *The farm is situated in a remote area.*

situation /ˌsɪtjuˈeɪʃən/ NOUN [plural **situations**]
the things that are happening in a place or affecting someone at a particular time 🖻 *We're in a difficult situation.* 🖻 *She handled the situation very well.* □ *They're trying to improve the situation for migrant workers.*
a formal word for the place or position where something is □ *Plant the sunflowers in a sunny situation.*

six /sɪks/ NUMBER [plural **sixes**] the number 6

sixteen /sɪksˈtiːn/ NUMBER the number 16
sixteenth /sɪksˈtiːnθ/ NUMBER 16th written as a word

sixth /sɪksθ/ ► NUMBER 6th written as a word
► NOUN [plural **sixths**] $\frac{1}{6}$; one of six equal parts of something

sixth form /ˌsɪksθ ˈfɔːm/ NOUN [plural **sixth forms**] in British schools, the classes in which students aged 16 to 18 study □ *Melanie's in the sixth form.*
• **sixth-former** /ˌsɪksθˈfɔːmə(r)/ NOUN [plural **sixth-formers**] a student in the sixth form at a British school

sixth sense /ˌsɪksθ ˈsens/ NOUN, NO PLURAL an ability that means you seem to be aware of things that cannot be seen, heard, touched, smelled or tasted □ *She always knows when there is going to be a storm - she seems to have a sixth sense about it.*

sixtieth /'sɪkstɪəθ/ NUMBER 60th written as a word

sixty /'sɪksti/ NUMBER [plural **sixties**]
1 the number 60
2 **the sixties** the years between 1960 and 1969

size /saɪz/ NOUN [plural **sizes**]
1 how big, small, long, wide, etc. something is. □ + *of* *The hole was the size of a tennis ball.* □ *They are less than 2 centimetres in size.* □ *We were disappointed by the small size of the bedrooms.* 🖻 *It's about the same size as a credit card.* 🖻 *There were boats of every size and shape.* □ *The government wants to reduce class sizes.*
2 one of the measurements that clothes, shoes and other objects are made in □ *Can I try a smaller size?* □ *I'm a size 12.*

✦ PHRASAL VERB [**sizes, sizing, sized**] **size something/someone up** to study someone or something to decide what they are like □ *He quickly sized up the situation.* □ *She sized up the two men.*
• **sizeable** /'saɪzəbəl/ or **sizable** ADJECTIVE quite big □ *a sizeable crowd* □ *He made a sizeable income from renting his land.*
• **-sized** /saɪzd/ SUFFIX -sized is added to the end of words to describe how big something is □ *a medium-sized company*

sizzle /'sɪzəl/ VERB [**sizzles, sizzling, sizzled**] to make a noise like food frying □ *Steaks were sizzling on the grill.*

skate /skeɪt/ ► NOUN [plural **skates**]
1 an ice skate
2 a roller skate

✦ IDIOM **get your skates on** an informal phrase used to tell someone to hurry □ *If you want to go, you'll need to get your skates on.*
► VERB [**skates, skating, skated**] to move wearing skates □ *The Russian pair skated well.*

skateboard /'skeɪtbɔːd/ NOUN [plural **skateboards**] a long narrow board with wheels on the bottom which you ride by standing on it
• **skateboarding** /'skeɪtbɔːdɪŋ/ NOUN, NO PLURAL the activity of riding on a skateboard

skater /'skeɪtə(r)/ NOUN [plural **skaters**] someone who skates on ice

skating /'skeɪtɪŋ/ NOUN, NO PLURAL the sport or activity of moving over ice wearing skates

skeletal /'skelɪtəl/ ADJECTIVE
1 extremely thin
2 to do with a skeleton

skeleton /'skelɪtən/ NOUN [plural **skeletons**]
1 the frame of bones inside the body of a person or an animal □ *They found a nearly complete dinosaur skeleton.*
2 a skeleton staff/crew, etc. fewer people than normal, but just enough to continue working □ *A skeleton staff will continue to maintain the building.*
◆ IDIOM a skeleton in the cupboard/closet a secret from your past that you do not want people to know about □ *He claims to have no skeletons in his cupboard.*

skeleton key /'skelɪtən 'ki:/ NOUN [plural **skeleton keys**] a key that will open several different locks

skeptic /'skeptɪk/ NOUN [plural **skeptics**] the US spelling of sceptic
● **skeptical** /'skeptɪkəl/ ADJECTIVE the US spelling of sceptical

sketch /sketʃ/ ► NOUN [plural **sketches**]
1 a drawing that is done quickly □ *a pencil sketch* □ *He drew a rough sketch of the house.*
2 a short, funny piece of acting 🔄 *a comedy sketch*
3 a short description of something without a lot of details □ *The book consists of biographical sketches of famous scientists.*
► VERB [**sketches, sketching, sketched**] to draw something quickly □ *She had sketched some designs.*
◆ PHRASAL VERB **sketch something out** to describe something quickly and without a lot of details □ *He sketched out the challenges ahead.*
● **sketchy** /'sketʃɪ/ ADJECTIVE [**sketchier, sketchiest**] not complete and without many details □ *Because the area is so remote, details of the incident are sketchy.*

skew /skju:/ VERB [**skews, skewing, skewed**]
1 to change or to influence facts or amounts so that they are not fair or accurate □ *This could skew the results.*
2 if something is skewed, it is not straight □ *His hat was skewed at an angle.*

skewer /'skju:ə(r)/ NOUN [plural **skewers**] a long thin pointed piece of metal or wood that you can cook small pieces of food on

ski /ski:/ ► NOUN [plural **skis**] one of two long narrow strips of wood or metal that you attach to boots and use for moving over snow 🔄 *a pair of skis*
► ADJECTIVE to do with the sport or activity of skiing □ *a ski resort* □ *the ski slopes*
► VERB [**skis, skiing, skied**] to move over snow on skis □ *They skied down together.* □ *I'm just learning to ski.*

skid /skɪd/ VERB [**skids, skidding, skidded**] to slide over a surface in a way that is not controlled □ *The plane skidded off the runway in heavy rain.*

skier /'ski:ə(r)/ NOUN [plural **skiers**] someone who skis

skies /skaɪz/ PLURAL NOUN the sky, used especially when talking about the weather □ *The forecast is for sunny skies and warm temperatures.*

skiing /'ski:ɪŋ/ NOUN, NO PLURAL the sport or activity of moving over snow on skis 🔄 *I would love to go skiing.* 🔄 *a skiing holiday*

skilful /'skɪlfʊl/ ADJECTIVE showing the ability to do something well □ *He's a very skilful player.* □ *She's very skilful at handling the media.*
● **skilfully** /'skɪlfʊlɪ/ ADVERB in a skilful way □ *They had skilfully avoided being caught.* □ *a skilfully edited programme*
● **skilfulness** /'skɪlfʊlnɪs/ NOUN, NO PLURAL the quality of being skilful

skill /skɪl/ NOUN [plural **skills**]
1 an ability to do something that you develop through training and practice 🔄 *It helps children develop their social skills.* 🔄 *Effective communication skills are essential.* 🔄 *They lack basic computer skills.*
2 no plural the ability to do something very well □ *His skill as a writer is in creating believable characters.* □ **+ in** *He showed great skill in handling the situation.* □ **+ at** *She was known for her skill at motivating workers.*
● **skilled** /skɪld/ ADJECTIVE
1 a skilled person is very good at what they do □ *Amanda's a skilled pianist.* 🔄 *a highly skilled workforce*
2 a skilled job needs special training and practice

skillful /'skɪlfʊl/ ADJECTIVE the US spelling of skilful
● **skillfully** /'skɪlfʊlɪ/ ADVERB the US spelling of skilfully

skim /skɪm/ VERB [**skims, skimming, skimmed**]
1 to move just above or just touching the surface of something □ *The birds flew low, skimming across the water.*
2 to remove something floating on the top of a liquid □ *Skim off any fat that floats to the surface.*
3 to read something quickly without paying attention to details □ *He quickly skimmed through the file.*

skimmed milk /'skɪmd 'mɪlk/ NOUN, NO PLURAL milk from which the cream has been removed

skim milk /'skɪm 'mɪlk/ NOUN, NO PLURAL the US word for skimmed milk

skimp /skɪmp/ VERB [**skimps, skimping, skimped**] buy or to use not enough of something □ *Don't skimp on the cream in the recipe.*
● **skimpy** /'skɪmpɪ/ ADJECTIVE [**skimpier, skimpiest**] skimpy clothes do not cover much of your body

skin /skɪn/ ► NOUN [plural **skins**]
1 the outside layer of your body 🔄 *She had blonde hair and very pale skin.* 🔄 *People with dark skin do burn as easily in the sun.* 🔄 *A moisturizing cream will help prevent dry skin.* □ *skin cancer*
2 the outside layer of a dead animal which is used for making something □ *the illegal trade in tiger skins*
3 the outside layer of some fruits and vegetables □ *banana skins* □ *grape skin*
4 a layer that forms on the top of some liquids □ *Warm milk develops a skin as it cools.*
5 something that you can use to change the appearance of information on a computer screen. computer word.
◆ IDIOMS do something by the skin of your teeth

informal phrase meaning to only just succeed in doing something □ *She caught the train by the skin of her teeth.* **make your skin crawl** to make you feel very uncomfortable because you are shocked or frightened □ *That noise makes my skin crawl*

▶ VERB [**skins, skinning, skinned**] to remove the skin from something □ *I've skinned the tomatoes.*

skincare /ˈskɪnkeə(r)/ NOUN, NO PLURAL keeping your skin in good condition □ *skincare products*

skinflint /ˈskɪnflɪnt/ NOUN [*plural* **skinflints**] an informal word meaning someone who does not like spending money

skinhead /ˈskɪnhed/ NOUN [*plural* **skinheads**] a man who has extremely short hair, especially one who also behaves violently

skinny /ˈskɪnɪ/ ADJECTIVE [**skinnier, skinniest**]
1 very thin □ *She's too skinny.*
2 skinny clothes fit your body very tightly □ *skinny jeans*
3 low in fat □ *a skinny latte*

skint /skɪnt/ ADJECTIVE having no money. An informal word □ *I can't afford the ticket. I'm totally skint.*

skin-tight /ˈskɪnˈtaɪt/ ADJECTIVE skin-tight clothes fit your body very tightly

skip /skɪp/ ▶ VERB [**skips, skipping, skipped**]
1 to move forward by jumping from one foot to the other foot □ *He skipped down the road.*
2 to jump over a rope that you are turning □ *The girls were skipping in the playground.*
3 to not do something that you should do □ *Children who skip breakfast find it more difficult to concentrate in class.* □ *He was being bullied and regularly skipped school.*
4 to avoid reading or mentioning something □ *The report skips over some essential issues.*

▶ NOUN [*plural* **skips**]
1 a large container for waste □ *We put a lot of broken furniture and bricks in the skip.*
2 a skipping movement

skipper /ˈskɪpə(r)/ NOUN [*plural* **skippers**]
1 the person in charge of a boat or ship
2 an informal word for the leader of a team □ *the former England skipper Alan Shearer*

skipping rope /ˈskɪpɪŋ ˈrəʊp/ NOUN [*plural* **skipping ropes**] a rope that you jump over as you are turning it

skirmish /ˈskɜːmɪʃ/ ▶ NOUN [*plural* **skirmishes**] a short fight or argument
▶ VERB [**skirmishes, skirmishing, skirmished**] to take part in a skirmish

skirmishing /ˈskɜːmɪʃɪŋ/ NOUN, NO PLURAL fighting or arguments that are not very serious

skirt /skɜːt/ ▶ NOUN [*plural* **skirts**] a piece of clothing for girls or women that hangs from the waist □ *Anja was wearing a black skirt.* □ *a short skirt*
▶ VERB [**skirts, skirting, skirted**]
to go around the edge of something □ *A small canal skirts the field.*
to avoid talking about something □ *He skirted the issue of immigration.*

skirting board /ˈskɜːtɪŋ ˈbɔːd/ NOUN [*plural* **skirting boards**] a narrow piece of wood fixed to the bottom of an inside wall where it meets the floor

skittle /ˈskɪtəl/ NOUN [*plural* **skittles**] an object in the shape of a bottle that you try to knock down with a ball as a game
● **skittles** /ˈskɪtəlz/ NOUN, NO PLURAL a game in which you use a ball to knock down objects in the shape of a bottle

skive /skaɪv/ VERB [**skives, skiving, skived**] an informal word meaning to not be at school or work when you should be □ *He skived off work to go and see a film.*
● **skiver** /ˈskaɪvə(r)/ NOUN [*plural* **skivers**] an informal word meaning someone who avoids work

skulduggery /skʌlˈdʌgərɪ/ NOUN, NO PLURAL activities that are intended to trick people

skulk /skʌlk/ VERB [**skulks, skulking, skulked**] to hide somewhere or move quietly in a way that makes you look guilty □ *He was skulking behind a parked car to avoid seeing her.*

skull /skʌl/ NOUN [*plural* **skulls**]
1 the structure of bones that form your head □ *He fell out of a tree and fractured his skull.*
2 **skull and crossbones** a picture of two crossed bones and a skull, often used as a warning sign, for example on poison

skull cap /ˈskʌl ˌkæp/ NOUN [*plural* **skull caps**] a small round hat that some men wear for religious reasons

skunk /skʌŋk/ NOUN [*plural* **skunks**] a small animal that produces an unpleasant smell if it is attacked

sky /skaɪ/ NOUN [*plural* **skies**] the area above the Earth where you can see the sun, moon, stars and clouds □ *There was a beautiful clear blue sky.* □ *She looked up at the cloudy sky.* □ *There were several stars in the sky.*
➡ go to **skies**

skydiving /ˈskaɪˌdaɪvɪŋ/ NOUN, NO PLURAL a sport in which people jump out of aeroplanes

skylight /ˈskaɪlaɪt/ NOUN [*plural* **skylights**] a window in a roof

skyline /ˈskaɪlaɪn/ NOUN [*plural* **skylines**] the shape made by buildings against the sky □ *the London skyline*

Skype /skaɪp/ NOUN, NO PLURAL an Internet system used for making telephone calls. A trademark.

skyscraper /ˈskaɪˌskreɪpə(r)/ NOUN [*plural* **skyscrapers**] a very tall building

slab /slæb/ NOUN [*plural* **slabs**] a thick flat piece of something □ *a slab of concrete*

slack /slæk/ ▶ ADJECTIVE [**slacker, slackest**]
1 loose or not pulled tight □ *The rope was too slack.*
2 not caring enough about doing something well □ *a slack attitude*
3 if business is slack, not many people are buying things
▶ VERB [**slacks, slacking, slacked**] to do less work than you should

• **slacken** /ˈslækən/ VERB [**slackens, slackening, slackened**]
1 to make something looser, or to become looser □ *His grip on her arm slackened.*
2 to become slower or less active, or to make something become slower or less active □ *The pace of economic growth has slackened.*

slacks /slæks/ PLURAL NOUN an old-fashioned word for an informal style of trousers

slain /sleɪn/ PAST PARTICIPLE OF slay

slalom /ˈslɑːləm/ NOUN [*plural* **slaloms**] a race in which people move from side to side between poles

slam /slæm/ ▶ VERB [**slams, slamming, slammed**]
1 to shut quickly with a loud noise, or to shut something quickly with a loud noise 🔁 *She walked angrily out of the room and slammed the door.* 🔁 *The gate slammed shut.*
2 to put something somewhere with a loud noise □ *He slammed the books down on the table.*
▶ NOUN [*plural* **slams**] the noise of something being slammed

slander /ˈslɑːndə(r)/ ▶ NOUN [*plural* **slanders**] the crime of saying bad things about someone which are not true
▶ VERB [**slanders, slandering, slandered**] to say bad things about someone which are not true
• **slanderous** /ˈslɑːndərəs/ ADJECTIVE not true, and with the intention of making people have a bad opinion of someone □ *slanderous remarks*

slang /slæŋ/ NOUN, NO PLURAL very informal words and phrases □ *'Brass' is a slang word for money.*
• **slangy** /ˈslæŋɪ/ ADJECTIVE [**slangier, slangiest**] using slang □ *slangy language*

slant /slɑːnt/ ▶ VERB [**slants, slanting, slanted**] to slope or to move in a sloping line □ *Sunlight slanted through the window.*
▶ NOUN [*plural* **slants**]
1 a way of writing or talking about something which shows a particular opinion □ *This was a new slant on an old argument.*
2 a slope

slap /slæp/ ▶ VERB [**slaps, slapping, slapped**] to hit something or someone with the flat part of your hand □ *She slapped him across the face.*
◆ PHRASAL VERB **slap something on** to quickly put something on a surface □ *Rachel slapped on some suncream.*
▶ NOUN [*plural* **slaps**] a hit made with the flat part of your hand
◆ IDIOM **a slap in the face** something someone does which upsets or insults you □ *The fare increases are a slap in the face for commuters.*

slap-bang /ˈslæpˈbæŋ/ ADVERB
1 exactly in a particular place □ *The theatre is slap-bang in the middle of Milan.*
2 directly and with force □ *He drove slap-bang into the wall.*

slapdash /ˈslæpdæʃ/ ADJECTIVE careless □ *slapdash work*

slapstick /ˈslæpstɪk/ NOUN, NO PLURAL a type of comedy in which the actors do silly things such as falling over or throwing things at each other

slash /slæʃ/ ▶ VERB [**slashes, slashing, slashed**]
1 to cut something quickly and violently □ *Vandals had slashed the car's tyres.*
2 an informal word meaning to reduce something by a large amount □ *Many stores are slashing the price of TVs.*
▶ NOUN [*plural* **slashes**]
1 a long deep cut
2 one of two punctuation marks (/) or (\), used especially in computing and in website addresses

slat /slæt/ NOUN [*plural* **slats**] one of several thin flat pieces of wood or plastic which are used for making furniture or for making a blind (=covering for a window)

slate /sleɪt/ ▶ NOUN [*plural* **slates**]
1 a type of grey stone that can be broken into thin layers
2 a piece of this stone used for making a roof
3 a piece of this stone that was used in the past to write on
▶ VERB [**slates, slating, slated**] an informal word meaning to criticize someone or something □ *The film was slated by critics.*

slate PC /sleɪt ˌpiːˈsiː/ NOUN [*plural* **slate PCs**] a small computer that you write on with a special pen

slaughter /ˈslɔːtə(r)/ ▶ VERB [**slaughters, slaughtering, slaughtered**]
1 to kill an animal, usually for its meat
2 to kill a lot of people very violently
3 an informal word meaning to defeat someone completely in a game or competition
▶ NOUN, NO PLURAL the act of slaughtering people or animals □ *Officials carried out a mass slaughter of cows to prevent the spread of the disease.* □ *The war has seen the slaughter of innocent civilians.*

slaughterhouse /ˈslɔːtəhaʊs/ NOUN [*plural* **slaughterhouses**] a place where animals are killed for their meat

slave /sleɪv/ ▶ NOUN [*plural* **slaves**]
1 someone who is owned by another person and has to work for them without being paid □ *My parents treat me like a slave.*
2 **be a slave to something** to be influenced by something too much □ *He was a slave to money.*
▶ VERB [**slaves, slaving, slaved**] an informal word meaning to work very hard □ *Don was slaving away the kitchen making dinner.*
• **slavery** /ˈsleɪvərɪ/ NOUN, NO PLURAL
1 the system of having slaves □ *The US did not abolish slavery until 1865.*
2 the state of being a slave □ *He had been sold into slavery.*

slay /sleɪ/ VERB [**slays, slaying, slew, slain**] a literary word meaning to kill a person or animal □ *The dragon was slain by Saint George.*

sleaze /'sli:z/ NOUN, NO PLURAL behaviour in business or politics that is dishonest or morally bad □ *The government is facing allegations of sleaze and corruption.*

• **sleazy** /'sli:zɪ/ ADJECTIVE [**sleazier, sleaziest**]
1 dirty, and attracting unpleasant people □ *a sleazy nightclub*
2 dishonest or morally bad □ *a sleazy businessman*

sledge /sledʒ/ or **sled** /sled/ ▶ NOUN [*plural* **sledges** or **sleds**]
1 a small vehicle with a flat bottom or long metal or wooden pieces under it, that you sit on to slide over snow
2 a larger vehicle that is pulled over snow by dogs or horses
▶ VERB [**sledges, sledging, sledged**] to ride on a sledge

sledgehammer /'sledʒ,hæmə(r)/ NOUN [*plural* **sledgehammers**] a large heavy hammer that you hold with both hands

sleek /sli:k/ ADJECTIVE [**sleeker, sleekest**]
1 smooth, soft and shiny □ *A mink has sleek dark-brown fur.*
2 looking fashionable and expensive
▶ PHRASAL VERB [**sleeks, sleeking, sleeked**] **sleek something back/down** to push something back or down to make it look smooth and shiny □ *She sleeked back her hair.*

sleep /sli:p/ ▶ NOUN [*plural* **sleeps**]
1 *no plural* the state when you are resting with your eyes closed and are naturally unconscious □ *I really need some sleep.* ▣ *I couldn't get to sleep.*
2 a period of time when you are sleeping □ *I managed to have a sleep this morning.* ▣ *She fell into a deep sleep.*
◆ **go to sleep** (a) to begin to sleep (b) if part of your body goes to sleep, you lose the feeling in it
◆ **put something to sleep** to kill an animal because it is old or ill
◆ IDIOM **lose sleep over something** to worry about something
▶ VERB [**sleeps, sleeping, slept**]
to become naturally unconscious and rest with your eyes closed □ *I hardly slept at all last night.* □ *She slept through the fire alarm* (=did not wake up). ▣ *After their long walk, they slept soundly* (=slept well).
if a place sleeps a particular number of people, it has enough space for that many people to sleep there
▶ PHRASAL VERB **sleep in** to sleep later than usual in the morning

sleeper /'sli:pə(r)/ NOUN [*plural* **sleepers**]
someone who is sleeping
a **light/heavy sleeper** someone who wakes easily/does not wake easily after they are asleep
a train with beds for passengers to sleep in

sleepily /'sli:pɪlɪ/ ADVERB in a tired way □ *'What time is it?' she asked sleepily.*

sleepiness /'sli:pɪnɪs/ NOUN, NO PLURAL when you feel tired and want to sleep

sleeping bag /'sli:pɪŋ 'bæg/ NOUN [*plural* **sleeping bags**] a large bag made of thick, warm cloth, used for sleeping in, especially when you are camping

sleeping pill /'sli:pɪŋ 'pɪl/ NOUN [*plural* **sleeping pills**] a pill containing a drug that makes you sleep

sleepless /'sli:plɪs/ ADJECTIVE if you have a sleepless night, you are unable to sleep

• **sleeplessness** /'sli:plɪsnɪs/ NOUN, NO PLURAL being unable to sleep

sleepover /'sli:pəʊvə(r)/ NOUN [*plural* **sleepovers**] when a child stays at a friend's house for the night

sleepwalk /'sli:pwɔ:k/ VERB [**sleepwalks, sleepwalking, sleepwalked**] to walk around while you are still asleep

• **sleepwalker** /'sli:p,wɔ:kə(r)/ NOUN [*plural* **sleepwalkers**] someone who sleepwalks

• **sleepwalking** /'sli:p,wɔ:kɪŋ/ NOUN, NO PLURAL when someone sleepwalks

sleepy /'sli:pɪ/ ADJECTIVE [**sleepier, sleepiest**] feeling tired and wanting to sleep

sleet /sli:t/ ▶ NOUN, NO PLURAL a mixture of rain and snow
▶ VERB [**sleets, sleeting, sleeted**] if it is sleeting, sleet is falling

sleeve /sli:v/ NOUN [*plural* **sleeves**] the part of a piece of clothing that covers your arm or part of your arm □ *a dress with wide sleeves*
◆ IDIOM **have something up your sleeve** to have a secret plan □ *I haven't persuaded them to come yet, but I've still got a few things up my sleeve.*

• **-sleeved** /sli:vd/ ADJECTIVE having sleeves of a particular length □ *a long-sleeved dress*

• **sleeveless** /'sli:vlɪs/ ADJECTIVE having no sleeves □ *a sleeveless top*

sleigh /sleɪ/ NOUN [*plural* **sleighs**] a vehicle that is pulled over snow by horses or other animals

sleight of hand /'slaɪt əv 'hænd/ NOUN, NO PLURAL
1 the skill of moving your hands in a quick and clever way so that other people cannot see what you are doing, for example when doing a magic trick
2 if something is done by sleight of hand it is done in a skilful but slightly dishonest way

slender /'slendə(r)/ ADJECTIVE
1 thin in an attractive way □ *a slender figure*
2 small or slight □ *His chances of winning are extremely slender.*

slept /slept/ PAST TENSE AND PAST PARTICIPLE OF sleep

sleuth /slu:θ/ NOUN [*plural* **sleuths**] a word sometimes used in books and films for someone who tries to solve crimes

slew /slu:/ PAST TENSE OF slay

slice /slaɪs/ ▶ NOUN [*plural* **slices**]
1 a thin or smaller piece cut from a larger piece of food □ *He cut himself a thick slice of chocolate cake.* □ *a slice of ham*
2 a part of something □ *He wanted to get a slice of the profits.*
▶ VERB [**slices, slicing, sliced**]

1 to cut something into slices □ *Slice the onions thinly.* □ *a tin of sliced peaches*
2 to cut something easily with a sharp blade or knife □ *He had the top of his finger sliced off in the accident.*

slick /slɪk/ ▶ ADJECTIVE [**slicker, slickest**]
1 done well and without seeming to involve much effort □ *a slick dance routine* □ *a slick election campaign*
2 clever at persuading people but probably not completely honest □ *a slick sales pitch*
▶ NOUN [*plural* **slicks**] a layer of oil that has been left on the surface of the sea
• **slickly** /slɪklɪ/ ADVERB skilfully and looking as if taking little effort □ *He passed the ball slickly forward.*

slide /slaɪd/ ▶ VERB [**slides, sliding, slid**]
1 to move over a surface quickly and smoothly, or to make something do this □ *The kids enjoyed sliding on the ice.* □ *a sliding door* □ *We slid the poles into place.*
2 to move quietly or make something move quietly □ *He slowly slid the gun out of his pocket.* □ *Karen slid into the back of the room without anyone noticing.*
3 to gradually become worse or get into a worse situation □ *We found ourselves gradually sliding into debt.* 🖫 *The restaurant had let standards slide since we were last there.*
▶ NOUN [*plural* **slides**]
1 a piece of play equipment on which children climb up steps and slide down a smooth sloping surface □ *Megan loves playing on the slide.*
2 a sliding movement □ *The car went into a slide on the wet road.*
3 a slow fall in level, price, quality etc. □ *the dollar's slide against the euro* □ *The film charts the family's gradual slide into poverty.*
4 a small transparent photograph that you shine light through to look at an image on a screen □ *a slide show*
5 a small clear piece of glass or plastic which you put something on so that you can look at it using a microscope (=scientific instrument for examining things)

slight /slaɪt/ ADJECTIVE [**slighter, slightest**]
1 small or not important □ *a slight increase in temperature* □ *There's a slight problem with your application.* □ *Lewis has a slight cold.*
2 a slight person is thin and light □ *He has a slight build.*
3 not in the slightest not at all □ *I'm not worried in the slightest by the news.*
• **slightly** /slaɪtlɪ/ ADVERB by only a small amount □ *Adam is slightly taller than Alex.* □ *I only know her slightly.*

slim /slɪm/ ▶ ADJECTIVE [**slimmer, slimmest**]
1 thin in an attractive way □ *His sister's a tall, slim girl with blonde hair.*
2 small □ *The chances of winning the lottery are very slim.*
▶ VERB [**slims, slimming, slimmed**] to become or try

to become thinner □ *I can't have any cake, I'm slimming.*
◆ PHRASAL VERBS **slim down** to become slimmer □ *He's slimmed down a lot in the last year.* **slim something down** to make an organization or business smaller, especially by employing fewer people

slime /slaɪm/ NOUN, NO PLURAL a thick, sticky, unpleasant liquid □ *When the flood subsided the carpets were covered in slime.*
slimmer /slɪmə(r)/ NOUN [*plural* **slimmers**] someone who is trying to become thinner
• **slimming** /slɪmɪŋ/ NOUN, NO PLURAL the process of trying to become thinner □ *a slimming club*
slimness /slɪmnɪs/ NOUN, NO PLURAL being attractively thin □ *A wide belt accentuated the slimness of her waist.*
slimy /slaɪmɪ/ ADJECTIVE [**slimier, slimiest**] covered with, or feeling like, slime (=thick, unpleasant liquid) □ *a slimy substance*

sling /slɪŋ/ ▶ VERB [**slings, slinging, slung**]
1 to throw something somewhere in a careless way □ *Just sling your rucksack in the corner.*
2 to put something in a position where it hangs down □ *She slung her bag over her shoulder and stalked out*
▶ NOUN [*plural* **slings**] a wide piece of cloth that is hung from someone's neck or shoulder to support a injured arm □ *Ken had his arm in a sling.*
slink /slɪŋk/ VERB [**slinks, slinking, slunk**] to move quietly, trying not to be noticed, often because you have done something wrong □ *He came slinking in well past midnight.*
slinky /slɪŋkɪ/ ADJECTIVE [**slinkier, slinkiest**] slinky clothing fits your body well and makes you look attractive □ *a slinky black top*

slip /slɪp/ ▶ VERB [**slips, slipping, slipped**]
1 to slide and lose your balance or fall □ *Gran had slipped on the ice and broken her hip.*
2 to fall out of position or out of your hands □ *The knife slipped and I nearly cut myself.* □ *I'm sorry, the cup just slipped out of my hands.*
3 to put something somewhere quickly □ *Dad slipp· a £10 note in my pocket.*
4 to go somewhere quietly and without anyone noticing you □ *I saw Polly slip out of the room.* □ *Th must have slipped away while we were watching th show.*
5 to become worse or lower in value, level, etc. □ *Profits have been slipping for months.* □ *I think support for the strike has slipped.*
6 if you slip a piece of clothing on or off, you put it or take it off quickly and easily □ *I'll just slip on a jacket.* □ *Slip off your shoes.*
◆ IDIOMS **let something slip** to tell someone someth· that is a secret by mistake □ *Annie let it slip that sh· been left a lot of money.* **slip your mind** if someth· slips your mind, you forget about it or forget to d □ *I'm so sorry about missing lunch yesterday – it completely slipped my mind.*

◆ PHRASAL VERBS **slip out** if something slips out, you say it without meaning to □ *I wasn't going to mention it but it just slipped out.* **slip up** to make a mistake or do something wrong □ *I'm afraid you slipped up on the first question.*

▶ NOUN [*plural* **slips**]

1 a small piece of paper □ *a slip of paper* □ *Fill in the green slip and give it back to me.*

2 a small mistake ⊞ *She made a couple of slips in her dance routine*

3 a **slip of the tongue** something that you say by mistake

4 an act of sliding or falling

5 a piece of thin clothing that a girl or woman wears under her dress or skirt

▸ IDIOM **give someone the slip** to escape from someone who is following you □ *He gave the police the slip near the tube station.*

slip-on /'slɪpɒn/ NOUN [*plural* **slip-ons**] a shoe that is easy to put on because it does not fasten □ *I prefer slip-ons to shoes with laces.*

slippage /'slɪpɪdʒ/ NOUN, NO PLURAL

1 the amount that something has slipped (=slid down)

2 the amount of time by which something that is being done has been delayed □ *There must not be any slippage on this project.*

slipped disc /'slɪpt 'dɪsk/ NOUN [*plural* **slipped discs**] a painful injury in which one of the layers of body tissue between the bones in your back moves out of place

slipper /'slɪpə(r)/ NOUN [*plural* **slippers**] a soft shoe for wearing indoors

slippery /'slɪpəri/ ADJECTIVE a slippery surface is smooth, wet or shiny and not easy to walk on or hold □ *The floor was slippery with grease.*

slip road /'slɪp 'rəʊd/ NOUN [*plural* **slip roads**] a narrow road used by traffic going on to or leaving a motorway

slipshod /'slɪpʃɒd/ ADJECTIVE careless and untidy □ *He's begun to demonstrate a slipshod approach to his work.*

slipstream /'slɪpstriːm/ NOUN [*plural* **slipstreams**] the flow of air behind someone or something that is moving very fast

slip-up /'slɪpʌp/ NOUN [*plural* **slip-ups**] a small mistake □ *I made an embarrassing slip-up when I addressed him as 'Madam Chairman'.*

slit /slɪt/ ▶ NOUN [*plural* **slits**] a long cut or narrow opening □ *Her tight black skirt had a slit up the side.*

▶ VERB [**slits, slitting, slit**] to make a long narrow cut in something □ *He quickly slit the letter open.*

slither /'slɪðə(r)/ VERB [**slithers, slithering, slithered**] to slide over a surface □ *The ice cubes slithered off the table.* □ *She saw a snake slithering through the grass.*

slithery /'slɪðəri/ ADJECTIVE unpleasantly smooth and difficult to hold

sliver /'slɪvə(r)/ NOUN [*plural* **slivers**] a long thin piece cut or broken from something □ *slivers of glass* □ *The cake was topped with slivers of chocolate.*

slob /slɒb/ NOUN [*plural* **slobs**] an informal word meaning a lazy, untidy person

slobber /'slɒbə(r)/ VERB [**slobbers, slobbering, slobbered**] to have saliva (=liquid from the mouth) coming out of your mouth □ *a slobbering bulldog*

● **slobbery** /'slɒbəri/ ADJECTIVE slobbery kisses or lips are unpleasantly wet

slog /slɒg/ ▶ VERB [**slogs, slogging, slogged**]

1 to work very hard for a long time □ *Tom spent hours slogging away at his revision.*

2 to walk or travel somewhere using a lot of effort □ *We slogged up the mountain.*

▶ NOUN, NO PLURAL

1 a period of hard or boring work □ *It was such a slog moving that piano.*

2 a difficult walk or journey □ *The climb up the hill was quite a slog.*

slogan /'sləʊgən/ NOUN [*plural* **slogans**] a phrase that is easy to remember and is used to advertise something or to emphasize the opinions of political parties, etc. □ *advertising slogans*

slop /slɒp/ VERB [**slops, slopping, slopped**] liquid slops when it moves around or comes out of its container □ *You've managed to slop soup down your front.*

slope /sləʊp/ ▶ VERB [**slopes, sloping, sloped**] to have one end higher than the other □ *The garden slopes upwards.* □ *a sloping roof*

▶ NOUN [*plural* **slopes**]

1 a surface that slopes □ *a steep slope* □ *a ski slope*

2 the amount that a surface slopes □ *a slope of 30 degrees*

3 the side of a hill or mountain □ *Sheep graze on the lower slopes of the mountains.*

sloppy /'slɒpi/ ADJECTIVE [**sloppier, sloppiest**]

1 careless or untidy □ *a sloppy piece of work*

2 showing emotions in a way that seems silly and embarrassing □ *a sloppy love story*

3 a sloppy substance has too much liquid in it

4 sloppy clothes are loose and do not have a clear shape □ *a sloppy jumper*

slosh /slɒʃ/ VERB [**sloshes, sloshing, sloshed**]

1 if you slosh a liquid, you throw it somewhere in a careless way □ *He sloshed cold water on his face.*

2 liquid sloshes when it moves around noisily in a container or over the edge of something □ *Water sloshed over the side of the boat.*

slot /slɒt/ ▶ NOUN [*plural* **slots**]

1 a small narrow opening, especially one that you put coins or bank cards into □ *There's a pound coin stuck in the slot.*

2 a period of time in an event or an activity when something particular is planned to happen □ *The new chat show will fill the early evening slot.*

▶ VERB [**slots, slotting, slotted**] to go into a slot or to put something into a slot □ *Slot the metal token in here.*

◆ PHRASAL VERBS **slot something in** to find a time to do something or be with someone □ *We can slot in an extra lesson after lunch.* **slot together** to fit together easily □ *The pieces of the storage unit just slot together.*

sloth /sləʊθ/ NOUN [*plural* **sloths**]
1 a South American animal that lives mostly in trees and moves very slowly
2 a literary word meaning being lazy
● **slothful** /ˈsləʊθful/ ADJECTIVE a literary word meaning lazy

slot machine /ˈslɒt məˈʃiːn/ NOUN [*plural* **slot machines**] a machine that you operate by putting in coins to try to win more money

slouch /slaʊtʃ/ VERB [**slouches, slouching, slouched**] to move, stand or sit with your back curved and your head hanging forward

slovenly /ˈslʌvənlɪ/ ADJECTIVE careless or untidy and dirty □ *The landlady was a plump, slovenly woman.*

slow /sləʊ/ ▶ ADJECTIVE [**slower, slowest**]
1 not fast or not moving or acting quickly □ *a slow march* □ *a slow reader* □ *We made slow progress through the crowds.*
2 not doing something immediately □ **+ to do something** *Social services had been slow to take any action to protect the child.* □ **+ in** *He was very slow in coming to the phone.*
3 not clever □ *She was put in a group with the slower students.*
4 not busy or not exciting □ *Business was slow in the restaurant last night.*
5 not exciting □ *I found the film very slow.*
6 if a clock or watch is slow, it shows a time earlier than the correct time □ *I think your clock's five minutes slow.*
▶ VERB [**slows, slowing, slowed**]
1 to become slower or to make something slower □ *The train slowed as we approached Birmingham.* □ *Increased hygiene has slowed the spread of disease.*
2 to become lower in amount or level, or to make something do this □ *Profit growth has slowed in recent months.*
◆ PHRASAL VERBS **slow down** to become less active □ *I've had to slow down a bit since my illness.* **slow (something) down** to become slower or to make something slower □ *You should slow down as you approach the bend.*

slowcoach /ˈsləʊkəʊtʃ/ NOUN [*plural* **slowcoaches**] an informal word for someone who takes a long time to do something

slowdown /ˈsləʊdaʊn/ NOUN [*plural* **slowdowns**] when an economy becomes less successful ⊞ *Experts predict an economic slowdown.*

slowly /ˈsləʊlɪ/ ADVERB
1 at a slow speed □ *He drove slowly past the house.* □ *She speaks very slowly.*
2 gradually □ *She is slowly recovering from her ordeal.*

slow motion /ˈsləʊ ˈməʊʃən/ NOUN, NO PLURAL a way of filming actions to make them seem much slower

than in real life □ *The bomb blast seemed to happen in slow motion.*
● **slow-motion** ADJECTIVE shown in slow motion □ *a slow-motion replay*

sludge /slʌdʒ/ NOUN, NO PLURAL thick soft mud or any similar substance □ *Sludge can build up in your radiators over time.*

slug[1] /slʌg/ NOUN [*plural* **slugs**] a creature with a long soft body and no legs, like a snail with no shell □ *Slugs had attacked our bean plants.*

slug[2] /slʌg/ VERB [**slugs, slugging, slugged**] to hit someone or something very hard

sluggish /ˈslʌgɪʃ/ ADJECTIVE not reacting or moving as quickly as usual □ *The heat made me feel tired and sluggish.* □ *There was only a sluggish flow of water from the tap.*
● **sluggishly** /ˈslʌgɪʃlɪ/ ADVERB in a sluggish way □ *The engine started rather sluggishly.*

slum /slʌm/ NOUN [*plural* **slums**] a part of a town or city where the buildings are dirty and in bad condition □ *She sang about her childhood in the slums of Naples.*
▶ VERB [**slums, slumming, slummed**] **slum it** an informal phrase meaning to live without the good conditions you are used to

slumber /ˈslʌmbə(r)/ ▶ VERB [**slumbers, slumbering, slumbered**] a literary word meaning to sleep
▶ NOUN [*plural* **slumbers**] a literary word meaning sleep

slump /slʌmp/ ▶ VERB [**slumps, slumping, slumped**]
1 to quickly go down to a much lower level □ *Business has slumped in the last few months.*
2 to fall or sit down suddenly because you feel weak or tired □ *He was slumped over his desk, fast asleep.* □ *She suddenly slumped back in her chair.*
▶ NOUN [*plural* **slumps**]
1 a big fall in sales, values, etc. □ *a slump in property prices*
2 a period when businesses are not selling many goods and a lot of people do not have jobs □ *The economy facing a slump.*

slung /slʌŋ/ PAST TENSE AND PAST PARTICIPLE OF sling

slunk /slʌŋk/ PAST TENSE AND PAST PARTICIPLE OF slink

slur /slɜː(r)/ ▶ VERB [**slurs, slurring, slurred**] to pronounce words in way that is not clear, usually because you are drunk or ill □ *The poor man was staggering and slurring his speech.*
▶ NOUN [*plural* **slurs**] an insult or remark that is likely to damage someone's reputation □ *racial slurs*

slurp /slɜːp/ VERB [**slurps, slurping, slurped**] to drink very noisily □ *The little boy was slurping his milkshake through a straw.*

slush /slʌʃ/ NOUN, NO PLURAL snow on the ground that is dirty and partly melted □ *By evening the thick snow had turned to slush.*
● **slushy** /ˈslʌʃɪ/ ADJECTIVE [**slushier, slushiest**]
1 soft and almost liquid, like partly melted snow □ *slushy pavement*
2 romantic in a silly way □ *a slushy novel*

sly /slaɪ/ ADJECTIVE [**slyer** or **slier**, **slyest** or **sliest**]
1 clever and good at tricking others □ *a sly and manipulative politician*
2 showing that you know something that other people do not know □ *a sly smile*
▶ NOUN, NO PLURAL **on the sly** if you do something on the sly you do it in secret because you should not be doing it □ *She was still texting her old boyfriend on the sly.*
• **slyly** /'slaɪli/ ADVERB in a sly way
• **slyness** /'slaɪnɪs/ NOUN, NO PLURAL being sly

smack /smæk/ ▶ VERB [**smacks, smacking, smacked**]
1 to hit someone with your hand flat □ *It is wrong to smack children.*
2 smack your lips to show that you are enjoying some food by making a loud noise with your lips or tongue
3 to hit something hard and make a loud noise □ *The car smacked into a wall.*
◆ PHRASAL VERB **smack of something** to seem to have an unpleasant quality □ *His reaction smacks of hypocrisy.*
▶ NOUN [*plural* **smacks**] a hit with a flat hand, or the sound made by this □ *I'll give you a smack if you aren't careful!*
▶ ADVERB exactly in a particular place □ *The ball landed smack in the middle of the pond.*

small /smɔːl/ ADJECTIVE [**smaller, smallest**]
1 little □ *a small country* ♫ *This coat is too small for you now.* □ *We're only interviewing a small number of applicants.*
2 very young □ *a playground for small children* □ *I used to love these books when I was small.*
3 not important or serious □ *a small problem*
4 feel/look small to feel or look silly and not important □ *He always made me feel small.*

small ad /'smɔːl æd/ NOUN [*plural* **small ads**] a short advertisement about something for sale, in a newspaper
small change /'smɔːl 'tʃeɪndʒ/ NOUN, NO PLURAL coins that are of low value □ *Can you lend me 10 pence? I don't have any small change.*
smallholder /'smɔːlˌhəʊldə(r)/ NOUN [*plural* **smallholders**] someone who has an area of land that they use as a very small farm
smallholding /'smɔːlˌhəʊldɪŋ/ NOUN [*plural* **smallholdings**] an area of land that is used as a very small farm
small intestine /'smɔːlɪn'testɪn/ NOUN [*plural* **small intestines**] the upper part of the body's system for digesting food where food is digested and taken into the body. A biology word.
small-minded /'smɔːl'maɪndɪd/ ADJECTIVE having a limited view of the world and not wanting to learn about different ideas or ways of doing things
smallness /'smɔːlnɪs/ NOUN, NO PLURAL how small something is when compared to other things
smallpox /'smɔːlpɒks/ NOUN, NO PLURAL a serious infectious disease which causes fever and marks on the skin □ *smallpox vaccination*

small print /'smɔːl 'prɪnt/ NOUN, NO PLURAL the details of a contract (=written legal agreement) that are often printed in very small letters ♫ *You should always read the small print before signing anything.*
small-scale /'smɔːl'skeɪl/ ADJECTIVE not very large or important □ *a small-scale operation*
small talk /'smɔːl 'tɔːk/ NOUN, NO PLURAL polite conversation about things that are not important, such as the weather ♫ *Danny's useless at making small talk.*
smarmy /'smɑːmi/ ADJECTIVE [**smarmier, smarmiest**] too pleasant and polite, in a way that is false □ *The head waiter has a very smarmy manner.*

smart /smɑːt/ ▶ ADJECTIVE [**smarter, smartest**]
1 clean and tidy □ *a pair of smart black shoes* □ *She looked really smart in her uniform.*
2 clever □ *a smart answer* □ *He's one of the smartest guys I know.*
3 fashionable and expensive □ *It's the smartest club in town.* □ *a smart flat on the river*
4 fast or strong □ *We walked at a smart pace.*
5 smart weapons, machines, etc. use computers to make them work □ *smart bombs*
▶ VERB [**smarts, smarting, smarted**] to feel a sharp, burning pain □ *The thick smoke made my eyes smart.*

smart card /'smɑːt 'kɑːd/ NOUN [*plural* **smart cards**] a small plastic card which stores information about a person □ *Swipe your smart card to get into the building.*
smarten /'smɑːtən/
◆ PHRASAL VERBS [**smartens, smartening, smartened**]
smarten something up to make something look better, for example by cleaning it or painting it □ *A coat of paint would smarten this room up.* **smarten (someone) up** to make someone look cleaner and tidier □ *I'd like to smarten up before we go out.*
smartly /'smɑːtli/ ADVERB
1 in a way that is tidy and fashionable □ *smartly dressed businessmen*
2 quickly or strongly □ *She tapped him smartly on the back.* □ *He marched smartly out of the room.*
smartness /'smɑːtnɪs/ NOUN, NO PLURAL being smart
smash /smæʃ/ ▶ VERB [**smashes, smashing, smashed**]
1 to break something into pieces, for example by dropping it □ *She smashed one of our best glasses.* □ *Mum, I've smashed a window.* □ *Police had to smash the door down.*
2 to break into pieces □ *The vase fell off the table and smashed.*
3 to hit something, or hit against it, with great force □ *The car smashed into a traffic island and overturned.*
4 to completely destroy a group or an organization □ *Police have smashed a drugs ring in South London.*
5 smash a record to do something better, faster, etc. than anyone has ever done it before
▶ NOUN [*plural* **smashes**]
1 the sound of something breaking
2 a road accident in which two vehicles hit each other and are damaged □ *There's been a bad smash on the M62.*

smash hit /ˈsmæʃ ˈhɪt/ NOUN [plural **smash hits**] a show, play, film, etc. that is very successful □ *This new musical is sure to be a smash hit.*

smashing /ˈsmæʃɪŋ/ ADJECTIVE an old-fashioned word that means very good or very enjoyable □ *That was a smashing meal.*

smattering /ˈsmætərɪŋ/ NOUN a smattering a small amount of something □ *George speaks German, Italian, and a smattering of French.*

smear /smɪə(r)/ ▶ VERB [**smears, smearing, smeared**]
1 to spread a soft or dirty substance on a surface □ *Her face was smeared with mascara.*
2 if a liquid such as paint or ink smears, it spreads in a way that is not intended
3 to say things about someone that are unpleasant and not true
▶ NOUN [plural **smears**]
1 a dirty mark made by spreading something sticky on something □ *smears of paint*
2 something unpleasant and not true that is said about someone □ *a smear campaign*

smear test /smɪə ˈtest/ NOUN [plural **smear tests**] a medical test for a woman, in which cells are taken from the entrance of the womb (=part where a baby grows) to check for cancer

smell /smel/ ▶ VERB [**smells, smelling, smelled** or **smelt**]
1 to notice or recognize something by using your nose □ *Can you smell burning?* □ *I could smell his sweaty trainers from across the room.*
2 to have a particular smell □ *Those scones smell delicious.* □ *+ of* *The sheets smelled of lavender.* □ *This chicken smells funny.*
3 to have a bad smell □ *His breath smells.*
▶ NOUN [plural **smells**]
1 *no plural* the ability to smell things ⬙ *The virus made him lose his sense of smell.*
2 the quality you notice by smelling □ *a strong smell of garlic* □ *These lilies have a lovely smell.*
3 the act of smelling something □ *Have a smell of this soup.*
• **smelly** /ˈsmelɪ/ ADJECTIVE [**smellier, smelliest**] having a strong or bad smell □ *smelly feet*

smelt¹ /smelt/ VERB [**smelts, smelting, smelted**] to melt rock to remove the metal it contains
smelt² /smelt/ PAST TENSE AND PAST PARTICIPLE OF smell

smile /smaɪl/ ▶ VERB [**smiles, smiling, smiled**] to show you are happy or think something is funny by making the corners of your mouth go up □ *The little girl smiled happily up at him.*

> ► Remember that you **smile at** someone. You do not 'smile to' someone:
> ✓ She turned and smiled at me.
> ✗ She turned and smiled to me.

▶ NOUN [plural **smiles**] an expression in which the corners of your mouth go up to show you are happy

□ *a broad smile* □ *'Can I help you?' she said with a smile.*

smiley /ˈsmaɪlɪ/ NOUN [plural **smileys**] an emoticon (= image of a face made with keyboard symbols), used in e-mails to express emotions

smirk /smɜːk/ ▶ VERB [**smirks, smirking, smirked**] to smile in an unpleasant or unkind way □ *He sat smirking at her in his new sports car.*
▶ NOUN [plural **smirks**] an unpleasant or unkind smile

smithereens /ˌsmɪðəˈriːnz/ PLURAL NOUN smash/blow something to smithereens to break something into very small pieces in a violent way □ *The building was blown to smithereens by a bomb.*

smitten /ˈsmɪtən/ ADJECTIVE very much in love with someone

smock /smɒk/ NOUN [plural **smocks**] a loose piece of clothing worn over other clothes to protect them □ *an artist's smock*

smog /smɒg/ NOUN, NO PLURAL a mixture of smoke and fog which hangs over some cities and towns

smoke /sməʊk/ ▶ NOUN, NO PLURAL
1 the grey or black gas that something produces when it is burning □ *I can smell smoke.*
□ *cigarette smoke* ⬙ *Firefighters battled thick smoke to rescue the children.* ⬙ *A cloud of smoke rose into the air.*
2 the act of smoking a cigarette □ *My grandmother enjoys a smoke.*
▶ VERB [**smokes, smoking, smoked**]
1 someone who smokes sucks smoke from cigarette □ *My parents don't smoke.* □ *Dan was smoking a cigarette.*
2 to produce smoke □ *The chimney was smoking.*
• **smoked** /sməʊkt/ ADJECTIVE smoked foods have been given a special flavour by being hung in smoke □ *smoked salmon*
• **smoker** /ˈsməʊkə(r)/ NOUN [plural **smokers**] someone who smokes cigarettes ⬙ *He used to be a heavy smoker* (=someone who smokes a lot of cigarettes).
• **smoking** /ˈsməʊkɪŋ/ NOUN, NO PLURAL the habit of smoking cigarettes ⬙ *My Dad wants to stop smoking.* □ *In England smoking is banned in public buildings.*
• **smoky** /ˈsməʊkɪ/ ADJECTIVE [**smokier, smokiest**]
1 filled with smoke □ *a smoky bar*
2 like smoke □ *a smoky grey colour*

smolder /ˈsməʊldə(r)/ VERB [**smolders, smoldering, smoldered**] the US spelling of smoulder

smooth /smuːð/ ▶ ADJECTIVE [**smoother, smoothest**]
1 having an even surface □ *She ran her fingers along the smooth surface of the wood.* □ *Babies have beautifully smooth, soft skin.*
2 a smooth substance has no lumps
□ *Stir the ingredients until a smooth paste is formed.*

3 happening without any problems ⌑ *Young people want a smooth transition from school to work.* ▢ *His recovery from the operation was relatively smooth.*
4 having no sudden movements ▢ *Larger boats provide a smoother ride than rowing boats.* ▢ *In one smooth movement, he climbed onto the horse.*
5 too polite and confident in a way that makes people not trust you ▢ *He is a very smooth talker.*
▶ VERB [**smooths, smoothing, smoothed**]
1 to move your hand across something in order to make it flat or smooth ▢ *She smoothed the bed covers and tidied her bedroom.*
2 to make something happen more easily ▢ *Schools are working to smooth the transition from primary school to high school.*
▶ PHRASAL VERB **smooth something over** to end a disagreement or problem, especially by talking to someone ▢ *She invited Antonio to dinner to try and smooth things over.*

smoothie /'smu:ði/ NOUN [*plural* **smoothies**] a thick drink made by crushing fruit

smoothly /'smu:ðli/ ADVERB
1 without any problems ⌑ *The event went very smoothly.* ▢ *The organization was running very smoothly.*
2 without any sudden movements ▢ *He pulled the knife smoothly out of its case.*
3 in a way that is too polite and confident ▢ *'Not at all, sir,' he replied smoothly.*

smother /'smʌðə(r)/ VERB [**smothers, smothering, smothered**]
1 to cover something with a substance ▢ *The little boy's hands were smothered in chocolate.* ▢ *She smothered him with kisses.*
2 to kill someone by putting something over their nose and mouth
3 to give someone too much love and attention ▢ *I felt she was smothering me.*
4 to stop something from happening ▢ *Maya smothered the urge to laugh.*
5 to stop a fire from burning by covering it

smoulder /'sməʊldə(r)/ VERB [**smoulders, smouldering, smouldered**]
1 to burn slowly, without a flame
2 to feel a strong emotion but not express it ▢ *He was smouldering with rage.*

SMS /ˌesem'es/ ABBREVIATION short message service; a system for sending text messages between mobile phones

smudge /smʌdʒ/ ▶ NOUN [*plural* **smudges**] a dirty mark where someone has touched something and it has spread
▶ VERB [**smudges, smudging, smudged**] to spoil the appearance of something by touching it and making it spread ▢ *She had smudged her lipstick.*

smug /smʌɡ/ ADJECTIVE [**smugger, smuggest**] too pleased with your abilities and achievements ▢ *a smug smile* ▢ *Jack looked very smug.*

smuggle /'smʌɡəl/ VERB [**smuggles, smuggling, smuggled**]
1 to bring something into a country illegally ▢ *The weapons had been smuggled into the country.*
2 to take something somewhere secretly ▢ *He smuggled the puppy into his room.*
● **smuggler** /'smʌɡlə(r)/ NOUN [*plural* **smugglers**] someone who brings something into a country illegally
● **smuggling** /'smʌɡlɪŋ/ NOUN, NO PLURAL the activity of bringing something into a country illegally ▢ *drug smuggling* ▢ *a smuggling operation*

smugly /'smʌɡli/ ADVERB in a way that shows you are too pleased with your own abilities and achievements ▢ *He smiled smugly when he heard he had won.*
● **smugness** /'smʌɡnɪs/ NOUN, NO PLURAL when you are too pleased with your own abilities and achievements

smutty /'smʌti/ ADJECTIVE [**smuttier, smuttiest**] slightly rude ▢ *He was telling smutty jokes.*

snack /snæk/ ▶ NOUN [*plural* **snacks**] a small meal, or a small amount of food that you eat between meals ⌑ *She had a snack during the morning.* ⌑ *Some people eat too many snack foods such as crisps and biscuits.*
▶ VERB [**snacks, snacking, snacked**] to eat food between your meals ▢ *Eating a big breakfast will help you not to snack.* ▢ **+ on** *You should try snacking on healthy food such as fruit and nuts.*

snack bar /'snæk bɑ:(r)/ NOUN [*plural* **snack bars**] a place where you can buy snacks

snag /snæɡ/ ▶ NOUN [*plural* **snags**] an informal word meaning a small problem ▢ *The process hit a snag.*
▶ VERB [**snags, snagging, snagged**] to become stuck on something sharp, or to damage something by getting it stuck on something sharp ▢ *Ellie had snagged her tights on a thorn.*

snail /sneɪl/ NOUN [*plural* **snails**]
1 a small creature with a soft body and a shell on its back
2 at a snail's pace very slowly ▢ *He was driving at a snail's pace.*

snail mail NOUN, NO PLURAL a humorous phrase for letters sent by post instead of by computer

snake /sneɪk/ ▶ NOUN [*plural* **snakes**] a long thin animal with no legs, which slides along the ground ▢ *There are several poisonous snakes in the region.*
▶ VERB [**snakes, snaking, snaked**] to move in a thin, curved line ▢ *The queue snaked round the building.*

snap /snæp/ ▶ VERB [**snaps, snapping, snapped**]
1 to break with a sudden, sharp noise or to break something with a sudden, sharp noise ▢ *The twig snapped.* ▢ *He snapped off a piece of his biscuit.*
2 to move into a particular position with a sudden, sharp noise, or to move something like this ▢ *She snapped the book shut.* ▢ *The two plastic parts snap together.*
3 snap your fingers to rub your finger and thumb

together in a quick movement to make a sudden, sharp noise

4 to speak to someone in an angry way □ *When I asked for a break, he snapped at me.*

5 to suddenly be unable to control your emotions, especially your anger □ *I put up with his untidiness, but when he flooded the bathroom, I just snapped.*

6 if an animal snaps, it tries to bite someone or something

7 an informal word meaning to take a photograph □ *He was snapped leaving the restaurant.*

♦ PHRASAL VERBS **snap out of something** to stop feeling angry or upset □ *Come on, snap out of it – you're ruining everyone's day.* **snap something up** to take or buy something quickly and enthusiastically □ *The new handbags were snapped up within days of getting into the shops.*

▶ NOUN [*plural* **snaps**]

1 a sudden, short sound □ *She shut her purse with a snap.*

2 an informal word for a photograph 🔁 *holiday snaps*

▶ ADJECTIVE done or decided very quickly, without much thought 🔁 *a snap decision/judgment*

• **snappy** /'snæpɪ/ ADJECTIVE [**snappier, snappiest**]

1 clever and interesting, and usually not using many words □ *It's a very snappy title for a book.*

2 fashionable □ *He was wearing a very snappy suit.*

3 if someone is snappy, they speak to people in a bad-tempered way

4 quick 🔁 *Get me a coffee, and make it snappy!*

snapshot /'snæpʃɒt/ NOUN [*plural* **snapshots**]

1 a photograph that you take quickly □ *There was a snapshot of him on the beach.*

2 something which gives you an idea of what something else is like □ *His songs were a snapshot of his life.*

snare /sneə(r)/ ▶ NOUN [*plural* **snares**] a device for catching animals

▶ VERB [**snares, snaring, snared**]

1 to catch an animal using a snare

2 to get someone or something which is difficult to get □ *He snared a gold medal in the competition.*

3 to get someone in a situation or place they do not want to be in by using tricks □ *They use these special offers to snare customers.*

snarl /snɑːl/ ▶ VERB [**snarls, snarling, snarled**]

1 to say something in an angry or threatening way □ *'I have no comment,' he snarled.*

2 if an animal snarls, it makes an angry sound and shows its teeth □ *The dog snarled every time he tried to move.*

3 to stop traffic from moving easily □ *The accident snarled traffic along the highway.*

▶ NOUN [*plural* **snarls**] an angry sound or expression in which a person or animal shows their teeth

snatch /snætʃ/ ▶ VERB [**snatches, snatching, snatched**]

1 to take something from someone suddenly and roughly □ *She snatched the book out of my hand.*

2 to quickly get or do something when you do not have much time □ *I managed to snatch an hour's sleep before the party.*

▶ NOUN [*plural* **snatches**] a snatch of something a short part of something such as a piece of music or a conversation □ *I only heard snatches of their conversation.*

sneak /sniːk/ ▶ VERB [**sneaks, sneaking, sneaked**]

1 to go somewhere quietly and secretly □ *Maggie sneaked out of the house.*

2 to take something somewhere secretly □ *He had sneaked his mobile phone into the exam room.*

3 sneak a look/glance at something to look at something quickly and secretly □ *Archie sneaked a look at his watch.*

4 to tell someone in authority something bad that another person has done

♦ PHRASAL VERB **sneak up on someone**

1 to walk towards someone without them seeing or hearing you □ *You scared me sneaking up on me like that.*

2 if an event sneaks up on you, it happens before you are ready for it

▶ NOUN [*plural* **sneaks**] someone who tells people in authority when someone else has done something bad

• **sneaker** /'sniːkə(r)/ NOUN [*plural* **sneakers**] a US word for a type of sports shoe 🔁 *Farooq was wearing a pair of sneakers.*

• **sneaking** /'sniːkɪŋ/ ADJECTIVE

1 have a sneaking feeling/suspicion to think that something is probably true □ *I had a sneaking suspicion that she was lying.*

2 have a sneaking admiration/regard, etc. for someone/something to like someone or something secretly although you do not want to admit it

• **sneaky** /'sniːkɪ/ ADJECTIVE [**sneakier, sneakiest**] clever but slightly unfair or dishonest □ *It was a very sneaky way of making money.*

sneer /snɪə(r)/ ▶ VERB [**sneers, sneering, sneered**] talk about someone or behave towards someone in an unpleasant way that shows that you do not admire them □ *John sneered at my attempt to write a story.* □ *'You're going to need lots of luck,' he sneered.*

▶ NOUN [*plural* **sneers**] a sneering expression or remark

sneeze /sniːz/ ▶ VERB [**sneezes, sneezing, sneezed**] to suddenly blow out air from your nose and mouth in a way that you cannot control □ *Dust always makes me sneeze.*

▶ NOUN [*plural* **sneezes**] the action and sound of sneezing

snide /snaɪd/ ADJECTIVE criticizing someone in a way that is unkind and not direct 🔁 *He kept making snide remarks about my cooking.*

sniff /snɪf/ ▶ VERB [**sniffs, sniffing, sniffed**]

1 to breathe in air through your nose noisily □ *He was crying and sniffing.*

2 to breathe in through your nose in order to smell something □ *Tess sniffed the air.*

▶ NOUN [plural **sniffs**] a quick loud breath through your nose

sniffle /'snɪfəl/ ▶ VERB [**sniffles, sniffling, sniffled**] to sniff several times, especially because you have a cold or are crying

▶ NOUN [plural **sniffles**] a slight cold

snigger /'snɪgə(r)/ ▶ VERB [**sniggers, sniggering, sniggered**] to laugh quietly in an unkind way

▶ NOUN [plural **sniggers**] a quiet unkind laugh

snip /snɪp/ ▶ VERB [**snips, snipping, snipped**] to cut something with a quick small cut using scissors □ She snipped the ends off.

▶ NOUN [plural **snips**] a quick small cut with scissors

snipe /snaɪp/ ▶ VERB [**snipes, sniping, sniped**]
1 to criticize someone in an unpleasant way □ She's always sniping at her colleagues.
2 to shoot at someone from a hidden place

▶ NOUN [plural **snipers**] someone who shoots at people from a hidden place

snippet /'snɪpɪt/ NOUN [plural **snippets**] a small piece of something such as news, information or conversation □ a snippet of information

snivel /'snɪvəl/ VERB [**snivels, snivelling, snivelled**] to cry and complain in a way that annoys other people

snob /snɒb/ NOUN [plural **snobs**] someone who thinks they are better than other people because they belong to a higher social class or because they know more □ Don't be such a snob!

snobbery /'snɒbərɪ/ NOUN, NO PLURAL the attitude or behaviour of a snob

snobbish /'snɒbɪʃ/ also **snobby** /'snɒbɪ/ ADJECTIVE behaving like a snob

snog /snɒg/ VERB [**snogs, snogging, snogged**] if people snog, they kiss each other for a long time. An informal word.

snooker /'snu:kə(r)/ NOUN, NO PLURAL a game played on a table, in which two players try to hit coloured balls into pockets □ a snooker player

snoop /snu:p/ VERB [**snoops, snooping, snooped**]
to look around a place secretly in order to find something □ Jane was snooping around to try to find my diary.
to try to find out information about someone in a secret way □ Mobile phone records allow officials to snoop on innocent citizens.

snooper /'snu:pə(r)/ NOUN [plural **snoopers**] someone who snoops

snooty /'snu:tɪ/ ADJECTIVE [**snootier, snootiest**] behaving in a rude and unfriendly way because you think you are better than other people

snooze /snu:z/ ▶ NOUN [plural **snoozes**] a short light sleep □ Grandad was having a snooze in his chair.
▶ VERB [**snoozes, snoozing, snoozed**] to sleep for a short time

snore /snɔ:(r)/ ▶ VERB [**snores, snoring, snored**] to make a loud noise when you breathe while you are sleeping □ My Dad snores and you can hear it all round the house.

▶ NOUN [plural **snores**] a loud noise that someone makes when they snore

snorkel /'snɔ:kəl/ ▶ NOUN [plural **snorkels**] a tube that allows you to breathe when you are swimming under water

▶ VERB [**snorkels, snorkelling/US snorkeling, snorkelled/US snorkeled**] to swim under water using a snorkel

snort /snɔ:t/ ▶ VERB [**snorts, snorting, snorted**] to make a noise through your nose □ The horses snorted, stamping their hooves. □ He snorted with laughter.
▶ NOUN [plural **snorts**] a loud noise made through your nose □ a snort of laughter

snout /snaʊt/ NOUN [plural **snouts**] a pig's nose

snow /snəʊ/ ▶ NOUN, NO PLURAL soft white pieces that fall from the sky when it is very cold 🔁 15 centimetres of snow fell in many areas. 🔁 Heavy snow affected much of the country. 🔁 The snow was starting to melt.

▶ VERB [**snows, snowing, snowed**]
1 if it snows, snow falls from the sky □ It's been snowing all night.
2 be **snowed in** to be unable to leave your house because there is so much snow
◆ IDIOM be **snowed under** to have too much work □ I'm snowed under with all my college work.

snowball /'snəʊbɔ:l/ ▶ NOUN [plural **snowballs**] a ball of snow that children make and throw at each other 🔁 The children were throwing snowballs. 🔁 a snowball fight

▶ VERB [**snowballs, snowballing, snowballed**] if a situation or a problem snowballs, it grows or develops quickly □ The strike snowballed and soon all the post offices were closed.

snowboarding /'snəʊbɔ:dɪŋ/ NOUN, NO PLURAL a sport in which you move over snow while standing on a board

snowbound /'snəʊbaʊnd/ ADJECTIVE unable to go anywhere because there is too much snow

snow-capped /'snəʊkæpt/ ADJECTIVE snow-capped mountains have snow on the top

snowdrift /'snəʊdrɪft/ NOUN [plural **snowdrifts**] a pile of snow which the wind has blown

snowdrop /'snəʊdrɒp/ NOUN [plural **snowdrops**] a small white flower that grows at the end of winter

snowfall /'snəʊfɔ:l/ NOUN [plural **snowfalls**] an occasion when snow falls from the sky, or the amount of snow which falls 🔁 There was a heavy snowfall overnight.

snowflake /'snəʊfleɪk/ NOUN [plural **snowflakes**] one of the soft white pieces that fall from the sky when it is very cold

snowman /'snəʊmæn/ NOUN [plural **snowmen**] a model of a person which children make from snow 🔁 The children have built a snowman.

snowplough /'snəʊplaʊ/ NOUN [plural **snowploughs**] a vehicle that moves snow off the roads

snowstorm /ˈsnəʊstɔːm/ NOUN [plural **snowstorms**] a storm with a lot of snow

snowy /ˈsnəʊɪ/ ADJECTIVE [**snowier, snowiest**] covered with snow, or involving snow □ snowy hills □ snowy weather

snub /snʌb/ ▶ VERB [**snubs, snubbing, snubbed**] to treat someone in a rude way, especially by ignoring them □ I tried to speak to him but he just snubbed me and turned away.
▶ NOUN [plural **snubs**] an act of snubbing someone □ The government saw the move as a deliberate snub.
▶ ADJECTIVE a snub nose is small and turns up at the end

snuff /snʌf/
◆ PHRASAL VERB [**snuffs, snuffing, snuffed**] snuff something out
1 an informal word meaning to end something in a sudden way □ Injury snuffed out his hopes of winning the competition.
2 to stop a candle burning

snuffle /ˈsnʌfəl/ VERB [**snuffles, snuffling, snuffled**] to breathe noisily through your nose

snug /snʌg/ ADJECTIVE [**snugger, snuggest**]
1 warm and comfortable □ We were all quite snug in our sleeping bags.
2 snug clothes fit quite tightly □ The jacket was a snug fit.

snuggle /ˈsnʌgəl/ VERB [**snuggles, snuggling, snuggled**] to get into a warm and comfortable position □ Sam snuggled up to his mother and soon fell asleep.

snugly /ˈsnʌglɪ/ ADVERB
1 in a warm and comfortable way □ They were all snugly dressed in thick coats.
2 tightly □ The jacket fits quite snugly.

so /səʊ/ ▶ ADVERB
1 used to emphasize the word that follows □ I was so happy to see her. □ I've never seen so many children. □ Thank you so much for all your help.
2 used to avoid repeating something that has just been said □ 'Are you coming to the party?' 'I hope so.' □ 'How do you know Emma's going camping?' 'Because she said so.' ⊞ When she won the competition, she was the first person over 40 to do so.
3 used to say that something is true for something or someone else □ She's tired and so am I. □ The accommodation was dreadful, and so was the food.
4 so far until now □ I'm enjoying the job so far.
5 or so used to show that a number or amount is not exact □ There were forty people or so at the party. □ I've been feeling ill for the last week or so.
6 used to get someone's attention when you want to talk about something □ So, who's ready for some food?
7 So what? used to show that you do not think something is important □ 'Sam will be cross if we're late.' 'So what? He can't do anything to us.'
8 and so on used to show that other similar things could be added to what you have just said □ Make sure you have plenty of pens, pencils, paper and so on.

9 so as to in order to □ We got there early so as to get good seats.
10 used to agree with something that you have just been shown or told □ 'Look, our tomato seeds are coming up.' 'Oh, so they are!'
11 used, often with a hand movement, to describe a size, position, etc. □ I saw a little boy about so high. □ Stretch your leg out so.
▶ CONJUNCTION
1 used to show that something was the reason for something else □ He asked me to come, so I did. □ S[o] they got married and lived happily ever after.
2 so (that) in order to make something happen □ I'v[e] washed my jeans so that I can wear them tomorrow.

soak /səʊk/ VERB [**soaks, soaking, soaked**]
1 to put something in liquid for a period of time □ [If] you soak your blouse, the stain might come out.
2 to make someone or something very wet □ Torrential rain soaked the city.
◆ PHRASAL VERB soak something up
1 if something soaks up a liquid, it takes it in □ I used [a] towel to soak up the spilt milk.
2 to enjoy experiencing something ⊞ We just sat there, soaking up the atmosphere.
● **soaked** /səʊkt/ ADJECTIVE very wet ⊞ It was rainin[g] and I was getting soaked.
● **soaking** /ˈsəʊkɪŋ/ or **soaking wet** /ˈsəʊkɪŋ ˈw[et]/ ADJECTIVE very wet □ Take your clothes off – they're[e] soaking.

so-and-so /ˈsəʊənˌsəʊ/ NOUN [plural **so-and-sos**]
1 used when referring to a person or thing without saying exactly which person or thing □ She's alway[s] gossiping about so-and-so getting married or so-an[d] so's new job.
2 used instead of calling someone a rude name □ S[he] can be a real so-and-so!

soap /səʊp/ NOUN [plural **soaps**]
1 no plural a substance that you use for washing ⊞ [a] bar of soap □ He washed his face with soap and wat[er]
2 a television programme about the lives of a group [of] people which is broadcast regularly □ Do you wat[ch] any of the soaps?

soap opera /ˈsəʊp ˈɒpərə/ NOUN [plural **soap operas**] a formal word for soap (=television programme)

soap powder /ˈsəʊp ˈpaʊdə(r)/ NOUN, NO PLURA[L] soap in the form of a powder, used for washing clot[hes]

soapy /ˈsəʊpɪ/ ADJECTIVE [**soapier, soapiest**] cove[red] in, full of, or similar to soap □ soapy water

soar /sɔː(r)/ VERB [**soars, soaring, soared**]
1 to increase very quickly to a high level □ The pri[ce of] petrol has soared over the last ten years.
2 to fly high in the air □ An eagle soared high ab[ove] their heads.
● **soaring** /ˈsɔːrɪŋ/ ADJECTIVE increasing very quick[ly] □ soaring prices

sob /sɒb/ ▶ VERB [**sobs, sobbing, sobbed**] to cry noisily □ *Lisa lay on her bed, sobbing.*

▶ NOUN [*plural* **sobs**] the sound of someone sobbing

sober /ˈsəʊbə(r)/ ADJECTIVE
1 not drunk
2 serious □ *a sober man*
3 plain and not brightly coloured □ *sober colours*

● **sobering** /ˈsəʊbərɪŋ/ ADJECTIVE making you become serious and think about a situation □ *The accident is a sobering reminder of how dangerous motorbikes can be.*

sob story /ˈsɒb ˌstɔːrɪ/ NOUN [*plural* **sob stories**] an informal word meaning a story that you tell someone to make them feel sorry for you □ *He gave me some sob story about his mother being ill.*

so-called /ˌsəʊˈkɔːld/ ADJECTIVE used for showing that you think a word used for describing someone or something is wrong □ *My so-called friend has stolen some money from me.*

soccer /ˈsɒkə(r)/ NOUN, NO PLURAL football □ *The children were playing soccer.* □ *a soccer ball*

sociable /ˈsəʊʃəbəl/ ADJECTIVE someone who is sociable enjoys being with other people □ *I'm quite a sociable person.*

social /ˈsəʊʃəl/ ADJECTIVE
1 to do with society □ *The programme is designed to tackle crime and other social problems.* □ *The school attracts students from all social backgrounds.*
2 to do with meeting and being friendly with other people □ *I always feel nervous in social situations.* □ *a social club* ⊞ *He didn't have very good social skills.*

socialism /ˈsəʊʃəlɪzəm/ NOUN, NO PLURAL the political belief that a country's main industries should be owned by the government, and that people should have equal opportunities

socialist /ˈsəʊʃəlɪst/ ▶ NOUN [*plural* **socialists**] someone who believes in socialism
▶ ADJECTIVE to do with socialism □ *socialist principles*

socialize *or* **socialise** /ˈsəʊʃəlaɪz/ VERB [**socializes, socializing, socialized**] to spend time with other people for fun □ *He doesn't socialize much.*

social life /ˈsəʊʃəl ˈlaɪf/ NOUN [*plural* **social lives**] the time when you do things with friends □ *She has a busy social life.*

socially /ˈsəʊʃəlɪ/ ADVERB
in a way that is to do with society □ *This is a socially conservative country.*
in a way that is connected with people meeting each other and being friendly □ *He never mixes socially with his colleagues.*

social networking /ˈsəʊʃəl ˈnetwɜːkɪŋ/ NOUN, NO PLURAL using websites to meet people and talk to them

social science /ˈsəʊʃəl ˈsaɪəns/ NOUN [*plural* **social sciences**] the study of society and the way it is organized

social security /ˈsəʊʃəl sɪˈkjʊərətɪ/ NOUN, NO PLURAL money that the government pays to people who are poor, ill, or unemployed

social services /ˈsəʊʃəl ˈsɜːvɪsɪz/ PLURAL NOUN the government department that provides help to people who have problems with their lives

social work /ˈsəʊʃəl ˈwɜːk/ NOUN, NO PLURAL work that the government pays for to help people who are poor, ill, or have problems

● **social worker** /ˈsəʊʃəl ˈwɜːkə(r)/ NOUN [*plural* **social workers**] someone whose job is to help people who are poor, ill, or have problems

society /səˈsaɪətɪ/ NOUN [*plural* **societies**]
1 all the people who live in a group or in a particular country or area □ *Racism still exists in British society.* □ *Australia is a more multicultural society.* ⊞ *We have a responsibility to support the weaker members of society.*
2 an organization for people with a particular interest □ *She joined the university's debating society.*

sociologist /ˌsəʊsɪˈɒlədʒɪst/ NOUN [*plural* **sociologists**] someone who studies how human societies are organized and how people behave

● **sociology** /ˌsəʊsɪˈɒlədʒɪ/ NOUN, NO PLURAL the study of societies and the way people behave

sock /sɒk/ NOUN [*plural* **socks**] a covering for your foot that you wear inside your shoe ⊞ *a pair of socks* ⊞ *She was wearing black socks.*

♦ IDIOM **pull your socks up** to try to improve your behaviour or work □ *You'll have to pull your socks up if you want to pass the exam.*

socket /ˈsɒkɪt/ NOUN [*plural* **sockets**]
1 the place on a wall where you connect electrical equipment to the electricity supply □ *an electric socket*
2 a hollow place that something fits into □ *She nearly pulled my arm out of its socket.*

soda /ˈsəʊdə/ NOUN, NO PLURAL water with bubbles in it that you mix with other drinks

sodden /ˈsɒdən/ ADJECTIVE very wet □ *The ground's sodden after all that rain.*

sodium /ˈsəʊdɪəm/ NOUN, NO PLURAL a chemical element found in salt. A chemistry word.

sofa /ˈsəʊfə/ NOUN [*plural* **sofas**] a long, comfortable seat for more than one person □ *Dan and Clare were sitting on the sofa watching television.*

sofa bed /ˈsəʊfə ˈbed/ NOUN [*plural* **sofa beds**] a sofa that you can pull out to make into a bed

soft /sɒft/ ADJECTIVE [**softer, softest**]
1 not hard or firm □ *a nice soft cushion* □ *soft ground*
2 smooth and pleasant to touch □ *She had soft silky hair.* □ *soft leather*
3 not severe enough with other people when they have done something wrong □ *He's far too soft with his children.* □ **+ on** *I think the government is too soft on crime.*
4 not loud □ *a soft voice*
5 not bright □ *Her bedroom is decorated in soft pastel colours.* □ *a soft light*
6 an informal word meaning easy and not involving much work ⊞ *The subject isn't a soft option.*

♦ IDIOM **have a soft spot for someone** an informal phrase meaning to like someone □ *I've always had a soft spot for Jenny.*

soft drink /'sɒft 'drɪŋk/ NOUN [plural **soft drinks**] a cold drink that does not contain alcohol

soften /'sɒfən/ VERB [**softens, softening, softened**]
1 to become soft or to make something soft □ *Soften the clay by working it with your hands.* □ *The cream softens the skin.*
2 to make the effect of something unpleasant slightly easier ᵇ *They tried to soften the blow of job losses by helping staff to retrain.*
3 to become more friendly, gentle or kind □ *Her face softened and she smiled.* □ *He appears to have softened his stance on the issue.*
4 to become or to make something become less strong, less bright, etc. □ *Her voice softened as she looked at the baby.*

soft fruit /'sɒft 'fruːt/ NOUN [plural **soft fruits** or **soft fruit**] a small fruit with no stone, for example a strawberry or a blackcurrant

softly /'sɒftlɪ/ ADVERB gently or quietly □ *Snow was falling softly in the moonlight.* □ *She stroked the cat softly.*

softness /'sɒftnɪs/ NOUN, NO PLURAL the quality of being soft, gentle or quiet □ *the softness of the pillows*

soft-spoken /'sɒft'spəʊkən/ ADJECTIVE having a quiet, gentle voice □ *his shy, soft-spoken manner*

soft toy /'sɒft 'tɔɪ/ NOUN [plural **soft toys**] a toy made from cloth, usually in the form of an animal

software /'sɒftweə(r)/ NOUN, NO PLURAL computer programs. A computing word. ᵇ *We've installed new software.* ᵇ *Users need to download a piece of software.*

soggy /'sɒgɪ/ ADJECTIVE [**soggier, soggiest**] unpleasantly wet and soft □ *soggy ground* □ *I had to walk back in soggy shoes.*

soil /sɔɪl/ ▶ NOUN, NO PLURAL
1 the top layer of the ground, that you can grow plants in □ *a soil sample* □ *Rice and corn grow well in the rich soil.* □ *He brushed the red, sandy soil off his trousers.*
2 used to talk about the land belonging to a particular country □ *It was his first win on American soil.*
▶ VERB [**soils, soiling, soiled**] a formal word meaning to make something dirty □ *soiled linen*

solace /'sɒləs/ NOUN, NO PLURAL a formal word meaning comfort from very sad feelings or disappointment ᵇ *She found some solace in writing poetry.*

solar /'səʊlə(r)/ ADJECTIVE
1 to do with the sun □ *a solar eclipse*
2 to do with energy from the sun □ *solar panels*

solar energy /'səʊlə(r) 'enədʒɪ/ or **solar power** /'səʊlə(r) 'paʊə(r)/ NOUN, NO PLURAL electricity that is made using the sun's light and heat

solar system /'səʊlə(r) sɪstəm/ NOUN [plural **solar systems**] the sun and the planets that move around it

sold /səʊld/ PAST TENSE AND PAST PARTICIPLE OF **sell**

solder /'səʊldə(r)/ ▶ VERB [**solders, soldering, soldered**] to join two pieces of metal with metal that has been melted
▶ NOUN, NO PLURAL melted metal used to join pieces of metal together

soldier /'səʊldʒə(r)/ NOUN [plural **soldiers**] someone who is in the army □ *Two soldiers from the same regiment were captured.*

sole [1] /səʊl/ ADJECTIVE
1 only □ *Her sole ambition was to be famous.* □ *A young boy was the sole survivor of the accident.*
2 belonging to only one person □ *He has sole ownership of the company.*

sole [2] /səʊl/ NOUN [plural **soles**] the bottom part of your foot or of a shoe ᵇ *The sand was hot on the soles of her feet.*

sole [3] /səʊl/ NOUN [plural **sole**] a flat fish that people can eat

solely /'səʊllɪ/ ADVERB only or alone □ *You are solely responsible for your own actions.* □ *The centre is run solely by volunteers.*

solemn /'sɒləm/ ADJECTIVE
1 serious and sometimes sad □ *a solemn expression* □ *a rather solemn little boy*
2 happening in a serious, formal way ᵇ *a solemn ceremony* □ *It was a solemn occasion.*
3 done or said in a serious and sincere way ᵇ *You've got to make me a solemn promise.*
• **solemnity** /sə'lemnətɪ/ NOUN, NO PLURAL the quality of being solemn
• **solemnly** /'sɒləmlɪ/ ADVERB in a solemn way □ *Jo nodded solemnly.*

solicit /sə'lɪsɪt/ VERB [**solicits, soliciting, solicited**] formal word meaning to ask someone for advice, help or money □ *The government is trying to solicit aid from other countries.*

solicitor /sə'lɪsɪtə(r)/ NOUN [plural **solicitors**] someone whose job is to give advice to people about the law and help them with legal work □ *a firm of solicitors*

solicitous /sə'lɪsɪtəs/ ADJECTIVE a formal word meaning showing that you care a lot about someone's comfort and happiness □ *She talked about you constantly and seemed most solicitous for your welfare.*

solid /'sɒlɪd/ ▶ ADJECTIVE
1 firm and with a fixed shape, not in the form of a liquid or a gas ᵇ *They scrambled through the mud to more solid ground.* □ *The river froze solid.*
2 not hollow or with no spaces inside □ *a solid chocolate egg* ᵇ *They had to cut through solid rock.*
3 able to be trusted □ *He's a solid and dependable leader.* ᵇ *We don't have any solid evidence.*
4 strong and well made □ *a solid piece of furniture*
5 solid gold, silver, etc. made only of gold, silver, □ *a solid gold pendant*

6 with no pauses in between □ *I've been working for six solid hours.*

7 good, but not excellent or special □ *I think it was a pretty solid performance.*

8 a solid shape has length, width, and height. A maths word. □ *A cube is a solid figure.*

▶ NOUN [*plural* **solids**]

1 something that is not a liquid or a gas □ *This element changes from a solid to a gas when heated.*

2 a shape that has length, width, and height. A maths word.

3 solids food in the form of solid substances, not liquids □ *Do not eat any solids for 24 hours.*

solidarity /ˌsɒlɪˈdærəti/ NOUN, NO PLURAL loyal support and agreement between members of a group ⬚ *The Scandinavian countries showed solidarity with Norway.*

solid fuel /ˌsɒlɪd ˈfjuəl/ NOUN [*plural* **solid fuels**] a type of fuel that is made from something solid, such as coal or wood

solidify /səˈlɪdɪfaɪ/ VERB [**solidifies, solidifying, solidified**]

1 to become solid or to make something solid □ *Let the butter cool and solidify slightly.*

2 a formal word meaning to become stronger or clearer □ *He has solidified his position as the group's spokesman.*

solidly /ˈsɒlɪdli/ ADVERB

1 strongly or firmly ⬚ *a solidly built structure* □ *He struck it solidly with his fist.*

2 continuously □ *We've been working solidly since nine o'clock this morning.* □ *It had been raining solidly for a week.*

3 supporting or believing something strongly □ *Public opinion is solidly against the move.*

4 well, but not in a special way □ *Hicks played solidly.*

solitary /ˈsɒlɪtəri/ ADJECTIVE

1 lonely or alone □ *She saw a solitary figure standing near the door.* □ *He lived a solitary existence.*

2 used to emphasize that there is only one person or thing □ *He could not remember a single solitary fact from the previous lesson.*

solitary confinement /ˌsɒlɪtəri kənˈfaɪnmənt/ NOUN, NO PLURAL if a prisoner is in solitary confinement, they are kept by themselves and are not allowed to communicate with others

solitude /ˈsɒlɪtjuːd/ NOUN, NO PLURAL when you are alone □ *She enjoyed the solitude of her little cottage by the lake.*

solo /ˈsəʊləʊ/ ▶ NOUN [*plural* **solos**] a piece of music or a song for one person to play or sing □ *a guitar solo* □ *Emma sang a solo in the Christmas concert.*

ADJECTIVE done or performed by one person alone □ *a solo flight* □ *a solo album* □ *He went on to have a career as a solo artist.*

ADVERB alone □ *It's the first time he's flown solo.*

soloist /ˈsəʊləʊɪst/ NOUN [*plural* **soloists**] someone who sings or plays a solo

solstice /ˈsɒlstɪs/ NOUN [*plural* **solstices**] one of the two days in the year when there are the most hours of light or darkness ⬚ *the summer/winter solstice*

soluble /ˈsɒljʊbəl/ ADJECTIVE

1 a soluble substance will dissolve in a liquid. A chemistry word □ *soluble aspirin* □ *The drug is soluble in water.*

2 a soluble problem can be solved

solution /səˈluːʃən/ NOUN [*plural* **solutions**]

1 an answer to a problem or a question □ **+ to** *It's difficult to offer simple solutions to a complex problem.* ⬚ *We must try to find a peaceful solution.*

2 a liquid with a substance dissolved in it. A chemistry word □ *a salt water solution* □ *a bottle of contact lens solution*

▶ Remember that 'solution' meaning 'an answer to a problem' is followed by the preposition to:
✓ There is no easy solution **to** the problem.
✗ There is no easy solution of the problem.

solve /sɒlv/ VERB [**solves, solving, solved**]

1 to find an answer to a problem or a difficult question □ *Solve the puzzle to win a prize.* ⬚ *A new bridge won't solve the traffic problem.*

2 to understand and explain how a mystery happened or a crime took place ⬚ *Scientists believe they have solved the mystery.* ⬚ *This information could help us to solve the crime.*

solvent[1] /ˈsɒlvənt/ NOUN [*plural* **solvents**] something that dissolves another substance. A chemistry word.

solvent[2] /ˈsɒlvənt/ ADJECTIVE having enough money to pay what you owe □ *At last they were financially solvent.*

somber /ˈsɒmbə(r)/ ADJECTIVE the US spelling of sombre

• **somberly** /ˈsɒmbəli/ ADVERB the US spelling of sombrely

sombre /ˈsɒmbə(r)/ ADJECTIVE

1 serious and sad □ *I found him in a sombre mood.* □ *a sombre ceremony*

2 dark in colour □ *sombre colours* □ *a sombre suit*

• **sombrely** /ˈsɒmbəli/ ADVERB in a serious and sad way □ *'It's a great shame,' he said sombrely.*

sombrero /sɒmˈbreərəʊ/ NOUN [*plural* **sombreros**] a Mexican hat with a wide brim

some /sʌm/ DETERMINER, PRONOUN

1 used to talk about a number or an amount without saying exactly how many or how much □ *It's all right; I've got some money.* □ *Would you like some more milk?* □ *I've made a cake – would you like some?*

2 used to talk about part of a larger amount or number of things or people □ **+ of** *Some of the apples were rotten.* □ *Some people have brought rain coats and some haven't.*

3 a fairly large amount of something, especially time or distance □ *It was some time before I noticed.* □ *We've still got some way to go.*

4 used to talk about a person or a thing when you do not know exactly who or what they are □ *He mentioned some letter that he had received.* □ *Some silly person forgot to close the gate.*

somebody /'sʌmbədɪ/ PRONOUN
1 used to talk about a person when you do not know who they are or it is not necessary to say their name □ *Somebody knocked at the door.* □ *They get money every time somebody downloads a song.* □ *She's somebody who's popular at school.* 🖰 *Let somebody else* (=another person) *do it for a change.*
2 an important person □ *He really thinks he's somebody in that big car.*

some day *or* **someday** /'sʌmdeɪ/ ADVERB at a time in the future although you are not sure exactly when □ *Prince William will be king some day.* □ *We'll go and visit them someday soon.*

somehow /'sʌmhaʊ/ ADVERB in a way that is not known or that you do not understand □ *Don't worry, we'll manage somehow.* □ *She'd somehow managed to get her finger caught in the mechanism.* □ *Somehow, it didn't seem very important.* 🖰 *He'll succeed in the end, somehow or other.*

someone /'sʌmwʌn/ PRONOUN used to talk about a person when you do not know who they are or it is not necessary to say their name □ *We'll have to find someone to replace him.* □ *I was having a conversation with someone at work about it.* □ *It could save someone's life.* 🖰 *It's good to have someone else* (=another person) *to blame.*

someplace /'sʌmpleɪs/ ADVERB a US word for somewhere □ *Are you going someplace?* □ *I left my glasses someplace around here.*

somersault /'sʌməsɔːlt/ ▶ NOUN [plural **somersaults**] when you turn your body over in the air so that your feet go over your head
▶ VERB [**somersaults, somersaulting, somersaulted**] to do a somersault □ *She somersaulted neatly into the water.*

something /'sʌmθɪŋ/ PRONOUN
1 used to talk about a thing or a fact when you do not know what it is, or when it is not necessary to say what it is □ *I've got something in my eye.* □ *Let's have something to eat before we go.* □ *She told me something else as well.* □ *The roof's leaking and we need to do something about it.*
2 used to show that what you have said is only a guess or an example □ *I think he's an actor or something like that.* □ *She speaks something like ten different languages.* 🖰 *We could take her some flowers or something.*
3 **have something to do with something** to be connected with something, or to be the cause of something □ *I think Alison had something to do with organizing the party.* □ *I'm not sure why they came*

home early, but the weather might have had something to do with it.

sometime /'sʌmtaɪm/ ▶ ADVERB used to talk about a time when you do not know when it is or it is not necessary to say exactly when it is □ *I'll talk to you about it sometime when you aren't so busy.* □ *They should arrive sometime soon.* □ *They left this neighbourhood sometime last year.*
▶ ADJECTIVE
1 used to talk about someone who had a particular position in the past, but not any longer □ *Dr Wilson, sometime member of Trinity College*
2 used to talk about someone who does something only part of the time, not always □ *He's a writer and sometime actor.*

sometimes /'sʌmtaɪmz/ ADVERB at times, but not always □ *I still see him sometimes.* □ *Sometimes I feel like giving up my job and moving away.*

somewhat /'sʌmwɒt/ ADVERB quite or slightly □ *The wind had died down somewhat.* □ *It came as somewhat of a surprise.*

somewhere /'sʌmweə(r)/ ADVERB
1 used to talk about a place when you do not know where it is, or when it is not necessary to say where it is □ *Let's go away somewhere for a few days.* □ *They live somewhere near Oxford.* □ *It must be around here somewhere.* □ *Put it somewhere safe.* 🖰 *If you don't like it, we can go somewhere else* (=to another place)
2 used to talk about an approximate amount, time, or number □ **+ between** *She must be somewhere between 35 and 40.* □ **+ around** *They generally cos somewhere around $30.*
3 **get somewhere** to make progress □ *I think we're getting somewhere with them.*

son /sʌn/ NOUN [plural **sons**] someone's male ch 🖰 *They have two young sons.* 🖰 *Her eldest son, Dav is at university.* □ **+ of** *He's the son of Algerian immigrants.*

sonar /'səʊnɑː(r)/ NOUN, NO PLURAL equipment tha uses sound waves to find out where things are und water

sonata /sə'nɑːtə/ NOUN [plural **sonatas**] a piece o classical music, in several parts, for one musical instrument

song /sɒŋ/ NOUN [plural **songs**]
1 a piece of music with words that you sing □ *a p song* □ *This is one of my favourite songs.* 🖰 *She mos sings folk songs.*
2 *no plural* songs in general or the activity of sing □ *A blackbird suddenly burst into song.* □ *a song a dance routine*
♦ IDIOM **make a song and dance about something** informal phrase meaning to treat something as be more difficult or more annoying than it really is □ *don't want to make a big song and dance about it*

songbird /'sɒŋbɜ:d/ NOUN [plural **songbirds**] a bird that sings

sonic /'sɒnɪk/ ADJECTIVE to do with sound. A physics word □ a sonic boom

son-in-law /'sʌnɪnlɔ:/ NOUN [plural **sons-in-law**] your daughter's husband

sonnet /'sɒnɪt/ NOUN [plural **sonnets**] a type of poem that has 14 lines

soon /su:n/ ADVERB [**sooner, soonest**]

1 in a short time from now □ It will soon be summer. □ I hope to see you soon. □ Soon we'll be reaching Liverpool □ I'd like the work done by Friday, or sooner if you can. 🔁 I'll do it as soon as I can.

2 too soon too early □ It's too soon to tell whether she'll recover. □ Help arrived not a moment too soon.

3 as soon as immediately □ As soon as I saw her, I knew something was wrong. □ He started shouting at us as soon as we arrived.

4 sooner or later used to say that you are certain that something will happen at some time in the future □ Sooner or later there's going to be an accident.

5 no sooner ... than used to talk about something that happens immediately after something else □ No sooner had we eaten than we were sent off to work again.

soot /sut/ NOUN, NO PLURAL the black powder that is produced when wood, coal, etc. burns

soothe /su:ð/ VERB [**soothes, soothing, soothed**]
to make someone feel calmer or happier □ She was unable to soothe her crying baby.
to make pain less strong □ I had a bath to soothe my sore muscles.

soothing /'su:ðɪŋ/ ADJECTIVE
making you feel calmer or happier □ soothing music 🔁 She had a soft, soothing voice.
making pain less strong □ a soothing massage

sooty /'suti/ ADJECTIVE [**sootier, sootiest**] covered in soot or like soot

sophisticated /sə'fɪstɪkeɪtɪd/ ADJECTIVE
knowing a lot about the world, culture, fashion, etc. a highly sophisticated audience □ It's a sophisticated and cosmopolitan city.
using new and clever ideas 🔁 highly sophisticated software

sophistication /sə,fɪstɪ'keɪʃən/ NOUN, NO PLURAL
the quality of being sophisticated □ a level of technical sophistication □ She preferred the sophistication of the French capital.

sopping /'sɒpɪŋ/ ADJECTIVE an informal word meaning very wet □ a sopping towel 🔁 They pulled off their sopping wet clothes.

soppy /'sɒpi/ ADJECTIVE [**soppier, soppiest**] showing too much emotion in a way that seems silly □ a soppy love song

soprano /sə'prɑ:nəu/ NOUN [plural **sopranos**]
a very high singing voice
a woman or young boy with a high singing voice

sorbet /'sɔ:beɪ/ NOUN [plural **sorbets**] a sweet food made with crushed ice, sugar and fruit

sorcerer /'sɔ:sərə(r)/ NOUN [plural **sorcerers**] a man in stories who can do magic

• **sorceress** /'sɔ:sərɪs/ NOUN [plural **sorceresses**] a woman in stories who can do magic

• **sorcery** /'sɔ:səri/ NOUN, NO PLURAL magic, or the ability to do magic

sordid /'sɔ:dɪd/ ADJECTIVE to do with behaviour which is dishonest or morally bad □ a sordid secret □ What was his role in this sordid affair?

sore /sɔ:(r)/ ► ADJECTIVE [**sorer, sorest**]

1 if a part of your body is sore, it is painful □ a sore finger 🔁 She woke up with a sore throat. 🔁 My legs feel sore today.

2 a sore point something which you are angry or upset about and do not want to talk about □ His job situation is a bit of a sore point at the moment.

► NOUN [plural **sores**] a red, painful place on your skin □ The horse had a nasty sore on its leg.

• **sorely** /'sɔ:li/ ADVERB very much or a lot 🔁 He was sorely disappointed. 🔁 Mr Watson will be sorely missed by his colleagues.

• **soreness** /'sɔ:nɪs/ NOUN, NO PLURAL when something is sore □ He has a lot of muscle soreness.

sorrow /'sɒrəu/ NOUN [plural **sorrows**]

1 a feeling of great sadness □ The President expressed his great sorrow. □ I couldn't find the words to comfort her in her sorrow.

2 something that makes you feel sad □ the joys and sorrows of parenthood

• **sorrowful** /'sɒrəful/ ADJECTIVE very sad □ a long, sorrowful face

• **sorrowfully** /'sɒrəfəli/ ADVERB in a sorrowful way □ She stared sorrowfully at the broken pieces.

sorry /'sɒri/ ADJECTIVE [**sorrier, sorriest**]

1 (I'm) sorry (a) something that you say when you have done something wrong, hurt someone, upset someone, etc. □ Sorry, I didn't mean to hurt you. □ I'm so sorry - I've spilt tea on your carpet. 🔁 He broke my chair and he never even said sorry. (b) something you say to be polite when you have to tell someone something they may not like □ Sorry, the shop's closing now. □ I'm sorry, but the tickets have all been sold. (c) something you say when you disagree or argue with someone □ I'm sorry, but this work just isn't good enough. □ I'm sorry, but I am not clearing up after you any more!

2 ashamed about something that you have done and wishing you had not done it □ She knows how much she upset us, and she's not even sorry. □ **+ that** I'm really sorry that I lied to you. □ **+ about** I'm sorry about forgetting your birthday. □ **+ for** He's truly sorry for spoiling your party.

3 feeling sympathy for someone □ I was sorry to hear about your father. □ **+ for** I feel really sorry for Anna, having to travel on her own. □ **+ that** I was sorry that you didn't get the job. 🕮 *It's time to stop feeling sorry for yourself and get on with your life.*

4 used to say that you wish a situation could have been different □ *+ that* *I was sorry that I never met her.* □ *+ to do something* *I think they were sorry to leave.* 🕮 *I'm sorry to say that I was not impressed by the restaurant.*

sort /sɔːt/ ► NOUN [*plural* **sorts**]

1 a type of thing or person □ *+ of* *What sort of books do you read?* □ *We won't tolerate that sort of behaviour here.* □ *It's the sort of shop that might sell matches.* 🕮 *There were all sorts of people there.* 🕮 *She needs to take up a hobby of some sort.* 🕮 *He enjoys skiing and that sort of thing.*

2 sort of similar, but not exactly what has been said □ *I think she'd sort of forgotten about us by then.* □ *The house was sort of cut out of the rock.*

3 of sorts used to describe something that acts as a particular thing, but is not as good as the usual thing □ *We made a bed of sorts from dried grass.* □ *He was able to claim a victory of sorts.*

► VERB [**sorts, sorting, sorted**]

1 to arrange things or people into groups or into a particular order □ *+ into* *We sorted the books into piles by subject.*

2 an informal word meaning to arrange or deal successfully with something □ *'What about accommodation?' 'Already sorted!'*

♦ PHRASAL VERBS **sort something out** to arrange or deal successfully with something □ *We've sorted out a new system for feeding the cattle.* □ *Did you manage to sort out Jackie's problem with her computer?* **sort through something** to look at a number of things in order to look for something or to organize them □ *It took us ages to sort through his correspondence.*

SOS /ˌesəʊˈes/ NOUN, NO PLURAL a signal that a ship or aircraft sends to ask for help

so-so /ˈsəʊsəʊ/ ADJECTIVE not very good but not very bad □ *The restaurant looked nice but the meal was so-so.*

sought /sɔːt/ PAST TENSE AND PAST PARTICIPLE OF seek

sought-after /ˈsɔːtɑːftə(r)/ ADJECTIVE if something is sought-after, many people want to have it and try hard to get it □ *His watercolours are now much sought-after.*

soul /səʊl/ NOUN [*plural* **souls**]

1 the part of a person that is not their body but which some people believe continues to exist after they die □ *the souls of the dead* □ *God rest his soul.*

2 your inner feelings and character 🕮 *She isn't one to bare her soul* (=express her inner feelings) *and rarely gives interviews.* 🕮 *I searched my soul, but I could not agree to her wishes.*

3 a type of pop music that expresses strong emotions, especially played by Black Americans 🕮 *a soul singer* 🕮 *He grew up listening to soul music.*

4 a person □ *The poor old soul got an awful shock.*

□ *A few brave souls waited in the rain.*

5 the special character of something □ *The market place is the soul of the city.*

soul-destroying /ˈsəʊldɪˈstrɔɪɪŋ/ ADJECTIVE very boring or upsetting, especially because of continuing for a long time □ *The work is absolutely soul-destroying.*

soulful /ˈsəʊlfʊl/ ADJECTIVE having or expressing deep feelings of sadness □ *The dog has large soulful eyes.*

● **soulfully** /ˈsəʊlfəlɪ/ ADVERB in a soulful way □ *He sang soulfully of the lost days of his youth.*

soulless /ˈsəʊllɪs/ ADJECTIVE

1 having no interesting or attractive features □ *a soulless modern hotel*

2 showing no emotion □ *She met my gaze with her soulless eyes.*

sound /saʊnd/ ► NOUN [*plural* **sounds**]

1 something that you can hear 🕮 *I could hear a fair sound.* □ *+ of* *We heard the sound of breaking glass.* 🕮 *Elspeth made a sound of disgust.* □ *There isn't a sound coming from the children's bedroom.*

2 the sound of something the way that something you read or hear about seems to you □ *I don't much like the sound of your new boss.* 🕮 *You need a holiday by the sound of it.*

► VERB [**sounds, sounding, sounded**]

1 if something sounds good, bad, etc., it seems that way from what you have heard or read □ *Tom's holiday sounds wonderful.* □ *I don't want to sound to negative.* □ *I don't think that sounds right. Are you sure?* 🕮 *You sound as though you know a lot about* 🕮 *You sound as if you're not certain.* 🕮 *That sound like a good idea.*

2 used to talk about a noise that you hear □ *His voi sounded shaky.* □ *All their songs sound exactly the same.* 🕮 *That sounds like Zoe's voice in the kitchen.*

3 to make a noise □ *Sound your horn before you tu the corner.* □ *If the fire alarm sounds, leave the building immediately.*

♦ PHRASAL VERBS **sound off** an informal phrase meaning to express your feelings and opinions, oft loudly and angrily □ *I shouldn't have sounded off you like I did this morning.* **sound someone out** ask for someone's opinion about something □ *Co you sound John out about my suggestion?*

► ADJECTIVE [**sounder, soundest**]

1 strong, firm or healthy □ *The walls of the old church were still sound.* □ *Her health was pretty sound.*

2 good, sensible and that you can trust 🕮 *It seem like sound advice.* □ *The recommendations are ba on scientifically sound evidence.*

3 a sound sleep is deep and difficult to wake up fr

4 good and complete □ *He has a sound knowledg French.*

► ADVERB **sound asleep** if someone is sound asle they are sleeping and it is difficult to wake them [ten o'clock I was still sound asleep.

sound barrier /'saʊnd 'bærɪə(r)/ NOUN, NO PLURAL the point at which an aircraft is travelling at the same speed as sound 🖻 *The jets can break the sound barrier.*

sound bite /'saʊndbaɪt/ NOUN [plural **sound bites**] a short statement made by a politician or someone famous that is reported in newspapers, on television, etc. because it is interesting, funny or clever

sound card /'saʊndkɑːd/ NOUN [plural **sound cards**] a small part in a computer that allows it to play sounds. A computing word.

sound effect /'saʊnd ɪ'fekt/ NOUN [plural **sound effects**] the sounds that are used in films and plays which are made artificially

soundly /'saʊndlɪ/ ADVERB

1 sleep soundly if you sleep soundly, you sleep well and nothing wakes you □ *Within a few minutes she was sleeping soundly.*

2 completely 🖻 *The party was soundly defeated in recent elections.*

3 in a way that is good, strong or sensible □ *The business is soundly managed.*

soundproof /'saʊndpruːf/ ADJECTIVE a soundproof material, structure, or room is made so that sound cannot pass through it

soundtrack /'saʊndtræk/ NOUN [plural **soundtracks**] a recording of the music from a film or television programme

soup /suːp/ NOUN [plural **soups**] a liquid food made from meat, fish or vegetables □ *a bowl of chicken soup*

sour /'saʊə(r)/ ► ADJECTIVE [**sourer, sourest**]
sour food has a bitter taste like a lemon, sometimes because it is bad □ *sour plums* □ *a sour taste* 🖻 *The milk had gone sour in the sun.*
unfriendly and unpleasant □ *He wore a sour expression.* 🖻 *The day started on a sour note.*

IDIOM **sour grapes** used to say that someone is criticizing something because they are jealous or disappointed □ *I'm not going to question the referee's decisions, because that would be sour grapes.*

► VERB [**sours, souring, soured**] to become unfriendly or unpleasant □ *The whole mood had soured.* 🖻 *The incident soured relations between the two countries.*

source /sɔːs/ NOUN [plural **sources**]
where something begins or comes from □ *renewable energy sources* □ *Nuts are a rich source of protein.* □ *Tourism is the island's main source of income.*
a person, book, etc. that you get information from □ *Police sources said that the attack was a suicide bombing.*
the original cause of something, especially a problem □ *Money is a major source of tension in many families.*
the place where a river starts

south /saʊθ/ ► NOUN
the direction that is to your right when you are facing towards the rising sun

2 the part of a country or the world that is in the south □ *We went on holiday to the south of France.*
► ADJECTIVE, ADVERB in or towards the south □ *the south coast* □ *The river flows south into the sea.*
• **southbound** /'saʊθbaʊnd/ ADJECTIVE moving or going towards the south 🖻 *southbound traffic*

south-east /'saʊθiːst/ ► NOUN
1 the direction between south and east
2 the part of a country between the south and the east □ *It's another sunny day in the south-east.*
► ADJECTIVE, ADVERB in or towards the south-east □ *the south-east coast*

southerly /'sʌðəlɪ/ ADJECTIVE coming from or going towards the south □ *Southerly gales are forecast.* □ *They were travelling in a southerly direction.*

southern /'sʌðən/ ADJECTIVE in or from the south □ *the southern states of the USA*
• **southerner** /'sʌðənə(r)/ NOUN [plural **southerners**] a person from the south

South Pole /'saʊθ 'pəʊl/ NOUN the South Pole the point on the Earth that is furthest South

southward /'saʊθwəd/ or **southwards** /'saʊθwədz/ ADVERB to or towards the south □ *We were soon heading southward down the motorway.*

south-west /'saʊθwest/ ► NOUN
1 the direction between south and west
2 the part of a country between the south and the west □ *the south-west of France*
► ADJECTIVE, ADVERB in or towards the south-west

souvenir /ˌsuːvə'nɪə(r)/ NOUN [plural **souvenirs**] something that you buy to help you remember a particular place or occasion □ **+ of** *We brought back some shells as souvenirs of our holiday.* 🖻 *a souvenir shop*

sovereign /'sɒvrɪn/ ► NOUN [plural **sovereigns**]
1 a king or queen
2 an old gold coin
► ADJECTIVE a sovereign state has its own independent government
• **sovereignty** /'sɒvrɪntɪ/ NOUN, NO PLURAL a formal word meaning when a country has independent political power to govern itself

sow[1] /səʊ/ VERB [**sows, sowing, sowed, sown**] to put seeds on or in the ground so that they will grow

sow[2] /saʊ/ NOUN [plural **sows**] a female pig

➤ This meaning of **sow** rhymes with **how**.

soya bean /'sɔɪə 'biːn/ NOUN [plural **soya beans**] a type of bean that can be cooked and eaten or used to make milk, oil and other foods

soya milk /'sɔɪə 'mɪlk/ NOUN, NO PLURAL a type of milk made from soya beans

soy sauce /'sɔɪ 'sɔːs/ NOUN, NO PLURAL a dark brown sauce made from soya beans, put on food to add flavour

spa /spɑː/ NOUN [plural **spas**]
1 a place where people can drink or bath in water that comes from the ground and is believed to be good for you
2 a place where people go to relax and have beauty treatments

space /speɪs/ ► NOUN [plural **spaces**]
1 no plural the area available to be used □ There isn't enough space to hold a party here. 🔁 Can you make space for one more person? 🔁 We created more space by removing all the shelves. 🔁 I don't have enough disk space.
2 an empty area □ Write your name in the space at the top of the sheet. 🔁 I couldn't find a parking space. 🔁 It is important for cities to have plenty of open spaces.
3 no plural the area outside the Earth's atmosphere, where the planets and stars are □ Another rocket was launched into space yesterday.
4 a period of time □ In the space of a month, he had completely reorganized the business. 🔁 She has achieved a lot in a short space of time.

> ► Remember that when you say 'space' meaning 'the area outside the Earth's atmosphere', you do not use the word 'the' before it:
> ✓ He's always been very interested in space.
> ✗ He's always been very interested in the space.

► VERB [**spaces, spacing, spaced**] to arrange things so that they have a particular distance or amount of time between them □ Helpers were spaced at intervals of roughly 5 kilometres. □ The journeys were spaced over a five year period.

space bar /speɪs ˈbɑː(r)/ NOUN [plural **space bars**] the long, narrow key at the front of a computer keyboard that lets you make a space between words. A computing word.

spacecraft /ˈspeɪskrɑːft/ NOUN [plural **spacecraft** or **spacecrafts**] a vehicle that can travel into space

spaceship /ˈspeɪsʃɪp/ NOUN [plural **spaceships**] a vehicle that can travel into space

space shuttle /ˈspeɪs ˈʃʌtəl/ NOUN [plural **space shuttles**] a vehicle like a plane that can travel into space and come back to Earth to be used again

space station /ˈspeɪs ˈsteɪʃən/ NOUN [plural **space stations**] a place in space where people can live and do experiments

spacesuit /ˈspeɪssuːt/ NOUN [plural **spacesuits**] a set of clothes worn by someone in space

spacious /ˈspeɪʃəs/ ADJECTIVE large and with a lot of room □ a spacious apartment

spade /speɪd/ NOUN [plural **spades**]
1 a tool with a wide flat part that you use for digging
2 spades one of the four types of playing card, which have the symbol (♠) printed on them □ the ace of spades
♦ IDIOM call a spade a spade to say exactly what you think, without worrying about whether you are being polite

spaghetti /spəˈɡetɪ/ NOUN, NO PLURAL a type of pasta that is like long thin string □ spaghetti with tomato sauce

spam /spæm/ ► NOUN, NO PLURAL e-mails that you do not want, especially e-mails trying to sell you things. A computing word.
► VERB [**spams, spamming, spammed**] to send spam to someone. A computing word.

span /spæn/ ► NOUN [plural **spans**]
1 the length of time that something lasts □ The country had changed completely within a span of twenty years. 🔁 Most toddlers have a very short attention span.
2 the width of something □ Its wings have a span of over 3 metres.
► VERB [**spans, spanning, spanned**]
1 to go across an area □ An old wooden bridge span the river.
2 to go all over an area □ The company's dealers now span the whole world.
3 to last for a particular period of time □ His singing career spanned three decades.

spangle /ˈspæŋɡəl/ NOUN [plural **spangles**] a small shiny piece of metal or plastic used as a decoration on clothes
● spangly /ˈspæŋɡlɪ/ ADJECTIVE covered with spangles □ a spangly scarf

spaniel /ˈspænjəl/ NOUN [plural **spaniels**] a type of dog with long ears that hang down □ a golden spaniel

spank /spæŋk/ VERB [**spanks, spanking, spanked**] to hit someone on the bottom with your hand flat, especially as a punishment

spanner /ˈspænə(r)/ NOUN [plural **spanners**] a metal tool used for turning nuts (=small pieces of metal holding things together) to take them off or make them tighter
♦ IDIOM put/throw a spanner in the works to cause a big problem in the progress of something □ We were due to fly to New York, but the airline strike put a spanner in the works.

spar /spɑː(r)/ VERB [**spars, sparring, sparred**]
1 to practise fighting with someone
2 to argue with someone

spare /speə(r)/ ► ADJECTIVE
1 extra and available to be used □ I stayed in Fiona's spare room. □ I've got a spare ticket for Saturday's concert, if you'd like it. □ Neither of us had any spare cash.
2 spare time time when you do not have to work and can do what you want □ What do you do in your spare time?
► VERB [**spares, sparing, spared**]
1 to be able to give or lend something to someone because you do not need it yourself □ Could you spare me a few pounds? □ We can't spare anyone to help out today.
2 if you can spare the time to do something, you have enough time to do it □ I'd love to come with you, but I just can't spare the time.

3 to prevent someone from experiencing something unpleasant □ *I tried to spare him the embarrassment of a public apology.*

4 to spare if you have something to spare, you have more of it than you need □ *We fed all 50 people and still had supplies to spare.*

5 to not harm or kill someone or something □ *In the violence that followed, not even the children were spared.*

6 spare no expense/effort to spend as much money/make as much effort as is needed to achieve something □ *We spared no expense to make the party a wonderful occasion.*

7 spare a thought for someone to think about someone who is in a difficult situation □ *When you sit down to dinner, spare a thought for some of the children who will not have anything to eat today.*

▶ NOUN [*plural* **spares**]

1 an extra thing that can be used if the one you are using or usually use is lost, broken, etc. □ *If you lose your compass, I've got a spare.*

2 a part of a machine or a vehicle that can be used to replace a broken part □ *It's not easy to get spares for these old cars.*

spare part /'speə 'pɑːt/ NOUN [*plural* **spare parts**] a part for a machine or car that is used to replace a part that is broken

sparing /'speərɪŋ/ ADJECTIVE using a very small amount □ *He is very sparing with his praise.*

sparingly /'speərɪŋlɪ/ ADVERB in very small amounts □ *These chillies are very hot, so use them sparingly.*

spark /spɑːk/ ▶ NOUN [*plural* **sparks**]

1 a very small burning piece that is sent out from a fire or made by rubbing two hard surfaces together □ *A shower of sparks shot out of the bonfire.*

2 a small amount of something such as enthusiasm or interest □ *There seemed to be no spark of life in the old woman.*

▶ VERB [**sparks, sparking, sparked**]

1 to make a spark

2 to cause something, especially anger or a fight □ *Her remark sparked off a huge argument.*

sparkle /'spɑːkəl/ ▶ VERB [**sparkles, sparkling, sparkled**] to shine, sending out a lot of points of bright light □ *Her jewels sparkled in the candlelight.*

▶ NOUN [*plural* **sparkles**] points of bright light □ *the sparkle of the sea*

sparkling /'spɑːklɪŋ/ ADJECTIVE

1 sending out points of bright light □ *sparkling eyes*

2 a sparkling drink has bubbles of gas in it □ *I'll have sparkling mineral water.*

3 full of energy and fun □ *sparkling conversation*

spark plug /'spɑːk 'plʌg/ NOUN [*plural* **spark plugs**] a small part in a car engine that produces an electrical spark (=very small flame) to make the fuel burn

sparrow /'spærəʊ/ NOUN [*plural* **sparrows**] a small brown bird

sparse /spɑːs/ ADJECTIVE [**sparser, sparsest**] if something is sparse, there is not much or not enough of it □ *sparse vegetation* □ *Information from the battle front is sparse.*

spasm /'spæzəm/ NOUN [*plural* **spasms**] a sudden movement of your muscles that you cannot control □ *The muscles of his leg had gone into spasm.*

spat /spæt/ PAST TENSE AND PAST PARTICIPLE OF **spit**

spate /speɪt/ NOUN, NO PLURAL a sudden large number or amount □ *There's been a spate of burglaries in the suburbs.*

spatter /'spætə(r)/ VERB [**spatters, spattering, spattered**] to cover something with small drops of liquid □ *His hair was spattered with paint.*

spatula /'spætjʊlə/ NOUN [*plural* **spatulas**] a kitchen tool with a wide, flat blade, used for spreading or mixing soft substances or lifting pieces of food

spawn /spɔːn/ ▶ VERB [**spawns, spawning, spawned**]

1 to cause or produce something □ *The children's cartoon spawned a multi-million pound empire.*

2 to lay eggs □ *The salmon return to the same places to spawn.*

▶ NOUN, NO PLURAL the eggs of frogs, toads or fish □ *frog spawn*

speak /spiːk/ VERB [**speaks, speaking, spoke, spoken**]

1 to say something □ **+ to** *Could I speak to you for a moment?* □ **+ about** *He never spoke publicly about his marriage.* □ *She was so tired she could hardly speak.* □ *We all sat there, and nobody spoke.*

2 to be able to talk in a particular language □ *Do you speak Greek?*

3 to make a speech □ **+ about** *She spoke for almost an hour about her work with lions.*

4 generally/strictly, etc. speaking used to show that you are talking in a general/exact, etc. way □ *They disapprove of parents helping with homework, generally speaking.* □ *Strictly speaking a spider is an animal.*

5 Speaking. something you say when someone on the telephone asks to speak to you □ *'May I speak to Mrs Kennedy?' 'Speaking.'*

♦ IDIOMS speak volumes to show a lot about someone or something □ *After such a major injury, this performance speaks volumes for the type of character he is.* speak your mind to say what you really think □ *She's not afraid to speak her mind.*

♦ PHRASAL VERBS speak out to speak about something in public, especially something that you have strong opinions about □ *He has spoken out against building wind farms in the area.* speak up **1** to say something more loudly □ *Could you speak up, please?* **2** to tell people your opinion about something □ *We all thought our boss was being unfair, but nobody was brave enough to speak up.* speak up for someone/ something to say something to support someone or something □ *I was grateful to Jenny for speaking up for me.*

• **speaker** /'spiːkə(r)/ NOUN [plural **speakers**]
1 a piece of equipment that the sound from a radio, CD player, etc. comes out of
2 someone who gives a speech ⊞ *Our guest speaker tonight is from Oxfam.*
3 someone who is speaking
4 someone who is able to speak a particular language □ *We need an Arabic speaker to work in our sales department.*

spear /spɪə(r)/ ► NOUN [plural **spears**] a long thin weapon with a sharp metal point
► VERB [**spears, spearing, speared**] to push a thin, sharp point into something □ *He speared a piece of meat with his fork.*

spearmint /'spɪəmɪnt/ NOUN, NO PLURAL a herb whose leaves are used to produce a flavour used in sweets and toothpaste (=substance for cleaning your teeth)

special /'speʃəl/ ADJECTIVE
1 unusual, and usually better than what is normal
⊞ *We've been saving this wine for a special occasion.* □ *My boyfriend always makes me feel really special.* ⊞ *We've all been making a special effort to be friendly.*
2 meant for or having a particular purpose □ *Special trains will take fans to the match.* □ *a special tool for making rugs*

• **specialist** /'speʃəlɪst/ NOUN [plural **specialists**] someone who knows a lot about a particular subject □ *My GP has referred me to a heart specialist.*

• **speciality** /ˌspeʃɪˈæləti/ NOUN [plural **specialities**] something that someone does very well □ *Birthday cakes are my speciality.*

specialization or **specialisation** /ˌspeʃəlaɪˈzeɪʃən/ NOUN, NO PLURAL when someone studies or works at one particular subject or job or one part of a subject or job □ *The new A levels were originally designed to reduce academic specialization.*

• **specialize** or **specialise** /'speʃəlaɪz/ VERB [**specializes, specializing, specialized**] to study or work at one particular subject or job or one part of a subject or job □ *Judy specializes in counselling the bereaved.* □ *Next door there's a little shop which specializes in old theatre posters.*

specially /'speʃəli/ ADVERB for one particular purpose □ *Jo's had her costume specially made for the party.*

special needs /'speʃəl 'niːdz/ PLURAL NOUN the needs of people who have physical or mental problems □ *special needs students*

species /'spiːʃiːz/ NOUN [plural **species**] a group of animals or plants whose members have similar features and that can produce young together □ *a rare species of orchid*

specific /spə'sɪfɪk/ ADJECTIVE
1 giving all the details about something in a clear way □ *Sarah's directions weren't very specific.*
2 exactly as has been stated or described □ *Each child has his own specific jobs to do.*

• **specifically** /spə'sɪfɪkəli/ ADVERB
1 for one particular purpose and no other □ *These flats were designed specifically for the elderly.*
2 clearly and exactly □ *I specifically told you not to go out tonight.*

specification /ˌspesɪfɪˈkeɪʃən/ NOUN [plural **specifications**] a clear description of how something should be made or done □ *The car was built to his own specifications.*

specify /'spesɪfaɪ/ VERB [**specifies, specifying, specified**] to state something clearly or in detail □ *Please specify the colour and size you require on the order form.*

specimen /'spesɪmən/ NOUN [plural **specimens**]
1 a small amount of blood, etc. that can be tested by doctors or scientists □ *a specimen of urine*
2 an example of a particular type of animal or plant □ *The specimens were arranged in cases, clearly labelled.*

speck /spek/ NOUN [plural **specks**]
1 a very small piece of something □ *a speck of dust*
2 a small spot or mark □ *a speck of paint*

speckle /'spekəl/ NOUN [plural **speckles**] one of several small spots □ *The egg was covered with speckles.*

• **speckled** /'spekəld/ ADJECTIVE covered in speckles □ *a speckled hen*

specs /speks/ PLURAL NOUN an informal word meaning glasses □ *Has anyone seen my specs?*

spectacle /'spektəkəl/ NOUN [plural **spectacles**]
1 something that is interesting, exciting or surprising to see □ *The opening ceremony of the games was a wonderful spectacle.*
2 **make a spectacle of yourself** to do something silly or embarrassing that a lot of people see

• **spectacles** /'spektəkəlz/ PLURAL NOUN an old-fashioned word for glasses □ *a pair of spectacles*

spectacular /spek'tækjulə(r)/ ADJECTIVE very interesting, exciting or surprising □ *a spectacular firework display* □ *The scenery was absolutely spectacular.*

• **spectacularly** /spek'tækjuləli/ ADVERB in a spectacular way or to a very great degree □ *a spectacularly successful film*

spectator /spek'teɪtə(r)/ NOUN [plural **spectators**] someone who is watching an event □ *United won the match in front of more than 60,000 spectators.*

specter /'spektə(r)/ NOUN [plural **specters**] the US spelling of spectre

spectre /'spektə(r)/ NOUN [plural **spectres**]
1 something unpleasant that people are frightened might happen again □ *The thunderstorms have raised the spectre of more flooding.*
2 a ghost (=spirit of a dead person)

spectrum /'spektrəm/ NOUN [plural **spectra** or **spectrums**]
1 a range of possible ideas, opinions or qualities ⊞ The conference brings together people with a wide spectrum of views.
2 all the different colours produced when light passes through glass or water

speculate /'spekjuleɪt/ VERB [speculates, speculating, speculated]
1 to make a guess about something that you do not know much about □ I wouldn't like to speculate about who might be the next president.
2 to buy and sell things with the aim of making money but with the possibility of losing it □ Many firms speculated on the financial markets rather than building factories.

speculation /,spekju'leɪʃən/ NOUN [plural speculations]
1 guesses about what will happen or why something happened ⊞ There's been a lot of speculation about how she died.
2 buying and selling things such as houses or shares in companies in order to make a large profit □ The rewards of financial speculation can be enormous.

speculative /'spekjulətɪv/ ADJECTIVE based on speculation □ The link between the virus and mental illness is purely speculative.

ped /sped/ PAST TENSE AND PAST PARTICIPLE OF speed □ A bullet sped past his ear.

speech /spiːtʃ/ NOUN [plural speeches]
1 a talk that you give in front of a group of people ⊞ The bride's father usually makes a speech.
2 no plural the ability to speak ⊞ He seemed to have lost the power of speech.
3 no plural the particular way that someone speaks □ She was so tired that her speech was slurred.
4 a set of words that one person says in a play □ The old king's final speech is very moving.

Note that when you speak formally in front of a group of people, you **make a speech**. You can also **give a speech**:
✓ I had to make/give a speech at the wedding.
✗ I had to do a speech at the wedding.

speechless /'spiːtʃlɪs/ ADJECTIVE unable to talk because you are so angry, shocked, upset, etc. □ The unfairness of his remarks left her speechless.

speed /spiːd/ ► NOUN [plural speeds]
1 how quickly someone or something moves □ He was driving at a speed of about 30 miles per hour. □ The train was travelling at speed when it hit the debris on the track. ⊞ What's the top speed of this model?
2 how quickly someone or something works or something happens □ Our new programs offer accuracy and speed. □ The managers are very pleased with the speed of her progress. ⊞ You'll gradually pick up speed as you learn the job.
► VERB [speeds, speeding, sped or speeded]
1 to move, go or pass quickly □ He sped off down the road on his bike. □ The hours sped by as we sat and chatted.
2 to drive faster than the law says you can □ I really didn't think I was speeding until I saw the police car.
♦ PHRASAL VERB speed (something) up to go faster or make something faster □ Accepting online applications should speed up the recruitment process.

speedboat /'spiːdbəʊt/ NOUN [plural speedboats] a small boat with a powerful engine that can go very fast

speed-dial /'spiːddaɪəl/ NOUN, NO PLURAL a feature on a telephone that allows you to telephone a number by pressing only one button

speeding /'spiːdɪŋ/ NOUN, NO PLURAL the offence of driving faster than the law says you can □ He's been fined for speeding three times.

speed limit /'spiːd 'lɪmɪt/ NOUN [plural speed limits] the fastest speed at which you are legally allowed to drive a vehicle on a particular road □ He was over the speed limit.

speedometer /spɪ'dɒmɪtə(r)/ NOUN [plural speedometers] a piece of equipment in a car that measures how fast you are travelling

speedway /'spiːdweɪ/ NOUN, NO PLURAL the sport of motorcycle racing, or the track that is used for this

speedy /'spiːdɪ/ ADJECTIVE [speedier, speediest] quick or fast □ Thanks for the speedy reply to my letter.

spell /spel/ ► VERB [spells, spelling, spelt or spelled]
1 to say or write the letters of a word in the correct order □ Could you spell your name for me? □ Adam was always good at spelling.
2 to make up a word □ L-i-g-h-t spells 'light'.
3 to mean that something bad is going to happen ⊞ A heavy fine will spell disaster for the company.
► NOUN [plural spells]
1 a short period of time □ The weather will be dull, with sunny spells.
2 a set of words that are used to make something magic happen ⊞ The wicked witch cast a spell on Snow White.

spellbound /'spelbaʊnd/ ADJECTIVE if you are spellbound by something, it is so interesting and good that all your attention is held by it □ The audience was spellbound for the whole two hours.

spellcheck /'speltʃek/ or **spellchecker** /'speltʃekə(r)/ NOUN [plural spellchecks or spellcheckers] a computer program that checks whether you have spelled words correctly. A computing word.
● **spellcheck** /'speltʃek/ VERB [spellchecks, spellchecking, spellchecked] to use a spellcheck on a document. A computing word.

spelling /'spelɪŋ/ NOUN [plural **spellings**]
1 the way that a word is spelt □ 'Donut' is the American spelling of 'doughnut'.
2 no plural the ability to spell □ His spelling is terrible.

spend /spend/ VERB [**spends, spending, spent**]
1 to use money to buy things 🖫 We spent a lot of money on our holiday. □ Try to cut down how much you spend.
2 to pass time doing something 🖫 Do you spend much time on the computer? 🖫 I used to spend hours reading in my room. 🖫 I spent ages decorating that cake. □ We spent the weekend at my sister's.

➤ Note that you spend money on someone or something:
✓ She spends a lot of money on clothes.
✗ She spends a lot of money for clothes.

• **spending** /'spendɪŋ/ NOUN, NO PLURAL the amount of money that a government, organization or person spends □ The government are taking steps to cut spending on prisons.

sperm /spɜːm/ NOUN [plural **sperm** or **sperms**] a cell from a man that joins with the egg from a woman to make a baby. A biology word.

spew /spjuː/ VERB [**spews, spewing, spewed**] to come out in large amounts, or to make something do this □ Great clouds of smoke and ash spewed from the volcano.

sphere /sfɪə(r)/ NOUN [plural **spheres**]
1 a solid object that is the shape of a ball
2 a particular area or subject of interest, activity, work, etc. □ He is well known within the political sphere.
• **spherical** /'sferɪkəl/ ADJECTIVE having the shape of a sphere

spice /spaɪs/ ▶ NOUN [plural **spices**]
1 a substance made from a plant that adds flavour to food □ herbs and spices □ Ginger is a spice.
2 something that adds excitement to a situation □ She took up hang-gliding to add a little spice to her life.
▶ VERB [**spices, spicing, spiced**] to add spice to food or drink □ apples spiced with cinnamon
♦ PHRASAL VERB **spice something up** to make something more exciting □ Producers decided to spice up the show with a live debate.
• **spiciness** /'spaɪsɪnɪs/ NOUN, NO PLURAL being spicy □ I would reduce the spiciness of the sauce.
• **spicy** /'spaɪsɪ/ ADJECTIVE [**spicier, spiciest**] tasting hot on your tongue □ spicy food

spider /'spaɪdə(r)/ NOUN [plural **spiders**] a small creature with eight legs that uses very thin threads to make a web for catching insects
• **spidery** /'spaɪdərɪ/ ADJECTIVE spidery writing is untidy with long, thin lines

spike /spaɪk/ NOUN [plural **spikes**] a hard, sharp point, usually made of metal or wood □ There were sharp spikes on top of the wall.
• **spiky** /'spaɪkɪ/ ADJECTIVE [**spikier, spikiest**] with sharp points □ a spiky hairstyle

spill /spɪl/ VERB [**spills, spilling, spilt** or **spilled**]
1 to come out of a container by accident or to make something, especially a liquid, do this □ Careful! You're going to spill your tea. □ She spilt a can of paint all over the carpet. □ The sack burst and the rice spilled out onto the floor.
2 if people spill out of a place they all leave it together □ Crowds were spilling out of the football ground and heading off home.
♦ IDIOM **spill the beans** to tell someone a secret □ Come on, spill the beans. What's going on?
♦ PHRASAL VERB **spill over** to spread from one place to another □ By now the rioting had spilled over into the neighbouring streets.
• **spillage** /'spɪlɪdʒ/ NOUN [plural **spillages**]
1 the act of spilling something □ The spillage of the lorry's load caused long tailbacks.
2 an amount that has been spilled □ Put a tray under the freezer to catch any spillages.

spin /spɪn/ ▶ VERB [**spins, spinning, spun**]
1 to turn round and round very quickly or make something do this □ The ballerina spun round and round on her toes. □ He can spin the basketball on his finger.
2 to make long, thin threads out of cotton, wool, or other material by pulling and twisting it
3 to remove water from clothes after washing them by turning them round very fast in a machine
♦ PHRASAL VERB **spin something out** to make something last a long time, often longer than is necessary □ She had to spin the story out till the end of the lesson.
▶ NOUN [plural **spins**]
1 when you make something spin □ Some tennis players can put a lot of spin on the ball.
2 a way of talking about something that makes it seem less bad than it really is □ political spin 🖫 It was impossible to put a positive spin on such a bad result.
3 an informal and slightly old-fashioned word for a short journey in a car 🖫 We went for a spin in Joe's new car.

spinach /'spɪnɪdʒ/ NOUN, NO PLURAL a vegetable with large dark green leaves

spinal /'spaɪnəl/ ADJECTIVE to do with your spine. A biology word. □ a spinal injury
spinal column /'spaɪnəl 'kɒləm/ NOUN [plural **spinal columns**] the bones and nerves that form your spine. A biology word.
spinal cord /'spaɪnəl 'kɔːd/ NOUN [plural **spinal cords**] the nerve cells inside your spine. A biology word.
spindly /'spɪndlɪ/ ADJECTIVE long, thin and not very strong 🖫 spindly legs

spin doctor /'spɪn 'dɒktə(r)/ NOUN [plural **spin doctors**] a politician who finds ways of talking about mistakes or problems in a positive way

spin drier or **spin dryer** /'spɪn 'draɪə(r)/ NOUN [plural **spin driers** or **spin dryers**] a machine that dries clothes by turning them round and round very fast

spine /spaɪn/ NOUN [plural **spines**]
1 the line of bones down the back of a person or animal
2 a stiff point that grows on some plants or animals such as a hedgehog □ the spines of a cactus
3 the narrow part of a book's cover that you can see when it is on a shelf

spine-chilling /'spaɪntʃɪlɪŋ/ ADJECTIVE a spine-chilling story, film or book is very frightening

spineless /'spaɪnlɪs/ ADJECTIVE weak and not brave enough to deal with something well □ The union was accused of being completely spineless.

spinning wheel /'spɪnɪŋ 'wiːl/ NOUN [plural spinning wheels] a piece of equipment for making thread, with a large wheel that turns round

spin-off /'spɪnɒf/ NOUN [plural **spin-offs**] a new product that is based on an older one, or something that is created as the result of something else □ The rapid commercial development of computers was one of the spin-offs of the space programme in the 1960s.

spinster /'spɪnstə(r)/ NOUN [plural **spinsters**] an old-fashioned word for a woman who is not married

spiral /'spaɪərəl/ ▶ NOUN [plural **spirals**]
1 a shape formed by a line that curves round and round a centre point □ The shell formed a perfect spiral.
2 a situation that gets worse in a way that is not controlled □ They were caught in a spiral of violence.
▶ ADJECTIVE in the shape of a spiral 🖻 a spiral staircase
▶ VERB [spirals, spiralling/US spiraling, spiralled/US spiraled]
1 to increase, fall or get worse very quickly □ House prices have spiralled recently.
2 to move in a spiral □ The smoke spiralled up through the trees.

spire /spaɪə(r)/ NOUN [plural **spires**] a tall pointed roof of a church tower

spirit /'spɪrɪt/ ▶ NOUN [plural **spirits**]
1 your attitude or the attitude of a group of people **+ of** The celebration was held in a spirit of friendship. □ Her adventurous spirit took her all over the world. □ Our town has a strong community spirit.
2 no plural enthusiasm and determination □ He showed real spirit during his illness.
3 enter/get into the spirit of something to take part in an event or activity in an enthusiastic and enjoyable way □ Everyone was dancing and getting into the spirit of the evening.
4 spirits your mood 🖻 She was in really high/low spirits (=a happy/sad mood).
5 the part of a person that some people believe continues to live after the body dies
6 a creature without a physical body that some people believe can influence our lives 🖻 evil spirits

7 a strong alcoholic drink, for example brandy or gin
▶ VERB [spirits, spiriting, spirited] to take someone or something somewhere without people noticing □ He was spirited into a waiting taxi.

• **spirited** /'spɪrɪtɪd/ ADJECTIVE enthusiastic and determined 🖻 She mounted a spirited defence of her husband's actions.

spirit level /'spɪrɪt 'levəl/ NOUN [plural **spirit levels**] a tool that you use to check whether a surface is level

spiritual /'spɪrɪtʃuəl/ ADJECTIVE
1 to do with someone's spirit, emotions and thoughts and not their body □ an intensely spiritual experience
2 to do with religion □ The poor looked to the church for spiritual leadership.

spit /spɪt/ ▶ VERB [spits, spitting, spat]
1 to force liquid or food out of your mouth □ She took one mouthful and then spat it out on to her plate.
2 if it is spitting, it is raining a little
▶ NOUN [plural **spits**]
1 the liquid inside your mouth
2 a thin metal bar that you put meat on to cook over a fire □ The ox was roasted on a spit.

spite /spaɪt/ NOUN, NO PLURAL
1 a feeling of wanting to hurt or upset someone □ He threw my picture away out of spite.
2 in spite of used to say that a fact or event makes something else that happens surprising □ We decided to go to the seaside in spite of the rain. □ He passed his exam in spite of doing no revision.

• **spiteful** /'spaɪtful/ ADJECTIVE doing or saying something unpleasant or cruel just to upset or hurt someone □ a spiteful remark
• **spitefully** /'spaɪtfulɪ/ ADVERB in a spiteful way
• **spitefulness** /'spaɪtfulnɪs/ NOUN, NO PLURAL being spiteful

spitting image /'spɪtɪŋ 'ɪmɪdʒ/ NOUN **be the spitting image of someone** to look exactly like someone else □ Tara's the spitting image of her mother.

splash /splæʃ/ ▶ VERB [splashes, splashing, splashed]
1 to put liquid on something with a quick movement □ Kate splashed some cold water on her face.
2 if a liquid splashes somewhere, it moves there and makes a noise □ The water splashed over the edge of the pan.
3 to move water around in a noisy way □ The baby was splashing happily in his bath.
◆ PHRASAL VERB **splash out** to spend a lot of money on something □ The singer has just splashed out on a mansion in Malibu.
▶ NOUN [plural **splashes**]
1 the sound that water makes when something hits it □ Kurt fell into the pool with a loud splash.
2 a mark made on something where a liquid has hit it □ Her jeans were covered in splashes of paint.
3 a splash of colour an area of colour that makes something look brighter □ A beautiful Chinese rug provided a splash of colour.

♦ IDIOM **make a splash** an informal phrase meaning to get a lot of attention □ *The group made a huge splash in Canada.*

splatter /'splætə(r)/ VERB [**splatters, splattering, splattered**] if a liquid splatters, drops of it fall all over something, and if you splatter a liquid, you make drops fall all over something □ *Blood was splattered on the walls.*

splay /spleɪ/ VERB [**splays, splaying, splayed**] to spread your legs, arms or fingers wide apart □ *He sat on the floor with his legs splayed.*

spleen /spli:n/ NOUN [*plural* **spleens**] an organ in your body which controls the quality of your blood. A biology word.

splendid /'splendɪd/ ADJECTIVE very good □ *a splendid idea*

● **splendour** /'splendə(r)/ NOUN, NO PLURAL the quality of being very beautiful and grand □ *the splendour of the royal palaces*

splint /splɪnt/ NOUN [*plural* **splints**] a piece of wood used to keep a broken bone in the right position

● **splinter** /'splɪntə(r)/ ► NOUN [*plural* **splinters**] a very small sharp piece of wood or glass □ *I got a splinter in my hand.*
► VERB [**splinters, splintering, splintered**] to break into very small sharp pieces □ *The wood had splintered.*

split /splɪt/ ► VERB [**splits, splitting, split**]
1 to break or tear apart □ *Your trousers have split down the back.*
2 to break something or tear it apart □ *The lightning had split the tree in two.*
3 to share something □ *We drove to Edinburgh and split the cost of the petrol.*
4 to cause a group to disagree and divide into smaller groups □ *The issue could split the Labour Party.*
5 to divide a group of people into smaller groups □ *I split the children into two groups.*
6 to end a marriage or relationship □ *I was three when my parents split.* □ *I've just split up with my boyfriend.*
♦ IDIOM **split hairs** to argue about small details that are not important
► NOUN [*plural* **splits**]
1 a tear or break in something □ *There's a long split in the wood.*
2 a disagreement that divides a group □ *This may leave a lasting split in the Republican Party.*

split second /'splɪt 'sekənd/ NOUN, NO PLURAL a very short time □ *For a split second I thought something awful had happened.*
● **split-second** ADJECTIVE taking a very short time □ *a split-second decision*

splutter /'splʌtə(r)/ VERB [**splutters, spluttering, spluttered**] to say something with difficulty because you are so angry or shocked □ *'I don't know what you're talking about!' he spluttered.*

spoil /spoɪl/ VERB [**spoils, spoiling, spoilt** or **spoiled**]
1 to make something less good □ *I had an argument*

with Adrian and it spoilt the whole evening. □ *Low cloud spoilt the view of the mountains.* □ *The weather was fairly awful but we didn't let it spoil our fun.*
2 to always allow a child to have or do what they want and cause them to become badly behaved □ *She spoils those children.*
3 to treat someone in a very nice way and give them nice things □ *Breakfast in bed! You're spoiling me!*
4 if food spoils, it starts to decay. A formal word.

spoilsport /'spoɪlspo:t/ NOUN [*plural* **spoilsports**] someone who does something that stops someone else enjoying themselves □ *Don't be such a spoilsport*

spoilt /spoɪlt/► PAST TENSE AND PAST PARTICIPLE OF spoil
► ADJECTIVE behaving badly because you have always been allowed to have or do what you want 🔁 *You're behaving like a spoilt child!*

spoke[1] /spəʊk/ PAST TENSE OF speak

spoke[2] /spəʊk/ NOUN [*plural* **spokes**] one of the thin metal pieces that connect the centre of a wheel with the edge

spoken /'spəʊkən/ PAST PARTICIPLE OF speak

spokesman /'spəʊksmən/ NOUN [*plural* **spokesmen**] a man who speaks officially for someone else

spokesperson /'spəʊks,pɜ:sən/ NOUN [*plural* **spokespeople**] someone who speaks officially for someone else □ *an army spokesperson*

spokeswoman /'spəʊks,wʊmən/ NOUN [*plural* **spokeswomen**] a woman who speaks officially for someone else

sponge /spʌndʒ/ ► NOUN [*plural* **sponges**]
1 a soft object, made from natural or artificial material, that you use to wash your body
2 a light cake
► VERB [**sponges, sponging, sponged**]
1 to wash something with a sponge □ *A nurse was sponging his face.*
2 an informal word meaning to try to get money from people without doing anything to help them □ *At ... he's still sponging off his parents.*

sponge bag /'spʌndʒ 'bæg/ NOUN [*plural* **sponge bags**] a bag that you carry things such as soap and toothbrush in when you are travelling

sponge cake /'spʌndʒ 'keɪk/ NOUN [*plural* **sponge cakes**] a light cake

spongy /'spʌndʒɪ/ ADJECTIVE [**spongier, spongiest**] something that is spongy feels soft when you press □ *spongy ground*

sponsor /'spɒnsə(r)/ ► VERB [**sponsors, sponsoring, sponsored**]
1 to pay for something such as an event or television programme, often as a way of advertising your company □ *A local company sponsors our football team.*
2 to agree to give someone money for a school, organization, etc. if they do something difficult □ *... you sponsor me to run in the race?*
► NOUN [*plural* **sponsors**] a person or company that sponsors someone or something □ *The company is ... official sponsor of the 2008 European Cup.*

sponsored /ˈspɒnsəd/ ADJECTIVE a sponsored swim/walk, etc. a swim or walk, etc. that you do to get money for a school or charity (=organization that helps people), in which people agree to give you money if you are successful

sponsorship /ˈspɒnsəʃɪp/ NOUN, NO PLURAL when someone sponsors someone or something ⊕ Toyota announced a five-year sponsorship deal with the American Football League.

spontaneity /ˌspɒntəˈneɪəti/ NOUN, NO PLURAL the quality of being spontaneous

spontaneous /spɒnˈteɪniəs/ ADJECTIVE happening naturally and not planned or organized □ spontaneous applause

spoof /spuːf/ NOUN [plural spoofs] a television programme, advertisement, etc. which copies the style of a serious one and makes it seem silly and funny

spooky /ˈspuːki/ ADJECTIVE [spookier, spookiest] an informal word that means frightening □ The forest is really spooky at night.

spool /spuːl/ NOUN [plural spools] an object that you wind thread, film, etc. around □ a spool of cotton

spoon /spuːn/ ▶ NOUN [plural spoons] an object with a handle and a curved part at one end that you use for lifting liquid food to your mouth □ a soup spoon □ a wooden spoon
▶ VERB [spoons, spooning, spooned] to lift up food on a spoon □ She was slowly spooning the cereal into the baby's mouth.

spoonful /ˈspuːnfʊl/ NOUN [plural spoonfuls] the amount a spoon will hold □ Jamila put a spoonful of sugar in her coffee.

sporadic /spəˈrædɪk/ ADJECTIVE happening in a few places, or happening sometimes but not regularly □ Sporadic violence continued across the country.

spore /spɔː(r)/ NOUN [plural spores] a cell that is produced by some plants, for example mushrooms, that develops into a new plant. A biology word.

sport /spɔːt/ ▶ NOUN [plural sports]
1 no plural games and physical activities like football, tennis and swimming □ Adam loves all kinds of sport. She watches a lot of sport on the television.
2 a particular game or activity □ Football is a very popular sport. ⊕ My Dad has played sports all his life. We have very good sports facilities at our school.
▶ VERB be sporting something to be wearing something, especially something unusual which people notice □ He arrived sporting a bright red shirt and orange shoes.

sporting /ˈspɔːtɪŋ/ ADJECTIVE to do with sport □ sporting events □ David Beckham was his sporting hero.

sports car /ˈspɔːts ˌkɑː(r)/ NOUN [plural sports cars] a small fast car that has two seats and no roof

sportsman /ˈspɔːtsmən/ NOUN [plural sportsmen] a man who takes part in sport

sportswoman /ˈspɔːtsˌwʊmən/ NOUN [plural sportswomen] a woman who takes part in sport

sporty /ˈspɔːti/ ADJECTIVE [sportier, sportiest]
1 good at sport □ She's very sporty.
2 designed to go fast and look attractive □ a sporty car

spot /spɒt/ ▶ NOUN [plural spots]
1 a place or position □ This is a lovely spot for a picnic. □ X marks the spot where the treasure is buried. □ She hopes to retain her number one spot in the championship.
2 a round shape that is often part of a pattern □ She wore a pink dress with white spots.
3 a small dirty mark on something □ There were spots of oil all over the table.
4 a red raised mark on your skin □ Teenagers often suffer from spots.
5 on the spot (a) immediately □ She threatened to sack me on the spot. (b) in the place where something happens □ There were several reporters on the spot when the plane landed. (c) in one place, without moving away □ We had to jog on the spot for ten minutes.
♦ IDIOM put someone on the spot to try to make someone answer a difficult or embarrassing question □ When I put him on the spot, he denied having met her.
▶ VERB [spots, spotting, spotted] to see or notice something or someone □ I suddenly spotted Ian over by the window. □ Social workers spotted signs of neglect in the girl.

spot check /ˈspɒt ˈtʃek/ NOUN [plural spot checks] a check that is done without warning to make sure something is good enough □ The organization does spot checks on nursing homes.

spotless /ˈspɒtləs/ ADJECTIVE completely clean □ a spotless white tablecloth

spotlessly /ˈspɒtləsli/ ADVERB spotlessly clean completely clean □ She keeps the house spotlessly clean.

spotlight /ˈspɒtlaɪt/ ▶ NOUN [plural spotlights]
1 a very bright light which you can direct at something
2 the spotlight a lot of attention that someone or something gets from newspapers, television, etc. □ Health care is in the spotlight again.
▶ VERB [spotlights, spotlighting, spotlighted] to make people give a lot of attention to something □ The report spotlighted failures in the police investigation.

spot-on /ˈspɒtˈɒn/ ADJECTIVE an informal word meaning completely right □ His judgement has always been spot-on.

spotted /ˈspɒtɪd/ ADJECTIVE having a pattern of spots □ a spotted handkerchief

spotty /ˈspɒti/ ADJECTIVE [spottier, spottiest]
1 having a lot of spots on your skin □ a spotty face
2 having a pattern of spots □ a spotty scarf

spouse /spaʊs/ NOUN [plural spouses] a formal word meaning your husband or wife

spout /spaʊt/ ▶ NOUN [plural spouts] the long thin part of a container, which you pour liquid out of □ The spout on the teapot was cracked.

▶ VERB [**spouts, spouting, spouted**]

1 if a liquid spouts, it comes out quickly with a lot of force □ *The oil came spouting up out of the ground.*

2 to talk a lot about something which other people think is boring or silly. An informal word □ *He was spouting a lot of nonsense about politics again.*

sprain /spreɪn/ ▶ VERB [**sprains, spraining, sprained**] to twist and injure a part of your body such as your ankle □ *Kelly fell and sprained her wrist.*

▶ NOUN [*plural* **sprains**] a painful injury when you twist a part of your body such as your ankle

● **sprained** /spreɪnd/ ADJECTIVE with a sprain □ *a sprained ankle*

sprang /spræŋ/ PAST TENSE OF spring

sprawl /sprɔːl/ ▶ VERB [**sprawls, sprawling, sprawled**]

1 to lie or sit with your legs and arms spread out in a relaxed way □ *The cat was sprawled on the grass in the sunshine.*

2 if a town sprawls, it covers a large area with no clear shape

▶ NOUN, NO PLURAL a large area of town without a clear shape □ *urban sprawl*

● **sprawling** /ˈsprɔːlɪŋ/ ADJECTIVE built over a large area with no clear shape □ *Sydney's sprawling suburbs*

spray /spreɪ/ ▶ VERB [**sprays, spraying, sprayed**] to cause a liquid to come out of a container in many very small drops □ *She sprayed herself with perfume.*

▶ NOUN [*plural* **sprays**]

1 many very small drops of liquid in the air □ *The spray from the waterfall wet their hair.*

2 liquid in a container which is forced out in very small drops □ *a perfume spray*

spread /spred/ ▶ VERB [**spreads, spreading, spread**]

1 to cover a larger area or to affect more and more people, or to make something do this □ *The cancer has spread to his lungs.* □ *The virus spread rapidly in the crowded conditions.* □ *I don't want to spread alarm.* □ *Fire spread throughout the building.*

2 to arrange something so that it covers a large area □ **+ out** *I spread the map out on the table.* □ *The bird spread its wings and flew off.* □ *Bits of machinery were spread all over the floor.*

3 if information spreads, or you spread it, it becomes known by more and more people □ *Rumours spread very quickly in this little village.* 🔊 *News of his death spread rapidly.* 🔊 *I always try to spread the word* (=tell people in a positive way) *about green energy.*

4 to put a layer of a soft substance onto a surface □ *She spread her toast thickly with butter.*

5 to separate something into parts so that it can be shared or so that it does not happen all at once □ **+ out** *Luckily, the exams were spread out over two whole weeks.* □ *They invested in several companies in order to spread the risk.*

6 if people or things are spread over an area, they are in several parts of that area □ *We have a dozen offices spread throughout Europe.*

◆ PHRASAL VERB **spread out** if people spread out, they move away from a group to cover a larger area □ *We all spread out to search for the boy.*

▶ NOUN [*plural* **spreads**]

1 when something covers a larger area or affects more and more people □ *We need to stop the spread of cholera.* □ *There has been a rapid spread of violence in the area.*

2 the area that something covers □ *You need to consider the geographical spread of these people.*

3 a type of soft food that you spread on bread □ *cheese/chocolate spread*

spreadsheet /ˈspredʃiːt/ NOUN [*plural* **spreadsheets**] a computer program that shows and calculates financial information. A computing word.

spree /spriː/ NOUN [*plural* **sprees**] a time when you d a lot of something that you enjoy □ *a shopping spree*

sprig /sprɪg/ NOUN [*plural* **sprigs**] a small stem of a plant that has leaves on it □ *a sprig of holly*

sprightly /ˈspraɪtlɪ/ ADJECTIVE an old person who is sprightly is very active □ *She's very sprightly for 85.*

spring /sprɪŋ/ ▶ NOUN [*plural* **springs**]

1 the season between winter and summer when plants start to grow □ *Daffodils flower in spring.* □ *There will be an election next spring.* □ *spring sunshi*

2 a twisted piece of wire which goes back to its original shape after you have pushed or pulled it □ *T. chair had some broken springs in it.*

3 a place where water flows out of the ground □ *a mountain spring* □ *spring water*

4 a jump or quick movement □ *With a spring, the fr landed right in front of them.*

▶ VERB [**springs, springing, sprang, sprung**]

1 to move or jump quickly □ *He sprang out of bed answer the door.*

2 spring to mind if something springs to mind, y immediately think of it □ *'Honest' isn't the first w that springs to mind when describing him.*

3 spring to life to suddenly become active, or to suddenly start doing something □ *Suddenly the fa machine sprang to life.*

◆ PHRASAL VERBS **spring from something** to deve from something else □ *His confidence springs from loving family background.* **spring something on someone** to suddenly tell someone something ask them to do something that they are not expect □ *I'm sorry to spring this on you, but could we co and stay at your house tonight?* **spring up** to app or start to exist very suddenly □ *New office build are springing up all over the city.*

springboard /ˈsprɪŋbɔːd/ NOUN [*plural* **springboards**]

1 something that helps another thing to happen

2 a board that you jump from into water

spring cleaning /ˌsprɪŋ ˈkliːnɪŋ/ NOUN, NO PLUR the process of cleaning a house with great care, w people sometimes do in spring

spring onion /'sprɪŋ 'ʌnjən/ NOUN [plural **spring onions**] a thin white onion with a green stem that is often eaten raw

springtime /'sprɪŋtaɪm/ NOUN, NO PLURAL the season of spring □ The bulbs flower in springtime.

springy /'sprɪŋi/ ADJECTIVE [**springier, springiest**] something that is springy is not hard and returns to its original shape after being pressed □ springy grass

sprinkle /'sprɪŋkəl/ VERB [**sprinkles, sprinkling, sprinkled**] to put small drops or pieces of something over a surface □ She sprinkled chocolate chips onto the cake.

sprinkler /'sprɪŋklə(r)/ NOUN [plural **sprinklers**]
1 a piece of equipment in the ceiling of a room that water comes out of if a fire starts
2 a piece of equipment that spreads small drops of water over an area □ He was using a sprinkler to water the lawn.

sprinkling /'sprɪŋklɪŋ/ NOUN, NO PLURAL a sprinkling of something a small amount of something spread on a surface □ There was a sprinkling of snow on top of the mountain.

sprint /sprɪnt/ ▶ VERB [**sprints, sprinting, sprinted**] to run fast for a short distance □ He sprinted down the street after her.
▶ NOUN [plural **sprints**] a short running race □ the 100 metre sprint

sprinter /'sprɪntə(r)/ NOUN [plural **sprinters**] someone who runs in a sprint

sprout /spraʊt/ ▶ VERB [**sprouts, sprouting, sprouted**] to start to grow, or to produce new leaves or flowers □ Buds were sprouting on the sycamore tree.
PHRASAL VERB **sprout up** to suddenly appear or start to exist □ New cafés are sprouting up everywhere.
▶ NOUN [plural **sprouts**]
a round green vegetable that looks like a very small cabbage
a part of a plant that is just starting to grow □ bean sprouts

spruce¹ /spru:s/ NOUN [plural **spruces**] a tall tree with leaves that look like needles

spruce² /spru:s/
PHRASAL VERB [**spruces, sprucing, spruced**] **spruce something/someone up** to make someone or something look cleaner and nicer □ They had spent a lot of money sprucing up the hotel. ADJECTIVE [**sprucer, sprucest**] clean and tidy □ You're looking very spruce in your new suit.

sprung /sprʌŋ/ PAST PARTICIPLE OF spring

spud /spʌd/ NOUN [plural **spuds**] an informal word for potato

spun /spʌn/ PAST PARTICIPLE OF spin

spur /spɜ:(r)/ ▶ NOUN [plural **spurs**]
something which encourages something else □ Hosting the Olympic Games was a spur to improve the city.
a sharp metal piece on a horse rider's boot that the rider presses against the horse to make it move faster
on the spur of the moment suddenly and

without planning □ It was a decision that was made on the spur of the moment.
▶ VERB [**spurs, spurring, spurred**]
1 to encourage someone to do something □ Winning the prize spurred her on to try even harder.
2 to make something happen □ The increase in sales was spurred by rising wages.

spurious /'spʊərɪəs/ ADJECTIVE a formal word meaning based on facts or reasons that are not correct □ The company had made spurious claims about the health benefits of its products.

spurn /spɜ:n/ VERB [**spurns, spurning, spurned**] a formal word meaning to refuse to accept something □ He spurned all her efforts to be friendly.

spurt /spɜ:t/ ▶ VERB [**spurts, spurting, spurted**] to flow quickly and forcefully □ Blood was spurting from a wound on his head.
▶ NOUN [plural **spurts**]
1 a sudden forceful flow of a liquid □ a spurt of blood
2 a sudden increase in something such as speed or development □ Children often have a growth spurt around this age.

sputter /'spʌtə(r)/ VERB [**sputters, sputtering, sputtered**]
1 to make several noises like very small explosions □ The engine sputtered and stopped.
2 to say something with difficulty because you are so angry or shocked □ 'You're a fool!' he sputtered.

spy /spaɪ/ ▶ NOUN [plural **spies**] someone whose job is to discover secret information about another country or company □ a former Russian spy
▶ VERB [**spies, spying, spied**]
1 to work as a spy □ Both men had been spying for the government.
2 a formal word meaning to notice someone or something □ He suddenly spied a man hiding behind the door.
◆ PHRASAL VERB **spy on someone** to secretly watch what someone is doing □ Hetty spent a lot of time spying on her neighbours.

squabble /'skwɒbəl/ ▶ VERB [**squabbles, squabbling, squabbled**] to argue about something that is not important □ The children were squabbling over who was going to sit in the front seat.
▶ NOUN [plural **squabbles**] an argument about something that is not important

squad /skwɒd/ NOUN [plural **squads**]
1 a part of a police force that tries to stop a particular type of crime □ the police fraud squad
2 a small group of soldiers who work together as a team
3 a sports team □ the England squad for the World Cup

squad car /'skwɒd ˌkɑ:(r)/ NOUN [plural **squad cars**] a car that police officers use

squadron /'skwɒdrən/ NOUN [plural **squadrons**] a group of soldiers or military vehicles □ a squadron of fighter planes

squalid /'skwɒlɪd/ ADJECTIVE dirty and unpleasant □ The refugees were living in squalid camps.

squall /skwɔːl/ NOUN [plural **squalls**] a sudden very strong wind

squalor /'skwɒlə(r)/ NOUN, NO PLURAL very dirty and unpleasant conditions □ The old man had been living alone in squalor.

squander /'skwɒndə(r)/ VERB [**squanders, squandering, squandered**] to waste something that is very valuable, especially time or money □ He squandered all his money on fast cars.

square /skweə(r)/ ▶ NOUN [plural **squares**]
1 a flat shape with four equal sides and four angles of 90 degrees
2 an open space with buildings on all four sides □ a tree-lined square □ There was a clock in the market square. □ Trafalgar Square
3 the result of multiplying a number by itself. A maths word □ The square of 4 is 16.
♦ IDIOM be back to square one to be back in the same situation as you were at the start of something □ I wasted all the money I won, and now I'm back to square one.
▶ ADJECTIVE
1 shaped like a square □ a square table
2 measuring a particular amount on each side □ The room was about 3 metres square.
3 a square metre/foot/mile, etc. the area of a square which has sides which are a metre, a foot, a mile, etc. long □ The tiles cost £20 a square metre. □ The building offers 65,000 square metres of office space.
4 (all) square (a) having the same number of points as someone else in a game □ The two teams were all square at half-time, at 3-3. (b) not owing each other any money □ If you pay for the coffee this week, we'll be square.
5 straight or level □ Keep the paper square with the edge of the table.
▶ VERB [**squares, squaring, squared**] to multiply a number by itself. A maths word □ Three squared is nine.
♦ PHRASAL VERBS **square with something** if two facts, ideas, reasons, etc. square with each other, they agree with each other □ These policies don't square with the government's claims to be concerned about the environment. **square up** to pay someone money that you owe □ If you buy the drinks, I'll square up with you later.
● **squarely** /'skweəlɪ/ ADVERB directly □ The judge's comments were aimed squarely at Ms Cisero. □ Susan looked at him squarely.

square meal /skweə 'miːl/ NOUN [plural **square meals**] a large meal of healthy food

square root /skweə 'ruːt/ NOUN [plural **square roots**] the number which makes another number when multiplied by itself. A maths word □ The square root of nine is three.

squash /skwɒʃ/ ▶ VERB [**squashes, squashing, squashed**]
1 to press something until it is flat □ Juliet squashed the empty can. 🖾 All the strawberries got squashed at the bottom of the bag.
2 to put a lot of people or things into a small space □ I was squashed in the back seat of the car with three other people. □ + into 12 of us squashed into two cars to travel into town.
▶ NOUN [plural **squashes**]
1 a squash a situation in which there are too many people or things in a place □ It was a bit of a squash fitting everything in the suitcase.
2 no plural a game in which you hit a small rubber ball against the walls of a court
3 no plural a sweet cold drink with a fruit flavour □ a glass of orange squash
4 a hard vegetable that grows on the ground
● **squashy** /'skwɒʃɪ/ ADJECTIVE soft and easy to press □ a big, squashy sofa

squat /skwɒt/ ▶ VERB [**squats, squatting, squatted**]
1 to bend your legs so that your bottom is close to the ground and balance on your feet □ He squatted down to talk to the child.
2 to live in a building without permission
▶ ADJECTIVE short and fat □ a rather squat little man
▶ NOUN [plural **squats**] a building that people are living in without permission
● **squatter** /'skwɒtə(r)/ NOUN [plural **squatters**] someone who is living in a building without permission

squawk /skwɔːk/ ▶ VERB [**squawks, squawking, squawked**] if a bird squawks, it makes a loud noise □ Seagulls were squawking.
▶ NOUN [plural **squawks**] a loud noise that a bird makes

squeak /skwiːk/ ▶ VERB [**squeaks, squeaking, squeaked**] to make a very high sound □ The door squeaked when he opened it.
▶ NOUN [plural **squeaks**] a very high sound
● **squeaky** /'skwiːkɪ/ ADJECTIVE [**squeakier, squeakiest**]
1 making a noise like a squeak □ a squeaky floorboard
2 squeaky clean very clean

squeal /skwiːl/ ▶ VERB [**squeals, squealing, squealed**] to make a long, loud, high sound □ The baby squealed with delight when he saw his mother.
▶ NOUN [plural **squeals**] a long, loud, high sound that someone makes □ a squeal of excitement

squeamish /'skwiːmɪʃ/ ADJECTIVE not liking to see unpleasant things, especially blood □ I couldn't be a nurse - I'm so squeamish.

squeeze /skwiːz/ ▶ VERB [**squeezes, squeezing, squeezed**]
1 to press something tightly □ She squeezed my hand encouragingly.
2 to try to move somewhere where there is very little space □ The cat tried to squeeze itself under the sofa. □ He was trying to squeeze into some very tight jeans.
3 to press something in order to get something out

□ *He squeezed the last of the toothpaste out of the tube.* □ *Emma was squeezing a lemon.*

▶ NOUN [*plural* **squeezes**]

1 the action of squeezing or pressing something 🔁 *She gave my hand a friendly squeeze.*

2 a (tight) squeeze a situation in which there is only just enough space □ *We all got into the car, but it was a tight squeeze.*

squelch /skwelt∫/ ▶ VERB [**squelches, squelching, squelched**] to make a noise when you move through something soft and wet like mud □ *The wet ground squelched under his feet.*

▶ NOUN [*plural* **squelches**] the noise you make when you move through something soft and wet like mud

squid /skwɪd/ NOUN [*plural* **squids**] a sea animal with a soft body and ten arms that is eaten as food

squiggle /'skwɪɡəl/ NOUN [*plural* **squiggles**] an informal word meaning a short, curly written line

squint /skwɪnt/ ▶ VERB [**squints, squinting, squinted**]

1 to close your eyes slightly when you are looking at something □ *She looked up at him, squinting in the sunlight.*

2 to have eyes that look in different directions

▶ NOUN [*plural* **squints**] a problem with your eyes that makes them look in different directions

squirm /skwɜːm/ VERB [**squirms, squirming, squirmed**] to move and twist your body because you are embarrassed, in pain, etc. □ *She squirmed when he remembered how rude she had been.*

squirrel /'skwɪrəl/ NOUN [*plural* **squirrels**] a small grey or red animal with a long, thick tail that lives in trees and eats nuts

squirt /skwɜːt/ VERB [**squirts, squirting, squirted**] to force out a stream of liquid □ *He squirted some ketchup on his fries.* □ *The kids were squirting each other with water.*

Snr /'siːnɪə(r)/ ABBREVIATION Senior; used after someone's name to show they are the older of two men in a family with the same name

St /seɪnt, striːt/ ABBREVIATION

1 Saint

2 street

stab /stæb/ ▶ VERB [**stabs, stabbing, stabbed**] to kill or to injure someone by pushing a knife or other sharp object into them □ *The woman was stabbed with a knife.*

▶ NOUN [*plural* **stabs**]

1 when you stab someone or something 🔁 *a stab wound*

2 a sudden, strong feeling □ *She felt a stab of pain in her leg.*

◆ IDIOM have/make/take a stab at something

1 an informal phrase meaning to try to do something you have not done before □ *I'd love to have a stab at running my own business.*

2 an informal phrase meaning to guess the answer to something □ *Go on, take a stab at it.*

• **stabbing** /'stæbɪŋ/ ▶ NOUN [*plural* **stabbings**] a crime in which someone is stabbed

▶ ADJECTIVE a stabbing pain is a sudden, strong pain

stability /stə'bɪlətɪ/ NOUN, NO PLURAL

1 when a situation stays the same and there are no sudden changes 🔁 *a period of economic stability* □ *Children need stability.*

2 when something is firm and strong and does not move

stabilize or **stabilise** /'steɪbəlaɪz/ VERB [**stabilizes, stabilizing, stabilized**]

1 to stop changing, or to make something do this □ *She's been very ill but her condition has stabilized.*

2 to make something firm and strong and not move □ *Put a book under the table leg to stabilize it.*

stable /'steɪbəl/ ▶ ADJECTIVE

1 firm, strong and not moving □ *This bracket will help to keep the shelf stable.*

2 not changing over a period of time 🔁 *The price has remained relatively stable over recent years.* 🔁 *He's in a stable condition in hospital.*

3 sensible and calm □ *She's a happy, emotionally stable young woman.*

▶ NOUN [*plural* **stables**] a building to keep horses in

stack /stæk/ ▶ NOUN [*plural* **stacks**]

1 a pile of things □ *a stack of books*

2 stacks of something an informal phrase meaning a lot of something □ *The phone has stacks of new features.*

▶ VERB [**stacks, stacking, stacked**] to put things into a stack □ *Stack the dishes in the sink and I'll wash them later.* 🔁 *He got a job stacking shelves in a supermarket.*

stadium /'steɪdɪəm/ NOUN [*plural* **stadiums** or **stadia**] a large open area for playing sports, with seats around it 🔁 *a football stadium* □ *They will face Real Madrid at the Bernabeu Stadium in the semi-finals.*

staff /stɑːf/ ▶ NOUN, NO PLURAL the people who work for a particular organization 🔁 *Six new members of staff are joining the school this term.* □ *The company has a staff of 150.* □ *There is a shortage of medical staff in many hospitals.*

▶ VERB [**staffs, staffing, staffed**] to work at a place or to provide workers for somewhere □ *More nurses are needed to staff these clinics.*

stag /stæɡ/ NOUN [*plural* **stags**] a male deer

stage /steɪdʒ/ ▶ NOUN [*plural* **stages**]

1 the raised area in a theatre where the actors and other performers perform □ *This is their first appearance on stage together.* 🔁 *As the band took the stage, the audience went wild.* 🔁 *I loved the stage show.*

2 one part of a process, or a period of time in the development of something □ *+ of The designs are at various stages of development.* 🔁 *The work is still in its early stages.* 🔁 *It's hard to predict what will happen at this stage.*

◆ IDIOM set the stage for something to make something possible □ *Hamilton's win last week sets the stage for a thrilling end to the season.*

▶ VERB [**stages, staging, staged**]
1 to organize a performance □ *They staged a charity pop concert in Rome.*
2 to organize and take part in something, especially a meeting to complain about something ⊞ *Students staged a noisy protest against his visit.*

stage fright /'steɪdʒ 'fraɪt/ NOUN, NO PLURAL strong feelings of fear or nervousness about performing in front of an audience

stagger /'stægə(r)/ VERB [**staggers, staggering, staggered**]
1 to walk moving from side to side in a way that looks as if you might fall □ *He staggered across the room and fell into a chair.*
2 if you are staggered, you are very surprised □ *I was staggered when they got married.*
3 to arrange events so that they do not all happen at the same time □ *We have to stagger our lunch breaks so that there's always someone in the office.*
• **staggering** /'stægərɪŋ/ ADJECTIVE very surprising □ *The amount of money collected was absolutely staggering.*

stagnant /'stægnənt/ ADJECTIVE
1 stagnant water is dirty because it does not flow □ *a stagnant pond*
2 not developing or changing □ *The economy remains stagnant.*
• **stagnate** /stæg'neɪt/ VERB [**stagnates, stagnating, stagnated**] to become stagnant □ *His career has stagnated.*

stag party /'stæg 'pɑːtɪ/ or **stag night** /'stæg 'naɪt/ NOUN [*plural* **stag parties** or **stag nights**] a party that a man has with his male friends just before he gets married

staid /steɪd/ ADJECTIVE serious and not willing to try new things □ *The organization is trying to get rid of its staid image.*

stain /steɪn/ ▶ VERB [**stains, staining, stained**]
1 to leave a mark that is difficult to remove □ *The coffee you spilt has stained the carpet.* □ **+ with** *His uniform was stained with blood.*
2 to paint wood with a special substance in order to change its colour
▶ NOUN [*plural* **stains**]
1 a dirty mark on something that is difficult to remove □ *His overalls were covered in oil stains.*
2 a substance you put on wood to change its colour

stained glass /'steɪnd 'glɑːs/ NOUN, NO PLURAL pieces of coloured glass used for making pictures in windows

stainless steel /'steɪnlɪs 'stiːl/ NOUN, NO PLURAL a type of steel (=strong metal) that does not rust (=become damaged by water) □ *stainless steel cutlery*

stair /steə(r)/ NOUN [*plural* **stairs**]
1 stairs a set of steps that go from one level in a building to another ⊞ *I climbed the stairs to the second*

floor. ⊞ *I always take the stairs instead of the lift.* ⊞ *A flight of stairs led down to the cellar.*
2 one of these steps □ *Alice sat on the bottom stair.*

staircase /'steəkeɪs/ NOUN [*plural* **staircases**] a set of stairs ⊞ *a spiral staircase* (=stairs which curl round and round)

stairway /'steəweɪ/ NOUN [*plural* **stairways**] a set of stairs inside or outside a building

stairwell /'steəwel/ NOUN [*plural* **stairwells**] the tall space in a building that contains the stairs

stake /steɪk/ ▶ NOUN [*plural* **stakes**]
1 at stake if something is at stake, you risk losing it □ *There's a lot at stake for both teams.* □ *There are people's lives at stake here.*
2 part of a business that you own □ *He bought a 24% stake in the company.*
3 a strong pointed stick, for example to support a fence □ *a wooden stake*
4 an amount of money that you risk by trying to guess the result of a competition □ *a £5 stake*
5 stakes the things you could lose in a situation or competition □ *The threat of a nuclear attack has raised the stakes in the dispute between the two countries.*
▶ VERB [**stakes, staking, staked**]
1 to risk losing something as a result of a situation o competition □ *He has staked his political future on th plan.* □ *I'll stake £10 on Paul winning.*
2 stake a/your claim to say publicly that somethin should belong to you □ *He's already staked his clai to be captain next year.*
◆ PHRASAL VERB **stake something out** to watch a place to see whether anyone leaves or enters □ *Poli staked out the building.*

stale /steɪl/ ADJECTIVE [**staler, stalest**]
1 not fresh □ *stale bread* □ *The air smelt stale ins the room.*
2 not new or interesting □ *The jokes seemed stale*

stalemate /'steɪlmeɪt/ NOUN, NO PLURAL
1 a situation in which progress is impossible becau the people or groups involved do not agree ⊞ *The ta are designed to break the stalemate between the t sides.*
2 a situation in a game of chess in which neither pla can make a move so neither player can win

stalk /stɔːk/ ▶ NOUN [*plural* **stalks**] the stem of a flower, leaf or fruit □ *an apple stalk*
▶ VERB [**stalks, stalking, stalked**]
1 to follow an animal quietly, in order to catch and it □ *The tigress stalked her prey.*
2 to follow and watch someone in a way that the find threatening □ *She is stalked by press photographers.*
3 to walk in a proud, often angry, way □ *She hac offended him so much that he stalked out of the ro*
• **stalker** /'stɔːkə(r)/ NOUN [*plural* **stalkers**] some who stalks another person

stall /stɔːl/ ▶ NOUN [*plural* **stalls**] a table or a s open shop where people sell things ⊞ *a market s*

□ *a roadside food stall* □ *The stalls sell fresh fruit and vegetables.*

➜ go to **stalls**

▶ VERB [**stalls, stalling, stalled**]
1 if a vehicle stalls, its engine suddenly stops while you are driving □ *The car stalled at traffic lights and she couldn't get it started again.*
2 to delay someone or to delay doing something □ *I'll try and stall her for a few minutes.*
3 to stop making progress □ *Peace talks have stalled again.*

stallion /'stælɪən/ NOUN [*plural* **stallions**] a male horse

stalls /stɔ:lz/ PLURAL NOUN the stalls the seats nearest to the stage in a theatre

stalwart /'stɔ:lwət/ ▶ NOUN [*plural* **stalwarts**] a strong, loyal supporter □ *a meeting of the party stalwarts*
▶ ADJECTIVE supporting someone or something in a strong and loyal way 🖭 *He's always been one of our most stalwart supporters.*

tamen /'steɪmən/ NOUN [*plural* **stamens**] the male part of a flower that makes pollen. A biology word.

tamina /'stæmɪnə/ NOUN, NO PLURAL the strength and energy to keep doing something for a long time □ *You need to do exercises to increase your stamina.*

tammer /'stæmə(r)/ ▶ VERB [**stammers, stammering, stammered**]
1 to have a speech problem that makes you stop or repeat some letters when you speak
2 to speak like this because you are frightened or nervous □ *'I'm s-s-sorry,' he stammered.*
▶ NOUN [*plural* **stammers**] a speech problem that makes you stammer

tamp /stæmp/ ▶ NOUN [*plural* **stamps**]
1 a small printed piece of paper that you buy and stick on letters before you post them 🖭 *a first-class stamp* □ *I noticed the Canadian stamp on the envelope.*
2 a tool that you use to stamp words, numbers or a design on something, or the mark it makes 🖭 *a rubber stamp* □ *a date stamp*
stamp of approval when someone publicly says they approve of something □ *The president gave his personal stamp of approval to the scheme.*
when you stamp your foot
IDIOM **put your stamp on something** to make changes to something in a way that shows your character □ *In his time as director, Murray has put his stamp on this organization.*
▶ VERB [**stamps, stamping, stamped**]
1 to bring your foot down firmly on the ground □ + *He stamped on the brake.* 🖭 *She stamped her feet to keep them warm.*
2 to print letters, numbers, or a design on something □ *The official stamped her passport.* □ + *with Each letter is stamped with the date we receive it.*
3 to put a stamp on a letter
PHRASAL VERB **stamp something out** to stop

something unpleasant or harmful from happening □ *We are determined to stamp out corruption.*

stamped addressed envelope /'stæmpt ə'drest 'envələup/ NOUN [*plural* **stamped addressed envelopes**] an envelope that you write your name and address on and stick a stamp on, so that someone can send you a reply

stampede /stæm'pi:d/ ▶ NOUN [*plural* **stampedes**] when a large group of people or animals suddenly go somewhere very quickly □ *The bell went and there was a stampede for the door.*
▶ VERB [**stampedes, stampeding, stampeded**] if a large group of people or animals stampede, they suddenly go somewhere very quickly

stance /stæns/ NOUN [*plural* **stances**]
1 someone's opinion about something □ *What's the company's stance on working from home?* 🖭 *They are taking a tough stance against illegal immigration.*
2 a formal word meaning the way someone is standing □ *He had a stiff, upright stance.*

stand /stænd/ ▶ VERB [**stands, standing, stood**]
1 to be in a vertical position on your feet, not sitting or lying □ *I was so tired I could barely stand.* □ *I stood on a chair to reach the shelf.* □ *He was standing next to his brother.*
2 to get up onto your feet after sitting or lying □ *Everyone stood when the queen entered.* □ + *up Stand up and let me look at you.*
3 to put your foot on something, often by accident □ + *on You stood on my finger.*
4 to be in a particular position □ *The train stood outside Waterloo for nearly an hour.* □ *Durham stands on the River Wear.*
5 to put something in a particular position □ *I stood the jug on the table.*
6 to be able to accept someone or something 🖭 *I can't stand her brother, Mark.* □ *Marie couldn't stand hearing her parents arguing any more.*
7 to continue to exist or to be used □ *The judge ordered that the sentence should stand.* 🖭 *His offer of money still stands.*
8 to be in a particular condition or situation 🖭 *As things stand* (=the way things are now), *we can't take on any more work.* 🖭 *At least with Tom you always know where you stand* (=know what he thinks and what he expects you to do).
9 to be strong enough to deal with something or not to be damaged by something □ *I left my last job because I couldn't stand the pressure.* □ *That dish won't stand the heat of an oven.*
10 to try to be elected □ + *for She's standing for parliament at the next election.*
11 stand a chance to have a chance of achieving something □ *I think he stands a good chance of winning.*
12 stand trial if someone stands trial, they go to a court where it is decided if they are guilty of a crime
➜ go to **stand your ground**

◆ PHRASAL VERBS **stand about/around** to stand somewhere and not do much □ *They've been standing around doing nothing all morning.* **stand aside 1** to leave a position in a business or an organization so that someone else can do it □ *I have decided to stand aside to allow one of my younger colleagues to take over.* **2** to move a short distance to the side □ *We stood aside to let him pass.* **stand at something** to be at a particular level or amount □ *Unemployment stands at over 4 million.* **stand back** to move a short distance away from someone □ *Stand back, please, so that the doctors can get through.* **stand by 1** to be ready to do something □ *Teams of doctors are standing by with medical equipment.* **2** to do nothing to prevent an unpleasant action or situation □ *The government is just standing by while its people starve.* **stand by someone** to continue to support someone □ *My parents stood by me all through the trial.* **stand by something** to continue to have the same opinion, or to not change a promise or an agreement □ *I stand by everything I said yesterday.* □ *I think they will stand by their promises.* **stand down** to leave a position in a business or an organization so that someone else can have it □ *+ as* *He offered to stand down as chairman.* **stand for something 1** if letters stand for something, that thing begins with those letters □ *What does BBC stand for?* **2** to support a particular idea □ *Our party stands for freedom and democracy.* **3** to be willing to accept a situation or someone's behaviour □ *I won't stand for laziness!* **stand in** to do someone else's job while they are not able to do it, for example because they are on holiday □ *+ for* *I'm standing in for their usual teacher, who's off sick.* **stand out 1** to be very easy to see or notice □ *The yellow flowers really stood out against the green background.* **2** to be better than other similar people or things □ *+ from* *He stood out from the other students because of his original mind.*

◆ go to **stand out like a sore** *thumb*
stand up to get up onto your feet after sitting or lying □ *She stood up and left the room.* **stand up for someone/something** to support someone or something that is being criticized or attacked □ *My brother always stands up for me when my parents tell me off.* **stand up to someone** to not allow yourself to be controlled or treated badly by someone, usually someone more powerful than you □ *Our manager is awful, but nobody dares to stand up to her.*

▶ NOUN [*plural* **stands**]
1 someone's opinion about something □ *+ on* *What's your head teacher's stand on school uniform?* 🔁 *He takes a tough stand on crime.*
2 make a stand to act in a strong way in order to achieve something or to prevent something □ *By refusing to buy battery farmed eggs, we are making a stand against cruelty.*

3 something that an object stands on □ *a large mirror on a stand*
4 a small shop with an open front, often that can be moved from place to place □ *There were lots of food stands at the fair.*
5 rows of seats where people sit to watch sports □ *Spectators were cheering from the stands.*
6 the stand the place in a court where people stand when they are being asked questions 🔁 *Her husband is due to take the stand* (=be questioned) *tomorrow.*

standard /ˈstændəd/ ▶ NOUN [*plural* **standards**]
1 a level of quality □ *+ of* *We hope to improve the standard of medical care.* 🔁 *The club has set high standards for itself this season.* 🔁 *Living standards have risen dramatically.* 🔁 *The facilities do not meet basic safety standards.* 🔁 *Standards have been slipping* (=getting worse) *recently.*
2 standards principles about what is acceptable behaviour □ *Standards aren't what they used to be.* □ *He has high moral standards.*
3 an official rule or system for measuring things □ *The kilogram is the international standard of weight.*
▶ ADJECTIVE normal or usual □ *the standard charge fo postage* 🔁 *All of this is standard police procedure.* □ *Chemotherapy is now a standard treatment for cancer.*
● **standardize** *or* **standardise** /ˈstændədaɪz/ VER [**standardizes, standardizing, standardized**] to mak or to keep things all the same □ *We're trying to standardize the filing system.*

standby /ˈstændbaɪ/ NOUN [*plural* **standbys**]
1 something or someone that you can use if you need them □ *I always keep some long-life milk as standby.*
2 on standby ready to travel or ready to do something if needed □ *Ambulance crews were on standby to treat any injuries.*

standing /ˈstændɪŋ/ ▶ NOUN [*plural* **standings**]
1 your position or people's opinion of you in a group society □ *This affair has damaged his international standing.*
2 the period of time that something continues or exists for □ *a relationship of several years standing*
▶ ADJECTIVE
1 to do with actions that are done standing up 🔁 speech received a *standing ovation* (=when an audience stands and claps). □ *She pulled herself up a standing position.*
2 permanent, regularly used, or continuing 🔁 *It's standing joke around the office.* □ *We have a stand invitation to visit.*

standing order /ˈstændɪŋ ˈɔːdə(r)/ NOUN [*plura* **standing orders**] an instruction to your bank to regularly pay a particular amount of money from y account to someone else

standing ovation /'stændɪŋ əʊ'veɪʃən/ NOUN [plural **standing ovations**] when everyone stands up and claps at the end of a performance, speech, etc.

stand-off /'stændɒf/ NOUN [plural **stand-offs**] a situation in which an argument or a fight stops because no one can win or achieve their aim □ a political stand-off

standpoint /'stændpɔɪnt/ NOUN [plural **standpoints**] a particular way of thinking about a situation □ From a political standpoint, it was a difficult decision.

standstill /'stændstɪl/ NOUN, NO PLURAL a complete stop 🔁 Icy roads brought traffic to a standstill.

tank /stæŋk/ PAST TENSE OF stink

taple¹ /'steɪpəl/ ► NOUN [plural **staples**] a type of food or product that you use a lot of □ staples such as milk and bread
► ADJECTIVE a staple food or product is one of the most basic and important ones 🔁 Their staple diet is rice.

taple² /'steɪpəl/ ► NOUN [plural **staples**] a bent piece of wire that you push through papers to fasten them together
► VERB [**staples, stapling, stapled**] to fasten papers together with a staple □ Staple the pages together.

stapler /'steɪplə(r)/ NOUN [plural **staplers**] a small tool for stapling papers together

tar /stɑː(r)/ ► NOUN [plural **stars**]
a mass of burning gas in the sky that you can see at ight as a point of light □ the brightest star in the night y □ There are billions of stars in our galaxy.
a famous person, especially a performer 🔁 a film star a pop star 🔁 He became one of Hollywood's biggest ars. □ + of He was married to Jennifer Aniston, star f the TV show 'Friends'.
a shape with five or more points □ a six-pointed star The EU symbol is a circle of gold stars on a blue ackground.
used to show the standard of something, especially hotel, restaurant, etc. □ a three-star hotel □ The sort received a top rating of four stars.
ADJECTIVE to do with a famous person or the best, ost famous, etc. person in a group □ a star rformance □ the club's star player
VERB [**stars, starring, starred**] to have the main part a film □ Tom Cruise is to star in the sequel. □ a new n starring Kate Winslet

rboard /'stɑːbəd/ NOUN, NO PLURAL the right side a ship or aircraft when you are facing the front

rch /stɑːtʃ/ ► NOUN [plural **starches**]
substance in foods such as potatoes, pasta and bread powder used to make clothes stiff
/ERB [**starches, starching, starched**] to make :hes stiff using starch □ a starched white shirt

archy /'stɑːtʃɪ/ ADJECTIVE containing a lot of starch void sugary and starchy foods.

dom /'stɑːdəm/ NOUN, NO PLURAL when someone ery famous □ She achieved international stardom supermodel.

stare /steə(r)/ ► VERB [**stares, staring, stared**] to look at someone or something for a long time □ What are you staring at?
► NOUN [plural **stares**] when you look at someone or something for a long time 🔁 Tony gave him a blank stare.

starfish /'stɑːfɪʃ/ NOUN [plural **starfish**] a sea animal with five arms

stark /stɑːk/ ► ADJECTIVE [**starker, starkest**]
1 unpleasant, clear and impossible to avoid 🔁 Scientists issued a stark warning about global warming. 🔁 She was faced with a stark choice.
2 complete and clear □ There were stark differences in the quality of service.
3 plain and empty □ a stark, barren landscape
► ADVERB **stark naked** wearing no clothes
● **starkly** /'stɑːklɪ/ ADVERB in a stark way □ a starkly furnished room □ The figures starkly show the financial problems we are facing.

starry /'stɑːrɪ/ ADJECTIVE [**starrier, starriest**] full of stars □ a starry sky

starry-eyed /'stɑːrɪ'aɪd/ ADJECTIVE full of dreams or hopes, especially ones that are not sensible □ She is starry-eyed about her future.

start /stɑːt/ ► VERB [**starts, starting, started**]
1 to begin doing something □ + **to do something** Suddenly, a bird started to sing. □ + **ing** What time did you start working this morning? □ I'm starting a new job next week.
2 to begin to happen or exist, or to make something happen or exist □ Work on the new bridge has started at last. □ He started an online art gallery. □ The fire started in the kitchen.
3 to begin an event, activity or period of time in a particular way □ My day started very badly. □ + **by** Shall we start by introducing ourselves? □ + **with** I'd like everyone to give their opinion. Let's start with Mel.
4 **to start with** (a) at the beginning of a period □ To start with, I wasn't sure if I'd get on with him. (b) used before you say the first thing in a list of things □ Why did I leave my job? Well, to start with, the money was awful.
5 to begin to work or to make a machine or a vehicle begin to work □ The car wouldn't start. □ I couldn't start the engine.
6 to be the lowest amount or level of something □ + **at** Prices start at £5.
◆ PHRASAL VERBS **start (something) off** to begin an activity or an event □ Let's start off with some gentle exercises. **start on something** to begin doing something □ Have you started on the cleaning yet? **start out 1** to begin as a particular thing or in a particular way □ + **as** I started out as a junior assistant. □ + **ing** He started out selling his photographs on a market stall. **2** to begin a journey □ We started out after dinner. **start over** a US word meaning to begin something again □ I burned the onions and had to start over. **start something up 1** to begin a business,

organization or activity □ *She started up a school for bullied children.*

2 to make a machine or a vehicle begin to work □ *He started up the engine and off we went.*

▶ NOUN [*plural* **starts**]

1 the beginning of something ⽥ *Right from the start, I knew I'd be happy here.* □ **+ of** *The runners lined up for the start of the race.*

2 the way something begins ⽥ *The business got off to a good start.* □ *After a shaky start, his performance was very good.*

3 make a start to begin doing something □ *I'm going to make a start on the cooking.*

4 for a start used to give the first of a list of reasons □ *For a start, I'm fed up with sharing a room with my sister.*

5 the beginning of a journey ⽥ *I must go to bed - we've got an early start tomorrow.*

6 the place where a race begins

• **starter** /'stɑːtə(r)/ NOUN [*plural* **starters**] the first part of a meal, eaten before the main part □ *We had soup as a starter.*

startle /'stɑːtəl/ VERB [**startles, startling, startled**] to suddenly frighten or shock someone □ *He was startled by a loud noise.*

• **startled** /'stɑːtəld/ ADJECTIVE shocked or surprised by something unexpected □ *a startled expression*

• **startling** /'stɑːtlɪŋ/ ADJECTIVE shocking because of being unusual or unexpected □ *Dr Jones made a startling discovery.*

starvation /stɑːˈveɪʃən/ NOUN, NO PLURAL when people are very hungry and have not got enough to eat □ *Thousands of people die of starvation every year.*

starve /stɑːv/ VERB [**starves, starving, starved**] to die or to suffer because you have not got enough to eat ⽥ *If they don't get food aid, these people are going to starve to death.*

♦ PHRASAL VERB **starve someone/something of something** if someone or something is starved of something they need, they do not have enough of it □ *His brain had been starved of oxygen.*

• **starving** /'stɑːvɪŋ/ ADJECTIVE

1 an informal word meaning very hungry □ *What's for dinner? I'm starving.*

2 dying because you do not have enough to eat □ *pictures of starving children*

stash /stæʃ/ ▶ VERB [**stashes, stashing, stashed**] an informal word meaning to hide something in a secret place □ *He had thousands of pounds stashed away under the floorboards.*

▶ NOUN [*plural* **stashes**] an informal word for an amount of something hidden in a secret place □ *He showed me his stash of secret files and photographs.*

state /steɪt/ ▶ NOUN [*plural* **states**]

1 the condition that someone or something is in □ *The house was in a very poor state.* □ **+ of** *She's always complaining about the state of our public transport.* ⽥ *I'm still in a state of shock.*

2 a country □ *the state of Israel* ⽥ *There was a meeting between heads of state* (=leaders of countries).

3 the state the government of a country □ *The state should provide for the sick and elderly.*

4 a part of a country that has its own government □ *New York state* □ **+ of** *the southern Indian state of Andhra Pradesh*

5 the States the US □ *He spent six weeks in the States.*

6 in a state very upset and worried □ *There's no point getting in a state about things.*

▶ ADJECTIVE

1 to do with the government of a country □ *a state pension* □ *a state school*

2 to do with a part of a country that has its own government □ *the state governor* □ *It's an offence under California state law.*

3 official and involving political leaders ⽥ *The Prince was on a state visit to India.*

▶ VERB [**states, stating, stated**] to formally say or write something □ *The letter clearly states that you must bring some identification with you.* □ *They were given an opportunity to state their views.*

• **stately** /'steɪtli/ ADJECTIVE

1 slow and formal □ *a stately procession* □ *The vehicle was moving at a stately pace.*

2 large and formal □ *We were shown into a stately living room.*

stately home /ˌsteɪtli 'həʊm/ NOUN [*plural* **stately homes**] a large, old house in the countryside where rich, important family live or lived

statement /'steɪtmənt/ NOUN [*plural* **statements**]

1 something that you say or write, especially formally or officially ⽥ *The police asked me to make a written statement of what I saw.* □ *A statement on his website said he had no plans to leave the band.*

2 a document showing how much money you have in your bank account and what you have spent ⽥ *Check your bank statements regularly.*

state of affairs /ˌsteɪt əv əˈfeəz/ NOUN, NO PLURAL situation, especially one that is bad □ *This is a sorry state of affairs.*

state-of-the-art /ˌsteɪt əv ðɪ 'ɑːt/ ADJECTIVE using the newest designs, ideas, technology, etc. □ *state-of-the-art medical facilities*

statesman /'steɪtsmən/ NOUN [*plural* **statesmen**] important political leader

static /'stætɪk/ ▶ ADJECTIVE not moving or changing □ *Crime levels have remained static.*

▶ NOUN, NO PLURAL electricity caused by rubbing surfaces together □ *You get static when you comb your hair with a plastic comb.*

station /'steɪʃən/ ▶ NOUN [*plural* **stations**]

1 a building where trains or buses stop to let people get on and off ⽥ *a railway station* ⽥ *a bus station* □ *meet you at the station.*

2 a building where some types of work take place 🗫 He was taken to the local police station. 🗫 a fire station 🗫 We stopped at a petrol station (=a place that sells petrol). 🗫 a nuclear power station
3 a company which makes and broadcasts television or radio programmes 🗫 The interview was broadcast by a Spanish television station.
▶ VERB [**stations, stationing, stationed**] to put or to send someone to a particular position or place □ They stationed a guard at each door.

stationary /'steɪʃnərɪ/ ADJECTIVE not moving □ a line of stationary traffic

stationery /'steɪʃnərɪ/ NOUN, NO PLURAL paper, pens, and other things you use to write with

statistical /stə'tɪstɪkəl/ ADJECTIVE to do with statistics □ All the statistical evidence supports our case.

statistically /stə'tɪstɪkəlɪ/ ADVERB using statistics □ His views have not been statistically proven.

statistics /stə'tɪstɪks/ PLURAL NOUN
1 information about something which is represented by numbers □ the official crime statistics 🗫 Statistics show that the number of births has increased by 2% over the last five years.
2 the study of information in the form of numbers

statue /'stætʃuː/ NOUN [*plural* **statues**] a large model of a person or animal made out of stone, metal or wood □ + of a huge statue of the Buddha □ a life-size bronze statue

statuesque /ˌstætju'esk/ ADJECTIVE tall and attractive □ a statuesque model and film star

stature /'stætʃə(r)/ NOUN, NO PLURAL
1 a formal word meaning importance and respect □ He is a political figure of international stature.
2 a formal word meaning size or height □ He was small in stature but had a strong personality.

status /'steɪtəs/ NOUN [*plural* **statuses**]
1 someone's position in a society or group compared to other people 🗫 Is success at school determined by social status?
2 the legal position of someone or something 🗫 The legal status of many websites is unclear. 🗫 There are questions about age, marital status (=whether you are married or not), etc.
3 the situation or condition of something at a particular time □ Call your airline to check on the status of your flight.

status quo /ˌsteɪtəs 'kwəʊ/ NOUN, NO PLURAL the situation as it is now, used especially when you are talking about possible changes □ Most countries want to maintain the status quo.

status symbol /'steɪtəs 'sɪmbəl/ NOUN [*plural* **status symbols**] something you own that shows you are rich or important

statute /'stætjuːt/ NOUN [*plural* **statutes**] a formal word meaning a law

statutory /'stætjʊtərɪ/ ADJECTIVE necessary or controlled by law □ statutory employment rights

staunch /stɔːntʃ/ ADJECTIVE [**stauncher, staunchest**] loyal □ a staunch supporter of the government

stave /steɪv/
◆ PHRASAL VERB [**staves, staving, staved**] stave something off to delay something happening □ We had a packet of crisps to stave off our hunger.

stay /steɪ/ ▶ VERB [**stays, staying, stayed**]
1 to remain in a place □ Make sure you stay inside the house. □ Would you like to stay for dinner? 🗫 He agreed to stay home and look after the children. 🗫 Stay there/here! □ I stayed in the same job for nearly twenty years.
2 to continue to be in a particular condition □ She tried to stay calm as they waited. □ I could hardly stay awake. □ Things can't stay the same for ever. 🗫 At the moment we are very happy together, and I hope it will stay that way.
3 to spend a period of time in a place □ + with I'm going to stay with my sister for a few days. □ + in We stayed in a wonderful hotel. 🗫 I stayed the night at a friend's house.
◆ IDIOMS stay put to remain in the same place □ My mother has decided to stay put because she has so many friends where she lives now. stay the course to continue doing something, even if it is difficult □ Do you think you will stay the course?
◆ PHRASAL VERBS stay away to not go somewhere □ The gardens are open to the public, but so far the crowds have stayed away. stay behind to remain in a place after other people have left □ I stayed behind to tidy up. stay in to remain in your house □ I stayed in on Saturday and watched TV. stay on to remain at a place, course, job, etc. for another period of time □ He's staying on at school to do his A levels. stay out to not come home at night, or to come home very late □ My parents don't like me staying out late. stay out of something to not become involved with an argument or in a difficult situation □ My brothers are always fighting, but I try to stay out of it. stay together if two people in a relationship stay together, they continue to live together stay up to not go to bed until later than usual □ We stayed up to watch the election results.
▶ NOUN [*plural* **stays**] a period of time that you spend at a place □ The trip includes an overnight stay in Bangkok.

steadfast /'stedfɑːst/ ADJECTIVE a formal word meaning not changing your opinion or what you are doing □ He remained steadfast in his refusal to negotiate.

steadily /'stedɪlɪ/ ADVERB
1 in a continuous and gradual way □ His performance has improved steadily. □ Costs have risen steadily.
2 without changing □ It's been raining steadily all week.

steady /'stedɪ/ ▶ ADJECTIVE [**steadier, steadiest**]
1 firm and not shaking □ You need a steady hand. □ Can you hold it steady for me?

2 continuous and gradual 🔁 *We're making steady progress.*

3 not changing □ *I tried to keep a steady pace.*

▶ VERB [**steadies, steadying, steadied**]

1 to stop something from moving or shaking □ *She tried to steady the tray.*

2 to become calmer, or to make someone become calmer □ *She waited until her voice had steadied.* 🔁 *I took several deep breaths to steady my nerves.*

3 steady yourself to stop yourself from falling, especially by holding onto something □ *Helen steadied herself against the wall.*

steak /steɪk/ NOUN [*plural* **steaks**] a thick piece of meat or fish, especially meat from a cow □ *He was eating steak and chips.* □ *tuna steaks*

steal /stiːl/ VERB [**steals, stealing, stole, stolen**]

1 to take something without the owner's permission □ *The thieves stole money and jewellery.* □ *It's wrong to steal.* □ **+ from** *Several valuable paintings were stolen from the house.* □ *a stolen car*

2 to move quietly □ *He stole out of the house to meet his girlfriend.*

➤ Remember that thieves **steal** money and objects. They **rob** people and places: □ *They stole his money and his watch.* □ *They were robbed in the street.* □ *They robbed a bank.*

stealth /stelθ/ NOUN, NO PLURAL a secret or quiet way of doing something □ *The government is introducing new taxes by stealth.*

● **stealthy** /stelθɪ/ ADJECTIVE [**stealthier, stealthiest**] doing something secretly or quietly □ *a stealthy killer*

steam /stiːm/ ▶ NOUN, NO PLURAL

1 the gas that is formed when you heat water □ *Steam was rising from the coffee pot.*

2 a steam train/engine etc. a train, engine, etc. that uses power from steam

◆ IDIOMS **let off steam** to say how angry you are feeling in a way that makes you feel better **run out of steam** to lose your energy or enthusiasm for something **under your own steam** without anyone else's help □ *He wanted to explore the city under his own steam.*

▶ VERB [**steams, steaming, steamed**]

1 to produce steam □ *A kettle was steaming on the stove.* □ *a steaming bowl of soup*

2 to cook food in steam □ *steamed vegetables*

◆ PHRASAL VERB **steam (something) up** to become covered in steam, or to cover something in steam □ *My glasses steamed up and I couldn't see a thing.*

● **steamer** /stiːmə(r)/ NOUN [*plural* **steamers**]

1 a pan used for cooking food in steam

2 a ship that uses steam for power

steamroller /stiːmˌrəʊlə(r)/ NOUN [*plural* **steamrollers**] a vehicle used for making road surfaces flat

steamy /stiːmɪ/ ADJECTIVE [**steamier, steamiest**] full of or covered in steam □ *a steamy rainforest*

steel /stiːl/ ▶ NOUN, NO PLURAL a very hard metal that is a mixture of iron and carbon 🔁 *Many knives and forks are made from stainless steel* (=steel that stays shiny).

▶ ADJECTIVE

1 made from steel □ *steel knives*

2 to do with making steel and steel objects □ *the steel industry*

▶ VERB [**steels, steeling, steeled**] steel yourself to prepare yourself for something difficult or bad □ *She steeled herself for the test results.*

● **steely** /stiːlɪ/ ADJECTIVE [**steelier, steeliest**] determined and strong □ *a steely gaze* □ *Her steely determination impressed many people.*

steep /stiːp/ ▶ ADJECTIVE [**steeper, steepest**]

1 a steep hill or slope goes up or down very quickly □ *steep hill* □ *The path was too steep for me to cycle up.* 🔁 *It was a steep climb to the top of the hill.*

2 a steep increase or decrease is very big 🔁 *There has been a steep rise in oil prices.* 🔁 *The company suffered a steep decline in sales.*

3 an informal word for expensive □ *Three pounds for a cup of coffee? That's a bit steep.*

▶ VERB be steeped in history/tradition/culture etc. to have a lot of a particular quality □ *China is a beautiful country, steeped in tradition and history.*

steeple /stiːpəl/ NOUN [*plural* **steeples**] a pointed tower on a church

steeply /stiːplɪ/ ADVERB in a way that is steep 🔁 *Oil prices have risen very steeply.*

steer /stɪə(r)/ VERB [**steers, steering, steered**]

1 to control the direction that a vehicle moves in □ *I steered the car through the narrow streets.* □ *The captain steered out of the harbour.*

2 to influence what someone does or the way something develops □ *He intended to steer the country from anarchy to peace.*

3 to put your hand on someone's arm or back and show them where to go □ *Penny steered me towards the house.*

4 steer clear of someone/something to avoid someone or something □ *It's best to steer clear of him when he's angry.*

steering wheel /stɪərɪŋ ˈwiːl/ NOUN [*plural* **steering wheels**] the wheel a driver holds to control a car's direction

stem /stem/ ▶ NOUN [*plural* **stems**] the long thin part of a plant, which the leaves grow on

▶ VERB [**stems, stemming, stemmed**] to stop something from continuing 🔁 *He used his scarf to stem the flow of blood.* □ *The government has failed to stem the violence.*

◆ PHRASAL VERB **stem from something** to happen or develop as a result of something □ *The charges arose from an incident in which he spat at a police officer.*

stench /stentʃ/ NOUN [*plural* **stenches**] a strong smell □ *the stench of rotting meat*

stencil /'stensəl/ ▶ NOUN [*plural* **stencils**] a piece of card with shapes cut out of it, which you paint over in order to make a pattern on something
▶ VERB [**stencils, stencilling, stencilled**] to use a stencil to decorate a surface

step /step/ ▶ NOUN [*plural* **steps**]

1 one of a series of actions involved in doing or achieving something ▣ *These talks are an important step in bringing peace to the region.* ▣ *For me, that school play was the first step towards becoming an actor.* ▣ *I shall take steps to prevent this happening again.* ▣ *Step by step* (=gradually) *she is learning to speak again.*

2 in step (a) having similar opinions or ways of doing things as someone else, or changing at the same speed as something else □ *Wages have not stayed in step with inflation.* (b) walking at the same speed as someone else □ *He fell in step with Daniel and they walked together.*

3 out of step having different opinions or ways of doing things from someone else, or changing at a different speed from something else

4 the action of lifting your foot off the ground and putting it down again in walking, running or dancing ▣ *He took a step forward.* □ *I'm sure I heard steps* (=the sound that steps make) *outside.*

5 a flat surface that you walk on to go up or down to a different level, often one of a series □ *The postman left the parcel on the front step.* □ *We climbed the steep steps to the monastery.*

6 a particular movement of the feet, for example in dancing □ *Try to learn these simple steps.*

IDIOM **one step ahead** slightly more successful than someone else, or having done something just before someone else □ *I like to stay one step ahead of the competition.*

▶ VERB [**steps, stepping, stepped**]
to take a step □ *He opened the door and stepped out.*

to put your foot on something, often by accident
+ on *He stepped on my toe!* □ **+ in** *I stepped in some mud.*

PHRASAL VERBS **step aside**
to leave a position in a business or an organization so that someone else can do it □ *She decided to step aside and let her daughters run the firm.*

to move a short distance away from someone □ *He stepped aside to let us past.* **step down** to leave a position in a business or an organization so that someone else can have it □ *He stepped down as president in 2007.* **step in** to become involved in a situation in order to try to deal with it □ *The army had to step in to halt the violence.* **step something up** to increase something that is being used or done □ *Security has been stepped up following the bomb scares.* □ *They stepped up his dose of painkillers.*

step- /step/ PREFIX step- is added to the beginning of words to show that people are related to you by a second marriage □ *stepfather* □ *stepdaughter*

stepbrother /'step,brʌðə(r)/ NOUN [*plural* **stepbrothers**] the son of a person who has married your mother or father, but who is not your brother

stepchild /'step,tʃaɪld/ NOUN [*plural* **stepchildren**] someone who is the child of your husband or wife, but is not your child

stepdaughter /'step,dɔːtə(r)/ NOUN [*plural* **stepdaughters**] the daughter of your husband or wife, who is not your daughter

stepfather /'step,fɑːðə(r)/ NOUN [*plural* **stepfathers**] the man who is married to your mother but is not your father

stepladder /'step,lædə(r)/ NOUN [*plural* **stepladders**] a small ladder (=something you use for reaching high places) that folds

stepmother /'step,mʌðə(r)/ NOUN [*plural* **stepmothers**] the woman who is married to your father but is not your mother

steppe /step/ NOUN the steppes a large area of hot, dry land with grass in Russia and Asia. A geography word.

stepping stone /'stepɪŋ 'stəʊn/ NOUN [*plural* **stepping stones**]

1 something which helps you achieve something else □ *Think of the job as a stepping stone to greater things.*

2 one of a line of stones that people walk on to cross a stream

stepsister /'step,sɪstə(r)/ NOUN [*plural* **stepsisters**] the daughter of a person who has married your mother or father, but who is not your sister

stepson /'stepsʌn/ NOUN [*plural* **stepsons**] the son of your husband or wife, who is not your son

stereo /'steriəʊ/ NOUN [*plural* **stereos**]

1 a piece of equipment for playing music which plays the sound through two speakers (=pieces of equipment that sound comes out of)

2 in stereo using a system that sends sound out through two speakers (=pieces of equipment that sound comes out of)

stereotype /'steriətaɪp/ ▶ NOUN [*plural* **stereotypes**] an idea about what a particular type of person is like, which may be wrong or unfair □ *The programme aims to challenge racial stereotypes.*

▶ VERB [**stereotypes, stereotyping, stereotyped**] to think that all women, all rich people, all white people, etc. have particular qualities

● **stereotypical** /,steriəʊ'tɪpɪkəl/ ADJECTIVE involving a stereotype □ *Many people have a very stereotypical view of old people.*

sterile /'steraɪl/ ADJECTIVE

1 completely clean, with no bacteria □ *A surgeon's instruments must be sterile.*

2 unable to have babies

● **sterilization** *or* **sterilisation** /,sterəlaɪ'zeɪʃən/ NOUN, NO PLURAL the treatment of something to destroy bacteria

• **sterilize** or **sterilise** /'sterəlaɪz/ VERB [**sterilizes, sterilizing, sterilized**] to make something clean by getting rid of bacteria □ *You need to sterilize babies' milk bottles.*

sterling /'stɜːlɪŋ/ ▶ NOUN, NO PLURAL the money used in Great Britain □ *She changed her euros into sterling.*
▶ ADJECTIVE very good □ *He has done some sterling work.*

stern /stɜːn/ ▶ ADJECTIVE [**sterner, sternest**] very serious and slightly angry □ *He had a stern expression on his face.* □ *a stern warning*
▶ NOUN [*plural* **sterns**] the back part of a ship

steroid /'stɪərɔɪd/ NOUN [*plural* **steroids**] a drug that doctors give people to treat swelling, or one that some people take illegally to improve their sports performance

stethoscope /'steθəskəʊp/ NOUN [*plural* **stethoscopes**] an instrument that a doctor uses to listen to your heart or breathing

stew /stjuː/ ▶ NOUN [*plural* **stews**] a mixture of vegetables and meat cooked slowly together in liquid □ *beef stew*
▶ VERB [**stews, stewing, stewed**] to cook something slowly in liquid □ *I stewed the apples.*

steward /'stjuəd/ NOUN [*plural* **stewards**]
1 a man whose job is to look after passengers on an aeroplane or a ship
2 an official at events such as races and concerts

stewardess /'stjuədɪs/ NOUN [*plural* **stewardesses**] an old-fashioned word for a woman whose job is to look after passengers on an aeroplane

stick¹ /stɪk/ VERB [**sticks, sticking, stuck**]
1 to push something thin or sharp into something, or to be pushed into something □ *We stuck pins into the cushion.* □ *Stop sticking your elbows into me!* □ *There was a thorn sticking in my skin.* □ *He stuck his fingers in his ears.*
2 to fix something to something else, or to become fixed to something □ *Never mind, we can always stick the pieces back together.* □ *We stuck labels on the jam jars.* □ *He had a piece of paper stuck on his back.*
3 to become unable to move □ *The car stuck in the mud.* □ *This drawer keeps sticking.*
4 an informal word meaning to put something somewhere □ *Just stick the shopping on the floor.* □ *He stuck his head round the door to say hello.*
♦ IDIOMS **stick to your guns** to refuse to change your decisions about something □ *Kat stuck to her guns and refused to sell the house.* **stick your neck out** to decide to do or say something although it might be wrong or make people angry □ *I'm going to stick my neck out here and say that this vase is worth at least £30,000.*
➡ *go to* **stick your *nose* in/into something**
♦ PHRASAL VERBS **stick around** an informal word meaning to stay in a place □ *He didn't stick around long enough to see his children grow up.* **stick at something** to continue to try to do something difficult □ *She found reading difficult, but she stuck at*

it and now she really enjoys it. **stick by someone** to continue to support someone, especially when they are having problems □ *My parents stuck by me when I was in prison.* **stick out 1** to come out further than a surface or an edge □ *His ears stick out.* □ *I could see an umbrella sticking out of her bag.* **2** to be easy to notice □ *The thing that stuck out most was the way they dressed.* □ *His work stuck out from all the rest.*
➡ *go to* **stick out like a sore *thumb***
stick something out to stretch a part of your body forward □ *They stuck out their hands for food.* 🖻 *She stuck her tongue out at me.* **stick to something 1** if you stick to a plan, decision, etc., you do not change it □ *They promised to stick to our original agreement.* **2** to continue using or doing something □ *They offered me a new car, but I prefer to stick to my bike.* □ *I've never been able to stick to a diet.* **stick together** to continue to stay together and support each other □ *We women have to stick together!* **stick up** to come up above a surface □ *My hair was sticking up.* **stick up for someone** to support someone who is asking for something or being criticized □ *If I ask the boss for a pay rise, I want you all to stick up for me.* **stick with someone/something** to continue using, doing or being with someone or something □ *The manager decided to stick with the same team.*

stick² /stɪk/ NOUN [*plural* **sticks**]
1 a thin piece of wood that has come from a tree □ *We searched for sticks to make a fire.*
2 a long thin piece of wood used for a particular purpose □ *a walking stick* □ *a hockey stick*
3 a long thin piece of something □ *a stick of rhuba...*

sticker /'stɪkə(r)/ NOUN [*plural* **stickers**] a sticky pie... of paper with a picture or writing on it □ *There we... lots of stickers on the back window of the car.*

sticking plaster /'stɪkɪŋ 'plɑːstə(r)/ NOUN [*plura...* **sticking plasters**] something that you stick on you... skin to cover a cut

stick insect /'stɪk ɪnsekt/ NOUN [*plural* **stick insec...** an insect with a long thin body and legs

stickler /'stɪklə(r)/ NOUN [*plural* **sticklers**] someon... who thinks that a particular thing is very importan... and that other people should think it is important ... □ *Rosie's a stickler for doing things properly.*

sticky /'stɪkɪ/ ADJECTIVE [**stickier, stickiest**]
1 designed or likely to stick to another surface 🖻 *Mend the book with some sticky tape.* 🖻 *sticky fingers*
2 difficult to deal with 🖻 *They found themselves ...* sticky situation.
3 sticky weather is hot with slightly wet air

stiff /stɪf/ ▶ ADJECTIVE [**stiffer, stiffest**]
1 difficult to bend □ *stiff cardboard* □ *stiff material*
2 if something is stiff, it is difficult or impossible ... move it in the usual way □ *I can't turn the tap on -* too stiff.

3 if part of your body is stiff, it hurts when you move it ▣ *I've got a stiff neck.* ▢ *stiff joints*
4 extreme ▢ *a stiff challenge* ▣ *The company is facing stiff competition from its Japanese rivals.* ▣ *People who break the law will face stiff penalties.*
5 a stiff wind is very strong ▢ *a stiff breeze*
6 not relaxed or friendly ▢ *She replied with stiff politeness.* ▢ *Baldwin gave a stiff nod.*
7 a stiff substance is thick ▢ *Whisk the cream until stiff.*
▶ ADVERB **bored/worried/scared stiff** an informal phrase meaning extremely bored, worried or frightened ▢ *I was bored stiff in the English lesson.*

stiffen /'stɪfən/ VERB [**stiffens, stiffening, stiffened**]
1 to suddenly stop moving because you are frightened, angry, etc. ▢ *She suddenly stiffened with fright.*
2 to make something stiff ▢ *You can stiffen cotton with starch.*

stiffly /'stɪflɪ/ ADVERB in a stiff way ▢ *Grandad got up stiffly from his chair.* ▢ *'No thank you,' she replied stiffly.*

stiffness /'stɪfnɪs/ NOUN, NO PLURAL the quality of being stiff ▢ *Massage can ease muscle stiffness.*

stifle /'staɪfəl/ VERB [**stifles, stifling, stifled**] to stop something from happening or developing ▣ *She stifled a yawn.*

stifling /'staɪflɪŋ/ ADJECTIVE very hot ▢ *stifling heat*

stigma /'stɪgmə/ NOUN [plural **stigmas**] a feeling that something is bad or embarrassing, especially when this is wrong ▣ *There used to be a stigma attached to being unemployed.*

stigmatize or **stigmatise** /'stɪgmətaɪz/ VERB [**stigmatizes, stigmatizing, stigmatized**] to think that something is bad or embarrassing, especially when this is wrong

stile /staɪl/ NOUN [plural **stiles**] a set of steps for climbing over a wall or fence in the countryside

stiletto /stɪ'letəʊ/ NOUN [plural **stilettos**]
a shoe with a thin, high heel (=part of a shoe under the back of the foot) ▢ *a pair of stilettos*
a thin, high heel on a shoe

still /stɪl/ ▶ ADVERB
up to a particular time and continuing ▢ *Are you still living in Tokyo?* ▢ *By Sunday she still hadn't replied to the invitation.* ▢ *I'm still hungry.*
despite what you have just said or done ▢ *She's treated me badly but she's still my daughter and I love her.* ▢ *It was raining but we still decided to go.*
used for saying that something is possible even now ▢ *You can still catch the bus if you leave now.*
better/worse/larger, etc. still used for emphasizing that something is even better, worse, etc. ▢ *You could come over tomorrow. Better still, why don't you bring Jane too?*
▶ ADJECTIVE [**stiller, stillest**]
not moving ▣ *Keep still while I brush your hair!*

2 calm ▢ *The city seems very still in the early morning.* ▢ *the still night air*
3 a still drink is without bubbles ▢ *still lemonade*

stillborn /'stɪlbɔːn/ ADJECTIVE a stillborn baby is born dead

still life /stɪl 'laɪf/ NOUN [plural **still lifes**] a painting of objects such as flowers or fruit

stillness /'stɪlnɪs/ NOUN, NO PLURAL the quality of being still ▢ *the stillness of early morning*

stilted /'stɪltɪd/ ADJECTIVE a stilted way of talking or writing is formal and not natural ▢ *a stilted conversation*

stilts /stɪlts/ PLURAL NOUN
1 a pair of long poles that you stand on and walk on
2 poles that support a building, raising it above the ground or water

stimulant /'stɪmjʊlənt/ NOUN [plural **stimulants**] a drug that gives you more energy ▢ *The caffeine in coffee is a stimulant.*

stimulate /'stɪmjʊleɪt/ VERB [**stimulates, stimulated, stimulating**]
1 to encourage something to grow and develop ▢ *The policy helped to stimulate economic growth.*
2 to encourage someone or make them feel excited ▢ *Good teaching should stimulate children and get them interested in a subject.*

• stimulating /'stɪmjʊleɪtɪŋ/ ADJECTIVE interesting, and making you think about new ideas ▢ *a stimulating discussion*

• stimulation /ˌstɪmjʊ'leɪʃən/ NOUN, NO PLURAL the act of stimulating someone or something ▢ *stimulation of the senses*

• stimulus /'stɪmjʊləs/ NOUN [plural **stimuli**] something that causes something else to happen or develop ▢ *Light is the stimulus that causes a flower to open.*

sting /stɪŋ/ ▶ VERB [**stings, stinging, stung**]
1 if an insect or plant stings you, it hurts your skin when it touches you ▢ *I was badly stung by nettles.* ▢ *Bees can sting.*
2 to feel a sudden pain in your eyes or skin, or to make someone feel a sudden pain in their eyes or skin ▢ *The shampoo made her eyes sting.* ▢ *Smoke stung his eyes.*
3 to make someone feel upset ▢ *He was stung by her criticism.*
▶ NOUN [plural **stings**]
1 the sudden pain you feel when an insect or plant stings you ▢ *a wasp sting*
2 a sudden pain in your eyes or skin

• stinging /'stɪŋɪŋ/ ADJECTIVE criticizing someone a lot ▢ *stinging criticism*

stingy /'stɪndʒɪ/ ADJECTIVE [**stingier, stingiest**] an informal word meaning not liking to spend money ▢ *He's very stingy with money.*

stink /stɪŋk/ ▶ NOUN [plural **stinks**] a bad smell ▢ *the stink of rotting fish*
◆ IDIOM **cause/create/kick up a stink** an informal phrase meaning to complain a lot about something

□ *You should kick up a stink if they won't give you your money back.*
▶ VERB [**stinks, stinking, stank** or **stunk, stunk**]
1 to have a bad smell □ *The house stinks of cats.*
2 an informal word meaning to be unfair or dishonest □ *The deal stinks.*

stint /stɪnt/ NOUN [*plural* **stints**] a period of time that you spend doing something □ *He did a five-year stint as party chairman.*

stipulate /'stɪpjʊleɪt/ VERB [**stipulates, stipulating, stipulated**] a formal word meaning to say that something should be done □ *The rules stipulate that all products must display a label showing country of origin.*
● **stipulation** /ˌstɪpjʊ'leɪʃən/ NOUN [*plural* **stipulations**] something that has been stipulated □ *He was given a temporary visa with the stipulation that he left the country when it ran out.*

stir /stɜː(r)/ ▶ VERB [**stirs, stirring, stirred**]
1 to mix something with a circular movement □ *He put sugar in his tea and stirred it.*
2 to move slightly, or to make something move slightly □ *The baby stirred in its sleep.* □ *The breeze stirred her hair.*
3 to cause an emotion in someone □ *The poem stirred powerful emotions in him.*
◆ PHRASAL VERB **stir something up**
1 to deliberately cause problems □ *He was always trying to stir up trouble.*
2 to make someone remember something, often something bad □ *The meeting had stirred up some painful memories for her.*
▶ NOUN, NO PLURAL
1 an act of stirring ⊞ *Now give the paint a stir.*
2 **cause/create a stir** to make people feel excited or interested □ *Their arrival caused quite a stir.*

stir-fry /'stɜː.fraɪ/ ▶ VERB [**stir-fries, stir-frying, stir-fried**] to cook small pieces of food very quickly in hot oil □ *stir-fried vegetables*
▶ NOUN [*plural* **stir-fries**] a meal made by cooking small pieces of food very quickly in hot oil

stirring /'stɜː.rɪŋ/ ADJECTIVE making you feel very strong emotions □ *a stirring speech*

stirrup /'stɪrəp/ NOUN [*plural* **stirrups**] a metal ring that you put your foot in when you are riding a horse

stitch /stɪtʃ/ ▶ NOUN [*plural* **stitches**]
1 a piece of thread on cloth that has been sewn □ *She sewed the hem with small neat stitches.*
2 a piece of thread that a doctor uses to repair injuries to your skin □ *He cut his hand and needed stitches in it.*
3 a bad pain in your side that you get when you are running □ *I've got a stitch.*
4 **in stitches** laughing a lot □ *We were all in stitches when we heard what had happened.*
▶ VERB [**stitches, stitching, stitching**] to sew □ *I stitched the button on to my coat.*
◆ PHRASAL VERB **stitch something up** to repair a hole in something by sewing

stoat /stəʊt/ NOUN [*plural* **stoats**] a small wild animal with a long thin body

stock /stɒk/ ▶ NOUN [*plural* **stocks**]
1 the goods that a shop has available □ *Buy now while stocks last!*
2 **out of/in stock** not available/available to buy in a particular shop □ *I'm sorry but the item is out of stock at the moment.*
3 a supply of something □ *a secret stock of weapons* □ *Fish stocks have declined in many seas.*
4 **stocks** shares in a company, which you can buy
5 a liquid in which meat or vegetables have been cooked □ *chicken stock*
6 **take stock of something** to think carefully about a situation □ *I needed time to take stock of my life.*
▶ VERB [**stocks, stocking, stocked**]
1 to have something available to buy □ *Most supermarkets now stock organic products.*
2 to fill a place with something so that you can use it later □ *He stocked the fridge with plenty of drinks.*
◆ PHRASAL VERB **stock up** to buy a lot of something □ *We stocked up on food for our trip.*
▶ ADJECTIVE a stock answer or phrase is one that someone always uses

stockade /stɒ'keɪd/ NOUN [*plural* **stockades**] a fence of strong posts put up round an area or building to protect or defend it

stockbroker /'stɒk.brəʊkə(r)/ NOUN [*plural* **stockbrokers**] someone whose job is to buy and sell company shares for other people

stock exchange /'stɒk ɪks'tʃeɪndʒ/ NOUN [*plural* **stock exchanges**] a place where company shares are bought and sold

stocking /'stɒkɪŋ/ NOUN [*plural* **stockings**] a very thin piece of clothing for a woman's foot and leg □ *a pair of stockings*

stock market /'stɒk 'mɑː.kɪt/ NOUN [*plural* **stock markets**]
1 a place where company shares are bought and sold
2 the business of buying and selling shares

stockpile /'stɒkpaɪl/ ▶ VERB [**stockpiles, stockpiling, stockpiled**] to collect a lot of things that you can use later □ *There are reports that weapons are being stockpiled.*
▶ NOUN [*plural* **stockpiles**] a large supply of something

stocktaking /'stɒk.teɪkɪŋ/ NOUN, NO PLURAL the process of counting all the goods in a shop or factory □ *The shop is closed for stocktaking.*

stocky /'stɒki/ ADJECTIVE [**stockier, stockiest**] a stocky person is wide and strong-looking but usually short

stodgy /'stɒdʒi/ ADJECTIVE [**stodgier, stodgiest**]
1 stodgy food is heavy and makes you feel full very quickly □ *a stodgy pudding*
2 serious and boring

stoical /'stəʊɪkəl/ or **stoic** /'stəʊɪk/ ADJECTIVE not complaining when bad things happen to you □ *She's clearly suffering but she's very stoical about it.*
● **stoicism** /'stəʊɪsɪzəm/ NOUN, NO PLURAL the quality of being stoical □ *I admire her stoicism.*

stoke /stəʊk/ VERB [stokes, stoking, stoked]
1 to put coal, wood, etc. on a fire
2 to make something increase, especially something bad □ *There are fears that this will stoke more violence.*

stole[1] /stəʊl/ PAST TENSE OF steal

stole[2] /stəʊl/ NOUN [plural **stoles**] a long piece of fur or cloth that a woman wears around her shoulders

stolen /ˈstəʊlən/ PAST PARTICIPLE OF steal

stomach /ˈstʌmək/ ▶ NOUN [plural **stomachs**]
1 the part inside your body where food goes when you have eaten it
2 the front part of your body below your chest □ *a flat stomach*
3 on an empty stomach without first eating something □ *You shouldn't take the pills on an empty stomach.*
4 not have the stomach for something to not be brave enough to do something □ *I don't have the stomach for dangerous sports.*
▶ VERB can't stomach something used for saying that someone does not like something □ *I can't stomach TV programmes that show real operations.*

stomach ache /ˈstʌmək ˈeɪk/ NOUN [plural **stomach aches**] a pain in the stomach

stomach bug /ˈstʌmək ˈbʌg/ NOUN [plural **stomach bugs**] an infectious illness that affects the stomach

stomp /stɒmp/ VERB [stomps, stomping, stomped] to walk in a heavy and noisy way □ *He shouted at us and stomped out of the room.*

stone /stəʊn/ ▶ NOUN [plural **stones**]
1 a small piece of rock ⊞ *The boys were throwing stones into the water.*
2 no plural the hard substance that rocks are made of □ *The house is built of stone.*
3 a small piece of valuable rock, used for making jewellery ⊞ *The necklace was made of gold and precious stones* (=valuable and rare stones).
4 a unit for measuring weight, equal to 6.35 kilograms (=14 pounds) □ *I weigh nine stone.*
5 the hard piece in the middle of some fruits □ *a peach stone*
◆ go to set in stone/concrete
▶ ADJECTIVE made of stone □ *stone walls* □ *a stone floor*
▶ VERB [stones, stoning, stoned]
1 to throw stones at someone □ *They had been stoned to death.*
2 to take the stones out of fruit

stone cold /ˈstəʊn ˈkəʊld/ ADJECTIVE very cold □ *The soup was stone cold.*

stone deaf /ˈstəʊn ˈdef/ ADJECTIVE completely deaf

stony /ˈstəʊni/ ADJECTIVE [stonier, stoniest]
1 full of, or covered with, stones □ *a stony beach*
2 unfriendly ⊞ *They sat in stony silence.* □ *a stony expression*

stood /stʊd/ PAST TENSE AND PAST PARTICIPLE OF stand

stool /stuːl/ NOUN [plural **stools**] a seat without a back □ *She was sitting on a stool in the kitchen.*

stoop /stuːp/ ▶ VERB [stoops, stooping, stooped] to bend your body forwards and down □ *The doorway was so low that she had to stoop to get through it.*
◆ PHRASAL VERB **stoop to doing something** to do something bad in order to get or achieve something □ *Surely he wouldn't stoop to stealing from his own mother!*
▶ NOUN, NO PLURAL a position in which your body is bent forwards □ *The old man walked with a stoop.*

stop /stɒp/ ▶ VERB [stops, stopping, stopped]
1 to prevent something happening or existing or someone from doing something □ **+ ing** *He'll never succeed but that won't stop him trying.* □ **+ from** *The barriers stop the crowd from pouring into the street.* □ *Nothing seems to stop the violence.*
2 to no longer do something □ **+ ing** *The wound has stopped bleeding.* □ *Please stop this nonsense.* ⊞ *Stop it! I'm trying to concentrate.*
3 to not happen or exist any more □ *It was lovely when the noise stopped.* □ *We're waiting for the rain to stop.*
4 to no longer move or to make something finish moving □ *A car stopped outside the house.* □ *He stopped the ball with his foot.*
5 if a public vehicle stops somewhere, it stays there for a short time for people to get on and off □ *Does this train stop at Chester?*
6 to no longer work □ *My watch has stopped.*
7 stop at nothing if someone will stop at nothing, they will do anything possible to achieve what they want
◆ IDIOM stop short of something to not do something, although you almost do it □ *His remarks stopped short of calling the minister a liar.*
◆ go to stop the rot
◆ PHRASAL VERB **stop off** to go to a place on your way to somewhere else □ *We stopped off at my son's house for a few days.*
▶ NOUN [plural **stops**]
1 a place where someone spends some time, often during a journey ⊞ *Our first stop was Las Vegas.* ⊞ *Next stop, Rome.*
2 a place where a public vehicle stops ⊞ *This train calls at all stops to Glasgow.*
3 a period of time when you stop somewhere ⊞ *We made a brief stop in Moscow.*
4 come to a stop to stop moving □ *The train came to a stop just outside Hull.*

stopgap /ˈstɒpgæp/ NOUN [plural **stopgaps**] something that is temporary ⊞ *This is a stopgap measure until a new headteacher can be found.*

stoplight /ˈstɒplaɪt/ NOUN [plural **stoplights**] the US word for traffic lights

stopover /ˈstɒpˌəʊvə(r)/ NOUN [plural **stopovers**] a short stay somewhere on a long plane journey □ *They* are flying from London to Sydney with a stopover in Singapore.

stoppage /ˈstɒpɪdʒ/ NOUN [plural **stoppages**]
1 a time when people stop working because they are angry about something □ Taxi drivers are staging a nationwide stoppage in protest at the new fare system.
2 a time when a game stops because a player is injured or because of bad weather □ Injury stoppages added six minutes to the end of the game.

stopper /ˈstɒpə(r)/ NOUN [plural **stoppers**] something that you push into the top of a bottle in order to close it

stopwatch /ˈstɒpwɒtʃ/ NOUN [plural **stopwatches**] a watch used for measuring exactly how long it takes someone to do something

storage /ˈstɔːrɪdʒ/ NOUN, NO PLURAL
1 the act of keeping things in a place until you need them □ the storage of goods ⊞ The apartment has plenty of storage space (=places where you can store things).
2 in storage if you put something in storage, you pay for it to be stored somewhere

store /stɔː(r)/ ▶ NOUN [plural **stores**]
1 a shop □ the village store □ an online store ⊞ The company opened its first store in 1930. ⊞ The store sells cards and gifts.
2 a supply of something which you keep to use when you need it □ + of Squirrels keep a store of food.
3 in store (for someone) going to happen to someone □ There may be some good news in store for her soon.
▶ VERB [**stores, storing, stored**]
1 to keep something somewhere □ Store the chocolate in a cool dry place. □ + away The books had been carefully stored away.
2 to keep information electronically □ All the information is stored on computers.
3 store up problems/trouble to do something that will cause problems in the future □ You're storing up health problems if you don't do any exercise.

storey /ˈstɔːri/ NOUN [plural **storeys**] one of the levels in a building □ a four-storey carpark

stork /stɔːk/ NOUN [plural **storks**] a bird with long legs and a long beak which walks in water

storm /stɔːm/ ▶ NOUN [plural **storms**]
1 a time when there is suddenly a lot of wind and rain ⊞ A huge storm hit New Orleans. ⊞ She waited indoors until the storm had passed. ⊞ a tropical storm
2 no plural a situation in which a lot of people disagree about something and are very angry □ + of The decision provoked a storm of protest.
▶ VERB [**storms, storming, stormed**]
1 to enter a place using force □ Troops stormed the embassy. □ Police stormed the building.
2 to walk somewhere in a very angry way □ She stormed out of the room.
• **stormy** /ˈstɔːmi/ ADJECTIVE [**stormier, stormiest**]

1 with a lot of strong winds and rain ⊞ stormy weather □ a stormy night
2 involving a lot of arguments □ a stormy relationship

story /ˈstɔːri/ NOUN [plural **stories**]
1 a description of events, which can be real or invented ⊞ The teacher was reading a story to the class. ⊞ The film is based on a true story. ⊞ The children were telling each other ghost stories. □ + of The book is the story of his life. □ + about It's a story about a Jewish boy growing up in London.
2 a report in a newspaper or on television about something that has happened ⊞ The paper published a front-page story about the singer's private life. ⊞ The murder was a big news story.
3 an explanation of what has happened, which may not be true ⊞ I don't think he's telling me the full story ⊞ The police didn't believe her story.
4 the US spelling of storey

stout /staʊt/ ADJECTIVE [**stouter, stoutest**]
1 fat □ He was a rather stout middle-aged man.
2 thick and strong □ stout boots

stove /stəʊv/ NOUN [plural **stoves**]
1 a piece of equipment for cooking on □ There was pan on the stove.
2 a piece of equipment that burns wood or coal and heats a room

stow /stəʊ/ VERB [**stows, stowing, stowed**] to put something in a place until you need it

stowaway /ˈstəʊəweɪ/ NOUN [plural **stowaways**] someone who hides on a ship or aeroplane in order travel secretly

straddle /ˈstrædəl/ VERB [**straddles, straddling, straddled**]
1 to stand or sit with one leg on each side of something □ Lori straddled the fence.
2 to be on both sides of a place □ The village straddl the border of Israel and Lebanon.

straggle /ˈstrægəl/ VERB [**straggles, straggling, straggled**] to walk more slowly than other people i group □ Some of the younger children were straggl behind.
• **straggler** /ˈstræglə(r)/ NOUN [plural **stragglers**] person who walks more slowly than the other peo in a group
• **straggly** /ˈstrægli/ ADJECTIVE [**stragglier, straggliest**] growing in an untidy way □ straggly

straight /streɪt/ ▶ ADJECTIVE [**straighter, straightest**]
1 not bent or curved □ a straight line □ straight
2 completely horizontal or vertical □ That picture i straight.
3 honest ⊞ Give me a straight answer!
4 tidy ⊞ I need to get this room straight before t students arrive.
5 one after another with nothing in between □ Juventus have now had five straight wins.
♦ IDIOMS get something straight to make sure that understand a situation correctly □ Now let's get

straight. *You want to borrow £3,000?* **keep a straight face** to manage to stop yourself laughing □ *When I saw her hat, I could hardly keep a straight face.*

▶ ADVERB

1 in a straight line □ *I was so tired, I couldn't walk straight.* □ *The lion ran straight towards him.* □ *She was looking straight at me.*

2 straight on without changing direction □ *Go straight on at the traffic lights.*

3 immediately □ *I came straight here.*

4 straight away immediately □ *Could you come to my office straight away, please?*

5 if you sit up straight, or stand up straight, you sit or stand with your back completely vertical

6 not think straight to be unable to think clearly, often because you are very tired, upset or excited

7 tell someone straight to tell someone something in a direct and honest way, even if it may upset them □ *I told him straight that if he didn't work harder he'd fail his exams.*

straighten /ˈstreɪtən/ VERB [**straightens, straightening, straightened**] to become straight or to make something straight □ *The road curved then straightened.* □ *He straightened his tie.*

PHRASAL VERBS **straighten something out** to deal with a problem or a complicated situation □ *I spent the whole day trying to straighten out my finances.*

straighten up to stand up straight

straightforward /ˌstreɪtˈfɔːwəd/ ADJECTIVE easy □ *a straightforward task* honest □ *He's fairly straightforward.*

strain /streɪn/ ▶ VERB [**strains, straining, strained**] to injure part of your body by using it too much *You'll strain your eyes reading in the dark.* to try hard to do something □ *He strained to look through a small hole in the wall.* to spoil a relationship by causing problems □ *The move has strained political relations with the US.* to separate solid parts from a liquid □ *Now strain the pasta.*

NOUN [*plural* **strains**] an injury to part of your body because you have used it too much □ *a muscle strain* the bad effects on your mind and body when you have too much work or too many worries □ *The strain of looking after four young children was too much for her.* □ *He's been under a lot of strain recently.* when something has a lot of pressure on it □ *The chain had burst under the strain.* type of a particular disease □ *a deadly strain of bird*

strained /streɪnd/ ADJECTIVE not friendly or relaxed □ *At that time relations between the two countries were very strained.* injured by being used too much □ *a strained knee ligament*

strainer /ˈstreɪnə(r)/ NOUN [*plural* **strainers**] a kitchen tool used for separating solids from a liquid

strait /streɪt/ NOUN [*plural* **straits**] a narrow area of sea that joins two larger seas. A geography word. □ *the Straits of Gibraltar*

straitjacket /ˈstreɪtˌdʒækɪt/ NOUN [*plural* **straitjackets**] a special jacket that is put on a violent person to stop them from moving their arms

strait-laced /ˌstreɪtˈleɪst/ ADJECTIVE old-fashioned and easy to shock □ *Her parents were very strait-laced.*

strand /strænd/ NOUN [*plural* **strands**]

1 a thin piece of something such as hair or thread □ *a strand of hair*

2 one of many parts to something □ *one strand of the business*

stranded /ˈstrændɪd/ ADJECTIVE being in a place that you cannot leave ⊞ *She was left stranded without money or passport.*

strange /streɪndʒ/ ADJECTIVE [**stranger, strangest**]

1 unusual □ *She's a very strange woman.* □ **+ that** *It's strange that he hasn't called.* ⊞ *The strange thing is that the burglars ignored all her jewellery.* ⊞ *That's strange - I wonder why she didn't tell you?*

2 not familiar □ *Being ill in a strange country was quite frightening.*

• **strangely** /ˈstreɪndʒli/ ADVERB

1 in a strange way □ *She looked at me strangely.*

2 used for saying that something is surprising ⊞ *Strangely enough, some actors are quite shy.*

• **stranger** /ˈstreɪndʒə(r)/ NOUN [*plural* **strangers**]

1 someone who you do not know □ *Children should never talk to strangers.* ⊞ *How many people would give £5000 to a complete stranger?*

2 someone who is in a place they do not know □ *I'm afraid I don't know where the station is. I'm a stranger here myself.*

3 be no stranger to something to have a lot of experience of something □ *She is no stranger to public attention.*

➤ Remember that a **stranger** is a person you do not know. It is not a person from another country. (The word for this is **foreigner**.)
✓ *Foreigners are usually very welcome in this region.*
✗ *Strangers are usually very welcome in this region.*

strangle /ˈstræŋɡəl/ VERB [**strangles, strangling, strangled**] to kill someone by putting something around their throat □ *She had been strangled with a piece of rope.*

strap /stræp/ ▶ NOUN [*plural* **straps**] a long narrow piece of leather or cloth used to hold things, fasten things or hang things on □ *a watch strap* □ *The bag had a shoulder strap.*

▶ VERB [**straps, strapping, strapped**] to fasten something with a strap □ *I usually strap my bag to my bike.*

• **strapless** /ˈstræplɪs/ ADJECTIVE a strapless dress or top has no pieces of material over the shoulders

strapping /'stræpɪŋ/ ADJECTIVE tall and strong □ *a strapping young man*

stratagem /'strætədʒəm/ NOUN [*plural* **stratagems**] a formal word meaning a plan for achieving something □ *political stratagems*

strategic /strə'tiːdʒɪk/ ADJECTIVE
1 done as part of a plan □ *strategic marketing decisions*
2 to do with fighting a war □ *The country was considered to be a strategic threat.*
3 a strategic position is one that is good for doing something □ *Cameras were installed at strategic locations.*

strategy /'strætɪdʒɪ/ NOUN [*plural* **strategies**] a plan for achieving something □ *a business strategy* □ *He had developed his own strategies for dealing with stress.*

straw /strɔː/ ► NOUN [*plural* **straws**]
1 long dried stems of crops which animals eat or sleep on □ *The cows need fresh straw.*
2 a thin tube used for sucking up a drink
◆ IDIOM the last/final straw the last in a series of unpleasant events, which makes you feel angry or makes you want to stop doing something □ *They all started laughing at her, and it was the last straw.*
► ADJECTIVE made of straw □ *a straw hat*

strawberry /'strɔːbərɪ/ NOUN [*plural* **strawberries**] a soft red fruit with many very small seeds on its surface □ *fresh strawberries* □ *strawberry ice cream*

stray /streɪ/ ► VERB [**strays, straying, strayed**] to go away from the place where you should be □ *Be careful not to stray from the path.* □ *The farmer was searching for some sheep that had strayed.*
► ADJECTIVE
1 a stray animal is lost or has no home □ *stray dogs*
2 separated from the rest □ *a stray bullet*
► NOUN [*plural* **strays**] a cat or dog that has no home

streak /striːk/ ► NOUN [*plural* **streaks**]
1 a long thin line or mark □ *hair with blonde streaks* □ *There were dirty streaks on the window.*
2 a part of someone's character, especially a bad one □ *He has a cowardly streak.*
3 a winning/losing streak a time when someone always wins/loses a game □ *The team are on a winning streak at the moment.*
► VERB [**streaks, streaking, streaked**]
1 to mark something with streaks □ *His face was streaked with black grease.*
2 to run or move very quickly □ *He streaked off down the hill.*

stream /striːm/ ► NOUN [*plural* **streams**]
1 a very narrow river □ *The children were paddling in the stream.*
2 a flow of something ⓖ *The museum had a steady stream of visitors.* ⓖ *There was a constant stream of traffic.*
► VERB [**streams, streaming, streamed**] to flow □ +

down *Tears streamed down her face* □ *The workers streamed out of the factory gates.*
● **streamer** /'striːmə(r)/ NOUN [*plural* **streamers**] a long narrow piece of coloured paper, used as a decoration

streamline /'striːmlaɪn/ VERB [**streamlines, streamlining, streamlined**]
1 to change something so that it happens more quickly and effectively □ *The company streamlined it production methods.*
2 to change the shape of something so that it move through air or water as easily as possible
● **streamlined** /'striːmlaɪnd/ ADJECTIVE
1 effective and wasting no time or money □ *a streamlined process*
2 designed to move through air or water as easily a possible □ *a streamlined jet*

street /striːt/ ► NOUN [*plural* **streets**] a road with buildings such as houses and shops on one or both sides ⓖ *Lincoln's main street was full of shoppers.* □ *There are a lot of shops on this street.* □ *She walke down the street to the library.* □ *I live at 32 Montgomery Street.*
◆ IDIOMS be right up someone's street an informal phrase meaning to be exactly what someone wants likes □ *The course will be right up your street.* be streets ahead to be much better than other people things □ *The company is streets ahead of its rivals i* terms of customer service. on the streets without home □ *With no family and no money, he ended up the streets.*
► ADJECTIVE to do with a street, or happening on a street ⓖ *A group of teenagers were standing on th street corner* (=the place where one street joins another street). □ *Street crime has increased.*

street lamp /'striːt ˌlæmp/ or **street light** /'striː ˌlaɪt/ NOUN [*plural* **street lamps** or **street lights**] a li at the top of a pole in the street

strength /streŋθ/ NOUN [*plural* **strengths**]
1 no plural when someone or something is stron ⓖ *He didn't have the strength to lift the box.* □ *soup gave her a little more strength.* □ *They tested strength of the metal.*
2 no plural when someone is brave and determir ⓖ *During her time in prison, she showed great stren of character.*
3 no plural how strong someone's beliefs and feel are □ *I was shocked by the strength of opposition the plans.*
4 a good quality or the ability to do something well □ *Her greatest strength is her sense of humo*
5 no plural how successful, good or powerful something is □ *The strength of the dollar has cat problems for some companies.* □ *The governmer should not underestimate the strength of the army.*
6 full strength when the correct number of pec

are present □ *The team will be back to full strength for next week's match.*

• **strengthen** /ˈstreŋθən/ VERB [**strengthens, strengthening, strengthened**] to become stronger or to make something stronger □ *He did exercises to strengthen his muscles.* □ *The wind strengthened.*

strenuous /ˈstrenjuəs/ ADJECTIVE
1 using a lot of effort or energy ⊞ *You should avoid strenuous exercise for six weeks after the operation.*
2 very strong and determined □ *strenuous objections to the proposal*

stress /stres/ ▶ NOUN [*plural* **stresses**]
1 the bad effect on your mind or body when you have too much work or too many worries □ *A lot of headaches are caused by stress.* ⊞ *He was suffering from stress and exhaustion.* ⊞ *Exercise is an effective way to reduce stress.* ⊞ *Students often have high stress levels around the time of exams.*
2 be under stress to have too much work or too many worries □ *I've been under a lot of stress recently.*
3 *no plural* special importance that is given to something ⊞ *The school lays great stress on the behaviour of its students.*
4 *no plural* physical pressure □ *The metal bends under stress.* □ *Jogging puts a lot of stress on your knee joints.*
5 the emphasis of a particular part of a word when you are saying it □ *In the word 'bedroom' the stress is on 'bed'.*
▶ VERB [**stresses, stressing, stressed**]
1 to say that something is important ⊞ *Her speech stressed the need for change.* □ + *that She stressed that she did not blame her father.*
2 to emphasize part of a word □ *When 'object' is a noun you stress the 'ob'.*
3 to worry about something □ *The meeting will be fine - you really mustn't stress over it!*

stressed /strest/ ADJECTIVE feeling extremely worried and tired □ *I'm really stressed at the moment.* □ *I get really stressed out when I do exams.*

stressful /ˈstresful/ ADJECTIVE making you feel very worried and tired □ *Starting a new job can be very stressful.*

stress mark /ˈstres ˌmɑːk/ NOUN [*plural* **stress marks**] a mark that shows which part of a word you would emphasize

stretch /stretʃ/ ▶ VERB [**stretches, stretching, stretched**]
1 to make something longer or wider, especially by pulling □ *Stretch this rope between the two posts.*
2 to become longer or wider □ *This material stretches. New shoes usually stretch a little.*
3 to push your arms or legs as far as you can □ *Amy got out of bed and stretched.* □ *She stretched her arms over her head.* □ + *over/across, etc. He stretched across me to get the book.*

4 to cover a large area □ *The mountains stretch from the north to the south of the country.*
5 to continue for a period of time □ + *into The trial stretched into its third week.*
◆ IDIOM **stretch your legs** to go for a walk after sitting for a long time
▶ NOUN [*plural* **stretches**]
1 an area of land or water □ + *of This is a very dangerous stretch of road.* □ *It's a deserted stretch of beach.*
2 a continuous period of time □ + *of You can't learn to drive in such a short stretch of time.*
3 at a stretch continuously □ *He had been working for 14 hours at a stretch.*
4 the action of stretching ⊞ *I always have a good stretch when I get out of bed.*

• **stretcher** /ˈstretʃə(r)/ NOUN [*plural* **stretchers**] a bed for carrying an ill or injured person □ *The stretcher was put into the back of the ambulance.*

• **stretchy** /ˈstretʃi/ ADJECTIVE [**stretchier, stretchiest**] able to stretch □ *stretchy fabric*

strew /struː/ VERB [**strews, strewing, strewed, strewn**] to drop a lot of things in an untidy way □ *Toys were strewn all over the floor.*

strict /strɪkt/ ADJECTIVE [**stricter, strictest**]
1 expecting people to obey your rules □ *a strict teacher* □ + *with He's very strict with the students.*
2 something that is strict must be obeyed ⊞ *The airport has strict rules on what you can and can't take on a plane.* ⊞ *There is a strict limit on the number of places available on the course.*
3 following all the rules of a particular belief or way of living □ *He's a strict vegetarian.*
4 exact □ *She's not depressed in the strict sense of the word.*

• **strictly** /ˈstrɪktli/ ADVERB
1 exactly ⊞ *It's not strictly true.* ⊞ *They are not refugees, strictly speaking* (=used for emphasizing that you are being exact).
2 in a way in which you are expected to obey rules □ *He was brought up very strictly.*
3 strictly prohibited/forbidden/banned used to emphasize that something is not allowed □ *Smoking is strictly prohibited.*
4 for a particular purpose or person □ *The spa was strictly women only.*

stride /straɪd/ ▶ VERB [**strides, striding, strode, stridden**] to walk with long steps □ *He strode up the path.*
▶ NOUN [*plural* **strides**] a long step you take when you walk
◆ IDIOMS **get into your stride** to start to do something well and confidently after a period of time □ *You'll soon get into your stride.* **take something in your stride** to deal with something difficult and not allow it to affect you □ *She's had a lot of health problems but she's taken them all in her stride.*

strident /ˈstraɪdənt/ ADJECTIVE
1 expressed in a forceful way □ *strident criticism*
2 loud and not pleasant to hear □ *a strident voice*

strife /straɪf/ NOUN, NO PLURAL a formal word meaning fighting or disagreement

strike /straɪk/ ▶ VERB [strikes, striking, struck]
1 to hit someone or something □ *The missile struck its target.* □ *My head struck the table.* □ *The house was struck by lightning.*
2 to attack someone or something suddenly □ *The enemy troops struck at dawn.* □ *Who knows when the terrorists may strike again?*
3 if a thought strikes you, you suddenly think of it □ + *that* *It suddenly struck me that the road would be closed.*
4 if you are struck by something, you notice it and think it is unusual, interesting, or good □ *He was struck by her beauty.*
5 if something unpleasant strikes, it happens suddenly □ *The earthquake struck in the evening.* ⊞ *Just as they reached the city, disaster struck.*
6 if you strike a match, you rub it against a rough surface to make it burn
7 if you strike an agreement, you make an agreement with someone ⊞ *Unions have struck a deal over pay.*
8 to refuse to work because of an argument with your employer □ + *for* *They were striking for higher wages.* □ + *over* *They are striking over their working conditions.*
9 if a clock strikes, it makes a number of sounds to show the time □ *The clock struck three.*
♦ PHRASAL VERBS **strike someone as something** to seem to someone to have a particular quality □ *He didn't strike me as particularly shy.* **strike back** to attack or criticize someone who has attacked or criticized you □ *The minister struck back at her critics, saying they did not know all the facts.* **strike someone down** if you are struck down by a disease, you are made very ill by it **strike something out** to draw a line through a word or phrase to remove it □ *She struck out the names of all those who had offended her.* **strike up something** to start something such as a conversation or a relationship □ *The two men struck up a friendship when they were in the army.*
▶ NOUN [plural strikes]
1 a period of time when workers refuse to work because of an argument with their employer ⊞ *The train drivers are threatening to go on strike.*
2 a sudden attack, especially a military one □ *The city has suffered repeated air strikes.*
● **striker** /ˈstraɪkə(r)/ NOUN [plural strikers]
1 a worker who is refusing to work because of an argument with their employer
2 in football, a player whose job is to try to score goals
● **striking** /ˈstraɪkɪŋ/ ADJECTIVE
1 ~~very noticeable~~ ⊞ *There are some striking similarities between the two boys.*

2 attractive in an unusual way that gets people's attention □ *She's a very striking woman.*

string /strɪŋ/ ▶ NOUN [plural strings]
1 no plural strong thread, used for tying things ⊞ *a ball of string*
2 a string of something (a) a series of things or a group of things □ *a string of disasters* □ *They have opened a string of nightclubs across Europe.* (b) several things which are on a piece of string □ *a string of beads*
3 a piece of wire used to make a sound on a musical instrument
4 the strings the people in an orchestra (=group of musicians) who play instruments with strings
5 strings special conditions that limit an offer or agreement ⊞ *The gift came with no strings attached.*
♦ IDIOM **pull strings** to use influence that you have with important people to get something done □ *I pulled a few strings to get him a job in the ministry.*
▶ VERB [strings, stringing, strung] to hang something somewhere using string □ *Coloured lights were strung across the ceiling.*
♦ PHRASAL VERBS **string someone along** to make someone believe something that is not true for a long time, especially something about your plans □ *He's never going to marry her - he's just stringing her along until he finds someone better.* **string something together** to use words in a way that other people can understand ⊞ *He can barely string a sentence together.*

stringent /ˈstrɪndʒənt/ ADJECTIVE stringent rules, laws or limits are very severe or strongly controlled □ *stringent security measures*

stringy /ˈstrɪŋɪ/ ADJECTIVE [stringier, stringiest]
1 looking like string □ *stringy hair*
2 stringy meat is hard and difficult to chew

strip /strɪp/ ▶ NOUN [plural strips] a long narrow piece of something □ + *of* *a strip of paper* □ *a narrow strip of land* □ *Slice the peppers into strips.*
▶ VERB [strips, stripping, stripped]
1 to remove a layer or covering from something □ *off* *You need to strip off the old paint first.*
2 to remove your clothes □ *He stripped and dived in the water.* □ + *off* *They stripped off their jackets.*
♦ PHRASAL VERB **strip someone of something** to take something away from someone as a punishment □ *The officer was stripped of his rank.*

stripe /straɪp/ NOUN [plural stripes] a line of colour □ *a T-shirt with black and white stripes*
● **striped** /straɪpt/ or **stripy** /ˈstraɪpɪ/ ADJECTIVE having stripes □ *a stripy shirt*

strive /straɪv/ VERB [strives, striving, strove, striven] a formal word meaning to try very hard to achieve something □ *The airline must strive to remain competitive.*
strode /strəʊd/ PAST TENSE OF stride
stroke /strəʊk/ ▶ NOUN [plural strokes]
1 a sudden illness in the brain that affects someone

ability to move and speak 🕮 *She had a stroke in August.*

2 the way you hit the ball in games such as tennis or golf □ *Both players produced a range of strokes.*

3 a way of moving your arms and legs when you swim □ *I usually do breast stroke.*

4 a stroke of luck something you are not expecting which is lucky □ *Police solved the crime by an incredible stroke of luck.*

5 a mark made by moving a pen or a brush across a surface 🕮 *His work is done with short brush strokes and intense colours.*

6 the sound made by a clock each hour □ *We arrived on the stroke of midnight.*

▶ VERB [**strokes, stroking, stroked**] to rub something gently with your hand □ *She was stroking the cat.*

stroll /strəʊl/ ▶ VERB [**strolls, strolling, strolled**] to walk in a slow, relaxed way □ *We strolled down to the beach.*

▶ NOUN [*plural* **strolls**] a relaxed walk □ *They went for a stroll in the park.*

strong /strɒŋ/ ADJECTIVE [**stronger, strongest**]

1 physically powerful □ *He is very strong.* □ *I have strong legs from cycling.*

2 not easy to damage or break □ *We tied the branches together with a strong rope.* □ *They have a very strong relationship.*

3 believed, felt or expressed in a deep and forceful way □ *He has very strong opinions about climate change.* □ *There has been strong opposition to the new airport.*

4 very noticeable 🕮 *There was a strong smell of fish in the room.* □ *She speaks with a strong French accent.*

5 successful and of good quality □ *We all benefit from a strong economy.* □ *There is strong evidence of his guilt.* 🕮 *We are in a strong position to win the contract* (=we are likely to win it).

6 if there is a strong chance or possibility of something, that thing is very likely

7 having or using a lot of power or force □ *I felt a strong pull on the rope.* 🕮 *strong winds*

8 brave and determined □ *Life is hard, but I try to stay strong for the sake of the children.*

9 a strong drink has a lot of a particular substance in it □ *He drinks really strong coffee.*

stronghold /strɒŋhəʊld/ NOUN [*plural* **strongholds**]

1 a place where a lot of people support a particular idea or political party □ *a Republican stronghold*

2 an area that is defended by a military group

strongly /strɒŋlɪ/ ADVERB

1 very much □ *I strongly recommend that you follow the instructions.* □ *He felt very strongly that there had been an error.* □ *We are strongly opposed to the plans.*

2 tasting or smelling of something a lot □ *The cheese strongly flavoured.*

strong-willed /strɒŋ'wɪld/ ADJECTIVE determined □ *Young children can be very strong-willed.*

stroppy /strɒpɪ/ ADJECTIVE [**stroppier, stroppiest**] an informal word meaning bad-tempered and difficult to

deal with □ *He got a bit stroppy when I asked him to leave.*

strove /strəʊv/ PAST TENSE OF strive

struck /strʌk/ PAST TENSE AND PAST PARTICIPLE OF strike

structural /'strʌktʃərəl/ ADJECTIVE to do with the structure of something □ *High winds caused structural damage to many buildings.*

● **structurally** /'strʌktʃərəlɪ/ ADVERB in a way that is to do with the structure of something □ *The building is structurally sound.*

structure /'strʌktʃə(r)/ ▶ NOUN [*plural* **structures**]

1 the way that the parts of something are arranged or organized □ + *of the structure of the story* □ *Crick and Watson discovered the structure of DNA.* □ *a new management structure*

2 something that has been built □ *The bridge was a massive steel structure.*

▶ VERB [**structures, structuring, structured**] to arrange or to plan something in an organized way □ *Many students have difficulty in structuring their essays.*

struggle /'strʌgəl/ ▶ VERB [**struggles, struggling, struggled**]

1 to try hard to do something that is difficult □ *She struggled to finish the work on time.*

2 to move somewhere with difficulty □ *She struggled up the stairs with her heavy suitcase.*

3 to turn and twist your body in order to try to escape □ *The child struggled in his arms.*

▶ NOUN [*plural* **struggles**]

1 when something is difficult to do or to achieve □ *It was a struggle, but I managed to get everything finished.*

2 a fight □ *the country's armed struggle for independence*

strum /strʌm/ VERB [**strums, strumming, strummed**] to play a musical instrument such as a guitar by moving your fingers across the strings

strung /strʌŋ/ PAST TENSE AND PAST PARTICIPLE OF string

strut /strʌt/ ▶ VERB [**struts, strutting, strutted**] to walk in a proud way

▶ NOUN [*plural* **struts**]

1 a proud way of walking

2 a long piece made of wood or metal which supports something

stub /stʌb/ ▶ NOUN [*plural* **stubs**] a short piece of something which is left when the rest has been used □ *cigarette stubs*

▶ VERB [**stubs, stubbing, stubbed**] stub your toe to hit your toe against something

◆ PHRASAL VERB **stub something out** to stop a cigarette burning by pressing it against something

stubble /'stʌbəl/ NOUN, NO PLURAL

1 short hairs on a man's face when he has not shaved

2 short stems of a crop such as corn left in the fields after it has been cut

stubborn /'stʌbən/ ADJECTIVE refusing to change your mind or do what other people tell you □ *a stubborn* man □ *I was frustrated by Tom's stubborn refusal to make any changes.*

• **stubbornly** /'stʌbənlɪ/ ADVERB in a stubborn way □ *She stubbornly refused to listen to my advice.*

• **stubbornness** /'stʌbənnɪs/ NOUN, NO PLURAL the quality of being stubborn

stuck /stʌk/ ► PAST TENSE AND PAST PARTICIPLE OF stick

► ADJECTIVE

1 unable to move 🔁 *The van got stuck in deep snow.*

2 in a situation that you do not like but cannot change □ *She was stuck at home looking after her younger brother.*

3 unable to do something because it is too difficult 🔁 *Ask the teacher to help you if you get stuck.*

stuck-up /'stʌk'ʌp/ ADJECTIVE an informal word that describes someone who thinks they are better than other people

stud /stʌd/ NOUN [plural **studs**]

1 a small, round piece of metal, used for decorating something such as clothes

2 a small, round earring (=jewellery for the ears)

3 a place where people keep and breed horses

student /'stju:dənt/ ► NOUN [plural **students**] someone who is studying, especially at a college or university □ *a law student* 🔁 *a part-time university student* □ **+ at** *He's a student at Harvard University.*

► ADJECTIVE

1 to do with students □ *student loans* □ *student accommodation*

2 studying to become something □ *a student nurse*

studio /'stju:dɪəʊ/ NOUN [plural **studios**]

1 a room from which radio or television programmes are broadcast 🔁 *a TV studio* □ *The programme's recorded in front of a live studio audience.*

2 a place where films are made, or a company that makes films 🔁 *an independent film studio* □ *Hollywood studios*

3 the room that an artist or photographer works in □ *She set up her own photographic studio.*

4 a small apartment with only one main room 🔁 *He moved into a tiny studio apartment.*

studious /'stju:dɪəs/ ADJECTIVE spending a lot of time reading and studying □ *a studious young man*

study /'stʌdɪ/ ► NOUN [plural **studies**]

1 when you spend time examining something to find out more about it □ *a scientific study* 🔁 *Researchers conducted a study on the effects of mobile phones.* 🔁 *A new study shows coffee-drinking does not increase the risk of heart disease.*

2 when you spend time learning about a subject □ **+ of** *the study of history* □ *He completed his undergraduate studies.*

3 a room used for studying or quiet work □ *She sat reading in her study.*

► VERB [**studies, studying, studied**]

1 to spend time learning about a subject □ *I'm studying French.* □ **+ for** *Sophie is studying for a*

degree in politics. □ **+ to do something** *She's studying to be a teacher.*

2 to spend time examining something to find out more about it □ *Researchers studied the effects of heat on the body.* □ *We must study the problem in detail.*

3 to look at something carefully □ *He studied the railway timetable.*

stuff /stʌf/ ► NOUN, NO PLURAL

1 used to talk about a substance, material or a group of objects □ *What's that black oily stuff on the beach?* □ *I've got too much stuff to carry.* □ *I need to buy some stuff for the party.*

2 used to talk about information, situations or things that people do, think or say □ *He told me all this stuff about his childhood.* □ *His book has some interesting stuff about India in it.*

♦ IDIOMS **know your stuff** to know a lot about a subject □ *When it comes to European law, he really knows his stuff.*

► VERB [**stuffs, stuffing, stuffed**]

1 to push something into a space, often in a quick, careless way □ *He stuffed the letter into his pocket.* □ *I stuffed tissue in my ears to block out the noise.* □ *All his old letters were stuffed into drawers.*

2 to fill something completely □ *She used feathers to stuff the cushions.* □ *Her suitcase was stuffed with clothes.*

3 to fill food such as meat, fish or vegetables with another kind of food, often a mixture of small pieces □ *peppers stuffed with rice*

4 to fill the body of a dead animal with a substance so that it looks as if it is still alive

♦ IDIOM **stuff your face** a very informal phrase meaning to eat a lot

• **stuffing** /'stʌfɪŋ/ NOUN, NO PLURAL

1 material used for putting inside things such as cushions (=soft, filled bags to sit on) or soft toys

2 food used for putting inside other food □ *We had turkey with an apricot stuffing.*

stuffy /'stʌfɪ/ ADJECTIVE [**stuffier, stuffiest**]

1 a stuffy place has no fresh air □ *How can you sit in this stuffy classroom all day?*

2 formal, boring and old-fashioned □ *The university has a very stuffy image.*

stumble /'stʌmbəl/ VERB [**stumbles, stumbling, stumbled**]

1 to almost fall while you are walking □ *He stumbled along the track in the dark.*

2 to make mistakes or to pause when you are speaking □ *She stumbled over the difficult words.*

♦ PHRASAL VERB **stumble across/on/upon something** to find something by chance □ *I stumbled across this book today.*

stumbling block /'stʌmblɪŋ ˌblɒk/ NOUN [plural **stumbling blocks**] a problem that makes it difficult to do something □ *High fees are the major stumbling block for many students.*

stump /stʌmp/ ► NOUN [plural **stumps**]

1 the part of something left after the main part has been taken away 🔁 *She sat on a tree stump.*

2 in cricket, one of the three wooden sticks that you throw the ball at

▶ VERB [**stumps, stumping, stumped**] an informal word meaning to be too difficult to answer or to understand □ *The problem has stumped scientists for years.*

◆ PHRASAL VERB **stump up (something)** to pay for something, slightly unwillingly □ *We had to stump up cash to pay the medical bills.*

● **stumpy** /'stʌmpɪ/ ADJECTIVE [**stumpier, stumpiest**] short and thick □ *The dog had a stumpy tail.*

stun /stʌn/ VERB [**stuns, stunning, stunned**]

1 if you are stunned by something, it surprises or shocks you very much □ *We were all stunned by the news of the accident.*

2 to make someone unconscious, usually by hitting them on the head

stung /stʌn/ PAST TENSE AND PAST PARTICIPLE OF sting

stunk /stʌŋk/ PAST TENSE AND PAST PARTICIPLE OF stink

stunning /'stʌnɪn/ ADJECTIVE

1 extremely attractive □ *She looked stunning.*

2 extremely surprising or shocking □ *a stunning announcement*

● **stunningly** /'stʌnɪnlɪ/ ADVERB in a stunning way □ *She was a stunningly beautiful woman.* □ *a stunningly simple idea*

stunt /stʌnt/ ▶ NOUN [*plural* **stunts**]

1 something exciting or unusual that someone does to attract attention 🔁 *The whole event was a big publicity stunt.*

2 something dangerous and exciting that someone does, especially in a film □ *The actor performs all his own stunts.*

▶ VERB [**stunts, stunting, stunted**] to stop something growing or developing normally □ *Lack of water stunted the plants.*

stunted /'stʌntɪd/ ADJECTIVE smaller than normal and often badly shaped □ *There were just a few stunted trees.*

stuntman /'stʌnt,mæn/ or **stuntwoman** /'stʌnt,wʊmən/ NOUN [*plural* **stuntmen** or **stuntwomen**] a man or woman who does dangerous things instead of an actor in a film

stupefied /'stju:pɪfaɪd/ ADJECTIVE so shocked or bored that you cannot think □ *He stood there with a stupefied look on his face.*

stupefying /'stju:pɪfaɪɪŋ/ ADJECTIVE making you so shocked or bored that you cannot think

stupendous /stju:'pendəs/ ADJECTIVE extremely good or large □ *The hotel is surrounded by stupendous mountains.*

stupid /'stju:pɪd/ ADJECTIVE

silly and not clever □ *It was a stupid thing to do!* □ *a stupid idea* □ *I felt rather stupid.*

used to show that you are annoyed □ *What's wrong with this stupid thing?* □ *What are you doing, you stupid idiot?*

stupidity /stju:'pɪdətɪ/ NOUN, NO PLURAL the quality of being stupid

● **stupidly** /'stju:pɪdlɪ/ ADVERB in a stupid way □ *I'd rather stupidly forgotten to bring a coat.* □ *Stupidly, I agreed to do it.*

sturdy /'stɜ:dɪ/ ADJECTIVE [**sturdier, sturdiest**] strong □ *sturdy shoes*

stutter /'stʌtə(r)/ ▶ VERB [**stutters, stuttering, stuttered**] to repeat some letters when you speak □ *'H-hello,' he stuttered.*

▶ NOUN [*plural* **stutters**] a speech problem that makes you repeat letters when you speak

sty[1] /staɪ/ NOUN [*plural* **sties**] a place where pigs are kept

sty[2] or **stye** /staɪ/ NOUN [*plural* **sties** or **styes**] an infection near your eye that makes it painful and swollen

style /staɪl/ ▶ NOUN [*plural* **styles**]

1 a particular way of doing something □ *a mix of musical styles* □ **+ of** *She has a wonderful style of writing.*

2 the design of something, especially clothes or buildings □ **+ of** *a new style of shoe* □ *We stayed in a traditional style chalet.*

3 *no plural* the quality of being attractive, fashionable, wearing nice clothes, etc. 🔁 *She has a real sense of style.*

4 in style in an attractive, exciting way, often spending a lot of money □ *They celebrated the New Year in style at a top hotel.*

▶ VERB [**styles, styling, styled**] to arrange or to design something, such as clothes or hair, in a particular style □ *I'm having my hair cut and styled.*

● **stylish** /'staɪlɪʃ/ ADJECTIVE attractive and fashionable □ *It's one of the city's most stylish hotels.* □ *She looked stylish in a simple black dress.*

● **stylishly** /'staɪlɪʃlɪ/ ADVERB in a stylish way □ *He was dressed very stylishly.*

suave /swɑ:v/ ADJECTIVE a suave man is very polite and confident

sub /sʌb/ NOUN [*plural* **subs**]

1 an informal word for submarine

2 an informal word for substitute

sub- /sʌb/ PREFIX sub- is added to the beginning of words to mean 'below' or 'under' □ *submarine* □ *sub-zero*

subatomic particle /ˌsʌbə'tɒmɪk pɑ:'tɪkəl/ NOUN [*plural* **subtomic particles**] a piece of matter that is smaller than an atom. A physics word.

subconscious /ˌsʌb'kɒnʃəs/ ▶ NOUN, NO PLURAL the part of your mind that contains thoughts and feelings which you are not aware of

▶ ADJECTIVE to do with your subconscious □ *subconscious fears*

● **subconsciously** /ˌsʌb'kɒnʃəslɪ/ ADVERB in a subconscious way

subdivide /ˌsʌbdɪ'vaɪd/ VERB [**subdivides, subdividing, subdivided**] to divide something into smaller parts □ *Each class is subdivided into groups according to ability.*

- **subdivision** /ˌsʌbdɪˈvɪʒən/ NOUN [plural subdivisions] a part made by subdividing

subdue /səbˈdjuː/ VERB [subdues, subduing, subdued] to control someone or something, especially using force □ Police used tear gas to subdue the crowd.

- **subdued** /səbˈdjuːd/ ADJECTIVE
1 quieter than usual, especially because you are unhappy □ You seem very subdued today.
2 not very loud or bright □ subdued voices

subheading /ˈsʌbˌhedɪŋ/ NOUN [plural subheadings] a title of one part of a text, not the main title

subject ► NOUN /ˈsʌbdʒɪkt/ [plural subjects]
1 the person or thing that a story, a conversation, etc. is about □ + of The affair has been the subject of many rumours. 🔊 He raised the subject of (=started talking about) security at the jail. 🔊 Can we change the subject (=talk about something different), please?
2 something that you study and learn about at school, university, etc. □ French is my favourite subject at school. □ Fewer students are now studying science subjects.
3 in grammar, the subject of a sentence is the person or thing that does something □ In the sentence 'John plays tennis.', 'John' is the subject.
► ADJECTIVE /ˈsʌbdʒɪkt/ **subject to something** (a) affected or controlled by something □ The soldiers there are not subject to Czech law. (b) only possible if something else or happens □ The plans are subject to approval by the government.
► VERB /səbˈdʒekt/ [subjects, subjecting, subjected] **subject someone to something** a formal word meaning to make someone suffer something unpleasant □ He was subjected to cruel treatment.

- **subjective** /səbˈdʒektɪv/ ADJECTIVE based on your own thoughts and feelings, and not facts □ a subjective opinion

subject matter /ˈsʌbdʒɪkt ˈmætə(r)/ NOUN, NO PLURAL the person or thing that you are talking about, writing about, painting, etc. □ His films varied in style and subject matter.

subjunctive /səbˈdʒʌŋktɪv/ NOUN, NO PLURAL a verb form used to express a doubt, a wish or something uncertain. For example, in English, we say 'if I were you', using were instead of was after I.

sublet /ˌsʌbˈlet/ VERB [sublets, subletting, sublet] to rent a house or a flat to someone when you are renting it from someone else

sublime /səˈblaɪm/ ADJECTIVE very great or beautiful □ a sublime performance

subliminal /ˌsʌbˈlɪmɪnəl/ ADJECTIVE a formal word meaning affecting your thoughts or behaviour in a way that you are not aware of 🔊 Are there subliminal messages hidden in the programme?

submarine /ˌsʌbməˈriːn/ ► NOUN [plural submarines] a ship that travels under water
► ADJECTIVE a formal word meaning to do with things under the sea □ submarine cables

submerge /səbˈmɜːdʒ/ VERB [submerges, submerging, submerged] to cover something with water, or to go under water □ Entire villages had been submerged.

- **submergence** /səbˈmɜːdʒəns/ or **submersion** /səbˈmɜːʃən/ NOUN, NO PLURAL when something submerges

submission /səbˈmɪʃən/ NOUN [plural submissions]
1 when someone is completely controlled by someone else □ They were beaten into submission.
2 something such as a plan or document that you give to someone so they can make a decision about it

submissive /səbˈmɪsɪv/ ADJECTIVE always willing to obey other people

submit /səbˈmɪt/ VERB [submits, submitting, submitted]
1 to give a plan, a document, etc. to someone so they can make a decision about it □ All competition entries must be submitted by Friday.
2 to agree to something or to accept someone's control, especially when you are being forced to □ The rebels were ordered to submit.

subnormal /ˌsʌbˈnɔːməl/ ADJECTIVE less intelligent than most other people

subordinate /səˈbɔːdɪnət/ ► ADJECTIVE a formal word meaning lower in position or less important □ hi subordinate officers
► NOUN [plural subordinates] a formal word meaning someone who has a less important position

subordinate clause /səˈbɔːdɪnət ˈklɔːz/ NOUN [plural subordinate clauses] in grammar, a part of a sentence which adds information but cannot exist on its own □ In the sentence 'The book that I got for m birthday was boring.', 'that I got for my birthday' is subordinate clause.

subscribe /səbˈskraɪb/ VERB [subscribes, subscribing, subscribed] to get a product or service b regularly paying money □ One in three Americans subscribe to cable television.
♦ PHRASAL VERB **subscribe to something** a forma phrase meaning to agree with something □ I don't subscribe to that view.

- **subscriber** /səbˈskraɪbə(r)/ NOUN [plural subscribers] someone who gets a product or servic by regularly paying money

- **subscription** /səbˈskrɪpʃən/ NOUN [plural subscriptions] money that you pay regularly to ge product or service or to be a member of an organization

subsequent /ˈsʌbsɪkwənt/ ADJECTIVE happening af something else □ The story is about the soldier's capture and subsequent escape.

- **subsequently** /ˈsʌbsɪkwəntlɪ/ ADVERB later □ S ate the shellfish and subsequently became ill.

subside /səbˈsaɪd/ VERB [subsides, subsiding, subsided]
1 to become less strong □ The pain gradually subsided.

2 if land or a building subsides, it starts to sink gradually into the ground
● **subsidence** /səb'saɪdəns, 'sʌbsɪdəns/ NOUN, NO PLURAL when land or a building subsides

subsidiary /səb'sɪdjərɪ/ NOUN [plural **subsidiaries**] a company that is controlled by a larger company

subsidize or **subsidise** /'sʌbsɪdaɪz/ VERB [**subsidizes, subsidizing, subsidized**] to pay part of the cost of something in order to help a person or an organization □ The government subsidizes the mining industry.

● **subsidy** /'sʌbsɪdɪ/ NOUN [plural **subsidies**] money given to help someone or something or to keep prices low □ farming subsidies

subsist /səb'sɪst/ VERB [**subsists, subsisting, subsisted**] a formal word meaning to live with only just enough food or money □ They subsisted on a diet of potatoes and milk.

subsistence /səb'sɪstəns/ NOUN, NO PLURAL when someone has or produces just enough for their needs □ subsistence farming

substance /'sʌbstəns/ NOUN [plural **substances**]
1 a liquid, a solid or a gas □ Glue is a sticky substance. □ a toxic substance
2 no plural a formal word meaning the quality of being true or important ⊞ There's no substance to the allegations. □ He said nothing of substance.
3 no plural the general or most important ideas of what someone says or writes □ + of The substance of her argument was that women are more intelligent than men.

substandard /,sʌb'stændəd/ ADJECTIVE not as good as it should be □ substandard housing

substantial /səb'stænʃəl/ ADJECTIVE
large in amount □ a substantial sum of money □ We have made substantial progress.
large and strong □ The leather bag was more substantial.

substantially /səb'stænʃəlɪ/ ADVERB
by a large amount □ Profits have increased substantially.
a formal word meaning in most ways □ The two reports are substantially the same.

substantiate /səb'stænʃɪeɪt/ VERB [**substantiates, substantiating, substantiated**] a formal word meaning to give facts that show that something is true □ There was no evidence to substantiate the claims.

substitute /'sʌbstɪtjuːt/ ► VERB [**substitutes, substituting, substituted**] to use one thing or person instead of something or someone else □ I substituted your name for mine on the list.
NOUN [plural **substitutes**]
a person or thing used instead of another ⊞ Use lemons as a substitute for limes.
a player who replaces another player in a team during a game □ James came on as a substitute at half-time.

substitution /,sʌbstɪ'tjuːʃən/ NOUN [plural

substitutions] when someone or something is substituted

subterranean /,sʌbtə'reɪnɪən/ ADJECTIVE a formal word meaning under the ground □ subterranean passages

subtitles /'sʌb,taɪtəlz/ PLURAL NOUN words at the bottom of a screen which show what the actors are saying in a film □ a French film with English subtitles

subtle /'sʌtəl/ ADJECTIVE [**subtler, subtlest**]
1 slight and difficult to notice or to describe ⊞ There have been subtle changes. ⊞ There is a subtle difference between the two birds.
2 a subtle flavour, smell, colour, etc. is pleasant and not very strong □ a subtle shade of green
3 clever □ They are finding more subtle ways of selling their products.

● **subtlety** /'sʌtəltɪ/ NOUN [plural **subtleties**] the quality of being subtle □ I love the subtlety of the colours in the painting.

● **subtly** /'sʌtlɪ/ ADVERB in a subtle way □ The picture has been subtly altered.

subtotal /'sʌb,təʊtəl/ NOUN [plural **subtotals**] the total of one set of numbers, but not the final total

subtract /səb'trækt/ VERB [**subtracts, subtracting, subtracted**] to take one number away from another. A maths word. □ + from If you subtract 4 from 6, you get 2.

● **subtraction** /səb'trækʃən/ NOUN [plural **subtractions**] when you subtract one number from another. A maths word.

subtropical /,sʌb'trɒpɪkəl/ ADJECTIVE connected to the parts of the Earth near the tropics (=very hot parts near the equator). A geography word.

● **subtropics** /,sʌb'trɒpɪks/ PLURAL NOUN the subtropics the subtropical areas of the Earth. A geography word.

suburb /'sʌbɜːb/ NOUN [plural **suburbs**] an area of houses at the edge of a town or city □ a suburb of Liverpool

● **suburban** /sə'bɜːbən/ ADJECTIVE to do with suburbs □ suburban housing

● **suburbia** /sə'bɜːbɪə/ NOUN, NO PLURAL the people who live in suburbs and the way they live

subversive /səb'vɜːsɪv/ ► ADJECTIVE intended to harm a government or political system □ a subversive organization
► NOUN [plural **subversives**] a subversive person

subvert /səb'vɜːt/ VERB [**subverts, subverting, subverted**] a formal word meaning to destroy a government or political system □ This is clearly an attempt to subvert democracy.

subway /'sʌbweɪ/ NOUN [plural **subways**]
1 a path under a busy road or railway
2 the US word for **underground** (=a railway under the ground)

sub-zero /'sʌb 'zɪərəʊ/ ADJECTIVE sub-zero temperatures are lower than 0°

succeed /sək'siːd/ VERB [succeeds, succeeding, succeeded]
1 to achieve something, or to have the effect you want □ If you try hard, I'm sure you'll succeed. □ Ravana's devious plan had succeeded. □ + in She succeeded in getting the job.
2 to do an important job after someone else □ + as She succeeded her father as manager of the company. □ He was succeeded by Lois Gallois.

> ▶ Note that succeed, meaning 'to achieve something' is followed by 'in doing' something':
> ✓ She finally succeeded in persuading him.
> ✗ She finally succeeded to persuade him.

success /sək'ses/ NOUN [plural successes]
1 no plural the achievement of what you tried to achieve □ Her success is due to determination and hard work. ⊞ He tried, without success, to pull her out of the water. ⊞ The project had little chance of success. □ + in Have you had any success in finding a job?
2 something that is popular or has the result that you want ⊞ The party had been a great success. ⊞ The film was a huge success.
• **successful** /sək'sesful/ ADJECTIVE
1 earning or achieving a lot in your work □ a successful businessman ⊞ Houlahan had a highly successful career training horses.
2 having the result you wanted □ a successful election campaign □ The policy has been very successful. □ + in He was successful in his attempt to buy the business.
3 very popular and making a lot of money ⊞ He starred in the hugely successful action film 'Die Hard'.
• **successfully** /sək'sesfuli/ ADVERB in a successful way □ Surgeons successfully removed a blood clot from his brain. □ She successfully completed all six races.
• **succession** /sək'seʃən/ NOUN, NO PLURAL
1 a series of things that happen one after the other □ He's suffered a succession of injuries recently.
2 in quick/rapid succession happening very quickly after each other □ She sneezed three times in quick succession.
3 when someone has an official job after someone else □ Some people challenged Brown's succession as Labour Party leader.
• **successive** /sək'sesɪv/ ADJECTIVE happening one after the other □ The team won three successive games.
• **successor** /sək'sesə(r)/ NOUN [plural successors] someone who has an important job after someone else □ The head teacher's successor will be Carolyn Robinson.

succinct /sək'sɪŋkt/ ADJECTIVE expressing something clearly using very few words □ His remarks were succinct and to the point.
• **succinctly** /sək'sɪŋktli/ ADVERB in a way that is succinct

succulent /'sʌkjulənt/ ADJECTIVE full of juice, and good to eat □ succulent peaches

succumb /sə'kʌm/ VERB [succumbs, succumbing, succumbed]
1 to be unable to stop something from affecting you. A formal word □ She succumbed to temptation and took the money.
2 to become very ill or to die from an illness. A formal word.

such /sʌtʃ/ DETERMINER, PRONOUN
1 such a used before a phrase with a noun for emphasizing a statement □ I was such a fool to believe him. □ This is such a waste of time. □ She's such a nice person.
2 such as used for giving an example □ Citrus fruits such as oranges and lemons contain a lot of vitamin C.
3 similar to someone or something that has already been mentioned □ Such things are difficult to find.
4 such ... that used for saying what the result of something is □ It was such an awful hotel that we decided to leave.
5 as such used in negative statements to say that the word you are using is not exactly correct □ He doesn't have a job as such, but he helps in the shop sometimes.
6 there's no such thing/person used for saying that something or someone does not exist □ There are no such things as monsters.

such-and-such /'sʌtʃəndsʌtʃ/ DETERMINER, PRONOUN used for referring to something without saying exactly which thing □ Let's suppose that you go into such-and-such a shop.

suck /sʌk/ ▶ VERB [sucks, sucking, sucked]
1 to take something into your mouth by pulling in air □ She was sucking lemonade through a straw. □ + Gerald sucked in his breath.
2 to hold something in your mouth while making pulling movements with your lips and tongue □ My sister still sucks her thumb. □ She was sucking a sweet □ + on The baby was sucking on a dummy.
3 if water or air sucks someone somewhere, it pulls them as it moves □ + under He was sucked under by wave.
◆ PHRASAL VERB **suck someone into something** someone is sucked into something bad, they become involved it □ He had been sucked into a life of crime
▶ NOUN [plural sucks] the action of sucking □ She took a suck of her lollipop.
• **sucker** /'sʌkə(r)/ NOUN [plural suckers]
1 an informal word for someone who is easy to tr because they believe everything that people tell them
2 a piece of rubber that sticks on a surface
• **suckle** /'sʌkəl/ VERB [suckles, suckling, suckled] feed a baby or young animal milk from the body □ cow suckled her calf.
• **suction** /'sʌkʃən/ NOUN, NO PLURAL when air or liq is removed from a space or container

sucrose /ˈsuːkrəʊz/ NOUN, NO PLURAL a type of sugar that is found in most plants. A biology word.

sudden /ˈsʌdən/ ADJECTIVE
1 happening quickly and unexpectedly □ The sudden death of his mother changed everything. □ Pat felt a sudden urge to laugh. □ The attack was so sudden that he hadn't been able to defend himself.
2 all of a sudden suddenly □ All of a sudden, he started to run towards the door.

• **suddenly** /ˈsʌdənlɪ/ ADVERB quickly and unexpectedly □ Suddenly a woman ran into the room, shouting. □ I suddenly felt very tired.

• **suddenness** /ˈsʌdənnɪs/ NOUN, NO PLURAL the quality of being sudden □ We were shocked by the suddenness of his death.

Sudoku /suːˈdəʊkuː/ NOUN [plural **Sudokus**] a number game in which you write a number in every small square of a larger 9 x 9 square

suds /sʌdz/ PLURAL NOUN soap bubbles

sue /suː/ VERB [**sues, suing, sued**] to start a law case to try to get money from a person or organization that has harmed you □ He sued the company for racial discrimination.

suede /sweɪd/ ► NOUN, NO PLURAL a type of leather with a rough surface
► ADJECTIVE made of suede □ a suede jacket

suet /ˈsuːɪt/ NOUN, NO PLURAL a hard fat from an animal used in cooking

suffer /ˈsʌfə(r)/ VERB [**suffers, suffering, suffered**]
1 to feel pain or unpleasant feelings ⌕ She suffered a lot of pain after the accident. □ I couldn't bear to see him suffering like that.
2 to be injured or suddenly have a health problem □ He suffered a heart attack at the age of 47. ⌕ She suffered serious head injuries in the accident.
3 to have a bad experience, such as a defeat, loss of money, etc. ⌕ The team suffered a defeat in the first round of the competition. □ The company suffered massive financial losses.
suffer from something to have a particular illness □ Her brother suffers from depression.
4 to become worse □ If you don't get enough sleep, your work will start to suffer.

sufferance /ˈsʌfərəns/ NOUN, NO PLURAL **on sufferance** if you do something on sufferance, you are allowed to do it by someone who would prefer that you did not do it. A formal phrase □ I was allowed to use his new camera but only on sufferance.

sufferer /ˈsʌfərə(r)/ NOUN [plural **sufferers**] someone who suffers from a particular illness □ asthma sufferers

suffering /ˈsʌfərɪŋ/ NOUN, NO PLURAL pain or unpleasant feelings ⌕ Years of civil war and drought have caused widespread human suffering.

suffice /səˈfaɪs/ VERB [**suffices, sufficing, sufficed**] a formal word meaning to be enough □ £50 should suffice.

sufficiency /səˈfɪʃənsɪ/ NOUN, NO PLURAL a formal word meaning enough of something □ There is a sufficiency of teachers in those subjects.

• **sufficient** /səˈfɪʃənt/ ADJECTIVE enough □ There is sufficient evidence to charge him with murder.

• **sufficiently** /səˈfɪʃəntlɪ/ ADVERB in a way that is enough □ He has a sufficiently large number of supporters to win the election.

suffix /ˈsʌfɪks/ NOUN [plural **suffixes**] a group of letters that is added to the end of a word to make another word

suffocate /ˈsʌfəkeɪt/ VERB [**suffocates, suffocating, suffocated**]
1 to kill someone by preventing them from getting enough oxygen □ The thick black smoke was suffocating him.
2 to die because of not getting enough oxygen □ Babies can suffocate if they sleep with a pillow.

• **suffocation** /ˌsʌfəˈkeɪʃən/ NOUN, NO PLURAL suffocating or being suffocated □ The cause of death was suffocation.

suffrage /ˈsʌfrɪdʒ/ NOUN, NO PLURAL a formal word meaning the right to vote

• **suffragette** /ˌsʌfrəˈdʒet/ NOUN [plural **suffragettes**] a woman who fought for women's right to vote

suffuse /səˈfjuːz/ VERB [**suffuses, suffusing, suffused**] if a place is suffused with light or colour, there is a lot of it all around. A literary word. □ The room was suffused with light.

sugar /ˈʃʊɡə(r)/ NOUN [plural **sugars**]
1 no plural white or brown grains that you add to food and drink to make them taste sweeter ⌕ Do you take sugar in your tea?
2 the amount of sugar that a small spoon holds □ I have two sugars in coffee.

sugar beet /ˈʃʊɡə ˌbiːt/ NOUN, NO PLURAL a plant that grows under the ground which sugar comes from

sugar cane /ˈʃʊɡə ˌkeɪn/ NOUN, NO PLURAL a tall tropical plant with stems that sugar comes from

sugary /ˈʃʊɡərɪ/ ADJECTIVE sweet □ sugary snacks

suggest /səˈdʒest/ VERB [**suggests, suggesting, suggested**]
1 to mention something as a possibility □ He suggested a picnic. □ **+ that** I suggest that we have lunch now. □ **+ ing** She suggested meeting outside the theatre.
2 to show that something may be true ⌕ The study suggests that drinking green tea could be good for your health. ⌕ Recent evidence suggests that this may not be true.
3 to say something in a way that is not direct □ **+ that** Are you suggesting that I'm too old for the job?
4 to tell someone about something that they might like or find useful □ Can you suggest a nice place to stay in Paris? □ **+ for** She suggested me for the job.

➤ Notice the examples in 'suggest' (*sense 1*). You
suggest that someone **does** something, or you
suggest doing something. You do not suggest 'to
do' something. ◻ *I suggest that we start now.*
✓ *I suggest starting now.*
✗ *I suggest to start now.*

● **suggestion** /sə'dʒestʃən/ NOUN [*plural*
suggestions]
1 an idea that you mention 🔁 *He made several helpful
suggestions.* 🔁 *Do you have any suggestions about
where we could go for a holiday?* 🔁 **+ that** *He rejected
suggestions that he had lied.*
2 *no plural* a sign that something is true ◻ **+ of** *There
was no suggestion of improper behaviour.* ◻ **+ that**
*There was some suggestion that he had been involved
in the fraud.*
3 a suggestion of something a very small amount
of something ◻ *There was a suggestion of anger in her
voice.*
● **suggestive** /sə'dʒestɪv/ ADJECTIVE **suggestive of
something** a formal phrase meaning making you
think of something ◻ *There was a smell suggestive of
onions.*

suicidal /su:ɪ'saɪdəl/ ADJECTIVE
1 wanting to kill yourself ◻ *He'd been feeling suicidal
for several weeks.*
2 likely to cause death ◻ *He was driving at a suicidal
speed.*
3 likely to cause serious problems or damage ◻ *The
policy will be politically suicidal.*
suicide /'su:ɪsaɪd/ NOUN [*plural* **suicides**]
1 the act of killing yourself deliberately 🔁 *He
committed suicide by jumping off a bridge.*
2 an action that is likely to cause serious problems for
you 🔁 *This sort of confession is political suicide.*

suit /su:t/ ➤ NOUN [*plural* **suits**]
1 a jacket and trousers or a jacket and skirt which are
made of the same cloth and are worn together 🔁 *He
was wearing a suit and tie.*
2 pieces of clothing that you wear for a particular
activity ◻ *a jogging suit*
3 one of the four types of cards in a set used for
playing games ◻ *The four suits are hearts, diamonds,
clubs and spades.*
4 a case in a law court 🔁 *She filed a suit (=started a
case) against the bank.*
➤ VERB [**suits, suiting, suited**]
1 if something suits you, it makes you look nice ◻ *Blue
really suits her.* ◻ *That dress suits you.*
2 to be convenient for someone ◻ *Would it suit you if I
called round this evening?* 🔁 *Another year here would
suit me fine.*
3 be well/ideally etc. suited to something to have
the right qualities for something ◻ *She's very well
suited to the job.*
4 Suit yourself! used for telling someone in an

annoyed way that they can do what they want ◻ *Suit
yourself! I'm going out now anyway.*
◆ IDIOM **suit someone down to the ground** to be
extremely suitable for someone ◻ *Being a model suits
her down to the ground.*
● **suitability** /ˌsu:tə'bɪlətɪ/ NOUN, NO PLURAL the
quality of being suitable ◻ *I am not sure of his
suitability for the role.*
● **suitable** /'su:təbəl/ ADJECTIVE right for a purpose,
person or occasion ◻ *Finding suitable accommodation
wasn't easy.* ◻ **+ for** *High-heeled shoes aren't suitable
for walking in the country.*
● **suitably** /'su:təblɪ/ ADVERB in a way that is suitable
◻ *Are you suitably dressed for the cold weather?*

suitcase /'su:tkeɪs/ NOUN [*plural* **suitcases**] a big
case with a handle, that you carry your clothes in when
you are travelling 🔁 *He packed his suitcase and went to
the airport.* 🔁 *I unpacked my suitcase as soon as I arrived*

suite /swi:t/ NOUN [*plural* **suites**]
1 a set of expensive rooms in a hotel ◻ *a hotel suite*
2 a set of furniture ◻ *a bathroom suite*
suitor /'su:tə(r)/ NOUN [*plural* **suitors**] an old-
fashioned word for a man who wants to marry a woman
sulfur /'sʌlfə(r)/ NOUN, NO PLURAL the US spelling of
sulphur
sulfuric acid /sʌl'fjuərɪk 'æsɪd/ NOUN, NO PLURAL the
US spelling of sulphuric acid
sulk /sʌlk/ ➤ VERB [**sulks, sulking, sulked**] to show that
you are angry by being silent ◻ *He's sulking because I
said he couldn't go out.*
➤ NOUN [*plural* **sulks**] a time when someone is sulking
◻ *He's in a sulk because his Dad said he couldn't have
an ice cream.*
● **sulky** /'sʌlkɪ/ ADJECTIVE [**sulkier, sulkiest**]
1 sulking ◻ *She's in a sulky mood.*
2 often sulking ◻ *a sulky child*
sullen /'sʌlən/ ADJECTIVE angry and silent ◻ *a sullen
young man*
sulphur /'sʌlfə(r)/ NOUN, NO PLURAL a yellow chemical
element which burns with a blue flame and has an
unpleasant smell. A chemistry word.
sulphuric acid /sʌl'fjuərɪk 'æsɪd/ NOUN, NO PLURAL
strong, colourless acid. A chemistry word.
sultan /'sʌltən/ NOUN [*plural* **sultans**] a ruler in some
Muslim countries ◻ *the Sultan of Brunei*
sultana /səl'tɑ:nə/ NOUN [*plural* **sultanas**]
1 a raisin (=dried grape) which is light in colour
2 a sultan's wife
sultry /'sʌltrɪ/ ADJECTIVE [**sultrier, sultriest**] sultry
weather is unpleasantly hot

sum /sʌm/ NOUN [*plural* **sums**]
1 an amount of money 🔁 *Huge sums were spent
repairing the building.* 🔁 *Some footballers earn vast
sums of money.*
2 the total when you add numbers together ◻ **+**
The sum of 2, 3 and 4 is 9.
3 a simple calculation ◻ *I was never any good at sums*
◆ PHRASAL VERBS [**sums, summing, summed**] **sum**

(something) up to end a discussion, speech, etc. by mentioning the main pieces of information in it □ *So to sum up, more money needs to be spent on education.* **sum someone up** if something that someone does sums them up, it is typical of their, usually bad, behaviour

summarize *or* **summarise** /'sʌməraɪz/ VERB [**summarizes, summarizing, summarized**] to give the main pieces of information about something □ *He summarized the arguments.*

summary /'sʌməri/ NOUN [*plural* **summaries**] a short statement which gives the main pieces of information about something □ *A summary of her speech was printed in the newspaper.*

summer /'sʌmə(r)/ NOUN [*plural* **summers**] the season between spring and autumn when the weather is warmest □ *People buy more ice cream in summer.* □ *My sister got married last summer.* □ *summer clothes* □ *summer holidays* □ *Summers are getting hotter.*

summer camp /'sʌmə(r) ˌkæmp/ NOUN [*plural* **summer camps**] a place where children can stay with other children in the summer holiday and do different activities

summer holiday /'sʌmə(r) ˈhɒlɪdeɪ/ NOUN [*plural* **summer holidays**] a period of time in the summer when children do not go to school

summer school /'sʌmə(r) ˌskuːl/ NOUN [*plural* **summer schools**] a course that you do in the summer at a school, college or university □ *He had attended a summer school for writers.*

summertime /'sʌmətaɪm/ NOUN, NO PLURAL the season of summer □ *The garden looks beautiful in summertime.*

summer vacation /'sʌmə(r) vəˈkeɪʃən/ NOUN [*plural* **summer vacations**] the period of time in the summer when people do not go to classes at university

summery /'sʌməri/ ADJECTIVE right for summer □ *summery weather*

summit /'sʌmɪt/ NOUN [*plural* **summits**]
1 the top of a hill or mountain ⊞ *He reached the summit of Mount Everest in 1970.*
2 a meeting between leaders of governments □ *The Prime Minister travelled to Brussels for an EU summit.*

summon /'sʌmən/ VERB [**summons, summoning, summoned**]
1 to order someone to come □ *The headteacher summoned me to her office.*
2 to find enough strength, courage, etc. to do something, although it is difficult □ *At last I summoned up the courage to ask her for a date.*

summons /'sʌmənz/ NOUN [*plural* **summonses**] a letter that says you must go to a court □ *He received a summons for a driving offence.*

sumptuous /'sʌmptʃuəs/ ADJECTIVE very expensive or of very high quality □ *a sumptuous meal*
sumptuously /'sʌmptʃuəsli/ ADVERB in a way that is sumptuous □ *a sumptuously decorated room*

sun /sʌn/ ▶ NOUN, NO PLURAL
1 the sun the yellow thing in the sky which gives light and heat to the Earth ⊞ *The sun shone brightly into the room.* ⊞ *The sun rose at 7.12 am.* ⊞ *The sun set at 8.24 pm.* □ *The Earth goes round the sun.*
2 the light and heat from the sun □ *We sat in the sun.*
▶ VERB [**suns, sunning, sunned**] **sun yourself** to sit or lie outside in the sun

sunbathe /'sʌnbeɪð/ VERB [**sunbathes, sunbathing, sunbathed**] to lie or sit in the sun so that your skin becomes darker □ *Lots of people were sunbathing on the beach.*
• **sunbathing** /'sʌnbeɪðɪŋ/ NOUN, NO PLURAL the activity of lying or sitting in the sun so that your skin becomes darker

sunbeam /'sʌnbiːm/ NOUN [*plural* **sunbeams**] a beam of light from the sun

sunbed /'sʌnbed/ NOUN [*plural* **sunbeds**]
1 a piece of equipment that you lie on to make your skin darker
2 a comfortable chair used for sitting or lying outside in the sun

sunblock /'sʌnblɒk/ NOUN [*plural* **sunblocks**] a cream that you put on your skin to stop the sun from burning it

sunburn /'sʌnbɜːn/ NOUN, NO PLURAL an area of sore, red skin caused by being in the sun for too long
• **sunburnt** /'sʌnbɜːnt/ ADJECTIVE having sore, red skin because you have been in the sun for too long □ *a sunburnt nose*

suncream /'sʌnkriːm/ NOUN, NO PLURAL cream that you put on your skin to protect it from the sun

sundae /'sʌndeɪ/ NOUN [*plural* **sundaes**] a dish of ice cream served with fruit, nuts and a sweet sauce

Sunday /'sʌndi/ NOUN [*plural* **Sundays**] the day of the week after Saturday and before Monday □ *I always go to church on Sundays.*

Sunday school /'sʌndi ˌskuːl/ NOUN [*plural* **Sunday schools**] a class on Sundays at a church, where children learn about the Christian religion

sundial /'sʌndaɪəl/ NOUN [*plural* **sundials**] an instrument that uses light from the sun and shadow to show you what time it is

sundry /'sʌndri/ ADJECTIVE
1 of many different types □ *sundry items*
2 all and sundry everyone

sunflower /'sʌnˌflaʊə(r)/ NOUN [*plural* **sunflowers**] a tall yellow flower with seeds that you can eat

sung /sʌŋ/ PAST PARTICIPLE OF **sing**

sunglasses /'sʌnˌglɑːsɪz/ PLURAL NOUN dark glasses that protect your eyes from the sun □ *She was wearing a pair of sunglasses.*

sunk /sʌŋk/ PAST PARTICIPLE OF **sink**
• **sunken** /'sʌŋkən/ ADJECTIVE
1 under water □ *sunken treasure*
2 lower than the surrounding area □ *a sunken bath*

sunlight /'sʌnlaɪt/ NOUN, NO PLURAL the light from the sun ⊞ *Driving can be difficult in bright sunlight* ⊞ *Keep babies out of direct sunlight.*

- **sunlit** /ˈsʌnlɪt/ ADJECTIVE lit up by the sun □ *a sunlit room*

sunny /ˈsʌnɪ/ ADJECTIVE [sunnier, sunniest]
1 full of light from the sun 🔊 *It's sunny outside.* 🔊 *It's a lovely sunny day.* □ *sunny weather*
2 happy □ *She has a very sunny nature.* □ *a sunny smile*

sunrise /ˈsʌnraɪz/ NOUN [plural sunrises]
1 the time when the sun appears in the morning □ *I was up at sunrise.*
2 the appearance of the sky at sunrise □ *There was a spectacular sunrise this morning.*

sunroof /ˈsʌnruːf/ NOUN [plural sunroofs] a window in the roof of a car that you can open

sunscreen /ˈsʌnskriːn/ NOUN [plural sunscreens] a cream that you put on your skin to stop the sun from burning it

sunset /ˈsʌnset/ NOUN [plural sunsets]
1 the time when the sun starts to disappear in the evening □ *We left the beach at sunset.*
2 the appearance of the sky at sunset □ *There was a beautiful golden sunset.*

sunshine /ˈsʌnʃaɪn/ NOUN, NO PLURAL the light and heat of the sun 🔊 *He was squinting in the bright sunshine.*

sunstroke /ˈsʌnstrəʊk/ NOUN, NO PLURAL an illness caused by spending too long in the sun

suntan /ˈsʌntæn/ NOUN [plural suntans] a brown skin colour that you get because you have been in the sun

- **sun-tanned** /ˈsʌntænd/ ADJECTIVE having a suntan □ *She came back from holiday looking very sun-tanned.*

suntan lotion /ˈsʌntæn ˈləʊʃən/ NOUN [plural suntan lotions] a cream that you put on your skin to stop the sun from burning it

super /ˈsuːpə(r)/ ▶ ADJECTIVE an old-fashioned word meaning extremely good □ *We had a super time at the fair.*
▶ ADVERB an informal word meaning very □ *I exercise a bit but I'm not super fit.*

super- /ˈsuːpə(r)/ PREFIX super- is added to the beginning of words to mean 'above' or 'extreme' □ *superhuman* □ *superpower*

superb /suːˈpɜːb/ ADJECTIVE extremely good □ *a superb performance*

- **superbly** /suːˈpɜːblɪ/ ADVERB in a way that is extremely good □ *They played superbly in the first-half.*

superbug /ˈsuːpəbʌg/ NOUN [plural superbugs] a type of bacteria that is very difficult to kill

supercilious /ˌsuːpəˈsɪlɪəs/ ADJECTIVE a formal word meaning treating other people as if they are not important □ *a supercilious smile*

superconductor /ˌsuːpəkənˈdʌktə(r)/ NOUN [plural superconductors] a substance that allows an

electrical current to pass through it easily at very low temperatures. A physics word.

superficial /ˌsuːpəˈfɪʃəl/ ADJECTIVE
1 affecting the surface only □ *The wound is only superficial.* □ *The building suffered superficial damage.*
2 without details □ *He had only a superficial knowledge of history.*
3 never thinking about things which are important o serious □ *He's very superficial.*

superfluous /suːˈpɜːfluəs/ ADJECTIVE a formal word meaning not necessary □ *superfluous equipment*

superhuman /ˌsuːpəˈhjuːmən/ ADJECTIVE superhuman strength or effort is much greater than ordinary human strength or ability □ *A superhuman effort will be needed if we are going to finish the project on time.*

superintendent /ˌsuːpərɪnˈtendənt/ NOUN [plural superintendents]
1 a police officer with a fairly high rank
2 someone who is in charge of something such as a building

superior /suːˈpɪərɪə(r)/ ▶ ADJECTIVE
1 better than something else 🔊 *This product is far superior to earlier versions.*
2 thinking that you are better than other people □ *can't stand her superior attitude.*
3 having a higher rank than someone else
▶ NOUN [plural superiors] a person who has a high rank than you at work □ *He made complaints to h superiors.*

- **superiority** /suː.ˌpɪərɪˈɒrətɪ/ NOUN, NO PLURAL bei superior □ *his superiority over others*

superlative /suːˈpɜːlətɪv/ ▶ ADJECTIVE in gramm the superlative form of an adjective or adverb is th form that usually ends with -est or is formed with most. For example, *hardest, worst* and *most difficu* are superlative forms.
▶ NOUN [plural superlatives] a superlative form of adjective or adverb

supermarket /ˈsuːpəˌmɑːkɪt/ NOUN [plural supermarkets] a large shop that sells food and ot goods

supermodel /ˈsuːpəˌmɒdəl/ NOUN [plural supermodels] a very successful model (=person v wear clothes to advertise them) who earns a lot o money

supernatural /ˌsuːpəˈnætʃərəl/ ▶ ADJECTIVE mysterious and impossible to explain □ *supernatu powers*
▶ NOUN the supernatural mysterious events or creatures that are impossible to explain

superpower /ˈsuːpəˌpaʊə(r)/ NOUN [plural superpowers] a country which has a lot of politic and military power

supersonic /ˌsuːpəˈsɒnɪk/ ADJECTIVE faster than speed of sound □ *a supersonic aeroplane*

superstar /'su:pəstɑ:(r)/ NOUN [*plural* **superstars**] a very famous actor, singer, person who plays sport, etc.

superstition /ˌsu:pə'stɪʃn/ NOUN [*plural* **superstitions**] a belief that some things or actions are lucky or unlucky

superstitious /ˌsu:pə'stɪʃəs/ ADJECTIVE believing in superstitions

supervise /'su:pəvaɪz/ VERB [**supervises, supervising, supervised**] to be in charge of a person or an activity □ *Someone has to be there to supervise the children.* □ *He was supervising the road repair work.*

supervision /ˌsu:pə'vɪʒən/ NOUN, NO PLURAL the act of supervising □ *The prisoner was kept under close supervision.*

supervisor /'su:pəvaɪzə(r)/ NOUN [*plural* **supervisors**] someone whose job is to make sure that other people do their work correctly

supper /'sʌpə(r)/ NOUN [*plural* **suppers**] a meal that you eat in the evening □ *He ate his supper and went to bed.*

supple /'sʌpəl/ ADJECTIVE able to bend and stretch easily □ *Yoga is great for keeping you fit and supple.* □ *supple leather*

supplement ▶ NOUN /'sʌplɪmənt/ [*plural* **supplements**]
a pill or liquid that you take when your food does not contain everything you need 🖰 *I always take a vitamin supplement.*
something extra that makes something better or bigger □ *They depended on this money as a supplement to their income.*
a separate part of a newspaper, magazine or book □ *The magazine published a special supplement on the Awards Ceremony.*
▶ VERB /'sʌplɪment/ [**supplements, supplementing, supplemented**] to add something in order to improve something or make it bigger □ *He supplements his wages by working in the evening.*

supplementary /ˌsʌplɪ'mentəri/ ADJECTIVE extra □ *a supplementary charge*

suppleness /'sʌpəlnɪs/ NOUN, NO PLURAL the ability to bend and stretch easily

supplier /sə'plaɪə(r)/ NOUN [*plural* **suppliers**] a company or country which supplies a product □ *In the 1990s, Australia was the world's largest supplier of coal.*

supply /sə'plaɪ/ ▶ NOUN [*plural* **supplies**]
an amount of something that you can use 🖰 *The lack of rain is threatening the city's water supply.* 🖰 *There is a limited supply of housing in the area.* 🖰 *A plentiful supply of restaurants and bars mean that tourists are well catered for.* □ *+ of a supply of food*
no plural the process of providing something □ *+ of the company is involved in the supply of weapons in the Middle East.*
supplies food, clothes, medicines, etc. that you need to live or to do something □ *A military plane loaded with medical supplies for the refugees.*
be in short/plentiful supply to have little/a lot of something available □ *Food was in short supply.*

▶ VERB [**supplies, supplying, supplied**] to provide something □ *Wind power could supply up to 20% of the country's electricity.* □ *+ with The farm supplies several major supermarkets with milk.* □ *+ to He supplied information to the police.*
▶ ADJECTIVE a supply teacher takes another teacher's place for a time

support /sə'pɔ:t/ ▶ VERB [**supports, supporting, supported**]
1 to agree with an idea, a person, etc. and want them to succeed □ *I support the idea in principle.* □ *Teachers did not support the proposal.*
2 to be under something and stop it from falling □ *The roof was supported by wooden beams.*
3 to show that a theory or statement is true □ *All the latest research supports this theory.* □ *There was no evidence to support his claim.*
4 to provide money for someone or something □ *She supports her family on a very low wage.*
5 to like a particular sports team and want them to win □ *Which football team do you support?*
▶ NOUN [*plural* **supports**]
1 no plural agreement with an idea or a person and wanting them to succeed 🖰 *The idea has received strong support from all the parties.* 🖰 *Klinsmann eventually won massive public support in Germany.* □ *+ for There was not much support for the war.*
2 no plural encouragement and help 🖰 *He called to offer support as soon as he heard about my accident.*
3 no plural money provided for someone 🖰 *A lack of financial support means that many students do not complete their courses.* □ *+ from The treatment costs £2000 a month but she receives no support from the government.*
4 an object under something, which stops it from falling □ *One of the supports of the bridge collapsed.*
● **supporter** /sə'pɔ:tə(r)/ NOUN [*plural* **supporters**]
1 someone who agrees with an idea or person and wants them to succeed 🖰 *He was a strong supporter of government policy.*
2 someone who likes a sports team and wants them to win □ *a Liverpool supporter*
● **supportive** /sə'pɔ:tɪv/ ADJECTIVE giving help and encouragement □ *Parents have been very supportive of the school.*

suppose /sə'pəuz/ VERB [**supposes, supposing, supposed**]
1 to think that something is probably true □ *+ that I suppose that all the tickets have been sold now?* 🖰 *I don't suppose we'll see him again.* □ *I suppose you'll be going to the concert.*
2 be supposed to do something (a) to be expected to do something, especially because of a rule □ *I'm supposed to look after my little sister on Saturdays.* □ *You're not supposed to walk on the grass.* (b) to be intended or expected to have a particular result or to happen in a particular way □ *The belts are supposed to support your back.* □ *He wasn't supposed to arrive until next week.*

3 I suppose used to say that you think something is possible, true or correct, although you are not sure or happy about it □ *We could get a taxi, I suppose.* □ *I suppose I deserve his criticism.* □ *I suppose the weather might improve.*

4 I suppose so (a) used to agree to something that you do not want to do or to happen □ *'Could you do the shopping this week?' 'I suppose so.'* (b) used to agree that something is possible, true or correct, but in a way that shows that you are not sure or happy about it □ *'We could always hire a gardener.' 'I suppose so, but it would be rather expensive.'*

5 be supposed to be something to be considered by many people to have a particular quality □ *That area is supposed to be really beautiful.* □ *He's supposed to be good at maths.*

6 used to tell someone to imagine that something is true so that a situation can be considered □ *Suppose you had £500,000 – what would you buy?* □ **+ that** *Supposing that you get the job – where will you live?*

• **supposed** /sə'pəʊzd/ ADJECTIVE believed by some people to exist or be true, although you think it may not □ *Why did none of her supposed friends help her?* □ *These people are a supposed threat to our security.*

• **supposedly** /sə'pəʊzɪdlɪ/ ADVERB according to what some people say, although you think it may not be true □ *He is supposedly one of the best doctors in the country.* □ *He charged me an extra £5, supposedly to cover postage.*

suppress /sə'pres/ VERB [**suppresses, suppressing, suppressed**]
1 to control a feeling so that you do not show it □ *She suppressed a smile.*
2 to stop people from complaining about a government, especially by using force □ *The rebellion was suppressed by government forces.*
3 to stop people from finding out about something important □ *The police were accused of trying to suppress evidence.*
4 to stop a physical process □ *The drug suppresses the growth of the tumour.*

• **suppression** /sə'preʃən/ NOUN, NO PLURAL the act of suppressing something □ *the suppression of protests*

supremacy /su'preməsɪ/ NOUN, NO PLURAL the state of being the most powerful □ *the supremacy of the president*

supreme /su:'pri:m/ ADJECTIVE
1 most powerful □ *the supreme ruler*
2 extreme □ *supreme courage*

• **supremely** /su'pri:mlɪ/ ADVERB extremely □ *She's supremely confident of her abilities.*

surcharge /'sɜ:tʃɑ:dʒ/ NOUN [plural **surcharges**] an extra amount of money that you have to pay □ *There's a surcharge if you exceed the airline's baggage limit.*

sure /ʃʊə(r)/ ▶ ADJECTIVE
1 certain □ **+ that** *I'm sure that we've met before.*
□ **+ about** *Alex is coming, but I'm not sure about Dan.*

□ **+ question word** *I'm not sure why he was so angry.*
□ **+ of** *I'll phone you when I'm sure of the date.* □ *Are you sure you want to leave?*
2 make sure (a) to do something to make it certain that something happens □ *Can you make sure all the doors are locked?* (b) to check that something is true □ *I think his birthday's on Saturday, but I'll just look in the diary to make sure.*
3 sure to do something certain to happen or be the result of something □ *He's sure to win.*
4 be sure to do something used to tell someone that they must do something □ *Be sure to take plenty of water with you.*
5 certain to be successful □ *A spoonful of sugar is a sure way to cure hiccups.*
6 certain to be true ⊞ *Well kept gardens are a sure sign of a good neighbourhood.*
▶ ADVERB
1 used to agree to something □ *'Could I borrow your hammer?' 'Sure!'*
2 for sure without any doubts □ *I think he's Polish but I don't know for sure.*
3 sure enough as was expected □ *I had an X-ray and sure enough, the bone was broken.*

• **surely** /'ʃʊəlɪ/ ADVERB
1 used to show surprise about something □ *Surely you're going to wash that fruit before you eat it!* □ *Surely he didn't just leave her there!*
2 used to show that you think something is very likely □ *Surely they'll phone if they're not coming.*
3 surely not used to show that you do not think something can be true □ *Sam punched someone? Surely not!*

surf /sɜ:f/ ▶ VERB [**surfs, surfing, surfed**]
1 to ride on a board on waves on the sea □ *Australia has some of the best places to surf.*
2 to look at a lot of different websites. A computer word. □ *He surfed the Internet for the best deals.*
▶ NOUN, NO PLURAL the white part at the top of waves on the sea

surface /'sɜ:fɪs/ ▶ NOUN [plural **surfaces**]
1 the outside or top layer of something □ *The leaf had a rough surface.* □ *The temperature of the Earth's surface has risen.* □ **+ of** *A light wind rippled the surface of the lake.*
2 no plural what someone or something seems to be like, especially when this is different from what they are really like □ *Beneath his calm surface there was a lot of anger.*
▶ VERB [**surfaces, surfacing, surfaced**]
1 to appear or become known about □ *The allegations of assault surfaced last week.*
2 to come up to the surface of water □ *The submarine surfaced close to the ship.*
3 to put a hard top layer on a road or path □ *Workmen were surfacing the road.*

surface area /'sɜːfɪs 'eərɪə/ NOUN, NO PLURAL the total area of the outside surface of something. A maths word.

surfboard /'sɜːfbɔːd/ NOUN [plural **surfboards**] a long board that you balance on and use for moving on the sea's waves

surfer /'sɜːfə(r)/ NOUN [plural **surfers**] a person who surfs the waves

surfing /'sɜːfɪŋ/ NOUN, NO PLURAL the sport of balancing on a board and moving on the sea's waves
🔄 We went surfing in Cornwall.

surge /sɜːdʒ/ ▶ VERB [surges, surging, surged]
1 to move in a particular direction with a lot of force
□ The crowd surged towards the fire exit. □ The storm surged up the coast.
2 to increase very quickly □ Oil prices surged.
▶ NOUN [plural **surges**]
1 a surge of excitement/anger, etc. a sudden, strong feeling □ He felt a surge of affection for her.
2 a sudden, large increase □ There's been a surge in gang violence.
3 a sudden movement in a particular direction

surgeon /'sɜːdʒən/ NOUN [plural **surgeons**] a doctor who does operations

surgery /'sɜːdʒərɪ/ NOUN [plural **surgeries**]
1 medical treatments which involve cutting into someone's body □ heart surgery
2 a place where you go to see a doctor or a dentist

surgical /'sɜːdʒɪkəl/ ADJECTIVE to do with medical operations □ surgical techniques

surgically /'sɜːdʒɪkəlɪ/ ADVERB involving an operation □ The lump will have to be surgically removed.

surly /'sɜːlɪ/ ADJECTIVE [surlier, surliest] bad-tempered and rude □ surly staff

surname /'sɜːneɪm/ NOUN [plural **surnames**] your last name or family name □ Smith is a common English surname. □ What's your surname?

surpass /sə'pɑːs/ VERB [surpasses, surpassing, surpassed]
1 a formal word meaning to be better than someone or something 🔄 His work surpassed my expectations.
2 to be greater than a particular limit or amount □ Donations have surpassed the 100,000 mark.

surplus /'sɜːpləs/ ▶ NOUN [plural **surpluses**] an extra amount that is more than you need □ This country produces a surplus of grain.
▶ ADJECTIVE extra and more than you need □ We have surplus food.

surprise /sə'praɪz/ ▶ NOUN [plural **surprises**]
1 no plural the feeling caused by something sudden or unexpected □ He stared at her in surprise. 🔄 To my surprise, I passed my driving test first time.
2 something sudden or unexpected □ Your letter was a nice surprise. 🔄 The news of their engagement came as a big surprise.
take/catch someone by surprise to happen

unexpectedly, and make you feel surprised □ The message had taken her by surprise.
▶ ADJECTIVE unexpected 🔄 I organized a surprise party for my Mum's 40th birthday. 🔄 The President made a surprise visit to Baghdad.
▶ VERB [surprises, surprising, surprised]
1 to make someone feel surprise □ He surprised me by turning up without calling. 🔄 It wouldn't surprise me if he'd committed other similar crimes.
2 to attack someone suddenly and without warning □ They surprised the enemy from the rear.
• **surprised** /sə'praɪzd/ ADJECTIVE having a feeling of surprise 🔄 Anna looked surprised when I told her. □ **+ that** I'm surprised that he agreed to come. □ **+ to do something** I was very surprised to hear that he had left. □ **+ at/by** She was surprised by the news.

> ► Notice the prepositions that follow the word **surprised**. You are **surprised at** or **by** something:
> ✓ I was surprised at/by his decision.
> ✗ I was surprised about his decision.

• **surprising** /sə'praɪzɪŋ/ ADJECTIVE making you feel surprise □ A surprising number of people voted for him. 🔄 It's surprising how many people believe in ghosts. 🔄 It's hardly surprising that (=it is not surprising that) people sometimes have arguments when they live together.
• **surprisingly** /sə'praɪzɪŋlɪ/ ADVERB in a way that surprises you □ She's surprisingly strong for such a small woman.

surreal /sə'rɪəl/ or **surrealistic** /sə,rɪə'lɪstɪk/ ADJECTIVE strange, and like something from a dream □ It was a surreal experience finding myself in a room full of people wearing 18th-century clothes.
• **surrealism** /sə'rɪəlɪzəm/ NOUN, NO PLURAL a style of art or literature in which different ideas or images are connected in a strange way
• **surrealist** /sə'rɪəlɪst/ ADJECTIVE to do with surrealism □ surrealist paintings

surrender /sə'rendə(r)/ ▶ VERB [surrenders, surrendering, surrendered]
1 to stop fighting or trying to escape because you know you will not be successful □ They surrendered to the enemy.
2 a formal word meaning to give something to someone in authority because they demand it □ He was forced to surrender his passport.
▶ NOUN, NO PLURAL an act of surrendering

surreptitious /,sʌrəp'tɪʃəs/ ADJECTIVE secret so that other people do not notice □ He took a surreptitious glance at his watch.
• **surreptitiously** /,sʌrəp'tɪʃəslɪ/ ADVERB in a secret way □ He surreptitiously put it in his pocket.

surrogate /'sʌrəgət/ ▶ ADJECTIVE taking the place of someone or something else 🔄 a surrogate mother (=a woman who has a baby for another woman)
▶ NOUN [plural **surrogates**] a person or thing that

takes the place of another person or thing □ *Robots are already used as surrogates for humans in some industrial processes.*

surround /səˈraʊnd/ VERB [**surrounds, surrounding, surrounded**]

1 to be or go all around something or someone □ *Fans surrounded the players.* □ *The city is surrounded by hills.*

2 if you are surrounded by something or someone, you have a lot of them near you □ *I'm surrounded by good friends who will help me.* □ *Losing weight is not easy when you are surrounded by food.*

3 if a feeling or quality surrounds something, it is connected with it □ *There is a lot of secrecy surrounding the organization.*

• **surrounding** /səˈraʊndɪŋ/ ADJECTIVE all around a place □ *People from the surrounding villages come to the market.* □ *Brisbane and the surrounding area became the fastest growing region in Australia.*

• **surroundings** /səˈraʊndɪŋz/ PLURAL NOUN the area around a person or place □ *The hotel is set in beautiful surroundings.* □ *He was glad to be back in his own surroundings.*

surveillance /sɜːˈveɪləns/ NOUN, NO PLURAL when people such as the police watch someone very closely □ *The FBI had been keeping him under surveillance for several months.*

survey ▶ NOUN /ˈsɜːveɪ/ [*plural* **surveys**]

1 a set of questions designed to find out people's opinions ▣ *We conducted a survey of students.* ▣ *The survey showed that parents and children both want more time together.*

2 an examination of a building in order to see its condition and value, especially when someone wants to buy it

▶ VERB /səˈveɪ/ [**surveys, surveying, surveyed**]

1 to ask people a set of questions in order to find out their opinions □ *60% of people surveyed felt that television was a bad influence on children.*

2 to look at something carefully ▣ *Residents surveyed the damage which the storm had caused to their homes.*

3 to examine a building or land

• **surveyor** /səˈveɪə(r)/ NOUN [*plural* **surveyors**] someone whose job is to examine the condition of a building or to look at the details of an area of land

survival /səˈvaɪvəl/ NOUN, NO PLURAL the fact of continuing to live or exist □ *His survival depended on finding fresh water.*

survive /səˈvaɪv/ VERB [**survives, surviving, survived**]

1 to continue to live after something bad has happened □ *He didn't survive long after the accident.* □ *Amazingly, the diver survived the shark attack.*

2 to continue to exist or live normally ▣ *Many companies are struggling to survive.* □ *They survive on only £100 a week.*

• **surviving** /səˈvaɪvɪŋ/ ADJECTIVE still alive or existing

after others have died or been destroyed □ *He is the last surviving soldier from the war.*

• **survivor** /səˈvaɪvə(r)/ NOUN [*plural* **survivors**] someone who continues to live after something bad has happened to them □ *He was the only survivor of the crash which killed the princess.*

susceptible /səˈseptəbəl/ ADJECTIVE likely to be affected by something □ *Children are more susceptible to colds.*

suspect ▶ NOUN /ˈsʌspekt/ [*plural* **suspects**] someone who may have committed a crime □ *terrorist suspects* ▣ *He's the prime suspect in the murder of Rachel Smith.*

▶ VERB /səˈspekt/ [**suspects, suspecting, suspected**]

1 to think that someone may have committed a crime □ *He's suspected of murdering two women.*

2 to think that something might be true □ *I suspect that she is hiding her true feelings.*

▶ ADJECTIVE /ˈsʌspekt/

1 difficult to trust ▣ *The country's election process highly suspect.*

2 looking dangerous or illegal ▣ *Four suspect packages were blown up by bomb squad officers.*

suspend /səˈspend/ VERB [**suspends, suspending, suspended**]

1 to stop something for a period of time □ *All busine will be suspended until after New Year.*

2 to make someone leave their job or a school for short time because they have done something wron □ *He was suspended from his job after allegations th he had bullied his staff.*

3 to hang something □ *The meat was suspended fro a hook.*

• **suspenders** /səˈspendə(r)z/ PLURAL NOUN

1 a piece of underwear that a woman wears to hold her stockings (=very thin leg coverings)

2 the US word for braces

suspense /səˈspens/ NOUN, NO PLURAL excitemen and nervousness because you are waiting for something to happen □ *We waited in suspense for result.*

suspension /səˈspenʃən/ NOUN [*plural* **suspensio**

1 when something stops for a period of time □ *T could lead to a suspension of the talks.*

2 when someone must leave a job, school or team a period of time because they have done somethi wrong □ *He faces a two-match suspension for dangerous play.*

3 the parts that are attached to a vehicle's wheels, make it more comfortable to ride in

suspension bridge /səˈspenʃən ˌbrɪdʒ/ NOUN [*plural* **suspension bridges**] a type of bridge that hangs from cables (=very thick, strong wires) attac to towers

suspicion /səˈspɪʃən/ NOUN [*plural* **suspicions**]

1 a feeling or a belief that someone has done something wrong or illegal ▣ *He was arrested or suspicion of drink-driving.* ▣ *His odd behaviour ra suspicions.*

2 a feeling that something is true 🔄 *I had a strong suspicion that it was broken.*

● **suspicious** /sə'spɪʃəs/ ADJECTIVE
1 feeling or showing that you do not completely trust someone □ *She gave him a suspicious glance.*
2 making you think that a crime might be involved □ *He died in suspicious circumstances.*

● **suspiciously** /sə'spɪʃəslɪ/ ADVERB in a suspicious way □ *She looked at him suspiciously.* □ *The boys were acting suspiciously.*

sustain /sə'steɪn/ VERB [**sustains, sustaining, sustained**]
1 to make something continue □ *It would be difficult to sustain such a fast pace.*
2 a formal word meaning to suffer something, such as an injury, damage, etc. 🔄 *He sustained head injuries in the accident.*
3 to keep someone healthy and strong □ *They don't have enough food to sustain them through the winter.*

sustainable /səs'teɪnəbəl/ ADJECTIVE
1 able to continue in the same way for a long time □ *sustainable economic growth*
2 not damaging the environment and so able to continue in the same way □ *sustainable farming practices*

sustainably /səs'teɪnəblɪ/ ADVERB in a sustainable way □ *a sustainably managed forest*

sustained /sə'steɪnd/ ADJECTIVE continuing in the same way □ *a sustained period of success*

sustenance /'sʌstɪnəns/ NOUN, NO PLURAL a formal word meaning food and drink

swab /swɒb/ ▶ NOUN [*plural* **swabs**] a piece of material used, for example, to clean injuries
▶ VERB [**swabs, swabbing, swabbed**] to clean something using a swab

swagger /'swægə(r)/ ▶ VERB [**swaggers, swaggering, swaggered**] to walk in a proud and confident way, moving your body from side to side □ *He swaggered along the street in his new suit.*
▶ NOUN [*plural* **swaggers**] a proud and confident way of walking

swallow /'swɒləʊ/ ▶ VERB [**swallows, swallowing, swallowed**]
1 to make food or drink go down your throat □ *Try to swallow the pill.* □ *She swallowed a large mouthful of water.*
2 to make a movement in your throat as if you are swallowing something □ *My throat hurts when I swallow.* □ *He swallowed hard and cleared his throat.*
3 to accept something difficult or unpleasant 🔄 *Being told you are losing your job is pretty hard to swallow.*
4 an informal word meaning to accept what someone tells you, especially when it is not true □ *She'll never swallow that story!*
5 to hide a feeling and not allow it to affect your behaviour 🔄 *He swallowed his pride and accepted the offer of help.*

● PHRASAL VERB **swallow something up** to make something disappear or to use all of something □ *The increase in profits has been swallowed up by rising wage bills.*
▶ NOUN [*plural* **swallows**]
1 when you swallow food or drink
2 a small bird with long pointed wings and a tail with two points

swam /swæm/ PAST TENSE OF **swim**

swamp /swɒmp/ ▶ NOUN [*plural* **swamps**] an area of land that is always very wet
▶ VERB [**swamps, swamping, swamped**]
1 to give someone more of something than they can deal with □ *I'm swamped with work.*
2 to cover something with water □ *A great wave swamped the deck.*

swan /swɒn/ NOUN [*plural* **swans**] a large white bird with a long neck which lives on rivers and lakes

swap /swɒp/ ▶ VERB [**swaps, swapping, swapped**] to exchange one thing for another thing □ *I took the dress back to the shop and swapped it for a bigger size.*
▶ NOUN [*plural* **swaps**] when you swap one thing for another 🔄 *He suggested that we do a swap.*

swarm /swɔ:m/ ▶ NOUN [*plural* **swarms**] a large group of insects which are flying or moving together □ *a swarm of bees*
▶ VERB [**swarms, swarming, swarmed**]
1 if a lot of people swarm somewhere, they quickly move there □ *Reporters swarmed around her as she left court.*
2 if a place is swarming with people or insects, there are a lot of them there □ *The area was swarming with police.*

swarthy /'swɔ:ðɪ/ ADJECTIVE [**swarthier, swarthiest**] with dark skin

swashbuckling /'swɒʃ,bʌklɪŋ/ ADJECTIVE full of adventure and excitement □ *a swashbuckling drama*

swat /swɒt/ VERB [**swats, swatting, swatted**] to hit and kill an insect

sway /sweɪ/ ▶ VERB [**sways, swaying, swayed**]
1 to move from side to side □ *The trees swayed in the wind.*
2 to persuade someone to change their opinion or decision □ *He wasn't swayed by threats.*
▶ NOUN, NO PLURAL **hold sway** a formal phrase meaning to have power or influence □ *He still holds sway in the party.*

swear /sweə(r)/ VERB [**swears, swearing, swore, sworn**]
1 to use words that are offensive □ *He was sent off for swearing at the referee.*
2 to promise □ *She swore never to do it again.*
3 used to say that you are certain about something 🔄 *I could have sworn I left the book on my desk.*
4 swear someone to secrecy to make someone promise that they will not tell people something
● PHRASAL VERBS **swear by something** to believe that something is very good and effective □ *She swears by her grandmother's recipe.* **swear someone in** if someone is sworn in, they make a public promise before they start an important job □ *The country's first elected female leader was sworn in last month.*

- swearing /'sweərɪŋ/ NOUN, NO PLURAL the use of offensive words

swear word /'sweə ˌwɜ:d/ NOUN [plural swear words] a word that is offensive

sweat /swet/ ► NOUN, NO PLURAL the salty liquid that comes out of your skin when you are hot □ He was dripping with sweat after his run.
► VERB [sweats, sweating, sweated] to give out sweat □ Exercise makes you sweat.

- sweater /'swetə(r)/ NOUN [plural sweaters] a piece of clothing for the top part of your body that you pull over your head □ He was wearing a blue sweater and jeans.

sweatshirt /'swetʃɜ:t/ NOUN [plural sweatshirts] a piece of clothing for the top part of your body, made of thick, soft cotton

sweaty /'swetɪ/ ADJECTIVE [sweatier, sweatiest] wet with sweat □ sweaty hands

swede /swi:d/ NOUN [plural swedes] a large round yellow vegetable that grows under the ground

sweep /swi:p/ ► VERB [sweeps, sweeping, swept]
1 to clean something using a brush □ He swept the floor. □ + up She swept up the broken glass.
2 to move someone or something somewhere with a quick, strong movement □ + away Whole villages were swept away by the flood. □ Tonnes of mud were swept down the hillside.
3 to quickly affect a large area □ The disease is sweeping through the country.
4 to go somewhere quickly and confidently □ She swept into my room without knocking.
♦ IDIOM sweep someone off their feet to quickly make someone love you
► NOUN [plural sweeps]
1 when you sweep something clean □ She gave the room a sweep.
2 a sweeping movement □ He indicated the damage with a sweep of his hand.

- sweeper /'swi:pə(r)/ NOUN [plural sweepers] in football, a player who stays behind the other players to stop the other team scoring

- sweeping /'swi:pɪŋ/ ADJECTIVE
1 affecting many people or things ⊞ The system has undergone sweeping changes.
2 too general to be true ⊞ That seems a rather sweeping statement.

sweepstake /'swi:psteɪk/ NOUN [plural sweepstakes] a system in which several people give money to guess the result of something and the person who guesses correctly wins all the money

sweet /swi:t/ ► ADJECTIVE [sweeter, sweetest]
1 tasting like sugar □ He loves sweet food.
2 pleasant in smell or sound □ the sweet smell of flowers
3 attractive and making you feel affection □ a sweet little boy

4 kind and friendly □ She seems very sweet. ⊞ It was sweet of him to offer.
► NOUN [plural sweets]
1 a small piece of sweet food, for example chocolate □ a packet of sweets
2 something sweet that people eat at the end of a meal

sweetcorn /'swi:tkɔ:n/ NOUN, NO PLURAL yellow grains of the maize plant, that you eat as a vegetable

sweeten /'swi:tən/ VERB [sweetens, sweetening, sweetened] to make something sweet □ Sweeten the raspberries with sugar.

- sweetener /'swi:tənə(r)/ NOUN [plural sweeteners]
1 a substance used instead of sugar to sweeten food and drinks
2 something that you offer to someone in order to persuade them to do something

sweetheart /'swi:thɑ:t/ NOUN [plural sweethearts]
1 a word used when talking to someone you love □ Sleep well, sweetheart.
2 a slightly old-fashioned word meaning a boyfriend or girlfriend ⊞ They were childhood sweethearts.

sweetie /'swi:tɪ/ NOUN [plural sweeties]
1 an informal word meaning a nice, kind person □ She's a real sweetie.
2 a word used for talking to someone you love □ There you are, sweetie.
3 a word used by children meaning a sweet □ Mum can I have a sweetie?

sweetly /'swi:tlɪ/ ADVERB in an attractive or friendly way □ She smiled sweetly.

sweetness /'swi:tnɪs/ NOUN, NO PLURAL
1 the quality of being sweet in taste or smell
2 the quality of being kind and friendly

sweet tooth /'swi:t 'tu:θ/ NOUN, NO PLURAL if you have a sweet tooth, you like sweet food

swell /swel/ ► VERB [swells, swelling, swelled, swollen]
1 to become bigger in size □ The wasp sting made my finger swell. □ + up My feet swelled up.
2 to increase in number □ The population has swelled by thirty percent.
► NOUN, NO PLURAL the movement of the sea as it goes up and down

- swelling /'swelɪŋ/ NOUN [plural swellings] a swollen part of the body

swelter /'sweltə(r)/ VERB [swelters, sweltering, sweltered] to be too hot □ Bus passengers sweltered in temperatures that hit 100 degrees.

- sweltering /'sweltərɪŋ/ ADJECTIVE unpleasantly hot □ It's sweltering today.

swept /swept/ PAST TENSE AND PAST PARTICIPLE OF sweep

swerve /swɜ:v/ ► VERB [swerves, swerving, swerved] to suddenly move to the right or left when you are driving □ The driver had to swerve to avoid hitting a dog.
► NOUN [plural swerves] when you swerve

swift /swɪft/ ADJECTIVE [swifter, swiftest] quick □ *I hope she makes a swift recovery.*
▸ **swiftly** /ˈswɪftlɪ/ ADVERB quickly
▸ **swiftness** /ˈswɪftnɪs/ NOUN, NO PLURAL the quality of being quick

swig /swɪg/ ▸ VERB [swigs, swigging, swigged] to drink something by taking a large amount into your mouth. An informal word. □ *He was swigging from a bottle of water.*
▸ NOUN [plural swigs] when you swig something. An informal word.

swill /swɪl/ ▸ VERB [swills, swilling, swilled] to wash something by moving water around quickly inside it □ *He swilled out the cups.*
▸ NOUN, NO PLURAL waste food which pigs eat

swim /swɪm/ ▸ VERB [swims, swimming, swam, swum]
1 to move through water using your arms and legs □ *Can you swim? □ He swam across the river.*
2 if your head swims, you feel confused or as if everything is moving around □ *He felt sick and his head was swimming.*
3 if something is swimming in a liquid, it is covered with it □ *The food was swimming in oil.*
▸ NOUN [plural swims] when you swim 🕮 *I think I'll go for a swim.*

swimmer /ˈswɪmə(r)/ NOUN [plural swimmers] someone or something that swims □ *an Olympic swimmer* 🕮 *She was a strong swimmer* (=able to swim well).

swimming /ˈswɪmɪŋ/ NOUN, NO PLURAL the activity or sport of moving through water using your arms and legs □ *Swimming is excellent exercise.* 🕮 *We went swimming at the local pool.*

swimming baths /ˈswɪmɪŋ ˌbɑːðz/ PLURAL NOUN a building with a pool inside which people can swim in

swimming costume /ˈswɪmɪŋ ˈkɒstjuːm/ NOUN [plural swimming costumes] a piece of clothing that women and girls wear for swimming

swimming pool /ˈswɪmɪŋ ˌpuːl/ NOUN [plural swimming pools] an area of water made for swimming in

swimming trunks /ˈswɪmɪŋ ˌtrʌŋks/ PLURAL NOUN a piece of clothing that men and boys wear for swimming

swimsuit /ˈswɪmsuːt/ NOUN [plural swimsuits] a piece of clothing that women and girls wear for swimming

swindle /ˈswɪndəl/ ▸ VERB [swindles, swindling, swindled] to trick someone in order to take their money □ *That shopkeeper has swindled me out of £2!*
▸ NOUN [plural swindles] when someone is swindled
swindler /ˈswɪndlə(r)/ NOUN [plural swindlers] a person who swindles other people

swine /swaɪn/ NOUN [plural swine]
1 a rude word for someone who treats others people badly
2 an old word for a pig

swing /swɪŋ/ ▸ VERB [swings, swinging, swung]
1 to move backwards and forwards through the air, or to make something do this □ *You swing your arms when you walk. □ The children were swinging on a rope hanging from a tree.*
2 to move in a smooth, wide curve, or to make something do this 🕮 *The door swung open.* □ *She sat up and swung her legs over the side of the bed.*
3 to try to hit something or someone □ **+ at** *She swung at the ball. □ Craig turned round and swung at my brother.*
4 to turn suddenly □ **+ round** *He swung round and stared at us.*
5 if moods, opinions, etc. swing, they suddenly change □ *Public opinion has swung against the war.*
6 **swing into action** to suddenly start doing something □ *A major rescue operation swung into action last night.*
▸ NOUN [plural swings]
1 a seat hanging from ropes or chains, that children sit on and move backwards and forwards
2 a sudden and big change 🕮 *She experienced dramatic mood swings.* □ *They recorded extreme swings in temperature.*
3 a swinging movement, especially to hit someone or something 🕮 *Simon took a swing at him and missed.* □ *He's been practising his golf swing.*
4 **in full swing** if an event or process is in full swing, it is happening and full of activity □ *The party was in full swing.*

swipe /swaɪp/ ▸ VERB [swipes, swiping, swiped]
1 an informal word meaning to hit or to try to hit someone or something □ *She swiped me across the face.*
2 to pull a plastic card through a device so electronic details can be read □ *You have to swipe your card in order to get into the building.*
3 an informal word meaning to steal something □ *The tapes had been swiped from his office.*
▸ NOUN [plural swipes]
1 an informal word meaning when you try to hit someone or something 🕮 *He took a swipe at the ball.*
2 an informal word meaning when you criticize someone 🕮 *The president took a swipe at his critics.*

swipe card /ˈswaɪp ˌkɑːd/ NOUN [plural swipe cards] a plastic card with electronic information on it which you pull through a device, especially to open a door

swirl /swɜːl/ ▸ VERB [swirls, swirling, swirled] to move quickly round in circles □ *Leaves swirled along the ground.*
▸ NOUN [plural swirls] a swirling movement

swish /swɪʃ/ ▶ VERB [swishes, swishing, swished] to move with a sound like cloth moving □ *Her long skirt swished as she danced.*
▶ NOUN [*plural* swishes] a swishing sound

switch /swɪtʃ/ ▶ VERB [switches, switching, switched]
1 to change from one thing to another thing □ *We switched channels to watch the news.* □ **+ from** *She switched from English to French effortlessly.* □ **+ to** *Many families have switched to cheaper gas suppliers.*
2 to exchange two things □ *Someone had switched the name tags.*
♦ PHRASAL VERBS **switch (something) on/off** to turn something on or off using a switch □ *I switched the light on.* □ *He'd forgotten to switch off the microphone.* **switch off** an informal phrase meaning to stop giving your attention to something □ *If it's boring, students just switch off.* **switch over 1** to change from one radio or television programme to another □ *I switched over to CNN.* **2** to start using a different system, product, etc. □ *Many airlines have switched over to electronic ticketing systems.*
▶ NOUN [*plural* switches]
1 a device that you press to make something work or stop working 🖰 *I can't find the light switch.* 🖰 *He flicked the switch on the kettle.*
2 a change from one thing to another □ **+ of/in** *We're considering a switch of location.* 🖰 *People are making the switch from CDs to digital downloads.*

switchboard /'swɪtʃbɔːd/ NOUN [*plural* switchboards] equipment for connecting telephone calls in an office building, a hospital, etc.

swivel /'swɪvəl/ VERB [swivels, swivelling/US swiveling, swivelled/US swiveled] to turn round quickly, or to turn something round quickly □ *I swivelled round to look at him.*

swollen /'swəʊlən/ ▶ ADJECTIVE bigger than usual □ *He had a swollen ankle after falling downstairs.* □ *Several swollen rivers burst their banks.*
▶ PAST PARTICIPLE OF swell

swoon /swuːn/ ▶ VERB [swoons, swooning, swooned] an old-fashioned word meaning to faint (=suddenly become unconscious)
▶ NOUN [*plural* swoons] an old-fashioned word meaning when you swoon

swoop /swuːp/ ▶ VERB [swoops, swooping, swooped]
1 to suddenly and quickly move down □ *The owl swooped down on its prey.*
2 if police officers swoop, they go somewhere without warning, in order to find someone or something □ *More than twenty police officers swooped on the house.*
▶ NOUN [*plural* swoops] when something or someone swoops

swop /swɒp/ ▶ VERB [swops, swopping, swopped] another spelling of swap
▶ NOUN [*plural* swops] another spelling of swap

sword /sɔːd/ NOUN [*plural* swords] a weapon with a long blade

swordfish /'sɔːdfɪʃ/ NOUN [*plural* swordfish or swordfishes] a large fish with a long pointed face

swore /swɔː(r)/ PAST TENSE OF swear

sworn /swɔːn/ ▶ PAST PARTICIPLE OF swear
▶ ADJECTIVE
1 made or given after you have officially promised that it is true □ *a sworn statement*
2 sworn enemies are people who will always hate each other

swot /swɒt/ ▶ NOUN [*plural* swots] an informal word for someone who studies too much
▶ VERB [swots, swotting, swotted] an informal word meaning to study hard
♦ PHRASAL VERB **swot up on something** an informal phrase meaning to learn as much as you can about something

swum /swʌm/ PAST PARTICIPLE OF swim

sycamore /'sɪkəmɔː(r)/ NOUN [*plural* sycamores] a tree with seeds in the shape of two wings

syllable /'sɪləbəl/ NOUN [*plural* syllables] a word or part of a word that is a single sound. For example, *pen* has one syllable and *pen-cil* has two syllables.

syllabus /'sɪləbəs/ NOUN [*plural* syllabuses or syllabi] a list of what students will learn in a subject

symbiosis /ˌsɪmbɪ'əʊsɪs/ NOUN, NO PLURAL when two living things live together and depend on each other. A biology word.

symbol /'sɪmbəl/ NOUN [*plural* symbols]
1 something that represents a more general idea □ **of** *The dove is a symbol of peace.* 🖰 *The statue became a symbol of freedom.*
2 a written sign or a letter that represents something □ **+ for** *H is the chemical symbol for hydrogen*
● **symbolic** /sɪm'bɒlɪk/ ADJECTIVE representing something 🖰 *The gift was a symbolic gesture of friendship.*
● **symbolism** /'sɪmbəlɪzəm/ NOUN, NO PLURAL the use of symbols to represent ideas, especially in art and literature □ *He uses a lot of religious symbolism in his work.*
● **symbolize** or **symbolise** /'sɪmbəlaɪz/ VERB [symbolizes, symbolizing, symbolized] to be a symbol of something □ *A ring symbolizes everlasting love.*

symmetrical /sɪ'metrɪkəl/ ADJECTIVE having two halves which are exactly the same □ *The two sides of a person's face are never completely symmetrical.*
● **symmetry** /'sɪmətrɪ/ NOUN, NO PLURAL the quality of being symmetrical □ *the symmetry of the building*

sympathetic /ˌsɪmpə'θetɪk/ ADJECTIVE
1 feeling or showing sympathy □ *a sympathetic smile*
2 showing someone or something in an attractive, positive way □ *It's a sympathetic portrait of the former president.*
3 supporting a person or idea □ *He was not sympathetic to their arguments.*

sympathetically /ˌsɪmpəˈθetɪkəlɪ/ ADVERB in a sympathetic way

sympathize or **sympathise** /ˈsɪmpəθaɪz/ VERB [**sympathizes, sympathizing, sympathized**]
1 to feel or to show sympathy for someone □ *I really sympathize with his family.*
2 to support someone's ideas or actions □ *She had sympathized with the aims of the French Revolution.*

sympathy /ˈsɪmpəθɪ/ NOUN [*plural* **sympathies**]
1 when you feel sorry for someone who is unhappy or suffering □ + *for* *I have great sympathy for the victims.* □ *She received many letters of sympathy when her husband died.* □ *He expressed his sympathies to the family.*
2 support for a group, an organization or a belief ⊞ *Are you in sympathy with the strikers?* □ *He's an actor with left-wing sympathies.*

symphony /ˈsɪmfənɪ/ NOUN [*plural* **symphonies**] a long piece of music for an orchestra (=large group of musicians)

symptom /ˈsɪmptəm/ NOUN [*plural* **symptoms**]
1 a sign that someone has a particular illness □ *Sore throat, blocked nose, and sneezing are the usual symptoms of a cold.*
2 a sign that a serious problem exists □ *Crime is often a symptom of problems in society.*

symptomatic /ˌsɪmptəˈmætɪk/ ADJECTIVE
1 showing that a more serious problem exists □ *His situation is symptomatic of a legal system which is failing to protect children.*
2 to do with the symptoms of an illness

synagogue /ˈsɪnəɡɒɡ/ NOUN [*plural* **synagogues**] a building where Jewish people go to pray

synchronization /ˌsɪŋkrənaɪˈzeɪʃən/ NOUN, NO PLURAL when things are synchronized

synchronize or **synchronise** /ˈsɪŋkrənaɪz/ VERB [**synchronizes, synchronizing, synchronized**] to make two things move or happen at the same time or speed

syndicate /ˈsɪndɪkət/ NOUN [*plural* **syndicates**] a group of people or organizations that work together □ *a banking syndicate*

syndrome /ˈsɪndrəʊm/ NOUN [*plural* **syndromes**] a medical condition which has a particular set of physical or mental problems □ *irritable bowel syndrome*

synonym /ˈsɪnənɪm/ NOUN [*plural* **synonyms**] a word that has the same meaning as another word

● **synonymous** /sɪˈnɒnɪməs/ ADJECTIVE
1 having the same meaning as another word
2 used to mean that two things are closely connected and people think of them together □ *Diamonds have always been synonymous with Hollywood glamour.*

synopsis /sɪˈnɒpsɪs/ NOUN [*plural* **synopses**] a short description of a book, play, etc.

syntax /ˈsɪntæks/ NOUN, NO PLURAL the set of grammatical rules about how words are arranged to make sentences

synthesis /ˈsɪnθəsɪs/ NOUN [*plural* **syntheses**]
1 a combination of things □ *His latest plan is a synthesis of old and new ideas.*
2 the production of something by a chemical or biological reaction. A chemistry or biology word.

● **synthesizer** or **synthesiser** /ˈsɪnθəsaɪzə(r)/ NOUN [*plural* **synthesizers**] an electronic musical instrument that makes the sounds of other musical instruments

● **synthetic** /sɪnˈθetɪk/ ADJECTIVE not made from natural substances □ *synthetic fabrics*

syphon /ˈsaɪfən/ ▶ NOUN [*plural* **syphons**] another spelling of siphon
▶ VERB [**syphons, syphoning, syphoned**] another spelling of siphon

syringe /sɪˈrɪndʒ/ NOUN [*plural* **syringes**] a tube used with a needle for taking blood out of your body or for putting drugs into your body

syrup /ˈsɪrəp/ NOUN [*plural* **syrups**] a thick, sticky substance made from sugar

system /ˈsɪstəm/ NOUN [*plural* **systems**]
1 an way of organizing or doing something ⊞ *the country's education system* ⊞ *the US legal system* □ + *of* *There's a system of checks already in place.* □ + *for* *We have a new system for processing applications.*
2 pieces of equipment that work together □ *a computer operating system* □ *There's a problem with the central heating system.*
3 parts of the body that work together to do something ⊞ *the body's immune system* ⊞ *The virus attacks the nervous system.*

● **systematic** /ˌsɪstəˈmætɪk/ ADJECTIVE using a particular method which you have planned carefully □ *Police carried out a systematic search of the area.*

● **systematically** /ˌsɪstəˈmætɪkəlɪ/ ADVERB in a way that you have planned carefully □ *He systematically killed his enemies.*

T t

T *or* **t** /ti:/ the 20th letter of the alphabet

ta /tɑ:/ EXCLAMATION an informal word for thank you

tab /tæb/ NOUN [*plural* **tabs**] a small piece of paper, metal, etc., used for opening something or marking the place of something □ *She pulled the tab on the drinks can.*

◆ IDIOM **keep (close) tabs on someone/something** an informal phrase meaning to watch someone or something to find out what they are doing or what is happening □ *Parents often give their children a mobile phone as a way of keeping tabs on them.*

tabby /'tæbɪ/ NOUN [*plural* **tabbies**] a cat with grey or brown stripes

tab key /'tæb ˌki:/ NOUN [*plural* **tab keys**] a key on a computer keyboard that you press to move several spaces forward in a line of text. A computing word.

table /'teɪbəl/ ▶ NOUN [*plural* **tables**]

1 a piece of furniture with a flat surface that you put things on 🔁 *They were sitting at the dining room/ kitchen table.* 🔁 *There was an alarm clock on the bedside table.*

2 lay/set the table to put the knives, forks, glasses, etc. on a table so that you are ready for a meal □ *The children offered to lay the table.*

3 a set of numbers or words that are arranged in rows □ *The table below shows which schools have the best results.*

◆ IDIOM **turn the tables on someone** to change a situation so that you have an advantage over someone after they had an advantage over you

▶ VERB [**tables, tabling, tabled**] to ask for something to be discussed at a formal meeting □ *They tabled proposals calling for the tax to be cut.*

tablecloth /'teɪbəlklɒθ/ NOUN [*plural* **tablecloths**] a cloth for covering a table

table manners /'teɪbəl ˌmænəz/ PLURAL NOUN the way you behave when you are eating a meal at a table □ *He had terrible table manners.*

tablespoon /'teɪbəlspu:n/ NOUN [*plural* **tablespoons**] a large spoon, often used for measuring things when you are cooking

● **tablespoonful** /'teɪbəlˌspu:nful/ NOUN [*plural* **tablespoonfuls**] the amount that a tablespoon will hold

tablet /'tæblɪt/ NOUN [*plural* **tablets**]

1 a pill 🔁 *She took a vitamin tablet.* □ *She takes sleeping tablets.*

2 a small, flat device attached to a computer that yc write on with a special pen. A computing word.

table tennis /'teɪbəl ˈtenɪs/ NOUN, NO PLURAL a gam in which people hit a ball over a net which is attache to a table

tabloid /'tæblɔɪd/ NOUN [*plural* **tabloids**] a small newspaper with lots of pictures and not much seriou news

taboo /tə'bu:/ ▶ NOUN [*plural* **taboos**] something that people must not do or talk about because it mig be offensive to other people □ *Divorce used to be social taboo in Britain.*

▶ ADJECTIVE not allowed because it might be offensi to other people □ *a taboo subject*

tabulate /'tæbjuleɪt/ VERB [**tabulates, tabulating, tabulated**] to arrange numbers or information in ro

tacit /'tæsɪt/ ADJECTIVE understood although not sa directly □ *They have given tacit approval for the pl*

tack /tæk/ ▶ NOUN [*plural* **tacks**]

1 a way of achieving something 🔁 *We aren't gett anywhere, so we need to try a different tack.*

2 a short nail with a flat top

3 the US word for drawing pin

▶ VERB [**tacks, tacking, tacked**] to fasten someth with tacks □ *She had a poster of David Beckham tacked to her wall.*

◆ PHRASAL VERB **tack something on** to add something, often something not planned or expec □ *The bank tacked on interest payments to the b*

tackle /'tækəl/ ▶ VERB [**tackles, tackling, tackled**]

1 to deal with something difficult 🔁 *The policy is designed to tackle the problem of pollution.* □ *T government has failed to tackle poverty.*

2 to try to get the ball from another player in ga such as football and hockey

3 to talk to someone because you are not happy their behaviour □ *I decided to tackle him about mess in the office.*

▶ NOUN [*plural* **tackles**]

1 an attempt to get the ball from another playe games such as football and hockey □ *He was sen after his tackle on Higgins.*

2 special equipment used for something □ *fishir tackle*

tacky /'tækɪ/ ADJECTIVE [tackier, tackiest]
1 an informal word meaning of bad quality, or showing no style □ *The shop sold tacky souvenirs.*
2 slightly wet or sticky □ *The paint is still tacky.*

tact /tækt/ NOUN, NO PLURAL the ability to be careful in what you do or say so that you do not upset or offend someone □ *She showed great tact in dealing with their complaints.*

tactful /'tæktfʊl/ ADJECTIVE careful in what you do or say so that you do not upset or offend someone □ *She was trying to think of a tactful way of asking him to leave.*

tactfully /'tæktfʊlɪ/ ADVERB in a tactful way □ *He handled the situation very tactfully.*

tactic /'tæktɪk/ NOUN [*plural* tactics] a way of doing something to achieve what you want 🖫 *The companies had used the same tactics for promoting their products.* □ *I've got a new tactic for persuading the children to walk.*

tactical /'tæktɪkəl/ ADJECTIVE to do with the methods you use to achieve what you want 🖫 *The government has made several tactical errors.*

tactless /'tæktlɪs/ ADJECTIVE doing or saying something that might offend or upset someone □ *a tactless remark*

tadpole /'tædpəʊl/ NOUN [*plural* tadpoles] a small creature that will become a frog (=a small green or brown animal that jumps, and lives near water)

taffeta /'tæfɪtə/ NOUN, NO PLURAL a type of stiff shiny cloth □ *She was wearing a black taffeta dress.*

tag /tæg/ ▶ NOUN [*plural* tags] a small piece of paper, plastic, etc. with information on it which is attached to something else 🖫 *She looked at the price tag on the jacket.*

▶ VERB [tags, tagging, tagged] to put a tag on something

PHRASAL VERB **tag along** an informal word meaning to go somewhere with someone, especially when they have not asked you to go □ *Do you mind if I tag along with you?*

tail /teɪl/ ▶ NOUN [*plural* tails]
1 the part that sticks out from the end of an animal's body 🖫 *The dog wagged its tail.*
2 the back part of an aeroplane □ *The aeroplane had a red and black symbol painted on its tail.*
3 **the tail end of something** the last part of something □ *It was the tail end of their holiday.*
4 **go to tails**

▶ VERB [tails, tailing, tailed] to follow someone in order to watch what they do or where they go □ *The police were tailing him.*

PHRASAL VERB **tail off** to gradually become quieter or weaker or to happen less often □ *Her voice tailed off as her eyes filled with tears.*

tailback /'teɪlbæk/ NOUN [*plural* tailbacks] a line of traffic that has stopped or is moving slowly □ *There were long tailbacks at junction 10.*

tailor /'teɪlə(r)/ ▶ NOUN [*plural* tailors] someone whose job is making men's clothes such as suits

▶ VERB [tailors, tailoring, tailored] to design something so that it is exactly what someone wants □ *The teaching is tailored to your child's particular needs.*

tails /teɪlz/ PLURAL NOUN the side of a coin that is opposite the side that has the head on it □ *Heads or tails?*

taint /teɪnt/ VERB [taints, tainting, tainted]
1 if a person or organization is tainted by something, it makes people have a bad opinion of them □ *The government has been tainted by corruption.*
2 to spoil something by adding a harmful substance □ *The main river running through the town is tainted with chemicals.*

take /teɪk/ VERB [takes, taking, took, taken]
1 to get something and often move it from one place to another □ *I took him some food.* □ *Make sure you take a coat with you.* □ *Who's taken all the milk?* □ **+ away** *His passport was taken away from him.* □ **+ back** *I must take Jo's book back.* □ **+ out** *He opened the case and took out a cloak.*
2 to accept something that you have been offered □ *She took a biscuit.* □ *Are you going to take the job?* □ *Do you take credit cards?*
3 to go somewhere with someone, especially to look after them or to provide transport for them □ *I took my mother to the hospital.* □ *I take my son swimming every week.*
4 to do or have a particular thing □ *Take a deep breath.* □ *Take a look at his work.* □ *She won't take any responsibility for the business.* □ *Sometimes, you have to take a chance.*
5 to need a particular amount of time to be done □ *I just need to finish this letter - it won't take long.* □ *It took him five years to finish his novel.*
6 to need something □ **+ to do something** *It takes a lot of courage to oppose your friends.* □ *It took five people to lift the piano.*
7 to travel somewhere using a particular form of transport □ *I took a ferry to Stockholm.*
8 to swallow medicine □ *I have to take these antibiotics for a week.*
9 to use something of a particular size or type □ *The printer only takes A4 paper.* □ *I take size 12 trousers.*
10 if you take a photograph, you use your camera to make a picture
11 if a space or container takes a certain amount, it has enough room for it □ *This jug takes nearly two pints.*

➡ *go to* take your *breath* away, take the *bull* by the horns, take your *eye* off something/someone, take your *mind* off something

◆ PHRASAL VERBS **take after someone** to be like an older person in your family □ *She's so emotional - she takes after her father.* **take something apart** to separate something into pieces □ *He took the bike apart and cleaned all the parts.* **take something down 1** to write something □ *He took down our names.* **2** to remove something from a wall or a position □ *They took down the posters.* **3** to remove something from a website □ *He had to take down those pages for legal reasons.* **take something forward** to make something develop or continue successfully □ *He is the best person to take our business forward.* **take something in** to understand something □ *I enjoyed the course but there was an awful lot to take in.* **take someone in 1** to allow someone to live with you □ *The children were taken in by a neighbour.* **2** if you are taken in by someone or something, they trick you □ *They used a very similar brand name, and a lot of customers were taken in.* **take something off** to remove a piece of clothing □ *He took off his jacket.* **take off 1** if an aircraft takes off, it leaves the ground at the beginning of a flight **2** to suddenly become successful □ *With all the extra publicity, our business really took off.* **take on something** to accept work, responsibility, etc. □ *We've taken on a lot of work this winter.* **take someone on 1** to begin to employ someone □ *We've had to take on more staff.* **2** to compete against someone □ *England are taking on France in the rugby.* **take someone out** to go somewhere with someone and pay for them □ *He's taking me out for a meal tonight.* **take something out on someone** to behave badly towards someone because you are upset, especially when it is not their fault □ *I know you had a bad day at work, but there's no need to take it out on me!* **take over (something) 1** to start doing something that someone else was doing □ *Could you take over the cooking while I make a phone call?* □ *+ from She took over from Annie as treasurer.* **2** to take control of something □ *The business was taken over by a French company.* **take to someone/something** to start to like someone or something □ *I took to Paul as soon as I met him.* **take something up 1** to start doing an activity □ *I've taken up judo.* **2** to use a particular amount of time or space □ *His piano takes up most of the front room.* **take someone up on something** to accept someone's offer □ *May I take you up on your offer of accommodation?*

takeaway /'teɪkəweɪ/ NOUN [plural **takeaways**]
1 a meal that you buy at a restaurant and take to eat somewhere else 🕮 *We got a Chinese takeaway.*
2 a shop that sells meals that you can take and eat somewhere else

taken /'teɪkən/ PAST PARTICIPLE OF take

take-off /'teɪkɒf/ NOUN [plural **take-offs**] the time when an aeroplane leaves the ground and goes up into the air □ *Please keep your seat belt fastened during take-off.*

takeover /'teɪk‚əʊvə(r)/ NOUN [plural **takeovers**] when a company takes control of another company 🕮 *The company accepted a takeover bid.*

takers /'teɪkəz/ PLURAL NOUN people who want to buy, do or accept something □ *She sent her work to several publishers, but there weren't any takers.*

takings /'teɪkɪŋz/ PLURAL NOUN the money that a shop or organization gets for selling things □ *Cinema takings have increased.*

talc /tælk/ or **talcum powder** /'tælkəm 'paʊdə(r)/ NOUN, NO PLURAL a powder that smells pleasant, which people put on their bodies after having a bath

tale /teɪl/ NOUN [plural **tales**] a story, often one that is difficult to believe □ *tales of great adventures*

talent /'tælənt/ NOUN [plural **talents**] a natural ability to do something well □ *Sarah had a talent for acting.*
● **talented** /'tæləntɪd/ ADJECTIVE having the ability to do something well □ *She's a talented young artist.*

talk /tɔːk/ ▶ VERB [**talks, talking, talked**]
1 to say words in order to communicate □ *+ to I talked to Molly on the phone yesterday.* □ *+ about He's always talking about football.* □ *I like him, but he talks too much.*
2 to discuss something, especially to try to plan something or solve an argument □ *+ about We need to talk about the housework.* □ *We agreed to meet and talk about the expedition.*
3 talk rubbish/nonsense, etc. to say things that are silly or not true
4 talk politics/sport, etc. to talk about a particular subject
◆ PHRASAL VERBS **talk about something** if people are talking about something, they are saying that they might do it or it might happen □ *They're talking about raising the school-leaving age.* **talk at someone** to talk to someone in a forceful way without allowing them to reply **talk down to someone** to talk to someone in a way that shows that you think you are more important or more clever than them **talk someone into/out of something** to persuade someone to do/not to do something □ *I never wanted to go skiing, but Ralf talked me into it.* **talk something over** to discuss something, especially a problem or a plan □ *There are a lot of issues to do with the business - we really need to talk things over.* **talk someone round** to persuade someone to agree to something □ *She didn't want to play in the concert, but her teacher talked her round.* **talk someone through something** to explain all the parts of a process to someone □ *I think I know how to set the alarm, but could you just talk me through it one more time?* **talk up someone/something** to talk about someone or something in a way that makes them seem successful or important □ *He was busy talking up his party's chances in the election.*
▶ NOUN [plural **talks**]
1 a conversation 🕮 *I need to have a talk with Julie.* **about** *We had a brief talk about school.*
2 talks formal meetings between people such as politicians, especially to try to make plans or solve arguments 🕮 *Ministers will be holding talks in Ger...* □ *+ between Talks between unions and employ... have broken down.*

3 when someone talks to a group of people about a particular subject 🕮 *He gave a talk about his work with gorillas.*

4 *no plural* when people talk about what might happen or be true □ + *of There was talk of an election in June.*

◆ IDIOM **be all talk (and no action)** to talk about what you are going to do, but never do it □ *I know he promised to resign, but he's all talk - he'll never do it.*

talkative /ˈtɔːkətɪv/ ADJECTIVE a talkative person talks a lot

talker /ˈtɔːkə(r)/ NOUN [plural **talkers**] a **smooth talker** someone who is good at persuading people by saying nice things

tall /tɔːl/ ADJECTIVE [**taller, tallest**]
1 bigger in height than most people or things 🕮 *a tall building* □ *He's tall for his age.* □ *tall trees*
2 used when talking about the height of someone or something □ *She's less than five feet tall.*

tally /ˈtælɪ/ ▶ NOUN [plural **tallies**] a record of how many points you have won, how much money you have spent, etc. 🕮 *He kept a tally of how many people had used the service.*
▶ VERB [**tallies, tallying, tallied**] if statements or numbers tally, they are the same □ *His answer tallied with mine.*
PHRASAL VERB **tally something up** to add things together □ *I tried to tally up everything we had spent.*

Talmud /ˈtælmʊd/ NOUN, NO PLURAL **the Talmud** a holy book of the Jewish religion

talon /ˈtælən/ NOUN [plural **talons**] a strong, curved nail of some birds

tambourine /ˌtæmbəˈriːn/ NOUN [plural **tambourines**] a flat, round musical instrument with small metal discs that make a noise when you shake it

tame /teɪm/ ▶ ADJECTIVE [**tamer, tamest**]
a tame animal is no longer wild, and has been trained to be near people
not exciting enough □ *The film was very tame.*
VERB [**tames, taming, tamed**]
to train a wild animal so that it can be near people *They had tried to tame the horse.*
to control something or someone that is difficult to control □ *She had spent a long time trying to tame her hair.*

tamper /ˈtæmpə(r)/
PHRASAL VERB [**tampers, tampering, tampered**]
tamper with something to make changes to something, especially in a way that stops it working correctly □ *Someone had tampered with the lock.*

tan /tæn/ ▶ NOUN [plural **tans**]
a brown colour on your skin because you have been in the sun 🕮 *Many people want to get a tan even though it is bad for your skin.*
light brown colour
VERB [**tans, tanning, tanned**] to get darker skin

because you have been in the sun □ *She tans very easily.*
▶ ADJECTIVE of a light brown colour □ *tan shoes*

tandem /ˈtændəm/ NOUN [plural **tandems**]
1 in tandem together with someone or something else □ *The two drugs work in tandem to fight the disease.*
2 a bicycle for two people

tang /tæŋ/ NOUN [plural **tangs**] a strong and pleasant taste or smell □ *He breathed in the salty tang of the sea air.*

tangent /ˈtændʒənt/ NOUN [plural **tangents**]
1 a straight line that touches a curve but does not go through it. A maths word.
2 in a triangle with one angle of 90°, the tangent is the length of the side opposite one of the angles of less than 90° divided by the length of the side next to it. A maths word.
◆ IDIOM **go off at a tangent** to start talking or thinking about a completely different subject

tangerine /ˌtændʒəˈriːn/ NOUN [plural **tangerines**] a type of small orange

tangible /ˈtændʒəbəl/ ADJECTIVE real enough to be seen, touched or measured □ *The policies were beginning to produce tangible results.*

tangle /ˈtæŋɡəl/ ▶ NOUN [plural **tangles**] a mass of wires, hair, string, etc. which are twisted together
▶ VERB [**tangles, tangling, tangled**] to become twisted together
● **tangled** /ˈtæŋɡəld/ ADJECTIVE twisted together □ *She ruffled his tangled hair.*

tango /ˈtæŋɡəʊ/ NOUN [plural **tangoes**] an energetic dance from South America, where the two dancers hold each other very tightly

tank /tæŋk/ NOUN [plural **tanks**]
1 a large container for liquids or gases 🕮 *The car's fuel tank was empty.* □ *an oxygen tank*
2 a large military vehicle with a gun on top, which moves on metal belts over wheels

tankard /ˈtæŋkəd/ NOUN [plural **tankards**] a large metal cup

tanker /ˈtæŋkə(r)/ NOUN [plural **tankers**] a ship or truck which carries liquids or gases 🕮 *an oil tanker*

tanned /tænd/ ADJECTIVE having brown skin because you have been in the sun □ *She came back from Spain looking fit and tanned.*

tantalizing *or* **tantalising** /ˈtæntəˌlaɪzɪŋ/ ADJECTIVE attractive and making you want something □ *She passed the bakery with its tantalizing smells of fresh bread and cakes.*

tantamount /ˈtæntəmaʊnt/ ADJECTIVE be **tantamount to something** to be as bad as something else □ *His actions are tantamount to cheating.*

tantrum /ˈtæntrəm/ NOUN [plural **tantrums**] when someone, especially a young child, behaves in a very angry way, often shouting 🕮 *Small children often have temper tantrums.*

tap /tæp/ ▶ NOUN [plural **taps**]
1 a device you use for controlling the flow of water or

gas from a pipe 🔷 *She turned on the tap to wash her hands.* 🔷 *The tap is dripping.* 🔷 *I always drink tap water rather than bottled water.* □ *the hot/cold tap*
2 a light knock □ *He felt a tap on his shoulder.*
3 on tap if something is on tap, it is easily available □ *Spain offers excellent leisure facilities and sunshine on tap.*
4 a device that is put on someone's telephone so someone can listen to what they are saying
▶ VERB [**taps, tapping, tapped**]
1 to knock gently □ **+ on** *He tapped on the window.* □ *She tapped me on the arm.*
2 to hit your fingers or feet gently against something 🔷 *He tapped his foot in time with the music.*
3 to secretly put a device on someone's telephone so someone can listen to what they are saying □ *The police had tapped his phone.*
♦ PHRASAL VERB **tap into something** to use something to help you □ *They tapped into this enthusiasm and made the project a success.*

tap dancing /'tæp ˈdɑːnsɪŋ/ NOUN, NO PLURAL a type of dancing in which you wear shoes that make a noise on the floor

tape /teɪp/ ▶ NOUN [*plural* **tapes**]
1 a long, thin piece of plastic for recording sounds or pictures, or the case that it is kept in 🔷 *They played a tape of the police interview.*
2 *no plural* a long, thin piece of plastic that is sticky on one side, used for fastening things □ *The door was sealed with yellow police tape.*
3 a thin piece of material used for tying things or for sewing onto things □ *I sewed name tapes into their clothes.*
4 the tape the strip of material that shows where a race finishes □ *She was the first through the tape.*
▶ VERB [**tapes, taping, taped**]
1 to record sounds and pictures onto tape □ *I taped the show to watch later.*
2 to fasten something somewhere using tape □ *The note was taped to the car's windscreen.*

tape measure /'teɪp ˈmeʒə(r)/ NOUN [*plural* **tape measures**] a long thin piece of cloth, plastic or metal with measurements on it, used for measuring things
taper /'teɪpə(r)/ VERB [**tapers, tapering, tapered**] to become gradually narrower at one end □ *The blade tapered to a sharp point.*
♦ PHRASAL VERB **taper off** to decrease gradually □ *Demand for the product has tapered off.*
tape recorder /'teɪp rɪˈkɔːdə(r)/ NOUN [*plural* **tape recorders**] a piece of equipment that records and plays sounds on tape
tapestry /'tæpɪstrɪ/ NOUN [*plural* **tapestries**] a piece of cloth with a design woven into it with coloured threads
tar /tɑː(r)/ NOUN, NO PLURAL a thick, black sticky substance which is used for covering roads
tarantula /təˈræntjʊlə/ NOUN [*plural* **tarantulas**] a large spider which is poisonous

target /'tɑːɡɪt/ ▶ NOUN [*plural* **targets**]
1 a person or thing that someone attacks 🔷 *Old people are an easy target for thieves.* □ *It is believed that the White House was the intended target of the terrorist attack.*
2 a person or thing that people criticize or joke about □ *Fletcher has been a constant target of criticism.* □ *He was the target of everyone's jokes.*
3 a level that you are trying to achieve 🔷 *The company won't reach its sales targets.*
4 be on target to be making progress at the expected rate □ *The project is on target to finish in May.*
5 a mark or object that people aim at when they are shooting 🔷 *I practised until I could hit the target.*
6 target audience/market the people that something is designed for □ *The magazine's target market is young men.*
▶ VERB [**targets, targeting, targeted**]
1 to try to attack a particular person or place □ *The attacker mainly targets young women.*
2 to put bombs or other weapons in a particular position □ *Two roadside bombs were targeted at police patrols.*
3 to be designed for a particular group □ *The programme is targeted at teenagers.*
tariff /'tærɪf/ NOUN [*plural* **tariffs**]
1 a list of prices □ *The website compares mobile phone tariffs.*
2 a tax on goods which come into a country □ *impo tariffs*
Tarmac /'tɑːmæk/ NOUN, NO PLURAL a mixture of t and small stones, used for covering a road. A trademark.
tarmac /'tɑːmæk/ NOUN, NO PLURAL the tarmac th area at an airport where the planes take off and lan □ *They walked out on to the tarmac towards the plan*
tarnish /'tɑːnɪʃ/ VERB [**tarnishes, tarnishing, tarnished**]
1 to make people have a worse opinion of someone something 🔷 *The affair tarnished his reputation.*
2 if metal tarnishes or something tarnishes it, it st being shiny
tarpaulin /tɑːˈpɔːlɪn/ NOUN [*plural* **tarpaulins**] a piece of strong material which is used to cover thi and protect them from rain
tart /tɑːt/ ▶ NOUN [*plural* **tarts**] a pastry case with top, filled with fruit, vegetables, etc. □ *a jam tart*
▶ ADJECTIVE tasting sour □ *The apples were tart.*
tartan /'tɑːtən/ NOUN [*plural* **tartans**] a tradition Scottish cloth with a pattern of coloured squares lines

task /tɑːsk/ NOUN [*plural* **tasks**] a job that you h to do 🔷 *The school is facing the difficult task of try to raise money.* 🔷 *He was so ill that he couldn't e perform simple tasks.* □ **+ of** *I was given the task helping the teacher carry the books to the office.*
♦ IDIOM **take someone to task** to criticize someor □ *The government has been taken to task for clo hospitals.*

taskbar /'tɑːskbɑː(r)/ NOUN [plural **taskbars**] on a computer screen, a row of words or pictures that shows you the different programs you have already opened. A computing word.

task force /'tɑːsk ˌfɔːs/ NOUN [plural **task forces**] a group of people or soldiers who work together to do a particular thing □ She headed a task force which was set up to deal with world pollution.

tassel /'tæsəl/ NOUN [plural **tassels**] a lot of threads tied together at one end, used as decoration

taste /teɪst/ ► NOUN [plural **tastes**]
1 the flavour of something, especially food or drink □ The seeds have a bitter taste.
2 no plural the ability to recognize flavours □ Smoking can affect your sense of taste.
3 the things that you like, for example clothes, music or food □ + for She developed a taste for luxury. □ + in He has unusual tastes in music. 🕭 She has rather expensive tastes.
4 no plural the ability to judge whether something such as clothing, art or behaviour is good and suitable for a situation 🕭 He has extremely good taste.
5 a small amount of food or drink to try 🕭 Can I have a taste of your cheese?
6 an experience of something □ + of They got a taste of what life is really like here.
IDIOM **leave a bad/bitter/nasty, etc. taste in your mouth** if an experience leaves a bad taste in your mouth, you are upset or angry about it afterwards
► VERB [**tastes, tasting, tasted**]
1 to have a particular flavour □ This sauce tastes salty.
2 to experience the flavour of something □ Can you taste the herbs in this?
3 to try a small amount of food or drink to judge its flavour □ Have you tasted this cheese?
4 to experience something for a short time □ They'd tasted victory for the first time and wanted more.

tasteful /'teɪstfʊl/ ADJECTIVE attractive or showing good judgment □ The ceremony was very tasteful.

tastefully /'teɪstfʊlɪ/ ADVERB in a tasteful way □ tastefully decorated

tasteless /'teɪstlɪs/ ADJECTIVE
1 showing bad judgment and likely to offend people □ a tasteless remark
2 having no flavour
3 not attractive □ cheap, tasteless decorations

tasting /'teɪstɪŋ/ NOUN [plural **tastings**] an event at which you can try a particular food or drink □ The shop offers free cheese tastings.

tasty /'teɪstɪ/ ADJECTIVE [**tastier, tastiest**] having a good flavour

tattered /'tætəd/ ADJECTIVE old and torn □ a tattered photograph □ tattered clothes

tatters /'tætəz/ PLURAL NOUN **in tatters** (a) very badly damaged or spoilt □ His career was in tatters. (b) badly torn □ Her dress was in tatters.

tattoo /tə'tuː/ ► NOUN [plural **tattoos**] a permanent picture made on someone's skin with ink
► VERB [**tattoos, tattooing, tattooed**] to put a tattoo on someone's skin

tatty /'tætɪ/ ADJECTIVE [**tattier, tattiest**] untidy, old and in bad condition □ a tatty old coat

taught /tɔːt/ PAST TENSE AND PAST PARTICIPLE OF teach

taunt /tɔːnt/ ► VERB [**taunts, taunting, taunted**] to say unkind things to someone to make them upset or angry □ Opposing football fans taunted each other.
► NOUN [plural **taunts**] something you say to taunt someone □ Some refugees suffered racist taunts.

taut /tɔːt/ ADJECTIVE [**tauter, tautest**] pulled or stretched tight □ Check that the rope is taut.

tavern /'tævən/ NOUN [plural **taverns**] an old word for a pub

tawdry /'tɔːdrɪ/ ADJECTIVE [**tawdrier, tawdriest**]
1 unpleasant and not moral □ The whole tawdry tale has now become public.
2 cheap and of bad quality □ tawdry ornaments

tax /tæks/ ► NOUN [plural **taxes**] money you pay to the government from your income or that is added to the price of goods you buy to pay for public services 🕭 Most pensioners don't pay tax. □ + on A company pays tax on its profits. 🕭 income tax rates
► VERB [**taxes, taxing, taxed**]
1 to charge tax on something □ There are plans to tax the profits of oil companies. □ Their income will be taxed at 40%.
2 if something taxes you, you find it difficult or tiring □ The matches so far haven't really taxed her physically.
• **taxable** /'tæksəbəl/ ADJECTIVE if something is taxable, you have to pay tax on it □ taxable income
• **taxation** /tæk'seɪʃən/ NOUN, NO PLURAL the system of tax or the amount of money the government gets in taxes

tax disc /'tæks ˌdɪsk/ NOUN [plural **tax discs**] a small round document on the window of a vehicle, that shows the owner has paid road tax

taxi /'tæksɪ/ ► NOUN [plural **taxis**] a car with a driver that you pay to take you from one place to another 🕭 They took a taxi to the airport. 🕭 Don't worry, I'll get a taxi home. 🕭 a taxi driver
► VERB [**taxis, taxiing, taxied**] an aeroplane taxis when it moves slowly along the ground after landing or before leaving

taxing /'tæksɪŋ/ ADJECTIVE difficult or needing a lot of effort □ He has a taxing schedule.

taxi rank /'tæksɪ ˌræŋk/ NOUN [plural **taxi ranks**] a place where taxis wait until people need them

taxonomy /tæk'sɒnəmɪ/ NOUN [plural **taxonomies**] a system of organizing things in groups of similar things, for example plants and animals. A biology word.

taxpayer /'tæksˌpeɪə(r)/ NOUN [plural **taxpayers**] someone who has to pay tax on the money they earn

tax year /'tæks ‚jɪə(r)/ NOUN [plural **tax years**] a period of twelve months that is used for calculating the tax you have to pay

TB /‚ti:'bi:/ ABBREVIATION tuberculosis

tbsp /'teɪbəlspu:n/ ABBREVIATION tablespoon

tea /ti:/ NOUN [plural **teas**]

1 a drink made by pouring boiling water on dried leaves, or the leaves you use to make this drink ⊞ *Can I have a cup of tea?* ⊞ *She sat and drank her tea.* □ *Two teas and a coffee, please.* □ *Do you serve peppermint tea?*

2 a light meal with tea that some people have in the afternoon ⊞ *We stopped in a café for afternoon tea.*

3 used by some people to refer to the meal they have in the early evening

teabag /'ti:bæg/ NOUN [plural **teabags**] a small bag of thin paper containing tea leaves that you pour boiling water over to make tea

teach /ti:tʃ/ VERB [**teaches, teaching, taught**]

1 to give lessons at a school, college or university □ *She taught at the local school.* □ *He teaches maths.* □ *Students are taught in small classes.*

2 to pass your knowledge, skills or experience on to another person □ **+ to do something** *Parents should teach their children to behave properly.* □ **+ question word** *Will you teach me how to sail a dinghy?* □ **+ about** *They are taught about healthy eating.*

3 if an experience teaches you something, you learn something new because of it □ *Recent experience had taught him to be cautious.*

• **teacher** /'ti:tʃə(r)/ NOUN [plural **teachers**] someone who teaches, usually as their job □ *She's an English teacher.* □ *He's the head teacher at the local school.*

• **teaching** /'ti:tʃɪŋ/ NOUN, NO PLURAL the work of a teacher □ *teaching methods* □ *language teaching materials* □ *We want to improve the quality of teaching in state schools.*

• **teachings** /'ti:tʃɪŋz/ PLURAL NOUN the ideas and beliefs of a particular person or group, especially about religion or politics

teacup /'ti:kʌp/ NOUN [plural **teacups**] a cup used for drinking tea

teak /ti:k/ NOUN, NO PLURAL a type of hard yellow-brown wood

tea leaf /'ti: ‚li:f/ NOUN [plural **tea leaves**] a dried leaf from a tea plant □ *Pour hot water over the tea leaves.*

team /ti:m/ ▶ NOUN [plural **teams**]

1 a group of people who play together against another group in a game or a sport □ *the England cricket team* □ *Which football team do you support?* ⊞ *He was selected for the national team.*

2 a group of people who work together □ **+ of** *a team of engineers* □ *the senior management team*

▶ VERB [**teams, teaming, teamed**] to put people or things together □ *She wore a dress teamed with boots.*

♦ PHRASAL VERB **team up (with someone)** to join with other people to achieve something by working together □ *He has teamed up with Nicole Kidman for two recent film projects.*

teammate /'ti:mmeɪt/ NOUN [plural **teammates**] someone who is in the same team as you

teamwork /'ti:mwɜ:k/ NOUN, NO PLURAL when people work together effectively □ *The aim of the project is to encourage teamwork.*

teapot /'ti:pɒt/ NOUN [plural **teapots**] a container for making tea in with a spout (=tube which the tea comes out of) and a handle

tear¹ /teə(r)/ ▶ VERB [**tears, tearing, tore, torn**]

1 to damage paper, cloth, etc. by pulling it apart or making a hole in it □ *You've torn your sleeve on the barbed wire.* □ *The cat tore a hole in the curtain.*

2 to pull or to remove something using force □ *a page torn from a notebook* □ *Liz tore open the envelope.* □ *He tore off a large chunk of bread.*

3 an informal word meaning to go somewhere very fast □ *Ellis tore down the left wing and scored.*

4 be torn between something if you are torn between two things or people, you do not know which one to choose or to support □ *She found herself torn between her family and her career.*

♦ PHRASAL VERBS **tear something apart**

1 to cause a group of people to argue or to fight with each other □ *The civil war is tearing the country apart.* **2** to badly damage or to destroy something □ *The explosion tore the building apart.* **tear someone apart** to make someone feel extremely upset or worried □ *Not knowing where she is is tearing me apart.* **tear someone away** to force someone to leave a place or to stop doing something □ *I'd like to talk to you if you can tear yourself away from the television for a minute.* **tear something down** knock down a building or a wall □ *The old buildings are being torn down.* **tear off something** if you tear off your clothes, you take them off very quickly and without care **tear through something** if an explosion, a storm, etc. tears through a place, it causes a lot of damage there □ *A tornado tore though the town.* **tear something up** to pull a piece of paper into many small pieces □ *She tore up the letter.*

▶ NOUN [plural **tears**] the place where something has been torn □ *There was a large tear in the fabric.*

tear² /tɪə(r)/ NOUN [plural **tears**]

1 a drop of liquid that comes from your eyes when you cry ⊞ *His mum burst into tears* (=started crying) □ *They cried tears of joy.*

2 in tears crying □ *We were all in tears at the end of the film.*

teardrop /'tɪədrɒp/ NOUN [plural **teardrops**] a single tear

tearful /'tɪəful/ ADJECTIVE crying or with people crying □ *We said a tearful goodbye.*

• **tearfully** /'tɪəfuli/ ADVERB in a tearful way □ *She apologized tearfully.*

tear gas /'tɪə(r) ‚gæs/ NOUN, NO PLURAL a gas which hurts people's eyes, especially used to control crowds

tear-stained /ˈtɪəˌsteɪnd/ ADJECTIVE covered in tears □ her tear-stained face

tease /tiːz/ VERB [**teases, teasing, teased**] to say or do something to make someone angry or embarrassed, or to make them believe something that is not true, either as a joke or to make them angry □ I didn't mean what I said. I was only teasing. □ Stop teasing the dog!

teaser /ˈtiːzə(r)/ NOUN [plural **teasers**] a difficult problem or question

teaspoon /ˈtiːspuːn/ NOUN [plural **teaspoons**] a small spoon used for mixing sugar in tea or for measuring small amounts

teaspoonful /ˈtiːˌspuːnfʊl/ NOUN [plural **teaspoonfuls**] the amount a teaspoon will hold

teat /tiːt/ NOUN [plural **teats**]
1 the part of a female animal that its babies suck to get milk
2 the rubber part on a feeding bottle that a baby sucks to get milk

teatime /ˈtiːtaɪm/ NOUN, NO PLURAL the time in the early evening when people have a meal

tea towel /ˈtiː taʊəl/ NOUN [plural **tea towels**] a cloth for drying dishes after they have been washed

technical /ˈteknɪkəl/ ADJECTIVE
1 to do with science and technology □ Does he have any technical training?
2 to do with the way a machine or a system works □ We're having some technical problems with our computers.
3 to do with special knowledge or skills in a particular subject or job ▣ a highly technical legal issue ▣ What is the technical term for your hip bone?
4 according to the details of a rule or the law □ This is a technical breach of the regulations.

technicality /ˌteknɪˈkælətɪ/ NOUN [plural **technicalities**] a detail of the law or a rule □ He was acquitted on a legal technicality.

technically /ˈteknɪklɪ/ ADVERB
1 to do with technology or practical skills □ The project is technically challenging. □ a technically gifted player
2 according to the details of a rule or the law □ Technically, it's not illegal. □ Technically speaking, he's right.

technician /tekˈnɪʃən/ NOUN [plural **technicians**] someone whose job is to do practical work in a laboratory or to use special equipment

technique /tekˈniːk/ NOUN [plural **techniques**] a particular method of doing something □ traditional painting techniques ▣ We've been using a new technique. □ + for There are improved techniques for DNA testing.

techno- /ˈteknəʊ/ PREFIX techno- is added to the beginning of words to mean 'to do with technology'

technological /ˌteknəˈlɒdʒɪkəl/ ADJECTIVE to do with technology □ technological advances

technologically /ˌteknəˈlɒdʒɪklɪ/ ADVERB in a way that is to do with technology □ technologically advanced

technology /tekˈnɒlədʒɪ/ NOUN [plural **technologies**] scientific knowledge, methods or equipment used in practical ways ▣ The system uses wireless technology. ▣ The company is investing in new technology.

teddy /ˈtedɪ/ NOUN [plural **teddies**] a toy in the shape of a bear with soft fur

tedious /ˈtiːdɪəs/ ADJECTIVE long and boring □ It was slow, tedious work.
• **tedium** /ˈtiːdɪəm/ NOUN, NO PLURAL when something is tedious

tee /tiː/ NOUN [plural **tees**]
1 the place where a golf ball is hit from to start part of a game of golf
2 a small plastic stick that you rest a golf ball on to hit it
♦ PHRASAL VERB [**tees, teeing, teed**] **tee off** to hit a golf ball from a tee

teem /tiːm/ VERB [**teems, teeming, teemed**] if it is teeming with rain, rain is falling very heavily □ Rain was teeming down.
♦ PHRASAL VERB **teem with something** if a place teems with people or animals, there are many of them moving around there □ The seafront was teeming with tourists.

teenage /ˈtiːneɪdʒ/ ADJECTIVE
1 aged between 13 and 19 ▣ a teenage girl ▣ a group of teenage boys □ They have a teenage son.
2 to do with people of this age □ teenage magazines
• **teenager** /ˈtiːnˌeɪdʒə(r)/ NOUN [plural **teenagers**] someone who is aged between 13 and 19 □ She's just a typical teenager. □ The site's popular with teenagers and young adults.
• **teens** /tiːnz/ PLURAL NOUN the years of your life between the ages of 13 and 19 □ He was in his teens when the family moved. ▣ The audience were mostly in their late teens and early twenties.

teeny /ˈtiːnɪ/ ADJECTIVE [**teenier, teeniest**] an informal word meaning very small

tee-shirt /ˈtiːʃɜːt/ NOUN [plural **tee-shirts**] another spelling of T-shirt

teeter /ˈtiːtə(r)/ VERB [**teeters, teetering, teetered**]
1 if something or someone teeters, they stand or move as if they are going to fall □ The vase was teetering on the edge of the shelf.
2 teeter on the brink/edge of something to be in a situation where it is possible that something bad could happen at any moment □ The country is teetering on the brink of civil war.

teeth /tiːθ/ PLURAL OF tooth □ Look after your teeth.

teethe /tiːð/ VERB [**teethes, teething, teethed**] a baby teethes when its first teeth start to grow

teething troubles /ˈtiːðɪŋ ˈtrʌbəlz/ PLURAL NOUN problems that happen at the beginning of a piece of work, or with a new piece of equipment □ We're *having teething troubles with the new computer system.*

teetotal /ti:ˈtəʊtəl/ ADJECTIVE someone who is teetotal does not drink any alcohol

- **teetotaller** /ti:ˈtəʊtələ(r)/ NOUN [*plural* **teetotallers**] someone who does not drink alcohol

TEFL /ˈtefəl/ ABBREVIATION teaching English as a foreign language

tele- /ˈtelɪ/ PREFIX
1 tele- is added to the beginning of words to mean 'over a long distance' □ *telepathic*
2 tele- is added to the beginning of words to mean 'using a telephone, radio, etc.' □ *telebanking*
3 tele- is added to the beginning of words to mean 'to do with the television' □ *teletext*

telebanking /ˈtelɪˌbæŋkɪŋ/ NOUN, NO PLURAL a system in which you move money into and out of your bank account by telephone

telecommunications /ˈtelɪkəˌmjuːnɪˈkeɪʃənz/ PLURAL NOUN sending information over long distances by telephone, radio or television □ *a telecommunications company*

telegram /ˈtelɪgræm/ NOUN [*plural* **telegrams**] a message sent by telegraph, used especially in the past for short, urgent messages

telegraph /ˈtelɪgrɑːf/ NOUN [*plural* **telegraphs**] a system used especially in the past for sending messages over long distances using radio signals

- **telegraphic** /ˌtelɪˈgræfɪk/ ADJECTIVE using telegraph

telemarketing /ˈtelɪˌmɑːkɪtɪŋ/ NOUN, NO PLURAL another word for telesales

telepathic /ˌtelɪˈpæθɪk/ ADJECTIVE able to know another person's thoughts without speaking or writing

- **telepathy** /tɪˈlepəθɪ/ NOUN, NO PLURAL the ability to know another person's thoughts without speaking or writing

telephone /ˈtelɪfəʊn/ ► NOUN [*plural* **telephones**]
1 *no plural* a system for speaking to someone in another place, using equipment connected by wires □ *I spoke to him by telephone yesterday.* ▣ *Kennedy made a telephone call.*
2 a piece of equipment that you use to make telephone calls ▣ *The telephone rang.* ▣ *Isabelle answered the telephone.* ▣ *Can I use your telephone?*
► VERB [**telephones, telephoning, telephoned**] to contact someone using the telephone □ *Her mother telephoned the police when she didn't return home.*

telephone box /ˈtelɪfəʊn ˌbɒks/ NOUN [*plural* **telephone boxes**] a small structure in a public place containing a telephone which you can pay to use

telephone number /ˈtelɪfəʊn ˈnʌmbə(r)/ NOUN [*plural* **telephone numbers**] the series of numbers that you use to call a particular telephone □ *Give me your telephone number, and I'll ring you tonight.*

telephoto lens /ˌtelɪˈfəʊtəʊ ˈlenz/ NOUN [*plural* **telephoto lenses**] a camera lens (=piece of curved glass) which produces large images of small objects o objects which are far away

telesales /ˈtelɪseɪlz/ NOUN, NO PLURAL the selling of goods and services by telephone

telescope /ˈtelɪskəʊp/ NOUN [*plural* **telescopes**] a piece of equipment with lenses (=curved pieces of glass) and mirrors inside that makes objects that are far away seem closer or larger

- **telescopic** /ˌtelɪˈskɒpɪk/ ADJECTIVE
1 to do with telescopes
2 with parts that can be pushed inside each other

teletext /ˈtelɪtekst/ NOUN, NO PLURAL a service that provides news and information in written form on your television screen. A trademark.

televise /ˈtelɪvaɪz/ VERB [**televises, televising, televised**] to broadcast something on television □ *T▮ event is being televised live.*

television /ˈtelɪˌvɪʒən/ NOUN [*plural* **televisions**
1 *no plural* a system for sending images and sounds the form of electrical signals, or programmes broadcast in this way ▣ *Children watch too much television.* □ *It was her first appearance on televisi▮* ▣ *a commercial television station*
2 the equipment which receives these pictures and sounds □ *a new flat-screen television* ▣ *an old bla▮ and-white television set* ▣ *He switched on the television.*

➤ Remember that people and things appear **on television**:
✓ *He's often on television these days.*
✗ *He's often in television these days.*

tell /tel/ VERB [**tells, telling, told**]
1 to give someone information by speaking □ *D▮ tell Mum I've lost my key.* □ *+ that* He told the c▮ that he was abroad at the time. □ *+ question w▮ Can you tell us why you disagree?* ▣ *He promised tell the truth.* ▣ *She accused us of telling lies ab▮ her.*
2 to order someone to do something □ *+ to do something* He told me to sit down. ▣ *I wish you▮ would do as you are told!*
3 if you can tell something, you know that it is tr▮ recognize the characteristics of someone or something ▣ *I couldn't tell if he was joking or not.▮ that* I could tell that she was upset. ▣ *Can you te▮ difference between butter and margarine?*
4 tell the time to be able to understand the information on a clock or watch

➤ Note that when you use the word **tell**, mear 'to speak to someone', you must say the per▮ that you are speaking to □ *I told Peter I wou▮ come.*
✓ *I told him I would come.*
✗ *I told that I would come.*

> PHRASAL VERBS **tell someone/something apart** to be able to see the difference between two people or things □ *There are two sisters, and I can never tell them apart.* **tell someone off** to speak angrily to someone who has done something wrong □ + *for He told me off for wasting water.*

telling /ˈtelɪŋ/ ADJECTIVE
1 showing the truth about something □ *Perhaps the most telling remark came from his brother.*
2 important or effective

telling-off /ˈtelɪŋˈɒf/ NOUN, NO PLURAL when you tell someone off □ *His teacher gave him a telling-off for being late again.*

telltale /ˈtelteɪl/ ADJECTIVE showing that something certainly exists or is true □ *The doctor spotted the telltale signs of the disease.*

telly /ˈtelɪ/ NOUN [plural **tellies**] an informal word for television

temp /temp/ ▶ NOUN [plural **temps**] someone who as a job for a short period of time, especially in an office □ *She was working as a temp.*
▶ VERB [**temps, temping, temped**] to do a job for a short period of time □ *I was temping at a law firm.*

temper /ˈtempə(r)/ NOUN [plural **tempers**] when someone becomes angry very easily ⊞ *My father had a really bad temper.* □ *He was known for his violent temper.* ⊞ *The little boy had a temper tantrum.*
lose/keep your temper to become angry/control your feelings □ *I'm afraid I lost my temper and shouted at him.* □ *He was trying to keep his temper.*
a person's mood □ *Don't ask him until he's in a better temper.*

temperament /ˈtempərəmənt/ NOUN [plural **temperaments**] your character, which affects the way you think and behave □ *Alex has a calm temperament.* □ *His fiery temperament often got him into trouble.*

temperamental /ˌtempərəˈmentəl/ ADJECTIVE
a temperamental person changes their mood suddenly and gets upset easily □ *Actors are notoriously temperamental.*
a temperamental machine, vehicle, etc. does not always work well □ *The shower's a bit temperamental.*

temperate /ˈtempərət/ ADJECTIVE with weather that never gets very cold or very hot. A geography word □ *a temperate climate* □ *a temperate region*

temperature /ˈtemprətʃə(r)/ NOUN [plural **temperatures**]
how hot or cold a place or a thing is □ *Average temperatures in spring are a pleasant 19-24°C.* □ + *of a temperature of minus 10°C* ⊞ *The furnace is heated to very high temperatures.* ⊞ *Serve at room temperature.*
how hot or cold a person's body is ⊞ *Flora woke up with a headache and a high temperature.* ⊞ *A nurse came in to take his temperature (=to measure it).*
have a temperature if someone has a temperature, their body is hotter than it should be because they are ill

tempest /ˈtempɪst/ NOUN [plural **tempests**] a violent storm with very strong wind

• **tempestuous** /temˈpestjuəs/ ADJECTIVE full of very strong emotions □ *a tempestuous relationship*

template /ˈtemplɪt/ NOUN [plural **templates**] something that is used as a pattern to make other things of the same kind ⊞ *This policy could provide a template for other cities to copy.*

temple /ˈtempəl/ NOUN [plural **temples**]
1 a building in which the members of some religions show respect for a god by praying, having religious ceremonies, etc. □ *a Hindu temple*
2 the area on the side of your head between the side of your eye and your hair □ *He rubbed his temples.*

tempo /ˈtempəʊ/ NOUN [plural **tempos** or **tempi**] the speed and rhythm of a piece of music

temporarily /ˈtempərərəlɪ/ ADVERB for a short or limited time only □ *The road was temporarily closed.* □ *He'd repaired the roof temporarily with a piece of plastic.* □ *The noise seems to have stopped, at least temporarily.*

• **temporary** /ˈtempərərɪ/ ADJECTIVE lasting or used only for a short or limited time □ *a temporary job* □ *The firm hires temporary workers in the summer.* ⊞ *He was put in charge of the team on a temporary basis.* ⊞ *Some families are living in temporary accommodation.*

tempt /tempt/ VERB [**tempts, tempting, tempted**]
1 to make someone want to do something or to have something □ *I was very tempted by their offer.* □ *Special deals are aimed at tempting people to switch banks.*
2 tempt fate to be too confident or to do something that might end your good luck □ *I didn't want to tempt fate by thinking too far ahead.*

• **temptation** /tempˈteɪʃən/ NOUN [plural **temptations**]
1 when you are tempted by something ⊞ *She resisted the temptation to open it straight away.*
2 something that tempts you □ *I'm on a diet, but those cakes were too much of a temptation.*

• **tempting** /ˈtemptɪŋ/ ADJECTIVE attractive and making you want to do or to have something □ *The food looks very tempting.* □ *a tempting offer*

ten /ten/ NUMBER [plural **tens**] the number 10

tenacious /tɪˈneɪʃəs/ ADJECTIVE determined not to stop doing something or trying to do something □ *He's a tenacious opponent.*

• **tenaciously** /tɪˈneɪʃəslɪ/ ADVERB in a tenacious way □ *She kept to her point tenaciously and would not give way.*

• **tenacity** /tɪˈnæsətɪ/ NOUN, NO PLURAL the quality of being tenacious □ *Everyone admires her tenacity.*

tenancy /'tenənsɪ/ NOUN [plural **tenancies**] the time when someone is a tenant or the agreement that makes someone a tenant

tenant /'tenənt/ NOUN [plural **tenants**] someone who pays rent to the owner of a house, building or land to use it □ *The table was left by the previous tenants.*

tend /tend/ VERB [**tends, tending, tended**]
1 tend to do something to often do something, happen, or be a particular way □ *She tends to be a bit moody.* □ *People tend not to talk about financial problems.*
2 a formal word meaning to look after someone or something □ *He spends most days tending his garden.* □ *A nurse tended to the injuries to his face.*
• **tendency** /'tendənsɪ/ NOUN [plural **tendencies**] when someone often does something or something often happens □ *Teenagers often have a tendency to get up late.*

tender /'tendə(r)/ ► ADJECTIVE
1 tender meat or vegetables are soft and easy to cut □ *Cook the beans until tender.*
2 kind and gentle □ *a tender smile* □ *They shared a tender moment.*
3 slightly painful when touched □ *The skin can be tender and red.* □ *My arm's quite tender to touch.*
4 sensitive and not very strong □ *These plants are too tender to be grown outside.*
► VERB [**tenders, tendering, tendered**]
1 to make a formal offer to do a particular job □ *Companies have been invited to tender for the contract.*
2 to formally offer something 🔁 *The minister has tendered his resignation.*
► NOUN [plural **tenders**] a formal offer to do a particular job □ *The company recently won the tender to install phones at Sydney Airport.*
• **tenderly** /'tendəlɪ/ ADVERB in a kind, gentle way □ *He smiled at her tenderly.*
• **tenderness** /'tendənɪs/ NOUN, NO PLURAL the quality of being tender

tendon /'tendən/ NOUN [plural **tendons**] strong body tissue that connects a muscle to a bone. A biology word.

tendril /'tendrəl/ NOUN [plural **tendrils**] a long, thin, curling stem of a plant, that winds around things

tenement /'tenəmənt/ NOUN [plural **tenements**] a large building with several floors divided into flats □ *a low-rent tenement building*

tenner /'tenə(r)/ NOUN [plural **tenners**] an informal word for ten pounds (=£10) or a ten pound note

tennis /'tenɪs/ NOUN, NO PLURAL a game played on a court with a net across the middle in which the players hit a small ball over the net using rackets (=objects held in the hand) 🔁 *We play tennis every weekend.* 🔁 *a professional tennis player* 🔁 *a tennis court*

tenor /'tenə(r)/ NOUN [plural **tenors**] a male singer who has quite a high voice

tenpin bowling /'tenpɪn 'bəʊlɪŋ/ NOUN, NO PLURAL a game in which you roll a heavy ball along the floor, and try to knock down ten wooden objects in the shape of bottles

tense¹ /tens/ NOUN [plural **tenses**] a form of a verb which shows whether the action of the verb happens now (the present tense), in the past (the past tense) or in the future (the future tense)

tense² /tens/ ► ADJECTIVE [**tenser, tensest**]
1 feeling nervous and unable to relax □ *He looked tense and exhausted.*
2 making you feel nervous or worried □ *There was tense atmosphere in the court.*
3 stretched tight □ *tense muscles*
► VERB [**tenses, tensing, tensed**] if you tense your muscles, you stretch them tight
• **tensely** /'tenslɪ/ ADJECTIVE in a way that is nervous and not relaxed □ *He stared tensely at the screen.*
• **tension** /'tenʃən/ NOUN [plural **tensions**]
1 the feeling when people do not trust each other 🔁 racial tension 🔁 *The two leaders are meeting in effort to ease tensions between the countries.*
2 a nervous or worried feeling □ *She could sense t tension in him.*
3 the state of being stretched tight

tent /tent/ NOUN [plural **tents**] a frame covered w cloth which you sleep in when you are camping 🔁 *pitched the tent (=put it up) next to the river.*

tentacle /'tentəkəl/ NOUN [plural **tentacles**] one the long arms of a sea animal such as an octopus

tentative /'tentətɪv/ ADJECTIVE
1 not certain yet □ *a tentative agreement*
2 not confident □ *She took a few tentative steps towards him.*

tenterhooks /'tentəhʊks/ PLURAL NOUN on tenterhooks nervous and excited because you ar waiting for something □ *We were on tenterhooks waiting for the exam results.*

tenth /tenθ/ ► NUMBER 10th written as a word
► NOUN [plural **tenths**] $\frac{1}{10}$; one of ten equal part something

tenuous /'tenjʊəs/ ADJECTIVE something that is tenuous is so uncertain that it almost does not e: □ *He had some tenuous links with the Royal Fam which he was always boasting about.*

tepid /'tepɪd/ ADJECTIVE tepid liquid is slightly war

term /tɜːm/ ► NOUN [plural **terms**]
1 in terms of something/in ... terms used for saying which part of a situation you are talking a □ *In financial terms, the company has been very successful.* □ *Families are doing a lot for the environment in terms of recycling.*
2 one of the periods of time that the school or co year is divided into □ *Students do exams in the summer term.*
3 a limited period of time □ *the president's terr*

office □ **+ of** *He was sent to prison for a term of 15 years.*

4 a word or expression with a particular meaning or used in a particular subject ⌗ *Patients don't understand complicated medical terms.* □ **+ for** *What is the term for someone who collects coins?* □ **+ of** *'Darling' is a term of affection.*

5 in the long/short term during a long/short period of time from now □ *Exposure to low levels of radiation increases the risk of ill health in the long term.*

6 terms the rules of an agreement □ *Under the terms of his contract, he is eligible for a payout of £2 million.*

7 be on good/bad/friendly etc. terms with someone used for saying what type of relationship you have with someone □ *She remained on good terms with her husband after their divorce.*

8 come to terms with something to accept and deal with a sad situation □ *The family are still coming to terms with his death.*

► **VERB** [terms, terming, termed] to use a particular word or phrase to describe someone or something □ *Dogs that are used for hunting are often termed 'hounds'.*

terminal /'tɜːmɪnəl/ ► **NOUN** [plural **terminals**]
1 a building where planes, boats, trains or buses arrive at and leave from ⌗ *Smoking is not allowed in the terminal building.* □ *Developers want to build a new terminal and runway at the airport.*
2 a computer screen and keyboard. A computing word.
► **ADJECTIVE** a terminal illness cannot be cured, and causes death ⌗ *Jane had terminal cancer.*

terminate /'tɜːmɪneɪt/ **VERB** [terminates, terminating, terminated] a formal word meaning to end, or to make something end ⌗ *His employers terminated his contract.*

termination /ˌtɜːmɪˈneɪʃən/ **NOUN** [plural **terminations**] a formal word meaning the act of ending something □ *The inquiry resulted in termination of the agreement.*

terminology /ˌtɜːmɪˈnɒlədʒɪ/ **NOUN** [plural **terminologies**] the words and phrases that are used in a particular subject □ *military terminology*

terminus /'tɜːmɪnəs/ **NOUN** [plural **termini** or **terminuses**] the place where a bus or train ends its journey

termite /'tɜːmaɪt/ **NOUN** [plural **termites**] an insect that eats wood

terrace /'terəs/ **NOUN** [plural **terraces**]
1 an area next to a building or on the roof of a building where you can sit □ *They sat and drank coffee on the terrace at the Hotel Duomo.*
2 a row of houses that are joined to each other
3 one of a series of flat areas cut into the side of a hill, where crops are grown

terraced house /'terəst 'haʊs/ **NOUN** [plural **terraced houses**] a house that is one of a row of houses which are joined together

terrain /teˈreɪn/ **NOUN, NO PLURAL** a particular type of land □ *rough terrain*

terrapin /'terəpɪn/ **NOUN** [plural **terrapins**] a small animal that lives in water and has a hard shell on its back

terrestrial /təˈrestrɪəl/ **ADJECTIVE**
1 terrestrial television, radio, etc. does not use signals from satellites (=devices in space) or cables (=thick wires)
2 to do with Earth and not space or other planets □ *terrestrial dust*
3 living on land and not water □ *terrestrial animals*

terrible /'terəbəl/ **ADJECTIVE** very bad or of very low quality □ *a terrible smell* □ *He made a terrible mistake.* □ *I'm terrible at remembering names.* ⌗ *I feel terrible about lying to my parents.*
• **terribly** /'terəblɪ/ **ADVERB**
1 extremely □ *I'm terribly sorry I broke your vase.* □ *I feel terribly guilty about it.*
2 very badly □ *His death has affected us terribly.*

terrier /'terɪə(r)/ **NOUN** [plural **terriers**] a type of small dog

terrific /təˈrɪfɪk/ **ADJECTIVE**
1 excellent □ *He's done a terrific job as team captain.* □ *The party was terrific.*
2 very great □ *The car was travelling at terrific speed.*
• **terrifically** /təˈrɪfɪklɪ/ **ADVERB** extremely □ *We were terrifically pleased to get the award.*

terrified /'terɪfaɪd/ **ADJECTIVE** very frightened □ *I was terrified of my history teacher.* □ *He is absolutely terrified that someone will break into the house while he is alone.*
• **terrify** /'terɪfaɪ/ **VERB** [terrifies, terrifying, terrified] to make someone feel very frightened □ *The thought of dying terrifies me.*
• **terrifying** /'terɪfaɪɪŋ/ **ADJECTIVE** making you feel very frightened □ *a terrifying ordeal*

territorial /ˌterɪˈtɔːrɪəl/ **ADJECTIVE** to do with land that a particular country controls □ *a territorial dispute*

territory /'terətrɪ/ **NOUN** [plural **territories**]
1 the land that a particular country controls ⌗ *The army was in enemy territory.* □ *The plane wasn't allowed to land on British territory.*
2 the area that an animal thinks is its own □ *Cats don't like it when other cats go into their territory.*
3 an area of knowledge or experience ⌗ *Technology was unfamiliar territory for me.*

terror /'terə(r)/ **NOUN, NO PLURAL**
1 a feeling of great fear □ *He ran away in terror.*
2 violence used by illegal groups to achieve political aims □ *Many people were killed in the September 11th terror attacks.* ⌗ *Police have arrested 15 terror suspects.*
• **terrorism** /'terərɪzəm/ **NOUN, NO PLURAL** violence used by illegal groups to achieve political aims □ *There has been a rise in global terrorism.*
• **terrorist** /'terərɪst/ **NOUN** [plural **terrorists**]

someone who uses terrorism ⊞ *a terrorist organization* □ *a suspected terrorist*

• **terrorize** *or* **terrorise** /'terəraɪz/ VERB [**terrorizes, terrorizing, terrorized**] to frighten someone by threatening to use violence □ *Gangs of teenagers terrorized the neighbourhood.*

test /test/ ▶ NOUN [*plural* **tests**]
1 an exam, usually a short one □ *a spelling test* ⊞ *You will need to pass a simple maths test.* ⊞ *I had to take a test to prove my French was good enough.* ⊞ *He failed his driving test.*
2 a medical examination of your body or part of your body □ *an eye/blood test* ⊞ *Tests showed she was suffering from a rare blood disease.*
3 something you do to check that something works correctly, is safe, etc. ⊞ *They will be conducting tests on the new aircraft over the next year.* ⊞ *nuclear tests*
4 a situation that proves the qualities of someone or something □ + *of* *The election will be a test of strength for the president.* ⊞ *She faces a real test of character in the months ahead.*
5 put someone/something to the test to do something that proves how good or effective someone or something is □ *The system will be put to the test next week.*

> ► Remember that you **do** or **take** a test (exam). You do not 'make' a test:
> ✓ I had to do a test in my interview.
> ✗ I had to make a test in my interview.

▶ VERB [**tests, testing, tested**]
1 to do something to check that something works correctly, is safe, etc. □ *After driving through water, you should test the brakes.* □ + *on* *The drugs are tested on volunteers.* □ *We need to design experiments to test our theories.*
2 to do a medical examination of your body or part of your body □ *I need to get my eyes tested.* □ + *for* *We are testing for anaemia.*
3 to give someone an exam, usually a short one □ + *on* *Can you test me on my verb endings?*
4 to prove the qualities of someone or something □ *These problems will test her ability to lead others.*

testament /'testəmənt/ NOUN [*plural* **testaments**]
testament to something a formal phrase meaning proof of something good □ *Her success is testament to all her hard work.*
testicle /'testɪkəl/ NOUN [*plural* **testicles**] one of the two organs under a man's penis. A biology word.
• **testicular** /tes'tɪkjulə(r)/ ADJECTIVE to do with the testicles. A biology word □ *testicular cancer*
testify /'testɪfaɪ/ VERB [**testifies, testifying, testified**] to give information in a court □ *He testified at the inquest into the Princess's death.*
testimonial /ˌtestɪ'məunɪəl/ NOUN [*plural* **testimonials**] a written statement about someone's character, skills and abilities

testimony /'testɪmənɪ/ NOUN [*plural* **testimonies**]
1 a formal statement that someone makes in a court
2 testimony to something a formal phrase meaning proof of something good □ *The huge profits are testimony to the confidence that people have in the company.*
testosterone /te'stɒstərəun/ NOUN, NO PLURAL a chemical substance that causes male characteristics to develop. A biology word.
test tube /'test ˌtju:b/ NOUN [*plural* **test tubes**] a thin glass tube which is closed at one end, used in scientific experiments
testy /'testɪ/ ADJECTIVE [**testier, testiest**] bad-tempered
tetanus /'tetənəs/ NOUN, NO PLURAL a serious disease that makes the muscles in your neck and face stiff, caused by bacteria that get into a cut on your skin
tetchy /'tetʃɪ/ ADJECTIVE [**tetchier, tetchiest**] getting annoyed easily □ *We had a rather tetchy meeting.*
tether /'teðə(r)/ ▶ VERB [**tethers, tethering, tethered**] to tie an animal to a tether
▶ NOUN [*plural* **tethers**] a rope or chain used for tying up an animal so that it can walk around but not escape
♦ IDIOM **be at/reach the end of your tether** to feel that you cannot deal with a bad situation any more □ *Some parents reach the end of their tether with badly behaved children.*

text /tekst/ ▶ NOUN [*plural* **texts**]
1 a written message sent to a mobile phone ⊞ *I send a text to my sister.* □ *She got a text from her boyfriend.*
2 no plural the writing in a book □ *The pictures were nice but the text wasn't very interesting.*
3 a book or piece of writing that people study □ *Indian ancient texts*
▶ VERB [**texts, texting, texted**] to send a written message to someone's mobile phone □ *Text me when you get to the station.*

textbook /'tekstbuk/ NOUN [*plural* **textbooks**] a book about a subject which you use at school or college □ *a biology textbook*
textile /'tekstaɪl/ NOUN [*plural* **textiles**] cloth □ *the textile industry*
text message /'tekst ˌmesɪdʒ/ NOUN [*plural* **text messages**] a text (=written message sent to a mobile phone)
texture /'tekstʃə(r)/ NOUN [*plural* **textures**] the way something feels when you touch it □ *the smooth texture of a baby's skin*

than /ðæn/ CONJUNCTION used when comparing things □ *The test was easier than I thought it would be.* □ *He can swim better than me.* □ *The dress cost less than £200.*

thank /θæŋk/ VERB [**thanks, thanking, thanked**]
1 to tell someone that you are grateful for something □ + *for* *He thanked me for the birthday present.* □ *I must thank Emma for helping me.*
2 thank goodness/thank heavens/thank God used for saying you are pleased about something □ *Thank goodness no one was seriously hurt.*

- **thankful** /ˈθæŋkfʊl/ ADJECTIVE pleased or grateful that something good has happened □ *I'm just thankful that someone found my dog.*

- **thankfully** /ˈθæŋkfʊli/ ADVERB used for saying that you are pleased because something good has happened □ *Thankfully, he managed to escape.*

- **thankless** /ˈθæŋklɪs/ ADJECTIVE a thankless task is one which is difficult and you do not get any praise for doing it ⓖ *She had the thankless task of deciding which schools would have to close.*

- **thanks** /θæŋks/ ▶ EXCLAMATION
  1 something you say to show that you are grateful □ *'I've made you a drink.' 'Thanks.'* ⓖ *'Here's an invitation to the party.' 'Oh, thanks very much.'* ⓖ *Many thanks for your letter.* □ + *for* *Thanks for the flowers. They're beautiful.* □ *Thanks for driving me to the airport.*
  2 used as a way of accepting an offer □ *'Would you like a sweet?' 'Thanks.'*
  3 no thanks used as a polite way of saying you do not want something □ *'Do you want to come with us?' 'No thanks, I'm busy on Saturday.'*
  ▶ PLURAL NOUN
  1 something you say or do to show that you are grateful □ *He expressed his thanks to everyone who had taken part.* □ *I got no thanks for helping him.*
  2 thanks to someone/something because of someone or something □ *We finished the project on time, thanks to everyone's hard work.* □ *Thanks to the strike, our flight was cancelled.*

- **Thanksgiving** /ˈθæŋksˌɡɪvɪŋ/ NOUN, NO PLURAL a holiday in the US and Canada in autumn, when families eat a special meal together

- **thank you** /ˈθæŋkjuː/ EXCLAMATION
  1 something you say to someone when you are grateful for something they have done or given you □ *'I've made you a cup of coffee.' 'Oh, thank you very much.'* □ + *for* *Thank you for the flowers. They're beautiful.* □ *Thank you for helping me yesterday.*
  2 used when answering a question in a polite way □ *'How are you?' 'I'm fine, thank you.'*
  3 used as a polite way of accepting or refusing someone's offer □ *'Would you like to come for a meal with us?' 'Thank you. That would be lovely.'* ⓖ *'Do you want another biscuit?' 'No, thank you.'*

  Note that you say **thank you for** something or **thank you for** + doing something □ *Thank you for your help.* □ *Thank you for helping.*

- **that** ▶ CONJUNCTION /ðət/
  1 used after some verbs, adjectives and nouns to start a new part of a sentence □ *He said that he hated it.* □ *We must make sure that we invite enough people.* □ *The fact that he earns so much means he can afford a big house.*
  2 used instead of 'who' or 'which' at the beginning of a clause (=part of a sentence) □ *People that know her*

well say she is very ambitious. □ *We are working with organizations that provide emergency aid.*
3 used after a superlative adjective for explaining more about the adjective □ *These clothes were the best that we could find.*
4 used after words to do with amounts of things, actions or people, for example 'nothing', 'anybody' and 'all' □ *We did everything that we could to help her.* □ *There was nothing that we could give him.*
▶ DETERMINER [plural **those**] used to talk about a person or thing that you have already talked about □ *Who is that girl over there?* □ *Pass me that towel, please.* □ *I left that job a year ago.*
▶ PRONOUN [plural **those**]
1 used to talk about something that you can see or that you have already talked about □ *I don't want to know that.* □ *Who is that at the door?*
2 that's it (a) used to say that someone has done something correctly □ *Put the wire through the loop - that's it.* (b) used to show that you are angry and will not continue with something □ *That's it! You can cook your own meals from now on!*
3 that's that used to say that something has happened or been decided and the situation cannot be changed □ *The taxi's broken down? Oh, well that's that then - we'll never catch our flight.* □ *He just walked out and that was that - we never saw him again.*
▶ ADVERB /ðæt/ to the amount or degree mentioned □ *I didn't think I'd run that far.* □ *The film wasn't that bad.*

- **thatched** /θætʃt/ ADJECTIVE having a roof that is made from straw (=dried stems of crops) or reeds (=a type of tall grass that grows in water) □ *a thatched cottage*

- **that'd** /ˈðætəd/ a short way to say and write that had or that would □ *That'd never happened before.* □ *That'd be nice.*

- **that'll** /ˈðætəl/ a short way to say and write that will □ *That'll be too big for you.*

- **that's** /ˈðæts/ a short way to say and write that is □ *That's not what I meant.*

- **thaw** /θɔː/ ▶ VERB [thaws, thawing, thawed]
  1 if something that is frozen thaws, it melts □ *The ice has thawed.*
  2 to become more friendly □ *Relations between the two men have thawed recently.*
  ▶ NOUN, NO PLURAL
  1 a period when the weather becomes warmer and ice melts
  2 when people who have had a bad relationship start to be more friendly

- **the** /ðə/ DETERMINER
  1 used before a noun to refer to a particular person or thing that has been mentioned or is known about □ *The bus arrived late, as usual.* □ *I opened the letter and read it.* □ *The men rode on horses and the women rode in carriages.*

2 used before a noun when there is only one of that thing □ *The moon was shining.* □ *Balloons floated up into the air.*
3 used to refer to part of a thing □ *Hold the box at the bottom.* □ *Come to the back of the building.*
4 used in dates □ *the third of June* □ *July the fourth*
5 used before nouns referring to actions, especially ones followed by 'of' □ *the introduction of new rules* □ *the abolition of slavery*

theater /ˈθɪətə(r)/ NOUN [*plural* **theaters**] the US spelling of theatre

theatre /ˈθɪətə(r)/ NOUN [*plural* **theatres**]
1 a building where plays are performed 🕮 *We went to the theatre last night.*
2 *no plural* the work of writing or performing plays □ *I've always wanted to work in theatre.* 🕮 *The Australian theatre company 'Back to Back' toured Europe with its production 'Small Metal Objects'.*
3 a room where operations are done in a hospital □ *He was in theatre for three hours.*
4 the US word for cinema
• **theatrical** /θɪˈætrɪkəl/ ADJECTIVE
1 to do with plays or acting □ *theatrical performances*
2 doing or saying things in an obvious and emotional way because you want people to notice you □ *She spread her arms in a theatrical gesture.*

thee /ðiː/ PRONOUN an old-fashioned word for you

theft /θeft/ NOUN [*plural* **thefts**] the crime of stealing something 🕮 *car thefts* □ **+ of** *The theft of a laptop from a government employee has raised concerns about security.* □ *She was jailed for theft.*

their /ðeə(r)/ DETERMINER belonging to or to do with them □ *Do you know their address?*
• **theirs** /ðeəz/ PRONOUN used to talk or write about things belonging to or to do with a group of people or things that have already been mentioned □ *They say it belongs to them, but I know it's not theirs.*

them /ðem/ PRONOUN
1 used for talking about two or more people or things that you have already mentioned □ *The girls waved to me and I waved back to them.* □ *'Do you like strawberries?' 'Yes, I love them.'*
2 used to avoid saying 'him' or 'her' □ *If anyone asks where I am, can you tell them I've gone to the dentist's.*

theme /θiːm/ NOUN [*plural* **themes**]
1 the main idea or subject in a book, film, discussion, etc. 🕮 *The country's history is the central theme of the book.*
2 theme song/tune/music the music that is played at the start and end of a television programme
theme park /ˈθiːm ˌpɑːk/ NOUN [*plural* **theme parks**] a place where you go for fun, where the entertainments and machines you ride on are based on one subject □ *Disney theme parks*

themselves /ðəmˈselvz/ PRONOUN
1 the reflexive form of they □ *They'd made themselves a cosy little shelter.*
2 used to show that two or more people do something without any help from other people □ *They'll have to work it out themselves.* 🕮 *They built the shelter all by themselves.*
3 used to emphasize the pronoun they □ *They themselves are innocent.*
4 by themselves not with or near other people □ *They sat by themselves and didn't talk to anyone else.*
5 to themselves without having to share with anyone else □ *They had the hall to themselves for the morning.*

then /ðen/ ▶ ADVERB
1 at that time, in the past or future □ *I didn't know yo* then. 🕮 *The rest of the kids should be here by then.* 🕮 *They can deliver the car by March, but we really need it before then.* 🕮 *Max and I met up in June, but haven't seen him since then.*
2 after that time or next □ *I went for a swim, and the I went home.* □ *Mix in the flour and then the fruit.*
3 because of that □ *If you can't be quiet, then you have to leave the room.* □ *'This carpet will last longe 'I think we'll have that then.'*
▶ ADJECTIVE at that time, but not now □ *I went the with my then boyfriend.*

theology /θɪˈɒlədʒɪ/ NOUN, NO PLURAL the study o God and religion

theorem /ˈθɪərəm/ NOUN [*plural* **theorems**] a rule maths that can be proved to be true. A maths wor

theoretical /ˌθɪəˈretɪkəl/ ADJECTIVE
1 based on ideas and not on practical situations □ *theoretical physics*
2 possible but not certain □ *The drug is not given pregnant women because of a theoretical risk to th unborn baby.*
• **theoretically** /ˌθɪəˈretɪklɪ/ ADVERB possibly but yet done or proved 🕮 *It is theoretically possible to the disease in its course.*

theory /ˈθɪərɪ/ NOUN [*plural* **theories**]
1 an idea which tries to explain why something happens □ **+ about** *There are many theories abo why children are getting fatter.* □ **+ of** *Newton's theory of gravity*
2 in theory used for saying what should be true may not be true □ *In theory you can get there in hours but there's often a lot of traffic.*
3 *no plural* the ideas and principles of an art or scie □ *economic theory*

therapeutic /ˌθerəˈpjuːtɪk/ ADJECTIVE
1 making you feel more relaxed and happy □ *I'v always found yoga very therapeutic.*
2 used for treating illnesses □ *therapeutic drugs*
therapist /ˈθerəpɪst/ NOUN [*plural* **therapists**] someone who treats physical or mental problem without drugs □ *a speech therapist*

therapy /ˈθerəpɪ/ NOUN [plural **therapies**]
1 the treatment of medical problems □ *There are many effective therapies for treating depression.*
2 in therapy having treatment for a mental or emotional problem

there /ðeə(r)/ ► PRONOUN used to start a statement about something that exists or happens □ *There is a mouse somewhere in this house.* □ *There's too much noise.* □ *There is plenty of milk in the fridge.* □ *I thought there would be more time for discussion.*
► ADVERB
1 at, in or to a place □ *I know someone who lives there.* □ *I'm going there tomorrow.* □ *When I got to work, Clive was already there.*
2 used to show someone something you are pointing to or want them to look at □ *You can leave your coats here.* □ *There's Dad.*
3 at a particular point in a process □ *Don't stop there. I was just beginning to enjoy the story.* □ *We've all worked hard - shall we leave it there for today?*
4 there and then immediately □ *I decided there and then that I wanted to be a doctor.*

thereabouts /ˈðeərəbaʊts/ ADVERB approximately □ *It will cost £50 or thereabouts.*

thereafter /ˌðeərˈɑːftə(r)/ ADVERB a formal word meaning after a particular time □ *The cost is £40 for the first session and £30 thereafter.*

thereby /ˌðeəˈbaɪ/ ADVERB in this way □ *Exercise lowers blood pressure thereby reducing the need for medication.*

therefore /ˈðeəfɔː(r)/ ADVERB because of that □ *She had been awake all that night and therefore was very tired the next day.*

thermal /ˈθɜːməl/ ADJECTIVE
1 using heat, or to do with heat. A physics word □ *thermal energy*
2 thermal clothes are made from a special cloth which keeps you warm

thermo- /ˈθɜːməʊ/ PREFIX used at the start of words to mean 'to do with or using heat' □ *thermometer*

thermometer /θəˈmɒmɪtə(r)/ NOUN [plural **thermometers**] an instrument for measuring the temperature of something or someone □ *The nurse used a thermometer to take his temperature.*

thermos /ˈθɜːmɒs/ NOUN [plural **Thermoses**] a container that keeps drinks hot or cold. A trademark. □ *Thermos flask*

thermostat /ˈθɜːməʊstæt/ NOUN [plural **thermostats**] a device that keeps a room or a machine at a particular temperature

thesaurus /θɪˈsɔːrəs/ NOUN [plural **thesauri** or **thesauruses**] a book that lists groups of words that have similar meanings

these /ðiːz/ ► DETERMINER used to talk about people or things that you have already talked about, or things you can see, usually near you □ *These cups are dirty.* □ *These athletes train very hard.* □ *These problems could have been avoided.*
► PRONOUN used to talk about things that you have already talked about, or that you can see, usually near you □ *I can't eat these.* □ *Are these yours?*

thesis /ˈθiːsɪs/ NOUN [plural **theses**] a long piece of writing that you do as part of an advanced university course □ *She wrote a thesis on the poetry of John Donne.*

they /ðeɪ/ PRONOUN
1 used to talk or write about two or more people or things that have already been mentioned □ *Apes are not monkeys. They don't have tails.* □ *What did they think of your idea?*
2 people in general, or people in authority □ *They say it's going to be a hot summer.* □ *They've raised taxes again.*

they'd /ðeɪd/ a short way to say and write they had or they would □ *They'd all had their lunch.* □ *They'd like to come with us.*

they'll /ðeɪl/ a short way to say and write they will or they shall □ *They'll be here tomorrow.*

they're /ðeə(r)/ a short way to say and write they are □ *They're going to the park after school.*

they've /ðeɪv/ a short way to say and write they have □ *They've never been skating before.*

thick /θɪk/ ► ADJECTIVE [**thicker, thickest**]
1 wide between the opposite sides or surfaces □ *Make sure you wear a thick coat.* □ *There was a thick layer of snow on the ground.*
2 having a particular width between sides or surfaces □ *The ice was two feet thick.*
3 made up of many parts that are very close together □ *thick hair*
4 a thick liquid does not flow easily □ *thick gravy*
5 thick smoke, fog, etc. fills the air and is difficult to see through
6 an informal word meaning stupid
► NOUN, NO PLURAL
1 in the thick of something to be involved in the most busy or important part of a situation or activity □ *They were in the thick of the battle.*
2 through thick and thin in all situations, even very difficult ones □ *We've stuck together through thick and thin.*
• **thicken** /ˈθɪkən/ VERB [**thickens, thickening, thickened**] to become thick or thicker or to make something thick or thicker □ *I used flour to thicken the sauce.*
• **thickly** /ˈθɪklɪ/ ADVERB in a thick layer or into thick pieces □ *thickly sliced bread*
• **thickness** /ˈθɪknɪs/ NOUN, NO PLURAL how thick something is □ *The thickness of the walls means that heat stays in the building.*

thickset /ˌθɪkˈset/ ADJECTIVE having a wide, heavy body □ *a thickset man*

thick-skinned /ˈθɪkˈskɪnd/ ADJECTIVE not easily upset if someone criticizes or insults you □ *Mary's very thick-skinned.*

thief /θiːf/ NOUN [plural **thieves**] someone who steals things ⊞ *car thieves* ⊞ *Thieves stole her handbag.*

thigh /θaɪ/ NOUN [plural **thighs**] the top part of your leg above your knee

thimble /ˈθɪmbəl/ NOUN [plural **thimbles**] a small, hard cover you put on your finger to protect it when you are sewing

thin /θɪn/ ► ADJECTIVE [**thinner**, **thinnest**]
1 not wide from one side to the other □ *He spread a thin layer of jam on the cake.* □ *Cut the potato into thin slices.*
2 a thin person or animal does not have much fat on their body ⊞ *She is painfully thin.*
3 a thin liquid flows very easily □ *They were given a bowl of thin soup.*
4 if you have thin hair, the hairs are not close together
5 thin air does not contain much oxygen
6 disappear/vanish into thin air to disappear suddenly and completely □ *He's just vanished into thin air - no one knows where he is.*
➡ go to **wear** thin
► VERB [**thins**, **thinning**, **thinned**]
1 to make a substance thin or thinner, for example by adding water or liquid to it
2 if your hair is thinning, you gradually have less of it
♦ PHRASAL VERB **thin something out** if a group of people or things thins out, or if someone thins them out, some of them are removed

thing /θɪŋ/ NOUN [plural **things**]
1 used to refer to an object without using its name □ *I bought a few things for the party when I was in town.* □ *Where's the thing for opening bottles?*
2 an action or event □ *I hope I haven't done the wrong thing.* □ *The same thing happened to me once.* ⊞ *It was a good thing Pia arrived.*
3 a fact, belief or idea □ *She said lots of nice things about you.* □ *He asked me a few things about my work.*
4 things a situation □ *Things improved when the new manager started.* □ *Things are a bit difficult for me at the moment.*
5 your things the objects that belong to you □ *He packed up his things and left.*
6 no such thing used to say that something does not exist □ *There's no such thing as ghosts.*
7 used to refer to a person or animal after an adjective that shows how you feel about them □ *You poor thing - you must be exhausted.* □ *I'm not having that filthy thing in the house!*
8 first/last thing at the beginning/end of the day □ *I always go for a run first thing in the morning.* □ *I lock all the doors last thing.*

think /θɪŋk/ VERB [**thinks**, **thinking**, **thought**]
1 to have an opinion about someone or something □ *I think there's too much salt in this soup.* □ **+ that**

I think that you should ask him to leave. □ **+ about** *What do you think about the death penalty?* □ **+ of** *What do you think of his new girlfriend?*
2 to believe that something is true, although you are not certain □ *I think Anna will be here soon.* □ **+ that** *We thought that there would be more people there.* ⊞ *'Do the trains run on Sunday?' 'I think so.'*
3 to consider something, especially in order to understand it or to decide what to do □ **+ about** *You need to think very carefully about which subjects to choose.* □ **+ of** *We need to think of a way to raise money.*
4 to remember someone or something □ **+ about** *was just thinking about the time we went to New York* □ **+ of** *I often think of my mother.*
5 to express words to yourself in your mind □ *I just remember thinking, 'I must stay calm'.*
6 if you are thinking of doing something, you are considering doing it □ **+ of** *I'm thinking of starting my own business.* □ **+ about** *They're thinking about sending their son to boarding school.*
7 not think much of someone/something to have a low opinion of someone or something □ *I don't think much of my new manager.*
8 think nothing of something to do something that other people would find difficult or strange in easy and natural way □ *He thinks nothing of cycling 50km to work every day.*
♦ IDIOM **think twice** to consider something carefully, often deciding not to do something you had intended to do □ *People would think twice about weekend breaks if air travel was more expensive.*
♦ PHRASAL VERBS **think ahead** to prepare for a possible situation in the future □ *You need to think ahead how many people will still want this kind of service 10 years time?* **think back** to remember something from the past □ *If you think back to when we were children, we were just as bad.* **think something** to consider all the parts of something carefully □ *I thought it all out - the timing, the finances, everything.* **think something over** to consider something before you make a decision □ *They offered him the job, but he's asked for a few days to think it over.* **think something through** to think about all the possible results of something □ *I didn't think it through properly and there were all sorts of problems with transport.* **think something up** to invent something such as an idea or a plan □ *We tried to think up a way to get her to come to London.*
● **thinking** /ˈθɪŋkɪŋ/ NOUN, NO PLURAL
1 when you think □ *You must do some serious thinking before you decide on a career.*
2 your opinion or thoughts about a particular subject □ *What's your thinking on this?* ⊞ *This whole plan is my way of thinking, a serious mistake.*
► ADJECTIVE intelligent and interested in serious subjects □ *a magazine for the thinking woman*

thinly /ˈθɪnlɪ/ ADVERB in a thin piece or layer □ *the onions thinly.*

third /θɜːd/ ► NUMBER 3ʳᵈ written as a word □ *That's the third time he's called today.* □ *She came third in an art competition.*
► NOUN [*plural* **thirds**] 1/3; one of three equal parts of something □ *The bottle holds a third of a litre.*

third party /ˈθɜːd ˈpɑːtɪ/ NOUN [*plural* **third parties**] someone who is not one of the two main people or organizations involved in something □ *There is a third party who saw the fight and can act as witness.*

third-party /ˈθɜːdˈpɑːtɪ/ ADJECTIVE third-party insurance protects you if you damage something belonging to someone else or injure another person

third person /ˈθɜːd ˈpɜːsən/ NOUN, NO PLURAL in grammar, the form of words used when you talk or write about someone who is not you and not the person you are talking or writing to □ *'He' is a third person pronoun.* 🕮 *The story is written in the third person.*

third-rate /ˈθɜːdˈreɪt/ ADJECTIVE of a very bad quality or standard □ *a third-rate spy film*

third World /ˈθɜːd ˈwɜːld/ ► NOUN, NO PLURAL the Third World a slightly old-fashioned name for the countries of the world that are the poorest and least developed □ *The work aims to improve health in the Third World.*
ADJECTIVE to do with the countries of the Third World □ *a Third World country*

thirst /θɜːst/ NOUN, NO PLURAL
1 the feeling that you need something to drink 🕮 *He used to quench his thirst (=have a drink) at a café.*
2 a thirst for something a feeling of wanting something very much □ *She has a thirst for knowledge.*

thirsty /ˈθɜːstɪ/ ADJECTIVE [**thirstier, thirstiest**] feeling that you need something to drink □ *They were tired, hungry and thirsty.* 🕮 *I felt incredibly thirsty.*

thirteen /ˌθɜːˈtiːn/ NUMBER the number 13

thirteenth /ˌθɜːˈtiːnθ/ NUMBER 13ᵗʰ written as a word
thirtieth /ˈθɜːtɪəθ/ NUMBER 30ᵗʰ written as a word
thirty /ˈθɜːtɪ/ NUMBER [*plural* **thirties**] the number 30
the thirties the years between 1930 and 1939

this /ðɪs/ ► DETERMINER [*plural* **these**]
1 used to talk about a person or thing that you have already talked about, or something that you can see, usually near you □ *This apple is sour.* □ *I've lived in this country for five years.* □ *This argument went on for weeks.*
2 used to refer to a present period of time, or the one that comes next □ *I went shopping this morning.* □ *I'll be seeing her this weekend.*
► PRONOUN
1 used to talk about something that you have already talked about, or that you can see, usually near you □ *I can't eat this.* □ *Where are you going after this?* □ *This is my bedroom.*

2 used to say who you are on the telephone □ *Hello, this is Ollie.*
3 this and that several different, usually not very important, things □ *'What have you been doing today?' 'Oh, this and that.'*
► ADVERB to the amount or degree mentioned □ *It wasn't this hot yesterday.* □ *I didn't know we'd used this much fuel already.*

thistle /ˈθɪsəl/ NOUN [*plural* **thistles**] a plant with sharp leaves and large purple flowers

thorax /ˈθɔːræks/ NOUN [*plural* **thoraxes** *or* **thoraces**]
1 the part of your body between the head and the waist. A biology word.
2 the middle part of an insect's body, where the wings are joined. A biology word.

thorn /θɔːn/ NOUN [*plural* **thorns**] a sharp point on the stems of some plants
✦ IDIOM a thorn in someone's side a problem or something annoying for someone that continues for a long time □ *The media were a thorn in his side.*
● **thorny** /ˈθɔːnɪ/ ADJECTIVE [**thornier, thorniest**]
1 covered with thorns □ *a thorny bush*
2 a thorny problem or question is difficult to deal with 🕮 *the thorny issue of illegal immigration*

thorough /ˈθʌrə/ ADJECTIVE
1 done carefully, paying attention to every detail □ *He made a thorough search.* 🕮 *We are conducting a thorough investigation into this incident.*
2 used to emphasize how bad or annoying something is □ *It was a thorough nuisance.*

thoroughbred /ˈθʌrəbred/ NOUN [*plural* **thoroughbreds**] a horse that has parents of the same high quality breed (=type), usually used for racing

thoroughfare /ˈθʌrəfeə(r)/ NOUN [*plural* **thoroughfares**] a public road, especially the main road through a town

thoroughly /ˈθʌrəlɪ/ ADVERB
1 with great care and attention to every detail □ *Clean all the kitchen surfaces thoroughly.* □ *The book has been thoroughly researched.*
2 completely 🕮 *We thoroughly enjoyed ourselves.* □ *She was feeling thoroughly fed up.* □ *They thoroughly deserve this victory.*

those /ðəʊz/ ► DETERMINER used to talk about several people or things already mentioned or that you can see, usually not near you □ *Who are those two boys?* □ *In those days, people didn't have cars.*
► PRONOUN used to talk about several things already mentioned or that you can see, usually not near you □ *What are those?* □ *Those are just some of the problems we face.*

thou /ðaʊ/ PRONOUN an old-fashioned word for you

though /ðəʊ/ ► ADVERB used to show that what you have just said is surprising or different from what you said before □ *It's a pity we didn't win. It was an exciting match, though.*
► CONJUNCTION

1 but □ *We only waited for half an hour, though it seemed like hours.* □ *He will continue his political work, though not necessarily with the same party.*
2 despite the fact that □ *He went out, though I told him not to.*

thought /θɔːt/ ▶ NOUN [*plural* **thoughts**]
1 an idea, opinion, word or image that you have in your mind □ **+ on** *Do you have any thoughts on the problem of transport?* □ **+ about** *I had a sudden thought about the garden.* □ **+ of** *I can't bear the thought of leaving you all.*
2 no plural the activity of thinking □ *This issue needs some careful thought.*
▶ PAST TENSE AND PAST PARTICIPLE OF **think**
• **thoughtful** /ˈθɔːtfʊl/ ADJECTIVE
1 a thoughtful person is kind and thinks of other people □ *It was very thoughtful of you to phone.*
2 if someone looks thoughtful, they look as if they are thinking
• **thoughtfully** /ˈθɔːtfʊli/ ADVERB in a thoughtful way □ *She stared thoughtfully at the letter.* □ *She'd very thoughtfully left drinks and sandwiches on the kitchen table for us.*
• **thoughtless** /ˈθɔːtləs/ ADJECTIVE a thoughtless person does things without thinking about how other people will be affected by their actions

thousand /ˈθaʊzənd/ NUMBER [*plural* **thousands**]
1 the number 1,000
2 thousands a large number. An informal word □ **+ of** *I've climbed that tree thousands of times.*

thousandth /ˈθaʊzəntθ/ ▶ NUMBER 1,000ᵗʰ written as a word
▶ NOUN [*plural* **thousandths**] 1/1,000; one of a thousand equal parts of something

thrash /θræʃ/ VERB [**thrashes, thrashing, thrashed**]
1 an informal word meaning to beat someone very easily in a game □ *His Croatia side thrashed Iceland 4-0.*
2 to make uncontrolled, violent movements □ *The fish thrashed around in the shallow water.*
3 to hit someone or something very hard, often repeatedly
◆ PHRASAL VERB **thrash something out** to continue discussing something until you reach an agreement □ *They've been in talks to thrash out a deal.*

thread /θred/ ▶ NOUN [*plural* **threads**]
1 a long, thin piece of cotton, wool, etc. used for sewing □ *fine silken threads* □ *His name was embroidered in red thread.*
2 the main idea that joins the parts of a story, a discussion, etc. ⊞ *A common thread runs though all of her work.*
3 a series of messages on a website about a particular subject
◆ IDIOM **lose the thread** to stop understanding what someone is saying, usually because you are not concentrating enough

▶ VERB [**threads, threading, threaded**]
1 to push something long and thin through a hole □ *He threaded a piece of wire through a hole in the top.*
2 to push a piece of thread through the hole in the to of a needle
3 to put objects with a hole in them onto a thread, wire, etc. □ *They were threading beads onto a string*
4 to move carefully through or between people or things ⊞ *He threaded his way through the crowd.*

threadbare /ˈθredbeə(r)/ ADJECTIVE a threadbare carpet or piece of cloth is thin because it has been use a lot

threat /θret/ NOUN [*plural* **threats**]
1 a warning that someone might hurt you or harm you, especially if you do not do what they say ⊞ *S has received death threats.* □ **+ against** *Militia leade have issued threats against the president.* □ **+ of** *H has a reputation for using threats of violence.*
2 something that might cause harm or problems ⊞ *The virus doesn't pose any threat to human heal.* □ **+ to** *These actions are a threat to international peace.*
3 the possibility that something bad might happe □ **+ of** *There's a threat of serious flooding.*
• **threaten** /ˈθretən/ VERB [**threatens, threatening threatened**]
1 to say that someone will be harmed or hurt, especially if they do not do something □ *His wife threatened with a knife.* □ **+ to do something** *Th kidnappers have threatened to kill the hostages.*
2 to be likely to cause harm or problems □ *Government cuts threaten the future of the serv*
3 to seem likely to happen □ *The situation threat to become a global crisis.*
• **threatening** /ˈθretənɪŋ/ ADJECTIVE likely to hurt or to cause harm □ *He became aggressive and threatening when the police arrived.* □ *She's bee receiving threatening phone calls.*
• **threateningly** /ˈθretənɪŋli/ ADVERB in a threatening way □ *He moved threateningly towa her.*

three /θriː/ NUMBER [*plural* **threes**] the numbe

three-dimensional /ˈθriːdɪˈmenʃənəl/ ADJECTIV three-dimensional shape is solid and has length, v and height that you can measure □ *a three-dimensional model of the building*

three-point turn /ˈθriːpɔɪnt ˈtɜːn/ NOUN [*plur* **three-point turns**] a movement to turn a car rou which you go forward, go back, and go forward

threshold /ˈθreʃhəʊld/ NOUN [*plural* **threshold**
1 a level at which something starts to happen □ *has been an increase in the threshold for tax.* □ *H a high pain threshold.*
2 on the threshold of something to be just to start something new □ *We're on the threshc incredible advances in technology.*

3 the floor at a door going into a building or a room □ *He crossed the threshold of his new home.*

threw /θru:/ PAST TENSE OF throw

thrift /θrɪft/ NOUN, NO PLURAL the quality of being careful about spending money

thrifty /ˈθrɪftɪ/ ADJECTIVE [thriftier, thriftiest] using money and other things carefully, without wasting any

thrill /θrɪl/ ► VERB [thrills, thrilling, thrilled] to make someone feel excited and very pleased □ *He thrilled the crowd with some dramatic shots.*

► NOUN [plural thrills] a feeling of excitement and pleasure, or the thing that gives you that feeling □ *She felt a thrill of excitement.* □ *Getting this job was a real thrill.*

thrilled /θrɪld/ ADJECTIVE excited and very pleased about something □ *We're absolutely thrilled about the news.* □ *She's thrilled with the result.*

thriller /ˈθrɪlə(r)/ NOUN [plural thrillers] a book, film or play with an exciting story, full of danger and frightening events ⛶ *He stars in a new crime thriller set in New York.*

thrilling /ˈθrɪlɪŋ/ ADJECTIVE very exciting □ *They played a thrilling match in the final round.*

thrive /θraɪv/ VERB [thrives, thriving, thrived] to grow strong and healthy, or to become successful □ *The business is thriving.* □ *These guys thrive on competition.*

thriving /ˈθraɪvɪŋ/ ADJECTIVE healthy or successful □ *The area has a thriving tourism industry.*

throat /θrəʊt/ NOUN [plural throats]

1 the top part of the tube that goes from your mouth down to your stomach □ *My throat felt dry and I couldn't speak.* □ *He got a piece of food stuck in his throat.* ⛶ *I had a headache and a sore throat.* ⛶ *The teacher cleared her throat.*

2 the front part of your neck □ *He put his hands round her throat.*

throb /θrɒb/ ► VERB [throbs, throbbing, throbbed]

1 to make a low sound with a strong rhythm □ *Music throbbed from passing cars.*

2 if part of your body throbs, you feel a strong, regular pain □ *My head was throbbing.*

3 if your heart throbs, it beats fast and hard

► NOUN [plural throbs] when something throbs □ *the throb of motorcycle engines*

throes /θrəʊz/ PLURAL NOUN in the throes of something involved in a difficult or painful situation □ *He was in the throes of a divorce.*

thrombosis /θrɒmˈbəʊsɪs/ NOUN [plural thromboses] a lump of blood that blocks the flow of blood in someone's body, often causing serious illness

throne /θrəʊn/ NOUN [plural thrones]

1 a special chair that a king or queen sits on

2 the throne the position of being a king or queen □ *The prince's daughter cannot take the throne.*

throng /θrɒŋ/ ► NOUN [plural throngs] a large crowd of people □ *She faced a throng of reporters as she came out.*

► VERB [throngs, thronging, thronged] to move around in a large crowd □ *Cheering supporters thronged the streets.*

throttle /ˈθrɒtəl/ ► NOUN [plural throttles] the part of an engine that controls fuel going into the engine

► VERB [throttles, throttling, throttled] to hold someone tightly round their neck so they cannot breath

through /θru:/ ► PREPOSITION

1 from one end or side of something to the other □ *He walked through the door.* □ *The pole fits through this hole.* □ *We walked through the woods.*

2 because of something or using something □ *He lost his home through no fault of his own.* □ *He contacted people through his website.*

3 for the whole of a period of time or activity □ *We drove through the night.* □ *We left half way through the film.* □ *She has lived through some terrible events.*

4 if information comes through someone, they tell you about it □ *I heard about the club through a friend.*

5 a US word meaning from one time to another time □ *He's staying with us Monday through Friday.*

► ADVERB

1 from one end or side of something to the other □ *He opened the hatch and stuck his head through.* □ *There are yellow stains on the ceiling where the water came through.*

2 connected by telephone ⛶ *Can you put me through to the manager, please?* ⛶ *I tried to ring Molly, but I couldn't get through.*

3 talk/think something through to talk/think carefully about something in order to decide what to do

4 soaked/wet through very wet

► ADJECTIVE

1 a through train does not stop at stations between the place it starts and the place it is going to

2 be through with something an informal phrase meaning to have finished doing or using something □ *Are you through with the paper yet?*

throughout /θru:ˈaʊt/ ► PREPOSITION

1 during a whole period of time □ *It rained throughout June and July.* □ *There will be regular news bulletins throughout the day.*

2 in every part of something □ *They have stores throughout the country.*

► ADVERB

1 during a whole period of time □ *The show was quite long, but the children behaved themselves throughout.*

2 in every part of something □ *It is a spacious apartment, with storage space throughout.*

throw /θrəʊ/ ► VERB [throws, throwing, threw, thrown]

1 to make something move through the air by pushing it with your hand □ *He threw the ball to me.* □ *They were throwing stones into the water.*

2 to put something somewhere very quickly and without care □ *She threw her bag down and rushed to* switch on the TV. □ *I threw a few clothes into a case and set off.*

3 to move your body or part of your body into a position quickly and with force □ *She threw herself to the floor.* □ *He threw his arms around me.*

4 to make someone confused □ *The new road signs really threw me.*

5 if someone is thrown into prison, they are put there in a rough way

6 to put someone in a bad state □ *We were thrown into confusion by his early arrival.*

➜ go to throw *light* on something, throw your *weight* around, throw your *weight* behind someone/something

♦ PHRASAL VERBS **throw something away**
1 to get rid of something you do not want □ *I threw away the rest of the food.* **2** to waste something □ *She threw away her career to follow her boyfriend.* **throw something in** to give a customer something extra for the same price □ *If you buy two duvets, we'll throw in two pillows free.* **throw something out** to get rid of something you do not want □ *I've thrown out all my old college books.* **throw someone out** to force someone to leave a place □ *My parents threw me out when I was seventeen.* **throw (something) up** an informal word meaning to vomit **throw something up** to cause a particular result □ *The experiments threw up more questions than they answered.*

▶ NOUN [*plural* **throws**] an act of throwing something □ *That was a great throw!*

throwaway /ˈθrəʊəˌweɪ/ ADJECTIVE
1 intended to be thrown away after use □ *a throwaway lighter*
2 a throwaway remark or act is said or done without thinking carefully □ *It was just a stupid throwaway remark.*

thrush /θrʌʃ/ NOUN [*plural* **thrushes**] a wild bird with brown feathers and a front with spots

thrust /θrʌst/ ▶ VERB [**thrusts, thrusting, thrust**] to push something somewhere quickly and with force □ *He thrust his hands into his coat pockets.* □ *Someone thrust a microphone at him.*

♦ PHRASAL VERB **thrust something on/upon someone** to suddenly make someone deal with something □ *The responsibility had been thrust on him.*

▶ NOUN [*plural* **thrusts**]
1 a quick and forceful push forward □ *He died from a single knife thrust.*
2 the thrust of something the main idea in what someone says or writes □ *The main thrust of his argument was that the policy is unfair.*

thud /θʌd/ ▶ NOUN [*plural* **thuds**] a sound made by something heavy falling or hitting something □ *He landed with a loud thud.*

▶ VERB [**thuds, thudding, thudded**] to make a thud □ *Waves thudded against the shore.*

thug /θʌg/ NOUN [*plural* **thugs**] a violent man □ *a gang of thugs*

thumb /θʌm/ ▶ NOUN [*plural* **thumbs**] the short, thick finger that is on the side of your hand □ *He injured his right thumb.* □ *She held it carefully between her thumb and forefinger.*

♦ IDIOMS a rule of thumb a simple, general rule that you can follow to do something ⊞ *As a rule of thumb, use double the amount of flour to butter.* stick/stand out like a sore thumb to be very noticeable because of being different from the other people or things around □ *With her blonde hair, she stuck out like a sore thumb* the thumbs up when someone says that they like something ⊞ *The show got the thumbs up from critics* under someone's thumb completely controlled by someone else □ *He's entirely under her thumb.*

▶ VERB [**thumbs, thumbing, thumbed**] thumb a lift ride to stand by the road and hold your hand out to ask cars to stop and take you somewhere

♦ PHRASAL VERB **thumb through something** to read something, looking quickly through the pages □ *She sat thumbing through a glossy magazine.*

thump /θʌmp/ ▶ VERB [**thumps, thumping, thumped**]
1 to hit someone or something hard, usually with your hand □ *He thumped the table for emphasis.*
2 if your heart thumps, it beats very hard or quickly □ *My heart was thumping.*
3 to fall or hit something with a loud, heavy noise □ *Their feet thumped on the wooden floor.*

▶ NOUN [*plural* **thumps**]
1 a loud, heavy noise □ *It fell to the floor with a loud thump.*
2 when you hit someone or something hard □ *She gave him a thump on the nose.*

thunder /ˈθʌndə(r)/ ▶ NOUN, NO PLURAL
1 the loud, deep sound that you hear in a storm after a flash of lightning (=bright light in the sky) ⊞ *thunder and lightning* ⊞ *There was a loud clap of thunder.*
2 a loud sound like thunder □ *the thunder of horses' hooves*

▶ VERB [**thunders, thundering, thundered**]
1 if it is thundering, there is a storm with thunder
2 to make a loud sound like thunder □ *The children thundered up the stairs.*
3 to talk in a very loud, angry voice □ *'What are you doing?' thundered Morris.*

thunderbolt /ˈθʌndəbəʊlt/ NOUN [*plural* **thunderbolts**] a flash of lightning (=bright light in the sky) that is followed immediately by thunder

thunderclap /ˈθʌndəklæp/ NOUN [*plural* **thunderclaps**] a sudden loud noise made by thunder

thunderous /ˈθʌndərəs/ ADJECTIVE very loud, like thunder □ *thunderous applause*

thunderstorm /ˈθʌndəstɔːm/ NOUN [*plural* **thunderstorms**] a storm with thunder and lightning (=bright light in the sky) □ *Thunderstorms were forecast for the afternoon.* □ *We arrived in the middle of a thunderstorm.*

thundery /ˈθʌndərɪ/ ADJECTIVE if the weather is thundery, there is or is likely to be thunder □ *The forecast is for thundery showers.*

Thursday /ˈθɜːzdɪ/ NOUN [plural **Thursdays**] the day of the week after Wednesday and before Friday □ *My piano lessons are on Thursday.*

thus /ðʌs/ ADVERB
1 a formal word meaning as a result of that □ *The drug thins the blood, thus preventing clotting.*
2 a formal word meaning in this or that way □ *The poem begins thus: 'I must go down to the sea again.'*
3 thus far a formal phrase meaning until now □ *Thus far, the agreement seems to be working.*

thwart /θwɔːt/ VERB [thwarts, thwarting, thwarted] to prevent someone from doing what they want to do □ *Police thwarted a car bomb attack.*

thy /ðaɪ/ DETERMINER an old-fashioned word for your □ *Thy will be done.*

thyme /taɪm/ NOUN, NO PLURAL a herb using in cooking with lots of very small leaves and flowers

thyroid /ˈθaɪrɔɪd/ NOUN [plural **thyroids**] an organ in your neck that produces a substance which controls how your body grows and works. A biology word ⊞ *the thyroid gland*

tiara /tɪˈɑːrə/ NOUN [plural **tiaras**] a piece of jewellery like a small crown

tick /tɪk/ ▶ NOUN [plural **ticks**]
1 a small written mark (✓) used to show that something is correct or to show which things on a list have been dealt with ⊞ *He put a tick in the box marked 'No'.* □ *The girl put a tick next to her name.*
2 the regular noise that a clock makes □ + *of* I could hear the tick of the clock in the hall.
3 an informal word meaning a very short time □ *Can you wait a tick while I get my coat?*
4 a small insect that sucks the blood of animals
▶ VERB [ticks, ticking, ticked]
5 to write a tick ⊞ *You just tick the boxes.*
6 to make a regular noise like a clock □ *a ticking clock*
IDIOM **what makes someone tick** what causes someone to behave the way they do □ *I don't understand what makes her tick.*
PHRASAL VERBS **tick away/by/down** used to say that time is passing □ *Time was ticking away fast.* □ *The clock is ticking down to Monday's deadline.* **tick something off** to write a tick next to something to show it has been dealt with □ *She ticked off the names on the list.* **tick someone off** an informal phrase meaning to talk to someone angrily because they have done something wrong □ *He ticked off the boys for throwing stones.* **tick over 1** to continue or to work in a slow, regular way □ *The business is ticking over nicely.* **2** if an engine is ticking over, it is working slowly while the vehicle is stopped

ticket /ˈtɪkɪt/ NOUN [plural **tickets**]
1 a small piece of printed paper that shows you have paid to do something ⊞ *She bought an airline ticket to*
Paris. ⊞ *a single/return ticket* □ + *for* He's got free tickets for the match.
2 an official notice saying that you have done something wrong while driving □ *a parking ticket*
• **ticketing** /ˈtɪkɪtɪŋ/ NOUN, NO PLURAL producing and selling tickets

tickle /ˈtɪkəl/ ▶ VERB [tickles, tickling, tickled]
1 to touch someone's body lightly so that they laugh □ *She tickled him under the arms.*
2 if something tickles you, it causes an uncomfortable, light feeling on your skin □ *The grass tickled her nose.*
3 to make someone feel pleased or to make them laugh □ *She was tickled by the suggestion.*
▶ NOUN [plural **tickles**] when something or someone tickles you
• **ticklish** /ˈtɪklɪʃ/ ADJECTIVE if you are ticklish, you laugh when someone tickles you
• **tickly** /ˈtɪklɪ/ ADJECTIVE [ticklier, tickliest] causing a tickling feeling

tidal /ˈtaɪdəl/ ADJECTIVE to do with tides (=the rise and fall of the sea) □ *a tidal current*

tidal wave /ˈtaɪdəl weɪv/ NOUN [plural **tidal waves**]
1 a very large wave that sometimes comes up onto the land
2 a very large amount of something that arrives suddenly □ *There was a tidal wave of criticism.*

tiddlywinks /ˈtɪdlɪwɪŋks/ NOUN, NO PLURAL a game in which you press a small coloured disc down on another one making it jump upwards and fall into a cup

tide /taɪd/ NOUN [plural **tides**]
1 the regular rise and fall of the level of the sea ⊞ *At high tide, the rocks are completely covered.* ⊞ *You can walk out to the island at low tide.*
2 an increase in the number or amount of something □ *the rising tide of crime* ⊞ *We need measures to stem the tide* (=stop the increase) *of people leaving the country.*
3 the way that most people think or behave ⊞ *He's trying to turn the tide of public opinion.*
♦ PHRASAL VERB [tides, tiding, tided] **tide someone over** to help someone get through a difficult time, especially by providing money □ *She had just enough to tide her over until she could get another job.*

tidily /ˈtaɪdɪlɪ/ ADVERB in a tidy way □ *They stacked the boxes tidily.* □ *She tied her hair back tidily.*
tidiness /ˈtaɪdɪnɪs/ NOUN, NO PLURAL the quality of being tidy
tidings /ˈtaɪdɪŋz/ PLURAL NOUN an old-fashioned word for news □ *glad tidings*

tidy /ˈtaɪdɪ/ ▶ ADJECTIVE [tidier, tidiest]
1 carefully ordered or arranged with everything in its correct place □ *Everything looked tidy.* ⊞ *He keeps his room tidy.*
2 a tidy person likes to keep things ordered and in their correct place □ *She's the tidiest person I know.*

3 an informal word used to talk about a large amount of money 🔂 *She's saved a tidy sum.* 🔂 *The event will make a tidy profit.*

▶ VERB [**tidies, tidying, tidied**] to put things back in their correct places and to make something tidy □ *Anne was tidying the kitchen.* □ **+ up** *Are you going to tidy up the mess you've made?* □ **+ away** *He tidied away his tools.*

---

tie /taɪ/ ▶ VERB [**ties, tying, tied**]

1 to join or to fasten things together using string, rope, etc. □ **+ together** *We tied the boats together.* □ **+ with** *a gift box tied with white ribbon* □ **+ to** *The riders tied their horses to a tree.* □ *She tied her long hair in a ponytail.* □ *Their hands were tied behind their backs.*
2 to twist pieces of rope, string, etc. together to make a knot 🔂 *Tie a knot in the end of the thread.* □ *He bent down to tie his shoe lace.* □ **+ around** *She had a silk scarf tied around her neck.*
3 if two teams or players tie, they each have the same number of points □ **+ for** *They tied for second place.* 🔂 *He came back to tie the score at 3-3.*
4 if two things are tied, they are connected, often in a way that cannot be changed □ **+ with** *Researchers have tied ocean heating directly with global warming.* □ **+ into** *Customers will be tied into an 18-month contract.*

♦ IDIOM **tie the knot** an informal phrase meaning to get married □ *The couple plan to tie the knot next summer.*

♦ PHRASAL VERBS **tie someone down** to limit someone's freedom □ *You're tied down by rules and regulations.* **tie in with something 1** to fit well with something □ *Her visit will tie in nicely with our plans.* **2** to provide more proof of something □ *That ties in with what we've found.* **tie someone/ something up 1** to fasten someone or something with rope, etc. so that they cannot move □ *The boat's tied up in the harbour.* □ *The kidnappers tied them both up.* **2** to keep someone or something busy so that they cannot be used for other things □ *This kind of incident ties up police resources.*

▶ NOUN [*plural* **ties**]
1 a narrow piece of cloth worn round your neck under your shirt collar and tied in a knot 🔂 *I have to wear a suit and tie for work* □ *James loosened his tie.*
2 a connection between two people or things □ **+ between** *He spoke of the close ties between the two countries.* □ **+ with** *She severed all ties with her former coach.*
3 a situation in which two teams or players each have the same number of points □ **+ for** *There was a tie for third place.*

---

tie-break /ˈtaɪbreɪk/ *or* **tie-breaker** /ˈtaɪbreɪkə(r)/ NOUN [*plural* **tie-breaks** *or* **tie-breakers**] an extra question or test that will decide the winner in a competition where two people or teams have the same score

tier /tɪə(r)/ NOUN [*plural* **tiers**]
1 one of several rows or layers, one above the other □ *a wedding cake with three tiers* □ *We had seats in the upper tier of the stadium.*
2 one of several layers in a system or an organization □ *the top tier of English football*

tiff /tɪf/ NOUN [*plural* **tiffs**] an informal word for an argument, especially one between friends 🔂 *He'd had a tiff with his brother.*

tiger /ˈtaɪɡə(r)/ NOUN [*plural* **tigers**] a large wild animal related to the cat with yellow fur and black stripes

tight /taɪt/ ▶ ADJECTIVE [**tighter, tightest**]
1 fitting very closely and difficult to move □ *I was wearing very tight jeans.* □ *The top on this jar is very tight.*
2 very firm and strong □ *Have you got a tight grip on that rope?* □ *a tight knot*
3 if something such as material or string is tight, it has been pulled or stretched so that it is straight □ *The piece of wood was held in place by four tight wires.*
4 controlled in a firm way □ *There are tight regulations about the sale of food.* 🔂 *Security at the event was extremely tight.*
5 a tight bend is a part of a road that suddenly curves a lot and is difficult to drive round
6 if money, time or space is tight, you do not have much of it 🔂 *We were on a very tight budget.*

➡ go to **keep a tight rein on something**

▶ ADVERB
1 very firmly 🔂 *Hold on tight!* □ *Make sure the belt pulled tight.*
2 **sit tight** if someone sits tight, they do not move take any action □ *Just sit tight - Mr Jones will be here a moment.*

● **tighten** /ˈtaɪtən/ VERB [**tightens, tightening, tightened**]
1 to become firmer and stronger or to make something firmer and stronger □ *He tightened his g* on my arm. □ *I tightened up the screws.*
2 to make something more firmly controlled □ *Security was tightened before the parade.* □ *The club rules have been tightened up.*
3 to pull something so that it is straighter or fits m closely □ *Now you can tighten the rope.*

tight-fisted /ˌtaɪtˈfɪstɪd/ ADJECTIVE an informal w meaning not willing to spend or to share your mo

tightly /ˈtaɪtli/ ADVERB
1 in a firm and strong way □ *She held her purse tightly.* □ *I pulled the door tightly shut.*
2 in a firmly controlled way □ *Access to the stag door is tightly controlled.*
3 closely □ *He wore a tightly fitting shirt.*

tightness /ˈtaɪtnɪs/ NOUN, NO PLURAL the state o feeling or being tight □ *He felt some tightness ac his chest.*

tightrope /ˈtaɪtrəʊp/ NOUN [*plural* **tightropes**] a piece of rope stretched tightly between two plac which someone walks along

tights /taɪts/ PLURAL NOUN a piece of women's clothing covering the feet, legs and bottom made of very thin material 🔊 *a pair of tights*

tigress /'taɪgrɪs/ NOUN [plural **tigresses**] a female tiger

tile /taɪl/ ▶ NOUN [plural **tiles**] a piece of hard, flat material such as clay or stone, used for covering roofs, walls or floors □ *red roof tiles* □ *shiny ceramic floor tiles* ▶ VERB [**tiles, tiling, tiled**] to fix tiles on a surface
tiled /taɪld/ ADJECTIVE covered with tiles □ *a tiled floor*

till¹ /tɪl/ PREPOSITION, CONJUNCTION until □ *We'll probably stay here till the end.* □ *It doesn't get dark till 10 o'clock in the summer.*

till² /tɪl/ NOUN [plural **tills**] a machine in a shop for counting what customers need to pay and for putting money in □ *She works at a supermarket behind the till.*

tilt /tɪlt/ VERB [**tilts, tilting, tilted**] to move something so that one side is lower than the other, or to move like this □ *He tilted his head to one side.*

timber /'tɪmbə(r)/ NOUN [plural **timbers**]
wood that is used for building things such as houses, or a piece of this wood
trees that can be used to provide wood for building

timbre /'tæmbrə, 'tɪmbə(r)/ NOUN [plural **timbres**]
the quality of sound that something makes □ *The timbre of his voice changed.*

time /taɪm/ ▶ NOUN [plural **times**]
no plural the way we measure minutes, hours, days, etc. □ *I was hardly aware of time passing.*
a particular moment in a day □ *What's the time? What would be a convenient time to meet?* 🔊 *What time does the show start?* 🔊 *Excuse me, have you got the time* (=can you tell me what time it is)? 🔊 *Can you tell the time* (=be able to read a clock) *yet?*
no plural an amount of time 🔊 *Do you spend a lot of time in London?* 🔊 *Ironing sheets is a complete waste of time.* 🔊 *We spent a long time talking about the past.* 🔊 *It takes a lot of time to learn a language well.*
a particular occasion □ *Do you remember the time Michael fell in the river?* □ *I've been to Morocco several times.* 🔊 *Next time you see Billy, can you remind him he still has my camera?* 🔊 *The first time we met, I thought he was really rude.*
no plural if it is time to do something or for something to happen, it should be done or happen now □ *It's time the children were in bed.* □ *Is it time to plant the tomatoes yet?*
in time not too late □ *We got there just in time to see the queen.* □ *I hope the present arrives in time for her birthday.*
on time not early or late □ *The trains are usually on time.*
a long enough period 🔊 *We don't have time to contact everyone.* □ *We can play tennis if there's time*

an experience, or a period in someone's life 🔊 *Did you have a nice time in Brighton?* □ *I had a dreadful time when the children were young.*
10 all the time (a) continuously □ *We monitor our staff all the time.* (b) very often □ *I love Crete - we go there all the time.*
11 one/two/five, etc. at a time one/two/five etc. on a particular occasion □ *He leaped up the steps three at a time.* □ *One at a time, we went to the front of the class.*
12 in an hour's/day's/year's, etc. time after a particular period of time □ *The work should be complete in three weeks' time.*

▶ Note that you **have** a good/great, etc. time somewhere. You do not **'spend'** a good/great, etc. time somewhere:
✓ *We had a great time in Paris.*
✗ *We spent a great time in Paris.*

▶ VERB [**times, timing, timed**]
1 to arrange for something to happen at a particular time □ *The meeting was timed to coincide with his visit.*
2 to measure how long something takes □ *He timed me running a mile.*

time-consuming /'taɪm,kənsjuːmɪŋ/ ADJECTIVE taking a long time to do □ *Doing the washing by hand is very time-consuming.*

time-honored /'taɪm,ɒnəd/ ADJECTIVE the US spelling of time-honoured

time-honoured /'taɪm,ɒnəd/ ADJECTIVE a time-honoured tradition is one that has been followed for a long time and is respected 🔊 *They celebrated in time-honoured fashion with champagne.*

timeless /'taɪmlɪs/ ADJECTIVE not affected by time or changing fashions □ *His novels are timeless.*

time limit /'taɪm 'lɪmɪt/ NOUN [plural **time limits**] a fixed length of time during which something must be done and finished □ *a 30-day time limit* 🔊 *No time limit has been set for this project.*

timely /'taɪmlɪ/ ADJECTIVE happening or done at the right time 🔊 *This serves as a timely reminder of the importance of preparation.*

timer /'taɪmə(r)/ NOUN [plural **timers**] a device for measuring how long something takes □ *a kitchen timer*

times /taɪmz/ PREPOSITION used in mathematics between the numbers you are multiplying □ *Two times four is eight.*

time scale /'taɪm ,skeɪl/ NOUN [plural **time scales**] the period of time during which an event or process happens □ *Evolution happens over a time scale of many thousands of years.*

timetable /'taɪm,teɪbəl/ NOUN [plural **timetables**]
1 a list of the times when public vehicles such as trains or buses arrive or leave
2 a list of the lessons at a school, college, etc. and the times they happen 🔊 *We want to see more practical subjects on the school timetable.*

3 a plan for when you expect or hope that things will happen □ **+ for** *We have set out a clear timetable for reform.*

time zone /'taɪm ˌzəʊn/ NOUN [plural **time zones**] one of the areas that the world is divided into, each of which uses one standard time

timid /'tɪmɪd/ ADJECTIVE nervous, shy and easily frightened □ *a timid child* □ *a timid smile*

• **timidity** /tɪ'mɪdəti/ NOUN, NO PLURAL the quality of being timid

• **timidly** /'tɪmɪdli/ ADVERB in a timid way □ *Oliver raised his hand timidly.*

timing /'taɪmɪŋ/ NOUN, NO PLURAL
1 the ability to choose the right time to do or say something □ *All comedians need to learn good timing.* ⊞ *Perfect timing - we were just about to order.*
2 the time when something happens □ *What was surprising was the timing of the announcement.*

timpani /'tɪmpəni/ PLURAL NOUN large drums that are usually used in an orchestra (=large group of musicians playing together)

tin /tɪn/ NOUN [plural **tins**]
1 a closed metal container which food is sold in □ **+ of** *a tin of tuna* □ *He opened a tin of tomato soup.*
2 a metal container with a lid, which you store food or other things in □ **+ of** *a tin of biscuits* □ *a tin of paint*
3 no plural a soft, silver metal □ *the tin roof of the garage* □ *a tin bucket*

tinder /'tɪndə(r)/ NOUN, NO PLURAL small, dry pieces of wood that can be used to light a fire

tinfoil /'tɪnfɔɪl/ NOUN, NO PLURAL very thin sheets of metal used for covering food

tinge /tɪndʒ/ NOUN [plural **tinges**] a slight amount of something, especially a colour or a feeling □ *white with a tinge of pink* □ *There was a tinge of sadness in her voice.*

• **tinged** /tɪndʒd/ ADJECTIVE containing a slight amount of a colour, feeling, etc. □ *Her eyes were tinged with red where she had been crying.*

tingle /'tɪŋgəl/ ▶ VERB [tingles, tingling, tingled] to feel a sharp, slightly uncomfortable feeling, especially on your skin □ *My face was tingling in the cold night air.*
▶ NOUN [plural **tingles**] a slight uncomfortable or excited feeling □ *I felt a tingle of excitement as the curtain went up.*

tinker /'tɪŋkə(r)/ VERB [tinkers, tinkering, tinkered] to try to repair or to improve a machine by making small changes □ *Phil spends hours tinkering with his motorbike.*

tinkle /'tɪŋkəl/ ▶ VERB [tinkles, tinkling, tinkled] to make a sound like small bells ringing
▶ NOUN [plural **tinkles**] a small, repeated ringing sound

tinned /tɪnd/ ADJECTIVE tinned food is sold and kept in closed metal containers □ *tinned soup*

tinnitus /tɪ'naɪtəs/ NOUN, NO PLURAL a medical condition in which you have a continuous ringing sound in your ears

tinny /'tɪni/ ADJECTIVE [tinnier, tinniest]
1 a tinny sound is thin, hard and high
2 a tinny object is made of thin or bad quality metal

tin opener /'tɪn ˌəʊpənə(r)/ NOUN [plural **tin openers**] a small tool for opening metal containers of food

tinsel /'tɪnsəl/ NOUN, NO PLURAL long pieces of shiny material that are used as a decoration at Christmas

tint /tɪnt/ ▶ NOUN [plural **tints**] a small amount of colour □ *His skin had a yellowish tint.*
▶ VERB [tints, tinting, tinted] to add a small amount of colour to something

tiny /'taɪni/ ADJECTIVE [tinier, tiniest] extremely small □ *a baby's tiny hands and feet* ⊞ *a tiny amount of water*

tip /tɪp/ ▶ NOUN [plural **tips**]
1 the point at the end or the top of something □ *The used arrows with poison tips.* □ *Point to it with the t. of your finger.*
2 a small extra amount of money for someone who has done a job for you ⊞ *Did you leave a tip?*
3 a piece of helpful advice □ *He gave me some usef tips on laying floor tiles.*
4 a place where you can take things you want to g rid of □ *I'm going to take the old carpet to the tip.*
5 an informal word meaning a very untidy place □ *Your bedroom's a tip.*
♦ IDIOMS **the tip of the iceberg** a small part of something, especially a serious problem □ *We hav seen six cases of the disease at our clinic, and that's j the tip of the iceberg.* **on the tip of your tongue** word is on the tip of your tongue, you cannot remember it but you feel that you are almost able remember it
▶ VERB [tips, tipping, tipped]
1 to move something so that it is not flat or vertica to move in this way □ *Tip the chairs forward agai the tables.* □ *The vehicle tipped onto its side.*
2 to pour something from a container □ *They just the rubbish over the side of the ship.* □ *She tippe bucket of water on my head.*
3 to give a small extra amount of money to some who has done a job for you □ *She tipped the tax driver.*
♦ PHRASAL VERBS **tip someone off** to give someo warning or some information, often secretly, so t they can prepare for something □ *His friends tipp him off before the police arrived.* **tip (somethir over** to push something onto its side or to fall on side □ *She tipped her drink over.* **tip somethin** to move a container so that things come out of it ▪ easily

tiptoe /'tɪptəʊ/ ▶ VERB [tiptoes, tiptoeing, tipt to walk somewhere very quietly or carefully on y toes □ *She tiptoed along the corridor, trying not wake the other guests.*

▶ NOUN **on tiptoe** standing or walking balanced on your toes □ *I can just see the sea if I stand on tiptoe.*

tirade /taɪˈreɪd/ NOUN [*plural* **tirades**] a long angry speech that criticizes someone or something □ *She launched into a long tirade against the government.*

tire /ˈtaɪə(r)/ VERB [**tires, tiring, tired**] to start feeling that you need a rest □ *Grandma tires easily nowadays.*

PHRASAL VERBS **tire of something** to become bored with something □ *We were beginning to tire of Nigel's stories.* **tire someone out** to make someone feel tired □ *Let's go to the park and tire the children out a bit.*

tired /ˈtaɪəd/ ADJECTIVE

1 feeling that you need a rest □ *You must be tired after your journey.* ▣ *I was getting really tired.* ▣ *He felt too tired and ill to continue.*

2 bored and often annoyed □ + **of** *I'm tired of wearing the same clothes every day.* ▣ *I'm sick and tired of people asking me questions.*

tiredness /ˈtaɪədnɪs/ NOUN, NO PLURAL the state of being tired □ *Tiredness is the main symptom of this virus.*

tireless /ˈtaɪəlɪs/ ADJECTIVE having a lot of energy and always continuing with something □ *He was a tireless campaigner for social justice.* □ *We admired her tireless efforts to raise money for charity.*

tirelessly /ˈtaɪəlɪslɪ/ ADVERB in a tireless way □ *They worked tirelessly for the cause.*

tiresome /ˈtaɪəsəm/ ADJECTIVE annoying or boring □ *Mona has a tiresome habit of finishing my sentences for me.*

tiring /ˈtaɪərɪŋ/ ADJECTIVE making you feel tired □ *It was a long and tiring trip.*

Notice the different meanings of **tiresome** and **tiring**. Tiresome means 'annoying'. It does not mean 'making you tired'. For this meaning, use the word 'tiring':
✓ Travelling is fun but it's tiring.
✗ Travelling is fun but it's tiresome.

tissue /ˈtɪʃuː/ NOUN [*plural* **tissues**]

1 the substance that animals and plants are made of. biology word □ *muscle tissue* □ *plant tissue*

2 a thin, soft piece of paper for cleaning your nose, etc. □ *She took out a tissue to wipe her face.*

3 very thin paper used for wrapping objects □ *a sheet of white tissue* ▣ *The glasses were wrapped in tissue paper.*

tit /tɪt/ NOUN [*plural* **tits**] a type of small bird

titbit /ˈtɪtbɪt/ NOUN [*plural* **titbits**]

1 a small piece of food

2 a small but interesting piece of information □ *a titbit of gossip*

title /ˈtaɪtəl/ ▶ NOUN [*plural* **titles**]

1 the name of something such as a book, song or film □ + **of** *What's the title of your poem?* □ *How did you choose the book's title?*

2 the position of being the winner of a sports competition ▣ *She won her first grand slam title last year.* □ *He's hoping to defend his Olympic 100-metre title.*

3 a word that you can use before your name, for example Ms or Professor □ *Her title is 'Doctor', not 'Mrs'.*

▶ VERB [**titles, titling, titled**] to give something a title □ *My new book is titled 'Missing'.*

titter /ˈtɪtə(r)/ ▶ VERB [**titters, tittering, tittered**] to laugh in a silly, nervous or embarrassed way

▶ NOUN [*plural* **titters**] a silly, nervous laugh

to /tuː/

1 used before a verb to make the infinitive form □ *I want to leave now.* □ *I forgot to tell him.*

2 used as part of the infinitive to show the purpose of something □ *I went to get a drink.* □ *I phoned her to invite her to the party.*

▶ PREPOSITION

1 used to say where someone or something goes □ *We went to the shops.* □ *I go to work by bus.* □ *The cup fell to the floor.*

2 used to say who is given something, told something, etc. □ *Give the letter to Clara.* □ *I spoke to her several times.*

3 connected or fixed □ *The cake was stuck to the tin.* □ *We nailed the chairs to the floor.*

4 facing or going in a particular direction □ *He had his back to me.* □ *Keep to the side of the woods.* □ *He pointed to the sign.*

5 used to say how someone's actions affect someone or something □ *He was always kind to me.* □ *What have you done to my car?*

6 from ... to (a) used to show a period of time □ *We are open from 9 to 6.* (b) used to show a range of something □ *Everyone was there, from young to old.*

7 used for saying the time up to thirty minutes before an hour □ *It's ten to three.*

▶ ADVERB

1 almost closed □ *Would you pull the door to?*

2 to and fro backwards and forwards □ *He was rocking to and fro.*

toad /təʊd/ NOUN [*plural* **toads**] a small brown animal that jumps using its long back legs

toadstool /ˈtəʊdstuːl/ NOUN [*plural* **toadstools**] a type of fungus (=plant with no leaves or flowers) that is often poisonous

toast /təʊst/ ▶ NOUN [*plural* **toasts**]

1 bread that has been made hard and slightly brown by heating □ *I had toast and marmalade for breakfast.* ▣ *a piece of toast*

2 when people lift their glasses and drink together to express good wishes to someone ▣ *I'd like to propose a toast to the bride and groom.*

▶ VERB [**toasts, toasting, toasted**]

1 to cook bread under a heat □ *a toasted sandwich*

2 to drink a toast to someone □ *They were soon toasting their success.*

- **toaster** /'təʊstə(r)/ NOUN [*plural* **toasters**] a machine for making toast

tobacco /tə'bækəʊ/ NOUN, NO PLURAL the leaves of a plant that are dried and used for smoking □ *tobacco smoke* □ *the tobacco industry*

- **tobacconist** /tə'bækənɪst/ NOUN [*plural* **tobacconists**]
  1 someone whose job is selling tobacco products
  2 tobacconist's a shop that sells tobacco products and sometimes sweets and newspapers

toboggan /tə'bɒgən/ NOUN [*plural* **toboggans**] a simple vehicle without wheels that you sit on to slide across snow

today /tə'deɪ/ ▶ ADVERB
1 on this day □ *I can't come today.* ⌨ *I spoke to Alan earlier today.* ⌨ *My parents are coming over later today.*
2 at or around the present time □ *People are taller today than they were a hundred years ago.*
▶ NOUN, NO PLURAL this day □ *Today is Tuesday.* □ *Today's announcement comes as no surprise.*

toddle /'tɒdəl/ VERB [**toddles, toddling, toddled**]
1 if a young child toddles, it is learning to walk □ *She's just starting to toddle.*
2 an informal word meaning to walk somewhere □ *Then she toddled off to bed.*

- **toddler** /'tɒdlə(r)/ NOUN [*plural* **toddlers**] a young child who is learning to walk □ *The children range from toddlers to young teens.* □ *a mother and toddler group*

toe /təʊ/ NOUN [*plural* **toes**]
1 one of the five parts at the end of your foot □ *Reach up high, standing on your toes.* ⌨ *He injured his left big toe.* ⌨ *She stubbed* (=hit) *her toe on the end of the bed.*
2 the closed end of a shoe or sock □ *a hole in the toe of my sock*

toenail /'təʊneɪl/ NOUN [*plural* **toenails**] the hard part at the end of each toe

toffee /'tɒfɪ/ NOUN [*plural* **toffees**] a hard, sticky sweet made of boiled butter and sugar □ *a piece of toffee* □ *a bag of toffees*

tog /tɒg/ NOUN [*plural* **togs**] a measurement of how warm a duvet (=bed cover) is □ *a 10.5 tog duvet*

together /tə'geðə(r)/ ADVERB
1 with or near each other □ *We work together.* □ *They spent the evening together watching television.* ⌨ *The houses are quite close together.*
2 touching, joined or mixed with each other □ *Mix the sugar and eggs together in a bowl.* □ *She pressed her hands together.* □ *Add all the numbers together.*
3 at the same time □ *All these things happened together.*
4 together with as well as or including □ *Keep the fruit, together with its juice, in the refrigerator.*

toggle /'tɒgəl/ ▶ NOUN [*plural* **toggles**]
1 a key on a computer that allows you to move between any documents or programs that you are using. A computing word.
2 a piece of wood or plastic that passes through a hole to fasten a coat or jacket
▶ VERB [**toggles, toggling, toggled**] to move from one document or program to another by pressing a key. A computing word.

toil /tɔɪl/ ▶ VERB [**toils, toiling, toiled**] a formal word meaning to work hard for a long time □ *Farm workers toiled in the fields.*
▶ NOUN, NO PLURAL a formal word meaning hard work

toilet /'tɔɪlɪt/ NOUN [*plural* **toilets**]
1 a large bowl that you sit on to get rid of waste from your body ⌨ *I need to go to the toilet.* ⌨ *He flushed the toilet and washed his hands in the sink.*
2 a room with a toilet in it ⌨ *a public toilet* □ *Excuse me, where are the ladies' toilets?*

toilet paper /'tɔɪlɪt 'peɪpə(r)/ NOUN, NO PLURAL the soft paper used for cleaning the body after using the toilet

toiletries /'tɔɪlɪtrɪz/ PLURAL NOUN products that you use to keep clean and to look and smell nice □ *She packed a toothbrush and toothpaste and a few other toiletries.*

toilet roll /'tɔɪlɪt ˌrəʊl/ NOUN [*plural* **toilet rolls**] a roll of toilet paper

token /'təʊkən/ NOUN [*plural* **tokens**]
1 a plastic or metal disc used in a machine instead of money □ *You need to buy special tokens for the coffee machine.*
2 a piece of paper that you can use instead of money ⌨ *a book token worth £10* □ *Just collect the tokens and get a free gift.*
3 a sign or a symbol of something ⌨ *Please accept this gift as a token of our thanks for all your hard work.*

told /təʊld/ PAST TENSE AND PAST PARTICIPLE OF **tell**

tolerable /'tɒlərəbəl/ ADJECTIVE
1 if something is tolerable, it is slightly unpleasant but you are willing to accept it □ *Air conditioning makes the summer heat more tolerable.*
2 acceptable but not very good

- **tolerably** /'tɒlərəblɪ/ ADVERB in a way that is acceptable but not very good □ *The system works tolerably well.*

tolerance /'tɒlərəns/ NOUN, NO PLURAL
1 when you are willing to accept other people's and behaviour, even when they are different from yours □ *Everyone needs to show tolerance.* ⌨ *His speech was about religious tolerance.*
2 the ability to experience something without serious bad effects □ *She had a very low tolerance for pain.* □ *We need crops with drought tolerance.*

- **tolerant** /'tɒlərənt/ ADJECTIVE
  1 showing tolerance towards different people □ *tolerant of different views and lifestyles.*
  2 able to experience something without serious

effects □ *Some plants are more tolerant of low temperatures.*

● **tolerate** /'tɒləreɪt/ VERB [**tolerates, tolerating, tolerated**]
1 to accept something even if you do not like it or agree with it □ *I can't tolerate this noise for much longer.* □ *We will not tolerate aggressive behaviour.*
2 to be able to experience something without serious bad effects □ *Older patients are less able to tolerate chemotherapy.*

toll /təʊl/ NOUN [*plural* **tolls**]
1 money you pay to cross a bridge or to use a road □ *a toll road*
2 the number of people killed or injured, or the damage caused in a bad accident or event ⑮ *The death toll was highest in the city centre.*
3 take a/its toll (on someone/something) to have a bad effect on someone or something □ *The heavy workload has taken its toll on her.*
▶ VERB [**tolls, tolling, tolled**] if a bell tolls, it rings slowly

tomato /tə'mɑːtəʊ/ NOUN [*plural* **tomatoes**] a soft, red fruit with a lot of juice that is used like a vegetable in salads, sauces, etc. □ *pasta with tomato sauce* □ *a cheese and tomato sandwich*

tomb /tuːm/ NOUN [*plural* **tombs**] a place where a dead body is buried, often with a stone structure

tombola /tɒm'bəʊlə/ NOUN [*plural* **tombolas**] a game of luck where people choose numbered tickets, some of which win prizes

tomboy /'tɒmbɔɪ/ NOUN [*plural* **tomboys**] a girl who likes energetic activities that boys usually enjoy

tombstone /'tuːmstəʊn/ NOUN [*plural* **tombstones**] a piece of stone with a dead person's name written on it at the end of a grave

tomcat /'tɒmkæt/ NOUN [*plural* **tomcats**] a male cat

tomorrow /tə'mɒrəʊ/ ▶ NOUN, NO PLURAL
1 the day after today □ *Tomorrow is Wednesday.* □ *He's arriving early tomorrow morning.* ⑮ *Will he be here for the game tomorrow night?* ⑮ *I'll be back the day after tomorrow.*
2 the future □ *Today's children are tomorrow's taxpayers.*
▶ ADVERB on the day after today □ *Let's have our meeting tomorrow.* □ *We'll be here tomorrow.*

ton /tʌn/ NOUN [*plural* **tons**]
1 a unit for measuring weight, equal to 2240 pounds in Britain or 2000 pounds in America □ *a truck carrying tons of coal*
2 tons of an informal phrase meaning a lot of something □ *She's got tons of clothes to choose from.* □ *I've got tons of things to do.*

tone /təʊn/ ▶ NOUN [*plural* **tones**]
1 the quality of a sound or of someone's voice ⑮ *I could tell she was angry from her tone of voice.* □ *a voice with a soft gentle tone*
2 the general feeling or atmosphere of a situation □ *His enthusiasm set the tone for the evening.*
3 a sound made by a machine, such as a telephone ⑮ *a mobile phone ring tone*
4 a particular type of colour □ *several tones of blue*
▶ VERB [**tones, toning, toned**]
1 to do exercises to make part of your body more healthy, stronger, etc. □ *It's a great way to tone your legs.*
2 to look good with something of a different colour □ *The red scarf tones in with the plum-coloured coat.*
♦ PHRASAL VERB **tone something down** to make something less strong, less offensive, etc. □ *He had to tone down his language with young children around.*

tone-deaf /'təʊn'def/ ADJECTIVE not able to hear the difference between different musical notes

tongs /tɒŋz/ PLURAL NOUN a tool with two long parts that are joined at one end, which you press together to pick something up

tongue /tʌŋ/ NOUN [*plural* **tongues**]
1 the soft part inside your mouth that you can move and that you use to speak, eat and taste □ *He ran his tongue across his teeth.* ⑮ *Tim stuck his tongue out at me.*
2 a formal word meaning a language ⑮ *He spoke in his native tongue of Punjabi.*
3 the piece of leather under the opening of a shoe or boot
♦ IDIOMS **bite/hold your tongue** to not say something, especially when you want to □ *There are times when I've had to bite my tongue.* **tongue in cheek** used to talk about something that someone says as a joke □ *His comments were tongue in cheek.*

tongue-tied /'tʌŋtaɪd/ ADJECTIVE too nervous, shy or embarrassed to speak

tongue twister /'tʌŋ 'twɪstə(r)/ NOUN [*plural* **tongue twisters**] a phrase or sentence that is difficult to say quickly

tonic /'tɒnɪk/ NOUN [*plural* **tonics**]
1 a clear drink with bubbles in it and a bitter taste □ *a glass of gin and tonic*
2 something that makes you feel stronger or gives you energy

tonight /tə'naɪt/ ▶ NOUN, NO PLURAL the night or evening of today □ *I'll have to miss tonight's class, I'm afraid.*
▶ ADVERB on the night or evening of today □ *I'm going to bed early tonight.* □ *The show is on BBC1 at 9pm tonight.*

tonne /tʌn/ NOUN [*plural* **tonnes**] a unit for measuring weight, equal to 1000 kilograms

tonsil /'tɒnsəl/ NOUN [*plural* **tonsils**] one of the soft parts on either side of the back of your throat. A biology word.

● **tonsillitis** /ˌtɒnsɪ'laɪtɪs/ NOUN, NO PLURAL an infection that causes your tonsils to swell and hurt

too /tuː/ ADVERB
1 more than necessary or more than is sensible □ *If the water is too hot, add some cold.* □ *The offer was*

too good to refuse. □ Don't spend too much. 🕮 You're driving much too fast!

2 also □ Can I come too? □ I was really shocked and I think Maria was too.

3 not too an informal phrase meaning 'not very' □ I hope it's not too serious. □ His health is not too good.

> ➤ Note that if something is **too** heavy/hot/old, etc. it is bad. It means that something is more heavy/hot/old, etc. than you want it to be □ It's too heavy - I can't lift it. □ The weather is too hot - I like it a bit cooler.

took /tʊk/ PAST TENSE OF take

tool /tuːl/ NOUN [plural **tools**]
1 a piece of equipment that you hold in your hand and use to do a particular job □ a set of gardening tools 🕮 Keep a basic tool kit in the car.
2 something that helps you to do or to achieve something □ The guidelines are a useful tool for parents.

toolbar /'tuːlbɑː(r)/ NOUN [plural **toolbars**] on a computer screen, a row of icons (=small pictures) that shows you all the different things you can do. A computing word.

toot /tuːt/ ➤ VERB [**toots, tooting, tooted**] to toot a horn on a vehicle is to make it sound
➤ NOUN [plural **toots**] the noise a horn on a vehicle makes

tooth /tuːθ/ NOUN [plural **teeth**]
1 one of the hard, white parts in your mouth that you use for biting □ He has one front tooth missing. 🕮 I brushed my teeth and washed my face. 🕮 That cat's got sharp teeth.
2 one of the row of sharp points that form one side of an object such as a comb (=thing used to tidy hair)

toothache /'tuːθeɪk/ NOUN, NO PLURAL a pain in or around your tooth 🕮 I had terrible toothache. □ He went to the dentist with toothache.

toothbrush /'tuːθbrʌʃ/ NOUN [plural **toothbrushes**] a small brush that you use for cleaning your teeth

toothpaste /'tuːθpeɪst/ NOUN, NO PLURAL a cream that you use to clean your teeth

top /tɒp/ ➤ NOUN [plural **tops**]
1 the highest point or part of something □ We climbed to the top of the tower. □ They were waiting at the top of the steps. □ Start reading at the top of the page.
2 the top the most successful position 🕮 He's determined to get to the top of his profession.
3 on (the) top on the upper surface of something □ I keep his photograph on top of the TV. □ I like pizza with lots of olives on top.
4 the lid or cover of a container □ Screw the top back on tightly.
5 a piece of clothing for the upper half of your body □ She was wearing green trousers and a black top.

◆ IDIOMS off the top of your head if you say something off the top of your head, you say the most correct thing you can without checking or thinking carefully □ I'm not sure how many people were there, but off the top of my head I'd say around 200. at the top of your voice shouting, singing, etc. as loudly as possible □ He was yelling at the top of his voice for them to come back. over the top an informal idiom meaning too extreme □ I know you were angry, but smashing the chair was a bit over the top.
▶ ADJECTIVE
1 most important or successful □ Safety is our top priority. 🕮 He came top in the exam. □ a top fashion designer
2 in the highest part of something 🕮 My office is on the top floor.
▶ VERB [**tops, topping, topped**]
1 to cover the upper surface of something □ Top the cake with fruit and whipped cream.
2 to be more important or successful than other things □ This album is expected to top the charts next week.
3 to be larger than a particular amount □ Sales of the DVD have topped 2 million.
◆ PHRASAL VERBS **top something off** to finish a successful event or activity with something □ He topped off a fine game with his third goal. **top (something) up 1** to add more of something to a container that already has something in it □ Let me top up your drink. **2** to add more of something so that it reaches a particular level □ Some restaurant owners use tips to top up waiters' wages.

topaz /'təʊpæz/ NOUN, NO PLURAL a type of valuable stone that is often yellow

top hat /ˌtɒp 'hæt/ NOUN [plural **top hats**] a tall, formal hat with a flat top for men

topic /'tɒpɪk/ NOUN [plural **topics**] a subject to study, write or talk about □ **+ of** The storms were the main topic of conversation. □ A range of topics were discussed. □ Immigration can be a sensitive topic.

topical /'tɒpɪkəl/ ADJECTIVE to do with things that are happening at the present time 🕮 The journal deals with topical issues. □ His remarks are highly topical.

topless /'tɒplɪs/ ADJECTIVE without any clothes on the top half of your body

topmost /'tɒpməʊst/ ADJECTIVE highest □ the topmost branches of the tree

top-notch /ˌtɒp'nɒtʃ/ ADJECTIVE of excellent quality □ We ate at a top-notch restaurant.

topping /'tɒpɪŋ/ NOUN [plural **toppings**] food that covers or decorates the top of a dish of food □ vegetable pie with cheese topping

topple /'tɒpəl/ VERB [**topples, toppling, toppled**]
1 to fall over or to make something fall over □ I knocked into a table and it toppled over. □ High winds toppled trees.

2 to make someone lose a position of power □ *The regime was toppled in 1932.*

top-secret /'tɒp'si:krɪt/ ADJECTIVE very secret and important □ *This is top-secret information.*

topsy-turvy /ˌtɒpsɪ'tɜ:vɪ/ ADJECTIVE, ADVERB an informal word meaning turned upside-down or very confused □ *It's been a bit of a topsy-turvy week.*

top-up /'tɒpʌp/ NOUN [*plural* **top-ups**]
1 when you put some more of a drink into someone's glass □ *Let me give you a top-up.*
2 an amount of money you pay to increase the level of another amount of money □ *a top-up loan*

top-up card /'tɒpʌp ˌkɑ:d/ NOUN [*plural* **top-up cards**] a card that you have that allows you to pay money to use your mobile phone

Torah /'tɔ:rə/ NOUN, NO PLURAL the holy books of the Jewish religion, especially the first five books of the Jewish Bible

torch /tɔ:tʃ/ ► NOUN [*plural* **torches**]
1 a small electric light that you carry in your hand ⊞ *Someone shone a torch into the tent.*
2 a long stick burning at one end that is carried □ *the Olympic torch*
► VERB [**torches, torching, torched**] an informal word meaning to burn something so that it is destroyed □ *Protesters torched cars.*

tore /tɔ:(r)/ PAST TENSE OF **tear**

torment ► VERB /tɔ:'ment/ [**torments, tormenting, tormented**]
1 to treat someone cruelly or to annoy them in an unkind way □ *A gang of youths had been tormenting the family.*
2 if you are tormented by something, you suffer for a long time because of it □ *She is still tormented by bad dreams.*
► NOUN /'tɔ:ment/ [*plural* **torments**] a formal word meaning very great pain or worry that continues for a long time □ *There were no signs of his inner torment.*

tormentor /tɔ:'mentə(r)/ NOUN [*plural* **tormentors**] a person who torments someone

torn /tɔ:n/ PAST PARTICIPLE OF **tear**

tornado /tɔ:'neɪdəʊ/ NOUN [*plural* **tornadoes**] a violent storm with a powerful wind with a circular movement that causes a lot of damage

torpedo /tɔ:'pi:dəʊ/ ► NOUN [*plural* **torpedoes**] a long thin bomb that moves quickly under water and explodes when it hits the thing it is aimed at
► VERB [**torpedoes, torpedoing, torpedoed**] to fire a torpedo at something

torrent /'tɒrənt/ NOUN [*plural* **torrents**]
1 a lot of water flowing or falling quickly □ *a torrent of water*
2 a large amount of something unpleasant ⊞ *He was subjected to a torrent of abuse.*

torrential /tə'renʃəl/ ADJECTIVE torrential rain is very heavy rain ⊞ *a day of torrential rain*

torso /'tɔ:səʊ/ NOUN [*plural* **torsos**] the main part of your body, not including your arms, legs or head

tortoise /'tɔ:təs/ NOUN [*plural* **tortoises**] an animal that moves slowly and has a hard shell covering its body

torture /'tɔ:tʃə(r)/ ► VERB [**tortures, torturing, tortured**] to hurt someone in a cruel way, usually as a punishment or to get information from them □ *He was interrogated and tortured by his captors.*
► NOUN, NO PLURAL
1 when someone is tortured □ *The European Convention on Human Rights bans all forms of torture.* □ *The men showed signs of torture.*
2 when something causes suffering □ *Not being able to see her children was torture.*
● **torturer** /'tɔ:tʃərə(r)/ NOUN [*plural* **torturers**] a person who tortures someone

Tory /'tɔ:rɪ/ ► NOUN [*plural* **Tories**] someone who supports or is a member of the Conservative Party in the UK
► ADJECTIVE to do with the Conservative Party □ *Tory policies* □ *Tory councillors*

toss /tɒs/ ► VERB [**tosses, tossing, tossed**]
1 to throw something lightly or without care □ *Toss the keys over here, would you?* □ *He tossed aside the magazine.*
2 to move repeatedly from side to side ⊞ *Alice spent the night tossing and turning restlessly.*
3 to throw a coin up in the air to see which side it falls on, in order to make a choice □ *We decided to toss for the front seat.* ⊞ *Why not just toss a coin?*
4 to mix food, especially so it is covered in a liquid □ *Toss the chicken with lemon juice and oil.*
► NOUN, NO PLURAL when you toss a coin to make a choice ⊞ *It was decided by the toss of a coin.*
⊞ *Williams won the toss and chose to serve first.*

toss-up /'tɒsʌp/ NOUN, NO PLURAL an informal word for a situation in which there are two possible choices which are difficult to decide between □ *It was a toss-up between Alex and Jon for captain.*

tot /tɒt/ NOUN [*plural* **tots**]
1 an informal word meaning a small child
2 a small glass of a strong alcoholic drink
◆ PHRASAL VERB [**tots, totting, totted**] **tot something up** to add numbers together □ *If you tot up all the costs, it comes to £347.*

total /'təʊtəl/ ► ADJECTIVE
1 complete □ *She was a total stranger.* □ *He showed a total lack of respect.* □ *The job must be done in total secrecy.*
2 including everything ⊞ *Two more people arrived yesterday, bringing the total number of guests to 12.* □ *the total cost of the project*
► NOUN [*plural* **totals**] the number or amount you get when you add everything together □ *+ of We've got a total of fifteen cats.* ⊞ *They raised a grand total of £940.* □ *There were thirty people in total.*
► VERB [**totals, totalling**/US **totaling, totalled**/US **totaled**] to be a particular number or amount when added together □ *Our collection totalled £320.*
● **totally** /'təʊtəlɪ/ ADVERB completely □ *Is she totally deaf?* □ *I agree with you totally.*

➤ **Totally** is only used before adjectives with very strong meanings. Before adjectives with less strong meanings, use **very** or **extremely** □ *I was totally exhausted.* □ *I was very tired.* □ *It's totally ridiculous.* □ *It's very silly.*

totem pole /ˈtəʊtəm ˌpəʊl/ NOUN [plural **totem poles**] a tall wooden pole with designs on it made by Native Americans

totter /ˈtɒtə(r)/ VERB [**totters, tottering, tottered**] to walk with small steps as if you are going to fall over □ *She tottered on high heels up the street.*

touch /tʌtʃ/ ► VERB [**touches, touching, touched**]
1 to put your hand or fingers on something □ *Please do not touch the items on the shelf.* □ *Can you touch the ceiling?*
2 if things touch, there is no space between them □ *We stood in a long line with our shoulders touching.*
3 if you are touched by someone's actions, you feel happy and grateful because they have been kind □ *I was touched by your kind letter.*
4 if someone's words or situation touch you, you feel sad for them □ *Who could fail to be touched by their stories of suffering?*
♦ PHRASAL VERBS **touch down** if an aircraft touches down, it lands **touch on/upon something** to mention a subject □ *He did briefly touch on the problems he is having.* **touch something up** to make small changes to improve something, especially its appearance □ *I need to touch up the paint on the windows.*
► NOUN [plural **touches**]
1 when you put your hands or fingers on something □ *You can start the engine at the touch of a button.* □ *I felt a touch on my shoulder.*
2 no plural the ability to feel □ *The fur was smooth to the touch.*
3 a touch is a small detail that makes something better □ *Matching flowers were a nice touch.* ⊞ *She added the finishing touches to the display.*
4 a particular quality that something adds to a situation □ *The story about his father gave the speech a personal touch.* □ *Her presence added a touch of glamour to the occasion.*
5 in touch (a) if you are in touch with someone, you communicate with them □ *I wish Sally would get in touch with me.* □ *I hope we can stay in touch.* (b) if you are in touch with a subject or a situation, you know the recent information about it □ *I like to keep in touch with what's going on in the world.*
6 lose touch to stop communicating with someone, usually not deliberately □ *We lost touch after we left university.*
7 out of touch if you are out of touch with a subject or a situation, you do not know the recent information about it □ *I didn't know Joe had got married - I'm rather out of touch these days.*

touch-and-go /ˌtʌtʃənd'ɡəʊ/ ADJECTIVE an informal word used to mean that the result of a situation is very uncertain and could be very bad □ *It was touch-and-go whether she'd survive.*

touchdown /ˈtʌtʃdaʊn/ NOUN [plural **touchdowns**]
1 when an aircraft or spacecraft lands on the ground □ *They announced the spacecraft's successful touchdown in the Arizona desert.*
2 when the ball is carried over a line to score points in rugby or American football

touching /ˈtʌtʃɪŋ/ ADJECTIVE making you feel sympathy □ *a touching story about a lost puppy*

touchpad /ˈtʌtʃpæd/ NOUN [plural **touchpads**] a small flat area on a laptop (=small computer you can carry around) that you touch to work the computer programs

touch screen /ˈtʌtʃ ˌskriːn/ NOUN [plural **touch screens**] a computer screen that you touch in order to make the computer do something

touchy /ˈtʌtʃɪ/ ADJECTIVE [**touchier, touchiest**]
1 easily annoyed □ *What's she so touchy about today?*
2 needing to be dealt with carefully because people are likely to become annoyed or upset □ *a touchy subject*

tough /tʌf/ ADJECTIVE [**tougher, toughest**]
1 difficult to deal with □ *It was a tough decision.* □ *He had a tough time in that job.*
2 very severe □ *Tough new measures have been introduced to reduce vandalism.* □ *We're very tough on students who do not work hard enough.*
3 physically or mentally strong □ *You need to be tough to succeed in business.*
4 not easy to cut or damage □ *You'll need a tough pair of shoes for climbing.* □ *The meat was a bit tough.*
• **toughen** /ˈtʌfən/ VERB [**toughens, toughening, toughened**]
1 to become physically or mentally stronger, or to make someone physically or mentally stronger □ *A year in the army has really toughened him up.*
2 to make something more severe □ *The government plans to toughen regulations on the sale of alcohol.*
• **toughness** /ˈtʌfnɪs/ NOUN, NO PLURAL being tough

tour /tʊə(r)/ ► NOUN [plural **tours**]
1 a visit to somewhere, stopping several times at places of interest □ **+ of** *We went on a tour of the wine region.* ⊞ *He takes visitors on guided tours of the city.*
2 a number of performances or matches in different places by a performer or sports team □ *a cricket tour of South Africa* □ *The singer's currently on tour in Europe.*
► VERB [**tours, touring, toured**] to go on a tour □ *We're going to tour the wine-making regions of France.* □ *We've hired a car to tour the city.*
• **tourism** /ˈtʊərɪzəm/ NOUN, NO PLURAL travelling and visiting places for enjoyment, or the business of providing holiday services ⊞ *the tourism industry*

□ *The program was set up to promote tourism on the island.*

● tourist /ˈtʊərɪst/ NOUN [*plural* **tourists**]
1 a person who is travelling for enjoyment or on holiday □ *a group of foreign tourists* 🔁 *a tourist attraction*
2 a player on a sports tour □ *The tourists won the first match in the series.*

:ournament /ˈtʊənəmənt/ NOUN [*plural* **tournaments**] a number of sports matches that make up a big competition 🔁 *a golf tournament* 🔁 *the US Open tennis tournament*

our operator /ˈtʊər ˈɒpəreɪtə(r)/ NOUN [*plural* **tour operators**] a company that organizes holidays for people

ousled /ˈtaʊzəld/ ADJECTIVE tousled hair is untidy

out /taʊt/ ▶ NOUN [*plural* **touts**] a person who tries to sell something, especially tickets for an event, usually illegally 🔁 *a ticket tout*
▶ VERB [**touts, touting, touted**]
◀ to try to persuade people that something is good or important □ *White is already being touted as a possible candidate.* □ *He is touting the benefits of preventive care.*
: to try to persuade people to buy something

●w /təʊ/ ▶ VERB [**tows, towing, towed**] to pull something behind you with a rope or chain □ *The car broke down and we had to be towed home.*
▶ NOUN [*plural* **tows**] when you tow something

ward /təˈwɔːd/ PREPOSITION a mainly US word for owards

owards /təˈwɔːdz/ PREPOSITION
◀ in the direction of someone or something □ *I ran towards her.* □ *The sign points towards the east.* □ *He oved his chair towards the window*
◀ used to talk about the way someone feels about omeone or something □ *I found his attitude towards oney strange.* □ *She feels a lot of bitterness towards r family.*
◀ near something □ *The bit about Cromwell is towards e end of the book.* □ *I hope to finish my book wards the end of the year.*
◀ for the purpose of achieving something □ *Nothing s been done towards organizing the party.*
◀ n order to help to pay for something □ *He made a nation towards the new roof.*
◀ sed to talk about how a situation is developing *he country is sliding towards civil war.*

wel /ˈtaʊəl/ ▶ NOUN [*plural* **towels**] a piece of t, thick cloth for drying yourself 🔁 *a bath towel* *She picked up the wet towel from the bathroom r.* 🔁 *She dried her hands using a paper towel.*
ERB [**towels, towelling, towelled**] to dry a thing or son with a towel □ *Towel your hair dry before lying the conditioner.*

welling /ˈtaʊəlɪŋ/ NOUN, NO PLURAL thick, soft on cloth that is good for drying things □ *a bath e made of towelling*

tower /ˈtaʊə(r)/ ▶ NOUN [*plural* **towers**] a tall narrow building or part of a building □ *a church tower* □ *the Eiffel Tower*
▶ VERB [**towers, towering, towered**] to be much taller than other things or people □ *William towers over all his colleagues.*

tower block /ˈtaʊə ˌblɒk/ NOUN [*plural* **tower blocks**] a very tall building where people live or work □ *a 20-storey tower block*

towering /ˈtaʊərɪŋ/ ADJECTIVE
1 very tall □ *towering office blocks*
2 very important and admired by many people □ *He was a towering literary figure.*

town /taʊn/ NOUN [*plural* **towns**]
1 a place where people live and work, bigger than a village and smaller than a city 🔁 *She comes from a small town in Ohio.* 🔁 *The wedding was in her home town of Hobart.*
2 the main part of a town where many shops and businesses are 🔁 *I'm going into town to do some shopping.*
◆ IDIOM go to town an informal phrase meaning to do something with a lot of effort, energy or money □ *She really went to town on the decorations.*

town centre /ˈtaʊn ˈsentə(r)/ NOUN [*plural* **town centres**] the part of a town where most of the shops, restaurants, etc. are

town hall NOUN [*plural* **town halls**] a building that contains local government offices

towpath /ˈtaʊpɑːθ/ NOUN [*plural* **towpaths**] a path next to a river or canal (=a passage filled with water, made for boats to travel on)

toxic /ˈtɒksɪk/ ADJECTIVE poisonous 🔁 *toxic chemicals* 🔁 *The river is polluted with toxic waste.*
● toxicity /tɒkˈsɪsəti/ NOUN, NO PLURAL the quality of being toxic
● toxin /ˈtɒksɪn/ NOUN [*plural* **toxins**] a substance that is poisonous

toy /tɔɪ/ NOUN [*plural* **toys**] an object made for someone, especially a child, to play with
◆ PHRASAL VERBS [**toys, toying, toyed**] toy with something **1** to consider an idea, but not in a very serious way □ *I'm toying with the idea of cutting my hair short.* **2** to keep touching or moving something, usually because you are nervous or upset □ *He was just toying with his food.* toy with someone to pretend that you love someone when you do not have serious feelings about them

trace /treɪs/ ▶ VERB [**traces, tracing, traced**]
1 to find someone or something by following information about where they have been □ *The man has been traced to a village in the south of the country.*
2 to discover the origin of something □ *She can trace her family back to the 13th century.*
3 to describe the development of something □ *The*

book traces his journey from farmer's son to famous explorer.

4 to copy a picture by covering it with a sheet of thin paper and drawing over the lines you can see through it

▶ NOUN [*plural* **traces**]

1 a mark or sign that someone or something leaves behind ⓖ *He disappeared without trace.*

2 a very small amount of something □ *There were traces of explosives on his shoes.*

trace element /'treɪs 'elɪmənt/ NOUN [*plural* **trace elements**] a chemical that an animal or plant needs very small amounts of to develop in a normal way. A biology or chemistry word.

trachea /trə'kiːə/ NOUN [*plural* **tracheas**] the tube that carries air to your lungs. A biology word.

tracing paper /'treɪsɪŋ 'peɪpə(r)/ NOUN, NO PLURAL very thin paper that you can see the lines of a picture through

track /træk/ ▶ NOUN [*plural* **tracks**]

1 a rough path or road □ *We followed a narrow track along the edge of the field.*

2 the long metal pieces that a train moves along □ *Repairs were needed to the track.*

3 an area of ground used for racing, often with a circular path

4 a mark on the ground left by a person, animal or thing that has been there □ *They followed the bear's tracks through the forest.*

5 one of the songs or pieces of music on a CD, record, etc.

6 on track likely to be successful □ *We are on track to finish the work by next year.*

7 on the right/wrong track trying to achieve something in a way that is likely to be successful/ unsuccessful □ *If she's hoping to be a professional musician, she's certainly on the right track.*

8 keep track to continue to have enough information about something □ *I can't keep track of all the new rules.*

9 lose track to no longer have enough information about something □ *I've lost track of the number of times I've had to give her money.*

▶ VERB [**tracks, tracking, tracked**]

1 to follow a person, animal or vehicle by looking for their marks or using special equipment □ *They use radar to track the aircraft's movements.*

2 to watch and record the progress or development of something □ *The report tracks the performance of several major companies.*

◆ PHRASAL VERB **track someone/something down** to find someone or something after looking for them for a long time □ *I'm trying to track down an old friend.* □ *The shop has tracked down the book you ordered.*

track and field /'træk ənd 'fiːld/ NOUN, NO PLURAL a mainly US phrase for sports such as running, jumping and throwing

track record /'træk 'rekɔːd/ NOUN [*plural* **track records**] all the things you have done in the past, by which people judge you □ *He has an excellent track record as an administrator.*

tracksuit /'træksuːt/ NOUN [*plural* **tracksuits**] comfortable trousers and a top that you wear for sport

tract /trækt/ NOUN [*plural* **tracts**]

1 a large area of land

2 a system of tubes and organs in the body. A biology word ⓖ *the digestive tract*

3 a piece of writing, especially about politics or religion

tractor /'træktə(r)/ NOUN [*plural* **tractors**] a powerful vehicle with large wheels, used on farms

trade /treɪd/ ▶ NOUN [*plural* **trades**]

1 *no plural* the buying and selling of goods, services or shares (=parts of a company that you can sell or buy) □ *international trade*

2 a particular area of business □ *She works in the diamond trade.*

3 a job using your hands that involves skill and training ⓖ *He learned the trade from his father.*

▶ VERB [**trades, trading, traded**]

1 to buy or sell goods, services or shares (=parts of a company that you can sell or buy) □ *+ with We will not trade with corrupt regimes.*

2 to exchange something for something else □ *+ for I traded my waterproof coat for a camera.*

◆ PHRASAL VERB **trade something in** to give something old as part of the payment for something new □ *We traded in our car for a newer model.*

trademark /'treɪdmɑːk/ NOUN [*plural* **trademarks**] a name, word or symbol that a company uses on its products and which legally belongs to that company

trade-off /'treɪdɒf/ NOUN [*plural* **trade-offs**] a situation where the advantage of one thing brings the disadvantage of another □ *There's a trade-off between cost and convenience.*

trader /'treɪdə(r)/ NOUN [*plural* **traders**] a person or company that buys and sells things

tradesman /'treɪdzmən/ NOUN [*plural* **tradesmen**]

1 a person who works with their hands in a skilled job

2 a person who sells something

trade union /'treɪd 'juːnjən/ NOUN [*plural* **trade unions**] an organization of workers that tries to get good pay and conditions for its members

trading /'treɪdɪŋ/ NOUN, NO PLURAL the activity of buying and selling goods, services or shares (=parts of a company that you can sell or buy) □ *High street trading has been hit by the recession.*

tradition /trə'dɪʃən/ NOUN [*plural* **traditions**] a custom that has continued for a long time □ *Having special birthday meals is a family tradition.* □ *He does not follow any religious tradition.*

◆ **traditional** /trə'dɪʃənəl/ ADJECTIVE

1 based on customs that have existed for a long time □ *They wore traditional costumes.*

2 based on what usually happens or what people

usually done □ *He did not follow the traditional career path.*

traditionally /trəˈdɪʃənəlɪ/ ADVERB based on what usually happens or what people have usually done □ *Traditionally, summer is a quiet time in politics.*

traffic /ˈtræfɪk/ ▶ NOUN, NO PLURAL
1 vehicles that are travelling ⊞ *We were stuck in heavy traffic* (=a lot of traffic).
2 the illegal buying and selling of goods □ *the traffic of weapons*
▶ VERB [**traffics, trafficking, trafficked**] to buy and sell things illegally

traffic circle /ˈtræfɪk ˈsɜːkəl/ NOUN [*plural* **traffic circles**] the US phrase for **roundabout**

traffic jam /ˈtræfɪk ˌdʒæm/ NOUN [*plural* **traffic jams**] a long line of vehicles that cannot move because the road is blocked

trafficker /ˈtræfɪkə(r)/ NOUN [*plural* **traffickers**] someone who buys or sells goods illegally □ *drug traffickers*

trafficking /ˈtræfɪkɪŋ/ NOUN, NO PLURAL buying and selling goods illegally

traffic lights /ˈtræfɪk laɪt/ PLURAL NOUN a set of red, yellow and green lights that tell vehicles when to stop or go

traffic warden /ˈtræfɪk ˈwɔːdn/ NOUN [*plural* **traffic wardens**] a person whose job is to check that vehicles have been parked legally

tragedy /ˈtrædʒədɪ/ NOUN [*plural* **tragedies**]
a very sad event, often where people die □ *The train driver could not be blamed for the tragedy.*
a very bad situation that makes people upset □ *It is a tragedy that so many children are becoming involved in crime.*
a story that has a sad ending, especially when the main character dies

tragic /ˈtrædʒɪk/ ADJECTIVE very sad, often because of death ⊞ *His death was a tragic accident.* □ *Her carelessness had tragic consequences.*

tragically /ˈtrædʒɪklɪ/ ADVERB in a way that is very □ *The poet died tragically young.*

trail /treɪl/ ▶ NOUN [*plural* **trails**]
series of marks or objects that someone or something leaves when they move somewhere *They left a trail of litter behind them.*
lot of damage or a series of bad events ⊞ *Their trucks had left a trail of destruction.*
path through the countryside
VERB [**trails, trailing, trailed**]
hang down from something or across something *er long coat trailed on the floor.* □ *Roses trailed the wall.*
walk slowly because you are tired or unhappy *he children trailed along behind their parents.*
be losing in a competition or an election □ *Their is trailing by 5 points.*

4 to leave a substance on the ground as you move □ *He's trailed mud all over the house.*
5 to follow someone secretly □ *He was trailed by the secret police for years.*
♦ PHRASAL VERB **trail away/off** if someone's words trail away/off, they gradually stop □ *His voice trailed off as she entered the room.*

• **trailer** /ˈtreɪlə(r)/ NOUN [*plural* **trailers**]
1 a container on wheels that is pulled behind another vehicle
2 a short part of a film or programme that is used as an advertisement for it

train¹ /treɪn/ NOUN [*plural* **trains**]
1 a vehicle that moves on a railway and carries passengers □ *I prefer to travel by train.* ⊞ *I caught the early train.*
2 a series of thoughts or events ⊞ *The sudden noise interrupted my train of thought.* ⊞ *Their argument set off a terrible train of events.*
3 the back part of a long dress that hangs on the floor

train² /treɪn/ VERB [**trains, training, trained**]
1 to teach a person or animal to do something □ + *to do something* *Veronica has trained her dog to carry her handbag.*
2 to learn to do a particular job □ + *as* *Andrew trained as a nurse when he left school.*
3 to prepare for a sports event □ *The team trains for three hours every day.*
4 to point a camera or gun in a particular direction □ + *on* *The enemy's guns are trained on the airport.*
• **trainee** /treɪˈniː/ NOUN [*plural* **trainees**] someone who is being trained to do a particular job
• **trainer** /ˈtreɪnə(r)/ NOUN [*plural* **trainers**]
1 someone who teaches people or animals to do something
2 trainers soft shoes that are used for sport
• **training** /ˈtreɪnɪŋ/ NOUN, NO PLURAL
1 the process of training people or being trained □ + *in* *We received very little training in how to use the equipment.* ⊞ *They run training courses for diving instructors.*
2 preparation for a sports event □ *The team will be in training for the next year.*

traipse /treɪps/ VERB [**traipses, traipsing, traipsed**]
1 to walk somewhere slowly □ *She traipsed up the hill carrying three heavy bags of shopping.*
2 to travel a long way □ *You can't expect them to traipse all the way to Scotland for a party.*

trait /treɪt/ NOUN [*plural* **traits**] a particular characteristic or quality that someone or something has □ *The test is supposed to reveal major character traits.*

traitor /ˈtreɪtə(r)/ NOUN [*plural* **traitors**] a person who is not loyal to their friends or country

trajectory /trəˈdʒektərɪ/ NOUN [*plural* **trajectories**] the curved line which something follows when it goes or is thrown into the air

tram /træm/ NOUN [*plural* **trams**] a type of electric bus that runs on metal tracks in the street

tramp /træmp/ ▶ NOUN [*plural* **tramps**] a person without a home who walks from place to place
▶ VERB [**tramps, tramping, tramped**] to walk with firm, heavy steps

trample /'træmpəl/ VERB [**tramples, trampling, trampled**] to walk on something with heavy steps, often causing damage □ *The sheep had trampled all over the wheat.*

trampoline /'træmpəli:n/ NOUN [*plural* **trampolines**] a piece of equipment that you jump up and down on for exercise or sport

trance /trɑ:ns/ NOUN [*plural* **trances**] a state when you are awake but not completely conscious of what is happening or what you are doing

tranquil /'træŋkwɪl/ ADJECTIVE quiet, calm and peaceful □ *The hotel is in a tranquil setting by a lake.*

• **tranquilize** /'træŋkwɪ,laɪz/ VERB [**tranquilizes, tranquilizing, tranquilized**] the US spelling of tranquillize

• **tranquilizer** /'træŋkwɪ,laɪzə(r)/ NOUN [*plural* **tranquilizers**] the US spelling of tranquillizer

• **tranquillity** /træŋ'kwɪlɪtɪ/ NOUN, NO PLURAL the state of being tranquil

• **tranquillize** *or* **tranquillise** /'træŋkwɪ,laɪz/ VERB [**tranquillizes, tranquillizing, tranquillized**] to give a person or animal a drug to make them calmer and more relaxed

• **tranquillizer** *or* **tranquilliser** /'træŋkwɪ,laɪzə(r)/ NOUN [*plural* **tranquillizers**] a drug that makes people feel calmer and more relaxed

trans- /trænz/ PREFIX
1 trans- is added to the beginning of words to mean 'across' □ *transatlantic*
2 trans- is added to the beginning of words to mean 'changing' □ *transformation*

transaction /træn'zækʃən/ NOUN [*plural* **transactions**] when something is bought or sold

transatlantic /,trænzət'læntɪk/ ADJECTIVE involving crossing the Atlantic Ocean □ *a transatlantic flight*

transfer ▶ VERB /træns'fɜ:(r)/ [**transfers, transferring, transferred**]
1 to move someone or something from one place to another □ *She transferred all her photos onto a CD.* □ *I transferred some money into his account.*
2 to change to a different job or place of work in the same organization, or to move someone to a different job or place of work in the same organization □ **+ to** *He transferred to the New York office.*
3 to change to a different vehicle as part of a journey □ *We transferred to an internal flight from Helsinki.*
4 to make someone able to speak to someone else instead of you on the telephone by connecting them □ **+ to** *I'll transfer you to our accounts department.*
5 to sell a sports player to another team
▶ NOUN /'trænsfɜ:(r)/ [*plural* **transfers**]
1 when someone moves to another job or place of

work in the same organization □ *The sergeant has asked for a transfer.*
2 the act of moving someone or something from one place to another □ *I am responsible for the transfer of supplies to the new base.*
3 when a sports player is sold to another team
4 a piece of paper with a design on one side that can be pressed on to another surface

• **transferable** /træns'fɜ:rəbəl/ ADJECTIVE able to be used by someone else or for a different purpose □ *This ticket is not transferable.*

transfix /træns'fɪks/ VERB [**transfixes, transfixing, transfixed**] if you are transfixed by something, it keeps your attention □ *The whole nation was transfixed by the drama.*

transform /træns'fɔ:m/ VERB [**transforms, transforming, transformed**] to change something completely □ *We could transform this room with a few tins of paint.*

• **transformation** /,trænsfə'meɪʃən/ NOUN [*plural* **transformations**] a complete change in someone or something ⊞ *The organization has undergone a complete transformation.*

• **transformer** /træns'fɔ:mə(r)/ NOUN [*plural* **transformers**] a device that changes the strength of an electric current. A physics word.

transfusion /træns'fju:ʒən/ NOUN [*plural* **transfusions**] when blood from someone else is put into the body of a person who is ill or injured

transient /'trænzɪənt/ ADJECTIVE
1 a formal word meaning lasting for only a short time □ *transient pleasures*
2 staying in one place for only a short time □ *a transient population*

transistor /træn'zɪstə(r)/ NOUN [*plural* **transistors**]
1 a small piece of electronic equipment used to control the flow of electricity in radios, televisions, computers, etc. A physics word.
2 a small radio

transit /'trænsɪt/ NOUN, NO PLURAL the activity of moving someone or something from one place to another □ *Their luggage has been lost in transit* (=while being moved).

transition /træn'zɪʃən/ NOUN [*plural* **transitions**] change from one state, situation or system to another □ *The transition from childhood to adulthood was difficult for her.* □ *We are trying to ensure a smooth transition to the new working methods.*

• **transitional** /træn'zɪʃənəl/ ADJECTIVE to do with transition ⊞ *During the transitional period either system may be used.*

transitive /'trænzɪtɪv/ ADJECTIVE a transitive verb always has as an object □ *In the sentence 'I carried Mary.', 'see' is a transitive verb.*

translate /træns'leɪt/ VERB [**translates, translates, translated**]
1 to change words into a different language □ **+** *Can you translate this into French?*

2 to cause something □ **+ into** *The company's success has translated into higher earnings for its staff.*

● **translation** /trænsˈleɪʃən/ NOUN [*plural* **translations**]

1 writing or speech that has been changed into a different language □ **+ of** *This is a new translation of her novel.*

2 *no plural* the process of translating something

● **translator** /trænsˈleɪtə(r)/ NOUN [*plural* **translators**] someone whose job is to change words into a different language

translucent /trænzˈluːsənt/ ADJECTIVE translucent objects allow light to pass through them but are not completely transparent

transmission /trænzˈmɪʃən/ NOUN [*plural* **transmissions**]

1 a television or radio broadcast, or the process of broadcasting □ *Transmissions from outside the region have been blocked.*

2 the process of sending something out from somewhere □ *the transmission of data*

3 the process of spreading a disease from one person to another

4 the part of a vehicle that takes power from the engine to turn the wheels

transmit /trænzˈmɪt/ VERB [**transmits, transmitting, transmitted**]

to broadcast programmes, information, etc. □ *The company plans to transmit live coverage of the match to mobile phones.*

to send something out from somewhere □ *The device transmits a radio signal.*

to spread a disease □ *The disease is transmitted by mosquitos.*

if a substance transmits light, heat, etc., it allows it to pass through

transparent /trænsˈpærənt/ ADJECTIVE

if something is transparent, you can see through it □ *The box is made of transparent plastic so that you can see all the wires inside.*

easy to understand and not keeping anything secret □ *Our system of expenses must be completely transparent.*

obviously not true □ *a transparent lie*

transpiration /ˌtrænspɪˈreɪʃən/ NOUN, NO PLURAL when a plant transpires. A biology word.

transpire /trænˈspaɪə(r)/ VERB [**transpires, transpiring, transpired**]

if it transpires that something happened, people discover that it has happened. A formal word □ *It later transpired that he had been in Paris all the time.*

if a plant transpires, water from its leaves goes back into the air. A biology word.

transplant ▶ NOUN /ˈtrænsˌplɑːnt/ [*plural* **transplants**] an operation to put an organ from one person's body into someone else □ *He had a heart transplant.*

▶ VERB /trænsˈplɑːnt/ [**transplants, transplanting, transplanted**]

1 to remove a part from one person's body and put it in someone else's

2 to move a plant that is growing in one place to somewhere else □ *The seedlings can be transplanted when they have four leaves.*

transport ▶ NOUN, NO PLURAL /ˈtrænspɔːt/

1 vehicles or a system used for taking people and goods from one place to another 🔊 *Older people have free travel on public transport.* 🔊 *Paris has a very efficient transport system.* 🔊 *Trains are a very safe form of transport.*

2 moving people or things from one place to another □ *The price includes the cost of transport.* □ **+ of** *The transport of farm animals was banned.*

➤ Remember that **transport** cannot be used in the plural:
✓ *Public transport is very good in the capital.*
✗ *Public transports are very good in the capital.*
➤ To talk about one particular type of transport, use the phrase **form of transport** □ *Train is probably the greenest form of transport.*

▶ VERB /trænsˈpɔːt/ [**transports, transporting, transported**] to move something from one place to another □ *The planes were used to transport prisoners.* □ *Red blood cells transport oxygen around the body.*

● **transportation** /ˌtrænspɔːˈteɪʃən/ NOUN, NO PLURAL

1 the process of moving people or things □ *transportation costs*

2 the US word for **transport** (sense 1)

● **transporter** /trænsˈpɔːtə(r)/ NOUN [*plural* **transporters**] a long vehicle that is usually used for taking a number of large objects, such as cars, to another place

transpose /trænsˈpəʊz/ VERB [**transposes, transposing, transposed**]

1 to make two things change places □ *The keyboarder had transposed two of the numbers.*

2 to play music in a different key to the one it is written in

trap /træp/ ▶ NOUN [*plural* **traps**]

1 a piece of equipment for catching animals □ *a mouse trap*

2 a clever plan that is designed to trick someone 🔊 *Police set a trap for the suspected thief.*

3 an unpleasant situation that is very difficult to escape from 🔊 *Many families are caught in the low-pay poverty trap.*

▶ VERB [**traps, trapping, trapped**]

1 if you are trapped in a bad place or situation, you cannot escape from it □ *Passengers were trapped as fire swept through the bus.* □ *He was trapped in a loveless marriage.*

2 to trick someone into doing or saying something □ *The suspect was trapped into admitting that he had been there.*

3 to catch an animal in a trap □ *The animals were trapped for their fur.*

trapdoor /'træpdɔ:(r)/ NOUN [*plural* **trapdoors**] a door in a floor or a ceiling

trapeze /trə'pi:z/ NOUN [*plural* **trapezes**] a short bar hanging between two ropes high up from the ground, on which someone moves backwards and forwards to entertain people

trapezium /trə'pi:ziəm/ NOUN [*plural* **trapeziums** or **trapezia**] a shape with four sides, two of which are parallel. A maths word.

trappings /'træpɪŋz/ PLURAL NOUN the nice things that someone has because of their position □ *Simon had all the trappings of success - a nice house, a boat, and three children at private school.*

trash /træʃ/ ► NOUN, NO PLURAL
1 an informal word meaning things that are of bad quality □ *There's a lot of trash on television.*
2 the US word for rubbish (=things that have been thrown away)
► VERB [**trashes, trashing, trashed**]
1 an informal word meaning to destroy something completely □ *Rioters trashed cars.*
2 an informal word meaning to criticize something badly

trashcan /'træʃkæn/ NOUN [*plural* **trashcans**] the US word for dustbin

trashy /'træʃi/ ADJECTIVE [**trashier, trashiest**] of very bad quality □ *trashy magazines*

trauma /'trɔ:mə/ NOUN [*plural* **traumas**] a very unpleasant experience that upsets someone a lot and for a long time □ *She never recovered from the trauma of losing her son.*

• **traumatic** /trɔ:'mætɪk/ ADJECTIVE very upsetting, unpleasant or frightening □ *a traumatic event*

• **traumatize** or **traumatise** /'trɔ:mətaɪz/ VERB [**traumatizes, traumatizing, traumatized**] to make someone feel very upset or frightened

travel /'trævəl/ ► VERB [**travels, travelling/US traveling, travelled/US traveled**]
1 to go from one place to another □ *Holly spent the summer travelling in the United States.* □ *Some people have to travel long distances to get to school.* 🔁 *She travels the world in her job.* □ **+ by** *I like travelling by train.*
2 to move at a particular speed □ *How fast does light travel?* □ *The vehicle was travelling too fast.*
► NOUN [*plural* **travels**]
1 *no plural* the activity of going from one place to another 🔁 *Cheap air travel has encouraged more people to fly.* 🔁 *Make sure you have travel insurance if you go abroad.*
2 **your travels** the journeys you make □ *Did you have good weather on your travels?*

travel agency /'trævəl 'eɪdʒənsi/ NOUN [*plural* **travel agencies**] a shop or business where you can buy holidays

travel agent /'trævəl 'eɪdʒənt/ NOUN [*plural* **travel agents**]

1 a person whose job is to arrange holidays for people
2 a travel agent's a travel agency

traveler /'trævələ(r)/ NOUN [*plural* **travelers**] the US spelling of **traveller**

traveler's check /'trævələ(r)z tʃek/ NOUN [*plural* **traveler's checks**] the US spelling of **traveller's cheque**

traveller /'trævələ(r)/ NOUN [*plural* **travellers**]
1 a person who is on a journey 🔁 *Air travellers faced delays due to bad weather.*
2 a person who lives in a vehicle and does not stay in one place

traveller's cheque /'trævələz ˌtʃek/ NOUN [*plural* **traveller's cheques**] a cheque for a fixed amount that you can change for local money when you are abroad

traverse /'trævəs, trə'vɜ:s/ VERB [**traverses, traversing, traversed**] to go from one side of a place or area to another

trawl /trɔ:l/ VERB [**trawls, trawling, trawled**]
1 to search something in order to find something □ *Detectives trawled through old police files.*
2 to catch fish by pulling a large net through the water

• **trawler** /'trɔ:lə(r)/ NOUN [*plural* **trawlers**] a boat that pulls a net along the bottom of the sea in order to catch fish

tray /treɪ/ NOUN [*plural* **trays**]
1 a flat object for carrying food, plates, cups, etc. or □ *The waiter was carrying a tray of drinks.*
2 a flat container □ *Put the paper in the paper tray*

treacherous /'tretʃərəs/ ADJECTIVE
1 very dangerous □ *Snow has caused treacherous driving conditions.* □ *treacherous mountains*
2 a treacherous person is not loyal and is willing to things that will harm you

• **treachery** /'tretʃəri/ NOUN, NO PLURAL when someone acts in a treacherous way

treacle /'tri:kəl/ NOUN, NO PLURAL a sweet, dark, sticky liquid made from sugar and used in cooking

tread /tred/ ► VERB [**treads, treading, trod, trodden**]
1 to put your foot on something □ *Don't tread on flowers.*
2 to walk in a particular way □ *We trod carefully around the broken glass.*
3 **tread carefully/warily** to be careful about what you say or do □ *We need to tread carefully.*
4 **tread water** to stay in one place in water by moving your legs up and down
► NOUN [*plural* **treads**]
1 the sound you make when you walk □ *He heard heavy tread of their boots on the bridge.*
2 the raised pattern on a tyre □ *The tread on this is completely worn away in parts.*

treason /'tri:zən/ NOUN, NO PLURAL the crime of being loyal to your country, for example by giving away secret information

treasure /'treʒə(r)/ ► NOUN [*plural* **treasures**]
1 valuable objects, especially if they have been hid □ *The children were hoping to find some buried treasure.*

2 a valuable and important object □ *The painting is a national treasure which must not be sold.*
▶ VERB [**treasures, treasuring, treasured**] to think that something is very special and important □ *These are memories which I shall always treasure.*

treasurer /'treʒərə(r)/ NOUN [*plural* **treasurers**] a person who looks after the money for an organization

treasury or **Treasury** /'treʒərɪ/ NOUN, NO PLURAL **the treasury** the part of a government that is responsible for a country's money

treat /triːt/ ▶ VERB [**treats, treating, treated**]
1 to behave in a particular way towards someone □ *I think Debbie treated Steve really badly.* □ *They treat their staff well.*
2 to deal with something in a particular way □ **+ as** *He treated my remark as a joke.* □ *We treat any form of racism very seriously.*
3 to give medicine or medical care to someone who is ill or injured □ *Doctors use all the latest methods to treat their patients.* □ **+ for** *She is being treated for shock.*
4 to put a substance on something to protect it □ *The material is treated with a spray to make it waterproof.*
5 to buy or do something special for someone □ **+ to** *I treated the children to a pizza on the way home.*
▶ NOUN [*plural* **treats**] something special that you do or buy for someone 🔊 *We're having dinner in front of the TV as a special treat.*

treatable /'triːtəbəl/ ADJECTIVE a treatable illness can be cured by medicine or medical care

treatment /'triːtmənt/ NOUN [*plural* **treatments**]
1 medicine or medical care □ *My treatment will last for about a month.* 🔊 *He is receiving treatment for a heart condition.* □ *They are trying out a new treatment for migraine.*
2 no plural the way you behave towards someone or deal with something □ *Will I get special treatment if I offer to pay more?*
3 when a substance is put on something to protect it, or the substance that is used □ *She recommended a good treatment for our floorboards.*

treaty /'triːtɪ/ NOUN [*plural* **treaties**] an official agreement between countries 🔊 *The two countries have signed a peace treaty.*

treble /'trebəl/ ▶ DETERMINER three times bigger or three times as much □ *House prices are treble what they were ten years ago.*
▶ VERB [**trebles, trebling, trebled**] to become or to make something three times as big or as much □ *Her salary has trebled over the last year.*
▶ NOUN [*plural* **trebles**]
1 the part that controls the highest sounds on a radio or other piece of equipment for playing music
2 a boy with a high singing voice

tree /triː/ NOUN [*plural* **trees**] a very tall plant with branches and leaves □ *an apple tree* □ *an oak tree*

🔊 *We planted a new tree.* 🔊 *The children were climbing trees.* 🔊 *a tree trunk*

trek /trek/ ▶ VERB [**treks, trekking, trekked**] to go on a long and difficult journey by walking □ *They were trekking in the Himalayas.*
▶ NOUN [*plural* **treks**] a long and difficult walk □ *They had to make a long trek to find water.*

trellis /'trelɪs/ NOUN [*plural* **trellises**] a wooden frame that a plant grows up

tremble /'trembəl/ ▶ VERB [**trembles, trembling, trembled**]
1 to shake because you are cold or frightened □ *Joe's hand trembled as he dialled the number.*
2 if your voice trembles, you sound weak, nervous or upset □ *Anna's voice trembled as she spoke.*
▶ NOUN [*plural* **trembles**] a shaking movement in part of the body □ *She had a slight tremble in her left hand.*

tremendous /trɪ'mendəs/ ADJECTIVE
1 very great □ *The car was travelling at a tremendous speed.*
2 very good □ *That's tremendous news!*
● **tremendously** /trɪ'mendəslɪ/ ADVERB extremely □ *We're tremendously grateful to you.*

tremor /'tremə(r)/ NOUN [*plural* **tremors**]
1 a small earthquake (=when the earth shakes) □ *The tremor lasted about a minute.*
2 a shaking movement in part of your body □ *There was a tremor in his hands.*

trench /trentʃ/ NOUN [*plural* **trenches**] a long narrow hole dug in the ground

trend /trend/ NOUN [*plural* **trends**] a gradual change or development □ *There's a new trend towards healthier eating.*
● **trendy** /'trendɪ/ ADJECTIVE [**trendier, trendiest**] fashionable □ *a trendy restaurant* □ *trendy clothes*

trepidation /ˌtrepɪ'deɪʃən/ NOUN, NO PLURAL a formal word meaning fear about something that is going to happen □ *Smith waited for his turn to jump with considerable trepidation.*

trespass /'trespəs/ VERB [**trespasses, trespassing, trespassed**] to go onto someone else's land without permission □ *No trespassing! This is private property.*
● **trespasser** /'trespəsə(r)/ NOUN [*plural* **trespassers**] someone who goes onto someone else's land without permission □ *Trespassers will be prosecuted.*

tri- /traɪ/ PREFIX tri- is added to the beginning of words to mean 'three' □ *triangle* □ *triathlon*

trial /'traɪəl/ ▶ NOUN [*plural* **trials**]
1 a legal process in which a court has to decide whether someone is guilty of a crime □ *a murder trial* 🔊 *She's on trial for the killing of her husband.* 🔊 *The suspect will now have to stand trial.* 🔊 *He had not been given a fair trial.*
2 a test that is done to find out how good or effective something is □ *The company is carrying out trials on new products.* 🔊 *Clinical trials of the anti-cancer drug have been successful.*
3 trial and error a way of achieving something by

trying lots of different methods and finding out which is successful □ *They solved the problem by trial and error.*

4 trials a sports competition that decides who will be included in a team □ *The Olympic trials were held last month.*

▶ ADJECTIVE done for a short time as a way of finding out what someone or something is like □ *The couple had a trial separation last year and have now decided to get divorced.* ⅏ *He was hired for a six-month trial period.*

triangle /ˈtraɪæŋgəl/ NOUN [plural **triangles**]
1 a flat shape with three sides and three angles □ *a right-angled triangle*
2 a musical instrument in the shape of a triangle that you hit with a metal stick

• **triangular** /traɪˈæŋgjʊlə(r)/ ADJECTIVE in the shape of a triangle □ *a triangular shape* □ *a triangular piece of cloth*

triathlon /traɪˈæθlɒn/ NOUN [plural **triathlons**] a sports competition that has three parts, usually swimming, running and cycling (=riding a bicycle)

tribal /ˈtraɪbəl/ ADJECTIVE to do with a tribe □ *tribal ceremonies*

tribe /traɪb/ NOUN [plural **tribes**] a group of families who have the same culture and language and have a traditional way of living a long way from cities □ *the Christian Arab tribes of the Syrian desert*

tribesman /ˈtraɪbzmən/ NOUN [plural **tribesmen**] a man who belongs to a particular tribe

tribulation /ˌtrɪbjuˈleɪʃən/ NOUN [plural **tribulations**] a problem in life ⅏ *She told me all the trials and tribulations of her work.*

tribunal /traɪˈbjuːnəl/ NOUN [plural **tribunals**] an official group of people whose job is to make a judgment about a particular problem, crime or disagreement □ *an employment tribunal* □ *a war crimes tribunal*

tributary /ˈtrɪbjʊtrɪ/ NOUN [plural **tributaries**] a stream or river that flows into a larger river. A geography word.

tribute /ˈtrɪbjuːt/ NOUN [plural **tributes**]
1 a speech or action that shows you admire someone □ *The film will be shown as a tribute to its star who died last week.*
2 pay tribute to someone/something to praise someone or something in public
3 be a tribute to someone/something to show how good or effective someone or something is □ *The success of the project is a tribute to her skill and determination.*

trick /trɪk/ ▶ NOUN [plural **tricks**]
1 an unfair or unpleasant thing that you do to someone as a joke, or in order to get an advantage for yourself ⅏ *The children were playing tricks on each other.* ⅏ *He accused the party of using dirty tricks in the election campaign.*
2 something that looks like magic which you do to

entertain people ⅏ *a magic trick* ⅏ *Ella was doing card tricks.*
3 an effective way of doing something □ *There's a trick to opening that door quietly.* ⅏ *The trick is to find the way you learn best.*
4 do the trick if something does the trick, it does what is needed to achieve something □ *I had a headache this morning but that tablet seems to have done the trick.*

▶ ADJECTIVE a trick question a question that is designed to make you give the wrong answer

▶ VERB [**tricks, tricking, tricked**] to make someone do what you want by using clever but unfair methods □ **into** *She was tricked into signing the papers.*

• **trickery** /ˈtrɪkərɪ/ NOUN, NO PLURAL the use of trick to get what you want

trickle /ˈtrɪkəl/ ▶ VERB [**trickles, trickling, trickled**] t flow in a slow, thin stream □ *Sweat trickled down h face.*

▶ NOUN [plural **trickles**] a slow, thin stream of liqu □ *The waterfall has become a trickle because there been so little rain.*

tricky /ˈtrɪkɪ/ ADJECTIVE [**trickier, trickiest**] difficult do or to deal with □ *a tricky situation*

tricycle /ˈtraɪsɪkəl/ NOUN [plural **tricycles**] a bicyc with three wheels

tried /traɪd/ PAST TENSE AND PAST PARTICIPLE OF try

trifle /ˈtraɪfəl/ NOUN [plural **trifles**]
1 a sweet food made from cake, fruit, cream and custard (=sauce of eggs and cream)
2 a trifle a small amount □ *It's a trifle hot in here*

◆ PHRASAL VERB [**trifles, trifling, trifled**] trifle with someone/something to treat someone in a w that is not serious □ *We played chess, but he is so good, he was just trifling with me.*

• **trifling** /ˈtraɪflɪŋ/ ADJECTIVE not at all important trifling matter

trigger /ˈtrɪgə(r)/ ▶ NOUN [plural **triggers**]
1 the part you pull to fire a gun ⅏ *He pointed the and pulled the trigger.*
2 something that causes something else to happe □ *Money is one of the most common triggers for arguments.*

▶ VERB [**triggers, triggering, triggered**] to make something start to happen □ *The announcement triggered violent protests around the country.*

trill /trɪl/ ▶ NOUN [plural **trills**] in music, when tw notes are played one after the other, very fast

▶ VERB [**trills, trilling, trilled**] to make a sound li trill □ *Birds were trilling in the high branches.*

trillion /ˈtrɪljən/ NUMBER [plural **trillions**] the nur 1,000,000,000,000

trilogy /ˈtrɪlədʒɪ/ NOUN [plural **trilogies**] a set of plays, books, poems, etc. that have the same subje the same characters

trim /trɪm/ ▶ VERB [**trims, trimming, trimmed**]
1 to cut a small amount off something □ *Get you trimmed.* □ *You'll need to trim that photo to get the frame.*

2 to decorate the edges of something □ *a coat trimmed with white fur*

3 to reduce something □ *The company has been forced to trim the number of employees.*

▶ NOUN [*plural* **trims**]

1 the act of cutting a small amount off something □ *Ask the hairdresser for a quick trim.*

2 a decoration that is added to something □ *The dress had a lace trim at the neck.*

▶ ADJECTIVE a trim person has a thin but healthy and attractive body

trimming /'trɪmɪŋ/ NOUN [*plural* **trimmings**]

a decoration on the edge of something

all the trimmings extra things added to a meal to make it more special or traditional □ *We had a Christmas dinner of roast turkey and all the trimmings.*

trinket /'trɪŋkɪt/ NOUN [*plural* **trinkets**] a piece of jewellery or a small pretty object which is not valuable

trio /'triːəʊ/ NOUN [*plural* **trios**] a group of three people or things, especially musicians

trip /trɪp/ ▶ NOUN [*plural* **trips**] a journey to a place and back again □ *There are boat trips around Lake Geneva.* 🖭 *a shopping trip* 🖭 *He has made several trips to Japan.* □ **+ to** *We went on a trip to the zoo.*

▶ VERB [**trips, tripping, tripped**]

1 to hit your foot on something and fall, or almost fall □ **+ over** *Caroline tripped over the edge of the carpet.* □ *Mind you don't trip on the step.*

2 to make someone fall by putting your foot in front of them □ **+ up** *One of the boys tripped me up.*

triple /'trɪpəl/ ▶ ADJECTIVE consisting of three parts □ *triple-glazed windows* □ *a triple somersault*

▶ VERB [**triples, tripling, tripled**] to become or to make something three times bigger in size or amount □ *The number of students has tripled this year.*

▶ DETERMINER three times as big, as many, or as much □ *We had triple the number of entries this year.*

triplet /'trɪplɪt/ NOUN [*plural* **triplets**] one of three children born to the same mother at the same time

tripod /'traɪpɒd/ NOUN [*plural* **tripods**] a piece of equipment with three legs, used for supporting something like a camera

trite /traɪt/ ADJECTIVE a trite remark, phrase, etc. is one that people have said so often that it is not interesting or original □ *It sounds trite to say that funerals 'bring people together', but it's true.*

triumph /'traɪəmf/ ▶ NOUN [*plural* **triumphs**]

1 a great success in a competition or fight □ *It was another triumph for the champions.* □ *England's only World Cup triumph was in 1966.*

2 the feeling of happiness you get when you have won or been successful □ *He felt a sense of triumph.*

▶ VERB [**triumphs, triumphing, triumphed**] to win or succeed □ *Yeltsin triumphed over his rivals again.*

triumphant /traɪˈʌmfənt/ ADJECTIVE very happy winning or succeeding □ *the triumphant medal-lers*

• **triumphantly** /traɪˈʌmfəntlɪ/ ADVERB in a triumphant way □ *She raised her arm triumphantly.*

trivia /'trɪvɪə/ NOUN, NO PLURAL facts and details that are not important □ *She knew a lot of sports trivia.*

• **trivial** /'trɪvɪəl/ ADJECTIVE not important or not serious □ *trivial details* □ *a trivial problem*

• **triviality** /ˌtrɪvɪˈælətɪ/ NOUN [*plural* **trivialities**]

1 something that is not important □ *I don't want to bore you with trivialities.*

2 the quality of not being important

• **trivialize** or **trivialise** /'trɪvɪəlaɪz/ VERB [**trivializes, trivializing, trivialized**] to make something seem less important than it really is □ *No one should trivialize this achievement.*

trod /trɒd/ PAST TENSE OF tread

trodden /'trɒdən/ PAST PARTICIPLE OF tread

trolley /'trɒlɪ/ NOUN [*plural* **trolleys**]

1 a container on wheels, used for carrying things □ *a supermarket trolley*

2 a table on wheels

3 the US word for tram

trombone /trɒmˈbəʊn/ NOUN [*plural* **trombones**] a metal musical instrument that you play by blowing, and by sliding a long part up and down

troop /truːp/ ▶ NOUN [*plural* **troops**]

1 troops soldiers □ *The US sent troops to Darfur.*

2 a group of people or animals □ *a troop of monkeys*

▶ VERB [**troops, trooping, trooped**] if a group of people troop somewhere, they go there □ *More than 7.5 million people trooped through the museum's doors last year.*

trophy /'trəʊfɪ/ NOUN [*plural* **trophies**] a prize such as a silver cup that you get for winning a competition □ *Helen won the junior tennis trophy three years running.*

tropical /'trɒpɪkəl/ ADJECTIVE in or to do with the tropics □ *a tropical rainforest*

tropics /'trɒpɪks/ PLURAL NOUN the tropics the hot areas near the equator (=line round the middle of the world). A geography word.

trot /trɒt/ ▶ VERB [**trots, trotting, trotted**]

1 if a horse trots, it moves more quickly than walking, but does not run □ *The horse trotted down the road.*

2 if a person trots somewhere, they walk with short, fast steps □ *They all trotted off to look at his paintings.*

• PHRASAL VERB **trot something out** to say something that has been said many times before □ *Politicians trot out the same old ideas at election time.*

▶ NOUN [*plural* **trots**]

1 on the trot happening one after the other □ *The team have won three games on the trot.*

2 a speed that is slightly faster than walking

trouble /'trʌbəl/ ▶ NOUN [*plural* **troubles**]

1 problems, difficulties or worries □ **+ ing** *She has trouble sleeping.* □ *He had financial troubles.* 🖭 *You'd have no trouble finding a better job.*

2 no plural extra effort 🖭 *A washing machine would save you a lot of trouble.* 🖭 *He took the trouble to*

thank everyone individually. 🔁 They went to so much trouble to make our visit pleasant.

3 no plural the thing about something that causes problems 🔁 The trouble is, I already have a meeting on that day. ▫ The trouble with Sarah is that she never stops to think.

4 no plural a problem with your health or with a machine or piece of equipment ▫ She has heart trouble. ▫ The car had some sort of engine trouble.

5 no plural a difficult or dangerous situation 🔁 Their ship got into trouble during a storm. 🔁 The business is in deep trouble.

6 no plural a situation where you will be punished or blamed 🔁 We got into trouble for talking in class. 🔁 If I'm late home, I'll be in big trouble.

7 no plural a situation where people are behaving badly, fighting, causing difficulties, etc. 🔁 Some people at the back of the hall started to cause trouble. 🔁 The trouble started when police tried to arrest the man.

▶ VERB [**troubles, troubling, troubled**] if something troubles you, it worries you ▫ They were troubled by reports of violence in the area.

• **troubled** /ˈtrʌbəld/ ADJECTIVE
1 suffering because you have a lot of problems in your life ▫ The troubled star returned home yesterday.
2 having a lot of problems ▫ We live in troubled times.

• **troublemaker** /ˈtrʌbəlˌmeɪkə(r)/ NOUN [plural **troublemakers**] someone who deliberately causes problems

• **troublesome** /ˈtrʌbəlsəm/ ADJECTIVE causing worry or problems ▫ He has a troublesome knee injury.

trough /trɒf/ NOUN [plural **troughs**] a long container that animals eat or drink from

trounce /traʊns/ VERB [**trounces, trouncing, trounced**] to defeat someone very easily

troupe /truːp/ NOUN [plural **troupes**] a group of performers who work together ▫ a troupe of acrobats

trouser /ˈtraʊzə(r)/ ADJECTIVE relating to trousers ▫ He put the money in his trouser pocket.

trousers /ˈtraʊzəz/ PLURAL NOUN a piece of clothing for the lower half of your body that covers each leg separately 🔁 She was wearing a pair of black trousers. ▫ leather trousers

trout /traʊt/ NOUN [plural **trout**] a type of fish that lives in rivers and lakes and is eaten

truancy /ˈtruːənsɪ/ NOUN, NO PLURAL the act of staying away from school without permission

• **truant** /ˈtruːənt/ NOUN [plural **truants**]
1 a student who stays away from school without permission
2 play truant to stay away from school without permission

truce /truːs/ NOUN [plural **truces**] an agreement to stop fighting or arguing 🔁 The political parties called a truce.

truck /trʌk/ NOUN [plural **trucks**] a large road vehicle for carrying goods ▫ He drove the truck into the yard ▫ Her Dad's a truck driver.

trudge /trʌdʒ/ VERB [**trudges, trudging, trudged**] to walk with slow, heavy steps ▫ They were trudging along in the snow.

true /truː/ ADJECTIVE [**truer, truest**]
1 real and not invented 🔁 Is it a true story? ▫ + that it true that you're moving to Tokyo?
2 real and not pretended ▫ Ben never showed his tru feelings. ▫ She's a true friend. ▫ He had finally four true love. ▫ He had a false passport to hide his true identity.
3 come true if something comes true, the thing yc have spoken about really happens ▫ I never though my wish to travel round the world would come true
4 be true to someone/something to be loyal tc someone or something, and do what you said you would do ▫ He had always been true to his principl

truffle /ˈtrʌfəl/ NOUN [plural **truffles**]
1 a soft sweet made of chocolate
2 a rare type of fungus (=plant with no leaves or flowers) that grows under the ground, which you can

truly /ˈtruːlɪ/ ADVERB
1 really ▫ Tell me what you truly want to do.
2 in a sincere way ▫ I'm truly sorry.

trump /trʌmp/ NOUN [plural **trumps**] a card that ha higher value than other cards in some card games
♦ IDIOM come up/turn up trumps to do something which helps you to succeed, especially when it is r expected ▫ Beckham came up trumps with a goal the last minute of the game.

trump card /ˈtrʌmp ˌkɑːd/ NOUN [plural **trump cards**] a usually secret advantage that will help yc succeed

trumped-up /ˈtrʌmptʌp/ ADJECTIVE deliberately invented in order to make someone seem guilty ▫ trumped-up evidence

trumpet /ˈtrʌmpɪt/ NOUN [plural **trumpets**] a m musical instrument that you blow into ▫ Millie is learning to play the trumpet.

truncheon /ˈtrʌntʃən/ NOUN [plural **truncheons**] short, thick stick that police officers carry

trundle /ˈtrʌndəl/ VERB [**trundles, trundling, trundled**]
1 to move slowly along on wheels or to move something like this ▫ Lorries were trundling thro the empty streets
2 to walk in a slow, heavy way ▫ Eventually, he trundled off down the road.

trunk /trʌŋk/ NOUN [plural **trunks**]
1 the thick main stem of a tree 🔁 a tree trunk
2 an elephant's long nose
3 a large box for storing things
4 the main part of a person's body, not including head, arms or legs
5 the US word for boot (=part of a car)

trunk road /ˈtrʌŋk ˌrəʊd/ NOUN [*plural* **trunk roads**] a main road between towns

trunks /trʌŋks/ PLURAL NOUN a piece of clothing that men or boys wear for swimming

trust /trʌst/ ▶ VERB [**trusts, trusting, trusted**]
1 to believe that someone is honest and loyal □ *The colonel picked out ten men he knew he could trust.*
2 to feel confident that someone will do something correctly and well or will look after something well □ **+ to do something** *I know I can trust you to choose a suitable present.*
3 to allow someone to have or use something that belongs to you because you think they will be careful with it □ **+ with** *Can I trust you with my new camera?*
4 Trust you/him/her, etc. used to say that a silly or annoying action is typical of someone □ *Trust Dan to be late!*
▶ NOUN [*plural* **trusts**]
1 *no plural* the belief that someone is honest and loyal 🔁 *The new manager will have to gain the trust of her staff.*
2 a legal arrangement in which someone looks after and controls money or property for someone else 🔁 *His inheritance was held in trust until he was twenty one.*

trustee /trʌsˈtiː/ NOUN [*plural* **trustees**]
1 someone who looks after and controls someone else's money or property in a legal arrangement
2 one of a group of people who manage a company or organization such as a school or hospital

trusting /ˈtrʌstɪŋ/ ADJECTIVE believing that other people are honest and good □ *She is a very trusting person.*

trustworthy /ˈtrʌstˌwɜːðɪ/ ADJECTIVE able to be trusted □ *I'm sure he's a trustworthy person.*

truth /truːθ/ NOUN [*plural* **truths**]
1 the truth the true facts 🔁 *I don't think he is telling the truth.* 🔁 *The simple truth is that she never really loved him.* □ **+ about** *I don't think we'll ever know the truth about what happened.*
2 *no plural* the quality of being true □ **+ in** *Do you think there's any truth in the rumours that he is planning to leave?*
3 a fact that people accept is true □ *People don't like being told uncomfortable truths.*

> Note that you **tell** the **truth**. You do not 'say the truth':
> ✓ *Tell me the truth: Do you like her?*
> ✗ *Say the truth: Do you like her?*

truthful /ˈtruːθfʊl/ ADJECTIVE honest □ *I don't think he's been completely truthful with me.* □ *a truthful answer*

truthfully /ˈtruːθfʊlɪ/ ADVERB in a truthful way □ *I don't think he answered truthfully.*

try /traɪ/ ▶ VERB [**tries, trying, tried**]
1 make an effort or an attempt to do something □ **+ to do something** *Please try to understand.* □ *We tried everything we could to save him.* 🔁 *He failed the exam, but he can always try again next year.*
2 to do or use something to see if you like it or if it works or is effective □ *Try this powder for a cleaner wash.* □ *I've never tried Chinese food.* □ **+ ing** *You could try phoning him.*
3 to find out if someone committed a crime by hearing all the evidence (=facts or statements given in a court of law) □ *They will be tried in the European Court of Human Rights.* □ **+ for** *She was tried for murder.*
♦ PHRASAL VERBS **try something on** to put on a piece of clothing to see if it fits or what it looks like on you □ *I tried on three summer dresses but I didn't like any of them.* **try something out** to use something to see if it works or is effective or if you like it □ *We're trying out a new type of carrot seed this year.*
➡ **go to** try your *luck*
▶ NOUN [*plural* **tries**]
1 an attempt to do something □ *That was a good try. Better luck next time.* 🔁 *I couldn't get the tyre off - could you have a try?*
2 when you do or use something to see if you like it or if it works or is effective 🔁 *I saw an advert for a sailing course, so I thought I'd give it a try.*
3 in the sport of rugby, a successful attempt to put the ball over the other team's goal line
● **trying** /ˈtraɪɪŋ/ ADJECTIVE difficult and annoying □ *He can be very trying sometimes.*

tsar /zɑː(r)/ NOUN [*plural* **tsars**] a ruler of Russia before 1917

T-shirt /ˈtiː ʃɜːt/ NOUN [*plural* **T-shirts**] a piece of clothing made from soft cotton which you wear on the top part of your body □ *She was wearing jeans and a white T-shirt.*

tsp /ˈtiːspuːn/ ABBREVIATION teaspoon

tsunami /tsuːˈnɑːmɪ/ NOUN [*plural* **tsunamis**] a very high, fast wave that is caused by an earthquake (=when the ground shakes) under the sea

tub /tʌb/ NOUN [*plural* **tubs**]
1 a container with a lid which has food in it □ *a tub of ice cream*
2 a round, deep container □ *The tub was full of bright red flowers.*
3 the US word for bath

tuba /ˈtjuːbə/ NOUN [*plural* **tubas**] a large metal musical instrument that you blow which plays very low notes

tubby /ˈtʌbɪ/ ADJECTIVE [**tubbier, tubbiest**] an informal word meaning slightly fat

tube /tjuːb/ NOUN [*plural* **tubes**]
1 a long, thin pipe □ *He was in hospital with a feeding tube in his stomach.*
2 a container for a soft substance which you press to get the substance out □ **+ of** *a tube of toothpaste*
3 *no plural* an underground railway system, especially

in London □ *We can easily get there by tube.* 🔊 *a tube station*

tuber /'tju:bə(r)/ NOUN [*plural* **tubers**] a swollen underground plant root that new plants can grow from. A biology word □ *Potatoes are tubers that you can eat or plant again.*

tuberculosis /tju:ˌbɜ:kjʊ'ləʊsɪs/ NOUN, NO PLURAL a serious infectious disease that affects your lungs

tuck /tʌk/ VERB [**tucks, tucking, tucked**]
1 to push the edge of something somewhere to make it tidy or firm □ *Tuck your shirt into your trousers.* □ *She tucked the flap into the envelope and sealed it with tape.*
2 to put something into a small space □ *She tucked the bag under her arm.*
♦ PHRASAL VERBS **tuck something away 1** to put something in a safe place □ *He quickly tucked the letter away when Ann walked into the room.*
2 if a place is tucked away, it is difficult to find or few people go there □ *The studio is tucked away at the top of the house.* **tuck in/tuck into something** an informal word meaning to start eating something enthusiastically □ *Joe tucked into a bowl of spaghetti.*
tuck someone in/up 1 to make someone comfortable in bed by putting the sheets over them □ *She went upstairs to tuck the children in.*
2 if you are tucked up in bed, you are lying comfortably in bed □ *He was tucked up in bed by 9pm.*

Tuesday /'tju:zdɪ/ NOUN [*plural* **Tuesdays**] the day of the week after Monday and before Wednesday □ *Kay's coming on Tuesday.*

tuft /tʌft/ NOUN [*plural* **tufts**] several pieces of grass or hair that are growing from the same place □ *The baby had a tuft of dark hair.*

tug /tʌg/ ► VERB [**tugs, tugging, tugged**] to pull something suddenly and firmly □ *She tugged her hand away from mine.* □ *James tugged on the rope.*
► NOUN [*plural* **tugs**]
1 a sudden firm pull 🔊 *I gave his arm a tug and he looked at me crossly.*
2 a tugboat

tugboat /'tʌgbəʊt/ NOUN [*plural* **tugboats**] a boat that is used for pulling other boats

tug-of-war /'tʌgəv'wɔ:(r)/ NOUN, NO PLURAL a competition in which two teams pull each end of a rope and try to pull each other over

tuition /tju:'ɪʃən/ NOUN, NO PLURAL teaching something, especially to one person or a small group □ *His parents paid for him to have private tuition in English.* 🔊 *Students have to pay tuition fees.*

tulip /'tju:lɪp/ NOUN [*plural* **tulips**] a type of flower in the shape of a cup that is often red or yellow

tumble /'tʌmbəl/ ► VERB [**tumbles, tumbling, tumbled**]
1 to fall somewhere □ *He tripped and tumbled down the stairs.*
2 if a price tumbles, it suddenly becomes lower □ *Oil prices tumbled last week.*

► NOUN [*plural* **tumbles**] a fall 🔊 *Lucy had taken a tumble* (=fallen) *over the doorstep.*

tumbledown /'tʌmbəldaʊn/ ADJECTIVE a tumbledown building is old and in bad condition

tumble-dry /'tʌmbəl'draɪ/ VERB [**tumble-dries, tumble-drying, tumble-dried**] to dry clothes in a tumble-dryer

● **tumble-dryer** *or* **tumble-drier** /'tʌmbəl'draɪə(r)/ NOUN [*plural* **tumble-dryers** *or* **tumble-driers**] a machine that dries clothes by turning them in hot a

tumbler /'tʌmblə(r)/ NOUN [*plural* **tumblers**] a glass with straight sides that you drink from

tummy /'tʌmɪ/ NOUN [*plural* **tummies**] an informal word for stomach

tumour /'tju:mə(r)/ NOUN [*plural* **tumours**] a group o cells in your body which are not growing in a norma way □ *He had an operation to remove a brain tumour.*

tumult /'tju:mʌlt/ NOUN [*plural* **tumults**] a formal word meaning a situation in which there is a lot of noise, confusion, or excitement □ *the tumult of batt*

● **tumultuous** /tju:'mʌltjʊəs/ ADJECTIVE
1 involving a lot of activity, violence, or confusion □ *had been a tumultuous year.*
2 noisy and excited □ *He walked on stage to tumultuous applause.*

tuna /'tju:nə/ NOUN [*plural* **tuna**] a large sea fish th you can eat □ *a tuna sandwich*

tundra /'tʌndrə/ NOUN, NO PLURAL a large area whe the ground is always frozen below the surface, and many plants can grow. A geography word.

tune /tju:n/ ► NOUN [*plural* **tunes**]
1 a series of musical notes that sound nice 🔊 *She playing some tunes on the piano.* 🔊 *a catchy tune* (=one that is easy to remember)
2 in tune playing or singing exactly the right sou □ *He can't sing in tune.*
3 out of tune playing or singing sounds which ar slightly wrong □ *The piano is out of tune.*
4 be in tune with someone/something to understand the way someone thinks and the thin that they want □ *She is very in tune with the need her students.*
5 be out of tune with someone/something to understand the way that someone thinks and the things that they want □ *The government is out of with the people in this country.*
♦ IDIOM **change your tune** to change your opinior surprising or sudden way □ *You've changed your*
► VERB [**tunes, tuning, tuned**]
1 to make small changes to a musical instrumen that it sounds right □ *Ben was tuning his guitar.*
2 if a radio or television is tuned to a particular programme, it is receiving it □ *You're tuned to F Gold.* 🔊 *Stay tuned* (=keep listening or watching) *chance to win £1,000.*
3 to make small changes to an engine so that it v better
♦ PHRASAL VERB **tune in** to listen to or watch a

particular radio or television programme □ Over 5 million viewers tuned in to watch the game.

tuneful /'tju:nfʊl/ ADJECTIVE tuneful music is nice to listen to

tuneless /'tju:nlɪs/ ADJECTIVE not having a pleasant tune

tunelessly /'tju:nlɪslɪ/ ADVERB in a tuneless way □ She was whistling tunelessly.

tunic /'tju:nɪk/ NOUN [plural tunics] a loose piece of clothing with no sleeves

tunnel /'tʌnəl/ ▶ NOUN [plural tunnels] a long underground passage □ There is a rail tunnel linking England and France. 🔄 There were plans to build a tunnel through the Alps.

▶ VERB [tunnels, tunnelling/US tunneling, tunnelled/ US tunneled] to make an underground passage □ Will they tunnel under the river or build a bridge over it?

turban /'tɜ:bən/ NOUN [plural turbans] a long piece of cloth that some men wrap around their heads for religious reasons

turbine /'tɜ:baɪn/ NOUN [plural turbines] a machine or engine that gets power when water or gas moves a wheel around

turbulence /'tɜ:bjʊləns/ NOUN, NO PLURAL movement in the water or air that makes ships or aircraft move suddenly □ There was a lot of turbulence in the flight so we had to stay in our seats.
when there are lot of sudden and confusing changes political turbulence

turbulent /'tɜ:bjʊlənt/ ADJECTIVE involving a lot of changes, confusion or disagreement □ It was a turbulent week for the government. □ a turbulent relationship
turbulent air or water moves suddenly and strongly

turf /tɜ:f/ ▶ NOUN, NO PLURAL short thick grass and the soil under it
▶ VERB [turfs, turfing, turfed] to put turf on an area of ground

▶ PHRASAL VERB **turf someone out** an informal word meaning to make someone leave a place □ He was turfed out of the club following an argument.

turkey /'tɜ:kɪ/ NOUN [plural turkeys]
a large bird that lives on farms and is eaten as food
no plural the meat from this bird □ roast turkey □ a turkey sandwich

turmoil /'tɜ:mɔɪl/ NOUN, NO PLURAL a state of worry and confusion □ Her mind was in turmoil. □ political turmoil

turn /tɜ:n/ ▶ VERB [turns, turning, turned]
to move your body or part of your body to face in another direction □ He turned and walked away. □ + round I turned around to look at them. □ + to She turned to her neighbour and whispered something. He turned his head slightly.
to move something so that it faces in another direction, or to move like this □ The car turned upside down. □ + over You must not turn the cards over

before the game starts. □ + round He turned the book round so that we could see the picture.

3 to make a circular movement around a central point, or to make something do this □ The wheels began to turn. □ Turn the handle to the right.

4 if you turn the page of a book, you move it so that you can see the next page

5 to change in a particular way □ She took one look and turned pale. □ Things turned nasty when the police arrived.

6 if your thoughts or your conversation turn to something, you start thinking or talking about that subject □ Later on, talk turned to the coming elections. 🔄 We need to turn our attention to the causes of these crimes.

◆ IDIOM **not turn a hair** to not show any emotion when something shocking happens

➡ go to **turn a blind eye** to something, **turn your nose up** at something, **turn the tables** on someone

◆ PHRASAL VERBS **turn (someone) against someone/something** to start to dislike someone or something and to stop supporting them, or to make someone do this □ My friends have all turned against me. **turn someone away** to say that someone cannot go into a place □ When they arrived at work the next day, they were turned away. **turn (someone) back** to stop a journey and go back again, or to make someone do this □ Their car was turned back at the border. **turn something down** to make a machine produce less sound, heat, etc. □ Could you turn the music down, please? □ I've turned down the heating. **turn someone/something down** to not accept an offer □ He asked her to marry him but she turned him down. □ I turned down a job in his company. **turn (someone/something) into someone/ something** to change into something different or to make someone or something do this □ His book is being turned into a movie. □ The caterpillar turns into a moth. **turn off (something)** to leave the road or path you are travelling on to go on another road or path □ Turn off the main road when you see a sign to the town hall. **turn something off** to move a switch so that a machine stops working or a supply of something is stopped □ Don't forget to turn off the lights. **turn something on** to move a switch so that a machine starts working or a supply of something is started □ I've turned on the heating. **turn out** to be found to have a particular reason, quality or result 🔄 It turned out that she'd never received the letter. 🔄 Conditions in the hotel turned out to be really bad. **turn over** to change to a different television programme **turn to someone** to go to someone for help □ I had lots of problems at work, and I felt there was nobody to turn to. **turn up 1** to arrive □ He didn't turn up for work this morning. **2** to be found □ My glasses turned up in the car. **turn something up** to make a machine produce more sound, heat, etc. □ Can you turn the volume up?

▶ NOUN [plural turns]

1 the time when you can or must do something, before or after someone else ⊞ *It's your/my turn next.* □ *Josh hasn't had a turn yet.*
2 take turns/take it in turns if people take turns, each person does something, one after the other
3 in turn one after the other □ *He tried each of the dishes in turn.*
4 a change of direction or a curve or corner in a road or path ⊞ *Take the first turn on the right.* ⊞ *a left/right turn*
5 when something is moved in a circle around a central point □ *I gave the screw another turn.*
6 when a situation changes ⊞ *Events took a dramatic turn when the president announced his resignation.* ⊞ *His health has taken a turn for the better/worse.*
7 a good turn something helpful or kind that you do for someone

turnaround /ˈtɜːnəraʊnd/ NOUN [*plural* **turnarounds**] a situation that changes from a bad one to a good one □ *In a remarkable turnaround, the team went on to win the competition.*

turning /ˈtɜːnɪŋ/ NOUN [*plural* **turnings**] a place where a car can leave a road and go onto another road ⊞ *Take the second turning on the right.* ⊞ *We took a wrong turning and ended up on a mud track.*

turning point /ˈtɜːnɪŋ ˌpɔɪnt/ NOUN [*plural* **turning points**] an important time which could change the future of something □ *He's reached a turning point in his career.*

turnip /ˈtɜːnɪp/ NOUN [*plural* **turnips**] a hard, round, white vegetable that grows under the ground

turnout /ˈtɜːnaʊt/ NOUN, NO PLURAL the number of people who go to an event or who go to vote in an election ⊞ *There was a low turnout in the election.*

turnover /ˈtɜːnˌəʊvə(r)/ NOUN [*plural* **turnovers**]
1 the value of the goods and services that a company sells during a particular time □ *The business has an annual turnover of more than $2.4 billion.*
2 the rate at which people leave and join a company or organization □ *The company has a high turnover of staff.*
3 a piece of pastry which is folded over fruit or jam □ *an apple turnover*

turnpike /ˈtɜːnpaɪk/ NOUN [*plural* **turnpikes**] a large road in America which drivers pay to use

turnstile /ˈtɜːnstaɪl/ NOUN [*plural* **turnstiles**] a gate that turns, allowing one person to go through at a time

turpentine /ˈtɜːpəntaɪn/ NOUN, NO PLURAL a liquid with a strong smell, used for removing paint

turquoise /ˈtɜːkwɔɪz/ ▶ NOUN, NO PLURAL a green-blue colour
▶ ADJECTIVE having a green-blue colour

turret /ˈtʌrɪt/ NOUN [*plural* **turrets**] a small tower on a castle

turtle /ˈtɜːtəl/ NOUN [*plural* **turtles**] an animal that usually lives in water and has a hard shell

tusk /tʌsk/ NOUN [*plural* **tusks**] one of the two long teeth that stick out of the mouth of some animals, such as elephants

tussle /ˈtʌsəl/ ▶ NOUN [*plural* **tussles**] a fight or argument between two people who want the same thing □ *They have been involved in a legal tussle over their daughter.*
▶ VERB [**tussles, tussling, tussled**] to argue or fight with someone over something you both want □ *The players were tussling for the ball.*

tut /tʌt/ or **tut-tut** /ˌtʌtˈtʌt/ ▶ EXCLAMATION a sound you make with your tongue to show disapproval
▶ VERB [**tuts, tutting, tutted**] to make a sound with your tongue to show disapproval

tutor /ˈtjuːtə(r)/ ▶ NOUN [*plural* **tutors**]
1 a teacher who teaches one person or a small group □ *He hired a private tutor to help him learn Japanese.*
2 a university teacher who works with a small group of students
▶ VERB [**tutors, tutoring, tutored**] to teach one person or a small group □ *He tutored children with learning difficulties.*

● **tutorial** /tjuːˈtɔːriəl/ NOUN [*plural* **tutorials**] a university class in which a small group of students discuss a subject □ *She had no lectures or tutorials that day.*

TV /ˈtiːˈviː/ NOUN [*plural* **TVs**] television ⊞ *She switched the TV on.* □ *What's on TV tonight?* ⊞ *I think the children watch too much TV.*

twang /twæŋ/ NOUN [*plural* **twangs**]
1 the sound of a tight string or wire being pulled □ *I listened to the twang of his guitar strings.*
2 someone's accent □ *His voice had a southern twang.*

tweak /twiːk/ ▶ VERB [**tweaks, tweaking, tweaked**]
1 to pull something quickly and suddenly □ *He tweaked my hair roughly.*
2 to make small changes to something □ *They have tweaked the words of the song.*
▶ NOUN [*plural* **tweaks**]
1 a quick and sudden pull
2 a small change that is made to something

tweed /twiːd/ NOUN [*plural* **tweeds**] a type of thick wool cloth □ *a tweed jacket*

tweezers /ˈtwiːzəz/ PLURAL NOUN a small tool consisting of two narrow pieces of metal that are joined at one end, used for picking up very small things or for pulling out hairs

twelfth /twelfθ/ NUMBER 12th written as a word

twelve /twelv/ NUMBER [*plural* **twelves**] the number 12

twentieth /ˈtwentɪəθ/ NUMBER 20th written as a word

twenty /ˈtwentɪ/ NUMBER [*plural* **twenties**]
1 the number 20
2 the twenties the years between 1920 and 1929

twice /twaɪs/ ADVERB two times □ *He sneezed twice.* □ *I could eat twice that amount.* □ *I visit my grandmother twice a week.*

twiddle /ˈtwɪdəl/ VERB [twiddles, twiddling, twiddled] to move something around several times in your hands, especially because you are bored □ *He was twiddling with his wedding ring.*

IDIOM **twiddle your thumbs** an informal phrase meaning to do nothing because you are waiting for something to happen □ *We were left twiddling our thumbs when the builder failed to arrive.*

twig /twɪg/ ► NOUN [plural twigs] a thin branch from a tree □ *We need a pile of dry twigs to start the fire.*
► VERB [twigs, twigging, twigged] an informal word meaning to suddenly understand something □ *Then I twigged what he meant.*

twilight /ˈtwaɪlaɪt/ NOUN, NO PLURAL the time in the evening just before it becomes completely dark

twin /twɪn/ ► NOUN [plural twins] one of two children born to the same mother at the same time □ *Paul and Jo are twins.* 🔁 *Our children are identical twins* (=they look exactly the same).
ADJECTIVE
twin sister/brother/daughters, etc. a sister, brother, etc. who is a twin □ *Bella's my twin sister.*
belonging to a pair of things that are very similar □ *twin beds* □ *The boat is powered by twin engines.*
VERB [twins, twinning, twinned] if a place is twinned with another place in a different country, the two places have a special relationship □ *Edinburgh is twinned with Munich.*

twine /twaɪn/ ► NOUN, NO PLURAL strong string
VERB [twines, twining, twined] to twist around something □ *Roses twined round the fence posts.*

twinge /twɪndʒ/ NOUN [plural twinges] a sudden unpleasant feeling □ *a twinge of pain* □ *Heidi felt a twinge of guilt.*

twinkle /ˈtwɪŋkəl/ ► VERB [twinkles, twinkling, twinkled]
1 if lights or stars twinkle, they shine in the dark, often in a way that looks as if their light is going on and off □ *The lights were twinkling along the shore.*
2 if someone's eyes twinkle, they look happy or as if they are joking
NOUN [plural twinkles]
1 bright shining light
2 look in your eyes that shows you are happy or joking □ *He had a mischievous twinkle in his eye.*

twirl /twɜːl/ ► VERB [twirls, twirling, twirled] to turn round and around very quickly, or to make something turn around and around very quickly □ *The leaders of the parade twirled their batons.*
NOUN [plural twirls] a fast turn around and around

twist /twɪst/ ► VERB [twists, twisting, twisted]
1 turn something using your hands □ *Twist the handle hard and then pull it to open the door.* □ *She twisted the lid of the jar.*
2 turn the top half of your body □ + *round/around* □ *Rory twisted round in his chair to look at me.*
3 bend something out of its correct shape □ *The wheel of the bike twisted when it hit the wall.*

4 **twist your ankle/knee, etc.** to hurt your ankle, knee, etc. by turning it suddenly
5 if a road or river twists, it has a lot of curves in it 🔁 *The road twisted and turned up the mountain.*
6 to change what someone has said in an unfair way 🔁 *He was angry about the way the media had twisted his words.*
♦ IDIOM **twist someone's arm** an informal phrase meaning to persuade someone to do something □ *OK then, I'll come - you've twisted my arm!*
► NOUN [plural twists]
1 a sudden and unexpected change in a story or situation □ *This announcement added a new and bizarre twist to his sudden death.*
2 a movement in which you turn something □ *Give the lid a twist.*
3 a piece of something that has been bent □ *She put a twist of lemon in the drink.*
4 a curve in a road or river

● **twisted** /ˈtwɪstɪd/ ADJECTIVE
1 bent □ *The car was a wreck of twisted metal after the crash.*
2 enjoying things which are cruel or shocking □ *The story looks inside a killer's twisted mind.*

twit /twɪt/ NOUN [plural twits] an informal word meaning a stupid person □ *Don't be such a twit!*

twitch /twɪtʃ/ ► VERB [twitches, twitching, twitched]
1 if part of your body twitches, it moves slightly in a way you cannot control □ *Her eyelid twitched.*
2 to make a small, sudden movement □ *I thought I saw the curtains twitch.*
► NOUN [plural twitches]
1 a slight movement of your body which you cannot control
2 a small, sudden movement

twitter /ˈtwɪtə(r)/ VERB [twitters, twittering, twittered] to make several high noises □ *Birds were twittering in the trees.*

two /tuː/ NUMBER [plural twos] the number 2
♦ IDIOMS **be in two minds** to not be able to decide between two possibilities □ *I'm in two minds about whether to sell my car.* **put two and two together** to guess the truth of something from things you have seen or heard □ *'How did you know she was going out with Tom?' 'Well, she seemed happier than usual, and when I saw them at the cinema, I put two and two together.'*

two-dimensional /ˈtuːdɪˈmenʃəl/ ADJECTIVE
1 a two-dimensional shape is flat
2 a two-dimensional character in a book, television programme, etc. does not seem real because their personality is not shown well enough

two-faced /ˈtuːˈfeɪst/ ADJECTIVE not sincere about your feelings or opinions, and telling people whatever will please them

twofold /ˈtuːfəʊld/ ► ADJECTIVE twice as much or as many 🔁 *There has been a twofold increase in crime rates.*

▶ ADVERB by twice as much or as many □ *Divorce has increased twofold.*

two-way /ˈtuːˈweɪ/ ADJECTIVE
1 moving or allowing movement in two opposite directions □ *a two-way street* □ *two-way traffic*
2 a two-way communication system is able to send and receive messages □ *a two-way radio*

tycoon /taɪˈkuːn/ NOUN [*plural* **tycoons**] a rich and successful person in business □ *She married a Texas oil tycoon.*

type /taɪp/ ▶ NOUN [*plural* **types**]
1 used for talking about people or things that have similar qualities and can be considered as a group ✋ *Research of this type has never been done before.* □ **+ of** *He's the type of person who never worries about anything.* □ *What type of dog have you got?* □ *There are many different types of cancer.*
2 someone who has particular interests or qualities □ *Kate's not the jealous type.*
3 be someone's type to be the kind of person that someone is attracted to □ *Andy's nice but he's not really my type.*
4 no plural printed letters and numbers □ *The title should be in bold type.*
▶ VERB [**types, typing, typed**] to write something using a keyboard on a computer or typewriter □ *Type your name and then your password.*

typewriter /ˈtaɪpˌraɪtə(r)/ NOUN [*plural* **typewriters**] an old-fashioned machine that prints words directly onto paper when you press keys

• **typewritten** /ˈtaɪpˌrɪtən/ ADJECTIVE produced using a typewriter □ *a typewritten letter*

typhoid /ˈtaɪfɔɪd/ NOUN, NO PLURAL a serious disease that you get from dirty food or water

typhoon /taɪˈfuːn/ NOUN [*plural* **typhoons**] a tropical storm with strong winds

typical /ˈtɪpɪkəl/ ADJECTIVE having the usual qualities of a particular person or thing ✋ *This is a typical example of a 17th-century cottage.* □ *Beth is a typical teenager.* □ *On a typical day, there are over 100,000 lorries on Britain's roads.* □ **+ of** *It was typical of Emi to offer to help.*

• **typically** /ˈtɪpɪkliː/ ADVERB
1 used for saying what is usually true or what usually happens □ *An insect typically has six legs and two pairs of wings.* □ *Schools in the area typically finish around 3pm.*
2 as you would expect from a particular person or thing □ *Typically, Tracy arrived late.* □ *He was behaving in a typically aggressive way.*

typist /ˈtaɪpɪst/ NOUN [*plural* **typists**] someone whose job is to type letters in an office

tyrannical /tɪˈrænɪkəl/ ADJECTIVE using power in a cruel and unfair way □ *a tyrannical leader*

tyranny /ˈtɪrəniː/ NOUN [*plural* **tyrannies**] a cruel and unfair way of using power

tyrant /ˈtaɪrənt/ NOUN [*plural* **tyrants**] a ruler who uses power in a cruel and unfair way

tyre /ˈtaɪə(r)/ NOUN [*plural* **tyres**] a piece of rubber around the edge of a wheel, which has air in it ✋ *had a flat tyre.*

U u

or u /juː/ the 21st letter of the alphabet

biquitous /juːˈbɪkwɪtəs/ ADJECTIVE seeming to be everywhere □ *the ubiquitous use of mobile phones*

dder /ˈʌdə(r)/ NOUN [*plural* **udders**] the part that hangs under a cow and produces milk

FO /juːefˈəʊ, ˈjuːfəʊ/ ABBREVIATION unidentified flying object; an object flying in the sky that cannot be explained and that some people think may come from another planet

gh /ʌg/ EXCLAMATION used to express disgust □ *'Ugh! It tastes horrible.'*

gliness /ˈʌglɪnɪs/ NOUN, NO PLURAL the state of being ugly

gly /ˈʌglɪ/ ADJECTIVE [**uglier, ugliest**]
not pleasant to look at □ *an ugly building* □ *a big ugly monster*
very unpleasant, and often involving violence □ *When the police arrived, things started to get ugly.*

People do not often use the word **ugly** to describe people as it sounds unkind. Sometimes the word **plain** (which has the same meaning) is used instead as it sounds less unkind.

T milk /ˈjuːeɪtʃtiːˈmɪlk/ NOUN, NO PLURAL milk that been heated to a very high temperature to make it stay fresh for longer

/juːˈkeɪ/ ABBREVIATION United Kingdom

er /ˈʌlsə(r)/ NOUN [*plural* **ulcers**] a small sore area your skin or inside your body □ *a mouth ulcer*

rior /ʌlˈtɪərɪə(r)/ ADJECTIVE ulterior motive a secret reason for doing something or behaving in a particular way □ *He's started being very helpful, but sure he's got an ulterior motive.*

nate /ˈʌltɪmət/ ▶ ADJECTIVE
happening at the end of a process □ *Our ultimate was to give up work.*
better, worse, greater, etc. than all others □ *He the ultimate sacrifice for his country.*
NOUN, NO PLURAL the ultimate in something the or greatest example of something □ *This sofa is ultimate in luxury.*

mately /ˈʌltɪmətlɪ/ ADVERB at the end of a ss □ *Ultimately, they were forced to admit* it.

atum /ˌʌltɪˈmeɪtəm/ NOUN [*plural* **ultimatums** imata] if you give someone an ultimatum, you ten something bad if they do not do what you

want □ *I gave her an ultimatum - either get rid of the dog or I'm leaving.*

ultra- /ˈʌltrə/ PREFIX ultra- is added to the beginning of words to mean 'extremely' □ *ultra-careful*

ultrasound /ˈʌltrəsaʊnd/ NOUN, NO PLURAL sound waves that are used to make a picture of the inside of someone's body □ *Many pregnant women have an ultrasound scan.*

ultraviolet /ˌʌltrəˈvaɪələt/ ADJECTIVE ultraviolet light is light you cannot see and which turns the skin darker. A physics word.

umbilical cord /ʌmˈbɪlɪkəl ˈkɔːd/ NOUN [*plural* **umbilical cords**] the tube that connects a baby to its mother while it is inside its mother's body. A biology word.

umbrella /ʌmˈbrelə/ NOUN [*plural* **umbrellas**] a frame with cloth over it that you hold above you for shelter when it rains

umpire /ˈʌmpaɪə(r)/ NOUN [*plural* **umpires**] the person in a game such as cricket, who makes sure the players obey the rules

umpteen /ˌʌmpˈtiːn/ DETERMINER an informal word meaning a large number □ *We've been there umpteen times.*
• **umpteenth** /ˌʌmpˈtiːnθ/ DETERMINER an informal word meaning the latest in a long number of things □ *For the umpteenth time, don't put banana skins in the waste paper basket!*

UN /juːˈen/ ABBREVIATION United Nations

un- /ʌn/ PREFIX un- is used at the beginning of words to mean 'not' □ *untidy* □ *unkind*

unable /ʌnˈeɪbəl/ ADJECTIVE unable to do something not able to do something □ *He stood completely still, unable to take his eyes off the bear.*

unacceptable /ˌʌnəkˈseptəbəl/ ADJECTIVE something unacceptable cannot be allowed to happen, exist or continue because it is wrong or not of a high enough standard □ *His behaviour is totally unacceptable.* □ *The bank decided that the financial risk was unacceptable.*
• **unacceptably** /ˌʌnəkˈseptəblɪ/ ADVERB of an unacceptable level or standard □ *There is an unacceptably high level of pollution in the river.*

unaccompanied /ˌʌnəˈkʌmpənɪd/ ADJECTIVE not having anyone with you □ *Unaccompanied children are not permitted at this event.*

unaccountable /ˌʌnəˈkaʊntəbəl/ ADJECTIVE
1 impossible to explain 🕀 *For some unaccountable reason, he decided to wear a velvet suit.*
2 someone who is unaccountable does not have to explain the reasons for their actions □ *Many of Scotland's services are run by people who are unaccountable to the public.*
• **unaccountably** /ˌʌnəˈkaʊntəblɪ/ ADVERB without an explanation □ *She was feeling unaccountably depressed.*

unaccounted for /ˌʌnəˈkaʊntɪd fɔː(r)/ ADJECTIVE if someone or something is unaccounted for, you do not know what has happened to them or how they have been used □ *Eight people were killed in the explosion and four people are still unaccounted for.*

unaccustomed /ˌʌnəˈkʌstəmd/ ADJECTIVE
1 not usual □ *We were in the unaccustomed position of having plenty of money.*
2 unaccustomed to something not used to something □ *I was unaccustomed to such luxury.*

unadulterated /ˌʌnəˈdʌltəreɪtɪd/ ADJECTIVE
1 pure, with nothing added □ *unadulterated drinking water.*
2 used to emphasize how good or bad something is □ *The holiday was two weeks of unadulterated pleasure.*

unaffected /ˌʌnəˈfektɪd/ ADJECTIVE not affected or changed by something □ *Most people working here have been unaffected by the changes in company policy.*

unaided /ʌnˈeɪdɪd/ ADJECTIVE without help □ *She is now able to walk unaided.*

unambiguous /ˌʌnæmˈbɪgjʊəs/ ADJECTIVE having only one, clear meaning □ *The law is quite unambiguous on this point.*

unanimity /ˌjuːnəˈnɪmətɪ/ NOUN, NO PLURAL the state of being unanimous

unanimous /juːˈnænɪməs/ ADJECTIVE agreed by everyone □ *a unanimous decision*
• **unanimously** /juːˈnænɪməslɪ/ ADVERB in a way that is unanimous □ *He was elected unanimously.*

unannounced /ˌʌnəˈnaʊnst/ ADJECTIVE, ADVERB if you arrive somewhere unannounced, you have not told anyone you are coming

unanswered /ʌnˈɑːnsəd/ ADJECTIVE
1 not having been answered or solved 🕀 *There are a lot of unanswered questions about the origins of the universe.*
2 unanswered letters, telephone calls, etc. have not been replied to

unapproachable /ˌʌnəˈprəʊtʃəbəl/ ADJECTIVE difficult to talk to because of being formal and unfriendly

unarmed /ʌnˈɑːmd/ ADJECTIVE without weapons □ *They attacked a group of unarmed civilians.*

unassuming /ˌʌnəˈsjuːmɪŋ/ ADJECTIVE having a pleasant, quiet manner, and not wanting to be notice

unattainable /ˌʌnəˈteɪnəbəl/ ADJECTIVE impossible t get or to achieve

unattended /ˌʌnəˈtendɪd/ ADJECTIVE not being looke after □ *Passengers are asked not to leave their luggag unattended.*

unattractive /ˌʌnəˈtræktɪv/ ADJECTIVE
1 not pleasant to look at □ *a rather unattractive modern house*
2 not pleasant or not enjoyable □ *Pride is one of h more unattractive qualities.*

unauthorized or **unauthorised** /ʌnˈɔːθəraɪzd/ ADJECTIVE done or produced without official permissi □ *an unauthorized biography*

unavailable /ˌʌnəˈveɪləbəl/ ADJECTIVE
1 not able to be somewhere or to speak to someo □ *I'm sorry, Dr Hughes is unavailable at the mome.*
2 impossible to get or buy □ *His book is unavailable the UK.*

unavoidable /ˌʌnəˈvɔɪdəbəl/ ADJECTIVE impossible avoid or prevent □ *I'm sorry to give you extra work, I I'm afraid it's unavoidable.*
• **unavoidably** /ˌʌnəˈvɔɪdəblɪ/ ADVERB for reason that could not be avoided □ *I was unavoidably delayed.*

unaware /ˌʌnəˈweə(r)/ ADJECTIVE not knowing about something □ *We were unaware of the danger.*
• **unawares** /ˌʌnəˈweəz/ ADVERB **catch/take** someone unawares to happen when someone d not expect it □ *Their arrival caught me unawares.*

unbearable /ʌnˈbeərəbəl/ ADJECTIVE too painful unpleasant to deal with □ *The pain was unbearal.*
• **unbearably** /ʌnˈbeərəblɪ/ ADVERB in a way tha impossible to accept or deal with □ *It is unbearably outside.*

unbeatable /ʌnˈbiːtəbəl/ ADJECTIVE better than others □ *Our catalogue offers unbeatable value money.*
• **unbeaten** /ʌnˈbiːtən/ ADJECTIVE never having b beaten in a game or competition 🕀 *Can United maintain its unbeaten record?*

unbelievable /ˌʌnbɪˈliːvəbəl/ ADJECTIVE
1 used to emphasize how bad, good, extreme, e something is □ *For me, seeing the whales was a unbelievable experience.*
2 difficult to believe □ *an unbelievable story*
• **unbelievably** /ˌʌnbɪˈliːvəblɪ/ ADVERB used to emphasize how bad, good, extreme, etc. somethi □ *She's unbelievably rich.*

unblock /ʌnˈblɒk/ VERB [**unblocks, unblocking, unblocked**] to remove something that is blockin something such as a pipe □ *I had to unblock th*

unborn /ʌnˈbɔːn/ ADJECTIVE not yet born 🕀 *an u child*

unbroken /ʌnˈbrəʊkən/ ADJECTIVE continuous has the longest unbroken run of wins in the spo

unbutton /ˌʌnˈbʌtən/ VERB [**unbuttons, unbuttoning, unbuttoned**] to open the buttons, especially on a piece of clothing □ *He unbuttoned his shirt.*

uncalled for /ˌʌnˈkɔːld fɔː(r)/ ADJECTIVE offensive and not fair □ *That remark was completely uncalled for.*

uncanny /ʌnˈkænɪ/ ADJECTIVE strange and difficult to explain □ *He had an uncanny ability to know what I was thinking.*

uncaring /ʌnˈkeərɪŋ/ ADJECTIVE not kind and not caring about bad things that happen to people

uncertain /ʌnˈsɜːtən/ ADJECTIVE
1 not sure what to decide □ *+ about* I was uncertain about what to do next.
2 not known ᵇ *The future is uncertain.* □ *+ question word* It is still uncertain whether he will be fit enough to play.

uncertainty /ʌnˈsɜːtəntɪ/ NOUN [*plural* **uncertainties**] when something is uncertain □ *There is a lot of uncertainty surrounding the event.*

unchanged /ʌnˈtʃeɪndʒd/ ADJECTIVE staying the same □ *Her condition remained unchanged overnight.*

uncharacteristic /ˌʌnˌkærəktəˈrɪstɪk/ ADJECTIVE not typical of someone or something □ *He spoke with uncharacteristic anger.*

uncharitable /ʌnˈtʃærɪtəbəl/ ADJECTIVE not kind □ *He made some rather uncharitable remarks about their work.*

uncivilized *or* **uncivilised** /ʌnˈsɪvɪlaɪzd/ ADJECTIVE
1 rude and offensive □ *Do you think it's uncivilized to eat with your fingers?*
2 an offensive word meaning not having a developed society or culture
3 an uncivilized time is a time that is not convenient, especially very early in the morning

uncle /ˈʌŋkəl/ NOUN [*plural* **uncles**]
1 the brother of one of your parents □ *My aunt and uncle live in Scotland.* □ *Uncle Douglas came to visit.*
2 your aunt's husband

unclean /ʌnˈkliːn/ ADJECTIVE
1 not morally good □ *After the experience, she felt unclean.*
2 dirty □ *unclean conditions*

unclear /ʌnˈklɪə(r)/ ADJECTIVE
1 not obvious or easy to understand □ *It's unclear why she left her job.* □ *The writing was rather unclear.*
2 if you are unclear about something, you do not completely understand it □ *I'm sorry; I'm still unclear on that point - could you explain it again?*

uncomfortable /ʌnˈkʌmftəbəl/ ADJECTIVE
1 not feeling comfortable □ *We were uncomfortable in the heat.*
2 causing you to feel uncomfortable □ *The seats were very uncomfortable.*
3 slightly embarrassed or slightly embarrassing □ *+ about* I feel uncomfortable about accepting money from her. □ *There were a lot of uncomfortable silences.*

• **uncomfortably** /ʌnˈkʌmftəblɪ/ ADVERB
1 in an uncomfortable way □ *Tom shifted uncomfortably in his seat.*
2 in a way that makes you feel worried or embarrassed □ *Inflation is still uncomfortably high.*

uncommon /ʌnˈkɒmən/ ADJECTIVE unusual or rare ᵇ *It is not uncommon for luggage to go missing.*

uncompromising /ʌnˈkɒmprəmaɪzɪŋ/ ADJECTIVE determined not to change your opinions or decisions □ *He has been uncompromising in his opposition to the government's plans.*

unconcerned /ˌʌnkənˈsɜːnd/ ADJECTIVE not worried about something □ *She was unconcerned about the prospect of months of unemployment.*

unconditional /ˌʌnkənˈdɪʃənəl/ ADJECTIVE not limited in any way □ *an unconditional surrender* ᵇ *My mother gave us unconditional love.*

• **unconditionally** /ˌʌnkənˈdɪʃənəlɪ/ ADVERB without any limits □ *It is required that you agree to these terms unconditionally.*

unconfirmed /ˌʌnkənˈfɜːmd/ ADJECTIVE unconfirmed information may not be true because there is no official proof yet ᵇ *There were unconfirmed reports that the man had been seen in Paris.*

unconnected /ˌʌnkəˈnektɪd/ ADJECTIVE not related in any way □ *His decision to resign was entirely unconnected to his illness.*

unconscious /ʌnˈkɒnʃəs/ ADJECTIVE
1 in a state like sleep where you are not aware of what is happening around you, because you are seriously ill or injured ᵇ *A brick hit his head and he was knocked unconscious.*
2 an unconscious thought or feeling is one that you are not aware of having □ *I think I must have had an unconscious desire to hurt my brother.*
3 if you are unconscious of something, you do not notice it □ *He was unconscious of the danger.*

• **unconsciously** /ʌnˈkɒnʃəslɪ/ ADVERB if you do something unconsciously, you are not aware that you are doing it □ *I must have been copying her unconsciously.*

• **unconsciousness** /ʌnˈkɒnʃəsnɪs/ NOUN, NO PLURAL the state of being unconscious

uncontrollable /ˌʌnkənˈtrəʊləbəl/ ADJECTIVE not possible to control ᵇ *She suddenly had an uncontrollable urge to kick something.*

• **uncontrollably** /ˌʌnkənˈtrəʊləblɪ/ ADVERB in an uncontrollable way □ *She sobbed uncontrollably at the funeral.*

unconventional /ˌʌnkənˈvenʃənəl/ ADJECTIVE different from what most people think is normal □ *He uses unconventional methods to train his animals.* □ *My parents were very unconventional.*

• **unconventionally** /ˌʌnkənˈvenʃənəlɪ/ ADVERB in an unconventional way □ *She likes to dress unconventionally.*

unconvincing /ˌʌnkən'vɪnsɪŋ/ ADJECTIVE
1 if something is unconvincing, you do not believe it or do not think it is correct □ *He produced a somewhat unconvincing excuse for being late.*
2 not seeming real □ *The plot and the characters are unconvincing.*

uncooperative /ˌʌnkəʊ'ɒpərətɪv/ ADJECTIVE not willing to help someone or to work with other people □ *He was being deliberately uncooperative.*

uncoordinated /ˌʌnkəʊ'ɔ:dɪneɪtɪd/ ADJECTIVE
1 an uncoordinated person moves their body in an awkward way □ *I'm too uncoordinated to be good at games.*
2 badly organized so that the parts of something do not work well together □ *The publicity campaign had been run in a hasty, uncoordinated fashion.*

uncount noun /ʌn'kaʊnt 'naʊn/ *or* **uncountable noun** /ʌn'kaʊntəbəl 'naʊn/ NOUN [*plural* **uncount nouns** *or* **uncountable nouns**] in grammar, a noun that does not have a plural form, e.g. *happiness, water* or *advice*

uncouth /ʌn'ku:θ/ ADJECTIVE rude and unpleasant □ *He is aggressive and uncouth.*

uncover /ʌn'kʌvə(r)/ VERB [**uncovers, uncovering, uncovered**]
1 to discover something that had been secret or hidden ⌨ *Police have uncovered new evidence relating to the murder.*
2 to remove a cover from something

undecided /ˌʌndɪ'saɪdɪd/ ADJECTIVE not having made a decision about something

undelete /ˌʌndɪ'li:t/ VERB [**undeletes, undeleting, undeleted**] on a computer, to make something that has been deleted (=removed) appear again

undeniable /ˌʌndɪ'naɪəbəl/ ADJECTIVE certainly true □ *It is undeniable that the Earth goes round the sun.*
• undeniably /ˌʌndɪ'naɪəblɪ/ ADVERB in a way that is certainly true

under /'ʌndə(r)/ ▶ PREPOSITION
1 below something □ *The bag is under the table.* □ *We walked under the bridge.*
2 covered by something □ *I found my glasses under a cushion.* □ *The mountains were under a thick layer of snow.*
3 less than an amount, level or age □ *All the clothes are under £20.* □ *The competition is open to anyone under 30.*
4 having a particular thing done, or affected by a particular thing ⌨ *Our troops came under attack.* ⌨ *He was under pressure to resign.* ⌨ *I think you should show her some sympathy under the circumstances* (=because of the situation).
5 controlled by a particular person, government, organization, etc. □ *The country was under military control.* □ *This issue does not come under my authority.*
6 according to a rule, law, etc. □ *Under the proposal, people would pay to have their rubbish removed.* □ *He will be allowed to continue on the course under certain conditions.*

7 used to show where to find or put information, books, documents, etc. □ *You'll find her books under 'history'.*
▶ ADVERB
1 in or to a lower place □ *We watched the divers go under.*
2 less than an amount, level or age □ *The play equipment is for children aged 6 and under.*

under- /'ʌndə(r)/ PREFIX
1 under- is added to the beginning of words to mean 'below' □ *underfoot* □ *underground*
2 under- is added to the beginning of words to mean 'not enough' □ *underdeveloped* □ *undernourished*

under-age /'ʌndər 'eɪdʒ/ ADJECTIVE not old enough to do something legally

underarm /'ʌndərɑ:m/ ▶ ADJECTIVE, ADVERB if you throw a ball underarm, you start with your hand in a low position and facing up
▶ NOUN [*plural* **underarms**] the area of your body under your arm

undercover /'ʌndə,kʌvə(r)/ ADJECTIVE working or done secretly □ *an undercover police operation*

underdeveloped /ˌʌndədɪ'veləpt/ ADJECTIVE an underdeveloped country or area is not modern and does not have much industry

underdog /'ʌndədɒg/ NOUN [*plural* **underdogs**] the person or team that will probably lose a competition

underdone /ˌʌndə'dʌn/ ADJECTIVE not cooked enough

underestimate /ˌʌndə'restɪmeɪt/ VERB [**underestimates, underestimating, underestimated**]
1 to think that something or someone is less important, valuable, powerful, etc. than they really are □ *You should not underestimate the importance of a good education.*
2 to think that an amount will be less than it is □ *The builder underestimated the number of bricks needed.* □ *I completely underestimated how much work the course would be.*

underfoot /ˌʌndə'fʊt/ ADVERB on the ground where you are walking □ *The stones underfoot grew slippy in the rain.*

undergo /ˌʌndə'gəʊ/ VERB [**undergoes, undergoing, underwent, undergone**] to experience something □ *He underwent an operation to mend his broken leg.*

undergraduate /ˌʌndə'grædʒuət/ NOUN [*plural* **undergraduates**] someone who is studying at a university and has not yet done their degree (=qualification)

underground ▶ ADJECTIVE /'ʌndəgraʊnd/
▶ ADVERB /ˌʌndə'graʊnd/
1 below the surface of the ground □ *Moles live underground.* □ *an underground stream*
2 existing or done secretly and often illegally □ *underground organization*
▶ NOUN /'ʌndəgraʊnd/ [*plural* **undergrounds**] a railway that is under the ground, usually in a large city □ *the London Underground*

undergrowth /ˈʌndəɡrəʊθ/ NOUN, NO PLURAL bushes and plants that cover the ground

underhand /ˌʌndəˈhænd/ ADJECTIVE secret and not honest □ *Some players use underhand tactics to confuse their opponents.*

underline /ˌʌndəˈlaɪn/ VERB [underlines, underlining, underlined]
1 to draw a line under something □ *Underline all the adjectives in these sentences.*
2 to emphasize that something is important or true □ *She underlined the need to be careful crossing the road.*

underlying /ˌʌndəˈlaɪɪŋ/ ADJECTIVE underlying reasons, problems, etc. are basic and important, but not easy to notice at first ⊞ *The underlying cause of these diseases is poverty.*

undermine /ˌʌndəˈmaɪn/ VERB [undermines, undermining, undermined] to make someone or something weaker, less confident or less effective □ *Her colleagues are always trying to undermine her.* □ *Reduced funding threatens to undermine our work.*

underneath /ˌʌndəˈniːθ/ ADVERB, PREPOSITION
under something □ *Look underneath the table!* □ *He was wearing a jumper with a shirt underneath.*
used to describe what someone or something is really like, when they seem different □ *Underneath the fierce exterior, he's a really kind person.*

undernourished /ˌʌndəˈnʌrɪʃt/ ADJECTIVE not healthy because of not eating enough good food

underpants /ˈʌndəpænts/ PLURAL NOUN underwear that men and boys wear under their trousers

underpass /ˈʌndəpɑːs/ NOUN [plural underpasses] a road or path under another road

underprivileged /ˌʌndəˈprɪvɪlɪdʒd/ ADJECTIVE having less money and fewer opportunities than other people

underrate /ˌʌndəˈreɪt/ VERB [underrates, underrating, underrated] to think that someone or something is less good than they really are □ *We would not underrate Australia's football team.*

underrated /ˌʌndəˈreɪtɪd/ ADJECTIVE of a higher quality than people think □ *He's a very underrated composer.*

understand /ˌʌndəˈstænd/ VERB [understands, understanding, understood]
to know what something means □ *I can't understand the instructions.* □ *Do you understand man?*
to know why something happens, how something works, or the effect or importance of something □ + **question word** *Doctors still don't understand how the disease is spread.* □ *We didn't understand the significance of his words at the time.*
to know why someone behaves and feels the way they do □ *I'll never understand him.* □ *I understood*

her anger. □ *I don't understand what you are trying to achieve.*
4 to think that something is true □ + **that** *I understood that you weren't coming.*

● **understandable** /ˌʌndəˈstændəbəl/ ADJECTIVE reasonable in a particular situation □ *His disappointment at not being in the football team was understandable.*

● **understandably** /ˌʌndəˈstændəblɪ/ ADVERB in a way that is reasonable in a particular situation □ *She was understandably upset.*

● **understanding** /ˌʌndəˈstændɪŋ/ ▶ NOUN [plural understandings]
1 *no plural* knowledge about something ⊞ *Scientists are trying to gain a better understanding of the origins of the universe.*
2 *no plural* when someone shows that they accept that your behaviour and feelings are reasonable, or when someone shows sympathy □ *My teachers showed great understanding when my father died.*
3 an agreement between two people, often one that is not spoken or written □ *We have an understanding. I cut his grass and he gives me apples.*
4 my/his/their, etc. understanding what I/he/they, etc. think is true □ *My understanding was that the meeting would still take place.*
5 on the understanding that used to say that you will do something if someone agrees to something □ *I will accept the post of chairman on the understanding that it will be for one year only.*
▶ ADJECTIVE able to understand other people's feelings or to forgive someone because of their situation □ *The illness makes me bad-tempered at times, but my family have been very understanding.*

understatement /ˌʌndəˈsteɪtmənt/ NOUN [plural understatements] when you describe something in a way that makes it seem less extreme than it really is □ *To say that his work is inadequate is an understatement.*

understood /ˌʌndəˈstʊd/ PAST TENSE AND PAST PARTICIPLE of **understand**

understudy /ˈʌndəˌstʌdɪ/ NOUN [plural understudies] someone who learns the part of another actor so they can play that part if the actor is ill

undertake /ˌʌndəˈteɪk/ VERB [undertakes, undertaking, undertook, undertaken]
1 to start to do a job or an activity, usually one that will take a long time □ *We all had to undertake extensive training.*
2 undertake to do something a formal word meaning to promise to do something □ *I undertook to ensure their safety.*

undertaker /ˈʌndəˌteɪkə(r)/ NOUN [plural undertakers] someone whose job is to arrange funerals

undertaking /ˌʌndəˈteɪkɪŋ/ NOUN [plural undertakings]
1 a difficult or long job or activity □ *It will be an enormous undertaking to equip every member of staff with their own terminal.*

2 a promise to do something ⊞ *The company has given an undertaking to protect jobs.*

undervalue /ˌʌndəˈvælju:/ VERB [**undervalues, undervaluing, undervalued**] to not understand how valuable, important, useful, etc. someone or something is □ *Sometimes we undervalue the contribution of artists to society.*

• **undervalued** /ˌʌndəˈvælju:d/ ADJECTIVE if something or someone is undervalued, people do not understand how valuable, important, useful, etc. they are □ *She felt undervalued in her last job.*

underwater /ˌʌndəˈwɔ:tə(r)/ ADJECTIVE, ADVERB under the surface of water □ *an underwater creature* □ *Can you swim underwater?*

underway /ˈʌndəˈweɪ/ ADJECTIVE happening or having started ⊞ *Work on the new motorway got underway last week.*

underwear /ˈʌndəweə(r)/ NOUN, NO PLURAL clothes you wear next to your skin and under your other clothes

underweight /ˌʌndəˈweɪt/ ADJECTIVE not heavy enough

underwent /ˌʌndəˈwent/ PAST TENSE OF **undergo**

underworld /ˈʌndəˌwɜ:ld/ NOUN, NO PLURAL
1 the criminals in a society and the lives they have
2 in stories, the place where people go when they die

undesirable /ˌʌndɪˈzaɪərəbəl/ ADJECTIVE unpleasant or harmful □ *She's mixing with some very undesirable friends.* □ *The drugs have undesirable side effects.*

undetected /ˌʌndɪˈtektɪd/ ADJECTIVE not discovered or seen ⊞ *The fraud went undetected for years.*

undid /ʌnˈdɪd/ PAST TENSE OF **undo**

undignified /ʌnˈdɪɡnɪfaɪd/ ADJECTIVE embarrassing or making you look silly □ *She landed in an undignified heap at the bottom of the steps.*

undisguised /ˌʌndɪsˈɡaɪzd/ ADJECTIVE undisguised feelings are not hidden □ *She watched her son receive his certificate with undisguised pride.*

undisputed /ˌʌndɪˈspju:tɪd/ ADJECTIVE not questioned or doubted by anyone □ *She is the undisputed leader in this area of research.*

undivided /ˌʌndɪˈvaɪdɪd/ ADJECTIVE complete ⊞ *You must give me your undivided attention.*

undo /ʌnˈdu:/ VERB [**undoes, undoing, undid, undone**]
1 to open something that is fastened □ *He undid his jacket.*
2 to get rid of the effect of something that has been done, so that something goes back to its original state □ *She's undone all the good work of the previous manager.*

undoing /ʌnˈdu:ɪŋ/ NOUN, NO PLURAL the thing that causes someone to fail □ *He's clever enough but greed was his undoing.*

undone /ʌnˈdʌn/ ▶ PAST PARTICIPLE OF **undo**
▶ ADJECTIVE
1 not fastened, closed or tied ⊞ *One of your shoelaces has come undone.*

2 not done □ *The kitchen was filthy and the washing had been left undone.*

undoubted /ʌnˈdaʊtɪd/ ADJECTIVE certain □ *Ellie has undoubted talent as a singer.*

• **undoubtedly** /ʌnˈdaʊtɪdlɪ/ ADVERB certainly □ *He is undoubtedly one of the best players.*

undress /ʌnˈdres/ VERB [**undresses, undressing, undressed**] to take your clothes off, or to take someone's clothes off

• **undressed** /ʌnˈdrest/ ADJECTIVE not wearing any clothes ⊞ *He was getting undressed.*

undue /ʌnˈdju:/ ADJECTIVE more than is necessary □ *undue alarm*

• **unduly** /ʌnˈdju:lɪ/ ADVERB more than is necessary □ *He did not seem unduly worried.*

unearth /ʌnˈɜ:θ/ VERB [**unearths, unearthing, unearthed**]
1 to discover something, especially something secret or hidden □ *Someone had unearthed some unpleasant facts about him.*
2 to find something by digging in the ground

unearthly /ʌnˈɜ:θlɪ/ ADJECTIVE strange and a bit frightening □ *an unearthly sound*

unease /ʌnˈi:z/ NOUN, NO PLURAL a feeling of being worried that something bad might happen □ *There growing unease about the military situation.*

• **uneasily** /ʌnˈi:zɪlɪ/ ADVERB in a way that shows ye are worried □ *John looked uneasily at his watch.*

• **uneasiness** /ʌnˈi:zɪnɪs/ NOUN, NO PLURAL anoth word for **unease**

• **uneasy** /ʌnˈi:zɪ/ ADJECTIVE
1 worried that something bad might happen □ *I fe uneasy about walking home so late at night.*
2 an uneasy situation or relationship could change a become worse at any time □ *At the moment, ther an uneasy peace in the area.*

unemployed /ˌʌnɪmˈplɔɪd/ ▶ ADJECTIVE withou job □ *My Dad's unemployed at the moment.*
□ *unemployed miners*
▶ NOUN **the unemployed** people who are unemplo

• **unemployment** /ˌʌnɪmˈplɔɪmənt/ NOUN, NO PLURAL
1 the number of people who do not have a job ⊞ *Unemployment has risen again.*
2 not having a job

unemployment benefit /ˌʌnɪmˈplɔɪmənt ˈbenɪfɪt/ NOUN, NO PLURAL money that the governm pays to people who do not have jobs

unending /ʌnˈendɪŋ/ ADJECTIVE seeming to cont for ever □ *Today was just an unending successior interruptions.*

unenthusiastic /ˌʌnɪnθju:zɪˈæstɪk/ ADJECTIVE n wanting to do something or not thinking that something is good □ *She was very unenthusiasti about the trip.*

• **unenthusiastically** /ˌʌnɪnθju:zɪˈæstɪklɪ/ AD in an unenthusiastic way □ *They agreed unenthusiastically to stay another day.*

unenviable /ˌʌnˈenvɪəbəl/ ADJECTIVE difficult and not pleasant 🕮 *I had the unenviable task of telling her that her work was not good enough.*

unequal /ˌʌnˈiːkwəl/ ADJECTIVE
1 different in size, amount or position □ *an unequal share of money*
2 not fair because of not being the same for everyone □ *The report claims that old people receive unequal treatment from doctors.*

unequivocal /ˌʌnɪˈkwɪvəkəl/ ADJECTIVE clearly stated so that there can be no doubt about what is meant □ *He has the party's unequivocal support.*

unequivocally /ˌʌnɪˈkwɪvəklɪ/ ADVERB in an unequivocal way □ *She has stated quite unequivocally that she will not resign.*

unerring /ˌʌnˈɜːrɪŋ/ ADJECTIVE always correct or accurate □ *She had an unerring talent for spotting promising youngsters.*

unethical /ˌʌnˈeθɪkəl/ ADJECTIVE morally wrong □ *He has acted in a most unethical manner.*

uneven /ˌʌnˈiːvən/ ADJECTIVE
not level or smooth □ *an uneven road*
not the same in size or amount □ *There is an uneven distribution of cancer cases in the country.*
not all of the same quality □ *Your work has been uneven this year.*

unevenly /ˌʌnˈiːvənlɪ/ ADVERB in an uneven way □ *The paint was applied unevenly.*

uneventful /ˌʌnɪˈventfʊl/ ADJECTIVE without anything interesting, surprising or important happening □ *The holidays were pretty uneventful.*

unexpected /ˌʌnɪkˈspektɪd/ ADJECTIVE surprising because of not being expected □ *an unexpected visitor* □ *an unexpected development*

unexpectedly /ˌʌnɪkˈspektɪdlɪ/ ADVERB in a way that you were not expecting □ *He was unexpectedly delayed.*

unexplained /ˌʌnɪkˈspleɪnd/ ADJECTIVE not yet having an explanation □ *unexplained deaths*

unfailing /ˌʌnˈfeɪlɪŋ/ ADJECTIVE an unfailing quality is always present and strong □ *Thanks to her unfailing good humour and encouragement we managed to get the crisis sorted out.*

unfair /ˌʌnˈfeə(r)/ ADJECTIVE
not right or reasonable □ *Some of her criticism was unfair.*
when a situation is unfair, people are not treated in an equal way, or do not have equal opportunities □ *His father's fame gives him an unfair advantage.*

unfairly /ˌʌnˈfeəlɪ/ ADVERB in a way that is unfair □ *We have been very unfairly treated.*

unfairness /ˌʌnˈfeənɪs/ NOUN, NO PLURAL being unfair

unfaithful /ˌʌnˈfeɪθfʊl/ ADJECTIVE not loyal or not keeping your promises

unfamiliar /ˌʌnfəˈmɪljə(r)/ ADJECTIVE
not known or seen before □ *an unfamiliar feeling* □ *an unfamiliar face*

2 **unfamiliar with something** not having any knowledge or experience of something □ *I was unfamiliar with the British legal system.*

unfashionable /ˌʌnˈfæʃənəbəl/ ADJECTIVE not fashionable or popular □ *Wide ties were becoming unfashionable.*

unfasten /ˌʌnˈfɑːsən/ VERB [unfastens, unfastening, unfastened] to open something that was fastened □ *She unfastened her coat.*

unfavorable /ˌʌnˈfeɪvrəbəl/ ADJECTIVE the US spelling of unfavourable

unfavourable /ˌʌnˈfeɪvrəbəl/ ADJECTIVE
1 not positive, or criticizing something □ *They came back with unfavourable reports of the resort.*
2 likely to cause problems or make it difficult to succeed □ *The company did well despite unfavourable economic conditions.*

unfeeling /ˌʌnˈfiːlɪŋ/ ADJECTIVE not feeling sympathy for other people □ *I'm sorry to seem unfeeling, but I can't solve your problems for you.*

unfinished /ˌʌnˈfɪnɪʃt/ ADJECTIVE not completed □ *The builders left the house unfinished when the money ran out.*

unfit /ˌʌnˈfɪt/ ADJECTIVE
1 not suitable or not good enough □ *The water is unfit to drink.*
2 not in good physical condition, especially because of not doing enough exercise

unfold /ˌʌnˈfəʊld/ VERB [unfolds, unfolding, unfolded]
1 to spread out something that was folded
2 if a situation unfolds, it develops and people start to know about it □ *The details of what happened began to unfold.*

unforeseen /ˌʌnfɔːˈsiːn/ ADJECTIVE not expected 🕮 *The flight has been cancelled due to unforeseen circumstances.*

unforgettable /ˌʌnfəˈgetəbəl/ ADJECTIVE impossible to forget, usually because of being enjoyable, interesting, etc. □ *Seeing the lions up close was a truly unforgettable experience.*

unforgivable /ˌʌnfəˈgɪvəbəl/ ADJECTIVE unforgivable behaviour is so bad that you cannot forgive it
● **unforgivably** /ˌʌnfəˈgɪvəblɪ/ ADVERB in a way that is unforgivable □ *She was unforgivably rude.*

unfortunate /ˌʌnˈfɔːtʃnət/ ADJECTIVE
1 caused by bad luck □ *an unfortunate accident*
2 if something is unfortunate, you wish it had not happened or been true □ *It was an unfortunate choice of words.*
● **unfortunately** /ˌʌnˈfɔːtʃnətlɪ/ ADVERB used to show that you wish something had not happened or been true □ *Unfortunately, I lost the ring.*

unfounded /ˌʌnˈfaʊndɪd/ ADJECTIVE not based on facts □ *The accusations against him have been proved to be unfounded.*

unfriendly /ˌʌnˈfrendlɪ/ ADJECTIVE not friendly □ *His sister was very unfriendly.*

unfurnished /ˌʌnˈfɜːnɪʃt/ ADJECTIVE with no furniture □ *We rented an unfurnished flat in Oxford.*

ungainly /ʌnˈɡeɪnlɪ/ ADJECTIVE moving in a way that is awkward and not attractive

ungrateful /ʌnˈɡreɪtfʊl/ ADJECTIVE not grateful □ *He was so ungrateful, I wished I hadn't helped him.*

• **ungratefully** /ʌnˈɡreɪtfʊlɪ/ ADVERB in a way that is ungrateful

unhappily /ʌnˈhæpɪlɪ/ ADVERB in a way that is not happy □ *He waited unhappily while the others played outside.*

unhappiness /ʌnˈhæpɪnɪs/ NOUN, NO PLURAL the state of being unhappy

unhappy /ʌnˈhæpɪ/ ADJECTIVE [**unhappier, unhappiest**]
1 sad or causing sadness 🕀 *Ben has been feeling unhappy for a long time.* □ *an unhappy marriage*
2 not pleased or not satisfied □ **+ about** *He was unhappy about the result of the meeting.* 🕀 *We were deeply unhappy about the quality of their work.*

unhealthy /ʌnˈhelθɪ/ ADJECTIVE [**unhealthier, unhealthiest**]
1 someone who is unhealthy is ill, or does not have good health □ *He looks very unhealthy.*
2 harmful for your health □ *an unhealthy lifestyle*
3 harmful for your mental state □ *She has an unhealthy obsession with death.*

unheard /ʌnˈhɜːd/ ADJECTIVE ignored or not heard by anyone 🕀 *Their pleas for help went unheard.*

unheard-of /ʌnˈhɜːdˌɒv/ ADJECTIVE if something is unheard-of, it has never happened before and is often shocking □ *Divorce was almost unheard-of in 19th-century England.*

unhurt /ʌnˈhɜːt/ ADJECTIVE not injured □ *The passengers were unhurt.*

uni- /juːnɪ/ PREFIX uni- is used at the beginning of words to mean 'having or being only one of something' □ *unilateral*

unicorn /ˈjuːnɪkɔːn/ NOUN [plural **unicorns**] in stories, an animal like a white horse with a horn on its head

unidentified /ˌʌnaɪˈdentɪfaɪd/ ADJECTIVE not recognized, known or named □ *An unidentified man was seen leaving the house.*

unification /ˌjuːnɪfɪˈkeɪʃən/ NOUN, NO PLURAL when two countries join together to form one country

unified /ˈjuːnɪfaɪd/ ADJECTIVE
1 with all people and groups working together and having the same opinions □ *We need a unified response to this threat.*
2 a unified country, organization, etc. has been formed by more than one country, organization, etc. joining together □ *The new unified company will employ hundreds of local people.*
3 the same in all places and situations □ *There is a unified system of registration for electricians.*

uniform /ˈjuːnɪfɔːm/ ► NOUN [plural **uniforms**] a set of clothes that shows you belong to a particular organization, job or school □ *a bus driver's uniform* 🕀 *school uniform*
► ADJECTIVE the same size, shape, standard, etc. □ *The company is trying to achieve uniform standards of training for all staff.*

• **uniformed** /ˈjuːnɪfɔːmd/ ADJECTIVE wearing a uniform □ *He was accompanied by two uniformed policemen.*

• **uniformity** /ˌjuːnɪˈfɔːmɪtɪ/ NOUN, NO PLURAL the state of being the same size, shape, standard, etc. □ *We need to bring some uniformity to the laws in th[...] region.*

• **uniformly** /ˈjuːnɪfɔːmlɪ/ ADVERB in a way that is th[...] same in all situations □ *The school has achieved uniformly high standards.*

unify /ˈjuːnɪfaɪ/ VERB [**unifies, unifying, unified**]
1 to make people, groups, countries, etc. feel that th[...] belong together □ *A sporting event like this can rea[...] unify a nation.*
2 if groups, organizations, countries, etc. unify, the[...] join together
3 to make something the same in all places and situations

unilateral /ˌjuːnɪˈlætərəl/ ADJECTIVE a unilateral act[...] or decision is one done or made by only one of th[...] people or groups involved □ *They agreed to a unilateral withdrawal of their troops.*

• **unilaterally** /ˌjuːnɪˈlætərəlɪ/ ADVERB in a unilate[...] way □ *Canada has acted unilaterally in banning fish[...] in this part of the Atlantic.*

unimaginable /ˌʌnɪˈmædʒɪnəbəl/ ADJECTIVE impossible to imagine because of being so extrem[...] so unusual 🕀 *This is a disaster of an almost unimaginable scale.*

unimaginative /ˌʌnɪˈmædʒɪnətɪv/ ADJECTIVE no[...] thinking of or not using new and interesting ideas[...] □ *Her house is decorated in a tasteful but unimaginative style.*

unimportance /ˌʌnɪmˈpɔːtəns/ NOUN, NO PLURA[...] fact of not being important

• **unimportant** /ˌʌnɪmˈpɔːtənt/ ADJECTIVE not important

uninhabitable /ˌʌnɪnˈhæbɪtəbəl/ ADJECTIVE if a [...] or a building is uninhabitable, it is impossible for people to live there □ *Pollution is making parts o[...] planet uninhabitable.*

uninhabited /ˌʌnɪnˈhæbɪtɪd/ ADJECTIVE an uninhabited place does not have people living in[...]

uninspired /ˌʌnɪnˈspaɪəd/ ADJECTIVE
1 not exciting or interesting □ *It was an uninspi[...] performance.*
2 not having any new or interesting ideas □ *I'm[...] supposed to be writing a poem, but I feel comp[...] uninspired.*

• **uninspiring** /ˌʌnɪnˈspaɪrɪŋ/ ADJECTIVE someth[...] that is uninspiring does not make you feel excit[...] enthusiastic or interested □ *Despite being one [...]*

London's most expensive restaurants, the food was pretty uninspiring.

uninstall /ˌʌnɪn'stɔːl/ VERB [**uninstalls, uninstalling, uninstalled**] to remove a program from a computer. A computing word.

unintelligible /ˌʌnɪn'telɪdʒəbəl/ ADJECTIVE impossible to understand

unintentional /ˌʌnɪn'tenʃənəl/ ADJECTIVE done by accident and not planned □ Any offence caused was entirely unintentional.

• **unintentionally** /ˌʌnɪn'tenʃənəli/ ADVERB in an unintentional way □ The film is unintentionally funny.

uninterested /ˌʌn'ɪntrəstɪd/ ADJECTIVE not interested □ I am totally uninterested in sport.

uninteresting /ˌʌn'ɪntrəstɪŋ/ ADJECTIVE boring

uninterrupted /ˌʌnˌɪntə'rʌptɪd/ ADJECTIVE
continuous □ We have had ten years of uninterrupted economic growth.
an uninterrupted view is not blocked by anything

uninvited /ˌʌnɪn'vaɪtɪd/ ADJECTIVE an uninvited guest has not been invited

union /'juːnɪən/ NOUN [**plural unions**]
another word for a trade union
a group of countries, organizations, etc. that join together
the process of joining people or things together

unionist /'juːnjənɪst/ NOUN [**plural unionists**] a member of a trade union

unique /juː'niːk/ ADJECTIVE
completely different from anyone or anything else
very special and unusual □ a unique opportunity
unique to something only happening or existing in one place □ The species is unique to this island.

• **uniquely** /juː'niːklɪ/ ADVERB in a unique way □ Is love a uniquely human emotion? □ He is uniquely placed to lead the party to victory.

unisex /'juːnɪseks/ ADJECTIVE intended for either men or women □ unisex clothes

unison /'juːnɪsən/ NOUN in unison if people do something in unison, they all do it together

unit /'juːnɪt/ NOUN [**plural units**]
a measure used to show an amount or level □ A metre is a unit of length. □ What is the unit of currency in Ecuador?
an organization or a part of an organization with a particular purpose, or the people that work in it □ They set up a specialist burns unit at the hospital. □ He is a member of an elite police unit.
a single thing that can be part of a larger group of things □ The book is divided into ten units.
a piece of furniture ⊞ They bought new kitchen units. □ They stock a range of storage units.
a building or part of a building □ Two hundred new residential units are to be built on the land.
a machine or part of a machine □ We had to put in an air conditioning unit.

unite /juː'naɪt/ VERB [**unites, uniting, united**]
if people or groups unite, they join together, often to achieve something □ Workers in the area have united to oppose the pay cuts.
2 to join people or groups together, often making them them feel that they belong together and have the same opinions □ We need a new leader to unite the party.

• **united** /juː'naɪtɪd/ ADJECTIVE
1 if people are united about something, they agree about it □ They are united in their opposition to the proposals.
2 with all the parts joined together □ Shall we see a united Ireland one day?

United Kingdom /juː'naɪtɪd 'kɪŋdəm/ NOUN the United Kingdom England, Scotland, Wales and Northern Ireland

United Nations /juː'naɪtɪd 'neɪʃənz/ NOUN the United Nations an organization of people from most countries of the world, that works to try to solve world problems

United States of America /juː'naɪtɪd 'steɪts əv ə'merɪkə/ NOUN the United States of America the 50 states that make the country of North America

unity /'juːnəti/ NOUN, NO PLURAL when people agree on things and act together □ She has called for unity within the party.

universal /ˌjuːnɪ'vɜːsəl/ ADJECTIVE
1 affecting or including everyone in the world
□ English may become a universal language that everyone can learn and use.
2 relating to everyone in a group □ He performed to universal applause.

• **universally** /ˌjuːnɪ'vɜːsəli/ ADVERB by everyone in a group or in the world □ He was universally admired.

universe /'juːnɪvɜːs/ NOUN the universe everything that exists anywhere, including the Earth, the sun and all the other planets and stars in space □ Somewhere in the universe there might be another world like ours.

university /ˌjuːnɪ'vɜːsəti/ NOUN [**plural universities**] a place where you go to study at the highest level after leaving school ⊞ I am hoping to go to university. □ university students

unjust /ˌʌn'dʒʌst/ ADJECTIVE not fair □ an unjust punishment

• **unjustifiable** /ˌʌndʒʌstɪ'faɪəbəl/ ADJECTIVE if something is unjustifiable, you cannot say that it is right or fair □ All acts of terrorism are morally unjustifiable.

• **unjustified** /ˌʌn'dʒʌstɪfaɪd/ ADJECTIVE not fair or having no good reason □ Her criticism was completely unjustified.

• **unjustly** /ˌʌn'dʒʌstli/ ADVERB not fairly □ He was treated very unjustly.

unkempt /ˌʌn'kempt/ ADJECTIVE not tidy □ unkempt hair

unkind /ˌʌn'kaɪnd/ ADJECTIVE [**unkinder, unkindest**] cruel and not kind □ It was unkind of you to tease her.

- **unkindly** /ʌnˈkaɪndlɪ/ ADVERB in an unkind way □ *They treated me unkindly.*
- **unkindness** /ʌnˈkaɪndnɪs/ NOUN, NO PLURAL being unkind

unknown /ʌnˈnəʊn/ ADJECTIVE
1 not known □ *The man's whereabouts are unknown.*
2 not famous □ *an unknown actor*

unlawful /ʌnˈlɔːfʊl/ ADJECTIVE illegal □ *A verdict of unlawful killing was reached.*

unleaded /ʌnˈledɪd/ ADJECTIVE unleaded petrol does not have lead (=a soft, grey metal) added to it and so causes less harm to the environment

unleash /ʌnˈliːʃ/ VERB [**unleashes, unleashing, unleashed**] to do something or cause something that has a strong and often violent effect □ *She unleashed a furious outburst against the media.*

unless /ənˈles/ CONJUNCTION except when, or except if □ *We always go for a walk on Sundays, unless it's raining.* □ *Don't come unless I phone you.*

unlike /ʌnˈlaɪk/ PREPOSITION
1 different from □ *I never saw twins who were so unlike each other.*
2 not usual for someone □ *It's unlike her to be so bad-tempered.*

unlikely /ʌnˈlaɪklɪ/ ADJECTIVE
1 not likely or expected to happen □ *+ that* *It's unlikely that she'll come.* □ *+ to do something* *We're unlikely to finish the work today.* ℗ *A victory for England now seems highly unlikely.*
2 probably not true □ *an unlikely tale*

unlimited /ʌnˈlɪmɪtɪd/ ADJECTIVE if something is unlimited, you can have or use as much of it as you want □ *This ticket allows unlimited travel on all train services for two months.* □ *The country does not have an unlimited amount of money to spend on health care.*

unload /ʌnˈləʊd/ VERB [**unloads, unloading, unloaded**]
1 to take things off or out of a vehicle □ *After we got back from the trip, our first job was to unload the car.*
2 if a vehicle unloads, things are taken off or out of it □ *The ship unloaded in Marseilles.*

unlock /ʌnˈlɒk/ VERB [**unlocks, unlocking, unlocked**] to open something that is locked □ *Unlock this door now!*

unloved /ʌnˈlʌvd/ ADJECTIVE not loved or liked □ *They have at last got rid of their unloved president.*

unlucky /ʌnˈlʌkɪ/ ADJECTIVE having bad luck, causing bad luck or caused by bad luck □ *I'm very unlucky at cards.* □ *It was an unlucky defeat.*

unmade /ʌnˈmeɪd/ ADJECTIVE an unmade bed has not had its covers arranged in a tidy way after being slept in

unmanageable /ʌnˈmænɪdʒəbəl/ ADJECTIVE very difficult to use or control □ *Her son has become completely unmanageable.*

unmanned /ʌnˈmænd/ ADJECTIVE unmanned vehicle or machines are controlled automatically, and do no have people in or near them to operate them □ *The use unmanned aircraft to gather information.*

unmarried /ʌnˈmærɪd/ ADJECTIVE not married □ *unmarried couples*

unmask /ʌnˈmɑːsk/ VERB [**unmasks, unmasking, unmasked**] to show the truth about someone or something, especially something bad □ *He was unmasked as a liar and a cheat.*

unmistakable /ʌnmɪˈsteɪkəbəl/ ADJECTIVE if something is unmistakable, you could not think that was anything else □ *I heard the unmistakable sound a Ferrari.*
- **unmistakably** /ʌnmɪˈsteɪkəblɪ/ ADVERB in an unmistakable way □ *It was unmistakably his handwriting.*

unmitigated /ʌnˈmɪtɪɡeɪtɪd/ ADJECTIVE used to emphasize how extreme something is ℗ *The performance was an unmitigated disaster.*

unmoved /ʌnˈmuːvd/ ADJECTIVE not affected emotionally □ *He appeared unmoved as the judge read out the sentence.*

unnatural /ʌnˈnætʃərəl/ ADJECTIVE not natural or normal □ *The animals were being fed an unnatura diet.*
- **unnaturally** /ʌnˈnætʃərəlɪ/ ADVERB in a strange unusual way □ *The building was unnaturally silent*

unnecessarily /ʌnˈnesəsərɪlɪ/ ADVERB in a way t is not necessary □ *We spent all that money unnecessarily.* □ *I thought you were unnecessarily rude.*

unnecessary /ʌnˈnesəsərɪ/ ADJECTIVE
1 something unnecessary is possible to avoid □ *Th measures will cause unnecessary suffering.* □ *We c afford any unnecessary expense.*
2 not needed □ *Any unnecessary clothing can be g to charity.*

unnerve /ʌnˈnɜːv/ VERB [**unnerves, unnerving, unnerved**] to make someone feel worried or ner □ *His silence unnerved me.*
- **unnerving** /ʌnˈnɜːvɪŋ/ ADJECTIVE causing you to worried or nervous

unnoticed /ʌnˈnəʊtɪst/ ADJECTIVE not noticed b anyone ℗ *His strange clothes did not go unnotic*

unobtrusive /ʌnəbˈtruːsɪv/ ADJECTIVE not attra much attention □ *He tried to be as unobtrusive possible.*
- **unobtrusively** /ʌnəbˈtruːsɪvlɪ/ ADVERB in an unobtrusive way □ *She slipped unobtrusively int room.*

unoccupied /ʌnˈɒkjʊpaɪd/ ADJECTIVE not being or lived in □ *These houses have been unoccupie years.*

unofficial /ʌnəˈfɪʃəl/ ADJECTIVE not done or al' by anyone in authority □ *Unofficial estimates s unemployment is still rising.*
- **unofficially** /ʌnəˈfɪʃəlɪ/ ADVERB in an unoffici

☐ Unofficially, I can tell you that you've passed your exams.

unorthodox /ˌʌnˈɔːθədɒks/ ADJECTIVE unorthodox behaviour or opinions are different from what is usual ☐ She used unorthodox methods of treating depression.

unpack /ˌʌnˈpæk/ VERB [unpacks, unpacking, unpacked] to take things out of a case, bag, box, etc. ☐ I've unpacked my case. ☐ Have you unpacked yet?

unpaid /ˌʌnˈpeɪd/ ADJECTIVE
not paid for doing work ☐ We are expected to do unpaid overtime.
not yet paid for ☐ unpaid debts

unpleasant /ʌnˈplezənt/ ADJECTIVE
if something is unpleasant, you do not like it or enjoy ☐ an unpleasant smell ☐ I found skiing a thoroughly unpleasant experience.
not polite, friendly or kind ☐ + to He was rather unpleasant to his students.

unpleasantly /ʌnˈplezəntlɪ/ ADVERB in an unpleasant way ☐ The weather was unpleasantly hot. ☐ She laughed rather unpleasantly when I asked for a cold drink.

unpleasantness /ʌnˈplezəntnɪs/ NOUN, NO PLURAL a situation in which people are angry, violent, upset, etc. ☐ His behaviour caused a great deal of unpleasantness at work.
being unpleasant

unplug /ʌnˈplʌɡ/ VERB [unplugs, unplugging, unplugged] to stop a piece of equipment from being connected to its supply of electricity by pulling out its plug (=device with small metal parts) ☐ I've unplugged the printer.

unpopular /ʌnˈpɒpjʊlə(r)/ ADJECTIVE disliked by many people ☐ His attitude makes him very unpopular at school.

unprecedented /ʌnˈpresɪdəntɪd/ ADJECTIVE if something is unprecedented, it has never happened or existed before ☐ Researchers have been given unprecedented access to the files.

unpredictable /ˌʌnprɪˈdɪktəbəl/ ADJECTIVE if someone or something is unpredictable, they change a lot so you cannot guess what they are going to be like or what they are going to do ☐ The weather can be very unpredictable.

unprepared /ˌʌnprɪˈpeəd/ ADJECTIVE not prepared for something or not expecting something ☐ We were unprepared for the racism we encountered there.

unprofessional /ˌʌnprəˈfeʃənəl/ ADJECTIVE not behaving in a way that is suitable for work or for a particular job ☐ Talking about her clients was extremely unprofessional.

unprofitable /ʌnˈprɒfɪtəbəl/ ADJECTIVE not making a profit ☐ We were forced to close our unprofitable branches.

unprovoked /ˌʌnprəˈvəʊkt/ ADJECTIVE an unprovoked attack is when someone is attacked for no reason

unqualified /ˌʌnˈkwɒlɪfaɪd/ ADJECTIVE
1 without the qualifications to do a particular job ☐ Concern was expressed about the increasing number of unqualified people offering medical treatment.
2 without the necessary experience to do something ☐ I am unqualified to advise you.
3 complete and not limited in any way ⊞ His performance was an unqualified success.

unquestionably /ˌʌnˈkwestʃənəblɪ/ ADVERB without any doubt ☐ He is, unquestionably, a great actor.

unravel /ʌnˈrævəl/ VERB [unravels, unravelling/US unraveling, unravelled/US unraveled]
1 to understand something complicated ☐ She was determined to unravel the mystery.
2 if complicated plans, arrangements, etc. unravel, they start to fail ☐ All my plans started to unravel.
3 if threads in a piece of cloth unravel, they stop being twisted together, and if you unravel them, you stop them from being twisted together

unreal /ʌnˈrɪəl/ ADJECTIVE not seeming to be true or real ☐ All this success still feels a bit unreal.
• **unrealistic** /ˌʌnrɪəˈlɪstɪk/ ADJECTIVE based on hopes or wishes that are not likely to be possible ☐ It's unrealistic to think that sales will go up.
• **unreality** /ˌʌnrɪˈælɪtɪ/ NOUN, NO PLURAL the state of being unreal ☐ All the time I was at the palace, I had a feeling of unreality.

unreasonable /ʌnˈriːzənəbəl/ ADJECTIVE
1 not fair, often because of wanting too much ☐ It's unreasonable to expect students to do so much homework. ☐ The unions were accused of making unreasonable demands.
2 not based on good reasons ☐ Their conclusions were not unreasonable.
• **unreasonably** /ʌnˈriːzənəblɪ/ ADVERB
1 in an unfair way ☐ I think you're behaving really unreasonably.
2 in a way that is not based on good reasons ☐ She believed, not unreasonably, that she would be paid for her work.

unrelated /ˌʌnrɪˈleɪtɪd/ ADJECTIVE if situations or events are unrelated, there is no connection between them ☐ The police say the murders are probably unrelated.

unreliable /ˌʌnrɪˈlaɪəbəl/ ADJECTIVE
1 not able to be trusted to do something ☐ He's totally unreliable. ☐ My car's a bit unreliable.
2 unreliable information may not be true

unremitting /ˌʌnrɪˈmɪtɪŋ/ ADJECTIVE never stopping or getting better ☐ We've had a year of unremitting gloom.

unrepresentative /ˌʌnreprɪˈzentətɪv/ ADJECTIVE not typical of a group of people or things ☐ The research was based on an unrepresentative sample.

unrest /ʌnˈrest/ NOUN, NO PLURAL when people are angry about something and may cause trouble ☐ The new tax sparked unrest all over the country.

unrestrained /ˌʌnrɪ'streɪnd/ ADJECTIVE not limited or controlled in any way □ *People were dancing with unrestrained joy.*

unripe /ˌʌn'raɪp/ ADJECTIVE unripe fruit is not ready to eat

unroll /ˌʌn'rəʊl/ VERB [unrolls, unrolling, unrolled] to open out something that has been rolled up and make it flat □ *He unrolled the map and put it on the ground.*

unruly /ˌʌn'ruːli/ ADJECTIVE
1 badly behaved and difficult to control □ *an unruly child*
2 unruly hair is untidy and difficult to control

unsafe /ˌʌn'seɪf/ ADJECTIVE dangerous □ *unsafe practices*

unsaid /ˌʌn'sed/ ADJECTIVE thought but not said ⊞ *Some things are better left unsaid.*

unsatisfactory /ˌʌnsætɪs'fæktəri/ ADJECTIVE not good enough

unsavoury /ˌʌn'seɪvəri/ ADJECTIVE unpleasant and morally bad □ *an unsavoury character*

unscathed /ˌʌn'skeɪðd/ ADJECTIVE without being harmed □ *They escaped from the burning building unscathed.*

unscrew /ˌʌn'skruː/ VERB [unscrews, unscrewing, unscrewed]
1 to remove something with a turning movement □ *Joe unscrewed the lid from the bottle and took a drink.*
2 to remove something by taking out a screw (=small pointed metal object) or screws □ *She unscrewed the cupboard door.*

unscrupulous /ˌʌn'skruːpjuləs/ ADJECTIVE willing to do dishonest or illegal things in order to make money, get an advantage, etc.

unseemly /ˌʌn'siːmli/ ADJECTIVE embarrassing and not suitable □ *unseemly behaviour*

unseen /ˌʌn'siːn/ ADJECTIVE, ADVERB not seen or not noticed □ *He managed to leave the house unseen.*

unselfish /ˌʌn'selfɪʃ/ ADJECTIVE thinking of other people's needs and feelings and not your own
• **unselfishly** /ˌʌn'selfɪʃli/ ADVERB in an unselfish way
• **unselfishness** /ˌʌn'selfɪʃnɪs/ NOUN, NO PLURAL being unselfish

unsettled /ˌʌn'setəld/ ADJECTIVE
1 if the weather is unsettled, it changes a lot
2 worried or upset in a situation

unshaven /ˌʌn'ʃeɪvən/ ADJECTIVE with hair growing on the face after not shaving recently

unsightly /ʌn'saɪtli/ ADJECTIVE not nice to look at □ *unsightly office blocks*

unskilled /ˌʌn'skɪld/ ADJECTIVE
1 without special skills or training ⊞ *unskilled workers*
2 unskilled work does not need special skills or training

unsociable /ˌʌn'səʊʃəbəl/ ADJECTIVE not wanting to be with other people

unsolicited /ˌʌnsə'lɪsɪtɪd/ ADJECTIVE given to you without you asking for it ⊞ *unsolicited advice*

unsolved /ˌʌn'sɒlvd/ ADJECTIVE having no solution or explanation □ *an unsolved murder*

unsound /ˌʌn'saʊnd/ ADJECTIVE
1 not safe □ *The building is structurally unsound.*
2 based on facts or ideas that cannot be trusted □ *unsound evidence*

unspeakable /ˌʌn'spiːkəbəl/ ADJECTIVE too bad to describe in words □ *unspeakable rudeness*

unspoiled /ˌʌn'spɔɪld/ or **unspoilt** /ˌʌn'spɔɪlt/ ADJECTIVE not spoiled or damaged in any way □ *the unspoiled beauty of the countryside*

unspoken /ˌʌn'spəʊkən/ ADJECTIVE understood, although not said in words □ *an unspoken agreeme.*

unstable /ˌʌn'steɪbəl/ ADJECTIVE
1 changing or likely to change over a period □ *a politically unstable region*
2 not firm or strong □ *This chair seems a bit unstabl.*
3 not calm and having moods that change sudden! □ *She seems a little unstable.*

unsteadily /ˌʌn'stediːli/ ADVERB in an unsteady wa.

unsteady /ˌʌn'stedi/ ADJECTIVE likely to fall and no firm □ *After the operation she was very unsteady o. her feet.*

unstoppable /ˌʌn'stɒpəbəl/ ADJECTIVE not able to stopped or prevented □ *an unstoppable force*

unstuck /ˌʌn'stʌk/ ADJECTIVE come unstuck to st. making progress, or to fail □ *I came unstuck with . last stage of the recipe.*

unsubscribe /ˌʌnsəb'skraɪb/ VERB [unsubscribes unsubscribing, unsubscribed] to remove your na. from an Internet mailing list (=all the people that organization sends information to)

unsubstantiated /ˌʌnsəb'stænʃieɪtɪd/ ADJECTIV not proved true □ *unsubstantiated rumours*

unsuccessful /ˌʌnsək'sesful/ ADJECTIVE not managing to do something you are trying to do ⊞ *Thieves made an unsuccessful attempt to steal the car.* □ *I tried to contact him but was unsuccessful.*
• **unsuccessfully** /ˌʌnsək'sesfuli/ ADVERB in an unsuccessful way □ *I tried unsuccessfully to pers. her.*

unsuitable /ˌʌn'suːtəbəl/ ADJECTIVE not right for purpose or occasion □ *unsuitable clothing*

unsung /ˌʌn'sʌŋ/ ADJECTIVE not praised or not far although you have done something very good ⊞ *unsung hero*

unsure /ˌʌn'ʃɔː(r)/ ADJECTIVE
1 not certain □ *I was unsure of the spelling.* □ *I a. if she was coming but he seemed unsure.*
2 be unsure of yourself to not be confident

unsuspecting /ˌʌnsə'spektɪŋ/ ADJECTIVE not aw that something bad is happening or going to ha

unsustainable /ˌʌnsə'steɪnəbəl/ ADJECTIVE
1 not able to continue in the same way for a long □ *unsustainable economic growth*
2 damaging the environment and so not able t. continue in the same way □ *unsustainable fam. practices*

unsympathetic /ˌʌnˌsɪmpəˈθetɪk/ ADJECTIVE
1 not caring about other people's problems □ *She was fairly unsympathetic when I had my accident.*
2 not showing support for a group or belief

untangle /ˌʌnˈtæŋgəl/ VERB [**untangles, untangling, untangled**]
1 to separate something that is twisted together or as knots in it
2 to try to solve a difficult problem

unthinkable /ˌʌnˈθɪŋkəbəl/ ADJECTIVE too bad or strange for you to be able to imagine

untidiness /ˌʌnˈtaɪdɪnɪs/ NOUN, NO PLURAL being untidy

untidy /ʌnˈtaɪdɪ/ ADJECTIVE [**untidier, untidiest**]
1 not carefully ordered or arranged □ *His flat is always untidy.*
2 an untidy person does not keep their home, office, etc. tidy

untie /ʌnˈtaɪ/ VERB [**unties, untying, untied**] to unfasten something that is tied in a knot □ *He untied his shoelaces.*

until /ənˈtɪl/ PREPOSITION, CONJUNCTION
1 continuing to a particular time but not after that □ *He'll be here until midday.* □ *I waited until she'd gone.*
2 continuing as far as somewhere □ *Carry on walking until you get to a bridge.*
3 not ... until not before □ *I won't start until you tell me.*

untimely /ʌnˈtaɪmlɪ/ ADJECTIVE
1 happening too soon □ *his untimely death*
2 happening at a time that is not convenient □ *her untimely return*

untold /ʌnˈtəʊld/ ADJECTIVE too great to be counted or measured □ *untold riches* □ *untold misery*

untoward /ˌʌntəˈwɔːd/ ADJECTIVE unexpected and not convenient. A formal word.

untrue /ʌnˈtruː/ ADJECTIVE false, not true □ *His story is completely untrue.*

untrustworthy /ʌnˈtrʌstˌwɜːðɪ/ ADJECTIVE not able to be trusted

untruth /ʌnˈtruːθ/ NOUN [*plural* **untruths**] a formal word meaning a lie

unused[1] /ʌnˈjuːzd/ ADJECTIVE not having been used or not used now □ *unused stamps*

unused[2] /ʌnˈjuːst/ ADJECTIVE be unused to sth to have little experience of something □ *I'm unused to cooking my own meals.*

unusual /ʌnˈjuːʒəl/ ADJECTIVE
1 not normal or not ordinary 🔁 *It's unusual for him to be late.* 🔁 *Police took the unusual step of issuing a photograph of the suspect.*
2 not like other things or people in a way that is interesting or attractive □ *They make some lovely, unusual jewellery.*

• unusually /ʌnˈjuːʒəlɪ/ ADVERB to a degree that is not normal or ordinary □ *It has been unusually cold for this time of year.*

unveil /ʌnˈveɪl/ VERB [**unveils, unveiling, unveiled**]
1 to announce a new plan to the public □ *The minister unveiled the plans at the conference this morning.*
2 to take a cover off something as part of a ceremony

unwanted /ˌʌnˈwɒntɪd/ ADJECTIVE not wanted □ *unwanted gifts*

unwarranted /ʌnˈwɒrəntɪd/ ADJECTIVE not deserved and not fair □ *unwarranted criticism*

unwary /ʌnˈweərɪ/ ADJECTIVE not aware of the dangers or risks in a situation □ *the unwary traveller*

unwelcome /ʌnˈwelkəm/ ADJECTIVE not wanted □ *unwelcome attention* □ *unwelcome news* □ *unwelcome visitors*

unwell /ʌnˈwel/ ADJECTIVE not healthy. A formal word.

unwieldy /ʌnˈwiːldɪ/ ADJECTIVE
1 large and awkward to carry
2 large, complicated and difficult to work with □ *an unwieldy system*

unwilling /ʌnˈwɪlɪŋ/ ADJECTIVE not wanting to do something □ **+ to do something** *They seem unwilling to help.*
• unwillingly /ʌnˈwɪlɪŋlɪ/ ADVERB in an unwilling way
• unwillingness /ʌnˈwɪlɪŋnɪs/ NOUN, NO PLURAL being unwilling □ **+ to do something** *His apparent unwillingness to discuss the problem made the situation very difficult.*

unwind /ʌnˈwaɪnd/ VERB [**unwinds, unwinding, unwound**]
1 to relax □ *Having a bath is a good way to unwind.*
2 to remove something that is wrapped around something else □ *He unwound the bandage.*

unwise /ʌnˈwaɪz/ ADJECTIVE not sensible □ *It would be unwise to spend all the money now.*

unworthy /ʌnˈwɜːðɪ/ ADJECTIVE
1 to be unworthy of something is to not deserve it □ *I felt I was unworthy of his love.*
2 if behaviour is unworthy of someone, it is bad and they would not do it for that reason

unwound /ʌnˈwaʊnd/ PAST TENSE AND PAST PARTICIPLE OF unwind

unwrap /ʌnˈræp/ VERB [**unwraps, unwrapping, unwrapped**] to open something that is wrapped □ *She carefully unwrapped the present.*

unzip /ʌnˈzɪp/ VERB [**unzips, unzipping, unzipped**]
1 to unfasten something using its zip (=fastening device with two rows of small parts that fit tightly together) □ *He unzipped his bag and took out a book.*
2 to make a computer file bigger again after it has been made smaller. A computing word.

up /ʌp/ ► ADVERB, PREPOSITION
1 towards or in a higher position □ *I walked up the stairs.* □ *We went up in a helicopter.* □ *He looked up and saw her.* □ *She threw the ball up in the air.*
2 to a greater amount or level □ *Prices have gone up again.* □ *Could you turn the volume up a bit?*

3 if you stand up or sit up, you move your body to a vertical position

4 up to less than or as much as a particular amount or level □ *The hall can hold up to 200 people.*

5 up to him/you, etc. if an action or decision is up to you, you are responsible for doing it or making it □ *It's up to you whether you come or not.*

6 used after verbs to show that something is finished or completely used □ *Eat up all your vegetables.*

7 if you go up to someone, you move close to them, often in order to speak to them □ *He came up to me and asked if I needed any help.*

8 further along a road, river, etc. □ *He lives just up the road from me.*

9 in or towards the north of a country □ *She lives up in Glasgow.*

10 be up to something to be doing something, usually something wrong or secret □ *The children are very quiet - what are they up to?*

▶ ADJECTIVE

1 not in bed □ *He's not up yet.* □ *I've been up half the night.*

2 if an amount or level is up, it is higher □ *Profits are up by 25% this year.* □ *They were two goals up at the end of the first half.*

3 if the sun is up, it has risen

4 if a period of time that something lasts for is up, it has finished □ *Bring the boats in now - your time is up.*

5 if something is up, there is a problem. An informal word ⊞ *What's up with you today?* □ *As soon as we reached the house, I knew something was up.*

6 if a computer is up, it is working. A computing word.

▶ NOUN [*plural* ups] ups and downs good experiences and situations and bad experiences and situations □ *We've been married over 30 years, and we've certainly had our ups and downs.*

▶ VERB [ups, upping, upped] to increase something □ *The doctors have upped his dose of painkillers.*

up-and-coming /ˌʌpəndˈkʌmɪŋ/ ADJECTIVE starting to become successful and famous □ *an up-and-coming young actor*

upbeat /ˈʌpbiːt/ ADJECTIVE positive and feeling hope □ *He seemed quite upbeat about his health.*

upbringing /ˈʌpˌbrɪŋɪŋ/ NOUN, NO PLURAL the way that your parents treat you when you are a child □ *We had a strict upbringing.*

update ▶ VERB /ʌpˈdeɪt/ [updates, updating, updated]

1 to add the latest information to something □ *When did we last update the website?*

2 to change something to make it more modern □ *I need to update my wardrobe.*

◆ PHRASAL VERB **update someone on something** to tell someone the latest information □ *Could you update me on any recent developments?*

▶ NOUN /ˈʌpdeɪt/ [*plural* updates] the latest information about a subject ⊞ *Dan gave me an update on the situation.*

upgrade ▶ VERB /ˌʌpˈɡreɪd/ [upgrades, upgrading, upgraded]

1 to improve a computer or machine, especially by adding or replacing parts

2 to give someone a more important job in the sam organization

▶ NOUN /ˈʌpɡreɪd/ [*plural* upgrades] a piece of software that makes a computer more powerful

upheaval /ʌpˈhiːvəl/ NOUN [*plural* upheavals] a gre change, involving activity and often problems □ *I ca face the upheaval of moving house.*

upheld /ʌpˈheld/ PAST TENSE AND PAST PARTICIPLE OF uphold

uphill ▶ ADJECTIVE /ˈʌphɪl/

1 going upwards □ *an uphill part of the track*

2 very difficult ⊞ *We face an uphill struggle gettir people to change their habits.*

▶ ADVERB /ˌʌpˈhɪl/ up a slope □ *We travelled uphill several miles.*

uphold /ʌpˈhəʊld/ VERB [upholds, upholding, uph to support or agree with a decision, especially in a court of law □ *The court upheld his complaint.*

upholstery /ʌpˈhəʊlstərɪ/ NOUN the soft parts of a chair or other seat □ *car uphols*

upkeep /ˈʌpkiːp/ NOUN, NO PLURAL the process or of keeping something such as a house or car in g condition

uplifting /ʌpˈlɪftɪŋ/ ADJECTIVE making you feel ha and full of hope □ *an uplifting film*

upload /ˌʌpˈləʊd/ VERB [uploads, uploading, uploaded] to copy computer programs or files fr small computer to a larger one or to the Interne computing word.

upmarket /ˈʌpmɑːkɪt/ ADJECTIVE expensive and high quality □ *an upmarket hotel*

upon /əˈpɒn/ PREPOSITION on. A formal word c *castle upon a high cliff*

upper /ˈʌpə(r)/ ADJECTIVE

1 being the higher of two things that are the sa □ *my upper lip*

2 at the top or towards the top □ *the upper flo the building*

3 of a higher social class or rank

upper class /ˈʌpə ˈklɑːs/ NOUN [*plural* upper cl people with the highest social class in a society

● **upper-class** /ˈʌpəklɑːs/ ADJECTIVE being from typical of the upper class □ *an upper-class acc*

uppermost /ˈʌpəməʊst/ ADJECTIVE

1 be uppermost in someone's mind to be the main thing that someone is thinking about

2 highest □ *the uppermost floors of the buildi*

upright /ˈʌpraɪt/ ▶ ADVERB vertical □ *He was upright in his cot.*

▶ ADJECTIVE

1 vertical □ *Make sure your seat is in an uprig position and fasten your seat belt.*

2 honest □ *an upright citizen*

uprising /ˈʌpˌraɪzɪŋ/ NOUN [plural **uprisings**] when a lot of people in a country use violence to try to change their government

uproar /ˈʌprɔː(r)/ NOUN, NO PLURAL when a lot of people criticize something very angrily

uproot /ʌpˈruːt/ VERB [**uproots, uprooting, uprooted**]
1 to make people move away from their homes □ Thousands of people were uprooted by the war.
2 to pull a plant and its roots out of the ground

upset ▶ VERB /ʌpˈset/ [**upsets, upsetting, upset**]
1 to make someone sad or worried □ I didn't mean to upset you.
2 to stop something from happening in the right way □ I don't want to upset your plans.
3 to knock something over by accident
4 upset your stomach to cause an illness in your stomach
▶ ADJECTIVE /ʌpˈset/
sad or worried about something that has happened □ He looked upset. □ + that She's upset that no one invited her. 🔁 She got upset looking at his photos.

upset stomach/tummy an illness affecting the stomach
▶ NOUN /ˈʌpset/ [plural **upsets**]
when a very good team or player is defeated by a less good team or player

stomach/tummy upset an illness affecting the stomach

when someone feels sad or worried

upsetting /ʌpˈsetɪŋ/ ADJECTIVE making you feel upset □ I found the whole experience very upsetting. upsetting news

upshot /ˈʌpʃɒt/ NOUN the upshot (of something) the final result of something □ The upshot of the discussion is that we've decided not to go.

upside down /ˈʌpsaɪd ˈdaʊn/ ADJECTIVE, ADVERB with the top part where the bottom should be and the bottom part where the top should be □ He was holding the book upside down.

upstage /ˌʌpˈsteɪdʒ/ VERB [**upstages, upstaging, upstaged**] to do something that makes people look at you instead of someone else

upstairs ▶ ADVERB /ˌʌpˈsteəz/ to or on a higher level of a building □ I went upstairs to get changed.
▶ ADJECTIVE /ˈʌpsteəz/ on a higher level of a building □ an upstairs bedroom

uptake /ˈʌpteɪk/ NOUN be slow/quick on the uptake to be slow/quick to understand what someone means

uptight /ˌʌpˈtaɪt/ ADJECTIVE nervous and often becoming angry □ You seem a bit uptight today.

up-to-date /ˌʌptəˈdeɪt/ ADJECTIVE
1 having the latest information □ an up-to-date news
2 new or modern □ up-to-date technology □ up-to-date fashions

upward /ˈʌpwəd/ ADJECTIVE
1 towards a higher place or position □ an upward climb
2 towards a higher level □ an upward trend
• **upwards** /ˈʌpwədz/ or **upward** /ˈʌpwəd/ ADVERB
1 towards a higher place or position □ He looked upwards and saw the sun.
2 towards a higher level

uranium /juˈreɪnjəm/ NOUN, NO PLURAL a metal that is used for making nuclear energy. A chemistry word.

urban /ˈɜːbən/ ADJECTIVE to do with a town or city □ urban areas □ urban planning

urge /ɜːdʒ/ ▶ VERB [**urges, urging, urged**] to advise someone strongly to do something □ If you haven't already filled in the form, I urge you to do so.
♦ PHRASAL VERB **urge someone on** to encourage someone as they are doing something □ I could hear the crowds urging me on as I ran the last few metres.
▶ NOUN [plural **urges**] a sudden, strong feeling of wanting to do something □ I felt an urge to shake him. 🔁 I resisted the urge to tell her (=did not tell her although I wanted to).

urgency /ˈɜːdʒənsɪ/ NOUN, NO PLURAL when something is very serious and needs action now □ I didn't realize the urgency of the situation.
• **urgent** /ˈɜːdʒənt/ ADJECTIVE very serious and needing action now 🔁 There is an urgent need for water and food supplies in the region. 🔁 He has called for urgent action to stop the killing.
• **urgently** /ˈɜːdʒəntlɪ/ ADVERB in an urgent way □ Medical supplies are needed urgently.

urinal /juəˈraɪnəl/ NOUN [plural **urinals**] a toilet, often fitted to a wall, that men and boys can urinate into

urinate /ˈjuərɪˌneɪt/ VERB [**urinates, urinating, urinated**] to pass urine out of your body. A formal word.
• **urine** /ˈjuərɪn/ NOUN, NO PLURAL the waste liquid passed out of the bodies of people and animals

URL /ˌjuːɑːˈrel/ ABBREVIATION Uniform Resource Locator; an Internet address. A computing word.

urn /ɜːn/ NOUN [plural **urns**]
1 a container for holding a dead person's ashes (=a powder that remains after a body is burnt)
2 a large metal container used for making large amounts of tea or coffee

US /ˌjuːˈes/ ABBREVIATION the United States of America

us /ʌs/ PRONOUN used as the object in a sentence to talk or write about yourself and at least one other person □ Do you want to come with us? □ They gave us coffee. □ The news surprised all of us.

USA /ˌjuːesˈeɪ/ ABBREVIATION the United States of America

usage /ˈjuːzɪdʒ/ NOUN [plural **usages**]
1 the way that words are used when they are spoken or written □ a book on English usage.
2 the way that something is used or how much of

something is used □ *Energy usage is at its highest at around 9pm.*

use ▶ VERB /juːz/ [**uses, using, used**]
1 to do something with something for a particular purpose □ *Use a knife to open it.* □ *He used words like 'disappointing' and 'shocking'.* □ *+ for I use these boxes for storing apples.* □ *+ as Dad uses this room as his office.*
2 to take an amount of something from a supply in order to do something with it □ *I've used all the milk now.* □ *You can use the logs from the shed.*
3 to treat someone in an unfair or unkind way in order to get something you want □ *He just used her to get to know her rich relatives.*
◆ PHRASAL VERB **use something up** to use all of a supply of something □ *We've used up all the paper.*
▶ NOUN /juːs/ [*plural* **uses**]
1 *no plural* when you use something □ *+ of We do not allow the use of calculators in the exam.* ⊞ *We were able to make use of the sports facilities.*
2 the purpose for which something is used □ *This knife has a lot of uses.* □ *They deny that the uranium is for military use.*
3 *no plural* if something is of use, it is useful or effective □ *Is this coat of any use to you?* ⊞ *What's the use of leaving messages when he never replies?* ⊞ *It's no use asking him for help - he's always busy.*
4 *no plural* the right or ability to use something □ *+ of He offered me the use of his car while he's away.* □ *She lost the use of her legs.*
• **used** /juːzd/ ADJECTIVE something that is used has been owned and used by someone else □ *He sells used cars.*

used to[1] /ˈjuːst tuː/ MODAL VERB used to talk about things that happened regularly in the past or things that were true in the past, especially when they no longer happen or are true □ *I used to visit her a lot when she lived in Germany.* □ *The fence used to be painted white.* □ *I used to be a teacher.*

▶ If you use **used to** in a question or a negative, you should use the form **use to** □ *Did you use to play the piano?* □ *I didn't use to like many vegetables.*

used to[2] /ˈjuːst tuː/ ADJECTIVE if you are used to something, you have often seen it or experienced it before, so it does not seem strange, difficult, etc. □ *I'm used to living on my own.* ⊞ *Working nights is difficult, but you get used to it.*

useful /ˈjuːsfʊl/ ADJECTIVE helpful for doing something or achieving something □ *The book gave me some useful information.* □ *+ for These little pots are useful for growing seedlings.* ⊞ *The contacts I made in that job proved useful later.*
• **usefully** /ˈjuːsfʊli/ ADVERB in a way that is helpful □ *How can we spend the money most usefully?* □ *There was nothing I could usefully do.*
• **usefulness** /ˈjuːsfʊlnɪs/ NOUN, NO PLURAL being

useful □ *He questioned the usefulness of their research.*

useless /ˈjuːslɪs/ ADJECTIVE
1 having no purpose, or not effective or working correctly □ *This knife's useless - it's completely blunt* □ *It's useless trying to explain to them.* □ *She wasted her money on useless ornaments.*
2 an informal word meaning without skill □ *I'm useless at maths.*
• **uselessly** /ˈjuːslɪsli/ ADVERB in a useless way □ *The cord flapped uselessly in the wind.*

user /ˈjuːzə(r)/ NOUN [*plural* **users**] a person who uses something □ *users of public transport*

user-friendly /ˈjuːzə ˈfrendli/ ADJECTIVE easy for anyone to use or understand □ *a user-friendly system*
username /ˈjuːzəˌneɪm/ NOUN [*plural* **usernames**] name that you type, together with a password (=secret word), so that you can use a computer system. A computing word.
usher /ˈʌʃə(r)/ ▶ NOUN [*plural* **ushers**] someone who shows people where to sit, especially at a theatre or wedding
▶ VERB [**ushers, ushering, ushered**] to go with someone and show them the way □ *The waiter ushered him to a table.*

usual /ˈjuːʒəl/ ADJECTIVE
1 done or happening most often □ *I had my usual coffee this morning.* □ *'What did you talk about?' '*the usual things.' □ *My walk to work took longer t*usual.*
2 as usual as happens most often □ *He was late* usual.*
• **usually** /ˈjuːʒəli/ ADVERB normally, on most occasions □ *I usually drink tea.* □ *We usually go holiday in August.* □ *Usually I'm in bed by ten o'c*

utensil /juːˈtensəl/ NOUN [*plural* **utensils**] a tool you use in the kitchen ⊞ *kitchen utensils*
uterus /ˈjuːtərəs/ NOUN [*plural* **uteri**] the organ i a woman's or female animal's body where her b grow until they are ready to be born. A biology
utility /juːˈtɪlɪti/ NOUN [*plural* **utilities**] a compa which supplies gas, electricity, water or another service
utilize or **utilise** /ˈjuːtɪlaɪz/ VERB [**utilizes, utiliz utilized**] a formal word for use □ *Old newspape utilized in the production of recycled paper.*
utmost /ˈʌtməʊst/ ▶ ADJECTIVE greatest possibl have the utmost respect for both players.*
▶ NOUN do your utmost to make the greates possible effort □ *She did her utmost to help hir*
utter[1] /ˈʌtə(r)/ VERB [**utters, uttering, uttered**] t something □ *She didn't utter a single word.*
utter[2] /ˈʌtə(r)/ ADJECTIVE complete □ *utter silen*
• **utterly** /ˈʌtəli/ ADVERB completely □ *I feel ut* exhausted.*

U-turn /'juːtɜːn/ NOUN [*plural* **U-turns**]
1 a turn in the shape of a U, made by a driver to go back the way he or she has just come

2 a complete change of plan or ideas □ *a U-turn in government policy*

UV /ˌjuːˈviː/ ABBREVIATION ultraviolet; a type of light from the sun which turns the skin darker

V v

V[1] *or* v /viː/ the 22nd letter of the alphabet

v[2] /viː/ ABBREVIATION
1 versus; used for saying which two players or teams are competing against each other □ *Arsenal v Manchester United*
2 very □ *v good* (=very good)

V[3] /viː/ ABBREVIATION volt; a unit for measuring how strong an electric current is

vacancy /ˈveɪkənsɪ/ NOUN [*plural* **vacancies**]
1 an available room in a hotel □ *Sorry, no vacancies.*
2 an available job
• **vacant** /ˈveɪkənt/ ADJECTIVE
1 if something is vacant, it is available because no one else is using it □ *a vacant seat* □ *a vacant office*
2 if a job is vacant, it is available because no one is doing it
3 looking as if you are not thinking about anything ⊞ *a vacant expression*
• **vacate** /vəˈkeɪt/ VERB [**vacates, vacating, vacated**] to leave somewhere or something so that it is available for someone else. A formal word □ *Hotel guests must vacate their rooms by midday.*

vacation /vəˈkeɪʃən/ NOUN [*plural* **vacations**]
1 the US word for holiday ⊞ *We're taking a vacation in the mountains this summer.*
2 on vacation taking a holiday. A US phrase.
3 a part of the year when a university is closed □ *the summer vacation*

vaccinate /ˈvæksɪneɪt/ VERB [**vaccinates, vaccinating, vaccinated**] to put a vaccine into someone's body to protect them from a disease
• **vaccination** /ˌvæksɪˈneɪʃən/ NOUN [*plural* **vaccinations**] the process of vaccinating someone

vaccine /ˈvæksiːn/ NOUN [*plural* **vaccines**] a substance containing bacteria or a virus, which is put into someone's body in order to protect them against a disease

vacuum[1] /ˈvækjʊəm/ NOUN [*plural* **vacuums**]
1 a space with no air or other gases in it
2 when something very important is missing from a situation

vacuum[2] /ˈvækjʊəm/ VERB [**vacuums, vacuuming, vacuumed**] to clean a floor using a vacuum cleaner

vacuum cleaner /ˈvækjʊəm ˌkliːnə(r)/ NOUN [*plural* **vacuum cleaners**] an electrical machine that sucks dust up from the floor

vacuum flask /ˈvækjʊəm ˌflɑːsk/ NOUN [*plural* **vacuum flasks**] a container for keeping drinks hot ⟨ cold

vacuum-packed /ˈvækjʊəmˈpækt/ ADJECTIVE in a container from which all the air has been removed □ *These nuts are vacuum-packed for freshness.*

vagina /vəˈdʒaɪnə/ NOUN [*plural* **vaginas**] the passage in a woman's body that connects her wor (=organ where a baby grows) to the outside of he body. A biology word.

vagrant /ˈveɪɡrənt/ NOUN [*plural* **vagrants**] a pers without a home who walks from place to place. A formal word.

vague /veɪɡ/ ADJECTIVE [**vaguer, vaguest**]
1 not clear and without details ⊞ *I have a vague* of where he lives. ⊞ *He had a vague memory of se her there.*
2 explaining something in a way that is not clear has no details □ *He was a bit vague about their pl*
• **vaguely** /ˈveɪɡlɪ/ ADVERB
1 in a way that is not clear and has no details ⊞ *vaguely remember saying that.*
2 slightly ⊞ *He looked vaguely familiar.*

vain /veɪn/ ADJECTIVE [**vainer, vainest**]
1 very pleased with your appearance and paying much attention to it
2 unsuccessful ⊞ *I made a vain attempt to get h stay.*
3 in vain without achieving what you want to *tried in vain to persuade him.*
• **vainly** /ˈveɪnlɪ/ ADVERB without achieving wha want to do □ *I turned over, vainly trying to get* comfortable.
➡ go to vanity

valentine /ˈvæləntaɪn/ NOUN [*plural* **valentine**
1 a card that you send on Valentine's Day (14 February) to show that you love someone
2 the person you send a valentine to

valet ► NOUN /ˈvæleɪ/ [*plural* **valets**]
1 a male servant who works for another man a looks after his clothes
2 someone who parks customers' cars at a hot restaurant, etc.
► VERB /ˈvælɪt/ [**valets, valeting, valeted**] to cle someone's car for payment

valiant /'væljənt/ ADJECTIVE a formal word meaning brave 🗎 *She made a valiant attempt to rescue the cat.*

valiantly /'væljəntlɪ/ ADVERB in a brave way

valid /'vælɪd/ ADJECTIVE
1 legally or officially acceptable and able to be used □ *a valid passport* □ *a valid ticket*
2 reasonable and acceptable □ *a valid excuse* □ *a valid argument*

validate /'vælɪdeɪt/ VERB [validates, validating, validated] to prove that something is true □ *Have these claims ever been validated?*

validity /və'lɪdətɪ/ NOUN, NO PLURAL the quality of being valid

valium /'vælɪəm/ NOUN, NO PLURAL a drug that people take to make them feel calm and less nervous. A trademark.

valley /'vælɪ/ NOUN [plural valleys] an area of low land between hills, often with a river running through it

valour /'vælə(r)/ NOUN, NO PLURAL a literary word that means courage, especially in a war

valuable /'væljuəbəl/ ADJECTIVE
worth a lot of money □ *valuable jewellery*
very useful □ *valuable advice* □ *She's a valuable member of the team.*

> Note that **valuable** does not have the same meaning as 'expensive'. If something is valuable, you could sell it for a lot of money. If something is expensive, it costs a lot of money: □ *valuable antiques/paintings* □ *expensive food/clothes*

valuables /'væljuəbəlz/ PLURAL NOUN things, especially things that you own, that are worth a lot of money

valuation /,vælju'eɪʃən/ NOUN [plural valuations]
the act of deciding how much money something is worth
the amount of money that someone decides something is worth

value /'vælju:/ ▶ NOUN [plural values]
the amount of money that something is worth □ *the paintings had an estimated value of $1.4 billion.* □ *The house has increased in value.*
how useful and important something is □ *This food has very little nutritional value.*
the quality or amount of something compared to its 🗎 *I thought the hotel was very good value.*
▶ VERB [values, valuing, valued]
think something is important and worth having □ *I really value my free time.* □ *I value your advice on this matter.*
say how much something is worth □ *The jewels were valued at three thousand dollars.*

values /'vælju:z/ PLURAL NOUN the things that you consider to be most important in life and that influence the way you treat other people

valve /vælv/ NOUN [plural valves] something that opens and shuts to control the flow of liquid, air or gas through a pipe

vampire /'væmpaɪə(r)/ NOUN [plural vampires] in stories, a dead person who comes out at night and sucks blood from people's necks

van /væn/ NOUN [plural vans] a road vehicle, like a small truck, used for carrying goods

vandal /'vændəl/ NOUN [plural vandals] someone who deliberately damages things in public places

• **vandalism** /'vændəlɪzəm/ NOUN, NO PLURAL the crime of deliberately damaging something such as a public building

• **vandalize** or **vandalise** /'vændəlaɪz/ VERB [vandalizes, vandalizing, vandalized] to deliberately damage something in a public place

vanguard /'vænɡɑːd/ NOUN, NO PLURAL in the vanguard of something creating new and original ideas and methods □ *They are very much in the vanguard of cancer research.*

vanilla /və'nɪlə/ NOUN, NO PLURAL a flavour that is used in a lot of sweet foods □ *vanilla ice cream*

vanish /'vænɪʃ/ VERB [vanishes, vanishing, vanished] to disappear suddenly, leaving nothing behind □ *He was standing in front of me a moment ago and suddenly he vanished.*

vanity /'vænətɪ/ NOUN, NO PLURAL when someone is very pleased with their own appearance and pays too much attention to it

vapor /'veɪpə(r)/ NOUN, NO PLURAL the US spelling of vapour

vapour /'veɪpə(r)/ NOUN, NO PLURAL many very small drops of liquid in the air □ *water vapour*

variable /'veərɪəbəl/ ADJECTIVE changing often and never staying the same □ *work of variable quality*

variant /'veərɪənt/ NOUN [plural variants] a different type of the same thing

• **variation** /,veərɪ'eɪʃən/ NOUN [plural variations] a change in the amount or level of something □ *variations in temperature*

varied /'veərɪd/ ADJECTIVE of many different types □ *He has varied interests, from comic books to bird watching.*

variety /və'raɪətɪ/ NOUN [plural varieties]
1 no plural a lot of different types □ *+ of* The chairs are available in a variety of colours.
2 no plural the quality of having many different things □ *You need variety in your diet.*
3 a type that is different from other similar things □ *a new variety of rose*

various /'veərɪəs/ ADJECTIVE many different □ *There were various types of cheese.* □ *There's been flooding in various parts of the country.*

varnish /'vɑːnɪʃ/ ▶ NOUN [plural **varnishes**] a liquid that you paint on wood to protect it and to give it a shiny surface
▶ VERB [**varnishes, varnishing, varnished**] to put varnish on wood

vary /'veərɪ/ VERB [**varies, varying, varied**]
1 if things of the same type vary, they are all different in some way □ Prices vary from shop to shop.
2 if something varies, it changes at different times □ Snowfall varies throughout the season.
3 to change something slightly □ You can vary the quantity that you order depending on your requirements at any given time.

vase /vɑːz/ NOUN [plural **vases**] a decorative container for flowers

vast /vɑːst/ ADJECTIVE extremely big □ a vast area of land
● **vastly** /'vɑːstlɪ/ ADVERB very much □ His work has improved vastly.

VAT /væt, ˌviːeɪ'tiː/ ABBREVIATION value added tax; a tax on goods and services in the UK

vat /væt/ NOUN [plural **vats**] a large container for liquids

vault /vɔːlt/ NOUN [plural **vaults**]
1 a room in a bank for storing valuable things
2 a room under a church where dead bodies are buried

VCR /ˌviːsiː'ɑː(r)/ ABBREVIATION video cassette recorder; a machine used for watching and recording videos

VDU /ˌviːdiː'juː/ ABBREVIATION visual display unit; a computer screen. A computing word.

veal /viːl/ NOUN, NO PLURAL meat from a baby cow

veer /vɪə(r)/ VERB [**veers, veering, veered**] to suddenly change direction, especially when moving fast □ The car suddenly veered to the left.

veg /vedʒ/ ABBREVIATION vegetables 🖃 fruit and veg

vegan /'viːgən/ ▶ NOUN [plural **vegans**] someone who does not eat anything that comes from an animal, such as meat, eggs or milk
▶ ADJECTIVE not eating or containing foods from an animal □ a vegan restaurant

vegetable /'vedʒtəbəl/ NOUN [plural **vegetables**] a plant that you can eat, especially one that is not sweet □ vegetables such as potatoes and carrots

➤ Note that although the word 'fruit' cannot be used in the plural, the word **vegetable** can:
✓ Eat more fruit and vegetables.
✗ Eat more fruit and vegetable.

vegetarian /ˌvedʒɪ'teərɪən/ ▶ NOUN [plural **vegetarians**] someone who does not eat meat or fish
▶ ADJECTIVE not eating or containing meat or fish □ vegetarian cookery

vegetation /ˌvedʒɪ'teɪʃən/ NOUN, NO PLURAL plants and trees

veggie /'vedʒɪ/ ▶ NOUN [plural **veggies**] an informa word that means vegetarian □ You're not a veggie, are you?
▶ ADJECTIVE not eating or containing meat or fish. A informal word. □ veggie food

vehement /'viːmənt/ ADJECTIVE expressing your opinion forcefully □ She was vehement in her condemnation of the practice.
● **vehemently** /'viːməntlɪ/ ADVERB forcefully □ Sh argued vehemently in support of the government.

vehicle /'viːɪkəl/ NOUN [plural **vehicles**] somethir that carries people or goods, especially on roads, fo example a car or a truck

veil /veɪl/ NOUN [plural **veils**] a piece of material th covers a woman's head or face
● **veiled** /veɪld/ ADJECTIVE
1 wearing a veil
2 not directly expressed □ veiled threats □ veiled criticism

vein /veɪn/ NOUN [plural **veins**] one of the thin tut inside the body that carry blood back to the heart

Velcro /'velkrəʊ/ NOUN, NO PLURAL a sticky mater that is used to fasten clothes. A trademark.

velocity /vɪ'lɒsətɪ/ NOUN, NO PLURAL the speed at which something moves. A physics word.

velvet /'velvɪt/ NOUN, NO PLURAL a thick cloth tha feels very soft on one side
● **velvety** /'velvɪtɪ/ ADJECTIVE feeling like velvet

vendetta /ven'detə/ NOUN [plural **vendettas**] w someone tries to harm someone else over a long period of time because they are angry about something that they did in the past

vending machine /'vendɪŋ mə'ʃiːn/ NOUN [plu **vending machines**] a machine that you can buy th from such as drinks and sweets

vendor /'vendɔː(r)/ NOUN [plural **vendors**] some who is selling something □ an ice cream vendor

veneer /və'nɪə(r)/ NOUN [plural **veneers**]
1 a thin layer of wood that provides an attractiv surface to something
2 a pleasant manner that is not sincere and that someone's real character

venetian blind /vɪ'niːʃən 'blaɪnd/ NOUN [plur **venetian blinds**] a covering for a window that is of long, horizontal pieces of metal or wood that turn to allow in or keep out light

vengeance /'vendʒəns/ NOUN, NO PLURAL punishment that you give to someone who has harmed you
● **vengeful** /'vendʒful/ ADJECTIVE wanting to pu someone because they have hurt you. A formal

venison /'venɪsən/ NOUN, NO PLURAL meat fro deer

Venn diagram /'ven 'daɪəgræm/ NOUN [plu **Venn diagrams**] a mathematical picture using which go over each other where the things in t share the same characteristics. A maths word.

enom /'venəm/ NOUN, NO PLURAL
1 the poison that some snakes produce
2 very strong hate and anger □ *His letters were full of* venom.

venomous /'venəməs/ ADJECTIVE
1 poisonous □ *a venomous snake*
2 full of hate and anger □ *a venomous attack*

ent /vent/ ▶ NOUN [*plural* **vents**] a small opening to llow air, gas or smoke to pass through
IDIOM **give vent to something** to express a feeling trongly, especially anger
▶ VERB [**vents, venting, vented**] to express your anger r other bad feeling strongly □ *He was just venting his* ustration with the situation.

ntilate /'ventɪleɪt/ VERB [**ventilates, ventilating, entilated**] to allow fresh air into a room or building
ventilation /ˌventɪ'leɪʃən/ NOUN, NO PLURAL when ou allow fresh air into a room or building
entilator /'ventɪˌleɪtə(r)/ NOUN [*plural* ntilators]
a machine that helps someone to breathe by forcing r into and out of their lungs
an opening or piece of equipment that allows air :o a room or building

ntricle /'ventrɪkəl/ NOUN [*plural* **ventricles**] one of e two lower parts of the heart. A biology word.

ntriloquism /ven'trɪləkwɪzəm/ NOUN, NO PLURAL e skill of speaking without moving your lips and aking it look as if a puppet (=toy in the shape of a 'son) is speaking

entriloquist /ven'trɪləkwɪst/ NOUN [*plural* ntriloquists] someone who has the skill of ntriloquism

ture /'ventʃə(r)/ ▶ NOUN [*plural* **ventures**] an vity, often a business activity ⊞ *It's his latest* iness venture.
▶ VERB [**ventures, venturing, ventured**] to go ewhere that involves a risk □ *The weather was so* I didn't venture out of the hotel for two days.

ue /'venju:/ NOUN [*plural* **venues**] the place re an event happens □ *The castle is used as a* ding venue.

nda /və'rændə/ NOUN [*plural* **verandas**] a red area next to a building where you can sit

) /vɜ:b/ NOUN [*plural* **verbs**] a word that says someone or something does. For example, *eat*, k and *be* are verbs.

al /'vɜ:bəl/ ADJECTIVE
oken and not written □ *a verbal agreement*
do with words □ *verbal communication*

ct /'vɜ:dɪkt/ NOUN [*plural* **verdicts**] a decision in a court of law saying whether someone is or not guilty of committing a crime
ntually the jury reached a verdict.

' /vɜ:dʒ/ NOUN [*plural* **verges**] the area at the of a road, usually covered in grass
on the verge of something going to do

something very soon □ *The company is on the verge of collapse.*

verify /'verɪfaɪ/ VERB [**verifies, verifying, verified**] to prove that something is true

veritable /'verɪtəbəl/ ADJECTIVE a formal word meaning real □ *The meal when it came was a veritable feast.*

vermin /'vɜ:mɪn/ PLURAL NOUN animals or insects that destroy crops or cause disease

verruca /və'ru:kə/ NOUN [*plural* **verrucas**] a small hard lump on the bottom of someone's foot

versatile /'vɜ:sətaɪl/ ADJECTIVE
1 useful for many different things □ *versatile clothes*
2 able to do many different things □ *a versatile actor*
● **versatility** /ˌvɜ:sə'tɪləti/ NOUN, NO PLURAL when someone or something is versatile

verse /vɜ:s/ NOUN [*plural* **verses**]
1 a set of lines that form one part of a song or poem
2 poetry and not ordinary writing

version /'vɜ:ʃən/ NOUN [*plural* **versions**]
1 one form of something when other forms of it exist
□ *I know three versions of this song.*
2 one person's description of something that happened ⊞ *I've only heard Debbie's version of events.*

versus /'vɜ:səs/ PREPOSITION used for saying which two players or teams are competing against each other □ *It's Scotland versus France tonight.*

vertebra /'vɜ:tɪbrə/ NOUN [*plural* **vertebrae**] one of the row of small bones down the middle of your back. A biology word.

vertebrate /'vɜ:tɪbreɪt/ NOUN [*plural* **vertebrates**] an animal that has a bone down the middle of its back. A biology word.

vertical /'vɜ:tɪkəl/ ADJECTIVE pointing straight up, at an angle of 90° to the ground □ *vertical lines*

vertigo /'vɜ:tɪgəʊ/ NOUN, NO PLURAL a feeling as if everything around you is moving when you are in a very high place

verve /vɜ:v/ NOUN, NO PLURAL excitement and energy

very /'veri/ ▶ ADVERB
1 to a great degree □ *I'm very tired.* □ *She was very pleased.* □ *It all happened very quickly.*
2 **not very good/nice/pleased, etc.** not good/nice/ pleased, etc. □ *She wasn't very pleased.*

➤ **Very** is not used before adjectives which have a strong meaning:
✓ *I was very tired.*
✗ *I was very exhausted.*
➤ If you are using an adjective with a strong meaning, put an adverb such as **completely** or **absolutely** before it □ *I was completely exhausted.*

▶ ADJECTIVE exact □ *At that very moment, the telephone rang.*

vessel /'vesəl/ NOUN [*plural* **vessels**]
1 a formal word that means a large boat or ship
2 a formal word that means a container for liquids

3 a tube that carries blood through your body. A biology word.

vest /vest/ NOUN [plural **vests**]
1 a piece of underwear without sleeves that covers the top part of the body
2 the US word for waistcoat

vested interest /ˈvestɪd ˈɪntrəst/ NOUN [plural **vested interests**] a feeling of wanting something to happen or succeed because you will get an advantage from it

vestige /ˈvestɪdʒ/ NOUN [plural **vestiges**] a very small amount of something that remains. A formal word.

vet /vet/ NOUN [plural **vets**] someone whose job is to treat animals that are ill or injured

veteran /ˈvetərən/ NOUN [plural **veterans**]
1 someone who has a lot of experience of something over many years
2 someone who fought in a war

veterinarian /ˌvetərɪˈneərɪən/ NOUN [plural **veterinarians**] the US word for vet

veterinary surgeon /ˈvetərɪnrɪ ˈsɜːdʒən/ NOUN [plural **veterinary surgeons**] a formal way of saying vet

veto /ˈviːtəʊ/ ▶ VERB [vetoes, vetoing, vetoed] to officially stop something from happening □ *The president vetoed the plan to lower taxes.*
▶ NOUN [plural **vetoes**] when someone officially stops something from happening

via /ˈvaɪə/ PREPOSITION
1 travelling through a place □ *The train goes to London via Birmingham.*
2 using a particular method or person to communicate □ *We keep in touch via e-mail.*

viable /ˈvaɪəbəl/ ADJECTIVE able to succeed □ *a viable option*

viaduct /ˈvaɪədʌkt/ NOUN [plural **viaducts**] a bridge that takes a railway over a road or river

vibrant /ˈvaɪbrənt/ ADJECTIVE
1 exciting and full of life □ *a vibrant city*
2 colourful and bright

vibrate /vaɪˈbreɪt/ VERB [vibrates, vibrating, vibrated] to make small, quick shaking movements □ *The floor was vibrating with the music.*
• **vibration** /vaɪˈbreɪʃən/ NOUN [plural **vibrations**] when something vibrates

vicar /ˈvɪkə(r)/ NOUN [plural **vicars**] in the Church of England, a priest
• **vicarage** /ˈvɪkərɪdʒ/ NOUN [plural **vicarages**] a house where a vicar lives

vicarious /vɪˈkeərɪəs/ ADJECTIVE a vicarious feeling is one that you get when someone else does something and not when you do something yourself
• **vicariously** /vɪˈkeərɪəslɪ/ ADVERB experienced when someone else does something

vice /vaɪs/ NOUN [plural **vices**]
1 a bad habit □ *vices such as smoking*
2 a crime that shows low moral standards
3 a tool for holding an object while you cut it, put glue on it, etc.

vice- /vaɪs/ PREFIX vice- is added to the beginning of words that refer to very important jobs to mean 'next in importance' □ *the vice-president of the company*

vice-president /ˌvaɪsˈprezɪdənt/ NOUN [plural **vice-presidents**] the person who is next in rank after a country's president □ *the vice-president of the United States*

vice versa /ˌvaɪsə ˈvɜːsə/ ADVERB used for saying that the opposite of what you have said is also true □ *I needed his help and vice versa.*

vicinity /vɪˈsɪnɪtɪ/ NOUN, NO PLURAL the area around a place □ *There are no schools in the vicinity.*

vicious /ˈvɪʃəs/ ADJECTIVE
1 extremely cruel and violent □ *a vicious attack*
2 extremely unkind □ *She could be vicious.*

vicious circle /ˈvɪʃəs ˈsɜːkəl/ NOUN, NO PLURAL a situation in which one problem causes another problem which then makes the first problem even worse

victim /ˈvɪktɪm/ NOUN [plural **victims**] someone who is harmed or killed by something bad, such as crime, disease, flood, etc. □ *victims of crime* □ *victims of the bombing* □ *murder victims*
• **victimize** or **victimise** /ˈvɪktɪmaɪz/ VERB [victimizes, victimizing, victimized] to treat one person unfairly because you do not like something about them

victor /ˈvɪktə(r)/ NOUN [plural **victors**] a formal word that means the person who has won a competition or fight

Victorian /vɪkˈtɔːrɪən/ ▶ ADJECTIVE from the period between 1837 and 1901, when Queen Victoria ruled the UK
▶ NOUN [plural **Victorians**] a person who lived during the time of Queen Victoria

victorious /vɪkˈtɔːrɪəs/ ADJECTIVE successful in a fight or competition
• **victory** /ˈvɪktərɪ/ NOUN [plural **victories**] success in a fight or competition □ *victory in the Cup Final for* □ *The game ended in victory for France.*

video /ˈvɪdɪəʊ/ ▶ NOUN [plural **videos**]
1 a recording of a film or television programme on videotape
2 a recording of an event that has been made using a video camera
3 a machine for playing videos
▶ VERB [videos, videoing, videoed]
1 to record a television programme onto video
2 to film an event using a video camera

video camera /ˈvɪdɪəʊ ˈkæmərə/ NOUN [plural **video cameras**] a piece of equipment that you record events onto videotape

video card /ˈvɪdɪəʊ ˌkɑːd/ NOUN [plural **video cards**] a small part in a computer that allows it to play videos. A computing word.

video game /ˈvɪdɪəʊ ˌɡeɪm/ NOUN [plural **video games**] an electronic game in which players move images on a computer or television screen

videotape /'vɪdɪəuteɪp/ NOUN [plural **videotapes**] magnetic tape that pictures and sounds can be recorded on

vie /vaɪ/ VERB [**vies, vying, vied**] to compete with other people to do something better or get more of something □ Children vie with each other for their mother's attention.

view /vju:/ ► NOUN [plural **views**]

1 your opinion □ + **on** What's your view on wind farms? □ + **about** He made his views about the government very clear. 🖰 I take the view that smacking children is wrong.

2 your ability to see things from a place □ The pillar spoilt my view of the concert. 🖰 Eventually, the lion came into view. 🖰 She tore up her work in full view of her teachers.

3 the things you can see from a place □ There's a fantastic view from the top of the hill.

4 in view of something because of something □ In view of the weather, we have cancelled the game.

5 on view if something is on view, it is in a place where people can go to look at it □ Several classic cars will be on view at the event.

with a view to doing something in order to make possible to do something □ He's moving to London with a view to finding a job.

► VERB [**views, viewing, viewed**]

to have a particular opinion about something or someone □ + **as** His ideas were viewed as a threat to society.

to look at something □ People came from all over the country to view his work.

viewer /'vju:ə(r)/ NOUN [plural **viewers**] someone who watches television □ The programme attracted more than a million viewers.

viewpoint /'vju:pɔɪnt/ NOUN [plural **viewpoints**] an opinion, especially one based on your situation □ Try to see the situation from her viewpoint.

vigil /'vɪdʒɪl/ NOUN [plural **vigils**] when someone stays quietly somewhere for a period, often in order to be with an ill person or to show their beliefs about something

vigilance /'vɪdʒɪləns/ NOUN, NO PLURAL being careful to notice any trouble or problems

vigilant /'vɪdʒɪlənt/ ADJECTIVE watching things carefully in order to notice any trouble or problems □ Police have urged the public to be vigilant after a series of bomb attacks in the region.

vigorous /'vɪgərəs/ ADJECTIVE very active and energetic □ vigorous exercise

vigorously /'vɪgərəslɪ/ ADVERB in an active and energetic way

vigour /'vɪgə(r)/ NOUN, NO PLURAL energy and strength

vile /vaɪl/ ADJECTIVE [**viler, vilest**] extremely unpleasant □ a vile taste

villa /'vɪlə/ NOUN [plural **villas**] a large house, especially one used for holidays

village /'vɪlɪdʒ/ NOUN [plural **villages**] an area where people live in the countryside, which is smaller than a town □ She lives in a village just outside Stratford.

• **villager** /'vɪlɪdʒə(r)/ NOUN [plural **villagers**] someone who lives in a village

villain /'vɪlən/ NOUN [plural **villains**] a bad person in a story, film, etc.

• **villainous** /'vɪlənəs/ ADJECTIVE behaving like a villain

vindicate /'vɪndɪkeɪt/ VERB [**vindicates, vindicating, vindicated**] to prove that something someone said or did is true or right after most people thought it was wrong

• **vindication** /ˌvɪndɪ'keɪʃən/ NOUN, NO PLURAL when someone is vindicated

vindictive /vɪn'dɪktɪv/ ADJECTIVE deliberately trying to harm or upset someone who has harmed or upset you

vine /vaɪn/ NOUN [plural **vines**] a plant that grapes (=small green or red fruit that grows in groups) grow on

vinegar /'vɪnɪgə(r)/ NOUN, NO PLURAL a sour liquid that is used for giving flavour to food

vineyard /'vɪnjəd/ NOUN [plural **vineyards**] a place where grapes (=small green or red fruit that grows in groups) are grown to produce wine

vintage /'vɪntɪdʒ/ ► NOUN [plural **vintages**] the wine that was produced in a particular year

► ADJECTIVE

1 typical of a particular time in the past □ vintage clothing

2 vintage wine is of the best quality and was produced several years ago

vintage car /'vɪntɪdʒ 'kɑː(r)/ NOUN [plural **vintage cars**] a car made between 1917 and 1930 that is still in very good condition

vinyl /'vaɪnɪl/ NOUN, NO PLURAL a type of strong plastic used for making furniture and floor coverings

viola /vɪ'əulə/ NOUN [plural **violas**] a musical instrument like a big violin (=instrument with four strings, which you hold under your chin)

violate /'vaɪəleɪt/ VERB [**violates, violating, violated**] to break a law or rule

• **violation** /ˌvaɪə'leɪʃən/ NOUN [plural **violations**] when a law or rule is broken

violence /'vaɪələns/ NOUN, NO PLURAL

1 actions intended to hurt or kill someone or to damage something □ Something must be done to stop the violence. □ + **against** violence against women

2 force and strength, often causing damage □ The violence of the storm shocked everyone.

• **violent** /'vaɪələnt/ ADJECTIVE

1 involving actions intended to hurt or kill someone or to damage something □ violent crime □ a violent film

2 with a lot of force and strength, causing damage □ a violent storm □ a violent explosion

3 extreme and impossible to control □ a violent coughing fit

• **violently** /'vaɪələntlɪ/ ADVERB in a violent way

violet /ˈvaɪələt/ ▶ NOUN [plural **violets**] a small purple flower

▶ ADJECTIVE having a pale purple colour

violin /ˌvaɪəˈlɪn/ NOUN [plural **violins**] a musical instrument with four strings, which you hold under your chin and play by pulling a bow (=long, thin piece of wood with hair stretched along it) across the strings

• **violinist** /ˌvaɪəˈlɪnɪst/ NOUN [plural **violinists**] someone who plays the violin

VIP /ˌviːaɪˈpiː/ ABBREVIATION very important person; someone who is treated very well because they are powerful or famous

viper /ˈvaɪpə(r)/ NOUN [plural **vipers**] a small poisonous snake

viral /ˈvaɪrəl/ ADJECTIVE caused by a virus □ *a viral infection*

virtual /ˈvɜːtʃuəl/ ADJECTIVE
1 almost a particular thing □ *He was a virtual prisoner in his own home.*
2 using computer images to make something that is not real seem real □ *a virtual tour of the museum*

• **virtually** /ˈvɜːtʃuəli/ ADVERB almost □ *Virtually all her friends have left.*

virtual reality /ˌvɜːtʃuəl rɪˈæləti/ NOUN, NO PLURAL the use of computer images and sounds to make something that is not real seem real

virtue /ˈvɜːtjuː/ NOUN [plural **virtues**]
1 a good quality in a person's character □ *Patience is a virtue.*
2 an advantage □ *The virtue of this approach is that it is quicker.*
3 a way of behaving that is morally good. A formal word. □ *a woman of virtue*
4 **by virtue of something** because of something, especially something good

virtuoso /ˌvɜːtjuˈəʊzəʊ/ NOUN [plural **virtuosos**] someone who is excellent at something, especially playing a musical instrument □ *a virtuoso pianist*

virtuous /ˈvɜːtʃuəs/ ADJECTIVE behaving well, in a way that is morally good

virus /ˈvaɪrəs/ NOUN [plural **viruses**]
1 a very small living thing that can enter the body and cause disease. A biology word.
2 an illness caused by a virus □ *He's been off work all week with a virus.*
3 a computer program that can send itself to many computers, for example by e-mail, and can destroy files on those computers. A computing word.

visa /ˈviːzə/ NOUN [plural **visas**] a document that you need to travel to and work in some countries

vis-à-vis /ˌviːzɑːˈviː/ PREPOSITION
1 to do with something □ *I spoke to Michael vis-à-vis the price increases.*
2 when compared with something

viscous /ˈvɪskəs/ ADJECTIVE a viscous liquid is thick. A biology word.

visibility /ˌvɪzɪˈbɪlɪti/ NOUN, NO PLURAL
1 how far and well you can see, for example in bad weather □ *poor visibility caused by heavy rain*
2 the fact of being easy to see □ *Visibility is importan* for cyclists.

• **visible** /ˈvɪzəbəl/ ADJECTIVE able to be seen □ *Is the house visible from the road?*

• **visibly** /ˈvɪzɪbli/ ADVERB in a way that you can see c notice □ *She was visibly upset by his remarks.*

vision /ˈvɪʒən/ NOUN [plural **visions**]
1 your ability to see □ *poor vision*
2 an idea of how something should be in the future □ *He talked about his vision for the school.*
3 the ability to think about the future and make plar that are clever and show imagination
4 **have visions of doing something** to imagine something happening □ *I had visions of turning up la and missing the train.*
5 an image that appears in front of someone during religious experience

visit /ˈvɪzɪt/ ▶ VERB [**visits, visiting, visited**]
1 to go and see a place or person □ *We're going to vi my aunt while we're in York.* □ *We visited a couple museums.*
2 to look at a website □ *It's one of the most visite* websites in the UK.

▶ NOUN [plural **visits**] the act of visiting a place o person ⏃ *I'm going to pay him a visit.*

• **visitor** /ˈvɪzɪtə(r)/ NOUN [plural **visitors**] someor who visits a place or person ⏃ *She had two visitor yesterday.*

visor /ˈvaɪzə(r)/ NOUN [plural **visors**]
1 the clear part of a helmet (=hard hat) that cove someone's face
2 a hat for protecting your eyes from the sun wh consists of a piece of plastic attached to a strip th goes around the head

visual /ˈvɪʒuəl/ ADJECTIVE to do with seeing □ *vis* signals

visual aid /ˌvɪʒuəl ˈeɪd/ NOUN [plural **visual aid** picture, film, etc. that helps you to understand a subject that you are learning about

visualize or **visualise** /ˈvɪʒuəlaɪz/ VERB [**visual** **visualizing, visualized**] to form a picture in your ▪ □ *I remember his name, but I can't visualize him*

visually /ˈvɪʒuəli/ ADVERB in a way that is to do seeing □ *Visually, it's a beautiful film.*

vital /ˈvaɪtəl/ ADJECTIVE necessary or extremely important □ *vital information* □ *He played a vita in the project.*

• **vitality** /vaɪˈtæləti/ NOUN, NO PLURAL energy a interest □ *A better diet will restore lost vitality.*

• **vitally** /ˈvaɪtəli/ ADVERB extremely ⏃ *vitally important information*

vitamin /ˈvɪtəmɪn/ NOUN [plural **vitamins**] a substance in food that you need to stay health □ *Oranges contain vitamin C.*

viva /'vaɪvə/ NOUN [plural **vivas**] a spoken exam at university

vivacious /vɪ'veɪʃəs/ ADJECTIVE full of energy, and enjoying meeting and speaking to people □ *a vivacious young woman*

vivid /'vɪvɪd/ ADJECTIVE
1 producing very clear ideas and pictures in your mind □ *a vivid description* □ *vivid memories*
2 very bright □ *vivid colours*
vividly /'vɪvɪdli/ ADVERB in a very clear way □ *I vividly remember meeting him.*

vivisection /ˌvɪvɪ'sekʃən/ NOUN, NO PLURAL when experiments are done on animals that are alive, usually for scientific reasons

vixen /'vɪksən/ NOUN [plural **vixens**] a female fox (=wild animal like a dog with red fur)

V-neck /'viː nek/ NOUN [plural **V-necks**]
a neck opening in a piece of clothing formed to make a point at the front
a piece of clothing for the upper half of the body with this neck opening
V-necked ADJECTIVE having a V-neck □ *a V-necked sweater*

vocabulary /və'kæbjuləri/ NOUN [plural **vocabularies**]
the range of words that someone knows and uses *She has a good vocabulary for a child of her age.*
all the words in a language

vocal /'vəukəl/ ADJECTIVE
to do with your voice □ *vocal quality*
saying your opinions strongly □ *her vocal opposition to the plan*

vocal cords /'vəukəl ˌkɔːdz/ PLURAL NOUN the part at the top of the throat that produces the voice

vocalist /'vəukəlɪst/ NOUN [plural **vocalists**] a singer, especially a singer of pop music

vocation /və'keɪʃən/ NOUN [plural **vocations**] a job that you feel you must do because you have the skills for it and because the work is very important □ *For her, teaching is a vocation.*

vocational /və'keɪʃənəl/ ADJECTIVE providing the skills needed for a particular job □ *vocational training*

vociferous /və'sɪfərəs/ ADJECTIVE saying your opinions in a strong, loud way □ *a vociferous group of protesters.*

vodka /'vɒdkə/ NOUN, NO PLURAL a strong clear alcoholic drink

vogue /vəug/ NOUN, NO PLURAL when something is fashionable or popular □ *There is a current vogue for Spanish films.*

voice /vɔɪs/ ▶ NOUN [plural **voices**]
the sound you make when you speak or sing □ *She has quite a low voice.* □ *Her singing voice is beautiful.*
I thought I heard voices.
lose your voice to stop being able to speak for a while because you are ill
no plural the chance to say your opinions □ *Poor people like this have no voice.*

4 no plural a person who says the opinions of a particular group □ *the voice of the people*
▶ VERB [**voices, voicing, voiced**] to express an opinion *Many people have voiced their concerns.*

void /vɔɪd/ ▶ ADJECTIVE not legally or officially acceptable and unable to be used □ *The contract was declared void.*
▶ NOUN, NO PLURAL
1 when something very important is missing from a situation □ *Her death has left a void in his life.*
2 a very large space with nothing in it

volatile /'vɒlətaɪl/ ADJECTIVE
1 a volatile person is likely to change their mood very quickly
2 a volatile situation could change very suddenly
3 a volatile liquid or substance changes quickly to a gas. A chemistry word.

volcanic /vɒl'kænɪk/ ADJECTIVE to do with a volcano □ *volcanic activity*

volcano /vɒl'keɪnəu/ NOUN [plural **volcanoes**] a mountain that sometimes sends out hot lava (=liquid rock) through a hole in its top

vole /vəul/ NOUN [plural **voles**] a small animal similar to a mouse

volley /'vɒli/ ▶ NOUN [plural **volleys**]
1 in some sports, for example tennis, when a ball is hit before it reaches the ground
2 a lot of bullets or weapons that are fired or thrown at the same time
▶ VERB [**volleys, volleying, volleyed**] in a sport such as tennis, to hit a ball before it reaches the ground

volleyball /'vɒlibɔːl/ NOUN, NO PLURAL a game in which two teams hit a ball over a high net with their hands

volt /vəult/ NOUN [plural **volts**] a unit for measuring the strength of an electric current
• **voltage** /'vəultɪdʒ/ NOUN [plural **voltages**] the amount of electrical force something has

volume /'vɒljuːm/ NOUN [plural **volumes**]
1 the level of sound that something makes *Can you turn the volume down on the TV, please?*
2 the space that something takes up or the amount of space that a container has
3 the amount of something □ **+ of** *The volume of trade has increased.*
4 a book, especially a book that is part of a set
➜ go to speak volumes

voluntary /'vɒləntri/ ADJECTIVE
1 done by choice and not because you have to □ *She took voluntary redundancy.*
2 done without payment *voluntary work*

volunteer /ˌvɒlən'tɪə(r)/ ▶ NOUN [plural **volunteers**]
1 someone who offers to do something □ *Do I have any volunteers to help me tidy up?*
2 someone who does work for no payment
3 someone who chooses to join the armed forces

▶ VERB [volunteers, volunteering, volunteered]
1 to offer to do something □ *Dana volunteered to take the children swimming.*
2 to choose to join the armed forces.
3 to give information or make a suggestion without being asked for it

vomit /ˈvɒmɪt/ ▶ VERB [vomits, vomiting, vomited]
to bring food back up from your stomach through your mouth
▶ NOUN, NO PLURAL food that someone has brought back from their stomach through their mouth

vote /vəʊt/ ▶ VERB [votes, voting, voted] to make a formal choice by secretly marking a piece of paper or putting your hand up to be counted □ **+ for** *Which candidate did you vote for in the local elections?* □ **+ to do something** *They voted to reject the offer.*
▶ NOUN [*plural* votes]
1 a choice you make by marking a piece of paper or putting your hand up to be counted ⊞ *The party offering to lower taxes will get my vote.*
2 the vote the right to vote in elections □ *They campaigned to be given the vote.*
• **voter** /ˈvəʊtə(r)/ NOUN [*plural* voters] someone who votes in an election

vouch /vaʊtʃ/
◆ PHRASAL VERB [vouches, vouching, vouched] vouch

for someone to say that you know from experience that someone is good and can be trusted

voucher /ˈvaʊtʃə(r)/ NOUN [*plural* vouchers]
1 a piece of paper that can be used instead of money to pay for something
2 a piece of paper that allows you to pay less than usual for something

vow /vaʊ/ ▶ VERB [vows, vowing, vowed] to promise in a very serious way
▶ NOUN [*plural* vows] a serious promise □ *marriage vows*

vowel /ˈvaʊəl/ NOUN [*plural* vowels]
1 one of the letters *a, e, i, o* or *u*
2 a speech sound you make that does not use your lips, teeth, or tongue to stop the flow of air

voyage /ˈvɔɪɪdʒ/ NOUN [*plural* voyages] a long journey by sea or in space

vulgar /ˈvʌlɡə(r)/ ADJECTIVE very rude

vulnerable /ˈvʌlnərəbəl/ ADJECTIVE easily hurt, upset or made ill □ *the protection of vulnerable children* □ *After surgery, people are more vulnerable to infection.*

vulture /ˈvʌltʃə(r)/ NOUN [*plural* vultures] a large bird that eats dead animals

W w

w or **w**[1] /'dʌbəlˌjuː/ the 23rd letter of the alphabet

W[2] /west/ ABBREVIATION west

wad /wɒd/ NOUN [plural **wads**]

1 a thick piece of soft material □ *She cleaned the wound with a wad of cotton wool.*

2 a pile of thin pieces of paper or paper money

waddle /'wɒdəl/ VERB [**waddles, waddling, waddled**] to walk moving from side to side, like a duck (=water bird with short legs)

wade /weɪd/ VERB [**wades, wading, waded**] to walk through water or mud □ *We waded across the stream.*

PHRASAL VERB **wade through something** to read or deal with a lot of complicated information □ *We had to wade through all his old files.*

wafer /'weɪfə(r)/ NOUN [plural **wafers**] a very thin biscuit, often eaten with ice cream

waffle /'wɒfəl/ ► NOUN [plural **waffles**]

1 a type of flat cake with a pattern of deep squares on it

2 talk or writing that does not say anything useful or interesting

► VERB [**waffles, waffling, waffled**] to talk or write a lot without saying anything useful or interesting

waft /wɑːft, wɒft/ VERB [**wafts, wafting, wafted**] to float through the air □ *The smell of freshly baked bread came wafting out of the window.*

wag /wæg/ VERB [**wags, wagging, wagged**]

1 if an animal wags its tail, it moves it from side to side □ *The dog ran backwards and forwards, wagging its tail.*

2 if you wag your finger, you move it from side to side, often when you are talking in an angry way or telling someone not to do something

3 if tongues wag, people talk together about a situation, often about someone's private life

wage /weɪdʒ/ ► NOUN [plural **wages**] money that someone is paid for doing their job □ *They pay our wages on Fridays.* □ *a wage increase/cut* □ *What's the average wage?*

► VERB [**wages, waging, waged**] to try hard to achieve something or fight against something □ *We are waging war on litter.* □ *to start a war or a fight*

wager /'weɪdʒə(r)/ ► NOUN [plural **wagers**] an agreement to risk money on the result of a competition or situation

► VERB [**wagers, wagering, wagered**] to make a wager

waggle /'wægəl/ VERB [**waggles, waggling, waggled**] to move something quickly from side to side or up and down, or to move in this way □ *Can you waggle your ears?*

wagon /'wægən/ NOUN [plural **wagons**]

1 a vehicle with four wheels that is pulled by horses □ *a hay wagon*

2 a container that is pulled by a train, used for carrying goods □ *a coal wagon*

waif /weɪf/ NOUN [plural **waifs**] someone, especially a child, who looks thin and poor and often has no home

wail /weɪl/ ► VERB [**wails, wailing, wailed**]

1 to cry loudly □ *A small child was wailing in the next room.*

2 to make a long, loud, high noise □ *The sirens wailed all night.*

► NOUN [plural **wails**] a loud cry or a long, loud, high noise

waist /weɪst/ NOUN [plural **waists**] the middle part of your body, where you wear a belt

waistband /'weɪstbænd/ NOUN [plural **waistbands**] the top part of a pair of trousers or a skirt that goes around your waist

waistcoat /'weɪskəʊt/ NOUN [plural **waistcoats**] a short jacket with no sleeves and usually with buttons up the front that is worn over a shirt

waistline /'weɪstlaɪn/ NOUN [plural **waistlines**]

1 the shape or size that you are round the waist □ *My waistline has expanded over the years.*

2 the part of a piece of clothing, especially a dress, that goes around your waist

wait /weɪt/ ► VERB [**waits, waiting, waited**]

1 to stay in a place until something happens, something or someone is ready, etc. □ *Several people were already waiting for the bus.* □ *He asked us to wait outside.* □ *We waited patiently for the show to begin.*

2 to not do something until something happens, someone arrives, etc. □ *I will wait until it stops raining before I leave.* □ *+ for* *We'd better wait for Jasmine before we start.*

3 to not do something or get something for a particular period of time □ *I had to wait 6 months for my operation.* □ *You'll have to wait a bit longer before you are old enough to be left alone.* □ *I decided to wait a while before making a decision.*

4 to expect that something will happen □ *We're all waiting for her to announce her engagement.*
5 can't wait/can hardly wait if you can't wait to do something or for something to happen, you are very excited about it □ *I can't wait for our holiday!*
6 wait a minute/second (a) used to tell someone to stop what they are doing or stay where they are for a short time □ *Wait a minute - I just need to get my keys.* (b) used for saying that you disagree with something or are angry about something □ *Wait a minute - I'm the boss round here, not you!*
♦ PHRASAL VERBS **wait on someone 1** to bring food to a customer in a restaurant **2** to do everything for someone that they ask you to □ *I'm not going to wait on my children.* **wait up** to not go to bed until someone comes home □ *I'll be late tonight - don't wait up for me.*
▶ NOUN [*plural* **waits**] a period of time when you are waiting 🔁 *We had a long wait for the bus.*
• **waiter** /ˈweɪtə(r)/ NOUN [*plural* **waiters**] someone who brings food to customers in a restaurant

waiting list /ˈweɪtɪŋ ˌlɪst/ NOUN [*plural* **waiting lists**] a list of people who are waiting to get or do something □ *hospital waiting lists*
waiting room /ˈweɪtɪŋ ˌruːm/ NOUN [*plural* **waiting rooms**] a room where people can wait, for example in a railway station or at the doctor's

waitress /ˈweɪtrɪs/ NOUN [*plural* **waitresses**] a woman who brings food to customers in a restaurant

waive /weɪv/ VERB [**waives, waiving, waived**]
1 to choose not to take or use something that is your right □ *He waived his right to remain anonymous.*
2 to allow someone not to obey a rule or not to pay money they owe you 🔁 *His solicitor agreed to waive his fee.*

wake¹ /weɪk/ VERB [**wakes, waking, woke, woken**] to stop sleeping, or to make someone stop sleeping □ *We woke the children early and set off.*
♦ PHRASAL VERBS **wake (someone) up** to stop sleeping, or to make someone stop sleeping □ *We were woken up by the dogs barking.* **wake up to something** to become aware of something □ *We need to wake up to the fact that global warming is getting worse.*

wake² /weɪk/ NOUN [*plural* **wakes**]
1 in the wake of something after something has happened and as a result of it □ *Many airlines went bankrupt in the wake of the disaster.*
2 the raised lines of water behind a moving boat
waken /ˈweɪkən/ VERB [**wakens, wakening, wakened**] to stop sleeping, or to make someone stop sleeping □ *A loud sound wakened me.*

walk /wɔːk/ ▶ VERB [**walks, walking, walked**]
1 to move by putting one foot in front of the other □ *The door opened and Simon walked in.* □ *I think I'll walk to work today.*

2 to go somewhere with someone on foot, to make sure they are safe □ *Dad will walk you home.*
3 if you walk a dog, you take it to get exercise
♦ IDIOMS **walk all over someone** to make someone do what you want, in a way that does not respect them **walk on eggshells** to be very careful not to upset or offend someone
♦ PHRASAL VERBS **walk off with something 1** to steal something □ *Someone's walked off with my umbrella.* **2** to win a prize □ *She walked off with fir prize for her oil painting.* **walk out 1** to leave a plac because you are angry or upset □ *Many of the audience walked out after what they described as rac jokes.* **2** to leave a person you are in a relationship with, or a job or a group of people you are working wit □ *My father walked out on us when we were little.*
▶ NOUN [*plural* **walks**]
1 a journey made by walking □ *It's just a short walk the newsagent's.* □ *I need to take the dog for a wa.*
2 the way someone walks □ *I recognized Ann by h walk.*
3 a route that you can walk for enjoyment □ *There lovely walk by the lake.*
4 from all walks of life if people in a group com from all walks of life, they have many different job social positions, etc.
• **walker** /ˈwɔːkə(r)/ NOUN [*plural* **walkers**] someo who walks, especially for enjoyment

walkie-talkie /ˌwɔːkiˈtɔːki/ NOUN [*plural* **walkie talkies**] a radio that you can carry with you to se and receive messages from someone with a simila radio
walking /ˈwɔːkɪŋ/ NOUN, NO PLURAL the activity c going for walks for enjoyment □ *walking boots*
walking stick /ˈwɔːkɪŋ ˌstɪk/ NOUN [*plural* **walk sticks**] a stick that you use for support when you walk
walkover /ˈwɔːkˌəʊvə(r)/ NOUN [*plural* **walkover** game, competition, etc. that has been won easily
walkway /ˈwɔːkweɪ/ NOUN [*plural* **walkways**] a that connects two places or buildings, especially that is above the ground

wall /wɔːl/ NOUN [*plural* **walls**]
1 any of the sides of a room or building □ *She h the new clock on the kitchen wall.*
2 a structure made of brick or stone that separa two areas or goes around an area □ *A high wall surrounds the school.*
♦ IDIOM **drive someone up the wall** an informal p meaning to make someone very angry □ *The ch were driving me up the wall.*

wallaby /ˈwɒləbi/ NOUN [*plural* **wallabies**] an a like a small kangaroo
walled /wɔːld/ ADJECTIVE surrounded by a wall ❚ *walled garden*
wallet /ˈwɒlɪt/ NOUN [*plural* **wallets**] a flat cor for money and credit cards, usually made of lea

wallflower /ˈwɔːlˌflaʊə(r)/ NOUN [plural **wallflowers**]
1 someone who does not have anyone to dance with at a social event
2 a plant which has flowers with a sweet smell

wallop /ˈwɒləp/ ▶ VERB [**wallops, walloping, walloped**] an informal word meaning to hit someone or something hard □ He walloped his head on the door as he came into the room.
▶ NOUN [plural **wallops**] an informal word meaning a hard hit

wallow /ˈwɒləʊ/ VERB [**wallows, wallowing, wallowed**]
1 to spend too much time feeling sad □ He did not wallow in self-pity but simply worked even harder.
2 to roll around in mud or water □ The hippos were wallowing in the mud.

wallpaper /ˈwɔːlˌpeɪpə(r)/ ▶ NOUN [plural **wallpapers**]
1 paper that you can use to cover and decorate the walls of a room
2 a pattern or picture that you choose to have on your main computer screen. A computing word.
▶ VERB [**wallpapers, wallpapering, wallpapered**] to put wallpaper onto the walls of a room

walnut /ˈwɔːlnʌt/ NOUN [plural **walnuts**] a large nut that you can eat, with many deep, curved lines in its surface

walrus /ˈwɔːlrəs/ NOUN [plural **walruses**] a large sea animal with tusks (=large curved teeth that come out of its mouth)

waltz /wɒls/ ▶ NOUN [plural **waltzes**] a dance for two people, with a rhythm of three repeated beats
▶ VERB [**waltzes, waltzing, waltzed**]
1 to dance a waltz
2 to walk somewhere in a confident way that annoys other people □ She just waltzed in and helped herself to our food.

WAN /wæn/ ABBREVIATION wide area network; a system that connects the computers of people who are in different places

wan /wɒn/ ADJECTIVE someone who is wan looks pale and tired

wand /wɒnd/ NOUN [plural **wands**] a long thin stick used for doing magic

wander /ˈwɒndə(r)/ ▶ VERB [**wanders, wandering, wandered**]
1 to go from one place to another without any clear aim or purpose □ We spent the summer wandering all around southern Italy.
2 if your mind or your thoughts wander, you start to think about other things instead of the thing you should be thinking about
PHRASAL VERB **wander off** to go away from a place, especially from the place you should be in □ The children wandered off again.
▶ NOUN [plural **wanders**] a short walk that has no plan or purpose □ Shall we go for a wander in the garden?

wane /weɪn/ ▶ VERB [**wanes, waning, waned**]
1 to become less strong □ Support for the movement is waning fast.
2 if the moon wanes, it seems to become smaller
▶ NOUN on the wane becoming less strong or successful □ Her career was on the wane.

wangle /ˈwæŋgəl/ VERB [**wangles, wangling, wangled**] to get something by persuading someone in a clever way □ Do you think you could wangle me a couple of free tickets to the concert?

wanly /ˈwɒnlɪ/ ADJECTIVE in a tired, sad way □ She smiled wanly.

want /wɒnt/ ▶ VERB [**wants, wanting, wanted**]
1 to feel that you would like to have something or do something, or to wish that something will happen □ Do you want some cake? □ Nobody wants higher taxes. □ **+ to do something** I didn't want anyone to know.
2 to need something □ Your hands want a good wash.
3 if something wants doing, it needs to be done □ The tomato plants want watering.
4 used to give someone advice or a warning □ Maps? You want to try the library. □ She has a lot of influence. You don't want to upset her.
▶ NOUN [plural **wants**]
1 no plural the state of being very poor or not having the things you need to live □ Many families are living in severe want.
2 for want of something because of something that is not done or not available □ He failed the test, but not for want of trying.
3 your wants are the things you need or would like to have □ The local shops are sufficient for our wants.
• **wanted** /ˈwɒntɪd/ ADJECTIVE
1 someone who is wanted is being searched for by the police 🔁 Pictures of the wanted man appeared in all the newspapers.
2 loved, needed, and cared for 🔁 Make your pet feel wanted by giving it plenty of attention.
• **wanting** /ˈwɒntɪŋ/ ADJECTIVE not of a high enough quality or standard 🔁 Against a much better side, the team was found wanting.

wanton /ˈwɒntən/ ADJECTIVE causing violence or damage for no reason □ We have seen the wanton destruction of our cities.

WAP /wæp/ ABBREVIATION wireless application protocol; a system that connects mobile phones to the Internet. A computing word.

war /wɔː(r)/ NOUN [plural **wars**]
1 fighting between two countries or groups, involving armies 🔁 War broke out (=started) between the two countries. 🔁 That was the year that war was declared (=announced). □ **+ between** the war between Britain and Argentina
2 at war fighting a war □ The two countries had been at war for years.
3 a series of activities intended to stop something bad from happening □ **+ on** the war on drugs

warble /ˈwɔːbəl/ VERB [**warbles, warbling, warbled**] if a bird warbles, it sings

ward /wɔːd/ NOUN [plural **wards**] a room with beds in a hospital □ *the children's ward*
◆ PHRASAL VERB [**wards, warding, warded**] **ward something off** to stop something bad from happening

warden /ˈwɔːdn/ NOUN [plural **wardens**] someone who is in charge of a building and the people in it

warder /ˈwɔːdə(r)/ NOUN [plural **warders**] someone who guards the prisoners in a prison

wardrobe /ˈwɔːdrəub/ NOUN [plural **wardrobes**]
1 a tall cupboard that you hang clothes inside
2 all of the clothes someone owns □ *my summer wardrobe*

warehouse /ˈweəhaus/ NOUN [plural **warehouses**] a big building where businesses store large amounts of things □ *a furniture warehouse*

wares /weəz/ PLURAL NOUN an old-fashioned word meaning things that are for sale

warfare /ˈwɔːfeə(r)/ NOUN, NO PLURAL fighting in a war □ *modern warfare*

warhead /ˈwɔːhed/ NOUN [plural **warheads**] the front part of a missile (=weapon that travels) that contains the explosive □ *a nuclear warhead*

warily /ˈweərɪlɪ/ ADVERB in a nervous way as if you do not trust someone □ *She eyed him warily.*

warlike /ˈwɔːlaɪk/ ADJECTIVE often starting wars

warm /wɔːm/ ▶ ADJECTIVE [**warmer, warmest**]
1 quite hot in a way that is pleasant □ *a nice warm bath* □ *Are you warm enough?* ⊞ *I tried to keep warm by jumping up and down.*
2 warm clothes make you feel warm □ *a warm winter coat*
3 friendly and showing good feelings towards other people ⊞ *a warm welcome* □ *She's a very warm person.*
▶ VERB [**warms, warming, warmed**] to make someone or something warm □ *She warmed her hands on the radiator.* □ *I'll just warm the sauce.*
◆ PHRASAL VERBS **warm to someone/something** to start to like someone or something after not liking them at the beginning □ *I've warmed to him over the months.* **warm (someone/something) up** to become warm, or to make someone or something warm □ *Put a sweater on and you'll soon warm up.* □ *Could you warm up the soup?* **warm up** to make your body ready to do a sport by doing gentle exercises □ *It's important to warm up before a run.*

warm-blooded /ˌwɔːmˈblʌdɪd/ ADJECTIVE a warm-blooded animal's temperature stays the same and does not change according to the temperature of the air around it. A biology word.

warm-hearted /ˌwɔːmˈhɑːtɪd/ ADJECTIVE kind and showing good feelings towards other people

warmly /ˈwɔːmlɪ/ ADVERB
1 in a warm way □ *Make sure you're warmly dressed for the walk.*
2 showing good feelings □ *She spoke very warmly of him.*

warmth /wɔːmθ/ NOUN, NO PLURAL
1 pleasant heat, or the state of being pleasantly warm □ *the warmth of the fire*
2 when someone is friendly and shows good feelings towards other people □ *the warmth of her welcome*

warm-up /ˈwɔːmʌp/ NOUN [plural **warm-ups**] a set of gentle exercises that make your body ready to do a sport

warn /wɔːn/ VERB [**warns, warning, warned**] to tell someone about a possible danger or something bad that may happen so that they can avoid it or prepare for it □ + *about* *I warned her about the icy roads.* □ + *that* *He warned me that it would be expensive.* □ + *do something* *I warned you to be careful!*
● **warning** /ˈwɔːnɪŋ/ NOUN [plural **warnings**]
1 a statement that tells you about a possible danger or something bad that may happen ⊞ *There are health warnings on all bottles of alcohol.* □ *There are flood warnings for the region.*
2 without warning if something bad happens without warning, it happens suddenly so that you do not know it is going to happen □ *The volcano erupted without any warning.*
3 when someone tells you that they will punish you if you do something again □ *Isabel got a warning from the teacher.*

warp /wɔːp/ VERB [**warps, warping, warped**] to become bent or twisted, or to make something do so □ *The wet weather had warped the door.*

warpath /ˈwɔːpɑːθ/ NOUN be on the warpath to be angry about something and wanting to punish the person who is responsible for it

warrant /ˈwɒrənt/ ▶ NOUN [plural **warrants**] a document that gives the police the right to arrest someone or search their property
▶ VERB [**warrants, warranting, warranted**] to be a good reason for an action □ *He made a mistake but didn't warrant such a harsh punishment.*

warranty /ˈwɒrəntɪ/ NOUN [plural **warranties**] a promise by a company that it will repair or replace a product if it breaks or stops working

warren /ˈwɒrən/ NOUN [plural **warrens**]
1 a group of underground passages where rabbits live
2 a place where you can easily get lost because there are so many passages

warring /ˈwɔːrɪŋ/ ADJECTIVE fighting against each other □ *the warring factions*

warrior /ˈwɒrɪə(r)/ NOUN [plural **warriors**] especially in the past, a soldier

warship /ˈwɔːʃɪp/ NOUN [plural **warships**] a ship with guns, used for fighting at sea

wart /wɔːt/ NOUN [plural **warts**] a small hard lump on the skin

wartime /ˈwɔːtaɪm/ NOUN, NO PLURAL a period when there is a war

wary /ˈweərɪ/ ADJECTIVE not wanting to do something or trust someone because you think it might cause problems □ *I'd be very wary of lending her money*

was /wɒz/ VERB the past tense of the verb be when it is used with **I**, **he**, **she** or **it** □ *I was surprised to see Rosie there.* □ *Mr Brock was my favourite teacher.*

wash /wɒʃ/ ▶ VERB [**washes, washing, washed**]
1 to clean something with water and soap □ *His mum still washes his clothes.*
2 to clean a part of your body □ *I washed before breakfast.* ♔ *Wash your hands before dinner.*
3 if water washes against something, it flows against it □ *Gentle waves were washing against the boat.*
▶ PHRASAL VERBS **wash something away** if something such as a building, tree or car is washed away, the force of the water carries it away □ *Whole trees were washed away in the storm.* **wash something down** to have a drink when you eat food or take medicine □ *I had a hamburger washed down with a milkshake.* **wash out** to disappear when you wash something □ *Luckily the coffee stains washed out.* **wash something out** to wash the inside of something **wash (something) up** to wash the plates, dishes, etc. that you have used for eating □ *It's my turn to wash up.*
▶ NOUN [*plural* **washes**]
1 when you wash yourself or wash something ♔ *I'll just have a wash.* □ *Could you give this shirt a wash?*
2 all the clothes that need to be washed □ *Your red shirt is in the wash.*
3 the waves that a boat causes as it moves

washable /ˈwɒʃəbəl/ ADJECTIVE able to be washed

washbasin /ˈwɒʃˌbeɪsən/ NOUN [*plural* **washbasins**] a bowl with taps (=objects you turn to get water) for washing your hands and face in

washer /ˈwɒʃə(r)/ NOUN [*plural* **washers**]
1 a flat ring made of metal or rubber that you put between a nut and a bolt (=objects used for fastening things)
2 an informal word for washing machine

washing /ˈwɒʃɪŋ/ NOUN, NO PLURAL all the clothes that need to be washed

washing machine /ˈwɒʃɪŋ məˈʃiːn/ NOUN [*plural* **washing machines**] a piece of electrical equipment that you wash clothes in

washing powder NOUN, NO PLURAL a powder that you use for washing clothes

washing-up /ˌwɒʃɪŋˈʌp/ NOUN, NO PLURAL
1 all the dishes, plates, etc. that need to be washed after cooking or eating
2 the activity of washing dishes and plates, etc. after cooking or eating ♔ *I'll do the washing-up.*

washout /ˈwɒʃaʊt/ NOUN, NO PLURAL an event that fails completely, often because no one goes to it. An informal word.

wasn't /ˈwɒzənt/ a short way to say and write was not □ *He wasn't there.*

wasp /wɒsp/ NOUN [*plural* **wasps**] an insect with a black and yellow body that can sting you (=hurt when it touches your skin)

waste /weɪst/ ▶ VERB [**wastes, wasting, wasted**]
1 to use too much of something, often in a way that means some of it is thrown away □ *I'm trying not to waste any paper.* □ *We waste far too much food.*
2 to use something, especially time or money, in a way that does not have good results □ *You're wasting your time.* ♔ *He wastes so much money.*
3 be wasted on someone if something of good quality is wasted on someone, they do not understand how good it is
♦ PHRASAL VERB **waste away** to become very thin
▶ NOUN [*plural* **wastes**]
1 *no plural* when too much of something is used, often so that some of it is thrown away □ *You should never throw away food - it's such a waste.*
2 *no plural* when something, especially time or money, is used in a way that does not have good results ♔ *I'm not going to clean this area - it's just a waste of time.* ♔ *The whole course was a complete waste of money.*
3 *no plural* rubbish or material that cannot be used for anything □ *industrial waste*
4 *usually plural* a large area of land where no crops grow □ *the frozen wastes of Siberia*
▶ ADJECTIVE
1 waste products or materials have no use now and can be thrown away □ *waste paper*
2 waste land has no buildings or crops on it

waste bin /ˈweɪst ˌbɪn/ NOUN [*plural* **waste bins**] a container for putting rubbish in

wasted /ˈweɪstɪd/ ADJECTIVE
1 achieving nothing □ *a wasted morning*
2 very thin, usually because of illness □ *her wasted arms*

wasteful /ˈweɪstfʊl/ ADJECTIVE causing things to be thrown away □ *It's so wasteful to use disposable plates.*

wasteland /ˈweɪstlænd/ NOUN [*plural* **wastelands**] an area of empty land where crops cannot grow

watch /wɒtʃ/ ▶ VERB [**watches, watching, watched**]
1 to look at someone or something for a while □ *Max is watching the football.* □ *I watched the children dancing.*
2 to be careful about something □ *Watch you don't trip over that step.*
3 to look after someone or something □ *Could you watch the baby for me while I go and wash my hands?*
♦ IDIOM **watch your step** to make sure you behave well or in a sensible way
♦ PHRASAL VERB **watch out** used for telling someone to be careful □ *Watch out! Don't bang your head!*
▶ NOUN [*plural* **watches**]
1 a small clock that you wear on your lower arm
2 keep a watch on something/someone to pay attention to something or someone, often to make sure that nothing bad happens
● **watchful** /ˈwɒtʃfʊl/ ADJECTIVE careful to notice what

is happening ⊞ *Molly kept a watchful eye on her little sister.*

---

water /'wɔːtə(r)/ ▶ NOUN, NO PLURAL

1 a clear liquid that falls from the sky as rain and is used for drinking, washing, etc. □ *a glass of water*

2 an area of water such as a part of a sea □ *I didn't go into the water.*

▶ VERB [**waters, watering, watered**]

1 to water a plant is to pour water on it so it will live and grow

2 if your eyes water, they produce tears □ *The smoke made her eyes water.*

3 if your mouth waters, it produces liquid because you see or smell something good to eat

♦ PHRASAL VERB **water something down** to add water to a liquid so that it is weaker

---

watercolour /'wɔːtəˌkʌlə(r)/ NOUN [*plural* **watercolours**]

1 a type of paint that is mixed with water, not oil

2 a painting done with watercolour paints

water cooler /'wɔːtə ˈkuːlə(r)/ NOUN [*plural* **water coolers**] a machine which provides cool water for people to drink

watercress /'wɔːtəkres/ NOUN, NO PLURAL a plant with round leaves that is eaten in salads

---

waterfall /'wɔːtəfɔːl/ NOUN [*plural* **waterfalls**] a place where a river or stream falls over a high rock onto rocks below

---

waterfront /'wɔːtəfrʌnt/ NOUN [*plural* **waterfronts**] the area along the edge of a lake, river or sea □ *waterfront apartments*

watering can /'wɔːtərɪŋ kæn/ NOUN [*plural* **watering cans**] a container with a handle, used for pouring water on plants

waterlogged /'wɔːtəlɒɡd/ ADJECTIVE waterlogged ground is so wet that you can see water on the surface □ *a waterlogged pitch*

watermark /'wɔːtəmɑːk/ NOUN [*plural* **watermarks**] a design on a piece of paper or a banknote (=piece of paper money) that you can only see when you hold it up against the light

watermelon /'wɔːtəˌmelən/ NOUN [*plural* **watermelons**] a large round fruit with a hard green skin and red flesh

waterproof /'wɔːtəpruːf/ ▶ ADJECTIVE waterproof material does not allow water through it

▶ NOUN [*plural* **waterproofs**] a coat or other piece of clothing made of waterproof material

waters /'wɔːtəz/ PLURAL NOUN used for talking about large areas of water, especially areas of the sea which belong to a particular country □ *The boat had entered Australian waters.*

watershed /'wɔːtəʃed/ NOUN [*plural* **watersheds**] a very important time which changes the future of something □ *a watershed in India's history*

water-ski /'wɔːtəskiː/ VERB [**water-skis, water-skiing, water-skied**] to travel over water on skis, pulled by a boat with a motor

● **water-skiing** /'wɔːtəskiːɪŋ/ NOUN, NO PLURAL the activity of travelling over water on skis, pulled by a boat with a motor

water sports /'wɔːtəspɔːtz/ PLURAL NOUN sports that are played on water or in water

water table /'wɔːtə ˌteɪbəl/ NOUN [*plural* **water tables**] the area under the Earth's surface where there is water. A geography word.

watertight /'wɔːtətaɪt/ ADJECTIVE

1 not allowing liquid in or out

2 a watertight excuse is a very good one that no one can say is not true

waterway /'wɔːtəweɪ/ NOUN [*plural* **waterways**] a river or canal (=artificial water passage) that a boat can travel along

watery /'wɔːtəri/ ADJECTIVE

1 containing too much water □ *watery soup*

2 filled with water □ *watery eyes*

watt /wɒt/ NOUN [*plural* **watts**] a unit of electrical power. This is often shortened to **W**.

● **wattage** /'wɒtɪdʒ/ NOUN, NO PLURAL electric power measured in watts

---

wave /weɪv/ ▶ NOUN [*plural* **waves**]

1 a raised line of water that moves across the sea or other area of water □ *The waves were huge.*

2 a movement of the hand to say hello or goodbye or to attract someone's attention ⊞ *She gave a cheery wave as the train left the station.*

3 a sudden, strong emotion or feeling □ *The pain comes in waves.* □ + *of* *A wave of sadness came over me.*

4 a lot of similar events happening in a short period of time, often bad events □ + *of* *the recent wave of violence* □ *a new wave of bombings*

5 a large group of people arriving somewhere together □ + *of* *Waves of protesters surrounded the building.*

6 the form that sound or light takes as it travels through the air □ *sound waves*

7 a curving shape in your hair □ *Your hair has a natural wave.*

▶ VERB [**waves, waving, waved**]

1 to move your hand in order to say hello or goodbye or to attract someone's attention ⊞ *She waved goodbye and then got on the train.*

2 to move in the wind □ *Flags were waving in the breeze.*

3 to move something from side to side in the air □ *waved a hanky at me.*

4 hair that waves is slightly curly □ *Mel's hair waves naturally.*

♦ PHRASAL VERB **wave someone off** to wave your hand to someone who is leaving □ *I felt so sad waving him off at the station.*

wavelength /ˈweɪvleŋθ/ NOUN [plural **wavelengths**]
1 the distance between one sound or light wave and the next
2 the length of radio wave that a radio station uses to broadcast programmes
▸ IDIOM be on the same wavelength to think in the same way as someone else so you are able to understand them

waver /ˈweɪvə(r)/ VERB [**wavers, wavering, wavered**]
1 to start to feel uncertain about a decision or belief □ She has never wavered in this belief.
2 to shake slightly □ His voice wavered, and tears filled his eyes.

wavy /ˈweɪvɪ/ ADJECTIVE [**wavier, waviest**]
1 a wavy line goes up and down in gentle curves
2 wavy hair has slight curls in it

wax /wæks/ ▸ NOUN, NO PLURAL a solid substance such as bees make, which becomes liquid when you heat it
▸ VERB [**waxes, waxing, waxed**]
to put wax on the surface of something
to remove hair from a part of the body by putting hot wax on the skin □ I had my legs waxed.
if the moon waxes, it seems to become bigger

waxwork /ˈwækswɜːk/ NOUN [plural **waxworks**] a model of a person, made of wax
waxworks /ˈwækswɜːks/ PLURAL NOUN a place where you can see models of famous people, made of wax
waxy /ˈwæksɪ/ ADJECTIVE [**waxier, waxiest**] like wax a waxy substance

way /weɪ/ ▸ NOUN [plural **ways**]
a method of doing something, or how someone does something □ + of We are trying out new ways of working. □ + to do something The best way to make new friends is to join a club. □ + that I like the way that she sings. ⌾ I've found a way to make cakes without eggs.
used to talk about a particular feature or characteristic of something ⌾ He's like his father in many ways. ⌾ In some ways I'd prefer it if I could work part time.
a route from one place to another □ + to Do you know the way to the station? ⌾ Sorry I'm late - I lost my way. ⌾ Can you manage to find your way to the main hall?
a distance, or a journey or movement from one place to another ⌾ It's quite a long way to the coast. ⌾ They have come all the way from Brazil ⌾ We made our way to the party on bikes.
an amount of time ⌾ The wedding still seems a long way off.
in his/its/my, etc. way coming towards a place □ Karen just phoned to say she's on her way. □ Dinner is on its way.
out of the way in/not in a position that stops someone seeing something or being able to move □ I couldn't see the stage - there was a pillar in my way. □ Could you get out of the way while I'm trying to cook, please?

8 used to talk about how much of something has happened or been done ⌾ We were half way through our dinner when the phone rang.
9 by the way used to add a piece of information □ By the way, have you heard the news about Alex?
10 no way (a) certainly not. An informal phrase. □ 'Are you giving any money towards Carlo's present?' 'No way!' (b) no possibility □ There's no way we'll be finished before June. (c) used to show surprise. An informal phrase. □ They're getting married? No way!
11 under way happening or being done now □ Plans are under way to modernize the centre.
12 way of life the things that someone usually does □ Marriage had changed his whole way of life.
▸ ADVERB used to emphasize the amount or level of something □ We have gone way over our budget. □ It was way too hot for running.

way out /weɪ ˈaʊt/ NOUN [plural **ways out**]
1 a door you go through to leave a public building
2 an excuse not to do something that you do not want to do

wayward /ˈweɪwəd/ ADJECTIVE behaving badly and not obeying other people

WC /ˌdʌbəljuːˈsiː/ NOUN [plural **WCs**] a toilet

we /wiː/ PRONOUN
1 used to talk or write about yourself and at least one other person □ We left home at about nine o'clock.
2 people in general □ We need to do more about global warming.

weak /wiːk/ ADJECTIVE [**weaker, weakest**]
1 not physically strong □ His illness has left him feeling very weak. □ She suffers from a weak heart.
2 not powerful □ a weak government/leader
3 not strong in character □ She's too weak to stand up to her boss.
4 likely to break □ The metal bolts were too weak to hold the structure. □ a weak bridge
5 not of a high quality or standard □ Her written work is very weak. □ The company's still weak on customer care.
6 weak liquids contain a lot of water, do not have a strong taste, or do not contain much alcohol □ a cup of weak tea
7 a weak argument, excuse, etc. is one that other people are not likely to believe or accept □ She put forward a very weak case against the plans.
8 a weak economy or currency (=system of money in a country) is not worth as much when compared with others □ + against The dollar is weak against the pound.
9 a weak light or sound is difficult to see or hear
● **weaken** /ˈwiːkən/ VERB [**weakens, weakening, weakened**]
1 to become weak or to make someone or something weak □ The metal had weakened because of rain and age. □ The illness weakened her heart.

2 to become less determined, or to make someone less determined □ *Dad said I couldn't have a new phone, but he's beginning to weaken.*
• **weakling** /'wiːklɪŋ/ NOUN [plural **weaklings**] a physically weak person
• **weakly** /'wiːklɪ/ ADVERB without much strength or force □ *She smiled weakly at his joke.*
• **weakness** /'wiːknɪs/ NOUN [plural **weaknesses**]
1 *no plural* when something or someone is not strong or forceful □ *The weakness of the frame meant that the building was dangerous.* □ *I was ashamed of my weakness.*
2 a feature of something that is not of a high quality or standard □ *His main weakness is that he does not react quickly enough.* □ *The plan has several major weaknesses.*
3 something that you like very much, often something that you think you should not have □ *Chocolate is my only weakness.* □ + *for* *I have a weakness for expensive shoes.*

wealth /welθ/ NOUN, NO PLURAL
1 when someone has a lot of money and expensive things □ *The wealth of these people is amazing.*
2 a wealth of something a lot of a good quality or thing □ *There's a wealth of talent in the team.*
• **wealthy** /'welθɪ/ ADJECTIVE [**wealthier, wealthiest**] rich □ *a wealthy businessman*

wean /wiːn/ VERB [**weans, weaning, weaned**] to gradually start feeding a baby on food and stop feeding it on its mother's milk

weapon /'wepən/ NOUN [plural **weapons**]
something that is used for fighting, such as a gun or a knife □ *The murder weapon was never found.*

wear /weə(r)/ ▶ VERB [**wears, wearing, wore, worn**]
1 to have clothes, jewellery, etc. on your body □ *Ann was wearing a red hat.* □ *How long have you worn glasses?* □ *He doesn't wear a wedding ring.*
2 to arrange your hair in a particular style □ *She usually wears her hair in a ponytail.*
3 to have a particular expression on your face □ *Ted wore an angry frown.*
4 if a material or surface wears, it gradually becomes thinner because of being used or rubbed, and if something wears it, it makes it thinner □ *His sleeves had worn through at the elbows.* 🖰 *My chair has worn a hole in the carpet.*

➤ Note that to **wear** clothes is to have them on your body. To say 'to start to wear clothes', use the phrasal verb **put on**:
✓ *I put on my coat and left.*
✗ *I wore my coat and left.*

♦ IDIOM **wear thin** to become less strong or less effective □ *He warned them that his patience was wearing thin.* □ *Her jokes were beginning to wear thin.*
♦ PHRASAL VERBS **wear (something) away** to disappear because of being used or rubbed, or to make

something do this □ *Over the years, the sea has worn away the rocks.* **wear someone down** to gradually make someone less strong or less determined □ *She keeps phoning me and writing me letters, trying to wear me down.* □ *They were worn down by years of struggle.* **wear off** if a feeling or the effect of something wears off, it gradually disappears □ *The anaesthetic should soon wear off.* **wear on** if time wears on, it passes □ *As the day wore on, we got more and more bored.* **wear (something) out** to use something so much that it becomes damaged and cannot be used any more, or to become damaged in this way □ *These shoes are completely worn out already.* **wear someone out** to make someone very tired □ *Walking so far completely wore me out.*
▶ NOUN, NO PLURAL
1 the amount that you use something over a period of time □ *The quality of carpet you need depends on how much wear it will have.*
2 damage caused by being used □ *There are signs of wear on the cables.*
3 clothes used in a particular situation or by particular people □ *evening wear*
4 wear and tear damage caused by being used
• **wearer** /'weərə(r)/ NOUN [plural **wearers**] someone who is wearing something

wearily /'wɪərɪlɪ/ ADVERB in a weary way □ *He sighed wearily.*
wearing /'weərɪŋ/ ADJECTIVE making you tired or making you lose your patience □ *Kids can be very wearing.*
weary /'wɪərɪ/ ADJECTIVE [**wearier, weariest**]
1 tired □ *He finally got home, weary after a long day*
2 annoyed or bored with something that has been happening for a long time □ *I'm rather weary of the whole situation.*
weasel /'wiːzəl/ NOUN [plural **weasels**] a small wild animal with a long thin body

weather /'weðə(r)/ ▶ NOUN, NO PLURAL the conditions outside, for example how hot, cold, wet, dry it is 🖰 *cold/hot weather* 🖰 *bad weather* □ *The weather's very warm for October.*
▶ VERB [**weathers, weathering, weathered**] to continue despite a bad situation □ *Somehow she managed to weather the crisis.*

weather-beaten /'weðəˌbiːtən/ ADJECTIVE having rough, dark skin caused by being often in the sun or wind □ *a weather-beaten face*
weather forecast /'weðə 'fɔːkɑːst/ NOUN [plural **weather forecasts**] a description of what the weather will be like during the next day, few days, etc.
weave /wiːv/ VERB [**weaves, weaving, wove, woven**]
1 to make cloth by passing threads under and over each other on a frame called a loom
2 to make something by twisting long pieces of thing together □ *She taught me how to weave baskets*

3 to move in and out between objects □ *The motorbike was weaving through the traffic.*

● **weaver** /ˈwiːvə(r)/ NOUN [*plural* **weavers**] someone who weaves cloth

web /web/ NOUN [*plural* **webs**]

1 a very thin net that a spider makes for catching insects

2 the Web the World Wide Web; all the websites on the Internet

webbed /webd/ ADJECTIVE webbed feet have skin joining the toes together

webcam /ˈwebkæm/ NOUN [*plural* **webcams**] a camera which allows you to see and hear on the internet moving pictures and sounds as they are happening. A computing word.

webcast /ˈwebkɑːst/ NOUN [*plural* **webcasts**] something that is broadcast on the Internet as it happens. A computing word.

web page /ˈweb ˌpeɪdʒ/ NOUN [*plural* **web pages**] a page on a website. A computing word.

website /ˈwebsaɪt/ NOUN [*plural* **websites**] a group of connected pages on the Internet about a particular company, organization, subject, etc. A computing word. □ *Rowling's official website* □ *He has his own website.*

we'd /wiːd/ a short way to say and write we had or we would □ *We'd better hurry up.* □ *We'd buy a new car if we had the money.*

wedding /ˈwedɪŋ/ NOUN [*plural* **weddings**] a marriage ceremony □ *I met her at Lucy and John's wedding.* □ *a wedding present*

wedge /wedʒ/ ▶ NOUN [*plural* **wedges**]

1 a piece of hard material that is thick at one end and thin at the other and is used to hold something in place □ *a door wedge*

2 something shaped like a wedge □ *He cut himself a thick wedge of cake.*

▶ VERB [**wedges, wedging, wedged**]

1 to hold something, often a door, in place with a wedge □ *She wedged the door open with a piece of cardboard.*

2 to push something firmly into a small space

wedlock /ˈwedlɒk/ NOUN, NO PLURAL the state of being married. An old-fashioned word.

Wednesday /ˈwenzdɪ/ NOUN [*plural* **Wednesdays**] the day of the week after Tuesday and before Thursday □ *Shall we meet again on Wednesday?*

wee /wiː/ ADJECTIVE an informal word used especially by Scottish people, meaning small □ *a wee boy*

weed /wiːd/ ▶ NOUN [*plural* **weeds**] a wild plant that grows where you do not want it to □ *The garden is overgrown with weeds.*

▶ VERB [**weeds, weeding, weeded**] to remove the weeds from a place □ *I spent an hour weeding the garden.*

● **weedy** /ˈwiːdɪ/ ADJECTIVE [**weedier, weediest**] an informal word meaning thin and weak

week /wiːk/ NOUN [*plural* **weeks**]

1 a period of seven days □ *Debbie teaches aerobics twice a week.* □ *I'll see you next week.*

2 in/during the week on the five days from Monday to Friday when many people go to work □ *I don't go out much during the week.*

weekday /ˈwiːkˌdeɪ/ NOUN [*plural* **weekdays**] any of the days from Monday to Friday □ *The office is only open on weekdays.*

weekend /ˌwiːkˈend/ NOUN [*plural* **weekends**] Saturday and Sunday □ *We're going to Oxford for the weekend.* □ *I like to go cycling at the weekend.*

weekly /ˈwiːklɪ/ ▶ ADJECTIVE happening or produced once every week □ *a weekly magazine*

▶ ADVERB once every week □ *In those days I used to get paid weekly.*

weep /wiːp/ VERB [**weeps, weeping, wept**] to cry □ *She wept when she heard the terrible news.*

weigh /weɪ/ ▶ VERB [**weighs, weighing, weighed**]

1 to measure how heavy something is □ *Brenda weighs herself every day.* □ *Weigh the ingredients carefully.*

2 to have a particular weight □ *My suitcase weighed 15 kilograms.*

3 to consider something carefully □ *We need to weigh all the facts before reaching a decision.*

◆ PHRASAL VERBS **weigh someone down**

1 to be heavy and make it difficult for someone to move □ *He was weighed down with luggage.*

2 to make someone feel worried or unhappy □ *He is weighed down with responsibility.* **weigh on someone** to make someone feel worried or unhappy ⊞ *Her fans' expectations weigh heavily on her.* **weigh something out** to measure an amount of something □ *I weighed out the flour and the sugar.* **weigh something up** to consider the advantages and disadvantages of something □ *We spent a long time weighing up the pros and cons of moving.*

● **weight** /weɪt/ NOUN [*plural* **weights**]

1 *no plural* how heavy someone or something is □ *My luggage was above the weight limit.* ⊞ *He has lost a lot of weight* (=got thinner) *recently.* ⊞ *I've put on weight* (=got fatter) *since I stopped cycling.*

2 *no plural* the quality of being heavy □ *The shelf bent under the weight of all those books.* ⊞ *I wasn't sure if the branch would bear my weight* (=not break).

3 *no plural* importance or influence ⊞ *His opinions carry a lot of weight in political circles.* ⊞ *The letters that have been found add weight to the argument that he was planning to leave.*

4 a heavy object □ *I put a 200g weight on the scales.*

5 weights heavy objects that you lift to make your muscles stronger □ *I spend the first ten minutes lifting weights.*

◆ IDIOMS **a weight off your mind** a problem or a worry

that has been solved □ *Having someone to help me with the work is a weight off my mind.* **throw your weight around** to try to make people do what you want in a rude and forceful way, especially when you have some power over them □ *Since he was been promoted, he's been throwing his weight around a bit.* **throw your weight behind someone/something** to support a plan □ *The government is throwing its weight behind a campaign to reduce knife crime.*
▶ VERB [**weights, weighting, weighted**] to put something heavy into or onto something □ *We weighted the sheet down with rocks.*
• **weightless** /'weɪtlɪs/ ADJECTIVE having no weight

weightlifter /'weɪt,lɪftə(r)/ NOUN [*plural* **weightlifters**] someone who competes in the sport of weightlifting
• **weightlifting** /'weɪt,lɪftɪŋ/ NOUN, NO PLURAL a sport in which people compete to lift the heaviest weight
weight training /'weɪt 'treɪnɪŋ/ NOUN, NO PLURAL a form of exercise in which people lift weights to make their muscles strong
weighty /'weɪtɪ/ ADJECTIVE [**weightier, weightiest**]
1 serious and important □ *They are discussing some weighty matters.*
2 heavy □ *a weighty volume of magic spells*
weir /wɪə(r)/ NOUN [*plural* **weirs**] a low wall across a river to control its flow
weird /wɪəd/ ADJECTIVE [**weirder, weirdest**] very strange □ *Something really weird just happened.*
• **weirdly** /'wɪədlɪ/ ADVERB in a weird way □ *The horses stood weirdly still and silent.*
• **weirdness** /'wɪədnɪs/ NOUN, NO PLURAL being weird

welcome /'welkəm/ ▶ ADJECTIVE
1 if someone or something is welcome, you are pleased about it □ *This fall in inflation is welcome news to home owners.* □ *We stopped for a very welcome rest.*
2 if you are welcome somewhere, people like you being there and make you feel happy and comfortable 🖥 *They made us very welcome in their home.* □ *He is no longer welcome at his parents' house.*
3 welcome to do something if someone is welcome to do something, you are happy to allow them to do it □ *You're welcome to borrow my bike when I'm not using it.*
4 You're welcome. used as a polite reply when someone has thanked you for something □ *'Thank you for all your help.' 'You're welcome.'*
5 welcome to something if you say that someone is welcome to something, you mean that they can have it because you do not want it □ *She stole my boyfriend, and frankly, she's welcome to him!*
▶ VERB [**welcomes, welcoming, welcomed**]
1 to meet someone and make them feel that you are happy to see them □ *The whole family turned out to welcome us at the airport.*
2 to be pleased about something □ *I would welcome*

the chance of a different job. □ *We welcome these new reforms.*
3 to be pleased to accept something □ *We would welcome suggestions from others.* □ *Applications from older people are welcomed.*
▶ NOUN [*plural* **welcomes**] the way that people treat someone when they arrive somewhere 🖥 *We received a very warm welcome in Berlin.*
▶ EXCLAMATION used for welcoming someone who has arrived somewhere □ **+ to** *Welcome to London!*
• **welcoming** /'welkəmɪŋ/ ADJECTIVE friendly and kind to someone who has just arrived □ *All the staff were very welcoming.*

weld /weld/ VERB [**welds, welding, welded**] to join together pieces of metal by heating them
• **welder** /'weldə(r)/ NOUN [*plural* **welders**] someone whose job is to weld metals
• **welding** /'weldɪŋ/ NOUN, NO PLURAL the activity of joining metal by heat

welfare /'welfeə(r)/ NOUN, NO PLURAL
1 health, happiness and safety □ *The police were concerned for the child's welfare.*
2 a US word for money given by the government to people who do not have enough money and cannot earn it

welfare state /'welfeə(r) 'steɪt/ NOUN, NO PLURAL a system in which a government provides services such as free health care and money for people who do not have enough money and cannot earn it
we'll /wiːl/ a short way to say and write we will □ *I'm sure we'll meet again.*

well¹ /wel/ ▶ ADVERB [**better, best**]
1 in a satisfactory, successful or correct way □ *Jan speaks French very well.* □ *Federer played really well* 🖥 *My students are all doing well.* 🖥 *Our meetings went well.*
2 completely □ *Mix the butter and sugar well before adding the flour.* □ *I know Marie really well.* □ *He is well aware of the situation.*
3 as well in addition □ *I'd like an ice cream as well.* □ *As well as his family, a lot of his colleagues were there.*
4 by a large amount □ *Profits are well up on last year.* □ *We need to be there well before the show starts.*
5 may as well/might as well used to make a suggestion because of a situation □ *If you're spending that much on rent, you might as well buy a flat.* □ *I may as well talk to them.*
6 well done used to praise someone for something they have done □ *You passed? Oh, well done!* □ *Well done for remembering the map!*
7 used to form compound adjectives (=adjectives in two parts). When they are used before nouns, they usually have hyphens, e.g. *a well-paid job* □ *The business was very well run.* □ *Their staff are well*
▶ ADJECTIVE [**better, best**]

1 healthy 🕮 *I don't feel very well.* 🕮 *You're looking well.* 🕮 *Get well soon!*

2 just as well used to say that something is lucky or convenient □ *It's just as well that I live so close to work, otherwise I'd be late every day.*

3 all is well everything about a situation is good or satisfactory □ *I hope all is well with you and your family.*

▶ EXCLAMATION

1 used at the beginning of a statement, especially a reply, often when you are explaining something, or expressing slight doubt or disagreement □ *'How did you make the sofa?' 'Well, I started with an old bed frame.'* □ *'Do you think he's suitable for the job?' 'Well, I've never worked with him, so it's hard to say.'* □ *'It's a great book, isn't it?' 'Well, I didn't enjoy it as much as you.'*

2 oh well used for accepting a bad situation □ *'Kiera is going to be late.' 'Oh well, we'll have to start without her.'*

well² /wel/ NOUN [plural **wells**] a deep hole in the ground where you can get water, oil or gas □ *an oil well*

PHRASAL VERB [**wells, welling, welled**] **well up**
1 if a liquid wells up, it comes to the surface and almost flows over it □ *Tears welled up in his eyes.*
2 if an emotion wells up, it becomes stronger □ *A feeling of rage welled up inside her.*

well-balanced /ˌwel'bælənst/ ADJECTIVE
1 containing a lot of things or parts that make a good combination □ *a well-balanced diet*
2 in a calm and happy mental state

well-behaved /ˌwelbɪ'heɪvd/ ADJECTIVE a well-behaved child is polite and behaves in a way that pleases people

well-being /ˌwel'biːɪŋ/ NOUN, NO PLURAL the state of being happy, safe, healthy, etc. □ *I'm only thinking of your well-being.*

well-built /ˌwel'bɪlt/ ADJECTIVE having a large, strong body □ *He was tall and well-built.*

well-dressed /ˌwel'drest/ ADJECTIVE wearing attractive clothes of good quality

well-earned /ˌwel'ɜːnd/ ADJECTIVE if something is well-earned, you deserve it 🕮 *She was enjoying a well-earned rest in Cyprus after several months' hard work.*

well-heeled /ˌwel'hiːld/ ADJECTIVE an informal word meaning rich

wellie /'welɪ/ NOUN [plural **wellies**] an informal word for a wellington

well-informed /ˌwelɪn'fɔːmd/ ADJECTIVE having a lot of knowledge about something

wellington /'welɪŋtən/ or **wellington boot** NOUN [plural **wellingtons** or **wellington boots**] a rubber boot that you wear to protect your feet from mud and water

well-intentioned /ˌwelɪn'tenʃənd/ ADJECTIVE trying to help, but sometimes causing problems □ *Well-intentioned offers of help just made me feel more stressed.*

well-known /ˌwel'nəʊn/ ADJECTIVE famous or known by many people □ *a well-known writer*

well-meaning /ˌwel'miːnɪŋ/ ADJECTIVE a well-meaning person wants to be helpful and kind, but sometimes causes problems □ *Well-meaning visitors gave the animals unsuitable food.*

well-off /ˌwel'ɒf/ ADJECTIVE [**better-off, best-off**]
1 having a lot of money □ *Only the better-off kids had bicycles.*
2 in a good situation □ *The trouble is, you don't realize when you're well-off.*

well-read /ˌwel'red/ ADJECTIVE a well-read person has read a lot of books

well-spoken /ˌwel'spəʊkən/ ADJECTIVE having a way of speaking that sounds educated and polite

well-timed /ˌwel'taɪmd/ ADJECTIVE done at a good or suitable moment □ *A few well-timed jokes kept the atmosphere friendly.*

well-to-do /ˌweltə'duː/ ADJECTIVE rich □ *Our customers are mostly quite well-to-do.*

well-wisher /'welˌwɪʃə(r)/ NOUN [plural **well-wishers**] someone who wants someone to be happy, successful, etc. □ *Her dressing room was filled with flowers from admirers and well-wishers.*

well-worn /ˌwel'wɔːn/ ADJECTIVE
1 used or worn a lot □ *a well-worn dictionary*
2 having been said many times before □ *a well-worn phrase*

Welsh /welʃ/ ▶ ADJECTIVE
1 belonging to or from Wales
2 to do with the Welsh language
▶ NOUN, NO PLURAL
1 the Celtic language of Wales
2 the Welsh the people of Wales

went /went/ PAST TENSE OF **go**

wept /wept/ PAST TENSE AND PAST PARTICIPLE OF **weep**

we're /wɪə(r)/ a short way to say and write we are □ *We're so pleased you could come.*

were /wɜː(r)/ PAST TENSE OF **be** when it is used with **you, we** or **they** □ *We were so relieved to see him.*

weren't /wɜːnt/ a short way to say and write were not □ *Weren't the acrobats amazing?*

werewolf /'wɪəwʊlf/ NOUN [plural **werewolves**] in stories, a person who changes into a wolf (=animal like a fierce dog) when there is a full (=completely round) moon

west /west/ ▶ NOUN, NO PLURAL
1 the direction in which the sun goes down
2 the countries in Europe and North America □ *The family moved to the West in 1998.*
3 the area of a country that is in the west □ *the west of Scotland*
▶ ADJECTIVE, ADVERB in or towards the west □ *the west coast of America* □ *We travelled west as far as the motorway.*

• **westerly** /'westəlɪ/ ADJECTIVE to or towards the west □ *a westerly breeze*

• **western** /'westən/ ▶ ADJECTIVE in or from the west □ *the western hills*

▶ NOUN [plural **westerns**] a book or film about cowboys (=men who ride horses and look after cows) in North America

• **westernized** or **westernised** /'westənaɪzd/ ADJECTIVE influenced by what is typical in America and Western Europe

• **westward** /'westwəd/ or **westwards** /'westwədz/ ADVERB to or towards the west □ We travelled westwards.

wet /wet/ ▶ ADJECTIVE [**wetter, wettest**]
1 full of water or covered with water □ wet clothes □ It's easy to skid on wet roads. 🔊 My trousers are soaking wet!
2 not dried □ wet paint
3 raining □ a wet afternoon
4 an informal word meaning having a weak character and not being brave □ Just jump - don't be so wet!
▶ VERB [**wets, wetting, wet**] to make something wet □ He wet his hair to flatten it down.

wetlands /'wetləndz/ PLURAL NOUN a large area of very wet land, often by a lake or river. A geography word.

wet suit /'wet ,su:t/ NOUN [plural **wet suits**] a rubber suit that you wear to keep you warm when you swim in cold water

we've /wi:v/ a short way to say and write we have □ We've got something to tell you.

whack /wæk/ ▶ VERB [**whacks, whacking, whacked**] to hit someone or something hard □ He whacked his brother on the head with a book.
▶ NOUN [plural **whacks**] a hard hit

whale /weɪl/ NOUN [plural **whales**] a very large mammal that lives in the sea
♦ IDIOM have a whale of a time to enjoy yourself very much

• **whaler** /'weɪlə(r)/ NOUN [plural **whalers**] a ship used for hunting whales

• **whaling** /'weɪlɪŋ/ NOUN, NO PLURAL the activity of hunting and killing whales

wharf /wɔ:f/ NOUN [plural **wharfs** or **wharves**] a place by the sea or by a river, where goods can be put on or taken off ships

what /wɒt/ ▶ DETERMINER, PRONOUN
1 used for asking for information about something □ What day is it today? □ What's your brother's name? □ What did that man want? □ What shall we do this evening?
2 used for referring to something □ This bag is just what I wanted. □ I saw what you did. □ I had no idea what to do.
3 what for used to ask about the purpose of something or the reason for something □ What's this handle for? □ What did you do that for?
4 an informal word used when you have not heard someone and want them to repeat what they have said □ 'Could you pass the bread?' 'What?'
5 an informal word used to ask what someone wants

when they speak to you or call to you □ 'Kate!' 'Yes, what?'
6 what if used to make people think about the result of a possible event or action □ What if nobody comes? □ What if it rains all day?
7 So what? used to show that you do not think something is important □ 'You'll be late for school.' 'So what?'
8 used to emphasize your feelings about something □ What a beautiful view!
▶ EXCLAMATION used to express surprise or shock □ 'The car repairs cost £400.' 'What! I had no idea it would be that much.'

whatever /wɒt'evə(r)/ PRONOUN, DETERMINER
1 any, anything or any amount □ I can give you whatever money you need. □ Choose whatever you like from the menu.
2 used to say that something will always be true and will not be affected by anything else □ You know we always love you, whatever happens. □ We'll be going whatever the weather.
3 used at the beginning of a question, especially to show that you are surprised, upset or shocked □ Whatever are you doing? □ Whatever does this thing do?
4 or whatever used after a list or an example to mean other things of the same type □ The children will be watching TV or whatever.
5 used when you do not know what something is □ I have one of those things for pulling nails out, whatever it's called. □ I'm talking to you, whatever your name

what'll /'wɒtəl/ a short way to say and write what will □ What'll happen to him?

what's /wɒts/ a short way to say and write what is or what has □ What's that noise? □ What's she got in hand?

whatsoever /,wɒtsəʊ'evə(r)/ ADJECTIVE used to emphasize a negative statement □ Your problems have nothing whatsoever to do with me.

what've /'wɒtəv/ a short way to say and write what have

wheat /wi:t/ NOUN, NO PLURAL a plant that produces grain that is used to make flour

wheedle /'wi:dəl/ VERB [**wheedles, wheedling, wheedled**] to try to persuade someone to do something, often by saying nice things to them □ I managed to wheedle some money out of my

wheel /wi:l/ ▶ NOUN [plural **wheels**]
1 a round object under a vehicle that turns to make the vehicle move 🔊 There's a spare wheel in the boot
2 at/behind the wheel driving a vehicle
3 a round part in a piece of machinery □ The wheel began to turn.
▶ VERB [**wheels, wheeling, wheeled**]
1 to push something along on wheels □ He got a puncture and had to wheel his bike home.
2 to move in a wide curve in the air □ Vultures wheeling overhead.

➤ PHRASAL VERBS **wheel around/round** to turn round quickly, often because you are surprised or angry □ *She wheeled around and slapped him.* **wheel something out** to show, use, or say something that has been shown, used or said many times before □ *He wheeled out some of his famous friends to say nice things about him.*

wheelbarrow /'wiːlˌbærəʊ/ NOUN [plural **wheelbarrows**] a container with a wheel at the front and handles at the back, used especially for carrying things in a garden

wheelchair /'wiːlˌtʃeə(r)/ NOUN [plural **wheelchairs**] a seat with wheels, used by people who cannot walk

wheeze /wiːz/ ➤ VERB [**wheezes, wheezing, wheezed**] to breathe with a rough noise, usually because you are ill
➤ NOUN [plural **wheezes**] the noise someone makes when they wheeze

when /wen/ ADVERB, CONJUNCTION
used for asking about the time something happened or will happen □ *When did you get home?* □ *When do you think they will arrive?* □ *When will the cakes be ready?*
used for talking about the time at which something happens or will happen □ *I'll go when I've had a shower.* □ *I'm not sure when the new store will open.*
used for talking about something that happens at the same time as something else □ *I was just going out when the phone rang.* □ *When I heard the news, I went straight to the airport.* □ *I was with her when she died.*
despite the fact that □ *Why do you need to buy the books when all the information is available online?* □ *How can you be busy when you don't have a job?*

whenever /wen'evə(r)/ CONJUNCTION, ADVERB
at any time □ *You can borrow my book whenever you want to.*
every time □ *They go swimming whenever they get the chance.*
used at the beginning of a question, especially to show that you are surprised □ *Whenever did you do all that?*

when's /wenz/ a short way to say and write when is □ *When's Layla coming?*

where /weə(r)/ ADVERB, CONJUNCTION
used for asking about a place or position □ *Where are we going?* □ *Where did you get that hat?* □ *Where can I park my car?* □ *Where do you come from?*
used for talking about a place or position □ *I know where you can buy really good fish.* □ *He told me where he lives.* □ *That is the place where I lost my camera.*
used for talking about a particular point in a process or event □ *I'm afraid this is where we must stop for today.* □ *I liked the part in the play where he murdered his wife.*

whereabouts ➤ ADVERB /ˌweərə'baʊts/ used to ask where someone or something is □ *Whereabouts in Texas do you come from?*
➤ NOUN, NO PLURAL /'weərəbaʊts/ the whereabouts of a person or thing is the place where they are □ *Do you know the whereabouts of your cousin?*

whereas /weər'æz/ CONJUNCTION used for comparing two things □ *He likes going out and meeting people, whereas I'm quite shy.*

whereby /weə'baɪ/ ADVERB using or according to which □ *We have an agreement whereby I look after the house and she looks after the garden.*

where's /weəz/ a short way to say and write where is or where has □ *Where's the cat?* □ *Where's he gone?*

whereupon /ˌweərə'pɒn/ CONJUNCTION a formal word meaning immediately after which □ *She interrupted him again, whereupon he stood up and walked out of the room.*

where've /'weəv/ a short way to say and write where have □ *Where've the children gone?*

wherever /weər'evə(r)/ CONJUNCTION, ADVERB
1 to or in any place □ *Wherever he is, I am sure he will come back soon.*
2 to or in every place □ *He follows me wherever I go.*
3 used to ask where someone or something is, especially when you are surprised or angry □ *Wherever did you get that hat?*
4 used to say that it does not matter where something is, where you go, etc., the result will be the same □ *Wherever I hide the biscuits, the children still find them.*
5 used to show that you do not know where something or someone is □ *He lives in Greenham, wherever that is.*

wherewithal /'weəwɪðɔːl/ NOUN the wherewithal the money or things that are needed to do something □ *We don't have the wherewithal to complete the project.*

whet /wet/ VERB [**whets, whetting, whetted**] whet your appetite to make you feel that you want something or want to do something □ *He'd seen a clip of the film, which had whetted his appetite to see more.*

whether /'weðə(r)/ CONJUNCTION
1 used to show that there is a choice between two possibilities □ *Whether we like it or not, we have to get up early.* □ *I couldn't decide whether to have the salmon or the pork.* □ *I wasn't sure whether or not to tell her.*
2 if □ *I'm not sure whether they're coming.*

which /wɪtʃ/ ADJECTIVE, DETERMINER
1 used for asking or talking about a choice between two or more people or things □ *Which hand do you think the coin is in?* □ *Which person is tallest?* □ **+ of** *Which of these books is yours?*
2 used for referring to something □ *I saw the letter*

which was lying on the table. □ *These are the rules which we have all agreed to.*

3 used for giving extra information about something □ *The cars, which were all luxury models, were available for us to use.* □ *I went to her party, which was very pleasant.*

whichever /wɪtʃˈevə(r)/ DETERMINER, PRONOUN

1 used to say that it is not important which thing or person happens, is chosen, etc., because the result will be the same □ *He'll be pleased, whichever one you give him.*

2 any of a group of things or people □ *Come on whichever day suits you.*

3 used to talk about the thing or person that has been chosen, has happened, etc. □ *You can come round on Monday or Tuesday, whichever suits you.* □ *Whichever person gets most points is the winner.*

whiff /wɪf/ NOUN [plural **whiffs**] a smell which you notice for a short time □ *a whiff of garlic*

while /waɪl/ ► CONJUNCTION

1 during the time that □ *Will you be going to Disneyland while you are in Florida?* □ *I had a cup of coffee while I was waiting.*

2 although □ *While I understand why you got angry, I think you should try to control your temper.*

3 used to compare two people or things □ *Bob is quite intellectual, while his brothers are more sporty.*

► Note that the word **while**, meaning 'during the time that' is never followed by a noun:
✓ *She got ill while we were on holiday.*
✗ *She got ill while the holiday.*

► NOUN **a while** a period of time □ *We waited inside for a while, but the rain didn't stop.* 🔁 *I haven't seen her for quite a while* (=a long time).

♦ PHRASAL VERB [**whiles, whiling, whiled**] **while something away** if you while away time, you do pleasant things to make the time pass, especially when you are waiting for something □ *We whiled away the evening chatting.*

whilst /waɪlst/ CONJUNCTION while □ *You could look at these magazines whilst you're waiting.*

whim /wɪm/ NOUN [plural **whims**] a sudden feeling that you want to have something or do something, usually something not very important □ *I phoned her on a whim.*

whimper /ˈwɪmpə(r)/ ► VERB [**whimpers, whimpering, whimpered**] to make a quiet crying sound because of pain or fear
► NOUN [plural **whimpers**] a quiet crying sound

whimsical /ˈwɪmzɪkəl/ ADJECTIVE slightly strange and humorous □ *Her pictures are detailed and whimsical.*

whine /waɪn/ ► VERB [**whines, whining, whined**]
1 to talk in a complaining voice □ *She's always whining about her job.*

2 a dog or other animal whines when it makes a long high sound
► NOUN [plural **whines**]
1 when someone whines □ *I had to listen to his whine about not having any money.*
2 the sound a dog or animal makes when it whines

whinge /wɪndʒ/ ► VERB [**whinges, whingeing, whinged**] to complain about things that are not important in a way that other people find annoying. An informal word.
► NOUN [plural **whinges**] an informal word meaning when someone whinges 🔁 *She was having a whinge about her neighbours.*

whinny /ˈwɪnɪ/ ► NOUN [plural **whinnies**] the high sound that a horse makes
► VERB [**whinnies, whinnying, whinnied**] if a horse whinnies, it makes a high sound

whip /wɪp/ ► NOUN [plural **whips**] a piece of leath or other material fastened to a handle and used to animals or people
► VERB [**whips, whipping, whipped**]
1 to hit someone or something with a whip
2 to move something very quickly □ *He whipped o a piece of paper and waved it at us.* □ *They whipp off the covers.*
3 to mix food, especially cream, very quickly to ma it become thick
♦ PHRASAL VERB **whip something up**
1 to make people feel strong emotions □ *His speec whipped up anger amongst the workers.*
2 to produce a meal very quickly □ *I can whip up so soup if you like.*

whir /wɜː(r)/ ► VERB [**whirs, whirring, whirred**] a mainly US spelling of whirr
► NOUN [plural **whirs**] a mainly US spelling of wh

whirl /wɜːl/ ► VERB [**whirls, whirling, whirled**]
1 to turn round and round very quickly or to mak someone or something do this □ *He picked up the and whirled him round.*
2 if your mind or thoughts are whirling, you feel confused or excited and not calm
♦ PHRASAL VERB **whirl around/round** to turn ro very quickly, often because of surprise or anger □ *whirled round and punched the man in the face.*
► NOUN [plural **whirls**]
1 a confused or excited situation, with a lot happe □ *The whole town was in a whirl of excitement.*
2 a very fast turning movement
♦ IDIOM **give something a whirl** to try an activity □ *invited me to go sailing with her, so I thought I'd g a whirl.*

whirlpool /ˈwɜːlpuːl/ NOUN [plural **whirlpools**] area of water where a strong current moves the in circles, often pulling things down into it

whirlwind /ˈwɜːlwɪnd/ ► NOUN [plural **whirlwi** powerful wind that has a circular movement an damage things
► ADJECTIVE
1 **a whirlwind tour/trip** a quick visit to a plac

2 a whirlwind romance a romantic relationship that starts very suddenly and develops very quickly

whirr /wɜː(r)/ ▶ VERB [whirrs, whirring, whirred] to make a continuous, low sound
▶ NOUN [plural whirrs] a continuous, low sound

whisk /wɪsk/ ▶ NOUN [plural whisks] a kitchen tool with curved wire parts, used for mixing things like cream or eggs and getting a lot of air into them
▶ VERB [whisks, whisking, whisked]
1 to mix food with a whisk
2 to make someone or something move somewhere quickly □ They whisked us off to meet their cousins. □ She whisked away the plates.

whisker /'wɪskə(r)/ NOUN [plural whiskers]
1 one of the long stiff hairs that grow on the faces of animals like mice, cats and dogs
2 a whisker an extremely small amount or distance □ He missed the ball by a whisker.

whisky /'wɪskɪ/ NOUN [plural whiskies] a strong alcoholic drink made from grain, or a glass of this drink

whisper /'wɪspə(r)/ ▶ VERB [whispers, whispering, whispered] to talk very quietly so that other people cannot hear □ My friend whispered the answer to me.
▶ NOUN [plural whispers] something said in a very quiet voice □ She answered in a whisper.

whistle /'wɪsəl/ ▶ VERB [whistles, whistling, whistled]
1 to make a high sound or musical notes by blowing air through your lips □ She was whistling a merry tune.
2 to make a high sound using a whistle □ The train whistled as it entered the tunnel. □ The referee whistled for the end of the game.
3 to make a high sound, often caused by air blowing □ The wind whistled round our legs.
4 to move very quickly □ A bullet whistled past his ear.
▶ NOUN [plural whistles]
1 a small object that makes a high sound when you blow in it
2 a piece of equipment that makes a loud, high sound, for example on a train
3 the sound made when someone or something whistles

white /waɪt/ ▶ ADJECTIVE
1 having the colour of snow □ He served the soup in white, white bowls. □ This powder will get your clothing really white.
2 white people are of a race that have pale skin □ He married a white woman.
3 white tea or coffee has milk in it
4 white wine is a pale yellow colour
▶ NOUN [plural whites]
1 the colour of snow □ The white of the walls reflected the sunlight.
2 the white of an egg is the clear substance around the yolk (=yellow part) which turns white if it is cooked

white blood cell /waɪt 'blʌd ,sel/ NOUN [plural white blood cells] white blood cells have a nucleus and many of them fight disease. A biology word.

whiteboard /'waɪtbɔːd/ NOUN [plural whiteboards] a big white screen which is connected to a computer. You write on it using a special pen which controls the computer. ▢ an interactive whiteboard

white-collar /'waɪt'kɒlə(r)/ ADJECTIVE white-collar workers have jobs in offices, not jobs involving physical work

white lie /waɪt 'laɪ/ NOUN [plural white lies] a lie that is not very serious, especially one used to avoid upsetting someone

whiten /'waɪtən/ VERB [whitens, whitening, whitened] to make something white or whiter □ She had her teeth whitened.

whitewash /'waɪtwɒʃ/ ▶ NOUN, NO PLURAL
1 something that is done to try to stop people discovering the truth about something □ This report is just a whitewash - it doesn't answer the most important questions.
2 a type of thin, white paint
▶ VERB [whitewashes, whitewashing, whitewashed] to paint whitewash on something

whizz /wɪz/ ▶ VERB [whizzes, whizzing, whizzed] to move somewhere very quickly □ We whizzed down the hill on our bikes.
▶ NOUN [plural whizzes] an informal word meaning someone who is extremely good at doing something □ She's a whizz at crosswords.

who /huː/ PRONOUN
1 used for asking about a person or people □ Who is your favourite actor? □ Who left the door open? □ Who are you going to London with?
2 used for referring to a person or people □ It was Malcolm who told me the news. □ It was the Italians who invented pizza. □ I know who has been offered the job.
3 used for giving extra information about a person or people □ Emily, who lives next door, is 12 years old.

who'd /huːd/ a short way to say and write who had or who would □ It was my Dad who'd told him. □ Who'd like another biscuit?

whodunit or **whodunnit** /,huː'dʌnɪt/ NOUN [plural whodunits or whodunnits] a book, play or film in which the story is about finding the person who did a murder

whoever /huː'evə(r)/ PRONOUN, CONJUNCTION
1 the person that has done something □ Would whoever it was that left the gate open please go and close it.
2 any person □ Bring whoever you like to the party.
3 used to say that it does not matter who does something, who is chosen, etc., because the result will be the same □ It'll take a long time, whoever does it.
4 used at the beginning of a question to show that you are surprised □ Whoever told you I was a doctor?
5 used to show that you do not know who someone is □ We need to talk to Mr Buckley, whoever he is.

whole /həʊl/ ▶ ADJECTIVE
1 containing or including every part of something

□ We spent the whole day on the beach. □ I drank a whole bottle of milk. □ Half the guests were late, and the whole thing was a disaster.

2 not broken into parts □ The cake is decorated with whole hazelnuts.

3 the whole point the most important reason for something □ For him, the whole point of owning a smart car is to be seen as successful.

▶ NOUN, NO PLURAL

1 a complete thing, especially one that is made up of different parts □ Two halves make a whole.

2 the whole of something all of something □ She spent the whole of her life in Wales. □ The Olympics will benefit the whole of the country.

3 on the whole used to talk about what something is usually or mostly like □ On the whole, I enjoy school. □ People were very kind to us on the whole.

4 as a whole considering all the parts of something, especially a group of people or an organization □ These scandals affect the industry as a whole.

▶ ADVERB

1 in one complete piece □ He swallowed the egg whole.

2 an informal word meaning completely □ We are trying a whole new approach to the problem.

wholefood /ˈhəʊlfuːd/ NOUN [plural **wholefoods**] a food that has not been changed to take away any part of it, and has not had any artificial substances added

wholehearted /ˌhəʊlˈhɑːtɪd/ ADJECTIVE enthusiastic and complete ⊞ He gave Clinton his wholehearted support.

wholemeal /ˈhəʊlmiːl/ ADJECTIVE made from flour which has been made from whole grains ⊞ wholemeal bread/flour

wholesale /ˈhəʊlseɪl/ ADJECTIVE

1 wholesale goods are bought in large amounts, often by businesses that sell them again

2 affecting every person or every part of something ⊞ We need to make wholesale changes to our education system.

wholesome /ˈhəʊlsəm/ ADJECTIVE

1 healthy and good for you □ wholesome food

2 having characteristics that people think are pleasant and morally good □ She had the image of a wholesome country girl.

who'll /huːl/ a short way to say and write who will □ Who'll help me to carry this box?

wholly /ˈhəʊlɪ/ ADVERB completely □ They were wholly committed to the team.

whom /huːm/ PRONOUN a formal word, used instead of 'who' when it is the object of a verb or a preposition □ He phoned his friend Andrew, whom he hadn't seen for years. □ To whom should I address the letter?

whoop /wuːp/ ▶ VERB [**whoops, whooping, whooped**] to give a loud shout of excitement

▶ NOUN [plural **whoops**] a loud shout of excitement

whooping cough /ˈhuːpɪŋ ˌkɒf/ NOUN, NO PLURAL a disease which makes it difficult to breathe and causes a loud, painful cough

whoops /wʊps/ EXCLAMATION something you say when you make a mistake or have a small accident

whopper /ˈwɒpə(r)/ NOUN [plural **whoppers**]

1 an informal word meaning something that is extremely big □ That fish was an absolute whopper.

2 an informal word meaning a lie

whopping /ˈwɒpɪŋ/ ADJECTIVE an informal word meaning extremely big □ a whopping 20% pay rise

who're /ˈhuːə(r)/ a short way to say and write who ar □ Who're you going with?

who's /huːz/ a short way to say and write who is o who has □ Who's coming for a walk? □ Who's got th TV guide?

whose /huːz/ ADJECTIVE, PRONOUN

1 used to say that something or someone belongs someone or is connected to them □ This is the boy whose family owns the farm. □ Cheeky, whose real name was Robert Ritchie, lived in Glasgow.

2 used to ask who something belongs to or is connected with □ Whose bike is this? □ Whose is t coat? □ Whose fault was it that we were late?

who've /huːv/ a short way to say and write who ha □ These are the members who've already paid the subscriptions.

why /waɪ/ ADVERB

1 used for asking and talking about the reason for something □ Why were you late? □ Why didn't th phone us? □ She explained why she had made the decision. □ I have no idea why he was so angry.

2 used for making a suggestion □ Why don't you Claire to come with you? □ Why doesn't he ask a doctor about it?

3 why not ...? (a) used for making a suggestion □ Why not make some soup with the vegetables have left? (b) used for agreeing to a suggestion □ 'Shall we invite Peter?' 'Yes, why not?'

why's /waɪz/ a short way to say and write why why has □ Why's she crying?

why've /waɪv/ a short way to say and write why □ Why've we got to wait?

wicked /ˈwɪkɪd/ ADJECTIVE

1 evil or morally wrong □ a wicked old witch □ Separating children from their parents is wicke

2 slightly unkind or badly behaved, but in a way makes people laugh □ He had a wicked sense of humour. □ a wicked grin

3 an informal word meaning very good □ He sco wicked goal.

● **wickedly** /ˈwɪkɪdlɪ/ ADJECTIVE

1 in a way that is slightly unkind or badly behave makes people laugh □ He told some wickedly f jokes.

2 in an evil way □ She treated them wickedly.

● **wickedness** /ˈwɪkɪdnɪs/ NOUN, NO PLURAL ev □ There is so much wickedness in the world.

wicker /'wɪkə(r)/ NOUN, NO PLURAL long, thin pieces of wood that are twisted together to make furniture, baskets, etc. □ *a wicker chair*

wicket /'wɪkɪt/ NOUN [plural **wickets**] in cricket, three vertical wooden sticks with two horizontal parts across the top

wide /waɪd/ ▶ ADJECTIVE [**wider, widest**]
1 a large distance from side to side □ *a wide river* □ *Floods affected a wide area.*
2 having a particular width □ *The river is nearly a mile wide at some points.*
3 including many different things 🔁 *They sell a wide range of products.* □ *The college offers a wide choice of subjects.*
4 very large □ *She has a wide circle of friends.* □ *They won the contest by a wide margin.*
5 if your eyes are wide, they are open as far as possible
6 if something that is aimed, for example a ball, is wide, it goes to the side of the thing it was aimed at □ *His shot was wide.*

▶ ADVERB [**wider, widest**]
1 with a large distance from top to bottom or side to side □ *The tiger opened his mouth wide, showing his enormous fangs.* 🔁 *The door was wide open.* 🔁 *She stood with her feet wide apart.*
2 wide awake completely awake
3 if something that is aimed, for example a ball, goes wide, it goes to the side of the thing it is aimed at
4 far and wide over a large area □ *They travelled far and wide.*

widely /'waɪdlɪ/ ADVERB
1 by many people or in many places □ *He was widely considered to be the best poet of his generation.* □ *The tour was widely advertised.*
2 by a large amount □ *Standards vary widely.*

widen /'waɪdən/ VERB [**widens, widening, widened**]
1 to make something wider or to become wider □ *The river widens as it reaches the sea.*
2 to become bigger or to make something bigger □ *We hope to widen the scope of our operation.*

widening /'waɪdənɪŋ/ ADJECTIVE becoming wider or bigger □ *There is a widening gap between rich and poor.*

wide-ranging /'waɪd'reɪndʒɪŋ/ ADJECTIVE dealing with many subjects or affecting many people or things □ *In a wide-ranging interview, she talks about her life and work.*

widespread /'waɪdspred/ ADJECTIVE found in a lot of places or among a lot of people □ *There is widespread use of these drugs.* □ *There has been widespread criticism of the law.*

widow /'wɪdəʊ/ NOUN [plural **widows**] a woman whose husband has died

widowed /'wɪdəʊd/ ADJECTIVE if someone is widowed, their husband or wife has died

widower /'wɪdəʊə(r)/ NOUN [plural **widowers**] a man whose wife has died

width /wɪdθ/ NOUN [plural **widths**] the width of something is how much it measures from side to side □ *This curtain material comes in several different widths.*

wield /wi:ld/ VERB [**wields, wielding, wielded**]
1 if you wield a tool or a weapon, you hold it as if you are going to use it □ *There is a portrait of him wielding a sword.*
2 to have power or influence

wife /waɪf/ NOUN [plural **wives**] the woman that a man is married to

WiFi /'waɪ,faɪ/ NOUN, NO PLURAL a system for connecting computers to the Internet that does not use wires

wig /wɪg/ NOUN [plural **wigs**] a covering of artificial hair that is worn on the head

wiggle /'wɪgəl/ ▶ VERB [**wiggles, wiggling, wiggled**] to make small movements from side to side, or to make something do this □ *Harriet was wiggling her loose tooth.*
▶ NOUN [plural **wiggles**] a small movement from side to side
● **wiggly** /'wɪglɪ/ ADJECTIVE [**wigglier, wiggliest**] a wiggly line has lots of small curves

wigwam /'wɪgwæm/ NOUN [plural **wigwams**] a tall tent shaped like a cone, used in the past by Native Americans

wild /waɪld/ ▶ ADJECTIVE [**wilder, wildest**]
1 wild animals or plants live in natural conditions and are not kept by human beings □ *wild salmon* □ *wild flowers*
2 a wild area of land is in a natural state and has not been used for houses, farming, etc.
3 not controlled, and often expressing strong emotions or a lot of energy and excitement 🔁 *When he came on stage, the audience went wild.* □ *The children were wild with excitement.* 🔁 *wild parties*
4 not based on facts or careful thought □ *He was making wild accusations.*
5 with strong wind and storms □ *It was a wild night.*
6 wild about something very enthusiastic about something or liking something very much □ *I'm not wild about the idea of camping.*
7 run wild to not be controlled □ *The children were allowed to run wild.*
▶ NOUN [plural **wilds**]
1 in the wild in a natural environment, not in a farm, zoo, etc. □ *These birds will not be able to survive in the wild.*
2 the wilds of somewhere the areas of a place that are very natural and far away from where people live

wild card /'waɪld ,kɑ:d/ NOUN [plural **wild cards**] a symbol used to represent any letter or number on a computer. A computing word.

wilderness /'wɪldənɪs/ NOUN [plural **wildernesses**] a wild area of a country with no roads, houses, etc.

wildfire /'waɪld,faɪə(r)/ NOUN, NO PLURAL spread like wildfire if a story, information, etc. spreads like wildfire, many people hear about it very quickly

wild-goose chase /'waɪld'gu:s ,tʃeɪs/ NOUN [plural **wild-goose chases**] a search for something that is impossible to find

wildlife /'waɪldlaɪf/ NOUN, NO PLURAL wild animals, birds, insects and plants

wildly /'waɪldlɪ/ ADVERB
1 in a way that is not controlled □ *Everyone was cheering wildly.*
2 extremely □ *They were wildly excited.*

wiles /waɪlz/ PLURAL NOUN tricks used to make people do what you want

wilful /'wɪlful/ ADJECTIVE
1 a wilful person is determined to do what they want □ *a wilful child*
2 deliberate □ *wilful damage*
• **wilfully** /'wɪlfulɪ/ ADVERB in a wilful way

will¹ /wɪl/ MODAL VERB
1 used to talk about the future □ *It will be winter soon.* □ *Will Tom be at the party?* □ *It won't take long to mend the hole.*
2 used to talk about whether someone is willing to do something □ *Will you hold this for me?* □ *I'll carry that bag for you.* □ *He won't lend me any money.*
3 used to talk about whether someone or something is able to do something □ *The car won't start.* □ *See if a drop of oil will help.*
4 used in conditional sentences that start with 'if' □ *If he is rude, I will leave straight away.* □ *If it rains, they will have to work indoors.*
5 used to show that you think something is true □ *Many of you will have seen me before.*

► Notice that instead of **will not**, people often say or write the short form **won't** □ *I won't tell her.*

---

will² /wɪl/ ► NOUN [plural **wills**]
1 the mental strength needed to achieve something □ *She has the will to succeed.* ⊞ *He had a very strong will.*
2 what you want to do or to happen □ *He signed the document against my will.* □ *We must listen to the will of the people.*
3 a legal document that says what you want to happen to your money and possessions when you die ⊞ *Have you made a will?*
► VERB [**wills, willing, willed**] if you will something to happen, you try to make it happen by wishing for it very much □ *We were willing our team to win.*

willful /'wɪlful/ ADJECTIVE the US spelling of wilful

willing /'wɪlɪŋ/ ADJECTIVE
1 willing to do something if you are willing to do something, you will do it if you are asked to □ *He will do well if he's willing to work hard.* □ *She wasn't willing to accept responsibility.*
2 eager and happy to do something □ *a willing helper*

• **willingly** /'wɪlɪŋlɪ/ ADVERB if you do something willingly, you do it in a happy and eager way
• **willingness** /'wɪlɪŋnɪs/ NOUN, NO PLURAL the state of being willing □ *I was impressed by his willingness to listen.*

willow /'wɪləu/ NOUN [plural **willows**] a tree with long thin branches and leaves that often grows near water

willpower /'wɪl,pauə(r)/ NOUN, NO PLURAL the mental strength needed to achieve something difficult, especially to stop yourself doing something bad □ *I know I should lose weight, but I haven't got any willpower.*

wilt /wɪlt/ VERB [**wilts, wilting, wilted**]
1 if a plant wilts, it hangs down towards the ground because it needs water or is dying
2 if a person wilts, they become weak or tired

wily /'waɪlɪ/ ADJECTIVE [**wilier, wiliest**] able to trick people in a clever way

wimp /wɪmp/ NOUN [plural **wimps**] an informal and insulting word for someone who is not strong or brave

win /wɪn/ ► VERB [**wins, winning, won**]
1 to beat everyone else in a game, competition, election, etc. ⊞ *We played tennis, and Sam won easily.* □ *They won the championship three times.*
2 to defeat the other side in a war, argument, etc.
3 to get something because of your skill or effort □ *took a long time to win their trust.* □ *The company has won a major contract.*
4 to get something because you have been successful in a game, competition, etc. □ *She won a gold medal at the 2008 Olympics.* □ *The film won two Oscars.*
5 you can't win used to say that nothing you do will be successful or please people □ *I can't win - if I offer help with his homework he says I'm interfering, and if I don't, he says I don't care about him.*
♦ PHRASAL VERB **win someone over/round** to persuade someone to agree with you or to like you □ *They won over their critics with offers of extra money.*
► NOUN [plural **wins**] when someone wins a game, competition, etc. □ *This is the team's third consecutive win.*

wince /wɪns/ VERB [**winces, wincing, winced**] to make a small, quick movement with your face because of sudden pain or thinking about something unpleasant □ *He winced when I reminded him of his mistake.*

winch /wɪntʃ/ ► NOUN [plural **winches**] a piece of equipment with a rope or chain, used for lifting or pulling something heavy
► VERB [**winches, winching, winched**] to use a winch to lift or pull something

wind¹ /wɪnd/ NOUN [plural **winds**]
1 a current of air ⊞ *Strong winds prevented the aircraft from landing.* ⊞ *The wind blew and snow fell.*
2 no plural if someone has wind, they have gas in their stomach, which makes them feel uncomfortable

wind² /waɪnd/ VERB [winds, winding, wound]

1 to twist or wrap something around something else □ **+ round** A turban is a long piece of cloth that is wound round the head.

2 if a road, path or river winds somewhere, it has a lot of curves or turns □ **+ through** A narrow path wound through the valley.

3 to turn a part of a machine or piece of equipment in order to make it work □ This watch has a battery, so you don't need to wind it. □ **+ up** He has a toy car that you wind up to make it go.

PHRASAL VERBS **wind down** to gradually become less busy or active □ We're winding down for the summer break. **wind (something) down** to end gradually, or to make something end gradually □ I've decided to wind down the business. **wind up** to end in a particular state or position □ **+ ing** He wound up having to apologize. □ You could wind up unemployed. **wind someone up 1** an informal word meaning to try to make someone believe something that is not true, usually for a joke □ He isn't really going to change you - he's just winding you up. an informal word meaning to make someone upset or angry □ It really winds me up when he's late. **wind something up** to end something □ He wound up the interview and left. □ She decided to wind up the company.

windfall /ˈwɪndfɔːl/ NOUN [plural **windfalls**] money that you get without expecting it

wind farm /ˈwɪnd ˌfɑːm/ NOUN [plural **wind farms**] a group of wind turbines (=tall, thin structures with long parts that turn in the wind) that produce electricity

winding /ˈwaɪndɪŋ/ ADJECTIVE a winding road, river, etc. has a lot of turns in it

wind instrument /ˈwɪnd ˌɪnstrʊmənt/ NOUN [plural **wind instruments**] an instrument in an orchestra (=large group of musicians) that is played by blowing into it

windmill /ˈwɪndmɪl/ NOUN [plural **windmills**] a building with large parts on the outside which are turned by the wind and provide power for crushing grain

window /ˈwɪndəʊ/ NOUN [plural **windows**]

1 an opening in the wall of a building or in a vehicle, with glass fitted in it ⊞ Could you open/close the window, please?

2 an area on a computer screen where you can work or see information. A computing word ⊞ I opened a new window.

window pane /ˈwɪndəʊ ˌpeɪn/ NOUN [plural **window panes**] a piece of glass in a window

window shopping /ˈwɪndəʊ ˌʃɒpɪŋ/ NOUN, NO PLURAL looking at things for sale in shop windows but not buying them

windowsill /ˈwɪndəʊsɪl/ NOUN [plural **windowsills**] a shelf at the bottom of a window

windpipe /ˈwɪndpaɪp/ NOUN [plural **windpipes**] the tube that goes from your mouth down your throat and into your lungs

windscreen /ˈwɪndskriːn/ NOUN [plural **windscreens**] the window at the front of a car or other vehicle

windscreen wiper /ˈwɪndskriːn ˈwaɪpə(r)/ NOUN [plural **windscreen wipers**] one of two long parts with a rubber edge that move across the windscreen of a vehicle to remove rain from it

windshield /ˈwɪndʃiːld/ NOUN [plural **windshields**] the US word for windscreen

windsurfing /ˈwɪndˌsɜːfɪŋ/ NOUN, NO PLURAL the sport of moving across the surface of water standing on a narrow board with a sail attached to it

windswept /ˈwɪndswept/ ADJECTIVE

1 a windswept place often has strong winds

2 looking untidy from being in the wind

wind turbine /ˈwɪnd tɜːbaɪn/ NOUN [plural **wind turbines**] a tall, thin structure with long parts that turn in the wind, used for producing electricity

windy /ˈwɪndɪ/ ADJECTIVE [**windier, windiest**] with a lot of wind □ a windy day

wine /waɪn/ NOUN [plural **wines**] an alcoholic drink usually made from grapes (=small green or purple fruits) ⊞ a glass of wine ⊞ red/white wine

wine bar /ˈwaɪn ˌbɑː(r)/ NOUN [plural **wine bars**] a place where people go to drink wine and often have a meal

wine glass /ˈwaɪn ˌglɑːs/ NOUN [plural **wine glasses**] a glass with a long stem, used for drinking wine

wing /wɪŋ/ NOUN [plural **wings**]

1 one of the parts of a bird or an insect's body that it uses to fly with ⊞ The owl flapped its wings.

2 one of the two long flat parts that stick out at either side of an aircraft

3 a part that sticks out from a main building □ They are repairing the east wing of the house.

4 one of the sides of a sports field, or a player who plays on this part in sports like football □ He's dribbling the ball down the wing.

5 a part of a political party or other organization with its own responsibilities or opinions □ He's a member of the party's military wing.

6 the wings the areas on either side of the stage in a theatre that are hidden from the audience

◆ IDIOM **take someone under your wing** to look after someone who has less experience of something than you

● **winged** /wɪŋd/ ADJECTIVE having wings □ a winged insect

● **winger** /ˈwɪŋə(r)/ NOUN [plural **wingers**] a player in a sports team whose place is on one of the wings

wink /wɪŋk/ ► VERB [**winks, winking, winked**]
1 to shut one of your eyes and open it again quickly, as a friendly or secret sign to someone
2 if a light winks, it goes off and on again quickly
► NOUN [*plural* **winks**] the action of winking

winner /'wɪnə(r)/ NOUN [*plural* **winners**] someone who wins a race, competition, election, etc. □ *This year's winner gets a £3,000 prize.*

winning /'wɪnɪŋ/ ADJECTIVE
1 describes the person, team, etc. that wins 🔁 *the winning entry*
2 a winning smile, manner, etc. is very attractive and makes people like you or do what you want
winnings /'wɪnɪŋz/ PLURAL NOUN the money that someone wins

winter /'wɪntə(r)/ NOUN [*plural* **winters**] the coldest season of the year, between autumn and spring □ *the winter months* □ *a winter coat*

wintertime /'wɪntətaɪm/ NOUN, NO PLURAL the period of winter □ *In wintertime these cottages get no sun at all.*

wintry /'wɪntri/ ADJECTIVE cold, like winter

wipe /waɪp/ ► VERB [**wipes, wiping, wiped**]
1 to rub the surface of something to clean it or dry it □ *I wiped my face with a tissue.* □ *We wiped all the tables.* 🔁 *Please wipe your feet* (=clean the dirt off your shoes) *before you come in.*
2 to remove something, for example dirt or water, from the surface of something by rubbing it □ *Wipe any mud off the potatoes.*
3 if you wipe a computer disk, video tape, etc., you remove all the information from it
◆ PHRASAL VERBS **wipe something down** to clean the surface of something by rubbing it □ *We wiped down all the cupboard doors.* **wipe something off something** to reduce the amount that something is worth by a lot □ *Millions of dollars were wiped off shares yesterday.* **wipe something out 1** to destroy something completely □ *These elephants were in danger of being wiped out by hunters.* **2** to clean the inside surface of something by rubbing it □ *Please wipe the bath out after you have used it.* **wipe someone out** to make someone feel very tired □ *The journey wiped him out.* **wipe something up** to clean away a substance, often a liquid, with a cloth
► NOUN [*plural* **wipes**]
1 an act of wiping something □ *I need to give my glasses a wipe.*
2 a piece of wet cloth or soft paper used to wipe things with
● **wiper** /'waɪpə(r)/ NOUN [*plural* **wipers**] a windscreen wiper

wire /'waɪə(r)/ ► NOUN [*plural* **wires**]
1 *no plural* metal that has been made into long, thin pieces, used for fastening things together, or for fences, etc. □ *a wire fence*

2 a piece of wire used for carrying electricity or telephone signals
◆ IDIOM **get your wires crossed** to become confused because you and the person you are talking to are talking about different things
► VERB [**wires, wiring, wired**]
1 to connect wires to a piece of electrical equipment □ *Do you know how to wire a plug?*
2 to fasten things together with wire

wireless /'waɪəlɪs/ ► ADJECTIVE not connected with wires □ *a wireless Internet connection*
► NOUN [*plural* **wirelesses**] an old-fashioned word for a radio

wiring /'waɪərɪŋ/ NOUN, NO PLURAL the wires that form the electrical system in a building or piece of equipment

wiry /'waɪəri/ ADJECTIVE [**wirier, wiriest**]
1 someone who is wiry has a thin, strong body
2 wiry hair is strong and stiff

wisdom /'wɪzdəm/ NOUN, NO PLURAL when someone understands a lot about life and is able to make good decisions and give good advice

wisdom tooth /'wɪzdəm ˌtuːθ/ NOUN [*plural* **wisdom teeth**] one of the big teeth at the back of your mouth that grow when you are an adult

wise /waɪz/ ADJECTIVE [**wiser, wisest**]
1 a wise person understands a lot about life and is able to make good decisions and give good advice
2 showing good judgment □ *a wise decision*
3 be none the wiser to still not understand something even when you have tried to find out or when someone has tried to explain it
4 wise to something knowing about something, especially a trick or something bad □ *We are wise to the tricks the photographers use.*

wisecrack /'waɪzkræk/ NOUN [*plural* **wisecracks**] clever joke

wish /wɪʃ/ ► VERB [**wishes, wishing, wished**]
1 to want something to happen, especially to want a situation to change □ *I wish it would stop raining.* ● **that** *I wish that I could go with you.* □ *I wish you wouldn't work so hard.*
2 wish to do something a formal word meaning to want to do something □ *Do you wish to pay now or later?*
3 used to say that you hope someone will have something or enjoy something 🔁 *We all wish you* □ *I wished her a happy birthday.*
4 to make a magic wish □ + **for** *I wished for a bicycle.*
► NOUN [*plural* **wishes**]
1 what you want to do or to happen 🔁 *We must respect his wishes* (=do what he wants). 🔁 *I have wish to see the document.*
2 something that you want to happen by magic 🔁 *Blow out the candles and make a wish!*

3 best wishes a polite way of ending a letter or e-mail

---

wishful thinking /ˈwɪʃful ˈθɪŋkɪŋ/ NOUN, NO PLURAL a belief that is based on what you want to be true and not what is likely to be true □ *I thought the rain was stopping, but I think it was just wishful thinking.*

wishy-washy /ˈwɪʃɪˌwɒʃɪ/ ADJECTIVE an informal word meaning weak □ *a wishy-washy approach to discipline*

wisp /wɪsp/ NOUN [plural **wisps**] a small, thin amount of something □ *a wisp of cloud* □ *a wisp of hair*

wispy /ˈwɪspɪ/ ADJECTIVE [**wispier, wispiest**] in the form of wisps ⑤ *She had rather wispy hair.*

wistful /ˈwɪstful/ ADJECTIVE
slightly sad, because you are remembering something good from the past □ *a wistful smile*
slightly sad because you cannot have something you want
wistfully /ˈwɪstfulɪ/ ADVERB in a wistful way □ *She gazed wistfully at the beautiful sports car.*

wit /wɪt/ NOUN, NO PLURAL the ability to say funny and clever things
go to wits

witch /wɪtʃ/ NOUN [plural **witches**] a woman in stories who has evil magic powers

witchcraft /ˈwɪtʃkrɑːft/ NOUN, NO PLURAL the use of magic, especially for evil purposes

witch doctor /ˈwɪtʃ ˈdɒktə(r)/ NOUN [plural **witch doctors**] in some cultures, a man who uses magic to try to cure illness

witch-hunt /ˈwɪtʃhʌnt/ NOUN [plural **witch-hunts**]
unfair attempt to punish a person or a group of people □ *The communist witch-hunt of the 1950s ruined many Hollywood careers.*

with /wɪð/ PREPOSITION
if something or someone is in a place with something or someone else, or doing something with someone or something else, they are together □ *Come with me.* □ *She keeps her diary on a shelf with her other books.* □ *He was playing football with his friends.*
holding or carrying □ *He arrived with a huge bunch of roses.*
using □ *The board was stuck down with glue.* □ *I chopped up the wood with an axe.*
having □ *Who is that man with the curly hair?* □ *The meeting was in the room with the large table.*
used to show what something refers to □ *What's wrong with your eye?* □ *I'm really pleased with my new computer.*
the result of □ *He was doubled up with pain.*
against □ *I'm always arguing with my parents.* □ *He was killed in the war with Spain.*
used to describe how something happens or is done □ *It is with great pleasure that I can announce the winner.* □ *She agreed with a smile.* □ *He stood with his hands behind his back.*
used after verbs to do with covering, filling or mixing □ *She covered the table with a sheet.* □ *Mix the dry ingredients with the milk in a large bowl.*

10 used after verbs to do with separating or finishing □ *I parted with them at the station.* □ *Have you finished with this magazine?*

withdraw /wɪðˈdrɔː/ VERB [**withdraws, withdrawing, withdrew, withdrawn**]
1 to take something away or to stop providing something □ *The council has withdrawn funding for the day centre.* □ *His father has withdrawn consent for the treatment.*
2 to not take part in something, or to say that someone cannot take part in something □ *The king's advisers have withdrawn from the negotiations.* □ *He began to withdraw from public life.*
3 to take money out of a bank account □ *I withdrew £100 for the weekend.*
4 if an army withdraws or is withdrawn, it leaves an area ⑤ *We plan to withdraw our forces from the area.*
5 to say that something you said earlier was not correct or true □ *I hope that he will withdraw these allegations.*
● **withdrawal** /wɪðˈdrɔːəl/ NOUN [plural **withdrawals**]
1 when something is taken away or not provided any more □ *The withdrawal of her support was a blow to the campaign.*
2 when someone does not take part in something □ *A knee injury forced her withdrawal from the tournament.*
3 an amount of money that you take out of your bank account, or the process of taking it out ⑤ *You can make a withdrawal at any bank.*
4 when an army leaves an area □ *We are hoping for a withdrawal of our troops by May.*
● **withdrawn** /wɪðˈdrɔːn/ ADJECTIVE a person who is withdrawn is shy and finds it difficult to communicate with other people

wither /ˈwɪðə(r)/ VERB [**withers, withering, withered**]
if a plant withers, it becomes dry and starts to die

withhold /wɪðˈhəʊld/ VERB [**withholds, withholding, withheld**] to refuse to give something to someone ⑤ *She was accused of withholding information from the police.*

within /wɪˈðɪn/ ► PREPOSITION
1 in less than a particular amount of time, or during a particular period of time □ *The police were called within minutes of the discovery.* □ *We'll be home within the hour.* □ *Within the last week there have been reports of fighting in the area.*
2 less than a particular distance or amount away from something ⑤ *A box of tissues was placed within reach.* □ *I have always lived within 20 miles of York.* □ *They are within two points of the championship.*
3 inside a place, group, organization or system □ *They took cover within the castle walls.* □ *I moved to another job within the same company.*
4 in the range that is possible because of a particular limit □ *We completed the project well within budget.* □ *This job should be well within his capability.*
5 if something is within the law, rules, etc., it is allowed

□ *The court decided that he had been acting within the law.* □ *We are within our rights to ask for compensation.*
▶ ADVERB
1 inside a place, organization, group or system □ *The notice on the restaurant window said: 'Waiters wanted. Apply within.'*
2 inside a person □ *Reading her poems, you could tell they truly came from within.*

without /wɪˈðaʊt/ ▶ PREPOSITION
1 not having something □ *I prefer my coffee without milk.* □ *It's a kind of bicycle without pedals.* □ *They left us without any food or water.* 🕮 *We had to do without cutlery.*
2 not with someone or something □ *Don't leave without me!*
3 not doing something □ *+ ing He left without saying goodbye.*
▶ ADVERB **do/go without** to manage when you do not have something □ *We only have two blankets, so the children will have to do without.*

withstand /wɪðˈstænd/ VERB [**withstands, withstanding, withstood**] to not be harmed by something □ *The buildings are specially designed to withstand earthquakes.*

witness /ˈwɪtnɪs/ ▶ NOUN [*plural* **witnesses**]
1 someone who sees an event such as an accident or a crime happening, and can tell other people about it
□ *+ to Were there any witnesses to the accident?*
2 someone who answers questions in a court about what they know about a crime
3 someone who watches somebody sign (=write their name on) an important document and writes their name there too
▶ VERB [**witnesses, witnessing, witnessed**]
1 to see something happening □ *Several people witnessed the shooting.*
2 to be a witness when someone signs (=writes their name on) an important document

witness box /ˈwɪtnɪs ˌbɒks/ NOUN [*plural* **witness boxes**] the place where a witness stands in a court
wits /wɪts/ PLURAL NOUN the ability to think quickly and make good decisions 🕮 *She made a fortune from her quick wits.* 🕮 *There are thieves about so you need to keep your wits about you* (=pay attention and be ready to react quickly).
◆ IDIOMS **be at your wits end** to be so upset or worried about something that you do not know what to do □ *I'm at my wits end trying to feed the family on my wages.* **frighten/scare the wits out** of someone to frighten someone very much **pit your wits against** someone to try to defeat someone by using your intelligence
witter /ˈwɪtə(r)/ VERB [**witters, wittering, wittered**] to talk a lot about things that are not important
witticism /ˈwɪtɪsɪzəm/ NOUN [*plural* **witticisms**] a funny and clever remark

wittily /ˈwɪtɪlɪ/ ADVERB in a funny and clever way
witty /ˈwɪtɪ/ ADJECTIVE [**wittier, wittiest**] clever and funny □ *My brother is very witty.* □ *a witty remark*
wives /waɪvz/ PLURAL OF **wife**
wizard /ˈwɪzəd/ NOUN [*plural* **wizards**]
1 in stories, a man with magic powers
2 someone who is very good at something □ *a computer wizard*
● **wizardry** /ˈwɪzədrɪ/ NOUN, NO PLURAL a high level skill at a difficult thing, or something that is made using a high level of skill □ *technical wizardry*
wizened /ˈwɪzənd/ ADJECTIVE having a lot of lines because of being old □ *a wizened face*
WMD /ˌdʌbəljuːemˈdiː/ ABBREVIATION weapons of mass destruction; weapons which kill many people a cause a lot of damage
wobble /ˈwɒbəl/ ▶ VERB [**wobbles, wobbling, wobbled**]
1 to move from side to side, or to make somethin move from side to side □ *This table wobbles.*
2 to become less strong or less confident □ *The do wobbled yesterday.*
3 if your voice wobbles, you sound as if you are go to cry
▶ NOUN [*plural* **wobbles**]
1 a movement from side to side
2 an informal word meaning a period of feeling le strong or less confident □ *I had prepared my spee but I had a bit of a wobble when I saw how many people were there.*
● **wobbly** /ˈwɒblɪ/ ADJECTIVE [**wobblier, wobbliest**]
1 moving from side to side □ *a wobbly tooth*
2 an informal word meaning not strong or not confident □ *He's still feeling a bit wobbly after hi defeat last week.*
wodge /wɒdʒ/ NOUN [*plural* **wodges**] an informa word meaning a thick piece or amount of someth □ *a wodge of papers*
woe /wəʊ/ NOUN [*plural* **woes**]
1 sadness
2 woes the things that make you sad or cause y problems □ *He told me all his woes.*
woeful /ˈwəʊfʊl/ ADJECTIVE
1 very bad and unsuccessful □ *a woeful attempt funny*
2 sad □ *a woeful sigh*
● **woefully** /ˈwəʊfʊlɪ/ ADVERB
1 used to emphasize how bad or unsuccessful something is □ *The building is woefully inadequ*
2 in an unhappy way □ *She stared woefully at* mess.
wok /wɒk/ NOUN [*plural* **woks**] a type of large shaped like a bowl, used to cook food in a Chinese
woke /wəʊk/ PAST TENSE OF **wake**
woken /ˈwəʊkən/ PAST PARTICIPLE OF **wake**
wolf /wʊlf/ NOUN [*plural* **wolves**] a wild animal large dog
◆ PHRASAL VERB [**wolfs, wolfing, wolfed**] **wolf**

something down to eat something very quickly because you are very hungry

woman /'wumən/ NOUN [plural **women**] an adult female person □ *There were three other women in the office.*

womanhood /'wumənhud/ NOUN, NO PLURAL the state of being a woman □ *When they reach womanhood, they are expected to marry.*

womanly /'wumənlɪ/ ADJECTIVE having the qualities that people expect a woman to have

womb /wu:m/ NOUN [plural **wombs**] the organ inside a woman's or female animal's body where her babies grow. A biology word.

wombat /'wɒmbæt/ NOUN [plural **wombats**] an Australian animal like a small bear

won /wʌn/ PAST TENSE AND PAST PARTICIPLE OF win

wonder /'wʌndə(r)/ ▶ VERB [wonders, wondering, wondered]

to want to know something □ + *question word* / *I wonder what Jack has bought me for Christmas.* □ *I wonder whether Susie is coming?*

used to ask someone something in a polite way □ *I wonder if you could tell me where the post office is?* □ *I was wondering if you would like to have dinner with me?*

NOUN [plural **wonders**]

no plural a feeling of great admiration and surprise □ *The comet filled people who saw it with wonder.* □ *We stared in wonder at the castle.*

something that makes you feel admiration and surprise □ *Now we can keep in touch all the time, with the wonders of modern technology.*

no wonder used to say that something does not surprise you □ *It's no wonder she gets cross if you have like that.*

wonderful /'wʌndəful/ ADJECTIVE extremely good □ *We had a wonderful view of the mountains.* □ *This is a wonderful opportunity for her.*

wonderfully /'wʌndəfulɪ/ ADVERB in a wonderful way □ *They played wonderfully well.*

wondrous /'wʌndrəs/ ADJECTIVE if something is wondrous, you like and admire it very much □ *a wondrous sight*

wonky /'wɒŋkɪ/ ADJECTIVE [wonkier, wonkiest] an informal word meaning not level or firm □ *Is that table ? It looks a bit wonky.*

won't /wəunt/ a short way to say and write will not □ *He won't tell me what he saw.*

woo /wu:/ VERB [woos, wooing, wooed] to try to persuade someone to support you or to buy something from you □ *The policy was intended to woo young voters.*

wood /wud/ NOUN [plural **woods**]

the hard substance that trees are made of □ *a piece of wood* □ *a wood floor* □ *They were chopping wood for the fire.*

2 also **woods** an area where a lot of trees grow closely together □ *We went for a walk in the woods.*

• **wooded** /'wudɪd/ ADJECTIVE a wooded area has trees growing on it

• **wooden** /'wudən/ ADJECTIVE

1 made of wood □ *wooden toys* □ *a wooden chair*

2 a wooden actor does not look natural and does not express enough emotion

woodland /'wudlənd/ NOUN [plural **woodlands**] land covered with trees

woodlouse /'wudlaus/ NOUN [plural **woodlice**] an insect that lives in rotten wood or slightly wet areas

woodpecker /'wud,pekə(r)/ NOUN [plural **woodpeckers**] a bird that uses its beak to make holes in trees

woodwind /'wudwɪnd/ NOUN, NO PLURAL the group of musical instruments that you play by blowing, for example flutes and clarinets

woodwork /'wudwɜ:k/ NOUN, NO PLURAL

1 the activity of making things from wood

2 the parts of a building that are made from wood

woodworm /'wudwɜ:m/ NOUN [plural **woodworm**] an insect that eats wood, or the damage that it causes

woody /'wudɪ/ ADJECTIVE [woodier, woodiest]

1 covered with trees

2 woody plants have a thick, hard stem

woof /wuf/ NOUN [plural **woofs**] the sound that a dog makes

wool /wul/ NOUN, NO PLURAL cloth or thread made from the hair of sheep 🔲 *a ball of wool* □ *a wool coat*

♦ IDIOM pull the wool over someone's eyes to trick someone

• **woollen** /'wulən/ ADJECTIVE made of wool □ *a woollen blanket*

• **woolly** /'wulɪ/ ADJECTIVE [woollier, woolliest] made of wool or a material similar to wool □ *a woolly hat*

woolen /'wulən/ ADJECTIVE the US spelling of woollen

• **wooly** /'wulɪ/ ADJECTIVE the US spelling of woolly

word /wɜ:d/ ▶ NOUN [plural **words**]

1 a unit of language that is written as a group of letters with spaces on either side □ *She asked me how to pronounce the word 'catastrophe'.* □ *He always uses lots of long words.*

2 words something that someone says □ *What were her exact words?* 🔲 *Tell us what happened in your own words.* 🔲 *Her last words were 'Always believe.'*

3 no plural a short conversation 🔲 *I'll have a word with my Dad and see if we can borrow the car.* 🔲 *I want a word with you.*

4 no plural a promise 🔲 *He gave me his word that he would be there.* 🔲 *I will always keep my word.*

5 no plural news or information about someone or something □ *Have you had any word of Danielle since she left?* □ + *from* *There's been no word from Suki.* 🔲 *We're having a party. Can you spread the word (=tell everyone)?*

6 in other words used when you say something in a

different way in order to explain it □ *Our expenditure is exceeding our income at the moment. In other words, we need more money.*

7 not believe/understand, etc. a word to not believe/understand, etc. any of what is said or written □ *I couldn't hear a word of what he was saying.* □ *She doesn't speak a word of English.*

8 take someone's word for it to believe what someone says about something □ *The movie's great, but you don't have to take my word for it - go and see it yourself.*

9 a word of advice/warning, etc. something that someone says to advise/warn, etc. you about something □ *Let me give you a word of advice - don't believe everything she tells you.*

10 word for word using exactly the same words □ *He copied the essay word for word from the Internet.*

▶ VERB [**words, wording, worded**] to choose particular words to express something □ *I wrote him a strongly worded letter of complaint.*

● **wording** /'wɜːdɪŋ/ NOUN, NO PLURAL the words that are used to express something □ *We argued about the precise wording of the letter.*

word-perfect /'wɜːd'pɜːfɪkt/ ADJECTIVE able to say something you have learnt, such as your part in a play, without any mistakes

word processing /'wɜːd 'prəʊsesɪŋ/ NOUN, NO PLURAL using a word processor to write documents

● **word processor** /'wɜːd 'prəʊsesə(r)/ NOUN [*plural* **word processors**] software or a computer that you use for writing documents

wordy /'wɜːdɪ/ ADJECTIVE [**wordier, wordiest**] using too many words □ *a wordy reply*

wore /wɔː(r)/ PAST TENSE OF wear

work /wɜːk/ ▶ VERB [**works, working, worked**]

1 to do something that needs effort or energy □ **+ on** *She's working on another novel.* □ **+ to do something** *We have been working to improve awareness of homelessness.* ⌨ *We all need to work hard to make this event a success.*

2 to have a job that you are paid to do □ **+ for** *He works for a shipping company.* □ **+ as** *I was working as a nurse at the time.*

3 to operate correctly □ *My e-mail isn't working at the moment.*

4 to be successful or effective □ *The new treatment seems to be working.* ⌨ *Our plan to trick him worked well.*

5 to operate a machine or a piece of equipment □ *I don't know how to work the heating.*

6 to gradually move into a different position ⌨ *These tiny particles can work their way into your lungs.* ⌨ *All the knots had begun to work loose.*

7 work your way to achieve something gradually □ *He worked his way up to the position of chairman.* □ *They have worked their way back into the competition.*

◆ PHRASAL VERBS **work at something** to try to improve something □ *I'm working at staying calm.*

work off something to get rid of something such as an emotion or food you have eaten □ *I went for a walk to work off my lunch.* **work on something** to try to improve something □ *He needs to work on his spoken English.* **work out 1** if a plan or a situation works out, it is successful □ *I hope everything works out for you.* **2** to end in a particular way □ *The arrangement worked out well for me.* **3** to do exercise to make your body stronger □ *I work out four times a week.* **work something out 1** to be able to understand something or make a decision about something □ **+ question word** *There was a message on the back, but I couldn't work out what it said.* □ *worked out how to put the tent up.* **2** to calculate something □ *I've worked out how much tax I owe.* □ *The doctors have worked out the correct dose for me.* **work out at something** to be the result of a calculation □ *The cost works out at £150 per person.* **work up something** to create something, especially a feeling □ *I can't work up the enthusiasm to phone him.* □ *Let's go for a walk to work up a bit of appetite.* **work up to something** to gradually prepare yourself to do something difficult □ *It took me over two years to work up to running a marathon.*

▶ NOUN [*plural* **works**]

1 *no plural* an activity that needs effort ⌨ *It was hard work clearing up after the party.* ⌨ *There's still a lot of work to do before the website will be ready.*

2 *no plural* someone's job, or the place they go to for it ⌨ *I go to work at 8.* □ *I usually go to the gym before work.* □ *My work involves talking to doctors.*

3 *no plural* the things that you create or do when you are working □ *I've done a lot of work with young people.* □ *Hand your work in to the teacher.*

4 something produced by an artist, musician, writer etc. □ *Her early works are quite different.*

5 get/set to work to start working □ *We set to work on the garden.*

● **workable** /'wɜːkəbəl/ ADJECTIVE a workable system or plan is practical and will be effective

workbench /'wɜːkbentʃ/ NOUN [*plural* **workbenches**] a table where you work with tools

workbook /'wɜːkbʊk/ NOUN [*plural* **workbooks**] a book for students which has questions, and space to write the answers

worked-up /'wɜːkt'ʌp/ ADJECTIVE very excited or upset

worker /'wɜːkə(r)/ NOUN [*plural* **workers**]

1 someone who works for a company or organization but who is not a manager □ *steel workers*

2 someone who works in a particular way □ *a good worker*

workforce /'wɜːkfɔːs/ NOUN, NO PLURAL all the people who work in a country or in a particular company

working /'wɜːkɪŋ/ ▶ ADJECTIVE

1 to do with your job ⌨ *They campaigned for*

working conditions. 🔄 He'd spent his whole working life in the same job. 🔄 He wanted to reduce his working hours.

2 having a job □ working mothers

3 a working knowledge of something a basic knowledge of something which is enough for you to do something effectively □ She had acquired a working knowledge of most European languages.

4 in working order working correctly, and not broken □ The clock isn't in working order.

▶ NOUN

1 no plural a particular way of working □ Parents of young children are allowed to request flexible working.

2 workings the way in which something works □ She tried to explain to me the mysterious workings of the stock market.

working class /'wɜːkɪŋ 'klɑːs/ ▶ NOUN [plural working classes] the social class that consists mainly of people who do physical work and do not have much money

▶ ADJECTIVE to do with the working class □ working class families

workload /'wɜːkləʊd/ NOUN [plural workloads] the amount of work that you have to do □ The workload of most teachers has increased.

workman /'wɜːkmən/ NOUN [plural workmen] a man who does work such as building or repairing things

workmanship /'wɜːkmənʃɪp/ NOUN, NO PLURAL the skill that is used for making something □ The workmanship was poor.

workmate /'wɜːkmeɪt/ NOUN [plural workmates] someone who you work with

work of art NOUN [plural works of art] something which an artist has painted or made □ The gallery houses the country's best-known works of art.

workout /'wɜːkaʊt/ NOUN [plural workouts] an occasion when you do exercises to make you stronger

work permit /'wɜːk 'pɜːmɪt/ NOUN [plural work permits] a document that gives you the right to work in a country

workplace /'wɜːkpleɪs/ NOUN [plural workplaces] a building or room where people work

workshop /'wɜːkʃɒp/ NOUN [plural workshops]

1 a meeting to learn more about something by discussing it and doing practical exercises □ a drama workshop

2 a place where things are built or repaired

workstation /'wɜːkˌsteɪʃən/ NOUN [plural workstations] a computer and the desk and area around it in an office

work surface or **worktop** /'wɜːktɒp/ NOUN [plural work surfaces or worktops] a flat surface in a kitchen for working on

world /wɜːld/ ▶ NOUN [plural worlds]

1 the world the Earth or all the people living on it □ He is the tallest man in the world. □ The whole world is affected by global warming. □ He longed to

travel the world. □ She really wants to change the world.

2 the people and things involved in a particular activity □ He is famous in the world of antiques.

3 an area of the world or a group of countries with a particular characteristic □ the Arab world □ Many of the goods we import are from the developing world.

4 a planet □ a creature from another world

5 a life or a place that has been invented □ His stories take us to a mysterious world of talking animals. 🔄 You're living in a fantasy world.

◆ IDIOM out of this world of extremely good quality □ The cream cakes are out of this world.

▶ ADJECTIVE relating to the whole world □ world peace □ a world record

world-class /'wɜːld'klɑːs/ ADJECTIVE being one of the best in the world □ world-class tennis players

world-famous /'wɜːld'feɪməs/ ADJECTIVE famous in many parts of the world □ a world-famous writer

worldly /'wɜːldlɪ/ ADJECTIVE [worldlier, worldliest]

1 a worldly person has a lot of experience of life

2 your worldly goods/possessions everything that you own

worldwide /'wɜːldwaɪd/ ADJECTIVE, ADVERB everywhere in the world □ The incident attracted worldwide attention. □ The virus has killed 144 people worldwide.

World Wide Web /'wɜːld waɪd 'web/ NOUN, NO PLURAL all the websites that exist on the Internet

worm /wɜːm/ ▶ NOUN [plural worms] a long, thin, soft creature with no bones or legs which lives in soil

▶ VERB [worms, worming, wormed] worm your way into something a disapproving phrase meaning to get into a situation by gradually making people like and trust you □ She had wormed her way into the job.

◆ PHRASAL VERB worm something out of someone to persuade someone to tell you something

worn /wɔːn/ ▶ PAST PARTICIPLE OF wear

▶ ADJECTIVE old and slightly damaged □ The carpet is worn and dirty.

worn-out /'wɔːn'aʊt/ ADJECTIVE

1 very tired

2 too old or damaged to use □ worn-out trousers

worried /'wʌrɪd/ ADJECTIVE thinking a lot about problems or bad things that could happen □ + about I'm worried about what will happen if I fail my exams. □ + that He was worried that Amy wouldn't like him. 🔄 She's worried sick about her son.

● **worrier** /'wʌrɪə(r)/ NOUN [plural worriers] a person who worries a lot

worry /'wʌrɪ/ ▶ VERB [worries, worrying, worried]

1 to keep thinking about a problem or something bad that might happen □ + about A lot of young people worry about the future. □ + that She worried that her children might be unhappy.

2 to make someone feel worried 🔄 It worries me that I might not be able to find a job.

3 Don't worry (a) said when trying to make someone

feel less worried □ *Don't worry. I'm sure things will improve.* (b) used to tell someone that they do not need to do something □ *Don't worry about getting the milk. I can get it on my way home from school.*

▶ NOUN [plural **worries**]

1 something that makes you worried ▣ *Lack of money is a real worry at the moment.*

2 *no plural* the feeling of being worried □ *Some medical tests can lead to unnecessary worry or anxiety.*

• **worrying** /ˈwʌrɪɪŋ/ ADJECTIVE making you feel worried □ *a worrying development*

• **worryingly** /ˈwʌrɪɪŋlɪ/ ADVERB □ *in a way that is worrying* □ *Water supplies are worryingly low.*

worse /wɜːs/ ▶ ADJECTIVE

1 of a lower standard, or more unpleasant ▣ *The situation will get worse.* □ **+ than** *The damage was worse than expected.*

2 more ill □ *I felt worse yesterday.*

▶ ADVERB

1 more badly, or more severely □ **+ than** *His headache had returned worse than ever.*

2 not as well □ **+ than** *Some of the children were treated worse than others.*

▶ NOUN, NO PLURAL

1 something more unpleasant □ *Worse was still to come.*

2 **for the worse** if a situation changes for the worse, it becomes more difficult or more unpleasant □ *He warned that things could change for the worse.*

• **worsen** /ˈwɜːsən/ VERB [**worsens, worsening, worsened**] to become worse, or to make something become worse □ *Increased traffic jams will worsen pollution.* □ *The situation is likely to worsen.*

worse off /ˈwɜːs ˈɒf/ ADJECTIVE

1 poorer or in a worse situation □ *Students are worse off than they were ten years ago.*

2 in a worse situation □ *You'd be even worse off without your car.*

worship /ˈwɜːʃɪp/ ▶ VERB [**worships, worshipping, worshipped**]

1 to show respect for a god by praying, having religious ceremonies, etc.

2 to admire someone so much that you do not see their faults

▶ NOUN, NO PLURAL religious services and other ways of worshipping ▣ *a place of worship* (=a church, mosque, etc.)

• **worshipper** /ˈwɜːʃɪpə(r)/ NOUN [plural **worshippers**] someone who is worshipping in a religious building

worst /wɜːst/ ▶ ADJECTIVE **the worst** most severe, most unpleasant, or most difficult □ *It was the worst storm we'd ever seen.*

▶ ADVERB most badly □ *I scored worst in the test.* □ *The area worst affected by the floods was the North.*

▶ NOUN

1 **the worst** the person or thing that is worse than all the others □ *I've had some pretty bad exams but this was the worst.*

2 **at (the) worst** used for saying what the most unpleasant or difficult situation would be □ *At worst, you might have to wait an hour for the bus.*

3 **if the worst comes to the worst** if a situation develops in the most unpleasant or difficult way □ *If the worst comes to the worst, I'll just have to work at the weekend too.*

worst-case /ˈwɜːstˈkeɪs/ ADJECTIVE **worst-case scenario** the worst thing that could possibly happen in a situation □ *The worst-case scenario is that we lose our home.*

worth /wɜːθ/ ▶ ADJECTIVE

1 having a particular value □ *The ring is worth £100.*

2 used for saying that something is useful, important or enjoyable □ *The museum is worth a visit.* □ **+ ing** *It would be worth asking a solicitor for advice.* ▣ *The project was hard work but it was worth it.*

▶ NOUN, NO PLURAL

1 **£10/$50, etc. worth of something** an amount of something that costs £10/$50, etc. to buy □ *About £10,000 worth of jewellery was stolen in the robbery.*

2 **a week's/a month's, etc. worth of something** an amount for a week/month, etc. □ *A month's worth of rain fell in less than 24 hours.*

3 how useful someone or something is ▣ *Since joining the team, he has proved his worth.*

• **worthless** /ˈwɜːθlɪs/ ADJECTIVE

1 not important or not useful □ *He felt worthless.*

2 having no financial value □ *The necklace is worthless.*

worthwhile /ˌwɜːθˈwaɪl/ ADJECTIVE if something is worthwhile, it is useful or enjoyable although you have to spend time or effort doing it □ *a worthwhile project*

worthy /ˈwɜːðɪ/ ADJECTIVE [**worthier, worthiest**]

1 deserving respect or support □ *The German team were worthy winners.* ▣ *She gives a lot of money to worthy causes.*

2 **be worthy of something** a formal phrase meaning to deserve something □ *The offer is certainly worthy of consideration.*

would /wʊd/ MODAL VERB

1 used to say what might happen in a particular situation □ *What would you do if you won a million dollars?* □ *What would happen if there was a fire?*

2 used as the past tense of will to talk about what is going to happen □ *I didn't think she would agree.* □ *I said he would come later.*

3 used as the past tense of will to talk about when someone or something was willing or able to do something □ *My camera wouldn't work.* □ *She wouldn't help me.*

4 used for talking about what you think is true, or what you think the reason for something is □ *You would find it very hard to get another job.* □ *It would be difficult to manage without a car.* □ *Why would I want to hurt them?*

5 would you used in polite questions and offers □ *Would you like a drink?* □ *Would you mind helping me with these boxes?*
6 would like/prefer, etc. used to say what you want or what you want to do □ *I would like to see a different doctor.* □ *I would really like a hot shower.*

would-be /'wʊdbi:/ ADJECTIVE describes what people would like to be or become □ *a group of would-be astronauts*

wouldn't /'wʊdənt/ a short way to say and write would not □ *She wouldn't go.*

would've /'wʊdəv/ a short way to say and write would have □ *It would've been nice to see her.*

wound¹ /waʊnd/ PAST TENSE AND PAST PARTICIPLE OF wind

wound² /wu:nd/ ► NOUN [plural **wounds**]
an injury, especially where the skin is broken □ *gunshot wounds*
harm to someone's emotions, a relationship, etc. □ *The party has tried to heal the wounds caused by the leadership contest.*
► VERB [**wounds, wounding, wounded**]
to injure a person or an animal, especially in a way that breaks their skin □ *She was seriously wounded in the attack.*
to make someone feel very upset □ *He was deeply wounded by the criticism of his work.*

wounded /'wu:ndɪd/ ADJECTIVE a wounded soldier or animal has been injured

wove /wəʊv/ PAST TENSE OF weave

woven /'wəʊvən/ PAST PARTICIPLE OF weave

wow /waʊ/ EXCLAMATION an informal word used to express surprise or admiration □ *Wow! You look great!*

WPC /,dʌbəlju:pi:'si:/ ABBREVIATION woman police officer; used before a female police officer's name □ *WPC Hobbs*

wrangle /'ræŋgəl/ ► VERB [**wrangles, wrangling, wrangled**] to argue with someone for a long time, often about something complicated □ *They're still wrangling over the divorce settlement.*
► NOUN [plural **wrangles**] an argument that goes on for a long time, often about something complicated □ *The club faces a legal wrangle over the sale of its ground.*

wrap /ræp/ VERB [**wraps, wrapping, wrapped**] to cover something by putting paper or another material around it □ *Would you like the chocolates wrapped?* □ *We wrapped all the glasses in tissue paper.*
• PHRASAL VERBS **wrap something around/round something 1** to put something such as paper or cloth around something to cover it □ *I wrapped an old blanket around the wound.* **2** if you wrap your arms, fingers or legs around something, you put them tightly around it **wrap up** to put on warm clothes □ *Make sure you wrap up warm.* **wrap something up** to cover something with paper or another material, especially a present □ *We wrapped up the toys.*

2 to finish an activity □ *We need to wrap up the meeting now.* **3 be wrapped up in something** to give a lot of attention to something, so that you do not have time for other things
• **wrapper** /'ræpə(r)/ NOUN [plural **wrappers**] a piece of paper or other material that something is wrapped in □ *sweet wrappers*

wrapping paper /'ræpɪŋ 'peɪpə(r)/ NOUN, NO PLURAL decorated paper used for wrapping presents

wrath /rɒθ/ NOUN, NO PLURAL a formal word meaning great anger

wreak /ri:k/ VERB [**wreaks, wreaking, wreaked**] to cause a lot of damage or harm □ *Rabbits can wreak havoc in your garden.*

wreath /ri:θ/ NOUN [plural **wreaths**] an arrangement of flowers and leaves in the shape of a ring, used as a decoration at Christmas or for a coffin (=container someone is buried in) or grave (=place someone is buried)

wreathe /ri:ð/ VERB [**wreathes, wreathing, wreathed**]
1 if something is wreathed in smoke, mist (=very small drops of water in the air), etc., it is surrounded by it
2 if someone is wreathed in smiles, they are smiling a lot

wreck /rek/ ► VERB [**wrecks, wrecking, wrecked**]
1 to destroy or badly damage something □ *He wrecked all our new furniture.* □ *A knee injury has wrecked his chance of playing in the final.*
2 if a ship is wrecked, it is damaged and sinks
► NOUN [plural **wrecks**]
1 a ship that has sunk
2 a badly damaged vehicle that has crashed
3 someone who looks or feels very tired and untidy
• **wreckage** /'rekɪdʒ/ NOUN, NO PLURAL the damaged pieces left after a vehicle has been wrecked □ *He was trapped in the wreckage for over an hour.*

wren /ren/ NOUN [plural **wrens**] a small bird with brown feathers and a short tail

wrench /rentʃ/ ► VERB [**wrenches, wrenching, wrenched**]
1 to pull or twist something very hard so that it comes out of its position □ *I managed to wrench the knife out of his hand.*
2 to hurt part of your body by twisting it □ *He fell and wrenched his ankle.*
► NOUN [plural **wrenches**]
1 when you feel sad because you must leave something or someone you like or love □ *Leaving Cambridge was a real wrench.*
2 a hard pull or twist
3 a tool used to turn things

wrestle /'resəl/ VERB [**wrestles, wrestling, wrestled**] to fight with someone by holding them and trying to throw them to the ground
• PHRASAL VERB **wrestle with something** to try to deal with a difficult problem, situation or emotion

□ *Some football clubs are still wrestling with the issue of racism.*

• **wrestler** /ˈreslə(r)/ NOUN [*plural* **wrestlers**]
someone who wrestles as a sport

• **wrestling** /ˈreslɪŋ/ NOUN, NO PLURAL the sport of fighting by holding someone and trying to throw them to the ground

wretch /retʃ/ NOUN [*plural* **wretches**] someone you feel sorry for because they are having problems □ *The poor wretch did not even own a pair of shoes.*

• **wretched** /ˈretʃɪd/ ADJECTIVE
1 annoying □ *Where's that wretched cat?*
2 very unpleasant or of bad quality □ *It was a wretched start to the day.*
3 very unhappy or ill □ *I felt wretched, knowing I had let her down.*

wriggle /ˈrɪgəl/ VERB [**wriggles, wriggling, wriggled**]
to make short, twisting movements □ *Stop wriggling about in your chair and sit still!*

♦ PHRASAL VERB **wriggle out of something** to avoid doing something you should do □ *She managed to wriggle out of the cooking.*

wring /rɪŋ/ VERB [**wrings, wringing, wrung**]
1 to twist a wet cloth or piece of clothing so that most of the water is forced out
2 **wring your hands** to twist your hands together because you are upset or nervous
3 **wring someone's neck** if you say you will wring someone's neck, you mean that you are very angry with them and want to punish them

wrinkle /ˈrɪŋkəl/ ▶ NOUN [*plural* **wrinkles**]
1 a line in your skin, caused by getting older
2 a line where something such as a piece of cloth is slightly folded
▶ VERB [**wrinkles, wrinkling, wrinkled**] to move part of your face, especially your nose, so that lines appear on your skin

• **wrinkly** /ˈrɪŋklɪ/ ADJECTIVE [**wrinklier, wrinkliest**]
having a lot of wrinkles

wrist /rɪst/ NOUN [*plural* **wrists**] the part of your body where your arm joins your hand

wristband /ˈrɪstbænd/ NOUN [*plural* **wristbands**]
1 a piece of thick material that you wear around your wrist when you play sport
2 a thin piece of material, usually plastic, that you wear around your wrist to show that you have particular opinions or support a particular person or group of people with problems

wristwatch /ˈrɪstwɒtʃ/ NOUN [*plural* **wristwatches**] a watch that you wear on your wrist

write /raɪt/ VERB [**writes, writing, wrote, written**]
1 to form letters, words or numbers, usually on paper using a pen or pencil □ *Write your name and address on the top of the paper.*
2 to use words to make a story, essay, book, letter, song, etc. □ *She has written four novels.* □ *I wrote a note and left it on the table,* □ *+ about She writes about gardening.*
3 to send a letter or a message to someone □ *+ to I*

wrote to the manager to complain. □ *We'll write in a week or two.*
4 if you write music, you put the symbols for the notes on special paper □ *He wrote his second symphony when he was fifteen.*
5 if you write a computer program, you create it

♦ PHRASAL VERBS **write something down** to write something on a piece of paper, especially so that you do not forget it □ *I wrote down his phone number.* **write off** to write to an organization in order to get something from it □ *We wrote off for tickets.* **write something/someone off** to think that something or someone is not useful or successful □ *When you get to fifty, most employers just write you off.* **write something off 1** to say officially that an amount money does not have to be paid or will not be paid □ *The company had to write off large debts.* **2** to damage a vehicle so badly that it cannot be used aga **write something up** to write an article, a report etc. using notes that you have made □ *We have to write up the results of our experiments.*

write-off /ˈraɪtɒf/ NOUN [*plural* **write-offs**] a vehi that has been so badly damaged in an accident that cannot be repaired

writer /ˈraɪtə(r)/ NOUN [*plural* **writers**]
1 someone who writes books, plays, newspaper articles, etc. as a job
2 someone who has written something

write-up /ˈraɪtʌp/ NOUN [*plural* **write-ups**] an article in a newspaper, magazine, etc. about someth such as a new performance, product, etc. □ *The Evening Herald gave the show an enthusiastic write-up.*

writhe /raɪð/ VERB [**writhes, writhing, writhed**] t twist your body because you feel uncomfortable o pain □ *He lay writhing in agony.*

writing /ˈraɪtɪŋ/ NOUN [*plural* **writings**]
1 the forming of letters and words on paper or o surfaces so that they can be read
2 your writing is the way you write
3 the things that a writer has written

writing paper /ˈraɪtɪŋ ˈpeɪpə(r)/ NOUN, NO PLU good quality paper for writing letters on

written /ˈrɪtən/ ▶ PAST PARTICIPLE OF **write**
▶ ADJECTIVE
1 using writing □ *He received a written warning.*
2 a written exam is one in which you have to w something

wrong /rɒŋ/ ▶ ADJECTIVE
1 if something is wrong, there is a problem □ *+ w there something wrong with David? He doesn't l happy.* □ *What's wrong? I thought you'd be pleas see me.*
2 not correct □ *That was the wrong answer.* □ made the wrong decision. □ *You're looking in th wrong place.* □ *+ about He was wrong about l*
3 not morally right □ *She has done nothing wr*

□ **+ to do something** *It would be wrong to deceive him.*
4 not suitable □ **+ with** *If you want flowers, what's wrong with roses?* □ **+ for** *The dress was wrong for a wedding.*
▶ IDIOM **get (hold of) the wrong end of the stick** to think that something is true when it is not □ *I think you've got the wrong end of the stick - you don't need to pay any extra.*
▶ ADVERB
1 in a way that is not correct □ *I think I have spelt your name wrong.* □ *He guessed wrong.*
2 **go wrong** (a) to stop working correctly □ *My watch has gone wrong.* (b) to stop being successful □ *Everything went wrong after Nik left.*
▶ NOUN, NO PLURAL
behaviour that is not morally correct 🗗 *He doesn't seem to know the difference between right and wrong.* □ *I accept that I did wrong.*

2 be in the wrong to be the person who is responsible for a mistake or doing something bad □ *The way she tells it, you'd think it was us that were in the wrong.*
● **wrongdoing** /ˈrɒŋˌduːɪŋ/ NOUN, NO PLURAL bad or illegal behaviour 🗗 *He denied any wrongdoing.*
● **wrongful** /ˈrɒŋful/ ADJECTIVE not correct, especially because of being unfair or illegal □ *He spent three years in jail following his wrongful conviction for murder.*
● **wrongly** /ˈrɒŋlɪ/ ADVERB not correctly □ *The plug had been fitted wrongly so the machine did not work.* □ *She was wrongly accused of fraud.*

wrote /rəʊt/ PAST TENSE OF write
wrung /rʌŋ/ PAST TENSE AND PAST PARTICIPLE OF wring
wry /raɪ/ ADJECTIVE [**wryer, wryest**] showing that you think a bad situation is slightly funny too □ *a wry smile* □ *a wry comment*
WWW /ˌdʌbəljuːdʌbəljuːˈdʌbəljuː/ or www ABBREVIATION World Wide Web; the Internet

X or **X** /eks/
1 the 24th letter of the alphabet
2 used when you do not know or do not want to say the name of a person or thing □ *The man was referred to as Mr X.*
3 used for representing a number or quantity that is not known. A maths word.
4 used for representing a kiss at the end of a letter

xenophobia /ˌzenəˈfəʊbɪə/ NOUN, NO PLURAL a dislike of foreign people and things

Xerox /ˈzɪərɒks/ ► NOUN [*plural* **Xeroxes**] a copy of a document made with a Xerox machine. A trademark.
► VERB [**Xeroxes, Xeroxing, Xeroxed**] to make a copy of a document with a Xerox machine

Xmas /ˈeksməs/ NOUN an informal short way of writing Christmas

XML /ˌeksemˈel/ ABBREVIATION extensible mark up language; a way of organizing information on a computer which makes the information easy to use different programs. A computing word.

X-ray /ˈeksreɪ/ ► NOUN [*plural* **X-rays**] a special ki of photograph that shows the inside parts of someone's body
► VERB [**X-rays, X-raying, X-rayed**] to make a pict of the inside of someone's body

xylophone /ˈzaɪləfəʊn/ NOUN [*plural* **xylophones** musical instrument made up of a set of wooden o metal bars that make different notes when you hit them with hammers

Y y

Y or **y** /waɪ/ the 25th letter of the alphabet

yacht /jɒt/ NOUN [plural **yachts**] a boat with sails that you use for racing or for pleasure

yachtsman /'jɒtsmən/ NOUN [plural **yachtsmen**] a man who sails a yacht

yachtswoman /'jɒts,wʊmən/ NOUN [plural **yachtswomen**] a woman who sails a yacht

yak /jæk/ NOUN [plural **yaks**] an animal like a cow with long hair and horns

yam /jæm/ NOUN [plural **yams**] a vegetable like a potato that grows in tropical countries

Yank /jæŋk/ NOUN [plural **Yanks**] an informal and slightly offensive word for someone from the United States

yank /jæŋk/ VERB [**yanks, yanking, yanked**] to suddenly pull something hard □ He yanked the book out of my hand.

yap /jæp/ ▶ VERB [**yaps, yapping, yapped**] if a dog yaps, it makes a quick, high sound
▶ NOUN [plural **yaps**] a quick, high sound that a dog makes

yard¹ /jɑːd/ NOUN [plural **yards**] a unit for measuring length, equal to 3 feet

yard² /jɑːd/ NOUN [plural **yards**]
a an area of land, often with a fence or wall around it, and often used for a particular purpose □ The dogs have a large exercise yard.
b a US word for a garden next to a house

yarn /jɑːn/ NOUN [plural **yarns**]
a thread made from wool, cotton, etc. used for making cloth
b an exciting story, which may not be true □ He told some great yarns about life in the army.

yashmak /'jæʃmæk/ NOUN [plural **yashmaks**] a piece of cloth that some Muslim women use to cover their face

yawn /jɔːn/ ▶ VERB [**yawns, yawning, yawned**] to open your mouth very wide and breathe in, because you are feeling tired or bored
▶ NOUN [plural **yawns**] the sound or action of someone yawning

yawning /'jɔːnɪŋ/ ADJECTIVE a yawning gap (a) a very large hole or place where something is missing □ There are yawning gaps in his knowledge. (b) a very big difference □ the yawning gap between rich and

yeah /jeə/ EXCLAMATION an informal way of saying yes

year /jɪə(r)/ NOUN [plural **years**]
1 a period of 365 or 366 days, marking the length of time it takes for the Earth to go around the sun, especially the period from 1 January to 31 December □ We're going to America next year. □ I spent a year working in Paris. □ In recent years, the building has not been used much.
2 three/sixteen/fifty, etc. years old used to talk about the age of someone or something □ He's only twelve years old. □ Our house is almost three hundred years old.
3 a three/sixteen/fifty year-old a person who is a particular age □ You're acting like a five year-old!
4 the academic/financial, etc. year a period of twelve months used by a particular organization, system, etc.
5 years a long period of time ⊞ I haven't been to Madrid for years.
6 the students at a school, college, etc. who start in the same year □ He was in my year at school. □ We studied the Egyptians in year 3.

> ➤ When saying how old someone is, do not say 'years'. Say only the number or a number + 'years old': □ She is eight.
> ✓ She is eight years old.
> ✗ She is eight years.

• **yearly** /'jɪəlɪ/ ADJECTIVE, ADVERB happening or done every year □ our yearly holiday □ Accounts must be prepared yearly.

yearn /jɜːn/ VERB [**yearns, yearning, yearned**] to want something very much □ As a teenager, I yearned for the big city.

yeast /jiːst/ NOUN, NO PLURAL a substance that is used to make bread rise

yell /jel/ ▶ VERB [**yells, yelling, yelled**] to shout something loudly □ 'Let me go!' she yelled.
▶ NOUN [plural **yells**] a loud shout

yellow /'jeləʊ/ ▶ ADJECTIVE having the colour of the sun or a lemon □ The garden was full of bright yellow flowers.
▶ NOUN [plural **yellows**] the colour of the sun or a lemon

yelp /jelp/ ▶ VERB [**yelps, yelping, yelped**] to make a short, high sound because of pain or excitement
▶ NOUN [*plural* **yelps**] a short, high sound

yes /jes/ EXCLAMATION
1 used to agree with someone, agree to do something, or to give a positive answer □ *'Are these shoes all right?' 'Yes, they're lovely.'* □ *'Could you help me with my homework?' 'Yes, no problem.'* □ *'Would you like a cup of coffee?' 'Yes, please.'*
2 used to disagree with a negative statement □ *'You haven't washed your hair.' 'Yes I have.'*

yesterday /ˈjestədeɪ/ ADVERB, NOUN the day before today □ *I saw Kim yesterday.* □ *He called me yesterday morning.* □ *Yesterday was her birthday.*

yet /jet/ ▶ ADVERB
1 used in questions or negative statements to mean before now or before the time you are talking about □ *Have you read her new book yet?* □ *No money has changed hands yet.* □ *I have not yet had the courage to challenge her.*
2 used in questions and negative statements to mean that something will not happen immediately but will happen in the future □ *Please don't leave yet.* □ *You can't go in yet.*
3 used to emphasize how often something exists or happens 🔂 *Yet again, they have let us down.*
🔂 *Apparently, Richard has bought yet another bicycle.*
4 the best/biggest/worst, etc. yet the best/biggest/worst, etc. that has ever happened or existed
5 used to say that something might happen in the future □ *Don't be too upset - she might yet turn up.*
6 used to show how long it will be until something happens □ *It'll be a few months yet before the new road is open.*
7 be/have yet to do something to have not done something, especially something you were expected to do □ *He has yet to apologize.*
▶ CONJUNCTION used to say something surprising after what has been said before □ *He was pleasant, yet failed to offer any real help.* □ *We claim to live in a civilized society, and yet we allow children to live in poverty.* □ *The decorations were colourful yet tasteful.*

yew /juː/ NOUN [*plural* **yews**] a tree with very dark green leaves, or the wood from this tree

Y-fronts /ˈwaɪfrʌntz/ PLURAL NOUN a piece of underwear for men and boys that covers the bottom and has a Y-shaped opening at the front. A trademark.

yield /jiːld/ ▶ VERB [**yields, yielding, yielded**]
1 to produce something useful □ *Negotiations have failed to yield results.* □ *The investment yielded a good profit.*
2 to produce a particular amount of a crop
3 to be forced to do something or agree to something, or to be defeated □ *The government yielded to pressure and delayed the tax rise.* □ *The army yielded to enemy forces.*
▶ NOUN [*plural* **yields**] the amount of something that

is produced □ *Farmers want cows with a high milk yield.*

yippee /jɪˈpiː/ EXCLAMATION a word that children use when they are pleased or excited about something

yob /jɒb/ NOUN [*plural* **yobs**] a young man who behaves in a rude and sometimes violent way

yoga /ˈjəʊɡə/ NOUN, NO PLURAL a type of exercise for the body and the mind, which involves stretching you body and doing breathing exercises

yogurt *or* **yoghurt** /ˈjɒɡət/ NOUN [*plural* **yogurts** o **yoghurts**] a thick, slightly sour liquid made from mil often with fruit added 🔂 *natural yoghurt (=with no sugar or fruit added)*

yolk /jəʊk/ NOUN [*plural* **yolks**] the yellow part in th middle of an egg

Yom Kippur /ˌjɒmkɪˈpʊə(r)/ NOUN, NO PLURAL a Jewish religious day when people do not eat or drin

yonder /ˈjɒndə(r)/ ADVERB, DETERMINER an old-fashioned word meaning in or towards a place far away from you □ *Take my sword, and go with it to yonder river.*

you /juː/ PRONOUN used to talk or write about th person or people that you are talking to □ *Do you l pizza?* □ *I'll ring you tomorrow night.* □ *Max is tall than you.*

you'd /juːd/ a short way to say and write you had you would □ *You'd better be careful.* □ *You'd be so if she left.*

you'll /juːl/ a short way to say and write you will □ *You'll never guess what happened next!*

young /jʌŋ/ ▶ ADJECTIVE [**younger, youngest**] n old □ *a young boy* □ *You're too young to stay up so l*
▶ PLURAL NOUN
1 the babies that an animal or bird has □ *a sparr feeding its young*
2 the young young people
• **youngster** /ˈjʌŋstə(r)/ NOUN [*plural* **youngster** young person

your /jɔː(r)/ DETERMINER
1 belonging to or to do with you □ *Can I borrow pen?*
2 belonging to or to do with people in general □ *school days are the happiest days of your life.*

you're /jɔː(r)/ a short way to say and write you □ *You're early!*

yours /jɔːz/ PRONOUN
1 used to talk or write about things belonging to do with the person or people you are talking to □ *Which glass is yours?*
2 used at the end of a letter, before your name *look forward to hearing from you. Yours, Amy.*

yourself /jɔːˈself/ PRONOUN [*plural* **yourselve**
1 the reflexive form of you □ *Careful you don't yourself on that knife.* □ *You'll have to dry your on your T-shirts.*
2 used to show that you do something withou'

help from other people □ *Did you really make that skirt yourself?* ⌑ *Have you done this work all by yourself?*
3 used to emphasize the pronoun *you* □ *You cannot film it yourselves, but you can buy a video.*
4 by yourself not with or near other people □ *It can be lonely living by yourself.*
5 to yourself without having to share with anyone else □ *You've got the house to yourself today.*

---

youth /juːθ/ NOUN [*plural* **youths**]
1 a young man □ *a gang of youths*
2 *no plural* the time in your life when you are young □ *She spent most of her youth abroad.*
3 *no plural* young people □ *the youth of today*

---

youth club /ˈjuːθ klʌb/ NOUN [*plural* **youth clubs**] a place where young people go for social activities

youthful /ˈjuːθfʊl/ ADJECTIVE typical of young people or seeming young □ *youthful energy*

youth hostel /ˈjuːθ ˈhɒstəl/ NOUN [*plural* **youth hostels**] a simple, quite cheap hotel for travellers, especially young people

you've /juːv/ a short way to say and write you have □ *You've left the door open again.*

yo-yo /ˈjəʊjəʊ/ NOUN [*plural* **yo-yos**] a small, round toy that goes up and down a piece of string

yummy /ˈjʌmɪ/ ADJECTIVE yummy food tastes very good. An informal word.

yuppie *or* **yuppy** /ˈjʌpɪ/ NOUN [*plural* **yuppies**] a disapproving word for someone who has a good job, is young, and has a high standard of life □ *Then came the yuppies with their designer ski wear and new fast cars.*

Zz

Z or **z** /zed/ the 26th letter of the alphabet

zany /'zeɪnɪ/ ADJECTIVE [zanier, zaniest] funny and unusual □ *She's full of zany ideas.*

zap /zæp/ VERB [zaps, zapping, zapped]
1 to destroy something quickly, often with a weapon □ *The game involves zapping aliens.*
2 to move quickly between television programmes using a remote control (=device you hold in your hand to change programmes) □ *She zapped to Channel One.*

zeal /ziːl/ NOUN, NO PLURAL great enthusiasm □ *The government is attacking poverty with zeal.*
• **zealous** /'zeləs/ ADJECTIVE very enthusiastic □ *He is one of the team's most zealous supporters.*

zebra /'zebrə, 'ziːbrə/ NOUN [plural zebras] an animal like a horse with black and white stripes

zebra crossing /'zebrə 'krɒsɪŋ, 'ziːbrə 'krɒsɪŋ/ NOUN [plural zebra crossings] a place where you can cross a road, marked with black and white stripes

zenith /'zenɪθ/ NOUN, NO PLURAL the most successful point of something □ *Scoring those five goals was the zenith of his career.*

zero /'zɪərəʊ/ NOUN [plural zeros]
1 nothing or the number 0 □ *There are six zeros in one million.*
2 no plural the temperature at which water freezes □ *It was three degrees below zero.*
3 no plural no amount at all □ *Politicians have zero job security.*

zest /zest/ NOUN, NO PLURAL enjoyment and enthusiasm □ *Joe had a great zest for life.*

zigzag /'zɪgzæg/ ► NOUN [plural zigzags] a line with many sharp angles where it changes direction □ *a zigzag pattern*
► VERB [zigzags, zigzagging, zigzagged] to have or make a zigzag pattern □ *The path zigzagged up the hillside.*

zinc /zɪŋk/ NOUN, NO PLURAL a blue-white metal. A chemistry word.

zip /zɪp/ ► NOUN [plural zips] a device for fastening clothes or bags that has two rows of small metal or plastic parts that fit tightly together when a sliding piece is pulled along them
► VERB [zips, zipping, zipped]
1 to fasten something with a zip □ *Zip up your jacket; it's cold.*
2 to make the information on a computer file fit into a much smaller space, so that it can be sent or stored more easily. A computing word. □ *I'll zip the file before I send it to you.*
3 to move somewhere very quickly, or to do something very quickly □ *The bullet zipped by his head.* □ *He zipped through the answers.*

zip code /'zɪp ˌkəʊd/ NOUN [plural zip codes] the US phrase for post code

zipper /'zɪpə(r)/ NOUN [plural zippers] the US word for zip

zodiac /'zəʊdɪæk/ NOUN, NO PLURAL the zodiac the twelve signs of the groups of stars that some people believe influence your life 🔁 *What sign of the zodiac are you?*

zombie /'zɒmbɪ/ NOUN [plural zombies]
1 in some religions or stories, a dead body that looks as if it is alive because of magic
2 someone who seems to be very slow or stupid, often because they are very tired

zone /zəʊn/ NOUN [plural zones] an area that has a particular feature or where a particular thing happens 🔁 *This is a danger zone because of landslides.* □ *a smoke-free zone* □ *a war zone*

zoo /zuː/ NOUN [plural zoos] a place where wild animals are kept for people to look at

zoological /ˌzəʊə'lɒdʒɪkəl/ ADJECTIVE to do with animals
• **zoology** /zəʊ'ɒlədʒɪ/ NOUN, NO PLURAL the study of animals

zoom /zuːm/ VERB [zooms, zooming, zoomed] to move somewhere very fast, especially with a loud noise □ *The rocket zoomed up into the air.*
♦ PHRASAL VERBS **zoom in** if a camera zooms in, it makes the thing being photographed look bigger
zoom out if a camera zooms out, it fits more into the picture

zoom lens /'zuːm lenz/ NOUN [plural zoom lenses] a lens (=curved piece of glass) on a camera that can make things look bigger or smaller

zucchini /zuː'kiːnɪ/ NOUN [plural zucchini] the US word for courgette

zygote /'zaɪgəʊt/ NOUN [plural zygotes] a cell which is formed when a male and a female cell join in reproduction (=process of producing babies). A biology word.